McDougal Littell
CLASSZONE

Visit **classzone.com** and get connected.

ClassZone resources provide instruction, planning and assessment support for teachers.

State-Specific Resources

- Select your state and access state-specific resources

Literature and Reading Center

- Selection-specific content includes vocabulary practice, research links, and extension activities for writing and critical thinking
- Author Online provides information about each author, as well as in-depth author studies on selected writers
- English Learner support for a variety of languages includes audio summaries of selections and a Multi-Language Academic Glossary

Vocabulary and Spelling Center

- Vocabulary practice and games
- Spelling lessons
- Multi-Language Academic Glossary

Writing and Grammar Center

- Quick-Fix Editing Machine provides grammar help in a student-friendly format
- Writing Templates and graphic organizers promote clear, orderly communication

Media Center

- Media Analysis Guides encourage critical thinking skills
- Project Ideas, Storyboards, and Production Templates inspire creative media projects

You have immediate access to the the online version of the textbook and *ClassZone* resources at **www.classzone.com**

MCDKLMLHLPIHU

Use this code to create your own user name and password.

McDougal Littell
Where Great Lessons Begin

McDougal Littell
LITERATURE

Built for **MARYLAND**

Maryland Essential Course of Study

Maryland Table of Contents

Maryland Student Guide

Embedded Standards Support

Full Standards Correlation

McDougal Littell
EVANSTON, ILLINOIS • BOSTON • DALLAS

ISBN 13: 978-0-618-94437-8   ISBN 10: 0-618-94437-0

Printed in China.

1 2 3 4 5 6 7 8 9—DSC—12 11 10 09 08 07

SENIOR PROGRAM CONSULTANTS

JANET ALLEN
Reading and Literacy Specialist, Lecturer, Consultant, and Author; Creator of the "It's Never Too Late for Literacy" institutes

JUDITH A. LANGER
Distinguished Professor at the University at Albany, State University of New York; Director of the Center on English Learning and Achievement; Director of the Albany Institute for Research in Education

ARTHUR N. APPLEBEE
Leading Professor, School of Education at the University at Albany, State University of New York; Director of the Center on English Learning and Achievement

ROBERT J. MARZANO
Senior Scholar at Mid-Continent Research for Education and Learning (McREL); Associate Professor at Cardinal Stritch University in Milwaukee, Wisconsin; President of Marzano & Associates

JIM BURKE
Lecturer and Author; Teacher of English at Burlingame High School, Burlingame, California

DONNA M. OGLE
Professor of Reading and Language at National-Louis University in Chicago, Illinois

DOUGLAS CARNINE
Professor of Education at the University of Oregon; Director of the Western Region Reading First Technical Assistance Center

CAROL BOOTH OLSON
Senior Lecturer in the Department of Education at the University of California, Irvine; Director of the UCI site of the National Writing Project

YVETTE JACKSON
Executive Director of the National Urban Alliance for Effective Education

CAROL ANN TOMLINSON
Professor of Educational Research, Foundations, and Policy at the University of Virginia; Co-Director of the University's Institutes on Academic Diversity

ROBERT T. JIMÉNEZ
Professor of Language, Literacy, and Culture at Vanderbilt University

ENGLISH LEARNER SPECIALISTS

MARY LOU McCLOSKEY
Director of Teacher Development
and Curriculum Design for Educo
in Atlanta, Georgia

LYDIA STACK
International ESL consultant

CURRICULUM SPECIALIST

WILLIAM L. McBRIDE
Lecturer and Author;
Curriculum Specialist

MEDIA SPECIALISTS

DAVID M. CONSIDINE
Professor of Instructional
Technology and Media Studies
at Appalachian State University
in North Carolina

LARKIN PAULUZZI
Teacher and Media Specialist;
trainer for the New Jersey
Writing Project

LISA K. SCHEFFLER
Teacher and Media Specialist

McDougal Littell

LITERATURE

Where Great
Lessons Begin

Great Lessons Begin with **You.**

You teach. You inspire. We help.

We help you with support for every standard, every selection, and every student.

RESOURCE MANAGER

McDougal Littell
LITERATURE

Resource Manager
Provides all-in-one
support for true
differentiation.

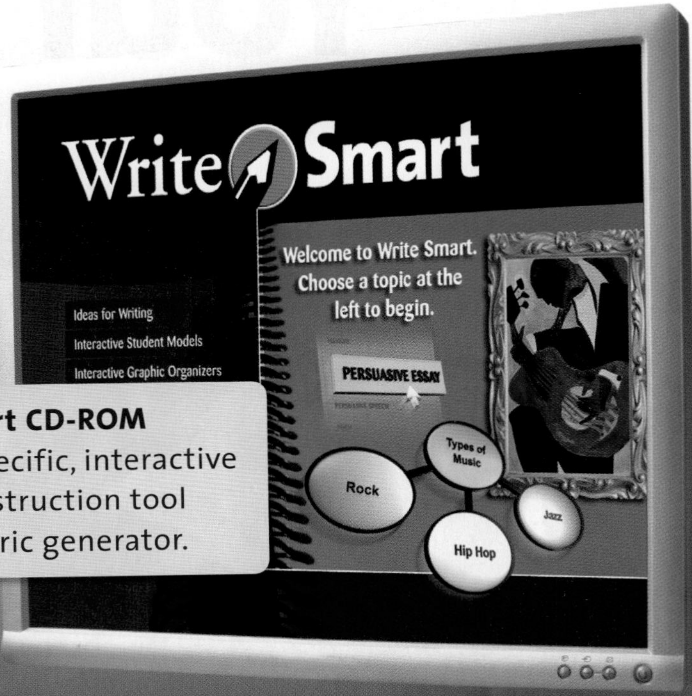

Write Smart

Welcome to Write Smart.
Choose a topic at the
left to begin.

Ideas for Writing
Interactive Student Models
Interactive Graphic Organizers

PERSUASIVE ESSAY

Rock
Types of Music
Jazz
Hip Hop

WriteSmart CD-ROM
A state-specific, interactive
writing instruction tool
with a rubric generator.

Vocabulary & Spelling
Literature
Grammar
Reading & Informational Texts
Media: Speaking & Listening
Writing, Research & Study Skills

STANDARDS LESSON FILE

McDougal Littell
LITERATURE

Standards Lesson File
Gives you a fast, organized
approach to teaching
every standard.

CONSULTANT'S CORNER

Bob Marzano
*McDougal Littell provides
maximum support to
teachers in terms of
instructional strategies
and addressing national and state
standards. Used well, this literature series
can dramatically enhance student
achievement while maximizing
teacher creativity.*

Great Lessons Begin with
Your Students.

They wonder. They question. We help.

We help your students become active readers, writers, and thinkers.

The **Student's Edition** helps engage and motivate students with a vibrant mix of selections.

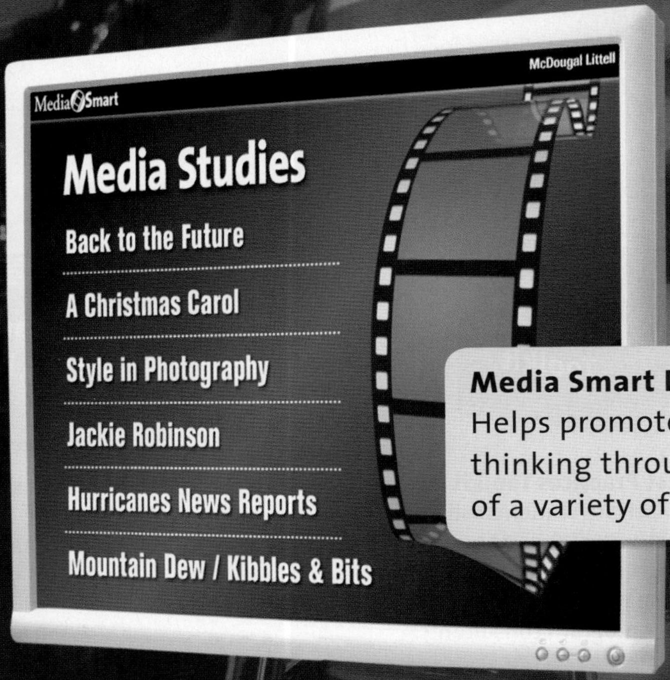

THE NOBLE EXPERIMENT

⭐ **Jackie Robinson**
as Told to Alfred Duckett

In 1910 Branch Rickey was a coach for Ohio Wesleyan. The team went to South Bend, Indiana, for a game. The hotel management registered the coach and team but refused to assign a room to a black player named Charley Thomas. In those days college ball had a few black players. Mr. Rickey took the manager aside and said he would move the entire team to another hotel unless the black athlete was accepted. The threat was a bluff because he knew the other hotels also would have refused accommodations to a black man. While the hotel manager was thinking about the threat, Mr. Rickey came up with a compromise. He suggested a cot be put in his own room, which he would share with the unwanted guest. The hotel manager wasn't happy about the idea, but he gave in.

Years later Branch Rickey told the story of the misery of that black player to whom he had given a place to sleep. He remembered that Thomas couldn't sleep.

"He sat on that cot," Mr. Rickey said, "and was silent for a long time. Then he began to cry, tears he couldn't hold back. His whole body shook with emotion. I sat and watched him, not knowing what to do until he began tearing at one hand with the other—just as if he were trying to scratch the skin off his hands with his fingernails. I was alarmed. I asked him what he was trying to do to himself.

"'It's my hands,' he sobbed. 'They're black. If only they were white, I'd be as good as anybody then, wouldn't I, Mr. Rickey? If only they were white.'

"'Charley,' Mr. Rickey said, 'the day will come when they won't have to be white.'"

810 UNIT 7: BIOGRAPHY AND AUTOBIOGRAPHY

ANALYZE VISUALS
What might you infer from the cover of this 1951 special edition comic book?

AUTOBIOGRAPHY
What does Robinson want the reader to know about the society in which Branch Rickey was coaching?

Media Smart DVD-ROM
Helps promote critical thinking through analysis of a variety of media.

Media Studies
- Back to the Future
- A Christmas Carol
- Style in Photography
- Jackie Robinson
- Hurricanes News Reports
- Mountain Dew / Kibbles & Bits

CONSULTANT'S CORNER

Janet Allen
In choosing to work on writing a literature program, I found a home with McDougal Littell because all our decisions could be based on students' needs and teachers' expertise. It was a perfect match for my interests and experience.

Carol Ann Tomlinson
Students come to us as a mixed set. They don't learn in the same ways, aren't motivated by the same things, and don't function at the same pace or depth. What I've always cared about is how teachers can help diverse learners succeed by teaching flexibly......that flexibility is built into this program.

Great Lessons Begin with
McDougal Littell

Teacher Resources

Time-saving, easy-to-use teacher resources make lesson planning and preparation simple.

Core Teacher Resources include:

Teacher's Edition

Easy Planner CD-Rom

Resource Manager

MediaSmart
Helps promote critical thinking through analysis of a variety of media.

WriteSmart
A state-specific, interactive writing instruction tool with a rubric generator.

Power Presentations
A collection of dynamic classroom presentation materials including leveled discussion questions, graphic organizers, and interactive vocabulary practice.

McDougal Littell Assessment System
Test Generator

Assessment File
Provides comprehensive opportunities to assess student progress with an array of tests including placement, selection, unit, and benchmark.

Best Practices Toolkit
Motivate students with engaging activities, over 200 graphic organizer transparencies, and research-based strategies from our program consultants.

Standards Lesson File
Stand-alone lessons ensure standards mastery.

Literature.

Student Resources

A complete program of technology and print resources provides support for differentiated student learning

InterActive Reader & Writer with Strategic Reading Support

InterActive Reader & Writer for Critical Analysis

Student's Edition

e-Edition includes Author Studies

Electronic Resources

Core Student Resources include:

Pupil Edition

eEdition online and CD-ROM

Interactive Reader & Writer
- **Strategic Reading Support**
- **Critical Analysis**

Both versions of the Interactive Reader & Writer include leveled readings, additional nonfiction, and test preparation.

Audio Anthology
Enables students to hear pronunciation, phrasing, and interpretations as they follow along in their textbook.

Multi-Language Academic Glossary Online
Facilitates comprehension of academic vocabulary with key terms and definitions in 10 languages.

Classzone.com
Provides a wealth of interactive resources for literature, reading, writing, grammar, vocabulary, spelling, and assessment.

Novels

Grammar for Writing

Grammar for Writing Workbook

Novels
Over 700 novels, works of nonfiction, and plays promote independent learning and reading

Grammar for Writing

Grammar for Writing Workbook
Supports systematic, student-friendly instruction in all aspects of grammar, usage, and mechanics.

Great Lessons Begin with
Your Maryland Customized Program

Welcome to the Maryland edition of McDougal Littell Literature. We hope that you will utilize all of the components whether print or technology to help your students become active readers, writers, speakers, and thinkers! This program was created to ensure mastery of the Maryland English/Language Arts Academic Standards while preparing for success on your different Maryland assessments. Please note that all of the components listed below are specifically customized for you!

Your customized Maryland program includes:

- **Maryland Student's Edition**
- **Maryland Teacher's Edition**
- **Maryland Resource Manager**
- **Maryland Standards Lesson File**
- **Targeted Instruction for Maryland Standards**
- **WriteSmart**
- **Test Generator**
- **McDougal Littell Assessment System**

For customized assessment use these resources:

Maryland Test Generator
Provides you with thousands of flexible test items correlated to Maryland Standards.

Assessment System

Available at **CLASSZONE.COM.**

The **McDougal Littell Assessment System (MLAS)** is a flexible, web-based program that allows you to use assessment as a teaching tool. This seamless testing and remediation system gives you a fast and easy way to:

TEST Unique testing is custom-built to Maryland Standards.

SCORE Automatic scoring gives you results in minutes.

REPORT Diagnostic reports show you what Maryland Standards were missed.

RETEACH Personalized remediation helps you target reteaching.

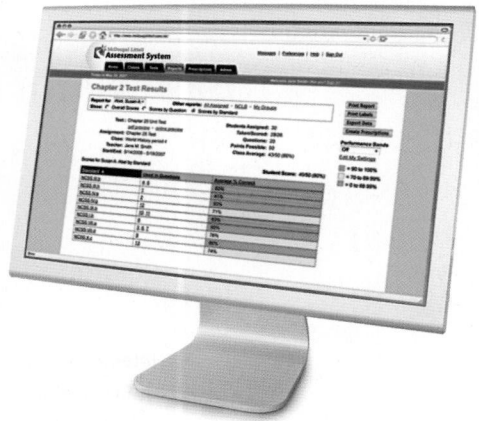

Introducing

The Maryland Essential Course of Study

So much to read and test with so little time! McDougal Littell helps you choose the lessons your students need to master critical skills that appear on formal assessments.

McDougal Littell provides two easy ways to find references for your use in the textbook.

- a complete listing of the Maryland Standards is located in the back of the Student's Edition.

- a complete correlation of the Maryland Standards to McDougal Littell Literature is available for your use in the back of the Teacher's Edition.

The Maryland Essential Course of Study on the pages that follow indicates which selections and workshops you should teach in order to cover key Maryland Standards that are tested on the English Language Arts Maryland Assessments. ▶

The Maryland Essential Course of Study

For a full listing of state standards see page S1.

	UNIT 1 Plot, Conflict, and Setting	**UNIT 2** Analyzing Character and Point of View	**UNIT 3** Understanding Theme	**UNIT 4** Mood, Tone, and Style	**UNIT 5** Appreciating Poetry
LITERATURE	Reader's Workshop: Parts of a Story *Seventh Grade* *The Last Dog* *Thank You, M'am* *An American Childhood* **1.E.3.a** Strategies during reading **1.E.4.c** Draw inferences **1.E.4.f** Connect **3.A.2.a** Analyze text features **3.A.3.b** Plot **3.A.3.c** Setting **3.A.3.g** Conflicts	Reader's Workshop: Character and Point of View *Zebra* *The Scholarship Jacket* *Retrieved Reformation* *The Three-Century Woman / Charles* **1.E.3.a** Strategies during reading **1.E.4.c** Draw inferences **1.E.4.d** Predictions **3.A.3.d** Characterization **3.A.3.i** Point of view	Reader's Workshop: Understanding Theme *Amigo Brothers* *What do Fish Have To Do With Anything?* *Spring Harvest of Snow Peas / Eating Alone* **1.E.3.a** Strategies during reading **3.A.6.a** Universal themes **3.A.6.b** Themes across texts **3.A.7.a** Language choices and meaning	Reader's Workshop: Mood, Tone, and Style *Dark They Were, and Golden-Eyed* *A Day's Wait* **1.D.2.b** Relationships between words **1.E.3.a** Strategies during reading **2.A.5** Analyze language **3.A.7.a** Style **3.A.7.b** Tone **3.A.7.d** Imagery	Reader's Workshop: Appreciating Poetry *The Names* *the earth is a living thing / Sleeping in the Forest / Gold* *The Charge of the Light Brigade/ The Highwayman* *Jabberwocky / Sarah Cynthia …/ Two Limericks* **1.E.3.a** Strategies during reading **1.E.4.c** Draw inferences **3.A.3.b** Conflict and plot **3.A.4.a** Types of poetry **3.A.4.c** Sound elements **3.A.7.c** Figurative language **3.A.7.d** Imagery
NONFICTION AND INFORMATIONAL MATERIAL	*The Unnatural Course of Time* **1.E.3.a** Strategies during reading **2.A.4.b** Author's viewpoint	*The Collected Grief of a Nation / A Mother's Words / U.S. Involvement in Vietnam* **1.E.4.c** Draw conclusions **2.A.4.g** Synthesize	*Homeless* **2.A.4.b** Author's perspective **4.A.2.d** Persuade	*How Hemingway Wrote The Only Girl …/ Breaking the Ice* **1.E.3.a** Strategies during reading **2.A.4.h** Fact and opinion **3.A.7.b** Tone **4.A.1.b.1** Organize information	
WRITING	Descriptive Essay **4.A.1** Prewriting **4.A.2.b** Describe in prose	Comparison-Contrast Essay **4.A.1** Prewriting **4.A.2.c** Inform		Interpretive Essay **4.A.1** Prewriting **4.A.2.c** Inform	
SPEAKING, LISTENING, AND MEDIA					

UNIT 6 Myths, Legends, and Tales	UNIT 7 Biography and Autobiography	UNIT 8 Information, Argument, and Persuasion	UNIT 9 The Power of Research	Student Resources Handbook
Reader's Workshop: Myths, Legends, and Tales *Prometheus / Orpheus* *Young Arthur* *Sally Ann ...* *Two Ways to Count to Ten/ The Race Between Toad and Donkey* **1.D.3.a** Use context **1.E.3.a** Strategies during reading **3.A.3.a** Types of narrative texts **3.A.6.a** Universal themes **3.A.6.b** Themes across texts **3.A.8.d** Structure and purpose	Reader's Workshop: Biography and Autobiography *Eleanor Roosevelt* *Noble Experiment* *Lucy Stone* **1.D.3.b** Use word structure **1.E.3.a** Strategies during reading **1.E.4.e** Summarize **3.A.3.a** Types of narrative texts **3.A.5** Elements of drama			
Serf on the Run/ Medieval Adventures **2.A.4.h** Fact and an opinion **4.A.2.c** Inform	*Letter to the President General of the Daughters of the American Revolution / The Autobiography of Eleanor Roosevelt* *Montreal Signs Negro Shortstop / Robinson Steals Home in Fifth* **1.E.4.c** Draw conclusions **1.E.4.e** Summarize **2.A.4** Analyze messages **4.A.7.a** Identify sources	Reader's Workshops: Information, Argument, and Persuasion *What Do You Know About Sharks?* *Great White Sharks* *Like Black Smoke / A World Turned ...* *Pro Athlete's .../ Do Professional ...* **1.E.3.a** Strategies **1.E.4.b** Explain information **1.E.4.a** Main idea **2.A.2.a** Print features **2.A.2.b** Graphic aids **2.A.3** Organizational **2.A.4.h** Fact and opinion **2.A.6.d** Argument **2.A.6.f** Persuade	Research Strategies Workshop **2.A.2** Analyze text features **4.A.7.b** Obtain information	Reading Handbook **2.A.1.a** Use primary and secondary sources **2.A.1.b** Use workplace and other real world documents **2.A.6** Read critically to evaluate
Cause-and-Effect Essay **4.A.1** Prewriting **4.A.2.c** Inform	Personal Narrative **4.A.1** Prewriting **4.A.2.a** Express personal ideas	Persuasive Essay **4.A.1** Prewriting **4.A.2.d** Persuade	Research Report **4.A.1** Prewriting **4.A.2.c** Inform **7.A.1.** Oral presentation	Summary **3.2.PO2** Write a summary
Formal Presentation **7.A.1.** Oral presentation		Persuasive Speech **7.A.1.** Oral presentation		

MARYLAND

McDougal Littell
LITERATURE

ACKNOWLEDGMENTS

INTRODUCTORY UNIT

The Barbara Hogenson Agency: Excerpt from *A Young Lady of Property* by Horton Foote. Copyright © 1955, 1983 by Horton Foote. Reprinted by arrangement with Horton Foote and The Barbara Hogenson Agency.

KidsHealth: Excerpt from "Stress" by the Memours Foundation, from KidsHealth.com. Copyright © by KidsHealth.com. Reprinted with permission.

Atheneum Books for Young Readers: Excerpt from "Shells," from *Every Living Thing* by Cynthia Rylant. Copyright © 1985 by Cynthia Rylant. Reprinted by permission of Atheneum Books for Young Readers, an imprint of Simon & Schuster Children's Publishing Division.

Continued on page R147

ART CREDITS

COVER, TITLE PAGE

Untitled (1986), Jerry N. Uelsmann. © 2003 Jerry N. Uelsmann.

Continued on page R151

ISBN 13: 978-0-618-94414-9   ISBN 10: 0-618-94414-1

Printed in the United States of America.

1 2 3 4 5 6 7 8 9—VJM—12 11 10 09 08 07

MARYLAND

McDougal Littell
LITERATURE

Janet Allen

Arthur N. Applebee

Jim Burke

Douglas Carnine

Yvette Jackson

Robert T. Jiménez

Judith A. Langer

Robert J. Marzano

Donna M. Ogle

Carol Booth Olson

Carol Ann Tomlinson

Mary Lou McCloskey

Lydia Stack

Baltimore, Maryland skyline © Jeremy Woodhouse/Getty Imageso

McDougal Littell

EVANSTON, ILLINOIS • BOSTON • DALLAS

SENIOR PROGRAM CONSULTANTS

JANET ALLEN Reading and Literacy Specialist; creator of the popular "It's Never Too Late"/"Reading for Life" Institutes. Dr. Allen is an internationally known consultant who specializes in literacy work with at-risk students. Her publications include *Tools for Content Literacy; It's Never Too Late: Leading Adolescents to Lifelong Learning; Yellow Brick Roads: Shared and Guided Paths to Independent Reading; Words, Words, Words: Teaching Vocabulary in Grades 4–12;* and *Testing 1, 2, 3 . . . Bridging Best Practice and High-Stakes Assessments.* Dr. Allen was a high school reading and English teacher for more than 20 years and has taught courses in both subjects at the University of Central Florida. She directed the Central Florida Writing Project and received the Milken Foundation National Educator Award.

ARTHUR N. APPLEBEE Leading Professor, School of Education at the University at Albany, State University of New York; Director of the Center on English Learning and Achievement. During his varied career, Dr. Applebee has been both a researcher and a teacher, working in institutional settings with children with severe learning problems, in public schools, as a staff member of the National Council of Teachers of English, and in professional education. Among his many books are *Curriculum as Conversation: Transforming Traditions of Teaching and Learning; Literature in the Secondary School: Studies of Curriculum and Instruction in the United States;* and *Tradition and Reform in the Teaching of English: A History.* He was elected to the International Reading Hall of Fame and has received, among other honors, the David H. Russell Award for Distinguished Research in the Teaching of English.

JIM BURKE Lecturer and Author; Teacher of English at Burlingame High School, Burlingame, California. Mr. Burke is a popular presenter at educational conferences across the country and is the author of numerous books for teachers, including *School Smarts: The Four Cs of Academic Success; The English Teacher's Companion; Reading Reminders; Writing Reminders;* and *ACCESSing School: Teaching Struggling Readers to Achieve Academic and Personal Success.* He is the recipient of NCTE's Exemplary English Leadership Award and was inducted into the California Reading Association's Hall of Fame.

DOUGLAS CARNINE Professor of Education at the University of Oregon; Director of the Western Region Reading First Technical Assistance Center. Dr. Carnine is nationally known for his focus on research-based practices in education, especially curriculum designs that prepare instructors of K-12 students. He has received the Lifetime Achievement Award from the Council for Exceptional Children and the Ersted Award for outstanding teaching at the University of Oregon. Dr. Carnine frequently consults on educational policy with government groups, businesses, communities, and teacher unions.

YVETTE JACKSON Executive Director of the National Urban Alliance for Effective Education. Nationally recognized for her work in assessing the learning potential of underachieving urban students, Dr. Jackson is also a presenter for the Harvard Principal Center and is a member of the Differentiation Faculty of the Association for Supervision and Curriculum Development. Dr. Jackson's research focuses on literacy, gifted education, and cognitive mediation theory. She designed the Comprehensive Education Plan for the New York City Public Schools and has served as their Director of Gifted Programs and Executive Director of Instruction and Professional Development.

ROBERT T. JIMÉNEZ Professor of Language, Literacy, and Culture at Vanderbilt University. Dr. Jiménez's research focuses on the language and literacy practices of Latino students. A former bilingual education teacher, he is now conducting research on how written language is thought about and used in contemporary Mexico. Dr. Jiménez has received several research and teaching honors, including two Fulbright awards from the Council for the International Exchange of Scholars and the Albert J. Harris Award from the International Reading Association. His published work has appeared in the *American Educational Research Journal, Reading Research Quarterly, The Reading Teacher, Journal of Adolescent and Adult Literacy,* and *Lectura y Vida.*

JUDITH A. LANGER Distinguished Professor at the University at Albany, State University of New York; Director of the Center on English Learning and Achievement; Director of the Albany Institute for Research in Education. An internationally known scholar in English language arts education, Dr. Langer specializes in developing teaching approaches that can enrich and improve what gets done on a daily basis in classrooms. Her publications include *Getting to Excellent: How to Create Better Schools* and *Effective Literacy Instruction: Building Successful Reading and Writing Programs*. She was inducted into the International Reading Hall of Fame and has received many other notable awards, including an honorary doctorate from the University of Uppsala, Sweden, for her research on literacy education.

ROBERT J. MARZANO Senior Scholar at Mid-Continent Research for Education and Learning (McREL); Associate Professor at Cardinal Stritch University in Milwaukee, Wisconsin; President of Marzano & Associates. An internationally known researcher, trainer, and speaker, Dr. Marzano has developed programs that translate research and theory into practical tools for K-12 teachers and administrators. He has written extensively on such topics as reading and writing instruction, thinking skills, school effectiveness, assessment, and standards implementation. His books include *Building Background Knowledge for Academic Achievement; Classroom Management That Works: Research-Based Strategies for Every Teacher;* and *What Works in Schools: Translating Research Into Action.*

DONNA M. OGLE Professor of Reading and Language at National-Louis University in Chicago, Illinois; Past President of the International Reading Association. Creator of the well-known KWL strategy, Dr. Ogle has directed many staff development projects translating theory and research into school practice in middle and secondary schools throughout the United States and has served as a consultant on literacy projects worldwide. Her extensive international experience includes coordinating the Reading and Writing for Critical Thinking Project in Eastern Europe, developing integrated curriculum for a USAID Afghan Education Project, and speaking and consulting on projects in several Latin American countries and in Asia. Her books include *Coming Together as Readers; Reading Comprehension: Strategies for Independent Learners; All Children Read;* and *Literacy for a Democratic Society.*

CAROL BOOTH OLSON Senior Lecturer in the Department of Education at the University of California, Irvine; Director of the UCI site of the National Writing Project. Dr. Olson writes and lectures extensively on the reading/writing connection, critical thinking through writing, interactive strategies for teaching writing, and the use of multicultural literature with students of culturally diverse backgrounds. She has received many awards, including the California Association of Teachers of English Award of Merit, the Outstanding California Education Research Award, and the UC Irvine Excellence in Teaching Award. Dr. Olson's books include *Reading, Thinking, and Writing About Multicultural Literature* and *The Reading/Writing Connection: Strategies for Teaching and Learning in the Secondary Classroom.*

CAROL ANN TOMLINSON Professor of Educational Research, Foundations, and Policy at the University of Virginia; Co-Director of the University's Institutes on Academic Diversity. An internationally known expert on differentiated instruction, Dr. Tomlinson helps teachers and administrators develop effective methods of teaching academically diverse learners. She was a teacher of middle and high school English for 22 years prior to teaching at the University of Virginia. Her books on differentiated instruction have been translated into eight languages. Among her many publications are *How to Differentiate Instruction in Mixed-Ability Classrooms* and *The Differentiated Classroom: Responding to the Needs of All Learners.*

MD5

ENGLISH LEARNER SPECIALISTS

MARY LOU McCLOSKEY Past President of Teachers of English to Speakers of Other Languages (TESOL); Director of Teacher Development and Curriculum Design for Educo in Atlanta, Georgia. Dr. McCloskey is a former teacher in multilingual and multicultural classrooms. She has worked with teachers, teacher educators, and departments of education around the world on teaching English as a second and foreign language. She is author of *On Our Way to English, Voices in Literature, Integrating English,* and *Visions: Language, Literature, Content.* Her awards include the Le Moyne College Ignatian Award for Professional Achievement and the TESOL D. Scott Enright Service Award.

LYDIA STACK International ESL consultant. Her areas of expertise are English language teaching strategies, ESL standards for students and teachers, and curriculum writing. Her teaching experience includes 25 years as an elementary and high school ESL teacher. She is a past president of TESOL. Her awards include the James E. Alatis Award for Service to TESOL (2003) and the San Francisco STAR Teacher Award (1989). Her publications include *On Our Way to English; Wordways: Games for Language Learning;* and *Visions: Language, Literature, Content.*

CURRICULUM SPECIALIST

WILLIAM L. McBRIDE Curriculum Specialist. Dr. McBride is a nationally known speaker, educator, and author who now trains teachers in instructional methodologies. A former reading specialist, English teacher, and social studies teacher, he holds a Masters in Reading and a Ph.D. in Curriculum and Instruction from the University of North Carolina at Chapel Hill. Dr. McBride has contributed to the development of textbook series in language arts, social studies, science, and vocabulary. He is also known for his novel *Entertaining an Elephant,* which tells the story of a burned-out teacher who becomes re-inspired with both his profession and his life.

MEDIA SPECIALISTS

DAVID M. CONSIDINE Professor of Instructional Technology and Media Studies at Appalachian State University in North Carolina. Dr. Considine has served as a media literacy consultant to the U.S. government and to the media industry, including Discovery Communications and Cable in the Classroom. He has also conducted media literacy workshops and training for county and state health departments across the United States. Among his many publications are *Visual Messages: Integrating Imagery into Instruction,* and *Imagine That: Developing Critical Viewing and Thinking Through Children's Literature.*

LARKIN PAULUZZI Teacher and Media Specialist; trainer for the New Jersey Writing Project. Ms. Pauluzzi puts her extensive classroom experience to use in developing teacher-friendly curriculum materials and workshops in many different areas, including media literacy. She has led media literacy training workshops in several districts throughout Texas, guiding teachers in the meaningful and practical uses of media in the classroom. Ms. Pauluzzi has taught students at all levels, from Title I Reading to AP English IV. She also spearheads a technology club at her school, working with students to produce media and technology to serve both the school and the community.

LISA K. SCHEFFLER Teacher and Media Specialist. Ms. Scheffler has designed and taught media literacy and video production curriculum, in addition to teaching language arts and speech. Using her knowledge of mass communication theory, coupled with real classroom experience, she has developed ready-to-use materials that help teachers incorporate media literacy into their curricula. She has taught film and television studies at the University of North Texas and has served as a contributing writer for the Texas Education Agency's statewide viewing and representing curriculum.

MARYLAND TEACHER ADVISORS

Tara Adams
Prince George's County Public Schools
Capital Heights, MD

Janice Albright
Esperanza Middle School
Lexington Park, MD

Gayle Brooks
Herbert Hoover Middle School
Potomac, MD

Elizabeth Burkes
Winston Middle School
Baltimore, MD

Rochelle Cooper
Northeast Middle School
Baltimore, MD

Stephanie Downes
Prince George's County Public Schools
Capital Heights, MD

Shelia Evans
Glenwood Elementary/Middle School
Baltimore, MD

Karen Kotchka
Lemmell Middle School
Baltimore, MD

Arlene Proto
Moravia Park Elementary/Middle School
Baltimore, MD

NATIONAL TEACHER ADVISORS

These are some of the many educators from across the country who played a crucial role in the development of the tables of contents, the lesson design, and other key components of this program:

Virginia L. Alford, MacArthur High School, San Antonio, Texas

Yvonne L. Allen, Shaker Heights High School, Shaker Heights, Ohio

Dave T. Anderson, Hinsdale South High School, Darien, Illinois

Kacy Colleen Anglim, Portland Public Schools District, Portland, Oregon

Beverly Scott Bass, Arlington Heights High School, Fort Worth, Texas

Jordana Benone, North High School, Torrance, California

Patricia Blood, Howell High School, Farmingdale, New Jersey

Marjorie Bloom, Eau Gallie High School, Melbourne, Florida

Edward J. Blotzer, Wilkinsburg Junior/Senior High School, Wilkinsburg, Pennsylvania

Stephen D. Bournes, Evanston Township High School, Evanston, Illinois

Barbara M. Bowling, Mt. Tabor High School, Winston-Salem, North Carolina

Kiala Boykin-Givehand, Duval County Public Schools, Jacksonville, Florida

Laura L. Brown, Adlai Stevenson High School, Lincolnshire, Illinois

Cynthia Burke, Yavneh Academy, Dallas, Texas

Hoppy Chandler, San Diego City Schools, San Diego, California

Gary Chmielewski, St. Benedict High School, Chicago, Illinois

Delorse Cole-Stewart, Milwaukee Public Schools, Milwaukee, Wisconsin

L. Calvin Dillon, Gaither High School, Tampa, Florida

Dori Dolata, Rufus King High School, Milwaukee, Wisconsin

Jon Epstein, Marietta High School, Marietta, Georgia

Helen Ervin, Fort Bend Independent School District, Sugarland, Texas

Sue Friedman, Buffalo Grove High School, Buffalo Grove, Illinois

Chris Gee, Bel Air High School, El Paso, Texas

Paula Grasel, The Horizon Center, Gainesville, Georgia

Christopher Guarraia, Centreville High School, Clifton, Virginia

Rochelle L. Greene-Brady, Kenwood Academy, Chicago, Illinois

Michele M. Hettinger, Niles West High School, Skokie, Illinois

Elizabeth Holcomb, Forest Hill High School, Jackson, Mississippi

Jim Horan, Hinsdale Central High School, Hinsdale, Illinois

James Paul Hunter, Oak Park-River Forest High School, Oak Park, Illinois

Susan P. Kelly, Director of Curriculum, Island Trees School District, Levittown, New York

Beverley A. Lanier, Varina High School, Richmond, Virginia

Pat Laws, Charlotte-Mecklenburg Schools, Charlotte, North Carolina

Diana R. Martinez, Treviño School of Communications & Fine Arts, Laredo, Texas

Natalie Martinez, Stephen F. Austin High School, Houston, Texas

Elizabeth Matarazzo, Ysleta High School, El Paso, Texas

Carol M. McDonald, J. Frank Dobie High School, Houston, Texas

Amy Millikan, Consultant, Chicago, Illinois

Terri Morgan, Caprock High School, Amarillo, Texas

Eileen Murphy, Walter Payton Preparatory High School, Chicago, Illinois

Lisa Omark, New Haven Public Schools, New Haven, Connecticut

Kaine Osburn, Wheeling High School, Wheeling, Illinois

Andrea J. Phillips, Terry Sanford High School, Fayetteville, North Carolina

Cathy Reilly, Sayreville Public Schools, Sayreville, New Jersey

Mark D. Simon, Neuqua Valley High School, Naperville, Illinois

Scott Snow, Sequin High School, Arlington, Texas

Jane W. Speidel, Brevard County Schools, Viera, Florida

Cheryl E. Sullivan, Lisle Community School District, Lisle, Illinois

Anita Usmiani, Hamilton Township Public Schools, Hamilton Square, New Jersey

Linda Valdez, Oxnard Union High School District, Oxnard, California

Nancy Walker, Longview High School, Longview, Texas

Kurt Weiler, New Trier High School, Winnetka, Illinois

Elizabeth Whittaker, Larkin High School, Elgin, Illinois

Linda S. Williams, Woodlawn High School, Baltimore, Maryland

John R. Williamson, Fort Thomas Independent Schools, Fort Thomas, Kentucky

Anna N. Winters, Simeon High School, Chicago, Illinois

Tonora D. Wyckoff, North Shore Senior High School, Houston, Texas

Karen Zajac, Glenbard South High School, Glen Ellyn, Illinois

Cynthia Zimmerman, Mose Vines Preparatory High School, Chicago, Illinois

Lynda Zimmerman, El Camino High School, South San Francisco, California

Ruth E. Zurich, Brown Deer High School, Brown Deer, Wisconsin

MARYLAND

OVERVIEW
Maryland Student's Edition

LESSONS WITH EMBEDDED STANDARDS INSTRUCTION

 Look for the Maryland symbol throughout the book. It highlights targeted objectives to help you succeed on your test.

Baltimore, Maryland skyline © Jeremy Woodhouse/Getty Images

MARYLAND CONTENTS

MARYLAND CONTENTS IN BRIEF

MD10

PART 3: NONFICTION WITH PURPOSE

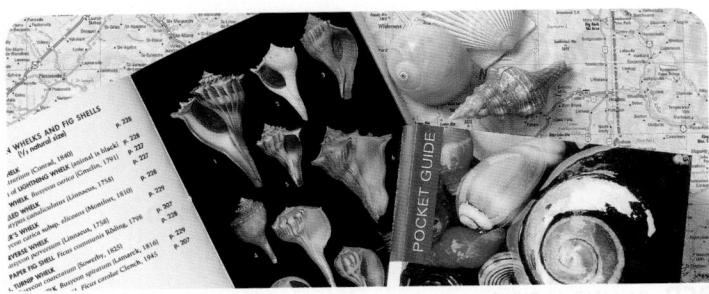

STUDENT RESOURCE BANK

READING HANDBOOK

WRITING HANDBOOK

GRAMMAR HANDBOOK

VOCABULARY AND SPELLING HANDBOOK

SPEAKING AND LISTENING HANDBOOK

MEDIA HANDBOOK

TEST-TAKING HANDBOOK

GLOSSARIES

Online LITERATURE
CLASSZONE.COM

LITERATURE AND READING CENTER
- Author Biographies
- Additional Selection Background
- Literary Analysis Frames
- Power Thinking Activities

WRITING AND GRAMMAR CENTER
- Writing Templates and Graphic Organizers
- Publishing Options
- Quick-Fix Editing Machine

VOCABULARY AND SPELLING CENTER
- Vocabulary Strategies and Practice
- Multi-Language Academic Vocabulary Glossary
- Vocabulary Flash Cards
- Spelling Lessons

MEDIA CENTER
- Production Templates
- Analysis Guides

RESEARCH CENTER
- Web Research Guide
- Citation Guide

ASSESSMENT CENTER
- MSA Practice and Test-Taking Tips
- SAT/ACT Practice and Tips

MORE TECHNOLOGY

eEdition
- Interactive Selections
- Audio Summaries

WriteSmart
- Writing Prompts and Templates
- Interactive Student Models
- Interactive Graphic Organizers
- Interactive Revision Lessons
- Rubric Generator

MediaSmart DVD
- Media Lessons
- Interactive Media Studies

MD11

UNIT 1
MARYLAND

Weaving a Story
PLOT, CONFLICT, AND SETTING
• IN FICTION • IN NONFICTION • IN POETRY • IN DRAMA • IN MEDIA

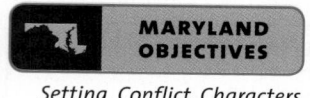

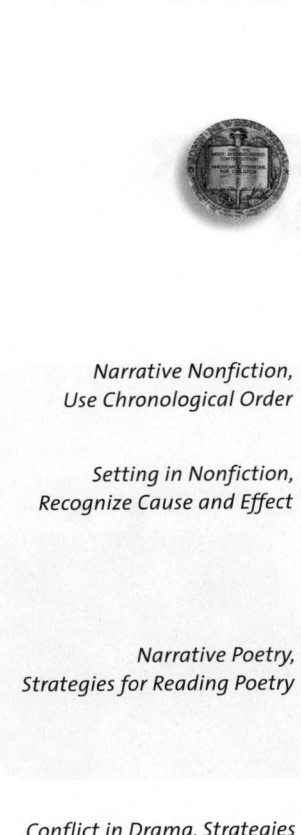
VOCABULARY STRATEGIES

Latin roots: *uni, p. 40*   Latin roots: *viv* and *vit, p. 90*
Antonyms as context clues, *p. 59*   Analogies, *p. 116*
Prefixes that mean "not," *p. 70*   Suffixes that form adjectives, *p. 127*

UNIT 2
MARYLAND

Personality Tests
ANALYZING CHARACTER AND POINT OF VIEW
- IN FICTION • IN NONFICTION • IN POETRY

MARYLAND OBJECTIVES

VOCABULARY STRATEGIES

Similes, *p. 206*

Context clues, *p. 225*

Multiple meaning words, *p. 238*

Latin roots: *cred, p. 256*

Using reference aids, *p. 266*

Idioms, *p. 278*

UNIT 3

MARYLAND

Lessons to Learn
UNDERSTANDING THEME

• IN FICTION • IN POETRY • IN DRAMA • IN MEDIA

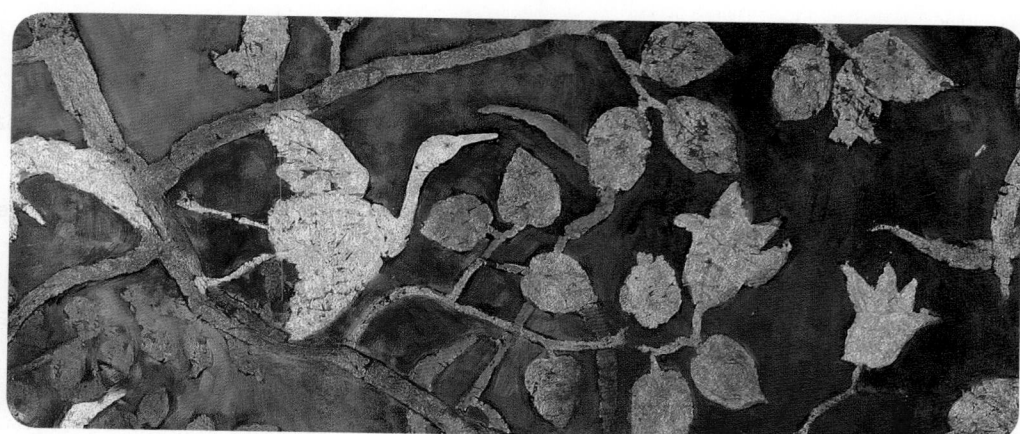

MARYLAND OBJECTIVES

MSA SKILLS
PRACTICE

VOCABULARY STRATEGIES

Latin roots: *pel, p. 324*   General context clues, *p. 354*

Denotations and connotations, *p. 336*   Forms of the prefix *in-, p. 373*

UNIT 4

MARYLAND

Finding a Voice
MOOD, TONE, AND STYLE

• IN FICTION • IN NONFICTION • IN POETRY • IN MEDIA

MARYLAND OBJECTIVES

VOCABULARY STRATEGIES

Latin roots: *pend, p. 464*

Synonyms, *p. 487*

Words for animal groups, *p. 474*

Literal and figurative meanings, *p. 506*

UNIT 5
MARYLAND

Picture the Moment
APPRECIATING POETRY

MARYLAND OBJECTIVES

Form, Speaker, Sound Devices, Imagery, Figurative Language

Free Verse, Imagery, Understand Historical Context

Lyric Poetry, Figurative Language, Make Inferences

Line and Stanza, Rhyme Scheme, Understand Speaker

MSA SKILLS PRACTICE

> **VOCABULARY STRATEGY**
>
> Connotations, *p. 580*

UNIT **6**

MARYLAND

Sharing Our Stories
MYTHS, LEGENDS, AND TALES

MARYLAND OBJECTIVES

VOCABULARY STRATEGIES

Latin roots: *fin, p. 645*

Homographs, *p. 658*

Compound words, *p. 668*

Easily confused words, *p. 684*

Latin words: *primus, p. 711*

Dictionary usage labels, *p. 721*

Writing a Life
BIOGRAPHY AND AUTOBIOGRAPHY
• IN NONFICTION • IN MEDIA • IN DRAMA • IN POETRY

MARYLAND
OBJECTIVES

*Characteristics of Biographies
and Autobiographies*

*Biography, Identify
Chronological Order*

Synthesize, Draw Conclusions

Personal Essay, Connect

Quotations, Make Inferences

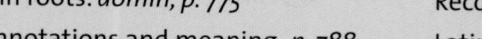

MSA SKILLS
PRACTICE

VOCABULARY STRATEGIES

Latin roots: *domin, p. 775*   Recognizing base words, *p. 801*
Connotations and meaning, *p. 788*   Latin roots: *spec, p. 821*

UNIT 8

MARYLAND

Face the Facts
INFORMATION, ARGUMENT, AND PERSUASION
• IN NONFICTION • IN MEDIA

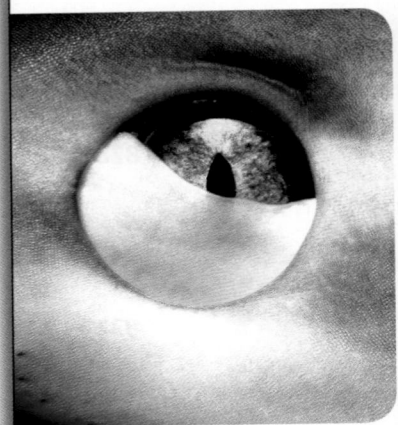

VOCABULARY STRATEGIES

Content-specific words, *p. 882*   Specialized vocabulary, *p. 906*   Greek roots: *aut, p. 935*

Prefixes and *vert, p. 893*   Idioms, *p. 926*   Acronyms, *p. 942*

UNIT 9
MARYLAND

Investigation and Discovery
THE POWER OF RESEARCH

SHELLS

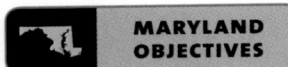

MARYLAND OBJECTIVES

Use Reference Materials and Technology, Evaluate Sources

Research, Synthesis

Student Resource Bank

Selections by Genre

FICTION

SHORT STORIES

ORAL TRADITION

NOVELS

NONFICTION

AUTOBIOGRAPHY/MEMOIR

BIOGRAPHY

ESSAYS

Selections by Genre

 LITERATURE CENTER at ClassZone.com

 WriteSmart

 MEDIA CENTER at ClassZone.com

 *MediaSmart* DVD

MARYLAND

STUDENT GUIDE TO MSA SUCCESS

MSA SUCCESS

Baltimore, Maryland skyline © Jeremy Woodhouse/Getty Images

Understanding the Maryland Voluntary State Curriculum

What is the Maryland Voluntary State Curriculum?

The Maryland Voluntary State Curriculum for Reading/English Language Arts outlines what you should know and be able to do at each grade level. Your teacher uses the Voluntary State Curriculum to design a course of instruction that will help you develop the skills and knowledge you are expected to have by the end of grade 7. The Maryland Voluntary State Curriculum for Reading/English Language Arts not only prepares you for success in taking tests like the Maryland School Assessment, but also prepares you for success in everyday life and the workplace.

How will I learn the material in the Maryland Voluntary State Curriculum?

Your textbook is closely aligned to the Maryland Voluntary State Curriculum for Reading/English Language Arts. Every time you learn new information or practice a skill, you are mastering one of the objectives in the curriculum. Each unit in the textbook, each reading selection, and each workshop connects to the Voluntary State Curriculum for Reading/English Language Arts. The objectives covered in each section of a unit are listed on the opening page of the section as well as in the table of contents.

The Maryland Voluntary State Curriculum for Reading/English Language Arts has seven standards. These standards are:

1. **General Reading Processes:** Phonemic Awareness, Phonics, Fluency, Vocabulary, and Comprehension
2. **Comprehension of Informational Text**
3. **Comprehension of Literary Text**
4. **Writing**
5. **Controlling Language**
6. **Listening**
7. **Speaking**

For a complete listing of the Maryland Voluntary State Curriculum for Reading/ English Language Arts, see pg. S1.

The standards are broken down into topics, indicators, and objectives. Topics describe in general terms the knowledge and skills that can be tested. Each topic is broken down into indicators, which focus on smaller areas of knowledge and particular skills that are part of each topic. Objectives are the particular goals or steps that help you meet the indicators. You must master the objectives and indicators in each topic to master the standard. Maryland uses a special numbering system to identify the standard, topic, indicator, and objective.

MARYLAND VOLUNTARY STATE CURRICULUM DECODER

3 . A . 7 . b

Indicates standard
3: Comprehension of Literary Text
Students will read, understand, interpret, analyze, and evaluate literary texts

Identifies the objective
b: Analyze language choices that create tone

Identifies the indicator
7: Analyze the author's purposeful use of language

Indicates topic A:
Comprehension of Literary Text

Embedded Assessment Practice

Each unit has a formatted practice test that covers specific standards-based skills.

Preparing for the MSA

What is the MSA?

MSA stands for the Maryland School Assessment. The MSA in Reading is a test that measures your understanding of the Maryland Voluntary State Curriculum for Reading/English Language Arts in every grade you have completed. The MSA is given to all grade 7 students in early March in two parts over two days. The test includes multiple-choice questions as well as questions that require written responses.

How can I be successful on the MSA?

Read the passages and questions on the following pages to prepare for the MSA in Reading. This section will familiarize you with the kinds of questions you can expect on the actual test. The tips and strategies highlighted in blue will guide you as you read the passages and answer the questions.

- Read the passages carefully, as well as the tips in the margins. The tips help you to focus on important ideas and details in the reading so that you will be better prepared to answer the questions that follow.

Barbara Jordan

Lawyer and U.S. Representative

From 1972 to 1978, Barbara Jordan served as congresswoman for Texas's 18th district. She was the first African-American woman that the Deep South sent to Congress.

As you read, notice facts and details that seem important.

Barbara Jordan (1936–1996) grew up in an African-American neighborhood in Houston, Texas. She became the first African American elected to serve in the Texas state senate since 1883. Jordan also became the first African-American woman from the Deep

at the time she "had no fixed notion of what that was."
Entering the White World In 1954, Jordan was in her junior year at Texas Southern University. That year, the Supreme Court decided, in the case *Brown v. Board of Education of Topeka*, that separate was not equal

- Each question tests a particular objective. Strategies highlighted in blue suggest ways to approach different kinds of questions on the MSA in Reading.

(1) What is the conflict between the magistrate and Ch'en Jung?
   A. Ch'en Jung does not finish the dragon painting.
   B. The magistrate does not like the dragon painting.
   C. The magistrate wants Ch'en Jung to paint eyes on the dragon.
   D. Ch'en Jung wants more money to paint the eyes on the dragon.

Objective: 3.A.3.b Analyze the conflict and the events of the plot.

Strategy: Review details from the passage where the magistrate and Ch'en Jung disagree. Ch'en Jung finishes the painting according to the agreement, so answer choice A is not correct. Answer choice B is incorrect because Narrator 1 states the "dragon was so grand and beautiful that no one made a sound." Answer choice D is also incorrect because Ch'en Jung does not ask for more money. The conflict between the magistrate and Ch'en Jung is about the eyes on the dragon. The correct answer is choice C.

(2) Irony is often used to create an unexpected outcome that reinforces a theme. What is an example of irony in this passage?
   A. Ch'en Jung paints left to right so the dragon's head meets the

MSA Strategies and Preparation

The following section introduces you to how the MSA in Reading will look and what kinds of questions you may encounter. Look for tips and strategies in the blue boxes throughout this section.

Eyes of the Dragon

By Margaret Leaf

NARRATOR 1: Long ago in China, there was a little village. The villagers there were afraid of wild beasts and wild men. So the head of the village, the magistrate, persuaded them to build a wall all around the village.

NARRATOR 4: The wall was strong and high, with a gate that could be locked. Now everyone felt safe, and they all slept soundly at night.

NARRATOR 2: The magistrate was especially proud of the wall. Every evening, he walked all around the village to admire it.

MAGISTRATE: How clever I was to think of the wall, and how beautiful it is.

NARRATOR 3: But one evening he noticed that the wall had no decoration.

MAGISTRATE: Perhaps it is a little plain.

NARRATOR 1: The next morning, he called a meeting of the village elders.

MAGISTRATE: Our wall is very strong and protects us well. However, I have decided we should have it decorated.

> As you read, notice clues about genre. Dragons are creatures from legend.

ELDER: We should have a portrait of the Dragon King painted on our wall. He controls the thunder and lightning, and could bring us rain for our fields if he were pleased.

MAGISTRATE: Exactly what I have been thinking.

ELDER: Ch'en Jung, the most famous dragon painter, lives in the city. I will gladly go and ask him to come.

NARRATOR 4: It was settled, and the elder set out that same day.

NARRATOR 2: Three days later, two figures were spied approaching the village. The magistrate hurried to the gate.

NARRATOR 3: Ch'en Jung was riding a little horse with a big box tied on behind the saddle. The magistrate bowed to Ch'en Jung and then led him into the village.

CH'EN: Before I start, I want your promise that I may paint your dragon in my own manner and that you will accept it. You must also pay me forty silver coins.

MAGISTRATE: We agree to your conditions.

NARRATOR 1: Ch'en Jung then opened his box of paint and brushes, and started to work. He began on the left side of the gate, carefully drawing the dragon's tail.

NARRATOR 4: He painted steadily, for days and days. Everyone in the village watched whenever they could. And the magistrate, of course, watched all day, looking very important.

NARRATOR 2: Little by little, the long body of the dragon appeared on the wall.

NARRATOR 3: Finally, the painter reached the right side of the gate, and the dragon's head met his tail.

ELDER: The painting is magnificent!

CH'EN: Yes, the Heavenly King will be pleased. I have finished. I will now accept your payment.

MAGISTRATE: Forty silver coins is no small amount, Ch'en Jung. We must first look at your dragon, to make certain he is as he should be.

NARRATOR 1: Ch'en Jung consented. Starting at the tail, he led the magistrate around the wall, with the other villagers following.

NARRATOR 4: The dragon's body was covered with fiery red scales like those of a fish. The magistrate counted carefully to be sure there were just eighty-one scales in each row, because eighty-one is nine times nine, and nine is a lucky number.

CH'EN: You will notice the feet on each of the four legs. They have the paws of a tiger and the claws of a hawk. Of course, your dragon has four claws on each foot. Only the Emperor's dragon may have five.

NARRATOR 2: As they walked around the wall, the dragon's body was bigger and bigger. The scales along his back looked like a row of mountains.

> Notice how the author uses figurative language to convey the large size of the painting.

NARRATOR 3:	Finally, they arrived at the great head shaped like a camel's, with heavy, shaggy eyebrows, the horns of a deer, the ears of an ox, sharp tusks in the mouth, and a pointed beard with long, streaming bristles. Under his chin, a large pearl glistened with all the colors of the rainbow.
NARRATOR 1:	The dragon was so grand and beautiful that no one made a sound.
CH'EN:	Now, the money, please.
MAGISTRATE:	But, wait! You have not finished! The dragon has no eyes!
CH'EN:	It would be dangerous to paint eyes on this dragon. And you promised to accept him as I painted him.
ELDER:	(*to the magistrate*) I think we should listen to the painter. Surely he knows best.
MAGISTRATE:	(*to Ch'en Jung*) Our dragon must have eyes! The silver coins shall not leave my hand until you have painted them!
CH'EN:	Very well, if you insist—even though you are breaking your word. The consequences will be of your own making.
NARRATOR 4:	The painter quickly filled in the empty spaces beneath the shaggy eyebrows. Then he took the bag of coins from the magistrate, packed his paints and brushes onto his horse, and left.
NARRATOR 2:	As the villagers stood and admired the dragon,
ELDER:	Look!
NARRATOR 2:	The newly painted eyes began to glow more and more brightly, as though there were fire within. A wisp of smoke curled up from the wide-open nostrils, and the scales began to glisten.
NARRATOR 3:	A great black cloud climbed the sky, and the wind began to howl.
NARRATOR 1:	Suddenly,
ELDER:	He moved!
NARRATOR 1:	The dragon shook himself, and little cracks appeared in the wall.
NARRATOR 4:	The black cloud moved overhead, lightning zigzagged across the sky, and there was a loud clap of thunder.
NARRATOR 2:	The dragon shook himself again. Then, with a scream, it rose into the air and disappeared into the black cloud.
NARRATOR 3:	The wall crumbled and fell in pieces.
CH'EN:	(*in the distance*) Hurry, my horse, hurry! Those fools, those fools!

The italicized text inside the parentheses contributes to the meaning of what's happening. In plays, this text feature is called a stage direction. Playwrights often use a different type style, such as italics, to distinguish stage directions from the dialogue.

(1) What is the conflict between the magistrate and Ch'en Jung?
   A. Ch'en Jung does not finish the dragon painting.
   B. The magistrate does not like the dragon painting.
   C. The magistrate wants Ch'en Jung to paint eyes on the dragon.
   D. Ch'en Jung wants more money to paint the eyes on the dragon.

Objective: 3.A.3.b Analyze the conflict and the events of the plot.

Strategy: Review details from the passage where the magistrate and Ch'en Jung disagree. Ch'en Jung finishes the painting according to the agreement, so answer choice *A* is not correct. Answer choice *B* is incorrect because Narrator 1 states the "dragon was so grand and beautiful that no one made a sound." Answer choice *D* is also incorrect because Ch'en Jung does not ask for more money. The conflict between the magistrate and Ch'en Jung is about the eyes on the dragon. The correct answer is choice *C*.

(2) What is the theme of this story?
   A. Artists need privacy to be creative.
   B. Walls make people feel safe.
   C. People long ago were superstitious.
   D. A person should not break a promise.

Objective: 3.A.6.a Analyze main ideas and universal themes.

Strategy: To answer this question correctly, ask yourself what message about life or people the author wants to convey. You can eliminate answer choice *A* because there is no evidence in the text to support that idea. The artist works just fine with everyone watching him. Answer choices *B* and *C* are not correct because they are not main ideas in the story. The legend is not about superstitions or walls, but about a painting and a broken promise. The correct answer is *D*. The painter warns that the broken promise will have great consequences, and the story shows that to be true.

(3) Which genre *best* describes the passage?

   A. Essay
   B. Poetry
   C. Folklore
   D. Nonfiction

Objective: 3.A.3.a
Distinguish among types of narrative texts.

Strategy: "Eyes of the Dragon" is an imaginative passage about a painting that comes to life. Answer choices *A* and *D* refer to nonfiction genres, so they cannot be correct. There is poetic language in the passage, but the lines are not in verse, so answer choice *B* is not the *best* answer. The correct answer is choice *C*.

(4) In "Eyes of the Dragon," the author uses parentheses and italics to

   A. show details not described in the narrative
   B. indicate the titles of books and magazines
   C. avoid using capital letters
   D. quote information from a different source

Objective: 3.A.2.a Analyze text features that contribute to meaning.

Strategy: Review the paragraphs that include parentheses and italics. Italics are commonly used for book and magazine titles, but there are no titles in this passage, so answer choice *B* is not correct. Similarly, parentheses may contain unpunctuated text and are often used for quotes from other sources. However, neither case is true for this passage, so answer choices *C* and *D* are also incorrect. The author uses this feature to show details not included in the narrative, such as *(in the distance)*. The correct answer is choice *A*.

(5) Read the last sentence from the passage and answer the following question.

CH'EN: (*in the distance*) Hurry, my horse, hurry! Those fools, those fools!

According to Ch'en, the fools are *most likely* the _____ .

A. painter
B. villagers
C. wild men
D. narrators

Objective: 1.E.4.c Draw inferences and/or conclusions and make generalizations.

Strategy: Read the question carefully; one answer is better than the others. Ch'en is the painter and he is not referring to himself, so answer choice *A* is incorrect. Answer choice *C* is unlikely because the wild men are not developed characters in the passage. The narrators are not characters at all; Ch'en would not refer to them, so answer choice *D* is also incorrect. Answer choice *B* is correct because the term "villagers" includes the elders and the magistrate.

(6) Summarize what happens in "Eyes of the Dragon." Use details from the passage to support your answer.

Rubric:

Score	Response
3	**The response demonstrates an understanding of the complexities of the text.** • Addresses the demands of the question • Effectively uses text-relevant information to clarify or extend understanding
2	**The response demonstrates a general understanding of the text.** • Partially addresses the demands of the question • Uses text-relevant information to show understanding
1	**The response demonstrates a minimal understanding of the text.** • Minimally addresses the demands of the question • Uses minimal information to show some understanding of the text in relation to the question
0	**The response is completely incorrect, irrelevant to the question, or missing.**

Objective: 1.E.4.e
Summarize or paraphrase.

Strategy: When you summarize a story, make sure you understand the difference between important actions and minor details. It is important to mention, for example, that the painter did not paint the dragon's eyes, but it is not necessary to mention the number and color of the dragon's scales or other details of its appearance.

(7) Describe how the author sets the tone in paragraphs 39–40. Include information from the passage to support your description.

Rubric:

Score	Response
3	**The response demonstrates an understanding of the complexities of the text.** • Addresses the demands of the question • Effectively uses text-relevant information to clarify or extend understanding
2	**The response demonstrates a general understanding of the text.** • Partially addresses the demands of the question • Uses text-relevant information to show understanding
1	**The response demonstrates a minimal understanding of the text.** • Minimally addresses the demands of the question • Uses minimal information to show some understanding of the text in relation to the question
0	**The response is completely incorrect, irrelevant to the question, or missing.**

Objective: 3.A.7.d Analyze imagery that contributes to meaning and/or creates style.

Strategy: To answer this question, reread paragraphs 39–40. They include descriptions of terrible beauty and comparisons to fire and storms. Think about the images, and then write about the emotional tone they create. Your response could include how you might feel if you were one of the villagers watching this occur.

Barbara Jordan

Lawyer and U.S. Representative

From 1972 to 1978, Barbara Jordan served as congresswoman for Texas's 18th district. She was the first African-American woman that the Deep South sent to Congress.

> As you read, notice facts and details that seem important.

▶ Barbara Jordan (1936–1996) grew up in an African-American neighborhood in Houston, Texas. She became the first African American elected to serve in the Texas state senate since 1883. Jordan also became the first African-American woman from the Deep South to serve in the U.S. Congress.

> It is important to notice how an author uses setting and background information. Consider how these details support the main idea.

▶ 2 When Jordan was growing up, opportunities for women were limited, and there was widespread discrimination against African Americans. In the South, segregation by race was still sanctioned by law. From grade school through college, Jordan received her education at all African-American schools. The ambitious young Texan doubted that the system would change any time soon. Even so, at Phillis Wheatley

> Notice that action verbs can help show people's motives.

▶ High School, Jordan decided she wanted to become a lawyer—though at the time she "had no fixed notion of what that was."

Entering the White World In 1954, Jordan was in her junior year at Texas Southern University. That year, the Supreme Court decided, in the case *Brown v. Board of Education of Topeka*, that separate was not equal when it came to education. But change came slowly.

When traveling in the South, Jordan's college debate team had to pack their own food and stay at black motels. Her coach recalled that in the North "we didn't eat at any fancy restaurants...But we could at least go in front doors to get something to eat."

Jordan left Texas to attend Boston University Law School. Jordan and Issie Shelton, a fellow Texan, were the only two black women among six first-year women students. Breaking

In law school, students usually *earn* law degrees, but the author says that Barbara Jordon *won* her law degree. Be sure to notice when authors choose language that helps you understand important emotions and events.

into the white, male world of law school was not easy. Jordan realized that "the best training available in an all-black...university was not equal." Jordan and Shelton rose to the challenge. Within three years, they had <u>won</u> their law degrees.

A Career in Politics After graduating, Jordan returned to Texas. In 1960, she volunteered to work for the election campaign of Democrats John F. Kennedy and Lyndon B. Johnson. At first, she addressed envelopes and licked stamps. But one night, Jordan had to fill in for a speaker who was ill. Jordan was a gifted speaker. "Right after that," she recalled, "they took me off licking and addressing."

7 After her work on the Kennedy campaign, Jordan entered politics. In 1966, she was elected state senator. Reporters were curious to see how an African-American woman would manage in this white-male stronghold. "As it turned out," Jordan said, "the Capitol stayed on its foundations and the star didn't fall off the top."

Jordan won a seat in the U.S. House of Representatives in 1972.

Just as she had once campaigned for him, former President Lyndon B. Johnson now returned the favor. LBJ said, "Wherever [Barbara Jordan] goes she is going to be at the top."

Jordan served on the House Judiciary Committee that held hearings on the impeachment of President Richard M. Nixon. In the course of the 1974 hearings, she delivered a speech on the Constitution that drew the world's admiration.

After serving three terms in the U.S. House of Representatives, Jordan returned to Texas. She later suffered from multiple sclerosis. Even so, she refused to let the crippling disease keep her from public service. Instead, she spoke from a wheelchair.

As head of the U.S. Commission on Immigration Reform in 1995, Jordan asked Congress not to deny citizenship to children born in the United States to illegal immigrants. "It was immigration that taught us, it does not matter where you came from, or who your parents were, what counts is who you are." Barbara Jordan died in January 1996.

As you read, look for information that the author includes in order to show a main idea. Here, the author wants readers to know that Barbara Jordan was important to a former president of the United States.

(8) What is the main idea of this passage?
A. Jordan became an important government official despite many obstacles in her path.
B. Jordan and Issie Shelton were pioneering students at Boston University Law School.
C. Jordan had an informed and opinionated view of the leaders who wrote the Constitution.
D. Jordan's career began with campaign work for John F. Kennedy and Lyndon B. Johnson.

Objective: 2.A.4.c State and support main ideas and messages.

Strategy: To answer this question correctly, review important details that you notice as you read. Answer choices *B*, *C*, and *D* all state an idea from a portion of the passage, but these are not main ideas because their focus is too narrow. They do not appear elsewhere in the passage and are not supported by other information. The correct answer is choice *A* because it is the overall message of the passage.

(9) Read these sentences from paragraph 7 of the passage.

In 1966, she was elected state senator. Reporters were curious to see how an African-American woman would manage in this white-male <u>stronghold</u>.

The author uses the word <u>stronghold</u> to emphasize the
A. kind nature of the political reporters
B. large salaries of many politicians
C. obstacles Jordan might encounter
D. intellectual power of state senators

Objective: 2.A.5.a Analyze specific word choice that contributes to the meaning and/or creates style.

Strategy: Other words and ideas offer clues to the meaning of this word in the sentence. The passage says that "reporters were curious" about how she would manage. "This white-male stronghold" describes the Senate, not the reporters. The passage does not compare Jordan's salary to other salaries, and her intellectual power is not in question. The author uses *stronghold* to emphasize the contrast between Jordan and the other senators, so the correct answer is choice *C*.

(10) Based on the information in the passage, the reader can conclude that

    A. Jordan studied immigration laws against her better judgment

    B. Jordan fiercely opposed the views of Lyndon B. Johnson

    C. Jordan earned her law degree one year before Issie Shelton

    D. Jordan used a wheelchair due to the effects of multiple sclerosis

Objective: 1.E.4.c Draw inferences and/or conclusions and make generalizations.

Strategy: Review important details from the passage. In the last paragraph, the quote shows Jordan's personal belief in favor of immigration reform, so answer choice *A* is not correct. You can immediately rule out answer choice *B* because the passage states that Barbara Jordan volunteered to work on Johnson's campaign. The passage also states that Jordan and Shelton won their law degrees together, so answer choice *C* is not correct. The correct answer is choice *D*.

(11) Read this sentence from paragraph 2 of the passage. Then choose the word that means the same as the underlined word.

In the South, segregation by race was still <u>sanctioned</u> by law.

<u>Sanctioned</u> means _____ .

    A. forgotten

    B. approved

    C. opposed

    D. mistaken

Objective: 1.D.3.a Use context to determine the meanings of words.

Strategy: Pay close attention to other words and clues in the sentence that can help you understand the word *sanctioned*. The adverb *still* implies that a situation has been going on already and has not ended, so it probably has not been forgotten. In the past, segregation had not been opposed, so it could not still be opposed. The sentence does not make sense if you try reading it with "mistaken" in place of *sanctioned*. Therefore, the correct answer is choice *B*.

(12) The author describes Barbara Jordan as ambitious in setting goals for her education. What information from the passage supports this description of Jordan?

Rubric:

Score	Response
3	**The response demonstrates an understanding of the complexities of the text.** • Addresses the demands of the question • Effectively uses text-relevant information to clarify or extend understanding
2	**The response demonstrates a general understanding of the text.** • Partially addresses the demands of the question • Uses text-relevant information to show understanding
1	**The response demonstrates a minimal understanding of the text.** • Minimally addresses the demands of the question • Uses minimal information to show some understanding of the text in relation to the question
0	**The response is completely incorrect, irrelevant to the question, or missing.**

Objective: 2.A.4.b Identify and explain the author's argument, viewpoint, or perspective.

Strategy: To answer this question correctly, pay close attention to details in the paragraphs that describe how and where Jordan earned her education. Consider which details support the author's description of her as "an ambitious young Texan."

(13) The author includes many reasons for Barbara Jordan's success. Evaluate whether the success was due *mostly* to good luck or *mostly* to personal courage. Include information from the passage and your own ideas to support your opinion.

Rubric:

Score	Response
3	**The response demonstrates an understanding of the complexities of the text.** • Addresses the demands of the question • Effectively uses text-relevant information to clarify or extend understanding
2	**The response demonstrates a general understanding of the text.** • Partially addresses the demands of the question • Uses text-relevant information to show understanding
1	**The response demonstrates a minimal understanding of the text.** • Minimally addresses the demands of the question • Uses minimal information to show some understanding of the text in relation to the question
0	**The response is completely incorrect, irrelevant to the question, or missing.**

Objective: 2.A.4.g
Synthesize ideas from text.

Strategy: To answer this question, review the passage and look for examples that suggest either that Barbara Jordan's success was due to good luck, or that it was due to personal courage. Based on your review, clearly state whether you think Barbara Jordan's success was due to good luck or to personal courage. Include lines from the passage in your response, and explain how they support your opinion.

George Washington Middle School
Grade 7 Spring Olympics Information Packet

Morning Events

8:00 A.M. — Opening Ceremonies (Auditorium)
Opening Remarks:
"Fit and Healthy For Life"
Mr. John Wolf, Principal

8:30 A.M. — Event Rotation*

Event Name:	Jump Rope Challenge (Gymnasium)	Obstacle Course (Athletic Field**)	50-Yard-Dash (Front Quad**)	Water Balloon Relay (Lunchroom)	Book Break (Media Center)
Session 1	Red Team	Orange Team	Yellow Team	Green Team	Blue Team
Session 2	Blue Team	Red Team	Orange Team	Yellow Team	Green Team
Session 3	Green Team	Blue Team	Red Team	Orange Team	Yellow Team
Session 4	Yellow Team	Green Team	Blue Team	Red Team	Orange Team
Session 5	Orange Team	Yellow Team	Green Team	Blue Team	Red Team

11:00 A.M. — Closing Ceremonies and Awards (Athletic Field**)

12:00 P.M. — Picnic Lunch on Athletic Field**

1:00 P.M. — Early Dismissal

Event Descriptions:

Jump Rope Challenge

Students will compete to see who can jump rope the longest. A special "Jump to It" winner will be awarded.

Obstacle Course

Science teachers created a course of climbing, running, and sliding. A "Rabbit" award will be given to the student who completes the course first!

50-Yard-Dash

English teachers will oversee four heats of foot races. Winners will compete against each other for the "School Swifty" award.

Water Balloon Relay

Try not to be "washed up" as the Math squad creates a wet and wild relay through the lunchroom. Team and individual awards will be presented.

Book Break

Ms. Clarkson will give students some rest and relaxation in between events. Students will have a chance to enjoy healthful treats—for body and mind!

Row and column labels can help you easily find information.

Pay close attention to features such as asterisks because they may lead you to more information.

* Each session will last 30 minutes. The start and end of each session will be noted over the loudspeaker.

** In the case of rain, these events will move to the Auditorium. The Picnic Lunch will take place in the Lunchroom.

Spring Olympics Team Assignments

Students will be divided up by last name and assigned to the teams listed below. There will be no team trades or substitutions. Coaches will take roll at each station.

Red Team	Orange Team	Yellow Team	Green Team	Blue Team
Coaches: Mr. Gregory Ms. Franco	Coach: Ms. Castellano Mr. Engle	Coach: Ms. Alexander Mr. Obisho	Coach: Mr. Seo Ms. Tangste	Coach: Ms. Assaf Mr. Gatsby
A–E	F–J	K–O	P–T	U–Z

Important Considerations for Our Spring Olympics Athletes

> Notice how the author uses a bulleted list to organize and highlight this information.

- Students should wear comfortable athletic shoes.
- Students should wear layered athletic clothing and plenty of sunscreen.
- Students should bring a water bottle to stay hydrated throughout the day.
- Students should leave all backpacks and school supplies in their lockers.
- Students should NOT bring lunches. Healthy sack lunches will be provided for all students.
- Participation in the Spring Olympics is part of our school's physical education program. Students who are unable to participate should bring a signed parent letter to their homeroom teacher by the morning of the event. Students who cannot participate physically will still be expected to cheer on their classmates during the event.

(14) According to the Spring Olympics Team Assignments, a student with the last name of Murray would be found on the

A. Orange Team
B. Yellow Team
C. Green Team
D. Blue Team

Objective: 2.A.1.b Read, use, and identify the characteristics of workplace and other real-world documents.

Strategy: A student with the last name of Murray would fall into the K–O team assignment. Answer choice A is incorrect because the Orange Team has students with last names that begin with F–J. The Green Team has students with names that begin with P–T, and the Blue Team has students with names that begin with U–Z, so answer choices C and D are also incorrect. Since the Yellow Team has students with last names that begin with K–O, the correct answer is choice B.

(15) After the Book Break, the Blue Team will go to the

A. Jump Rope Challenge
B. Obstacle Course
C. 50-Yard-Dash
D. Water Balloon Relay

Objective: 2.A.3.c Use organizational pattern to locate specific information.

Strategy: Look at the schedule of events. The Blue Team is in the Book Break for session 1. Look in the next row to find the event the Blue Team will go to for session 2. Answer choice B is incorrect because the Blue Team does the Obstacle Course in session 3. The Blue Team will be in the 50-Yard-Dash in session 4, so answer choice C is also incorrect. Answer choice D is incorrect because the Blue Team will be part of the Water Balloon Relay during the last session. The Jump Rope Challenge is the next event for the Blue Team, so the correct answer is choice A.

(16) According to the Event Rotation, session 3 will begin at
   A. 9:00 A.M.
   B. 9:30 A.M.
   C. 10:00 A.M.
   D. 10:30 A.M.

Objective: 2.A.2.c Analyze informational aids that contribute to meaning.

Strategy: Look for information related to the Event Rotation heading. The passage says the rotations will begin at 8:30 A.M., and the first footnote states each session will last 30 minutes. Answer choice A is incorrect because that is when session 2 begins. Session 4 begins at 10:00 A.M. so answer choice C is not correct. Answer choice D gives the start time for session 5, not session 3. The correct answer is choice B.

(17) The author's purpose for writing this passage is *most likely* to
   A. explain to parents why the school was holding a special event
   B. provide rules and directions for early dismissal from the event
   C. supply teachers with a list of equipment and policies for the event
   D. inform students about the schedule and expectations for the event

Objective: 2.A.4.a Identify and explain the author's/text's purpose and intended audience.

Strategy: Think about who would be *most likely* to use this passage. It includes a schedule and team assignments for the event. Answer choice A is incorrect because the passage does not provide any information to parents about why the event is being held. Similarly, the passage does not include any rules or directions for early dismissal other than the time, so answer choice B is also incorrect. Answer choice C is incorrect because there is no list of equipment and policies for teachers. This passage is *most likely* intended for students because it informs them about what to expect at the event. The correct answer is choice D.

(18) Under which heading would a reader find information describing the Book Break?

    A. Event Rotation

    B. Closing Ceremonies and Awards

    C. Event Descriptions

    D. Spring Olympics Team Assignments

Objective: 1.E.4.b Identify and explain information directly stated in text.

Strategy: Review the passage to find a description of the Book Break. Answer choice *A* has information about *when* the Book Break takes place for each team, but not about *what* it is, so choice *A* is incorrect. Answer choices *B* and *D* do not contain any information about the Book Break and are both incorrect. The boxes under Event Descriptions include information about every event. The correct answer is choice *C*.

(19) Read the heading from the passage.

Important <u>Considerations</u> for Our Spring Olympics Athletes

<u>Considerations</u> means _____ .

    A. events

    B. matters

    C. schedules

    D. organizers

Objective: 1.D.2.b Explain relationships between and among words.

Strategy: Look for the heading in the passage, and read the bullet points under it. They list several things that students need to think about before participating. Answer choice *A* is incorrect because the bullet points do not describe events. The bullet points do not refer to schedules, so answer choice *C* is also incorrect. Answer choice *D* is not correct because the bullet points do not mention the organizers of the Spring Olympics. The bullet points are about important matters and issues that students should keep in mind for the Spring Olympics. The correct answer is choice *B*.

Life

By Paul Laurence Dunbar

A crust of bread and a corner to sleep in,
A minute to smile and an hour to weep in,
A pint of joy to a peck of trouble,
And never a laugh but the moans come double;
5   And that is life!

A crust and a corner that love makes precious,
With a smile to warm and the tears to refresh us;
And joy seems sweeter when cares come after,
And a moan is the finest of foils for laughter;
10   And that is life!

> Writers of prose use paragraphs to tell readers that a new idea is coming, and poets use stanzas in the same way.

> Use context clues to help you determine the meaning of unfamiliar words, such as *foils*. Poets may make comparisons that help readers understand new words.

Sea Fever

By John Masefield

I must go down to the seas again, to the lonely sea
      and the sky,
And all I ask is a tall ship and a star to steer her by,
And the wheel's kick and the wind's song and the
5   white sail's shaking,
      And a gray mist on the sea's face, and a gray
      dawn breaking.

I must go down to the seas again, for the call of the
      running tide
10   Is a wild call and a clear call that may not be denied;
      And all I ask is a windy day with the white clouds
      flying,
      And the flung spray and the blown spume, and
      the sea-gulls crying.

15   I must go down to the seas again, to the vagrant
      gypsy life,
      To the gull's way and the whale's way where the
      wind's like a whetted knife;
      And all I ask is a merry yarn from a laughing
20   fellow-rover,
      And quiet sleep and a sweet dream when the long

> Poets use sound to emphasize words and ideas and to create a musical quality. Notice the repetition of the *w* sound in these lines.

trick's over.

(20) Read line 9 of "Life" below.

And a moan is the finest of foils for laughter;

<u>Foils</u> means_____.
A. greetings
B. contrasts
C. complements
D. remedies

Objective: 3.A.4.b Analyze language and structural features to determine meaning.

Strategy: Think about the relationship between a moan and laughter. They represent two opposite emotions. Replace the word *foils* with each of the answer choices, then choose the answer that fits within the context of the line. Answer choices *A* and *C* are incorrect. A moan is neither the finest greeting for laughter nor is it a complement to laughter. Answer choice *D* is not correct because in general, no remedy is required for laughter. A moan and laughter are opposites, and opposites contrast. The correct answer is choice *B*.

(21) Read line 3 of "Life" and complete the sentence below.

"A pint of joy to a peck of trouble" means life contains
A. more unhappiness than happiness
B. more happiness than unhappiness
C. equal amounts of joy and trouble
D. nothing but trouble

Objective: 3.A.7.c Analyze figurative language that contributes to meaning and/or creates style.

Strategy: Most readers will probably not be familiar with the word "peck" as it is used in the poem. Think about the main idea of the poem, and how the poet compares the amounts of joy and trouble. Answer choice *B* describes more joy than trouble, and answer choice *C* describes equal amounts, so both are incorrect. Answer choice *D* describes all trouble and no joy, so it is also incorrect. Therefore, the correct answer is choice *A*.

(22) Read lines 4 and 5 of "Sea Fever" below.

And the wheel's kick and the wind's song and the
white sail's shaking,

These lines contain an example of which sound element?

A. Rhyme

B. Assonance

C. Alliteration

D. Onomatopoeia

Objective: 3.A.4.c Analyze sound elements of poetry that contribute to meaning.

Strategy: Note the repetition of the *w* sound. Rhyme and assonance (near or partial rhyme) are not present in these lines, so answer choices *A* and *B* are incorrect. The words do not sound like the things they represent, so answer choice *D* is also incorrect. The repetition of initial consonant sounds is called alliteration. Answer choice *C* is correct.

(23) "Life" and "Sea Fever" describe how each speaker looks at life. Compare or contrast the main ideas of the speakers in these two poems. Include examples from both poems to support your response.

Rubric:

Score	Response
3	**The response demonstrates an understanding of the complexities of the text.** • Addresses the demands of the question • Effectively uses text-relevant information to clarify or extend understanding
2	**The response demonstrates a general understanding of the text.** • Partially addresses the demands of the question • Uses text-relevant information to show understanding
1	**The response demonstrates a minimal understanding of the text.** • Minimally addresses the demands of the question • Uses minimal information to show some understanding of the text in relation to the question
0	**The response is completely incorrect, irrelevant to the question, or missing.**

Objective: 3.A.6.b Analyze similar themes across multiple texts.

Strategy: A comparison describes how two things are alike; a contrast shows how they are different. To answer this question, begin by identifying the main idea of each poem. Find examples from the poems that illustrate the main ideas. Then describe how the main ideas are alike or different, using the examples to support you answer.

(24) Some critics believe the main message in "Life" and "Sea Fever" is that hardships help people to appreciate life more. Explain whether you agree or disagree with this viewpoint. Use information from both poems and your own ideas to support your response.

Rubric:

Score	Response
3	**The response demonstrates an understanding of the complexities of the text.** • Addresses the demands of the question • Effectively uses text-relevant information to clarify or extend understanding
2	**The response demonstrates a general understanding of the text.** • Partially addresses the demands of the question • Uses text-relevant information to show understanding
1	**The response demonstrates a minimal understanding of the text.** • Minimally addresses the demands of the question • Uses minimal information to show some understanding of the text in relation to the question
0	**The response is completely incorrect, irrelevant to the question, or missing.**

Objective: 3.A.6.a Analyze main ideas and universal themes.

Strategy: To answer this question, review both passages and look for lines that emphasize either happiness or hardship. Based on your review, state whether you agree or disagree with the viewpoint that hardships make people appreciate life more. Include lines from the poems that support your position in your response.

(25) Choose the word that means the same, or about the same, as the underlined word.

The athlete followed a <u>strict</u> routine.

<u>Strict</u> means _____ .
A. firm
B. detailed
C. weekly
D. complicated

Objective: 1.D.2.b Explain relationships between and among words.

Strategy: Words that mean the same are synonyms. The word *strict* can mean either "stern" or "exact." Answer choices *B, C,* and *D* do not fall within either definition. The correct answer is choice *A*.

(26) Choose the word that means the opposite, or nearly the opposite, of the underlined word.

A <u>violent</u> reaction is the opposite of a(n) _____ reaction.
A. mean
B. angry
C. intense
D. peaceful

Objective: 1.D.2.b. Explain relationships between and among words.

Strategy: This question is asking for a word that means the opposite (antonym) of the word *violent.* The word *violent* can mean "vicious" or "strong." Answer choices *A* and *B* are similar to "vicious." Answer choice *C* can mean the same thing as "strong." "Peaceful" means "calm." It is not part of either definition and does not belong with the other three choices. The correct answer is choice *D*.

(27) Read the sentence below, and then answer the question that follows.

The student felt <u>tense</u> during the spelling bee.

In which sentence does the word <u>tense</u> mean the same thing as in the sentence above?

A. The balloon string pulled <u>tense</u> in the wind.
B. The reporter wrote the article in present <u>tense</u>.
C. The mood was <u>tense</u> in the school gymnasium.
D. The verb <u>tense</u> showed when the contest happened.

Objective: 1.D.3.a Use context to determine the meanings of words.

Strategy: Think about multiple meanings for the word *tense*. It can mean "tight" or "nervous," or it can be a reference to grammar. The sentence in question uses the second definition: "nervous." Answer choice *A* uses the word as if it means "tight," which is incorrect. Answer choices *B* and *D* refer to grammar and are also incorrect. The correct answer is choice *C*.

(28) Choose the word which correctly completes both sentences below.

The choir sang the _____ twice.

Please _____ from talking during the program.

A. cease
B. refrain
C. persist
D. anthem

Objective: 1.D.3.a Use context to determine the meanings of words.

Strategy: Some answers may have unfamiliar words with multiple meanings. Read the sentences for clues. The first sentence includes *the* before the blank, so the correct answer must be a noun. The second sentence needs a verb in order to make sense. Answer choice *A* is a verb and completes the second sentence only, so choice *A* is incorrect. "Persist" does not make sense with either sentence, so answer choice *C* is not correct. Answer choice *D* is incorrect because it only makes sense with the first sentence. A refrain is a noun that means "part of a song" and also a verb that means "to avoid doing." The correct answer is choice *B*.

(29) Read the sentence below, and then choose the correct definition.

The school <u>re</u>cycles all glass and plastic containers.

In the word <u>re</u>cycles, <u>re</u> means _____ .

A. down
B. under
C. again
D. never

Objective: 1.D.3.b Use word structure to determine the meanings of words.

Strategy: To answer this question correctly, think about what it means to recycle. To recycle means "to reuse" or "use again." Answer choices *A* (cycles down), *B* (cycles under), and *D* (cycles never) do not make sense in the sentence. The meaning of the word *recycles* means "cycles again." The correct answer is choice *C*.

(30) Read the sentence below, and then complete the sentence about the underlined word.

The state of Maryland is in the northern <u>hemisphere</u>.
The word <u>hemisphere</u> includes the _____ .

A. prefix <u>hemi</u> and the suffix <u>sphere</u>
B. suffix <u>hemi</u> and the prefix <u>sphere</u>
C. base word <u>hemi</u> and the suffix <u>sphere</u>
D. prefix <u>hemi</u> and the base word <u>sphere</u>

Objective: 1.D.3.b Use word structure to determine the meanings of words.

Strategy: To answer this question correctly, break the word *hemisphere* into two parts: hemi and sphere. Prefixes and suffixes are word parts that don't make sense on their own. Base words have complete meanings when used by themselves. *Sphere* is a complete word, not a prefix or suffix, so answer choices *A*, *B*, and *C* are incorrect. The correct answer is choice *D*.

The Power of Ideas

INTRODUCING THE ESSENTIALS

- Literary Genres Workshop
- Reading Strategies Workshop
- Writing Process Workshop

1

About the Art The images on this page are (clockwise from top right) a still image from the feature film *Back to the Future* (see page 151), a photograph of the "Tribute in Light" commemorating September 11 (see page 550), and an illustration by Leo and Diane Dillon for Virginia Hamilton's *The People Could Fly* (see page 483).

For help using this Introductory Unit, see

R RESOURCE MANAGER—Introductory Unit
p. 1

What Are Life's Big Questions?

This page will help you introduce students to the concept of **key ideas** and how they can be explored in literature. Use approaches such as these to stimulate students' thinking about ideas:

- As a class, define the word *idea*. You might begin by listing several concrete concepts and asking what idea connects all of them.

Concrete concepts	Idea
• A parent works long hours to make money to care for his or her family.	love
• A teenager spends a whole weekend making a special gift for a friend.	
• A child hugs a puppy and pets it gently.	

Lead the class to conclude that an idea is an abstract concept that allows people to see patterns and connections in the concrete world of things and actions.

- Remind students of the title of this unit, **The Power of Ideas.** Ask: How can ideas have power? *(Possible answers: Ideas are powerful tools for thinking about the world. Ideas can also influence the way people act and feel.)*

- Challenge students to think of powerful ideas that have had an impact on history, society, and their own lives.

Read aloud the introductory paragraph on this page. Ask students if they have read stories, poems, or works of nonfiction that have helped them answer important questions in their lives. Then explain that because certain universal issues affect many people, authors often explore those themes and offer their own interpretations and answers.

Have students take turns reading aloud the **Big Questions** on these pages. Discuss with students their first thoughts and reactions to each one. Then explain that these questions span cultures and historical time periods, applying to people in all places and eras.

The Power of Ideas

What Are Life's Big Questions?

We all wrestle with the big questions in life, including the ones shown here. That's because such questions prompt us to think about key ideas—for example, love, growing up, and loss—that affect all our lives, no matter who we are or where we come from. Through our experiences, we come closer to answering these questions, making sense of the world, and understanding ourselves. But powerful literature holds some answers too.

What is COURAGE?

Courage helps people face big challenges, such as protecting their families or fighting life-threatening illnesses. It can also take courage to do something small, like talk to someone who intimidates you. This book is filled with brave characters—among them a pet mongoose and a shy seventh grader—who can teach you what true courage is.

Is life always FAIR?

If you've ever single-handedly lost a team championship or gotten blamed for something that wasn't your fault, you've probably realized that life can feel completely unfair. Read Ernest Lawrence Thayer's poem "Casey at the Bat" or Chaim Potok's story "Zebra," and you'll discover that you're not alone in feeling this way.

Introductory Unit Resources

 RESOURCE MANAGER
Note Taking pp. 2–4

BEST PRACTICES TOOLKIT

Graphic Organizers/Strategies
Venn Diagram • Jigsaw • Read Aloud/Think Aloud • Making Inferences • Story Map

Reading Support
Audio Anthology CD*

Technology
ClassZone.com

---

* Resources for Differentiation

After the class has discussed the questions on pages 2 and 3, have students think of other **Big Questions.** Explain that every lesson in this anthology will begin with a **Big Question** that will allow them to explore important ideas in depth and make connections between the literature and their own lives.

Where is HOME?

"Home is where the heart is," as the old saying goes. The place you call home doesn't have to be the house where you live. Rather, home can be wherever you feel most comfortable and secure. Think about all the places that people might call home—for example, a certain country or a hiding place that nobody else knows about. Then ask yourself: Where is home?

Can we achieve the IMPOSSIBLE?

In many Hollywood action movies, the hero emerges victorious despite impossible odds. Some stories in this book star real-life heroes whose astonishing achievements can make us believe that anything is possible. However, tales as ancient as Greek myths warn us about what can happen if we set our sights too high. Is the impossible really within our reach?

- understand the types and characteristics of different literary genres
- become familiar with the academic vocabulary used to write about and discuss literature

The Genres

Determine Readiness Read the introductory paragraphs aloud and review the genres in the chart. To determine students' level of readiness, have them turn to these selections and classify each one:

- "The Monsters Are Due on Maple Street," page 138 *(drama)*
- *Exploring the* Titanic, page 100 *(nonfiction)*
- "Casey at the Bat," page 130 *(poetry)*
- *Back to the Future,* described on pages 150–151 *(media; feature film)*
- "The Last Dog," page 44 *(fiction)*

Discuss the characteristics of each selection that help reveal its genre.

Discuss and Review Ask students to cite other examples of each genre. To prompt them, you might display some titles from last year's anthology, such as "All Summer in a Day" *(fiction),* "The Dog of Pompeii" *(nonfiction),* and "I'm Nobody! Who Are You?" *(poetry).* Point out how different genres allow writers and readers to explore ideas through a variety of approaches and perspectives.

If students need help . . . Have them use the note-taking frame for this unit to help them focus on important ideas.

R RESOURCE MANAGER—Copy Master
Note Taking pp. 2–4

Literary Genres Workshop

Exploring Ideas in Literature

The big questions in life are not easy to answer, but that doesn't stop people from trying. For centuries, writers have searched for answers to such questions, exploring their ideas through stories, poems, and plays. As readers, we turn to literature to understand how others see the world and to learn about ourselves.

The Genres

Literature includes a variety of genres, including the ones shown here. Some are meant to be read; others are meant to be performed. Formats such as blockbuster movies and advertisements are not what you would expect to find in a literature book. They are important to analyze, though, since they communicate many ideas and messages in today's world.

In this book you will explore questions and ideas in many genres. By reading everything from dramas and newspaper articles to poetry and short stories, you will be able to discuss and write about such key ideas as survival and happiness. First, review the characteristics of each genre.

GENRES AT A GLANCE

FICTION
Fiction refers to made-up stories about characters and events.
- short stories
- novels
- novellas
- folk tales

POETRY
Poetry is a type of literature in which words are chosen and arranged in a compact, precise way to create specific effects.
- haiku
- limericks
- narrative poems

DRAMA
Dramas are stories that are meant to be performed.
- comedies
- historical dramas
- teleplays

NONFICTION
Nonfiction tells about real people, places, and events.
- autobiographies
- essays
- news articles
- biographies
- speeches
- feature articles

TYPES OF MEDIA

The word *media* refers to communication that reaches many people.
- feature films
- advertising
- news media

4   THE POWER OF IDEAS

DIFFERENTIATED INSTRUCTION

FOR LESS–PROFICIENT READERS

Concept Support Use a chart to help students classify the information on this page. Have students fill out their own copies, and instruct them to add examples of each genre.

> Genres—major kinds of literature or communication

| Fiction | Poetry | Drama | Nonfiction | Media |

| short story | novel | novella | folk tale |

FOR ENGLISH LEARNERS

Vocabulary: Cognates Point out that students who speak Spanish can use their knowledge of cognates to understand these key terms: *fiction (ficción), drama (drama),* and *communication (communicación).* Encourage students to look for other cognates as they read the text.

FICTION

Whether it is a book by your favorite author or a story that your friend invented, a work of fiction starts as an idea in someone's imagination. Sometimes fiction is also inspired by real people and events.

A good work of fiction keeps readers interested by weaving together many elements. These elements include **plot** (the action of the story), **characters** (the persons or animals involved in the action), **setting** (where and when the action takes place), and **theme** (the big idea behind the story—what the story is *really* about). Three types of fiction are short stories, novels, and novellas.

- A **short story** is a brief work of fiction that can usually be read in one sitting. It often focuses on a single event or a few main characters.
- A **novel** is a much longer work of fiction that can take several days or even weeks to read. Because they are longer than short stories, novels have room to develop more complex characters and plots.
- A **novella** is longer than a short story but shorter than a novel.

Read the Model In the novel *The Cay,* a young boy named Phillip and his mother flee their home in the Caribbean. After their ship is attacked, Phillip goes blind from an injury and gets lost at sea. Soon he finds himself stranded on a remote island. His only companions are an island man named Timothy and a cat. Notice the elements of fiction that the author uses to explore the **key idea** of survival.

from
The Cay

Novel by **Theodore Taylor**

The palm fronds above me rattled in the breeze, and there were other noises from the underbrush. I knew Stew Cat was around somewhere, but it didn't sound like him.

I wondered if Timothy had checked for snakes. There were also
5 scorpions on most Caribbean islands, and they were deadly. I wondered if there were any on our cay.

During those first few days on the island, the times I spent alone were terrible. It was, of course, being unable to see that made all the sounds so frightening. I guess if you are born blind, it is not so bad. You grow
10 up knowing each sound and what it means.

Suddenly, the tears came out. I knew it was not a manly thing to do, something my father would have frowned on, but I couldn't stop.

Close Read

1. Using terms from the Academic Vocabulary list, describe what's happening in this scene.

2. **Key Idea: Survival** Phillip will probably have to overcome his fear if he wants to **survive.** What qualities might help him stay alive on this solitary island?

DIFFERENTIATED INSTRUCTION

FOR LESS—PROFICIENT READERS

Concept Support Use a graphic organizer such as this one to help students relate details from the story to the elements of fiction.

Element	Story Details	What I Learn
point of view	"above me" "I knew"	The point of view is first person. The character Phillip tells the story.
character	"being unable to see ... made all the sounds so frightening"; "the tears came out ... not a manly thing to do"	Phillip, who is blind, is trying to be brave but feels frightened and alone.
setting		

FICTION

- Record the **Academic Vocabulary for Fiction** on the board.
- Have students read this section of the text in pairs. Have them look for the definitions of the vocabulary terms.
- Define the terms as a class.
- Then have students work in small groups to respond to these prompts:

  Think of a story with an exciting **plot.** What happens? What is the major **conflict?**

  Who is the most memorable **character** you have met in your reading?

  Describe an unusual **setting** from a work of fiction you have read.
- Invite groups to share some of their responses.

Read the Model Have students read the introductory paragraph. Then read the model aloud as students follow along silently. Have students answer the **Close Read** questions.

Close Read

1. *Possible answer: The **setting** is on a remote island in the Caribbean. The **characters** Phillip (the narrator) and Timothy are stranded on the island. This is the main **conflict** driving the **plot.** The scene occurs during the first few days of Phillip's time on the island. He is terrified of his surroundings, especially since he can't see. He is probably also very homesick. The novel is told from Phillip's **point of view.** While it is not possible to determine the **theme** of a novel from only a few paragraphs, the excerpt suggests that the theme may involve courage and survival.*

2. *Students may say that courage, physical and emotional strength, resourcefulness, a sense of adventure, fearlessness, and an ability to remain calm might help Phillip survive.*

If students need help ... Read each paragraph of the model aloud. Pause to ask students questions such as *Who is telling the story?* that will help them identify the important elements of fiction.

CHECK UNDERSTANDING In what ways is a novel different from a short story?

POETRY

- Preview the **Academic Vocabulary for Poetry** by writing several nursery rhymes—such as "Little Miss Muffet," "As I Was Going to St. Ives," and "Hey Diddle Diddle"—on the board. Use the poems to illustrate the concepts of **lines, stanzas, rhyme, rhythm, speaker,** and **imagery.**

- Have students read the first two paragraphs on page 6. Ask volunteers to summarize how the form of a poem differs from other kinds of writing, and what sound devices add to a poem.

Read the Model Remind students that poetry is meant to be listened to as well as read. Then read the poem "Thumbprint" once while students listen. Next read the poem again as they follow along in their books. Remind students that readers should not pause at the end of a line unless there is punctuation. Then have them answer the **Close Read** questions. The complete poem is also available on the *Audio Anthology CD.*

Close Read

1. *Possible answer: You can tell that this is a poem and not fiction because its form is very different from that of the fiction excerpt on page 5. "Thumbprint" is made up of 20 lines that are grouped together into one stanza. The lines vary in length, giving the poem an interesting rhythm. Certain words at the ends of lines rhyme, such as alone / own (lines 4 and 5) and brain / rain (lines 16 and 18).*

2. *Students may say that personality, appearance, sense of humor, way of laughing, manner of walking, and talents all help to make someone an individual.*

CHECK UNDERSTANDING What are some sound devices that a poet might use?

POETRY

Poetry is all around you—in the nursery rhymes you learned as a child, in the lyrics of the songs you listen to, in greeting-card messages, and in this book. You already know that poetry is very different from fiction, starting with the way words are arranged on the page. In poetry, ideas are expressed through a series of **lines,** which are often grouped into **stanzas.**

Many poems are meant to be heard, not just read. For that reason, the way a poem sounds is as important as the way it looks on the page. Poets often experiment with sound devices, including **rhythm** and **rhyme,** to emphasize important words and create musical effects.

Read the Model A powerful poem can make readers look at something ordinary—a thumbprint, for example—in a new way. Read this poem aloud so that you can hear its rhythm and rhyme. What is the poet saying about the **key idea** of individuality?

ACADEMIC VOCABULARY FOR POETRY

- form
- line
- stanza
- rhythm
- rhyme
- speaker
- imagery

Thumbprint

Poem by **Eve Merriam**

On the pad of my thumb
are whorls, whirls, wheels
in a unique design:
mine alone.
5 What a treasure to own!
My own flesh, my own feelings.
No other, however grand or base,
can ever contain the same.
My signature,
10 thumbing the pages of my time.
My universe key,
my singularity.
Impress, implant,
I am myself,
15 of all my atom parts I am the sum.
And out of my blood and my brain
I make my own interior weather,
my own sun and rain.
Imprint my mark upon the world,
20 whatever I shall become.

Close Read

1. How can you tell that "Thumbprint" is a poem? Cite specific details to support your answer.

2. **Key Idea: Individuality** A thumbprint is one of many things that distinguishes one person from another. What other qualities or characteristics make an **individual** unique?

DIFFERENTIATED INSTRUCTION

FOR LESS-PROFICIENT READERS

Concept Support Review the definition of *imagery.* Then give pairs of students a starter set of adjectives, adverbs, verbs, and nouns on separate slips of paper. (For example, one set might include words such as *glittering, chewed, velvet, spongy, crystals, juicy, scarlet, draped, strawberries, moss, statue.*) Have students create their own examples of imagery using these words and some of their own. Ask pairs to share their examples. Discuss the senses to which each image appeals.

FOR ENGLISH LEARNERS

Culture: Connect Have students choose short poems from their cultures. Ask them to print each poem in its original language on a large poster and illustrate it. Have students read their poems to the class and explain what they are about. Then display the posters around the room.

Vocabulary Support Define challenging words in "Thumbprint," such as "whorls" (line 2), "base" (line 7), "singularity" (line 12), and "implant" (line 13), before students read the poem.

DRAMA

At the heart of both fiction and drama are good stories. Unlike fiction, though, drama is meant to be performed before an audience. As a result, a drama does not include long descriptions of settings or characters' thoughts. Instead, the story is developed through **dialogue** and actions—what the characters say and do. The structure of a drama is also different from that of a short story or novel. A drama is made up of **scenes** and **acts,** rather than chapters and parts.

A drama also includes notes to help the actors and the director perform it as the writer intended. These instructions, or **stage directions,** describe the setting and how the characters should look, talk, and act. Stage directions are often printed in *italic* type.

Read the Model *A Young Lady of Property* is about Wilma, a teenager who dreams of leaving her home and becoming a movie star. Wilma also wants to leave so that she doesn't have to deal with Mrs. Leighton, her father's girlfriend. In this excerpt Wilma reveals her plan to her father. As you read, think about the **key idea** of ambition.

> **ACADEMIC VOCABULARY FOR DRAMA**
> - plot
> - character
> - act
> - scene
> - dialogue
> - stage directions

from A Young *Lady* of Property
Drama by **Horton Foote**

Lester. Say hello to Mrs. Leighton.

Wilma (*most ungraciously*). Hello, Mrs. Leighton.

Mrs. Leighton (*most graciously*). Hello, Wilma.

Lester. What are you doing hanging around the streets, Wilma?

5 **Wilma.** Waiting to see if I have a letter.

Lester. What kind of letter, Wilma?

Wilma. About getting into the movies. Arabella and I saw an ad in the *Houston Chronicle* about a Mr. Delafonte who is a famous Hollywood director.

10 **Lester.** Who is Mr. Delafonte?

Wilma. The Hollywood director I'm trying to tell you about. He's giving screen tests in Houston to people of beauty and talent, and if they pass they'll go to Hollywood and be in the picture shows.

Lester. Well, that's all a lot of foolishness, Wilma. You're not going to
15 Houston to take anything.

Wilma. But, Daddy . . . I . . .

Lester. You're fifteen years old and you're gonna stay home. . . .

Close Read

1. How does Wilma treat Mrs. Leighton? How does Mrs. Leighton act toward Wilma? Explain how you can tell.

2. **Key Idea: Ambition** Wilma's desire to become a movie star is an **ambition** that many other teens may share. What other ambitions do young people have? Explain why such ambitions are appealing.

DRAMA

- Poll students to find out how many have seen or acted in plays before. Draw on students' prior knowledge to discuss some of the characteristics of plays before they read the first two paragraphs on this page.

- Define each term under **Academic Vocabulary for Drama.** Point out that drama shares some terms with fiction, such as *character* and *plot*. Then use the model to identify examples of dialogue and stage directions.

Read the Model Introduce the model by reading the background paragraph aloud. Have students read the excerpt silently, and then have volunteers read the parts aloud. Afterwards, have students answer the **Close Read** questions.

Close Read

1. *Possible answer: Wilma is not very polite to Mrs. Leighton. According to the stage directions, she greets her "most ungraciously." Mrs. Leighton, however, is more polite and friendly. The stage directions say that Mrs. Leighton greets Wilma "most graciously."*

2. *Students may say that teens have ambitions such as becoming famous athletes, politicians, musicians, video game programmers, inventors, or movie producers or directors. These aspirations are appealing because of the fame, fans, power, and fortune that come with them. Or, teens might have goals such as entering the medical profession, becoming a lawyer, or working with people in some way. These careers are appealing because they involve helping others.*

CHECK UNDERSTANDING What is the purpose of stage directions?

DIFFERENTIATED INSTRUCTION

FOR LESS–PROFICIENT READERS

Concept Support Have students work in small groups to compare and contrast the characteristics of fiction and drama in a Venn Diagram. Then use the groups' input to complete a class diagram.

 BEST PRACTICES TOOLKIT—Transparency
Venn Diagram p. A26

- Remind students that nonfiction deals mostly with facts. This type of writing tells about people, places, and events in the real world.

- Record the **Academic Vocabulary for Nonfiction** on the board. With the class, develop a working definition for each term. Then discuss how each term relates to nonfiction. For example, the writer of a nonfiction work can have **purposes** that include informing, persuading, and entertaining readers. The **organization** of a nonfiction work helps the writer achieve his or her purpose by presenting ideas in a clear, powerful way. The writer's **main idea** must be supported by relevant facts and details. In writing that is intended to persuade, the writer's main idea is an **argument**—a statement that the writer supports with reasons and facts.

- Read the introductory paragraph aloud. Tell students that **literary nonfiction** often engages readers' emotions by describing real events in an exciting or moving way. **Informational text** is intended purely to convey facts or instructions clearly.

- Have students take turns reading the descriptions of the various kinds of nonfiction. Draw students' attention to the purpose of each form. Then ask students to classify these examples:

  — A brief article describing a sunset and how it affected the writer (*essay*)

  — A book written by a famous athlete describing his struggle with a serious illness (*autobiography*)

  — A book written about a famous athlete who survived a serious illness (*biography*)

  — A Web page with instructions for downloading and installing software (*consumer document*)

  — A factual account in a newspaper about a recent hurricane (*news article*)

  — A text in which the writer argues for less homework, intended to be read aloud to the school board (*speech*)

CHECK UNDERSTANDING How are autobiographies and biographies similar and different?

NONFICTION AND INFORMATIONAL TEXT

Through **literary nonfiction,** such as autobiographies and speeches, you can learn about historic events, inspiring people, and ground-breaking topics. **Informational text,** such as instruction manuals, magazine articles, and other writing that conveys factual information, is also an important source for learning about the world. For these reasons, you need to become a critical reader of all types of nonfiction.

ACADEMIC VOCABULARY FOR NONFICTION

- purpose
- organization
- main idea
- argument

TYPE OF NONFICTION	CHARACTERISTICS	
AUTOBIOGRAPHY/ BIOGRAPHY The true story of a person's life, told by that person (autobiography) or by someone else (biography)	• Helps readers learn about events and experiences in a person's life • Is told from the first-person point of view (autobiography) or the third-person point of view (biography)	
ESSAY A short piece of writing about a single, focused subject	• Has one or more of the following purposes: to express feelings, to inform, to entertain, to persuade • Uses either formal or informal language	
SPEECH An oral presentation of the speaker's ideas or beliefs	• Is intended to express feelings, to inform, to entertain, or to persuade • Achieves its power through well-chosen language as well as the speaker's voice and gestures	
NEWS/FEATURE ARTICLES Informational writing in newspapers and magazines. News articles report on recent events. Feature articles provide in-depth coverage of interesting people, topics, and trends.	• Are primarily intended to inform or entertain • Often use examples, statistics, quotations from sources, and graphic aids to present information	
CONSUMER DOCUMENTS Printed materials that usually accompany products and services	• Are intended to inform consumers about how to use a product or service • Often include illustrations, diagrams, and step-by-step directions	

DIFFERENTIATED INSTRUCTION

FOR LESS–PROFICIENT READERS

Concept Support Divide students into Jigsaw groups. Provide each group with a different example of nonfiction. Have students read their sample and chart its important features, using the information on page 8 as a guide. Then ask groups to read their examples to the class and share their charts.

 BEST PRACTICES TOOLKIT
Jigsaw p. A1

FOR ENGLISH LEARNERS

Vocabulary: Word Parts Explain to students that knowing the meanings of word parts can help them define unfamiliar words. Write these word parts and their definitions on the board: *auto* ("self"), *bio* ("life"), *non* ("not"). Have students work in small groups to define the key terms *autobiography, biography,* and *nonfiction.*

MODEL 1: AUTOBIOGRAPHY

As you read this excerpt from an autobiography by author Walter Dean Myers, notice how he describes his feelings. Through his descriptions, what do you learn about the **key idea** of overcoming obstacles?

from
BAD BOY

Autobiography by
Walter Dean Myers

I knew in my heart that I would have some difficulties in life because of my speech problems, and I also knew that I wouldn't always be able to solve them by punching somebody out. But I didn't want to make my speech the focus of my life. If I couldn't speak well, I could
5 still communicate by writing. If the words didn't come easily from my mouth, they would, I hoped, eventually come from my writing.

I never understood my speech problem. The words I spoke sounded clear to me. When a teacher or classmate asked me to say something more clearly, I didn't know what to do. Reading aloud in front of an
10 audience was especially difficult for me. After a while I dreaded reading even a sports page to my friends. My stomach would tighten up, and I would become so nervous I could hardly read at all.

Close Read

1. What challenges did young Myers face because of his speech problem? Look for descriptions of his feelings.

2. **Key Idea: Overcoming Obstacles** Myers realized early on that he had to deal with his problem. Do you think that all **obstacles** can be **overcome** with enough effort? Why or why not?

MODEL 2: FEATURE ARTICLE

Stress, the **key idea** in this article, is something that many people experience. How does the article help you understand the reactions that Myers describes in his autobiography?

Stress
HEALTH WATCH

Everyone experiences stress at times—adults, teens, and even kids. But there are things you can do to minimize stress and manage the stress that's unavoidable.

What Is Stress? Stress is a feeling that's created when we react
5 to particular events. It's the body's way of rising to a challenge and preparing to meet a tough situation with focus, strength, stamina, and heightened alertness.

The events that provoke stress are called *stressors,* and they cover a whole range of situations—everything from outright physical danger to
10 making a class presentation. . . .

Close Read

1. How are the boxed details in this article different from the kinds of details that Myers uses to describe the stress he felt as a child?

2. **Key Idea: Stress** Life is full of stressful situations. What other events or factors in life can cause **stress?**

9

DIFFERENTIATED INSTRUCTION

FOR LESS–PROFICIENT READERS

Comprehension Support On the board, list the characteristics of an autobiography (describes events in a real person's life; is told from first-person point of view) and a feature article (informs or entertains; uses examples, statistics, quotes, graphics). Have students work in small groups to find examples of these characteristics in each model. Discuss their observations.

MODEL 1: AUTOBIOGRAPHY

Read **Model 1** aloud. Then have students answer the questions.

Close Read

1. *Possible answer: Myers could not make people understand what he was saying and became increasingly nervous about trying to communicate through talking. He "dreaded" reading aloud, even in front of friends (lines 10–11). He became angry and would sometimes lash out at others who made fun of his speech (lines 2–3).*

2. *Students may say that determination can help people overcome or manage most obstacles in their lives. For example, Myers may not have been able to overcome his speech problems entirely, but he realized he could "still communicate by writing." So, instead of letting his speech become the focus of his life, he channeled his energies into his writing.*

MODEL 2: FEATURE ARTICLE

Read the introduction to **Model 2** aloud. Have students answer the questions after reading the model silently.

Close Read

1. *Possible answer: The boxed details are more factual and objective than the details that Myers provides in his autobiography. The details in "Stress" help to define stress and explain what causes it. In contrast, the details in Myers's autobiography focus on the author's personal thoughts and feelings about the stress he experienced as a result of his speech problem.*

2. *Students may say that circumstances such as family problems, exams, athletic competitions, arguments, pressure to excel in school, or illness can also cause stress.*

CHECK UNDERSTANDING What is the purpose of the first model? What is the purpose of the second?

TYPES OF MEDIA

- Read the first paragraph aloud. Ask students how they think media influences their thoughts and attitudes. For example, have they ever wanted to buy something after seeing it advertised?

- Work together to define the **Academic Vocabulary for Media.** Discuss these points:

  — **Medium** is the format in which ideas are conveyed. In art, oil painting and marble sculpture are two kinds of medium. *Media* (the plural form of *medium*) refers to newspapers, TV programs, advertisements, and other methods of presenting information to many people at once.

  — A **message** is an idea conveyed through the media. For example, a soap opera might convey the message that beauty and romantic love make life worth living. An advertisement might send the message that wearing a particular brand of clothing can make a person more popular. In a feature film, a message is usually called a theme.

  — The **purpose** of media is to communicate information and ideas to a wide audience. Each kind of media has a slightly different purpose—to inform, to persuade, to entertain, and so on.

  — Many kinds of media are aimed at a particular **target audience.** An animated feature film might have children as its target audience. The target audience for a luxury car ad might be wealthy adults.

- Have volunteers read aloud the description of each type of media. Discuss the purpose of each medium as it is described in the first bulleted item in each row. Encourage students to use the **Academic Vocabulary** terms to summarize the format and purpose of each medium.

CHECK UNDERSTANDING Which forms of media have the primary purpose of entertaining?

TYPES OF MEDIA

Movies allow you to experience everything from time travel to heroic adventures. The news informs you about what's happening in the world. Ads promise that your life will improve if you buy certain products. Media messages like these influence your life in many ways. That's why you need to become **media literate**—that is, learn how to "read" the media as carefully as you would a work of literature.

ACADEMIC VOCABULARY FOR MEDIA
- medium
- message
- purpose
- target audience

TYPE OF MEDIA	CHARACTERISTICS	
FEATURE FILMS Motion pictures that tell stories	• Are meant to entertain and to make a profit • Use camera shots, sound effects, music, actors, and sets to tell stories • Are at least one hour long	
NEWS MEDIA Reports of recent events in newspapers and magazines and on TV, the radio, and the Web	• Are intended to inform and to create a loyal audience • Medium (TV, radio, or print) affects how information is presented • Need to be closely examined for accuracy and bias	 LIVE ET BARBARA PINTO NEWS Punta Gorda, Florida
TV SHOWS Dramas, sitcoms, and other programs broadcast on television	• Are meant to inform and entertain • Use visuals, sound effects, and music to create entertaining stories • Are usually 30 to 60 minutes long	
ADVERTISING The promotion of products, services, and ideas using print and broadcast media	• Is designed to persuade a target audience to buy a product or agree with an idea • Uses persuasive techniques, visuals, and sounds to convey a message	
WEB SITES Collections of pages on the World Wide Web	• Use text, graphics, audio, and video to present information • Include hyperlinks and menus that allow users to navigate to the information they are looking for	

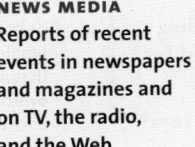
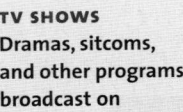
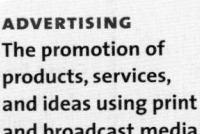

DIFFERENTIATED INSTRUCTION

FOR ENGLISH LEARNERS

Comprehension: Concept Support Show students examples of each type of media. Point out how the characteristics of each help to achieve its purpose. For example,

- *Back to the Future* (clip from feature film is on Media*Smart* DVD)—exciting, humorous story entertains audiences as ticket sales make money for movie's producers

- newspaper article—information is presented in a factual way, informing readers while earning their trust and loyalty to the paper

- TV shows—a documentary informs audiences about history, nature, or other topics; a sitcom entertains viewers with funny situations and dialogue

- Mountain Dew ad (on Media*Smart* DVD)—fast pace and sound effects make the product, a soft drink, seem exciting so that people will want to buy it

- Web site—hyperlinks and menus organize information, making it easy for users to find exactly what they want

Strategies That Work: Literature

❶ Ask Yourself the Right Questions

One skill that can help you analyze any work of literature is the ability to ask good questions. This book will show you what good questions are, so that you can begin to craft them yourself.

Kinds of Questions	Where to Look
Big questions about key ideas	▶ **Before Reading** pages (at the beginning of every selection)
Questions about literary elements and analysis	▶ Side notes (alongside each selection) and **After Reading** pages (following each selection)
Questions to ask when reading different genres	▶ **Analysis Frames** (Literature Center at Classzone.com)

❷ Make Connections

For literature to have real meaning for you, you have to make connections. Here are some ways to do just that:

- **Connect to Your Life** What does it take to survive? What makes an individual unique? Consider how experiences in your own life can help you explore big questions like these and the key ideas at the heart of them.

- **Connect to Other Subjects** Surviving on an island, managing stress, living in ancient times—the subjects you read about can help you learn about the world. If a subject interests you, research it on the Web.

❸ Record Your Reactions

Jot down your thoughts and impressions in a **Reader's Notebook**, both while and after you read. Consider using these formats.

JOURNAL
Capture your thoughts as you read.

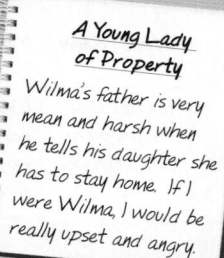

A Young Lady of Property

Wilma's father is very mean and harsh when he tells his daughter she has to stay home. If I were Wilma, I would be really upset and angry.

GRAPHIC ORGANIZER
After reading, create a graphic organizer to help you understand characters and events.

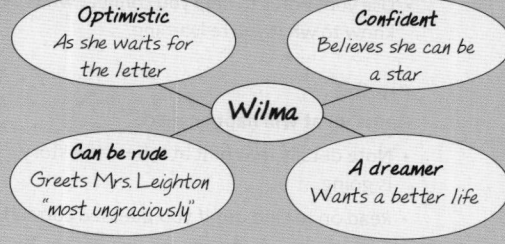

Optimistic
As she waits for the letter

Confident
Believes she can be a star

Wilma

Can be rude
Greets Mrs. Leighton "most ungraciously"

A dreamer
Wants a better life

Strategies That Work: Literature

Discuss how any activity that students enjoy—sports, art, music, or drama—involves strategies, or ways of helping them become better at the activity. Explain that, similarly, using certain strategies will help students get the most out of the literature that they read and make it more exciting to them.

1. **Ask Yourself the Right Questions** Tell students that asking themselves questions and looking for the answers will help them focus and think about what they are reading. This strategy will also help them remember what they have read. Turn to a selection in the pupil edition and point out the **Before Reading** feature, the side notes, and the **After Reading** pages.

2. **Make Connections** Ask students if they have ever met someone that they knew could be a friend. They may have felt an immediate connection or bond with the person. Explain that good literature often triggers the same reaction in readers. Readers recognize their own feelings or experiences through the characters or the words of the author. They use these connections to think more deeply about their lives. Discuss the two kinds of connections that students might make while reading literature.

3. **Record Your Reactions** Tell students that literature can be a stepping stone to learning more about themselves and the world around them. Keeping a **Reader's Notebook** can help them reflect on what they have read and understand its significance in their lives more fully. In addition, they will be able to compare how different authors approach similar big questions. Encourage them to use the formats suggested on page 11, as well as recording the questions, reactions, and connections that might occur to them as they read.

DIFFERENTIATED INSTRUCTION

FOR ENGLISH LEARNERS

Comprehension: Task Support Provide students with a template for their **Reader's Notebook** entries. The template may be adapted for different types of literature.

Title _____ Date _____

Connections Chart

Characters, Events, and Ideas	My Feelings, Thoughts, and Questions

Journal Entry

This _____ was about _____.

I liked _____.

I didn't like _____.

The best part was _____ because _____.

OBJECTIVES

- become familiar with the skills and strategies needed for active reading
- practice reading skills and strategies, such as **visualize, monitor, make inferences,** and **connect**

Explain to students that, like explorers discovering new worlds, active readers use different skills and strategies to learn what they need to know in a text until they have thoroughly explored its contents. Even when they have finished, active readers will continue to share and explore new ideas.

Model for students the strategies they might use to explore this page. For example, they should **preview** the layout of the page, noting the chart format and the various skills covered. They should **set a purpose.** Are they reading to become informed or for some other reason? What **prior knowledge** on this topic can they recall to help them understand what they are reading?

Read the text aloud as students follow along silently.

CHECK UNDERSTANDING What are three ways in which readers can monitor their understanding?

Becoming an Active Reader

A science fiction story, a biography of an athlete, a news article about a faraway country—every kind of text offers a world of ideas for you to explore. Active reading skills and strategies can help you tap into those ideas. Most of the skills and strategies you will practice throughout this book are already familiar to you. Which ones do you recognize?

SKILLS AND STRATEGIES FOR ACTIVE READING

Preview
Get your bearings before you read.
- Scan the title, graphics, and subheadings.
- Skim the first paragraph to get a sense of what the text is about.

Set a Purpose
Think about *why* you are reading a text.
- Ask: Am I reading to learn, to be entertained, or for another reason?
- Decide how this purpose affects your reading. Pay close attention or simply enjoy?

Connect
Take the text personally.
- Think about whether any situations described remind you of experiences in your own life.
- Ask: If I were this character, how would I feel?

Use Prior Knowledge
Recall what you already know about a topic.
- Jot down any facts, descriptions, and impressions before you read.
- Use your notes to help you connect what you know to what you're learning.

Predict
Guess what will happen next.
- Note details that hint at where the story is going.
- Read on to find out if you guessed correctly.

Visualize
Picture in your mind what is being described.
- Note descriptions of characters and settings.
- Use these details to help you form a clear mental image.

Monitor
Check your understanding as you read.
- **Question** what is happening and why.
- Reread difficult parts or ask for help to **clarify** your understanding.
- **Evaluate** yourself as a reader. Ask: How well am I understanding the text?

Make Inferences
Make logical guesses based on details in the text and your own experiences.
- Record important details about characters, settings, and events.
- Ask: How can what I know help me "read between the lines"? (This chart shows how one student made an inference about a character in the story on the next page.)

Details in "Shells"	What I Know	My Inference
Both of Michael's parents died six months ago.	It takes time for people to deal with loss.	Michael's anger and sadness won't last forever.

DIFFERENTIATED INSTRUCTION

FOR LESS–PROFICIENT READERS
Concept Support Distribute a short informational article that includes some text features, or ask students to turn to "What Do You Know About Sharks?" on page 874 of the pupil edition. Have students read one or two pages of the article silently. Then use a Read Aloud/Think Aloud strategy to model how to apply the various skills described on this page.

 **BEST PRACTICES TOOLKIT—Transparency**
Read Aloud/Think Aloud p. A34

FOR ENGLISH LEARNERS
Comprehension: Self-Monitor Suggest these steps to check reading comprehension:

1. Students should write down what they do not understand on sticky notes and place the notes near the confusing text.
2. They should reread difficult passages.
3. After completing the text, they should return to the troublesome sections and try to answer their earlier questions.
4. They should then ask a partner or teacher to answer any remaining questions.

MODEL: SHORT STORY

This story is about a boy named Michael who goes to live with his aunt Esther after his parents die. Will Michael ever break out of his lonely shell and overcome his anger toward Esther? As you read this excerpt, use the **Close Read** questions to practice the skills and strategies you just learned.

from

Shells

Short story by **Cynthia Rylant**

"I can't make you happy, Michael. You just refuse to be happy here. And you punish me every day for it."

"*Punish* you?" Michael gawked at her. "I don't punish you! I don't care about you! I don't care what you eat or how you dress or where you
5 go or what you think. Can't you just leave me alone?"

He slammed down the glass, scraped his chair back from the table and ran out the door.

"Michael!" yelled Esther.

They had been living together, the two of them, for six months.
10 Michael's parents had died and only Esther could take him in—or, only she had offered to. Michael's other relatives could not imagine dealing with a fourteen-year-old boy. They wanted peaceful lives.

Esther lived in a condominium in a wealthy section of Detroit. Most of the area's residents were older (like her) and afraid of the world they
15 lived in (like her). They stayed indoors much of the time. They trusted few people.

Esther liked living alone. She had never married or had children. She had never lived anywhere but Detroit. She liked her condominium. But she was fiercely loyal to her family, and when her only sister had
20 died, Esther insisted she be allowed to care for Michael. And Michael, afraid of going anywhere else, had accepted.

Oh, he was lonely. Even six months after their deaths, he still expected to see his parents—sitting on the couch as he walked into Esther's living room, waiting for the bathroom as he came out of the
25 shower, coming in the door late at night. He still smelled his father's Old Spice somewhere, his mother's talc.

Sometimes he was so sure one of them was somewhere around him that he thought maybe he was going crazy. His heart hurt him. He wondered if he would ever get better.

Close Read

1. **Set a Purpose** People often read short stories for enjoyment. Here, you also have another purpose—to practice active reading skills and strategies. Have a notebook ready in which you can record your observations.

2. **Monitor** Reread the boxed text. Why did Esther insist on taking care of Michael?

MODEL: SHORT STORY

- The full text of the story is available on the *Audio Anthology CD*.
- Explain to students that reading the model will provide them with the opportunity to practice the **Skills and Strategies for Active Reading** listed on page 12. Ask them to pay attention to how each strategy provides different information about and insights into the text.
- Have students silently read the excerpt from "Shells" and work on the questions in pairs.

Close Read

1. *Point out that each **Close Read** question is labeled with one of the active reading skills and strategies that students are meant to be practicing. Have students record their answers to the questions in their notebooks. Make sure that they cite details from the story to support their answers.*

2. *Possible answer: Esther is a very family-minded person. In line 19, she is described as "fiercely loyal to her family." Even though she liked living alone, she felt compelled to care for Michael after her only sister (Michael's mother) died.*

If students need help . . . Remind them that when they are reading for the purpose of answering questions, they may need to read more slowly or reread certain passages.

DIFFERENTIATED INSTRUCTION

FOR LESS–PROFICIENT READERS

Comprehension Support Have students work in pairs to read the selection aloud and employ some of the reading strategies introduced on the previous page, such as connecting, using prior knowledge, visualizing, and monitoring. Circulate throughout the room to check on students' progress and their grasp of the strategies.

FOR ENGLISH LEARNERS

Comprehension: Self-Monitor Provide students with sticky notes. Ask them to write out questions they have as they read or listen to the selection. They should place their notes near the part of the story that needs clarifying. After they have read the selection, have them work in groups to try to answer the questions before discussing them as a class.

3. *Possible answer: Michael is lonely, extremely sad, and scared. He misses his parents and wonders whether he will ever "get better" (lines 28–29). Despite the fact that Esther is trying very hard to make Michael happy and comfortable in his new home, he is mean to her, probably out of grief and fear. Students may infer that anger is Michael's way of dealing with these intense emotions. Also, it is easy for Michael to "hate" Esther because she seems so different from his parents (lines 30–31).*

4. *Students should give examples of specific details. For example, the phrases "She was having tea and a crescent roll and seemed cheerful" (line 52) and "poked the long, shiny nail of her little finger at the crab's claws" (lines 54–55) reveal the change in Esther's mood and her interest in Michael's new pet. The detail "Michael showed her the crab's eyes peering through the small opening of the shell" (lines 57–58) helps readers picture the hermit crab hiding. Michael seems to be warming up to Esther. His mood is conveyed through his willingness to show Esther the crab as well as his body language: "Michael grinned and shrugged his shoulders" (line 64).*

5. *Students' predictions will vary, but many may guess that Esther and Michael will eventually find a way to get along. In the last part of the excerpt, they seem to be getting along better, though they are still rather awkward with each other. Readers may guess that this is the first positive step in their becoming more of a family and trusting each other.*

If students need help . . . Complete a Making Inferences chart to help students understand how to use details from the text to make logical guesses.

BEST PRACTICES TOOLKIT—Transparency
Making Inferences p. A13

---

30   And though he denied it, he did hate Esther. She was so different from his mother and father. Prejudiced—she admired only those who were white and Presbyterian. Selfish—she wouldn't allow him to use her phone. Complaining—she always had a headache or a backache or a stomachache.

35   He didn't want to, but he hated her. And he didn't know what to do except lie about it.

     Michael hadn't made any friends at his new school, and his teachers barely noticed him. He came home alone every day and usually found Esther on the phone. She kept in close touch with several other women

40 in nearby condominiums.

     Esther told her friends she didn't understand Michael. She said she knew he must grieve for his parents, but why punish her? She said she thought she might send him away if he couldn't be nicer. She said she didn't deserve this.

45   But when Michael came in the door, she always quickly changed the subject.

     One day after school Michael came home with a hermit crab. He had gone into a pet store, looking for some small, living thing, and hermit crabs were selling for just a few dollars. He'd bought

50 one, and a bowl.

     Esther, for a change, was not on the phone when he arrived home. She was having tea and a crescent roll and seemed cheerful. Michael wanted badly to show someone what he had bought. So he showed her.

     Esther surprised him. She picked up the shell and poked the long,

55 shiny nail of her little finger at the crab's claws.

     "Where is he?" she asked.

     Michael showed her the crab's eyes peering through the small opening of the shell.

     "Well, for heaven's sake, come out of there!" she said to the crab,

60 and she turned the shell upside down and shook it.

     "Aunt Esther!" Michael grabbed for the shell.

     "All right, all right." She turned it right side up. "Well," she said, "what does he do?"

     Michael grinned and shrugged his shoulders.

65   "I don't know," he answered. "Just grows, I guess."

     His aunt looked at him.

     "An attraction to a crab is something I cannot identify with. However, it's fine with me if you keep him, as long as I can be assured that he won't grow out of that bowl." She gave him a hard stare.

70   "He won't," Michael answered. "I promise." . . .

3. Make Inferences Why do you think Michael treats his aunt the way he does? Explain how the details in lines 22–34 help you to understand his behavior at the beginning of the story.

4. Visualize Reread lines 51–64 and try to picture the scene in your mind. Cite specific details that helped you to see the characters, the setting, and the action.

5. Predict Do you think Michael and his aunt will ever find a way to get along? Try to guess what will happen to their relationship.

DIFFERENTIATED INSTRUCTION

FOR LESS–PROFICIENT READERS

Concept Support Have students write their reactions to "Shells" in their **Reader's Notebooks.** Encourage them to make connections to key ideas or to note topics that they would like to know more about. Have them write a journal entry and use a graphic organizer to examine the theme, characters, or other elements. Invite students to share some of their ideas in small groups.

Strategies That Work: Reading

❶ Know Your Purpose

Before you delve into any selection, make sure you know *why* you are reading. Then choose the strategy that best suits your purpose. Consider these strategies.

Purpose	Strategy
For enjoyment	▶ Take your time and read at your own pace.
To learn or become informed	▶ Take notes on the main ideas and supporting details to help you remember what you've learned.
For research	▶ Use text features, such as subheadings and graphic aids, to help you locate the information you're looking for.
To follow directions	▶ Follow each step carefully, using any photographs or illustrations as your guide.

❷ Take Notes

Recording your observations as you read can help you better understand a selection. Try creating a two-column chart. In one column, record details or quotations from the selection. In the other, write your thoughts and impressions.

"Shells"	My Thoughts
Esther likes living by herself, and she never had children of her own.	No wonder Esther is frustrated with Michael. She can't seem to make him feel better, *and* she's not used to taking care of someone else.

❸ Create a Personal Word List

Keep track of new words you encounter as you read. This is a good habit to continue to practice.

- **Pick your words.** You may decide to list the vocabulary words for each selection, as well as any other words you find particularly challenging.
- **Don't stop with the definitions.** Write synonyms, antonyms, and sentences to help the words really stick in your mind.
- **Practice makes perfect.** Visit the **Vocabulary Center** at **ClassZone.com** for interactive exercises.
- **Use them or lose them.** Weave new words into your speaking and writing before you forget what you learned.

Word	Meaning
gawked (v.) "Shells," line 3	**Definition:** stared at long and hard in amazement **Synonym:** gaped **Antonym:** glanced **Sentence:** As they entered the lobby, the family *gawked* at the magnificent hotel.

INTRODUCING THE ESSENTIALS **15**

Strategies That Work: Reading

Explain that certain strategies can help students get the most out of whatever they are reading, whether it is fiction or nonfiction, short or long.

1. **Know Your Purpose** Read the various purposes and strategies aloud. Ask students for examples of when they might use each strategy.
2. **Take Notes** Remind students that they might take different kinds of notes depending upon their purpose. For example, if they are reading to become informed, their notes might consist of important facts from the text. Take this opportunity to show students some of the note-taking formats from the Toolkit that they might use.
3. **Create a Personal Word List** Help students access the **Vocabulary Center** at **ClassZone.com.** Suggest that they set aside several pages in their **Reader's Notebooks** for vocabulary, and select a new word each day or week to use at least five times.

CHECK UNDERSTANDING What is a helpful strategy to use when you are reading something for the purpose of learning?

DIFFERENTIATED INSTRUCTION

FOR LESS—PROFICIENT READERS

Comprehension Support Reinforce students' understanding of note-taking techniques by having them work in small groups to fill out a Story Map with details from "Shells." Have groups volunteer details from their maps for a class organizer. Remind students that taking good notes as they read will help them recall important details.

🧰 BEST PRACTICES TOOLKIT—Transparency
Story Map p. D16

FOR ENGLISH LEARNERS

Vocabulary Support Have students choose words from "Shells" for a class word list. Record them on the board. Then return to the text and model how to define them from context. Write definitions next to the words before having small groups check the definitions in the dictionary. Encourage students to transfer the words to their **Reader's Notebooks.** Work together to compose new sentences for the words.

OBJECTIVES

- understand the relationship between **purpose, audience,** and **format**
- become familiar with the stages of the writing process
- become familiar with the key traits of effective writing
- understand how rubrics can be used to evaluate writing

Consider Your Options

Read aloud the introductory paragraph and the ideas under **Purpose, Audience,** and **Format.** Then draw this diagram on the board:

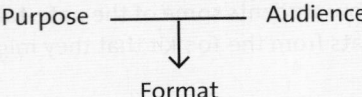

Explain that in most cases, writers consider their purpose and audience first, and then they pick an appropriate format. To illustrate, have students imagine they are going to write about a disastrous camping trip. If their purpose is to entertain and their audience is a friend, an appropriate format would be a humorous letter or e-mail. Change the audience to classmates and teachers, and the format would also need to change—perhaps to a narrative essay. Have students select other purposes and audiences from the chart and discuss which formats would work with each combination.

CHECK UNDERSTANDING Which formats are most often used for the purpose of conveying information?

Expressing Ideas in Writing

Writing is a way of sharing your ideas with others and learning more about what you really think. Whether you're writing a diary entry for your eyes alone or creating a Web site intended for millions of visitors, the power of words is in your hands.

Consider Your Options

All writers must make some important choices *before* they start giving shape to their ideas. You might want to describe a hilarious incident, write a letter of complaint about a damaged CD, or post a movie review to an online database. No matter what your topic is, you should begin by considering your **purpose, audience,** and **format.**

PURPOSE	AUDIENCE	FORMAT
Why am I writing?	**Who are my readers?**	**Which format will best suit my purpose and audience?**
• to entertain • to inform or explain • to persuade • to describe • to express thoughts and feelings	• classmates • teachers • friends • myself • community members • Web users • customer service at a company	• essay • journal entry • letter • research paper • poem • script • short story • power presentation • review • Web site • speech

DIFFERENTIATED INSTRUCTION

FOR LESS–PROFICIENT READERS

Concept Support Have students complete this chart to practice matching purpose, audience, and format. Discuss their responses.

Purpose	Audience	Format
give information about science fair	school community	
persuade people to take action		letter to the editor about litter in the city
	other classmates	poem about the first snowfall of the season

FOR ENGLISH LEARNERS

Vocabulary Support Make sure students understand that the word *audience* refers to readers as well as to people who attend performances or presentations.

Continue the Process

There is no single right way to write. Every writer does it a little differently. The **Writing Workshops** in this book will help you discover the process that works best for you. First, though, familiarize yourself with the basic process. Then you can move forward according to your own working style.

THE WRITING PROCESS

What Should I Do?	What Does It Look Like?
PREWRITING Explore your ideas and decide what you want to write about. Once you have considered the options on the preceding page, try some of these strategies: **freewriting, brainstorming,** and **questioning.** See page 19 for more strategies.	**FREEWRITING** _The Cay_ _It must be terrifying to be stranded on an island. This scenario is often shown as being exciting (on TV, at least). Maybe I will write about what it takes to keep going in that situation._
DRAFTING Turn your ideas into a rough draft. If you are doing some informal or personal writing, you might **draft to discover**—jump in without a formal outline to guide you. If you are writing an essay for school, you may want to **draft from an outline.** If you are writing a short story, create a **story map.**	**OUTLINE** _I. Survival depends on both physical and emotional strength._ _A. Phillip has a serious physical problem—can't see_ _B. Needs to get his emotions under control_
REVISING AND EDITING Review what you've written. Think about how you might improve the ideas, style, and structure of your writing. • Use a **rubric** to make sure you are on track (page 18). • Have a classmate review your draft. • **Proofread** for errors in spelling and grammar.	**PEER SUGGESTIONS** _It's all about survival. Phillip in_ The Cay _is in a terribly position. Luckily, he has the qualities he needs to pull through._ _**Suggestion:** Could you make the first sentence clearer? Also, it is too informal. Try: "What does it take to survive when your life is threatened?"_
PUBLISHING Get your writing out where it can be read. Choose a publishing option suited to your **purpose, audience,** and **format.** Visit the **Writing Center** at Classzone.com for specific publishing options.	**PUBLISHING OPTIONS**  

Continue the Process

Review the stages of the writing process listed under **What Should I Do?**

Determine Readiness Have students give examples or explanations of each boldfaced term in the chart. For example,

- **freewriting:** allowing your mind to move from one idea to another as you jot down each idea; the goal is to discover new ideas through a creative thinking process

- **brainstorming:** starting from a specific topic and thinking of as many related ideas or subtopics as possible

- **questioning:** asking yourself questions about a topic to see if they lead to a writing idea

- **draft to discover:** write the first version of a paper without planning its structure in advance; then you can analyze your first draft to see what works and what doesn't

- **draft from an outline:** plan the order in which you will present your ideas and then follow this plan, or outline, as you write

- **story map:** a chart that outlines the major elements in a story—setting, characters, conflict, plot, resolution, and theme

- **rubric:** list of qualities that a strong piece of writing should have

- **proofread:** reread something you've written to find and correct any errors in spelling, grammar, and punctuation

Ask volunteers for examples of when they have used these strategies. Then explain that **Writing Workshops** throughout the book will help them learn more about these stages of the writing process.

DIFFERENTIATED INSTRUCTION

FOR LESS-PROFICIENT READERS

Concept Support Present students with a writing prompt, such as one of the big questions from pages 2 and 3. Divide students into three groups. Have the members of each group identify possible approaches to the topic by practicing one of the prewriting techniques described on this page—freewriting, brainstorming, or questioning. Have group members share their ideas. Discuss the usefulness of each strategy.

FOR ENGLISH LEARNERS

Comprehension: Task Support Summarize the writing process as a series of steps. Explain and model each one.

1. Think of possible topics.
2. Choose one topic.
3. List ideas to include.
4. Organize ideas.
5. Write.
6. Revise.
7. Publish.

Do a Self-Check

Discuss each of the **Key Traits** in the chart. Make certain that students understand the meaning and purpose of each trait.

- **Ideas** Make sure that the main idea is thoroughly developed. Details should be specific and related to the central topic.

- **Organization** Choose the method of organization that is most logical for the kinds of details and purpose. Patterns of organization include chronological, comparison and contrast, cause and effect, and spatial order.

- **Voice** Choose words and sentence structure to convey voice.

- **Word Choice** Avoid imprecise pronouns and vague adjectives and adverbs. Use vocabulary that makes sense in context and sounds natural.

- **Sentence Fluency** Include different sentence types, including simple, compound, and complex. Ask some questions to keep the reader's interest.

- **Conventions** Take the time to correct spelling, punctuation, and grammar.

Reinforce the importance of these traits by comparing them to the ingredients of a cake. If one ingredient is missing or spoiled, then the cake will not turn out very well. In the same way, if one of these areas is weak, then the quality of the overall piece will be affected.

CHECK UNDERSTANDING What qualities does well-organized writing have?

Do a Self-Check

Knowing the key traits of effective writing can help you at every step of the process. Stay on track by checking your draft against this rubric.

KEY TRAITS RUBRIC

		Strong	*Average*	*Weak*
Ideas	1	• has a clear topic • supports statements with relevant details	• has a topic that needs more focus • includes some details but not enough	• has no clear topic • lacks details or includes ones that are unrelated to the topic
Organization	2	• begins with an interesting introduction and ends with a satisfying conclusion • uses transitions between ideas	• has an introduction and a conclusion, but they could be more interesting • needs more transitions to connect ideas	• has no introduction or conclusion • presents a confusing jumble of unrelated ideas
Voice	3	• reflects the writer's unique personality • has a tone that fits the audience and purpose	• shows a lack of interest in the topic • sounds too formal or informal at times	• has no life • uses a completely inappropriate tone
Word Choice	4	• uses vivid words • expresses ideas in a way that sounds natural	• uses words that are correct, but ordinary • sounds forced or awkward at times	• uses words that are too general or incorrect • fails to make the meaning clear
Sentence Fluency	5	• includes sentences of varying length and type	• varies sentence length and type somewhat, but not enough	• includes mostly short or overly long sentences
Conventions	6	• has few errors in grammar, usage, and mechanics	• includes some errors, but readers can still follow the ideas	• has so many errors that the writing is hard to understand

DIFFERENTIATED INSTRUCTION

FOR LESS–PROFICIENT READERS

Concept Support Create a simple checklist for students to use, based on the **Key Traits.** Generate one or two questions for each trait that will help students evaluate their own work or that of others. Use questions such as these:

- Do I state my main idea clearly?

- Are all of my details related to the same main idea?

- Do I use transitions? (Examples: *first, next, then; on the right, on the left*)

- Is there a definite beginning, middle, and end?

- Are my words precise? (Examples: *darted, crept*, or *seeped* instead of *moved*; *poodle* or *German shepherd* instead of *dog*)

- Do I use different kinds of sentences?

Distribute and discuss the checklist. Encourage students to add more examples.

Strategies That Work: Writing

❶ Use Prewriting Strategies

Try different strategies to help you get a strong start.

- **Freewrite.** Jot down whatever pops into your head.
- **Picture it.** Use a graphic organizer to capture your ideas.
- **Brainstorm with classmates.** Generate topics and supporting details with others.
- **Observe your surroundings.** Venture into the world with your notebook. Write notes about interesting people, events, and places.
- **Question yourself.** "What if I were president?" The answer to a silly or serious "what if" question could be your topic.

❷ Get Friendly Feedback

You can ask other writers for help at any stage of the writing process. Keep these guidelines in mind.

When You're the Writer	When You're the Reader
• Be clear about the feedback you want. Should readers comment on your ideas or proofread for errors? • Listen politely to readers' comments and suggestions. • Ask your readers to clarify suggestions that you find confusing.	• Be respectful and positive when you talk about the writer's work. • Support your opinions with reasons, and try to give specific suggestions for improvement. • Don't rewrite the work yourself. Let the writer make the final changes.

❸ Read, Read, Read

Reading other people's writing can help you develop your own style. Here are some sources.

LITERATURE
Take advantage of the literature in this book. Also, don't forget about novels, magazines, and newspapers that interest you.

WRITING COMMUNITY
Form a writing group with other students to share your writing processes and products.

ONLINE RESOURCES
Visit the **Writing Center** at **ClassZone.com** for links to blogs and student publication sites.

Strategies That Work: Writing

Explain that the techniques on this page can help students with any kind of writing.

1. **Use Prewriting Strategies** Read the various strategies aloud. Ask students which ones they have used in the past and which they have found helpful.

2. **Get Friendly Feedback** After students have read the tips, talk about the advantages of getting feedback. Explain that writers are sometimes too involved with what they write to look at it objectively. That is why having someone else look at their work can help to identify parts that need clarification or improvement. Then point out the need to be respectful and courteous when critiquing someone else's work.

3. **Read, Read, Read** Tell students that the more they read, the more easily they will be able to recognize and produce good writing. Have students form small groups to create lists of some of their most recent reading outside of class. Ask groups to share their lists and talk about the merits of the various examples. Encourage students to start their own writing groups. If possible, offer to help students access online resources, particularly the **Writing Center** at **ClassZone.com.**

DIFFERENTIATED INSTRUCTION

FOR LESS–PROFICIENT READERS

Concept Support Provide students with samples of weak writing. (You might retype some examples from last year's class to conceal the writers' identities.) Have students jot down what they might say to the writer to help him or her improve the quality of the writing. Then have students work in pairs to role-play giving this feedback. Observe students' performances and comment generally on the process at the end of the exercise.

UNIT 1

Weaving a Story

PLOT, CONFLICT, AND SETTING

- In Fiction
- In Nonfiction
- In Poetry
- In Drama
- In Media

21

About the Art The painting above illustrates the selection from *An American Childhood* by Annie Dillard. See page 120.

For help in planning this unit, see

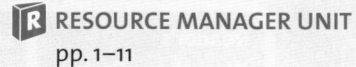 RESOURCE MANAGER UNIT 1
pp. 1–11

INTRODUCE THE UNIT

A well-written story is like a tapestry, with colorful strands of thread woven together to make a compelling picture. The sturdy threads that form the foundation of a tapestry are called the warp. The basic elements that form the foundation of a story are **plot, conflict,** and **setting.**

Ask students to think about an important event in their lives. What details about this experience strike them as they look back on it? Do the details include where and when the experience happened, who was involved, a difficult challenge they faced, or a surprising or exciting moment? Ask students to consider these ideas as they discuss the pictures on this page. To elicit responses, ask

- What is each person doing? How do you think each person might look back on the event shown? What lessons might they learn from their experiences?
- How would you describe the mood of each picture based on the setting? How do the actions of each person affect the mood?
- What challenge or struggle does each person face? What is different about each person's struggle?
- What events do you think led up to the scenes shown? What events might follow?

Discuss with students which information led to their conclusions. Tell students that just as each picture tells a story, each story is made up of many parts. In this unit, students will examine how **plot, conflict,** and **setting** are woven together to make a memorable story.

UNIT 1
Standards Skills Trace

MARYLAND

SKILLS STRAND	1.E.1.b, 3.A.3.b, 3.A.3.c, 3.A.8.b, 3.A.3.d **Reader's Workshop: Parts of a Story** pp. 24–29	1.D.3.b, 1.E.4.f, 3.A.3.b, 5.A.2.c **Seventh Grade** pp. 30–41 Short Story *Level: Easy*	1.D.2.b, 1.E.3.a, 3.A.3.c, 5.A.2.c **The Last Dog** pp. 42–61 Short Story *Level: Challenging*	1.D.3.b, 1.E.4.c, 3.A.3.g, 5.C.2.b **Thank You, M'am** pp. 62–71 Short Story *Level: Easy*	1.D.3.b, 1.E.3.a, 3.A.3.h, 5.B.2.b **Rikki-tikki-tavi** pp. 72–91 Short Story *Level: Easy*	1.E.1.b, 3.A.1.b **Great Reads:** *from* **Holes** pp. 92–97 Adventure Novel *Level: Easy*
Literary Analysis	Stages of Plot pp. 26–29 Internal and External Conflict pp. 24–25, 28–29 Setting pp. 24–25, 28	Stages of Plot pp. 31, 32, 34, 36, 37, 38, 39	Setting pp. 43, 44, 47, 48, 51, 55, 57, 58 Review: Plot p. 47	Internal and External Conflict pp. 63, 64, 66, 69	Suspense pp. 73, 76, 79, 80, 81, 82, 84, 85, 87, 89 Review: Conflict pp. 80, 84, 88	Form (Adventure Novel) p. 92
Reading and Informational Texts	Analyze the Literature pp. 25, 27–29	Connect pp. 31, 34, 36, 37, 39	Identify Sequence pp. 43, 46, 50, 52, 54, 56, 58 Review: Compare and Contrast p. 49 Read an Online Article p. 61	Make Inferences pp. 63, 66, 67, 68, 69 Read a Poem p. 68	Predict pp. 73, 74, 79, 81, 83, 87, 89 Review: Cause and Effect pp. 76, 83, 86	
Vocabulary	Academic Vocabulary pp. 24, 26	Word Acquisition pp. 31, T31, 40 Context Clues p. T31 Latin Roots (*uni*) p. 40	Word Acquisition pp. 43, T43, 59 Context Clues p. T43 Antonyms as Context Clues p. 59	Word Acquisition pp. 63, T63, 70 Word Questioning Map p. T63 Prefixes That Mean "Not" (*dis-, in-, un-, mis-, non-*) p. 70	Word Acquisition pp. 73, T73, 90 Context Clues p. T73 Latin Roots (*viv* and *vit*) p. 90	
Writing, Grammar, and Style		Ways to Correct Sentence Fragments p. 41 Subjects, Predicates, and Complete Sentences p. 41	Ways to Correct Run-on Sentences p. 60	Punctuation of Possessives p. 71	Pronoun-Antecedent Agreement p. 91	
Speaking, Listening, Viewing, and Media	Discuss pp. 24–27	Discuss pp. 30, T32–T38, 39 Analyze Visuals pp. 32, T35, T36	Discuss pp. 42, T44–T57, 58, T61 Analyze Visuals pp. 44, 49, 52, T56	Discuss pp. 62, T64–T68, 69 Analyze Visuals pp. 64, T67	Discuss pp. 72, T74–T88, 89 Present a Picture p. 72 Analyze Visuals pp. 74, 78, T82, T86	Discuss pp. 92, T97

Assessment-Based Planning: Skills in red are assessed on the Unit 1 Test. **T** = Teacher's Edition page

1.D.2.b, 1.E.3.a, 3.A.3, 5.B.2.b	**1.D.3.b, 1.E.3.a, 3.A.3.c**	**3.A.4.a, 3.A.4.c**	**3.A.3.b, 3.A.5.c**	**6.A.2**	**1.E.3.a, 2.A.4.b**	**4.A.1, 4.A.2.b, 4.A.3.c**
				Linked selections		
from **Exploring the *Titanic*** pp. 98–117 Narrative Nonfiction *Level: Average*	*from* **An American Childhood** pp. 118–127 Memoir *Level: Average*	**Casey at the Bat** pp. 128–133 Narrative Poem *Level: Challenging*	**The Monsters Are Due on Maple Street** pp. 134–149 Teleplay *Level: Average*	**Media Study:** *from* **Back to the Future** pp. 150–153 Film Clip	**The Unnatural Course of Time** pp. 154–157 Movie Review *Level: Challenging*	**Writing Workshop: Descriptive Essay** pp. 158–165
Narrative Nonfiction pp. 99, 102, 103, 105, 108, 109, 110, 112, 113, 114, 115 Review: Suspense pp. 106, 108, 111	Setting in Nonfiction pp. 119, 122, 123, 126	Narrative Poetry pp. 129, 130, 132, 133	Conflict in Drama pp. 135, T138, T140, T141, T143, T144, T146, T148, 149		Characteristics of a Movie Review pp. 155, 157	
Identify Chronological Order pp. 99, 100, 106, 107, 109, 111, 115 Review: Make Inferences pp. 110, 112, 115	Recognize Cause and Effect pp. 119, 120, 122, 123, 126 Review: Make Inferences pp. 123, 125, 126	Strategies for Reading Poetry pp. 129, 130, 132 Review: Make Inferences p. 132	Strategies for Reading a Teleplay pp. 135, T136, T138, T139, T140, T142, T144, T146, T147, T148, 149		Analyze a Writer's Position pp. 154, 155, 156, 157 Compare and Contrast Opinions p. 157	Analyze a Focused Description pp. 159–160, 164
Word Acquisition pp. 99, T99, 116 Context Clues p. T99 Analogies p. 116	Word Acquisition pp. 119, T119, 127 Context Clues p. T119 Suffixes That Form Adjectives p. 127		Word Acquisition pp. 135, T135 Classify Words p. T135	Academic Vocabulary (Film) p. 151		
Correct Pronoun Case p. 117						Write a Focused Description pp. 158–165 Sensory Details pp. 158, 159, 161, 162 Comma Usage p. 164
Discuss pp. 98, T100–T114, 115 Analyze Visuals pp. 100, 103, 105, T107, T111, T113	Discuss pp. 118, T120–T125, 126 Analyze Visuals pp. 120, T124	Discuss pp. 128, T130–T132, 133 Analyze Visuals p. 130	Discuss pp. 134, T136–T148, 149 Analyze Visuals pp. T136, T139, T140, T143, T144	Discuss pp. 150, 153 Analyze Film Elements pp. 151–152 Create a Storyboard p. 153	Discuss pp. 154, T155–T156, 157	Discuss pp. 158–160 Produce a Radio Dramatization p. 165

Skills Assessed on the Unit 1 Test:

Literary Analysis
- Identify and analyze stages of plot
- Analyze and evaluate setting

Reading and Informational Texts
- Identify sequence
- Identify patterns of organization
- Recognize cause-and-effect relationships
- Make inferences

Vocabulary
- Understand and use Latin roots
- Understand and use prefixes and suffixes
- Complete analogies

Writing, Grammar, and Style
- Write a focused description
- Use end marks, commas and coordinating conjunctions, and semicolons to correct run-on sentences
- Correctly use apostrophes to punctuate possessives
- Maintain pronoun-antecedent agreement
- Use correct pronoun case
- Additional writing and grammar skills

For additional lesson planning help, see **Easy Planner DVD.**

21B

OBJECTIVES
- establish prior knowledge about **plot, conflict,** and **setting**
- discuss plot, conflict, and setting in familiar stories

What makes a STORY *unforgettable?*

Ask students to describe stories they like and dislike. Record details on the board as they describe them. Work with students to categorize the details according to story elements such as plot, conflict, and setting. Then have them draw conclusions about what was effective in the stories they enjoyed and what was missing from those they didn't like.

ACTIVITY Encourage students to list specific details about their chosen story. Help students understand how their answers relate to plot, conflict, and setting. Explain that in a good story, all of these factors work together to hold a reader's interest.

CHECK UNDERSTANDING Have students identify the common parts of a story and tell how these elements help make a story **unforgettable.**

What makes a STORY *unforgettable?*

Whether it's a spellbinding mystery, a heartwarming true story, or a tale from your grandmother's past, an **unforgettable story** has a certain "something" that sets it apart from other tales. The story might have a riveting plot, a mysterious setting, or a powerful ending, but whatever that certain something is, an unforgettable story stays with you long after you've read or heard it.

ACTIVITY Think of an unforgettable story that you've read or heard. It might be a classic piece of fiction, such as *The Black Stallion,* or a family story that has been passed down for generations. With a group of classmates, discuss the following questions:

- What makes the story unforgettable?
- What do your reasons have in common?
- After your discussion, how would you answer the original question: What makes a story unforgettable?

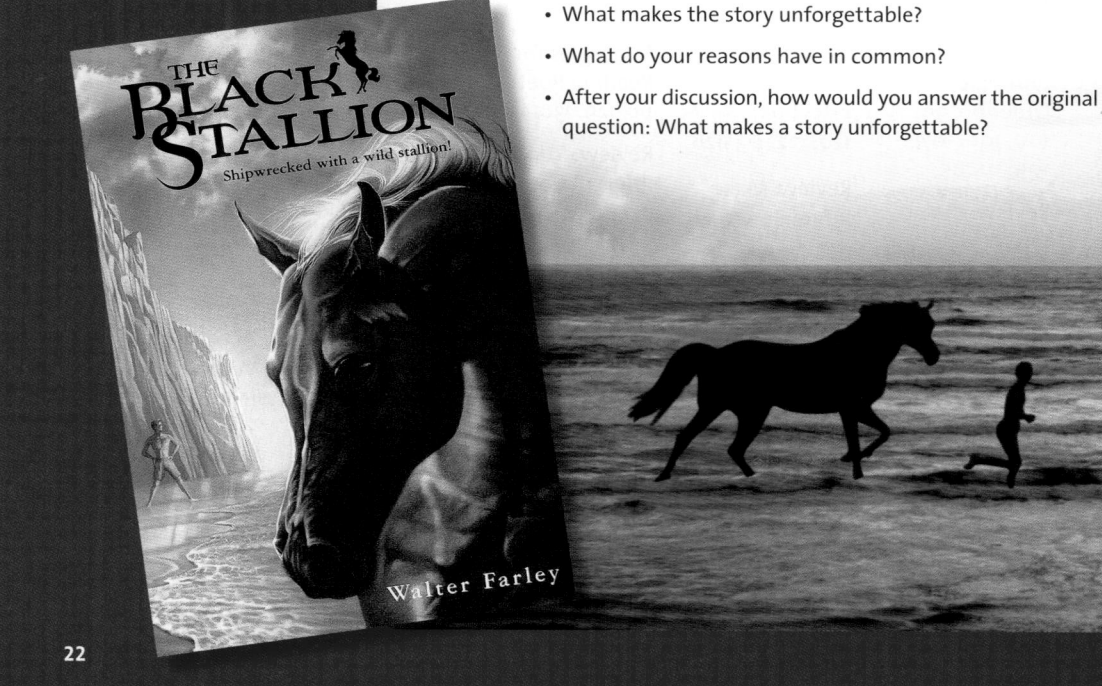

Unit Resources

 RESOURCE MANAGER UNIT 1
 BEST PRACTICES TOOLKIT
STANDARDS LESSON FILE

- Easy Planner DVD
- WriteSmart CD
- ClassZone.com
- Audio Anthology CD
- Multi-Language Academic Vocabulary Online

- eEdition CD & Online
- McDougal Littell Assessment System
- Test Generator CD
- MediaSmart DVD

 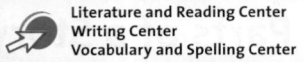
MARYLAND OBJECTIVES

Preview Unit Goals

LITERARY ANALYSIS
- Identify stages of plot; analyze plot development
- Identify and analyze setting
- Identify conflict, flashback, and foreshadowing

READING
- Use reading strategies, including connecting and predicting
- Identify sequence and cause-and-effect relationships
- Identify patterns of organization, including chronological order

WRITING AND GRAMMAR
- Write a description
- Avoid sentence fragments and run-on sentences
- Punctuate possessives correctly
- Maintain pronoun-antecedent agreement in number

SPEAKING, LISTENING, AND VIEWING
- Identify and analyze visual and sound elements in film
- Analyze film techniques that establish plot and setting
- Compare personal opinions with a reviewer's opinion
- Produce a radio dramatization

VOCABULARY
- Understand and use prefixes, suffixes, and word roots

ACADEMIC VOCABULARY
- plot
- conflict
- setting
- sequence
- foreshadowing
- flashback
- cause and effect
- prefix, suffix, word root

23

DIFFERENTIATED INSTRUCTION

FOR ENGLISH LEARNERS
Academic Vocabulary Students will study and practice using these vocabulary terms throughout the unit.

1. Read each word aloud and discuss its meaning. Encourage students to volunteer their own definitions and examples.

2. Allow students to work in pairs to complete the sentences on the Academic Vocabulary copy master and answer the questions.

3. Reconvene to review students' responses.

Additional Academic Vocabulary Use the second copy master to help students study these terms from the unit: *exposition, rising action, climax, falling action, resolution, suspense, pronoun, antecedent, run-on sentence.* Have students take turns reading aloud the terms and examples. Then have students work individually to write their definitions and complete Part B. Discuss answers as a class.

RESOURCE MANAGER—Copy Masters
Academic Vocabulary p. 9
Additional Academic Vocabulary p. 10

Preview Unit Goals

Draw students' attention to the color-coding provided for each skill strand. Explain that throughout the unit, the skills taught within a strand match the color of that strand. Encourage students to consider their ability to use each strategy as they read the page.

Suggest that students write the Academic Vocabulary terms in their journals and define them as they read the unit. Encourage students to use these terms in their discussions and writings about the selections.

ADDITIONAL UNIT GOALS
These skills will be taught in this unit but are not the major focus of the unit:

Literary Analysis
- Identify and evaluate characteristics of narrative nonfiction
- Identify and analyze narrative elements in poetry
- Evaluate theme
- Recognize sound development in a poem, including repetition, rhyme, and rhythm
- Study a variety of genres: short story, narrative nonfiction, poetry, teleplay, adventure fiction, film review

Reading
- Apply strategies for reading poetry
- Understand the function of stage directions in a teleplay
- Make inferences

Writing and Grammar
- Use sensory details
- Use correct pronoun case
- Correctly use apostrophes to punctuate possessives
- Use subject and object pronouns correctly

Speaking, Listening, and Viewing
- Create a storyboard
- Read a film review
- Analyze a writer's position

Vocabulary
- Use context clues to determine word meaning
- Complete analogies

Focus and Motivate

OBJECTIVES

- identify stages of plot
- analyze plot development
- identify internal and external conflict
- analyze and evaluate setting

Teach

Part 1: What Drives a Story?

Setting Explain that the time and place of a story's action are not always clearly stated. Use this activity to illustrate how readers must "add up" details about setting:

1. Have each student write a list of details about a familiar setting, such as the classroom, a room at home, or a local park. Then have students form pairs and read aloud a few details at a time to each other.

2. Ask students to notice how their view of the setting changes with each detail. Ask how their mental image of the place would change if certain details were left out.

Characters Tell students that characters may be revealed through their appearance, speech, thoughts, and actions. Some characters are complex and change during a story, while others have only a few traits and do not change. Ask students to recall a character from a movie or book they know. Ask them what traits and actions make the character memorable.

Conflict Point out that a story may contain several conflicts, but it is the main conflict that ties events together and keeps the action moving forward. Using a story everyone knows, ask these questions:

- Who is the main character?

- What problems or conflicts does this character face? List as many as you can.

- Which conflict is most important in the story? What events happen as a result of this main conflict?

- Is the main conflict inside the character's mind (internal), or is it between the character and an outside force (external)?

 BEST PRACTICES TOOLKIT—Transparencies
Analysis Frame: Plot, Setting pp. D23, D30, D32

 **MARYLAND OBJECTIVES**

LITERATURE STANDARDS
3.A.3.b Analyze conflict and plot
3.A.3.c Analyze setting

Parts of a Story

What makes you willing to spend two hours at the movie theater or a week finishing a book? Is it the thrill of action-packed events or a connection to the characters? Is it a fascination with the setting, such as a faraway galaxy? Setting, characters, conflict, and plot all play a role in holding your interest in a story. Looking closely at these parts can help you understand what makes a story worthwhile.

Part 1: What Drives a Story?

Even the best-built car doesn't cruise on its own. A car needs an engine and a good set of wheels. In the same way, a writer can invent an interesting story, but without the following key parts, that story would sputter to a stop.

- **Setting** is the time and place of the action. The time might be the historical era, the season, or the time of day. The place might be a country, a neighborhood, or a room. In many stories, setting affects the action and the characters' feelings.
- **Characters** are the people, animals, or imaginary creatures that take part in a story. The characters' behavior directly affects what happens.
- **Conflict** is a struggle between different forces. It is the fuel that keeps the action moving forward. A conflict can be external or internal.

TYPE OF CONFLICT	EXAMPLE
External Conflict is a struggle between a character and an outside force. This force might be another character, a group of characters, or nature. 	A sea captain attempts to guide his boat to shore in the middle of a deadly storm. ▶ **(sea captain vs. nature)** *Other Examples* • A boxer faces an opponent. • A girl has a fight with friends.
Internal Conflict is a struggle within a character's mind. This kind of conflict happens when a character must deal with opposing thoughts or feelings.	A girl strongly disagrees with her friends, but she wants them to like her. Should she speak her mind or stay silent? ▶ **(girl vs. herself)** *Other Examples* • Admit needing help or do it alone? • Take a risk or play it safe?

DIFFERENTIATED INSTRUCTION

FOR ALL STUDENTS
For general guidelines on differentiating instruction, see

 BEST PRACTICES TOOLKIT
Differentiated Instruction pp. 31–38

FOR LESS–PROFICIENT READERS
Note Taking Use the copy master Note Taking: What Drives a Story? to help students understand, record, and retain the information on page 24.

 RESOURCE MANAGER—Copy Master
Note Taking p. 15

Illustrate Setting Have students work in small groups to create an illustrated map of the scene in **Model 1** (p. 25). Encourage them to include a legend with symbols for the forest, plain, trails, and Cambodia-Thailand border.

MODEL 1: SETTING

This author draws you into the story by providing specific details about the setting. How might the setting affect what happens?

from The Clay Marble
Novel by **Minfong Ho**

The last rays of afternoon sun were filtering through the forest as we approached the Border. Gradually the trees thinned out and the path widened. Several trails merged into ours. It seemed as if all the paths out of Cambodia were converging on this one spot on the Thai border.

5   I could barely contain my excitement. I imagined mountains of rice lining the horizon, and piles of tools and fishnets everywhere. Perhaps there would even be mounds of sweet moist coconut cakes and banana fritters. "Hurry," I urged my brother.

    Yet, as we finally emerged from the forest, all we could see was a vast 10 barren plain dotted with shrubs and scraggly trees, flat and desolate.

Close Read

1. What details about the setting do you find in lines 1–4? One detail has been boxed.

2. Describe what the narrator expects to see when she crosses the border. Then describe what she actually sees. How might the actual setting affect the narrator and the story?

MODEL 2: CONFLICT

Here, a girl watches from the deck of a ship as her brother is left on a deserted island. What do you learn about the conflict in this excerpt?

from Island of the Blue Dolphins
Novel by **Scott O'Dell**

Against my will, I screamed.

Chief Matasaip grasped my arm.

"We cannot wait for Ramo," he said. "If we do, the ship will be driven on the rocks."

5   "We must!" I shouted. "We must!"

    "The ship will come back for him on another day," Matasaip said. "He will be safe. There is food for him to eat and water to drink and places to sleep."

    "No," I cried.

10 Matasaip's face was like stone. He was not listening.

Close Read

1. Describe the conflict the girl experiences.

2. Is the girl's conflict internal or external? Explain how you know.

MODEL 1: SETTING
Close Read

1. *Possible answer:*
   - *It is late afternoon at the edge of a forest in Cambodia near the Thai border.*
   - *The narrator is at a spot where the trees have thinned out.*
   - *The path she is on gets wider as many paths come together.*

2. *Possible answer: The narrator expects to find a rich country with plenty of food and jobs. Instead she finds a wide, flat plain with little vegetation. She will most likely be disappointed and discouraged by what she sees. Events in the story may further show that Thailand is not at all what she expected it to be.*

   If students need help . . . Draw the two scenes on the board as students identify details from the text. Label the scenes "What she expects" and "What she finds." As a class, discuss differences between the two scenes and how these differences might affect the narrator and the story.

MODEL 2: CONFLICT
Close Read

1. *Possible answer: The girl is aboard a ship that is leaving a deserted island without her brother, Ramo. She begs Chief Matasaip to wait, but he refuses.*

2. *Possible answer: The girl's conflict is external because her struggle is with another character. Clues include the verbal disagreement between the girl and the chief (lines 3–9) and the girl's thoughts expressing frustration with the chief (line 10).*

FOR ENGLISH LEARNERS
Concept Support: Characters and Conflict

1. List these characters on the board: Ramo, the narrator, and Chief Matasaip.
2. Have volunteers share what they can tell about each character based on the text.
3. Help students understand how each character relates to the conflict.

FOR ADVANCED LEARNERS/PRE–AP*
Identify and Discuss Conflict Have students read the workshop independently. Then assign groups of three or four a previously read selection or an appropriate short story that they can all read quickly. Have each group identify the main conflict, tell whether it is an internal or external conflict, and discuss how the characters and setting relate to the conflict.

Build a Story Have students form small groups and work together to build a story.

1. One student begins by describing a setting and several characters.
2. A second student tells what conflict the characters face.
3. A third tells what events happen as a result of the conflict.
4. A fourth tells how the conflict is resolved.
5. The group refines and presents its story.

Teach

Part 2: Stages of Plot

Plot Tell students that listing the major events in a story and details related to the plot stages can be a helpful technique in understanding a story. Point out these devices that authors may use to add complexity to a story's plot:

- A story may begin in the middle of the action, revealing details about the setting and characters as events unfold.

- The sequence of events may be interrupted to tell about an event in the past or to hint at something that might happen in the future.

- A story may include one or more subplots that make the main plot more interesting or complicated.

- A **climax** may occur at or near the end of the story, leaving the reader with unanswered questions about the characters and conflict.

As a class, identify a story or movie with which all students are familiar. Use a Plot Diagram to outline the stages of the plot.

Exposition
Setting: _____
Characters: _____
Potential Conflicts: _____

Climax:

Rising Action: *Falling Action:*

_____   _____
_____   _____
_____   _____
_____   *Resolution:*
_____
          _____
          _____

Then discuss these questions:

- Did the story fit neatly in the diagram?
- Did the author use any of the devices we discussed to make the plot more complex?
- How would the story be different if the events were arranged differently?

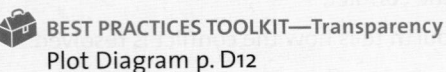 **BEST PRACTICES TOOLKIT—Transparency**
Plot Diagram p. D12

Part 2: Stages of Plot

No matter who the characters are, where the action takes place, or what conflicts occur, a story has a plot. A **plot** is the series of events in a story. Usually a story begins by introducing a main character who has a conflict. As the story moves on, the conflict becomes more complicated, and the character must find a solution. Once the problem is solved, the character adjusts, and the story ends.

A typical plot can be broken down into five stages. By understanding these stages, you can follow a story more closely and know what to look for at all times. For example, at the beginning—or **exposition**—of a story, pay attention to the details that tell you about the characters, the setting, and any potential conflicts that may arise.

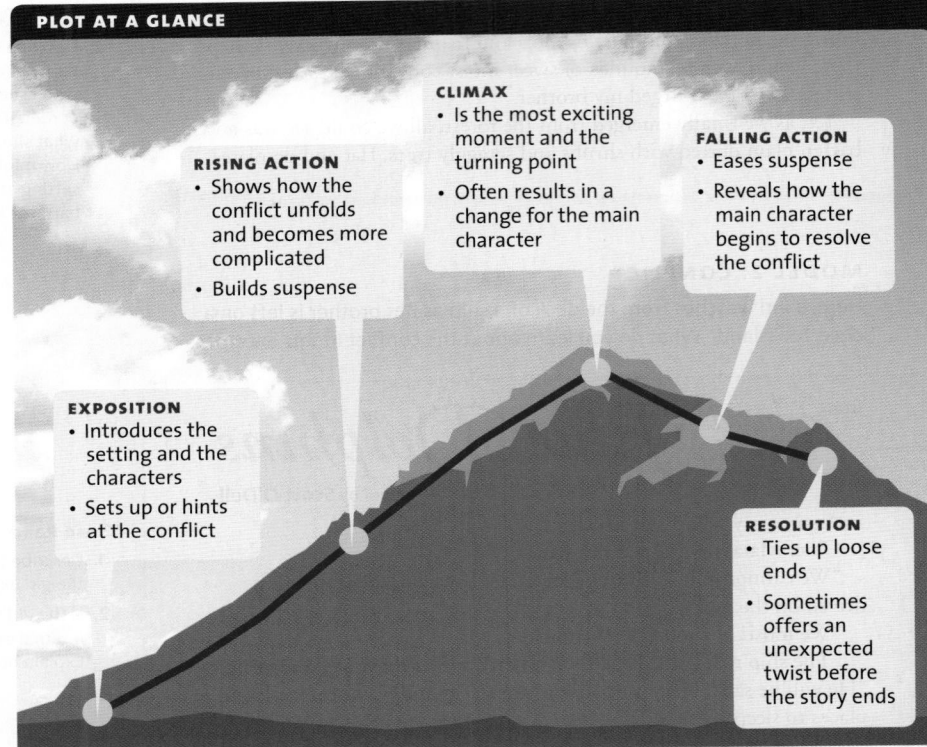

PLOT AT A GLANCE

CLIMAX
- Is the most exciting moment and the turning point
- Often results in a change for the main character

RISING ACTION
- Shows how the conflict unfolds and becomes more complicated
- Builds suspense

FALLING ACTION
- Eases suspense
- Reveals how the main character begins to resolve the conflict

EXPOSITION
- Introduces the setting and the characters
- Sets up or hints at the conflict

RESOLUTION
- Ties up loose ends
- Sometimes offers an unexpected twist before the story ends

DIFFERENTIATED INSTRUCTION

FOR LESS–PROFICIENT READERS

Note Taking For students who need help with note taking, hand out the Note Taking: Stages of Plot copy master. Read and discuss the first paragraph on page 26. Assist students, as needed, in completing the first item on the copy master. Then have students read the rest of the page and take notes on the five stages of plot.

RESOURCE MANAGER—Copy Master
Note Taking p. 16

FOR ENGLISH LEARNERS

Reading Support: Setting and Verb Tense
To clarify when the actions take place in **Model 1**, help students identify verb tenses.

- *Present tense—narrator begins his story in the present time (lines 1–4).*
- *Past tense—narrator goes back to the past to tell about a winter afternoon with his mother (lines 5–6).*
- *Past perfect tense—the use of* had *shows that the narrator is telling what happened before he saw his mother (lines 4, 7–9).*

MODEL 1: EXPOSITION

What do you learn about the setting and the conflict in the exposition of this story?

from
Last Cover
Short story by **Paul Annixter**

I'm not sure I can tell you what you want to know about my brother; but everything about the pet fox is important, so I'll tell all that from the beginning.

It goes back to a winter afternoon after I'd hunted the woods all
5 day for a sign of our lost pet. I remember the way my mother looked up as I came into the kitchen. Without my speaking, she knew what had happened. For six hours I had walked, reading signs, looking for a delicate print in the damp soil or even a hair that might have told of a red fox passing that way—but I had found nothing.

Close Read

1. What can you tell about the setting in which the main character lives? Find specific details that describe the setting.

2. Review the boxed details. Describe the conflict that the main character faces. What does this conflict suggest the story will be about?

MODEL 2: RISING ACTION

At the beginning of this story, lonely Mr. Peters is granted three wishes. He uses his first wish to ask for a wife. In the rising action, what do you learn about the conflict that results from this wish?

from
THE THIRD WISH
Short story by **Joan Aiken**

One evening he was returning home along the river path when he saw Leita in front of him, down by the water. A swan had sailed up to the verge and she had her arms round its neck and the swan's head rested against her cheek. She was weeping, and as he came nearer he
5 saw that tears were rolling, too, from the swan's eyes.

"Leita, what is it?" he asked, very troubled.

"This is my sister," she answered. "I can't bear being separated from her."

Now he understood that Leita was really a swan from the forest, and
10 this made him very sad because when a human being marries a bird it always leads to sorrow.

Close Read

1. Reread the boxed text. What conflict is Mr. Peters facing?

2. The rising action leads toward the climax. What decision or action might this situation be building toward?

MODEL 1: EXPOSITION
Close Read

1. *Possible answer: The setting is a winter afternoon. The narrator lives in a rural area with a moderate climate. Details include "winter afternoon" and "woods" (line 4), "six hours I had walked" (line 7), and "damp soil" (line 8).*

2. *Possible answer: The conflict faced by the narrator is that his family's pet, a red fox, is missing. The story will probably have something to do with his search for the fox and what happens to it.*

MODEL 2: RISING ACTION
Close Read

1. *Possible answer: Mr. Peters realizes that he actually married a swan from the forest, after wishing for a wife.*

2. *Possible answer: Mr. Peters will probably have to make an important decision at the climax: Should he stay married to Leita, even though she is unhappy, or should he use another wish to have Leita transformed back into a swan?*

If students need help . . . Point out this phrase that helps clarify the conflict: "when a human being marries a bird" (line 10).

FOR LESS–PROFICIENT READERS

Identify Characters and Rising Action List these words from "The Third Wish" in the first column of a T Chart. Work with students to identify each character, based on clues in the passage and in the introductory paragraph.

- "he" (line 1), *possible answers: the husband of Leita, the main character, Mr. Peters*
- "Leita" (line 2), *the wife of Mr. Peters*
- "A swan. . . . She was weeping" (lines 2–4), *Leita's sister*

Then have students draw a simple cartoon showing the characters and what is happening in this part of the rising action.

 BEST PRACTICES TOOLKIT—Transparency T Chart p. A25

FOR ADVANCED LEARNERS/PRE–AP

Predict Outcome of Story Have students predict an outcome for **Model 2.** Encourage them to include events that lead to a climax, falling action, and a resolution. You might challenge them to add some interesting twists to their outcomes, such as a subplot involving Leita's sister, a flashback to earlier events, or a surprise ending. Suggest that they keep in mind the title, "The Third Wish."

Practice and Apply

Part 3: Analyze the Literature

Close Read
Exposition (Lines 1–13)

1. **Possible answer:** *The story takes place at a dinner party at an up-country station in India (lines 1–2). Since the party is given by "a colonial official and his wife" (line 2), the story is probably set sometime in the late nineteenth or early twentieth century. (The British government controlled India as a colony between 1858 and 1947.)*

2. **Possible answer:** *The young girl argues that modern women have greater control over their behavior and emotions than women of earlier generations (lines 6–8). The colonel argues that men still have more control than women (lines 8–9, 11–13).*

Close Read
Rising Action (Lines 14–36)

3. **Possible answer:** *Details include "he sees a strange expression come over the face of the hostess" (lines 15–16), "staring straight ahead" and "muscles of her face contracting slightly" (lines 16–17), and "The boy's eyes widen: he turns quickly and leaves the room" (line 19).*

Part 3: Analyze the Literature

In this story, an elegant dinner party turns dangerous when an uninvited "guest" makes an appearance. As you read, use what you've just learned about plot, conflict, and setting to analyze the story.

The Dinner Party

Short story by
Mona Gardner

The country is India. A large dinner party is being given in an up-country station by a colonial official[1] and his wife. The guests are army officers and government attachés[2] and their wives, and an American naturalist.[3]

5   At one side of the long table a spirited discussion springs up between a young girl and a colonel. The girl insists women have long outgrown the jumping-on-a-chair-at-the-sight-of-a-mouse era, that they are not as fluttery as their grandmothers. The colonel says they are, explaining that women haven't the actual nerve control of men. The other men at 10 the table agree with him.

   "A woman's unfailing reaction in any crisis," the colonel says, "is to scream. And while a man may feel like it, yet he has that ounce more of control than a woman has. And that last ounce is what counts!"

   The American scientist does not join in the argument, but sits 15 watching the faces of the other guests. As he looks, he sees a strange expression come over the face of the hostess. She is staring straight ahead, the muscles of her face contracting slightly. With a small gesture she summons the native boy standing behind her chair. She whispers to him. The boy's eyes widen: he turns quickly and leaves the room.

---

1. **colonial official:** a person holding a position in the British government ruling India.
2. **attachés** (ăt′ə-shāz′): people who assist an ambassador.
3. **naturalist:** a person who studies living things by observing them directly.

Close Read
Exposition (Lines 1–13)

1. What do you learn about the setting in the exposition?

2. What are the young girl and the colonel arguing about in lines 5–13?

Close Read
Rising Action (Lines 14–36)

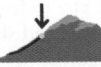

3. Find two details in lines 14–19 that hint at a possible conflict. One detail has been boxed.

DIFFERENTIATED INSTRUCTION

FOR LESS–PROFICIENT READERS

Concept Support For students who have trouble identifying the plot stages, suggest that they act out the events in the story. Encourage them to focus on facial expressions, gestures, and speech in order to recognize how the tension builds and then eases. Compare this building and easing of tension to the process of climbing a mountain, as shown in the diagram on page 26.

FOR ENGLISH LEARNERS

Vocabulary Support: Phrasal Verbs Guide students in using context clues to understand the meanings of these phrasal verbs. Use the activity as an opportunity to clarify what is happening in the story.

- *springs up* (line 5), "begins"
- *come over* (line 16), "change"
- *comes to* (line 22), "suddenly understands what is happening"
- *make for* (line 39), "move toward"

20 No one else sees this, nor the boy when he puts a bowl of milk on the verandah[4] outside the glass doors.

The American comes to with a start. In India, milk in a bowl means only one thing. It is bait for a snake. He realizes there is a cobra in the room.

25 He looks up at the rafters[5]—the likeliest place—and sees they are bare. Three corners of the room, which he can see by shifting only slightly, are empty. In the fourth corner a group of servants stand, waiting until the next course can be served. The American realizes there is only one place left—under the table.

30 His first impulse is to jump back and warn the others. But he knows the commotion will frighten the cobra and it will strike. He speaks quickly, the quality of his voice so arresting that it sobers everyone.

"I want to know just what control everyone at this table has. I will count three hundred—that's five minutes—and not one of you is to

35 move a single muscle. The persons who move will forfeit 50 rupees.[6] Now! Ready!"

The 20 people sit like stone images while he counts. He is saying ". . . two hundred and eighty . . ." when, out of the corner of his eye, he sees the cobra emerge and make for the bowl of milk. Four or five

40 screams ring out as he jumps to slam shut the verandah doors.

"You certainly were right, Colonel!" the host says. "A man has just shown us an example of real control."

"Just a minute," the American says, turning to his hostess, "there's one thing I'd like to know. Mrs. Wynnes, how did you know that cobra was

45 in the room?"

A faint smile lights up the woman's face as she replies. "Because it was lying across my foot."

---

4. **verandah:** a long porch, usually roofed, along the side of a building.

5. **rafters:** wooden beams that support a roof.

6. **rupees** (rōō-pēz'): Indian units of money.

4. Reread lines 22–24. What is the main conflict? Explain whether it is internal or external.

Close Read
Climax (Lines 37–40)

5. What happens at the climax, or the most exciting moment?

Close Read
Falling Action and Resolution (Lines 41–47)

6. At what point in the falling action does the tension begin to ease? Explain.

7. What surprise is revealed in the resolution?

---

4. *Possible answer: The main conflict is that there is a deadly cobra hiding somewhere in the room. The conflict is external, between the dinner guests and the snake.*

Close Read
Climax (Lines 37–40)

5. *Possible answer: The climax occurs when the snake slithers out of the room and the naturalist slams the door behind it. Several people scream as they see the snake.*

Close Read
Falling Action and Resolution (Lines 41–47)

6. *Possible answer: The tension eases once the door has been shut. The host makes light of the event by relating it to the dinner conversation.*

7. *Possible answer: Mrs. Wynnes reveals that the cobra had been lying across her foot. To everyone's surprise, she has quietly disproven the colonel's argument about women's nerves.*

Assess and Reteach

Assess

Have students identify the characters, setting, and conflict in "The Dinner Party" and briefly summarize the plot.

Reteach

For students who are unable to apply the workshop skills to "The Dinner Party," select from these reteaching options:

1. Have students review their Note Taking copy masters for homework. Have them list an example of each term based on a story they have read or a movie they have seen.

2. Divide students into four groups. Assign each group a section of "The Dinner Party" (lines 1–13, lines 14–36, lines 37–40, or lines 41–47). Have each group read the section and summarize the plot stages. When they have finished, have groups share their summaries.

FOR ADVANCED LEARNERS/PRE–AP

Extension Activities Assign one of these activities to students who have mastered the workshop content:

• Have students write a brief essay explaining how the dinner conversation relates to the conflict, and how the author ties this in with a surprise twist at the story's end.

• Have students complete a Plot Diagram like the one on page 26 for a previously read or newly assigned short story. When they have finished, have them write a brief evaluation of the plot structure, telling whether they thought it was effective, what they did or didn't like about it, and what they might change if they were going to tell the story differently.

OBJECTIVES

Literary Analysis
- explore the key idea of making a good **impression**
- identify stages of a plot
- analyze plot development
- read a short story

Reading
- make connections to a story

Vocabulary
- build vocabulary for reading and writing
- understand and use the Latin root *uni* (also an EL language objective)

Grammar and Writing
- avoid sentence fragments
- use writing to analyze literature

SUMMARY

Victor enters seventh grade determined to make Teresa "his girl." During French class, he tries to impress her by claiming to know the language. His teacher, realizing Victor's motive, does not expose him. As a result, Teresa thinks Victor knows French and asks him to help her study. Victor happily assents.

How do you make a good IMPRESSION?

Ask students what the word *impress* means. Discuss why someone might want to make an **impression** on another person, and how they might go about it. After students complete the *LIST IT* activity, have students share their best ideas.

Seventh Grade
Short Story by Gary Soto

How do you make a good IMPRESSION?

MARYLAND OBJECTIVES

READING/LIT STANDARDS
1.E.4.f Connect text to personal experience
3.A.3.b Analyze plot

KEY IDEA All of us have times when we're eager to make a good **impression**—to win the approval of parents, teachers, or friends. But influencing how others see us isn't always easy. In "Seventh Grade," a boy finds that trying to make a good impression can lead to some embarrassing moments.

LIST IT What tips have you heard about how to make a good impression? Create a list of the suggestions you think are most effective.

How to Make a Good Impression
1. Stand up straight.
2.
3.

30

* Resources for Differentiation   † Also in Spanish   ‡ In Haitian Creole and Vietnamese

LITERARY ANALYSIS: PLOT

A **plot** is what happens in a story, and usually consists of five stages.

- The **exposition** introduces the characters, the setting, and often the conflict, or struggle between forces.
- The **rising action** shows how the conflict gets more complicated.
- The **climax** is the moment of greatest interest.
- The **falling action** and **resolution** reveal the outcome.

As you read "Seventh Grade," notice how the events in the story lead up to the climax.

READING STRATEGY: CONNECT

In almost any story, you can find some common ground with the characters by relating your knowledge and experiences to theirs. This is called **connecting**, and it helps you enter into the story. As you read the selection, use a chart like the one shown to connect what is happening in "Seventh Grade" to your own life.

What's Happening in the Story	Connection to My Life
Victor is daydreaming about traveling to France.	I daydream about the world outside my neighborhood too.

▲ VOCABULARY IN CONTEXT

The boldfaced words help tell the story of a day in the life of a seventh grader. After reading the sentences, write the definitions of the boldfaced words with which you are familiar.

1. A student may **quiver** when tests are handed back.
2. Feel free to **linger** after class if you have a question.
3. Sam loves to eat; he is rather **portly.**
4. The athlete's **ferocity** was praised.
5. She smiled **sheepishly** as she admitted to staying up late.
6. The class recited poems in **unison.**

Author Online

Gary Soto
born 1952

A Neighborhood's Influence
Gary Soto fills his fiction and poetry for young adults with lively details of his upbringing in a Mexican-American neighborhood. Soto wants his work to help others appreciate his old neighborhood's values. But, he says, "I am really writing about the feelings and experiences of most American kids: having a pet, going to the park for a family cookout ... getting a bee sting!"

The Power of Reading Soto has said that as a child he never thought about being a writer. Today, though, he meets with young people to encourage their curiosity about reading and writing. The award-winning author explains, "I believe in literature and the depth it adds to all our lives."

 MORE ABOUT THE AUTHOR
For more on Gary Soto, visit the **Literature Center** at **ClassZone.com.**

Background

Fresno, California "Seventh Grade" is set in Fresno, California, where Gary Soto grew up. Fresno is located southeast of San Francisco. Its dry, hot summers and cool, humid winters are excellent for growing grapes. A large number of Latinos, whose families are originally from Spanish-speaking countries, are employed in Fresno's vineyards.

Teach

STANDARDS FOCUS

LITERARY ANALYSIS

● **PLOT**

Read this example aloud:

> Latisha stood nervously on stage. She had to sing well tonight to impress the talent scout. She took a deep breath and stopped. The microphone was not on. She began again. Her voice soared. Later, the talent scout said, "We'd like to offer you a contract."

Have students identify the plot elements. *Possible answer: Conflict: Latisha is nervous but must sing well.* **Rising action:** *Microphone is off.* **Climax:** *She sings well.* **Resolution:** *She gets a contract.*

CHECK UNDERSTANDING Have students identify plot elements of a familiar story.

READING STRATEGY

■ **CONNECT**

Ask students whether they enjoy stories about people their own age. If so, ask them to explain why such stories interest them. *Students may say they can identify with the experiences and feelings of characters their own age.*

CHECK UNDERSTANDING Ask students how they might connect with characters in a story called "Seventh Grade."

 RESOURCE MANAGER—Copy Master
Connect p. 29 (for student use while reading the selection)

VOCABULARY SKILL

▲ VOCABULARY IN CONTEXT

DIAGNOSE WORD KNOWLEDGE To determine preteaching needs, have all students complete **Vocabulary in Context.** Check their answers against those on the selection pages: *quiver* (p. 34), *linger* (p. 34), *portly* (p. 35), *ferocity* (p. 34), *sheepishly* (p. 37), *unison* (p. 35).

PRETEACH VOCABULARY Use the Vocabulary Study copy master to help students determine meanings for each boldfaced word, using context clues.

1. Read the first paragraph aloud, emphasizing *linger.*
2. Point out the phrase "take too long." Elicit possible meanings for *linger,* such as "delay."
3. Repeat the procedure for the rest of the passage.

 RESOURCE MANAGER—Copy Master
Vocabulary Study p. 31

For general guidelines on differentiating vocabulary instruction and for alternative vocabulary activities for students not needing vocabulary preteaching, see

BEST PRACTICES TOOLKIT
Scaffolding Vocabulary Instruction pp. 43–46

ⓘ Vocabulary Center at **ClassZone.com**

ANALYZE VISUALS

Possible answer: *The expression on the girl's face suggests that she is happy, relaxed, and friendly.*

LITERARY ANALYSIS

Ⓐ PLOT: EXPOSITION

Record students' answers in a list. **Possible answer:**

- *Victor is a student on his first day of school.*
- *He speaks English and Spanish.*
- *He lives in Fresno where it's hot.*
- *He dreams of traveling to France one day.*

Extend the Discussion Why does the author present this information about Victor in the first paragraph of the story?

Seventh Grade
Gary Soto

> On the first day of school, Victor stood in line half an hour before he came to a wobbly card table. He was handed a packet of papers and a computer card on which he listed his one elective, French. He already spoke Spanish and English, but he thought some day he might travel to France, where it was cool; not like Fresno, where summer days reached 110 degrees in the shade. There were rivers in France, and huge churches, and fair-skinned people everywhere, the way there were brown people all around Victor. Ⓐ
>
> Besides, Teresa, a girl he had liked since they were in catechism classes[1]
> 10 at Saint Theresa's, was taking French, too. With any luck they would be in the same class. Teresa is going to be my girl this year, he promised himself as he left the gym full of students in their new fall clothes. She was cute. And good in math, too, Victor thought as he walked down the hall to his homeroom. He ran into his friend, Michael Torres, by the water fountain that never turned off.

ANALYZE VISUALS
What might you **infer** about the girl from her expression?

❶ **Targeted Passage**

Ⓐ **PLOT: EXPOSITION**
What background information do you learn about Victor in the first paragraph?

---

1. **catechism** (kăt′ĭ-kĭz′əm) **classes:** formal classes in religious instruction.

DIFFERENTIATED INSTRUCTION

FOR ALL STUDENTS

Journals Victor arrives at school with several goals in mind. Setting goals, whether they are social, academic, artistic, or athletic, can have a powerful effect on your life. Someone with clear goals is more likely to take the actions needed to reach his or her aims. Ask students to reflect in their journals on the goals they would like to achieve this year.

FOR LESS–PROFICIENT READERS

In combination with the *Audio Anthology CD*, use one or more Targeted Passages (pp. 32, 37, 38) to ensure that students focus on key story events, concepts, and skills.

❶ **Targeted Passage [Lines 1–12]**

This passage begins the story's exposition. It introduces the main character (Victor), the setting (first day of school in Fresno), and Victor's motivation for taking French (to be in class with Teresa).

BACKGROUND

Picking Grapes In this story, Victor and his friend Michael both earn money for new school clothes by picking grapes. They compare the experience to "living in Siberia, except hot and more boring" (lines 30–31). The timing of the harvest is vital because grapes do not ripen once they are removed from the vine, so they must be picked at their peak. Although more and more grape harvesting is being done by machine, some grapes are still picked by hand. Table grapes—those meant to be eaten fresh—are cut in clusters and then packed for shipment. They must be handled carefully so that they do not bruise. Grapes that will become raisins are cut and placed on drying trays in the sun. The fruit is turned about halfway through the two to three weeks it takes to complete the drying process.

- Who are two main characters in the story?
- When and where does the story take place?
- Why did Victor sign up for French?
- What does Victor hope will happen this year?

FOR ENGLISH LEARNERS

Key Academic Vocabulary Have students complete Word Squares for these words: *grade* (title; line 182), *principal* (line 43), *period* (lines 47, 51, 152), *finally* (line 91), *eventually* (line 109).

 BEST PRACTICES TOOLKIT—Transparency
Word Squares p. E10

Prereading For prereading instruction for English learners, see

 BEST PRACTICES TOOLKIT
Scaffolding Reading Instruction pp. 43–46

FOR ADVANCED LEARNERS/PRE–AP

Pre-AP exercises in the bottom channel provide additional challenge for your advanced students. Use them for small groups or individuals.

ADDITIONAL GUIDELINES

For more help with differentiation and tips for classroom management, see

 BEST PRACTICES TOOLKIT
Differentiated Instruction pp. 31–38

B CONNECT

Have students write their answers in the chart from page 31. **Possible answers:**

In the Story	My Life
Victor and Michael shake hands raz-a-style and do a saludo de vato.	When I meet a friend, I might wave, slap the person on the back, or just smile.

CULTURAL CONNECTION

Greetings People from various cultures have different ways of greeting each other. In lines 16–17, Michael and Victor say hello in a way that reflects their Mexican-American background. Across the globe in Cambodia, it is customary for people to place their hands together and bow. The Maoris of New Zealand sometimes greet each other with a hug, or they may perform the more traditional salutation, known as the hongi. They press their noses together with their eyes closed and make a quiet humming sound. While strangers and acquaintances shake hands in Turkey, close friends often kiss both cheeks.

C PLOT: EXPOSITION

Possible answer: *The girls might be impressed, or they might be wondering why the boys are wearing such strange expressions.*

Extend the Discussion What kind of impression is Michael trying to create by scowling?

They shook hands, *raza*-style,[2] and jerked their heads at one another in a *saludo de vato*.[3] "How come you're making a face?" asked Victor. **B**

"I ain't making a face, *ese*.[4] This *is* my face." Michael said his face had changed during the summer. He had read a GQ[5] magazine that his older
20 brother had borrowed from the Book Mobile and noticed that the male models all had the same look on their faces. They would stand, one arm around a beautiful woman, and *scowl*. They would sit at a pool, their rippled stomachs dark with shadow, and *scowl*. They would sit at dinner tables, cool drinks in their hands, and *scowl*.

"I think it works," Michael said. He scowled and let his upper lip **quiver.** His teeth showed along with the **ferocity** of his soul. "Belinda Reyes walked by a while ago and looked at me," he said.

Victor didn't say anything, though he thought his friend looked pretty strange. They talked about recent movies, baseball, their parents, and the
30 horrors of picking grapes in order to buy their fall clothes. Picking grapes was like living in Siberia,[6] except hot and more boring.

"What classes are you taking?" Michael said, scowling.

"French. How 'bout you?"

"Spanish. I ain't so good at it, even if I'm Mexican."

"I'm not either, but I'm better at it than math, that's for sure."

A tinny, three-beat bell propelled students to their homerooms. The two friends socked each other in the arm and went their ways, Victor thinking, man, that's weird. Michael thinks making a face makes him handsome.

On the way to his homeroom, Victor tried a scowl. He felt foolish,
40 until out of the corner of his eye he saw a girl looking at him. Umm, he thought, maybe it does work. He scowled with greater conviction. **C**

In homeroom, roll was taken, emergency cards were passed out, and they were given a bulletin to take home to their parents. The principal, Mr. Belton, spoke over the crackling loudspeaker, welcoming the students to a new year, new experiences, and new friendships. The students squirmed in their chairs and ignored him. They were anxious to go to first period. Victor sat calmly, thinking of Teresa, who sat two rows away, reading a paperback novel. This would be his lucky year. She was in his homeroom, and would probably be in his English and math classes. And,
50 of course, French.

The bell rang for first period, and the students herded noisily through the door. Only Teresa **lingered,** talking with the homeroom teacher.

---

2. *raza* (rä'sä)-**style** *Spanish:* in the manner that Mexican Americans greet each other.
3. *saludo de vato* (sä-lōō'dō dě bä'tō) *Spanish:* greeting between Mexican-American friends.
4. *ese* (ě'sě) *Spanish:* a slang term used in addressing someone, as in "Hey, man."
5. *GQ: Gentleman's Quarterly*, a magazine of men's styles and fashions.
6. **Siberia:** a cold, isolated region of northern Russia.

B CONNECT
How do you greet your friends when you see them in the hall?

quiver (kwĭv'ər) *v.* to shake with a slight, rapid movement

ferocity (fə-rŏs'ĭ-tē) *n.* fierceness; extreme intensity

C PLOT: EXPOSITION
Reread lines 25–27 and lines 39–41. When the boys scowl, they see girls look at them. What might the girls be thinking?

linger (lĭng'gər) *v.* to continue to stay; delay leaving

DIFFERENTIATED INSTRUCTION

FOR LESS–PROFICIENT READERS
Reading Strategy Follow-Up: Connect
Lead students in a discussion of what they have been able to connect to so far in the story. Students might identify the setting, the anticipation about the new school year, or the hope that someone will be in one of their classes. Have students then find two details on this page to which they can connect. Have them record these references in their charts and state their connection to them.

Possible answers:

What's Happening in the Story	Connection to My Life
Victor's friend Michael developed a new scowling look over the summer.	I had my hair cut in a new style this year. I wanted a new look for this school year.
Victor and Michael had to earn the money for their new school clothes.	I have certain chores that I do to earn my allowance. Clothes seem expensive when I'm spending my own money.

"So you think I should talk to Mrs. Gaines?" she asked the teacher. "She would know about ballet?"

"She would be a good bet," the teacher said. Then added, "Or the gym teacher, Mrs. Garza."

60 Victor lingered, keeping his head down and staring at his desk. He wanted to leave when she did so he could bump into her and say something clever.

He watched her on the sly. As she turned to leave, he stood up and hurried to the door, where he managed to catch her eye. She smiled and said, "Hi, Victor."

He smiled back and said, "Yeah, that's me." His brown face blushed. Why hadn't he said, "Hi, Teresa," or "How was your 70 summer?" or something nice?

As Teresa walked down the hall, Victor walked the other way, looking back, admiring how gracefully she walked, one foot in front of the other. So much for being in the same class, he thought. As he trudged to English, he practiced scowling.

In English they reviewed the parts of speech. Mr. Lucas, a **portly** man, waddled down the aisle, asking, "What is a noun?"

"A person, place, or thing," said the class in **unison**.

80 "Yes, now somebody give me an example of a person—you, Victor Rodriguez."

"Teresa," Victor said automatically. Some of the girls giggled. They knew he had a crush on Teresa. He felt himself blushing again.

"Correct," Mr. Lucas said. "Now provide me with a place."

Mr. Lucas called on a freckled kid who answered, "Teresa's house with a kitchen full of big brothers."

After English, Victor had math, his weakest subject. He sat in the back by the window, hoping he would not be called on. Victor understood most of the problems, but some of the stuff looked like the teacher made 90 it up as she went along. It was confusing, like the inside of a watch.

After math he had a fifteen-minute break, then social studies, and, finally, lunch. He bought a tuna casserole with buttered rolls, some fruit cocktail, and milk. He sat with Michael, who practiced scowling between bites.

Girls walked by and looked at him.

portly (pôrt'lē) *adj.* stout or overweight

unison (yōo'nĭ-sən) *n.* harmony or agreement; as with one voice

SEVENTH GRADE   **35**

ANALYZE VISUALS

Activity Ask students how this image helps them connect to the story. *Possible answer: It helps them visualize the setting and compare it to their own school.*

Lines 59–70
REINFORCE *KEY IDEA:* IMPRESSION

Discuss What does Victor think will make a good **impression** on Teresa? *Possible answer: Victor thinks she will be impressed if he says clever things. He wants to show her that he's smart and nice.*

Lines 66–76
DISCUSSION PROMPTS

Use these prompts to help students understand how Victor's mood changes after talking with Teresa:

Connect Think about a time when you wanted to say something clever but couldn't think of the right words until it was too late. Based on that experience, how do you think Victor feels after talking to Teresa? *Students might say that Victor feels disappointed in himself and is worried that Teresa isn't able to see what an interesting person he really is.*

Analyze What does the verb *trudged* (line 76) suggest about Victor's feelings? *Possible answer: He has lost his original lightheartedness and feels weighed down by his failure in that crucial first encounter.*

Synthesize Why does Victor return to practicing his scowling? *Possible answer: He thinks Michael's approach may be better after all, so he tries to change his appearance rather than making clever conversation.*

FOR ENGLISH LEARNERS

Vocabulary Support Assign mixed-ability groups several school-related words and phrases from the story. Have each group define the words and report back to the class.

- *elective* (line 3)
- *taking French* (line 10)
- *gym* (lines 12, 57)
- *homeroom* (line 14)
- *roll was taken, emergency cards* (line 42)
- *bulletin, principal* (line 43)
- *loudspeaker* (line 44)

- *first period* (line 47); *bell rang for* (line 51)
- *desk* (line 60)
- *English [class]* (line 76)
- *called on* (lines 85, 88)
- *subject* (line 87)
- *campus* (line 101)
- *bag lunch* (line 103)
- *chalkboard* (line 119); *blackboard* (line 142); *board* (line 149); *erasing the board* (line 154)
- *metal shop* (line 179)
- *textbooks* (line 181)

FOR ADVANCED LEARNERS/PRE–AP

Illustrate Plot Assign each student a section of the story to illustrate in a four-panel cartoon strip. Then have students combine their strips and discuss the plot elements represented by each one. Possible sections are lines 14–38, 59–76, 77–100, 101–115, 116–151, 152–182.

ANALYZE VISUALS

Activity Ask students to write a caption for this image that connects it to what is happening in the story. ***Possible answer:*** *Victor's English teacher asks him for an example of a person, and Victor immediately says, "Teresa" (lines 80–82).*

LITERARY ANALYSIS

Ⓓ PLOT: RISING ACTION

You may want to record students' answers in a list or place them on a plot diagram similar to the one on page 39. **Possible answer:**

- *Teresa spends time talking with the teacher after homeroom, which makes it difficult for Victor to talk to her.*
- *Victor thought he would have more classes with Teresa, but she isn't in any of his morning classes.*
- *Teresa is not eating lunch inside.*

If students need help . . . Have students work in small groups to diagram the elements of plot identified so far. Ask groups to contribute to a class diagram of the plot.

READING STRATEGY

Ⓔ CONNECT

Remind students to record their answers in their charts from page 31. **Possible answer:**

In the Story	My Life
Victor feels frustrated about not being able to find Teresa.	I was supposed to meet a friend at the movies. It was so crowded that I couldn't find her for a long time. I felt pretty frustrated.

"See what I mean, Vic?" Michael scowled. "They love it."

"Yeah, I guess so."

They ate slowly, Victor scanning the horizon for a glimpse of Teresa. He didn't see her. She must have brought lunch, he thought, and is eating outside. Victor scraped his plate and left Michael, who was busy scowling 100 at a girl two tables away. Ⓓ

The small, triangle-shaped campus bustled with students talking about their new classes. Everyone was in a sunny mood. Victor hurried to the bag lunch area, where he sat down and opened his math book. He moved his lips as if he were reading, but his mind was somewhere else. He raised his eyes slowly and looked around. No Teresa.

He lowered his eyes, pretending to study, then looked slowly to the left. No Teresa. He turned a page in the book and stared at some math problems that scared him because he knew he would have to do them eventually. He looked to the right. Still no sign of her. He stretched 110 out lazily in an attempt to disguise his snooping. Ⓔ

Then he saw her. She was sitting with a girlfriend under a plum tree. Victor moved to a table near her and daydreamed about taking her to a movie. When the bell sounded, Teresa looked up, and their eyes met. She smiled sweetly and gathered her books. Her next class was French, same as Victor's.

36 UNIT 1: PLOT, CONFLICT, AND SETTING

Ⓓ **PLOT: RISING ACTION**
What obstacles are getting in the way of Victor making Teresa "his girl"?

Ⓔ **CONNECT**
What experiences have you had that help you understand how Victor might be feeling as he looks for Teresa?

DIFFERENTIATED INSTRUCTION

FOR ENGLISH LEARNERS

Language: Pronoun Referents Explain that sometimes the noun to which a pronoun refers is not actually stated. For example, in line 95, Michael says, "They love it." *It* refers to his scowling. In other cases, the noun to which the pronoun refers is in a separate sentence. Point out line 102. *Everyone* (line 102) refers to *students* in line 101. Have pairs of students find the missing noun for these pronouns: *her* (line 111), *They* (line 116), *She* (line 163).

FOR ADVANCED LEARNERS/PRE–AP

Analyze Point of View Point out that this story is told from a third-person limited point of view. The narrator is able to describe only Victor's thoughts. Challenge students to rewrite a scene in the story from another character's point of view, giving details about that character's thoughts and feelings. Then discuss how students' versions of the scene differ from Gary Soto's version. Does Victor seem like a different person when described from the other character's point of view?

They were among the last students to arrive in class, so all the good desks in the back had already been taken. Victor was forced to sit near the front, a few desks away from Teresa, while Mr. Bueller wrote French words on the chalkboard. The bell rang, and Mr. Bueller wiped his hands,
120 turned to the class, and said, *"Bonjour."* [7]

"Bonjour," braved a few students.

"Bonjour," Victor whispered. He wondered if Teresa heard him. **F**

Mr. Bueller said that if the students studied hard, at the end of the year they could go to France and be understood by the populace.

One kid raised his hand and asked, "What's 'populace'?"

"The people, the people of France."

Mr. Bueller asked if anyone knew French. Victor raised his hand, wanting to impress Teresa. The teacher beamed and said, *"Très bien. Parlez-vous français?"* [8]

130 Victor didn't know what to say. The teacher wet his lips and asked something else in French. The room grew silent. Victor felt all eyes staring at him. He tried to bluff his way out by making noises that sounded French.

"La me vave me con le grandma," he said uncertainly. **G**

Mr. Bueller, wrinkling his face in curiosity, asked him to speak up.

Great rosebushes of red bloomed on Victor's cheeks. A river of nervous sweat ran down his palms. He felt awful. Teresa sat a few desks away, no doubt thinking he was a fool. Without looking at Mr. Bueller, Victor mumbled, "Frenchie oh wewe gee in September."

Mr. Bueller asked Victor to repeat what he said.

140 "Frenchie oh wewe gee in September," Victor repeated.

Mr. Bueller understood that the boy didn't know French and turned away. He walked to the blackboard and pointed to the words on the board with his steel-edged ruler. **2 Targeted Passage**

"Le bateau," he sang.

"Le bateau," the students repeated.

"Le bateau est sur l'eau," [9] he sang.

"Le bateau est sur l'eau."

Victor was too weak from failure to join the class. He stared at the board and wished he had taken Spanish, not French. Better yet, he
150 wished he could start his life over. He had never been so embarrassed. He bit his thumb until he tore off a sliver of skin.

The bell sounded for fifth period, and Victor shot out of the room, avoiding the stares of the other kids, but had to return for his math book. He looked **sheepishly** at the teacher, who was erasing the board, then

---

F PLOT: RISING ACTION
Why does the tension increase now that Victor and Teresa are in the same class together?

G CONNECT
Think of a time when you said you knew something that you really didn't. **Compare and contrast** how it made you feel with how Victor is feeling now.

sheepishly (shē′pĭsh-lē) *adv.* with a bashful or embarrassed look

---

7. *Bonjour* (bôn′zhōōr) *French:* Good day.
8. *Très bien. Parlez-vous français?* (trĕ byăn pär′lā vōō frän′sĕ) *French:* Very good. Do you speak French?
9. *Le bateau est sur l'eau* (lə bä′tō ĕ sür lō) *French:* The boat is on the water.

F PLOT: RISING ACTION

Possible answer: This is Victor's chance to get Teresa's attention and make an impression on her.

If students need help . . . Remind them that Victor has been trying all day to find an opportunity to impress Teresa. Ask students what they think he will try to do in class.

G CONNECT

Possible answer: Students might say that based on their own experience, they think Victor is probably feeling very uncomfortable and trapped. He most likely doesn't know what to do next. Students may contrast Victor's reaction—trying to bluff his way out of the situation—with their own—confessing they didn't know the answer.

Lines 135–138
REINFORCE *KEY IDEA*:
IMPRESSION

Discuss Is Victor's idea of how to make an **impression** on Teresa a good one? Why or why not? *Possible answers:*

- *No. He pretends to be something he is not and finds himself caught in an embarrassing situation.*

- *Yes. She will be impressed with his creativity and courage, even if she knows he is bluffing.*

FOR LESS–PROFICIENT READERS

2 Targeted Passage [Lines 127–143]

This passage leads into the climax of the story as Victor seizes the moment to try to make an impression on Teresa.

- Does Victor know French? Why does he raise his hand?
- How does Victor respond when Mr. Bueller asks him a question in French?
- Does Victor think he has succeeded in impressing Teresa?

FOR ADVANCED LEARNERS/PRE–AP

Analyze Characters A *sympathetic character* is one that readers find likable. When reading about a sympathetic character, the reader might exclaim, "Yeah, I can see why he (or she) did that." Have students do a quickwrite to answer these questions:

- How does the author make Victor a sympathetic character?
- Which other characters in the story do you find sympathetic or not sympathetic, and why?

LITERARY ANALYSIS

ⓗ PLOT: CLIMAX

Possible answer: *Teresa is impressed that Victor appears to speak French.*

If students need help . . . Apply a Read Aloud/Think Aloud strategy to clarify why this part of the plot is the climax.

🧰 BEST PRACTICES TOOLKIT—Transparency Read Aloud/Think Aloud p. A34

LITERARY ANALYSIS

ⓘ PLOT: FALLING ACTION

Possible answer: *Mr. Bueller is not going to correct Teresa's impression; he is thinking about a time when he himself misled a girl in an effort to impress her (lines 162–166). This gives Victor another chance to make Teresa "his girl."*

LITERARY ANALYSIS

ⓙ PLOT: RESOLUTION

Possible answer: *By the end of the day, Victor has succeeded in impressing Teresa, and it looks as if they'll be spending more time together.*

SELECTION WRAP–UP

REFLECT Have students think about how the story would have been different if Victor had admitted his deception to Teresa. How might she have reacted?

⭐ **CRITIQUE** Ask students to evaluate the credibility of the characters in this story. Does the author succeed in making them believable seventh graders?

READING FLUENCY

Distribute the copy masters and have students work in pairs to practice fluency.

📕 RESOURCE MANAGER—Copy Master Reading Fluency p. 37

---

widened his eyes in terror at Teresa who stood in front of him. "I didn't know you knew French," she said. "That was good." ⓗ

Mr. Bueller looked at Victor, and Victor looked back. Oh please, don't say anything, Victor pleaded with his eyes. I'll wash your car, mow your lawn, walk your dog—anything! I'll be your best student, and I'll clean
160 your erasers after school.

Mr. Bueller shuffled through the papers on his desk. He smiled and hummed as he sat down to work. He remembered his college years when he dated a girlfriend in borrowed cars. She thought he was rich because each time he picked her up he had a different car. It was fun until he had spent all his money on her and had to write home to his parents because he was broke. ⓘ

Victor couldn't stand to look at Teresa. He was sweaty with shame. "Yeah, well, I picked up a few things from movies and books and stuff like that." They left the class together. Teresa asked him if he would help
170 her with her French.

"Sure, anytime," Victor said.

"I won't be bothering you, will I?"

"Oh no, I like being bothered."

"Bonjour," Teresa said, leaving him outside her next class. She smiled and pushed wisps of hair from her face.

"Yeah, right, *bonjour*," Victor said. He turned and headed to his class. The rosebushes of shame on his face became bouquets of love. Teresa is a great girl, he thought. And Mr. Bueller is a good guy.

He raced to metal shop. After metal shop there was biology, and after
180 biology a long sprint to the public library, where he checked out three French textbooks.

He was going to like seventh grade. � ⓙ

③ Targeted Passage

ⓗ PLOT: CLIMAX
Why is this the moment of greatest interest in the story?

ⓘ PLOT: FALLING ACTION
How do Mr. Bueller's actions affect the plot at this point?

ⓙ PLOT: RESOLUTION
How has Victor's life changed by the end of the day?

DIFFERENTIATED INSTRUCTION

FOR LESS–PROFICIENT READERS
③ Targeted Passage [Lines 155–171]

This passage reveals the story's climax and resolution: Teresa is impressed with Victor, and the two plan to study together.

- How does Teresa show that she was impressed by Victor's behavior in class?
- How does Mr. Bueller's presence create tension or suspense?
- What does Teresa ask Victor to do?

FOR ENGLISH LEARNERS
Comprehension: Task Support Clarify that Victor does not know French; he makes up the words in lines 133 and 138 and says them with a French accent. After Teresa's comment to Victor in lines 155–156, Mr. Bueller can either expose Victor as a fake or allow Victor to take care of the situation in his own way. Help students understand that in lines 161–166, Mr. Bueller thinks back to when he was young and tried to impress a girl. This memory makes him sympathize with Victor.

Comprehension

1. **Recall** What is the main reason Victor wants to take French?

2. **Recall** How does Victor respond when Teresa talks to him after homeroom?

3. **Summarize** Explain the events that happen after Victor tells Mr. Bueller that he speaks French.

Literary Analysis

4. **Connect** Review the chart you created as you read. How do the connections you made help you understand the characters and events that take place in the story? Note specific examples.

5. **Compare and Contrast** Compare and contrast Michael's efforts to impress girls with Victor's efforts to impress Teresa. Give examples from the story. How do their efforts give the story tension—and humor?

6. **Make Inferences** The French teacher, Mr. Bueller, realizes that Victor is faking his knowledge of French. Why does he keep the truth to himself?

7. **Analyze Plot** The plot of "Seventh Grade" centers on Victor's attempts to win Teresa over. Go back through the story and make a list of the important events. Then use a diagram like the one shown, and fill in what happens at each stage of the plot.

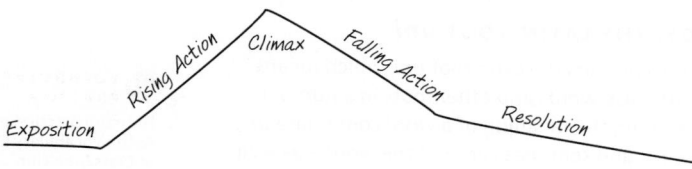

8. **Make Judgments** Victor is finally able to impress Teresa. Do you think it matters that this **impression** is based on something that isn't true? Explain your answer.

Extension and Challenge

9. **Readers' Circle** In a group, discuss what Teresa might be thinking at each stage in the plot. Draw a diagram like the one shown in question 7, and note on it the thoughts and feelings your group identifies for her.

10. **Creative Project: Writing** Imagine that Victor and Michael both work as personalities on a radio talk show. A boy calls in, asking for their opinions about how to impress girls. Write the response each of the boys would give.

MARYLAND OBJECTIVES

LITERATURE STANDARD
3.A.3.b Analyze plot

Practice and Apply

After Reading

For additional support of post-reading questions, use these copy masters:

R RESOURCE MANAGER—Copy Masters

Reading Check p. 34 (to check understanding of the selection)

Plot p. 27 (for practice of literary analysis standards focus)

Question Support p. 35 (**After Reading** questions adapted for English learners and less-proficient readers)

Additional selection questions are provided for teachers on page 21.

For additional activities to challenge students, see

i Power Thinking at **ClassZone.com**

ANSWERS

Comprehension

1. *Victor wants to take French because Teresa is taking it.*

2. *Victor can't look at her and says something awkward.*

3. *Victor makes up some words and says them in a French accent. Mr. Bueller knows the truth but doesn't say anything. After class, Teresa is impressed with Victor and wants to study with him.*

Literary Analysis

Possible answers:

4. **STANDARDS FOCUS Connect** *Students may say that when they can relate to what a character is going through, they are more interested in the story.*

5. *Michael's efforts are all about appearances. Victor, at first, makes a real effort to communicate with Teresa, although in the end he tries to impress her by faking knowledge. Both boys' efforts are rather awkward, making the story amusing and suspenseful.*

6. *Mr. Bueller sympathizes with Victor; he remembers his own efforts to impress a girl.*

---

7. ● **STANDARDS FOCUS** *Plot*
Exposition: Victor wants to make Teresa "his girl." Rising action: Obstacles keep Victor from talking to Teresa. Climax: Victor pretends to speak French in order to impress her. Falling action: Teresa tells Victor his French was good. The teacher keeps Victor's secret. Resolution: Teresa asks Victor to help her study. He's happy.

8. *Students may say that Victor has created a false impression of himself as someone who knows French. Therefore, their friendship is based on a lie. Others may say that Victor will live up to the impression he created, thus becoming a better person.*

Extension and Challenge

9. *Diagrams should demonstrate an understanding of Teresa's character and of the stages of the plot.*

10. *Responses should reflect an understanding, based on details in the story, of what the boys believe impresses girls.*

ANSWERS

Vocabulary in Context

VOCABULARY PRACTICE

1. *(c) gentleness*
2. *(c) stiffen*
3. *(b) boldly*
4. *(b) hurry*
5. *(c) thin*
6. *(a) separation*

 RESOURCE MANAGER—Copy Master
Vocabulary Practice p. 32

VOCABULARY IN WRITING

Students can use a Cluster Diagram to brainstorm details about their first days of seventh grade this year. Suggest that students include both incidents and emotions.

 BEST PRACTICES TOOLKIT—Transparency
Cluster Diagram p. B18

VOCABULARY STRATEGY: THE LATIN ROOT
uni (also an EL language objective)

Before students embark on the exercise, say each word in the web aloud. Then remind students to look at the other parts of each word to help them figure out its meaning.

Answers:
1. *unicorn*
2. *unicycle*
3. *uniform*
4. *union*
5. *unique*

 **RESOURCE MANAGER—Copy Master**
Vocabulary Strategy p. 33

ⓘ Vocabulary Center at ClassZone.com
Additional Vocabulary Activities

Vocabulary in Context

VOCABULARY PRACTICE

Choose the word in each group that is most nearly opposite in meaning to the boldfaced word.

1. **ferocity:** (a) fear, (b) bravery, (c) gentleness
2. **quiver:** (a) tremble, (b) vibrate, (c) stiffen
3. **sheepishly:** (a) shyly, (b) boldly, (c) easily
4. **linger:** (a) struggle, (b) hurry, (c) prolong
5. **portly:** (a) fluid, (b) heavy, (c) thin
6. **unison:** (a) separation, (b) company, (c) time

VOCABULARY IN WRITING

Write a paragraph about what things were like for you during your first few days of seventh grade. Include at least three vocabulary words. Here is a sample of how you might begin your paragraph.

> **EXAMPLE SENTENCE**
>
> *As I walked up the school steps that first day, I just wanted to __linger__ outside the door forever.*

MARYLAND OBJECTIVES

READING STANDARD
1.D.3.b Use word structure to determine meaning

VOCABULARY STRATEGY: THE LATIN ROOT *uni*

The vocabulary word *unison* contains the Latin root *uni,* which means "one." *Uni* is combined with base words and other roots in a number of English words. To understand the meaning of a word containing *uni,* use context clues—the words and sentences around the word—as well as your knowledge of the root.

ⓥ VOCABULARY PRACTICE
For more practice, go to the **Vocabulary Center** at **ClassZone.com.**

PRACTICE Choose the word from the web that best completes each sentence. Be ready to explain how *uni* helps give meaning to each word.

1. The _____, a creature with one horn, exists only in fairy tales.
2. The clown rode in circles, balanced unsteadily on a _____.
3. Each team member stood out from the crowd in his bright purple _____.
4. The colonists banded together to form a new _____.
5. She claims her ring is _____, but I've seen others like it.

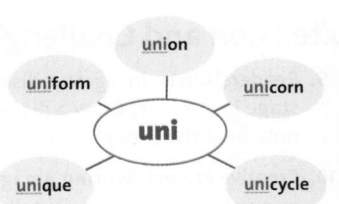

DIFFERENTIATED INSTRUCTION

FOR ENGLISH LEARNERS

Vocabulary Strategy Point out that some of the choices in the web are similar to the Spanish words for the same idea, such as *union* and *uniform.* Have speakers of Latin-based languages use a T Chart to compare the word forms of all of the choices in the web. Ask students to present their charts.

 BEST PRACTICES TOOLKIT—Transparency
T Chart p. A25

FOR ADVANCED LEARNERS/PRE–AP

Vocabulary Strategy Have students work in teams to create new words by adding *uni* to these bases: *cellular, color, dimensional, directional, lingual.* Ask teams to define the new words that they form, based on their knowledge of the word parts. Have teams check their definitions in a dictionary.

Reading-Writing Connection

Increase your understanding of "Seventh Grade" by responding to these prompts. Then complete the **Grammar and Writing** exercise.

WRITING PROMPTS	SELF-CHECK
A. Short Response: Describe an Expression Victor's friend Michael has some interesting opinions about what kind of facial expression **impresses** girls. Write a **one-paragraph description** of Michael's scowl.	*A strong description will . . .* • include details about Michael's facial expression • use words and phrases that appeal to the sense of sight
B. Extended Response: Write a Journal Entry What would Victor write in a journal about his first day of seventh grade? Write a **two- or three-paragraph journal entry** from Victor's point of view.	*A creative journal entry will . . .* • relate events and feelings described in the story • use words that Victor would use

GRAMMAR AND WRITING

AVOID SENTENCE FRAGMENTS Every complete sentence has a subject and a predicate. The complete subject includes all the words that tell whom or what the sentence is about. The complete predicate includes the verb and all the words that go with it. If a sentence is missing a subject, a predicate, or both, then it is a **sentence fragment.** The missing part(s) must be added in order to make the sentence complete.

 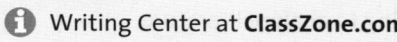

MARYLAND OBJECTIVES

LANGUAGE STANDARD
5.A.2.c Differentiate complete sentences from nonsentences

> *Original:* I had French class today. In Mr. Bueller's room.
> *("In Mr. Bueller's room" is a sentence fragment because it is missing a subject and a predicate.)*
>
> *Revised:* I had French class today. It was in Mr. Bueller's room.
> *(This is now a complete sentence because it contains the subject "It" and the predicate "was in Mr. Bueller's room.")*

PRACTICE Decide whether the following sentence fragments (in bold) are missing a subject, a predicate, or both. Then insert the missing parts.

1. I went to homeroom. **Then to English class.**
2. **Saw Teresa in the hall.** She walked the other way.
3. After English class, I had math. **My weakest subject.**
4. Teresa and I get along well. **In most ways.**

For more help with sentence fragments, see page R64 in the **Grammar Handbook.**

FOR LESS–PROFICIENT WRITERS

For Prompt A:

1. Have students work in pairs. While one partner scowls, the other should write down words and phrases that describe the look on the scowling student's face. Pairs should then reverse roles.
2. Have partners share their words and expressions with the class. Choose those that best convey the mental image.
3. Then have each student write his or her own description.

For Prompt B:

1. Limit the length of the assignment to one paragraph.
2. Discuss the incident in French class and how Victor felt during and after that event. Encourage students to review that part of the story if necessary.
3. Have students focus their journal entry on that major event.

Reading-Writing Connection

WRITING PROMPTS

• For **Prompt A,** have students first draw a picture of Michael scowling and then brainstorm words and phrases that would help create that mental image in a reader's mind.

• For **Prompt B,** remind students that journal entries use first-person point of view. Suggest that students skim the story and jot down details from Victor's day as well as words and phrases used in the story to describe the events or his feelings about them.

For an extended Reading-Writing Connection activity, see

ℹ Writing Center at **ClassZone.com**

GRAMMAR AND WRITING

• Point out that sometimes authors use sentence fragments to create a mood, establish a rhythm, or convey realism. In students' writing, however, fragments are to be avoided.

• Write the fragments on the board. Have students suggest corrections.

Possible answers:

1. *[subject and predicate] Then I went to English class.*
2. *[subject] I saw Teresa in the hall.*
3. *[subject and predicate] It is my weakest subject.*
4. *[subject and predicate] We are alike in most ways.*

R RESOURCE MANAGER—Copy Master
Avoid Sentence Fragments p. 36

Assess and Reteach

Assess

R RESOURCE MANAGER—Copy Masters
Selection Tests A, B/C pp. 39–40, 41–42
💿 Test Generator CD

Reteach

S STANDARDS LESSON FILE
Literature Lesson 5: Elements of Plot
Vocabulary Lesson 1: Base Words, Prefixes, Suffixes, and Roots
Grammar Lesson 1: Avoiding Sentence Fragments

OBJECTIVES

Literary Analysis
- explore the key idea of **companionship**
- analyze and evaluate setting
- identify flashback
- read a short story and an online article

Reading
- identify sequence

Vocabulary
- build vocabulary for reading and writing
- use antonyms as context clues (*also an EL language objective*)

Grammar and Writing
- use punctuation to correct run-on sentences
- use writing to analyze literature

SUMMARY

In this story set sometime in the future, Brock's society lives inside a dome and believes that Earth is too poisoned to support life. One day, Brock goes outside the dome and finds a puppy. Scientists want to experiment on her, so he decides to leave the dome permanently. Once outside, he realizes that Earth is habitable. He and his puppy start a new life.

Why are pets good COMPANIONS?

To lead into the *KEY IDEA,* ask volunteers to share stories about their pets that illustrate **companionship.** Challenge them to explain the saying "A dog is a man's best friend." Then have students complete the *LIST IT* activity.

The Last Dog
Short Story by Katherine Paterson

Why are pets good COMPANIONS?

MARYLAND OBJECTIVES

READING/LIT STANDARDS
1.E.3.a Select and apply appropriate strategies during reading
3.A.3.c Analyze setting

KEY IDEA For many of us, pets are an important part of our lives. We feed them and care for them and often consider them to be a part of the family, but what do we get in return? Some would say that pets reward us with their **companionship**—their affection, loyalty, and good company. In "The Last Dog," a boy's powerful bond with a puppy helps teach him an important lesson.

LIST IT In a small group, make a list of reasons pets are good companions. To get started, use a list like the one shown. Then share your list with other groups.

Why Are Pets
Good Companions?
1. Pets are fun to play with.
2.
3.
4.

42

![R] RESOURCE MANAGER UNIT 1

Plan and Teach pp. 43–50

Literary Analysis
Summary pp. 51*, 52‡*
Setting pp. 53, 54†*
Question Support p. 61*

Reading
Identify Sequence pp. 55, 56†*
Reading Check p. 60
Reading Fluency p. 63

Vocabulary
Study p. 57*
Practice p. 58
Strategy p. 59

Grammar and Writing
Avoid Run-on Sentences p. 62

Assessment
Selection Tests A, B/C pp. 65*, 67*
Test Generator CD

🧰 BEST PRACTICES TOOLKIT

Differentiated Instruction
pp. 31–38*

Scaffolding Instruction pp. 43–46*

Graphic Organizers/Strategies
Spider Map • Word Questioning • Read Aloud/Think Aloud • Venn Diagram • T Chart • Sequence Chart

Reading Support

Audio Anthology CD*

Technology

ℹ️ Literature and Vocabulary Centers at ClassZone.com

WriteSmart CD

---

* Resources for Differentiation   † Also in Spanish   ‡ In Haitian Creole and Vietnamese

● LITERARY ANALYSIS: SETTING

Setting is where and when a story happens. Sometimes the setting of a story is obvious. In the story you're about to read, however, you will need to look for details to help you understand the setting. Here are some details to look for:

- details about scenery and weather
- details about buildings, clothing, culture, and technology

As you read, note these and other details about where and when the story takes place.

Review: **Plot**

■ READING SKILL: IDENTIFY SEQUENCE

A plot is made up of many events. The **sequence,** or order, of the events is important to understanding the story. These words and phrases are often clues to the sequence of events:

first	then	later	in the past

While events are often presented in the order in which they occur, sometimes the action is interrupted to present a scene from an earlier time. This is called a **flashback.** When you come across a flashback, notice any new information.

As you read, keep track of the sequence by recording important events on a sequence chart like the one shown.

Review: **Compare and Contrast**

▲ VOCABULARY IN CONTEXT

Katherine Paterson uses the following words in her story about a futuristic world. See how many you know. Make a chart like the one shown, and put each vocabulary word in the appropriate column.

WORD LIST		
copious	foray	posterity
disembodied	foresighted	reproof
evasive	languish	

Know Well	Think I Know	Don't Know at All

Author Online

"A Weird Little Kid"
Sometimes an outsider has an interesting way of looking at things. Katherine Paterson is convinced that as the child of U.S. missionaries in China, she learned valuable lessons about life. But

Katherine Paterson
born 1932

being an outsider wasn't always easy. After returning to the United States at the age of five, Paterson and her family moved 18 times. She remembers feeling "small, poor, and foreign" on the playground. She was, in her own words, "a weird little kid," but she states today that "there are few things, apparently, more helpful to a writer than having once been a weird little kid."

> **MORE ABOUT THE AUTHOR**
> For more on Katherine Paterson, visit the **Literature Center** at ClassZone.com.

Background

Science Fiction In a work of science fiction, a writer combines real scientific information with elements from his or her imagination to create an altered universe. Science fiction stories typically take place in the distant future—in outer space or on a changed Earth. Plots often center on challenges characters face in these unusual settings.

THE LAST DOG   **43**

Teach

STANDARDS FOCUS

LITERARY ANALYSIS

● SETTING

Read aloud this example:

> The little dog leaped high into the blue sky, snatching the ball from the air. Across the park, his owner whistled. The dog sped toward her, past beds of yellow daffodils and bright red tulips.

Ask students to identify the setting from this passage. *Possible answer: It is a sunny spring day in the park.*

CHECK UNDERSTANDING Have students share details of setting from science fiction stories or movies they know.

READING SKILL

■ IDENTIFY SEQUENCE

Have students review **Author Online** on page 43. Ask these questions:

- Where did the author live before she returned to America at the age of five? *Answer: She lived in China.*
- What happened after the author returned to America? *Answer: Her family moved 18 times.*

CHECK UNDERSTANDING Ask students to list the sequence of events from the time they woke up to right now.

> **R** RESOURCE MANAGER—Copy Master
> Identify Sequence p. 55 (for student use while reading the selection)

VOCABULARY SKILL

▲ VOCABULARY IN CONTEXT

DIAGNOSE WORD KNOWLEDGE To determine preteaching needs, have all students complete **Vocabulary in Context.** Determine which words students need to have clarified. Provide definitions from the selection pages: *copious* (p. 54), *disembodied* (p. 44), *evasive* (p. 46), *foray* (p. 46), *foresighted* (p. 50), *languishing* (p. 51), *posterity* (p. 54), *reproof* (p. 53).

PRETEACH VOCABULARY Help students determine meanings for each boldfaced word on the Vocabulary Study copy master.

1. Read the first sentence aloud, emphasizing *copious*.
2. Point out the phrase "testing every possible function." Elicit possible meanings for *copious*, such as "many" or "plentiful."
3. Have students check their definitions against the text in the third column.
4. Repeat for each remaining word.

 RESOURCE MANAGER—Copy Master
Vocabulary Study p. 57

For general guidelines on differentiating vocabulary instruction and for alternative vocabulary activities for students not needing vocabulary preteaching, see

 BEST PRACTICES TOOLKIT
Scaffolding Vocabulary Instruction pp. 43–46

ⓘ Vocabulary Center at **ClassZone.com**

ANALYZE VISUALS

Possible answer: *The barren landscape, purple sky, and odd dome building make the setting appear futuristic and somewhat eerie.*

About the Art Artist Ericka O'Rourke works in both traditional and digital mediums. She is skilled in acrylics, watercolors, pen and ink, and photography. Many of her photographs capture the natural beauty of Allentown, New Jersey, where she lives, and coastal Maine. For her digital illustrations, O'Rourke often combines her photographs and paintings with found objects and uses various software programs to achieve her desired effect.

LITERARY ANALYSIS

Ⓐ SETTING

Possible answer: *The story may be set in the future or in a technologically advanced society.*

If students need help... Work together to record important details about setting on a class Spider Map.

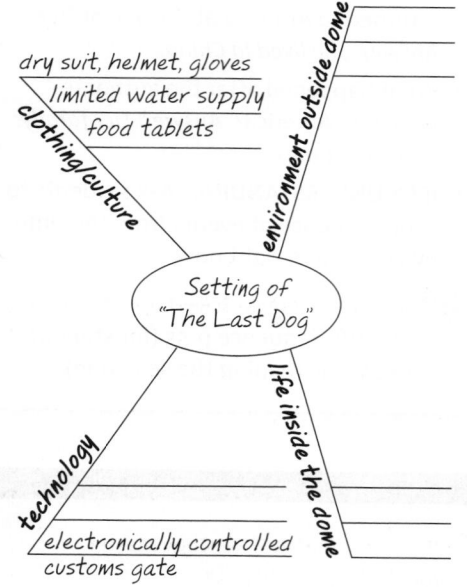

Extend the Discussion What inference can you draw about conditions on the "outside" based on details in lines 1–17?

 BEST PRACTICES TOOLKIT—Transparency Spider Map p. B22

THE LAST DOG
KATHERINE PATERSON

Brock approached the customs gate. Although he did not reach for the scanner, a feeling it might have labeled "excitement" made him tremble. His fingers shook as he punched in his number on the inquiry board. "This is highly irregular, Brock 095670038," the **disembodied** voice said. "What is your reason for external travel?"

Brock took a deep breath. "Scientific research," he replied. He didn't need to be told that his behavior was "irregular." He'd never heard of anyone doing research outside the dome—actual rather than virtual research. "I— I've been cleared by my podmaster and the Research Team. . . ."

10 "Estimated time of return?" So, he wasn't to be questioned further. "Uh, 1800 hours."

"Are you wearing the prescribed dry suit with helmet and gloves?"

"Affirmative."[1]

"You should be equipped with seven hundred fifty milliliters of liquid and food tablets for one day travel."

"Affirmative." Brock patted the sides of the dry suit to be sure. Ⓐ

"Remember to drink sparingly. Water supply is limited." Brock nodded. He tried to lick his parched lips, but his whole mouth felt dry. "Is that understood?"

20 "Affirmative." Was he hoping customs would stop him? If he was, they didn't seem to be helping him. Well, this was what he wanted, wasn't it? To go outside the dome.

"Turn on the universal locator, Brock 095670038, and proceed to gate."

Why weren't they questioning him further? Were they eager for him to go? Ever since he'd said out loud in group speak that he wanted to go outside the dome, people had treated him strangely—that session with the podmaster and then the interview with the representative

---

1. **affirmative** (ə-fûr′mə-tĭv): formal or scientific word for *yes*.

44 UNIT 1: PLOT, CONFLICT, AND SETTING

ANALYZE VISUALS
How would you describe the **setting** shown in this painting?

disembodied (dĭs′ĕm-bŏ′dĕd) *adj.* separated from or lacking a body **disembody** *v.*

❶ **Targeted Passage**

Ⓐ **SETTING**
Reread lines 1–16. What does the unusual technology in the dome suggest about the time in which the story takes place?

DIFFERENTIATED INSTRUCTION

FOR ALL STUDENTS

Enhancing Learning Styles Provide independent projects for various learning styles.

- **Spatial** Draw a blueprint of the dome.
- **Verbal** Complete a story map for an original science fiction story.
- **Kinesthetic** Have pairs debate the merits of dome life versus life outside the dome.

For further details on these projects, see

 RESOURCE MANAGER
Ideas for Extension pp. 48–49

FOR LESS–PROFICIENT READERS

In combination with the *Audio Anthology CD*, use one or more Targeted Passages (pp. 44, 51, 55, 57) to ensure that students focus on key story events, concepts, and skills.

❶ **Targeted Passage [Lines 1–22]**

This passage introduces the main character, Brock, and builds understanding of the futuristic setting.

- In what kind of place does Brock live?
- Where is Brock going?

BACKGROUND

Environmental Pollution The setting of this story appears to be a post-environmental wasteland of Earth. The characters live in an environmentally controlled dome, believing that Earth remains uninhabitable after an earlier disaster destroyed much of the population (lines 171–175). As with many works of science fiction, there is much truth to this story: environmental pollution to air, land, and water is a serious problem, and it increases as technology, industry, and the world's population continue to grow.

In the United States, the Environmental Protection Agency (EPA) was formed in 1970 to oversee all antipollution efforts, including activities to combat the two forms of environmental pollution discussed in "The Last Dog"—global warming and a threatened water supply. There is increasing worldwide demand to phase out the production of substances that deplete the ozone layer. Without these efforts, more ultraviolet rays will penetrate the earth, resulting in skin cancer, eye problems, and damage to crops. The EPA also enforces the laws that keep our water safe for drinking, recreation, and fishing by setting quality standards, aiding wastewater treatment facilities, and protecting watersheds and water sources.

- What is he wearing?
- What is he taking with him?
- How does Brock feel about his journey?

FOR ENGLISH LEARNERS

Key Academic Vocabulary Have pairs complete a Word Questioning sheet for one of these words: *research* (lines 6, 8), *virtual* (lines 8, 33), *environment* (lines 52, 334), *normal* (lines 54, 210), *monitor* (lines 240, 413), *unique* (line 344).

 BEST PRACTICES TOOLKIT—Transparency
Word Questioning p. E9

Prereading For prereading instruction for English learners, see

 BEST PRACTICES TOOLKIT
Scaffolding Reading Instruction pp. 43–46

FOR ADVANCED LEARNERS/PRE–AP
Pre-AP exercises in the bottom channel provide additional challenge for your advanced students. Use them for small groups or individuals.

ADDITIONAL GUIDELINES
For more help with differentiation and tips for classroom management, see

 BEST PRACTICES TOOLKIT
Differentiated Instruction pp. 31–38

from Research. Did they think he was a deviant?[2] Deviants sometimes disappeared. The word was passed around that they had "gone outside," but no one really knew. No deviant had ever returned.

The gate slid open. Before he was quite ready for it, Brock found himself outside the protection of the dome. He blinked. The sun—at least it was what was called "the sun" in virtual lessons—was too bright for his eyes even inside the tinted helmet. He took a deep breath, one last backward look at the dome, which, with the alien sun gleaming on it, was even harder to look at than the distant star, and started across an expanse of brown soil [was it?] to what he recognized from holograms as a line of purplish mountains in the distance. **B**

It was, he pulled the scanner from his outside pouch and checked it, "hot." Oh, that was what he was feeling. Hot. He remembered "hot" from a virtual lesson he'd had once on deserts. He wanted to take off the dry suit, but he had been told since he could remember that naked skin would suffer irreparable burning outside the protection of the dome. He adjusted the control as he walked so that the unfamiliar perspiration would evaporate. He fumbled a bit before he found the temperature adjustment function. He put it on twenty degrees centigrade[3] and immediately felt more comfortable. No one he really knew had ever left the dome (stories of deviants exiting the dome being hard to verify), but there was all this equipment in case someone decided to venture out. He tried to ask the clerk who outfitted him, but the woman was **evasive**. The equipment was old, she said. People used to go out, but the outside environment was threatening, so hardly anyone (she looked at him carefully now), hardly anyone ever used it now.

Was Brock, then, the only normal person still curious about the outside? Or had all those who had dared to venture out perished, discouraging further **forays**? Perhaps he *was* a deviant for wanting to see the mountains for himself. When he'd mentioned it to others, they had laughed, but there was a hollow sound to the laughter.

If he never returned, he'd have no one to blame but himself. He knew that. While his podfellows played virtual games, he'd wandered into a subsection of the historical virtuals called "ancient fictions." Things happened in these fictions more—well, more densely than they did in the virtuals. The people he met there—it was hard to describe—but somehow they were more *actual* than dome dwellers. They had strange names like Huck Finn and M. C. Higgins the Great.[4] They were even a little scary. It was their insides. Their insides were very loud. But even

---

2. **deviant** (dē'vē-ənt): a person who does not follow customary or accepted behavior.

3. **twenty degrees centigrade:** a temperature equivalent to 68 degrees Fahrenheit.

4. **Huck Finn and M. C. Higgins the Great:** the main characters in two books that are often read by young adults.

hologram *n.* a three-dimensional picture made by laser light

B SEQUENCE
What happens after Brock goes through the customs gate? As you read, use your chart to record the events described.

evasive (ĭ-vā'sĭv) *adj.* tending or trying to avoid

foray (fôr'ā') *n.* a trip into an unknown area

B SEQUENCE

Record students' answers in a sequence chart similar to the one on page 43.

Possible answers:

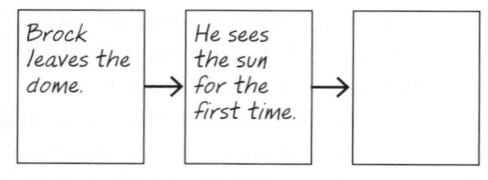

Brock leaves the dome. → He sees the sun for the first time. →

Lines 59–70
DISCUSSION PROMPTS

Use these prompts to help students understand why Brock leaves the dome:

Connect What are some ways to satisfy your curiosity about unknown places or experiences? *Students may say that they ask questions, do research, or investigate for themselves.*

Apply Why did reading books such as *The Adventures of Huckleberry Finn* make Brock curious about the outside world? *Possible answer: Brock says that the characters' "insides were very loud" (line 66). In other words, the characters seemed to have much more of an emotional life than the people Brock knows in the dome. Brock became curious about the world that produced these vivid characters.*

Evaluate Is Brock fulfilled by his life in the dome? How do you know? *Possible answer: No, he is not fulfilled. Brock keeps going back to these stories because he longs for something beyond what the dome can offer. He seems to feel there should be more to life.*

DIFFERENTIATED INSTRUCTION

FOR LESS–PROFICIENT READERS

Vocabulary Support Tell students that, like many science fiction writers, Paterson invents words to bring alive her unique setting. Students must use context clues to infer the meanings of these words. In some cases, they will need to read on to gather more clues—for example, students may not understand what a *scanner* is, but its various functions are described throughout the story (lines 1–3, 39–40, 124–125, and so on). Suggest that they keep a list of unusual words and their meanings as they read.

- *scanner* (line 2)
- *podmaster* (line 9)
- *deviant* (line 28)
- *virtual lessons* (line 33)
- *podfellows* (line 60)
- *fictions* (line 61)
- *robopet* (line 100)

FOR ENGLISH LEARNERS

Comprehension: Concept Support Help students understand the author's frequent use of the word *virtual*. Explain that "virtual reality" refers to an artificial experience generated by a computer to stimulate the senses. Direct students to reread lines 31–75, keeping a list of all the phrases they find with the word *virtual*. Have pairs work together to create definitions for their phrases. Then invite volunteers to share their ideas with the class.

though the people in the ancient fictions frightened him a bit, he couldn't get enough of them. When no one was paying attention, he went back again and again to visit them. They had made him wonder about that
70 other world—that world outside the dome. **G**

Perhaps, once he had realized the danger the ancient fictions posed, he should have left them alone, but he couldn't help himself. They had made him feel hollow, hungry for something no food pellet or even virtual experience could satisfy. And now he was in that world they spoke of and the mountains of it were in plain view. **D**

He headed for the purple curves. Within a short distance from the dome, the land was clear and barren, but after he had been walking for an hour or so he began to pass rusting hulks and occasional ruins of what might have been the dwellings of ancient peoples that no one
80 in later years had cleared away for recycling or vaporization.[5]

He checked the emotional scanner for an unfamiliar sensation. "Loneliness," it registered. He rather liked having names for these new sensations. It made him feel a bit "proud," was it? The scanner was rather interesting. He wondered when people had stopped using them. He hadn't known they existed until, in that pod meeting, he had voiced his desire to go outside.

The podmaster had looked at him with a raised eyebrow and a sniff. "Next thing you'll be asking for a scanner," he said.

"What's a scanner?" Brock asked.
90 The podmaster requisitioned one from storage, but at the same time, he must have alerted Research, because it was the representative from Research who had brought him the scanner and questioned him about his expressed desire for an Actual Adventure—a journey outside the dome.

"What has prompted this, uh—unusual ambition?" the representative had asked, his eyes not on Brock but on the scanner in his hand. Brock had hesitated, distracted by the man's fidgeting with the strange instrument. "I—I'm interested in scientific research," Brock said at last.

So here he was out of the pod, alone for the first time in his life. Perhaps, though, he should have asked one of his podfellows to come along. Or
100 even the pod robopet. But the other fellows all laughed when he spoke of going outside, their eyes darting back and forth. Nothing on the outside, they said, could equal the newest Virtual Adventure. He suddenly realized that ever since he started interfacing[6] with the ancient fictions, his fellows had given him that look. They did think he was odd—not quite the same as a regular podfellow. Brock didn't really vibe with the pod robopet.

---

5. **vaporization** (vā'pər-ĭ-zā'shən): the process of making a thing disappear by changing it into a fog or mist.

6. **interfacing** (ĭn'tər-fā'sĭng): making connections.

G SETTING
Reread lines 54–70. What do these details tell you about the place where the story is set?

D PLOT
What experiences led Brock to decide to leave the dome?

G SETTING

Possible answer: The story seems to be taking place on Earth, in the United States. The characters Brock meets in the "ancient fictions" (line 61) are from real books written by the American authors Mark Twain and Virginia Hamilton.

LITERARY ANALYSIS: *Review*

D PLOT

Possible answer: Brock became curious about the outside world after experiencing "ancient fictions," or novels from the past. These stories showed him a world that was much more exciting than life in the dome.

If students need help . . . Point out that lines 59–70 describe a flashback, or scene from the past. Help students see the relationship between this earlier event and what Brock is doing now by adding this information to the sequence chart started on page 46. Place this box in front of the first one already filled in.

FOR LESS–PROFICIENT READERS

Reading Skill Follow-Up: Sequence Use Read Aloud/Think Aloud to clarify sequence. Read aloud lines 81–97. Note that the main action of the story is told in the past tense. Point out verb forms that signal a flashback sequence, such as "hadn't known" (line 84), "had voiced" (line 85), and "had brought" (line 92). Record events in the sequence chart as you read.

Review: Plot Remind students that plot is the series of events in a story. Review the definition of *flashback* ("a description of events that happened before the main action of a story") and explain that authors often use flashback to show the causes of present events. Have pairs discuss how the events in lines 60–70 caused Brock to end up in his current situation, exploring the outside world.

BEST PRACTICES TOOLKIT—Transparency
Read Aloud/Think Aloud p. A34

Lines 115–129
DISCUSSION PROMPTS

Use these prompts to help students understand the importance of the discoveries that Brock is making:

Connect Have you ever visited a place that is very different from your home? Was the experience more exciting or more fearsome? *Students may say that they felt many different emotions, depending on the experience.*

Analyze In what way is nature outside the dome different from what Brock has been taught? *Possible answer: He has been taught that the world outside cannot support life. However, he has found living trees (line 115) and a flowing brook (line 126) not far from the dome.*

Evaluate Why do you think dome scientists and leaders have not updated their information about the outside environment? *Possible answer: The dome leaders do not want to lose members of their population to the outside world. The dome dwellers are imprisoned by their fear of what might be outside. They are too comfortable inside the dome.*

LITERARY ANALYSIS

Ⓔ SETTING

Possible answer: Most students will say that grass, brooks, and trees can also be found in their own natural setting. One difference might be the absence of people in the area outside of the dome.

LITERARY ANALYSIS

Ⓕ SETTING

Possible answer: Living in the dome has made Brock fearful of nature and of new situations. He suppresses his desire to dip his finger in the brook (lines 129–130) and to breathe the outside air (lines 133–134).

Extend the Discussion What event may have caused the supposed poisoning of Earth?

It was one of the more modern ones, and when they'd programmed its artificial intelligence they'd somehow made it too smart. The robopet in the children's pod last year was older, stupider, and more "fun" to have around.

110 He'd badly underestimated the distance to the mountains. The time was well past noon, and he had at least three kilometers to go. Should he signal late return or turn about now? He didn't have much more than one day's scant supply of water and food tablets. But he was closer to the hills than to the dome. He felt a thrill ["excitement"] and pressed on.

There were actual trees growing on the first hill. Not the great giants of virtual history lessons, more scrubby and bent. But they were trees, he was sure of it. The podmaster had said that trees had been extinct for hundreds of years. Brock reached up and pulled off a leaf. It was green and had veins. In some ways it looked like his own hand. He put the leaf in
120 his pack to study later. He didn't want anyone accusing him of losing his scientific objectivity.[7] Only deviants did that. Farther up the hill he heard an unfamiliar burbling sound. No, he knew that sound. It was water running. He'd heard it once when the liquid dispenser had malfunctioned. There'd been a near panic in the dome over it. He checked the scanner. There was no caution signal, so he hurried toward the sound. Ⓔ

It was a—a "brook"—he was sure of it! Virtual lessons had taught that there were such things outside in the past but that they had long ago grown poisonous, then in the warming climate had dried up. But here was a running brook, not even a four-hour journey from his dome. His
130 first impulse was to take off his protective glove and dip a finger in it, but he drew back. He had been well conditioned to avoid danger. He sat down clumsily on the bank. Yes, this must be grass. There were even some tiny flowers mixed in the grass. Would the atmosphere poison him if he unscrewed his helmet to take a sniff? He punched the scanner to read conditions, but the characters on the scanner panel danced about uncertainly until, at length, the disembodied voice said "conditions unreadable." He'd better not risk it. Ⓕ

He pushed the buttons now for liquid and pellets. A tube appeared in his mouth. It dropped a pellet on his tongue. From the tube he sucked
140 liquid enough to swallow his meal. What was it they called outside nourishment in the history virtuals? *Pecnec*? Something like that. He was having a *pecnec* in the *woods* by a *brook*. A hasty consulting of the scanner revealed that what he was feeling was "pleasure." He was very glad he hadn't come with an anxious podfellow or, worse, an advanced robopet that would, no doubt, be yanking at his suit already, urging him back toward the dome.

---

7. **scientific objectivity:** a way of looking upon a situation and remaining true to scientific facts.

48 UNIT 1: PLOT, CONFLICT, AND SETTING

Ⓔ **SETTING**
Compare and contrast the setting outside the dome with the natural setting where you live. How familiar does the setting outside the dome seem to you?

Ⓕ **SETTING**
Reread lines 126–137. Notice how Brock reacts to nature. How do you think Brock's time in the dome is influencing his reactions?

DIFFERENTIATED INSTRUCTION

FOR ENGLISH LEARNERS
Language: Compound Words Point out the words "podmaster" in line 117 and "podfellow" in line 144. Sketch or show students a picture of peas in a pod and discuss how the peas look alike. Help them understand that in the context of the story, *pod* refers to a small group of people who have been raised together in a kind of family. Ask pairs to use this information to define each word formed with *pod* in this part of the story.

FOR ADVANCED LEARNERS/PRE–AP
Compare and Contrast Have students read another science fiction story, such as "The Sand Castle" by Alma Luz Villanueva or a selection by Ray Bradbury or Isaac Asimov. Ask them to use a Venn Diagram to compare elements of setting in each story and then make generalizations about the view of science fiction writers toward the future. Have students share their generalizations.

 BEST PRACTICES TOOLKIT—Transparency
Venn Diagram p. A26

It was then, in the middle of post-*pecnec* satisfaction, that he heard the new sound. Like that programmed into a robopet, yet different. He struggled to his feet. The dry suit from storage was certainly awkward when you wanted
150 to stand up or sit down. Nothing on the scanner indicated danger, so he went into the scrubby woods toward the sound. And stopped abruptly.

Something was lying under the shadow of a tree. Something about a meter long. It was furred and quite still. The sound was not coming from it. And then he saw the small dog—the puppy. He was sure it was a puppy, nosing the stiff body of what must once have been its mother, making the little crying sounds that he'd heard from the brook. Later, much later, he realized that he should have been wary. If the older dog had died of some extradomal disease, the puppy might have been a carrier. But at the time, all he could think of was the puppy, a small creature who had lost its mother. **G**
160 He'd found out about mothers from the Virtuals. Mothers were extinct in the dome. Children were conceived and born in the lab and raised in units of twelve in the pods, presided over by a bank of computers and the podmaster. Nuclear families, as everyone knew, had been wasteful of time, energy, and space. There was an old proverb: The key to survival is efficiency. So though Brock could guess the puppy was "sad" (like that fictions person, Jo, whose podmate expired), he didn't know what missing a mother would feel like. And who would whimper for a test tube?

Brock had never seen a dog, of course, but he'd seen plenty of dog breed descriptions on the science/history virtuals. Dogs had been
170 abundant once. They filled the ancient fictions. They even had names

THE LAST DOG   **49**

ANALYZE VISUALS
What do the details in the painting tell you about the **setting?**

G COMPARE AND CONTRAST
How has Brock's attitude about his adventure and his safety changed since he left the dome?

ANALYZE VISUALS
Possible answer: Life is evident in the flowing stream, growing trees, and shining sun.

READING SKILL: Review

G COMPARE AND CONTRAST
Possible answer: Brock has become less afraid of the outside and has started to feel more human emotions.

If students need help . . .

1. Ask a volunteer to read aloud lines 156–159, starting with "Later, much later, he realized that he should have been wary. . . ."

2. Ask students to consider Brock's dependence on the scanner up to this point. Why doesn't he need it to help him interpret the puppy?

3. Have students contrast Brock's behavior toward the flowers (lines 133–137) to his encounter with the puppy. Why does he decide to "risk it" now, when he didn't before?

Extend the Discussion How would Brock's attitudes have been affected if he had brought a podfellow or robopet on his adventure? Why is being alone important to his character's change and growth?

FOR LESS–PROFICIENT READERS
Review: Compare and Contrast Remind students that when they compare and contrast, they look for differences and similarities. Explain the concept of "nuclear families" (line 163)—family units consisting of parents and their children. Then have students work in pairs to compare the structure of nuclear families to the dome's social organization as described in lines 160–167. Discuss the differences they identify.

FOR ENGLISH LEARNERS
Language: Punctuation and Print Cues Explain that the author uses quotation marks and italics to draw attention to emotions, objects, and activities that Brock has been taught in the dome but has never experienced before in real life. Have students make a list of examples they find on pages 47–49. Point out that the word "*pecnec*" (line 141) is a deliberate misspelling of *picnic.* Then have pairs come up with synonyms for each example they find.

- "loneliness" (line 82)
- "proud" (line 83)
- "fun" (line 108)
- "excitement" (line 114)
- "brook" (line 126)
- *pecnec* (line 141)
- *woods* (line 142)
- "pleasure" (line 143)
- "sad" (line 165)

REINFORCE *KEY IDEA*: COMPANIONSHIP

Discuss What details suggest that Brock is already enjoying the **companionship** of the puppy? *Possible answer:*

- *He laughs when the puppy wrinkles its nose at the pellet (lines 198–199).*
- *He feels pleasure when the puppy licks his hand and looks at him (lines 199–201).*
- *He talks to the puppy (line 202).*

READING SKILL

H SEQUENCE

Students may add these events to their sequence charts:

Possible answer:

- *The puppy is hungry but doesn't like the smell or taste of Brock's glove (lines 191–192).*
- *Brock takes off his glove and holds out a food pellet (lines 195–197).*
- *The puppy licks Brock's hand (line 198).*

---

there—Lassie, Toto, Sounder. But now dogs were extinct, gone during the dark ages when the atmosphere had become warm and poisonous. The savages who had not had the intelligence or wealth to join the **foresighted** dome crafters had killed all animals wild or domesticated for food before they had eventually died out themselves. It was all in one of the very first virtual lessons. He had seen that one many times. He never confessed to anyone how, well, sad it made him feel.

But obviously, dogs were not quite extinct. Cautiously, he moved toward the small one.

180 "Alert. Alert. Scanning unknown object."

Brock pushed the off button. "Are you sure you want to turn off scanner?"

"Affirmative." He stuck the scanner into his pouch.

The puppy had lifted its head at the sound of his voice. It looked at him, head cocked, as though deciding whether to run or stay.

"It's all right, dog," Brock said soothingly. "I won't hurt you." He stayed still. He didn't want to frighten the little beast. If it ran, he wasn't sure he'd be able to catch it in his clumsy dry suit.

Slowly he extended his gloved hand. The dog backed away anxiously, but when Brock kept the hand extended, the puppy slowly crept toward him 190 and sniffed, making whimpering sounds. It wasn't old enough to be truly afraid, it seemed. The pup licked his glove tentatively, then backed away again. It was looking for food, and plasticine gloves weren't going to satisfy.

Brock looked first at the dead mother whose source of nourishment must have long dried up, then around the landscape. What would a dog eat? A puppy on its own? He took off his glove and reached through his pouch into the inside pocket that held his pellet supply. Making every move slow and deliberate so as not to startle the dog, he held out a pellet. The dog came to his hand, licked it, then the pellet. It wrinkled its nose. Brock laughed. He didn't need the scanner now to tell him that what he 200 felt was "pleasure." He loved the feel of the rough tongue on his palm and the little furred face, questioning him.

"It's all right, fellow. You can eat it." **H**

As though understanding, the pup gulped down the pellet. Then looked around for more, not realizing that it had just bolted down a whole meal. When the dog saw there was no more coming, it ran over to the brook. Brock watched in horror as it put its head right down into the poisonous stream and lapped noisily.

"Don't!" Brock cried.

The puppy turned momentarily at the sound, then went back to 210 drinking, as though it was the most normal thing in the world. Well, it was, for the dog. Where else would a creature in the wild get liquid? If the streams were not all dried up, they must have learned to tolerate the water. But then, it was breathing the poisoned atmosphere, wasn't it?

foresighted (fôr'sī'tĭd) *adj.* having the ability to anticipate the future and prepare for it

H SEQUENCE
What sequence of events leads to Brock's touching the puppy?

DIFFERENTIATED INSTRUCTION

FOR ADVANCED LEARNERS/PRE–AP

Analyze Character Have students consider whether they would describe Brock as a risk-taker. Ask them to support their opinions with examples from the story. Also have them predict what Brock may do in the future, based on their observations of Brock's behavior so far.

Why hadn't it hit Brock before? This was a fully organic creature on the outside *without any life support system.* What could that mean? Some amazing mutation[8] must have occurred, making it possible for at least some creatures to breathe the outside atmosphere and drink its poisoned water. Those who couldn't died, those who could survived and got stronger. Even the ancient scientist Darwin[9] knew that. And Brock had
220 come upon one of these magnificent mutants! ❶

The puppy whimpered and looked up at Brock with large, trusting eyes. How could he think of it as a mutant specimen? It was a puppy. One who had lost its mother. What would it eat? There was no sign of food for a carnivore.[10] Perhaps way back in the mountains some small mammals had also survived, keeping the food chain going, but the puppy would not live long enough to find its way there, much less know how to hunt with its mother gone. For the first time in his life something deep inside Brock reached out toward another creature. The thought of the puppy **languishing** here by the side of its dead parent until it, too . . .
230 "Your name is Brog, all right?" The ancient astronomers had named stars after themselves. He had discovered something just as wonderful. Didn't he have the right to name it sort of after himself while preserving the puppy's uniqueness? "Don't worry, Brog. I won't let you starve."

Which is why Brock appeared at the customs portal after dark, the front of his dry suit stained, carrying a wriggling *Canis familiaris*[11] of uncertain breed.

If there had been any way to smuggle the dog in, Brock would have. But he couldn't for the life of him figure out how. As it was, every alarm in the area went off when he stepped into the transitional cubicle.[12]
240 The disembodied voice of the monitor queried him:
"Welcome back, Brock 095670038. You're late."
"Affirmative."
"And you are carrying contraband."
"I pulled a leaf."
"Deposit same in quarantine bins."
"Affirmative."
"Sensors denote warm-blooded presence not on official roster."
"I found a dog," Brock mumbled.

---

8. **mutation** (myōō-tā′shən): a change within a creature's genes that results in a new trait or characteristic.
9. **Darwin:** Charles Darwin (1809–1882) was a British naturalist who founded the theory of evolution based on natural selection.
10. **carnivore** (kär′nə-vôr′): a flesh-eating animal.
11. *Canis familiaris* (kā′nĭs fə-mĭl-ê-âr′əs): the scientific name for the domesticated, or household, dog.
12. **transitional cubicle:** a small compartment where one is examined before moving from one environment into the next.

❶ **SETTING**
Reread lines 209–220. How is finding the puppy changing what Brock has always believed about the outside?

languish (lăng′gwĭsh) v. to remain unattended or be neglected

❷ **Targeted Passage**

LITERARY ANALYSIS

❶ **SETTING**

Possible answer: *Brock realizes that living creatures still exist outside the dome and that the world outside may not be as poisonous as the dome dwellers believe.*

If students need help . . . Fill in a T Chart with what the dome dwellers believe about the world outside and what Brock is discovering.

Beliefs of Dome Dwellers	Brock's Discoveries
Trees are extinct (lines 117–118).	He sees trees (line 115).
Earth's water is poisoned (lines 126–128).	The puppy drinks water from the stream (lines 209–210).
Earth's atmosphere is poisoned (line 171).	Brock's hand is unharmed when he removes his glove (line 195).
No animals or people survived outside the dome (lines 173–175).	He finds a puppy (lines 152–154).

Extend the Discussion What conclusions can you draw about the environment outside the dome, based on details in the story?

 BEST PRACTICES TOOLKIT—Transparency T Chart p. A25

Lines 227–233
REINFORCE *KEY IDEA:* COMPANIONSHIP

Discuss What does Brock promise the puppy? What do his actions reveal about the **companionship** between people and dogs? ***Possible answer:*** *Brock promises that he won't let the puppy starve. Humans have a responsibility to take care of their canine companions.*

ANALYZE VISUALS

Possible answer:

• *The boy looks excited and happy. He is fascinated with the puppy and enjoys playing with it.*

• *The boy's facial expression mimics the puppy's. This suggests that he identifies with and feels close to the dog.*

Lines 253–267
DISCUSSION PROMPTS

Use these prompts to help students understand what happens when Brock and Brog arrive at quarantine inspection:

Connect Think about a time when you had to request permission for something very important to you. How do those thoughts help you understand Brock's feelings toward the officials during the quarantine inspection? *Students might say that although Brock may have been nervous, he needed to be assertive and persuasive for the puppy's sake.*

Analyze How do the inspectors react to Brog? Why do you think they react this way? *Possible answer: The inspectors are nervous at first but then become interested in Brog. The puppy is much more alive and interactive than a robopet. The puppy may inspire in them the same warm, protective feelings that Brock has toward it.*

Synthesize How does the chief inspector's decision affect the story? *Possible answer: Brog is allowed to stay, so Brock will have more time to study and get to know the puppy.*

READING SKILL

▣ SEQUENCE

Possible answer:

• *Brock takes the puppy back to the dome (lines 234–236).*

• *The quarantine inspectors decide that the puppy can stay but must go to Research (line 262).*

• *Brock takes the puppy to Research (lines 265–267).*

"Repeat."

250   "A dog."

"*Canis familiaris* is extinct."

"Well, maybe it's just a robopet that got out somehow."

"Correction. Robopets are bloodless. Leave dry suit for sterilization and proceed to quarantine inspection."

The officials in quarantine inspection, who rarely had anything to inspect, were at first nervous and then, as they watched the puppy happily licking Brock's face, interested despite themselves. An actual dog! None of them had ever seen one, of course, and Brock's dog was so much, well, more vital than a robopet. And although, on later reflection,

260 they knew they should have terminated or expelled it, they couldn't quite bring themselves to do so that night.

"It will have to go to Research," the chief inspector finally declared.

"Permission requested to hand carry the dog known as Brog to Research," Brock said. There was a bit of an argument about that. Several inspectors sought the honor, but the chief declared that Brock, having shed his dry suit and being already contaminated, should be placed with the dog in a hermetically sealed air car and transported to Research. ▣

The scientists in Research were predictably amazed to see a live *Canis familiaris*. But being scientists and more objective than the lower-grade

270 quarantine inspectors, they kept a safe distance both physically and psychically[13] from the creature. Only the oldest scientist, dressed in proper protective clothing, came into the laboratory with Brock and the dog.

---

13. **psychically** (sī'kĭk-lē): in a manner related to the mind or spirit.

ANALYZE VISUALS
Look at the boy's expression. What can you **infer** about his feelings toward the puppy?

▣ **SEQUENCE**
What events happen after Brock finds the puppy? As you read, record the sequence on your chart.

DIFFERENTIATED INSTRUCTION

FOR ADVANCED LEARNERS/PRE–AP

Analyze Setting Have students consider the various aspects of the dome society where Brock and the dome dwellers live, including the physical, emotional, societal, and educational details. Challenge students to create a new plan for domed life that allows its inhabitants to live fuller, more interesting lives. Invite volunteers to present their plans, including visuals that highlight key attributes.

He scanned and poked and prodded the poor little fellow until it began to whimper in protest.

"Brog needs to rest," said Brock, interrupting the scientist in the midst of his inspection. "She's (for by this time gender had been indisputably established) had a hard day. And if there's some actual food available—she's not used to pellets."

"Of course, of course," said one of the researchers through the speaker
280 in the observation booth. "How thoughtless. Send someone out for a McLike burger without sauce. She may regard it as meat. Anyhow, it will seem more like food to her than a pellet, affirmative, Brock?"

The scientists, Brock soon realized, were looking to him for advice. He was, after all, the discoverer of the last dog. It gave him sudden scientific status. Brock had sense enough to take advantage of this. After Brog had swallowed the McLike burger in three quick gulps, Brock insisted that he be allowed to stay with Brog, so that he might interact and sleep with her. "She's not like us," he explained. "She's used to tumbling about and curling up with other warm bodies. In the old myths," he added, "puppies
290 separated from their litters cried all night long. She will need constant interaction with another warm-blooded creature or she might well die of," he loved using his new vocabulary, "'loneliness.'"

The scientists agreed. After all, research was rather like quarantine, and since Brock had touched the dog ungloved and unprotected, he might well have picked up some germ from her. It was better to keep them both isolated in the research lab where proper precautions would be taken.

For nearly a week, Brock lived with Brog in the research center, eating McLike burgers, playing "fetch," teaching Brog to "sit," "heel," "come"—all the commands he could cull from the ancient texts. The dog quickly
300 learned to obey Brock's commands, but it wasn't the automatic response of a robopet. Brog delighted in obedience. She wanted to please Brock, and those few times when she was too busy nosing about the lab and failed to obey instantly, those times when Brock's voice took on a sharp tone of **reproof,** the poor little thing put her tail between her legs, looked up at him with sorrowful eyes, begging to be forgiven. Brock was tempted to speak sharply to her even when there was no need, for the sight of her drooping ears and tail, her mournful eyes was so dear to him that he did what Travis Coates had done to Old Yeller.[14] He hugged her. There was no other way to explain it. He simply put his arms around her and held
310 her to his chest while she beat at him with her tail and licked his face raw. Out of the corner of his eye he was aware that one of the scientists was watching. Well, let him watch. Nothing was as wonderful as feeling this warmth toward another creature.

reproof (rĭ-prōōf′) *n.*
criticism for a fault

---

14. **Travis Coates...Old Yeller:** In the novel *Old Yeller,* Old Yeller is a stray dog who becomes friends with 14-year-old Travis.

THE LAST DOG 53

Lines 297–313
DISCUSSION PROMPTS

Use these prompts to help students understand the growing bond between Brock and Brog:

Connect What do people find rewarding about the process of training a pet? *Students may say that training a pet helps people learn more about their animal and how to handle it. They may also say that watching an animal learn a skill is fun.*

Analyze Why is Brog better than a robopet in Brock's mind? *Possible answer: Although a robopet is always obedient, it has no personality or feelings. Brog may not always follow commands, but she can show affection and other emotions.*

Synthesize How is the growing bond between Brog and Brock unusual in the dome society? How might the dome dwellers respond to this bond? *Possible answer: Life within the dome is very controlled. Emotions do not have a place in the society. Therefore, the affection and loyalty growing between Brock and Brog may be perceived as a threat.*

FOR LESS–PROFICIENT READERS

Concept Support After students read page 53, have them describe ways in which Brog is becoming a companion to Brock. Refer students back to the list they wrote before reading the selection.

FOR ENGLISH LEARNERS

Language: Pronouns Remind students that pronouns such as *he, she,* and *it* stand for other words. Explain that it can be tricky to identify a pronoun when it stands for an idea instead of a specific noun. Discuss these examples with students:

- *it* (line 281) stands for "McLike burger" in preceding sentence
- *it* (line 360) stands for "the list" (line 358)

- *it* (line 284) means "the fact that Brock discovered the dog"—must be inferred from context
- "It was better to" (line 295) is an idiomatic use of *it*—sentence could be rephrased as "Keeping them both isolated was better than letting Brock leave the lab."

Have student pairs discuss what *it* means in the context of lines 300, 309, 318, 324, 341, 367, 395, and 426.

Possible answers: They have been living in the research facility of the dome for about a week.

If students need help . . . A sequence clue is given at the start of the paragraph (line 314): "For the first week." Readers can infer that Brock wakes up in the middle of the night about a week into his stay.

READING SKILL

L SEQUENCE

Possible answers: The scientists are planning to experiment on Brog. Their experiments will probably hurt and might even kill Brog.

Lines 349–351
REINFORCE *KEY IDEA*: COMPANIONSHIP

Discuss Which of the puppy's less desirable traits does Brock love because the dog's **companionship** is so valuable to him? What does this reveal about the importance of close social connections? *Possible answer: Brock doesn't mind the "terrible smell of her breath" or the sound of her snoring. Friends see the best in each other, and don't expect perfection. You can always be yourself among true friends.*

For the first week, the researchers seemed quite content to observe dog and boy from their glass-paneled observation booth and speak **copious** notes into their computers. Only the oldest of them would come into the lab and actually touch the alien creature, and he always wore a sterile protective suit with gloves. The others claimed it would interfere with objectivity if they got close to the dog, but they all seemed to behave 320 positively toward Brog. No mention was made to Brock of his own less than objective behavior. So Brock was astounded to awake in the middle of the night to the sounds of an argument. Someone had forgotten to turn off the communication system. **K**

"Cloning[15]—it's the only thing to do. If she's the last, we owe it to **posterity** to keep the line going."

"And how are we going to raise a pack of dogs in a dome? One is nearly eating and drinking us out of test tube and petri dish. We can't go on this way. As drastic as it may seem, we have to be realistic. Besides, no one has had the chance to do actual experiments since the dark ages. Haven't you 330 ever, just once, yearned to compare virtual research with actual?"

"What about the boy? He won't agree. Interfacing daily with the dog, he's become crippled by primal urges."

"Can you think what chaos might ensue if a flood of primordial emotions[16] were to surface in a controlled environment such as ours?" another asked. "Apparently, emotions are easily triggered by interactions with primitive beasts, like dogs."

"Shh. Not now. The speaker is—" The system clicked off. **L**

But Brock had already heard. He knew he had lost anything resembling scientific objectivity. He was no longer sure objectivity was a desirable 340 trait. He rather enjoyed being flooded by "primordial emotions." But he was more worried for Brog than for himself. It wasn't hard to figure out what the scientists meant by "actual experiments." Cloning would be bad enough. Ten dogs who looked just like Brog so no one would know how special, how truly unique Brog was. But experiments! They'd cut her open and examine her internal organs, the way scientists had in the dark ages. They'd prod her with electric impulses and put chips in her brain. They'd try to change her personality or modify her behavior. They'd certainly try to make her eat and drink less!

In the dark, he put his arm around Brog and drew her close. He loved 350 the terrible smell of her breath and the way she snored when she slept. They'd probably fix that, too.

The next day he played sick. Brog, faithful dog that she was, hung around him whimpering, licking his face. The scientists showed no

copious (kō′pē-əs) *adj.* more than enough; plentiful

K SEQUENCE
How long have Brock and Brog been living in the dome when the argument occurs?

posterity (pŏ-stĕr′ĭ-tē) *n.* future generations

L SEQUENCE
What are the scientists planning to do to Brog? As you read, note on your chart the events that follow.

---

15. **cloning:** the scientific process of creating several identical plants or animals from a single ancestor.
16. **primal urges . . . primordial** (prī-môr′dē-əl) **emotions:** feelings or desires that have existed from the beginning of humankind.

particular concern. They were too busy plotting what they might do with Brog.

Brock crept to the nearest terminal in the lab. It was already logged in. The scientists had been doing nothing but research on *Canis familiaris.* COMMON CANINE DISEASES. Brock scrolled down the list with descriptions. No, *distemper* wouldn't do. The first symptom was loss of appetite. He couldn't make Brog fake that. On and on it went—no, *heartworms* wouldn't do. What he needed was a disease that might affect *Homo sapiens*[17] as well as *Canis familiaris.* Here it was! "Rabies: A viral disease occurring in animals and humans, esp. in dogs and wolves. Transmitted by bite or scratch. The early stages of the disease are most dangerous, for an otherwise healthy and friendly appearing animal will suddenly bite without provocation."

Rabies was it! Somehow he would have to make Brog bite him. There was no antirabies serum in the dome, he felt sure. There were no animals in the dome. Why would they use precious space to store an unneeded medication? So they'd have to expel him as well as Brog for fear of spreading the disease. He shivered, then shook himself. No matter what lay on the outside, he could not stand to go back to the life he had lived in the dome before he met Brog. Ⓜ

③ Targeted Passage

Ⓜ **SETTING**
How does the setting inside the dome help Brock make his decision?

He crept back to bed, pulling the covers over Brog. When one of the scientists came into the observation booth, Brock pinched Brog's neck as hard as he could. Nothing. He pinched again, harder. Brog just snuggled closer, slobbering on his arm.

Disgusted, Brock got out of bed. Brog hopped down as well, rubbing against his leg. Pinching obviously was not going to do it. While the scientist on duty in the booth was bending over a computer terminal, Brock brought his foot down on Brog's paw. A tiny *yip* was all he got from that cruel effort—not enough sound even to make the man look up.

"Feeling better, Brock 095670038?" The oldest researcher had come into the lab.

"Affirmative," Brock answered.

"And how are you, puppy-wuppy?" The old man tickled Brog under her chin with his gloved hand. *If I were a dog, I'd bite someone like that,* thought Brock, but Brog, of course, simply licked the researcher's glove and wagged her tail.

That was when he got his great idea. He waited to execute it until the proper moment. For the first time, all the scientists had gathered in the lab, all of them in protective garb, some of them twitching nervously in their chairs. They were sitting in a circle around Brock and Brog, explaining what must be done.

17. ***Homo sapiens*** (hō'mō sā'pē-ənz): the scientific name for the species of human beings now on Earth.

Lines 367–373
REINFORCE *KEY IDEA:* COMPANIONSHIP

Discuss How important has Brog's **companionship** become to Brock? ***Possible answer:*** *Brock is willing to risk being expelled from the dome to prevent the scientists from experimenting on Brog. His relationship with the dog has become the most important thing in his life.*

LITERARY ANALYSIS

Ⓜ SETTING

Possible answer: *Everything is controlled in the dome. There is no room for emotions or imperfections. Brock cannot return to that sterile life after experiencing the fun and happiness of having Brog.*

BACKGROUND

Rabies Every year, thousands of people and millions of mammals around the world die from rabies. Rabies is a serious disease caused by a virus and spread through saliva (usually from the bite of an infected animal). Only mammals—such as raccoons, skunks, foxes, bats, dogs, cats, cattle, and humans—can get rabies. Rabid animals may behave strangely—wild animals may appear tame and approach humans, while once-friendly pets may snap or bite. If someone is bitten by a rabid animal, getting a vaccine from a doctor can keep the person from developing rabies. If left untreated, rabies slowly attacks the brain and spinal cord and destroys the central nervous system.

DIFFERENTIATED INSTRUCTION

FOR LESS–PROFICIENT READERS

③ Targeted Passage [Lines 356–373]

This passage develops the story's conflict as Brock devises a plan to save Brog from the scientists who wish to experiment on her.

- Why is Brog looking up dog diseases on the computer?
- What does he find out about rabies?
- What does he hope will happen if he manages to make Brog bite him?

Activity Have students compare this image to the one on page 45. Ask them how the differences between the two illustrations show the differences in Brock. *Possible answers: In the first illustration, the boy is wearing a protective suit. In this image, the boy is standing unprotected in the environment. He is less confined. He is free, like Brock at the end of the story.*

Lines 404–413
DISCUSSION PROMPTS

Use these prompts to help students understand the values of the dome scientists:

Connect Have you ever made a decision that was not popular with your family or a group of friends? How do those thoughts help you understand Brock's behavior toward the researchers? *Possible answer: Students may say that going against group mentality is difficult and feels strange. To do what is right for oneself takes courage and determination.*

Analyze How do the scientists act as Brock is leaving the dome? What does this suggest about relationships among people in the dome? *Possible answer: No one seems sad or concerned that Brock is leaving. People in the dome probably do not have caring personal relationships with each other.*

Synthesize Based on the scientists' reaction, what has become most important to the people living in the dome? *Possible answer: Survival has become most important. It is valued even above knowledge and love.*

◻N SEQUENCE

Record students' answers in the sequence chart from page 43.

Possible answer:

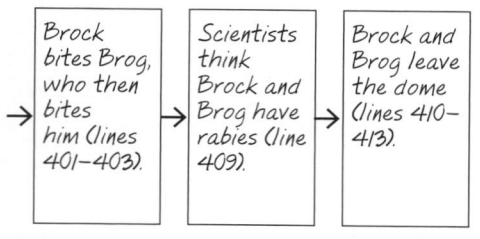

"It has to be done for the sake of science," they began. Then they went on to, "For the sake of the dome community, which is always, as you well know, short on food, and particularly short on water." Brock listened to their arguments, nodding solemnly, pretending to agree. "It won't be as if she'll really be gone, you know. We've made virtuals of her—a special series 400 just for you to keep. You can virtually play with her whenever you like."

That was the cue. Brock turned and bit Brog on the tail so hard that the blood started. Brog, surprised and enraged, spun around and bit Brock on the nose.

There was a shocked silence. Every scientist leaned backward, body pressed hard against his or her chair back. Every eye was on the two of them.

"I—I don't know what got into me," Brock said. "I've been feeling very weird." The scientists continued to stare. "I was checking the historical records. . . ."

All of the scientists fled the room. Someone ran to a computer terminal. 410 When Brock offered to take Brog out of the dome and let her loose in the mountains, no one argued. Neither did they say, "Hurry back," or even, "Take care." No one came close as he loaded his pouch with water and food pellets. The customs gate monitor asked no questions. ◻N

Out of sight of the dome, Brog was delirious with joy, jumping and running about in circles around Brock's boots. Why wasn't the

◻N SEQUENCE
How does Brock get the scientists to release him and Brog?

DIFFERENTIATED INSTRUCTION

FOR ADVANCED LEARNERS/PRE–AP

Analyze Discuss how some works of science fiction act as a warning to people about what could happen if they ignore signs of danger or refuse to change their ways. Ask students to work in pairs to create a graphic organizer that identifies practices or attitudes in modern society that might lead to the world described in "The Last Dog." Have students summarize in a statement what they think is the author's main warning.

atmosphere choking Brog if it was as poisonous as the dome dwellers claimed? His heart beating rapidly, Brock unscrewed his helmet just enough to let in a little of the outside atmosphere. Nothing happened. In fact, he seemed to be breathing perfectly normally. He took off the helmet entirely. He was still breathing freely. But his heart was beating
20 so hard, he couldn't be sure. He waited for the choking sensation he had been warned of. It didn't occur. Could they be wrong? Could the outside world have healed itself? Perhaps—perhaps the reason the scanner had so much trouble reading the outside atmosphere was because it wasn't within the range of computerized expectations.

Could it be? Could it be that fear had kept the dome dwellers prisoner many years longer than a poisoned environment would have?

He unfastened the dry suit and slowly stepped out of it into the sunlight.

It was wonderful how much faster he could walk without the clumsy suit.
30 "Who knows?" Brock said to a frisking Brog. "Who knows, maybe out here you aren't the last dog. Your mother had to come from somewhere."

Brog barked happily in reply.

"And maybe, just maybe, where there are dogs, there are humans as well."

They stopped at the brook where they'd met, and both of them had a long drink. Brock no longer carried a scanner, but he knew what he felt was excitement. The water was delicious. ~ ◎

④ Targeted Passage

◎ SETTING
How are Brock's questions about the world outside the dome beginning to be answered?

THE LAST DOG   **57**

FOR LESS–PROFICIENT READERS

④ Targeted Passage [Lines 417–436]

This passage resolves the story's conflict as Brock overcomes his fear of the environment.

- What internal conflict does Brock face as he takes off his helmet? What does he fear?

- What does Brock learn about the air and water outside the dome?

- What does Brock think he and Brog might find eventually?

- Does Brock regret leaving the dome?

FOR ENGLISH LEARNERS

Comprehension: Task Support Assign groups to review these passages about what Brock was taught about the outside world:

- sun (lines 41–43)

- water (lines 126–128)

- air, dogs (lines 171–172)

- people, animals (lines 173–175)

Have them search page 57 to find out how Brock's actual experiences differ from these ideas. Then have groups share their results.

LITERARY ANALYSIS

◎ SETTING

Possible answer:

- *In lines 421–423, Brock wonders whether the outside world might have healed itself. When he breathes the air (lines 417–420) and drinks the water (lines 434–436), he finds that the environment does not seem poisonous.*

- *Brock was taught that all animals and people perished outside the dome (lines 173–175). Having discovered Brog, he wonders if there might be other dogs and even people living in the outside world (lines 430–433).*

SELECTION WRAP–UP

REFLECT Have students think about the events that led Brock to leave the dome permanently. If he had not found Brog, would he have been content to stay inside forever? Or, would he eventually have left anyway?

⭐ **CRITIQUE** Ask students to evaluate the effectiveness of setting in helping to convey the author's message. Would the story have had the same impact if the events took place in a different time and place?

READING FLUENCY

Distribute the copy masters and have students practice fluency.

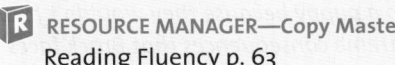 **RESOURCE MANAGER—Copy Master**
Reading Fluency p. 63

THE LAST DOG   **57**

Practice and Apply

After Reading

For additional support of post-reading questions, use these copy masters:

R RESOURCE MANAGER—Copy Masters

Reading Check p. 60 (to check understanding of the selection)

Setting p. 53 (for practice of literary analysis standards focus)

Question Support p. 61 (**After Reading** questions adapted for English learners and less-proficient readers)

Additional selection questions are provided for teachers on page 47.

ANSWERS

Comprehension

1. *Brock checks a scanner to find out what he is feeling.*

2. *Pretending to have rabies is the only way for both Brock and Brog to get out of the dome.*

3. *Meeting Brog allows Brock to feel a connection to another living being. He realizes that the outside world is where he wants to be.*

Literary Analysis

Possible answers:

4. *The setting seems to be Earth in the future. The dome is technologically advanced, but its dwellers are human. There are references to products, such as a "McLike" burger, and novels that are part of Earth's culture. The landscape outside of the dome resembles Earth.*

5. ■ **STANDARDS FOCUS** *Identify Sequence The flashbacks reveal Brock's conversations with dome officials about leaving the dome to explore the outside world. Readers learn of Brock's curiosity and the suspicion with which people view his leaving the dome.*

6. ● **STANDARDS FOCUS** *Setting Students' diagrams will vary. However, the setting affects the plot because when Brock finds a puppy, he is forced to leave the only home he has ever known. In their diagrams, students might say that they would be able to keep a puppy because they wouldn't face the extreme consequences that Brock faces.*

Comprehension

MARYLAND OBJECTIVES

LITERATURE STANDARD
3.A.3.c Analyze setting

1. **Recall** In the first half of the story, how does Brock know what emotions he is feeling?

2. **Clarify** Why does Brock fool the scientists into thinking he and Brog have rabies?

3. **Summarize** How does meeting Brog change Brock's life?

Literary Analysis

4. **Make Inferences** What would you say is the **setting** of the story? Give details from the text about both the time and the place.

5. **Identify Sequence** Review the chart you created as you read. Which event or events occur as a **flashback**? What new information about the people in the dome do you learn in the flashback?

6. **Analyze Setting** One way to consider the importance of setting to a story is to imagine the same story happening in a different time or place. Think about what might happen if you found a puppy. How would your experience be different from Brock's? Use a Venn diagram to **compare and contrast** which details might stay the same and which details might be different. Explain what your diagram suggests about the influence of setting on a story.

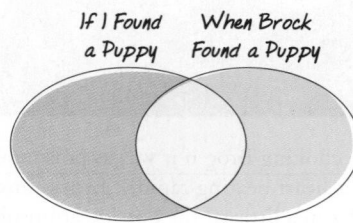

7. **Draw Conclusions** Why do you think the people in the dome live the way they do? Think about their food, their fears, and their attitude about the outside world. Then consider how their history and their environment might be affecting them. Support your answer with details from the story.

8. **Evaluate** Go back and review the list you created to answer the question on page 42. Think about what you might add to your list after reading the story. What do you think Brock got from Brog that he wasn't getting from people? Explain your answer.

Extension and Challenge

9. **SCIENCE CONNECTION** Read the article "'Spot' Goes High-Tech" on page 61. Then do research to find out what other kinds of tasks or functions robots are being asked to perform. Note at least three. In a small group, discuss how new technologies might have both a positive and a negative impact on our lives.

> **RESEARCH LINKS**
> For more on robots, visit the **Research Center** at ClassZone.com.

---

7. *Students may say that some catastrophic event forced people into the dome. This is suggested by their fears of the poisoned environment and the abandoned structures that Brock passes (lines 78–80). Once settled in the dome, they became too afraid to leave it. They have lost all curiosity about the outside world, calling those who show a desire to push the boundaries "deviants."*

8. *Answers will vary. Students may say that Brog is warmer and more responsive to Brock than any human in Brock's life. Brog plays with Brock, trusts him, and loves him.*

Extension and Challenge

9. **SCIENCE CONNECTION** *Students' discussions should show evidence of research. Opinions should be supported with facts.*

Vocabulary in Context

VOCABULARY PRACTICE

For each item, choose the word that differs most in meaning from the other words.

1. (a) journey, (b) expedition, (c) foray, (d) climb
2. (a) perceptive, (b) foresighted, (c) careless, (d) prophetic
3. (a) evasive, (b) clever, (c) bright, (d) knowledgeable
4. (a) numerous, (b) copious, (c) plentiful, (d) thin
5. (a) trail, (b) ail, (c) languish, (d) suffer
6. (a) separated, (b) apart, (c) disembodied, (d) together
7. (a) ancestor, (b) posterity, (c) grandfather, (d) veteran
8. (a) blame, (b) reproof, (c) position, (d) criticism

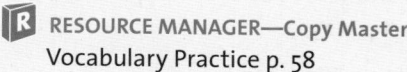

copious
disembodied
evasive
foray
foresighted
languish
posterity
reproof

VOCABULARY IN WRITING

Pretend you are Brock. People from the dome are searching for you, and you're on the run. Use four or more vocabulary words to write a paragraph about what happens next. You could start like this.

> **EXAMPLE SENTENCE**
>
> To escape the searchers, I must make certain **_evasive_** moves now.

VOCABULARY STRATEGY: ANTONYMS AS CONTEXT CLUES

Context clues can often be found in the words and sentences that surround an unfamiliar word. These clues can help you figure out the meaning of the word. **Antonyms,** or words that mean the opposite of each other, can be one kind of context clue. For example, a sentence in "The Last Dog" talks of "actual rather than virtual research." The words *rather than* signal that *virtual* is an antonym of *actual*. Since you know *actual*, you can figure out *virtual*.

PRACTICE Identify the antonym of each boldfaced word. Then define the word.

1. Though he tried to **facilitate** the cleanup process, he complicated it instead.
2. Her costume was **ostentatious**, but her cousin's was quite plain.
3. You should praise your brother, rather than continually **disparaging** him.
4. Unlike Isabel, who had an **antipathy** to snakes, Luisa seemed to love them.
5. Jeremy was as **pugnacious** as his brother was peace loving.

MARYLAND OBJECTIVES

READING STANDARD
1.D.2.b Explain relationships between words

 VOCABULARY PRACTICE
For more practice, go to the **Vocabulary Center** at ClassZone.com.

DIFFERENTIATED INSTRUCTION

FOR ENGLISH LEARNERS
Vocabulary in Writing

1. Have students write three sentences about Brock or about any part of the story using three words from the vocabulary list.
2. Have students share their sentences in small groups.

FOR ADVANCED LEARNERS/PRE–AP

Vocabulary in Writing Have students develop their paragraphs into a new ending for the story. Encourage students to adapt characteristics of the author's style and to keep their new conclusion consistent with the plot, setting, and characters of the original story.

ANSWERS

Vocabulary in Context
VOCABULARY PRACTICE

1. *(d) climb*
2. *(c) careless*
3. *(a) evasive*
4. *(d) thin*
5. *(a) trail*
6. *(d) together*
7. *(d) veteran*
8. *(c) position*

R RESOURCE MANAGER—Copy Master
Vocabulary Practice p. 58

VOCABULARY IN WRITING

Students can use a Sequence Chain to organize the events they would like to include in their paragraph. Students might wish to explain how the search will end and then fill in the events leading up to that conclusion.

BEST PRACTICES TOOLKIT—Transparency
Sequence Chain p. B21

VOCABULARY STRATEGY: ANTONYMS AS CONTEXT CLUES *(also an EL language objective)*

Tell students that other words also signal the presence of **antonyms.** Remind students to look for words or phrases such as *but, though, unlike, although,* and *in contrast.*

Possible answers:

1. *make easier*
2. *fancy; showy*
3. *criticizing*
4. *hatred*
5. *argumentative; aggressive*

R RESOURCE MANAGER—Copy Master
Vocabulary Strategy p. 59

i Vocabulary Center at **ClassZone.com**
Additional Vocabulary Activities

Reading-Writing Connection

WRITING PROMPTS

- For **Prompt A,** students might list story details about how Brock has prepared for his trip and what he thinks about his unusual desire to leave the dome.

- For **Prompt B,** have students use a T Chart to list the advantages of each kind of pet and examples from the article. To plan their responses, they should review the chart and decide how the two pets are similar and different and which one has more benefits.

 **BEST PRACTICES TOOLKIT—Transparency**
T Chart p. A25

For ideas for writing, see
🛈 Writing Center at **ClassZone.com**

GRAMMAR AND WRITING

- Use all three methods of correction shown on the model to demonstrate how each works.

- Write the run-ons on the board. Have students suggest corrections.

Possible answers:

1. *Both types of pets make people feel needed. People like feeling needed.*

2. *Robot pets are just machines, but animal pets really do need us.*

3. *How can a metal dog take the place of a warm, furry one? You can't hug a robot.*

4. *It might help to have a robotic dog, but it can't take the place of a real one.*

🅡 **RESOURCE MANAGER—Copy Master**
Avoid Run-On Sentences p. 62

Assess and Reteach

Assess

🅡 RESOURCE MANAGER—Copy Masters
Selection Tests A, B/C pp. 65–66, 67–68

💿 Test Generator CD

Reteach

🅢 STANDARDS LESSON FILE
Literature Lesson 7: Flashbacks
Vocabulary Lesson 18: Synonyms and Antonyms
Grammar Lesson 2: Avoiding Run-Ons

Reading-Writing Connection

Explore the ideas presented in "The Last Dog" by responding to these prompts. Then complete the **Grammar and Writing** exercise.

WRITING PROMPTS	SELF-CHECK

A. Short Response: Make a Prediction
Reread pages 44–46, lines 10–30. What might Brock be thinking he could find on the outside? Write a **one-paragraph prediction,** taking into account why Brock is worried about being labeled a deviant and why deviants never return.

A strong prediction will . . .
- use clues in the text to predict what Brock thinks might happen
- note qualities of the setting that could influence events

B. Extended Response: Write Across Texts
Look again at "'Spot' Goes High-Tech" on page 61. Both Brock and the elderly people in the article enjoy having the **companionship** of a pet, be it an animal pet or a robot. Is a robot pet as good as an animal pet? Using examples from both selections, write a **two- or three-paragraph response,** describing the benefits of each pet.

A detailed response will . . .
- use examples from both texts
- explain whether robots are as good as animal pets

GRAMMAR AND WRITING

AVOID RUN-ON SENTENCES A run-on sentence, sometimes simply called a run-on, is two or more sentences written as though they were a single sentence. Use one of these methods to correct a run-on:

- Insert an **end mark** and start a new sentence.
- Insert a **coordinating conjunction,** such as *and, but,* or *so,* after a comma.
- Change a comma to a **semicolon.**

> Original: Some people like having an animal companion, others may think a robot is just as good.
>
> Revised: Some people like having an animal companion, but others may think a robot is just as good.

MARYLAND OBJECTIVES

LANGUAGE STANDARD
5.A.2.c Differentiate complete sentences from comma splices

PRACTICE Rewrite the following sentences so that they are no longer run-ons.

1. Both types of pets make people feel needed people like feeling needed.
2. Animal pets really do need us, robot pets are just machines.
3. How can a metal dog take the place of a furry one, you can't hug a robot.
4. It might help to have a robotic dog it can't take the place of a real one.

*For more help with run-ons, see pages R64–R65 in the **Grammar Handbook.***

DIFFERENTIATED INSTRUCTION

FOR LESS–PROFICIENT WRITERS

For Prompt A:
1. Help students identify clues from the story that help them predict what Brock might be thinking
2. Help students write topic sentences for their prediction paragraphs.
3. Then have each student write his or her own prediction based on the text clues.

For Prompt B:
1. Limit the assignment to one paragraph.
2. Help students list the benefits of both pets and decide which pet is better.
3. Help students write a topic sentence that states their opinion about the better pet.
4. Then have them complete the paragraph by explaining their reasons for choosing that pet.

ONLINE ARTICLE Robotic pets, such as the ones in the dome, are not just futuristic fantasy. This news article describes a contemporary project that is testing whether robotic dogs can bring joy to senior citizens.

BACK   FORWARD   STOP   REFRESH   HOME   PRINT

E-mail This   Print This   Save This   Subscribe

'Spot' Goes High-Tech

Researchers Try Robotic Pets as Companions for the Elderly

Researchers in Indiana are trying to find out if robots—which no one has to feed or walk—can do the same job as flesh and blood animals.

Rosewalk Common is an assisted living community for seniors in Lafayette, Indiana. Rose Lawson, 90, has lived at Rosewalk for four years and recently joined other residents to meet "Aibo" (pronounced "I-bo"), a frisky, silver and black robotic dog.

Aibo made its way around a circle of seated residents, playing fetch, responding to spoken commands, sitting in laps to be petted—and winning friends.

"Do you like me? Do you like me?" Lawson asked Aibo. The robot responded with an electronic "Ohhh," winning a big smile from Lawson....

Can Robots Make People Happier?

The robotic dogs were brought to Rosewalk by researchers at Indiana's Purdue University as part of a **project** to determine whether robots can make people happier.

Alan M. Beck, a professor at Purdue and director of the **Center for Human-Animal Bond** at the university's veterinary school, said one possible benefit may be better socialization.

"We find people who in nursing home settings might be socially isolated and don't routinely chat with each other have something to talk about together, to have fun, to have reminiscences," said Beck....

Programmed to Generate Human Feelings

Robotic dogs are programmed to respond to commands, to wag their tails if told they are "good." All of this is supposed to lull humans into feeling ... attached—to a robot.

The very concept of robots that seduce people into thinking they are real is just too much for sociologist Sherry Turkle, director of the **Initiative on Technology and Self** at the Massachusetts Institute of Technology.

"I think we should take it as a wake-up call and really say, 'Now, why are we giving robot pets to old people?' And the answer, I think, is that we really have been struggling to figure out how to give enough people to old people."

Assistant professor Nancy Edwards, of the Purdue School of Nursing, acknowledges the preference of human contact. But she still sees value in the Aibo study. "We know human interaction is best, we know human-animal [interaction] is probably second, but if these people are having no interaction, what we're saying is, will some interaction with a robot help in some way?"

"You can see smiling, laughing, remembering of good things, and talking among each other," said Beck. "This is more than just diversion. This is kind of a therapeutic event, where people really, I think, benefit from the experience."

DIFFERENTIATED INSTRUCTION

FOR ENGLISH LEARNERS
Vocabulary Support Point out that the word *Spot* in the title is an allusion, and represents a typical American name for a dog. (See line 171 of "The Last Dog" for additional typical dog names.) Then help students understand these words and phrases:

- "assisted living community" refers to a place where older adults live and receive personal care
- "seniors" refers to older, elderly, or retired people

FOR ADVANCED LEARNERS/PRE–AP
Make Judgments After students have read the article, ask them to decide whether interaction with a robot is better for older people than no interaction at all. Have them debate the issue in class, bringing in evidence from the text and their own observations to support their opinions.

This selection provides support for Writing Prompt B on page 60. You can also use it as a mini-lesson on reading for information.

READING FOR INFORMATION
Point out that "'Spot' Goes High-Tech" is an online article. Have students preview the article by reading the headings. Ask them what they might expect to learn about in this article.
Possible answer: This article gives information about real robotic pets that are being used as companions for the elderly. The idea is to make people feel happier by having them interact with the robotic pets.

DISCUSSION PROMPTS
Use these prompts to help students understand how the technological advances in the story "The Last Dog" may not be as far in the future as the author imagined:

Connect Did you know that robotic pets had been invented? What is your opinion of real-life robopets? *Students may say that they were unaware of this technological advance. They may not like the idea of robopets but might be able to understand their usefulness in society. After reading this article, some may think that robopets can be cute and even lovable to a certain extent.*

Analyze Would the positive effects of a robotic pet last? Why or why not? *Possible answers:*

- *No. Just as Brock found, robotic pets become predictable. They do not change, and therefore people would lose interest in them eventually.*
- *Yes. People might become very fond of them because they act like real animals.*

Evaluate Do you think the use of robotic pets is the first step toward a society like the one described in "The Last Dog"? Explain. *Possible answers:*

- *No. Using robotic pets in a limited way will not erase people's love for real animal companions.*
- *Yes. Because of cell phones, video conferencing, and automated services at many businesses, our society is already becoming impersonal and sterile. This use of robotic pets could indicate a further disturbing trend.*

Focus and Motivate

OBJECTIVES

Literary Analysis
- explore the key idea of **potential**
- identify internal and external conflict
- read a short story and a poem

Reading
- make inferences

Vocabulary
- build vocabulary for reading and writing
- understand and use prefixes that mean "not" *(also an EL language objective)*

Grammar and Writing
- punctuate possessive nouns correctly
- use writing to analyze literature

SUMMARY

In "Thank You, M'am," Roger tries to steal Mrs. Jones's purse. She thwarts his attempt and drags him home with her instead. There, she forces him to wash his face and comb his hair before they eat dinner together. She then gives him ten dollars to buy the shoes he wants and sends him on his way.

Who sees the BEST *in you?*

Discuss the question. To lead into the *KEY IDEA,* ask students for their definitions of *potential.* Have them think about a time when they did their best or reached their potential because someone else believed that they could. Then have students complete the *QUICKWRITE* activity.

Selection Resources

Thank You, M'am
Short Story by Langston Hughes

Who sees the BEST *in you?*

MARYLAND OBJECTIVES

READING/LIT STANDARDS
1.E.4.c Draw inferences
3.A.3.g Analyze conflicts

KEY IDEA Have you ever gone through a time when it seemed like you couldn't do anything right? If so, then you know how important it is to have someone have faith in you. When a friend, a family member, or a teacher believes you can do better, it can help you try harder instead of giving up. In "Thank You, M'am," a woman sees **potential**—or possibility—where others might see a problem.

QUICKWRITE Create a web of people you know who see the best in you. Then explain why you have included these people. In what ways do they show their belief in you?

Mr. Simpson

Who Sees My Best?

62

---

* Resources for Differentiation   † Also in Spanish   ‡ In Haitian Creole and Vietnamese

LITERARY ANALYSIS: CONFLICT

There is no story without plot, and there is no plot without **conflict.** A story's plot centers on conflict, or the struggle between opposing forces.

- An **external conflict** is a character's struggle against an outside force. For example, a character may struggle against nature or against another character.
- An **internal conflict** takes place inside the character. For example, a character may struggle between wanting something and knowing that taking it is wrong.

Stories often contain more than one conflict. As you read "Thank You, M'am," look for examples of both types of conflict.

READING SKILL: MAKE INFERENCES

When you make an **inference,** you use your reason and experience to guess at what a writer doesn't say directly. Combining clues in a passage with your own knowledge helps you understand what characters are feeling and thinking. As you read "Thank You, M'am," make inferences to better understand the characters. Record your inferences on a chart like the one shown.

Detail About Character	What I Infer
Mrs. Jones holds Roger but lets him stoop to pick up her purse.	Mrs. Jones is trying to decide whether to trust Roger.

VOCABULARY IN CONTEXT

The following words helped Langston Hughes write a story about a boy facing a serious conflict. To see how many words you already know, use them to complete the sentences.

> **WORD LIST**   barren   frail   mistrust   presentable

1. Don't _____ him; he will keep his promise.
2. Because he was _____, the hard work tired him.
3. The _____ room was a source of loneliness.
4. He wanted to look _____ for the assembly.

Author Online

A Fascinating Journey
As a child being raised by his grandmother in Lawrence, Kansas, Langston Hughes began a lifelong exploration of literature and blues music. He later went to Columbia University, worked

**Langston Hughes
1902–1967**

in hotels, and traveled the world as a cook's assistant on freighters. Hughes was first recognized as a poet while working as a busboy. He left his poems at a table where the poet Vachel Lindsay was dining. Lindsay promoted the young poet's work, and Hughes's career was launched. Langston Hughes went on to become an influential writer of the 20th century.

The People's Poet After being discovered, Hughes went on to write novels, short stories, and plays as well as poems. Hughes's work shows a special understanding of everyday people—people who may not be famous or rich but whose lives are inspiring and valuable nonetheless.

 MORE ABOUT THE AUTHOR
For more on Langston Hughes, visit the **Literature Center** at ClassZone.com.

Background
Harlem "Thank You, M'am" takes place in Harlem, a section of New York City. In the early 1900s, Harlem attracted many African-American writers. The stimulating community had a deep influence on their work.

THANK YOU, M'AM **63**

Teach

STANDARDS FOCUS

LITERARY ANALYSIS

● **CONFLICT**

Read aloud this example and have students identify an internal conflict and an external conflict:

> Twenty miles into the marathon, Maria's muscles felt like putty. The wind blew fiercely against her. Then she saw her family holding a sign that said, "We believe in you, Maria!" She knew she couldn't give up.

Possible answer: *The internal conflict is Maria's exhaustion versus her desire to complete the race. She is also fighting the wind, an external conflict.*

CHECK UNDERSTANDING Have students identify conflicts from stories they know.

READING SKILL

■ **MAKE INFERENCES**

Reread the example above. Ask students to identify details that help them infer that Maria has a supportive family.
Possible answer: *Her family is there at the race and holding a sign.*

CHECK UNDERSTANDING Ask students to make inferences about the situation in the photograph on page 62.

R RESOURCE MANAGER—Copy Master
Make Inferences p. 81 (for student use while reading the selection)

VOCABULARY SKILL

▲ **VOCABULARY IN CONTEXT**

DIAGNOSE WORD KNOWLEDGE To determine preteaching needs, have all students complete **Vocabulary in Context.** Check students' answers. (**1.** *mistrust;* **2.** *frail;* **3.** *barren;* **4.** *presentable*)

PRETEACH VOCABULARY Use the Vocabulary Study copy master to help students analyze the meaning of each boldfaced word.

  1. Read item 1 aloud, emphasizing *barren.*

2. Point out the words "transformed" and "beautiful, flourishing garden." Discuss what *barren* might mean, what it is and is not, examples, and related words.

3. Have students record their ideas on the Word Questioning Map.

4. Repeat the procedure for items 2–4.

R RESOURCE MANAGER—Copy Master
Vocabulary Study p. 83

For general guidelines on differentiating vocabulary instruction and for alternative vocabulary activities for students not needing vocabulary preteaching, see

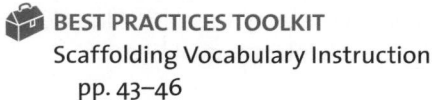 **BEST PRACTICES TOOLKIT**
Scaffolding Vocabulary Instruction pp. 43–46

ⓘ Vocabulary Center at **ClassZone.com**
Additional Vocabulary Activities

Lines 12–23
DISCUSSION PROMPTS

Use these prompts to help students understand the character of Mrs. Jones:

Connect Have you ever had to make a quick decision under pressure? Do you think you would react to an attempted robbery the same way that Mrs. Jones does? *Students may say that they would be afraid and would try to get away as quickly as possible or find a police officer.*

Analyze What qualities does Mrs. Jones possess? *Possible answer: She is physically strong. She has quick reactions. She has courage. She is a no-nonsense lady.*

Synthesize Why doesn't Mrs. Jones want the boy to run away? *Possible answer: She wants to talk to him. She wants to take him to jail. She wants to contact his parents.*

LITERARY ANALYSIS

Ⓐ CONFLICT

Possible answer: The boy and the woman are in conflict. The boy is trying to steal the woman's purse, and she is preventing him.

If students need help . . . Tell them that another way to look at conflict is to see it as problems faced by characters. Ask them

- What problem does the woman have?
- What problem does the boy have?
- How are these problems related? Can both the woman and the boy have what they want?

ANALYZE VISUALS

Possible answer: The woman looks kind, patient, and wise.

About the Art The American painter Alice Neel (1900–1984) is best known for her portraits, such as this one of fellow artist Faith Ringgold. She portrays her subjects with great honesty. Like Mrs. Jones in the story, the artist Alice Neel recognizes people's intrinsic qualities.

Thank You, M'am
Langston Hughes

She was a large woman with a large purse that had everything in it but hammer and nails. It had a long strap, and she carried it slung across her shoulder. It was about eleven o'clock at night, and she was walking alone, when a boy ran up behind her and tried to snatch her purse. The strap broke with the single tug the boy gave it from behind. But the boy's weight and the weight of the purse combined caused him to lose his balance so, instead of taking off full blast as he had hoped, the boy fell on his back on the sidewalk, and his legs flew up. The large woman simply turned around and kicked him right square in his blue-jeaned sitter. Then
10 she reached down, picked the boy up by his shirt front, and shook him until his teeth rattled. Ⓐ

After that the woman said, "Pick up my pocketbook, boy, and give it here."

She still held him. But she bent down enough to permit him to stoop and pick up her purse. Then she said, "Now ain't you ashamed of yourself?"

Firmly gripped by his shirt front, the boy said, "Yes'm."

The woman said, "What did you want to do it for?"

The boy said, "I didn't aim to."

20 She said, "You a lie!"

By that time two or three people passed, stopped, turned to look, and some stood watching.

"If I turn you loose, will you run?" asked the woman.

① Targeted Passage

Ⓐ CONFLICT
Who is in conflict and why?

ANALYZE VISUALS
Look at the woman in the painting. What might you **infer** about her personality?

Faith Ringgold (1977), Alice Neel. Oil on canvas, 48″ × 36″. Private collection. © 2004 Estate of Alice Neel/Courtesy Robert Miller Gallery, New York/Philadelphia Museum of Art, Special Exhibition.

64 UNIT 1: PLOT, CONFLICT, AND SETTING

DIFFERENTIATED INSTRUCTION

FOR ALL STUDENTS
Expert Groups Write these topics on the board and allow students to work independently or in groups to research topics that interest them. When they have completed their research, student experts may present their information to the class, using visuals as appropriate.

- Harlem
- community or school mentoring programs

FOR LESS–PROFICIENT READERS
In combination with the *Audio Anthology CD*, use one or more Targeted Passages (pp. 64, 66, 68) to ensure that students focus on key story events, concepts, and skills.

① Targeted Passage [Lines 1–11]

This passage sets up the story by introducing the main characters and the conflict.

- What two characters do you meet in this paragraph? Describe them.
- What happens when the boy grabs the purse?

BACKGROUND

Harlem The outpouring of African-American creativity in the early 1900s in Harlem, New York City, signaled an important shift in American life. This cultural movement, known as the Harlem Renaissance, brought the works of many African-American writers, artists, playwrights, musicians, and political thinkers new attention and respect. The artists involved in the Harlem Renaissance embraced art as a powerful tool to bring about change. They used various media to articulate and convey an honest exploration of African-American life and culture. Instead of imitating and following convention, they innovated, experimented, and celebrated their heritage. Their efforts succeeded in giving voice to a people long denied freedom of self-expression, as well as opening new doors of opportunity for African Americans.

- What does the woman do to the boy?
- In what way are the woman and the boy in conflict with each other?

FOR ENGLISH LEARNERS

Key Academic Vocabulary Have students use New Word Analysis to study this academic vocabulary from the story: *release* (line 25), *contact* (lines 39, 40), *job* (line 105).

 BEST PRACTICES TOOLKIT—Transparency
New Word Analysis p. E8

Prereading For prereading instruction for English learners, see

 BEST PRACTICES TOOLKIT
Scaffolding Reading Instruction pp. 43–46

FOR ADVANCED LEARNERS/PRE–AP

Pre-AP exercises in the bottom channel provide additional challenge for your advanced students. Use them for small groups or individuals.

ADDITIONAL GUIDELINES

For more help with differentiation and tips for classroom management, see

BEST PRACTICES TOOLKIT
Differentiated Instruction pp. 31–38

B MAKE INFERENCES

Record the details from the passage and students' inferences in a chart like the one from page 63. *Possible answers:*

Detail About Character	What I Infer
The boy says he is sorry (line 26).	He is honest. He is afraid of the woman.
The boy's face is dirty and there is no one at home to tell him to wash it (lines 27–29).	He is not well cared for at home.

Extend the Discussion How are the woman's values revealed through what she says to the boy in lines 27–30?

LITERARY ANALYSIS

C CONFLICT

Possible answer: Roger's internal conflict is his struggle to decide whether to make a run for it. He looks at the door and then goes to the sink. He chooses to stay, probably because he is shocked and confused about the way Mrs. Jones is treating him.

Lines 54–56
ADDITIONAL TEACHING OPPORTUNITY

Conflict Resolution Explain that the conflicts in a story are often—though not always—resolved. Read aloud lines 54–56 and elicit how Roger resolves his inner conflict about whether to leave or stay. *(When Roger goes to the sink, it is clear that he has decided to stay.)* Ask students to suggest how these other conflicts in the story are resolved:

- Mrs. Jones's external conflict of being robbed (lines 4–11), *She saves her purse when the boy falls.*
- Roger's inner conflict of wanting blue suede shoes (lines 64–66, 110–111), *Mrs. Jones gives him money for them.*

"Yes'm," said the boy.

"Then I won't turn you loose," said the woman. She did not release him.

"I'm very sorry, lady, I'm sorry," whispered the boy.

"Um-hum! And your face is dirty. I got a great mind to wash your face for you. Ain't you got nobody home to tell you to wash your face?"

"No'm," said the boy.

30 "Then it will get washed this evening," said the large woman starting up the street, dragging the frightened boy behind her. **B**

He looked as if he were fourteen or fifteen, **frail** and willow-wild, in tennis shoes and blue jeans.

The woman said, "You ought to be my son. I would teach you right from wrong. Least I can do right now is to wash your face. Are you hungry?"

"No'm," said the being-dragged boy. "I just want you to turn me loose."

"Was I bothering *you* when I turned that corner?" asked the woman.

"No'm."

"But you put yourself in contact with *me*," said the woman. "If you

40 think that that contact is not going to last awhile, you got another thought coming. When I get through with you, sir, you are going to remember Mrs. Luella Bates Washington Jones."

Sweat popped out on the boy's face and he began to struggle. Mrs. Jones stopped, jerked him around in front of her, put a half nelson about his neck, and continued to drag him up the street. When she got to her door, she dragged the boy inside, down a hall, and into a large kitchenette-furnished room at the rear of the house. She switched on the light and left the door open. The boy could hear other roomers laughing and talking in the large house. Some of their doors were open, too, so he

50 knew he and the woman were not alone. The woman still had him by the neck in the middle of her room.

She said, "What is your name?"

"Roger," answered the boy.

"Then, Roger, you go to that sink and wash your face," said the woman, whereupon she turned him loose—at last. Roger looked at the door— looked at the woman—looked at the door—*and went to the sink.* **C**

"Let the water run until it gets warm," she said. "Here's a clean towel."

"You gonna take me to jail?" asked the boy, bending over the sink.

"Not with that face, I would not take you nowhere," said the woman.

60 "Here I am trying to get home to cook me a bite to eat and you snatch my pocketbook! Maybe you ain't been to your supper either, late as it be. Have you?"

"There's nobody home at my house," said the boy.

"Then we'll eat," said the woman. "I believe you're hungry—or been hungry—to try to snatch my pocketbook."

B MAKE INFERENCES
Reread lines 18–31. From the details presented so far, what can you guess about the boy's background and personality? Add this information to your chart.

frail (frāl) *adj.* delicate; weak and fragile

2 Targeted Passage

C CONFLICT
What is Roger's internal conflict?

DIFFERENTIATED INSTRUCTION

FOR LESS–PROFICIENT READERS
2 Targeted Passage [Lines 43–62]

This passage advances the plot and increases understanding of the characters by showing how they interact in Mrs. Jones's home.

- Where does Mrs. Jones take the boy?
- What does she tell Roger to do once they get there?
- Why does she ask Roger if he has eaten yet? How does she seem to feel toward him?

FOR ENGLISH LEARNERS
Language: Conversational English Patterns
Explain that the author uses some dialect and slang—the speech patterns of a certain area—to reflect the way real people speak. For example, in line 20 Mrs. Jones says, "You a lie" ("You are lying"). Have mixed language-ability Jigsaw groups reword any nonstandard English in their assigned sections. Then have groups share their dialogue.

 **BEST PRACTICES TOOLKIT**
Jigsaw p. A1

"I wanted a pair of blue suede shoes," said the boy.

"Well, you didn't have to snatch *my* pocketbook to get some suede shoes," said Mrs. Luella Bates Washington Jones. "You could of asked me."

70 "M'am?"

The water dripping from his face, the boy looked at her. There was a long pause. A very long pause. After he had dried his face and not knowing what else to do dried it again, the boy turned around, wondering what next. The door was open. He could make a dash for it down the hall. He could run, run, run, run, *run!*

The woman was sitting on the day-bed.[1] After a while she said, "I were young once and I wanted things I could not get."

80 There was another long pause. The boy's mouth opened. Then he frowned, but not knowing he frowned.

The woman said, "Um-hum! You thought I was going to say *but,* didn't you? You thought I was going to say, *but I didn't snatch people's pocketbooks.* Well, I wasn't going to say that." Pause. Silence. "I have done things, too, which I would not tell you, son—neither tell God, if he didn't already know. So you set down while I fix us something to eat. You might run that comb through your hair so you will look **presentable.**"

90 In another corner of the room behind a screen was a gas plate and an icebox. Mrs. Jones got up and went behind the screen. The woman did not watch the boy to see if he was going to run now, nor did she watch her purse which she left behind her on the day-bed. But the boy took care to sit on the far side of the room where he thought she could easily see him out of the corner of her eye, if she wanted to. He did not trust the woman *not* to trust him. And he did not want to be **mistrusted** now.

"Do you need somebody to go to the store," asked the boy, "maybe to get some milk or something?"

"Don't believe I do," said the woman, "unless you just want sweet milk 100 yourself. I was going to make cocoa out of this canned milk I got here."

"That will be fine," said the boy. **D**

She heated some lima beans and ham she had in the icebox, made the cocoa, and set the table. The woman did not ask the boy anything about where he lived, or his folks, or anything else that would embarrass him. Instead, as they ate, she told him about her job in a hotel beauty shop that stayed open late, what the work was like, and how all kinds of women

---

1. **day-bed:** a couch or sofa that can also serve as a bed.

Gamin (about 1929), Augusta Savage. Painted plaster, 9" × 5³/₄" × 4³/₈". Smithsonian American Art Museum, Gift of Benjamin and Olya Margolin.

presentable
(prĭ-zĕn'tə-bəl) *adj.*
fit to be seen
by people

mistrust (mĭs-trŭst')
v. to think of without
confidence or trust

D MAKE INFERENCES
Why does Roger want
to go to the store for
Mrs. Jones? Add this
information to your
chart.

E MAKE INFERENCES

Possible answers: Roger may have wanted to say how much the encounter meant to him, and how good it felt to have her see potential in him—even when he didn't see it in himself. He may have wanted to promise that he would never do anything dishonest again.

Lines 1–7 (Poem)
DISCUSSION PROMPTS

Use these prompts to help students understand how the poem relates to Mrs. Jones's actions in the story:

Connect How do you think the world would change if everyone adopted the attitude expressed in the poem? *Students might say the world would be a better place because people would try to help each other.*

Analyze How does the poet make her message relevant to ordinary people? ***Possible answer:*** *She does not suggest grand, heroic gestures but gives examples of actions on a small scale that anyone would be able to do.*

Evaluate Based on the ideas in this poem, would Mrs. Jones be able to say that she has not lived "in vain"? ***Possible answer:*** *Yes. She reached out and recognized Roger's potential at a difficult time in his life.*

SELECTION WRAP–UP

★ **CRITIQUE** Ask students whether the fact that Roger never meets Mrs. Jones again is a strength or a weakness of the story. Have students consider why the author might have chosen to write this last line of the story.

READING FLUENCY

Distribute the copy masters and have students work in pairs to practice fluency.

[R] RESOURCE MANAGER—Copy Master
Reading Fluency p. 89

---

came in and out, blondes, red-heads, and Spanish. Then she cut him a half of her ten-cent cake.

"Eat some more, son," she said.

110   When they were finished eating she got up and said, "Now, here, take this ten dollars and buy yourself some blue suede shoes. And next time, do not make the mistake of latching onto *my* pocketbook *nor nobody else's*—because shoes come by devilish like that will burn your feet. I got to get my rest now. But I wish you would behave yourself, son, from here on in."

She led him down the hall to the front door and opened it. "Goodnight! Behave yourself, boy!" she said, looking out into the street.

The boy wanted to say something else other than "Thank you, m'am" to Mrs. Luella Bates Washington Jones, but he couldn't do so as he turned at the **barren** stoop and looked back at the large woman in the door.

120 He barely managed to say "Thank you" before she shut the door. And he never saw her again. ∿ E

❸ Targeted Passage

barren (băr'ən) *adj.*
empty; lacking interest or charm

E MAKE INFERENCES
What else might Roger have wanted to say?

Connect: Poem

If I can
stop one Heart
from **breaking**

Emily Dickinson

If I can stop one Heart from breaking
I shall not live in vain
If I can ease one Life the Aching
Or cool one Pain

5 Or help one fainting Robin
Unto his Nest again
I shall not live in Vain.

DIFFERENTIATED INSTRUCTION

FOR LESS–PROFICIENT READERS

❸ Targeted Passage [Lines 110–121]

This passage resolves the conflicts in the story.

- What does Mrs. Jones do after they finish eating? What advice does she give Roger?
- What does Roger say as he leaves?
- How do you think Roger will act from this point on?
- Recall the conflict between Mrs. Jones and Roger. How has it been resolved?

FOR ADVANCED LEARNERS/PRE–AP

Analyze Setting Tell students that this story is set in the 1950s. Have groups discuss how changing the setting to the current time would affect the plot. Have them consider whether Mrs. Jones could behave similarly in today's society and what the author might have to change in order to communicate a similar theme.

Comprehension

1. **Recall** What happens when Roger tries to steal Mrs. Jones's purse?

2. **Clarify** What does Mrs. Jones say will happen to Roger if he gets the shoes through dishonest means?

3. **Summarize** What details do you learn about Roger and his life?

MARYLAND OBJECTIVES

LITERATURE STANDARD
3.A.3.g Analyze conflicts

Literary Analysis

4. **Identify Conflict** Using a chart like the one shown, go back through the story and record examples of **internal** and **external conflict.** Which conflict is the most important conflict in the story?

Conflict	Internal	External
Roger tries to steal Mrs. Jones's purse.		

5. **Make Inferences** Review the chart you created as you read. Use the inferences you made to answer the following question: Why does Mrs. Jones treat Roger the way she does? Give details from the story to support your answer.

6. **Analyze a Character** Reread lines 71–101, looking specifically at what Roger says and does. What might Roger's behavior suggest about his future **potential?** Give evidence to support your answer.

7. **Compare Literary Works** Reread Emily Dickinson's poem on page 68. Which lines remind you of the way Mrs. Jones might think? Explain why.

8. **Evaluate Theme** The theme of a story is a message about life or human nature that the writer shares with readers. What theme do you think Hughes communicates in "Thank You, M'am"? Do you agree with him? Explain your answer.

Extension and Challenge

9. **Readers' Circle** There's an African proverb that says, "It takes a village to raise a child." With your group, discuss how this proverb applies to "Thank You, M'am." Start by talking about whether the story supports or contradicts the statement.

10. **Creative Project: Writing** Choose one of the characters in this story and write a poem, song, or rap from his or her perspective. Refer to the events in the story, to the character's past, and to the character's imagined hopes for the future.

7. *Students might note lines 3–4: "If I can ease one Life the Aching / Or cool one Pain." Mrs. Jones seems to know that one person's efforts can make a great difference in another's life.*

8. *Students might say Hughes's theme is "People live up to the expectations that others have of them." Students should support their opinions about the message with specific examples.*

Extension and Challenge

9. *Students might say that the story supports the proverb because it shows a woman taking responsibility for a boy she doesn't know. Or, they might note that the story contradicts the proverb because it shows that an individual has greater influence than a group.*

10. *Students' poems, songs, or raps should draw on valid inferences about the characters.*

Practice and Apply

After Reading

For additional support of post-reading questions, use these copy masters:

R RESOURCE MANAGER—Copy Masters
Reading Check p. 86 (to check understanding of the selection)
Conflict p. 79 (for practice of literary analysis standards focus)
Question Support p. 87 (**After Reading** questions adapted for English learners and less-proficient readers)

Additional selection questions are provided for teachers on page 73.

For additional activities to challenge students, see

i Power Thinking at **ClassZone.com**

ANSWERS

Comprehension

1. *The strap breaks, he falls down, and Mrs. Jones grabs him and confronts him.*

2. *They will burn his feet. In other words, his guilt will make the shoes uncomfortable.*

3. *Roger has no supervision. He is thin and frail and appears to eat irregularly. There seems to be no one in his life who really cares about him. He has little money.*

Literary Analysis

Possible answers:

4. ● **STANDARDS FOCUS** *Conflict Internal conflicts include Mrs. Jones's consideration of what to do with Roger (lines 23–31) and Roger's struggle over whether to run away (lines 54–56, 72–76). The major external conflict, the physical struggle between the characters (lines 1–11), may be the most important since it sets the plot in motion.*

5. ● **STANDARDS FOCUS** *Make Inferences Mrs. Jones treats Roger with compassion because she has been in his situation (lines 78–79). She knows that people can change if someone believes in them, which is why she gives Roger her faith and her money.*

6. *Roger decides not to run away (lines 72–76), sits where Mrs. Jones can see him (lines 93–95), and asks if she needs him to go to the store (lines 97–98). He wants to deserve her trust. This shows he has the potential to live up to others' expectations.*

ANSWERS

Vocabulary in Context

VOCABULARY PRACTICE

1. *(c) proper*
2. *(a) empty*
3. *(d) weak*
4. *(b) doubt*

 RESOURCE MANAGER—Copy Master
Vocabulary Practice p. 84

VOCABULARY IN WRITING

Suggest that students collect details from the story about Mrs. Jones's treatment of Roger and the effect it has on him before they form their opinions. Students should include some of their details as support for their opinions.

VOCABULARY STRATEGY: PREFIXES THAT MEAN "NOT" *(also an EL language objective)*

• Ask student volunteers to read each prefix and its meaning. Have students think of familiar words that use each prefix. *(disappoint, inside, unaware, misspell, nonsense)*

• Point out the two meanings of the prefix *in-*. Tell students that they must use the context of a word with this prefix in order to determine which meaning is intended.

Possible answers:

1. *nonviolence—lack of violence*
2. *unpaid—not paid; volunteer*
3. *inaccurate—not correct or not accurate*
4. *disappeared—passed out of sight*
5. *mistreated—treated badly*

 RESOURCE MANAGER—Copy Master
Vocabulary Strategy p. 85

ⓘ Vocabulary Center at **ClassZone.com**
Additional Vocabulary Activities

Vocabulary in Context

VOCABULARY PRACTICE

Choose the letter of the word that means the same, or nearly the same, as the boldfaced word.

1. **presentable** clothing: (a) old-fashioned, (b) tattered, (c) proper, (d) sturdy
2. a **barren** house: (a) empty, (b) dark, (c) private, (d) lovely
3. **frail** patients: (a) unconscious, (b) friendly, (c) nervous, (d) weak
4. to **mistrust** someone's advice: (a) accept, (b) doubt, (c) seek, (d) believe

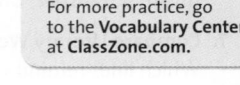

barren
frail
mistrust
presentable

VOCABULARY IN WRITING

Do you think that Mrs. Jones takes the right approach toward Roger? Write a paragraph explaining your opinion. Use at least two vocabulary words in your paragraph. Here is a sample of how you might begin.

MARYLAND OBJECTIVES

READING STANDARD
1.D.3.b Use word structure to determine meaning

> **EXAMPLE SENTENCE**
> *At first, Mrs. Jones is right to* **mistrust** *Roger.*

VOCABULARY STRATEGY: PREFIXES THAT MEAN "NOT"

A **prefix** is a word part that appears at the beginning of a base word to form a new word, as in the vocabulary word *mistrust* (mis + trust). *Mis-* is one of several prefixes that mean "not." Look at the chart to see some other prefixes that mean "not" and to see what other meanings these prefixes may have. If you can identify the base word that a prefix is combined with, you can usually figure out the meaning of the new word.

➜ **VOCABULARY PRACTICE**
For more practice, go to the **Vocabulary Center** at ClassZone.com.

PRACTICE One word in each sentence contains a prefix that can mean "not." Write the word and the word's definition.

1. Martin Luther King Jr. preached nonviolence.
2. Our school district has many unpaid teachers' aides.
3. It is probably inaccurate to say that the universe contains only one solar system.
4. The missile slipped behind the cloud and disappeared from sight.
5. It's common sense that animals should not be mistreated.

Prefix	Meanings
dis-	not; opposite of
in-	not; in
un-	not
mis-	not; incorrect or badly
non-	not; opposite of

DIFFERENTIATED INSTRUCTION

FOR ENGLISH LEARNERS
Vocabulary Strategy

• Assign groups one prefix from the chart.
• Have students place the prefix in the center of a Cluster Diagram and fill the surrounding ovals with words containing the prefix that they find in the textbook or other materials.
• Have groups share their diagrams. Help them define each word based on prefix and root.

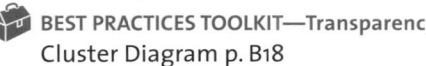 **BEST PRACTICES TOOLKIT—Transparency**
Cluster Diagram p. B18

FOR ADVANCED LEARNERS/PRE–AP

Vocabulary Bee Have students search for words that include each prefix in the **Vocabulary Strategy** chart. Students should record the root of each word on one side of a large card and write the prefix and definition on the back. Then conduct a vocabulary "bee" in which teams of students present their root words. Other teams should try to figure out which prefix meaning "not" is appropriate and to define the entire word.

Reading-Writing Connection

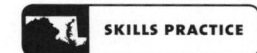

Show your understanding of the characters in "Thank You, M'am" by responding to these prompts. Then complete the **Grammar and Writing** exercise.

WRITING PROMPTS	SELF-CHECK
A. Short Response: Describe a Character's Life Go back to the story and find details that describe Mrs. Jones's job, her house, and what she is able to give Roger. From these details, what can you infer about her life? Write **one paragraph** to describe Mrs. Jones's situation.	*A successful description will . . .* • include a topic sentence that tells what you infer about Mrs. Jones's life • provide specific details to support the topic sentence
B. Extended Response: Compare and Contrast Write **two or three paragraphs** comparing how Roger behaves on the street with how he behaves after spending some time with Mrs. Jones. Explain how Mrs. Jones's belief in his **potential** helps Roger show his best self.	*An effective compare-and-contrast response will . . .* • show an understanding of Roger's actions before and after he gets to know Mrs. Jones • give an example that shows how Roger values Mrs. Jones's trust

GRAMMAR AND WRITING

PUNCTUATE POSSESSIVES CORRECTLY When forming a possessive noun, be sure to put the **apostrophe** in the correct place. To help keep your writing clear, follow these guidelines for punctuating possessive nouns:

Singular nouns: Add an apostrophe and *s*, even if the word ends in *s* (*book's cover, waitress's tray*).

Plural nouns ending in *s*: Add an apostrophe (*songs' melodies, bees' honey*).

Plural nouns not ending in *s*: Add an apostrophe and *s* (*women's sports, people's health*).

> *Original:* In the beginning, Rogers' potential is not easy to see.
>
> *Revised:* In the beginning, Roger's potential is not easy to see.

PRACTICE Correct the possessive nouns in the following sentences.

1. Mrs. Jones' treatment of Roger shows her sympathy toward him.
2. She proves that you cannot always prejudge childrens' actions.
3. She knows that many boy's actions do not reflect their true personalities.
4. Roger understands that it is wrong to take someone elses' money.

*For more help with apostrophes, see page R50 in the **Grammar Handbook**.*

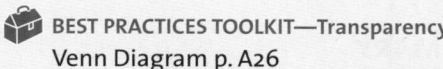

MARYLAND OBJECTIVES

LANGUAGE STANDARD
5.C.2.b Use an apostrophe to designate possession

DIFFERENTIATED INSTRUCTION

FOR LESS–PROFICIENT WRITERS

For Prompt A:

1. As a class, list the details that describe Mrs. Jones's house, job, and gifts to Roger.
2. Help students use the details to make an inference about her life.

For Prompt B:

• Limit the assignment to one paragraph. Have students give one example of how Roger behaves on the street and one example of how he behaves at Mrs. Jones's.

• Before students write their paragraphs, have them work in pairs to choose "before" and "after" examples.

• Prepare students for writing by discussing why Mrs. Jones has a good effect on Roger.

Reading-Writing Connection

WRITING PROMPTS

• For **Prompt A,** remind students to note details that indirectly describe Mrs. Jones's life. For example, she is walking home, not taking a taxi or driving a car. She does not finish work until eleven o'clock. Significant inferences can be made from such details.

• For **Prompt B,** have students use a Venn Diagram to show the differences and similarities in Roger's behavior. Have them draw conclusions about the contrast to support their view of how Mrs. Jones's belief in Roger affects him.

📦 **BEST PRACTICES TOOLKIT—Transparency**
   Venn Diagram p. A26

For an extended Reading-Writing Connection activity, see

ℹ️ Writing Center at **ClassZone.com**

GRAMMAR AND WRITING

• Have the class read each rule aloud.
• Write the **Practice** sentences on the board. Have students cite each rule as they make corrections.

Possible answers:

1. *Mrs. Jones's treatment . . .*
2. *. . . prejudge children's actions.*
3. *She knows that many boys' actions . . .*
4. *. . . take someone else's money.*

R **RESOURCE MANAGER—Copy Master**
   Punctuate Possessives Correctly p. 88

Assess and Reteach

Assess

R **RESOURCE MANAGER—Copy Masters**
   Selection Tests A, B/C pp. 91–92, 93–94

💿 Test Generator CD

Reteach

S **STANDARDS LESSON FILE**
   Literature Lesson 6: Conflict
   Reading Lesson 8: Making Inferences
   Vocabulary Lesson 2: Prefixes (negation and number)

Focus and Motivate

OBJECTIVES

Literary Analysis
- explore the key idea of being **brave**
- recognize and analyze suspense
- read a short story

Reading
- predict

Vocabulary
- build vocabulary for reading and writing
- use the Latin roots *viv* and *vit* to help unlock meaning (*also an EL language objective*)

Grammar and Writing
- maintain pronoun-antecedent agreement
- use writing to analyze literature

SUMMARY

In "Rikki-tikki-tavi," a young mongoose comes to live with a British family in colonial India. When he learns that there are cobras in the garden, Rikki-tikki knows it is his destiny to fight and kill them. In a series of exciting encounters, he outsmarts and outmaneuvers the cobras Nag and Nagaina, killing them and also destroying their nest of eggs.

What makes you BRAVE?

Discuss the question with students. To lead into the *KEY IDEA,* encourage students to expand their idea of what it means to be **brave.** Suggest that they think of telling the truth, standing up to peer pressure, or overcoming a personal fear. Then have students do the *PRESENT* activity.

Selection Resources

Rikki-tikki-tavi

Short Story by Rudyard Kipling

What makes you B R A V E?

MARYLAND OBJECTIVES

READING/LIT STANDARDS
1.E.3.a Select and apply appropriate strategies during reading
3.A.3.h Analyze the author's approach to issues of time

KEY IDEA You see a small child stepping in front of a speeding car. . . . You get the chance to sing in front of a thousand people. . . . Your best friend needs help standing up to a bully. . . . All of these are occasions that might make you feel **brave**—full of energy and courage to meet a tough challenge. In the story you're about to read, you will see bravery in action.

PRESENT Think of a time when you felt brave. Create a picture of the occasion, including a caption explaining what was happening and why it made you brave. Share your picture with the class.

September 12, 2006

Belleville Herald

Local Teen Rescues Five Children

By Terry Jones Staff Reporter

A thirteen-year-old student from Oakdale Elementary School won praise from local community groups for her bravery this Tuesday when fire alarms in her building went off. Cathy Gutierrez was caring for two small brothers at the time and knew there were also young children in the apartment next door. At the sound of the alarms, Cathy rounded up the children, calmed them, and took them to the stairwell designated for evacuations by the Belleville Fire Department. The alarm turned out to be . . .

72

RESOURCE MANAGER UNIT 1

Plan and Teach pp. 95–102

Literary Analysis
Summary pp. 103†*, 104‡*
Suspense pp. 105, 106†*
Question Support p. 113*

Reading
Predict pp. 107, 108†*
Reading Check p. 112
Reading Fluency p. 115

Vocabulary
Study p. 109*
Practice p. 110
Strategy p. 111

Grammar and Writing
Maintain Pronoun-Antecedent
  Agreement p. 114

Assessment
Selection Tests A, B/C pp. 117*, 119*
Test Generator CD

 **BEST PRACTICES TOOLKIT**

Differentiated Instruction
  pp. 31–38*
Scaffolding Instruction pp. 43–46*

Graphic Organizers/Strategies
Cause-and-Effect Chain • New
Word Analysis • T Chart • Word
Squares • Venn Diagram •
Character Map

Reading Support
Audio Anthology CD*

Technology
Literature and Vocabulary
  Centers at **ClassZone.com**

Write*Smart* CD

LITERARY ANALYSIS: SUSPENSE

When you feel growing tension and excitement as you read or watch a movie, that feeling is called **suspense.** Sometimes writers build suspense by using **foreshadowing,** hints or clues about events that will happen later. Foreshadowing can occur when a character makes an unusual statement or issues a strong warning. As you read "Rikki-tikki-tavi," notice how the author builds suspense and makes you want to keep reading. Also notice examples of foreshadowing.

Review: **Conflict**

READING STRATEGY: PREDICT

A **prediction** is a reasonable guess about what will happen over the course of a story. Predicting helps you stay involved as you read. To make predictions, ask yourself:

* What do I already know about the setting and plot?
* On the basis of their words and actions, what might characters do in the future? What events might result?

As you read, write predictions in a chart like the one shown.

Clues from the Story	Predictions
Teddy's mother takes Rikki-tikki home.	Rikki-tikki will become a part of Teddy's family.

Review: **Cause and Effect**

VOCABULARY IN CONTEXT

Rudyard Kipling uses the following boldfaced words in telling his tale of bravery. Restate each sentence, using a different word or phrase for the boldfaced word.

1. She made a **valiant** effort to overcome hardship.
2. She tried to **revive** the unconscious woman.
3. He **cunningly** outsmarted the other contestants.
4. Do not **cower** in scary situations.
5. The dog had a peculiar limping **gait.**
6. The **fledgling** made its first trip outside the nest.
7. We offered them **consolation** in their sorrow.
8. Be careful not to **singe** the hair on your arms.

Author Online

A Man of Two Countries
When Rudyard Kipling was five, he left India, where he had been born, to go to school in England. India, however, would always be a powerful attraction for Kipling; he lived there again for a while

Rudyard Kipling
1865–1936

as an adult, and many of his stories take place there. In works such as *The Jungle Book*, Kipling introduced a vivid cast of animal and human characters. Kipling's adventure stories gained worldwide popularity. In 1907, he received the Nobel Prize in literature.

 MORE ABOUT THE AUTHOR
For more on Rudyard Kipling, visit the **Literature Center** at ClassZone.com.

Background

The Mongoose and the Cobra The mongoose and the cobra are a pair of natural enemies—a pair that will fight to the death. The mongoose, a mammal growing to a length of only 16 inches, seems hardly a match for the poisonous cobra, a snake that averages six feet in length. But the mongoose's speed and agility make it a powerful fighter.

Life in Colonial India This story is set in India during the late 1800s, when Great Britain ruled India. Many British families lived in bungalows—open, airy houses that permitted snakes to enter easily. In such an environment, mongooses were valuable assets.

Teach

STANDARDS FOCUS

LITERARY ANALYSIS

● SUSPENSE

Read aloud this example:

> Tamara slowly pushed open the rusty gate. The garden was so overgrown it looked like a jungle. "There could be all kinds of strange creatures hiding in this place," she thought.

Ask students how this passage creates a feeling of suspense. *Possible answer: The image of a jungle and "strange creatures" suggest hidden dangers.*

CHECK UNDERSTANDING Ask students to name stories or experiences that have given them a feeling of suspense.

READING STRATEGY

■ PREDICT

Encourage students to give examples of predicting from their own lives, such as guessing who will win a game or what gifts they might receive for their birthday. Have them tell what kinds of clues help them make accurate predictions.

CHECK UNDERSTANDING Reread the Suspense example and ask students to predict what might happen to Tamara.

 RESOURCE MANAGER—Copy Master
Predict p. 107 (for student use while reading the selection)

▲ VOCABULARY IN CONTEXT

DIAGNOSE WORD KNOWLEDGE To determine preteaching needs, have all students complete **Vocabulary in Context.** *Possible answers:*
1. *brave* (p. 83); **2.** *wake up* (p. 74); **3.** *cleverly* (p. 85); **4.** *back down* (p. 77); **5.** *way of walking* (p. 79); **6.** *baby bird* (p. 78); **7.** *comfort* (p. 84); **8.** *burn* (p. 83)

PRETEACH VOCABULARY Use the Vocabulary Study copy master to help students assess their

knowledge and predict possible meanings of each boldfaced word, using context clues.

1. Read item 1 in Part A aloud, emphasizing *revive.*
2. Ask students to identify clues to the meaning of *revive,* such as "lost consciousness" and "almost drowned."
3. Repeat the procedure for items 2–8.

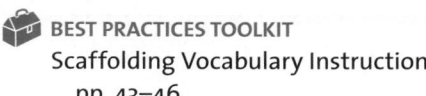 **RESOURCE MANAGER—Copy Master**
Vocabulary Study p. 109

For general guidelines on differentiating vocabulary instruction and for alternative vocabulary activities for students not needing vocabulary preteaching, see

BEST PRACTICES TOOLKIT
Scaffolding Vocabulary Instruction pp. 43–46

Vocabulary Center at **ClassZone.com**
Additional Vocabulary Activities

ANALYZE VISUALS

Possible answer: *They probably have a lot of money to live in such a nice house with such a big garden. They must also like flowers.*

About the Art Pennsylvania-born Jerry Pinkney (b. 1939) is an award-winning illustrator and artist. He began illustrating children's books in 1964 and has more than 75 works to his credit. Pinkney is known for doing meticulous research to make his watercolor paintings realistic and also for creating distinctive personalities in his art. "Rikki-tikki-tavi" was one of Pinkney's favorite stories as a child.

READING STRATEGY

A PREDICT

Possible answer:

Clues from the Story	Predictions
• Rikki-tikki is a mongoose (line 7). • The mongoose and the cobra are natural enemies (**Background**, p. 73).	Rikki-tikki will go to war with a cobra.

If students need help . . .

1. Ask students what kind of animal Rikki-tikki is *(a mongoose)*.

2. Reread the **Background** section aloud. Have students note clues in the passage that relate to the idea of war. *(The mongoose and the cobra are natural enemies who will fight to the death.)*

3. Direct them to conclude with whom Rikki-tikki will go to war *(a cobra)*.

Extend the Discussion Rikki-tikki's war was fought "through the bathrooms of the big bungalow" (line 2). Why might the fighting have happened there?

Rikki-*tikki*-tavi
Rudyard Kipling

This is the story of the great war that Rikki-tikki-tavi fought single-handed, through the bathrooms of the big bungalow in Segowlee cantonment.[1] Darzee, the tailorbird, helped him, and Chuchundra,[2] the muskrat, who never comes out into the middle of the floor but always creeps round by the wall, gave him advice; but Rikki-tikki did the real fighting.

He was a mongoose, rather like a little cat in his fur and his tail but quite like a weasel in his head and his habits. His eyes and the end of his restless nose were pink; he could scratch himself anywhere he pleased
10 with any leg, front or back, that he chose to use; he could fluff up his tail till it looked like a bottle-brush, and his war cry as he scuttled through the long grass was: *Rikk-tikk-tikki-tikki-tchk!* Ⓐ

One day, a high summer flood washed him out of the burrow where he lived with his father and mother and carried him, kicking and clucking, down a roadside ditch. He found a little wisp of grass floating there and clung to it till he lost his senses. When he **revived,** he was lying in the hot sun on the middle of a garden path, very draggled indeed, and a small boy was saying, "Here's a dead mongoose. Let's have a funeral."

"No," said his mother, "let's take him in and dry him. Perhaps he isn't
20 really dead."

---

1. **Segowlee** (sə-gou'lē) **cantonment:** area in India that was home to a British military base.
2. **Chuchundra** (chə-chōōn'drə).

74 UNIT 1: PLOT, CONFLICT, AND SETTING

Illustrations © 1997 by Jerry Pinkney.

ANALYZE VISUALS
What might you **infer** about the people who live in this house?

① Targeted Passage

Ⓐ PREDICT
Recall the information in the **Background** section on page 73. Whom will Rikki-tikki go to war with? Record this and other predictions in your chart as you read.

revive (rĭ-vīv') *v.*
to return to life or consciousness

DIFFERENTIATED INSTRUCTION

FOR ALL STUDENTS

Interest Stations Post suggested assignments for students to work on independently.

- **Victory Song** Write a song that Darzee could sing to celebrate Rikki-tikki's victory.
- **Colonial Life** Research and report on life in northern India in the 1800s.
- **Story Illustration** Choose an unillustrated scene from the story and illustrate it.

For further details on these projects, see

Ⓡ RESOURCE MANAGER
Ideas for Extension pp. 100–101

FOR LESS–PROFICIENT READERS

In combination with the *Audio Anthology CD,* use one or more Targeted Passages (pp. 74, 81, 82–83, 88) to ensure that students focus on key story events, concepts, and skills.

① Targeted Passage [Lines 1–20]

This passage introduces the story's setting, conflict, and main character.

- When and where does this story take place?
- Who is Rikki-tikki-tavi? What is he like?
- What kind of conflict will Rikki-tikki face?

BACKGROUND

Anthropomorphism The word *anthropomorphism* is derived from the Greek words *anthropos*, meaning "human being," and *morph*, meaning "shape." It is the attribution of human feelings, characteristics, or behavior to objects or animals. In this story, Rudyard Kipling combines his knowledge of the plants and animals of India with a tradition of tales about animals who exhibit human characteristics. Rikki-tikki and the other animals not only talk to one another but have the same kinds of relationships (husband and wife), emotions (anger, fear, hatred, heartbreak), and motivations (curiosity, revenge, protecting loved ones) that humans do. The mongoose and cobra are natural enemies, but a real mongoose would be unlikely to protect a human family from cobras. Nor would a cobra plan an attack on humans as described in the story (lines 224–239 and 374–397). While some people in Asia make pets of the mongoose, it is not an easy animal to control. Many countries, including the United States, limit the importation of mongooses because they tend to kill too many native animals, not just the rats and snakes they were intended to kill.

FOR ENGLISH LEARNERS
Options for Reading

- Preview the illustrations with students and discuss words such as *bungalow, veranda, garden path, bushes, tailorbird, nest, cobra, hood, mongoose,* and *eggs.*

- Have students listen to the story on the *Audio Anthology CD.* Consider pausing the CD at appropriate places to talk about the feeling of suspense or to predict what might happen next.

Prereading For prereading instruction for English learners, see

 BEST PRACTICES TOOLKIT
Scaffolding Reading Instruction pp. 43–46

FOR ADVANCED LEARNERS/PRE–AP

Pre-AP exercises in the bottom channel provide additional challenge for your advanced students. Use them for small groups or individuals.

ADDITIONAL GUIDELINES

For more help with differentiation and tips for classroom management, see

 BEST PRACTICES TOOLKIT
Differentiated Instruction pp. 31–38

RIKKI-TIKKI-TAVI   **75**

B CAUSE AND EFFECT

You might record students' answers in a cause-and-effect chart. ***Possible answer:***

```
A flood washes Rikki-tikki     Cause
away from his parents.
              |
              v
A human family finds           Effect/Cause
him in their garden.
              |
              v
The family takes Rikki-        Effect
tikki into the bungalow.
```

Extend the Discussion Why does Rikki-tikki decide to stay in the house with the family?

LITERARY ANALYSIS

C SUSPENSE

Possible answer: *The father's warning might foreshadow a snake entering the house and endangering the family.*

Extend the Discussion Why does Teddy's father say that Teddy is safer with Rikki-tikki than he would be with a dog like a bloodhound watching him?

They took him into the house, and a big man picked him up between his finger and thumb and said he was not dead but half choked; so they wrapped him in cotton wool and warmed him over a little fire, and he opened his eyes and sneezed. "Now," said the big man (he was an Englishman who had just moved into the bungalow), "don't frighten him, and we'll see what he'll do."

It is the hardest thing in the world to frighten a mongoose, because he is eaten up from nose to tail with curiosity. The motto of all the mongoose family is "Run and Find Out"; and Rikki-tikki was a true mongoose. He looked at the cotton wool, decided that it was not good to eat, ran all round
30 the table, sat up and put his fur in order, scratched himself, and jumped on the small boy's shoulder.

"Don't be frightened, Teddy," said his father. "That's his way of making friends."

"Ouch! He's tickling under my chin," said Teddy.

Rikki-tikki looked down between the boy's collar and neck, snuffed at his ear, and climbed down to the floor, where he sat rubbing his nose.

"Good gracious," said Teddy's mother, "and that's a wild creature! I suppose he's so tame because we've been kind to him."

"All mongooses are like that," said her husband. "If Teddy doesn't pick
40 him up by the tail or try to put him in a cage, he'll run in and out of the house all day long. Let's give him something to eat."

They gave him a little piece of raw meat. Rikki-tikki liked it immensely; and when it was finished, he went out into the veranda and sat in the sunshine and fluffed up his fur to make it dry to the roots. Then he felt better.

"There are more things to find out about in this house," he said to himself, "than all my family could find out in all their lives. I shall certainly stay and find out." **B**

He spent all that day roaming over the house. He nearly drowned himself
50 in the bathtubs, put his nose into the ink on a writing table, and burnt it on the end of the big man's cigar, for he climbed up in the big man's lap to see how writing was done. At nightfall he ran into Teddy's nursery to watch how kerosene lamps were lighted, and when Teddy went to bed, Rikki-tikki climbed up too; but he was a restless companion, because he had to get up and attend to every noise all through the night and find out what made it. Teddy's mother and father came in, the last thing, to look at their boy, and Rikki-tikki was awake on the pillow.

"I don't like that," said Teddy's mother; "he may bite the child."

"He'll do no such thing," said the father. "Teddy is safer with that little
60 beast than if he had a bloodhound to watch him. If a snake came into the nursery now—" **C**

But Teddy's mother wouldn't think of anything so awful.

VISUAL VOCABULARY

veranda *n.* a long, open porch, usually with a roof

B CAUSE AND EFFECT
How does Rikki-tikki come to live in the bungalow?

C SUSPENSE
What might the father's words be **foreshadowing**?

DIFFERENTIATED INSTRUCTION

FOR LESS–PROFICIENT READERS

Review: Cause and Effect Distribute copies of the transparency. Remind students that a *cause* is an event that brings about another event, known as the *effect* or result. Have students work in pairs to reread lines 13–48 and fill out a Cause-and-Effect Chain that starts with the summer flood and ends with Rikki-tikki coming to live in the bungalow.

BEST PRACTICES TOOLKIT—Transparency
Cause-and-Effect Chain pp. B16, B39

FOR ENGLISH LEARNERS

Language: Punctuation and Print Cues Remind students that a dash indicates a pause in the flow of a sentence. Explain that a dash can be used after a word to show interruption (line 61) or between two words to emphasize what follows (line 88). Dashes can link clauses (line 84) or enclose interrupting elements (lines 140–141). Have students practice reading aloud sentences with dashes on pages 81 and 82.

Early in the morning Rikki-tikki came to early breakfast in the veranda, riding on Teddy's shoulder, and they gave him banana and some boiled egg; and he sat on all their laps one after the other, because every well-brought-up mongoose always hopes to be a house mongoose some day and have rooms to run about in; and Rikki-tikki's mother (she used to live in the general's house at Segowlee) had carefully told Rikki what to do if ever he came across white men.

70 Then Rikki-tikki went out into the garden to see what was to be seen. It was a large garden, only half-cultivated, with bushes, as big as summerhouses, of Marshal Niel roses, lime and orange trees, clumps of bamboos, and thickets of high grass. Rikki-tikki licked his lips. "This is a splendid hunting ground," he said, and his tail grew bottlebrushy at the thought of it; and he scuttled up and down the garden, snuffing here and there till he heard very sorrowful voices in a thorn bush. It was Darzee, the tailorbird, and his wife. They had made a beautiful nest by pulling two big leaves together and stitching them up the edges with fibers and had filled the hollow with cotton and downy fluff. The nest swayed to and fro, 80 as they sat on the rim and cried.

"What is the matter?" asked Rikki-tikki.

"We are very miserable," said Darzee. "One of our babies fell out of the nest yesterday, and Nag ate him."

"H'm!" said Rikki-tikki, "that is very sad—but I am a stranger here. Who is Nag?"

Darzee and his wife only **cowered** down in the nest without answering, for from the thick grass at the foot of the bush there came a low hiss—a horrid, cold sound that made Rikki-tikki jump back two clear 90 feet. Then inch by inch out of the grass rose up the head and spread hood[3] of Nag, the big black cobra, and he was five feet long from tongue to tail. When he had lifted one-third of himself clear of the ground, he stayed, balancing to and fro exactly as a dandelion tuft balances in the wind; and he looked at Rikki-tikki with the wicked snake's eyes that never change their expression, whatever the snake may be thinking of.

"Who is Nag?" said he. "*I* am Nag. The great god Brahm[4] put his mark upon all our people when 100 the first cobra spread his hood to keep the sun off Brahm as he slept. Look, and be afraid!"

---

3. **hood:** an expanded part on or near the head of an animal.

4. **Brahm** (bräm): another name for Brahma, creator of the universe in the Hindu religion.

cower (kou'ər) *v.* to crouch or shrink down in fear

SOCIAL STUDIES CONNECTION

Between the early 1600s and 1757, the British East India Company gained control of much of India. In 1858, the British government took direct control, and India became a British colony ruled by parliament. The main British leader in India was the viceroy, who was supported by about 1,500 British government officials throughout the country. As more Indians became educated and took jobs in government, they wanted to have more say in how their country was run. The Indian National Congress was created in 1885. Shortly after World War I, Mahatma Gandhi became a leader in the fight for Indian independence, which was achieved in 1947.

Lines 81–101
DISCUSSION PROMPTS

Use these prompts to help students understand the character of Nag and how the other characters respond to him:

Connect How do you respond when someone you meet for the first time acts very tough and superior? *Students may say that they dislike such people and try to avoid them.*

Analyze Compare how Darzee and his wife and Rikki-tikki respond to Nag. *Possible answer: All three characters understand that Nag is dangerous. The birds' response is to shrink in fear (lines 86–87). Rikki-tikki is curious when he hears Nag's name (lines 84–85), but then jumps back when he hears the snake's hiss (lines 88–90).*

Synthesize How does the author's description of Nag show that he is the villain of the story? *Possible answer:*

- *Darzee says that Nag has killed a baby bird (lines 82–83).*

- *The author describes Nag's "horrid cold sound" (lines 88–89) and his "wicked snake's eyes" (line 96).*

- *Nag speaks in an arrogant, intimidating manner (lines 98–101).*

FOR ENGLISH LEARNERS

Vocabulary: Idioms and Sayings Use New Word Analysis to teach the meanings of these idioms and sayings from the story:

- *eaten up . . . with* (line 27), "consumed by, full of"

- *to and fro* (lines 94, 182, 253, 277), "in one direction then the other, back and forth"

- *make an end of* (line 120), "kill"

BEST PRACTICES TOOLKIT—Transparency
New Word Analysis p. E8

Vocabulary: Word Associations Have pairs of students use context clues to predict the meanings of these word combinations: *cotton wool* (line 23), "cotton batting, like quilt lining"; *hunting ground* (line 74), "place for finding animals"; *natural history* (line 137), "study of nature"; *melon bed* (line 233), "place where melons grow"; *watch spring* (lines 425–426), "coiled metal inside a windup watch"; *town crier* (line 467), "person who spreads the news." Clarify understanding as needed.

ANALYZE VISUALS

Possible answer:

- *The snake looks brave because it is raised up tall and baring its teeth.*

- *The mongoose looks brave because it is looking right at the snake and has its feet planted so it can jump.*

Lines 102–114
REINFORCE *KEY IDEA:* BRAVE

Discuss What does this passage suggest about the relationship between being afraid and being **brave**? *Possible answer: Being brave doesn't necessarily mean you are not afraid. In fact, it may mean that you take the right action in spite of feeling afraid. Both Rikki-tikki and Nag are afraid, but they don't run away or back down.*

He spread out his hood more than ever, and Rikki-tikki saw the spectacle mark on the back of it that looks exactly like the eye part of a hook-and-eye fastening. He was afraid for the minute, but it is impossible for a mongoose to stay frightened for any length of time; and though Rikki-tikki had never met a live cobra before, his mother had fed him on dead ones, and he knew that all a grown mongoose's business in life was to fight and eat snakes. Nag knew that too, and at the bottom of his cold heart, he was afraid.

"Well," said Rikki-tikki, and his tail began to fluff up again, "marks or
110 no marks, do you think it is right for you to eat **fledglings** out of a nest?"

Nag was thinking to himself and watching the least little movement in the grass behind Rikki-tikki. He knew that mongooses in the garden meant death sooner or later for him and his family; but he wanted to get Rikki-tikki off his guard. So he dropped his head a little, and put it on one side.

"Let us talk," he said. "You eat eggs. Why should not I eat birds?"

"Behind you! Look behind you!" sang Darzee.

Rikki-tikki knew better than to waste time in staring. He jumped up in the air as high as he could go, and just under him whizzed by the head of

fledgling (flĕj′lĭng) *n.* a young bird that has recently grown its flight feathers

DIFFERENTIATED INSTRUCTION

FOR ADVANCED LEARNERS/PRE–AP

Analyze Behavior Have students analyze Rikki-tikki's response to Darzee's warning (lines 116–118). Darzee says, "Look behind you!" Instead of looking, though, Rikki-tikki jumps up in the air immediately.

- How does Rikki-tikki's behavior show what he knows about cobras?

- What does Rikki-tikki's behavior show about his understanding of whom he can trust?

Nagaina,[5] Nag's wicked wife. She had crept up behind him as he was
talking, to make an end of him; and he heard her savage hiss as the stroke
missed. He came down almost across her back, and if he had been an old
mongoose, he would have known that then was the time to break her back
with one bite; but he was afraid of the terrible lashing return stroke of the
cobra. He bit, indeed, but did not bite long enough; and he jumped clear
of the whisking tail, leaving Nagaina torn and angry. **D**

"Wicked, wicked Darzee!" said Nag, lashing up as high as he could
reach toward the nest in the thorn bush; but Darzee had built it out of
reach of snakes, and it only swayed to and fro.

Rikki-tikki felt his eyes growing red and hot (when a mongoose's eyes
grow red, he is angry), and he sat back on his tail and hind legs like a
little kangaroo and looked all around him and chattered with rage. But
Nag and Nagaina had disappeared into the grass. When a snake misses
its stroke, it never says anything or gives any sign of what it means to do
next. Rikki-tikki did not care to follow them, for he did not feel sure that
he could manage two snakes at once. So he trotted off to the gravel path
near the house and sat down to think. It was a serious matter for him. **E**

If you read the old books of natural history, you will find they say that
when the mongoose fights the snake and happens to get bitten, he runs
off and eats some herb that cures him. That is not true. The victory is only
a matter of quickness of eye and quickness of foot—snake's blow against
mongoose's jump—and as no eye can follow the motion of a snake's head
when it strikes, this makes things much more wonderful than any magic
herb. Rikki-tikki knew he was a young mongoose, and it made him all the
more pleased to think that he had managed to escape a blow from behind.
It gave him confidence in himself, and when Teddy came running down
the path, Rikki-tikki was ready to be petted. But just as Teddy was stooping,
something wriggled a little in the dust, and a tiny voice said, "Be careful.
I am Death!" It was Karait,[6] the dusty brown snakeling that lies for choice
on the dusty earth; and his bite is as dangerous as the cobra's. But he is so
small that nobody thinks of him, and so he does the more harm to people.

Rikki-tikki's eyes grew red again, and he danced up to Karait with the
peculiar rocking, swaying motion that he had inherited from his family.
It looks very funny, but it is so perfectly balanced a **gait** that you can fly
off from it at any angle you please; and in dealing with snakes this is an
advantage.

If Rikki-tikki had only known, he was doing a much more dangerous
thing than fighting Nag; for Karait is so small and can turn so quickly,

---

5. **Nagaina** (nä'gə-ē'nə).
6. **Karait** (kə-rīt').

D SUSPENSE
Reread lines 111–125.
Which details of
Nagaina's attack
on Rikki-tikki create
tension?

E PREDICT
As you read, check the
predictions you make.
Was the prediction
you made on page 74
correct?

gait (gāt) *n.* a manner
of walking or moving
on foot

Possible answer: *Rikki-tikki doesn't know that he must bite Karait very close to the back of his head, or else the small snake will be able to twist around and bite Rikki on the eye or lip (lines 158–159).*

Extend the Discussion How does the author build tension by giving readers this information?

LITERARY ANALYSIS: *Review*

G CONFLICT

You might use a chart to record students' answers. **Possible answer:**

Character	Evidence of Conflict
Darzee and wife	Nag ate their baby (lines 82–83).
Rikki-tikki	Nagaina and Karait attack him (lines 117–121, 161).
Teddy's family	Parents are worried about snakes (lines 60–61); father hits Karait with a stick (lines 174–175).

that unless Rikki bit him close to the back of the head, he would get the return stroke in his eye or his lip. But Rikki did not know: his eyes were 160 all red, and he rocked back and forth, looking for a good place to hold. Karait struck out. Rikki jumped sideways and tried to run in, but the wicked little dusty gray head lashed within a fraction of his shoulder, and he had to jump over the body, and the head followed his heels close. **F**

Teddy shouted to the house, "Oh, look here! Our mongoose is killing a snake"; and Rikki-tikki heard a scream from Teddy's mother. His father ran out with a stick, but by the time he came up, Karait had lunged out once too far, and Rikki-tikki had sprung, jumped on the snake's back, dropped his head far between his forelegs, bitten as high up the back as he could get hold, and rolled away.

170 That bite paralyzed Karait, and Rikki-tikki was just going to eat him up from the tail, after the custom of his family at dinner, when he remembered that a full meal makes a slow mongoose; and if he wanted all his strength and quickness ready, he must keep himself thin. He went away for a dust bath under the castor-oil bushes, while Teddy's father beat the dead Karait. "What is the use of that?" thought Rikki-tikki; "I have settled it all."

And then Teddy's mother picked him up from the dust and hugged him, crying that he had saved Teddy from death; and Teddy's father said that he was a providence,[7] and Teddy looked on with big scared eyes. Rikki-tikki was rather amused at all the fuss, which, of course, he did 180 not understand. Teddy's mother might just as well have petted Teddy for playing in the dust. Rikki was thoroughly enjoying himself. **G**

That night at dinner, walking to and fro among the wineglasses on the table, he might have stuffed himself three times over with nice things; but he remembered Nag and Nagaina, and though it was very pleasant to be patted and petted by Teddy's mother and to sit on Teddy's shoulder, his eyes would get red from time to time, and he would go off into his long war cry of *"Rikk-tikk-tikki-tikki-tchk!"*

Teddy carried him off to bed and insisted on Rikki-tikki sleeping under his chin. Rikki-tikki was too well-bred to bite or scratch, but as soon as 190 Teddy was asleep, he went off for his nightly walk around the house; and in the dark he ran up against Chuchundra, the muskrat, creeping around by the wall. Chuchundra is a brokenhearted little beast. He whimpers and cheeps all the night, trying to make up his mind to run into the middle of the room; but he never gets there.

"Don't kill me," said Chuchundra, almost weeping. "Rikki-tikki, don't kill me!"

"Do you think a snake killer kills muskrats?" said Rikki-tikki scornfully.

F SUSPENSE
Reread lines 156–163. What doesn't Rikki-tikki realize about Karait?

G CONFLICT
Which characters in this story have conflicts with the snakes in the garden?

---

7. **providence:** blessing; something good given by God.

DIFFERENTIATED INSTRUCTION

FOR LESS–PROFICIENT READERS
Review: Conflict Remind students that conflict is a struggle between opposing forces.

- Ask students whether Rikki-tikki's conflict is with an outside force (external conflict) or within his own mind (internal conflict). *(external conflict against snakes)*
- How is the story's conflict related to its plot? *(The plot revolves around how Rikki-tikki is going to deal with the snakes and whether he will win.)*

FOR ENGLISH LEARNERS
Language: Punctuation and Print Cues Help students use commas and semicolons as cues to break down Kipling's long sentences into smaller meaningful chunks.

1. Write lines 170–173 on the board, with each clause on a separate line. Help students paraphrase each piece and then the whole sentence.

2. Allow pairs to practice with lines 182–187. Clarify understanding as needed.

"Those who kill snakes get killed by snakes," said Chuchundra, more sorrowfully than ever. "And how am I to be sure that Nag won't mistake
200 me for you some dark night?"

"There's not the least danger," said Rikki-tikki; "but Nag is in the garden, and I know you don't go there."

"My cousin Chua,[8] the rat, told me—" said Chuchundra, and then he stopped.

"Told you what?"

"H'sh! Nag is everywhere, Rikki-tikki. You should have talked to Chua in the garden."

"I didn't—so you must tell me. Quick, Chuchundra, or I'll bite you!"

Chuchundra sat down and cried till the tears rolled off his whiskers.
210 "I am a very poor man," he sobbed. "I never had spirit enough to run out into the middle of the room. H'sh! I mustn't tell you anything. Can't you *hear*, Rikki-tikki?"

Rikki-tikki listened. The house was as still as still, but he thought he could just catch the faintest *scratch-scratch* in the world—a noise as faint as that of a wasp walking on a windowpane—the dry scratch of a snake's scales on brickwork. **H**

"That's Nag or Nagaina," he said to himself, "and he is crawling into the bathroom sluice.[9] You're right, Chuchundra; I should have talked to Chua."

He stole off to Teddy's bathroom, but there was nothing there, and
220 then to Teddy's mother's bathroom. At the bottom of the smooth plaster wall, there was a brick pulled out to make a sluice for the bath water, and as Rikki-tikki stole in by the masonry curb where the bath is put, he heard Nag and Nagaina whispering together outside in the moonlight.

"When the house is emptied of people," said Nagaina to her husband, "*he* will have to go away, and then the garden will be our own again. Go in quietly, and remember that the big man who killed Karait is the first one to bite. Then come out and tell me, and we will hunt for Rikki-tikki together."

"But are you sure that there is anything to be gained by killing the people?" said Nag.

230 "Everything. When there were no people in the bungalow, did we have any mongoose in the garden? So long as the bungalow is empty, we are king and queen of the garden; and remember that as soon as our eggs in the melon bed hatch (as they may tomorrow), our children will need room and quiet." **I**

"I had not thought of that," said Nag. "I will go, but there is no need that we should hunt for Rikki-tikki afterward. I will kill the big man and his

---

8. **Chua** (chōō′ə).
9. **bathroom sluice** (slōōs): an opening in a wall through which the water in a bathtub can be drained outdoors.

H SUSPENSE
Reread lines 203–216. What details make the conversation between Chuchundra and Rikki-tikki suspenseful?

2 Targeted Passage

I PREDICT
Think about what Nag and Nagaina are planning to do. How do you think Rikki-tikki might respond?

Lines 195–212
REINFORCE *KEY IDEA*: BRAVE

Discuss Does Chuchundra act **brave** in this scene? Cite evidence from the story. *Possible answer: Chuchundra does not act brave.*

- He is afraid of Rikki-tikki (lines 195–196) and of Nag (lines 199–200).
- He's afraid to tell Rikki-tikki what Chua said; he just sits and cries (lines 203–209).
- He admits that he isn't even brave enough to go out into the middle of the room (lines 210–211).

LITERARY ANALYSIS

H SUSPENSE

Possible answer: Chuchundra's terror at being overheard by Nag makes the scene suspenseful. The way he repeats "H'sh!" and says, "Nag is everywhere" (line 206) and "I mustn't tell you anything" (line 211) creates tension by making readers feel his fear.

READING STRATEGY

I PREDICT

Possible answer: Nag and Nagaina plan to kill all the people in the house and then kill Rikki-tikki (lines 224–227). Students may predict that Rikki-tikki will try to kill the snakes before they can carry out their plan.

Extend the Discussion How does what you know about Rikki-tikki help you predict what he will do?

FOR LESS–PROFICIENT READERS

2 Targeted Passage [Lines 213–234]

This passage builds suspense and advances the plot by revealing the cobras' plan to kill the human family and Rikki-tikki.

- What is the *scratch-scratch* sound Rikki-tikki hears?
- What are the snakes planning to do?
- Why are the cobras anxious to get rid of Rikki-tikki?

FOR ADVANCED LEARNERS/PRE–AP

Evaluate Have students review lines 224–234. Ask them to discuss whether this passage makes Nag and Nagaina seem more sympathetic as characters. Can students empathize with their situation? Have students hold an informal debate about whether the cobras have any less right to raise their family safely than the human family does.

Activity Before they read the text on this page, have students study the illustration and predict what is going to happen next.

Possible answer: Rikki-tikki is going to fight Nag by biting him on the back of the neck.

LITERARY ANALYSIS

❿ SUSPENSE

Possible answer: Rikki-tikki is not sure of the best place to bite Nag. He hopes to break Nag's back, but if he isn't able to do this quickly, Nag will put up a terrible fight.

Extend the Discussion How does reading what Rikki-tikki is thinking help build suspense?

Lines 249–280
DISCUSSION PROMPTS

Use these prompts to help students understand the planning process that Rikki-tikki goes through:

Connect Think about whether you could stay completely still for an hour. Would it be easier or harder if your life, or the lives of others, depended on it? *Students' responses should acknowledge the difficulty of the task. Students may say that they could do it if lives depended on it.*

Analyze Compare how Rikki-tikki plans his attack on Nag with how Nag plans his attack on the man. *Possible answer: Both look for the most advantageous place to stage the attack. Nag decides on the bath because the man will not have his "stick" there. Rikki-tikki decides to wait until Nag is asleep around the water jar.*

Evaluate Rikki-tikki is just a young mongoose. What is your opinion of his skills? Explain, citing evidence from the story. *Students may say that he is very skillful at killing snakes. He is fit, alert, brave, and agile. He killed Karait, he made a good plan to kill Nag, and he carried out his plan.*

---

wife, and the child if I can, and come away quietly. Then the bungalow will be empty, and Rikki-tikki will go."

240   Rikki-tikki tingled all over with rage and hatred at this, and then Nag's head came through the sluice, and his five feet of cold body followed it. Angry as he was, Rikki-tikki was very frightened as he saw the size of the big cobra. Nag coiled himself up, raised his head, and looked into the bathroom in the dark, and Rikki could see his eyes glitter.

   "Now, if I kill him here, Nagaina will

250 know; and if I fight him on the open floor, the odds are in his favor. What am I to do?" said Rikki-tikki-tavi.

   Nag waved to and fro, and then Rikki-tikki heard him drinking from the biggest water jar that was used to fill the bath. "That is good," said the snake. "Now, when Karait was killed, the big man had a stick. He may have that stick still, but when he comes in to bathe in the morning, he will

260 not have a stick. I shall wait here till he comes. Nagaina—do you hear me?—I shall wait here in the cool till daytime."

   There was no answer from outside, so Rikki-tikki knew Nagaina had gone away. Nag coiled himself down, coil by coil, around the bulge at the bottom of the water jar, and Rikki-tikki stayed still as death. After an hour he began to move, muscle by muscle, toward the jar. Nag was asleep, and Rikki-tikki looked at his big back, wondering which would be the best place for a good hold. "If I don't break his back at the first jump," said Rikki, "he can still fight; and if he fights—O Rikki!" He looked at the thickness of the neck below the hood, but that was too much for him;

270 and a bite near the tail would only make Nag savage. ❿

   "It must be the head," he said at last; "the head above the hood. And, when I am once there, I must not let go."

   Then he jumped. The head was lying a little clear of the water jar, under the curve of it; and, as his teeth met, Rikki braced his back against the bulge of the red earthenware to hold down the head. This gave him just one second's purchase,[10] and he made the most of it. Then he was battered to and fro as a rat is shaken by a dog—to and fro on the floor, up

❸ Targeted Passage

❿ SUSPENSE
Why is the outcome of Rikki-tikki's fight with Nag uncertain?

---

10. **purchase:** an advantage, such as a firm hold, to be used when applying power.

DIFFERENTIATED INSTRUCTION

FOR LESS–PROFICIENT READERS

❸ Targeted Passage [Lines 262–287]

This passage presents the climax of Rikki-tikki's conflict with Nag.

- Where does Rikki-tikki fight Nag?
- Why is it important for Rikki-tikki to bite Nag in just the right place?
- What happens after Rikki-tikki bites Nag?
- How does Nag finally die?
- Is the main conflict of the story now resolved?

and down, and round in great circles; but his eyes were red, and he held on as the body cart-whipped over the floor, upsetting the tin dipper and the
280 soap dish and the flesh brush, and banged against the tin side of the bath. **K**

As he held, he closed his jaws tighter and tighter, for he made sure he would be banged to death; and, for the honor of his family, he preferred to be found with his teeth locked. He was dizzy, aching, and felt shaken to pieces when something went off like a thunderclap just behind him; a hot wind knocked him senseless, and red fire **singed** his fur. The big man had been awakened by the noise and had fired both barrels of a shotgun into Nag just behind the hood.

Rikki-tikki held on with his eyes shut, for now he was quite sure he was dead; but the head did not move, and the big man picked him up and said,
290 "It's the mongoose again, Alice; the little chap has saved *our* lives now." **L**

Then Teddy's mother came in with a very white face and saw what was left of Nag, and Rikki-tikki dragged himself to Teddy's bedroom and spent half the rest of the night shaking himself tenderly to find out whether he really was broken into forty pieces, as he fancied.

W hen morning came, he was very stiff but well pleased with his doings. "Now I have Nagaina to settle with, and she will be worse than five Nags, and there's no knowing when the eggs she spoke of will hatch. Goodness! I must go and see Darzee," he said.
300 Without waiting for breakfast, Rikki-tikki ran to the thorn bush where Darzee was singing a song of triumph at the top of his voice. The news of Nag's death was all over the garden, for the sweeper had thrown the body on the rubbish heap.

"Oh, you stupid tuft of feathers!" said Rikki-tikki angrily. "Is this the time to sing?"

"Nag is dead—is dead—is dead!" sang Darzee. "The **valiant** Rikki-tikki caught him by the head and held fast. The big man brought the bang stick, and Nag fell in two pieces! He will never eat my babies again."

"All that's true enough; but where's Nagaina?" said Rikki-tikki, looking carefully round him.
310 "Nagaina came to the bathroom sluice and called for Nag," Darzee went on; "and Nag came out on the end of a stick—the sweeper picked him up on the end of a stick and threw him upon the rubbish heap. Let us sing about the great, the red-eyed Rikki-tikki!" And Darzee filled his throat and sang.

"If I could get up to your nest, I'd roll your babies out!" said Rikki-tikki. "You don't know when to do the right thing at the right time. You're

❸ **Targeted Passage**

K PREDICT
Thinking about how the **plot** has unfolded so far, predict what will happen next.

singe (sĭnj) *v.* to burn lightly

L CAUSE AND EFFECT
What happens because of Rikki-tikki's tight hold on Nag?

valiant (văl'yent) *adj.* brave; courageous

FOR LESS-PROFICIENT READERS
Vocabulary Support Kipling uses words from his 19th-century British background that may be unfamiliar to students. Have students work in pairs and use context clues to predict the meanings of the following: *flesh brush* (line 280), "bath brush"; *chap* (line 290), "fellow"; *fancied* (line 294), "imagined"; *doings* (line 296), "actions"; *rubbish heap* (line 302), "trash pile"; *bother* (line 324), "forget about." Allow students to check their predictions by using a dictionary.

K PREDICT

Possible answers: *Students may predict that Rikki-tikki will be successful because he's bitten Nag in the right place and is holding on tight. They may also predict that the noise will wake up the family and someone will come to help Rikki-tikki.*

If students need help . . . Have them review lines 273–280 and say what is happening. Lead them to the idea that the fight is making a lot of noise and ask what might happen as a result of this.

L CAUSE AND EFFECT
Record students' responses in a cause-and-effect chain. ***Possible answer:***

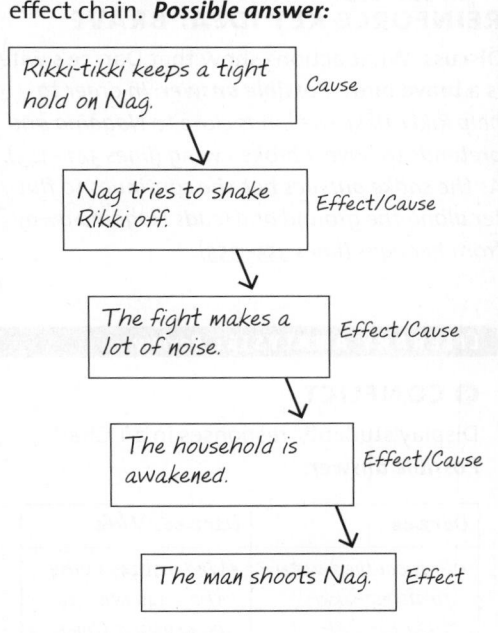

Rikki-tikki keeps a tight hold on Nag.	Cause
Nag tries to shake Rikki off.	Effect/Cause
The fight makes a lot of noise.	Effect/Cause
The household is awakened.	Effect/Cause
The man shoots Nag.	Effect

Extend the Discussion How do you think Nag's death will affect Nagaina?

safe enough in your nest there, but it's war for me down here. Stop singing a minute, Darzee."

"For the great, the beautiful Rikki-tikki's sake I will stop," said Darzee.
320 "What is it, O Killer of the terrible Nag?"

"Where is Nagaina, for the third time?"

"On the rubbish heap by the stables, mourning for Nag. Great is Rikki-tikki with the white teeth."

"Bother my white teeth! Have you ever heard where she keeps her eggs?"

"In the melon bed, on the end nearest the wall, where the sun strikes nearly all day. She hid them there weeks ago."

"And you never thought it worthwhile to tell me? The end nearest the wall, you said?"

"Rikki-tikki, you are not going to eat her eggs?"

330 "Not 'eat' exactly, no. Darzee, if you have a grain of sense, you will fly off to the stables and pretend that your wing is broken and let Nagaina chase you away to this bush. I must get to the melon bed, and if I went there now, she'd see me." **Ⓜ**

Darzee was a featherbrained little fellow who could never hold more than one idea at a time in his head; and just because he knew that Nagaina's children were born in eggs like his own, he didn't think at first that it was fair to kill them. But his wife was a sensible bird, and she knew that cobra's eggs meant young cobras later on; so she flew off from the nest and left Darzee to keep the babies warm and continue his song about the death
340 of Nag. Darzee was very like a man in some ways.

She fluttered in front of Nagaina by the rubbish heap and cried out, "Oh, my wing is broken! The boy in the house threw a stone at me and broke it." Then she fluttered more desperately than ever.

Nagaina lifted up her head and hissed, "You warned Rikki-tikki when I would have killed him. Indeed and truly, you've chosen a bad place to be lame in." And she moved toward Darzee's wife, slipping along over the dust.

"The boy broke it with a stone!" shrieked Darzee's wife.

"Well! It may be some **consolation** to you when you're dead to know that I shall settle accounts[11] with the boy. My husband lies on the rubbish heap
350 this morning, but before night the boy in the house will lie very still. What is the use of running away? I am sure to catch you. Little fool, look at me!"

Darzee's wife knew better than to do *that,* for a bird who looks at a snake's eyes gets so frightened that she cannot move. Darzee's wife fluttered on, piping sorrowfully, and never leaving the ground, and Nagaina quickened her pace. **Ⓝ**

Rikki-tikki heard them going up the path from the stables, and he raced for the end of the melon patch near the wall. There, in the warm litter above

11. **settle accounts:** even things out by getting revenge.

84 UNIT 1: PLOT, CONFLICT, AND SETTING

Ⓜ SUSPENSE
Why does Rikki-tikki's impatience with Darzee lend suspense to this scene?

consolation
(kŏn′sə-lā′shən) *n.*
a comfort

Ⓝ CONFLICT
How do Darzee and his wife differ in their approach to the conflict with Nagaina?

LITERARY ANALYSIS

Ⓜ SUSPENSE

Possible answer: Rikki-tikki's impatience reminds readers that Nagaina is still on the loose and that Rikki must stop her before she gets to Teddy's family.

Lines 334–355
REINFORCE *KEY IDEA:* BRAVE

Discuss What actions show that Darzee's wife is a **brave** bird? *Possible answer: In order to help Rikki-tikki, she lands close to Nagaina and pretends to have a broken wing (lines 341–343). As the snake pursues her, she continues to flutter along the ground and leads Nagaina away from her eggs (lines 353–355).*

LITERARY ANALYSIS: *Review*

Ⓝ CONFLICT

Display students' responses in a T Chart.
Possible answer:

Darzee	Darzee's Wife
• Preoccupied with praising Rikki-tikki for killing Nag (lines 299–314) • Not sure Rikki-tikki should crush Nagaina's eggs (lines 335–337)	• Understands why the eggs need to be crushed (lines 337–338) • Confronts Nagaina in order to help Rikki-tikki (lines 341–343)

BEST PRACTICES TOOLKIT—Transparency
T Chart p. A25

DIFFERENTIATED INSTRUCTION

FOR LESS–PROFICIENT READERS

Reading Strategy Follow-Up: Predict Have students work in pairs to read lines 324–355 and update their prediction charts. Encourage them to predict what Rikki-tikki is planning to do (*destroy the eggs, lines 324–330*), what Nagaina is going to do to Darzee's wife (*kill her, lines 344–346*), and what might happen to Teddy (*he might die from a snake bite, lines 348–350*). Have teams compare their charts.

Clues from the Story	Predictions
Rikki-tikki wants to find Nagaina's eggs (line 324).	Rikki-tikki will destroy the eggs.

the melons, very **cunningly** hidden, he found twenty-five eggs, about the size of
360 a bantam's eggs[12] but with whitish skins instead of shells.

"I was not a day too soon," he said, for he could see the baby cobras curled up inside the skin, and he knew that the minute they were hatched they could each kill a man or a mongoose. He bit off the tops of the eggs as fast as he could, taking care to crush the young cobras, and turned over the litter from time to time to see
370 whether he had missed any. At last there were only three eggs left, and Rikki-tikki began to chuckle to himself when he heard Darzee's wife screaming.

"Rikki-tikki, I led Nagaina toward the house, and she has gone into the veranda and—oh, come quickly—she means killing!"

Rikki-tikki smashed two eggs and tumbled backward down the melon bed with the third egg in his mouth and scuttled to the veranda as hard as he could put foot to the ground. Teddy and his mother and father were there at early breakfast; but Rikki-tikki saw that they were
380 not eating anything. They sat stone still, and their faces were white. Nagaina was coiled up on the matting by Teddy's chair, within easy striking distance of Teddy's bare leg; and she was swaying to and fro, singing a song of triumph.

"Son of the big man that killed Nag," she hissed, "stay still. I am not ready yet. Wait a little. Keep very still, all you three! If you move, I strike, and if you do not move, I strike. Oh, foolish people who killed my Nag!"

Teddy's eyes were fixed on his father, and all his father could do was to whisper, "Sit still, Teddy. You mustn't move. Teddy, keep still." ◉

Then Rikki-tikki came up and cried, "Turn round, Nagaina; turn
390 and fight!"

"All in good time," said she, without moving her eyes. "I will settle my account with you presently. Look at your friends, Rikki-tikki. They are still and white. They are afraid. They dare not move, and if you come a step nearer, I strike."

"Look at your eggs," said Rikki-tikki, "in the melon bed near the wall. Go and look, Nagaina!"

The big snake turned half round and saw the egg on the veranda. "Ah-h! Give it to me," she said.

cunningly (kŭn′ĭng-lē) *adv.* in a clever way that is meant to trick or deceive

◉ **SUSPENSE**
At this point in the story, what questions are you waiting to have answered?

---

12. **bantam's eggs:** the eggs of a small hen.

Activity Invite students to do a quickwrite about what Jerry Pinkney's illustrations add to their experience of reading "Rikki-tikki-tavi."

READING SKILL: *Review*

P CAUSE AND EFFECT

Possible answer: To distract Nagaina and save Teddy, Rikki-tikki points out the egg on the veranda (lines 395–396) and then tells Nagaina it's the last one (line 401).

Rikki-tikki put his paws one on each side of the egg, and his eyes were
400 blood-red. "What price for a snake's egg? For a young cobra? For a young
king cobra? For the last—the very last of the brood? The ants are eating
all the others down by the melon bed."

Nagaina spun clear round, forgetting everything for the sake of the one
egg; and Rikki-tikki saw Teddy's father shoot out a big hand, catch Teddy
by the shoulder, and drag him across the little table with the teacups, safe
and out of reach of Nagaina. **P**

"Tricked! Tricked! Tricked! *Rikk-tck-tck!*" chuckled Rikki-tikki. "The boy
is safe, and it was I—I—I that caught Nag by the hood last night in the
bathroom." Then he began to jump up and down, all four feet together,

P CAUSE AND EFFECT
Reread lines 395–406.
What does Rikki-tikki
do to save Teddy?

DIFFERENTIATED INSTRUCTION

FOR ENGLISH LEARNERS

Language: Conversational English Patterns
Read Rikki-tikki's four questions in lines
400–401 aloud. Point out that the words
would you pay are left out but understood in
the first question. Ask students what words
are left out of the next three questions *(what
price would you pay)*. Ask students why they
think the author wrote the dialogue this
way. ***Possible answer:*** *It makes the dialogue
move faster and sound more interesting than
repeating the phrase over and over.*

410 his head close to the floor. "He threw me to and fro, but he could not shake me off. He was dead before the big man blew him in two. I did it! *Rikki-tikki-tck-tck!* Come then, Nagaina. Come and fight with me. You shall not be a widow long."

Nagaina saw that she had lost her chance of killing Teddy, and the egg lay between Rikki-tikki's paws. "Give me the egg, Rikki-tikki. Give me the last of my eggs, and I will go away and never come back," she said, lowering her hood.

"Yes, you will go away, and you will never come back, for you will go to the rubbish heap with Nag. Fight, widow! The big man has gone for his
420 gun! Fight!"

Rikki-tikki was bounding all round Nagaina, keeping just out of reach of her stroke, his little eyes like hot coals. Nagaina gathered herself together and flung out at him. Rikki-tikki jumped up and backwards. Again and again and again she struck, and each time her head came with a whack on the matting of the veranda, and she gathered herself together like a watch spring. Then Rikki-tikki danced in a circle to get behind her, and Nagaina spun round to keep her head to his head, so that the rustle of her tail on the matting sounded like dry leaves blown along by the wind.

He had forgotten the egg. It still lay on the veranda, and Nagaina came
430 nearer and nearer to it, till at last, while Rikki-tikki was drawing breath, she caught it in her mouth, turned to the veranda steps, and flew like an arrow down the path, with Rikki-tikki behind her. When the cobra runs for her life, she goes like a whiplash flicked across a horse's neck. Rikki-tikki knew that he must catch her, or all the trouble would begin again. **Q**

She headed straight for the long grass by the thorn bush, and as he was running, Rikki-tikki heard Darzee still singing his foolish little song of triumph. But Darzee's wife was wiser. She flew off her nest as Nagaina came along and flapped her wings about Nagaina's head. If Darzee had helped, they might have turned her; but Nagaina only lowered her hood
440 and went on. Still, the instant's delay brought Rikki-tikki up to her, and as she plunged into the rat hole where she and Nag used to live, his little white teeth were clenched on her tail, and he went down with her—and very few mongooses, however wise and old they may be, care to follow a cobra into its hole. **R**

It was dark in the hole; and Rikki-tikki never knew when it might open out and give Nagaina room to turn and strike at him. He held on savagely and stuck out his feet to act as brakes on the dark slope of the hot, moist earth.

Then the grass by the mouth of the hole stopped waving, and Darzee
450 said, "It is all over with Rikki-tikki! We must sing his death song. Valiant Rikki-tikki is dead! For Nagaina will surely kill him underground."

Q SUSPENSE
Reread lines 429–434. How does the suspense increase at this point?

R PREDICT
What problem does Rikki-tikki now face? On the basis of the details you've learned, what do you predict?

RIKKI-TIKKI-TAVI **87**

So he sang a very mournful song that he made up on the spur of the minute;[13] and just as he got to the most touching part, the grass quivered again, and Rikki-tikki, covered with dirt, dragged himself out of the hole leg by leg, licking his whiskers. Darzee stopped with a little shout. Rikki-tikki shook some of the dust out of his fur and sneezed. "It is all over," he said. "The widow will never come out again." And the red ants that live between the grass stems heard him and began to troop down one after another to see if he had spoken the truth.

460   Rikki-tikki curled himself up in the grass and slept where he was— slept and slept till it was late in the afternoon, for he had done a hard day's work. **⑤**

④ **Targeted Passage**

⑤ **CONFLICT**
How is the conflict between Rikki-tikki and the cobras resolved?

"Now," he said, when he awoke, "I will go back to the house. Tell the coppersmith, Darzee, and he will tell the garden that Nagaina is dead."

The coppersmith is a bird who makes a noise exactly like the beating of a little hammer on a copper pot; and the reason he is always making it is because he is the town crier to every Indian garden and tells all the news to everybody who cares to listen. As Rikki-tikki went up the path, he heard his "attention" notes like a tiny dinner gong, and then the steady

470   *"Ding-dong-tock! Nag is dead—dong! Nagaina is dead! Ding-dong-tock!"* That set all the birds in the garden singing and the frogs croaking, for Nag and Nagaina used to eat frogs as well as little birds.

When Rikki got to the house, Teddy and Teddy's mother (she looked very white still, for she had been fainting) and Teddy's father came out and almost cried over him; and that night he ate all that was given him till he could eat no more and went to bed on Teddy's shoulder, where Teddy's mother saw him when she came to look late at night.

"He saved our lives and Teddy's life," she said to her husband. "Just think, he saved all our lives."

480   Rikki-tikki woke up with a jump, for the mongooses are light sleepers.

"Oh, it's you," said he. "What are you bothering for? All the cobras are dead; and if they weren't, I'm here."

Rikki-tikki had a right to be proud of himself; but he did not grow too proud, and he kept that garden as a mongoose should keep it, with tooth and jump and spring and bite, till never a cobra dared show its head inside the walls. ✣

---

13. **on the spur of the minute:** on a sudden impulse, without previous thought or planning.

LITERARY ANALYSIS: *Review*

⑤ CONFLICT

Possible answer: *Rikki-tikki wins his fight with the cobras by killing Nagaina and presumably destroying the final egg.*

SELECTION WRAP–UP

REFLECT Have students think about how the author's use of animals with human characteristics affected their response to the story. How were they able to relate to the characters? What did they think of the relationship between the family and Rikki-tikki?

★ **CRITIQUE** Ask students to evaluate how successful the author was at maintaining suspense throughout the story. Have them discuss which parts they found most suspenseful and why.

READING FLUENCY

Distribute the copy masters and have students work in pairs to practice fluency.

📕 RESOURCE MANAGER—Copy Master
Reading Fluency p. 115

DIFFERENTIATED INSTRUCTION

FOR LESS–PROFICIENT READERS

④ **Targeted Passage [Lines 452–462]**

This passage resolves the conflict between the mongoose and the cobras: Rikki-tikki kills Nagaina and destroys her last egg.

- What does Rikki-tikki mean when he says, "The widow will never come out again"?
- Why does Rikki-tikki need to sleep so long after emerging from the cobras' hole?
- How is the main conflict in this story finally resolved?

FOR ADVANCED LEARNERS/PRE–AP

Make Judgments In lines 1–2, Kipling writes that Rikki-tikki fought the war against the snakes "single-handed." Have students discuss whether they agree with this statement and find evidence in the story to support their opinions.

Comprehension

1. **Recall** Why is Rikki-tikki grateful to Teddy's family?

2. **Recall** Why does Rikki-tikki destroy Nagaina's eggs?

3. **Represent** At first, Teddy's mother doesn't want the mongoose too close to Teddy. Use a timeline to show the events that help Rikki-tikki prove himself.

Literary Analysis

4. **Predict** Check the predictions you wrote in your chart against what happened. What details helped you guess correctly or misled you?

5. **Analyze Suspense** Go back through the story and write down clues that **foreshadow** Rikki-tikki's ultimate victory. Then write down details that led you to believe Rikki might be defeated. How did the combination of the two kinds of details help create suspense?

6. **Compare Literary Works** Both "Rikki-tikki-tavi" and "The Last Dog" have exciting plots and **brave** main characters. How else are the two stories similar? How are they different? To present your answer, add details to a Venn diagram like the one shown.

"Rikki-tikki-tavi"   "The Last Dog"

Humans are protected by an animal.   Animal/human friendship   An animal is protected by a human.

7. **Make Judgments** "Rikki-tikki-tavi" is regarded as one of the great adventure stories. Does it deserve this reputation? Explain your answer.

Extension and Challenge

8. **Creative Response: Drama** Plan an oral reading of a scene from the story. Some students can perform the parts of the characters and the narrator, while other students provide sound effects. Rehearse your performance and tape-record it for other classes.

9. **SOCIAL STUDIES CONNECTION** This story takes place in colonial India. With a partner, do research to find out more about India under British rule, from 1858 to 1947. What are two long-lasting effects that resulted from Britain's control of India? Present your findings to the class.

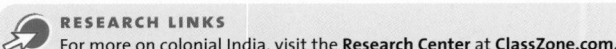

RESEARCH LINKS
For more on colonial India, visit the **Research Center** at **ClassZone.com**.

MARYLAND OBJECTIVES

LITERATURE STANDARD
3.A.3.h Analyze the author's approach to issues of time

---

6. *Possible comparisons for Venn diagram: In "Rikki-tikki-tavi," an animal (a snake) threatens people and other animals. In "The Last Dog," people threaten an animal. In both stories, there are animals in danger.*

7. *Students' responses should reflect their understanding that an adventure story is one in which the hero triumphs over some kind of danger. Students should support their judgments about "Rikki-tikki-tavi" with specific examples from the story.*

Extension and Challenge

8. *Students should use different tones of voice to represent different characters and the narrator, as well as to create suspense. Sound effects should be based on details in the story or valid inferences.*

9. **SOCIAL STUDIES CONNECTION** *Students' findings should reflect research in reliable sources. Possible long-lasting effects include the parliamentary form of government, many educated people who speak English, and the creation of Pakistan and Bangladesh out of Indian territory.*

Practice and Apply

After Reading
For additional support of post-reading questions, use these copy masters:

R RESOURCE MANAGER—Copy Masters
Reading Check p. 112 (to check understanding of the selection)
Suspense p. 105 (for practice of literary analysis standards focus)
Question Support p. 113 (**After Reading** questions adapted for English learners and less-proficient readers)

Additional selection questions are provided for teachers on page 99.

For additional activities to challenge students, see

i Power Thinking at **ClassZone.com**

ANSWERS
Comprehension

1. *Rikki-tikki is grateful to the family for rescuing him and for letting him live in the bungalow.*

2. *Rikki-tikki destroys the eggs to avoid more cobras in the garden.*

3. *A timeline should show events from the story that help Rikki-tikki prove his worth, such as: Rikki kills Karait (line 170); Rikki fights Nag (lines 273–287); Rikki kills Nagaina (lines 466–467).*

Literary Analysis
Possible answers:

4. ■ **STANDARDS FOCUS Predict** *Students should point to specific examples from their charts where details in the story helped them make accurate predictions or influenced them to make incorrect ones.*

5. ● **STANDARDS FOCUS Suspense**
   • *Clues that foreshadow Rikki's victory: opening lines of story, Nag's being afraid of Rikki, Rikki's enjoyment of fighting and self-confidence*
   • *Details that suggest Rikki will have a tough time: Rikki's inexperience in fighting snakes; Rikki's own fear that he will not be able to bite and kill Nag; Rikki's worry that he won't trap Nagaina in time*

   Students may say that the combination of both kinds of details leaves the reader anxious and guessing.

ANSWERS

Vocabulary in Context

VOCABULARY PRACTICE

1. *revive*
2. *singe*
3. *fledgling*
4. *cower*
5. *gait*
6. *consolation*
7. *cunningly*
8. *valiant*

 RESOURCE MANAGER—Copy Master
Vocabulary Practice p. 110

VOCABULARY IN WRITING

Suggest that students reread the scene in which Rikki-tikki kills Nag (lines 262–290). Encourage them to consider how each vocabulary word might be used to describe the scene and choose the words that work best for writing their paragraphs.

VOCABULARY STRATEGY: THE LATIN ROOTS viv AND vit *(also an EL language objective)*

- Have students use context clues to decide which word would fit best in each sentence. For example, in the first sentence, "food and water" are necessary for people to live. Figuring out what part of speech is called for may also help.
- Point out that *vitality* contains the word *vital* and that *survive* is similar in structure (prefix + root) to *revive*. Such clues will help students figure out the words' meanings.

Answers:

1. *survive* or continue to "live"
2. *vivacious* or "lively"
3. *vitamins* are important for a healthy "life"
4. *vitality* or sense of "aliveness"
5. *vivid* or "lively"

 RESOURCE MANAGER—Copy Master
Vocabulary Strategy p. 111

Vocabulary Center at ClassZone.com
Additional Vocabulary Activities

Vocabulary in Context

VOCABULARY PRACTICE

Choose the vocabulary word that makes the most sense in each sentence.

1. After Rikki-tikki almost drowned, the family put him by the fire to _____ him.
2. The fire accidentally began to _____ his fur, and he quickly woke up.
3. Nag would not hesitate to eat a _____.
4. Though Darzee would _____ in fear at the sight of Nag, Rikki was not afraid.
5. He walked with a proud _____ that showed how brave he felt.
6. Rikki's killing Nag was a great _____ to the frightened family.
7. Rikki also _____ discovered Nagaina's eggs hidden among the melons.
8. Because of his _____ actions, everyone admired Rikki's courage.

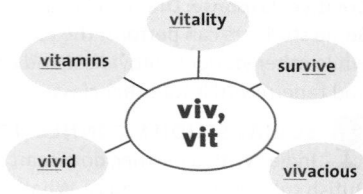

consolation
cower
cunningly
fledgling
gait
revive
singe
valiant

VOCABULARY IN WRITING

Using three or more vocabulary words, write a paragraph to describe how Rikki killed Nag. Here is a sample of how you might begin.

EXAMPLE SENTENCE
Rikki **cunningly** *waited until Nagaina had left her husband alone.*

MARYLAND OBJECTIVES

READING STANDARD
1.D.3.b Use word structure to determine meaning

VOCABULARY STRATEGY: THE LATIN ROOTS viv AND vit

The vocabulary word *revive* contains the Latin root *viv*, which means "live." Another Latin root, *vit*, has the same meaning. *Viv* and *vit* occur in a number of English words. To understand the meaning of words with *viv* or *vit*, use context clues and your knowledge of what these roots mean.

VOCABULARY PRACTICE
For more practice, go to the **Vocabulary Center** at **ClassZone.com**.

PRACTICE Choose the word from the web that best completes each sentence. Then tell how *viv* or *vit* helps give meaning to each word.

1. People cannot _____ without food and water.
2. She was a _____ hostess who threw lively parties.
3. _____ can provide some of the substances our bodies need to be healthy.
4. He lost much of his _____ after the accident.
5. The artist used _____ colors in her painting.

vitality
vitamins
survive
viv, vit
vivid
vivacious

DIFFERENTIATED INSTRUCTION

FOR ENGLISH LEARNERS

Vocabulary: Roots Tell students that in English *live* is both a verb (pronounced with short *i*) and an adjective (pronounced with long *i*), short for *alive*. As a root it forms the basis for many common words, such as *livable, livelihood, lively, livestock,* and *relive*. Assign pairs of students one of these words and have them create a Word Square for it. Then have teams share their Word Squares.

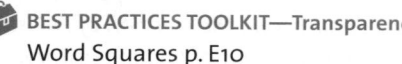 **BEST PRACTICES TOOLKIT—Transparency**
Word Squares p. E10

FOR ADVANCED LEARNERS/PRE–AP

Vocabulary in Writing Have students use as many of the vocabulary words as possible to write a paragraph describing the fight between Rikki-tikki and Nag as if Nag were the hero of the story.

Reading-Writing Connection

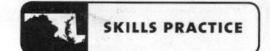

Deepen your understanding of "Rikki-tikki-tavi" by responding to these prompts. Then complete the **Grammar and Writing** exercise.

WRITING PROMPTS

A. Short Response: Write a Scene
Most of the characters, but not all, consider Rikki-tikki to be a hero. In **one paragraph,** write a scene from the story from Nagaina's perspective. What does she think and feel about Rikki-tikki?

B. Extended Response: Give an Evaluation
Is Rikki-tikki the **bravest** character in this story? Choose a brave character. Decide whether the character shows more or less bravery than Rikki. Write **two or three paragraphs** to evaluate the bravery of your chosen character and of Rikki.

SELF-CHECK

A creative scene will . . .
- include details about events in the story
- include a convincing portrait of Nagaina

An effective evaluation will . . .
- describe scenes that show each character's bravery
- show similarities and differences between Rikki-tikki and the other character

GRAMMAR AND WRITING

MAINTAIN PRONOUN–ANTECEDENT AGREEMENT You may recall that an antecedent is the noun or pronoun that a pronoun refers to. For example, in the following sentence, notice how the plural pronoun *their* refers to the plural antecedent *friends: My friends grabbed their bags.* Be especially careful when using antecedents like *each, someone,* and *no one.* These words should always be paired with singular pronouns. In the revised sentence, notice how the pronouns (in yellow) and the antecedent (in green) **agree in number.**

MARYLAND OBJECTIVES

LANGUAGE STANDARD
5.B.2.b Apply pronoun/antecedent agreement

> *Original:* Someone had to take control. They would need to kill the snakes.
>
> *Revised:* Someone had to take control. He or she would need to kill the snakes.

PRACTICE Correct the pronoun-antecedent error in each sentence.

1. Each snake wants the garden for themselves.
2. No one in the family wants to have their life threatened by the snakes.
3. Rikki-tikki stands up to the snakes and gets rid of its eggs.
4. Each person has their own space again!

*For more help with pronoun-antecedent agreement, see pages R52–R53 in the **Grammar Handbook**.*

FOR LESS–PROFICIENT WRITERS

For Prompt A:

1. Have pairs create a Character Map for Nagaina based on story details.
2. Direct them to lines 321–322 to see her first reaction to Nag's death.
3. As they write, encourage students to focus on Nagaina's feelings for Nag and her desire for revenge against Rikki-tikki.

BEST PRACTICES TOOLKIT—Transparency
Character Map p. D8

For Prompt B:

1. Place students in groups based on their chosen characters. Have them brainstorm examples of the character's bravery.
2. Allow groups to debate the relative bravery of their character and Rikki-tikki.
3. Encourage students to begin by writing a statement about what it means to be brave, followed by examples of each character's bravery, and a conclusion.

Reading-Writing Connection

WRITING PROMPTS

- For **Prompt A,** encourage students to put themselves in Nagaina's place. How would they feel if someone close to them were killed? What might they think of the killer?
- For **Prompt B,** direct students to review scenes in which their character and Rikki-tikki show bravery. Then have them use a Venn Diagram to list similarities and differences between them.

BEST PRACTICES TOOLKIT—Transparency
Venn Diagram p. A26

For an extended Reading-Writing Connection activity, see

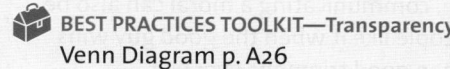 Writing Center at **ClassZone.com**

GRAMMAR AND WRITING

- Explain that the antecedent can also be changed to match the pronoun. For example, item 1 might be rewritten "The snakes want the garden for themselves."
- Challenge students to rewrite item 2 to avoid having to use "his or her." ***Possible answer:*** *The family members are upset about having their lives threatened by snakes.*

Answers:
1. *snake/itself;* 2. *No one/his or her life;*
3. *snakes/their eggs;* 4. *members/their house*

RESOURCE MANAGER—Copy Master
Maintain Pronoun-Antecedent Agreement p. 114

Assess and Reteach

Assess

RESOURCE MANAGER—Copy Masters
Selection Tests A, B/C pp. 117–118, 119–120

Test Generator CD

Reteach

STANDARDS LESSON FILE
Literature Lesson 8: Foreshadowing and Suspense
Reading Lesson 1: Predicting
Vocabulary Lesson 10: Latin Roots (active verbs)
Grammar Lesson 8: Pronoun-Antecedent Agreement

Introduce

OBJECTIVE
- read adventure fiction

Meet Louis Sachar

Sachar says that his books teach a moral, or lesson, in the sense that they always deal with right and wrong. He stresses, however, that he writes his books mainly to make reading enjoyable for his readers. His goal when he sits down to write is to make reading fun and interesting. Sachar also says, "If a book is well written, communicating a moral can also be fun. People like it when the good guy wins and when good triumphs over evil."

Try an Adventure Novel

An adventure can take place in any kind of setting. Many adventure novels take readers to faraway or unusual times and places. Other adventures are set in modern times, in a city or neighborhood similar to the reader's own. Ask students to name some adventure stories they have heard or read. One famous tale of adventure is *Treasure Island* by Robert Louis Stevenson. This 1883 novel is about a hunt for a treasure that involves pirates and a daring voyage. Other adventure stories include

- J. D. Wyss's *Swiss Family Robinson,* about a family that becomes shipwrecked on a tropical island

- Gary Paulsen's *Hatchet,* about a boy who must survive on his own in a remote wilderness after his plane crashes

- Avi's *The True Confessions of Charlotte Doyle,* about a girl who takes charge during a difficult journey at sea

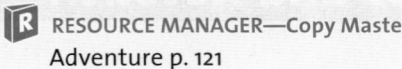

R RESOURCE MANAGER—Copy Master
Adventure p. 121

Holes

Novel by Louis Sachar

**Louis Sachar
born 1954**

Other Books by Louis Sachar
- *The Boy Who Lost His Face*
- *Dogs Don't Tell Jokes*
- *Sixth Grade Secrets*
- *Someday Angeline*

Meet Louis Sachar

Louis Sachar knows what it's like to be a kid. As a writer, he tries to share with his readers the thoughts and feelings he had when he was their age. "When I write," he says, "I'm always putting myself in the shoes of the character and always reacting to how I would feel about something if I were that character." Sachar also says that as he writes, he's "constantly doing it in fear that the reader is going to close the book at any second." Fearing that his readers might get bored inspires Sachar to keep his plots interesting.

Sachar worked as a teacher's aide at an elementary school while he was in college, and that gave him the idea to try writing books for young readers. He even used the names of his students in the first stories he wrote. He went to law school after college, but he found that he was more interested in writing than in practicing law.

Try an Adventure Novel

Holes is an example of an **adventure novel.** This type of fiction focuses on a main character who is usually on a mission and is facing many challenges and choices. There is often physical danger involved. In *Holes,* the main character and his friend face what seem at times to be overwhelming obstacles, but they do so with great courage.

DIFFERENTIATED INSTRUCTION

FOR LESS–PROFICIENT READERS

Reading Support Before students begin reading, review the teaching notes on pages 93–97 and select those that you think would be most helpful to them. You might read the selection aloud with students and discuss the relevant notes. Stop occasionally to answer questions, give an explanation, or hold a discussion.

Read a Great Book

Stanley Yelnats, the main character in *Holes*, gets teased in school, has no friends, and lives in a smelly apartment. He also has some unfortunate family history. Stanley is suffering from a curse dating back to the time of his great-great-grandfather, a "no-good-dirty-rotten-pig-stealing" character whose reputation continues to haunt Stanley. In an episode of bad luck, Stanley lands at Camp Green Lake, "a camp for bad boys." And so the adventure begins.

from

HOLES

LOUIS SACHAR

There is no lake at Camp Green Lake. There once was a very large lake here, the largest lake in Texas. That was over a hundred years ago. Now it is just a dry, flat wasteland.

There used to be a town of Green Lake as well. The town shriveled and dried up along with the lake, and the people who lived there.

During the summer the daytime temperature hovers around ninety-five degrees in the shade—if you can find any shade. There's not much shade in a big dry lake.

The only trees are two old oaks on the eastern edge of the "lake."
10 A hammock is stretched between the two trees, and a log cabin stands behind that.

The campers are forbidden to lie in the hammock. It belongs to the Warden. The Warden owns the shade.

Out on the lake, rattlesnakes and scorpions find shade under rocks and in the holes dug by the campers.

Here's a good rule to remember about rattlesnakes and scorpions: If you don't bother them, they won't bother you.

Usually.

Being bitten by a scorpion or even a rattlesnake is not the worst
20 thing that can happen to you. You won't die.

Usually.

Read

Read a Great Book

Louis Sachar approached the writing of *Holes* differently than he approached the writing of his other books. Several years before he began writing it, he heard novelist Patricia MacLachlan speak at a conference for writers. During her talk she said that setting was the most important aspect of a novel. Sachar had never thought of setting as being as important as character and plot.

When he began writing *Holes,* he started with its setting—Camp Green Lake, a juvenile correctional facility in which boys are required to dig holes under the hot Texas sun. They work hard every day—always fearful of encountering rattlesnakes and deadly yellow-spotted lizards. Sachar had no idea what would happen at Camp Green Lake and who his main character would be. He knew, however, that many great stories could grow out of such a strong setting.

SHARE WORD MEANINGS

A *scorpion* (line 14) is an animal related to a spider. It has a segmented, curved tail and a poisonous stinger. In legends and fables, scorpions often represent something harmful or evil.

FOR ENGLISH LEARNERS

Read Aloud Preread part of the excerpt and have students continue reading in pairs or small groups. Alternatively, read aloud all or part of the excerpt and stop occasionally to answer questions, hold a discussion, or give an explanation.

Listen to the *Audio Anthology CD* Have students listen to the excerpt as they read along. Then have them read the text independently. Lead them in a follow-up discussion.

Jigsaw Reading Give students an introduction to and a summary of the excerpt. Then have students meet in small groups for Jigsaw reading. Each person should read part of the excerpt and explain it to the others.

 BEST PRACTICES TOOLKIT
Jigsaw p. A1

Sometimes a camper will try to be bitten by a scorpion, or even a small rattlesnake. Then he will get to spend a day or two recovering in his tent, instead of having to dig a hole out on the lake.

But you don't want to be bitten by a yellow-spotted lizard. That's the worst thing that can happen to you. You will die a slow and painful death.

Always.

If you get bitten by a yellow-spotted lizard, you might as well
30 go into the shade of the oak trees and lie in the hammock.

There is nothing anyone can do to you anymore.

The reader is probably asking: Why would anyone go to Camp Green Lake?

Most campers weren't given a choice. Camp Green Lake is a camp for bad boys.

If you take a bad boy and make him dig a hole every day in the hot sun, it will turn him into a good boy.

That was what some people thought.

Stanley Yelnats was given a choice. The judge said, "You may
40 go to jail, or you may go to Camp Green Lake."

Stanley was from a poor family. He had never been to camp before.

Stanley Yelnats was the only passenger on the bus, not counting the driver or the guard. The guard sat next to the driver with his seat turned around facing Stanley. A rifle lay across his lap.

Stanley was sitting about ten rows back, handcuffed to his armrest. His backpack lay on the seat next to him. It contained his toothbrush, toothpaste, and a box of stationery his mother had given him. He'd promised to write to her at least once a week.

He looked out the window, although there wasn't much to see—
50 mostly fields of hay and cotton. He was on a long bus ride to nowhere. The bus wasn't air-conditioned, and the hot, heavy air was almost as stifling as the handcuffs.

Stanley and his parents had tried to pretend that he was just going away to camp for a while, just like rich kids do. When Stanley was younger he used to play with stuffed animals, and

pretend the animals were at camp. Camp Fun and Games he called it. Sometimes he'd have them play soccer with a marble. Other times they'd run an obstacle course, or go bungee jumping off a table, tied to broken rubber bands. Now Stanley tried to pretend he was
60 going to Camp Fun and Games. Maybe he'd make some friends, he thought. At least he'd get to swim in the lake.

He didn't have any friends at home. He was overweight and the kids at his middle school often teased him about his size. Even his teachers sometimes made cruel comments without realizing it. On his last day of school, his math teacher, Mrs. Bell, taught ratios. As an example, she chose the heaviest kid in the class and the lightest kid in the class, and had them weigh themselves. Stanley weighed three times as much as the other boy. Mrs. Bell wrote the ratio on the board, 3:1, unaware of how much embarrassment she had caused
70 both of them.

Stanley was arrested later that day.

He looked at the guard who sat slumped in his seat and wondered if he had fallen asleep. The guard was wearing sunglasses, so Stanley couldn't see his eyes.

Stanley was not a bad kid. He was innocent of the crime for which he was convicted. He'd just been in the wrong place at the wrong time.

It was all because of his no-good-dirty-rotten-pig-stealing-great-great-grandfather!
80 He smiled. It was a family joke. Whenever anything went wrong, they always blamed Stanley's no-good-dirty-rotten-pig-stealing-great-great-grandfather.

Supposedly, he had a great-great-grandfather who had stolen a pig from a one-legged Gypsy, and she put a curse on him and all his descendants. Stanley and his parents didn't believe in curses, of course, but whenever anything went wrong, it felt good to be able to blame someone.

Things went wrong a lot. They always seemed to be in the wrong place at the wrong time.
90 He looked out the window at the vast emptiness. He watched the rise and fall of a telephone wire. In his mind he could hear his father's gruff voice softly singing to him.

SHARE A READING TIP

Sachar repeats the term "dirty-rotten-pig-stealing-great-great-grandfather" (lines 78–79, 81–82, 108) to add some humor to Stanley's difficult situation. The term is hyphenated because it is all part of one noun. The extreme length of the term, as well as the added detail about stealing a pig, makes it humorous. Have students look for other examples of humor as they continue reading.

A word, phrase, sentence, or number that reads the same backwards and forwards—such as "Stanley Yelnats"—is known as a palindrome. Other examples include "Was it a cat I saw?" and the date 1881. Sachar says he planned to use the name "Yelnats" for Stanley only until he thought of a better last name, but then he decided to keep it.

"If only, if only," the woodpecker sighs,
"The bark on the tree was just a little bit softer."
While the wolf waits below, hungry and lonely,
He cries to the moo—oo—oon,
"If only, if only."

It was a song his father used to sing to him. The melody was sweet and sad, but Stanley's favorite part was when his father would howl
100 the word "moon."

The bus hit a small bump and the guard sat up, instantly alert.

Stanley's father was an inventor. To be a successful inventor you need three things: intelligence, perseverance, and just a little bit of luck.

Stanley's father was smart and had a lot of perseverance. Once he started a project he would work on it for years, often going days without sleep. He just never had any luck.

Every time an experiment failed, Stanley could hear him cursing his dirty-rotten-pig-stealing-great-grandfather.

Stanley's father was also named Stanley Yelnats. Stanley's father's
110 full name was Stanley Yelnats III. Our Stanley is Stanley Yelnats IV.

Everyone in his family had always liked the fact that "Stanley Yelnats" was spelled the same frontward and backward. So they kept naming their sons Stanley. Stanley was an only child, as was every other Stanley Yelnats before him.

All of them had something else in common. Despite their awful luck, they always remained hopeful. As Stanley's father liked to say, "I learn from failure."

But perhaps that was part of the curse as well. If Stanley and his father weren't always hopeful, then it wouldn't hurt so much every
120 time their hopes were crushed.

"Not every Stanley Yelnats has been a failure," Stanley's mother often pointed out, whenever Stanley or his father became so discouraged that they actually started to believe in the curse. The first Stanley Yelnats, Stanley's great-grandfather, had made a fortune in the stock market. "He couldn't have been too unlucky."

At such times she neglected to mention the bad luck that befell the first Stanley Yelnats. He lost his entire fortune when he was moving from New York to California. His stagecoach was robbed by the outlaw Kissin' Kate Barlow.

130   If it weren't for that, Stanley's family would now be living in a mansion on a beach in California. Instead, they were crammed in a tiny apartment that smelled of burning rubber and foot odor.
    If only, if only . . .
    The apartment smelled the way it did because Stanley's father was trying to invent a way to recycle old sneakers. "The first person who finds a use for old sneakers," he said, "will be a very rich man."
    It was this latest project that led to Stanley's arrest.
    The bus ride became increasingly bumpy because the road was no longer paved.

140   Actually, Stanley had been impressed when he first found out that his great-grandfather was robbed by Kissin' Kate Barlow. True, he would have preferred living on the beach in California, but it was still kind of cool to have someone in your family robbed by a famous outlaw.
    Kate Barlow didn't actually kiss Stanley's great-grandfather. That would have been really cool, but she only kissed the men she killed. Instead, she robbed him and left him stranded in the middle of the desert.
    "He was *lucky* to have survived," Stanley's mother was quick

150 to point out.
    The bus was slowing down. The guard grunted as he stretched his arms.
    "Welcome to Camp Green Lake," said the driver.
    Stanley looked out the dirty window. He couldn't see a lake. And hardly anything was green. ✎

Keep Reading

Now you have a sense of the bad situation Stanley is in. Which part of the description of the camp surprised you most? To find out how Stanley will handle the situation, read the rest of the story. As the plot of *Holes* unfolds, Stanley experiences many challenges and obstacles, some because of the harsh setting and others because of some harsh people. Through it all, he learns a few things about himself.

Discuss

SHARE AN FYI

Some businesses have found a way to recycle old sneakers. The shoes are ground up and used to make new sports surfaces such as soccer fields, tennis and basketball courts, and running tracks.

Keep Reading

Share these discussion questions with students after they have finished the excerpt. You might use the questions to lead a class discussion or have students form small groups to discuss them.

- Have you read this book? If yes, would you recommend it to others? Why? If no, what questions are you hoping the rest of the book will answer?

- What do you find most interesting about the character of Stanley?

- Do you believe Stanley's family could have a curse? Why?

- What crimes do you think Stanley could have been accused of committing?

- What do you think life will be like for Stanley at Camp Green Lake? What details give you an idea of what Camp Green Lake is like?

Focus and Motivate

OBJECTIVES

Literary Analysis
- explore the key idea of a **disaster**
- identify and evaluate characteristics of narrative nonfiction
- read narrative nonfiction

Reading
- identify patterns of organization: chronological order

Vocabulary
- build vocabulary for reading and writing
- complete analogies (*also an EL language objective*)

Grammar and Writing
- use subject and object pronouns correctly
- use writing to analyze literature

SUMMARY

This excerpt details the loss of the famous—and allegedly unsinkable—*Titanic*. Survivors recall the wonder and excitement surrounding its launch. The author describes how the *Titanic* was ill-equipped for a disaster, and how iceberg warnings were ignored or mishandled before the ship's fatal collision with an iceberg.

What can we learn from DISASTERS?

Discuss the question. Ask students what **disasters** they have heard about. Could people have been better prepared? Then have students form small groups for the **CHART IT** activity. Afterward, ask volunteers to share their key ideas about learning from disasters.

from **Exploring the *Titanic***
Narrative Nonfiction by Robert D. Ballard

What can we learn from DISASTERS?

MARYLAND OBJECTIVES

READING/LIT STANDARDS
1.E.3.a Select and apply appropriate strategies during reading
3.A.3 Analyze elements of narrative text

KEY IDEA Have you ever learned a lesson the hard way? Unfortunately, sometimes it takes a **disaster** to teach us to properly plan for danger. In the selection you're about to read, people on an "unsinkable" ship encounter terrible danger at sea—without enough lifeboats for everyone.

CHART IT When a disaster happens, we try to find out what went wrong so that we know how to be better prepared in the future. Using a chart like the one shown, list different types of disasters and things we can learn from them. Compare your chart with those of your classmates.

Disasters	What We Can Learn from Them
Fires	We can learn to build safer buildings.
	More fire drills will help people know what to do in emergencies.

98

Selection Resources

* Resources for Differentiation   † Also in Spanish   ‡ In Haitian Creole and Vietnamese

LITERARY ANALYSIS: NARRATIVE NONFICTION

Narrative nonfiction uses literary elements, such as plot, setting, and conflict, to tell a story. Unlike fiction, though, narrative nonfiction tells a true story about events that really happened. To be accurate, narrative nonfiction relies on source material, such as quotations from real people, facts from reliable accounts, and photographs. As you read *Exploring the* Titanic, notice how literary elements and source material help create a compelling narrative.

Review: **Suspense**

READING SKILL: USE CHRONOLOGICAL ORDER

When writers use **chronological order,** or time order, they present events in the order in which they happened. To help you recognize time order, look for

- calendar dates, such as *Wednesday, April 10, 1912*
- clock time, such as *shortly after noon* and *8:03 P.M.*
- words and phrases that show time order, such as *before, later, around lunchtime,* and *for the next ten months*

Use a timeline to track the events of the *Titanic*'s final day.

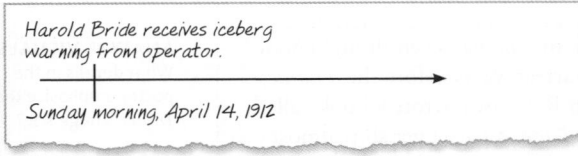

> Harold Bride receives iceberg warning from operator.
>
> Sunday morning, April 14, 1912

Review: **Make Inferences**

VOCABULARY IN CONTEXT

The boldfaced words help tell the story of this disaster. Use context clues to give a definition for each word.

1. The elegant **accommodations** thrilled the passengers.
2. **Adjoining** rooms kept families together.
3. There were **moderate** prices for less luxurious rooms.
4. Travelers enjoyed the **novelty** of the ship's first voyage.
5. Some believed they had heard a **prophecy** of tragedy.
6. The crews worked **feverishly** to avoid a collision.
7. They were unable to prevent a **ghastly** disaster at sea.
8. Rescue ships were delayed **indefinitely.**

Author Online

Robert D. Ballard
born 1942

Underwater Explorer
Robert D. Ballard, a pioneer of deep-sea exploration, traces his interest in the ocean to childhood walks on the beach in San Diego. He was so fascinated by sea lore and by the crabs washed in by the tide that he decided to spend his life by the water. Ballard is trained as a marine geologist, a geophysicist (a mapper of land and oceans), and a Navy commander. After years of searching, he found one of the most important shipwrecks in history— the remains of the *Titanic*.

A World Beneath the Water
The oxygen-poor water at the bottom of the ocean keeps shipwrecks in excellent condition. "There's probably more history now preserved underwater than in all the museums of the world combined," Ballard has observed. To help excavate that history, Ballard organizes expeditions to areas rich in shipwrecks. He explores the depths with the help of robots and submersibles, or minisubmarines.

Mysteries Solved Ballard's discovery solved many mysteries about the *Titanic*'s last hours. For instance, pieces on the ocean floor reveal that the ship broke in two before sinking.

 MORE ABOUT THE AUTHOR
For more on Robert D. Ballard, visit the **Literature Center** at ClassZone.com.

Teach

STANDARDS FOCUS

LITERARY ANALYSIS

● NARRATIVE NONFICTION

Have students read **Author Online.**

- Which elements could be used in a narrative nonfiction account of Ballard's life? *Possible answer: facts about his childhood and career, the direct quotation, the photograph*
- Why is this text *not* an example of narrative nonfiction? *Possible answer: There is no plot or conflict.*

CHECK UNDERSTANDING Ask students to name some real historical events that authors have retold as stories.

READING SKILL

■ USE CHRONOLOGICAL ORDER

Help students see that using chronological order requires organization and attention to detail. Display a calendar showing the last seven days. Ask students to record events from the prior week, noting specific dates and times for each event.

CHECK UNDERSTANDING As a class, work together to put the students' data into a chronological master list for a specific day, or track the weekly occurrence of a specific event.

R RESOURCE MANAGER—Copy Master
Use Chronological Order p. 135 (for student use while reading the selection)

VOCABULARY SKILL

▲ VOCABULARY IN CONTEXT

DIAGNOSE WORD KNOWLEDGE To determine preteaching needs, have all students complete **Vocabulary in Context.** Check students' definitions against those on the selection pages: *accommodations* (p. 102), *adjoining* (p. 103), *feverishly* (p. 111), *ghastly* (p. 114), *indefinitely* (p. 105), *moderate* (p. 105), *novelty* (p. 106), *prophecy* (p. 100).

PRETEACH VOCABULARY Use the Vocabulary Study copy master to help students explore the vocabulary words in another context.

1. Read aloud the sentences in Part A through the first boldfaced word (*feverishly*). Emphasize the boldfaced word.
2. Ask students to imagine the scene that is described. Elicit possible meanings for *feverishly,* such as "in an emotional way."
3. Repeat the procedure for each of the other boldfaced words.

R RESOURCE MANAGER—Copy Master
Vocabulary Study p. 137
For general guidelines on differentiating vocabulary instruction and for alternative vocabulary activities for students not needing vocabulary preteaching, see

BEST PRACTICES TOOLKIT
Scaffolding Vocabulary Instruction pp. 43–46

ⓘ Vocabulary Center at **ClassZone.com**

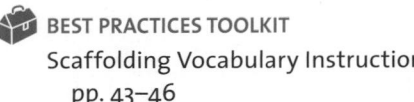

ANALYZE VISUALS

Possible answer:

- The Titanic *fills nearly the entire poster.*
- *Nearby boats look very small by comparison.*
- *The passengers behind the railings look tiny.*
- *Showing the ship move toward the viewer makes it seem even larger.*
- *The words* Olympic *and* Titanic *emphasize the ship's great size.*

About the Art Grand, stylish, and confident, this advertising poster conveys the ambitions of the White Star Line. By the early 1900s, fortunes had been made from building transatlantic passenger ships, and competition was intense. Shipping lines tried to outdo each other with ever larger and more elegant ships; as a result, the transatlantic route had the finest ships at sea. In 1906, the launch of the Cunard Line's *Mauretania* and *Lusitania,* with their great size and hotel-like accommodations, heralded a new age of luxury travel. As the poster indicates, by 1912 the White Star Line ships were the largest in the world, and they offered the largest accommodations as well.

READING SKILL

A CHRONOLOGICAL ORDER

Possible answer: The "eerie prophecy" grabs readers' attention and foreshadows what will happen to the Titanic. *Readers can use the story of the* Titan *to make predictions about the shipwreck of the* Titanic.

If students need help . . .

- Remind them that foreshadowing is when a writer hints at events that will happen later in a story.
- Ask them how learning about *The Wreck of the* Titan affects them as readers. Are they eager to find out how the true story of the *Titanic* might be similar?

Exploring the
TITANIC

Robert D. Ballard

The story of the *Titanic* began before anyone had even thought about building the great ship. In 1898, fourteen years before the *Titanic* sank, an American writer named Morgan Robertson wrote a book called *The Wreck of the* Titan.[1] In his story, the *Titan,* a passenger ship almost identical to the *Titanic,* and labeled "unsinkable," sails from England headed for New York. With many rich and famous passengers on board, the *Titan* hits an iceberg in the North Atlantic and sinks. Because there are not enough lifeboats, many lives are lost.

The story of the *Titan* predicted exactly what would happen to the *Titanic* fourteen years later. It was an eerie **prophecy** of terrible things to come. **A**

In 1907, nearly ten years after *The Wreck of the* Titan was written, two men began making plans to build a real titanic ship. At a London dinner party, as they relaxed over coffee and cigars, J. Bruce Ismay, president of the White Star Line of passenger ships, and Lord Pirrie, chairman of Harland & Wolff shipbuilders, discussed a plan to build three enormous

ANALYZE VISUALS
What **details** in the poster emphasize the *Titanic's* huge size?

1 Targeted Passage

prophecy (prŏf'ĭ-sē) *n.* a prediction of the future

A CHRONOLOGICAL ORDER
Why do you think Ballard begins his narrative with a reference to *The Wreck of the* Titan?

---

1. **Titan:** In Greek mythology, the Titans were a race of giants. The word *titanic* has come to be applied to any person or thing of great size or power.

Titanic, Olympic, White Star Line (1912). Montague B. Black. Christie's Images/Corbis.

DIFFERENTIATED INSTRUCTION

FOR ALL STUDENTS

Learning Center Set up a learning center on the *Titanic* disaster with books and pictures on topics such as Ballard's *Titanic* expedition, famous shipwrecks, and safety regulations for ships today. Provide a variety of independent projects, such as a scientific diagram of how icebergs form, a short *Titanic* survivor biography, and a film review of *A Night to Remember* (1958).

FOR LESS–PROFICIENT READERS

In combination with the *Audio Anthology CD,* use one or more Targeted Passages (pp. 100, 102–103, 109, 111, 114) to ensure that students focus on key story events, concepts, and skills.

1 Targeted Passage [Lines 1–11]

This passage tells a story that foreshadows the main narrative of this selection—the launch and wreck of the *Titanic.*

BACKGROUND

Steamship Travel The Atlantic crossing was a legendary journey, bringing famous explorers and millionaires as well as millions of immigrants from Europe to North America. For centuries, it was also a very dangerous journey because of rough waters, Antarctic icebergs, and fog. Many transatlantic sailing ships were wrecked or lost at sea. Although the steamships that became the norm by the mid-1800s were quicker and safer than sailing ships, the Atlantic Ocean still posed risks. In the spring of 1912, for example, when the *Titanic* was launched, a warm winter had caused an unusually high number of icebergs to break from the Arctic glaciers.

Airplane travel finally brought an end to the age of steamships. The introduction of transatlantic passenger flights aboard commercial jets in October 1958 meant that the journey could be completed in less than seven hours—rather than six days by steamship—and without the risk of icebergs.

- In Robertson's story, where is the *Titan* launched? Where is it headed?

- What causes the *Titan* to sink? Why are so many lives lost?

- How is the story of the *Titan* related to the real-life story of the *Titanic*?

FOR ENGLISH LEARNERS

Key Academic Vocabulary Have students use New Word Analysis to learn and practice this academic vocabulary: *relax* (lines 14, 93, 155), *goal* (line 17), *enormous* (lines 39, 109, 120), *series* (119), *occur* (line 230), *abandon* (line 359).

 BEST PRACTICES TOOLKIT—Transparency New Word Analysis p. E8

Prereading For prereading instruction for English learners, see

 BEST PRACTICES TOOLKIT Scaffolding Reading Instruction pp. 43–46

FOR ADVANCED LEARNERS/PRE–AP

Pre-AP exercises in the bottom channel provide additional challenge for your advanced students. Use them for small groups or individuals.

ADDITIONAL GUIDELINES

For more help with differentiation and tips for classroom management, see

 BEST PRACTICES TOOLKIT Differentiated Instruction pp. 31–38

ocean liners. Their goal was to give the White Star Line a competitive edge in the Atlantic passenger trade with several gigantic ships whose **accommodations** would be the last word in comfort and elegance.

20 The two men certainly dreamed on a grand scale.[2] When these floating palaces were finally built, they were so much bigger than other ships that new docks had to be built on each side of the Atlantic to service them. Four years after that London dinner party, the first of these huge liners, the *Olympic,* safely completed her maiden voyage.[3]

On May 31, 1911, the hull of the *Titanic* was launched at the Harland & Wolff shipyards in Belfast, Ireland, before a cheering crowd of 100,000. Bands played, and people came from miles around to see this great wonder of the sea. Twenty-two tons of soap, grease, and train oil were used to slide her into the water. In the words of one eyewitness, 30 she had "a rudder as big as an elm tree . . . propellers as big as a windmill. Everything was on a nightmare scale." **B**

For the next ten months the *Titanic* was outfitted and carefully prepared down to the last detail. The final size and richness of this new ship was astounding. She was 882 feet long, almost the length of four city blocks. With nine decks, she was as high as an eleven-story building.

Among her gigantic features, she had four huge funnels, each one big enough to drive two trains through. During construction an astonishing three million rivets had been hammered into her hull. Her three enormous anchors weighed a total of thirty-one tons—the weight of 40 twenty cars. And for her maiden voyage, she carried enough food to feed a small town for several months.

As her name boasted, the *Titanic* was indeed the biggest ship in the world. Nicknamed "the Millionaires' Special," she was also called "the Wonder Ship," "the Unsinkable Ship," and "the Last Word in Luxury" by newspapers around the world. **C**

The command of this great ocean liner was given to the senior captain of the White Star Line, Captain Edward J. Smith. This proud, white-bearded man was a natural leader and was popular with both crew members and passengers. Most important, after thirty-eight years' service 50 with the White Star Line, he had an excellent safety record. At the age of fifty-nine, Captain Smith was going to retire after this last trip, a perfect final tribute to a long and successful career.

On Wednesday, April 10, 1912, the *Titanic*'s passengers began to arrive in Southampton for the trip to New York. Ruth Becker was dazzled as she boarded the ship with her mother, her younger sister, and two-year-old brother, Richard. Ruth's father was a missionary in India. The rest of the

---

2. **on a grand scale:** in a large or impressive way.

3. **maiden voyage:** very first trip.

---

accommodations
(ə-kŏm′ə-dā′shənz)
n. rooms and food, especially in a hotel or on a ship or train

B NARRATIVE NONFICTION
What details help you picture the **setting** of the *Titanic*'s launch?

2 Targeted Passage

C NARRATIVE NONFICTION
What do the newspaper quotations add to your understanding?

DIFFERENTIATED INSTRUCTION

FOR LESS—PROFICIENT READERS

2 Targeted Passage [Lines 42–70]

This passage introduces the *Titanic* and two young passengers, Ruth Becker and Jack Thayer. It also sets up the ship's launching.

- What are the *Titanic*'s nicknames?
- On what date do the passengers arrive? Where are they launching from?
- Who is the captain of the *Titanic*?
- Why are Ruth and Jack on board? Do they have the same class of tickets?

Review: Narrative Review the literary term *narrative* (writing that tells a story). Remind students that narrative nonfiction tells a story about real events. Have students work in pairs to identify these literary elements on page 102:

- characters
- setting
- events

FOR ENGLISH LEARNERS

Vocabulary: Synonyms Have pairs sort these italicized words from the story into three groups of synonyms:

- *great* (line 2), *titanic* (line 13), *enormous* (line 16), *gigantic* (line 18), *grand* (line 20), *huge* (line 23)—words that mean "big"
- *astounding* (line 34), *astonishing* (line 37), *fantastic* (line 70), *magnificent* (line 143)—words that mean "wonderful"
- *dazzled* (line 54), *delighted* (line 60), *impressed* (line 61)—words that mean "amazed"

Ruth Becker

Jack Thayer

Illustration of grand staircase © Ken Marschall, from *On Board the Titanic*, a Hyperion/Madison Press Book.

family was sailing to New York to find medical help for young Richard, who had developed a serious illness in India. They had booked second-class tickets on the *Titanic*.

60 Twelve-year-old Ruth was delighted with the ship. As she pushed her little brother about the decks in a stroller, she was impressed with what she saw. "Everything was new. New!" she recalled. "Our cabin was just like a hotel room, it was so big. The dining room was beautiful—the linens, all the bright, polished silver you can imagine."

Meanwhile, seventeen-year-old Jack Thayer from Philadelphia was trying out the soft mattress on the large bed in his cabin. The first-class rooms his family had reserved for themselves and their maid had thick carpets, carved wooden panels on the walls, and marble sinks. As his parents were getting settled in their **adjoining** stateroom,[4] Jack decided 70 to explore this fantastic ship. **D**

On A Deck, he stepped into the Verandah and Palm Court and admired the white wicker furniture and the ivy growing up the trellised walls. On the lower decks, Jack discovered the squash court,[5] the swimming pool, and the Turkish bath[6] decorated like a room in a sultan's palace. In the gymnasium, the instructor was showing passengers the

---

4. **stateroom:** a private cabin on a ship.

5. **squash court:** a walled court or room for playing squash, in which a rubber ball is hit off the walls.

6. **Turkish bath:** steam bath.

ANALYZE VISUALS
The photographs of Ruth Becker and Jack Thayer are **source material.** How does seeing the faces of these young passengers affect the way you read the selection?

 Targeted Passage

adjoining (ə-joi′nĭng) *adj.* next to or in contact with **adjoin** *v.*

D NARRATIVE NONFICTION
What details about the **setting** do you learn from firsthand observations of people on the ship?

ANALYZE VISUALS

About the Art Ken Marschall is world-renowned for his images of the *Titanic*. He drew his first picture of the ship at age 16 and for more than 30 years has devoted himself to researching and depicting its voyage. Combining photograph-like detail with dramatic force, his paintings have brought the ship to life for many viewers. His work inspired James Cameron, director of the 1997 movie *Titanic*. Marschall was a consultant on the film.

Activity Ask students how seeing what Ruth and Jack look like affects how they read lines 60–70. *Possible answer: Because the pictures show that Ruth and Jack were real people, it makes their words seem more real. Ruth and Jack are close in age to the students, which makes it easier for students to imagine the setting through their eyes.*

LITERARY ANALYSIS

D NARRATIVE NONFICTION

Possible answer:
- *the ship was new*
- *everything was shiny and spacious*
- *the first-class accommodations were very fancy*

If students need help . . . Have them reread lines 62–75 and point out the details that Ruth and Jack noticed. Ask them why these details might have drawn Ruth's and Jack's attention: In what ways might the ship have been very different from their everyday lives at home?

FOR ENGLISH LEARNERS

Vocabulary: Idioms Use New Word Analysis to teach these idioms from the excerpt: *the last word* (lines 19 and 44), *close call* (line 130), *what the matter was* (lines 270 and 281), and *every man for himself* (line 360). Then have each student complete a Word Square for one of these idioms.

 BEST PRACTICES TOOLKIT—Transparencies
New Word Analysis p. E8
Word Squares p. E10

Idiom: *Every man for himself*	Symbol:
My meaning: *Every person has to take care of his or her own needs*	Sentence: *Abuela put out the food, gave us plates, and said, "It's every man for himself."*

FOR ADVANCED LEARNERS/PRE–AP

Use Imagery Have students work independently to write a letter from Ruth to her father in India about her impressions of the *Titanic*. Students should bear in mind what they have heard of Ruth's voice (lines 62–64) and use imagery (words that appeal to the senses).

Lines 78–94
DISCUSSION PROMPTS

Use these prompts to help students understand how significant the *Titanic* was in its day:

Connect Imagine that an extremely luxurious means of transportation—perhaps the world's fanciest airplane—was being launched today. Who might want to have tickets for its first journey? *Possible answers: political leaders, celebrities, people who are successful in sports or business*

Analyze Are the first-class passengers on the *Titanic* treated differently than the other passengers? Cite evidence. *Possible answer: First-class passengers do receive special treatment. They have their own reception room (line 79), where the ship's band plays for them (line 80), and they are greeted by the president of the shipping line (lines 91–92). One first-class passenger has even been allowed to bring a car on board (lines 89–90).*

Evaluate Do you think J. Bruce Ismay would give the same attention to the second- and third-class passengers? Why or why not?

Possible answers:

- *No, because Ismay cares most about the comfort and happiness of the wealthy people whose money could help make his new luxury ship profitable.*

- *No, but he might still give some attention to the other passengers so that he will make a good impression on everyone and create good publicity.*

First-class promenade

First-class cabins

Third-class cabins

Second-class cabins

Second-class dining room

Engine rooms

Propellers

Illustration © Ken Marschall, from *On Board the Titanic*, a Hyperion/Madison Press Book.

latest in exercise equipment, which included a mechanical camel you could ride on, stationary bicycles, and rowing machines.

Daylight shone through the huge glass dome over the Grand Staircase as Jack went down to join his parents in the first-class reception room.

80　　There, with the ship's band playing in the background, his father pointed out some of the other first-class passengers. "He's supposed to be the world's richest man," said his father of Colonel John Jacob Astor, who was escorting the young Mrs. Astor. He also identified Mr. and Mrs. Straus, founders of Macy's of New York, the world's largest department store. Millionaire Benjamin Guggenheim was aboard, as were Jack's parents' friends from Philadelphia, Mr. and Mrs. George Widener and their son, Harry. Mr. Widener had made a fortune building streetcars. Mr. and Mrs. William Carter were also friends of the Thayers. Stowed in one of the holds below was a new Renault car that they were bringing

90　　back from England.

J. Bruce Ismay, president of the White Star Line, moved about the room saying hello to people. He wanted to make sure that his wealthy passengers were comfortable, that they would feel relaxed and safe aboard his floating palace.

DIFFERENTIATED INSTRUCTION

FOR LESS–PROFICIENT READERS

Reading Support Have students create a Classification Chart to help them understand the differences among the social classes on board the *Titanic*. Copies of the transparency can be adapted for this purpose by crossing out the second tier of boxes.

 BEST PRACTICES TOOLKIT—Transparency Classification Chart p. B17

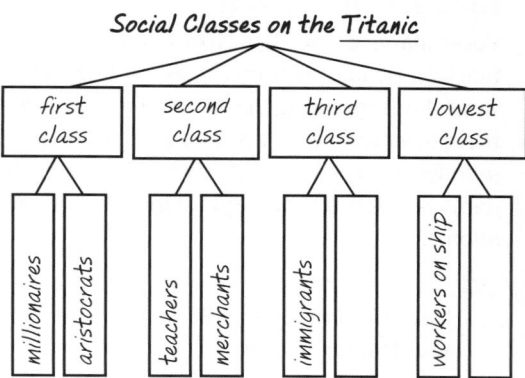

Social Classes on the *Titanic*

| first class | second class | third class | lowest class |

millionaires | aristocrats | teachers | merchants | immigrants | workers on ship

Gymnasium
Grand staircase
Crow's nest
Morse lamp
First-class lounge
Wireless room
Bridge
Third-class cabins
Third-class dining room
First-class dining room
Boiler rooms

ANALYZE VISUALS
Identify which parts of the boat are dedicated to the first-, second-, and third-class passengers. What differences do you note?

Indeed, when Ruth Becker's mother had asked one of the second-class staff about the safety of the ship, she had been told that there was absolutely nothing to worry about. The ship had watertight compartments that would allow her to float **indefinitely.** There was much talk among the passengers about the *Titanic* being unsinkable.

100   In 1912, people were divided into social classes according to background, wealth, and education. Because of these class lines, the *Titanic* was rather like a big floating layer cake. The bottom layer consisted of the lowly manual workers sweating away in the heat and grime of the boiler rooms and engine rooms. The next layer was the third-class passengers, people of many nationalities hoping to make a new start in America. After that came the second class—teachers, merchants, and professionals of **moderate** means like Ruth's family. Then, finally, there was the icing on the cake in first class: the rich and the aristocratic. The differences between these groups were enormous. While the wealthy brought their maids and valets[7]
110   and mountains of luggage, most members of the crew earned such tiny salaries that it would have taken them years to save the money for a single first-class ticket. **E**

indefinitely
(ĭn-dĕf'ə-nĭt-lē) *adv.* for an unlimited length of time

moderate (mŏd'ər-ĭt) *adj.* not excessive or extreme; average

E NARRATIVE NONFICTION
Why is it important to understand the way social class influenced the people on the ship?

---

7. **valets** (vă-lāz'): gentlemen's personal servants.

ANALYZE VISUALS

Possible answer: First-class passengers have the largest facilities in the best locations.

- *First-class cabins are above the ship's deck, where they would have windows and a view of the ocean. First-class facilities, including a lounge and a promenade (place for walking), are located mostly above decks and in the center of the ship.*

- *Second-class cabins are smaller and located near the back of the ship. The second-class dining room looks less fancy than the first-class one.*

- *Third-class cabins are very small and located at the extreme ends of the ship. The third-class dining room looks very plain with its long rows of tables and benches.*

LITERARY ANALYSIS

E NARRATIVE NONFICTION

Possible answer: Understanding social class
- *helps the reader understand how the ship was organized*
- *informs the reader about the era in which the* Titanic *sailed*

Extend the Discussion How might social class affect how the captain, crew, and passengers respond to a disaster?

FOR ADVANCED LEARNERS/PRE–AP

Analyze Simile The author uses a simile of a layer cake (lines 101–108) to describe the class divisions on the ship. Have students discuss or illustrate why the simile works. Invite students to suggest other similes that the author may have considered using.

SCIENCE CONNECTION

The wireless telegraph, which uses radio waves to send messages over long distances, was invented by Italian physicist Guglielmo Marconi in 1896. (Earlier telegraph technology used wires to transmit electrical signals.) Some mathematicians believed that the curvature of the Earth would limit radio communication to 200 miles or less. Marconi disproved this theory in 1901, when he transmitted a signal across the Atlantic Ocean from England to Newfoundland.

LITERARY ANALYSIS: Review

F SUSPENSE

Possible answer:

- *The description of the near-collision is tense and dramatic.*

- *The phrases "not a good sign," "close call," and "bad omen" (lines 128–130) suggest that worse events are yet to come.*

- *This foreshadowing creates suspense about how the terrible events will unfold.*

Extend the Discussion How could the *Titanic's* size pose a problem for the crew?

READING SKILL

G CHRONOLOGICAL ORDER

Answer: *He picks up the iceberg warning on Sunday, April 14.*

Point out that as the narrative continues, many events will happen in a short time. Students will need to label timeline events with times of day, not just dates.

If students need help . . . Point out that the *Titanic* began its voyage on April 10 (line 113). Bride picked up the message on the fourth day of the voyage (line 140).

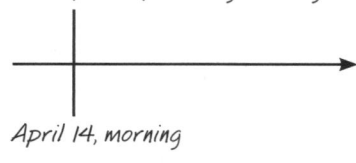

Bride picks up iceberg warning.

April 14, morning

At noon on Wednesday, April 10, the *Titanic* cast off. The whistles on her huge funnels were the biggest ever made. As she began her journey to the sea, they were heard for miles around.

Moving majestically down the River Test,[8] and watched by a crowd that had turned out for the occasion, the *Titanic* slowly passed two ships tied up to a dock. All of a sudden, the mooring ropes holding the passenger liner *New York* snapped with a series of sharp cracks like fireworks going
120 off. The enormous pull created by the *Titanic* moving past her had broken the *New York's* ropes and was now drawing her stern toward the *Titanic.* Jack Thayer watched in horror as the two ships came closer and closer. "It looked as though there surely would be a collision," he later wrote. "Her stern could not have been more than a yard or two from our side. It almost hit us." At the last moment, some quick action by Captain Smith and a tugboat captain nearby allowed the *Titanic* to slide past with only inches to spare.

It was not a good sign. Did it mean that the *Titanic* might be too big a ship to handle safely? Those who knew about the sea thought that such
130 a close call at the beginning of a maiden voyage was a very bad omen. **F**

Jack Phillips, the first wireless operator on the *Titanic,* quickly jotted down the message coming in over his headphones. "It's another iceberg warning," he said wearily to his young assistant, Harold Bride. "You'd better take it up to the bridge." Both men had been at work for hours in the *Titanic's* radio room, trying to get caught up in sending out a large number of personal messages. In 1912, passengers on ocean liners thought it was a real **novelty** to send postcard-style messages to friends at home from the middle of the Atlantic.

Bride picked up the iceberg message and stepped out onto the boat deck.
140 It was a sunny but cold Sunday morning, the fourth day of the *Titanic's* maiden voyage. The ship was steaming at full speed across a calm sea. Harold Bride was quite pleased with himself at having landed a job on such a magnificent new ship. After all, he was only twenty-two years old and had just nine months' experience at operating a "wireless set," as a ship's radio was then called. As he entered the bridge area, he could see one of the crewmen standing behind the ship's wheel steering her course toward New York. **G**

Captain Smith was on duty in the bridge, so Bride handed the message to him. "It's from the *Caronia,*[9] sir. She's reporting icebergs and pack ice ahead." The captain thanked him, read the message, and then posted
150 it on the bulletin board for other officers on watch to read. On his way

---

8. **the River Test:** a river flowing into the English Channel at Southampton, the city in England from which the *Titanic* set sail.

9. *Caronia* (kə-rō'nē-ə).

SCIENCE CONNECTION

An important technological advancement used on the *Titanic* was the wireless. A wireless telegraph is a machine used for transmitting and receiving messages.

F SUSPENSE
Reread lines 116–130. How does the author use **foreshadowing** to create suspense?

novelty (nŏv'əl-tē) *n.* something new, original, or unusual

G CHRONOLOGICAL ORDER
Reread lines 139–141. What day does Bride pick up the iceberg warning from the operator? Begin your timeline by recording this event. As you read on, record each major event that follows.

DIFFERENTIATED INSTRUCTION

FOR LESS–PROFICIENT READERS

Review: Suspense Write *suspense* on the board. Ask students what words, feelings, and examples (stories or movies) they associate with this word. Create a word web with their responses. If necessary, use the word in context.

In that movie the suspense was almost unbearable! I wanted to know what would happen next, but I was also a little scared to find out.

Develop a definition of *suspense*, such as "a feeling of wanting to know what will happen next."

Harold Bride

Illustration © Ken Marschall, from *On Board the Titanic*, a Hyperion/Madison Press Book.

back to the radio room, Bride thought the captain had seemed quite unconcerned by the message. But then again, he had been told that it was not unusual to have ice floating in the sea lanes during an April crossing. Besides, what danger could a few pieces of ice present to an unsinkable ship?

Elsewhere on board, passengers relaxed on deck chairs, reading or taking naps. Some played cards, some wrote letters, while others chatted with friends. As it was Sunday, church services had been held in the morning, the first-class service led by Captain Smith. Jack Thayer spent most of the day walking about the decks getting some fresh air with his parents.

160 Two more ice warnings were received from nearby ships around lunch time. In the chaos of the radio room, Harold Bride only had time to take one of them to the bridge. The rest of the day passed quietly. Then, in the late afternoon, the temperature began to drop rapidly. Darkness approached as the bugle call announced dinner.

Jack Thayer's parents had been invited to a special dinner for Captain Smith, so Jack ate alone in the first-class dining room. After dinner, as he was having a cup of coffee, he was joined by Milton Long, another passenger going home to the States. Long was older than Jack, but in the easy-going atmosphere of shipboard travel, they struck up a conversation

170 and talked together for an hour or so. **H**

At 7:30 P.M., the radio room received three more warnings of ice about fifty miles ahead. One of them was from the steamer *Californian* reporting three large icebergs. Harold Bride took this message up to the bridge, and it was again politely received. Captain Smith was attending the dinner party being held for him when the warning was delivered. He never got

H CHRONOLOGICAL ORDER
Reread lines 160–170. About how much time passes between these iceberg warnings and Jack's conversation?

EXPLORING THE *TITANIC* **107**

ANALYZE VISUALS

Activity Ask students how the illustration helps build suspense. *Possible answer: The* Titanic *is shown moving through an ice field on a very dark night. The painting shows how difficult it would be to spot one of these icebergs in time to avoid hitting it.*

Lines 139–154
REINFORCE *KEY IDEA:* DISASTER

Discuss The radio operators and other workers on the *Titanic* do not seem concerned about how "a few pieces of ice" could harm the "unsinkable" ship. How could this attitude make a **disaster** worse? *Possible answer: Because they are not especially concerned, they might not be prepared for the possibility of a disaster. Lack of concern may also cause them to overlook signs of danger.*

READING SKILL

H CHRONOLOGICAL ORDER

Possible answer: About six or seven hours passed.

Students may add these events to their timelines:

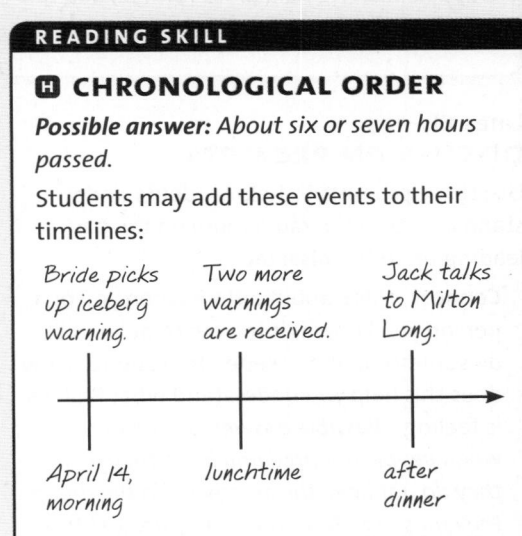

Bride picks up iceberg warning.

Two more warnings are received.

Jack talks to Milton Long.

April 14, morning

lunchtime

after dinner

FOR ENGLISH LEARNERS
Vocabulary: Prefixes

1. Point out the words *unconcerned* (line 152), *unusual* (line 153), and *unsinkable* (line 154). Explain that their common prefix *un-* means "not." Discuss how these words are used to show that there does not seem to be much worry among the ships' workers about the iceberg reports.

2. Form mixed language-ability pairs. Ask students to brainstorm other words that use the prefix *un-*. Then ask them to take apart each word by separating the prefix, the base word, and any suffix. Discuss how understanding the meaning of the word parts can help them understand the meaning of the whole word.

FOR ADVANCED LEARNERS/PRE–AP

Compare and Contrast Setting Have pairs of students discuss the contrast in setting between the radio room (lines 131–136) and the deck (lines 155–159). Challenge them to imagine another setting where workers and vacationers could be near one another yet have very different experiences. Ask them to jot down details for these settings:

- Dining room: *music, nice chairs, air conditioning*
- Kitchen: *yelling, running around, hot ovens*

① NARRATIVE NONFICTION

Possible answer: The images and feelings Jack Thayer recalls help readers imagine how carefree it felt on deck that night.

Images
- *no moon (line 183)*
- *sparkling stars (line 184)*

Feelings
- *cold (line 182)*
- *glad to be alive (line 185)*

① SUSPENSE

Possible answer: Details about the operators' exhaustion (lines 187–189), their dismissal of the final ice warning (lines 189–191), and the Californian's *being trapped in an ice field (lines 191–192) add to a feeling of dread.*

Lines 187–197
DISCUSSION PROMPTS

Use these prompts to help students understand events in the radio room on the day leading up to the **disaster**:

Connect Think about a time when you or a person you know felt too overwhelmed to do something that needed to be done. How does this help you understand what Phillips is feeling? *Possible answer: Sometimes, when people are tired and busy, they feel they do not have the energy to do the things they must do. Sometimes they are just too tired to care.*

Analyze What factors probably contribute to the way Phillips responds to the message from the* Californian*? *Possible answer: Phillips is working alone. He feels tired, busy, and overwhelmed.*

Synthesize Do you think Bride and Phillips played a role in the disaster? Why or why not? *Possible answers: Yes, because they were too tired and too busy to fulfill the responsibilities of their jobs. No, because they could not control the fact that the icebergs were there, and they were not responsible for steering the ship.*

to see it. Then, around 9:00 P.M., the captain excused himself and went up to the bridge. He and his officers talked about how difficult it was to spot icebergs on a calm, clear, moonless night like this with no wind to kick up white surf around them. Before going to bed, the captain ordered
180 the lookouts to keep a sharp watch for ice.

After trading travel stories with Milton Long, Jack Thayer put on his coat and walked around the deck. "It had become very much colder," he said later. "It was a brilliant, starry night. There was no moon, and I have never seen the stars shine brighter . . . sparkling like diamonds. . . . It was the kind of night that made one feel glad to be alive." At eleven o'clock, he went below to his cabin, put on his pajamas, and got ready for bed. ①

In the radio room, Harold Bride was exhausted. The two operators were expected to keep the radio working twenty-four hours a day, and Bride lay down to take a much-needed nap. Phillips was so busy with
190 the passenger messages that he actually brushed off the final ice warning of the night. It was from the *Californian*. Trapped in a field of ice, she had stopped for the night about nineteen miles north of the *Titanic*. She was so close that the message literally blasted in Phillips's ears. Annoyed by the loud interruption, he cut off the *Californian*'s radio operator with the words, "Shut up, shut up. I'm busy."

The radio room had received a total of seven ice warning messages in one day. It was quite clear that floating icebergs lay ahead of the *Titanic*. ①

High up in the crow's nest on the forward mast, Fred Fleet had passed a quiet watch. It was now 11:40 P.M., and he and his fellow lookout were
200 waiting to be relieved so they could head below, perhaps for a hot drink before hopping into their warm bunks. The sea was dead calm. The air was bitterly cold.

Suddenly, Fleet saw something. A huge, dark shape loomed out of the night directly ahead of the *Titanic*. An iceberg! He quickly sounded the alarm bell three times and picked up the telephone.

Illustration by Ken Marschall © 1992 from *Titanic: An Illustrated History*. Hyperion/Madison Press Books.

① NARRATIVE NONFICTION
How does the inclusion of **primary source material**—Jack Thayer's firsthand observation—help you better understand what it must have been like on the ship that night?

① SUSPENSE
Reread lines 187–197. What details in these lines create a sense of worry and dread?

"What did you see?" asked the duty officer.

"Iceberg right ahead," replied Fleet.

Immediately, the officer on the bridge ordered the wheel turned as far as it would go. The engine room was told to reverse the engines, while 210 a button was pushed to close the doors to the watertight compartments in the bottom of the ship.

The lookouts in the crow's nest braced themselves for a collision. Slowly the ship started to turn. It looked as though they would miss it. But it was too late. They had avoided a head-on crash, but the iceberg had struck a glancing blow along the *Titanic*'s starboard bow. Several tons of ice fell on the ship's decks as the iceberg brushed along the side of the ship and passed into the night. A few minutes later, the *Titanic* came to a stop. **K**

Many of the passengers didn't know the ship had hit anything. Because it was so cold, almost everyone was inside, and most people had already gone 220 to bed. Ruth Becker and her mother were awakened by the dead silence. They could no longer hear the soothing hum of the vibrating engines from below. Jack Thayer was about to step into bed when he felt himself sway ever so slightly. The engines stopped. He was startled by the sudden quiet.

Sensing trouble, Ruth's mother looked out of the door of their second-class cabin and asked a steward[10] what had happened. He told her that nothing was the matter, so Mrs. Becker went back to bed. But as she lay there, she couldn't help feeling that something was very wrong.

Jack heard running feet and voices in the hallway outside his first-class cabin. "I hurried into my heavy overcoat and drew on my slippers. All 230 excited, but not thinking anything serious had occurred, I called in to my father and mother that I was going up on deck to see the fun."

On deck, Jack watched some third-class passengers playing with the ice that had landed on the forward deck as the iceberg had brushed by. Some people were throwing chunks at each other, while a few skidded about playing football with pieces of ice.

Down in the very bottom of the ship, things were very different. When the iceberg had struck, there had been a noise like a big gun going off in one of the boiler rooms. A couple of stokers[11] had been immediately hit by a jet of icy water. The noise and the shock of cold water had sent them 240 running for safety. **L**

Twenty minutes after the crash, things looked very bad indeed to Captain Smith. He and the ship's builder, Thomas Andrews, had made a rapid tour below decks to inspect the damage. The mail room was filling up with water, and sacks of mail were floating about. Water was also pouring into some of the forward holds and two of the boiler rooms.

---

10. **steward:** a worker on a ship who attends to the needs of the passengers.

11. **stokers:** workers who tended the boilers that powered steamships.

B Targeted Passage

K CHRONOLOGICAL ORDER
What is the time order of the events that happen after Fleet spots the iceberg? Record the events on your timeline.

L NARRATIVE NONFICTION
In lines 218–240 the author describes how the passengers react after the collision. **Compare and contrast** the responses of the passengers and the workers in different areas of the ship.

READING SKILL

K CHRONOLOGICAL ORDER
Possible answer:
- *11:40 P.M.—Fleet spots the iceberg.*
- *The officer orders the wheel turned.*
- *The engine room is told to reverse the engines and a button is pushed to close doors in the bottom of the ship.*
- *The ship turns.*
- *The ship hits the iceberg.*
- *Ice falls on the ship's decks.*
- *The* Titanic *comes to a stop.*

Lines 212–215
REINFORCE *KEY IDEA*: DISASTER

Discuss The *Titanic*'s collision with an iceberg sets the **disaster** in motion. Could this event have been avoided? *Possible answer: If the ship had turned more quickly, the collision— and the disaster—might have been avoided. However, the lookout reported the iceberg as soon as he saw it (lines 204–205), and the officer on the bridge reacted immediately. The crew could have been better prepared if they had paid attention to the warnings all day.*

LITERARY ANALYSIS

L NARRATIVE NONFICTION
Record students' answers in a chart.
Possible answer:

Passengers Upstairs	Workers Downstairs
did not feel the collision	felt the collision
calm, most unconcerned	panicked
sleeping	running for safety

DIFFERENTIATED INSTRUCTION

FOR LESS-PROFICIENT READERS

B Targeted Passage [Lines 206–223]

This passage describes a turning point in the narrative: the moment at which the *Titanic* collides with an iceberg.
- Where does Fleet see the iceberg?
- How does the crew try to avoid a disaster?
- How does the ship run into the iceberg?
- Why do many passengers not know about the collision right away?

FOR ENGLISH LEARNERS

Language: Phrasal Verbs Explain that *brush off* (line 190) means "to ignore", whereas *brush along* (line 216) and *brush by* (line 233) mean "to touch lightly." Assign pairs other words to look up in a dictionary and have them share their definitions: *cast off* (line 113), *turn out* (line 117), *kick up* (lines 178–179), *cut off* (line 194), *put on* (line 276), and *hung on* (line 382).

FOR ADVANCED LEARNERS/PRE-AP

Analyze Mood Have pairs of students read lines 181–202 and discuss these questions:
- How would you describe the feeling the author creates in this passage?
- What words and phrases create this feeling?
- How would the excerpt be different without these four paragraphs and the mood the paragraphs create?

Ⓜ NARRATIVE NONFICTION

Possible answer: *The people aboard the ship face two conflicts. They are struggling against nature—an external force—as the ship sinks into the ocean. They also face internal conflict, and must decide whether or not to remain on the ship.*

Lines 246–253
REINFORCE *KEY IDEA:*
DISASTER

Discuss If the *Titanic* has been described as unsinkable, why does flooding threaten to make the ship sink? What could other ship builders learn from this **disaster**? *Possible answer: Only some of the ship's compartments are watertight. When the other compartments flood, the ship will sink. To avoid this, other ship builders could make ships that have more watertight compartments.*

Ⓝ MAKE INFERENCES

Possible answer: *He probably felt shocked and guilty. He had thought the ship was unsinkable, but this disaster revealed a flaw in his design. Now many people's lives were at risk.*

Extend the Discussion Why do you think Thomas Andrews spoke "in a low voice"? If you were Thomas Andrews, with whom would you have shared this information, and how?

Captain Smith knew that the *Titanic*'s hull was divided into a number of watertight compartments. She had been designed so that she could still float if only the first four compartments were flooded, but not any more than that. But water was pouring into the first five compartments. And when the water filled them, it would spill over into the next compartment. One by one all the remaining compartments would flood, and the ship would eventually sink. Andrews told the captain that the ship could last an hour, an hour and a half at the most. Ⓜ

Harold Bride had just awakened in the radio room when Captain Smith stuck his head in the door. "Send the call for assistance," he ordered.

"What call should I send?" Phillips asked.

"The regulation international call for help. Just that." Then the captain was gone. Phillips began to send the Morse code[12] "CQD" distress call, flashing away and joking as he did it. After all, they knew the ship was unsinkable.

Five minutes later, the captain was back. "What are you sending?" he asked.

"CQD," Phillips answered. Then Bride cut in and suggested that they try the new SOS[13] signal that was just coming into use. They began to send out the new international call for help—it was one of the first SOS calls ever sent out from a ship in distress.

Ruth and her family had stayed in their bunks for a good fifteen minutes or so after the room steward had told them nothing was wrong. But Ruth's mother couldn't stop worrying as she heard the sound of running feet and shouting voices in the hallway. Poking her head out of the cabin, she found a steward and asked what the matter was.

"Put on your things and come at once," said the steward.

"Do we have time to dress?" she asked.

"No, madam. You have time for nothing. Put on your life jackets and come up to the top deck."

Ruth helped her mother dress the children quickly. But they only had time to throw their coats over their nightgowns and put on their shoes and stockings. In their rush, they forgot to put on their life jackets.

Just after midnight, Captain Smith ordered the lifeboats uncovered. The ship's squash court, which was thirty-two feet above the keel,[14] was now completely flooded. Jack Thayer and his father came into the first-class lounge to try to find out exactly what the matter was. When Thomas Andrews, the ship's builder, passed by, Mr. Thayer asked him what was going on. He replied in a low voice that the ship had not much more than an hour to live. Jack and his father couldn't believe their ears. Ⓝ

Ⓜ NARRATIVE NONFICTION
What **conflict** do the people aboard the ship now face?

Ⓝ MAKE INFERENCES
What can you infer about how Thomas Andrews, the ship's builder, might have felt as he passed through the passenger lounge?

---

12. **Morse code:** a system used in wireless telegraphy in which numbers and letters are represented by sets of long and short sounds or flashes of light.

13. **CQD ... SOS:** standard international distress calls used by ships at sea.

14. **keel:** the main timber or steel piece that extends the whole length of the bottom of a ship.

DIFFERENTIATED INSTRUCTION

FOR LESS–PROFICIENT READERS

Review: Make Inferences Remind students that making an inference means using information from the text plus what they already know to draw a conclusion. Their background knowledge might come from other reading or from personal experience. Use a Making Inferences chart to lead students through the process of inferring Thomas Andrews's feelings in this situation.

🧰 BEST PRACTICES TOOLKIT—Transparency
Making Inferences p. A13

Detail from Excerpt:		What I Know:		My Inference:
• Andrews built the ship (line 282). • The ship is sinking (lines 283–284).	+	People feel responsible for things they have made.	=	Andrews must feel guilty that the ship is sinking.

FOR ADVANCED LEARNERS/PRE–AP

Evaluate Have students work in small groups to discuss Captain Smith's behavior in the radio room (lines 254–258). When he told Bride and Phillips to send the call for assistance, should he also have told them the ship was sinking? How might this information have affected Bride and Phillips? Why might the captain have chosen not to share this information with them?

This telegraph message was sent by Bride and Phillips as a call for help.

Illustration © Ken Marschall from *Titanic, an Illustrated History*, a Hyperion/Madison Press Book.

From the bridge of the *Titanic*, a ship's lights were observed not far away, possibly the *Californian*'s. Captain Smith then ordered white distress rockets fired to get the attention of the nearby ship. They burst high in the air with a loud boom and a shower of stars. But the rockets made no difference. The mystery ship in the distance never answered.

290   In the radio room, Bride and Phillips now knew how serious the accident was and were **feverishly** sending out calls for help. A number of ships heard and responded to their calls, but most were too far away to come to the rescue in time. The closest ship they had been able to reach was the *Carpathia*,[15] about fifty-eight miles away. Immediately, the *Carpathia* reported that she was racing full steam to the rescue. But could she get there in time? ◎

Not far away, the radio operator of the *Californian* had gone to bed for the night and turned off his radio. Several officers and crewmen on the deck of the *Californian* saw rockets in the distance and reported them
300 to their captain. The captain told them to try to contact the ship with a Morse lamp. But they received no answer to their flashed calls. No one thought to wake up the radio operator. ℗

On board the *Titanic*, almost an hour after the crash, most of the passengers still did not realize the seriousness of the situation. But Captain Smith was a very worried man. He knew that the *Titanic* only carried lifeboats for barely half the estimated twenty-two hundred people on board. He would have to make sure his officers kept order to avoid any panic among the passengers. At 12:30 Captain Smith gave the orders

feverishly
(fē'vər-ĭsh-lē) *adv.* in a way marked by intense emotion or activity

④ **Targeted Passage**

◎ **SUSPENSE**
Given what you already know about the *Titanic*, what details help create suspense?

℗ **CHRONOLOGICAL ORDER**
Record the *Californian*'s response on your timeline. At this point, how might disaster still have been minimized?

15. *Carpathia* (kär-pā'thē-ə).

FOR LESS–PROFICIENT READERS

④ **Targeted Passage [Lines 290–307]**

This passage builds suspense by describing the crew's response to the disaster and by clarifying the shortage of lifeboats.

- What do the radio operators do when they realize the *Titanic* is sinking fast?
- How does the *Carpathia* respond? How does the *Californian* respond?
- Why is Captain Smith worried about the lifeboats?

FOR ENGLISH LEARNERS

Language: Conversational English Patterns
Read aloud these bits of dialogue: "Send the call" (line 255) and "Put on your things" (line 271). Explain that in an English command (or imperative), the subject is usually not stated. Read aloud other dialogue on pages 110 and 113 and ask the students to identify the commands. Ask students how commands are stated in other languages (e.g., for the *tú* command in Spanish, the verb is usually third person).

Activity Ask students to examine the art on this page closely. What details from pages 110–112 of the excerpt are reflected in the art?
Possible answer:

- *People in lifeboats are wearing life jackets (lines 273–274).*
- *The ship's bow is sinking (lines 309–310).*
- *People are being loaded into lifeboats in a calm, orderly way (lines 316–317).*
- *Some women in the closest lifeboat wear fancy hats, suggesting they are first- or second-class passengers (lines 342–344).*
- *The telegraph has nearly the same message quoted in lines 348–349.*

LITERARY ANALYSIS: *Review*

◎ **SUSPENSE**

Possible answer: Readers already know that there are not enough lifeboats for all the passengers (lines 7–10), and that the Titanic *will sink in a little over an hour (lines 283–284). These details build suspense about what will happen as the disaster unfolds:*

- *There is another ship close by, and the* Titanic *has fired distress rockets (lines 285–287).*
- *Bride and Phillips are sending out calls for help (lines 290–291).*
- *The* Carpathia *is 58 miles away and is speeding to the scene (lines 293–295).*

READING SKILL

℗ **CHRONOLOGICAL ORDER**

Possible answer: If someone on the Californian *had decided to turn on the radio, the ship could have received the* Titanic's *distress calls and come to the rescue in time to save lives.*

DISCUSSION PROMPTS

Use these prompts to help students understand how the *Titanic's* passengers reacted shortly after the collision:

Connect Think about a time when you or a person you know strongly believed in something. How does this help you understand the passengers' reluctance to leave the sinking ship? ***Possible answer:*** *Sometimes, when people are convinced that what they believe is true, it is hard to accept any other alternative—especially a negative one.*

Speculate What effects may the musicians' "lively tunes" have had on the passengers? ***Possible answer:*** *The music made the night feel like a party, and may have falsely assured people that there was no cause for alarm.*

Evaluate Was Captain Smith's resolve to keep order and avoid panic in the passengers' best interest? Why or why not? ***Possible answers:*** *Yes, because the lifeboats were able to launch without much chaos. No, because people did not realize how serious the situation was until too late.*

LITERARY ANALYSIS

Q NARRATIVE NONFICTION

Possible answer: The main conflict is external, between people and nature. This scene shows, however, that people also struggled among themselves. Mrs. Becker's internal resolve not to leave her children leads her to plead with the crew.

READING SKILL: *Review*

R MAKE INFERENCES

Possible answer: Since there are lifeboats for only about half of the people on board, those who got on deck last probably found there were no lifeboats left.

---

to start loading the lifeboats—women and children first. Even though
310 the *Titanic* was by now quite noticeably down at the bow and listing[16] slightly to one side, many passengers still didn't want to leave the huge, brightly lit ship. The ship's band added to a kind of party feeling as the musicians played lively tunes.

About 12:45 the first lifeboat was lowered. It could carry sixty-five people, but left with only twenty-eight aboard. Indeed, many of the first boats to leave were half empty. Ruth Becker noticed that there was no panic among the crowds of passengers milling about on the decks. "Everything was calm, everybody was orderly." But the night air was now biting cold. Ruth's mother told her to go back to their cabin to get some
320 blankets. Ruth hurried down to the cabin and came back with several blankets in her arms. The Beckers walked toward one of the lifeboats, and a sailor picked up Ruth's brother and sister and placed them in the boat.

"That's all for this boat," he called out. "Lower away!"

"Please, those are my children!" cried Ruth's mother. "Let me go with them!" **Q**

The sailor allowed Mrs. Becker to step into the lifeboat with her two children. She then called back to Ruth to get into another lifeboat. Ruth went to the next boat and asked the officer if she could get in. He said, "Sure," picked her up, and dumped her in.

330 Boat No. 13 was so crowded that Ruth had to stand up. Foot by foot it was lowered down the steep side of the massive ship. The new pulleys shrieked as the ropes passed through them, creaking under the weight of the boat and its load of sixty-four people. After landing in the water, Ruth's lifeboat began to drift. Suddenly Ruth saw another lifeboat coming down right on top of them! Fearing for their lives, the men in charge of her boat shouted, "Stop!" to the sailors up on the deck. But the noise was so great that nobody noticed. The second lifeboat kept coming down, so close that they could actually touch the bottom of it. All of a sudden, one of the men in Ruth's boat jumped up, pulled out a knife, and cut them
340 free of their lowering ropes. Ruth's boat pushed away from the *Titanic* just as boat No. 15 hit the water inches away from them.

Below, in the third-class decks of the ship, there was much more confusion and alarm. Most of these passengers had not yet been able to get above decks. Some of those who did finally make it out had to break down the barriers between third and first class. **R**

By 1:30 the bow was well down, and people were beginning to notice the slant of the decks. In the radio room, Bride and Phillips were still desperately sending out calls for help: "We are sinking fast . . . women and children in boats. We cannot last much longer." The radio signal

---

16. **listing:** tilting; leaning.

Q NARRATIVE NONFICTION
How does Ruth's mother's pleading with the sailor add to the **conflict?**

R MAKE INFERENCES
Given the lifeboat situation, what do delays in getting above decks mean for the third-class passengers?

DIFFERENTIATED INSTRUCTION

FOR LESS–PROFICIENT READERS

Reading Skill Follow-Up: Chronological Order
Have students create a timeline of Ruth's escape from the boat that begins with Ruth's mother telling her to go get blankets (lines 319–320). Then have the students explain the chronology in their own words, using words that show time order (such as *first, then, next, after that,* and *finally*).

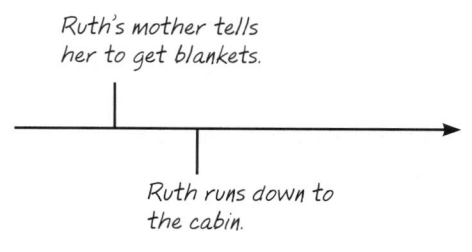

Ruth's mother tells her to get blankets.

Ruth runs down to the cabin.

🧰 BEST PRACTICES TOOLKIT—Transparency
Timeline p. B23

Illustration © Ken Marschall from *Titanic, an Illustrated History*, a Hyperion/Madison Press Book.

350 gradually got weaker and weaker as the ship's power faded out. Out on the decks, most passengers now began to move toward the stern[17] area, which was slowly lifting out of the water.

By 2:05 there were still over 1,500 people left on the sinking ship. All the lifeboats were now away, and a strange stillness took hold. People stood quietly on the upper decks, bunching together for warmth, trying to keep away from the side of the tilting ship.

Captain Smith now made his way to the radio room and told Harold Bride and Jack Phillips to save themselves. "Men, you have done your full duty," he told them. "You can do no more. Abandon your cabin. Now it's 360 every man for himself." Phillips kept working the radio, hanging on until the very last moment. Suddenly Bride heard water gurgling up the deck outside the radio room. Phillips heard it, too, and cried, "Come on, let's clear out."

Near the stern, Father Thomas Byles had heard confession and given absolution[18] to over one hundred passengers. Playing to the very end, the members of the ship's brave band finally had to put down their instruments and try to save themselves. In desperation, some of the passengers and crew began to jump overboard as the water crept up the slant of the deck. ⑤

⑤ NARRATIVE NONFICTION
Recall the **conflict** you identified on page 110. How do the various people on the ship respond to the conflict?

---

17. **stern:** the rear end of the ship.

18. **heard confession . . . absolution:** Father Byles had conducted a Roman Catholic religious ceremony in which a priest listens to people confess their sins and then declares them forgiven.

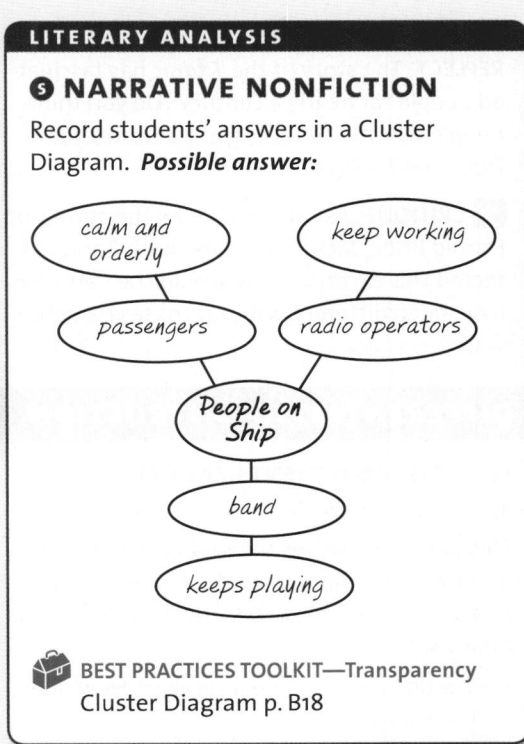

Jack Thayer stood with his friend Milton Long at the railing to keep
370 away from the crowds. He had become separated from his father in
the confusion on deck. Now Jack and his friend heard muffled thuds
and explosions deep within the ship. Suddenly the *Titanic* began to slide
into the water. The water rushed up at them. Thayer and Long quickly
said goodbye and good luck to each other. Then they both jumped.

As he hit the water, Jack Thayer was sucked down. "The cold was
terrific. The shock of the water took the breath out of my lungs. Down
and down I went, spinning in all directions." When he finally surfaced,
gasping for air and numbed by the water, the ship was about forty feet
away from him. His friend Milton Long was nowhere to be seen. Jack
380 would never see him again.

Jack Thayer was lucky. As he struggled in the water, his hand came
to rest on an overturned lifeboat. He grabbed hold and hung on, barely
managing to pull himself up out of the water. Harold Bride had been
washed overboard and now also clung to this same boat.

Both Jack and Harold witnessed the mighty ship's last desperate
moments. "We could see groups of . . . people aboard, clinging in clusters
or bunches, like swarming bees; only to fall in masses, pairs, or singly,
as the great part of the ship . . . rose into the sky. . . ." said Thayer.
"I looked upwards—we were right under the three enormous propellers.
390 For an instant, I thought they were sure to come right down on top of us.
Then . . . she slid quietly away from us into the sea."

Out in the safety of her lifeboat, Ruth Becker also witnessed the end
of the *Titanic*. "I could look back and see this ship, and the decks were
just lined with people looking over. Finally, as the *Titanic* sank faster,
the lights died out. You could just see the stern remaining in an upright
position for a couple of minutes. Then . . . it disappeared."

⑤ Targeted Passage

Then, as Ruth recalled, "there fell upon the ear the most terrible noise
that human beings ever listened to—the cries of hundreds of people
struggling in the icy cold water, crying for help with a cry we knew could
400 not be answered." In Thayer's words, they became "a long continuous
wailing chant." Before long this **ghastly** wailing stopped, as the freezing
water took its toll.[19] **❼**

Jack Thayer and Harold Bride and a number of other survivors clung
to their overturned lifeboat, inches away from an icy death in the North
Atlantic. Numb from the cold and not daring to move in case the boat
sank under their weight, they prayed and waited for help. Then, as the
first light of dawn crept on the horizon, a rocket was seen in the distance.
The *Carpathia* had come to their rescue. ❧

ghastly (găst′lē) *adj.*
terrifyingly horrible

**❼ NARRATIVE
NONFICTION**
Reread lines 385–402
and decide which
quotation is most
memorable. Why
do you think so?

---

19. **took its toll:** claimed passengers' lives.

LITERARY ANALYSIS

❼ NARRATIVE NONFICTION

*Students should provide logical reasons as
to why their chosen quotations are memorable. Reasons might include the emotional
impact of a quotation or the mental image
it creates.*

SELECTION WRAP–UP

REFLECT The story of the *Titanic* has fascinated people for nearly a century. Do you think
people will still be talking about it 100 years
from now? Why?

★ **CRITIQUE** Ask students how the stories of
Harold Bride, Jack Thayer, and Ruth Becker affected this excerpt. How would the narrative
have been different without these characters?

DIFFERENTIATED INSTRUCTION

FOR LESS–PROFICIENT READERS
⑤ Targeted Passage [Lines 381–396]

This passage resolves the main conflict in the
narrative, describing how the featured characters survive the shipwreck and how the *Titanic*
finally sinks.

- How do Jack and Harold survive? How does
  Ruth survive?
- What happens to the people who are still on
  board the *Titanic*?
- What event do Jack and Ruth witness?

Note Sensory Details Have students take Sensory Notes to help them pay close attention to
the details of the shipwreck.

Most Important Image or Thought

I see . . . ship disappearing

I hear . . . people wailing

I feel . . . cold and scared

I think . . . Will they be rescued?

 **BEST PRACTICES TOOLKIT—Transparency**
Sensory Notes p. B9

FOR ADVANCED LEARNERS/PRE–AP
Analyze Use of Source Material The sinking
of the *Titanic* is described entirely through
quotations from source material. Discuss what
effect this has on the reader, and how the effect would have been different if the author
had simply described the sinking. Have pairs of
students write an imaginary eyewitness report
of the sinking. Invite volunteers to share their
reports with the class.

Comprehension

1. **Recall** Why was Captain Smith given command of the *Titanic*?

2. **Recall** What kinds of accommodations did the ship have for first-class, second-class, and third-class passengers?

3. **Summarize** What safety precautions did Captain Smith and other crew members take before and after the collision?

Literary Analysis

4. **Understand Chronological Order** Using the timeline you made as you read and other information in the selection, determine about how much time passed between the ship's hitting the iceberg and the survivors' being rescued.

5. **Make Inferences** Harold Bride and Captain Smith both received iceberg warnings before the *Titanic* sank. Use a graphic organizer like the one shown to note how they reacted to the warnings and why they might have reacted the way they did.

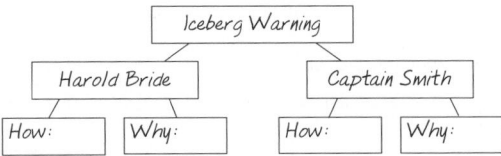

Iceberg Warning → Harold Bride (How: / Why:) — Captain Smith (How: / Why:)

6. **Identify Cause and Effect** Events are often related by cause and effect— that is, one event brings about another. Referring to your timeline, note which events caused others to happen.

7. **Evaluate Narrative Nonfiction** Ballard could have written his account as a piece of informational text, presenting just the facts of what happened the day the *Titanic* sank. Instead he wrote a piece of narrative nonfiction; he added **foreshadowing** and **suspense,** and he included the words and experiences of people on the ship. In your opinion, is Ballard's telling an effective way of involving readers in the story? Explain your answer.

Extension and Challenge

8. **Readers' Circle** The sinking of the *Titanic* has inspired many movies and books. In a group, discuss why this **disaster** lends itself to storytelling. Find details in the selection to support your views.

TITANIC

MARYLAND OBJECTIVES

READING STANDARD
1.E.3.a Select and apply appropriate strategies during reading

---

Practice and Apply

After Reading

For additional support of post-reading questions, use these copy masters:

R RESOURCE MANAGER—Copy Masters
Reading Check p. 140 (to check understanding of the selection)
Narrative Nonfiction p. 133 (for practice of literary analysis standards focus)
Question Support p. 141 (**After Reading** questions adapted for English learners and less-proficient readers)

Additional selection questions are provided for teachers on page 127.

ANSWERS

Comprehension

1. *Captain Smith was the senior captain of the White Star Line. He was a popular leader with an excellent safety record. This was to be his last trip before retirement.*

2. *The ship had luxurious first-class accommodations, new and spacious second-class accommodations, and new but crowded third-class accommodations.*

3. *The operators gave Captain Smith some (but not all) of the iceberg warnings. Smith posted them but seemed unconcerned. Before going to bed, he asked others to keep watch. A lookout saw an iceberg, and crew members responded quickly, but the ship could not turn fast enough to avoid a collision. After the collision, the radio operators frantically sent out SOS calls. The captain and crew tried to ensure a calm and orderly evacuation, despite lacking enough lifeboats for all on board.*

Literary Analysis

Possible answers:

4. ■ **STANDARDS FOCUS** *Use Chronological Order The iceberg was hit at about midnight and the survivors were rescued at dawn, so five or six hours passed.*

5. **Bride—How:** *didn't take all the warnings to the bridge;* **Why:** *He was tired and busy from handling passengers' requests. He also believed the ship was unsinkable.*
Smith—How: *posted the first warning, but seemed unconcerned;* **Why:** *He was busy socializing with passengers and he, too, believed the ship was unsinkable.*

---

6. *After ignoring some warnings, the ship hit an iceberg, which caused water to flow into compartments in the hull of the ship. This caused the ship to sink.*

7. ● **STANDARDS FOCUS** *Narrative Nonfiction Literary elements such as plot, setting, foreshadowing, and suspense effectively reveal the drama of the event. The firsthand accounts and photographs Ballard uses help readers become emotionally involved and feel as if they were there.*

Extension and Challenge

8. *Students should note that the tension, fast-paced action, and crises that occur as the result of a disaster are dramatic and thus lend themselves to storytelling. The luxurious atmosphere of the Titanic and showy style of its richest passengers contribute fairy tale–like elements that would be especially interesting on film. In addition, the contrast between the wealthy passengers and the poor workers and immigrants who are on the same ship offers dramatic possibilities.*

ANSWERS
Vocabulary in Context
VOCABULARY PRACTICE

1. *(a) innovation*
2. *(c) frantically*
3. *(b) average*
4. *(b) lodging*
5. *(a) prediction*
6. *(b) endlessly*
7. *(c) terrible*
8. *(d) connected*

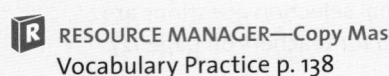 **RESOURCE MANAGER**—Copy Master
Vocabulary Practice p. 138

VOCABULARY IN WRITING

Ask students to imagine what a reporter would have said about the *Titanic*. What was most impressive? How was it different from other ships? Suggest that students brainstorm ideas in a Cluster Diagram first.

 BEST PRACTICES TOOLKIT—Transparency
Cluster Diagram p. B18

VOCABULARY STRATEGY: ANALOGIES *(also an EL language objective)*

Have students read aloud each analogy and then state the relationship between the first two words. For example, what is the relationship between *low* and *high*? (Low *means the opposite of* high.)

Answers:
1. *girl*
2. *well-known*
3. *worried*
4. *stingy*

 **RESOURCE MANAGER**—Copy Master
Vocabulary Strategy p. 139

Vocabulary Center at ClassZone.com
Additional Vocabulary Activities

Vocabulary in Context

VOCABULARY PRACTICE

Choose the letter of the word that has the same, or nearly the same, meaning as the boldfaced word.

1. an exciting **novelty**: (a) innovation, (b) discussion, (c) solution, (d) occasion
2. working **feverishly**: (a) steadily, (b) carelessly, (c) frantically, (d) sickly
3. have **moderate** success: (a) huge, (b) average, (c) surprising, (d) little
4. elegant **accommodations**: (a) clothes, (b) lodging, (c) manners, (d) jewelry
5. a disturbing **prophecy**: (a) prediction, (b) crash, (c) party, (d) curse
6. to wait **indefinitely**: (a) patiently, (b) endlessly, (c) silently, (d) anxiously
7. a **ghastly** accident: (a) traffic, (b) slight, (c) terrible, (d) funny
8. in **adjoining** rooms: (a) carpeted, (b) decorated, (c) large, (d) connected

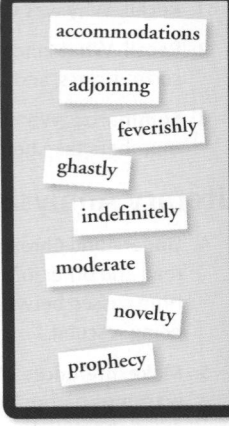

VOCABULARY IN WRITING

Use details from the selection to write a paragraph describing the *Titanic*. Include three or more vocabulary words. Below is a sample beginning.

> **EXAMPLE SENTENCE**
>
> The first-class **accommodations** on the *Titanic* were extravagant.

VOCABULARY STRATEGY: ANALOGIES

An **analogy** presents relationships between pairs of words. To complete an analogy, identify the relationship between the words in the first pair. The words in the second pair should relate to each other in the same way.

MARYLAND OBJECTIVES

READING STANDARD
1.D.2.b Explain relationships between words

- If the words in the first pair relate to each other as **antonyms** (words with opposite meanings), the words in the second pair should also relate as antonyms.
- If the words in the first pair relate to each other as **synonyms** (words with the same meaning), the words in the second pair should also relate as synonyms.

Analogies often follow the format *low : high :: wild : tame*. If the analogy is read aloud, one would say, "Low **is to** high **as** wild **is to** tame."

PRACTICE Choose a word from the box to complete each analogy.

1. man : woman :: boy : _____
2. foolish : silly :: famous : _____
3. amazed : astonished :: concerned : _____
4. freezing : boiling :: generous : _____

worried	stingy
girl	well-known

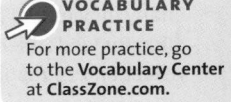
VOCABULARY PRACTICE
For more practice, go to the **Vocabulary Center** at **ClassZone.com**.

DIFFERENTIATED INSTRUCTION

OR LESS PROICIENT READERS

Comprehension Support: Analogies Ask students to think of two pairs of antonyms or two pairs of synonyms. First model the process for them.

1. Write a sentence that states the relationship between the pairs of words. Hot *is the opposite of* cold, *just as* clean *is the opposite of* dirty.
2. Rewrite the sentence in analogy format. HOT : COLD :: CLEAN : DIRTY

OR ADVANCED LEARNERS PRE AP

Vocabulary in Writing Give students the following words that describe the *Titanic*: *famous, huge,* and *luxurious.* Have students use these to create word pairs that relate as either antonyms or synonyms. Then have students brainstorm three words about a subject in current events and use those words to create word pairs that would complete the analogies. Example: *FAMOUS : UNKNOWN :: EXTINCT : LIVING*

Reading-Writing Connection

Deepen your understanding of the excerpt from *Exploring the* Titanic by responding to these prompts. Then complete the **Grammar and Writing** exercise.

WRITING PROMPTS	SELF-CHECK
A. Short Response: Write a Description How would you describe the state of mind of the passengers and crew when the *Titanic* first set sail? Write **one paragraph,** describing how people felt that day. Include details from the selection.	*An effective description will...* • include passengers' impressions of the ship • include quotations from eye-witnesses or newspapers
B. Extended Response: Give an Evaluation What was your opinion of the behavior of the *Titanic*'s builder, captain, and crew before and during the **disaster?** Could more lives have been saved if responses to warnings or evacuation efforts had been conducted differently? Write **two or three paragraphs,** giving your evaluation.	*A convincing evaluation will...* • make a judgment about whether more lives could have been saved • give reasons and evidence why or why not

GRAMMAR AND WRITING

USE CORRECT PRONOUN CASE People often confuse the **subject** and **object cases** of personal pronouns. If a pronoun is functioning as a subject, then you should use a **subject pronoun,** such as *I, she, he, we,* or *they.* If a pronoun is functioning as an object, then you should use an **object pronoun,** such as *me, her, him, us,* or *them.* (*You* and *it* function as both subject and object pronouns.)

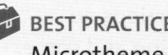

MARYLAND OBJECTIVES

LANGUAGE STANDARD
5.B.2.b Apply appropriate use of the case of pronouns

> *Original:* Him and his crew should have been more careful.
>
> *Revised:* He and his crew should have been more careful.
> (*The pronoun is a subject, so it should be* he, *not* him.)

PRACTICE Choose the correct pronouns in the following sentences.

1. The crew knew about the icebergs. The captain had warned (they, them) about the possibility of floating ice.
2. Despite everything, the crew didn't pay attention to (he, him).
3. The radio operator was especially to blame. (Him, He) and his assistant didn't pass on messages to the captain.
4. (They, Them) should've communicated better with each other.

*For more help with pronoun cases, see page R53 in the **Grammar Handbook**.*

DIFFERENTIATED INSTRUCTION

FOR LESS-PROFICIENT WRITERS

For Prompt A:

1. Identify two features of the *Titanic*.
2. Brainstorm two adjectives and two feeling words for each feature.
3. Use these words to make up two quotes from an eyewitness or a newspaper.
4. Suggest that students organize the paragraph by first describing the setting, then using the two quotes, and closing with a statement about what the journey is expected to be like.

For Prompt B:

1. Limit the length of the response to two paragraphs.
2. Use Think-Pair-Share with students to help them develop their opinions.
3. Have students work in pairs to identify their main points and review the selection for evidence.

 BEST PRACTICES TOOLKIT—Transparency
Think-Pair-Share p. A18

Reading-Writing Connection

WRITING PROMPTS

• For **Prompt A,** encourage students to reread lines 60–70 to recall how passengers felt about the ship. Ask them to imagine how the passengers would have felt on the day the long-awaited journey of the *Titanic* began.

• For **Prompt B,** have students review their timelines. Ask them at what points something could have been done differently. Before writing, ask them to complete a Microtheme that includes their opinion, their main points, and the supporting evidence.

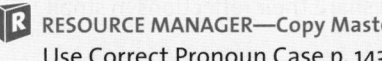 BEST PRACTICES TOOLKIT—Transparency
Microtheme p. C13

For an extended Reading-Writing Connection activity, see

🛈 Writing Center at **ClassZone.com**

GRAMMAR AND WRITING

Write these sentences on the board. Ask students to choose the correct pronoun case.

> Ballard's training as a marine geologist helps [he, him] understand the current and floor of the ocean. [He, Him] found the shipwreck of the *Titanic*. [He, Him] leads explorations that allow [he, him] to keep learning about history.

Answers:
1. *them;* **2.** *him;* **3.** *He;* **4.** *They*

📋 RESOURCE MANAGER—Copy Master
Use Correct Pronoun Case p. 143

Assess and Reteach

Assess

📋 RESOURCE MANAGER—Copy Masters
Selection Tests A, B/C pp. 145–146, 147–148

💿 Test Generator CD

Reteach

🔲 STANDARDS LESSON FILE
Reading Lesson 6: Recognizing Sequence and Chronological Order
Vocabulary Lesson 23: Analogies
Grammar Lesson 13: Pronoun Case with Compound Objects and Subjects

Focus and Motivate

OBJECTIVES

Literary Analysis
- explore the key idea of a **thrill**
- analyze and evaluate setting
- read narrative nonfiction

Reading
- understand cause-and-effect relationships

Vocabulary
- build vocabulary for reading and writing
- understand and use suffixes that form adjectives *(also an EL language objective)*

SUMMARY

In this memoir, the author describes an incident from her childhood. She and some neighborhood boys are throwing snowballs at cars. Suddenly, one of the cars stops. The driver gets out and chases the author and one of her friends for over ten blocks. He finally catches the children and yells at them, but this is anticlimactic. It is the chase itself that remains in the author's memory as one of the most exhilarating experiences of her life.

When do you feel most ALIVE?

Introduce the question to students and discuss the *KEY IDEA*. Ask students if a **thrill** can result only from doing something challenging or if people can feel a thrill looking at a beautiful sunset or hearing a favorite piece of music. Then have students complete the *QUICKWRITE* activity and share their reflections in small groups.

Selection Resources

---

from An American Childhood
Memoir by Annie Dillard

When do you feel most ALIVE?

MARYLAND OBJECTIVES

READING/LIT STANDARDS
1.E.3.a Select and apply appropriate strategies during reading
3.A.3.c Analyze setting

KEY IDEA We all have something that makes us appreciate the wonder and excitement of life. It might be a tense basketball game, a rocky roller-coaster ride, or the **thrill** of an unexpected snowstorm. The author Annie Dillard has said that nothing makes her feel alive like facing a tough challenge. This selection is about one of the most exciting challenges she ever faced.

QUICKWRITE When do you feel most alive? Reflect on this question in a journal entry. Other questions you might ask yourself are these: When do I feel the happiest? What makes me feel great about my life? When am I glad to be me? Explain your answers.

118

 **RESOURCE MANAGER UNIT 1**

Plan and Teach pp. 149–156

Literary Analysis
Summary pp. 157†*, 158‡*
Setting in Nonfiction pp. 159, 160†*
Question Support p. 167*

Reading
Recognize Cause and Effect
    pp. 161, 162†*
Reading Check p. 166
Reading Fluency p. 168

Vocabulary
Study p. 163*
Practice p. 164
Strategy p. 165

Assessment
Selection Tests A, B/C pp. 169*, 171*
Test Generator CD

BEST PRACTICES TOOLKIT

Differentiated Instruction
    pp. 31–38*

Scaffolding Instruction pp. 43–46*

Graphic Organizers/Strategies
Word Squares • Making Inferences • Draw It

Reading Support
Audio Anthology CD*

Technology
Literature and Vocabulary Centers at **ClassZone.com**

Write*Smart* CD

---

* Resources for Differentiation   † Also in Spanish   ‡ In Haitian Creole and Vietnamese

LITERARY ANALYSIS: SETTING IN NONFICTION

In the memoir you're about to read, Annie Dillard tells a true story from her childhood. The **setting,** the time and place in which events occur, is the 1950s in suburban Pittsburgh, Pennsylvania, where Dillard grew up.

As you read, look for details that help you understand and picture where the selection takes place.

We were standing up to our boot tops in snow on a front yard on trafficked Reynolds Street . . .

Then look for ways the setting affects events.

READING SKILL: RECOGNIZE CAUSE AND EFFECT

Events are often related as **cause and effect:** one event brings about the other. The event that happens first is the cause; the one that follows is the effect. Often an effect becomes the cause of another effect, forming a chain of causes and effects.

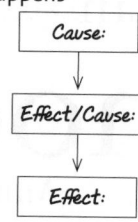

As you read "An American Childhood," record causes and effects in a chain like the one shown.

Review: **Make Inferences**

VOCABULARY IN CONTEXT

The following words help Annie Dillard tell about her exciting experience. How many of the words do you know? Create a chart like the one shown, and place each word in the appropriate column. As you read the selection, look for definitions of words that you've listed in the third column.

WORD LIST		
improvise	revert	spherical
perfunctorily	righteous	translucent
redundant	simultaneously	

Know Well	Think I Know	Don't Know at All

Author Online

Annie Dillard
born 1945

Childhood Memories
Pulitzer Prize–winner Annie Dillard frequently writes about events in her life when she was growing up. Her parents shared with her and her sisters their favorite books and music and told stories and jokes. The young Dillard, full of curiosity, spent hours studying small pond creatures with her microscope. But despite a childhood filled with happy memories, as Dillard reached her late teens, she began to rebel and yearned to get away.

A Fulfilling Life Dillard got her wish for a new adventure when she went away to college and began to focus on writing. Since then, she has written essays, a memoir, poetry, and a Western novel. Dillard spends a great deal of time alone in the wilderness, and she frequently writes about nature. One might think a nature writer would tend to be serious, but Dillard loves to laugh. She keeps an "index of jokes" and says that ". . . irony has the highest place . . ." in literature.

 MORE ABOUT THE AUTHOR
For more on Annie Dillard, visit the **Literature Center** at ClassZone.com.

Teach

STANDARDS FOCUS

LITERARY ANALYSIS

● SETTING IN NONFICTION

Ask students to think of a story they've read this year, such as "The Last Dog." Have them identify ways in which the setting affected events in the story. Then discuss how setting in a nonfiction selection might have a similar impact.

CHECK UNDERSTANDING Have students jot down details of setting they could use in nonfiction writing about their own lives.

READING SKILL

■ RECOGNIZE CAUSE AND EFFECT

Have students read about Annie Dillard on page 119. Ask these questions:

- What were some results of Dillard's reaching her late teens? *Possible answer: She began to rebel and wanted to leave home.*

- What changes caused the author to settle down? *Possible answer: She went to college and began to write.*

CHECK UNDERSTANDING Have students imagine that they missed their ride to school this morning. Ask them to chart the subsequent events as a cause-and-effect chain.

 RESOURCE MANAGER—Copy Master
Recognize Cause and Effect p. 161 (for student use while reading the selection)

VOCABULARY SKILL

▲ VOCABULARY IN CONTEXT

DIAGNOSE WORD KNOWLEDGE To determine preteaching needs, have all students complete **Vocabulary in Context.** Students may check their understanding of word meanings against definitions on the selection pages: *improvising* (p. 123), *perfunctorily* (p. 125), *redundant* (p. 125), *revert* (p. 122), *righteous* (p. 125), *simultaneously* (p. 123), *spherical* (p. 122), *translucent* (p. 122).

PRETEACH VOCABULARY Use the Vocabulary Study copy master to help students predict the meaning of each boldfaced word.

1. Read item 1. Emphasize *improvising.*
2. Point out the context phrase "making up shortcuts." Elicit possible meanings for *improvise,* such as "make up or invent."
3. Have students record their predictions.
4. Repeat for items 2–8. Then remind students to look for the words as they read the selection.

 RESOURCE MANAGER—Copy Master
Vocabulary Study p. 163

For general guidelines on differentiating vocabulary instruction and for alternative vocabulary activities for students not needing vocabulary preteaching, see

BEST PRACTICES TOOLKIT
Scaffolding Vocabulary Instruction pp. 43–46

① Vocabulary Center at **ClassZone.com**

ANALYZE VISUALS

Possible answer: *Not knowing the source of the snowballs causes the viewer to wonder who is throwing the snowballs and where these people might be hiding.*

Lines 1–13
DISCUSSION PROMPTS

Use these prompts to help students understand the character of the author:

Connect Do you think playing football requires more courage than other sports do? Why or why not? *Students may say that because football is a physically aggressive sport, it requires more courage. Others may say that sports such as mountain climbing or scuba diving require more courage because there's a greater chance of being killed while doing them.*

Speculate Why does the author like playing football? *Possible answer: It is an all-or-nothing sport. It requires fearlessness and bold action.*

Synthesize What does the author's attitude toward football suggest about her approach to life? *Possible answer: She seeks out challenges that require her to show courage and use her abilities and energy.*

READING SKILL

A CAUSE AND EFFECT

Record students' answers in a cause-and-effect chain like the one on page 119.

Possible answer:

> **Cause:** *Fresh snow falls.*

↓

> **Effect/Cause:** *Children decide to throw snowballs at passing cars.*

↓

If students need help ... List words and phrases that indicate a cause-and-effect relationship, such as *because, as a result of, since,* and *so.* Have students identify the clue word in lines 15–17 (*so*).

An American Childhood

Annie Dillard

Some boys taught me to play football. This was fine sport. You thought up a new strategy for every play and whispered it to the others. You went out for a pass, fooling everyone. Best, you got to throw yourself mightily at someone's running legs. Either you brought him down or you hit the ground flat out on your chin, with your arms empty before you. It was all or nothing. If you hesitated in fear, you would miss and get hurt: you would take a hard fall while the kid got away, or you would get kicked in the face while the kid got away. But if you flung yourself wholeheartedly at the back of his knees—if you gathered and joined body and soul and pointed them diving fearlessly—then you likely wouldn't get hurt, and you'd stop the ball. Your fate, and your team's score, depended on your concentration and courage. Nothing girls did could compare with it.

Boys welcomed me at baseball, too, for I had, through enthusiastic practice, what was weirdly known as a boy's arm. In winter, in the snow, there was neither baseball nor football, so the boys and I threw snowballs at passing cars. I got in trouble throwing snowballs, and have seldom been happier since. **Ⓐ**

ANALYZE VISUALS
Why is it interesting to see the snowballs flying through the air but not see who threw them?

① **Targeted Passage**

Ⓐ CAUSE AND EFFECT
What effect does the snow have on the children's activities? Begin creating your chain here.

120   UNIT 1: PLOT, CONFLICT, AND SETTING

DIFFERENTIATED INSTRUCTION

FOR ALL STUDENTS
Enhancing Learning Styles Provide independent projects for various learning styles.

- **Mathematical** Collect and graph data on snowfall amounts.
- **Verbal** Write a brief memoir about a memorable event.
- **Auditory** Develop running commentary on a footrace.

For further details on these projects, see

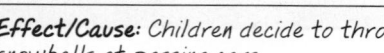 **RESOURCE MANAGER**
Ideas for Extension pp. 154–155

FOR LESS-PROFICIENT READERS
In combination with the *Audio Anthology CD,* use one or more Targeted Passages (pp. 120, 122, 125) to ensure that students focus on key story events, concepts, and skills.

① Targeted Passage [Lines 1–18]

This passage introduces the author and foreshadows the future conflict.

- Why does the author enjoy playing football? How would you describe the way she plays?

BACKGROUND

Winters in Pittsburgh In this memoir, the snow and cold weather are important elements of the setting. In Pittsburgh, winters tend to be cold and snowy—a setting that provides ample opportunity for children to engage in snow sports and activities. Pittsburgh typically receives around 43 inches of snow each year—with the most, 11 inches, falling in January. Hats, mittens, and warm winter coats are essential in Pittsburgh during the winter, where the average high temperature just reaches the mid-30s Fahrenheit. In March of 1993, Pittsburgh was blanketed in 25 inches of snow in three days, by a blizzard that was coined the "Storm of the Century." This fast-moving storm dropped the largest band of snow on record across the country, affecting 26 states and 50 percent of the United States' population.

- What do the author and the neighborhood boys like to do when it snows?
- What kind of conflict do you think the author might face in this selection?

FOR ENGLISH LEARNERS

Key Academic Vocabulary Have pairs complete Word Squares for this vocabulary: *target* (lines 22, 48), *intervals* (line 35), *project* (line 42), *adult* (lines 53, 78, 118), *route* (line 83), *drama* (line 114).

 BEST PRACTICES TOOLKIT—Transparency
Word Squares p. E10

Prereading For prereading instruction for English learners, see

 BEST PRACTICES TOOLKIT
Scaffolding Reading Instruction pp. 43–46

FOR ADVANCED LEARNERS/PRE–AP

Pre-AP exercises in the bottom channel provide additional challenge for your advanced students. Use them for small groups or individuals.

ADDITIONAL GUIDELINES

For more help with differentiation and tips for classroom management, see

 BEST PRACTICES TOOLKIT
Differentiated Instruction pp. 31–38

On one weekday morning after Christmas, six inches of new snow had
20 just fallen. We were standing up to our boot tops in snow on a front yard
on trafficked Reynolds Street, waiting for cars. The cars traveled Reynolds
Street slowly and evenly; they were targets all but wrapped in red ribbons,
cream puffs. We couldn't miss.

I was seven; the boys were eight, nine, and ten. The oldest two Fahey
boys were there—Mikey and Peter—polite blond boys who lived near
me on Lloyd Street, and who already had four brothers and sisters. My
parents approved Mikey and Peter Fahey. Chickie McBride was there,
a tough kid, and Billy Paul and Mackie Kean, too, from across Reynolds,
where the boys grew up dark and furious, grew up skinny, knowing, and
30 skilled. We had all drifted from our houses that morning looking for
action, and had found it here on Reynolds Street.

It was cloudy but cold. The cars' tires laid behind them on the snowy
street a complex trail of beige chunks like crenellated[1] castle walls. I had
stepped on some earlier; they squeaked. We could have wished for more
traffic. When a car came, we all popped it one. In the intervals between
cars we **reverted** to the natural solitude of children. **B**

I started making an iceball—a perfect iceball, from perfectly white
snow, perfectly **spherical,** and squeezed perfectly **translucent** so no
snow remained all the way through. (The Fahey boys and I considered
40 it unfair actually to throw an iceball at somebody, but it had been known
to happen.)

I had just embarked on the iceball project when we heard tire chains
come clanking from afar. A black Buick was moving toward us down
the street. We all spread out, banged together some regular snowballs,
took aim, and, when the Buick drew nigh, fired.

A soft snowball hit the driver's windshield right before the driver's face.
It made a smashed star with a hump in the middle.

Often, of course, we hit our target, but this time, the only time in
all of life, the car pulled over and stopped. Its wide black door opened;
50 a man got out of it, running. He didn't even close the car door.

He ran after us, and we ran away from him, up the snowy Reynolds
sidewalk. At the corner, I looked back; incredibly, he was still after us.
He was in city clothes: a suit and tie, street shoes. Any normal adult
would have quit, having sprung us into flight and made his point. This
man was gaining on us. He was a thin man, all action. All of a sudden,
we were running for our lives. **C**

Wordless, we split up. We were on our turf; we could lose ourselves
in the neighborhood backyards, everyone for himself. I paused and

---

1. **crenellated** (krĕn′ə-lā′tĭd): notched at the top.

B SETTING

Possible answer: The snow is indented in the pattern of a snow tire. The snow is not pure white but beige—where the cars have driven on it.

If students need help ... Suggest that they visualize a castle made of stone. Ask a volunteer to draw a castle tower with notches at the top. Then ask students how this image compares to the way tire tracks in fresh snow look.

READING SKILL

C CAUSE AND EFFECT

Add students' answers to the cause-and-effect chain.

Possible answer:

↓

Effect/Cause: Children decide to throw snowballs at passing cars.

↓

Effect/Cause: Snowball hits black Buick.

↓

Effect/Cause: Driver gets out and chases children.

↓

---

revert (rĭ-vûrt′) *v.*
to return to a former condition

B SETTING
How do you think the tire tracks look on the snowy street? Referring to the footnote might help you **visualize** the scene.

spherical (sfîr′ĭ-kəl) *adj.*
having the shape of a sphere or round ball

translucent (trăns-loo′sənt) *adj.*
allowing light to pass through

2 **Targeted Passage**

C CAUSE AND EFFECT
What happens when the children hit the Buick? Record the effect in your chain.

DIFFERENTIATED INSTRUCTION

FOR LESS–PROFICIENT READERS

2 Targeted Passage [Lines 42–56]

This passage introduces the narrative's main conflict: the children hit a car with a snowball, and the driver gets out to chase them.

- What do the children do to the black Buick?
- How does the car's driver react?
- What do the children do when the driver runs toward them?
- How does this passage set up a conflict?

FOR ENGLISH LEARNERS

Vocabulary: Idioms and Sayings List these idiomatic and slang expressions on the board:

- *cream puffs* (line 23), "easy targets"
- *popped it one* (line 35), "threw snowballs at the car"
- *banged together* (line 44), "quickly made"
- *on our turf* (line 57), "in our personal territory"

Have small groups use context to define these and similar expressions from the selection.

considered. Everyone had vanished except Mikey Fahey, who was just
rounding the corner of a yellow brick house. Poor Mikey—I trailed him.
The driver of the Buick sensibly picked the two of us to follow. The man
apparently had all day.

He chased Mikey and me around the yellow house and up a backyard
path we knew by heart: under a low tree, up a bank, through a hedge,
down some snowy steps, and across the grocery store's delivery driveway.
We smashed through a gap in another hedge, entered a scruffy backyard,
and ran around its back porch and tight between houses to Edgerton
Avenue; we ran across Edgerton to an alley and up our own sliding
woodpile to the Halls' front yard; he kept coming. We ran up Lloyd
Street and wound through mazy backyards toward the steep hilltop at
Willard and Lang. **D**

He chased us silently, block after block. He chased us silently over
picket fences, through thorny hedges, between houses, around garbage
cans, and across streets. Every time I glanced back, choking for breath,
I expected he would have quit. He must have been as breathless as we
were. His jacket strained over his body. It was an immense discovery,
pounding into my hot head with every sliding, joyous step, that this
ordinary adult evidently knew what I thought only children who trained
at football knew: that you have to fling yourself at what you're doing,
you have to point yourself, forget yourself, aim, dive. **E**

Mikey and I had nowhere to go, in our own neighborhood or out of
it, but away from this man who was chasing us. He impelled us forward;
we compelled him to follow our route. The air was cold; every breath tore
my throat. We kept running, block after block; we kept **improvising,**
backyard after backyard, running a frantic course and choosing it
simultaneously, failing always to find small places or hard places to slow
him down, and discovering always, exhilarated, dismayed, that only bare
speed could save us—for he would never give up, this man—and we were
losing speed.

He chased us through the backyard labyrinths of ten blocks before
he caught us by our jackets. He caught us and we all stopped. **F**

We three stood staggering, half blinded, coughing, in an obscure
hilltop backyard: a man in his twenties, a boy, a girl. He had released
our jackets, our pursuer, our captor, our hero: he knew we weren't going
anywhere. We all played by the rules. Mikey and I unzipped our jackets.
I pulled off my sopping mittens. Our tracks multiplied in the backyard's
new snow. We had been breaking new snow all morning. We didn't look
at each other. I was cherishing my excitement. The man's lower pant
legs were wet; his cuffs were full of snow, and there was a prow of snow
beneath them on his shoes and socks. Some trees bordered the little flat

---

D **SETTING**
Reread lines 63–71.
In what way does the
children's familiarity
with the neighborhood
help them?

E **MAKE INFERENCES**
Dillard uses the word
joyous to describe the
difficulty of the chase.
What does this choice
of words suggest
about her?

improvise (ĭm′prə-vīz′) *v.*
to make up on the spur
of the moment, without
preparation

simultaneously
(sī′məl-tā′nē-əs-lē)
adv. at the same time

F **CAUSE AND EFFECT**
What happens because
the children lose speed?
List the effect in your
chain.

LITERARY ANALYSIS

D **SETTING**

*Possible answer: The children know short-
cuts and back routes that help them stay
ahead of the man who's chasing them.*

READING SKILL: *Review*

E **MAKE INFERENCES**

*Possible answer: She is daring and loves the
excitement of facing a difficult challenge.*

Lines 76–80
REINFORCE *KEY IDEA*: THRILL

Discuss Dillard is **thrilled** to be chased by
a man who does not give up. Why does his
determination add to her thrill? *Possible
answer: It is completely unexpected and out of
the ordinary. She relishes having more time to
fling herself fearlessly and wholeheartedly into
the chase.*

READING SKILL

F **CAUSE AND EFFECT**

Add students' answers to the cause-and-
effect chain.

Possible answer:

• *Effect/Cause: The children become tired
and slow down.*

• *Effect: The man catches the children.*

FOR LESS—PROFICIENT READERS

Reading Skill Follow-Up: Cause and Effect Ask
students to identify other cause-and-effect
relationships that they find on these pages by
completing these simple charts:

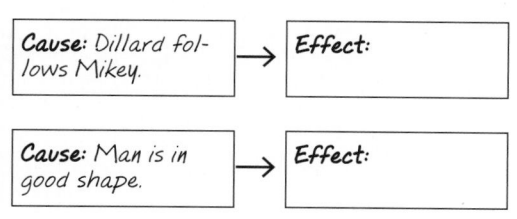

Review: Make Inferences Remind students that
readers make inferences based on text details
and prior knowledge. Work as a class to make
inferences from these details:

• The man leaves his car door open (line 50).

• The man is wearing a suit and tie (line 53).

• The man is able to keep up with the children
(lines 72–74).

• The chase goes on for ten blocks (line 90).

 BEST PRACTICES TOOLKIT—Transparency
Making Inferences p. A13

ANALYZE VISUALS

Activity Have students discuss which elements of this image help create the impression that the children are enjoying themselves.

Possible answer:

- *the artist's use of bright colors*
- *the movement of the children*
- *the smile on the boy's face*

backyard, some messy winter trees. There was no one around: a clearing in a grove, and we the only players.

It was a long time before he could speak. I had some difficulty at first recalling why we were there. My lips felt swollen; I couldn't see out of the sides of my eyes; I kept coughing.

"You stupid kids," he began **perfunctorily**.

We listened perfunctorily indeed, if we listened at all, for the chewing out was **redundant**, a mere formality, and beside the point. The point was that he had chased us passionately without giving up, and so he had caught us. Now he came down to earth. I wanted the glory to last forever.

B ut how could the glory have lasted forever? We could have run through every backyard in North America until we got to Panama. But when he trapped us at the lip of the Panama Canal, what precisely could he have done to prolong the drama of the chase and cap its glory? I brooded about this for the next few years. He could only have fried Mikey Fahey and me in boiling oil, say, or dismembered us piecemeal, or staked us to anthills. None of which I really wanted, and none of which any adult was likely to do, even in the spirit of fun. He could only chew us out there in the Panamanian jungle, after months or years of exalting pursuit. He could only begin, "You stupid kids," and continue in his ordinary Pittsburgh accent with his normal **righteous** anger and the usual common sense. **G**

If in that snowy backyard the driver of the black Buick had cut off our heads, Mikey's and mine, I would have died happy, for nothing has required so much of me since as being chased all over Pittsburgh in the middle of winter—running terrified, exhausted—by this sainted, skinny, furious redheaded man who wished to have a word with us. I don't know how he found his way back to his car. ❧

---

perfunctorily
(pər-fŭngk′tə-rĭ-lē)
adv. in a mechanical or unconcerned way

redundant (rĭ-dŭn′dənt)
adj. not needed; more than necessary

3 Targeted Passage

righteous (rī′chəs) *adj.* based on one's sense of what is right

G MAKE INFERENCES
Reread lines 111–122. Why does Dillard say that the man's response would have been the same even if he had finally caught them in Panama?

AN AMERICAN CHILDHOOD   **125**

FOR LESS–PROFICIENT READERS

3 Targeted Passage [Lines 106–128]

This passage resolves the conflict and explores why the incident was significant to the author.

- How is the conflict of the chase resolved?
- What does the man do when he catches the children?
- Why is the author disappointed when the chase ends?
- Why is this incident a highlight in her life?

FOR ENGLISH LEARNERS

Comprehension: Task Support Have students work in pairs to draw three or four pictures that summarize the main events in this selection and their causal relationships. Ask students to include short captions for their pictures. Then have pairs present their pictorial summaries in small groups, explaining how the events are related.

🧰 BEST PRACTICES TOOLKIT
Draw It p. A2

G MAKE INFERENCES

Possible answer: The chase was so exciting that the man could do nothing to top it—except fry them in oil (lines 115–116) or something equally unlikely. In reality, no matter where or when the children were caught, the man could only yell at them.

Extend the Discussion What do you think the man actually said to the children? Did the author make a good decision in letting readers infer what he said rather than quoting his whole speech?

Lines 123–128
REINFORCE *KEY IDEA*: THRILL

Discuss Dillard is so **thrilled** by the chase that she claims she "would have died happy" right then and there. Why did this thrill add so much to her life? *Possible answer: In giving all of herself, she felt an intense, heightened awareness of what it means to be truly alive—to risk, to face danger, and to utterly commit to reaching a goal. She realizes that the outcome—getting caught—doesn't even matter. For her, the dizzying excitement and demanding challenge of the chase revealed more to her about life and herself than she ever expected.*

SELECTION WRAP–UP

REFLECT Have students consider whether the author's attitude toward life as seen in this selection is admirable or dangerous. In what way could her attitude lead to problems? In what way could it solve problems?

⭐ **CRITIQUE** Ask students whether the author succeeds in bringing this incident to life for her readers. Have them discuss the reasons for their opinions.

READING FLUENCY

Distribute the copy masters and have students work in pairs to practice fluency.

📖 RESOURCE MANAGER—Copy Master
Reading Fluency p. 168

Practice and Apply

After Reading

For additional support of post-reading questions, use these copy masters:

R RESOURCE MANAGER—Copy Masters
Reading Check p. 166 (to check understanding of the selection)
Setting in Nonfiction p. 159 (for practice of literary analysis standards focus)
Question Support p. 167 (**After Reading** questions adapted for English learners and less-proficient readers)

Additional selection questions are provided for teachers on page 153.

For additional activities to challenge students, see

i Power Thinking at **ClassZone.com**

ANSWERS
Comprehension

1. *The man chased the children because they threw snowballs at his car.*

2. *He yelled at them for throwing snowballs.*

3. *Sketches should show details such as the snowy sidewalk (lines 51–52), a thin man (line 55) running in his city clothes (line 53), and children running for their lives (line 56).*

Literary Analysis
Possible answers:

4. ◼ STANDARDS FOCUS *Recognize Cause and Effect Students may say that the man's stopping to chase the children was most important. The chase was the highlight of the author's childhood—and of her later life.*

5. *Students may say that Dillard is adventurous, energetic, brave, and tough. Some may not understand why Dillard enjoys being in trouble. Others may see that she takes risks to experience thrilling excitement.*

6. *Students may reference these details:*
   - *The man is wearing a suit, tie, and street shoes (line 53). Inference: He is on his way to work in an office.*
   - *He knew the kids weren't going anywhere (lines 94–95). Inference: He may have been in chases like this when he was a kid.*
   - *He yells at the author and Mikey (lines 106–108). Inference: As an adult, he is not tolerant of mischievous behavior.*

Comprehension

 MARYLAND OBJECTIVES

LITERATURE STANDARD
3.A.3.c Analyze setting

1. **Recall** Why did the man chase Dillard and her friend?

2. **Recall** What happened when he caught up with them?

3. **Represent** Reread the paragraph that begins at line 51 on page 122. Using details from the paragraph, sketch the scene.

Literary Analysis

4. **Recognize Cause and Effect** Look over the chain you created as you read. What was the most important effect in the story? Why?

5. **Connect** What do you learn about Dillard from her reaction to being chased? Do you understand this reaction? Explain your answer.

6. **Make Inferences** What do you think the man who chased Dillard might be like? Use details from the selection and your own knowledge to fill out a chart like the one shown.

The Man	Details	Inference
What work might the man do?		
What might he have been like as a kid?		
What might he be like now?		

7. **Evaluate Setting** Go through the selection and find passages that describe Dillard's neighborhood and the weather there on the day of the chase. Which details are especially effective at conveying setting? Explain your answer.

8. **Analyze the Ending** Reread lines 111–128. Why do you think Dillard ended the piece this way, rather than just ending at line 110? Explain what information the last section provides and why Dillard included it.

Extension and Challenge

9. **Big Question Activity** Survey a small group of people to find out when they feel most alive. Then combine your findings with those of your classmates to create a master list of answers. What experiences **thrill** people? What generalizations can you make about these experiences, on the basis of your survey results?

10. **Inquiry and Research** In the first paragraph, Dillard says that when she was growing up, nothing girls did could compare with playing football. Do research to find out how women's sports have changed and grown over the last 50 years. What team sport might Dillard play if she were growing up today? Share your findings with the class.

> **RESEARCH LINKS**
> For more on women's sports, visit the **Research Center** at **ClassZone.com**.

---

7. ● STANDARDS FOCUS *Setting in Nonfiction Six inches of new snow had just fallen (lines 19–20), it was cloudy and cold, the chunks of snow squeaked (lines 32–34), the backyards of the houses were like a maze (line 70), and there were gaps in hedges, fences, and alleys that allowed the kids to keep running (lines 66–69).*

8. *The ending explains what the author learned from this incident: that taking on any task with passion and determination is an experience that makes life worth living.*

Extension and Challenge

9. *Students' generalizations should be supported by the information they collect in the survey.*

10. *Students' reports should show evidence of research and identify a number of team sports open to women, such as basketball, hockey, rowing, softball, and so on.*

Vocabulary in Context

VOCABULARY PRACTICE

Show that you understand the vocabulary words by deciding if each statement is true or false.

1. A **redundant** explanation is one that's already been given.
2. You can expect a **spherical** object to roll.
3. A tightly woven wool scarf is **translucent.**
4. If two events occur **simultaneously,** they happen one after the other.
5. If you clean your room **perfunctorily,** you do a very careful job.
6. If I **revert** to telling lies, I am going back to an old habit.
7. A speaker following carefully prepared notes will **improvise.**
8. A **righteous** person tends to act in a moral way.

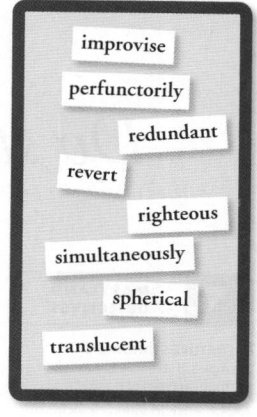

improvise
perfunctorily
redundant
revert
righteous
simultaneously
spherical
translucent

VOCABULARY IN WRITING

What is your opinion of the end of this selection? Write a one-paragraph answer, using two or more vocabulary words. You could start like this.

> **EXAMPLE SENTENCE**
>
> I was surprised at the end of the chase when the man reacted so _**perfunctorily**_.

VOCABULARY STRATEGY: SUFFIXES THAT FORM ADJECTIVES

A **suffix** is a word part that appears at the end of a root or base word to form a new word. Some suffixes, such as those in _righteous_ and _spherical_, can be added to nouns to form adjectives. If you can recognize the noun that a suffix is attached to, you can often figure out the meaning of the adjective formed from it. See the chart for common suffixes and their meanings.

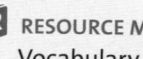

MARYLAND OBJECTIVES

READING STANDARD
1.D.3.b Use word structure to determine meaning

Suffixes	Meanings
-ate, -ous, -eous, -ial, -ical	like; having to do with; showing

PRACTICE Identify the noun in each boldfaced word. Then define the adjective.

1. The science experiment produced a **gaseous** cloud.
2. Their pet dog is gentle and **affectionate.**
3. Many famous people write **autobiographical** books or articles.
4. Pollution has a **ruinous** effect on our environment.
5. His **facial** features included a long, thin nose.

VOCABULARY PRACTICE
For more practice, go to the **Vocabulary Center** at ClassZone.com.

DIFFERENTIATED INSTRUCTION

FOR ENGLISH LEARNERS

Vocabulary in Writing Provide students with sentence stems and have them fill in the blanks with the appropriate vocabulary words. For example:

1. The man's scolding seemed _____.
   He had already taught the children a lesson by catching them.

2. The man almost forgot he was an adult when he chased the children. He seemed to _____ to his childhood self.

FOR ADVANCED LEARNERS/PRE–AP

Vocabulary in Writing Have students use the vocabulary words and some of their ideas from the paragraph to develop a conversation that the man might have had with someone at work or at home about this incident. Ask volunteers to share their dialogues.

ANSWERS

Vocabulary in Context

VOCABULARY PRACTICE

1. *true;* **2.** *true;* **3.** *false;* **4.** *false;* **5.** *false;* **6.** *true;* **7.** *false;* **8.** *true*

 **RESOURCE MANAGER**—Copy Master
Vocabulary Practice p. 164

VOCABULARY IN WRITING

Students might brainstorm their reactions and opinions before they begin writing. Encourage students to link vocabulary words with the ideas they record.

VOCABULARY STRATEGY: SUFFIXES THAT FORM ADJECTIVES *(also an EL language objective)*

Point out that there is no spelling change when a **suffix** beginning with a vowel is added to a word ending with a consonant. When a word ends with a vowel, that vowel is usually dropped before a suffix is added.

Possible answers:

1. *gas*—"having qualities of gas"; **2.** *affection*—"showing affection"; **3.** *autobiography*—"like an autobiography"; **4.** *ruin*—"leading to ruin" **5.** *face*—"having to do with the face"

RESOURCE MANAGER—Copy Master
Vocabulary Strategy p. 165

Vocabulary Center at **ClassZone.com**
Additional Vocabulary Activities

Assess and Reteach

Assess

RESOURCE MANAGER—Copy Masters
Selection Tests A, B/C pp. 169–170, 171–172

Test Generator CD

Reteach

STANDARDS LESSON FILE
Literature Lesson 9: Setting and Its Roles
Reading Lesson 7: Recognizing Cause and Effect
Vocabulary Lesson 7: Suffixes (adjective, adverb)

Focus and Motivate

OBJECTIVES

Literary Analysis
- explore the key idea of **fans**
- identify and analyze narrative elements in poetry
- recognize sound devices: repetition, rhyme, rhythm
- read a poem

Reading
- read poetry

SUMMARY

"Casey at the Bat" tells the story of the dramatic last inning of a baseball game in Mudville. The home team is behind by two runs. With two men out, two batters manage to get on base. Then the team's best hitter, Casey, comes up to bat, representing the winning run—or the final out. Casey lets two pitches go by without swinging. Then he takes a mighty swing at the third pitch but strikes out. The Mudville fans are devastated.

Do sports FANS *care too much?*

Discuss the question and the **KEY IDEA.** Ask students what they believe motivates sports **fans:** love of the game, competition, the players, or something else. Explain that this intensity can add much joy to a fan's life and can unite families, friends, and cities. At the same time, however, fans may take their passion too far. Extend the discussion by having students do the **WEB IT** activity. Invite volunteers to share their ideas with the class.

Selection Resources

Casey at the Bat
Poem by Ernest Lawrence Thayer

Do sports FANS *care too much?*

MARYLAND OBJECTIVES

LITERATURE STANDARDS
3.A.4.a Use structural features to distinguish types of poetry
3.A.4.c Analyze sound elements of poetry

KEY IDEA Sports **fans** love their teams. They dress in the teams' colors, cheer wildly when great plays are made, and boo when things don't go their way. Is this a good thing, or do sports fans care too much about winning? In "Casey at the Bat," the fans expect only the best from their mighty hitter.

WEB IT Create an idea web of what can happen when fans care too much. List things you have read about or witnessed happening at sporting events.

Fights can break out.

What happens when fans care too much?

128

 RESOURCE MANAGER UNIT 1

Plan and Teach pp. 173–180

Literary Analysis
Narrative Poetry pp. 181, 182†*
Question Support p. 185*

Reading
Reading Poetry pp. 183, 184†*
Reading Fluency p. 187

Assessment
Selection Tests A, B/C pp. 189*, 191*
Test Generator CD

 BEST PRACTICES TOOLKIT

Differentiated Instruction pp. 31–38*

Scaffolding Instruction pp. 43–46*

Graphic Organizers/Strategies
Spider Map • Draw It • Making Inferences

Reading Support
Audio Anthology CD*

Technology
Literature and Vocabulary Centers at **ClassZone.com**
Write*Smart* CD

* Resources for Differentiation   † Also in Spanish

LITERARY ANALYSIS: NARRATIVE POETRY

Like fiction, poetry can tell stories. Poems that do so are called **narrative poems.** Just as any other story, a narrative poem has characters, a plot, and a setting. It presents a conflict and might also include suspense.

As you read "Casey at the Bat," identify its setting, characters, and main plot events in a diagram like the one shown. Also note the suspense that builds as you read the story.

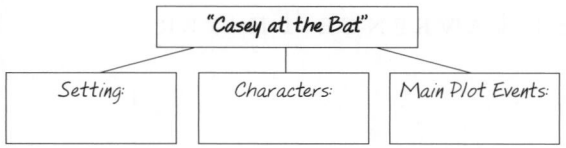

"Casey at the Bat"
- Setting:
- Characters:
- Main Plot Events:

READING STRATEGY: READING POETRY

In addition to the elements that all stories have, narrative poems include poetic elements that add meaning and interest. Much of the energy and excitement of "Casey at the Bat" comes from the poet's use of **sound devices,** such as repetition, rhyme, and rhythm.

- **Repetition** is the repeating of a sound, word, phrase, or line to emphasize something in a poem.

  For <u>Casey</u>, mighty <u>Casey</u>, was advancing to the bat.

- **Rhyme** is the repetition of sounds at the ends of words.

  It looked extremely rocky for the Mudville nine that <u>day</u>;
  The score stood two to four, with but an inning
      left to <u>play</u>.

- **Rhythm** is a pattern of stressed (´) and unstressed (˘) syllables in a line of poetry.

  Thĕn frŏm thĕ gláddĕnĕd múltĭtŭde wĕnt úp ă
      jóyŏŭs yéll—

As you read the poem, pay attention to the sound devices. Reading the poem aloud may help you.

Review: **Make Inferences**

Author Online

Ernest Lawrence Thayer
1863–1940

One-Hit Wonder
Although Ernest Lawrence Thayer wrote many poems for newspapers, he is remembered for just one: "Casey at the Bat." Thayer was educated at Harvard University. Being known among his classmates as a very funny person probably helped him become editor, and later president, of the university's humor magazine, the *Lampoon.*

Crowd Pleaser After graduation, Thayer joined the staff of the *San Francisco Examiner,* where in 1887 he began writing a poem for each Sunday issue. "Casey at the Bat" was first printed in the paper in 1888. By the time of Thayer's death in 1940, "Casey at the Bat" had become an American favorite.

 MORE ABOUT THE AUTHOR
For more on Ernest Lawrence Thayer, visit the **Literature Center** at ClassZone.com.

Background
America's Sport Baseball began in the United States in the mid-1800s. Small towns and large cities formed teams and clubs. The first baseball game with set rules was played in 1846 between Cartwright's Knickerbockers and the New York Baseball Club. By the early 1900s, going to baseball games was a favorite pastime of people throughout the United States.

Teach

STANDARDS FOCUS

LITERARY ANALYSIS

● NARRATIVE POETRY

Tell students that "Casey at the Bat" tells a story about baseball. Ask them to predict where the poem might be set, who the main characters might be, and what the plot might include. ***Possible answer:*** *Setting*—a baseball field; *Characters*—baseball players, fans; *Plot*—events that happen during a baseball game

CHECK UNDERSTANDING Ask students how a narrative poem is like a short story.

READING STRATEGY

■ READING POETRY

Review the definitions of *repetition, rhyme,* and *rhythm* on page 129.

- Have students read aloud the **Repetition** example, omitting the repetition. Which version is stronger, and why?
- Read aloud the **Rhyme** example. Ask students to suggest other rhymes for *day,* including multi-syllable words.
- Do a choral reading of the **Rhythm** example, having students clap on stressed syllables.

CHECK UNDERSTANDING Ask students to briefly define the terms *repetition, rhyme,* and *rhythm* as they apply to poetry.

 RESOURCE MANAGER—Copy Master
Reading Poetry p. 183 (for student use while reading the selection)

DIFFERENTIATED INSTRUCTION

FOR ALL STUDENTS
For general guidelines on differentiating instruction, see

 BEST PRACTICES TOOLKIT
Differentiated Instruction pp. 43–46

FOR LESS–PROFICIENT READERS
Comprehension Support Poets often change the regular order of words to aid rhythm and rhyme. Have students look for the subject of each sentence in lines 11, 17, 23–24, 31, 37, and 42 and provide a paraphrase.

Poets also choose words to fit the rhythm and rhyme of a particular line. For example, Thayer uses *multititude* in lines 11 and 17 to mean "crowd." Have students look for words used to mean "ball" in lines 29 and 39.

FOR ENGLISH LEARNERS
Vocabulary: Baseball Terms Give students the following baseball terms and concepts from the poem: *nine* (line 1); *inning* (line 2); *bat* (line 8); *single* (line 13); *ball* (line 14); *second, third* (line 16); *pitcher* (line 27); *strike, umpire* (line 32); *plate* (line 46); *struck out* (line 52). Have pairs

work together to organize these words using a Spider Map; the four legs off the center topic, *baseball,* should be *people, equipment, verbs,* and *concepts.* Then have students record a brief definition next to each word. Invite volunteers to share their maps and definitions. Discuss and clarify words as necessary.

BEST PRACTICES TOOLKIT—Transparency
Spider Map p. B22

LITERARY ANALYSIS

Ⓐ NARRATIVE POETRY

Possible answer: The setting of the poem is a baseball game in Mudville, in the bottom of the ninth (last) inning.

- *Because the people in the stands are upset about Mudville's being close to losing (line 4), readers know the game is being played in Mudville.*
- *The poet says there is only "an inning left to play" (line 2).*
- *Since the home team always bats last, it must be the bottom (second half) of the ninth (last) inning.*

Extend the Discussion How do these four lines create a feeling of tension and suspense?

ANALYZE VISUALS

Possible answer: He looks proud and confident.

READING STRATEGY

Ⓑ READING POETRY

Possible answer: Casey's name is repeated because he is the main character and Mudville's last hope to win the game. The phrase "mighty Casey" also adds two stressed syllables to make this line match the rhythm of all the others.

If students need help . . . Have them reread lines 9–14, paying attention to how Casey's teammates are described (Flynn is a "pudd'n"; Blake is a "fake" and "much-despised"). Explain that introducing Casey as "mighty" and repeating his name in line 20 serves to set him apart as the hero of the team.

Casey at the Bat

ERNEST LAWRENCE THAYER

It looked extremely rocky for the Mudville nine that day;
The score stood two to four, with but an inning left to play.
So, when Cooney died at second, and Burrows did the same,
A pallor wreathed the features of the patrons of the game. Ⓐ

5 A straggling few got up to go, leaving there the rest,
With that hope which springs eternal within the human breast.
For they thought: "If only Casey could get a whack at that,"
They'd put even money now, with Casey at the bat.

But Flynn preceded Casey, and likewise so did Blake,
10 And the former was a pudd'n, and the latter was a fake.
So on that stricken multitude[1] a deathlike silence sat;
For there seemed but little chance of Casey's getting to the bat.

But Flynn let drive a "single," to the wonderment of all.
And the much-despised Blakey "tore the cover off the ball."
15 And when the dust had lifted, and they saw what had occurred,
There was Blakey safe at second, and Flynn a-huggin' third.

Then from the gladdened multitude went up a joyous yell—
It rumbled in the mountaintops, it rattled in the dell;[2]
It struck upon the hillside and rebounded on the flat;
20 For Casey, mighty Casey, was advancing to the bat. Ⓑ

---

1. **stricken multitude:** a crowd of people affected by great trouble.
2. **dell:** valley.

Ⓐ **NARRATIVE POETRY**
What is the **setting** of this poem? How do you know?

ANALYZE VISUALS
Look at the picture. What can you **infer** about the baseball player's attitude?

Ⓑ **READING POETRY**
Reread line 20. Why do you think Casey's name is repeated?

DIFFERENTIATED INSTRUCTION

FOR LESS–PROFICIENT READERS

Reading Strategy Follow-Up: Reading Poetry
Have students reread lines 1–20.

- Encourage students to find the pattern in the poet's use of rhyme. *(In each stanza, the first two lines rhyme and the last two lines rhyme.)* Which word is rhymed in more than one stanza? *(bat)*
- Have students find words that rhyme but have different ways of spelling the rhyming sounds. *(rest/breast, occurred/third)*

- Have students read along to the *Audio Anthology CD* and tap the stressed and unstressed syllables of each line.
- Ask students why they think the phrases "at the bat" and "to the bat" are repeated. *(Possible answer: It creates anticipation that Casey's turn at bat will change the outcome of the game.)*
- Which two sound devices does the poet combine in lines 18–19? *(repetition and rhythm)*

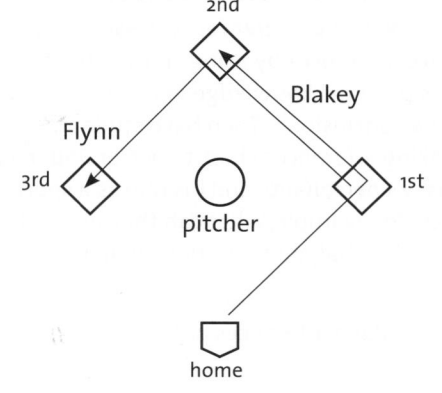

BACKGROUND

The Road to Immortality How does a poem become an American classic? For Thayer's "Casey at the Bat," it took everything from famous friends, to an unofficial press agent, to a comedian, to professional baseball clubs! Thayer joined the *San Francisco Examiner* staff at the urging of a Harvard classmate—William Randolph Hearst—who inherited the newspaper from his father. When the poem was first published in June of 1888, it was read and presumably forgotten by all. But a well-read novelist, Archibald C. Gunter, clipped it out. Instead of just saving it, Gunter soon found a chance to share the poem. He read that the New York and Chicago baseball clubs would be at a comedy performance in New York. Gunter had a feeling that the little poem might amuse the players, so he passed it along to his friend—the professional comedian. The road to immortality? Luck, coincidence, and a great poem.

CULTURAL CONNECTION

A Worldwide Pastime Almost as soon as baseball became popular in the United States, it spread to other countries. Cuban students who had studied in the United States took the game back to their home country in 1864. From there baseball spread throughout the Caribbean and to Mexico. At about the same time a teacher from the United States introduced baseball to Japan. Today baseball is also popular in Canada, Australia, Taiwan, Korea, and parts of Europe. Players born in other countries now routinely play on major-league baseball teams in the United States. Invite students to share their knowledge of baseball or other bat and ball games in different cultures.

FOR ENGLISH LEARNERS

Options for Reading Use Draw It as you read aloud the first 20 lines of the poem. Use a diagram of a baseball diamond to help students understand the actions that lead to the main plot event of the poem: Casey's turn at bat. Next have students listen to the *Audio Anthology CD* and note any unfamiliar words. Clarify understanding as needed. Then do an echo reading of the poem with students.

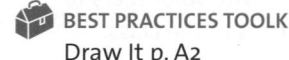
BEST PRACTICES TOOLKIT
Draw It p. A2

2nd

Blakey

Flynn

3rd   pitcher   1st

home

FOR ALL STUDENTS

Learning Center Set up a baseball learning center with materials on important games of the past, famous players, how technology is used to train players today, and so on. Provide a variety of independent projects, such as a statistical comparison of legendary players like Babe Ruth with today's top players, a newspaper editorial suggesting changes to the local team, and a review of a baseball movie.

132 UNIT 1: PLOT, CONFLICT, AND SETTING

READING SKILL: *Review*

C MAKE INFERENCES

Possible answer:

- *Casey is the best hitter on the team (lines 7–8, 20).*
- *He is confident in his ability to win the game (lines 21–22).*
- *He has a good relationship with his fans (line 23).*

LITERARY ANALYSIS

D NARRATIVE POETRY

Possible answer: The main conflict is between Casey and the pitcher. There is also a conflict between the fans and the umpire.

If students need help . . . Have students review the list of characters in their diagrams (introduced on page 129). Ask:

- Who is the main character?
- What does the main character want to do?
- Who or what is opposing the character as he tries to reach his goal?

READING STRATEGY

E READING POETRY

Possible answer: The rhymes put strong words at the ends of the lines, making the reader wonder what's going to happen next. The rhythm sets up a slow unfolding of the events by having pauses in the middle of each line until line 44.

SELECTION WRAP-UP

REFLECT Have students describe the range of emotions the **fans** in the poem feel. Might losing actually increase their appreciation and happiness when their team wins?

⭐ **CRITIQUE** Have students evaluate whether the poet did an effective job of describing an intense sporting competition.

READING FLUENCY

Distribute the copy masters and have students work in groups to practice fluency.

RESOURCE MANAGER—Copy Master
Reading Fluency p. 187

There was ease in Casey's manner as he stepped into his place,
There was pride in Casey's bearing and a smile on Casey's face;
And when responding to the cheers he lightly doffed his hat,
No stranger in the crowd could doubt 'twas Casey at the bat. **C**

25 Ten thousand eyes were on him as he rubbed his hands with dirt,
Five thousand tongues applauded when he wiped them on his shirt;
Then when the writhing pitcher ground the ball into his hip,
Defiance glanced in Casey's eye, a sneer curled Casey's lip.

And now the leather-covered sphere came hurtling through the air,
30 And Casey stood a-watching it in haughty grandeur[3] there.
Close by the sturdy batsman the ball unheeded sped;
"That ain't my style," said Casey. "Strike one," the umpire said.

From the benches, filled with people, there went up a muffled roar,
Like the beating of the storm waves on the stern and distant shore.
35 "Kill him! Kill the umpire!" shouted someone on the stand;
And it's likely they'd have killed him had not Casey raised his hand. **D**

With a smile of honest charity great Casey's visage[4] shone;
He stilled the rising tumult, he made the game go on;
He signaled to the pitcher, and once more the spheroid[5] flew;
40 But Casey still ignored it, and the umpire said, "Strike two."

"Fraud!" cried the maddened thousands, and the echo answered "Fraud!"
But one scornful look from Casey and the audience was awed;
They saw his face grow stern and cold, they saw his muscles strain,
And they knew that Casey wouldn't let the ball go by again. **E**

45 The sneer is gone from Casey's lips, his teeth are clenched in hate,
He pounds with cruel vengeance his bat upon the plate;
And now the pitcher holds the ball, and now he lets it go,
And now the air is shattered by the force of Casey's blow.

Oh, somewhere in this favored land the sun is shining bright,
50 The band is playing somewhere, and somewhere hearts are light;
And somewhere men are laughing, and somewhere children shout,
But there is no joy in Mudville: Mighty Casey has struck out.

---

3. **haughty grandeur:** proud majesty and splendor.
4. **visage** (vĭz′ĭj): face.
5. **spheroid** (sfĭr′oid′): in this instance, another name for a baseball.

132 UNIT 1: PLOT, CONFLICT, AND SETTING

C MAKE INFERENCES
What inferences can you make about Casey from what you've read so far?

D NARRATIVE POETRY
What is the **conflict** in this poem?

E READING POETRY
Reread lines 37–44. How does the poet's use of **rhyme** and **rhythm** increase the suspense in the poem?

DIFFERENTIATED INSTRUCTION

FOR LESS-PROFICIENT READERS
Review: Make Inferences Review how to make inferences by using clues in the text plus personal knowledge and experiences to draw conclusions. Then have students use a Making Inferences chart to better understand Casey's personality and his role as a sports star. For example, what can they infer when he says, "That ain't my style," in line 32?

BEST PRACTICES TOOLKIT—Transparency
Making Inferences p. A13

FOR ADVANCED LEARNERS/PRE-AP
Analyze Character Have students review the poem and identify moments when readers learn something about Casey from his words, looks, and actions and from how others react to him. Challenge students to create a cartoon strip depicting one or more of these key scenes in the poem. Encourage them to add thought balloons, filled with their own hypotheses, that disclose what Casey was thinking and feeling. Invite volunteers to explain their comic strips to the class.

Comprehension

1. **Recall** What events occur to allow Casey a final turn at bat?

2. **Recall** How does Casey approach the last pitch?

3. **Represent** Review the poem and figure out what some of the game statistics are in the ninth inning. Include the score for each team and the number of hits and men left on base for "the Mudville nine."

	Score	Hits	Men Left on Base
Home			
Visitor			

Literary Analysis

4. **Draw Conclusions** How would you describe Casey's overall response to his team's situation? Consider his interactions with his **fans,** the pitcher, and the umpire.

5. **Make Judgments About a Character** What is your opinion of Casey by the end of the poem? Explain.

6. **Analyze Narrative Poetry** Review the notes about setting, characters, and plot that you included in your diagram as you read. How does the setting affect the characters' actions and emotions?

7. **Analyze Repetition** A **stanza** is a group of lines that form a unit within a poem. Reread the last stanza and notice the word that is repeated in lines 50–51. What idea does the repeated word seem to emphasize?

8. **Evaluate the Poem** Why do you think this poem has remained popular for so many years?

Extension and Challenge

9. **Speaking and Listening** With a small group, practice reading the poem aloud in a way that captures the excitement and suspense of the game. Then discuss how the sound devices help you add drama to your oral reading.

10. **Inquiry and Research** Choose a famous baseball player—such as Babe Ruth, Lou Gehrig, or Hank Aaron—whose accomplishments have made history. Research the player to find out what team he played for and when, what records he broke, and what his fans and teammates had to say about him.

Babe Ruth
1895–1948

CASEY AT THE BAT   133

MARYLAND OBJECTIVES

LITERATURE STANDARD
3.A.4.a Use structural features to distinguish types of poetry

Practice and Apply

After Reading

For additional support of post-reading questions, use these copy masters:

R RESOURCE MANAGER—Copy Masters
Narrative Poetry p. 181 (for practice of literary analysis standards focus)
Question Support p. 185 (**After Reading** questions adapted for English learners and less-proficient readers)

Additional selection questions are provided for teachers on page 177.

ANSWERS

Comprehension

1. *With two men out, Flynn and Blake each get base hits. Casey bats after them.*

2. *Casey is angry and determined to get a hit. He swings hard at the pitch.*

3. *Score: Home 2, Visitor 4. For Mudville, after Flynn there was one hit and one man on base; after Blakey there were two hits and two men left on base.*

Literary Analysis

Possible answers:

4. *Casey seems calm and in control; he is confident that he can get a hit (lines 21–22). He quiets the fans down when they get upset with the umpire (lines 35–38).*

5. *He seems arrogant and overconfident when he doesn't swing at the first two pitches (lines 32, 40). He lets his emotions get in the way when he faces the last pitch with "hate" and "vengeance" (lines 45–46).*

6. ● **STANDARDS FOCUS** *Narrative Poetry* *It's the last inning and the home team is losing (lines 1–4). As a result, the players and fans are charged up to do something to turn the game around.*

7. ■ **STANDARDS FOCUS** *Reading Poetry* *Repetition of the word "somewhere" suggests that life still goes on, although in Mudville it feels like the end of the world when Casey strikes out.*

8. *Baseball is still very popular. Also, people can identify with the suspense of the situation and relate to the idea of a sports star and the feelings of the fans who desperately want their team to win.*

Extension and Challenge

9. *Students' discussions should give specific examples of repetition, rhyme, and rhythm that help make their oral reading of the poem exciting and interesting.*

10. *Students should use reliable sources to gain information about each chosen player, including facts about his career and statements that show what fans and teammates thought of the player.*

Assess and Reteach

Assess

R RESOURCE MANAGER—Copy Masters
Selection Tests A, B/C pp. 189–190, 191–192

◎ Test Generator CD

Reteach

S STANDARDS LESSON FILE
Literature Lesson 16: Narrative vs. Lyric Poetry
Literature Lesson 19: Rhyme and Rhyme Scheme
Literature Lesson 20: Rhythm and Meter

Focus and Motivate

OBJECTIVES

Literary Analysis
- explore the key idea of a **mob**
- recognize conflict in drama
- analyze a teleplay

Reading
- read stage directions for a teleplay

Vocabulary
- build vocabulary for reading and writing

SUMMARY

The residents of Maple Street are first puzzled and then frightened when all the machines in their neighborhood stop working. After a boy suggests that aliens from outer space are behind the odd events, everyone's prejudices come to the fore. The crowd quickly becomes a mob, turning its accusing eye from one person to the next. The climax occurs when one neighbor kills another. Meanwhile, the real "monsters" observe the scene and comment on how easy it is to make humans destroy each other.

What turns a crowd into a MOB?

Introduce the question and discuss the **KEY IDEA.** Ask students if they have ever been in a crowd that began to act irrationally or aggressively. Talk about the concepts of "mob mentality" and "safety in numbers." Then have students do the **DISCUSS** activity to help them explore the circumstances that might create a **mob**.

Selection Resources

The Monsters Are Due on Maple Street
Teleplay by Rod Serling

What turns a crowd into a MOB?

MARYLAND OBJECTIVES

LITERATURE STANDARDS
3.A.3.b Analyze conflict
3.A.5.c Analyze stage directions

KEY IDEA People in a crowd often act differently than they do when they're alone. In a big group, people might laugh louder, feel braver, or get angrier. Sometimes a crowd can even become dangerous. When it does—as in the teleplay you're about to read—it becomes a **mob**.

DISCUSS With a small group, share stories you may have heard about crowds turning into mobs. Think about how some fans react after a favorite sports team wins a championship or about what can happen when frustrated people take the law into their own hands. Continue your discussion by creating a list of things that can turn a crowd into a mob.

What Can Turn a Crowd into a Mob?
1. Feeling of victory
2.
3.
4.

Selection Resources

RESOURCE MANAGER UNIT 1

Plan and Teach pp. 193–200

Literary Analysis
Summary pp. 201†*, 202‡*
Conflict in Drama pp. 203, 204†*
Question Support p. 209*

Reading
Reading a Teleplay pp. 205, 206†*
Reading Check p. 208
Reading Fluency p. 210

Vocabulary
Study p. 207*

Assessment
Selection Tests A, B/C pp. 211*, 213*
Test Generator CD

BEST PRACTICES TOOLKIT

Differentiated Instruction
pp. 31–38*

Scaffolding Instruction pp. 43–46*

Graphic Organizers/Strategies
New Word Analysis • T Chart •
Read Aloud/Think Aloud • Jigsaw
• Open Mind

Reading Support
Audio Anthology CD*

Technology
Literature and Vocabulary Centers at **ClassZone.com**

WriteSmart CD

---

* Resources for Differentiation   † Also in Spanish   ‡ In Haitian Creole and Vietnamese

LITERARY ANALYSIS: CONFLICT IN DRAMA

Like any story, a drama has a plot that centers on a **conflict.** Since drama is meant to be performed by actors, a drama's conflict usually unfolds through dialogue (conversation between characters) and action that you picture taking place on a stage or screen.

As you read "The Monsters Are Due on Maple Street," make notes about the story's conflict in a conflict map like the one shown.

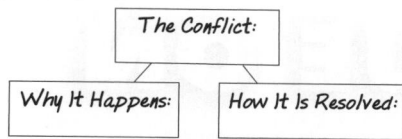

The Conflict:

Why It Happens: How It Is Resolved:

READING STRATEGY: READING A TELEPLAY

To best understand the dialogue and action in a drama, it's important to read the **stage directions.** Stage directions are instructions for the actors, the director, and the reader. They often appear in italics within parentheses. In a **teleplay,** a drama written specifically for television, stage directions also include directions for the camera, such as the following:

The camera moves slowly across the various porches . . .

As you read this teleplay, use all the stage directions to help you imagine the story as it might be presented on television.

VOCABULARY IN CONTEXT

Rod Serling uses these words to help show the conflict unfolding. See how many of them you can match with their numbered definitions.

WORD LIST	assent	converging	optimistic
	antagonism	defiant	revelation
	contorted	incriminate	

1. hopeful about the future; confident
2. willing to stand up to opposition; bold
3. hostility
4. something made known
5. agreement
6. to cause to appear guilty
7. twisted or pulled out of shape
8. moving toward one point

Author Online

Social Issues
During his extraordinary career, Rod Serling won six Emmy awards, the highest honors given to those in the television industry. Known to the public as a creator of exciting television shows, Serling was sometimes referred to by his friends and business associates as "the angry young man of television." Serling wanted to write teleplays about important social issues, but television executives often thought his topics were too controversial.

Rod Serling
1924–1975

Science Fiction Frustrated by this lack of support, Serling turned to writing science fiction and fantasy. He created an eerie series called *The Twilight Zone,* which became one of the most popular shows in television history during its 1959–1964 run. Because the teleplays for this series were not realistic, Serling had more freedom to deal with issues such as prejudice and intolerance. "The Monsters Are Due on Maple Street" first appeared in 1960 as an episode of *The Twilight Zone.*

 MORE ABOUT THE AUTHOR
For more on Rod Serling, visit the
Literature Center at ClassZone.com.

135

Teach

STANDARDS FOCUS

LITERARY ANALYSIS

● CONFLICT IN DRAMA

Read aloud this example:

> **Speaker 1:** Do you hear what those fans are yelling at the players?
>
> **Speaker 2:** I'm nervous. This crowd is getting out of control.
>
> **Speaker 1:** Let's leave before they stampede onto the field.

Have students describe the conflict. *Possible answer: The speakers do not want to get caught up in an angry crowd.*

CHECK UNDERSTANDING Have students identify conflicts in movies or television shows that they have seen recently.

READING STRATEGY

■ READING A TELEPLAY

Read these **stage directions** aloud and ask what each example tells readers about setting, mood, characters, and conflict:

- *We see a full moon over a clock tower. It is two minutes before midnight.*
- *The man smiles and tips his hat.*
- *The two women lock eyes and glare at each other.*

CHECK UNDERSTANDING Ask students what the stage directions might say for a scene from their favorite TV show.

 RESOURCE MANAGER—Copy Master
Reading a Teleplay p. 205 (for student use while reading the selection)

VOCABULARY SKILL

▲ VOCABULARY IN CONTEXT

ANSWERS 1. *optimistic;* **2.** *defiant;* **3.** *antagonism;* **4.** *revelation;* **5.** *assent;* **6.** *incriminate;* **7.** *contorted;* **8.** *converging*

PRETEACH VOCABULARY As you preteach vocabulary, using the Vocabulary Study copy master, supply these definitions:

antagonism (ăn-tăg′ə-nĭz′əm) *n.* hostility; resistance

assent (ə-sĕnt′) *n.* agreement; consent

contorted (kən-tôr′tĭd) *adj.* twisted or pulled out of shape

converging (kən-vûrj′ĭng) *v.* moving toward one point

defiant (dĭ-fī′ənt) *adj.* willing to stand up to opposition; boldly resisting

incriminate (ĭn-krĭm′ə-nāt′) *v.* to cause to appear guilty of a crime or fault

optimistic (ŏp′tə-mĭs′tĭk) *adj.* hopeful about the future; confident

revelation (rĕv′ə-lā′shən) *n.* something made known

RESOURCE MANAGER—Copy Master
Vocabulary Study p. 207

For alternative vocabulary activities, see

ⓘ Vocabulary Center at **ClassZone.com**
Additional Vocabulary Activities

ANALYZE VISUALS

About the Art Much of the work of Belgian artist René Magritte (1898–1967) is characterized by the use of contrast and paradox. In this painting a blue sky, one of the recurring motifs in Magritte's art, spreads out over a night scene below. Many interpretations of this painting are possible, including several ideas also suggested by the teleplay. Darkness may lie under a pleasant and sunny exterior, and things are not always as they seem.

Activity Have students do a quickwrite about

- any unusual elements they notice in the painting on page 137
- the overall effect the painting creates

Students may point out that although the sky is blue and sunlit, the area around the house is dark. The only light comes from the street lamp. The mood created by this contrast is quite eerie. The painting suggests unusual circumstances.

READING STRATEGY

■ READING A TELEPLAY

The first character listed is the narrator. What function might the narrator perform in this drama? *Possible answer: The narrator may add background information or explain some of the events that are occurring.*

THE MONSTERS ARE DUE ON MAPLE STREET

ROD SERLING

CHARACTERS

Narrator	Voice Five
Tommy	Pete Van Horn
Steve Brand	Charlie
Don Martin	Sally, Tommy's mother
Myra Brand, Steve's wife	Man One
Woman	Les Goodman
Voice One	Ethel Goodman, Les's wife
Voice Two	Man Two
Voice Three	Figure One
Voice Four	Figure Two

Empire of Lights (1954), René Magritte. Oil on canvas, 146 cm × 114 cm. Musée d'Art Moderne, Brussels. © Photothèque R. Magritte-ADAGP/Artists Rights Society, New York/Art Resource, New York.

DIFFERENTIATED INSTRUCTION

FOR ALL STUDENTS

Anchor Activity Provide opportunities for independent learning on the key idea of **mobs.** Have individual students or groups research historic events made famous by mobs, such as the St. Bartholomew's Day Massacre, the storming of the Bastille, the Boston Tea Party, the Boxer Rebellion, and the Bolshevik revolution. For further details on this project, see

R RESOURCE MANAGER
Ideas for Extension pp. 198–199

FOR LESS–PROFICIENT READERS

In combination with the *Audio Anthology CD,* use one or more Targeted Passages (pp. 138, 142, 145, 146, 148) to ensure that students focus on key story events, concepts, and skills.

Comprehension Support Have students preview these elements on page 136:

- the title, which gives a setting clue (Maple Street) and creates suspense (monsters are "due")
- the list of characters that shows family relationships (Steve's wife, Tommy's mother)

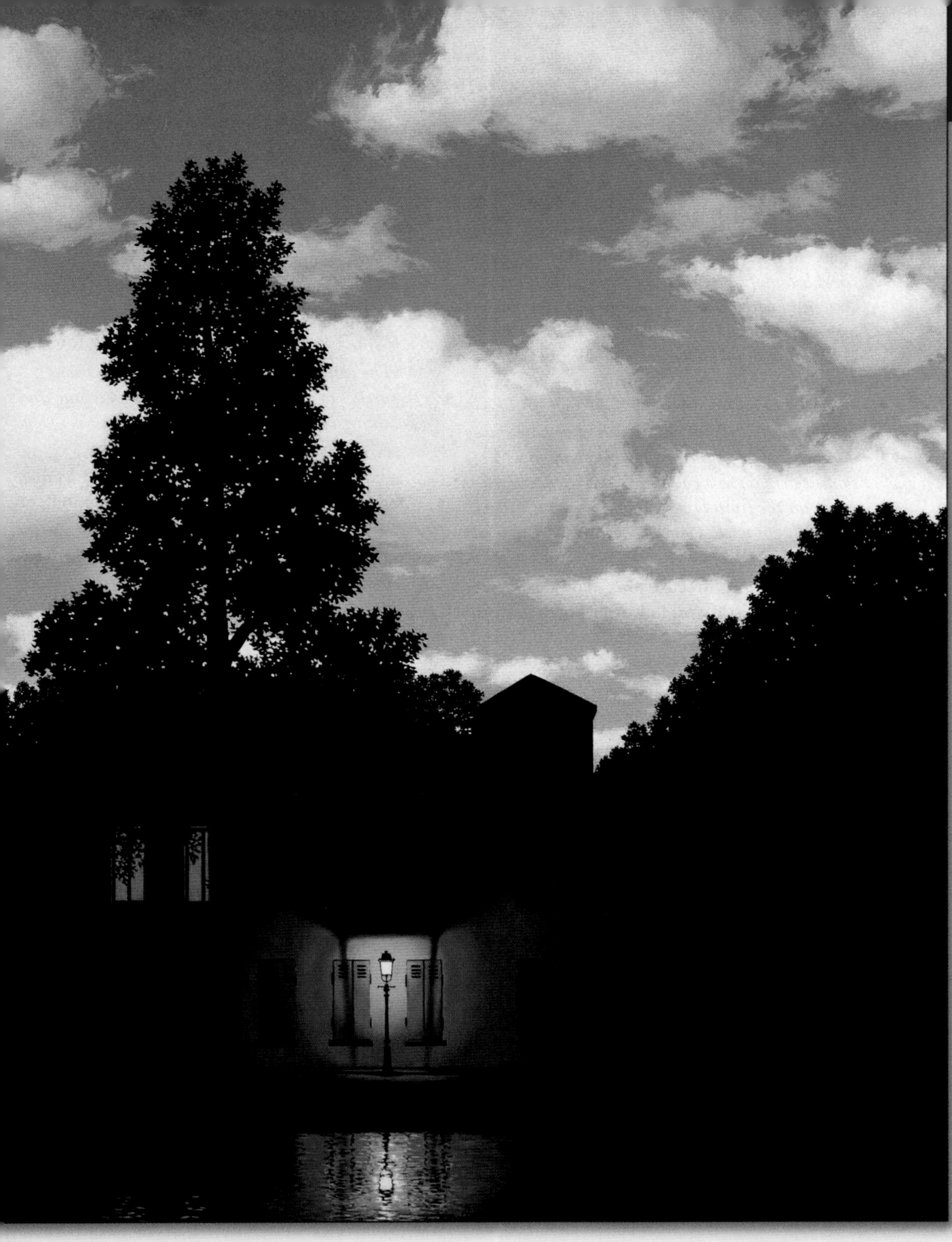

BACKGROUND

Meteors In this teleplay, the residents of Maple Street are busy pursuing their summer evening activities when they hear a "screeching roar" and see a "flash of light" (lines 30–31). They decide that a meteor must have caused the disturbance. Meteors are the streaks of light that can be seen when debris from a comet or asteroid enters Earth's atmosphere. The high speed at which the fragment is traveling, and its friction with molecules in the atmosphere, usually cause it to burn up, producing the light trail. If it is large enough and has a slightly lower velocity, the solid object, called a meteoroid, may survive into lower altitudes. At this point, it might produce a sound like thunder or a sonic boom. Most meteoroids that are not destroyed before reaching Earth's surface fall unnoticed. They make only a slight whistling sound and a thud when they hit the ground. At the point of contact with Earth, the meteoroid becomes known as a meteorite.

FOR ENGLISH LEARNERS

Vocabulary: Technical Language Preview some of the specialized language used in the stage directions of a teleplay, such as

- *"shot"* (Act 1 line 1)
- *"camera moves slowly across"* (Act 1 line 3)
- *"camera takes us"* (Act 1 line 55)
- *"scene slowly fades to black"* (Act 1 line 371)
- *"camera starts to pull away"* (Act 2 line 266)
- *"bringing into focus"* (Act 2 line 270)
- *"silhouetted"* (Act 2 line 274)

Key Academic Vocabulary Use New Word Analysis to help students learn this vocabulary: *intense* (Act 1 line 154), *approaches* (Act 1 line 271), *circumstances* (Act 2 lines 22, 23), *trigger* (Act 2 line 148), *attitudes* (Act 2 line 298).

BEST PRACTICES TOOLKIT—Transparency
New Word Analysis p. E8

Prereading For prereading instruction for English learners, see

BEST PRACTICES TOOLKIT
Scaffolding Reading Instruction pp. 43–46

FOR ADVANCED LEARNERS/PRE–AP

Pre-AP exercises in the bottom channel provide additional challenge for your advanced students. Use them for small groups or individuals.

ADDITIONAL GUIDELINES

For more help with differentiation and tips for classroom management, see

BEST PRACTICES TOOLKIT
Differentiated Instruction pp. 31–38

READING STRATEGY

■ READING A TELEPLAY

Visualize the camera shot described in lines 1–5 of the stage directions. If you were watching this teleplay on TV, what would the image of the night sky make you think of? **Possible answer:** *The night sky makes viewers think of outer space. This opening shot suggests that what happens on Maple Street has something to do with outer space.*

If students need help . . . Set up a T Chart and record the first image described by the stage directions. Discuss what students see in their minds and what the effect is intended to be.

Stage Directions	Effect
image of the night sky and then Maple Street in the daytime (lines 1–5)	makes viewers think of outer space; connects outer space to Maple Street

Extend the Discussion What might this opening shot foreshadow about the "monsters" on Maple Street?

 BEST PRACTICES TOOLKIT—Transparency
T Chart p. A25

LITERARY ANALYSIS

● CONFLICT IN DRAMA

What problem are the people on Maple Street experiencing?

Record students' answers in the chart from page 135. **Possible answer:**

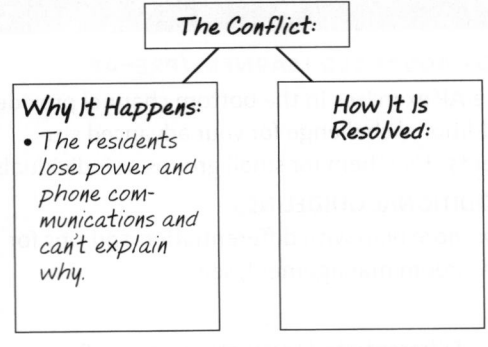

The Conflict:

Why It Happens:
• The residents lose power and phone communications and can't explain why.

How It Is Resolved:

ACT 1

Targeted Passage ①

(*Fade in¹ on a shot of the night sky. The various heavenly bodies stand out in sharp, sparkling relief. The camera moves slowly across the heavens until it passes the horizon and stops on a sign that reads "Maple Street." It is daytime. Then we see the street below. It is a quiet, tree-lined, small-town American street. The houses have front porches on which people sit and swing on gliders, talking across from house to house. Steve Brand is polish-* 10 *ing his car, which is parked in front of his house. His neighbor,* Don Martin, *leans against the fender watching him. An ice-cream vendor riding a bicycle is just in the process of stopping to sell some ice cream to a couple of kids. Two women gossip on the front lawn. Another man is water-ing his lawn with a garden hose. As we see these various activities, we hear the* Narrator's *voice.*)

Narrator. Maple Street, U.S.A., late summer. A tree-lined little world of front-porch gliders, 20 hopscotch, the laughter of children, and the bell of an ice-cream vendor.

(*There is a pause, and the camera moves over to a shot of the ice-cream vendor and two small boys who are standing alongside just buying ice cream.*)

Narrator. At the sound of the roar and the flash of the light, it will be precisely six-forty-three P.M. on Maple Street.

(*At this moment* Tommy, *one of the two boys buy-ing ice cream from the vendor, looks up to listen* 30 *to a tremendous screeching roar from overhead. A flash of light plays on the faces of both boys and then moves down the street and disappears. Various people leave their porches or stop what they are doing to stare up at the sky.* Steve Brand, *the man who has been polishing his car, stands there transfixed, staring upwards. He looks at* Don Martin, *his neighbor from across the street.*)

Steve. What was that? A meteor?

Don. That's what it looked like. I didn't hear 40 any crash though, did you?

Steve. Nope. I didn't hear anything except a roar.

Myra (*from her porch*). What was that?

Steve (*raising his voice and looking toward the porch*). Guess it was a meteor, honey. Came awful close, didn't it?

Myra. Too close for my money! Much too close.

(*The camera moves slowly across the various porches to people who stand there watching and* 50 *talking in low conversing tones.*)

Narrator. Maple Street. Six-forty-four P.M. on a late September evening. (*He pauses.*) Maple Street in the last calm and reflective moment (*pause*) before the monsters came!

(*The camera takes us across the porches again. A man is replacing a light bulb on a front porch. He gets off his stool to flick the switch and finds that nothing happens. Another man is working on an electric power mower. He plugs in the plug,* 60 *flicks the switch of the mower off and on, but noth-ing happens. Through a window we see a woman pushing her finger up and down on the dial hook of a telephone. Her voice sounds far away.*)

Woman. Operator, operator, something's wrong on the phone, operator! (*Myra Brand comes out on the porch and calls to* Steve.)

Myra (*calling*). Steve, the power's off. I had the soup on the stove, and the stove just stopped working.

70 **Woman.** Same thing over here. I can't get anybody on the phone either. The phone seems to be dead.

(*We look down again on the street. Small, mildly disturbed voices are heard coming from below.*)

Voice One. Electricity's off.

Voice Two. Phone won't work.

---

1. **fade in:** cause the television image to appear gradually.

DIFFERENTIATED INSTRUCTION

FOR LESS–PROFICIENT READERS

① **Targeted Passage [Act 1 Lines 18–72]**

This passage establishes the setting and the inciting incident for the main conflict: a strange power outage on Maple Street.

• What kind of place is Maple Street?
• What do the residents of Maple Street see and hear at 6:43 P.M.?
• What happens to the electricity and phones?
• What does the narrator say is coming? How does this statement affect the audience?

FOR ENGLISH LEARNERS

Culture: Clarify Make sure students under-stand that the residents of Maple Street are doing ordinary summer evening activities. Explain terms such as *"front-porch gliders,"* *"hopscotch,"* and *"ice-cream vendor"* (lines 19–21) that might be unfamiliar to students. Tell them that the setting is meant to repre-sent any street in a typical town in America, to show that what happens there can happen anywhere.

Voice Three. Can't get a thing on the radio.

Voice Four. My power mower won't move, won't work at all.

80 **Voice Five.** Radio's gone dead!

(*Pete Van Horn, a tall, thin man, is seen standing in front of his house.*)

Pete. I'll cut through the back yard to see if the power's still on, on Floral Street. I'll be right back!

(*He walks past the side of his house and disappears into the back yard. The camera pans[2] down slowly until we are looking at ten or eleven people standing around the street and overflowing to the* 90 *curb and sidewalk. In the background is* Steve *Brand's car.*)

Steve. Doesn't make sense. Why should the power go off all of a sudden and the phone line?

Don. Maybe some kind of an electrical storm or something.

Charlie. That don't seem likely. Sky's just as blue as anything. Not a cloud. No lightning. No thunder. No nothing. How could it be a storm?

---

2. **pans:** turns.

Woman. I can't get a thing on the radio. Not 100 even the portable.

(*The people again begin to murmur softly in wonderment.*)

Charlie. Well, why don't you go downtown and check with the police, though they'll probably think we're crazy or something. A little power failure and right away we get all flustered and everything—

Steve. It isn't just the power failure, Charlie. If it was, we'd still be able to get a broadcast 110 on the portable.

(*There is a murmur of reaction to this.* Steve *looks from face to face and then at his car.*)

Steve. I'll run downtown. We'll get this all straightened out.

(*He gets in the car and turns the key. Looking through the open car door, we see the crowd watching* Steve *from the other side. He starts the engine. It turns over sluggishly and then stops dead. He tries it again, and this time he can't get* 120 *it to turn over. Then very slowly he turns the key back to "off" and gets out of the car. The people stare at* Steve. *He stands for a moment by the car and then walks toward them.*)

THE MONSTERS ARE DUE ON MAPLE STREET **139**

LITERARY ANALYSIS

● CONFLICT IN DRAMA

Why does Tommy try to prevent the men from going downtown?

Add students' answers to the lower left box of the chart from page 135. **Possible answer:**

Why It Happens:

- *Tommy says that "they" do not want anyone to leave.*

If students need help . . . Remind them of the roar and flash of light in the beginning of Act 1 (lines 28–32). Then have them reread lines 151–152. Help them infer what Tommy believes caused that disturbance and connect his idea to what he is saying to the men.

Extend the Discussion How do Tommy's words increase tension in this situation?

Lines 156–162

READING STRATEGY

■ READING A TELEPLAY

Reread the stage directions in lines 158–160. What is Steve's response to Tommy's idea? **Possible answer:** *He thinks it is foolish, but he is trying to remain calm and pleasant.*

ANALYZE VISUALS

Activity Have students look carefully at the camera angles and focus in this shot. Ask students what the viewer's attention is meant to be on and why. **Possible answer:** *The focus is on the men in the foreground. The crowd is a little blurred. The viewer is meant to pay attention to how the men are interacting; in this scene, the crowd is not central to the action.*

Steve. I don't understand it. It was working fine before—

Don. Out of gas?

Steve (*shakes his head*). I just had it filled.

Woman. What's it mean?

Charlie. It's just as if (*pause*) as if everything
130 had stopped. (*Then he turns toward* Steve.) We'd better walk downtown.

(*Another murmur of* **assent** *to this.*)

Steve. The two of us can go, Charlie. (*He turns to look back at the car.*) It couldn't be the meteor. A meteor couldn't do this.

(*He and* Charlie *exchange a look. Then they start to walk away from the group.* Tommy *comes into view. He is a serious-faced young boy in spectacles. He stands halfway between the group and the two*
140 *men, who start to walk down the sidewalk.*)

Tommy. Mr. Brand—you'd better not!

Steve. Why not?

Tommy. They don't want you to.

(Steve *and* Charlie *exchange a grin, and* Steve *looks back toward the boy.*)

Steve. *Who* doesn't want us to?

Tommy (*jerks his head in the general direction of the distant horizon*). Them!

Steve. Them?

150 **Charlie.** Who are them?

Tommy (*intently*). Whoever was in that thing that came by overhead.

(Steve *knits his brows for a moment, cocking his head questioningly. His voice is intense.*)

Steve. What?

Tommy. Whoever was in that thing that came over. I don't think they want us to leave here.

(Steve *leaves* Charlie, *walks over to the boy, and puts his hand on the boy's shoulder. He forces his*
160 *voice to remain gentle.*)

Steve. What do you mean? What are you talking about?

Tommy. They don't want us to leave. That's why they shut everything off.

Steve. What makes you say that? Whatever gave you that idea?

Woman (*from the crowd*). Now isn't that the craziest thing you ever heard?

DIFFERENTIATED INSTRUCTION

FOR ENGLISH LEARNERS

Language: Contractions Explain that contractions are used often in casual conversation, such as the dialogue in this play. Have small groups identify contractions and the words that form each one, such as

- *don't* (line 124), "do not"
- *What's* (line 128), "What does"
- *It's* (line 129), "It is"
- *We'd* (line 131), "We had"
- *couldn't* (line 135), "could not"
- *you'd* (line 141), "you had"
- *isn't* (line 167), "is not"
- *He's* (line 175), "He has"
- *you'll* (line 180), "you will"
- *Floral Street's* (line 246), "Floral Street has"
- *Let's* (line 289), "Let us"
- *What's* (line 302), "What is"
- *Nothing's* (line 303), "Nothing is"
- *I've* (line 313), "I have"
- *We're* (line 321), "We are"

Tommy (*persistent but a little frightened*). It's always that way, in every story I ever read about a ship landing from outer space.

Woman (*to the boy's mother, Sally, who stands on the fringe of the crowd*). From outer space yet! Sally, you better get that boy of yours up to bed. He's been reading too many comic books or seeing too many movies or something!

Sally. Tommy, come over here and stop that kind of talk.

Steve. Go ahead, Tommy. We'll be right back. And you'll see. That wasn't any ship or anything like it. That was just a . . . a meteor or something. Likely as not— (*He turns to the group, now trying very hard to sound more **optimistic** than he feels.*) No doubt it did have something to do with all this power failure and the rest of it. Meteors can do some crazy things. Like sunspots.

Don (*picking up the cue*). Sure. That's the kind of thing—like sunspots. They raise Cain³ with radio reception all over the world. And this thing being so close—why, there's no telling the sort of stuff it can do. (*He wets his lips and smiles nervously.*) Go ahead, Charlie. You and Steve go into town and see if that isn't what's causing it all.

(Steve *and* Charlie *walk away from the group down the sidewalk as the people watch silently.* Tommy *stares at them, biting his lips, and finally calls out again.*)

Tommy. Mr. Brand!

(*The two men stop.* Tommy *takes a step toward them.*)

Tommy. Mr. Brand . . . please don't leave here.

(Steve *and* Charlie *stop once again and turn toward the boy. In the crowd there is a murmur of irritation and concern, as if the boy's words—even though they didn't make sense—were*

bringing up fears that shouldn't be brought up. Tommy *is both frightened and **defiant**.*)

Tommy. You might not even be able to get to town. It was that way in the story. Nobody could leave. Nobody except—

Steve. Except who?

Tommy. Except the people they sent down ahead of them. They looked just like humans. And it wasn't until the ship landed that—

(*The boy suddenly stops, conscious of the people staring at him and his mother and of the sudden hush of the crowd.*)

Sally (*in a whisper, sensing the **antagonism** of the crowd*). Tommy, please son . . . honey, don't talk that way—

Man One. That kid shouldn't talk that way . . . and we shouldn't stand here listening to him. Why this is the craziest thing I ever heard of. The kid tells us a comic book plot, and here we stand listening—

(Steve *walks toward the camera and stops beside the boy.*)

Steve. Go ahead, Tommy. What kind of story was this? What about the people they sent out ahead?

Tommy. That was the way they prepared things for the landing. They sent four people. A mother and a father and two kids who looked just like humans . . . but they weren't.

(*There is another silence as* Steve *looks toward the crowd and then toward* Tommy. *He wears a tight grin.*)

Steve. Well, I guess what we'd better do then is to run a check on the neighborhood and see which ones of us are really human.

(*There is laughter at this, but it's a laughter that comes from a desperate attempt to lighten the*

---

3. **raise Cain:** cause trouble; create a disturbance. (In the Bible, Adam and Eve's son Cain becomes the first murderer when he kills his brother Abel.)

REINFORCE *KEY IDEA:* MOB

Discuss Who almost becomes a victim of the **mob**? Why? *Possible answer: Les almost becomes a victim of the mob. Everyone is surprised that Les's car starts while no one else's car will (lines 263–270). Don points out that Les did not come out to see what had caused the noise and flash of light (lines 273–277). This behavior makes Les seem different and therefore suspicious in the eyes of the crowd.*

Lines 307–311

READING STRATEGY

■ READING A TELEPLAY

What do the stage directions in lines 307–311 indicate about the change in the crowd's mood? *Possible answer: The crowd is chanting rather than murmuring. They are moving closer to Les. They are angry more than puzzled or confused. They are looking for someone to blame for the odd events that have happened.*

---

atmosphere. The people look at one another in the middle of their laughter.)

Charlie (*rubs his jaw nervously*). I wonder if Floral Street's got the same deal we got. (*He looks past the houses.*) Where is Pete Van Horn anyway? Isn't he back yet?

(*Suddenly there is the sound of a car's engine*
250 *starting to turn over. We look across the street toward the driveway of Les Goodman's house. He is at the wheel trying to start the car.*)

Sally. Can you get started, Les?

(*Les Goodman gets out of the car, shaking his head.*)

Les. No dice.[4]

(*He walks toward the group. He stops suddenly as, behind him, the car engine starts up all by itself. Les whirls around to stare at the car. The car idles*
260 *roughly, smoke coming from the exhaust, the frame shaking gently. Les's eyes go wide, and he runs over to his car. The people stare at the car.*)

Man One. He got the car started somehow. He got *his* car started!

(*The people continue to stare, caught up by this* **revelation** *and wildly frightened.*)

Woman. How come his car just up and started like that?

Sally. All by itself. He wasn't anywheres near it.
270 It started all by itself.

(*Don Martin approaches the group and stops a few feet away to look toward Les's car.*)

Don. And he never did come out to look at that thing that flew overhead. He wasn't even interested. (*He turns to the group, his face taut and serious.*) Why? Why didn't he come out with the rest of us to look?

Charlie. He always was an oddball. Him and his whole family. Real oddball.

280 **Don.** What do you say we ask him?

---

4. **no dice:** no success.

(*The group starts toward the house. In this brief fraction of a moment, it takes the first step toward changing from a group into a mob. The group members begin to head purposefully across the street toward the house. Steve stands in front of them. For a moment their fear almost turns their walk into a wild stampede, but Steve's voice, loud, incisive, and commanding, makes them stop.*)

Steve. Wait a minute . . . wait a minute! Let's
290 not be a mob!

(*The people stop, pause for a moment, and then, much more quietly and slowly, start to walk across the street. Les stands alone facing the people.*)

Les. I just don't understand it. I tried to start it, and it wouldn't start. You saw me. All of you saw me.

(*And now, just as suddenly as the engine started, it stops, and there is a long silence that is gradually intruded upon by the frightened*
300 *murmuring of the people.*)

Les. I don't understand. I swear . . . I don't understand. What's happening?

Don. Maybe you better tell us. Nothing's working on this street. Nothing. No lights, no power, no radio, (*then meaningfully*) nothing except one car—yours!

(*The people's murmuring becomes a loud chant filling the air with accusations and demands for action. Two of the men pass Don and head*
310 *toward Les, who backs away from them against his car. He is cornered.*)

Les. Wait a minute now. You keep your distance—all of you. So I've got a car that starts by itself—well, that's a freak thing—I admit it. But does that make me a criminal or something? I don't know why the car works—it just does!

(*This stops the crowd momentarily, and Les, still backing away, goes toward his front porch. He goes up the steps and then stops, facing the mob.*)

②

Targeted Passage

DIFFERENTIATED INSTRUCTION

FOR LESS–PROFICIENT READERS

② Targeted Passage [Act 1 Lines 249–293]

This passage reveals a turning point in the story: the crowd becomes a mob, and the conflict between the neighbors begins.

- Why are people surprised when Les's car starts?
- What do Don and Charlie say about Les?
- How has the mood of the crowd changed?
- Why does Steve say, "Let's not be a mob!" (lines 289–290)?

FOR ADVANCED LEARNERS/PRE–AP

Analyze Have small groups research the McCarthy era. Pose these questions to guide their research:

- Who was Joseph McCarthy?
- Of what did he accuse people?
- What was his proof?
- How could the accused prove their innocence?
- What brought the McCarthy era to an end?

Discuss how many people in the early 1950s saw communists as monsters of a sort. They were ready to believe that anyone who was a little different might be a communist. Ask students to find parallels between McCarthy's tactics and the actions of the characters in this play as they try to establish guilt or prove their innocence. Have students identify themes that the playwright might have intended to convey through these parallels.

320 Les. What's it all about, Steve?

Steve (*quietly*). We're all on a monster kick, Les. Seems that the general impression holds that maybe one family isn't what we think they are. Monsters from outer space or something. Different from us. Aliens from the vast beyond. (*He chuckles.*) You know anybody that might fit that description around here on Maple Street?

Les. What is this, a gag? (*He looks around the group again.*) This a practical joke or something?

330 (*Suddenly the car engine starts all by itself, runs for a moment, and stops. One woman begins to cry. The eyes of the crowd are cold and accusing.*)

Les. Now that's supposed to **incriminate** me, huh? The car engine goes on and off, and that really does it, doesn't it? (*He looks around at the faces of the people.*) I just don't understand it . . . any more than any of you do! (*He wets his lips, looking from face to face.*) Look, you all know me. We've lived here five years. Right in this **340** house. We're no different from any of the rest of you! We're no different at all. . . . Really . . . this whole thing is just . . . just weird—

Woman. Well, if that's the case, Les Goodman, explain why— (*She stops suddenly, clamping her mouth shut.*)

Les (*softly*). Explain what?

Steve (*interjecting*). Look, let's forget this—

Charlie (*overlapping him*). Go ahead, let her talk. What about it? Explain what?

350 Woman (*a little reluctantly*). Well . . . sometimes I go to bed late at night. A couple of times . . . a couple of times I'd come out here on the porch, and I'd see Mr. Goodman here in the wee hours of the morning standing out in front of his house . . . looking up at the sky. (*She looks around the circle of faces.*) That's right, looking up at the sky as if . . . as if he were waiting for something, (*pauses*) as if he were looking for something.

360 (*There's a murmur of reaction from the crowd again as* Les *backs away.*)

Les. She's crazy. Look, I can explain that. Please . . . I can really explain that. . . . She's making it up anyway. (*Then he shouts.*) I tell you she's making it up!

(*He takes a step toward the crowd, and they back away from him. He walks down the steps after them, and they continue to back away. Suddenly he is left completely alone, and he looks like a* **370** *man caught in the middle of a menacing circle as the scene slowly fades to black.*)

THE MONSTERS ARE DUE ON MAPLE STREET   **143**

FOR LESS–PROFICIENT READERS
Reading Strategy Follow-Up: Reading a Teleplay Use Read Aloud/Think Aloud to show students the significance of the stage directions within lines 281–371. Reading only the italicized text, point out how the camera stays focused on the crowd and what that reveals about the changes taking place within the group. Have students use the strategy to analyze stage directions in the next act.

 BEST PRACTICES TOOLKIT—Transparency
Read Aloud/Think Aloud p. A34

Activity Have students do a quickwrite of the thoughts that are going through the mind of the character pictured here (Les). Ask students to share their ideas.

Lines 321–361
DISCUSSION PROMPTS

Use these prompts to help students understand the emotions and views of the characters as the conflict becomes realized:

Connect Have you ever worried that other people might think that something about you was odd or different? How does this help you understand how Les is feeling? *Students might say that Les feels frightened and nervous. Everyone seems to be against him for reasons he cannot understand. He feels he must defend his actions, even though he's done nothing wrong.*

Analyze What is Steve's strategy for saving Les from the crowd's judgment? *Possible answer: He makes fun of the theory that there may be aliens in the neighborhood. Through humor, he is trying to show how ridiculous the idea is.*

Synthesize How do fear and a mob mentality change the way people interpret the behavior of others? *Possible answer: Any behavior can seem strange or suspicious to people who are scared and acting as a mob.*

Lines 350–361
LITERARY ANALYSIS

● **CONFLICT IN DRAMA**

How does the woman's description of Les's activities increase tension and deepen the conflict? *Possible answer: She describes his looking at the night sky. In the context of the crowd's fear of aliens, this activity seems suspicious. The neighbors quickly jump to the conclusion that Les is associated with aliens, which makes him their enemy.*

Activity Ask students to pick out dialogue from the play that matches this image.
Possible answer: The image shows Charlie, Myra, and Steve in lines 108–117.

Lines 1–10

■ READING A TELEPLAY

What mood is created by the stage directions at the beginning of Act 2, Scene 1?
Possible answer: The neighbors are suspicious and appear to be waiting for something to happen.

If students need help . . . Return to the T Chart (page 138). Identify significant details in the stage directions. For example, *"At the end of each conversation they look toward Les Goodman's house"* (lines 3–4). Also, there is candlelight but no electricity (line 5). Discuss the effect of these details.

Lines 17–33

● CONFLICT IN DRAMA

What major conflict is revealed through the dialogue of Charlie and Les in lines 17–33?

You might record students' answers in the top box of the conflict map from page 135.
Possible answer:

The Conflict:
The neighbors turn against each other.

Extend the Discussion Is this conflict one that can be easily resolved? Explain.

ACT 2
Scene One

(*Fade in on Maple Street at night. On the sidewalk, little knots of people stand around talking in low voices. At the end of each conversation they look toward Les Goodman's house. From the various houses, we can see candlelight but no electricity. The quiet that blankets the whole area is disturbed only by the almost whispered voices of the people standing around. In one group* Charlie *stands staring across at the Goodmans' house. Two men stand*
10 *across the street from it in almost sentrylike[5] poses.*)

Sally (*in a small, hesitant voice*). It just doesn't seem right, though, keeping watch on them. Why . . . he was right when he said he was one of our neighbors. Why, I've known Ethel Goodman ever since they moved in. We've been good friends—

Charlie. That don't prove a thing. Any guy who'd spend his time lookin' up at the sky early in the morning—well, there's something wrong
20 with that kind of person. There's something that ain't legitimate. Maybe under normal circumstances we could let it go by, but these aren't normal circumstances. Why, look at this street! Nothin' but candles. Why, it's like goin' back into the Dark Ages[6] or somethin'!

(Steve *walks down the steps of his porch, down the street to the Goodmans' house, and then stops at the foot of the steps.* Les *is standing there;* Ethel Goodman *behind him is very frightened.*)

30 **Les.** Just stay right where you are, Steve. We don't want any trouble, but this time if anybody sets foot on my porch—that's what they're going to get—trouble!

Steve. Look, Les—

Les. I've already explained to you people. I don't sleep very well at night sometimes. I get up and I take a walk and I look up at the sky. I look at the stars!

---

5. **sentrylike:** resembling those of guards.
6. **Dark Ages:** a period from about A.D. 400 to 1000, when learning and culture in Western Europe were decreasing.

144 UNIT 1: PLOT, CONFLICT, AND SETTING

DIFFERENTIATED INSTRUCTION

FOR ENGLISH LEARNERS

Language: Conversational English Patterns
Tell students that in casual speech, people often use sentence fragments. When people are talking with each other, they are able to fill in any blanks from the context of the conversation. Because the dialogue in this play is meant to suggest informal conversation, there are many sentence fragments throughout.

Assign mixed language-ability Jigsaw groups the task of using context clues to complete these fragments and others they find throughout the play:

- "Nothin' but candles." (line 24)
- "Or you, Charlie. . . . From age eight on up!" (lines 48–50)
- "Steve, please." (line 98)
- "No more talk, Steve." (lines 143–144)

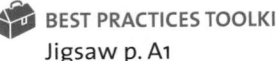

BEST PRACTICES TOOLKIT
Jigsaw p. A1

Ethel. That's exactly what he does. Why, this
40 whole thing, it's . . . it's some kind of madness
or something.

Steve (*nods grimly*). That's exactly what it is—
some kind of madness.

Charlie's Voice (*shrill, from across the street*).
You best watch who you're seen with, Steve!
Until we get this all straightened out, you ain't
exactly above suspicion yourself.

Steve (*whirling around toward him*). Or you,
Charlie. Or any of us, it seems. From age eight
50 on up!

Woman. What I'd like to know is—what are
we gonna do? Just stand around here all night?

Charlie. There's nothin' else we *can* do! (*He
turns back, looking toward* Steve *and* Les *again.*)
One of 'em'll tip their hand. They got to.

Steve (*raising his voice*). There's something
you can do, Charlie. You can go home and
keep your mouth shut. You can quit strutting
around like a self-appointed judge and climb
60 into bed and forget it.

Charlie. You sound real anxious to have that
happen, Steve. I think we better keep our eye
on you, too!

Don (*as if he were taking the bit in his teeth, takes
a hesitant step to the front*). I think everything
might as well come out now. (*He turns toward*
Steve.) Your wife's done plenty of talking,
Steve, about how odd you are!

Charlie (*picking this up, his eyes widening*).
70 Go ahead, tell us what she's said.

(Steve *walks toward them from across the street.*)

Steve. Go ahead, what's my wife said? Let's get it
all out. Let's pick out every idiosyncrasy[7] of every
single man, woman, and child on the street. And
then we might as well set up some kind of citizens' court. How about a firing squad at dawn,
Charlie, so we can get rid of all the suspects.
Narrow them down. Make it easier for you.

Don. There's no need gettin' so upset, Steve.
80 It's just that . . . well . . . Myra's talked about
how there's been plenty of nights you spent
hours down in your basement workin' on some
kind of radio or something. Well, none of us
have ever seen that radio—

(*By this time* Steve *has reached the group.
He stands there defiantly.*)

Charlie. Go ahead, Steve. What kind of "radio
set" you workin' on? I never seen it. Neither
has anyone else. Who do you talk to on that
90 radio set? And who talks to you?

Steve. I'm surprised at you, Charlie. How come
you're so dense all of a sudden? (*He pauses.*)
Who do I talk to? I talk to monsters from
outer space. I talk to three-headed green men
who fly over here in what look like meteors.

(Myra Brand *steps down from the porch, bites
her lip, calls out.*)

Myra. Steve! Steve, please. (*Then looking around,
frightened, she walks toward the group.*) It's just a
100 ham radio[8] set, that's all. I bought him a book
on it myself. It's just a ham radio set. A lot of
people have them. I can show it to you. It's right
down in the basement.

Steve (*whirls around toward her*). Show them
nothing! If they want to look inside our
house—let them go and get a search warrant.

Charlie. Look, buddy, you can't afford to—

Steve (*interrupting him*). Charlie, don't start
telling me who's dangerous and who isn't and
110 who's safe and who's a menace. (*He turns to
the group and shouts.*) And you're with him,
too—all of you! You're standing here all set

---

7. **idiosyncrasy** (ĭd´ē-ō-sĭng´krə-sē): personal way of acting; odd
mannerism.

8. **ham radio:** a two-way radio with which an amateur broadcaster
communicates with other amateurs.

FOR LESS–PROFICIENT READERS

③ **Targeted Passage [Act 2 Lines 61–90]**

This passage shows how a mob turns its attention quickly from one victim to another as
Steve becomes the focus of accusations.

- Why does Charlie say the neighbors should
  keep an eye on Steve (lines 62–63)?
- Why does Don think Steve is odd?
- To whom does Charlie think Steve talks on
  his radio?
- What does this passage show about how a
  mob operates?

Comprehension Support Make sure students
understand the sarcasm in Steve's comments
in lines 72–78 and 91–95. When he talks
about a "citizens' court" (lines 75–76) and
communicating "with three-headed green
men" (line 94), he feels these ideas are so
absurd that no one could possibly take him
seriously. Read these lines aloud, using your
voice to show Steve's sarcastic, mocking tone.

Lines 108–117
REINFORCE *KEY IDEA:* MOB

Discuss What does Steve say a **mob** needs? Why? *Possible answer: Steve says that a mob needs a scapegoat. They need someone to focus their anger on.*

Lines 122–127

READING STRATEGY

■ READING A TELEPLAY

Imagine the scene described in these stage directions. What feeling would it convey to viewers? *Possible answers: The shadowy figure that approaches with slow, regular footsteps creates a feeling of menace or danger.*

Lines 143–160

LITERARY ANALYSIS

● CONFLICT IN DRAMA

The climax of a story occurs when the conflict reaches its most intense moment. Do you think Charlie's shooting Pete Van Horn is the climax of the play? Explain. *Possible answers:*

- *Yes. The mob's fear and suspicion have finally led one neighbor to kill another. The playwright has made his point about the damage that mobs can do.*

- *No. The plot may become even more exciting if there are actual monsters or if the mob turns on Charlie.*

---

to crucify—all set to find a scapegoat[9]—all desperate to point some kind of a finger at a neighbor! Well now, look, friends, the only thing that's gonna happen is that we'll eat each other up alive—

(*He stops abruptly as* Charlie *suddenly grabs his arm.*)

120 **Charlie** (*in a hushed voice*). That's not the only thing that can happen to us.

(*Down the street, a figure has suddenly materialized in the gloom. In the silence we hear the clickety-clack of slow, measured footsteps on concrete as the figure walks slowly toward them. One of the women lets out a stifled cry. Sally grabs her boy, as do a couple of other mothers.*)

Tommy (*shouting, frightened*). It's the monster! It's the monster!

130 (*Another woman lets out a wail, and the people fall back in a group staring toward the darkness and the approaching figure. The people stand in the shadows watching. Don Martin joins them, carrying a shotgun. He holds it up.*)

Don. We may need this.

Steve. A shotgun? (*He pulls it out of* Don's *hand.*) No! Will anybody think a thought around here! Will you people wise up. What good would a shotgun do against—

140 (*The dark figure continues to walk toward them as the people stand there, fearful, mothers clutching children, men standing in front of their wives.*)

Charlie (*pulling the gun from* Steve's *hands*). No more talk, Steve. You're going to talk us into a grave! You'd let whatever's out there walk right over us, wouldn't yuh? Well, some of us won't!

(Charlie *swings around, raises the gun, and suddenly pulls the trigger. The sound of the shot explodes in the stillness. The figure suddenly lets*

150 *out a small cry, stumbles forward onto his knees,*

---

9. **scapegoat:** a person or thing made to bear the blame for the mistakes of others.

---

and then falls forward on his face. Don, Charlie, and Steve race forward to him. Steve is there first and turns the man over. The crowd gathers around them.)

Steve (*slowly looks up*). It's Pete Van Horn.

Don (*in a hushed voice*). Pete Van Horn! He was just gonna go over to the next block to see if the power was on—

Woman. You killed him, Charlie. You shot

160 him dead!

Charlie (*looks around at the circle of faces, his eyes frightened, his face* **contorted**). But . . . but I didn't know who he was. I certainly didn't know who he was. He comes walkin' out of the darkness—how am I supposed to know who he was? (*He grabs* Steve.) Steve—you know why I shot! How was I supposed to know he wasn't a monster or something? (*He grabs* Don.) We're all scared of the same thing. I was just tryin'

170 to . . . tryin' to protect my home, that's all! Look, all of you, that's all I was tryin' to do. (*He looks down wildly at the body.*) I didn't know it was somebody we knew! I didn't know—

(*There's a sudden hush and then an intake of breath in the group. Across the street all the lights go on in one of the houses.*)

Woman (*in a hushed voice*). Charlie . . . Charlie . . . the lights just went on in your house. Why did the lights just go on?

180 **Don.** What about it, Charlie? How come you're the only one with lights now?

Les. That's what I'd like to know.

(*Pausing, they all stare toward* Charlie.)

Les. You were so quick to kill, Charlie, and you were so quick to tell us who we had to be careful of. Well, maybe you had to kill. Maybe Pete there was trying to tell us something. Maybe he'd found out something and came

④

Targeted Passage

DIFFERENTIATED INSTRUCTION

FOR LESS-PROFICIENT READERS

④ **Targeted Passage [Act 2 Lines 122–160]**

This passage represents the climax of the play: the mob becomes violent when Charlie shoots Pete Van Horn.

- Who or what do people think the dark figure is?
- What does Charlie do? Why?
- Who is the figure?
- Does Charlie's action resolve the play's conflict?

FOR ENGLISH LEARNERS

Vocabulary: Idioms and Slang Have pairs of students use context clues to define idiomatic and slang expressions found in the teleplay, such as

- *eat each other up alive* (lines 116–117), "destroy each other"
- *wise up* (line 138), "think"
- *walk right over us* (lines 145–146), "take advantage of us" or "take control"
- *pulling a gag* (line 195), "playing a joke"

FOR ADVANCED LEARNERS/PRE-AP

Explore the Concept of a Scapegoat Have students use a dictionary or other source to investigate the historical origin of the word *scapegoat* (line 113). *(In the Bible, Aaron confessed the sins of his entire community over the head of a goat and then sent the goat into the wilderness. The word* scape *is a variant of* escape.*)* Have them share what they find and relate it to the concept of a mob.

back to tell us who there was amongst us we
190 should watch out for—

(Charlie *backs away from the group, his eyes wide with fright.*)

Charlie. No . . . no . . . it's nothing of the sort! I don't know why the lights are on. I swear I don't. Somebody's pulling a gag or something.

(*He bumps against* Steve, *who grabs him and whirls him around.*)

Steve. A gag? A gag? Charlie, there's a dead man on the sidewalk, and you killed him!
200 Does this thing look like a gag to you?

(Charlie *breaks away and screams as he runs toward his house.*)

Charlie. No! No! Please!

(*A man breaks away from the crowd to chase* Charlie. *As the man tackles him and lands on top of him, the other people start to run toward them.* Charlie *gets up, breaks away from the other man's grasp, and lands a couple of desperate punches that push the man aside. Then he forces his way, fight-*
210 *ing, through the crowd and jumps up on his front porch.* Charlie *is on his porch as a rock thrown from the group smashes a window beside him, the broken glass flying past him. A couple of pieces cut him. He stands there perspiring, rumpled, blood running down from a cut on the cheek. His wife breaks away from the group to throw herself into his arms. He buries his face against her. We can see the crowd*
220 **converging** *on the porch.*)

Voice One. It must have been him.

Voice Two. He's the one.

Voice Three. We got to get Charlie.

(*Another rock lands on the porch.* Charlie *pushes his wife behind him, facing the group.*)

Charlie. Look, look, I swear to you . . . it isn't me . . . but I do know who

it is . . . I swear to you, I do know who it is.
230 I know who the monster is here. I know who it is that doesn't belong. I swear to you I know.

Don (*pushing his way to the front of the crowd*). All right, Charlie, let's hear it!

(Charlie's *eyes dart around wildly.*)

Charlie. It's . . . it's . . .

Man Two (*screaming*). Go ahead, Charlie.

Charlie. It's . . . it's the kid. It's Tommy. He's the one!

(*There's a gasp from the crowd as we see* Sally
240 *holding the boy.* Tommy *at first doesn't understand and then, realizing the eyes are all on him, buries his face against his mother.*)

Sally (*backs away*). That's crazy! He's only a boy.

Woman. But he knew! He was the only one! He told us all about it. Well, how did he know? How could he have known?

(*Various people take this up and repeat the question.*)

THE MONSTERS ARE DUE ON MAPLE STREET **147**

Lines 180–190
REINFORCE *KEY IDEA*: MOB

Discuss What is ironic about the fact that Les is now accusing Charlie of being dangerous? What characteristic of a **mob** is revealed through Les's comments? *Possible answer: Les was the accused person just a few minutes ago. Now he is the accuser. The sympathies of a mob are unstable and likely to change at any time.*

Lines 201–220

READING STRATEGY

READING A TELEPLAY

What actions are described in lines 201–220? What do these actions reveal about the situation on Maple Street now? *Possible answer: There is a burst of violent activity as the mob chases Charlie to his porch and someone throws a rock at him. All control on the part of the neighbors is now gone.*

Lines 221–223
REINFORCE *KEY IDEA*: MOB

Discuss Why is this dialogue spoken by nameless voices? What happens when people become part of a **mob**? *Possible answer: The fact that no name is given to either speaker shows that it doesn't matter at this point who is speaking—the mob mentality has taken over. People lose their identity when they become part of a mob. They can act differently because they are almost anonymous.*

FOR ADVANCED LEARNERS/PRE–AP

Explore Characters Have students form pairs to locate a scene in which Charlie and Steve interact. One student should complete an Open Mind organizer for Charlie, imagining what thoughts are in his mind, while the other completes the organizer for Steve. Then have students compare what they wrote or drew and discuss why the two characters reacted so differently to situations in the play.

 BEST PRACTICES TOOLKIT—Transparency
Open Mind p. D11

READING STRATEGY

■ READING A TELEPLAY

Use the stage directions to help you imagine the beginning of Act 2, Scene Two. What is the effect of leaving the aliens in silhouette rather than showing their appearances clearly? ***Possible answer:*** *Viewers are left to imagine what the aliens look like. The mystery of who and what they are is not fully resolved.*

LITERARY ANALYSIS

● CONFLICT IN DRAMA

Review the end of Scene One (lines 249–268), and then read Figure One's dialogue in lines 288–292. How will the play's conflict eventually be resolved?

Record students' answers in the third box of the conflict chart from page 135. ***Possible answer:***

How It Is Resolved:
The conflict will spread from one neighborhood to another until all the humans have destroyed each other.

SELECTION WRAP–UP

SYNTHESIZE Have students discuss what they think the major theme of this play is. Ask students to support their conclusions with evidence from the selection. ***Possible answer:*** *"People become their own worst enemies when they act as a mob."*

★ **CRITIQUE** Ask students to evaluate the impact of having actual space aliens be responsible for the chaos on Maple Street. Would the point have been made as effectively or more so if some other circumstance had caused the power and communications failures?

READING FLUENCY

Distribute the copy masters and have students work in groups to practice fluency.

R **RESOURCE MANAGER—Copy Master** Reading Fluency p. 210

Voice One. How could he know?

250 **Voice Two.** Who told him?

Voice Three. Make the kid answer.

(*The crowd starts to converge around the mother, who grabs* Tommy *and starts to run with him. The crowd starts to follow, at first walking fast, and then running after him. Suddenly Charlie's lights go off and the lights in other houses go on, then off.*)

Man One (*shouting*). It isn't the kid . . . it's Bob Weaver's house.

Woman. It isn't Bob Weaver's house, it's Don 260 Martin's place.

Charlie. I tell you it's the kid.

Don. It's Charlie. He's the one.

(*People shout, accuse, and scream as the lights go on and off. Then, slowly, in the middle of this nightmarish confusion of sight and sound, the camera starts to pull away until, once again, we have reached the opening shot looking at the Maple Street sign from high above.*)

Scene Two

(*The camera continues to move away while* 270 *gradually bringing into focus a field. We see the metal side of a spacecraft that sits shrouded in darkness. An open door throws out a beam of light from the illuminated interior. Two figures appear, silhouetted against the bright lights. We get only a vague feeling of form.*)

Figure One. Understand the procedure now? Just stop a few of their machines and radios and telephones and lawn mowers. . . . Throw them into darkness for a few hours, and then 280 just sit back and watch the pattern.

Figure Two. And this pattern is always the same?

Figure One. With few variations. They pick the most dangerous enemy they can find . . . and it's themselves. And all we need do is sit back . . . and watch.

Figure Two. Then I take it this place . . . this Maple Street . . . is not unique.

Figure One (*shaking his head*). By no means. Their world is full of Maple Streets. And we'll 290 go from one to the other and let them destroy themselves. One to the other . . . one to the other . . . one to the other—

Scene Three

(*The camera slowly moves up for a shot of the starry sky, and over this we hear the* Narrator's *voice.*)

Narrator. The tools of conquest do not necessarily come with bombs and explosions and fallout. There are weapons that are simply thoughts, attitudes, prejudices—to be found only in the minds of men. For the record, 300 prejudices can kill and suspicion can destroy. A thoughtless, frightened search for a scapegoat has a fallout all its own for the children . . . and the children yet unborn, (*a pause*) and the pity of it is . . . that these things cannot be confined to . . . The Twilight Zone!

(*Fade to black.*)

S **Targeted Passage**

DIFFERENTIATED INSTRUCTION

FOR LESS–PROFICIENT READERS

S **Targeted Passage [Act 2 Lines 269–306]**

This passage resolves the conflict for readers by revealing that aliens really are seeking to destroy humankind, although indirectly.

- Who are Figure One and Figure Two?
- What did the aliens actually do?
- What does Figure One say always happens when people are frightened and confused?
- What is the goal of the aliens?

FOR ENGLISH LEARNERS

Comprehension: Concept Support Read aloud the narrator's speech at the end of the play (lines 295–305). Explain that this speech summarizes a major theme of the play, which is that suspicion and prejudice are more destructive than bombs and other weapons. Ask students for examples from the play that show how suspicion can damage relationships and lead to great harm.

Comprehension

1. **Recall** When do the neighbors first sense something is wrong?

2. **Clarify** How is Pete Van Horn killed?

3. **Clarify** Why do the neighbors become suspicious of Tommy?

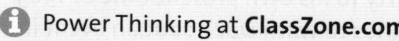

MARYLAND OBJECTIVES

LITERATURE STANDARD
3.A.5.c Analyze stage directions

Literary Analysis

4. **Identify Conflict** Review the conflict map you created as you read. Then explain what you think is the main conflict in the story. What do their reactions to the conflict reveal about the characters?

5. **Analyze the Teleplay** How did the stage directions help you **visualize** the teleplay? Record your answers on a chart like the one shown.

Stage Direction	Its Effect
Fade in on a shot of the night sky.	It makes you focus on outer space.

6. **Analyze Foreshadowing** Foreshadowing is a technique a writer uses to hint at something that will occur later in a story. Reread what the narrator says in lines 51–54 of Act 1. How does this example of foreshadowing affect you as a reader?

7. **Draw Conclusions** At various points in the teleplay, the **mob** thinks different people are the monsters in their midst. Make a list of these people, and consider the moments when the mob turns on them. What conclusions can you draw about how the mob picks its victims?

8. **Make Judgments** In your opinion, who are the monsters referred to in the title? Give reasons for your answer.

Extension and Challenge

9. **Creative Project: Drama** With a small group, review the information about Rod Serling on page 135. Then act out a part of the teleplay that your group thinks communicates a message about prejudice and fear. Remember to follow stage directions as you act out your scene. After your performance, explain why your group chose that particular scene.

10. **Big Question Activity** Look again at the big question on page 134. Not all of the characters in this teleplay are equally quick to go along with the crowd. Identify a character who urges people to think calmly and reasonably, and write three paragraphs describing his or her efforts. Include a sentence that tells why the character isn't successful in preventing the crowd from becoming a mob.

THE MONSTERS ARE DUE ON MAPLE STREET **149**

Extension and Challenge

9. *Students should choose scenes that clearly communicate a message about prejudice and fear, such as lines 249–319 (Act 1).*

10. *Most students will choose Steve. Their paragraphs should describe how he remains unmoved by the suspicions sweeping the others and how he stands up against the mob. He is not successful primarily because there are too many others who want to believe the accusations.*

Assess and Reteach

Assess

 RESOURCE MANAGER—Copy Masters
Selection Tests A, B/C pp. 211–212, 213–214

Test Generator CD

Reteach

STANDARDS LESSON FILE
Literature Lesson 6: Conflict

Practice and Apply

After Reading

For additional support of post-reading questions, use these copy masters:

RESOURCE MANAGER—Copy Masters
Reading Check p. 208 (to check understanding of the selection)
Conflict in Drama p. 203 (for practice of literary analysis standards focus)
Question Support p. 209 (**After Reading** questions adapted for English learners and less-proficient readers)

Additional selection questions are provided for teachers on p. 197.

For additional activities to challenge students, see

Power Thinking at **ClassZone.com**

ANSWERS

Comprehension

1. *The neighbors sense that something is wrong when all the power sources fail.*

2. *Charlie thinks that Pete is a monster and shoots him.*

3. *The neighbors begin to suspect Tommy when Charlie points out that Tommy was the first to mention the idea of aliens.*

Literary Analysis

Possible answers:

4. ● **STANDARDS FOCUS** *Conflict in Drama* The major conflict is among the neighbors or between aliens and humans. Charlie, Don, Les, and the others fight for survival by accusing their neighbors. Only Steve does not do this.

5. ■ **STANDARDS FOCUS** *Reading a Teleplay* Students may select such lines as 6–9 and 144–145 (both from Act 1) that describe where the action occurs and what people are doing.

6. *These lines heighten suspense and motivate readers to read further.*

7. *Students' lists should support the idea that there are no facts to support any of the accusations; the mob turns its attention wildly from one victim to another.*

8. *Some students may say that the aliens are the monsters. However, the narrator's comments at the end suggest that the humans are the real monsters.*

THE MONSTERS ARE DUE ON MAPLE STREET **149**

Focus and Motivate

OBJECTIVES

Media Literacy

- explore the key idea of **imagination**
- identify and analyze visual and sound elements in film
- analyze film techniques that establish plot and setting
- create a storyboard

SUMMARY

In this clip from *Back to the Future*, Doc has devised a way to harness energy from a lightning bolt that will strike at a precise moment in 1955. The energy will fuel a time machine to return Marty to his own present time of 1985. As Marty tries to warn Doc about an event in the future, the storm knocks down a cable, and the pair must scramble to reconnect it. Doc connects the cable just as the lightning strikes, and Marty and the time machine disappear in a burst of light.

What makes your IMAGINATION *soar?*

Discuss the question. Point out that people use their **imaginations** to answer questions that begin with "What if . . . ?" After students read the *KEY IDEA* paragraph, ask them to name stories or movies with fantastic settings and plots. Which stories do the best job of engaging their imaginations, and why?

BACKGROUND

Marty McFly first winds up in 1955 when terrorists come to claim the plutonium Doc has stolen to fuel his time machine. Marty jumps into the car to flee these dangerous men. When he hits the critical speed of 88 miles per hour, he is sent back 30 years.

The car used for the time machine in the movie is a DeLorean. The initials DMC, for DeLorean Motor Car, can be seen in the car's grill. The DMC-12 had an unpainted stainless-steel exterior and gull-wing doors. The first draft of the movie script included a modified refrigerator as the time machine. Director Robert Zemeckis and producer Steven Spielberg dropped that idea for fear it would give children the idea to climb into refrigerators.

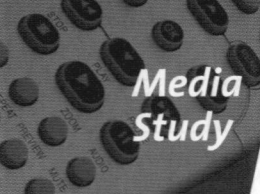

Media Study

from Back to the Future
Film Clip on  Media*Smart* DVD

What makes your IMAGINATION *soar?*

MARYLAND OBJECTIVES

LISTENING STANDARD
6.A.2 Apply comprehension and literary analysis strategies for a variety of listening purposes

KEY IDEA One of the keys to a good story is how it is told. Storytellers of all kinds know how satisfying a story can be when it taps into your sense of wonder and your willingness to believe in fantastic happenings and places. To explore how a movie can bring an unusual plot and setting to life, you'll watch a scene from a movie that has captured the **imagination** of millions of people.

Background

From Time to Time The movie *Back to the Future* is a science fiction adventure about time travel. Seventeen-year-old Marty McFly has a scientist friend, Dr. Emmett L. Brown, who has been experimenting with ways to travel across time. Doc, as Marty calls him, has invented a time machine that looks like a stylish, specially equipped car.

To escape sudden danger, Marty leaps into the car and speeds 30 years into the past—to 1955. He soon learns that having the power to control time comes with certain risks.

150

Media Study Resources

 RESOURCE MANAGER UNIT 1

Plan and Teach pp. 215–218

Media Analysis
Summary pp. 219†*, 220‡*
Viewing Guide p. 221
Close Viewing p. 222
Viewing Activity p. 223
Produce Your Own Media p. 224

S STANDARDS LESSON FILE

Media Lesson 4: Analyzing Visuals in Film
Media Lesson 5: Analyzing Sound Elements in Film
Media Lesson 6: Analyzing Editing in Film and TV

ℹ️ Media Center at **ClassZone.com**

MEDIA VIEWING
🔘 Media*Smart* DVD

---

* **Resources for Differentiation**   † **Also in Spanish**   ‡ **In Haitian Creole and Vietnamese**

Media Literacy: Plot and Setting in Movies

Moviemakers tell stories by using visual and sound techniques. These techniques are used to help viewers follow the events of a plot. In addition, the techniques help to make the setting and the actions within it seem very real.

MOVIE TECHNIQUES	STRATEGIES FOR VIEWING	
Visual Techniques A movie director uses carefully chosen camera shots to support important elements of the plot. A **shot** is the continuous recording of a scene or image.	Watch for carefully chosen **camera shots.** • A **close-up shot** is a close view of a person or an object. It is often used to show a character's emotions or reactions. • A **reaction shot** shows a character responding in some way to what he or she sees. • A **low-angle shot,** in which the camera looks up at the subject, can help create the impression of height or distance.	
Editing The careful selection and arrangement of shots is called **editing.** Moviemakers put shots together in ways that help you follow the action of a story or show relationships between place and events.	• Single shots, when put together, can form a **sequence.** For example, a shot of someone tossing a ball, a shot of the same ball in mid-air, and then a shot of someone catching the ball fit together to form a complete action. • Look for shots that set up a cause-and-effect sequence. In movies with lots of actions, these shots add excitement.	
Sound Techniques Moviemakers use sound to make a setting or action believable. In addition, sound techniques can affect the audience's emotions as events unfold.	• Listen to the **sounds,** which in a movie consist of **music, sound effects,** and **dialogue.** • Be aware of what **sound effects** add to images. Seeing a flash of lightning is one thing, but hearing the clap of thunder helps viewers experience the setting and react to it.	

MEDIA STUDY **151**

MEDIA STUDY: TEACHING OPTIONS

Teaching Option 1: The Basics (1–2 Days)

1. Begin the Media Study using the material provided on pages 150–151.

2. Show the Introduction on Media*Smart.* Then show the First Viewing. As they watch, have students use the Viewing Guide on page 152, along with the corresponding copy master on page 221 of the Resource Manager. Discuss their responses.

3. Return to the pupil edition for the extension activities on page 153.

Teaching Option 2: In-Depth Study (2–3 Days)

1. Begin the Media Study using pages 150–151.

2. Show the Introduction and First Viewing from Media*Smart.*

3. Continue on Media*Smart* with the Media Lessons, using the teacher notes available in the Resources section.

4. Show the Guided Analysis presentation. Have students record their observations on the Student Viewing Guide available in the Resources section from Media*Smart.*

5. Return to the pupil edition, page 153.

Teach

MEDIA LITERACY

Review the terms *plot* and *conflict* and ask students to describe some conflicts faced by characters in movies they have seen. Ask if they recall any scenes in which characters engaged in a "race against time." What makes this kind of scene exciting for movie viewers? Then discuss the chart on page 151.

- **Visual Techniques** Have students explain how the first image on page 151 could be an example of all three kinds of shot—**close-up, reaction,** and **low-angle.** Ask how the effect would be different if this character were shown from a distance or from a high angle. Would viewers see the emotion on the actor's face? Might the actor look small and helpless from a high angle?

- **Editing** Tell students that the scenes in a movie are usually shot out of sequence. After the shooting is completed, the director and the editor arrange the shots in a logical way to tell the story. Also tell students that *pace* refers to the length of time each shot stays on the screen. Ask: What effect could a film editor create by putting together many quick shots in a fast-paced scene?

- **Sound Techniques** Have students imagine several different settings and tell what sound effects would make each one realistic. For example,

  —an afternoon at the seashore *(waves crashing)*

  —midnight in a deserted old house *(creaking floor boards)*

  —a battle scene in the Civil War *(cannon fire)*

  —a busy space station in A.D. 2700 *(computer sounds)*

  Also have them consider what kinds of music might enhance each setting.

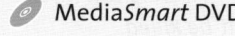 STANDARDS LESSON FILE

> Media Lesson 4: Analyzing Visuals in Film
> Media Lesson 5: Analyzing Sound Elements in Film
> Media Lesson 6: Analyzing Editing in Film and TV

 Media*Smart* DVD

MEDIA STUDY **151**

VIEWING GUIDE

1. As students prepare to view the clips, tell them that they will be asked to explain how specific techniques are used to present the movie's plot and setting. Encourage them to watch and listen for these elements:

   - **camera shots** that establish the setting and focus attention on key events
   - careful **editing** that results in a sequence of logical, fast-paced events
   - **sound effects** that help viewers imagine the setting, and **music** that creates a certain mood
   - **dialogue** that advances the plot and develops characters

2. As students view this action-packed scene, they may have difficulty focusing on the technical aspects. Suggest that they first view the clip without sound to focus on visual elements, and then listen without watching to focus on sound. To help them appreciate the fast pace of the scene, suggest that they watch the clip again and keep a tally sheet, adding a tick mark each time a new shot begins.

   R **RESOURCE MANAGER—Copy Masters**
   Viewing Guide p. 221
   Close Viewing p. 222
   Viewing Activity p. 223

   ⊘ Media*Smart* DVD

ANSWERS

FIRST VIEWING: Comprehension

1. *The time machine must reach a speed of exactly 88 miles per hour and make contact with a wire at the precise moment lightning strikes the clock tower.*

2. *Doc tears up Marty's envelope without reading the information inside.*

CLOSE VIEWING: Media Literacy

Possible answers:

3. *The low-angle shots emphasize how far from the ground Doc is. Viewers can infer that if he falls, he might be killed.*

4. *Sound effects include*
   - *thunder and wind*
   - *Doc tearing Marty's envelope*
   - *falling tree*

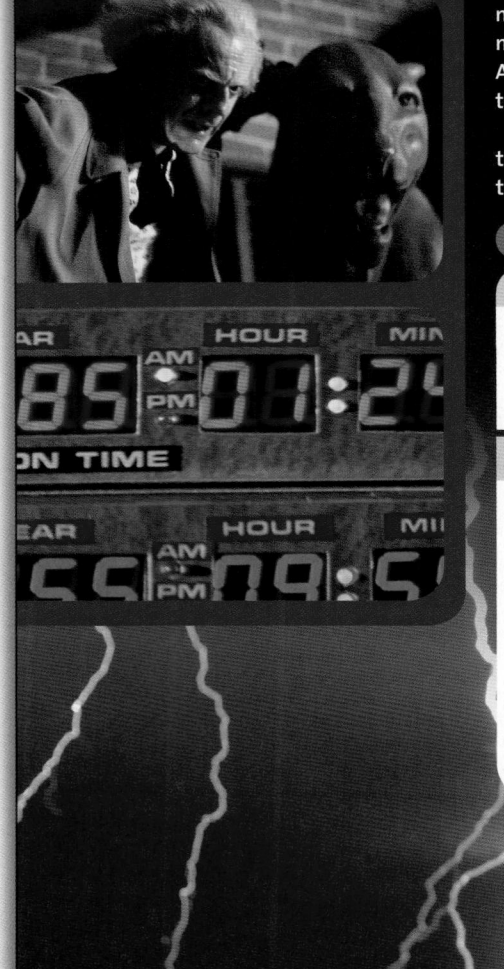

⊙ **MediaSmart** DVD
- **Film Clip:** *Back to the Future*
- **Director:** Robert Zemeckis
- **Rating:** PG
- **Genre:** Sci-fi adventure
- **Running Time:** 8 minutes

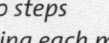
152

- *cable falling onto steps*
- *clock hands moving each minute*
- *clock ringing on the hour*
- *car's engine revving and tires screeching*
- *electronic controls inside time machine*
- *car's starter refusing to turn over*
- *ledge crumbling under Doc's feet*
- *hem of Doc's pants tearing*
- *alarm clock ringing*
- *disconnected cable hitting lamppost*
- *electric current running down wire*

Students may also note the use of music to heighten the drama of the scene.

Viewing Guide for
Back to the Future

At this point in the movie, Marty has realized that his presence in the past has caused a disturbance in time. He has found Dr. Brown, who is 30 years younger, and convinced the inventor to help. If Marty can't leave the year 1955 within the next few minutes, his family will lose its place in the future. He and Doc make speedy preparations in the middle of a lightning storm. As they say their goodbyes, Marty feels he must take a moment to share some important information.

Watch the clip several times. Take as much time as you need to see the events unfold and to spot different visual and sound techniques. Use these questions to help you.

NOW VIEW

FIRST VIEWING: Comprehension

1. **Summarize** What has to happen for the time machine to leave 1955?

2. **Recall** What does Doc do with the information from Marty?

CLOSE VIEWING: Media Literacy

3. **Analyze Camera Shots** The director uses many **low-angle shots** to show Doc at work at the top of the clock tower. How do the low-angle shots help you believe Doc is in danger?

4. **Analyze Sound** Identify at least three **sound effects** that add excitement to the scene.

5. **Analyze Techniques** The clip from *Back to the Future* includes many shots of clocks—both old-fashioned and digital. Why do you think the director uses so many shots that focus on the time?

5. *Time is crucial to both setting and plot. The story revolves around Marty's use of a time machine. Also, the scene in the clip is a race against time before the lightning strikes.*

Write or Discuss

Evaluate the Film Clip In this lesson, you've explored several moviemaking techniques that are used to spark an audience's imagination. Consider the clip from *Back to the Future*. How close did you come to believing the amazing events? Give at least two reasons for your response. Think about

- how you reacted to the events at your first viewing
- how well the moviemakers use such techniques as camera shots and music and other sounds to create excitement

Produce Your Own Media

Storyboard a Race Against Time A **storyboard** is a device used to plan the shooting of a movie. A storyboard is made up of drawings and brief descriptions of what is happening in each shot of a scene. The drawings of a storyboard help moviemakers visualize how a finished scene might look before the scene is filmed. Create a storyboard for a part of the *Back to the Future* clip that you think shows a tense moment. Work with a partner to decide what part of the clip to present.

HERE'S HOW Here are two suggestions for making the storyboard:

- Show what happens in four to six individual frames.
- Show Marty and Doc's race against time. Include a shot or two that includes their quick actions.

> **MEDIA TOOLS**
> For help with creating a storyboard, visit the **Media Center at ClassZone.com.**

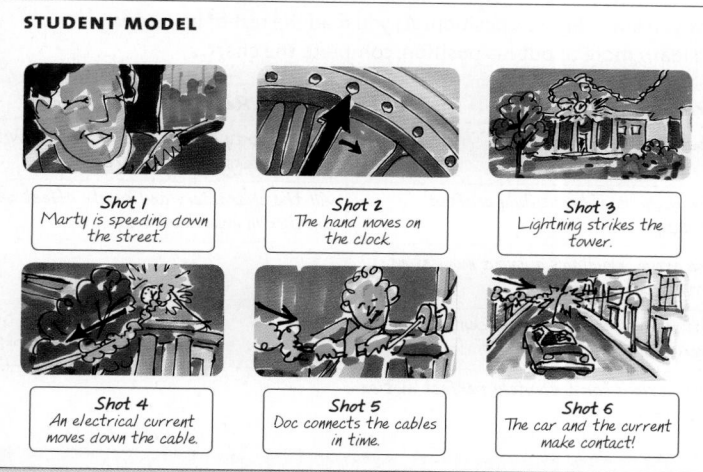

STUDENT MODEL

Shot 1	Shot 2	Shot 3
Marty is speeding down the street.	The hand moves on the clock.	Lightning strikes the tower.
Shot 4	Shot 5	Shot 6
An electrical current moves down the cable.	Doc connects the cables in time.	The car and the current make contact!

Tech Tip
Try using a computer drawing program to make the frames for the storyboard.

Write or Discuss

Evaluate the Film Clip In their evaluations, students should discuss how the filmmakers used camera shots, music, and sound effects to help viewers imagine the unusual events of the story. For example, the last shot of Doc shows his amazed reaction as Marty and the time machine disappear. Viewers identify with the character and tend to believe Marty has indeed gone "back to the future." Sound effects such as the loud thunder and buzzing electrical currents support the idea that Doc has harnessed the awesome power of nature to do amazing things. Students may also note that the fast-paced editing and dramatic music drew them into the excitement of the scene, helping them suspend their disbelief about a story involving a time machine.

Produce Your Own Media

Rubric A strong storyboard should have

- four to six drawings that show the sequence of shots in a scene
- a brief caption for each drawing
- one or two quick shots to indicate the fast pace at which events are happening
- well-chosen shots that show a logical sequence of events linked by cause and effect

R RESOURCE MANAGER—Copy Master
Produce Your Own Media p. 224

MediaSmart DVD

MEDIA STUDY WRAP—UP

Summarize Ask students to summarize the techniques filmmakers use to establish setting and to show action or plot. Have them provide specific examples from the *Back to the Future* film clip they have viewed. Prompt them, if necessary, to focus on the use of various camera shots, the editing of shots to create scenes, and sound techniques such as music, sound effects, and dialogue.

RETEACH

S STANDARDS LESSON FILE
Media Lesson 4: Analyzing Visuals in Film
Media Lesson 5: Analyzing Sound Elements in Film
Media Lesson 6: Analyzing Editing in Film and TV

Focus and Motivate

OBJECTIVES

Reading for Information

- analyze a writer's position
- compare and contrast personal opinions with a reviewer's opinions
- read a movie review

SUMMARY

Daniel Briney writes an enthusiastic review of *Back to the Future*, praising its plot, characters, theme, and cinematic devices. He applauds the fact that the movie is both entertaining and uplifting.

What's the Connection?

Begin a KWL chart on *Back to the Future* to prepare students for the selection. (Plan to complete it at the end of the lesson.) Then have them do a quickwrite of their ideas about the film clip before they read Briney's review. Ask them to consider these questions:

- What did you like best—and least—about the film clip? Why?
- How well did you relate to the characters and the plot?
- Did the film clip make you want to see the whole film? Why or why not?

 BEST PRACTICES TOOLKIT—Transparency
KWL p. A20

Teach

Skill Focus: Analyze a Writer's Position

Explain that a writer's position is his or her opinion about a particular issue. Ask these questions to guide students to the specific reasons and evidence that support each of Briney's positions in the chart:

- What key word(s) in each statement must be supported by evidence?
- What kind of evidence would best support each statement? For example, what would make a movie "thoughtful"?
- Note the boldness of the author's opinions. How strong does the evidence need to be to support them?

Possible chart entries appear on page 156.

 RESOURCE MANAGER—Copy Master
Analyze a Writer's Position p. 233

The Unnatural Course of Time
Movie Review

Use with the *Back to the Future* Media Study, page 150.

 MARYLAND OBJECTIVES

READING/INFO TEXT STANDARDS
1.E.3.a Select and apply appropriate strategies during reading
2.A.4.b Identify and explain the author's viewpoint

What's the Connection?

Did you enjoy the film clip from *Back to the Future*? Find out what Daniel Briney thought of the entire film by reading his movie review, "The Unnatural Course of Time."

Skill Focus: Analyze a Writer's Position

If someone were to say, "That was a great movie! Go see it!" you might ask, "What makes it so good?" and "What's it about?"

When you run across a movie review, read to find out the reviewer's opinion of the film. But don't stop there. Read on to learn specific reasons and evidence for the reviewer's opinion. Then you can decide whether you might agree.

You can usually find the writer's opinion, or **position,** stated in the first paragraph. In the following review, Daniel Briney uses the first paragraph to express his position on the film. He writes

> *Back to the Future* is a thoughtful, beautifully crafted fantasy that maintains a joyous momentum from beginning to end. The movie succeeds so magnificently in everything it sets out to do as to be an absolutely perfect motion picture.

Now you know Briney's position. As you read the rest of his review and learn more about his position, complete the chart.

Briney's Position	Specific Reasons and Evidence
The movie is "thoughtful."	"Fox's Marty McFly is a genuine kid, with genuine fears for his future."
The movie is a "beautifully crafted fantasy."	All the characters and events affect one another in important ways.
The movie "maintains a joyous momentum from beginning to end."	
The movie succeeds "magnificently in everything it sets out to do."	
The movie is "an absolutely perfect motion picture."	

Selection Resources

 RESOURCE MANAGER UNIT 1

Plan and Teach pp. 225–229

Reading
Summary pp. 231†*, 232‡*
Analyze a Writer's Position pp. 233, 235†*
Reading Check p. 237
Compare and Contrast pp. 234, 236†*
Question Support p. 239*

Assessment
Selection Tests A, B/C pp. 241*, 243*
 Test Generator CD

Reading Support
 Audio Anthology CD*

BEST PRACTICES TOOLKIT
KWL • Reciprocal Teaching • New Word Analysis

* Resources for Differentiation   † Also in Spanish   ‡ In Haitian Creole and Vietnamese

The Unnatural Course of Time

Review by **Daniel Briney**

Back to the Future is a thoughtful, beautifully crafted fantasy that maintains a joyous momentum from beginning to end. The movie succeeds so magnificently in everything it sets out to do as to be an absolutely perfect motion picture. **Ⓐ**

Its hero is Marty McFly (Michael J. Fox), an average American 17-year-old of the '80s—filled with youthful hopes for his future, and fearful that they may not come to pass. . . . One night, an encounter with his friend Dr. Emmett L. Brown's (Christopher Lloyd) time machine throws Marty into a struggle for his very existence. . . . He's deposited in the year 1955, where his home town Hill Valley is cleaner and brighter, Doc Brown is a younger man only beginning to probe the fourth dimension, and Marty's own parents are high school students with their whole lives before them. . . . But by coming to the past, Marty has accidentally altered something with profound ramifications for his future: his parents' first meeting. A photo of Marty and his siblings, whose images are fading away one by one, is an ominous sign of what this turn of events means. Of course, if his parents never meet and fall in love, he can never be born. . . . Marty has exactly a week to somehow bring them together, or be erased for all time. **Ⓑ**

Fox's Marty McFly is a genuine kid, with genuine fears for his future—and as we are introduced to the other members of his family, failures all, his otherwise-normal teenage anxieties take on a greater urgency. . . . It's in this context that his friendship with Doc Brown makes such perfect sense.

Fox and Lloyd both turn in outstanding performances here—the personalities of these two and the excellent comic and dramatic chemistry

Ⓕ OCUS ON FORM
"The Unnatural Course of Time" is a **movie review,** a short essay in which a writer presents and supports his or her opinions about a movie.

Ⓐ ANALYZE A WRITER'S POSITION
Judging by his opening paragraph, what do you expect Daniel Briney to discuss in the rest of the review?

Ⓑ MOVIE REVIEW
A movie review usually gives a short description of the movie's main plot and conflict. Briefly summarize Briney's description of *Back to the Future.*

READING FOR INFORMATION **155**

FOCUS ON FORM

Discuss with students the purpose of a movie review and these main characteristics:

- content is nonfiction
- style is journalistic or promotional (newspaper, magazine, or Web site)
- topic is a particular movie
- usually includes a short description of the setting, characters, conflict, and plot
- purpose is to present a writer's opinion of a movie with supporting evidence to help viewers evaluate the movie

Invite students to brainstorm what they think makes a good movie review. As movie viewers and as critical readers, what would they be looking for?

INFORMATIONAL ANALYSIS

Ⓐ ANALYZE A WRITER'S POSITION

Possible answer: He will give examples from the movie that support his opinion that the movie is completely successful in every way.

LITERARY ANALYSIS

Ⓑ MOVIE REVIEW

Possible answer: The movie focuses on a 17-year-old of the 1980s named Marty McFly who is sent back in time and somehow changes his parents' first meeting in a way that could prevent his ever being born.

If students need help . . . Have students reread the passage and identify the setting, the main character, and the problem he faces.

DIFFERENTIATED INSTRUCTION

FOR LESS–PROFICIENT READERS

Comprehension Support Model Reciprocal Teaching on the first paragraph (lines 1–6). Sample responses include

- **Summarize:** *Briney is enthusiastic about every aspect of the movie.*
- **Question:** *In what specific ways does the movie succeed magnificently?*
- **Clarify:** *A movie has "momentum" (line 3) if it has a lot of action and isn't boring.*

- **Predict:** *In the next paragraphs, Briney will provide evidence for his opinion.*

Have pairs of students use the technique as they read the rest of the review.

BEST PRACTICES TOOLKIT—Transparency Reciprocal Teaching p. A35

FOR ENGLISH LEARNERS

Options for Reading Make sure students understand that *position* is a synonym for *opinion,* an expression of the author's beliefs and feelings. *Evidence* may include reasons, examples, or facts. Have students read along as they listen to the selection on the *Audio Anthology CD.* Clarify unfamiliar words as needed.

between them are crucial to *Back to the Future*'s great appeal. . . . **C**
The characters' relationship is best communicated by the major conflict
30 that erupts between them: that of future knowledge. Doc is adamant
that *no one* should be allowed information about his own future, lest
that knowledge endanger the same future—just as Marty's has been
endangered. Marty faces a heart-rending decision over whether to heed
the scientist's warnings or ignore them. . . . And even if there were an
easy way to tell him, Doc won't listen. . . . In this, one of the movie's
most touching scenes, Doc rebuffs his friend's attempt to save him:

DOC: Marty, I'm going to be really sad to see you go. You've made
a real difference in my life; you've given me something to shoot for.
Just *knowing* that I'm going to be around to see *1985,* that I'm going
40 to succeed in *this,* that I'm going to have a chance to travel through time
. . . It's going to be really hard waiting thirty years before I can talk
to you about everything that's happened in the past few days. I'm really
going to miss you, Marty.

MARTY: I'm really going to miss you. (*a beat*) Doc, *about* the future . . .

DOC: *No!* Marty, we've already agreed that having information about
the future can be extremely dangerous! Even if your intentions are *good,*
it can backfire drastically. Marty, whatever you have to tell me, I'll find
out through the natural course of *time.*

Of course, the film deserves a great deal of praise for its action
50 sequences, most of which feature the bizarrely modified, impossibly cool
DeLorean time machine. There is a great deal of excitement in Marty's . . .
pursuit through the town square by an enraged bully, and a superbly
realized, adrenaline-fueled climax in which Doc Brown dangles
precipitously from the courthouse clock tower. . . . **D**

But it is *Back to the Future*'s ultimate message—that we can change our
lives for the better—that is at the very heart of its enormous success. . . .

Back to the Future is a unique coming-of-age story that hits every mark
in spectacular fashion and leaves us not only thoroughly entertained, but
heartened. We don't need to believe in real-life time machines for it to
60 successfully remind us that all things are possible—and that we are our
own second chances.

DIFFERENTIATED INSTRUCTION

FOR ENGLISH LEARNERS

Vocabulary: Idioms Use New Word Analysis to teach these idiomatic expressions:

- "something to shoot for" (line 38), *"a goal to work toward"*
- "coming-of-age story" (line 57), *"story about a young person growing up"*
- "hits every mark" (line 57), *"achieves all its goals"*

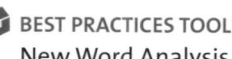 BEST PRACTICES TOOLKIT—Transparency
New Word Analysis p. E8

FOR ADVANCED LEARNERS/PRE–AP

Analyze Writing Style Some reviewers refrain from writing "rave reviews" because they think that too many superlatives raise doubts in readers' minds. Readers may think, "It can't be *that* good." Have students make a quick list of adjectives that Briney uses to describe the movie. Then have them share their opinions about whether or not these descriptions convince them of the movie's excellence.

Comprehension

1. **Recall** What does Daniel Briney say is the main message of *Back to the Future*?

2. **Summarize** In his movie review, Briney includes a touching scene between Doc and Marty. Summarize what happens in this scene.

Critical Analysis

3. **Examine a Movie Review** Reread the notes next to the movie review. Besides providing a writer's opinions of a movie and support for those opinions, what else does a movie review usually provide? Tell why you think this might be helpful to a reader.

4. **Analyze a Writer's Position** Review the chart you completed. Does Briney support each part of his position?

Read for Information: Compare and Contrast

MARYLAND OBJECTIVES

READING/INFO TEXT STANDARDS
1.E.3.a Select and apply appropriate strategies during reading
2.A.4.b Identify and explain the author's viewpoint

WRITING PROMPT

In the review you just read, Daniel Briney describes the clock-tower scene as "a superbly realized, adrenaline-fueled climax" (lines 52–53). Do you agree with his opinions of this scene? In a paragraph, compare and contrast your opinions of this scene with Briney's.

To answer this prompt, first decide on your own opinions of the clock-tower scene by jotting them down. Then follow these steps:

1. Use a Venn diagram to record your opinions and Daniel Briney's.

2. Look at your diagram to see whether there are more similarities or more differences.

My Opinions   Briney's Opinions

Similarities

3. In a sentence, tell whether your opinions and Briney's are very similar or quite different. Then support the sentence by pointing out the specific similarities and differences.

4. If your opinion of the clock-tower scene is very different from Briney's, consider explaining the reasons for your opinion.

FOR LESS–PROFICIENT WRITERS

Read for Information Before students begin making their Venn diagrams, help them paraphrase Briney's descriptive phrase. Encourage students to restate "a superbly realized, adrenaline-fueled climax" in their own words, or with the help of a dictionary or thesaurus. Sample paraphrases may read:

- "a well put-together, energy-powered turning point"

- "a fantastically accomplished, intensity-driven moment of greatest interest"

FOR ENGLISH LEARNERS

Writing: Task Support Make sure students understand that the point of the **Writing Prompt** is to compare and contrast their opinions with Briney's position. Provide the following sentence frames to help students organize their thoughts and structure their responses:

- Briney thinks that _____. However, I disagree because _____.

- I agree with Briney when he says _____. This is a strong argument because _____.

Practice and Apply

For additional support of post-reading questions, use these copy masters:

 RESOURCE MANAGER—Copy Masters
Reading Check p. 237
Question Support p. 239
Compare and Contrast p. 234

For additional questions, see p. 228.

ANSWERS

Comprehension

1. *"that we can change our lives for the better" (lines 55–56)*

2. *Possible answer: Doc and Marty say goodbye and that they will miss each other. Marty tries to share information about the future, but Doc won't let him (lines 37–48).*

Critical Analysis

3. *Examine a Movie Review **Possible answer:** A review usually describes the movie's main conflict and plot to help readers decide if they would enjoy the movie.*

4. ■ STANDARDS FOCUS *Analyze a Writer's Position Students should be able to point to evidence that supports each part. Some may question whether Briney's claim that the movie is "absolutely perfect" is fully supported.*

Read for Information: Compare and Contrast

Writing Prompt *Students' paragraphs should clearly state how their opinions are similar to or different from Briney's and include specific examples. Students who differ from Briney significantly should explain their reasons.*

Assess and Reteach

Assess

RESOURCE MANAGER—Copy Masters
Selection Tests A, B/C pp. 241–242, 243–244
Test Generator CD

Reteach

STANDARDS LESSON FILE
Informational Texts Lesson 16: Evaluating Evidence

Focus and Motivate

OBJECTIVES

- analyze a student model that reflects the key traits of a focused description of a place
- use the writing process to produce a descriptive essay
- use sensory details
- revise and edit, using a rubric for descriptive writing
- produce a radio dramatization

WRITER'S ROAD MAP

WRITING PROMPTS 1 AND 2

Help students choose a prompt by brainstorming a list of places they know well, or unusual or special places they have visited. Students might also brainstorm details about places from stories they have read.

ADDITIONAL PROMPTS

Use these prompts for practice with writing descriptive essays:

WRITING PROMPT 3

Writing for the Real World Write descriptive text about a special place for a travel brochure or a travel Web site.

Subjects to Consider
- a place you have visited
- a place you hope to visit

WRITING PROMPT 4

Writing from a Picture Write a focused description of a scene from a painting or photograph.

Places to Consider
- an urban or rural scene from a magazine, book, or online source
- a personal photograph of a familiar place

For additional writing prompts, see

 WriteSmart CD

 Writing Center at **ClassZone.com**

KEY TRAITS

Review the six **KEY TRAITS** with students, focusing primarily on ideas and organization. Compare the list of traits with the rubric on page 164.

Writing Workshop

Descriptive Essay

The literature in this unit includes vivid descriptions that make you feel as if you're right there with the characters. Now you have a chance to describe the world as you see it. Check out the **Writer's Road Map** for details on writing a focused description—a detailed explanation of what a certain place is like.

WRITER'S ROAD MAP

Describing People and Places

WRITING PROMPT 1

Writing from Your Life Write a focused description of a special place. Your description should be richly detailed and should explain why the place is important to you.

Places to Consider
- an unusual or special place you have visited
- a place in your everyday life, such as a park or mall
- a place that was important in your past

WRITING PROMPT 2

Writing from Literature Choose a place from a story you have read. Describe the place in that story from a character's point of view. You may invent details about the place, as long as they make sense in the story. Be sure to explain which story and character you chose and why you chose them.

Places to Consider
- Mrs. Jones's room from the point of view of Roger ("Thank You, M'am")
- Victor's school, from his point of view ("Seventh Grade")

 WRITING TOOLS
For prewriting, revision, and editing tools, visit the **Writing Center** at ClassZone.com.

KEY TRAITS

1. IDEAS
- Identifies the **place**
- Explains why the place is **significant**

2. ORGANIZATION
- Follows a clear **organizational pattern,** with an introduction, a body, and a conclusion
- Uses **transitions** to connect ideas
- Provides **background information** for the reader, if it is needed

3. VOICE
- Shows the writer's or the character's personality and **style**

4. WORD CHOICE
- Uses **sensory details** to show the reader what the place is like

5. SENTENCE FLUENCY
- Holds reader interest by using different **sentence lengths**

6. CONVENTIONS
- Uses **correct grammar, spelling, and punctuation**

Writing Workshop Resources

 RESOURCE MANAGER UNIT 1

Plan and Teach pp. 245–248
Prewriting–Editing pp. 249–253
Writing Rubric p. 254
Publishing with Technology p. 255
Writing Support p. 256*

STANDARDS LESSON FILE
Writing Lesson 27: Descriptive Writing
Writing Lesson 39: Sensory Details
Grammar Lesson 20: Commas

BEST PRACTICES TOOLKIT

Scaffolding Writing Instruction pp. 43–46*
Observation Chart • Cluster Diagram

TECHNOLOGY

- Easy Planner DVD
- Writing Center at **ClassZone.com**
- WriteSmart CD

* **Resources for Differentiation**

Part 1: Analyze a Student Model

Rico Alvarez
Draper School

Sammy's: My Special Place

If you ask friends to name a special place, they'll probably say some fancy spot that costs a lot of money to visit. I'm different. One of my special places is a tiny little diner with peeling paint and small, crowded tables. For four years, I went to Sammy's Place every day after school to
5   wait for my mom and to see my grandma. For about five hours a week almost every week, Sammy's Place was my place.

The first thing I'd notice on my way to Sammy's was the smells. Sammy's was known for its fried chicken, hamburgers, and pizza. It was also known for gyros, which is a kind of sandwich made with lamb. As I
10 got close to the diner, the smell of meat on the grill would always greet me first. Before I entered the door, my nose would tell me if lamb was roasting in the oven. I could usually smell peppers and onions frying. Sometimes, I knew something sizzling and crispy had just come out of the deep fryer. On Fridays, the smells of garlic, sauce, and fresh pizza
15 crust drifted onto the street from the pizza oven.

When I stepped inside the door, the same scene always greeted me. I'd see the line of tables, some filled with diners. At that time of day, though, most sat like empty boxes, waiting for people to fill them. There was always some music playing, too—some old '90s stuff, only the
20 violin version. The best part of walking in, though, was the people who greeted me. "Rico!" Sammy's voice would sing out. She'd say it like a song, with a long *REEEE* and a short, short *ko,* the way she'd learned it from my grandma. A huge smile would crack her face from cheek to cheek. Sammy was really Samantha Stavros, the owner and the cook.

KEY TRAITS IN ACTION

Introduction identifies the **place** and explains why it is **significant** to the writer.

Description includes **transitions** and has a clear **organization**— on the way to the diner, at the diner, leaving the diner. **Background information** (the explanation of gyros) helps the reader understand.

Sensory details involving sound and sight give the reader a "you are there" feeling.

Teach

Part 1: Analyze a Student Model

Have students read the **Student Model** and **Key Traits in Action.** Then discuss the model with the class, pointing out specific examples of each trait and building on what students have already noted. You may also wish to incorporate the following activities:

- **Introduction** Ask students to identify the place that is the subject of the student model and why it is significant to the writer. Where did the writer put this information? *Possible answer: The place is a diner called Sammy's Place. It is significant to the writer because he used to go there every day after school and has fond memories of it. The writer identifies the name of the place in his introduction, the first paragraph of the description.*

- **Transitions** Help students recognize how transitions are used in the model. Ask these questions:

  How does the writer smoothly connect the first and second paragraphs? *Possible answer: He has introduced the topic of Sammy's in the first paragraph. He begins the second paragraph with the transition "The first thing I'd notice" and then describes the delicious smells he experienced when approaching the place.*

  What transition words are used in the third paragraph? *Possible answer: "When" (line 16), "At that time of day" (line 17), "always" (lines 19, 27), "As" (line 28)*

DIFFERENTIATED INSTRUCTION

FOR ALL STUDENTS

For general guidelines on differentiating writing instruction, see

 BEST PRACTICES TOOLKIT
Scaffolding Writing Instruction
pp. 43–46

FOR ENGLISH LEARNERS

Language: Skill Words Write these terms on the board and review them with students:

- *topic:* the subject or main idea of a conversation or a piece of writing

- *significant:* important

- *organizational pattern:* the way a writer puts ideas together for a reader

- *sensory details:* details that help a reader understand how something looks, smells, tastes, sounds, or feels

- *style:* a writer's unique way of giving information or talking about a topic. In this model, the writer uses a relaxed, personal style. Share this example (lines 16–20): "When I stepped inside the door, the same scene always greeted me. I'd see the line of tables, some filled with diners. . . . There was always some music playing, too—some old '90s stuff, only the violin version."

- **Sensory Details** Have students find sensory details in the second and third paragraphs. *Possible answer:*
  - *Paragraph 2: "the smell of meat on the grill" (line 10), "lamb . . . roasting in the oven" (lines 11–12), "peppers and onions frying" (line 12), "something sizzling and crispy" (line 13), "smells of garlic, sauce, and fresh pizza" (line 14)*
  - *Paragraph 3: "line of tables, some filled with diners" (line 17), "like empty boxes" (line 18), "some old '90s stuff, only the violin version" (lines 19–20), "give me a hug" (line 27), "coffee spills or sauce stains" (lines 28–29)*
- **Style** To illustrate the author's style, work with students to look through the piece for passages that reveal the writer's personality.
  - *"If you ask friends to name a special place, they'll probably say some fancy spot that costs a lot of money to visit. I'm different. One of my special places is a tiny little diner with peeling paint and small, crowded tables." (lines 1–4)*
  - *"I loved the slightly salty taste of the tuna. Yum! I'd eat the sour pickle last and wash it all down with cold milk." (lines 33–35)*

Talk about the informal style of this piece. Ask students why they think this style works well in an example of personal writing.

For interactive student models, see

WriteSmart CD

Writing Center at **ClassZone.com**

---

25 Better than hearing Sammy, though, was seeing my grandma. Even if she was in the middle of waiting on a customer, her face would brighten, and she'd always come over and give me a hug. "How's my little man?" she'd ask. As I hugged her back, her apron, with its coffee spills or sauce stains, would tell me part of the story of her day.

30 Then I'd sit down. I always sat at the right end of the counter on a tall silver stool with a soft, red leather seat. That was close to where Sammy flipped burgers. I'd almost always order my favorite, a gooey tuna melt, with cheese dripping out of the toasted bread. I loved the slightly salty taste of the tuna. Yum! I'd eat the sour pickle last and wash

35 it all down with cold milk. As long as it wasn't busy, my grandma would take her break then and sit with me. She'd ask me about my day and tell me about customers. Then my mom would arrive. I'd hug Grandma goodbye, and Sammy would call out, "Take care of your mama!" It was always the same.

40 I don't go to Sammy's Place anymore. I'm old enough to be on my own now, and besides, I have track or math club most days. The strange thing is how much I miss that old diner, though. I can still see that counter and smell the cooking smells. Maybe that's because, for a few years, Sammy's Place was the next best thing to home.

Different **sentence lengths** help keep the description lively and interesting.

Entire description has a relaxed, informal **style** that shows the writer's personality.

2

DIFFERENTIATED INSTRUCTION

FOR ENGLISH LEARNERS

Comprehension: Transitions Use this activity to illustrate how a writer might use transitional terms to describe a scene.

1. Write three or four sentences on the board that describe your arrival at school this morning. Use transitional words suggested in the chart on page 163.

   First I got out of my car. Then I followed the sidewalk to the front door. When I opened the front door, I heard the sound of students talking and walking.

2. With students, underline the transitional words.

3. Next use spatial-order words to describe the classroom.

   When you walk through the door, you notice students' artwork on the walls. On the right are student desks. On the left is the teacher's desk and a chalkboard.

4. Have students point out the transitional words.

5. Use the copy master to provide students with further practice using transitions.

   RESOURCE MANAGER—Copy Master
   Writing Support p. 256

Part 2: Apply the Writing Process

 **WRITING STANDARD**
4.A.1 Compose text using prewriting and drafting strategies

PREWRITING

What Should I Do?	**What Does It Look Like?**
1. Generate ideas. List places that are special to you. Try to see, hear, or otherwise experience each one in your mind. Which one comes to life best? Put an asterisk next to it. **TIP** Are you short on ideas? Look through old photo albums, scrapbooks, post cards, or souvenirs.	▶ the beach near Uncle Dave's house • hot sand, cold water, big waves the baseball field in the park • shouts, cheers, dust *Sammy's Place, where I went after school • food, smells of cooking
2. Decide on your focus. Now ask yourself how you can make your topic interesting to your reader.	▶ Sammy's Place I went there every school day for four years! Sammy is really Samantha. Lots of great smells and tastes.
3. Think about sensory details. Make a cluster of details related to sights, sounds, smells, tastes, and textures. **TIP** Some memories don't include certain senses, such as taste. However, if you can't come up with plenty of sensory details, choose a new topic.	▶ sights — empty tables, tall stools / sounds — Sammy calling "Rico", sizzle of deep fryer / Sammy's Place / tastes — sour pickles / smells — garlic, meat on the grill / textures — soft seat
4. Freewrite as you observe your topic or picture it in your mind. If you can, observe the place again, or try studying pictures of your subject. Otherwise, call your subject to mind. Then just start writing.	▶ I can smell the garlic and pizza crust baking before I even go in. Peppers frying, too. Hamburgers on the grill, lamb roasting. Grandma smiling!

FOR ENGLISH LEARNERS

Deciding on a Focus and Gathering Sensory Details Have students use these prompts to focus their topics and choose sensory details to describe their subjects:

- My description is about _____.
- This topic is interesting to me because _____.
- I will describe these sights: _____.
- I will describe these sounds: _____.
- I will describe how _____ smells or tastes.
- I will describe how _____ feels.

Provide copies of the Observation Chart and encourage students to record details about their topic in the chart. Then they can meet with a partner to share their charts and continue to talk about their topics.

 **BEST PRACTICES TOOLKIT—Transparency**
Observation Chart p. C7

Practice and Apply

To support students during the writing process, use these copy masters:

RESOURCE MANAGER—Copy Masters
Prewriting–Editing pp. 249–253
Writing Rubric p. 254
Publishing with Technology p. 255
Writing Support p. 256 (for English learners)

Part 2: Apply the Writing Process

PREWRITING

1. **Generate ideas.** If students need help gathering ideas, bring their attention to the **TIP** in the first step. Have students discuss their best ideas with partners. As each student talks about his or her description, the partner should list the details that are most interesting. Partners should also ask questions about things that are unfamiliar or missing from the description.

2. **Decide on your focus.** Encourage students to begin by writing a first draft of an introduction. The introduction should identify a topic and capture the reader's attention with interesting details. Have students meet in pairs to exchange introductions and offer suggestions to each other.

3. **Think about sensory details.** Have students work in small groups to make a cluster of details related to sights, sounds, smells, tastes, and textures in the classroom or school. Then have students work individually to complete the Cluster Diagrams for their own pieces. If students are having trouble coming up with sensory details, point out the **TIP** in step 3.

BEST PRACTICES TOOLKIT—Transparency
Cluster Diagram p. B18

4. **Freewrite as you observe your topic or picture it in your mind.** Encourage students to think about walking into the place for the first time. What stands out to them? What makes this place unique or interesting? Explain that looking at their subject with fresh eyes will help them notice details that are worth including in their writing.

For interactive graphic organizers, see

WriteSmart CD

Writing Center at **ClassZone.com**

DRAFTING

1. Get organized. Discuss the advantages and challenges of each type of organization. With **spatial order,** both the writer and the reader focus on one part or aspect at a time. However, it might be difficult to view the "big picture"—the person or place as a whole. With **order of impression,** the reader is more likely to feel that he or she is really there. The writer must be careful, though, to include transitions and have a clear organization.

2. Start out strong. Encourage students to experiment with different kinds of "hooks" for their pieces. Have them meet in pairs or small groups to share their introductions and figure out which works best. Point out the **TIP** to students who are struggling.

3. Use sensory details. As students write, they should pause at each descriptive passage and think about the five senses. For example, if the description involves an outdoor place, can you smell flowers or the ocean? Can you hear birds or frogs? What does it feel like to sit on a hard bench or feel sand between your toes?

4. Wrap it up. Students should reflect back on their introductions to focus on what they want to say. Encourage them to experiment with different endings and then share their ideas with a partner.

Write*Smart* CD

Writing Center at ClassZone.com

DRAFTING

What Should I Do?	**What Does It Look Like?**
1. Get organized. There are many ways to organize a description. Here are two: • **Spatial Order** Describes qualities in the order they appear, such as top to bottom, left to right, inside to outside • **Order of Impression** Discusses details in the order in which the writer experiences them	**SPATIAL ORDER** **Left**—grill area and kitchen (smell meat on grill, hear sizzle) **Middle**—tables (see empty tables, hear old 1990s music) **Right**—doorway and cash register (see people coming in, hear beeps of register) **ORDER OF IMPRESSION** **Outside the door** (smell meat, onions, pizza crust) **When I come in** (see people, hear Sammy and Grandma) **When I sit down** (feel soft seat, taste tuna melt)
2. Start out strong. Start your description with a "hook" to interest your reader. You can do that with emotion, surprise, humor, a question, a contrast, or vivid details. **TIP** If you have trouble writing your introduction, write your body and conclusion first.	*Vivid details* I can still smell the roasting meat and hear the sizzling peppers of Sammy's Place. *A contrast* If you ask friends to name a special place, they'll probably say some fancy spot that costs a lot of money to visit. I'm different.
3. Use sensory details. Don't stop with how something looks. Tell how it smells, tastes, sounds, or feels. Use language that lets your reader share the experience. **See page 164:** Avoid Clichés	My nose would tell me if lamb was roasting in the oven. I could usually smell peppers and onions frying. ⟩ Sensory details: smell
4. Wrap it up. Is there a final detail or thought that could help your reader understand why this subject matters to you?	The strange thing is how much I miss that old diner. Maybe that's because, for a few years, Sammy's Place was the next best thing to home. ⟩ Why it matters

---

DIFFERENTIATED INSTRUCTION

FOR LESS–PROFICIENT WRITERS

Getting Organized To help students describe details in the order of impression, provide this frame and explain that it represents the organization of the student model. Have students follow this model to plan their own descriptive pieces:

Introduction

• Introduce the topic.

• Begin to show why the topic is important or interesting to you.

Middle Paragraphs—Order of Impression (number will vary)

• Talk about what a person would notice or do first.
  —Include sensory details.
  —Provide any necessary background information.

• Talk about what happens next.
  —Include sensory details.
  —Provide background information.

• Continue describing what you or your character experiences using sensory details.

Final Thoughts

• Mention again the topic of your essay. For example, in the student model, the writer begins the final paragraph by repeating the name of the diner.

• Include a final detail or idea that shows, again, why this topic is important or interesting to you.

REVISING AND EDITING

What Should I Do?	What Does It Look Like?

1. Check your organization.
- <u>Underline</u> transitional words and phrases. Transitions include *first, next, then, when, after, on the right, on the left, at the top, next to,* and *below,* and any other words and phrases that link ideas.
- Do you have enough transitions to help your reader move easily from detail to detail and idea to idea?

See page 292: Add Transitions

▶ <u>As I got close to the diner,</u> the smell of meat on the grill would always greet me <u>first.</u>
~~Before I entered the door,~~
∧ My nose would tell me if lamb was roasting in the oven.

2. Add background information.
- Ask a peer reader to [bracket] words or references that are confusing or unfamiliar.
- Add details or explanations that make your description clear.

See page 164: Ask a Peer Reader

▶ It was also known for [gyros.] That's a kind of sandwich made with lamb.

3. Make your voice heard.
- Because this is personal writing, you want your reader to get a sense of your **voice**— your style and personality. (If you chose prompt 2, you want your reader to get a sense of the character's voice.)
- Read your description aloud. Does it sound like a textbook? If so, add details that put you (or the character) in the picture.

▶ For four years, I went to Sammy's Place every day after school ∧ to wait for my mom and to see my grandma. For about five hours a week almost every week, Sammy's Place was my place.

4. Add variety to your sentences.
- Are all your sentences about the same length?
- Try mixing in some short and long sentences for a change of pace.

▶ ~~I'd almost always order my favorite. It was a gooey tuna melt. It had cheese dripping out of the toasted bread. I really liked it.~~

I'd almost always order my favorite, a gooey tuna melt, with cheese dripping out of the toasted bread. Yum!

REVISING AND EDITING

1. **Check your organization.** Have students form pairs for peer reading. Readers should answer these questions: Does the writing flow smoothly from one idea to the next? Where do I get stuck or feel confused? Have writers consider whether transitions could improve these parts.

2. **Add background information.** Remind students to put themselves in the place of the reader who does not know the place being described. What details and explanations will the reader need? Suggest that students use the **Ask a Peer Reader** questions on page 164 to make sure they have included enough support.

3. **Make your voice heard.** Remind students that personal writing can use informal language that they might not see in a textbook or formal essay. This might include using contractions, slang expressions, or interjections (such as "Yum!" in line 34 of the student model). Give examples of words or sentences and ask students to tell whether the language is formal or informal. Then have students work with a partner to find places where they could do a better job of putting themselves or their character in the picture.

4. **Add variety to your sentences.** Students should refer back to selections in the unit to find out how other writers add variety to their sentences. For example, they might examine lines 90–98 of "Thank You, M'am" (p. 67). Have students consider using introductory phrases and inverted syntax (lines 90–91), combining short sentences (lines 91–93), and using direct quotations (lines 97–98).

For interactive revision tools, see

⊘ Write*Smart* CD

ℹ Writing Center at **ClassZone.com**

FOR LESS–PROFICIENT WRITERS

Revising and Editing Provide an outline to help students revise their writing. They can complete the outline with a peer reader.

- I am including transition words such as _____, _____, and _____.
- This word/idea needs background information: _____. I will say _____.
- This detail/word shows my (or a character's) personality: _____.
- I changed the sentence _____ to add more variety. It now reads _____.

FOR ADVANCED LEARNERS/PRE–AP

Experiment with Point of View Remind students that point of view is the vantage point from which something is described. Explain that the same place or situation can look completely different when told from a different person's point of view. Ask students to rewrite their descriptions from the point of view of a different person. The new person or character should express a very different attitude toward what he or she sees.

Preparing to Publish

Support for meeting the goals in the writing rubric is supplied throughout the **Writing Workshop** on pages 158–163.

For Rubric Bank, see

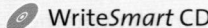 Write*Smart* CD

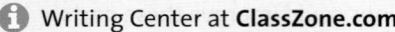 Writing Center at **ClassZone.com**

Assess and Reteach

After reading and assessing students' descriptive essays, you might use these lessons to reteach key skills:

 STANDARDS LESSON FILE

Writing Lesson 27: Descriptive Writing
Writing Lesson 39: Sensory Details
Grammar Lesson 20: Commas

Apply the Rubric

A strong description of a place . . .

☑ identifies the place being described

☑ tells why the place matters

☑ is well organized, with an introduction, a body, and a conclusion

☑ uses transitions to connect ideas

☑ uses details that appeal to the senses

☑ varies the lengths of sentences

☑ explains information that might be unclear to the reader

☑ has a style that shows the writer's or character's personality

Ask a Peer Reader

• What is my subject, and why is it important to me?

• As you read, what can you see? hear? taste? touch? smell?

• Is anything unclear? What do I need to explain?

Avoid Clichés

Cliché	Replacement
home sweet home	my place
like night and day	as different as waking and dreaming
dry as a bone	dry as dune grass in the sun
as tough as nails	steely, strong, unyielding

Check Your Grammar

• Use commas to separate items in a series.

> *garlic, sauce, and fresh pizza crust*

• Use a comma after an introductory phrase or clause.

> *For four years, I went to Sammy's Place every day after school.*

See page R49: Quick Reference: Punctuation

Writing On|ine

PUBLISHING OPTIONS
For publishing options, visit the **Writing Center** at ClassZone.com.

ASSESSMENT PREPARATION
For writing and grammar assessment practice, go to the **Assessment Center** at ClassZone.com.

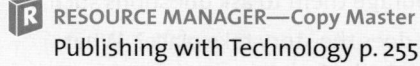

WRITING STANDARD
4.A.3.c Prepare the final product for presentation to an audience

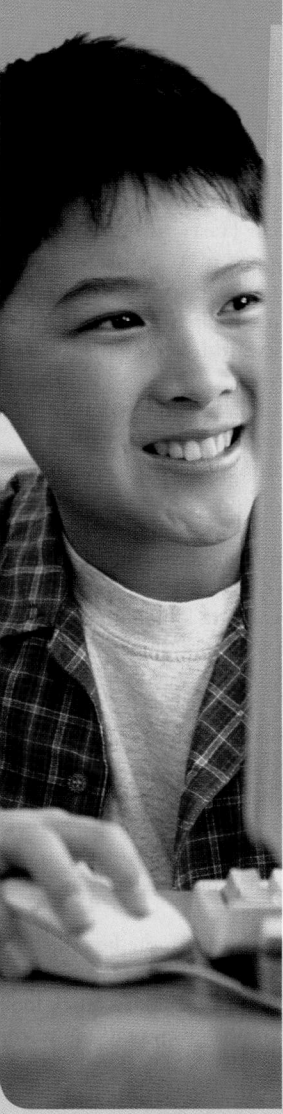

Producing a Radio Dramatization

To turn all or part of your description into a radio segment, all you need is a tape recorder, sound effects, and imagination.

Preparing the Dramatization

1. **Sound it out.** A radio segment needs words, sound effects, and, usually, a narrator. To get started, try making a chart.

Narrator	Words	Sound Effects
Rico tells own story	"I walk into Sammy's Place."	dishes clinking, pop music playing (violin version)
	"Sammy always says hello."	Sammy's voice saying "REEEEko"
	"It's not very busy now."	background voices of diners

2. **Write a script.** A radio script is more than words and sound effects. It includes information on emotions, pauses, interruptions, and sensory details. It also tells how—for example, loud or soft, fast or slow.

> RICO: Grandma would always come over and give me a hug.
> GRANDMA (cheerfully): How's my little man?
> (Sound effects: glasses and silverware clinking, people talking in background)

Presenting the Dramatization

1. **Cast your segment.** Choose your actors and narrator. Put some other classmates in charge of sound effects.

2. **Rehearse.** Run through the presentation. Look for ways to make it more interesting, more dramatic, and more entertaining. Add or change sounds and words.

3. **Record and air your segment.** Record your segment on audiotape. Then play it for your classmates or for family members. Get their feedback on your descriptive powers.

WRITING WORKSHOP **165**

PUBLISHING WITH TECHNOLOGY

Ask students to read this page to get an overview of how to create a radio dramatization.

Before students begin working, review this rubric with them so that they understand their goals:

Rubric A strong radio dramatization

- uses realistic-sounding words, or dialogue
- includes sound effects
- has a clear narrator who helps the listener understand the segment
- is based on a script that includes words, sound effects, and information about how the actors should read their lines (pauses, emotions, and so on)
- is presented by a well-organized cast and crew
- has been rehearsed and critiqued

R RESOURCE MANAGER—Copy Master
Publishing with Technology p. 255

FOR LESS–PROFICIENT WRITERS

Producing a Radio Dramatization Have students compare the radio script sample to lines 27–28 on page 160. Note that

- Rico is the narrator and describes events as he experiences them
- Grandma's dialogue is taken directly from the description
- the script describes how Grandma's voice sounds ("cheerfully")
- the script lists sound effects for the diner

Have students use a chart like the one on page 165 to organize ideas for their own radio scripts. Have them consider these questions:

- Who will be my narrator?
- What words will the narrator say? (Use a highlighter to show which parts of your description the narrator will read.)
- What sound effects will help listeners feel as if they are "on the scene"?
- Should any other characters have dialogue?

Assessment Practice

CHECK READINESS

Read aloud the paragraph under **ASSESS** and stress to students that this is not the full Unit Test but a way for them to check their readiness for it. Then have students examine the skills listed under **REVIEW** and look back in the unit or in the Handbook for any they need to study.

READ THE SELECTION

Remind students to keep Unit Goals in mind as they read the passage, paying particular attention to

- plot stages
- setting
- sequence
- cause and effect

To help students focus on the **plot** while reading, encourage them to ask questions such as

- Where does the story take place? What conflict do the father and son face?
- How does Rocky the parrot come into the story? What sequence of events leads to the story's climax?

ANSWER THE QUESTIONS

Direct students to pages R93–R99 of the Test-Taking Handbook to review test-taking strategies. Remind them not to choose the first alternative that seems to fit when answering a multiple-choice question. Instead, students should read through all the choices, eliminate any that are clearly wrong, and then choose the best answer—the one that is most accurate and complete.

Explain to students the importance of understanding the directions for every question—before attempting to answer it. A good way to measure comprehension is to try to paraphrase, or say in your own words, what the directions ask. After completing the first question, remind students to reread the directions, just to be sure they are on target.

Reading Comprehension

ASSESS
The practice test items on the next few pages match skills listed on the Unit Goals page (page 23) and addressed throughout this unit. Taking this practice test will help you assess your knowledge of these skills and determine your readiness for the Unit Test.

REVIEW
After you take the practice test, your teacher can help you identify any skills you need to review.

- Plot Stages
- Setting
- Sequence
- Cause and Effect
- Latin Roots
- Prefixes
- Suffixes
- Possessives
- Pronoun-Antecedent Agreement
- Run-On Sentences

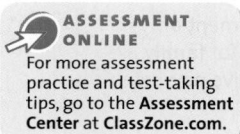

ASSESSMENT ONLINE
For more assessment practice and test-taking tips, go to the **Assessment Center** at ClassZone.com.

DIRECTIONS *Read this selection and answer the questions that follow.*

Papa's Parrot

Cynthia Rylant

Though his father was fat and merely owned a candy and nut shop, Harry Tillian liked his papa. Harry stopped liking candy and nuts when he was around seven, but, in spite of this, he and Mr. Tillian had remained friends and were still friends in the year Harry turned twelve.

For years, after school, Harry had always stopped in to see his father at work. Many of Harry's friends stopped there, too, to spend a few cents choosing penny candy from the giant bins or to sample Mr. Tillian's latest batch of roasted peanuts. Mr. Tillian looked forward to seeing his son and his son's friends every day. He liked the company.

10 When Harry entered junior high school, though, he didn't come by the candy and nut shop as often. Nor did his friends. They were older and they had more spending money. They went to a burger place. They played video games. They shopped for records. None of them were much interested in candy and nuts anymore.

A new group of children came to Mr. Tillian's shop now. But not Harry Tillian and his friends.

The year Harry turned twelve was also the year Mr. Tillian got a parrot. He went to a pet store one day and bought one for more money than he could really afford. He brought the parrot to his shop, set its cage near the

20 sign for maple clusters and named it Rocky.

Harry thought this was the strangest thing his father had ever done, and he told him so, but Mr. Tillian just ignored him.

Rocky was good company for Mr. Tillian. When business was slow, Mr. Tillian would turn on a small color television he had sitting in a corner, and he and Rocky would watch the soap operas. Rocky liked to scream when the romantic music came on, and Mr. Tillian would yell at him to shut up, but they seemed to enjoy themselves.

The more Mr. Tillian grew to like his parrot, and the more he talked to it instead of to people, the more embarrassed Harry became. Harry would

30 stroll past the shop, on his way somewhere else, and he'd take a quick look inside to see what his dad was doing. Mr. Tillian was always talking to the bird. So Harry kept walking.

DIFFERENTIATED INSTRUCTION

FOR ENGLISH LEARNERS

Assessment Practice: Work Backwards
Prepare students for the assessment by having them read the questions before reading the text passage. Have pairs follow these steps to learn unfamiliar words in the test directions and questions:

- Find words you don't recognize and write each one on an index card.
- Look up the meaning in a dictionary.
- Write the meaning on the back of the card.
- Use your word cards to teach and practice the vocabulary with your partner and another pair.

At home things were different. Harry and his father joked with each other at the dinner table as they always had—Mr. Tillian teasing Harry about his smelly socks; Harry teasing Mr. Tillian about his blubbery stomach. At home things seemed all right.

But one day, Mr. Tillian became ill. He had been at work, unpacking boxes of caramels, when he had grabbed his chest and fallen over on top of the candy. A customer had found him, and he was taken to the hospital
40 in an ambulance.

Mr. Tillian couldn't leave the hospital. He lay in bed, tubes in his arms, and he worried about his shop. New shipments of candy and nuts would be arriving. Rocky would be hungry. Who would take care of things?

Harry said he would. Harry told his father that he would go to the store every day after school and unpack boxes. He would sort out all the candy and nuts. He would even feed Rocky.

So, the next morning, while Mr. Tillian lay in his hospital bed, Harry took the shop key to school with him. After school he left his friends and walked to the empty shop alone. In all the days of his life, Harry had
50 never seen the shop closed after school. Harry didn't even remember what the CLOSED sign looked like. The key stuck in the lock three times, and inside he had to search all the walls for the light switch.

The shop was as his father had left it. Even the caramels were still spilled on the floor. Harry bent down and picked them up one by one, dropping them back in the boxes. The bird in its cage watched him silently.

Harry opened the new boxes his father hadn't gotten to. Peppermints. Jawbreakers. Toffee creams. Strawberry kisses. Harry traveled from bin to bin, putting the candies where they belonged.

"Hello!"
60 Harry jumped, spilled a box of jawbreakers.

"Hello, Rocky!"

Harry stared at the parrot. He had forgotten it was there. The bird had been so quiet, and Harry had been thinking only of the candy.

"Hello," Harry said.

"Hello, Rocky!" answered the parrot.

Harry walked slowly over to the cage. The parrot's food cup was empty. Its water was dirty. The bottom of the cage was a mess.

Harry carried the cage into the back room.

"Hello, Rocky!"

ITEM ANALYSIS

COMPREHENSION AND BRIEF CONSTRUCTED RESPONSE	ITEMS	UNIT PAGES
Plot Stages	2, 4, 6, 7, 10	26, 31
Setting	1, 3, 9	43, 119
Sequence	2, 3, 5	43
Cause and Effect	4, 8, 10	119

VOCABULARY	ITEMS	UNIT PAGES
Latin Roots	1, 2, 3	40, 90
Prefixes	4, 5	70
Suffixes	6, 7	127

WRITING AND GRAMMAR	ITEMS	UNIT PAGES
Possessives	3, 5	71
Pronoun-Antecedent Agreement	4, 6	91, 117
Run-On Sentences	1, 2	60

FOR LESS-PROFICIENT READERS

Assessment Support Consider these options for completing the **Assessment Practice:**

- Have students "work backwards," reviewing the questions before reading the passage.
- Select random questions in the assessment and have students demonstrate how and where to look for the answers.
- Ask students to locate unfamiliar vocabulary words in the assessment. Elicit their meanings from the class.
- Have students record useful testing words and definitions in their journals for later reference.
- Read the selection or parts of it aloud to aid in student comprehension.

McDougal Littell Assessment System

After checking student readiness with this Assessment Practice, you may administer the complete Unit 1 Test, which matches the structure and format of the MSA.

Comprehension

Model a thinking process for answering multiple-choice questions.

1. **B is correct.** *Mr. Tillian's candy and nut shop is where most of the stages of plot are revealed. A is incorrect because the Tillian home is mentioned only in lines 33–36. C is incorrect, since Harry and his father have only one conversation in the hospital. D is incorrect because the pet store is mentioned only in line 18.*

2. **C is correct.** *The conflict between Mr. Tillian and Harry starts when Harry enters junior high (lines 10–11), not when he is seven, as in A. B and D are incorrect because the story's conflict begins before Mr. Tillian buys his parrot.*

3. **A is correct.** *Describing Harry's behavior when he was younger sets up a contrast to his behavior as a twelve-year-old. B is incorrect because the story never mentions Mr. Tillian's becoming less talkative. C is incorrect because Harry's friends did like the shop (lines 6–7). Although Rocky does eventually play a role in helping Harry realize his father's loneliness, D is incorrect because it has no relation to the story's starting when Harry is seven.*

4. **D is correct.** *Mr. Tillian faces an internal conflict: he misses his son's companionship when Harry stops visiting the shop. A is incorrect because while Mr. Tillian and his parrot do argue, his conflict is with Harry, not Rocky. B is incorrect because Mr. Tillian buys a parrot and grows very fond of it. C is incorrect because the store's financial status is not discussed in the story.*

5. **D is correct.** *Mr. Tillian buys the parrot after Harry enters junior high because he misses his son and wants some company. A is incorrect because Harry and his friends have stopped visiting the shop when Mr. Tillian buys the parrot. B is incorrect because Mr. Tillian has owned the shop since Harry was a small boy. C is untrue, since Mr. Tillian gets sick after he has had Rocky for a while.*

---

70   "Is that all you can say, you dumb bird?" Harry mumbled. The bird said nothing else.

Harry cleaned the bottom of the cage, refilled the food and water cups, then put the cage back in its place and resumed sorting the candy.

"Where's Harry?"

Harry looked up.

"Where's Harry?"

Harry stared at the parrot.

"Where's Harry?"

Chills ran down Harry's back. What could the bird mean? It was like
80   something from *The Twilight Zone.*

"Where's Harry?"

Harry swallowed and said, "I'm here. I'm here, you stupid bird."

"You stupid bird!" said the parrot.

Well, at least he's got one thing straight, thought Harry.

"Miss him! Miss him! Where's Harry? You stupid bird!"

Harry stood with a handful of peppermints.

"*What?*" he asked.

"Where's Harry?" said the parrot.

"I'm *here,* you stupid bird! I'm here!" Harry yelled. He threw the
90   peppermints at the cage, and the bird screamed and clung to its perch.

Harry sobbed, "I'm here." The tears were coming.

Harry leaned over the glass counter.

"Papa." Harry buried his face in his arms.

"Where's Harry?" repeated the bird.

Harry sighed and wiped his face on his sleeve. He watched the parrot. He understood now: someone had been saying, for a long time, "Where's Harry? Miss him."

Harry finished his unpacking, then swept the floor of the shop. He checked the furnace so the bird wouldn't get cold. Then he left to go visit
100   his papa.

Comprehension

DIRECTIONS *Answer these questions about the story "Papa's Parrot."*

1. Most of the story takes place at the
   - **A.** Tillian home
   - **B.** candy shop
   - **C.** hospital
   - **D.** pet store

2. The conflict in the story begins when
   - **A.** Harry is seven years old
   - **B.** Rocky screams at the television
   - **C.** Harry turns twelve years old
   - **D.** Rocky says, "Where's Harry?"

168

---

6. **A is correct.** *Although Harry does not like nuts and candy, as in B, his feelings of embarrassment are what keep him from visiting the shop (lines 28–32). C and D are incorrect, as shown by lines 10–14, for Harry appears happy with his friends, spends his free time after school with them, and clearly would have time to work if he wanted to.*

7. **D is correct.** *The moment of greatest interest is when Harry understands that his father has been missing him (lines 86–91). A is incorrect, because this detail is part of the story's exposition. B is incorrect, since it is part of the rising action. C is incorrect because it only develops the character of Rocky.*

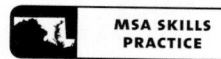 **MSA SKILLS PRACTICE**

3. The author probably begins the story when Harry is seven to show that
   A. Harry liked visiting his father at the shop for many years
   B. Mr. Tillian became less talkative at that time
   C. Harry's friends did not like the shop
   D. Rocky changed Harry's feelings about the shop

4. Which conflict does Mr. Tillian struggle with in the story?
   A. His parrot argues with him.
   B. He does not like birds.
   C. His store is losing money.
   D. He misses his son's company.

5. When does Mr. Tillian buy the parrot?
   A. when Harry and his school friends visit the nut shop
   B. when he first buys the candy and nut shop
   C. after he gets sick and has to go to the hospital
   D. after Harry stops visiting the shop every day

6. Which of the following is the cause of Harry's conflict?
   A. He is embarrassed by his father.
   B. He does not like candy.
   C. He is unhappy with his friends.
   D. He cannot work after school.

7. The climax of the story occurs when
   A. Harry and his friends stop visiting the store
   B. Mr. Tillian buys a parrot
   C. the parrot watches television
   D. Harry realizes that his father has been lonely

Constructed Response

8. Why are Harry's friends less interested in the shop after they turn twelve?

9. Why can Harry and his father joke together at home but not at the store?

10. Discuss how the parrot brings about the climax of the story. What does Harry learn about his father when he takes care of the shop and Rocky?

 **GO ON**

169

Brief Constructed Response

Evaluate student writing using the Maryland writing rubrics in the back of the book.

Possible responses:

8. *Harry's friends have outgrown the candy shop—they are older and have more spending money (lines 11–12). They have new interests, such as video games and records, and they like to stop at a burger place to eat (lines 12–13). They have lost interest in candy and nuts.*

9. *Harry and his father can still joke together at home because they are more comfortable there. Harry's friends are not around, so he is not embarrassed about his father or self-conscious about his relationship with his father. Mr. Tillian's feelings about Harry never change, so he can easily continue his tradition of joking with his son. They still love each other, but their relationship is more complicated than it once was.*

10. *The response should note that when Harry goes to take care of the shop after Mr. Tillian gets sick, Rocky the parrot says, "Where's Harry?" over and over and then says, "Miss him" several times (lines 74–83). Further details of this exchange may show that at first, Harry thinks it is a little scary that the bird is asking him where he is (lines 77–78), then he gets angry at the bird for repeatedly asking him the same question, and then he throws peppermints at it (lines 87–88). Finally, Harry realizes that Rocky is just repeating what his father has been saying to it (lines 94–95).*

   Students should explain that the climax of the story is when Harry realizes how much his father has missed him, and he begins to cry (lines 87–91). At this point, Harry understands that his father became lonely when Harry stopped visiting the shop after school. It had not occurred to Harry how important his companionship was to his father. Now Harry realizes that his father bought Rocky because he missed his son. When the parrot reveals what Mr. Tillian has been saying to it, Harry understands how his father felt.

DIFFERENTIATED INSTRUCTION

FOR ENGLISH LEARNERS

Test-Taking Strategies: Read Directions Read aloud with students the directions on pages 168–171.

- Check that students know the vocabulary, especially the words *comprehension* ("understanding") and *passage* ("text").
- Have students locate the text to which each set of directions applies.
- Model answering one question under each set of directions; then have students demonstrate answering a second question.

Assessment Vocabulary Give students these words from the questions on pages 168–169: *conflict* (2, 4, 6); *cause* (6); *climax* (7, 10). Refer students to the plot diagram on page 26 and have pairs use the words to describe the basic structure of a story. (For example: A story has a *conflict* or problem that *causes* events to happen. The events lead to a *climax*, which is the most exciting part of the story.) Then have pairs come together to share and compare their descriptions.

ANSWERS

Vocabulary

1. **C is correct.** Since the Latin word ambulare implies movement, and A, B, and D do not relate to movement, C is the best answer. Also, the spelling of ambulance most closely resembles the Latin word.

2. **C is correct.** Although company can be used to mean "guests" (as in A), people may entertain guests in their homes (as in B), and friends may be considered guests (as in D), C is the best answer. The spelling of hospital builds upon the original Latin word hospes, and a hospital's patients are guests requiring medical attention.

3. **B is correct.** Since the Latin word fornax implies heat and warmth, we can eliminate A and C, which have unrelated meanings. D is incorrect because while food may be cooked in an oven, food is not a source of heat like an oven. Also, the spelling of furnace (as in B) closely resembles fornax.

4. **A is correct.** In line 3, the word around is used to approximate Harry's age. A is the best answer because it implies coming close to, and encircling, a precise number. B and C are incorrect, since both would negate the idea of being close to Harry's age. D is also incorrect, since the idea of "under" does not fit this context.

5. **A is correct.** In lines 37–38, we can infer that Mr. Tillian is moving the caramels out of their containers or boxes and into "giant bins" where customers can see them (line 7). B is incorrect, since it implies that an action was not completed. Mr. Tillian is not redoing an action, as in C, or putting the caramels away, as in D.

6. **A is correct.** Adding the suffix -al, which means "relating to," correctly turns the noun music into the adjective musical. B is incorrect, since -able is usually added to verbs, not nouns, and because "musicable" is not a word. Likewise, "musicial" and "musiceous" are not words (as in C and D).

7. **D is correct.** Adding the suffix -y, which means "full of," changes the base word room into the adjective roomy, meaning "having plenty of room." A and B are incorrect, since they both mean "like, having to do with, or showing." C is incorrect, since -ly usually forms adverbs, not adjectives.

Vocabulary

DIRECTIONS *Use your knowledge of Latin word roots to answer the following questions.*

1. The Latin word *ambulare* means "to go about." Which word in the story most likely comes from the word *ambulare*?

   A. business
   B. caramels
   C. ambulance
   D. customer

2. The Latin word *hospes* means "guest." Which word in the story most likely comes from the word *hospes*?

   A. company
   B. home
   C. hospital
   D. friends

3. The Latin word *fornax* means "oven." Which word in the story most likely comes from the word *fornax*?

   A. forward
   B. furnace
   C. afford
   D. food

DIRECTIONS *Use your knowledge of prefixes and suffixes to answer the following questions.*

4. The word *round* means "circle." What is the most likely meaning of the prefix *a-*, which is used to form *around* in line 3?

   A. in   C. without
   B. not   D. under

5. The word *pack* means "to put into a container." What is the most likely meaning of the prefix *un-*, which is used to form *unpacking* in line 37?

   A. the opposite of   C. again
   B. not done   D. away

6. Which suffix can be added to the noun *music* in line 26 to form an adjective that means "skilled in music"?

   A. -al   C. -ial
   B. -able   D. -eous

7. Which suffix can be added to the noun *room* in line 68 to form an adjective that means "having plenty of room"?

   A. -ate   C. -ly
   B. -ial   D. -y

DIFFERENTIATED INSTRUCTION

FOR ENGLISH LEARNERS

Assessment Support: Latin Roots Point out to students who speak Romance languages that they can use their knowledge of cognates to answer questions 1–3. For example:

Spanish
- *ambulancia* ("ambulance"); *ambulante* ("walking" or "traveling")
- *hospital* ("hospital"); *hospitalidad* ("hospitality")

French
- *ambulance* ("ambulance"); *ambulatoire* ("ambulatory")
- *hôpital* ("hospital"); *hospitalité* ("hospitality")
- *fourneau* ("furnace")

Italian
- *ambulanza, autoambulanza* ("ambulance")
- *ospitalità* ("hospitality"); *ospitale* ("hospitable")
- *fornace* ("furnace"); *forno* ("furnace" or "oven")

Writing & Grammar

DIRECTIONS *Read this passage and answer the questions that follow.*

> (1) Nature can do some amazing things, sometimes, people even get to watch.
> (2) In 1995, a new island formed as part of the Tonga Islands. (3) An active
> volcano erupted at Metis Shoal this eruption caused a heavy flow of lava.
> (4) As the <u>volcanos</u> lava bubbled up, it built a new island. (5) Fortunately,
> someone used <u>their</u> video camera to record this event. (6) According to many
> <u>scientists</u> accounts, Metis Shoal had erupted before with similar results.
> (7) The volcano produced new islands when <u>they</u> erupted in 1968 and 1979.

1. Choose the correct way to rewrite sentence 1 so that it is no longer a run-on sentence.

   A. Nature can do some amazing things, sometimes people. Even get to watch.

   B. Nature can do some amazing things sometimes people even get to watch.

   C. Nature can do some amazing things sometimes, people; even get to watch.

   D. Nature can do some amazing things; sometimes, people even get to watch.

2. Choose the correct way to rewrite sentence 3 so that it is no longer a run-on sentence.

   A. An active volcano erupted at Metis Shoal, and this eruption caused a heavy flow of lava.

   B. An active volcano erupted at Metis Shoal this eruption. Caused a heavy flow of lava.

   C. An active volcano erupted but at Metis Shoal this eruption caused a heavy flow of lava.

   D. An active volcano; erupted at Metis Shoal this eruption caused a heavy flow of lava.

3. Choose the correct way to write the possessive form of the underlined word in sentence 4.

   A. volcano's'   C. volcano's

   B. volcanos'   D. volcanos's

4. To maintain pronoun-antecedent agreement in sentence 5, change "their" to

   A. her   C. its

   B. they   D. theirs

5. Choose the correct way to write the possessive form of the underlined word in sentence 6.

   A. scientists's   C. scientist's

   B. scientists'   D. scientist's'

6. To maintain pronoun-antecedent agreement in sentence 7, change "they" to

   A. he   C. theirs

   B. them   D. it

STOP

171

INTRODUCE *MORE GREAT READS*

In Unit 1, students have discussed a number of big questions. Invite students to tell which question they found most intriguing and why. Then focus attention on the three questions that appear on this page. Discuss the recommended books and their summaries, pointing out how each book connects to the related question. Encourage students to choose one or more of these "great reads" to read independently.

ⓘ ClassZone.com

To find additional books that match students' interests and ability levels, visit the Literature Center at **ClassZone.com**.

UNIT 1

More Great Reads

Ideas for Independent Reading

Which questions from Unit 1 made an impression on you? Continue exploring them with these books.

How do you make a good impression?

The Ghost in the Tokaido Inn
by Dorothy Hoobler
What do you long to be? Seikei wants to be a samurai, but he knows that as a merchant's son, the chances are slim. Will Seikei achieve his life's dream? Read this award-winning book and find out.

The Great Turkey Walk
by Kathleen Karr
It is 1860. Fifteen-year-old Simon likes and respects his teacher. One day she tells him it's time he left her class to venture out into the real world. But what will become of him in the rough world of this frontier setting?

No Man's Land
by Susan Bartoletti
Fourteen-year-old Thrasher lies about his age, joins the Confederate Army, and begins his courageous adventure. Along the way, Thrasher comes to know that enemies are people too.

Who sees the best in you?

Bearstone
by Will Hobbs
A troubled Native American teen is sent to work on a ranch in the mountains of Colorado. There the elderly owner provides the steadying influence the boy needs, but complications arise.

Good Night, Mr. Tom
by Michelle Magorian
Young Willie is among thousands of children evacuated from London because of the bombing raids at the brink of World War II. When a wise old man named Mr. Tom adopts him, Willie learns to trust his world again.

Nobody's Daughter
by Susan Pfeffer
Eleven-year-old Emily is packed off to an orphanage but dreams of finding her sister, who has been adopted. Harsh reality greets her in the form of Miss Browne, the director. Whom can she turn to?

What makes you brave?

North by Night
by Katherine Ayres
This story centers on the 1850 Fugitive Slave Act. Through her letters and journal entries, 16-year-old Lucinda tells of her family's attempts to turn their Ohio farm into an Underground Railroad station.

The Dark Is Rising
by Susan Cooper
Eleven-year-old Will Stanton struggles to overcome the powers of the Dark. Will must search for the six magical signs needed in the great battle between the Dark and the Light. Can he find them in time?

The Clay Marble
By Minfong Ho
After fleeing war-torn Cambodia in 1980, Dara, her older brother, and her mother find sanctuary on the Thailand border in a refugee camp. Then fighting erupts, and Dara is separated from her family.

UNIT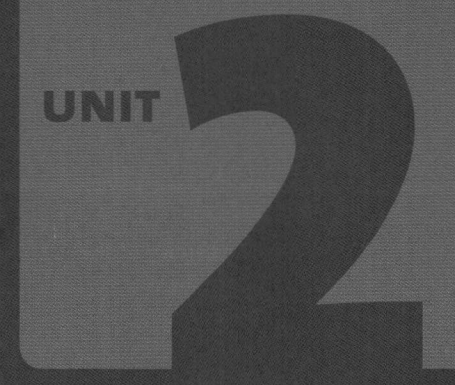

Personality Tests

ANALYZING CHARACTER AND POINT OF VIEW

- **In Fiction**
- **In Nonfiction**
- **In Poetry**

173

About the Art The painting above by Robert Henri appears as an illustration for "The Scholarship Jacket," by Marta Salinas. For more information, see page 218 of the teacher's edition.

For help in planning this unit, see

 RESOURCE MANAGER UNIT 2
pp. 1–11

INTRODUCE THE UNIT

A flamboyant style of dress, a brazen attitude, a soft-spoken voice, or a muscular build—certain things about passersby can tell a lot about their personalities. Suggest to students that as they get to know people, their first impressions of them might change. Explain that authors must develop a character's personality in the same way we might learn about someone in real life.

Invite students to share experiences they may have had in getting to know someone. Then ask them to think about these ideas as they discuss the pictures on this page. To spark a discussion, ask

- Based on the pictures, in what time period do you think each person might live?
- How is each person dressed? What does that tell you?
- What do the characters' expressions tell you about their personalities? What do you think they are thinking and feeling?
- If you were going to write a story about these characters, what would each story be about?

Discuss which responses are direct observations and which are opinions. Explain that in literature, readers make inferences about characters based on information in the story and prior knowledge. In this unit, students will explore how **character** and **point of view** help make a story come alive.

UNIT 2
Standards Skills Trace

MARYLAND

SKILLS STRAND	Reader's Workshop: Character and Point of View pp. 176–181 3.A.3.d, 3.A.3.i	Zebra pp. 182–207 Short Story Level: Challenging 1.D.3.a, 1.E.3.a, 3.A.3.d, 5.B.2.c	The Legacy of the Vietnam War pp. 208–215 Feature Article, Letter, Timeline Level: Average 1.E.4.c, 2.A.4.g	The Scholarship Jacket pp. 216–225 Short Story Level: Easy 1.D.3.a, 1.E.4.c, 3.A.3.i	A Retrieved Reformation pp. 226–239 Short Story Level: Challenging 1.D.3.a, 1.E.4.d, 3.A.3.i, 5.B.2
Literary Analysis	Point of View pp. 176–177, 181 Methods of Characterization pp. 178–180, 181	Character pp. 183, 186, 187, 188, 190, 191, 196, 197, 200, 201, 203, 205	Characteristics of a Feature Article pp. 209, 211	First-Person Point of View pp. 217, 218, 220, 223, 224	Omniscient Point of View pp. 227, 228, 231, 233, 234, 237
Reading and Informational Texts	Analyze the Literature pp. 177, 179–181	Visualize pp. 183, 184, 187, 193, 196, 202, 205 Review: Make Inferences pp. 183, 186, 191, 193 Read a Poem p. 204	Synthesize pp. 208, 209, 210, 211, 212, 213, 214, 215 Draw Conclusions p. 215	Make Inferences pp. 217, 220, 222, 223, 224	Predict pp. 227, 231, 232, 233, 236, 237 Review: Make Inferences pp. 227, 232, 235, 236
Vocabulary	Academic Vocabulary pp. 176, 178	Word Acquisition pp. 183, T183, 206 Context Clues p. T183 Similes as Context Clues p. 206		Word Acquisition pp. 217, T217, 225 Context Clues p. T217 Context Clues (Definition and Synonym) p. 225	Word Acquisition pp. 227, T227, 238 Categorize Words p. T227 Words with Multiple Meanings p. 238
Writing, Grammar, and Style		Correct Verb Tense p. 207			Comparative and Superlative Forms p. 239
Speaking, Listening, Viewing, and Media	Discuss pp. 176–180	Discuss pp. 182, T184–T204, 205 Analyze Visuals pp. 184, 189, 192, T197, T199, 203	Discuss pp. 208, T209–T214, 215	Discuss pp. 216, T218–T223, 224 Analyze Visuals pp. 218, 222	Discuss pp. 226, T228–T236, 237 Analyze Visuals pp. 228, T232, 234

Linked selections

Assessment-Based Planning: Skills in red are assessed on the Unit 2 Test. **T** = Teacher's Edition page

1.D.3.b, 1.E.3.a, 3.A.3.d, 3.A.3.e	1.D.3.c, 1.E.4.f, 3.A.3.d	1.D.3.a, 1.E.3.a, 3.A.3.i, 5.B.2.c	3.A.3.d, 3.A.4.a	4.A.1, 4.A.2.c, 6.A.1.b
The Three-Century Woman / Charles pp. 240–257	**Encounter with Martin Luther King Jr.** pp. 258–267	**Dirk the Protector** pp. 268–279	**It Was a Long Time Before / Abuelito Who** pp. 280–285	**Writing Workshop: Comparison-Contrast Essay** pp. 286–293
Short Stories *Level: Average*	Autobiography *Level: Challenging*	Memoir *Level: Average*	Poems *Level: Average*	
Characterization pp. 241, 242, 244, 245, 248, 249, 250, 251, 253, 255	Characterization in Nonfiction pp. 259, 260, 263, 264, 265	Point of View in a Memoir pp. 269, 272, 273, 275, 277	Characterization in Poetry pp. 281, 283, 285	
Set a Purpose for Reading p. 241 Compare Characters pp. 249, 255 Review: Make Inferences pp. 245, 246, 248, 252, 254, 255	Connect pp. 259, 263, 264, 265 Read a Memorandum p. 267	Identify Cause-and-Effect Relationships pp. 269, 270, 273, 274, 276, 277	Strategies for Reading Poetry pp. 281, 283, 284, 285	Analyze a Comparison-Contrast Essay pp. 287–288, 292
Word Acquisition pp. 241, T241, 256 Context Clues p. T241 Latin Roots (*cred*) p. 256	Word Acquisition pp. 259, T259, 266 Context Clues p. T259 Reference Aids p. 266	Word Acquisition pp. 269, T269, 278 Context Clues p. T269 Idioms p. 278		
Write for Assessment p. 257		Misplaced Modifiers p. 279 Prepositional Phrases p. 279		Write a Comparison-Contrast Essay pp. 286–293 Organization pp. 286, 287, 290 Transitions pp. 288, 290, 292 Run-On Sentences p. 292
Discuss pp. 240, T242–T248, 249, T250–T254, 255 Analyze Visuals pp. 242, 247, 250	Discuss pp. 258, T260–T264, 265, T267 Analyze Visuals p. 260	Discuss pp. 268, T270–T276, 277 Analyze Visuals pp. 270, T275	Discuss pp. 280, T282–T284, 285 Analyze Visuals p. 282	Discuss pp. 286–288 Conduct an Interview p. 293

Skills Assessed on the Unit 2 Test:

Literary Analysis
- Recognize character traits
- Recognize and analyze point of view
- Identify and analyze characterization

Reading and Informational Texts
- Visualize
- Make inferences
- Draw conclusions
- Predict

Vocabulary
- Use figurative language (simile) to understand words
- Use context clues to determine the meaning of idioms
- Identify idioms

Writing, Grammar, and Style
- Write a comparison-contrast essay
- Use past, present, and future tenses of verbs correctly
- Use comparative and superlative forms of adjectives and adverbs correctly
- Correct misplaced modifiers
- Connect ideas with transitions
- Additional writing and grammar skills

For additional lesson planning help, see **Easy Planner DVD.**

173B

OBJECTIVES

- establish prior knowledge about **character** and **characterization**
- discuss great characters

What makes a great CHARACTER?

Ask students to describe characters they have met in literature and felt strongly about. As you discuss the characters, ask students to consider why their feelings were so strong. Do they think the author intended this reaction? Did they identify with certain qualities the character possessed? Did the character remind them of someone they knew? Conclude by eliciting from students that being able to evoke a strong response from an audience is one sign of a great character.

ACTIVITY Suggest that students list as many details about each character as they can think of. Then guide them in categorizing their responses in terms of appearance, actions, speech, personality, and what they learn about the character's life through the story. Point out that writers must consider all of these elements in creating a great character.

CHECK UNDERSTANDING Have students identify the qualities that make a **character** seem life-like. You might name a specific character, such as Yoda (shown on page 174), and have them explain what makes this fantastic creature seem real to moviegoers. What details in the *Star Wars* films help bring Yoda to life?

What makes a great CHARACTER?

An eccentric inventor, an orphaned boy, and a spider—hard to imagine what these three characters have in common, isn't it? But once you know their names—Willy Wonka, Harry Potter, and Charlotte—the connection becomes clearer. All three are examples of **great characters**—figments of authors' imaginations that are so lifelike they seem to pop off the page and into our own world.

ACTIVITY With a partner, brainstorm a list of great characters from stories, TV shows, and movies. Then discuss the following questions:

- Why did you choose these characters? Next to each name, jot down what makes him or her (or it!) great.
- What similarities do you notice about your reasons for selecting these characters?
- On the basis of your discussion, what advice would you give a first-time author about how to create great characters?

174

Unit Resources

- **R** RESOURCE MANAGER UNIT 2
- **BEST PRACTICES TOOLKIT**
- **S** STANDARDS LESSON FILE

- Easy Planner DVD
- Write*Smart* CD
- ClassZone.com
- Audio Anthology CD
- Multi-Language Academic Vocabulary Online

- eEdition CD & Online
- McDougal Littell Assessment System
- Test Generator CD
- Media*Smart* DVD

 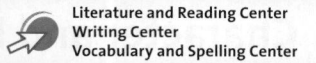
 **MARYLAND OBJECTIVES** ## Preview Unit Goals

LITERARY ANALYSIS	• Recognize character traits
	• Identify and analyze characterization
	• Recognize point of view, including first person, limited third person, and omniscient
	• Identify and compare characters
READING	• Use reading strategies, including visualizing, predicting, and connecting
	• Make inferences, draw conclusions, and synthesize
	• Identify cause-effect relationships
WRITING AND GRAMMAR	• Write a comparison-contrast essay
	• Correctly use present, past, and future verb tenses
	• Correctly use comparative and superlative forms of adjectives and adverbs
SPEAKING, LISTENING, AND VIEWING	• Conduct an interview
VOCABULARY	• Use context clues to determine the meaning of words and idioms
ACADEMIC VOCABULARY	• character traits • omniscient point of view
	• characterization • inferences
	• first-person point of view • context clues

175

Preview Unit Goals

This page provides an overview of the skills and strategies covered in this unit. Draw students' attention to the color-coding. Explain that throughout the unit, each skill within a strand matches the color of that strand. Encourage students to consider their ability to use each skill and strategy as they study this page.

Suggest that students write the Academic Vocabulary terms in their journals and define them as they read the unit. Encourage students to use these terms as they discuss and write about the selections.

ADDITIONAL UNIT GOALS

These skills will be taught in this unit but are not the major focus of the unit.

Literary Analysis
• Analyze characters
• Recognize main and minor characters
• Identify static and dynamic characters
• Study a variety of genres: short story, poetry, memoir

Reading
• Apply strategies for reading poetry, feature articles, letters, timelines, and memos
• Use strategies to set a purpose for reading
• Use reading strategies such as synthesizing

Writing and Grammar
• Use correct verb tense
• Compare correctly
• Avoid misplaced modifiers
• Connect ideas with transitions
• Use prepositions and prepositional phrases correctly

Vocabulary
• Use figurative language such as similes as a context clue to determine word meanings
• Use context clues to determine the meanings of multiple-meaning words
• Understand and use the Latin root *cred*
• Identify idioms
• Use reference aids such as a thesaurus or a dictionary to locate synonyms

DIFFERENTIATED INSTRUCTION

FOR ENGLISH LEARNERS

Academic Vocabulary Students will study and practice using these terms throughout the unit. Use the Academic Vocabulary copy master to introduce the terms.

• Read each word aloud and discuss its meaning. Ask students if they have heard any of these words and in what context.

• Allow students to work in pairs to complete the sentences and the activities. Then discuss student answers as a class.

Additional Academic Vocabulary Use the second copy master to help students study these terms from the unit: *main character, minor character, verb tense, simile, idiom.*

• Divide the class into five groups.

• Have each group discuss one term, think of examples, and explain it to the class.

• Have students complete Part B individually.

R RESOURCE MANAGER—Copy Masters
Academic Vocabulary p. 9
Additional Academic Vocabulary p. 10

175

Focus and Motivate

OBJECTIVES

- recognize character traits
- recognize and analyze point of view, including first person, omniscient, and limited
- identify and analyze characterization

Teach

Part 1: Point of View

Narrator Explain that in choosing the narrator, an author controls how information is shared with readers. The narrator may be a major or minor character or an outsider. Ask a volunteer to tell about an event in the news. Have students identify other people who could have told about this event, such as eyewitnesses or the people involved. Then discuss what information each person would be able to share about the event.

Point of View Tell students that when analyzing a story it is important to consider the objectivity and reliability of the narrator. They should ask themselves how a story might differ if it were told by an impartial observer or another character. Use this activity to show how point of view can affect a story:

- Have students brainstorm a list of stories with which they are familiar.
- Have students list the stories in a chart, identifying the narrator and point of view of each. Then ask students to discuss how each story might change if the author used a different narrator and point of view.

Story	Narrator	Point of View

 BEST PRACTICES TOOLKIT—Transparency
Analysis Frame: Character pp. D23, D28

Character and Point of View

Bossy and loud, sensitive and shy, athletic and adventurous—what qualities make you admire one person and dislike another? When you meet characters in literature, you are likely to form strong impressions, just as you do with people in real life. By looking closely at character and point of view, you can understand your reactions to the people you meet on the page.

 **MARYLAND OBJECTIVES**

LITERATURE STANDARDS
3.A.3.d Analyze characterization
3.A.3.i Analyze point of view

Part 1: Point of View

Imagine watching three videotapes of a soccer game. One was taken from the sidelines; you can see all the players in action. The second was taped by someone running alongside one player. The third was taken *by* a player; you can see the game through her eyes. In literature, the **narrator** holds the camera—that is, tells the story. A writer's choice of narrator is referred to as **point of view.**

Just how much can point of view affect a story? Find out by examining these examples from a comical take on the familiar tale "Cinderella."

FIRST-PERSON POINT OF VIEW

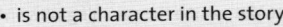

The Narrator

- is a character in the story
- uses the pronouns *I* and *me* to refer to himself or herself
- describes his or her own thoughts, feelings, and impressions
- does not know what other characters are thinking and feeling

Example

Cinderella was the last girl in the world I would want to marry. I mean, who wears glass slippers to a ball? I only picked up that lost slipper because it was a safety hazard. And it seemed like a princely thing to do.

THIRD-PERSON POINT OF VIEW

The Narrator

- is not a character in the story
- is called **limited** if he or she tells the thoughts and feelings of only one character
- is called **omniscient,** or all-knowing, if he or she reveals the thoughts and feelings of all the characters

Examples

Limited: Cinderella ran down the steps, losing a slipper along the way. The prince thought to himself, "She's going to break an ankle."

Omniscient: Cinderella hated to lose her slipper but knew she was running out of time. Watching her, the prince shook his head and thought, "There's an accident waiting to happen!"

---

176 UNIT 2: ANALYZING CHARACTER AND POINT OF VIEW

DIFFERENTIATED INSTRUCTION

FOR ALL STUDENTS

For general guidelines on differentiating instruction, see

 BEST PRACTICES TOOLKIT
Differentiated Instruction pp. 31–38

FOR LESS–PROFICIENT READERS

Note Taking Hand out the Note Taking: Point of View copy master and have students read page 176 silently. Then have students take notes on the copy master as you discuss the information.

 RESOURCE MANAGER—Copy Master
Note Taking p. 15

Use Point of View Organize students into groups of three. Tell each group that they will tell a story about a recent event at school. Allow students a few minutes to discuss the event, describing what happened and focusing on two or three main participants, such as themselves, other students, or teachers. Then have each group member tell the story from a different point of view.

MODEL 1: FIRST-PERSON POINT OF VIEW

This story is told by a teenage boy. What do you learn about him from what he says and thinks?

from

An HOUR with Abuelo

Short story by **Judith Ortiz Cofer**

My grandfather is in a nursing home in Brooklyn, and my mother wants me to spend some time with him, since the doctors say that he doesn't have too long to go now. *I* don't have much time left of my summer vacation, and there's a stack of books next to my bed I've
5 got to read if I'm going to get into the AP English class I want. I'm going stupid in some of my classes, and Mr. Williams, the principal at Central, said that if I passed some reading tests, he'd let me move up.

Besides, I hate the place, the old people's home, especially the way it smells like industrial-strength ammonia and other stuff I won't
10 mention, since it turns my stomach.

Close Read

1. Copy any sentence, then circle the pronouns that show the first-person point of view.

2. Describe two things you learn about the narrator from what he tells you about himself.

MODEL 2: THIRD-PERSON POINT OF VIEW

In a story told from the third-person limited point of view, the narrator reveals the thoughts of one character. Here, the character is a dog named Buck.

from

THE CALL OF THE *Wild*

Novel by **Jack London**

Dazed, suffering intolerable pain from throat and tongue, with the life half throttled out of him, Buck attempted to face his tormentors. But he was thrown down and choked repeatedly, till they succeeded in filing the heavy brass collar from off his neck. Then the rope was
5 removed, and he was flung into a cagelike crate.

There he lay for the remainder of the weary night, nursing his wrath and wounded pride. He could not understand what it all meant. What did they want with him, these strange men? Why were they keeping him pent up in this narrow crate? He did not know why,
10 but he felt oppressed. . . .

Close Read

1. Find two places where the narrator reveals Buck's thoughts. One example has been boxed.

2. What more might an omniscient narrator be able to tell you?

MODEL 1: FIRST-PERSON POINT OF VIEW

Close Read

1. *Possible answers:*
   - sentence 1 (lines 1–3): *My, my, me*
   - sentence 2 (lines 3–5): *I, my, my, I've, I'm, I*
   - sentence 3 (lines 5–7): *I'm, my, I, me*
   - sentence 4 (lines 8–10): *I, I, my*

2. *Possible answer: The narrator is hoping to get into an advanced English class (line 5), and he hates the nursing home in which his grandfather lives (line 8).*

MODEL 2: THIRD-PERSON POINT OF VIEW

Close Read

1. *Possible answers: Buck's thoughts as revealed by the narrator include*
   - *"Dazed, suffering intolerable pain" (line 1)*
   - *"nursing his wrath and wounded pride" (lines 6–7)*
   - *"Why were they keeping him pent up in this narrow crate?" (lines 8–9)*
   - *"He did not know why, but he felt oppressed" (lines 9–10)*

2. *Possible answer: An omniscient narrator might tell what the men want with the dog and why they are keeping him in the crate.*

   If students need help . . . Have them reread the passage and underline any references to other characters. Then ask students what they might learn if they knew what these characters were thinking and feeling.

FOR ENGLISH LEARNERS

Concept Support: First-Person Point of View

1. Have students underline words and phrases in the first passage about the mother and the grandfather.

2. Ask them to think about how these characters might feel about the situation described by the narrator.

3. Have students write a brief paragraph from the point of view of either the mother or the grandfather.

FOR ADVANCED LEARNERS/PRE–AP

Change Point of View Have students rewrite the first passage from the third-person omniscient point of view, revealing the thoughts of the mother, the grandfather, and the school principal. Encourage them to describe other characters, such as the boy's English teacher or people who work at the nursing home.

Teach

Part 2: Methods of Characterization

Traits Clarify for students that while a narrator might expressly point out certain character traits, in most cases it is up to the reader to make inferences about characters based on evidence in the text. Ask students to think about a memorable character from one of their favorite movies or stories. Have them use a chart like this to describe the character, supplying evidence from the story or movie that supports their description:

Traits	Supporting Evidence

Methods of Characterization After students read the chart on page 178, encourage them to use the information in the examples to make judgments about the fairy godmother. In addition to the questions in the chart, encourage students to also consider these questions when analyzing the methods of characterization:

- What does the character's appearance reveal about his or her personality?

- What are the reasons behind what the character does, says, or thinks? How do you feel about the character's thoughts, speech, or actions?

- What history does the character have with the other characters? What are the reasons behind other characters' reactions to the character? How do you feel about other character's reactions to the character?

- Is the narrator a character in the story? If so, do his or her opinions affect his or her comments about the character? If not, what is the significance of the narrator's comments about the character?

Part 2: Methods of Characterization

When you meet people, how do you figure out what they are like? You might make judgments based on how they look or how they behave. You may also find out information from others. In literature, these kinds of details are clues to a character's personality. As a reader, you can use these clues to infer a character's **traits,** or qualities, such as sloppiness or bravery. By knowing what to look for, you can get to know the **main characters,** or the most important ones. You may even learn something about the **minor characters,** or less important ones, too.

Writers use four **methods of characterization** to bring their characters to life. What do you learn about Cinderella's fairy godmother from each example?

METHOD OF CHARACTERIZATION	EXAMPLE
PHYSICAL APPEARANCE Appearances can tell you a great deal about a character. Ask: • What does the character look like? • What are his or her expressions, gestures, or body language?	The fairy godmother was wearing greasy overalls with a rusty garden fork sticking out of one back pocket. She brushed some dirt off her hands and smiled.
 **THOUGHTS, SPEECH, AND ACTIONS** A character's words and actions can reveal his or her personality. Ask: • What does the character think, say, or do? • How does he or she treat others? • What kinds of things are important to him or her?	The fairy godmother thought to herself, "I'd better get to work! I have only eight hours to get Cinderella ready for the ball. And from what I've seen of her, I'll need every second of it."
 **OTHER CHARACTERS** Other characters' reactions to a character can also serve as clues. Ask: • What do others say about the character? • How do they treat him or her?	Cinderella's wicked stepsister shrieked when she saw the fairy godmother. "What is this disgusting woman doing in my home? Have her removed at once!"
NARRATOR'S COMMENTS Sometimes the narrator tells you directly about a character. Ask: • What does the narrator say about the character? • Does the narrator respect the character or criticize him or her?	The fairy godmother knew how to handle wicked people! In fact, she was frighteningly clever.

DIFFERENTIATED INSTRUCTION

FOR LESS—PROFICIENT READERS

Note Taking For students who need help with note taking, hand out the Note Taking: Methods of Characterization copy master. Read and discuss the information on page 178. Assist students, as needed, in completing the copy master.

 RESOURCE MANAGER—Copy Master
Note Taking p. 16

Illustrate a Character Have students list the details that describe the mother's appearance in *Homecoming*. Then have them use the details to draw a picture of the mother. Encourage them to incorporate as many details as they can into their drawings. Then ask students what they might think about this woman if she passed by them at a shopping center.

METHOD 1: PHYSICAL APPEARANCE

In this novel, a girl finds herself abandoned with her younger siblings in a car outside a shopping mall. What do you learn about their mother from this one brief glimpse?

from

Homecoming

Novel by **Cynthia Voigt**

The woman put her sad moon-face in at the window of the car. "You be good," she said. "You hear me? You little ones, mind what Dicey tells you. You hear?"

"Yes, Momma," they said.

5 "That's all right then." She slung her purse over her shoulder and walked away, her stride made uneven by broken sandal thongs, thin elbows showing through holes in the oversized sweater, her jeans faded and baggy. When she had disappeared into the crowd of Saturday morning shoppers entering the side doors of the mall, the three younger
10 children leaned forward onto the front seat.

Close Read

1. Find three details that describe the mother's appearance. One example has been boxed for you.

2. What do you learn about the mother from these details?

METHOD 2: THOUGHTS, SPEECH, AND ACTIONS

Here, a girl at her piano lesson notices an umbrella that was left behind by Eugenie, an older student she admires and envies.

from

The White Umbrella

Short story by **Gish Jen**

I stared at the umbrella. I wanted to open it, twirl it around by its slender silver handle; I wanted to dangle it from my wrist on the way to school the way the other girls did. I wondered what Miss Crosman would say if I offered to bring it to Eugenie at school tomorrow. She
5 would be impressed with my consideration for others; Eugenie would be pleased to have it back; and I would have possession of the umbrella for an entire night. I looked at it again, toying with the idea of asking for one for Christmas. I knew, however, how my mother would react.

"Things," she would say. "What's the matter with a raincoat? All you
10 want is things, just like an American."

Close Read

1. The boxed text suggests that the girl wants to fit in at school. What do her other thoughts tell you about her?

2. What do the girl's thoughts in lines 7–10 reveal about her relationship with her mother?

METHOD 1: PHYSICAL APPEARANCE

Close Read

1. *Possible answers:*
   - *"sad moon-face" (line 1)*
   - *"purse over her shoulder" (line 5)*
   - *"stride made uneven by broken sandal thongs" (line 6)*
   - *"thin elbows showing through" (lines 6–7)*
   - *"jeans faded and baggy" (lines 7–8)*

2. *Possible answer: The mother's appearance is disheveled, and she is probably depressed and struggling financially. She may feel overwhelmed with the burden of raising four children.*

METHOD 2: THOUGHTS, SPEECH, AND ACTIONS

Close Read

1. *Possible answer: The girl longs for things she doesn't have (lines 1–2, 9–10) and is concerned about what other people think of her, including the other girls at school (line 3), her teacher (lines 3–4), Eugenie (lines 5–6), and her mother (line 8).*

2. *Possible answer: The girl's thoughts reveal a conflict between her and her mother. The girl thinks about asking for an umbrella for Christmas (lines 7–8) but she knows that her mother will reject the idea as frivolous and materialistic (lines 9–10). The girl wants to be more like the other girls at school, while her mother wishes her daughter would embrace her own individuality and culture.*

DIFFERENTIATED INSTRUCTION

FOR ENGLISH LEARNERS

Concept Support: Characterization

1. Have students name characters from stories they have read in class. Choose an especially memorable one and write his or her name in the center of a concept web.

2. Draw four outer ovals labeled *appearance; thoughts, speech, and actions; other characters;* and *narrator's comments*.

3. Have student volunteers write details about the character extending from each oval.

FOR ADVANCED LEARNERS/PRE–AP

Static and Dynamic Characters Tell students that some characters are static, or remain the same over the course of a story, while others are dynamic, undergoing a major change in personality or developing a different outlook by the story's end. Ask students to write two endings for "The White Umbrella"—the first continuing the story about the girl as she is portrayed in the excerpt, and the second shaping the girl into a dynamic character.

METHOD 3: OTHER CHARACTERS

Close Read

1. **Possible answer:** *Gracey Pearson doesn't seem to like Cassie, since she objects to Cassie sitting next to her, claiming that the seat is saved for another classmate (line 3).*

2. **Possible answer:** *The way in which Cassie describes Miss Crocker glaring down at her (line 6) with an accusatory expression (lines 7–8) suggests that Cassie may have had problems with the teacher.*

3. **Possible answer:** *It seems as if Cassie is a bit of a troublemaker and has a history of confrontations with both her classmates and her teacher.*

METHOD 4: NARRATOR'S COMMENTS

Close Read

1. **Possible answers:**

   • *Mack is a promising and talented baseball player (lines 1–3).*

   • *He is well-liked, but mainly because of his athletic success (lines 4–5).*

   • *He is arrogant and expects recognition for his talents wherever he goes (lines 5–7).*

   • *He is smart but he makes a point of showing that he is not concerned with his grades (lines 8–9).*

2. **Possible answers:**

   • *Yes, the narrator admires Mack for his athletic ability and intelligence.*

   • *No, the narrator thinks Mack is shallow and arrogant.*

METHOD 3: OTHER CHARACTERS

In this excerpt, a girl named Cassie walks into her classroom and faces her classmates and her teacher. As you read, observe how others react to Cassie. Does she seem to be well liked?

from
ROLL OF THUNDER, HEAR MY CRY
Novel by **Mildred Taylor**

I hurried to the rear of the building, turned to the right, and slid into a third-row bench occupied by Gracey Pearson and Alma Scott. "You can't sit here," objected Gracey. "I'm saving it for Mary Lou." I glanced back at Mary Lou Wellever depositing her lunch pail on
5 a shelf in the back of the room and said, "Not any more you ain't."

Miss Daisy Crocker, yellow and buckeyed, glared down at me from the middle of the room with a look that said, "Soooooooo, it's you, Cassie Logan."

Close Read

1. Does Gracey Pearson like Cassie? Explain.

2. Reread the boxed sentence about Miss Crocker, Cassie's teacher. How does Miss Crocker feel about Cassie?

3. What impression do you get of Cassie from other characters' reactions to her?

METHOD 4: NARRATOR'S COMMENTS

Here, the narrator tells you directly about a character named Mack. What do you learn about Mack from the narrator's comments?

from
Kitty and Mack: A Love Story
Short story by **Walter Dean Myers**

He was eighteen and one newspaper article about him said that he could be in the major leagues by the time he was nineteen. That's how good he was. Naturally the baseball coach loved him. That was the thing about Mack, the people who liked him usually liked him because
5 he was a star. Mack had an attitude problem. He thought he could just show up and everybody was supposed to fall down and go crazy or something.

He was pretty smart, too, but he made this big show of not caring about grades.

Close Read

1. On the basis of the narrator's comments, how would you describe Mack?

2. Do you think the narrator admires Mack? Support your opinion with evidence.

DIFFERENTIATED INSTRUCTION

FOR LESS-PROFICIENT READERS

Analysis Support: Characterization Suggest that students act out the scene described in the excerpt from *Roll of Thunder, Hear My Cry.* Encourage them to use exaggerated tones and gestures to emphasize the edgy relationships between the characters.

FOR ENGLISH LEARNERS

Analysis Support: "Kitty and Mack: A Love Story" Have student pairs role-play as sports announcers during one of Mack's baseball games. Have them describe Mack's actions both on and off the field, discuss his prospects as an athlete and student, and comment on his relationships with others. Encourage students to exhibit differing opinions about Mack in their commentary.

Part 3: Analyze the Literature

In this story, a girl named Katie spends her birthday visiting her dying mother in the hospital. Among her presents is one from her mother. It's a box—a beautiful, empty box. Katie is upset by the present and by her mother's last words to her: "It's you." As you read, use what you have learned to analyze both Katie and her mother.

from
BIRTHDAY BOX

Short story by **Jane Yolen**

. . . For about a year I cried at anniversaries, like Mama's birthday or mine, at Thanksgiving, on Mother's Day. I stopped writing. I stopped reading except for school assignments. I was pretty mean to my half brothers and totally rotten to my stepmother and Dad. I felt empty and
5 angry, and they all left me pretty much alone.

And then one night, right after my first birthday without Mama, I woke up remembering how she had said, "It's you." Not, "It's for you," just "It's you." Now Mama had been a high school English teacher and a writer herself. She'd had poems published in little magazines. She didn't
10 use words carelessly. In the end she could hardly use any words at all. So—I asked myself in that dark room—why had she said, "It's you"? Why were they the very last words she had ever said to me, forced out with her last breath?

I turned on the bedside light and got out of bed. The room was full
15 of shadows, not all of them real.

Pulling the desk chair over to my closet, I climbed up and felt along the top shelf, and against the back wall, there was the birthday box, just where I had thrown it the day I had moved in with my dad.

I pulled it down and opened it. It was as empty as the day I had put
20 it away.

"It's you," I whispered to the box.

And then suddenly I knew.

Mama had meant *I* was the box, solid and sturdy, maybe even beautiful or at least interesting on the outside. But I had to fill up the
25 box to make it all it could be. And I had to fill me up as well. She had guessed what might happen to me, had told me in a subtle way. In the two words she could manage.

I stopped crying and got some paper out of the desk drawer. I got out my fountain pen. I started writing, and I haven't stopped since.

Close Read

1. From what point of view is this story told? Explain how you can tell.

2. Reread the boxed paragraph. How does Katie react to her mother's death?

3. What do you learn about Katie's mother from what Katie tells you in lines 6–13?

4. Reread lines 23–27. Given what you know about the characters, why do you think Katie's mother would have chosen to deliver her message in this way?

5. How would you describe the character of Katie? Support your answer.

Practice and Apply

Part 3: Analyze the Literature
Close Read

1. *Possible answer: The story is told from the daughter's first-person point of view. The narrator is a character; uses the pronouns* I, me, *and* my; *describes her own feelings; and is unaware of her mother's thoughts (lines 11–13).*

2. *Possible answer: Katie is distraught over her mother's death, feeling empty and angry (lines 4–5), and often becoming depressed on anniversaries (lines 1–2). She stops doing things she once enjoyed (lines 2–3).*

3. *Possible answer: Katie's mother was a high school English teacher and a published writer (lines 8–9). She became very sick as her death neared (line 10), and before she died had given her daughter something and forced out the carefully chosen last words, "It's you" (lines 11–13).*

4. *Possible answer: Katie's mother probably knew that Katie would reflect on the words later. She may have felt that Katie was not ready to hear the message at the time but would make the discovery on her own as part of the healing process.*

5. *Possible answer: Katie's relationship with her mother and her guilt about treating her family badly shows that she is caring and sensitive. Her ability to decipher her mother's message shows her inner strength, and her writing shows that she is creative.*

Assess and Reteach

Assess

Have students characterize Katie based on the excerpt. Then have them identify which methods of characterization they used.

Reteach

Use this activity for students who have trouble applying the workshop skills:

1. Have small groups review the copy masters, sharing their examples.

2. Have students work together to come up with examples of the four methods of characterization.

3. Have them make inferences about the characters based on their examples.

DIFFERENTIATED INSTRUCTION

FOR LESS–PROFICIENT READERS
Analysis Support: Character Have students list the characters mentioned by Katie, the narrator in "The Birthday Box." Ask students what they can tell about Katie based on her relationships with these characters. Have them write a brief paragraph describing the relationships and how these characters have influenced Katie.

FOR ADVANCED LEARNERS/PRE–AP
Analyze Character Have students write a brief essay analyzing the character of Katie and discussing the meaning of the birthday box.

Focus and Motivate

OBJECTIVES

Literary Analysis
- explore the key idea of ways to **heal**
- analyze characters
- recognize main and minor characters
- read a short story and a poem

Reading
- visualize

Vocabulary
- build vocabulary for reading and writing
- use similes as context clues to help unlock meaning *(also an EL language objective)*

Grammar and Writing
- use correct verb tense
- use writing to analyze literature

SUMMARY

"Zebra" is the story of a seventh-grade boy whose nickname is based on his love of running. One year ago, Zebra was hit by a car while running. His injured leg and hand are slow to heal. Taking a summer art class taught by a Vietnam veteran who lost an arm helps Zebra heal both his body and his spirit. In turn, one of Zebra's drawings is part of the veteran's own healing process after the war.

What has the power to HEAL?

Discuss the question. Expand the **KEY IDEA** by encouraging students to think about words that they associate with **heal.** Possible words include *fix, repair, mend, cure, recover, get well, health,* and *make whole.* Then have students do the **LIST IT** activity.

Selection Resources

Zebra
Short Story by Chaim Potok

What has the power to HEAL?

MARYLAND OBJECTIVES

READING/LIT STANDARDS
1.E.3.a Select and apply appropriate strategies during reading
3.A.3.d Analyze characterization

KEY IDEA You never know what kind of wounds will cause the greatest damage. An argument with a friend can cause as much pain as a broken leg. Likewise, a physical injury can also scar the spirit. In "Zebra," you will read about a boy your age who needs to **heal** both his body and his mind.

LIST IT With a partner, create two lists. In the first, list three to five ways people cope with physical injuries or disabilities. In the second, identify at least three ways that people deal with emotional pain.

182

R RESOURCE MANAGER UNIT 2

Plan and Teach pp. 17–24

Literary Analysis
Summary pp. 25†*, 26‡*
Character pp. 27, 28†*
Question Support p. 35*

Reading
Visualize pp. 29, 30†*
Reading Check p. 34
Reading Fluency p. 37

Vocabulary
Study p. 31*
Practice p. 32
Strategy p. 33

Grammar and Writing
Use Correct Verb Tense p. 36

Assessment
Selection Tests A, B/C pp. 39*, 41*
⊙ Test Generator CD

BEST PRACTICES TOOLKIT

Differentiated Instruction
pp. 31–38*

Scaffolding Instruction pp. 43–46*

Graphic Organizers/Strategies
Word Questioning • Making
Inferences • Timeline • Jigsaw •
T Chart • New Word Analysis •
Spider Map • Cause-and-Effect
Chain • Think-Pair-Share •
Character Map

Reading Support
⊘ Audio Anthology CD*

Technology
ℹ Literature and Vocabulary
Centers at **ClassZone.com**

⊘ Write*Smart* CD

---

* Resources for Differentiation   † Also in Spanish   ‡ In Haitian Creole and Vietnamese

LITERARY ANALYSIS: CHARACTER

The people who appear in stories are called **characters.** A short story usually focuses on one or two **main characters.** To identify who they are, ask yourself:

- Who are the most important characters in the story?
- Who changes or grows over the course of the story?

Minor characters help the reader learn more about the main characters. As you read, notice each character's role.

READING STRATEGY: VISUALIZE

How would you like to view every story in this book as a movie? If you **visualize** while you read, you might come close. To visualize, use descriptions from the selection and your knowledge and imagination to form mental pictures. As you read, record these descriptions in a chart and then sketch the mental pictures they help you form.

Descriptions	Mental Picture
"They were odd-looking creatures, like stubby horses, short-legged, thick-necked, with dark and white stripes."	

Review: **Make Inferences**

VOCABULARY IN CONTEXT

Chaim Potok uses the boldfaced words to help tell a story of pain and healing. To see how many you know, substitute a different word or phrase for each one.

1. He tried not to **grimace** in pain.
2. It was hard to unwrap the **intricate** bandage.
3. She is a firm **disciplinarian.**
4. The animal looked **gaunt** and underfed.
5. They skipped **jauntily** down the path.
6. He **winced** when he got a flu shot.
7. A cast might **chafe** your skin.
8. We saw the **contour** of the jagged mountain.
9. She appeared **somber** when she heard the bad news.
10. They applauded our team **exuberantly.**

Author Online

Chaim Potok
1929–2002

Early Days
While growing up in New York City, Chaim Potok lived the strict life of a Hasidic Jew. His parents wanted him to be a religious scholar. But by the time he was 16, Potok had started reading literature other than traditional Jewish texts. The more he read, the more he struggled between religious learning and the call to become a creative artist.

Coming to Terms Potok eventually left the Hasidic community for the Conservative movement of Judaism. He became a rabbi and published his first novel in 1967. Much of Potok's writing centers on characters who try to live in both the spiritual world and the secular world of everyday life.

 MORE ABOUT THE AUTHOR
For more on Chaim Potok, visit the **Literature Center** at **ClassZone.com.**

Background

Vietnam War One of the characters in this story is a veteran of the Vietnam War. U.S. troops fought in Vietnam from 1965 until 1973. Approximately 58,000 Americans died there, and more than 300,000 were wounded. In 1982, the Vietnam Veterans Memorial was unveiled in Washington, D.C., to honor the men and women who served in the war. A black granite wall bears the names of those who died.

ZEBRA **183**

Teach

STANDARDS FOCUS

● CHARACTER

Ask students to describe the main character of "Zebra" based on reading the **Key Idea** paragraph on page 182 *(a seventh-grade boy who needs healing).* Invite students to predict who some of the minor characters might be in the story. ***Possible answers:*** *doctors, nurses, parents, teachers, friends*

CHECK UNDERSTANDING Ask students for examples of major and minor characters from stories, movies, or TV shows.

■ VISUALIZE

Explain that when they try to visualize, students should look for descriptions and details that appeal to all their senses. They should ask themselves, "When I read this, what do I see, hear, smell, feel, or taste that helps me create a picture in my mind?" Sense descriptions can help them relate an unfamiliar topic to their own knowledge and experience.

CHECK UNDERSTANDING Ask students to use words that appeal to their senses to describe the picture on page 182.

RESOURCE MANAGER—Copy Master
Visualize p. 29 (for student use while reading the selection)

▲ VOCABULARY IN CONTEXT

DIAGNOSE WORD KNOWLEDGE To determine preteaching needs, have all students complete **Vocabulary in Context.** *Students' responses will vary.* **Possible answers:** 1. *make a face (p. 197);* 2. *complex (p. 192);* 3. *rule enforcer (p. 189);* 4. *thin (p. 187);* 5. *happily (p. 197);* 6. *jerked back (p. 188);* 7. *rub (p. 190);* 8. *shape (p. 194);* 9. *sad (p. 198);* 10. *enthusiastically (p. 187)*

PRETEACH VOCABULARY Use the Vocabulary Study copy master to help students explore the meaning of each boldfaced word.

1. Read item 1 aloud, emphasizing *chafe.*
2. Point out the context clues *uncomfortable* and *when he moved his arm.* Elicit possible meanings for *chafe,* such as "to hurt."
3. Have students record their predictions.
4. Repeat the procedure for items 2–10.

 **RESOURCE MANAGER—Copy Master**
Vocabulary Study p. 31

For general guidelines on differentiating vocabulary instruction and for alternative vocabulary activities for students not needing vocabulary preteaching, see

 **BEST PRACTICES TOOLKIT**
Scaffolding Vocabulary Instruction pp. 43–46

ⓘ Vocabulary Center at **ClassZone.com**

ANALYZE VISUALS

Possible answers: a person running, his shadow, and zebras running

---

READING STRATEGY

Ⓐ VISUALIZE

Possible answers: "Africa," "zebras," "hundreds," "thundering," "grassy plain," "dust rising in boiling brown clouds"

If students need help . . . Have students reread lines 8–10 and identify the words that appeal to their senses. Suggest that students think about the kinds of information each sense takes in. Ask which sense is involved in each part of the sentence.

ZEBRA

CHAIM POTOK

> **H**e couldn't remember when he began to be called by that name. Perhaps they started to call him Zebra when he first began running. Or maybe he began running when they started to call him Zebra.
>
> He loved the name and he loved to run.
>
> When he was very young, his parents took him to a zoo, where he saw zebras for the first time. They were odd-looking creatures, like stubby horses, short-legged, thick-necked, with dark and white stripes.
>
> Then one day he went with his parents to a movie about Africa, and he saw zebras, hundreds of them, thundering across a grassy plain, dust
> 10 rising in boiling brown clouds. Ⓐ

ANALYZE VISUALS
Examine the photograph. What images can you identify?

① Targeted Passage

Ⓐ VISUALIZE
Reread lines 8–10. What words help you picture the scene in the movie?

184 UNIT 2: ANALYZING CHARACTER AND POINT OF VIEW

DIFFERENTIATED INSTRUCTION

FOR ALL STUDENTS

Expert Groups Encourage individual students or groups to choose one of these topics on which to become experts:

- art therapy
- "found art"—art from found objects
- anatomy of the hand
- helicopters in the Vietnam War

FOR LESS–PROFICIENT READERS

In combination with the *Audio Anthology CD*, use one or more Targeted Passages (pp. 184, 186, 198, 201, 202, 203) to ensure that students focus on key story events, concepts, and skills.

① Targeted Passage [Lines 1–10]

This passage introduces the story's main character: it describes Zebra and tells how he got his nickname and learned about zebras.

BACKGROUND

Zebras Zebras are similar to horses and live in open areas of southern and eastern Africa. At their shoulders they are about four to five feet high. Different species have different striping patterns. Young zebras play by running and chasing one another, and sometimes by chasing other animals. Zebras often travel with herds of antelopes. Antelopes can run up to 40 miles an hour when they are being hunted. The number of zebras has declined as their habitat has been destroyed and they have been hunted for their skins. Two species are endangered, but zebras breed well in captivity. The offspring of captive zebras might provide a source of animals that could be reintroduced to the wild.

- How might Zebra have received his name?
- When did Zebra first see zebras?
- What do you learn about zebras from the opening page?

FOR ENGLISH LEARNERS

Key Academic Vocabulary Use Word Questioning for these words: *emerge* (lines 36, 74, 170), *injure* (lines 44, 387, 394), *remove* (lines 93, 412), *grade* (lines 185, 342, 580), *rigid* (lines 391, 482).

 BEST PRACTICES TOOLKIT—Transparency
Word Questioning p. E9

Prereading For prereading instruction for English learners, see

 BEST PRACTICES TOOLKIT
Scaffolding Reading Instruction pp. 43–46

FOR ADVANCED LEARNERS/PRE–AP

Pre-AP exercises in the bottom channel provide additional challenge for your advanced students. Use them for small groups or individuals.

ADDITIONAL GUIDELINES

For more help with differentiation and tips for classroom management, see

 BEST PRACTICES TOOLKIT
Differentiated Instruction pp. 31–38

Was he already running before he saw that movie, or did he begin to run afterward? No one seemed able to remember.

He would go running through the neighborhood for the sheer joy of feeling the wind on his face. People said that when he ran he arched his head up and back, and his face kind of flattened out. One of his teachers told him it was clever to run that way, his balance was better. But the truth was he ran that way, his head thrown back, because he loved to feel the wind rushing across his neck.

20 Each time, after only a few minutes of running, his legs would begin to feel wondrously light. He would run past the school and the homes on the street beyond the church. All the neighbors knew him and would wave and call out, "Go, Zebra!" And sometimes one or two of their dogs would run with him awhile, barking.

He would imagine himself a zebra on the African plain. Running. **B**

There was a hill on Franklin Avenue, a steep hill. By the time he reached that hill, he would feel his legs so light it was as if he had no legs at all and was flying. He would begin to descend the hill, certain as he ran that he needed only to give himself the slightest push and off he would go, and instead of a zebra he would become the bird he had once seen 30 in a movie about Alaska, he would swiftly change into an eagle, soaring higher and higher, as light as the gentlest breeze, the cool wind caressing his arms and legs and neck.

*T*hen, a year ago, racing down Franklin Avenue, he had given himself that push and had begun to turn into an eagle, when a huge rushing shadow appeared in his line of vision and crashed into him and plunged him into a darkness from which he emerged very, very slowly. . . .

"Never, never, *never* run down that hill so fast that you can't stop at the corner," his mother had warned him again and again.

His schoolmates and friends kept calling him Zebra even after they all 40 knew that the doctors had told him he would never be able to run like that again. **C**

His leg would heal in time, the doctors said, and perhaps in a year or so the brace would come off. But they were not at all certain about his hand. From time to time his injured hand, which he still wore in a sling, would begin to hurt. The doctors said they could find no cause for the pain.

One morning, during Mr. Morgan's geography class, Zebra's hand began to hurt badly. He sat staring out the window at the sky. Mr. Morgan, a stiff-mannered person in his early fifties, given to smart suits and dapper bow ties, called on him to respond to a question. Zebra stumbled about 50 in vain for the answer. Mr. Morgan told him to pay attention to the geography inside the classroom and not to the geography outside.

B CHARACTER
Reread lines 13–24. How does Zebra feel about running?

2 Targeted Passage

C MAKE INFERENCES
What happened to Zebra a year ago? What details tell you this?

LITERARY ANALYSIS

B CHARACTER

Possible answer: Zebra loves to run ("sheer joy," line 13). He loves to feel the wind on his face and neck (lines 14, 18) and to feel the lightness of his legs (lines 19–20).

Extend the Discussion How much of Zebra's identity is related to his running?

READING SKILL: *Review*

C MAKE INFERENCES

Possible answer: Zebra ran very quickly into the street. He was hit by something (probably a car), knocked unconscious, and hurt his legs. Details include that he felt like he was turning "into an eagle," "a huge rushing shadow . . . crashed into him and plunged him into a darkness" (lines 33–36). The doctors said that "he would never be able to run like that again" (lines 40–41).

Extend the Discussion How do you think Zebra feels after hearing the doctors' comments?

DIFFERENTIATED INSTRUCTION

FOR LESS–PROFICIENT READERS

2 Targeted Passage [Lines 25–45]

This passage sets up the story's plot: it reveals why Zebra is in need of healing.

- How does Zebra feel when he runs down Franklin Avenue?
- What is the "huge rushing shadow" that comes into Zebra's line of vision?
- Why had Zebra's mother warned him about running too fast on Franklin Avenue?
- What two parts of Zebra's body need healing?

Review: Make Inferences Review how to make inferences *(draw conclusions based on your personal experience and clues from the text).* Distribute copies of the Making Inferences chart. Have students work in pairs to reread lines 33–41 and use the graphic organizer to help them figure out what happened to Zebra a year ago.

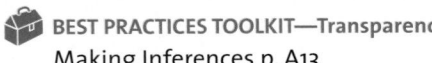 **BEST PRACTICES TOOLKIT—Transparency**
Making Inferences p. A13

"In this class, young man, you will concentrate your attention upon the earth, not upon the sky," Mr. Morgan said.

*L*ater, in the schoolyard during the midmorning recess, Zebra stood near the tall fence, looking out at the street and listening to the noises behind him.

His schoolmates were racing about, playing **exuberantly,** shouting and laughing with full voices. Their joyous sounds went ringing through the quiet street.

60 Most times Zebra would stand alongside the basketball court or behind the wire screen at home plate and watch the games. That day, because his hand hurt so badly, he stood alone behind the chain-link fence of the schoolyard. **D**

That's how he happened to see the man. And that's how the man happened to see him.

One minute the side street on which the school stood was strangely empty, without people or traffic, without even any of the dogs that often roamed about the neighborhood—vacant and silent, as if it were already in the full heat of summer. The red-brick ranch house that belonged to 70 Mr. Morgan, and the white clapboard two-story house in which Mrs. English lived, and the other homes on the street, with their columned front porches and their back patios, and the tall oaks—all stood curiously still in the warm golden light of the mid-morning sun. **E**

Then a man emerged from wide and busy Franklin Avenue at the far end of the street.

Zebra saw the man stop at the corner and stand looking at a public trash can. He watched as the man poked his hand into the can and fished about but seemed to find nothing he wanted. He withdrew the hand and, raising it to shield his eyes from the sunlight, glanced at the street sign on 80 the lamppost.

He started to walk up the street in the direction of the school.

He was tall and wiry, and looked to be about forty years old. In his right hand he carried a bulging brown plastic bag. He wore a khaki army jacket, a blue denim shirt, blue jeans, and brown cowboy boots. His **gaunt** face and muscular neck were reddened by exposure to the sun. Long brown hair spilled out below his dark-blue farmer's cap. On the front of the cap, in large orange letters, were the words LAND ROVER.[1]

He walked with his eyes on the sidewalk and the curb, as if looking for something, and he went right past Zebra without noticing him.

90 Zebra's hand hurt very much. He was about to turn away when he saw the man stop and look around and peer up at the red-brick wall of

---

1. **Land Rover:** British automaker known for producing four-wheel-drive vehicles.

ZEBRA **187**

exuberantly
(ĭg-zōō′bər-ənt-lē) *adv.*
in a manner showing
enthusiasm or joy

D CHARACTER
Why does Zebra stand
alone and watch the
other students run
and play?

E VISUALIZE
Reread lines 66–73.
What descriptions help
you see the street in
your mind? Record
them in your chart.

gaunt (gônt) *adj.* thin
and bony

LITERARY ANALYSIS

D CHARACTER

Possible answer: Zebra's hand hurts too much for him to stand and watch his schoolmates play.

Extend the Discussion Why might Zebra's physical pain make him want to be alone?

READING STRATEGY

E VISUALIZE

Possible answer: Potok describes the street as "strangely empty," "vacant and silent, as if it were already in the full heat of summer." There are tall oak trees. One house is a "red-brick ranch" and another is a "white clapboard two-story." The other houses have "columned front porches" and "back patios." The "mid-morning sun" warms up the street and casts a "golden light." Everything is "curiously still."

Extend the Discussion What do you think it would be like to live in the neighborhood the author describes?

FOR ENGLISH LEARNERS

Comprehension: Sequence Explain that the story has quickly covered the time from when Zebra was a young child up to the present, in order to explain how he got his nickname and why he is in need of healing. Now a new character is introduced to the story. Have pairs of students use a timeline to chart the events described on pages 184–187. Point out that the exact time when Zebra got his name and began running is not stated.

Culture: Clarify Lines 69–72 describe home styles common in American towns and suburbs.

- Ranch houses are built on one level and became widely popular after World War II.
- A two-story house has an upstairs and downstairs.
- "White clapboard" refers to houses with horizontal wooden siding.
- Porches are attached structures with a separate roof supported by columns or pillars.
- Patios are open areas, often paved, at the back or side of a house.

📖 **BEST PRACTICES TOOLKIT—Transparency**
Timeline p. B23

the school. The man set down the bag and took off his cap and stuffed it into a pocket of his jacket. From one of his jeans pockets he removed a handkerchief, with which he then wiped his face. He shoved the handkerchief back into the pocket and put the cap back on his head. **F**

Then he turned and saw Zebra.

He picked up the bag and started down the street to where Zebra was standing. When the man was about ten feet away, Zebra noticed that the left sleeve of his jacket was empty.

100 The man came up to Zebra and said in a low, friendly, shy voice, "Hello."

Zebra answered with a cautious "Hello," trying not to look at the empty sleeve, which had been tucked into the man's jacket pocket.

The man asked, with a distinct Southern accent, "What's your name, son?"

Zebra said, "Adam."

"What kind of school is this here school, Adam?"

"It's a good school," Zebra answered.

"How long before you-all begin your summer vacation?"

110 "Three days," Zebra said.

"Anything special happen here during the summer?"

"During the summer? Nothing goes on here. There are no classes."

"What do you-all do during the summer?"

"Some of us go to camp. Some of us hang around. We find things to do."

Zebra's hand had begun to tingle and throb. Why was the man asking all those questions? Zebra thought maybe he shouldn't be talking to him at all. He seemed vaguely menacing in that army jacket, the dark-blue cap with the words LAND ROVER on it in orange letters, and the empty sleeve.

120 Yet there was kindness in his gray eyes and ruddy features.

The man gazed past Zebra at the students playing in the yard. "Adam, do you think your school would be interested in having someone teach an art class during the summer?"

That took Zebra by surprise. "An *art* class?"

"Drawing, sculpting, things like that."

Zebra was trying *very hard* not to look at the man's empty sleeve. "I don't know. . . ."

"Where's the school office, Adam?"

"On Washington Avenue. Go to the end of the street and turn right."

130 "Thanks," the man said. He hesitated a moment. Then he asked, in a quiet voice, "What happened to you, Adam?"

"A car hit me," Zebra said. "It was my fault."

The man seemed to **wince.**

F CHARACTER
Reread lines 74–95. What are your first impressions of this new character?

wince (wĭns) *v.* to draw back, as in pain or distress

DIFFERENTIATED INSTRUCTION

FOR ENGLISH LEARNERS
Language: Conversational English Patterns
Point out that the man speaks with "a distinct Southern accent" (line 104) and explain that this affects his speech pattern. For example, many Southerners say "you-all" (line 109) instead of *you.* Another distinctive phrase the character uses is "this here" (line 107) instead of *this.*

In addition, sometimes words are left out but understood in things he and other characters say. For example, the word *does* is understood at the beginning of line 111.

1. Assign mixed language-ability Jigsaw groups to review the dialogue in the rest of the story, noting examples of these speech patterns and filling in missing words.

2. Have groups report their findings to the class.

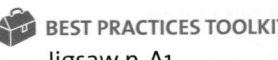 BEST PRACTICES TOOLKIT
Jigsaw p. A1

ANALYZE VISUALS

Possible answer: The way he's standing alone and looking through the fence suggests he's thinking about something; maybe he's lonely or sad. Looking across the water toward the city suggests there may be something there he wants. The fingers on his left hand are not spread in the same way as those on the right. They may be injured.

For a flash of a second, Zebra thought to ask the man what had happened to *him*. The words were on his tongue. But he kept himself from saying anything.

The man started back up the street, carrying the brown plastic bag. Zebra suddenly called, "Hey, mister."

The man stopped and turned. "My name is John Wilson," he said softly.

40 "Mr. Wilson, when you go into the school office, you'll see signs on two doors. One says 'Dr. Winter,' and the other says 'Mrs. English.' Ask for Mrs. English."

Dr. Winter, the principal, was a **disciplinarian** and a grump. Mrs. English, the assistant principal, was generous and kind. Dr. Winter would probably tell the man to call his secretary for an appointment. Mrs. English might invite him into her office and offer him a cup of coffee and listen to what he had to say.

ANALYZE VISUALS
What might you **infer** from this figure's body language?

disciplinarian
(dĭs′ə-plə-nâr′ē-ən) *n.* someone who enforces strict discipline, or rules

ZEBRA **189**

FOR LESS–PROFICIENT READERS

Identify Character Traits Explain that on pages 188–189, the author shows the traits or qualities of Zebra and John Wilson by describing their appearance, speech, thoughts, and actions. He also shows their character traits through the ways they talk and act toward one another. Have pairs of students read the two pages and fill out the chart showing traits and story evidence. Traits may be physical or expressions of personality.

	Zebra	John Wilson
Trait	injured	injured
Evidence	hand hurts very much; tingles and throbs	left sleeve is empty
Trait	polite	kind
Evidence	tries not to look at the empty sleeve and doesn't ask about it; calls him Mr. Wilson	friendly, shy voice; kindness in eyes and features; asks about Zebra's injury
Trait	helpful	artistic
Evidence	tells Mr. Wilson to ask for Mrs. English	suggests a summer art class at the school

Ⓖ CHARACTER

Possible answer: John Wilson has been friendly and has shown empathy about Zebra's accident. Zebra may also be curious about the art class and wants John Wilson to succeed. Perhaps Zebra identifies with Wilson's physical injury.

Lines 169–183
DISCUSSION PROMPTS

Use these prompts to help students understand the character of Mrs. English:

Connect How would you react to a teacher like Mrs. English? *Students' responses should reflect their understanding of Mrs. English's personality traits or her background and interests.*

Analyze What do you think is the outcome of the meeting between Mrs. English and Mr. Wilson? Cite evidence. *Possible answer: Mr. Wilson will be teaching an art class at the school during the summer. Mrs. English nods and smiles when she shakes Mr. Wilson's hand (line 172) and refers to their meeting as "an important matter" (line 179).*

Synthesize Why might Mrs. English be seen as a character who represents the author in the story? *Possible answer: She was a writer of short stories and probably became a teacher to share her interest in stories and writing. Her name suggests her interests, which she shares with the author.*

The man hesitated, looking at Zebra.

"Appreciate the advice," he said. Ⓖ

150   Zebra watched him walk to the corner.

Under the lamppost was a trash can. Zebra saw the man set down the plastic bag and stick his hand into the can and haul out a battered umbrella.

The man tried to open the umbrella, but its metal ribs were broken. The black fabric dangled flat and limp from the pole. He put the umbrella into the plastic bag and headed for the entrance to the school.

A moment later, Zebra heard the whistle that signaled the end of recess. He followed his classmates at a distance, careful to avoid anyone's bumping against his hand.

160   **H**e sat through his algebra class, copying the problems on the blackboard while holding down his notebook with his left elbow. The sling **chafed** his neck and felt warm and clumsy on his bare arm. There were sharp pains now in the two curled fingers of his hand.

Right after the class he went downstairs to the office of Mrs. Walsh, a cheerful, gray-haired woman in a white nurse's uniform.

She said, "I'm sorry I can't do very much for you, Adam, except give you two Tylenols."

He swallowed the Tylenols down with water.

On his way back up to the second floor, he saw the man with the dark-170 blue cap emerge from the school office with Mrs. English. He stopped on the stairs and watched as the man and Mrs. English stood talking together. Mrs. English nodded and smiled and shook the man's hand.

The man walked down the corridor, carrying the plastic bag, and left the school building.

Zebra went slowly to his next class.

The class was taught by Mrs. English, who came hurrying into the room some minutes after the bell had rung.

"I apologize for being late," she said, sounding a little out of breath. "There was an important matter I had to attend to."

180   Mrs. English was a tall, gracious woman in her forties. It was common knowledge that early in her life she had been a journalist on a Chicago newspaper and had written short stories, which she could not get published. Soon after her marriage to a doctor, she had become a teacher.

This was the only class Mrs. English taught.

Ten students from the upper school—seventh and eighth grades—were chosen every year for this class. They met for an hour three times a week

Ⓖ **CHARACTER**
Why did Zebra give Mr. Wilson advice?

chafe (chāf) *v.* to irritate by rubbing

DIFFERENTIATED INSTRUCTION

FOR LESS–PROFICIENT READERS

Reading Strategy Follow-Up: Visualize Have students work in pairs to read lines 150–174 and update their charts, introduced on page 183. Remind students to look for words and phrases that appeal to their senses, and to notice when a scene shifts to a different image. There are five distinct scenes described in these lines. Afterwards, have teams compare their charts and discuss how visualizing helps them understand the story better.

Descriptions	Mental Picture
Lines 154–155: "The man tried to open the umbrella, but its metal ribs were broken. The black fabric dangled flat and limp from the pole."	

and told one another stories. Each story would be discussed and analyzed by Mrs. English and the class.

Mrs. English called it a class in the *imagination*.

90 Zebra was grateful he did not have to take notes in this class. He had only to listen to the stories.

That day, Andrea, the freckle-faced, redheaded girl with very thick glasses who sat next to Zebra, told about a woman scientist who discovered a method of healing trees that had been blasted apart by lightning.

Mark, who had something wrong with his upper lip, told in his quavery[2] voice about a selfish space cadet who stepped into a time machine and met his future self, who turned out to be a hateful person, and how the cadet then returned to the present and changed himself.

Kevin talked in blurred, high-pitched tones and often related parts
00 of his stories with his hands. Mrs. English would quietly repeat many of his sentences. Today he told about an explorer who set out on a journey through a valley filled with yellow stones and surrounded by red mountains, where he encountered an army of green shadows that had been at war for hundreds of years with an army of purple shadows. The explorer showed them how to make peace.

When it was Zebra's turn, he told a story about a bird that one day crashed against a closed windowpane and broke a wing. A boy tried to heal the wing but couldn't. The bird died, and the boy buried it under a tree on his lawn.

10 When he had finished, there was silence. Everyone in the class was looking at him.

"You always tell such sad stories," Andrea said.

The bell rang. Mrs. English dismissed the class.

In the hallway, Andrea said to Zebra, "You know, you are a very gloomy life form."

"Andrea, get off my case," Zebra said. ⬤

He went out to the schoolyard for the midafternoon recess. On the other side of the chain-link fence was the man in the dark-blue cap. Zebra went over to him.

20 "Hello again, Adam," the man said. "I've been waiting for you."

"Hello," said Zebra.

"Thanks much for suggesting I talk to Mrs. English."

"You're welcome."

"Adam, you at all interested in art?"

"No."

---

2. **quavery** (kwā'vər-ē): quivering or trembling.

ZEBRA   **191**

H MAKE INFERENCES
What do all the students in Mrs. English's class have in common with Zebra? Cite details to support your answer.

I CHARACTER
What does Andrea's comment tell you about Zebra?

READING SKILL: *Review*

H MAKE INFERENCES

Possible answer: All of the students have their own physical disabilities. Andrea has "very thick glasses." Mark has "something wrong with his upper lip" and speaks in a "quavery voice." Kevin "talked in blurred high-pitched tones."

If students need help . . . Have students use a T Chart to identify the students in Mrs. English's class and note how the author describes each one. Then have them compare the other students to Zebra.

Character	Description
Zebra	injured hand and leg
Andrea	Lines 192–193: "freckle-faced, redheaded girl with very thick glasses"
Mark	Line 195: "something wrong with his upper lip" Line 196: "quavery voice"
Kevin	Line 199: "talked in blurred, high-pitched tones"

💼 BEST PRACTICES TOOLKIT—Transparency
T Chart p. A25

LITERARY ANALYSIS

I CHARACTER

Possible answer: Andrea's comment reflects other people's perception of Zebra, who is depressed because of his injuries.

FOR ENGLISH LEARNERS
Vocabulary: Idioms and Sayings Use New Word Analysis to teach the following idioms and sayings from the story:

- *get off my case* (line 216), "leave me alone"
- *suit yourself* (line 233), "do what you want"
- *off and on* (line 315), "with some breaks"
- *for heaven's sake* (line 388), expression of exasperation and emphasis, roughly "for the good of everyone"

- *odds and ends* (line 506), "various items that don't belong together"

 BEST PRACTICES TOOLKIT—Transparency
New Word Analysis p. E8

FOR ADVANCED LEARNERS/PRE–AP
Analyze Character Explain that the author reveals Zebra's character in a variety of ways, and many of them require the reader to make inferences. For example, the story Zebra tells in Mrs. English's class (lines 206–209) is a metaphor for his own situation. Have students use a Spider Map to note the ways Potok presents information about Zebra's character.

 BEST PRACTICES TOOLKIT—Transparency
Spider Map p. B22

ANALYZE VISUALS

Possible answer: *Students' responses should refer to specific details in the sketch that are similar to or different from their mental image. Since there hasn't been any description of Zebra's face in the story, students' mental images will be influenced by what they've learned in the story about his character and perhaps by earlier visuals.*

Lines 226–257
DISCUSSION PROMPTS

Use these prompts to help students understand the way Zebra and Mr. Wilson feel about art:

Connect What is your opinion about art? Is your approach to art more like Zebra's or like Mr. Wilson's? *Student responses should reflect their own experience with art, and they should be able to say where they fall in the spectrum between Zebra's dislike of art and Mr. Wilson's passion for it.*

Analyze What does the description of Mr. Wilson in this scene tell you about him as an artist? Cite evidence. *Possible answer: The description of his tongue, the wrinkles around his eyes, and the sweat on his forehead show that he is concentrating very hard on his work (lines 247–254). The ink and colors on his hand show that he spends a lot of time drawing and painting (lines 256–257).*

Synthesize Why does Mr. Wilson ask Zebra to help him? *Possible answer: By asking Zebra to hold his pad, Mr. Wilson subtly reminds Zebra that he still has one good hand. He's also bringing Zebra closer to the creative process so he can see how Wilson works with one hand to create art.*

"You ever try your hand at it?"

"I've made drawings for class. I don't like it."

"Well, just in case you change your mind, I'm giving an art class in your school during the summer."

230 "I'm going to camp in August," Zebra said.

"There's the big long month of July."

"I don't think so," Zebra said.

"Well, okay, suit yourself. I'd like to give you something, a little thank-you gift."

He reached into an inside pocket and drew out a small pad and a pen. He placed the pad against the fence.

"Adam, you want to help me out a little bit here? Put your fingers through the fence and grab hold of the pad."

Extending the fingers of his right hand, Zebra held the pad to the fence 240 and watched as the man began to work with the pen. He felt the pad move slightly.

"I need you to hold it real still," the man said.

He was standing bent over, very close to Zebra. The words LAND ROVER on his cap shone in the afternoon sunlight. As he worked, he glanced often at Zebra. His tongue kept pushing up against the insides of his cheeks, making tiny hills rise and fall on his 250 face. Wrinkles formed **intricate** spidery webs in the skin below his gray eyes. On his smooth forehead, in the blue and purple shadows beneath the peak of his cap, lay glistening beads of sweat. And his hand—how dirty it was, the fingers and palm smudged with black ink and encrusted with colors.

Then Zebra glanced down and noticed the plastic bag near the man's 260 feet. It lay partly open. Zebra was able to see a large pink armless doll, a dull metallic object that looked like a dented frying pan, old newspapers, strings of cord, crumpled pieces of red and blue cloth, and the broken umbrella.

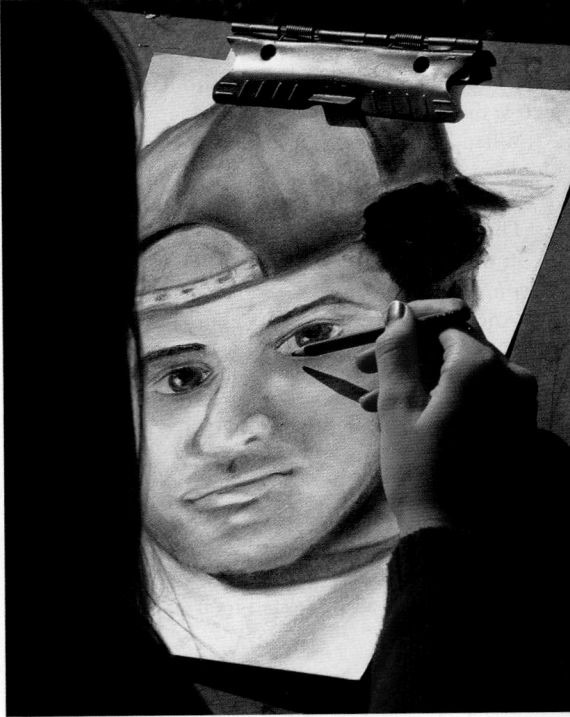

ANALYZE VISUALS
How does the sketch in this photo **compare** with your mental image of Zebra?

intricate (ĭn′trĭ-kĭt) *adj.* arranged in a complex way; elaborate

---

DIFFERENTIATED INSTRUCTION

FOR ENGLISH LEARNERS

Vocabulary: Shades of Meaning Help students use context clues to understand the slightly different meanings of the word *give* in lines 228 and 233. *Giving* a class means "teaching, leading, or presenting" the class. When Mr. Wilson says, "I'd like to give you something, a little thank-you gift" he means that he wants to present a gift to Zebra. Point out the different pronunciation of the verb *present* and the noun *present*.

FOR ADVANCED LEARNERS/PRE–AP

Hypothesize Have students quickwrite or quickdraw about what they think the items in the plastic bag (lines 258–265) might be used for, based on what they now know about Mr. Wilson. Encourage students to think about how this information relates to their initial impressions of him, based on earlier descriptions of Mr. Wilson searching in trash cans. Invite students to share their writing with a partner and to verify their prediction as they read.

"One more minute is all I need," the man said.

He stepped back, looked at the pad, and nodded slowly. He put the pen back into his pocket and tore the top page from the pad. He rolled up the page and pushed it through the fence. Then he took the pad 70 from Zebra.

"See you around, Adam," the man said, picking up the plastic bag.

Zebra unrolled the sheet of paper and saw a line drawing, a perfect image of his face. **J**

He was looking at himself as if in a mirror. His long straight nose and thin lips and sad eyes and gaunt face; his dark hair and smallish ears and the scar on his forehead where he had hurt himself years before while roller skating.

In the lower right-hand corner of the page the man had written: "To Adam, with thanks. John Wilson."

80 Zebra raised his eyes from the drawing. The man was walking away.

Zebra called out, "Mr. Wilson, all my friends call me Zebra."

The man turned, looking surprised.

"From my last name," Adam said. "Zebrin. Adam Martin Zebrin. They call me Zebra."

"Is that right?" the man said, starting back toward the fence. "Well, in that case you want to give me back that piece of paper."

He took the pad and pen from his pocket, placed the page on the pad, and, with Zebra holding the pad to the fence, did something to the page and then handed it back.

90 "You take real good care of yourself, Zebra," the man said.

He went off toward Franklin Avenue.

Zebra looked at the drawing. The man had crossed out Adam and over it had drawn an animal with a stubby neck and short legs and a striped body.

A zebra!

Its legs were in full gallop. It seemed as if it would gallop right off the page.

A strong breeze rippled across the drawing, causing it to flutter like a flag in Zebra's hand. He looked out at the street.

00 The man was walking slowly in the shadows of the tall oaks. Zebra had the odd sensation that all the houses on the street had turned toward the man and were watching him as he walked along. How strange that was: the windows and porches and columns and front doors following intently the slow walk of that tall, one-armed man—until he turned into Franklin Avenue and was gone. **K**

J MAKE INFERENCES
Why do you think Mr. Wilson drew the picture of Zebra?

K VISUALIZE
Reread lines 300–305. What images do you see in your mind?

FOR ADVANCED LEARNERS/PRE–AP

Analyze Character Encourage students to update their Spider Maps with the information about Zebra that they learn from Mr. Wilson's drawing of him (lines 274–277).

J MAKE INFERENCES

Possible answer: Mr. Wilson is trying to reach out to Zebra, and show friendship and thanks. Mr. Wilson may express himself better through art than through words. He may also be trying to open up Zebra, who expresses a dislike of art in line 227, to the wonder and beauty of art.

If students need help . . .

1. Have students review lines 222–234 to help them remember why Mr. Wilson might want to thank Zebra, and how their views on art differ.

2. Ask students to consider why Mr. Wilson chose to draw Zebra's face, instead of any other subject. How does this personal gift show Mr. Wilson's emotions?

READING STRATEGY

K VISUALIZE

Possible answer: Students' responses should relate to the descriptions of Mr. Wilson as tall and one-armed, walking down the street in the shadows, and also to Zebra's image of the houses on the street noticing Mr. Wilson and turning toward him as he walks down the street.

Lines 278–290

ADDITIONAL TEACHING OPPORTUNITY

Character Motivation Just as in life, people in stories have reasons—or **motivation**—for acting the way they do. Explain that writers sometimes state a character's motivation directly. More often, however, readers need to infer why a character acts a certain way. Ask students what Zebra's motivation is for telling Mr. Wilson his nickname. *(Zebra appreciates the lifelike portrait that Mr. Wilson drew of him and wants his treasured nickname to appear on it.)*

Use these prompts to help students understand how Zebra responds to Mr. Wilson's drawing:

Connect What do you know about people imagining unusual things when they are sick? *Students' responses may be based on their own experience or what they have heard about people hearing or seeing things when they are ill.*

Analyze Why does Zebra imagine that he sees the zebra galloping? *Possible answer: In his fevered state, Zebra imagines the drawing of the zebra actually running because that's how he most often thought of zebras—and because he thought of himself as running like a zebra.*

Evaluate Why does the author include this event in the story? *Possible answers: Because he wants to reinforce the idea that Zebra's need for healing is serious, and he also wants to show how much the drawing means to Zebra. The scene also shows how much Zebra still thinks about running even though he can't run anymore.*

The whistle blew, and Zebra went inside. Seated at his desk, he slipped the drawing carefully into one of his notebooks.

From time to time he glanced at it.

Just before the bell signaled the end of the school day, he looked at it again.

310 Now *that* was strange!

He thought he remembered that the zebra had been drawn directly over his name: the head over the A and the tail over the M. Didn't it seem now to have moved a little beyond the A?

Probably he was running a fever again. He would run mysterious fevers off and on for about three weeks after each operation on his hand. Fevers sometimes did that to him: excited his imagination.

He lived four blocks from the school. The school bus dropped him off at his corner. In his schoolbag he carried his books and the notebook with the drawing.

320 His mother offered him a snack, but he said he wasn't hungry. Up in his room, he looked again at the drawing and was astonished to discover that the zebra had reached the edge of his name and appeared poised to leap off.

It *had* to be a fever that was causing him to see the zebra that way. And sure enough, when his mother took his temperature, the thermometer registered 102.6 degrees.

She gave him his medicine, but it didn't seem to have much effect, because when he woke at night and switched on his desk light and peered at the drawing, he saw the little zebra galloping across the page, along the **contours** of his face, over the hills and valleys of his eyes and nose and

330 mouth, and he heard the tiny clickings of its hooves as cloudlets of dust rose in its wake.

He knew he was asleep. He knew it was the fever working upon his imagination.

But it was so real.

The little zebra running . . .

When he woke in the morning the fever was gone, and the zebra was quietly in its place over ADAM.

contour (kŏn'tŏŏr') *n.* the outline of a figure or body

Later, as he entered the school, he noticed a large sign on the bulletin board in the hallway:

340
SUMMER ART CLASS
The well-known American artist Mr. John Wilson will conduct an art class during the summer for students in 7th and 8th grades. For details, speak to Mrs. English. There will be no tuition fee for this class.

DIFFERENTIATED INSTRUCTION

FOR LESS–PROFICIENT READERS
Comprehension Support Make sure students understand that the events described in lines 300–337 contain a combination of things that are really happening and things that Zebra is imagining because he has a fever. Display the T Chart transparency. Encourage students to create their own T charts listing the things that really happened in one column and things that Zebra imagined in the other.

 BEST PRACTICES TOOLKIT—Transparency T Chart p. A25

FOR ENGLISH LEARNERS
Vocabulary: Word Associations Have pairs of students use context clues to figure out the meaning of these word combinations:

- *run a fever* (line 314), "have a body temperature above 98.6°F"
- *over supper* (line 380), "during the evening meal"
- *went off* (line 564), "went away." Remind students that *went* is the past tense of *go*. The phrase *go off* has several different meanings.

During the morning, between classes, Zebra ran into Mrs. English in the second-floor hallway.

"Mrs. English, about the summer art class . . . is it okay to ask where—um—where Mr. Wilson is from?"

"He is from a small town in Virginia. Are you thinking of signing
350 up for his class?"

"I can't draw," Zebra said.

"Drawing is something you can learn."

"Mrs. English, is it okay to ask how did Mr. Wilson—um—get hurt?"

The school corridors were always crowded between classes. Zebra and Mrs. English formed a little island in the bustling, student-jammed hallway.

"Mr. Wilson was wounded in the war in Vietnam," Mrs. English said. "I would urge you to join his class. You will get to use your imagination."

For the next hour, Zebra sat impatiently through Mr. Morgan's geography class, and afterward he went up to the teacher.

360 "Mr. Morgan, could I—um—ask where is Vietnam?"

Mr. Morgan smoothed down the jacket of his beige summer suit, touched his bow tie, rolled down a wall map, picked up his pointer, and cleared his throat.

"Vietnam is this long, narrow country in southeast Asia, bordered by China, Laos, and Cambodia.[3] It is a land of valleys in the north, coastal plains in the center, and marshes in the south. There are barren mountains and tropical rain forests. Its chief crops are rice, rubber, fruits, and vegetables. The population numbers close to seventy million people. Between 1962 and 1973, America fought a terrible war there to prevent
370 the south from falling into the hands of the communist north. We lost the war."

"Thank you."

"I am impressed by your suddenly awakened interest in geography, young man, though I must remind you that your class is studying the Mediterranean," said Mr. Morgan.

During the afternoon recess, Zebra was watching a heated basketball game, when he looked across the yard and saw John Wilson walk by, carrying a laden plastic bag. Some while later, he came back along the street, empty-handed.

380 Over supper that evening, Zebra told his parents he was thinking of taking a summer art class offered by the school.

His father said, "Well, I think that's a fine idea."

"Wait a minute. I'm not so sure," his mother said.

---

3. **Laos** (lous) . . . **Cambodia** (kăm-bō′dē-ə): countries in southeast Asia.

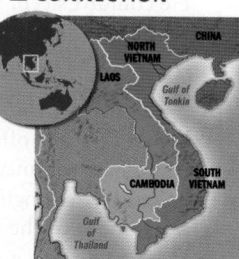

SOCIAL STUDIES CONNECTION

In 1976 North Vietnam and South Vietnam were reunited into one country, the Socialist Republic of Vietnam

SOCIAL STUDIES CONNECTION
Vietnam had been part of French Indochina since the mid-1800s. After World War II, Communists in Vietnam fought the French for control of the country. A treaty in 1954 ended French rule and temporarily divided the country into Communist North Vietnam and the Republic of South Vietnam. The United States sent military advisers to help train the South Vietnamese army in 1962, but the Communists gained control of large parts of South Vietnam. In 1965 the first U.S. combat troops arrived in South Vietnam, growing to a force of more than 500,000 by 1968. Despite this large number of troops and extensive bombing in North and South Vietnam, the United States was not able to defeat the Communist guerrilla forces. The war deeply divided the United States, and growing antiwar protests helped pressure President Lyndon Johnson to begin peace talks in 1968. Although U.S. troop strength was reduced beginning in 1969, the war continued to spread, including air and ground raids into neighboring Cambodia and Laos under President Richard Nixon. A treaty was finally signed in January 1973, and remaining U.S. forces left the country. The Communists gained control of South Vietnam with the fall of Saigon in April 1975, and the country was reunited.

FOR ENGLISH LEARNERS

Language: Conversational English Patterns
Read lines 347–348 aloud and point out the use of the ellipses and the word *um* to indicate Zebra's hesitant speech. Also note his saying "is it okay to ask" and explain that he's not sure if it's proper for him to be asking for personal information about an adult. Have students read lines 353, 360, and 403 and note how the author indicates hesitation in those lines.

Comprehension: Cause-Effect Help students see the chain of events (lines 224–381) that lead Zebra to change his mind about the art class.

1. Distribute copies of the Cause-and-Effect Chain.

2. Fill in the first two boxes as a group *(Zebra tells Mr. Wilson he doesn't like art; Mr. Wilson draws a picture of Zebra).* Explain how the two events are connected.

3. Have pairs read the rest of the text and fill in their charts. Clarify understanding as needed.

 BEST PRACTICES TOOLKIT—Transparency Cause-and-Effect Chain pp. B16, B39

L VISUALIZE

Possible answer: Students' answers should cite words and phrases from the passage:

• *"like dead leaves that never fell" (lines 390–391)*

• *"rigid and curled" (line 391)*

• *"barely moved" (line 392)*

Extend the Discussion Why does Zebra say that his hand *"was a dread and a mystery to him" (lines 389–390)?*

LITERARY ANALYSIS

M CHARACTER

Possible answer: Mrs. English tells Zebra that John Wilson was a helicopter pilot in Vietnam.

"It'll get him off the streets," his father said. "He'll become a Matisse[4] instead of a lawyer like his dad. Right, Adam?"

"Just you be very careful," his mother said to Adam. "Don't do anything that might injure your hand."

"How can drawing hurt his left hand, for heaven's sake?" said his father.

That night, Zebra lay in bed looking at his hand. It was a dread and 390 a mystery to him, his own hand. The fingers were all there, but like dead leaves that never fell, the ring and little fingers were rigid and curled, the others barely moved. The doctors said it would take time to bring them back to life. So many broken bones. So many torn muscles and tendons. So many injured nerves. The dark shadow had sprung upon him so suddenly. How stupid, stupid, *stupid* he had been! **L**

He couldn't sleep. He went over to his desk and looked at John Wilson's drawing. The galloping little zebra stood very still over ADAM.

*E*arly the following afternoon, on the last day of school, Zebra went to Mrs. English's office and signed up for John Wilson's summer art class.
400 "The class will meet every weekday from ten in the morning until one," said Mrs. English. "Starting Monday."

Zebra noticed the three plastic bags in a corner of the office.

"Mrs. English, is it okay to ask what Mr. Wilson—um—did in Vietnam?"

"He told me he was a helicopter pilot," Mrs. English said. "Oh, I neglected to mention that you are to bring an unlined notebook and a pencil to the class." **M**

"That's all? A notebook and a pencil?"

Mrs. English smiled. "And your imagination."

When Zebra entered the art class the next Monday morning, he
410 found about fifteen students there—including Andrea from his class with Mrs. English.

The walls of the room were bare. Everything had been removed for the summer. Zebra noticed two plastic bags on the floor beneath the blackboard.

He sat down at the desk next to Andrea's.

She wore blue jeans and a yellow summer blouse with blue stripes. Her long red hair was tied behind her head with a dark-blue ribbon. She gazed at Zebra through her thick glasses, leaned over, and said, "Are you going to make gloomy drawings, too?"

Just then John Wilson walked in, carrying a plastic bag, which he put
420 down on the floor next to the two others.

He stood alongside the front desk, wearing a light-blue long-sleeved shirt and jeans. The left shirtsleeve had been folded back and pinned to the shirt.

---

4. **Matisse** (mə-tēs´) (1869–1954): a French painter who was one of the best-known artists of the 20th century.

---

196   UNIT 2: ANALYZING CHARACTER AND POINT OF VIEW

L VISUALIZE
Reread lines 389–395. Notice the description of Zebra's hand. What words help you visualize how it looks?

M CHARACTER
What does Mrs. English tell Zebra about Mr. Wilson?

DIFFERENTIATED INSTRUCTION

FOR ENGLISH LEARNERS
Language: Contractions and Possessives
Remind students that an apostrophe may signal a contraction or a possessive.

1. Have pairs of students read lines 384–407 and find all the words with apostrophes.

2. Have students use copies of the T Chart to classify the contractions and possessives.

3. Help students use context clues to figure out the meaning of each word.

BEST PRACTICES TOOLKIT—Transparency
T Chart p. A25

FOR ADVANCED LEARNERS/PRE–AP
Analyze Metaphor Invite students to discuss whether they think the phrase "paper into faces and garbage into people" (line 426) might have a more symbolic meaning in the story beyond the creation of drawings and sculpture from trash. Have them cite evidence from the story and their own observations to support their opinions about what it might mean.

The dark-blue cap with the words LAND ROVER sat **jauntily** on his head.

"Good morning to you-all," he said, with a shy smile. "Mighty glad you're here. We're going to do two things this summer. We're going to make paper into faces and garbage into people. I can see by your expressions that you don't know what I'm talking about, right? Well, I'm about to show you."

He asked everyone to draw the face of someone sitting nearby.

430 Zebra hesitated, looked around, then made a drawing of Andrea. Andrea carefully drew Zebra.

He showed Andrea his drawing.

"It's awful." She **grimaced.** "I look like a mouse."

Her drawing of him was good. But was his face really so sad?

John Wilson went from desk to desk, peering intently at the drawings. He paused a long moment over Zebra's drawing. Then he spent more than an hour demonstrating with chalk on the blackboard how they should not be thinking *eyes* or *lips* or *hands* while drawing, but should think only *lines* and *curves* and *shapes*; how they should be looking at

440 where everything was situated in relation to the edge of the paper; and how they should not be looking *directly* at the edges of what they were drawing but at the space *outside* the edges.

jauntily (jôn′tə-lē) *adv.* in a light and carefree way

grimace (grĭm′ĭs) *v.* to twist one's face to show pain or disgust

N CHARACTER
How does Andrea's drawing affect Zebra?

ANALYZE VISUALS

Activity What is the first thing you notice about this image? *Most students will say they notice the reflection of the helicopters in the mirrored sunglasses.*

LITERARY ANALYSIS

N CHARACTER

Possible answer: Zebra seems to notice for the first time how sad he has become.

FOR LESS–PROFICIENT READERS

Predict Have students do a Think-Pair-Share activity to discuss what they think Mr. Wilson means when he says, in lines 425–426, "We're going to make paper into faces and garbage into people." Have students write down their predictions and check them as they read on in the story.

 **BEST PRACTICES TOOLKIT—Transparency** Think-Pair-Share p. A18

FOR ADVANCED LEARNERS/PRE–AP

Analyze Character Encourage students consider Zebra's thoughts in line 395 and the description of Andrea's drawing (line 434) and think about what they learn about Zebra's emotional state. Have students update their Spider Maps and then share their diagrams in small groups. Invite the groups to discuss how Zebra's emotions might be affecting his healing.

DISCUSSION PROMPTS

Use these prompts to help students understand what Mr. Wilson is doing in his art class:

Connect Would you enjoy being in Mr. Wilson's art class? Give reasons for your reply. *Students' responses should indicate what they might like or dislike about being in the class, with references to specific activities such as drawing or creating sculptures.*

Analyze How does Mr. Wilson help the students learn to "see in a new way" in this scene? *Possible answer: He's showing them how to look at common objects in a different way, to consider how they might be combined into sculptures.*

Evaluate How well does Mr. Wilson do his job as an art teacher? Cite evidence to support your evaluation. *Possible answer: He does a good job because he is able to explain and demonstrate what he wants students to do. The students' artwork shows that they are learning the techniques he is teaching them.*

Zebra stared in wonder at how fast John Wilson's hand raced across the blackboard, and at the empty sleeve rising and falling lightly against the shirt.

"You-all are going to learn how to *see* in a new way," John Wilson said. They made another drawing of the same face.

"Now I look like a horse," Andrea said. "Are you going to add stripes?"

"You are one big pain, Andrea," Zebra said.

450　Shortly before noon, John Wilson laid out on his desk the contents of the plastic bags: a clutter of junked broken objects, including the doll and the umbrella.

Using strips of cloth, some lengths of string, crumpled newspaper, his pen, and his one hand, he swiftly transformed the battered doll into a red-nosed, umbrella-carrying clown, with baggy pants, a tattered coat, a derby hat, and a **somber** smile. Turning over the battered frying pan, he made it into a pedestal, on which he placed the clown.

"That's a sculpture," John Wilson said, with his shy smile. "Garbage into people."

460　The class burst into applause. The clown on the frying pan looked as if it might take a bow.

(3) **Targeted Passage**

somber (sŏm'bər) *adj.* serious; gloomy

"You-all will be doing that, too, before we're done," John Wilson said. "Now I would like you to sign and date your drawings and give them to me."

When they returned the next morning the drawings were on a wall.

Gradually, in the days that followed, the walls began to fill with drawings. Sculptures made by the students were looked at with care, discussed by John Wilson and the class, and then placed on shelves along the walls: a miniature bicycle made of wire; a parrot made of an 470 old sofa cushion; a cowboy made of rope and string; a fat lady made of a dented metal pitcher; a zebra made of glued-together scraps of cardboard.

"I like your zebra," Andrea said.

"Thanks," Zebra said. "I like your parrot."

One morning John Wilson asked the class members to make a contour drawing of their right or left hand. Zebra felt himself sweating and trembling as he worked.

"That's real nice," John Wilson said, when he saw Andrea's drawing. He gazed at the drawing made by Zebra.

480　"You-all were looking at your hand," he said. "You ought to have been looking at the edge of your hand and at the space outside."

Zebra drew his hand again. Strange and ugly, the two fingers lay rigid and curled. But astonishingly, it looked like a hand this time.

DIFFERENTIATED INSTRUCTION

FOR LESS–PROFICIENT READERS

(3) **Targeted Passage [Lines 450–461]**

This passage shows a key turning point in the story: John Wilson demonstrates how to turn discarded items into valuable art objects. This scene suggests that anything broken can be given new life.

• What does Wilson use to make the clown?

• His sculpture is full of life—what does this suggest about broken things?

• How might the students in Wilson's class connect to his art?

Reading Strategy Follow-Up: Visualize

Encourage students to update their charts, introduced on page 183, to help them picture what is happening in the art class described on page 198 (lines 450–474). Remind them to look for sensory details. Have students choose a description to sketch that will help them focus on what is happening in the class. Allow time for students to share their sketches with a partner.

One day, a few minutes before the end of class, John Wilson gave everyone an assignment: draw or make something at home, something very special that each person *felt deeply* about. And bring it to class.

Zebra remembered seeing a book titled *Incredible Cross-Sections* on a shelf in the family room at home. He found the book and took it into his room.

490 There was a color drawing of a rescue helicopter on one of the Contents pages. On pages 30 and 31, the helicopter was shown in pieces, its complicated insides displayed in detailed drawings. Rotor blades, control rods, electronics equipment, radar scanner, tail rotor, engine, lifeline, winch—all its many parts.

Zebra sat at his desk, gazing intently at the space outside the edges of the helicopter on the Contents page.

He made an outline drawing and brought it to class the next morning.

John Wilson looked at it. Was there a stiffening of his muscular neck, a sudden tensing of the hand that held the drawing?

ZEBRA **199**

FOR ENGLISH LEARNERS

Culture: Clarify Explain to students that a "family room" (line 489) is a common room in many American homes that is used for a variety of casual family activities such as watching television, reading, or playing games. Such a room is also sometimes called a recreation room or a rumpus room. Many homes also have a living room that might be used for similar activities, or might be furnished in a more formal way and used for entertaining guests.

Lines 484–499
DISCUSSION PROMPTS

Use these prompts to help students understand how Zebra is responding to the art class:

Connect How would you respond if you were given an assignment like the one Mr. Wilson gave his students? *Some students may say that they would enjoy having the opportunity to create artwork about something that was important to them. Others might say they would find it challenging.*

Analyze Why does Zebra choose to draw a helicopter as something he "felt deeply" about? *Possible answer: Zebra wanted to let Mr. Wilson know he felt badly about the fact that Mr. Wilson had lost his arm while flying helicopters in Vietnam. It shows how much Zebra cares about Mr. Wilson.*

Synthesize Why might Mr. Wilson have tensed up when he saw Zebra's drawing? *Possible answer: He was probably surprised that Zebra chose a helicopter as his subject, and he might also have had unexpected memories of Vietnam come back to him.*

ANALYZE VISUALS

Activity Have students compare this drawing with the earlier description of Zebra's hand (lines 390–392). *Possible answer: Students should note how the drawing is similar to or different from the way they pictured Zebra's hand from the earlier description. They might note that the drawing shows a right hand but it is Zebra's left hand that is hurt.*

He took the drawing and tacked it to the wall.

The next day he gave them all the same home assignment: draw or make something they *felt very deeply* about.

That afternoon, Zebra went rummaging through the trash bin in his kitchen and the garbage cans that stood near the back door of his home. He found some sardine cans, a broken eggbeater, pieces of cardboard, chipped buttons, bent bobby pins, and other odds and ends.

With the help of epoxy glue, he began to make of those bits of garbage a kind of helicopter. For support, he used his desktop, the floor, his knees, the elbow of his left arm, at one point even his chin. Struggling with the
510 last piece—a button he wanted to position as a wheel—he realized that without thinking he had been using his left hand, and the two curled fingers had straightened slightly to his needs. ◉

His heart beat thunderously. There had been so many hope-filled moments before, all of them ending in bitter disappointment. He would say nothing. Let the therapist or the doctors tell him. . . .

The following morning, he brought the helicopter to the class.

"Eeewwww, what is *that*?" Andrea grimaced.

"Something to eat you with," Zebra said.

"Get human, Zebra. Mr. Wilson will have a laughing fit over that."
520 But John Wilson didn't laugh. He held the helicopter in his hand a long moment, turning it this way and that, nodded at Zebra, and placed it on a windowsill, where it shimmered in the summer sunlight.

The next day, John Wilson informed everyone that three students would be leaving the class at the end of July. He asked each of those students to make a drawing for him that he would get to keep. Something to remember them by. All their other drawings and sculptures they could take home.

Zebra lay awake a long time that night, staring into the darkness of his room. He could think of nothing to draw for John Wilson.
530 In the morning, he sat gazing out the classroom window at the sky and at the helicopter on the sill.

"What are you going to draw for him?" Andrea asked.

Zebra shrugged and said he didn't know.

"Use your imagination," she said. Then she said, "Wait, what am I seeing here? Are you able to move those fingers?"

"I think so."

"You *think* so?"

"The doctors said there was some improvement."

Her eyes glistened behind the thick lenses. She seemed genuinely happy. ℗

◉ CHARACTER
What effect is John Wilson's art class having on Zebra?

℗ CHARACTER
How have Andrea's feelings toward Zebra changed?

LITERARY ANALYSIS

◉ CHARACTER

Possible answer: Zebra is changing. He is becoming a more skilled artist and is feeling excited about something again. He's getting absorbed in the art the way he was once absorbed in running. His hand is healing and he is healing mentally as well.

If students need help . . . Remind students that another word for "effect" is *result*, and ask them to think about how Zebra has changed as a result of taking the art class.

LITERARY ANALYSIS

℗ CHARACTER

Possible answer: Instead of being critical of Zebra for being gloomy and sad and making nasty comments about his drawings, she is showing that she cares about him as a friend and is happy to see his improvement.

If students need help . . . Suggest that they reread lines 212–216, 433, 448–449, and 473–474 to see how Andrea has reacted to Zebra in the past.

Extend the Discussion How might Mr. Wilson's reactions to Zebra's artwork have had an influence on Andrea's reactions to Zebra?

DIFFERENTIATED INSTRUCTION

FOR ENGLISH LEARNERS

Language: Compound Nouns Lines 503–522 contain a number of compound nouns; some are two words, such as *trash bin*, while others are one word made up of two words, such as *eggbeater*. Have pairs of students locate the passage's compound nouns, using New Word Analysis to figure out their meaning. Explain that *bobby pins* (line 506) is difficult to figure out from context; a bobby pin is a bent-wire hairpin made popular in the early 1930s.

 BEST PRACTICES TOOLKIT—Transparency
New Word Analysis p. E8

FOR ADVANCED LEARNERS/PRE–AP

Synthesize Have students work independently to create a web diagram to show the references to imagination throughout the story. Invite students to share their diagrams in small groups and to discuss why the author has so many characters talk about the importance of using imagination.

200 UNIT 2

He sat looking out the window. Dark birds wheeled and soared. There was the sound of traffic. The helicopter sat on the windowsill, its eggbeater rotor blades ready to move to full throttle.

Later that day, Zebra sat at his desk at home, working on a drawing. He held the large sheet of paper in place by pressing down on it with the palm and fingers of his left hand. He drew a landscape: hills and valleys, forests and flatlands, rivers and plateaus. Oddly, it all seemed to resemble a face.

Racing together over that landscape were a helicopter and a zebra.

It was all he could think to draw. It was not a very good drawing. He signed it: "To John Wilson, with thanks. Zebra." ◐

The next morning, John Wilson looked at the drawing and asked Zebra to write on top of the name "John Wilson" the name "Leon."

"He was an old buddy of mine, an artist. We were in Vietnam together. Would've been a much better artist than I'll ever be."

Zebra wrote in the new name.

"Thank you kindly," John Wilson said, taking the drawing. "Zebra, you have yourself a good time in camp and a good life. It was real nice knowing you."

He shook Zebra's hand. How strong his fingers felt!

"I think I'm going to miss you a little," Andrea said to Zebra after the class.

"I'll only be away a month."

"Can I help you carry some of those drawings?"

"Sure. I'll carry the helicopter."

Zebra went off to a camp in the Adirondack Mountains.[5] He hiked and read and watched others playing ball. In the arts and crafts program he made some good drawings and even got to learn a little bit about watercolors. He put together clowns and airplanes and helicopters out of discarded cardboard and wood and clothing. From time to time his hand hurt, but the fingers seemed slowly to be coming back to life.

"Patience, young man," the doctors told him when he returned to the city. "You're getting there."

One or two additional operations were still necessary. But there was no urgency. And he no longer needed the leg brace.

On the first day of school, one of the secretaries found him in the hallway and told him to report to Mrs. English.

"Did you have a good summer?" Mrs. English asked.

"It was okay," Zebra said.

---

5. **Adirondack** (ăd′ə-rŏn′dăk′) **Mountains:** mountains covering a large area of northeast New York State.

④ Targeted Passage

◐ **CHARACTER**
Why does Zebra thank John Wilson?

LITERARY ANALYSIS

◐ **CHARACTER**

Possible answer: Zebra understands that John Wilson has helped him recover.

If students need help . . . Remind students that not all gifts are things. Encourage students to think about what Zebra has received from John Wilson.

Extend the Discussion How does Zebra's drawing bring together previous ideas and images associated with John Wilson and himself?

Lines 564–573
REINFORCE *KEY IDEA:* HEAL

Discuss How does this passage show how much Zebra has been able to **heal**? *Possible answer: His leg is strong enough for him to go hiking and his hand hurts less. He is able to use his fingers more and creates a variety of art projects. His doctors confirm that his hand is much better, and he no longer needs to wear a leg brace. He seems to be enjoying life again.*

FOR LESS–PROFICIENT READERS

④ **Targeted Passage [Lines 540–558]**
This gift-exchange passage reveals important growth in Zebra's character—his relationship with Mr. Wilson is helping him heal, both physically and emotionally.

- What does Zebra draw for Mr. Wilson?
- How does Zebra use his hand when he's working on the art project?
- What does Mr. Wilson ask Zebra to add to the drawing?

FOR ENGLISH LEARNERS

Comprehension: Sequence Have students review lines 523–576 and use a calendar to identify what Zebra does in July *(takes the art class)*, August *(goes to camp)*, and September *(returns to school)*.

READING STRATEGY

R VISUALIZE

Possible answer: Students' sketches should reflect an understanding of these details: John Wilson kneels by a black, shiny wall wearing the same clothing that Zebra remembers. The drawing Zebra made for John Wilson is framed now and is leaning against the wall.

Lines 590–601
REINFORCE *KEY IDEA*: HEAL

Discuss How do John Wilson's visits to the wall help him to **heal**? *Possible answer: He goes to the wall to pay his respects and to feel close to his friend. These visits and the gifts he takes to the wall and keeps in his studio seem to help him heal the painful memories and losses from the war.*

"This came for you in the mail."

She handed him a large brown envelope. It was addressed to Adam
580 Zebrin, Eighth Grade, at the school. The sender was John Wilson, with a return address in Virginia.

"Adam, I admit I'm very curious to see what's inside," Mrs. English said. She helped Zebra open the envelope.

Between two pieces of cardboard were a letter and a large color photograph.

The photograph showed John Wilson down on his right knee before a glistening dark wall. He wore his army jacket and blue jeans and boots, and the cap with the words LAND ROVER. Leaning against the wall to his right was Zebra's drawing of the helicopter and the zebra racing together across a facelike landscape. The drawing was enclosed in a narrow frame.
590 The wall behind John Wilson seemed to glitter with a strange black light. R

Zebra read the letter and showed it to Mrs. English.

> *Dear Zebra,*
>
> *One of the people whose names are on this wall was among my very closest friends. He was an artist named Leon Kellner. Each year I visit him and leave a gift—something very special that someone creates and gives me. I leave it near his name for a few hours, and then I take it to my studio in Virginia, where I keep*
600 *a collection of those gifts. All year long I work in my studio, but come summer I go looking for another gift to give him.*
>
> *Thank you for your gift.*
>
> > *Your friend,*
> > *John Wilson*
>
> *P.S. I hope your hand is healing.*

Mrs. English stood staring awhile at the letter. She turned away and touched her eyes. Then she went to a shelf on the wall behind her, took down a large book, leafed through it quickly, found what she was searching for, and held it out for Zebra to see.

Zebra found himself looking at the glistening black wall of the
610 Vietnam Memorial in Washington, D.C. And at the names on it, the thousands of names. . . .

*L*ater, in the schoolyard during recess, Zebra stood alone at the chain-link fence and gazed down the street toward Franklin Avenue. He thought how strange it was that all the houses on this street had seemed to turn toward John Wilson that day, the windows and porches and columns and doors, as if saluting him.

Had that been only his imagination?

5 Targeted Passage

R **VISUALIZE**
Reread lines 585–592. Sketch the photo Zebra found in the envelope.

DIFFERENTIATED INSTRUCTION

FOR LESS–PROFICIENT READERS
5 **Targeted Passage [Lines 578–611]**

This passage reveals what Mr. Wilson did with the drawing Zebra made for him and gives more detail about Mr. Wilson's character.

• What was in the package that Zebra received from John Wilson?

• What had John Wilson done with Zebra's drawing?

• What is the wall in the picture and what is on it?

• How does Mrs. English react to the picture and the letter?

ANALYZE VISUALS
Look carefully at this photograph. How do you think it was taken? What feelings was the photographer trying to show?

Maybe, Zebra thought, just maybe he could go for a walk to Franklin Avenue on Saturday or Sunday. He had not walked along Franklin
620 Avenue since the accident; had not gone down that steep hill. Yes, he would walk carefully down that hill to the corner and walk back up and past the school and then the four blocks home.

Andrea came over to him.

"We didn't get picked for the story class with Mrs. English," she said. "I won't have to listen to any more of your gloomy stories."

Zebra said nothing.

"You know, I think I'll walk home today instead of taking the school bus," Andrea said.

"Actually, I think I'll walk, too," Zebra said. "I was thinking maybe
630 I could pick up some really neat stuff in the street."

"You are becoming a pleasant life form," Andrea said. ∿ ❺

ⓖ **Targeted Passage**

❺ **CHARACTER**
Reread lines 618–631. How has Zebra changed since the beginning of the story?

FOR LESS–PROFICIENT READERS

ⓖ **Targeted Passage [Lines 618–631]**

This passage concludes the story: it shows how much Zebra has healed and how the change affects his relationship with others.

- Why is Zebra thinking of taking a walk along Franklin Avenue?
- What do Zebra and Andrea plan to do on the walk home from school?
- What does Andrea think of Zebra now?

FOR ADVANCED LEARNERS/PRE–AP

Analyze Symbol Franklin Avenue is referred to many times throughout the story (lines 25–36, 74, 291, 305, 612–613, and 618–622). Ask students to work independently to identify the references to Franklin Avenue and to note the importance of each to the story. Then have students form small groups and discuss what Franklin Avenue symbolizes to Zebra in both a positive and a negative way, citing evidence from the text to support their opinions.

ANALYZE VISUALS

Possible answer: The photographer shot the picture to show the wall and the reflection of people standing in front of it, as well as the reflection of the Washington Monument. The photographer was trying to show feelings of respect and sadness at remembering all those who had died.

LITERARY ANALYSIS

❺ **CHARACTER**

Possible answer: Zebra has built up the courage to revisit the scene of his accident; he no longer needs to be in the special story class; and his spirits have improved.

SELECTION WRAP–UP

REFLECT Encourage students to think about what it added to the story to have Mr. Wilson be a disabled veteran rather than an art teacher without a disability. Have them discuss what Zebra and the other students learned besides art from Mr. Wilson.

⭐ **CRITIQUE** Have students think about how the author developed the characters of Zebra and Mr. Wilson. Were they well developed and believable? Have students cite story evidence to support their opinions.

READING FLUENCY

Distribute the copy masters and have students practice fluency.

🅡 RESOURCE MANAGER—Copy Master
Reading Fluency p. 37

DISCUSSION PROMPTS

Use these prompts to help students understand the connection between "The Rider" and the need for emotional healing discussed in "Zebra":

Connect Do you think trying to run away from emotional pain, such as loneliness or sadness, is a good solution? Why or why not? *Some students may say that being involved in an intense physical activity like roller-skating, bicycling, or running is a good way to deal with emotional pain because it takes their mind off the problem. Others may say it's not a good solution because it doesn't deal with the real reason for the pain.*

Compare How are roller-skating and bicycling alike? How are the images of roller-skating and bicycling different from the image of the azaleas? *Possible answer: Both roller-skating and bicycling involve moving quickly. The azaleas are rooted in one place and their flower petals fall slowly.*

Synthesize How does the image of the azaleas suggest another way to heal emotional pain? *Possible answer: The azaleas seem to be full of beauty and are content just being. The falling petals are part of a natural cycle of growth and decay.*

The Rider

NAOMI SHIHAB NYE

A boy told me
if he rollerskated fast enough
his loneliness couldn't catch up to him,

the best reason I ever heard
5 for trying to be a champion.

What I wonder tonight
pedaling hard down King William Street
is if it translates to bicycles.

A victory! To leave your loneliness
10 panting behind you on some street corner
while you float free into a cloud of sudden azaleas,
luminous pink petals that have never felt loneliness,
no matter how slowly they fell.

204 UNIT 2: ANALYZING CHARACTER AND POINT OF VIEW

DIFFERENTIATED INSTRUCTION

FOR LESS–PROFICIENT READERS

Vocabulary Support Point out that the author plays with the words *pedal* (*pedaling*, line 7) and *petal* (line 12), which are close in sound and spelling but have different meanings. Encourage students to use context clues such as *bicycles* and *azaleas* (a type of flowering bush) to figure out the meaning of each.

FOR ENGLISH LEARNERS

Option for Reading Have students listen to the *Audio Anthology CD* while they read along with the poem. Then do an echo reading of the poem with students. Help students paraphrase the poem to make sure they understand what the poet is saying.

Comprehension

1. **Recall** How does Zebra get his name?

2. **Recall** What does John Wilson do with Zebra's drawing?

3. **Represent** On the basis of the description in the story, sketch Zebra's drawing of a helicopter and a zebra racing together over a landscape.

Literary Analysis

4. **Visualize** Choose three sketches from the chart you made while reading "Zebra." Which of the author's words helped you draw these sketches?

5. **Identify Static and Dynamic Characters** A static character doesn't change throughout a story. A dynamic character changes as a result of events in a story. Do you think John Wilson is a static or dynamic character? Give examples to support your answer.

6. **Analyze Characters** Complete a chart like the one shown by classifying each character as a main character or a minor character.

Characters	Main or Minor	Explanation
Zebra		
John Wilson		
Mrs. English		
Andrea		

7. **Analyze Point of View** When a story is told from third-person limited point of view, the narrator tells us what only one character sees, thinks, and feels. "Zebra" is told from third-person limited point of view. Find a place in the story where the narrator reveals Zebra's thoughts and feelings.

8. **Compare Literary Works** Consider the character Zebra and the speaker in "The Rider" on page 204. How are they alike? How are they different?

Extension and Challenge

9. **Creative Project: Art** Choose three characters from this story and decide what everyday things you would use to make a "sculpture" of each of them. For each character, list the objects and tell why you chose them.

10. **SOCIAL STUDIES CONNECTION** What challenges did Vietnam veterans like John Wilson face when they came home? Research what aid and resources were available to them as they sought help in the **healing** process. Share your findings with the class.

> **RESEARCH LINKS**
> For more on the aid and resources available to Vietnam veterans, visit the **Research Center** at ClassZone.com.

Downhearted by Janine Hilder is an example of a found objects sculpture.

ZEBRA **205**

---

7. *Possible scenes: running (lines 13–32), first meeting with Mr. Wilson (lines 116–119), looking at his hand in bed (lines 389–395), in art class (lines 443–445, 475–483), after receiving the letter (lines 612–622).*

8. *They both enjoy the feeling of moving quickly and both experience some kind of emotional pain. They differ in that Zebra runs because he loves the feeling of the wind against his face and the lightness. The speaker in the poem rides fast because he or she is trying to escape loneliness.*

Extension and Challenge

9. *Students' lists should include objects that they can relate to the physical description of each character, such as body shape, hair color, clothing, or other physical description.*

10. SOCIAL STUDIES CONNECTION *Students' findings should reflect research in reliable sources on the kinds of aid available to help veterans deal with the physical and emotional challenges they faced when they came home.*

After Reading

For additional support of post-reading questions, use these copy masters:

R RESOURCE MANAGER—Copy Masters
Reading Check p. 34 (to check understanding of the selection)
Character p. 27 (for practice of literary analysis standards focus)
Question Support p. 35 (**After Reading** questions adapted for English learners and less-proficient readers)

Additional selection questions are provided for teachers on page 21.

For additional activities to challenge students, see

i Power Thinking at **ClassZone.com**

ANSWERS

Comprehension

1. *Zebra gets his name because his last name is Zebrin and he loves to run as zebras do.*

2. *He frames the drawing and places it next to his good friend's name on the Vietnam memorial; then he takes it to his studio.*

3. *Students' sketches should reflect details from the description in the selection.*

Literary Analysis

Possible answers:

4. ■ **STANDARDS FOCUS** *Visualize* *Students should point to specific words and phrases that are reflected in each of their sketches.*

5. ● **STANDARDS FOCUS** *Character Static— He has been touched by his relationship with Zebra, but it hasn't changed him significantly. Wilson's letter suggests he has taught similar classes before.*

6. ● **STANDARDS FOCUS** *Character Information for chart: **Zebra, Main,** Zebra is the focus of the story and the plot revolves around him. He changes over the course of the story. **John Wilson, Main,** His relationship with Zebra drives the plot and causes Zebra to change. His character is well developed, and he is central to the story. **Mrs. English, Minor,** She provides information about John Wilson and encourages Zebra, but she is not the story's focus. **Andrea, Minor,** Her relationship with Zebra merely provides information about him.*

ANSWERS

Vocabulary in Context

VOCABULARY PRACTICE

1. *(d) plain*
2. *(b) glumly*
3. *(c) gaunt*
4. *(b) grimace*
5. *(c) angry*
6. *(c) approach*
7. *(a) disciplinarian*
8. *(b) slowly*
9. *(c) color*
10. *(d) bless*

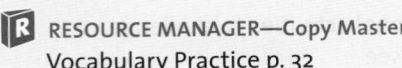 RESOURCE MANAGER—Copy Master
Vocabulary Practice p. 32

VOCABULARY IN WRITING

Suggest that students review the vocabulary words to see which ones might describe Zebra before he met Mr. Wilson and which ones might be used to describe how Mr. Wilson helped change some of those things about Zebra.

VOCABULARY STRATEGY: SIMILES *(also an EL language objective)*

- Point out that a simile is generally introduced by the word *like* or *as*. Have students identify what is being compared in each sentence.
- Encourage students to figure out what the simile is describing and then think of a synonym for the boldfaced word in each sentence.

Answers:

1. *set free*
2. *stalemate* or *unsolvable conflict*
3. *jump back in fear or horror*
4. *mysterious* or *puzzling*
5. *unwilling to give in or let go*

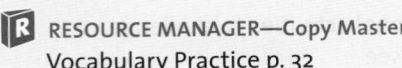 RESOURCE MANAGER—Copy Master
Vocabulary Strategy p. 33

ⓘ Vocabulary Center at **ClassZone.com**
Additional Vocabulary Activities

Vocabulary in Context

VOCABULARY PRACTICE

For each set, choose the word that differs most in meaning from the other words. Refer to a dictionary if you need help.

1. (a) elaborate, (b) ornate, (c) intricate, (d) plain
2. (a) joyously, (b) glumly, (c) delightedly, (d) exuberantly
3. (a) thick, (b) fat, (c) gaunt, (d) full
4. (a) smile, (b) grimace, (c) grin, (d) laugh
5. (a) somber, (b) dreary, (c) angry, (d) depressing
6. (a) cringe, (b) flinch, (c) approach, (d) wince
7. (a) disciplinarian, (b) counselor, (c) advisor, (d) guide
8. (a) jauntily, (b) slowly, (c) lightheartedly, (d) cheerfully
9. (a) outline, (b) contour, (c) color, (d) shape
10. (a) scrape, (b) chafe, (c) rub, (d) bless

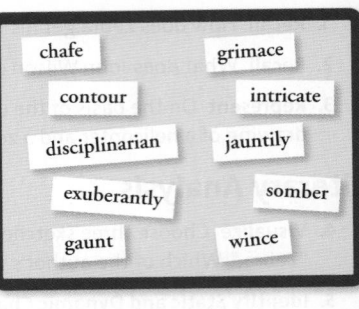

VOCABULARY IN WRITING

What role did John Wilson play in Zebra's healing process? Write a paragraph about this, using three or more vocabulary words. You could start like this.

> **EXAMPLE SENTENCE**
>
> *Before meeting John Wilson, Zebra's injury made him **somber** and sad.*

VOCABULARY STRATEGY: SIMILES

Writers sometimes use **similes** to compare two things (using the words *like* or *as*) that are not alike. In this story, Zebra's fingers are said to be "rigid and curled," "**like** dead leaves that never fell." This simile helps you see his fingers in a new way.

Similes can also provide context clues to help you figure out the meaning of unknown words. If you can visualize dead leaves, you can understand the meaning of *rigid*.

PRACTICE Use the simile in each sentence as a context clue to help you define the boldfaced word.

1. Teresa felt as **emancipated** as a prisoner recently released from jail.
2. Like a dam bursting, the **impasse** between the enemies was finally broken.
3. The sight of his destroyed home made him **recoil** like a snake.
4. The clues to the robbery were as **enigmatic** as unidentified ruins found in a desert.
5. Tom was as **tenacious** in business as a survivor hanging on to a lifeboat.

READING STANDARD
1.D.3.a Use context to determine the meanings of words

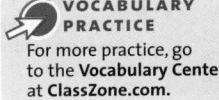
VOCABULARY PRACTICE
For more practice, go to the **Vocabulary Center** at **ClassZone.com**.

DIFFERENTIATED INSTRUCTION

FOR ENGLISH LEARNERS

Vocabulary Support Encourage students to identify the vocabulary word in each set in the **Vocabulary Practice** exercise. Ask if they can recall how the word was used in the story. If necessary, allow them to refer back to the usage in the story and use those context clues to help them choose the word in each set that differs most from the meaning of the other three.

FOR ADVANCED LEARNERS/PRE–AP

Vocabulary Strategy Challenge students to create new sentences with different similes for the boldfaced words.

Reading-Writing Connection

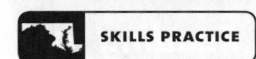 **SKILLS PRACTICE**

Demonstrate an understanding of the characters in "Zebra" by responding to these prompts. Then complete the **Grammar and Writing** exercise.

WRITING PROMPTS	SELF-CHECK
A. Short Response: Write a Character Sketch When Zebra and John Wilson first notice each other, the author gives a long description of John Wilson. Now it's your turn. Describe Zebra in **one paragraph.**	*A strong description will . . .* • include details about how Zebra looks, acts, and talks • use specific details from the story
B. Extended Response: Write a Letter Write a **two- or three-paragraph letter** that Zebra might send in response to John Wilson's letter. It should include a description of how the art class and their friendship helped **heal** his hand and spirits.	*An interesting letter will . . .* • respond to details in John Wilson's letter • include descriptions that Zebra would be likely to make

GRAMMAR AND WRITING

 **MARYLAND OBJECTIVES**

LANGUAGE STANDARD
5.B.2.c Recognize and correct incorrect use of verbs

USE CORRECT VERB TENSE **Verb tense** indicates the time that an action takes place. The three basic verb tenses are **present, past,** and **future.** In your writing, be sure to use the same verb tense when describing actions that happen at the same time. Only make a change in verb tense if actions are happening at different times.

> *Original:* I **am** grateful for your encouragement. I **looked** forward to seeing you again. (Am *is present tense, and* looked *is past tense.*)
>
> *Revised:* I **am** grateful for your encouragement. I **look** forward to seeing you again. (*Since both actions are happening in the present, both verbs should be present tense.*)

PRACTICE Choose the correct verb tense to complete the sentence.

1. I feel good when I work on my art. It (reflected, reflects) my creativity.
2. Art inspires me. It (helps, helped) me to focus my energy.
3. After the accident, I never thought my hand would get better. Now I (knew, know) I'll be fine.
4. I will always remember you and (will try, tried) to keep in touch.

For more help with verb tenses, see pages R56–R57 in the ***Grammar Handbook.***

FOR LESS–PROFICIENT WRITERS

For Prompt A:

1. Have students write sentences summarizing each aspect of their Character Map.
2. After students write an opening sentence that states their main idea, tell them to organize their other supporting sentences to present a full description of Zebra. They may need to combine sentences or create transitions to make the text flow logically.

For Prompt B:

Students may organize their letters in this way:

• **First paragraph:** focus on how Zebra felt after receiving John Wilson's letter.
• **Second paragraph:** focus on how Zebra felt during the art class and how he begins to heal.
• **Third paragraph:** focus on events since the art class that show Zebra continuing to heal.

Reading-Writing Connection

WRITING PROMPTS

• For **Prompt A,** encourage students to create a Character Map about Zebra based on what they recall from the story. Suggest that they begin their paragraphs with a physical description and move on to personality traits.

• For **Prompt B,** direct students to review John Wilson's letter to note specific details they want to respond to. Suggest they think about what Zebra might say about the class and what he might do after getting the letter.

🧰 BEST PRACTICES TOOLKIT—Transparency
Character Map p. D8

For an extended Reading-Writing Connection activity, see

ℹ️ Writing Center at **ClassZone.com**

GRAMMAR AND WRITING

• Explain that in items 1, 2, and 4, both verbs represent action that takes place at the same time. Ask students to identify the tense in each item (*1 and 2, present; 4, future*).

• In item 3 the action in the two sentences takes place at different times. Ask students to identify clue words and verb tenses (*"after the accident"—past; "now"—present*).

Answers:
1. *reflects;* **2.** *helps;* **3.** *know;* **4.** *will try*

R RESOURCE MANAGER—Copy Master
Use Correct Verb Tense p. 36

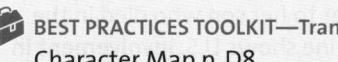 **Assess and Reteach**

Assess

R RESOURCE MANAGER—Copy Masters
Selection Tests A, B/C pp. 39–40, 41–42

💿 Test Generator CD

Reteach

S STANDARDS LESSON FILE
Literature Lesson 1: Types of Characters and Character Traits
Literature Lesson 4: Character Development
Grammar Lesson 16: Basic Verb Tenses

Focus and Motivate

OBJECTIVES

Reading for Information

- synthesize
- draw conclusions
- read a feature article, a letter, and a timeline

SUMMARY

The legacy of the Vietnam War is explored through a feature article, a letter, and a timeline. The article describes an exhibit of mementos left at the Vietnam Veterans Memorial. One such memento is a letter written by a mother to her son who died in the war. The timeline shows U.S. involvement in Vietnam from the 1950s through the 1990s.

What's the Connection?

Use an Anticipation Guide to prepare students. Write these statements on the transparency. Have students determine the accuracy of each one, before and after reading.

- The Vietnam War was a short war. *(false)*
- Many American soldiers died in Vietnam. *(true)*
- The Wall is only meaningful to veterans from the war. *(false)*
- Many Americans protested the war. *(true)*

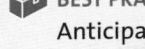 **BEST PRACTICES TOOLKIT—Transparency**
Anticipation Guide p. A14

Teach

Skill Focus: Synthesize

Explain that synthesizing is like putting together a jigsaw puzzle. When ideas from the various pieces are put together, a more complete picture emerges. Give students the following suggestions to follow as they read:

- State complex ideas or phrases in your own words to make sure you understand them.
- Summarize the main idea of each piece.
- Compare and contrast the pieces to see how they present the topic.
- Connect the ideas in each piece to what you already know about the topic.
- Look at the pieces as a group to see what they tell you about the topic.

Possible chart entries appear on page 214.

 RESOURCE MANAGER—Copy Master
Synthesize p. 51

test

Reading for Information

The Legacy of the Vietnam War

- Feature Article, page 209
- Letter, page 212
- Timeline, page 214

Use with "Zebra," page 184.

What's the Connection?

In "Zebra" you read about a veteran of the Vietnam War. In the following selections, you will learn more about the war and the Vietnam Veterans Memorial.

 MARYLAND OBJECTIVES

READING/INFO TEXT STANDARDS
1.E.4.c Draw conclusions
2.A.4.g Synthesize ideas from text

Skill Focus: Synthesize

Have you ever seen a movie about something—knights, for example—and then read about that topic in a textbook? What happened? Chances are you put together what you learned from the movie with what you learned from your book and wound up understanding knights even better than before.

When you put together information from different sources to get a fuller understanding of a topic, you are **synthesizing**. You probably synthesize information automatically all the time, but now you're going to practice doing it more purposefully. Here's how:

- Summarize what you learned about the Vietnam War and the Vietnam Veterans Memorial from reading "Zebra."
- Read the following three selections, and note any new information you learn from each one.
- Jot down any particular details or information you especially want to remember.

To help you in synthesizing, record this information in a chart like the one started here. As you read, add the titles of the other selections to the chart.

Source	Ideas and Information About the Vietnam War and the Memorial
"Zebra"	Some veterans lost limbs in the war. Some veterans bring gifts to friends whose names are written on the Wall.
"The Collected Grief of a Nation"	

Selection Resources

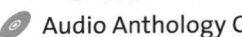 **RESOURCE MANAGER UNIT 2**

Plan and Teach pp. 43–47

Reading
Summary pp. 49†*, 50‡*
Synthesize pp. 51, 53†*
Reading Check p. 55
Draw Conclusions pp. 52, 54†*
Question Support p. 57*

Assessment
Selection Tests A, B/C pp. 59*, 61*

 Test Generator CD

Reading Support

Audio Anthology CD*

BEST PRACTICES TOOLKIT

Anticipation Guide • Cluster Diagram • Word Squares • Venn Diagram

* Resources for Differentiation   † Also in Spanish   ‡ In Haitian Creole and Vietnamese

The Collected Grief of a Nation

AN EXHIBIT OF MEMENTOS FROM THE VIETNAM WALL

by Judith Weinraub

At 19 Duery Felton Jr. was drafted and sent to Vietnam.

At 20 the D.C. native, assigned to the 1st Infantry Division, was badly wounded—so badly he refuses to discuss the details. "I was almost a name on the Wall," he says simply.

Decades later, Felton has made the Vietnam Wall—or more properly, the tens of thousands of objects that have been left there since it was dedicated in 1982—the center of his life. From dog tags to combat boots, letters to prayers, he looks after them, he researches them, he speaks for them.

And the objects have become a collection of war memorabilia
20 unlike any other.

"It's a living collection," says Felton. "People are leaving keepsakes at a public site—things normally passed on to their children.". . . **A**

No one would have predicted the memorial would engender such an outpouring of feeling.

READING FOR INFORMATION **209**

F **FOCUS ON FORM**
"The Collected Grief of a Nation" is a **feature article,** a nonfiction article found in a newspaper or magazine that gives readers information about an interesting topic. Unlike news articles, feature articles do not need to focus on current events.

A **SYNTHESIZE**
In "Zebra" you learned that a veteran brought a boy's drawing to the Vietnam Veterans Memorial. Now you're learning about gifts people have actually brought to the memorial. In your chart, jot down these items, along with your thoughts about what each might represent.

Practice and Apply

FOCUS ON FORM

Discuss the purpose and these main characteristics of a feature article with students:

- nonfiction
- journalistic (newspaper or magazine)
- does not need to focus on current events
- may focus on human interest stories or cover topics in more depth or from different angles than a news story does
- purpose is to provide information about an interesting topic

Invite students to brainstorm topics that might make interesting feature articles.

INFORMATIONAL ANALYSIS

A SYNTHESIZE

Possible answer: People leave dog tags, combat boots, letters, prayers, and other keepsakes they would normally pass on to their children. Dog tags (soldiers' metal ID tags worn on a chain around the neck) and combat boots are things the soldiers would have worn while in Vietnam. Letters and prayers are ways of communicating thoughts and feelings about the soldiers who have died, and perhaps about the war itself.

DIFFERENTIATED INSTRUCTION

FOR LESS-PROFICIENT READERS
Concept Support Explain that the legacy of the war refers to the lasting effects of this event from the past. Use a Cluster Diagram to explore students' associations with the word *memory.* The article contains many words with similar roots that refer to ways of remembering war veterans—*mementos, memorabilia, memorial, tokens of remembrance. Keepsakes* is a synonym for *mementos.*

🧰 **BEST PRACTICES TOOLKIT—Transparency**
Cluster Diagram p. B18

FOR ENGLISH LEARNERS
Background Explain that the word *drafted* means that men were required to serve in the army. The words *feature* and *article* have multiple meanings when used alone. When they are combined, they refer to a type of story in a newspaper or magazine.

Options for Reading Have students listen to the selections on the *Audio Anthology CD.* Then have them read the selections with a partner and fill in the graphic organizer.

B SYNTHESIZE

Possible answers:

- *flags and flowers (line 57)*
- *a wooden cross with a crown of thorns made of barbed wire (lines 57–59)*
- *wedding rings (line 59)*
- *Purple Hearts (line 60)*
- *a varsity letter (line 60)*
- *a replica of a POW "tiger" cage (line 61)*
- *POW-MIA bracelets (line 62)*
- *an IV bag (line 62)*
- *a menorah (line 63)*

Extend the Discussion What was unusual about the objects that were being left at the Vietnam Veterans Memorial?

B SYNTHESIZE
Add to the list of gifts you started in your chart. If any item is unfamiliar, circle it and make a note to find out what it is some other time.

In 1981 Maya Lin's proposed
30 design—two long walls of black granite meeting in a V, with the names of the dead chiseled in chronological order, set into the gradual incline of a site near the Lincoln Memorial—ignited a hue and cry.

But over the years, as millions of visitors viewed their reflections in the polished granite and left
40 behind their tributes to the dead, the black gash has become a mirror of America. . . .

It was that way with the Vietnam Veterans Memorial almost from the start. In the first two years, according to Donna Donaldson, chief of visitor services for the National Park Service, some 600 tokens of remembrance were left.
50 As time went on, the number grew.

It is still growing. "It became obvious that we couldn't just leave them sitting there," says Donaldson. "Something different was happening at this memorial."

And the offerings weren't just flags and flowers. . . . A wooden cross with a crown of thorns made of barbed wire. Wedding rings.
60 Purple Hearts. A varsity letter. A replica of a POW "tiger" cage. . . . POW-MIA bracelets. An IV bag. A menorah. B

"The objects were different from anything else we'd ever collected," says Pamela West, the regional curator for the Park Service's National Capital region. "It took on its own momentum.
70 We decided to keep these things as a museum collection and treat it as such.". . .

DIFFERENTIATED INSTRUCTION

FOR LESS-PROFICIENT READERS

Vocabulary Support Assign one of these words or phrases to pairs of students and have them create Word Squares: *dog tags, combat boots, a wooden cross with a crown of thorns made of barbed wire, wedding ring, Purple Heart, varsity letter, IV bag, menorah.* Students can use a dictionary to look up unfamiliar terms. Have teams teach their Word Squares to the class.

Comprehension Support Have a volunteer look up the acronyms *POW* and *MIA* in a dictionary. Help students infer that POW-MIA bracelets (line 62) were worn in memory of those who were prisoners of war or missing in action. Explain that POW "tiger" cages (line 61) were bamboo cages in which some prisoners were kept.

 BEST PRACTICES TOOLKIT—Transparency
Word Squares p. E10

Felton got involved one day while visiting the Lanham warehouse where the objects were stored. A reporter also there that day asked about certain objects. Only Felton knew what they were. . . .

By 1984, the collection had become overwhelming, and someone in the Park Service remembered Duery Felton. He began as a volunteer, working a couple of hours a day. Felton assumed responsibility for the collection in 1988. **C**

Felton now has a small staff and an army of volunteers. He has witnessed the changing American reaction to the war from the time he was evacuated to Walter Reed Army Medical Center in 1968 until today. "I feel the memorial meets a felt need," he says. "It has

become America's bulletin board, a protest site—whatever you want to say, you can say at that site.". . . **D**

When asked what single object left at the Wall shocked him the most, he points to a black beret from the 101st Airborne Division reconnaissance unit ambushed in November 1967. "It was left by the sole surviving member of a 12-man unit some 20 years after the fact," he says, shaking his head.

At the Wall, the Capitol and the Washington Monument look postcard-perfect in the distance. And as Lincoln—the symbol of this country's other divisive war—looks down from his majestic perch nearby, people are still bringing offerings to the Wall.

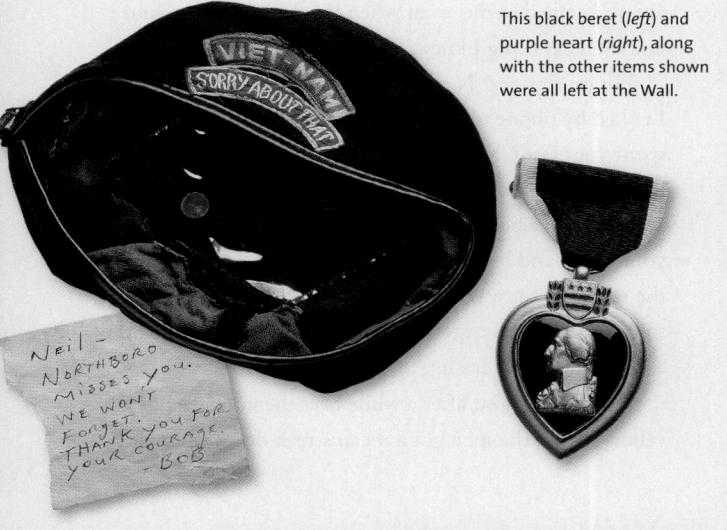

This black beret (*left*) and purple heart (*right*), along with the other items shown were all left at the Wall.

C SYNTHESIZE
In your chart, jot down the service Duery Felton performs at the Wall.

D FEATURE ARTICLE
Reread Felton's thoughts about the Wall. Then reread **Focus on Form** on page 209. What makes the Wall such a good topic for a feature article?

C SYNTHESIZE

Possible answer: Duery Felton is a Vietnam veteran who takes care of all the items that are left at the Wall, researches information about them, and tells their stories.

If students need help . . . Have students reread lines 9–17 to understand what it means for Duery Felton to have "assumed responsibility for the collection" (lines 85–86).

D FEATURE ARTICLE

Possible answers: Feature articles cover topics of interest that aren't necessarily current news. The Vietnam Veterans Memorial has become a place for many Americans to express their feelings about the war and the soldiers who fought there, so the story would interest many people. It's also a story that spans a long period of time; it wouldn't be headline news.

If students need help . . . Have students think about why "America's bulletin board" (line 95), or a place where people can say whatever they want, would be of interest to many people.

FOR ENGLISH LEARNERS
Culture: Clarify Explain that the U.S. Capitol (where Congress meets) and the Washington Monument (in honor of President George Washington) are famous landmarks in Washington, D.C. (lines 108–109). The photo on page 203 shows the Washington Monument reflected in the Wall. "Lincoln" refers to the Lincoln Memorial, which is located nearby (lines 35, 111). The country's "other divisive war" (lines 112–113) is the American Civil War, 1861–1865, when Lincoln was president.

FOR ADVANCED LEARNERS/PRE–AP
Analyze Form Have students review the lead to this story (lines 1–20) and contrast it with the lead to a news story. Encourage them to think about the "5 Ws and an H" that are important to cover at the beginning of a news article. Invite them to write a lead for a news story announcing Duery Felton's appointment as curator of the collection of articles left at the Vietnam Wall. Invite students to share their writing with a partner and to discuss the differences between the two kinds of articles.

A Mother's Words

Mrs. Eleanor Wimbish of Glen Burnie, Maryland, is the mother of William R. Stocks, who died in the Vietnam War. For years she left letters to her son under his name on the Vietnam Veterans Memorial in Washington, D.C.

Dear Bill,

Today is February 13, 1984. I came to this black wall again to see and touch your name, and as I do I wonder if anyone ever stops to realize that next to your name, on this black wall, is your mother's heart. A heart broken 15 years ago today, when you lost your life in Vietnam. **E**

And as I look at your name, William R. Stocks, I think of how many, many times I used to wonder how scared and homesick you must have been in that strange country called Vietnam. And if and how it might have changed you, for you were the most happy-go-lucky kid in the world, hardly ever sad or unhappy. And until the day I die, I will see you as you laughed at me, even when I was very mad at you, and the next thing I knew, we were laughing together.

But on this past New Year's Day, I had my answer. I talked by phone to a friend of yours from Michigan, who spent your last Christmas and the last four months of your life with you. Jim told me how you died, for he was there and saw the helicopter crash. He told me how you had flown your quota and had not been scheduled to fly that day. How the regular pilot was unable to fly and had been replaced by someone with less experience. How they did not know the exact cause of the crash. . . .

He told me how, after a while over there, instead of a yellow streak, the men got a mean streak down their backs.

E SYNTHESIZE
Why do you think Bill's mother comes to the Wall? Note her purpose for coming in your chart.

INFORMATIONAL ANALYSIS

E SYNTHESIZE

Possible answer: *Bill's mother misses her son. She comes to the wall to feel close to him, especially on the anniversary of his death.*

If students need help . . .

- Have students reread line 3 to notice what Bill's mother does at the Wall, and lines 5–6 to see how she feels—and why the date is special to her.
- Guide students to infer why Bill's mother comes to the Wall.

DIFFERENTIATED INSTRUCTION

FOR ENGLISH LEARNERS

Vocabulary: Slang In lines 24–25 Jim uses slang and an analogy to describe how the fighting in Vietnam affected many of the soldiers. *Yellow* is slang, meaning "cowardly." The "mean streak down their backs" alludes to the image of a skunk, which has a white streak down its back, and the common simile, "mean as a skunk." Skunks are not actually mean but do let off a powerful, unpleasant odor when they are frightened or attacked.

Each day the streak got bigger and the men became meaner.
Everyone but you, Bill. He said how you stayed the same,
happy-go-lucky guy that you were when you arrived in
Vietnam. How your warmth and friendliness drew the
30 guys to you. How your lieutenant gave you the nickname
of "Spanky," and soon your group, Jim included, were all
known as "Spanky's gang." How when you died it made it
so much harder on them for you were their moral support.
And he said how you of all people should never have been
the one to die. **F**

How it hurts to write this. But I must face it and then
put it to rest. I know after Jim talked to me, he must have
relived it all over again and suffered so. Before I hung up the
phone I told Jim I loved him. Loved him for just being your
40 close friend, and for being there with you when you died.
How lucky you were to have him for a friend, and how
lucky he was to have had you. . . .

They tell me the letters I write to you and leave here at this
memorial are waking others up to the fact that there is still
much pain left, after all these years, from the Vietnam War. **G**

But this I know. I would rather have had you for 21
years, and all the pain that goes with losing you, than never
to have had you at all.

Mone

F SYNTHESIZE
Reread lines 24–30.
Clarify what Bill's friend
said about the effects
that fighting in Vietnam
had on the soldiers.

G SYNTHESIZE
In what way do you
think Bill's mother
benefits from writing
letters to her son?

INFORMATIONAL ANALYSIS

F SYNTHESIZE

Possible answer: *Jim said that fighting in Vietnam tended to make most of the soldiers act in a mean way.*

Extend the Discussion Why do you think many of the men "became meaner" the longer they were in Vietnam?

INFORMATIONAL ANALYSIS

G SYNTHESIZE

Possible answer: *Writing the letters enables Bill's mother to share her feelings instead of bottling them up inside. She may also feel good knowing that the letters are helping educate others about the long-lasting pain caused by the Vietnam War.*

FOR ENGLISH LEARNERS
Culture: Clarify Spanky and Our Gang was a
popular American musical group from 1967
to 1969. They were known for light, upbeat
songs that seem to fit the personality of Bill
Stocks (lines 27–32). The group's lead singer
was Elaine "Spanky" McFarlane. The group's
name alluded to a popular children's TV show
of the 1950s and 1960s, *The Little Rascals,* featuring comic films from the 1920s to 1940s.
One of the characters was named Spanky.

FOR ADVANCED LEARNERS/PRE–AP
Compare and Contrast Have students use a
three-way Venn Diagram to chart the similarities and differences of John Wilson from
"Zebra," Duery Felton from the feature article,
and Bill Stocks from this letter. Encourage
students to think about when each was in
Vietnam, what they did there, what happened to each of them, and how they are
connected to the Vietnam Wall.

 BEST PRACTICES TOOLKIT—Transparency
Venn Diagram p. A26

BACKGROUND

Communism Communist governments tightly control their economies and allow little political freedom. After World War II, the Soviet Union wanted to extend the influence of communism to eastern Europe. Communists also gained control of China in 1949. The Cold War was the struggle between the Soviet Union and the United States and their allies that lasted from 1945 until 1991. During this time, U.S. foreign policy was driven by the desire to contain the spread of communism. The U.S. government feared that if South Vietnam fell to communism, other countries of Asia would soon follow.

INFORMATIONAL ANALYSIS

Ⓗ SYNTHESIZE

Possible answer: Many U.S. citizens at home protested the war.

Skill Focus: Synthesize

Possible answers for the chart on page 208:

"The Collected Grief of a Nation": Tens of thousands of keepsakes have been left at the Wall, including dog tags, combat boots, letters, prayers, flags, flowers, and other personal items, described in lines 14–15, 56–63. A Vietnam veteran named Duery Felton Jr. takes care of these items, which are treated as a museum collection. The Wall has become a place to express a variety of feelings about the war.

"A Mother's Words": Bill's mother comes to the Wall to heal the pain she feels over her son's death.

Timeline: U.S. troops fought in Vietnam from 1965 to 1973. Many U.S. citizens protested the war. The Wall was dedicated in 1982. The two countries renewed full diplomatic relations in 1995.

Timeline: U.S. Involvement in Vietnam

The seeds of the Vietnam War were planted in 1858 when France attacked Vietnam for control of the government. After decades of frustration under foreign rule, many Vietnamese began supporting the Communist movement against the French. Meanwhile, the United States struggled against the spread of communism worldwide.

USA	VIETNAM
1950s	
1950 The United States sends economic aid to the French forces in Vietnam.	**1954** The French are defeated. Vietnam divides into Communist North and non-Communist South.
	1957 Communist rebels (the Viet Cong) fight for control of South Vietnam.
1960s	
1965 Antiwar protests become widespread.	**1965** The United States bombs North Vietnam. The first U.S. combat troops arrive in South Vietnam.
1968 U.S. citizens begin to think the war cannot be won.	**1968** The number of U.S. troops in Vietnam reaches its peak. The North Vietnamese and the Viet Cong launch the Tet offensive, a series of surprise attacks.
1970s	
1970 Four students are killed at an antiwar demonstration in Ohio. Ⓗ	**1973** All U.S. troops leave Vietnam.
	1975 South Vietnam surrenders to the Communists. The U.S. Embassy in Vietnam is evacuated.

	1978 Thousands of refugees flee Vietnam to escape poverty and punishment for aiding the United States during the war.
1980s	
1982 The Vietnam Veterans Memorial is dedicated in Washington, D.C.	**1986** The Vietnamese government begins economic restructuring.
1990s	
1995 The United States and Vietnam restore full diplomatic relations.	

Ⓗ SYNTHESIZE
While the Vietnam War was being fought, how were U.S. citizens at home responding to the conflict? Note the information you learn about the war in your chart.

DIFFERENTIATED INSTRUCTION

FOR LESS–PROFICIENT READERS
Comprehension Support Guide students to understand how this timeline is organized. The columns show events that happened in the United States and Vietnam over a 40-year period. Point out that each row reflects a decade and that they should read across both columns to follow the sequence of events in that time period. Ask students to note that in the 1960s, events in the same years are shown in both columns.

FOR ADVANCED LEARNERS/PRE–AP
Draw Conclusions Have students review the timeline and draw conclusions about how events in one country are connected to events in the other, or how events from a previous decade affected events in the next. Encourage students to write their conclusions as a third column and to include at least one conclusion for each decade from the 1950s through the 1980s. Allow students to share their conclusions with a small group.

Comprehension

1. **Recall** When did the last U.S. combat troops leave Vietnam?

2. **Clarify** What kind of person was Bill Stocks?

3. **Summarize** In general, how would you describe the "tokens of remembrance" people leave at the Wall?

Critical Analysis

4. **Analyze** In the feature article, the Wall is described as a "black gash," a "mirror of America," a "bulletin board," and a "protest site." Pick one of these phrases and explain what it suggests about the Wall.

5. **Synthesize** Review your chart. What information did you get from reading the selections that you had not learned from reading "Zebra"?

Read for Information: Draw Conclusions

MARYLAND OBJECTIVES

READING/INFO TEXT STANDARDS
1.E.4.c Draw conclusions
2.A.4.g Synthesize ideas from text

> **WRITING PROMPT**
>
> In a paragraph, state and support a **conclusion** you have reached about one of the following topics:
> - the importance of the Vietnam Veterans Memorial to those who visit it
> - the effects of the Vietnam War on veterans and their friends and family
> - how people heal after suffering a loss

A **conclusion** is a judgment or belief about something. To reach a solid conclusion, you need sound reasoning, evidence, and experience to support it. The steps below can help you state and support a conclusion.

1. Choose a topic and jot down ideas or information about it. Ask yourself what this information leads you to conclude about your topic.

2. From two or more selections, pick out details that support your conclusion. If you can't find enough support, you might need to revisit your conclusion.

3. State your conclusion in a topic sentence. Then present the reasons and evidence that led you to this conclusion.

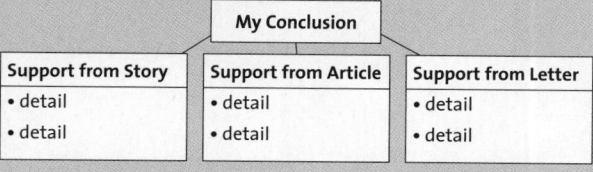

My Conclusion		
Support from Story	**Support from Article**	**Support from Letter**
• detail	• detail	• detail
• detail	• detail	• detail

Practice and Apply

For additional support of post-reading questions, use these copy masters:

R RESOURCE MANAGER—Copy Masters
Reading Check p. 55
Question Support p. 57
Draw Conclusions p. 52

For additional questions, see p. 46.

ANSWERS

Comprehension

1. *The last U.S. troops left Vietnam in 1973.*

2. *Bill was easygoing, friendly, and well liked.*

3. *Possible answer: Some objects are symbols of love and attachment; some are associated with the soldiers' war experiences.*

Critical Analysis

4. *Possible answers: "Black gash"—the Vietnam War is a wound in the nation; "Mirror of America"—reflects what average Americans feel; "Bulletin board"—people leave notes to remind others of important events; "Protest site"—people express their feelings about the war.*

5. ■ **STANDARDS FOCUS** *Synthesize Possible answers: Students should note that they learned more about the Wall and how people respond to it, as well as more about the war and how it affected soldiers and people at home.*

Read for Information: Draw Conclusions

Writing Prompt *Students' paragraphs should focus on one of the topics and state their conclusion as a topic sentence that is supported with evidence and reasons from at least two of the selections.*

FOR LESS–PROFICIENT WRITERS
Read for Information

- Divide students into groups based on the topics they choose. Have them brainstorm ideas and discuss their conclusions.

- Assign one or two students in each group to review one selection (story, article, or letter) for evidence to support their conclusion. Have them share their findings with other group members and use the pooled information to write their paragraphs.

FOR ADVANCED LEARNERS/PRE–AP

Read for Information Encourage students to find an additional example of a feature article that is pertinent to their chosen topic. Have students include evidence from that source, as well as from the assigned selections, when they write their paragraphs. Allow students to expand their writing to more than one paragraph.

Assess and Reteach

Assess

R RESOURCE MANAGER—Copy Masters
Selection Tests A, B/C pp. 59–60, 61–62
⊘ Test Generator CD

Reteach

S STANDARDS LESSON FILE
Reading Lesson 9: Drawing Conclusions
Reading Lesson 14: Synthesizing Information

Focus and Motivate

OBJECTIVES

Literary Analysis
- explore the key idea of **obstacles**
- recognize first-person point of view
- read a short story

Reading
- make inferences

Vocabulary
- build vocabulary for reading and writing
- use context clues to determine the meanings of words (also an EL language objective)

SUMMARY

With straight-A grades, Martha has earned the scholarship jacket given to the top eighth-grade student. She is devastated to learn that unless she pays fifteen dollars, the honor will go to the daughter of an influential school board member. Martha informs the principal that her grandfather refuses to pay. Shamed by this act of integrity, the principal decides to give Martha the jacket anyway.

What stands in the way of your DREAMS?

Discuss the question and **KEY IDEA.** Then ask students what **obstacles** they have overcome in the past to reach a dream. Ask them what advice they would give someone about facing and overcoming obstacles, based on their own experiences. Then have students form small groups to complete the **QUICKWRITE** activity.

Selection Resources

The Scholarship Jacket
Short Story by Marta Salinas

What stands in the way of your DREAMS?

MARYLAND OBJECTIVES

READING/LIT STANDARDS
1.E.4.c Draw inferences
3.A.3.i Analyze point of view

KEY IDEA Your dream may be to go to camp, to be a star on the basketball court, to be class president, or to go to college someday. Whatever it is, hard work and luck can help you fulfill that dream. But, like the narrator of "The Scholarship Jacket," you may encounter **obstacles** that block your progress.

QUICKWRITE With a small group of classmates, discuss your dream for the future. What obstacles might you encounter while working to make your dream come true? Then, in your journal, write one or two ways to overcome each obstacle.

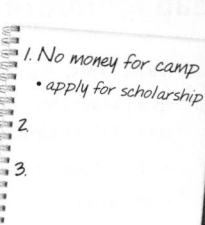

1. No money for camp
   • apply for scholarship
2.
3.

216

---

* Resources for Differentiation   † Also in Spanish   ‡ In Haitian Creole and Vietnamese

LITERARY ANALYSIS: FIRST-PERSON POINT OF VIEW

When you listen to a friend talk, you can learn a great deal about him or her. Your friend's personality, experiences, and opinions all come through. The same is true when you read a story from one character's point of view. When a story is told from the **first-person point of view,** the narrator

- is a character in the story
- tells the story using the pronouns *I, me, we,* and *us*
- tells the story as he or she experiences it

As you read "The Scholarship Jacket," notice how the information you receive is limited to what the narrator sees, hears, thinks, and feels.

READING SKILL: MAKE INFERENCES

One way to get the most out of what you read is to make logical guesses, or **inferences,** about things that are not directly stated. Base your inferences on details in the story and on your own knowledge and experiences. As you read "The Scholarshic Jacket," record each inference you make in an equation like the one shown.

Details from the Text	My Experiences	Inference
Martha couldn't play sports because of cost. **+**	I couldn't go to playoffs because of expense. **=**	Martha's grand-parents don't have extra money.

VOCABULARY IN CONTEXT

These words help tell the story of a girl facing obstacles. Write the word that best completes each sentence.

WORD LIST	agile	dismay	falsify
	despair	eavesdrop	vile

1. She unhappily swallowed the _____ medicine.
2. He would often _____ on his parents' conversations.
3. He tried not to _____ over the terrible news.
4. She climbed the tree in a very _____ manner.
5. There was a look of _____ when she received the news.
6. Don't _____ the records to hide the truth.

Author Online

California Native
Marta Salinas was born in Coalinga, California, and received a degree in creative writing from the University of California at Irvine. "The Scholarship Jacket" is one of several short stories Salinas has published in journals and collections.

**Marta Salinas
born 1949**

Background

Texas History The main character in "The Scholarship Jacket" is a Mexican-American girl who lives in Texas. The history of Tejanos, or Texas Mexicans, dates back more than 200 years. As early as 1731, Tejanos established a ranch community in what was then northeastern Mexico. About 100 years later, Mexico invited immigrants from the United States to settle in the region. The Tejanos and the immigrants eventually joined forces to fight for their independence from Mexico, and in 1845, Texas became part of the United States. Mexicans continued migrating to Texas, but they often faced discrimination. Today, over seven million residents of Texas are Mexican Americans.

 MORE ABOUT THE AUTHOR AND BACKGROUND
To learn more about Marta Salinas and Tejano history and culture, visit the **Literature Center** at **ClassZone.com.**

Teach

STANDARDS FOCUS

LITERARY ANALYSIS

● FIRST—PERSON POINT OF VIEW

Read aloud this example:

> I slammed my sneakers into the locker, upset that the track meet had been postponed again. I would never get the chance to earn the title I deserved!

Ask students what clues and evidence reveal the narrator's point of view. *Possible answer: The passage uses the pronoun* I, *and all the information comes from the narrator, who is in the story. We learn only what the narrator thinks and feels—not how others feel.*

CHECK UNDERSTANDING Ask students to explain how reading a story told from the first-person point of view is similar to reading someone's journal or diary.

READING SKILL

■ MAKE INFERENCES

Ask students to make inferences about the narrator's character in the passage above. *Possible answer: The narrator is angry.*

CHECK UNDERSTANDING Ask students what they might infer if they saw all their friends taking home their science text-books.

R RESOURCE MANAGER—Copy Master
Make Inferences p. 75 (for student use while reading the story)

VOCABULARY SKILL

▲ VOCABULARY IN CONTEXT

DIAGNOSE WORD KNOWLEDGE To determine preteaching needs, have all students complete **Vocabulary in Context.** Check students' answers. *(**1.** vile; **2.** eavesdrop; **3.** despair; **4.** agile; **5.** dismay; **6.** falsify)*

PRETEACH VOCABULARY Use the Vocabulary Study copy master to help students explore the meaning of each boldfaced word.

1. Read the first sentence of the passage aloud, emphasizing *agile.*

2. Point out the phrase *quick enough.* Elicit possible meanings for *agile,* such as "fast" or "able to react quickly."

3. Repeat the procedure for the rest of the passage.

 RESOURCE MANAGER—Copy Master
Vocabulary Study p. 77

For general guidelines on differentiating vocabulary instruction and for alternative vocabulary activities for students not needing vocabulary preteaching, see

BEST PRACTICES TOOLKIT
Scaffolding Vocabulary Instruction pp. 43–46

ℹ Vocabulary Center at **ClassZone.com**
Additional Vocabulary Activities

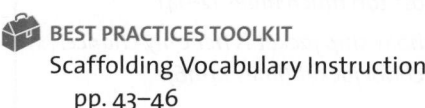

ANALYZE VISUALS

Possible answer:

- *The girl is looking sideways, suggesting that she feels uncertain or shy.*
- *The girl has a serious expression, as if she is thinking deeply about something.*
- *The firm set of the girl's jaw makes her seem calm and determined.*

About the Art American artist Robert Henri (1865–1929) painted people from many walks of life in urban America. He aimed for realism and freedom of expression in his work. He believed that each artist perceived the sitter's inner state differently, depending on the emotions of the artist at the time. In this painting, Henri communicates his impression of the subject through the use of color, form, and gesture.

LITERARY ANALYSIS

Ⓐ FIRST–PERSON POINT OF VIEW

You might record students' answers in a list or cluster chart. *Possible answers:*

- *The narrator is an eighth-grader at a small Texas school (lines 1, 8).*
- *She has an older sister, Rosie, who won the scholarship jacket (line 7).*
- *She has straight-As and expects to win the scholarship jacket this year (lines 8–9).*
- *Her father is a farm laborer and too poor to care for all eight children, so she lives with her grandparents (lines 10–12).*
- *She does not participate in sports because they cost too much (lines 12–14).*
- *The scholarship jacket is her only chance for a school jacket (lines 14–16).*

The Scholarship Jacket

Marta Salinas

The small Texas school that I went to had a tradition carried out every year during the eighth-grade graduation: a beautiful gold and green jacket (the school colors) was awarded to the class valedictorian, the student who had maintained the highest grades for eight years. The scholarship jacket had a big gold S on the left front side and your name written in gold letters on the pocket.

My oldest sister, Rosie, had won the jacket a few years back, and I fully expected to also. I was fourteen and in the eighth grade. I had been a straight A student since the first grade and this last year had looked
10 forward very much to owning that jacket. My father was a farm laborer who couldn't earn enough money to feed eight children, so when I was six I was given to my grandparents to raise. We couldn't participate in sports at school because there were registration fees, uniform costs, and trips out of town; so, even though our family was quite **agile** and athletic there would never be a school sports jacket for us. This one, the scholarship jacket, was our only chance. Ⓐ

In May, close to graduation, spring fever had struck as usual with a vengeance.[1] No one paid any attention in class; instead we stared out the windows and at each other, wanting to speed up the last few weeks of

---

1. **with a vengeance** (vĕn′jəns): to an extreme degree.

ANALYZE VISUALS
On the basis of the **details** in the painting, how do you think the girl is feeling?

① **Targeted Passage**

agile (ăj′əl) *adj.* quick and light in movement

Ⓐ **FIRST-PERSON POINT OF VIEW**
Who is the narrator? What have you learned from her so far?

Bernadita (1922), Robert Henri. Oil on canva 24¹/₈″ × 20¹/₈″. Gift of the San Diego Wednesda Club. © San Diego Museum of Art (1926:138

DIFFERENTIATED INSTRUCTION

FOR ALL STUDENTS

Expert Groups Write these topics on the board and allow individual students or groups to select topics to research. Then have student experts share their information with the class.

- graduation traditions
- types of scholarships
- the process of growing beans
- history of Mexicans in Texas
- role of a school board

FOR LESS–PROFICIENT READERS

In combination with the *Audio Anthology CD*, use one or more Targeted Passages (pp. 218, 220–221, 222–223) to ensure that students focus on key story events, concepts, and skills.

① Targeted Passage [Lines 1–16]

This passage introduces the narrator and provides background on her character: she is looking forward to receiving the scholarship jacket for her academic achievement.

BACKGROUND

Farm Laborers In this story, the narrator's father is a farm laborer in Texas "who couldn't earn enough money to feed eight children" (line 11). So, the narrator was given to her grandparents to raise. Although the number of American farm laborers has decreased over recent years, they still struggle with difficult working and living conditions. Field workers earn a low minimum wage. Because their wages have not kept up with inflation, farm laborers can actually buy less with their earnings today than they could buy 20 years ago. Many do not have health insurance and cannot afford good health care on their own. As a result, the rate of infant mortality is high, and the life expectancy for adults is significantly lower than the national average.

- What is the scholarship jacket? Who gets this jacket each year?

- Why does the narrator live with her grandparents?

- What is one reason the scholarship jacket is important to the narrator?

FOR ENGLISH LEARNERS

Key Academic Vocabulary Have pairs use New Word Analysis to learn this vocabulary found in the story: *tradition* (line 1), *participate* (line 12), *fees* (line 13), *team* (line 30), *policy* (line 60), *appreciate* (line 80).

 BEST PRACTICES TOOLKIT—Transparency
New Word Analysis p. E8

Prereading For prereading instruction for English learners, see

 BEST PRACTICES TOOLKIT
Scaffolding Reading Instruction pp. 43–46

FOR ADVANCED LEARNERS/PRE–AP

Pre-AP exercises in the bottom channel provide additional challenge for your advanced students. Use them for small groups or individuals.

ADDITIONAL GUIDELINES

For more help with differentiation and tips for classroom management, see

 BEST PRACTICES TOOLKIT
Differentiated Instruction pp. 31–38

Lines 31–49
DISCUSSION PROMPTS

Use these prompts to help students understand the major conflict in the story:

Connect Have you ever accidentally overheard someone talking about you? Based on this experience, how do you think Martha feels as she listens to the teachers' conversation? *Students may say that she probably feels embarrassed and a little guilty about eavesdropping, but she is also curious to know what the teachers are saying about her.*

Infer What kind of records is Mr. Schmidt being asked to falsify? Why? *Possible answer: He is being asked to adjust the academic records of his history class to say that Joann has a higher average than Martha. This would allow Joann to get the scholarship jacket.*

Evaluate How important are Joann and Martha's different backgrounds in this argument about who should get the jacket? *Possible answer: They are very important. Joann's father is influential and wants the jacket for his daughter (lines 44–45). There also seems to be resistance to giving the jacket to the daughter of a Mexican-American farm laborer (line 47).*

LITERARY ANALYSIS

B FIRST–PERSON POINT OF VIEW

Possible answer: Martha is so shaken, the rest of her day is a blur. She hides her crying at night.

Extend the Discussion What does Martha's reaction to the overheard conversation reveal about her character?

READING SKILL

C MAKE INFERENCES

Possible answer: The principal is unhappy because he must give Martha a dishonest excuse for why she cannot have the scholarship jacket.

If students need help ... Remind them about the conversation between Mr. Boone and Mr. Schmidt that Martha overheard the day before. Help students make connections between what the teachers were discussing and what the principal is about to tell her.

---

20 school. I **despaired** every time I looked in the mirror. Pencil thin, not a curve anywhere. I was called "beanpole" and "string bean," and I knew that's what I looked like. A flat chest, no hips, and a brain; that's what I had. That really wasn't much for a fourteen-year-old to work with, I thought, as I absent-mindedly wandered from my history class to the gym. Another hour of sweating in basketball and displaying my toothpick legs was coming up. Then I remembered my P.E. shorts were still in a bag under my desk where I'd forgotten them. I had to walk all the way back and get them. Coach Thompson was a real bear if someone wasn't dressed for P.E. She had said I was a good forward and even tried to talk Grandma
30 into letting me join the team once. Of course Grandma said no.

    I was almost back at my classroom door when I heard voices raised in anger as if in some sort of argument. I stopped. I didn't mean to **eavesdrop**, I just hesitated, not knowing what to do. I needed those shorts and I was going to be late, but I didn't want to interrupt an argument between my teachers. I recognized the voices: Mr. Schmidt, my history teacher, and Mr. Boone, my math teacher. They seemed to be arguing about me. I couldn't believe it. I still remember the feeling of shock that rooted me flat against the wall as if I were trying to blend in with the graffiti written there.

40   "I refuse to do it! I don't care who her father is, her grades don't even begin to compare to Martha's. I won't lie or **falsify** records. Martha has a straight A-plus average and you know it." That was Mr. Schmidt and he sounded very angry. Mr. Boone's voice sounded calm and quiet.

    "Look. Joann's father is not only on the Board, he owns the only store in town: we could say it was a close tie and—"

    The pounding in my ears drowned out the rest of the words, only a word here and there filtered through. " . . . Martha is Mexican . . . resign . . . won't do it . . . . " Mr. Schmidt came rushing out and luckily for me went down the opposite way toward the auditorium, so he didn't see me.
50 Shaking, I waited a few minutes and then went in and grabbed my bag and fled from the room. Mr. Boone looked up when I came in but didn't say anything. To this day I don't remember if I got in trouble in P.E. for being late or how I made it through the rest of the afternoon. I went home very sad and cried into my pillow that night so Grandmother wouldn't hear me. It seemed a cruel coincidence that I had overheard that conversation. **B**

    The next day when the principal called me into his office I knew what it would be about. He looked uncomfortable and unhappy. I decided I wasn't going to make it any easier for him, so I looked him straight in the eyes. He looked away and fidgeted with the papers on his desk. **C**
60   "Martha," he said, "there's been a change in policy this year regarding the scholarship jacket. As you know, it has always been free." He cleared

despair (dĭ-spâr') *v.* to lose hope

eavesdrop (ēvz'drŏp') *v.* to listen secretly to a private conversation of others

falsify (fôl'sə-fī') *v.* to make false by adding to or changing

B FIRST-PERSON POINT OF VIEW Reread lines 46–55. How does the argument between Mr. Schmidt and Mr. Boone make Martha feel?

C MAKE INFERENCES Why is the principal unhappy?

2 Targeted Passage

DIFFERENTIATED INSTRUCTION

FOR LESS–PROFICIENT READERS
Reading Skill Follow-Up: Make Inferences
Help students make inferences about Martha from these and other details in the text. Have students record their inferences in equations similar to the one on page 217.

- "I despaired every time I looked in the mirror." (line 20)
- "She had said I was a good forward and even tried to talk Grandma into letting me join the team." (lines 29–30)
- "I looked him straight in the eyes." (lines 58–59)

Details from the Text	My Experiences	Inference
Martha does not show how upset she is in the principal's office (lines 64–69). +	It is hard not to react emotionally after a shock. =	Martha is level-headed and strong. She has a lot of pride.

his throat and continued. "This year the Board has decided to charge fifteen dollars, which still won't cover the complete cost of the jacket."

I stared at him in shock, and a small sound of **dismay** escaped my throat. I hadn't expected this. He still avoided looking in my eyes.

"So if you are unable to pay the fifteen dollars for the jacket it will be given to the next one in line." I didn't need to ask who that was.

Standing with all the dignity I could muster, I said, "I'll speak to my grandfather about it, sir, and let you know tomorrow." I cried on the walk home from the bus stop. The dirt road was a quarter mile from the highway, so by the time I got home, my eyes were red and puffy.

"Where's Grandpa?" I asked Grandma, looking down at the floor so she wouldn't ask me why I'd been crying. She was sewing on a quilt as usual and didn't look up.

"I think he's out back working in the bean field."

I went outside and looked out at the fields. There he was. I could see him walking between the rows, his body bent over the little plants, hoe in hand. I walked slowly out to him, trying to think how I could best ask him for the money. There was a cool breeze blowing and a sweet smell of mesquite[2] fruit in the air, but I didn't appreciate it. I kicked at a dirt clod. I wanted that jacket so much. It was more than just being a valedictorian and giving a little thank you speech for the jacket on graduation night. It represented eight years of hard work and expectation. I knew I had to be honest with Grandpa; it was my only chance. He saw my shadow and looked up.

He waited for me to speak. I cleared my throat nervously and clasped my hands behind my back so he wouldn't see them shaking. "Grandpa, I have a big favor to ask you," I said in Spanish, the only language he knew. He still waited silently. I tried again. "Grandpa, this year the principal said the scholarship jacket is not going to be free. It's going to cost fifteen dollars, and I have to take the money in tomorrow, otherwise it'll be given to someone else." The last words came out in an eager rush. Grandpa straightened up tiredly and leaned his chin on the hoe handle. He looked out over the field that was filled with the tiny green bean plants. I waited, desperately hoping he'd say I could have the money.

He turned to me and asked quietly, "What does a scholarship jacket mean?"

I answered quickly; maybe there was a chance. "It means you've earned it by having the highest grades for eight years and that's why they're giving it to you." Too late I realized the significance of my words.

---

2. **sweet smell of mesquite** (mĕ-skēt'): Mesquite, a small tree or shrub native to hot, dry regions of North America, has small flowers and large super-rich pods that give off a sweet smell.

THE SCHOLARSHIP JACKET **221**

2 Targeted Passage

dismay (dĭs-mā') *n.* distress caused by trouble or something unexpected

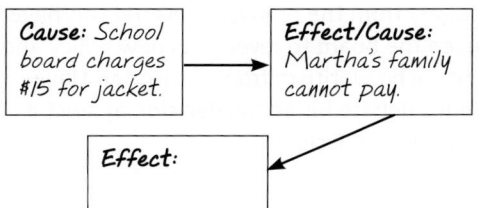

Lines 81–84
REINFORCE *KEY IDEA:* OBSTACLES

Discuss What **obstacle** may prevent Martha from getting the scholarship jacket? *Possible answer: The school has decided that the recipient must pay fifteen dollars. She does not think her grandfather will give her the money.*

Lines 86–100
DISCUSSION PROMPTS

Use these prompts to help students understand the narrator's internal conflict:

Connect Think of a time when you wanted someone to grant you a favor but didn't think the person would agree. How does this experience help you understand how Martha feels talking to her grandfather? *Students may say that Martha probably feels very nervous because she wants to phrase her request just right and make her arguments convincing.*

Analyze Why is Martha willing to ask for the money even though she doubts her grandfather will give it to her? *Possible answer: She wants the jacket so badly that she's willing to pay for it.*

Evaluate What is the difference between a scholarship jacket that you pay for and one that is given for free? *Possible answer: A jacket that is paid for is not an honor. The scholarship jacket has special meaning because it must be earned through academic achievement.*

FOR LESS–PROFICIENT READERS

2 Targeted Passage [Lines 60–71]

This passage establishes the story's major conflict: Martha will not receive the jacket unless she pays fifteen dollars.

- Why does the principal tell Martha that she must pay for the scholarship jacket? What is the real reason?
- Why does Martha cry on the way home?
- What do you think her grandfather will do?

FOR ENGLISH LEARNERS

Comprehension: Cause and Effect To help students understand what the school board hopes will happen as a result of their policy change, complete this cause-and-effect chain with them.

Cause: School board charges $15 for jacket. → **Effect/Cause:** Martha's family cannot pay.

Effect:

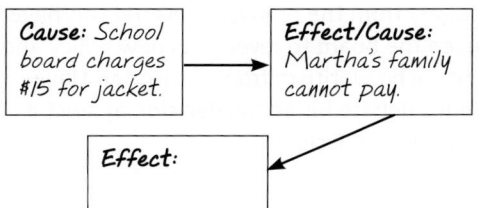

THE SCHOLARSHIP JACKET **221**

Possible answer: *I imagine Martha's grandfather to be a hard worker, with weathered hands and face, much like the man in the painting. Because her grandfather spends long hours working outside in the sun, I picture him wearing a wide brimmed hat.*

About the Art Dutch artist Vincent van Gogh (1853–1890) left behind hundreds of paintings and drawings, all completed in ten years. He began painting in 1880 in a heavy and dark style. By 1888, at the time this portrait was done, he had been influenced by the Impressionists and was using bright, saturated colors to convey meaning in his work.

Portrait of Patience Escalier (1888), Vincent van Gogh. Oil on canvas. Private collection. © Lefevre Fine Art Ltd., London/Bridgeman Art Library.

ANALYZE VISUALS
How does the man shown **compare** with your image of Martha's grandfather?

READING SKILL

Ⓓ MAKE INFERENCES

Possible answers: *Grandpa is determined to stand on principle. Even by Martha's description (lines 98–100), a scholarship is something given as an award for achievement. If it is paid for, it is not a scholarship.*

If students need help . . . Use an analogy to help them see that paying for the jacket takes away its honor: if a car company's salesperson of the year wins a car, but is told that he or she must pay for it, the contest is a farce—for it mocks the salesperson's achievement.

Extend the Discussion Does her grandfather regret having to give Martha this answer? How do you know?

Grandpa knew that I understood it was not a matter of money. It wasn't that. He went back to hoeing the weeds that sprang up between the delicate little bean plants. It was a time-consuming job; sometimes the small shoots were right next to each other. Finally he spoke again as I turned to leave, crying.

"Then if you pay for it, Marta, it's not a scholarship jacket, is it? Tell your principal I will not pay the fifteen dollars." Ⓓ

I walked back to the house and locked myself in the bathroom for a long time. I was angry with Grandfather even though I knew he was
110 right, and I was angry with the Board, whoever they were. Why did they have to change the rules just when it was my turn to win the jacket? Those were the days of belief and innocence.

I t was a very sad and withdrawn girl who dragged into the principal's office the next day. This time he did look me in the eyes.

"What did your grandfather say?"

I sat very straight in my chair.

"He said to tell you he won't pay the fifteen dollars."

The principal muttered something I couldn't understand under his breath and walked over to the window. He stood looking out

Ⓓ MAKE INFERENCES
Why won't Martha's grandfather pay the money for the jacket?

❸ Targeted Passage

DIFFERENTIATED INSTRUCTION

FOR ADVANCED LEARNERS/PRE–AP

Hypothesize Have students review lines 86–107. Ask students to consider whether Grandfather made the best decision, or if a more active response was needed. For example, what if he had demanded an apology from the principal? Would this have forced the board to reverse its new policy and kept such favoritism from recurring? Have groups debate his actual decision against a hypothetical decision.

Evaluate Narrator A first-person narrator filters information through his or her own perceptions. Therefore, some details may not be totally objective or accurate. Ask students to create a checklist for Martha's reliability. Have them provide text evidence for areas such as

- portrays herself honestly
- presents other characters and events objectively
- helps readers understand the story

120 at something outside. He looked bigger than usual when he stood up; he was a tall, gaunt man with gray hair, and I watched the back of his head while I waited for him to speak. **E**

"Why?" he finally asked. "Your grandfather has the money. He owns a two-hundred acre ranch."

I looked at him, forcing my eyes to stay dry. "I know, sir, but he said if I had to pay for it, then it wouldn't be a scholarship jacket." I stood up to leave. "I guess you'll just have to give it to Joann." I hadn't meant to say that, it had just slipped out. I was almost to the door when he stopped me.

"Martha—wait."

130 I turned and looked at him, waiting. What did he want now? I could feel my heart pounding loudly in my chest and see my blouse fluttering where my breasts should have been. Something bitter and **vile** tasting was coming up in my mouth; I was afraid I was going to be sick. I didn't need any sympathy speeches. He sighed loudly and went back to his big desk. He watched me, biting his lip.

"Okay. We'll make an exception in your case. I'll tell the Board, you'll get your jacket." **F**

I could hardly believe my ears. I spoke in a trembling rush. "Oh, thank you, sir!" Suddenly I felt great. I didn't know about adrenalin³ in those
140 days, but I knew something was pumping through me, making me feel as tall as the sky. I wanted to yell, jump, run the mile, do something. I ran out so I could cry in the hall where there was no one to see me.

At the end of the day, Mr. Schmidt winked at me and said, "I hear you're getting the scholarship jacket this year."

His face looked as happy and innocent as a baby's, but I knew better. Without answering I gave him a quick hug and ran to the bus. I cried on the walk home again, but this time because I was so happy. I couldn't wait to tell Grandpa and ran straight to the field. I joined him in the row where he was working, and without saying anything I crouched down and
150 started pulling up the weeds with my hands. Grandpa worked alongside me for a few minutes, and he didn't ask what had happened. After I had a little pile of weeds between the rows, I stood up and faced him.

"The principal said he's making an exception for me, Grandpa, and I'm getting the jacket after all. That's after I told him what you said."

Grandpa didn't say anything; he just gave me a pat on the shoulder and a smile. He pulled out the crumpled red handkerchief that he always carried in his back pocket and wiped the sweat off his forehead.

"Better go see if your grandmother needs any help with supper."

I gave him a big grin. He didn't fool me. I skipped and ran back
60 to the house whistling some silly tune. ◞

---

3. **adrenalin** (ə-drĕn′ə-lĭn): a hormone that speeds up the heartbeat and increases bodily energy. The body produces adrenalin when a person experiences emotions such as excitement or fear.

THE SCHOLARSHIP JACKET **223**

---

③ Targeted Passage

E FIRST-PERSON POINT OF VIEW
Reread lines 118–122. How does the first-person point of view limit your understanding of what the principal is thinking?

vile (vīl) adj. disgusting; unpleasant

F MAKE INFERENCES
Why do you think the principal changed his mind?

LITERARY ANALYSIS

E FIRST–PERSON POINT OF VIEW

Possible answers: Readers know only what Martha knows. She can see only the back of the principal's head, so readers don't even know what his facial expression is. The principal mutters something, but Martha cannot hear him, so that information is not revealed to readers.

READING SKILL

F MAKE INFERENCES

Possible answers:

- *The principal changed his mind because he realizes that Martha knows the truth (lines 127–129).*

- *He changed his mind because he admires Martha and her grandfather for sticking to their principles (lines 123–126). He knows he should have done the same in refusing the policy change.*

Lines 134–137
REINFORCE KEY IDEA: OBSTACLES

Discuss What **obstacles** might the principal face in order to keep his promise to Martha?
Possible answer: The principal will have to tell the school board that he has decided to give Martha the jacket even though she won't pay the fifteen dollars. He may face opposition because the Board probably pressured him into the original policy change (lines 44–45, 57–63).

SELECTION WRAP–UP

★ **CRITIQUE** Have students evaluate whether the principal's decision to give Martha the jacket after all is a logical and satisfying conclusion. Ask if the conflict could have been resolved in another way.

FOR LESS–PROFICIENT READERS

③ Targeted Passage [Lines 117–137]

This passage presents the climax of the story: the principal gives Martha the jacket even though she refuses to pay for it.

- What does the principal say when Martha first tells him that her grandfather refuses to pay?
- How does he react when she explains their reason for not paying?
- What is the principal's final decision?

FOR ENGLISH LEARNERS

Comprehension: Task Support Make sure students understand that inferences can be made from characters' gestures and facial expressions. In a T Chart, list significant body language used by the characters, such as the principal's initial refusal to look at Martha (line 59). In the right column, help students make inferences about the character's feelings as expressed by this body language.

🧰 **BEST PRACTICES TOOLKIT—Transparency** T Chart p. A25

Practice and Apply

After Reading

For additional support of post-reading questions, use these copy masters:

R RESOURCE MANAGER—Copy Masters
Reading Check p. 80 (to check understanding of the selection)
First-Person Point of View p. 73 (for practice of literary analysis standards focus)
Question Support p. 81 (**After Reading** questions adapted for English learners and less-proficient readers)

Additional selection questions are provided for teachers on page 67.

ANSWERS

Comprehension

1. *Martha could not earn a jacket through sports because her family could not afford the fees. So, winning a scholarship jacket was the only way to obtain one.*

2. *The teachers argue over whether to falsify records that would result in Joann getting the jacket instead of Martha.*

3. *The principal seems angry. He mutters and looks out the window as if to calm himself.*

4. *Martha wants the jacket because it represents eight years of hard work and expectation (line 83). She feels she has earned it.*

Literary Analysis

Possible answers:

5. ■ **STANDARDS FOCUS** *Make Inferences Some of students' inferences may change as a result of information learned later in the story. For example, they may have inferred that the principal was a hard man but revised their inference after he gives the jacket to Martha.*

6. *If Mr. Boone made that statement, it could mean that Martha should not get the jacket because she is Mexican. If Mr. Schmidt said it, it could be a warning that they should not discriminate against Martha because she is Mexican.*

7. **Mr. Boone:** *reveals the reason that Martha may not get the jacket;* **Mr. Schmidt:** *defends Martha and shows that there is another side to the argument;* **The grandfather:** *teaches Martha to stand by her principles;* **The principal:** *is the antagonist of the story who establishes the conflict.*

After Reading

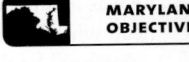

Comprehension

1. **Recall** Why does Martha call the scholarship jacket "our only chance"?

2. **Clarify** What do Mr. Boone and Mr. Schmidt argue about?

3. **Clarify** How does the principal respond when Martha says her grandfather will not pay for the jacket?

4. **Summarize** Tell why the scholarship jacket is so important to Martha. Cite evidence from the story.

Literary Analysis

5. **Make Inferences** Review the inferences that you recorded in equations. Have any of your inferences changed after reading the entire story? If necessary, write a revised inference next to the equation. Be prepared to explain your reasons for changing an inference or keeping the original.

6. **Interpret** Reread lines 47–48. During the teachers' argument, one of the teachers says, "Martha is Mexican." What could he mean by this?

7. **Analyze Character** Martha is the main character in the story. Use a web to describe how the minor characters interact with Martha and what effect they have on the story.

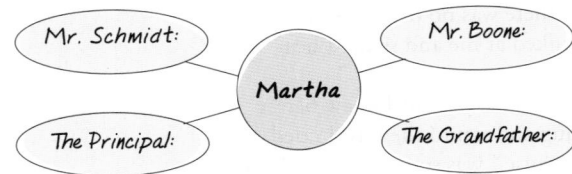

8. **Draw Conclusions** Martha's grandfather says little, but his words and actions mean much to Martha. What does Martha learn from him? Explain how you came to this conclusion.

9. **Evaluate First-Person Point of View** Think about how the story might change if you knew everyone's thoughts and feelings. In what ways would the story be different?

Extension and Challenge

10. **Big Question Activity** How would Martha answer the Big Question on page 216? Write a thank-you speech for Martha to give when she receives her scholarship jacket. In the speech, mention the **obstacles** Martha had to overcome in order to achieve this award.

---

8. *Martha learns that she should not compromise her principles. When her grandfather asks what the scholarship jacket means (lines 96–97), he helps her see that she should never need to buy something that she has already earned.*

9. ● **STANDARDS FOCUS** *First-Person Point of View The effect of the story might be different if readers knew what other characters were thinking and feeling. For example, the principal might come across as a more sympathetic character.*

Extension and Challenge

10. *Students' speeches should be written from Martha's point of view. They should include an acknowledgment of the honor of receiving a scholarship jacket and should also mention the valuable lesson she learned through refusing to compromise her principles in order to achieve her dream.*

Vocabulary in Context

VOCABULARY PRACTICE

Answer each question to show your understanding of the vocabulary words.

1. Which is a way to **falsify**—forging a signature or correcting an error?
2. Would an **agile** person be more likely to sing well or run quickly?
3. If I began to **despair**, would I more likely mingle with others or keep to myself?
4. Which is the more **vile** material—rotting garbage or rose petals?
5. Would losing one's glasses or having lunch with friends more likely cause **dismay**?
6. If you were going to **eavesdrop**, would you talk on the phone or listen behind a door?

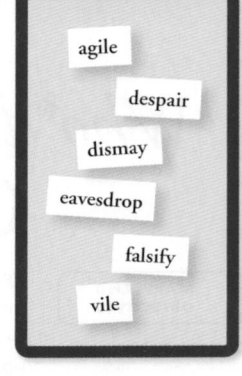

agile

despair

dismay

eavesdrop

falsify

vile

VOCABULARY IN WRITING

If someone asked you to summarize this story, what would you say? Use at least three vocabulary words in your account of the story's events. Here is a sample beginning.

> **EXAMPLE SENTENCE**
> Martha did not mean to **eavesdrop**, but she overheard an argument.

VOCABULARY STRATEGY: CONTEXT CLUES

Sometimes writers tell you directly what difficult words mean. This kind of context clue, a **definition**, usually follows the difficult word. It is set off by commas or dashes or by expressions like *that is*. Look for a definition of *valedictorian* on page 218 of this story.

Sometimes the definition might be in the form of a **synonym**, a word that has the same or similar meaning. Look for *falsify* and its synonym in the same sentence on page 220 of this story.

PRACTICE Define the boldfaced words. Identify context clues that helped you understand the meaning of the word.

1. Loretta is a **polygot**—that is, someone who knows several languages.
2. The hurricane began as an **amorphous** mass—a shapeless group of clouds.
3. When I **disparaged** him, he put me down in the same way.
4. She was not simply happy to receive the gift; she was **euphoric**.
5. The sleep clinic treats **somnambulists**, people who walk in their sleep.

 MARYLAND OBJECTIVES

READING STANDARD
1.D.3.a Use context to determine the meanings of words

 VOCABULARY PRACTICE
For more practice, go to the **Vocabulary Center** at ClassZone.com.

THE SCHOLARSHIP JACKET **225**

DIFFERENTIATED INSTRUCTION

FOR ENGLISH LEARNERS
Vocabulary in Writing

1. Help students list the major story events in a chart.
2. Work together to write a summary of the story.
3. Give pairs of students two of the sentences from the summary to rewrite, using vocabulary words.

FOR ADVANCED LEARNERS/PRE–AP
Vocabulary Practice Have students work together to write clues and create a crossword for the vocabulary words. Have pairs exchange their crosswords to see if they can complete each other's puzzles.

ANSWERS

Vocabulary in Context
VOCABULARY PRACTICE

1. *forging a signature;* **2.** *run quickly;* **3.** *keep to myself;* **4.** *rotting garbage;* **5.** *losing one's glasses;* **6.** *listen behind a door*

 **RESOURCE MANAGER—Copy Master**
Vocabulary Practice p. 78

VOCABULARY IN WRITING

Suggest that students organize the main story events in a Story Map to help them figure out where best to use the words.

BEST PRACTICES TOOLKIT—Transparency
Story Map p. D16

VOCABULARY STRATEGY: CONTEXT CLUES
(also an EL language objective)

Remind students that sometimes synonyms for unfamiliar words occur in an introductory clause in the same sentence or in a preceding or later sentence.

Answers:
1. *someone who knows several languages*
2. *shapeless*
3. *put down*
4. *happy*
5. *people who walk in their sleep*

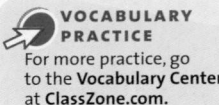 **RESOURCE MANAGER—Copy Master**
Vocabulary Strategy p. 79

i Vocabulary Center at **ClassZone.com**
Additional Vocabulary Activities

Assess and Reteach

Assess

RESOURCE MANAGER—Copy Masters
Selection Tests A, B/C pp. 83–84, 85–86

Test Generator CD

Reteach

STANDARDS LESSON FILE
Literature Lesson 10: Narrator
Literature Lesson 11: Point of View
Reading Lesson 8: Making Inferences
Vocabulary Lesson 13: Context Clues
(definition and restatement)

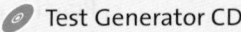 THE SCHOLARSHIP JACKET **225**

Focus and Motivate

OBJECTIVES

Literary Analysis
- explore the key idea of a second **chance**
- recognize and analyze omniscient point of view
- read a short story

Reading
- predict

Vocabulary
- build vocabulary for reading and writing
- use context clues to determine the meanings of multiple-meaning words *(also an EL language objective)*

Grammar and Writing
- use comparatives and superlatives
- use writing to analyze literature

SUMMARY

Jimmy Valentine, a notorious safecracker, is released from prison and falls in love with Annabel, a banker's daughter. He forges a new and honest identity for himself. Shortly before their wedding, Annabel's niece is accidentally locked in the bank vault. Jimmy saves her, and in a surprising twist, the detective who has come to arrest him lets him go.

Who deserves a second CHANCE?

Have students read the *KEY IDEA* paragraph, and then discuss the question. Ask students who might decide to give someone a second **chance.** Elicit that it might be an individual, a group, or society as a whole. Then have students complete the *DISCUSS* activity.

Selection Resources

A Retrieved Reformation
Short Story by O. Henry

Who deserves a second CHANCE?

MARYLAND OBJECTIVES

READING/LIT STANDARDS
1.E.4.d Confirm, refute, or make predictions
3.A.3.i Analyze point of view

KEY IDEA Everybody makes mistakes—sometimes bad ones. But some people, if they're lucky, are given a **chance** to redeem themselves. In "A Retrieved Reformation," a man has the opportunity to change his scheming ways. Will he take it?

DISCUSS With a small group, think of one or two individuals who could have used a second chance. Perhaps it's a coach who had a losing season. Maybe it's someone who betrayed a friend's secret. What criteria could be used to determine whether that person deserves another chance?

226

RESOURCE MANAGER UNIT 2

Plan and Teach pp. 87–94

Literary Analysis
Summary pp. 95†*, 96‡*
Omniscient Point of View pp. 97, 98†*
Question Support p. 105*

Reading
Predict pp. 99, 100†*
Reading Check p. 104
Reading Fluency p. 107

Vocabulary
Study p. 101*
Practice p. 102
Strategy p. 103

Grammar and Writing
Compare Correctly p. 106

Assessment
Selection Tests A, B/C pp. 109*, 111*
Test Generator CD

BEST PRACTICES TOOLKIT

Differentiated Instruction
pp. 31–38*

Scaffolding Instruction pp. 43–46*

Graphic Organizers/Strategies
Word Squares • New Word Analysis • T Chart • Read Aloud/Think Aloud • Comparison Matrix • Cluster Diagram

Reading Support
Audio Anthology CD*

Technology
Literature and Vocabulary Centers at **ClassZone.com**

Write*Smart* CD

---

* Resources for Differentiation   **† Also in Spanish**   **‡ In Haitian Creole and Vietnamese**

UNIT 2: ANALYZING CHARACTER AND POINT OF VIEW

LITERARY ANALYSIS: OMNISCIENT POINT OF VIEW

What would it be like to know what all your friends are thinking? The feeling would be similar to reading a story written in the **third-person omniscient point of view.** An omniscient, or all-knowing, narrator

- tells the story using the pronouns *he, she, it,* and *they*
- is aware of what all the characters in the story are thinking and doing

As you read "A Retrieved Reformation," notice when you have more information than the characters do.

READING STRATEGY: PREDICT

One way to make reading a story even more interesting is to **predict** what will happen next. Your predictions won't always be correct, but finding out whether they are correct or not can be fun. As you read "A Retrieved Reformation," record your predictions in a chart like the one shown.

My Prediction	Reason for Prediction
Jimmy will keep cracking safes.	

Review: **Make Inferences**

VOCABULARY IN CONTEXT

The boldfaced words help tell the story of a man who is given another chance. Figure out the meaning of each word by using the context clues in each of the phrases.

1. **saunter** casually through the park
2. might **balk** and change his mind at the last minute
3. friendly neighbors chatting **genially**
4. an upright, **virtuous** individual
5. **compulsory** attendance with no excuses allowed
6. slipped away like an **elusive** butterfly
7. tried to **rehabilitate** the injured man
8. honored to have such an **eminent** guest
9. a suitcase in the corner **unperceived** by anyone
10. promised **retribution** if the offender was caught

Author Online

An Early Reader
How could one of the most famous short story writers of all time die with only 23 cents in his pocket? That is what happened to William Sydney Porter, better known as O. Henry. Porter's adventures

O. Henry
1862–1910

began in the home of his aunt, who raised him. She encouraged the young boy's love of reading, writing, and drawing caricatures, which are comically exaggerated representations of people. The sense of humor seen in his drawings often appears in his writing.

No Ordinary Life Porter continued writing and illustrating throughout his adult life in addition to working as a pharmacist, ranch hand, cook, and bank teller. Several years after leaving his position at the First National Bank of Austin, Texas, he was convicted of stealing money from the bank. He published several short stories from jail, using the pen name O. Henry in order to conceal his criminal record.

A Real Character Porter's vast experiences serve as the inspiration for most of his stories. The main character in "A Retrieved Reformation" is based on a safecracker (someone who breaks into safes) who Porter met in prison.

 MORE ABOUT THE AUTHOR
For more on O. Henry, visit the **Literature Center** at **ClassZone.com**.

A RETRIEVED REFORMATION **227**

Teach

STANDARDS FOCUS

● OMNISCIENT POINT OF VIEW

Read aloud this example:

> The guidance counselor felt relieved as he read the teacher's note. The student sitting in front of him, nervously wondering what was to happen to her, would get a second chance after all.

Ask students how they know that the point of view is third-person omniscient. *Possible answer: Third-person pronouns are used. The narrator knows what each character thinks and feels.*

CHECK UNDERSTANDING Ask students to think of a fairy tale or myth. Is it told from an omniscient point of view? How do they know?

READING STRATEGY

■ PREDICT

Explain that when readers predict, they combine information from the text with their prior knowledge to guess what might happen next. Ask students to predict how the student in the example above will feel when she hears the news. *Possible answer: She will be happy.*

CHECK UNDERSTANDING Ask students to make a prediction about this story based on its title and the facts on page 227.

 RESOURCE MANAGER—Copy Master
Predict p. 99 (for student use while reading the selection)

▲ VOCABULARY IN CONTEXT

DIAGNOSE WORD KNOWLEDGE To determine preteaching needs, have all students complete **Vocabulary in Context.** Check students' answers against the definitions in the text: *saunter* (p. 235), *balk* (p. 230), *genially* (p. 231), *virtuous* (p. 230), *compulsory* (p. 230), *elusive* (p. 231), *rehabilitate* (p. 230), *eminent* (p. 230), *unperceived* (p. 235), *retribution* (p. 231).

PRETEACH VOCABULARY Use the Vocabulary Study copy master to help students explore the meaning of each boldfaced word.
1. Read item 1 aloud, emphasizing *balk*.
2. Point out the phrase *refusal to move.* Elicit possible meanings for *balk*, such as "stop."
3. Discuss in which category of Part B the word *balk* belongs.
4. Repeat the procedure for items 2–10.

 RESOURCE MANAGER—Copy Master
Vocabulary Study p. 101

For general guidelines on differentiating vocabulary instruction and for alternative vocabulary activities for students not needing vocabulary preteaching, see

BEST PRACTICES TOOLKIT
Scaffolding Vocabulary Instruction pp. 43–46

Vocabulary Center at **ClassZone.com**

ANALYZE VISUALS

Possible answer: The man has a strong chin, chiseled features, and a direct gaze. These aspects make him appear determined and forthright. He is dressed nicely and looks very respectable.

About the Art The American artist Norman Rockwell (1894–1978) is perhaps best known for his magazine cover illustrations, most notably for the *Saturday Evening Post*. His art creates vivid impressions of common people, such as the man shown here, and of everyday life in small towns in America.

Lines 1–11
DISCUSSION PROMPTS

Use these prompts to help students begin to build a picture of Jimmy Valentine's character:

Connect When you are required to do something, how does that affect your attitude toward the task? Does it surprise you that Jimmy works so hard and carefully at his prison job? Explain. *Students may say they are surprised, because being required to do a job can take all the fun out of it. They might expect Jimmy to put in the least possible effort.*

Analyze What can you infer from the fact that Jimmy has many friends on the "outside"? *Possible answer: He is likeable. He may do favors for people.*

Evaluate Based on the warden's words, is Jimmy Valentine a tough, hardened criminal? Why or why not? *Possible answer: The warden says that Jimmy has a good heart and could live a law-abiding existence if he wanted to (lines 10–11). Those words suggest that the warden does not see Jimmy as being past redemption.*

LITERARY ANALYSIS

Ⓐ OMNISCIENT POINT OF VIEW

Possible answer: Jimmy's friends on the outside will make sure he doesn't have to stay in jail for his whole sentence.

A *Retrieved* REFORMATION

O. Henry

A guard came to the prison shoe shop, where Jimmy Valentine was assiduously stitching uppers,[1] and escorted him to the front office. There the warden handed Jimmy his pardon, which had been signed that morning by the governor. Jimmy took it in a tired kind of way. He had served nearly ten months of a four-year sentence. He had expected to stay only about three months, at the longest. When a man with as many friends on the outside as Jimmy Valentine had is received in the "stir"[2] it is hardly worthwhile to cut his hair. Ⓐ

"Now, Valentine," said the warden, "you'll go out in the morning.
10 Brace up, and make a man of yourself. You're not a bad fellow at heart. Stop cracking safes, and live straight."

"Me?" said Jimmy, in surprise. "Why, I never cracked a safe in my life."

"Oh, no," laughed the warden. "Of course not. Let's see, now. How was it you happened to get sent up on that Springfield job? Was it because you wouldn't prove an alibi for fear of compromising somebody in extremely high-toned society? Or was it simply a case of a mean old jury that had it in for you? It's always one or the other with you innocent victims."

---

1. **assiduously** (ə-sĭj′ōō-əs-lē) **stitching uppers:** carefully and industriously sewing together the top portions of shoes.
2. **"stir":** a slang term for prison.

ANALYZE VISUALS
What do the details in the painting help you **infer** about this man?

① **Targeted Passage**

Ⓐ **OMNISCIENT POINT OF VIEW**
Writers sometimes use the omniscient point of view to make general comments about life. Reread lines 6–8. What does this comment mean?

Detail of *Tides of Memory* (1936), Norman Rockwell. Oil on board, 18¾″ × 15¼″

DIFFERENTIATED INSTRUCTION

FOR ALL STUDENTS
Enhancing Learning Styles Provide independent projects for various learning styles.

- **Spatial** Draw a diagram of the story plot on a large poster board.
- **Visual** Create a "wanted" poster for Jimmy.
- **Linguistic** Write an alternate ending to the story. If possible, include a surprise twist.

For further details on these projects, see

R RESOURCE MANAGER
Ideas for Extension pp. 92–93

FOR LESS–PROFICIENT READERS
In combination with the *Audio Anthology CD*, use one or more Targeted Passages (pp. 228, 231, 233, 236) to ensure that students focus on key story events, concepts, and skills.

① Targeted Passage [Lines 1–11]

This passage introduces the main character (Jimmy Valentine) and presents the essential facts of his situation: he is a safecracker who has a second chance to live an honest life.

Safecracking The main character in this story, Jimmy Valentine, is a safecracker. He opens safes illegally and steals the money and other valuables stored inside. There are different ways to crack a safe. One method is by determining the combination of the lock, sometimes done by listening to clicks of the lock and graphing the results. A second and more common procedure for opening a safe illegally is by drilling. Jimmy Valentine has his own set of tools, including "the latest designs in drills" (line 52), indicating that this is the method he prefers. Using explosives is a crude but often effective third way to penetrate a safe (line 226).

- How long has Jimmy been in prison?
- What is his prison job?
- What crime did Jimmy commit, according to the prison warden?
- What does the warden tell Jimmy to do with his life?

FOR ENGLISH LEARNERS

Key Academic Vocabulary Have students create Word Squares to learn this vocabulary: *panel* (line 49), *designs* (line 52), *currency* (line 70), *community* (line 142), *implements* (line 240).

 BEST PRACTICES TOOLKIT—Transparency Word Squares p. E10

Prereading For prereading instruction for English learners, see

 BEST PRACTICES TOOLKIT Scaffolding Reading Instruction pp. 43–46

FOR ADVANCED LEARNERS/PRE–AP

Pre-AP exercises in the bottom channel provide additional challenge for your advanced students. Use them for small groups or individuals.

ADDITIONAL GUIDELINES

For more help with differentiation and tips for classroom management, see

 BEST PRACTICES TOOLKIT Differentiated Instruction pp. 31–38

Lines 45–56
DISCUSSION PROMPTS

Use these prompts to help students identify important characteristics of Ben Price and Jimmy Valentine that will help them make accurate future predictions:

Connect How does Jimmy feel about his burglary tools? How can you tell? *Students may say that the tools are Jimmy's most prized possession. They are the first thing he looks for when he gets back to his room. He gazes at them "fondly" and takes pride in the tools he invented himself. They are worth a lot of money.*

Infer What is Jimmy's attitude toward safe-cracking? What does this tell you about his personality? *Possible answer: He takes safe-cracking seriously and enjoys doing it well. He is probably a person who likes to take risks and challenge himself with difficult tasks.*

Compare Ben Price is described as "that eminent detective" (line 47). What might he and Jimmy have in common? *Possible answer: Both men are very good at what they do, although one is a thief and the other is a law officer.*

"Me?" said Jimmy, still blankly **virtuous.** "Why, warden, I never was in Springfield in my life!"

20 "Take him back, Cronin," smiled the warden, "and fix him up with outgoing clothes. Unlock him at seven in the morning, and let him come to the bull-pen. Better think over my advice, Valentine."

At a quarter past seven on the next morning Jimmy stood in the warden's outer office. He had on a suit of the villainously fitting, ready-made clothes and a pair of the stiff, squeaky shoes that the state furnishes to its discharged **compulsory** guests.

The clerk handed him a railroad ticket and the five-dollar bill with which the law expected him to **rehabilitate** himself into good citizenship and prosperity. The warden gave him a cigar, and shook hands. Valentine, 30 9762, was chronicled[3] on the books "Pardoned by Governor," and Mr. James Valentine walked out into the sunshine.

Disregarding the song of the birds, the waving green trees, and the smell of the flowers, Jimmy headed straight for a restaurant. There he tasted the first sweet joys of liberty in the shape of a broiled chicken and a bottle of white wine—followed by a cigar a grade better than the one the warden had given him. From there he proceeded leisurely to the depot. He tossed a quarter into the hat of a blind man sitting by the door, and boarded his train. Three hours set him down in a little town near the state line. He went to the café of one Mike Dolan and shook hands with 40 Mike, who was alone behind the bar.

"Sorry we couldn't make it sooner, Jimmy, me boy," said Mike. "But we had that protest from Springfield to buck against, and the governor nearly **balked.** Feeling all right?"

"Fine," said Jimmy. "Got my key?"

He got his key and went upstairs, unlocking the door of a room at the rear. Everything was just as he had left it. There on the floor was still Ben Price's collar-button that had been torn from that **eminent** detective's shirt-band when they had overpowered Jimmy to arrest him.

Pulling out from the wall a folding-bed, Jimmy slid back a panel in the 50 wall and dragged out a dust-covered suitcase. He opened this and gazed fondly at the finest set of burglar's tools in the East. It was a complete set, made of specially tempered steel, the latest designs in drills, punches, braces and bits, jimmies, clamps, and augers, with two or three novelties invented by Jimmy himself, in which he took pride. Over nine hundred dollars they had cost him to have made at _____, a place where they make such things for the profession.

---

3. **chronicled** (krŏn′ĭ-kəld): written down in a record book or ledger book.

virtuous
(vûr′chōo-əs) *adj.*
morally good; honorable

compulsory
(kəm-pŭl′sə-rē) *adj.*
forced; required

rehabilitate
(rē′hə-bĭl′ĭ-tāt′) *v.* to restore to useful life, as through therapy and education

balk (bôk) *v.* to refuse to move or act

eminent (ĕm′ə-nənt) *ad...* famous; well-respected

DIFFERENTIATED INSTRUCTION

FOR ENGLISH LEARNERS

Vocabulary: Idioms and Slang Explain that many expressions in this story are idioms or slang from the late 1800s. Have small groups use New Word Analysis to identify the meanings of these and other phrases: *cracking safes, live straight* (line 11), "opening safes illegally," "live respectably"; *set him down in* (line 38), "took him to"; *buck against* (line 42), "fight against"; *got anything on* (line 60), "do you have a job planned."

 BEST PRACTICES TOOLKIT—Transparency
New Word Analysis p. E8

FOR ADVANCED LEARNERS/PRE–AP

Analyze Irony Verbal irony means saying something contrary to the truth to make a point— what is stated is not what is meant. Dramatic irony occurs when the audience knows more information than the characters. Distribute copies of a T Chart that students can use to record and explain examples of irony that they identify throughout the story. Have students share their completed charts.

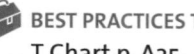 BEST PRACTICES TOOLKIT—Transparency
T Chart p. A25

Example of Irony	Why It Is Ironic
describing the inmates of prison as "guests" (line 26)	"Guest" suggests being invited to a place you want to be, which is the opposite of prison.
Jimmy immediately takes out his safe-cracking kit. (lines 49–56)	He has been out of prison only a few hours and is already planning his return to a "life of crime."

In half an hour Jimmy went downstairs and through the café. He was now dressed in tasteful and well-fitting clothes, and carried his dusted and cleaned suitcase in his hand. **B**

60 "Got anything on?" asked Mike Dolan, **genially.**

"Me?" said Jimmy, in a puzzled tone. "I don't understand. I'm representing the New York Amalgamated Short Snap Biscuit Cracker and Frazzled Wheat Company."

This statement delighted Mike to such an extent that Jimmy had to take a seltzer-and-milk on the spot. He never touched "hard" drinks.

A week after the release of Valentine, 9762, there was a neat job of safe-burglary done in Richmond, Indiana, with no clue to the author. A scant eight hundred dollars was all that was secured. Two weeks after that a patented, improved, burglar-proof safe in Logansport was
70 opened like a cheese to the tune of fifteen hundred dollars, currency; securities and silver untouched. That began to interest the rogue catchers.[4] Then an old-fashioned bank safe in Jefferson City became active and threw out of its crater an eruption of banknotes amounting to five thousand dollars. The losses were now high enough to bring the matter up into Ben Price's class of work. By comparing notes, a remarkable similarity in the methods of the burglaries was noticed. Ben Price investigated the scenes of the robberies, and was heard to remark: "That's Dandy Jim Valentine's autograph. He's resumed business. Look at that combination knob—jerked out as easy as pulling up a radish in wet weather. He's got
80 the only clamps that can do it. And look how clean those tumblers were punched out! Jimmy never has to drill but one hole. Yes, I guess I want Mr. Valentine. He'll do his bit next time without any short-time or clemency foolishness."[5]

Ben Price knew Jimmy's habits. He had learned them while working up the Springfield case. Long jumps, quick get-aways, no confederates,[6] and a taste for good society—these ways had helped Mr. Valentine to become noted as a successful dodger of **retribution.** It was given out that Ben Price had taken up the trail of the **elusive** cracksman, and other people with burglar-proof safes felt more at ease. **C**

90 One afternoon Jimmy Valentine and his suitcase climbed out of the mailhack in Elmore, a little town five miles off the railroad down in the blackjack country of Arkansas. Jimmy, looking like an athletic young senior just home from college, went down the board sidewalk toward the hotel.

---

4. **rogue** (rōg) **catchers:** people who chase after criminals.

5. **He'll do his bit . . . foolishness:** He'll serve his full term in prison without anyone shortening the length of it or pardoning him.

6. **confederates** (kən-fĕd′ər-ĭts): accomplices or associates in crime.

2 Targeted Passage

B PREDICT
On the basis of Jimmy's actions in this paragraph, what do you predict he will do?

genially (jēn′yəl-lē) *adv.* in a pleasant, friendly manner

retribution (rĕt′rə-byōō′shən) *n.* punishment for bad behavior

elusive (ĭ-lōō′sĭv) *adj.* tending to elude capture

C OMNISCIENT POINT OF VIEW
Reread lines 84–89. What information does the narrator share with you that the main character, Jimmy, doesn't know?

A RETRIEVED REFORMATION **231**

B PREDICT

Record students' answers in the chart from page 227.

Possible answer:

My Prediction	Reason for Prediction
Jimmy will return to a life of crime.	Jimmy picks up his safecracking tools the minute he is released from prison.

If students need help . . . Model how to make predictions by applying the Read Aloud/Think Aloud strategy to lines 49–63.

🧰 BEST PRACTICES TOOLKIT—Transparency Read Aloud/Think Aloud p. A34

Lines 66–83
REINFORCE *KEY IDEA*: CHANCE

Discuss What has Jimmy done with the second **chance** he received? Do you think the warden was wrong when he said Jimmy is "not a bad fellow at heart"? *Possible answer: Jimmy has gone right back to safecracking after getting out of prison. Some students may say the warden was wrong about Jimmy, who seems to feel no shame about his criminal behavior. Others may argue that Jimmy simply doesn't know any other way to make a living, and that his crimes are not violent.*

LITERARY ANALYSIS

C OMNISCIENT POINT OF VIEW

Possible answer: Ben Price is chasing Jimmy.

Extend the Discussion What details support the inference that Ben Price has a good chance of catching Jimmy Valentine?

BACKGROUND

The "blackjack country of Arkansas" (line 92) refers to the western part of the state, near its border with Oklahoma. The blackjack oak tree, a member of the red oak family with black bark, is common in this region. The town of Elmore, Arkansas, is fictional.

FOR LESS–PROFICIENT READERS

2 Targeted Passage [Lines 66–83]

This passage sets up the major conflict: Ben Price is out to capture Jimmy for robberies committed after Jimmy's release from prison.

• How many safecracking jobs does Jimmy carry out in the few months after his release?

• How does the detective Ben Price know that Jimmy committed these crimes?

• What is Ben Price determined to do?

FOR ADVANCED LEARNERS/PRE–AP

Analyze Author's Craft Point out the simile in lines 69–70 that shows the effortlessness with which Jimmy carries out his burglaries. Have students identify the other figures of speech on this page. Then challenge them to create original similes or metaphors that convey the same idea. List examples on the board and have the class vote on which ones capture the tone and style of O. Henry most closely.

A young lady crossed the street, passed him at the corner, and entered a door over which was the sign "The Elmore Bank." Jimmy Valentine looked into her eyes, forgot what he was, and became another man. She lowered her eyes and colored slightly. Young men of Jimmy's style and looks were scarce in Elmore.

100 Jimmy collared a boy that was loafing on the steps of the bank as if he were one of the stockholders, and began to ask him questions about the town, feeding him dimes at intervals. By and by the young lady came out, looking royally unconscious of the young man with the suitcase, and went her way.

"Isn't that young lady Miss Polly Simpson?" asked Jimmy, with specious guile.[7]

"Naw," said the boy. "She's Annabel Adams. Her pa owns this bank. What'd you come to Elmore for? Is that a gold watch-chain? I'm going to get a bulldog. Got any more dimes?" D

110 Jimmy went to the Planters' Hotel, registered as Ralph D. Spencer, and engaged a room. He leaned on the desk and declared his platform to the clerk. He said he had come to Elmore to look for a location to go into business. How was the shoe business, now, in the town? He had thought of the shoe business. Was there an opening? E

The clerk was impressed by the clothes and manner of Jimmy. He, himself, was something of a pattern of fashion to the thinly gilded youth of Elmore, but he now perceived his shortcomings. While trying to figure out Jimmy's manner of tying his four-in-hand[8] he cordially gave information.

120 Yes, there ought to be a good opening in the shoe line. There wasn't an exclusive shoe store in the place. The dry-goods and general stores handled them. Business in all lines was fairly good. Hoped Mr. Spencer would decide to locate in Elmore. He would find it a pleasant town to live in, and the people 130 very sociable.

Eleanor (1907), Frank Weston Benson. Oil on canvas, 64.13 cm × 76.83 cm. The Hayden Collection–Charles Henry Hayden Fund. © Museum of Fine Arts, Boston (08.326).

---

7. **specious guile** (spē'shəs gīl): innocent charm masking real slyness.

8. **four-in-hand:** a necktie tied in the usual way, that is, in a slipknot with the ends left hanging.

DIFFERENTIATED INSTRUCTION

FOR LESS–PROFICIENT READERS

Reading Strategy Follow-Up: Predict Point out that readers make predictions based on details in the text as well as prior knowledge. Then have small groups of students use these details to predict what Jimmy will do next: *Jimmy made shoes in prison; Jimmy is attracted to Annabel; Jimmy changes his name; Jimmy asks the clerk about shoe stores in Elmore.* Have students share their predictions and read further to verify them.

Review: Make Inferences List the facts that are known about Annabel Adams. Then discuss the position of young ladies in the late 1800s. Using these ideas, help students make inferences about the character of Annabel. *(She leads a sheltered life, her parents most likely make important decisions for her, she has little independence, and she must behave in a respectable way.)* Then ask students to infer the kind of man she would be expected to marry and what that means for Jimmy.

Mr. Spencer thought he would stop over in the town a few days and look over the situation. No, the clerk needn't call the boy. He would carry up his suitcase, himself; it was rather heavy.

Mr. Ralph Spencer, the phoenix[9] that arose from Jimmy Valentine's ashes—ashes left by the flame of a sudden and alterative attack of love—remained in Elmore, and prospered. He opened a shoe store and secured a good run of trade. **F**

Socially he was also a success and made many friends. And he accomplished the wish of his heart. He met Miss Annabel Adams, 140 and became more and more captivated by her charms.

At the end of a year the situation of Mr. Ralph Spencer was this: he had won the respect of the community, his shoe store was flourishing, and he and Annabel were engaged to be married in two weeks. Mr. Adams, the typical, plodding, country banker, approved of Spencer. Annabel's pride in him almost equaled her affection. He was as much at home in the family of Mr. Adams and that of Annabel's married sister as if he were already a member.

One day Jimmy sat down in his room and wrote this letter, which he mailed to the safe address of one of his old friends in St. Louis:

150 *Dear Old Pal:*

I want you to be at Sullivan's place, in Little Rock, next Wednesday night, at nine o'clock. I want you to wind up some little matters for me. And, also, I want to make you a present of my kit of tools. I know you'll be glad to get them—you couldn't duplicate the lot for a thousand dollars. Say, Billy, I've quit the old business—a year ago. I've got a nice store. I'm making an honest living, and I'm going to marry the finest girl on earth two weeks from now. It's the only life, Billy—the straight one. I wouldn't touch a dollar of another man's money now for a million. After I get married I'm
160 *going to sell out and go West, where there won't be so much danger of having old scores brought up against me. I tell you, Billy, she's an angel. She believes in me; and I wouldn't do another crooked thing for the whole world. Be sure to be at Sully's, for I must see you. I'll bring along the tools with me.* **G**

> *Your old friend,*
> *Jimmy*

---

9. **phoenix** (fē'nĭks): a mythological bird that lived for 500 years and then burned itself to death, only to rise from its own ashes to live another long life.

Sidebar annotations (story margin)

F OMNISCIENT POINT OF VIEW
Who in the story knows that Ralph Spencer is also Jimmy Valentine?

3 Targeted Passage

G PREDICT
Do you think Jimmy will ever crack another safe? Why or why not?

LITERARY ANALYSIS

F OMNISCIENT POINT OF VIEW

Possible answer: Only Jimmy himself knows about his assumed identity.

Lines 134–147
REINFORCE *KEY IDEA*: CHANCE

Discuss What events have given Jimmy another **chance** to redeem himself? Do you think his reformation will last? *Possible answer: Falling in love with Annabel and opening a shoe store have allowed Jimmy to turn his life around. Some students may say that his reformation will last because of his devotion to Annabel. Others may say that he could slip back into his old ways if he gets the urge to crack a safe or if his business starts to fail.*

READING STRATEGY

G PREDICT

You may wish to record students' answers in the chart from page 227. Discuss the evidence that supports their predictions. *Possible answer:*

My Prediction	Reason for Prediction
No. He will not crack another safe.	He is giving away his tools. He has stayed away from crime for a year, even though he has access to Annabel's father's bank.

FOR LESS–PROFICIENT READERS

3 Targeted Passage [Lines 148–166]

This passage is an important turning point in the story: Jimmy has reformed and wants to give away his safecracking tools.

- To whom is Jimmy giving his tools? Why?
- Why does he want to go out West after he and Annabel marry?
- Why does he say he won't ever do a dishonest thing again?

FOR ENGLISH LEARNERS

Comprehension: Concept Support Make sure students understand that Valentine and Spencer are the same person with different lifestyles. Help students compare the two identities by completing a Comparison Matrix. Label the two parts "Before Meeting Annabel" and "After." Include similarities, such as Jimmy's work ethic, sense of style, and charming personality, in the center space.

BEST PRACTICES TOOLKIT—Transparency
Comparison Matrix p. A24

ANALYZE VISUALS

Possible answer: The bright elements of the painting—the blue sky and the sunlight touching the pedestrians, buggy, and car—create an optimistic and cheerful mood, suggesting the progress of humankind. At the same time, the darker shadows and colors may suggest some uncertainty about the future and the many changes to daily life it will bring.

About the Art American artist John Sloan (1871–1951) was a leader in the American Social Realism movement and a founding member of the Ashcan School. The Ashcan artists painted scenes of New York City around the turn of the 20th century, when the city was rapidly changing into a modern metropolis. Sloan is well known for his street scenes, such as this one, in which he tells stories through contrasts. *Hill Street* shows an automobile speeding past a horse-drawn cart, illustrating just one way in which urban life was changing in the early 1900s.

Hill Street (1916), John Sloan. The Parrish Art Museum Collection, Southhampton, New York.

On the Monday night after Jimmy wrote this letter, Ben Price jogged unobtrusively into Elmore in a livery buggy.[10] He lounged about town in his quiet way until he found out what he wanted to know. From the
170 drugstore across the street from Spencer's shoe store he got a good look at Ralph D. Spencer.

"Going to marry the banker's daughter are you, Jimmy?" said Ben to himself, softly. "Well, I don't know!"

The next morning Jimmy took breakfast at the Adamses. He was going to Little Rock that day to order his wedding suit and buy something nice for Annabel. That would be the first time he had left town since he came to Elmore. It had been more than a year now since those last professional "jobs," and he thought he could safely venture out. ❶
After breakfast quite a family party went down together—Mr. Adams,
180 Annabel, Jimmy, and Annabel's married sister with her two little girls,

ANALYZE VISUALS
What **mood** do the colors in the painting suggest?

❶ OMNISCIENT POINT OF VIEW
What do you know that Jimmy doesn't know at this point?

---

10. **livery** (lĭv'ə-rē) **buggy:** a hired horse and carriage.

234 UNIT 2: ANALYZING CHARACTER AND POINT OF VIEW

DIFFERENTIATED INSTRUCTION

FOR ENGLISH LEARNERS
Vocabulary: Multiple-Meaning Words Have students form mixed-ability pairs to determine the meanings of these words in context, using a dictionary as necessary.

- *jogged* (line 167), "rode slowly in a horse-drawn carriage"
- *lounged* (line 168), "moved in a relaxed way"
- *party* (line 179), "group of people"
- *boarded* (line 181), "lived in a hotel"

- *bubbling* (line 189), "showing an excess of emotion"
- *express* (line 194), "involving rapid delivery"
- *engaged* (line 204), "involved in doing something"
- *stand* (line 223), "endure or survive"
- *pet* (line 243), "favorite"

FOR ADVANCED LEARNERS/PRE–AP
Make Judgments Have students quickwrite to predict whether Jimmy's reformation is sincere. Ask them to find evidence from the text and formulate reasons that support their view. Then have them keep reading to see if their predictions are correct.

aged five and nine. They came by the hotel where Jimmy still boarded, and he ran up to his room and brought along his suitcase. Then they went on to the bank. There stood Jimmy's horse and buggy and Dolph Gibson, who was going to drive him over to the railroad station.

All went inside the high, carved oak railings into the banking room—Jimmy included, for Mr. Adams's future son-in-law was welcome anywhere. The clerks were pleased to be greeted by the good-looking, agreeable young man who was going to marry Miss Annabel. Jimmy set his suitcase down. Annabel, whose heart was bubbling with happiness and lively youth, put on Jimmy's hat and picked up the suitcase. "Wouldn't I make a nice drummer?"[11] said Annabel. "My! Ralph, how heavy it is. Feels like it was full of gold bricks."

"Lot of nickel-plated shoehorns in there," said Jimmy, coolly, "that I'm going to return. Thought I'd save express charges by taking them up. I'm getting awfully economical."

The Elmore Bank had just put in a new safe and vault. Mr. Adams was very proud of it, and insisted on an inspection by everyone. The vault was a small one, but it had a new patented door. It fastened with three solid steel bolts thrown simultaneously with a single handle, and had a time lock. Mr. Adams beamingly explained its workings to Mr. Spencer, who showed a courteous but not too intelligent interest. The two children, May and Agatha, were delighted by the shining metal and funny clock and knobs. **□**

While they were thus engaged Ben Price **sauntered** in and leaned on his elbow, looking casually inside between the railings. He told the teller that he didn't want anything; he was just waiting for a man he knew.

Suddenly there was a scream or two from the women, and a commotion. **Unperceived** by the elders, May, the nine-year-old girl, in a spirit of play, had shut Agatha in the vault. She had then shot the bolts and turned the knob of the combination as she had seen Mr. Adams do.

The old banker sprang to the handle and tugged at it for a moment. "The door can't be opened," he groaned. "The clock hasn't been wound nor the combination set."

Agatha's mother screamed again, hysterically.

"Hush!" said Mr. Adams, raising his trembling hand. "All be quiet for a moment. Agatha!" he called as loudly as he could. "Listen to me." During the following silence they could just hear the faint sound of the child wildly shrieking in the dark vault in a panic of terror.

"My precious darling!" wailed the mother. "She will die of fright! Open the door! Oh, break it open! Can't you men do something?"

---

11. **drummer:** an old-fashioned word for traveling salesman.

□ MAKE INFERENCES
Why does "Mr. Spencer" show a "courteous but not too intelligent interest" in the new safe and vault?

saunter (sôn'tər) v. to stroll in a casual manner

unperceived (ŭn-pər-sēvd') adj. not seen or noticed

Line 229–256

READING STRATEGY

J PREDICT

Possible answers:

- *Jimmy will open the safe to save Annabel's niece.*
- *Jimmy will do nothing in order to keep his criminal past hidden from Annabel.*

READING SKILL: *Review*

K MAKE INFERENCES

Possible answer: Jimmy is planning to unlock the safe. He wants Annabel's rose as a reminder of her because he expects to lose her when she learns he is a safecracker.

Line 229–256

REINFORCE *KEY IDEA:* CHANCE

Discuss How does Jimmy earn one more **chance** at an honest life? Do you think he will take it? Why? *Possible answer: Jimmy's selfless act inspires Ben to give him another chance. Jimmy may decide that the honest life is best, or he may go back to safecracking because he has lost everything else.*

READING SKILL: *Review*

L MAKE INFERENCES

Possible answer: Price understands that Jimmy's act of selflessness proves Jimmy has really changed.

SELECTION WRAP–UP

SYNTHESIZE Why does Ben Price stay to see Jimmy even though he has decided not to arrest him? *Possible answer: He wants Jimmy to know that at least one person recognizes his redemption and sacrifice.*

⭐ **CRITIQUE** Ask students to evaluate the effectiveness of third-person omniscient point of view in this story. What would the story lose or gain with a different narrator?

READING FLUENCY

Distribute the copy masters and have students work in pairs to practice fluency.

R RESOURCE MANAGER—Copy Master
Reading Fluency p. 107

"There isn't a man nearer than Little Rock who can open that door," said Mr. Adams, in a shaky voice. "My God! Spencer, what shall we do? That child—she can't stand it long in there. There isn't enough air, and, besides, she'll go into convulsions from fright." **J**

Agatha's mother, frantic now, beat the door of the vault with her hands. Somebody wildly suggested dynamite. Annabel turned to Jimmy, her large eyes full of anguish, but not yet despairing. To a woman nothing seems quite impossible to the powers of the man she worships.

"Can't you do something, Ralph—try, won't you?"

230 He looked at her with a queer, soft smile on his lips and in his keen eyes.

"Annabel," he said, "give me that rose you are wearing, will you?"

Hardly believing that she had heard him aright, she unpinned the bud from the bosom of her dress, and placed it in his hand. Jimmy stuffed it into his vest pocket, threw off his coat and pulled up his shirt sleeves. With that act Ralph D. Spencer passed away and Jimmy Valentine took his place. **K**

"Get away from the door, all of you," he commanded, shortly.

He set his suitcase on the table, and opened it out flat. From that time on he seemed to be unconscious of the presence of anyone else. He laid
240 out the shining, queer implements swiftly and orderly, whistling softly to himself as he always did when at work. In a deep silence and immovable, the others watched him as if under a spell.

In a minute Jimmy's pet drill was biting smoothly into the steel door. In ten minutes—breaking his own burglarious record—he threw back the bolts and opened the door.

Agatha, almost collapsed, but safe, was gathered into her mother's arms.

Jimmy Valentine put on his coat, and walked outside the railings toward the front door. As he went he thought he heard a faraway voice that he once knew call "Ralph!" But he never hesitated. At the door a
250 big man stood somewhat in his way.

"Hello, Ben!" said Jimmy, still with his strange smile. "Got around at last, have you? Well, let's go. I don't know that it makes much difference, now."

And then Ben Price acted rather strangely.

"Guess you're mistaken, Mr. Spencer," he said. "Don't believe I recognize you. Your buggy's waiting for you, ain't it?"

And Ben Price turned and strolled down the street. 〜 **L**

J PREDICT
On the basis of everything you know about Jimmy, what do you think he will do?

K MAKE INFERENCES
What is Jimmy preparing to do? How does he expect it to affect his relationship with Annabel?

④ Targeted Passage

L MAKE INFERENCES
Why does Ben Price let Jimmy go free?

DIFFERENTIATED INSTRUCTION

FOR LESS–PROFICIENT READERS

④ **Targeted Passage [Lines 237–256]**

This passage resolves major conflicts and presents the surprise ending: Ben Price does not arrest Jimmy.

- How long does it take Jimmy to open the safe?
- Who calls after Jimmy? Why doesn't he answer?
- What does Jimmy say to Ben Price? What does he mean?
- What is surprising about Price's response?

FOR ENGLISH LEARNERS

Vocabulary: Prefixes Point out the words *impossible* (line 228), *unpinned* (line 232), *unconscious* (line 239), and *immovable* (line 241). Explain that the prefixes *im-* and *un-* mean "not." Help students use their knowledge of the base words and the meanings of the prefixes to define each word.

Comprehension

1. **Recall** What successes does Jimmy achieve in Elmore?

2. **Recall** How does Ben Price react when Jimmy cracks the safe?

3. **Summarize** How has Jimmy changed?

Literary Analysis

4. **Predict** Review the prediction chart you made as you read. How close were your predictions to what actually happens to Jimmy?

5. **Analyze Omniscient Point of View** Skim the story from lines 196–236. Use a graphic organizer like the one shown to note the information the reader knows that Jimmy does not.

6. **Identify Irony** Irony is a contrast between what is expected and what actually happens. What is ironic about the turn of events in this story?

7. **Make Judgments** At the end of the story, it's not clear how Annabel and her family will react to Jimmy's safecracking tools and skills. How do you think they should react? Support your opinion with details from the story.

8. **Evaluate the Title** A reformation is a change for the better. The word *retrieve* means "to rescue or regain something." Think about what the title refers to. Do you think it is a good title for this story? Why or why not?

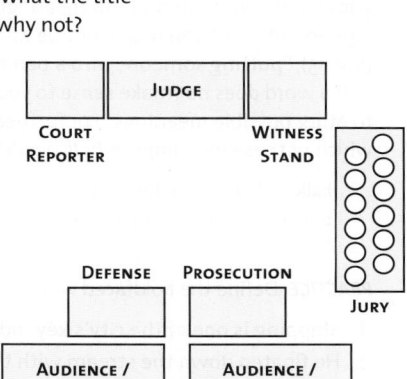

I Know

Jimmy Knows

Extension and Challenge

9. **Speaking and Listening** Do you agree with Ben Price's decision to let Jimmy go free? Hold a classroom trial to decide Jimmy's fate. Choose who will be Jimmy's defense lawyer, the prosecutor, the judge, the witnesses, the jury, the audience, and the court reporter. The defense will argue that Jimmy be granted a second **chance** and the prosecution will argue that he should be sent back to prison. The closing arguments should be presented to the classroom jury. Your arguments must be supported with evidence from the text.

JUDGE

COURT REPORTER

WITNESS STAND

DEFENSE   PROSECUTION

JURY

AUDIENCE / WITNESSES   AUDIENCE / WITNESSES

Typical courtroom layout

MARYLAND OBJECTIVES

READING STANDARD
1.E.4.d Confirm, refute, or make predictions

A RETRIEVED REFORMATION   237

---

7. *Some students may say the family should forgive Jimmy his past because he made a selfless gesture in saving Agatha. Others may say that the family should be grateful that he saved the child but should not trust him after all the lies he has told them.*

8. *It is an appropriate title because Jimmy is close to going back to jail and forfeiting his pardon. But, he retrieves or salvages his reformation by rescuing Agatha.*

Extension and Challenge

9. *Students' arguments should be well organized and supported. Arguments for giving Jimmy a second chance should include details of his success in Elmore as well as his self-sacrificing act of saving Agatha. Arguments in favor of sending him back to jail should refer to the lack of remorse he showed upon leaving jail and his immediate resumption of his safecracking career.*

Practice and Apply

After Reading

For additional support of post-reading questions, use these copy masters:

RESOURCE MANAGER—Copy Masters
Reading Check p. 104 (to check understanding of the selection)
Omniscient Point of View p. 97 (for practice of literary analysis standards focus)
Question Support p. 105 (**After Reading** questions adapted for English learners and less-proficient readers)

Additional selection questions are provided for teachers on page 91.

For additional activities to challenge students, see

ℹ️ Power Thinking at **ClassZone.com**

ANSWERS

Comprehension

1. *He opens a successful shoe store, he makes friends and is accepted into society, and he becomes engaged to Annabel.*

2. *Ben pretends not to recognize Jimmy, calling him Mr. Spencer instead.*

3. *At the beginning of the story, Jimmy seems to care mostly about himself and money. At the end of the story, he saves Agatha, showing that he cares more about Annabel and her family than himself.*

Literary Analysis

Possible answers:

4. ■ **STANDARDS FOCUS** *Predict Some students may have predicted that Ben Price would arrest Jimmy. Others may have foreseen that Ben Price would let Jimmy go.*

5. ● **STANDARDS FOCUS** *Omniscient Point of View I Know: Ben Price is in the bank and plans to arrest Jimmy. Jimmy Knows: Agatha is locked in the vault; Jimmy has the skills to save the child.*

6. *One ironic turn of events is that Jimmy's skills as a safecracker end up being used for good, but only after he has decided never to use those skills again. Another irony is that by using his criminal expertise, he ends up escaping punishment for past crimes.*

ANSWERS

Vocabulary in Context

VOCABULARY PRACTICE

1. *antonyms*
2. *synonyms*
3. *synonyms*
4. *synonyms*
5. *antonyms*
6. *synonyms*
7. *antonyms*
8. *synonyms*
9. *synonyms*
10. *antonyms*

 RESOURCE MANAGER—Copy Master
Vocabulary Practice p. 102

VOCABULARY IN WRITING

Distribute copies of the Cluster Diagram. Suggest that students use the diagram to organize Ben Price's qualities. Then have them identify those details that could be expressed using vocabulary words. Encourage students to organize their paragraphs logically.

BEST PRACTICES TOOLKIT—Transparency
Cluster Diagram p. B18

VOCABULARY STRATEGY: WORDS WITH MULTIPLE MEANINGS (*also an EL language objective*)

Point out that the way a word is used in a sentence can help show which meaning is intended. For example, if the word is placed in front of a noun, it may be an adjective. Therefore, its possible meanings are narrowed down.

Possible answers:

1. *important; main*
2. *part of a body of water that moves continuously in a certain direction*
3. *plan; put together*
4. *prominence due to contrast*
5. *amount of space occupied by a three-dimensional object*

RESOURCE MANAGER—Copy Master
Vocabulary Strategy p. 103

Vocabulary Center at ClassZone.com
Additional Vocabulary Activities

Vocabulary in Context

VOCABULARY PRACTICE

Synonyms are words that have the same meaning, and **antonyms** are words that have the opposite meaning. Decide whether the words in each pair are synonyms or antonyms.

1. compulsory—voluntary
2. elusive—slippery
3. virtuous—honorable
4. saunter—stroll
5. balk—agree
6. retribution—punishment
7. eminent—unknown
8. rehabilitate—restore
9. unperceived—unnoticed
10. genially—disagreeably

balk   rehabilitate
compulsory   retribution
elusive   saunter
eminent   unperceived
genially   virtuous

VOCABULARY IN WRITING

What were some of Ben Price's qualities? Write a paragraph describing Ben, using four or more vocabulary words. You could start like this.

> **EXAMPLE SENTENCE**
> *Ben Price often spoke genially, but he always took his job seriously.*

VOCABULARY STRATEGY: WORDS WITH MULTIPLE MEANINGS

Many English words have more than one meaning. For example, you might know that *compromising* can mean "giving in by both sides to reach an agreement." But you might not be familiar with its meaning in this story (line 15), "putting someone into a bad position or situation."

If a word does not make sense to you, look at the words around it for clues to other possible meanings. For further help, check a dictionary. For example, which of these meanings of *balk* would you expect to find in a baseball article?

> **balk** (bôk) *v.* **1.** to refuse to move or act: *The horse balked at jumping the fence.* **2.** to make an illegal motion as a pitcher, especially to start a throw and not finish it.

PRACTICE Define the boldfaced words using context clues or a dictionary.

1. Shipping is one of the city's **key** industries.
2. He floated down the stream with the **current.**
3. Several town officials helped to **frame** the new law.
4. The stars stood out in sharp **relief** against the sky.
5. What numbers must you multiply to figure out the **volume** of a room?

MARYLAND OBJECTIVES

READING STANDARD
1.D.3.a Use context to determine the meanings of words

VOCABULARY PRACTICE
For more practice, go to the **Vocabulary Center** at **ClassZone.com**.

DIFFERENTIATED INSTRUCTION

FOR ENGLISH LEARNERS
Vocabulary in Writing

1. Have students who speak Romance languages pick out three or four of the vocabulary words that resemble words familiar to them from their own languages (*virtuous, eminent, rehabilitate, genial*).
2. Ask students to explain the meaning of each word they chose.
3. Have students use each word in a sentence about the story or about Ben Price.

FOR ADVANCED LEARNERS/PRE–AP
Vocabulary Strategy Have students write sentences using a different meaning of each boldfaced word. Encourage them to include context clues. Then ask them to exchange papers and define the words as they are used in the new sentences.

eading-Writing Connection

Demonstrate an understanding of the characters in "A Retrieved Reformation" by responding to these prompts. Then complete the **Grammar and Writing** exercise.

WRITING PROMPTS	SELF-CHECK

A. Short Response: Compare Characters
Jimmy Valentine and Ben Price both make surprising decisions at the end of "A Retrieved Reformation." Using details and examples from the text, write **one paragraph** in which you compare the two characters.

▶ *A strong comparison will ...*
- use transition words and phrases such as *like* and *similarly*
- conclude with a clear statement about the characters

B. Extended Response: Write a Personal Letter
How will Jimmy Valentine explain his actions to Annabel? Write a **two- or three-paragraph letter** to Annabel in which Jimmy describes his past and asks for a second **chance.**

▶ *A successful letter will ...*
- show an understanding of Jimmy Valentine's character
- be written in personal letter format

GRAMMAR AND WRITING

COMPARE CORRECTLY When making comparisons, follow these guidelines:

- To compare only two people or things, use the **comparative form** (stronger; more quickly). Never use *more* and *-er* together.
- To compare three or more people or things, use the **superlative form** (strongest; most quickly). Never use *most* and *-est* together.

PRACTICE Choose the comparative or superlative form to correctly complete each sentence.

1. Of the two men, Jimmy is the (smarter, smartest).
2. Annabel is the (sweeter, sweetest) person in the world to him.
3. Jimmy must decide what he wants (more, most)— the life of a safecracker or the life of a family man.
4. Ben Price can see that Jimmy has become the (more, most) reformed of all the crooks he has known.

For more help with comparative and superlative forms, see page R58 in the Grammar Handbook.

 **MARYLAND OBJECTIVES**

LANGUAGE STANDARD
5.B.2 Apply standard English usage

FOR LESS—PROFICIENT WRITERS

For Prompt A:

- Help students write a topic sentence in which they state how Jimmy and Ben are alike.
- Help students write three sentences in which they explain and give examples of the similarities.
- Remind students to conclude with a restatement of the topic sentence in different words.

For Prompt B:

Limit the length of the letter to one paragraph. Suggest that students organize their letters in this way:

Beginning: Jimmy asks Annabel to give him a second chance.

Middle: Jimmy tells Annabel about his past and explains how meeting her changed his life.

Closing: Jimmy tells her why he was willing to sacrifice his freedom for her.

Reading-Writing Connection

WRITING PROMPTS

- For **Prompt A,** encourage students to outline the similarities before they begin to write their paragraphs. Remind them to begin with a strong topic sentence that states what is important about the comparison.

- For **Prompt B,** encourage students to reread the letter from Jimmy to his friend, lines 150–166, to familiarize themselves with Jimmy's writing style. Also remind them that Jimmy's goal is to obtain Annabel's forgiveness. They should choose their details accordingly.

For an extended Reading-Writing Connection activity, see

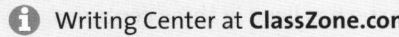 Writing Center at **ClassZone.com**

GRAMMAR AND WRITING

Tell students that *more* or *most* often precedes adjectives and adverbs with more than two syllables, while *-er* or *-est* is added to the end of shorter adjectives and adverbs.

Possible answers:
1. *smarter*
2. *sweetest*
3. *more*
4. *most*

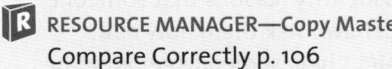 **RESOURCE MANAGER**—Copy Master
Compare Correctly p. 106

Assess and Reteach

Assess

 **RESOURCE MANAGER**—Copy Masters
Selection Tests A, B/C pp. 109–110, 111–112

Test Generator CD

Reteach

S STANDARDS LESSON FILE
Literature Lesson 11: Types of Point of View
Reading Lesson 1: Predicting
Vocabulary Lesson 19: Multiple-Meaning Words
Grammar Lesson 19: Confusing Comparisons

Focus and Motivate

OBJECTIVES

Literary Analysis
- explore the key idea of **behavior**
- identify and compare characters
- read two short stories

Reading
- set a purpose for reading

Vocabulary
- build vocabulary for reading and writing
- understand and use the Latin root *cred* (also an EL language objective)

Grammar and Writing
- write a compare-contrast response paper

SUMMARY

In "The Three-Century Woman," Great-Grandma Breckenridge is interviewed for TV because she has lived in three centuries. When the reporter annoys her, she invents memories involving famous historical events. In "Charles," the narrator's son, Laurie, begins kindergarten. He comes home each day with stories about an outrageous troublemaker in his class named Charles. At a PTA meeting, Laurie's mother finds out that *he* is Charles.

Why do people MISBEHAVE?

Discuss the question and the **KEY IDEA.** Ask students to identify reasons that someone might misbehave. Ask them how bad **behavior** might help someone get what he or she wants, and what that might be. After students complete the **LIST IT** activity, have them share their ideas in small groups.

Selection Resources

 RESOURCE MANAGER UNIT 2

Plan and Teach pp. 113–122

Literary Analysis
Summary pp. 123†*, 124‡*; 130†*, 131‡*
Question Support pp. 128*; 133*

Reading
Set a Purpose for Reading pp. 125, 126†*
Reading Check pp. 127; 132
Reading Fluency pp. 129; 134

Vocabulary
Study p. 135*
Practice p. 136
Strategy p. 137

Grammar and Writing
Writing for Assessment p. 138

Assessment
Selection Tests A, B/C
  pp. 139*, 141*

 Test Generator CD

 BEST PRACTICES TOOLKIT
Differentiated Instruction
  pp. 31–38*
Scaffolding Instruction
  pp. 43–46*

Graphic Organizers/Strategies
New Word Analysis • Venn Diagram • Read Aloud/Think Aloud • T Chart

Reading Support
🎧 Audio Anthology CD*

Technology
ℹ️ Literature and Vocabulary Centers at **ClassZone.com**

💿 Write*Smart* CD

* Resources for Differentiation   † Also in Spanish   ‡ In Haitian Creole and Vietnamese

---

The Three-Century Woman
Short Story by Richard Peck

Charles
Short Story by Shirley Jackson

Why do people MISBEHAVE?

 MARYLAND OBJECTIVES

READING/LIT STANDARDS
1.E.3.a Select and apply appropriate strategies during reading
3.A.3.d Analyze characterization

KEY IDEA No one's **behavior** is always perfect. When we misbehave, sometimes we do so for a reason—although that doesn't mean it's a good one. In the stories you are about to read, an elderly woman and a young boy misbehave at important milestones in their lives.

LIST IT Make a list of ways you've seen people misbehave. Did someone make a face in a yearbook picture? Did someone disrupt a serious ceremony? After making your list, discuss with classmates why you think those individuals may have acted as they did.

240

LITERARY ANALYSIS: CHARACTERIZATION

Literary characters have personalities just as real people do. How a writer creates and develops these personalities is known as **characterization.** For example, a writer may

- describe a character's physical appearance
- present a character's thoughts, words, and actions
- present the thoughts, words, and reactions of other characters
- make direct comments about a character's personality

As you read the following two stories, note what the characters say and do and what is said about them.

READING STRATEGY: SET A PURPOSE FOR READING

When you **set a purpose** for reading, you choose specific reasons for reading one or more works. Your purpose for reading "The Three-Century Woman" and "Charles" is to find similarities and differences between the two main characters. After the first story, begin filling in the chart.

	Great-Grandma	Laurie
What does each character look like?		
How does each character behave?		
How do others see each character?		
How would you describe each character's personality?		

Review: **Make Inferences**

VOCABULARY IN CONTEXT

The listed words help reveal the characters' personalities. For each word, choose the numbered term closest in meaning.

WORD LIST	cynically	insolently	renounce
	incredulously	raucous	venerable

1. noisy
2. disrespectfully
3. sarcastically
4. skeptically
5. well-respected
6. give up

Author Online

Richard Peck: Inspired Teacher
Teaching high school English brought out the writer in Richard Peck. As he says, "I found my future readers right there in the roll book." Although Peck has written novels for adults, he is best known and loved for his young-adult fiction.

Richard Peck
born 1934

Shirley Jackson: Rebel with a Cause
From an early age, Shirley Jackson rebelled against what she considered her wealthy family's selfish lifestyle. Instead of taking part in social events, she would

Shirley Jackson
1919–1965

disappear into her journals. After she married, Jackson moved to a small town in Vermont and adopted a much different way of life. She wrote many novels, essays, and short stories. Jackson's friends and critics described the reclusive author as the "Madame of Mystery," referring to the dark humor and strange twists found in her stories. Sadly, Jackson died at 45 from a heart attack.

 MORE ABOUT THE AUTHOR
For more on the authors, visit the
Literature Center at **ClassZone.com**.

241

Teach

STANDARDS FOCUS

LITERARY ANALYSIS

● **CHARACTERIZATION**

Read aloud this example and ask students to identify how the author builds character:

> With an impish grin, the petite curly-haired girl wrestled her brother's truck from his grip. Just as he opened his mouth to cry, she yelled, "Mom, Jack is trying to take my truck!"

Possible answer: The author describes what the girl looks like and tells what she does and says.

CHECK UNDERSTANDING Have students explain why a character from a previous reading stands out in their minds.

READING STRATEGY

■ **SET A PURPOSE FOR READING**

Help students understand the various purposes for reading, such as for enjoyment or to find out information. Point out that sometimes the purpose is more specific and may require them to use a graphic organizer and adjust their reading rate.

CHECK UNDERSTANDING Ask students to identify something they might read for information.

 RESOURCE MANAGER—Copy Master
Set a Purpose for Reading p. 125
(for student use while reading the selections)

VOCABULARY SKILL

▲ **VOCABULARY IN CONTEXT**

DIAGNOSE WORD KNOWLEDGE To determine preteaching needs, have all students complete **Vocabulary in Context.** Check students' answers. (**1.** *raucous;* **2.** *insolently;* **3.** *cynically;* **4.** *incredulously;* **5.** *venerable;* **6.** *renounce*)

PRETEACH VOCABULARY Use the Vocabulary Study copy master to help students explore the meaning of each boldfaced word.

1. Read the first set of sentences aloud, emphasizing *cynically.*
2. Point out the context clues *boasts* and *did not believe a word.* Elicit possible meanings for *cynically,* such as "with disbelief."
3. Have students record their definition in the chart.
4. Repeat for the rest of the words.

 RESOURCE MANAGER—Copy Master
Vocabulary Study p. 135

For general guidelines on differentiating vocabulary instruction and for alternative vocabulary activities for students not needing vocabulary preteaching, see

 **BEST PRACTICES TOOLKIT**
Scaffolding Vocabulary Instruction
pp. 43–46

ⓘ Vocabulary Center at **ClassZone.com**
Additional Vocabulary Activities

ANALYZE VISUALS

Possible answers: The color of her hat suggests that this woman is quite daring. Her face has kind lines and eyes that seem wise. She looks gentle yet strong.

ANALYZE VISUALS

Possible answers: The color of her hat suggests that this woman is quite daring. Her face has kind lines and eyes that seem wise. She looks gentle yet strong.

About the Art American artist Deidre Scherer has worked with fabric and thread since the late 1970s. She often portrays members of the older generation, as in *Red Hat*, in an effort to highlight issues related to aging and mortality.

LITERARY ANALYSIS

Ⓐ CHARACTERIZATION

Record students' answers in a list.

Possible answers:

- *The narrator is fourteen years old.*
- *She doesn't like to do homework.*
- *She likes to spend time at the mall.*

Extend the Discussion Do these details make the narrator seem like a believable character? Explain.

The Three-Century Woman

Richard Peck

"I guess if you live long enough," my mom said to Aunt Gloria, "you get your fifteen minutes of fame."

Mom was on the car phone to Aunt Gloria. The minute Mom rolls out of the garage, she's on her car phone. It's state of the art and better than her car.

We were heading for Whispering Oaks to see my Great-Grandmother Breckenridge, who's lived there since I was a little girl. They call it an Elder Care Facility. Needless to say, I hated going.

The reason for Great-Grandma's fame is that she was born in 1899.
10 Now it's January 2001. If you're one of those people who claim the new century begins in 2001, not 2000, even you have to agree that Great-Grandma Breckenridge has lived in three centuries. This is her claim to fame.

We waited for a light to change along by Northbrook Mall, and I gazed fondly over at it. Except for the Multiplex, it was closed because of New Year's Day. I have a severe mall habit. But I'm fourteen, and the mall is the place without homework. Aunt Gloria's voice filled the car. Ⓐ

"If you take my advice," she told Mom, "you'll keep those Whispering Oaks people from letting the media in to interview Grandma. Interview
20 her my foot! Honestly. She doesn't even know where she is, let alone how many centuries she's lived in. The poor old soul. Leave her in peace. She's already got one foot in the—"

"Gloria, your trouble is you have no sense of history." Mom gunned across the intersection. "You got a C in History."

"I was sick a lot that year," Aunt Gloria said.

"Sick of history," Mom murmured.

ANALYZE VISUALS
What can you **infer** about the personality of the woman in the red hat on the basis of her appearance?

Ⓘ **Targeted Passage**

Ⓐ **CHARACTERIZATION**
Reread lines 14–17. What do you learn about the narrator here?

Red Hat (2003), Deidre Scherer. Fabric and thread. © Deidre Scherer.

DIFFERENTIATED INSTRUCTION

FOR ALL STUDENTS

Interest Stations Post suggested projects for students to work on independently.

- **Timeline** Research and create a timeline of historical milestones from 1889 to 2001.
- **Historical Fiction** Write a short story about an historic event in your lifetime.
- **Comic Strip** Draw an event in "Charles."

For further details on these projects, see

Ⓡ RESOURCE MANAGER
  Ideas for Extension pp. 120–121

FOR LESS–PROFICIENT READERS

In combination with the *Audio Anthology CD*, use one or more Targeted Passages (pp. 242, 245, 248, 250, 251, 254) to ensure that students focus on key story events, concepts, and skills.

Ⓘ **Targeted Passage [Lines 3–17]**

This passage begins to build understanding of the characters and their relationship: the narrator is a fourteen-year-old girl going with her mother to visit her great-grandmother in an elder care facility.

- What is the narrator's great-grandmother's claim to fame?
- How does the narrator feel about visiting her great-grandmother?
- Where would the narrator rather be?

BACKGROUND

Elder Care In this story, the narrator is on her way to the elder care facility in which her 102-year-old great-grandmother lives. Once more commonly known as nursing homes, these institutions provide assistance and medical care for the elderly. About 20 percent of Americans over the age of 85 live in elder care facilities. The majority of residents are female. Women live an average of seven years longer than men and have more chronic illnesses that require care.

CULTURAL CONNECTION

Traditional Care In China, elderly people most often live with family members, who accept the responsibility for their aged relatives' welfare as an important tradition. This situation may change, however, as more young Chinese are forced to move away from their homes to find jobs, and as the number of elderly increases disproportionately compared to the number of young people.

FOR ENGLISH LEARNERS

Options for Reading Read the first Targeted Passage of each selection aloud. Discuss what readers learn about characters and plot. Then have pairs read the rest of each story along with the *Audio Anthology CD*.

Reading: Predict Encourage students to make predictions based on what they learn from each initial Targeted Passage. For example, will the narrator enjoy visiting her great-grandmother? Will Laurie do well in kindergarten?

Key Academic Vocabulary Have students use New Word Analysis to study these words: *media* (line 19), *trace* (line 79), *technology* (line 85), *attribute* (line 95), *predict* (line 184).

🧰 BEST PRACTICES TOOLKIT—Transparency
New Word Analysis p. E8

Prereading For prereading instruction for English learners, see

🧰 BEST PRACTICES TOOLKIT
Scaffolding Reading Instruction pp. 43–46

FOR ADVANCED LEARNERS/PRE–AP

Pre-AP exercises in the bottom channel provide additional challenge for your advanced students. Use them for small groups or individuals.

ADDITIONAL GUIDELINES

For more help with differentiation and tips for classroom management, see

🧰 BEST PRACTICES TOOLKIT
Differentiated Instruction pp. 31–38

DISCUSSION PROMPTS

Use these prompts to help students understand the narrator's initial attitude toward her great-grandmother and the elderly in general:

Connect What impression do you have of old-age homes? *Students might say that they think of old-age homes as being depressing places where most of the people suffer from poor health and loneliness. Others might have a more positive view.*

Analyze According to the narrator, how is Whispering Oaks better than the stereotypical old-age home? *Possible answers: The home smells all right. There is a real Christmas tree.*

Evaluate What does the language that the narrator uses in this passage suggest about her feelings toward the elderly? *Possible answers: She uses phrases such as "get so old," "have to be put away," and "keep the inmates from escaping." These word choices reveal a negative and almost callous feeling toward the elderly.*

LITERARY ANALYSIS

Ⓑ CHARACTERIZATION

Possible answer: The narrator's mother is assertive and not afraid to say what is on her mind.

"I heard that," Aunt Gloria said.

They bickered on, but I tuned them out. Then when we turned in at Whispering Pines, a sound truck from IBC-TV was blocking the drive.

30 "Good grief," Mom murmured. "TV."

"I told you," Aunt Gloria said, but Mom switched her off. She parked in a frozen rut.

"I'll wait in the car," I said. "I have homework."

"Get out of the car," Mom said.

If you get so old you have to be put away, Whispering Oaks isn't that bad. It smells all right, and a Christmas tree glittered in the lobby. A real tree. On the other hand, you have to push a red button to unlock the front door. I guess it's to keep the inmates from escaping, though Great-Grandma Breckenridge wasn't going anywhere and hadn't for

40 twenty years.

When we got to her wing, the hall was full of camera crews and a woman from the suburban newspaper with a notepad.

Mom sighed. It was like that first day of school when you think you'll be okay until the teachers learn your name. Stepping over a cable, we stopped at Great-Grandma's door, and they were on to us.

"Who are you people to Mrs. Breckenridge?" the newspaperwoman said. "I want names."

These people were seriously pushy. And the TV guy was wearing more makeup than Mom. It dawned on me that they couldn't get into Great-

50 Grandma's room without her permission. Mom turned on them.

"Listen, you're not going to be interviewing my grandmother," she said in a quiet bark. "I'll be glad to tell you anything you want to know about her, but you're not going in there. She's got nothing to say, and . . . she needs a lot of rest."

"Is it Alzheimer's?"[1] the newswoman asked. "Because we're thinking Alzheimer's."

"Think what you want," Mom said. "But this is as far as you get. And you people with the camera and the light, you're not going in there either. You'd scare her to death, and then I'd sue the pants off you." Ⓑ

60 They pulled back.

But a voice came wavering out of Great-Grandma's room. Quite an eerie, echoing voice.

"Let them in!" the voice said.

Ⓑ **CHARACTERIZATION**
Reread lines 41–59. What do you learn about the narrator's mother from how she talks to the reporters?

---

1. **Alzheimer's** (älts'hī-mərz): a disease of the brain that causes confusion and may lead to total loss of memory.

DIFFERENTIATED INSTRUCTION

FOR LESS–PROFICIENT READERS

Reading Strategy Follow-Up: Set a Purpose for Reading Remind students that their purpose in reading this selection is to learn about Great-Grandma Breckenridge in order to compare her to the character in the second story. As students read the text, have them place sticky notes next to important details about the main character. Create a class list of the ideas they identify, or place the ideas in the chart from page 241.

FOR ENGLISH LEARNERS

Vocabulary: Idioms and Sayings On the board, list some of the idiomatic and slang expressions in the selection: *my foot* (line 20), expression of disgust meaning "I don't think so"; *she's already got one foot in the [grave]* (line 22), "she's close to death"; *tuned them out* (line 28), "stopped listening"; *good grief* (line 30), "oh, no"; *were on to us* (line 45), "knew who we were." Have small groups work on defining these and other similar expressions from context.

It had to be Great-Grandma Breckenridge. Her roommate had died. "Good grief," Mom murmured, and the press surged forward.

Mom and I went in first, and our eyes popped. Great-Grandma was usually flat out in the bed, dozing, with her teeth in a glass and a book in her hand. Today she was bright-eyed and propped up. She wore a fuzzy pink bed jacket. A matching bow was stuck in what remained of her hair.

70 "Oh for pity's sake," Mom murmured. "They've got her done up like a Barbie doll."

Great-Grandma peered from the bed at Mom. "And who are you?" she asked.

"I'm Ann," Mom said carefully. "This is Megan," she said, meaning me.

"That's right," Great-Grandma said. "At least you know who you are. Plenty around this place don't." **C**

The guy with the camera on his shoulder barged in. The other guy turned on a blinding light.

80 Great-Grandma blinked. In the glare we noticed she wore a trace of lipstick. The TV anchor elbowed the woman reporter aside and stuck a mike in Great-Grandma's face. Her claw hand came out from under the covers and tapped it.

"Is this thing on?" she inquired.

"Yes, ma'am," the TV anchor said in his broadcasting voice. "Don't you worry about all this modern technology. We don't understand half of it ourselves." He gave her his big, five-thirty news smile and settled on the edge of her bed. There was room for him. She was tiny.

"We're here to congratulate you for having lived in three centuries— for being a Three-Century Woman! A great achievement."

90 Great-Grandma waved a casual claw. "Nothing to it," she said. "You sure this mike's on? Let's do this in one take."

The cameraman snorted and moved in for a closer shot. Mom stood still as a statue, wondering what was going to come out of Great-Grandma's mouth next. **D**

"Mrs. Breckenridge," the anchor said, "to what do you attribute your long life?"

"I was only married once," Great-Grandma said. "And he died young." The anchor stared. "Ah. And anything else?"

"Yes. I don't look back. I live in the present."

100 The camera panned around the room. This was all the present she had, and it didn't look like much.

"You live for the present," the anchor said, looking for an angle, "even now?"

C CHARACTERIZATION
Consider Great-Grandma's appearance and words. What is your first impression of her?

② Targeted Passage

D MAKE INFERENCES
Reread lines 77–94. How do you think Megan feels about the reporters?

LITERARY ANALYSIS

C CHARACTERIZATION

Record students' answers in the chart from page 241. **Possible answers:**

	Great-Grandma
What does each character look like?	Great-Grandma is sitting up in bed. She is wearing a pink bed jacket and a bow in her hair.
How does each character behave?	She appears alert and interested in what is going on around her. She makes astute comments. She takes control and says to let the media come in.
How do others see each character?	
How would you describe each character's personality?	

READING SKILL: *Review*

D MAKE INFERENCES

Possible answer: *Megan does not like the news people. She says the cameraman "barged in" (line 77) and the anchor "elbowed the woman reporter aside and stuck a mike in Great-Grandma's face" (lines 80–81).*

FOR LESS–PROFICIENT READERS

② Targeted Passage [Lines 79–99]

This passage develops the character of Great-Grandma Breckenridge: it shows her sense of humor and her attitude toward the media.

- Why is Great-Grandma Breckenridge wearing lipstick?
- Is she nervous about the media interviewing her? What does she say to the reporter when he congratulates her on living so long?
- What does Great-Grandma give as reasons she has lived so long? Is she serious?

FOR ENGLISH LEARNERS

Vocabulary: Media Terms Clarify that "the media" (line 19) refers to newspapers and TV news programs. Have mixed-ability pairs define these terms related to the media:

- *camera crews* (line 41)
- *the press* (line 65)
- *TV anchor* (line 80)
- *mike* (line 81)
- *five-thirty news* (line 86)
- *one take* (line 91)
- *closer shot* (line 92), *close-up* (line 137)
- *panned* (line 100)
- *network ratings* (line 183)
- *a wrap* (line 187)

FOR ADVANCED LEARNERS/PRE–AP

Analyze Author's Craft Discuss how one aspect of this author's style is humor. Ask small groups to find examples of humor in the story. Then have students evaluate how this device affects the impact of the story and the author's purpose. Ask groups to share their examples and insights.

Lines 99–110
DISCUSSION PROMPTS

Use these prompts to help students understand why Great-Grandma says the things she does to the interviewer:

Connect Do you think that Great-Grandma's philosophy of living in the present is a good idea for someone her age? Explain. *Students may say that living in the present helps older people stay interested in life. It is better than thinking about sad things in the past, such as loved ones who have already died.*

Analyze What is the anchor's attitude toward Great-Grandma's present life? *Possible answer: He seems to think her life in the present is too boring to talk about (lines 100–103).*

Synthesize What does Great-Grandma realize after she tells the anchor about the bed pan incident? *Possible answer: She sees that he has no sense of humor and is uninterested in her as a person.*

READING SKILL: Review

E MAKE INFERENCES

Possible answers: Great-Grandma's claim to fame is that she has lived for over 100 years. Therefore, he believes that her stories of what she has seen and done over that time period and the changes she has lived through could be interesting.

SOCIAL STUDIES CONNECTION

San Francisco Earthquake At approximately 5:12 A.M. on April 18, 1906, the San Andreas Fault slipped, resulting in severe tremors in San Francisco and areas as far south as Los Angeles and as far north as Oregon. The earthquake caused more than 30 fires to break out in San Francisco. Because the water lines were damaged, these fires burned for four days and destroyed over 500 city blocks. Thousands were killed and left homeless as a result of the dual disasters.

Great-Grandma nodded. "Something's always happening. Last night I fell off the bed pan."

Mom groaned.

The cameraman pulled in for a tighter shot. The anchor seemed to search his mind. You could tell he thought he was a great interviewer, though he had no sense of humor. A tiny smile played around Great-
110 Grandma's wrinkled lips.

"But you've lived through amazing times, Mrs. Breckenridge. And you never think back about them?" **E**

Great-Grandma stroked her chin and considered. "You mean you want to hear something interesting? Like how I lived through the San Francisco earthquake—the big one of oh-six?"

Beside me, Mom stirred. We were crowded over by the dead lady's bed. "You survived the 1906 San Francisco earthquake?" the anchor said.

Great-Grandma gazed at the ceiling, lost in thought.

"I'd have been about seven years old. My folks and I were staying at
120 that big hotel. You know the one. I slept in a cot at the foot of their bed. In the middle of the night, that room gave a shake, and the chiffonier walked right across the floor. You know what chiffonier is?"

"A chest of drawers?" the anchor said.

"Close enough," Great-Grandma said. "And the pictures flapped on the walls. We had to walk down twelve flights because the elevators didn't work. When we got outside, the streets were ankle-deep in broken glass. You never saw such a mess in your life."

Mom nudged me and hissed: "She's never been to San Francisco. She's never been west of Denver. I've heard her say so."

130 "Incredible!" the anchor said.

"Truth's stranger than fiction," Great-Grandma said, smoothing her sheet.

"And you never think back about it?"

Great-Grandma shrugged her little fuzzy pink shoulders. "I've been through too much. I don't have time to remember it all. I was on the Hindenburg when it blew up, you know."

Mom moaned, and the cameraman was practically standing on his head for a close-up.

"The Hindenburg?"

"That big gas bag the Germans built to fly over the Atlantic Ocean.
140 It was called a zeppelin. Biggest thing you ever saw—five city blocks long. It was in May of 1937, before your time. You wouldn't remember. My husband and I were coming back from Europe on it. No, wait a minute."

Great-Grandma cocked her head and pondered for the camera.

E MAKE INFERENCES
Why do you think the reporter wants Great-Grandma to talk about her memories?

SOCIAL STUDIES CONNECTION

On April 18, 1906, an earthquake devastated San Francisco, California. It is still considered one of the worst natural disasters in the history of the United States.

DIFFERENTIATED INSTRUCTION

FOR LESS–PROFICIENT READERS

Concept Support Make sure students know that Great-Grandma is lying to the news anchor about the earthquake. Although she supplies many specific details, the narrator's mother says that Great-Grandma has never been farther west than Denver (lines 128–129). Use a map to show east, west, Denver, and San Francisco. Help students understand why Great-Grandma tells this story, and ask them to predict whether she was really on the *Hindenburg* when it exploded.

FOR ENGLISH LEARNERS

Vocabulary: Multiple Meanings Explain that both the word *anchor* and the word *present* in line 102 have more than one meaning. Tell students that in the story an *anchor* is "the narrator of a newscast" and *present* means "now" or "a moment in time between past and future." Have mixed-ability groups identify one other meaning for each word and use each word in a sentence that shows the second meaning. Ask groups to share their sentences.

"My husband was dead by then. It was some other man. Anyway, the two of us were coming back on the Hindenburg. It was smooth as silk. You didn't know you were moving. When we flew in over New York, they stopped the ball game at Yankee Stadium to see us passing overhead."

Great-Grandma paused, caught up in memories.

"And then the Hindenburg exploded," the anchor said, prompting her.

150 She nodded. "We had no complaints about the trip till then. The luggage was all stacked, and we were coming in at Lakehurst, New Jersey. I was wearing my beige coat—beige or off-white, I forget. Then whoosh! The gondola² heated up like an oven, and people peeled out of the windows. We hit the ground and bounced. When we hit again, the door fell off, and I walked out and kept going. When they caught up with me in the parking lot, they wanted to put me in the hospital. I looked down and thought I was wearing a lace dress. The fire had about burned up my coat. And I lost a shoe."

"Fantastic!" the anchor breathed. "What detail!" Behind him the
160 woman reporter was scribbling away on her pad.

"Never," Mom muttered. "Never in her life."

"Ma'am, you are living history!" the anchor said. "In your sensational span of years you've survived two great disasters!"

"Three." Great-Grandma patted the bow on her head. "I told you I'd been married."

"And before we leave this **venerable** lady," the anchor said, flashing a smile for the camera, "we'll ask Mrs. Breckenridge if she has any predictions for this new twenty-first century ahead of us here in the Dawn of the Millennium."

170 "Three or four predictions," Great-Grandma said, and paused again, stretching out her airtime. "Number one, taxes will be higher. Number two, it's going to be harder to find a place to park. And number three, a whole lot of people are going to live as long as I have, so get ready for us."

"And with those wise words,"
180 the anchor said, easing off the bed, "we leave Mrs. Breck—"

---

2. **gondola** (gŏn'dl-ə): a car that hangs under an airship and contains equipment and controls.

venerable
(vĕn'ər-ə-bəl) *adj.*
deserving respect because of age, character, or importance

ANALYZE VISUALS
What do you notice about the fabric patterns used in this quilt of the Hindenburg?

THE THREE-CENTURY WOMAN   **247**

Lines 139–148
REINFORCE *KEY IDEA:*
BEHAVIOR

Discuss What does Great-Grandma's **behavior** during the interview reveal about her personality? *Possible answers: She is very comfortable in front of the camera, suggesting that she is an actress at heart. She is an accomplished storyteller. She is insightful enough to realize that the anchor will not suspect her of having the wits to invent such tales. She does not want to be overlooked or talked down to. She is quite mischievous.*

ANALYZE VISUALS

Possible answer: The searing red and orange blasts erupting from the Hindenburg capture the disaster of the burning blimp. The bright blues of the sky and the green of the earth suggest that the world was sunny and bright before the disaster.

Lines 109–163
ADDITIONAL TEACHING OPPORTUNITY

Character Motivation Recall that a character's **motivation** is the reason why he or she acts a certain way. Ask students what Great-Grandma's motivation is for making up her stories to the reporters. *Possible answer: Great-Grandma is annoyed by the reporters who are pushy, inconsiderate, and condescending. Since the reporters expect her to be slow and dotty, she instead makes up extraordinary stories about her life.*

FOR ENGLISH LEARNERS
Comprehension: Concept Support Help students distinguish between literal and figurative meanings of words used in this story. Point out the word *claw* in line 90. Explain that Great-Grandma's hand is not a claw; it just resembles one because it is bony and bent. Identify these other words and phrases used figuratively in the text: *lost in thought* (line 118), *walked* (line 122), *withered-up leaf of a lady* (line 216). Discuss the idea that each is meant to convey.

FOR ADVANCED LEARNERS/PRE–AP
Synthesize Have students choose one of these activities to explore the character of the TV anchor:

• Role-play the conversation the anchor has with his camera crew as they drive back to the station after the interview.
• Write an email that the anchor might send to his boss describing the interview and why it will be good for the five-thirty news.

F MAKE INFERENCES

Possible answer: This last prediction shows that Great-Grandma dislikes the anchor.

Extend the Discussion What does Great-Grandma's knowledge of Web sites prove about her mental state?

Lines 206–209
REINFORCE *KEY IDEA*: BEHAVIOR

Discuss What led to Great-Grandma's **behavior** during the interview? *Possible answer: She did not like the anchor. He didn't see her as a person with ideas, only as a source of memories that could make an interesting news story.*

LITERARY ANALYSIS

G CHARACTERIZATION

Possible answers: In the beginning, Megan is reluctant to visit her great-grandmother. She thinks of her as an inmate of the facility and usually sees her dozing, with her teeth in a glass. After this visit, Megan sees her great-grandmother's sense of humor and says that she would like to spend more time with her.

If students need help . . . Identify words and phrases from the beginning and end of the story that show Megan's attitude. Record them in a Venn Diagram to show the change.

 BEST PRACTICES TOOLKIT—Transparency Venn Diagram p. A26

SELECTION WRAP–UP

REFLECT Have students think about the lesson that the narrator learns in this story. In what way does Great-Grandma's misbehavior help the narrator see her as a real person rather than a stereotype?

⭐ **CRITIQUE** Ask students to evaluate the believability of the characters. Have them discuss which characters are most realistic and which seem less credible.

READING FLUENCY

Distribute the copy masters and have students work in pairs to practice fluency.

R RESOURCE MANAGER—Copy Master Reading Fluency p. 129

"And one more prediction," she said. "TV's on the way out. Your network ratings are already in the basement. It's all websites now. Son, I predict you'll be looking for work." **F**

And that was it. The light went dead. The anchor, looking shaken, followed his crew out the door. When TV's done with you, they're done with you. "Is that a wrap?" Great-Grandma asked.

But now the woman from the suburban paper was moving in on her. "Just a few more questions, Mrs. Breckenridge."

190 "Where you from?" Great-Grandma blinked pink-eyed at her.

"*The Glenview Weekly Shopper.*"

"You bring a still photographer with you?" Great-Grandma asked.

"Well, no."

"And you never learned shorthand either, did you?"

"Well . . . no."

"Honey, I only deal with professionals. There's the door."

So then it was just Mom and Great-Grandma and I in the room. Mom planted a hand on her hip. "Grandma. Number one, you've never been to San Francisco. And number two, you never *saw* one of
200 those zeppelin things."

Great-Grandma shrugged. "No, but I can read." She nodded to the pile of books on her nightstand with her spectacles folded on top. "You can pick up all that stuff in books."

"And number three," Mom said. "Your husband didn't die young. I can *remember* Grandpa Breckenridge."

"It was that TV dude in the five-hundred-dollar suit who set me off," Great-Grandma said. "He dyes his hair, did you notice? He made me mad, and it put my nose out of joint.[3] He didn't notice I'm still here. He thought I was nothing but my memories. So I gave him some."

210 Now Mom and I stood beside her bed.

"I'll tell you something else," Great-Grandma said. "And it's no lie."

We waited, holding our breath to hear. Great-Grandma Breckenridge was pointing her little old bent finger right at me. "You, Megan," she said. "Once upon a time, I was your age. How scary is that?"

Then she hunched up her little pink shoulders and winked at me. She grinned and I grinned. She was just this little withered-up leaf of a lady in the bed. But I felt like giving her a kiss on her little wrinkled cheek, so I did.

"I'll come to see you more often," I told her. **G**

"Call first," she said. "I might be busy." Then she dozed. ∾

---

3. **put my nose out of joint:** got me into a bad mood.

F MAKE INFERENCES How does Great-Grandma feel about the anchorman?

VISUAL VOCABULARY

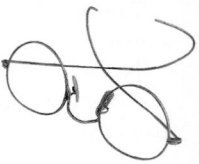

spectacles (spĕk′tə-kəls) *n.* eyeglasses

3 Targeted Passage

G CHARACTERIZATION How has Megan's opinion of Great-Grandma changed?

DIFFERENTIATED INSTRUCTION

FOR LESS–PROFICIENT READERS

3 Targeted Passage [Lines 206–219]

This passage reveals a change in Megan's perception of her great-grandmother: she sees her as someone who still has a lot to offer.

- In what way is Megan's attitude at the beginning of the story the same as the anchor's?
- What does Great-Grandma tell Megan?
- What is Megan's reaction?
- What has Megan realized about her great-grandmother?

FOR ADVANCED LEARNERS/PRE–AP

Analyze Theme Have students reexamine the interactions between the anchor and Great-Grandma and the change in the narrator's perspective on her great-grandmother. Ask them to state one possible theme conveyed by these parts of the story. Have pairs share and defend their interpretations of theme.

Comprehension

1. **Recall** Where does Great-Grandma live?

2. **Recall** Why are the reporters interviewing Great-Grandma?

3. **Clarify** Why does Great-Grandma make up the stories?

MARYLAND OBJECTIVES

LITERATURE STANDARD
3.A.3.d Analyze characterization

Literary Analysis

4. **Examine the Main Character** How would you describe Great-Grandma to someone who hasn't read "The Three-Century Woman"?

5. **Analyze Minor Characters** Even though the anchorman is a minor character, he plays an important role in the story. How do his interactions with Great-Grandma affect the plot?

6. **Evaluate the Main Character** In line 99, Great-Grandma says, "I don't look back. I live in the present." Is this true? Support your opinion with examples from the story.

7. **Make Judgments** Skim "The Three-Century Woman" and look for examples where each of the characters **misbehaves.** Who misbehaves the most in this story?

Comparing Characters

Now that you know more about Great-Grandma, start filling in your chart. Add information that helps you understand Great-Grandma's character.

	Great-Grandma	Laurie
What does each character look like?		
How does each character behave?	She makes up stories for the news anchor.	
How do others see each character?		
How would you describe each character's personality?		

Comparing Characters

■ **STANDARDS FOCUS** *Set a Purpose for Reading*

	Great-Grandma
What does each character look like?	Great-Grandma is sitting up in bed. She is wearing a pink bed jacket and a bow in her hair.
How does each character behave?	She appears alert and interested in what is going on around her. She makes astute comments. She takes control and says to let the media come in.
How do others see each character?	At first, Megan and her mother think Great-Grandma is too old to know what is going on. After the interview, Megan realizes that her great-grandmother is still an interesting person.
How would you describe each character's personality?	Great-Grandma is sharp, observant, funny, and quick-witted.

Practice and Apply

After Reading

For additional support of post-reading questions, use these copy masters:

R RESOURCE MANAGER—Copy Masters
Reading Check p. 127 (to check understanding of the selection)
Question Support p. 128 (**After Reading** questions adapted for English learners and less-proficient readers)

Additional selection questions are provided for teachers on page 118.

ANSWERS

Comprehension

1. *Great-Grandma lives at Whispering Oaks, an elder care facility.*

2. *Reporters are interviewing her because she has lived in three centuries.*

3. *She makes up stories because she does not like the anchor's treatment of her.*

Literary Analysis

Possible answers:

4. *Great-Grandma is sharp and perceptive. She has a good sense of humor. She keeps up with what is going on around her.*

5. *The anchor's disregard for Great-Grandma as a person is the catalyst for her misbehavior.*

6. ● **STANDARDS FOCUS** *Characterization*
Students may say that based on the details in the story, Great-Grandma does live in the present. Her statement about television being replaced by Web sites (lines 182–183) shows that she is well aware of current events. She uses current terms, such as "TV dude," "wrap," and "take." She explains her irritation at the anchor by saying, "He didn't notice I'm still here" (line 208).

7. *Students may say that Great-Grandma misbehaves most because she deliberately makes up stories. If it is found out that the interview is based on lies, the anchor will be in serious trouble. Others may say the anchor misbehaves most because he stereotypes Great-Grandma and is aggressive toward her.*

Practice and Apply

ANALYZE VISUALS

Possible answer: The school bus and fenced yard suggest that families with young children live in this neighborhood. The neighborhood is probably middle-class since the man and woman are dressed as if they work in offices.

LITERARY ANALYSIS

Ⓐ CHARACTERIZATION

Record students' answers in the chart from page 241. **Possible answer:**

	Laurie
What does each character look like?	
How does each character behave?	Laurie has become bold and independent.
How do others see each character?	
How would you describe each character's personality?	

If students need help ... Use Read Aloud/Think Aloud to help students draw conclusions from this first paragraph about the changes in Laurie.

 BEST PRACTICES TOOLKIT—Transparency Read Aloud/Think Aloud p. A34

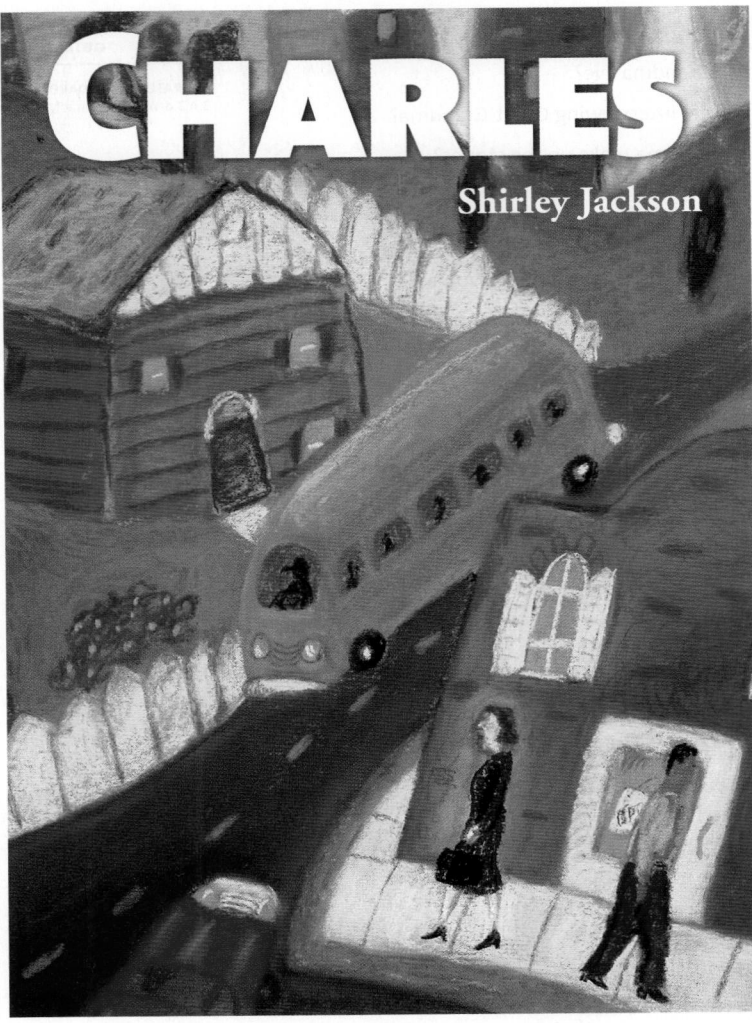

CHARLES
Shirley Jackson

ANALYZE VISUALS
Make an **inference** about what kind of people live in this neighborhood. What details support your inference?

The day my son Laurie started kindergarten he **renounced** corduroy overalls with bibs and began wearing blue jeans with a belt; I watched him go off the first morning with the older girl next door, seeing clearly that an era of my life was ended, my sweet-voiced nursery-school tot replaced by a long-trousered, swaggering character who forgot to stop at the corner and wave goodbye to me. Ⓐ

④ **Targeted Passage**
renounce (rĭ-nouns´) *v.* to give up

Ⓐ **CHARACTERIZATION**
What does the narrator imply about how Laurie's personality has changed recently?

250 UNIT 2: ANALYZING CHARACTER AND POINT OF VIEW

DIFFERENTIATED INSTRUCTION

FOR LESS–PROFICIENT READERS
④ **Targeted Passage [Lines 1–6]**

This passage introduces the main character (Laurie) and describes important changes: he turns from a sweet nursery school child to a swaggering kindergartener.

- Who is Laurie? How is he related to the narrator?
- Where is Laurie going?
- How has Laurie's behavior changed now that he's in kindergarten?

FOR ENGLISH LEARNERS
Culture: Connect Explain that like many American parents, the narrator sees her son's entrance into kindergarten as an indication that he is growing up and away from her. She knows that once he is in school, he will develop his own life and identity and become more independent. This thought makes her sad. Ask students what events have a similar significance in their cultures or mark important milestones in growing up.

He came home the same way, the front door slamming open, his cap on the floor, and the voice suddenly become **raucous** shouting, "Isn't anybody *here?*"

10   At lunch he spoke **insolently** to his father, spilled his baby sister's milk, and remarked that his teacher said we were not to take the name of the Lord in vain.

"How *was* school today?" I asked, elaborately casual.

"All right," he said.

"Did you learn anything?" his father asked.

Laurie regarded his father coldly. "I didn't learn nothing," he said.

"Anything," I said. "Didn't learn anything."

"The teacher spanked a boy, though," Laurie said, addressing his bread and butter. "For being fresh," he added, with his mouth full.

20   "What did he do?" I asked. "Who was it?"

Laurie thought. "It was Charles," he said. "He was fresh. The teacher spanked him and made him stand in a corner. He was awfully fresh."

"What did he do?" I asked again, but Laurie slid off his chair, took a cookie, and left, while his father was still saying, "See here, young man."

The next day Laurie remarked at lunch, as soon as he sat down, "Well, Charles was bad again today." He grinned enormously and said, "Today Charles hit the teacher."

"Good heavens," I said, mindful of the Lord's name, "I suppose he got spanked again?"

30   "He sure did," Laurie said. "Look up," he said to his father.

"What?" his father said, looking up.

"Look down," Laurie said. "Look at my thumb. Gee, you're dumb." He began to laugh insanely. **B**

"Why did Charles hit the teacher?" I asked quickly.

"Because she tried to make him color with red crayons," Laurie said. "Charles wanted to color with green crayons so he hit the teacher and she spanked him and said nobody play with Charles but everybody did."

The third day—it was Wednesday of the first week—Charles bounced a see-saw onto the head of a little girl and made her bleed, and the teacher 40 made him stay inside all during recess. Thursday Charles had to stand in a corner during story-time because he kept pounding his feet on the floor. Friday Charles was deprived of blackboard privileges because he threw chalk.

On Saturday I remarked to my husband, "Do you think kindergarten is too unsettling for Laurie? All this toughness, and bad grammar, and this Charles boy sounds like such a bad influence."

"It'll be all right," my husband said reassuringly. "Bound to be people like Charles in the world. Might as well meet them now as later."

raucous (rô′kəs) *adj.* loud and harsh-sounding

insolently (ĭn′sə-lənt-lē) *adv.* boldly and insultingly

5 Targeted Passage

B CHARACTERIZATION
What do you learn about Laurie from how he treats his parents?

CHARLES   **251**

Lines 10–12
REINFORCE *KEY IDEA:* BEHAVIOR

Discuss What is Laurie's **behavior** like when he comes home from school after the first morning? *Possible answer: He speaks insolently to his father and spills his sister's milk.*

LITERARY ANALYSIS

B CHARACTERIZATION
Record students' answers in the "How does each character behave?" row of the chart. *Possible answer: Laurie is rude and willful.*

Lines 30–45
DISCUSSION PROMPTS
Use these prompts to help students understand the attitude of Laurie's parents toward his misbehavior:

Connect If you were Laurie's father, would you have found his little joke (lines 30–33) amusing? Explain. *Students might say that they would have been amused because it would sound cute coming from a five-year-old. Other students might say that they would be irritated at Laurie's boldness and rudeness.*

Analyze What consequences are there for Laurie when he misbehaves at home? *Possible answer: There do not appear to be any consequences.*

Evaluate Do you agree with the narrator that school and Charles are the causes of Laurie's toughness? Explain. *Possible answers:*

- *No. Laurie showed signs of toughness and rudeness even before he went to school on the first day. He was described as swaggering and not waving to his mother. He also behaved badly at lunchtime after the very first morning.*
- *Yes. Laurie may have wanted to assume a tougher identity when he got to kindergarten, but it's unlikely his behavior would change so drastically if something or someone were not influencing him.*

FOR LESS–PROFICIENT READERS
5 Targeted Passage [Lines 18–37]
This passage introduces a second important character (Charles) and sets up an important parallel between Laurie and Charles: they both behave badly.
- Who is Charles?
- How does Charles behave at school?
- How does Laurie treat his parents?
- In what ways are Laurie and Charles similar?

FOR ENGLISH LEARNERS
Culture: Clarify Point out the word *fresh* in lines 19, 21, and 22. Explain that in this context *fresh* means "rude" or "disrespectful." Although American classrooms may be less formal than those in some other cultures, being rude is not acceptable. Therefore, Charles is spanked. Tell students that at the time the story was written, teachers were allowed to discipline their students by hitting them on the hand or the back of their legs.

On Monday Laurie came home late, full of news. "Charles," he shouted as he came up the hill; I was waiting anxiously on the front steps.
50 "Charles," Laurie yelled all the way up the hill, "Charles was bad again."

"Come right in," I said, as soon as he came close enough. "Lunch is waiting."

"You know what Charles did?" he demanded, following me through the door. "Charles yelled so in school they sent a boy in from first grade to tell the teacher she had to make Charles keep quiet, and so Charles had to stay after school. And so all the children stayed to watch him."

"What did he do?" I asked.

"He just sat there," Laurie said, climbing into his chair at the table. "Hi, Pop, y'old dust mop."

60 "Charles had to stay after school today," I told my husband. "Everyone stayed with him."

"What does this Charles look like?" my husband asked Laurie. "What's his other name?"

"He's bigger than me," Laurie said. "And he doesn't have any rubbers[1] and he doesn't ever wear a jacket."

Monday night was the first Parent-Teachers meeting, and only the fact that the baby had a cold kept me from going; I wanted passionately to meet Charles's mother. On Tuesday Laurie remarked suddenly, "Our teacher had a friend come to see her in school today." **C**

70 "Charles's mother?" my husband and I asked simultaneously.

"Naaah," Laurie said scornfully. "It was a man who came and made us do exercises, we had to touch our toes. Look." He climbed down from his chair and squatted down and touched his toes. "Like this," he said. He got solemnly back into his chair and said, picking up his fork, "Charles didn't even do exercises."

"That's fine," I said heartily. "Didn't Charles want to do exercises?"

"Naaah," Laurie said. "Charles was so fresh to the teacher's friend he wasn't *let* do exercises."

"Fresh again?" I said.

80 "He kicked the teacher's friend," Laurie said. "The teacher's friend told Charles to touch his toes like I just did and Charles kicked him."

"What are they going to do about Charles, do you suppose?" Laurie's father asked him.

Laurie shrugged elaborately. "Throw him out of school, I guess," he said.

---

1. **rubbers:** low-cut overshoes once commonly worn when it rained.

C MAKE INFERENCES
Why do you think Laurie's mother wanted to meet Charles's mother?

C MAKE INFERENCES

Possible answer: Laurie's mother is curious about who could have raised such a badly behaved child and how a mother copes with such a difficult child.

Line 84
REINFORCE *KEY IDEA:* BEHAVIOR

Discuss What does Laurie think might happen to Charles if he continues to misbehave? What does his comment suggest about a possible motive for bad **behavior** at school?
Possible answer: Laurie thinks Charles might be thrown out of school. Laurie's idea suggests that perhaps the child who is misbehaving does not want to be in school and is trying to get thrown out.

DIFFERENTIATED INSTRUCTION

FOR ENGLISH LEARNERS

Language Modifiers Explain that adverbs are used to better describe a verb, an adjective, or another adverb, and often end in *-ly.* Ask students to create a three-column chart with these headings: *Adverb, Word(s) Modified, Definition of Adverb.* As they reread lines 46–87, have them fill in their charts, using context clues or a dictionary to define their adverbs. Have small groups compare their charts.

- *anxiously* (line 49)
- *passionately* (line 67)
- *suddenly* (line 68)
- *simultaneously* (line 70)
- *scornfully* (line 71)
- *solemnly* (line 74)
- *heartily* (line 76)
- *elaborately* (line 84)

Wednesday and Thursday were routine; Charles yelled during story hour and hit a boy in the stomach and made him cry. On Friday Charles stayed after school again and so did all the other children.

90 **W**ith the third week of kindergarten Charles was an institution in our family;[2] the baby was being a Charles when she cried all afternoon; Laurie did a Charles when he filled his wagon full of mud and pulled it through the kitchen; even my husband, when he caught his elbow in the telephone cord and pulled the telephone and a bowl of flowers off the table, said, after the first minute, "Looks like Charles."

During the third and fourth weeks it looked like a reformation in Charles; Laurie reported grimly at lunch on Thursday of the third week, "Charles was so good today the teacher gave him an apple."

"What?" I said, and my husband added warily, "You mean Charles?"

"Charles," Laurie said. "He gave the crayons around and he picked up the books afterward and the teacher said he was her helper."

00 "What happened?" I asked **incredulously**.

"He was her helper, that's all," Laurie said, and shrugged.

"Can this be true, about Charles?" I asked my husband that night. "Can something like this happen?"

"Wait and see," my husband said **cynically**. "When you've got a Charles to deal with, this may mean he's only plotting." He seemed to be wrong. For over a week Charles was the teacher's helper; each day he handed things out and he picked things up; no one had to stay after school.

"The PTA meeting's next week again," I told my husband one evening. "I'm going to find Charles's mother there."

10 "Ask her what happened to Charles," my husband said. "I'd like to know."

"I'd like to know myself," I said.

On Friday of that week things were back to normal. "You know what Charles did today?" Laurie demanded at the lunch table, in a voice slightly awed. "He told a little girl to say a word and she said it and the teacher washed her mouth out with soap and Charles laughed."

"What word?" his father asked unwisely, and Laurie said, "I'll have to whisper it to you, it's so bad." He got down off his chair and went around to his father. His father bent his head down and Laurie whispered joyfully. His father's eyes widened.

20 "Did Charles tell the little girl to say *that?*" he asked respectfully.

"She said it *twice*," Laurie said. "Charles told her to say it *twice*." **D**

"What happened to Charles?" my husband asked.

"Nothing," Laurie said. "He was passing out the crayons."

2. **an institution in our family:** something that has become a significant part of family life.

incredulously
(ĭn-krĕj′ə-ləs-lē) *adv.* in a way that shows doubt or disbelief

cynically (sĭn′ĭ-kəl-lē) *adv.* in a way that shows mistrust in the motives of others

D CHARACTERIZATION
Reread lines 112–121, paying close attention to how Laurie describes Charles's antics. How does Laurie feel about Charles?

Lines 94–107
DISCUSSION PROMPTS
Use these prompts to help students examine the change in Charles and its effect upon Laurie:

Connect If you were the teacher, what feelings would you have about Charles's transformation? *Students might say that they would be grateful for each day of good behavior. However, they might be suspicious about how long it would last.*

Analyze Why does Laurie report Charles's apparent transformation "grimly"? *Possible answers: Charles's good behavior is not as exciting to report. He is not sure why Charles has changed or how his parents will react when he tells them.*

Synthesize Based on what the narrator does *not* say in this part of the story, how is Laurie's behavior at home during these weeks? *Possible answer: The narrator does not report any of Laurie's misdeeds, suggesting that he, too, is well behaved.*

LITERARY ANALYSIS

D CHARACTERIZATION

Possible answer: Charles's behavior impresses Laurie. The narrator uses phrases such as "in a voice slightly awed" (lines 113–114) and "whispered joyfully" (lines 118-119) to describe how Laurie talks about Charles.

Extend the Discussion In what way is Charles a hero to Laurie?

FOR ENGLISH LEARNERS
Culture: Clarify Explain that because bad words are thought to be "dirty," a typical punishment for children who said bad words used to be washing their mouths out with soap (lines 115, 125). Children would be forced to swish soapy water around in their mouths to "clean" them. Because soapy water tastes so horrible, the belief was that the punishment would deter the children from saying bad things ever again.

FOR ADVANCED LEARNERS/PRE–AP
Synthesize Ask students to think about why Laurie's parents are so fascinated by Charles. Have students work in pairs to list three reasons. Then have students make some inferences about the narrator and her husband from their lists.

E MAKE INFERENCES

Possible answer: *Laurie is Charles.*

If students need help . . . Have students work in small groups to identify ways in which Laurie and Charles are similar. List those similarities to help students arrive at the correct inference.

1. Both are rude to adults and will not do what they are told.
2. Both enjoy getting into trouble. Laurie laughs "insanely" after he insults his father by telling him he is dumb (line 33).
3. Both appear quite rough. Laurie swaggers (line 5) slams doors (line 7), and spills his sister's milk (line 10). Charles bounces a see-saw off a child's head (lines 38–39), throws chalk (line 42), and kicks people (line 80).
4.

Extend the Discussion Why does Laurie create Charles?

SELECTION WRAP–UP

REFLECT Have students consider how the narrator might react after hearing that there is no Charles in the class. What emotions might she feel? What might she say to the teacher?

★ CRITIQUE Ask students to evaluate the ending of the story. Ask them to propose alternate endings that might have worked in the story.

READING FLUENCY

Distribute the copy masters and have students work in pairs to practice fluency.

R RESOURCE MANAGER—Copy Master
Reading Fluency p. 134

Monday morning Charles abandoned the little girl and said the evil word himself three or four times, getting his mouth washed out with soap each time. He also threw chalk.

M y husband came to the door with me that evening as I set out for the PTA meeting. "Invite her over for a cup of tea after the meeting," he said. "I want to get a look at her."

130 "If only she's there," I said prayerfully.

"She'll be there," my husband said. "I don't see how they could hold a PTA meeting without Charles's mother."

At the meeting I sat restlessly, scanning each comfortable matronly face, trying to determine which one hid the secret of Charles. None of them looked to me haggard enough. No one stood up in the meeting and apologized for the way her son had been acting. No one mentioned Charles.

After the meeting I identified and sought out Laurie's kindergarten teacher. She had a plate with a cup of tea and a piece of chocolate cake; I had a plate with a cup of tea and a piece of marshmallow cake.

140 We maneuvered up to one another cautiously, and smiled.

"I've been so anxious to meet you," I said. "I'm Laurie's mother."

"We're all so interested in Laurie," she said.

"Well, he certainly likes kindergarten," I said. "He talks about it all the time."

"We had a little trouble adjusting, the first week or so," she said primly, "but now he's a fine little helper. With occasional lapses, of course."

"Laurie usually adjusts very quickly," I said. "I suppose this time it's Charles's influence."   **⑥ Targeted Passage**

"Charles?"

150 "Yes," I said, laughing, "you must have your hands full in that kindergarten, with Charles."

"Charles?" she said. "We don't have any Charles in the kindergarten." ꙮ E

E MAKE INFERENCES
Who is Charles?

DIFFERENTIATED INSTRUCTION

FOR LESS–PROFICIENT READERS
⑥ Targeted Passage [Lines 141–153]
This passage presents the surprise ending of the story: Laurie is Charles.

- What does the teacher say about Laurie's first few weeks of school?
- What does she mean when she says he has "occasional lapses"?
- What surprising news does the teacher have about Charles?
- Who is Charles?

FOR ADVANCED LEARNERS/PRE–AP
Evaluate Although the revelation that Laurie is Charles may come as a shock to Laurie's mother, the author has prepared the readers by using ample foreshadowing. For example, Laurie hesitates before naming Charles (line 21) and often arrives home late (lines 56 and 87). Have pairs of students create a flowchart of clues that hint that Charles and Laurie are the same person. Ask students to compare their charts and discuss how foreshadowing affects the overall impact of the story.

Comprehension

1. **Recall** Who is the narrator of the story?

2. **Recall** Reread lines 25–45. Why does Laurie's mother think kindergarten is "unsettling" for Laurie?

3. **Clarify** According to Laurie, do the other students tend to side with Charles or the teacher?

Literary Analysis

4. **Examine Characterization** What have you learned about Laurie's mother from how she behaves, what she thinks, and what she says?

5. **Make Inferences** Why doesn't Laurie's mother realize that he is Charles?

6. **Analyze the Main Character** Why do you think Laurie **misbehaves?** Support your opinion with details from the story.

7. **Make Judgments** How do you think Laurie's parents should have responded to the "toughness" Laurie displayed around his family and to the tales he told about school?

MARYLAND OBJECTIVES

LITERATURE STANDARD
3.A.3.d Analyze characterization

Comparing Characters

Now that you have read the second short story, finish filling in your chart. Add the final questions and answer them.

	Great-Grandma	Laurie
What does each character look like?		He wears blue jeans and a belt.
How does each character behave?	She makes up stories for the news anchor.	
How do others see each character?		
How would you describe each character's personality?		
In what ways are the characters similar? In what ways are they different?		

Comparing Characters

■ **STANDARDS FOCUS** *Set a Purpose for Reading* Students' charts should include details such as the following about Laurie:

Row 1: He wears blue jeans and a belt.

Row 2: He's bold and independent. He is rude and willful. He makes up stories about Charles.

Row 3: The narrator sees Laurie as basically good but influenced by Charles. The teacher sees Laurie as a challenge.

Row 4: Laurie is naughty and spoiled. He is also clever and creative.

Similarities: Both are clever and quick-witted, make up very convincing stories, and misbehave in public. Both want attention.

Differences: Great-Grandma is not mean or rude. She misbehaves because she is provoked. Laurie misbehaves in many ways. He may be naughty, anxious about kindergarten, or wanting attention.

Practice and Apply

After Reading

For additional support of post-reading questions, use these copy masters:

R RESOURCE MANAGER—Copy Masters
Reading Check p. 132 (to check understanding of the selection)
Question Support p. 133 (**After Reading** questions adapted for English learners and less-proficient readers)

Additional selection questions are provided for teachers on page 119.

ANSWERS
Comprehension

1. *Laurie's mother is the narrator.*

2. *Laurie is acting tough and using bad grammar.*

3. *The students seem to side with Charles, playing with him when they are not supposed to (line 37).*

Literary Analysis
Possible answers:

4. ● **STANDARDS FOCUS** *Characterization Laurie's mother is somewhat naïve because she does not realize Laurie is Charles. She is involved in Laurie's life, asking about Charles, making him lunch, and waiting for him after school. She is sad that Laurie is growing up. She is not a strict parent.*

5. *She does not seem to see Laurie as poorly behaved so does not connect Charles with him. Also, Laurie's stories about Charles are very convincing.*

6. *He wants attention. He does not want to be in school. He is not used to rules and regulations. He likes to shock his parents.*

7. *Students may say that his parents should have been stricter with him at home and imposed rules of behavior. Some may think that the parents should have gone in to see the teacher to discuss Charles's influence on Laurie.*

ANSWERS
Vocabulary in Context

VOCABULARY PRACTICE

1. *false*
2. *true*
3. *false*
4. *false*
5. *false*
6. *true*

 **RESOURCE MANAGER—Copy Master**
Vocabulary Practice p. 136

VOCABULARY IN WRITING

Suggest that students quickly brainstorm the reasons that one of the characters was surprising. Then have them choose three of their reasons and rephrase them using vocabulary words.

VOCABULARY STRATEGY: THE LATIN ROOT
cred (also an EL language objective)

Remind students that suffixes often determine the part of speech of the word. Knowing the part of speech may make it easier to define the word. For example, *-ence* forms nouns, and *-ible* forms adjectives.

Answers:

1. *credible*
2. *discredit*
3. *credit cart*
4. *credentials*
5. *credence*

 **RESOURCE MANAGER—Copy Master**
Vocabulary Strategy p. 137

ⓘ Vocabulary Center at **ClassZone.com**
Additional Vocabulary Activities

Vocabulary in Context

VOCABULARY PRACTICE

Show that you understand the boldfaced words. Decide if each statement is true or false.

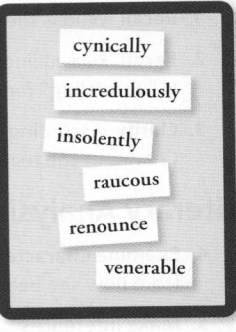

1. At a **raucous** party, most guests sit quietly and talk.
2. You will most likely get in trouble if you speak **insolently** to the principal.
3. A **venerable** individual is usually between the ages of 9 and 12.
4. Dressing **cynically** is a good way to be safe on a long hike.
5. If you **renounce** your bad habits, you plan to continue them.
6. People respond **incredulously** to things they do not believe.

VOCABULARY IN WRITING

Which character in these stories was most surprising to you? Write an explanation, using three or more vocabulary words. Here is a sample beginning.

> **EXAMPLE SENTENCE**
>
> I expected that Great-Grandma would talk like a **venerable** old lady.

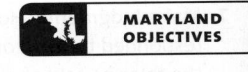

READING STANDARD
1.D.3.b Use word structure to determine meaning

VOCABULARY STRATEGY: THE LATIN ROOT *cred*

The Latin root *cred* means "believe." This root is combined with various prefixes and suffixes to form a number of English words. For example, you already know that the vocabulary word *incredulously* means "in a way that shows doubt or disbelief." To understand the meaning of other words with *cred*, use context clues and your knowledge of what this root means.

PRACTICE Choose a word from the web that best completes each sentence.

1. If the witness is not _____ , the jury will not believe her.
2. The opposition tried to _____ the candidate by making false statements about him.
3. Many banks offer customers a _____ , which allows them to buy things without using cash.
4. When you come to the job interview, please bring all your _____ with you.
5. She gossips so much that it is hard to put any _____ in what she says.

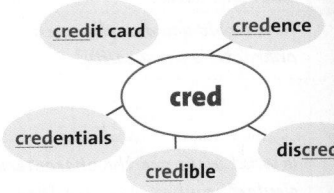

DIFFERENTIATED INSTRUCTION

FOR ENGLISH LEARNERS
Vocabulary Practice

1. Have students work in pairs to create a chart listing each vocabulary word and the definition given in the text.
2. Using their chart and context clues, pairs should identify each statement as true or false.
3. Discuss responses and point out clues in the sentences.

FOR ADVANCED LEARNERS/PRE–AP

Vocabulary in Writing Have students develop their argument for one character or the other. Then have volunteers form teams to debate the issue in class, presenting their reasons and evidence from the text. Have listening students evaluate the persuasiveness of each side's argument.

Writing for Assessment

1. READ THE PROMPT

In writing assessments, you will often be asked to compare and contrast two works that are similar in some way, such as two short stories with similar **characters**.

> **PROMPT**
>
> In four or five paragraphs, compare and contrast Great-Grandma from "The Three-Century Woman" and Laurie from "Charles." Identify the characters' similarities and differences, citing details from the two stories to support your ideas. Then state whether you think the characters are more alike than they are different.

◄ **STRATEGIES IN ACTION**

1. I have to **tell** the **similarities** **and differences** between the characters.

2. I need to **give examples** that show how the characters are **alike** and how they are **different**.

3. I need to **decide** whether the characters are more alike than they are different.

2. PLAN YOUR WRITING

Using your chart, identify the ways in which the characters are alike and the ways they are different. Then think about how to best present these similarities and differences.

- Write a position statement that presents your main idea.
- Review the stories to find quotations and details that support the similarities and the differences you have identified.
- Create an outline to organize your ideas. This sample outline shows one way to organize your paragraphs.

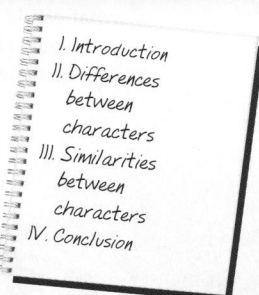

I. Introduction
II. Differences between characters
III. Similarities between characters
IV. Conclusion

3. DRAFT YOUR RESPONSE

Introduction   Introduce the characters you are comparing, the titles of the stories in which the characters appear, and your reason for comparing the characters. Also include your position statement.

Body   Present the characters' similarities and differences, using your outline as a guide. Make clear whether you think the similarities or differences are more important.

Conclusion   State whether you think the characters are more alike than different. Leave your readers with a final thought about the two characters.

Revision   Make sure each point of your comparison is supported by an example .

DIFFERENTIATED INSTRUCTION

FOR LESS–PROFICIENT WRITERS

Drafting Your Response

- To help students focus their essays before beginning to write, record similarities and differences on the board.

- Discuss which are more important in bringing out character and helping to reveal theme. Then provide a writing template to help students structure their responses.

  Introduction: Give titles and authors, introduce characters, and state the main idea.

Middle paragraphs: Explain the similarities in one paragraph and the differences in the other. Whichever is more significant should be discussed last.

- State one similarity or difference at a time.
- Support each idea with evidence.

Conclusion: Tell whether the characters are more alike or more different and explain why.

Writing for Assessment

1. **READ THE PROMPT**

   - Read the prompt aloud. Ask volunteers to identify key words that define the task.

   - Discuss the third **Strategy in Action**. Distinguish between superficial differences such as appearance and significant details such as motives for their actions.

2. **PLAN YOUR WRITING**

   - Students can use a T Chart with the column headings *Similarities* and *Differences* to organize their details.

   - Have students express the main idea of their essay in a strong position statement. Give them an example, such as "Although Great-Grandma Breckenridge and Laurie both invent stories, their motives and the consequences of their actions differ."

   - Give students this alternative outline:

     First paragraph: introduction

     Second paragraph: the less significant similarities (or differences)

     Third paragraph: the more important differences (or similarities)

     Fourth paragraph: conclusion

   🧰 BEST PRACTICES TOOLKIT—Transparency
   T Chart p. A25

3. **DRAFT YOUR RESPONSE**

   Remind students to begin each body paragraph with a strong topic sentence.

   📖 RESOURCE MANAGER—Copy Master
   Writing for Assessment p. 138

Assess and Reteach

Assess

📖 RESOURCE MANAGER—Copy Masters
Selection Tests A, B/C pp. 139–140, 141–142

💿 Test Generator CD

Reteach

🗂 STANDARDS LESSON FILE
Literature Lesson 3: Characterization
Reading Lesson 12: Comparing and Contrasting
Vocabulary Lesson 10: Latin Roots (active verbs)

Focus and Motivate

OBJECTIVES

Literary Analysis
- explore the key idea of **heroes**
- identify and analyze characterization in nonfiction
- read a memoir and a memorandum

Reading
- connect

Vocabulary
- build vocabulary for reading and writing
- use reference aids to locate synonyms (also an EL language objective)

SUMMARY

In "Encounter with Martin Luther King Jr." writer Maya Angelou describes her first meeting with King when she was working for the Southern Christian Leadership Conference. During their conversation he shows understanding of her background and sympathy for the plight of her brother Bailey, who is in jail. Angelou reveals that this personal response gave her hope for the future of African Americans.

What if you could meet your H E R O ?

Discuss the question with students. To lead into the *KEY IDEA,* ask students what qualities make someone a **hero.** Extend the discussion by having students do the *QUICKWRITE.* After the activity, invite volunteers to identify their hero and share one of the questions they would like to ask.

Selection Resources

Encounter with Martin Luther King Jr.

Autobiography by Maya Angelou

What if you could meet your H E R O ?

MARYLAND OBJECTIVES

READING/LIT STANDARDS
1.E.4.f Connect text to personal experience
3.A.3.d Analyze characterization

KEY IDEA You see them on TV, read about them in magazines and newspapers, and even watch movies that tell the stories of their accomplishments. But for most of us, meeting our famous **heroes** in person is something that only happens in daydreams. In this selection, Maya Angelou recounts an unforgettable private meeting with her larger-than-life hero, Martin Luther King Jr.

QUICKWRITE If a hero of yours walked into your home tomorrow, what would you say to him or her? In your journal, note whom you would like to meet in this way. Then write five questions you would ask if you had the chance.

258

---

* Resources for Differentiation   † Also in Spanish   ‡ In Haitian Creole and Vietnamese

LITERARY ANALYSIS: CHARACTERIZATION IN NONFICTION

To help her readers understand what Martin Luther King Jr. was like, Maya Angelou uses methods of **characterization** that fiction writers use. She reveals King's personality by

- making direct statements about his personality
- describing his appearance and actions
- showing how others acted toward him
- sharing what he said and what others said about him

As you read the selection, notice the ways in which Angelou conveys what King was like in person.

READING STRATEGY: CONNECT

Whenever you find similarities between your life and someone else's, you are connecting with that person. You can **connect** with what you are reading by comparing the events described with experiences you are familiar with. As you read, keep a log to record connections between you and Angelou.

Angelou	Me
Angelou was so surprised to see King that she didn't shake his hand right away.	When I saw my teacher at the grocery store, I was so surprised that I didn't say hello right away.

VOCABULARY IN CONTEXT

The boldfaced words help Angelou convey the African-American experience in the 1960s. To see how many of them you know, restate each sentence, using a different word or words for the boldfaced term.

1. He did not allow his bitterness to **fester** and ruin his life.
2. For King, nonviolence was the key to winning the **fray.**
3. She is **punctual** and in her seat before the bell rings.
4. His kindness helped to **redeem** her from sadness.
5. For some, a **shanty** was the only affordable housing.

Author Online

An Early Activist
At age 16, Maya Angelou wanted to become a streetcar conductor in San Francisco. However, the railway would not hire female or African-American drivers. Supported by organizations that backed her cause, Angelou went to the railway office every day. After three weeks, she became San Francisco's first female African-American streetcar driver.

Maya Angelou
born 1928

Renaissance Woman Angelou eventually moved on to many other pursuits. She has been a dancer, an actor, a mother, a poet, and a songwriter as well as the author of six autobiographies, each covering a different time in her life.

 MORE ABOUT THE AUTHOR
For more on Maya Angelou, visit the **Literature Center at ClassZone.com.**

Background

Civil Rights Supporter Under the leadership of Rev. Martin Luther King Jr., the Southern Christian Leadership Conference (SCLC) promoted nonviolent protest as a way to gain civil rights for African Americans. In 1960, Angelou wrote and co-produced a musical to raise funds for the organization. She later became the Northern coordinator for the group. King was just becoming famous when Maya Angelou met him at the SCLC office.

259

Teach

STANDARDS FOCUS

LITERARY ANALYSIS

● CHARACTERIZATION IN NONFICTION

Have students review **An Early Activist** on page 259. Ask what Angelou's actions reveal about her as a person. ***Possible answer:*** *She was not afraid to be the first person to do something. She did not give up and sought support from others to help her achieve her goal.*

CHECK UNDERSTANDING Ask students to identify which method of characterization the writer of the paragraph used to show what Angelou was like.

READING STRATEGY

■ CONNECT

Direct students to read **Renaissance Woman** on page 259 and ask them to make a connection to their own lives. *Students may relate to one of Angelou's achievements as something they would like to do, they may say they've wanted to be many different things when they grow up, or they may say they know someone who does many things well.*

CHECK UNDERSTANDING Have students make a connection to the photograph on page 258.

R **RESOURCE MANAGER—Copy Master**
Connect p. 155 (for student use while reading the selection)

VOCABULARY SKILL

▲ VOCABULARY IN CONTEXT

DIAGNOSE WORD KNOWLEDGE To determine preteaching needs, have all students complete **Vocabulary in Context.** *Students' responses will vary.* ***Possible answers:*** *1. grow stronger (p. 263); 2. battle (p. 264); 3. on time (p. 264); 4. save (p. 264); 5. tiny house (p. 262)*

PRETEACH VOCABULARY Help students determine meanings for each boldfaced word on the Vocabulary Study copy master.

1. Read the first sentence in Part A aloud, emphasizing *fester.*
2. Point out the context clues *pain* and *make him bitter.* Elicit possible meanings for *fester.*
3. Repeat the procedure for the other words.

 RESOURCE MANAGER—Copy Master
Vocabulary Study p. 157

For general guidelines on differentiating vocabulary instruction and for alternative vocabulary activities for students not needing vocabulary preteaching, see

BEST PRACTICES TOOLKIT
Scaffolding Vocabulary Instruction pp. 43–46

ℹ Vocabulary Center at **ClassZone.com**
Additional Vocabulary Activities

ANALYZE VISUALS

Possible answers: King's expression suggests that he is imagining a brighter future. His upward gaze makes him look like a visionary. The background photo also suggests that he is concerned about a variety of civil rights issues.

About the Art The photograph of Martin Luther King Jr. on page 261 was taken in 1964. Those on pages 262–263 are from 1967. The crowd scenes are from the August 1963 March on Washington at which King delivered his famous "I have a dream" speech.

LITERARY ANALYSIS

Ⓐ CHARACTERIZATION

Possible answer: He is short, young, friendly, and powerful.

Extend the Discussion Why did Angelou find King's "easy friendliness . . . unsettling"?

Encounter with

Martin Luther King Jr.

Maya Angelou

I returned from lunch. In the outer office Millie Jordan was working over a table of papers. Hazel was busy on the telephone. I walked into my office and a man sitting at my desk, with his back turned, spun around, stood up and smiled. Martin Luther King said, "Good afternoon, Miss Angelou. You are right on time."

The surprise was so total that it took me a moment to react to his outstretched hand.

I had worked two months for the SCLC, sent out tens of thousands of letters and invitations signed by Rev. King, made hundreds of statements 10 in his name, but I had never seen him up close. He was shorter than I expected and so young. He had an easy friendliness, which was unsettling. Looking at him in my office, alone, was like seeing a lion sitting down at my dining-room table eating a plate of mustard greens. Ⓐ

"We're so grateful for the job you all are doing up here. It's a confirmation for us down on the firing line."[1]

---

1. **a confirmation . . . line:** proof to us in the middle of the struggle that we are doing the right thing.

ANALYZE VISUALS
What might you **infer** about the expression on King's face?

❶ **Targeted Passage**

Ⓐ **CHARACTERIZATION**
Reread lines 10–13. What do you learn about King from Angelou's description of him?

DIFFERENTIATED INSTRUCTION

FOR ALL STUDENTS

Learning Center Set up a learning center on the Civil Rights movement with books and pictures on these high-interest topics: Martin Luther King Jr., Malcolm X or James Farmer (other civil rights leaders), and the status of civil rights today. Provide a variety of independent projects, such as creating a timeline of key events, designing a civil rights rally poster, and listening to King's speeches.

FOR LESS–PROFICIENT READERS

In combination with the *Audio Anthology CD*, use one or more Targeted Passages (pp. 260, 263, 264) to ensure that students focus on key selection events, concepts, and skills.

❶ **Targeted Passage [Lines 1–13]**

This passage sets up the selection: it describes how Angelou first met King.

• How does Martin Luther King surprise Maya Angelou?

• How does Angelou first respond to him?

• How is King different than Angelou expected him to be?

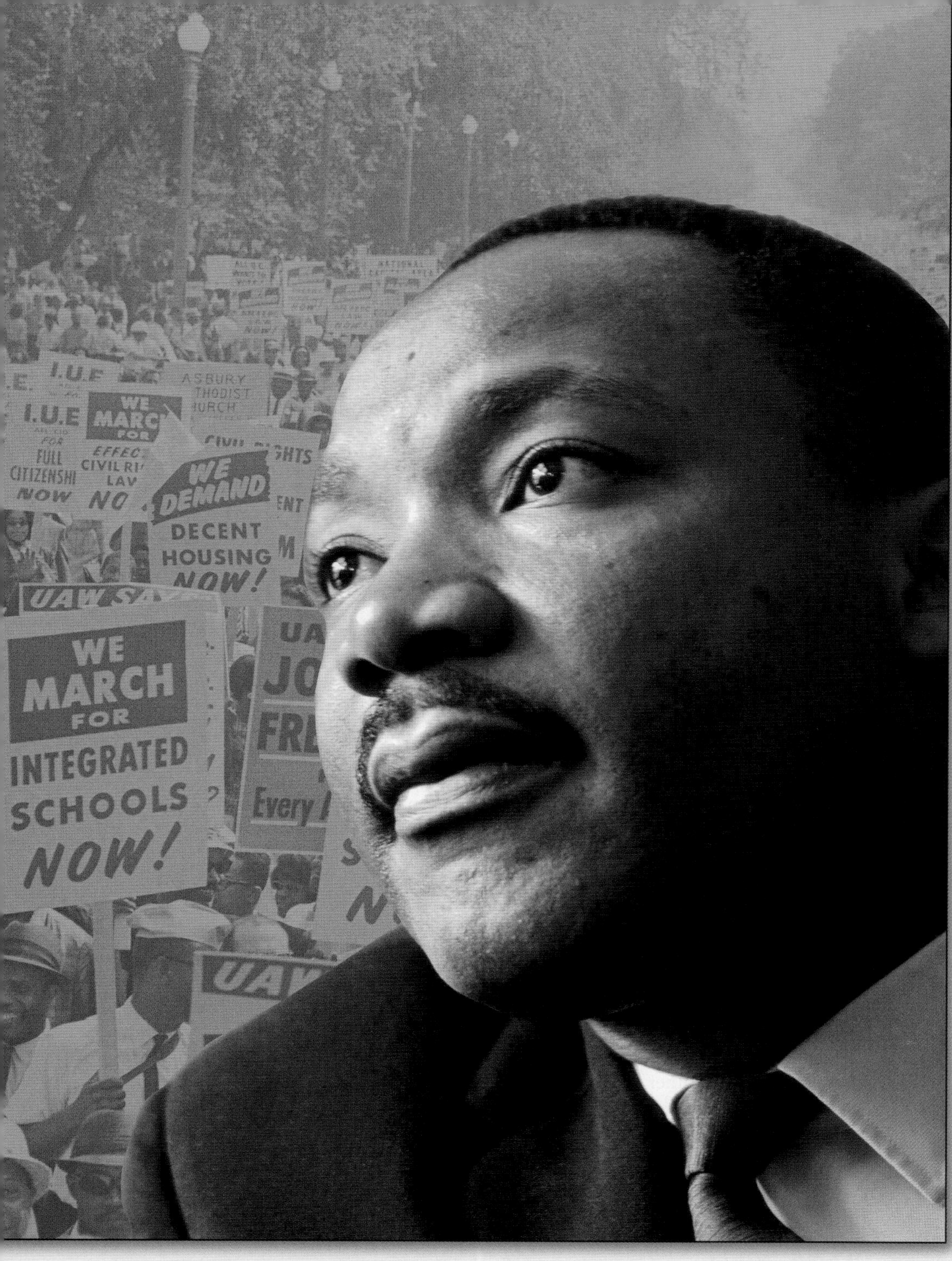

BACKGROUND

Southern Christian Leadership Conference (SCLC) The bus boycott in Montgomery, Alabama (1955–1956), ended the city's segregation in public transportation. This success inspired Martin Luther King and others who had worked on that campaign to create the SCLC. They founded the organization in 1957 to help local groups use nonviolence to achieve racial equality in housing, education, employment, and voting. The organization's headquarters were in Atlanta, Georgia, and most of its leaders were Protestant ministers.

Maya Angelou succeeded Bayard Rustin as coordinator of the SCLC's northern office. This office helped gain support for the fight against segregation in the South and also fought against unfair housing practices in the North. The organization's greatest successes were the ending of segregation in Birmingham, Alabama, in 1963; the 1963 March on Washington; and securing the passage of the Civil Rights Act of 1964 and the Voting Rights Act of 1965. After King was assassinated in 1968, the organization became less visible and was marked by conflicts between its leaders. The SCLC was at the forefront of the push for a national holiday to mark Martin Luther King Jr.'s birthday.

FOR ENGLISH LEARNERS

Options for Reading Read the first Targeted Passage aloud and explain that an encounter is a meeting. Then have students read along while listening to the *Audio Anthology CD*.

Key Academic Vocabulary Use New Word Analysis to provide instruction and practice for this academic vocabulary: *react* (line 6), *job* (lines 14, 35), *finally* (line 16), *benefit* (line 64), *relax* (line 65), *constant* (line 83).

BEST PRACTICES TOOLKIT—Transparency
New Word Analysis p. E8

Prereading For prereading instruction for English learners, see

BEST PRACTICES TOOLKIT
Scaffolding Reading Instruction pp. 43–46

FOR ADVANCED LEARNERS/PRE–AP

Pre-AP exercises in the bottom channel provide additional challenge for your advanced students. Use them for small groups or individuals.

ADDITIONAL GUIDELINES

For more help with differentiation of a nonfiction selection and tips for classroom management, see

BEST PRACTICES TOOLKIT
Differentiated Instruction pp. 31–38

Lines 20–32
DISCUSSION PROMPTS

Use these prompts to help students understand how Martin Luther King helps Maya Angelou feel comfortable talking with him:

Connect Think about how you would feel if you unexpectedly met a famous person you admire. How do you think Maya Angelou felt when she met Martin Luther King? *Students' responses should reflect an understanding that Angelou was very surprised and may have felt shy or nervous.*

Analyze How did King's questions and change in speaking style help Angelou feel more at ease with him? *Possible answers: His questions about her background showed his genuine interest in her as a person. Because he had dropped the "church way of talking" (line 21), Angelou was able to see him as an ordinary person whom she could talk with more easily.*

Synthesize What did King do to encourage Angelou to keep telling him more about her background? *Possible answers: He said he was familiar with the area around her hometown and continued to ask her questions to draw her out. He nodded and smiled to show he related to what she was saying.*

Lines 27–32
REINFORCE *KEY IDEA:* HEROES

Discuss "Mamma" is the term Angelou uses to refer to her grandmother (line 28). How might Mamma be a **hero** to Angelou? *Possible answer: Angelou might think of her grandmother as a hero because she raised Angelou and her brother in difficult conditions.*

I was finally able to say how glad I was to meet him.

"Come on, take your seat back and tell me about yourself."

I settled gratefully into the chair and he sat on the arm of the old sofa across the room.

20 "Stanley says you're a Southern girl. Where are you from?" His voice had lost the church way of talking and he had become just a young man asking a question of a young woman. I looked at him and thought about the good-looking . . . school athlete, who was invariably the boyfriend of the . . . cheerleader.

I said, "Stamps, Arkansas. Twenty-five miles from Texarkana."

He knew Texarkana and Pine Bluff, and, of course, Little Rock. He asked me the size and population of Stamps and if my people were farmers. I said no and started to explain about Mamma and my crippled uncle who raised me. As I talked he nodded as if he knew them 30 personally. When I described the dirt roads and **shanties** and the little schoolhouse on top of the hill, he smiled in recognition. When I mentioned my brother Bailey, he asked what he was doing now.

The question stopped me. He was friendly and understanding, but if I told him my brother was in prison, I couldn't be sure how long his

shanty (shăn'tē) *n.* a rundown house; a shack

DIFFERENTIATED INSTRUCTION

FOR LESS–PROFICIENT READERS

Reading Strategy Follow-Up: Connect

1. Read lines 20–24. Point out how Angelou connects King to a type of person she knows.

2. Ask students to record this connection in their charts. (See sample at right.)

3. Read lines 27–32 and ask students to think about King's responses to what Angelou says.

4. Have students record another connection. Remind them that connections may involve differences as well as similarities.

Maya Angelou	Me
Maya Angelou compares Dr. King to a popular boy in school.	When I met my friend's cousin he reminded me of the smartest boy in science class.

understanding would last. I could lose my job. Even more important, I might lose his respect. Birds of a feather and all that, but I took a chance and told him Bailey was in Sing Sing.[2]

He dropped his head and looked at his hands. **②** **Targeted Passage**

40 "It wasn't a crime against a human being." I had to explain. I loved my brother and although he was in jail, I wanted Martin Luther King to think he was an uncommon criminal. "He was a fence. Selling stolen goods. That's all." **B**

He looked up. "How old is he?"

"Thirty-three and very bright. Bailey is not a bad person. Really."

"I understand. Disappointment drives our young men to some desperate lengths." Sympathy and sadness kept his voice low. "That's why we must fight and win. We must save the Baileys of the world. And Maya, never stop loving him. Never give up on him. Never deny him. And remember, he is freer than those who hold him behind bars." **C**

50 Redemptive[3] suffering had always been the part of Martin's argument which I found difficult to accept. I had seen distress **fester** souls and bend

---

2. **Sing Sing:** a prison in New York State.
3. **redemptive:** earning freedom or salvation.

B CONNECT
Have you ever felt the need to explain or defend the actions of someone you love? Why do you think Angelou might have done this?

C CHARACTERIZATION
Reread lines 45–49. What does King's statement suggest about him?

fester (fĕs'tər) v. to become an increasing source of irritation or poisoning

---

B CONNECT

Students' responses will vary. They may say that Angelou explained her brother's actions because she loved him and wanted King to understand that Bailey was basically a good person who hadn't hurt anyone else. She wanted King to think her brother was better than a common criminal.

If students need help ... Have them focus on lines 39–41. What does Angelou say after she says "I had to explain"?

Extend the Discussion What do you learn about Maya Angelou as a person from this scene?

C CHARACTERIZATION

Possible answer: He is understanding, cares about others, and does not judge them. He also sees individual problems as part of a bigger struggle.

If students need help ... Ask these questions:

- What does King's first comment, "I understand," say about the kind of person he is?
- How does Angelou describe King's voice, and what feelings does she see in him (line 46)?
- What does King's advice to Angelou (line 48) reveal about what he considers important?

FOR LESS–PROFICIENT READERS

② Targeted Passage [Lines 39–49]

In this passage Angelou reveals King's personality by describing his response to learning that her brother is in jail.

- Why is Maya Angelou's brother in jail?
- How does Angelou feel about her brother?
- How does King feel about Bailey's being in jail?
- What advice does King give Angelou?

FOR ENGLISH LEARNERS

Language: Idioms and Sayings Explain that Angelou's statement "Birds of a feather and all that" (line 36) refers to the saying "Birds of a feather flock together," which means that birds of the same species or type gather in groups. Applied to people, this means that people who have things in common tend to spend time together. In this case, Angelou is afraid that King may think that she, too, might break the law.

peoples' bodies out of shape, but I had yet to see anyone **redeemed** from pain, by pain.

There was a knock at the door and Stanley Levison entered.

"Good afternoon, Maya. Hello, Martin. We're about ready."

Martin stood and the personal tenderness disappeared. He became the fighting preacher, armed and ready for the public **fray.**

He came over to my desk. "Please accept my thanks. And remember, we are not alone. There are a lot of good people in this nation. White
60 people who love right and are willing to stand up and be counted."
His voice had changed back to the mellifluous Baptist cadence[4] raised for the common good. **D**

We shook hands and I wondered if his statement on the existence of good whites had been made for Stanley's benefit.

At the door, he turned. "But we cannot relax, because for every fair-minded white American, there is a Bull Connor[5] waiting with his shotgun and attack dogs."

I was sitting, mulling over the experience, when Hazel and Millie walked in smiling.
70 "Caught you that time, didn't we?"

I asked her if she had set up the surprise. She had not. She said when Martin came in he asked to meet me. He was told that I was due back from lunch and that I was fanatically **punctual.** He offered to play a joke by waiting alone in my office.

Millie chuckled. "He's got a sense of humor. You never hear about that, do you?"

Hazel said, "It makes him more human somehow. I like a serious man to be able to laugh. Rounds out the personality." **E**

Martin King had been a hero and a leader to me since the time when
80 Godfrey and I heard him speak and had been carried to glory on his wings of hope. However, the personal sadness he showed when I spoke of my brother put my heart in his keeping forever, and made me thrust away the small constant worry which my mother had given me as a part of an early parting gift: Black folks can't change because white folks won't change. ✍ **F**

---

4. **mellifluous** (mə-lĭf′lōō-əs) **Baptist cadence** (kād′ns): the smooth rhythms of speech characteristic of Baptist preachers.

5. **Bull Connor:** an official in Birmingham, Alabama, best known for ordering police officers to use fire hoses and police dogs to break up a civil rights demonstration in 1963.

UNIT 2: ANALYZING CHARACTER AND POINT OF VIEW

---

redeem (rĭ-dēm′) v. to set free

fray (frā) n. a fight; a heated dispute

D CHARACTERIZATION
Reread lines 56–62. Describe the shift in King's attitude. What can you **infer** about why he is different in private than he is in public?

punctual (pŭngk′chōō-əl) adj. on time; prompt

E CHARACTERIZATION
What do you learn about King through Millie's and Hazel's words?

3 Targeted Passage

F CONNECT
Think about how Angelou feels toward King. Who has touched your heart or mind in a similar way?

LITERARY ANALYSIS

D CHARACTERIZATION

Possible answers: He shifts from having a personal conversation and showing his feelings to speaking in a more general way. The public side of him must be strong, fearless, and ready to fight in order to achieve his goals.

LITERARY ANALYSIS

E CHARACTERIZATION

Possible answers: He has a sense of humor and is not always serious.

READING STRATEGY

F CONNECT

Students' answers will vary and should reflect an understanding that Angelou was inspired by King and was also impressed with his sympathy and kindness.

SELECTION WRAP–UP

REFLECT Have students think about how this piece affected their perceptions of Martin Luther King Jr. Ask them to give examples of things that surprised or touched them.

★ **CRITIQUE** Ask students to evaluate how well the author succeeded in portraying Martin Luther King as an individual. What techniques did she use to do this?

READING FLUENCY

Distribute the copy masters and have students work in pairs to practice fluency.

R **RESOURCE MANAGER—Copy Master**
Reading Fluency p. 162

DIFFERENTIATED INSTRUCTION

FOR LESS–PROFICIENT READERS
3 Targeted Passage [Lines 79–85]

This passage concludes the selection by revealing how the encounter changed Maya Angelou.

• When did King first become Maya Angelou's hero?
• What made her give her heart to him?
• What had Angelou's mother made her worry about?
• How did the conversation with King affect Angelou's worry?

FOR ADVANCED LEARNERS/PRE–AP

Analyze Language Some of Angelou's descriptions of King are poetic or metaphorical: "a lion sitting down at my dining-room table" (lines 12–13), "the good-looking . . . school athlete" (line 23), and "carried to glory on his wings of hope" (lines 80–81). Challenge students to write statements using different comparisons to convey the same meaning. Have students share their statements in small groups.

264 UNIT 2

Comprehension

1. **Recall** What joke does King play on Maya Angelou?

2. **Recall** Why is Angelou afraid to tell King about her brother?

3. **Clarify** Why did King want to meet Angelou?

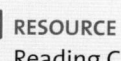

MARYLAND OBJECTIVES

LITERATURE STANDARD
3.A.3.d Analyze characterization

Literary Analysis

4. **Examine Connections** Review the notes you made in your log. What events were you able to connect with? Note which connection surprised you the most.

5. **Interpret Meaning** Reread lines 12–13. When Angelou enters her office and sees King, she describes her **hero** as a "lion sitting down at my dining-room table eating a plate of mustard greens." What does she mean by this?

6. **Analyze Characterization** What three words or phrases would you use to describe King's personality? Write them in a chart like the one shown. Below each word or phrase, cite several details from the selection to support it.

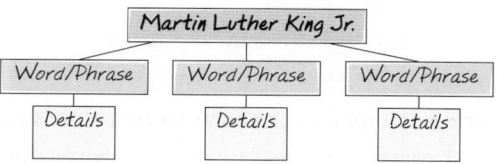

Martin Luther King Jr.

Word/Phrase	Word/Phrase	Word/Phrase
Details	Details	Details

7. **Make Inferences** Reread the last paragraph. Why do you think King's comments about Angelou's brother helped Angelou stop worrying so much, or, in her words, "thrust away the small constant worry" she had felt since her mother left her?

8. **Draw Conclusions** Which side of King, the "fighting preacher" or the tender young man, do you think meant the most to Angelou? Give examples from the text to support your answer.

Extension and Challenge

9. **Speaking and Listening** If King were to give a speech to persuade people not to give up on family members who made mistakes like Angelou's brother, Bailey, what would he say? Prepare a short speech and present it to the class.

10. 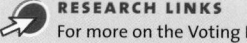 **SOCIAL STUDIES CONNECTION** Read the memorandum from Martin Luther King Jr. on page 267. Why were King and the SCLC concerned about the African-American vote in the South? What was the result of their efforts? Research the Voting Rights Act of 1965 to find the answers. Also note how the law changed voting practices.

> **RESEARCH LINKS**
> For more on the Voting Rights Act of 1965, visit the **Research Center** at ClassZone.com.

8. *King's private side meant the most to Angelou. Although his preaching made him her hero, it was his "personal sadness" about her brother that gained her loyalty forever and made her hope for change (lines 79–85).*

Extension and Challenge

9. *Students' speeches should reflect the ideas that King expressed in lines 45–49. They might also include his thoughts in lines 58–60.*

10. **SOCIAL STUDIES CONNECTION**
Possible answer: *They were concerned because Southern states had passed laws that limited African Americans' right to vote. Their efforts resulted in passage of the Voting Rights Act of 1965, which outlawed the use of literacy tests and allowed the federal government to supervise voter registration to make sure it was fair.*

Practice and Apply

After Reading

For additional support of post-reading questions, use these copy masters:

RESOURCE MANAGER—Copy Masters
Reading Check p. 160 (to check understanding of the selection)
Characterization in Nonfiction p. 153 (for practice of literary analysis standards focus)
Question Support p. 161 (**After Reading** questions adapted for English learners and less-proficient readers)

Additional selection questions are provided for teachers on page 147.

ANSWERS

Comprehension

1. *King surprises her by sitting in her chair with his back to the door so she won't know who it is when she returns from lunch.*

2. *She is afraid of how he will react if she tells him that her brother is in jail. She thinks he might fire her or lose respect for her.*

3. *He wanted to thank her for her work and get to know a little about her.*

Literary Analysis

Possible answers:

4. ■ **STANDARDS FOCUS** *Connect Answers will vary, but students' responses should reflect a deeper understanding of their experiences through identifying with Maya Angelou's experiences in some way.*

5. *It feels strange to see a man she considers a hero sitting in her office. Like a lion, he is powerful and fearless. He looks out of place in this everyday setting.*

6. ● **STANDARDS FOCUS** *Characterization in Nonfiction Answers will vary, but students' charts should reflect an understanding of King's character. Possible words include strong, compassionate, and wise. Details should support each word or phrase.*

7. *His understanding of her brother's situation proved to her that he was very aware of the challenges faced by African Americans. Angelou's confidence in King's ability helped her stop worrying that people's racist attitudes would not change.*

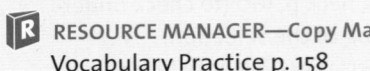

ANSWERS
Vocabulary in Context
VOCABULARY PRACTICE

1. *(c)*; 2. *(b)*; 3. *(a)*; 4. *(a)*; 5. *(b)*

 RESOURCE MANAGER—Copy Master
Vocabulary Practice p. 158

VOCABULARY IN WRITING

Distribute copies of the Cause-and-Effect Diagram. Students can use it to chart the multiple effects that meeting King had on Angelou. Then have students review the vocabulary words and connect them with the effects to help them write their descriptions.

BEST PRACTICES TOOLKIT—Transparency
Cause-and-Effect Diagram pp. B16, B38

VOCABULARY STRATEGY: USING REFERENCE AIDS *(also an EL language objective)*

Explain that a thesaurus contains lists of synonyms but does not usually define words. A dictionary does not list synonyms for every entry, but it gives the meanings of words and may help students infer a synonym.

Possible answers:
1. *end*; 2. *release*; 3. *dominate*; 4. *greedy.*
Example sentence: The Voting Rights Act of 1965 made states end the use of literacy tests.

RESOURCE MANAGER—Copy Master
Vocabulary Strategy p. 159

Vocabulary Center at ClassZone.com
Additional Vocabulary Activities

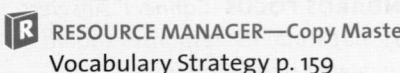

Assess
RESOURCE MANAGER—Copy Masters
Selection Tests A, B/C pp. 163–164, 165–166
Test Generator CD

Reteach
STANDARDS LESSON FILE
Literature Lesson 3: Characterization

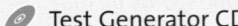
266 UNIT 2

Vocabulary in Context
VOCABULARY PRACTICE

Choose the letter of the term that is most closely related to the boldfaced word.

1. **shanty:** (a) mansion, (b) abode, (c) hut
2. **fester:** (a) improve, (b) disturb, (c) go away
3. **redeem:** (a) rescue, (b) enslave, (c) preserve
4. **fray:** (a) conflict, (b) converse, (c) sew
5. **punctual:** (a) lazy, (b) on time, (c) late

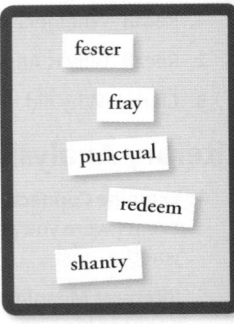

VOCABULARY IN WRITING

Using two or more vocabulary words, write a paragraph describing how Maya Angelou's encounter with Dr. King affected her. You might start like this.

> **EXAMPLE SENTENCE**
> Maya Angelou was always **punctual**.

VOCABULARY STRATEGY: USING REFERENCE AIDS

To express ideas clearly and accurately, you need to choose just the right words. Reference aids, or resources of information, can improve your writing by providing synonyms for words you already know. **Synonyms** are words with similar meanings. For example, a synonym for *shanty* is *shack*. To find a synonym for a word, look in a reference aid.

MARYLAND OBJECTIVES
READING STANDARD
1.D.3.c Use resources to gather information about words

- A **thesaurus** is a reference book of synonyms. Also, many word processing programs contain an electronic thesaurus tool.

  shanty *noun* hovel, hut, lean-to, shack

- A **dictionary** lists synonyms after the definitions of some words.

  shanty (shăn'tē) *n., pl.* **-ties** a rundown house: *The shanty collapsed after years of neglect.* **syn** HOVEL, HUT, LEAN-TO, SHACK

PRACTICE Use a reference aid to find a synonym for each word. Note the synonym and the reference aid you used to find it. Then use each synonym in a sentence that matches its shade of meaning.

1. abolish   3. monopolize
2. extricate   4. voracious

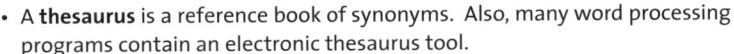
VOCABULARY PRACTICE
For more practice, go to the **Vocabulary Center** at **ClassZone.com**.

DIFFERENTIATED INSTRUCTION

FOR ENGLISH LEARNERS
Vocabulary Strategy

1. Have students work in pairs to look up each word in a dictionary to understand its meaning.
2. Direct students to use a thesaurus to look up synonyms for each word. Invite them to clarify shades of meaning of the synonyms by looking them up in a dictionary.
3. Have students use each of the synonyms in a sentence.

FOR ADVANCED LEARNERS/PRE–AP
Vocabulary Strategy

- Challenge students to list synonyms for each word before they look up the word in a thesaurus.
- Invite students to use different synonyms for each word in sentences to show their different shades of meaning.

Reading for Information

MEMORANDUM Following is a memo that Dr. King sent to the people organizing the opening-day rallies for the Crusade for Citizenship, a drive to register African Americans to vote. Notice the phrases that reflect Dr. King's fairness and leadership.

FROM: M. L. King Jr., President
TO: Speakers, Local Contacts, Participants in S. C. L. C.
RE: Crusade for Citizenship Mass Meeting, February 12, 1958

UNITY OF EMPHASIS

At our executive committee meeting on Thursday, Jan. 30, 1958, many expressed the hope that all persons would leave the Mass Meetings with a clear picture of the aims and purposes of the Southern Christian Leadership Conference, with a firm determination to register and vote, and with a sense of being part of a southwide "crusade."

To help achieve this unity of aim and direction, we are urging you to make certain that the following points are clearly and simply made from the platform by some responsible person during the mass meeting:

1. The Crusade for Citizenship is a southwide movement. These meetings express this. The list should be read. It should be clear that this is the opening step in a long and hard, but necessary and glorious struggle.

2. The Crusade has two aims:
   (a) to double the number of Negroes who vote in the South
   (b) and thus, to help liberate all Southerners, Negro and white, to extend democracy in our great nation. When Negroes can vote, white people will have greater economic and political freedom. The South can have a real two party system— a necessity for real democracy.

3. The Crusade will place emphasis on preparing spiritually and tactically for registration prior to the 1958 and 1960 elections.

4. The Crusade is non-partisan. Its major purpose is to get men and women to realize that voting is a "moral" and "political" duty to God, to the nation, to themselves, and to their children; then to help them learn how to register and to want to vote. The Crusade will not engage in partisan politics. We urge people to vote: we do not want to influence them to vote for any particular party. We believe in the people. When they are aroused to vote, they will vote intelligently. No one need tell them where their political interest lies. This is morally the right approach.

5. The right to vote is related to all other rights. When Negroes have won and fully exercise their right to vote many changes can then occur:
   (a) segregated buses will disappear
   (b) wages will be increased
   (c) police brutality will be a thing of the past
   (d) men who believe in justice will be sent to congress
   (e) "mob violence" will fade away
   (f) justice will be established in the courts.

These things will come about because the mayors, city councilmen, police commissioners, the governors, congressmen and even the President will know that they must do the right things or be turned out of office when the people go to the ballot box. . . .

This selection provides support for question 10 on page 265. You can also use it as a mini-lesson on reading for information.

READING FOR INFORMATION

Explain that a memorandum is a workplace document, often called a memo, used to communicate information. Ask students what the header (FROM, TO, RE) tells them. (Clarify that *RE* is short for *Regarding*.) **Answer:** *The header identifies the writer (M. L. King Jr.), the audience (speakers and organizers of the SCLC), and the topic (mass meeting to be held on February 12).*

BACKGROUND

Negro The term *Negro* had been used since the 1500s to refer to black people. In the late 1960s, *black* became the more accepted term, and in the 1980s, *African American* also became common. Many people now consider the term *Negro* to be offensive because of its links to slavery.

DISCUSSION PROMPTS

Use these prompts to help students understand how King uses the memorandum to communicate his ideas:

Connect How does King's use of numbered and lettered points help you understand his ideas more easily? *Students may say that it is easier to read and understand text in which the main points are organized in outline form.*

Analyze How does the way the memorandum is organized help King communicate his ideas? *Possible answer: The title and the first paragraph set out his goals. The body then outlines those ideas step by step.*

Synthesize How does King link the registration of African-American voters to benefits for all U.S. citizens? Give examples of specific sections of the memorandum. *Possible answer: In points 2 and 5, King states that increasing the number of African-American voters will help spread democracy and increase economic and political freedom for all, and he outlines the other rights and benefits that will follow.*

DIFFERENTIATED INSTRUCTION

FOR LESS-PROFICIENT READERS

Comprehension Support: Preview Have students preview the underlined points that King wishes to communicate in the memo. Ask them to write one or two sentences to summarize what they think the memorandum is about and to confirm their ideas after they read the complete text.

FOR ENGLISH LEARNERS

Language: Word Roots Explain that the word *crusade* comes from the Latin root *crux,* meaning "cross." The Crusades were Christian expeditions to recapture parts of the Holy Land in the 11th to 13th centuries. The word is also used to describe any strong movement in support of a cause. King also uses other words to reinforce the moral aspect of the campaign, including "necessary and glorious struggle," "spiritually," and "voting is a moral . . . duty to God."

Focus and Motivate

OBJECTIVES

Literary Analysis
- explore the key idea of what a person needs to **survive**
- identify point of view in a memoir
- read a memoir

Reading
- identify causes and effects

Vocabulary
- build vocabulary for reading and writing
- identify idioms *(also an EL language objective)*

Grammar and Writing
- avoid misplaced modifiers
- use prepositional phrases correctly

SUMMARY

"Dirk the Protector" is a memoir of a teenage boy struggling to survive on his own. He lives alone in the basement of a building, works odd jobs, and often becomes the target of bullies. One night he shares his food with a stray dog who, in gratitude, becomes his bodyguard. The two are close companions for nearly a year, until the dog is adopted by a farmer.

What do you need to SURVIVE?

Discuss the question. Ask students what they know about emergency kits for home and car safety. What supplies are essential for nourishment? For warmth? What about for pets? After students complete the *LIST IT* activity, have pairs compare their lists of what it takes to **survive.**

Dirk the Protector
Memoir by Gary Paulsen

What do you need to SURVIVE?

MARYLAND OBJECTIVES

READING/LIT STANDARDS
1.E.3.a Select and apply appropriate strategies during reading
3.A.3.i Analyze point of view

KEY IDEA Hunger, fear, injury, turmoil—it's amazing what people can withstand when they must. But there's a limit. Every human being needs certain things to **survive.** In "Dirk the Protector," a chance encounter provides a young Gary Paulsen with what he needs to survive life alone on the streets.

LIST IT What if you woke up tomorrow and all the adults had vanished? Brainstorm a list of items you would need to survive. Remember, no one would know how to operate electrical plants, manufacture products in factories, or purify drinking water. You may use the list that is shown to get started. When you're finished, compare your list with those of your classmates.

Items to Survive a World Without Adults
1. *Flashlight*
2. *Gallons of*
   purified water
3.
4.

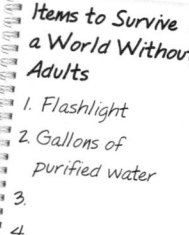

268

Selection Resources

---

* Resources for Differentiation   † Also in Spanish   ‡ In Haitian Creole and Vietnamese

LITERARY ANALYSIS: POINT OF VIEW IN A MEMOIR

In a **memoir,** the writer gives a true account of experiences in his or her life. Because the writer has participated in the events, he or she writes from the **first-person point of view,** using the pronoun *I.* However, that doesn't mean the writer states everything directly. As you read "Dirk the Protector," note when Gary Paulsen says something openly about himself and when he only hints at his true meaning.

READING SKILL: IDENTIFY CAUSE AND EFFECT

To fully understand what you read, you need to know why things happen. Often, a writer tells you that one event (the **cause**) made another event (the **effect**) happen. In this example, Paulsen directly states that troubles with his parents caused him to leave home:

For a time in my life I became a street kid. It would be nice to put it another way but what with the drinking at home and the difficulties it caused with my parents I couldn't live in the house.

Other times you have to infer cause-and-effect relationships on the basis of clues in the text and your knowledge.

As you read "Dirk the Protector," note other cause-and-effect relationships and record them in a diagram like the one shown.

Cause		Effect
Trouble with parents at home.	→	Paulsen moves into basement.

VOCABULARY IN CONTEXT

Make a chart like the one shown. Put each vocabulary word in the appropriate column, and then write a brief definition of each word you are familiar with.

WORD LIST			
cohort	forerunner	predatory
conventional	hustle	puny
decoy	impasse	

Know Well	Think I Know	Don't Know at All

Author Online

**Gary Paulsen
born 1939**

A Young Survivor
Gary Paulsen was born to a family that faced many problems. As a boy, Paulsen often had to work and take care of himself. While delivering newspapers one cold evening, he went into a library to warm up. The librarian offered him a book and a library card. Paulsen recalls, "The most astonishing thing happened. This silly little card with my name on it gave me an identity." In the library, it did not matter what he wore, who liked him, or how much money he had.

Reader and Writer Paulsen still reads a lot, and he is a very hardworking writer. He has published more than 150 books for children, young adults, and adults. His childhood experiences and outdoor adventures are frequent subjects in his writing.

Devoted to Dogs "Dirk the Protector" is from Paulsen's memoir *My Life in Dog Years.* He gives the reader a peek into his own life by sharing memories of his dogs. Paulsen has said, "I've always thought of dogs as people.... They have personalities and likes and dislikes and humor and anger and great heart and spirit."

 MORE ABOUT THE AUTHOR
For more on Gary Paulsen, visit the **Literature Center** at **ClassZone.com.**

DIRK THE PROTECTOR **269**

Teach

STANDARDS FOCUS

● POINT OF VIEW IN A MEMOIR

Read aloud this example:

As I rubbed my icy fingers, I hoped desperately that someone would find us soon. Perhaps other hikers had seen our tiny fire or heard our calls for help.

Ask students what readers know and don't know because of the first-person point of view. *Possible answer: Readers know what the narrator thinks and feels, but they don't know if help is on the way.*

CHECK UNDERSTANDING Ask students why a memoir is always told from the first-person point of view.

■ IDENTIFY CAUSE AND EFFECT

Have students review **A Young Survivor** on page 269. Ask these questions:

- What caused Paulsen to have to take care of himself as a child? *Possible answer: His family had troubles.*

- A librarian offered Paulsen a library card. How did he feel as a result? *Possible answer: He had "an identity."*

CHECK UNDERSTANDING Ask students to explain a topic in the news, using words such as *because, since,* and *therefore.*

 RESOURCE MANAGER—Copy Master Identify Cause and Effect p. 179 (for student use while reading the selection)

▲ VOCABULARY IN CONTEXT

DIAGNOSE WORD KNOWLEDGE To determine preteaching needs, have all students complete **Vocabulary in Context.** Check students' definitions against those on the selection pages: *cohort* (p. 275), *conventional* (p. 270), *decoy* (p. 273), *forerunner* (p. 272), *hustle* (p. 275), *impasse* (p. 273), *predatory* (p. 272), *puny* (p. 273).

PRETEACH VOCABULARY Use the Vocabulary Study copy master to help students determine the meaning of each boldfaced word.

1. Read aloud the sentences in Part A. Emphasize each boldfaced word.

2. Ask students to think about the way the word is used. Discuss possible meanings for *cohort,* such as "pal" or "colleague."

3. Repeat the procedure for each of the other sentences.

 RESOURCE MANAGER—Copy Master Vocabulary Study p. 181

For general guidelines on differentiating vocabulary instruction and for alternative vocabulary activities for students not needing vocabulary preteaching, see

🧰 BEST PRACTICES TOOLKIT
Scaffolding Vocabulary Instruction pp. 43–46
ℹ️ Vocabulary Center at **ClassZone.com**

ANALYZE VISUALS

Possible answers:

- *The fact that he is by himself on a rooftop implies that he is an outsider.*
- *Life is hard for the boy; it is winter and he is in an outdoor place, rather than a cozy indoor place.*
- *He appears to be thinking; maybe he needs to rely upon himself and his wits.*
- *The golden colors and the orange in the boy's hands may suggest that he does have some bright spots in his life, or some hope within him.*

About the Art *Boy with Orange* is an oil painting by Canadian artist Murray Kimber (born 1964). In Kimber's art, the setting may be the element that tells most about what is going on; characters often do not make eye contact and are depicted in simple, frontal views against complex backgrounds with emotionally expressive colors. Kimber has worked on a variety of projects, including billboards, postage stamps, and children's books.

READING SKILL

A CAUSE AND EFFECT

Remind students to record their answers in the cause-and-effect diagram.

Possible answer:

Cause	Effect
Paulsen must support himself.	He takes the only job he can find in town working at the bowling alley.

Dirk *the* PROTECTOR

Gary Paulsen

For a time in my life I became a street kid. It would be nice to put it another way but what with the drinking at home and the difficulties it caused with my parents I couldn't live in the house.

I made a place for myself in the basement by the furnace and hunted and fished in the woods around the small town. But I had other needs as well—clothes, food, school supplies—and they required money.

I was not afraid of work and spent most of my summers working on farms for two, three and finally five dollars a day. This gave me enough for school clothes, though never for enough clothes or the right kind; I was never cool or in. But during the school year I couldn't leave town to work the farms. I looked for odd jobs but most of them were taken by the boys who stayed in town through the summer. All the **conventional** jobs like working in the markets or at the drugstore were gone and all I could find was setting pins in the small bowling alley over the Four Clover Bar. **A**

It had just six alleys and they were busy all the time—there were leagues each night from seven to eleven—but the pay for truly brutal

10

ANALYZE VISUALS
Examine this painting. What can you **infer** about the boy's life?

① Targeted Passage

conventional
(kən-vĕn'shə-nəl) *adj.*
usual; traditional

A CAUSE AND EFFECT
What causes Paulsen to take the job at the bowling alley? Keep reading to find an effect of working this job.

Boy with Orange, Murray Kimber
© Murray Kimber/Illustrationworks.com

DIFFERENTIATED INSTRUCTION

FOR ALL STUDENTS

Expert Groups Write these topics on the board and invite students to research topics that interest them. Suggest they use visuals when they present to the class.

- survival memoirs
- books or movies that feature significant relationships between dog and person
- ways that dogs work to help humans (guide dogs; search-and-rescue dogs; police dogs)

FOR LESS–PROFICIENT READERS

In combination with the *Audio Anthology CD*, use one or more Targeted Passages (pp. 270, 275, 276) to ensure that students focus on key selection events, concepts, and skills.

① Targeted Passage [Lines 1–14]

This passage introduces the author and the conflict he faced at this point in his life: the struggle to survive alone on the streets.

- Why did Paulsen become "a street kid"?

BACKGROUND

Homeless Teens As many as 1.5 million U.S. teens are homeless. No one is certain of the actual number because homeless teens generally hide the fact that they are homeless; many move from the home of one friend or relative to another and try to avoid the intervention of social services. Others, finding nowhere else to go, live on the street. Some have been thrown out of their homes, but many are runaways. Teens who run away often do so in response to family troubles. Since they may be too young to hold jobs legally or secure housing on their own, homeless teens often find it hard to earn money and may face violence, harassment, and other dangers on the streets. In addition to basic safety concerns, homeless teens confront difficulties in accessing health care, acquiring job skills, and staying in school.

- Where does he live?
- What kind of work does he do in the summer? Why doesn't he do this work the rest of the year?

FOR ENGLISH LEARNERS

Key Academic Vocabulary Have students use Word Questioning to learn this vocabulary: *income* (line 22), *target* (line 30), *area* (line 40), *policy* (line 79), *remove* (lines 118 and 192), *constant* (line 185).

 BEST PRACTICES TOOLKIT—Transparency Word Questioning p. E9

Prereading For prereading instruction for English learners, see

 BEST PRACTICES TOOLKIT Scaffolding Reading Instruction pp. 43–46

FOR ADVANCED LEARNERS/PRE–AP

Pre-AP exercises in the bottom channel provide additional challenge for your advanced students. Use them for small groups or individuals.

ADDITIONAL GUIDELINES

For more help with differentiation and tips for classroom management, see

 BEST PRACTICES TOOLKIT Differentiated Instruction pp. 31–38

REINFORCE *KEY IDEA:* SURVIVE

Discuss Paulsen repeatedly risks his physical safety in order to **survive** on his own. Do survival stories always involve an element of risk? Explain. ***Possible answer:*** *A survival story must feature a character at risk of something—such as starvation, freezing, or being caught by an enemy. It is the struggle to carry on or stay alive despite the risk that makes it a survival story.*

LITERARY ANALYSIS

B POINT OF VIEW

Possible answer: Paulsen felt discouraged because he was outnumbered and because he thought the authorities would not think he was worth helping.

If students need help . . . Read aloud lines 35–37, emphasizing words and phrases that convey Paulsen's sense of discouragement ("tried . . . but," "couldn't win," "wrong side," "didn't think," "hopeless").

---

work was only seven cents a line. There weren't many boys willing to do the work but with so few alleys, it was still very hard to earn much money. A dollar a night was not uncommon and three was outstanding.

20 To make up the difference I started selling newspapers in the bars at night. This kept me up and out late, and I often came home at midnight. But it added to my income so that I could stay above water.[1]

Unfortunately it also put me in the streets at a time when there was what might be called a rough element. There weren't gangs then, not exactly, but there were groups of boys who more or less hung out together and got into trouble. They were the **<u>forerunners</u>** of the gangs we have now, but with some singular differences. They did not have firearms— but many carried switchblade knives.

These groups were **<u>predatory,</u>** and they hunted the streets at night.

30 I became their favorite target in this dark world. Had the town been larger I might have hidden from them, or found different routes. But there was only a small uptown section and it was impossible for me to avoid them. They would catch me walking a dark street and surround me and with threats and blows steal what money I had earned that night.

I tried fighting back but there were usually several of them. I couldn't win. Because I was from "the wrong side of the tracks"[2] I didn't think I could go to the authorities. It all seemed hopeless. **B**

And then I met Dirk.

*T*he bowling alley was on a second floor and had a window in back
40 of the pit area. When all the lanes were going, the heat from the pin lights made the temperature close to a hundred degrees. Outside the window a ladder led to the roof. One fall evening, instead of leaving work through the front door, I made my way out the window and up the ladder onto the roof. I hoped to find a new way home to escape the boys who waited for me. That night one of the league bowlers had bowled a perfect game—300—and in celebration had bought the pit boys hamburgers and Cokes. I had put the burger and Coke in a bag to take back to my basement. The bag had grease stains and smelled of toasted buns, and my mouth watered as I moved from the roof of the bowling
50 alley to the flat roof over the hardware store, then down a fire escape that led to a dark alcove[3] off an alley.

There was a black space beneath the stairs and as I reached the bottom and my foot hit the ground I heard a low growl. It was not loud, more a rumble that seemed to come from the earth and so full of menace that it stopped me cold, my foot frozen in midair.

---

1. **stay above water:** survive.
2. **"the wrong side of the tracks":** the less desirable part of town.
3. **alcove** (ăl'kōv'): a small hollow space in a wall.

forerunner (fôr'rŭn'ər) *n.* person or thing that came before

predatory (prĕd'ə-tôr'ē) *adj.* given to stealing from or hurting others for one's own gain

B POINT OF VIEW
Reread lines 35–37. What does Paulsen tell the reader about his attitude toward himself and his situation?

DIFFERENTIATED INSTRUCTION

FOR LESS–PROFICIENT READERS
Comprehension Support To clarify the demands of Paulsen's day, ask students to help you jot down his weekday schedule in a T Chart.

Time	Activity
Morning	Goes to school
Afternoon	School, works in bowling alley
Evening	Works in bowling alley and bars
Midnight	Walks home alone

Visualizing Use Draw It to help students visualize lines 39–55. Talk aloud as you illustrate the scene, while students read along and give you cues for what to draw next. Use a dotted line to show Paulsen's route up the ladder, along the rooftops, and down the fire escape ladder to where the dog is hiding.

BEST PRACTICES TOOLKIT—Transparency
T Chart p. A25
Draw It p. A2

FOR ENGLISH LEARNERS
Vocabulary: Prefixes Point out the words *midnight* (line 21) and *midair* (line 55). Explain that their common prefix *mid-* means "middle" and that it is usually combined with a noun to indicate a time or place. Ask students to recall or build other words that begin with *mid-*, such as *midsummer* and *midtown*.

I raised my foot and the growl stopped.

I lowered my foot and the growl came again. My foot went up and it stopped.

60 I stood there, trying to peer through the steps of the fire escape. For a time I couldn't see more than a dark shape crouched back in the gloom. There was a head and a back, and as my eyes became accustomed to the dark I could see that it had scraggly, scruffy hair and two eyes that glowed yellow. **C**

We were at an **impasse.** I didn't want to climb up the ladder again but if I stepped to the ground it seemed likely I would be bitten. I hung there for a full minute before I thought of the hamburger. I could use it as a **decoy** and get away.

The problem was the hamburger smelled so good and I was so hungry.

I decided to give the beast under the stairs half a burger. I opened the sack, unwrapped the tinfoil and threw half the sandwich under the steps, 70 then jumped down and ran for the end of the alley. I was just getting my stride, legs and arms pumping, pulling air with a heaving chest, when I rounded the corner and ran smack into the latest group of boys who were terrorizing me.

There were four of them, led by a thug—he and two of the others would ultimately land in prison—named, absurdly, "Happy" Santun.

Happy was built like an upright freezer and had just about half the intelligence but this time it was easy. I'd run right into him.

"Well—lookit here. He came to us this time. . . ."

Over the months I had developed a policy of flee or die—run as fast 80 as I could to avoid the pain, and to hang on to my hard-earned money. Sometimes it worked, but most often they caught me.

This time, they already had me. I could have handed over the money, taken a few hits and been done with it, but something in me snapped and I hit Happy in the face with every ounce of strength in my **puny** body.

He brushed off the blow easily and I went down in a welter of blows and kicks from all four of them. I curled into a ball to protect what I could. I'd done this before, many times, and knew that they would stop sometime—although I suspected that because I'd hit Happy it might take longer than usual for them to get bored hitting me. **D**

90 Instead there was some commotion that I didn't understand and the kicks stopped coming. There was a snarling growl that seemed to come from the bowels of the earth, followed by the sound of ripping cloth, screams, and then the fading slap of footsteps running away.

For another minute I remained curled up, then opened my eyes to find that I was alone.

But when I rolled over I saw the dog.

C CAUSE AND EFFECT
Reread lines 52–62. Make an **inference** about what kind of beast is under the stairs. What's causing the beast to growl?

impasse (ĭm'păs') n. a situation in which no progress can be made; a deadlock

decoy (dē'koi') n. a person or thing used to distract others or lead them in a different direction

puny (pyōō'nē) adj. weak and small

D POINT OF VIEW
Reread lines 79–89. As Paulsen describes the attack, what else does the reader learn about him?

C CAUSE AND EFFECT

Inferences about what kind of beast it is will vary but should be based on evidence in the text (such as the setting in a town, the growling noise, and the "scruffy hair"). Ideas about causes may include

- *The beast growls when it sees Paulsen's foot.*
- *The beast is trying to protect its hiding place.*

Lines 56–66
DISCUSSION PROMPTS

Use these prompts to help students understand the author's lonely predicament in this scene:

Connect What would go through your mind in this situation? What would you do? *Students may say they would think they had disturbed a wild animal and would fear for their lives. Most may say that they would run away from it.*

Analyze Why doesn't Paulsen go back up the ladder and eat his burger on the roof? *Possible answer: It is so late that he just wants to get home. He is too tired and startled to think clearly. Maybe he doesn't know another way down.*

Evaluate How does the author use details about the passage of time to create a mood of tension? *Possible answer: As Paulsen's foot goes up and then down, the growl stops and then starts again. He stares into the dark "for a time" before the beast's shape becomes clear. He hangs "for a minute" trying to come up with an escape plan.*

D POINT OF VIEW

Possible answers: Paulsen has been the subject of attacks over several months (line 79), and he has suffered pain and had his money stolen (line 80). He has learned to protect himself by curling up to shield himself from blows (lines 86–89).

FOR ENGLISH LEARNERS

Vocabulary: Words with -ing Explain that the ending -ing is used to form the progressive verb tense that describes an action that is (or was) in the process of happening. An example is "I was just getting my stride" (lines 70–71). Point out that verb forms with -ing can also be used as nouns and adjectives, and that some words ending in -ing are not verb forms at all. Have students locate and discuss examples such as the following.

- **Progressive tense:** *pulling* (line 71), *terrorizing* (line 73), *staring* (line 111)
- **Adjectives:** *willing* (line 17), *bowling alley* (line 39), *ripping cloth* (line 92)
- **Nouns:** *fighting* (35), *setting* (123)
- **Not verb forms at all:** *outstanding* (line 19), *evening* (line 42), *something* (line 83)

It was the one that had been beneath the stairs. Brindled, patches of hair gone, one ear folded over and the other standing straight and notched from fighting. He didn't seem to be any particular breed. Just big and
100 rangy, right on the edge of ugly, though I would come to think of him as beautiful. He was Airedale crossed with hound crossed with alligator.

Alley dog. Big, tough, mean alley dog. As I watched he spit cloth—it looked like blue jeans—out of his mouth.

"You bit Happy, and sent them running?" I asked.

He growled, and I wasn't sure if it was with menace, but he didn't bare his teeth and didn't seem to want to attack me. Indeed, he had saved me.

"Why?" I asked. "What did I do to deserve . . . oh, the hamburger."

I swear, he pointedly looked at the bag with the second half of hamburger in it.

110 "You want more?" **E**

He kept staring at the bag and I thought, Well, he sure as heck deserves it. I opened the sack and gave him the rest of it, which disappeared down his throat as if a hole had opened into the universe.

He looked at the bag.

"That's it," I said, brushing my hands together. "The whole thing."

A low growl.

"You can rip my head off—there still isn't any more hamburger."

I removed the Coke and handed him the bag, which he took, held on the ground with one foot and deftly ripped open with his teeth.

120 "See? Nothing." I was up by this time and I started to walk away. "Thanks for the help . . ."

He followed me. Not close, perhaps eight feet back, but matching my speed. It was now nearly midnight and I was tired and sore from setting pins and from the kicks that had landed on my back and sides.

"I don't have anything to eat at home but crackers and peanut butter and jelly," I told him. I kept some food in the basement of the apartment building, where I slept near the furnace.

He kept following and, truth be known, I didn't mind. I was still half scared of him but the memory of him spitting out bits of Happy's pants
130 and the sound of the boys running off made me smile. When I arrived at the apartment house I held the main door open and he walked right in. I opened the basement door and he followed me down the steps into the furnace room.

I turned the light on and could see that my earlier judgment had been correct. He was scarred from fighting, skinny and flat sided and with patches of hair gone. His nails were worn down from scratching concrete.

"Dirk," I said. "I'll call you Dirk." I had been trying to read a detective novel and there was a tough guy in it named Dirk. "You look like somebody named Dirk."

brindled (brĭn´dld): *adj.* light brownish yellow o grayish with streaks or spots of a darker color

E CAUSE AND EFFECT
Reread lines 105–110. What is the cause-and-effect relationship Paulsen explains here?

READING SKILL

E CAUSE AND EFFECT

Possible answer:

Cause		Effect
Paulsen shares his hamburger with the dog.	>	The dog defends Paulsen, hoping for more hamburger.

DIFFERENTIATED INSTRUCTION

FOR LESS–PROFICIENT READERS

Reading Skill Follow-Up: Identify Cause and Effect Have students work in pairs to complete a cause-and-effect diagram for the remainder of page 274. Suggest that they begin with Paulsen's giving the dog the rest of his burger. Have pairs of students compare their completed charts. Discuss the different and equally valid ways of describing causes and effects in this sequence of events.

FOR ENGLISH LEARNERS

Language: Plurals Remind students that when a noun ends in *ch, s, sh, x,* or *z,* the plural usually is formed by adding *-es,* not just *-s.* Draw students' attention to *patches* (line 136), *boxes* (lines 141 and 149), and *sandwiches* (line 206).

FOR ADVANCED LEARNERS/PRE–AP

Analyze Simile Point out the simile Paulsen uses in lines 112–113 to show how hungry Dirk is: the burger "disappeared down his throat as if a hole had opened into the universe." Challenge students to identify another characteristic of Dirk or Paulsen and use an original simile to describe it. Have students share their similes with the class.

And so we sat that first night. I had two boxes of Ritz crackers I'd **hustled** somewhere, a jar of peanut butter and another one of grape jelly, and a knife from the kitchen upstairs. I would smear a cracker, hand it to him—he took each one with great care and gentleness—and then eat one myself. We did this, back and forth, until both boxes were empty and my stomach was
50 bulging; then I fell asleep on the old outdoor lounge I used for furniture.

The next day was a school day. I woke up and found Dirk under the basement stairs, watching me. When I opened the door he trotted up the steps and outside—growling at me as he went past—and I started off to school.

He followed me at a distance, then stopped across the street when I went
60 into the front of the school building. I thought I'd probably never see him again.

But he was waiting when I came out that afternoon, sitting across the street by a mailbox. I walked up to him.

"Hi, Dirk." I thought of petting him but when I reached a hand out he growled. "All right—no touching."

I turned and made my way toward the bowling alley. It was Friday and sometimes on Friday afternoon there were people who wanted to bowl
70 early and I could pick up a dollar or two setting pins.

Dirk followed about four feet back—closer than before—and as I made my way along Second Street and came around the corner by Ecker's Drugstore I ran into Happy. He had only two of his **cohorts** with him and I don't think they had intended to do me harm, but I surprised them and Happy took a swing at me.

Dirk took him right in the middle. I mean bit him in the center of his stomach, hard, before Happy's fist could get to me. Happy screamed and doubled over and Dirk went around and ripped into his rear and kept tearing at it even as Happy and his two companions fled down the street.
80 It was absolutely great. Maybe one of the great moments in my life. **F**
I had a bodyguard.

Street Corner (1991), Daniel Bennett Schwartz. Oil on canvas, 91.4 cm × 71.1 cm. Private collection. © Bridgeman Art Library.

hustle (hŭs´əl) *v.* to gain by energetic effort

2 Targeted Passage

cohort (kō´hôrt´) *n.* a companion or associate

F POINT OF VIEW
On the basis of what you know about Paulsen, why does he say it was "one of the great moments in my life"?

Lines 140–151
DISCUSSION PROMPTS
Use these prompts to help students understand how the relationship between Paulsen and Dirk grows:

Connect In your experience, is sharing always part of building a friendship? Explain. *Students may say that sharing and friendship tend to go together. Friends may share interests and experiences as well as their thoughts, problems, and secrets.*

Analyze Compare the interaction between Paulsen and Dirk in this paragraph with the their first encounter. How are these interactions different? *Possible answer: Paulsen and Dirk are beginning to trust each other. Paulsen loses his fear—in fact, he falls asleep near Dirk.*

Synthesize Besides Dirk's coming to his rescue, what do you think accounts for Paulsen's change in attitude toward the dog? *Possible answer: He is touched when the dog follows him home. In the light, he sees how skinny and roughed-up the dog is. Perhaps he identifies with the dog and wants to help him.*

ANALYZE VISUALS

About the Art American illustrator Daniel Bennett Schwartz (born 1929) is known for his portraits and realistic images of contemporary life. His work has appeared in many magazines and on movie posters.

Activity Ask students how the image relates to Dirk's life in the selection. *Possible answers: The dog is alone on the street, as Dirk was. His posture hints that he is wary; he crouches slightly as he looks around, and he seems to be on the move. Like Dirk, he seems to be a cautious dog. The shadows may suggest lurking danger or loneliness—two factors in Dirk's life on the street.*

LITERARY ANALYSIS

F POINT OF VIEW

Possible answer: Paulsen was used to taking care of himself. Now he had someone else to protect him.

REINFORCE *KEY IDEA:* SURVIVE

Discuss How do Paulsen and Dirk help each other to **survive?** *Possible answer: Paulsen gives food to Dirk. Dirk acts as a bodyguard for Paulsen. They offer companionship to each other.*

READING SKILL

G CAUSE AND EFFECT

Possible answer:

Cause		Effect
Dirk acts as Paulsen's body-guard for about a year.	→	The bullies never bother Paulsen again.

SELECTION WRAP–UP

REFLECT Ask students to consider what the selection suggests about the things a person needs to survive. Besides offering him protection, how did Paulsen's relationship with Dirk help him to get by?

⭐ **CRITIQUE** Ask students whether they found the narrator believable. Why or why not? Were there any elements of the memoir that seemed exaggerated or hard to believe?

It was as close to having a live nuclear weapon as you can get. I cannot say we became friends. I touched him only once, when he wasn't looking—I petted him on the head and received a growl and a lifted lip for it. But we became constant companions. Dirk moved into the basement with me, and I gave him a hamburger every day and hustled up dog food for him and many nights we sat down there eating Ritz crackers and he watched me working on stick model airplanes.

190   He followed me to school, waited for me, followed me to the bowling alley, waited for me. He was with me everywhere I went, always back three or four feet, always with a soft growl, and to my great satisfaction every time he saw Happy—every time—Dirk would try to remove some part of his body with as much violence as possible.

He caused Happy and his mob to change their habits. They not only stopped hunting me but went out of their way to avoid me, or more specifically, Dirk. In fact after that winter and spring they never bothered me again, even after Dirk was gone. **G**

D irk came to a wonderful end. I always thought of him as a street dog—surely nobody owned him—and in the summer when I was 200 hired to work on a farm four miles east of town I took him with me. We walked all the way out to the farm, Dirk four feet in back of me, and he would trot along beside the tractor when I plowed, now and then chasing the hundreds of seagulls that came for the worms the plow turned up.

The farmer, whose name was Olaf, was a bachelor and did not have a dog. I looked over once to see Dirk sitting next to Olaf while we ate some sandwiches and when Olaf reached out to pet him Dirk actually—this was the first time I'd seen it—wagged his tail.

He'd found a home.

I worked the whole summer there and when it came time to leave, 210 Dirk remained sitting in the yard as I walked down the driveway. The next summer I had bought an old Dodge for twenty-five dollars and I drove out to Olaf's to say hello and saw Dirk out in a field with perhaps two hundred sheep. He wasn't herding them, or chasing them, but was just standing there, watching the flock.

"You have him with the sheep?" I asked Olaf.

He nodded. "Last year I lost forty-three to coyotes," he said. "This year not a one. He likes to guard things, doesn't he?"

I thought of Dirk chasing Happy down the street, and later spitting out bits of his pants, and I smiled. "Yeah, he sure does."

G CAUSE AND EFFECT
What is the long-term effect Dirk has on the young Paulsen's life?

③ Targeted Passage

DIFFERENTIATED INSTRUCTION

FOR LESS–PROFICIENT READERS

③ Targeted Passage [Lines 194–217]

This passage shows the resolution of the memoir: it summarizes the effects Dirk had on Paulsen's life and tells what happened to the dog.

- What effects does Dirk have on Happy and his cohorts?
- Who is Olaf? How does Dirk seem to feel about Olaf?
- What does Dirk do after Paulsen leaves the farm? How does Paulsen learn this?

FOR ENGLISH LEARNERS

Reading Comprehension: Sequence To clarify when events took place and how much time has elapsed, have students scan page 276 for words that relate to the seasons. Remind students that Paulsen and Dirk met in the fall (line 42). Distribute copies of the Timeline transparency. Have students make a time-line that indicates where Dirk is during each season mentioned.

🧰 **BEST PRACTICES TOOLKIT—Transparency** Timeline p. B23

Comprehension

1. **Recall** What keeps Paulsen out late at night?
2. **Recall** What does Paulsen do to take care of Dirk?
3. **Clarify** What are two challenges that Paulsen faces?

Literary Analysis

4. **Analyze Point of View** On the left side of a two-column chart, list information you know about Paulsen because he states it directly. On the right, list the questions you have about Paulsen after reading the memoir.

What I Know About Paulsen	Questions I Have About Paulsen
He lived by himself in a basement.	Did his parents know he was there?

5. **Analyze Cause and Effect** Compare the cause-and-effect relationships you recorded with those recorded by another classmate. With that classmate, choose the one cause-and-effect relationship that you think influenced Paulsen's life the most, and explain why you think so.

6. **Analyze Character** Writers often give animals character traits that appear human. On the basis of the details Paulsen provides about Dirk, describe the dog's "personality."

7. **Compare and Contrast** Reread the first two paragraphs of "Dirk the Protector" and then the last three. How is Paulsen's life the same in the end, and how has it changed?

8. **Draw Conclusions** Dirk's protection ended the attacks against Paulsen. Why don't the attacks start up again after Dirk stays at the farm?

Extension and Challenge

9. **Big Question Activity** Now that you've read "Dirk the Protector," think about the advice Paulsen might give you to enable you to survive in the world without the help of adults. If necessary, revise the list you made in the activity on page 268. Then create a **survival** manual based on your new list.

10. **Readers' Circle** One way to think about the complexity of a cause-and-effect relationship is to ask, What if . . . ? For example, what if the man had not bowled a perfect game? In a group discussion, talk about how the story might have turned out differently. Then, create another what-if question for another group to answer.

Extension and Challenge

9. A survival manual might include advice about working hard, taking care of yourself, helping out someone else, and finding good friends.

10. The discussion might cover these points:

- If the bowler had not won a perfect game, Paulsen would not have had a burger to share, and the dog might not have been motivated to help him.

- If Paulsen hadn't lived alone in the basement, he wouldn't have had a place where Dirk could stay, and they might not have become so close.

Other questions: What if Paulsen had not been attacked that night? What if one of the other boys had had a dog?

After Reading

For additional support of post-reading questions, use these copy masters:

RESOURCE MANAGER—Copy Masters
Reading Check p. 184 (to check understanding of the selection)
Point of View in Memoir p. 177 (for practice of literary analysis standards focus)
Question Support p. 185 (**After Reading** questions adapted for English learners and less-proficient readers)

Additional selection questions are provided for teachers on page 171.

ANSWERS

Comprehension

1. *Paulsen makes extra money by selling newspapers in the bars late at night.*
2. *He gives the dog food and shelter every day.*
3. *He needs to make money to buy clothes, school supplies, and food. He is always being attacked by bullies who steal his money.*

Literary Analysis

Possible answers:

4. ● **STANDARDS FOCUS** *Point of View in a Memoir* Answers will vary. Students may say that they know Paulsen hunted in the woods, but wonder how he did so; they may know that he was in school, but wonder how old he was.

5. ■ **STANDARDS FOCUS** *Identify Cause and Effect* Answers will vary. Students may say that the most central cause-and-effect relationship was that Paulsen fed Dirk and then received the dog's protection as a result.

6. *The dog is loyal, protective, ferocious, and tough.*

7. *Same: He still needs to work and take care of himself.* *Different: He is a little older and he has enough money to buy a car. He seems happier and more self-assured.*

8. *There may be something different about Paulsen himself. Maybe he became more confident. Maybe he could take better care of himself when he was able to keep the money he earned.*

MARYLAND OBJECTIVES

LITERATURE STANDARD
3.A.3.i Analyze point of view

ANSWERS

Vocabulary in Context

VOCABULARY PRACTICE

1. *conventional*
2. *predatory*
3. *puny*
4. *hustle*
5. *impasse*
6. *decoy*
7. *cohort*
8. *forerunner*

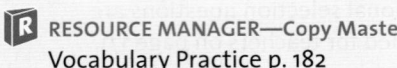
RESOURCE MANAGER—Copy Master
Vocabulary Practice p. 182

VOCABULARY IN WRITING

Ask students to think about the sort of life Dirk had with Paulsen. How was it different from the life Dirk could have with Olaf?

VOCABULARY STRATEGY: IDIOMS *(also an EL language objective)*

Have students read aloud each idiom and discuss what sort of image the idiom creates. For example, what picture does "kicked around a few ideas" bring to mind? "Kick around" may make students think of playing a game. To "kick around" ideas implies playing with, or considering, them.

Answers:
1. *kicked around, "played with or considered"*
2. *changed her tune, "changed her opinion"*
3. *on the level, "fair or straightforward"*
4. *take me under your wing, "support or take care of me"*
5. *hang in there, "don't give up"*

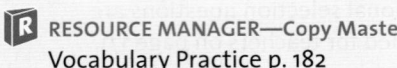
RESOURCE MANAGER—Copy Master
Vocabulary Strategy p. 183

ⓘ Vocabulary Center at **ClassZone.com**
Additional Vocabulary Activities

Vocabulary in Context

VOCABULARY PRACTICE

Choose the vocabulary word that best completes each sentence.

1. The boy tried to get a(n) _____ job but could only find an unusual one.
2. He was frequently beaten up by members of a(n) _____ gang.
3. Unlike the big, strong gang members, he was _____.
4. He had to _____ all day for one solid meal.
5. There he met Dirk, and they stared each other down into a(n) _____.
6. The boy used his hamburger as a(n) _____ to distract the dog.
7. Dirk became the boy's protector and _____.
8. Is Dirk the _____ of other protectors in the boy's future?

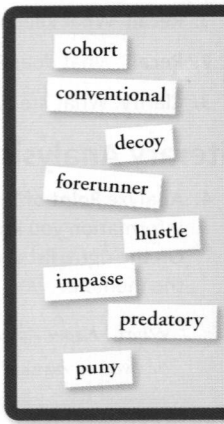

cohort
conventional
decoy
forerunner
hustle
impasse
predatory
puny

VOCABULARY IN WRITING

Were you surprised that Dirk stayed with Olaf? Using two or more vocabulary words, write a paragraph to explain how you thought the memoir might have ended. Here is an example of how you might begin.

> **EXAMPLE SENTENCE**
>
> I thought that Dirk would always want to remain the boy's **cohort**.

VOCABULARY STRATEGY: IDIOMS

An **idiom** is an expression in which the overall meaning of the words in it is different from the meanings of the individual words. For example, in this story, Paulsen says that working at a certain job helped him "stay above water." *Stay above water* is an idiomatic expression because Paulsen was never in fear of drowning. We know Paulsen means that the job helped him survive.

Language is full of idioms. If you encounter an unfamiliar one, you can often use context clues to figure out its meaning. Otherwise, consult a dictionary.

PRACTICE Identify the idiom in each sentence and give a definition for it.

1. They kicked around a few ideas about how to make scenery for the play.
2. She changed her tune once she found out the cost of the project.
3. I don't trust Jackson, but his friend seems on the level.
4. Will you take me under your wing if I decide to join the chorus?
5. Getting all this work done will be tough, but hang in there and we'll finish it.

MARYLAND OBJECTIVES

READING STANDARD
1.D.3.a Use context to determine the meanings of words

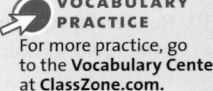

VOCABULARY PRACTICE
For more practice, go to the **Vocabulary Center** at **ClassZone.com.**

DIFFERENTIATED INSTRUCTION

FOR ENGLISH LEARNERS

Vocabulary: Idioms Direct students' attention to these two common idioms used in the selection: "stay above water" (line 22) and "wrong side of the tracks" (line 36). Explain that in American towns, railroad tracks sometimes literally separated poor neighborhoods from wealthier ones. Discuss the images created by these idioms and challenge students to use each idiom in a sentence.

FOR ADVANCED LEARNERS/PRE–AP

Vocabulary Strategy Have students write a paragraph from Paulsen's point of view that uses at least three of the idioms presented in the **Vocabulary Strategy** exercise.

Reading-Writing Connection

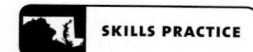

SKILLS PRACTICE

Deepen your understanding of "Dirk the Protector" by responding to these prompts. Then complete the **Grammar and Writing** exercise.

WRITING PROMPTS	SELF-CHECK
A. Short Response: Analyze Cause and Effect Paulsen **survived** many things in addition to attacks from Happy and his friends. Use details from the text to describe in **one paragraph** how Paulsen's choices made his survival possible.	*A strong analysis will . . .* • include more than one choice • explain how each choice made a difference
B. Extended Response: Explore Point of View In the memoir, we learn only as much about Dirk as Paulsen knows. If Dirk could talk, what kind of story might he tell? In **two or three paragraphs**, retell a part of the story from Dirk's point of view.	*An interesting response will . . .* • use the pronouns *I, me, we,* and *us* • reveal something about the boy and the dog

GRAMMAR AND WRITING

AVOID MISPLACED MODIFIERS A **prepositional phrase** is a group of words that begins with a preposition, such as *from, in, on, under,* or *with,* and ends with a noun or pronoun. A prepositional phrase is used to modify, or give information about, another word in the sentence. When you use this kind of phrase in your writing, place it close to the word it modifies. Otherwise, you may end up with something confusing or unintentionally funny.

MARYLAND OBJECTIVES

LANGUAGE STANDARD
5.B.2.c Recognize and correct misplaced modifiers

> Original: He ran into the boys who had been terrorizing him with a hamburger in each hand. (*Were the boys terrorizing him with hamburgers?*)
>
> Revised: With a hamburger in each hand, he ran into the boys who had been terrorizing him. (*It is the boy, himself, who has the hamburgers.*)

PRACTICE Move each misplaced prepositional phrase to the correct place.

1. While some waited, others punched him in his stomach on the sidewalk.
2. I bit one of the boys on the leg with blond hair.
3. I spit out pieces onto the sidewalk of his jeans.
4. I pulled a piece of hamburger from the bag with ketchup on it.

For more help with prepositional phrases, see page R60 in the **Grammar Handbook.**

DIRK THE PROTECTOR **279**

DIFFERENTIATED INSTRUCTION

FOR LESS–PROFICIENT WRITERS

For Prompt A:

1. Identify two choices Paulsen made in the interests of survival and identify one thing that Paulsen gained from each choice.

2. Have students write a topic sentence and then two sentences to describe each choice and explain its effect.

For Prompt B:

• Limit the response to two paragraphs.

• Have students fill in a Sequence Chain for a scene to better organize their response.

• Encourage students to use transition words to help the reader follow what is happening.

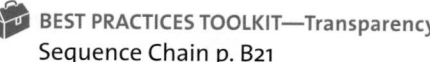 BEST PRACTICES TOOLKIT—Transparency
Sequence Chain p. B21

Reading-Writing Connection

WRITING PROMPTS

• For **Prompt A,** encourage students to reread lines 4–22 to recall the choices Paulsen made.

• For **Prompt B,** display the Reporter's Questions transparency. Suggest that students begin by answering reporter's questions from Dirk's point of view.

 BEST PRACTICES TOOLKIT—Transparency
Reporter's Questions p. C9

For ideas for writing, see

ⓘ Writing Center at **ClassZone.com**

GRAMMAR AND WRITING

Possible answers:

1. While some waited on the sidewalk, others punched him in his stomach.

2. I bit one of the boys with blond hair on the leg.

3. I spit out pieces of his jeans onto the sidewalk.

4. I pulled a piece of hamburger with ketchup on it from the bag.

ℝ RESOURCE MANAGER—Copy Master
Avoid Misplaced Modifiers p. 186

Assess and Reteach

Assess

ℝ RESOURCE MANAGER—Copy Masters
Selection Tests A, B/C pp. 187–188, 189–190

◎ Test Generator CD

Reteach

Ⓢ STANDARDS LESSON FILE
Literature Lesson 11: Types of Point of View
Reading Lesson 7: Recognizing Cause and Effect
Vocabulary Lesson 22: Idioms

Focus and Motivate

OBJECTIVES

Literary Analysis
- explore the key idea of **generations**
- identify and analyze characterization in poetry

Reading
- use strategies for reading poetry

SUMMARY

"It Was a Long Time Before" describes memories of the speaker's grandmother, a strong and traditional Laguna woman. In "Abuelito Who," a series of images builds an impression of the speaker's grandfather—his vitality and his sad decline.

What do we learn from our E L D E R S ?

Discuss the question with students. Ask students for specific examples of what they have learned from a member of the older **generation.** Have them think about why they value this knowledge. To lead into the **KEY IDEA,** ask students what they would want to hand down to the next generation. Then have them complete the **LIST IT** activity and share what they have written in small groups.

It Was a Long Time Before
Poem by Leslie Marmon Silko

Abuelito Who
Poem by Sandra Cisneros

What do we learn from our E L D E R S ?

MARYLAND OBJECTIVES

LITERATURE STANDARDS
3.A.3.d Analyze characterization
3.A.4.a Use structural features to distinguish types of poetry

KEY IDEA Between you, your parents, and your grandparents, the **generations** of your family may span a hundred years or more. As you move into the future, what will you take with you from the past? What will you take with you from the present? In the poems "It Was a Long Time Before" and "Abuelito Who," memories and more connect the generations.

LIST IT Think of someone in another generation who spends time with you. Brainstorm a list of the activities you do together. Reread the list, then write one way that person has affected your life or one thing that person has taught you.

280

Selection Resources

RESOURCE MANAGER UNIT 2
Plan and Teach pp. 191–198
Literary Analysis
Characterization in Poetry pp. 199, 200†*
Question Support p. 203*
Reading
Reading Poetry pp. 201, 202†*
Reading Fluency p. 204

Assessment
Selection Tests A, B/C pp. 205*, 207*
Test Generator CD

BEST PRACTICES TOOLKIT
Differentiated Instruction pp. 31–38*
Scaffolding Instruction pp. 43–46*
Graphic Organizers/Strategies
Spider Map • T Chart

Reading Support
Audio Anthology CD*
Technology
Literature and Vocabulary Centers at **ClassZone.com**
WriteSmart CD

* Resources for Differentiation   † Also in Spanish

LITERARY ANALYSIS: CHARACTERIZATION IN POETRY

When poets describe people in their writing, they usually **characterize** them in fewer words than fiction writers do. An image, a phrase, or a telling detail—in a poet's hand, these can suggest an entire personality.

In "Abuelito Who," Sandra Cisneros characterizes her grandfather as someone "who throws coins like rain." This statement gives the reader the impression that the grandfather is generous. You might even be able to picture an elderly man making a ritual of tossing bright coins onto the floor for his grandchildren to scoop up. As you read "It Was a Long Time Before" and "Abuelito Who," pay attention to what else the poets' language suggests about the people in the poems.

READING STRATEGY: READING POETRY

Some poems contain complete sentences with standard punctuation. Other poems don't. But all poems are divided into **lines,** and where they are divided is important to the poems' meaning and rhythm. For example, read the following lines from "It Was a Long Time Before." The poet is telling the reader why she affectionately called her grandmother "Grandma A'mooh."

> I had been hearing her say
>   "a'moo'ooh"
> which is the Laguna expression of endearment
> for a young child
> spoken with great feeling and love.

Notice that all of these words, put together, create a sentence, but each line read separately has its own effect. Since "a'moo'ooh" appears on its own line, the reader lingers on it, letting its cultural and emotional importance sink in. As you read the two poems, pay attention to how each poet uses lines, sentences, and punctuation to give meaning to each poem.

Author Online

Leslie Marmon Silko: Native American Storyteller Leslie Marmon Silko was raised on the Laguna Pueblo reservation in New Mexico. As she grew up, female relatives taught her traditional

Leslie Marmon Silko
born 1948

Native American stories and legends. Today Silko considers herself part of the global community. She says, "I am writing to the world, not to the United States alone."

Sandra Cisneros: Latina Writer When Sandra Cisneros was a child, she and her family moved frequently between Chicago and her father's birthplace in Mexico. She often spoke English to

Sandra Cisneros
born 1954

her Mexican-American mother and Spanish to her father. For Cisneros, writing is a way to deal with the poverty, loneliness, and instability she faced in her childhood. She incorporates the Spanish language in her writing "to say things in English that have never been said before."

 MORE ABOUT THE AUTHOR
For more on Leslie Marmon Silko and Sandra Cisneros, visit the **Literature Center** at ClassZone.com.

Teach

STANDARDS FOCUS

LITERARY ANALYSIS

● **CHARACTERIZATION IN POETRY**

Read aloud this example from Robert Burns: "My love is like a red, red rose." Ask students to use the simile to identify traits of the woman. ***Possible answer:*** *The woman is beautiful, special, and delicate.*

CHECK UNDERSTANDING Ask students to analyze how Burns and Cisneros develop characterization in the given examples— by describing the character's appearance, actions, or speech?

READING STRATEGY

■ **READING POETRY**

Ask students how the excerpt about Grandma A'mooh would be punctuated if it were prose instead of poetry. How would the poem's effect be altered if the punctuation were added? ***Possible answer:*** *In prose, commas would be added after "a'moo'ooh" and "young child." Such punctuation could interrupt the rhythm and flow of the poem.*

CHECK UNDERSTANDING Ask students why the poet may have placed this phrase on its own line: "spoken with great feeling and love."

 RESOURCE MANAGER—Copy Master
Reading Poetry p. 201 (for student use while reading the poems)

DIFFERENTIATED INSTRUCTION

FOR ALL STUDENTS

Expert Groups List these topics and have students work together or independently to find information about them. The class experts should then present what they find to the class.

- different names for grandparents around the world
- yucca roots—how they are grown and used
- Pueblo peoples

For general guidelines on differentiating instruction, see

 BEST PRACTICES TOOLKIT
Differentiated Instruction pp. 31–38

FOR LESS—PROFICIENT READERS

Concept Support To prepare students for reading the poems, preview and pronounce difficult words and names in advance. Point out terms defined in the footnotes. Then read each poem aloud as students follow along.

FOR ENGLISH LEARNERS

Options for Reading Provide students with a brief overview of each poem. Then have them read the poems as they listen to the *Audio Anthology CD.* Pause the CD frequently to monitor students' understanding and answer questions.

Practice and Apply

ANALYZE VISUALS

Possible answers: The woman appears to be dressed in her best clothes. This suggests that she has a sense of pride in who she is. Her skin is weathered as if she has spent a lot of time outdoors. Her hair is gray, showing her age. Yet she sits upright and looks directly into the camera, revealing her strength and fearlessness.

About the Art The photographs of Native American photographer Lee Marmon (born 1925) chronicle the lives and traditions of members of the Laguna and Acoma groups of New Mexico. His photographs are often used to complement the poetry of his daughter Leslie Marmon Silko.

Lines 1–11
DISCUSSION PROMPTS

Use these prompts to help students understand the relationship between the grandmother and the speaker of the poem:

Connect Do you have a special name that you call a family member? How did the name originate? *Students may say they have a special name that originated from a mistake, such as their inability to pronounce a word correctly when they were little.*

Analyze Why does a strong bond develop between the grandmother and the speaker? *Possible answer: The grandmother looks after the speaker while her mother works.*

Synthesize How does the grandmother feel about her grandchild? How do you know? *Possible answer: The grandmother loves her grandchild. She calls her grandchild "a'moo'ooh," a term that shows great affection (line 11).*

It Was a Long Time Before

Leslie Marmon Silko

Rosita Johnson (1958), Lee Marmon. Laguna, New Mexico. © Lee Marmon.

It was a long time before
I learned that my Grandma A'mooh's
real name was Marie Anaya Marmon.
I thought her name really was "A'mooh."
5 I realize now it had happened when I was a baby
and she cared for me while my mother worked.
I had been hearing her say
    "a'moo'ooh"
which is the Laguna[1] expression of endearment
10 for a young child
spoken with great feeling and love.

ANALYZE VISUALS
What do the **details** in the photograph tell you about the woman?

---

1. **Laguna** (lə-gōō′nə): dialect of the Keres language spoken by the Laguna people, whose home is in rural New Mexico.

282   UNIT 2: ANALYZING CHARACTER AND POINT OF VIEW

DIFFERENTIATED INSTRUCTION

FOR LESS–PROFICIENT READERS

Comprehension Support Use Spider Maps to help students organize the details they learn about each grandparent through their reading and discussion. Complete a map after each poem, and then compare and contrast the two grandparents in an end-of-class discussion.

 BEST PRACTICES TOOLKIT—Transparency
Spider Map p. B22

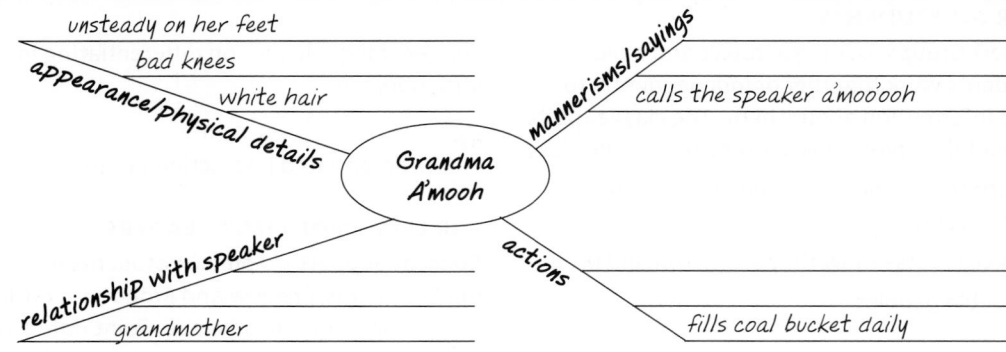

unsteady on her feet
bad knees
appearance/physical details
white hair

mannerisms/sayings
calls the speaker a'moo'ooh

Grandma A'mooh

relationship with speaker
grandmother

actions
fills coal bucket daily

Her house was next to ours
and as I grew up
I spent a lot of time with her
15 because she was in her eighties
and they worried about her falling.
So I would go check up on her—which was really
an excuse to visit her.
After I had to go to school
20 I went to carry in the coal bucket
which she still insisted on filling.
I slept with her
in case she fell getting up in the night. **A**

She still washed her hair with yucca[2] roots
25 or "soap weed" as she called it. She said
it kept white hair like hers from yellowing.
She kept these yucca roots on her windowsill
and I remember I was afraid of them for a long time
because they looked like hairy twisted claws.

30 I watched her make red chili on the grinding stone
the old way, even though it had gotten difficult for her
to get down on her knees.
She used to tell me and my sisters
about the old days when they didn't have toothpaste
35 and cleaned their teeth with juniper[3] ash,
and how, instead of corn flakes, in the old days they ate
"*maaht'zini*"[4] crushed up with milk poured over it. **B**

Her last years they took her away to Albuquerque[5]
to live with her daughter, Aunt Bessie.
40 But there was no fire to start in the morning
and nobody dropping by.
She didn't have anyone to talk to all day
because Bessie worked.
She might have lived without watering morning glories
45 and without kids running through her kitchen
but she did not last long
without someone to talk to.

---

2. **yucca** (yŭk'ə): a plant that grows in warm regions, chiefly those of western North America. Yucca have long sword-shaped leaves, a woody base, and white flowers.

3. **juniper** (jōō'nə-pər) a pleasant-smelling evergreen shrub.

4. **maaht'zini** (mät-zē-nē) *Keres, one of numerous Pueblo languages:* thin, flaky bread made of finely ground blue corn flour.

5. **Albuquerque** (ăl'bə-kûr'kē): the largest city in New Mexico.

IT WAS A LONG TIME BEFORE **283**

A READING POETRY
Do the sentences in this poem follow standard patterns of grammar and punctuation? Where do the sentences begin and end?

B CHARACTERIZATION IN POETRY
Reread lines 24–37. What do the details and descriptions tell you about Grandma A'mooh?

READING STRATEGY

A **READING POETRY**

Possible answer: Sentences follow standard patterns. Although they may run for several lines, they usually start at the beginning of a line and conclude at the end of a line.

Extend the Discussion What effect is produced by the use of standard sentence structure throughout the poem?

LITERARY ANALYSIS

B **CHARACTERIZATION IN POETRY**

You might record students' answers in a cluster chart or list.

Possible answers:

• *Grandma A'mooh has white hair that she washes with yucca roots (lines 24–26).*

• *She is traditional (lines 30–31).*

• *Her knees cause her pain (lines 31–32).*

• *She likes to share her memories of the past (lines 33–37).*

Lines 30–37
REINFORCE *KEY IDEA:* GENERATIONS

Discuss What values is Grandma A'mooh passing on to younger **generations?** *Possible answer: She is showing the importance of remembering the past and honoring tradition.*

FOR LESS–PROFICIENT READERS
Reading Strategy Follow-Up: Reading Poetry Work with students to divide the poem into sets of lines expressing complete thoughts. Assign pairs of students one or two sets. Ask them to write a short sentence stating the main idea of each. Then have pairs read their statements in sequence.

FOR ADVANCED LEARNERS/PRE–AP
Analyze Have small groups examine the speakers and their importance to the poems. Direct students to consider these relationships in their analysis:

• the language of the poem and the age of the speaker

• the probable age of the speaker and his or her perspective on the subject

• the perspective of the speaker and the kinds of details included about the subject

DISCUSSION PROMPTS

Use these prompts to help students understand the contrasting images of Abuelito:

Connect Recall some happy memories involving people you care about. Which images in lines 1–18 give you similar feelings? *Students may say that the images in lines 1, 3–5, 7–8, and 12 give them a cheerful feeling.*

Analyze What are the first signs that something is wrong with Abuelito? *Possible answer: First, he is too sad to come downstairs (line 6). Then he cannot come out to play because he sleeps in his room all day (lines 10–11). Then he stops laughing (line 12).*

Speculate What does the speaker mean in line 18 when she refers to Abuelito "who talks to me inside my head"? *Possible answer: Abuelito has died. The speaker has only her memories of Abuelito to give her comfort.*

READING STRATEGY

C READING POETRY

Possible answer: In the early lines, Abuelito is alive and the words can be read as if they are coming from him. The ending lines contain the only punctuation in the poem, a question mark. Abuelito has died, but the speaker still feels his presence, as the sound of falling rain reminds her of his question.

If students need help . . . Read the lines aloud so that they can hear the urgency in the last lines.

SELECTION WRAP–UP

⭐ **CRITIQUE** Ask students to evaluate the effectiveness of the characterization in each poem. Ask them what other kinds of details the poets might have included.

READING FLUENCY

Distribute the copy masters and have students work in groups to practice fluency.

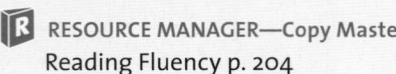 RESOURCE MANAGER—Copy Master
Reading Fluency p. 204

Abuelito Who

Sandra Cisneros

Abuelito[1] who throws coins like rain
and asks who loves him
who is dough and feathers
who is a watch and glass of water
5 whose hair is made of fur
is too sad to come downstairs today
who tells me in Spanish you are my diamond
who tells me in English you are my sky
whose little eyes are string
10 can't come out to play
sleeps in his little room all night and day
who used to laugh like the letter k
is sick
is a doorknob tied to a sour stick
15 is tired shut the door
doesn't live here anymore
is hiding underneath the bed
who talks to me inside my head
is blankets and spoons and big brown shoes
20 who snores up and down up and down up and down again
is the rain on the roof that falls like coins
asking who loves him
who loves him who? **C**

C **READING POETRY**
Reread line 2 and lines 22–23. How does the phrase at the end of the poem differ from the phrase at the beginning?

---

1. **Abuelito** (ä-bwe-lē′tō) *Spanish:* an affectionate term for a grandfather.

DIFFERENTIATED INSTRUCTION

FOR ENGLISH LEARNERS

Comprehension: Concept Support Explain that this poem describes Abuelito when he was healthy and happy, and also as he became sick. Help students understand what the speaker is saying about Abuelito's character by filling in a T Chart that examines the meaning of each line.

 BEST PRACTICES TOOLKIT—Transparency
T Chart p. A25

Line from Poem	Meaning
Abuelito who throws coins like rain	He is generous.
and asks who loves him	He is affectionate and outgoing.
who is dough and feathers	He is soft to hug and gentle.

Comprehension

1. **Recall** What language did each grandparent speak to his or her grandchildren?

2. **Recall** In "It Was a Long Time Before," why did Grandma A'mooh take care of her grandchild?

3. **Clarify** By the end of each poem, what has happened to each grandparent?

Literary Analysis

4. **Make Inferences** In "It Was a Long Time Before," why did Grandma A'mooh still insist on filling the coal bucket?

5. **Recognize Characterization** Reread lines 3, 9, and 12 of "Abuelito Who." What do these descriptions tell you about Abuelito?

6. **Analyze Point of View** From what point of view is each of these poems written? How does the point of view affect the meaning of each poem?

7. **Examine Poetry** Note the differences in the ways each poet uses sentences and punctuation. How does the use of lines, sentences, and punctuation affect the way you read and understand the poems?

8. **Compare and Contrast** Use a Venn diagram like the one shown, compare and contrast Grandma A'mooh with Abuelito. To complete the diagram, draw on inferences you made about the characters as well as on details from the poems.

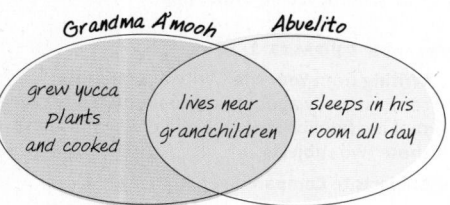

Grandma A'mooh — Abuelito

- grew yucca plants and cooked
- lives near grandchildren
- sleeps in his room all day

Extension and Challenge

9. **Big Question Activity** How would the speaker of each poem answer the Big Question on page 280? Choose one of the poems, and write a note to the grandparent from the speaker's point of view. Tell the grandparent what you learned from him or her.

10. **SOCIAL STUDIES CONNECTION** Laguna Pueblo is one of many Pueblo communities located in New Mexico. Do some research to find out more about the Pueblo people. Look for information about their traditional culture and values and how they are reflected today.

> **RESEARCH LINKS**
> For more on the Pueblo people, visit the **Research Center** at **ClassZone.com**.

Extension and Challenge

9. *Students' responses should be written in the form of friendly letters and include specific details and images from the poem.*

10. **SOCIAL STUDIES CONNECTION** *Students may choose to write a report or develop an oral presentation with visual aids. Students should include specific examples of how the Pueblo culture influences the lives of the people today.*

Assess and Reteach

Assess

RESOURCE MANAGER—Copy Masters
Selection Tests A, B/C pp. 205–206, 207–208

Test Generator CD

Reteach

STANDARDS LESSON FILE
Literature Lesson 3: Characterization

Practice and Apply

After Reading

For additional support of post-reading questions, use these copy masters:

RESOURCE MANAGER—Copy Masters
Characterization in Poetry p. 199 (for practice of literary analysis standards focus)
Question Support p. 203 (**After Reading** questions adapted for English learners and less-proficient readers)

Additional selection questions are provided for teachers on page 195.

ANSWERS

Comprehension

1. *Grandma A'mooh spoke in Laguna, Keres, and probably English; Abuelito spoke in Spanish and English.*

2. *The child's mother was working.*

3. *Both have died.*

Literary Analysis

Possible answers:

4. *Grandma A'mooh clung to traditions, lighting a fire each day for cooking.*

5. ● **STANDARDS FOCUS** *Characterization in Poetry Abuelito was soft and cuddly. He had narrow eyes. His laugh was loud and wholehearted.*

6. *The poems are written from the first-person point of view. The speakers are grandchildren who love and miss their grandparents, making the poems personal and emotional.*

7. ■ **STANDARDS FOCUS** *Reading Poetry The first poem reads more like a story, for the poet uses standard grammar and punctuation. The second poem lacks standard punctuation and grammar, which prompts the reader to study each line for its individual meaning. Words and images run together to show how memories from the poet's past flow into the present.*

8. *Similarities: Both grandparents had strong bonds with their grandchildren. Both die and are missed by their grandchildren. Difference: Memories of Grandma A'mooh include stories about the past and traditional ways of doing things. Abuelito leaves memories of his place in the household and his personality.*

Focus and Motivate

OBJECTIVES

- analyze a student model that reflects the key traits of comparison-contrast writing
- use the writing process to produce a comparison-contrast essay
- revise and edit, using a rubric for comparison-contrast writing
- connect ideas with transitions
- conduct an interview

WRITER'S ROAD MAP

WRITING PROMPTS 1 AND 2

Help students choose a prompt by reviewing interesting characters from the unit or by brainstorming pairs of familiar people, places, and objects. Point out that subjects should be similar enough to compare but different enough for an interesting contrast.

ADDITIONAL PROMPTS

Use these prompts for practice with writing comparison-contrast essays:

WRITING PROMPT 3

Writing for the Real World Write a consumer report that compares and contrasts two products. Your article should include concrete details about your two subjects.

Subjects to Consider

- two restaurants
- two brands of clothing
- two convenience foods

WRITING PROMPT 4

Writing About Music Write a two-minute speech that compares two musicians, bands, singers, or types of music.

Ideas to Consider

- two musicians, bands, or singers who perform the same type of music
- a contemporary performer or band and a performer or band from another era
- two contemporary styles of music

For additional writing prompts, see

- WriteSmart CD
- Writing Center at **ClassZone.com**

KEY TRAITS

Review the six **KEY TRAITS,** focusing primarily on ideas and organization. Compare these traits with the rubric on page 292.

Comparison-Contrast Essay

If you look at something long enough, you'll begin to see it in a new way. When you look for similarities and differences between characters, people, places, or objects, you start examining more deeply, exploring more fully. Use the **Writer's Road Map** to help you develop this skill.

WRITER'S ROAD MAP

Comparison-Contrast Essay

WRITING PROMPT 1

Writing from Literature Write an essay that compares and contrasts two characters from literature. Your essay should explain why you chose those characters.

Characters to Compare

- Roger and Mrs. Luella Bates Washington Jones in "Thank You, M'am"
- Roger in "Thank You, M'am" and Zebra in "Zebra"
- Jimmy Valentine/Ralph D. Spencer and Ben Price in "A Retrieved Reformation"

WRITING PROMPT 2

Writing from Your Life Write a comparison-contrast essay about two people, places, or objects that are familiar to you. Explain why you chose those two subjects.

Subjects to Compare

- two people you know well or two famous people whose work is familiar to you
- two places you have lived or visited
- your favorite type of music and your least favorite type of music

WRITING TOOLS
For prewriting, revision, and editing tools, visit the **Writing Center** at ClassZone.com.

KEY TRAITS

1. IDEAS

- Identifies the **characters** or **subjects** being compared and contrasted
- Includes a **thesis statement** that identifies similarities and differences
- Supports key ideas with **examples**

2. ORGANIZATION

- Includes a strong **introduction** and a satisfying **conclusion**
- Follows a clear **organizational pattern**
- Connects ideas with **transitions**

3. VOICE

- Uses language that is **appropriate** for the audience and purpose

4. WORD CHOICE

- Uses **precise words** to explain similarities and differences

5. SENTENCE FLUENCY

- Varies **sentence beginnings**

6. CONVENTIONS

- Uses **correct grammar, spelling, and punctuation**

Writing Workshop Resources

 **RESOURCE MANAGER UNIT 2**

Plan and Teach pp. 209–212
Prewriting–Editing pp. 213–217
Writing Rubric p. 218
Speaking and Listening p. 219
Writing Support p. 220*

STANDARDS LESSON FILE

Writing Lesson 29: Comparison-Contrast Essay
Writing Lesson 19: Transitions
Grammar Lesson 2: Avoiding Run-Ons

 BEST PRACTICES TOOLKIT

Scaffolding Writing Instruction pp. 43–46*
Venn Diagram • Y Chart • Analysis Frames • Writing Templates

TECHNOLOGY

- Easy Planner DVD
- Writing Center at **ClassZone.com**
- WriteSmart CD

* Resources for Differentiation

Part 1: Analyze a Student Model

Priya Mahapatra
Jefferson Middle School

Martha and Roger: Different People, Different Lives

Did you ever long for a special item of clothing? In "The Scholarship Jacket" by Marta Salinas, Martha wants a jacket that her school awards for good grades. In "Thank You, M'am" by Langston Hughes, Roger wants a pair of blue suede shoes. The two characters are about the
5 same age, and it's easy to sympathize with them both because they are struggling to grow up in an unfair world. Martha and Roger are very different characters, however, because they have different reasons for what they want, different ways of trying to get it, and different lives at home.

10 Martha and Roger want special items of clothing for different reasons. In "The Scholarship Jacket," Martha feels she has to have the jacket because it is supposed to go to the best student in the school. At the beginning of the story, she reflects, "I had been a straight A student since the first grade and this last year had looked forward very much to
15 owning that jacket." Because she earned the best grades, Martha deserves the jacket. It represents years of hard work. On the other hand, Roger in "Thank You, M'am" hasn't earned blue suede shoes. He just wants them desperately. The story doesn't explain why he wants them so much, so the reader assumes that Roger wants the shoes because they are in style.

20 Martha and Roger also use different methods to get what they want. Although Martha is not sure what to do at first, she responds as best as she can when the principal tells her that she has to pay for the

KEY TRAITS IN ACTION

Introduction identifies the **characters** being contrasted.

Thesis statement identifies differences that will be discussed.

Uses **point-by-point organization.** This paragraph discusses the characters' different reasons. Varied **sentence beginnings** help keep the essay interesting.

Introduces the **second point,** the characters' different methods.

Teach

Part 1: Analyze a Student Model

Have students read the **Student Model** and **Key Traits in Action.** Then discuss the model with the class, pointing out specific examples of each trait and building on what students have already noted. You may also wish to incorporate the following activities:

- **Introduction** Write the following weak thesis statement on the board:

  > Martha in "The Scholarship Jacket" and Roger in "Thank You, M'am" are similar in some ways but different in other ways.

  Ask a student to read this statement and then lines 4–9 of the **Student Model** aloud. Ask students to compare the two. *(The thesis statement on the board does not provide any details about the characters' similarities and differences. The thesis statement in the model points out ways in which the two characters are similar and then identifies three specific differences between them.)*

- **Organization** To illustrate point-by-point organization, have students identify the topic of each body paragraph in the model.

  > Paragraph 2: *the reasons the characters want special items of clothing*

  > Paragraph 3: *the methods the characters use to get what they want*

  > Paragraph 4: *the characters' homes*

DIFFERENTIATED INSTRUCTION

FOR ALL STUDENTS
For general guidelines on differentiating writing instruction, see

 BEST PRACTICES TOOLKIT
Scaffolding Writing Instruction
pp. 43–46

FOR ENGLISH LEARNERS
Language: Skill Words Write these terms on the board and review them with students:

- *subject:* a person or thing being discussed or written about. For example, two people or two places may be the subjects of a comparison.

- *point of comparison:* a feature that is being compared—for example, the home lives of two characters

- *thesis statement:* one or two sentences stating the main idea of an essay. In a comparison-contrast essay, the thesis statement names the subjects and points of comparison. Share this example:

  > Martha in "The Scholarship Jacket" and Roger in "Thank You, M'am" both struggle toward a goal. However, they have different reasons for what they want and different ways of trying to get it.

- **Precise Words** To illustrate the importance of using precise words, write the following sentence pair on the board:

  It's easy to sympathize with them both because they are growing up in the world.

  It's easy to sympathize with them both because they are struggling to grow up in an unfair world.

  Have students discuss differences in the two sentences. Ask them to point out the precise words in the second sentence (*struggling, unfair*). Talk about how the second sentence gives more information about the characters and their situations.

- **Transitions** Tell students that they can find a list of transitions useful for comparison-contrast writing in the chart on page 292. Point out that words like *in contrast, however,* and *unlike* help readers understand relationships between ideas.

  Point out the words highlighted in lines 27–30. Then ask students to find additional transitions that signal comparisons.

  Line 43: *while*

  Line 44: *both*

  Line 46: *alike*

- **Examples** The writer includes evidence from the literature to support her ideas about the characters. Ask students to look through the essay to find at least three examples of statements supported by quotations or examples. *(lines 11–15, 21–26, 33–36)*

For interactive student models, see

🔘 Write*Smart* CD

ℹ️ Writing Center at **ClassZone.com**

---

jacket. She doesn't yell or whine. Instead, she calmly says she will speak with her grandfather. Then she goes to her grandfather for help. She
25 realizes, "I knew I had to be honest with Grandpa; it was my only chance." The end of the story shows that turning to her grandfather was the right choice. In contrast, Roger in "Thank You, M'am" tries snatching a purse to solve his problem. He is not successful, however. When Mrs. Jones asks him why he did that, he lies. "I didn't aim to,"
30 he says. Unlike Martha, Roger does not tell the truth until he becomes a little more comfortable with Mrs. Jones.

Another difference between Martha and Roger is their homes. Martha goes home to her grandma and grandpa. Martha appears to have a good home. She knows she can turn to her grandpa for help.
35 He gives her good advice about the jacket when he says, "Then if you pay for it, Marta, it's not a scholarship jacket, is it?" Unlike Martha, Roger appears to have no one at home. When Mrs. Jones asks, "Ain't you got nobody home to tell you to wash your face?" he says, "No'm." Although it's late at night, Mrs. Jones finds out that Roger hasn't eaten
40 any supper. He explains, "There's nobody home at my house." No one makes sure that Roger washes or eats. No one seems to care about him.

Martha and Roger have different reasons and methods for getting what they want. Martha gets help at home, while Roger finds help by luck. Despite their differences, both characters end up getting excellent
45 advice. A close look at the characters reveals another way that the stories are alike. Both stories show the importance of having someone who cares. Both Roger and Martha get help and support from a caring older person.

Precise words make the essay clear and interesting.

Transitions introduce contrasts. The language is **appropriate** for the audience (teacher and classmates) and purpose (formal essay).

Introduces the **third point,** the characters' different homes.

Supports key ideas with **examples** from the story

Conclusion summarizes the main points and includes a thoughtful comment about a similarity in the stories.

2

DIFFERENTIATED INSTRUCTION

FOR ENGLISH LEARNERS

Comprehension: Transitions If students are not familiar with the transitional words they need for a comparison-contrast essay, use this activity to illustrate the concepts of likeness and similarity.

- Hold up pictures of two farm animals, such as a horse and a cow.

- Using the words and phrases in the chart on page 292, provide model sentences that compare and contrast the animals.

The horse is dark brown. The cow, **however,** is light brown.

Both animals walk on all four legs.

Another way in which the animals are **alike** is that **both** have tails.

Unlike the cow, the horse has a mane.

- Hold up two new pictures and repeat the exercise, this time asking students to provide the sentences.

📕 RESOURCE MANAGER—Copy Master
Writing Support p. 220

WRITING STANDARD
4.A.1 Compose text using prewriting and drafting strategies

Part 2: Apply the Writing Process

PREWRITING

What Should I Do?

1. Analyze the prompt.
Look back at the prompt you chose. ⟨Circle⟩ the form your writing should take, such as an essay, a letter, or a report. Identify your audience. <u>Underline</u> words that describe your purpose, such as explaining or persuading.

TIP If your audience is not stated, assume that you are writing for your teacher and your classmates.

2. Brainstorm comparison-contrast ideas.
Use a Venn diagram or two-column chart to explore the ways in which two subjects are alike and the ways in which they differ.

TIP If you can't think of interesting similarities or differences, try different subjects.

3. Find support for key points.
Remember that you need to explain and support each of your main points. List some examples that explain your comparisons and/or contrasts. If you are writing from literature, also look for exact words in the literature that explain your points.

4. Write a working thesis.
State your main points in a single sentence. Write your main points in the order you will cover them in your essay. You can revise your thesis later to make it clearer or more accurate.

What Does It Look Like?

▶ **WRITING PROMPT** Write an⟨essay⟩that <u>compares and contrasts</u> two characters from literature. Your essay should <u>explain why you chose those characters.</u>

The audience isn't stated, so I know this essay is for my teacher and classmates. I have to compare and contrast two characters in a way that explains why I chose them.

▶

Martha — earns the jacket; asks Grandpa for help; has support at home

Both — want an item of clothing; get help from an older person

Roger — wants the shoes; tries to steal money; has no one at home

▶ *Martha*
• "I'll speak to my grandfather about it, sir."
• gets good advice from him
Roger
• "There's nobody home at my house."
• has no one to make sure he washes, eats

▶ *Working Thesis:*
Roger and Martha want things for different reasons, try different ways to get what they want, and have different lives at home.

FOR ENGLISH LEARNERS
Planning a Thesis Give students the following sentence starters to help them create a working thesis and gather support for their main ideas:

• My subjects are _____ and _____.
• The thesis, or main idea, is _____.
• The points I want to compare are _____.
• For my first point, my evidence is _____.
• For my second point, my evidence is _____.

FOR ADVANCED LEARNERS/PRE–AP
Analyze Challenge students to explore their subjects in greater depth and write thesis statements that reflect deeper analysis. Analysis Frames can help students generate ideas. Students who are writing about characters, people, or places may use the frames for character or setting.

🧰 **BEST PRACTICES TOOLKIT—Transparencies**
Analysis Frame: Character pp. D23, D28
Analysis Frame: Setting pp. D23, D32

Practice and Apply

To support students during the writing process, use these copy masters:

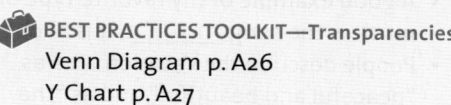 **RESOURCE MANAGER—Copy Masters**
Prewriting–Editing pp. 213–217
Writing Rubric p. 218
Speaking and Listening p. 219
Writing Support p. 220 *(for English learners)*

Part 2: Apply the Writing Process

PREWRITING

1. Analyze the prompt. Be sure that students understand what the prompt they chose is asking them to produce. Students who have chosen the same prompt can talk about what form their writing will take and what purpose their essays will have. Students should also identify their audience, noting the **TIP** in the first step.

2. Brainstorm comparison-contrast ideas. This activity works well for paired and small-group work. Encourage students to work together to experiment with Venn Diagrams or different kinds of charts to help them generate and organize ideas.

🧰 **BEST PRACTICES TOOLKIT—Transparencies**
Venn Diagram p. A26
Y Chart p. A27

3. Find support for key points. Encourage students to list the main points they want to make in their essays. Then have them list examples that explain each main point. You might want to suggest that students review lines 10–19 of the **Student Model** one more time before they begin searching for examples. Point out that quotations and specific details are often very effective for supporting ideas.

4. Write a working thesis. Check students' plans, making sure each student has a valid outline before beginning to write. You might want each student to share a working thesis and outline with a partner or in a small group. Students can give each other feedback and help each other to clarify what they want to say in their pieces.

For interactive graphic organizers, see

📀 Write*Smart* CD
ℹ️ Writing Center at **ClassZone.com**

DRAFTING

1. **Organize your thoughts.** Help students understand some of the advantages and challenges of each type of organization.

   - A writer who uses **subject-by-subject** organization can focus on one subject at a time. However, a reader might find it harder to keep track of the comparisons and contrasts.

   - A writer who uses **point-by-point** organization can stay focused on the comparisons and the contrasts throughout the essay. This organization can be easier for a reader to follow, but the writer must be sure to use helpful transitional words and phrases.

2. **Explain and support your points.** Encourage students to show, not just tell, when they are writing about similarities and differences. They can do this by using concrete details, examples, and/or quotations. Provide the following examples from different types of comparison-contrast essays:

   - No one makes sure that Roger washes or eats. No one seems to care about him.
   - A good example of my favorite type of music is the song _____. It is about . . .
   - People describe the vacation area as "peaceful and beautiful" and as "the perfect getaway" . . .

3. **Use transitions.** Remind students that transitional words help readers follow the main points of a comparison-contrast essay. Suggest that they review how transitional words and phrases were used in the **Student Model.**

   Before students begin to revise, point out the **TIP** provided with step 3.

For comparison-contrast essay writing templates, see

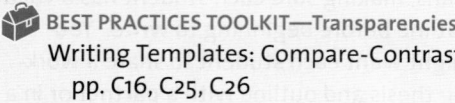 BEST PRACTICES TOOLKIT—Transparencies
Writing Templates: Compare-Contrast
pp. C16, C25, C26

WriteSmart CD

Writing Center at **ClassZone.com**

DRAFTING

What Should I Do?	What Does It Look Like?

1. Organize your thoughts.
Here are two ways to organize a comparison-contrast essay. You can try each way to see which one works best for you.

- **Subject-by-Subject Organization**
  Discusses all the points in relation to the first subject, then moves on to the second subject

- **Point-by-Point Organization**
  Discusses the points one by one, explaining how they relate to each subject

SUBJECT-BY-SUBJECT ORGANIZATION

Subject A: Martha
  Reason: deserves jacket
  Method: asks for help
  Home life: caring
Subject B: Roger
  Reason: wants to be in style?
  Method: tries to steal
  Home life: nobody seems to care

POINT-BY-POINT ORGANIZATION

Point 1: Reason
  Martha: deserves jacket
  Roger: wants to be in style?
Point 2: Method
  Martha: asks for help
  Roger: tries to steal
Point 3: Home Life
  Martha: caring
  Roger: nobody seems to care

2. Explain and support your points.
Use facts and details to back up what you say. For example, if you say that Martha has a good home, you might explain how she can turn to her grandfather for good advice. Then you might quote the advice he gives.

Martha appears to have a good home. ⎱ Key point
She knows she can turn to her grandpa for help. ⎱ Support (explanation)
He gives her good advice about the jacket when he says, "Then if you pay for it, Marta, it's not a scholarship jacket, is it?" ⎱ Support (quotation)

3. Use transitions.
Some transitional words and phrases show likeness. They include _both, similarly,_ and _like_. Other transitional words and phrases show contrast, such as _on the other hand, instead,_ and _however_.

See page 292: Add Transitions

TIP Before you revise, look at the **key traits on page 286** and at the **rubric and peer-reader questions on page 292.**

The two characters are about the same age, and it's easy to sympathize with them both because they are struggling to grow up in an unfair world.

In contrast, Roger in "Thank You, M'am" tries snatching a purse to solve his problem. He is not successful, however.

DIFFERENTIATED INSTRUCTION

FOR LESS—PROFICIENT WRITERS

Organize Your Thoughts Explain that the **Student Model** is a good example of point-by-point organization. Provide the following frame to help students with subject-by-subject organization:

Beginning Paragraph
- Introduce the two subjects.
- In your thesis, clearly state the similarities and differences between your subjects.

Middle Paragraphs (Number will vary.)
- Present the first subject and all points relating to the first subject.
- Present the second subject and all points relating to the second subject.
- Explain all ideas fully.
- Back up all ideas with evidence from the text.

End Paragraph
- Briefly restate the subjects and their similarities and differences.
- Offer a fresh observation and state your conclusion.

REVISING AND EDITING

What Should I Do?	What Does It Look Like?
1. Make your introduction strong. • Reread your first sentence. Does it create interest or draw the reader in? • If not, add an interesting detail, question, or quotation.	▶ *Did you ever long for a special item of clothing?* *ʌIn "The Scholarship Jacket" by Marta Salinas, Martha wants a jacket that her school awards for good grades. In "Thank You, M'am" by Langston Hughes, Roger wants a pair of blue suede shoes.*

2. Use appropriate language.
 • Read your essay aloud. Listen for and [bracket] words and phrases that are too casual or slangy.
 • Replace them with words that are appropriate for an essay that your teacher will read.
	▶ *The story doesn't explain why he wants*
	      the reader assumes
	 them so much, soʌ[I figure] that Roger wants
	      in style.
	 the shoes because they areʌ[totally the in thing.]

3. Be precise.
 • <u>Underline</u> vague words and phrases, such as *really, many, a lot,* and *nice*.
 • Replace them with more precise words.
 	
 TIP Replace weak, state-of-being verbs like *is, has,* and *was*, too. Use strong action verbs instead.
	▶ *earned*
	 Because she ~~has~~ the best grades,
	     deserves
	 Martha ~~really, truly should get~~ the jacket.
	     represents
	 It ~~is for~~ years of hard work.
	 Roger hasn't earned blue suede shoes. He just
	 wants them ~~a lot~~ desperately.

4. Improve your conclusion. • Ask a peer reader to tell how your conclusion adds some new but related idea. • If it doesn't, add an explanation of how your comparisons and/or contrasts deepened your understanding of the subjects. **See page 292:** Ask a Peer Reader	▶ *Despite their differences, both characters end up getting excellent advice. A close look at the characters reveals another way that the stories are alike. Both stories show the importance of having someone who cares. Both Roger and Martha get help and support from a caring older person.*

REVISING AND EDITING

1. **Make your introduction strong.** Suggest that students share their introductions with peer readers. Remind them of these techniques they can use to capture the interest of a reader:

   • Begin with a question (as in the **Student Model**).
   • Begin with an interesting detail about the subjects.
   • Begin with a quotation that gets the reader interested in the topic of the essay.

2. **Use appropriate language.** Before students begin revising for appropriate language, give them examples of words or sentences and have them tell whether the language is casual and slangy or formal. You might have students give their own examples of appropriate and inappropriate language for a classroom essay.

3. **Be precise.** Point out the **TIP** provided with step 3. Have students work in pairs or small groups to brainstorm a list of precise words and phrases and strong action verbs that would work in their essays. Then meet as a class to share the changes that students made to individual essays.

4. **Improve your conclusion.** Suggest that students reread their introductions. Students' conclusions should reflect back on the ideas introduced at the beginning of the essay.

For interactive revision tools, see

⊘ Write*Smart* CD

ⓘ Writing Center at **ClassZone.com**

FOR ENGLISH LEARNERS

Comprehension: Transitions Provide sentence frames such as the following to help students use transitions in their essays.

• Both [subject A] and [subject B] _____.
• While [subject A] _____, [subject B] _____.
• Unlike [subject A], [subject B] _____.
• However, they both _____.
• [Subject A] _____; however, [subject B] _____.
• [Subject A] _____; similarly, [subject B] _____.

Preparing to Publish

Support for meeting the goals in the writing rubric is supplied throughout the **Writing Workshop** on pages 286–291.

For Rubric Bank, see

 Write*Smart* CD

ℹ Writing Center at **ClassZone.com**

Assess and Reteach

After reading and assessing students' essays, you might use these lessons to reteach key skills:

S STANDARDS LESSON FILE
Writing Lesson 29: Comparison-Contrast Essay
Writing Lesson 19: Transitions
Grammar Lesson 2: Avoiding Run-Ons

Apply the Rubric

A strong comparison-contrast essay . . .

☑ has an interesting introduction that names the subjects or characters to be compared and/or contrasted

☑ has a focused thesis statement

☑ is well organized

☑ uses transitions to connect ideas

☑ supports points with explanations, details, and quotations

☑ uses appropriate language and precise words

☑ varies sentence beginnings to keep reader interest

☑ has a satisfying conclusion

Ask a Peer Reader

- What main points did I make about my two subjects?
- Where should I add more details?
- What else could I say in my conclusion?

Add Transitions

For Comparing	For Contrasting
also	although
another	despite
both	however
in addition to	in contrast
like	nevertheless
likewise	on the other hand
similarly	unlike

Check Your Grammar

- Use a comma to set off an introductory phrase from the rest of the sentence.

> On the other hand , Roger in "Thank You, Ma'm" hasn't earned blue suede shoes.

See page R49: Quick Reference: Punctuation

- Correct run-on sentences.

> She doesn't yell or whine ⋀ instead, she calmly says she will speak with her grandfather.

See pages R64–R65: Correcting Run-On Sentences

Writing On|ine

PUBLISHING OPTIONS
For publishing options, visit the **Writing Center** at **ClassZone.com**.

ASSESSMENT PREPARATION
For writing and grammar assessment practice, go to the **Assessment Center** at **ClassZone.com**.

LISTENING STANDARD
6.A.1.b Gather information from listening to a speaker

Conducting an Interview

In this unit, you have read fiction and nonfiction from different points of view. Another way to see the world from someone else's point of view is to conduct an interview.

Planning the Interview

1. **Determine your purpose.** An interview can be a chance to learn firsthand about someone's life, work, or thoughts. Sometimes, an interview helps you understand an event. Decide what subject you want to learn about.

   TIP Want some practice with interviewing before you start your real interview? Try having a classmate role-play a character in literature.

2. **Identify people you might interview.** For example, if you want to learn about pets, list veterinarians, people who work at shelters, dog walkers, and pet owners.

3. **Contact your first choice.** Identify yourself and your purpose. If you want to audiotape or videotape, ask for permission.

4. **Write your questions.** Avoid questions that lead to simple yes or no answers. Anticipate possible answers so that you can write follow-up questions. Research your topic to find out what to ask.

Conducting the Interview

1. **Listen carefully and take notes.** Even if you are taping, it is still a good idea to take notes.

2. **Be flexible.** You don't have to ask every question you planned. On the other hand, new questions might occur to you on the spot. Be sure to ask follow-up questions if you are not sure you understand what you hear.

3. **Say thanks.** Thank the person for the interview. Send a thank-you note promptly.

4. **Summarize the interview.** Your teacher will determine how you should do this. You might produce a written summary, a partial transcript (that is, a written word-for-word re-creation of what was said), or an audio or video presentation.

   See page R82: Evaluate an Interview

WRITING WORKSHOP **293**

SPEAKING AND LISTENING

Ask students to read this page to get an overview of how to conduct an interview.

Before students begin working, review this rubric with them so that they understand their goals:

Rubric A strong interview

- includes questions that achieve a purpose
- avoids simple yes or no questions
- is flexible and anticipates possible answers and follow-up questions
- is well researched
- includes note-taking and careful listening
- is polite and includes sending a prompt thank-you note
- can be summarized with a written summary, a partial transcript, or a presentation

R RESOURCE MANAGER—Copy Master
Speaking and Listening p. 219

S STANDARDS LESSON FILE
Speaking and Listening Lesson 9: Interview

DIFFERENTIATED INSTRUCTION

FOR LESS–PROFICIENT WRITERS

Writing Interview Questions Explain that the goal of an interview is to inspire the subject to share what he or she knows about a topic. Help students recognize effective questions by discussing these examples:

- Do dogs make good pets? *(This question can be answered with one word—yes or no.)*

- What are some reasons that dogs make good pets? *(This question is open-ended and requires the person to provide specific information. He or she may talk for several minutes.)*

Have students work in pairs to develop some good interview questions they might ask a veterinarian or other expert about pets. Have each pair share one question with the class. Write the question in a chart like the one at right, and work with students to develop follow-up questions based on two possible answers.

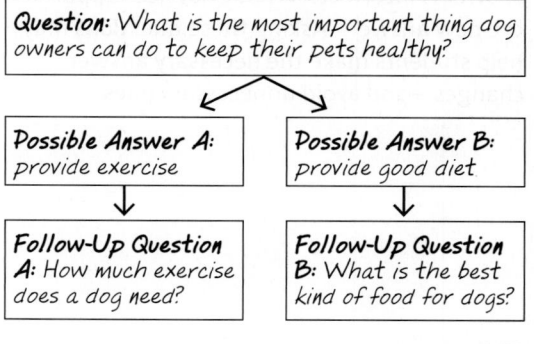

Question: What is the most important thing dog owners can do to keep their pets healthy?

Possible Answer A: provide exercise

Possible Answer B: provide good diet

Follow-Up Question A: How much exercise does a dog need?

Follow-Up Question B: What is the best kind of food for dogs?

Assessment Practice

CHECK READINESS

Read aloud the paragraph under **ASSESS** and stress to students that this is not the full Unit Test, but a way for them to check their readiness for it. Then have students examine the skills listed under **REVIEW** and look back in the unit or in the Handbook for any they need to study.

READ THE SELECTIONS

Remind students to keep unit goals in mind as they read each passage, paying particular attention to

- character traits and characterization
- point of view
- their own inferences

To help students focus on **character traits** while reading, encourage them to ask questions such as

- Who are the main characters in "The Man Who Was a Horse" and "A Mother in Mannville"? How are they introduced? How would you describe them?
- How do the characters change or grow during the passages?

ANSWER THE QUESTIONS

Direct students to pages R93–R99 of the Test-Taking Handbook to review test-taking strategies. Remind them not to choose the first alternative that seems to fit when answering a multiple-choice question. Instead, they should read through all the choices, eliminate any that are clearly wrong, and then choose the *best* answer—the one that is most accurate and complete.

During tests, students may be tempted to go back to questions and change their responses. Encourage students to approach such changes with caution: are they sure that their first answer is incorrect? What evidence supports the new answer? Asking these questions may help students make the necessary answer changes—and avoid unnecessary ones.

Assessment Practice

ASSESS
The practice test items on the next few pages match skills listed on the Unit Goals page (page 175) and addressed throughout this unit. Taking this practice test will help you assess your knowledge of these skills and determine your readiness for the Unit Test.

REVIEW
After you take the practice test, your teacher can help you identify any skills you need to review.

- Character Traits
- Characterization
- Point of View
- Make Inferences
- Idioms
- Similes
- Verb Tenses
- Comparative and Superlative Forms

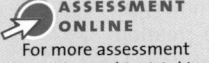

ASSESSMENT ONLINE
For more assessment practice and test-taking tips, go to the **Assessment Center** at **ClassZone.com.**

Reading Comprehension

DIRECTIONS *Read these selections and answer the questions that follow.*

Bob Lemmons is a cowboy who is able to capture a herd of mustangs single-handedly.

from The Man Who Was a Horse
Julius Lester

He had been seeing the wild horses since he could remember. The first time had been at dusk one day. He had been playing near the corral when he happened to look toward the mesa and there, standing atop it, was a lone stallion. The wind blew against it and its mane and tail flowed in the breeze like tiny ribbons. The horse stood there for a long while; then, without warning, it suddenly wheeled and galloped away. Even now Bob remembered how seeing that horse had been like looking into a mirror. He'd never told anyone that, sensing that they would perhaps think him a little touched in the head. Many people thought it odd enough that he
10 could bring in a herd of mustangs by himself. But, after that, whenever he saw one mustang or a herd, he felt like he was looking at himself.

One day several of the cowboys went out to capture a herd. The ranch was short of horses and no one ever thought of buying horses when there were so many wild ones. He had wanted to tell them that he would bring in the horses, but they would have laughed at him. Who'd ever heard of one man bringing in a herd? So he watched them ride out, saying nothing. A few days later they were back, tired and disgusted. They hadn't even been able to get close to a herd.

That evening Bob timidly suggested to Mr. Hunter that he be allowed
20 to try. Everyone laughed. Bob reminded them that no one on the ranch could handle a horse like he could, that the horses came to him more than anyone else. The cowboys acknowledged that that was true, but it was impossible for one man to capture a herd. Bob said nothing else. Early the next morning he rode out alone, asking the cook to leave food in a saddlebag for him on the fence at the north pasture every day. Three weeks later the cowboys were sitting around the corral one evening and looked up to see a herd of mustangs galloping toward them, led by Bob. Despite their amazement, they moved quickly to open the gate and Bob led the horses in.
30 That had been some twenty years ago, and long after Bob left the Hunter Ranch he found that everywhere he went he was known.

DIFFERENTIATED INSTRUCTION

FOR ENGLISH LEARNERS
Assessment Practice: Work Backwards
Prepare students for the assessment by having them read the questions before reading the text passage. Have pairs follow these steps to learn unfamiliar words in the test directions and questions:

1. Find words you don't recognize and write each one on an index card.

2. Look up the meaning in a dictionary.

3. Write the meaning on the back of the card.

4. Use your word cards to teach and practice the vocabulary with your partner and another pair.

from A Mother in Mannville

Marjorie Kinnan Rawlings

When I took the cabin, I asked for a boy or man to come and chop wood for the fireplace. The first few days were warm, I found what wood I needed about the cabin, no one came, and I forgot the order.

I looked up from my typewriter one late afternoon, a little startled. A boy stood at the door, and my pointer dog, my companion, was at his side and had not barked to warn me. The boy was probably twelve years old, but undersized. He wore overalls and a torn shirt, and was barefooted.

He said, "I can chop some wood today."

I said, "But I have a boy coming from the orphanage."

"I'm the boy."

"You? But you're small."

"Size don't matter, chopping wood," he said. "Some of the big boys don't chop good. I've been chopping wood at the orphanage a long time."

I visualized mangled and inadequate branches for my fires. I was well into my work and not inclined to conversation. I was a little blunt.

"Very well. There's the ax. Go ahead and see what you can do."

I went back to work, closing the door. At first the sound of the boy dragging brush annoyed me. Then he began to chop. The blows were rhythmic and steady, and shortly I had forgotten him, the sound no more of an interruption than a consistent rain. I suppose an hour and a half passed, for when I stopped and stretched, and heard the boy's steps on the cabin stoop, the sun was dropping behind the farthest mountain, and the valleys were purple with something deeper than the asters.

The boy said, "I have to go to supper now. I can come again tomorrow evening."

I said, "I'll pay you now for what you've done," thinking I should probably have to insist on an older boy. "Ten cents an hour?"

"Anything is all right."

We went together back of the cabin. An astonishing amount of solid wood had been cut. There were cherry logs and heavy roots of rhododendron, and blocks from the waste pine and oak left from the building of the cabin.

"But you've done as much as a man," I said. "This is a splendid pile."

I looked at him, actually, for the first time. His hair was the color of the

 GO ON

ITEM ANALYSIS

COMPREHENSION AND BRIEF CONSTRUCTED RESPONSE	ITEMS	UNIT PAGES
Character Traits	8, 9, 10	178
Characterization	1, 3, 4, 7, 11	178, 241, 259, 281
Point of View	2, 5, 6	176, 217, 227, 269
Make Inferences	1, 8, 11	217

VOCABULARY	ITEMS	UNIT PAGES
Idioms	1, 2, 3	278
Similes	4, 5, 6	206

WRITING AND GRAMMAR	ITEMS	UNIT PAGES
Verb Tenses	1, 4, 5	207
Comparative and Superlative Forms	2, 3, 6	239

FOR LESS–PROFICIENT READERS

Assessment Support Consider these options for completing the **Assessment Practice:**

- Have students "work backwards," reviewing the questions before reading the passage.

- Select random questions in the assessment and have students demonstrate how and where to look for the answers.

- Ask students to locate unfamiliar vocabulary in the assessment. Elicit the meanings of these words from the class.

- Have students record useful test words and definitions in their journals for later reference.

- Read the selections or parts of them aloud to aid in student comprehension.

MSA PREPARATION

 McDougal Littell **Assessment System**

After checking student readiness with this Assessment Practice, you may administer the complete Unit 2 Test, which matches the structure and format of the MSA.

Comprehension

Model a thinking process for answering multiple-choice questions.

1. **B is correct.** *Bob sees himself reflected in the horses—much as family members identify with and respond to one another. Although the horses are wild, as in A, Bob's character is not; rather, he is sensitive and timid. C and D are completely untrue, as these ideas are not mentioned in the story.*

2. **C is correct.** *The narrator reveals the thoughts and feelings of one character— Bob. The thoughts of the other cowboys are not revealed, as in A. B is incorrect because the narrator is outside the story. D is incorrect because the narrator describes Bob's thoughts, not his or her own.*

3. **D is correct.** *Bob's ability to handle horses and win their trust sets him apart from other cowboys. We can eliminate A, B, and C because they do not reveal Bob's physical or emotional skills with horses.*

4. **C is correct.** *Bob's action—suggesting that he bring in the herd—causes the other characters to laugh. We can eliminate A and D, because physical appearance is not discussed in these lines. B is incorrect because the narrator is simply describing Bob's actions, not commenting on them.*

5. **B is correct.** *Knowing that the narrator lives in a cabin and works on a typewriter (lines 1–4, 14–15), we can infer that the narrator is a writer. The boy from the orphanage is not the narrator, as in A, but is the character Jerry. C is incorrect because the narrator is within the story and uses first-person pronouns such as I and me. D is incorrect because the narrator does not mention having a child.*

6. **C is correct.** *A narrator who is within the story and refers to him- or herself as "I" gives a first-person point of view. A, B, and D are incorrect because they appear to be from a third-person point of view.*

7. **B is correct.** *The boy's facial features, which the narrator notes for the first time, reveal new dimensions of his character. In her description, there is no dialogue, as in A, nor are there any descriptions of characters' reactions or the boy's actions, as in C and D.*

---

corn shocks and his eyes, very direct, were like the mountain sky when rain is pending—gray, with a shadowing of that miraculous blue. As I spoke, a light came over him, as though the setting sun had touched him with the same suffused glory with which it touched the mountains. I gave him a quarter.

40 "You may come tomorrow," I said, "and thank you very much."

He looked at me, and at the coin, and seemed to want to speak, but could not, and turned away.

"I'll split kindling tomorrow," he said over his thin ragged shoulder. "You'll need kindling and medium wood and logs and backlogs."

At daylight I was half wakened by the sound of chopping. Again it was so even in texture that I went back to sleep. When I left my bed in the cool morning, the boy had come and gone, and a stack of kindling was neat against the cabin wall. He came again after school in the afternoon and worked until time to return to the orphanage. His name was Jerry; he

50 was twelve years old, and he had been at the orphanage since he was four. I could picture him at four, with the same grave gray-blue eyes and the same—independence? No, the word that comes to me is "integrity."

Comprehension

DIRECTIONS *Answer these questions about the excerpt from "The Man Who Was a Horse."*

1. What can you infer about Bob from his thoughts in lines 6–11?

   A. Bob is as wild as a horse.

   B. Bob feels a kinship with horses.

   C. Bob loves to run through the hills.

   D. Bob has big ears and a long face.

2. You can tell that this story is told from a third-person limited point of view because the narrator

   A. reveals the thoughts of all characters

   B. is a character in the story

   C. reveals one character's thoughts

   D. describes his own thoughts

3. Which sentence from the story shows that Bob is a talented horseman?

   A. "He had been playing near the corral when he happened to look toward the mesa and there, standing atop it, was a lone stallion."

   B. "But, after that, whenever he saw one mustang or a herd, he felt like he was looking at himself."

   C. "He had wanted to tell them that he would bring in the horses, but they would have laughed at him."

   D. "Bob reminded them that no one on the ranch could handle a horse like he could, that the horses came to him more than anyone else."

296

---

8. **C is correct.** *Jerry first arrives at the cabin on his own, chops wood as well as a strong man, and returns to the orphanage for supper. He comes back the next day, as promised (lines 43–45). He is not thoughtless, as in A, nor irritable, as in B; rather, he is thoughtful and polite. D is incorrect because Jerry says very little and seems speechless when the narrator gives him a quarter (lines 41–42).*

9. **A is correct.** *Both Bob and Jerry are dependable—when they say they will do a job, they do it swiftly and competently. B is incorrect because both characters are shy and timid, not bold. C is incorrect because neither character behaves in a reckless way. D is incorrect because the passages do not provide evidence about either character's optimism or lack of it.*

4. Which methods of characterization are used in lines 19–20?

A. descriptions of characters' thoughts and physical appearance

B. narrator's comments and descriptions of other characters' reactions

C. descriptions of a character's actions and other characters' reactions

D. descriptions of a character's physical appearance and other characters' reactions

DIRECTIONS *Answer these questions about the excerpt from "A Mother in Mannville."*

5. The narrator of the story is

A. a boy who lives in an orphanage

B. a writer who lives in a cabin

C. a voice outside the story

D. the mother of a young boy

6. Which sentence shows that this excerpt is told in the first person?

A. "The boy was probably twelve years old, but undersized."

B. "He said, 'I can chop some wood today.'"

C. "I went back to work, closing the door."

D. "An astonishing amount of solid wood had been cut."

7. Which method of characterization does the author use in lines 34–36?

A. the boy's own words

B. a description of his physical appearance

C. a description of other characters' reactions

D. a description of his actions

8. Which of the following words best describes Jerry?

A. thoughtless

B. irritable

C. reliable

D. talkative

DIRECTIONS *Answer this question about both selections.*

9. Which character trait do Bob and Jerry have in common?

A. dependability

B. boldness

C. recklessness

D. optimism

Brief Constructed Response

10. Name two character traits of Bob Lemmons in "The Man Who Was a Horse." Give details from the story that reveal these traits.

11. Reread lines 33–44 of the excerpt from "A Mother in Mannville." What can you infer about the boy from his reaction to the narrator's praise? Support your answer with details from the excerpt.

GO ON ➡

297

Brief Constructed Response

Evaluate student writing using the Maryland writing rubrics in the back of the book.

Possible responses:

10. *Bob Lemmons is **shy**, as shown when he timidly suggests that he be allowed to try to capture the herd of horses (lines 19–20). He is **self-assured** and **confident**—when the other cowboys laugh at him, he reminds them that he can handle horses better than anyone else (lines 20–21). He is **responsible**—he wants to capture the herd for the ranch, and he returns with the horses three weeks after setting out. He is also **self-reliant**, as shown when he rides out alone, asking only that the cook leave food for him each day (lines 24–25).*

11. *From the boy's reaction to the narrator's praise, readers can infer that he is glad to help someone and is very happy that his work is appreciated. This is shown by the way his face lights up when he hears the compliment (lines 36–37). Readers might also infer that he is not used to receiving many compliments, since this one seems to affect him so deeply. The way the boy looks at the narrator and the coin but says nothing, although he appears to want to say something (lines 41–42), suggests that he is shy. He is finally able to talk to the narrator after he has turned away (lines 43–44). The way he talks about the work he plans to do the next day suggests that the boy is proud of his work and feels responsible for making sure the narrator's needs are met. The details he provides about the different kinds of firewood (line 44) suggest that the boy is skilled at and knowledgeable about chopping wood.*

DIFFERENTIATED INSTRUCTION

FOR ENGLISH LEARNERS

Assessment Vocabulary On the board, write the following academic vocabulary listed in italics. Then give the definitions and examples in random order and have students classify them. Continue by eliciting examples from students.

- *infer:* to make a logical guess based on text clues and your own knowledge and experience

- *character traits:* responsible; timid; modest; stubborn; lazy; eager

- *third-person limited point of view:* "Sonia was anxious to leave, but her brother kept talking and didn't seem to notice."

- *narrator:* the person telling a story

- *first-person point of view:* "I stopped by the farm stand on my way home. I wanted to surprise everyone with fresh corn on the cob for dinner."

Vocabulary

1. **A is correct.** Bob keeps his visions to himself, for fear that others might think he is crazy. We can eliminate B, C, and D, because they do not help explain why Bob chooses not to share his ideas with others.

2. **B is correct.** To fall "short of" something means not having enough. The ranch does not have enough horses, so the cowboys plan to capture some wild horses (lines 12–14). We can eliminate C because it does not refer to quantity or amounts. A is incorrect because no specific type of horse is mentioned. D refers to the result of being "short of horses"—the cowboys look for more.

3. **C is correct.** An idea that "comes to mind" arrives suddenly. The idiom suggests a new thought that does not relate to remembering, as in A. It also does not develop over time, as in B, or need to be learned, as in D; rather, it comes in a flash, without trying to learn or study anything.

4. **A is correct.** Similes use *like* or *as* to compare two unlike things, as in this comparison of a horse's mane and tail to ribbons in the breeze. B, C, and D do not compare two different ideas. In C, *like* is used as a conjunction, meaning "in the same way that."

5. **D is correct.** Bob sees himself reflected in the horse; he connects and identifies with it. The simile is not just about horses, as in A, nor is it a literal comparison, as in B. The simile implies an emotional connection, not physical closeness, as in C.

6. **C is correct.** The unlike things compared in this simile are "his eyes" and "the mountain sky when rain is pending." We can eliminate A, B, and D because these sentences do not create a comparison between two unlike things or ideas.

Vocabulary

DIRECTIONS *Use context clues and your knowledge of idioms to answer the following questions.*

1. In "The Man Who Was a Horse," Bob does not want people to think he is "a little touched in the head" (line 9). This idiom refers to someone who
   A. behaves in a crazy way
   B. talks only to horses
   C. has an injured head
   D. makes reckless decisions

2. In line 13 in "The Man Who Was a Horse," the narrator says the ranch is "short of horses." The idiom *short of* means
   A. needing one type
   B. having too few
   C. being apart from
   D. looking for more

3. In line 52 in "A Mother in Mannville," the narrator says "the word that comes to me is 'integrity.'" The idiom *comes to me* means that something
   A. is easy to remember
   B. develops over time
   C. occurs to someone
   D. needs to be learned

DIRECTIONS *Use context clues and your knowledge of similes to answer the following questions.*

4. Which expression from "The Man Who Was a Horse" contains a simile?
   A. "its mane and tail flowed in the breeze like tiny ribbons"
   B. "Who'd ever heard of one man bringing in a herd?"
   C. "no one on the ranch could handle a horse like he could"
   D. "A few days later they were back, tired and disgusted."

5. In "The Man Who Was a Horse," Bob says "seeing that horse had been like looking into a mirror" (line 7). This simile means that
   A. the horse looks like other horses
   B. Bob looks like the horse
   C. Bob and the horse are always together
   D. Bob identifies with the horse

6. Which expression from "A Mother in Mannville" contains a simile?
   A. "I visualized mangled and inadequate branches for my fires."
   B. "An astonishing amount of solid wood had been cut."
   C. "his eyes, very direct, were like the mountain sky when rain is pending"
   D. "I could picture him at four, with the same grave gray-blue eyes"

298

DIFFERENTIATED INSTRUCTION

FOR ENGLISH LEARNERS

Review Academic Vocabulary Point out the words *idioms* and *similes* in the directions on page 298. Discuss the meanings of these terms and provide examples. Ask students to think of their own examples.

- *idiom*—an expression that means something different than the literal meaning of the words. Examples:
  — *hit the hay* ("go to sleep" or "rest")
  — *hold your horses* ("slow down")
  — *shake a leg* ("hurry up")

- *simile*—a comparison between two things that are very different but share one trait in common. Examples:
  — *The horse stood as still as a statue.* (Both are very still and do not move.)
  — *The sound of the boy's chopping was like a steady rain on the roof.* (Both are steady and regular.)
  — *The boy and the dog walked in together like two old friends.* (Both pairs are comfortable with each other.)

Writing & Grammar

DIRECTIONS *Read the passage and answer the questions that follow.*

> (1) A hundred years ago, methods of transportation <u>are</u> very different.
> (2) It was <u>more tougher</u> to get around at that time than it is now. (3) Traveling
> by foot, horse, or wagon was usually <u>more slower</u> than using bicycles,
> streetcars, or trains. (4) Transportation <u>will improve</u> greatly when the
> automobile and airplane were invented. (5) It took a few decades for them to
> become common, but once they did, everything <u>will change</u>. (6) Today, these
> two modes of transportation are often the <u>more convenient</u> of all.

1. Choose the correct verb tense to replace the underlined word in sentence 1.

A. will be

B. is

C. were

D. are becoming

2. Choose the correct comparative to replace the underlined words in sentence 2.

A. most toughest

B. tougher

C. most tougher

D. toughest

3. Choose the correct comparative to replace the underlined word in sentence 3.

A. slower

B. slowest

C. most slower

D. most slowest

4. Choose the correct verb tense to replace the underlined words in sentence 4.

A. improved

B. improves

C. is improving

D. will be improved

5. Choose the correct verb tense to replace the underlined words in sentence 5.

A. was changing

B. changes

C. would be changing

D. changed

6. Choose the correct superlative to replace the underlined words in sentence 6.

A. most convenient

B. most convenientest

C. convenienter

D. more convenientest

STOP

299

DIFFERENTIATED INSTRUCTION

FOR ENGLISH LEARNERS

Review Academic Vocabulary Discuss the definitions and examples of these terms.

- *verb tense* (items 1, 4, 5)—a form of a verb that tells when the action happens. Examples:
  — present tense *(he walks, we eat, she is sleeping)*
  — past tense *(he walked, we ate, she was sleeping, I had forgotten)*
  — future tense *(he will walk, we will be eating)*

- *comparative* (items 2, 3)—an adjective that compares two things. Examples:
  — Sheila is *taller* than Mario.
  — My mom's car is *more dependable* than my dad's car.

- *superlative* (item 6)—an adjective that compares three or more things. Examples:
  — Marla is the *tallest* girl in our class.
  — That was the *most beautiful* sunset I have ever seen.

ANSWERS

Writing & Grammar

1. **C is correct.** *The context clue "a hundred years ago" reveals that something from the past is being discussed, and the second clause therefore requires the past tense of the verb* to be. *We can eliminate* A, B, *and* D *because they are verbs in the present or future tense.*

2. **B is correct.** *Since* tough *is a one-syllable word, its comparative form requires just the suffix* -er. A, C, *and* D *are incorrect because they improperly combine the superlative elements of* -est *and* most.

3. **A is correct.** *Slow is a one-syllable word, so its comparative form is made by adding* -er. B *is incorrect because the superlative form should not be used when only two sets of things are compared.* C *is incorrect because it contains the unnecessary superlative word* most. D *is incorrect because it contains the two superlative elements* -est *and* most.

4. **A is correct.** *The second clause of the sentence has a past-tense verb,* were, *which is a clue that the verb in the first clause should also be past tense. We can eliminate* B *and* C *because they are in the present tense, and* D *because it is in the future tense.*

5. **D is correct.** *The past tense of the verb* change *is needed, because the sentence discusses events from past decades.* A *is incorrect because it is in the past progressive tense, suggesting action that is ongoing, but the context clue "once they did" suggests that the action was completed.* B *is incorrect because it is in the present tense.* C *is incorrect because it is a conditional tense, but the sentence does not discuss the conditions under which everything "would be changing."*

6. **A is correct.** *Convenient is a multi-syllable word, so its superlative form is made by adding* most *before it, with no* -est, *as in* B *and* D, *and no* -er, *as in* C.

INTRODUCE *MORE GREAT READS*

In Unit 2, students have discussed a number of big questions. Invite students to tell which question they found most intriguing and why. Then focus attention on the three questions that appear on this page. Discuss the recommended books and their summaries, pointing out how each connects to the related question. Encourage students to choose one or more of these "great reads" to read independently.

ⓘ ClassZone.com

To find additional books that match students' interests and ability levels, visit the Literature Center at **ClassZone.com**.

More Great Reads

UNIT 2

Ideas for Independent Reading

Which questions from Unit 2 made an impression on you? Continue exploring them with these books.

What has the power to heal?

Crazy Lady!
by Jane Leslie Conly
Does friendship have the power to heal? In this book, a woman's love for her son serves as a beacon of hope for a troubled youth.

Getting Near to Baby
by Audrey Couloumbis
Twelve-year-old Willa and Little Sister take to escaping to the roof of their aunt's house when their baby sister dies. Their mother, suffering from depression, can offer them nothing. Will time heal their wounds?

The Birthday Room
by Kevin Henkes
When Ben Hunter receives two unique gifts, he tells his mom that he'd prefer a trip to see his estranged uncle. Why would he choose an uncle he hasn't seen for ten years? Read this compelling story of one family's forgiveness.

What stands in the way of your dreams?

The Midwife's Apprentice
by Karen Cushman
Alyce is a homeless girl living in medieval England. The town's midwife offers to teach her the art of delivering babies. She learns a great deal, but will she be able to make herself independent?

Charlie Pippin
by Candy Dawson Boyd
Charlie's dad rarely shows her any affection. Now she's in trouble with the principal at school. Will father and daughter ever come to understand and appreciate each other?

Number the Stars
by Lois Lowry
Life in Copenhagen is very different now that Nazi soldiers have marched into town. When the Jews of Denmark are "relocated," ten-year-old Ellen moves in with her best friend's family so that her own life is spared.

Who deserves a second chance?

Spider Boy
by Ralph Fletcher
When Bobby Ballenger moves from the Midwest to New York, he has a difficult time adjusting. The cruelty of his classmates makes him long for his former friends. Will he face the bullies and earn a second chance?

Spinners
by Donna Jo Napoli and Richard Tchen
Napoli and Tchen retell a classic tale to give insights into the lives of Rumpelstiltskin and his daughter. Love, pride, avarice, and revenge are all a part of this delightful new version.

The Fire Pony
by Rodman Philbrick
Roy is happiest when he's with his older brother Joe, who has a fiery temper and a special gift for healing horses. All seems well when Joe rescues Roy from a foster home, but before long, Joe reveals a darker side.

UNIT 3

Lessons to Learn

UNDERSTANDING THEME

- In Fiction
- In Poetry
- In Drama
- In Media

301

About the Art Barbara Weldon painted *Birds XII* in 2003. For more information, see page 382 of the teacher's edition.

For help in planning this unit, see

 RESOURCE MANAGER UNIT 3
pp. 1–11

INTRODUCE THE UNIT

A big test, a special holiday, a decisive victory, or a heartbreaking loss—we learn important lessons through our experiences. Ask students what the word *lesson* brings to mind for them. Do they recall making a mistake and learning from it? Do they remember things their parents or other adults have taught them? Then have students discuss what makes a lesson "stick." For example, are they more likely to remember a lesson learned through experience, or one taught by someone they respect?

Ask students to keep the idea of lessons in mind as they discuss the pictures on this page. To elicit ideas, ask

- Why do you think this painter was inspired to paint birds? What might she have learned by observing birds?
- What do the photograph and the painting have in common?
- What has happened to the bird in the photograph? How is the man trying to help the bird?
- What lesson might people learn from what happened to the bird?

Discuss how the information in the pictures led to an idea or lesson about people's relationship to nature. Let students know that in this unit they will explore **themes** in stories, poems, and plays. Themes in literature are often like lessons. In searching for themes, students may discover valuable insights into their own lives.

MARYLAND

SKILLS STRAND	3.A.3.a, 3.A.6.b, 3.A.6.b	1.D.3.b, 1.E.3.a, 3.A.6.a, 5.C.2	1.D.2.b, 1.E.3.a, 3.A.6.a	*Linked selections* 1.D.3.a, 1.E.4.c, 3.A.7.a, 5.A.2.d	2.A.4.b, 4.A.2.d	1.D.3.b, 1.E.3.a, 3.A.3.e
	Reader's Workshop: Understanding Theme pp. 304–309	**Amigo Brothers** pp. 310–325 Short Story *Level: Average*	**The War of the Wall** pp. 326–337 Short Story *Level: Average*	**What Do Fish Have to Do with Anything?** pp. 338–355 Short Story *Level: Average*	**Homeless** pp. 356–361 Problem-Solution Essay *Level: Easy*	**A Crush** pp. 362–373 Short Story *Level: Average*
Literary Analysis	Understanding Theme pp. 304–309	Theme versus Topic pp. 311, 315, 316, 318, 319, 322, 323	Theme pp. 327, 328, 332, 334, 335	Symbol pp. 339, 343, 345, 346, 352, 353	Characteristics of a Problem-Solution Essay pp. 357, 359, 360	Theme and Character pp. 363, 367, 368, 370, 371, 372
Reading and Informational Texts	Analyze the Literature pp. 305, 307–309	Compare and Contrast pp. 311, 312, 320, 323	Monitor pp. 327, 330, 332, 333, 335 Read a Magazine Article p. 337	Make Inferences pp. 339, 342, 344, 349, 352, 353 Review: Compare and Contrast pp. 349, 353	Identify Author's Perspective pp. 356, 359, 360, 361 Support an Opinion p. 361	Identify Cause-and-Effect Relationships pp. 363, 364, 368, 371, 372
Vocabulary	Academic Vocabulary pp. 304, 306	Word Acquisition pp. 311, T311, 325 Context Clues p. T311 Latin Roots (*pel*) p. 324	Word Acquisition pp. 327, T327, 336 Context Clues p. T327 Denotations and Connotations p. 336	Word Acquisition pp. 339, T339, 354 Context Clues p. T339 General Context Clues p. 354		Word Acquisition pp. 363, T363, 373 Context Clues p. T363 Prefixes (*in-*) p. 373
Writing, Grammar, and Style		Punctuation in Dialogue p. 325		Sentence Combining p. 355 Coordinating Conjunctions p. 355		
Speaking, Listening, Viewing, and Media	Discuss pp. 304–306	Discuss pp. 310, T312–T322, 323 Analyze Visuals pp. 312, 315, 317, 320	Discuss pp. 326, T328–T334, 335, T337 Analyze Visuals pp. 328, T333	Discuss pp. 338, T340–T352, 353 Analyze Visuals pp. 340, 345, 347, 351	Discuss pp. 356, T357–T360, 361	Discuss pp. 362, T364–T371, 372 Analyze Visuals pp. 364, T371, 374

Assessment-Based Planning: Skills in red are assessed on the Unit 3 Test. **T** = Teacher's Edition page

1.E.1.b, 3.A.1.b	1.E.3.a, 3.A.6.b	1.E.3.a, 3.A.6.a, 5.A.2.d	3.A.6.a	4.A.1, 4.A.2.a
Great Reads: *from* **The Giver** pp. 374–379 Fantasy Novel *Level: Average*	**Spring Harvest of Snow Peas / Eating Alone** pp. 380–385 Poems *Level: Average*	**A Christmas Carol** pp. 386–415 Drama *Level: Challenging*	**Media Study:** *from* **A Christmas Carol** pp. 416–419 Film Clips	**Writing Workshop: Short Story** pp. 420–427
Form (Fantasy Novel) p. 374 Form (Fantasy Novel) p. 374	Recurring Theme pp. 381, 382, 383, 384	Theme in Drama pp. 387, T389, T390, T392, T393, T394, T396, T400, T401, T404, T405, T406, T410, 414		
	Set a Purpose for Reading p. 381 Compare and Contrast Themes pp. 384, 385	Analyze Sequence pp. 387, T390, T396, T397, T398, T400, T402, T406, T409, T412, 414 Read an Online Article p. 413		Analyze a Short Story pp. 421–422, 426
		Word Acquisition pp. 387, T387 Context Clues p. T387	Academic Vocabulary (Film) p. 417	
	Write for Assessment p. 385	Dependent and Independent Clauses p. 415		Write a Short Story pp. 420–427 Dialogue pp. 420, 422, T422, 424, 425 Pronoun-Antecedent Agreement p. 426
Discuss pp. 374, T379	Discuss pp. 380, T382–T383, 384 Analyze Visuals p. T382	Discuss pp. 386, T388–T413, 414 Analyze Visuals pp. T389, T391, T395, T397, T399, T403, T404, T407, T408, T411	Discuss pp. 416, 419 Theme in Movies pp. 417–418 Design a DVD Cover p. 419	Discuss pp. 420–422, 424, 425, 426 Dramatize a Short Story p. 427

Skills Assessed on the Unit 3 Test:

Literary Analysis
- Identify theme
- Identify and interpret symbol

Reading and Informational Texts
- Understand cause-and-effect relationships
- Make inferences
- Compare and contrast
- Identify author's perspective

Vocabulary
- Understand and use denotation and connotation of words
- Use context clues to understand word meaning

Writing, Grammar, and Style
- Write a short story
- Punctuate dialogue correctly
- Combine dependent and independent clauses to avoid sentence fragments
- Use coordinating conjunctions to join sentences
- Additional writing and grammar skills

For additional lesson planning help, see **Easy Planner DVD.**

301B

OBJECTIVES

- establish prior knowledge about **theme**
- discuss themes in familiar books and movies

What's the
BIG IDEA?

To introduce the page, ask students to think of stories (either books or movies) that have lingered in their memories because they conveyed strong messages about life. These messages might involve love, courage, kindness, or honesty. Help students state each message in a sentence, such as "Love is more important than any amount of money" or "Courage means doing the right thing even when you feel afraid." Discuss how the characters and events in each story reveal the theme.

ACTIVITY Remind students that a story can have more than one theme. Encourage them to consider several theme ideas for each story and then decide which is the strongest or most important.

CHECK UNDERSTANDING Have students tell what a theme is and describe how a theme can be expressed through the characters and events in a story.

What's the
BIG IDEA?

"Things are not always what they seem." "There's no place like home." These are examples of **themes,** or messages about life and human nature that writers convey to their readers. Often, these ideas are what remain with you long after you've read the last page.

ACTIVITY Pick two or three of your all-time favorite books or movies. For each, reflect on what message the writer or director is trying to express about life and human nature. Get together with a small group and talk about your choices and your responses to these questions:

- What lessons do the characters learn?
- What message did you take away from the book or movie?
- How do you see this big idea, or message, apply to your own life?

302

Unit Resources

 **RESOURCE MANAGER UNIT 3**

 **BEST PRACTICES TOOLKIT**

S **STANDARDS LESSON FILE**

- Easy Planner DVD
- Write*Smart* CD
- ClassZone.com
- Audio Anthology CD
- Multi-Language Academic Vocabulary Online

- eEdition CD & Online
- McDougal Littell Assessment System
- Test Generator CD
- Media*Smart* DVD

 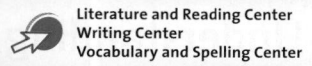
Preview Unit Goals

MARYLAND OBJECTIVES

LITERARY ANALYSIS
- Distinguish topic from theme
- Identify theme, including universal and recurring theme
- Compare and contrast themes and characters
- Identify and interpret symbols

READING
- Use reading strategies, including monitoring and setting a purpose for reading
- Make inferences
- Identify and analyze cause and effect and sequence

WRITING AND GRAMMAR
- Write a short story
- Use coordinating conjunctions to join sentences
- Combine dependent and independent clauses

SPEAKING, LISTENING, AND VIEWING
- Compare a film with a play
- Design a DVD cover
- Dramatize a short story

VOCABULARY
- Understand and use denotation and connotation of words
- Use general context clues to understand word meaning

ACADEMIC VOCABULARY
- topic
- theme
- symbol
- cause and effect
- sequence
- make inferences
- compare and contrast
- clauses

303

Preview Unit Goals

This page provides a quick overview of the skills and strategies covered in the unit. Make sure students are aware of the color-coding used to identify each skill strand. This color-coding is used wherever skills are taught in the unit. As students read the page, encourage them to think about their ability to use each skill or strategy.

Suggest that students copy the Academic Vocabulary terms in their journals and define them in their own words as they work through the unit. Encourage students to use these words as they discuss and write about the selections.

ADDITIONAL UNIT GOALS

These skills will be taught in this unit but are not the major focus of the unit:

Literary Analysis
- Identify how character growth and change reveal theme
- Identify theme in drama
- Read a problem-solution essay
- Support an opinion
- Study a variety of genres: short story, poetry, play, science fiction/fantasy, problem-solution essay

Reading
- Compare and contrast
- Set a purpose for reading

Writing and Grammar
- Use dialogue to show characters' personalities
- Combine sentences to avoid choppy writing

Vocabulary
- Understand and use the Latin root *pel*
- Understand and use the prefix *in-*

DIFFERENTIATED INSTRUCTION

FOR ENGLISH LEARNERS

Academic Vocabulary Use the Academic Vocabulary copy master to introduce students to the terms listed on page 303.

1. To fill in the chart, students may work in pairs to brainstorm forms of each word and to complete the definitions.

2. Have students complete Part B independently.

3. Meet as a class to discuss students' answers.

Additional Academic Vocabulary Use the second copy master to help students learn these academic terms from the unit: *connotation, context clues, coordinating conjunction, denotation, monitor, perspective.*

1. Read aloud each term in Part A and discuss the example with students.

2. Have students complete the page and then discuss their answers in groups.

R RESOURCE MANAGER—Copy Masters
Academic Vocabulary p. 9
Additional Academic Vocabulary p. 10

303

Focus and Motivate

OBJECTIVES

- distinguish topic from theme
- identify theme

Teach

Part 1: Themes in Literature

Topics and Themes Point out that literature often deals with complex topics such as love and death. Topics like these can support many themes. Two authors might write about the same topic but express completely different ideas about it. Use this activity to help students explore the way many themes can grow from a single topic.

- Write a topic word on the board, such as *love, death,* or *friendship.*
- Ask students to brainstorm theme statements related to the topic. Suggest they consider what they would want to teach a younger sibling about the topic. Use students' sentences to create a web diagram.

A good friend sticks with you through hard times.

Trust is the basis of any true friendship.

Friendship

Friends must allow each other to grow and change.

Some friendships last only a short time, but they are still valuable.

- Challenge students to think of well-known stories from books, movies, or television that express the themes in the web diagram. If they think of stories that express other themes on the same topic, add these themes to the diagram.

 BEST PRACTICES TOOLKIT—Transparency
Analysis Frame: Theme pp. D23, D34

Understanding Theme

The Wizard of Oz could be described as a story about a lost girl who finds her way home. But that description doesn't tell you what the story is really *about*. There is more to a story than what happens and whom it happens to. Often there is a deeper meaning, or theme. A **theme** is a message about life that a writer wants you to understand. A story usually has at least one theme and sometimes more. By figuring out a theme, you can learn a little about human nature.

 MARYLAND OBJECTIVES

LITERATURE STANDARDS
3.A.6.a Analyze universal themes
3.A.6.b Analyze themes across multiple texts

Part 1: Themes in Literature

It's easy to confuse a story's theme with its topic. Here's a way to tell the difference: A topic can be summed up in a word or two, such as "taking risks." A theme, however, is a writer's message *about* a topic. It usually takes at least one complete sentence to express a theme—for example, "Life's biggest rewards come from taking risks."

Stories can mean different things to different people. Two people reading a story might describe its theme differently or find different themes.

EXAMPLES OF THEMES IN LITERATURE

Thank You, M'am

Unit 1
pages 64–68

PLOT SUMMARY

Mrs. Luella Bates Washington Jones catches Roger trying to steal her purse. She drags him to her home, makes him wash up, and feeds him. Then she gives him the ten dollars he was trying to steal.

TOPIC

- Second chances

POSSIBLE THEMES

- Everyone deserves a second chance.
- An act of kindness can make a difference in a person's life.

Casey at the Bat

Unit 1
pages 130–132

PLOT SUMMARY

When the hometown baseball hero Casey comes to bat, there are two outs and two men on base. Instead of winning the game with a home run, Casey strikes out, and his team loses.

TOPIC

- Baseball

POSSIBLE THEMES

- Even a hero can fail.
- Overconfidence can lead to failure.

DIFFERENTIATED INSTRUCTION

FOR ALL STUDENTS

For general guidelines on differentiating instruction, see

 BEST PRACTICES TOOLKIT
Differentiated Instruction pp. 31–38

FOR LESS–PROFICIENT READERS

Note Taking For students who need help with note taking, hand out the Note Taking: Themes in Literature copy master and have students read page 304 silently. Then discuss the information and have students record notes on the copy master.

 RESOURCE MANAGER—Copy Master
Note Taking p. 15

Find Evidence for Themes Discuss the themes provided for "Thank You, Ma'm" and "Casey at the Bat." Have students provide text evidence for each theme. For example, the theme "Everyone deserves a second chance" is supported by the ending in which Mrs. Jones helps Roger.

MODEL 1: THEME IN A STORY

Fables often convey themes about human nature through the actions of animal characters. What lesson can readers learn from this fable?

The **LION** and the M O U S E

Fable by **Aesop**

A lion was idling in the sun, pretending to sleep, when he felt a tickle on his nose. He opened one eye and, with a swipe of his huge paw, caught a small mouse trying to run away. The lion roared angrily and tossed the mouse into the air. The mouse cried, "Please don't hurt
5 me! If only you will spare my life, I promise I will repay you." Surprised and amused by the little creature's earnest promise, the lion laughed and let the mouse go.

Time passed, and then one day the lion became ensnared in a trap. As he struggled to free himself, the ropes tightened around him until
10 he couldn't move. The little mouse was close by and heard the lion's roars. She came and set the lion free by gnawing through the ropes. "When you kindly spared my life," said the mouse, "you laughed at the idea that one day I would repay you."

Close Read

1. What does the lion decide to do after capturing the mouse? Explain how the mouse repays the lion.

2. What lesson can readers learn from the way the lion and the mouse treat each other?

MODEL 2: THEME IN A POEM

In this poem, the writer presents a strong message about family.

LiTTLE SiSTER

Poem by **Nikki Grimes**

little sister
holds on tight.
My hands hurt
from all that squeezing,
5 but I don't mind.
She thinks no one will bother her
when I'm around,
and they won't
if I can help it.
10 And even when I can't
I try
'cause she believes in me.

Close Read

1. How does the little sister rely on the speaker of the poem? Explain how the speaker feels about his or her sister.

2. Reread the boxed lines. Which statement best expresses the theme?
   a. When family members believe in you, it makes you stronger.
   b. Families should spend more time together.

MODEL 1: THEME IN A STORY
Close Read

1. *Possible answer:* *Amused by the mouse's plea, the lion decides to free the mouse. Later, when the lion is caught in a trap with ropes, the mouse gnaws through the ropes to free the lion.*

2. *Possible answers:* *People should treat others in the same way that they want to be treated. Also, people never really know in advance who may prove to be a great friend.*

MODEL 2: THEME IN A POEM
Close Read

1. *Possible answer:* *The little sister relies on the speaker for protection and support; she believes that the speaker can keep her safe from people who "bother her" (lines 6–7). The speaker seems to like being looked up to. The speaker wants to help his or her sister because the sister "believes in me."*

2. *Possible answer:* *"When family members believe in you, it makes you stronger."*

If students need help . . . Direct their attention to lines 10–12, which suggest that the little sister's trust makes the speaker try harder instead of just giving up.

FOR ENGLISH LEARNERS

Concept Support Help students determine the theme of "The Lion and the Mouse" by having them identify the main event in each paragraph. What message (theme) can the reader take from these events? Chart their responses in a graphic organizer.

Paragraph 1: The big guy (lion) saves the little guy (mouse).

↓

Paragraph 2: Later, the little guy saves the big guy.

↓

Theme: You never know who will prove to be a valuable friend.

FOR ADVANCED LEARNERS/PRE–AP

Identify and Discuss Themes Have students read the workshop independently. Then

1. Have students form small groups to select several stories, books, or movies whose themes they will discuss.
2. Students should then work independently to identify possible themes.
3. Finally, students should meet to discuss the themes and give evidence to support their opinions.

Teach

Part 2: A Closer Look at Theme

Clues to Theme Discuss each kind of clue in reference to stories students know. Here are some questions relating to selections in Unit 1.

- **TITLE** Which titles in Unit 1 reflect the topic of the selection? *Possible answers: "The Dinner Party," "Seventh Grade," "The Last Dog,"* Exploring the *Titanic,* An American Childhood, *"Casey at the Bat"*

- **TITLE** What is one theme in "The Dinner Party"? What new title could you give the story to reflect this theme? *Possible answers: One theme is "Stereotypes are often not true." The story could be called "The Proof Is in the Action" or "The Gentle Hostess with Nerves of Steel."*

- **PLOT** In "The Last Dog," what two ways of living must Brock choose between? How does he feel about his decision at the end? What theme does this plot suggest? *Possible answers: Brock must choose between a life in the controlled dome and one in the natural world. He is happy and excited with his choice. The theme could be stated, "Freedom and truth can be scary, but they are worth it."*

- **CHARACTERS** How does Roger in "Thank You, Ma'm" change during the story? What theme does this change suggest? *Possible answers: At the beginning of the story, Roger tries to steal a purse. He is desperate and self-centered. At the end, he feels gratitude for Mrs. Jones's kindness. This suggests the theme "Kindness can make a difference to another person."*

- **SETTING** What is the setting of "The Monsters Are Due on Maple Street"? What does the setting suggest about where mob action can happen? *Possible answers: The setting is an average, normal neighborhood. This suggests that mob action can happen anywhere.*

Part 2: A Closer Look at Theme

Sometimes the theme of a story is stated directly by the narrator or a character. Most often, though, a theme is implied—hinted at but not stated directly. In such a case, you need to **infer** the theme by finding clues in the text. This chart tells you where to look for those clues. Use the questions shown to help you uncover the theme of any story you read.

CLUES TO THEME

TITLE	The title may reflect a story's topic, its theme, or both. Ask
	• What does each word in the title mean? • What ideas does the title emphasize?

PLOT	A story's plot often revolves around a conflict that is important to the theme. Ask
	• What conflicts do the characters face? • How are the conflicts resolved?

CHARACTERS	What characters do and learn can reflect a theme. Ask
	• What are the main characters like? (Analyze their speech, thoughts, and actions.) • How do the characters respond to the conflicts? • How do the characters change? • What lessons do the characters learn?

SETTING	A setting can suggest a theme because of what it means to the characters. Ask
	• How does the setting influence the characters? • How does the setting affect the conflicts? • What might the setting represent? (For example, a character's childhood home might represent safety for him or her.)

DIFFERENTIATED INSTRUCTION

FOR LESS-PROFICIENT READERS

Note Taking For students who need help, hand out the Note Taking: A Closer Look at Theme copy master. Read and discuss the first paragraph on page 306. Help students complete the sentences on the top part of the copy master. Then have students read the rest of the page and take notes on the four kinds of clues. Pairs or small groups may then compare their notes.

RESOURCE MANAGER—Copy Master
Note Taking p. 16

FOR ENGLISH LEARNERS

Vocabulary: Synonyms Point out that writers use synonyms (words with nearly the same meaning) to avoid repeating the same word. Discuss these synonyms used on page 306.

- *imply, hint at, suggest*—"to express or show indirectly"
- *infer, uncover*—"to reveal something that is hidden or expressed indirectly"
- *reflect, represent*—"stand for something else"
- *influence, affect*—"cause to happen"

Part 3: Analyze the Literature

In this story, two brothers respond to a challenge by making very different choices. As you read, use the clues in the story to help you understand what the writer is saying about their choices.

THE TWO BROTHERS

Short story by **Leo Tolstoy**

Two brothers set out on a journey together. At noon they lay down in a forest to rest. When they woke up they saw a stone lying next to them. There was something written on the stone, and they tried to make out what it was.

5 "Whoever finds this stone," they read, "let him go straight into the forest at sunrise. In the forest a river will appear; let him swim across the river to the other side. There he will find a she-bear and her cubs. Let him take the cubs from her and run up the mountain with them, without once looking back. On the top of the mountain

10 he will see a house, and in that house will he find happiness."

Close Read

1. The title of this story suggests that the two brothers are central to the theme. As you read, think about the differences in the brothers' outlooks on life.

2. What challenge do the brothers face? Predict how they might respond to the challenge.

Part 3: Analyze the Literature
Close Read

2. ***Possible answer:*** *The brothers find a stone that tells them they can find happiness if they overcome several challenges, including going into a forest, swimming across a river, seizing cubs from a she-bear, and running up to the top of a mountain. Students may predict that the brothers will be excited and intrigued by this challenge and the prospect of finding happiness. Others may predict that the brothers will be wary of the dangers posed by the challenges.*

DIFFERENTIATED INSTRUCTION

FOR LESS–PROFICIENT READERS

Understand Genre Clarify that this short story by Tolstoy has elements of a folk tale, such as fantastic events. Ask students to identify things that seem beyond the realm of the ordinary on page 307. ***Possible answer:*** *the appearance of a stone with complex instructions written on it*

FOR ENGLISH LEARNERS

Language Support Understanding the wording of the instructions on the stone may be difficult for English learners. Ask them to put the instructions in their own words. Provide this sample paraphrase for the first instruction (lines 5–6):

If you find this stone, go straight into the forest at sunrise.

3. *Possible answer:* The elder brother responds to the challenges by focusing on the dangers and refusing to go ahead. His reaction shows that he is practical, cautious, and fearful. He tends to focus on the negative rather than the positive.

If students need help . . . Read the passage aloud, using your voice and facial expressions to convey the elder brother's anxiety. Then ask students to describe the kind of character you portrayed.

4. *Possible answer:* The elder brother's outlook on life could be summarized as "If it seems too good to be true, it's probably not true." He does not believe in magical solutions to the problems of life. The younger brother's outlook is more adventurous. He believes that amazing things can happen if a person has faith and is willing to take risks.

When they had read what was written on the stone, the younger brother said:

"Let us go together. We can swim across the river, carry off the bear cubs, take them to the house on the mountain, and together 15 find happiness."

"I am not going into the forest after bear cubs," said the elder brother, "and I advise you not to go. In the first place, no one can know whether what is written on this stone is the truth—perhaps it was written in jest. It is even possible that we have not read it 20 correctly. In the second place, even if what is written here is the truth— suppose we go into the forest and night comes, and we cannot find the river. We shall be lost. And if we do find the river, how are we going to swim across it? It may be broad and swift. In the third place, even if we swim across the river, do you think it is an easy 25 thing to take her cubs away from a she-bear? She will seize us, and, instead of finding happiness, we shall perish, and all for nothing. In the fourth place, even if we succeeded in carrying off the bear cubs, we could not run up a mountain without stopping to rest. And, most important of all, the stone does not tell us what kind of 30 happiness we should find in that house. It may be that the happiness awaiting us there is not at all the sort of happiness we would want."

"In my opinion," said the younger brother, "you are wrong. What is written on the stone could not have been put there without reason. And it is all perfectly clear. In the first place, no harm will come to 35 us if we try. In the second place, if we do not go, someone else will read the inscription on the stone and find happiness, and we shall have lost it all. In the third place: if you do not make an effort and try hard, nothing in the world will succeed. In the fourth place: I should not want it thought that I was afraid of anything."

40 The elder brother answered him by saying: "The proverb says: 'In seeking great happiness small pleasures may be lost.' And also: 'A bird in the hand is worth two in the bush.'"

3. Reread the boxed text The setting—the forest the river, the bears, and the mountain—all represent danger to the elder brother. What does his reaction to the setting's challenges tel you about him?

4. Reread lines 16–39. How are the brothers' attitudes different? Describe each brother's outlook on life.

DIFFERENTIATED INSTRUCTION

FOR ENGLISH LEARNERS

Analysis Support: Character Remind students that characters often give clues to a story's theme. Have them use web diagrams to analyze the two brothers' approaches to life. Point out that the phrases *in the first place, in the second place,* and so on indicate each brother's arguments for or against following the stone's instructions. Have them summarize each argument on a spoke, as shown.

words on stone may be false (lines 17–18)

might get lost or drown in river (lines 21–23)

Elder Brother

might be eaten by bear (lines 24–26)

hard to run up mountain (line 28)

FOR ADVANCED LEARNERS/PRE–AP

Synthesize Have students consider the two brothers and the differences in their outlooks on life. Ask them to list occupations that would suit each brother (engineer, astronaut, poet, teacher, and so on) and to give reasons for each job match. Then have students write cover letters to potential employers in the voice of each brother, describing what kind of job he is looking for and why he'd be good at it.

The younger brother replied: "I have heard: 'He who is afraid of the leaves must not go into the forest.' And also: 'Beneath a stone
45 no water flows.'"
    Then the younger brother set off, and the elder remained behind.

No sooner had the younger brother gone into the forest than he found the river, swam across it, and there on the other side was the she-bear, fast asleep. He took her cubs, and ran up the
50 mountain without looking back. When he reached the top of the mountain the people came out to meet him with a carriage to take him into the city, where they made him their king.
    He ruled for five years. In the sixth year, another king, who was stronger than he, waged war against him. The city was conquered,
55 and he was driven out.
    Again the younger brother became a wanderer, and he arrived one day at the house of the elder brother. The elder brother was living in a village and had grown neither rich nor poor. The two brothers rejoiced at seeing each other, and at once began telling
60 of all that had happened to them.
    "You see," said the elder brother, "I was right. Here I have lived quietly and well, while you, though you may have been a king, have seen a great deal of trouble."
    "I do not regret having gone into the forest and up the mountain,"
65 replied the younger brother. "I may have nothing now, but I shall always have something to remember, while you have no memories at all."

Close Read

5. How do the brothers resolve their conflict?

6. Reread lines 61–66. How does each brother feel about the choice he made? Explain whether the brothers' attitudes have changed.

7. Consider what the writer might be saying about the choices people make. (Hint: Is there always a right or wrong choice?) Write a statement that expresses the theme of the story.

Close Read

5. **Possible answer:** *Each one follows his own instincts: the younger brother goes off to the forest and the elder one stays behind (line 46).*

6. **Possible answer:** *Each brother is happy with the choice he made. Neither brother has experienced a change in attitude.*

7. **Possible answer:** *The writer is probably saying that people make choices based on what they are comfortable with, and as long as they are happy, all is well. "Different strokes for different folks" is one way to express this theme. Students may state the theme in any of these ways:*

   • *There are no absolutely right or wrong choices in life.*

   • *Individuals must decide what is right for them and what makes them happy.*

   • *People make choices that suit their personalities.*

Assess and Reteach

Assess

Have students briefly summarize the story of the two brothers and tell what lesson it teaches about making good choices in life.

Reteach

For students who are unable to apply the workshop skills to "The Two Brothers," select from these reteaching options:

1. Have students review the story and fill in a Venn diagram to show differences between the two brothers. Prompt them to fill in the center section to indicate that both want happiness. Then ask what the diagram shows about happiness in general.

2. Divide students into four groups. Assign each a clue category—title, plot, characters, or setting. Have each group discuss how the questions on page 306 apply to "The Two Brothers." They may refer to the **Close Read** questions for help. Then have each group report its answers to the class. Guide the class toward a consensus on the main theme of the story.

📓 **BEST PRACTICES TOOLKIT—Transparency**
Venn Diagram p. A26

DIFFERENTIATED INSTRUCTION

FOR LESS–PROFICIENT READERS
Comprehension Support

• The elder brother's proverbs (lines 40–42) mean the same thing. Have students use the literal meaning of the first to infer the metaphorical meaning of the second.

• Help students rephrase the proverbs in lines 43–45 as lessons about human life. **Possible answers:** *"A person who fears small things cannot tackle large challenges." "A person must take action to make things happen."*

FOR ADVANCED LEARNERS/PRE–AP

Write a New Ending Have students think about how the ending of the story relates to its theme. Challenge them to write a new ending for the story (starting at line 47) that presents a different theme. For example, the new ending might show that one brother's approach to life is clearly better than the other's.

OBJECTIVES

Literary Analysis
- explore the key idea of **competition**
- distinguish topic from theme
- identify theme
- read a short story

Reading
- compare and contrast

Vocabulary
- build vocabulary for reading and writing
- use the Latin root *pel* to help unlock meaning (*also an EL language objective*)

Grammar and Writing
- use quotation marks, commas, and periods correctly in dialogue
- use writing to analyze literature

SUMMARY

Antonio and Felix are Puerto Rican teenagers in New York who share a love of boxing. Their **competition** for a spot in the Golden Gloves tournament threatens their close friendship. On the night of their fight they are evenly matched, and both are fiercely determined to win. The ending of the story leaves the winner unnamed, but the boys' friendship is intact.

What happens when friends COMPETE?

Discuss the question and the **KEY IDEA**. Ask students why **competition** might strain a friendship. After students do the **QUICKWRITE**, invite volunteers to give examples of how competition affected a friendship.

Amigo Brothers
Short Story by Piri Thomas

What happens when friends
COMPETE?

MARYLAND OBJECTIVES

READING/LIT STANDARDS
1.E.3.a Select and apply appropriate strategies during reading
3.A.6.a Analyze universal themes

KEY IDEA We face **competition** all the time, whether we are competing for someone's attention or for the best grade. And while some competitions are friendly and even fun, others can be brutal. In "Amigo Brothers," best friends Antonio and Felix find out if their deep friendship can survive an explosive competition.

QUICKWRITE Jot down a list of times when you competed with one or more friends. When you are done, review your list. Decide which of those experiences helped or hurt your friendship. Reflect on one of those experiences in a journal entry.

310

 **RESOURCE MANAGER UNIT 3**

Plan and Teach pp. 17–24

Literary Analysis
Summary pp. 25†*, 26‡*
Theme Versus Topic pp. 27, 28†*
Question Support p. 35*

Reading
Compare and Contrast pp. 29, 30†*
Reading Check p. 34
Reading Fluency p. 37

Vocabulary
Study p. 31*
Practice p. 32
Strategy p. 33

Grammar and Writing
Punctuate Dialogue Correctly p. 36

Assessment
Selection Tests A, B/C pp. 39*, 41*

 Test Generator CD

BEST PRACTICES TOOLKIT
Differentiated Instruction pp. 31–38*
Scaffolding Instruction pp. 43–46*

Graphic Organizers/Strategies
Word Questioning • T Chart • New Word Analysis • Making Inferences • Read Aloud/ Think Aloud • Timeline

Reading Support
Audio Anthology CD*

Technology
Literature and Vocabulary Centers at **ClassZone.com**

Write*Smart* CD

---

* Resources for Differentiation   † Also in Spanish   ‡ In Haitian Creole and Vietnamese

LITERARY ANALYSIS: THEME VERSUS TOPIC

A story's **theme** is a message about life or human nature that the writer wants readers to understand. Sometimes readers confuse the theme with the subject, or **topic,** of the story. One way to tell topic and theme apart is to remember that a topic can be stated in just one or two words. A theme is often expressed as a sentence.

	Length	Example
Topic	one or two words	growing up
Theme	sentence	Growing up brings new responsibilities.

One topic of "Amigo Brothers" is friendship. As you read the story, you'll find a deeper message as its theme.

READING SKILL: COMPARE AND CONTRAST

Comparing and contrasting characters can help you better understand a story. When you **compare** two or more people or things, you look for ways they are similar. When you **contrast** them, you look for ways they are different. As you read "Amigo Brothers," note similarities and differences between Felix and Antonio in a Venn diagram like the one shown.

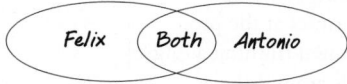

Felix   Both   Antonio

VOCABULARY IN CONTEXT

The boldfaced terms help tell this story about **competition.** Restate each sentence, using a different word or words.

1. He received a **barrage** of criticism for his comments.
2. The report shows the **devastating** effects of the illness.
3. She considered the offer **pensively.**
4. The crowd burst into a **torrent** of laughter.
5. He can't stand her **perpetual** complaining.
6. We were surprised at their **unbridled** enthusiasm.
7. They worked hard to **dispel** my concerns.
8. It was a noisy classroom, where **bedlam** reigned.
9. His arms began to **flail** as he lost his balance.
10. She has remarkable **clarity** for a person her age.

Author Online

A Troubled Beginning
In the 1950s, Piri Thomas realized that he was getting into too much trouble with the law and needed to turn his life around. He said to himself, "Man, where am I at? I got a mind; let's see if I can use it." He says he then "jumped into books." For him, writing became a tool to discover who he really was and to portray his Puerto Rican and African-American heritage.

Piri Thomas born 1928

A Rich Heritage Thomas's writings are all set where he grew up, in New York City. He writes about neighborhoods that are heavily populated with Puerto Ricans and African Americans, such as Spanish Harlem and the Lower East Side of Manhattan. Thomas's writing celebrates the strength and determination of the people in his community.

 MORE ABOUT THE AUTHOR For more on Piri Thomas, visit the **Literature Center** at ClassZone.com.

Background

Golden Gloves In this story, Felix and Antonio compete to participate in a Golden Gloves tournament, a famous amateur boxing competition. Past winners who went on to fame and fortune include Sugar Ray Robinson, George Foreman, and Muhammad Ali.

Teach

STANDARDS FOCUS

LITERARY ANALYSIS

● THEME VERSUS TOPIC

Read aloud this example:

> **Competition** encourages people to give their best performance.

Ask students whether this is a theme or a topic and how they know. ***Possible answer:*** *This is a theme on the topic of competition. It is a sentence with a message about human nature.*

CHECK UNDERSTANDING Ask students to suggest other possible themes on the topic of competition.

READING SKILL

■ COMPARE AND CONTRAST

Have students compare and contrast the two people in the photograph on page 310. Remind students that comparing means looking for what is the same, and contrasting means looking at what is different. ***Possible answer:*** *Same: African-American girls, basketball players, intense gaze; Different: uniforms, height*

CHECK UNDERSTANDING Have pairs list similarities and differences between themselves, such as their food preferences.

R **RESOURCE MANAGER—Copy Master** Compare and Contrast p. 29 (for student use while reading the story)

VOCABULARY SKILL

▲ VOCABULARY IN CONTEXT

DIAGNOSE WORD KNOWLEDGE To determine preteaching needs, have all students complete **Vocabulary in Context.** *Possible answers:* **1.** *large amount;* **2.** *destructive;* **3.** *thoughtfully;* **4.** *streams;* **5.** *constant;* **6.** *unlimited;* **7.** *eliminate;* **8.** *confusion;* **9.** *flap wildly;* **10.** *clearness*

PRETEACH VOCABULARY Use the Vocabulary Study copy master to help students predict meanings for each boldfaced word.

1. Read the first two sentences aloud, emphasizing *devastating.*
2. Point out the words *moved across town* and *afraid.* Elicit possible meanings for *devastating,* such as "very harmful."
3. Repeat the procedure as you read through the passage.

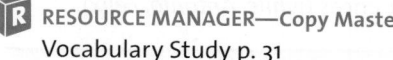 **RESOURCE MANAGER—Copy Master** Vocabulary Study p. 31

For general guidelines on differentiating vocabulary instruction and for alternative vocabulary activities for students not needing vocabulary preteaching, see

BEST PRACTICES TOOLKIT Scaffolding Vocabulary Instruction pp. 43–46

 Vocabulary Center at **ClassZone.com**

Practice and Apply

ANALYZE VISUALS

Possible answers: Red and orange make me think of anger and blood. The dark background makes me think of fear and of being alone in the dark.

About the Art British painter and illustrator Roger Coleman (born 1930) lived and worked in London in the 1960s and lived for a time in Sussex in the 1970s. The latter experience led to a book of watercolors depicting life in a small rural village.

Tempera, the medium used for *The Boxers*, was first created by mixing pigment with egg yolk and water. Before oil painting became common during the Renaissance, tempera was used to paint everything from Egyptian mummy cases to medieval manuscripts. Twentieth-century artists such as Andrew Wyeth and Ben Shahn revived tempera painting. Tempera dries quickly, so rather than mixing colors on the surface of the painting, artists lay down layers of colors.

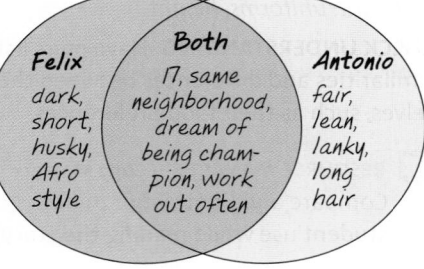
Amigo BROTHERS

PIRI THOMAS

Antonio Cruz and Felix Vargas were both seventeen years old. They were so together in friendship that they felt themselves to be brothers. They had known each other since childhood, growing up on the lower east side of Manhattan in the same tenement building[1] on Fifth Street between Avenue A and Avenue B.

Antonio was fair, lean, and lanky, while Felix was dark, short, and husky. Antonio's hair was always falling over his eyes, while Felix wore his black hair in a natural Afro style.

Each youngster had a dream of someday becoming lightweight champion
10 of the world. Every chance they had the boys worked out, sometimes at the Boys Club on 10th Street and Avenue A and sometimes at the pro's gym on 14th Street. Early morning sunrises would find them running along the East River Drive, wrapped in sweatshirts, short towels around their necks, and handkerchiefs Apache style around their foreheads. **A**

While some youngsters were into street negatives, Antonio and Felix slept, ate, rapped, and dreamt positive. Between them, they had a collection of *Fight* magazines second to none, plus a scrapbook filled with torn tickets to every boxing match they had ever attended and some clippings of their own. If asked a question about any given fighter, they
20 would immediately zip out from their memory banks divisions,[2] weights, records of fights, knockouts, technical knockouts, and draws or losses.

Each had fought many bouts representing their community and had won two gold-plated medals plus a silver and bronze medallion. The difference was in their style. Antonio's lean form and long reach made him the better boxer, while Felix's short and muscular frame

---

1. **tenement building:** a rundown apartment building in which mostly poor families live.
2. **divisions:** weight groups into which boxers are separated.

ANALYZE VISUALS
What do the colors in this painting make you think of?

1 Targeted Passage

A COMPARE AND CONTRAST
Reread lines 1–14 and use your Venn diagram to note similarities and differences between the two boys. Add more notes to your diagram as you continue reading

The Boxers, Roger Coleman
Tempera. Private collection. Pho
© The Bridgeman Art Librar

DIFFERENTIATED INSTRUCTION

FOR ALL STUDENTS

Learning Center Set up a learning center on boxing. Stock it with books and pictures that cover a range of students' interests, such as the rules of boxing, boxing history, and the lives of famous boxers. Provide various projects that students may complete independently, such as writing an illustrated report, collecting photos and writing descriptive captions, or preparing an oral report on the life of a boxer.

FOR LESS–PROFICIENT READERS

In combination with the *Audio Anthology CD*, use one or more Targeted Passages (pp. 312, 314, 318, 322) to ensure that students focus on key story events, concepts, and skills.

1 Targeted Passage [Lines 1–14]

This passage sets up the story by introducing the boys, their common love of boxing, and their desire to be champions. It shows that they are evenly matched.

BACKGROUND

Period Details "Amigo Brothers" is set in the 1970s. Certain period details give clues to the story's setting. Antonio's long hair (line 7) and Felix's "natural Afro style" (line 8) both became popular in the late 1960s. The Afro was the bushy hairstyle adopted by many African Americans with the rise of the "black is beautiful" movement. The story's reference to how the boys wore their handkerchiefs around their heads as "Apache style" (line 14) shows the influence of the American Indian movement. When Thomas says that Antonio and Felix "rapped" (line 16), he is most likely not referring to rap music, as students might assume, but is using the common slang for "talked." The boys' avid interest in boxing is in tune with the renewed interest in the sport that began with the career of Muhammad Ali in the 1960s. Puerto Rican writers coined the term *Loisaida* (line 201) in 1974.

- Why are Antonio and Felix such good friends?
- What is the dream that the two boys share?
- What do they do to make their dream a reality?

FOR ENGLISH LEARNERS

Key Academic Vocabulary Use Word Questioning for these academic vocabulary words: *community* (lines 22, 177), *style* (lines 24, 77), *scheduled* (lines 29, 158, 165), *finally* (lines 52, 316), *challenger* (lines 111, 114, 120), *affect* (line 137).

 BEST PRACTICES TOOLKIT—Transparency Word Questioning p. E9

Prereading For prereading instruction for English learners, see

BEST PRACTICES TOOLKIT Scaffolding Reading Instruction pp. 43–46

FOR ADVANCED LEARNERS/PRE–AP

Pre-AP exercises in the bottom channel provide additional challenge for your advanced students. Use them for small groups or individuals.

ADDITIONAL GUIDELINES

For more help with differentiation and tips for classroom management, see

 BEST PRACTICES TOOLKIT Differentiated Instruction pp. 31–38

SOCIAL STUDIES CONNECTION

The Lower East Side in New York City has been home to successive waves of immigrants drawn to the neighborhood's inexpensive housing. In the 1960s, the northern part of the area, where the story is set, became known as the East Village.

Lines 28–61
DISCUSSION PROMPTS

Use these prompts to help students explore how **competition** is affecting the boys' friendship:

Connect How does it feel when something is making it hard to talk openly to a friend? *Students may say that it's uncomfortable not to be able to share their thoughts and feelings as they normally would.*

Analyze How are things the same between the boys, and how are they different? *Possible answer: They continue working out together (lines 32, 35–38), but the coming fight makes them think about possibly hurting each other (lines 46–48, 56–59).*

Evaluate How does the author use specific language to establish both the closeness and the competitiveness of the boys? *Possible answers: He calls them "ace boon buddies" (line 47) and has them call each other "bro" and "panín" (lines 44, 56). He also says they will be "blasting each other" (line 48), and Felix says, "we both are cheverote fighters and we both want to win" (line 60).*

---

made him the better slugger. Whenever they had met in the ring for sparring sessions,[3] it had always been hot and heavy.

Now, after a series of elimination bouts,[4] they had been informed that they were to meet each other in the division finals that were scheduled
30 for the seventh of August, two weeks away—the winner to represent the Boys Club in the Golden Gloves Championship Tournament.

The two boys continued to run together along the East River Drive. But even when joking with each other, they both sensed a wall rising between them.

One morning less than a week before their bout, they met as usual for their daily workout. They fooled around with a few jabs at the air, slapped skin, and then took off, running lightly along the dirty East River's edge.

Antonio glanced at Felix, who kept his eyes purposely straight ahead,
40 pausing from time to time to do some fancy leg work while throwing one-twos followed by upper cuts to an imaginary jaw. Antonio then beat the air with a **barrage** of body blows and short **devastating** lefts with an overhand, jawbreaking right.

After a mile or so, Felix puffed and said, "Let's stop for awhile, bro. I think we both got something to say to each other."

Antonio nodded. It was not natural to be acting as though nothing unusual was happening when two ace boon buddies were going to be blasting each other within a few short days.

They rested their elbows on the railing separating them from the river.
50 Antonio wiped his face with his short towel. The sunrise was now creating day.

Felix leaned heavily on the river's railing and stared across to the shores of Brooklyn. Finally, he broke the silence.

"Man. I don't know how to come out with it."

Antonio helped. "It's about our fight, right?"

"Yeah, right." Felix's eyes squinted at the rising orange sun.

"I've been thinking about it too, *panín*.[5] In fact, since we found out it was going to be me and you, I've been awake at night, pulling punches[6] on you, trying not to hurt you."

"Same here. It ain't natural not to think about the fight. I mean,
60 we both are *cheverote*[7] fighters, and we both want to win. But only one of us can win. There ain't no draws in the eliminations."

---

3. **sparring sessions:** practice boxing matches.
4. **elimination bouts:** matches to determine which boxers advance in a competition.
5. *panín* (pä-nēn') *American Spanish:* pal; buddy.
6. **pulling punches:** holding back in delivering blows.
7. *cheverote* (chĕ-vĕ-rô'tĕ) *American Spanish:* great or fantastic.

314 UNIT 3: UNDERSTANDING THEME

SOCIAL STUDIES CONNECTION

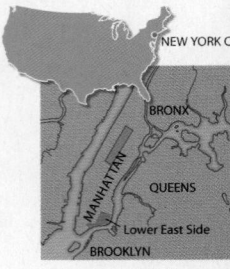

Antonio and Felix grew up on the Lower East Side of Manhattan.

2 Targeted Passage

barrage (bə-räzh') *n.* a rapid, heavy attack

devastating (dĕv'ə-stā'tĭng) *adj.* very effective in causing pain or destruction **devastate** *v.*

DIFFERENTIATED INSTRUCTION

FOR LESS–PROFICIENT READERS
2 Targeted Passage [Lines 28–48]

This passage sets up the central conflict as it shows how the boys' friendship will be tested.

- Why must Felix and Antonio fight each other?
- What does the author mean when he says the boys "sensed a wall rising between them"?
- Why do the boys stop in the middle of their workout? What do they feel is "not natural"?
- How might the boys solve this problem?

FOR ADVANCED LEARNERS/PRE–AP
Compile a Glossary Challenge students to compile an illustrated glossary of boxing terms used in the story. Have them add to their list of terms as they continue reading and decide which terms should be illustrated. Possible terms include

- *bouts* (line 22)
- *throwing one-twos* (lines 40–41)
- *upper cuts* (line 41)
- *body blows* (line 42)
- *short lefts* (line 42)
- *overhand right* (line 43)
- *draws* (line 61)
- *ring* (line 64)
- *welterweight size* (line 69)
- *pulling punches* (line 73)

314 UNIT 3: UNDERSTANDING THEME

Left, Moose (1956), Alice Neel. © Estate of Alice Neel. Courtesy Robert Miller Gallery, New York. *Right, Call Me Joe* (1955), Alice Neel. Oil on canvas, 34″× 32″. © Estate of Alice Neel. Courtesy Robert Miller Gallery, New York.

Felix tapped Antonio gently on the shoulder. "I don't mean to sound like I'm bragging, bro. But I wanna win, fair and square."

Antonio nodded quietly. "Yeah. We both know that in the ring the better man wins. Friend or no friend, brother or no . . ."

Felix finished it for him. "Brother. Tony, let's promise something right here. Okay?"

"If it's fair, *hermano*,[8] I'm for it." Antonio admired the courage of a tugboat pulling a barge five times its welterweight[9] size.

"It's fair, Tony. When we get into the ring, it's gotta be like we never met. We gotta be like two heavy strangers that want the same thing, and only one can have it. You understand, don'tcha?" **B**

"*Sí*, I know." Tony smiled. "No pulling punches. We go all the way."

"Yeah, that's right. Listen, Tony. Don't you think it's a good idea if we don't see each other until the day of the fight? I'm going to stay with my Aunt Lucy in the Bronx.[10] I can use Gleason's Gym for working out. My manager says he got some sparring partners with more or less your style."

---

8. **hermano** (ĕr-mä′nô) *Spanish:* brother.
9. **welterweight:** one of boxing's weight divisions, with a maximum weight of 147 pounds.
10. **the Bronx:** a borough of New York City, north of Manhattan.

ANALYZE VISUALS
Compare and contrast these pictures with your own mental images of Felix and Antonio.

B THEME
What **characters** say can offer clues about a story's theme. What does the boys' **dialogue**, or conversation, tell you about their friendship?

Vocabulary: Multiple-Meaning Words
Explain that *blasting* (line 48) means "hitting hard" in this context. It can also mean "using an explosive" or "playing music loudly." Assign pairs of students one or two words from this list: *draws* (line 61), *ring* (line 64), *heavy* (lines 71, 90, 136), *split* (lines 86, 131), *boring* (line 226). Have them try to figure out the meaning from context and then check a dictionary. Have them note which meanings are labeled as slang, or casual language.

Culture: Connect If there are Spanish speakers in your class, ask them to elaborate on American Spanish words used throughout the story, such as *panín* (line 56) and *cheverote* (line 60). These words are defined in footnotes in the pupil edition, but students may be able to provide more information. Ask: In what situation would you use this word? Does the way it's used in the story sound natural?

ANALYZE VISUALS
Possible answers: If the two boys in the paintings were Tony and Felix, the boy on the left would be Tony because he is bigger and taller than the boy on the right. However, the boy called Moose is not as fair as I pictured Tony, and his hair doesn't hang over his eyes. The boy in Call Me Joe is less husky in the face than I imagined Felix, and his hair is not as big as Felix's Afro would be.

About the Art American artist Alice Neel (1900–1984) is known for her unflinching portraits that show insight into her subjects' character and empathy for their lives. Neel lived in Spanish Harlem in New York City between 1938 and 1962. During that time she painted many of her neighbors, such as the two young men in these portraits. The portraits show the dignity of boys who, like Felix and Antonio, grow up in the face of poverty and prejudice.

LITERARY ANALYSIS

B THEME

Possible answer: Their conversation shows that they both value their friendship and are worried about how the competition might hurt their relationship.

If students need help . . . Use a T Chart to list some things from the conversation that show each boy's concern about the situation and their friendship.

Felix	Antonio
wants to talk about the fight	calls Felix "panín" and "hermano"
calls Antonio "bro"	is worried about hurting Felix
wants to win fairly, not because his friend is holding back	agrees that they will both fight all out, even though they are friends

 BEST PRACTICES TOOLKIT—Transparency T Chart p. A25

DISCUSSION PROMPTS

Use these prompts to help students understand how the boys are mentally preparing themselves for the fight:

Connect How do you prepare yourself for a difficult task? *Students may mention practicing, studying, visualizing themselves performing a task, or distracting themselves so they don't worry.*

Analyze Why do the boys have a lot of "psyching up" to do before the fight? *Possible answers: They know it might not be easy to fight fiercely against a close friend. They want to win and still maintain their friendship.*

Evaluate What does the difference in the boys' ways of preparing for the fight suggest about their characters? *Possible answers: Tony chooses to be alone and tries not to think about Felix. He seems more thoughtful and calm than Felix. Felix watches a violent boxing movie and visualizes himself in the role of champion. He walks the street but can't relax. He seems more excitable than Tony.*

LITERARY ANALYSIS

ⒸTHEME

Possible answer: Antonio is struggling with how to win the competition without hurting his best friend.

Extend the Discussion What does Antonio think about his chances of winning?

Tony scratched his nose **pensively.** "Yeah, it would be better for our heads." He held out his hand, palm upward. "Deal?"

80 "Deal." Felix lightly slapped open skin.

"Ready for some more running?" Tony asked lamely.

"Naw, bro. Let's cut it here. You go on. I kinda like to get things together in my head."

"You ain't worried, are you?" Tony asked.

"No way, man." Felix laughed out loud. "I got too much smarts for that. I just think it's cooler if we split right here. After the fight, we can get it together again like nothing ever happened."

The *amigo*[11] brothers were not ashamed to hug each other tightly.

"Guess you're right. Watch yourself, Felix. I hear there's some

90 pretty heavy dudes up in the Bronx. *Suavecito,*[12] okay?"

"Okay. You watch yourself too, *sabe?*"[13]

Tony jogged away. Felix watched his friend disappear from view, throwing rights and lefts. Both fighters had a lot of psyching up to do before the big fight.

The days in training passed much too slowly. Although they kept out of each other's way, they were aware of each other's progress via the ghetto grapevine.[14]

The evening before the big fight, Tony made his way to the roof of his tenement. In the quiet early dark, he peered over the ledge.

100 Six stories below, the lights of the city blinked, and the sounds of cars mingled with the curses and the laughter of children in the street. He tried not to think of Felix, feeling he had succeeded in psyching his mind. But only in the ring would he really know. To spare Felix hurt, he would have to knock him out, early and quick. Ⓒ

Up in the South Bronx, Felix decided to take in a movie in an effort to keep Antonio's face away from his fists. The flick was *The Champion* with Kirk Douglas, the third time Felix was seeing it.

The champion was getting beat, his face being pounded into raw, wet hamburger. His eyes were cut, jagged, bleeding, one eye swollen,

110 the other almost shut. He was saved only by the sound of the bell.

Felix became the champ and Tony the challenger.

The movie audience was going out of its head, roaring in blood lust at the butchery going on. The champ hunched his shoulders, grunting and sniffing red blood back into his broken nose. The challenger, confident that he had the championship in the bag, threw a left. The champ countered with a dynamite right that exploded into the challenger's brains.

---

11. *amigo* (ä-mē'gô) *Spanish:* friend.
12. *Suavecito* (swä-vĕ-sē'tô) *American Spanish:* Take it easy.
13. *sabe* (sä'bĕ) *Spanish:* you know.
14. **ghetto grapevine:** the chain of gossip that spreads through the neighborhood.

pensively (pĕn'sĭv-lē) *adv.* thoughtfully

Ⓒ **THEME**
Understanding a story's **conflict** can help you understand its theme. An **internal conflict** is a struggle within a character's mind. Reread lines 102–104. What is Antonio's internal conflict?

DIFFERENTIATED INSTRUCTION

FOR LESS–PROFICIENT READERS

Reading Skill Follow-Up: Compare and Contrast
Have students use Venn diagrams (as introduced on page 311) to compare and contrast Felix and Antonio on the night before the fight (lines 98–124). Encourage students to notice where each boy is and what he is doing, thinking, and feeling. When students have completed their diagrams, ask volunteers to share with the class. Clarify understanding as needed.

Felix watches a movie

Both think about the fight

Antonio goes to the rooftop

FOR ENGLISH LEARNERS

Culture: Clarify Explain that youth gangs exist in many places and cultures. *Gang colors* (line 126) refers to any common insignia or clothing such as shirts, jackets, or hats. *Turf* (line 127) refers to what the gang considers to be its territory. Point out that here Thomas uses the term *brothers* (line 130) because that is how gang members often refer to themselves. This is different from the way it is used to describe the close relationship between Felix and Tony.

Felix's right arm felt the shock. Antonio's face, superimposed on the screen, was shattered and split apart by the awesome force of the killer blow. Felix saw himself in the ring, blasting Antonio against the ropes.

20 The champ had to be forcibly restrained. The challenger was allowed to crumble slowly to the canvas, a broken, bloody mess.

When Felix finally left the theatre, he had figured out how to psyche himself for tomorrow's fight. It was Felix the Champion vs. Antonio the Challenger.

He walked up some dark streets, deserted except for small pockets of wary-looking kids wearing gang colors. Despite the fact that he was Puerto Rican like them, they eyed him as a stranger to their turf. Felix did a last shuffle, bobbing and weaving, while letting loose a **torrent**

30 of blows that would demolish whatever got in its way. It seemed to impress the brothers, who went about their own business.

torrent (tôr′ənt) *n.* a violent, rushing stream

Still Open (1994), Douglas Safranek. Egg tempera on panel, 4⅛′ × 4′. © Museum of the City of New York.

ANALYZE VISUALS
How does this picture **compare** with the description of the **setting** given in lines 98–101?

ANALYZE VISUALS
Possible answers:

- It shows a view from rooftop level looking down on the street, as Tony is doing.
- It shows the lights of the city at night.
- Most of the tenements are about six stories high, as the passage describes.
- There are cars on the street and people on the sidewalk, including someone on a bicycle. They might be children.

About the Art *Still Open* is one of many views looking down on New York City created by American artist Douglas Safranek (born 1956). This particular view shows what the artist saw when looking out his window in the Greenpoint section of Brooklyn. Like Antonio, Safranek likes to look at the city from above street level in order to gain a sense of order and calm.

FOR ENGLISH LEARNERS

Language: Idioms and Slang Use New Word Analysis to teach these idiomatic and slang expressions from the story:

- *slapped skin* (line 37), "hit their hands together"
- *come out with it* (line 53), "say what I'm thinking"
- *same here* (line 59), "I feel the same way"
- *fair and square* (line 63), "without any cheating or special arrangements"
- *I'm for it* (line 68), "I agree with the idea"
- *watch yourself* (line 91), "be careful"

- *psyching up* (line 93), "getting excited and ready to win"
- *flick* (line 106), "movie"
- *in the bag* (line 115), "already won"
- *finding no takers* (line 131), "finding no one to fight with"
- *cold, hard cash* (lines 150–151), "real money"
- *on the line* (line 151), "at risk"
- *sucker* (line 268), "trick or lure"
- *ate it up* (line 304), "loved it"

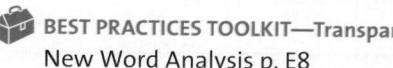 **BEST PRACTICES TOOLKIT—Transparency**
New Word Analysis p. E8

Lines 146–153
REINFORCE *KEY IDEA:*
COMPETITION

Discuss How has the **competition** between Felix and Antonio affected other people in the neighborhood? *Possible answers:*

- *Many people in the neighborhood are interested in who will win the upcoming fight.*
- *Many are placing bets on their favorite fighter.*
- *Backers of Felix and Antonio think each has strengths that will allow him to win.*

LITERARY ANALYSIS

Ⓓ THEME

Possible answer: *Antonio still thinks of Felix primarily as his friend, even though today they are also opponents in a boxing match.*

If students need help . . . Use an inference chart to guide students through the process of inferring Antonio's attitude.

Detail from Story: Antonio waves at someone he thinks is Felix.	+	What I Know: Waving to someone is a friendly gesture.

=	My Inference: Antonio still considers Felix his friend.

 BEST PRACTICES TOOLKIT—Transparency
Making Inferences p. A13

Finding no takers, Felix decided to split to his aunt's. Walking the streets had not relaxed him, neither had the fight flick. All it had done was to stir him up. He let himself quietly into his Aunt Lucy's apartment and went straight to bed, falling into a fitful sleep with sounds of the gong for Round One.

Antonio was passing some heavy time on his rooftop. How would the fight tomorrow affect his relationship with Felix? After all, fighting was like any other profession. Friendship had nothing to do with it. A gnawing doubt crept in. He cut negative thinking real quick by doing 140 some speedy fancy dance steps, bobbing and weaving like mercury. The night air was blurred with **perpetual** motions of left hooks and right crosses. Felix, his *amigo* brother, was not going to be Felix at all in the ring. Just an opponent with another face. Antonio went to sleep, hearing the opening bell for the first round. Like his friend in the South Bronx, he prayed for victory via a quick, clean knockout in the first round.

Large posters plastered all over the walls of local shops announced the fight between Antonio Cruz and Felix Vargas as the main bout.

The fight had created great interest in the neighborhood. Antonio and Felix were well liked and respected. Each had his own loyal following. 150 Betting fever was high and ranged from a bottle of Coke to cold, hard cash on the line.

Antonio's fans bet with **unbridled** faith in his boxing skills. On the other side, Felix's admirers bet on his dynamite-packed fists.

Felix had returned to his apartment early in the morning of August 7th and stayed there, hoping to avoid seeing Antonio. He turned the radio on to salsa music sounds and then tried to read while waiting for word from his manager.

The fight was scheduled to take place in Tompkins Square Park. It had been decided that the gymnasium of the Boys Club was not 160 large enough to hold all the people who were sure to attend. In Tompkins Square Park, everyone who wanted could view the fight, whether from ringside or window fire escapes or tenement rooftops.

The morning of the fight, Tompkins Square was a beehive of activity with numerous workers setting up the ring, the seats, and the guest speakers' stand. The scheduled bouts began shortly after noon, and the park had begun filling up even earlier.

The local junior high school across from Tompkins Square Park served as the dressing room for all the fighters. Each was given a separate classroom, with desktops, covered with mats, serving as resting tables. Antonio 170 thought he caught a glimpse of Felix waving to him from a room at the far end of the corridor. He waved back just in case it had been him. Ⓓ

③ Targeted Passage

perpetual
(pər-pĕch′ōō-əl) *adj.* continual; unending

unbridled (ŭn-brīd′ld) *adj.* lacking restraint or control

Ⓓ **THEME**
What can you **infer** about Antonio's attitude toward Felix on the day of the fight?

DIFFERENTIATED INSTRUCTION

FOR LESS–PROFICIENT READERS
③ Targeted Passage [Lines 136–145]

This passage clearly states Antonio's internal conflict: How will the fight affect his relationship with Felix?

- What is Antonio having doubts about?
- How does he deal with negative thinking?
- What does he think it will be like to see Felix in the boxing ring tomorrow?
- What do both Antonio and Felix pray for?

Comprehension Support Explain that authors often describe things by comparing them to something else. Point out these examples of figurative language and help students use context clues to interpret them: *bobbing and weaving like mercury* (line 140), "moving quickly"; *dynamite-packed fists* (line 153), "powerful punching"; and *a beehive of activity* (line 163), "a busy place." Have them list other examples as they continue reading (*lines 224, 252, 269–270, 278, 279, 316*).

The fighters changed from their street clothes into fighting gear. Antonio wore white trunks, black socks, and black shoes. Felix wore sky blue trunks, red socks, and white boxing shoes. Each had dressing gowns to match their fighting trunks with their names neatly stitched on the back.

The loudspeakers blared into the open window of the school. There were speeches by dignitaries, community leaders, and great boxers of yesteryear. Some were well prepared, some improvised on the spot. They all carried the same message of great pleasure and honor at being part of such a historic event. This great day was in the tradition of champions emerging from the streets of the lower east side.

Interwoven with the speeches were the sounds of the other boxing events. After the sixth bout, Felix was much relieved when his trainer, Charlie, said, "Time change. Quick knockout. This is it. We're on."

Waiting time was over. Felix was escorted from the classroom by a dozen fans in white T-shirts with the word FELIX across their fronts. Antonio was escorted down a different stairwell and guided through a roped-off path.

As the two climbed into the ring, the crowd exploded with a roar. Antonio and Felix both bowed gracefully and then raised their arms in acknowledgment.

Antonio tried to be cool, but even as the roar was in its first birth, he turned slowly to meet Felix's eyes looking directly into his. Felix nodded his head and Antonio responded. And both as one, just as quickly, turned away to face his own corner. **E**

Bong, bong, bong. The roar turned to stillness.

"Ladies and Gentlemen, *Señores y Señoras.*"[15]

The announcer spoke slowly, pleased at his bilingual efforts.

"Now the moment we have all been waiting for—the main event between two fine young Puerto Rican fighters, products of our lower east side."

"*Loisaida,*"[16] called out a member of the audience.

"In this corner, weighing 131 pounds, Felix Vargas. And in this corner, weighing 133 pounds, Antonio Cruz. The winner will represent the Boys Club in the tournament of champions, the Golden Gloves. There will be no draw. May the best man win."

The cheering of the crowd shook the windowpanes of the old buildings surrounding Tompkins Square Park. At the center of the ring, the referee was giving instructions to the youngsters.

"Keep your punches up. No low blows. No punching on the back of the head. Keep your heads up. Understand. Let's have a clean fight. Now shake hands and come out fighting."

---

15. *Señores y Señoras* (sĕ-nyô'rĕs ē sĕ-nyô'räs) *Spanish:* Ladies and Gentlemen.

16. *Loisaida* (loi-sĭ'dä) *American Spanish:* Lower East Side.

AMIGO BROTHERS **319**

E THEME
Reread lines 192–195. How do you think the boys feel at this moment?

LITERARY ANALYSIS

E THEME

Possible answers:

- *They are probably feeling a bit nervous at finally facing each other in the ring.*
- *They show their respect by nodding and acknowledging their friendship.*
- *They feel the need to stay focused on the match, so they turn quickly away.*

If students need help . . . Help students find clues in the descriptions of the characters' actions to imagine how they might be feeling. For example:

- "Antonio tried to be cool." *(He's not feeling cool.)*
- When Antonio turns, he finds Felix looking at him. *(Both boys wonder what the other is thinking.)*
- They nod and then turn quickly away. *(They don't want to focus on their friendship but on the fight.)*

Extend the Discussion How do you think the noise of the crowd affects the fighters?

FOR ENGLISH LEARNERS

Comprehension: Sequence Use Read Aloud/Think Aloud to clarify sequence.

1. Read aloud lines 158–185.

2. Point out verb forms that signal different time periods, such as *was scheduled* (line 158), *had been decided* (line 159), and *were sure to attend* (line 160).

3. Point out clue words about the sequence of events on the day of the fight (lines 163–166, 182–185).

4. Have pairs of students create timelines to show the sequence of events described in the passage. Direct them to start with "Planners schedule the fight in the park" and end with "The fight begins."

5. Review student timelines and clarify understanding as needed.

BEST PRACTICES TOOLKIT—Transparencies
Read Aloud/Think Aloud p. A34
Timeline p. B23

Both youngsters touched gloves and nodded. They turned and danced quickly to their corners. Their head towels and dressing gowns were lifted neatly from their shoulders by their trainers' nimble fingers. Antonio crossed himself. Felix did the same.

BONG! BONG! ROUND ONE. Felix and Antonio turned and faced each other squarely in a fighting pose. Felix wasted no time. He came in fast, head low, half hunched toward his right shoulder, and lashed out with a straight left. He missed a right cross as Antonio slipped the punch
220 and countered with one-two-three lefts that snapped Felix's head back, sending a mild shock coursing through him. If Felix had any small doubt about their friendship affecting their fight, it was being neatly **dispelled**.

Antonio danced, a joy to behold. His left hand was like a piston pumping jabs one right after another with seeming ease. Felix bobbed and weaved and never stopped boring in. He knew that at long range he was at a disadvantage. Antonio had too much reach on him. Only by coming in close could Felix hope to achieve the dreamed-of knockout.

Antonio knew the dynamite that was stored in his *amigo* brother's fist. He ducked a short right and missed a left hook. Felix trapped him
230 against the ropes just long enough to pour some punishing rights and lefts to Antonio's hard midsection. Antonio slipped away from Felix, crashing two lefts to his head, which set Felix's right ear to ringing.

Bong! Both *amigos* froze a punch well on its way, sending up a roar of approval for good sportsmanship.

Felix walked briskly back to his corner. His right ear had not stopped ringing. Antonio gracefully danced his way toward his stool none the worse, except for glowing glove burns, showing angry red against the whiteness of his midribs.

"Watch that right, Tony." His trainer talked into his
240 ear. "Remember Felix always goes to the body. He'll want you to drop your hands for his overhand left or right. Got it?"

Antonio nodded, spraying water out between his teeth. He felt better as his sore midsection was being firmly rubbed.

Felix's corner was also busy.

"You gotta get in there, fella." Felix's trainer poured water over his curly Afro locks. "Get in there or he's gonna chop you up from way back."
250 *Bong! Bong!* Round two. Felix was off his stool and rushed Antonio like a bull, sending a hard right to his head. Beads of water exploded from Antonio's long hair.

dispel (dĭ-spĕl') *v.* to get rid of

F COMPARE AND CONTRAST
Reread lines 223–227. Compare and contrast the boys' boxing styles.

ANALYZE VISUALS
Describe the feeling this sculpture conveys.

Seated Fighter (1985), Joseph Sheppard. Bronze, height 21″.

F COMPARE AND CONTRAST

Possible answer: Both boys are fighting aggressively. Antonio is graceful, quick, and has a longer reach. Felix, however, can deliver more powerful blows.

If students need help . . . Have them use the Venn diagram introduced on page 311 to organize details from the text. Encourage them to use information from the diagram to develop a few sentences summarizing how the boys' styles are similar and different.

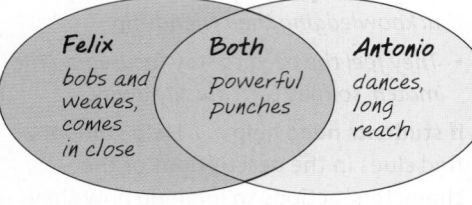

Felix
bobs and weaves, comes in close

Both
powerful punches

Antonio
dances, long reach

ANALYZE VISUALS

Possible answer: The sculpture conveys the power in the boxer's arms and shoulders. His bowed head suggests a feeling of tiredness from fighting hard.

About the Art Maryland-born Joseph Sheppard (born 1930) is sometimes called a Renaissance man because of his ability to work in multiple mediums and his dedication to the classical portrayal of the human figure. Paintings of fighters were among Sheppard's best-known early works. He began to develop his sculpture more fully in the 1980s while living in Italy. Looking at *Seated Fighter*, one can imagine Felix and Antonio catching their breath between rounds.

DIFFERENTIATED INSTRUCTION

FOR ADVANCED LEARNERS/PRE–AP

Analyze Figurative Language Figurative language is the use of words in an imaginative way to emphasize ideas and to evoke emotions. Ask students to analyze the following metaphors from the story. Have them list what qualities may have made the author choose these images. Afterwards, invite students to share their lists.

- *dynamite that was stored in his* amigo *brother's fist* (lines 228–229)

- *rushed Antonio like a bull* (line 251)

- *bedlam broke loose* (line 264)

- *the powerful bombs he carried in each fist* (lines 268–269)

- *grunting like a bull* (line 278)

- *in a fog* (line 289)

Antonio, hurt, sent back a blurring barrage of lefts and rights that only meant pain to Felix, who returned with a short left to the head followed by a looping right to the body. Antonio countered[17] with his own flurry, forcing Felix to give ground. But not for long.

Felix bobbed and weaved, bobbed and weaved, occasionally punching his two gloves together.

260 Antonio waited for the rush that was sure to come. Felix closed in and feinted[18] with his left shoulder and threw his right instead. Lights suddenly exploded inside Felix's head as Antonio slipped the blow and hit him with a pistonlike left, catching him flush on the point of his chin.

Bedlam broke loose as Felix's legs momentarily buckled. He fought off a series of rights and lefts and came back with a strong right that taught Antonio respect.

Antonio danced in carefully. He knew Felix had the habit of playing possum when hurt, to sucker an opponent within reach of the powerful bombs he carried in each fist.

270 A right to the head slowed Antonio's pretty dancing. He answered with his own left at Felix's right eye that began puffing up within three seconds.

Antonio, a bit too eager, moved in too close, and Felix had him entangled into a rip-roaring, punching toe-to-toe slugfest that brought the whole Tompkins Square Park screaming to its feet.

Rights to the body. Lefts to the head. Neither fighter was giving an inch. Suddenly a short right caught Antonio squarely on the chin. His long legs turned to jelly, and his arms **flailed** out desperately. Felix, grunting like a bull, threw wild punches from every direction. Antonio, groggy, bobbed and weaved, evading most of the blows.

280 Suddenly his head cleared. His left flashed out hard and straight catching Felix on the bridge of his nose.

Felix lashed back with a haymaker,[19] right off the ghetto streets. At the same instant, his eye caught another left hook from Antonio. Felix swung out, trying to clear the pain. Only the frenzied screaming of those along ringside let him know that he had dropped Antonio. Fighting off the growing haze, Antonio struggled to his feet, got up, ducked, and threw a smashing right that dropped Felix flat on his back.

Felix got up as fast as he could in his own corner, groggy but still game.[20] He didn't even hear the count. In a fog, he heard the roaring of the crowd,
290 who seemed to have gone insane. His head cleared to hear the bell sound at the end of the round. He was very glad. His trainer sat him down on the stool.

---

17. **countered:** gave a blow after receiving or blocking his opponent's blow.
18. **feinted:** made a pretend attack to draw attention from his real purpose.
19. **haymaker:** a powerful blow.
20. **groggy but still game:** unsteady and shaky but willing to proceed.

bedlam (bĕd'ləm) *n.* a noisy confusion

flail (flāl) *v.* to wave wildly

Lines 323–329
REINFORCE KEY IDEA: COMPETITION

Discuss As the **competition** ends, Felix and Antonio are both described as champions, yet only one is the winner. What is the difference between a champion and a winner? *Possible answer: A champion is someone who performs with skill and determination, who puts forth his or her best effort. The winner is the one the judges decide has done the best job. While there can only be one winner of the fight, both Felix and Antonio have competed like champions because they gave it all they had.*

LITERARY ANALYSIS

G THEME

*Possible answer: During the intense **competition,** each boy is focused on his desire to win. They both forget everything else during the match, including their friendship.*

SELECTION WRAP-UP

REFLECT Have students think about whether Antonio and Felix did a good job of balancing the demands of friendship and **competition** in the story. Ask them for examples of ways the boys might have acted differently. How might different behaviors have changed the outcome of the story?

★ **CRITIQUE** Ask students to evaluate how the author ended this story. Have them discuss why they think the author ended the story as he did.

READING FLUENCY

Distribute the copy masters and have students work in pairs to practice fluency.

R RESOURCE MANAGER—Copy Master
Reading Fluency p. 37

In his corner, Antonio was doing what all fighters do when they are hurt. They sit and smile at everyone.

The referee signaled the ring doctor to check the fighters out. He did so and then gave his okay. The cold-water sponges brought **clarity** to both *amigo* brothers. They were rubbed until their circulation ran free.

Bong! Round three—the final round. Up to now it had been tick-tack-toe, pretty much even. But everyone knew there could be 300 no draw and that this round would decide the winner.

This time, to Felix's surprise, it was Antonio who came out fast, charging across the ring. Felix braced himself but couldn't ward off the barrage of punches. Antonio drove Felix hard against the ropes.

The crowd ate it up. Thus far the two had fought with *mucho corazón.*[21] Felix tapped his gloves and commenced his attack anew. Antonio, throwing boxer's caution to the winds, jumped in to meet him.

Both pounded away. Neither gave an inch, and neither fell to the canvas. Felix's left eye was tightly closed. Claret red blood poured from Antonio's nose. They fought toe-to-toe.

310 The sounds of their blows were loud in contrast to the silence of a crowd gone completely mute. The referee was stunned by their savagery.

Bong! Bong! Bong! The bell sounded over and over again. Felix and Antonio were past hearing. Their blows continued to pound on each other like hailstones.

Finally the referee and the two trainers pried Felix and Antonio apart. Cold water was poured over them to bring them back to their senses. **G**

They looked around and then rushed toward each other. A cry of alarm surged through Tompkins Square Park. Was this a fight to the death 320 instead of a boxing match?

The fear soon gave way to wave upon wave of cheering as the two *amigos* embraced.

No matter what the decision, they knew they would always be champions to each other.

Bong! Bong! Bong! "Ladies and Gentlemen. *Señores* and *Señoras.* The winner and representative to the Golden Gloves Tournament of Champions is . . ."

The announcer turned to point to the winner and found himself alone. Arm in arm, the champions had already left the ring. ❧

clarity (klăr′ĭ-tē) *n.* clearness of mind

4 Targeted Passage

G THEME
Reread lines 313–317. Why do such good friends keep fighting after the bell rings?

---

21. **mucho corazón** (mōō′chô kô-rä-sôn′) *Spanish:* a lot of heart; great courage.

DIFFERENTIATED INSTRUCTION

FOR LESS-PROFICIENT READERS

4 Targeted Passage [Lines 298–329]
This passage concludes the story by describing what happens at the end of the fight.

- Why is round three so important?
- How do the boys fight during round three?
- Why are people alarmed when Antonio and Felix rush toward each other after the end of the fight?
- Once the fight is over, what is most important to the boys?

FOR ADVANCED LEARNERS/PRE-AP

Complete the Glossary Have students complete their glossaries with additional terms from the story. These may include:

- *knock him out* (line 104)
- *challenger* (line 111)
- *the ropes* (line 119)
- *slipped the punch* (line 219)
- *countered* (line 220)
- *too much read on him* (line 226)

Comprehension

 MARYLAND OBJECTIVES

LITERATURE STANDARD
3.A.6.a Analyze universal themes

1. **Recall** Why is this fight so important to Felix and Antonio?

2. **Recall** What happens at the end of the fight?

3. **Summarize** Describe how the two boys fight during the boxing match. What strengths does each boy demonstrate?

Literary Analysis

4. **Make Inferences** Felix draws an **analogy,** or point-by-point comparison, between *The Champion* and his upcoming fight with Antonio. How does this analogy help Felix deal with his **internal conflict?**

5. **Compare and Contrast Characters** Look back at the Venn diagram you created as you read "Amigo Brothers." Which are more important, the similarities or the differences? Why?

6. **Draw Conclusions** What effect does the boxing competition have on Felix and Antonio's relationship? Support your answer with examples from the story.

7. **Identify Theme** Draw a graphic organizer like the one shown. Note details from the story about the boys' **friendship.** Then write a theme statement about friendship.

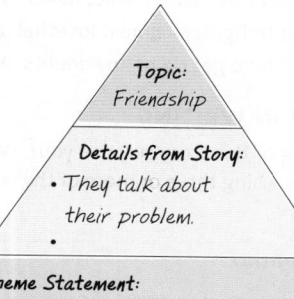

Topic:
Friendship

Details from Story:
• They talk about their problem.
•

Theme Statement:

8. **Evaluate** Given that the boys know each other so well, do you think it is easier or harder for them to fight each other? Use examples from the story to support your answer.

Extension and Challenge

9. **Creative Project: Music** Filmmakers often use music to enhance a movie's **theme.** Suppose you were asked to pick five songs for a film version of "Amigo Brothers." What would they be? Present your list to the class. Explain how each song reflects a theme of the selection.

Oscar de la Hoya

10. **Inquiry and Research** Find out about the early life of a Golden Gloves champion who later became a professional boxer, such as Oscar de la Hoya or Muhammad Ali. How was the person you researched like Felix and Antonio? Present your findings to the class.

> **RESEARCH LINKS**
> For more on Golden Glove champions, visit the **Research Center** at **ClassZone.com.**

---

7. ● **STANDARDS FOCUS Theme Versus Topic** Details: They agree to fight fairly; they don't wait to hear the winner announced. Theme: Friendship is more important than winning.

8. It is easier because they know each other's boxing styles, strengths, and weaknesses (lines 225–229, 267–269). It is harder because they do not want to hurt each other (lines 56–59, 102–104).

Extension and Challenge

9. Students should be able to explain how songs on their lists are related to themes involving friendship and competition.

10. Student presentations should include information about a particular Golden Gloves champion and compare the person to the characters in the story. They might focus on the person's background, character or personality, and fighting style.

Practice and Apply

After Reading

For additional support of post-reading questions, use these copy masters:

® RESOURCE MANAGER—Copy Masters
Reading Check p. 34 (to check understanding of the selection)
Theme Versus Topic p. 27 (for practice of literary analysis standards focus)
Question Support p. 35 (**After Reading** questions adapted for English learners and less-proficient readers)

Additional selection questions are provided for teachers on page 21.

For additional activities to challenge students, see

ℹ Power Thinking at **ClassZone.com**

ANSWERS

Comprehension

1. *The winner will represent the Boys Club in the Golden Gloves tournament.*

2. *The boys leave the ring before the winner is announced.*

3. *Possible answer: Both boys fight hard. Antonio has a long reach and dances around a lot. Felix is a powerful slugger.*

Literary Analysis

Possible answers:

4. *Watching the movie helps Felix solve his internal conflict. The movie puts him in a competitive frame of mind—thinking of himself as a champion and Antonio as just another opponent, not his best friend.*

5. ■ **STANDARDS FOCUS Compare and Contrast** *Some students may say that the boys' similarities are more important because their similarities are what make them such good friends. Others may say the boys' differences are more important because the differences make each boy unique and make the friendship more interesting.*

6. *The competition puts some strain on the friendship but eventually makes it stronger. Before the fight they find it hard to act naturally with one another and decide not to see each other for the last week. The fact that they leave the ring without knowing who won shows that their friendship means more to them than the fight's outcome.*

ANSWERS

Vocabulary in Context

VOCABULARY PRACTICE

1. *devastating*
2. *perpetual*
3. *unbridled*
4. *bedlam*
5. *pensively*
6. *flail*
7. *barrage*
8. *torrent*
9. *clarity*
10. *dispel*

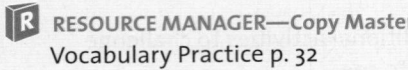 **RESOURCE MANAGER—Copy Master**
Vocabulary Practice p. 32

VOCABULARY IN WRITING

Suggest that students list words that describe how they felt at the end of the story, such as *shocked, surprised, happy, angry, puzzled.* Have them think about why they felt this way and then review the vocabulary words in the context of those reactions.

VOCABULARY STRATEGY: THE LATIN ROOT
pel (also an EL language objective)

- Point out that many of the words combine a prefix with the root. Encourage students to break words into parts to figure out meanings.

- Have students use context clues to decide which word would fit best in each sentence. For example, in the first sentence the missing word means "something that will drive insects away."

Answers:

1. *repellent*
2. *impulsive*
3. *expel*
4. *propeller*

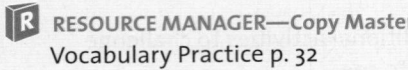 **RESOURCE MANAGER—Copy Master**
Vocabulary Strategy p. 33

Vocabulary Center at ClassZone.com
Additional Vocabulary Activities

Vocabulary in Context

VOCABULARY PRACTICE

For each sentence, choose the vocabulary word that is similar in meaning to the boldfaced word or phrase.

1. In the ring, both fighters were **extremely good at causing pain.**
2. Felix was in **continual** motion on his feet.
3. Antonio's fans cheered with **uncontrolled** emotion.
4. The **noise** in the gym was so loud that Felix couldn't hear himself think.
5. The trainer sat **deep in thought.**
6. Antonio began to **wave his arms crazily** about.
7. Felix came at Antonio with a **concentrated attack** of punches.
8. Antonio responded with a **wild, never-ending stream** of blows.
9. At times, both fighters almost lost their **ability to think clearly.**
10. Felix was able to **get rid of** any doubts about his friend.

barrage	flail
bedlam	pensively
clarity	perpetual
devastating	torrent
dispel	unbridled

VOCABULARY IN WRITING

Did the ending of this story surprise you? Write a paragraph explaining your reactions, using three or more of the vocabulary words. You might start like this.

> **EXAMPLE SENTENCE**
>
> *I expected the ending to **dispel** the question of who the better fighter was.*

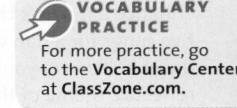 **MARYLAND OBJECTIVES**

READING STANDARD
1.D.3.b Use word structure to determine meaning

VOCABULARY STRATEGY: THE LATIN ROOT *pel*

The vocabulary word *dispel* contains the Latin root *pel*, which means "drive" or "push." This root, which is sometimes spelled *puls*, is found in many English words. To understand the meaning of words with *pel* or *puls*, use context clues and your knowledge of the root's meaning.

VOCABULARY PRACTICE
For more practice, go to the **Vocabulary Center** at **ClassZone.com.**

PRACTICE Choose the word from the web that best completes each sentence.

1. Use insect _____ before you hike through the woods.
2. A person who is _____ often doesn't think before acting.
3. She threatened to _____ any club member who missed more than two meetings.
4. A plane's _____ helps it move through the air.

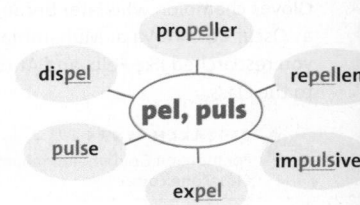

propeller
dispel — repellent
pel, puls
pulse — impulsive
expel

DIFFERENTIATED INSTRUCTION

FOR ENGLISH LEARNERS

Vocabulary: Prefixes and Suffixes Tell students that a prefix goes before a root while a suffix goes after a root.

1. Assign each student a word—*dispel, propeller, repellent, impulsive,* or *expel.*

2. Have students break their words into parts and look them up to see how prefixes and suffixes affect the meanings of the roots.

3. Have students meet in pairs or small groups to share their words.

FOR ADVANCED LEARNERS/PRE–AP

Vocabulary in Writing Have students use as many of the vocabulary words as possible to write a paragraph by one of the judges of the fight. The paragraph should indicate who the winner is and the reasons for the judge's decision.

Reading-Writing Connection

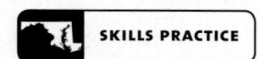

Increase your understanding of "Amigo Brothers" by responding to these prompts. Then complete the **Grammar and Writing** exercise.

WRITING PROMPTS

A. Short Response: Analyze the Message
Some people believe boxing is too brutal to be an appropriate sport for young people. Others disagree. Which side of this debate is presented in "Amigo Brothers"? Using details and examples from the story, write **one paragraph** explaining your response.

B. Extended Response: Write Dialogue
What do you suppose Antonio and Felix talk about as they walk away from the boxing ring? Keep in mind the big question about **competition** on page 310 and what you know about the boys' friendship. Write their conversation as a **one-page dialogue.**

SELF-CHECK

A strong response will . . .
- include a clear opening statement
- use specific details and examples from the story to support the statement

An effective dialogue will . . .
- demonstrate the nature of the boys' friendship
- include language that fits each character

GRAMMAR AND WRITING

MARYLAND OBJECTIVES

LANGUAGE STANDARD
5.C.2 Apply standard English punctuation

PUNCTUATE DIALOGUE CORRECTLY Dialogue is a conversation between two or more speakers. If you don't punctuate it correctly, readers might be confused about who is speaking. To avoid confusion, use **quotation marks** at the beginning and end of a speaker's words. Place end marks, such as **periods,** inside closing quotation marks. Use **commas** to set off a speaker's words from the rest of a sentence. Notice the placement of the comma and quotation marks in the revised sentence.

> *Original:* Antonio said Felix, you will always be my *amigo* brother.
>
> *Revised:* Antonio said, "Felix, you will always be my *amigo* brother."

PRACTICE Fix the misplaced punctuation marks in the following dialogue and insert any missing marks.

1. Felix replied, Same here, bro. No way I would let anything come between us.
2. "So, I feel good about our decision", Antonio said.
3. Felix shrugged and said Yeah. Me, too.
4. "Brother, boxing will never mean more to me than our friendship does".

For more help with punctuating dialogue, see page R50 in the Grammar Handbook.

FOR LESS—PROFICIENT WRITERS

For Prompt A:

1. Have students work in small groups to write a statement of Thomas's attitude toward boxing for young people.
2. Have jigsaw groups review the story for evidence to support this statement.

For Prompt B:

1. Allow students to work in pairs in which they assume the roles of Felix and Tony.
2. Student One writes a sentence congratulating the other on a good fight.

3. Student Two responds to that statement. Students continue taking turns in this way to create a dialogue.
4. Encourage students to end their dialogue with each boy affirming the value of their friendship.

Reading-Writing Connection

WRITING PROMPTS

- For **Prompt A,** have students review the story for clues to Thomas's position. Lines 15–21 and 125–130 provide evidence that he thinks boxing is good for young people.
- For **Prompt B,** have students reread lines 44–91 to recall how the boys speak.

For an extended Reading-Writing Connection activity, see

ⓘ Writing Center at **ClassZone.com**

GRAMMAR AND WRITING

- On the board, write the sample sentence with this punctuation: *"Antonio," said Felix, "you will always be my* amigo *brother."* Discuss how the meaning is changed.
- Have students work individually or in pairs to fix the practice sentences. **Answers:**

1. *Felix replied, "Same here, bro. No way would I let anything come between us."*
2. *"So, I feel good about our decision," Antonio said.*
3. *Felix shrugged and said, "Yeah. Me, too."*
4. *"Brother, boxing will never mean more to me than our friendship does."*

R RESOURCE MANAGER—Copy Master
Punctuate Dialogue Correctly p. 36

Assess and Reteach

Assess

R RESOURCE MANAGER—Copy Masters
Selection Tests A, B/C pp. 39–40, 41–42

💿 Test Generator CD

Reteach

S STANDARDS LESSON FILE
Literature Lesson 13: Theme
Reading Lesson 12: Comparing and Contrasting
Writing Lesson 48: Writing Dialogue
Vocabulary Lesson 10: Latin Roots (active verbs)

Focus and Motivate

OBJECTIVES

Literary Analysis
- explore the key idea of **community**
- identify theme
- read a short story and a magazine article

Reading
- monitor reading comprehension by asking questions

Vocabulary
- build vocabulary for reading and writing
- understand and use denotations and connotations of words to unlock shades of meaning *(also an EL language objective)*

SUMMARY

When an artist from New York begins painting on a wall in their small Southern town, the narrator and his cousin are outraged. The boys plan to take back their wall by painting graffiti over the woman's work. However, they change their minds when they see her mural honoring African-American history. The mural links the residents of this small town to a much broader cultural **community.**

What makes a COMMUNITY?

Discuss the question with students. To lead into the *KEY IDEA,* brainstorm words that students associate with **community.** After students complete the *DISCUSS* activity, have them share their ideas about welcoming a new person to a community.

Selection Resources

The War of the Wall
Short Story by Toni Cade Bambara

What makes a COMMUNITY?

MARYLAND OBJECTIVES

READING/LIT STANDARDS
1.E.3.a Select and apply appropriate strategies during reading
3.A.6.a Analyze universal themes

KEY IDEA Belonging to a **community** can give people feelings of identity and security. What things in the community help contribute to those feelings? In "The War of the Wall," an "outsider" comes to a town and challenges its residents' idea of what it means to be a community.

DISCUSS Think about the different communities, or groups, that you belong to, such as your school, your neighborhood, and your town. With a group of classmates, discuss how you would welcome someone new to your school or town.

326

 RESOURCE MANAGER UNIT 3

Plan and Teach pp. 43–50

Literary Analysis
Summary pp. 51†*, 52‡*
Theme pp. 53, 54†*
Question Support p. 61*

Reading
Monitor pp. 55, 56†*
Reading Check p. 60
Reading Fluency p. 62

Vocabulary
Study p. 57*
Practice p. 58
Strategy p. 59

Assessment
Selection Tests A, B/C pp. 63*, 65*
 Test Generator CD

 BEST PRACTICES TOOLKIT

Differentiated Instruction
 pp. 31–38*
Scaffolding Instruction
 pp. 43–46*

Graphic Organizers/Strategies
Word Squares • New Word
Analysis • Making Inferences

Reading Support
 Audio Anthology CD*

Technology
 Literature and Vocabulary Centers at **ClassZone.com**
 Write*Smart* CD

---

* Resources for Differentiation   † Also in Spanish   ‡ In Haitian Creole and Vietnamese

LITERARY ANALYSIS: THEME

By paying attention to a story's **theme,** or message, you can learn things about human nature that you might never get a chance to learn from experience. You can determine a story's main theme by

- noting the **setting** of the story and how it might relate to the theme
- making inferences about why the **narrator** and other **characters** say and do things and about how they feel
- noting what **conflicts** arise and how they are resolved

As you read "The War of the Wall," keep these tips in mind in order to identify the story's theme.

READING STRATEGY: MONITOR

Active readers check, or **monitor,** their understanding as they read. One way to monitor your understanding is to pause occasionally and ask yourself questions. Sometimes you'll need to reread to find the answer. Other times you'll want to read on, because your question might be answered later in the story. Either way, asking questions will help you focus on and better understand what you are reading.

As you read "The War of the Wall," record questions and answers about what is happening and why characters act the way they do. Use a chart like the one shown.

My Questions	Answers
What is the lady painting on the wall?	

VOCABULARY IN CONTEXT

The following phrases could be newspaper headlines for articles about the artist's painting in "The War of the Wall." Write a definition of each boldfaced word.

1. **Aroma** of Paint Was Promise of Future Beauty
2. Artist's **Masterpiece** Creates Sensation
3. Viewers in **Trance** over Splendid Work
4. Colors and Subject Matter **Beckon** to Wide Audience
5. **Inscription** on Mural Provides Dedication

Author Online

Creative Beginnings
Born Miltona Mirkin Cade, Toni Cade Bambara announced at five years old that she was changing her name to Toni. Her mother, who supported all of Bambara's creative efforts, agreed. Bambara began writing as a child and never stopped. She went on to become an award-winning author, teacher, filmmaker, and a leading activist in the African-American community. Although set in a small town, "The War of the Wall" was inspired by Bambara's memories of growing up in the Harlem neighborhood of New York City.

Toni Cade Bambara
1939–1995

 MORE ABOUT THE AUTHOR
For more on Toni Cade Bambara, visit the **Literature Center** at **ClassZone.com.**

Background
Murals A mural is a large picture painted on an interior or exterior wall of a building. Many murals illustrate scenes from history or reflect the people of local communities. In the 1960s, African-American artists began a "wall of respect" movement. They painted murals as symbols of their respect for different groups. Walls of respect appeared everywhere from Eastern cities such as New York to Western cities such as Los Angeles. They were also painted in small Southern towns such as the one in which "The War of the Wall" takes place.

Teach

STANDARDS FOCUS

LITERARY ANALYSIS

● **THEME**

After students read the information about the author, have them imagine a profile or biography based on Bambara's childhood. Ask: What theme might this story have?
Possible answers: Nurturing creative talent can pay off well. Childhood memories provide the material for creative work later in life.

CHECK UNDERSTANDING Ask students to identify details on page 327 that support the themes they suggested.

READING STRATEGY

■ **MONITOR**

Remind students that they can check their understanding by asking themselves questions that start with *who, what, when, where, why,* or *how.* To help them formulate questions as they read, provide these examples:

- What is making the character upset?
- Why does the character act like this?

CHECK UNDERSTANDING Have students read the **Background** note and develop two questions to share with the class.

 RESOURCE MANAGER—Copy Master
Monitor p. 55 (for student use while reading the selection)

▲ VOCABULARY IN CONTEXT

DIAGNOSE WORD KNOWLEDGE To determine preteaching needs, have all students complete **Vocabulary in Context.** *Possible answers:*
1. *smell;* 2. *great work;* 3. *daze;* 4. *call;* 5. *writing*

PRETEACH VOCABULARY Use the Vocabulary Study copy master to help students explore the meaning of each boldfaced word.
  1. Read the first pair of sentences in Part A aloud, emphasizing *aroma.*

2. Point out the context clues *fresh-baked bread* in the first sentence and *roses* in the second sentence. Elicit possible meanings for *aroma,* such as "scent" or "fragrance."

3. Repeat the procedure for items b–e.

RESOURCE MANAGER—Copy Master
Vocabulary Study p. 57

For general guidelines on differentiating vocabulary instruction and for alternative vocabulary activities for students not needing vocabulary preteaching, see

BEST PRACTICES TOOLKIT
Scaffolding Vocabulary Instruction pp. 43–46

Vocabulary Center at ClassZone.com
Additional Vocabulary Activities

ANALYZE VISUALS

Possible answer: The painting shows a vital urban community (Harlem). Details of the setting include tenement apartments, neighborhood stores, a horse-drawn vegetable wagon, a fire hydrant, 1930s vehicles, and clotheslines criss-crossing rooftops. Several people in the scene are involved in various activities, such as playing checkers on the sidewalk, hoisting a piano with a pulley, hanging laundry, walking dogs, jumping rope, and looking out windows.

About the Art Jacob Lawrence (1917–2000), one of the most acclaimed African-American artists of the 20th century, moved to Harlem, New York, at the age of 13. From 1942 to 1943, he painted a series of 30 Harlem paintings, including the painting shown on page 329. Lawrence used bold, bright colors to capture the vitality and expressive moods of Harlem.

LITERARY ANALYSIS

A THEME

Possible answer: There is going to be trouble between the narrator and Lou and the "painter lady." She is painting the wall and they don't like it.

Extend the Discussion Why don't the boys think Mr. Eubanks has a right to give the woman permission to paint on the wall?

THE WAR OF THE WALL

TONI CADE BAMBARA

Me and Lou had no time for courtesies. We were late for school. So we just flat out told the painter lady to quit messing with the wall. It was our wall, and she had no right coming into our neighborhood painting on it. Stirring in the paint bucket and not even looking at us, she mumbled something about Mr. Eubanks, the barber, giving her permission. That had nothing to do with it as far as we were concerned. We've been pitching pennies against that wall since we were little kids. Old folks have been dragging their chairs out to sit in the shade of the wall for years. Big kids have been playing handball against
10 the wall since so-called integration[1] when the crazies 'cross town poured cement in our pool so we couldn't use it. I'd sprained my neck one time boosting my cousin Lou up to chisel Jimmy Lyons's name into the wall when we found out he was never coming home from the war in Vietnam to take us fishing. **A**

"If you lean close," Lou said, leaning hipshot against her beat-up car, "you'll get a whiff of bubble gum and kids' sweat. And that'll tell you something—that this wall belongs to the kids of Taliaferro Street." I thought Lou sounded very convincing. But the painter lady paid us no mind. She just snapped the brim of her straw hat down and
20 hauled her bucket up the ladder.

"You're not even from around here," I hollered up after her. The license plates on her old piece of car said "New York." Lou dragged me away because I was about to grab hold of that ladder and shake it. And then we'd really be late for school.

When we came from school, the wall was slick with white. The painter lady was running string across the wall and taping it here and there. Me and Lou leaned against the gumball machine outside the pool hall and watched. She had strings up and down and back and forth. Then she began chalking them with a hunk of blue chalk.

ANALYZE VISUALS
Look closely at this picture. What details of **setting** does it include?

1 Targeted Passage

A THEME
After reading the first few lines of this story, what do you think the main **conflict** will be? As you continue reading, think about what message this conflict might communicate.

---

1. **since so-called integration:** from the time in the 1960s when segregation, the separation of the races in public places, was outlawed. The narrator is being sarcastic, suggesting that integration has not been successful.

Harlem Street Scene (1942), Jacob Lawrence. Gouache on paper, 21" × 20¾". Private collection. © The Jacob and Gwendolyn Lawrence Foundation/Art Resource, New York. Artists Rights Society (ARS), New York.

DIFFERENTIATED INSTRUCTION

FOR ALL STUDENTS

Expert Groups Encourage students to choose one of these topics on which to become experts. Students may work in groups or independently to research their topics. Suggest that they use visuals in their presentations.

- civil rights movement
- Vietnam Memorial in Washington, D.C.
- Southern cooking
- murals

FOR LESS–PROFICIENT READERS

In combination with the *Audio Anthology CD*, use one or more Targeted Passages (pp. 328, 332–333, 334) to ensure that students focus on key story events, concepts, and skills.

1 Targeted Passage [Lines 1–14]

This passage is critical to explaining the theme of the story because it introduces the story's main characters and sets up the main conflict.

- Who is the "painter lady"? What is she doing in the narrator's town?
- How does the narrator feel about the painter's project? Why?
- Why is the wall so important to the community?

Segregation In the southern United States, racial segregation between blacks and whites was enforced by law from the late 1800s until the 1950s. There were separate schools and public facilities, including transportation, restaurants, and hotels. Through Supreme Court rulings and federal civil rights laws in the 1950s and 1960s, the practice was declared illegal. However, there was often strong resistance from whites to ending segregation. In line 10 the narrator refers to "so-called integration" when people from another part of town damaged the community's pool. Even after segregation became illegal, *de facto* (actual) segregation continued in both the North and the South as African Americans still faced discrimination in housing and jobs.

Cultural Connection Segregation has existed in many places and times when a powerful group sought to control a minority. Segregation may be based on racial, religious, or national differences. Jews in Europe were often forced to live in separate areas and had limited rights during the Middle Ages. Koreans living in Japan are the victims of segregation. In South Africa, racial segregation was known as apartheid and was ended only after strong international pressure in the 1990s.

FOR ENGLISH LEARNERS

Key Academic Vocabulary Use Word Squares for these academic vocabulary words that occur in the story: *convincing* (line 18), *tape* (line 44), *shifted* (line 83), *definitely* (line 140), *scheme* (line 165), *section* (line 200).

 BEST PRACTICES TOOLKIT—Transparency Word Squares p. E10

Prereading For prereading instruction for English learners, see

 BEST PRACTICES TOOLKIT Scaffolding Reading Instruction pp. 43–46

FOR ADVANCED LEARNERS/PRE–AP

Pre-AP exercises in the bottom channel provide additional challenges for your advanced students. Use them for small groups or individuals.

ADDITIONAL GUIDELINES

For more help with differentiation and tips for classroom management, see

BEST PRACTICES TOOLKIT Differentiated Instruction pp. 31–38

REINFORCE *KEY IDEA:* COMMUNITY

Discuss Different members of a **community** can respond to outsiders, such as the painter, in different ways. How do the Morris twins represent one way, while the narrator and Lou represent another? ***Possible answer:*** *The twins represent a welcoming response, while the narrator and Lou represent a suspicious response.*

You might collect story evidence in a chart.

Twins	Narrator and Lou
• bring dinner and lemonade	• question what she's doing
• make her feel welcome	• act angry and suspicious

READING STRATEGY

B MONITOR

Possible answer: The painter is so focused on painting that she completely ignores everyone around her. The image of the gophers suggests that the local people seem low and insignificant to her. The narrator feels hurt and not respected.

If students need help . . .

- Reread lines 35–36. What does the narrator's action tell you about how he is feeling?

- Reread lines 43–44 and 54–58. How does the painter react to those around her? How might that make you feel?

- Reread lines 58–60. What does the narrator's reaction to Lou's comment tell you about his feelings?

Extend the Discussion Do you think the narrator might change his mind about the painter by the end of the story? Why or why not?

---

30 The Morris twins crossed the street, hanging back at the curb next to the beat-up car. The twin with the red ribbons was hugging a jug of cloudy lemonade. The one with yellow ribbons was holding a plate of dinner away from her dress. The painter lady began snapping the strings. The blue chalk dust measured off halves and quarters up and down and sideways too. Lou was about to say how hip it all was, but I dropped my book satchel on his toes to remind him we were at war.

Some good **aromas** were drifting our way from the plate leaking pot likker[2] onto the Morris girl's white socks. I could tell from where I stood that under the tinfoil was baked ham, collard greens, and candied yams.
40 And knowing Mrs. Morris, who sometimes bakes for my mama's restaurant, a slab of buttered cornbread was probably up under there too, sopping up some of the pot likker. Me and Lou rolled our eyes, wishing somebody would send us some dinner. But the painter lady didn't even turn around. She was pulling the strings down and prying bits of tape loose.

Side Pocket came strolling out of the pool hall to see what Lou and me were studying so hard. He gave the painter lady the once-over, checking out her paint-spattered jeans, her chalky T-shirt, her floppy-brimmed straw hat. He hitched up his pants and glided over toward the painter lady, who kept right on with what she was doing.
50 "Whatcha got there, sweetheart?" he asked the twin with the plate.

"Suppah," she said all soft and countrylike.

"For her," the one with the jug added, jerking her chin toward the painter lady's back.

Still she didn't turn around. She was rearing back on her heels, her hands jammed into her back pockets, her face squinched up like the **masterpiece** she had in mind was taking shape on the wall by magic. We could have been gophers crawled up into a rotten hollow for all she cared. She didn't even say hello to anybody. Lou was muttering something about how great her concentration was. I butt him with
60 my hip, and his elbow slid off the gum machine. ■ **B**

"Good evening," Side Pocket said in his best ain't-I-fine voice. But the painter lady was moving from the milk crate to the step stool to the ladder, moving up and down fast, scribbling all over the wall like a crazy person. We looked at Side Pocket. He looked at the twins. The twins looked at us. The painter lady was giving a show. It was like those old-timey music movies where the dancer taps on the tabletop and then starts jumping all over the furniture, kicking chairs over and not skipping a beat. She didn't even look where she was stepping. And for a minute there, hanging on the ladder to reach a far spot, she looked like she was going
70 to tip right over.

---

2. **pot likker:** the broth or liquid in which meat or vegetables have been cooked.

aroma (ə-rō′mə) *n.* a smell; odor

masterpiece (măs′tər-pēs′) *n.* a great work of art

B MONITOR
Why do you think the **narrator** says, "We could have been gophers . . . for all she cared"? How is the narrator feeling?

DIFFERENTIATED INSTRUCTION

FOR LESS–PROFICIENT READERS

Reading Strategy Follow-Up: Monitor Advise students that on this page the author introduces new characters who respond to the painter in their own ways. This is a good time for students to review and update their monitoring charts. Have them work in pairs to read lines 30–56 and list at least three new questions. If they have found answers to any of their questions, they should fill those in. Then have teams compare charts.

My Questions	Answers
• What was the lady doing with string and chalk?	• marking out sections on the wall
• Why are the twins carrying food and lemonade?	• to offer them to the painter

"Ahh," Side Pocket cleared his throat and moved fast to catch the ladder. "These young ladies here have brought you some supper."

"Ma'am?" The twins stepped forward. Finally the painter turned around, her eyes "full of sky," as my grandmama would say. Then she stepped down like she was in a **trance.** She wiped her hands on her jeans as the Morris twins offered up the plate and the jug. She rolled back the tinfoil, then wagged her head as though something terrible was on the plate.

"Thank your mother very much," she said, sounding like her mouth was full of sky too. "I've brought my own dinner along." And then,
80 without even excusing herself, she went back up the ladder, drawing on the wall in a wild way. Side Pocket whistled one of those oh-brother breathy whistles and went back into the pool hall. The Morris twins shifted their weight from one foot to the other, then crossed the street and went home. Lou had to drag me away, I was so mad. We couldn't wait to get to the firehouse to tell my daddy all about this rude woman who'd stolen our wall.

A ll the way back to the block to help my mama out at the restaurant, me and Lou kept asking my daddy for ways to run the painter lady out of town. But my daddy was busy talking about the trip to the country
90 and telling Lou he could come too because Grandmama can always use an extra pair of hands on the farm.

Later that night, while me and Lou were in the back doing our chores, we found out that the painter lady was a liar. She came into the restaurant and leaned against the glass of the steam table, talking about how starved she was. I was scrubbing pots and Lou was chopping onions, but we could hear her through the service window. She was asking Mama was that a ham hock in the greens, and was that a neck bone in the pole beans, and were there any vegetables cooked without meat, especially pork.

"I don't care who your spiritual leader is," Mama said in that way of
100 hers. "If you eat in the community, sistuh, you gonna eat pig by-and-by, one way or t'other."

Me and Lou were cracking up in the kitchen, and several customers at the counter were clearing their throats, waiting for Mama to really fix her wagon³ for not speaking to the elders when she came in. The painter lady took a stool at the counter and went right on with her questions. Was there cheese in the baked macaroni, she wanted to know? Were there eggs in the salad? Was it honey or sugar in the iced tea? Mama was fixing Pop Johnson's plate. And every time the painter lady asked a fool question, Mama would dump another spoonful of rice on the pile. She
10 was tapping her foot and heating up in a dangerous way. But Pop Johnson

trance (trăns) n.
a condition of daydreaming or being unconscious of one's surroundings

---

3. **fix her wagon:** a slang expression meaning "put her in her place; bring about her downfall."

Lines 61–91
DISCUSSION PROMPTS
Use these prompts to help students explore the development of the conflict between the **community** and the painter:

Connect Has someone new ever joined a community or group to which you belonged and started making changes you didn't like? How might you feel toward the new person in a situation like that? *Students may say that they would feel resentful toward the new person or would want the person to leave.*

Analyze Which character is most upset with the painter? How do you know? *Possible answers: The narrator is the angriest. Side Pocket and the twins leave the scene. Lou has to drag the narrator away. The narrator says he is "so mad," describes the painter as "rude," and says she's "stolen our wall" (lines 84–86). The narrator's father shows little interest in the painter's offenses (lines 87–91).*

Synthesize What could the painter do to ease the growing conflict? *Possible answers: She could explain to the boys what she's doing or at least be friendlier to them. She could accept gifts like the food offered by the Morris twins.*

FOR ENGLISH LEARNERS

Language: Conversational English Patterns
Point out that the narrator uses *me and Lou* or *Lou and me* as the subject of some sentences and clauses (lines 42, 45, 87, 92, 102) rather than the grammatically correct *Lou and I.* This style reflects how a young boy living in this small town might actually speak. Ask students to notice when the narrator correctly uses *I* (singular) or *we* (plural) rather than *me and Lou.*

Language: Contractions Explain that contractions are used to make characters' dialogue sound more natural.

1. Display some common contractions such as *we've, couldn't, you'll,* and *it's.* Show what words have been combined to form them.

2. Point out other contractions used in this story: *'cross* (line 10), "across"; *t'other* (line 101), "the other"; *'cause* (line 204), "because."

C THEME

Possible answers:

- *She has different tastes in food—she doesn't want to eat cheese, eggs, or meat, especially pork (lines 96–98, 106–107).*

- *She may have different religious beliefs that prevent her from eating pork (line 99).*

- *She doesn't understand the importance of "speaking to the elders" to show her respect (lines 102–104).*

Extend the Discussion How do these details explain the painter's reaction to the food the twins offered (lines 76–77)?

READING STRATEGY

D MONITOR

Possible answers:

- *Why is the painter having such a hard time ordering her food?*

- *Why is Mama upset with the painter?*

- *What are the people in town going to do about the painter now?*

LITERARY ANALYSIS

E THEME

Possible answers: The story is set in a small Southern town, and the painter is a stranger from the North. She and the members of this community don't understand each other's culture. The conflict develops from that.

If students need help . . . Have students say what they know about where the story takes place. Ask them to find the clue word that has to do with place (*North, line 132*). Guide them to see how the passage suggests that the North and South have different cultures.

was happy as he could be. Me and Lou peeked through the service window, wondering what planet the painter lady came from. Who ever heard of baked macaroni without cheese, or potato salad without eggs? **C**

"Do you have any bread made with unbleached flour?" the painter lady asked Mama. There was a long pause, as though everybody in the restaurant was holding their breath, wondering if Mama would dump the next spoonful on the painter lady's head. She didn't. But when she set Pop Johnson's plate down, it came down with a bang.

120 When Mama finally took her order, the starving lady all of a sudden couldn't make up her mind whether she wanted a vegetable plate or fish and a salad. She finally settled on the broiled trout and a tossed salad. But just when Mama reached for a plate to serve her, the painter lady leaned over the counter with her finger all up in the air.

"Excuse me," she said. "One more thing." Mama was holding the plate like a Frisbee, tapping that foot, one hand on her hip. "Can I get raw beets in that tossed salad?"

"You will get," Mama said, leaning her face close to the painter lady's, "whatever Lou back there tossed. Now sit down." And the painter lady sat back down on her stool and shut right up. **D**

130 All the way to the country, me and Lou tried to get Mama to open fire on the painter lady. But Mama said that seeing as how she was from the North, you couldn't expect her to have any manners. Then Mama said she was sorry she'd been so impatient with the woman because she seemed like a decent person and was simply trying to stick to a very strict diet. Me and Lou didn't want to hear that. Who did that lady think she was, coming into our neighborhood and taking over our wall? **E**

"Wellllll," Mama drawled, pulling into the filling station so Daddy could take the wheel, "it's hard on an artist, ya know. They can't always get people to look at their work. So she's just doing her work in the open, that's all."

140 Me and Lou definitely did not want to hear that. Why couldn't she set up an easel downtown or draw on the sidewalk in her own neighborhood? Mama told us to quit fussing so much; she was tired and wanted to rest. She climbed into the back seat and dropped down into the warm hollow Daddy had made in the pillow.

All weekend long, me and Lou tried to scheme up ways to recapture our wall. Daddy and Mama said they were sick of hearing about it. Grandmama turned up the TV to drown us out. On the late news was a story about the New York subways. When a train came roaring into the station all covered from top to bottom, windows too, with writings and drawings done with

150 spray paint, me and Lou slapped five. Mama said it was too bad kids in New York had nothing better to do than spray paint all over the trains. Daddy said that in the cities, even grown-ups wrote all over the trains and buildings too. Daddy called it "graffiti." Grandmama called it a shame.

C THEME
Reread lines 96–113. How is the painter different from the people who live in the community?

D MONITOR
What **questions** do you have about what is happening in this scene? Record them in your monitoring chart.

E THEME
Reread lines 130–136. What does the **setting** have to do with the **conflict** between the community and the painter?

2 Targeted Passage

DIFFERENTIATED INSTRUCTION

FOR ENGLISH LEARNERS

Culture: Clarify Explain that the North and the South are two U.S. regions with different cultural histories. In the mid-1800s the South was mostly rural. Its large African-American population was mostly enslaved. In the North, many people lived in cities and worked in factories. Differences between these regions, especially over slavery, led to the Civil War. Mama's remark shows that some people still see real differences between the regions.

Language: Idioms and Slang Use New Word Analysis to teach these idioms and slang expressions: *paid us no mind* (lines 18–19), "ignored us"; *gave . . . the once-over* (line 46), "looked at closely"; *cracking up* (line 102), "laughing"; *open fire on* (lines 130–131), "speak against"; *right off* (line 179), "immediately"; *laying down a heavy rap* (line 181), "saying something important or serious."

 BEST PRACTICES TOOLKIT—Transparency
New Word Analysis p. E8

W e couldn't wait to get out of school on Monday. We couldn't find any black spray paint anywhere. But in a junky hardware store downtown we found a can of white epoxy[4] paint, the kind you touch up old refrigerators with when they get splotchy and peely. We spent our whole allowance on it. And because it was too late to use our bus passes, we had to walk all the way home lugging our book satchels and gym 160 shoes, and the bag with the epoxy.

When we reached the corner of Taliaferro and Fifth, it looked like a block party or something. Half the neighborhood was gathered on the sidewalk in front of the wall. I looked at Lou, he looked at me. We both looked at the bag with the epoxy and wondered how we were going to work our scheme. The painter lady's car was nowhere in sight. But there were too many people standing around to do anything. Side Pocket and his buddies were leaning on their cue sticks, hunching each other. Daddy was there with a lineman[5] he catches a ride with on Mondays. Mrs. Morris had her arms flung around the shoulders of the twins on 170 either side of her. Mama was talking with some of her customers, many of them with napkins still at the throat. Mr. Eubanks came out of the barbershop, followed by a man in a striped poncho, half his face shaved, the other half full of foam.

"She really did it, didn't she?" Mr. Eubanks huffed out his chest. Lots of folks answered right quick that she surely did when they saw the straight razor in his hand. **F**

Mama **beckoned** us over. And then we saw it. The wall. Reds, greens, figures outlined in black. Swirls of purple and orange. Storms of blues and yellows. It was something. I recognized some of the faces right off. There 180 was Martin Luther King, Jr. And there was a man with glasses on and his mouth open like he was laying down a heavy rap. Daddy came up alongside and reminded us that that was Minister Malcolm X. The serious woman with a rifle I knew was Harriet Tubman because my grandmama has pictures

2 **Targeted Passage**

F MONITOR
Reread lines 171–176. Why do people agree with Mr. Eubanks so quickly?

beckon (bĕk'ən) v. to summon or call, usually by a gesture or nod

---

4. **epoxy** (ĭ-pŏk'sē): a plastic used in glues and paints.
5. **lineman**: a person who repairs telephone or power lines.

© Andre Jenny/Alamy.

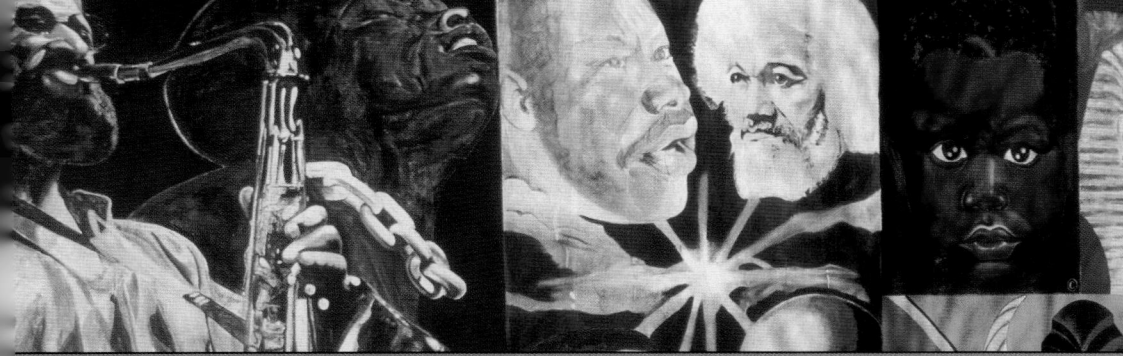

Lines 161–179
REINFORCE *KEY IDEA:* COMMUNITY

Discuss What effect does the painter's work have on the narrator's **community?** *Possible answer: The community gathers to appreciate her work. The painting gives them something to look at, think about, and talk about.*

READING STRATEGY

F MONITOR

Possible answer: The people agree with him because he has a razor in his hand, although he doesn't seem to be actually threatening them.

Extend the Discussion Why does Mr. Eubanks seem to take personal pride in the painter's work?

ANALYZE VISUALS

Activity Invite students to do a quickwrite about how they think one of the characters in the story might respond to this piece of art. As an option, students might do a quickdraw to suggest other visuals that could be added to this mural.

FOR LESS–PROFICIENT READERS
2 Targeted Passage [Lines 145–166]

This passage reveals a turning point in the story. It shows how the narrator and Lou plan to win their conflict with the painter and how their plan is defeated.

- Why do the narrator and Lou want to buy black spray paint?
- What do they find when they return to the wall?
- How does this change their plans?

FOR ADVANCED LEARNERS/PRE–AP
Analyze Motivation [paired activity option]
Have students recall what they know about the narrator's relationship to Jimmy Lyons (lines 11–14). Challenge them to create a flashback scene involving these two characters that would help explain why the narrator made such an effort to chisel Jimmy's name in the wall. Their scenes should also help explain why the narrator resents the painter's work so strongly.

SOCIAL STUDIES CONNECTION

Harriet Tubman (c. 1820–1913) was a runaway slave who led many slaves to freedom on the Underground Railroad in the 1850s. Martin Luther King Jr. (1929–1968) used nonviolent protest to help African Americans win their civil rights in the 1950s and 1960s. Malcolm X (1925–1965) was a spokesman for black pride who eventually believed that blacks and whites could live together in harmony. Fannie Lou Hamer (1917–1977) worked for voting rights for African Americans and tried to integrate the Democratic Party in Mississippi in the 1960s.

LITERARY ANALYSIS

ⓖ THEME

Possible answer: She portrays the children in the community as smart and full of potential. She illustrates the kinds of things the community cares about, especially the children's future.

SELECTION WRAP–UP

SYNTHESIZE Why do you think the painter calls her work a "wall of respect"? **Possible answer:** *The wall honors the sacrifice that her cousin Jimmy made, and more generally it conveys respect for African-American people and culture.*

⭐ **CRITIQUE** Ask students to evaluate how well the author succeeded in creating a vivid picture of life in this **community.** What techniques did she use to do this?

READING FLUENCY

Distribute the copy masters and have students work in pairs to practice fluency.

Ⓡ RESOURCE MANAGER—Copy Master
Reading Fluency p. 62

---

of her all over the house. And I knew Mrs. Fannie Lou Hamer 'cause a signed photograph of her hangs in the restaurant next to the calendar.

Then I let my eyes follow what looked like a vine. It trailed past a man with a horn, a woman with a big white flower in her hair, a handsome dude in a tuxedo seated at a piano, and a man with a goatee holding a book. When I looked more closely, I realized that what had looked like
190 flowers were really faces. One face with yellow petals looked just like Frieda Morris. One with red petals looked just like Hattie Morris. I could hardly believe my eyes.

"Notice," Side Pocket said, stepping close to the wall with his cue stick like a classroom pointer. "These are the flags of liberation," he said in a voice I'd never heard him use before. We all stepped closer while he pointed and spoke. "Red, black and green," he said, his pointer falling on the leaflike flags of the vine. "Our liberation flag.[6] And here Ghana, there Tanzania. Guinea-Bissau, Angola, Mozambique."[7] Side Pocket sounded very tall, as though he'd been waiting all his life to give this lesson.

200 Mama tapped us on the shoulder and pointed to a high section of the wall. There was a fierce-looking man with his arms crossed against his chest guarding a bunch of children. His muscles bulged, and he looked a lot like my daddy. One kid was looking at a row of books. Lou hunched me 'cause the kid looked like me. The one that looked like Lou was spinning a globe on the tip of his finger like a basketball. There were other kids there with microscopes and compasses. And the more I looked, the more it looked like the fierce man was not so much guarding the kids as defending their right to do what they were doing. ⓖ

Then Lou gasped and dropped the paint bag and ran forward, running
210 his hands over a rainbow. He had to tiptoe and stretch to do it, it was so high. I couldn't breathe either. The painter lady had found the chisel marks and had painted Jimmy Lyons's name in a rainbow.

"Read the **inscription,** honey," Mrs. Morris said, urging little Frieda forward. She didn't have to urge much. Frieda marched right up, bent down, and in a loud voice that made everybody quit oohing and ahhing and listen, she read,

To the People of Taliaferro Street
I Dedicate This Wall of Respect
Painted in Memory of My Cousin
220   *Jimmy Lyons* ❧

---

6. **Red, black and green ... liberation flag:** a banner of red, black, and green horizontal stripes has been used in the United States as well as Africa to stand for the liberation, or freedom, sought by people of African heritage.

7. **Ghana ... Tanzania. Guinea-Bissau, Angola, Mozambique** (mō′zəm-bēk′): countries in southern and western Africa.

● SOCIAL STUDIES CONNECTION

Martin Luther King Jr., Malcolm X, Harriet Tubman, and Fannie Lou Hamer (shown here) were all African Americans who fought for freedom and equality.

③ Targeted Passage

ⓖ THEME

Reread lines 200–208. Here you see the story's main **characters** through the painter's eyes. How does this show that she understands the community?

inscription
(ĭn-skrĭp′shən) *n.* something written, carved, or engraved on a surface

---

DIFFERENTIATED INSTRUCTION

FOR LESS–PROFICIENT READERS

③ **Targeted Passage [Lines 200–220]**
This passage ends the story and resolves the conflict by revealing what the artist was painting on the wall and why she did it.

- How did the painter portray the children of the community?
- What causes Lou to drop the paint bag?
- Why did the artist decide to paint this wall?

FOR ADVANCED LEARNERS/PRE–AP

Analyze a Minor Character Have students review the scenes in which Side Pocket appears (lines 45–82 and 193–199) and develop a brief character sketch of this colorful minor character. They might fill out a chart with these categories:

- personality
- manners
- favorite pastimes
- favorite section of the library
- role in the story

Comprehension

1. **Recall** Why is the wall special to the narrator and Lou?

2. **Represent** Who is related to whom in this story? Use web diagrams to show the family relationships mentioned.

3. **Clarify** Why don't Lou and the narrator carry out their plan to recapture the wall?

Literary Analysis

4. **Monitor** Review the chart you filled in as you read. Which questions and answers were most important for understanding the story? Why?

5. **Make Inferences** Reread lines 209–220. How do you think Lou and the narrator feel about the paint they've bought once they read the inscription on the wall?

6. **Analyze Characters** Mama's reaction to the painter seems to change over the course of the story. Her first impression of the painter seems to be negative. Why does she then defend the painter to the narrator and Lou?

7. **Identify Theme** Given what the **characters** learn about themselves and the painter, what do you think the theme of the story is?

8. **Evaluate** Was the painter an outsider or part of the **community**? Use examples from the story to support your answer.

Extension and Challenge

9. **Readers' Circle** "The War of the Wall" is told from the **first-person point of view.** Everything we learn about the characters and plot comes from what the narrator chooses to tell us. For that reason, we don't know very much about the painter's thoughts and feelings. With a small group of classmates, talk about what the painter may have been thinking about the **community.** Support your responses with evidence from the story.

10. ⚫ **SOCIAL STUDIES CONNECTION** Read the article "Back to the Wall" on page 337 about the artist Judith Baca's mural restoration project. What are the similarities and differences between Los Angeles's Great Wall and the mural in the story? Think about the subject matter of each mural and the way each was created.

MARYLAND OBJECTIVES

READING STANDARD
1.E.3.a Select and apply appropriate strategies during reading

THE WAR OF THE WALL **335**

---

8. *An outsider—she's from New York and doesn't relate well to the local people. Part of the community—her cousin Jimmy grew up there, and she painted the wall to show respect for him and the community.*

Extension and Challenge

9. *Student discussion should use evidence from the painter's behavior to infer her thoughts. The mural shows that she thought the people in the community cared about their children's futures. It also shows her respect for the community's*

culture. She was probably touched by the Morris twins offering food and by her cousin's name being carved into the wall.

10. ⚫ **SOCIAL STUDIES CONNECTION**
Possible answer: Both murals reflect the history and culture of their communities. In the story, one woman painted the mural by herself. In Los Angeles, the painter supervised many young people from the community in creating the mural.

Practice and Apply

After Reading

For additional support of post-reading questions, use these copy masters:

📖 **RESOURCE MANAGER—Copy Masters**
Reading Check p. 60 (to check understanding of the selection)
Theme p. 53 (for practice of literary analysis standards focus)
Question Support p. 61 (**After Reading** questions adapted for English learners and less-proficient readers)

Additional selection questions are provided for teachers on page 47.

For additional activities to challenge students, see

ℹ️ Power Thinking at **ClassZone.com**

ANSWERS

Comprehension

1. *They had been playing games against it since they were young. They carved their friend's name in it after he died in Vietnam.*

2. *Webs should show the following relationships: Mama, Daddy, Grandma, narrator, and Lou; Jimmy Lyons and the painter; Mrs. Morris, Frieda, and Hattie.*

3. *Possible answer: Once they see the value of the painting, they no longer want to destroy it.*

Literary Analysis
Possible answers:

4. ⬛ **STANDARDS FOCUS** *Monitor The most important relate to the main conflict and to the theme of the story. Examples: What was the lady painting on the wall? Why was she painting it? What are Lou and the narrator going to do to the wall? How does the community respond to the painting?*

5. *They're sorry about the paint because they no longer want to ruin the painting.*

6. *Mama's attitude toward the painter softens after she thinks about how hard it is to be an artist and to be an outsider.*

7. ⬤ **STANDARDS FOCUS** *Theme Students' responses should reflect an understanding that the community had misjudged the painter. Example: "Making hasty judgments about people can cause problems."*

THE WAR OF THE WALL **335**

ANSWERS

Vocabulary in Context

VOCABULARY PRACTICE

1. *c*; 2. *b*; 3. *c*; 4. *a*; 5. *b*

 RESOURCE MANAGER—Copy Master
Vocabulary Practice p. 58

VOCABULARY IN WRITING

Students can use a Making Inferences chart to help them describe the painter as a character. Then have students review the vocabulary words and connect them with their inferences.

 BEST PRACTICES TOOLKIT—Transparency
Making Inferences p. A13

VOCABULARY STRATEGY: DENOTATIONS AND CONNOTATIONS *(also an EL language objective)*

Suggest that students first consider what meaning the two words have in common. Then have them think of different contexts in which they have seen or heard each word used.

Answers:
1. *gathering*; 2. *slender*; 3. *chuckle*; 4. *petite*; 5. *inquiring*; 6. *chat*; 7. *self-confident*; 8. *youthful*
Example sentence: *The gathering in front of the wall reminded Lou of a block party.*

 RESOURCE MANAGER—Copy Master
Vocabulary Strategy p. 59

ℹ Vocabulary Center at **ClassZone.com**
Additional Vocabulary Activities

Assess and Reteach

Assess

 RESOURCE MANAGER—Copy Masters
Selection Tests A, B/C pp. 63–64, 65–66

🖴 Test Generator CD

Reteach

📄 **STANDARDS LESSON FILE**
Literature Lesson 13: Theme
Reading Lesson 2: Monitoring
Vocabulary Lesson 17: Denotation and Connotation

336 UNIT 3: UNDERSTANDING THEME

Vocabulary in Context

VOCABULARY PRACTICE

Choose the letter of the situation that you would associate with each boldfaced vocabulary word.

1. **aroma:** (a) arguing with a friend, (b) writing a letter, (c) smelling a rose
2. **masterpiece:** (a) a game of catch, (b) a prize-winning play, (c) a stormy day
3. **trance:** (a) walking a dog, (b) snoring loudly, (c) not paying attention
4. **beckon:** (a) hailing a taxicab, (b) passing a test, (c) eating lunch
5. **inscription:** (a) military service, (b) words on a tombstone, (c) parts of a car

VOCABULARY IN WRITING

What kind of person is the painter? Write a brief character description of her, using two or more vocabulary words. Here is an example of how you might begin.

> **EXAMPLE SENTENCE**
>
> *The painter seems to know from the beginning that she is creating a **masterpiece**.*

VOCABULARY STRATEGY: DENOTATIONS AND CONNOTATIONS

A word's **denotation** is its literal meaning—that is, the meaning found in a dictionary definition. A word's **connotation** comes from the shades of meaning it has beyond its definition. For example, a stubborn person could also be described as *strong-willed* or *pig-headed*. But *strong-willed* connotes "independent in thinking and acting," while *pig-headed* connotes "inflexible." Recognizing connotations can improve both your reading and your writing.

PRACTICE Choose the word in each pair that has a positive connotation. Then use the word in a sentence.

1. gathering—mob
2. skinny—slender
3. chuckle—snicker
4. petite—puny
5. inquiring—prying
6. gossip—chat
7. self-confident—arrogant
8. immature—youthful

MARYLAND OBJECTIVES

READING STANDARD
1.D.2.b Explain relationships between words

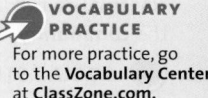

VOCABULARY PRACTICE
For more practice, go to the **Vocabulary Center** at **ClassZone.com**.

336 UNIT 3: UNDERSTANDING THEME

DIFFERENTIATED INSTRUCTION

FOR ENGLISH LEARNERS
Vocabulary: Denotations and Connotations

1. Provide students with context clues by using each word in a sentence.
2. Ask students what the two words have in common and which sounds more positive.
3. Encourage students to use the more positive word in a new sentence.

FOR ADVANCED LEARNERS/PRE–AP

Vocabulary in Writing Have students use at least three vocabulary words to write a brief newspaper article about the mural and the community's reaction to it. They should include facts and comments from story characters in their article.

MAGAZINE ARTICLE In "The War of the Wall," a woman paints a mural in a Southern town. In the following article, you'll read about the real-life artist Judith Baca and the people who helped her create and restore a large mural in Los Angeles, California.

Back to the Wall

from **People**

Working in a city known more for freeways than museums, Judith Baca may be the quintessential Los Angeles artist, painting not on canvas but on concrete. Since 1974 she has overseen the creation of roughly 550 murals in public spaces, providing summer work for inner-city kids while she brings color and life to highway underpasses and parks. "I want it to continue," Baca, 58, says of her work. "I want future generations to see it."

One of her most famous pieces is the 13-foot-high, half-mile-long Great Wall, which depicts world and L.A. history on a flood-channel wall. Some 400 youths—many from poor, crime-ridden areas—worked on the mural, and 30 years later, some of their kids worked on its restoration. "People come first for Judy," says Priscilla Becker, 40, who, as a teen from a poor family, worked with Baca for three summers. Now CEO of a software company, Becker adds, "From Judy I learned that dreams are not just dreams."

Baca was teaching art in an inner-city park when she began planning murals to build bridges between rival gangs. She still wants her projects to meet the same goal. "All these people made the wall together," she says. "That's the story—what they made together."

DIFFERENTIATED INSTRUCTION

FOR ENGLISH LEARNERS
Culture: Clarify
- Explain that Los Angeles, or L.A., is the largest city in California. Many interstate highways run through the city. These highways are called freeways, because drivers don't have to pay tolls, or expressways, because they are designed to get drivers from place to place quickly. The areas underneath the highways are called underpasses.

- The term *inner city* refers to the older, central part of certain cities. With the increase in the number of cars and highways in the 1950s, many people chose to move to suburbs farther from the center of the city. Often this movement left the inner city inhabited by ethnic minorities, including new immigrants who could not afford to live elsewhere. Many inner-city neighborhoods have problems with poverty and crime.

This selection provides support for question 10 on page 335. You can also use it as a mini-lesson on reading for information.

READING FOR INFORMATION
Point out that "Back to the Wall" is a magazine article. Ask students what the title, the photograph, and the source of the article tell them about the content of the article. *Possible answer: The title and photograph suggest that the story will be about a mural painted on a wall. The magazine* People *features articles about interesting people, so the story will likely focus on the artist.*

DISCUSSION PROMPTS
Use these prompts to help students understand how art helps strengthen **communities:**

Connect How has this article affected your ideas about the role of outdoor art in communities? *Accept all responses that show students' understanding that it's important to have art in places other than museums in order to make it accessible to more people. Public art, such as murals, can help bring communities together.*

Analyze What effect has creating murals had on the young people of Los Angeles? *Possible answer: The murals have provided summer work and positive experiences for young people in Los Angeles. The murals have also helped them feel pride in their history and have enriched their environment.*

Synthesize How would "The War of the Wall" be different if the painter were someone like Judith Baca? *Possible answer: There probably would not have been a "war" because Judith Baca would have involved the narrator and others in the community in creating the mural instead of keeping her intentions to herself. There might still have been conflicts, but they would have been different ones.*

Focus and Motivate

OBJECTIVES

Literary Analysis
- explore the key idea of **unhappiness**
- identify and interpret symbols
- read a short story

Reading
- make inferences

Vocabulary
- build vocabulary for reading and writing
- use general context clues to understand word meaning (*also an EL language objective*)

Grammar and Writing
- use coordinating conjunctions to join sentences
- use writing to analyze literature

SUMMARY

Sixth-grader Willie Markham gives a homeless man nickels and cake and asks him about a cure for **unhappiness.** The interaction gives Willie the answer he seeks. However, when he tries to share it with his unhappy mother, she refuses to listen and has the police remove the man.

What is the cure for
UNHAPPINESS?

Before discussing the question, draw a cluster chart on the board and ask students for ideas related to **unhappiness.** Then ask them if they think there is one cure for unhappiness or several different cures. To extend the discussion, have students do the *QUICKWRITE* activity.

Selection Resources

What Do Fish Have to Do with Anything?
Short Story by Avi

What is the cure for
UNHAPPINESS?

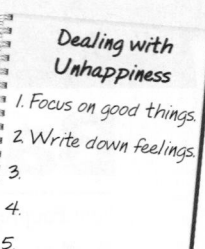

MARYLAND OBJECTIVES

READING/LIT STANDARDS
1.E.4.c Draw inferences
3.A.7.a Analyze how specific language choices contribute to meaning

KEY IDEA What helps you through sad times? Is it talking to another person? Is it listening to music by yourself? Everyone deals with **unhappiness** in his or her own way. In "What Do Fish Have to Do with Anything?" a young boy searches for a cure to the unhappiness he sees all around him.

QUICKWRITE With a partner or small group, brainstorm a list of strategies that can help people overcome unhappiness. You may use the list shown to get started. Then record the most effective strategies in your journal.

Dealing with Unhappiness
1. Focus on good things.
2. Write down feelings.
3.
4.
5.

338

Selection Resources

RESOURCE MANAGER UNIT 3

Plan and Teach pp. 67–74

Literary Analysis
Summary pp. 75†*, 76‡*
Symbol pp. 77, 78†*
Question Support p. 85*

Reading
Make Inferences pp. 79, 80†*
Reading Check p. 84
Reading Fluency p. 87

Vocabulary
Study p. 81*
Practice p. 82
Strategy p. 83

Grammar and Writing
Combine Sentences p. 86

Assessment
Selection Tests A, B/C pp. 89*, 91*
Test Generator CD

BEST PRACTICES TOOLKIT

Differentiated Instruction
pp. 31–38*

Scaffolding Instruction pp. 43–46*

Graphic Organizers/Strategies
Reciprocal Teaching • Word Questioning • Making Inferences • T Chart • Read Aloud/Think Aloud • Venn Diagram • Jigsaw • Sequence Chain/Sequence Circle

Reading Support
Audio Anthology CD*

Technology
Literature and Vocabulary Centers at **ClassZone.com**

WriteSmart CD

---

* Resources for Differentiation   † Also in Spanish   ‡ In Haitian Creole and Vietnamese

LITERARY ANALYSIS: SYMBOL

When you see a dove, do you think of peace? Many people do, because a dove is a well-known **symbol** for peace. A symbol is a person, place, or thing that stands for something beyond itself. To find symbols in a story, try the following:

- Look for people, places, things, or actions that the writer emphasizes or mentions over and over.
- Think about whether any repeated symbol might be a clue to identifying the overall **theme** of the story.
- Keep the title in mind as you read, because writers often provide clues there.

As you read "What Do Fish Have to Do with Anything?" ask yourself what is being used as a symbol.

READING SKILL: MAKE INFERENCES

An **inference** is a logical guess based on clues in the text plus your own knowledge. Making inferences about characters, what they learn, and how they change will help you understand the message of the story. As you read the story, record each inference you make about the characters in an equation such as the one shown.

Details or Evidence from Story	+	What I Know from Reading or Experience	=	Inference About Character

Review: **Compare and Contrast**

VOCABULARY IN CONTEXT

The words in column A help Avi tell his story about **unhappiness.** Match each word with the word in column B that is closest in meaning.

Column A	Column B
1. contemplate	a. unavoidably
2. inevitably	b. distracted
3. preoccupied	c. reply
4. retort	d. necessity
5. threshold	e. consider
6. urgency	f. entrance

Author Online

Early Challenges
Avi Wortis has written over 30 books for children and young adults, but he had to overcome a huge challenge to do so. As a boy, Avi had trouble spelling. But he loved reading—

Avi
born 1937

anything from comic books to histories. He later found out that he had a learning disability called dysgraphia, which caused him to reverse letters and misspell words. Although that affected his ability to write, Avi was determined to be a writer. He had no intention of giving up.

Success! Today, Avi is one of the most well-known and respected writers for young adults and has the awards to prove it. His advice to readers: "Don't be satisfied with answers others give you. Don't assume that because everyone believes a thing, it is right or wrong. Reason things out for yourself. Work to get answers on your own." Avi includes this idea in "What Do Fish Have to Do with Anything?"

Homelessness Avi's parents worked to promote civil rights and other social justice issues. As an adult, Avi has shared their concerns. His writing often addresses social problems. In this story, a homeless man plays a positive role in a young boy's life.

 MORE ABOUT THE AUTHOR
For more on Avi, visit the **Literature Center** at **ClassZone.com.**

339

Teach

LITERARY ANALYSIS

● SYMBOL

Draw a "happy face" on the board. Discuss how this image stands for something more than what it is. People recognize it as a symbol of happiness. Ask students to describe how this symbol could be changed to represent **unhappiness.** *Possible answer:* turn the smile upside down

CHECK UNDERSTANDING Ask students to identify symbols displayed in the school or classroom and explain their significance. They might start with the school mascot— often an animal considered to have admirable traits.

READING SKILL

■ MAKE INFERENCES

Discuss with students that inferences must be based on details from the story as well as on their own knowledge. Have students review the information on page 339. Ask: What detail from the text supports the inference that Avi is a hard worker? *Possible answer: He is a writer even though a learning disability makes it hard for him.*

CHECK UNDERSTANDING Ask students what kind of behavior might help them to infer that a character in a story is unhappy.

 RESOURCE MANAGER—Copy Master
Make Inferences p. 79 (for student use while reading the selection)

VOCABULARY SKILL

▲ VOCABULARY IN CONTEXT

DIAGNOSE WORD KNOWLEDGE To determine preteaching needs, have all students complete **Vocabulary in Context.** Check students' answers. (**1.** *e;* **2.** *a;* **3.** *b;* **4.** *c;* **5.** *f;* **6.** *d*)

PRETEACH VOCABULARY Use the Vocabulary Study copy master to help students determine meanings for each boldfaced word.

  1. Read the first sentence in Part A aloud, emphasizing *threshold.*

2. Point out the phrases *his mother's room* and *enter.* Elicit possible meanings for *threshold,* such as "entrance" or "doorway."

3. Have students record their definitions.

4. Repeat the procedure for items 2–6.

 RESOURCE MANAGER—Copy Master
Vocabulary Study p. 81

For general guidelines on differentiating vocabulary instruction and for alternative vocabulary activities for students not needing vocabulary preteaching, see

📦 BEST PRACTICES TOOLKIT
  Scaffolding Vocabulary Instruction
    pp. 43–46

ℹ Vocabulary Center at **ClassZone.com**
  Additional Vocabulary Activities

Practice and Apply

WHAT DO FISH HAVE TO DO WITH ANYTHING?

AVI

E very day at three o'clock Mrs. Markham waited for her son, Willie, to come out of school. They walked home together. If asked why she did it, Mrs. Markham would say, "Parents need to watch their children."

As they left the schoolyard, Mrs. Markham **inevitably** asked, "How was school?"

Willie would begin to talk, then stop. He was never sure his mother was listening. She seemed **preoccupied** with her own thoughts. She had been like that ever since his dad had abandoned them six months ago. No one knew where he'd gone. Willie had the feeling that his mother
10 was lost too. It made him feel lonely.

One Monday afternoon, as they approached the apartment building where they lived, she suddenly tugged at him. "Don't look that way," she said.

"Where?"

"At that man over there."

Willie stole a look over his shoulder. A man, whom Willie had never seen before, was sitting on a red plastic milk crate near the curb. His matted, streaky gray hair hung like a ragged curtain over his dirty face. His shoes were torn. Rough hands lay upon his knees. One hand was palm up. No one seemed to pay him any mind. Willie was certain he
20 had never seen a man so utterly alone. It was as if he were some spat-out piece of chewing gum on the pavement.

"What's the matter with him?" Willie asked his mother in a hushed voice.

Keeping her eyes straight ahead, Mrs. Markham said, "He's sick." She pulled Willie around. "Don't stare. It's rude."

"What kind of sick?"

inevitably
(ĭn-ĕv′ĭ-tə-blē) *adv.* unavoidably; without fail

preoccupied
(prē-ŏk′yə-pīd′) *adj.* lost in thought; distracted

① **Targeted Passage**

ANALYZE VISUALS
What is the first thing you notice about this image? What sense does it give you about the person?

Gregory, Los Angeles, March 31s 1982, David Hockney. Composit Polaroid, 14¹/₂″ × 13¹/₄″. Phot © David Hockney/The Davi Hockney No. 1 U.S. Trus

340 UNIT 3: UNDERSTANDING THEME

Gregory.   Los Angeles.   March 31st 1982   M.

BACKGROUND

Homelessness in America One of the characters in this story is a homeless man. In the United States, between 2.3 and 3.5 million people are homeless at some time during a year. The major causes of homelessness are poverty and the inability to obtain affordable housing. Someone earning minimum wage in the United States is unable to afford the average rent on a small apartment.

CULTURAL CONNECTION

A Global Issue Homelessness is a problem around the world. In the past decade, Japan has seen its first homeless villages spring up in public parks. Most of Japan's estimated 25,000 homeless had jobs and led stable lives until recent economic problems put them out of work.

FOR ENGLISH LEARNERS

Key Academic Vocabulary Display a Word Questioning transparency. Begin filling out the organizer for one of these academic vocabulary words: *abandoned* (line 8), *approached* (line 11), *images* (line 38), *requirements* (line 43), *portion* (lines 43, 286, 292, 293), *persisted* (lines 186, 221). Have small groups complete the organizer and create a second one for a different word.

Options for Reading Read aloud the first Targeted Passage. Discuss the characters and the conflict: Mrs. Markham is very protective of Willie and does not want him to go near the homeless man. Have students continue reading along with the *Audio Anthology CD,* or assist groups in using Reciprocal Teaching.

📋 BEST PRACTICES TOOLKIT—Transparencies
   Word Questioning p. E9
   Reciprocal Teaching p. A35

Prereading For prereading instruction for English learners, see

📋 BEST PRACTICES TOOLKIT
   Scaffolding Reading Instruction pp. 43–46

FOR ADVANCED LEARNERS/PRE–AP

Pre-AP exercises in the bottom channel provide additional challenge for your advanced students. Use them for small groups or individuals.

ADDITIONAL GUIDELINES

For more help with differentiation and tips for classroom management, see

📋 BEST PRACTICES TOOLKIT
   Differentiated Instruction pp. 31–38

A MAKE INFERENCES

Possible answer: She is strict and very sad, but she wants to take good care of Willie.

If students need help ... Display the transparency for the **Make Inferences** graphic organizer introduced on page 339. Fill in the Inference box. Then have students work in pairs to find evidence from lines 34–53 to support each inference. Have students add what they know from their own experience to the middle box.

Evidence from Story:		What I Know:		Inference:
does not let him have a bigger piece of cake; has trained him to be neat	+	people who set lots of rules are strict	=	strict

Additional entries:

- **Inference:** unhappy; **Evidence from Story:** "She was staring sadly at the cake box." (lines 55–56); **What I Know:** people who look sad are unhappy

- **Inference:** takes good care of Willie; **Evidence from Story:** cuts him a piece of cake and gives him milk, makes sure he does his homework; **What I Know:** good parents take care of their children

Extend the Discussion Why is Mrs. Markham so strict with Willie?

 BEST PRACTICES TOOLKIT—Transparency Making Inferences p. A13

As Mrs. Markham searched for an answer, she began to walk faster. "He's unhappy," she said.

"What's he doing?"

"Come on, Willie, you know perfectly well. He's begging."

30 "Do you think anyone gave him anything?"

"I don't know. Now, come on, don't look."

"Why don't you give him anything?"

"We have nothing to spare."

When they got home, Mrs. Markham removed a white cardboard box from the refrigerator. It contained pound cake. Using her thumb as a measure, she carefully cut a half-inch piece of cake and gave it to Willie on a clean plate. The plate lay on a plastic mat decorated with images of roses with diamondlike dewdrops. She also gave him a glass of milk and a folded napkin. She moved slowly.

40 Willie said, "Can I have a bigger piece of cake?"

Mrs. Markham picked up the cake box and ran a manicured pink fingernail along the nutrition information panel. "A half-inch piece is a portion, and a portion contains the following health requirements. Do you want to hear them?"

"No."

"It's on the box, so you can believe what it says. Scientists study people, then write these things. If you're smart enough you could become a scientist. Like this." Mrs. Markham tapped the box. "It pays well."

Willie ate his cake and drank the milk. When he was done he took 50 care to wipe the crumbs off his face as well as to blot his milk mustache with the napkin. His mother liked him to be neat.

His mother said, "Now go on and do your homework. Carefully. You're in sixth grade. It's important." **A**

Willie gathered up his books that lay on the empty third chair. At the kitchen entrance he paused and looked back at his mother. She was staring sadly at the cake box, but he didn't think she was seeing it. Her unhappiness made him think of the man on the street.

"What *kind* of unhappiness do you think he has?" he suddenly asked.

"Who's that?"

60 "That man."

Mrs. Markham looked puzzled.

"The begging man. The one on the street."

"Oh, could be anything," his mother said, vaguely. "A person can be unhappy for many reasons." She turned to stare out the window, as if an answer might be there.

A MAKE INFERENCES Reread lines 34–53. Judging by what Mrs. Markham says and does, how would you describe her?

DIFFERENTIATED INSTRUCTION

FOR ENGLISH LEARNERS

Background Bring in the nutrition facts from a box of cookies or a cake. Explain the kinds of data in the chart. Clarify that Mrs. Markham is following the guidelines on the box label (lines 41–44). She gives Willie exactly one portion, even though he wants a bigger piece. (A portion, or serving, is the amount one person should eat at one meal.) Discuss why these guidelines are set and how people are supposed to use them.

"Is unhappiness a sickness you can cure?"

"I wish you wouldn't ask such questions."

"Why?"

After a moment she said, "Questions that have no answers shouldn't
70 be asked."

"Can I go out?"

"Homework first."

Willie turned to go again.

"Money," Mrs. Markham suddenly said. "Money will cure a lot
of unhappiness. That's why that man was begging. A salesman once said
to me, 'Maybe you can't buy happiness, but you can rent a lot of it.'
You should remember that."

"How much money do we have?"

"Not enough."

80 "Is that why you're unhappy?"

"Willie, do your homework." **B**

Willie started to ask another question, but decided he would not get
an answer. He left the kitchen.

The apartment had three rooms. The walls were painted mint green.
Willie walked down the hallway to his room, which was at the front of
the building. By climbing up on the windowsill and pressing against the
glass he could see the sidewalk five stories below. The man was still there.

It was almost five when he went to tell his mother he had finished his
school assignments. He found her in her dim bedroom, sleeping. Since
90 she had begun working the night shift at a convenience store—two weeks
now—she took naps in the late afternoon.

For a while Willie stood on the **threshold,** hoping his mother would
wake up. When she didn't, he went to the front room and looked
down on the street again. The begging man had not moved.

Willie returned to his mother's room.

"I'm going out," he announced—softly.

Willie waited a decent interval[1] for his mother to waken. When she did
not, he made sure his keys were in his pocket. Then he left the apartment.

By standing just outside the building door, he could keep his eyes on
100 the man. It appeared as if he had still not moved. Willie wondered how
anyone could go without moving for so long in the chill October air.
Was staying still part of the man's sickness?

During the twenty minutes that Willie watched, no one who passed
looked in the beggar's direction. Willie wondered if they even saw the
man. Certainly no one put any money into his open hand.

---

1. **interval:** amount of time.

● SYMBOL
What might money
symbolize to Mrs.
Markham?

threshold (thrĕsh′ōld′) *n.*
a doorway or entrance

Line 66
REINFORCE *KEY IDEA:* UNHAPPINESS

Discuss Is **unhappiness** a sickness? Why might Willie want to believe that it is? ***Possible answers:*** *Some people might consider long-term unhappiness a sickness. Being sad makes people unable to function or interact with others as they usually do. It drains their energy. If unhappiness is a sickness, it might be curable or at least controllable. That thought gives Willie hope.*

LITERARY ANALYSIS

● SYMBOL

You might record students' answers in a list.

Possible answers:

- *happiness*
- *her husband's presence*
- *security*
- *freedom from worries*

If students need help . . . Write this sentence on the board: "If I had a lot of money, I would _____." Have students complete the sentence. Use their responses to connect what money can provide with the ideas of happiness, opportunity, freedom, power, control, and so on.

FOR LESS–PROFICIENT READERS

Reading Skill Follow-Up: Make Inferences Use Read Aloud/Think Aloud to help students infer the reason that Mrs. Markham doesn't answer Willie's question in line 80. Model: "Hmm, I know that people sometimes change the subject when they don't want to answer a question. I wonder why she doesn't want to answer Willie's question." Invite students to use their own experience and story clues to infer the reason. *(Possible answer: She may feel embarrassed about being unhappy and may not want to let Willie know.)*

 BEST PRACTICES TOOLKIT—Transparency
Read Aloud/Think Aloud p. A34

FOR ADVANCED LEARNERS/PRE–AP

Make Judgments Discuss the meaning of the salesman's comment repeated by Mrs. Markham in line 76. Have students decide whether they agree or disagree with it. Ask students to support their opinions with evidence from the text and their own observations. Have students hold a short, informal debate on the topic.

A lady leading a dog by a leash went by. The dog strained in the direction of the man sitting on the crate. His tail wagged. The lady pulled the dog away. "Heel!" she commanded.

The dog—tail between his legs—scampered to the lady's side. Even so,
110 the dog twisted around to look back at the beggar.

Willie grinned. The dog had done exactly what Willie had done when his mother told him not to stare.

Pressing deep into his pocket, Willie found a nickel. It was warm and slippery. He wondered how much happiness you could rent for a nickel.

Squeezing the nickel between his fingers, Willie walked slowly toward the man. When he came before him, he stopped, suddenly nervous. The man, who appeared to be looking at the ground, did not move his eyes. He smelled bad.

"Here." Willie stretched forward and dropped the coin into the man's
120 open right hand. **C**

"God bless you," the man said hoarsely as he folded his fingers over the coin. His eyes, like high beams on a car, flashed up at Willie, then dropped.

Willie waited for a moment, then went back up to his room. From his window he looked down on the street. He thought he saw the coin in the man's hand, but was not sure.

2 Targeted Passage

C MAKE INFERENCES
Reread lines 113–120. What does Willie's action tell you about his **character**?

After supper Mrs. Markham readied herself to go to work, then kissed Willie good night. As she did every night, she said, "If you have regular problems, call Mrs. Murphy downstairs. What's her number?"

"274-8676," Willie said.
130 "Extra bad problems, call Grandma."

"369-6754."

"Super special problems, you can call me."

"962-6743."

"Emergency, the police."

"911."

"Lay out your morning clothing."

"I will."

"Don't let anyone in the door."

"I won't."
140 "No television past nine."

"I know."

"But you can read late."

"You're the one who's going to be late," Willie reminded her.

"I'm leaving," Mrs. Markham said.

After she went, Willie stood for a long while in the hallway. The empty apartment felt like a cave that lay deep below the earth. That day in school Willie's teacher had told the class about a kind of fish that lived

---

READING SKILL

C MAKE INFERENCES

Remind students to fill in their inferences about Willie in a chart similar to the one on page 339.

Possible answers:

Evidence from Story:		What I know:		Inference:
Willie gives the man his only nickel.	+	It is hard to give away money when you do not have very much.	=	Willie is caring and wants to help the homeless man.

Lines 145–156
DISCUSSION PROMPTS

Use these prompts to help students understand the importance of the blind fish to Willie:

Connect How do people feel when the lights go out and it is too dark to see? *Possible answer: They may feel helpless, floundering, uncertain, and scared.*

Apply How does Willie feel when he thinks about the blind fish? Why? *Possible answer: His question to the teacher suggests that Willie is disturbed by the idea of these blind fish. He sees a parallel between his mother and himself and these fish.*

Synthesize What answer does Willie want from the teacher about whether the eyes of the fish will return? Why? *Possible answer: He wants to hear that once the fish emerge into the light, their eyes return. He wants to believe that the darkness, or sadness, that he and his mother experience will not follow them when things get better.*

DIFFERENTIATED INSTRUCTION

FOR LESS–PROFICIENT READERS
2 Targeted Passage [Lines 113–125]

This passage shows an important turning point in the story: Willie's first encounter with the homeless man.

- How does Willie feel as he gets closer to the man?
- Why does Willie give the man a nickel?
- How does the man respond when Willie puts the nickel in his hand?

FOR ENGLISH LEARNERS
Language: Conversational English Patterns
Read lines 127–144 aloud. Point out that when people speak informally, they don't always use complete sentences. Explain what Mrs. Markham is doing in this part of the story. Have students discuss why she asks Willie these same questions each night.

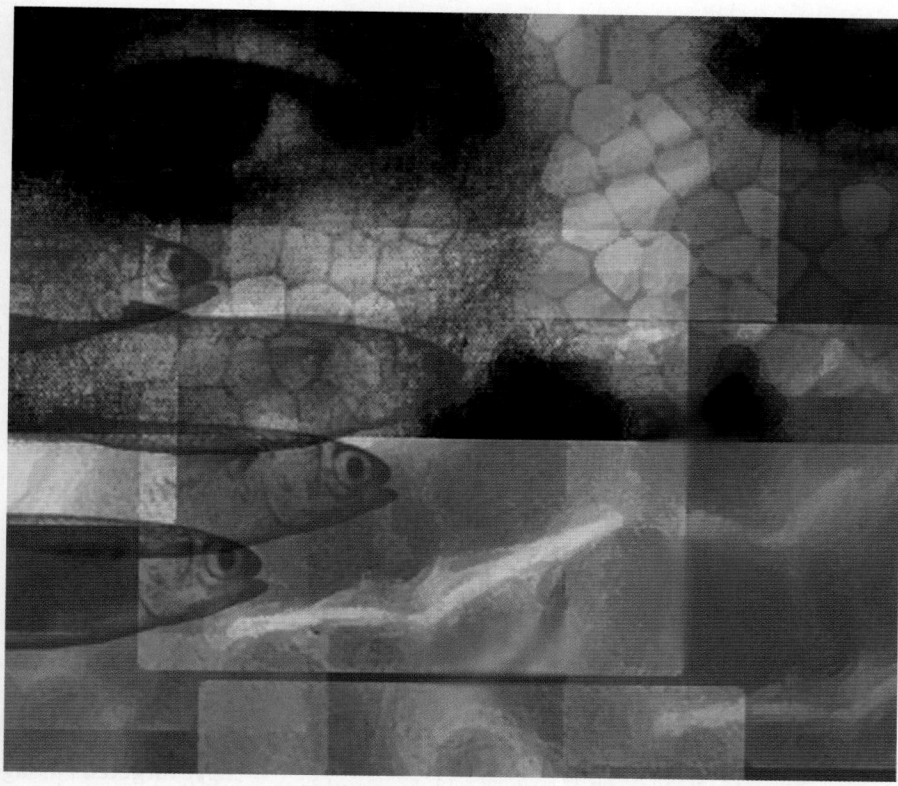

At the Aquarium (2003), Jim Macbeth. Digital collage. Photo © Jim Macbeth/SuperStock.

in caves. These fish could not see. They had no eyes. The teacher had said it was living in the dark cave that made them like that.

Willie had raised his hand and asked, "If they want to get out of the cave, can they?"

"I suppose."

"Would their eyes come back?"

"Good question," she said, but did not give an answer. **D**

Before he went to bed, Willie took another look out the window. In the pool of light cast by the street lamp, Willie saw the man.

On Tuesday morning when Willie went to school, the man was gone. But when he came home from school with his mother, he was there again.

"*Please* don't look at him," his mother whispered with some **urgency.**

During his snack, Willie said, "Why shouldn't I look?"

"What are you talking about?"

ANALYZE VISUALS
How do the details in this image connect with the story?

D SYMBOL
Reread lines 145–154. What makes Willie think of the story about the fish with no eyes?

urgency (ûr′jən-sē) *n.* a condition of pressing importance; necessity

ANALYZE VISUALS

Possible answer: Eyes are featured prominently in this image: several fish with large, round eyes seem to be swimming past the eyes of a human face. These fish, unlike the ones Willie learned about, can see. However, it is questionable whether the human and the fish really see each other clearly.

About the Art The artist Jim Macbeth began his career as a fisheries biologist. Many of his works feature fish, freshly caught and digitally scanned. To create a multi-layered effect, he combines these fish images with various artifacts and backgrounds.

LITERARY ANALYSIS

D SYMBOL

Possible answer: The dark, empty apartment feels like a cave, which is the habitat of the sightless fish.

If students need help... Discuss how even an apartment high above the street can feel like a cave beneath the earth. Depending on one's viewpoint, the hollow sense of emptiness can be the same in both places.

FOR ADVANCED LEARNERS/PRE–AP

Draw Conclusions Pose these questions: *Who can truly see in the story? Who cannot?* Have students work independently to trace the references to light/darkness and eyes/sight throughout the story. Have them use a chart to keep track of characters associated with each image. (See sample chart at right.) Then ask students to regroup and discuss the questions. Encourage them to use details from their charts to support their answers.

Mrs. Markham	Willie	Homeless man
Line 23: Mrs. Markham keeps her eyes straight ahead when they walk past the homeless man.	Lines 99–105: Willie keeps his eye on the man and watches him carefully.	Line 122: "His eyes, like high beams on a car, flashed up at Willie."
Lines 55–57: She stares sadly at the cake but doesn't really see it.		
Line 89: She sleeps in a dim room.		

DISCUSSION PROMPTS

Use these prompts to help students understand Mrs. Markham's character:

Connect Have you noticed that people interact differently with other people on days when they feel unhappy? Do you think it is embarrassing for most people to be unhappy? *Students may say that when people are unhappy they may be impatient with other people. Some people may feel embarrassed to show their unhappiness.*

Analyze Why does Mrs. Markham believe that people are ashamed of being unhappy? *Possible answers: She is ashamed of the situation that has led to her unhappiness. She feels she is somehow to blame for her unhappiness.*

Synthesize Why do you think Mrs. Markham is sometimes reluctant to answer Willie's questions about unhappiness? *Possible answers: Speaking about unhappiness makes her uneasy. She may want to hide her unhappiness from Willie, but his questions make her realize that she cannot. His questions also force her to think about a painful subject that she would rather not remember.*

Line 195
REINFORCE *KEY IDEA:* UNHAPPINESS

Discuss What will happen if Mrs. Markham never thinks about her **unhappiness**? *Possible answer: It may be harder for her to come to terms with her feelings or move past them.*

LITERARY ANALYSIS

E SYMBOL

Possible answer: The fish have no eyes because they live in a dark cave. Willie and his mother have had a lot of darkness (sadness) in their lives since Dad left, and Mrs. Markham has become "blind" (unwilling to look at problems). Willie does not want to be blind to the world around him, so he asks a lot of questions. He wishes his mother would remember how to "see," too.

Extend the Discussion What does Willie fear might happen to his mother and himself?

"That man. On the street. Begging."

"I told you. He's sick. It's better to act as if you never saw him. When people are that way they don't wish to be looked at."

"Why not?"

Mrs. Markham pondered for a little while. "People are ashamed of being unhappy."

Willie looked thoughtfully at his mother. "Are you sure he's unhappy?"

"You don't have to ask if people are unhappy. They tell you all the time."

170 "How?"

"The way they look."

"Is that part of the sickness?"

"Oh, Willie, I don't know. It's just the way they are."

Willie **contemplated** the half-inch slice of cake his mother had just given him. A year ago his parents seemed to be perfectly happy. For Willie, the world seemed easy, full of light. Then his father lost his job. He tried to get another but could not. For long hours he sat in dark rooms. Sometimes he drank. His parents began to argue a lot. One day, his father was gone.

180 For two weeks his mother kept to the dark. And wept.

Willie looked at his mother. "You're unhappy," he said. "Are *you* ashamed?"

Mrs. Markham sighed and closed her eyes. "I wish you wouldn't ask that."

"Why?"

"It hurts me."

"But are you ashamed?" Willie persisted.

He felt it was urgent that he know. So that he could do something. She only shook her head.

Willie said, "Do you think Dad might come back?"

190 She hesitated before saying, "Yes, I think so."

Willie wondered if that was what she really thought.

"Do you think Dad is unhappy?" Willie asked.

"Where do you get such questions?"

"They're in my mind."

"There's much in the mind that need not be paid attention to."

"Fish who live in caves have no eyes."

"What are you talking about?"

"My teacher said it's all that darkness. The fish forget how to see. So they lose their eyes." **E**

200 "I doubt she said that."

"She did."

"Willie, you have too much imagination."

contemplate
(kŏn'təm-plāt') *v.* to consider carefully and at length

3 Targeted Passage

E SYMBOL
Reread lines 189–199. What is the connection between the questions Willie is asking his mother and the story about the fish?

DIFFERENTIATED INSTRUCTION

FOR LESS–PROFICIENT READERS

3 Targeted Passage [Lines 174–191]

This passage identifies the underlying cause for the story characters' unhappiness: the fact that Willie's father left his family behind.

- Why did Willie's father leave his family?
- How does Willie's mother react to her husband's leaving?
- Is Willie's mother honest with Willie?

FOR ENGLISH LEARNERS

Comprehension: Transitions Point out that the action in lines 174–180 jumps to the past. This is called a *flashback.* In line 174, Willie is thinking about the cake his mother just gave him. Then he starts thinking about his past family life. The phrase *A year ago* (line 175) signals the shift. Have students find other time words in this passage (*Then, For long hours, Sometimes, One day, For two weeks*) and tell where the story returns to the present (*line 181*).

After his mother went to work, Willie gazed down onto the street. The man was there. Willie thought of going down, but he knew he was not supposed to leave the building when his mother worked at night. He decided to speak to the man the next day.

That afternoon—Wednesday—Willie stood before the man. "I don't have any money," Willie said. "Can I still talk to you?"

The man lifted his face. It was a dirty face with very tired eyes.
10 He needed a shave.

"My mother," Willie began, "said you were unhappy. Is that true?"

"Could be," the man said.

"What are you unhappy about?"

The man's eyes narrowed as he studied Willie intently. He said, "How come you want to know?"

ANALYZE VISUALS
Compare this man with how you picture the man in the story.

FOR ADVANCED LEARNERS/PRE–AP

Infer Feelings and Meaning Have students read the dialogue between Willie and his mother in lines 162–202. Point out that Mrs. Markham often gives answers that are evasive—avoiding the point. Ask students to work in pairs to rewrite Mrs. Markham's part of the dialogue so she says directly what she means. Then have them reread their new dialogues aloud. Provide clarification if students disagree about what Mrs. Markham was really thinking.

ANALYZE VISUALS

Possible answer:

Man in Story	Both	Man in Picture
• Line 17: shaggy gray hair • Line 18: poor and ragged	• Line 16: sitting outdoors • Line 20: appear lonely • Line 117: avoid eye contact	• balding • neatly dressed

DISCUSSION PROMPTS

Use these prompts to help students understand the interaction between Willie and the homeless man:

Connect How might you feel if a stranger asked you the kinds of questions Willie is asking the man? *Students might say that they would feel defensive or irritated. Some might say they would feel curious or interested.*

Analyze Why does the homeless man finally start talking with Willie? *Possible answer: He begins to trust Willie. He thinks Willie is sincere in the questions he is asking.*

Evaluate Do you think this man is a good source of advice for Willie? Explain. *Possible answers:*

- *No; if the homeless man knew the cure for unhappiness, he would not still be unhappy.*

- *Yes; he is an expert on unhappiness and has probably learned a lot through his experiences. Even if he cannot cure his own unhappiness, his insights might be helpful to Willie.*

Willie shrugged.

"I think you should go home, kid."

"I am home." Willie gestured toward the apartment. "I live right here. Fifth floor. Where do you live?"

220 "Around."

"*Are* you unhappy?" Willie persisted.

The man ran a tongue over his lips. His Adam's apple bobbed. "A man has the right to remain silent," he said, and closed his eyes.

Willie remained standing on the pavement for a while before retreating back to his apartment. Once inside he looked down from the window. The man was still there. For a moment Willie was certain the man was looking at the apartment building and the floor where Willie lived.

The next day, Thursday—after dropping a nickel in the man's palm—Willie said, "I've never seen anyone look so unhappy as you do.

230 So I figure you must know a lot about it."

The man took a deep breath. "Well, yeah, maybe."

Willie said, "And I need to find a cure for it."

"A *what?*"

"A cure for unhappiness."

The man pursed his cracked lips and blew a silent whistle. Then he said, "Why?"

"My mother is unhappy."

"Why's that?"

"My dad went away."

240 "How come?"

"I think because he was unhappy. Now my mother's unhappy too—all the time. So if I found a cure for unhappiness, it would be a good thing, wouldn't it?"

"I suppose. Hey, you don't have anything to eat on you, do you?"

Willie shook his head, then said, "Would you like some cake?"

"What kind?"

"I don't know. Cake."

"Depends on the cake."

On Friday Willie said to the man, "I found out what kind of cake it is."

250 "Yeah?"

"Pound cake. But I don't know why it's called that."

"Long as it's cake it probably don't matter."

Neither spoke. Then Willie said, "In school my teacher said there are fish who live in caves and the caves are so dark the fish don't have eyes. What do you think? Do you believe that?"

"Sure."

"You do? How come?"

"Because you said so."

DIFFERENTIATED INSTRUCTION

FOR LESS–PROFICIENT READERS

Make Inferences Readers get clues about characters by studying their looks, words, and actions. Have students reread lines 218–237 to pick up clues about the homeless man. Ask them these questions to guide their inferential thinking:

- **Looks/Actions** Why do you think the homeless man closes his eyes (line 223)? *(Possible answer: It's his way of saying, Stop—don't ask me any more questions.)*

- **Actions** What action leads you to think that the homeless man is curious about Willie after he leaves? *(He looks up at Willie's apartment in lines 226–227.)*

- **Words** Why does the homeless man speak with emphasis in line 233? *(He is surprised at Willie's question.)*

- **Actions** What might the man be "saying" by blowing a "silent whistle" in line 235? *(Possible answer: Whoa, that's a big, complex question!)*

FOR ENGLISH LEARNERS

Language: Idioms Help students use context clues to figure out the meanings of these idioms from the story:

- Line 240: "How come?" (*"Why?"*)

- Line 244: "have anything to eat on you?" (*"Are you carrying any food?"*)

- Line 289: "Hold it!" (*"Stop!"*)

"You mean, just because someone *said* it you believe it?"

60 "Not someone. You." **F**

Willie was puzzled. "But, well, maybe it *isn't* true."

The man grunted. "Hey, do you believe it?"

Willie nodded.

"Well, you're not just anyone. You got eyes. You see. You ain't no fish."

"Oh." Willie was pleased.

"What's your name?" the man asked.

"Willie."

"That's a boy's name. What's your grown-up name?"

"William."

70 "And that means another thing."

"What?"

"I'll take some of that cake."

Willie started.[2] "You will?" he asked, surprised.

"Just said it, didn't I?"

Willie suddenly felt excited. It was as if the man had given him a gift. Willie wasn't sure what it was except that it was important and he was glad to have it. For a moment he just gazed at the man. He saw the lines on the man's face, the way his lips curved, the small scar on the side of his chin, the shape of his eyes, which he now saw were blue. **G**

80 "I'll get the cake," Willie cried and ran back to the apartment. He snatched the box from the refrigerator as well as a knife, then hurried back down to the street. "I'll cut you a piece," he said, and he opened the box.

"Hey, that don't look like a pound of cake," the man said.

Willie, alarmed, looked up.

"But like I told you, it don't matter."

Willie held his thumb against the cake to make sure the portion was the right size. With a poke of the knife he made a small mark for the proper width.

Just as he was about to cut, the man said, "Hold it!"

90 Willie looked up. "What?"

"What were you doing there with your thumb?"

"I was measuring the size. The right portion. A person is supposed to get only one portion."

"Where'd you learn that?"

"It says so on the box. You can see for yourself." He held out the box.

The man studied the box then handed it back to Willie. "That's just lies," he said.

"How do you know?"

"William, how can a box say how much a person needs?"

---

2. **started:** jumped or gave a sudden jerk in surprise.

F COMPARE AND CONTRAST
Why do you think the man believes Willie but his own mother doesn't? How are the man and the mother different?

G MAKE INFERENCES
Reread lines 275–279. What "gift" has the man given Willie?

READING SKILL: *Review*

F COMPARE AND CONTRAST

Possible answers: Mrs. Markham is so unhappy that she has no energy to discuss Willie's ideas about the fish. Willie has been kind to the man, so the man trusts him (lines 259–265). The man also sees Willie more objectively, as an honest and curious person. Willie's mother sees him only as a child she must protect (lines 266–269).

READING SKILL

G MAKE INFERENCES

Possible answer: By accepting the cake, the man has broken through his usual wall of suspicion and has allowed Willie to share a friendly moment with him. The man's trust feels like a gift to Willie.

If students need help ... Ask them how they might feel after someone who has been shutting people out suddenly opens up to a friendly gesture. Relate their feelings to Willie's.

Lines 266–279
DISCUSSION PROMPTS

Use these prompts to help students understand how Willie is affected by his conversation with the man:

Connect Would you feel more adult if people called you by your "grown-up" name instead of a nickname? What other things make you feel more adult? *Students may say using a grown-up name, being allowed to voice opinions, and making their own decisions makes them feel like an adult.*

Apply How might seeing himself as a grown-up help Willie cope with his situation at home? *Possible answers: He might feel more self-confident and more sure of his ability to understand and solve problems.*

Synthesize What is significant about the way Willie looks at the man in lines 277–279? *Possible answer: Willie takes the time to really look at the man. He sees him as a person with value, not someone to be ignored or hurried past. Willie proves that he "ain't no fish" (line 264) because he truly sees the man.*

FOR LESS–PROFICIENT READERS

Review Compare and Contrast Discuss how finding similarities and differences between characters can help readers understand each character and the author's purpose more fully. Have students work together to complete a Venn diagram to compare and contrast several aspects of Mrs. Markham and the homeless man.

 BEST PRACTICES TOOLKIT—Transparency
Venn Diagram p. A26

FOR ENGLISH LEARNERS

Language: Conversational English Patterns
Point out that the word *Do* is left off of the beginning of the sentence "You mean, just because someone *said* it you believe it?" (line 259). Explain that in dialogue, words are often left out but are understood. Have mixed language-ability Jigsaw groups study the dialogue in the rest of the story, fill in missing words, and report back to the class.

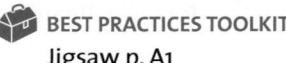 **BEST PRACTICES TOOLKIT**
Jigsaw p. A1

Celia, Los Angeles, April 10th, 1982, David Hockney. Composite Polaroid, 18″ × 30″. Photo © David Hockney/The David Hockney No. 1 U.S. Trust.

DIFFERENTIATED INSTRUCTION

FOR ADVANCED LEARNERS/PRE–AP

Synthesize Discuss how Avi uses similes to convey both physical and emotional impressions of his characters. Ask what the simile in lines 20–21, "as if he were some spat-out piece of chewing gum on the pavement," says about the homeless man. *(He is emotionally isolated and physically broken down.)* Have students write two similes to describe the physical and emotional state of a character at some point in the story. Ask them to share their examples.

"But it does. The scientists say so. They measured, so they know. Then they put it there."

"Lies," the man repeated.

Willie began to feel that this man knew many things. "Well, then, how much should I cut?" he asked.

The man said, "You have to look at me, then at the cake, and then you're going to have to decide for yourself."

"Oh." Willie looked at the cake. The piece was about three inches wide. Willie looked up at the man. After a moment he cut the cake into two pieces, each an inch and a half wide. He gave one piece to the man and kept the other in the box.

"God bless you," the man said as he took the piece and laid it in his left hand. He began to break off pieces with his right hand and put them in his mouth one by one. Each piece was chewed thoughtfully. Willie watched him eat.

When the man was done, he licked the crumbs on his fingers.

"Now I'll give you something," the man said.

"What?" Willie said, surprised.

"The cure for unhappiness."

"You know it?" Willie asked, eyes wide.

The man nodded.

"What is it?"

"It's this: What a person needs is always more than they say."

"Who's *they?*" Willie asked.

The man pointed to the cake box. "The people on the box," he said.

In his mind Willie repeated what he had been told, then he gave the man the second piece of cake.

The man took it, saying, "Good man," and he ate it.

Willie grinned.

The next day was Saturday. Willie did not go to school. All morning he kept looking down from his window for the man, but it was raining and he did not appear. Willie wondered where he was, but could not imagine it.

Willie's mother woke about noon. Willie sat with her while she ate her breakfast. "I found the cure for unhappiness," he announced.

"Did you?" his mother said. She was reading a memo from the convenience store's owner.

"It's 'What a person needs is always more than they say.'"

His mother put her papers down. "That's nonsense. Where did you hear that?"

ANALYZE VISUALS
Compare the image on page 350 with the one on page 341. What similarities and differences do you see?

FOR ENGLISH LEARNERS

Language: Pronoun Referents Explain that the pronoun *it* in line 300 refers to the box mentioned in the previous sentence, and *they* refers to the scientists. Remind students to look back to previous sentences if the referent to a pronoun is unclear. Have students work in mixed-ability groups to identify referents for the pronouns in lines 319 and 337.

Lines 300–310
DISCUSSION PROMPTS

Use these prompts to help students understand the symbolism in the story:

Connect How much cake would you have given to the man? Why? *Students may say that they would have given him all the cake because he appeared very hungry.*

Analyze What does the cake symbolize? *Possible answers: Willie's compassion; Willie's initiative; Willie's insight*

Synthesize Why is Willie's decision about how much cake to give the man important? *Possible answers: He begins to think for himself instead of being guided by the opinions of others. He shows that he is willing to break the unwritten rules in order to help a fellow human being.*

Lines 318–324
REINFORCE *KEY IDEA*:
UNHAPPINESS

Discuss What is the cure for **unhappiness,** according to the homeless man? What does this statement mean? *Possible answers: The man says that what a person needs is always more than "they" say (line 322). Experts do not know what makes a person happy. Giving love, compassion, or help might cure the unhappiness of another.*

ANALYZE VISUALS

Possible answer: Both images are connected and divided by a grid of lines, suggesting the multiple dimensions of people. Both subjects look pensive and appear to be gazing at something in the distance.

About the Art This photo collage, *Celia, Los Angeles, April 10th, 1982,* is one of Hockney's earliest efforts. He used a Polaroid camera for his first photo collages, which he called "joiners." Even with this relatively simple camera, Hockney is able to suggest strong emotion in this composition, just as Avi uses words and mental images to show the complexity of his characters' feelings.

"That man."

"What man?"

"On the street. The one who was begging. You said he was unhappy. So I asked him."

"Willie, I told you I didn't want you to even look at that man."

"He's a nice man. . . ."

"How do you know?"

"I've talked to him."

"When? How much?"

Willie shrank down. "I did, that's all."

350 "Willie, I forbid you to talk to him. Do you understand me? Do you? Answer me!" She was shrill.

"Yes," Willie said, but he'd already decided he would talk to the man one more time. He needed to explain why he could not talk to him anymore.

On Sunday, however, the man was not there. Nor was he there on Monday.

"That man is gone," Willie said to his mother as they walked home from school.

"I saw. I'm not blind."

"Where do you think he went?"

360 "I couldn't care less. But you might as well know, I arranged for him to be gone."

Willie stopped short. "What do you mean?"

"I called the police. We don't need a nuisance³ like that around here. Pestering kids."

"He wasn't pestering me."

"Of course he was."

"How do you know?"

"Willie, I have eyes. I can see."

Willie glared at his mother. "No, you can't. You're a fish. You live 370 in a cave." Ⓗ

"Fish?" **retorted** Mrs. Markham. "What do fish have to do with anything? Willie, don't talk nonsense."

"My name isn't Willie. It's William. And I know how to keep from being unhappy. I do!" He was yelling now. "What a person needs is always more than they say! *Always!*" Ⓘ

He turned on his heel and walked back toward the school. At the corner he glanced back. His mother was following. He kept going. She kept following. ✎

④ **Targeted Passage**

Ⓗ **SYMBOL**
Reread lines 356–370. Why does Willie compare his mother to the fish living in the cave?

retort (rĭ-tôrt′) *v.* to reply sharply

Ⓘ **MAKE INFERENCES**
Reread lines 373–375. Why does Willie now insist that his name is William, not Willie?

---

3. **nuisance:** someone who is bothersome.

LITERARY ANALYSIS

Ⓗ SYMBOL

Possible answer: The cave fish cannot see. Willie thinks that his mother is like the cave fish because she is blind to the feelings of others, such as the homeless man.

READING SKILL

Ⓘ MAKE INFERENCES

Possible answer: Willie feels that he has grown up a lot and wants to be called by his grown-up name now. The homeless man called him William.

SELECTION WRAP–UP

REFLECT Have students think about the changes in Willie throughout the story. In what ways has he grown? What important truths has he come to realize by the end of the story?

⭐ **CRITIQUE** Ask students to evaluate how the author ended this story. Have them discuss why the story ends in this way and what it means.

READING FLUENCY

Distribute the copy masters and have students work in pairs to practice fluency.

Ⓡ **RESOURCE MANAGER—Copy Master**
Reading Fluency p. 87

DIFFERENTIATED INSTRUCTION

FOR LESS–PROFICIENT READERS

④ **Targeted Passage [Lines 363–378]**

This passage resolves the story's plot and helps show how Willie has changed.

- What has Willie's mother done?
- How does Willie feel about his mother's action?
- How does the end of the story differ from the way the story began?
- What is Willie trying to show his mother by walking away from her?

FOR ADVANCED LEARNERS/PRE–AP

Predict Ask students if they see the incident at the end of the story as a turning point in Willie's relationship with his mother. Have them predict how Willie will interact with his mother from this point on.

Comprehension

1. **Recall** What do Willie and his class learn about a certain kind of fish that lives in caves?

2. **Recall** What does Willie's mother say is wrong with the homeless man?

3. **Retell** Use your own words to retell how the story ends.

MARYLAND OBJECTIVES

LITERATURE STANDARD
3.A.7.a Analyze how specific language choices contribute to meaning

Literary Analysis

4. **Interpret Symbols** The type of fish with no eyes is mentioned many times in this story. What do you think it symbolizes? Now reread lines 34–48 and 286–310. What do you think the pound cake symbolizes?

5. **Make Inferences** Look over the equations you created as you read. What inferences did you make about the **characters** in the story?

6. **Compare and Contrast Characters** The two people in the story who have the greatest influence on Willie are his mom and the homeless man. Compare and contrast how these two characters try to help Willie.

7. **Analyze Theme** Use a chart to help you identify clues the writer provides about the theme of the story. What do you think the theme is?

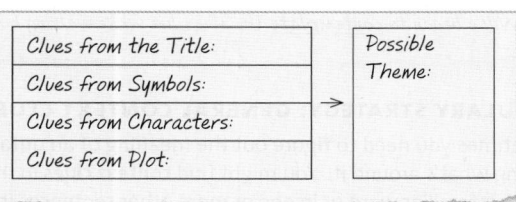

Clues from the Title:		Possible Theme:
Clues from Symbols:	→	
Clues from Characters:		
Clues from Plot:		

8. **Evaluate** Willie's mother says, "Parents need to watch their children." Given what you know about her character, do you think she was right or wrong to call the police about the man?

Extension and Challenge

9. **Big Question Activity** Suppose Willie came to you for a cure for **unhappiness.** Using what you learned about Willie, what advice would you give him? Try giving him advice on specific areas in his life, such as his dad's leaving or his mom's lack of "seeing." Use examples from the story to explain your suggestions. Present your advice to the class.

10. **SOCIAL STUDIES CONNECTION** Find out about organizations and volunteer programs in your community or a nearby city that help people who are homeless or living in poverty. Call or write to one of these organizations to ask for more information about what they do and how young people can help.

6. *His mother tries to help Willie by taking good physical care of him. She makes sure that he is well fed, does his homework, and is safe. The man helps Willie by listening to him and answering his questions.*

7. *Charts will vary. One theme is that people should not be so focused on themselves that they become blind to the needs of others.*

8. *Some students may say that she was right to follow her own principles of how to keep Willie safe. The homeless man was a stranger and the mother did not know if he was dangerous or not. Other students may* say that she was wrong to call the police without talking to Willie first. She assumes the man is "pestering" Willie, when he is actually helping Willie.

Extension and Challenge

9. *Students' responses should show their understanding of Willie and his mother and should include specific references to the text.*

10. **SOCIAL STUDIES CONNECTION** *Students may find it helpful to work with a librarian to locate directories of social service organizations.*

Practice and Apply

After Reading

For additional support of post-reading questions, use these copy masters:

RESOURCE MANA E R Copy Masters

Reading Check p. 84 (to check understanding of the selection)

Symbol p. 77 (for practice of literary analysis standards focus)

Question Support p. 85 (**After Reading** questions adapted for English learners and less-proficient readers)

Additional selection questions are provided for teachers on page 71.

For additional activities to challenge students, see

Power Thinking at Class one.com

ANSWERS

Comprehension

1. *Willie's class learns that these fish have no eyes. The fish have lost their eyes because of living in total darkness.*

2. *Willie's mother says that the man is sick.*

3. *Paraphrases will vary. Willie finds out that his mother called the police to move the man. Willie is so angry that he tells her she is just like the blind fish. The two argue, and Willie turns to go back to school. His mother follows him.*

Literary Analysis

Possible answers:

4. ● **STANDARDS FOCUS Symbol** *The fish are a symbol for people who are so focused on the sad things in their own lives that they become blind to the needs of others. The cake symbolizes sharing and taking care of other people's needs.*

5. ■ **STANDARDS FOCUS Make Inferences** *Mrs. Markham is too unhappy to see what her son needs. She uses routine to control her unhappiness. Willie is kind, generous, and compassionate. He wants to emerge from the darkness that he and his mother live in. The homeless man is insightful. His eyes have seen a lot of life, and he has learned from experience.*

Vocabulary in Context

VOCABULARY PRACTICE

1. *true*
2. *false*
3. *true*
4. *false*
5. *false*
6. *true*

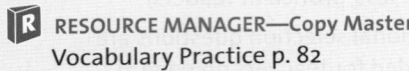 **RESOURCE MANAGER—Copy Master**
Vocabulary Practice p. 82

VOCABULARY IN WRITING

Before writing their paragraphs, students can use Sequence Chains/Sequence Circles to identify the specific events through which Willie comes to know the homeless man.

 BEST PRACTICES TOOLKIT—Transparency
Sequence Chain/Sequence Circle p. B21

VOCABULARY STRATEGY: GENERAL CONTEXT CLUES *(also an EL language objective)*

Context clues may appear before or after an unfamiliar word. Remind students that a context clue might restate the meaning of the word or even be a synonym for the word.

Answers:
1. *small fishing boat*
2. *able to make errors*
3. *calm down; make less angry*
4. *people who contribute generously to charities and other worthy groups*
5. *the study of stamps*

 RESOURCE MANAGER—Copy Master
Vocabulary Strategy p. 83

ⓘ Vocabulary Center at **ClassZone.com**
Additional Vocabulary Activities

Vocabulary in Context

VOCABULARY PRACTICE

Choose *true* or *false* for each statement.

1. If something happens **inevitably,** there is probably no way to avoid it.
2. A **preoccupied** person is one who lives in a house that was previously occupied.
3. A **threshold** can be found at the front of a house.
4. A person walking slowly communicates a feeling of **urgency.**
5. People who **contemplate** art tend to have little respect for culture.
6. If someone **retorts,** he or she is probably irritated or impatient.

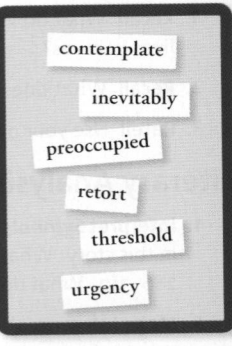

VOCABULARY IN WRITING

Using two or more vocabulary words, write a paragraph explaining how Willie came to know the man on the street. You might start like this.

> **EXAMPLE SENTENCE**
>
> *Willie began to **contemplate** the man's life while walking home.*

VOCABULARY STRATEGY: GENERAL CONTEXT CLUES

Sometimes you need to figure out the meaning of an unfamiliar word by reading what's around it. You might find **context clues** in the same sentence as the unfamiliar word or in one or more other sentences in the paragraph. For example, a clue to the meaning of *preoccupied* in this story comes in the previous sentence, which says that Willie "was never sure his mother was listening." From this, we know she is often lost in thought, or preoccupied.

PRACTICE Use context clues to determine the definition of each boldfaced word. Then write its definition.

1. Tossing about on their **skiff** in open waters, the passengers got drenched by the thunderstorm.
2. Lola actually made a mistake in counting the election results. She showed that she is **fallible** after all.
3. Mom could not **placate** Peter, no matter how hard she tried. He was determined to remain angry.
4. Wealthy **philanthropists** contribute large sums to charities.
5. Tobias became interested in **philately** once he saw my stamp collection.

MARYLAND OBJECTIVES

READING STANDARD
1.D.3.a Use context to determine the meanings of words

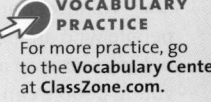
VOCABULARY PRACTICE
For more practice, go to the **Vocabulary Center** at **ClassZone.com.**

DIFFERENTIATED INSTRUCTION

FOR LESS—PROFICIENT READERS

Write Context Sentences Have students write an original sentence for each of the vocabulary words. Ask students to include context clues in their sentences. For example, *Zara was so preoccupied and lost in thought that she did not hear the bell ring.* Have students exchange papers and identify the context clues in each other's sentences.

FOR ENGLISH LEARNERS

Vocabulary Strategy Tell students that if they do not understand a word, they should continue reading. Often the word's meaning will become clear as they read on.

1. Have students identify unfamiliar words from the short story.
2. Assign pairs of students one or two words to define with context clues.
3. Have students share their definitions and explain the clues that helped them.

Reading-Writing Connection

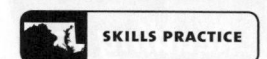

Demonstrate your understanding of "What Do Fish Have to Do with Anything?" by responding to these prompts. Then complete the **Grammar and Writing** exercise.

WRITING PROMPTS

A. Short Response: Write a Letter
Even though Willie might never see the homeless man again, their brief relationship has made a huge difference in Willie's life. Write a **one-paragraph letter** in which Willie thanks the man for all he did for him.

SELF-CHECK

A well-written letter will . . .
- clearly explain why Willie is thanking the man
- use details from the story to clarify his reasons

B. Extended Response: Evaluate a Symbol
On page 339, you learned that writers often use symbols to help them support ideas they want to share with their readers. Avi chose the fish with no eyes as his main symbol in this story. How does this symbol relate to the idea of **unhappiness?** Write a **two- or three-paragraph response.**

A strong response will . . .
- include a clear position statement
- use examples from the story to support this position

GRAMMAR AND WRITING

COMBINE SENTENCES You can avoid choppy writing by combining two or more short sentences into one. Use the **coordinating conjunction** *and, but, or, nor, yet, so,* or *for* to join sentences that relate to the same topic. Remember to always put a comma before the coordinating conjunction.

 **MARYLAND OBJECTIVES**

LANGUAGE STANDARD
5.A.2.d Compose compound sentences

> *Original:* You were friendly. I liked talking to you.
>
> *Revised:* You were friendly, and I liked talking to you.

PRACTICE Join these sentences by using the correct coordinating conjunctions.

1. You listened to me. You answered my questions.
2. My mom didn't want me to talk to you. I did it anyway.
3. I wanted you to stick around. My mom sent you away.
4. You could come back to stay for good. You could just come for a visit.
5. I miss my conversations with you. I want you to come back.

For more help with coordinating conjunctions, see page R47 in the Grammar Handbook.

FOR LESS–PROFICIENT WRITERS

For Prompt A:
1. Help students write two sentences, each giving a reason that Willie is grateful.
2. Help students identify one example or detail from the story to support each reason.
3. Suggest that students organize their letters in this way:
   - Beginning: general statement of gratitude
   - Middle: details and examples
   - End: summary of significance of events

For Prompt B:
1. Help students state how the blind fish relate to the story's theme.
2. Have pairs locate references to the fish.
3. In a single paragraph, have students use their statement from step 1 as a topic sentence and then explain two examples.

Reading-Writing Connection

WRITING PROMPTS
- For **Prompt A,** encourage students to reread the passage in which Willie gives the man the cake. Have them write what Willie gains from this exchange.
- For **Prompt B,** have students first state the story's theme about **unhappiness.** Then have students use a T chart to list all the references to the blind fish and the significance of each one.

BEST PRACTICES TOOLKIT—Transparency
   T Chart p. A25

For ideas for writing, see

Writing Center at **ClassZone.com**

GRAMMAR AND WRITING
Explain that some coordinating conjunctions set up a contrast (*but, nor, yet*), some show a cause-and-effect relationship (*so*), and some extend the same idea (*and*).

1. *Possible answer: You listened to me, and you answered my questions.*

Possible conjunctions for remaining items:

2. *but;* **3.** *but;* **4.** *or;* **5.** *and*

RESOURCE MANAGER—Copy Master
   Combine Sentences p. 86

Assess and Reteach

Assess
RESOURCE MANAGER—Copy Masters
   Selection Tests A, B/C pp. 89–90, 91–92
Test Generator CD

Reteach
STANDARDS LESSON FILE
   Reading Lesson 8: Making Inferences
   Literature Lesson 29: Symbol and
      Symbolism
   Vocabulary Lesson 16: Context Clues
      (using all types)

Focus and Motivate

OBJECTIVES

Reading for Information

- identify author's perspective
- support an opinion
- read a problem-solution essay

SUMMARY

In this essay, the author reflects on the concept of home and presents her view of homelessness in the United States. She believes the solution is to look at each person without a home as an individual and to avoid seeing homelessness as just another political issue.

What's the Connection?

Use an Anticipation Guide to prepare students for the selection. Write these statements on the transparency. Have students respond to each one before and after reading.

- "You are where you live."
- Homelessness is the most serious problem facing the nation.
- Building more shelters would solve the homeless problem.

 BEST PRACTICES TOOLKIT—Transparency
Anticipation Guide p. A14

Teach

Skill Focus: Identify Author's Perspective

Guide students through the process of identifying Quindlen's perspective on homelessness. In the first column of the chart, have students note opinions, descriptive words and phrases, and supporting details. Then ask them to consider these questions as they fill in the second column:

- Why does Quindlen share this opinion? For example, does she want to connect with her readers or emphasize a particular idea?
- What impression or feeling is created by Quindlen's use of words in this sentence?
- Is this detail a fact, statistic, example, or reflection? How does this kind of supporting detail affect readers' understanding of the main idea?

Possible chart entries appear on page 360.

 RESOURCE MANAGER—Copy Master
Identify Author's Perspective p. 101

Homeless
Problem-Solution Essay

Use with "What Do Fish Have to Do with Anything?" on page 340.

 MARYLAND OBJECTIVES

INFO TEXT/WRITING STANDARDS
2.A.4.b Identify and explain the author's perspective
4.A.2.d Compose to persuade

What's the Connection?

In the short story you just read, a mother instructs her son not to look at a homeless man who is begging. In the problem-solution essay you are about to read, Anna Quindlen notes that this is often the way people react to "the homeless," but she recommends a different response.

Skill Focus: Identify Author's Perspective

Your view, or perspective, on a topic is influenced by your experiences, beliefs, and values. For example, if you've had dogs, you might think they're fun. If you haven't, you might be scared of them. Likewise, an **author's perspective**—that is, the way a writer looks at a topic—is influenced by his or her experiences, beliefs, and values.

Here's how to identify Quindlen's perspective on homelessness:

- Notice which parts of the topic Quindlen focuses on.
- Write down direct statements she makes about herself as well as the way she thinks or feels about the topic.
- Note words and details she uses to describe the topic.
- Think about what these elements of her essay tell you about her perspective on being homeless.

As you read Quindlen's essay, use these tips to help you complete a chart like the one started here.

Direct Statements, Descriptive Words, and Other Details	What These Details Tell Me About Quindlen's Perspective
She introduces a homeless woman by name, emphasiz-ing that this woman has a name and is a human being like any one of us.	She views this woman as an individual person first, homeless second.
"I've never been very good at looking at the big picture, taking the global view."	

Selection Resources

 RESOURCE MANAGER UNIT 3

Plan and Teach pp. 93–97

Reading
Summary pp. 99†*, 100‡
Identify Author's Perspective pp. 101, 103†*
Reading Check p. 105
Support an Opinion pp. 102, 104†*
Question Support p. 106*

Assessment
Selection Tests A, B/C pp. 109*, 111*

Test Generator CD

Reading Support

Audio Anthology CD*

BEST PRACTICES TOOLKIT

Anticipation Guide • Think-Pair-Share • Cluster Diagram

* Resources for Differentiation   † Also in Spanish   ‡ In Haitian Creole and Vietnamese

Homeless

by Anna Quindlen

Her name was Ann, and we met in the Port Authority Bus Terminal several Januarys ago. I was doing a story on homeless people. She said I was wasting my time talking to her; she was just passing through, although she'd been passing through for more than two weeks. To prove to me that this was true, she rummaged through a tote bag and a manila envelope and finally unfolded a sheet of typing paper and brought out her photographs.

They were not pictures of family, or friends, or even a dog or cat, its eyes brown-red in the flash-bulb's light. They were pictures of a house. It was like a thousand 20 houses in a hundred towns, not suburb, not city, but somewhere in between, with aluminum siding and a chainlink fence, a narrow driveway running up to a one-car

READING FOR INFORMATION   **357**

F OCUS ON FORM
"Homeless" is a **problem-solution essay,** a short work of nonfiction in which a writer presents a problem and offers a reasonable solution.

Practice and Apply

BACKGROUND

The Homeless in Port Authority Bus Terminal
The Port Authority Bus Terminal in New York City is a hub for the nation's major bus lines, serving about 56 million passengers a year in the largest city in the United States. Its vast size and its location draw many homeless people. To help this population, the Port Authority has set up various programs in partnership with social service agencies. A drop-in center for the homeless operates across the street from the terminal. Under another program, social workers identify vulnerable people in the station so that they can receive the services they need.

FOCUS ON FORM

Problem-Solution Essay Discuss the purpose and characteristics of a problem-solution essay. This type of essay

- describes a real-life problem
- presents one or more solutions
- appears in newspapers or magazines (journalistic in tone)
- is a short work of nonfiction

As students read the essay, have them identify parts (lines 46–60, 95–107) where Quindlen describes the problem (homelessness) and parts (lines 149–157) where she suggests solutions.

Lines 1–19
DISCUSSION PROMPTS

Use these prompts to help students explore the importance of Ann in the essay:

Connect Think about a time when you met someone whose life seemed very different from yours. How does that experience help you understand the interaction between Quindlen and Ann, the homeless woman? *Students may say that people from different backgrounds look for experiences or values they share to help them relate to each other.*

Interpret Do you believe that Ann is just passing through? *Students may say that if she were truly passing through, she would not still be there after two weeks.*

Synthesize Why do you think the author included this information about Ann in her essay? ***Possible answer:*** *The author wants to put a human face on a serious problem and wants to increase readers' empathy by showing that the homeless are people like themselves.*

READING FOR INFORMATION   **357**

DIFFERENTIATED INSTRUCTION

FOR LESS–PROFICIENT READERS
Concept Support Help students distinguish between facts and opinions by listing some of the clue words or phrases that signal an opinion (*I think, it seems, probably, most, all*). Have students work in pairs to locate statements in the text that contain these clues. Ask students to record three of these opinions in the first column of their chart like the one on page 356.

FOR ENGLISH LEARNERS
Options for Reading Make sure students understand the terms *problem* and *solution*. Prepare students to read this essay by discussing or charting its organization: the author describes the problem by talking to a homeless person, sharing her own feelings about a home, and explaining what homeless people need and want. Then she presents a solution. Students may read the selection along with the *Audio Anthology CD*.

Lines 29–40
DISCUSSION PROMPTS

Use these prompts to help students understand more about the author's character and how it influences her views on homelessness:

Connect Have you ever realized that your ideas about a person were based only on how they looked or what they wore? How do you think this realization affects Quindlen's understanding of Ann? *Students may say that realizing you have something in common with another person makes his or her outward appearance less important in shaping your opinion of the person.*

Analyze What does the author's reaction to Ann's photographs reveal about her character? *Possible answer: She knows immediately what Ann is trying to tell her, showing that she is a person of insight. She also feels a bond with Ann, revealing her ability to see Ann as a fellow human being.*

Synthesize If the author believes that "you are where you live," how does she most likely view homelessness? *Possible answer: Quindlen most likely views homelessness with horror. This statement indicates that she believes a person's home is part of his or her identity. It anchors a person and makes him or her "somebody" instead of "nobody." A home gives someone a voice in society. Without a home, a person is invisible.*

garage and a patch of backyard. The house was yellow. I looked on the back for a date or a name, but neither was there. There was no need for discussion. I knew what 30 she was trying to tell me, for it was something I had often felt. She was not adrift, alone, anonymous, although her bags and her raincoat with the grime shadowing its creases had made me believe she was. She had a house, or at least once upon a time had had one. Inside were curtains, a couch, a stove, potholders. You are where 40 you live. She was somebody.

I've never been very good at looking at the big picture, taking the global view, and I've always been a person with an overactive sense of place, the legacy[1] of an Irish grandfather. So it is natural that the thing that seems most wrong with the world to me right now is that there are so many people with no 50 homes. I'm not simply talking about shelter from the elements, or three square meals a day or a mailing address to which the welfare[2] people can send the check—although I know that all these are important for survival. I'm talking about a

1. **legacy** (lĕg'ə-sē): something handed down from an ancestor or from the past.
2. **welfare**: a program of financial aid provided by the government to people in need.

DIFFERENTIATED INSTRUCTION

FOR LESS–PROFICIENT READERS
Comprehension Support

- Help students identify the author's direct statement of the problem (lines 46–50). Make sure students understand the connection between the information about Ann and the problem as it is stated.

- Have students use Think-Pair-Share to answer selected discussion prompts.

   BEST PRACTICES TOOLKIT—Transparency
   Think-Pair-Share p. A18

FOR ADVANCED LEARNERS/PRE–AP
Analyze Have students discuss the opening paragraphs of the essay (lines 1–40).

- How does Quindlen's anecdote about Ann help make the author's point about homelessness come alive?

- What important elements in the opening help it to achieve the author's purpose?

home, about precisely those kinds of feelings that have wound up in cross-stitch and French knots on samplers[3] over the years. **A**

Home is where the heart is. There's no place like it. I love my home with a ferocity totally out of proportion to its appearance or location. I love dumb things about it: the hot-water heater, the plastic rack you drain dishes in, the roof over my head, which occasionally leaks. And yet it is precisely those dumb things that make it what it is—a place of certainty, stability,[4] predictability, privacy, for me and for my family. It is where I live. What more can you say about a place than that? That is everything. **B**

Yet it is something that we have been edging away from gradually during my lifetime and the lifetimes of my parents and grandparents. There was a time when where you lived often was where you worked and where you grew the food you ate and even where you were buried. When that era passed, where you lived at least was where your parents had lived and where you would live with your children when you became enfeebled.[5] Then, suddenly, where you lived was where you lived for

three years, until you could move on to something else and something else again.

And so we have come to something else again, to children who do not understand what it means to go to their rooms because they have never had a room, to men and women whose fantasy is a wall they can paint a color of their own choosing, to old people reduced to sitting on molded plastic chairs, their skin blue-white in the lights of a bus station, who pull pictures of houses out of their bags. Homes have stopped being homes. Now they are real estate. **C**

People find it curious that those without homes would rather sleep sitting up on benches or huddled in doorways than go to shelters. Certainly some prefer to do so because they are emotionally ill, because they have been locked in before and they are damned if they will be locked in again. Others are afraid of the violence and trouble they may find there. But some seem to want something that is not available in shelters, and they will not compromise, not for a cot, or oatmeal, or a shower with special soap that kills the bugs. "One room," a woman with a baby who

---

3. **in cross-stitch and French knots on samplers:** spelled out in fancy stitching and embroidered decorations.

4. **stability:** a condition of being reliable or permanent.

5. **enfeebled:** deprived of strength; made weak.

A AUTHOR'S PERSPECTIVE
What does Quindlen think is most wrong in the world right now? Name two facts she shares about herself to help readers understand her perspective on this issue.

B PROBLEM-SOLUTION ESSAY
Restate the point that Quindlen makes in this paragraph.

C AUTHOR'S PERSPECTIVE
Reread lines 95–109. What does Quindlen say homes have become? What does she mean by this?

INFORMATIONAL ANALYSIS

A AUTHOR'S PERSPECTIVE

Possible answer: Quindlen thinks the world's biggest problem is that there are so many people without homes. Two reasons she gives for her perspective are (1) she's "never been very good at looking at the big picture, taking the global view" and (2) she's "always been a person with an overactive sense of place, the legacy of an Irish grandfather."

If students need help . . . Read lines 41–46 aloud. Work with students to define *big picture, global view,* and *overactive sense of place* in this context.

LITERARY ANALYSIS

B PROBLEM–SOLUTION ESSAY

Possible answer: A home is a person's most treasured place. It gives one security, privacy, and refuge.

INFORMATIONAL ANALYSIS

C AUTHOR'S PERSPECTIVE

You might record students' answers in the chart from page 356.
Possible answer:

Direct Statements and Details	What These Details Tell Me
Quindlen says that homes have become real estate.	She thinks that homes have lost their identities as places of comfort and refuge. They are now just investments, valued only for how much money they're worth.

FOR LESS–PROFICIENT READERS

Comprehension Support One clue to the author's feelings about homelessness is her attitude toward her own home. Have students reread lines 61–76, in which she defines what a home is to her. Work together on a Cluster Diagram to summarize Quindlen's views about her home. Discuss how these feelings influence her opinion on homelessness.

FOR ENGLISH LEARNERS

Culture: Connect Point out line 61, "Home is where the heart is." Explain that this saying means that a home is a place someone loves and feels comfortable in or in which beloved friends and family are found. Ask students to design a plaque that illustrates a saying about home from their own culture. Have students include images that show what the saying means.

BEST PRACTICES TOOLKIT—Transparency
Cluster Diagram p. B18

LITERARY ANALYSIS

D PROBLEM—SOLUTION ESSAY

Possible answer: She believes most people think of homeless people not as individuals but as examples of an issue that needs to be solved. We turn "Ann" and "the man who lives in the box" into "the homeless"—a nameless, faceless problem.

LITERARY ANALYSIS

E PROBLEM—SOLUTION ESSAY

Possible answers: She recommends that we stop thinking about homelessness in "broad strokes" and concentrate on the details. In other words, we might begin to improve the situation if we remember that "the homeless" are individuals who are trying to live without all the things a home can provide.

Skill Focus: Identify Author's Perspective

Possible entries for chart on page 356:

Direct Statements and Details	What These Details Tell Me
"the thing that seems most wrong" (lines 46–47)	Quindlen's choice of words shows how seriously she takes the problem of homelessness.
"It is where I live. . . . That is everything." (lines 73–76)	These sentences show Quindlen's passionate feelings about her home, even though it is quite ordinary.
"old people reduced to sitting on molded plastic chairs, their skin blue-white in the lights of a bus station" (lines 102–106)	These details emphasize the hardships of homelessness and suggest it is a terrible way for our elders to live.
"'One room,' a woman with a baby . . . once told me, 'painted blue.'" (lines 125–128)	This specific example reinforces the idea that the homeless are individuals, with their own special needs and desires.

D PROBLEM-SOLUTION ESSAY
Reread lines 132–148. How does Quindlen think most people "work around" the problem of homelessness?

E PROBLEM-SOLUTION ESSAY
What does Quindlen recommend that readers do to start addressing the problem she has introduced?

was sleeping on her sister's floor, once told me, "painted blue." That was the crux[6] of it; not size or location, but pride of ownership. Painted blue.

This is a difficult problem, and some wise and compassionate people are working hard at it. But in the main I think we work around it, just as we walk around it when it is lying on the sidewalk or sitting in the bus terminal—the problem, that is. It has been customary to take people's pain and lessen our own participation in it by turning it into an issue, not a collection of human beings. We turn an adjective into a noun: the poor, not poor people; the homeless, not Ann or the man who lives in the box or the woman who sleeps on the subway grate. **D**

Sometimes I think we would be better off if we forgot about the broad strokes and concentrated on the details. Here is a woman without a bureau. There is a man with no mirror, no wall to hang it on. They are not the homeless. They are people who have no homes. No drawer that holds the spoons. No window to look out upon the world. My God. That is everything. **E**

---

6. **crux:** the most important point or element.

DIFFERENTIATED INSTRUCTION

FOR LESS—PROFICIENT READERS

Concept Support Have pairs of students complete their chart from page 356. They should include three opinions as directed on page 357. Encourage them also to include one or two words or phrases that evoke a particular feeling in the reader. As a class, analyze what the details tell the reader about Quindlen's perspective.

FOR ADVANCED LEARNERS/PRE—AP

Apply Have students work in small groups to identify practical applications for the solution Quindlen suggests in her essay. Ask each group to present their best proposal to the class.

Comprehension

1. **Recall** In Quindlen's opinion, what was Ann trying to tell her by sharing her carefully protected pictures of a house? Explain.

2. **Recall** What do some homeless people want that they cannot get at a shelter? Explain.

Critical Analysis

3. **Analyze Author's Perspective** Review the direct statements and details you noted in your chart. Then pick one and explain what it tells you about Quindlen's perspective on homelessness.

4. **Evaluate a Problem-Solution Essay** A strong problem-solution essay does all of the following: gives a clear picture of the problem, explores its causes and effects, recommends a solution, and explains how to put the solution into effect. Would you say that this essay is a strong problem-solution essay? Why or why not?

Read for Information: Support an Opinion

MARYLAND OBJECTIVES

INFO TEXT/WRITING STANDARDS
2.A.4.b Identify and explain the author's perspective
4.A.2.d Compose to persuade

WRITING PROMPT

In "What Do Fish Have to Do with Anything?" a homeless man tells the main character, "What a person needs is always more than they say" (line 322). Do you think Quindlen would agree with this statement? Why or why not? Support your opinion with evidence from "Homeless."

To answer this prompt, first clarify what the man is saying. You might need to go back to the story to figure this out. Then do as follows:

1. Review your chart to see what you have learned about Quindlen's perspective.

2. Then, keeping her perspective in mind, decide whether she would agree or disagree with the man's statement.

3. Look for evidence in "Homeless" to support your conclusion. For example, you might check whether Quindlen in any way suggests that Ann or the woman with the baby needs more than "they" say.

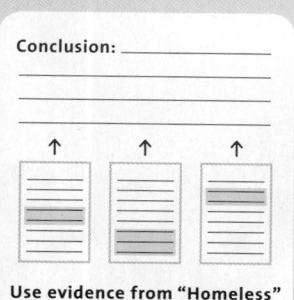

Conclusion: _____

↑   ↑   ↑

Use evidence from "Homeless" to support your conclusion.

DIFFERENTIATED INSTRUCTION

FOR LESS–PROFICIENT WRITERS
Read for Information

1. Ask students to review their charts. What needs of homeless people does Quindlen point out? (*Possible answers: lines 69–76: stability, predictability, privacy; line 130: pride of ownership*)

2. Discuss students' opinions about whether Quindlen would agree with the quotation.

3. Guide students in giving specific examples from the essay to support their opinions.

FOR ADVANCED LEARNERS/PRE–AP
Read for Information Have students develop their opinion statement into a short speech that the author might give to a group considering solutions for the problem of homelessness. Have them use the quotation as the central idea of their speech and then support or refute its validity as applied to the issue of the homeless. Ask students to present their speeches to a small group of their peers and evaluate each other's effectiveness.

Practice and Apply

For additional support of post-reading questions, use these copy masters:

R RESOURCE MANAGER—Copy Masters
Reading Check p. 105
Question Support p. 106
Support an Opinion p. 102

For additional questions, see p. 96.

ANSWERS
Comprehension

1. *Possible answer: Ann was saying that she is "somebody." Her photos prove that she is not just another homeless person.*

2. *Possible answer: They want to feel the pride of ownership and have the freedom to make choices.*

Critical Analysis

3. ■ **STANDARDS FOCUS** *Analyze Author's Perspective* **Possible answer:** *"I love my home with a ferocity totally out of proportion to its appearance or location" (lines 62–65). This statement explains why Quindlen would view homelessness as the most serious problem in society.*

4. *Evaluate a Problem-Solution Essay* *Students may say that this essay is a strong problem-solution essay because Quindlen gives a clear picture of the homelessness problem, explores its effects, and recommends a solution, although it is not a practical solution.*

Read for Information: Support an Opinion

Writing Prompt *Students' opinions should be clearly stated and offer specific and relevant evidence from the text.*

Assess and Reteach

Assess

R RESOURCE MANAGER—Copy Masters
Selection Tests A, B/C pp. 109–110, 111–112
💿 Test Generator CD

Reteach

S STANDARDS LESSON FILE
Literature Lesson 39: Author's Perspective

Focus and Motivate

OBJECTIVES

Literary Analysis
- explore the key idea of a **gift**
- identify theme
- identify how character growth and change reveal theme
- read a short story

Reading
- understand cause-and-effect relationships

Vocabulary
- build vocabulary for reading and writing
- understand and use prefix *in-* *(also an EL language objective)*

SUMMARY

In "A Crush," a mentally disabled man named Ernie admires Dolores from afar. Dolores, who works in a hardware store, appears to most townspeople as an unlikely choice for a crush. However, Ernie's deep feelings inspire him to use his most valued possession—a box of seed packages—to grow flowers for her. With help from his friend Jack, Ernie secretly delivers a bouquet to the store each week.

What makes a GIFT special?

Discuss the question with students. Ask if they've heard the saying "It is better to give than to receive." Challenge them to explain what it means. Then have students form small groups for the **DISCUSS** activity. After the group discussions, ask volunteers to share their key points about **gift**-giving with the class.

Selection Resources

A Crush
Short Story by Cynthia Rylant

What makes a GIFT *special?*

MARYLAND OBJECTIVES

READING/LIT STANDARDS
1.E.3.a Select and apply appropriate strategies during reading
3.A.3.e Analyze relationships between characters, setting, and events

KEY IDEA Everyone loves presents, right? Receiving a special **gift** is always a treat, but sometimes giving a gift can be even more rewarding. In the story "A Crush," simple but generous gifts bring about positive changes for both the recipients and the givers.

DISCUSS Gather in a small group to talk about gifts. Consider the following questions: What is the most special gift you have ever received? What is the most special gift you have ever given? How does gift giving make you feel? Do gifts have to cost a lot of money to be special? After your discussion, jot down one or two key points about gifts and giving.

362

Selection Resources

R RESOURCE MANAGER UNIT 3

Plan and Teach pp. 111–118

Literary Analysis
Summary pp. 119†*, 120‡*
Theme and Character pp. 121, 122†*
Question Support p. 129*

Reading
Identify Cause and Effect pp. 123, 124†*
Reading Check p. 128
Reading Fluency p. 130

Vocabulary
Study p. 125*
Practice p. 126
Strategy p. 127

Assessment
Selection Tests A, B/C pp. 131*, 133*
⊘ Test Generator CD

BEST PRACTICES TOOLKIT

Differentiated Instruction pp. 31–38*

Scaffolding Instruction pp. 43–46*

Graphic Organizers/Strategies
Word Questioning • Cluster Diagram • Read Aloud/Think Aloud • Timeline

Reading Support
⊘ Audio Anthology CD*

Technology
ℹ Literature and Vocabulary Centers at **ClassZone.com**

⊘ Write*Smart* CD

* Resources for Differentiation   † Also in Spanish   ‡ In Haitian Creole and Vietnamese

362 UNIT 3: UNDERSTANDING THEME

LITERARY ANALYSIS: THEME AND CHARACTER

Paying attention to what **characters** say, do, think, and feel can help you identify a story's **theme,** or message about life. The following questions can guide you:

- What important statements are made by the characters or about the characters?
- What lessons do the characters learn?
- Do any characters change over the course of the story? If so, how do they change?

As you read "A Crush," keep these questions in mind to help you determine the story's theme.

READING SKILL: IDENTIFY CAUSE AND EFFECT

Seeing how things are related can help you understand them. Events in a plot are often related to each other by **cause and effect.** Sometimes, an effect becomes the cause of another event, and so on until the end of the story. This is called a cause-and-effect chain. As you read "A Crush," record events in a chain graphic organizer like the one shown.

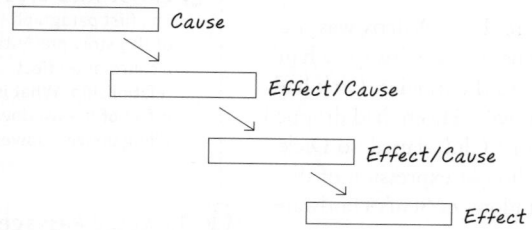

Cause
↓
| Effect/Cause |
↓
| Effect/Cause |
↓
| Effect |

VOCABULARY IN CONTEXT

The words in column A help tell Rylant's story about **giving.** For each word, choose the word or phrase in column B that is related in meaning.

Column A	Column B
1. cherish	a. overflow
2. usher	b. tall tale
3. improbable	c. Valentine card
4. excess	d. escort
5. taut	e. barely noticed
6. discreetly	f. strong knot

Author Online

Cynthia Rylant born 1954

Humble Beginnings Award-winning author Cynthia Rylant grew up in the mountains of West Virginia. Rylant lived with her grandparents for four years while her mother was in nursing school. Her grandfather was a coal miner, and the family lived in a small house with no plumbing. When Rylant's mother finished school, she found an apartment for herself and her daughter. Rylant says she "felt rich" living there because the building had running water and an indoor bathroom.

 MORE ABOUT THE AUTHOR For more on Cynthia Rylant, visit the **Literature Center at ClassZone.com.**

Background

Inspiration In Kent, Ohio, where Cynthia Rylant once lived, a man sometimes brought flowers to the waitresses at a little diner. He was Rylant's inspiration for one of the main characters in "A Crush." Next to the diner was a hardware store. "That's where my imagination found Dolores," said Rylant, referring to another character in the story. Rylant says she enjoys taking "people who don't get any attention in the world and making them really valuable in my fiction—making them absolutely shine with their beauty!"

A CRUSH   **363**

Teach

> ### LITERARY ANALYSIS
>
> ● **THEME AND CHARACTER**
>
> Read aloud this example:
>
> > For Dad's birthday, George bakes a batch of Dad's favorite cookies. His sister, Marla, wraps a CD that she never listens to and gives it to Dad.
>
> Ask what students learn about George and Marla from their **gifts. *Possible answer: George is more thoughtful than Marla.***
>
> **CHECK UNDERSTANDING** Have students name TV or movie characters and tell what their actions reveal about them. What are the themes of these shows and movies?

> ### READING SKILL
>
> ■ **IDENTIFY CAUSE AND EFFECT**
>
> Have students review the information on page 363. Ask these questions:
>
> - What caused Rylant to feel rich? *Possible answer: Her apartment had running water, unlike her previous house.*
> - Rylant knew a man who brought flowers to waitresses. How did this affect her? *Possible answer: She wrote "A Crush."*
>
> **CHECK UNDERSTANDING** Ask students to name an important event and chart its effects in a cause-and-effect chain.
>
> **R** **RESOURCE MANAGER—Copy Master** Identify Cause and Effect p. 123 (for student use while reading the story)

▲ **VOCABULARY IN CONTEXT**

DIAGNOSE WORD KNOWLEDGE To determine preteaching needs, have all students complete **Vocabulary in Context.** Check students' answers. (**1.** *c;* **2.** *d;* **3.** *b;* **4.** *a;* **5.** *f;* **6.** *e*)

PRETEACH VOCABULARY Use the Vocabulary Study copy master to help students predict meanings for each boldfaced word.

1. Read the first sentence aloud, emphasizing the word *cherish.*

2. Point out the phrases *loved flowers* and *take good care of it.* Elicit possible meanings for *cherish,* such as "to love or value."

3. Repeat for the other words in the chart.

4. Have students uncover or unfold their papers and check their definitions.

R **RESOURCE MANAGER—Copy Master** Vocabulary Study p. 125

For general guidelines on differentiating vocabulary instruction and for alternative vocabulary activities for students not needing vocabulary preteaching, see

BEST PRACTICES TOOLKIT Scaffolding Vocabulary Instruction pp. 43–46

ℹ Vocabulary Center at **ClassZone.com** Additional Vocabulary Activities

Practice and Apply

READING SKILL

Ⓐ CAUSE AND EFFECT

Possible answer: The immediate effect is that the townspeople know something has happened. Because the flowers are fresh and arranged in jars, people know that no one has died. So, they assume that whoever is leaving the flowers has a crush on someone else.

If students need help . . . Work together to complete a cause-and-effect chain for the first paragraph of the story.

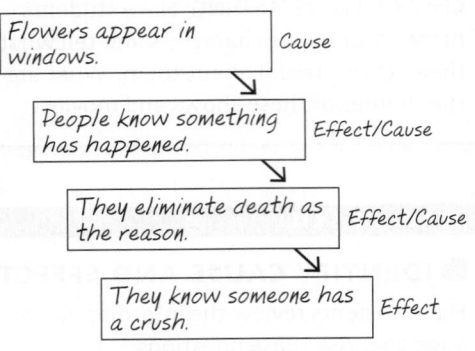

Flowers appear in windows. — *Cause*

People know something has happened. — *Effect/Cause*

They eliminate death as the reason. — *Effect/Cause*

They know someone has a crush. — *Effect*

Extend the Discussion What exactly is "a crush"? What else might someone with a crush do?

ANALYZE VISUALS

Possible answer: The artist wanted to create a general impression of a hardware store in a small town. The store could be in any town, so the specific details are not important.

About the Art The paintings of Virginian Bill Firestone are known for their vivid colors and bold brushwork, suggesting light and movement. Firestone took naturally to drawing and painting as a young child. During his later studies at Virginia Commonwealth University, he was influenced by the abstract expressionist style. Firestone's work has appeared on magazine covers and posters as well as on the walls of public and private collections.

A CRUSH

CYNTHIA RYLANT

When the windows of Stan's Hardware started filling up with flowers, everyone in town knew something had happened. **Excess** flowers usually mean death, but since these were all real flowers bearing the aroma of nature instead of floral preservative, and since they stood bunched in clear Mason jars[1] instead of impaled on Styrofoam crosses,[2] everyone knew nobody had died. So they all figured somebody had a crush and kept quiet. Ⓐ

There wasn't really a Stan of Stan's Hardware. Dick Wilcox was the owner, and since he'd never liked his own name, he gave his store half
10   the name of his childhood hero, Stan Laurel[3] in the movies. Dick had been married for twenty-seven years. Once, his wife, Helen, had dropped a German chocolate cake on his head at a Lion's Club dance, so Dick and Helen were not likely candidates for the honest expression of the flowers in those clear Mason jars lining the windows of Stan's Hardware, and speculation had to move on to Dolores.

Dolores was the assistant manager at Stan's and had worked there for twenty years, since high school. She knew the store like a mother knows her baby, so Dick—who had trouble keeping up with things like prices and new brands of drywall compound[4]—tried to keep himself busy in
20   the back and give Dolores the run of the floor. This worked fine because the carpenters and plumbers and painters in town trusted Dolores and took her advice to heart. They also liked her tattoo.

excess (ĭk-sĕs') *adj.* too much or too many

Ⓐ CAUSE AND EFFECT
The first paragraph of this story presents a cause-and-effect relationship. What is the effect of the windows' filling up with flowers?

① Targeted Passage

ANALYZE VISUALS
Why do you think the artist used a "blurry" style for this image?

1. **Mason jars:** glass jars with tight lids, used for canning or preserving foods.
2. **impaled on Styrofoam crosses:** pinned onto crosses made of a lightweight plastic material.
3. **Stan Laurel:** a comedian who with his partner, Oliver Hardy, made comedy films from the 1920s to the 1950s.
4. **drywall compound:** a mixture used to install or repair wallboard, of which the interior walls of many houses are made.

© Bill Firestone.

DIFFERENTIATED INSTRUCTION

FOR ALL STUDENTS

Enhancing Learning Styles Provide these independent projects for various learning preferences.

- **Musical** Compose a song that expresses what Ernie might want to say if he could.
- **Verbal** Create a journal entry in Dolores's voice on the day she finds the flowers.
- **Tactile** Create a flower box for the classroom, starting from seeds.

Ⓡ **RESOURCE MANAGER**
Ideas for Extension pp. 116–117

FOR LESS–PROFICIENT READERS

In combination with the *Audio Anthology CD*, use one or more Targeted Passages (pp. 364, 367, 369, 371) to ensure that students focus on key story events, concepts, and skills.

① Targeted Passage [Lines 1–22]

This passage sets up the story by introducing the mystery of the flowers and Dolores, one of the main characters.

BACKGROUND

Mental Retardation In this story, the character Ernie suffers from mental retardation. People with mental retardation have below-average intellectual abilities and limited communication, self-care, and/or social skills. The signs of mental retardation appear before the age of 18. Children with mental retardation can learn new skills, but they develop more slowly than other children. Rylant writes that "Ernie would not be able to speak in sentences until he was six years old. He would not be able to count the apples in a bowl until he was eight" (lines 76–78). In many cases, the cause of a person's mental retardation is unknown. However, some known causes include head injuries, infectious diseases, genetic abnormalities, lead poisoning, and malnutrition.

- How do the people in town explain the flowers in the store windows?
- Why is it unlikely that Dick and his wife are exchanging the flowers?
- Who is Dolores? What is she like?

FOR ENGLISH LEARNERS

Key Academic Vocabulary Have students use Word Questioning for *assistant* (line 16), *theory* (line 47), *mentally* (line 49), *uniform* (line 89), *resident* (line 125), and *attached* (line 220).

 BEST PRACTICES TOOLKIT—Transparency
Word Questioning p. E9

Prereading For prereading instruction for English learners, see

BEST PRACTICES TOOLKIT
Scaffolding Reading Instruction pp. 43–46

FOR ADVANCED LEARNERS/PRE–AP

Pre-AP exercises in the bottom channel provide additional challenge for your advanced students. Use them for small groups or individuals.

ADDITIONAL GUIDELINES

For more help with differentiation and tips for classroom management, see

 BEST PRACTICES TOOLKIT
Differentiated Instruction pp. 31–38

DISCUSSION PROMPTS

Use these prompts to help students explore how people react to someone who is different:

Connect Have you ever known someone who was different, as Dolores is with her tattoo? How do other people react to such a person? *Students may say that people are puzzled by those who act or look different, or that they have false ideas or prejudices regarding such individuals.*

Analyze Why do the women who sell cosmetics want to change Dolores's hair, face, and clothing? *Possible answers: They think she would be happier if she fit in with everyone else and had a boyfriend. They are uncomfortable with someone who does not accept their own standards of beauty.*

Evaluate Do you agree with the conclusion that Dolores does not want love? Why? *Possible answers: Yes, because her appearance is keeping others away, and she could easily make some changes. No, because most people do want love, and Dolores may simply have a different idea of what is attractive.*

Dolores was the only woman in town with a tattoo. On the days she went sleeveless, one could see it on the **taut** brown skin of her upper arm: "Howl at the Moon." The picture was of a baying coyote, which must have been a dark gray in its early days but which had faded to the color of the spackling paste[5] Dolores stocked in the third aisle. Nobody had gotten out of Dolores the true story behind the tattoo. Some of the men who came in liked to show off their own, and they'd roll up their
30 sleeves or pull open their shirts, exhibiting bald eagles and rattlesnakes and Confederate flags, and they'd try to coax out of Dolores the history of her coyote. All of the men had gotten their tattoos when they were in the service, drunk on weekend leave and full of the spitfire of young soldiers. Dolores had never been in the service, and she'd never seen weekend leave, and there wasn't a tattoo parlor anywhere near. They couldn't figure why or where any half-sober woman would have a howling coyote ground into the soft skin of her upper arm. But Dolores wasn't telling.

That the flowers in Stan's front window had anything to do with Dolores seemed completely **improbable.** As far as anyone knew,
40 Dolores had never been in love, nor had anyone ever been in love with her. Some believed it was the tattoo, of course, or the fine dark hair coating Dolores's upper lip which kept suitors away. Some felt it was because Dolores was just more of a man than most of the men in town, and fellows couldn't figure out how to court someone who knew more about the carburetor of a car or the back side of a washing machine than they did. Others thought Dolores simply didn't want love. This was a popular theory among the women in town who sold Avon and Mary Kay cosmetics. Whenever one of them ran into the hardware for a package of light bulbs or some batteries, she would mentally pluck every
50 one of the black hairs above Dolores's lip. Then she'd wash that grease out of Dolores's hair, give her a good blunt cut, dress her in a decent silk-blend blouse with a nice Liz Claiborne skirt from the Sports line, and, finally, tone down that swarthy, longshoreman look[6] of Dolores's with a concealing beige foundation,[7] some frosted peach lipstick, and a good gray liner for the eyes.

Dolores simply didn't want love, the Avon lady would think as she walked back to her car carrying her little bag of batteries. If she did, she'd fix herself up.

taut (tôt) *adj.* not loose or flabby

improbable (ĭm-prŏb′ə-bəl) *adj.* not likely

---

5. **spackling paste:** a substance used to repair holes or cracks in plaster.
6. **swarthy, longshoreman look:** darkly tanned skin, like that of a worker who unloads ships all day.
7. **concealing beige foundation:** a liquid makeup that covers skin flaws.

DIFFERENTIATED INSTRUCTION

FOR LESS–PROFICIENT READERS
Comprehension Support Direct students' attention to lines 48–55. Ask them to clarify what is happening in this passage. Make sure they understand that Dolores's makeover is not actually happening. The passage describes what the women who sell cosmetics *imagine* doing to change Dolores's appearance.

FOR ENGLISH LEARNERS
Culture: Clarify Make sure students know what a tattoo is (line 23) and understand its cultural significance in this story. Tattoos have become much more common among American teenagers in recent years. However, in the small town where Dolores lives, very few women have tattoos. Also explain that the Confederate flag (line 31) is a symbol of the South from the American Civil War (1861–1865).

Vocabulary: Phrasal Verbs Explain that words like *up* and *down* can change the meaning of a verb. Assign phrasal verbs for pairs of students to look up in a dictionary: *tone down* (line 53), *fix up* (line 58), *pull up* (line 89), *set down* (line 91), *pick up* (line 93). Point out that context also affects meaning—for example, you can *pull up* your socks or *pull up* to the curb in a car.

The man who was in love with Dolores and who brought her zinnias and cornflowers and nasturtiums and marigolds and asters and four-o'clocks in clear Mason jars did not know any of this. He did not know that men showed Dolores their tattoos. He did not know that Dolores understood how to use and to sell a belt sander.[8] He did not know that Dolores needed some concealing beige foundation so she could get someone to love her. The man who brought flowers to Dolores on Wednesdays when the hardware opened its doors at 7:00 A.M. didn't care who Dolores had ever been or what anyone had ever thought of her. He loved her, and he wanted to bring her flowers. **B**

Ernie had lived in this town all of his life and had never before met Dolores. He was thirty-three years old, and for thirty-one of those years he had lived at home with his mother in a small dark house on the edge of town near Beckwith's Orchards. Ernie had been a beautiful baby, with a shock of shining black hair and large blue eyes and a round, wise face. But as he had grown, it had become clearer and clearer that though he was indeed a perfectly beautiful child, his mind had not developed with the same perfection. Ernie would not be able to speak in sentences until he was six years old. He would not be able to count the apples in a bowl until he was eight. By the time he was ten, he could sing a simple song. At age twelve, he understood what a joke was. And when he was twenty, something he saw on television made him cry.

Ernie's mother kept him in the house with her because it was easier, so Ernie knew nothing of the world except this house. They lived, the two of them, in tiny dark rooms always illuminated by the glow of a television set, Ernie's bags of Oreos and Nutter Butters littering the floor, his baseball cards scattered across the sofa, his heavy winter coat thrown over the arm of a chair so he could wear it whenever he wanted, and his box of Burpee[9] seed packages sitting in the middle of the kitchen table.

These Ernie **cherished.** The seeds had been delivered to his home by mistake. One day a woman wearing a brown uniform had pulled up in a brown truck, walked quickly to the front porch of Ernie's house, set a box down, and with a couple of toots of her horn, driven off again. Ernie had watched her through the curtains and, when she was gone, had ventured onto the porch and shyly, cautiously, picked up the box. His mother checked it when he carried it inside. The box didn't have their name on it, but the brown truck was gone, so whatever was in the box was theirs to keep. Ernie pulled off the heavy tape, his fingers trembling, and found inside the box more little packages of seeds than he could count. He lifted them out, one by one, and examined the beautiful photographs of

---

8. **belt sander:** a machine that uses a rough-textured moving belt to smooth surfaces.
9. **Burpee:** W. Atlee Burpee and Co. is the world's largest mail-order seed company.

B THEME AND CHARACTER
How is the man who loves Dolores different from other people in town?

2 Targeted Passage

cherish (chĕr′ĭsh) *v.*
to care for deeply

LITERARY ANALYSIS

B THEME AND CHARACTER

Possible answer: The man who loves Dolores thinks she is perfect just as she is. Others in town are judgmental of Dolores.

If students need help . . . Have them reread lines 23–68 and cluster details of townspeople's reactions to Dolores. Have them rate each reaction as positive or negative and compare it to the admiration of the flower sender.

BEST PRACTICES TOOLKIT—Transparency
Cluster Diagram p. B18

Lines 89–97
REINFORCE *KEY IDEA:* GIFT

Discuss In what sense is the box of seed packages a **gift**? Does a gift always have to come from another person? *Possible answer: The seeds are a gift because Ernie receives them without asking for them or paying for them. Sometimes people receive "gifts" that do not come from other people. Such gifts include unexpected events or insights that can change a person's life.*

FOR LESS-PROFICIENT READERS

Comprehension Support Use Read Aloud/Think Aloud to clarify sequence in lines 65–91. Note that the main action of the story is told in the past tense. Point out verb forms that signal a flashback sequence, such as *had lived* (line 69) and *had been delivered* (line 88). Have students place key events on a timeline.

BEST PRACTICES TOOLKIT—Transparencies
Read Aloud/Think Aloud p. A34
Timeline p. B23

2 Targeted Passage [Lines 65–82]

This passage introduces the main character, Ernie, and sets up the theme of love and **gift**-giving.

- Who has been bringing flowers to Dolores? Why does he do it?

- Where does Ernie live? Why has he never met Dolores before?

- How was Ernie different from most other children?

FOR ADVANCED LEARNERS/PRE-AP

Character Study Have students write a paragraph in response to this question: *What details in the story thus far support the view that it seemed "completely improbable" (line 39) that the flowers at Stan's were for Dolores?* Invite students to compare their responses.

flowers on each. His mother was not interested, had returned to the
100 television, but Ernie sat down at the kitchen table and quietly looked
at each package for a long time, his fingers running across the slick paper
and outlining the shapes of zinnias and cornflowers and nasturtiums and
marigolds and asters and four-o'clocks, his eyes drawing up their colors. **C**

T wo months later Ernie's mother died. A neighbor found her at the
mailbox beside the road. People from the county courthouse came
out to get Ernie, and as they **ushered** him from the home he would never
see again, he picked up the box of seed packages from his kitchen table
and passed through the doorway.

Eventually Ernie was moved to a large white house near the main
110 street of town. This house was called a group home, because in it lived
a group of people who, like Ernie, could not live on their own. There
were six of them. Each had his own room. When Ernie was shown the
room that would be his, he put the box of Burpee seeds—which he had
kept with him since his mother's death—on the little table beside the bed,
and then he sat down on the bed and cried.

Ernie cried every day for nearly a month. And then he stopped. He dried
his tears, and he learned how to bake refrigerator biscuits and how to dust
mop and what to do if the indoor plants looked brown. **D**

Ernie loved watering the indoor plants, and it was this pleasure which
120 finally drew him outside. One of the young men who worked at the
group home—a college student named Jack—grew a large garden in
the back of the house. It was full of tomato vines and the large yellow
blossoms of healthy squash. During his first summer at the house,
Ernie would stand at the kitchen window, watching Jack and sometimes
a resident of the home move among the vegetables. Ernie was curious
but too afraid to go into the garden.

368 UNIT 3: UNDERSTANDING THEME

**C THEME AND
CHARACTER**
Reread lines 98–103.
Why do you think the
seeds are so interestin[g]
to Ernie?

usher (ŭsh′ər) v. to guid[e]
in a certain direction

D CAUSE AND EFFEC[T]
Reread lines 104–118.
How does the death of
Ernie's mother affect
Ernie's life?

LITERARY ANALYSIS

C THEME AND CHARACTER

*Possible answer: Ernie has been very
sheltered all his life and hasn't experienced
many things. The surprise gift of something
colorful and beautiful is very special to him.*

Extend the Discussion Do you think Ernie
knows what is inside the seed packages?

READING SKILL

D CAUSE AND EFFECT

Possible answers:

- *Ernie is moved to a group home. (lines
  109–112)*
- *He cries for almost a month. (line 116)*
- *He learns to do new tasks. (lines 117–118)*
- *He cares for indoor plants. (line 119)*

Extend the Discussion How do you think
living in the group home will affect Ernie?

DIFFERENTIATED INSTRUCTION

FOR LESS–PROFICIENT READERS

Reading Skill Follow-Up: Cause and Effect
Have students create a cause-and-effect chain
(as introduced on page 363) that begins with
the death of Ernie's mother. Students may
work in pairs to select events for their charts.
Afterward, have pairs compare their charts.
Discuss any differences between charts, emphasizing the importance of accurate causal
relationships rather than minor details.

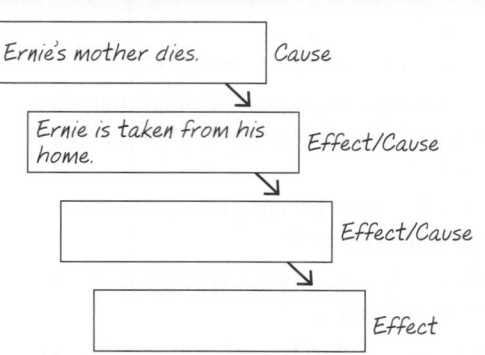

FOR ENGLISH–LEARNERS

Language: Pronoun Referents Explain that
sometimes a pronoun can be rephrased as an
adjective plus a noun. For example, in line 112,
"Each" can be rephrased as "Each person." Have
students work in pairs to supply the missing
noun (the referent) for these pronouns:

- *his* (line 113), "his room"
- *this* (line 139), "this idea"
- *those* (line 153), "those people"

Then one day when Ernie was watching through the window, he noticed that Jack was ripping open several slick little packages and emptying them into the ground. Ernie panicked and ran to his room.
30 But the box of Burpee seeds was still there on his table, untouched. He grabbed it, slid it under his bed, then went back through the house and out into the garden as if he had done this every day of his life.

He stood beside Jack, watching him empty seed packages into the soft black soil, and as the packages were emptied, Ernie asked for them, holding out his hand, his eyes on the photographs of red radishes and purple eggplant. Jack handed the empty packages over with a smile and with that gesture became Ernie's first friend.

Jack tried to explain to Ernie that the seeds would grow into vegetables, but Ernie could not believe this until he saw it come true. And when
40 it did, he looked all the more intently at the packages of zinnias and cornflowers and the rest hidden beneath his bed. He thought more deeply about them, but he could not carry them to the garden. He could not let the garden have his seeds.

That was the first year in the large white house.

The second year, Ernie saw Dolores, and after that he thought of nothing else but her and of the photographs of flowers beneath his bed.

Jack had decided to take Ernie downtown for breakfast every Wednesday morning to ease him into the world outside that of the group home. They left very early, at 5:45 A.M., so there would be few
50 people and almost no traffic to frighten Ernie and make him beg for his room. Jack and Ernie drove to the Big Boy restaurant which sat across the street from Stan's Hardware. There they ate eggs and bacon and French toast among those whose work demanded rising before the sun: bus drivers, policemen, nurses, mill workers. Their first time in the Big Boy, Ernie was too nervous to eat. The second time, he could eat, but he couldn't look up. The third time, he not only ate everything on his plate, but he lifted his head and he looked out the window of the Big Boy restaurant toward Stan's Hardware across the street. There he saw a dark-haired woman in jeans and a black T-shirt unlocking the front door of
60 the building, and that was the moment Ernie started loving Dolores and thinking about giving up his seeds to the soft black soil of Jack's garden.

Love is such a mystery, and when it strikes the heart of one as mysterious as Ernie himself, it can hardly be spoken of. Ernie could not explain to Jack why he went directly to his room later that morning, pulled the box of Burpee seeds from under his bed, then grabbed Jack's hand in the kitchen and walked with him to the garden, where Ernie

③ Targeted Passage

Lines 133–161
DISCUSSION PROMPTS

Use these prompts to help students understand how Ernie's life is changed by his friendship with Jack:

Connect How do you know when someone is a true friend? How does a friend make you feel? *Students may say that a friend is someone you like and trust. Friends make you feel comfortable. They accept you for who you are.*

Analyze Would you say that Jack is a true friend to Ernie? Why? **Possible answer:** *Yes, because he is kind to Ernie and makes Ernie feel comfortable. Ernie trusts Jack. Jack understands that Ernie is afraid of new situations, so he figures out a way to ease him into the wider world (lines 147–151).*

Synthesize How is Ernie's life changed by his friendship with Jack? **Possible answer:** *Ernie's world expands through his friendship with Jack. He learns about gardening, and he starts to experience the world outside the group home. Jack's example of kindness and generosity inspires Ernie to want to grow flowers for Dolores.*

FOR LESS–PROFICIENT READERS
③ Targeted Passage [Lines 156–163]

This passage represents a turning point in the story, when Ernie falls in love and decides to give up his seeds in order to grow flowers for Dolores.

• How does Ernie feel the first time he sees Dolores from the Big Boy restaurant?

• Why does seeing Dolores make Ernie think about giving up his flower seeds?

• How does falling in love change Ernie?

E THEME AND CHARACTER

Possible answer: He has a crush on Dolores. He thinks he is in love with her because he feels something special when he first sees her. This feeling makes him want to give her something special. The seed packages are also very special to him.

Extend the Discussion What sacrifice does Ernie make when he plants the seeds? Do all gifts involve some kind of sacrifice?

Lines 200–206
REINFORCE *KEY IDEA:* GIFT

Discuss Why do both Ernie and Jack smile as they watch Dolores pick up Ernie's **gift?**
Possible answer: Both of them feel good about the gift. Ernie is happy because he has found a way to express his love for Dolores. Jack is glad to have helped Ernie do something that was important to him.

---

had come to believe things would grow. Ernie handed the packets of seeds one by one to Jack, who stood in silent admiration of the lovely photographs before asking Ernie several times, "Are you sure you want
170 to plant these?" Ernie was sure. It didn't take him very long, and when the seeds all lay under the moist black earth, Ernie carried his empty packages inside the house and spent the rest of the day spreading them across his bed in different arrangements. **E**

That was in June. For the next several Wednesdays at 7:00 A.M. Ernie watched every movement of the dark-haired woman behind the lighted windows of Stan's Hardware. Jack watched Ernie watch Dolores and **discreetly** said nothing.

When Ernie's flowers began growing in July, Ernie spent most of his time in the garden. He would watch the garden for hours,
180 as if he expected it suddenly to move or to impress him with a quick trick. The fragile green stems of his flowers stood uncertainly in the soil, like baby colts on their first legs, but the young plants performed no magic for Ernie's eyes. They saved their shows for the middle of the night and next day surprised Ernie with tender small blooms in all the colors the photographs had promised.

The flowers grew fast and hardy, and one early Wednesday morning when they looked as big and bright as their pictures on the empty packages, Ernie pulled a glass canning jar off a dusty shelf in the basement of his house. He washed the jar, half filled it with water,
190 then carried it to the garden, where he placed in it one of every kind of flower he had grown. He met Jack at the car and rode off to the Big Boy with the jar of flowers held tight between his small hands. Jack told him it was a beautiful bouquet.

When they reached the door of the Big Boy, Ernie stopped and pulled at Jack's arm, pointing to the building across the street. "OK," Jack said, and he led Ernie to the front door of Stan's Hardware. It was 6:00 A.M., and the building was still dark. Ernie set the clear Mason jar full of flowers under the sign that read "Closed," then he smiled at Jack and followed him back across the street to get breakfast.
200 When Dolores arrived at seven and picked up the jar of zinnias and cornflowers and nasturtiums and marigolds and asters and four-o'clocks, Ernie and Jack were watching her from a booth in the Big Boy. Each had a wide smile on his face as Dolores put her nose to the flowers. Ernie giggled. They watched the lights of the hardware store come up and saw Dolores place the clear Mason jar on the ledge of the front window. They drove home still smiling.

E THEME AND CHARACTER
Reread lines 162–173. Why does Ernie suddenl[y] want to grow flowers after he sees Dolores?

discreetly (dĭ-skrēt′lē)
adv. in a manner that shows caution and good judgment

VISUAL VOCABULAR[Y]

Mason jar *n.* a jar with a wide opening and a twist-on lid, used for canning and preserving foods

---

DIFFERENTIATED INSTRUCTION

FOR ENGLISH LEARNERS

Comprehension: Sequence Pages 370–371 contain words relating to months, seasons, times of day, and weekly events. Use these activities to help students clarify sequence:

- Have pairs of students create timelines showing the months of the year and how they break down into winter, spring, summer, and fall. Students can add translations of these English words, especially *June, July, September,* and *summer.*

- Have students show on a calendar what is meant by *the next several Wednesdays* (line 174), *every Wednesday morning* (lines 207–208), and *late September* (line 218).

- Explain that *at 7:00 a.m.* (line 174) can be substituted for *at seven* (line 200). "At seven o'clock" is another way to express this.

 **BEST PRACTICES TOOLKIT—Transparency** Timeline p. B23

All the rest of that summer Ernie left a jar of flowers every Wednesday morning at the front door of Stan's Hardware. Neither Dick Wilcox nor Dolores could figure out why the flowers kept coming, and each of them assumed somebody had a crush on the other. But the flowers had an effect on them anyway. Dick started spending more time out on the floor making conversation with the customers, while Dolores stopped wearing T-shirts to work and instead wore crisp white blouses with the sleeves rolled back off her wrists. Occasionally she put on a bracelet. **F**

By summer's end Jack and Ernie had become very good friends, and when the flowers in the garden behind their house began to wither, and Ernie's face began to grow gray as he watched them, Jack brought home one bright day in late September a great long box. Ernie followed Jack as he carried it down to the basement and watched as Jack pulled a long glass tube from the box and attached this tube to the wall above a table. When Jack plugged in the tube's electric cord, a soft lavender light washed the room.

"Sunshine," said Jack. **G**

Then he went back to his car for a smaller box. He carried this down to the basement, where Ernie still stood staring at the strange light. Jack handed Ernie the small box, and when Ernie opened it, he found more little packages of seeds than he could count, with new kinds of photographs on the slick paper.

"Violets," Jack said, pointing to one of them.

Then he and Ernie went outside to get some dirt. ❧

④ Targeted Passage

F CAUSE AND EFFECT
Reread lines 207–214. What effect do the flowers have on Dick and Dolores?

G THEME AND CHARACTER
How is Jack's gift to Ernie like Ernie's gift to Dolores?

© Bill Firestone.

READING SKILL

F CAUSE AND EFFECT
Possible answer: The flowers serve as a symbol to Dolores that she is special. She starts to feel good about herself and takes more care with her appearance. Likewise, Dick starts being more friendly toward his customers.

LITERARY ANALYSIS

G THEME AND CHARACTER
Possible answer: Each is a genuine gift to make another person happy, with no expectation of getting something in return.

If students need help . . . Use two web diagrams to record students' ideas about each gift. Then look for similarities in the webs.

Light and Seeds   Flowers

ANALYZE VISUALS

Activity Ask students to compare and contrast the painting with their own mental images of Ernie's garden. *Possible answers: It is similar to Ernie's garden because it is bright and cheerful. It is different because it has only one kind of flower, whereas Ernie grew many.*

SELECTION WRAP–UP

★ **CRITIQUE** Ask students to evaluate how the author ended this story. Have them discuss whether the ending is both emotionally satisfying and believable.

READING FLUENCY

Distribute the copy masters and have students use them to practice fluency.

 **RESOURCE MANAGER—Copy Master**
Reading Fluency p. 130

FOR LESS–PROFICIENT READERS
④ Targeted Passage [Lines 207–214]
This passage sums up the positive effects of Ernie's **gift** and evokes a major theme of the story.

• How do Ernie's flowers affect Dick?
• How do the flowers affect Dolores?
• In general, how do gifts affect the people who receive them? State your idea in a sentence that could be a theme of this story.

FOR ADVANCED LEARNERS/PRE–AP
Evaluate Use of Dialogue [paired activity option] Have pairs review the story and find all the dialogue (*lines 169–170, 195, 223, 229*). Then have them discuss these questions:

• Why did the author choose not to write any dialogue for Ernie?
• How do readers learn about Ernie's thoughts and feelings without "hearing" his voice?
• Would the story be improved if Ernie had some dialogue? Why or why not?

A CRUSH **371**

Practice and Apply

After Reading

For additional support of post-reading questions, use these copy masters:

R RESOURCE MANAGER—Copy Masters
Reading Check p. 128 (to check understanding of the selection)
Theme and Character p. 121 (for practice of literary analysis standards focus)
Question Support p. 129 (**After Reading** questions adapted for English learners and less-proficient readers)

Additional selection questions are provided for teachers on page 115.

ANSWERS

Comprehension

1. *Ernie is mentally challenged.*
2. *Students' drawings will differ, but all should show Ernie and Jack by a window in the restaurant and Dolores opening up the hardware store across the street.*
3. *He gives Ernie a special light to grow flowers in the winter.*

Literary Analysis

Possible answers:

4. *Jack helps Ernie feel comfortable in the garden and then takes him to a restaurant to get used to being in public places. He gives Ernie the gifts of kindness and friendship and helps him find a sense of purpose.*
5. *Beginning: Ernie has no experience with the outside world and is afraid of new situations. Middle: After his mother's death, Ernie begins to adjust to life in the group home. End: Ernie has become friends with Jack and fallen in love with Dolores. He grows flowers and leaves them for her every Wednesday.*
6. ■ **STANDARDS FOCUS** *Identify Cause and Effect Cause: Ernie moves to group home. Effect/Cause: Ernie meets Jack. Effect/Cause: Ernie goes to restaurant and sees Dolores. Effect/Cause: Ernie falls in love (has biggest effect). Effect/Cause: Ernie gives flowers to Dolores. Effect: Dolores and Ernie are both happier as a result of Ernie's gift (reason it was important).*

Comprehension

1. **Recall** How is Ernie different from other people?
2. **Represent** Using stick figures with labels to represent **characters,** draw the scene in which Ernie first gets a crush on Dolores.
3. **Clarify** How does Jack help Ernie at the end of the story?

Literary Analysis

4. **Make Inferences** Reflect on Jack's character. What gifts does he give Ernie in addition to seeds and a light?

5. **Analyze Character** Ernie changes a great deal from the time he receives the box of seeds to the end of the story. Note details about significant changes in his life and his behavior in a diagram such as the one shown. Using your notes, analyze how Ernie's behavior changes.

Ernie's Changing Character

Beginning		Middle		End
☐	→	☐	→	☐

6. **Analyze Cause and Effect** Look at the cause-and-effect chain you created as you read. On the basis of your notes, which event would you say had the most significant effect on Ernie's life? Why?

7. **Identify Theme** Review the questions you asked yourself as you read (see page 363). What did the characters learn in this story? Restate the lesson or lessons as a theme.

8. **Evaluate Point of View** This story is told from a **third-person omniscient point of view,** in which the narrator is an invisible observer who can get into the minds of all the characters. Why is that the best point of view for the author to use in "A Crush"?

Extension and Challenge

9. **Big Question Activity** Newspapers often include stories about local events like those that take place in this story. Write a newspaper article about how Dolores's life changes because of the anonymous gifts of flowers. Think about how she might answer the discussion questions on page 362, about what makes a **gift** special. Remember to include a catchy headline for your article!

MARYLAND OBJECTIVES

LITERATURE STANDARD
3.A.3.e Analyze relationships between characters, setting, and events

DAILY HERALD

STAN'S HARDWARE STORE BLOOMS
Jack B. Nimble

A local woman found herself the focus of a romantic mystery recently when an unidentified person began leaving flowers at her workplace every Wednesday morning. Dolores, who has worked at Stan's Hardware for nearly twenty years, is surprised by all the attention she's been getting since the flowers started arriving. "It's like one day no one noticed me, and the next day everyone did," she commented. "I suddenly feel so special." Dolores's friends and neigh- bors say... remarkable change in her since the mystery crush began. "She's a new woman," said Helen Wilcox, the wife of the store's owner. "It's been great to see the changes in her ... and in my husband."

Dick Wilcox, who was originally believed to be the focus of the anonymous crush, is said to have become much friendlier toward customers. Sales at the hardware store have increased significantly in recent weeks, keeping Wilcox very b...

7. ● **STANDARDS FOCUS** *Theme and Character Simple acts of kindness can make a positive difference in people's lives.*

8. *The two main characters in "A Crush," Ernie and Dolores, do not know each other. If Ernie were the narrator, he would not be able to tell much about Dolores. Dolores could not tell anything about Ernie. The third-person omniscient point of view allows readers to see into the minds and lives of all the characters.*

Extension and Challenge

9. *Students' responses should be written in the form of newspaper articles, with appropriate headlines and text written in an informational style. Articles should begin with a summary of the major events and should also employ details, such as quotations from Dolores and Dick. Articles should clearly address the idea of gifts.*

Vocabulary in Context

VOCABULARY PRACTICE

Use context clues to identify the vocabulary word that best completes each sentence.

1. Dolores was a hard-working woman with _____ muscles.
2. For Ernie to fall in love with Dolores at one glance might seem _____.
3. Nevertheless, he began to _____ her from the first day he saw her.
4. Jack kindly helped to _____ Ernie into the world of gardening.
5. Ernie made a large bouquet of flowers, but he still had _____ flowers in his garden.
6. Not wanting to be noticed, Ernie _____ delivered it early in the morning.

cherish
discreetly
excess
improbable
taut
usher

VOCABULARY IN WRITING

How many people's lives do you think Ernie affected? Write a paragraph explaining your opinion, using two or more vocabulary words. Here is a sample opening sentence.

> **EXAMPLE SENTENCE**
> The way that Ernie **cherished** Dolores affected several people.

VOCABULARY STRATEGY: FORMS OF THE PREFIX *in-*

As you have learned, the prefix *in-* often means "not." This prefix may have various spellings, depending on the letter that follows it.

- When added to words beginning with *b, m,* or *p,* it is spelled *im-,* as in the vocabulary word *improbable.*
- For words beginning with *l,* it is spelled *il-,* as in the word *illogical.*
- For words beginning with *r,* it is spelled *ir-,* as in the word *irreversible.*

Learning to recognize this prefix with its various spellings can help you figure out the meanings of many words.

PRACTICE Choose the word in each group that contains a correctly spelled prefix meaning "not." Then use the word in a sentence.

1. inproper, inperfect, impossible
2. irresponsible, irelevant, iregular
3. imcapable, imhospitable, intolerant
4. imature, imobile, immortal
5. iladvisable, illegal, inlogical
6. ireparable, irreplaceable, iresistible

MARYLAND OBJECTIVES

READING STANDARD
1.D.3.b Use word structure to determine meaning

 VOCABULARY PRACTICE
For more practice, go to the **Vocabulary Center** at ClassZone.com.

A CRUSH **373**

ANSWERS

Vocabulary in Context
VOCABULARY PRACTICE
1. *taut;* 2. *improbable;* 3. *cherish;* 4. *usher;*
5. *excess;* 6. *discreetly*

R RESOURCE MANAGER—Copy Master
Vocabulary Practice p. 126

VOCABULARY IN WRITING

Students can use a Cluster Diagram to list all the people who might be affected by Ernie's actions. Then they can consider which words tell something about the diagram.

BEST PRACTICES TOOLKIT—Transparency
Cluster Diagram p. B18

VOCABULARY STRATEGY: FORMS OF THE PREFIX *in-* (also an EL language objective)

Point out that the base word to which a prefix is attached should be complete (not missing its first letter). For example, words formed with *ir-* should have a double *r,* as in *irreversible.*

Answers:
1. *impossible;* 2. *irresponsible;* 3. *intolerant;*
4. *immortal;* 5. *illegal;* 6. *irreplaceable*
Example sentence: It is impossible *to know exactly why Ernie fell in love with Dolores.*

R RESOURCE MANAGER—Copy Master
Vocabulary Strategy p. 127

i Vocabulary Center at **ClassZone.com**
Additional Vocabulary Activities

Assess and Reteach

Assess

R RESOURCE MANAGER—Copy Masters
Selection Tests A, B/C pp. 131–132, 133–134

Test Generator CD

Reteach

S STANDARDS LESSON FILE
Reading Lesson 7: Recognizing Cause and Effect
Literature Lesson 13: Theme
Vocabulary Lesson 2: Prefixes (negation, number)

DIFFERENTIATED INSTRUCTION

FOR ENGLISH LEARNERS
Vocabulary: Prefixes Tell students that English has several other prefixes that also mean "not."

1. Assign each student the prefix *non-, un-,* or *dis-.*
2. Have each student look up a word with his or her assigned prefix and write the word with its definition.
3. Have students meet in pairs or small groups to share their words.

FOR ADVANCED LEARNERS/PRE-AP
Vocabulary in Writing Have students brainstorm words that rhyme with the vocabulary words. Then challenge them to write poems on the theme of gift giving, using several vocabulary words to create rhymes.

A CRUSH **373**

Introduce

OBJECTIVE

- read fantasy

Meet Lois Lowry

Lowry's books cover many different topics. Most, however, deal with the same basic theme: the importance of people staying connected to each other and to the world around them. Lowry says, "I try, through writing, to convey my passionate awareness that we live intertwined on this planet and that our future depends upon our caring more, and doing more, for one another."

Try a Fantasy Novel

Some fantasies are almost completely fanciful and unreal, with characters, settings, and events that could not possibly exist in the real world. Examples of this type of fantasy include Lewis Carroll's books *Alice's Adventures in Wonderland* and *Through the Looking-Glass*; L. Frank Baum's series about the land of Oz, which was the basis for the 1939 movie *The Wizard of Oz*; and *The Hobbit* and *The Lord of the Rings* by J.R.R. Tolkien. Other fantasies have a more balanced mix of realistic and fanciful details. For example, *Mary Poppins* by P. L. Travers and *Tuck Everlasting* by Natalie Babbitt are grounded in realistic settings but feature imaginary characters and events. In *The Giver*, many of the characters seem like ordinary people. The novel's setting and main events, however, are anything but ordinary.

 **RESOURCE MANAGER—Copy Master**
Fantasy p. 135

Great Reads

The Giver

Fantasy Novel by Lois Lowry

Lois Lowry
born 1937

**Other Books
by Lois Lowry**
- *Anastasia Krupnik*
- *Gathering Blue*
- *Messenger*
- *Number the Stars*
- *Rabble Starkey*
- *A Summer to Die*

Meet Lois Lowry

By the time she was three, Lois Lowry had already learned to read, so books played an important role in her childhood. "I was a solitary child who lived in the world of books and my own vivid imagination," she says. "That is how I write—I go back to the child I was and see things through those eyes."

Though she always loved reading and writing stories, Lowry didn't begin writing full-time until after she went to college, married, and raised her four children. She is now the author of over 30 books and has won many awards for her work.

It's no wonder people like Lowry's books so much. To her, there are stories in the most ordinary of life's events. Because of this Lowry's readers find themselves able to identify with the characters she creates and the things that happen to them in her stories.

Try a Fantasy Novel

Many of Lowry's books are a type of literature called **fantasy.** In a fantasy novel, you can travel to a different world where you'll find at least one element that is completely unreal and could exist only in the imagination. The setting might be strange, events might sound impossible, or you might read about characters with superhuman abilities.

DIFFERENTIATED INSTRUCTION

FOR LESS—PROFICIENT READERS

Reading Support Before students begin reading, review pages 375–379 in the teacher's edition and select the reading tips and other notes that you think would be most helpful to them. You might read the selection aloud with students and discuss the relevant notes. Stop occasionally to answer questions, give an explanation, or hold a discussion.

Read a Great Book

Lois Lowry puts her astonishing imagination to work in *The Giver*, a novel about a 12-year-old boy named Jonas, who lives in a world without fear of pain, hunger, poverty, or crime. Community leaders control everything, including what individuals are allowed to say and do. Upon turning 12, children are given specific roles in the community, based on their abilities.

In the following section from the book, the day of assignments has arrived. Jonas anxiously awaits the decision of the Elders.

from the Giver

Now Father sat beside Mother in the audience. Jonas could see them applauding dutifully as the Nines, one by one, wheeled their new bicycles, each with its gleaming nametag attached to the back, from the stage. . . .

Finally the Nines were all resettled in their seats, each having wheeled a bicycle outside where it would be waiting for its owner at the end of the day. Everyone always chuckled and made small jokes when the Nines rode home for the first time. "Want me to show you how to ride?" older friends would call. "I know you've never
10 been on a bike before!" But invariably the grinning Nines, who in technical violation of the rule had been practicing secretly for weeks, would mount and ride off in perfect balance, training wheels never touching the ground.

Then the Tens. Jonas never found the Ceremony of Ten particularly interesting—only time-consuming, as each child's hair was snipped neatly into its distinguishing cut: females lost their braids at Ten, and males, too, relinquished their long childish hair and took on the more manly short style which exposed their ears.

Laborers moved quickly to the stage with brooms and swept away
20 the mounds of discarded hair. Jonas could see the parents of the new Tens stir and murmur, and he knew that this evening, in many dwellings, they would be snipping and straightening the hastily done haircuts, trimming them into a neater line.

GREAT READS **375**

Read a Great Book

One of the main themes of *The Giver* is the importance of memory. In order for the characters in the book to live in their world without fear of pain, hunger, poverty, or crime, their memories of these unpleasant parts of life are removed. Lowry's questions about whether it is important for people to remember painful experiences as well as pleasant ones shaped this novel. She said in her 1994 Newbery Medal acceptance speech, "We can forget pain, I think. And it is comfortable to do so. But I also wonder briefly: is it safe to do that, to forget?" Lowry wonders if people need memories of past experiences to learn, grow, and be complete human beings. In the same 1994 speech she said, "We can't live in a walled world, in an 'only us, only now' world where we are all the same and feel safe. We would have to sacrifice too much." This is an idea for students to think about as they read.

SHARE A READING TIP

The Giver is narrated in the third person ("he said" instead of "I said"), and only the thoughts and feelings of Jonas are described. So, throughout the book, all descriptions of the community are based on how Jonas sees his community.

FOR ENGLISH LEARNERS

Use these options to help English learners enjoy the selection:

Jigsaw Reading Give students an introduction to and a summary of the excerpt. Then have students meet in small groups for Jigsaw reading. Each person should read part of the excerpt and explain the content to the others.

BEST PRACTICES TOOLKIT
Jigsaw p. A1

Read Aloud Preread part of the text and have students continue reading in pairs or small groups. Alternatively, read all of the text aloud and stop occasionally to answer questions, hold a discussion, or give an explanation.

Listen to the *Audio Anthology CD* Have students listen to the excerpt as they read along. Then have them read the text independently. Lead them in a follow-up discussion.

In this excerpt, Jonas and the other characters use capitalized words and phrases that are unique to their community. For example, groups of children are called *Nines, Tens,* and *Elevens.* Students will also notice terms such as *Elsewhere, Ceremony of Release, Matching of Spouses, Committee of Elders,* and *Naming.* Suggest that they use the background information on page 375, clues within the text, and their understanding of Jonas's community to figure out what these words and phrases mean.

Elevens. It seemed a short time ago that Jonas had undergone the Ceremony of Eleven, but he remembered that it was not one of the more interesting ones. By Eleven, one was only waiting to be Twelve. It was simply a marking of time with no meaningful changes. There was new clothing: different undergarments for the females, whose bodies were beginning to change; and longer trousers for the males, with a specially shaped pocket for the small calculator that they would use this year in school; but those were simply presented in wrapped packages without an accompanying speech.

Break for midday meal. Jonas realized he was hungry. He and his groupmates congregated by the tables in front of the Auditorium and took their packaged food. Yesterday there had been merriment at lunch, a lot of teasing, and energy. But today the group stood anxiously separate from the other children. Jonas watched the new Nines gravitate toward their waiting bicycles, each one admiring his or her nametag. He saw the Tens stroking their new shortened hair, the females shaking their heads to feel the unaccustomed lightness without the heavy braids they had worn so long.

"I heard about a guy who was absolutely certain he was going to be assigned Engineer," Asher muttered as they ate, "and instead they gave him Sanitation Laborer. He went out the next day, jumped into the river, swam across, and joined the next community he came to. Nobody ever saw him again."

Jonas laughed. "Somebody made that story up, Ash," he said. "My father said he heard that story when *he* was a Twelve."

But Asher wasn't reassured. He was eyeing the river where it was visible behind the Auditorium. "I can't even swim very well," he said. "My swimming instructor said that I don't have the right boyishness or something."

"Buoyancy," Jonas corrected him.

"Whatever. I don't have it. I sink."

"Anyway," Jonas pointed out, "have you ever once known of anyone—I mean really known for sure, Asher, not just heard a story about it—who joined another community?"

"No," Asher admitted reluctantly. "But you can. It says so in the rules. If you don't fit in, you can apply for Elsewhere and be released. My mother says that once, about ten years ago, someone applied and

was gone the next day." Then he chuckled. "She told me that because I was driving her crazy. She threatened to apply for Elsewhere."

"She was joking."

"I know. But it was true, what she said, that someone did that once. She said that it was really true. Here today and gone tomorrow. Never seen again. Not even a Ceremony of Release."

Jonas shrugged. It didn't worry him. How could someone not fit in? The community was so meticulously ordered, the choices so carefully made.

70   Even the Matching of Spouses was given such weighty consideration that sometimes an adult who applied to receive a spouse waited months or even *years* before a Match was approved and announced. All of the factors—disposition, energy level, intelligence, and interests—had to correspond and to interact perfectly. Jonas's mother, for example, had a higher intelligence than his father, but his father had a calmer disposition. They balanced each other. Their match, which like all Matches had been monitored by the Committee of Elders for three years before they could apply for children, had always been a successful one.

80   Like the Matching of Spouses and the Naming and Placement of newchildren, the Assignments were scrupulously thought through by the Committee of Elders.

He was certain that his Assignment, whatever it was to be, and Asher's too, would be the right one for them. He only wished that the midday break would conclude, that the audience would reenter the Auditorium, and the suspense would end.

As if in answer to his unspoken wish, the signal came and the crowd began to move toward the doors.

Now Jonas's group had taken a new place in the Auditorium, 90   trading with the new Elevens, so that they sat in the very front, immediately before the stage.

They were arranged by their original numbers, the numbers they had been given at birth. The numbers were rarely used after the Naming. But each child knew his number, of course. Sometimes parents used them in irritation at a child's misbehavior, indicating that mischief made one unworthy of a name. Jonas always chuckled

Lowry once referred to Elsewhere in trying to explain the power of reading. She said, "Each time a child opens a book, he pushes open the gate that separates him from Elsewhere. It gives him choices. It gives him freedom."

SHARE WORD MEANINGS

Meticulously (line 68) means "carefully and precisely" or "thoroughly."

In this community, only a certain number of children are born each year. These children are born to Birthmothers—who don't raise their offspring or even see them—and they spend the first year of life in a Nurturing Center with the other "newchildren" born that year. They are then assigned to families.

SHARE WORD MEANINGS

A *tunic* (line 124) is a type of long, usually knee-length, shirt or jacket.

when he heard a parent, exasperated, call sharply to a whining toddler, "That's *enough,* Twenty-three!"

Jonas was Nineteen. He had been the nineteenth newchild born
100 his year. It had meant that at his Naming, he had been already standing and bright-eyed, soon to walk and talk. It had given him a slight advantage the first year or two, a little more maturity than many of his groupmates who had been born in the later months of that year. But it evened out, as it always did, by Three.

After Three, the children progressed at much the same level, though by their first number one could always tell who was a few months older than others in his group. Technically, Jonas's full number was Eleven-nineteen, since there were other Nineteens, of course, in each age group. And today, now that the new Elevens
110 had been advanced this morning, there were *two* Eleven-nineteens. At the midday break he had exchanged smiles with the new one, a shy female named Harriet.

But the duplication was only for these few hours. Very soon he would not be an Eleven but a Twelve, and age would no longer matter. He would be an adult, like his parents, though a new one and untrained still.

Asher was Four, and sat now in the row ahead of Jonas. He would receive his Assignment fourth.

Fiona, Eighteen, was on his left; on his other side sat Twenty,
120 a male named Pierre whom Jonas didn't like much. Pierre was very serious, not much fun, and a worrier and tattletale, too. "Have you checked the rules, Jonas?" Pierre was always whispering solemnly. "I'm not sure that's within the rules." Usually it was some foolish thing that no one cared about—opening his tunic if it was a day with a breeze; taking a brief try on a friend's bicycle, just to experience the different feel of it.

The initial speech at the Ceremony of Twelve was made by the Chief Elder, the leader of the community who was elected every ten years. The speech was much the same each year: recollection
130 of the time of childhood and the period of preparation, the coming responsibilities of adult life, the profound importance of Assignment, the seriousness of training to come.

Then the Chief Elder moved ahead in her speech.

"This is the time," she began, looking directly at them, "when we acknowledge differences. You Elevens have spent all your years till now learning to fit in, to standardize your behavior, to curb any impulse that might set you apart from the group.

"But today we honor your differences. They have determined your futures."

140 She began to describe this year's group and its variety of personalities, though she singled no one out by name. She mentioned that there was one who had singular skills at caretaking, another who loved newchildren, one with unusual scientific aptitude, and a fourth for whom physical labor was an obvious pleasure. Jonas shifted in his seat, trying to recognize each reference as one of his groupmates. The caretaking skills were no doubt those of Fiona, on his left; he remembered noticing the tenderness with which she had bathed the Old. Probably the one with scientific aptitude was Benjamin, the male who had devised new, important equipment

150 for the Rehabilitation Center.

He heard nothing that he recognized as himself, Jonas.

Finally the Chief Elder paid tribute to the hard work of her committee, which had performed the observations so meticulously all year. The Committee of Elders stood and was acknowledged by applause. Jonas noticed Asher yawn slightly, covering his mouth politely with his hand.

Then, at last, the Chief Elder called number One to the stage, and the Assignments began. ∽

Keep Reading

You've just gotten a sense of the community Jonas lives in. What details about the group seemed strange to you? To learn more about this strange community, read more of *The Giver*. You'll discover how Jonas is assigned to become the new Receiver of Memory for his community and begins training with a man known as The Giver. Once Jonas learns the truth about his society and how it compares to the larger world, he finds that he has some difficult choices to make.

Discuss

SHARE WORD MEANINGS

To *standardize behavior* (line 136) is to make it "normal" or the same as everyone else's behavior.

Keep Reading

Share these discussion questions with students after they have finished the excerpt. You might use the questions to lead a class discussion or have students form small groups to discuss them.

- Have you read this book? If yes, would you recommend it to others? Why? If no, what questions are you hoping the rest of the book will answer?

- How is Jonas's community different from your community? How is it similar?

- Would you want to live in a community where your role in life was decided for you? Why? What would be some advantages and disadvantages?

- What do you think Jonas's assignment might be?

Focus and Motivate

Comparing Themes

Spring Harvest of Snow Peas
Poem by Maxine Hong Kingston

Eating Alone
Poem by Li-Young Lee

OBJECTIVES

Literary Analysis
- explore the key idea of being **lonely**
- identify recurring theme
- read poetry
- compare and contrast themes

Reading
- set a purpose for reading

SUMMARY

In "Spring Harvest of Snow Peas," the speaker walks through her garden and carefully picks snow peas. She enjoys her solitude in nature, her happy memories of her mother, and her task. In "Eating Alone," the speaker pulls up the last of the year's onions. He uses them to prepare a delicious meal, but his satisfaction is marred by the fact that he misses his father and must eat alone.

Can you be alone and not LONELY?

Introduce the question and encourage students to make the distinction between being alone and being **lonely**. Lead into the *KEY IDEA* by telling students that there is a saying that a person can be lonely in a crowd. Ask them if they would agree. Follow up by having students do the *DISCUSS* activity.

Comparing Themes

Spring Harvest of Snow Peas
Poem by Maxine Hong Kingston

Eating Alone
Poem by Li-Young Lee

Can you be alone and not LONELY?

MARYLAND OBJECTIVES

READING/LIT STANDARDS
1.E.3.a Select and apply appropriate strategies during reading
3.A.6.b Analyze themes across multiple texts

KEY IDEA Some people love to be alone. Others get bored or sad when no one else is around or feel **lonely** even when they are with other people. In the two poems you are about to read, the speakers share their thoughts and feelings about being alone.

DISCUSS What advice would you give to someone who is feeling lonely when alone? Work with a partner to list ways to overcome loneliness. Then share your insights with the class to come up with a master list of "loneliness busters."

1. Write in a journal.
2.
3.
4.
5.

Selection Resources

 **RESOURCE MANAGER UNIT 3**

Plan and Teach pp. 137–144

Literary Analysis
Question Support p. 147*

Reading
Set a Purpose for Reading pp. 145, 146†*

Grammar and Writing
Writing for Assessment p. 148

Assessment
Selection Tests A, B/C pp. 149*, 151*

 Test Generator CD

 BEST PRACTICES TOOLKIT

Differentiated Instruction
  pp. 31–38*
Scaffolding Instruction
  pp. 43–46*

Graphic Organizers/Strategies
Cluster Diagram • Think-Pair-Share • Read Aloud/Think Aloud • Venn Diagram • Main Idea and Details

Reading Support
Audio Anthology CD*

Technology
Literature Center at **ClassZone.com**

Write*Smart* CD

---

* Resources for Differentiation   † Also in Spanish

LITERARY ANALYSIS: RECURRING THEME

How many stories and poems have you read that conveyed the message "Love is all you need" or "Growing up is difficult"? You've probably come across these themes fairly often. When the same theme is presented in more than one piece of literature, it is called a **recurring theme.**

The two poems you are about to read have a common theme, but the poets express it differently. As you read each poem, pay attention to the following elements. They will help you find the poems' shared message.

- title
- subjects presented
- words and phrases that describe the speaker's feelings
- **images,** or words and phrases that help you know how things look, feel, smell, sound, or taste

READING STRATEGY: SET A PURPOSE FOR READING

Sometimes your purpose for reading might be to relax with a good book. At other times it might be to get information. In this lesson, your **purpose for reading** the two poems is to identify the recurring theme and compare the ways the poets communicate it.

After you've read "Spring Harvest of Snow Peas" and "Eating Alone," read the poems again. This time, fill in a chart like the one shown. You will be asked to do more with this chart after you finish reading.

	"Spring Harvest of Snow Peas"	"Eating Alone"
What idea is described in the title?		
What subjects are presented?	garden, mother, food	garden, father, food
How is the speaker feeling?		
What important images can you find?		

Author Online

Maxine Hong Kingston: Lifelong Poet Maxine Hong Kingston grew up listening to her mother's bedtime stories and began writing poetry when she was in the fourth grade. She has since become one of the best-known Asian-American writers of nonfiction, fiction, and poetry. As the child of Chinese immigrants, Kingston often focuses her writing on her cultural heritage.

Maxine Hong Kingston born 1940

Li-Young Lee: Master of Imagery Li-Young Lee's first language was Chinese. He didn't speak English until he moved to the United States in 1964 with his parents. Yet Lee's artistic mastery of English is clear in his award-winning poetry, which has been praised for its imagery and the "brave honesty" of its language.

Li-Young Lee born 1957

 MORE ABOUT THE AUTHOR For more on Maxine Hong Kingston and Li-Young Lee, visit the **Literature Center** at **ClassZone.com.**

Teach

STANDARDS FOCUS

LITERARY ANALYSIS

● RECURRING THEME

Discuss how themes in literature often repeat, suggesting new ways of thinking about common feelings or experiences. Ask students to identify selections from previous units with a common theme. *Possible answers: Doing what is right takes a special kind of courage ("A Retrieved Reformation," "The Scholarship Jacket"); everyone has the potential to be someone's hero ("Thank You, Ma'm," "Rikki-tikki-tavi").*

CHECK UNDERSTANDING Ask students for examples of songs or movies that share the same theme.

READING STRATEGY

■ SET A PURPOSE FOR READING

Discuss how the purpose for reading affects how students might read a poem.

- Students reading for pleasure may stop to savor the images and feelings that the words evoke.
- Students reading a poem for a specific purpose, such as identifying a theme, may read slowly and then reread to look for key words and literary devices.

To get the most from reading a poem, the first reading should always be for pleasure.

CHECK UNDERSTANDING Have students summarize how to read for a purpose.

 RESOURCE MANAGER—Copy Master Set a Purpose for Reading p. 146 (for student use while reading the poems)

DIFFERENTIATED INSTRUCTION

FOR ALL STUDENTS

For general guidelines on differentiating instruction, see

BEST PRACTICES TOOLKIT Differentiated Instruction pp. 31–38

FOR LESS–PROFICIENT READERS

Concept Support Identify characteristics of poetry in a class Cluster Diagram. Then have groups of students read the poems aloud and discuss which features they find.

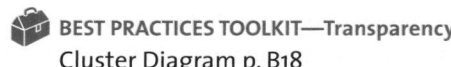 **BEST PRACTICES TOOLKIT—Transparency** Cluster Diagram p. B18

FOR ENGLISH LEARNERS

Options for Reading Read each poem aloud before beginning discussion. (A reading of "Eating Alone" is available on the *Audio Anthology CD.*) Have students use Think-Pair-Share to answer important questions about each work, especially the two questions about theme that appear on pages 382 and 383.

 BEST PRACTICES TOOLKIT—Transparency Think-Pair-Share p. A18

Practice and Apply

ANALYZE VISUALS

About the Art American artist Barbara Weldon expresses an attunement to nature through her art. Common motifs, seen in her *Birds* series on these pages, include vines, gardens, and wings.

Activity Ask students to compare and contrast the elements of each image on this spread. Discuss what they might predict about each poem from the choice of image. *Possible answer: The content of the images is the same, but the color spectrum changes from vibrant to subdued, to match the mood of each poem.*

LITERARY ANALYSIS

Ⓐ THEME

Possible answer: The speaker is relaxed and enjoying her activities, tasting and picking the snow peas. Being in the garden brings back happy memories of her parents.

If students need help . . . Work together to pick out phrases and images—such as "taste and eat," "blue blossoms wave above me and touch my neck," "reach for more," "eat and sing"—that show the speaker's attitude toward her task.

Lines 1–17
DISCUSSION PROMPTS

Use these prompts to help students develop insight into the significance of the speaker's act in this poem:

Connect What feelings might you have if you were picking fruits or vegetables that you had grown yourself? *Students might say that they would feel the pride of achievement. The task would be more enjoyable than simply buying food in a store.*

Analyze Why is the act of growing snow peas important to the speaker? *Possible answer: The activity connects her to her parents, to her neighbors, and to nature.*

Synthesize Is the speaker alone, lonely, or both? *Possible answer: Although the speaker is by herself, she is befriended by her memories and the energy of nature. She is connected to others through the bounty of the snow peas. She is alone but not lonely.*

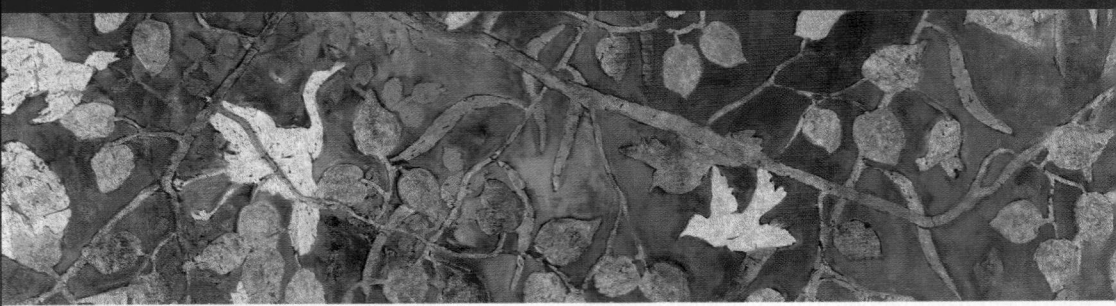

Detail of *Birds XII* (2003), Barba... Weldon. Oil, gold leaf, and wax o... canvas, 60˝ × 72...

spring harvest
of snow peas

Maxine Hong Kingston

They're taller than me.
I taste and eat as I pick along,
choose the flat big ones and baby ones,
and leave the bulging pods for shelling or seed.
5 The purple and lavender blossoms
and the blue blossoms wave above me
and touch my neck.
I stand on the ledge of the box, reach for more,
and remember my mother and father growing
10   snow peas[1] every season. Ⓐ
When she could hardly see anymore, my mother
      showed me
by feel how to plant 3 seeds per mound.
Every day, enough for dinner, and for leaving
15   at neighbors' doors.
The birds surround me and eat and sing. I am
      unequivocally happy.

Ⓐ **THEME**
Reread lines 1–10.
How does the speaker
seem to feel about bein...
in the garden?

---

1. **snow peas:** peas of a type having a soft outer pod.

DIFFERENTIATED INSTRUCTION

FOR LESS–PROFICIENT READERS
Vocabulary Support

- Explain that the first word of the Kingston poem, *They're,* refers to the snow pea plants. Guide students to see that reading on to find clues in lines 4–6 can help them figure out this meaning.

- Explain that the word *unequivocally* in line 17 of the Kingston poem means "without any doubt; wholeheartedly." Have students use *unequivocally* in an original sentence to modify a different adjective.

FOR ENGLISH LEARNERS
Language: Punctuation and Print Cues

Point out that in a poem, a complete thought sometimes ends in the middle or even near the beginning of a line. Use Read Aloud/Think Aloud to show how to identify complete thoughts within the first stanzas of "Eating Alone." Have pairs of students apply the strategy to the rest of the poem.

 BEST PRACTICES TOOLKIT—Transparency
Read Aloud/Think Aloud p. A34

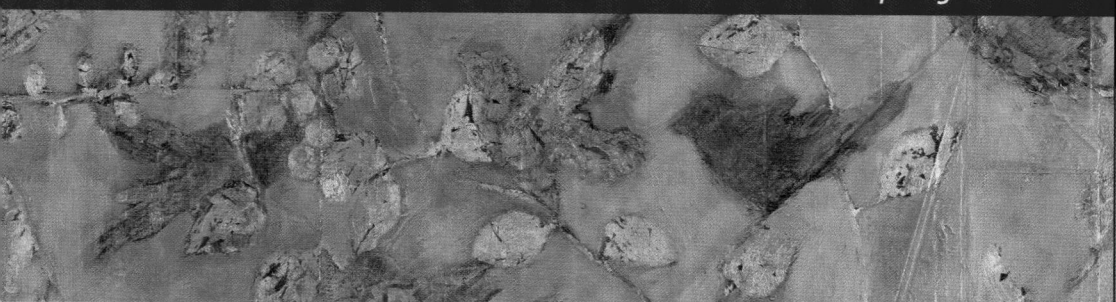

EATiNGalone

Li-Young Lee

Detail of *Birds III* (2002), Barbara
Weldon. Oil, gold leaf, and wax
on canvas, 40″ × 40″.

I've pulled the last of the year's young onions.
The garden is bare now. The ground is cold,
brown and old. What is left of the day flames
in the maples at the corner of my
5 eye. I turn, a cardinal vanishes.
By the cellar door, I wash the onions,
then drink from the icy metal spigot.

Once, years back, I walked beside my father
among the windfall pears. I can't recall
10 our words. We may have strolled in silence. But
I still see him bend that way—left hand braced
on knee, creaky—to lift and hold to my
eye a rotten pear. In it, a hornet
spun crazily, glazed in slow, glistening juice.

15 It was my father I saw this morning
waving to me from the trees. I almost
called to him, until I came close enough
to see the shovel, leaning where I had
left it, in the flickering, deep green shade. **B**

20 White rice steaming, almost done. Sweet green peas
fried in onions. Shrimp braised in sesame
oil and garlic. And my own loneliness.
What more could I, a young man, want.

B THEME
Reread lines 8–19.
Note what the speaker
remembers about
his father. Are they
positive memories?

SPRING HARVEST OF SNOW PEAS / EATING ALONE   **383**

Lines 20–23
REINFORCE *KEY IDEA*: LONELY

Discuss How does the speaker's **lonely** feeling
affect him? *Possible answer: It makes all of his
feelings more intense, including his awareness
of the delicious food.*

LITERARY ANALYSIS

B THEME

*Possible answer: He remembers the time he
and his father spent together in the garden
and the things his father showed him. His
memories are positive.*

Extend the Discussion Why do you think
the author included the image of the pear
and the hornet?

SELECTION WRAP–UP

REFLECT Have students think about how the
two speakers relate to the natural world. In
what ways does nature play a similar role in
both speakers' lives? In what ways is it different for each speaker?

⭐ **CRITIQUE** Point out that Lee uses many
more descriptive words (adjectives and adverbs) than Kingston. Ask students to discuss
which style appeals to them more, and why.

FOR LESS–PROFICIENT READERS
Comprehension Support Using the chart
from page 381, discuss and record what students learned about the speaker in the first
poem. Then ask these questions about the
speaker in the second poem:

- What kind of mood do the adjectives *bare,
  cold, brown,* and *old* create?

- What time of year is the poem's setting?

- What does the speaker feel as he sits down
  to eat his dinner?

FOR ADVANCED LEARNERS/PRE–AP
Compare and Contrast Have students work
in pairs to analyze the style of each poet.
They should focus on aspects of style including use of literary devices (imagery, figurative
language, sound devices, symbolism, and
so on), development of mood and speaker,
line length, rhythm, rhyme, and word choice.
They may organize their ideas in a Venn
diagram.

 BEST PRACTICES TOOLKIT—Transparency
Venn Diagram p. A26

Practice and Apply

After Reading

For additional support of post-reading questions, use these copy masters:

 RESOURCE MANAGER—Copy Masters

Question Support p. 147 (**After Reading** questions adapted for English learners and less-proficient readers)

Additional selection questions are provided for teachers on page 141.

ANSWERS

Comprehension

1. *The speaker is in the garden harvesting snow peas.*

2. *His father, who used to live there with him, is no longer alive.*

3. *In the last stanza, the speaker is eating a meal that includes onions he pulled up from the garden (first stanza).*

Literary Analysis

4. *Possible answers:*

   - *She was a strong person who continued planting and harvesting her snow peas even after she went blind.*

   - *She was a kind person who not only took care of her family's needs but was generous with her neighbors as well.*

   - *She wanted to pass on her knowledge to her daughter.*

5. *The speaker seems to enjoy cooking and eating things from his garden. "White rice steaming," "sweet green peas," "shrimp braised in sesame oil" are phrases that show his attention to the food he prepares. At the same time, the word "loneliness" indicates that he misses his father.*

6. *Students may say that food symbolizes fulfillment and a connection to the past or to special memories.*

7. *In Kingston's poem, the season is spring. This choice conveys the speaker's happiness and the idea of the rebirth of her mother's traditions through her own actions. In Lee's poem, the season is fall. This adds to the sense that the speaker is still adjusting to his loneliness after his father's death.*

Comprehension

1. **Recall** Where is the speaker in "Spring Harvest of Snow Peas"?

2. **Recall** What is one reason why the speaker in the second poem is eating alone?

3. **Clarify** How does the last stanza of "Eating Alone" connect with the first stanza?

Literary Analysis

4. **Make Inferences** Reread lines 11–15 of "Spring Harvest of Snow Peas." What do you learn about the speaker's mother?

5. **Draw Conclusions** How do you think the speaker in "Eating Alone" feels about the meal he is fixing? Note the words or phrases that give you clues about his feelings.

6. **Identify Symbols** What does the food in each poem symbolize, or stand for beyond its usual meaning?

7. **Analyze** Note which season it is in each poem. How does the choice of season affect the meaning of each poem?

Comparing Themes

Now that you've read both poems, finish filling in the chart. Then use the answers to the questions to help you identify the **recurring theme** in the poems.

	"Spring Harvest of Snow Peas"	"Eating Alone"
What idea is described in the title?		
What subjects are presented?	garden, mother, food	garden, father, food
How is the speaker feeling?		
What important images can you find?		
What theme do the poems have in common?		

MARYLAND OBJECTIVES

LLITERATURE STANDARD
3.A.6.b Analyze themes across multiple texts

Comparing Themes Possible answers:	"Spring Harvest of Snow Peas"	"Eating Alone"
What idea is described in the title?	new life and abundance	solitude and reflection
What subjects are presented?	garden, mother, food	garden, father, food
How is the speaker feeling?	content and happy	lonely
What important images can you find?	descriptions of snow pea and blossoms; singing of birds	bare, cold ground; father picking up pear; foods prepared by speaker
What theme do the poems have in common?	Nature can be a source of spiritual and physical nourishment. Loneliness is influenced by many factors, including events in the past and present.	

Writing for Assessment

1. READ THE PROMPT

In writing assessments, you will often be asked to compare selections that share a **recurring theme**.

> **PROMPT**
>
> While "Spring Harvest of Snow Peas" and "Eating Alone" share a recurring theme, Maxine Hong Kingston and Li-Young Lee express the theme differently. In four or five paragraphs, compare and contrast the ways the poets get the theme across. Support your response with details from the poems.

◀ **STRATEGIES IN ACTION**

1. I have to make sure I understand what **message** the poems share.
2. I need to identify the **similarities and differences** in the ways the poets express the message.
3. I should include **details** from the poems to show what I mean.

2. PLAN YOUR WRITING

Using the chart you filled out for the poems, note how each poet develops the theme. Write a position statement that expresses the main similarities and differences you find in the poets' methods. Then decide how you will set up your response.

- Do you want to focus on one poem first and then show how the other poem is similar and different, as shown in the sample outline?
- Do you want to compare each element—title, subject, feelings, and images—in a separate paragraph?

Once you have decided, put your ideas into outline form.

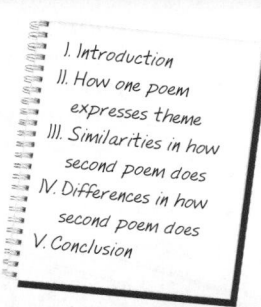

I. Introduction
II. How one poem expresses theme
III. Similarities in how second poem does
IV. Differences in how second poem does
V. Conclusion

3. DRAFT YOUR RESPONSE

Introduction Include the titles and poets' names for the poems you will be comparing, and state the theme that the poems share. Also include your position statement.

Body Paragraphs If using an outline like the one shown, explain everything you want to about the first poem. Then start a new paragraph before you discuss how the second poem is similar or different.

Conclusion Wrap up your response with a restatement of your main idea and a thought about why the theme might appeal to different poets.

Revision Check to see whether adding transitions such as *similarly, unlike,* or *however* can help you make your comparisons and contrasts clearer.

DIFFERENTIATED INSTRUCTION

FOR LESS–PROFICIENT WRITERS

Draft Your Response Provide a template to help students structure their responses.

Introduction
- Give titles and names of poets.
- State main idea of your response.

Middle paragraphs
- Explain how first poet develops theme.
  —Describe mood of first poem.
  —Discuss images that show life and joy.
  —Describe how the speaker feels and why.
- Explain how second poet develops theme.
  —Describe mood of second poem.
  —Discuss images that show life and also sadness and loss.
  —Describe how the speaker feels and why.
- Point out similarities. (Both poems involve a garden; both speakers are nourished by vegetables and by memories of parents.)
- Summarize major differences.

Conclusion
- Restate main idea.

Writing for Assessment

1. READ THE PROMPT

Read the prompt aloud. Ask volunteers to identify key words that define the task. *(recurring theme, four or five paragraphs, compare and contrast, details from the poems)*

2. PLAN YOUR WRITING

- Have students incorporate their themes in strong main idea statements. Give them an example: "Although both Kingston and Lee convey the idea that nature is a source of nourishment and life, they develop this theme very differently." Explain that this statement belongs in an introduction.

- Have students extract details from their charts to support their main ideas. They might use a main idea chart to gather ideas.

- After students have decided how to organize their essays, suggest that they write relevant details in the appropriate sections of their outlines. Encourage them to include direct quotations from the poems.

 **BEST PRACTICES TOOLKIT—Transparency**
Main Idea and Details p. B6

3. DRAFT YOUR RESPONSE

Remind students to begin each body paragraph with a strong topic sentence. For example: "In Kingston's poem, the speaker is nourished both physically and emotionally by nature." "In Lee's poem, nature is seen as a cycle of abundance and loss."

R RESOURCE MANAGER—Copy Master
Writing for Assessment p. 148

Assess and Reteach

Assess

R RESOURCE MANAGER—Copy Masters
Selection Tests A, B/C pp. 149–150, 151–152

 Test Generator CD

Reteach

S STANDARDS LESSON FILE
Literature Lesson 13: Theme
Writing Lesson 29: Comparison-Contrast Essay

OBJECTIVES

Literary Analysis
- explore the key idea of **money**
- identify theme in drama
- read a play and an online article

Reading
- identify and analyze sequence

Vocabulary
- build vocabulary for reading and writing

Grammar and Writing
- use dependent and independent clauses to form complete sentences
- use writing to analyze literature

SUMMARY

In this dramatic version of Dickens's tale, Ebenezer Scrooge journeys through time with the ghosts of Christmas past, present, and yet to come. He sees the innocent, happy person he was and the miserly, sad old man he has become. When he awakens on Christmas Day, he begins to mend his ways, sending a feast to his clerk's house, giving money to the poor, and celebrating the day with his nephew.

How important is MONEY?

Discuss what **money** can and cannot do. List students' ideas in a two-column chart, and, as a class, draw some conclusions about the importance of money. Then have student pairs discuss the sayings in the *KEY IDEA* paragraph before they begin the *QUOTE IT* activity. Have small groups share their sayings.

A Christmas Carol
Novel by Charles Dickens
Dramatized by Frederick Gaines

How important is MONEY?

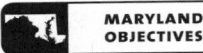

MARYLAND OBJECTIVES

READING/LIT STANDARDS
1.E.3.a Select and apply appropriate strategies during reading
3.A.6.a Analyze universal themes

KEY IDEA People say, "**Money** makes the world go round," "Show me the money," and "Time is money." But they also say, "You can't buy happiness." There are many sayings about what money can and can't do, about what it is and what it isn't. In *A Christmas Carol*, the main character's opinion about what it means to be wealthy changes drastically by the end of the play.

QUOTE IT Read over the four sayings quoted in the previous paragraph. In a chart, jot down your ideas about what each saying means. Then write your own saying on the last line, expressing your thoughts about money.

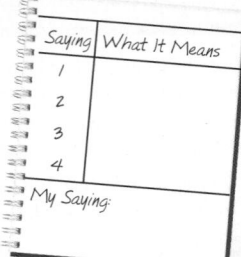

Saying	What It Means
1	
2	
3	
4	

My Saying:

386

R RESOURCE MANAGER UNIT 3

Plan and Teach pp. 153–160

Literary Analysis
Summary pp. 161†*, 162‡*
Theme in Drama pp. 163, 164†*
Question Support p. 169*

Reading
Analyze Sequence pp. 165, 166†*
Reading Check p. 168
Reading Fluency p. 171

Vocabulary
Study p. 167*

Grammar and Writing
Independent and Dependent Clauses p. 170

Assessment
Selection Tests A, B/C pp. 173*, 175*
Test Generator CD

BEST PRACTICES TOOLKIT
Differentiated Instruction pp. 31–38*

Scaffolding Instruction pp. 43–46*

Graphic Organizers/Strategies
Read Aloud/Think Aloud • Cluster Diagram • Microtheme

Reading Support
Audio Anthology CD*

Technology
Literature and Vocabulary Centers at **ClassZone.com**

WriteSmart CD

* Resources for Differentiation   † Also in Spanish   ‡ In Haitian Creole and Vietnamese

LITERARY ANALYSIS: THEME IN DRAMA

Just as short stories, novels, and poems communicate **themes,** so do dramas. To identify the message in a drama, you can use some of the same methods you use with other works: read closely and think about what larger meaning the writer is suggesting. Also pay special attention to

- descriptions of the setting, events, and characters in the **stage directions**
- **dialogue** between characters

As you read *A Christmas Carol,* try to focus not only on what the characters say and do but also on how and why they say and do those things. Then ask yourself questions about what message the playwright is sharing.

READING SKILL: ANALYZE SEQUENCE

Knowing the order of events in a work of literature helps you better understand the work's theme. Events are not always presented in the order in which they happen. The reader may be taken backward or forward in time.

In a drama, clues about the order, or **sequence,** of events often appear in the stage directions. The titles of the scenes also provide clues about the sequence of events.

As you read *A Christmas Carol,* use a sequence wheel to help you keep track of the unusual sequence of events.

Key Events

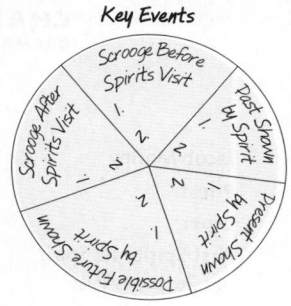

VOCABULARY IN CONTEXT

The following words all help tell the story of a man who is too concerned with **money.** How many words can you match with their definition?

1. accost	a. abrupt or blunt in speaking
2. anonymous	b. made very angry
3. brusque	c. not having one's name known
4. currency	d. to approach and speak unpleasantly to
5. incoherent	e. money
6. infuriated	f. confused

Author Online

Unhappy Childhood

Charles Dickens 1812–1870

Charles Dickens's childhood in England provided material for many of his stories. When Dickens was 12 and living with his family in London, his father was put in prison for not paying his debts. Young Dickens had to leave school to work in a rat-infested factory to help earn money for his family. The hopelessness and shame he felt there affected him deeply.

 MORE ABOUT THE AUTHOR
For more on Charles Dickens, visit the **Literature Center at ClassZone.com.**

Background

A Plea for the Poor When Frederick Gaines wrote the play you are about to read, he based it on a novel by the same name that Charles Dickens first published in 1843. At that time, about one-third of the people in London were living in poverty and hunger. The city was dirty and overcrowded, and jobs and houses were in short supply. Many children were forced to work instead of staying in school.

Charles Dickens wanted his novel *A Christmas Carol* to be "a plea for the poor." The book was instantly and widely popular, and as Dickens had hoped, it and his other writings did affect how his readers felt about the social conditions of their time.

Teach

STANDARDS FOCUS

● THEME IN DRAMA

Read aloud this example:

Speaker 1: You look great! Have you been on a vacation?

Speaker 2: No, I gave my fortune away to charity. I've never been happier!

Have students identify a theme revealed in this dialogue. Suggest they review the sayings on page 386. ***Possible answer:*** *"Money can't buy happiness."*

CHECK UNDERSTANDING Have students think of movies or plays that convey a theme about money.

■ ANALYZE SEQUENCE

Explain that in a play, stage directions may include sequence words such as *first, next, then,* and *after.* A change of setting, special sound effects, or special visual effects may also indicate a transition to an earlier or a later time. Point out that knowing the sequence of events in a character's life can help readers understand the character and related themes.

CHECK UNDERSTANDING Ask students how they might know, when watching a movie, that the setting has changed to an earlier time.

R RESOURCE MANAGER—Copy Master
Analyze Sequence p. 165 (for student use while reading the selection)

▲ VOCABULARY IN CONTEXT

ANSWERS 1. *d;* 2. *c;* 3. *a;* 4. *e;* 5. *f;* 6. *b*

PRETEACH VOCABULARY To preteach vocabulary, use the Vocabulary Study copy master, which provides a teacher-directed activity. Supply these definitions as needed:

accost (ə-kôst′) *v.* to approach and speak unpleasantly to

anonymous (ə-nŏn′ə-məs) *adj.* not having one's name known

brusque (brŭsk) *adj.* abrupt or blunt in speaking

currency (kûr′ən-sē) *n.* money in any form

incoherent (ĭn′-kō-hîr′ənt) *adj.* lacking connection; confused

infuriated (ĭn-fyŏŏr′ē-āt-ĭd) *v.* made very angry; enraged

R RESOURCE MANAGER—Copy Master
Vocabulary Study p. 167

For general guidelines on differentiating vocabulary instruction and for alternative vocabulary activities for students not needing vocabulary preteaching, see

 **BEST PRACTICES TOOLKIT**
Scaffolding Vocabulary Instruction pp. 43–46

ⓘ Vocabulary Center at **ClassZone.com** Additional Vocabulary Activities

Practice and Apply

BACKGROUND

Industrial Revolution in England The Industrial Revolution of the 19th century made possible the manufacture of cheaper toys and goods for people to exchange with each other. It created a class of poor factory workers who lived in miserable, crowded conditions, and it also created a class of wealthy business owners. In *A Christmas Carol*, Dickens urged these wealthy citizens to give to the poor at Christmas, helping to establish the tradition of charity during this holiday season.

CULTURAL CONNECTION

Christmas Traditions *A Christmas Carol,* the novel by Charles Dickens upon which this play is based, is credited with reviving an interest in Christmas celebrations, such as decorating Christmas trees and giving gifts. Other Christmas traditions can be traced to cultures around the world. The Norse people, pre-Christian Celtic and Germanic tribes, believed that the sun was a wheel, or hweol, that rolled toward and then away from the Earth. When they celebrated the winter solstice, they burned the "hweol," or Yule, log. Today, the Yule log mostly refers to a symbolically decorated cake that is served at Christmas. The poinsettia, a plant with large red flowers favored at Christmas, came from Mexico. In 1828, Joel R. Poinsett, the U.S. minister to Mexico, brought home the first poinsettia and encouraged its cultivation.

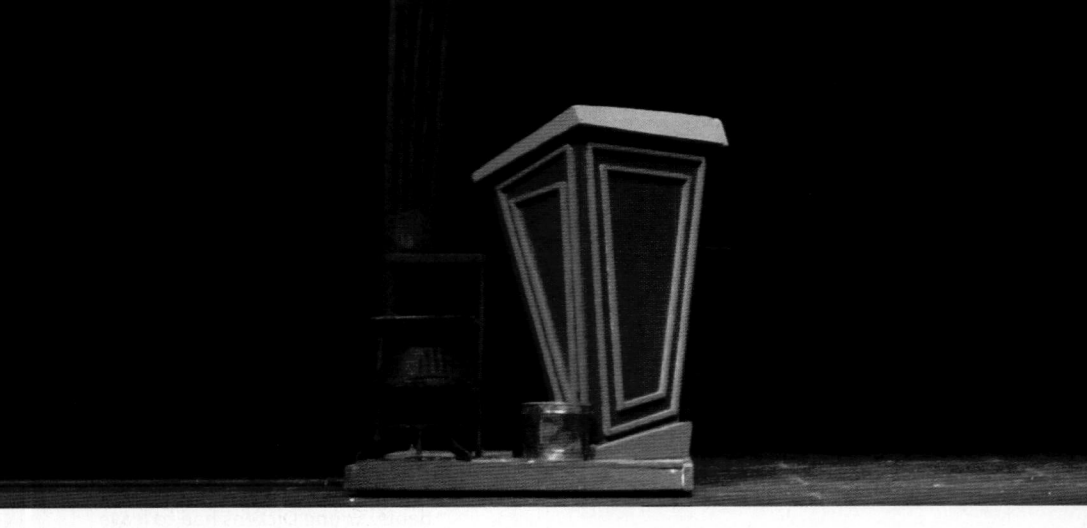

A CHRISTMAS CAROL

CHARLES DICKENS
DRAMATIZED BY FREDERICK GAINES

CHARACTERS

Carolers, Families, Dancers
First Boy
Second Boy
Third Boy
Girl with a doll
Ebenezer Scrooge
Bob Cratchit, Scrooge's clerk
Fred, Scrooge's nephew
Gentleman Visitor
Warder and Residents of the Poorhouse
Sparsit, Scrooge's servant
Cook
Charwoman

Jacob Marley
Priest
Leper
First Spirit, the Spirit of Christmas Past
Jack Walton
Ben Benjamin
Child Scrooge
Fan, Scrooge's sister
Fezziwig
Young Ebenezer
Dick Wilkins
Sweetheart of Young Ebenezer

Second Spirit, the Spirit of Christmas Present
Poorhouse Children
Mrs. Cratchit
Several Cratchit Children
Tiny Tim
Beggar Children, Hunger and Ignorance
Third Spirit, the Spirit of Christmas Yet to Come
Peter, a Cratchit child
Boy
Butcher
Coachman

DIFFERENTIATED INSTRUCTION

FOR ALL STUDENTS

Expert Groups Write these topics on the board. Encourage groups or individuals to become experts by researching topics that interest them. Suggest that students use visuals when they present their information to the class.

- a typical Christmas dinner menu in Victorian England
- debtors' prisons and workhouses
- London in the mid-1800s

FOR LESS–PROFICIENT READERS

In combination with the *Audio Anthology CD,* use one or more Targeted Passages (pp. 390, 396, 400, 405, 410) to help students focus on key story events, concepts, and skills.

FOR ENGLISH LEARNERS

Key Academic Vocabulary Discuss how to use the meanings of prefixes to define unfamiliar words. List these prefixes and their meanings: *re-* ("back or again"), *trans-* ("change"). Have small groups define these academic vocabulary words from the selection using their knowledge of the prefixes and roots: *transformed* (sc. 1 line 7), *recovers* (sc. 2 line 24), *responds* (sc. 2 line 85), *release* (sc. 3 line 166), *resource* (sc. 4 line 173), *removes* (sc. 5 line 59).

© Louisiana Tech University
School of Performing Arts.

PROLOGUE

The play begins amid a swirl of street life in Victorian London. Happy groups pass; brightly costumed carolers *and* families *call out to one another and sing "Joy to the World." Three* boys *and a* girl *are grouped about a glowing mound of coal. As the* carolers *leave the stage, the lights dim and the focus shifts to the mound of coals, bright against the dark. Slowly, the children begin to respond to the warmth. A piano plays softly*
10 *as the children talk.*

First Boy. I saw a horse in a window. (*pause*) A dapple . . . gray and white. And a saddle, too . . . red. And a strawberry mane down to here. All new. Golden stirrups. (*People pass by the children, muttering greetings to one another.*)

Second Boy. Christmas Eve.

Third Boy. Wish we could go.

First Boy. So do I.

Third Boy. I think I'd like it.

20 **First Boy.** Oh, wouldn't I . . . wouldn't I!

Second Boy. We're going up onto the roof. (*The* boys *look at him quizzically.*) My father has a glass. Telescope. A brass one. It opens up and it has twists on it and an eyepiece that you put up to look through. We can see all the way to the park with it.

Third Boy. Could I look through it?

Second Boy. Maybe . . . where would you look? (*The* third boy *points straight up.*) Why there?

30 **Third Boy.** I'd like to see the moon. (*The* boys *stand and look upward as the* girl *sings to her doll. One of the* boys *makes a snow angel on the ground.*)

Girl (*singing*).
Christ the King came down one day,
Into this world of ours,
And crying from a manger bed,
Began the Christmas hour.
(*speaking*)
40 Christ the King, my pretty one,
Sleep softly on my breast,
Christ the King, my gentle one,
Show us the way to rest.
(*She begins to sing the first verse again. As snow starts to fall on the* boy *making the snow angel, he stands up and reaches out to catch a single flake.*)

A CHRISTMAS CAROL **389**

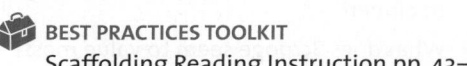

Lines 19–27

LITERARY ANALYSIS

● **THEME IN DRAMA**

Why is Scrooge disgusted with Christmas?

Possible answer: He thinks it is foolish for people to feel merry, since they are no richer on Christmas than on any other day.

Extend the Discussion How does Scrooge's attitude contrast with his nephew's?

Lines 41–43

READING SKILL

■ **ANALYZE SEQUENCE**

What event happens in lines 41–43? Suggest that students record their answers in the first segment of the sequence wheel from page 387.

Possible answer:

Scrooge Before Spirits Visit

1. Refuses invitation to Christmas dinner from nephew Fred
2.

The percussion[1] thunders. Scrooge hurls himself through the descending snowflakes and sends the children scattering. They retreat, watching. Cratchit comes in. He takes some coal from the mound and puts it into a small bucket; as he carries it to a corner of the stage, the stage area is transformed from street to office. Scrooge's nephew Fred enters, talks with the children, gives them coins, and sends them away with 10 *a "Merry Christmas."*

Fred. A Merry Christmas, Uncle! God save you!

Scrooge. Bah! Humbug!

Fred. Christmas a humbug, Uncle? I hope that's meant as a joke.

Scrooge. Well, it's not. Come, come, what is it you want? Don't waste all the day, Nephew.

Fred. I only want to wish you a Merry Christmas, Uncle. Don't be cross.

Scrooge. What else can I be when I live in such 20 a world of fools as this? Merry Christmas! Out with Merry Christmas! What's Christmas to you but a time for paying bills without money, a time for finding yourself a year older and not an hour richer. If I could work my will, every idiot who goes about with "Merry Christmas" on his lips should be boiled with his own pudding and buried with a stake of holly through his heart.

Fred. Uncle!

Scrooge. Nephew, keep Christmas in your own 30 way and let me keep it in mine.

Fred. But you don't keep it.

Scrooge. Let me leave it alone then. Much good may it do you. Much good it has ever done you.

Fred. There are many things from which I

might have derived good by which I have not profited, I daresay, Christmas among the rest. And though it has never put a scrap of gold in my pocket, I believe it has done me good and will do me good, and I say, God bless it!

40 **Scrooge.** Bah!

Fred. Don't be angry, Uncle. Come! Dine with us tomorrow.

Scrooge. I'll dine alone, thank you.

Fred. But why?

Scrooge. Why? Why did you get married?

Fred. Why, because I fell in love with a wonderful girl.

Scrooge. And I with solitude. Good afternoon.

Fred. Nay, Uncle, but you never came to 50 see me before I was married. Why give it as a reason for not coming now?

Scrooge. Good afternoon.

Fred. I am sorry with all my heart to find you so determined; but I have made the attempt in homage to Christmas, and I'll keep that good spirit to the last. So, a Merry Christmas, Uncle.

Scrooge. Good afternoon!

Fred. And a Happy New Year!

Scrooge. Good afternoon! (*Fred hesitates as* 60 *if to say something more. He sees that* Scrooge *has gone to get a volume down from the shelf, and so he starts to leave. As he leaves, the doorbell rings.*) Bells. Is it necessary to always have bells? (*The gentleman visitor enters, causing the doorbell to ring again.*) Cratchit!

Cratchit. Yes, sir?

Scrooge. The bell, fool! See to it!

Cratchit. Yes, sir. (*He goes to the entrance.*)

❶ **Targeted Passage**

---

1. **percussion:** noise made by loudly striking objects, such as drums or cymbals.

DIFFERENTIATED INSTRUCTION

FOR LESS–PROFICIENT READERS

❶ **Targeted Passage** [Scene 1, Lines 17–43]

This passage introduces two main characters and sets up the play's basic conflict: Scrooge's internal struggle involving his love of money.

- How does Scrooge feel about Christmas?
- What is Fred's feeling about the holiday?
- How does Scrooge react to Fred's invitation to dinner?
- What does Scrooge seem to value most?

Drama Basics Explain the parts of a play and have students find examples of each.

- Dialogue is the conversation between characters.
- Stage directions are instructions that tell the actors where to move or how to speak. They also describe the setting, sound effects, and props (items that characters use).
- Scenes and acts are the divisions within a play. Each scene has a different setting.

ANALYZE VISUALS

Activity Tell students that all the images in this selection are from a stage production of *A Christmas Carol.* Ask them what impression of Scrooge the image on page 391 creates and why. ***Possible answer:*** *Scrooge seems to be warning the children away. The image suggests that he has no tolerance or patience for children and is somewhat bad-tempered.*

FOR ADVANCED LEARNERS/PRE–AP

Analyze a Dynamic Character Explain that a dynamic character is one who changes during the course of a story. Often the way a character changes is connected to the theme of the story. Have students create a chart to track how Scrooge has changed over the course of his life. At the end of the play, have them predict how Scrooge may continue to change in the future, and discuss how these changes reveal a message about life.

Ebenezer Scrooge

Childhood	Young Manhood	Present	Future
What the changes in Scrooge teach about life:			

DISCUSSION PROMPTS

Use these prompts to help students understand how Scrooge's exchange with the gentleman visitor reinforces major themes:

Connect If you were collecting money to help the poor, would you ask Ebenezer Scrooge to contribute? Explain. ***Possible answers: Yes, because Scrooge is a wealthy business owner. No, because he does not seem very friendly.***

Analyze Why does Scrooge feel justified in turning down the visitor's request for a donation? ***Possible answer: He feels that he already supports government institutions that help the poor, such as workhouses.***

Evaluate Which character makes a more convincing argument about the situation of the poor? What message or theme does this dialogue suggest? ***Possible answer: The visitor makes a more convincing argument. He seems to appreciate how miserable life can be for the poor. The scene conveys the message that it is right to treat other people with compassion and generosity.***

Lines 133–141

LITERARY ANALYSIS

● THEME IN DRAMA

What does Scrooge mean when he says, "If they would rather die, they had better do it and decrease the surplus population" (lines 133–134)? ***Possible answer: He thinks the poor should be satisfied with whatever they are given. Scrooge does not care what happens to the "idle" poor, and he does not feel responsible for helping them with their problems. He cares only about his own business affairs (lines 135–136).***

Scrooge (*muttering*). Merry Christmas . . .
70 Wolves howling and a Merry Christmas . . .

Cratchit. It's for you, sir.

Scrooge. Of course it's for me. You're not receiving callers, are you? Show them in.

Cratchit. Right this way, sir. (*The gentleman visitor approaches Scrooge.*)

Scrooge. Yes, yes?

Gentleman Visitor. Scrooge and Marley's, I believe. Have I the pleasure of addressing Mr. Scrooge or Mr. Marley?

80 **Scrooge.** Marley's dead. Seven years tonight. What is it you want?

Gentleman Visitor. I have no doubt that his liberality is well represented by his surviving partner. Here, sir, my card. (*He hands Scrooge his business card.*)

Scrooge. Liberality? No doubt of it? All right, all right, I can read. What is it you want? (*He returns to his work.*)

Gentleman Visitor. At this festive season
90 of the year . . .

Scrooge. It's winter and cold. (*He continues his work and ignores the gentleman visitor.*)

Gentleman Visitor. Yes . . . yes, it is, and the more reason for my visit. At this time of the year it is more than usually desirable to make some slight provision for the poor and destitute² who suffer greatly from the cold. Many thousands are in want of common necessaries; hundreds of thousands are in
100 want of common comforts, sir.

Scrooge. Are there no prisons?

Gentleman Visitor. Many, sir.

Scrooge. And the workhouse?³ Is it still in operation?

---

2. **destitute:** people lacking the necessities of life.
3. **workhouse:** an establishment in which poor people are housed and required to do work.
4. **abundance rejoices:** those with wealth are happy.

Gentleman Visitor. It is; still, I wish I could say it was not.

Scrooge. The poor law is still in full vigor then?

Gentleman Visitor. Yes, sir.

Scrooge. I'm glad to hear it. From what
110 you said, I was afraid someone had stopped its operation.

Gentleman Visitor. Under the impression that they scarcely furnish Christian cheer of mind or body to the multitude, a few of us are endeavoring to raise a fund to buy the poor some meat and drink and means of warmth. We choose this time because it is the time, of all others, when want is keenly felt and abundance rejoices.⁴ May I put you down for
120 something, sir?

Scrooge (*retreating into the darkness temporarily*). Nothing.

Gentleman Visitor. You wish to be **anonymous**?

Scrooge. I wish to be left alone. Since you ask me what I wish, sir, that is my answer. I don't make merry myself at Christmas, and I can't afford to make idle people merry. I help support the establishments I have mentioned . . . they cost enough . . . and those who are poorly off
130 must go there.

Gentleman Visitor. Many can't go there, and many would rather die.

Scrooge. If they would rather die, they had better do it and decrease the surplus population. That is not my affair. My business is. It occupies me constantly. (*He talks both to the gentleman visitor and to himself while he thumbs through his books.*) Ask a man to give up life and means . . . fine thing. What is it, I want to know? Charity?
140 . . . (*His nose deep in his books, he vaguely hears the dinner bell being rung in the workhouse; he*

DIFFERENTIATED INSTRUCTION

FOR ENGLISH LEARNERS

Vocabulary: Context Clues Point out that some of the dialogue may be difficult to understand because the characters use terms and phrases common in the mid-1800s that are no longer in general use. Explain how to look for context clues in surrounding text to figure out the meanings of difficult terms or phrases. Then have students work in pairs to determine the meanings of these phrases:

- *are in want of* (line 98), "need"

- *is . . . in full vigor* (line 107), "is in effect; is working"

- *the multitude* (line 114), "most people"

- *endeavoring* (line 115), "trying"

- *want is keenly felt* (line 118), "poverty or need is very painful"

- *put you down for something* (lines 119–120), "write your name on the list of donors"

- *I don't make merry myself* (line 126), "I don't celebrate"

looks up as if he has heard it but never focuses on the actual scene. The warder *of the poorhouse stands in a pool of light at the far left, slowly ringing a bell.*)

Warder. Dinner. All right. Line up. (*The poorly clad, dirty residents of the poorhouse line up and file by to get their evening dish of gruel,[5] wordlessly accepting it and going back to eat listlessly in the gloom. Scrooge returns to the business of his office.* 160 *The procession continues for a moment, then the image of the poorhouse is obscured by darkness. The dejected gentleman visitor exits.*)

Scrooge. Latch the door, Cratchit. Firmly, firmly. Draft as cold as Christmas blowing in here. Charity! (*Cratchit goes to the door, starts to close it, then sees the little girl with the doll. She seems to beckon to him; he moves slowly toward her, and they dance together for a moment. Scrooge continues to work. Suddenly* carolers *appear on the* platform, *and a few phrases of their carol, "Angels We Have Heard on High," are heard. Scrooge looks up.*) Cratchit! (*As soon as Scrooge shouts, the* girl *and the* carolers *vanish and* Cratchit *begins to close up the shop.*) Cratchit!

Cratchit. Yes, sir.

Scrooge. Well, to work then!

Cratchit. It's evening, sir.

Scrooge. Is it?

Cratchit. Christmas evening, sir.

170 **Scrooge.** Oh, you'll want all day tomorrow off, I suppose.

Cratchit. If it's quite convenient, sir.

Scrooge. It's not convenient, and it's not fair. If I was to deduct half a crown[6] from your salary for it, you'd think yourself ill-used, wouldn't you? Still you expect me to pay a day's wage for a day of no work.

Cratchit. It's only once a year, sir.

---

5. **gruel:** a thin, watery food made by boiling ground grain in water or milk.

6. **half a crown:** until 1971, an amount of British money equal to one-eighth of a pound. The pound is the basic unit of British money.

Scrooge. Be here all the earlier the next morning.

Cratchit. I will, sir.

180 **Scrooge.** Then off, off.

Cratchit. Yes, sir! Merry Christmas, sir!

Scrooge. Bah! (*As soon as* Cratchit *opens the door, the sounds of the street begin, very bright and loud.* Cratchit *is caught up in a swell of people hurrying through the street. Children pull him along to the top of an ice slide, and he runs and slides down it, disappearing in darkness as the stage suddenly is left almost empty. Scrooge goes around the room blowing out the candles, talking to himself.*) Christmas 190 Eve. Carolers! Bah! There. Another day. (*He opens his door and peers out.*) Black, very black. Now where are they? (*The children are heard singing carols for a moment.*) Begging pennies for their songs, are they? Oh, boy! Here, boy! (*The little* girl *emerges from the shadows. Scrooge hands her a dark lantern, and she holds it while he lights it with an ember from the pile of coals.*)

© Louisiana Tech University School of Performing Arts.

A CHRISTMAS CAROL **393**

Lines 140–152

LITERARY ANALYSIS

● **THEME IN DRAMA**

When and where does the scene of the poorhouse take place in relation to Scrooge's conversation with the visitor? *Possible answer: The poorhouse is located nearby, somewhere in London. The dinner scene takes place just as Scrooge is dismissing the visitor; he looks up when he hears the bell.*

Extend the Discussion How do the stage directions describing the poorhouse scene further reveal Scrooge's attitude toward the poor?

Lines 173–179
REINFORCE *KEY IDEA:* MONEY

Discuss How important is **money** to Scrooge at this point in the play? *Possible answer: Scrooge cares more about money than he does about making others happy or about Christmas itself.*

FOR ENGLISH LEARNERS

Language: Conversational English Patterns
Point out that in line 154 the words *A* and *is* are missing from the sentence: *[A] draft as cold as Christmas [is] blowing in here.* Explain that in dialogue, words are often left out but are understood. Guide students to supply missing words in line 166 (*let's get*); line 169 (*It's*); line 180 (*go*); line 190 (*is over*); line 191 (*It's . . . outside*).

Comprehension: Monitor Have students write on index cards any lines from the play that they do not understand or any questions that they have. Collect the cards when students are finished. Assign small groups one or more questions or sets of lines to discuss. Have groups share their ideas in a whole-class discussion.

FOR ADVANCED LEARNERS/PRE–AP

Explore Setting Challenge students to re-create lines 153–188 in a modern setting. Have small groups discuss Bob Cratchit's subservient relationship to his boss and the meaning of his dance with the little girl (lines 155–158). Ask them to describe a similar scene that could take place today, including the kind of job Cratchit might have and how he might dream of escaping the drudgery.

A CHRISTMAS CAROL **393**

● THEME IN DRAMA

Why do you think the image of Marley, Scrooge's former partner, appears to Scrooge? *Possible answers: He is on Scrooge's mind because he died seven years ago on Christmas Eve. Scrooge feels guilty about Marley. The past is coming back to haunt Scrooge.*

If students need help . . . Return to Scene 1, line 80, to identify Marley and the date of his death. Discuss how the anniversary of a person's death often brings that person to mind.

Lines 44–52
REINFORCE *KEY IDEA:* MONEY

Discuss What does Scrooge's refusal to give his servants **money** at Christmas reveal about his priorities? *Possible answer: He cares little about treating his servants fairly or trying to win their affection. He cares only about hoarding his own money.*

SCENE 2
~ SCROOGE GOES HOME ~

Scrooge (*talking to the little* girl). Hold it quiet! There. Off now. That's it. High. Black as pitch. Light the street, that's it. You're a bright lad! Good to see that. Earn your supper, boy. You'll not go hungry this night. Home. You know the way, do you? Yes, that's the way. The house of Ebenezer Scrooge. (*As the two find their way to Scrooge's house, the audience sees and hears a brief image of a cathedral interior with a*
10 *living crèche[7] and a large choir singing "Amen!"; the image ends in a blackout. The lights come up immediately, and* Scrooge *is at his door.*) Hold the light up, boy, up. (*The girl with the lantern disappears.*) Where did he go? Boy? No matter. There's a penny saved. Lantern's gone out. No matter. A candle saved. Yes, here's the key. (*He turns with the key toward the door, and* Marley's *face swims out of the darkness.* Scrooge *watches, unable to speak. He fumbles for a match,*
20 *lights the lantern, and swings it toward the figure, which melts away. Pause.* Scrooge *fits the key in the lock and turns it as the door suddenly is opened from the inside by the porter,* Sparsit. Scrooge *is startled, then recovers.*) Sparsit?

Sparsit. Yes, sir?

Scrooge. Hurry, hurry. The door . . . close it.

Sparsit. Did you knock, sir?

Scrooge. Knock? What matter? Here, light me up the stairs.

30 **Sparsit.** Yes, sir. (*He leads* Scrooge *up the stairs. They pass the* cook *on the way.* Scrooge *brushes by her, stops, looks back, and she leans toward him.*)

Cook. Something to warm you, sir? Porridge?

Scrooge. Wha . . . ? No. No, nothing.

Cook (*waiting for her Christmas coin*). Merry Christmas, sir. (Scrooge *ignores the request and the* cook *disappears. Mumbling,* Scrooge *follows* Sparsit.)

Scrooge (*looking back after the* cook *is gone*). Fright a man nearly out of his life . . . Merry
40 Christmas . . . bah!

Sparsit. Your room, sir.

Scrooge. Hmmm? Oh, yes, yes. And good night.

Sparsit (*extending his hand for his coin*). Merry Christmas, sir.

Scrooge. Yes, yes . . . (*He sees the outstretched hand; he knows what* Sparsit *wants and is* **infuriated.**) Out! Out! (*He closes the door after* Sparsit, *turns toward his chamber, and discovers*
50 *the* charwoman *directly behind him.*)

Charwoman. Warm your bed for you, sir?

Scrooge. What? Out! Out!

Charwoman. Aye, sir. (*She starts for the door.* Marley's *voice is heard mumbling something unintelligible.*)

Scrooge. What's that?

Charwoman. Me, sir? Not a thing, sir.

Scrooge. Then, good night.

Charwoman. Good night. (*She exits, and*
60 Scrooge *pantomimes shutting the door behind her. The voice of* Marley *over an offstage microphone whispers and reverberates:[8] "Merry Christmas, Scrooge!" Silence.* Scrooge *hears the voice but cannot account for it. He climbs up to open a window and looks down. A cathedral choir singing "O Come, All Ye Faithful" is heard in the distance.* Scrooge *listens a moment, shuts the window,*

---

7. **a cathedral interior with a living crèche:** the inside of a large church in which real people pose for the Christmas manger scene.

8. **reverberates** (rĭ-vûr′bə-rāts′): echoes.

394 UNIT 3: UNDERSTANDING THEME

DIFFERENTIATED INSTRUCTION

FOR LESS–PROFICIENT READERS

Mood Explain that the story takes place in the days before electric street lights. The flickering light cast by gas street lights was insufficient, so Scrooge arranges to pay a child to carry a lantern (lines 1–24). Scrooge seems to feel uncomfortable about the darkness. As he walks home, the alternating images of light and darkness set the anxious, nervous mood for the scene. Scrooge doesn't seem to know if what he sees is real or if he is imagining things.

FOR ENGLISH LEARNERS

Language: Punctuation Cues Explain that ellipses can be used to indicate missing letters or words in text. Sometimes ellipses show that a sentence is deliberately incomplete. Work with students to paraphrase the missing letters or words indicated by these ellipses:

- Line 26: "The door . . ." *(is open)*
- Line 34: "Wha . . . ?" *(What did you say?)*
- Lines 39–40: *(All these idiots are wishing me a)* ". . . Merry Christmas"
- Line 40: *(All I have to say is)* ". . . bah!"

LITERARY ANALYSIS

● THEME IN DRAMA

What does Marley's chain symbolize? *Possible answer: Marley must wear his chain as punishment for the greedy life he led. The chain symbolizes the money that was so important to him in life. In death, it traps him and weighs him down.*

Lines 115–131

READING SKILL

■ ANALYZE SEQUENCE

What events are foreshadowed by Marley's message (lines 115–129)? *Possible answer: Three spirits will visit Scrooge on the next three nights. They will give Scrooge a chance to change his life so that he can avoid the fate of Marley.*

Remind students to continue adding important events to the sequence wheel. *Possible answers:*

Scrooge Before Spirits Visit

1. Refuses invitation to Christmas dinner from nephew Fred
2. *Refuses to give money for the poor*
3. *Is prepared by Marley for the spirits' visits*

Extend the Discussion Why is Marley's visit important?

---

and prepares for bed. As soon as he has shut the sound out of his room, figures appear; they seem
70 *to be coming down the main aisle of a church, bearing gifts to the living crèche. The orchestra plays "O Come, All Ye Faithful" as the procession files out.* Scrooge, *ready for bed, warms himself before the heap of coals. As he pulls his nightcap from a chair, a small hand-bell tumbles off onto the floor. Startled, he picks it up and rings it for reassurance; an echo answers it. He turns and sees the little* girl *on the street; she is swinging her doll, which produces the echo of his bell.* Scrooge
80 *escapes to his bed; the* girl *is swallowed up in the darkness. The bell sounds grow to a din,* **incoherent** *as in a dream, then suddenly fall silent.* Scrooge *sits up in bed, listens, and hears the chains of* Marley *coming up the stairs.* Scrooge *reaches for the bell pull to summon* Sparsit. *The bell responds with a gong, and* Marley *appears. He and* Scrooge *face one another.*)

Scrooge. What do you want with me?

Marley (*in a ghostly, unreal voice*). Much.

90 **Scrooge.** Who are you?

Marley. Ask who I was.   **Targeted Passage** ②

Scrooge. Who were you?

Marley. In life, I was your partner, Jacob Marley.

Scrooge. He's dead.

Marley. Seven years this night, Ebenezer Scrooge.

Scrooge. Why do you come here?

Marley. I must. It is commanded me. I must wander the world and see what I can no longer share, what I would not share when I walked
100 where you do.

Scrooge. And must go thus?

Marley. The chain? Look at it, Ebenezer, study it. Locks and vaults and golden coins. I forged it, each link, each day when I sat in these chairs,

commanded these rooms. Greed, Ebenezer Scrooge, wealth. Feel them, know them. Yours was as heavy as this I wear seven years ago, and you have labored to build it since.

Scrooge. If you're here to lecture, I have
110 no time for it. It is late; the night is cold. I want comfort now.

Marley. I have none to give. I know not how you see me this night. I did not ask it. I have sat invisible beside you many and many a day. I am commanded to bring you a chance, Ebenezer. Heed it!

Scrooge. Quickly then, quickly.

Marley. You will be haunted by three spirits.

Scrooge (*scoffing*). Is that the chance?

120 **Marley.** Mark it.

Scrooge. I do not choose to.

Marley (*ominously*). Then you will walk where I do, burdened by your riches, your greed.

Scrooge. Spirits mean nothing to me.

Marley (*slowly leaving*). Expect the first tomorrow, when the bell tolls one, the second on the next night at the same hour, the third upon the next night when the last stroke of twelve has ended. Look to see me no more.
130 I must wander. Look that, for your own sake, you remember what has passed between us.

Scrooge. Jacob . . . Don't leave me! . . . Jacob! Jacob!

Marley. Adieu,[9] Ebenezer. (*At Marley's last words a funeral procession begins to move across the stage. A boy walks in front; a* priest *follows, swinging a censer;[10] sounds of mourning and the suggestion of church music are heard.* Scrooge *calls out, "Jacob, don't leave me!" as if talking in the midst*
140 *of a bad dream. At the end of the procession is the little* girl, *swinging her doll and singing softly.*)

---

9. **adieu** (ə-dyōō'): farewell.

10. **censer:** a container in which incense is burned.

DIFFERENTIATED INSTRUCTION

FOR LESS–PROFICIENT READERS

② **Targeted Passage [Scene 2, Lines 112–131]**

This passage predicts important events that will follow, and it highlights a major theme in the play: the consequences Scrooge will face if he continues his life of greed.

- In what way is Marley being punished?
- Who, beside Marley, is going to visit Scrooge? When?
- How does Scrooge react to Marley's message?

FOR ENGLISH LEARNERS

Vocabulary: Multiple-Meaning Words Explain that the word *spirit* has more than one meaning. Have students turn to page 390 and use context clues to determine what Fred means by the "good spirit" of Christmas in lines 55–56 (*meaning or essence*). Then point out Marley's statement on page 396 that Scrooge will be "haunted by three spirits" (line 118). Help them think of a synonym for *spirit* in this sense (*ghost, specter*).

© Louisiana Tech University School of Performing Arts.

Girl.
Hushabye, don't you cry,
Go to sleep, little baby.
When you wake, you shall have
All the pretty little horses,
Blacks and bays, dapples and grays,
All the pretty little horses.

(*She stops singing and looks up at* Scrooge; *their
eyes meet, and she solemnly rings the doll in greeting.* Scrooge *pulls shut the bed curtains, and the
girl exits. The bell sounds are picked up by the bells
of a* leper[11] *who enters, dragging himself along.*)

Leper (*calling out*). Leper! Leper! Stay the way!
Leper! Leper! Keep away! (*He exits and the clock

---

11. **leper:** a person who has leprosy, a skin disease once
thought to be highly contagious.

begins to chime, ringing the hours.* Scrooge *sits
up in bed and begins to count the chimes.*)

Scrooge. Eight . . . nine . . . ten . . . eleven . . .
it can't be . . . twelve. Midnight? No. Not twelve.
160 It can't be. I haven't slept the whole day through.
Twelve? Yes, yes, twelve noon. (*He hurries to the
window and looks out.*) Black. Twelve midnight.
(*pause*) I must get up. A day wasted. I must get
down to the office. (*Two small chimes are heard.*)
Quarter past. But it just rang twelve. Fifteen
minutes haven't gone past, not so quickly.
(*Again two small chimes are heard.*) A quarter
to one. The spirit . . . It's to come at one. (*He
hurries to his bed as the chimes ring again.*) One.

READING SKILL

■ ANALYZE SEQUENCE

What part of his life is Scrooge reliving in this scene?

Have students record their answers in the sequence wheel from page 387. **Possible answer:**

Past Shown by Spirit

1. *Sees himself as a boy at boarding school, left there for the holidays*

Lines 31–62
DISCUSSION PROMPTS

Use these prompts to help students compare and contrast the characters of young and old Scrooge:

Connect How would a child feel if he or she were left somewhere while everyone else went home? *Students may say that the child would feel lonely and sad.*

Analyze What does young Scrooge's choice of reading material reveal about his character? *Possible answers: He liked adventure and fantasy. He had an active imagination. He liked to read to escape.*

Synthesize In what ways are the young and old characters of Scrooge the same and different? *Possible answers: Young Scrooge is lonely. Old Scrooge is also cut off from others, only he has brought it on himself. Young Scrooge is gentle and imaginative. Old Scrooge is harsh. He has no time for anything but business.*

SCENE 3
~ THE SPIRIT OF CHRISTMAS PAST ~

The hour is struck again by a large street clock, and the first spirit *appears. It is a figure dressed to look like the little girl's doll.*

Scrooge. Are you the spirit whose coming was foretold to me?

First Spirit. I am.

Scrooge. Who and what are you?

First Spirit. I am the Ghost of Christmas Past.

Scrooge. Long past?

10 **First Spirit.** Your past.

Scrooge. Why are you here?

First Spirit. Your welfare. Rise. Walk with me.

Scrooge. I am mortal still. I cannot pass through air.

First Spirit. My hand. (Scrooge *grasps the* spirit's *hand tightly, and the doll's bell rings softly. Scrooge remembers a scene from his past in which two boys greet each other in the street.)*

First Voice. Halloo, Jack!

20 **Second Voice.** Ben! Merry Christmas, Ben!

Scrooge. Jack Walton. Young Jack Walton. Spirits . . . ?

First Voice. Have a good holiday, Jack.

Scrooge. Yes, yes, I remember him. Both of them. Little Ben Benjamin. He used to . . .

First Voice. See you next term, Jack. Next . . . term . . .

Scrooge. They . . . they're off for the holidays and going home from school. It's Christmas
30 time . . . all of the children off home now . . . No . . . no, not all . . . there was one . . .

---

12. **Ali Baba:** in the *Arabian Nights*, a poor woodcutter who discovers a treasure.

13. **Robinson Crusoe:** a shipwrecked sailor who survives for years on a small island in the novel *Robinson Crusoe*.

(*The* spirit *motions for* Scrooge *to turn, and he sees a young boy playing with a teddy bear and talking to it.*) Yes . . . reading . . . poor boy.

First Spirit. What, I wonder?

Scrooge. Reading? Oh, it was nothing. Fancy, all fancy and make-believe and take-me-away. All of it. Yes, nonsense.

Child Scrooge. Ali Baba.[12]

40 **Scrooge.** Yes . . . that was it . . .

Child Scrooge. Yes, and remember . . . and remember . . . remember Robinson Crusoe?[13]

Scrooge. And the parrot!

Child Scrooge. Yes, the parrot! I love him best.

Scrooge (*imitating the parrot*). With his stripy green body and yellow tail drooping along and couldn't sing—awk—but could talk, and a thing like a lettuce growing out the top of his head . . . and he used to sit on the very top of the tree—up there.

50 **Child Scrooge.** And Robinson Crusoe sailed around the island, and he thought he had escaped the island, and the parrot said, the parrot said . . .

Scrooge (*imitating the parrot*). Robinson Crusoe, where you been? Awk! Robinson Crusoe, where you been?

Child Scrooge. And Robinson Crusoe looked up in the tree and saw the parrot and knew he hadn't escaped and he was still there, still all alone there.

60 **Scrooge.** Poor Robinson Crusoe.

Child Scrooge (*sadly replacing the teddy bear*). Poor Robinson Crusoe.

Scrooge. Poor child. Poor child.

First Spirit. Why poor?

Scrooge. Fancy . . . fancy . . . (*He tries to mask his feelings by being* **brusque**.) It's his way, a child's

---

DIFFERENTIATED INSTRUCTION

FOR LESS–PROFICIENT READERS

Reading Skill Follow-Up: Analyze Sequence
Use Read Aloud/Think Aloud to help students understand the flashback in lines 15–38. Point out that Scene 3 starts out with Scrooge meeting the first spirit. Discuss how these elements show that the scene has shifted to Scrooge's childhood:

• stage directions (lines 15–18)

• dialogue (lines 19–31)

• new characters, Jack and Ben (lines 19–21)

 BEST PRACTICES TOOLKIT—Transparency
Read Aloud/Think Aloud p. A34

ANALYZE VISUALS

Activity Ask students what kinds of reactions adults might have to seeing themselves as young boys and girls. What does the expression upon the face of the actor playing Scrooge reveal about Scrooge's feelings?

Possible answers: Some people would feel sad at the innocence and hopefulness that they have lost since they were children. Others might be happy because they feel they are still much the same inside. Scrooge looks terrified at the thought of traveling into the past and seeing himself as he used to be.

FOR ENGLISH LEARNERS

Language: Punctuation Explain that most of the ellipses on this page indicate incomplete thoughts that reflect the dreamlike mood. Work with students to paraphrase the missing words indicated by these ellipses:

- Line 22: "Spirits . . . ?" *(are what I'm seeing)*
- Line 25: "He used to . . .?" *(be at school with me)*
- Line 34: "Yes . . . *(he was)* reading . . . *(I feel sorry for the)* poor boy."

Lines 66–72
REINFORCE *KEY IDEA:* MONEY

Discuss What did **money** replace in Scrooge's life? *Possible answer: Money took the place of his dreams.*

Lines 131–141

LITERARY ANALYSIS

● THEME IN DRAMA

How does Scrooge feel about seeing Mr. Fezziwig? Explain. *Possible answer: Scrooge is pleased to see Fezziwig because he liked Fezziwig and was happy while working for him.*

Extend the Discussion Why is the spirit showing Scrooge scenes from his past?

Lines 100–109

READING SKILL

▪ ANALYZE SEQUENCE

When did Scrooge know Fezziwig? What did Fezziwig represent to him? *Possible answer: Scrooge was Fezziwig's apprentice when he was a boy. Fezziwig represents a time when Scrooge felt happy.*

Suggest that students add this event to their sequence wheels. *Possible answer:*

Past Shown by Spirit
2. *Sees himself as a young employee and remembers what a good master Fezziwig was*

---

way to . . . to lose being alone in . . . in dreams, dreams . . . Never matter if they are all nonsense, yes, nonsense. But he'll be all right, grow out
70 of it. Yes. Yes, he did outgrow it, the nonsense. Became a man and left there, and he became, yes, he became a man and . . . yes, successful . . . rich! (*The sadness returns.*) Never matter . . . never matter. (Fan *runs in and goes to* Child Scrooge.) Fan!

Fan. Brother, dear brother! (*She kisses* Child Scrooge.)

Child Scrooge. Dear, dear Fan.

Fan. I've come to bring you home, home for good and ever. Come with me, come now. (*She takes his hand, and they start to run off, but*
80 *the* spirit *stops them and signals for the light on them to fade. They look at the* spirit, *aware of their role in the* spirit's *"education" of* Scrooge.)

Scrooge. Let me watch them go? Let them be happy for a moment! (*The* spirit *says nothing.* Scrooge *turns away from them, and the light goes out.*) A delicate, delicate child. A breath might have withered her.

First Spirit. She died a woman and had, as I remember, children.

Scrooge. One child.
90 **First Spirit.** Your nephew.

Scrooge. Yes, yes, Fred, my nephew. (Scrooge *pauses, then tries to bluster through.*) Well? Well, all of us have that, haven't we? Childhoods? Sadnesses? But we grow and we become men, masters of ourselves. (*The* spirit *gestures for music to begin. It is heard first as from a great distance, then* Scrooge *becomes aware of it.*) I've no time for it, Spirit. Music and all of your Christmas folderol.[14] Yes, yes, I've learnt what you have
100 to show me. (Fezziwig, Young Ebenezer, *and* Dick *appear, busily preparing for a party.*)

Fezziwig. Yo ho, there! Ebenezer! Dick!

---

14. **folderol** (fŏl'-də-rŏl'): foolishness; nonsense.

15. **'prenticed:** short for *apprenticed,* here meaning "learned a trade while working."

16. **macabre** (mə-kä'brə) **dance to discordant sounds:** a bizarre, ghastly dance with unharmonious music.

Targeted Passage

③

Scrooge. Fezziwig! It's old Fezziwig that I 'prenticed[15] under.

First Spirit. Your master?

Scrooge. Oh, aye, and the best that any boy could have. There's Dick Wilkins! Bless me. He was very much attached to me was Dick. Poor Dick. Dear, dear.

110 **Fezziwig.** Yo ho, my boys! No more work tonight. Christmas Eve, Dick! Christmas, Ebenezer! Let's have the shutters up before a man can say Jack Robinson! (*The music continues. Chandeliers are pulled into position, and mistletoe, holly, and ivy are draped over everything by bustling servants. Dancers fill the stage for Fezziwig's wonderful Christmas party. In the midst of the dancing and the gaiety servants pass back and forth through the crowd*
120 *with huge platters of food. At a pause in the music,* Young Ebenezer, *who is dancing, calls out.*)

Young Ebenezer. Mr. Fezziwig, sir, you're a wonderful master!

Scrooge and Young Ebenezer. A wonderful master!

Scrooge (*echoing the phrase*). A wonderful master! (*The music changes suddenly, and the* dancers *jerk into distorted postures and then begin to move in slow motion. The celebrants slowly exit, performing a macabre*
130 *dance to discordant sounds.[16]*)

First Spirit. Just because he gave a party? It was very small.

Scrooge. Small!

First Spirit. He spent a few pounds of your "mortal" money, three, four at the most. Is that so much that he deserves this praise?

Scrooge. But it wasn't the money. He had the power to make us happy, to make our service light or burdensome. The happiness he gives

---

DIFFERENTIATED INSTRUCTION

FOR LESS–PROFICIENT READERS

③ Targeted Passage [Scene 3, Lines 77–118]
This passage contrasts the young Scrooge with the adult character and reveals significant relationships in his past.

- What was Scrooge's relationship with his sister like?

- What happened to his sister?

- How does Scrooge describe Fezziwig?

- What did Fezziwig do for his employees on Christmas Eve?

FOR ADVANCED LEARNERS/PRE–AP

Analyze Tone Have students focus on lines 125–150 and discuss the tone of the spirit's remarks. Why does he contradict everything Scrooge says? Is he teasing Scrooge? Whose ideas is the spirit mocking? Have student pairs read these lines aloud to show how actors could portray the two characters. You might have them perform the dialogue for the class.

40 is quite as great as if it cost a fortune. That's what . . . a good master is.

First Spirit. Yes?

Scrooge. No, no, nothing.

First Spirit. Something, I think.

Scrooge. I should like to be able to say a word or two to my clerk just now, that's all.

First Spirit. But this is all past. Your clerk, Cratchit, couldn't be here.

Scrooge. No, no, of course not, an idle thought.
50 Are we done?

First Spirit (*motioning for the waltz music to begin*). Nearly.

Scrooge (*hearing the waltz and remembering it*). Surely it's enough. Haven't you tormented me enough? (*Young Ebenezer is seen waltzing with his* Sweetheart.)

First Spirit. I only show the past, what it promised you. Look. Another promise.

Scrooge. Oh. Oh, yes. I had forgotten . . . her. Don't they dance beautifully? So young, so
60 young. I would have married her if only . . .

Sweetheart. Can you love me, Ebenezer? I bring no dowry[17] to my marriage, only me, only love. It is no **currency** that you can buy and sell with, but we can live with it. Can you? (*She pauses, then returns the ring* Scrooge *gave her as his pledge.*) I release you, Ebenezer, for the love of the man you once were. Will that man win me again, now that he is free?

Scrooge (*trying to speak to her*). If only you had
70 held me to it. You should not have let me go. I was young; I did love you.

Sweetheart (*speaking to* Young Ebenezer). We have never lied to one another. May you be happy in the life you have chosen. Good-bye. (*She runs out.* Young Ebenezer *slowly leaves.*)

Scrooge. No, no, it was not meant that way . . . !

---

17. **dowry** (dou'rē): money or property brought by a bride to her husband when they marry.

First Spirit. You cannot change now what you would not change then. I am your mistakes, Ebenezer Scrooge, all of the things you could
180 have done and did not.

Scrooge. Then leave me! I have done them. I shall live with them. As I have, as I do; as I will.

First Spirit. There is another Christmas, seven years ago, when Marley died.

Scrooge. No! I will not see it. I will not! He died. I could not prevent it. I did not choose for him to die on Christmas Day.

First Spirit. And when his day was chosen, what did you do then?

190 **Scrooge.** I looked after his affairs.

First Spirit. His business.

Scrooge. Yes! His business! Mine! It was all that I had, all that I could do in this world. I have nothing to do with the world to come after.

First Spirit. Then I will leave you.

Scrooge. Not yet! Don't leave me here! Tell me what I must do! What of the other spirits?

First Spirit. They will come.

Scrooge. And you? What of you?

200 **First Spirit.** I am always with you. (*The little* girl *appears with her doll; she takes* Scrooge's *hand and gently leads him to bed. Numbed, he follows her. She leans against the foot of the bed, ringing the doll and singing. The* first spirit *exits as she sings.*)

Girl.
When you wake, you shall have
All the pretty little horses,
Blacks and bays, dapples and grays,
All the pretty little horses.

210 (*She rings the doll, and the ringing becomes the chiming of* Scrooge's *bell. The* girl *exits.* Scrooge *sits upright in bed as he hears the chimes.*)

Scrooge. A minute until one. No one here. No one's coming. (*A larger clock strikes one o'clock.*)

LITERARY ANALYSIS

● **THEME IN DRAMA**

What does Scrooge realize about being a good master? Does he live up to his own description of one? *Possible answer: He says that a good master makes his employees happy and their labor light (line 138). It has nothing to do with money. He realizes that he does not live up to his own description.*

If students need help . . .

- Describe Scrooge's grasping and greedy attitude toward **money** as revealed so far in the play.

- Have students reread lines 137–141. Discuss what Scrooge says about money in these lines. Point out how Scrooge hesitates on line 140 and help students see that he may suddenly realize he has not been a good master himself.

Extend the Discussion What do you think Scrooge wants to say to Cratchit as he watches this scene from his past?

Lines 161–176
REINFORCE *KEY IDEA:* MONEY

Discuss How does Scrooge's life change when he chooses **money** over love? Would he make the same decision again? *Possible answer: He loses the woman he loves and is destined to lead a sad and lonely existence. His words of regret in lines 170–171 and 176 indicate that he would not let her go again.*

FOR LESS-PROFICIENT READERS
Monitor Comprehension

- Lines 139–146: To help students understand the "something" that Scrooge is thinking about, have them recall his stingy, sour encounter with his clerk Cratchit on page 393 (lines 166–181).

- Lines 161–168: Guide students to understand that when his sweetheart pauses on line 165, she is waiting for Scrooge to say that her lack of money is not important to him. He does not answer, so she returns his ring.

READING SKILL

■ ANALYZE SEQUENCE

When do the events in this scene take place? *Possible answer: The events take place in the present on Christmas Eve (lines 20–21). Scrooge is with the Ghost of Christmas Present*

Lines 40–58
DISCUSSION PROMPTS

Use these prompts to help students understand the significance of Scrooge's trip into the present:

Connect If you were Scrooge, would you view a trip into the present as more or less frightening than a trip into the past? Why? *Students might say they would be less anxious about a trip into the present. Because they live in the present, they would know what to expect.*

Analyze What is the significance of the funeral procession of children from the poorhouse following the coffin of a child? *Possible answers: The funeral might be a reminder to Scrooge of Marley's warning. The purpose of the child's coffin might be to make Scrooge feel guilty about his refusal to give to the poor.*

SCENE 4
~ THE SPIRIT OF CHRISTMAS PRESENT ~

A light comes on. Scrooge *becomes aware of it and goes slowly to it. He sees the* second spirit, *the Spirit of Christmas Present, who looks like* Fezziwig.

Scrooge. Fezziwig!

Second Spirit. Hello, Scrooge.

Scrooge. But you can't be . . . not Fezziwig.

Second Spirit. Do you see me as him?

Scrooge. I do.

10 **Second Spirit.** And hear me as him?

Scrooge. I do.

Second Spirit. I wish I were the gentleman, so as not to disappoint you.

Scrooge. But you're not . . . ?

Second Spirit. No, Mr. Scrooge. You have never seen the like of me before. I am the Ghost of Christmas Present.

Scrooge. But . . .

Second Spirit. You see what you will see, Scrooge, 20 no more. Will you walk out with me this Christmas Eve?

Scrooge. But I am not yet dressed.

Second Spirit. Take my tails, dear boy, we're leaving.

Scrooge. Wait!

Second Spirit. What is it now?

Scrooge. Christmas Present, did you say?

Second Spirit. I did.

Scrooge. Then we are traveling here? In this 30 town? London? Just down there?

Second Spirit. Yes, yes, of course.

---

18. **bob:** a British slang term for shillings. (There were 20 shillings in a pound.)

Scrooge. Then we could walk? Your flying is . . . well, too sudden for an old man. Well?

Second Spirit. It's your Christmas, Scrooge; I am only the guide.

Scrooge (*puzzled*). Then we can walk? (*The* spirit *nods.*) Where are you guiding me to?

Second Spirit. Bob Cratchit's.

Scrooge. My clerk?

40 **Second Spirit.** You did want to talk to him? (Scrooge *pauses, uncertain how to answer.*) Don't worry, Scrooge, you won't have to.

Scrooge (*trying to change the subject, to cover his error*). Shouldn't be much of a trip. With fifteen bob[18] a week, how far off can it be?

Second Spirit. A world away, Scrooge, at least that far. (Scrooge *and the spirit start to step off a curb when a funeral procession enters with a child's coffin, followed by the* poorhouse 50 children, *who are singing. Seated on top of the coffin is the little* girl. *She and* Scrooge *look at one another.*) That is the way to it, Scrooge. (*The procession follows the coffin offstage;* Scrooge *and the* spirit *exit after the procession. As they leave, the lights focus on* Mrs. Cratchit *and her* children. Mrs. Cratchit *sings as she puts* Tiny Tim *and the other* children *to bed, all in one bed. She pulls a dark blanket over them.*)

Mrs. Cratchit (*singing*).
60 When you wake, you shall have
All the pretty little horses,
Blacks and bays, dapples and grays,
All the pretty little horses.
To sleep now, all of you. Christmas tomorrow (*She kisses them and goes to* Bob Cratchit, *who is b[y] the hearth.*) How did our little Tiny Tim behave?

Bob Cratchit. As good as gold and better. He told me, coming home, that he hoped the

© Louisiana Tech University School of Performing Ar[t]

DIFFERENTIATED INSTRUCTION

FOR ENGLISH LEARNERS
Comprehension: Sequence Review the sequence wheel from page 387 that students have been filling in. Explain that the trip into the present also takes place on Christmas Eve. Guide students to add to the sequence wheel. *Possible answers:*

Present Shown by Spirit

1. *Scrooge is guided to Bob Cratchit's house.*

2. *Scrooge sees a funeral procession for a child.*

FOR ADVANCED LEARNERS/PRE–AP
Author's Craft Have students work in pairs to examine how, in addition to the dialogue, the playwright uses sounds and sights to elicit strong feelings. Note the examples of the sight of the child's coffin and the sad singing of the funeral song. Have students track and list other strong visuals and sounds in the play.

ANALYZE VISUALS

Activity Have small groups discuss these questions:

- Of the three ghosts that have appeared so far, which one is the scariest?
- Why do you think Dickens made one ghost much scarier than the others?

Possible answers: Students may say that Marley is the scariest ghost. Dickens may have made him the scariest to impress on Scrooge what would happen to him if he failed to change his greedy ways.

Activity Have students discuss the way Scrooge appears in this image. What emotions or attitudes are suggested by the actor's facial expression and body language? *Possible answer: Scrooge stands very still, completely absorbed in whatever he is observing. His expression suggests attentiveness, disappointment, and sadness.*

Lines 88–102

LITERARY ANALYSIS

● **THEME IN DRAMA**

What does Christmas mean to Bob Cratchit? How can you tell? *Possible answer: For Cratchit, Christmas is a time to be kind and charitable toward everyone (line 102). He wishes Scrooge well even though Scrooge treats him badly. Instead of feeling bitter that Scrooge pays him so little, he expresses gratitude that Scrooge pays him at all.*

people saw him in church because he was
70 a cripple and it might be pleasant to them
to remember upon Christmas Day who made
the lame to walk and the blind to see.

Mrs. Cratchit. He's a good boy. (*The* second spirit *and* Scrooge *enter.* Mrs. Cratchit *feels a sudden draft.*) Oh, the wind. (*She gets up to shut the door.*)

Second Spirit. Hurry. (*He nudges* Scrooge *in before* Mrs. Cratchit *shuts the door.*)

Scrooge. Hardly hospitable is what I'd say.

Second Spirit. Oh, they'd say a great deal more,
80 Scrooge, if they could see you.

Scrooge. Oh, they should, should they?

Second Spirit. Oh yes, I'd think they might.

Scrooge. Well, I might have a word for them . . .

Second Spirit. You're here to listen.

Scrooge. Oh. Oh yes, all right. By the fire?

Second Spirit. But not a word.

Bob Cratchit (*raising his glass*). My dear, to Mr. Scrooge. I give you Mr. Scrooge, the
90 founder of the feast.

Mrs. Cratchit. The founder of the feast indeed! I wish I had him here! I'd give him a piece of my mind to feast upon, and I hope he'd have a good appetite for it.

Bob Cratchit. My dear, Christmas Eve.

Mrs. Cratchit. It should be Christmas Eve, I'm sure, when one drinks the health of such an odious,[19] stingy, hard, unfeeling man as Mr. Scrooge. You know he is, Robert! Nobody
100 knows it better than you do, poor dear.

Bob Cratchit. I only know one thing on Christmas: that one must be charitable.

Mrs. Cratchit. I'll drink to his health for your sake and the day's, not for his. Long life to him! A Merry Christmas and a Happy New

---

19. **odious** (ō′dē-əs): causing or deserving strong dislike.

© Louisiana Tech University School of Performing Arts.

DIFFERENTIATED INSTRUCTION

FOR LESS–PROFICIENT READERS
Comprehension Support Guide students in finding references to Tiny Tim's illness (lines 70, 114, and 127) and to his cheerful, hopeful character (lines 66–73, and 112–120).

FOR ENGLISH LEARNERS
Comprehension: Clarify

- Make sure students understand that the Second Spirit and Scrooge cannot be seen or heard by the Cratchits. However, Scrooge can hear and see the Cratchits perfectly well.

- Ask students to identify what Scrooge overhears about himself from Mrs. Cratchit (lines 98–99) and Mr. Cratchit (line 108).

Year. He'll be very merry and very happy, I have no doubt.

Bob Cratchit. If he cannot be, we must be happy for him. A song is what is needed. Tim!

Mrs. Cratchit. Shush! I've just gotten him down, and he needs all the sleep he can get.

Bob Cratchit. If he's asleep on Christmas Eve, I'll be much mistaken. Tim! He must sing, dear; there is nothing else that might make him well.

Tiny Tim. Yes, Father?

Bob Cratchit. Are you awake?

Tiny Tim. Just a little.

Bob Cratchit. A song then! (*The* children *awaken and, led by* Tiny Tim, *sit up to sing "What Child Is This?" As they sing,* Scrooge *speaks.*)

Scrooge. (*He holds up his hand; all stop singing and look at him.*) I . . . I have seen enough. (*When the spirit signals to the* children, *they leave the stage, singing the carol quietly.* Tiny Tim *remains, covered completely by the dark blanket, disappearing against the black.*) Tiny Tim . . . will he live?

Second Spirit. He is very ill. Even song cannot keep him whole through a cold winter.

Scrooge. But you haven't told me!

Second Spirit (*imitating* Scrooge). If he be like to die, he had better do it and decrease the surplus population. (Scrooge *turns away.*) Erase, Scrooge, those words from your thoughts. You are not the judge. Do not judge, then. It may be that in the sight of heaven you are more worthless and less fit to live than millions like this poor man's child. Oh God! To hear an insect on a leaf pronouncing that there is too much life among his hungry brothers in the dust. Good-bye, Scrooge.

Scrooge. But is there no happiness in Christmas Present?

Second Spirit. There is.

Scrooge. Take me there.

Second Spirit. It is at the home of your nephew . . .

Scrooge. No!

Second Spirit (*disgusted with* Scrooge). Then there is none.

150 **Scrooge.** But that isn't enough . . . You must teach me!

Second Spirit. Would you have a teacher, Scrooge? Look at your own words.

Scrooge. But the first spirit gave me more . . . !

Second Spirit. He was Christmas Past. There was a lifetime he could choose from. I have only this day, one day, and you, Scrooge. I have nearly lived my fill of both. Christmas Present must be gone at midnight. That is near now.
160 (*He speaks to two* beggar children *who pause shyly at the far side of the stage. The* children *are thin and wan; they are barefoot and wear filthy rags.*) Come. (*They go to him.*)

Scrooge. Is this the last spirit who is to come to me?

Second Spirit. They are no spirits. They are real. Hunger, Ignorance. Not spirits, Scrooge, passing dreams. They are real. They walk your streets, look to you for comfort. And you
170 deny them. Deny them not too long, Scrooge. They will grow and multiply, and they will not remain children.

Scrooge. Have they no refuge, no resource?

Second Spirit (*again imitating* Scrooge). Are there no prisons? Are there no workhouses? (*tenderly to the* children) Come. It's Christmas Eve. (*He leads them offstage.*)

④ **Targeted Passage**

Lines 126–140

LITERARY ANALYSIS

● **THEME IN DRAMA**

How do Scrooge's earlier words come back to haunt him? *Possible answer: In Scene 1, Scrooge said that the poor might as well die and reduce the surplus population. Now he cannot bear to think of Tiny Tim dying.*

If students need help . . . Invite volunteers to locate the passages in Scene 1 in which Scrooge said the words that the ghost is now repeating (Scene 1, lines 133–134).

Lines 160–177
DISCUSSION PROMPTS

Use these prompts to help students understand how the spirits are urging Scrooge to take responsibility for others:

Connect How do you feel when you say something foolish or thoughtless and someone repeats it back to you later? *Possible answer: It is embarrassing to have someone repeat your words back to you when you have said something foolish or thoughtless.*

Analyze In what way are these children different from those in the prologue? *Possible answer: The children in the prologue were not described as poor or filthy. They represented the innocence of Christmas. These children represent Hunger and Ignorance.*

Synthesize In what way are these children a further progression from the children of the funeral procession? *Possible answer: The children of the funeral procession were from the poorhouse. Without the help that Scrooge has denied them, they may become very similar to the children the spirit labels as Hunger and Ignorance.*

FOR LESS–PROFICIENT READERS

④ **Targeted Passage [Scene 4, Lines 120–157]**

This passage reveals the lesson of Christmas Present and shows Scrooge an unsettling view of the present.

• How does Scrooge begin to show concern for another person?

• What tone does Christmas Present take with Scrooge?

FOR ADVANCED LEARNERS/PRE–AP

Evaluate Have students discuss in small groups why Scrooge refuses to go to his nephew's house (line 147). Ask students if his refusal might signify a change in his attitude and understanding or might show that he has not yet changed at all. Have students support their opinions with reasons and evidence from the text.

DISCUSSION PROMPTS

Use these prompts to help students understand the portrayal of Christmas Yet to Come:

Connect How would you feel about journeying into the future? Why? *Students might say that they would be excited about seeing their lives years from now or nervous about the changes that might be revealed.*

Analyze Why does the Ghost of Christmas Yet to Come have no visible physical features? *Possible answer: The future has not happened yet, so it is not possible to know what it looks like.*

Evaluate Why is Scrooge being shown the future? Do you agree that people can determine their future? *Possible answers: Scrooge is being shown the future in the hope that he will change what he does in the present. People's choice of present action can determine the future to a degree. Some events are beyond people's control, however.*

Lines 25–40

READING SKILL

■ ANALYZE SEQUENCE

What does this scene (lines 25–40) suggest is in Scrooge's future?

You might record students' answers in the sequence wheel. *Possible answer:*

Possible Future Shown by Spirit

1. *Scrooge dies, and his servants strip his body and home of all valuables.*

Lines 27–28

LITERARY ANALYSIS

● THEME IN DRAMA

What does the charwoman mean when she says that Scrooge "ain't been alive in deed for half his life"? *Possible answer: She means that he has been dead in spirit, not truly living life. For many years, he has done nothing except hoard his money.*

SCENE 5

~ THE SPIRIT OF CHRISTMAS YET TO COME ~

Scrooge *is entirely alone for a long moment. He is frightened by the darkness and feels it approaching him. Suddenly he stops, senses the presence of the* third spirit, *turns toward him, and sees him. The* spirit *is bent and cloaked. No physical features are distinguishable.*

Scrooge. You are the third. (*The* spirit *says nothing.*) The Ghost of Christmas Yet to Come. (*The* spirit *says nothing.*) Speak to me. Tell me
10 what is to happen—to me, to all of us. (*The* spirit *says nothing.*) Then show me what I must see. (*The* spirit *points. Light illumines the shadowy recesses of* Scrooge's *house.*) I know it. I know it too well, cold and cheerless. It is mine. (*The* cook *and the* charwoman *are dimly visible in* Scrooge's *house.*) What is . . . ? There are . . . thieves! There are thieves in my rooms! (*He starts forward to* **accost** *them, but the* spirit *beckons for him to stop.*) I cannot. You cannot tell me that
20 I must watch them and do nothing. I will not. It is mine still. (*He rushes into the house to claim his belongings and to protect them. The two women do not notice his presence.*)

Cook. He ain't about, is he? (*The* charwoman *laughs.*) Poor ol' Scrooge 'as met 'is end.[20] (*She laughs with the* charwoman.)

Charwoman. An' time for it, too; ain't been alive in deed for half his life.

Cook. But the Sparsit's nowhere, is he . . . ?

30 **Sparsit** (*emerging from the blackness*). Lookin' for someone, ladies? (*The* cook *shrieks, but the* charwoman *treats the matter more practically, anticipating competition from* Sparsit.)

Charwoman. There ain't enough but for the two of us!

Sparsit. More 'an enough . . . if you know where to look.

Cook. Hardly decent is what I'd say, hardly decent, the poor old fella hardly cold and
40 you're thievin' his wardrobe.

Sparsit. You're here out of love, are ya?

Charwoman. There's no time for that. (Sparsit *acknowledges* Scrooge *for the first time, gesturing toward him as if the living* Scrooge *were the corpse.* Scrooge *stands as if rooted to the spot, held there by the power of the* spirit.)

Sparsit. He ain't about to bother us, is he?

Charwoman. Ain't he a picture?

Cook. If he is, it ain't a happy one.
50 (*They laugh.*)

Sparsit. Ladies, shall we start? (*The three of them grin and advance on* Scrooge.) Cook?

Cook (*snatching the cuff links from the shirt* Scrooge *wears*). They're gold, ain't they?

Sparsit. The purest, madam.

Charwoman. I always had a fancy for that nightcap of his. My old man could use it. (*She takes the nightcap from* Scrooge's *head.* Sparsit *playfully removes* Scrooge's *outer garment, the coat
60 or cloak that he has worn in the previous scenes.*)

Sparsit. Bein' a man of more practical tastes, I'll go for the worsted[21] and hope the smell ain't permanent. (*The three laugh.*) Cook, we go round again.

Cook. Do you think that little bell he's always ringing at me is silver enough to sell? (*The three of them move toward the nightstand, and* Scrooge *cries out.*)

---

20. **'as met 'is end:** a dialect pronunciation of "has met his end."
21. **worsted:** a smooth woolen fabric.

© Louisiana Tech University School of Performing Arts

DIFFERENTIATED INSTRUCTION

FOR ENGLISH LEARNERS

Language: Conversational English Patterns
Explain that the servants speak in an informal dialect. Their dialogue includes letters dropped from words (as in line 25, "Poor ol' Scrooge 'as met 'is end") and the frequent use of *ain't*, which means "is not" or "are not." Assign various lines to student pairs. Ask them to rewrite the dialogue in standard English and share their rewrites with the class.

Scrooge. No more! No more! (*As the* spirit *directs* Scrooge's *attention to the tableau*²² *of the three thieves standing poised over the silver bell,* Scrooge *bursts out of the house, clad only in his nightshirt.*) I cannot. I cannot. The room is . . . too like a cheerless place that is familiar. I won't see it. Let us go from here. Anywhere. (*The* spirit *directs his attention to the Cratchit house; the* children *are sitting together near* Mrs. Cratchit, *who is sewing a coat.* Peter *reads by the light of the coals.*)

80 **Peter.** "And he took a child and set him in the midst of them."

Mrs. Cratchit (*putting her hand to her face*). The light tires my eyes so. (*pause*) They're better now. It makes them tired to try to see by firelight, and I wouldn't show reddened eyes to your father when he comes home for the world. It must be near his time now.

Peter. Past it, I think, but he walks slower than he used to, these last few days, Mother.

90 **Mrs. Cratchit.** I have known him to walk with . . . I have known him to walk with Tiny Tim upon his shoulder very fast indeed. (*She catches herself, then hurries on.*) But he was very light to carry and his father loved him, so that it was no trouble, no trouble. (*She hears* Bob Cratchit *approaching.*) Smiles, everyone, smiles.

Bob Cratchit (*entering*). My dear, Peter . . . (*He greets the other* children *by their real* 100 *names.*) How is it coming?

Mrs. Cratchit (*handing him the coat*). Nearly done.

---

22. **tableau** (tăb′lō′): a portion of a play where the actors momentarily freeze in their positions for dramatic effect.

© Louisiana Tech University School of Performing Arts.

Bob Cratchit. Yes, good, I'm sure that it will be done long before Sunday.

Mrs. Cratchit. Sunday! You went today then, Robert?

Bob Cratchit. Yes. It's . . . it's all ready. Two o'clock. And a nice place. It would have done you good to see how green it is. But you'll see it often. I promised him that, that I would walk there on Sunday . . . often.

Mrs. Cratchit. We mustn't hurt ourselves for it, Robert.

Bob Cratchit. No. No, he wouldn't have wanted that. Come now. You won't guess who I've seen. Scrooge's nephew, Fred. And he asked after us and said he was heartily sorry and to give his respect to my good wife. How he ever knew that, I don't know.

Mrs. Cratchit. Knew what, my dear?

Bob Cratchit. Why, that you were a good wife.

Peter. Everybody knows that.

Bob Cratchit. I hope that they do. "Heartily sorry," he said, "for your good wife, and if I can be of service to you in any way—" and he gave me his card—"that's where I live"—and Peter, I shouldn't be at all surprised if he got you a position.

Mrs. Cratchit. Only hear that, Peter!

Bob Cratchit. And then you'll be keeping company with some young girl and setting up for yourself.

Peter. Oh, go on.

Bob Cratchit. Well, it will happen, one day, but remember, when that day does come—as it must—we must none of us forget poor Tiny Tim and this first parting in our family.

Scrooge. He died! No, no! (*He steps back and the scene disappears; he moves away from the* spirit.)

Lines 134–139

READING SKILL

■ ANALYZE SEQUENCE

What does Scrooge learn about Tiny Tim in this visit to the future? How does he react?

Encourage students to record their answers in the sequence wheel. ***Possible answer:***

Possible Future Shown by Spirit

2. *Tiny Tim dies. Scrooge is horrified.*

Lines 6–15

● THEME IN DRAMA

Has Scrooge come to understand the true spirit of Christmas? Explain. **Possible answer:** *Yes. He sees the errors of his former ways. He vows to keep the spirit of generosity and charity in his heart year round.*

If students need help . . . Return to Scene 1 and review Scrooge's mean-spirited words. Contrast his attitude then with his attitude now, as revealed in lines 6–15. Help students connect the changes to a theme, such as "There are more important things in life than money."

Lines 49–68
DISCUSSION PROMPTS

Use these prompts to help students explore the changes in Scrooge:

Connect If you had been through everything Scrooge went through with the spirits, how would you feel about finally waking up in your own bed? *Many students will say that they would feel relieved, overjoyed, and hopeful about the future.*

Analyze Describe the changes in Scrooge's behavior. *Possible answers: Scrooge now likes children (line 49), he is friendly (line 54), and he is generous (lines 60–63 and 65–68).*

Synthesize What important lessons did Scrooge learn from each of the spirits? *Possible answers:*

- *Christmas Past: Scrooge's love of money isolated him from friends and family.*
- *Christmas Present: People around him were suffering because of his stinginess.*
- *Christmas Yet to Come: All his wealth would be useless to him after death.*

SCENE 6
~ SCROOGE'S CONVERSION ~

Scrooge. Because he would not . . . no! You cannot tell me that he has died, for that Christmas has not come! I will not let it come! I will be there . . . It was me. Yes, yes, and I knew it and couldn't look. I won't be able to help. I won't. (*pause*) Spirit, hear me. I am not the man I was. I will not be that man that I have been for so many years. Why show me all of this if I am past all hope? Assure me that I yet may change these
10 shadows you have shown me. Let the boy live! I will honor Christmas in my heart and try to keep it all the year. I will live in the Past, the Present, and the Future. The spirits of all three shall strive within me. I will not shut out the lessons that they teach. Oh, tell me that I am not too late! (*A single light focuses on the little* girl, *dressed in a blue cloak like that of the Virgin Mary. She looks up, and from above a dove is slowly lowered in silence to her; she takes it and encloses*
20 *it within her cloak, covering it. As soon as she does this, a large choir is heard singing "Gloria!" and the bells begin to ring. Blackout. When the lights come up again,* Scrooge *is in bed. The* third spirit *and the figures in the church have disappeared.* Scrooge *awakens and looks around his room.*) The curtains! They are mine and they are real. They are not sold. They are here. I am here; the shadows to come may be dispelled. They will be. I know they will be. (*He dresses himself hurriedly.*) I don't
30 know what to do. I'm as light as a feather, merry as a boy again. Merry Christmas! Merry Christmas! A Happy New Year to all the world! Hello there! Whoop! Hallo! What day of the month is it? How long did the spirits keep me? Never mind. I don't care. (*He opens the window and calls to a* boy *in the street below.*) What's today?

Boy. Eh?

Scrooge. What's the day, my fine fellow?

Boy. Today? Why, Christmas Day!

40 **Scrooge.** It's Christmas Day! I haven't missed it! The spirits have done it all in one night. They can do anything they like. Of course they can. Of course they can save Tim. Hallo, my fine fellow!

Boy. Hallo!

Scrooge. Do you know the poulterers[23] in the next street at the corner?

Boy. I should hope I do.

Scrooge. An intelligent boy. A remarkable boy.
50 Do you know whether they've sold the prize turkey that was hanging up there? Not the little prize; the big one.

Boy. What, the one as big as me?

Scrooge. What a delightful boy! Yes, my bucko!

Boy. It's hanging there now.

Scrooge. It is? Go and buy it.

Boy. G'wan!

Scrooge. I'm in earnest! Go and buy it and tell 'em to bring it here that I may give them
60 the direction where to take it. Come back with the butcher and I'll give you a shilling. Come back in less than two minutes and I'll give you half a crown!

Boy. Right, guv! (*He exits.*)

Scrooge. I'll send it to Bob Cratchit's. He shan't know who sends it. It's twice the size of Tiny Tim and such a Christmas dinner it will make. (Carolers *suddenly appear singing "Hark! The Herald Angels Sing." Scrooge leans*

⑤ Targeted Passage

---

23. **poulterers** (pōl′tər-ərz): people who sell poultry, such as chickens and turkeys.

© Louisiana Tech University School of Performing Arts

DIFFERENTIATED INSTRUCTION

FOR LESS–PROFICIENT READERS

⑤ Targeted Passage [Scene 6, Lines 1–36]

This passage shows the turning point in the play: Scrooge changes from a miserly man to a kind one.

- What does Scrooge promise he will do if Tiny Tim is allowed to live?
- Why is Scrooge relieved when he awakens?
- How can you tell that Scrooge is a changed man?

FOR ADVANCED LEARNERS/PRE–AP

Analyze In lines 13–15 Scrooge says, "The spirits of all three shall strive within me. I will not shut out the lessons that they teach." Invite students to do a quickwrite on the lessons that Scrooge learned from each of the spirits. Then challenge them to think of a modern saying that summarizes each lesson. (For example, the lesson from the spirit of Christmas Yet to Come may be summarized as "Where there's a will, there's a way.")

ANALYZE VISUALS

Activity Ask students to contrast this image of Scrooge and Tiny Tim with the image on page 391. How does the contrast suggest a theme of the play? *Possible answers: In the first image, Scrooge sits behind a podium and tells the children to go away. In the second, he holds Tiny Tim in his arms and is surrounded by friends and family. This contrast suggests that happiness comes not from working to make money but from enjoying human relationships.*

FOR ENGLISH LEARNERS

Culture: Connect Explain to students that many people eat turkey (line 51) at Christmas time. Scrooge is sending the boy he sees in the street to buy the largest turkey that the butcher has. Ask students to describe some of the special foods eaten for the special holidays of their cultures.

FOR ADVANCED LEARNERS/PRE–AP

Analyze Minor Characters Have students complete their charts of minor characters (introduced on page 391). Ask students to share their analyses of the roles of the characters and discuss how they help to convey theme or develop understanding of Scrooge's character.

REINFORCE KEY IDEA: MONEY

Discuss What has become more important than **money** to Scrooge? *Possible answer: People have become more important to Scrooge.*

Lines 83–132

READING SKILL

◼ ANALYZE SEQUENCE

At the end of the play, Scrooge comes "full circle" by interacting with the same people he did at the beginning of the play. How does this sequence help to reveal the theme? *Possible answer: The audience can compare his previous attitude with his re-formed outlook on life and see that Scrooge has realized that money has no value unless it is used to help others.*

If students need help . . . Complete and review the sequence wheel. Discuss how the same people who appear in Scene 1 are also in Scene 6, in reverse order. Scrooge's previous conflict with each person is resolved, showing his transformation and bringing closure to the events.

SELECTION WRAP–UP

REFLECT Have students discuss whether visiting only the future would have brought about the change in Scrooge or whether all three spirits were necessary.

⭐ **CRITIQUE** Have students evaluate whether Scrooge's conversion in the play is believable and explain why or why not.

READING FLUENCY

Distribute the copy masters and have students work in groups to practice fluency.

RESOURCE MANAGER—Copy Master
Reading Fluency p. 171

---

70 *out the window and joins them in the song.*) I must dress, I must. It's Christmas Day! I must be all in my best for such a day. Where is my China silk shirt? (*The boy and the butcher run in with the turkey.*) What? Back already? And such a turkey. Why, you can't carry that all the way to Cratchit's. Here, boy, here is your half a crown and here an address in Camden Town. See that it gets there. Here, money for the cab, for the turkey, and for you, good man! (*The* 80 boy *and the* butcher, *delighted, catch the money and run out. Scrooge sees the* gentleman visitor *walking by the window.*) Halloo, sir!

Gentleman Visitor (*looking up sadly, less than festive*). Hello, sir.

Scrooge. My dear sir, how do you do? I hope you succeeded yesterday. It was very kind of you to stop by to see me.

Gentleman Visitor (*in disbelief*). Mr. Scrooge?
Scrooge. Yes, that is my name, and I fear it may 90 not be pleasant to you. Allow me to ask your pardon, and will you have the goodness to add this (*throwing him a purse*) to your good work!

Gentleman Visitor. Lord bless me! My dear Mr. Scrooge, are you serious?

Scrooge. If you please, not a penny less. A great many back payments are included in it, I assure you. Will you do me that favor?

Gentleman Visitor. My dear sir, I don't know what I can say to such generosity . . .
100 **Scrooge.** Say nothing! Accept it. Come and see me. Will you come and see me?

Gentleman Visitor. I will.

Scrooge. Thank 'ee. I am much obliged to you. I thank you fifty times. God bless you and Merry Christmas!

---

24. **finale** (fə-năl'ē): conclusion.

Gentleman Visitor. Merry Christmas to you, sir!

Scrooge (*running downstairs, out of his house, and onto the street*). Now which is the way 110 to that nephew's house. Girl! Girl!

Girl (*appearing immediately*). Yes, sir?

Scrooge. Can you find me a taxi, miss?

Girl. I can, sir. (*She rings her doll, and a* coachman *appears.*)

Scrooge (*handing the* coachman *a card*). Can you show me the way to this home?

Coachman. I can, sir.

Scrooge. Good man. Come up, girl. (*They mount to the top of the taxi. This action may* 120 *be stylistically suggested.*) Would you be an old man's guide to a Christmas dinner?

Girl. I would, sir, and God bless you!

Scrooge. Yes, God bless us every one! (*raising his voice almost in song*) Driver, to Christmas! (*They exit, all three singing "Joy to the World." Blackout. The lights come up for the finale*[24] *at Fred's house. The* Cratchits *are there with* Tiny Tim. *All stop moving and talking when they see* Scrooge *standing in the center,* 130 *embarrassed and humble.*) Well, I'm very glad to be here at my nephew's house! (*He starts to cry.*) Merry Christmas! Merry Christmas!

All (*softly*). Merry Christmas. (*They sing "Deck the Halls," greeting one another and exchanging gifts.* Scrooge *puts* Tiny Tim *on his shoulders.*)

Tiny Tim (*shouting as the carol ends*). God bless us every one!

Scrooge (*to the audience*). Oh, yes! God bless us every one!

DIFFERENTIATED INSTRUCTION

FOR ENGLISH LEARNERS

Vocabulary Support Point out the title of Scene 6. Place the word *conversion* in the center of a Cluster Diagram. Fill in the outer circles with ideas students associate with a conversion, based on Scrooge's behavior in this scene. Then have students look up the word in a dictionary and choose the definition that best matches its use in this play.

 BEST PRACTICES TOOLKIT—Transparency
Cluster Diagram p. B18

Reading for Information

ONLINE ARTICLE In the play *A Christmas Carol,* you read about a man named Scrooge, who was stingy with his money. In the following article, you'll read about why Charles Dickens wrote *A Christmas Carol* and how some real-life Scrooges took advantage of Dickens.

BACK   FORWARD   STOP   REFRESH   HOME   PRINT

Dickens and Too Many Scrooges

DICKENS BIOGRAPHY → BOOKS BY DICKENS → THE STORY BEHIND A CHRISTMAS CAROL

Story Line

Biography

About Us

Links

Scrooge at his office with Bob Cratchit

Dickens' cherished little Christmas story, the best loved and most read of all of his books, began life as the result of the author's desperate need of money. In the fall of 1843 Dickens and his wife, Kate, were expecting their fifth child. Requests for money from his family, a large mortgage on his Devonshire Terrace home, and lagging sales from the monthly installments of *Martin Chuzzlewit* had left Dickens seriously short of cash.

As the idea for the story took shape and the writing began in earnest, Dickens became engrossed in the book. He wrote that as the tale unfolded he "wept and laughed, and wept again" and that he "walked about the black streets of London fifteen or twenty miles many a night when all sober folks had gone to bed."

At odds with his publishers, Dickens paid for the production costs of the book himself and insisted on a lavish design that included a gold-stamped cover and four hand-colored etchings. He also set the price at 5 shillings so that the book would be affordable to nearly everyone.

The book was published during the week before Christmas 1843 and was an instant sensation but, due to the high production costs, Dickens' earnings from the sales were lower than expected. In addition to the disappointing profit from the book, Dickens was enraged that the work was instantly the victim of pirated editions. Copyright laws in England were often loosely enforced, and a complete lack of international copyright law had been Dickens' theme during his trip to America the year before. He ended up spending more money fighting pirated editions of the book than he was making from the book itself.

Despite these early financial difficulties, Dickens' Christmas tale of human redemption has endured beyond even Dickens' own vivid imagination. It was a favorite during Dickens' public readings of his works late in his lifetime and is known today primarily due to the dozens of film versions and dramatizations which continue to be produced every year.

READING FOR INFORMATION   413

DISCUSSION PROMPTS

Use these prompts to help students understand Dickens's motives for writing *A Christmas Carol:*

Connect How does knowing the reason that Dickens wrote the original novel affect your reaction to the play? *Students may say that they appreciate it more knowing the sacrifices he made to have it published.*

Analyze What details from the article suggest that *A Christmas Carol* meant more to Dickens than just a way to make money? *Possible answers: Dickens paid for the production costs himself. He included expensive features such as a gold-stamped cover and etchings when he had it printed. He priced it affordably.*

Synthesize How did Dickens's feelings about money, as described in the article, compare with Scrooge's feelings about money in the play? *Possible answers: Like Scrooge, Dickens felt that money was important. He worked hard to make money and protect the profits from his books. In contrast to the early Scrooge, Dickens priced* A Christmas Carol *cheaply so that poor people could afford to buy it.*

Practice and Apply

After Reading

For additional support of post-reading questions, use these copy masters:

R RESOURCE MANAGER—Copy Masters

Reading Check p. 168 (to check understanding of the selection)

Theme in Drama p. 163 (for practice of literary analysis standards focus)

Question Support p. 169 (**After Reading** questions adapted for English learners and less-proficient readers)

Additional selection questions are provided for teachers on page 157.

For additional activities to challenge students, see

ⓘ Power Thinking at **ClassZone.com**

ANSWERS

Comprehension

1. *Marley was Scrooge's business partner. Like Scrooge, he lived a greedy life. Marley's spirit comes to warn Scrooge that three other spirits will visit him and to show Scrooge what punishment awaits him if he doesn't change his ways.*

2. *Scrooge sends the Cratchits a huge turkey for their dinner.*

3. *Scrooge is mean and stingy at the beginning of the play. By the end, he has become a generous person, cheerfully spending money to make others happy.*

Literary Analysis

Possible answers:

4. ■ STANDARDS FOCUS *Analyze Sequence*
Students' summaries should indicate that the play does not follow a strict chronological sequence but moves from present to past to present to future to present.

5. *The past can never be completely left behind; the memories remain within us always and shape who we are as individuals.*

6. *Scrooge feels guilty. He knows he might have done something to save Tiny Tim if he had not been so selfish and miserly.*

7. *Students may identify the young girl as a symbol of hope and youth, Marley's chain as the consequences of his greed, or the dove as peace.*

Comprehension

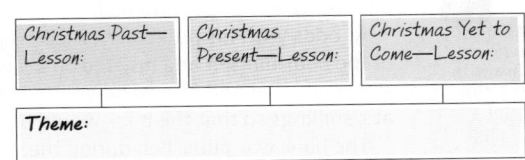

MARYLAND OBJECTIVES

LITERATURE STANDARD
3.A.6.a Analyze universal themes

1. **Recall** Who was Jacob Marley, and why does his spirit visit Scrooge?

2. **Recall** What does Scrooge do for the Cratchit family at the play's end?

3. **Clarify** How does Scrooge's view of **money** change from the beginning of the play to the end?

Literary Analysis

4. **Analyze Sequence** Review the sequence wheel you created as you read. Number the sections according to the order in which the time periods are presented in the play. Use your numbers to summarize the **sequence** of events in *A Christmas Carol*.

5. **Make Inferences** What does the Spirit of Christmas Past mean by saying, "I am always with you"? Explain your answer.

6. **Draw Conclusions** Why do you think Tiny Tim's death affects Scrooge so deeply?

7. **Analyze Symbols** In the play there are a number of things used as symbols, such as the little girl with the doll, Marley's chains, and a dove. Reread lines 102–108 in Scene 2, lines 200–212 in Scene 3, and lines 18–22 in Scene 6. Choose one symbol and analyze its meaning.

8. **Identify Theme** Use a diagram like the one shown to describe what lesson each spirit teaches Scrooge. Based on these lessons, what do you think the **theme** of the play is?

Christmas Past— Lesson:	Christmas Present—Lesson:	Christmas Yet to Come—Lesson:

Theme:

Extension and Challenge

9. **Creative Project: Drama** With a small group, choose the scene or part of a scene that you feel best reflects Dickens's message. Act out the scene for the rest of the class. Then explain why your group chose it.

10.  **SOCIAL STUDIES CONNECTION** What was it like to live in Victorian England (1837–1901)? Find out by researching one element of the time period: the Poor Law of 1834, workhouses, prisons, leprosy, how wealthy people lived, or how poor people lived. Present your research to the class.

 RESEARCH LINKS
For more on Victorian England, visit the **Research Center** at ClassZone.com.

---

8. ● STANDARDS FOCUS *Theme in Drama*
Christmas Past teaches charity, sympathy, generosity, and the enjoyment of life. Christmas Present teaches Scrooge to live fully and experience the happiness the world has to offer. Christmas Yet to Come shows that Scrooge has the power to influence what happens to himself and others. One theme is that money does not buy happiness; happiness comes from connecting and sharing with others.

Extension and Challenge

9. *Students' choice of scene should be a valid reflection of Dickens's central message about the importance of love and generosity. The explanation should link what happens in the scene to this central idea.*

10. *Encourage students to use printed materials as well as online sources for their research. Suggest that they use visual aids in their presentation.*

Reading-Writing Connection

Demonstrate your understanding of *A Christmas Carol* by responding to these prompts. Then complete the **Grammar and Writing** exercise.

WRITING PROMPTS

A. Short Response: Write a Journal Entry
Return to the opening activity on page 386. How has reading the play affected your beliefs about the importance of **money?** Write a **one-paragraph journal entry** explaining how the play changed or supported your original ideas.

SELF-CHECK

A well-written entry will . . .
- state your original ideas about money
- tell whether your ideas changed and why or why not

B. Extended Response: Evaluate a Statement
In lines 12–13 of Scene 6, Scrooge declares, "I will live in the Past, the Present, and the Future." In a **two- or three-paragraph response,** explain what Scrooge means by this statement. Also describe what steps he takes to accomplish his goal.

A strong response will . . .
- show an understanding of the statement
- use specific details or examples from the play

GRAMMAR AND WRITING

COMBINE CLAUSES A clause is a group of words that contains a subject and a verb. Clauses can be **independent** or **dependent** (also known as subordinate). An independent clause expresses a complete thought and can stand on its own as a sentence, but a dependent clause cannot. To help avoid sentence fragments, join dependent clauses to independent clauses. Here is an example, with the independent clause highlighted in yellow and the dependent clause highlighted in green.

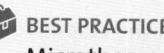

MARYLAND OBJECTIVES

LANGUAGE STANDARD
5.A.2.d Compose complex sentences

> *Original:*   We can help people in need. Although we don't have much money.
>
> *Revised:*   We can help people in need, although we don't have much money.

PRACTICE Combine the following independent and dependent clauses.

1. I still like money. Although reading the play changed my mind a little.
2. While money can be important. Helping people is even more important.
3. Scrooge found that out. Even though it took him a long time.
4. After he discovered this. He became a better person.

For more help with independent and dependent clauses, see pages R63–R64 in the **Grammar Handbook.**

DIFFERENTIATED INSTRUCTION

FOR LESS–PROFICIENT WRITERS

For Prompt A:
1. Have students list some of the reasons they think money is or is not important.
2. Help students craft a topic sentence stating their opinion. Then ask them to list three reasons or examples from the play that show why they feel this way. Example: A small amount of money can make someone happy (lines 74–81).

For Prompt B:
Limit the assignment to one paragraph.
1. Discuss what Scrooge's statement means, referring to charts used during reading.
2. Have students work in pairs to pick out examples from Scene 6 that show how Scrooge is trying to meet his goal.

Reading-Writing Connection

WRITING PROMPTS

- For **Prompt A,** suggest that students list ways their original ideas may have changed. Then they can look back through the play to find passages that caused the changes.
- For **Prompt B,** have pairs identify lessons Scrooge learned from the past, present, and future. Have them match up at least one action from Scene 6 that shows the implementation of a lesson. Students may organize their ideas in the Microtheme outline.

 BEST PRACTICES TOOLKIT—Transparency
   Microtheme p. C13

For an extended Reading-Writing Connection activity, see

ⓘ Writing Center at **ClassZone.com**

GRAMMAR AND WRITING

- List common subordinating conjunctions on the board: *although, if, even though, after, before, because, until, as soon as, unless.*
- Write the clauses on the board. Have students suggest corrections. Point out the use of commas to join clauses.

Possible answers:
1. *I still like money, although . . .*
2. *While money can be important, helping . . .*
3. *Scrooge found that out, even though . . .*
4. *After he discovered this, he became . . .*

ⓡ RESOURCE MANAGER—Copy Master
   Independent and Dependent Clauses
   p. 170

Assess and Reteach

Assess

ⓡ RESOURCE MANAGER—Copy Masters
   Selection Tests A, B/C pp. 173–174, 175–176

⊘ Test Generator CD

Reteach

Ⓢ STANDARDS LESSON FILE
   Literature Lesson 13: Theme
   Reading Lesson 6: Recognizing Sequence and Chronological Order

Focus and Motivate

OBJECTIVES

Media Literacy

- explore the key idea of **themes**
- analyze visual elements in a film
- compare a film and a play
- analyze film elements used to create theme
- analyze actors' performances for characterization
- design a DVD cover using visual elements

SUMMARY

In this series of four clips from the classic 1951 film version of *A Christmas Carol,* Ebenezer Scrooge is transformed from a mean and miserly man into a good and generous man. In the opening clip, Scrooge turns away two men who are collecting for a charity, saying that the poor and destitute would be better off dead. Then he and the Spirit of Christmas Present observe the loving Cratchit family, and Scrooge learns that Tiny Tim is going to die. Later, Scrooge awakens a changed man. He's generous to everyone he meets, he gives Bob Cratchit a raise, and he helps save Tiny Tim's life.

What's the MESSAGE?

Ask students if they have ever read a book and then seen a movie version of the same story. Have them cite examples and discuss how the two versions were similar and different. Ask them whether the book and movie versions presented the same messages or **themes**, and what parts of the movie conveyed its themes.

BACKGROUND

The 1951 British film version of *A Christmas Carol* was originally titled *Scrooge.* Many viewers consider Alastair Sim (1900–1976), a Scottish-born character actor known for his comic roles, to be their favorite Scrooge. Before he became an actor, Sim taught elocution (public speaking) at Edinburgh University. Later in his acting career, Sim appeared frequently as Captain Hook in stage productions of *Peter Pan.* The Scrooge who appears on page 417 is Reginald Owen, from the 1938 version of the tale. He was a last-minute replacement for the ailing Lionel Barrymore.

Media Study

from A Christmas Carol
Film Clips on *MediaSmart* DVD

What's the MESSAGE?

MARYLAND OBJECTIVES

LITERATURE STANDARD
3.A.6.a Analyze universal themes

KEY IDEA You've explored a play version of a timeless tale and have discovered its **themes,** or messages about life. Now experience the tale in a different way as you watch selected scenes from a classic movie version of *A Christmas Carol.*

Background

Classic Scrooge The images throughout this lesson are taken from two different movie versions of *A Christmas Carol.* Many stage plays, movies, cartoons, and television specials have been based on the story. This may be because the public enjoys revisiting the tale's timeless themes. An even bigger attraction may be the simple pleasure of seeing Scrooge's personality change.

You'll see four clips from a movie that was filmed many decades ago in black and white and yet remains a popular holiday classic.

416

Media Study Resources

RESOURCE MANAGER UNIT 3

Plan and Teach pp. 177–180

Media Analysis
Summary pp. 181†*, 182‡*
Viewing Guide p. 183
Close Viewing p. 184
Viewing Activity p. 185
Produce Your Own Media p. 186

STANDARDS LESSON FILE

Media Lesson 4: Analyzing Visuals in Film and TV
Media Lesson 5: Analyzing Sound in Film and TV

 Media Center at **ClassZone.com**

MEDIA VIEWING
MediaSmart DVD

* Resources for Differentiation   † Also in Spanish   ‡ In Haitian Creole and Vietnamese

Media Literacy: Theme in Movies

Characters need to grow up! As you know from your understanding of *A Christmas Carol* and the character Scrooge, themes are often conveyed through a character's growth and change. To discover a theme in a written story, you look at the words for clues. To identify the theme of a movie, you must focus on the images and sounds. Moviemakers—in particular, the director—use the following techniques to make sure you get the message.

THEME DELIVERY	STRATEGIES FOR VIEWING	
The Director's Plan A director makes basic decisions about how to transfer a well-known tale to the screen and what themes to portray.	• Be aware that a director usually presents the same **themes** that appeared in the original work. • Be prepared to find a theme expressed (or repeated) in the key scenes the director presents.	
The Director's Tools In presenting certain images important to the theme, a director uses film techniques to highlight the message.	• Study the **camera shots** that show more than one character. These shots bring an audience close enough to see the ways characters react to each other. • The **lighting** of characters can reveal a theme in an indirect way. For example, soft lighting can represent goodness or warm moments between characters. • Listen for verbal clues. A director can state a theme directly through **dialogue.** You can also listen to the narration of a **voice-over,** the voice of an unseen narrator who provides important information about the story.	
The Actor's Performance An actor can indicate a theme by showing changes in the behavior of his or her character.	• Notice an actor's **body movements.** An actor can portray a character's personality change by using different **gestures** or **facial expressions.** • Focus on the **tone of voice** of the actors. Think of how a voice can change to show surprise, anger, or weariness.	

Teach

MEDIA LITERACY

Ask a volunteer to summarize how the change in Scrooge's character conveys a message about life, or a **theme.** *(Possible answer: People are more important than money.)* Then discuss the chart on page 417.

- **The Director's Plan** Ask students to recall the most memorable scenes from the play version of *A Christmas Carol.* List these on the board and discuss how each one conveys themes of the story. Then ask students whether, as film directors, they would include each of these scenes in a movie version. Why or why not?

- **The Director's Tools** Return to your list of key scenes. Ask students to describe how each scene would look and sound in a movie version that they were directing. Would the camera shots be up close or from a distance? Would the lighting be bright or dark? How could dialogue and voice-overs convey themes?

- **The Actor's Performance** Have students think about the characters who appear in each of their scenes. As movie directors, they would need to help the actors show what the characters are like and how they change. How could the actors move their bodies and use facial expressions to portray these characters? How could they use their voices to reveal the characters?

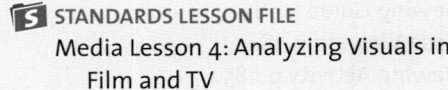 STANDARDS LESSON FILE
  Media Lesson 4: Analyzing Visuals in
     Film and TV

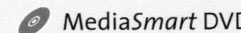 Media*Smart* DVD

MEDIA STUDY: TEACHING OPTIONS

Teaching Option 1: The Basics (1–2 Days)

1. Begin the Media Study using the material provided on pages 416–417.

2. Show the Introduction on Media*Smart.* Then show the First Viewing. As they watch, have students use the Viewing Guide on page 418, along with the corresponding copy master on page 183 of the Resource Manager. Discuss their responses.

3. Return to the pupil edition for the extension activities on page 419.

Teaching Option 2: In-Depth Study (2–3 Days)

1. Begin the Media Study using pages 416–417.

2. Show the Introduction and First Viewing from Media*Smart.*

3. Continue on Media*Smart* with the Media Lessons, using the teacher notes available in the Resources section.

4. Show the Guided Analysis presentation. Have students record their observations on the Student Viewing Guide available in the Resources section from Media*Smart.*

5. Return to the pupil edition, page 419.

VIEWING GUIDE

1. As students prepare to view the clips, remind them that they will be asked to explain how specific techniques are used to convey themes. Encourage them to watch and listen for these elements:

   - scenes that express a **theme** by showing how Scrooge's life changes when he learns to have compassion for others
   - **camera shots** that allow viewers to see how characters relate to each other
   - ways of **lighting** different scenes to show changes in Scrooge's life
   - the use of **dialogue** and **voice-over** to highlight themes
   - Alastair Sim's use of **body movements, facial expressions,** and **tone of voice** to show how Scrooge's attitudes change

2. Give students a theme statement for *A Christmas Carol,* such as "People are more important than money," and suggest that they keep it handy as they analyze the clips. After each viewing, they can refer to the theme statement and ask themselves how the clip conveys some part of that theme through the techniques described on page 417. Students may also view the clips without sound to focus on visual elements, or listen without watching to focus on sound.

📑 RESOURCE MANAGER—Copy Masters
   Viewing Guide p. 183
   Close Viewing p. 184
   Viewing Activity p. 185

💿 MediaSmart DVD

ANSWERS

FIRST VIEWING: Comprehension

1. *Scrooge says this at the beginning of the third clip, as he is awakening from his experience with the spirits.*

2. *The voice-over tells viewers that Tiny Tim "lived and got well again" as Scrooge became like a second father to him.*

💿 **MediaSmart** DVD
- **Film Clip:** *A Christmas Carol*
- **Director:** Brian Desmond Hurst
- **Genre:** Fantasy/Drama
- **Running Time:** 12 minutes

418

Viewing Guide for
A Christmas Carol

Since you've read the play version of *A Christmas Carol,* you already know all that happens to Ebenezer Scrooge. Watch the four movie clips one at a time. Each clip focuses either on Scrooge or on others who are part of his life-changing experience. Try to spot the movie techniques and acting techniques that were carefully designed to deliver Charles Dickens's themes.

View each clip several times and take as much time as you need to observe the events that take place. Keep these questions in mind as you view.

NOW VIEW

FIRST VIEWING: Comprehension

1. **Recall** At what point does Scrooge declare, "I am not the man I was"?

2. **Summarize** What happens to Tiny Tim, according to the voice-over narration at the end?

CLOSE VIEWING: Media Literacy

3. **Compare Lighting Techniques** The lighting in Scrooge's office in clip 1 is dark and dreary. The lighting of Scrooge's home when he awakes in clip 3 is bright and cheerful. What comparison do you think the director is making between Scrooge's old way of looking at the world and his new way?

4. **Interpret Acting** Scrooge goes from being cold-hearted to being softhearted. Beyond his dialogue, how do you know he has changed? Respond by using a chart like the one shown.

Scrooge's Behavior

	Clip 1	Clip 2	Clip 3	Clip 4
Facial expression				
Body movements				
Tone of voice				

CLOSE VIEWING: Media Literacy
Possible answers:

3. *In clip 1, Scrooge's life is focused only on making money, and he takes no pleasure in his relationships with other people. When he awakens in clip 3, he has realized that loving relationships give life meaning, and he is grateful to have a chance to improve his relationships.*

4. *Clip 1: Scrooge scowls at people, moves slowly as if tired, and speaks in a low, stern voice. Clip 2: Scrooge's expression is compassionate and concerned as he observes the Cratchits;* *he asks about Tiny Tim's fate in a soft voice. Clip 3: Scrooge's eyes light up; he dances around his room; he giggles and speaks in a joyous, childlike voice. Clip 4: Scrooge smiles and giggles as he talks to Bob Cratchit; he waves to people in town and swings Tiny Tim into his arms; his tone of voice is happy and kind.*

Assess and Reteach

Write or Discuss

Compare Play and Film Versions You've read a play version of the Dickens tale and watched scenes from a movie version. What did you enjoy about reading the play as compared to watching the movie scenes? Use evidence from either version to support your answer. Think about

- the portrayal of the character Scrooge in both versions
- how well each version delivers Dickens's basic themes
- the details in the stage directions of the play and the visual representation of the scenes

Produce Your Own Media

Design a DVD Cover Imagine you're part of a team promoting a new, up-to-date version of *A Christmas Carol.* Create a DVD cover that presents the highlights of this retelling. Follow the instructions on the Design Guide to help you position words and pictures on the DVD cover.

HERE'S HOW Use the Design Guide and these tips as you create the cover:

- Think of a modern-day setting and a basic story line that make it clear that this version happens in a very different time and place.
- Who's Scrooge? Brainstorm a cast list.
- Brainstorm what images to use on the cover, where to place them, and what colors to use.
- Write a blurb—a brief description of the version to appear on the back of the cover. Be sure to include within the blurb a statement that reflects a theme of the tale. Also create a rating and a critic's one-line comment about the version.

> **MEDIA TOOLS**
> For help with designing a DVD cover, visit the **Media Center at ClassZone.com.**

DESIGN GUIDE

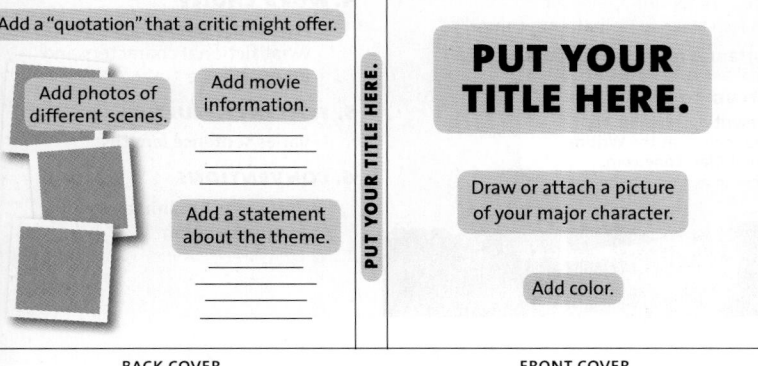

Add a "quotation" that a critic might offer.

Add photos of different scenes.

Add movie information.

Add a statement about the theme.

PUT YOUR TITLE HERE.

PUT YOUR TITLE HERE.

Draw or attach a picture of your major character.

Add color.

BACK COVER   FRONT COVER

Tech Tip
You can choose colored typefaces for your title and other text. Also, try arranging the elements in a unique way. For example, try your title at the bottom.

RETEACH

S STANDARDS LESSON FILE
Media Lesson 4: Analyzing Visuals in Film and TV
Media Lesson 5: Analyzing Sound in Film and TV

Write or Discuss

Compare Play and Film Versions Students should discuss how Alastair Sim's performance as Scrooge compares with the play, how scenes in each version help express **themes**, and how lighting is used in both versions. For example, some of the dialogue in the film is nearly the same as in the play, but Sim's vocal and facial expressions bring this dialogue to life in a unique and memorable way. The scene in clip 4 is not included in the play, but it shows Scrooge's transformation by highlighting his sense of humor as well as his generosity. The voice-over at the end of the film tells viewers exactly how Scrooge helps Tiny Tim, while the play version only hints at it. Lines in the play that are especially relevant include Scene 1, lines 72–140; Scene 4, lines 53–177; and Scene 6, lines 1–82.

Produce Your Own Media

Rubric A strong DVD cover should have

- front and back covers and a title on the spine (between the two covers)
- a clearly presented, logical concept for a modern-day setting and plot
- a cast list for all major characters
- images appropriate to the plot and the **themes**
- a back-cover blurb that describes the new version and indicates its central **theme**

 RESOURCE MANAGER—Copy Master
Produce Your Own Media p. 186

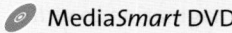 Media*Smart* DVD

MEDIA STUDY WRAP—UP

Summarize Ask students to summarize how directors and actors can present **themes** in a movie. Have them provide specific examples from the film clips of *A Christmas Carol* they have viewed. Prompt them, if necessary, to focus on the choice of scenes, the use of camera shots, the lighting, the dialogue, the voice-over, and the actors' performances.

Focus and Motivate

OBJECTIVES

- analyze a student model that reflects the key traits of a short story
- use the writing process to produce a short story
- revise and edit, using a rubric for short story writing
- use dialogue to show characters' personalities
- dramatize a short story

WRITER'S ROAD MAP

WRITING PROMPTS 1 AND 2

Help students choose a prompt by brainstorming unusual settings or by reviewing theme-related questions from the unit. When they find an idea that intrigues them, suggest that students brainstorm characters and events related to that setting or question.

ADDITIONAL PROMPTS

Use these prompts for writing about real-life experiences and about art:

WRITING PROMPT 3

Writing from Your Life Write a short story about a person, a place, or an experience from your own life.

Ideas to Consider
- an interesting friend or family member
- a special place you've visited
- a vacation adventure

WRITING PROMPT 4

Writing About Fine Art Locate a picture of a painting or a sculpture at an online museum or in a book. Use your imagination to write a story based on the art.

Possible Subjects
- a painting of a city scene or a natural scene
- a sculpture of a person
- a painting of a battle

For additional writing prompts, see

 Write*Smart* CD

 Writing Center at **ClassZone.com**

KEY TRAITS

Review the six **KEY TRAITS** with students, focusing primarily on ideas and organization. Compare the list of traits with the rubric on page 426.

Writing Workshop

Short Story

Did the stories and characters in this unit surprise you, make you think, or remind you of someone you know? Good stories can draw you into other worlds. In this workshop, you will invent your own combination of characters, setting, and plot. Use the **Writer's Road Map** to guide your creative journey.

WRITER'S ROAD MAP

Short Story

WRITING PROMPT 1

Writing from Your Imagination Write a story that is set in an unusual time or location. Make sure that your story has a plot, a conflict, and one or more characters.

Settings to Consider
- an extreme environment, such as Antarctica or the Sahara
- another time, such as ancient Egypt or the distant future
- a place you have always wanted to visit, such as the Grand Canyon or the Great Wall of China

WRITING PROMPT 2

Writing from Literature Choose a "big question" from this unit that really made you think. Then write a short story related to that question. Create a plot, a conflict, a setting, and one or more characters.

Questions to Make You Think
- What happens when friends compete? ("Amigo Brothers")
- What is the cure for unhappiness? ("What Do Fish Have to Do with Anything?")
- How important is money? (*A Christmas Carol*)

 WRITING TOOLS
For prewriting, revision, and editing tools, visit the **Writing Center** at **ClassZone.com**.

KEY TRAITS

1. IDEAS
- Has an interesting **plot** and one or more **characters**
- Develops and resolves a **central conflict**
- Includes **descriptive details** that reveal the setting and characters
- Uses **dialogue** to show characters' personalities

2. ORGANIZATION
- **Introduces** the characters, the setting, or the action in a way that gets a reader's attention
- Follows a clear **sequence of events**
- Resolves the conflict with a convincing **conclusion**

3. VOICE
- Shows the writer's individual **style**

4. WORD CHOICE
- Uses **sensory language** to show what fictional characters and places are like

5. SENTENCE FLUENCY
- Varies **sentence lengths**

6. CONVENTIONS
- Uses **correct grammar, spelling, and punctuation**

Writing Workshop Resources

 RESOURCE MANAGER UNIT 3

Plan and Teach pp. 187–190
Prewriting–Editing pp. 191–195
Writing Rubric p. 196
Speaking and Listening p. 197
Writing Support p. 198*

STANDARDS LESSON FILE

Writing Lessons 9, 28, 48
Grammar Lesson 8

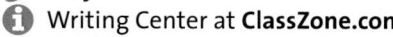 **BEST PRACTICES TOOLKIT**

Scaffolding Writing Instruction pp. 43–46*
Sequence Chain • Cluster Diagram • Spider Map • Reporter's Questions • Story Frame • Writing Template

TECHNOLOGY
- Easy Planner DVD
- Writing Center at **ClassZone.com**
- Write*Smart* CD

* **Resources for Differentiation**

Part 1: Analyze a Student Model

WRITING STANDARD
4.A.2.a Compose to express personal ideas

Angela Tressler
Jane Addams Middle School

The Trap

Panic! That's what I was feeling. My friend Jack and I were riding bikes after school. After about an hour I realized that nothing looked familiar anymore.

"Hey, Jack? Any idea where we are?"

5 "Well," he answered, "it must be a new subdivision or something."

"Must be. Let's see if we can find our way out."

We kept riding. Soon it started getting dark. "Maybe we better ask someone where we are."

The first person we saw was a guy about our age. "Excuse me,
10 how do we get out of this subdivision?" Jack asked him.

"Subdivision?" he asked us. "Funny, I haven't heard that one in a while." Then he started laughing and making fun of us.

Soon we came across this old lady sitting on her front porch with her cats. "Ma'am," I called out, "could you please tell us how
15 to get out of here?"

"Child, you'll have to hurry. Once it gets dark, there's no way of ever leaving."

Suddenly, all the pieces started falling into place. Jack and I had ridden into the Time-To-Relive-Actuality-Permanently area, also called
20 Time Trap for short.

I remember reading about this. As soon as you cross the border of our town, if you're going in the right direction, and the sun is about half set, you'll end up in the Time Trap. Once you're in, you can only get out before the sun sets completely the same day.

KEY TRAITS IN ACTION

Introduces two **characters** in an attention-getting way.

Develops a **central conflict** (being lost).

Has an interesting, unusual **plot**. Writer varies **sentence lengths** throughout story.

Descriptive details add excitement.

Teach

Part 1: Analyze a Student Model

Have students read the **Student Model** and **Key Traits in Action.** Then discuss the model, pointing out specific examples of each trait. You may also use the following activities:

- **Central Conflict** Have students reread lines 7–8 and note the central conflict of being lost. Then ask how the writer deepens the plot by making the conflict more scary in lines 18–24. **Possible answer:** *The writer describes the Time Trap and tells why it's difficult to get out. The characters are in a race against the clock, and if they don't escape, they'll be trapped forever.*

- **Descriptive Details** Write this sentence on the board:

    When you go outside our town, you can end up in the Time Trap and not get out.

Have students compare the sentence to the last paragraph on page 421. What descriptive details make the student model more interesting? **Possible answer:** *To enter the Time Trap, a person must be traveling in a certain direction when the sun is about half set (lines 22–23). To escape, the person must get out before the sun sets that same day (lines 23–24).*

Have students find additional descriptive details as they read. **Possible answers:**

- *Lines 13–14: "Soon we came across this old lady sitting on her front porch with her cats."*

- *Lines 35–37: "We followed Yellow Mill to the creek...."*

DIFFERENTIATED INSTRUCTION

FOR ALL STUDENTS
For general guidelines on differentiating writing instruction, see

 BEST PRACTICES TOOLKIT
Scaffolding Writing Instruction
pp. 43–46

FOR ENGLISH LEARNERS
Language: Skill Words Write these terms on the board and review them with students.

- *central conflict:* a struggle between characters, or between characters and a situation, that creates the action in a story

- *plot:* the events or action of a story

- *descriptive details:* words and phrases that help a reader picture what the characters are doing and where they are

- *dialogue:* words spoken by characters in a story (example in line 4: "Hey, Jack? Any idea where we are?")

- *sequence:* the order of events in a story

- *sensory language:* words or phrases that appeal to a reader's sense of sight, hearing, taste, touch, or smell. In line 37, readers can see what the characters see: "The sun had disappeared almost completely...."

- *conclusion:* the ending of a story

- **Dialogue** Throughout the story, the writer uses dialogue to add excitement, to move the events of the story forward, and to show the characters' personalities. Have students look through the story and find at least three examples of dialogue that are important to the story. Ask students what the lines of dialogue add to the story. **Possible answers:**

  - *Lines 11–12: "'Subdivision?' he asked us. 'Funny, I haven't heard that one in a while.'" (reveals that main characters are in an unfamiliar place)*
  - *Lines 16–17: "'Child, you'll have to hurry. Once it gets dark, there's no way of ever leaving.'" (shows personality of woman and adds excitement)*
  - *Line 43: "'Come on, Jack, we can still make it!'" (adds excitement)*

- **Sequence** To illustrate the clarity of the sequence of events in this story, ask students to briefly explain the events in the order in which they happen. You might list their answers in a Sequence Chain.

  📦 BEST PRACTICES TOOLKIT—Transparency
  Sequence Chain p. B21

- **Conclusion** Discuss the central conflict of the story and how it is resolved. *(The conflict is resolved in lines 44–45 when readers learn that the characters are caught in the Time Trap and will never escape.)* Ask students what makes the conclusion of the story a surprise for the reader. Have them talk about how they expected events to unfold as they were reading.

For interactive student models, see

🖉 Write*Smart* CD

ℹ️ Writing Center at **ClassZone.com**

---

25   "No way, lady, this can't be happening."

"Hush up, child. Only your believing me can save you now. If you get out of here and back to your neighborhood before the sun disappears in the sky, you will have escaped the curse. If you don't make it, every day will be identical for the rest of your immortal life."

30   "So all we have to do is go back the way we came?" I asked.

"Not quite. You have to go back by going the exact opposite way you came. It sounds odd, I know, but trust me—it's your only way home."

"So what's the opposite way?" Jack asked.

"Come in. I'll show you on a map."

35   We followed Yellow Mill to the creek just like she said, but we must have made a wrong turn after that, because we were nowhere near where we should've been. The sun had disappeared almost completely, and we knew that within a half-hour it would be dark.

After quite a while we started to see some familiar things, like
40   the lady's house. Sure enough, she was still sitting on her front porch.

"Quick, just tell us what to do after the creek!"

"You turn right, then left at the next stop."

"OK, we've got it now. Come on, Jack, we can still make it!" I cried.

As we rode away, the old lady muttered, "The idiots—don't they
45   realize they've been doing the same thing for 15 years?"

Dialogue shows characters' personalities. This writer's **style** is fast-paced and dramatic.

Follows a clear **sequence of events**. **Sensory language** adds suspense.

The writer resolves the conflict in a surprising **conclusion**.

2

DIFFERENTIATED INSTRUCTION

FOR ENGLISH LEARNERS

Comprehension: Transitions Point out words used to indicate sequence: *before* (line 27), *after that* (line 36), *after quite a while* (line 39). Ask students for examples of other sequence words, such as *first, next, then, soon,* and *suddenly,* and list them on the board. Then use the following activity to illustrate sequence:

1. Write a brief paragraph on the board that describes something you did that morning. Include appropriate sequence words.

2. Read the paragraph aloud. Underline the sequence words.

   First, I went to the kitchen. Then I made breakfast. Soon, it was time to leave.

3. Repeat this exercise. This time ask student volunteers to use sequence words to describe what they did this morning.

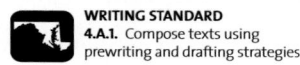

WRITING STANDARD
4.A.1. Compose texts using prewriting and drafting strategies

Part 2: Apply the Writing Process

PREWRITING

What Should I Do?	*What Does It Look Like?*

1. Brainstorm ideas.
Freewrite about places, people, or "big questions" that interest you. Then (circle) one or more ideas that might make a good story.

TIP Are you out of ideas? Choose a picture from a book or magazine and freewrite about the person, place, or event shown.

See page 426: Brainstorm Topics

▶ My friends and I shoot hoops most days after school, and nothing happens.

We ride our bikes around a lot, and it's the same old neighborhood day after day.

⟨What if we went back in time?⟩ Or to the future?

2. Focus your ideas.
Identify your characters. The writer of the student model decided to make herself a character in the story. She used **first-person point of view** ("That's what I was feeling" rather than "That's what she was feeling").

Next, decide on your setting. Start to think through what happens to the characters—that is, jot down your first ideas about your **plot.**

▶
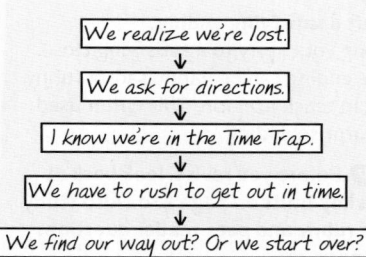

Characters	Setting	Plot
me	a strange	We ride our
Jack, my	neighborhood,	bikes too
friend	starting to	far and end
	get dark	up getting
people we		lost, maybe
meet on		going to
our trip		another time
		or place?
		Ask the
		people there
		for help?

3. Make a story map.
Don't start to write your story until you have mapped out a plot that includes a **conflict** and at least two or three events.

TIP Remember that some ideas will come to you as you write. You can also make changes as you draft.

▶
We realize we're lost.
↓
We ask for directions.
↓
I know we're in the Time Trap.
↓
We have to rush to get out in time.
↓
We find our way out? Or we start over?

FOR ENGLISH LEARNERS

Planning a Story Have students use these sentence starters to help them focus their ideas before they begin writing:

• My story is about _____.

• The conflict in my story is _____.

• My characters are _____.

• My story takes place _____.

Students can then meet with partners to create their story maps. One student in the pair can read his or her story ideas. The partner should ask questions that will help the writer add details and revise his or her ideas. Then the partners can reverse roles.

Using Descriptive Language To help students develop descriptive language for their stories, have them use the copy master.

R RESOURCE MANAGER—Copy Master
Writing Support p. 198

Practice and Apply

To support students during the writing process, use these copy masters:

R RESOURCE MANAGER—Copy Master
Prewriting–Editing pp. 191–195
Writing Rubric p. 196
Speaking and Listening p. 197
Writing Support p. 198 (for English learners)

Part 2: Apply the Writing Process

PREWRITING

1. Brainstorm ideas. Students can do this activity individually or in pairs or small groups. If students are struggling for ideas, be sure they have noted the **TIP** in the first step. Also encourage students to experiment with various graphic organizers to help them generate ideas.

BEST PRACTICES TOOLKIT—Transparencies
Cluster Diagram p. B18
Spider Map p. B22

2. Focus your ideas. Talk about the difference between **first-person** and **third-person point of view.** Use the model and other stories in the unit as examples. Discuss the advantages of using each point of view. (For example, a first-person point of view allows readers to know the thoughts and feelings of the character telling the story.) Encourage students to keep their characters in mind as they gather details related to setting and plot.

3. Make a story map. To help students get started on their maps, encourage them to ask themselves: What happens in my story? Who is involved? How is it resolved? Students can practice answering these questions using the student model. Be sure to point out the **TIP** in the third step. Suggest some graphic organizers students can use at this stage.

BEST PRACTICES TOOLKIT—Transparencies
Reporter's Questions p. C9
Sequence Chain p. B21
Story Frame p. C10

For interactive graphic organizers, see

💿 Write*Smart* CD

ℹ️ Writing Center at **ClassZone.com**

DRAFTING

1. **Start with a "hook."** Encourage students to experiment with possible story beginnings. Have them write three passages for their stories: one that incorporates sensory language, one that includes dialogue, and one that includes descriptive details about setting. Then ask students to meet in pairs to read aloud their opening sentences and get feedback about which opening is the best "hook."

2. **Develop your characters.** Tell students that good dialogue can make their characters sound natural. Ask them to think about how real people speak and to recall a recent conversation with friends or with family. Then have them review the dialogue in the model.
   - Lines 4 and 6: *"Any idea where we are?"*; *"Must be."* (People often use casual, shortened language when they speak, rather than complete sentences.)
   - Lines 11 and 16: *haven't, you'll* (When people speak, they often use contractions.)
   - Lines 26 and 44: *"Hush up, child"*; *"The idiots—"* (Sometimes a character has a particular way of speaking that reveals something about his or her personality.)

3. **Make sure the sequence of events is clear.** Remind students to make sure that readers can understand the order of events in a story. Direct them once again to the model to review how the author of "The Trap" lets readers know what happens when. Encourage students to practice writing sentences for their own stories that use sequence words like those listed in the third step.

4. **Craft a satisfying ending.** Have students discuss which of the two possible endings for "The Trap" is most satisfying and why. Then encourage students to brainstorm two or three possible endings for their own stories. Have them share their endings with a partner and discuss which works best.

For a short-story writing template, see

    BEST PRACTICES TOOLKIT—Transparency
      Writing Template: Short Story pp. C16, C42

    Write*Smart* CD

    Writing Center at ClassZone.com

DRAFTING

What Should I Do?	What Does It Look Like?
1. Start with a "hook." Right from the first sentence, get your readers' attention. You can do this with **sensory language,** exciting **dialogue, descriptive details,** or a surprising statement.	**Sensory language** *My friend Jack and I rode down street after street, past old houses with peeling paint and some mutt yapping its head off.* **A surprising statement** *Panic! That's what I was feeling.*
2. Develop your characters. Use **dialogue** to make the people in your story seem real.	*"Hey, Jack? Any idea where we are?"* *"Well," he answered, "it must be a new subdivision or something."* *"Must be. Let's see if we can find our way out."*
3. Make sure the sequence of events is clear. Use words and phrases such as *first, next, then, soon,* and *suddenly* to help your reader understand what happens when.	*The first person we saw was a guy about our age....* *Soon we came across this old lady....* *Suddenly, all the pieces started falling into place.*
4. Craft a satisfying ending. Bring your story to a satisfying close. The ending can be happy, sad, or funny. It can teach a lesson. This writer used a surprise ending. **TIP** Before you revise, look back at the **key traits on page 420.** Also study the **rubric** and **peer-reader questions** on **page 426.**	**A dramatic finish** *When it was almost dark, the glowing yellow Time Trap gate appeared. As we rushed through, we heard the old lady yell, "Goodbye, and don't come back!"* **A surprise ending** *As we rode away, the old lady muttered, "The idiots— don't they realize they've been doing the same thing for 15 years?"*

DIFFERENTIATED INSTRUCTION

FOR ENGLISH LEARNERS

Vocabulary: Sensory Words On the board, write a list of words that appeal to the five senses. Discuss the words with students.

1. Assign each student one of the senses. Ask them to come up with at least two sensory words for that sense.

2. Ask them to write one or two sentences for their stories that include these words.

3. Have students meet in pairs or small groups to share their sentences.

FOR ADVANCED LEARNERS/PRE–AP

Explore Flashback Challenge students to experiment with sequence. Explain that some stories begin in the middle of the action or after an important event has already occurred. In this situation, the writer can use a technique called flashback to give readers background information. Ask students to think about stories or movies that use this technique. Then encourage them to try using it in their stories.

REVISING AND EDITING

What Should I Do?	What Does It Look Like?
1. Match the dialogue to the character. • Ask a peer reader to <u>underline</u> dialogue that seems phony or unnatural. • Revise to include contractions, slang, or exclamations that match the character's age and personality. **See page 426: Ask a Peer Reader**	▶ ~~"I cannot accept that this is happening."~~ "No way, lady, this can't be happening." ~~"Jack, it is time to go."~~ "Come on, Jack, we can still make it!"
2. Vary sentence lengths. • If all your sentences are short, they may seem choppy or immature. If all your sentences are long, your writing may be boring or hard to understand. • Revise your story to create a mix of long and short sentences.	▶ ~~"It sounds odd. I know that. Trust me. It's your only way home."~~ "It sounds odd, I know, but trust me—it's your only way home." After quite a while we started to see some familiar things, like the lady's house, and she was still sitting on her front porch. *(Sure enough,)*
3. Show your style. • Dialogue and word choice are parts of a writer's style. Do you want your style to be fast paced or relaxed, formal or fun filled? • This writer revised her story to make it more dramatic. She added colorful words and phrases (*hush up, save you*) and an important detail (*before the sun disappears in the sky*). You will learn more about style in Unit 4.	▶ ~~"If you get out of here, you will escape the curse."~~ "Hush up, child. Only your believing me can save you now. If you get out of here and back to your neighborhood before the sun disappears in the sky, you will have escaped the curse."
4. Brainstorm the right title. • Your title should interest a reader but not give away the whole story. If you wish, ask a peer reader for suggestions. • This writer chose a simple, dramatic title.	▶ ~~Riding Around Forever~~ *The Trap ~~Lost in Time~~ ~~Saved Just in Time~~

REVISING AND EDITING

1. **Match the dialogue to the character.** Encourage students and peer readers to read lines of dialogue aloud. Listening will help them make sure words and phrases sound like real speech.

2. **Vary sentence lengths.** Tell students they can use these techniques to vary sentence lengths and make their writing more interesting:
   - combine short sentences
   - break up long, complicated sentences
   - add dialogue to long descriptive passages

   Tell students that reading sentences aloud can help them listen for natural pauses and for places where sentences should be combined.

3. **Show your style.** Students should read though their stories and mark places where dialogue and colorful language could be added. Suggest that they ask themselves these questions:
   - What words and phrases would each character use?
   - Does the language in my story work well for the kind of story I am telling? (For example, are there any places where my language is too formal for a story that is supposed to be light and funny?)

4. **Brainstorm the right title.** Have students glance through the stories in the unit for examples of titles. Encourage students to list possible titles for their story and then give their list to a peer reader who is unfamiliar with the story. The peer reader should say what each title brings to mind or what questions each title raises.

For interactive revision tools, see

⊘ Write*Smart* CD

ⓘ Writing Center at **ClassZone.com**

FOR LESS—PROFICIENT WRITERS

Varying Sentence Lengths Give students additional instruction in editing their work to include sentences of varied lengths. On the board, write this paragraph:

I walked to the busy park. It was one sunny day. I spotted a friend. She was an old friend. I couldn't believe I saw this person. I called out to her. I called out hello to my friend.

Work with students to add sentence variety to the paragraph. Remind them that combining sentences and adding dialogue are two ways of changing sentence length. **(Possible answer:** *I walked to the busy park one sunny day and spotted an old friend. I couldn't believe it! I called out, "Hello!"*)

Have students work in pairs to vary sentence lengths in their own stories.

Preparing to Publish

Support for meeting the goals in the writing rubric is supplied throughout the **Writing Workshop** on pages 420–425.

For Rubric Bank, see

 Write*Smart* CD

ℹ Writing Center at **ClassZone.com**

Assess and Reteach

After reading and assessing students' stories, you might use these lessons to reteach key skills:

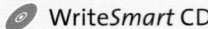 STANDARDS LESSON FILE

Writing Lesson 9: Creating Sentence Variety
Writing Lesson 28: Short Story
Writing Lesson 48: Writing Dialogue
Grammar Lesson 8: Pronoun-Antecedent Agreement

Apply the Rubric

A strong short story . . .

- ☑ begins in an attention-getting way
- ☑ includes an interesting plot and at least one character
- ☑ has a central conflict
- ☑ uses descriptive details, sensory language, and dialogue to reveal the setting and characters
- ☑ has its own style
- ☑ follows a clear sequence of events
- ☑ uses a variety of sentence lengths
- ☑ has a satisfying conclusion

Ask a Peer Reader

- What is the conflict in my story?
- How could I make the dialogue more convincing?
- What three words would you use to describe my style?
- What did you like or dislike about the story's ending?

Brainstorm Topics

What if a disaster separated family members in a strange place?

What if a character slipped into another time or reality?

What if enemies had to work together to find their way out of a cave, a jungle, or a forest?

What if characters had to race against time to get to safety?

Check Your Grammar

Make sure each pronoun matches its antecedent (the noun or pronoun to which it refers). In this example, the pronoun *her* matches the antecedent *old lady*.

Soon we came across this old lady sitting
                                        her
on ^their front porch.

See page R52: Agreement with Antecedent

Writing On*l*ine

 PUBLISHING OPTIONS
For publishing options, visit the **Writing Center** at **ClassZone.com**.

ASSESSMENT PREPARATION
For writing and grammar assessment practice, go to the **Assessment Center** at **ClassZone.com**.

WRITING STANDARD
4.A.2.a Compose to express personal ideas

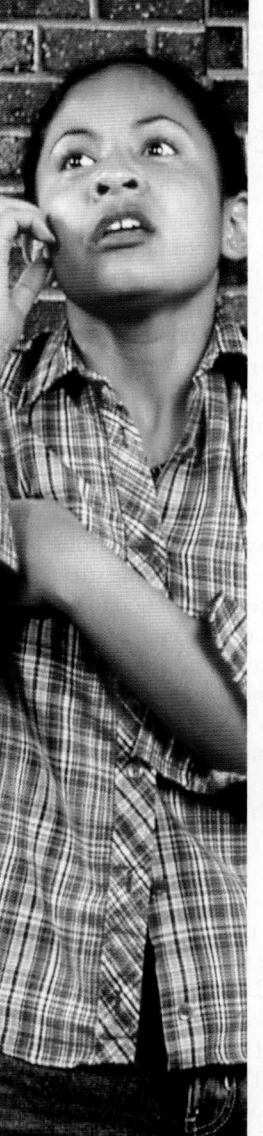

Dramatizing a Short Story

This is your chance to sit in the director's chair. Turn your story, "The Trap," or another story from this unit into a play. Then work with classmates to perform it.

Planning the Dramatization

1. **Identify the mood you want to create.** Should the story make audience members laugh, examine their own lives, feel surprise, or shiver with fear? Keep the mood in mind as you follow the other step.

2. **Write your script.** Dialogue is what moves the action along in most plays, so consider using more of it. You may also want to add a narrator, or even more characters if needed. Remember that a script includes stage directions. You should also add ideas for music and sound effects.

> **Jack** (fear in his voice). So what's the opposite way?
>
> **Old Lady** (in a serious voice). Come in. I'll show you on a map.
>
> The three characters walk though a door that creaks. The lights go down. After a moment, the bike riders appear in dim spotlight, stage left.
>
> **Narrator.** They followed Yellow Mill to the creek. . . .

Presenting the Dramatization

1. **Choose your cast and crew.** Decide on the actors. Put other people in charge of music, sound effects, and props. You might also need help with lighting, costumes, and other details.

2. **Rehearse.** Invite someone to listen when you rehearse. Ask for feedback. Actors may need to speak the words more clearly, or you may need to add dialogue.

3. **Act it out.** Present your play to your classmates and/or family members. Soak up the applause! If possible, ask someone to videotape the presentation so you can evaluate its strengths and weaknesses.

   See page R80: Evaluate an Oral Interpretation

SPEAKING AND LISTENING

Ask students to read this page to get an overview of how to create a dramatization of a short story.

Before students begin working, review this rubric with them so that they understand their goals:

Rubric A strong dramatization

- connects with the audience by conveying a particular mood
- features realistic dialogue that moves the action of the play forward
- has characters and/or a narrator to convey information and make the words of the play come alive
- includes clear stage directions and ideas for music and sound effects
- is presented by an organized cast and crew
- has been rehearsed before being presented to an audience

R RESOURCE MANAGER—Copy Master
Speaking and Listening p. 197

S STANDARDS LESSON FILE
Speaking and Listening Lesson 8: Oral Interpretation

DIFFERENTIATED INSTRUCTION

FOR LESS–PROFICIENT WRITERS

Dramatizing a Short Story Have students read the script sample and compare it to lines 33–35 on page 422. Make sure they note that

- the first two lines of dialogue are taken directly from the story
- stage directions ("fear in his voice," "The three characters walk . . .") have been added to the script
- a narrator has been added to describe some of the action

Direct students' attention to lines 1–8 on page 421. Work with them to dramatize this section. Prompt them with questions such as

- What lines of dialogue can be used in the script?
- Would a narrator be helpful? What things should the narrator describe?
- What should the stage directions say? Think about what the characters are doing and how they are feeling.

Assessment Practice

CHECK READINESS

Read aloud the paragraph under **ASSESS** and stress to students that this is not the full Unit Test, but a way for them to check their readiness for it. Then have students examine the skills listed under **REVIEW** and look back in the unit or in the Handbook for any they need to study.

READ THE SELECTION

Remind students to keep unit goals in mind as they read the passage, paying particular attention to

- theme and symbols
- their inferences about the text
- causes and effects
- comparisons and contrasts

To help students focus on **theme** while reading, encourage them to ask questions such as

- What message about life is expressed through the events in "The Hummingbird That Lived Through Winter"? What does the hummingbird symbolize?
- What lessons do the characters learn from the hummingbird, and from each other?

ANSWER THE QUESTIONS

Direct students to pages R93–R99 of the Test-Taking Handbook to review test-taking strategies. Remind students not to choose the first alternative that seems to fit when answering a multiple-choice question. Instead, they should read through all the choices, eliminate any that are clearly wrong, and then choose the best answer—the one that is most accurate and complete.

Also encourage students to quickly look over the entire test before they begin—noting the directions, the different types of questions asked, and which questions may take longer than others. Explain that this strategy will help them budget their time and plan how long to spend on each question.

ASSESS
The practice test items on the next few pages match skills listed on the Unit Goals page (page 303) and addressed throughout this unit. Taking this practice test will help you assess your knowledge of these skills and determine your readiness for the Unit Test.

REVIEW
After you take the practice test, your teacher can help you identify any skills you need to review.

- Theme
- Symbol
- Make Inferences
- Cause and Effect
- Compare and Contrast
- Context Clues
- Connotation and Denotation
- Independent and Dependent Clauses
- Coordinating Conjunctions

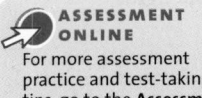

ASSESSMENT ONLINE
For more assessment practice and test-taking tips, go to the **Assessment Center** at **ClassZone.com**.

Reading Comprehension

DIRECTIONS *Read the selection and answer the questions that follow.*

from The Hummingbird That Lived Through Winter

William Saroyan

There was a hummingbird once which in the wintertime did not leave our neighborhood in Fresno, California.

I'll tell you about it.

Across the street lived old Dikran, who was almost blind. He was past eighty and his wife was only a few years younger. They had a little house that was as neat inside as it was ordinary outside—except for old Dikran's garden, which was the best thing of its kind in the world. Plants, bushes, trees—all strong, in sweet black moist earth whose guardian was old Dikran. All things from the sky loved this spot in our poor neighborhood,

10 and old Dikran loved *them*.

One freezing Sunday, in the dead of winter, as I came home from Sunday School I saw old Dikran standing in the middle of the street trying to distinguish what was in his hand. Instead of going into our house to the fire, as I had wanted to do, I stood on the steps of the front porch and watched the old man. He would turn around and look upward at his trees and then back to the palm of his hand. He stood in the street at least two minutes and then at last he came to me. He held his hand out, and in Armenian he said, "What is this in my hand?"

I looked.

20 "It is a hummingbird," I said half in English and half in Armenian. Hummingbird I said in English because I didn't know its name in Armenian.

"What is that?" old Dikran asked.

"The little bird," I said. "You know. The one that comes in the summer and stands in the air and then shoots away. The one with the wings that beat so fast you can't see them. It's in your hand. It's dying."

"Come with me," the old man said. "I can't see, and the old lady's at church. I can feel its heart beating. Is it in a bad way? Look again, once."

I looked again. It was a sad thing to behold. This wonderful little

30 creature of summertime in the big rough hand of the old peasant. Here

---

DIFFERENTIATED INSTRUCTION

FOR ENGLISH LEARNERS

Assessment Practice: Work Backwards
Prepare students for the assessment by having them "work backwards," reading the questions before reading the passage. Have pairs follow these steps to learn unfamiliar words in the test directions and questions:

1. Find words you don't recognize and write each one on an index card.

2. Look up the meaning in a dictionary.

3. Write the meaning on the back of the card.

4. Use your word cards to teach and practice the vocabulary with another pair.

it was in the cold of winter, absolutely helpless and pathetic, not suspended in a shaft of summer light, not the most alive thing in the world, but the most helpless and heartbreaking.

"It's dying," I said.

The old man lifted his hand to his mouth and blew warm breath on the little thing in his hand which he could not even see. "Stay now," he said in Armenian. "It is not long till summer. Stay, swift and lovely."

We went into the kitchen of his little house, and while he blew warm breath on the bird he told me what to do.

40 "Put a tablespoonful of honey over the gas fire and pour it into my hand, but be sure it is not too hot."

This was done.

After a moment the hummingbird began to show signs of fresh life. The warmth of the room, the vapor of the warm honey—and, well, the will and love of the old man. Soon the old man could feel the change in his hand, and after a moment or two the hummingbird began to take little dabs of the honey.

"It will live," the old man announced. "Stay and watch."

The transformation was incredible. The old man kept his hand
50 generously open, and I expected the helpless bird to shoot upward out of his hand, suspend itself in space, and scare the life out of me—which is exactly what happened. The new life of the little bird was magnificent. It spun about in the little kitchen, going to the window, coming back to the heat, suspending, circling as if it were summertime and it had never felt better in its whole life.

The old man sat on the plain chair, blind but attentive. He listened carefully and tried to see, but of course he couldn't. He kept asking about the bird, how it seemed to be, whether it showed signs of weakening again, what its spirit was, and whether or not it appeared to be restless;
60 and I kept describing the bird to him.

When the bird was restless and wanted to go, the old man said, "Open the window and let it go."

"Will it live?" I asked.

"It is alive now and wants to go," he said. "Open the window."

I opened the window, the hummingbird stirred about here and there,

ASSESSMENT PRACTICE **429**

ITEM ANALYSIS

COMPREHENSION AND BRIEF CONSTRUCTED RESPONSE	ITEMS	UNIT PAGES
Theme	5, 10, 11	302, 304, 306, 311, 327, 363, 381, 387
Symbol	1, 8, 9	339
Make Inferences	5, 6, 10	339
Cause and Effect	2, 3, 12	363
Compare and Contrast	4, 7, 13	311

VOCABULARY	ITEMS	UNIT PAGES
Context Clues	1, 2, 3, 4	354
Denotation and Connotation	5, 6, 7	336

WRITING AND GRAMMAR	ITEMS	UNIT PAGES
Independent and Dependent Clauses	1, 2	415
Coordinating Conjunctions	3, 4	355

FOR LESS–PROFICIENT READERS

Assessment Support Consider these options for completing the **Assessment Practice**:

- Have students "work backwards" to review the test questions before reading the passage.

- Select random questions in the assessment and have students demonstrate how and where to look for the answers.

- Ask students to locate unfamiliar vocabulary in the assessment. Elicit word meanings from the class.

- Have students record useful testing words and definitions in their journals for later reference.

- Read the selection or parts of it aloud to aid in student comprehension.

MSA PREPARATION

McDougal Littell
Assessment System

After checking student readiness with this Assessment Practice, you may administer the complete Unit 3 Test, which matches the structure and format of the MSA.

Comprehension

Model a thinking process for answering multiple-choice questions.

1. **D is correct.** *Dikran's garden is full of life and loved by wild creatures. A is incorrect, since the garden is strong and alive. B is incorrect, since the story's theme is life in nature, not Armenia. C is incorrect, since Dikran appears to be as comfortable in his house as he is in his garden.*

2. **C is correct.** *The narrator is so puzzled by Dikran that he stands in the cold watching him. A is incorrect, since the narrator mentions no cars. B is incorrect, as shown in lines 13–15. D is incorrect, since the narrator at first does not know what Dikran holds in his hand.*

3. **D is correct.** *After the hummingbird eats the warm honey, it is filled with new life. A is incorrect, since the hummingbird flies out the window the same day it is taken inside. B is incorrect, since it is the characters' actions that warm and nourish the hummingbird. C is incorrect, since the narrator opens the window only after the hummingbird has revived.*

4. **B is correct.** *The hummingbird's transformation, from near death to fully alive, is an amazing sight. A and C are incorrect, as shown by lines 28–29, since they describe the hummingbird before it is taken inside. D is incorrect, since the narrator makes this observation the following summer.*

5. **C is correct.** *Once the hummingbird becomes restless, Dikran knows they must set it free. A is incorrect, for Dikran cannot know for sure what will happen in the future. B is incorrect, since the story is set "in the dead of winter" (line 11). D is incorrect, since Dikran does not consider caring for the wild creature any further.*

6. **B is correct.** *Dikran's love for nature and gentle ways make him well suited to care for living things. Dikran is not unhappy about his vision, as in A, for he uses his other senses to care for the hummingbird. C is incorrect, since Dikran's motivation is to help the hummingbird. D is only partly true, for above any individual, Dikran cherishes all life (line 81).*

---

feeling the cold from the outside, suspended itself in the area of the open window, stirring this way and that, and then it was gone.

"Close the window," the old man said.

We talked a minute or two and then I went home.

70 The old man claimed the hummingbird lived through that winter, but I never knew for sure. I saw hummingbirds again when summer came, but I couldn't tell one from the other.

One day in the summer I asked the old man.

"Did it live?"

"The little bird?" he said.

"Yes," I said. "That we gave the honey to. You remember. The little bird that was dying in the winter. Did it live?"

"Look about you," the old man said. "Do you see the bird?"

"I see humming*birds*," I said.

80 "Each of them is our bird," the old man said. "Each of them, each of them," he said swiftly and gently.

Comprehension

DIRECTIONS *Answer the following questions about the selection.*

1. Dikran's garden symbolizes
   - **A.** the certainty of death
   - **B.** his homeland of Armenia
   - **C.** an escape from his house
   - **D.** the abundance of nature

2. Seeing Dikran in the street causes the narrator to
   - **A.** worry that a car will hit Dikran
   - **B.** run to his own house to get warm by the fire
   - **C.** watch Dikran to find out what he is doing
   - **D.** look for birds suffering from the cold

3. Which action helps cause the hummingbird to revive?
   - **A.** keeping the bird inside all winter
   - **B.** asking questions about the bird
   - **C.** opening the window
   - **D.** feeding the bird warm honey

4. Compare and contrast the hummingbird's behavior before and after Dikran takes it inside. Which of the following statements best describes the change in behavior?
   - **A.** "It was a sad thing to behold."
   - **B.** "The transformation was incredible."
   - **C.** "I can feel its heart beating."
   - **D.** "I saw hummingbirds again. . . ."

430

---

7. **A is correct.** *Both characters value the life that surrounds them. Although B and C are true, they are minor details, and not the most important similarities shared by the characters. D is incorrect, since although they both appreciate nature, it is not clear if either the young boy or old man is an expert.*

8. **B is correct.** *The hummingbird, with its boundless summer energy, symbolizes the life in nature. A is incorrect, since the hummingbirds are alive. C and D are incorrect, since Dikran is enjoying the summer moment, and not dwelling on winter or the past.*

5. Dikran lets the hummingbird go because he knows that

A. it will survive the winter now

B. spring will come soon

C. it is wild and needs to be free

D. he can't take care of it

6. What can you infer about Dikran from the way he cares for the hummingbird?

A. He is unhappy that he can't see very well.

B. He loves caring for living things.

C. He wants to make the narrator feel good.

D. He thinks that this bird is special.

7. What is the most important way in which the narrator and Dikran are similar?

A. They appreciate nature and life.

B. They are Armenian.

C. They live in the same poor neighborhood.

D. They know a lot about nature.

8. What does the hummingbird symbolize to Dikran at the end of the story?

A. death   **C.** memories

B. life   **D.** winter

9. Which of the following descriptions best shows what the hummingbird symbolizes?

A. "wonderful little creature of summertime"

B. "absolutely helpless and pathetic"

C. "the most alive thing in the world"

D. "the one with the wings that beat so fast"

10. Which statement best describes a theme of the story?

A. The life force is powerful.

B. Nature is very fragile.

C. Elderly people deserve respect.

D. Life is full of hardships.

11. Which lines from the story best demonstrate its theme?

A. "There was a hummingbird once which in the wintertime did not leave our neighborhood in Fresno, California."

B. "He listened carefully and tried to see, but of course he couldn't."

C. "I saw hummingbirds again when summer came, but I couldn't tell one from the other."

D. "'Each of them is our bird,' the old man said. 'Each of them, each of them,' he said swiftly and gently."

Brief Constructed Response

12. Name two things Dikran does to cause the hummingbird to revive.

13. Reread lines 24–33. What is the hummingbird like? Compare its wintertime appearance with how hummingbirds look and act in the summer.

GO ON ➡

9. **C is correct.** *Although A, B, and D do describe the hummingbird at different times in the story, C captures the larger symbolic meaning of the hummingbird, with its energy, life, and vigor.*

10. **A is correct.** *As Dikran and the narrator discover, the life force in even the smallest of creatures is powerful. B is incorrect, since the hummingbird's resilience is emphasized over its fragility. C and D, although true statements in general, are incorrect because they do not describe a theme of this story.*

11. **D is correct.** *The theme—that life's energy and power endure—can be seen in all the hummingbirds. A is incorrect, since it merely sets up the plot of the story. B is incorrect, since it only describes the character of Dikran. C is incorrect, since it just shows the narrator's emotions in a specific scene.*

Brief Constructed Response

Evaluate student writing using the Maryland writing rubrics in the back of the book.

Possible responses:

12. *Dikran does many things to help revive the hummingbird. First, he brings it into his house (line 38). Then he blows warm breath on it (lines 38–39). He feeds it warm honey (lines 40–41). The narrator says that Dikran's "will and love" also bring the hummingbird back to life (line 45).*

13. *The response should describe the hummingbird as a small, fragile creature that is wild and free-spirited. In the winter, this hummingbird is helpless and half-dead from the cold; its heart is beating, but it is dying. It is a "sad thing to behold" (line 29). It stays still in Dikran's hand until it has eaten some honey and warms up; then it behaves as it does in summer—shooting up, darting about, and suspending itself in space. In the summer the hummingbird usually arrives, "stands in the air and then shoots away" (line 25). It is "the most alive thing in the world" (lines 32–33). It circles and hovers on "wings that beat so fast you can't see them" (lines 25–26).*

DIFFERENTIATED INSTRUCTION

FOR ENGLISH LEARNERS

Test-Taking Strategies: Preview Test and Budget Time Have pairs take turns reading aloud the directions on pages 430–433. Ask them to record any unfamiliar terms. Then have pairs look at the different types of questions on the assessment. Ask them to discuss which questions they will need to leave more time for than others, and why. As a class, discuss unfamiliar words and invite volunteers to share ideas on how to budget time during the assessment.

Assessment Vocabulary Give students the following words from the questions on pages 430–431. Ask them to record a definition for each. Then have small groups compare their definitions and write sentences with each word. Invite groups to share their sentences.

- *symbolize* (items 1, 8, 9)
- *cause* (items 2, 3, 12)
- *compare, contrast* (items 4, 13)
- *infer* (item 6)
- *theme* (items 10, 11)

Vocabulary

1. **B is correct.** *Dikran could be attempting to hold, caress, or save something, as in A, C, and D. However, B is the best answer, since we know that Dikran is "almost blind" (line 4) and that he is "trying" (line 13) to figure out what he has in his hand.*

2. **A is correct.** *The bird is also described as "helpless" (lines 31 and 33) and "heartbreaking" (line 33), so pathetic must have a similar meaning. B and C have no connection to these words. D is also incorrect, since the bird is dying from the "cold of winter" (line 31), not from being broken.*

3. **C is correct.** *The narrator expects the hummingbird to "shoot upward" into space (lines 50–51), so it must be doing something visible in the air. A and B have no relation to this context. D is incorrect, since the hummingbird's flight (lines 53–55) is energetic, but not out of control.*

4. **D is correct.** *Dikran wants to know whether the hummingbird is "weakening" or "restless" (lines 58–59). We can eliminate A, B, and C because they do not help to measure the hummingbird's recovery.*

5. **C is correct.** *Dikran's house is small and in a poor neighborhood, as in A and B. However, C is the best answer because the word except (line 6) sets up a contradiction to the house's appearance, and calling the garden "the best thing of its kind in the world" (line 7) makes the contrast between the lovely garden and plain house clear. D is incorrect because the house is lived in.*

6. **B is correct.** *Since the context involves a garden that is "strong" and "loved" (lines 8–9), and has "moist" (line 8) earth, we know that sweet must be a positive word to describe soil. We can eliminate A because soil is not eaten, C because it is a negative word, and D because it does not help explain why the soil is so fruitful.*

7. **A is correct.** *The sentence contrasts the delicate little bird and Dikran's "big rough hand" (line 30). C is incorrect because it does not support the contrast. B and D are incorrect because these words have negative connotations; Dikran may be rough on the outside, but he has a kind heart.*

Vocabulary

DIRECTIONS *Use context clues to answer the following questions.*

1. Which is the most likely meaning of *distinguish* in line 13?
   A. hold
   B. see
   C. caress
   D. save

2. Which is the most likely meaning of *pathetic* in line 31?
   A. pitiful
   B. lost
   C. small
   D. broken

3. Which is the most likely meaning of *suspend* in line 51?
   A. disappear from sight
   B. stop breathing for a short time
   C. hang in the air without falling
   D. spin out of control

4. Which is the most likely meaning of *spirit* as it is used in line 59?
   A. a strong loyalty
   B. the quality that sets something apart
   C. an emotional tendency
   D. the energy of a living thing

DIRECTIONS *Use context clues and your knowledge of connotation and denotation to answer the following questions.*

5. The denotation of *ordinary* in line 6 is "usual." Which word below best describes its connotation?
   A. poor
   B. small
   C. plain
   D. deserted

6. The denotation of *sweet* in line 8 is "free of acid or acidity." Which word below best describes its connotation?
   A. tasty
   B. good
   C. cheap
   D. perfumed

7. Which connotation does the word *peasant* have in line 30?
   A. coarseness
   B. vulgarity
   C. hostility
   D. rudeness

DIFFERENTIATED INSTRUCTION

FOR ENGLISH LEARNERS
Assessment Support: Context Clues

- Point out the term *context clues* in the directions for items 1–4. Remind students that context clues are words and ideas in the surrounding text that can help them figure out the meaning of an unfamiliar word.

- Have students read lines 35–47. Ask them to define *vapor* (line 44) using context clues. *(The bird is able to smell the warm honey. Vapor means "mist" or "steam.")*

Assessment Support: Denotation and Connotation

- Read aloud the directions for items 5–7. Explain that a word's denotation is its literal meaning from a dictionary. A word's connotation includes related ideas or feelings that affect the word's meaning.

- Give the denotation for *stay* (lines 36, 37): "to stop going forward." Ask students to suggest the word's connotation in this context. *("live"; "fight to stay alive")*

Writing & Grammar

DIRECTIONS *Read this passage and then answer the questions that follow.*

> (1) Last summer, our family drove to Mexico. (2) Where my mom was born. (3) We saw the places where she played as a little girl and visited her home. (4) Her old neighborhood has narrow streets. (5) That wind past the houses. (6) My mom remembered her friends, although she didn't find any of them living there anymore. (7) She looked for the anthill she had loved to watch as a child. (8) Like her friends, the anthill was gone. (9) Still, Mom was happy we went. (10) We'll probably go back again sometime.

1. Combine sentence 1 and fragment 2 to form one sentence with an independent clause and a dependent clause.

  A. Last summer, our family drove to Mexico and where my mom was born.

  B. Last summer, our family drove to Mexico, where my mom was born.

  C. Last summer, our family drove to Mexico; my mom was born there.

  D. Our family drove to Mexico last summer to my mom's birthplace.

2. Combine sentence 4 and fragment 5 to form one sentence with an independent clause and a dependent clause.

  A. Her old neighborhood has narrow streets; that wind past the houses.

  B. Her old neighborhood has narrow streets that wind past the houses.

  C. Her old neighborhood has narrow streets—and the streets wind past the houses.

  D. Her old neighborhood has narrow streets, and furthermore, these streets wind past the houses.

3. Choose the correct coordinating conjunction to combine sentences 7 and 8.

  A. so

  B. but

  C. for

  D. or

4. Choose the correct coordinating conjunction to combine sentences 9 and 10.

  A. for

  B. but

  C. yet

  D. and

STOP

433

ANSWERS

Writing & Grammar

1. **B is correct.** *The words "where my mom was born" are a dependent clause because they do not form a complete thought. A is incorrect because it contains the unnecessary coordinating conjunction* and. *C is incorrect because it is two independent clauses joined by a semicolon. D is incorrect because it contains only one (independent) clause; the fragment has been rewritten as a prepositional phrase.*

2. **B is correct.** *The words "that wind past the houses" are a dependent clause. A is incorrect because a semicolon should only link two independent clauses. Neither C nor D includes a dependent clause.*

3. **B is correct.** *The conjunction* but *sets up a contrast between what the mother tries to do (find the anthill) and what actually happens (she doesn't find it). The coordinating conjunctions in A, C, and D do not correctly link the ideas expressed in the two sentences.*

4. **D is correct.** *D is the best answer because sentence 10 continues the positive thought established in sentence 9. A is incorrect because* for *implies an illogical cause-and-effect relationship—the mother is happy they went because they will go back sometime. B and C are incorrect because* but *and* yet *imply that Mom did not enjoy the visit.*

DIFFERENTIATED INSTRUCTION

FOR ENGLISH LEARNERS
Review Academic Vocabulary

1. Write this academic vocabulary on the board and have groups brainstorm what they know about each topic:
   coordinating conjunctions
   independent clauses
   dependent clauses

2. Have students read lines 71–73. Ask them how the meaning of each sentence would change if *but* was substituted with

another coordinating conjunction (*and, or, not, yet, so, for*).

3. Then have students identify the dependent and independent clauses in the sentences. *(dependent—"when summer came"; independent—"The old man claimed the hummingbird lived through that winter," "I never knew for sure," "I saw hummingbirds again," "I couldn't tell one from the other")*

More Great Reads

UNIT 3

Ideas for Independent Reading

Which questions from Unit 3 made an impression on you? Continue exploring them with these books.

What happens when friends compete?

Wolf Shadows
by Mary Casanova

As hunting season approaches, 12-year-old Seth finds himself disagreeing with his best friend, Matt, over the protection of wolves. On opening day, Matt wounds a wolf. Can Seth resolve his conflicting emotions before it's too late?

Friends and Enemies
by LouAnn Gaeddert

William and Jim are best friends. But when World War II breaks out, Jim refuses to support the war. Angered by his friend's stance, William joins classmates in attacking Jim. Will Jim ever forgive him?

End of the Race
by Dean Hughes

Two 12-year-olds find their friendship is tested when they represent their school in a track race. Jared feels he has to be the great athlete his dad was, while Davin, who is African American, considers their rivalry a racial conflict.

What is the cure for unhappiness?

Roll of Thunder, Hear My Cry
by Mildred D. Taylor

Cassie Logan, growing up in a loving family, has never had reason to suspect that anyone would wish her harm. All that changes when her community comes under constant threat from "night riders."

Because of Winn-Dixie
by Kate DiCamillo

If you were suddenly uprooted to a distant place, would you be able to adjust? India Opal Buloni's (pronounced "baloney") first summer in the little town of Naomi is action packed— all thanks to a big, ugly dog named Winn-Dixie.

Mick Harte Was Here
by Barbara Park

Can one ever feel happy after the death of a brother or sister? Thirteen-year-old Phoebe describes the stages of grief her family suffers after her brother Mick dies in an accident. Finally, she comes to terms with his death.

Can you be alone and not lonely?

The Wanderer
by Sharon Creech

Thirteen-year-old Sophie takes a risk when she travels to England aboard a 45-foot sailboat. In journal entries, she describes destructive storms, close quarters, and the secrets she discovers about her past.

Island of the Blue Dolphins
by Scott O'Dell

Karana, a 12-year-old Native American girl, finds herself alone on a rocky island. For 18 years, she forages on land and in the ocean, clothes herself, secures shelter, and finds strength and serenity.

Lone Wolf
by Kristine L. Franklin

After Perry's parents divorce, his dad moves him to an isolated wooded area. He adapts to his dad's harsh new rules by tramping through the woods. Then a family who moves in nearby changes everything.

UNIT 4

Finding a Voice

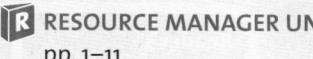

MOOD, TONE, AND STYLE

- In Fiction
- In Nonfiction
- In Poetry
- In Media

435

About the Art The painting above is a detail from *Mural Painting for the Terrace Plaza Hotel, Cincinnati,* by Joan Miró. For more information, see page 517 of the teacher's edition.

For help in planning this unit, see

R RESOURCE MANAGER UNIT 4
pp. 1–11

INTRODUCE THE UNIT

Each of us has many different voices, and we've learned to use these voices to suit different occasions and purposes. At a baseball game, our voices may be high and loud; when holding a baby, our voices are probably low and soft; when leading others, our voices might be strong and commanding. Ask students to share ideas about the tone of voice and style of speaking that people use in different situations. Invite students to think about these ideas as they discuss the pictures on this page. To spark a discussion, ask

- How do the facial expressions in each picture differ? What do you think each character is thinking or feeling?
- How would you describe the voice that is being expressed in each picture?
- If you were going to write a caption for each picture, what would you say?

Discuss the value and importance of finding a voice and using it. Explain that just as we use a certain tone of voice in particular speaking situations, an author can create a voice to express his or her message or ideas in writing. In this unit, students will explore how authors use **mood, tone,** and **style** to communicate their ideas to readers.

UNIT 4
Standards Skills Trace

SKILLS STRAND	Reader's Workshop: Mood, Tone, and Style pp. 438–443 3.A.7.a, 3.A.7.b, 3.A.7.d	Dark They Were, and Golden-Eyed pp. 444–465 Science Fiction Level: Average 1.D.3.b, 1.E.3.a, 3.A.7.a, 5.B.2.a	A Day's Wait pp. 466–475 (Linked selections) Short Story Level: Average 1.D.3.c, 1.E.3.a, 3.A.7.a, 5.B.2.a	How Hemingway Wrote pp. 476–479 (Linked selections) Informative Article Level: Average 2.A.4.h, 4.A.1.b.1	The People Could Fly pp. 480–487 Folk Tale Level: Challenging 1.D.3.c, 1.E.4.e, 3.A.7.e	Great Reads: from Out of the Dust pp. 488–493 Novel in Verse Level: Average
Literary Analysis	Mood and Tone pp. 438–439, 442–443 Style pp. 440–443	Mood pp. 445, 446, 448, 449, 452, 454, 455, 459, 463 Characteristics of Science Fiction p. 445	Style pp. 467, 470, 473		Style in Folk Tales pp. 481, 482, 485, 486	Form (Novel in Verse) p. 488
Reading and Informational Texts	Analyze the Literature pp. 439, 441–443	Strategies for Reading Science Fiction pp. 445, 448, 450, 451, 452, 453, 458, 460, 463 Review: Make Inferences pp. 453, 456, 457, 460, 463 Read a Magazine Article p. 462	Understand Dialogue pp. 467, 468, 470, 473	Distinguish Fact from Opinion pp. 476, 477, 478, 479 Characteristics of an Informative Article p. T477	Summarize pp. 481, 484, 485, 486	
Vocabulary	Academic Vocabulary pp. 438, 440	Word Acquisition pp. 445, T445, 464 Context Clues p. T445 Latin Roots (*pend*) p. 464	Word Acquisition pp. 467, T467, 474 Context Clues p. T467 Specialized Vocabulary (Animal Groups) p. 474		Word Acquisition pp. 481, T481, 487 Context Clues p. T481 Synonyms p. 487	
Writing, Grammar, and Style		Subject-Verb Agreement (Number) p. 465	Subject-Verb Agreement (Using Compound Subjects) p. 475	Write Instructions p. 479		
Speaking, Listening, Viewing, and Media	Discuss pp. 438–441	Discuss pp. 444, T446–T462, 463 Analyze Visuals pp. 446, 451, 454, 458, 461	Discuss pp. 466, T468–T472, 473 Analyze Visuals pp. 468, 471	Discuss pp. 476, T477–T478, 479	Discuss pp. 480, T482–T485, 486 Analyze Visuals p. 482	Discuss pp. 488, T493

Assessment-Based Planning: Skills in red are assessed on the Unit 4 Test. **T** = Teacher's Edition page

MARYLAND STANDARDS

For a full listing of state standards see page S1.

1.D.3.a, 1.E.3.a, 3.A.7.b	3.A.4.b, 3.A.7.e	1.E.3.a, 3.A.7.e	3.A.7.e	4.A.1, 4.A.2.c, 7.A.1
The Only Girl in the World for Me / Breaking the Ice pp. 494–507 Essays *Level: Average*	**One Perfect Rose / Song for an April Dusk** pp. 508–513 Poems *Level: Average*	**maggie and milly and molly and may / who are you,little i / old age sticks** pp. 514–519 Poems *Level: Challenging*	**Media Study: Style and Mood in Photographs** pp. 520–523 Image Collections	**Writing Workshop: Interpretive Essay** pp. 524–531
Tone pp. 495, 496, 498, 499, 500, 501, 503, 504, 505	Irony pp. 509, 510, 512, 513	Style in Poetry pp. 515, 516, 517, 518, 519		
Set a Purpose for Reading p. 495 Compare Tone pp. 505, 507	Analyze Form in Poetry pp. 509, 510, 512, 513	Monitor pp. 515, 516, 517, 518, 519		Analyze an Interpretive Essay pp. 525–526, 530
Word Acquisition pp. 495, T495, 506 Context Clues p. T495 Literal and Figurative Meanings p. 506			Academic Vocabulary (Photography) p. 521	
Write for Assessment p. 507				Write an Interpretive Essay pp. 524–531 Punctuation Marks p. 530
Discuss pp. 494, T496–T500, 501, T502–T504, 505 Analyze Visuals pp. T497, 502	Discuss pp. 508, T510–T512, 513	Discuss pp. 514, T516–T518, 519 Analyze Visuals pp. T517, T518	Discuss pp. 520, 523 Analyze Style and Mood in Photography pp. 521–522 Create Style in a Photograph p. 523	Discuss pp. 524–526, 530 Produce and Edit a Video p. 531

Skills Assessed on the Unit 4 Test:

Literary Analysis
- Identify and analyze mood
- Identify and analyze elements of style (word choice, sentence structure)
- Identify and analyze tone
- Compare and contrast tone

Reading and Informational Texts
- Monitor understanding (clarify)
- Summarize a story
- Distinguish fact from opinion
- Understand dialogue

Vocabulary
- Identify and use synonyms
- Identify and use literal and figurative meanings of words

Writing, Grammar, and Style
- Write an interpretive essay
- Maintain subject-verb agreement in number
- Maintain subject-verb agreement when using compound subjects
- Additional writing and grammar skills

⊘ For additional lesson planning help, see **Easy Planner DVD.**

OBJECTIVES

- identify and analyze elements of **style**
- compare and contrast

What's your STYLE?

Ask students to describe people whose style they admire. Have students describe specific details that appeal to them. What do they like about the person's hairstyle, clothes, or way of walking and talking? What do these things say about the person? Discuss how details combine to create an overall impression about a person.

ACTIVITY Tell students to list details about each person. Guide them in analyzing and comparing the elements of personal style, such as clothing, hairstyle, voice, attitude, and lifestyle. Help students understand that in writing, style consists of choosing elements such as tone, language, and point of view. A writer puts these elements together to create a unique style of writing.

CHECK UNDERSTANDING Have students summarize what they have learned about **style.**

What's your STYLE?

When we get ready for an important event, we usually start by figuring out what we are going to wear. Why do you think that is? What can our clothing and hairstyle say about us? By making choices about these things, each of us can create a personal style. In things such as writing, filmmaking, and art, **style** refers to the way a person expresses a message. Some people are even known for their unique style.

ACTIVITY Think of three people with distinct personal styles. They can be people you know and admire or people you have seen in movies or on television. Evaluate their styles by thinking about these questions:

- What made you notice each person?
- How do their styles differ?
- Which style is most similar to your own?

After answering these questions, write a description of your own style.

436

Unit Resources

 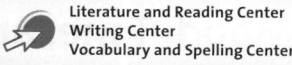
Preview Unit Goals

This page provides an overview of the skills and strategies covered in this unit. Point out that each skill strand is a different color, and that throughout the unit, each skill within a strand matches that color. Encourage students to consider their ability to use each skill and strategy as they read this page.

Suggest that students copy the Academic Vocabulary terms in their journals and define them in their own words as they read the unit. Encourage students to use these terms as they discuss and write about the selections.

ADDITIONAL UNIT GOALS

These skills will be taught in this unit but are not the major focus of the unit.

Literary Analysis
- Identify characteristics of science fiction
- Identify characteristics of a folk tale
- Evaluate science fiction
- Evaluate style in a folk tale
- Study a variety of genres: science fiction, short story, folk tale, poetry, magazine article, essay

Reading
- Develop strategies for reading science fiction
- Develop strategies for reading poetry
- Evaluate style in a folk tale

Writing and Grammar
- Write a compare-and-contrast response paper
- Write an interpretive essay
- Support thesis and major ideas with evidence
- Punctuate quotes, clauses, and compound sentences correctly

Speaking, Listening, and Viewing
- Analyze style in photography
- Analyze visual elements (framing, composition, lighting)
- Analyze color, shape, line, and texture
- Use aesthetic techniques to create style in a photograph
- Produce and edit a video

Vocabulary
- Understand and use the Latin root *pend*
- Understand and use specialized vocabulary (animal groups)

MARYLAND OBJECTIVES

Preview Unit Goals

LITERARY ANALYSIS
- Identify and analyze mood, tone, and irony
- Compare and contrast tone
- Identify and analyze elements of style, including word choice, sentence structure, imagery, and dialogue
- Understand form in poetry

READING
- Use reading strategies, including monitoring and setting a purpose for reading
- Summarize a story
- Distinguish fact from opinion

WRITING AND GRAMMAR
- Write a set of instructions
- Write an interpretive essay
- Maintain subject-verb agreement in number
- Maintain subject-verb agreement when using compound subjects

SPEAKING, LISTENING, AND VIEWING
- Analyze visual elements in media
- Produce and edit a video

VOCABULARY
- Identify and use synonyms
- Identify and use literal and figurative meanings of words

ACADEMIC VOCABULARY
- mood
- tone
- style
- monitor
- summarize
- interpretive essay
- subject-verb agreement
- fact
- opinion

437

DIFFERENTIATED INSTRUCTION

FOR ENGLISH LEARNERS

Academic Vocabulary Students will study and practice using these terms throughout the unit. Use the Academic Vocabulary copy master to introduce the terms.

1. Read each word aloud and discuss its meaning. Ask students if they have heard any of these words and in what context.

2. Allow students to work in pairs to complete the sentences and the activities. Then discuss students' answers as a class.

Additional Academic Vocabulary Use the second copy master to teach *synonyms, literal meaning, figurative meaning, dialogue, compound subject, irony,* and *word choice.* Divide the class into five groups. Have each group discuss one term, think of examples, and explain it to the class. Then have students complete Part B individually.

R RESOURCE MANAGER—Copy Masters
Academic Vocabulary p. 9
Additional Academic Vocabulary p. 10

Focus and Motivate

OBJECTIVES
- identify and analyze mood and tone
- identify and analyze elements of style (word choice, sentence structure, imagery, dialogue, non-standard speech)

Teach

Part 1: Mood and Tone

Mood Tell students that a good way to identify mood in a story is to notice how they feel as they read. Explain that a story's mood is often shaped by its setting, but that other factors also contribute. Readers should pay attention to word choice, foreshadowing, and the way characters behave toward each other. Use this activity with a story that everyone knows to help students understand how a mood conveys a feeling to readers:

1. Ask students how they felt as they read the story. What adjectives would they use to describe its mood? Write the adjectives in the center of a Cluster Diagram.

2. In the outside circles, note details that created the mood. Ask students to recall times when descriptions, dialogue, and other elements affected how they felt.

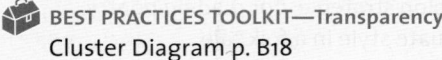 **BEST PRACTICES TOOLKIT—Transparency** Cluster Diagram p. B18

Tone Explain that different tones are appropriate for different kinds of writing. The topic of a piece of writing or its intended audience often demands a certain tone. Read aloud these examples and ask students to select adjectives from the **Words to Describe Tone** list that suit each example:

- poem about a kitten who befriends a baby bird (*humorous*)
- essay about children suffering from disease in a poor country (*sympathetic, serious*)
- letter to the editor protesting a cut in school funding (*serious, angry*)

 **BEST PRACTICES TOOLKIT—Transparency** Analysis Frame: Author's Craft pp. D23, D26

Mood, Tone, and Style

Think of a story as a homemade meal. You've learned about the basic ingredients: plot, characters, setting, and theme. What gives a writer's work a unique flavor? What makes you tear hungrily through one story, while another is hard to digest? The answer is the blend of spices known as mood, tone, and style.

MARYLAND OBJECTIVES

LITERATURE STANDARDS
3.A.7.a Analyze how specific language choices create style
3.A.7.b Analyze language choices that create tone
3.A.7.d Analyze imagery

Part 1: Mood and Tone

Mood is a feeling that a writer creates for readers. **Tone** is a writer's attitude toward his or her subject. What's the difference? Imagine this scenario: You and a friend venture into a haunted house, advertised as "spine-tinglingly scary." As you enter the shadowy house, your stomach tightens. You hear eerie howling. Suddenly, your friend sneers, "Spine-tingling. *Right*. This is as spine-tingling as a laundromat."

The mood of the haunted house was terrifying (at least for you!), but your friend's tone was sarcastic. As a reader, think of mood as the feeling the writer creates—the overall atmosphere. Tone, however, is how you imagine the writer "sounds." Often, you can identify a mood or tone by looking at the writer's choice of words and details.

MOOD	TONE
Words to Describe Mood	**Words to Describe Tone**
• cheerful • wondrous • peaceful • romantic • eerie • silly • somber • terrifying • thoughtful	• humorous • serious • disgusted • sarcastic • sincere • admiring • sympathetic • mocking • angry
▼	▼
Example The highlighted words and phrases reveal the gloomy setting and create an eerie mood.	**Example** The highlighted words and details help you almost "hear" the author's mocking tone.
A wind had sprung up, driving the dust of the weeks-dry road before it, when they entered the street on which they lived, and the leaves rustled ominously. Lightning flickered. —from "Rain, Rain, Go Away" by Isaac Asimov	I went to a British school and every morning we sang "God Save the King." Of course the British children loved singing about their gracious king. Ian Forbes stuck out his chest and sang as if he were saving the king all by himself. —from *Homesick* by Jean Fritz

DIFFERENTIATED INSTRUCTION

FOR ALL STUDENTS
For general guidelines on differentiating instruction, see

 BEST PRACTICES TOOLKIT Differentiated Instruction pp. 31–38

FOR LESS–PROFICIENT READERS
Note Taking For students who need help with note taking, hand out the Note Taking: Mood and Tone copy master and have students read page 438 silently. Then have students record their notes on the copy

master as you discuss the information.

 RESOURCE MANAGER—Copy Master Note Taking p. 15

Illustrate Mood Have students create a picture that conveys the mood of the first excerpt on page 439 or the story that was explored in the Cluster Diagram. They should use evidence from the text. Suggest that they use color and line to help show the mood.

MODEL 1: MOOD

Here, you see a New England autumn through the eyes of a girl from Barbados. Notice the words and details that are used to describe the setting. What mood do they help to create?

from
The Witch of Blackbird Pond
Novel by **Elizabeth George Speare**

... The October sun filled the world with mellow warmth. Before Kit's eyes a miracle took place, for which she was totally unprepared. She stood in the doorway of her uncle's house and held her breath with wonder. The maple tree in front of the doorstep burned like a gigantic
5 red torch. The oaks along the roadway glowed yellow and bronze. The fields stretched like a carpet of jewels, emerald and topaz and garnet. Everywhere she walked the color shouted and sang around her. The dried brown leaves crackled beneath her feet and gave off a delicious smoky fragrance. No one had ever told her about autumn in New
10 England. The excitement of it beat in her blood.

Close Read

1. Find two details that the writer uses to describe the setting. Then identify two details that tell you how Kit feels about her surroundings. One of each is boxed.

2. Judging by the details you found, how would you describe the mood?

MODEL 2: TONE

When Roald Dahl was a boy, he spent a lot of time at the local candy shop. In this excerpt from his autobiography, Dahl tells you more than you would ever want to know about the shop's owner, Mrs. Pratchett.

from
BOY: Tales of Childhood
Autobiography by **Roald Dahl**

But by far the most loathsome thing about Mrs. Pratchett was the filth that clung around her. Her apron was grey and greasy. Her blouse had bits of breakfast all over it, toast crumbs and tea stains and splotches of dried egg yolk. It was her hands, however, that disturbed us most.
5 They were disgusting. They were black with dirt and grime. They looked as though they had been putting lumps of coal on the fire all day long. And do not forget, please, that it was these very hands and fingers that she plunged into the sweet jars. ...

Close Read

1. This excerpt is full of words that have negative **connotations,** or feelings, attached to them. One example has been boxed. Find three more words.

2. Review the words you identified. How would you describe Dahl's tone, or his attitude toward Mrs. Pratchett?

MODEL 1: MOOD
Close Read
1. Possible answers:

Details that describe the setting

- *"The maple tree ... burned like a gigantic red torch." (lines 4–5)*
- *"The oaks along the roadway glowed yellow and bronze." (line 5)*
- *"The fields stretched like a carpet of jewels" (lines 5–6)*
- *"The dried brown leaves crackled beneath her feet and gave off a delicious smoky fragrance." (lines 7–9)*

Details that tell readers how Kit feels about her surroundings

- *"Before Kit's eyes a miracle took place" (lines 1–2)*
- *"the color shouted and sang around her" (line 7)*
- *"The excitement of it beat in her blood." (line 10)*

2. *Answers will vary; students may describe the mood with words like* joyful, wondrous, *and* excited.

MODEL 2: TONE
Close Read

1. Possible answer: *Words that have negative connotations include "filth," "greasy," "stains," "disturbed," "disgusting," and "grime."*

2. *Answers will vary; students may describe the tone with words like* disgusted, horrified, *and* disapproving.

FOR ENGLISH LEARNERS
Concept Support: Mood and Tone

1. Read aloud part of each model, using your tone of voice and facial expressions to emphasize expressive language.

2. After each reading, ask students what feelings you expressed. Discuss how these feelings relate to mood and tone.

3. Have volunteers read aloud from each model in an expressive manner while students listen carefully to detect the emotions being conveyed.

FOR ADVANCED LEARNERS/PRE–AP
Identify and Discuss Mood Have students read the workshop independently. Then assign pairs previously read selections and have them complete the graphic organizer for each one.

Mood	Details That Show Mood	How I Felt

Teach

Part 2: What Is Style?

Word Choice Point out that the highlighted words in the **Word Choice** example create a visual image. Use this activity to help students create visual images:

1. Name a visual feature of the classroom. Use Whip Around to collect words that describe it. List the words on the board.

2. Ask volunteers to help you choose words from the list to create sentences that describe the classroom feature. Discuss how the words you collected can be used to create images. For example:

   Books on the shelf
   - Colorful books rest on the sagging shelf.
   - The sunlit shelf groans under the heavy books.

 BEST PRACTICES TOOLKIT
Whip Around p. B1

Sentence Structure Use this exercise to help students understand how sentence structures must reflect the subject:

1. Ask a volunteer to read aloud the example under **Sentence Structure.** Discuss how the short phrases joined by commas mirror the fluid action of a basketball game.

2. Then read aloud this example:

   Sara relaxed in a chair with her book, which was about yoga, which she was eager to explore. She read for a while, dozed off, woke up, yawned, stretched, and decided to make herself a cup of tea—*yummy!*

3. Discuss why this sentence structure is not as effective for this subject. *(**Possible answer:** To make this subject interesting, readers would want more descriptive details. The quick list of verbs does not reflect the slow pace of the scene.)*

Imagery Remind students that imagery is not always visual—imagery can be used to appeal to any of the reader's senses. Ask students to name the senses. For each one, brainstorm topics that could be explored using imagery that appeals to that sense. For example:

   Taste
   - hot sauce
   - cookies fresh from the oven
   - ocean water

Part 2: What Is Style?

Mood and tone can affect the way you feel about a work of literature. Style, though, is often what brings you back again and again to the writing of a particular author. In literature, **style** is the way something is written—not what is said, but *how* it's said. A writer's style can be chatty, flowery, or overly formal. It all depends on certain elements, such as a writer's tone, sentence structures, and choice of words. Is the tone silly or serious? Does the writer use fancy words, like *expectorate,* or everyday words, like *spit?*

The celebrated author Gary Soto is known for his unique style of writing. Notice how three key elements help to create his one-of-a-kind style.

GARY SOTO'S STYLE

Soto sees himself as "someone who paints a vivid picture." He says, "Most of my writing is descriptive. You come away with clear pictures of the scene. . . ." Notice how Soto's style shines through in the examples from his novel *Taking Sides.*

Word Choice
Style begins with **word choice,** a writer's use of words. With just a few descriptive verbs and adjectives, Soto puts you at the scene of a basketball practice.

> **Example**
> Shafts of afternoon sunlight glared on the polished gym floor.

Sentence Structure
Sentence structure refers to whether sentences are short and simple or long and complex. Notice how these sentences reflect the fast pace of a basketball game.

> **Example**
> Lincoln passed to James, who passed to Durkins, who took a shot and missed from the top of the key. But Lincoln pulled the ball down, chambered, and shot—*swish.*

Imagery
At the heart of Soto's style is **imagery,** words and phrases that appeal to readers' senses. Here, Soto appeals to the sense of sight with a unique description of a city boy.

> **Example**
> Lincoln was a star basketball player, tall but not thin. When he made a fist, his forearm tightened with muscles. His stomach was muscle, his legs muscle. His face was brown, like coffee laced with cream, and his hair black as a chunk of asphalt.

440 UNIT 4: MOOD, TONE, AND STYLE

DIFFERENTIATED INSTRUCTION

FOR LESS–PROFICIENT READERS

Note Taking For students who need help with note taking, hand out the Note Taking: What Is Style? copy master. Read and discuss the first paragraph on page 440. Assist students, as needed, in completing the first item on the copy master. Then have students read the rest of the page and take notes on the three featured elements of Gary Soto's style.

RESOURCE MANAGER—Copy Master
Note Taking p. 16

FOR ADVANCED LEARNERS/PRE–AP

Use Imagery to Create a Portrait Have students create a portrait of a friend or family member, using words and phrases that appeal to the senses.

MODEL 1: STYLE IN SCIENCE FICTION

Many writers, including H. G. Wells, have crafted science fiction stories about time travel. Wells, who wrote *The Time Machine* in 1895, is known for his formal style and use of vivid imagery.

from
The Time Machine

Novel by **H. G. Wells**

. . . I made good my retreat to the narrow tunnel. But I had scarce entered this when my light was blown out, and in the blackness I could hear the Morlocks rustling like wind among leaves, and pattering like the rain, as they hurried after me.

5 In a moment I was clutched by several hands, and there was no mistaking that they were trying to haul me back. I struck another light, and waved it in their dazzled faces. You can scarce imagine how nauseatingly inhuman they looked—those pale, chinless faces and great, lidless, pinkish-grey eyes!—as they stared in their blindness
10 and bewilderment.

Close Read

1. Certain words and phrases, such as those in the boxed example, contribute to Wells's formal style. Find two more examples.

2. Identify three images that help you see and hear the Morlocks.

MODEL 2: STYLE IN SCIENCE FICTION

Here is an excerpt from another science fiction story, this one by a contemporary author with a much more informal style.

from
Future Tense

Short story by **Robert Lipsyte**

A half hour later, Mr. Smith called Gary out of Spanish. There was no expression on his regular features. He said, "I'm going to need some help with you."

Cold sweat covered Gary's body as Mr. Smith grabbed his arm and led
5 him to the new vice-principal. She read the composition while they waited. Gary got a good look at her for the first time. Ms. Jones was . . . just there. She looked as though she'd been manufactured to fit her name. Average. Standard. Typical. The cold sweat turned into goose pimples.

How could he have missed the clues? Smith and Jones were aliens!

Close Read

1. Look at the boxed phrases. How does Lipsyte's choice of words compare with Wells's?

2. What is the most striking difference between these two authors' styles? Consider word choice, sentence structure, and imagery.

MODEL 1: STYLE IN SCIENCE FICTION

Close Read

1. *Possible answers:*
   - "I had scarce entered" (lines 1–2)
   - "there was no mistaking" (lines 5–6)
   - "You can scarce imagine" (line 7)

2. *Possible answers:*
   - "rustling like wind among leaves, and pattering like the rain" (lines 3–4)
   - "pale, chinless faces and great, lidless, pinkish-grey eyes!" (lines 8–9)
   - "stared in their blindness and bewilderment" (lines 9–10)

MODEL 2: STYLE IN SCIENCE FICTION

Close Read

1. *Possible answer:* The words Lipsyte uses are more casual than those Wells uses. Lipsyte's words are ones that people might use in everyday conversation.

2. Answers will vary, but students may say that the most striking difference lies in the two authors' choice of words (Wells's formality versus Lipsyte's ordinary speech). Students may also point out that Wells uses long, complex sentences and detailed imagery, while Lipsyte uses short sentences and not much imagery.

DIFFERENTIATED INSTRUCTION

FOR LESS-PROFICIENT READERS

Analysis Support: Style Have students analyze the second paragraph of the "Future Tense" excerpt using the elements explained on page 440. Have them note at least one example of each. *Possible answers:*

- **Word Choice:** *"just there"; "typical"*
- **Sentence Structure:** *In line 7, a long sentence is followed by a one-word sentence.*
- **Imagery:** *"cold sweat"; "grabbed his arm"*

FOR ENGLISH LEARNERS

Concept Support: Vocabulary Have students use context clues to determine the meanings of these verbs in the *Time Machine* excerpt: *rustling* (line 3), *pattering* (line 3), *hurried* (line 4), *clutched* (line 5), *haul* (line 6). Ask volunteers to mime these meanings, and then discuss how Wells's choice of verbs reveals his style and helps create an image of the Morlocks.

Part 3: Analyze the Literature

Close Read

1. Possible answers:

- "bright morning" (line 2)
- "all was well with the world" (lines 2–3)
- "this best of all days" (line 3)
- "the sun warm and good" (lines 3–4)
- "the very precise tie that belonged with the day and the sun and his comfortable feet" (lines 5–6)
- "world just a wonderful place" (line 7)

2. Possible answer: *The first sentence is very long—seven lines—and complex. Its rambling rhythm matches Mr. Johnson's carefree mood and rambling train of thought.*

3. Possible answer: *The writer's tone, or attitude toward her subject (Mr. Johnson), is mocking rather than admiring. All of the boxed text points to flaws in Mr. Johnson and his surroundings.*

Part 3: Analyze the Literature

A man goes out for a walk. What situation could be simpler? Both of the following excerpts begin with this setup. However, you will see how a story's mood, tone, and style can make even the most similar situations seem very different.

from

One Ordinary Day, with Peanuts

Short story by **Shirley Jackson**

Mr. John Philip Johnson shut his front door behind him and went down his front steps into the bright morning with a feeling that all was well with the world on this best of all days, and wasn't the sun warm and good, and didn't his shoes feel comfortable after the resoling,
5 and he knew that he had undoubtedly chosen the very precise tie that belonged with the day and the sun and his comfortable feet, and, after all, wasn't the world just a wonderful place? In spite of the fact that he was a small man, and though the tie was perhaps a shade vivid, Mr. Johnson radiated a feeling of well-being as he went down the steps
10 and onto the dirty sidewalk, and he smiled at people who passed him, and some of them even smiled back. He stopped at the newsstand on the corner and bought his paper, saying, "*Good* morning" with real conviction to the man who sold him the paper and the two or three other people who were lucky enough to be buying papers when Mr.
15 Johnson skipped up. He remembered to fill his pockets with candy and peanuts, and then he set out to get himself uptown. He stopped in a flower shop and bought a carnation for his buttonhole, and stopped almost immediately afterward to give the carnation to a small child in a carriage, who looked at him dumbly, and then smiled, and Mr. Johnson
20 smiled, and the child's mother looked at Mr. Johnson for a minute and then smiled, too.

Close Read

1. What words and details in lines 1–7 help to create a cheerful mood?

2. Read the first sentence aloud. How would you describe its length and rhythm? Notice how the sentence structure reflects Mr. Johnson's carefree attitude.

3. Look at the boxed details. Would you describe the author's tone, or attitude toward Mr. Johnson, as mocking or admiring? Explain.

DIFFERENTIATED INSTRUCTION

FOR LESS–PROFICIENT READERS

Analysis Support: Tone Have students review lines 1–10 and use a T Chart to contrast Mr. Johnson's view of the scene with the author's. Ask what this contrast suggests about the author's attitude toward her subject.

Mr. Johnson's View	Author's View
tie is perfect	tie is too bright
world is wonderful	sidewalk is dirty

 BEST PRACTICES TOOLKIT—Transparency
T Chart p. A25

FOR ADVANCED LEARNERS/PRE–AP

Use Tone to Describe a Scene As a class, brainstorm two or three events that start a typical student day, such as waking up, eating breakfast, and waiting for the bus. Challenge pairs of students to write a scene describing these events in a specific tone, which you secretly assign to them. Examples of tone words include *humorous, annoyed, eerie, anxious,* and so on. Then have pairs share their scenes while the rest of the group tries to guess the tone word they were assigned.

In this excerpt, Rip Van Winkle leaves his nagging wife and goes for a hike with his dog, Wolf. It won't take you long to notice the different "feeling" of this story. Read closely to find out what the author has done to create such a contrasting effect.

from

RIP VAN WINKLE

Short story by **Washington Irving**

. . . He looked down into a deep mountain glen, wild, lonely, and shagged, the bottom filled with fragments from the impending cliffs, and scarcely lighted by the reflected rays of the setting sun. For some time Rip lay musing[1] on this scene; evening was gradually advancing;

5 the mountains began to throw their long blue shadows over the valleys; he saw that it would be dark long before he could reach the village, and he heaved a heavy sigh when he thought of encountering the terrors of Dame Van Winkle.

As he was about to descend, he heard a voice from a distance,

10 hallooing, "Rip Van Winkle! Rip Van Winkle!" He looked around, but could see nothing but a crow winging its solitary flight across the mountain. He thought his fancy[2] must have deceived him, and turned again to descend, when he heard the same cry ring through the still evening air; "Rip Van Winkle! Rip Van Winkle!"—at the

15 same time Wolf bristled up his back, and giving a low growl, skulked[3] to his master's side, looking fearfully down into the glen. Rip now felt a vague apprehension stealing over him; he looked anxiously in the same direction, and perceived a strange figure slowly toiling up the rocks, and bending under the weight of something he carried on his back.

---

1. **musing:** thinking or reflecting.
2. **fancy:** imagination.
3. **skulked:** moved fearfully.

Close Read

1. Examine the boxed words and details. What mood do they help to create?

2. Read lines 3–8 aloud and try to hear how the author "sounds" while describing Rip's thoughts. Is the author's tone serious or mocking? Explain.

3. Washington Irving is known for his use of formal words and phrases and long, complex sentences. Find two examples of each in this excerpt.

Close Read

1. *Answers will vary. Students may use words like* threatening, tense, *and* mysterious *to describe the mood.*

2. *Possible answer: The writer's attitude toward his subject (Rip) seems to be serious. The descriptions of the setting ("long blue shadows"), Rip's feelings ("he heaved a heavy sigh"), and Rip's home life ("the terrors of Dame Van Winkle") are all somber and thus help to convey this tone.*

3. *Possible answer: Formal words: "scarcely lighted" (line 3), "lay musing on this scene" (line 4), "evening was gradually advancing" (line 4), "slowly toiling up the rocks" (line 18). Sentence structures: The last sentence of each paragraph is long and complex, as is the sentence that begins "He thought his fancy" (line 12).*

Assess and Reteach

Assess

Have students briefly summarize the mood, tone, and style of the excerpts on pages 442 and 443.

Reteach

For students who are unable to apply the workshop skills to the excerpts, select from these reteaching options:

1. Review with students the note-taking copy masters for this lesson. Have pairs

   - compare the information they recorded
   - explain each term to one another, using their own words
   - question each other to clarify understanding
   - share their insights and challenges with the class

2. Refer students to a story the class has read recently. Have students describe the mood and how the author seemed to feel about the subject. Ask them what evidence helped them form these impressions. Then have students look back through the story and describe the author's style, using the elements described on page 440.

DIFFERENTIATED INSTRUCTION

FOR LESS–PROFICIENT READERS

Analysis Support: Mood Have students complete a Cluster Diagram like the one described on page 438 of the teacher's edition to identify the mood of the "Rip Van Winkle" excerpt.

 BEST PRACTICES TOOLKIT—Transparency Cluster Diagram p. B18

FOR ENGLISH LEARNERS

Analysis Support: Mood

1. Clarify the setting described in the first paragraph: a deep valley between crumbling cliffs, overgrown plants, the late afternoon sun casting dark shadows. Invite students to draw what they visualize.

2. Ask students to visualize a single crow flying overhead in this setting (line 11). What feeling does the crow create? Have them use their own words to describe the mood of the excerpt as a whole.

Focus and Motivate

OBJECTIVES

Literary Analysis
- explore the key idea of **change**
- analyze mood
- read a short story and an interview

Reading
- read science fiction

Vocabulary
- build vocabulary for reading and writing
- recognize the Latin root *pend* (also an EL language objective)

Grammar and Writing
- maintain subject-verb agreement
- use writing to analyze literature

SUMMARY

The Bitterings, an American family, move to Mars and become stranded there after a nuclear war stops all rockets from Earth. Despite Mr. Bittering's desperate struggle to retain his identity, he and his family gradually adopt Martian ways and the Martian language. When an Earth rocket finally arrives more than five years later, they are no longer recognizable as human.

Can where you are
C H A N G E *who you are?*

Discuss the question. Ask students if they know or have read about anyone whose move to a new place **changed** the way he or she lived or viewed the world. How did the new place shape the person's life? After students complete the *DISCUSS* activity, ask small groups to compare their charts.

Selection Resources

Dark They Were, and Golden-Eyed
Science Fiction by Ray Bradbury

Can where you are
CHANGE *who you are?*

MARYLAND OBJECTIVES

READING/LIT STANDARDS
1.E.3.a Select and apply appropriate strategies during reading
3.A.7.a Analyze how specific language choices contribute to meaning

KEY IDEA Your hobbies, interests, and habits often depend on the climate you are used to and the people and places you encounter every day. If you were to move away from everything you know, how much of who you are would **change**, and how much would stay the same? In "Dark They Were, and Golden-Eyed," a family moves to a very different environment and gets the chance to find out.

DISCUSS With a group, discuss your thoughts about the question at the top of the page. Take turns answering the question and explaining your reasons. Record the group's responses on a chart like the one shown.

Can Where You Are Change Who You Are		
Name	Yes or No	Why or Why Not?

444

RESOURCE MANAGER UNIT 4

Plan and Teach pp. 17–24

Literary Analysis
Summary pp. 25†*, 26‡*
Mood pp. 27, 28†*
Question Support p. 35*

Reading
Read Science Fiction pp. 29, 30†*
Reading Check p. 34
Reading Fluency p. 37

Vocabulary
Study p. 31*
Practice p. 32
Strategy p. 33

Grammar and Writing
Maintain Subject-Verb Agreement p. 36

Assessment
Selection Tests A, B/C pp. 39*, 41*
⊘ Test Generator CD

BEST PRACTICES TOOLKIT

Differentiated Instruction pp. 31–38*

Scaffolding Instruction pp. 43–46*

Graphic Organizers/Strategies
Word Questioning • Read Aloud/Think Aloud • Draw It • Cluster Diagram • Open Mind • Timeline • Venn Diagram • Brainstorming

Reading Support
⊘ Audio Anthology CD*

Technology
ⓘ Literature and Vocabulary Centers at **ClassZone.com**

⊘ Write*Smart* CD

---

* Resources for Differentiation   † Also in Spanish   ‡ In Haitian Creole and Vietnamese

LITERARY ANALYSIS: MOOD

Has a story ever made you feel hopeful, nervous, or completely terrified? The feeling you get from a story is called the **mood**. Writers create a mood by

- carefully choosing words to describe the **plot, setting,** and **characters**
- showing what characters think and how they talk

Identifying mood can help you understand a story. As you read "Dark They Were, and Golden-Eyed," notice how it makes you feel, and think about which words may have made you feel that way.

READING STRATEGY: READING SCIENCE FICTION

In **science fiction,** writers often explore what life might be like in the future. They do so by blending scientific facts and theories and familiar elements of real life with their own ideas to create imaginary worlds and unique situations.

Science fiction writers often use their stories to comment on present-day problems. As you read Ray Bradbury's story, use a chart to note the elements of science fiction.

Elements of Science Fiction	Examples in the Story
known scientific information	
familiar elements of life today	
imaginary worlds and situations	

Review: Make Inferences

VOCABULARY IN CONTEXT

Bradbury's **word choice** affects the **mood** of his story. Match each numbered word or phrase with a vocabulary word.

WORD LIST	convivial	forlorn	recede
	dwindle	muse	subtly
	flimsy	pendulum	

1. friendly
2. indirectly
3. hanging weight
4. decrease
5. become distant
6. daydream
7. lonely
8. breakable

Author Online

An Early Start
Ray Bradbury credits his mother for encouraging his imagination. She loved films and started taking her son to see them when he was only 3. By age 8, Bradbury had developed a love for both science fiction and the planet Mars. Bradbury wrote his first Martian stories when he was 12. Just before his 21st birthday, Bradbury sold his first story. That began a career filled with bestsellers, awards, and a lasting love of writing.

Ray Bradbury
born 1920

Man with a Mission Bradbury believes that one purpose of science fiction is to warn about negative things that might happen in the future if care is not taken in the present. Some of his writing reflects his worries about where our society is headed.

 MORE ABOUT THE AUTHOR
For more on Ray Bradbury, visit the
Literature Center at ClassZone.com.

Background

Red Planet Mars has been the setting of many science fiction films and stories, including "Dark They Were, and Golden-Eyed." Films and stories about Mars rarely give a realistic description of the planet, but they often incorporate elements of actual scientific research and developments in space travel.

DARK THEY WERE, AND GOLDEN-EYED **445**

Teach

STANDARDS FOCUS

LITERARY ANALYSIS

● **MOOD**

Read aloud this example:

> Hawaii has become my home, Jesenia thought as she floated easily over the coral reef, the soft pulse of the waves carrying her gently back and forth.

Ask students what kind of mood is created. *Possible answer: The example has a pleasant mood. Words like "easily," "soft," and "gently" create a relaxed feeling.*

CHECK UNDERSTANDING Ask students to think of details in a movie that created a scary, happy, or sad mood.

READING STRATEGY

■ **READING SCIENCE FICTION**

Read aloud this example:

> Because Eduardo knew that Venus was closer to the sun than Earth, he packed sunglasses for his vacation there.

Ask students which details are scientific, which are familiar, and which are imaginary. *Possible answer: Scientific: Venus closer to sun; Familiar: wearing sunglasses; Imaginary: vacation on Venus*

CHECK UNDERSTANDING Ask students what familiar details could be included in a story about a trip to another planet.

 RESOURCE MANAGER—Copy Master
Reading Science Fiction p. 29 (for student use while reading the selection)

VOCABULARY SKILL

▲ VOCABULARY IN CONTEXT

DIAGNOSE WORD KNOWLEDGE To determine preteaching needs, have all students complete **Vocabulary in Context.** Check students' answers. (**1.** *convivial*; **2.** *subtly*; **3.** *pendulum*; **4.** *dwindle*; **5.** *recede*; **6.** *muse*; **7.** *forlorn*; **8.** *flimsy*)

PRETEACH VOCABULARY Use the Vocabulary Study copy master to help students determine the meaning of each boldfaced word.

1. Read aloud the first sentence on the copy master. Emphasize the boldfaced word.

2. Ask students to think about the way the word is used. Discuss possible meanings for *convivial,* such as "cheerful" or "friendly."

3. Repeat for each of the other sentences.

 RESOURCE MANAGER—Copy Master
Vocabulary Study p. 31

For general guidelines on differentiating vocabulary instruction and for alternative vocabulary activities for students not needing vocabulary preteaching, see

🧰 **BEST PRACTICES TOOLKIT**
Scaffolding Vocabulary Instruction
pp. 43–46

ℹ️ Vocabulary Center at **ClassZone.com**
Additional Vocabulary Activities

Practice and Apply

ANALYZE VISUALS

Possible answers:

- *The person feels alone; no one sits with her, and the sky is big and empty. There is little sign of other life in the landscape.*

- *She seems overwhelmed by her surroundings, which take up almost all of the image and feature striking, intense colors.*

- *The person may feel thoughtful. The viewer cannot see her face, but she is sitting in what looks like a comfortable and quiet way. Maybe she is thinking about the strangeness of the landscape.*

About the Art *Sugar Sphinx* is by Spanish painter Salvador Dali (1904–1989). Dali was part of an artistic movement known as surrealism, which explores dreamlike imagery sometimes nightmarish or laden with symbols. In one of Dali's most famous paintings, *The Persistence of Memory* (1931), clocks melt in an eerie, barren seaside landscape. In addition to painting, Dali experimented with film, sculpture, writing, and set design.

LITERARY ANALYSIS

Ⓐ MOOD

Possible answer: The mood is tense. The man seems to have an uneasy feeling about Mars. He

- *feels "the tissues of his body draw tight" (line 5)*

- *imagines his family blowing away (lines 6–8)*

- *tells his wife he wants to go back (line 12)*

DARK THEY WERE, AND Golden-Eyed

RAY BRADBURY

The rocket metal cooled in the meadow winds. Its lid gave a bulging *pop.* From its clock interior stepped a man, a woman, and three children. The other passengers whispered away across the Martian meadow, leaving the man alone among his family.

The man felt his hair flutter and the tissues of his body draw tight as if he were standing at the center of a vacuum. His wife, before him, seemed almost to whirl away in smoke. The children, small seeds, might at any instant be sown to all the Martian climes.

The children looked up at him, as people look to the sun to tell
10 what time of their life it is. His face was cold.

"What's wrong?" asked his wife.

"Let's get back on the rocket." Ⓐ

"Go back to Earth?"

"Yes! Listen!"

ANALYZE VISUALS
What can you **infer** about how the person in the painting might be feeling?

① Targeted Passage

Ⓐ MOOD
How would you describe the man's first impression of Mars? Think about how his feelings affect the mood of the story.

Sugar Sphinx (1933), Salvador Dali. Oil on canvas
© Salvador Dali. Gala-Salvador Dali Foundation/ARS

446 UNIT 4: MOOD, TONE, AND STYLE

DIFFERENTIATED INSTRUCTION

FOR ALL STUDENTS

Learning Center Set up a center on space exploration with books and pictures on these high-interest topics: Mars; famous astronauts (Mae Jemison, Sally Ride, John Glenn); the International Space Station. Give a variety of independent projects, such as creating a timeline of key events in the space race, watching science fiction films, and drawing blueprints for a space station.

FOR LESS–PROFICIENT READERS

In combination with the *Audio Anthology CD,* use one or more Targeted Passages (pp. 446, 453, 457, 459, 460) to ensure that students focus on key story events, concepts, and skills.

① Targeted Passage [Lines 1–13]

This passage introduces the main characters and their science fiction setting—an Earth family on Mars—and establishes a mood of tension and uncertainty.

- Where has the family arrived?
- Where has the family come from?
- How did they make their trip?
- How does the father feel about Mars?

BACKGROUND

Mars Mars has long been a favorite setting for science fiction. Scientists know more about Mars than any other planet except for Earth because the thin atmosphere of Mars makes it relatively easy to observe. Besides being just one planet farther from the sun than Earth, the red planet (so called for the rust-colored iron particles in its atmosphere) has some things in common with our blue planet. Like Earth, Mars has a day of about twenty-four hours and experiences four seasons. Images of Mars taken during the 1970s indicate that rivers and streams once flowed on its surface, as they do on Earth. Some scientists—and many science fiction writers—have been interested in the idea that some form of life has existed on Mars.

FOR ENGLISH LEARNERS

Options for Reading Read aloud the first three paragraphs. Make sure students understand that "Martian" refers to the planet Mars. Students may continue reading along with the *Audio Anthology CD.*

Key Academic Vocabulary Have students use Word Questioning to learn these vocabulary words: *cease* (line 51), *remove* (line 116), *construct* (line 205), *abandon* (lines 409 and 474), *suspend* (line 441), *odd* (line 455).

 BEST PRACTICES TOOLKIT—Transparency Word Questioning p. E9

Prereading For prereading instruction for English learners, see

 BEST PRACTICES TOOLKIT Scaffolding Reading Instruction pp. 43–46

FOR ADVANCED LEARNERS/PRE–AP

Pre-AP exercises in the bottom channel provide additional challenge for your advanced students. Use them for small groups or individuals.

ADDITIONAL GUIDELINES

For more help with differentiation and tips for classroom management, see

 BEST PRACTICES TOOLKIT Differentiated Instruction pp. 31–38

Ⓑ MOOD

Possible answer: The description of the setting uses eerie, surreal words and phrases to create a negative feeling about Mars. Words and phrases that help to create this feeling include

- *"air might draw his soul" (line 16)*
- *"submerged" (line 17)*
- *"burn away" (line 18)*
- *"crushing pressure of years" (lines 19–20)*
- *"lost" (line 20)*
- *"lying like children's delicate bones" (lines 20–21)*
- *"no answer but the racing hiss of wind" (line 25)*

READING STRATEGY

Ⓒ READING SCIENCE FICTION

Have students record their responses in the chart introduced on page 445, under "familiar elements of life today." *Possible answer:*

- *The Bitterings are awakened every day by an alarm clock.*
- *Their home has a hearth and potted geraniums.*
- *The morning paper is delivered every day.*

Extend the Discussion What imaginary world or situation does the author describe on page 448?

ADDITIONAL TEACHING OPPORTUNITY

Compare Settings Explain that science fiction stories are usually set in the future and involve technology that doesn't exist today. Ask students to **compare the setting** of "Dark They Were, and Golden-Eyed" with the setting of "The Last Dog" in Unit 1. How are the two settings similar and different? *(Similar: Both are set in the future and have invented technologies. Both settings create an eerie mood. Different: "Dark They Were" is set on Mars in a windswept landscape of stiff grass. "The Last Dog" is set on Earth in a barren landscape.)*

The wind blew as if to flake away their identities. At any moment the Martian air might draw his soul from him, as marrow comes from a white bone. He felt submerged in a chemical that could dissolve his intellect and burn away his past.

20 They looked at Martian hills that time had worn with a crushing pressure of years. They saw the old cities, lost in their meadows, lying like children's delicate bones among the blowing lakes of grass.

"Chin up, Harry," said his wife. "It's too late. We've come over sixty million miles."

The children with their yellow hair hollered at the deep dome of Martian sky. There was no answer but the racing hiss of wind through the stiff grass. Ⓑ

He picked up the luggage in his cold hands. "Here we go," he said—a man standing on the edge of a sea, ready to wade in and be drowned.

They walked into town.

30 Their name was Bittering. Harry and his wife Cora; Dan, Laura, and David. They built a small white cottage and ate good breakfasts there, but the fear was never gone. It lay with Mr. Bittering and Mrs. Bittering, a third unbidden partner at every midnight talk, at every dawn awakening.

"I feel like a salt crystal," he said, "in a mountain stream, being washed away. We don't belong here. We're Earth people. This is Mars. It was meant for Martians. For heaven's sake, Cora, let's buy tickets for home!"

But she only shook her head. "One day the atom bomb will fix Earth. Then we'll be safe here."

"Safe and insane!"

40 *Tick-tock, seven o'clock* sang the voice-clock; *time to get up.* And they did. Something made him check everything each morning—warm hearth, potted blood-geraniums—precisely as if he expected something to be amiss. The morning paper was toast-warm from the 6 A.M. Earth rocket. He broke its seal and tilted it at his breakfast place. He forced himself to be **convivial.** Ⓒ

"Colonial days all over again," he declared. "Why, in ten years there'll be a million Earthmen on Mars. Big cities, everything! They said we'd fail. Said the Martians would resent our invasion. But did we find any Martians? Not a living soul! Oh, we found their empty cities, but no one 50 in them. Right?"

A river of wind submerged the house. When the windows ceased rattling Mr. Bittering swallowed and looked at the children.

"I don't know," said David. "Maybe there're Martians around we don't see. Sometimes nights I think I hear 'em. I hear the wind. The sand hits my window. I get scared. And I see those towns way up in the mountains where the Martians lived a long time ago. And I think I see things moving

Ⓑ MOOD
Reread lines 15–26. On the basis of Bradbury's description of the **setting,** decide whether you have a positive or negative feeling about Mars. What words contribute to your feeling?

convivial
(kən-vĭv′ē-əl) *adj.* enjoying the company of others; sociable

Ⓒ READING SCIENCE FICTION
Reread lines 40–45. What are three examples of how Bradbury brings present-day life into this futuristic **setting?**

DIFFERENTIATED INSTRUCTION

FOR ENGLISH LEARNERS
Language: Pronoun Referents Explain the referents for the pronouns, shown in italics, in line 44: "*He* (Mr. Bittering) broke *its* (the newspaper's) seal and tilted *it* (the newspaper) at *his* (Mr. Bittering's) breakfast place." Then have students work in mixed language-ability groups to identify referents for other pronouns in the breakfast scene.

Vocabulary: Idioms Explain that "Chin up" (line 22) is from the common idiom "Keep your chin up," meaning to stay positive in hard times.

FOR ADVANCED LEARNERS/PRE–AP
Analyze Similes Note how the similes in lines 15–18 and 34–35 use comparisons with natural processes to express Harry's feeling that he is losing his sense of self. Challenge students to come up with an original simile that uses organic imagery to convey Harry's feelings at this point in the story.

around those towns, Papa. And I wonder if those Martians *mind* us living here. I wonder if they won't do something to us for coming here."

"Nonsense!" Mr. Bittering looked out the windows. "We're clean, decent people." He looked at his children. "All dead cities have some kind of ghosts in them. Memories, I mean." He stared at the hills. "You see a staircase and you wonder what Martians looked like climbing it. You see Martian paintings and you wonder what the painter was like. You make a little ghost in your mind, a memory. It's quite natural. Imagination." He stopped. "You haven't been prowling up in those ruins, have you?"

"No, Papa." David looked at his shoes.

"See that you stay away from them. Pass the jam."

"Just the same," said little David, "I bet something happens."

Something happened that afternoon. Laura stumbled through the settlement, crying. She dashed blindly onto the porch.

"Mother, Father—the war, Earth!" she sobbed. "A radio flash just came. Atom bombs[1] hit New York! All the space rockets blown up. No more rockets to Mars, ever!"

"Oh, Harry!" The mother held onto her husband and daughter.

"Are you sure, Laura?" asked the father quietly.

Laura wept. "We're stranded on Mars, forever and ever!"

For a long time there was only the sound of the wind in the late afternoon.

Alone, thought Bittering. Only a thousand of us here. No way back. No way. No way. Sweat poured from his face and his hands and his body; he was drenched in the hotness of his fear. He wanted to strike Laura, cry, "No, you're lying! The rockets will come back!" Instead, he stroked Laura's head against him and said, "The rockets will get through someday."

"Father, what will we do?"

"Go about our business, of course. Raise crops and children. Wait. Keep things going until the war ends and the rockets come again."

The two boys stepped out onto the porch.

"Children," he said, sitting there, looking beyond them, "I've something to tell you."

"We know," they said.

In the following days, Bittering wandered often through the garden to stand alone in his fear. As long as the rockets had spun a silver web

1. **atom bombs:** In 1945 the United States dropped atomic bombs over the cities of Hiroshima and Nagasaki, in Japan, killing over 100,000 people and injuring many thousands more.

SCIENCE CONNECTION

Robotic equipment sent to Mars to gather data has shown that the planet has no signs of civilization, though there is some evidence of water on its surface.

SCIENCE CONNECTION

The Mars Exploration Rover Mission placed two robotic landers, Spirit and Opportunity, on the surface of Mars in January 2004. As of mid-December 2005, both had been exploring the planet for a full Martian year (687 Earth days). The two rovers explore opposite sides of the planet using cameras, rock-grinding tools, spectrometers, and magnets. The exploration strategy is to "follow the water," because water is almost always linked with life on Earth. Both rovers have found evidence that water once existed on Mars. In fact, Opportunity discovered signs that a shallow sea once covered part of the planet. Still, the first real life on Mars may be human, if people decide to travel there on future missions.

Lines 71–76
REINFORCE *KEY IDEA:* CHANGE

Discuss How does the loss of the Earth rockets affect the way the Bitterings think about being on Mars? Do you think this loss makes it more likely that Mars will **change** them? Why? *Possible answer: Now the Bitterings can't go back to Earth. They must think of Mars as their home and accept living there, at least for awhile. This acceptance could make it more likely that they will adapt to their new place—and that it will change them.*

LITERARY ANALYSIS

Ⓓ MOOD

Possible answer: *Sentence fragments ("Alone. . . . Only a thousand of us here") and repeated words ("No way back. No way. No way.") show Bittering's panic, creating a tense and fearful mood.*

If students need help . . . Write Bittering's thoughts on the board in a complete sentence without repeated words. For example:

> *We are alone, Bittering thought. There are only a thousand of us here, and we have no way back.*

Ask students how the mood of this sentence is different from the original. In which version do Bittering's thoughts seem more calm and clear?

Ⓓ **MOOD**
Reread lines 79–84. Note that Bradbury uses sentence fragments to portray Bittering's thoughts. How does this help create a mood?

FOR ADVANCED LEARNERS/PRE–AP

Evaluate Gesture Have small groups of students read aloud the dialogue in lines 59–66 and 89–90 and notice how the characters look away from each other as they speak. Ask students to consider what this suggests about what the characters really think or feel. Then have students say these lines to each other, first maintaining eye contact and then looking away. Invite them to perform both interpretations for the class and receive feedback about how the mood is different in each.

across space, he had been able to accept Mars. For he had always told himself: Tomorrow, if I want, I can buy a ticket and go back to Earth.

But now: The web gone, the rockets lying in jigsaw heaps of molten girder and unsnaked wire. Earth people left to the strangeness of Mars, the cinnamon dusts and wine airs, to be baked like gingerbread shapes in Martian summers, put into harvested storage by Martian winters.

100 What would happen to him, the others? This was the moment Mars had waited for. Now it would eat them.

He got down on his knees in the flower bed, a spade in his nervous hands. Work, he thought, work and forget.

He glanced up from the garden to the Martian mountains. He thought of the proud old Martian names that had once been on those peaks. Earthmen, dropping from the sky, had gazed upon hills, rivers, Martian seats left nameless in spite of names. Once Martians had built cities, named cities; climbed mountains, named mountains; sailed seas, named seas. Mountains melted, seas drained, cities tumbled. In spite of this, the Earthmen had felt

110 a silent guilt at putting new names to these ancient hills and valleys. **E**

Nevertheless, man lives by symbol and label. The names were given.

Mr. Bittering felt very alone in his garden under the Martian sun, anachronism[2] bent here, planting Earth flowers in a wild soil.

Think. Keep thinking. Different things. Keep your mind free of Earth, the atom war, the lost rockets.

He perspired. He glanced about. No one watching. He removed his tie. Pretty bold, he thought. First your coat off, now your tie. He hung it neatly on a peach tree he had imported as a sapling from Massachusetts.

He returned to his philosophy of names and mountains. The Earthmen

120 had changed names. Now there were Hormel Valleys, Roosevelt[3] Seas, Ford Hills, Vanderbilt Plateaus, Rockefeller[4] Rivers, on Mars. It wasn't right. The American settlers had shown wisdom, using old Indian prairie names: Wisconsin, Minnesota, Idaho, Ohio, Utah, Milwaukee, Waukegan, Osseo. The old names, the old meanings.

Staring at the mountains wildly, he thought: Are you up there? All the dead ones, you Martians? Well, here we are, alone, cut off! Come down, move us out! We're helpless!

The wind blew a shower of peach blossoms.

He put out his sun-browned hand and gave a small cry. He touched

130 the blossoms and picked them up. He turned them, he touched them again and again. Then he shouted for his wife.

"Cora!"

She appeared at a window. He ran to her.

---

2. **anachronism** (ə-năk′rə-nĭz′əm): something placed outside of its proper time period.

3. **Roosevelt:** most likely refers to Franklin Delano Roosevelt, the 32nd president of the United States.

4. **Hormel…Ford…Vanderbilt…Rockefeller:** names of industrial and financial "giants" in American history.

 READING SCIENCE FICTION
Reread lines 107–110. On the basis of these past accomplishments, consider the similarities between Martian and human civilizations. What comment about present-day human civilization might Bradbury be making through this comparison?

Lines 112–121
DISCUSSION PROMPTS

Use these prompts to help students understand how the Earth people have attempted to cope with having moved to a new planet:

Connect Imagine that you are moving to an entirely unfamiliar place. What would you need to bring with you in order to feel like yourself? *Students may say that their clothing, music, books, and photographs would help them feel like themselves in a new place.*

Analyze Why would Harry wear a coat and tie in the heat of Mars? *Possible answer: This is what he wears during the day back on Earth. Wearing familiar clothing helps him feel like his old self.*

Evaluate Do you think it is a good idea for the Earth people to bring their plants and new place names to Mars? Explain. *Possible answers:*

- *It is a good idea because it helps them adjust to their new surroundings.*
- *It is a bad idea because the new plants may become invasive; also, the Earth people should respect the history of the planet by preserving its traditional place names.*

DIFFERENTIATED INSTRUCTION

FOR LESS–PROFICIENT READERS
Comprehension Support Use Read Aloud/Think Aloud for lines 96–101 to help students understand Bradbury's figurative language. Explain that

- the web and the personification of a hungry Mars are images in Harry's anxious mind
- "cinnamon" and "wine" refer to the red color of Mars
- "baked" in summer and "put into harvested storage" in winter express the fact that the climate is extreme

BEST PRACTICES TOOLKIT—Transparency
Read Aloud/Think Aloud p. A34

FOR ENGLISH LEARNERS
Culture: Clarify As Bradbury notes, numerous town and city names come from American Indian words, as do about half of state names. For example, *Chicago* means "garlic place," and *Illinois* comes from the word *Illiniwek,* meaning "people."

Shellfish Flowers (1929), Max Ernst. Oil on canvas, 129 cm × 129 cm. Inv.: R 19 P. Photo Jean-Francois Tomasian. Musée National d'Art Moderne, Centre Georges Pompidou, Paris. Photo © CNAC/MNAM/Dist. Réunion des Musées Nationaux/Art Resource, New York.

ANALYZE VISUALS
Compare these flowers to the ones on Mars in the story. How are they similar?

"Cora, these blossoms!"

She handled them.

"Do you see? They're different. They've changed! They're not peach blossoms any more!"

"Look all right to me," she said.

"They're not. They're wrong! I can't tell how. An extra petal, a leaf,
40 something, the color, the smell!"

The children ran out in time to see their father hurrying about the garden, pulling up radishes, onions, and carrots from their beds.

"Cora, come look!"

They handled the onions, the radishes, the carrots among them.

"Do they look like carrots?"

"Yes . . . no." She hesitated. "I don't know."

"They're changed."

"Perhaps."

"You know they have! Onions but not onions, carrots but not carrots.
50 Taste: the same but different. Smell: not like it used to be." He felt his heart pounding, and he was afraid. He dug his fingers into the earth. "Cora, what's happening? What is it? We've got to get away from this." He ran across the garden. Each tree felt his touch. "The roses. The roses. They're turning green!" **F**

F **READING SCIENCE FICTION**
Think of what you know about plants. Do you think it's possible for plants to change like they do in this story, or is it purely imaginary?

DARK THEY WERE, AND GOLDEN-EYED **451**

ANALYZE VISUALS
Possible answer: *The flowers look otherworldly. Like Mr. Bittering's peach blossoms, they are identifiable as flowers, but their mottled colors and transparency make them unlike flowers you would see in real life. Likewise, Mr. Bittering's flowers are different from others he has known.*

About the Art German painter Max Ernst (1891–1976) is known for his contributions to surrealism. Artists in this movement create imaginative, unrealistic images that might seem as if they had emerged from a dream. Ernst was interested in textures in nature and sometimes used rubbings of organic materials, such as leaves, in his work.

READING STRATEGY

F **READING SCIENCE FICTION**
Possible answer: *Plants adapt slowly, over many generations, not as quickly as in this story. On the other hand, fertilizer or other additives can dramatically affect how a plant grows—for example, adding aluminum to the soil can make hydrangea blossoms turn from pink to blue.*

Lines 136–154
DISCUSSION PROMPTS
Use these prompts to help students understand the significance of the changes in the plants from Earth:

Connect Imagine that a familiar plant looked strangely different one day. Would you be able to believe your eyes or, like Harry, would you seek another opinion? Why? ***Possible answer:*** *You would need another opinion because such a thing would be so unexpected or might seem impossible.*

Analyze What could have caused the changes in Harry's plants? ***Possible answer:*** *The changes might have been caused by the water or soil on Mars, or by the air itself.*

Synthesize If the plants are changing, what predictions can you make about what could happen to the Bitterings and other Earth people? ***Possible answer:*** *They might begin to change physically, too.*

G MOOD

Possible answer: Bittering's new fear—that he and his family will change—makes the mood of the story feel threatening. Now it seems that they may be at the mercy of strange forces they do not understand.

Lines 182–193
DISCUSSION PROMPTS

Use these prompts to help students explore how the characters react to the changes occurring on Mars:

Connect Think about a time when someone ignored or laughed at something you took very seriously. How does such an interaction make you feel? *Students may say this is a frustrating experience. It can make you angry; sometimes it can also make you doubt your own thoughts.*

Analyze How does the author use language and gesture to express the men's lack of concern? *Possible answer: They speak in a relaxed, casual way—"Sure. Sure, Harry"; "Why, yes, Harry"; "Can't recall that it did much"—and seem to be in agreement. They nod and laugh.*

Speculate Why aren't the men on the stoop more concerned? *Possible answer: The changes don't bother them. Perhaps the food and air on Mars are already turning them into compliant Martians, or perhaps they accept the changes because they do not wish to return to Earth.*

H MOOD

Possible answer: The fact that the other characters are so easygoing about the changes is creepy, because that might mean they are turning into Martians. On the other hand, readers may wonder if Harry really is overreacting.

And they stood looking at the green roses.

And two days later Dan came running. "Come see the cow. I was milking her and I saw it. Come on!"

They stood in the shed and looked at their one cow.

It was growing a third horn.

160 And the lawn in front of their house very quietly and slowly was coloring itself like spring violets. Seed from Earth but growing up a soft purple.

"We must get away," said Bittering. "We'll eat this stuff and then we'll change—who knows to what? I can't let it happen. There's only one thing to do. Burn this food!" G

"It's not poisoned."

"But it is. **Subtly,** very subtly. A little bit. A very little bit. We mustn't touch it."

He looked with dismay at their house. "Even the house. The wind's done something to it. The air's burned it. The fog at night. The boards,
170 all warped out of shape. It's not an Earthman's house any more."

"Oh, your imagination!"

He put on his coat and tie. "I'm going into town. We've got to do something now. I'll be back."

"Wait, Harry!" his wife cried. But he was gone.

In town, on the shadowy step of the grocery store, the men sat with their hands on their knees, conversing with great leisure and ease.

Mr. Bittering wanted to fire a pistol in the air.

What are you doing, you fools! he thought. Sitting here! You've heard the news—we're stranded on this planet. Well, move! Aren't you
180 frightened? Aren't you afraid? What are you going to do?

"Hello, Harry," said everyone.

"Look," he said to them. "You did hear the news, the other day, didn't you?"

They nodded and laughed. "Sure. Sure, Harry."

"What are you going to do about it?"

"Do, Harry, do? What *can* we do?"

"Build a rocket, that's what!"

"A rocket, Harry? To go back to all that trouble? Oh, Harry!"

"But you *must* want to go back. Have you noticed the peach blossoms,
190 the onions, the grass?"

"Why, yes, Harry, seems we did," said one of the men.

"Doesn't it scare you?"

"Can't recall that it did much, Harry." H

"Idiots!"

"Now, Harry."

G MOOD

When he sees that the plants and animals are changing, Mr. Bittering becomes afraid that he and his family will change too. What impact does this **plot** turn have on the mood of the story?

subtly (sŭt'lē) *adv.* not obviously; in a manner hard to notice o perceive

H MOOD

How do the **characters'** reactions to the situation make you feel?

DIFFERENTIATED INSTRUCTION

FOR LESS–PROFICIENT READERS

Reading Strategy Follow-Up: Reading Science Fiction Ask students to use the chart introduced on page 445 to note scientific, familiar, and imaginary elements in the description of the Bitterings' yard. *Possible answers:*

- *Scientific information: grass grows from seed*
- *Familiar elements: people milk cows*
- *Imaginary worlds: cows grow third horns, green roses*

Bittering wanted to cry. "You've got to work with me. If we stay here, we'll all change. The air. Don't you smell it? Something in the air. A Martian virus, maybe; some seed, or a pollen. Listen to me!"

They stared at him.

"Sam," he said to one of them.

"Yes, Harry?"

"Will you help me build a rocket?"

"Harry, I got a whole load of metal and some blueprints. You want to work in my metal shop on a rocket, you're welcome. I'll sell you that metal for five hundred dollars. You should be able to construct a right pretty rocket, if you work alone, in about thirty years."

Everyone laughed.

"Don't laugh."

Sam looked at him with quiet good humor.

210 "Sam," Bittering said. "Your eyes—"

"What about them, Harry?"

"Didn't they used to be gray?"

"Well now, I don't remember."

"They were, weren't they?"

"Why do you ask, Harry?"

"Because now they're kind of yellow-colored."

"Is that so, Harry?" Sam said, casually.

"And you're taller and thinner—"

"You might be right, Harry."

220 "Sam, you shouldn't have yellow eyes." **I**

"Harry, what color eyes have *you* got?" Sam said.

"My eyes? They're blue, of course."

"Here you are, Harry." Sam handed him a pocket mirror. "Take a look at yourself."

Mr. Bittering hesitated, and then raised the mirror to his face.

There were little, very dim flecks of new gold captured in the blue of his eyes.

"Now look what you've done," said Sam a moment later. "You've broken my mirror." **J**

230 Harry Bittering moved into the metal shop and began to build the rocket. Men stood in the open door and talked and joked without raising their voices. Once in a while they gave him a hand on lifting something. But mostly they just idled and watched him with their yellowing eyes.

"It's suppertime, Harry," they said.

His wife appeared with his supper in a wicker basket.

---

② **Targeted Passage**

I **READING SCIENCE FICTION**
Are the changes in Sam's appearance realistic according to the laws of science, or is Bradbury using his imagination here?

J **MAKE INFERENCES**
Why did Sam's mirror break?

I **READING SCIENCE FICTION**

Possible answer: Bradbury is using his imagination. People's eye color does not change—especially not to yellow—and people do not grow taller so quickly.

J **MAKE INFERENCES**

Possible answer: Harry has broken the mirror. When he sees the gold in his own eyes, he drops the mirror in shock, fear, or anger.

Lines 175–229
ADDITIONAL TEACHING OPPORTUNITY

Analyze Characters Explain that different characters may see a situation in different ways. Noticing this can help readers understand story events. Ask students to compare Harry's views of the changes on Mars with the views of the other men in town. Help them see that Harry's dread of the changes on Mars is in sharp contrast to the "great leisure and ease" that the other men feel. Harry's dread helps readers understand how drastic the changes on Mars really are.

FOR LESS–PROFICIENT READERS

② **Targeted Passage [Lines 210–227]**

This passage builds suspense by heightening the central conflict between the main character and his setting: it becomes apparent that the Earth people have begun to change physically on Mars.

- What are the physical signs of change?
- What does Harry notice about himself?

Review: Make Inferences An inference is a logical conclusion based on evidence. A reader can make inferences about what happened to Sam's mirror (lines 228–229) based on what Harry saw when he looked in the mirror and how he had been feeling about the changes around him. Readers may also use their own experiences with feeling shocked or afraid to make an inference about how Harry reacted to what he saw.

FOR ADVANCED LEARNERS/PRE–AP

Plan and Visualize Ask students to sketch the rocket Harry wants to build. Have them label key features and include a list of steps that Harry should take to prepare for the journey and avoid contaminating Earth with Martian material.

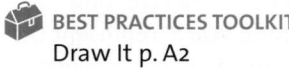 **BEST PRACTICES TOOLKIT**
Draw It p. A2

REINFORCE *KEY IDEA:* CHANGE

Discuss Mr. Bittering has already experienced physical **changes** as a result of his new environment; now he suddenly uses a Martian word. What does this new development suggest about how Mars is changing who he is? *Possible answer: Mars is changing him on the inside as well as the outside. It has begun to shape the way he thinks and the language he uses.*

LITERARY ANALYSIS

Ⓚ MOOD

Possible answer: A feeling of eeriness is created by words such as

- *"shifted"*
- *"melted"*
- *"burnt"*
- *"roaring"*
- *"shaking"*

The unusual sentence structure contributes to an eerie feeling. This sort of structure is sometimes used with a ghost story or other scary tale.

If students need help ... Rewrite this passage on the board using pared-down description and straightforward syntax.

> *Mr. Bittering lay in bed. He felt that his bones were becoming different.*

Discuss how the mood of the passage is affected by these changes.

ANALYZE VISUALS

Possible answer: Students may say that the figure farthest to the left would represent Harry: it stands out from the others and looks more grounded. Its form also seems clearer. The others look more like they have been transformed.

About the Art The Swiss sculptor and painter Alberto Giacometti (1901–1966) was best known for his bronze sculptures of rough-surfaced, elongated figures. It has been suggested that these thin and haunting figures, which Giacometti began creating after the horrors of World War II, represent the fragility of humankind in an uncertain world.

"I won't touch it," he said. "I'll eat only food from our Deepfreeze. Food that came from Earth. Nothing from our garden."

His wife stood watching him. "You can't build a rocket."

240 "I worked in a shop once, when I was twenty. I know metal. Once I get it started, the others will help," he said, not looking at her, laying out the blueprints.

"Harry, Harry," she said, helplessly.

"We've *got* to get away, Cora. We've got to!"

The nights were full of wind that blew down the empty moonlit sea meadows past the little white chess cities lying for their twelve-thousandth year in the shallows. In the Earthmen's settlement, the Bittering house shook with a feeling of change.

Lying abed, Mr. Bittering felt his bones shifted, shaped, melted like gold.
250 His wife, lying beside him, was dark from many sunny afternoons. Dark she was, and golden-eyed, burnt almost black by the sun, sleeping, and the children metallic in their beds, and the wind roaring **forlorn** and changing through the old peach trees, the violet grass, shaking out green rose petals. Ⓚ

The fear would not be stopped. It had his throat and heart. It dripped in a wetness of the arm and the temple and the trembling palm.

A green star rose in the east.

A strange word emerged from Mr. Bittering's lips.

"Iorrt. Iorrt." He repeated it.

260 It was a Martian word. He knew no Martian.

In the middle of the night he arose and dialed a call through to Simpson, the archaeologist.

"Simpson, what does the word *Iorrt* mean?"

"Why that's the old Martian word for our planet Earth. Why?"

forlorn (fər-lôrn') *adj.* appearing lonely or sad

Ⓚ **MOOD**
Reread lines 249–253. Notice Bradbury's **word choice** and unusu[al] **sentence structure.** What word would you use to describe the feeling this paragraph conveys?

ANALYZE VISUALS
If this sculpture had bee[n] made specifically for thi[s] story, which figure woul[d] represent Harry?

The Forest (1950), Alberto Giacometti. Bronze, painted, 22″ × 24″ × 29¼″. Gift of Enid Haupt. National Gallery of Art, Washington. © National Gallery of Art, Washington.

DIFFERENTIATED INSTRUCTION

FOR LESS–PROFICIENT READERS

Reading Strategy Follow-Up: Reading Science Fiction Have students review lines 245–256 to look for elements of ordinary life and imaginary situations. Have students note these elements in the chart:

- *Familiar elements: people sleeping in beds, grass growing*
- *Imaginary worlds: ancient cities on Mars, purple grass*

FOR ENGLISH LEARNERS

Vocabulary: Multiple-Meaning Words Point out that in line 253, *rose* is a noun that means a kind of flower, while in line 256, *rose* is a verb that means "moved upward." Ask students for help in composing two new sentences for *rose* that show each of its meanings in context. Then do the same for other multiple-meaning words in the selection, such as *temple* (line 255), *mean* (line 266), *show, left* (both line 320), *still, film* (both line 357).

"No special reason."

The telephone slipped from his hand.

"Hello, hello, hello, hello," it kept saying while he sat gazing out at the green star. "Bittering? Harry, are you there?"

The days were full of metal sound. He laid the frame of the rocket with the reluctant help of three indifferent men. He grew very tired in an hour or so and had to sit down.

"The altitude," laughed a man.

"Are you *eating,* Harry?" asked another.

"I'm eating," he said, angrily.

"From your Deepfreeze?"

"Yes!"

"You're getting thinner, Harry."

"I'm not!"

"And taller."

"Liar!"

His wife took him aside a few days later. "Harry, I've used up all the food in the Deepfreeze. There's nothing left. I'll have to make sandwiches using food grown on Mars."

He sat down heavily.

"You must eat," she said. "You're weak."

"Yes," he said.

He took a sandwich, opened it, looked at it, and began to nibble at it.

"And take the rest of the day off," she said. "It's hot. The children want to swim in the canals and hike. Please come along."

"I can't waste time. This is a crisis!"

"Just for an hour," she urged. "A swim'll do you good."

He rose, sweating. "All right, all right. Leave me alone. I'll come."

"Good for you, Harry."

The sun was hot, the day quiet. There was only an immense staring burn upon the land. They moved along the canal, the father, the mother, the racing children in their swimsuits. They stopped and ate meat sandwiches. He saw their skin baking brown. And he saw the yellow eyes of his wife and his children, their eyes that were never yellow before. A few tremblings shook him, but were carried off in waves of pleasant heat as he lay in the sun. He was too tired to be afraid.

"Cora, how long have your eyes been yellow?"

She was bewildered. "Always, I guess."

"They didn't change from brown in the last three months?"

She bit her lips. "No. Why do you ask?"

"Never mind."

 MOOD
Reread lines 301–304. Note how different Harry's attitude is now than it was before. What effect does this change have on you as a reader?

LITERARY ANALYSIS

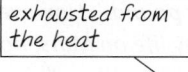 **MOOD**

Possible answer: Harry is becoming less resistant to the forces of Mars. The reader may feel sorry for Harry's plight and worry that if Harry—the most vocal opponent of change—stops resisting Mars, more dramatic changes will be yet to come.

Extend the Discussion Why might Harry's attitude be changing? Have students cluster possible causes of Harry's attitude change. Ask students how considering these causes helps them sympathize with Harry.

exhausted from the heat	feels powerless to change things

Harry begins to accept changes.

lacks support from others	might be hungry

💼 **BEST PRACTICES TOOLKIT—Transparency**
Cluster Diagram p. B18

FOR LESS-PROFICIENT READERS

Concept Support Reread lines 305–309. Discuss how a change can occur so gradually that it is barely perceptible day by day—for example, over the years a tree seedling will become a big tree, yet during that time it may look generally the same from one day or week to the next. Ask students for other examples.

FOR ENGLISH LEARNERS

Language: Modifiers Point out the adverbs *angrily* (line 278), *heavily* (line 288), and *easily* (line 318). Explain that each is formed by dropping the final letter from an adjective ending in *y* and then adding *-ily.* Remind students that many adverbs are formed simply by adding *-ly,* such as *seriously* (line 331) and *slowly* (line 346).

DISCUSSION PROMPTS

Use these prompts to help students understand Mr. Bittering's acceptance of this new situation:

Connect If you were Dan's parent, would you let him change his name? Why or why not? *Students may say that Dan has the right to change his own name. Or, they may say that such a name change shows the dangerous power of Mars, and as a result should not be permitted.*

Analyze How does Mr. Bittering feel about Dan's name change? Explain your answer. *Possible answer: Mr. Bittering is alarmed; his body is cold and his heart pounds. However, he has been worn down by life on Mars; not only his rocket but his own identity—"himself alone even among his family"—seem pointless. He lacks the will to resist.*

Synthesize If the Bitterings were able to return to Earth, do you think Dan's parents would accept his name change? Why? *Possible answer: If they believed they would return to Earth, Dan's parents might not permit him to change his name, because they would be trying harder to hold on to their old identities.*

READING SKILL: *Review*

Ⓜ MAKE INFERENCES

Possible answer: Dan is becoming a Martian. He feels that his old name no longer fits him and he wants a Martian name instead.

---

310 They sat there.

"The children's eyes," he said. "They're yellow, too."

"Sometimes growing children's eyes change color."

"Maybe *we're* children, too. At least to Mars. That's a thought." He laughed. "Think I'll swim."

They leaped into the canal water, and he let himself sink down and down to the bottom like a golden statue and lie there in green silence. All was water-quiet and deep, all was peace. He felt the steady, slow current drift him easily.

If I lie here long enough, he thought, the water will work and eat away 320 my flesh until the bones show like coral. Just my skeleton left. And then the water can build on that skeleton—green things, deep water things, red things, yellow things. Change. Change. Slow, deep, silent change. And isn't that what it is up *there*?

He saw the sky submerged above him, the sun made Martian by atmosphere and time and space.

Up there, a big river, he thought, a Martian river; all of us lying deep in it, in our pebble houses, in our sunken boulder houses, like crayfish hidden, and the water washing away our old bodies and lengthening the bones and—

330 He let himself drift up through the soft light.

Dan sat on the edge of the canal, regarding his father seriously.

"*Utha,*" he said.

"What?" asked his father.

The boy smiled. "You know. *Utha's* the Martian word for 'father.'"

"Where did you learn it?"

"I don't know. Around. *Utha!*"

"What do you want?"

The boy hesitated. "I—I want to change my name."

"Change it?"

340 "Yes."

His mother swam over. "What's wrong with Dan for a name?"

Dan fidgeted. "The other day you called Dan, Dan, Dan. I didn't even hear. I said to myself, That's not my name. I've a new name I want to use."

Mr. Bittering held to the side of the canal, his body cold and his heart pounding slowly. "What is this new name?"

"Linnl. Isn't that a good name? Can I use it? Can't I, please?" Ⓜ

Mr. Bittering put his hand to his head. He thought of the silly rocket, himself working alone, himself alone even among his family, so alone.

350 He heard his wife say, "Why not?"

He heard himself say, "Yes, you can use it."

"Yaaa!" screamed the boy. "I'm Linnl, Linnl!"

Ⓜ **MAKE INFERENCES**
Why does Dan want to change his name?

DIFFERENTIATED INSTRUCTION

FOR LESS–PROFICIENT READERS

Comprehension Support Direct students' attention to lines 319–322. Point out that Mr. Bittering is using figurative language when he compares his bones to coral. Explain that coral grows slowly in warm, shallow water and that new life grows on its skeleton bit by bit until, over time, it takes a new form. This is what Mr. Bittering feels is happening to him on Mars.

FOR ADVANCED LEARNERS/PRE–AP

Analyze Setting In lines 315–346, the Bitterings are drifting or immersed in water. How would the mood of the scene and the conversation have been different if the family had been seated indoors? What if the season had been different? Have student pairs discuss and make notes about how a different setting could have changed the mood—and perhaps the conclusion—of this scene. Ask them to compare their notes with those of another pair.

Racing down the meadowlands, he danced and shouted.

Mr. Bittering looked at his wife. "Why did we do that?"

"I don't know," she said. "It just seemed like a good idea."

They walked into the hills. They strolled on old mosaic paths, beside still pumping fountains. The paths were covered with a thin film of cool water all summer long. You kept your bare feet cool all the day, splashing as in a creek, wading.

350 They came to a small deserted Martian villa with a good view of the valley. It was on top of a hill. Blue marble halls, large murals, a swimming pool. It was refreshing in this hot summertime. The Martians hadn't believed in large cities.

"How nice," said Mrs. Bittering, "if we could move up here to this villa for the summer."

"Come on," he said. "We're going back to town. There's work to be done on the rocket."

But as he worked that night, the thought of the cool blue marble villa entered his mind. As the hours passed, the rocket seemed

370 less important.

In the flow of days and weeks, the rocket **receded** and **dwindled.** The old fever was gone. It frightened him to think he had let it slip this way. But somehow the heat, the air, the working conditions—

He heard the men murmuring on the porch of his metal shop.

"Everyone's going. You heard?"

"All going. That's right."

Bittering came out. "Going where?" He saw a couple of trucks, loaded with children and furniture, drive down the dusty street.

"Up to the villas," said the man.

380 "Yeah, Harry. I'm going. So is Sam. Aren't you Sam?"

"That's right, Harry. What about you?"

"I've got work to do here."

"Work! You can finish that rocket in the autumn, when it's cooler."

He took a breath. "I got the frame all set up."

"In the autumn is better." Their voices were lazy in the heat.

"Got to work," he said.

"Autumn," they reasoned. And they sounded so sensible, so right.

"Autumn would be best," he thought. "Plenty of time, then."

No! cried part of himself, deep down, put away, locked tight,

390 suffocating. No! No!

"In the autumn," he said.

"Come on, Harry," they all said.

"Yes," he said, feeling his flesh melt in the hot liquid air. "Yes, in the autumn. I'll begin work again then."

VISUAL VOCABULARY

mosaic (mō-zā´ĭk) *adj.* formed from pieces of stone or glass that are inlaid to make a design

 **MAKE INFERENCES**
Why is the rocket becoming less important to Harry?

recede (rĭ-sēd´) *v.* to become fainter or more distant

dwindle (dwĭn´dl) *v.* to become less, until little remains

3 **Targeted Passage**

FOR LESS–PROFICIENT READERS

3 **Targeted Passage [Lines 360–394]**

This passage shows a turning point in the plot: the Bitterings decide, like the others, to leave the homes they built and live in the old Martian villas.

- Who used to live in the villas the Earth people are moving to?

- How long do the Earth people plan to live in the villas?

- What does Harry decide to do? How does he seem to feel about his decision?

Comprehension Support Distribute copies of the Open Mind graphic organizer and have students use the organizer to imagine what is going through Harry's mind when he agrees to move his family to the villas. Students may wish to draw images, such as a rocket frame and a faraway Earth, and write thoughts, such as "It's so nice and cool up in the villas."

BEST PRACTICES TOOLKIT—Transparency Open Mind p. D11

Detail from *Figures Crossing River on Gold Coins*, Andrew Judd. ©Andrew Judd/Masterfile.

ANALYZE VISUALS

Possible answer: The lonely, mysterious, and rather haunted mood of this painting detail is created by

- *an entirely barren landscape*
- *an empty river intertwining with an empty highway*
- *the snaking of the highway up a desolate mountain*
- *the disappearance of the river into the landscape*

About the Art The diverse work of Canadian painter Andrew Judd (born 1958) encompasses landscapes, still lifes, and portraiture done in both traditional and abstract styles.

Lines 409–415
REINFORCE *KEY IDEA:* CHANGE

Discuss The Bitterings have decided to leave behind things they brought all the way from Earth. What does this choice suggest about how they have **changed?** *Possible answer: Their old things no longer suit them. Now they want to have new things that fit their new lives.*

READING STRATEGY

○ READING SCIENCE FICTION

Possible answers: The fact that people are changing the names shows that they are adapting to life on Mars. The Martian history and culture are beginning to seem more meaningful to them than the history and cultures of Earth.

Extend the Discussion Names and naming are important in most cultures. What does changing the name of a person or place say about that person or place?

"I got a villa near the Tirra Canal," said someone.

"You mean the Roosevelt Canal, don't you?"

"Tirra. The old Martian name."

"But on the map—"

"Forget the map. It's Tirra now. Now I found a place in the Pillan
400 Mountains—"

"You mean the Rockefeller Range," said Bittering.

"I mean the Pillan Mountains," said Sam.

"Yes," said Bittering, buried in the hot, swarming air. "The Pillan Mountains."

Everyone worked at loading the truck in the hot, still afternoon of the next day.

Laura, Dan, and David carried packages. Or, as they preferred to be known, Ttil, Linnl, and Werr carried packages. ○

The furniture was abandoned in the little white cottage.

410 "It looked just fine in Boston," said the mother. "And here in the cottage. But up at the villa? No. We'll get it when we come back in the autumn."

Bittering himself was quiet.

"I've some ideas on furniture for the villa," he said after a time. "Big, lazy furniture."

"What about your encyclopedia? You're taking it along, surely?"

ANALYZE VISUALS
What is the **mood** of this painting? Explain what elements help create this mood.

○ READING SCIENCE FICTION
Why is it significant that the people are changing the names of the landmarks and themselves?

DIFFERENTIATED INSTRUCTION

FOR LESS–PROFICIENT READERS

Comprehension Support Ask students to help you make a list on the board of changes that have occurred in the Bitterings' lives since their move to Mars. *Possible answers:*

- *no more rockets from Earth*
- *children have new names*
- *decided to leave their house and furniture*

Mr. Bittering glanced away. "I'll come and get it next week."

They turned to their daughter. "What about your New York dresses?"

The bewildered girl stared. "Why, I don't want them any more."

420 They shut off the gas, the water, they locked the doors and walked away. Father peered into the truck.

"Gosh, we're not taking much," he said. "Considering all we brought to Mars, this is only a handful!" **P**

He started the truck.

Looking at the small white cottage for a long moment, he was filled with a desire to rush to it, touch it, say good-bye to it, for he felt as if he were going away on a long journey, leaving something to which he could never quite return, never understand again.

Just then Sam and his family drove by in another truck.

430 "Hi, Bittering! Here we go!"

The truck swung down the ancient highway out of town. There were sixty others traveling in the same direction. The town filled with a silent, heavy dust from their passage. The canal waters lay blue in the sun, and a quiet wind moved in the strange trees.

"Good-bye, town!" said Mr. Bittering.

"Good-bye, good-bye," said the family, waving to it.

They did not look back again.

Summer burned the canals dry. Summer moved like flame upon the meadows. In the empty Earth settlement, the painted houses flaked
440 and peeled. Rubber tires upon which children had swung in back yards hung suspended like stopped clock **pendulums** in the blazing air.

At the metal shop, the rocket frame began to rust.

In the quiet autumn Mr. Bittering stood, very dark now, very golden-eyed, upon the slope above his villa, looking at the valley.

"It's time to go back," said Cora.

"Yes, but we're not going," he said quietly. "There's nothing there any more."

"Your books," she said. "Your fine clothes."

"Your *llles* and your fine *ior uele rre*," she said.

450 "The town's empty. No one's going back," he said. "There's no reason to, none at all."

The daughter wove tapestries and the sons played songs on ancient flutes and pipes, their laughter echoing in the marble villa.

Mr. Bittering gazed at the Earth settlement far away in the low valley. "Such odd, such ridiculous houses the Earth people built."

"They didn't know any better," his wife **mused.** "Such ugly people. I'm glad they've gone."

P MOOD
Reread lines 416–423. What effect does this **dialogue** have on the overall mood of the story?

pendulum (pĕn′jə-ləm) *n.* a weight hung so that it can swing freely, sometimes used in timing the workings of certain clocks

4 Targeted Passage

muse (myōōz) *v.* to say thoughtfully

DARK THEY WERE, AND GOLDEN-EYED **459**

LITERARY ANALYSIS

P MOOD

Possible answer: *Earlier in the story, an anxious mood characterized the Bitterings' feelings about Mars. However, when the Bitterings admit to each other that they are leaving behind their Earth things, the mood becomes eerily calm. They seem to be accepting that Mars will change them.*

Lines 438–451
DISCUSSION PROMPTS

Use these prompts to help students understand how the Bitterings' viewpoints have changed:

Connect Think about a time when you outgrew or lost interest in something that had been important to you. What does it feel like afterward to look back on that thing?
Possible answer: *It can be hard to remember why something was so important after it has lost its meaning in your life.*

Analyze Compare the Earth settlement and the Martian villas in autumn. Which one seems more like a ruin? Explain your answer.
Possible answer: *The Earth settlement has become a lifeless ruin. The settlement is empty (line 439) and the houses are decaying (lines 439–440). Meanwhile, the Martian villas are inhabited again.*

Evaluate Mr. Bittering says that "there's no reason to" go back to the Earth settlement (lines 450–451). Do you agree? Explain.
Possible answer: *They are no longer Earth people, so it doesn't make sense for them to live in Earth houses and use their old Earth things. On the other hand, if they adapt completely to Mars, they cannot return to Earth if that becomes a possibility again.*

FOR LESS–PROFICIENT READERS
4 Targeted Passage [Lines 443–457]

This passage reveals the story's climax: after their summer in the Martian villas, the Bitterings no longer think of themselves as Earth people.

- What do the Bitterings decide to do in autumn? How do they seem to feel about this decision?
- Who lives in the Earth settlement now?
- Whom does Mrs. Bittering mean when she says "they" (line 456)?

FOR ADVANCED LEARNERS/PRE–AP

Analyze Mood Have students reread line 437 and discuss what feeling this line leaves with the reader. Challenge them to come up with a line that would end the scene with a different feeling. (Example: "Weeping, the children covered their faces with their hands.")

DARK THEY WERE, AND GOLDEN-EYED **459**

Q READING SCIENCE FICTION

Possible answers:

- *Their skin color has changed; they look younger, or perhaps have become ageless.*

- *The Bitterings seem unable to remember what happened to the people they once were: "Where did they go?" (line 460).*

It is possible that the Bitterings are no longer human. The dialogue shows only their perspective, but they do not seem to think of themselves as human.

Lines 475–476
REINFORCE KEY IDEA: CHANGE

Discuss What does the lieutenant's report tell you about how the Bitterings were **changed** by their environment? *Possible answer: The lieutenant's report confirms that the colonists have turned into Martians. The Bitterings themselves seem to have stopped being aware that they were changing.*

READING SKILL: *Review*

R MAKE INFERENCES

Possible answer: Like the Bitterings, in time they will turn into Martians.

If students need help ... Point out that conflict is unlikely, as the rocket men and the Martians have already had a friendly encounter. Ask students to summarize what happened to the Bitterings and other Earth people.

They both looked at each other, startled by all they had just finished saying. They laughed.

460 "Where did they go?" he wondered. He glanced at his wife. She was golden and slender as his daughter. She looked at him, and he seemed almost as young as their eldest son. **Q**

"I don't know," she said.

"We'll go back to town maybe next year, or the year after, or the year after that," he said, calmly. "Now—I'm warm. How about taking a swim?"

They turned their backs to the valley. Arm in arm they walked silently down a path of clear-running spring water.

F ive years later a rocket fell out of the sky. It lay steaming in the
470 valley. Men leaped out of it, shouting.

"We won the war on Earth! We're here to rescue you! Hey!"

But the American-built town of cottages, peach trees, and theaters was silent. They found a **flimsy** rocket frame rusting in an empty shop.

The rocket men searched the hills. The captain established headquarters in an abandoned bar. His lieutenant came back to report.

"The town's empty, but we found native life in the hills, sir. Dark people. Yellow eyes. Martians. Very friendly. We talked a bit, not much. They learn English fast. I'm sure our relations will be most friendly with them, sir."

"Dark, eh?" mused the captain. "How many?"

480 "Six, eight hundred, I'd say, living in those marble ruins in the hills, sir. Tall, healthy. Beautiful women."

"Did they tell you what became of the men and women who built this Earth settlement, Lieutenant?"

"They hadn't the foggiest notion of what happened to this town or its people."

"Strange. You think those Martians killed them?"

"They look surprisingly peaceful. Chances are a plague did this town in, sir."

"Perhaps. I suppose this is one of those mysteries we'll never solve.
490 One of those mysteries you read about." **R**

The captain looked at the room, the dusty windows, the blue mountains rising beyond, the canals moving in the light, and he heard the soft wind in the air. He shivered. Then, recovering, he tapped a large fresh map he had thumbtacked to the top of an empty table.

"Lots to be done, Lieutenant." His voice droned on and quietly on as the sun sank behind the blue hills. "New settlements. Mining sites, minerals to be looked for. Bacteriological specimens[5] taken. The work, all the work.

---

5. **bacteriological specimens:** samples of different kinds of single-celled living things.

flimsy (flĭm'zē) *adj.* not solid or strong

5 Targeted Passage

DIFFERENTIATED INSTRUCTION

FOR LESS–PROFICIENT READERS

5 Targeted Passage [Lines 468–490]

This passage includes the resolution of the story: after five years on Mars, the Earth people have been so changed by their environment that they are no longer recognizable as human.

- When does the rocket come? What is its mission?

- What do the people in the hills look like? How do they react to the lieutenant?

- What happened to the people in the Earth settlement?

Review: Make Inferences Point out that in lines 486–488 the captain and the lieutenant are making inferences. They are making logical guesses, based on observations and their own prior knowledge, about what happened to the Earth people.

The Whole City (1935), Max Ernst. Oil on canvas, 60 cm × 81 cm. Kunsthaus, Zurich, Switzerland/Artists Rights Society (ARS), New York.

And the old records were lost. We'll have a job of remapping to do, renaming the mountains and rivers and such. Calls for a little imagination.

"What do you think of naming those mountains the Lincoln Mountains, this canal the Washington Canal, those hills—we can name those hills for you, Lieutenant. Diplomacy. And you, for a favor, might name a town for me. Polishing the apple.[6] And why not make this the Einstein Valley, and farther over . . . are you *listening*, Lieutenant?"

The lieutenant snapped his gaze from the blue color and the quiet mist of the hills far beyond the town.

"What? Oh, *yes*, sir!" ✺

ANALYZE VISUALS
Does the place at the top of the hill look inviting to you? Why or why not?

---

6. **polishing the apple:** acting in a way to get on the good side of another person.

ANALYZE VISUALS
Possible answer: Some students may say that the brilliant sun, rich colors, and interesting stepped form of the landscape make the place at the top of the hill look inviting. Others may feel that the knotty vegetation and apparent isolation of the place make it look uninviting.

About the Art This painting is by German surrealist Max Ernst, who also created *Shellfish Flowers* on page 451. Like the flowers in that painting, the finely detailed but somewhat mysterious flora in *The Whole City* reveals Ernst's interest in organic textures. The landscape, too, features intricate, unreal patterns.

SELECTION WRAP-UP

REFLECT Have students think about whether the Bitterings' lives seem better or worse after they change into Martians. What might be some of the benefits of adapting to an environment? What might be some of the dangers?

⭐ **CRITIQUE** Which element of the story do you think the author developed most effectively: the plot, the characters, or the setting? Explain.

READING FLUENCY

Distribute copy masters and have students work in pairs to practice fluency.

 RESOURCE MANAGER—Copy Master
Reading Fluency p. 37

FOR ENGLISH LEARNERS
Reading Comprehension: Sequence Lines 464–468 contain references to years. Distribute copies of the Timeline transparency. Have students create a timeline of at least five years of life on Mars (they can make up the year the timeline begins). Ask them to show events in the lives of the Bitterings.

 BEST PRACTICES TOOLKIT—Transparency
Timeline p. B23

FOR ADVANCED LEARNERS/PRE-AP
Analyze Mood Have students reread lines 505–506. Ask them to think about how the author describes what the lieutenant sees and what the mood suggests about what the lieutenant is feeling. Distribute copies of the Venn Diagram transparency. Have students use the diagram to compare and contrast the lieutenant's feelings with the feelings Harry had when he arrived on Mars.

BEST PRACTICES TOOLKIT—Transparency
Venn Diagram p. A26

READING FOR INFORMATION

Point out that the magazine article features an interview—a conversation with author Ray Bradbury. Ask students what impression of Bradbury they get from the picture. **Possible answer:** *He looks like a creative person who enjoys his work. The table or desk is covered with a mess of interesting things, including a toy robot.*

DISCUSSION PROMPTS

Use these prompts to help students understand Ray Bradbury's creative process:

Connect Think of a time when an idea stimulated your mind or imagination. How does this help you understand Ray Bradbury's desire to write? *Students may say that when an idea takes hold of your mind, you want to keep thinking about it and then express your thoughts about it. Ray Bradbury does this by writing.*

Analyze Bradbury says that he would tell a beginning writer to "Fill your life with metaphors. And then explode." What does he mean? **Possible answer:** *When you have lots of ideas and images in your mind, you will be likely to feel creative. By "explode," Bradbury means a writer should go with that feeling and see what happens.*

Synthesize How might being "a collector of metaphors" help an artist write a story, draw a picture, or choreograph a dance? Explain. **Possible answer:** *Metaphors are creative; they are efforts to understand something in a different way by using the imagination. A metaphor can help an artist think through ideas and can serve as a starting point for creating something new.*

Reading for Information

MAGAZINE ARTICLE As you read this interview, you'll find out how Ray Bradbury views himself as an author, how he writes stories like "Dark They Were, and Golden-Eyed," and what advice he has for beginning writers.

Section 3   THE CHARLOTTE OBSERVER

An Interview with
RAY BRADBURY

Q: You don't consider yourself a science fiction writer, even though others call you that. How do you see yourself?

A: I am a collector of metaphors. Any idea that strikes me I run with. . . .

I wrote *The October Country,* which is weird fantasy. There is no science fiction there. And *Halloween Tree,* which is a history of Halloween. And *Dandelion Wine,* which is my childhood in Illinois. *Something Wicked This Way Comes,* which is also my childhood plus fantasy. So when you look at the spread of things, there is only one novel that is science fiction. And that's *Fahrenheit 451.* In other words, science fiction is the art of the possible, not the art of the impossible. As soon as you deal with things that can't happen you are writing fantasy.

Q: Walk me through your daily inspiration and writing process.

A: I just wake up with ideas every morning from my subconscious percolating. At 7 in the morning I lie in bed and I watch all the fragments of ideas swarming around in my head and these voices talk to me. And when they get to a certain point, I jump out of bed and run to the typewriter. So I'm not in control. Two hours later I have a new short story or an essay or part of a play. . . .

Q: What kind of advice would you give beginning writers?

A: Explode. Don't intellectualize. Get passionate about ideas. Cram your head full of images. Stay in the library. Stay off the Internet. Read all the great books. Read all the great poetry. See all the great films. Fill your life with metaphors. And then explode. And you're bound to do something good.

462 UNIT 4: MOOD, TONE, AND STYLE

DIFFERENTIATED INSTRUCTION

FOR LESS-PROFICIENT READERS
Concept Support Remind students that a work of fantasy is one that includes at least one unreal element. Ask them to name works of fantasy and recall unreal or impossible elements in them.

FOR ENGLISH LEARNERS
Language: Conjunctions Explain that in conversational English, conjunctions are often used to show relationships between sentences. For example, in the first answer, Bradbury uses the conjunction *and* to connect "I wrote [a book that is not science fiction]" with titles in later sentences: "And *Halloween Tree.* . . . And *Dandelion Wine.* . . ." Have mixed language-ability pairs skim the interview for other conjunctions that show relationships between sentences and describe those relationships.

FOR ADVANCED LEARNERS/PRE-AP
Figurative Language Have small groups of students reread the interview to note what metaphors Bradbury uses in conversation. Suggest that students look up any unfamiliar words in a dictionary. Have them discuss what each metaphor adds to their understanding and then share their ideas with another group. (Example: "percolating": keeps popping up. He can't control it.)

Comprehension

1. **Recall** Why do the Bitterings settle on Mars?

2. **Recall** Why do the rockets from Earth stop coming to Mars?

3. **Represent** Create a timeline of the main events of the story, including the physical changes Harry notices in the people and things around him.

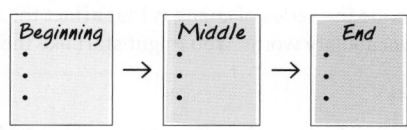

MARYLAND OBJECTIVES

LITERATURE STANDARD
3.A.7.a Analyze how specific language choices contribute to meaning

Literary Analysis

4. **Identify Mood** Before you read the story, you were asked to consider, as you read, how Bradbury's choice of words affected the way you felt. Now think of the story as a whole. What words would you use to describe the overall mood of the story? Cite descriptions of plot elements, setting, or characters and examples of dialogue to support your response.

5. **Interpret Foreshadowing** Writers use foreshadowing to provide hints of what might happen later in the story. Reread lines 15–18. How do Harry's thoughts upon first arriving on Mars foreshadow later events in the story?

6. **Analyze Character** Harry changes throughout the story. Using an organizer like the one shown, record his attitude and appearance at the beginning, middle, and end of the story.

Beginning		Middle		End
• • •	→	• • •	→	• • •

7. **Make Inferences** Who do you think will resist change the most, the captain or the lieutenant? Use examples from the story to support your answer.

8. **Evaluate Science Fiction** Reread Bradbury's first answer from the interview on page 462. Note that he does not consider himself a science fiction writer. In light of this information, do you think it is right to label "Dark They Were, and Golden-Eyed" as science fiction? Explain your answer, using support from the selection, the chart you created as you read, and the interview.

Extension and Challenge

9. **Big Question Activity** Reread the Big Question on page 444. Suppose you are Harry Bittering. Write a journal entry in which you answer the question about **change** from his point of view after he has moved up to the villa.

10.  **SCIENCE CONNECTION** Find out more about Mars by visiting the library in your school or neighborhood. What do we now know about the planet? What plans are scientists making to study it further? Focus your research on what interests you most. Report your findings to the class.

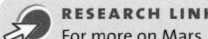 **RESEARCH LINKS**
For more on Mars, visit the **Research Center** at ClassZone.com.

Practice and Apply

After Reading

For additional support of post-reading questions, use these copy masters:

R RESOURCE MANAGER—Copy Masters
Reading Check p. 34 (to check understanding of the selection)
Mood p. 27 (for practice of literary analysis standards focus)
Question Support p. 35 (**After Reading** questions adapted for English learners and less-proficient readers)

Additional selection questions are provided for teachers on page 21.

For additional activities to challenge students, see

ⓘ Power Thinking at **ClassZone.com**

ANSWERS

Comprehension

1. *The Bitterings settle on Mars to escape a predicted atomic war on Earth.*

2. *The rockets are destroyed in an Earth war.*

3. *Timelines should include all major events.*

Literary Analysis
Possible answers:

4. ● **STANDARDS FOCUS** *Mood Students may say that the mood is tense, eerie, scary, or suspenseful. Supporting examples will vary.*

5. *Just as Harry fears, the Bitterings lose their identities.*

6. *Beginning: scared, fights changes, blue eyes; Middle: accepts some changes, eyes turn golden, uses Martian words; End: abandons belongings, calls humans "others"*

7. *The captain will resist the changes more because he wants to bring Earth culture to Mars, shown by his effort to rename places.*

8. ■ **STANDARDS FOCUS** *Reading Science Fiction Some students may say yes, because it fits criteria in their charts. Others may say no, because it is impossible, and Bradbury says science fiction is "the art of the possible."*

Extension and Challenge

9. *Students' responses should be written in the form of journal entries and use the first-person point of view. They may or may not presume that Harry can remember that he has changed, but all should clearly address the idea of whether where you are can change who you are.*

10.  **SCIENCE CONNECTION** *Students' reports should include a thesis statement and evidence from multiple sources that supports that thesis. When reporting findings to the class, students should introduce the topic, present the information logically, and offer a conclusion. Presenters should make sure that they communicate the significance of the topic.*

ANSWERS

Vocabulary in Context

VOCABULARY PRACTICE

1. *(a) a grandfather clock*
2. *(c) a lonely child*
3. *(a) your supply of money*
4. *(b) a gradually dimming light*
5. *(b) a friendly crowd*
6. *(b) a weak argument*
7. *(a) a plane flying away*
8. *(b) a person considering choices*

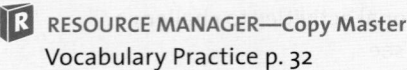 **RESOURCE MANAGER—Copy Master**
Vocabulary Practice p. 32

VOCABULARY IN WRITING

Ask students to recall some of the most significant changes. Have them think about how the changes occurred and what the Bitterings felt at the time.

VOCABULARY STRATEGY: THE LATIN ROOT
pend (also an EL language objective)

Help students look for context clues, such as "wears" and "around her neck" in sentence 1. Encourage students to break the word into parts and use familiar prefixes or suffixes, such as *-ful* ("full of"), to help figure out the meaning of the word.

Answers:

1. *pendant*
2. *dependent*
3. *suspenseful*
4. *suspenders*
5. *impending*

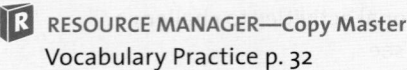 **RESOURCE MANAGER—Copy Master**
Vocabulary Strategy p. 33

ℹ️ **Vocabulary Center at ClassZone.com**
Additional Vocabulary Activities

Vocabulary in Context

VOCABULARY PRACTICE

Write the letter of the phrase that has a connection to each vocabulary word.

1. **pendulum:** (a) a grandfather clock, (b) a racing motorcycle, (c) a gossiping man
2. **forlorn:** (a) a heavy snowfall, (b) a bitter quarrel, (c) a lonely child
3. **dwindle:** (a) your supply of money, (b) your age, (c) your science textbook
4. **subtly:** (a) a fireworks show, (b) a gradually dimming light, (c) a long bus ride
5. **convivial:** (a) a dog and a squirrel, (b) a friendly crowd, (c) a curving staircase
6. **flimsy:** (a) a stuffed chair, (b) a weak argument, (c) a party in a yard
7. **recede:** (a) a plane flying away, (b) an arriving plane, (c) a plane parked at a gate
8. **muse:** (a) a noisy band, (b) a person considering choices, (c) a windy day

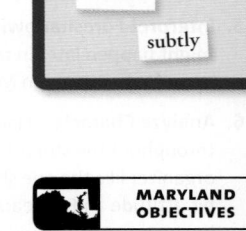

convivial

dwindle

flimsy

forlorn

muse

pendulum

recede

subtly

VOCABULARY IN WRITING

In a paragraph, describe the series of changes that affect the Bitterings. Use three or more vocabulary words. You might start like this.

> **EXAMPLE SENTENCE**
>
> The changes that gradually overtake the Bitterings begin **subtly**.

 **MARYLAND OBJECTIVES**

READING STANDARD
1.D.3.b Use word structure to determine meaning

VOCABULARY STRATEGY: THE LATIN ROOT *pend*

The vocabulary word *pendulum* contains the Latin root *pend*, which means "hang." This root, which is sometimes spelled *pens*, is found in many English words. To understand the meaning of words with *pend* or *pens*, use context clues and your knowledge of the root's meaning.

 **VOCABULARY PRACTICE**
For more practice, go to the **Vocabulary Center** at **ClassZone.com**.

PRACTICE Choose the word from the web that best completes each sentence. Then explain how the root *pend* relates to the meaning of the word.

1. She wears that _____ around her neck every day.
2. My choice is _____ on what you decide to do.
3. The book was so _____ that he couldn't stop reading it.
4. To hold up his pants, Dad prefers _____ to belts.
5. They could not shake off their feeling of _____ trouble.

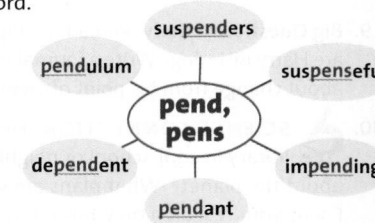

DIFFERENTIATED INSTRUCTION

FOR ENGLISH LEARNERS

Vocabulary: Cognates Encourage students who speak Latin-based languages to brainstorm words containing the Latin root *pend*, such as the Spanish cognates *suspense* and *suspensión*. Ask them to skim the story and note three other words that are similar to those in a Latin-based language.

FOR ADVANCED LEARNERS/PRE–AP

Vocabulary Strategy Have students write a descriptive paragraph about the story's setting or mood using at least three words that contain the Latin root *pend*.

Reading-Writing Connection

Increase your understanding of "Dark They Were, and Golden-Eyed" by responding to these prompts. Then complete the **Grammar and Writing** exercise.

WRITING PROMPTS	SELF-CHECK

A. Short Response: Write a Letter
Bradbury originally named "Dark They Were, and Golden-Eyed" "The Naming of Names." Which title do you think is more appropriate? Using details and examples from the story, write a **one-paragraph letter** to the author to explain your choice.

A strong letter will . . .
- directly address Ray Bradbury
- include a well-supported opinion

B. Extended Response: Evaluate Ideas
Should all **change** be feared and resisted, or does it depend on the types of changes and why they are happening? Write a **two- or three-paragraph response,** citing examples from the story and from your own experiences.

An effective response will . . .
- show an understanding of the question
- use evidence from the story as support

GRAMMAR AND WRITING

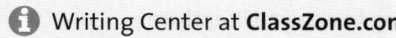 **MARYLAND OBJECTIVES**

LANGUAGE STANDARD
5.B.2.a Apply appropriate subject/verb agreement

MAINTAIN SUBJECT-VERB AGREEMENT In any sentence you write, a verb must **agree in number** with its subject. *Number* refers to whether a word is singular or plural. Be especially careful when you form a sentence that is a question or when you use the word *doesn't* or *don't* in a sentence.

> *Original:* The human don't seem to notice the changes.
>
> *Revised:* The human doesn't seem to notice the changes.
> *(The subject* human *is singular, so the verb should be too.)*

PRACTICE Choose the verb form that agrees in number with each subject.

1. Harry Bittering resists these changes, but he (don't, doesn't) convince the others to resist.
2. Soon the adults and children (starts, start) to use Martian names.
3. How (does, do) Harry and his family cope with these changes?
4. The Bittering family and the other humans (move, moves) into villas on the hill.

*For more help with subject-verb agreement in number, see pages R65–R67 in the **Grammar Handbook.***

FOR LESS–PROFICIENT WRITERS

For Prompt A:

- Have students decide which title is more appropriate.
- Help students to recall and then locate two supporting examples from the story.
- Have them summarize each example in two sentences that make a clear connection between the example and the choice of title.
- Suggest that students open the letter with a statement of opinion, followed by the examples.

For Prompt B:

- Limit the response to two paragraphs.
- Help students form a statement of opinion.
- Have each student list three examples that support the opinion.
- Allow pairs to compare and develop their opinions and examples.

Reading-Writing Connection

WRITING PROMPTS

- For **Prompt A,** have students focus on finding examples that support their choice of title. Ask them to skim the story for details about naming or physical changes and think about the effect of these details.

- For **Prompt B,** have students brainstorm using a concept map that shows relationships between ideas and evidence. Suggest that students begin their response with an example that dramatically illustrates their opinion.

For an extended Reading-Writing Connection activity, see

ⓘ Writing Center at **ClassZone.com**

GRAMMAR AND WRITING

Write these sentences on the board. Ask students to choose the verb form that agrees with each subject.

> The eyes of the Martian (shine, shines) gold in the evening light. *(shine)*
>
> The rocket men (was, were) surprised to meet the natives. *(were)*

R RESOURCE MANAGER—Copy Master
Maintain Subject-Verb Agreement p. 36

Assess and Reteach

Assess

R RESOURCE MANAGER—Copy Masters
Selection Tests A, B/C pp. 39–40, 41–42

Test Generator CD

Reteach

S STANDARDS LESSON FILE
Literature Lesson 36: Mood
Vocabulary Lesson 10: Latin Roots (active verbs)
Grammar Lesson 3: Agreement in Number

Focus and Motivate

OBJECTIVES

Literary Analysis
- explore the key idea of being **brave**
- identify and analyze elements of style
- read a short story

Reading
- understand dialogue

Vocabulary
- build vocabulary for reading and writing
- understand and use specialized vocabulary
  (also an EL language objective)

Grammar and Writing
- maintain subject-verb agreement when using compound subjects
- use writing to analyze literature

SUMMARY

In "A Day's Wait," a young boy with a temperature of 102 degrees has heard that a temperature of 44 degrees is high enough to kill someone. He spends the day waiting to die, while his father, unaware of his fears, hunts quail. Finally, the boy learns that the 44 degrees refers to Celsius, not Fahrenheit.

Is it B R A V E *to suffer in silence?*

Discuss the question and **KEY IDEA** with students. Take a class vote on whether it is more **brave** to suffer in silence than to voice one's fears. Record the tally to compare with a vote to be taken after students have read the story. Then have them do the **QUICKWRITE** activity.

Selection Resources

A Day's Wait
Short Story by Ernest Hemingway

Is it B R A V E
to suffer in silence?

MARYLAND OBJECTIVES

READING/LIT STANDARDS
1.E.3.a Select and apply appropriate strategies during reading
3.A.7.a Analyze how specific language choices create style

KEY IDEA Whether from an injury or a broken heart, everyone suffers at times. Some people try hard to keep their pain to themselves, while others believe it is better to share their thoughts and feelings with others. In "A Day's Wait," a young boy tries to be **brave** while suffering from an illness.

QUICKWRITE Do you consider it an act of bravery to face pain on your own, or does it take more courage for you to open up to other people? In a journal entry, explain your answers to these questions.

466

---

* Resources for Differentiation   † Also in Spanish   ‡ In Haitian Creole and Vietnamese

LITERARY ANALYSIS: STYLE

Style is a writer's unique way of communicating ideas. It is often not only what writers say but how they say it that gives stories meaning and makes them memorable. To identify a writer's style, focus on these elements:

- **Word choice,** or the author's choice of language. Hemingway strives to use vivid verbs and precise nouns rather than using many adjectives and adverbs.
- **Sentence structure** and variety. In this story, Hemingway often uses long sentences for descriptions and short sentences when characters are talking.
- **Dialogue,** or conversations between characters. Hemingway relies heavily on realistic dialogue to "tell" his stories.

As you read "A Day's Wait," notice how these elements help create Hemingway's unique writing style.

READING SKILL: UNDERSTAND DIALOGUE

Characters reveal much about themselves by what they say or don't say. When reading **dialogue,** note that

- each speaker's words are framed by quotes
- the line is indented when someone new is speaking

As you read "A Day's Wait," keep track of who's speaking by using a chart like the one shown.

Line	Speaker
"What's the matter, Schatz?"	narrator

VOCABULARY IN CONTEXT

Each of the boldfaced terms reflects Hemingway's **word choice** in "A Day's Wait." How many of these words do you know? Try to figure out the meaning of each.

1. People were there, but he felt **detached** from them.
2. There is a serious flu **epidemic** this winter.
3. He had **slack** muscles from lack of exercise.
4. It was **evidently** too much for him to deal with.
5. The man observed a **covey** of partridges.

Author Online

An Adventurous Life
Ernest Hemingway lived a life full of adventure. He was one of a group of writers called the Lost Generation. These writers rejected what they saw as an American focus on acquiring

Ernest Hemingway
1899–1961

many possessions. Along with being one of America's most famous writers, Hemingway was a fisherman, a hunter, and a fan of bullfighting. He participated in both world wars. Many of his works are based on his experiences in Europe and Cuba.

An Influential Style Hemingway and other Lost Generation writers, including F. Scott Fitzgerald and Sherwood Anderson, expressed their ideas in writing styles that were new and different. Hemingway's writing style, particularly his method of writing dialogue, has influenced many other writers. He is one of the most often imitated writers of the 1900s.

Fact Becomes Fiction Like much of Hemingway's writing, "A Day's Wait" is based on actual events in Hemingway's life. While Hemingway was living in France, his son came down with a high fever and reacted similarly to the boy in the story you will read.

 MORE ABOUT THE AUTHOR
For more on Ernest Hemingway, visit the **Literature Center** at **ClassZone.com.**

Teach

STANDARDS FOCUS

● STYLE

Read aloud this example:

> The boy's knuckles gleamed white. His jaw clenched, holding in his cries. All the while, the silver needle flashed in and out, stitching the flaps of his skin together. When asked how he was doing, his reply was, "Fine, thank you."

Ask students to describe the writer's style, in terms of word choice and sentence structure. *Possible answer: The writer uses strong verbs ("gleamed," "clenched," "flashed") to show the boy's distress. Commas link the details in quick succession, making the flow of his experience seem more realistic.*

CHECK UNDERSTANDING Ask students how they think the boy is really feeling.

READING SKILL

■ UNDERSTAND DIALOGUE

Ask students what they learn about the boy's character from his dialogue in the passage above. *Possible answer: He is polite. He is determined not to reveal his pain.*

CHECK UNDERSTANDING Ask students for examples of memorable dialogue from movies they have seen.

 RESOURCE MANAGER—Copy Master
Understand Dialogue p. 55 (for student use while reading the selection)

VOCABULARY SKILL

▲ VOCABULARY IN CONTEXT

DIAGNOSE WORD KNOWLEDGE To determine preteaching needs, have all students complete **Vocabulary in Context.** Check students' answers against the definitions in the story: *detached* (p. 470), *epidemic* (p. 470), *slack* (p. 472), *evidently* (p. 472), *covey* (p. 471).

PRETEACH VOCABULARY Use the Vocabulary Study copy master to help students explore the meaning of each boldfaced word.

1. Read sentence 1 aloud, emphasizing *slack*.
2. Point out the context word "tightened." Discuss possible meanings for *slack,* such as "loose or relaxed."
3. Help students predict how the word might relate to one of the story elements.
4. Repeat the procedure for sentences 2–5.

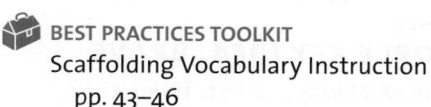 RESOURCE MANAGER—Copy Master
Vocabulary Study p. 57

For general guidelines on differentiating vocabulary instruction and for alternative vocabulary activities for students not needing vocabulary preteaching, see

BEST PRACTICES TOOLKIT
Scaffolding Vocabulary Instruction pp. 43–46
ⓘ Vocabulary Center at **ClassZone.com**
Additional Vocabulary Activities

ANALYZE VISUALS

Possible answer: The boy's expression conveys worry and preoccupation.

About the Art The American artist Alice Kent Stoddard (ca. 1885–1976) specialized in portraits, such as the one shown here. She is particularly well known for her paintings of prominent citizens.

READING SKILL

Ⓐ DIALOGUE

Point out that the narrator is the first speaker. Tell students that speakers usually alternate in a passage of dialogue. Review the speakers that they identify in their charts. *Possible answers:*

Line	Speaker
"What's the matter, Schatz?" (line 4)	narrator
"I've got a headache." (line 5)	Schatz
"You better go back to bed." (line 6)	narrator
"No. I'm all right." (line 7)	Schatz
"You go to bed. I'll see you when I'm dressed." (line 8)	narrator

Extend the Discussion What does Schatz's reaction to his headache reveal about his character?

Lines 12–13
REINFORCE *KEY IDEA:* BRAVE

Discuss In what way is Schatz trying to be **brave?** Why do you think he is behaving like this? *Possible answer: He is saying that he feels all right even though he doesn't. He may not want the narrator to worry.*

A DAY'S WAIT

ERNEST HEMINGWAY

He came into the room to shut the windows while we were still in bed and I saw he looked ill. He was shivering, his face was white, and he walked slowly as though it ached to move.

"What's the matter, Schatz?"[1]

"I've got a headache."

"You better go back to bed."

"No. I'm all right."

"You go to bed. I'll see you when I'm dressed." Ⓐ

But when I came downstairs he was dressed, sitting by the fire, looking
10 a very sick and miserable boy of nine years. When I put my hand on his forehead I knew he had a fever.

"You go up to bed," I said, "you're sick."

"I'm all right," he said.

When the doctor came he took the boy's temperature.

"What is it?" I asked him.

"One hundred and two."

---

1. **Schatz** (shäts): German term of affection meaning "my treasure," used here as a nickname.

Contemplation (1930), Alice Kent Stoddard. Oil on canvas

ANALYZE VISUALS
Consider the expression on this boy's face. What **mood** does it convey?

① **Targeted Passage**

Ⓐ **DIALOGUE**
Reread the dialogue in lines 4–8. Notice that Hemingway does not always tell the reader who is speaking. Use your chart to keep track of the different speakers.

DIFFERENTIATED INSTRUCTION

FOR ALL STUDENTS

Interest Stations Create these interest stations and post suggested assignments for students to work on independently:

- **Survey on Bravery** Create a survey about bravery and conduct a poll.
- **Influenza Research** Investigate and create a bulletin board about this disease.
- **Dialogue** Write realistic dialogue that could be used in a story.

R RESOURCE MANAGER
Ideas for Extension pp. 48–49

FOR LESS–PROFICIENT READERS

In combination with the *Audio Anthology CD*, use one or more Targeted Passages (pp. 468, 470, 472) to ensure that students focus on key story events, concepts, and skills.

① **Targeted Passage [Lines 1–11]**

This passage relies mostly on dialogue to introduce the main characters (the narrator and Schatz) and the conflict: Schatz is sick.

- How can the narrator tell that Schatz is sick?
- What does the narrator tell Schatz to do?

BACKGROUND

Influenza In this story, the main character Schatz has influenza. Influenza, or the flu, as it is commonly called, has a variety of symptoms including fever, headache, tiredness, and body aches, all of which Schatz suffers from. However, it is the fever that most concerns the boy. In fact, fever is not a sickness. A mild fever is one way the body fights off infection. By raising the temperature a few degrees above normal, the body can create an environment in which it is too warm for many kinds of bacteria and viruses to survive.

• Why do you think Schatz refuses to do what the narrator tells him?

FOR ENGLISH LEARNERS

Key Academic Vocabulary Have groups use New Word Analysis to study this vocabulary: *areas* (line 29), *commenced* (line 84), *normal* (line 98), *relaxed* (lines 103, 104).

 BEST PRACTICES TOOLKIT—Transparency
New Word Analysis p. E8

Prereading For prereading instruction for English learners, see

BEST PRACTICES TOOLKIT
Scaffolding Reading Instruction pp. 43–46

FOR ADVANCED LEARNERS/PRE–AP

Pre-AP exercises in the bottom channel provide additional challenge for your advanced students. Use them for small groups or individuals.

ADDITIONAL GUIDELINES

For more help with differentiation and tips for classroom management, see

 BEST PRACTICES TOOLKIT
Differentiated Instruction pp. 31–38

B STYLE

Possible answer: The narrator is revealed as Schatz's father through this dialogue. The author's style is to reveal details in a natural way as the story unfolds, rather than to provide a lot of explanation at the beginning of the story.

READING SKILL

C DIALOGUE

Students should fill in their charts from page 467 with the lines of dialogue in this passage. *Answer:*

- line 27—narrator
- line 28—Schatz
- line 33—narrator
- line 34—Schatz
- line 39—narrator
- line 40—Schatz
- lines 41–42—Schatz
- line 43—narrator
- line 44—Schatz

LITERARY ANALYSIS

D STYLE

Possible answer: The description conveys a treacherous, threatening setting. Hemingway's words create a vivid image of a frozen world encased in ice.

If students need help ... List the descriptive words and phrases that Hemingway uses in this passage: *bright, cold, sleet, frozen, varnished with ice, frozen, glassy surface, slipped, slithered, hard, slide away.* Classify each word or phrase as either positive or negative.

Extend the Discussion How is Hemingway's style in the narrative passages, such as this one, different from the way he writes dialogue?

Downstairs, the doctor left three different medicines in different-colored capsules with instructions for giving them. One was to bring down the fever, another a purgative,[2] the third to overcome an acid 20 condition. The germs of influenza can only exist in an acid condition, he explained. He seemed to know all about influenza and said there was nothing to worry about if the fever did not go above one hundred and four degrees. This was a light **epidemic** of flu and there was no danger if you avoided pneumonia.

Back in the room I wrote the boy's temperature down and made a note of the time to give the various capsules.

"Do you want me to read to you?"

"All right. If you want to," said the boy. His face was very white and there were dark areas under his eyes. He lay still in the bed and seemed 30 very **detached** from what was going on.

I read aloud from Howard Pyle's *Book of Pirates;*[3] but I could see he was not following what I was reading.

"How do you feel, Schatz?" I asked him.

"Just the same, so far," he said.

I sat at the foot of the bed and read to myself while I waited for it to be time to give another capsule. It would have been natural for him to go to sleep, but when I looked up he was looking at the foot of the bed, looking very strangely.

"Why don't you try to go to sleep? I'll wake you up for the medicine."

40 "I'd rather stay awake."

After a while he said to me, "You don't have to stay in here with me, Papa, if it bothers you." **B**

"It doesn't bother me."

"No, I mean you don't have to stay if it's going to bother you." **C**

I thought perhaps he was a little lightheaded and after giving him the prescribed capsules at eleven o'clock I went out for a while.

It was a bright, cold day, the ground covered with a sleet that had frozen so that it seemed as if all the bare trees, the bushes, the cut brush, and all the grass and the bare ground had been varnished with ice. I took the 50 young Irish setter for a little walk up the road and along a frozen creek, but it was difficult to stand or walk on the glassy surface and the red dog slipped and slithered and I fell twice, hard, once dropping my gun and having it slide away over the ice. **D**

---

2. **purgative** (pûr'gə-tĭv): laxative.

3. **Howard Pyle's *Book of Pirates:*** a collection of tales about real and fictional pirates, very popular when it was published in the 1920s.

---

epidemic (ĕp'ĭ-dĕm'ĭk) *n.* an outbreak of a disease that spreads quickly among many people

detached (dĭ-tăcht') *adj.* separated; disconnected **detach** *v.*

② Targeted Passage

B STYLE
Reread lines 41–42. Hemingway reveals the narrator through dialogue. What does this tell you about his style?

C DIALOGUE
Use your chart to track the speakers in the dialogue in lines 27–44.

D STYLE
Do the words Hemingway uses to describe the **setting** convey a positive or negative atmosphere? Explain.

DIFFERENTIATED INSTRUCTION

FOR LESS–PROFICIENT READERS

② Targeted Passage [Lines 27–46]

This passage highlights the author's use of dialogue to develop the plot: Schatz is struggling with an unnamed internal conflict.

- How does Schatz react when his father reads to him?
- What does Schatz do instead of sleeping?
- Why does the narrator think Schatz is lightheaded? What might be causing the boy to behave so strangely?

Reading Skill Follow-Up: Understand Dialogue Review students' charts with them. Make sure that they have correctly identified the speaker of each line of dialogue. Point out that when the order of speakers changes from every other line, the author usually inserts a tag, such as "he said." Draw students' attention to lines 40–42. Schatz speaks two lines in a row. The second line is introduced by "After a while he said to me" so readers understand who is speaking.

ANALYZE VISUALS
How does this painting convey the passing of time?

covey (kŭv'ē) *n.* a small group or flock of birds, especially partridges or quail

We flushed a <u>**covey**</u> of quail under a high clay bank with overhanging brush and I killed two as they went out of sight over the top of the bank. Some of the covey lit in trees, but most of them scattered into brush piles and it was necessary to jump on the ice-coated mounds of brush several times before they would flush. Coming out while you were poised unsteadily on the icy, springy brush, they made difficult shooting and I killed two, missed five, and started back pleased to have found a covey close to the house and happy there were so many left to find on another day.

FOR LESS–PROFICIENT READERS

Language: Pronoun Referents Help students understand what the pronoun *it* refers to as used throughout lines 47–57. Rewrite these phrases on the board: *It was a bright, cold day* ("The day was bright and cold"); *so that it seemed . . .* ("so that the trees, bushes, brush, . . . seemed varnished with ice"); *but it was difficult to stand or walk* ("but standing or walking was difficult"); *it was necessary to jump* ("I needed to jump").

FOR ADVANCED LEARNERS/PRE–AP

Evaluate Discuss how the relationship between the father and the son is central to the story's plot. Distribute copies of the Making Inferences chart. Ask students to use details in the story to make inferences about the way the father and son understand each other, how close they are, and the strengths and weaknesses of their relationship. Have students share their charts in small groups.

🧰 **BEST PRACTICES TOOLKIT—Transparency**
Making Inferences p. A13

ANALYZE VISUALS

Possible answer: *The passing of time is suggested by the light and shadow falling across the chair.*

Lines 54–62
DISCUSSION PROMPTS

Use these prompts to help students examine and understand the importance of the narrator's character to the story:

Connect Do you enjoy being outdoors on a cold day? How does your experience help you understand how the narrator reacts to the cold weather? Does he enjoy it? *Students might say that being out in the cold can be energizing. The narrator must enjoy cold weather or he would not have decided to go hunting.*

Infer What do you learn about the narrator's character from his attitude toward hunting? ***Possible answers:*** *He is quite persistent and not easily discouraged. He enjoys challenges. He accepts the outcome. He is hardy and tough.*

Synthesize What values do you think the narrator has passed on to his son, based on what you learn about him in this passage? ***Possible answer:*** *The narrator's character suggests that he values perseverance, endurance, and strength.*

Lines 86–95
DISCUSSION PROMPTS

Use these prompts to help students understand the reasons for Schatz's internal conflict:

Connect Do you sometimes avoid talking about something that frightens you? Why or why not? *Students may respond that saying something frightening aloud makes it seem more real.*

Infer Why do you think Schatz finally asks his father when he is going to die? ***Possible answers:*** *He didn't think it would take so long. He feels puzzled at his father's casual attitude. He wants to make the most of his remaining time.*

Synthesize How does the narrator feel when he realizes what his son has been going through? ***Possible answer:*** *He feels sorry for his son. He may also feel amazed that his son did not share his thoughts sooner.*

 SCIENCE CONNECTION

The Celsius, or centigrade, scale is commonly used in most countries, although not the United States. The formula for converting Fahrenheit to Celsius is $C = 5/9 (F − 32)$. Using this formula, Schatz's temperature is about 39 degrees C.

Lines 103–105
REINFORCE *KEY IDEA:* BRAVE

Discuss Why is there no longer a need for Schatz to be **brave**? ***Possible answers:*** *Now he knows he is not going to die. The relief after being so worried is too much for him.*

SELECTION WRAP–UP

REFLECT Have students think about how the narrator's expectations of his son influence Schatz's reactions to his illness.

⭐ **CRITIQUE** Ask students to evaluate the believability of the father-and-son relationship in this story. How does it compare to other similar relationships students know of?

READING FLUENCY

Distribute the copy masters and have students work in groups to practice fluency.

R **RESOURCE MANAGER—Copy Master**
Reading Fluency p. 63

At the house they said the boy had refused to let anyone come into the room.

"You can't come in," he said. "You mustn't get what I have."

I went up to him and found him in exactly the position I had left him, white-faced, but with the tops of his cheeks flushed by the fever, staring still, as he had stared, at the foot of the bed.

I took his temperature.

70 "What is it?"

"Something like a hundred," I said. It was one hundred and two and four tenths.

"It was a hundred and two," he said.

"Who said so?"

"The doctor."

"Your temperature is all right," I said. "It's nothing to worry about."

"I don't worry," he said, "but I can't keep from thinking."

"Don't think," I said. "Just take it easy."

"I'm taking it easy," he said and looked straight ahead. He was

80 **evidently** holding tight onto himself about something.

"Take this with water."

"Do you think it will do any good?"

"Of course it will."

I sat down and opened the *Pirate* book and commenced to read, but I could see he was not following, so I stopped.

"About what time do you think I'm going to die?" he asked.

"What?"

"About how long will it be before I die?"

"You aren't going to die. What's the matter with you?"

90 "Oh, yes, I am. I heard him say a hundred and two."

"People don't die with a fever of one hundred and two. That's a silly way to talk."

"I know they do. At school in France the boys told me you can't live with forty-four degrees. I've got a hundred and two."

He had been waiting to die all day, ever since nine o'clock in the morning.

"You poor Schatz," I said. "Poor old Schatz. It's like miles and kilometers. You aren't going to die. That's a different thermometer. On that thermometer thirty-seven is normal. On this kind it's ninety-eight."

"Are you sure?"

100 "Absolutely," I said. "It's like miles and kilometers. You know, like how many kilometers we make when we do seventy miles in the car?"

"Oh," he said.

But his gaze at the foot of the bed relaxed slowly. The hold over himself relaxed too, finally, and the next day it was very **slack** and he cried very easily at little things that were of no importance. ✍

evidently (ĕv′ĭ-dənt-lē) *adv.* obviously; clearly

 **SCIENCE CONNECTION**

On the Celsius scale, water freezes at 0° and boils at 100°. On the Fahrenheit scale, water freezes at 32° and boils at 212°.

3 **Targeted Passage**

slack (slăk) *adj.* not firm or tight; loose

DIFFERENTIATED INSTRUCTION

FOR LESS–PROFICIENT READERS
3 Targeted Passage [Lines 86–105]

The climax, turning point, and resolution unfold when the main character's internal conflict is revealed: Schatz finds out that he is not going to die.

- Why does Schatz think he is going to die?
- What does his father explain to him?
- How does Schatz feel when he learns the truth?
- What internal conflict is resolved in this passage?

FOR ENGLISH LEARNERS
Comprehension: Self-Monitor Help students check their understanding of the story by using a Reciprocal Teaching strategy to summarize it. Mixed-ability groups should work through the steps of summarizing, questioning, and clarifying. After group discussion, address any areas of confusion that members are unable to clear up or any remaining questions that students have.

 BEST PRACTICES TOOLKIT—Transparency
Reciprocal Teaching p. A35

Comprehension

1. **Recall** Why does the boy think he is going to die?

2. **Clarify** Why does the father spend the afternoon hunting instead of staying with his worried son?

3. **Summarize** How does the story end?

Literary Analysis

4. **Understand Dialogue** Look over the dialogue chart you created as you read. At which points do the father and son not seem to understand each other?

5. **Analyze Character** In what ways does the boy show concern for others?

6. **Draw Conclusions** Why does the boy cry so much the next day?

7. **Make Judgments** Do you think the boy's actions show **bravery?** Why or why not? Support your answer with examples from the story. Use a diagram like the one shown to record your support. Use line numbers when referring to parts of the story.

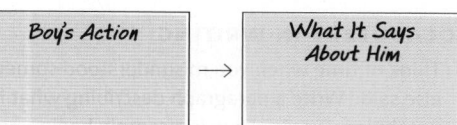

Boy's Action → What It Says About Him

8. **Identify Style** Reread lines 65–83. Note Hemingway's **word choice, sentence structure,** and use of **dialogue.** Why is this passage a good example of Hemingway's style? Explain your answer, using evidence from the passage.

Extension and Challenge

9. **Creative Project: Drama** Most of this story is told through **dialogue** between the father and son. With a partner, choose one of their conversations to act out. Use details from the scene to accurately portray the characters. Practice on your own, and then present the dialogue to the class.

10. **Readers' Circle** With a small group, discuss what clues the story gives you about the relationship between the boy and his father. Consider whether this experience is likely to affect their relationship in any way. If so, how?

MARYLAND OBJECTIVES

LITERATURE STANDARD
3.A.7.a Analyze how specific language choices create style

Practice and Apply

After Reading

For additional support of post-reading questions, use these copy masters:

 RESOURCE MANAGER—Copy Masters

Reading Check p. 60 (to check understanding of the selection)

Style p. 53 (for practice of literary analysis standards focus)

Question Support p. 61 (**After Reading** questions adapted for English learners and less-proficient readers)

Additional selection questions are provided for teachers on page 47.

For additional activities to challenge students, see

i Power Thinking at **ClassZone.com**

ANSWERS

Comprehension

1. *The boy's fever is 102 degrees. He has heard a temperature of over 44 degrees is fatal. He does not know that 44 refers to Celsius and his temperature is Fahrenheit.*

2. *The father figures he can go out for a short time while the boy rests. He does not know that Schatz thinks he is dying.*

3. *The father explains the misunderstanding, and the boy is relieved. The boy cries often the next day.*

Literary Analysis

Possible answers:

4. ■ **STANDARDS FOCUS** *Understand Dialogue Students may point out lines 39–44. Schatz says that his father can leave if "it" bothers him, meaning watching his son die. The father thinks "it" means just sitting with the boy.*

5. *He keeps his fear of dying to himself. He excuses his father from staying with him. He won't let others in the room in case they catch what he has.*

6. *The boy waits a whole day before telling his father his fear of dying. Once he knows he is not going to die, he can release the emotions that he had kept to himself.*

7. *Boy's Action: He keeps his fears to himself so that he does not upset his father (lines 28–30). What It Says: He is brave and kind, but also a bit foolish.*

---

8. ● **STANDARDS FOCUS** *Style This passage is a good example because it shows realistic dialogue, such as "Something like a hundred" (line 71). It creates vivid images through precise words, such as "white-faced, but with the tops of his cheeks flushed by the fever" (line 67). It also illustrates Hemingway's characteristic style of using long sentences for narrative and short sentences for dialogue.*

Extension and Challenge

9. *Students should choose one of the major passages of dialogue, such as lines 27–44 or 70–101, to perform.*

10. *Students' discussions should bring out the idea that although there seems to be affection between the boy and his father, their relationship is distant. They act more like two adults than a father and son. The experience might teach the father to try to be more understanding and sensitive and might teach the boy to share more.*

ANSWERS

Vocabulary in Context

VOCABULARY PRACTICE

1. *true*
2. *false*
3. *true*
4. *true*
5. *false*

 RESOURCE MANAGER—Copy Master
Vocabulary Practice p. 58

VOCABULARY IN WRITING

Students may find it helpful to brainstorm incidents first. Distribute copies of the Reporter's Questions transparency to help students identify important details to include in their paragraphs. Students should then relate two of the vocabulary words to the details they have noted.

📦 **BEST PRACTICES TOOLKIT—Transparency**
Reporter's Questions p. C9

VOCABULARY STRATEGY: WORDS FOR ANIMAL GROUPS *(also an EL language objective)*

Tell students that when they do a matching activity, they should narrow down their choices by matching the terms they know first. Students can then make educated guesses or use a dictionary to figure out the meanings of the remaining words.

Answers:

1. *e*
2. *f*
3. *a*
4. *c*
5. *b*
6. *d*

 RESOURCE MANAGER—Copy Master
Vocabulary Strategy p. 59

ℹ️ **Vocabulary Center at ClassZone.com**
Additional Vocabulary Activities

Vocabulary in Context

VOCABULARY PRACTICE

Show that you understand the boldfaced words by deciding whether each statement is true or false.

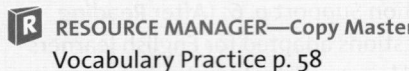

1. If something is **evidently** true, it has been proven through a series of experiments.
2. A **covey** is a place where birds and small mammals go to spend the winter.
3. An **epidemic** generally affects a large number of people.
4. If you are **detached** from a situation, you are probably not very concerned about it.
5. Tightened muscles around someone's lips and jaw are typical of a **slack** expression.

VOCABULARY IN WRITING

Think of time when you misunderstood something important that someone else said. Write a paragraph describing what happened, using at least two vocabulary words. Here is a sample beginning.

> **EXAMPLE SENTENCE**
>
> *At camp I thought I heard, "It's time for nights out," but I was **evidently** wrong.*

VOCABULARY STRATEGY: WORDS FOR ANIMAL GROUPS

There are many names for groups of animals. Some, like the vocabulary word *covey*, are used mainly with one or two specific types of animals. Others, like *herd*, are used when describing animals in certain categories, such as large animals that move or feed together (a herd of elephants, a herd of antelope). Knowing the correct word for an animal group can enrich both your reading and your writing.

PRACTICE Match each numbered word for an animal group with the type of animal it is usually associated with. Refer to a dictionary if you need help.

1. pride   **a.** cattle
2. swarm   **b.** fish
3. drove   **c.** wolves
4. pack   **d.** birds
5. school   **e.** lions
6. flock   **f.** bees

MARYLAND OBJECTIVES

READING STANDARD
1.D.3.c Use resources to confirm definitions

VOCABULARY PRACTICE
For more practice, go to the **Vocabulary Center** at **ClassZone.com.**

DIFFERENTIATED INSTRUCTION

FOR ENGLISH LEARNERS
Vocabulary Strategy

1. Have students make flashcards for each of the words in column 1.
2. Explain that they should draw a picture on one side of the card and write the correct term on the back.
3. Have students test each other with their flashcards.

FOR ADVANCED LEARNERS/PRE–AP

Vocabulary Strategy Challenge students to find and define additional terms for groups of animals (for example, *bevy, cete, covert, gaggle, murder, pod,* and so on). Have students put together a small, illustrated glossary of the words they find as well as the vocabulary words.

Reading-Writing Connection

Increase your understanding of "A Day's Wait" by responding to these prompts. Then complete the **Grammar and Writing** exercise.

WRITING PROMPTS

A. Short Response: Evaluate Characterization
According to Hemingway, "A writer should create living people; people not characters." Do you think he creates real people in "A Day's Wait"? Write a **one-paragraph response,** using details from the story to support your opinion.

B. Extended Response: Write a Letter
Imagine how Schatz would remember this day 20 years later. Write a **two- or three-paragraph letter** from Schatz to his father in which he reminds his father about the misunderstanding and how it affected him.

SELF-CHECK

An effective evaluation will . . .
• include a clear position statement
• use specific details and examples from the story that support the statement

A creative response will . . .
• summarize the events of the story
• show an understanding of how the boy felt that day

GRAMMAR AND WRITING

MAINTAIN SUBJECT-VERB AGREEMENT A **compound subject** is made up of two or more subjects joined by a conjunction, such as *and, or,* or *nor.* When you write a sentence with a compound subject joined by *and,* you should usually use a plural verb. When you write a sentence with a compound subject joined by *or* or *nor,* use a verb that agrees in number with the subject.

MARYLAND OBJECTIVES

LANGUAGE STANDARD
5.B.2.a Apply appropriate subject/verb agreement

Original: Because Schatz is constantly worrying, neither the capsules nor rest seem to help him.

Revised: Because Schatz is constantly worrying, neither the capsules nor rest seems to help him.

PRACTICE Choose the verb form that agrees with each compound subject.

1. Parents and children sometimes (have, has) a problem talking to one another.

2. Often, the parents or the child (get, gets) confused about some information.

3. In the story, neither the father nor the boy (realize, realizes) the misunderstanding until later on.

4. Once they understand the problem, the boy and his father (relax, relaxes).

*For more help with subject-verb agreement with compound subjects, see pages R65–R66 in the **Grammar Handbook.***

DIFFERENTIATED INSTRUCTION

FOR LESS–PROFICIENT WRITERS

For Prompt A:

• In a T Chart, list traits of real people. Then match ways the characters show those traits. For example, real people often speak in fragments and do not always say what they feel.

• Help students write a position statement to explain some similarities from their charts.

BEST PRACTICES TOOLKIT—Transparency
T Chart p. A25

For Prompt B:

• Limit the letter to two paragraphs.

• Suggest that students organize their letters in this way:

First paragraph: Schatz recounts the incident and asks his father if he remembers it.

Second paragraph: Schatz explains how it affected him at the time and later in life.

Reading-Writing Connection

Reading-Writing Connection

WRITING PROMPTS

• For **Prompt A,** encourage students to consider the way the characters speak and interact with each other, the insights into their personalities that the author gives, and their reactions to events.

• For **Prompt B,** have students first list all of the ways the events might have affected Schatz. Ask them to pick the most important effects and to include those in the letter. Remind students to maintain the tone of a friendly letter from an adult son to his father.

For an extended Reading-Writing Connection activity, see

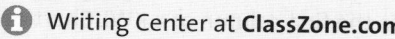 Writing Center at **ClassZone.com**

GRAMMAR AND WRITING

• After students examine the revised model, rewrite the sentence on the board with the two parts of the subject reversed. Point out that the verb must change to match the plural subject, which is now closer to it (". . . neither rest nor the **capsules seem** to help . . .").

• Before students begin the exercise, it might be helpful to identify the subjects and the conjunction in each sentence.

Answers:
1. *have*
2. *gets*
3. *realizes*
4. *relax*

RESOURCE MANAGER—Copy Master
Maintain Subject-Verb Agreement p. 62

Assess and Reteach

Assess

RESOURCE MANAGER—Copy Masters
Selection Tests A, B/C pp. 65–66, 67–68
Test Generator CD

Reteach

STANDARDS LESSON FILE
Literature Lesson 38: Style
Literature Lesson 35: Dialogue and Dialect
Grammar Lesson 4: Verb Agreement with Compound Subjects

Focus and Motivate

OBJECTIVES

Reading for Information
- distinguish fact from opinion
- write a set of instructions
- read a magazine article

SUMMARY

In this article, the writer explains Hemingway's creative process. He quotes advice that the author gave and received and presents insights based on Hemingway's work.

What's the Connection?

To help prepare students for the selection, record what they know about Hemingway's style of writing in the first column of a KWL Chart. For the second column, have students list questions about Hemingway's style or process. As students read the article, pause occasionally to record details in the last column.

 BEST PRACTICES TOOLKIT—Transparency
KWL Chart p. A21

Teach

Skill Focus: Distinguish Fact from Opinion

- Have volunteers read each column of the chart aloud. Ask students to give examples of facts and opinions.
- Point out that to be a fact, the information does not have to be accurate, but it must be verifiable. In other words, it must be possible to check or prove whether the information is accurate.
- Discuss and add these ideas to the opinion column: (1) Judgment words—words that show personal feeling—often indicate opinions. (2) Words such as *all, never, none,* and *always* often signal opinions.

Possible chart entries appear on page 478.

 RESOURCE MANAGER—Copy Master
Distinguish Fact from Opinion p. 75

Reading for Information

Use with "A Day's Wait," page 468.

 MARYLAND OBJECTIVES

INFO TEXT/WRITING STANDARDS
2.A.4.h Distinguish between a fact and an opinion
4.A.1.b.1 Organize information logically

How Hemingway Wrote
Informative Article

What's the Connection?

You've just read a short story by Ernest Hemingway, an author whose style is so distinct and admired that writers often try to copy it. Now you will read an **informative article** that explains how Hemingway approached writing.

Skill Focus: Distinguish Fact from Opinion

An **opinion** is a statement of belief or feeling, such as "I think everyone should read Hemingway's stories." A **fact** is a statement that can be proved, such as "Hemingway wrote many stories."

When you read informative articles, it's important to distinguish facts from opinions. If you mistake an opinion for a fact, you run the risk of basing your conclusions on someone's personal beliefs rather than on provable information. The opinions of experts can be good sources of information, but you should always know whether you are reading a fact or an opinion.

As you read Bruce Rettman's article, list the facts in one column and Rettman's opinions in another. Use the tips on the chart to help you distinguish facts from opinions.

FACT OR OPINION?

Is it a fact?	Is it an opinion?
Watch Out • Words and phrases often used to state facts: *the fact that, in fact, indeed, the truth is,* and *as a matter of fact.* • The same words and phrases used to state facts *may* be used to disguise opinions as facts. ▼	**Watch Out** Words and phrases often used to express opinions: *I think, I believe, perhaps,* and *maybe.* ▼
Can I prove it by • consulting a reliable source, such as a print or online encyclopedia? • interviewing a recognized expert in the field? • checking the statement against what I observe or know to be true? *If the answer is "yes" . . .* The statement is a **fact.**	**Ask yourself:** • Can this statement be debated? • Might people disagree with the statement? *If the answer is "yes" . . .* The statement is probably an **opinion.**

Selection Resources

 RESOURCE MANAGER UNIT 4

Plan and Teach pp. 69–72

Reading
Summary pp. 73†*, 74‡*
Distinguish Fact from Opinion pp. 75, 77†*
Create Instructions for Writers pp. 76, 78†*
Reading Check p. 79
Question Support p. 80*

Assessment
Selection Tests A, B/C pp. 81*, 83*

 Test Generator CD

Reading Support

Audio Anthology CD*

BEST PRACTICES TOOLKIT
KWL Chart • Jigsaw

* Resources for Differentiation   † Also in Spanish   ‡ In Haitian Creole and Vietnamese

How Hemingway Wrote. Ⓐ

by Bruce Rettman

Hemingway is shown here working on a story.

Ernest Hemingway said that the best writing advice he ever got came from the writing guidelines he received as a young reporter working for the *Kansas City Star*. These guidelines began as follows: "Use short sentences. Use short first paragraphs. Use vigorous English, not forgetting to strive for smoothness." Anyone who reads Hemingway's simple and direct sentences built on strong nouns and verbs—not "extravagant adjectives"—can see that he took those guidelines to heart. Ⓑ

Hemingway's own advice for becoming a good writer is also informative. "When people 20 talk, listen completely," said Hemingway to a young writer. "Don't be thinking what you're going to say. Most people never listen. Nor do they observe." In other words, Hemingway advises young writers to write from life, blending fact and fiction. The short story "A Day's Wait," for example, 30 is based on an actual time when Hemingway's first child had a fever.

READING FOR INFORMATION **477**

Ⓕ **OCUS ON FORM**
"How Hemingway Wrote" is an **informative article**, a nonfiction article written to provide information or to explain something about a topic.

Ⓐ **INFORMATIVE ARTICLE**
Now that you have read the title, what do you think this informative article will explain?

Ⓑ **DISTINGUISH FACT FROM OPINION**
To check whether the statements in lines 1–16 are accurate, who might you contact or what source might you consult?

Practice and Apply

FOCUS ON FORM

Discuss the purpose and characteristics of an informative article. This type of article

- is nonfiction
- provides useful factual information about real people, places, and events
- is easy to follow
- appears in magazines
- is based on primary and secondary sources

Ask students if they have read any informative articles recently. Invite them to list possible topics for this type of article.

LITERARY ANALYSIS

Ⓐ INFORMATIVE ARTICLE

Possible answers: This article will explain how Ernest Hemingway wrote. It will analyze Hemingway's writing process.

INFORMATIONAL ANALYSIS

Ⓑ DISTINGUISH FACT FROM OPINION

Possible answer: One place to check would be the Kansas City Star *newspaper, if it still exists. Their newspaper guidelines might verify this information. Another option would be to consult a reference librarian or do an online search for information.*

If students need help ... Have them work in small groups to review the kinds of resources that can be used to check facts when going to the source (in this case the newspaper) is not possible. List groups' ideas on the board.

Extend the Discussion Why does the writer place quotation marks around the guidelines?

DIFFERENTIATED INSTRUCTION

FOR LESS–PROFICIENT READERS
Concept Support Write key sentences (lines 1–6, 11–16, 17–19, 28–32) from the first page of the article on a transparency. Help students distinguish between facts and opinions by prefacing each with "Could I prove that ..." For example, "Could I prove that Hemingway once said that the best advice ...?" Explain that if the answer is yes, the statement should go in their fact column. If no, it should be placed in their opinion column.

FOR ENGLISH LEARNERS
Options for Reading Tell students that in this article they will learn more about how Hemingway wrote his stories. Have students read the selection in pairs or read along with the *Audio Anthology CD*.

C DISTINGUISH FACT FROM OPINION

Possible answer: The last sentence is an expert's opinion. It is an opinion because it is introduced by the phrase "I would suggest." It is an expert's opinion because Rettman arrives at the opinion after studying Hemingway's manuscripts.

If students need help ... Clarify that an expert is someone who has studied a subject or who has experience in a particular field. Direct students' attention to lines 37–49. Ask them to summarize why Rettman might be considered an expert on Hemingway's writing process.

D DISTINGUISH FACT FROM OPINION

Possible answer: Some readers might disagree with the last statement, which seems to suggest that writing like Hemingway can be accomplished by a series of practical steps unrelated to talent.

Skill Focus: Distinguish Fact from Opinion

Possible answers for the chart on page 476:

Facts

- *"Ernest Hemingway ... Kansas City Star." (lines 1–6)*
- *"These guidelines began ... smoothness." (lines 6–11)*
- *"The short story ... a fever." (lines 28–32)*
- *"What I've discovered is ... were more often additions than cuts." (lines 42–45)*
- *"He was a fisherman ... parts of the United States." (lines 89–95)*

Opinions

- *"Anyone who ... to heart." (lines 11–16)*
- *"Hemingway's own ... is also informative." (lines 17–19)*
- *"There's another ... to writing." (lines 56–59)*
- *"Then, maybe ... like Hemingway." (lines 97–101)*

So, are you getting a sense of how Hemingway approached writing? Well, there's still more to learn from Hemingway's manuscripts. I've studied them to learn how he wrote his sto-ries. I've paid particular atten-40 tion to his revisions to see how they changed the meaning of a story. What I've discovered is the surprising fact that his revi-sions were more often additions than cuts. He added details for clarity and depth. Like a painter, Hemingway added to his can-vas until the picture was how he wanted it. From this observation 50 I would suggest that to approach writing as Hemingway did, you could start with the bare mini-mum and build, going back over your writing to see where details might add interest and clarity. **C**

There's another piece of information you need to have to begin to understand Heming-way's approach to writing. In 60 Hemingway's stories, dialogue is very important. For example, in "A Day's Wait," after the doctor takes the boy's temperature, the brief exchange that occurs be-tween the doctor and the boy's father is what triggers the boy's day of suffering:

C DISTINGUISH FACT FROM OPINION

Is the last sentence in this paragraph a fact, an opinion, or an expert's opinion? Give reasons for your answer.

D DISTINGUISH FACT FROM OPINION

Which statement in this paragraph might people disagree about?

"What is it?" I asked him.
"One hundred and two."

70 At times Hemingway cut his description of a character's thoughts in order to rely more heavily on dialogue.

You might also want to keep in mind Hemingway's other bit of advice to a young writer: "Get in somebody else's head for a change. If I bawl you out, try to figure what I'm thinking about 80 as well as how you feel about it." In other words, try to see every event from all sides.

Now, perhaps, you are ready to start writing stories of your own. Of course, you have to have something to write about. Hemingway's life experi-ences were a rich source of material. He was a fisherman 90 and a hunter, went to bullfights, and experienced both World War I and World War II. He lived in Europe, Cuba, and different parts of the United States. I'm not suggesting that you need to do similar things. Just embrace life. Then, may-be, after a time—and if you follow all this advice—you 100 can be a successful writer like Hemingway. **D**

DIFFERENTIATED INSTRUCTION

FOR ENGLISH LEARNERS

Comprehension Support Explain that each paragraph in this article develops one main idea related to the topic of how Hemingway wrote. Have students work in mixed-ability Jigsaw groups. Assign each group a para-graph and have them identify and state the main idea in their own words before sharing it with the class.

 BEST PRACTICES TOOLKIT
Jigsaw p. A1

FOR ADVANCED LEARNERS/PRE–AP

Synthesize Direct students to reread lines 74–82. Explain that the advice on getting "in somebody else's head for a change" can not only make one a stronger writer, it can also help one make better decisions in life and de-velop healthier relationships. Have students write a journal entry incorporating this advice into an important decision or relationship in their lives. Ask them to anticipate, consider, and record the thoughts and feelings of the others involved.

Comprehension

1. **Recall** Hemingway is known for writing what kinds of sentences?

2. **Clarify** What actual event in Hemingway's life helped inspire "A Day's Wait"?

Critical Analysis

3. **Distinguish Fact from Opinion** Review the facts and opinions you identified in the informative article. Then identify one of each, and explain why you identified it as you did.

4. **Identify Topic Sentences** A topic sentence is one that tells what a paragraph is about. Not all paragraphs have a topic sentence, but when it is present, it is often the first or second sentence in the paragraph. Identify three topic sentences in this informative article.

5. **Evaluate an Informative Article** A strong informative article is easy to follow, interesting, and useful. Would you say that "How Hemingway Wrote" is a strong informative article? Explain.

Read for Information: Create Instructions for Writers

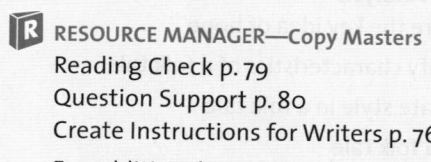

MARYLAND OBJECTIVES

INFO TEXT/WRITING STANDARDS
2.A.4.h Distinguish between a fact and an opinion
4.A.1.b.1 Organize information logically

WRITING PROMPT

In the informative article you just read, Bruce Rettman explains how to approach writing as Ernest Hemingway did. Now use these ideas to create a set of instructions for writers. To help explain your instructions, include examples from "A Day's Wait" or Rettman's article.

To answer this prompt, do as follows:

1. Scan Rettman's article to find six things a person can do to approach writing as Hemingway did.

2. Arrange the six directions in a logical order.

3. Illustrate at least two or three of these directions with examples from "A Day's Wait" or Rettman's article.

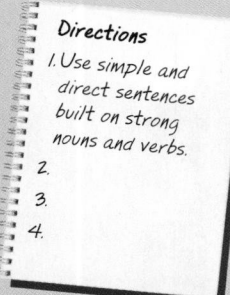

Directions
1. Use simple and direct sentences built on strong nouns and verbs.
2.
3.
4.

FOR LESS–PROFICIENT WRITERS

Read for Information

- Help students phrase each point as a brief instruction on an index card.

- Then have them find one example to illustrate each point from "A Day's Wait."

- Have students write each example on the relevant index card. Students should then put their cards in the order of Rettman's article or choose an organizational pattern, such as least to most important, before copying their instructions onto their paper.

FOR ADVANCED LEARNERS/PRE–AP

Read for Information Challenge students to develop their instructions and examples into a writing workshop lesson plan that includes short activities to allow participants to practice the skill.

Practice and Apply

For additional support of post-reading questions, use these copy masters:

R RESOURCE MANAGER—Copy Masters
Reading Check p. 79
Question Support p. 80
Create Instructions for Writers p. 76
For additional questions, see p. 71.

ANSWERS

Comprehension

1. *Possible answer: Hemingway is known for simple and direct sentences.*

2. *Possible answer: A fever suffered by Hemingway's first child inspired the short story (lines 28–32).*

Critical Analysis

3. ■ **STANDARDS FOCUS** *Distinguish Fact from Opinion* Students' examples will vary. *Possible answers: Fact*—Kansas City Star *guidelines said to use short sentences (quoted directly from source in lines 7–8);* *Opinion*—it is "surprising" (line 43) that Hemingway made more additions than cuts (some people may not find this surprising).

4. *Possible answer: Students may choose from among these topic sentences: lines 1–6, 17–19, 35–37, 59–61, 85–86.*

5. *Possible answer: Evaluations will vary but should be supported with evidence from the article.*

Read for Information: Create Instructions for Writers

Writing Prompt *Possible answer: A strong answer will restate the six principles as directions, present them in a logical order, and give examples.*

Assess and Reteach

Assess

R RESOURCE MANAGER—Copy Masters
Selection Tests A, B/C pp. 81–82, 83–84
⊘ Test Generator CD

Reteach

S STANDARDS LESSON FILE
Reading Lesson 5: Distinguishing Fact from Opinion

Focus and Motivate

OBJECTIVES

Literary Analysis
- explore the key idea of **hope**
- identify characteristics of a folk tale
- evaluate style in a folk tale
- read a folk tale

Reading
- summarize a story

Vocabulary
- build vocabulary for reading and writing
- identify and use synonyms *(also an EL language objective)*

SUMMARY

"The People Could Fly" is a folk tale about enslaved African Americans who once knew how to fly in Africa and have kept this power, although they have lost their wings. When Sarah and her baby are whipped, an old man named Toby says magic words, and she is able to fly away. Eventually, all the enslaved people who once knew how to fly use their power to escape from the plantation. Those who are not able to fly tell the story to their children.

Where do people find HOPE?

Discuss the question with students. To lead into the *KEY IDEA*, ask students to think about how **hope** links the present and the future. Extend the discussion by having students do the *WEB IT* activity. After the activity, invite volunteers to share their thoughts about hope with the class.

Selection Resources

The People Could Fly
Folk Tale retold by Virginia Hamilton

Where do people find HOPE?

MARYLAND OBJECTIVES

READING/LIT STANDARDS
1.E.4.e Summarize
3.A.7.e Analyze elements of style

KEY IDEA What is **hope?** Why do we need it? Where can we find it? How can we give hope to others? In her retelling of "The People Could Fly," Virginia Hamilton shares a story that gave people hope for freedom when little else did.

WEB IT With a partner, discuss the questions posed in the previous paragraph. Record ideas from your conversation in a word web like the one shown, adding to it as necessary.

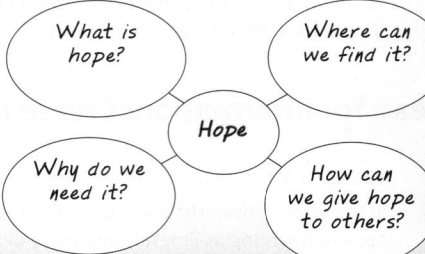

What is hope?

Where can we find it?

Hope

Why do we need it?

How can we give hope to others?

480

RESOURCE MANAGER UNIT 4

Plan and Teach pp. 85–92

Literary Analysis
Summary pp. 93†*, 94‡*
Style in Folk Tales pp. 95, 96†*
Question Support p. 103*

Reading
Summarize pp. 97, 98†*
Reading Check p. 102

Vocabulary
Study p. 99*
Practice p. 100
Strategy p. 101

Assessment
Selection Tests A, B/C pp. 105, 107
⊘ Test Generator CD

BEST PRACTICES TOOLKIT

Differentiated Instruction pp. 31–38*
Scaffolding Instruction pp. 43–46*

Graphic Organizers/Strategies
Jigsaw • Word Questioning • Comparison Matrix • T Chart • New Word Analysis

Reading Support
⊘ Audio Anthology CD*

Technology
ⓘ Literature and Vocabulary Centers at **ClassZone.com**

⊘ Write*Smart* CD

---

* Resources for Differentiation   † Also in Spanish   ‡ In Haitian Creole and Vietnamese

LITERARY ANALYSIS: STYLE IN FOLK TALES

The selection you are about to read is a **folk tale,** a story that has been passed from generation to generation by word of mouth. In writing the folk tale down, Virginia Hamilton chose to use a **style** that reflects how the story would sound if told aloud. That style includes

- nonstandard spellings that match how people might say certain words
- sentence structure that matches how people might talk

As you read, notice how Hamilton uses language to re-create the sound of speech. It may help you to read parts of the story aloud, as it was originally meant to be told.

READING SKILL: SUMMARIZE

One way to check your understanding of what you are reading is to **summarize** it. A summary is a brief retelling, in your own words, of the main ideas of a story. When you summarize a story, include

- the characters, setting, conflict, and resolution
- key details, so that someone who has not read the story understands your summary

As you read "The People Could Fly," collect the information you'll need to give a summary. Note the main elements in a story map like the one shown.

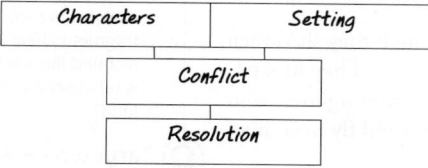

VOCABULARY IN CONTEXT

The boldfaced words all help tell a story of hardship and **hope.** Try to figure out what each word means in the context of the numbered phrases.

1. **croon** a lullaby
2. **snagged** by a tree branch
3. slide and **shuffle** to the left
4. **glinty** diamond

Author Online

A Storytelling Family
Virginia Hamilton grew up listening to her parents, grandparents, and others tell stories of their past. She has since realized that "they were passing along heritage and culture and a pride in their history."

Virginia Hamilton
1936–2002

From Listener to Writer Hamilton put these stories in writing and added some of her own, publishing more than 35 books. Many of her books, including *The People Could Fly,* deal with African-American history and culture.

Background

Slavery Between the 1500s and 1800s, about 12 million Africans were sent to North and South America as enslaved people. Colonists in the Americas wanted a cheap labor force to support their large-scale farming. People were kidnapped in Africa and sent overseas as enslaved people to be sold.

A Hopeful Community Despite the hardships they faced, enslaved people held on to a sense of community and tradition. They passed on stories, folk tales, and legends from generation to generation. The folk tale "The People Could Fly" is one example of these stories of hope and tradition.

 MORE ABOUT THE AUTHOR AND BACKGROUND
To learn more about Virginia Hamilton and African-American oral tradition, visit the **Literature Center** at **ClassZone.com.**

Teach

STANDARDS FOCUS

LITERARY ANALYSIS

● STYLE IN FOLK TALES

Read aloud this example:

"Hey, how ya doin'?"

"Real good. And you?"

Ask students to restate the dialogue in a more formal style using correct spelling and complete sentences. ***Possible answer:*** *"Hello, how are you doing?" "I'm very well. How are you doing?"*

CHECK UNDERSTANDING Ask students for other examples of spoken language that might be different from formal writing.

READING SKILL

■ SUMMARIZE

Explain that a summary contains only the main idea and most important details, re-stated in one's own words. Direct students to read the two paragraphs about Virginia Hamilton on page 481 and summarize them in one sentence. ***Possible answer:*** *Virginia Hamilton learned traditional stories from her family and then used them in her writing to reflect pride in her culture.*

CHECK UNDERSTANDING Have students summarize the background information on page 481 in two sentences.

 RESOURCE MANAGER—Copy Master
Summarize p. 97 (for student use while reading the selection)

VOCABULARY SKILL

▲ VOCABULARY IN CONTEXT

DIAGNOSE WORD KNOWLEDGE To determine preteaching needs, have all students complete **Vocabulary in Context.** *Students' responses will vary.* ***Possible answers:*** **1.** *sing;* **2.** *caught;* **3.** *step;* **4.** *sparkling*

PRETEACH VOCABULARY Use the Vocabulary Study copy master to help students assess their knowledge and predict possible meanings of each boldfaced word using context clues.

1. Read item 1 in Part A aloud, emphasizing *croon.*

2. Ask students to identify words that give a clue to the meaning of *croon,* such as "song" and "comfort him and help him fall sleep."

3. Repeat the procedure for items 2–4.

 RESOURCE MANAGER—Copy Master
Vocabulary Study p. 99

For general guidelines on differentiating vocabulary instruction and for alternative vocabulary activities for students not needing vocabulary preteaching, see

BEST PRACTICES TOOLKIT
Scaffolding Vocabulary Instruction
pp. 43–46

① Vocabulary Center at **ClassZone.com**
Additional Vocabulary Activities

ANALYZE VISUALS

Possible answer: The people are floating above the buildings and trees. They are up in the clouds without wings or anything else to hold them up.

About the Art Leo and Diane Dillon are award-winning artists who have been illustrating children's books since 1970. When they won the Caldecott Medal in 1976 for *Why Mosquitoes Buzz in People's Ears,* Leo became the first African-American artist to win the award. As the people's clothing in this illustration shows, the artists are dedicated to reflecting accurate content and pay careful attention to detail in their work. They work on every piece together, each one contributing in ways that produce a final illustration that cannot be identified with either artist individually.

LITERARY ANALYSIS

Ⓐ STYLE

Possible answer: Sentence fragments make the story sound more casual and more natural. They create the rhythm of someone telling the story out loud by presenting short thoughts with frequent pauses.

If students need help . . .

- Make sure students can identify the sentence fragments. Remind them that a sentence must have a subject and a verb.
- Have students read the passage aloud so they can hear what it sounds like.
- Ask them to think about how the story would be different if it were written with only complete sentences.

The People Could Fly

Virginia Hamilton

*T*hey say the people could fly. Say that long ago in Africa, some of the people knew magic. And they would walk up on the air like climbin' up on a gate. And they flew like blackbirds over the fields. Black, shiny wings flappin' against the blue up there.

Then, many of the people were captured for Slavery. The ones that could fly shed their wings. They couldn't take their wings across the water on the slave ships. Too crowded, don't you know. Ⓐ

The folks were full of misery, then. Got sick with the up and down of the sea. So they forgot about flyin' when they could no longer breathe
10 the sweet scent of Africa.

Say the people who could fly kept their power, although they shed their wings. They kept their secret magic in the land of slavery. They looked the same as the other people from Africa who had been coming over, who had dark skin. Say you couldn't tell anymore one who could fly from one who couldn't.

One such who could was an old man, call him Toby. And standin' tall, yet afraid, was a young woman who once had wings. Call her Sarah. Now Sarah carried a babe tied to her back. She trembled to be so hard worked and scorned.

20 The slaves labored in the fields from sunup to sundown. The owner of the slaves callin' himself their Master. Say he was a hard lump of clay. A hard, **glinty** coal. A hard rock pile, wouldn't be moved. His Overseer[1]

---

1. **Overseer:** a person who directs the work of others; a supervisor. During the time of slavery, the overseer was usually a white man.

482 UNIT 4: MOOD, TONE, AND STYLE

ANALYZE VISUALS
Folk tales often include supernatural elements. What supernatural element does this illustration show?

Ⓐ STYLE
Reread lines 1–7. Note the sentence fragments. How does Hamilton's use of sentence fragments help make it sound like someone is telling the story out loud?

① **Targeted Passage**

glinty (glĭn'tē) *adj.* sparkling

From *The People Could Fly* Illustrations © 1985 by Leo and Diane Dillon. Used by permission of Alfred A. Knopf, an imprint of Random House Children's Books, a division of Random House, Inc.

DIFFERENTIATED INSTRUCTION

FOR ALL STUDENTS

Enhance Learning Styles Provide independent projects for various learning styles.

- **Mathematical** Create a timeline showing highlights of African-American history.
- **Visual** Sketch the setting of the story.
- **Verbal** Evaluate the importance of your own oral history.

For further details on these projects, see

R RESOURCE MANAGER
Ideas for Extension pp. 90–91

FOR LESS–PROFICIENT READERS

In combination with the *Audio Anthology CD,* use one or more Targeted Passages (pp. 482, 484, 485) to ensure that students focus on key story events, concepts, and skills.

① Targeted Passage [Lines 1–19]

This passage sets up the folk tale: it introduces two main characters (Toby and Sarah) and sets up the premise that certain enslaved Africans have the power to fly.

- What magic were certain people in Africa able to do?
- What did these people lose when they were taken into slavery? What did they keep?
- Describe two of the enslaved people who were able to fly.

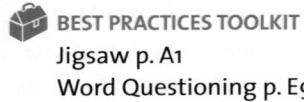

BACKGROUND

Slave Ships The tragic journey of enslaved Africans across the Atlantic Ocean from Africa to the Americas was known as the Middle Passage. Captains from many European countries and from the colonies journeyed to West Africa with goods to trade for enslaved Africans. In order to maximize their profits, most captains packed the area between their decks with as many Africans as possible, ranging from 150 to 600 depending on the size of the ship (lines 5–10). The enslaved people were usually shackled together and often chained to the deck as well. They were frequently forced to lie down in a space only 16 inches wide. They were not able to change their position and could not sit or stand up straight. The journey lasted from three weeks to three months or more. It is estimated that 13 percent of Africans died during the Middle Passage due to starvation or disease caused by a lack of adequate nutrition, ventilation, and sanitation.

FOR ENGLISH LEARNERS

Options for Reading Have students silently read along as they listen to the *Audio Anthology CD*. Divide students into Jigsaw groups and assign one Targeted Passage to each. Allow each group to do a choral reading of their assigned passage.

Key Academic Vocabulary Use Word Questioning to provide instruction and practice for the word *labored* (line 20).

 BEST PRACTICES TOOLKIT
Jigsaw p. A1
Word Questioning p. E9

Prereading For prereading instruction for English learners, see

BEST PRACTICES TOOLKIT
Scaffolding Reading Instruction pp. 43–46

FOR ADVANCED LEARNERS/PRE–AP

Pre-AP exercises in the bottom channel provide additional challenge for your advanced students. Use them for small groups or individuals.

ADDITIONAL GUIDELINES

For more help with differentiation and tips for classroom management, see

BEST PRACTICES TOOLKIT
Differentiated Instruction pp. 31–38

Possible answer:

- **Characters:** Toby, Sarah, Sarah's baby, Master, Overseer, Driver
- **Setting:** fields in America during the time of slavery

If students need help . . . Remind them that setting is where and when a story takes place and that characters are the people involved in the action of a story.

Extend the Discussion What was life like for the enslaved Africans?

READING SKILL

C SUMMARIZE

Possible answer: *The conflict is between Sarah and the Overseer and Driver. The men are angry because Sarah's baby is crying.*

If students need help . . . Remind them that conflict is a struggle between opposing forces. Ask which characters are opposed to one another in this scene.

Lines 54–58
REINFORCE *KEY IDEA:* HOPE

Discuss How might Sarah's flight give **hope** to the other enslaved people? *Possible answers: They might feel it is possible for them to escape from the pain of slavery themselves. Some might remember that they, too, know how to fly.*

---

on horseback pointed out the slaves who were slowin' down. So the one called Driver cracked his whip over the slow ones to make them move faster. That whip was a slice-open cut of pain. So they did move faster. Had to. **B**

Sarah hoed and chopped the row as the babe on her back slept.

Say the child grew hungry. That babe started up bawling too loud. Sarah couldn't stop to feed it. Couldn't stop to soothe and quiet it down. She let it cry. She didn't want to. She had no heart to **croon** to it.

30 "Keep that thing quiet," called the Overseer. He pointed his finger at the babe. The woman scrunched low. The Driver cracked his whip across the babe anyhow. The babe hollered like any hurt child, and the woman fell to the earth. **C**

The old man that was there, Toby, came and helped her to her feet. "I must go soon," she told him.

"Soon," he said.

Sarah couldn't stand up straight any longer. She was too weak. The sun burned her face. The babe cried and cried, "Pity me, oh, pity me," say it sounded like. Sarah was so sad and starvin', she sat down in the row.

40 "Get up, you black cow," called the Overseer. He pointed his hand, and the Driver's whip snarled around Sarah's legs. Her sack dress tore into rags. Her legs bled onto the earth. She couldn't get up.

Toby was there where there was no one to help her and the babe.

"Now, before it's too late," panted Sarah. "Now, Father!"

"Yes, Daughter, the time is come," Toby answered. "Go, as you know how to go!"

He raised his arms, holding them out to her. *"Kum . . . yali, kum buba tambe,"* and more magic words, said so quickly, they sounded like whispers and sighs.

50 The young woman lifted one foot on the air. Then the other. She flew clumsily at first, with the child now held tightly in her arms. Then she felt the magic, the African mystery. Say she rose just as free as a bird. As light as a feather.

The Overseer rode after her, hollerin'. Sarah flew over the fences. She flew over the woods. Tall trees could not **snag** her. Nor could the Overseer. She flew like an eagle now, until she was gone from sight. No one dared speak about it. Couldn't believe it. But it was, because they that was there saw that it was.

*S*ay the next day was dead hot in the fields. A young man slave fell
60 from the heat. The Driver come and whipped him. Toby come over and spoke words to the fallen one. The words of ancient Africa once heard are never remembered completely. The young man forgot them as soon as he heard them. They went way inside him. He got up and rolled over on the air. He rode it awhile. And he flew away.

484 UNIT 4: MOOD, TONE, AND STYLE

B SUMMARIZE
Note the **setting** and the names of the **characters** in your story map.

croon (kro͞on) *v.* to sing softly

C SUMMARIZE
What is the **conflict?** Record it in your story map.

2 Targeted Passage

snag (snăg) *v.* to catch and tear

DIFFERENTIATED INSTRUCTION

FOR LESS–PROFICIENT READERS

2 Targeted Passage [Lines 37–58]

This passage describes the conflict and a partial resolution: Toby helps Sarah fly away with her baby after she is whipped by the Driver.

- Why is Sarah unable to keep working?
- What does the Driver do to Sarah?
- How does Toby help Sarah?
- What was it that "no one dared speak about" (line 57)?

Reading Skill Follow-Up: Summarize

Encourage students to add details about the conflict to their story maps after reading lines 37–42. Then direct students to read lines 45–64 and record information about the resolution of this conflict. *Possible answers:*

- **Conflict:** *The Overseer and the Driver get angrier with Sarah, who is too weak to keep working. They whip her and she can't get up.*

- **Resolution:** *Toby says magic words that help Sarah and a young man fly away to freedom.*

Another and another fell from the heat. Toby was there. He cried out to the fallen and reached his arms out to them. *"Kum kunka yali, kum . . . tambe!"* Whispers and sighs. And they too rose on the air. They rode the hot breezes. The ones flyin' were black and shinin' sticks, wheelin' above the head of the Overseer. They crossed the rows, the fields, the fences, the streams, and were away.

"Seize the old man!" cried the Overseer.

"I heard him say the magic *words*. Seize him!"

The one callin' himself Master come runnin'. The Driver got his whip ready to curl around old Toby and tie him up. The slave owner took his hip gun from its place. He meant to kill old black Toby. **D**

But Toby just laughed. Say he threw back his head and said, "Hee, hee! Don't you know who I am? Don't you know some of us in this field?" He said it to their faces. "We are ones who fly!"

And he sighed the ancient words that were a dark promise. He said them all around to the others in the field under the whip, ". . . *buba yali . . . buba tambe . . .*"

There was a great outcryin'. The bent backs straightened up. Old and young who were called slaves and could fly joined hands. Say like they would ring-sing. But they didn't **shuffle** in a circle. They didn't sing. They rose on the air. They flew in a flock that was black against the heavenly blue. Black crows or black shadows. It didn't matter, they went so high. Way above the plantation, way over the slavery land. Say they flew away to *Free-dom*.

And the old man, old Toby, flew behind them, takin' care of them. He wasn't cryin'. He wasn't laughin'. He was the seer. His gaze fell on the plantation where the slaves who could not fly waited. **E**

"Take us with you!" Their looks spoke it, but they were afraid to shout it. Toby couldn't take them with him. Hadn't the time to teach them to fly. They must wait for a chance to run.

"Goodie-bye!" the old man called Toby spoke to them, poor souls! And he was flyin' gone.

So they say. The Overseer told it. The one called Master said it was a lie, a trick of the light. The Driver kept his mouth shut.

The slaves who could not fly told about the people who could fly to their children. When they were free. When they sat close before the fire in the free land, they told it. They did so love firelight and *Free-dom,* and tellin'.

They say that the children of the ones who could not fly told their children. And now, me, I have told it to you. ❧

D STYLE
In line 73 there is an example of **dialect,** a form of language spoken in a certain place or by a certain group of people. Why might Hamilton use dialect in this story?

③ Targeted Passage

shuffle (shŭf′əl) *v.* to slide the feet along the ground while walking

E SUMMARIZE
What role does Toby play in the **resolution** of the conflict?

SOCIAL STUDIES CONNECTION

Folk tales and other stories that were first told orally rather than written down make up what is called the **oral tradition** of many cultures throughout the world.

D STYLE

Possible answer: She wants to make the folk tale sound as if it is being told by someone who witnessed the events or who heard the story as passed down by witnesses.

E SUMMARIZE

Possible answer: Toby says the words that remind the people that they can fly. He helps them fly away. Toby watches over them as they fly.

SOCIAL STUDIES CONNECTION
Oral tradition involves the passing along of stories, common history, folk wisdom, games, and songs from one generation to the next—without writing. Since speaking precedes writing, all cultures were at one time oral. In cultures where written language was slower to develop or literacy less widespread, the oral tradition remained stronger. People who live more closely connected to their cultural roots have a more direct link to their oral tradition. Yet all people have some connection to oral tradition, not just through folk tales, but through the passing down of family or group customs and stories.

SELECTION WRAP–UP

★ CRITIQUE Ask students to evaluate how successfully Virginia Hamilton captured the feeling of a story being told out loud. What techniques did she use to do this?

FOR LESS–PROFICIENT READERS

③ Targeted Passage [Lines 73–103]

This passage presents the climax and resolution of the conflict: the slave owner threatens Toby, but he and all the enslaved people who are able to fly escape.

- What do the Driver and the slave owner want to do to Toby?
- How does Toby respond to them?
- What do the other enslaved people do when Toby says the magic words?
- Why are some enslaved people left behind?

FOR ADVANCED LEARNERS/PRE–AP

Analyze Language Hamilton describes Toby as "the seer" (line 90). Invite students to consider how this word is connected to the word *Overseer*. Distribute copies of the Comparison Matrix and have students use it to contrast Toby as the seer with the Overseer. Encourage them to think about how Toby and the Overseer each view the enslaved people and how this difference affects their actions.

BEST PRACTICES TOOLKIT—Transparency Comparison Matrix p. A24

Practice and Apply

After Reading

For additional support of post-reading questions, use these copy masters:

R RESOURCE MANAGER—Copy Masters

Reading Check p. 102 (to check understanding of the selection)

Style in Folk Tales p. 95 (for practice of literary analysis standards focus)

Question Support p. 103 (**After Reading** questions adapted for English learners and less-proficient readers)

Additional selection questions are provided for teachers on page 89.

ANSWERS

Comprehension

1. *Some Africans had the power to fly.*

2. *The Driver whips Sarah and her baby.*

3. *The enslaved people who could not fly away tell the story to their children.*

Literary Analysis

Possible answers:

4. ■ **STANDARDS FOCUS** *Summarize*
   Summaries should be in students' own words and include main ideas and details about the setting of the story, the main characters, the significant conflicts, and the resolution of the conflicts.

5. *There had to be an explanation for why some people were still enslaved, and there needed to be some people left behind to tell and hear the story.*

6. *Responses should focus on the need for and power of hope. The people who first heard the story would be proud of their heritage and hopeful that one day they, too, could rise up and obtain freedom.*

7. ● **STANDARDS FOCUS** *Style in Folk Tales*
   Spellings:** outcryin', takin', cryin', laughin', flyin';* ***Sentence Fragments: *"Say like they would ring-sing." "Black crows or black shadows." "Way above the plantation, way over the slavery land." "Say they flew away to Free-dom." "Hadn't the time to teach them to fly."* ***Effective style:*** *story sounds like it is being told aloud and creates familiarity with the culture of the people who created the story.* ***Not effective:*** *makes the story more difficult to read.*

Comprehension

1. **Recall** What special power did some of the people in Africa have?

2. **Recall** What does the Driver do to Sarah and her baby?

3. **Clarify** After Toby is gone, who tells the story of the people who could fly?

Literary Analysis

4. **Summarize** Use the story map you created as you read to summarize the story. Compare your summary with that of a classmate.

5. **Draw Conclusions** Why do you think the people who first told this **folk tale** did not have all the slaves fly away?

6. **Analyze Theme** What do you think this story meant to the people who first heard it told?

7. **Evaluate Style in a Folk Tale** Reread lines 82–96. In a graphic like the one shown, note examples of Hamilton's style that appear in this section. Do you think this is an effective style for telling this story, or would you prefer to read it with standard spellings and complete sentences? Explain.

Hamilton's Style	
Spellings	Sentence Fragments
• _____	• _____
• _____	• _____
• _____	• _____

Extension and Challenge

8. **Big Question Activity** Revisit the Web It activity on page 480. This time, consider how either Toby or Sarah would answer the questions about **hope**. Use details from the folk tale and your own knowledge and experiences to answer the questions as he or she would.

9. **SOCIAL STUDIES CONNECTION** The African-American **oral tradition** has its roots in Africa—particularly West Africa. Research to find out about griots (grē-ōz') West African storytellers, and their role in the local culture.

RESEARCH LINKS
For more on griots, visit the **Research Center** at **ClassZone.com.**

Extension and Challenge

8. *Students' responses should reflect both Toby's and Sarah's belief that one day they will escape slavery. Both may have hope based on the knowledge that they have the power to fly. Students may point to the way the community and the story give hope to the enslaved people. Toby and Sarah may have slightly different hopes based on their circumstances. Toby may hope to help the other slaves. Sarah may have hope for her baby's future.*

9. ● **SOCIAL STUDIES CONNECTION**
   Possible answer: *Griots were the people in West Africa responsible for learning and telling their community's history. They memorized the family connections, praised important people and deeds, and gave advice to the rulers. The rulers wanted the griots to travel with them so they could tell the people what the ruler had done. Griots used both words and music in telling their stories and might speak for hours or days.*

Vocabulary in Context

VOCABULARY PRACTICE

Use **context clues** to choose a vocabulary word to complete each sentence.

croon

glinty

shuffle

snag

1. Though they tried not to _____ them, people often ripped their clothes while doing hard labor in the fields.
2. They had no money for jewelry or _____ things.
3. They would _____ with their heads down to keep the Overseer from noticing them.
4. At night, the mothers might _____ to their weeping children to comfort them.

VOCABULARY IN WRITING

In your opinion, is this story more about sadness or hope? In a paragraph, tell what you think. Use two or more vocabulary words. You could start this way.

> **EXAMPLE SENTENCE**
>
> *The people in this story had to **shuffle** from one place of hardship to another.*

VOCABULARY STRATEGY: USE THE BEST SYNONYM

One way writers make their stories come alive is by using well-chosen words. Common words like *sing* have many **synonyms,** or words with similar meanings. However, not all synonyms are interchangeable. In this story, for example, the verb *croon* gives a much more precise sense of the scene than the more common verb *sing* would convey. In a **thesaurus**—a book or electronic tool used to find synonyms—*croon* might be grouped with words like *hum, murmur,* and *chant.*

PRACTICE Choose the synonym in parentheses that best replaces each boldfaced word. If you need help, consult a thesaurus or a dictionary.

1. His sleeves got **dirty** from the leaking printer ink. (smudged, dingy)
2. Little children often **frown** if they don't get their way. (glare, pout)
3. Al Capone was a **famous** criminal. (distinguished, notorious)
4. She was so hungry that she **ate** everything in sight. (devoured, dined on)
5. The frightened field mouse **ran** across the kitchen floor. (scampered, jogged)

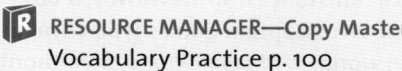

MARYLAND OBJECTIVES

READING STANDARD
1.D.3.c Use resources to gather further information about words

 VOCABULARY PRACTICE
For more practice, go to the **Vocabulary Center** at ClassZone.com.

DIFFERENTIATED INSTRUCTION

FOR ENGLISH LEARNERS
Vocabulary Strategy: Synonyms

- Use New Word Analysis to help students identify context clues and use them to figure out the shades of meaning of the synonyms in each sentence.
- Allow students to work in pairs to consult a thesaurus or dictionary if they need additional help.

 **BEST PRACTICES TOOLKIT—Transparency**
New Word Analysis p. E8

FOR ADVANCED LEARNERS/PRE–AP
Vocabulary Strategy: Synonyms

- Encourage students to list additional synonyms for each of the boldfaced words.
- After students have chosen the correct synonym in each sentence, challenge them to create sentences for the unselected words: *dingy, glare, distinguished, dined on,* and *jogged.*

ANSWERS

Vocabulary in Context
VOCABULARY PRACTICE

1. *snag*
2. *glinty*
3. *shuffle*
4. *croon*

R RESOURCE MANAGER—Copy Master
Vocabulary Practice p. 100

VOCABULARY IN WRITING

Distribute copies of the T Chart transparency. Students can list the things in the story that relate to sadness in one column and those that relate to **hope** in the other. Then have students review the vocabulary words in relation to the opinion they form from the chart.

BEST PRACTICES TOOLKIT—Transparency
T Chart p. A25

VOCABULARY STRATEGY: USE THE BEST SYNONYM *(also an EL language objective)*

Explain that students should use context clues in the sentences to help them choose the best synonym. Allow them to use a reference aid if they need additional help.

Answers:

1. *smudged*
2. *pout*
3. *notorious*
4. *devoured*
5. *scampered*

R RESOURCE MANAGER—Copy Master
Vocabulary Strategy p. 101

i Vocabulary Center at **ClassZone.com**
Additional Vocabulary Activities

Assess and Reteach

Assess

R RESOURCE MANAGER—Copy Masters
Selection Tests A, B/C pp. 105–106, 107–108
Test Generator CD

Reteach

S STANDARDS LESSON FILE
Literature Lesson 38: Style
Vocabulary Lesson 18: Synonyms and Antonyms

Introduce

Out of the Dust

Novel in Verse by Karen Hesse

OBJECTIVES

- read poetry
- read an excerpt from a novel in verse

Meet Karen Hesse

In many of Hesse's books, young people grapple with challenges that arise from their historical circumstances. In *Stowaway*, a boy narrowly survives Captain Cook's 1768 voyage around the world; in *Phoenix Rising*, a Vermont girl copes with the aftermath of a nuclear accident. Hesse puts a high value on compassion. In her Newbery Medal acceptance speech, she said that historical fiction "helps us understand that . . . sometimes there are no answers, sometimes there is only forgiveness."

Try a Novel in Verse

A novel in verse combines the narrative sweep of a novel with the vivid images of poetry. It tells a story in few words and with a distinctive voice and style. In *Heartbeat* by Sharon Creech, the *thump-thump* of a girl's beating heart and running feet make a steady rhythm while all else is changing around her. In *Shakespeare Bats Cleanup* by Ron Koertge, various forms of verse by a teenage athlete show his emerging gift for poetry. Novels in verse are especially effective at capturing emotions and creating moods. Robert Cormier's *Frenchtown Summer* follows a lonely boy as he uncovers disturbing local secrets while on his paper route; Sonya Sones's *Stop Pretending* relates the confusing experience of watching a sister become mentally ill.

 RESOURCE MANAGER—Copy Master
Novel in Verse p. 109

Karen Hesse
born 1952

Other Books by Karen Hesse

- *Aleutian Sparrow*
- *Letters from Rifka*
- *A Light in the Storm*
- *The Music of Dolphins*
- *Phoenix Rising*
- *Stowaway*
- *A Time of Angels*
- *Witness*

Meet Karen Hesse

Karen Hesse has worked as a librarian, teacher, secretary, proofreader, waitress, and nanny, but at heart she's always been a writer. "I love writing," she says. "I can't wait to get to my keyboard every morning." She also loves books and has shared that passion with her two daughters.

Hesse had a troubled childhood, but she feels that her experiences have strengthened her skills as a writer. "My work reflects the bumps and knocks that I've experienced," she explains. "I write the kinds of books that I would've wanted as a child."

Try a Novel in Verse

Most novels are written in prose, the ordinary form of written language, but they can also be written as poetry. Hesse wrote *Out of the Dust* as a series of **free verse** poems, which are poems written without regular rhyme or rhythm. As personal journal entries, these poems provide a window into what the main character is thinking and feeling.

Before Hesse began writing *Out of the Dust*, she spent several months researching the 1930s, the era in U.S. history in which her novel in verse is set. She used real places and events from the era to create her story.

488

DIFFERENTIATED INSTRUCTION

FOR LESS—PROFICIENT READERS

Reading Support Before students begin reading, review the teaching notes on pages 489–493 and select those that you think would be most helpful to them. You might read the selection aloud with students and discuss the relevant notes. Stop occasionally to answer questions, give an explanation, or hold a discussion.

Read a Great Book

Thirteen-year-old Billie Jo and her family of farmers are barely surviving the hardships of the Dust Bowl in Oklahoma in the 1930s. Drought and strong winds have ruined their crops. Dust covers everything, and money is scarce. Every day is a struggle. The only source of joy in Billie Jo's life is her talent for playing the piano.

from

Out of the Dust

Fields of Flashing Light

I heard the wind rise,
and stumbled from my bed,
down the stairs,
out the front door,
5 into the yard.
The night sky kept flashing,
lightning danced down on its spindly legs.

489

Read a Great Book

One of the most powerful images in *Out of the Dust* is the dust itself: swirling, choking storms of dust that coat everything they touch. The Dust Bowl certainly earned its name. During the 1930s, fierce summer winds in the western Great Plains lifted the topsoil, which had been damaged by extreme drought and overcultivation, into devastating storms of dust. Many farmers in hard-hit states—Kansas, Oklahoma, Texas, New Mexico, Colorado—were left with nothing. In *Out of the Dust,* the speaker's family farm has been nearly destroyed. As fits a setting where people must make every resource count, Hesse uses brief chapters and carefully chosen language to express the hardships of daily life. Says Hesse, "I never attempted to write this book any other way than in free verse. The frugality of the life, the hypnotically hard work of farming, the grimness of conditions during the dust bowl demanded an economy of words."

SHARE WORD MEANINGS

Out of the Dust is written in verse. Suggest that students try reading it aloud to get a feeling for how it sounds. Point out that they should take a breath when they come to a comma and pause when they come to a period. Listening for the rhythms of a poem helps readers understand the thoughts and images it expresses.

FOR ENGLISH LEARNERS

Use these options to help English learners enjoy the selection:

Read Aloud Use Read Aloud/Think Aloud to preread part of the selection. Describe how you heed end punctuation and how you try to visualize images. Have students continue reading in pairs.

 BEST PRACTICES TOOLKIT—Transparency
Read Aloud/Think Aloud p. A34

Listen to the *Audio Anthology CD* Have students read along as they listen to the excerpt. Then have them read the text independently. Lead them in a follow-up discussion.

Echo Reading Read aloud one sentence at a time, pausing at line breaks. Have students echo back each sentence after you read it.

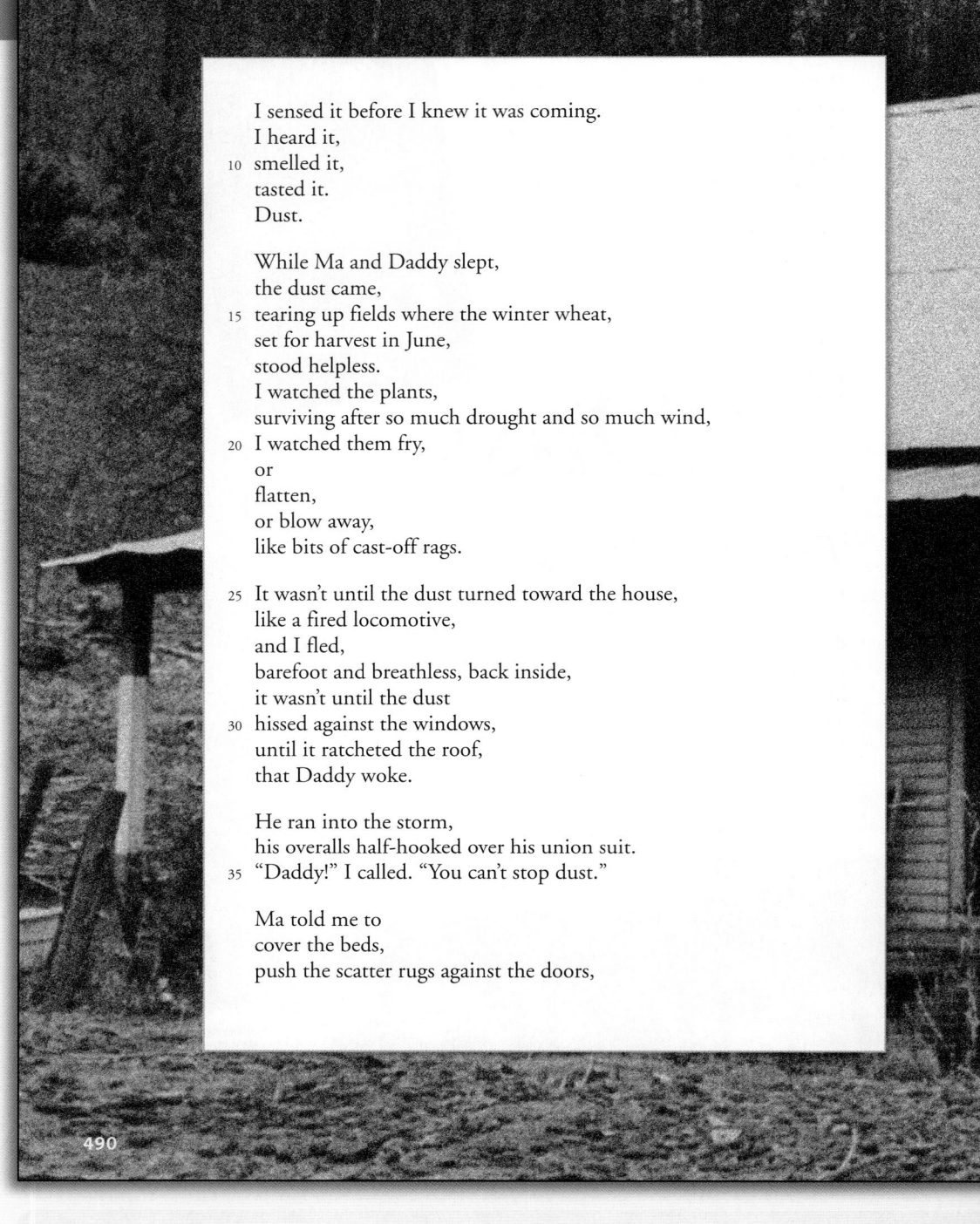

I sensed it before I knew it was coming.
I heard it,
10 smelled it,
tasted it.
Dust.

While Ma and Daddy slept,
the dust came,
15 tearing up fields where the winter wheat,
set for harvest in June,
stood helpless.
I watched the plants,
surviving after so much drought and so much wind,
20 I watched them fry,
or
flatten,
or blow away,
like bits of cast-off rags.

25 It wasn't until the dust turned toward the house,
like a fired locomotive,
and I fled,
barefoot and breathless, back inside,
it wasn't until the dust
30 hissed against the windows,
until it ratcheted the roof,
that Daddy woke.

He ran into the storm,
his overalls half-hooked over his union suit.
35 "Daddy!" I called. "You can't stop dust."

Ma told me to
cover the beds,
push the scatter rugs against the doors,

490

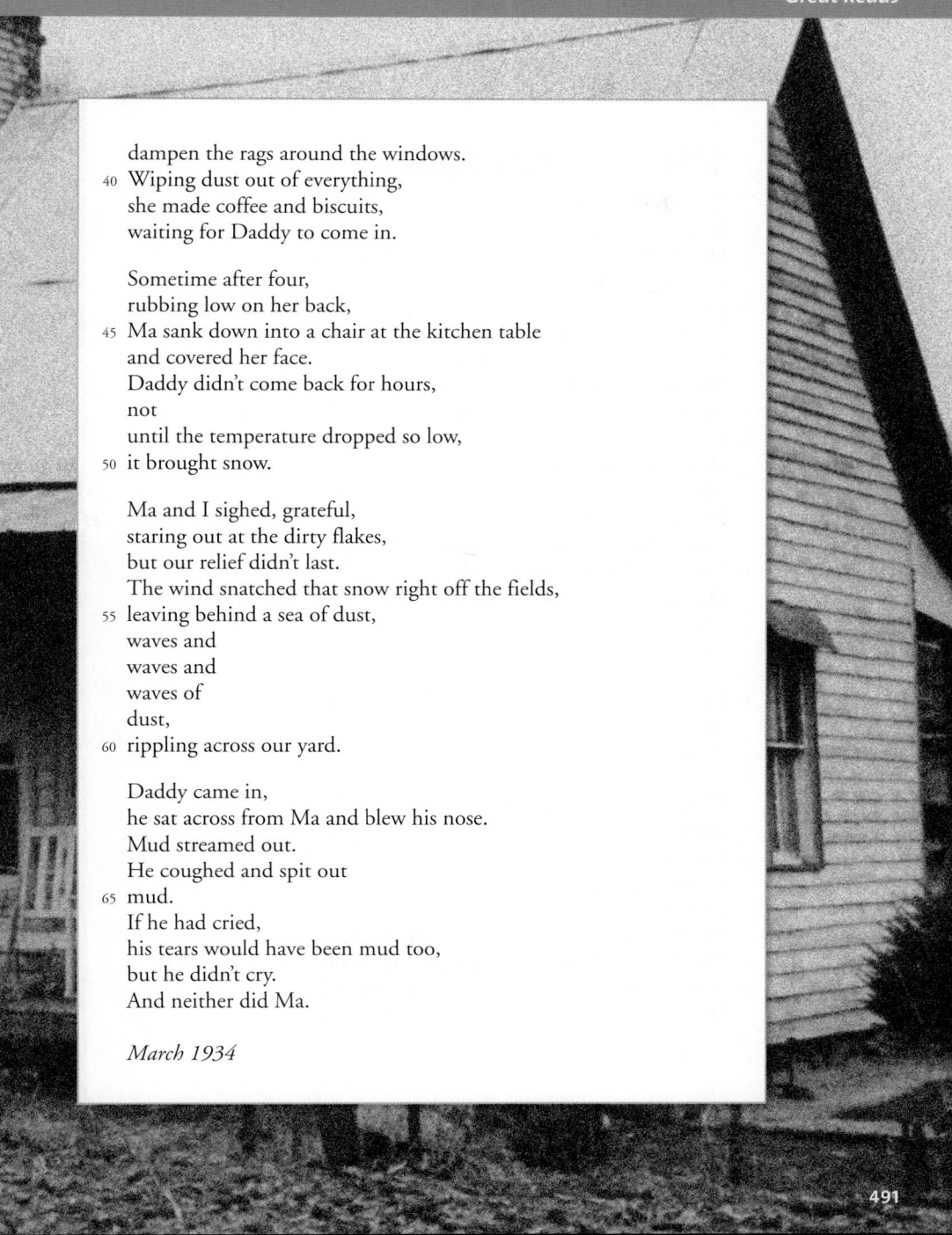

dampen the rags around the windows.
40 Wiping dust out of everything,
she made coffee and biscuits,
waiting for Daddy to come in.

Sometime after four,
rubbing low on her back,
45 Ma sank down into a chair at the kitchen table
and covered her face.
Daddy didn't come back for hours,
not
until the temperature dropped so low,
50 it brought snow.

Ma and I sighed, grateful,
staring out at the dirty flakes,
but our relief didn't last.
The wind snatched that snow right off the fields,
55 leaving behind a sea of dust,
waves and
waves and
waves of
dust,
60 rippling across our yard.

Daddy came in,
he sat across from Ma and blew his nose.
Mud streamed out.
He coughed and spit out
65 mud.
If he had cried,
his tears would have been mud too,
but he didn't cry.
And neither did Ma.

March 1934

491

SHARE AN FYI

Biscuits (line 41) are very popular in Oklahoma and in the South in general. Among Oklahoma's state symbols is an "Official State Meal" that includes biscuits served with gravy.

SHARE A READING TIP

Sometimes a poet or author uses gestures or posture to show what a character is feeling, as Hesse does in lines 45–46. When students notice this, they should make an effort to visualize what the character is doing, or try out a gesture or posture themselves to see how it feels. This can help students understand the content and the emotions being expressed.

SHARE WORD MEANINGS

"Much obliged" (line 22) is an old-fashioned way of saying "thank you." It is a shortened form of "I am much obliged to you," which means "I feel that I owe you a debt because of your kindness to me."

Wild Boy of the Road

A boy came by the house today,
he asked for food.
He couldn't pay anything, but Ma set him down
and gave him biscuits
5 and milk.
He offered to work for his meal,
Ma sent him out to see Daddy.
The boy and Daddy came back late in the afternoon.
The boy walked two steps behind,
10 in Daddy's dust.
He wasn't more than sixteen.
Thin as a fence rail.
I wondered what
Livie Killian's brother looked like now.
15 I wondered about Livie herself.
Daddy asked if the boy wanted a bath,
a haircut,
a change of clothes before he moved on.
The boy nodded.
20 I never heard him say more than "Yes, sir" or
"No, sir" or
"Much obliged."

We watched him walk away
down the road,
25 in a pair of Daddy's mended overalls,
his legs like willow limbs,
his arms like reeds.
Ma rested her hands on her heavy stomach,
Daddy rested his chin on the top of my head.
30 "His mother is worrying about him," Ma said.
"His mother is wishing her boy would come home."

Lots of mothers wishing that these days,
while their sons walk to California,
where rain comes,
35 and the color green doesn't seem like such a miracle,
and hope rises daily, like sap in a stem.
And I think, some day I'm going to walk there too,
through New Mexico and Arizona and Nevada.
Some day I'll leave behind the wind, and the dust
40 and walk my way West
and make myself to home in that distant place
of green vines and promise.

July 1934

Keep Reading

This is just a small part of the story about the life of a family during the Great Depression and Dust Bowl of the 1930s. Which descriptions stand out most vividly in your mind? To find out more about Billie Jo and her family, read more of *Out of the Dust*. You'll read about Billie Jo's struggles, why she thinks about running away to a place "where rain comes," and how she finds hope for a better future.

GREAT READS **493**

Discuss

SHARE AN FYI

In the 1930s, many people in the Dust Bowl left their homes to seek work in the West; California, with its booming agriculture, was the most popular destination (line 33). Some Dust Bowl states lost nearly half their population during this time.

SHARE A READING TIP

Ask if students can visualize the route from Oklahoma to California that the speaker describes (line 38). If not, have them look at a map of the United States.

Keep Reading

Share these discussion questions with students after they have finished the excerpt. You might use the questions to lead a class discussion or have students form small groups to discuss them.

- Have you read this book? If yes, would you recommend it to others? Why? If no, what questions are you hoping the rest of the book will answer?

- What images did the excerpt leave in your mind?

- How do you think Billie Jo felt when she could sense the dust coming?

- What other natural disasters does the dust storm make you think of?

- What do you think might happen to the "wild boy of the road"?

- Who do you think has more reason to feel hopeful: Billie Jo or the "wild boy"? Why?

- What impression of California does Billie Jo give you?

OBJECTIVES

Literary Analysis
- explore the key idea of **humor**
- identify and analyze tone
- compare and contrast tone
- read two essays

Reading
- set a purpose for reading

Vocabulary
- build vocabulary for reading and writing
- identify and use literal and figurative meanings of words (also an EL language objective)

Grammar and Writing
- write a compare-contrast response paper

SUMMARY

In both essays, the authors humorously describe the events leading up to their awkward first dates. Bill Cosby writes notes to the friend of the girl he likes, who acts as an intermediary for him. Dave Barry relies on his friend Phil Grant to arrange his date for him. Both authors take their dates to the movies, but each has a different perspective on the experience.

What makes us L A U G H ?

Discuss the question and the *KEY IDEA* of **humor.** Then have students think of the funniest person they know and analyze why that person is humorous. Use the traits students identify to develop a list of what makes someone funny. Then have students complete the *QUOTE IT* activity and share their ideas in small groups.

The Only Girl in the World for Me
Essay by Bill Cosby

Breaking the Ice
Essay by Dave Barry

What makes us L A U G H ?

MARYLAND OBJECTIVES

READING/LIT STANDARDS
1.E.3.a Select and apply appropriate strategies during reading
3.A.7.b Analyze language choices that create tone

KEY IDEA There have probably been times when you told a joke and nobody laughed. Maybe you heard a joke that made other people laugh but that you didn't think was funny. Each person has a unique sense of **humor,** and everyone has a different way of being funny. The essay writers you are about to read have built careers out of making people laugh.

QUOTE IT "Laughter is the best medicine." "Laugh and the world laughs with you." "Laughter is the closest distance between two people." There are dozens of quotes about laughter. Now it is your turn to add to the list. Think of the kinds of things that make you laugh and how laughing makes you feel. Then write your own quote about laughter.

494

Selection Resources

 RESOURCE MANAGER UNIT 4

Plan and Teach pp. 111–118
Literary Analysis
Summary pp. 119†*, 120‡*; 125†*, 126‡*
Question Support pp. 124*; 128*

Reading
Set a Purpose for Reading
pp. 121, 122†*
Reading Check pp. 123; 127

Vocabulary
Study p. 129*
Practice p. 130
Strategy p. 131

Grammar and Writing
Writing for Assessment p. 132

Assessment
Selection Tests A, B/C pp. 133*, 135*
Test Generator CD

BEST PRACTICES TOOLKIT

Differentiated Instruction
pp. 31–38*

Scaffolding Instruction pp. 43–46*

Graphic Organizers/Strategies
Storyboard • Word Questioning •
T Chart • Comparison Matrix

Reading Support
Audio Anthology CD*

Technology
Literature and Vocabulary Centers at **ClassZone.com**

WriteSmart CD

* Resources for Differentiation   † Also in Spanish   ‡ In Haitian Creole and Vietnamese

LITERARY ANALYSIS: TONE

Have you ever been told, "Don't use that tone with me"? If so, the person speaking probably didn't like your attitude. In literature, **tone** is a writer's attitude toward a topic. Tone is part of a writer's **style** and often can be described in one word, such as *sarcastic* or *sentimental*.

The two essays you are about to read relate humorous stories about dating experiences, but each has a different tone. As you read each essay, do the following:

- Identify the topic. Ask: "What is the writer writing about?"
- Notice significant words and phrases. Do most of them convey a similar attitude?
- Notice images and descriptions. Are they exaggerated, silly, or frightening?

These clues will help you identify the tone of each essay.

READING STRATEGY: SET A PURPOSE FOR READING

In this lesson, your **purpose for reading** is to compare tone. As you read, take notes, writing them in a chart like the one shown. You will be asked to add more rows to this chart later.

	"The Only Girl in the World for Me"	"Breaking the Ice"
Topic of the essay		
Words and phrases that display an attitude	"for one golden moment our eyes met"	"Never risk direct contact with the girl in question."
Vivid images and descriptions		

VOCABULARY IN CONTEXT

Descriptive words help Bill Cosby create **humor** in his essay. For each boldfaced word, use context clues to figure out its meaning.

1. I made the **transition** from grade school to junior high.
2. She experienced the **heady** feeling of success.
3. It was an **agonizing** day in the hot, blazing sun.
4. A library is a **reservoir** of information.
5. He was **suppressing** the news and not publicizing it.

Author Online

Bill Cosby: Class Clown
Bill Cosby began his comedy career long before he was getting paid for it. "I thought that if people laughed at what you said, that meant they liked you," he has said. Cosby was always the class clown. By the time he was in college, he was a professional comedian. He continued his schooling and earned two advanced degrees in education from the University of Massachusetts. Cosby is also a television star, a musician, and an award-winning author.

Bill Cosby
born 1937

Dave Barry: Journalism's Funny Man
Pulitzer Prize–winning writer Dave Barry is best known for the columns he has written for the *Miami Herald* newspaper. Barry's columns, including "Breaking the Ice," often exaggerate and poke fun at the daily life of his readers. As one reviewer put it, Barry has a gift for "squeezing every ounce of humor out of a perfectly ordinary experience."

Dave Barry
born 1947

 MORE ABOUT THE AUTHOR
For more on Bill Cosby and Dave Barry, visit the **Literature Center** at **ClassZone.com.**

495

Teach

STANDARDS FOCUS

● TONE

Read aloud this example:

> Here's a foolproof way to get noticed at a new school. First, trip and fall flat coming off the bus. Then drop your books down the stairs. Finally, tip your lunch tray over the vice-principal. I guarantee that everyone will know who you are by the end of the day.

Ask students to describe the author's tone. *Possible answer: The tone is ironic and humorous.*

CHECK UNDERSTANDING Ask students to identify the clues to tone in the passage.

■ SET A PURPOSE FOR READING

Explain that to fulfill a specific purpose for reading, such as comparing tone, students may have to adjust their reading rate, reread passages, and pause to review their graphic organizers.

CHECK UNDERSTANDING Ask students to set a purpose for reading the author information and use reading strategies to achieve the purpose.

 RESOURCE MANAGER—Copy Master
Set a Purpose for Reading p. 121 (for student use while reading the selections)

VOCABULARY SKILL

▲ VOCABULARY IN CONTEXT

DIAGNOSE WORD KNOWLEDGE To determine preteaching needs, have all students complete **Vocabulary in Context.** Check students' definitions against those on the selection pages: *transition* (p. 499), *heady* (p. 496), *agonizing* (p. 498), *reservoir* (p. 499), *suppressing* (p. 498).

PRETEACH VOCABULARY Use the Vocabulary Study copy master to help students explore the meaning of each boldfaced word.

1. Read item 1 aloud, emphasizing *agonizing*.
2. Point out the context clues "as well as" and "times of great happiness." Elicit possible meanings for *agonizing*, such as "painful or unhappy."
3. Have students record their predictions.
4. Repeat the procedure for items 2–5.

 RESOURCE MANAGER—Copy Master
Vocabulary Study p. 129

For general guidelines on differentiating vocabulary instruction and for alternative vocabulary activities for students not needing vocabulary preteaching, see

📦 BEST PRACTICES TOOLKIT
Scaffolding Vocabulary Instruction pp. 43–46

ℹ Vocabulary Center at **ClassZone.com**
Additional Vocabulary Activities

Practice and Apply

Lines 1–12

DISCUSSION PROMPTS

Use these prompts to help students understand the impact that falling in love for the first time has on Cosby's life:

Retell Have students describe what was important to the author about the first girl he fell in love with. *Students should use their own words to tell how the smell of the girl's hair pomade and cold cream impressed him, and how he dreamed of marrying her and taking care of her.*

Analyze In what way does falling in love change the author? *Possible answers: He starts taking several baths a day in an effort to improve his appearance. He begins to feel the thrill of romance.*

Synthesize How do you know that the author still treasures the memory of his first love? *Possible answer: He still recalls vivid details such as the smell of her cold cream (lines 3–4) and how he used to wash his belt until it was white (line 11). He describes his memories with positive, sentimental language such as "honeysuckle for me" (line 4), "only girl in the world" (line 5), and "take care of her forever in a palace" (line 6).*

LITERARY ANALYSIS

Ⓐ TONE

Direct students to record their answers in the first row of their chart from page 495. *Possible answer: The topic of the essay is Cosby's first love.*

The Only Girl in the World for Me
Bill Cosby

I can't remember where I have left my glasses, but I can still remember the smell of the first girl I ever fell in love with when I was twelve: a blend of Dixie Peach pomade[1] on her hair and Pond's cold cream on her skin; together they were honeysuckle for me. And just as **heady** as her scent was the thought that I was in love with the only girl in the world for me and would marry her and take care of her forever in a palace in North Philadelphia. Because I wanted to make a wondrous impression on this girl, grooming was suddenly important to me. Before puberty, happiness in appearance for me was pants that didn't fall down and a football that

10 stayed pumped; but now I started taking three long baths a day and washing my own belt until it was white and shining my shoes until I could see in them a face that was ready for romance. Ⓐ

The first time I saw her, she was crossing the street to the schoolyard and for one golden moment our eyes met. Well, maybe the moment was closer to bronze because she made no response. But at least she had seen me, just about the way that she saw lampposts, hydrants, and manholes. Or was there something more? I began to dream; and later that day, when I was playing with the boys in the yard, it seemed that she was looking at me and the world was suddenly a better place, especially Twelfth and Girard.

20 However, we still never talked, but just traded silent unsmiling looks whenever we passed. For several days, just her look was enough of a lift for me; but a higher altitude was coming, for one night at a party, we met and I actually danced with her. Now I was certain that I was in love and was going to win her.

I began my conquest with a combination of sporting skill and hygiene: I made my jump shots and my baths as dazzling as they could be. Oddly enough, however, although I saw her every day at school and on the weekends too, I never spoke to her. I had what was considered one of the faster mouths in Philadelphia, but I still wasn't ready to talk to

30 her because I feared rejection. I feared:

---

heady (hĕd′ē) *adj.* tending to make one feel really happy or excited

Ⓐ TONE
Reread lines 1–12. On the basis of the title and the first paragraph, what do you think the **topic** of the essay is?

① Targeted Passage

---

1. **pomade** (pŏ-mād′): a perfumed ointment for the scalp and hair.

DIFFERENTIATED INSTRUCTION

FOR ALL STUDENTS

Hands-On Learning Have students work in mixed-ability groups to create a storyboard for each of the two selections. Each group can choose one of their storyboards as the basis for a movie, radio play, or skit. Display the storyboards and set aside time after reading the selections for groups to perform their productions.

 BEST PRACTICES TOOLKIT—Transparency Storyboard p. C11

FOR LESS–PROFICIENT READERS

In combination with the *Audio Anthology CD* (for the Dave Barry piece only), use one or more Targeted Passages (pp. 496, 499, 503, 504) to ensure that students focus on key selection events, concepts, and skills.

① Targeted Passage [Lines 13–19]

This passage establishes the attitude of the author toward the subject: he looks back with fondness on the memory of his first love.

- What does the phrase "golden moment" (line 14) mean to you? Why does Cosby use it here?
- How does Cosby's view of the world change after he sees the girl?

ANALYZE VISUALS

Activity Have students identify the body language clues that reveal the feelings of the girl and boy in the photograph. ***Possible answers:*** *The girl and boy are not looking at each other. Their linked hands are almost hidden. Their crossed arms signal an unwillingness to be open. Neither one looks very happy. These clues suggest that they are a little awkward with each other and with their relationship.*

BACKGROUND

Hindenburg In this essay, Cosby alludes to the *Hindenburg* disaster. After hearing that the girl he likes already has a boyfriend, he says, "the air left me faster than it left the *Hindenburg*" (lines 66–67). The *Hindenburg* was the largest airship ever built. It was over 800 feet long and was used to carry passengers across the Atlantic between Europe and the United States. In 1937, while landing in New Jersey, the ship caught fire and was destroyed within seconds, leaving nearly a third of the passengers dead.

FOR ENGLISH LEARNERS

Options for Reading Read the first essay aloud, pausing frequently to monitor students' comprehension. For the second essay, have students read along with the *Audio Anthology CD* in small groups. Make sure that students understand that in both essays, the narrators are looking back at their first dating experiences and describing them humorously.

Key Academic Vocabulary Have groups complete Word Questioning organizers for this vocabulary from "Breaking the Ice": *mature* (lines 1, 13), *emerge* (line 4), *intense* (line 46), *communicate* (line 60).

 BEST PRACTICES TOOLKIT—Transparency
Word Questioning p. E9

Prereading For prereading instruction for English learners, see

 BEST PRACTICES TOOLKIT
Scaffolding Reading Instruction pp. 43–46

FOR ADVANCED LEARNERS/PRE–AP

Pre-AP exercises in the bottom channel provide additional challenge for your advanced students. Use them for small groups or individuals.

ADDITIONAL GUIDELINES

For more help with differentiation and tips for classroom management, see

 BEST PRACTICES TOOLKIT
Differentiated Instruction pp. 31–38

COSBY: I like you very much. Will you be my girlfriend?
GODDESS: *(Doing a poor job of **suppressing** a laugh)* I'd rather have some cavities filled. **Ⓑ**

All I did, therefore, was adore her in silent cleanliness. Each Sunday night, I took a bath and then prepared my shirt and pants for display to her. On Monday morning, I took another bath (Bill the Baptist,[2] I should have been called) and then brushed my hair, my shoes, and my eyelashes and went outside to await the pang of another silent passage.

At last, deciding that I could no longer live this way, I sat down one
40 Sunday night and wrote a note that was almost to her. It was to her constant girlfriend and it said:

> *Please don't tell her, but find out what she thinks of me.*
>
> *Bill*

The following morning, I slipped the note to the girlfriend and began the longest wait of my life.

Two **agonizing** days later, the girlfriend slipped me an answer, but I put it into my pocket unread. For hours, I carried it around, afraid to read it because I didn't happen to be in the mood for crushing rejection that day. At last, however, I summoned the courage to open the note and read:

> *She thinks you're cute.*

50 Not even malaria[3] could have taken my temperature to where it went. I had been called many things, but cute was never one of them.

An even lovelier fever lay ahead, for the next time I saw her, she smiled at me, I smiled at her, and then I composed my next winged message to her friend:

> *I think she's cute too. Does she ever talk about me?*

The answer to this one came return mail and it sounded like something by Keats:

> *She talks about you a lot. She knows it when you come around her.*

And the angels sang! Imagine: She actually *knew* it when I came around
60 her! The fact that she also knew it when gnats came around her in no way dampened my ecstasy. **Ⓒ**

And so, we continued to smile as we passed, while I planned my next move. My Western Union[4] style had clearly been charming the pants off her (so to speak) and now I launched my most courageous question yet:

---

2. **Bill the Baptist:** a reference to John the Baptist, a prophet who baptized his followers by submerging them in water.
3. **malaria** (mə-lâr′ē-ə): a disease characterized by chills and fever.
4. **Western Union:** a company that once operated a telegraph service.

498 UNIT 4: MOOD, TONE, AND STYLE

suppressing (sə-prĕ′sĭn)
n. keeping in; holding back **suppress** *v.*

Ⓑ TONE
Reread lines 25–33 and think about what make this passage funny. Wh did Cosby use the word "goddess" instead of the girl's real name?

agonizing (ăg′ə-nī′zĭng)
adj. resulting in great pain or deep sadness **agonize** *v.*

VISUAL VOCABULARY

John Keats (1795–1821), a English Romantic poet

Ⓒ TONE
Cosby's writing **style** shows us his sense of humor. Reread lines 50–61. Record two examples of funny sentences or phrases that affect the tone of the essay.

DIFFERENTIATED INSTRUCTION

FOR ENGLISH LEARNERS

Culture: Clarify Explain that *girlfriend* (line 41) has two meanings. It is used in this line to refer to a friend who happens to be a girl. *Girlfriend* can also mean a romantic companion. Cosby wants the girl he likes to become his romantic companion.

Background Clarify that Western Union telegraph messages (line 63) tended to be very brief because people paid for them by the word.

FOR ADVANCED LEARNERS/PRE–AP

Evaluate Discuss the various devices that Cosby uses to create humor in this essay, such as quirky allusions, subtle irony, and exaggeration, among others. Have students work in small groups to identify and chart examples of the major devices. Ask groups to decide which device contributes most to the humorous tone of the essay.

Does she have a boyfriend?

When I opened the answer the next day in school, the air left me faster than it left the *Hindenburg:*[5]

Yes.

Trying to recover from this deflation,[6] I told myself that I was still cute. I was the cutest man in second place. But perhaps my beloved wasn't aware of the glory she kept passing by. Once more, I sat down and wrote:

How much longer do you think she'll be going with him? And when she's finished with him, can I be next?

Note the elegance and dignity of my appeal. My dignity, however, did have some trouble with the reply:

She thinks she's going to break up with him in about a week, but she promised Sidney she would go with him next. **D**

Suddenly, my aching heart found itself at the end of a line. But it was like a line at a bank: I knew it was leading to a payoff. I also knew that I could cream Sidney in cuteness.

Once she had made the **transition** to Sidney, I patiently began waiting for her to get sick of him. I had to be careful not to rush the illness because Sidney belonged to a tough gang and there was a chance that I might not be walking around too well when the time came for me to inherit her.

And then, one magnificent morning, I received the magic words:

She would like to talk to you.

I wrote back to see if she would wait until I had finished duty at my post as a school crossing guard. Yes, she would wait; I could walk her home. We were going steady now; and how much more torrid our passion would be when I began to *talk* to her.

At last, the words came and I chose them with care. As I walked her home from school, I reached into my **reservoir** of romantic thoughts, smiled at her soulfully, and said, "How you doing?"

Her response was equally poetic: "All right."

"So we're going steady now?"

"You want to?"

"Yeah. Give me your books."

And now, as if our relationship were not already in the depths of desire, I plunged even deeper by saying, "You wanna go to a movie on Saturday?"

"Why not?"

---

5. ***Hindenburg:*** an airship filled with hydrogen gas that caught fire and blew up following a transatlantic flight in 1937.

6. **deflation** (dĭ-flā'shən): the act or process of losing confidence.

D TONE
What is Cosby's attitude toward the notes that are being passed around? Identify the words and descriptions that suggest his attitude.

transition (trăn-zĭsh'ən) *n.* change from one place or condition to another

2 Targeted Passage

reservoir (rĕz'ər-vwär') *n.* a place where anything is collected and stored

---

LITERARY ANALYSIS

D TONE

Possible answer: *The letters are a safe go-between method that he sees as very romantic and that helps him achieve his goal at the time (line 40: "almost to her"; line 53: "winged message"). In retrospect, he sees the idea as somewhat ridiculous (line 63: "my Western Union style") and is gently sarcastic about the method (line 74: "Note the elegance and dignity of my appeal").*

If students need help . . . Read lines 62–75 aloud to enable students to hear the tone.

Lines 76–79
REINFORCE *KEY IDEA*: HUMOR

Discuss How does the contrast between the way romance is usually viewed and the way it is portrayed in these lines create **humor?**
Possible answers: *The girl's businesslike attitude is unexpected. Instead of being swept off her feet, the girl approaches romance cold-bloodedly, as if she is negotiating a business deal. Cosby, the great romantic, is willing to accept this approach, even though it reminds him of waiting in a bank line.*

FOR LESS–PROFICIENT READERS
2 Targeted Passage [Lines 78–97]

This passage highlights the tone of the essay: Cosby humorously recounts the turning point of his relationship.

- Why is Cosby content to wait for the girl's relationship with Sidney to run its course?
- How does Cosby find out that it's his turn to date the girl?
- What is funny about Cosby's describing their relationship as "going steady"?

FOR ENGLISH LEARNERS

Vocabulary: Idioms and Slang Have students work in pairs to figure out the meanings of these and other phrases in the essay. Remind students to use context clues and their own knowledge to help define each phrase.

- *going with him* (line 72), "involved with him romantically"
- *break up with him* (line 76), "stop dating him"
- *cream Sidney* (line 80), "outshine him"

- *get sick of him* (line 82), "become tired of him"
- *going steady* (line 89), "dating each other and no one else"
- *smooth opening move* (line 114), "elegant way to begin getting closer to the girl"

There might have been reasons. Some people were looking at us now because she was so beautiful, people possibly wondering what she was doing with me; but I knew that I was someone special to be the love of a vision like this, no matter how nearsighted that vision might be.

When we reached her door, I said, "Well, I'll see you Saturday."

"Right," she replied as only she could say it.

"What time?"

"One o'clock."

110 When this day of days finally arrived, I took her to a theater where I think the admission was a dime. As we took our seats for the matinee, two basic thoughts were in my mind: not to sit in gum and to be a gentleman.

Therefore, I didn't hold her hand. Instead, I put my arm around the top of her seat in what I felt was a smooth opening move. Unfortunately, it was less a move toward love than toward gangrene.[7] With my blood moving uphill, my arm first began to tingle and then to ache. I could not, however, take the arm down and let my blood keep flowing because such a lowering would mean I didn't love her; so I left it up there, its muscles full of pain, its fingertips full of needlepoints. **E**

120 Suddenly, this romantic agony was enriched by a less romantic one: I had to go to the bathroom. Needless to say, I couldn't let her know about this urge, for great lovers never did such things. The answer to "Romeo, Romeo, wherefore art thou, Romeo?"[8] was not "In the men's room, Julie."

What a prince of passion I was at this moment: My arm was dead, my bladder was full, and I was out of money too; but I desperately needed an excuse to move, so I said, "You want some popcorn?"

"No," she said.

"Fine, I'll go get some."

When I tried to move, every part of me could move except my arm: It
130 was dead. I reached over and pulled it down with the other one, trying to be as casual as a man could be when pulling one of his arms with the other one.

"What's the matter?" she said.

"Oh, nothing," I replied. "I'm just taking both of my arms with me."

A few minutes later, as I came out of the bathroom, I was startled to meet her: She was coming from the bathroom *too*. How good it was to find another thing that we had in common. With empty bladders and full hearts, we returned to our seats to continue our love. **F**

---

7. **gangrene** (găng′grēn′): tissue decay in a part of the body.

8. **"Romeo . . . Romeo?":** approximate quote of a question asked by Juliet in William Shakespeare's play *Romeo and Juliet*.

500 UNIT 4: MOOD, TONE, AND STYLE

E TONE
Reread lines 113–119. In your chart, record examples of Cosby's unusual descriptive phrases.

F TONE
In what way does the last paragraph convey a sense of innocence?

---

omprehension

1. **Recall** How old is Bill Cosby when the events in the essay take place?

2. **Recall** Where do young Cosby and the girl go on their date?

3. **Summarize** Why is he uncomfortable on the date?

terary Analysis

4. **Make Inferences** Why does Cosby pass notes with the girl's best friend rather than talking to the girl directly? Explain your answer.

5. **Examine Word Choice** Cosby uses formal-sounding phrases such as "and the angels sang" and "this day of days" in this essay. Reread lines 87–94 to find other formal language. How does this language add **humor** to the essay?

6. **Analyze Tone** What seems to be Cosby's attitude toward his first love? Give examples of the words, images, and descriptions that convey this tone.

7. **Draw Conclusions** Why do you think Cosby never names or provides much description about his first love?

omparing Tone

Now that you've read "The Only Girl in the World for Me," add more information to your chart.

	"The Only Girl in the World for Me"	"Breaking the Ice"
Topic of the essay		
Words and phrases that display an attitude	"for one golden moment our eyes met"	"Never risk direct contact with the girl in question."
Vivid images and descriptions		
Adjectives that describe the tone		

Comparing Tone

■ **STANDARDS FOCUS** *Set a Purpose for Reading*

	"The Only Girl in the World for Me"
Topic of the essay	Cosby's first love
Words and phrases that display an attitude	"adore her in silent cleanliness" (line 34); "And the angels sang!" (line 59); "I reached into my reservoir of romantic thoughts, smiled at her soulfully" (lines 92–93)
Vivid images and descriptions	"brushed my hair, my shoes, and my eyelashes" (line 37); "crushing rejection" (line 47); "the air left me faster than it left the Hindenburg" (lines 66–67); "fingertips full of needlepoints" (line 119); "with empty bladders and full hearts" (line 136)
Adjectives that describe the tone	humorous, gently ironic, sentimental

---

Practice and Apply

After Reading

For additional support of post-reading questions, use these copy masters:

R RESOURCE MANAGER—Copy Masters

Reading Check p. 123 (to check understanding of the selection)

Question Support p. 124 (**After Reading** questions adapted for English learners and less-proficient readers)

Additional selection questions are provided for teachers on page 115.

ANSWERS

Comprehension

1. *Cosby is 12 years old at the time the events in the essay take place (line 2).*

2. *Cosby and his girlfriend go to a movie.*

3. *Cosby puts his arm around the back of her chair, and his arm falls asleep. He doesn't want to lower his arm because she might misinterpret it. He also needs to go to the restroom but is embarrassed to say so.*

Literary Analysis

Possible answers:

4. *He's not sure whether she'll reject him, so he communicates through her best friend to avoid an embarrassing situation.*

5. *The language emphasizes the seriousness with which he took his first love, but it is out of proportion to the situation. The exaggeration adds humor to the situation.*

6. ● **STANDARDS FOCUS** *Tone He looks back at his first romance and laughs at himself but in a heart-warming and sentimental way. Some examples of words and phrases that convey this tone include "just her look was enough of a lift for me" (lines 21–22) and "adore her in silent cleanliness" (line 34).*

7. *The subject is not about the specific girl but rather about Cosby's first experience with love. He doesn't need to name her because she is meant to represent everyone's first love.*

Lines 1–6
DISCUSSION PROMPTS

Use these prompts to help students determine the author's purpose and approach to his subject:

Connect How did you think this comparison between the author and the mother fish was going to end? What is your reaction to the conclusion? *Students may say that they thought the mother would continue caring for her young, not eat them. They may have been surprised or shocked.*

Interpret What might you predict about the rest of this essay based on this first passage? *Possible answer: Barry might surprise readers by including unexpected events or conclusions.*

Synthesize What do you learn about the author's purpose from reading the introduction? *Possible answer: Barry is warning readers that anyone looking for helpful information probably will not find it in this essay. His purpose is to entertain.*

ANALYZE VISUALS

Possible answer: The essay will be about a boy making an important phone call, maybe to a girl.

About the Art Chinese-American artist Diana Ong (b. 1940) works in several media, including watercolors, acrylics, pen and ink, and wood. She also generates art by computer. Her art has graced the covers of many books.

BREAKING THE ICE
DAVE BARRY

A s a mature adult, I feel an obligation to help the younger generation, just as the mother fish guards her unhatched eggs, keeping her lonely vigil day after day, never leaving her post, not even to go to the bathroom, until her tiny babies emerge and she is able, at last, to eat them. "She may be your mom, but she's still a fish" is a wisdom nugget that I would pass along to any fish eggs reading this column.

But today I want to talk about dating. This subject was raised in a letter to me from a young person named Eric Knott, who writes:

ANALYZE VISUALS
As you look at this picture, **predict** what the essay will be about.

DIFFERENTIATED INSTRUCTION

FOR LESS–PROFICIENT READERS
Reading Strategy Follow-Up: Set a Purpose for Reading Read the first six lines aloud. Have students return to their charts from page 495 and work in pairs to record words and phrases that reveal the author's attitude toward his subject. Use these details to identify the tone of this initial passage.

FOR ADVANCED LEARNERS/PRE–AP
Evaluate As they read, have students chart examples of the devices that Barry uses to create humor, including exaggeration, irony, comparisons, and allusions. Ask students to discuss in small groups which technique contributes most to the tone of the essay.

Compare After students read the essay, have them use their evaluations to compare the authors' styles in a Comparison Matrix.

 BEST PRACTICES TOOLKIT—Transparency
Comparison Matrix p. A24

	Cosby	Barry
Irony	mild/subtle Example: "She was coming from . . . in common." (lines 135–136)	sharp/caustic Example: "a fun first date . . . real-estate closing" (lines 68–69)
Allusions	mostly historical (John the Baptist, John Keats, Hindenburg)	popular culture (Chip 'n' Dale)

I have got a big problem. There's this girl in my English class who is *really* good-looking. However, I don't think she knows I exist. I want to ask her out, but I'm afraid she will say no, and I will be the freak of the week. What should I do? **Ⓐ**

Eric, you have sent your question to the right mature adult, because as a young person I spent a lot of time thinking about this very problem. Starting in about eighth grade, my time was divided as follows:

Academic Pursuits: 2 percent.
Zits: 16 percent.
Trying to Figure Out How to Ask Girls Out: 82 percent.

The most sensible way to ask a girl out is to walk directly up to her on foot and say, "So, you want to go out? Or what?" I never did this. I knew, as Eric Knott knows, that there was always the possibility that the girl would say no, thereby leaving me with no viable option[1] but to leave Harold C. Crittenden Junior High School forever and go into the woods and become a bark-eating hermit whose only companions would be the gentle and understanding woodland creatures.

"Hey, ZITFACE!" the woodland creatures would shriek in cute little Chip 'n' Dale voices while raining acorns down upon my head. "You wanna DATE? HAHAHAHAHAHA." **Ⓑ**

So the first rule of dating is: Never risk direct contact with the girl in question. Your role model should be the nuclear submarine, gliding silently beneath the ocean surface, tracking an enemy target that does not even begin to suspect that the submarine would like to date it. I spent the vast majority of 1960 keeping a girl named Judy under surveillance,[2] maintaining a minimum distance of 50 lockers to avoid the danger that I might somehow get into a conversation with her, which could have led to disaster:

JUDY: Hi.
ME: Hi.
JUDY: Just in case you have ever thought about having a date with me, the answer is no.
WOODLAND CREATURES: HAHAHAHAHAHA.

The only problem with the nuclear-submarine technique is that it's difficult to get a date with a girl who has never, technically, been asked. This is why you need Phil Grant. Phil was a friend of mine who had the

---

1. **viable option:** choice that has a possibility of working.
2. **surveillance** (sər-vā'ləns): close observation.

Ⓐ TONE
Reread lines 1–12. What is the **topic** of the essay?

❸ Targeted Passage

Ⓑ TONE
Reread lines 26–28. What is Barry's attitude toward his younger self? Note how the **style** of using capital letters helps communicate this attitude.

Ⓐ TONE
Record students' answers in the chart from page 495. *Possible answer: The topic is dating—specifically, asking girls out.*

Ⓑ TONE
Possible answer: The author is somewhat critical of his younger self. The capitalization emphasizes the self-mocking tone.

If students need help... Read lines 26–28 aloud, emphasizing the capitalized words and projecting the tone.

Lines 32–36
REINFORCE *KEY IDEA*: HUMOR

Discuss What is the source of the **humor** in this image of the author keeping his distance from Judy? *Possible answer: He uses exaggeration to emphasize the irony of the situation—saying he doesn't want to be closer than 50 lockers away from the girl he wants to date.*

FOR LESS–PROFICIENT READERS
❸ Targeted Passage [Lines 19–36]

This passage shows Barry's use of exaggeration and irony to produce a mocking tone.

- What does Barry say is the sensible way to ask for a date? What does he actually do?
- What does he say he would have done if he were turned down for a date?
- What are some examples of exaggeration in this passage?

FOR ENGLISH LEARNERS
Culture: Clarify Explain these references:

- "zits" (line 17): This is a slang term for acne, raised red bumps on the skin.
- "bark-eating hermit" (line 24): This is a reference to someone who keeps to himself, foraging for food in the woods.
- "Chip 'n' Dale" (line 27): These are two cartoon chipmunks that speak in high voices.

❸ TONE

Remind students to include details from this paragraph in their charts before answering the question. *Possible answer: The tone of this paragraph is quite sarcastic. The author uses exaggeration to make the situation of arranging a date seem complex and very serious.*

Extend the Discussion What is Barry's purpose in projecting this tone?

---

❹ TONE

Guide students to add these words and phrases to their charts: "extremely quiet drive" (line 55); "hideously embarrassing" (line 56); "sitting in the backseat about 75 feet apart" (line 59); "After what seemed like several years" (line 61). *Possible answer: These words and phrases indicate that Barry did not enjoy the ride to the movie theater.*

SELECTION WRAP–UP

REFLECT Have students think about how Barry has made his particular experience relevant to many readers. To which parts of his essay might readers most easily connect?

⭐ **CRITIQUE** Have students evaluate whether Barry accomplishes his purpose in this essay. Ask students what he could have included to make his essay more entertaining.

---

ability to talk to girls. It was a mysterious superhuman power he had, comparable to X-ray vision. So, after several thousand hours of intense discussion and planning with me, Phil approached a girl he knew named Nancy, who approached a girl named Sandy, who was a direct personal friend of Judy's and who passed the word back to Phil via
50 Nancy that Judy would be willing to go on a date with me. This procedure protected me from direct humiliation. . . . ❸

Thus it was that, finally, Judy and I went on an actual date, to see a movie in White Plains, New York. If I were to sum up the romantic ambience[3] of this date in four words, those words would be: "My mother was driving." This made for an extremely quiet drive, because my mother, realizing that her presence was hideously embarrassing, had to pretend she wasn't there. If it had been legal, I think she would have got out and sprinted alongside the car, steering through the window. Judy and I, sitting in the backseat about 75 feet apart, were also silent, unable
60 to communicate without the assistance of Phil, Nancy, and Sandy. ❹

After what seemed like several years we got to the movie theater, where my mother went off to sit in the Parents and Lepers Section. The movie was called *North to Alaska,* but I can tell you nothing else about it because I spent the whole time wondering whether it would be necessary to amputate my right arm, which was not getting any blood flow as a result of being perched for two hours like a petrified snake on the back of Judy's seat exactly one molecule away from physical contact.

So it was definitely a fun first date, featuring all the relaxed spontaneity of a real-estate closing,[4] and in later years I did regain some feeling in
70 my arm. My point, Eric Knott, is that the key to successful dating is self-confidence. I bet that good-looking girl in your English class would LOVE to go out with you. But YOU have to make the first move. So just do it! Pick up that phone! Call Phil Grant. ◕

④ **Targeted Passage**

❸ TONE
Reread lines 44–51. Note Barry's description of Phil Grant's "superhuman" abilities. How would you describe the tone of this paragraph?

❹ TONE
Does Barry seem to enjoy the drive to the movie theater? Note words and phrases that give his description of the ride either a positive or a negative tone.

---

3. **ambience** (ăm′bē-əns): atmosphere; environment.
4. **spontaneity of a real-estate closing:** A real-estate closing is a meeting where a piece of property transfers from a seller to a buyer. Many required documents are signed, in a very formal, un-spontaneous way.

DIFFERENTIATED INSTRUCTION

FOR LESS–PROFICIENT READERS
④ **Targeted Passage [Lines 61–70]**

This passage illustrates Barry's use of comparisons to convey his attitude toward his first date: he does not enjoy the date.

- To what does Barry compare his arm? Is this a positive or negative image?
- To what does he compare the date?
- Does Barry have a more or less romantic view of his experience than Cosby?

FOR ENGLISH LEARNERS
Comprehension: Concept Support Make sure students understand the humor of the conclusion. Read lines 70–73 aloud, pausing before the last sentence. Explain that most readers would be expecting the author to urge Eric to call the girl himself. Instead, he says to call Phil Grant, the same person who arranged Barry's first date. The surprise of this suggestion and the reintroduction of Phil Grant create a humorous conclusion.

---

omprehension

1. **Recall** How does Dave Barry ask Judy out on a date?

2. **Recall** Where do they go on their date?

3. **Clarify** Why is Barry uncomfortable on the date?

terary Analysis

4. **Make Inferences** Reread Barry's advice to Eric Knott in lines 70–71. Does Barry himself display self-confidence during his first date? Cite details from the essay to support your answer.

5. **Analyze Style** On the basis of this example of Barry's style, how would you describe his sense of **humor** to someone who hasn't read anything by him?

6. **Compare Descriptions** Compare how Cosby and Barry describe being at a movie with a girl, focusing not only on what each author says about his experience but how he says it. Cite key words and phrases.

7. **Draw Conclusions** Which author seems to have enjoyed his teenage years more? Give clues from each essay that led you to your conclusion.

8. **Evaluate Humor** Consider which essay made you laugh more. What did you think was the most effective part of the funnier essay? Why?

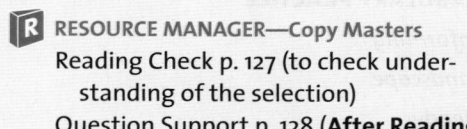

MARYLAND OBJECTIVES

LITERATURE STANDARD
3.A.7.b Analyze language choices that create tone

omparing Tone

Finish filling in your chart with information on "Breaking the Ice." Now add the final question to your chart and try answering it.

	"The Only Girl in the World for Me"	"Breaking the Ice"
Topic of the essay		
Words and phrases that display an attitude	"for one golden moment our eyes met"	"Never risk direct contact with the girl in question."
Vivid images and descriptions		
Adjectives that describe the tone		
In what ways are the essays similar or different in tone?		

Comparing Tone

■ **STANDARDS FOCUS** *Set a Purpose for Reading* The third column of students' charts should include the following details:

Row 1: dating—specifically, asking a girl out

Row 2: "I spent the vast majority of 1960 keeping a girl named Judy under surveillance, maintaining a minimum distance of 50 lockers" (lines 32–34); "This procedure protected me from direct humiliation" (lines 50–51); "it was definitely a fun first date, featuring all the relaxed spontaneity of a real-estate closing" (lines 68–69)

Row 3: "bark-eating hermit" (line 24); "ZITFACE" (line 26); "nuclear-submarine technique" (line 42); "It was a mysterious superhuman power he had, comparable to X-ray vision" (line 45); "Parents and Lepers Section" (line 62); "like a petrified snake" (line 66); "exactly one molecule away from physical contact" (lines 67–68)

Row 4: sarcastic, humorous

Similarities: Both are humorous.

Differences: Cosby's tone is more sentimental, gentle, and understanding. Barry's tone is sharp and very ironic.

Practice and Apply

After Reading

For additional support of post-reading questions, use these copy masters:

R **RESOURCE MANAGER—Copy Masters**
Reading Check p. 127 (to check understanding of the selection)
Question Support p. 128 (**After Reading** questions adapted for English learners and less-proficient readers)

Additional selection questions are provided for teachers on page 115.

ANSWERS

Comprehension

1. *Barry asks a friend, who asks Judy's friend, who asks Judy.*

2. *The author and Judy go to a movie.*

3. *His arm goes numb from resting on the back of Judy's seat.*

Literary Analysis

Possible answers:

4. *Barry displays no self-confidence. He is too afraid of rejection to ask Judy out himself. He endures physical pain at the movie theater rather than risk offending her by moving his arm.*

5. ● **STANDARDS FOCUS** *Tone Barry's humor is dry, sarcastic, and witty. Readers must "read between the lines" to get all of his jokes.*

6. *Both boys put their arms around the back of the girl's chair. Each one's arm falls asleep. Cosby's description glorifies his suffering—it was all for love. He uses phrases such as "lowering would mean I didn't love her" (line 118) and "romantic agony" (line 120). Barry's description is more negative—"wondering whether it would be necessary to amputate my right arm" (lines 64–65), "perched . . . like a petrified snake" (lines 66–67).*

7. *Cosby seems to have more positive memories, whereas Barry seems happy to have moved out of an awkward phase ("zitface," "disaster," "humiliation").*

8. *Students' responses will vary and should include specific reasons and text examples.*

ANSWERS

Vocabulary in Context

VOCABULARY PRACTICE

1. *informing*
2. *landscape*
3. *heady*
4. *notice*
5. *restoring*

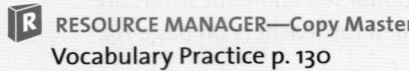 **RESOURCE MANAGER—Copy Master**
Vocabulary Practice p. 130

VOCABULARY IN WRITING

Suggest that students skim the essay and jot down possible best and worst moments. They should then survey their list to decide which ideas might be incorporated into a paragraph and described using vocabulary words.

VOCABULARY STRATEGY: LITERAL AND FIGURATIVE MEANINGS *(also an EL language objective)*

- Remind students to use the context of the word to help them identify the meaning that is intended.
- Explain that a comparison is implied by the use of a figurative word. Tell them that rephrasing the sentence as a comparison might help them to define the word figuratively. For example, "After the windstorm, the leaves covered the ground like a blanket."

Possible answers:

1. *figurative: covering*
2. *figurative: unable to think logically*
3. *figurative: situation with many complicated parts*
4. *literal: legal way to remove debt*
5. *figurative: something to be overcome*

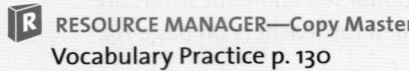 **RESOURCE MANAGER—Copy Master**
Vocabulary Strategy p. 131

ⓘ **Vocabulary Center at ClassZone.com**
Additional Vocabulary Activities

Vocabulary in Context

VOCABULARY PRACTICE

In each item, choose the word that differs most in meaning from the other words. Refer to a dictionary or thesaurus if you need help.

1. (a) concealing, (b) suppressing, (c) informing, (d) hiding
2. (a) container, (b) trunk, (c) landscape, (d) reservoir
3. (a) concerned, (b) heady, (c) worried, (d) agitated
4. (a) transition, (b) change, (c) passage, (d) notice
5. (a) painful, (b) tormenting, (c) restoring, (d) agonizing

VOCABULARY IN WRITING

Decide what was the best or the worst part of Cosby's romance as he describes it. Write a paragraph explaining your ideas, using two or more vocabulary words. Here is a sample opening sentence.

> **EXAMPLE SENTENCE**
>
> *The most **agonizing** part of the romance was waiting for it to start.*

VOCABULARY STRATEGY: LITERAL AND FIGURATIVE MEANINGS

MARYLAND OBJECTIVES

READING STANDARD
1.D.3.a Use context to determine the meanings of words

Many words have multiple meanings. Some meanings are straightforward, or **literal**, while others are more symbolic, or **figurative.** For example, there are two meanings of the word *reservoir*:

- literal definition: an artificial lake used to collect and store water
- figurative definition: a place where *anything* is collected or stored

When you encounter words that have both a literal and a figurative meaning, it is important to recognize which meaning the writer intends.

PRACTICE For each sentence, tell whether the boldfaced word has a literal or figurative meaning. Then give the meaning of the word as it is used.

1. After the windstorm, a **blanket** of leaves covered the ground.
2. Franklin was **blinded** by bitterness and envy.
3. Mrs. Nelson had to go through a **maze** of confusing letters and bills.
4. When they could no longer make their payments, they went **bankrupt.**
5. Catching a cold just before the debate was one more **hurdle** for Janice.

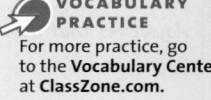
VOCABULARY PRACTICE
For more practice, go to the **Vocabulary Center** at **ClassZone.com.**

DIFFERENTIATED INSTRUCTION

FOR ENGLISH LEARNERS

Vocabulary in Writing

1. Ask students to pick out the part of Cosby's romance that was *heady* and the part that was *agonizing.*
2. Have them write two sentences explaining each part and using the vocabulary words appropriately.

FOR ADVANCED LEARNERS/PRE–AP

Vocabulary Strategy Have students list other words and expressions that might be used figuratively in everyday speech or writing. Have students contribute to a class list. Define each example and have volunteers use it in a sentence.

Writing for Assessment

1. READ THE PROMPT

In writing assessments, you might be asked to compare the **tones** of essays—even humorous essays like the ones you just read.

> **PROMPT**
>
> Both "The Only Girl in the World for Me" and "Breaking the Ice" focus on the sometimes amusing, sometimes painful topic of love. However, each author has used a unique tone to present his experience. In four or five paragraphs, describe the tone of each essay, and then compare how each author developed that tone. Support your response with details from the two essays.

◄ **STRATEGIES IN ACTION**

1. I need to **describe the attitude** each author has toward his subject.
2. I have to show the **similar and different** ways each author makes his attitude known.
3. I should **give examples** from the essays to help explain my ideas.

2. PLAN YOUR WRITING

Review the chart you filled out on page 505. Use the information to help you describe the tone of each essay and identify the similarities and differences in the words, images, and descriptions that convey the tone. Then think about how you will set up your response.

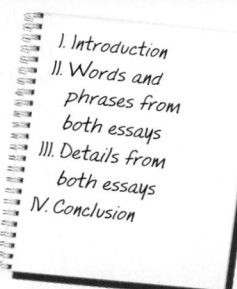

I. Introduction
II. Words and phrases from both essays
III. Details from both essays
IV. Conclusion

- Do you want to describe the first essay and then point out similarities and differences in the second essay?
- Do you want to compare the words and phrases of both essays in one paragraph and the details of both essays in another paragraph? The sample outline shows this way of organizing.

Once you have decided, outline the order of your paragraphs.

3. DRAFT YOUR RESPONSE

Introduction Include the titles and authors' names for the essays. Identify the tone of each essay, and provide an overview of the similarities and differences in how the authors communicate tone.

Body Stay focused on the points you want to make in each paragraph. Make sure you support each point with an example from one of the essays.

Conclusion Restate your main idea and leave the reader with a final thought about tone and humor.

Revision Check to see that your paragraphs flow smoothly. If they don't, add transitional phrases such as *on the other hand*, or *while both essays*.

Writing for Assessment

1. **READ THE PROMPT**
   - Read the prompt aloud. Ask volunteers to identify key words and phrases that define the task.
   - Discuss each strategy. Help students brainstorm a list of words they could use to **describe** an author's **attitude**, such as *fond* and *sarcastic*.

2. **PLAN YOUR WRITING**
   - Direct students to use their charts from page 505. The chart should include most of the information that they need to write the response.
   - Guide students to keep their focus on the development of tone and not to stray into a comparison of experiences.
   - Students may find it easier to use a block method of comparison, discussing the way tone is developed in Cosby's essay before moving into examination of Barry's essay. With this model, the conclusion might be used to highlight similarities and differences between the development of tone in each essay.

3. **DRAFT YOUR RESPONSE**
   - Remind students to begin each body paragraph with a strong topic sentence.
   - List transitions on the board that might strengthen the unity within each paragraph and between paragraphs, such as *in addition, unlike, in contrast,* and *similarly.*

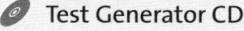 RESOURCE MANAGER—Copy Master
Writing for Assessment p. 132

Assess and Reteach

Assess

RESOURCE MANAGER—Copy Masters
Selection Tests A, B/C pp. 133–134, 135–136

Test Generator CD

Reteach

STANDARDS LESSON FILE
Literature Lesson 37: Tone
Vocabulary Lesson 19: Multiple-Meaning Words

DIFFERENTIATED INSTRUCTION

FOR LESS–PROFICIENT WRITERS

Plan Your Writing

- Review charts from page 505.
- Discuss the details that best show tone. Have students circle those ideas on their charts and include them in their essays.

Draft Your Response

Give students this template for writing their responses:

Introduction The tone of [title of essay] by [author] is [adjective from chart]. In contrast, the tone of [title of essay] by [author] is [adjective from chart].

Middle paragraphs

- [First author] creates this tone by using vivid words and phrases. [Explain examples.] He also uses details to show his attitude. [Explain examples.]
- [Second author] also uses language and details to convey tone. [Explain examples.]

Conclusion [Explain similarities and differences.]

Focus and Motivate

OBJECTIVES

Literary Analysis
- explore the key idea of **sentimental**
- identify and analyze irony
- identify and analyze elements of style
- read poetry

Reading
- develop strategies for reading poetry

SUMMARY

These two poems by Dorothy Parker present an ironic view of romance. In "One Perfect Rose," the first two stanzas describe the gift of a rose to symbolize love. In the final stanza, the speaker reveals she'd rather have a limousine. In "Song for an April Dusk," the speaker evokes romantic stories with images of nature and mythical creatures. In the final line, the speaker says that such stories bore her.

Does everyone LOVE *being in love?*

Discuss the question with students. To help students understand the **KEY IDEA,** point out the context clues that help them understand the meaning of **sentimental.** Then have students do the **DISCUSS** activity. Conclude by discussing the question "Is our society in love with love?"

Selection Resources

One Perfect Rose
Song for an April Dusk
Poems by Dorothy Parker

Does everyone LOVE *being in love?*

MARYLAND OBJECTIVES

LITERATURE STANDARDS
3.A.4.b Analyze language and structural features
3.A.7.e Analyze elements of style

KEY IDEA Love is a popular subject in songs, books, and movies. In fact, romance novels make up nearly half of all adult paperback fiction sales in the United States. But some people prefer things that aren't too "mushy," overly emotional, or **sentimental.** Dorothy Parker's poems give readers a sense of whether she would love being in love.

DISCUSS One of the most popular holidays for cards is Valentine's Day. Why do you think this is so? Talk about the reasons people send Valentine's Day cards. Also, talk about other holidays that are popular for sending cards.

508

 **RESOURCE MANAGER UNIT 4**

Plan and Teach pp. 137–144
Literary Analysis
Irony pp. 145, 146†*
Question Support p. 149*
Reading
Form in Poetry pp. 147, 148†*
Reading Fluency p. 150

Assessment
Selection Tests A, B/C pp. 151*, 153*
 Test Generator CD

BEST PRACTICES TOOLKIT

Differentiated Instruction
pp. 31–38*
Graphic Organizers
Comparison Matrix • T Chart

Reading Support
Audio Anthology CD*

Technology
Literature Center at
ClassZone.com

WriteSmart CD

---

* Resources for Differentiation   † Also in Spanish

LITERARY ANALYSIS: IRONY

In the two poems you are about to read, the poet uses irony. **Irony** is a contrast between what is expected and what actually happens. Dorothy Parker creates irony in her poetry by

- starting with romantic images
- using form and language to set the poem's **tone,** creating what the reader thinks is Parker's attitude toward the subject
- revealing a different attitude at the end of the poem, taking the reader by surprise

Parker's ironic shifts in attitude add humor to her poems. Her use of irony also allows her to challenge a common assumption. As you read her poems, think about the expectation that women will always respond in the same way. Then notice how the **speaker,** or voice that talks to the reader, responds to romance.

READING STRATEGY: FORM IN POETRY

An important part of understanding poetry comes from understanding its form. A poem's **form** is the way it is laid out on the page. Traditional poems follow regular, or repeated, patterns.

- The length of each **line** in a poem helps create the poem's **rhythm** and meaning.
- Lines might be grouped into **stanzas,** which often express a single idea or **theme.**
- The pattern of lines and stanzas often creates a pattern of **rhyming** words.

Poets choose the form that best suits the intended message of a particular poem. Parker purposely chooses a traditional form for her ironic poems. As you read, make notes about the poems' lines, stanzas, and rhyming words. Use a chart like the one shown.

One Perfect Rose	
Line length	3 the same length, 1 shorter
Number of stanzas	
Rhyming words	

Author Online

Dorothy Parker
1893–1967

Harsh Humor
After being fired from *Vanity Fair* magazine in New York City for writing reviews that were considered too harsh, Dorothy Parker started writing poetry. With several other writers, she founded a literary group called the Algonquin Round Table. Parker and the rest of the group became known for their humorous and lively conversations.

A New Attitude As a young woman, Parker read the sentimental poetry that was popular in the Victorian era. When writing poetry of her own, Parker blended traditional poetic forms with the "challenge everything" attitude of her time. This new style was a hit. Her first book of poetry, *Enough Rope* (1926), was a bestseller.

Social Critic The 1920s are often symbolized by "flappers"—independent women who challenged what was considered a woman's proper role in society. Parker used her sharp humor to express her independent spirit and to help her comment on issues such as materialism and the limited roles available to women in the 1920s.

 MORE ABOUT THE AUTHOR
For more on Dorothy Parker, visit the **Literature Center at ClassZone.com.**

509

Teach

STANDARDS FOCUS

LITERARY ANALYSIS

● **IRONY**

- Ask students why a fire station burning down is ironic. ***Possible answer:*** *One would expect fire fighters to be able to put out a fire in their own workplace.*
- Encourage students to predict what they might expect from a poem filled with romantic images—and what irony it might contain. ***Possible answer:*** *One would expect the poem to praise romance. It would be ironic if the poem expressed a different attitude.*

CHECK UNDERSTANDING Ask students for other examples of ironic situations in which reality contrasts with expectations.

READING STRATEGY

■ **FORM IN POETRY**

Review the boldfaced terms on page 509. Explain that Parker's traditional form includes all the qualities noted there. Point out that a **stanza** is like a paragraph in a prose story. Encourage students to look for the main idea of each stanza.

CHECK UNDERSTANDING Have students explain what lines and stanzas are in their own words.

® **RESOURCE MANAGER—Copy Master**
Form in Poetry p. 147 (for student use while reading the poems)

DIFFERENTIATED INSTRUCTION

FOR ALL STUDENTS
For general guidelines on differentiating instruction, see

 BEST PRACTICES TOOLKIT
Differentiated Instruction pp. 31–38

FOR LESS—PROFICIENT READERS
Concept Support Help students understand Parker's use of irony by drawing two doors on the board, one labeled *sentimental* and the other *uncaring.* Explain that a poem would be ironic if readers thought they were heading for one door but then suddenly found themselves standing in front of the other. For example, a writer might start out using words and images that suggest a sentimental attitude but then, near the end of the poem, unexpectedly reveal an uncaring attitude.

FOR ENGLISH LEARNERS
Options for Reading Read "One Perfect Rose" aloud and help students paraphrase the main idea of each stanza. Make sure students understand the irony in the last stanza. Next have students listen to the *Audio Anthology CD* as they read along. Then do an echo reading of the poem with students. Repeat this procedure with "Song for an April Dusk."

Practice and Apply

REINFORCE *KEY IDEA*:
SENTIMENTAL

Discuss How does the speaker describe the rose in a **sentimental** way? *Possible answer: She describes it as a messenger of love (line 2) and as a magic charm that holds the heart of the person who sent it (lines 5–8).*

READING STRATEGY

Ⓐ FORM IN POETRY

Have students include this information in their charts (introduced on page 509). *Possible answer: The first and third lines rhyme and the second and fourth lines rhyme. The pattern is the same in the other stanzas.*

If students need help ...

1. Write this list on the board:

   line 1: *met*

   line 2: *chose*

   line 3: *wet*

   line 4: *rose*

2. Label line 1 "a." Ask students which line rhymes with it *(line 3)*. Label line 3 "a."

3. Label line 2 "b," and follow the same procedure as above.

4. Direct students to conclude the poem's rhyme pattern is *abab*. Have them find examples of the pattern in other stanzas.

LITERARY ANALYSIS

Ⓑ IRONY

Possible answer: The use of the word limousine *in line 10 shifts the tone of the poem; the straightforward question begun in line 9 suggests the shift of tone.*

If students need help ...

1. Remind them that **tone** is the expression of the writer's attitude.

2. Have students reread the first two stanzas and look for words and details that suggest tone. Ask them to describe the tone in a single word *(sentimental; romantic)*.

3. Ask what word or detail in the third stanza suggests a different attitude *("limousine," "Ah no," "just my luck")*.

One PERFECT *Rose*

Dorothy Parker

A single flow'r he sent me, since we met.
  All tenderly his messenger he chose;
Deep-hearted, pure, with scented dew still wet—
  One perfect rose. Ⓐ

5 I knew the language of the floweret;
  "My fragile leaves," it said, "his heart enclose."
Love long has taken for his amulet[1]
  One perfect rose.

Why is it no one ever sent me yet
10   One perfect limousine, do you suppose?
Ah no, it's always just my luck to get
  One perfect rose. Ⓑ

Ⓐ FORM IN POETRY
Notice which lines **rhyme** in the first **stanza**. Is the pattern of rhyme the same in stanzas 2 and 3?

Ⓑ IRONY
In which line does the **tone** of the poem change?

---

1. **amulet:** an object worn as a magic charm.

DIFFERENTIATED INSTRUCTION

FOR LESS–PROFICIENT READERS
Reading Strategy Follow-Up: Form in Poetry
Have students examine the way the lines are laid out on the page. Explain that extra space between the groupings of four lines indicates that the groupings are separate stanzas. Have students include this information in their charts from page 509. Direct students to place information about the rhyme pattern in their charts as well.

FOR ADVANCED LEARNERS/PRE–AP
Analyze Tone To help students contrast the techniques Parker uses to convey tone, distribute copies of the Comparison Matrix. Encourage them to find words from both poems that allude to sentimental Victorian poetry and others that suggest the more modern tone of the 1920s. Invite students to identify sentence structures that reinforce each tone. Allow small groups to share their charts.

 BEST PRACTICES TOOLKIT—Transparency
Comparison Matrix p. A24

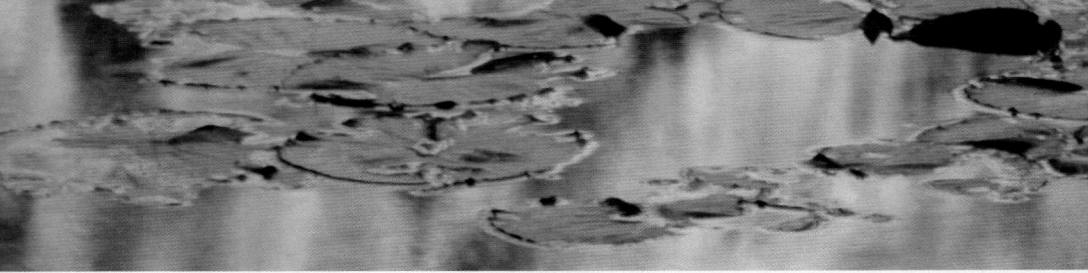

C FORM IN POETRY

Possible answer: Every pair of lines is a sentence, with the second line usually slightly shorter than the first. Most pairs begin with the words "Tell me." This repetition of form and phrase makes the poem monotonous and predictable, and it moves along with a fairly quick, regular rhythm.

If students need help ... Remind students that the consistent length of each pair of lines (one longer line followed by one shorter line) helps create the poem's rhythm. Ask them to notice what words are repeated at the beginning of many lines. Read the poem aloud to help them feel the rhythm.

LITERARY ANALYSIS

D IRONY

Possible answer: Throughout the poem the speaker has been describing a series of romantic images, leading readers to believe that the speaker likes romantic stories. In the last line, the speaker reveals that such stories bore her.

If students need help ... Have students summarize the meaning of each stanza up through line 22. Then ask students what is different about the last two lines.

SELECTION WRAP–UP

⭐ **CRITIQUE** Ask students to evaluate how effective Parker is in building up a romantic attitude in the poems and then shifting to a different attitude at the end of each poem. Encourage them to give examples to support their opinions.

READING FLUENCY

Distribute the copy masters and have students work in groups to practice fluency.

📄 RESOURCE MANAGER—Copy Master
Reading Fluency p. 150

Song for an APRIL DUSK
Dorothy Parker

Tell me tales of a lilied pool
    Asleep beneath the sun.
Tell me of woodlands deep and cool,
    When chuckling satyrs[1] run.
5 Tell me, in light and tinkling words,
    Of rippling, lilting streams.
Tell me of radiant-breasted birds,
    Who sing their amorous[2] dreams.
Tell of the doomed butterfly
10   That flings his hour away.
Fated to live and love and die
    Before the death of day. **C**

Tell me tales of the moon-pale sprites[3]
    Whose beauty none may know.
15 Tell me of secret, silver nights
    When great red stars are low.
Tell of the virgin Spring, the fair,
    Who roams the circling years.
Rain-drops strung in her fragrant hair,
20   Her eyes a-mist with tears.
Tell me of elves, who leap to kiss,
    Who trip the velvet sward.[4]
Tell me stories of things like this,
    And, boy, will I be bored! **D**

---

1. **satyrs** (sā′tərs): in Greek mythology, woodland spirits in the male form, but with the ears and tail of a horse or goat.
2. **amorous** (ăm′ər-es): filled with love.
3. **sprites:** elves or fairies.
4. **trip the velvet sward:** skip along a smooth lawn.

C FORM IN POETRY
Describe the **rhythm** of this poem. How does **repetition** add to the rhythm?

D IRONY
How does the last line change the meaning of the poem?

DIFFERENTIATED INSTRUCTION

FOR LESS–PROFICIENT READERS
Reading Strategy Follow-Up: Form in Poetry
Help students add information about this poem to their charts. Point out that this poem has only two stanzas. Each twelve-line stanza has three four-line sets in which every other line rhymes. The pattern repeats, but no rhymes are repeated. Ask students why the longer stanzas work in this poem. *(The main idea—romance and myth in nature—is the same in each stanza, though the setting moves from day [first stanza] to night [second stanza].)*

FOR ENGLISH LEARNERS
Vocabulary Support Explain that rhyme depends on sound rather than spelling. Have students work in pairs to identify rhyming pairs in which the rhyming vowels are spelled the same *(pool/cool)* as well as pairs with a similar sound but different spelling *(words/birds)*. Have students use a T Chart to list the different kinds of rhymes in two columns. Clarify understanding as needed.

🧰 BEST PRACTICES TOOLKIT—Transparency
T Chart p. A25

Comprehension

1. **Clarify** In "One Perfect Rose," what gift would the **speaker** prefer to receive?

2. **Summarize** What is the second poem about?

3. **Represent** Choose any pair of lines from "Song for an April Dusk" and illustrate them.

Literary Analysis

4. **Identify Irony** For each poem, complete a chart like the one shown. Record what the first part of the poem leads you to expect, and what actually happens at the end.

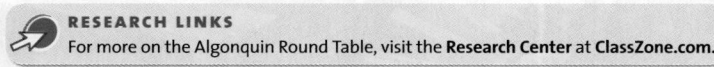

Title: _____	
What We Expect	What Happens

5. **Compare and Contrast** In one to three sentences, compare and contrast the attitudes about romance expressed in "One Perfect Rose" and "Song for an April Dusk." How are they similar and different?

6. **Analyze Poetic Form** Look back at the notes you made about the poet's use of **lines, stanzas,** and **rhyme.** Explain how Parker's use of traditional form reinforces the **irony** in her poetry.

7. **Analyze Irony** Did the ending of each poem change your understanding of the poem's meaning? Explain your response, using evidence from the poems. Note which ending you found to be more surprising.

8. **Evaluate Style** Parker is known as a witty and humorous writer. On the basis of these poems, do you think she deserves this reputation? Explain, using examples from the poems.

Extension and Challenge

9. **Creative Project: Poetry** Try writing a short, **ironic** poem about love. You may use Parker's poems as a model, if you wish, or follow a different form.

10. **Inquiry and Research** Research to find out who else was in Parker's literary group, the Algonquin Round Table. Investigate what the group did when they met and how long the group was together. Share your opinion as to how this group may have influenced Parker's writing and style.

> **RESEARCH LINKS**
> For more on the Algonquin Round Table, visit the **Research Center** at **ClassZone.com.**

Members of the Algonquin Round Table

Practice and Apply

After Reading

For additional support of post-reading questions, use these copy masters:

R RESOURCE MANAGER—Copy Masters
Irony p. 145 (for practice of literary analysis standards focus)
Question Support p. 149 (**After Reading** questions adapted for English learners and less-proficient readers)

Additional selection questions are provided for teachers on page 141.

ANSWERS
Comprehension

1. *The speaker would prefer a limousine.*

2. *The speaker describes a long list of images that are common in romantic stories. Then the speaker says those stories are boring.*

3. *Students' drawings should reflect specific details described in the lines they chose.*

Literary Analysis
Possible answers:

4. ● **STANDARDS FOCUS** *Irony*
"Rose"—Expect: The speaker will express her love for the person who gave her the rose; Happens: She wishes the rose were a limousine. "Dusk"—Expect: The speaker wants to hear stories full of romantic images; Happens: The speaker says such stories are boring.

5. *Both poems reflect a dislike of romance. In the first, the speaker seems to care more for wealth than for love. In the second, the speaker opposes romantic fantasy in stories but doesn't comment on love in real life.*

6. ■ **STANDARDS FOCUS** *Form in Poetry*
Because the form is traditional, the reader expects that the ideas will be traditional as well. Therefore, the ironic ending comes as a great surprise.

7. *To support their opinions, students should cite evidence of romantic images that contrasted with the surprising endings.*

8. *The endings of these poems show Parker's wit by using such unexpected images (limousine) and language ("just my luck"; "boy, will I be bored") that the reader laughs at the contrast with the intense romantic descriptions that preceded them.*

Extension and Challenge

9. *Students' poems should reflect an understanding of irony by using words and images to create one attitude that is then shifted, by the ending of the poem, to create a different meaning.*

10. *Students should name other writers who regularly met for lunch during the 1920s and 1930s and who were known for witty conversations about literature and society. They influenced Parker by encouraging her use of humor for social criticism.*

Assess and Reteach

Assess
R RESOURCE MANAGER—Copy Masters
Selection Tests A, B/C pp. 151–152, 153–154
Test Generator CD

Reteach
S STANDARDS LESSON FILE
Literature Lesson 33: Irony
Literature Lesson 17: Structure of Poetry

Focus and Motivate

OBJECTIVES

Literary Analysis
- explore the key idea of **connections**
- identify and analyze elements of style
- read poetry

Reading
- monitor

SUMMARY

In the first poem, four girls go to the beach to play. Each has a different experience according to who they are and what they value. In the second poem, the beauty of a November sunset makes a lasting impression on a small child. The third poem focuses on the perennial conflict between the young and the old and the ironic cycle of life in which the young become the old.

Are all things
CONNECTED?

Discuss the question and **KEY IDEA** with students. Challenge students to think of ways in which humans and nature are **connected.** Then have them complete the **WEB IT** activity.

Selection Resources

---

maggie and milly and molly and may
who are you,little i
old age sticks

Poems by E. E. Cummings

Are all things
CONNECTED?

MARYLAND OBJECTIVES

READING/LIT STANDARDS
1.E.3.a Select and apply appropriate strategies during reading
3.A.7.e Analyze elements of style

KEY IDEA A snowflake always has six sides. An insect always has six legs. The moon you see at night is the same moon seen by people in Brazil. In a world of infinite variety, scientists, artists, and writers—including the poet whose work you are about to read—can reveal unexpected **connections**.

WEB IT Think of a plant or an animal, an object, and a very old or very young person that you share connections with. Use a word web to describe each connection. Then compare the connections you noted with those your classmates noted.

Me

My Tomato Plant

I water the plant and give it soil. The plant gives me tomatoes.

514

Selection Resources

**RESOURCE MANAGER UNIT 4**

Plan and Teach pp. 155–162

Literary Analysis
Style in Poetry pp. 163, 164†*
Question Support p. 167*

Reading
Monitor pp. 165, 166†*

Assessment
Selection Tests A, B/C pp. 169*, 171*
Test Generator CD

BEST PRACTICES TOOLKIT

Differentiated Instruction pp. 31–38*

Graphic Organizers/Strategies
Reciprocal Teaching • Read Aloud/ Think Aloud • T Chart

Reading Support
Audio Anthology CD*

Technology
Literature and Vocabulary Centers at **ClassZone.com**

WriteSmart CD

LITERARY ANALYSIS: STYLE IN POETRY

Poet E. E. Cummings has one of the most recognizable **styles** in literature. As with many writers, his style is not in what he says, but in how he says it. To identify the poet's unique style, focus on the following elements:

- **Word Choice** Cummings often invented new words or used familiar words in an unfamiliar way.
- **Form** Cummings often created unusual line breaks in his poetry. Sometimes he even broke a line in the middle of a word. He also arranged the lines of some poems in order to create a visual pattern on the page.
- **Punctuation, Capitalization, and Spacing** Cummings used punctuation in new ways and rarely used capital letters. He sometimes eliminated the space between two words, as well.

As you can see, Cummings broke many "rules." Watch for examples of his style as you read three of his poems.

READING STRATEGY: MONITOR

To get the most meaning out of what you are reading, it is good to occasionally check, or **monitor,** your understanding. One part of monitoring is to **clarify,** or pause to reflect on what you know so far and use clues in the selection to make inferences about meaning. When reading poetry, rephrasing lines in your own words can help make the meaning more clear.

After you read each poem once, read it again. This time, pause to clarify the meaning of the lines as you go. For each poem, it may help you to create a chart like the one shown.

"maggie and milly and molly and may"		
Line Numbers	Poet's Words	My Words
5–6	"milly befriended a stranded star / whose rays five languid fingers were"	Milly discovered a starfish with five arms.

Author Online

An American Original
Beginning at age eight, E. E. Cummings wrote a poem a day. While attending Harvard University, he switched from traditional to modern forms of poetry. He frequently traveled to Paris, where he was exposed to modern forms of literature and art.

E. E. Cummings
1894–1962

A Lot of Style Cummings experimented with a writing style that would later make him famous. While the style of Cummings's poems was new and different, his subject matter and themes were often traditional. He frequently wrote about childhood, relationships, and nature. Cummings was also an accomplished visual artist whose work was frequently exhibited at galleries in New York City.

 MORE ABOUT THE AUTHOR
For more on E. E. Cummings, visit the **Literature Center at ClassZone.com.**

Background

Breaking It Down Cummings wrote during a period of literary and artistic experimentation. He was influenced by writers such as Gertrude Stein and artists such as Pablo Picasso. These writers and artists were trying to break down language and images into their most basic elements. Cummings frequently broke up his poems on the page, with the aim of making their appearance add to their meaning.

515

Teach

STANDARDS FOCUS

LITERARY ANALYSIS

● STYLE IN POETRY

On the board, write a simple nursery rhyme such as "Hickory Dickory Dock." Next to it, rewrite lines using some of Cummings's techniques as described on this page. For example, arrange the words going up and then down to show the route of the mouse. Or leave out the spaces in "ran up the clock" to show the mouse's speed.

CHECK UNDERSTANDING Ask students how the style changes affect their reading of the familiar poem and their reaction to it.

READING STRATEGY

■ MONITOR

Explain that two additional methods readers might use to **clarify** information are rereading a passage or reading it aloud. Reading a poem aloud can be especially helpful because the way it sounds relates closely to its meaning.

CHECK UNDERSTANDING Have partners use one or both methods to **monitor** their understanding as they read the author information on this page.

 RESOURCE MANAGER—Copy Master
Monitor p. 165 (for student use while reading the poems)

DIFFERENTIATED INSTRUCTION

FOR ALL STUDENTS

For general guidelines on differentiating instruction, see

 BEST PRACTICES TOOLKIT
Differentiated Instruction pp. 31–38

FOR LESS–PROFICIENT READERS

Comprehension Support Briefly identify the topic of each poem. Display this in a chart to help students keep it in mind. Then have students listen to the *Audio Anthology CD.*

Title	Topic
"maggie and milly and molly and may"	playing at the beach
"who are you, little i"	looking at a November sunset
"old age sticks"	youth versus old age

FOR ENGLISH LEARNERS

Options for Reading Read each poem aloud before beginning a discussion, or have students listen to the *Audio Anthology CD.* Use a Reciprocal Teaching strategy to supplement class discussion of the poems and to help students monitor their understanding.

 BEST PRACTICES TOOLKIT—Transparency
Reciprocal Teaching p. A35

Practice and Apply

Ⓐ STYLE IN POETRY

Possible answer: The lines are traditional in their arrangement on the page, their rhythm, and their rhyme. They are unusual in the lack of capital letters for the girls' names and in the absence of space between punctuation and words ("beach" and the parenthesis in line 2, the comma and "and" in line 4, the colon and "and" in line 8, and "lose" and the parenthesis in line 11).

Extend the Discussion What impression of the characters is conveyed by using lower-case letters instead of capital letters for their names?

Ⓑ MONITOR

Have students record their rewritten lines in the chart from page 515. ***Possible answer:***

"maggie and milly and molly and may"		
Line Numbers	**Poet's Words**	**My Words**
11–12	"For whatever we lose(like a you or a me) / it's always ourselves we find in the sea"	Nature can help us find ourselves again.

Lines 11–12
REINFORCE *KEY IDEA:* CONNECTIONS

Discuss What **connections** exist between nature and humans, according to the poet? *Possible answers: Humans look to nature for answers. Nature gives gifts to humans.*

maggie and milly and molly and may

E. E. Cummings

maggie and milly and molly and may
went down to the beach(to play one day) Ⓐ

and maggie discovered a shell that sang
so sweetly she couldn't remember her troubles,and

5 milly befriended a stranded star
whose rays five languid[1] fingers were;

and molly was chased by a horrible thing
which raced sideways while blowing bubbles:and

may came home with a smooth round stone
10 as small as a world and as large as alone.

For whatever we lose(like a you or a me)
it's always ourselves we find in the sea Ⓑ

Ⓐ **STYLE IN POETRY**
In what ways are lines 1–2 both traditional and unusual?

Ⓑ **MONITOR**
Clarify by restating the meaning of the last two lines.

---

1. **languid** (lăng′gwĭd): lacking energy; drooping.

DIFFERENTIATED INSTRUCTION

FOR LESS-PROFICIENT READERS
Reading Strategy Follow-Up: Monitor Model how to monitor understanding by using a Read Aloud/Think Aloud strategy for the first poem. Uncover the literal meaning by asking questions (What do the girls do at the beach?); clarifying (a star with five fingers must be a starfish); rereading, and pausing to make inferences (I think the way each girl looks at the world reflects her experience).

📋 BEST PRACTICES TOOLKIT—Transparency
Read Aloud/Think Aloud p. A34

FOR ADVANCED LEARNERS/PRE-AP
Analyze Symbols Have volunteers summarize the literal meaning of the first poem. Then challenge students to use the symbolic images of the sea, and of each character's experience there, to probe the deeper meaning the poet intends to convey. Have small groups use copies of the T Chart to note the significance of each symbol. Have groups present their charts and defend their interpretations.

📋 BEST PRACTICES TOOLKIT—Transparency
T Chart p. A25

Mural Painting for the Terrace Plaza Hotel, Cincinnati (1947), Joan Miró. Oil on canvas. Cincinnati Art Museum, Cincinnati, Ohio. Gift of Thomas Emery's Sons, Inc. Photo by Tony Walsh. © 2004 Successio Miró/Artists Rights Society (ARS), NY/ADAGP, Paris.

who are you,little i

E. E. Cummings

who are you,little i **C**

(five or six years old)
peering from some high

window;at the gold

5 of November sunset

(and feeling:that if day
has to become night

this is a beautiful way) **D**

C STYLE IN POETRY
What is the effect of having unusual **line breaks?**

D MONITOR
Clarify what the word *this* refers to in line 8.

ANALYZE VISUALS

Activity Like some of Cummings's poems, the mural is made up of elements that at first look randomly placed and unrelated to a central meaning. Ask students to explain steps that might help them analyze both the mural and Cummings's poetry. ***Possible answer:** First, get a general impression of the work by looking at the whole. Then analyze each element. Finally, relate the parts to each other and to the work as a whole.*

About the Art Spanish artist Joan Miró (1893–1983) is well known for his abstract style of art. His paintings are characterized by the use of a few bright colors and highly symbolic shapes, as seen in this work. In his art, he often represents the timelessness of nature through symbols, and he sometimes uses his work to express social criticism.

LITERARY ANALYSIS

C STYLE IN POETRY

***Possible answer:** Unusual line breaks emphasize words in a particular line. They force readers to pay more attention to what they are reading.*

If students need help . . . Write each line of the poem on a strip of transparency (or have students write them on strips of paper). Move the lines around so that the stanzas are broken differently. Discuss how changing the way the lines are spaced changes the emphasis on particular words or ideas.

READING STRATEGY

D MONITOR

***Possible answer:** "This" refers to the sunset.*

Students may record their answers in their charts.

- ***Line Numbers:** line 8*
- ***Poet's Words:** "this is a beautiful way"*
- ***My Words:** the sunset is a beautiful ending to the day*

FOR LESS–PROFICIENT READERS
Concept Support Point out the phrase "little i" in the first line. Tell students that Cummings's use of the word *little* and the lowercase *i* suggest two meanings. First, the "little i" can be seen as a young child, who is five or six years old. Also, the "little i" might be the speaker's younger self. In that case, the poem might be a memory of something the speaker experienced.

FOR ENGLISH LEARNERS
Comprehension: Concept Support To help students understand "who are you,little i," divide it into three sets of lines (lines 1–3, 4–5, 6–8). Record them in the second column of the chart from page 515. Then provide students with these sentence frames to help them paraphrase each set: *A little child is standing at ____. The child sees a ____. The child thinks that ____.* Have groups complete the frames. Discuss their responses.

Activity What does the smaller figure appear to be doing to the larger figure? How does this image relate to the poem? *Possible answer: The smaller figure appears to be shouting at or talking loudly to the taller figure. This reflects the conflict between young and old in the poem.*

READING STRATEGY

E MONITOR

Have students record their ideas in their charts from page 515. *Possible answer: Old people make rules and set boundaries, but young people ignore the rules and limits.*

LITERARY ANALYSIS

F STYLE IN POETRY

Possible answer: Cummings capitalizes only the words associated with old age, perhaps to indicate that "old age" keeps forceful rules.

Lines 17–19
REINFORCE *KEY IDEA:* CONNECTIONS

Discuss What are the **connections** between the young and the old? *Possible answer: The young eventually become the old.*

SELECTION WRAP–UP

SYNTHESIZE Based on his style of writing, with which character in "old age sticks" do you think Cummings would most identify? Explain. *Possible answer: Cummings would identify with youth because he is constantly challenging and breaking the conventional rules of grammar and spelling. His approach to poetry is playful and experimental.*

★ **CRITIQUE** Have students evaluate the effectiveness of the form of each poem. Could Cummings have written any of the poems differently and produced a similar effect?

Painting (1953), Joan Miró. Oil on canvas, 75 ⅞″ × 51″. Collection Mr. and Mrs. Richard K. Weil, St. Louis, Missouri/ARS.

old
age
sticks

E. E. Cummings

old age sticks
up Keep
Off
signs)&

5 youth yanks them
down(old
age
cries No

Tres)&(pas)
10 youth laughs
(sing E
old age

scolds Forbid
den Stop
15 Must
n't Don't F

&)youth goes
right on
gr
20 owing old

E MONITOR
To **clarify**, rephrase what the poet says in lines 1–11.

F STYLE IN POETRY
Note which words are **capitalized** in the poem. Why do you think Cummings chose to capitalize these words?

DIFFERENTIATED INSTRUCTION

FOR LESS–PROFICIENT READERS
Comprehension Support Encourage students to review their charts for each poem and note questions that they still have on index cards. Collect students' questions and work together to clarify areas of confusion.

FOR ADVANCED LEARNERS/PRE–AP
Analyze Line Breaks Ask students to look at the line divisions in "old age sticks." Point out how the juxtaposition of words in some lines gives a dual meaning, as in the first line. The poet could be saying that old age is irreversible. Ask students to find other lines that convey two different meanings as a result of the line breaks. Have small groups discuss their observations.

Comprehension

1. **Recall** According to the poem "maggie and milly and molly and may," what do we find in the sea?

2. **Recall** What does little i see out the window?

3. **Clarify** In lines 9 and 11 of "old age sticks," what familiar word is disguised by Cummings's style?

Literary Analysis

4. **Monitor** Look back at the charts you created as you read. For each poem, choose one line or one set of lines and explain what clues helped you rephrase it as you did.

5. **Make Inferences** In the poem "who are you,little i," who do you think little i is in relation to the **speaker,** or voice that talks to the reader?

6. **Identify Irony** When what happens in a poem is different than what is expected, the poet has used irony. How is the ending of "old age sticks" ironic?

7. **Identify Recurring Theme** When a similar message, or theme, appears in multiple pieces of writing, it is called a recurring theme. What theme appears in all three of these poems?

8. **Analyze Style** Reread the poems and identify three characteristics of Cummings's style that the poems all share. Using a chart like the one shown, note examples of each characteristic.

Style	Examples	Effects
Does not use capital letters		

Extension and Challenge

9. **SCIENCE CONNECTION** Cummings's poem "who are you, little i" mentions the connection between day and night. The poem "maggie and milly and molly and may" says "it's always ourselves we find in the sea." What other **connections** or cycles can you see in nature? Brainstorm ideas with a small group of your classmates.

10. **Speaking and Listening** How would Cummings's **punctuation** and line breaks affect a reading of his poetry? Prepare to read one of the poems for the class. Practice different ways of reading the poem until you feel your reading clearly expresses its meaning.

Practice and Apply

After Reading

For additional support of post-reading questions, use these copy masters:

R RESOURCE MANAGER—Copy Masters
Style in Poetry p. 163 (for practice of literary analysis standards focus)
Question Support p. 167 (**After Reading** questions adapted for English learners and less-proficient readers)

Additional selection questions are provided for teachers on page 159.

ANSWERS

Comprehension

1. *We find ourselves in the sea.*

2. *The child sees a gold sunset in November.*

3. *The word* trespassing *is disguised.*

Literary Analysis

Possible answers:

4. ■ **STANDARDS FOCUS** *Monitor Students will explain different lines. Students may say that the use of parentheses in lines 9 and 11 in the third poem helped them put* trespassing *together and understand that "old age cries 'No Trespassing.'"*

5. *The "little i" in the second poem may be the younger version of the speaker. The poem may be a memory.*

6. *The ending is ironic because throughout the poem, the emphasis is on the differences between the young and the old. Yet at the end, the young become the old.*

7. *All three poems present images of cycles— the tides of the sea, sunsets, the young growing old. One theme might be that there is a rhyme and reason to our existence. Our lives follow a pattern.*

8. ● **STANDARDS FOCUS** *Style in Poetry*

- *Style: Does not use capital letters*
  Examples: the pronoun i, *"maggie and milly and molly and may"*
  Effect: emphasizes youth and innocence

- *Style: Uses parentheses in new ways*
  Example: lines 6–8 in "who are you"
  Effect: suggests inner thoughts; groups ideas

- *Style: Breaks up words*
  Example: "old age / scolds Forbid / den Stop" (lines 12–14)
  Effect: emphasizes; adds levels of meaning

Extension and Challenge

9. **SCIENCE CONNECTION**
Encourage students to check resources if they need to get additional ideas. They might mention the water cycle or the change of the seasons, for example.

10. *Students' readings should help reinforce the meaning of the poem. Remind them to pay attention to commas, semicolons, and periods used in a way that signals a pause.*

Assess and Reteach

Assess

R RESOURCE MANAGER—Copy Masters
Selection Tests A, B/C pp. 169–170, 171–172

💿 Test Generator CD

Reteach

S STANDARDS LESSON FILE
Literature Lesson 38: Style
Reading Lesson 2: Monitoring

Style and Mood in Photographs

Image Collection on **MediaSmart** DVD

OBJECTIVES

Media Literacy

- analyze style in **photography**
- analyze visual elements (framing, composition, lighting)
- analyze color, shape, line, and texture
- use aesthetic techniques to create style in a photograph

SUMMARY

This series of photographs, taken by Ferdinando Scianna and Robert Doisneau, demonstrates the power of photography to express meaning and ideas that go beyond the literal representation of the subject. Scianna creates a dramatic effect in his work through his use of light and shadows, repetition, and through his unusual angles of perspective. Doisneau adds humor to many of his photographs. His work startles the viewer into seeing everyday objects in a new light.

When is a P H O T O *more than a picture?*

Discuss the question. Point out that while many people take snapshots to remember special moments, **photography** can also be a form of art. After students read the *KEY IDEA* paragraph, have them discuss the photos on pages 42, 118, 338, and 514 of their textbooks. How does each photo use light or perspective to convey a feeling or idea?

BACKGROUND

Italian artist Ferdinando Scianna (born 1946) lived in Sicily for the first 22 years of his life before moving to Milan and taking up photography for the weekly *L'Europea*. In 1989 Scianna became a member of Magnum, a prestigious photographic cooperative whose members chronicle world events and issues in their work.

Robert Doisneau (1912–1994) became one of France's best known and most prolific photographers. In addition to his whimsical Parisian vignettes, Doisneau produced images for newspapers, magazines, and advertising agencies. His portrait work includes images of important modern artists, such as Braque, Cocteau, and Picasso.

When is a P H O T O *more than a picture?*

MARYLAND OBJECTIVES

LITERATURE STANDARD
3.A.7.e Analyze elements of style

KEY IDEA The saying "A picture is worth a thousand words" is perhaps the best way to describe the power of **photography.** Photographs create meaning beyond the images they contain. In this lesson, you'll discover how two imaginative photographers use their individual styles to make ordinary subjects extraordinary.

Background

Picture This! Imagine you've just received your first camera. What images would you shoot? Would you take pictures of family and friends or of places in your neighborhood? What would you do to make your photographs special?

The Sicilian photographer Ferdinando Scianna (făr'dĕ-nän'dō shä'nə) is known for capturing people and things in quiet moments. Instead of shooting a subject from the usual direct angle, he sometimes uses unusual points of view. Robert Doisneau (rō-bare' dwä-no') is a famous French photographer. He is known for capturing everyday moments in the streets of Paris and for adding a humorous twist to his photographs.

520

Media Study Resources

R RESOURCE MANAGER UNIT 4	**S** STANDARDS LESSON FILE
Plan and Teach pp. 173–176	Media Lesson 19: Analyzing Visuals
Media Analysis	**i** Media Center at **ClassZone.com**
Summary pp. 177†*, 178‡*	
Viewing Guide p. 179	**MEDIA VIEWING**
Close Viewing p. 180	**MediaSmart** DVD
Viewing Activity p. 181	
Produce Your Own Media p. 182	

* **Resources for Differentiation**   † **Also in Spanish**   ‡ **In Haitian Creole and Vietnamese**

Media Literacy: Style in Photography

Photographers not only take a picture; they create one. Before shooting a picture, photographers decide what they want to include in a frame. The **frame** is what the camera sees. When **composing,** or arranging a subject within a frame, photographers consider the effects of these elements:

- the position of a subject and its background
- the camera angles, such as low and high angles
- the lighting, which can change the way people or objects appear

Study the photographs closely to learn how Ferdinando Scianna experimented with the camera to create his unique style. To see larger versions of these photographs, please access the DVD.

STRATEGIES FOR ANALYZING A PHOTOGRAPH

- Consider how photographs tell a story or convey a message. Once photographers find a subject, they experiment with the subject and its background. They may move closer to or farther away from a subject, depending on the message or mood they want to create. Look at the picture of the balconies. What is your impression of the building?

- Notice how Scianna composed the photographs, shooting from an unusual **angle** or directly to create a dramatic effect. Where do you think the camera was placed?

- Observe the effects of **lighting.** Photographers experiment with lighting to create a **mood** or a dramatic effect, to draw attention to something, or to create a contrast between two or more things. For example, direct sunlight creates shadows that can make a person or object appear mysterious, threatening, or gloomy. What is the effect of the shadows in the second photograph?

MEDIA LITERACY

Review the concept of artistic **style,** which involves arranging and presenting elements in a way that expresses the artist's unique vision and the emotions and ideas that he or she wants to convey. Ask students to cite examples of style from different media, such as animation. Discuss what makes each example unique, and then have students focus on the images on page 521.

- **Angles** Have students explain where Scianna placed his camera in relation to the building and why he might have chosen that position. Point out that the angles in both images create repeating parallel lines that establish a rhythm.

- **Lighting** Lighting is a critical factor in all photography. Photographers make use of both natural light from the sun and artificial lights. They can manipulate light by varying the amount of time they expose the film. Scianna most likely used sunlight for his images, choosing the camera position, exposure, and external conditions (time of day, weather, and so on) that let him create the textures and contrasts he sought.

- **Mood** Explain that mood is the feeling created by a work of art. Ask students to speculate on the mood that Scianna creates in these photos. Point out that Scianna is noted for his fascination with figures asleep. He has thousands of images of people and animals sleeping in a variety of locations.

S STANDARDS LESSON FILE
Media Lesson 19: Analyzing Visuals

Media*Smart* DVD

MEDIA STUDY: TEACHING OPTIONS

Teaching Option 1: The Basics (1–2 Days)

1. Begin the Media Study using the material provided on pages 520–521.

2. Show the Introduction on Media*Smart.* Have students use the Viewing Guide on page 522, along with the corresponding copy master on page 179 of the Resource Manager. Discuss their responses.

3. Return to the pupil edition for the extension activities on page 523.

Teaching Option 2: In-Depth Study (2–3 Days)

1. Begin the Media Study using pages 520–521.

2. Show the Introduction from Media*Smart.*

3. Continue on Media*Smart* with the Media Lessons, using the teacher notes available in the Resources section.

4. Show the Guided Analysis presentation. Have students record their observations on the Student Viewing Guide available in the Resources section from Media*Smart.*

5. Return to the pupil edition, page 523.

Practice and Apply

VIEWING GUIDE

1. As students prepare to view the photos, tell them that they will be asked to explain the techniques the photographer used to create certain effects. Encourage them to consider

   - the **composition,** including the frame and camera angle, that the photographer used to create effects
   - how **lighting** draws attention to the subject and contributes to meaning
   - the **mood** that the photographer conveys through the images

2. Some students may have difficulty focusing on the technical aspects of photography. Suggest that they first concentrate on literal meaning and on their own personal responses to the images. Once they've defined the ideas and subjective feelings that the photographs invoke, ask them to look for ways in which the photographer might have tried to express those feelings.

RESOURCE MANAGER—Copy Masters
Viewing Guide p. 179
Close Viewing p. 180
Viewing Activity p. 181

Media*Smart* DVD

ANSWERS

FIRST VIEWING: Comprehension

1. *In the first photograph, a man protects a cello from the rain with an umbrella. In the second, a cellist plays from a score atop a mountain under a stormy sky.*

2. *The musician appears in an unusual alpine setting. The chair and music stand heighten this incongruity.*

CLOSE VIEWING: Media Literacy

Possible answers:

3. *On the one hand, Doisneau creates a whimsical mood through the comic elements of his compositions; on the other, he makes a serious comment about the dedication and aspirations of musicians.*

4. *It evokes the personal sacrifices that the musician is willing to make for his art, and the human-like shape of the cello case hints at the musician's strong feelings about the instrument.*

Media*Smart* DVD
- **Photograph Pair 1 :** "Milan" and "Coney Island" by Ferdinando Scianna
- **Photograph Pair 2:** "Musician in the Rain" and "The Cellist" by Robert Doisneau
- **Genre:** Photography

522 UNIT 4: MOOD, TONE, AND STYLE

Viewing Guide for
Image Collection

The photographs shown on this page were taken by Robert Doisneau. Doisneau is known for his storytelling talents. His photographs celebrate the daily lives of children, artists, sailors, and others who are willing to tell their stories.

To help you explore the following questions, use the DVD to study larger sizes of the photographs.

NOW VIEW

FIRST VIEWING: Comprehension

1. **Summarize** What is happening in the photographs?
2. **Clarify** What do you think is unusual about the musician's position in "The Cellist"?

CLOSE VIEWING: Media Literacy

3. **Make Inferences** Photographers can create a **mood** that will make viewers feel happy, sad, curious, or even confused. What mood does Doisneau create in these photographs?
4. **Analyze Style** What is the effect of placing an umbrella over the cello in the photograph entitled "Musician in the Rain"?
5. **Analyze Lighting** How do you think the meaning of the photographs would change if they had been taken on a sunny day? How would the meaning change if they had been taken at night?
6. **Analyze Composition** How would the meaning of "The Cellist" change if the photographer had taken a **close-up shot** of the cello player?

---

5. *A sunny day would have made the musician's use of an umbrella appear foolish. In "The Cellist," swirling storm clouds create a tension that sunny skies could not replicate. Night-time shots would have eliminated the importance of the background in both photos. The silhouette effect that gives the umbrella and cello case their prominence in "Musician in the Rain" would vanish, as would the linear patterns created by the railings. Given the impossibility of lighting mountains properly at night, "The Cellist" would lose its meaning entirely.*

6. *A close-up shot of the cellist would not have allowed the photographer to include the background, thereby destroying the mood and meaning created by the odd juxtaposition of the subject and the setting.*

Write or Discuss

Analyze Style In this lesson, you've studied two very distinctive photographic styles. On the DVD, you'll find additional photographs taken by Scianna and Doisneau. Choose one photographer. In your own words, describe his style. As you prepare your response, consider the following:

• Whom or what do you see in each photograph?
• What mood do you think the photographs suggest?
• What elements of composition do you see in the photographs?
• How does the composition reflect the photographer's style?

Produce Your Own Media

Experiment with Photography Here's your opportunity to be the next Doisneau or Scianna. Take a few pictures that show your personal style.

HERE'S HOW The sample photograph was taken by a student in the stairwell of her high school. Notice how she experimented with light and shadow. The photograph was taken from an unusual angle to show the photographer's perspective. Before taking your photographs, follow these suggestions:

• Choose a subject that interests you.
• Determine what you want to keep in and leave out of each photograph.
• Experiment with the position of your subject, camera angles, and lighting.

MEDIA TOOLS

For help with taking photographs, visit the **Media Center** at **ClassZone.com.**

STUDENT MODEL

Tech Tip

If you have access to photo-editing software, experiment with shades of color. See how different shades, including black and white tones, change the **mood** of your photographs.

Assess and Reteach

Write or Discuss

Analyze Style In their responses, students should discuss how the photographers used composition, camera angles, and lighting to convey meaning and establish mood. Make sure that students understand the decisions a photographer makes about where to position the camera, what to include in the frame, and how to use light to enhance meaning. In addition, students should include their own personal responses to the photos and cite evidence to support their opinions.

Produce Your Own Media

Rubric A strong photograph should contain

• a well-chosen subject and frame
• a composition that supports meaning beyond the literal image
• controlled, creative use of lighting
• an original perspective and style

R RESOURCE MANAGER—Copy Master
Produce Your Own Media p. 182

MediaSmart DVD

MEDIA STUDY WRAP—UP

Summarize Photographic Techniques Ask students to summarize the techniques photographers use to express ideas and to establish mood. Have them provide specific examples from the work of Scianna and Doisneau. Prompt them, if necessary, to focus on the way that composition, camera angles, and lighting can be used to create effects.

RETEACH

S STANDARDS LESSON FILE
Media Lesson 19: Analyzing Visuals

Focus and Motivate

OBJECTIVES

- analyze a student model that reflects the key traits of an interpretive essay
- use the writing process to produce an interpretive essay
- revise and edit, using a rubric for interpretive writing
- support thesis and points with evidence
- punctuate quotations, clauses, and compound sentences correctly
- produce and edit a video

WRITER'S ROAD MAP

WRITING PROMPTS 1 AND 2

Help students choose a prompt by reviewing stories from the unit that convey a strong theme, or by listing recent movies or TV shows with a worthwhile message.

ADDITIONAL PROMPTS

Use these prompts for practice with business writing and writing in the humanities:

WRITING PROMPT 3

Writing from the Real World Prepare a brief speech for a media class, interpreting the meaning of images and text in a print ad or a commercial. Find your subject on television, on a billboard, or in a magazine.

Possible Subjects
- consumer product ad
- lifestyle ad
- public service announcement

WRITING PROMPT 4

Writing About Fine Art Prepare the text for an audio guide that explains the meaning of a work of art in a museum. Find your subjects at an online museum or in a book.

Possible Subjects
- a well-known abstract painting
- a frieze from an ancient building
- a modern sculpture

For additional writing prompts, see

 WriteSmart CD

Writing Center at **ClassZone.com**

KEY TRAITS

Review the six **KEY TRAITS,** focusing primarily on ideas and organization. Compare these traits with the rubric on page 530.

Writing Workshop

Interpretive Essay

In the stories in Unit 4, reality does some shifting, sliding, and squirming. To get a grip on it, you needed to figure out key details as you read. You'll do that same kind of work in this workshop as you interpret, or explain the meaning of, a story. The **Writer's Road Map** will help you.

WRITER'S ROAD MAP

Interpretive Essay

WRITING PROMPT 1

Writing from Literature Interpreting a work of literature involves examining it closely and figuring out meanings that you did not notice at first. Choose a short story and write an interpretive essay that helps the reader find new meanings in it. Examine one or two literary elements in the story, such as plot, characters, conflict, setting, mood, dialogue, or point of view.

Literature to Consider
- conflict in "The People Could Fly"
- character and dialogue in "A Day's Wait"
- setting in "The War of the Wall"

WRITING PROMPT 2

Writing from the Real World Powerful stories are everywhere, not just in literature. Think of a memorable story that you recently viewed or read. Write an essay that briefly summarizes the story and examines its deeper meaning or overall message.

Places to Look
- television dramas with strong characters
- movies that show conflicts
- magazine articles that describe real-life people or settings

 WRITING TOOLS
For prewriting, revision, and editing tools, visit the **Writing Center** at ClassZone.com.

KEY TRAITS

1. IDEAS
- Includes a **thesis statement** that identifies the key points the writer will discuss
- Supports key points with **evidence**—details, examples, or quotations from the story

2. ORGANIZATION
- Identifies the author and title of the work in an interesting **introduction**
- Provides **plot details** as needed to help the reader understand the interpretation
- Summarizes the interpretation in a **conclusion** and tells why the story is interesting or important

3. VOICE
- Has an appropriate **tone** for the audience and purpose

4. WORD CHOICE
- Uses **precise language** to examine and explain the work

5. SENTENCE FLUENCY
- Varies **sentence structures**

6. CONVENTIONS
- Uses **correct grammar, spelling, and punctuation**

Writing Workshop Resources

 RESOURCE MANAGER UNIT 4
Plan and Teach pp. 183–186
Prewriting–Editing pp. 187–191
Writing Rubric p. 192
Publishing with Technology p. 193
Writing Support p. 194*

STANDARDS LESSON FILE
Writing Lessons 9, 33, 46
Grammar Lesson 20
Media Lesson 20

BEST PRACTICES TOOLKIT
Scaffolding Writing Instruction pp. 43–46*
Analysis Frame: Theme • Writing Template: Literary Analysis

TECHNOLOGY
- Easy Planner DVD
- Writing Center at **ClassZone.com**
- WriteSmart CD

* Resources for Differentiation

Part 1: Analyze a Student Model

Erika Herzoff
Concord Regional School

Changed They Were, and Terrified

What if your family decided to live on Mars? What would life be like? Would you ever adjust? Perhaps the move would change you in strange and unexpected ways, as it changes Harry Bittering in "Dark They Were, and Golden-Eyed" by Ray Bradbury. In this story about
5 an Earth family that moves to Mars, Bradbury uses mood and dialogue to tell a chilling tale about how an environment can change a person.

The story sets the mood at the beginning by making Mars seem like an eerie and forbidding place. Bradbury uses the word "alone" to describe the Bitterings' new situation. A strange, unsettling wind blows, creating
10 a mood of uncertainty in the story. It is a wind of change, a wind that makes Harry Bittering feel as if "at any moment the Martian air might draw his soul from him." Later Harry reflects, "We don't belong here. . . . This is Mars. It was meant for Martians." Harry is afraid. The reader feels sympathy because the family is alone and scared. The reader's spine also
15 tingles in fear of what might happen to this Earth family.

In the middle of the story, Harry goes to town, where there are other settlers from Earth. They are "conversing with great leisure and ease." They seem at home on Mars. Harry, however, is jumpy and tense because he can sense an unwanted change coming over him and his family. The
20 mood of unrest increases when Sam says, "You've broken my mirror." The reader knows that the shock of seeing his own golden eyes made Harry drop the mirror. Those golden eyes terrify Harry because the Martians had golden eyes and now he does too. Harry and the others thought they could change Mars to make it like Earth. Instead, Mars
25 is changing them.

KEY TRAITS IN ACTION

Interesting **introduction** states the title and author. The **thesis statement** names two literary elements, mood and dialogue.

Uses quotations and details as **evidence** to support the key points—mood and dialogue.

Includes **plot details** to help the reader understand the interpretation.

Uses **precise language** when interpreting story events.

Teach

Part 1: Analyze a Student Model

Have students read the student model and **Key Traits in Action.** Then discuss the model with the class, helping students find specific examples of each trait. You may also wish to incorporate the following activities:

- **Thesis Statement** Write this weak thesis statement on the board:

  This story has a lot of meaning that the author brings out in many ways.

  Ask a student to read this statement and then lines 5–6 of the student model aloud. Ask students to compare the two. **Possible answer:** *The thesis statement on the board is vague and general. It provides no direction for the reader or the writer of the essay. The thesis statement in the model not only identifies the two literary elements that will be examined, but it also states the meaning that the two elements reveal.*

- **Plot Details** Point out that this writer avoids summarizing the plot. She includes only those details that provide necessary background, as in line 5, or that support the main idea. Ask students to identify the plot details used in the model to show the effect of the environment on Harry Bittering.

  Paragraph 2: *A strange wind constantly blows, creating unease in the characters.*

  Paragraph 3: *The character Harry goes to town and talks to other settlers from Earth who appear relaxed. He drops a mirror when he sees that his eyes are turning golden, the color of Martian eyes.*

  Paragraph 4: *Harry stops building a rocket to take him back to Earth and starts accepting the Martian way of life.*

DIFFERENTIATED INSTRUCTION

FOR ALL STUDENTS

For general guidelines on differentiating writing instruction, see

 BEST PRACTICES TOOLKIT
   Scaffolding Writing Instruction
      pp. 43–46

FOR ENGLISH LEARNERS

Language: Skill Words Write these terms on the board and review them with students:

- *interpretation:* the explanation of the meaning of a story, a poem, or a work of art or music

- *key points:* the main ideas that will be discussed in an essay

- *thesis statement:* one or two sentences that state the main ideas or key points. In an interpretive essay, the thesis states the meaning of

the work and the ways in which this meaning is shown. Share this example:

   In "A Day's Wait," Hemingway uses dialogue and characterization to show how simple misunderstandings can lead to great anxiety.

- *tone:* the attitude that the writer shows toward his or her subject. For example, in this kind of essay, the writer's tone should be serious.

- **Sentence Structures** Explain that using different kinds of sentences helps keep readers interested and can show relationships between ideas. Point out that in this paragraph the writer has used a combination of simple sentences ("Harry becomes more relaxed on Mars") and complex sentences ("The colonists begin to prefer the Martians' old homes, which are 'refreshing' and 'cool'"). Ask students to find another example of each type of sentence in paragraph 4.

  Simple sentences: *"The narrator explains, 'The old fever was gone.' Harry has been taken over. Anyone else who comes to Mars will be taken over, too."*

  Complex sentences: *"As the story nears its end and Harry changes, the mood of the story becomes less eerie and less fearful. After Harry lives in a Martian home for a while, he thinks that Earth people built 'such odd ridiculous houses.'"*

- **Conclusion** One effective way to end an interpretive essay is to show how the meaning of the story relates to the readers. Ask students to identify the sentences in the conclusion of the model in which the writer connects the important ideas in the story to the readers' own lives. *("Like so many people, he thought he was in control of everything and could rename and change his world. Instead, it changed him.")*

For interactive student models, see

📀 Write*Smart* CD

ℹ️ Writing Center at **ClassZone.com**

As the story nears its end and Harry changes, the mood of the story becomes less eerie and less fearful. Harry becomes more relaxed on Mars. The colonists begin to prefer the Martians' old homes, which are

30 "refreshing" and "cool." Harry gives up building the rocket that might take him back to Earth. The narrator explains, "The old fever was gone." After Harry lives in a Martian home for a while, he thinks that Earth people built "such odd, ridiculous houses." Harry has been taken over. Anyone else who comes to Mars will be taken over too.

The mood and dialogue in this story help tell how Harry Bittering's

35 environment has changed him. Like so many people, he thought he was in control of everything and could rename and change his new world. Instead, it changed him. At the end of the story, he no longer feels lost and alone, which is how most people feel when they move to a foreign place. His loneliness and fears have been "drawn from him."

40 The reader doesn't know if there's anything left of the real Harry. The environment has changed him in strange and terrifying ways.

> Varies **sentence structures** so that ideas flow smoothly. Uses a serious **tone** that matches the purpose (to interpret a short story) and the audience (teacher and classmates).

> **Conclusion** summarizes the essay and tells why the story is interesting.

2

DIFFERENTIATED INSTRUCTION

FOR ENGLISH LEARNERS

Comprehension: Transitions Explain that an interpretive essay may use different types of transitions.

1. First point out the sequence words in the essay: *later* (line 12), *now* (line 23), *after* (line 31).

2. Ask students if they can think of other words that show the order in which events happen. List suggestions on the board. Be sure to include *first, next, then, before,* and *finally.*

3. Write these sentences on the board:

   The humans landed on Mars.
   They built houses.
   They planted crops.
   They went back to Earth.

   Have pairs use sequence transitions to show a time relationship among these actions.

4. Next point out the comparison-contrast transitions used in the essay: *however* (line 18), *instead* (line 24), *like* (line 35).

5. Have students suggest other words that show similarities or differences. Be sure to include *both, unlike,* and *in contrast to.*

6. Hold up pictures of two flowers or other items. Ask students to work in small groups to write two or three sentences that explain differences or similarities between the two.

📘 RESOURCE MANAGER—Copy Master
Writing Support p. 194

Part 2: Apply the Writing Process

WRITING STANDARD
4.A.1. Compose texts using prewriting and drafting strategies

Practice and Apply

PREWRITING

What Should I Do?	What Does It Look Like?

1. Read (or watch) the story again.
What did you like about it? What parts really made you think? List some of the story's elements, such as its characters, setting, plot, and conflict. Start breaking the story into parts you can interpret.

▶

Characters	Setting	Plot
Harry, his family, others	house, town, Martians' homes	new colony, changes, worries, new people

Conflict: past vs. present, Earth vs. Mars

2. Freewrite to find big ideas.
Just start writing! Jot down your thoughts and feelings about the story. Ask questions too. Write what comes to mind.

▶

Harry is really scared about his new world (scared of changing?), but by the end of the story, when he seems to be a Martian, he doesn't even care anymore! What happened to him?

3. Develop a working thesis.
It doesn't have to be perfect, but it should provide a key idea that you can develop.

TIP Find your focus by referring to the writing prompt. For prompt 1, your paper must interpret one or two literary elements, so be sure your thesis names them.

▶

Working Thesis
Harry is afraid of change and worried that something bad will happen, as you can tell from the mood and the dialogue. He wants to change his environment, but the environment may change him instead.

4. Find evidence to support your thesis.
Before you go further, be sure you have some support for your ideas. List examples, details, and quotations from the story that will help you make your point.

▶

Mood	Dialogue
• the wind: weird • Harry's feelings of panic • refreshing, cool Martian homes	• "We don't belong here." • "odd, ridiculous houses" of settlers

---

FOR ENGLISH LEARNERS
Developing a Thesis Have students use these sentence starters to help them arrive at their thesis statements:

- I think this story is interesting because _____.
- It made me think about _____.
- I think an important meaning of this story is _____.
- The parts of the story that help me figure out the meaning are _____ and _____.

FOR ADVANCED LEARNERS/PRE–AP
Analyze Theme Distribute copies of the Analysis Frame: Theme. Have students use the frame to help them explore the meaning of their stories in depth or to stimulate other thoughts about how to interpret the works.

📦 **BEST PRACTICES TOOLKIT—Transparency**
Analysis Frame: Theme pp. D23, D34

To support students during the writing process, use these copy masters:

R **RESOURCE MANAGER—Copy Masters**
Prewriting–Editing pp. 187–191
Writing Rubric p. 192
Publishing with Technology p. 193
Writing Support p. 194 *(for English learners)*

Part 2: Apply the Writing Process

PREWRITING

1. **Read (or watch) the story again.** Have students who have chosen the same story work together to fill out a chart, highlighting its elements.

2. **Freewrite to find big ideas.** Before students start writing, have them review their charts. Ask them to highlight points that seem interesting, such as characters' feelings, their relationships, or ways in which they change. Encourage group members to discuss possible big ideas.

3. **Develop a working thesis.** Have students return to the model to identify the components of a good thesis statement. Tell them that their first thesis may be wordy, but as they develop their ideas, they will be able to refine it. Their thesis should state the meaning of the work as they see it at this point.

4. **Find evidence to support your thesis.** Encourage students to collect their evidence in graphic organizers that will help them to order their essays. For example, a chart with three columns and two rows will enable students to trace the development of meaning through both literary elements in the beginning, middle, and end of the story. Suggest that students write their thesis in the center oval of the organizer or across the chart to help them keep focused on their main idea.

For interactive graphic organizers, see

🖉 Write*Smart* CD

ℹ️ Writing Center at **ClassZone.com**

DRAFTING

1. **Plan your essay.** Discuss the advantages and challenges of each type of organization.

   - Story order may make it easier for the writer to show how meaning is revealed as the story progresses. However, the writer must avoid summarizing the story and stay focused on the two chosen elements without any irrelevant details.
   - The element-by-element organization helps guide the writer's choice of supporting details. It may be harder to avoid repetition, however, while discussing the significance of each set of details.

2. **Add plot details to help your reader.** Encourage students to include a brief plot overview in the introduction. Review line 5 of the student model. Then have students practice writing a sentence that provides the necessary background. Ask pairs to critique each other's sentences.

3. **Back up your key points with evidence.** Have students point out examples of direct quotations in the model. Discuss what is revealed by each and how the writer weaves them into the text of her essay, preceding some with an explanation (lines 10–12) and others with an introductory phrase (line 12). In other cases she quotes single words or short phrases (lines 8, 29, 32).

For an interpretive essay writing template, see

 WriteSmart CD

 Writing Center at **ClassZone.com**

DRAFTING

What Should I Do?

1. **Plan your essay.**
   Create an informal outline before you start drafting. This writer organized her ideas in the order in which events occur in the story (option 1). You can also discuss one literary element at a time (option 2) or discuss the most important ideas first.

What Does It Look Like?

1. STORY ORDER

1. Beginning
- Mood: strange, unsettling wind
- Dialogue: "We don't belong here."

2. Middle
- Mood: others calm, Harry tense
- Dialogue: "You've broken my mirror."

3. End
- Mood: calmer as Harry changes
- Dialogue: "odd, ridiculous houses"

2. ELEMENT BY ELEMENT

1. Mood
- Beginning: strange, unsettling wind
- Middle: others calm, Harry tense
- End: calmer as Harry changes

2. Dialogue
- Beginning: "We don't belong here."
- Middle: "You've broken my mirror."
- End: "odd, ridiculous houses"

2. **Add plot details to help your reader.** Provide information about the story to help your reader understand your interpretation.

In the middle of the story, Harry goes to town, where there are other settlers from Earth. They are "conversing with great leisure and ease."

3. **Back up your key points with evidence.** You don't need to discuss every line of the story. You do need to find a few good **details** and **quotations** in the story that support your key ideas.

   See page 530: Check Your Grammar

   TIP Before you revise, look back at the key traits on page 524 and the rubric and peer-reader questions on page 530.

The story sets the mood at the beginning by making Mars seem like an eerie and forbidding place. — Key point

Bradbury uses the word "alone" to describe the Bitterings' new situation. — Support

---

DIFFERENTIATED INSTRUCTION

FOR LESS–PROFICIENT WRITERS

Plan Your Essay Encourage students to choose story order. Guide them with these steps:

1. Have students write the meaning of the story, referring back to the thesis.

2. Ask them to list all the details from the story that show the meaning. Have students put them in the order they occur in the story.

3. Have pairs share their lists and decide if most details are related to plot, character, setting, or another element. Suggest that

students focus on one element if possible.

4. Give students this outline for their essays.

   Beginning
   - Name the title and author and, in a few words, tell what the story is about.
   - Explain what you think the story means and what literary element shows that meaning.

   Middle
   - Talk about the meaning shown at the start of the story and what evidence supports it.
   - Discuss the meaning that emerges in the

middle of the story. Provide supporting details.
   - Point out how the ending is important in completing the reader's understanding of the story's meaning.

   Conclusion
   - Restate your interpretation.
   - Make a connection to real life or explain why the story's meaning is interesting.

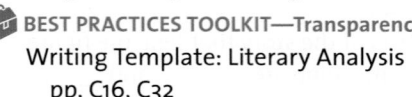 **BEST PRACTICES TOOLKIT—Transparency**
   Writing Template: Literary Analysis
      pp. C16, C32

REVISING AND EDITING

What Should I Do?	**What Does It Look Like?**
1. Find the right tone. • Remember, the tone has to be right for your audience and purpose. • Read your essay aloud. <u>Underline</u> words that sound too informal or slangy. Instead, choose words that you find in formal, published writing.	~~The reader also gets a little freaked out about what's about to go down for these Earth people.~~ The reader's spine also tingles in fear of what might happen to this Earth family.
2. Use exact, specific words. • Exact words include strong adverbs and adjectives. (Circle) *very, really, good, bad, nice,* and other weak and imprecise adverbs and adjectives. • Replace them with better, bolder modifiers.	The story sets the mood at the beginning by making Mars seem like an eerie forbidding ~~a very strange~~ and ~~really weird~~ place.
3. Vary your sentence structures. • Read your essay aloud again, this time looking for sentences that are short and choppy. • Combine short sentences to make them smoother and more sophisticated.	~~The story is coming to an end. Harry is changing. The mood changes too. It becomes less eerie and less fearful.~~ As the story nears its end and Harry changes, the mood of the story becomes less eerie and less fearful.
4. Tell why it matters. • Ask a peer reader to draw a box around phrases and sentences that explain why the story is important, interesting, or meaningful. • If there are few or no boxes, add ideas about the story's significance. **See page 530:** Ask a Peer Reader	Like so many people, Harry thought he was in control of everything and could rename and change his new world. Instead, it changed him. At the end of the story, he no longer feels lost and alone, which is how most people feel when they move to a foreign place.

FOR ENGLISH LEARNERS

Vary Your Sentence Structures Provide students with these explanations and models:

1. Put two complete sentences together that develop the same idea: *The Martians had golden eyes, and now he does too.* [sentence A], **and** [sentence B].

2. Put two complete sentences together that show opposite ideas: *They seem at home on Mars, but Harry is jumpy and tense.* [sentence A], **but** [sentence B].

3. Put together sentences explaining earlier and later actions: *After Harry lives in a Martian home for a while, he thinks that Earth people built such "odd ridiculous houses."*
After [earlier action], [later action].
Before [later action], [earlier action].

4. Put sentences together that show a cause and effect: *The reader feels sympathy because the family is alone and scared.* [effect] **because** [cause].
[cause], **so** [effect].

REVISING AND EDITING

1. **Find the right tone.**
   • Have students check their essays for adjectives used in place of adverbs (such as *real quickly, awful sad, he did good*). Remind them that the way they talk is often not the way they should write.
   • Ask students for some expressions that they might use in everyday language to describe or explain something. Write them on the board and have pairs think of more formal ways to convey the same ideas.

2. **Use exact, specific words.** Point out that precise verbs also convey meaning more effectively. Have students find examples of strong verbs in the model (*tingles, sense, terrify*) and work with partners to think of verbs they might use in their own essays.

3. **Vary your sentence structures.**
   • Caution students to convey the relationship between ideas accurately when they make a sentence subordinate to another independent clause.
   • Remind students to use semicolons or conjunctions and commas when they create compound sentences.
   • Tell students that sometimes short, simple sentences are good for drawing attention to an idea or adding emphasis.

4. **Tell why it matters.** Have peer readers look not only at the conclusion but also at the details in the rest of the essay. Ask them to circle details that do not seem to be explained adequately. Encourage writers to add explanation of these details or, if the details are not significant enough to analyze, drop them.

For interactive revision tools, see

⊘ Write*Smart* CD

ℹ Writing Center at **ClassZone.com**

Preparing to Publish

Support for meeting the goals in the writing rubric is supplied throughout the **Writing Workshop** on pages 524–529.

For Rubric Bank, see

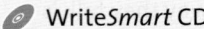 WriteSmart CD

 Writing Center at ClassZone.com

Assess and Reteach

After reading and assessing students' essays, you might use these lessons to reteach key skills:

STANDARDS LESSON FILE

Writing Lesson 9: Creating Sentence Variety

Writing Lesson 33: Writing About Literature

Writing Lesson 46: Choosing a Tone

Grammar Lesson 20: Missing or Misplaced Commas

Media Lesson 20: Producing a Video

Apply the Rubric

A strong interpretive essay . . .

☑ has an attention-getting introduction that identifies the author and title of the work

☑ includes a clear thesis statement that lists the key points of the essay

☑ uses evidence from the text to support key points

☑ provides plot details when needed for clarity

☑ uses an appropriate tone for the audience and purpose

☑ uses precise language

☑ varies sentence structures

☑ has a conclusion that summarizes the interpretation and reflects on why the story is important or interesting

Ask a Peer Reader

• How can I make my thesis clearer?

• Where do I need more support or explanation?

• Where in my essay do I explain what makes the story interesting or meaningful?

Check Your Grammar

• Place quotation marks at the beginning and end of any words you copy directly from a story.

> They are " conversing with great leisure and ease."

• Periods and commas always go inside the quotation marks.

> The colonists begin to prefer the Martians' old homes, which are "refreshing" and "cool."

• Use a comma to separate independent clauses in a compound sentence.

> Harry is tense , but the men in town seem calm.

• The comma always comes before—not after—the coordinating conjunction.

> Harry cannot control his world, and he is taken over.

See pages R49–R50: Quick Reference: Punctuation

Writing Online

 PUBLISHING OPTIONS
For publishing options, visit the **Writing Center** at ClassZone.com.

ASSESSMENT PREPARATION
For writing and grammar assessment practice, go to the **Assessment Center** at ClassZone.com.

Producing and Editing a Video

Here's how to produce a video that shows style and has style.

Planning the Video

1. **Select story parts.** Go back to the story you just wrote about. If possible, read or view other stories by the same author. Find words, sentences, or sections that show the author's style. Think about choice of words, tone, figurative language, and sentence length.

2. **Find or create images.** For example, if you've chosen a paragraph in which Ray Bradbury describes the Martian landscape, you might make a drawing or collage of the colors, shapes, and feelings that the writing suggests.

3. **Make a plan.** Write a script or storyboard. You might include narration, dramatic readings, onscreen text, music, or sound effects. You may also want to cast actors and create backdrops, costumes, and props.

IMAGE 1: dusty, swirling, sandy landscape of the planet Mars

SFX: eerie, whooshing sounds

IMAGE 2: man next to spacecraft on this landscape

NARRATOR: "The man felt his hair flutter and the tissues of his body draw tight.... His face was cold."

Making the Video

1. **Shoot the video.** Try to include close-ups, medium shots, and long shots. Remember that you are re-creating the author's style, so your video has to sound and look like something that the author created or suggested.

2. **Put it all together.** Use editing software to assemble the video the way you planned it in your script or storyboard.

3. **Show your stuff.** Screen your video for classmates or friends. Ask what they learned about the author's style.

PUBLISHING WITH TECHNOLOGY

Ask students to read this page to get an overview of how to create a video. Students who choose this option should then familiarize themselves with the editing software they will use by taking advantage of the tutorial option that is usually included.

R RESOURCE MANAGER—Copy Master
Publishing with Technology p. 193

S STANDARDS LESSON FILE
Media Lesson 20: Producing a Video
Media Lesson 21: Creating a Web Site
Media Lesson 22: Creating a Power Presentation

Before students begin working, review this rubric with them so that they understand their goals:

Rubric A strong video

- contains specific and strong examples of style
- has a well-organized script
- includes appropriate sound effects, narration, onscreen text, and visuals
- is easy to follow
- captures and keeps the attention of the audience
- has a variety of camera shots and angles
- is carefully edited
- conveys a vivid sense of the author's style

DIFFERENTIATED INSTRUCTION

FOR LESS–PROFICIENT WRITERS

Planning the Video Have students work in pairs to complete these steps:

1. Have them choose four passages from the story they wrote about that create vivid images in their minds.

2. Have them draw the pictures that the words create.

3. Ask them to choose music that fits the pictures they have illustrated.

4. Have them put the pictures, text, and music ideas on a storyboard. Suggest that the order in which the passages appear in the story might be a good way to organize their own presentation. Point out the storyboard example on page 531. Their storyboards should resemble that one. Have them label the text or passages from the story as the narrator's part.

Assessment Practice

CHECK READINESS

Read aloud the paragraph under **ASSESS** and stress to students that this is not the full Unit Test but a way for them to check their readiness for it. Then have students examine the skills listed under **REVIEW** and look back in the unit or in the Handbook for any skills they need to study.

READ THE SELECTION

Remind students to keep unit goals in mind as they read the passage, paying particular attention to

- mood
- style
- tone

To help students focus on **mood** while reading, encourage them to ask questions such as

- Where does the story take place?
- Who are the main characters? What words are used to describe them?
- What questions are raised by the characters' actions?
- What feelings do descriptions create in the reader?

ANSWER THE QUESTIONS

Direct students to pages R93–R99 of the Test-Taking Handbook to review test-taking strategies. Remind students not to choose the first alternative that seems to fit when answering a multiple-choice question. Instead, they should read through all the choices, eliminate any that are clearly wrong, and then choose the best answer—the one that is most accurate and complete.

Explain to students the importance of referring back to the selections as needed. There is no point in guessing at answers. Skimming the selection for key words or terms is a good way to locate information that will help to answer questions.

Reading Comprehension

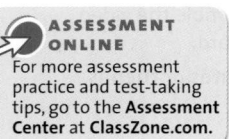

DIRECTIONS *Read this selection and answer the questions that follow.*

Mrs. Barrymore and her husband are servants at Baskerville Hall. Sherlock Holmes's friend, Dr. Watson, is describing the couple in a letter to the famou[s] detective.

from The Hound of the Baskerville[s]
Sir Arthur Conan Doy[le]

Mrs. Barrymore is of interest to me. She is a heavy, solid person, very limited, intensely respectable, and inclined to be puritanical. You could hardly conceive a less emotional subject. Yet I have told you how, on the firs[t] night here, I heard her sobbing bitterly, and since then I have more than once observed traces of tears upon her face. Some deep sorrow gnaws ever at her heart. Sometimes I wonder if she has a guilty memory which haunts her, and sometimes I suspect Barrymore of being a domestic tyrant. I have always felt that there was something singular and questionable in this man['s] character, but the adventure of last night brings all my suspicions to a head[.]

10 And yet it may seem a small matter in itself. You are aware that I am not a very sound sleeper, and since I have been on guard in this house my slumbers have been lighter than ever. Last night, about two in the morning, I was aroused by a stealthy step passing my room. I rose, opened my door, and peeped out. A long black shadow was trailing down the corridor. It was thrown by a man who walked softly down the passage with a candle held in his hand. He was in shirt and trousers, with no covering to his feet. I could merely see the outline, but his height told me that it was Barrymore. He walked very slowly and circumspectly, and there was something indescribably guilty and furtive in his whole appearance.

20 I have told you that the corridor is broken by the balcony which runs round the hall, but that it is resumed upon the farther side. I waited unti[l] he had passed out of sight and then I followed him. When I came round the balcony he had reached the end of the farther corridor, and I could se[e] from the glimmer of light through an open door that he had entered one of the rooms. Now, all these rooms are unfurnished and unoccupied, so that his expedition became more mysterious than ever. The light shone

---

DIFFERENTIATED INSTRUCTION

FOR ENGLISH LEARNERS
Assessment Practice: Active Reading Strategies Remind students to use active reading strategies, asking questions as they read and making notes on scrap paper.

- Students can check their understanding by asking questions such as "What did the character do? Why?"

- They can jot down their impressions of characters, noting descriptive words that the author uses.

- Students can check comprehension by stopping after every few paragraphs and summarizing what they have read, using their own words.

steadily as if he were standing motionless. I crept down the passage as noiselessly as I could and peeped round the corner of the door.

Barrymore was crouching at the window with the candle held against the glass. His profile was half turned towards me, and his face seemed to be rigid with expectation as he stared out into the blackness of the moor. For some minutes he stood watching intently. Then he gave a deep groan and with an impatient gesture he put out the light. Instantly I made my way back to my room, and very shortly came the stealthy steps passing once more upon their return journey. Long afterwards when I had fallen into a light sleep I heard a key turn somewhere in a lock, but I could not tell whence the sound came. What it all means I cannot guess, but there is some secret business going on in this house of gloom which sooner or later we shall get to the bottom of. I do not trouble you with my theories, for you asked me to furnish you only with facts. I have had a long talk with Sir Henry this morning, and we have made a plan of campaign founded upon my observations of last night. I will not speak about it just now, but it should make my next report interesting reading.

ITEM ANALYSIS

COMPREHENSION AND BRIEF CONSTRUCTED RESPONSE	ITEMS	UNIT PAGES
Mood	1, 3, 4, 5	438, 445
Style	6, 7, 8, 11, 12	436, 438, 440, 467, 481, 495, 515, 521, 529
Summarize	2, 9, 10	481

VOCABULARY	ITEMS	UNIT PAGES
Synonyms	1, 2, 3	487
Literal and Figurative Meanings	4, 5, 6	506

WRITING AND GRAMMAR	ITEMS	UNIT PAGES
Subject-Verb Agreement	1, 2, 3, 4, 5, 6	465, 475

MSA PREPARATION

After checking student readiness with this Assessment Practice, you may administer the complete Unit 4 Test, which matches the structure and format of the MSA.

FOR LESS–PROFICIENT READERS

Assessment Support Consider these options for completing the **Assessment Practice:**

- Have students "work backwards," reviewing the test questions before reading the passage.

- Select random questions in the assessment and have students demonstrate how and where to look for the answers.

- Ask students to locate unfamiliar vocabulary in the assessment. Elicit the meanings of these words from the class.

- Have students record useful test words and definitions in their journals for later reference.

- Read the selection or parts of it aloud to aid in student comprehension.

Comprehension

Model a thinking process for answering multiple-choice questions.

1. **B is correct.** The mood is suspenseful because readers wonder what Mr. Barrymore will do next and why he is behaving so strangely. The action is not fast and exciting, as suggested by A. C is incorrect because Mr. Barrymore seems restless, not peaceful. D is incorrect because both Mr. and Mrs. Barrymore seem upset.

2. **D is correct.** While Mrs. Barrymore appears to be under control, Watson has observed that she cries often (lines 3–5). A and C are incorrect because she is described as very unemotional (line 3). B is incorrect because nothing is said about her being unexpectedly severe and cold.

3. **B is correct.** The "stealthy step" suggests danger and makes readers wonder who is in the hall and why, adding to the mood of suspense. A, C, and D are all straightforward statements that do not suggest danger or raise puzzling questions.

4. **D is correct.** The words guilty and furtive raise questions about why Mr. Barrymore is sneaking around. We can eliminate A, B, and C because none of these words have connotations that cast doubt on Barrymore's character or actions.

5. **B is correct.** The description of Barrymore's face as "rigid with expectation" suggests that he is fearful of what he might see. There is no suggestion of relief, as in A. C is incorrect because his actions are puzzling and nothing is made clear. D is incorrect because Barrymore seems fearful, not hopeful.

6. **C is correct.** In the excerpt, the author does not interject any ideas other than the ones that Watson expresses, so the tone is neutral, or detached. For the author's tone to be vengeful, as in A, ironic, as in B, or suspicious, as in D, the author would have needed to add comments of his own.

7. **A is correct.** These simple words describe actions objectively. The words in B suggest a tone of suspicion, the words in C suggest puzzlement, and the words in D suggest a mysterious tone.

Comprehension

DIRECTIONS *Answer these questions about the excerpt from* The Hound of the Baskervilles.

1. Which word best describes the mood of this passage?
   A. thrilling
   B. suspenseful
   C. peaceful
   D. comforting

2. Which statement is the best summary of Dr. Watson's impression of Mrs. Barrymore?
   A. She is intensely moral, sometimes emotional, and not likeable at all.
   B. She is reliable, trustworthy, and yet unexpectedly severe and cold.
   C. She wants people to feel sorry for her, so she makes a show of crying at night.
   D. She gives an appearance of being under control, but something is upsetting her.

3. Which sentence contributes most clearly to the mood of this excerpt?
   A. "You could hardly conceive a less emotional subject."
   B. "Last night, about two in the morning, I was aroused by a stealthy step passing my room."
   C. "He was in shirt and trousers, with no covering to his feet."
   D. "I do not trouble you with my theories, for you asked me to furnish you only with facts."

4. Which words in lines 18–19 contribute most to the mood of the story?
   "He walked very slowly and circumspectly, and there was something indescribably guilty and furtive in his whole appearance."
   A. walked, slowly
   B. circumspectly, indescribably
   C. something, appearance
   D. guilty, furtive

5. The description of Barrymore's actions in lines 29–31 affects the mood of the story by
   A. providing relief
   B. increasing the tension
   C. making everything clear
   D. adding hope

6. What is the author's tone toward Watson's investigation in this excerpt?
   A. vengeful   C. detached
   B. ironic   D. suspicious

7. Which words from the excerpt give Watson's report an objective tone?
   A. heard, observed
   B. wonder, suspect
   C. asked, guess
   D. felt, crept

534

---

8. **B is correct.** The style is formal because the author uses formal vocabulary and correct sentence patterns. The use of the pronoun you (lines 10, 20, 39–40) indicates a conversational style. There is no flowery or symbolic language, as in A, nor are there any references to scientific facts, as in C; instead, the passage contains descriptive observations of characters. D is incorrect because there is no dialogue in the passage, and therefore no use of natural speech patterns.

9. **A is correct.** This summary of Dr. Watson's actions is reflected at the end of the passage (lines 40–42). Choices B, C, and D are incorrect because each statement describes a single event that happened before that morning.

8. Which one of the following descriptions best characterizes Conan Doyle's style in this excerpt?

   A. a formal, flowery style that relies on symbolic language

   B. a formal, conversational style that relies on descriptive observations

   C. an objective, journalistic style that relies on scientific facts

   D. an informal, folksy style that relies on natural speech patterns

9. Which statement is the best summary of Dr. Watson's actions on the morning after he sees Barrymore?

   A. Dr. Watson reports what he saw to Sir Henry and they come up with a plan of action.

   B. Dr. Watson hears a key turning in a lock, but he doesn't know where.

   C. Dr. Watson barely makes it back to his room before he hears steps coming back again.

   D. Dr. Watson hears someone weeping miserably in the house.

Brief Constructed

10. Briefly summarize Dr. Watson's report to Sherlock Holmes. Identify the characters and the setting in your summary.

11. What is Conan Doyle's attitude toward the character Watson? Give an example from the excerpt to support your answer.

12. Reread the descriptions of Mr. and Mrs. Barrymore in the excerpt. Describe the author's style based on his words, sentences, and tone.

GO ON ➡

Brief Constructed Response

Evaluate student writing using the Maryland writing rubrics in the back of the book.

Possible responses:

10. *In his report to Holmes, Dr. Watson describes how he hears Mrs. Barrymore crying at night. He says he thinks that she is often unhappy. Watson gives a detailed description of Mr. Barrymore's mysterious nighttime activities at Baskerville Hall and says that he is suspicious of Mr. Barrymore's character.*

    Students could list the following main events:

    - *Watson hears Mrs. Barrymore sobbing in her room.*
    - *Watson observes Mr. Barrymore sneaking through the house.*
    - *Barrymore looks out the window for a few minutes and groans.*
    - *Watson reports his observations to Sir Henry, and they devise a plan to get to the heart of the matter.*

11. *The author portrays Watson as a reliable and sharp observer of people. He shows Watson observing and investigating the situation. Although he has Watson mention his suspicions, the emphasis is on Watson's observations rather than his opinions or guesses. For example, he has Watson say, "I do not trouble you with my theories, for you asked me to furnish you only with facts" (lines 39–40).*

12. *The word choice, tone, and sentence structure work together to create a style that is formal, objective, analytical, and detached. Students' responses should include examples of word choice, sentence structure, and tone from the passage and should explain how the examples demonstrate the author's style.*

DIFFERENTIATED INSTRUCTION

FOR ENGLISH LEARNERS

Organize Information To help students respond to question 12, have them use a graphic organizer to list examples of the author's word choice, sentence structure, and tone. Then, based on their examples, have students draw conclusions about the author's style.

	Examples	Style
Word Choice	"She is a heavy, solid person" (line 1) "You could hardly conceive" (lines 2–3)	objective formal
Sentence Structure	Long sentences: "You are aware that I am not a very sound sleeper..." (lines 10–12)	formal
Tone	"is of interest to me" (line 1) "sometimes I suspect" (line 7)	detached analytical

ANSWERS

Vocabulary

1. **D is correct.** *Words that are synonyms have similar meanings. In this sentence, Watson is pointing out that it would be difficult to think of or imagine a person who is less emotional than Mrs. Barrymore. We can eliminate A, B, and C because none of these words has a meaning similar to "think of" or "imagine."*

2. **B is correct.** *In this sentence, traces means "evidence" or "something left behind." "Traces of tears" would be faint marks left on the face after someone had stopped crying. We can eliminate A and D because "edges of tears" and "shades of tears" do not have this meaning. C is incorrect because "puddles of tears" would be seen on someone's face only if the person was actively crying.*

3. **C is correct.** *The word* intently *suggests that the person was watching in a very focused or careful way. We can eliminate A and B because the sentence does not suggest the emotion of anger or sadness. D is incorrect because it is possible to stare at something intently without having any intelligent thoughts about it.*

4. **D is correct.** *The figurative expression "gnaws ever at" means "constantly eats away at" and describes the feeling of being troubled. A, B, and C are incorrect because "deep sorrow" calls up the image of a troubled heart rather than a sickened, frightened, or angry heart.*

5. **C is correct.** *The sentence mentions Barrymore in the context of being a husband, and the word* domestic *refers to the family or the household. A, B, and D can be eliminated because they refer to political roles.*

6. **B is correct.** *Gloom* and *sadness are synonyms, so A, C, and D can be eliminated.*

Vocabulary

DIRECTIONS *Use context clues and your knowledge of synonyms to answer the following questions.*

1. Which word is a **synonym** for the underlined word in this sentence from lines 2–3?

   "You could hardly <u>conceive</u> a less emotional subject."

   A. understand   **C.** plan

   B. see   **D.** imagine

2. Which word is a **synonym** for the underlined word in this sentence from lines 3–5?

   "Yet I have told you how, on the first night here, I heard her sobbing bitterly, and since then I have more than once observed <u>traces</u> of tears upon her face."

   A. edges   **C.** puddles

   B. streaks   **D.** shades

3. Which word is a **synonym** for the underlined word in this sentence from line 32?

   "For some minutes he stood watching <u>intently</u>."

   A. angrily   **C.** carefully

   B. sadly   **D.** intelligently

DIRECTIONS *Use context clues and your knowledge of literal and figurative meanings to answer the following questions.*

4. Which expression is the most likely meaning of the underlined words in the following sentence from lines 5–6?

   "Some deep sorrow <u>gnaws ever at her heart</u>."

   A. sickens her   **C.** angers her

   B. frightens her   **D.** troubles her

5. Which expression is the most likely meaning of the underlined term in the following sentence from lines 6–7?

   "Sometimes I wonder if she has a guilty memory which haunts her, and sometime I suspect Barrymore of being a <u>domestic tyrant</u>."

   A. a strict national ruler

   B. a local official

   C. a harsh husband

   D. a native-born dictator

6. Which word is the most likely meaning of the underlined word in this sentence from lines 37–39?

   "What it all means I cannot guess, but there is some secret business going on in this house of <u>gloom</u> which sooner or later we shall get to the bottom of."

   A. confusion   **C.** danger

   B. sadness   **D.** cruelty

536

DIFFERENTIATED INSTRUCTION

FOR ENGLISH LEARNERS

Language Support Clarify the meanings of these words:

- *conceive* (item 1), "think of"
- *traces* (item 2), "small signs"
- *gnaws* (item 4), "chews or eats at"
- *domestic* (item 5), "relating to the home or family"

MSA SKILLS PRACTICE

Writing & Grammar

DIRECTIONS *Read this passage and answer the questions that follow.*

(1) <u>Historians tells</u> us that for thousands of years, cultures preserved bodies by embalming them. (2) Ancient <u>Egyptians was</u> among the most well-known embalmers, using a process called mummification. (3) The ancient historian <u>Herodotus and modern archaeologists has taught</u> us much about this process. (4) An embalmer would remove internal organs, dry out the body, and wrap it in linen. (5) <u>Herbs and salt was</u> two ingredients the embalmer would use as part of the drying process. (6) Next, <u>linen or other materials was placed</u> inside the body to fill it out. (7) Such careful <u>preparations shows</u> how important burial was to the Egyptians.

1. To maintain subject-verb agreement in sentence 1, change the underlined words to

A. Historian tells

B. Historian tell

C. Historians tell

D. Historians is telling

2. To maintain subject-verb agreement in sentence 2, change the underlined words to

A. Egyptian are   **C.** Egyptians is

B. Egyptians were   **D.** Egyptian were

3. To maintain subject-verb agreement in sentence 3, change the underlined words to

A. Herodotus and modern archaeologists is teaching

B. Herodotus and modern archaeologists teaches

C. Herodotus and modern archaeologists was teaching

D. Herodotus and modern archaeologists have taught

4. To maintain subject-verb agreement in sentence 5, change the underlined words to

A. Herb and salts was

B. Herbs and salts was

C. Herbs and salt were

D. Herb and salt was

5. To maintain subject-verb agreement in sentence 6, change the underlined words to

A. linen or other material were placed

B. linen or other materials were placed

C. linens or other materials was placed

D. linens or other material were placed

6. To maintain subject-verb agreement in sentence 7, change the underlined words to

A. preparations show

B. preparation show

C. preparation do show

D. preparations was showing

STOP

537

ANSWERS

Writing & Grammar

1. **C *is correct.*** *For sense, the subject should be plural, which requires the plural verb* tell *for subject-verb agreement. We can eliminate A and B because the singular subject does not make sense in the sentence. D is incorrect because the plural subject does not agree in number with the singular verb.*

2. **B *is correct.*** *Both the subject and the verb should be plural. A and D can be eliminated because they each use a singular subject with a plural verb. C is incorrect because it has a plural subject and a singular verb.*

3. **D *is correct.*** *The compound subject calls for a plural verb. A, B, and C are incorrect because they have singular verbs. In addition, B is present tense, which does not make sense because Herodotus has been dead for centuries.*

4. **C *is correct.*** *The compound subject calls for a plural verb. A, B, and D are incorrect because they have singular verbs.*

5. **B *is correct.*** *The compound subject includes a singular noun and a plural noun. It requires the verb to agree in number with the noun that is closest to the verb. A and D are incorrect because in each item the singular noun does not agree with the plural verb. C is incorrect because the plural noun does not agree with the singular verb.*

6. **A *is correct.*** *The subject and the verb are both plural and they agree in number. B and C are incorrect because each has a singular subject and a plural verb. D is incorrect because the subject is plural but the verb is singular. Also, the verb tense does not make sense in the sentence.*

INTRODUCE *MORE GREAT READS*

In Unit 4, students have discussed a number of big questions. Invite students to tell which question they found most intriguing and why. Then focus attention on the three questions that appear on this page. Discuss the recommended books and their summaries, pointing out how each connects to the related question. Encourage students to choose one or more of these "great reads" to read independently.

ClassZone.com

To find additional books that match students' interests and ability levels, visit the Literature Center at **ClassZone.com**.

More Great Reads

Ideas for Independent Reading

Which of the questions in Unit 4 made an impression on you? Continue exploring them with these books.

Can where you are change who you are?

Skellig
by David Almond

What if you discovered an ailing being in an old garage in your new neighborhood? This happens to Michael, who shares his find with his neighbor, Mina, and the two embark on a secret mission to save Skellig.

Dragonwings
by Laurence Yep

In the early 1900s, a Chinese boy named Moon Shadow travels to San Francisco. There he joins his father, Windrider, whom he has never met. The two survive poverty, loneliness, and an earthquake as they work to fulfill a long-held dream.

Shabanu: Daughter of the Wind
by Suzanne Staples

Shabanu is the 11-year-old daughter of a nomadic family in Pakistan. When it becomes apparent that the family's only chance to survive is to pledge Shabanu in marriage, she has to make a decision. Where will she go?

Is it brave to suffer in silence?

Blackwater
by Eve Bunting

Thirteen-year-old Brodie feels he may have caused the accidental death of Pauline and Otis. It all started out innocently enough, but then there was a fall into the rushing current of the Blackwater River. Should Brodie tell what he knows?

The Window
by Michael Dorris

Rayona, who is part Native American and part African American, has suffered a childhood of neglect and secrets. When her father sends her to live with her grandmother in Kentucky, she finally finds some security and happiness.

The Voices of Silence
by Bel Mooney

When you live in a totalitarian society, keeping silent means staying alive. Does that make you brave? Thirteen-year-old Flora Popescu confronts this question as she comes of age in Communist Romania.

What makes us laugh?

Bud, Not Buddy
by Christopher Curtis

During the Great Depression, ten-year-old Bud escapes from a terrible foster home and hits the road in search of his real dad. The humorous way he tells about his travels across Michigan might make you laugh out loud.

Squashed
by Joan Bauer

Ellie's future prize-winning pumpkin needs to gain 200 pounds in time for the Rock River Pumpkin Weigh-In, and Ellie thinks she needs to lose 20 pounds. Whathallenges she sets for herself is her sense of humor.

A Long Way from Chicago
by Richard Peck

Each summer Joey and his sister, Mary Alice, travel to downstate Illinois for a visit with Grandma Dowdel. This year, her tendency to stretch the truth and hatch wild schemes creates hilarious adventures.

Picture the Moment

5

APPRECIATING POETRY

539

For help in planning this unit, see

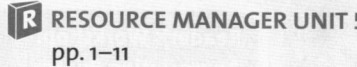

RESOURCE MANAGER UNIT 5
pp. 1–11

INTRODUCE THE UNIT

For the most part, our lives move along at a steady pace, but every once in a while, something special makes us want to freeze the action and concentrate on the moment. Ask students to describe mental pictures of important moments they have experienced in life, in movies, on TV, or in books. Point out that, like a mental picture, a poem can allow readers to experience a moment, tap into emotions, or even tell a story. Invite students to think about these ideas as they discuss the pictures on this page. To spark a discussion, ask

- What is similar about the two pictures? What is different?
- How would you describe the mood of each picture? What details help create the mood?
- How might a photograph of the place shown in the larger image differ from the artist's interpretation? How might an artist interpret the place shown in the photograph?
- What message does each image convey?

Point out that, like artists and photographers, poets use special forms and techniques to create images that express their own ideas and perceptions. In this unit, students will learn how **appreciating poetry** can open doors to understanding not only the poet's experiences, but also their own experiences.

About the Art Vanessa Julian painted *Hacienda* in 2002. For more information, see page 559 of the teacher's edition.

UNIT 5
Standards Skills Trace

SKILLS STRAND	Reader's Workshop: Appreciating Poetry pp. 542–547 — 3.A.4.a, 3.A.4.c, 3.A.7.c	The Names pp. 548–553 — 3.A.4.a, 3.A.7.d — Poem *Level: Average*	the earth is a living thing / Sleeping in the Forest / Gold pp. 554–561 — 1.E.4.c, 3.A.7.c, 5.A.2.d — Poems *Level: Average*	Scaffolding / The World Is Not a Pleasant Place to Be / Annabel Lee pp. 562–569 — 3.A.4.b, 3.A.4.c — Poems *Level: Challenging*	The Charge of the Light Brigade / The Highwayman pp. 570–581 — 1.D.2.b, 3.A.3.b, 3.A.4.c, 5.B.2.b — Narrative Poem/Ballad *Level: Average*
Literary Analysis	Form and Speaker pp. 542–543, 547 Sound Devices pp. 544–545, 547	Characteristics of Free Verse pp. 549, 551, 552 Imagery pp. 549, 550, 551, 552	Characteristics of Lyric Poetry pp. 555, 558, 560 Figurative Language pp. 555, 556, 558, 559, 560	Line and Stanza pp. 563, 564, 566, 568, 569 Sound Devices (Rhyme Scheme) pp. 563, 567, 568, 569	Rhythm and Meter pp. 571, 572, 574, 577, 579 Characteristics of a Narrative Poem p. 571 Review: Mood p. 578
Reading and Informational Texts	Analyze the Literature pp. 543, 545, 547	Understand Historical Context pp. 549, 551, 552 Read an Article p. 553	Make Inferences pp. 555, 558, 559, 560	Understand Speaker pp. 563, 564, 567, 569	Strategies for Reading a Narrative Poem pp. 571, 574, 575, 577, 578, 579
Vocabulary	Academic Vocabulary pp. 542, 544–546				Word Acquisition pp. 571, T571, 580 Context Clues p. T571 Connotations p. 580
Writing, Grammar, and Style			Sentence Types p. 561 End Punctuation p. 561		Active Voice p. 581
Speaking, Listening, Viewing, and Media	Discuss pp. 542–546	Discuss pp. 548, T550–T551, 552 Analyze Visuals p. 550	Discuss pp. 554, T556–T559, 560 Analyze Visuals pp. 556, T558, T559	Discuss pp. 562, T564–T568, 569 Analyze Visuals pp. 564, T566, T567	Discuss pp. 570, T572–T578, 579 Analyze Visuals pp. 572, T575

Assessment-Based Planning: Skills in red are assessed on the Unit 5 Test. **T** = Teacher's Edition page

MARYLAND STANDARDS

For a full listing of state standards see page S1.

Linked selections				
Two Haiku / Fireflies / Fireflies in the Garden pp. 582–587	**Stars with Wings** pp. 588–591	**Jabberwocky / Sarah Cynthia Sylvia Stout Would Not Take the Garbage Out / Two Limericks** pp. 592–599	**The Delight Song of Tsoai-Talee / Four Skinny Trees** pp. 600–607	**Writing Workshop: Personal Response to a Poem** pp. 608–615
Poems *Level: Easy*	Science Article *Level: Challenging*	Humorous Poems *Level: Challenging*	Poems *Level: Average*	
Characteristics of Haiku pp. 583, 584, 587 Symbol pp. 583, 584, 586, 587		Characteristics of Humorous Poetry pp. 593, 597, 599 Sound Devices pp. 593, 594, 596, 598, 599	Mood and Figurative Language pp. 601, 602, 604, 606 Review: Repetition p. 602	
Visualize pp. 583, 585, 587	Use Text Features to Locate Information pp. 588, 589, 591 Connect Nonfiction and Poetry p. 591 Read a Science Article pp. 589–590	Monitor pp. 593, 594, 597, 599	Set a Purpose for Reading p. 601 Compare Mood p. 606	Analyze a Personal Response to a Poem pp. 609–610, 614
			Write for Assessment p. 607	Write a Personal Response to a Poem pp. 608–615 Precise Literary Terms pp. 608, 609, T613 Sentence Fragments p. 614
Discuss pp. 582, T584–T586, 587 Analyze Visuals p. T584	Discuss pp. 588, T589–T590, 591	Discuss pp. 592, T594–T598, 599 Analyze Visuals p. 594	Discuss pp. 600, T602–T605, 606 Analyze Visuals pp. 602, 604	Discuss pp. 608–610 Oral Interpretation of a Poem p. 615

Skills Assessed on the Unit 5 Test:

Literary Analysis
- Understand poetic form
- Identify the characteristics of various poetic forms
- Identify and interpret imagery
- Identify and interpret figurative language
- Identify and interpret sound devices (rhyme, rhyme scheme, repetition, onomatopoeia, alliteration)

Reading and Informational Texts
- Make inferences
- Understand speaker
- Use strategies for reading a narrative poem

Vocabulary
- Understand and use connotative meanings of words

Writing, Grammar, and Style
- Write a personal response to a poem
- Identify and correctly punctuate types of sentences
- Use correct sentence types to convey purpose and meaning
- Use active voice
- Additional writing and grammar skills

For additional lesson planning help, see **Easy Planner DVD.**

OBJECTIVES
- identify and analyze characteristics of **poetry**
- make inferences

What is a
POEM?

Discuss different types of poems. What kinds of poems do students like or dislike? Do they like poems that rhyme? poems that tell a story? poems that are sad, serious, or funny? List students' responses on the board and take an informal survey of favorite types of poetry.

ACTIVITY To help students recall poems, provide a poetry anthology for students to page through, or have them review poems they have read in earlier units (pages 68, 130–132, 204, 282–284, 382–383, 510–512, 516–518). Write memorable lines that students suggest on the board. Guide students in comparing the poetry and the song lyrics, pointing out any images or special devices and comparing the mood.

CHECK UNDERSTANDING Have students tell what a **poem** is and explain how reading a poem is a way of sharing experiences.

What is a
POEM?

There are almost as many **poems** as there are people. Some poem are very formal, and others are more playful. Some rhyme, and some don't. Some are published in beautiful books, and others are written on sidewalks. But the thing that makes all poems alike is that each expresses the writer's imagination and feelings in a creative way.

ACTIVITY Think of the poems you've read in the past. Can you remember a particular one that you enjoyed? Now think about th lyrics of your favorite song. With a partner, share the name of the poem and song you chose. Then compare the poem and the song lyrics by considering the following questions:

- What is the most memorable line of the poem or song?
- Are the lines grouped in any particular way?
- Do any of the lines rhyme?

Discuss whether the song lyrics you chose should be considered a poem.

540

Unit Resources

 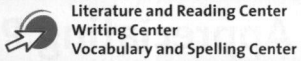

MARYLAND OBJECTIVES — Preview Unit Goals

LITERARY ANALYSIS	• Understand form in poetry
	• Identify characteristics of free verse, lyric poetry, narrative poetry, ballads, and haiku
	• Identify and interpret imagery and figurative language
	• Identify and interpret sound devices, such as rhyme, repetition, and alliteration
	• Identify and compare mood
READING	• Make inferences
	• Use text features to locate and comprehend information
	• Use reading strategies, including monitoring and visualizing
WRITING AND GRAMMAR	• Write a personal response to a poem
	• Support key points with quotes and details
	• Identify and correctly punctuate various types of sentences
	• Use active voice
SPEAKING, LISTENING, AND VIEWING	• Give an oral interpretation of a poem
VOCABULARY	• Understand and use connotative meanings of words
ACADEMIC VOCABULARY	• imagery • form
	• figurative language • personal response
	• sound devices • connotation

541

Preview Unit Goals

This page provides an overview of the skills and strategies covered in the unit. Make sure students are aware of the color coding used to identify each strand. This color coding is used wherever skills are taught in the unit. As students read this page, encourage them to think about their ability to use each skill or strategy.

Suggest that students copy the Academic Vocabulary terms in their journals and define them as they read the unit. Encourage students to use these terms as they discuss and write about the selections.

ADDITIONAL UNIT GOALS

These skills will be taught in this unit but are not the major focus of the unit:

Literary Analysis
• Identify characteristics of humorous poetry
• Read limericks
• Identify and interpret personification, metaphor, and simile
• Identify and interpret meter
• Identify and interpret symbols
• Read and understand a scientific article

Reading
• Use strategies to read a narrative poem
• Set a purpose for reading
• develop strategies for reading science fiction
• Understand and analyze historical context
• Understand speaker

Writing and Grammar
• Use correct sentence type to convey purpose and meaning
• Write a compare-contrast paper

DIFFERENTIATED INSTRUCTION

FOR ENGLISH LEARNERS

Academic Vocabulary Students will study and practice using these terms throughout the unit. Use the Academic Vocabulary copy master to introduce the terms.

1. Read each word aloud and discuss the example. Ask students if they have heard any of these words and in what context.

2. Allow students to work in pairs to write the definitions and complete the activities. Then discuss students' answers as a class.

Additional Academic Vocabulary Use the second copy master to teach additional academic vocabulary that students will use during the unit.

1. Divide the class into small groups.

2. Have each group brainstorm and list other forms of each word.

3. Ask students to complete the definitions and Part B individually.

R RESOURCE MANAGER—Copy Masters
Academic Vocabulary p. 9
Additional Academic Vocabulary p. 10

Focus and Motivate

OBJECTIVES
- identify and analyze poetry form and speaker
- identify free verse characteristics
- identify and analyze rhyme and rhythm
- identify and interpret imagery
- identify and interpret forms of figurative language

Teach

Part 1: The Basics

Form Tell students that a stanza in a poem is similar to a paragraph in a story. Each stanza conveys an idea that contributes to the poem's overall message. The poet also considers the look of the lines on the page. For example, a poet may use a **free verse** form that is not broken into stanzas in order to convey a continuous train of thought or create a special visual effect. Another poet may use a **traditional form** to create a specific effect with regular rhythm and rhyme. Use this activity to help students explore traditional form:

- Read aloud the first stanza of "A Minor Bird" as students follow along in their books.
- Point out that traditional poems have a regular rhythm. Have students tap out the beats (four stressed syllables per line) as you reread lines 1–2.

  ˘ ´ ˘ ´ ˘ ˘ ´ ˘ ´
  I have wished a bird would fly away,

  ˘ ´ ˘ ´ ˘ ´ ˘ ´
  And not sing by my house all day;

- Ask students to notice the end rhymes in the first stanza (*away* and *day*).
- Read the entire poem aloud. Ask students what patterns are repeated throughout the poem. *(two-line stanzas with end rhyme, four beats per line, capital letter at start of each line, standard punctuation)*

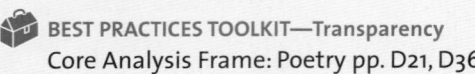 **BEST PRACTICES TOOLKIT—Transparency**
Core Analysis Frame: Poetry pp. D21, D36

 MARYLAND OBJECTIVES

LITERATURE STANDARDS
3.A.4.a Use structural features to distinguish types of poetry
3.A.4.c Analyze sound elements of poetry
3.A.7.c Analyze figurative language

Appreciating Poetry

What makes a song unforgettable? Perhaps it's the rhythm of the music or the catchy lyrics. A song might also speak to you because it reminds you of something in your own life. Like a song, a poem can capture your imagination with what it says and how it sounds. In this workshop, you will learn what gives poetry this special power.

Part 1: The Basics

How does a poem speak to you from the page? Aside from its unique sound, a poem also conveys meaning through its form and its speaker.

Form is the way a poem's words and lines are laid out on the page. Lines may or may not be complete sentences and can vary in length. In some poems, the lines are arranged into groups, called **stanzas.** Each stanza helps to convey a poem's overall message.

Some poems have **traditional,** or **structured,** forms. Traditional poems follow fixed rules; for instance, they might have a certain number of lines or a repeating pattern of rhythm or rhyme. Poems that do not follow set rules are called **free verse.**

A poem's personality depends on its speaker as well as its form. The **speaker** in a poem is the voice that talks to the reader. The speaker may be the poet, or it may be a character created by the poet—a child, for example. In Carl Sandburg's famous poem "Grass," the speaker is actually the grass.

Examine the elements of form and speaker in this traditional poem.

A MINOR BIRD
Poem by **Robert Frost**

I have wished a bird would fly away,
And not sing by my house all day;

Have clapped my hands at him from the door
When it seemed as if I could bear no more.

5 The fault must partly have been in me.
The bird was not to blame for his key.

And of course there must be something wrong
In wanting to silence any song.

EXAMINE THE POEM
- Notice that this poem is made up of four two-line stanzas.
- Look at the four pairs of rhyming words.
- Read the poem aloud to hear its singsong rhythm.
- Note that the speaker is the "I" in the poem but may not be the poet. We don't know if the poet shares the speaker's attitude toward the bird.

DIFFERENTIATED INSTRUCTION

FOR ALL STUDENTS
For general guidelines on differentiating instruction, see

 BEST PRACTICES TOOLKIT
Differentiated Instruction pp. 31–38

FOR LESS—PROFICIENT READERS
Note Taking For students who need help with note taking, hand out the Note Taking: Poetry Basics copy master and have students read page 542 silently. Then have students record their notes on the copy master as you discuss the information.

Identify Speaker Have partners list at least four adjectives to create a character sketch of the speaker in "A Minor Bird." Suggest that they think of one adjective for each stanza. To get them started, suggest these adjectives: *annoyed, reflective, impatient.*

 RESOURCE MANAGER—Copy Master
Note Taking p. 15

MODEL: FORM AND SPEAKER

The following poem is written in free verse. Because it has no regular pattern of rhythm or rhyme, the poem sounds like everyday speech. Read it aloud to hear what the speaker is saying about his or her special hiding place.

UNDER
THE
BACK
PORCH

Poem by **Virginia Hamilton**

> [Our house] is two stories high
> shaped like a white box.
> There is a yard stretched around it
> and in back
> 5   a wooden porch.
>
> [Under the back porch is my place.]
> I rest there.
> I go there when I have to be alone.
> It is always shaded and damp.
> 10   Sunlight only slants through the slats
> in long strips of light,
> and the smell of the damp
> is moist green,
> like the moss that grows here.
>
> 15   My sisters and brothers
> can stand on the back porch
> and never know
> [I am here
> underneath.]
> 20   It is my place.
> All mine.

Close Read

1. Describe the focus of each stanza. (What do you "see"?) Look at the [boxed] details for clues.

2. What do you learn about the speaker of this poem? Cite details that help you understand his or her age, personality, and family life.

3. Notice the last four lines of the poem. What effect does their short length help to create? (Hint: Think about where the speaker is at this point in the poem.)

MODEL: FORM AND SPEAKER
Close Read

1. *Possible answers:* The **first stanza** describes the speaker's house and yard. The **second stanza** focuses on the back porch—the speaker's special place. The speaker describes the sights and smells that he or she experiences while resting there. In the **third stanza,** the speaker describes how private it is underneath the porch. Readers can picture the speaker resting under the porch with the sisters and brothers on the porch above, unaware of the speaker's presence.

2. *Possible answer:* The speaker is a child from a large family ("my sisters and brothers," line 15). Privacy is probably rare, but the speaker likes to be alone sometimes (line 8). The speaker also seems proud to have found a hiding place that is "All mine" (line 21) and does not have to be shared.

3. *Possible answer:* The short length of the last four lines makes it seem as if the speaker is whispering these thoughts from the hiding place. The arrangement of lines in the third stanza, with the longer second line, almost looks like a side view of a back porch, with the boxed lines representing the child hiding underneath.

FOR ENGLISH LEARNERS
Reading Support: Setting Use a Draw It strategy to help students visualize the setting of "Under the Back Porch."

1. Read the poem aloud, pausing to think aloud as you sketch the two-story house, yard, and back porch on the board. Also sketch the speaker sitting under the porch and the speaker's siblings standing above.

2. Have students help you add these labels to the sketch: *house, yard, porch, speaker, sisters and brothers.*

3. Discuss the details in lines 10–14—the strips of sunlight and the damp smell—and indicate these in the sketch as well.

4. Encourage students to make their own sketches to help them visualize the setting and remember the vocabulary.

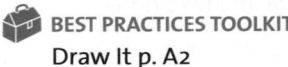 **BEST PRACTICES TOOLKIT**
Draw It p. A2

FOR ADVANCED LEARNERS/PRE–AP
Synthesize Have students read the workshop independently. Then have them apply their understanding of poetic form by rewriting all or part of "A Minor Bird" as free verse, or by rewriting all or part of "Under the Back Porch" in traditional form. Remind them that traditional form is not necessarily rhymed couplets but should have a regular rhythm and rhyme scheme. Have students share their work in a poetry reading.

Part 2: Special Effects

Rhyme Work with students to analyze the rhyme scheme of "Faults."

1. Point out the color-coded words at the end of each line. Ask students to identify the end word that rhymes with *me (see), one (done),* and *before (more).*

2. Explain that traditional poems have a pattern of rhyming words called the rhyme scheme. Each rhyme is assigned a letter. The rhyme scheme of "A Minor Bird" (p. 542) is *aa bb cc dd.* Have students assign a letter to each pair of rhyming words in "Faults."

3. Ask students to use the letter code to write out the rhyme scheme of "Faults" (*abbcac*). Point out that although the rhyming pattern is irregular (as opposed to *ababab,* for example), each line ends with a rhyming word.

Rhythm Have students read aloud "Faults" together, emphasizing the stressed syllables to create an upbeat mood. Point out that the rhythm is so regular that students can tap their feet or clap their hands to it.

Repetition To help students hear how repetition establishes a mood and creates focus in "Winter Moon," conduct an oral reading of the poem with these parts:

- **Half of the class:** reads "How thin and sharp"
- **Other half:** reads "moon tonight"
- **Teacher:** reads the remaining words

Alliteration Read aloud these examples of alliteration and ask students to identify the repeated consonant sounds and the mood that each creates:

- "a lovely, lilting lullaby" (*Possible answers: pleasant, calm, happy*)

- "the droning, deadly drumbeat" (*Possible answers: threatening, ominous*)

Part 2: Special Effects

You've seen how filmmakers use special effects to transport you to new worlds, affect your emotions, and keep you on the edge of your seat. Poets use special effects too. Sound devices can make a poem seem as peaceful as ocean waves lapping on the shore or as intense as a close race. Imagery and figurative language create word pictures that help you imagine things as vividly as if you were seeing them unfold on a movie screen.

SOUND DEVICES

Sound devices give poems a musical quality, but they can also create a mood and emphasize important ideas or words. Here are a few of the sound devices poets use.

SOUND DEVICES	EXAMPLES
RHYME the repetition of sounds at the end of words, as in *me* and *see*	Notice how the rhythm and rhyme in this poem help to create a playful, upbeat mood.
RHYTHM the pattern of stressed (´) and unstressed (˘) syllables in each line (A poem with a repeating pattern has what is called a meter.)	They came to tell your faults to me, They named them over one by one; I laughed aloud when they were done, I knew them all so well before,— Oh, they were blind, too blind to see Your faults had made me love you more. —"Faults" by Sara Teasdale
REPETITION the use of a word, phrase, or line more than once	The repeated phrases and the alliteration in the last line help to emphasize the moon's shape.
ALLITERATION the repetition of consonant sounds at the beginning of words, such as the *c* in *curved crook*	How thin and sharp is the moon tonight! How thin and sharp and ghostly white Is the slim curved crook of the moon tonight! —"Winter Moon" by Langston Hughes

---

DIFFERENTIATED INSTRUCTION

FOR LESS—PROFICIENT READERS

Note Taking For students who need help with note taking, hand out the Note Taking: Special Effects copy master. Read and discuss the first paragraph on page 544. Assist students, as needed, in completing the first item on the copy master. Then have students read the rest of the page and take notes.

 RESOURCE MANAGER—Copy Master
Note Taking p. 16

MODEL 1: RHYME AND RHYTHM

As you read this short poem aloud, notice how Emily Dickinson uses rhyme and rhythm to emphasize the most important words.

A word is dead

Poem by **Emily Dickinson**

A word is dead
When it is said,
Some say.

Ĭ say it just
5 Bĕgins to live
Thăt daý.

Close Read

1. One pair of rhyming words is boxed. Find the other pair.

2. Stressed and unstressed syllables are marked in the second stanza. How does the rhythm in this stanza compare with that in the first stanza?

MODEL 2: OTHER SOUND DEVICES

This free-verse poem is filled with sound devices: repetition, rhyme, alliteration, and **onomatopoeia**—the use of words (made-up or real) whose sounds suggest their meanings. How do these sound devices help you experience the snow?

Cynthia in the Snow

Poem by **Gwendolyn Brooks**

It SUSHES.
It hushes
The loudness in the road.
It flitter-twitters,
5 And laughs away from me.
It laughs a lovely whiteness,
And whitely whirs away,
To be
Some otherwhere,
10 Still white as milk or shirts.
So beautiful it hurts.

Close Read

1. What onomatopoeic words does the poet use to suggest the silencing effect of falling snow?

2. The use of alliteration in the boxed line helps to create a light, joyful mood. Find another example of alliteration.

3. Identify three pairs of rhymes. For one pair, explain what qualities of snow the rhyme helps to emphasize.

MODEL 1: RHYME AND RHYTHM
Close Read

1. *The second pair of rhyming words is* say *and* day *(lines 3 and 6).*

2. **Possible answers:** *The rhythm of the first stanza mirrors that of the second. The only variation is in line 1, where the words* word *and* dead *are stressed, and* A *and* is *are unstressed.*

MODEL 2: OTHER SOUND DEVICES
Close Read

1. **Possible answers:** *"Sushes" (a made-up word) and "hushes" suggest the silencing effect of falling snow.*

2. **Possible answer:** *Another example of alliteration is in lines 6–7—"a lovely whiteness, / And whitely whirs away." The* wh *sound is repeated.*

3. **Possible answers:** *Three pairs of rhymes are:* sushes/hushes, flitter/twitters, *and* shirts/hurts. *Students may say that the rhyme in* sushes/hushes *helps to emphasize the silence that accompanies a snowfall; that the rhyme in* flitter/twitters *suggests snowflakes dancing through the air; and that the rhyme in* shirts/hurts *helps to emphasize the cold, stark beauty of pure white snow.*

DIFFERENTIATED INSTRUCTION

FOR ENGLISH LEARNERS

Concept Support: Vocabulary Explain that in **Model 2** the words *sushes* (line 1), *flitter-twitters* (line 4), *whitely* (line 7), and *otherwhere* (line 9) are inventions of the poet. Help students identify the part of speech for each word (sushes *and* flitter-twitters, *verb;* whitely, *adverb;* otherwhere, *noun*). Have students use context clues to determine the intended meanings of these words and describe the special effects they create.

Concept Support: Onomatopoeia To show the sound effects of onomatopoeia, provide a list of words whose sounds echo their meanings (*chirp, buzz, whir, gargle, murmur*). Have students list the words in a two-column chart. Say each word, using exaggeration to communicate the meaning/sound correspondence. (For example, use a high-pitched voice for *chirp;* emphasize the *z*'s in *buzz*.) In their charts, have students sketch the image that each word brings to mind.

Imagery and Figurative Language Explain that imagery and figurative language in a poem are similar to special effects in a movie. They grab attention and help describe people, emotions, and events. They also help create a mood or feeling. For example, an image of a ruined, abandoned house in the woods can evoke feelings of sadness or loneliness.

Tell students that to get the most out of the imagery in a poem, they should try to create mental pictures of the images. As they read the poem or listen to it being read aloud, they can imagine a video that might accompany the poem. What images would appear in the video? Have students use copies of the T Chart transparency as they read the examples on page 546. Students should

- use the left column to jot down words and phrases from the poem that appeal to the senses of sight, sound, smell, or touch

- use the right column to record their reactions to the images—ideas or feelings

Images from Poem	Reactions

 BEST PRACTICES TOOLKIT—Transparency
T Chart p. A25

IMAGERY AND FIGURATIVE LANGUAGE

Imagery is language that appeals to the five senses—sight, hearing, smell, taste, and touch. "Cynthia in the Snow" focuses on the sense of hearing, but it also helps you see the snow as it "whitely whirs away." With a few vivid images, the poet draws you into the winter scene.

One way poets create imagery is through **figurative language.** Figurative language uses creative comparisons to help readers picture ordinary things in new ways. For example, the snow is not just white but "white as milk or shirts." Here are three types of figurative language.

TYPE	EXAMPLE
SIMILE a comparison between two unlike things, using the word *like* or *as*	This simile compares a cat's coloring to spilled milk. The word *as* signals the comparison. He's white As spilled milk, My cat who sleeps With his belly Turned toward The summer sky. —from "Ode to Mi Gato" by Gary Soto
METAPHOR a comparison between two unlike things that does not contain the word *like* or *as*	This metaphor compares fame to a bee. It conveys both the good and the bad side of fame. Fame is a bee. It has a song— It has a sting— Ah, too, it has a wing. —by Emily Dickinson

PERSONIFICATION a description of an object, an animal, a place, or an idea as if it were human or had human qualities	Here, "proud words" are given human qualities.
	
	 Look out how you use proud words.
	 When you let proud words go, it is
	     not easy to call them back.
	 They wear long boots, hard boots; they
	 walk off proud; they can't hear you
	     calling—
	 Look out how you use proud words.
	
	 —"Primer Lesson" by Carl Sandburg

DIFFERENTIATED INSTRUCTION

FOR LESS–PROFICIENT READERS
Comprehension Support: Figurative Language Have students review the examples and use a T Chart to list what is being compared.

Figurative Language	__ compared to __
simile	cat compared to milk
metaphor	fame compared to bee
personification	proud words compared to people

 BEST PRACTICES TOOLKIT—Transparency
T Chart p. A25

FOR ADVANCED LEARNERS/PRE–AP
Illustrate Figurative Language Have small groups create a quick reference chart to post in the classroom to help students identify different types of figurative language. Charts should be easy to read and should include definitions and examples of simile, metaphor, and personification. They may also include illustrations.

Part 3: Analyze the Literature

In this poem, the speaker reflects on her mother's courage, a quality that she has missed since her mother died. Use what you've learned in this workshop to analyze the elements—form, speaker, sound devices, figurative language, and imagery—that help to create a picture of a remarkable parent.

The COURAGE
That My Mother Had
Poem by **Edna St. Vincent Millay**

The courage that my mother had
Went with her, and is with her still:
Rock from New England quarried;[1]
Now granite in a granite hill.

5 The golden brooch[2] my mother wore
She left behind for me to wear;
I have no thing I treasure more:
Yet, it is something I could spare.

Oh, if instead she'd left to me
10 The thing she took into the grave!—
That courage like a rock, which she
Has no more need of, and I have.

1. **quarried:** dug up from the ground.
2. **brooch:** a piece of jewelry that can be fastened to clothing.

Close Read

1. Describe two characteristics that make this a traditional poem. Think about the number of lines in each stanza and the patterns of rhythm and rhyme.

2. One example of alliteration is boxed. Find another example.

3. Identify the simile in the third stanza. What does it suggest about the mother's personality?

4. How would you describe the speaker of this poem? Think about how she views herself, what she admires about her mother, and what she seems to value.

Practice and Apply

Part 3: Analyze the Literature
Close Read
1. **Possible answer:** All three stanzas have the same number of lines (four) and follow the same rhyme pattern, with end-rhyming words in the second and fourth lines (abab). The stanzas follow a similar rhythm.

2. **Possible answers:** "Went with her" (line 2); "my mother" (line 5); "something I could spare" (line 8)

3. **Possible answer:** The simile occurs in line 11: "That courage like a rock." It suggests how courageous, brave, and emotionally strong the mother was.

4. **Possible answers:** The speaker values internal qualities such as courage over material things such as jewelry (the "golden brooch"). She seems to miss her mother tremendously. The speaker does not view herself as courageous or strong; she wishes she could be more like her mother.

Assess and Reteach

Assess
Have students briefly summarize the form, speaker, and special effects used in the poems on pages 545 and 547.

Reteach
Select from these options for students who have trouble applying the workshop skills:
1. Review with students their note-taking copy masters. Then have pairs
   - compare the information they recorded
   - explain each term to one another
   - question each other to clarify ideas
   - share their insights and challenges
2. Refer students to a poem the class has read recently. Discuss these questions:
   - What poetic form has the poet used? Is it a sonnet, haiku, lyric, or free verse?
   - How are the lines arranged on the page?
   - How do stanzas and punctuation affect your understanding of the poem?
   - What do sound devices—such as rhyme, rhythm, repetition, and alliteration—add to the poem's meaning or effect?

DIFFERENTIATED INSTRUCTION

FOR LESS–PROFICIENT READERS
Analysis Support: Poetry Elements Work with students to complete a Cluster Diagram analyzing the elements of "The Courage That My Mother Had." **Possible map details:**
- **form**—traditional
- **speaker**—daughter whose mother has died
- **sound devices**—alliteration ("my mother"); rhyme scheme abab cdcd efef
- **imagery**—rock/granite (lines 3–4, 11)
- **figurative language**—simile ("courage like a rock")

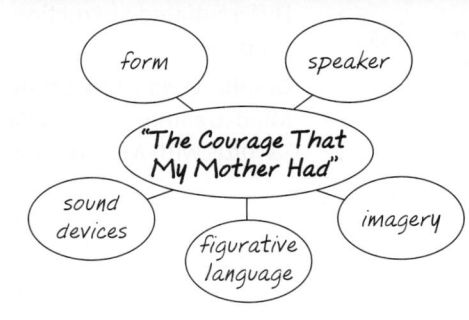

BEST PRACTICES TOOLKIT—Transparency
Cluster Diagram p. B18

Focus and Motivate

OBJECTIVES

Literary Analysis
- explore the key idea of a **memorial**
- identify characteristics of free verse
- identify and interpret imagery
- read a poem and an article

Reading
- understand and analyze historical context

SUMMARY

"The Names" pays tribute to the people who lost their lives in the terrorist attacks of September 11. Collins weaves an A-to-Z list of names of the dead among descriptions of everyday sights and imagery to suggest a sense of loss. The speaker conveys the feeling that the losses of that single day—"So many names"—are too great to express.

Why do we need MEMORIALS?

Have students read the question and the *KEY IDEA* paragraph. Ask them what monuments exist locally and what **memorials** they know of elsewhere. What events do these memorials commemorate? Why is it important to remember these events and the people associated with them? Bring the discussion back to the big question—*Why do we need memorials?*—before students pursue the *QUICKWRITE* activity.

Selection Resources

R RESOURCE MANAGER UNIT 5
Plan and Teach pp. 17–24
Literary Analysis
Imagery pp. 25, 26†*
Question Support p. 29*
Reading
Understand Historical Context
    pp. 27, 28†*
Reading Fluency p. 30

Assessment
Selection Tests A, B/C pp. 31*, 33*
  Test Generator CD

BEST PRACTICES TOOLKIT
Differentiated Instruction
    pp. 31–38*
Graphic Organizers/Strategies
Mindstreaming • Think-Pair-Share
• Words with Multiple Meanings

Reading Support
  Audio Anthology CD*
Technology
  Literature Center
    at ClassZone.com
  WriteSmart CD

* Resources for Differentiation   † Also in Spanish

The Names
Poem by Billy Collins

Why do we need MEMORIALS?

MARYLAND OBJECTIVES

LITERATURE STANDARDS
3.A.4.a Use structural features to distinguish types of poetry
3.A.7.d Analyze imagery

KEY IDEA When tragedy strikes, putting the incident behind you as soon as possible might at first seem like the quickest route to recovery. In reality, many people find that creating a **memorial** to remember and reflect on a loss can provide great comfort. Read the memorial poem "The Names" to find out how, in a time of grief, one poet used his work to help others heal.

QUICKWRITE Consider your own experience with loss, or an experience that you've observed. Why do you think remembering a sad event might help the healing process? Reflect on this question in a journal entry.

548

POETIC FORM: FREE VERSE

The way a poem looks on the page is the poem's **form**. Poetry with no regular pattern of rhyme, rhythm, or line length is written in a form called **free verse**. When poets write free verse, they don't have to follow set rules. They can create whatever lines, rhythms, and rhymes they feel best communicate the ideas they want to express.

LITERARY ANALYSIS: IMAGERY

Imagery consists of words and phrases that appeal to your senses of sight, hearing, smell, taste, and touch. Poets use imagery not only to vividly describe things, but also to communicate feelings and ideas. For example, look at the opening lines of "The Names":

Yesterday, I lay awake in the palm of the night.

A soft rain stole in, unhelped by any breeze,

The images "palm of the night" and "soft rain" appeal to your senses of sight and touch. These phrases also suggest a sense of troubled thoughtfulness and perhaps a feeling of change. As you read "The Names," use a word web to identify these and other examples of imagery.

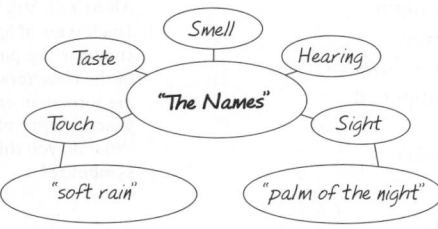

READING SKILL: UNDERSTAND HISTORICAL CONTEXT

Many works of literature seem easier to understand once you know their historical context—the real events and situations that influenced them. Billy Collins wrote "The Names" as a tribute to the more than 3,000 people who died in the terrorist attacks of September 11, 2001. Before you read the poem, read the **Background** on this page. The information can help you better appreciate the imagery Collins uses.

Author Online

A Popular Poet
Poet Billy Collins is a spellbinding performer. His readings have helped spark a renewed hunger for poetry in America. Collins served as the U.S. poet laureate from 2001 to 2003.

Billy Collins
born 1941

Background

A City Grieves Collins was born and raised in New York City. His hometown suffered heavy losses on September 11, 2001, when terrorists flew planes into the World Trade Center, causing its two towers to collapse. In the following days, signs, posters, and photographs showing the dead or missing were posted all over the city and the surrounding area. These postings often turned into memorials, with passersby adding notes, flowers, and mementos as it became clear that few of the missing had survived.

A Poem of Remembrance When asked on the day of the attacks what poem was appropriate to the tragedy, Collins replied, "Any poem." Asked to explain, Collins stated that good poetry affirms life. Collins read "The Names" in a special session of Congress in New York City on September 6, 2002.

 MORE ABOUT THE AUTHOR AND BACKGROUND
To learn more about Billy Collins and September 11, 2001, visit the **Literature Center** at ClassZone.com.

Teach

POETIC FORM

● FREE VERSE

Write this example on the board:

> I crush the sprig of blue-green juniper,
>
> Coarse needles yielding a crisp scent,
>
> And smile, remembering Grandpa's yard.

Ask students how they can tell it is free verse. *Possible answer: The words do not rhyme and there is no regular rhythm.*

CHECK UNDERSTANDING Ask students what a free verse poem might look like on the page.

LITERARY ANALYSIS

● IMAGERY

Referring to the example above, ask students to which senses the words appeal. *Possible answers: "Crush" and "coarse" appeal to touch; "sprig," "blue-green," and "yard" appeal to sight; "crisp scent" appeals to smell.*

CHECK UNDERSTANDING Ask students to name an example from a song of imagery that appeals to a sense.

 RESOURCE MANAGER—Copy Master Imagery p. 25 (for student use while reading the poem)

READING SKILL

■ UNDERSTAND HISTORICAL CONTEXT

Ask students how the historical context of the September 11 attacks might influence a poem set in New York City just after that time. *Possible answer: The poem might deal with sadness and loss, and it might mention details or images that relate to the events of September 11.*

CHECK UNDERSTANDING Ask students to identify the historical context of a movie they know. How did this context affect the action?

DIFFERENTIATED INSTRUCTION

FOR ALL STUDENTS

For general guidelines on differentiating instruction, see

 BEST PRACTICES TOOLKIT
Differentiated Instruction pp. 31–38

FOR LESS-PROFICIENT READERS

Concept Support To build background on the historical context, have pairs use Mindstreaming to tell each other what they know about how people responded to the September 11 attacks.

 BEST PRACTICES TOOLKIT—Transparency
Mindstreaming p. A16

FOR ENGLISH LEARNERS

Options for Reading Prepare students to look for imagery by asking them to listen for words and phrases that tell how something looks, feels, or sounds. Allow students to read along with the *Audio Anthology CD*. Then ask for volunteers to take turns reading aloud from the poem; have each volunteer read one sentence (1–6 lines each).

ANALYZE VISUALS

About the Photograph The lights of this **memorial** were first lit on March 11, 2002, the six-month anniversary of the September 11 attacks. Two banks of searchlights, each creating a 50-foot-square column of light, were set up about a block from where the Twin Towers once stood. The display was called the "Tribute in Light."

Activity What things might the lights symbolize? *Possible answers: The lights may symbolize*

- *the Twin Towers that fell*
- *the people who died*
- *the spirit of hope*

Lines 1–10
DISCUSSION PROMPTS

Use these prompts to help students explore the imagery used by the poet:

Connect How does it feel to lie awake at night? What kinds of thoughts might a person lying awake at night have? *Possible answer: It can feel odd and wrong to lie awake at night. A person may reflect on his or her memories and concerns.*

Analyze Willow trees (line 10) are a symbol of mourning. What other words and phrases in lines 1–10 suggest sadness? *Possible answer: Sadness may be suggested by images of darkness and night (lines 1, 7, 8) and water (lines 2, 7, 9, 10), which may represent tears.*

Evaluate What image in lines 1–10 do you think best expresses a feeling of grief? *Possible answers: "droplets fell through the dark" (line 7); "Names printed on the ceiling of the night" (line 8); "Names slipping around a watery bend" (line 9); "willows on the banks of a stream" (line 10)*

LITERARY ANALYSIS

Ⓐ IMAGERY

Possible answers: Images appealing to sight and touch include

- *"walked out barefoot" (line 11)*
- *"thousands of flowers / Heavy with dew like the eyes of tears" (lines 12–13)*
- *"[a name] inscribed on a yellow petal" (line 15)*

The NAMES

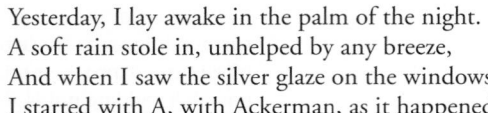

Billy Collins

Yesterday, I lay awake in the palm of the night.
A soft rain stole in, unhelped by any breeze,
And when I saw the silver glaze on the windows,
I started with A, with Ackerman, as it happened,
5 Then Baxter and Calabro,
Davis and Eberling, names falling into place
As droplets fell through the dark.

Names printed on the ceiling of the night.
Names slipping around a watery bend.
10 Twenty-six willows on the banks of a stream.

In the morning, I walked out barefoot
Among thousands of flowers
Heavy with dew like the eyes of tears,
And each had a name—
15 Fiori inscribed on a yellow petal
Then Gonzalez and Han, Ishikawa and Jenkins. Ⓐ

ANALYZE VISUALS
The towers of light shown in the picture of the New York skyline are turned on each year on September 11. What do you think they **symbolize?**

Ⓐ IMAGERY
Reread lines 11–16. Which images appeal to your senses of sight and touch? Record the images in your web. Then think about how they affect the poem's meaning.

DIFFERENTIATED INSTRUCTION

FOR LESS–PROFICIENT READERS

Comprehension Support Read aloud lines 11–18. Ask students to clarify what the speaker is expressing. Make sure they understand that when he refers to a name that is written on a petal (line 15) or in the air (line 17), he does not actually see written names. He is using figurative language to communicate the feeling that everywhere he goes, he is aware of and thinking about the fact that so many individual people have been lost.

Concept Support Have students use Think-Pair-Share to answer the Discussion Prompts on this page.

 BEST PRACTICES TOOLKIT—Transparency Think-Pair-Share p. A18

Names written in the air
And stitched into the cloth of the day.
A name under a photograph taped to a mailbox.
20 Monogram[1] on a torn shirt,
I see you spelled out on storefront windows
And on the bright unfurled awnings of this city.
I say the syllables as I turn a corner—
Kelly and Lee,
25 Medina, Nardella, and O'Connor. **B**

When I peer into the woods,
I see a thick tangle where letters are hidden
As in a puzzle concocted for children.
Parker and Quigley in the twigs of an ash,
30 Rizzo, Schubert, Torres, and Upton,
Secrets in the boughs of an ancient maple.

Names written in the pale sky.
Names rising in the updraft[2] amid buildings.
Names silent in stone
35 Or cried out behind a door. **C**
Names blown over the earth and out to sea.

In the evening— weakening light, the last swallows.
A boy on a lake lifts his oars.
A woman by a window puts a match to a candle,
40 And the names are outlined on the rose clouds—
Vanacore and Wallace,
(let X stand, if it can, for the ones unfound)
Then Young and Ziminsky, the final jolt of Z.
Names etched on the head of a pin.
45 One name spanning a bridge, another undergoing a tunnel.
A blue name needled into the skin. **D**

Names of citizens, workers, mothers and fathers,
The bright-eyed daughter, the quick son.
Alphabet of names in green rows in a field.
50 Names in the small tracks of birds.
Names lifted from a hat
Or balanced on the tip of the tongue.
Names wheeled into the dim warehouse of memory.
So many names, there is barely room on the walls of the heart.

---

1. **monogram:** the initials of one's name combined into a design.

2. **updraft:** an upward movement of air.

B HISTORICAL CONTEXT
Consider what you learned in the **Background** section on page 549. What can you **infer** about the people Collins is naming?

C FREE VERSE
Reread lines 34–35. Why do you think Collins broke this sentence fragment into two short lines instead of writing it as one line?

D IMAGERY
Reread lines 37–46. Identify images that strike you as particularly powerful. Note what senses they appeal to. What feelings do the images suggest?

READING SKILL

B HISTORICAL CONTEXT
Possible answer: The names represent the many people who died on September 11.

Lines 32–36
REINFORCE KEY IDEA: MEMORIAL
Discuss How might including names of people in a **memorial** help to comfort their loved ones? *Possible answers: Including names can help people feel that the dead will not be forgotten. It may make them feel that their personal loss is being honored by the larger society.*

POETIC FORM

C FREE VERSE
Possible answers:
- *The pause created by the broken line emphasizes a feeling of loss.*
- *The pause suggests the silence of "silent in stone" (line 34).*
- *The break emphasizes the contrast between "silent" and "cried out."*

LITERARY ANALYSIS

D IMAGERY
Remind students to record their ideas in their word webs. *Answers will vary but should include specific evidence. Students may say that the images suggest that loss is everywhere and might be evoked by any everyday sight or experience.*

SELECTION WRAP–UP

REFLECT Ask students how the names in the poem reflect the diversity of New Yorkers and Americans in general.

★ **CRITIQUE** Have students evaluate whether the poet's inclusion of names from A to Z was effective in memorializing the losses of September 11.

READING FLUENCY

Distribute the copy masters and have students work in groups to practice fluency.

R RESOURCE MANAGER—Copy Master
Reading Fluency p. 30

FOR ENGLISH LEARNERS
Vocabulary: Multiple-Meaning Words Have pairs use a dictionary to find the part of speech and definition for one of these words as used in the poem. Then have them write a sentence with another meaning for the word.

- *palm* (line 1)
- *turn* (line 23)
- *bend* (line 9)
- *letters* (line 27)
- *banks* (line 10)
- *tracks* (line 50)

BEST PRACTICES TOOLKIT—Transparency
Words with Multiple Meanings p. E31

FOR ADVANCED LEARNERS/PRE–AP
Analyze Imagery Draw students' attention to some of the many places the speaker notices names, such as "in the pale sky" (line 32) or "blown over the earth" (line 36). Challenge them to create an original image of another place where names might be perceived.

Names in the clatter of chopsticks on a plate.

Practice and Apply

After Reading

For additional support of post-reading questions, use these copy masters:

R RESOURCE MANAGER—Copy Masters
Understand Historical Context p. 27 (for practice of reading standards focus)

Question Support p. 29 (**After Reading** questions adapted for English learners and less-proficient readers)

Additional selection questions are provided for teachers on page 21.

ANSWERS

Comprehension

1. *The letter X stands for those people or victims who have not been found.*

2. *Possibilities include "on the ceiling of the night" (line 8), on flowers (line 15), in trees (line 29), in the sky (line 32), on clouds (line 40), and on skin (line 46).*

3. *The names belong to people who died in the September 11 attacks.*

Literary Analysis

Possible answers:

4. ● **STANDARDS FOCUS** *Imagery Answers will vary. Students should explain how the images they consider effective relate to their ideas about the meaning of the poem.*

5. *Subject: the victims of September 11; Images: names appearing everywhere, such as in the night sky (line 8) and on flower petals (line 15); Words: "Heavy with dew like the eyes of tears" (line 13), "So many names, there is barely room on the walls of the heart" (line 54); Theme: Since each person's life is unique and precious, the many lives lost on September 11 are a tragedy almost too great to comprehend.*

6. ■ **STANDARDS FOCUS** *Understand Historical Context Answers will vary. Students may say that at the anniversary of the attacks, Collins expressed the sense of loss that listeners felt and assured them that the dead would not be forgotten.*

7. ● **STANDARDS FOCUS** *Free Verse Answers will vary. Students may say that the naturalness of free verse helps them connect with the speaker's experience.*

Comprehension

MARYLAND OBJECTIVES

LITERATURE STANDARD
3.A.7.d Analyze imagery

1. **Recall** According to the poem, what does the letter *X* stand for?

2. **Recall** In what places does the speaker of the poem see the names? Describe three.

3. **Clarify** Whom do the names in the poem belong to?

Literary Analysis

4. **Understand Imagery** Look at the word web you created as you read. Which images from the poem do you consider especially effective? How do these images strengthen the meaning of the poem? Explain your answer.

5. **Identify Theme** The theme of a poem is its basic message about life or human nature. Think about the subject of this poem, the key images, and the words that are emphasized or repeated. What do you think is the overall message about September 11, 2001, that Billy Collins wishes to convey in "The Names"? Collect your thoughts in a graphic like the one shown.

Subject:	Images:	Words:

Theme:

6. **Analyze Historical Context** Recall that Billy Collins read this **memorial** poem when Congress met in New York City nearly one year after the attacks. Choose three lines or sections of the poem and tell why they might have been particularly meaningful to the people hearing them on that day.

7. **Evaluate Free Verse** Read the poem aloud as naturally as you can. Do you think this free verse poem is successful at communicating ideas and emotions? Explain why or why not.

Extension and Challenge

8. **Creative Project: Art** Choose a visual image in the poem that you find particularly powerful. Draw or sketch the image, and explain to the class how the poet's words guided your work.

9. 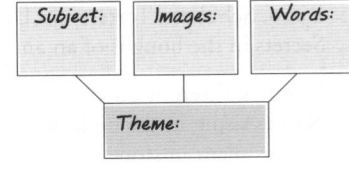 **SOCIAL STUDIES CONNECTION** Read the article "A Nation Mourns" on page 553. Then reread "The Names." In what ways does the information in the article deepen your appreciation of the poem? Share your answer with a small group, being sure to point out at least two specific ways that knowing about the events of September 11 helped to broaden your understanding of the poem.

Extension and Challenge

8. *Students should be able to explain how their representation connects to a particular visual image in the poem.*

9. **SOCIAL STUDIES CONNECTION**
Students may say that the article gives a sense of the terrible shock of the tragedy as well as the efforts to help victims, survivors, and rescuers. It also describes how the casualties included immigrants from many nations.

Assess and Reteach

Assess

R RESOURCE MANAGER—Copy Masters
Selection Tests A, B/C pp. 31–32, 33–34

Test Generator CD

Reteach

S STANDARDS LESSON FILE
Literature Lesson 17: Structure of Poetry
Literature Lesson 26: Imagery

ARTICLE Can the worst in humanity bring out the best in humanity? "The Names" reflects on the lives lost on September 11, 2001. Read this article to find out more about that day and the way people responded to the tragedy.

Enemies Attack: *A Nation Mourns*

Between 7:58 A.M. and 8:10 A.M. on September 11, 2001, four passenger planes left the Boston, Newark, and Washington, D.C., airports. In a matter of minutes, each of these planes was hijacked by terrorists. One of the worst attacks on the United States was underway.

Just seconds after 8:46 A.M., Eastern Standard Time, the first of these planes flew into Tower One of the World Trade Center in New York City; about fifteen minutes later, a second plane flew into Tower Two. Both towers collapsed less than two hours after the attacks. A third plane struck the Pentagon just outside of Washington, D.C. The fourth plane crashed in a Pennsylvania field. Its intended target remains unknown. In all, more than 3,000 civilians, firefighters, and police officers were killed that morning, and thousands were wounded.

The nation and most of the world responded with an outpouring of sympathy and good will. Immediately, volunteers in and around New York City and Washington, D.C., arranged services for the survivors and the rescuers. Around the country, people organized charities to aid the families of victims. Improvised memorials sprung up near the sites of the attacks and the victims' homes, and communities held vigils to pay tribute to the dead and comfort the grieving.

Newspapers published profiles of the deceased, revealing people of all ages and professions, from corporate executives to firefighters. The victims included immigrants from more than 80 nations.

Many of the spontaneous memorials that dotted the country in the weeks following the incident have since been replaced by permanent memorials. In Bucks County, Pennsylvania, a Garden of Reflection provides a peaceful place to pay respect. In Sherwood Island State Park in Connecticut, a Living Memorial granite monument and garden now stands. And where the World Trade Center once stood, several different memorials pay tribute to the victims and their families, as well as to the relief workers whose efforts to aid survivors endure as an example of the best in people.

READING FOR INFORMATION   **553**

This selection provides support for question 9 on page 552. You can also use it as a mini-lesson on reading for information.

DISCUSSION PROMPTS

Use these prompts to help students explore how people used **memorials** to help cope with grief caused by the September 11 attacks:

Interpret Memorials can allow people to share their grief. How might sharing grief help a person to cope with loss? *Possible answer: Sharing grief can help a person feel that others understand their experience and that they are not alone.*

Analyze What purpose might the improvised memorials have served? Why do you think many of these were replaced with permanent memorials? *Possible answer: Improvised memorials helped people express and share their feelings right away. They might also have satisfied a need to "do something." They might have been replaced by permanent memorials to acknowledge the fact that grief would continue and to honor the memories of the dead in a more lasting way.*

Evaluate How might a "peaceful place" such as one of the gardens mentioned in the article support the purpose of a memorial? *Possible answers: A peaceful place can help bring about the reflecting and remembering that a memorial is often intended to encourage. Because a peaceful place is calm and pleasant, it can help people think. Many people are especially comforted by feeling close to nature in a garden.*

DIFFERENTIATED INSTRUCTION

FOR ENGLISH LEARNERS
Comprehension: Sequence Have students note phrases in the first five sentences that indicate time order. Have them show on a clock what each phrase means.

- *between 7:58 A.M. and 8:10 A.M.*
- *in a matter of minutes*
- *just seconds after 8:46 A.M.*
- *about fifteen minutes later*
- *less than two hours after*

Vocabulary: Cognates Have students scan for cognates. Spanish cognates in the title and first sentence of the article include

- *enemy/el enemigo(a)*
- *to attack/atacar*
- *nation/la nación*
- *passenger/el pasajero(a)*
- *airport/el aeropuerto*

Students might also notice words that look the same but are used differently, such as *plane/el plano.*

Focus and Motivate

OBJECTIVES

Literary Analysis
- explore the key idea of **nature**
- identify characteristics of lyric poetry
- identify and interpret figurative language (personification, metaphor, simile)
- read poetry

Reading
- make inferences

Grammar and Writing
- identify and correctly punctuate types of sentences
- use correct sentence types to convey purpose and meaning
- use writing to analyze poetry

SUMMARY

These three lyric poems explore aspects of nature. In "the earth is a living thing," the planet is compared to wild creatures and to a beloved child. In "Sleeping in the Forest," the speaker becomes immersed in the sensory world of a forest at night. "Gold" joyfully expresses the beauty of a desert landscape at sunset.

What is our place in NATURE?

Discuss the question. Ask students to think of a time when they felt connected to **nature.** Where were they—in a park, on a hike, near a lake or ocean, or in someone's yard? Have students recall what made an impression on their senses. Encourage them to keep this memory in mind as they complete the *SKETCH IT* activity.

Selection Resources

RESOURCE MANAGER UNIT 5

Plan and Teach pp. 35–42

Literary Analysis
Figurative Language pp. 43, 44†*
Question Support p. 47*

Reading
Make Inferences pp. 45, 46†*

Grammar and Writing
Use Correct Sentence Type p. 49

Assessment
Selection Tests A, B/C pp. 51*, 53*
Test Generator CD

BEST PRACTICES TOOLKIT

Differentiated Instruction
pp. 31–38*

Graphic Organizers/Strategies
Read Aloud/Think Aloud •
Sensory Notes • Draw It

Reading Support
Audio Anthology CD*

Technology
Literature Center at
ClassZone.com

Write*Smart* CD

* Resources for Differentiation   † Also in Spanish

---

the earth is a living thing
Poem by Lucille Clifton

Sleeping in the Forest
Poem by Mary Oliver

Gold
Poem by Pat Mora

What is our place in NATURE?

MARYLAND OBJECTIVES

READING/LITERATURE STANDARDS
1.E.4.c Draw inferences
3.A.7.c Analyze figurative language

KEY IDEA When you left the house to go to school this morning, was the sky clear or cloudy? How did the air feel? Did you hear birds singing or see an insect darting by? **Nature** surrounds us, but sometimes we forget to notice.

SKETCH IT In a small group, discuss how you fit in with the natural world. In what ways does nature affect your life? Do you think people are part of nature or separate from it? Give concrete examples to support your opinion. Then make a sketch that shows your place in nature.

554

POETIC FORM: LYRIC POETRY

A **lyric poem** is a short poem in which a single speaker expresses personal thoughts and feelings. Lyric poems cover many subjects, from love and death to everyday experiences. Like many other lyric poems, each of those you're about to read creates a strong, unified impression.

LITERARY ANALYSIS: FIGURATIVE LANGUAGE

Literal language is language that reflects the dictionary definition of words. It forms a factual statement, such as "a tree sheds its leaves in autumn." **Figurative language** expresses an idea through a more imaginative use of words: "A tree mourns its lost leaves in autumn."

Here are some types of figurative language poets frequently use:

- **Personification** gives human qualities to an animal, an object, or an idea. (*whispering trees, angrily marching ants*)
- **Similes** compare two unlike things using the word *like* or *as*. (*The stars flamed like torches.*)
- **Metaphors** compare two unlike things without using the word *like* or *as*. (*The stars were torches.*)

READING SKILL: MAKE INFERENCES

To understand poetry, you will have to **make inferences,** or make logical guesses, about images and figurative language. Base these guesses on both the details of the poem and your own knowledge and experience. As you read, use charts like the one shown to record striking or puzzling lines or phrases from each poem. Then record your inferences.

Title: "Sleeping in the Forest"		
Lines and Phrases	What I Know from Reading or Experience	Inference
"I slept/as never before, a stone/on the riverbed"	The speaker compares herself to a stone. Stones are completely still.	The speaker slept soundly, without moving.

Author Online

Lucille Clifton: An Original Voice
Though Lucille Clifton was always comfortable when it came to writing, she says, "I had to learn that poetry could sound like me." After writing in traditional forms, Clifton discovered that good poetry could sound like everyday speech.

Lucille Clifton born 1936

Mary Oliver: Nature's Poet
Mary Oliver finds her inspiration in exploring nature. Oliver describes the writer's life as "an unstoppable urge toward that life of the imagination. I don't think I have been bored one day in my life, you know, or an hour."

Mary Oliver born 1935

Pat Mora: Poetry Pioneer
Pat Mora, who is Mexican American, has helped pioneer poetry about the Mexican-American experience. Since she grew up outside of El Paso, Texas, she also loves to write about the desert.

Pat Mora born 1942

 MORE ABOUT THE AUTHOR
For more on these poets, visit the **Literature Center** at ClassZone.com.

555

Teach

STANDARDS FOCUS

POETIC FORM

● **LYRIC POETRY**
Write this example on the board:

> My puppy is velvet
> She wiggles and licks
> And tumbles to my arms
> Like a leaf in the wind

Ask what makes this a lyric poem. ***Possible answer:*** *The poem is short, shares the thoughts and feelings of the speaker, and creates a strong impression of its subject—the puppy.*

CHECK UNDERSTANDING Ask students to name subjects from their own experience that would be appropriate for a lyric poem.

LITERARY ANALYSIS

● **FIGURATIVE LANGUAGE**
Referring to the example above, ask students what figurative language is used. ***Possible answer:*** *"[The] puppy is velvet" is a metaphor. "And tumbles . . . / Like a leaf" is a simile.*

CHECK UNDERSTANDING Ask students to explain how similes, personification, and metaphors are similar and different.

READING SKILL

■ **MAKE INFERENCES**
Ask students what inferences they can make about how the puppy in the example moves. ***Possible answer:*** *It is compared to a leaf in the wind. The puppy, like a blowing leaf, may seem to fly easily from place to place.*

CHECK UNDERSTANDING Ask students to explain in their own words the process of making inferences.

 RESOURCE MANAGER—Copy Master
Make Inferences p. 45 (for student use while reading the poems)

DIFFERENTIATED INSTRUCTION

FOR ALL STUDENTS
For general guidelines on differentiating instruction, see

 BEST PRACTICES TOOLKIT
Differentiated Instruction pp. 31–38

FOR LESS–PROFICIENT READERS
Comprehension Support Point out that "the earth is a living thing" is a series of predicates—different ways to complete the same sentence. Help students find the subject (*the earth*), which appears in the title only.

FOR ENGLISH LEARNERS
Options for Reading Allow students to read along with the *Audio Anthology CD.* Then have pairs of students take turns reading the poems aloud to each other. Encourage them to read slowly and listen for repeated words and sounds.

LITERARY ANALYSIS

Ⓐ FIGURATIVE LANGUAGE

Answer: *The earth is compared to a bear (line 1), a hawk (line 4), a fish (line 7), and a diamond (line 8).*

LITERARY ANALYSIS

Ⓑ FIGURATIVE LANGUAGE

Possible answer: *The image of the earth as a "favorite child" of the universe (line 10), having its hair stroked and "brushed clean" (lines 12–14), suggests a close and loving parent-child relationship between the earth and the universe.*

ANALYZE VISUALS

Possible answers:

Bear with Houses	Hacienda
• black, green, and blue	• mostly orange and red
• large, strong form	• smaller, more detailed shapes
• looms in foreground	• recedes in background

Students' answers about which picture is more realistic may vary.

About the Art The work of American illustrator Michael Wertz has appeared in national magazines and newspapers, as well as on movie trailers and book covers. In addition to working with pastels, as he did for *Bear with Houses*, Wertz uses collage, screen printing, and digital art to create his colorful and dynamic images.

the earth
is a living thing
Lucille Clifton

is a black shuffling bear
ruffling its wild back and tossing
mountains into the sea

is a black hawk circling
5 the burying ground circling the bones
picked clean and discarded[1]

is a fish black blind in the belly of water
is a diamond blind in the black belly of coal Ⓐ

is a black and living thing
10 is a favorite child
of the universe
feel her rolling her hand
in its kinky hair
feel her brushing it clean Ⓑ

Ⓐ **FIGURATIVE LANGUAGE**
Reread the title and lines 1–8. To what four things is the earth being compared?

Ⓑ **FIGURATIVE LANGUAGE**
Reread lines 10–14. What relationship between the earth and the universe is suggested by this use of **personification?**

ANALYZE VISUALS
Compare the style of this art with the style of the art on page 559. Which is more realistic?

---

1. **discarded** (dĭ-skärd'ĕd): thrown away; gotten rid of.

Bear with Houses, Michael Wertz
Pastel. © Michael Wertz

DIFFERENTIATED INSTRUCTION

FOR LESS–PROFICIENT READERS

Comprehension Support Explain that a poet may ignore rules of grammar and punctuation to create a particular sound or feeling. Use Read Aloud/Think Aloud to clarify a thought in "the earth is a living thing." Then have students help you rewrite the thought in standard sentence form. Read aloud both versions. Discuss the differences and what a poet might gain from ignoring grammatical rules.

Line 7
The earth is a fish that can't see anything deep inside the water.

 BEST PRACTICES TOOLKIT—Transparency
Read Aloud/Think Aloud p. A34

FOR ENGLISH LEARNERS

Vocabulary: Cognates Have students scan the poems for cognates. Spanish cognates in "the earth is a living thing" include

- *mountain/la montaña* (line 3)
- *diamond/el diamante* (line 8)
- *favorite/favorito(a)* (line 10)
- *universe/el universo* (line 11)

Ask students to look for other cognates in this poem and those on pages 558–559.

BACKGROUND

Wonders of Nature In "the earth is a living thing," Lucille Clifton mentions a few of nature's many wonders. The swift, smooth flight of a hawk circling in search of prey, for instance (line 4), is a sight that inspires awe. With vision eight times as sharp as human sight, a hawk can spot food from high in the air. Fish may live at depths where almost no light penetrates (line 7), yet their specially adapted eyes permit them to detect food even in near-total darkness. Hard, brilliant diamonds and dark, combustible coal (line 8) both form in the earth's crust from the same element—carbon.

FOR ENGLISH LEARNERS

Language: Pronoun Referents Make sure students understand that the subject *the earth* (or the pronoun *it*) is implied at the start of each stanza. Then explain the referents for these pronouns.

- "feel her rolling her hand" (line 12)—"her" refers to the universe (line 11). English nouns usually do not have gender, but here the universe is personified as a mother.

- "its kinky hair" (line 13)—"its" refers to the earth, which is personified as a child (line 10).

Ask students to identify the referents for the pronouns in the last line of the poem. *("Her" refers to the universe; "it" refers to the "child's" hair.)*

FOR ADVANCED LEARNERS/PRE–AP

Analyze Personification Ask students which example of personification in this poem they find most effective and why. Then challenge them to create an original example of personification in which they compare the earth to a living thing.

DISCUSSION PROMPTS

Use these prompts to help students explore the figurative language used by the poet:

Connect Think about a time and place you felt deeply at home. How does this help you understand the feeling the speaker describes? *Possible answer: When you feel at home, you feel safe and comfortable.*

Analyze What words and images create a secure and peaceful feeling? *Possible answer: The words "remembered" and "tenderly" evoke this feeling, as does the care implied by "arranging."*

Evaluate How do the references to memory ("remembered" and "[take] me back") make the image more powerful? *Possible answer: They may connect the speaker to memories of the past.*

LITERARY ANALYSIS

ⓒ FIGURATIVE LANGUAGE

Possible answer: The earth is being personified as a caring mother.

READING SKILL

ⓓ MAKE INFERENCES

Possible answer: The speaker may be suggesting that being one with nature— "vanishing"—is better and more fulfilling than life in human society.

POETIC FORM

ⓔ LYRIC POETRY

Possible answer: The speaker conveys the idea that in the forest the separation between him- or herself and the natural world dissolves. The speaker's thoughts are "light" (line 10) and are in tune with the "small kingdoms" of animals (line 12).

ANALYZE VISUALS

About the Art Much of artist Peter Davidson's work features intensely colored images of nature. Davidson, born in Wales, studied art and shipbuilding. Later he moved to Canada, where he taught art for more than 20 years.

Activity Is this image a good fit for the poem? Why? *Possible answer: The dark colors and leaves are like trees at night. The floating leaves may seem magical or mystical.*

The Orchard (1997), Peter Davidson. Oil on paper, 37.5 cm × 44 cm. Private collection. Photo © Bridgeman Art Library.

Sleeping in the FOREST

Mary Oliver

I thought the earth
remembered me, she
took me back so tenderly, arranging
her dark skirts, her pockets
5 full of lichens[1] and seeds. I slept ⓒ
as never before, a stone
on the riverbed, nothing
between me and the white fire of the stars
but my thoughts, and they floated
10 light as moths among the branches
of the perfect trees. All night
I heard the small kingdoms breathing
around me, the insects, and the birds
who do their work in the darkness. All night
15 I rose and fell, as if in water, grappling[2]
with a luminous doom. By morning
I had vanished at least a dozen times
into something better. ⓓ ⓔ

---

1. **lichens** (lī′kəns): fungi that grow together with algae and form crustlike growths on rocks or tree trunks.
2. **grappling**: struggling.

ⓒ **FIGURATIVE LANGUAGE**
Reread lines 1–5. What is being **personified?**

ⓓ **MAKE INFERENCES**
Reread the last sentence in the poem. What do you think the speaker means by "something better"?

ⓔ **LYRIC POETRY**
What thoughts and feelings is the speaker conveying in this poem?

DIFFERENTIATED INSTRUCTION

FOR LESS–PROFICIENT READERS

Comprehension Support Remind students that using their senses can help them understand what they are reading. Have them make Sensory Notes for "Sleeping in the Forest." Encourage them to note both what the poet says and the impressions that form in their own imaginations.

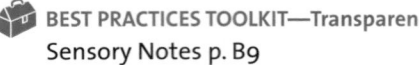 **BEST PRACTICES TOOLKIT—Transparency** Sensory Notes p. B9

Sense	Example
sight	white stars (line 8)
hearing	insects in the night (lines 12–13)
touch	smooth seeds (line 5)

G○LD
Pat Mora

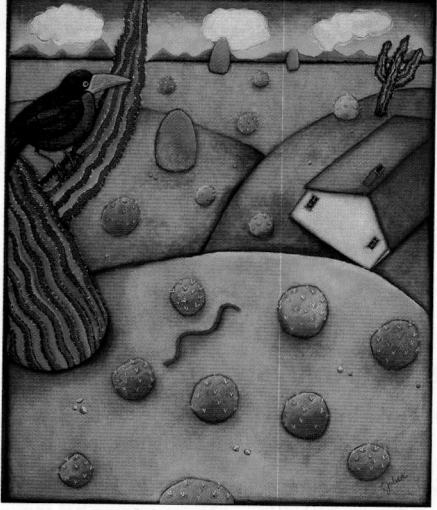

Hacienda (2002), Vanessa Julian. Acrylic on matteboard, 23″ × 19″.
© Vanessa Julian.

When Sun paints the desert
with its gold,
I climb the hills.
Wind runs round boulders, ruffles
5 my hair. I sit on my favorite rock,
lizards for company, a rabbit,
ears stiff in the shade
of a saguaro.[1]
In the wind, we're all
10 eye to eye. **F**

Sparrow on saguaro watches
rabbit watch us in the gold
of sun setting.
Hawk sails on waves of light, sees
15 sparrow, rabbit, lizards, me,
our eyes shining,
watching red and purple
    sand rivers stream down the hills.

I stretch my arms wide as the sky
20 like hawk extends her wings
in all the gold light of this, home. **G**

F MAKE INFERENCES
Reread lines 1–10. What can you **infer** about the speaker's connection to nature?

G FIGURATIVE LANGUAGE
Reread lines 19–21. What two **similes** are used to describe the speaker's arms?

---

1. **saguaro** (sə-gwär'ō): a tall, branching cactus found in the southwestern United States and northern Mexico.

ANALYZE VISUALS

About the Art In the paintings of American artist Vanessa Julian, landscapes seem to exert a force of their own. For a while Julian lived in Montana, where she was inspired by that state's great natural beauty.

Activity How does the picture make you feel? Why? *Possible answer: It suggests a happy feeling; the colors are cheerful and bright, the house looks cozy, and the shapes are playful.*

Lines 5–8
REINFORCE *KEY IDEA*: NATURE

Discuss In lines 5–8 of "Gold," what does the speaker show about the place of living things in **nature**? *Possible answer: Each creature has its place. Lizards lie on rocks (lines 5–6); the rabbit seeks shade (lines 6–7); a saguaro grows in the desert (line 8); the speaker has chosen to sit on a rock (line 5).*

READING SKILL

F MAKE INFERENCES

Have students enter their responses in the chart begun on page 555. *Possible answer: The speaker feels a connection to nature.*

- *The speaker has a "favorite" spot (line 5), so he or she must know the place well.*
- *The speaker perceives the animals as "company" (line 6).*
- *In the outdoors, the different species seem to be "all / eye to eye" (lines 9–10).*

LITERARY ANALYSIS

G FIGURATIVE LANGUAGE

Possible answer: When stretched wide, the speaker's arms are compared to the sky (line 19) and to the wings of a hawk (line 20).

SELECTION WRAP–UP

⭐ **CRITIQUE** Ask students which poem has the most vivid and memorable images of nature. Which image seems most striking?

FOR LESS–PROFICIENT READERS

Reading Skill Follow-Up: Make Inferences
Ask students to read the description in "Gold" of the hawk's flight (line 14). Use the chart begun on page 555 to make an inference about what the speaker means.

Lines and Phrases	What I Know	Inference
"Hawk sails on waves of light"	Sun rays may waver like water.	The hawk seems to sail on sun waves.

Reading Support Help students visualize the scene in "Gold" of different species in quiet coexistence by using Draw It to show how the species observe each other (lines 11–16). Draw shapes or write names—for example, "hawk"—in relative locations on the board, and then connect them with arrows to represent who sees or watches whom.

sparrow ⟶ rabbit ⟶ speaker

 **BEST PRACTICES TOOLKIT**
Draw It p. A2

Practice and Apply

After Reading

For additional support of post-reading questions, use these copy masters:

📋 RESOURCE MANAGER—Copy Masters

Figurative Language p. 43 (for practice of literary analysis standards focus)

Question Support p. 47 (**After Reading** questions adapted for English learners and less-proficient readers)

Additional selection questions are provided for teachers on page 39.

ANSWERS

Comprehension

1. *The earth is compared to a bear, a hawk, a fish, a diamond, and a favorite child.*

2. *The "small kingdoms" are the colonies of forest-dwelling creatures such as insects and birds.*

3. *The speaker is in the desert at sunset.*

Literary Analysis

Possible answers:

4. ■ STANDARDS FOCUS *Make Inferences Answers will vary. Students should use their own experience or knowledge to make inferences about lines or phrases in the poems.*

5. ● STANDARDS FOCUS *Figurative Language Students may say that the comparisons and personification helped them visualize what they read and understand the meaning each poet wanted to convey.*

6. *Students may find the use of the word "doom" in line 16 surprising, as well as the idea that losing oneself completely in nature would be better than normal life. Students may say that in lines 14–18 the speaker is evoking the dream world of sleep.*

7. *Students' diagrams will vary. Students may say that "Sleeping . . ." and "Gold" are most similar because they relate the experience of one person in a specific natural setting.*

8. ● STANDARDS FOCUS *Lyric Poetry Students may point out the bold personification in Clifton's poem, the evocative descriptions of night in Oliver's poem, or the joyful celebration in Mora's poem to support their opinions.*

After Reading

Comprehension

1. **Recall** What living things is the earth compared to in "the earth is a living thing"?

2. **Clarify** What are the "small kingdoms" that the speaker hears in "Sleeping in the Forest"?

3. **Represent** Where, and at what time of day, does the poem "Gold" take place? Make a drawing illustrating the setting described in lines 5–18.

Literary Analysis

4. **Make Inferences** Review the charts you created as you read. Which inferences most helped you understand the poems? Explain your answers.

5. **Examine Figurative Language** What **similes, metaphors,** or examples of **personification** in these poems helped you see **nature** in a fresh way? Give three examples. For each one, tell what type of figurative language was used and why you found it to be effective.

6. **Interpret Meaning** Did the ending of "Sleeping in the Forest" surprise you? Reread lines 14–18. Then tell what feeling you think these lines try to capture.

7. **Compare and Contrast** Use a Venn diagram like the one shown to examine similarities and differences among the three poems. Think about such things as the setting, the speaker, and the **mood,** or feeling, of each poem. Then decide which two poems you think are most similar.

8. **Evaluate Lyric Poetry** Which of the poems do you think was most successful at capturing the speaker's thoughts and feelings? Include specific details from the poem to support your answer.

Venn diagram labeled: "the earth . . ." / "Sleeping . . ." / "Gold" / nature

Extension and Challenge

9. **Big Question Activity** Reread the question on page 554. How would the speaker of each poem answer this question? After you've decided, consider whether the speakers' attitudes have affected how you feel about your own place in nature.

10. **Speaking and Listening** Lyric poems are known for their strong, melodic rhythms. They often use repetition to emphasize emotional experiences. In a group, take turns reading each poem aloud. Which of the poems do you think has an especially appealing sound or rhythm? Discuss your answer.

Extension and Challenge

9. *The **speaker in "the earth . . ."** might say that his or her place is as an observer of nature; the **speaker in "Sleeping . . ."** might express a desire to be one with nature; the **speaker in "Gold"** might say his or her role is to rejoice in nature. All would probably say that they seek to be aware of and admire the natural world.*

10. *To support their opinions about the poem with the most appealing sound, students may mention*

• *in "the earth . . .," the repetition of b and l sounds*

• *in "Sleeping . . .," the long, flowing sentences beginning with "I" (lines 1, 5), "All night" (lines 11, 14), and "By morning" (line 16)*

• *in "Gold," the short lines and straightforward language*

eading-Writing Connection

Explore the poems further by responding to these prompts. Then complete the **Grammar and Writing** exercise.

WRITING PROMPTS	SELF-CHECK
A. Short Response: Write a Poem Write a **short poem** about an aspect of **nature** that you find especially inspiring, dramatic, or appealing. Include at least two types of figurative language in your poem.	*A creative poem will . . .* • use vivid details and imagery to create a strong impression in the reader's mind • use figurative language to enhance the meaning
B. Extended Response: Analyze Metaphors Reread "the earth is a living thing." Select three specific metaphors to explore further. Write **two or three paragraphs** explaining what view of **nature** is suggested by each metaphor.	*An effective analysis will . . .* • explain how the metaphors relate to the poem's meaning • give reasons and evidence to support the explanation

GRAMMAR AND WRITING

 **MARYLAND OBJECTIVES**

USE CORRECT SENTENCE TYPE In order for your sentences to serve their correct purposes and reflect the emotions you intend, be sure to use the correct sentence type. A **declarative** sentence makes a statement and ends with a period. An **interrogative** sentence asks a question and ends with a question mark. An **imperative** sentence makes a request or gives a command (with the understood subject being *you*) and usually ends with a period. An **exclamatory** sentence shows strong feeling and ends with an exclamation point.

LANGUAGE STANDARD
5.A.2.d Compose simple, compound, complex, and compound-complex sentences

> Original: How long has this mountain been here.
> I can't believe its beauty.
>
> Revised: How long has this mountain been here?
> I can't believe its beauty!

PRACTICE Identify each sentence type and punctuate it correctly.

1. Its peak rises into the clouds like a skyscraper
2. How wonderful it looks
3. Can you hear how the wind whispers around it
4. Listen carefully

For more help with sentence types, see page R60 in the Grammar Handbook.

DIFFERENTIATED INSTRUCTION

FOR LESS–PROFICIENT WRITERS

For Prompt A:

1. Ask students to identify an aspect of nature that they would like to describe. It could be a plant, a landscape, a season, or an animal.
2. Have students visualize their subjects and then make notes about what they see in their mind's eye. Ask them to also note details relating to other senses.
3. Suggest that students focus on using one type of figurative language.

For Prompt B:

1. Limit the assignment to two metaphors.
2. Have each student identify one quality shared by the two things being compared.
3. Ask students what feelings or ideas this quality brings to mind, and how these could relate to the speaker's view of nature.

Reading-Writing Connection

WRITING PROMPTS

• For **Prompt A,** suggest that students begin by brainstorming sensory details that describe the aspect they have chosen. Then have them use those details to make comparisons that will help them create original figurative language.

• For **Prompt B,** have students identify the qualities that are shared by the things being compared in each metaphor. Ask students to consider what clues these qualities could provide about the speaker's view of nature.

For ideas for writing, see

ℹ️ Writing Center at **ClassZone.com**

GRAMMAR AND WRITING

Write these sentences on the board. Ask students to punctuate them correctly.

> Bats are truly astonishing *(!)*
> Did you know they are the only winged mammals *(?)*

Answers:

1. *declarative; . . . skyscraper.*
2. *exclamatory; . . . looks!*
3. *interrogative; . . . around it?*
4. *imperative; . . . carefully.*

R **RESOURCE MANAGER—Copy Master**
Use Correct Sentence Type p. 49

Assess and Reteach

Assess

R **RESOURCE MANAGER—Copy Masters**
Selection Tests A, B/C pp. 51–52, 53–54

💿 Test Generator CD

Reteach

S **STANDARDS LESSON FILE**
Literature Lesson 16: Narrative vs. Lyric Poetry
Literature Lesson 27: Simile and Metaphor
Reading Lesson 8: Making Inferences

Focus and Motivate

OBJECTIVES

Literary Analysis
- explore the key idea of **relationship**
- identify lines and stanzas
- analyze repetition and rhyme scheme
- read poetry

Reading
- understand speaker

SUMMARY

"Scaffolding" develops a comparison between a loving relationship and the construction of a building. Once solid walls are built, the scaffolding is no longer necessary. "The World Is Not a Pleasant Place to Be" expresses the importance of having someone in the world to care about and who cares in return. In "Annabel Lee," the speaker talks about his love for his wife. Although she has died, he remains faithful to their love and keeps a vigil by her tomb each night.

Whom do you feel CLOSEST *to?*

Discuss the question with students. To lead into the *KEY IDEA,* ask students for examples of strong **relationships** depicted in recent movies or books that they have read. Have students explain why each relationship is a good one. Then have them examine their own relationships and complete the *QUICKWRITE* activity.

Selection Resources

Before Reading

Scaffolding
Poem by Seamus Heaney

The World Is Not a Pleasant Place to Be
Poem by Nikki Giovanni

Annabel Lee
Poem by Edgar Allan Poe

Whom do you feel CLOSEST *to?*

MARYLAND OBJECTIVES

LITERATURE STANDARDS
3.A.4.b Analyze structural features
3.A.4.c Analyze sound elements of poetry

KEY IDEA Think about a family member or friend with whom you have a close **relationship**. Chances are you've fought with this person, yet he or she still brings you comfort and joy. Why do you think this is? The poems you're about to read explore the mysteries of strong relationships.

QUICKWRITE What are your two or three most important relationships? Note them in your journal. Then write about what makes each a good relationship. What keeps your bonds strong when difficulties arise?

562

 RESOURCE MANAGER UNIT 5

Plan and Teach pp. 55–62

Literary Analysis
Rhyme Scheme pp. 63, 64†*
Question Support p. 67*

Reading
Understand Speaker pp. 65, 66†*
Reading Fluency p. 68

Assessment
Selection Tests A, B/C pp. 69*, 71*
📀 Test Generator CD

 BEST PRACTICES TOOLKIT

Differentiated Instruction
pp. 31–38*

Graphic Organizer
Sequence Chain

Reading Support
📀 Audio Anthology CD*

Technology
ℹ️ Literature Center at **ClassZone.com**

📀 Write*Smart* CD

POETIC FORM: LINE AND STANZA

The **line** is the main unit of a poem. Lines can be organized into **stanzas,** groups of two or more lines that form longer units within a poem. Sometimes, as in this example from "The World Is Not a Pleasant Place to Be," you have to read the whole stanza to learn the speaker's complete thought:

the world is not a pleasant place

to be without

someone to hold and be held by

LITERARY ANALYSIS: RHYME SCHEME

Poets use **sound devices** to convey meaning and create emphasis. One sound device is **rhyme,** the repetition of sounds at the end of words. The **rhyme scheme** is the pattern of rhyme at the ends of lines in a poem. You can track the rhyme by assigning a letter to each line. The first line gets the letter *a.* Each following line that rhymes with it also gets an *a.* The first line that doesn't rhyme gets the letter *b,* as do the other lines that rhyme with that line. Each new rhyme gets a new letter.

And this was the reason that, long <u>ago</u> ,	*a*
In this kingdom by the <u>sea</u> ,	*b*
A wind blew out of a cloud by <u>night</u>	*c*
Chilling my Annabel <u>Lee</u> ;	*b*

As you read "Scaffolding" and "Annabel Lee," use letters to identify each poem's rhyme scheme.

READING SKILL: UNDERSTAND SPEAKER

In poetry, the **speaker** is the voice that "talks" to the reader. To understand a poem, you have to decide who the speaker is and how he or she feels about the subject of the poem. Complete a chart like the one shown as you read each of the selections.

	Poem 1	Poem 2	Poem 3
Who is the speaker?			
How do I know?			
How does he/she feel?			

Author Online

Seamus Heaney: Celebrated Irishman
Nobel Prize winner Seamus Heaney's poetry is celebrated throughout the world. Describing how he felt when he wrote his first successful poem, Heaney said, "I felt that I had let down a shaft into real life."

Seamus Heaney born 1939

Nikki Giovanni: Storyteller Poet
Nikki Giovanni gained popularity as a poet after the release of an album of her readings, *Truth Is on Its Way.* She says that in her poetry, "I use a very natural rhythm; I want my writing to sound like I talk."

Nikki Giovanni born 1943

Edgar Allan Poe: Literary Giant
Edgar Allan Poe has fascinated generations of readers with his haunting poetry and tales of horror. He and his adored young wife, Virginia, were poor and often sick. "Annabel Lee" is believed to be Poe's tribute to Virginia.

Edgar Allan Poe 1809–1849

 MORE ABOUT THE AUTHOR
For more on these poets, visit the **Literature Center** at ClassZone.com.

563

Teach

STANDARDS FOCUS

POETIC FORM

● LINE AND STANZA

Tell students that stanzas in poetry are similar to paragraphs in prose. Each stanza usually develops a different aspect of the main idea or topic.

CHECK UNDERSTANDING Have students review some poems they have read—such as the three on pages 556–559—to compare and contrast how lines and stanzas are used in the poems.

LITERARY ANALYSIS

● RHYME SCHEME

Read aloud this poem, leaving out the last word:

Just before you turn on the TV,
Ask, Is this where I really should be?
With my friends I could talk,
Read a book, take a walk—
There's so much that my eyes ought
to _____ !

Ask students to provide the last word (*see*), and to explain how the rhyme scheme helped them figure it out. *Possible answer: The rhyme scheme leads listeners to expect a word that rhymes with* TV *and* be.

CHECK UNDERSTANDING Write the poem on the board and have students use letters to identify the rhyme scheme.

READING SKILL

■ UNDERSTAND SPEAKER

Remind students not to confuse the speaker with the poet. The speaker is like a character invented by the poet.

CHECK UNDERSTANDING Ask students to identify speakers in other poems they have read this year.

 RESOURCE MANAGER—Copy Master
Understand Speaker p. 65 (for student use while reading the poems)

DIFFERENTIATED INSTRUCTION

FOR ALL STUDENTS

For general guidelines on differentiating instruction, see

 BEST PRACTICES TOOLKIT
Differentiated Instruction pp. 31–38

FOR LESS–PROFICIENT READERS

Concept Support Help students implement these steps when they read each poem.

1. Read the poem aloud or listen to it.
2. Try to picture the images mentally.
3. Identify the speaker.
4. Focus on important words and phrases.
5. Think about the poem's overall meaning.
6. Reread the poem to discover ideas that you overlooked the first time.

FOR ENGLISH LEARNERS

Options for Reading Have students listen to each poem on the *Audio Anthology CD.* Then have small groups practice reading assigned passages aloud before the class discussion.

ANALYZE VISUALS

Possible answer: People are positioned on a structure that is similar to scaffolding.

About the Art The painting *Stages II* could be a metaphor for the career of American artist Paul Davis. He has moved through many stages in his career. His early art reflected the bleakness of the world. Then he realized that he could create whatever vision of life he wanted. His works are characterized by many layers of paint as well as layers of meaning.

POETIC FORM

Ⓐ LINE AND STANZA

Possible answer: This couplet (lines 3–4) gives directions for building a strong scaffold.

READING SKILL

Ⓑ SPEAKER

Possible answers:

	"Scaffolding"
Who is the speaker?	someone in a loving relationship
How do I know?	The speaker addresses the other person as "my dear."
How does he/she feel?	The speaker loves the person and wants to keep their relationship strong.

Line 7–10
REINFORCE *KEY IDEA*: RELATIONSHIP

Discuss What does the speaker say might sometimes happen in the **relationship?** Does the speaker feel that this is a cause for concern?

Possible answer: The speaker says that old bridges sometimes break, meaning that the two people may have disagreements or go through changes. Because their relationship is strong, the speaker knows that they can handle these situations.

SCAFFOLDING
SEAMUS HEANEY

Masons,[1] when they start upon a building,
Are careful to test out the scaffolding;

Make sure that planks won't slip at busy points,
Secure all ladders, tighten bolted joints.[2] Ⓐ

5 And yet all this comes down when the job's done
Showing off walls of sure and solid stone.

So if, my dear, there sometimes seem to be
Old bridges breaking between you and me

Never fear. We may let the scaffolds fall
10 Confident that we have built our wall. Ⓑ

ANALYZE VISUALS
How does this painting reflect the **title** of the poem?

Ⓐ LINE AND STANZA
A stanza that consists of two rhyming lines is called a **couplet.** What is being described in this couplet?

Ⓑ SPEAKER
Reread lines 7–10. Whom is the speaker addressing? In your chart, note how the speaker feels about this person.

---

1. **masons** (mā'sənz): wallers who build with brick or stone.
2. **joints** (joints): places where two parts or pieces join together.

Stages II, Paul Davis. Oil, 10" × 8
Courtesy Coda Gallery. © Paul Dav

DIFFERENTIATED INSTRUCTION

FOR LESS–PROFICIENT READERS

Comprehension Use a graphic organizer to help students comprehend the central metaphor of the poem and to make parallels between the stages of a relationship and the stages of construction.

Construction	Relationship
Scaffolding provides support for workers. It allows them to build strong walls.	A strong relationship is built by investing time and energy in it.
↓	↓
Strong walls will not crumble.	A strong relationship can survive problems and changes.

Scaffolding The poem "Scaffolding" is based on an extended metaphor. A strong relationship is compared to a solid wall that is supported during the building process by scaffolding. Scaffolding is constructed from wood or metal. It consists of a vertical frame that supports planks or platforms upon which the workers stand.

Water Cycle Lines 8–10 of "The World Is Not a Pleasant Place to Be" ("an ocean would never laugh / if clouds weren't there / to kiss her tears") refer to the water cycle. Oceans provide much of the water in the atmosphere. Water evaporates, forming clouds, which later drop precipitation back into the ocean and over the land in the form of rain or snow.

FOR ENGLISH LEARNERS

Comprehension: Clarify

- Show students a picture of a scaffold to help them visualize lines 1–6.
- Make sure students understand the basic comparison: a strong relationship is like a well-built wall. If two people have built their relationship carefully, it can survive changes and problems, just as a strong wall survives the removal of scaffolding.
- Ask students to identify the lines that summarize this main idea *(lines 7–10)*.

FOR ADVANCED LEARNERS/PRE–AP

Make Judgments Discuss some of the characteristics of conventional love poetry—flowery and elaborate language, references to nature, lofty comparisons. Then ask students if they would classify "Scaffolding" as a love poem. Have them draw up a list of reasons and details from the poem that support their view that it is or is not a love poem. Have students meet in small groups and present their ideas.

ANALYZE VISUALS

About the Art The artist Colin Bootman moved from Trinidad to the United States at a young age. Art became a way for him to cope with adjusting to a new culture and later led him to a career as an illustrator of children's books.

Activity What do the expressions on the people's faces suggest about their relationship? *Possible answer: They are happy in each other's company.*

Lines 1–7
DISCUSSION PROMPTS

Use these prompts to help students understand important ideas in the poem:

Connect Think about the relationships you identified in the **QUICKWRITE** activity. In what ways do they make the world a more pleasant place for you to be? *Students may say that their relationships give them comfort, security, or joy.*

Analyze Into what does a river normally flow? How does the poem say a river would be affected if "only a stream were there to receive" its flow (lines 5–7)? *Possible answer: A river normally flows into a larger body of water, such as an ocean or a larger river. The poem suggests that if a smaller waterway like a stream were at the receiving end, the river would have to stop flowing and dry up, because there would be nowhere for the water to go.*

Synthesize What point about human relationships is the poet making through the image of the river? *Possible answer: People need to give and receive love—"to hold and be held by" someone (line 3). If a person does not have someone to love, his or her love will dry up, like a river that has nowhere to deposit its water.*

THE WORLD IS NOT A PLEASANT PLACE TO BE

Nikki Giovanni

Detail of *Family in the Park* (1999), Colin Bootman. Oil on canvas. Private collection. Photo © Bridgeman Art Library.

> the world is not a pleasant place
> to be without
> someone to hold and be held by
>
> a river would stop
> 5 its flow if only
> a stream were there
> to receive it
>
> an ocean would never laugh
> if clouds weren't there
> 10 to kiss her tears
>
> the world is not
> a pleasant place to be without
> someone ●

● LINE AND STANZA
Repetition is the repeating of a sound, word, phrase, or line to emphasize an idea. Notice how the last stanza echoes the first with one small difference. What effect is created by this change?

DIFFERENTIATED INSTRUCTION

FOR ADVANCED LEARNERS/PRE–AP

Analyze Poetic Form In each stanza, the poet uses words that establish a sense of loss, lack, or contradiction—such as "not," "without," "stop," "if only," "never," and "weren't." Discuss how this style affects the poem's message. Challenge students to rewrite the poem using only positive words and ideas ("the world *is* a pleasant place / to be *with* / someone to hold and be held by"). Have students compare their drafts in small groups. Which poem do they prefer, and why?

The Seashore (1900), William Henry Margetson. Oil on canvas. Private collection.
Photo © The Maas Gallery, London/Bridgeman Art Library.

Annabel Lee

Edgar Allan Poe

It was many and many a year ago,
    In a kingdom by the sea,
That a maiden there lived whom you may know
    By the name of Annabel Lee;—
5 And this maiden she lived with no other thought
    Than to love and be loved by me. **D**

She was a child and *I* was a child,
    In this kingdom by the sea,
But we loved with a love that was more than love—
10   I and my Annabel Lee—
With a love that the wingéd seraphs[1] of Heaven
    Coveted[2] her and me. **E**

---

1. **seraphs** (sĕr′əfs): any of the highest order of angels.
2. **coveted** (kŭv′ĭ-tĭd): envied.

D RHYME SCHEME
What rhyme scheme is used in the first stanza?

E SPEAKER
What is the speaker's relationship to Annabel Lee?

LITERARY ANALYSIS

D RHYME SCHEME

Answer: The rhyme scheme is ababcb.

If students need help . . . Write the last word of each line on the board vertically. Assign *a* to the first sound (the long *o*), and *b* to the second sound (the long *e*). Then have students work in pairs to identify where each sound repeats.

Extend the Discussion What feeling is created by the regular rhyme scheme in this first stanza?

READING SKILL

E SPEAKER

Possible answer: The speaker is a person who had a strong and loving relationship with Annabel Lee.

Extend the Discussion What does the description of their relationship suggest about the speaker's feelings for Annabel Lee?

ANALYZE VISUALS

About the Art This painting by British artist William Henry Margetson (1861–1940) shows his hallmark style. He is noted for his pictures of beautiful solitary women in various settings.

Activity Ask students what mood is created by this image. **Possible answer:** *The mood is calm and reflective.*

FOR LESS–PROFICIENT READERS
Comprehension Support

- Explain that "Annabel Lee" has many musical qualities, and when read aloud, sounds much like a song. Have pairs take turns reading or singing the stanzas aloud, listening for the story that unfolds.

- Remind students that punctuation not only signals a break in ideas, but can also suggest different moods and emotions.

FOR ENGLISH LEARNERS

Vocabulary Support To help students prepare to read this poem, preview some of the more archaic vocabulary it contains. Define words and phrases such as

- *maiden* (line 3), "unmarried girl or woman"
- *high-born kinsmen* (line 17), "relatives of noble birth"
- *bore her away* (line 18), "carried her away"
- *demons* (line 31), "evil spirits"

Lines 21–26
REINFORCE *KEY IDEA:* RELATIONSHIP

Discuss How does the speaker say the angels view his **relationship** with Annabel Lee? What insight into his frame of mind do the speaker's thoughts in these lines give the reader?
Possible answer: According to the speaker, the angels were jealous of his love, so they killed Annabel Lee. His thoughts show that he is unbalanced by grief.

POETIC FORM

F LINE AND STANZA

Possible answer: The words that are repeated include "love," "of . . . than we," and "soul." The effect is to emphasize the strength of the connection between the speaker and Annabel Lee.

POETIC FORM

G LINE AND STANZA

Possible answer: The longer lines and stanzas emphasize that the speaker's love will endure for all time. The earlier stanzas tell about past events, but the speaker has more to say when he is describing his reaction to Annabel Lee's death.

SELECTION WRAP–UP

REFLECT Ask students to think about the role of the speaker in each poem and whether or not the speaker's personality influences students' reactions to the poem.

⭐ **CRITIQUE** Have students evaluate the images used in each poem to represent or bring out ideas about **relationships.** Which images help them understand the poet's point most clearly?

READING FLUENCY

Distribute the copy masters and have students work in groups to practice fluency.

R RESOURCE MANAGER—Copy Master
Reading Fluency p. 68

And this was the reason that, long ago,
　　In this kingdom by the sea,
15 A wind blew out of a cloud by night
　　Chilling my Annabel Lee;
So that her high-born kinsmen came
　　And bore her away from me,
To shut her up in a sepulcher³
20　　In this kingdom by the sea.

The angels, not half so happy in Heaven,
　　Went envying her and me;
Yes! that was the reason (as all men know,
　　In this kingdom by the sea)
25 That the wind came out of the cloud chilling
　　And killing my Annabel Lee.

But our love it was stronger by far than the love
　　Of those who were older than we—
　　Of many far wiser than we—
30 And neither the angels in Heaven above
　　Nor the demons down under the sea
Can ever dissever⁴ my soul from the soul
　　Of the beautiful Annabel Lee:— **F**

For the moon never beams without bringing me dreams
35　　Of the beautiful Annabel Lee;
And the stars never rise but I feel the bright eyes
　　Of the beautiful Annabel Lee;
And so, all the night-tide, I lie down by the side
Of my darling, my darling, my life and my bride
40　　In her sepulcher there by the sea—
　　In her tomb by the side of the sea. **G**

F LINE AND STANZA
Reread this stanza. Identify words and phrases that are repeated. What emphasis does this **repetition** create?

G LINE AND STANZA
The last two stanzas are among the longest in the poem. What ideas and emotions does the poet emphasize by ending the poem with long stanzas?

---

3. **sepulcher** (sĕp′əl-kər): a place for burial; tomb.
4. **dissever** (dĭ-sĕv′ər): separate; tear apart.

DIFFERENTIATED INSTRUCTION

FOR ENGLISH LEARNERS
Comprehension: Task Support To help students understand the meaning of "Annabel Lee," explain that it begins by describing a young couple in love. When the woman dies, the speaker tries to make sense of her death, but ultimately he is still sick with grief. Have student pairs complete a Sequence Chain of key events (noting the lines). Have pairs contribute ideas to a class sequence chart.

 BEST PRACTICES TOOLKIT—Transparency Sequence Chain p. B21

FOR ADVANCED LEARNERS/PRE–AP
Analyze Poe likely began composing this musical tribute to his young wife, Virginia, during the long, five-year illness that preceded her death. Challenge students to find out more about the background of "Annabel Lee." For example, when was the poem published, and by whom? When did Poe and Virginia marry? To what illness did Virginia succumb? What was the topic Poe believed to be most worthy of poetry? Have student groups present their findings to the class.

Comprehension

1. **Recall** Why does the speaker in "Scaffolding" say that the scaffolds in his relationship could be allowed to fall?

2. **Recall** In "The World Is Not a Pleasant Place to Be," what is the relationship between the ocean and the clouds?

3. **Clarify** What happened to Annabel Lee and the person who loved her?

MARYLAND OBJECTIVES

LITERATURE STANDARD
3.A.4.c Analyze sound elements of poetry

Literary Analysis

4. **Identify Rhyme Scheme** Determine the rhyme scheme in "Scaffolding." Why do you think Seamus Heaney might have chosen this rhyme scheme for a poem about a couple's relationship?

5. **Analyze a Stanza** Reread the first stanza of "The World Is Not a Pleasant Place to Be." How does the meaning of the first line change as you read the rest of the stanza? Find one other example of a line break that you think affects the meaning of the words in an important way.

6. **Draw Conclusions About Speakers** Review the chart you created as you read. Based on the details you recorded and your understanding of the poems, what conclusions can you draw about each speaker's attitude about relationships? Give evidence from the poem to support your conclusions.

7. **Make Judgments** Go back and reread "Annabel Lee." In a chart, note words and details that make the speaker seem romantic and those that make him seem grief stricken. Are his feelings and attitudes understandable? Support your opinion with examples from your chart.

Romantic	Grief Stricken
"...we loved with a love that was more than love—"	

Extension and Challenge

8. **Big Question Activity** With a partner, role-play an interview between a television reporter and the **speaker** of one of the poems, about what keeps **relationships** strong. Discuss specific details from the poem in your interview.

9. **Creative Project: Art** As you read the poems, which visual images seemed especially beautiful or powerful? Draw a sketch of one of these images, and explain how it helped draw you into the poem.

Extension and Challenge

8. *Students' interviews should be based on details from one of the poems and show understanding of main ideas.*

9. *Students' images should reflect important ideas contained in one of the poems.*

Assess and Reteach

Assess

RESOURCE MANAGER—Copy Masters
Selection Tests A, B/C pp. 69–70, 71–72

Test Generator CD

Reteach

STANDARDS LESSON FILE
Literature Lesson 17: Structure of Poetry
Literature Lesson 19: Rhyme and Rhyme Scheme
Reading Lesson 9: Drawing Conclusions

Practice and Apply

After Reading

For additional support of post-reading questions, use these copy masters:

RESOURCE MANAGER—Copy Masters
Rhyme Scheme p. 63 (for practice of literary analysis standards focus)
Question Support p. 67 (**After Reading** questions adapted for English learners and less-proficient readers)

Additional selection questions are provided for teachers on page 59.

ANSWERS

Comprehension

1. *The scaffolding may be removed because the wall—the strong relationship—is already built.*

2. *The ocean is replenished by the rain that falls from the clouds.*

3. *Annabel Lee dies, and the speaker keeps a vigil at her tomb.*

Literary Analysis

Possible answers:

4. ● **STANDARDS FOCUS** *Rhyme Scheme The rhyme scheme is aa bb cc dd ee. Each stanza is a couplet, which emphasizes the couple's close, strong relationship.*

5. *Line 1 says that "the world is not a pleasant place," but the rest of the stanza explains that this is true only if a person has no one "to hold and be held by." The last stanza ends each line with a negative word ("not," "without") that signals a shift in meaning.*

6. ■ **STANDARDS FOCUS** *Understand Speaker The **first speaker** believes that strong relationships can handle problems. The **second speaker** believes relationships give meaning to life. **The third speaker** is focused only on his lost relationship.*

7. *Romantic: "With a love that the wingéd seraphs of Heaven / Coveted her and me," "our love it was stronger . . . than we," "beautiful Annabel Lee." Grief Stricken: "The angels, not half so happy . . . Went envying her and me," "neither the angels . . . Nor the demons . . . Can ever dissever my soul from the soul / Of the beautiful Annabel Lee," "And so, all the night-tide, I lie down by the side / Of my darling, my darling, my life and my bride"*

Focus and Motivate

OBJECTIVES

Literary Analysis
- explore the key idea of **honor**
- identify characteristics of a narrative poem
- identify and interpret rhythm and meter
- read narrative poetry

Reading
- use strategies for reading a narrative poem

Vocabulary
- build vocabulary for reading and writing
- understand and use connotative meanings of words *(also an EL language objective)*

Grammar and Writing
- use active voice
- use writing to analyze literature

SUMMARY

"The Charge of the Light Brigade" tells the true story of how a mistake in orders caused hundreds of British soldiers to lose their lives in a disastrous charge against Russian gunners. "The Highwayman" tells of a young woman who kills herself with a musket to warn her love that the king's troops have set a trap for him. He escapes but returns to avenge his love and dies in the attempt.

What is HONOR?

Discuss the question with students. To lead into the *KEY IDEA,* list students' definitions of **honor** on the board and have students keep these definitions in mind as they complete the *DISCUSS* activity and read the poems.

Selection Resources

The Charge of the Light Brigade
Poem by Alfred, Lord Tennyson

The Highwayman
Poem by Alfred Noyes

What is HONOR?

MARYLAND OBJECTIVES

LITERATURE STANDARDS
3.A.3.b Analyze the conflict and the events of the plot
3.A.4.c Analyze sound elements of poetry

KEY IDEA When you think of **honor,** who or what comes to mind? Do you picture a person you respect, or do you remember a noble sacrifice that somebody made? In "The Charge of the Light Brigade" and "The Highwayman," the characters give up their lives for very different reasons. It is up to you to decide whether their causes were honorable.

DISCUSS With a small group, discuss people who have acted honorably. On the basis of this conversation, how would you define honor? Be ready to share your definition with the class.

570

RESOURCE MANAGER UNIT 5

Plan and Teach pp. 73–80

Literary Analysis
Rhythm and Meter pp. 81, 82†*
Question Support p. 88*

Reading
Reading a Narrative Poem pp. 83, 84†*
Reading Fluency p. 90

Vocabulary
Study p. 85*
Practice p. 86
Strategy p. 87

Grammar and Writing
Use the Active Voice p. 89

Assessment
Selection Tests A, B/C pp. 91*, 93*
Test Generator CD

BEST PRACTICES TOOLKIT

Differentiated Instruction pp. 31–38*
Scaffolding Instruction pp. 43–46*

Graphic Organizers/Strategies
Reciprocal Teaching • Plot Diagram • Think-Pair-Share • Making Inferences • Draw It • T Chart • Reporter's Questions

Reading Support
Audio Anthology CD*

Technology
Literature and Vocabulary Centers at **ClassZone.com**
Write*Smart* CD

---

* Resources for Differentiation   † Also in Spanish

LITERARY ANALYSIS: RHYTHM AND METER

Rhythm is the pattern of stressed and unstressed syllables in a line of poetry. Rhythm that follows a regular pattern from line to line is called **meter.**

When you "scan" a line of poetry, you analyze its rhythm, marking the syllables that are stressed (´) and those that are unstressed (˘). This system is called scansion. Read these lines from "The Highwayman" out loud. Concentrate on the stressed and unstressed syllables.

Thĕ wínd wăs ă tórrĕnt ŏf dárknĕss ămóng thĕ gústy̆ trées.
Thĕ móon wăs ă ghóstly̆ gálleŏn tóssĕd ŭpón clóudy̆ séas.

As you read the following selections, notice each poem's rhythm and meter and the effect they create.

Review: **Mood**

READING STRATEGY: READING A NARRATIVE POEM

"The Highwayman" and "The Charge of the Light Brigade" are **narrative poems,** which means they tell stories. Like novels and short stories, narrative poems have characters, a setting, and a plot. As you read each poem, keep track of these elements in a story map.

> **"The Charge of the Light Brigade"**
>
> | Characters: | Setting: |
> |---|---|
>
> Conflict:
>
> Event 1:
> Event 2:

VOCABULARY IN CONTEXT

The boldfaced vocabulary words can help you picture the scenes in these poems. Match each word in Column A to the word or phrase in Column B that is closest in meaning.

Column A	Column B
1. cascade	a. twist
2. claret	b. tan
3. tawny	c. waterfall
4. writhe	d. dark red

Author Online

Alfred, Lord Tennyson: Victorian Poet Tennyson's best friend died in 1833, and the shock to Tennyson was severe. However, it was during this time of incredible grief that Tennyson wrote some of his best poetry. These

Alfred, Lord Tennyson
1809–1892

poems were so popular that he was named poet laureate, or court poet, by Queen Victoria.

Alfred Noyes: Popular Poet
English poet Alfred Noyes wrote "The Highwayman" when he was only 24. Readers loved it, but critics didn't. Regardless of the critics, Noyes still earned his living from poetry.

Alfred Noyes
1880–1958

Background

A Tragic Battle "The Charge of the Light Brigade" was inspired by a real-life battle in the Crimean War between England and Russia (1854–1856). A group of British troops called the Light Brigade, armed only with swords, was ordered to charge a unit of Russian gunners. Though the British lost this battle, they eventually won the war.

 MORE ABOUT THE AUTHOR AND BACKGROUND
To learn more about these poets and the Crimean War, visit the **Literature Center at ClassZone.com.**

571

Teach

STANDARDS FOCUS

LITERARY ANALYSIS

● RHYTHM AND METER
Write the first few lines of the nursery rhyme "Jack and Jill" on the board and read them aloud. Have students listen and pick out the stressed syllables. Mark the stressed syllables on the board. Ask students how they determined the rhythm. *Possible answers: by knowing the normal pronunciation of each word; by sensing the singsong rhythm of the nursery rhyme as a whole*

CHECK UNDERSTANDING Have pairs of students read aloud parts of other poems and describe the rhythm they hear.

READING STRATEGY

■ READING A NARRATIVE POEM
Remind students that a narrative structure usually consists of exposition, rising action, climax, falling action, and resolution.

CHECK UNDERSTANDING Have students identify the plot elements in a narrative poem, a folk song (such as "Puff, the Magic Dragon"), or a story that they know.

 RESOURCE MANAGER—Copy Master
Reading a Narrative Poem p. 83 (for student use while reading the poems)

▲ VOCABULARY IN CONTEXT

DIAGNOSE WORD KNOWLEDGE To determine preteaching needs, have all students complete **Vocabulary in Context.** Check students' answers. *(1. c; 2. d; 3. b; 4. a)*

PRETEACH VOCABULARY Use the Vocabulary Study copy master to help students explore the meaning of each boldfaced word.

1. Read the first set of sentences aloud, emphasizing *cascade*.

2. Point out the context clues *flowed* and *dark water*. Elicit possible meanings for *cascade*, such as "waterfall."

3. Have students record their definitions in the chart.

4. Repeat the procedure for the remaining words.

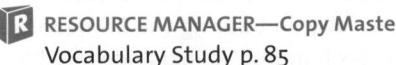 RESOURCE MANAGER—Copy Master
Vocabulary Study p. 85

For general guidelines on differentiating vocabulary instruction and for alternative vocabulary activities for students not needing vocabulary preteaching, see

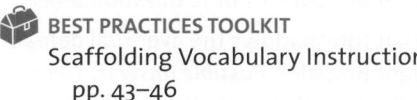 BEST PRACTICES TOOLKIT
Scaffolding Vocabulary Instruction
pp. 43–46

ℹ Vocabulary Center at **ClassZone.com**
Additional Vocabulary Activities

Ⓐ RHYTHM AND METER

Possible answer: *There are two stressed syllables in line 1, two in line 2, three in line 3, and two in line 4.*

If students need help . . . Write out the first four lines of the poem. Read each line aloud, pausing to check with students about which syllables they hear as stressed. Mark the lines accordingly.

Half a league, half a league,

Half a league onward,

All in the valley of Death

Rode the six hundred.

Extend the Discussion What mood does the rhythm create?

ANALYZE VISUALS

Possible answer: *The images very closely match many details from the scene of the poem: soldiers on horseback fight frantically with swords, the chaotic battle appears to take place in a valley, and a cannon and rifle are featured prominently in the foreground.*

Lines 9–17
DISCUSSION PROMPTS

Use these prompts to help students understand the major conflict of the poem:

Connect Have you ever been told to do something that you feared would lead to disaster? Is it brave or foolhardy to proceed in such cases? *Students may say that it depends on what is at stake, and what consequences they might face for their actions.*

Analyze Why do you think the poet chose to repeat the phrase "Theirs not to . . ." in lines 13–15? *Possible answer: The repetition suggests a lesson that the soldiers have been taught over and over—not to question orders.*

Infer What foreshadows the eventual defeat of the Light Brigade? *Possible answer: They are described as riding "Into the valley of Death" (line 16), which suggests that few will emerge alive.*

The CHARGE OF THE LIGHT BRIGADE

ALFRED, LORD TENNYSON

Half a league,[1] half a league,
Half a league onward,
All in the valley of Death
    Rode the six hundred.
5 "Forward, the Light Brigade!
Charge for the guns!" he said:
Into the valley of Death
    Rode the six hundred. Ⓐ

"Forward, the Light Brigade!"
10 Was there a man dismay'd?
Not tho' the soldier knew
    Some one had blunder'd:[2]
Theirs not to make reply,
Theirs not to reason why,
15 Theirs but to do and die:
Into the valley of Death
    Rode the six hundred.

Cannon to right of them,
Cannon to left of them,

Ⓐ **RHYTHM AND METER**
Reread lines 1–4, tapping your desk with each stressed syllable. How many stressed syllables are in each line?

ANALYZE VISUALS
How well do the **images** in this painting match the scene described in the poem? Explain your answer.

---

1. **league:** a distance of three miles.
2. **blunder'd:** made a mistake.

Detail of *The Charge of the Light Brigade.* © Getty Images

DIFFERENTIATED INSTRUCTION

FOR ALL STUDENTS

For general guidelines on differentiating instruction, see

🧰 **BEST PRACTICES TOOLKIT**
Differentiated Instruction pp. 31–38

FOR LESS–PROFICIENT READERS

Interpret Meaning Explain that the poem describes a brave but doomed attack by a British cavalry unit during the Crimean War in 1854. Six hundred soldiers ride into battle, even though the order to attack is a mistake.

Ask students to find lines that show the men are brave and lines that foreshadow that the attack is doomed. *Possible answers:*

- **Brave attack:** *"Forward . . . Charge" (lines 5–6); "not to make reply . . . not to reason why" (lines 13–14)*
- **Doomed attack:** *"valley of Death" (line 3); "but to do and die" (line 15); "Cannon to the right of them, / Cannon to the left of them" (lines 18–19)*

The Crimean War Tennyson was inspired to write his narrative poem after reading a newspaper account of the battle at Balaklava (in southern Ukraine). The details of this battle caught Tennyson's attention and imagination, because the Light Brigade's unfailing courage in the face of near-certain defeat seemed to capture the best of the English spirit.

Just what went wrong for the Light Brigade? During the battle, the English and Russians both held certain parts of the valley and surrounding hills. The English battle commanders, from their position high atop a hill, suddenly saw Russian soldiers taking guns from an artillery post on another hill, under English control. The Light Brigade was sent a message to disrupt these Russians—but the order was unclear, and the Light Brigade charged down into the valley instead of toward the few Russians by the artillery post. As a result, the brigade suffered heavy casualties.

FOR ENGLISH LEARNERS

Options for Reading Introduce the basic plot of each poem to the students. Then have them listen to the poems on the *Audio Anthology CD* and use the Reciprocal Teaching strategy in small groups to work through each selection.

 BEST PRACTICES TOOLKIT—Transparency Reciprocal Teaching p. A35

Prereading For prereading instruction for English learners, see

 BEST PRACTICES TOOLKIT Scaffolding Reading Instruction pp. 43–46

Language: Word Order Help students navigate through the poem's unusual word order by analyzing the first four lines together. The subject (*the six hundred*) and verb (*Rode*) are inverted and follow introductory details.

Language: Punctuation Point out that 19th-century poets often replaced the letter *e* with an apostrophe in past-particle forms of verbs, as in "dismay'd" (line 10) and "blunder'd" (line 12). Explain to students that this does not affect the pronunciation of the word.

FOR ADVANCED LEARNERS/PRE–AP

Make Judgments Have students write a paragraph reacting to the assertion that the soldiers of the Light Brigade should be honored for their charge. Does blind devotion to duty equal honor? Do the soldiers of the Light Brigade deserve honor? Can someone who merely follows orders earn honor? Invite students to share their paragraphs.

READING STRATEGY

B READING A NARRATIVE POEM

Possible answer: The climax of the poem occurs in the fourth stanza, when the British soldiers break through the Russian line.

If students need help . . . Chart the events on a Plot Diagram to show the event that is the point of highest suspense or tension. *(Rising action—order to attack is given; six hundred soldiers ride into the valley; soldiers fight fiercely. Climax—soldiers break through the line. Falling action— a few survivors ride back.)*

 BEST PRACTICES TOOLKIT—Transparency
Plot Diagram p. D12

LITERARY ANALYSIS

C RHYTHM AND METER

Possible answer: The Light Brigade soldiers, armed only with sabers, are being shot at by cannons. There are two stressed syllables in each line. The emphasis on the first syllable of cannon *conveys the sound the cannons would make. The short lines move quickly, showing the fast pace of battle.*

Extend the Discussion These lines repeat lines 18–21 with a slight difference. What is the poet showing by this change?

Lines 50–55
REINFORCE *KEY IDEA:* HONOR

Discuss Why does the poet believe that the Light Brigade deserves **honor**? *Possible answer: The story told in this poem suggests that the Light Brigade should be honored because the soldiers fought with their whole hearts in the face of overwhelming odds.*

---

20 Cannon in front of them
    Volley'd and thunder'd;
  Storm'd at with shot and shell,
  Boldly they rode and well,
  Into the jaws of Death,
25 Into the mouth of Hell
    Rode the six hundred.

  Flash'd all their sabers[3] bare,
  Flash'd as they turn'd in air
  Sabring the gunners there,
30 Charging an army, while
    All the world wonder'd:
  Plunged in the battery[4] smoke,
  Right thro' the line they broke;
  Cossack and Russian
35 Reel'd from the saber-stroke,
    Shatter'd and sunder'd.[5]
  Then they rode back, but not,
    Not the six hundred. **B**

  Cannon to right of them,
40 Cannon to left of them,
  Cannon behind them
    Volley'd and thunder'd;
  Storm'd at with shot and shell,
  While horse and hero fell,
45 They that had fought so well
  Came thro' the jaws of Death,
  Back from the mouth of Hell,
  All that was left of them,
    Left of six hundred. **C**

50 When can their glory fade?
  O, the wild charge they made!
    All the world wonder'd.
  Honor the charge they made!
  Honor the Light Brigade,
55   Noble six hundred!

---

3. **sabers:** heavy, slightly curved swords.
4. **battery:** related to guns and cannons used together.
5. **sunder'd:** broken apart; split into pieces.

574 UNIT 5: APPRECIATING POETRY

B READING A NARRATIVE POEM
Since narrative poems have a plot, they also have a **climax,** or point of greatest excitement. What is the climax of this poem?

C RHYTHM AND METER
Reread lines 39–42 aloud. What is happening to the 600 soldiers? Explain how the meter of these lines matches the event being depicted.

DIFFERENTIATED INSTRUCTION

FOR LESS–PROFICIENT READERS
Reading Strategy Follow-Up: Reading a Narrative Poem Have students use Think-Pair-Share to compare the details they added to their story maps. Before beginning the next poem, gather information from the groups to compile a class story map.

 BEST PRACTICES TOOLKIT—Transparency
Think-Pair-Share p. A18

"The Charge of the Light Brigade"

Characters: 600 Light Brigade soldiers; Russian soldiers	**Setting:** A chaotic battle scene, in a valley
Conflict: British soldiers battle Russian soldiers	
Event 1: British, armed with swords, are shot at by cannons	
Event 2: British charge the enemy line and break it, but suffer great casualties	

Detail of *Equestrian Portrait of a Man with a Page* (1600s), Thomas de Keyser. Oil on canvas, 94.6 cm × 77.2 cm. Private collection. Photo © Bridgeman Art Library.

The Highwayman
Alfred Noyes

Part One

The wind was a torrent of darkness among the gusty trees.
The moon was a ghostly galleon[1] tossed upon cloudy seas.
The road was a ribbon of moonlight over the purple moor,[2]
And the highwayman came riding—
⁵   Riding—riding—
The highwayman came riding, up to the old inn-door. **D**

He'd a French cocked-hat on his forehead, a bunch of lace at his chin,
A coat of the **claret** velvet, and breeches of brown doeskin.
They fitted with never a wrinkle. His boots were up to the thigh.
¹⁰ And he rode with a jeweled twinkle,
    His pistol butts a-twinkle.
His rapier hilt[3] a-twinkle, under the jeweled sky.

---
1. **galleon** (gǎl′ē-ən): a large sailing ship.
2. **moor:** a wide, rolling open area, usually covered with low-growing shrubs.
3. **rapier** (rā′pē-ər) **hilt:** sword handle.

D READING A NARRATIVE POEM
What is the **setting** of this poem? Note the setting and the **characters** in your story map.

claret (klăr′ĭt) *adj.* dark red

ANALYZE VISUALS

About the Art Dutch artist Thomas de Keyser (1596–1667) specialized in portraits. Interestingly, he was an architect and stone dealer by profession and painted only as an avocation. In many of his portraits, the subject is doing something active—in this case, riding a horse.

Activity What details suggest that the rider is experienced? *Possible answer: Although his horse is rearing up, the rider appears relaxed and in control.*

READING STRATEGY

D READING A NARRATIVE POEM

Have students record their answers in the story map from page 571. *Possible answers:*

Characters:	Setting:
Highwayman riding a horse	dark windy night upon a moor, long ago; an old inn

If students need help . . . Point out that this poem has two parts. Part One is the exposition. It introduces the setting, characters, and conflict.

Extend the Discussion What might be foreshadowed by the description of the setting?

FOR LESS–PROFICIENT READERS

Comprehension Support Help students interpret the metaphors in lines 1–3 of "The Highwayman" to form a mental image of the setting. Ask students what images are created by these comparisons:

1. *wind* compared to a *torrent* ("a swiftly moving stream") *of darkness*
2. *moon* compared to a *ghostly galleon*
3. *road* compared to a *ribbon of moonlight*

Then have them summarize the setting of the poem (*windy moonlit night, an inn on the edge of a moor*).

FOR ENGLISH LEARNERS

Comprehension: Clarify

• Point out that *highway* is another word for *road*. Tell students that long ago in England, a *highwayman* (line 4) was a robber who stopped travelers on the roads and stole their money and jewelry. A related expression in modern English is *highway robbery*, which refers to charging such a high price for something that the seller is practically stealing from the buyer.

• Read the second stanza aloud for students, pausing to define these unfamiliar terms: *cocked-hat* (line 7), "hat with brim turned up to give three-corner look"; *velvet* (line 8), "soft, smooth fabric"; *breeches* (line 8), "pants"; *doeskin* (line 8), "soft leather." Point out how attractive the image of the highwayman is. Encourage students to use these details to figure out what the poet wants readers to think about the highwayman.

Over the cobbles[4] he clattered and clashed in the dark inn-yard.
He tapped with his whip on the shutters, but all was locked and barred.
15 He whistled a tune to the window, and who should be waiting there
But the landlord's black-eyed daughter,
    Bess, the landlord's daughter,
Plaiting[5] a dark red love-knot into her long black hair.

And dark in the dark old inn-yard a stable wicket[6] creaked
20 Where Tim the ostler[7] listened. His face was white and peaked.
His eyes were hollows of madness, his hair like moldy hay,
But he loved the landlord's daughter,
    The landlord's red-lipped daughter.
Dumb as a dog he listened, and he heard the robber say—

25 "One kiss, my bonny sweetheart, I'm after a prize tonight,
But I shall be back with the yellow gold before the morning light;
Yet, if they press me sharply, and harry me through the day,
Then look for me by moonlight,
    Watch for me by moonlight,
30 I'll come to thee by moonlight, though hell should bar the way."

He rose upright in the stirrups. He scarce could reach her hand,
But she loosened her hair in the casement.[8] His face burnt like a brand
As the black **cascade** of perfume came tumbling over his breast;
And he kissed its waves in the moonlight,
35   (O, sweet black waves in the moonlight!)
Then he tugged at his rein in the moonlight, and galloped away to
    the west.

Part Two

He did not come in the dawning. He did not come at noon;
And out of the **tawny** sunset, before the rise of the moon,
When the road was a gypsy's ribbon, looping the purple moor,
40 A redcoat troop came marching—
    Marching—marching—
King George's men came marching, up to the old inn-door.

---

4. **cobbles:** rounded stones used for paving roads.
5. **plaiting:** braiding.
6. **wicket:** a small door or gate.
7. **ostler** (ŏs'-lər): a worker who takes care of horses at an inn.
8. **casement:** a window that opens outward on side hinges.

With the cry of "Stand and deliver!" highwaymen halted and robbed the carriages of the upper class in 17th- and 18th-century England. Like Robin Hood, highwaymen were admired by ladies and celebrated by the poor, who often felt oppressed by the rich.

cascade (kă-skād') *n.* a waterfall or something that resembles a waterfall

tawny (tô'nē) *adj.* a warm, sandy shade of brownish orange

SOCIAL STUDIES CONNECTION

Highwaymen Highwaymen existed before the 1600s, but their numbers notably increased during this century in England. When King Charles I was executed in 1649, he left behind numerous soldiers. Unwanted by the new government, many of these men became highwaymen to support themselves. Some tried to avoid violence, using their charm and cunning to persuade their victims to hand over money and jewels. Others relied on force. By the 1800s, the presence of paid police reduced the threat of highwaymen to travelers.

Lines 19–30
DISCUSSION PROMPTS

Use these prompts to help students understand the significance of Tim's eavesdropping:

Interpret What is Tim's relationship to Bess? How do you think Tim feels as he sees the interaction between Bess and the highwayman? *Possible answer: Tim loves Bess from afar (line 22). He probably feels very jealous and resentful when he sees that Bess and the highwayman are lovers.*

Analyze Why is it dangerous for someone to overhear the highwayman's plans? *Possible answer: The highwayman's activities are illegal. He could be in danger if his plans are revealed.*

Synthesize What conflict is foreshadowed by the description of Tim's character, the highwayman's plan for that night, and the words of the highwayman in line 30? *Possible answer: Tim will cause a problem for the highwayman, preventing him from keeping his promise to Bess.*

DIFFERENTIATED INSTRUCTION

FOR ENGLISH LEARNERS
Comprehension: Predict Ask students to predict what role Tim will play in the highwayman's future. Help them infer from clues in lines 19–24 that Tim is in love with Bess and probably jealous of the highwayman. He may do something to keep them apart or to get the highwayman into trouble.

FOR ADVANCED LEARNERS/PRE–AP
Critique the Poem "The Highwayman" has fans who love it and critics who don't. Have students work in pairs to list the best and worst features of the poem. Then have one student write a brief "thumbs up" review and the other a brief "thumbs down" review. Students may present their reviews to the class and invite other students to share their opinions.

They said no word to the landlord. They drank his ale instead.
But they gagged his daughter, and bound her, to the foot of her
      narrow bed.
45 Two of them knelt at her casement, with muskets at their side!
There was death at every window;
   And hell at one dark window;
For Bess could see, through her casement, the road that *he* would ride.

They had tied her up to attention, with many a sniggering jest.
50 They had bound a musket beside her, with the muzzle beneath her breast!
"Now, keep good watch!" and they kissed her. She heard the doomed
      man say—
Look for me by moonlight;
   Watch for me by moonlight;
I'll come to thee by moonlight, though hell should bar the way! **E**

55 She twisted her hands behind her; but all the knots held good!
She **writhed** her hands till her fingers were wet with sweat or blood!
They stretched and strained in the darkness, and the hours crawled by
      like years,
Till, now, on the stroke of midnight,
   Cold, on the stroke of midnight,
60 The tip of one finger touched it! The trigger at least was hers!

The tip of one finger touched it. She strove no more for the rest.
Up, she stood up to attention, with the muzzle beneath her breast.
She would not risk their hearing; she would not strive again;
For the road lay bare in the moonlight;
65   Blank and bare in the moonlight;
And the blood of her veins, in the moonlight, throbbed to her
      love's refrain.

Tlot-tlot; tlot-tlot! Had they heard it? The horse hoofs ringing clear;
Tlot-tlot, tlot-tlot, in the distance? Were they deaf that they did not hear? **F**
Down the ribbon of moonlight, over the brow of the hill,
70 The highwayman came riding—
   Riding—riding—
The redcoats looked to their priming![9] She stood up, straight and still.

---

9. **looked to their priming:** prepared their muskets by pouring in the gunpowder used to fire them.

E READING A NARRATIVE POEM
How did the redcoats find out about Bess and the highwayman? Explain how you made this **inference.** Then note the main **conflict** in your story map.

writhe (rīth) *v.* to twist or move painfully

F RHYTHM AND METER
On a piece of paper, scan lines 67–68, noting the stressed and unstressed syllables in each line. Why is this meter perfectly suited to the action that's taking place?

G READING A NARRATIVE POEM

Have students record their answers on the story map from page 571. *Possible answer: Bess kills herself to warn the highwayman that the soldiers are waiting for him at the inn.*

LITERARY ANALYSIS: *Review*

H MOOD

Possible answer: The images "spurred like a madman" (line 85) and "white road smoking behind him" (line 86) convey the speed with which the highwayman returns to the inn, which creates a mood of excitement. "Blood-red were his spurs" and "wine-red was his velvet coat" (line 87) create an ominous mood.

Lines 85–87
REINFORCE *KEY IDEA:* HONOR

Discuss Does the highwayman's reaction show him to be a man of **honor**? *Possible answers:*

- *Yes. The highwayman could have escaped. He is honorable because he wants to avenge Bess's death.*
- *No. The highwayman is acting out of passion and rage, not honor.*

SELECTION WRAP–UP

REFLECT Ask students to think about whether the characters in the poems die in vain. Do they accomplish anything with their deaths?

★ **CRITIQUE** Ask students if they found both poems to be equally suspenseful, or if one poem was more exciting. Have students explain their opinions.

READING FLUENCY

Distribute the copy masters and have students practice fluency.

R **RESOURCE MANAGER—Copy Master**
Reading Fluency p. 90

Tlot-tlot, in the frosty silence! *Tlot-tlot*, in the echoing night!
Nearer he came and nearer. Her face was like a light.
75 Her eyes grew wide for a moment; she drew one last deep breath,
Then her finger moved in the moonlight,
Her musket shattered the moonlight,
Shattered her breast in the moonlight and warned him—with her death. **G**

He turned. He spurred to the west; he did not know who stood
80 Bowed, with her head o'er the musket, drenched with her own blood!
Not till the dawn he heard it, his face grew grey to hear
How Bess, the landlord's daughter,
The landlord's black-eyed daughter,
Had watched for her love in the moonlight, and died in the
darkness there.

85 Back, he spurred like a madman, shouting a curse to the sky,
With the white road smoking behind him and his rapier brandished high.
Blood-red were his spurs in the golden noon; wine-red was his velvet coat;
When they shot him down on the highway,
Down like a dog on the highway,
90 And he lay in his blood on the highway, with a bunch of lace at
his throat. **H**

And still of a winter's night, they say, when the wind is in the trees,
When the moon is a ghostly galleon tossed upon cloudy seas,
When the road is a ribbon of moonlight over the purple moor,
A highwayman comes riding—
95 *Riding—riding—*
A highwayman comes riding, up to the old inn-door.

Over the cobbles he clatters and clangs in the dark inn-yard.
He taps with his whip on the shutters, but all is locked and barred.
He whistles a tune to the window, and who should be waiting there
100 *But the landlord's black-eyed daughter,*
Bess, the landlord's daughter,
Plaiting a dark red love-knot into her long black hair.

G READING A NARRATIVE POEM
What just happened? Note the event on your story map.

H MOOD
Reread lines 85–90. Note the images that stand out to you. What mood, or feeling, do they help create?

DIFFERENTIATED INSTRUCTION

FOR ENGLISH LEARNERS
Comprehension: Task Support Assign each student one stanza in "The Highwayman." Ask them to reread the stanza and then draw what is happening or described. Have students exchange completed drawings. Partners should locate the passage that is illustrated and write a caption for it. Have students then share their drawings in sequence.

BEST PRACTICES TOOLKIT
Draw It p. A2

FOR ADVANCED LEARNERS/PRE–AP
Visualize Would "The Highwayman" work as a movie? Have students sketch a plan, in words or pictures, for adapting the poem for the big screen. Suggest they think of a clever way to incorporate the last two stanzas.

Analyze Color Imagery Have students review the poem for references to color. Then have them make a chart or key that explains the significance of various colors.

Comprehension

1. **Clarify** What is the outcome of the Light Brigade's charge?

2. **Recall** Where does Bess wait for the highwayman?

3. **Summarize** In your own words, explain how Bess and the highwayman each die.

Literary Analysis

4. **Compare and Contrast Characters** For each poem, make a list of the **character traits** the soldiers display. Are the soldiers in the two poems similar or different? Explain your answer.

5. **Analyze a Ballad** "The Highwayman" is a special type of **narrative poem** called a ballad. Ballads have the same features as narrative poems, but they were originally meant to be sung or read out loud. What elements of "The Highwayman" make it an exciting poem to read aloud? Give examples.

6. **Reading a Narrative Poem** Look back at the story map you created as you read "The Charge of the Light Brigade." How do you think a short story about the same battle might be different from this poem? What added information might the story include, and what effects might be missing?

7. **Evaluate Rhythm and Meter** Choose a few lines from each poem and read them to yourself, exaggerating the emphasis on the stressed syllables. Write the lines in a chart like the one shown and mark the stressed and unstressed syllables in each. Then explain how the rhythm of each line contributes to its overall effect.

"The Charge of the Light Brigade"	
Lines from Poem	Effect
Half a league, half a league, Half a league onward,	sounds like a galloping horse

Extension and Challenge

8. **SOCIAL STUDIES CONNECTION** Research the true story behind the legendary Light Brigade. When and where did the battle described in the poem occur? How many soldiers lost their lives? Share your findings with the class.

9. **Big Question Activity** Think back to the discussion of honor on page 570. Who acted with the most **honor**—Bess, the highwayman, or the soldiers of the Light Brigade? Explain your answer.

> **RESEARCH LINKS**
> For more on the Light Brigade, visit the **Research Center** at ClassZone.com.

7. ● **STANDARDS FOCUS** *Rhythm and Meter* Answers will vary. **Possible answers:**
   - **Rhythm of "Charge":** few stressed syllables in each line; **Effect:** emphasizes lack of hesitation with which the soldiers fought and their unflinching courage
   - **Rhythm of "Highwayman":** regular, with numerous stressed syllables; **Effect:** adds suspense and drama to the poem

Extension and Challenge

8.  **SOCIAL STUDIES CONNECTION** Students might present their facts in a short report or in a visual organizer.

9. Students' answers may vary. Some may say that Bess died honorably, sacrificing herself to save someone she loved. Others may say that the soldiers of the Light Brigade lived and died honorably, doing the job that they had sworn to do.

Practice and Apply

After Reading

For additional support of post-reading questions, use these copy masters:

R RESOURCE MANAGER—Copy Masters
Rhythm and Meter p. 81 (for practice of literary analysis standards focus)
Question Support p. 88 (**After Reading** questions adapted for English learners and less-proficient readers)

Additional selection questions are provided for teachers on page 77.

ANSWERS

Comprehension

1. *Though the soldiers of the Light Brigade fight bravely, many are killed.*

2. *Bess waits by the window of the inn that her father owns.*

3. *Bess shoots herself to warn the highwayman that soldiers are waiting for him. The highwayman flees, but he returns to avenge Bess and is shot by the soldiers.*

Literary Analysis

Possible answers:

4. *"The Charge of the Light Brigade": The soldiers act with honor, riding bravely into battle. "The Highwayman": The soldiers act in a cowardly way, abusing the landlord and his daughter (lines 43–44, 49–51) and using a civilian (Bess) to lure the highwayman to his death.*

5. *The poem's romantic theme, urgent rhythm, repetition, and colorful word choice make it exciting to read aloud. Students should offer examples of these elements from the poem.*

6. ■ **STANDARDS FOCUS** *Reading a Narrative Poem A prose narrative might give a clearer account of the events of the battle and might include more about the soldiers' thoughts. The poetic language, vivid imagery, and driving rhythm of the poem help convey the feel of the battle. Such aspects might be missing from a prose account.*

MARYLAND OBJECTIVES

LITERATURE STANDARD
3.A.4.c Analyze sound elements of poetry

ANSWERS

Vocabulary in Context

VOCABULARY PRACTICE

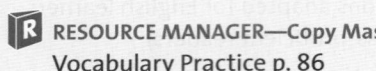

1. *tawny*
2. *writhe*
3. *claret*
4. *cascade*

 RESOURCE MANAGER—Copy Master
Vocabulary Practice p. 86

VOCABULARY IN WRITING

Students might find it helpful to organize details about their character in a chart with a column for physical appearance and one for character traits. Students can then think about how to express their ideas using vocabulary words.

BEST PRACTICES TOOLKIT—Transparency
T Chart p. A25

VOCABULARY STRATEGY: CONNOTATIONS
(also an EL language objective)

• Have students point out context clues in the sentences that can help them determine connotation and meaning.

• Ask students to describe the feelings that they associate with each word that is familiar to them.

Answers:
1. *negative*
2. *positive*
3. *negative*
4. *positive*

RESOURCE MANAGER—Copy Master
Vocabulary Strategy p. 87

ⓘ Vocabulary Center at **ClassZone.com**
Additional Vocabulary Activities

Vocabulary in Context

VOCABULARY PRACTICE

Choose the word from the list that best fits each sentence.

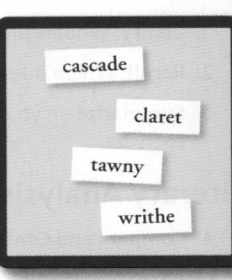

1. The hiker looked at the _____ glow of the setting sun and began to worry.
2. Not watching where he was walking, he tripped and fell, which made him _____ in pain.
3. A thin, _____-colored stream of blood trickled down his face.
4. He heard a _____ of water far in the distance and tried not to think about his growing thirst.

VOCABULARY IN WRITING

Which character could you see most clearly in your mind as you read these poems? Write a paragraph describing that character, using at least two vocabulary words. You might start like this.

> **EXAMPLE SENTENCE**
>
> I pictured Bess most clearly, especially her **cascade** of long black hair.

VOCABULARY STRATEGY: CONNOTATIONS

Poets use language carefully. They consider not only the dictionary definition of each word, but also its connotation. The connotation of a word includes all the thoughts or feelings the word may bring to people's minds. Words can have a positive, a negative, or a neutral connotation. For example, the vocabulary word *cascade* has a positive connotation that suggests something grand or picturesque.

PRACTICE For each sentence below, tell whether the boldfaced word has a positive, a negative, or a neutral connotation. Then explain the meaning of the word.

1. She didn't like the waiter's **prim** manner and the restaurant's overly formal atmosphere.
2. Because the coach was **decisive,** the players knew exactly what to do.
3. With one look at his **haggard** face, they knew he had been experiencing sleepless nights.
4. She was so interesting and **vivacious** that everyone at the dinner party wanted to sit by her.

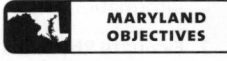

READING STANDARD
1.D.2.b Explain relationships between words

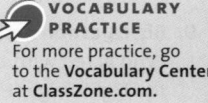
VOCABULARY PRACTICE
For more practice, go to the **Vocabulary Center** at **ClassZone.com.**

DIFFERENTIATED INSTRUCTION

FOR ENGLISH LEARNERS

Vocabulary in Writing Have students return to "The Highwayman" and find the line in which each vocabulary word is used. Ask students to write a sentence based on the idea in the line, using the vocabulary word as it is used there. For example, *The highwayman wore a claret-colored velvet jacket* (line 8).

FOR ADVANCED LEARNERS/PRE–AP

Vocabulary Strategy Have students return to the poems and pick out three or four examples of words that evoke either a positive or a negative association. Have students replace those words with synonyms and compare the effect of the substitution on the reader's understanding of the poem. Give students an example: Replacing *moldy* with *old* in "hair like moldy hay" (line 21) makes Tim seem less disgusting.

eading-Writing Connection

Increase your appreciation of "The Charge of the Light Brigade" and "The Highwayman" by responding to these prompts. Then complete the **Grammar and Writing** excercise.

WRITING PROMPTS	SELF-CHECK
A. Short Response: Write a Dialogue Both Bess and the soldiers of the Light Brigade stand up to something more powerful. Write a **half-page dialogue** between Bess and a soldier of the Light Brigade in which they discuss their ideas of **honor**.	*A realistic dialogue will . . .* • use language appropriate for each character • include details from the poems that support each character's ideas
B. Extended Response: Write a News Article Pretend you are a reporter writing a front-page story about a recent tragedy. Choose one of the poems and write a journalistic account of its events in **three to five paragraphs.** Include a headline that will grab your readers' attention.	*A successful article will . . .* • describe all the important events of the poem • use descriptive words and phrases to make the event come alive for the reader

GRAMMAR AND WRITING

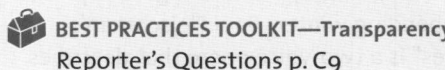

USE THE ACTIVE VOICE A verb can be in either the active voice or the passive voice. In a sentence that uses the **active voice,** the subject *performs* the verb's action. In a sentence that uses the **passive voice,** the subject of the sentence *receives* the verb's action.

LANGUAGE STANDARD
5.B.2.b Apply consistent and appropriate use of active and passive voice

> Active: The officers commanded the British soldiers.
> *(The subject* officers *performs the action of the verb* commanded.*)*
>
> Passive: The British soldiers were commanded by the officers.
> *(The subject* officers *receives the action of the verbs* were commanded.*)*

PRACTICE Rewrite each of these sentences using the active voice.

1. The officers' commands were obeyed by the Light Brigade.
2. Sabers were the weapons used by the British soldiers.
3. Soldiers and horses alike were killed by the Russians.
4. The Light Brigade will be remembered by the world.

For more help with active and passive voice, see page R57 in the Grammar Handbook.

Reading-Writing Connection

WRITING PROMPTS

• For **Prompt A,** suggest that before writing the dialogue students list the reasons that each character sacrifices his or her life. Suggest that students decide how each character would converse.

• For **Prompt B,** suggest that students use the Reporter's Questions organizer to gather the facts they need for their article. Remind them to include a lead paragraph.

 **BEST PRACTICES TOOLKIT—Transparency** Reporter's Questions p. C9

For ideas for writing, see

ℹ Writing Center at **ClassZone.com**

GRAMMAR AND WRITING

Tell students to use the active voice to make their writing more dynamic and lively.

Possible answers:
1. *The Light Brigade obeyed the officers' commands.*
2. *The British soldiers used sabers.*
3. *The Russians killed soldiers and horses alike.*
4. *The world will remember the Light Brigade.*

R RESOURCE MANAGER—Copy Master Use Active Voice p. 89

Assess and Reteach

Assess

R RESOURCE MANAGER—Copy Masters Selection Tests A, B/C pp. 91–92, 93–94

⊘ Test Generator CD

Reteach

S STANDARDS LESSON FILE
Literature Lesson 20: Rhythm and Meter
Vocabulary Lesson 17: Denotation and Connotation
Writing Lesson 10: Using Active and Passive Voice

FOR LESS–PROFICIENT WRITERS

For Prompt A:

1. Help students list the reasons that each character gives up his or her life and how he or she might feel about the sacrifice.

2. Have students write two or three sentences from the point of view of each character, using the list of details.

3. Have students put their sentences in dialogue form with alternating speakers. Help them add transitions to tie the sentences together.

For Prompt B:

• Limit the length of the assignment to two paragraphs.

• Fill out a Five Ws and an H organizer together, using the facts from "The Charge of the Light Brigade."

• Tell students to identify the event, time, place, and participants in the first paragraph and then explain the results in the second paragraph.

Focus and Motivate

OBJECTIVES

Literary Analysis
- explore the key idea of **seasons**
- identify characteristics of haiku
- identify and interpret symbols
- read poetry

Reading
- visualize

SUMMARY

Two haiku by Bashō present images of spring and impending winter. Paul Fleischman's "Fireflies" is a two-voice poem that describes the actions of fireflies against the backdrop of night. Robert Frost's "Fireflies in the Garden" is a comparison between stars and fireflies in which the insects are seen to mimic but fall far short of the celestial bodies.

How do the SEASONS *affect you?*

Discuss the question and *KEY IDEA* with students. Challenge them to draw an image that captures what they feel or think about each of the **seasons**. Have students share their images before completing the *SURVEY* activity.

Selection Resources

Two Haiku
Poems by Matsuo Bashō

Fireflies
Poem by Paul Fleischman

Fireflies in the Garden
Poem by Robert Frost

How do the SEASONS *affect you?*

MARYLAND OBJECTIVES

LITERATURE STANDARDS
3.A.4.a Use structural features to distinguish types of poetry
3.A.7.a Analyze how language choices contribute to meaning

KEY IDEA With shelters, cars, and climate controls of all kinds, it can sometimes be easy to overlook the dramatic changes that occur on the earth each year. But the **seasons** still determine the daily rhythms of our lives. As the poems you're about to read show, the changing seasons can even affect our emotions. How do the seasons make you feel?

SURVEY Conduct a survey of your classmates. Ask them for one or two words or phrases that they associate with each of the four **seasons.** Record their answers in a graphic organizer like the one shown. Review your data when you are done. What patterns do you see?

	Spring	Summer	Fall	Winter
Student 1				
Student 2				

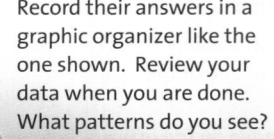

582

 **RESOURCE MANAGER UNIT 5**
Plan and Teach pp. 95–102
Literary Analysis
Symbol pp. 103, 104†*
Question Support p. 107*
Reading
Visualize pp. 105, 106†*

Assessment
Selection Tests A, B/C pp. 109*, 111*
Test Generator CD

 BEST PRACTICES TOOLKIT
Differentiated Instruction pp. 31–38*
Graphic Organizers/Strategies
Think-Pair-Share • Cluster Diagram • Read Aloud/Think Aloud

Reading Support
Audio Anthology CD*

Technology
ℹ️ Literature Center at **ClassZone.com**
WriteSmart CD

---

* Resources for Differentiation   † Also in Spanish

POETIC FORM: HAIKU

Haiku is a form of poetry that originated hundreds of years ago in Japan. In haiku, poets seek to create a clear picture with few words. There are three key points to remember about traditional haiku.

- The entire poem consists of just 17 syllables arranged in three lines.
- The first and third lines each contain 5 syllables, and the second line has 7 syllables.
- Haiku centers on a symbol that instantly reminds its readers of a season.

The haiku by Bashō on page 584 are classics of the form.

LITERARY ANALYSIS: SYMBOL

Are you aware that you are surrounded by symbols? For example, you may have a U.S. flag in your classroom or a company logo on your backpack. A **symbol** is a person, place, object, or activity that stands for something beyond itself.

- Some symbols are unique to certain cultures. In Japan, for example, plum blossoms symbolize early spring. The crow symbolizes late autumn or the coming winter.
- Some symbols are understood across cultures. For instance, in most cultures, a heart represents love.

By using symbols, poets are able to communicate rich and complex ideas quickly. As you read the poems, identify the symbols and think about what ideas they express.

READING STRATEGY: VISUALIZE

Poets create images by using **sensory details**—words and phrases that appeal to the reader's senses of sight, touch, taste, smell, and hearing. Details that appeal to your sense of sight help you **visualize**, or create mental pictures of, the poet's words.

As you read each poem, list the sensory details that help you "see" the pictures created by the poem.

	Sensory Details
"Fireflies"	1. flickering
	2. glimmering
	3.

Author Online

Matsuo Bashō: Japan's Master Poet
Matsuo Bashō first pursued a career as a samurai before devoting himself to the poetry that he had loved in his youth. He created a new style that raised haiku to the level of serious literature.

Matsuo Bashō
1644–1694

Paul Fleischman: A Musician of Words
Poet Paul Fleischman gives as much attention to the sound of his words as to their meaning. Fleischman grew up playing piano with his mother and listening to his father, an author, read aloud.

Paul Fleischman
born 1952

Robert Frost: A Legendary Poet
Robert Frost is one of the most beloved poets of the 20th century. As a young man, Frost ran a New Hampshire farm. The New England farmers Frost met were rich sources for his poetry. He won his first of four Pulitzer Prizes in 1924.

Robert Frost
1874–1963

 MORE ABOUT THE AUTHOR
For more on these poets, visit the **Literature Center** at ClassZone.com.

583

Teach

STANDARDS FOCUS

POETIC FORM

● HAIKU

Explain that each word used by a haiku poet is like an artist's brushstroke that helps paint a complete image. Write this example on the board:

> Warm, gentle breeze brings
> The fragrance of new flowers—
>   Spring blows softly in.

Ask students to identify the elements that make this passage a haiku. **Possible answers:** *There are three lines with a total of seventeen syllables; the warm, fragrant breeze is a symbol of spring.*

CHECK UNDERSTANDING Have students name other images or symbols relating to seasons that could be used in a haiku.

LITERARY ANALYSIS

● SYMBOL

Read aloud this example:

> With dread, she watched the geese
> form their perfect *V* to fly south.
> Already, the wind seemed colder
> and the fields more barren.

What does the southern migration of the geese symbolize? **Possible answer:** *It symbolizes the coming of winter.*

CHECK UNDERSTANDING Have students explain symbols in stories or poems they have read.

READING STRATEGY

◼ VISUALIZE

Read aloud a descriptive passage from a work such as "The Highwayman" (page 575). Ask students what they hear, see, feel, taste, or smell.

CHECK UNDERSTANDING Have students draw the image they "see" in the passage.

 RESOURCE MANAGER—Copy Master
Visualize p. 105 (for student use while reading the poems)

Practice and Apply

ANALYZE VISUALS

About the Art Utagawa Hiroshige (1797–1858) is considered to be one of Japan's greatest artists. His first woodblock prints were mostly of actors, warriors, and beautiful women. Later, he began to depict landscapes, such as the one seen here. His work had a major influence on future Western artists, such as the impressionist Van Gogh.

Activity Have students identify the mood of the print and explain how the artist creates that mood. *Possible answers: The mood is calm and serene. The soft colors and the distance between the tree and the figures help to create this mood.*

POETIC FORM

Ⓐ HAIKU

Possible answer: Plum blossoms symbolize and evoke spring. The mountain path might be interpreted as a symbol of new possibilities, the future, or excitement.

LITERARY ANALYSIS

Ⓑ SYMBOL

Possible answer: The crow's arrival may symbolize the coming of winter.

Extend the Discussion What other symbol might have been used to evoke the same meaning?

REINFORCE *KEY IDEA:* SEASONS

Discuss Based on the images in both haiku, what emotions does the poet associate with the different **seasons**? *Possible answer: Spring is associated with hope and expectation, as shown by the image of the plum blossoms and the sun rising. Late autumn is associated with desolation, as shown by the bareness of the branch and the image of evening.*

TWO HAIKU

MATSUO BASHŌ

Plum Garden, Kameido from *One Hundred Views of Famous Places in Edo* (1857), Utagawa Hiroshige. Photo © Christie's Images/Corbis.

On sweet plum blossoms[1]
The sun rises suddenly.
Look, a mountain path! Ⓐ

A crow
has settled on a bare branch—
autumn evening. Ⓑ

Ⓐ **HAIKU**
Identify at least one symbol in this poem. Also note what season the poem evokes.

Ⓑ **SYMBOL**
What does the crow's arrival **symbolize?**

---

1. When haiku is translated from the original Japanese into English, the number of syllables per line sometimes changes slightly.

DIFFERENTIATED INSTRUCTION

FOR LESS—PROFICIENT READERS

Comprehension Support Use a Cluster Diagram to explore the symbolism in each haiku. Complete the first map together, asking students to identify each possible symbol and volunteer ideas about what it represents. Encourage students to identify more than one meaning. Have pairs complete maps for the second haiku before sharing ideas.

 BEST PRACTICES TOOLKIT—Transparency Cluster Diagram p. B18

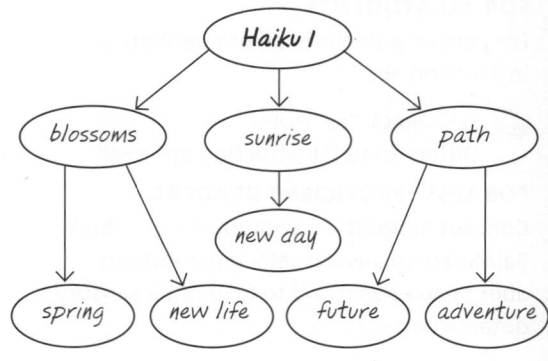

Fireflies

PAUL FLEISCHMAN

Light	Light
	is the ink we use
Night	Night
is our parchment[1]	
5	We're
	fireflies
fireflies	flickering
flitting	
	flashing
10 fireflies	
glimmering	fireflies
	gleaming **C**
glowing	
Insect calligraphers[2]	Insect calligraphers
15 practicing penmanship	
	copying sentences
Six-legged scribblers	Six-legged scribblers
of vanishing messages,	
	fleeting[3] graffiti
20 Fine artists in flight	Fine artists in flight
adding dabs of light	
	bright brush strokes
Signing the June nights	Signing the June nights
as if they were paintings	as if they were paintings **D**
25	We're
flickering	fireflies
fireflies	flickering
fireflies.	fireflies.

C VISUALIZE
Reread lines 1–12. What words help you see the fireflies in your mind?

D VISUALIZE
Reread lines 20–24. Notice the **simile** comparing the "June nights" to paintings. What do you picture when you visualize the image presented in lines 20–24?

---

1. **parchment:** fine-quality paper, usually made from the skin of goats or sheep.
2. **calligraphers** (kə-lĭg′rə-fərz): creators of beautiful, elaborate handwriting.
3. **fleeting:** passing swiftly; soon gone.

BACKGROUND

Firefly Communication Fleischman's poem describes the "flickering," "flashing," "glimmering" light of the fireflies. Individual species of fireflies use their own unique flashing patterns to communicate. Males light up as they fly; females stay perched and light up in response to a prospective mate.

Reading the Poem "Fireflies" is set up like a musical duet for two readers. One reads the lines on the right and the other reads the lines on the left. Lines on the same level are read simultaneously.

READING STRATEGY

C VISUALIZE
Record students' answers in the chart from page 583. *Possible answers:*

Poem	Sensory Details
"Fireflies"	1. flickering
	2. flitting
	3. glimmering
	4. gleaming
	5. glowing
	6. dabs of light
	7. bright brush strokes

READING STRATEGY

D VISUALIZE
Possible answer: Students may say that they can see the large and small movements of fireflies against a dark backdrop.

Lines 1–28
DISCUSSION PROMPTS

Use these prompts to help students understand the effect of the poem's arrangement on the page:

Interpret Based on the way the poem is laid out on the page, how many fireflies are "speaking"? *Possible answer: There are two fireflies communicating with each other.*

Analyze When you read the poem, how does the arrangement in two columns make you feel as if you're watching the fireflies? *Possible answer: The reader's eyes move constantly back and forth, as if catching glimpses of firefly lights in the night sky.*

FOR LESS–PROFICIENT READERS
Reading Skill Follow-Up: Visualize Play "Fireflies" from the *Audio Anthology CD.* As students listen, have them shut their eyes and concentrate on the mental images brought out by the words. Then ask them to draw what they see. Have students compare sketches in small groups and point out details in the poem that helped them visualize their drawings.

FOR ADVANCED LEARNERS/PRE–AP
Metaphors A metaphor is a figure of speech that compares two unlike things. Unlike a simile, it does not use the word *like* or *as.* Point out the first metaphor in "Fireflies": "Light is the ink we use" (lines 1–2). Ask students to identify other metaphors in the poem and what they represent. Then have them write one or two additional metaphors that would work in "Fireflies." Afterward, invite them to work together to create and illustrate a collage of their original metaphors.

Lines 1–6
DISCUSSION PROMPTS

Use these prompts to help students understand important ideas in the poems:

Interpret What adjectives are used to describe stars and fireflies? How do they compare? *Possible answer:* Real *is used to describe stars.* Emulating *describes flies. The speaker suggests that fireflies' brilliance cannot compete with stars.*

Analyze How does the poet develop his description of fireflies? What is the effect of this approach? *Possible answer: The poet points out all the traits of stars that fireflies do not have. This honest approach reveals the true nature and role of fireflies.*

Evaluate What point is the poet making about nature? *Possible answers: The poet is pointing out that all parts of nature—stars, fireflies, and humans—have a distinct and defined role. The nature of stars is to provide long-lasting brilliance, whereas fireflies and humans cannot aspire to such heavenly magnificence.*

LITERARY ANALYSIS

ⓔ SYMBOL

Possible answer: The fireflies might represent creatures on Earth, including humans. Humans may have a spark of greatness, but they are imperfect and mortal.

SELECTION WRAP–UP

SYNTHESIZE Ask students to consider all four poems. How do the poems show the profound effect that **seasons** can have on people? *Possible answer: The change of seasons and the experiences people have in each season can give people fresh insights into human life.*

⭐ **CRITIQUE** Have students decide which poet uses symbols most effectively and explain why.

Fireflies
in the Garden
Robert Frost

Here come real stars to fill the upper skies,
And here on earth come emulating[1] flies,
That though they never equal stars in size,
(And they were never really stars at heart)
5 Achieve at times a very star-like start.
Only of course they can't sustain[2] the part. ⓔ

> ⓔ **SYMBOL**
> Reread the poem and think about what the fireflies might symbolize.

---

1. **emulating:** imitating.
2. **sustain:** keep up; prolong.

DIFFERENTIATED INSTRUCTION

FOR LESS–PROFICIENT READERS
Concept Support Use a chart to explore the symbolism in the Frost poem.

Symbol	Ideas from Poem	Meaning
fireflies	• live on Earth, not in heavens • not as brilliant or dazzling as stars	• imitation of something greater • imperfect humans

FOR ENGLISH LEARNERS
Comprehension: Clarify Use a Read Aloud/ Think Aloud strategy to help students understand these aspects of the poem:

- the compare/contrast organization
- references to the flies throughout as "they"
- the tone conveyed by comparisons and word choice ("real," "emulating," "of course")
- the main idea

 BEST PRACTICES TOOLKIT—Transparency Read Aloud/Think Aloud p. A34

Comprehension

1. **Recall** In the first haiku, what does the rising sun reveal? In the second haiku, where does the crow settle?

2. **Clarify** In "Fireflies," what is the "ink" the fireflies use?

3. **Summarize** In what ways are the fireflies in "Fireflies in the Garden" unlike the stars they try to copy?

MARYLAND OBJECTIVES

LITERATURE STANDARD
3.A.7.a Analyze how language choices contribute to meaning

Literary Analysis

4. **Visualize** Look back at the list of sensory details that helped you visualize. For each poem, choose the details that most helped you visualize an image from that poem. Sketch one of these images.

5. **Examine Haiku** Which haiku gives you a more hopeful feeling? Explain.

6. **Evaluate Sound Devices** In "Fireflies," Fleischman repeats many words and phrases. What are the words he repeats the most? What other example of **repetition** do you notice? Tell how this repetition reflects the subject of the poem.

7. **Analyze Symbol** In "Fireflies in the Garden," Robert Frost contrasts the stars in the "upper skies" with the fireflies "here on earth." Use a chart like the one shown to explore the comparison more closely. What **theme** or larger idea about life might Frost be trying to express by using the fireflies as a symbol?

Details About the Fireflies	My Thoughts
The flies copy the stars.	
The stars are in the sky, and the flies are on earth.	
The flies were "never really stars at heart."	
The flies can shine like stars, but they "can't sustain the part."	

Extension and Challenge

8. **Speaking and Listening** "Fireflies" is written for two voices. Work with a partner and prepare an oral reading of the poem. One of you should read the words in the left column at the same time the other reads the words in the right. Perform your reading for the class. What images in the poem does reading aloud help to reinforce?

9. **Creative Project: Writing** Write a traditional haiku. Pick one **season** and try to express how it affects you. (You might look back at the words and phrases you collected in the survey on page 582 for ideas.)

Extension and Challenge

8. *Students' paired readings should bring out the repetition of the words and phrases, emphasizing the quick and momentary movements of the fireflies.*

9. *Students' poems should express a central idea about a season and should include one or more symbols that relate to this central idea.*

Assess and Reteach

Assess

RESOURCE MANAGER—Copy Masters
Selection Tests A, B/C pp. 109–110, 111–112

Test Generator CD

Reteach

STANDARDS LESSON FILE
Literature Lesson 14: Haiku
Literature Lesson 29: Symbol and Symbolism

Practice and Apply

After Reading

For additional support of post-reading questions, use these copy masters:

RESOURCE MANAGER—Copy Masters
Symbol p. 103 (for practice of literary analysis standards focus)
Question Support p. 107 (**After Reading** questions adapted for English learners and less-proficient readers)

Additional selection questions are provided for teachers on page 99.

ANSWERS

Comprehension

1. *The rising sun reveals a mountain path. The crow settles on a bare branch.*

2. *The fireflies' "ink" is light.*

3. *The fireflies are not the size of stars, nor can they sustain their light for as long as stars. The fireflies also lack the essence of stars—they are not "stars at heart" (line 4).*

Literary Analysis

Possible answers:

4. ■ **STANDARDS FOCUS** *Visualize Students' sketches should reflect details in the poem.*

5. *The first haiku is more hopeful. The rising sun and the blossoms suggest new beginnings. The last line suggests an unexpected and delightful discovery.*

6. *Repetition: The most often repeated words are "fireflies," "light," "night," and "flickering." Other examples are "insect calligraphers," "six-legged scribblers," "fine artists in flight," "signing the June nights," and "as if they were paintings." Effect: The repetition of words mimics the repetition of the fireflies' flickering lights.*

7. ● **STANDARDS FOCUS** *Symbol*
My Thoughts: row 1—a cheap imitation; row 2—it's more impressive to be in the sky; row 3—the flies are imposters; row 4—the flies fizzle out, but the stars keep shining. Possible themes: Imitations never live up to the real thing. Humans can never hope to achieve perfection.

Focus and Motivate

OBJECTIVES

Reading for Information

- use **text features** to locate and comprehend information
- make connections between nonfiction and poetry
- read and understand a science article

SUMMARY

This article provides information about the insect commonly known as the lightning bug or firefly. It explains the chemical reactions that produce the firefly's light as well as the eating habits, life cycle, and habitat of the insect.

What's the Connection?

Use a KWL chart to help prepare students for the selection. List what students know about fireflies in the first column—details such as *insects, active in summer,* and *flickering light.* Then identify questions that students have about other aspects of fireflies. As students read the article, pause occasionally to record answers to their questions in the last column, add new questions, or revise details in the first column.

 BEST PRACTICES TOOLKIT—Transparency
KWL p. A21

Teach

Skill Focus: Use Text Features

Guide students through the process of identifying the treatment and scope of a text.

- What do I learn about the general organization of the article from previewing the text features?
- For what purposes are text features used in this article?
- The subheadings are all in the same type size. What does that tell me about the importance of the information under each subheading?
- Are there other text features, such as footnotes or italicized terms? If so, what can I expect to find out from those elements?

Possible chart entries appear on page 590.

 RESOURCE MANAGER—Copy Master
Use Text Features p. 119

Reading for Information

Stars with Wings

Science Article

Use with "Fireflies," page 585.

 MARYLAND OBJECTIVES

INFO TEXT/WRITING STANDARDS
2.A.2 Analyze text features
4.A.2.c Compose to inform

What's the Connection?

The more you know about fireflies, the more easily you can spot the clever ways poet Paul Fleischman has imitated them in his poem "Fireflies." Take the time to learn more about these creatures by reading the science article "Stars with Wings."

Skill Focus: Use Text Features

Think about how all of the signs you see each day, even signs such as Do Not Walk on the Grass, communicate important information.

Text features are like signs. They help you figure out where you are in an article, and they tell you what is especially important to know. For example, consider what these text features reveal:

- A **title** identifies the text and its topic.
- An **introductory question** following the title may reveal the writer's focus or main idea.
- A **subheading,** which is a heading within the text, signals the start of a new topic or section and identifies what it will be about
- **Graphic aids**—such as illustrations, maps, and diagrams—help you visualize people, places, things, and ideas.

As you read the science article that follows, look for these text features and notice what you learn from them. Use two-column notes, such as the ones started here, to record your ideas.

Text Feature	What I Learn or Infer
Title and art: "Stars with Wings" with a picture of a firefly	The article will be about fireflies.
Introductory question:	
Subheadings: 1. A Beetle, Actually	1. Fireflies are not bugs or flies. They are beetles.
2.	2.
3.	3.
Graphic aids:	

588 UNIT 5: APPRECIATING POETRY

Selection Resources

RESOURCE MANAGER UNIT 5

Plan and Teach pp. 113–116

Reading
Summary pp. 117†*, 118‡*
Use Text Features pp. 119, 121†*
Reading Check p. 123
Connect Nonfiction and Poetry pp. 120, 122†*
Question Support p. 124*

Assessment
Selection Tests A, B/C pp. 125*, 127*

Test Generator CD

Reading Support

Audio Anthology CD*

BEST PRACTICES TOOLKIT

KWL • Concept Cards • Jigsaw

* Resources for Differentiation † Also in Spanish ‡ In Haitian Creole and Vietnamese

Stars with Wings

by Therese Ciesinski

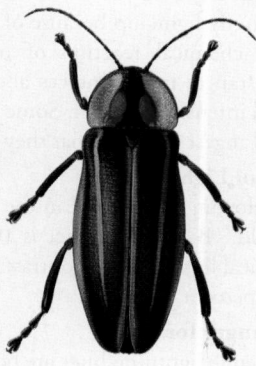

Who needs summer fireworks when you have a backyard display of lightning bugs? **A**

Nature holds many wondrous sights, but few are as magical or close to home as a backyard busy with the luminous meanderings of fireflies. On sultry July evenings, adults ease back in lawn chairs while children race about and capture the pulsating glow of these lightning bugs in a glass jar. "I wonder how many amateur entomologists[1] first became interested in science and insects as the result of collecting fireflies," muses Greg Hoover, an entomologist at Pennsylvania State University in State College, Pennsylvania. Hoover, one of the folks who helped the firefly species Photuris *pennsylvanica* (illustrated here) become the official insect of Pennsylvania, remembers fly-fishing one evening and watching fireflies arise from the woods and reeds along the water's edge. "It was really neat. It looked like the New York City skyline at night," he recalls. Call them fireflies or lightning bugs, these marvelous insects are more than just aesthetic wonders. They're also good for the garden, consuming slugs and other critters who hunger for your vegetables.

- **A Beetle, Actually B**
  Neither bug nor fly, a firefly is a soft-bodied beetle belonging to the family Lampyridae, Latin for "shining fire." There are 124 species in North America, mostly in the eastern states and provinces. Lightning bugs are usually brown or black with light-colored markings and grow about an inch in length.

---

1. **entomologists:** scientists who specialize in the study of insects.

Practice and Apply

FOCUS ON FORM

Discuss the purpose and characteristics of a science article. Explain that in addition to the characteristics described, science articles may also

- include specialized vocabulary
- use formal sentence structure
- appear in journals or science sections of the newspaper
- quote experts in the field

As students read the article, have them identify five new facts or terms that they learn.

INFORMATIONAL ANALYSIS

A USE TEXT FEATURES

Possible answers:

Text Feature	What I Learn or Infer
Introductory question: Who needs summer fireworks when you have a backyard display of lightning bugs?	This introductory question connects the title "Stars with Wings" to fireflies. It reveals that the writer thinks the insects are as interesting, exciting, and beautiful as fireworks.

INFORMATIONAL ANALYSIS

B USE TEXT FEATURES

Have volunteers identify all of the remaining subheadings in the article. *(Light My Fire, Cool Light, Hungry for Slugs, Grounded, Time to Shine, Water Lovers)* Have students predict what kind of information might be provided in each section.

F OCUS ON FORM
A **science article** is a short piece of nonfiction writing on a scientific subject. The **author's purpose** for writing a science article is usually to inform or explain. Science articles often use **text features** to present information clearly.

A USE TEXT FEATURES
What do you learn from the question between the title and first line of this article? Add this information to your chart.

B USE TEXT FEATURES
Preview the rest of the article to identify the other **subheadings** in it. Write these on your chart. Then, as you read the article, jot down what you learn from the text that follows each subheading.

DIFFERENTIATED INSTRUCTION

FOR LESS-PROFICIENT READERS

Comprehension Support Use Concept Cards to help students preview the article and use the text features to make predictions about its content. As students read the article, have them find and record answers to their questions in the KWL chart.

 BEST PRACTICES TOOLKIT—Transparency
Concept Cards p. A19

FOR ENGLISH LEARNERS

Options for Reading Point out the various text features included in the article. Have students read the article along with the *Audio Anthology CD,* or provide students with a brief summary of the content. Then have Jigsaw groups read assigned sections of the text and report back on the information they discover.

 BEST PRACTICES TOOLKIT
Jigsaw p. A1

DISCUSSION PROMPTS

Use these prompts to help students understand aspects of the writer's style:

Interpret Why doesn't the writer begin the article with facts? *Possible answer: The writer wants to relate the subject to readers' experience, so she first describes the sight of fireflies in a backyard.*

Analyze How does the writer introduce new scientific terms, such as *bioluminescence?* *Possible answer: She italicizes each term to draw readers' attention to it. Then she defines the term, so that readers can clearly understand the information.*

Synthesize How might the writer explain her style and approach to scientific articles? *Possible answer: She makes her facts engaging and easy for readers to follow.*

LITERARY ANALYSIS

C SCIENCE ARTICLE

Possible answer: The writer's primary purpose is to inform and explain. Her secondary purpose is to entertain readers and make them feel interested in her subject.

Extend the Discussion How does the writer accomplish each purpose in this article?

Skill Focus: Use Text Features

Possible answers for chart on page 588:

Subheadings

Light My Fire: The reaction of oxygen, luciferin, and luciferase in fireflies' abdomens produces their light.

Cool Light: Fireflies are cool to the touch. Bioluminescence gives off no heat.

Hungry for Slugs: Young fireflies eat garden pests. Adult fireflies may eat pollen and nectar or nothing at all.

Grounded: Fireflies go through many different stages over the course of a year, including spending the winter underground.

Time to Shine: Fireflies are most active in July and August. They glow off and on from dusk to midnight.

Water Lovers: Fireflies need damp places to breed.

Graphic aids: *The illustration on page 589 shows what a firefly looks like.*

- **Light My Fire**
  A firefly lights up because of *bioluminescence,* a natural glow caused by the chemical reaction of oxygen and *luciferin* and *luciferase,* two substances in the insect's abdomen. Cells within the abdomen reflect and intensify the light. Some frogs love the bitter taste of lightning bugs and ingest so many that they begin to glow themselves.

- **Cool Light**
  30   A glowing firefly held in the hand won't burn its captor, as the light is "cold." Bioluminescence is 100 percent efficient, giving off no heat. A typical lightbulb, by contrast, emits 10 percent of its energy as light and 90 percent as heat. . . .

- **Hungry for Slugs**
  Juvenile lightning bugs are beneficial insects. The larvae[2] dine on snails, slugs, and aphids.[3] . . . At adulthood, some species don't eat at all; others eat only pollen and nectar.

- **Grounded**
  The light-show portion of a firefly's life—about 3 to 8 weeks—is only a 40   small span of its existence. The life cycle begins when females lay eggs on swampy terrain. The larvae—nicknamed *glowworms* because they give off a faint light—hatch in late summer. After feeding for a few weeks, they burrow underground to escape the winter cold. Emerging in spring, the glowworms feed and later seal themselves within a cell of soil. After 2 weeks they emerge as adult, air-worthy lightning bugs.

- **Time to Shine**
  Lightning bugs are most active in July and August. The light show begins at dusk and usually ends around midnight. In the daytime, you'll find fireflies clinging to tree trunks and branches. "Most people see them in 50   the day but don't realize what they are," says Hoover. "Fireflies like to hang out in crevices in tree bark."

- **Water Lovers**
  Drought and the loss of wetlands impact firefly populations. The beetles need soggy places with low vegetation to breed and thrive. "Soil moisture determines the abundance of fireflies in any given year," Hoover says. "Gardeners may notice a decrease in the amount of fireflies after a drought." **C**

C SCIENCE ARTICLE
What do you think the **author's purpose** was for writing this article?

---

2. **larvae** (lär′vē): insects at a stage during which they are newly hatched and often wormlike.

3. **aphids** (ā′fĭdz): small, soft-bodied insects of the family Aphididae that have mouthparts specially adapted for feeding on sap from plants.

DIFFERENTIATED INSTRUCTION

FOR ADVANCED LEARNERS/PRE–AP
Synthesize Explain the function of other text features, such as captions (text that provides information about a graphic aid), overview (short summary that previews the text), sidebars (additional information set in a box alongside or within an article), and pullout text (important or memorable facts or quotes, often set in large, colorful type). Ask students to create one or two of these features for the article and then share their additions in small groups.

Reading for Information

Comprehension

1. **Recall** What causes fireflies to light up?
2. **Clarify** Why is neither *firefly* nor *lightning bug* an accurate name?

Critical Analysis

3. **Identify Characteristics of a Science Article** What are three characteristics of a science article? Give an example of each one from "Stars with Wings."
4. **Analyze Text Features** Review the chart you completed while reading this science article. What did learn from the text features? Choose one type of text feature and explain how it was useful to you.

Read for Information: Connect Nonfiction and Poetry

MARYLAND OBJECTIVES

INFO TEXT/WRITING STANDARDS
2.A.2 Analyze text features
4.A.2.c Compose to inform

WRITING PROMPT

When poets write about the natural world in their poems, they sometimes relate scientifically accurate details. However, poets might also decide to use imaginative details to create images and express ideas that get at a less literal truth. Explain which poem, "Fireflies" or "Fireflies in the Garden," uses more accurate details.

To answer this prompt, follow these steps:

1. Reread "Fireflies" and "Fireflies in the Garden." Note which lines appear to relate scientifically accurate details.
2. Review "Stars with Wings" and your notes on the article to find out whether the details are accurate. Note passages from the article that support or contradict the lines from the poems.
3. Write a paragraph explaining which poem is more accurate and a paragraph explaining which poem takes more liberties with the facts. Use quotations from the poems as well as the article to support your explanation.

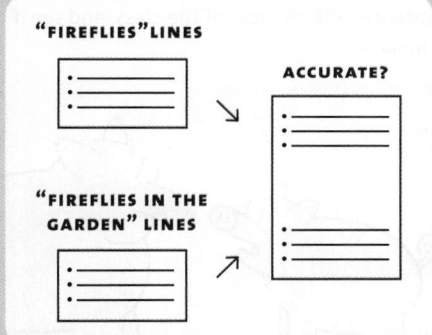

"FIREFLIES" LINES

ACCURATE?

"FIREFLIES IN THE GARDEN" LINES

READING FOR INFORMATION **591**

FOR LESS-PROFICIENT WRITERS
Read for Information

1. Have students reread "Fireflies" and "Fireflies in the Garden" by themselves.
2. Have pairs paraphrase the poems together, noting the details each poet sees and imagines about fireflies.
3. As a class, list the connections made between the poems' details and the details from the scientific article.

Possible answers:

- In "Fireflies," the poet calls fireflies "Insect calligraphers / practicing penmanship" (lines 14–15), who scribble messages and graffiti (lines 17–19) on June nights (line 23). The article says a chemical reaction makes them glow, mostly in July and August.
- "Fireflies in the Garden" gives brief but accurate details. It notes that fireflies look like stars but are smaller and eventually fade out (lines 3–6).

Practice and Apply

For additional support of post-reading questions, use these copy masters:

RESOURCE MANAGER—Copy Masters
Reading Check p. 123
Question Support p. 124
Connect Nonfiction and Poetry p. 120

For additional questions, see p. 115.

ANSWERS

Comprehension

1. *Oxygen, luciferin, and luciferase react in the firefly's abdomen to produce light.*
2. *A firefly is actually a soft-bodied beetle.*

Critical Analysis

3. *Possible answers: Author's purpose—The purpose of "Stars with Wings" is to give information, such as "A firefly lights up because of bioluminescence" (line 24). **Text features**—The article has a title, an introductory question, subheadings, and a graphic aid (the illustration on page 589). **Short nonfiction**—The article is short and includes facts and firsthand observations about fireflies.*
4. ■ **STANDARDS FOCUS** *Use Text Features* *Possible answer: The subheadings organize a lot of information into manageable segments. They tell what each part will be about.*

Read for Information: Connect Nonfiction and Poetry

Writing Prompt *A strong response will contain two paragraphs, each developing a main idea. Students should include relevant quotations that support their topic sentences.*

Assess and Reteach

Assess

RESOURCE MANAGER—Copy Masters
Selection Tests A, B/C pp. 125–126, 127–128
Test Generator CD

Reteach

STANDARDS LESSON FILE
Informational Texts Lesson 1: Text Features

READING FOR INFORMATION **591**

OBJECTIVES

Literary Analysis
- explore the key idea of **nonsense**
- identify characteristics of humorous poetry (rhyme, repetition, onomatopoeia, alliteration)
- identify and interpret sound devices
- read humorous poetry, including limericks

Reading
- monitor reading comprehension (clarify and question)

SUMMARY

In Carroll's nonsense poem, the hero slays a beast known as the Jabberwock. In Silverstein's poem, Sarah Stout will not take the garbage out. It piles up, leading to her premature demise. The first of Lear's limericks recounts the tale of an old man with a light who dances all night. The second tells of an old man who is cold.

When does NONSENSE *make sense?*

Discuss the question. To lead into the **KEY IDEA,** point out the cartoon. Tell students that the caption is written in pig Latin, an invented language that appears to be **nonsense** to someone who does not know the key. To form pig Latin, the first consonant sound of a word is moved to the end, and then the suffix *-ay* is added. Have students complete the **BRAINSTORM** activity and share their invented words. Discuss whether any of their words are onomatopoetic, or sound like what they mean.

Selection Resources

Jabberwocky
Poem by Lewis Carroll

Sarah Cynthia Sylvia Stout Would Not Take the Garbage Out
Poem by Shel Silverstein

Two Limericks
Poems by Edward Lear

When does NONSENSE *make sense?*

MARYLAND OBJECTIVES

READING/LIT STANDARDS
1.E.3.a Select and apply appropriate strategies during reading
3.A.4.c Analyze sound elements of poetry

KEY IDEA Is there a strong feeling that you just can't put into words or a hilarious sight that is impossible to describe? What if you could invent a new word that would capture the idea exactly? A **nonsense** word, like some of those used in the poems that follow, might be just what you need.

BRAINSTORM With a partner, think of something you've never been able to describe clearly. It might be the bouncy movement a squirrel uses when it hops along a fence or the emotion you feel when a bully gets suspended. Invent a nonsense word that captures the idea perfectly, and then write a sentence that uses that word. Share your sentence with the rest of the class, and see if others can guess what it means.

"Ommymay, why do we alktay so unnyfay?"

© Shannon Burns/www.CartoonStock.com

592

RESOURCE MANAGER UNIT 5

Plan and Teach pp. 129–136

Literary Analysis
Sound Devices pp. 137, 138†*
Question Support p. 141*

Reading
Monitor pp. 139, 140†*

Assessment
Selection Tests A, B/C pp. 143*, 145*
Test Generator CD

BEST PRACTICES TOOLKIT

Differentiated Instruction pp. 31–38*

Graphic Organizers/Strategies
Read Aloud/Think Aloud • Cluster Diagram

Reading Support
Audio Anthology CD*

Technology
Literature Center at **ClassZone.com**
WriteSmart CD

* Resources for Differentiation   † Also in Spanish

POETIC FORM: HUMOROUS POETRY

The selections you are about to read are examples of **humorous poetry.** This type of poetry is often written for young people and may contain the following:

- sound devices that make the poems fun to read aloud
- descriptions that are exaggerated for comic effect
- elements of fantasy that sweep readers into another world

LITERARY ANALYSIS: SOUND DEVICES

Poets use **sound devices** to make their poems both musical and memorable. As you read these poems, be on the lookout for the following sound devices:

- **Rhyme** is the repetition of the sounds at the end of words. (b<u>aloney</u> and mac<u>aroni</u>)
- **Repetition** is the use of a word or phrase more than once.
- **Onomatopoeia** is the use of words that sound like their meanings. (*buzz, whisper, squish*)
- **Alliteration** is the repetition of consonant sounds at the beginning of words. (<u>t</u>wenty <u>t</u>ame <u>t</u>igers)

Think about what these devices add to the poems.

READING STRATEGY: MONITOR

As you read these humorous poems, pause regularly to check, or **monitor,** how well you are understanding them.

- Try rereading confusing lines silently or aloud and discussing your ideas with classmates.
- If you get stuck on an unfamiliar or made-up word, use **context clues,** or information in the surrounding lines, to help you guess the word's meaning.
- As you read each poem, use a chart like the one shown to record notes about language or ideas you clarify.

"Jabberwocky"	
Lines from Poem	My Notes
"Twas brillig, and the slithy toves ..." (line 1)	"Brillig" might describe a time of day or the weather. "Slithy" reminds me of "slimy". "Toves" sounds like "toads".

Author Online

Lewis Carroll: Math Magician Lewis Carroll was an Oxford University mathematician when he began making up children's stories. Before Carroll published his books *Alice's Adventures in Wonderland* and *Through the Looking Glass,* people believed children's books should instruct, not entertain. Carroll, however, offers readers pure delight.

Lewis Carroll
1832–1898

Shel Silverstein: Cartoonist and Poet Shel Silverstein began his artistic career as a child. "I would much rather have been a good baseball player," he says. "But I couldn't play ball.... So I started to draw and write."

Shel Silverstein
1932–1999

Edward Lear: Limerick Master The limerick is a type of poem that first appeared in England in the mid-1700s. Edward Lear became a master of the form and helped make limericks popular.

Edward Lear
1812–1888

 MORE ABOUT THE AUTHOR
For more on these poets, visit the **Literature Center** at ClassZone.com.

593

STANDARDS FOCUS

POETIC FORM

● HUMOROUS POETRY

Explain that the main purpose of humorous poetry is to entertain, although it may also convey a serious theme.

CHECK UNDERSTANDING Ask students to define *exaggeration* and *fantasy,* and tell how they could add humor to a poem.

LITERARY ANALYSIS

● SOUND DEVICES

Have students identify the sound devices in these lines from "The Highwayman":

"Tlot-tlot; tlot-tlot! Had they heard it? The horse hoofs ringing clear; / Tlot-tlot, tlot-tlot, in the distance? Were they deaf that they did not hear?"

Possible answers: *"Tlot-tlot, tlot-tlot"—repetition and onomatopoeia; "horse hoofs"—alliteration; "clear", "hear"—rhyme*

CHECK UNDERSTANDING Have students find sound devices in other poems.

READING STRATEGY

■ MONITOR

Have students share monitoring strategies they have used. List them on the board.

CHECK UNDERSTANDING Have students monitor their reading of **Author Online.**

 RESOURCE MANAGER—Copy Master Monitor p. 139 (for student use while reading the poems)

DIFFERENTIATED INSTRUCTION

FOR ALL STUDENTS

For general guidelines on differentiating instruction, see

 BEST PRACTICES TOOLKIT
Differentiated Instruction pp. 31–38

FOR LESS—PROFICIENT READERS

Concept Support As students read "Jabberwocky," fill in a chart with examples of sound devices from the poem.

Sound Devices	Stanza 1	Stanza 2
alliteration		claws that catch
onomatopoeia		
repetition		Beware the ...
rhyme	toves/ borogoves, wabe/ outgrabe	son/shun, catch/ Bandersnatch

FOR ENGLISH LEARNERS

Options for Reading Before beginning each poem, explain what it is about. Then read the poem aloud or have students read along silently as they listen to the *Audio Anthology CD.*

A MONITOR

Record students' answers in the chart from page 593. *Possible answer:*

"Jabberwocky"	
Lines from poem	**My Notes**
"Beware the Jabberwock, my son! / The jaws that bite, the claws that catch!"	The father tells the son to beware of the Jabberwock. This warning and the details that it bites and has claws suggest that the Jabberwock is a dangerous beast.

B SOUND DEVICES

Answer: *Burbled* *is an example of* *onomatopoeia.*

Extend the Discussion What impression of the Jabberwock does the word *burbled* create? Is the word humorous in any way?

ANALYZE VISUALS

Possible answers: Adjectives might include scaly, rainbow-colored, fierce, *and* serpent-like.

About the Art American artist Greg Spalenka (b. 1958) uses both acrylic paints and a computer to produce unique and highly engaging art. Science fiction and fantasy stories influence his work, as can be seen in this example.

Lines 17–24
REINFORCE *KEY IDEA:* NONSENSE

Discuss What are some of the **nonsense** words in these lines? How do they convey meaning? *Possible answers: Nonsense words include* vorpal, snicker-snack, beamish, frab-jous, *and* Callooh! Callay! *(Galumphing and chortle were also nonsense words when Carroll wrote this poem, but they have since become accepted words in English.) The way the words are used and the way they sound help bring out their meaning.*

JABBERWOCKY
LEWIS CARROLL

'Twas brillig, and the slithy toves
Did gyre[1] and gimble in the wabe:
All mimsy were the borogoves,
And the mome raths outgrabe.

5 "Beware the Jabberwock, my son!
The jaws that bite, the claws that catch! **A**
Beware the Jubjub bird, and shun
The frumious Bandersnatch!"

He took his vorpal sword in hand:
10 Long time the manxome foe he sought—
So rested he by the Tumtum tree,
And stood awhile in thought.

And, as in uffish thought he stood,
The Jabberwock, with eyes of flame,
15 Came whiffling through the tulgey wood,
And burbled as it came! **B**

One, two! One, two! And through and through
The vorpal blade went snicker-snack!
He left it dead, and with its head
20 He went galumphing back.

"And hast thou slain the Jabberwock?
Come to my arms, my beamish boy!
O frabjous day! Callooh! Callay!"
He chortled in his joy.

25 'Twas brillig, and the slithy toves
Did gyre and gimble in the wabe:
All mimsy were the borogoves,
And the mome raths outgrabe.

1. **gyre** (jīr): whirl.

A MONITOR
What do lines 5–6 tell you about the Jabberwock? Using **context clues,** explain what you think a Jabberwock is.

B SOUND DEVICES
Which word in line 16 is an example of **onomatopoeia?** Say the word aloud.

ANALYZE VISUALS
What three **adjectives** best describe the beast on page 595?

Dragon, Greg Spalenka. © Greg Spalenk

DIFFERENTIATED INSTRUCTION

FOR ENGLISH LEARNERS
Comprehension: Task Support

1. Hand out a list of all the nonsense words in the poem. Tell students that the class will define these words later, and encourage them to read around the unknown words.

2. Explain that the first stanza describes the setting of the poem. Have students focus on lines 5–24. Briefly summarize the events in these stanzas: *"He" in line 9 is the hero who kills the monster known as the Jabberwock.*

3. Have pairs of students locate information about each of these points:
   - description of the Jabberwock
   - what the hero does before he meets the Jabberwock
   - how the hero kills the Jabberwock
   - how the hero's father reacts

4. Help students use context clues to understand some of the key nonsense words (*manxome, whiffling, burbled, snicker-snack, beamish, frabjous, Callooh! Callay!*).

BACKGROUND

Nonsense Words in "Jabberwocky" The poem "Jabberwocky" appears in the first chapter of Lewis Carroll's book *Through the Looking-Glass and What Alice Found There.* To read the poem, Alice must hold it up to the looking-glass, or mirror. Even then, she really cannot understand it. In the sixth chapter, however, Alice meets Humpty Dumpty, who explains some of the words to her:

- *brillig:* four o'clock in the afternoon (the time to begin broiling things for dinner)
- *slithy:* a combination of *slimy* and *lithe*
- *tove:* a kind of badger
- *gimble:* to make holes like a gimlet—a tool used for boring holes
- *wabe:* the area around a sundial
- *mimsy:* a combination of *miserable* and *flimsy*
- *borogove:* a decrepit-looking bird with its feathers sticking out
- *mome raths:* green pigs who have lost their way from home
- *outgrabe:* made a sound rather like shouting and whistling with a sneeze in the middle

---

FOR LESS–PROFICIENT READERS

Reading Strategy Follow-Up: Monitor Use Read Aloud/Think Aloud to model using context clues and prior knowledge to define nonsense words in lines 5–16. Point out that how a word is used gives clues to its meaning. For example, *frumious* is an adjective. It looks like the word *furious.* Have small groups finish the poem using Read Aloud/Think Aloud. Afterward, discuss any questions.

BEST PRACTICES TOOLKIT—Transparency
Read Aloud/Think Aloud p. A34

FOR ADVANCED LEARNERS/PRE–AP

Evaluate Nonsense Words Which of Lewis Carroll's invented words should be added to the English language next? Ask students to consider what qualities helped *galumph* and *chortle* find their way into people's everyday speech and writing. Then have them select another word from "Jabberwocky" that seems equally deserving. Have them write a letter to the publisher of a dictionary explaining what the word means, why it is useful, and why it should be included in the next edition.

DISCUSSION PROMPTS

Use these prompts to help students understand the elements of the poem that make it humorous:

Describe How would you describe the character Sarah Cynthia Sylvia Stout? *Possible answer: Sarah is a young person who doesn't mind helping around the house but absolutely refuses to take out the garbage.*

Analyze What is funny about this poem so far? *Possible answers: Sarah's long, alliterative name and the fact that she does all kinds of other chores but draws the line at taking out the garbage make her a quirky, humorous character. The descriptions of specific items of garbage piling up to the ceilings (lines 7–10) create a humorous image in readers' minds.*

Speculate What humorous events might happen later in the poem? *Possible answer: The garbage will continue to pile up, forcing Sarah to come up with a creative solution.*

LITERARY ANALYSIS

Ⓒ SOUND DEVICES

Possible answer: Examples of alliteration include

- "Sarah Cynthia Sylvia Stout" (line 1)
- "scour," "scrape"; "pots," "pans" (line 3)
- "potato peelings" (line 8)
- "brown bananas" (line 9)

The alliteration emphasizes the phrases in which it is used, adds humor to the description, and gives the poem a song-like quality that makes it fun to read aloud.

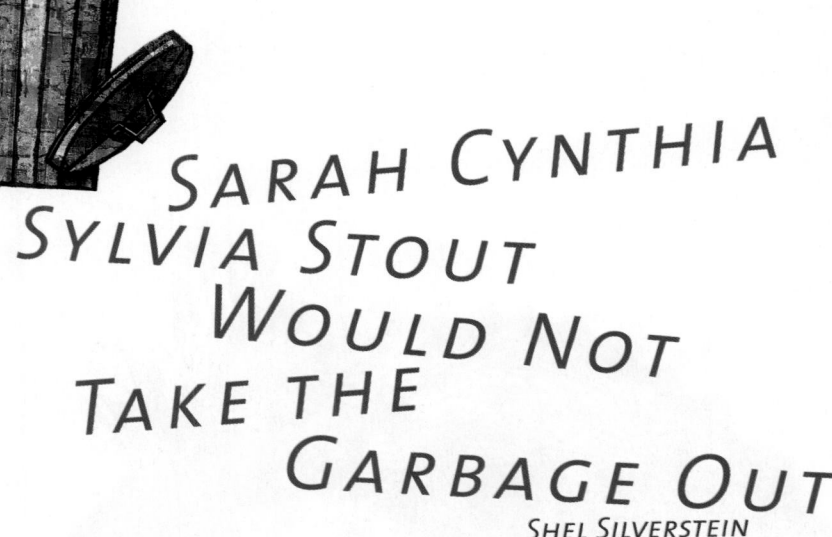

SARAH CYNTHIA SYLVIA STOUT WOULD NOT TAKE THE GARBAGE OUT

SHEL SILVERSTEIN

Sarah Cynthia Sylvia Stout
Would not take the garbage out!
She'd scour the pots and scrape the pans,
Candy the yams and spice the hams,
5 And though her daddy would scream and shout,
She simply would not take the garbage out.
And so it piled up to the ceilings:
Coffee grounds, potato peelings,
Brown bananas, rotten peas,
10 Chunks of sour cottage cheese. Ⓒ
It filled the can, it covered the floor,
It cracked the window and blocked the door

Ⓒ SOUND DEVICES
Find two examples of **alliteration** in lines 1–10. What do you think the alliteration adds to this disgusting description?

DIFFERENTIATED INSTRUCTION

FOR LESS–PROFICIENT READERS
Concept Support

1. Reinforce the idea that alliteration refers to the repetition of sound, not necessarily the repetition of the same consonant letter.

2. Have students work in teams to locate as many examples of alliteration in the poem as they can.

FOR ENGLISH LEARNERS
Comprehension: Clarify

1. Divide the poem into four sections: lines 1–6, 7–32, 33–38, 39–47.

2. Have mixed-ability groups fill out their chart from page 593, recording ideas about each of these sets of lines.

3. Use groups' input to complete a class chart.

With bacon rinds and chicken bones,
Drippy ends of ice cream cones,
15 Prune pits, peach pits, orange peel,
Gloppy glumps of cold oatmeal,
Pizza crusts and withered greens,
Soggy beans and tangerines,
Crusts of black burned buttered toast,
20 Gristly bits of beefy roasts . . .
The garbage rolled on down the hall,
It raised the roof, it broke the wall . . .
Greasy napkins, cookie crumbs,
Globs of gooey bubble gum,
25 Cellophane from green baloney,
Rubbery blubbery macaroni,
Peanut butter, caked and dry,
Curdled milk and crusts of pie,
Moldy melons, dried-up mustard,
30 Eggshells mixed with lemon custard,
Cold french fries and rancid meat,
Yellow lumps of Cream of Wheat. **D**
At last the garbage reached so high
That finally it touched the sky.
35 And all the neighbors moved away,
And none of her friends would come to play.
And finally Sarah Cynthia Stout said,
"OK, I'll take the garbage out!" **E**
But then, of course, it was too late . . .
40 The garbage reached across the state,
From New York to the Golden Gate.
And there, in the garbage she did hate,
Poor Sarah met an awful fate,
That I cannot right now relate.
45 Because the hour is much too late.
But children, remember Sarah Stout
And always take the garbage out!

D HUMOROUS POETRY
Silverstein lists 33 types
of garbage in this poem.
How does this add to
the humor of the poem?

E MONITOR
Reread lines 33–38. Why
does Sarah finally take
the garbage out?

SARAH CYNTHIA SYLVIA STOUT . . .   **597**

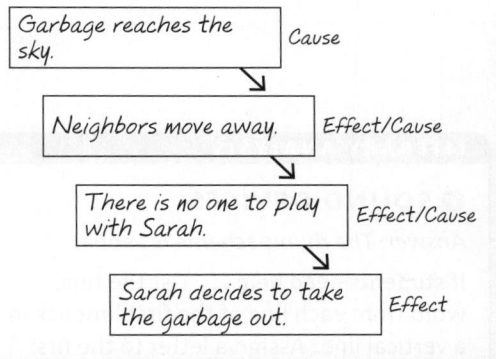

Activity After students finish reading both limericks, ask them to explain which one is illustrated by the drawing. Does the mood of the art match the mood of the limerick?

Possible answer: The drawing illustrates the first limerick, capturing these details: "old man"; "dressed in a garment of white"; "held a small candle, / With never a handle"; "danced." Both the art and the limerick have a lighthearted, comical, and whimsical mood.

About the Art Alberto Ruggieri lives in Rome, Italy, where he works as a painter and an advertising and editorial illustrator.

LITERARY ANALYSIS

F SOUND DEVICES

Answer: *The rhyme scheme is* aabba.

If students need help . . . List the final word from each line of the first limerick in a vertical line. Assign a letter to the first sound and have students fill in the rest of the rhyme scheme.

SELECTION WRAP–UP

⭐ **CRITIQUE** Have students evaluate the effectiveness of the sound devices used by each poet. Do they enhance or detract from readers' understanding of each poem?

TWO LIMERICKS
EDWARD LEAR

Old Man. Illustration by Alberto Ruggieri.

There was an old man with a light,
Who was dressed in a garment of white;
He held a small candle,
With never a handle,
5 And danced all the merry long night.

There was an old man who made bold,
To affirm[1] that the weather was cold;
So he ran up and down,
In his grandmother's gown,
5 Which was woollen, and not very old. **F**

---
1. **affirm** (ə-fûrm′): to declare or prove true.

F SOUND DEVICES
All true limericks have the same **rhyme scheme,** or pattern of rhyming words. What is the pattern?

DIFFERENTIATED INSTRUCTION

FOR LESS–PROFICIENT READERS

Concept Support Have students reread both limericks. Use a Cluster Diagram to help students develop an understanding of the characteristics of limericks as seen in these examples.

 BEST PRACTICES TOOLKIT—Transparency
Cluster Diagram p. B18

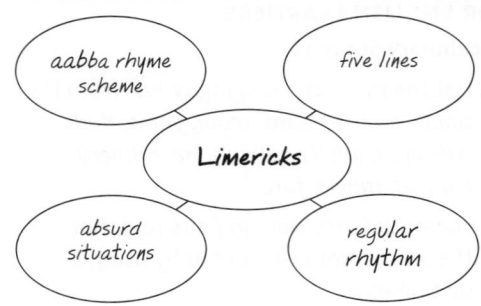

Comprehension

1. **Recall** How does the Jabberwock die?

2. **Recall** What happens when Sarah finally agrees to take the garbage out?

3. **Recall** In the second limerick, why does the old man run around in his "grandmother's gown"?

Literary Analysis

4. **Monitor** Review the information you recorded as you read "Jabberwocky." Does *frabjous* (line 23) mean "good" or "bad"? How can you tell?

5. **Identify Sensory Details** Silverstein uses sensory details—details that appeal to the five senses—to make you see, smell, and even feel the heaping mass of foul garbage in Sarah's house. Find four sensory details in the poem and explain which sense each appeals to.

6. **Analyze a Limerick** Limericks usually have a specific **rhythm,** or pattern of stressed and unstressed syllables. Reread the first limerick aloud. How many stressed syllables are in each line? Now read the second limerick. How similar is the rhythm to that in the first poem?

7. **Analyze Sound Devices** Reread "Sarah Cynthia Sylvia Stout Would Not Take the Garbage Out." As you read, look for several examples of rhyme, repetition, onomatopoeia, and alliteration. Create a chart like the one shown to record what you find. In your opinion which device most adds to the humor of the piece?

Sound Devices in "Sarah Cynthia ..."			
Rhyme	Repetition	Onomatopoeia	Alliteration
"Rubbery blubbery" (line 26)			

8. **Evaluate Humorous Poetry** Pick the poem you thought was funniest. Review the characteristics of humorous poetry listed on page 593. Which characteristics helped to make your favorite poem so funny? Give examples to support your answer.

Extension and Challenge

9. **Big Question Activity** Try writing your own **nonsense** poem. Think back to the activity on page 592 and the nonsense word you made up. Write a short, funny poem that explains what your word means.

10. **Inquiry and Research** The word *chortle* didn't exist until Carroll included it in "Jabberwocky." Using a dictionary or the Internet, find this word's definition. Do you think this former nonsense word makes sense?

MARYLAND OBJECTIVES

LITERATURE STANDARD
3.A.4.c Analyze sound elements of poetry

Practice and Apply

After Reading

For additional support of post-reading questions, use these copy masters:

R RESOURCE MANAGER—Copy Masters
Sound Devices p. 137 (for practice of literary analysis standards focus)
Question Support p. 141 (**After Reading** questions adapted for English learners and less-proficient readers)

Additional selection questions are provided for teachers on page 133.

ANSWERS

Comprehension

1. *The son (lines 5, 21–23) cuts off the Jabberwock's head (lines 18–19).*

2. *By the time Sarah takes out the garbage, it's too late. She meets an "awful fate."*

3. *The old man wants to prove that the weather is cold.*

Literary Analysis
Possible answers:

4. ■ **STANDARDS FOCUS** *Monitor Frabjous means "good" or "great." Readers know this from the fact that the son has slain the awful Jabberwock and his father "chortled in his joy" (line 24).*

5. *The image of "brown bananas" (line 9) appeals to sight. "Gloppy glumps of cold oatmeal" (line 16) appeals to sight and touch. The detail "chunks of sour cottage cheese" (line 10) appeals to sight and smell, and "cold French fries and rancid meat" (line 31) appeals to smell, sight, and touch.*

6. *Lines 1, 2, and 5 have three stressed syllables; lines 3 and 4 have two. The second limerick follows the same pattern.*

7. ● **STANDARDS FOCUS** *Sound Devices Repetition: "would not take the garbage out" (lines 2, 6); Onomatopoeia: "gloppy glumps" (line 16); Alliteration: "black burned buttered toast" (line 19). Students may say that alliteration adds the most to the humor.*

8. ● **STANDARDS FOCUS** *Humorous Poetry Students may cite the sound devices or the exaggeration as the major contributor to the humor of the poem they choose. Be sure students offer specific examples.*

Extension and Challenge

9. *Students' poems may or may not have rhyme or other sound devices but should be humorous and provide context clues to the meaning of the nonsense word.*

10. *The word* chortle *means "a snorting, joyful laugh or chuckle." It is a combination of* chuckle *and* snort. *Students may say that this word makes sense because many people snort when they laugh.*

Assess and Reteach

Assess

R RESOURCE MANAGER—Copy Masters
Selection Tests A, B/C pp. 143–144, 145–146

💿 Test Generator CD

Reteach

S STANDARDS LESSON FILE
Literature Lessons 15, 19, 21, 23
Reading Lesson 2: Monitoring

Focus and Motivate

OBJECTIVES

Literary Analysis
- explore the key idea of **comparison**
- identify mood
- identify and interpret figurative language (metaphor, personification)
- read poetry and prose

Reading
- set a purpose for reading

Grammar and Writing
- write a compare-contrast paper
- use writing to analyze literature

SUMMARY

In "The Delight Song of Tsoai-Talee," the speaker metaphorically compares himself to elements of nature, including fish, stars, rain, and geese. His song is a celebration of the fact that he is alive. In "Four Skinny Trees," the narrator describes the tenacity of four trees trapped in the city and compares their struggle for survival to her own.

How would you D E S C R I B E *yourself?*

Discuss the question and **KEY IDEA.** Point out that **comparisons** are used frequently in everyday conversation to help communicate ideas. For example, people might describe someone as having "nerves of steel" or "a heart of gold." Ask students for other examples of common metaphorical expressions. Talk about what each means. Then have students complete the **WEB IT** activity and share their responses.

Selection Resources

RESOURCE MANAGER UNIT 5

Plan and Teach pp. 147–154

Literary Analysis
Question Support p. 157*

Reading
Set a Purpose for Reading pp. 155, 156†*

Grammar and Writing
Writing for Assessment p. 158

Assessment
Selection Tests A, B/C pp. 159*, 161*
Test Generator CD

BEST PRACTICES TOOLKIT

Differentiated Instruction pp. 31–38*

Graphic Organizers/Strategies
T Chart • Spider Map • Read Aloud/Think Aloud

Reading Support
Audio Anthology CD*

Technology
Literature Center at **ClassZone.com**

Write*Smart* CD

* Resources for Differentiation   † Also in Spanish

Comparing Mood

The Delight Song of Tsoai-Talee
Poem by N. Scott Momaday

Four Skinny Trees
Vignette by Sandra Cisneros

How would you DESCRIBE *yourself?*

MARYLAND OBJECTIVES

READING/LIT STANDARDS
1.E.3.a Select and apply appropriate strategies during reading
3.A.7.c Analyze figurative language

KEY IDEA If someone were to ask you to describe yourself, what would you say? Often, we describe ourselves in **comparison** to something or someone. In the selections you're about to read, people compare themselves to the natural world.

WEB IT Comparing yourself to an element in nature, such as a blooming sunflower or a powerful tiger, can convey a vivid sense of who you are. Create a word web like the one shown. In it show what in nature you would compare yourself to, and why.

600

LITERARY ANALYSIS: MOOD AND FIGURATIVE LANGUAGE

Have you ever described a story with a word like *mysterious, creepy, joyful,* or *cheerful?* Then you've described the **mood,** or the feeling that a writer creates for the reader. One way writers create mood is through **figurative language,** which is language used in imaginative ways to express ideas that are not literally true.

- A **metaphor** is a comparison between two unlike things. It does not use the word *like* or *as. (I am an antelope.)*
- **Personification** is a comparison that gives human qualities to an object, animal, or idea. *(My shoes punished the pavement.)*

In "The Delight Song of Tsoai-Talee," N. Scott Momaday uses metaphors; in "Four Skinny Trees," Sandra Cisneros uses personification. As you read, notice how the figurative language helps to set the mood of each piece.

Review: **Repetition**

READING STRATEGY: SET A PURPOSE FOR READING

Every time you read something, you read with a purpose. Sometimes that purpose might be just to have fun. Other times it might be to learn specific information.

In this lesson, your **purpose for reading** is to compare the moods of two pieces. To help you do this, look closely at the figurative language in each poem.

After you read "The Delight Song of Tsoai-Talee" and "Four Skinny Trees," read the selections again. You will then be asked to fill in a chart like the one shown.

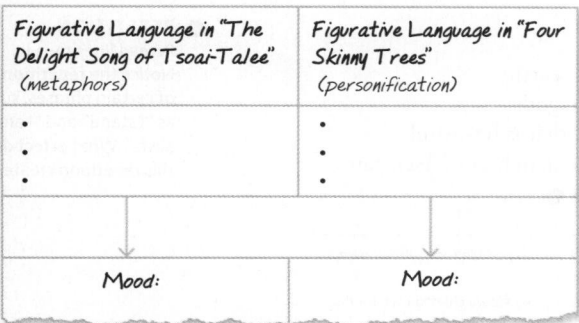

Figurative Language in "The Delight Song of Tsoai-Talee" (metaphors)	Figurative Language in "Four Skinny Trees" (personification)
•	•
•	•
•	•

| Mood: | Mood: |

Author Online

N. Scott Momaday: Rock Tree Boy
Pulitzer Prize–winning poet N. Scott Momaday was born to Kiowa and Cherokee parents. He spent his childhood on Native American reservations throughout the Southwest. Momaday's Kiowa name, Tsoai-Talee, means "Rock Tree Boy" and refers to an 865-foot volcanic butte that is sacred to the Kiowa people.

N. Scott Momaday born 1934

Sandra Cisneros: Writer on the Move
Sandra Cisneros grew up as the only daughter in a large Mexican-American family. The family frequently moved back and forth between the United States and Mexico. "I

Sandra Cisneros born 1954

didn't like school because we moved so much," she says. Despite her awkwardness in class, Cisneros read and wrote a great deal on her own. Around the time she published her first novel, *The House on Mango Street,* she was also teaching and counseling high-school dropouts. The stories her students told her about their lives greatly influenced her writing.

MORE ABOUT THE AUTHOR
For more on N. Scott Momaday and Sandra Cisneros, visit the **Literature Center** at **ClassZone.com.**

601

Teach

STANDARDS FOCUS

LITERARY ANALYSIS

● MOOD AND FIGURATIVE LANGUAGE

Display and read this passage: *The sun smiled on flowers dancing merrily to the tune of the breeze. Above, wisps of pure white meringue floated across the blue sky.* Ask students to identify figurative language and mood. *Possible answers: Personification*—*"sun smiled," "flowers dancing"; Metaphor*—*"tune of the breeze," "wisps of . . . meringue"; Mood*—*happy*

CHECK UNDERSTANDING Ask students how the sun, wind, and sky could be described to create a scary or sad mood.

READING STRATEGY

■ SET A PURPOSE FOR READING

Have students read **Author Online** to find the answers to these questions:

- What is N. Scott Momaday's Kiowa name? What does it mean?
- Why was school hard for Cisneros?

Possible answers: Momaday's name is Tsoai-Talee. It means "Rock Tree Boy." Cisneros's family moved often, so she was constantly readjusting.

CHECK UNDERSTANDING Ask students their purpose for reading **Author Online.**

RESOURCE MANAGER—Copy Master
Set a Purpose for Reading p. 155 (for student use while reading the selections)

DIFFERENTIATED INSTRUCTION

FOR ALL STUDENTS

For general guidelines on differentiating instruction, see

 BEST PRACTICES TOOLKIT
Differentiated Instruction pp. 31–38

FOR LESS–PROFICIENT READERS
Concept Support

Before reading, help students distinguish between literal and figurative meanings.

- In a T Chart, list several familiar sayings, such as "It's raining cats and dogs," "I'm so hungry

I could eat a horse," and "I wished the ground would swallow me up." Invite students to think of others.

- Together, record the interpretation of each saying in the second column.
- Assign pairs of students to draw the literal meaning of each expression. Have students present and explain their drawings to the class.

 BEST PRACTICES TOOLKIT—Transparency
T Chart p. A25

FOR ENGLISH LEARNERS

Options for Reading One approach to these selections is to have students read them along with the *Audio Anthology CD.* Another option is to practice echo reading, giving students a chance to absorb an impression of mood through their repetition of the lines.

Practice and Apply

ANALYZE VISUALS

Possible answer: In addition to people's faces, the collage includes aspects of nature such as a bird, a tree, a cow, a wolf or dog, and a fish.

About the Art In her art, Native American artist Jaune Quick-to-See Smith addresses issues facing Native Americans in contemporary society. Her work shows the influence of abstract artists as well as Native American pictograms. She often uses the collage format, as seen here, to convey her message.

LITERARY ANALYSIS

Ⓐ MOOD AND FIGURATIVE LANGUAGE

Have students record the metaphors and description of mood in their chart from page 601. *Possible answers: These metaphors create a sense of power, exhilaration, and beauty.*

If students need help ...

- List these words and phrases on the board: *feather, bright, blue horse, runs, fish, rolls, shining, light, lustre, eagle playing with the wind.*

- Point out that many of the words suggest movement and light. Help students arrive at a description of mood based on the feeling of these words.

Lines 10–17
REINFORCE *KEY IDEA:* COMPARISON

Discuss What do all the **comparisons** in lines 10–17 have in common? What important idea is brought out by these comparisons? *Possible answer: All of the comparisons are based on nature. The speaker is emphasizing his closeness to nature, his sense of belonging to the earth.*

LITERARY ANALYSIS: *Review*

Ⓑ REPETITION

Possible answer: The repetition adds to the feeling of exultation, celebration, and connection with other living things.

Extend the Discussion In addition to reinforcing mood, what other functions does the repetition serve in the poem?

THE DELIGHT SONG OF TSOAI-TALEE

N. Scott Momaday

I am a feather on the bright sky
I am the blue horse that runs in the plain
I am the fish that rolls, shining, in the water
I am the shadow that follows a child
5 I am the evening light, the lustre of meadows
I am an eagle playing with the wind Ⓐ
I am a cluster of bright beads
I am the farthest star
I am the cold of the dawn
10 I am the roaring of the rain
I am the glitter on the crust of the snow
I am the long track of the moon in a lake
I am a flame of four colors
I am a deer standing away in the dusk
15 I am a field of sumac and the pomme blanche[1]
I am an angle of geese in the winter sky
I am the hunger of a young wolf
I am the whole dream of these things

You see, I am alive, I am alive
20 I stand in good relation to the earth
I stand in good relation to the gods
I stand in good relation to all that is beautiful
I stand in good relation to the daughter of Tsen-tainte[2]
You see, I am alive, I am alive Ⓑ

---

1. **pomme blanche** (pôm bläɴsh): a plant with heavy edible roots, also known as breadroot.

2. **Tsen-tainte:** a heroic and respected 19th-century Kiowa chief known for his bold raids on both white and Native American settlements.

ANALYZE VISUALS

List the **images** you see in this collage. Which images portray aspects of nature?

Ⓐ MOOD AND FIGURATIVE LANGUAGE

Reread lines 1–6. Note the first several things that the poet compares himself to. What mood do these **metaphors** create?

Ⓑ REPETITION

Reread lines 19–24. Notice the **repetition** of certain phrases, such as "I stand" and "I am alive." What effect does this repetition create?

Details of Four Directions (1995), Jaune Quick-to-*
Smith. Lithograph with linocut collage, 44.5″ × 3*
Courtesy The Lawrence Lithography Worksh*
© Jaune Quick-to-See Smi*

DIFFERENTIATED INSTRUCTION

FOR LESS–PROFICIENT READERS

Comprehension Support Help students focus on the metaphors in this poem by completing a Spider Map like this one. Use the contents of the map to draw some conclusions about mood.

📦 **BEST PRACTICES TOOLKIT—Transparency** Spider Map p. B22

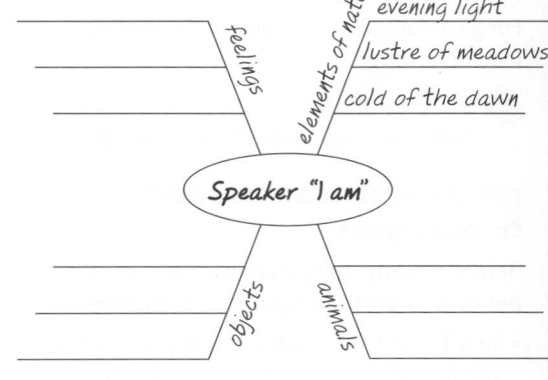

feelings
elements of nature
evening light
lustre of meadows
cold of the dawn
Speaker "I am"
objects
animals

BACKGROUND

Kiowas By the mid-1700s, the Kiowas had migrated from Montana to the southern plains. They were buffalo hunters as well as fierce warriors who frequently raided other settlements, carrying off horses and prisoners. In 1868, they moved onto a reservation in Oklahoma.

Tsen-Tainte Unhappy at the agreement that forced them onto the reservation, White Horse, or Tsen-Tainte, and others fought back. In the early 1870s, Tsen-Tainte led numerous raids on Texas settlements and engaged in battles with soldiers. His activities came to an end on April 19, 1875, when Texan troops overpowered the warriors during a battle. After being released from prison, Tsen-Tainte lived peacefully on the reservation until his death in 1892.

FOR ENGLISH LEARNERS
Comprehension: Task Support

1. Have students work in small groups. Assign each group a set of lines between 1 and 18.

2. Have students draw the images that the speaker compares himself to. Encourage students to use colors in a meaningful way.

3. Ask each group to display its set of images in order. Use the colors and figures in the drawings to help students arrive at a sense of the mood of the poem.

FOR ADVANCED LEARNERS/PRE–AP

Synthesize Have students write journal entries in which they do one of the following:

• describe their reaction to the poem
• use a line or image as a starting point for reflection
• identify connections between themselves and the text or between this poem and another work they have read
• explore the poem's theme

Invite students to share some of their entries in small groups.

LITERARY ANALYSIS

C MOOD AND FIGURATIVE LANGUAGE

Possible answers: *The trees*

- *"understand" the narrator (line 1)*
- *have "skinny necks," "pointy elbows," "hairy toes," and "violent teeth" (lines 2–3, 8)*
- *grab the earth with their toes and bite the sky (lines 7–8)*

By giving the trees human traits, the author is conveying the feeling of anger.

REINFORCE *KEY IDEA:* **COMPARISON**

Discuss Explain the narrator's **comparison** between a tree growing in a city and an angry person. What qualities do the tree and the person have in common? *Possible answers: Both are in a situation that is making them uncomfortable or unhappy. Both are ready to fight for their survival if necessary.*

LITERARY ANALYSIS

D MOOD AND FIGURATIVE LANGUAGE

Possible answer: *The mood created by this passage is one of determination.*

ANALYZE VISUALS

Possible answers: *The colors are bright and vigorous, suggesting energy and liveliness. The trees are a warm yellow-orange color against a cool background, making them stand out and seem brilliantly alive.*

Four Skinny Trees

Sandra Cisneros

They are the only ones who understand me. I am the only one who understands them. Four skinny trees with skinny necks and pointy elbows like mine. Four who do not belong here but are here. Four raggedy excuses planted by the city. From our room we can hear them, but Nenny just sleeps and doesn't appreciate these things.

Their strength is secret. They send ferocious roots beneath the ground. They grow up and they grow down and grab the earth between their hairy toes and bite the sky with violent teeth and never quit their anger. This is how they keep. **C**

10 Let one forget his reason for being, they'd all droop like tulips in a glass, each with their arms around the other. Keep, keep, keep, trees say when I sleep. They teach.

When I am too sad and too skinny to keep keeping, when I am a tiny thing against so many bricks, then it is I look at trees. When there is nothing left to look at on this street. Four who grew despite concrete. Four who reach and do not forget to reach. Four whose only reason is to be and be. **D**

C MOOD AND FIGURATIVE LANGUAGE
Reread lines 1–9. What human qualities do the trees have? What emotion is **personified**?

D MOOD AND FIGURATIVE LANGUAGE
Reread lines 13–17. What words and phrases stand out to you? Consider the **mood** and meaning these words and phrases create.

ANALYZE VISUALS
What feeling or emotion do the colors of this image suggest to you?

Detail of *Houses, Trees, Bike*, Anne Lavina Dimeur
© Anne Lavina Dimeur/Images.com

DIFFERENTIATED INSTRUCTION

FOR LESS–PROFICIENT READERS
Monitor Reading

1. Read aloud lines 1–5, pausing to make connections between the examples of personification and the mood.

2. Have pairs continue reading, following the same steps. Each partner should read and think aloud a few lines at a time.

3. Have students record their insights and any questions for follow-up discussion.

 **BEST PRACTICES TOOLKIT—Transparency**
Read Aloud/Think Aloud p. A34

FOR ENGLISH LEARNERS
Comprehension: Clarify

1. Draw a simple picture of a tree on the board. Have students help label the parts that would be the neck, the elbows, the teeth (biting the sky), and the toes.

2. Discuss how naming the parts of the tree in this way makes the tree seem like a person.

Lines 10–17
DISCUSSION PROMPTS

Use these prompts to help students understand the narrator's feelings:

Connect Think about a time when you felt discouraged. What helps people get over feelings of discouragement? *Students may say that the help of others or noticing someone else's example can help a person rebound.*

Interpret What does the narrator mean by saying, "When I am too sad and too skinny to keep keeping" (line 13)? ***Possible answer:*** *The phrase "keep keeping" means to keep going. The narrator says that sometimes it's just too difficult to continue to try.*

Synthesize Why is the narrator inspired by the trees? ***Possible answer:*** *The trees inspire the narrator because they can grow through concrete. They are able to survive even in the least favorable conditions. This gives the narrator hope and determination to overcome difficulties.*

SELECTION WRAP–UP

REFLECT Have students think about the importance of nature in both works. How does each writer use images from nature to help convey his or her main idea?

⭐ **CRITIQUE** Have students evaluate the style used by the author of "Four Skinny Trees" and explain whether or not they think it is effective. Does the use of incomplete sentences help bring out the author's ideas more clearly or not?

FOR ADVANCED LEARNERS/PRE–AP
Create a New Personification What if the "skinny trees" are not angry after all? Challenge students to personify the trees in a different way, perhaps using the art on page 605 as an inspiration. They might begin by thinking of another adjective to replace *skinny.* Have them write a brief response in the voice of one of the trees, refuting the narrator's points of comparison and providing a new interpretation. What new lesson might the trees impart?

Practice and Apply

After Reading

For additional support of post-reading questions, use this copy master:

R RESOURCE MANAGER—Copy Master Question Support p. 157 (**After Reading** questions adapted for English learners and less-proficient readers)

Additional selection questions are provided for teachers on page 151.

ANSWERS

Comprehension

1. *The speaker compares himself to a horse, a fish, an eagle, a deer, geese, and a wolf.*

2. *The narrator looks at the trees when feeling "too sad" and "too skinny."*

3. *Students' sketches should show an urban landscape with lots of brick and four thin trees.*

Literary Analysis

Possible answers:

4. ● **STANDARDS FOCUS** *Mood and* **Figurative Language** *Metaphors will vary. Students may say that the metaphors convey a sense of the power, playfulness, unpredictability, or loveliness of nature. The overall mood may be one of exhilaration, celebration, connection, or joy.*

5. *Momaday wishes to proclaim his membership in the Kiowa tribe or his good relations with the Kiowa people. He is proud that his people survived their historical conflicts with white settlers.*

6. *Both the trees and the narrator are skinny and tough. Both feel out of place in their cityscape. The narrator, determined to survive and hang on, identifies with the trees. The narrator admires the trees' strength and tenacity.*

7. *Students may say that the mood is determined.* **Personification:** *They "grab the earth between their hairy toes," they "bite the sky with violent teeth," and they "never quit their anger" (lines 7–8).*

Comprehension

MARYLAND OBJECTIVES

LITERATURE STANDARD
3.A.7.c Analyze figurative language

1. **Recall** In "The Delight Song of Tsoai-Talee," what animals does Tsoai-Talee compare himself to?

2. **Recall** In "Four Skinny Trees," when does the narrator look at the trees?

3. **Represent** What does the narrator's street look like? Make a sketch illustrating the scene.

Literary Analysis

4. **Analyze Figurative Language** In "The Delight Song of Tsoai-Talee," what three **metaphors** are especially vivid or imaginative? Explain the feeling you think each metaphor creates.

5. **Interpret Meaning** Reread "The Delight Song of Tsoai-Talee," N. Scott Momaday's biography on page 601, and footnote 2 on page 602. On the basis of this information, how do you interpret the meaning of lines 23–24?

6. **Make Inferences** In "Four Skinny Trees," which details about the trees could also be used to describe the narrator? Explain why the narrator might respond to the trees as she does.

7. **Analyze Mood** Is the overall mood of "Four Skinny Trees" sad, determined, hopeful, or something in between? Explain your opinion by citing three examples of **personification** that contribute to the mood.

Comparing Mood

Now that you've read both selections and answered some questions about them, fill in a chart like the one shown.

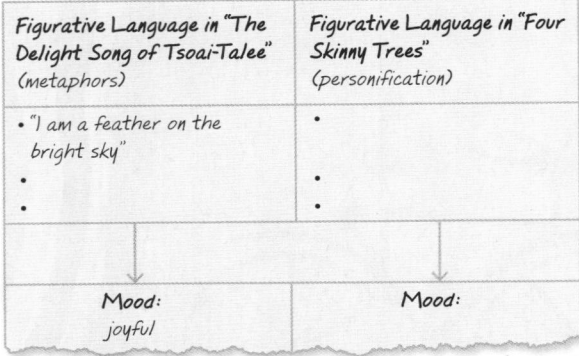

Figurative Language in "The Delight Song of Tsoai-Talee" (metaphors)	Figurative Language in "Four Skinny Trees" (personification)
• "I am a feather on the bright sky" • •	• • •
↓	↓
Mood: joyful	Mood:

Comparing Mood

■ **STANDARDS FOCUS** *Set a Purpose for* **Reading** *Students' charts should include details such as the following:*

Metaphors in "Delight Song": *"I am . . .*

- *the blue horse that runs . . .*
- *the fish that rolls . . .*
- *a cluster of bright beads . . .*
- *the farthest star . . .*
- *the glitter on the crust of the snow . . .*
- *a flame of four colors . . .*
- *an angle of geese . . ."*

Mood: *joyful, lively, energetic*

Personification in "Four Skinny Trees":

- *"They . . . understand me."*
- *"Four skinny trees with skinny necks and pointy elbows like mine."*
- *"They . . . grab the earth . . . and bite the sky . . . and never quit their anger."*
- *"Let one forget his reason for being, they'd all droop . . . each with their arms around the other."*
- *"Keep, keep, keep, trees say when I sleep."*
- *"They teach."*

Mood: *defiant, determined*

Writing for Assessment

1. READ THE PROMPT

In writing assessments, you will often be asked to explore how writers use language to create a mood. In this essay, you will focus on figurative language.

> **PROMPT**
>
> The poem "Tsoai-Talee" and the vignette "Four Skinny Trees" convey two very different moods. In four or five paragraphs, contrast the moods and explore how each author uses figurative language to help create that feeling. Support your ideas with details from both selections.

◀ **STRATEGY**

1. I have to describe the **feeling** each selection creates.

2. I need to tell the similarities and differences between the feelings.

3. I should **give examples** of the **figurative language** that create the different moods.

2. PLAN YOUR WRITING

Referring to your chart, note the figurative language and mood you identified for each selection. Then follow these steps.

- Write a statement that identifies the moods and describes the kinds of figurative language used to create each one.
- Use your chart to collect evidence to support your statement.
- Decide on a logical way to present your ideas, then make an outline. One example of how you might organize your paragraphs is shown here.

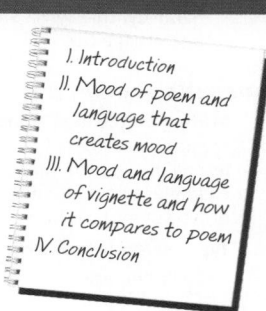

I. Introduction
II. Mood of poem and language that creates mood
III. Mood and language of vignette and how it compares to poem
IV. Conclusion

3. DRAFT YOUR RESPONSE

Introduction Introduce the selections and tell why you are comparing them. Include your statement of your main idea.

Body If you're using an outline similar to the one shown, explain how the language of the first selection creates a specific mood. Then start a new paragraph by telling how the second selection is similar or different.

Conclusion Leave your reader with a final thought about the way each author uses figurative language to create a specific mood.

Revision Make sure that the paragraphs after your introduction support the main idea you stated. If they don't, make changes to one or the other.

DIFFERENTIATED INSTRUCTION

FOR LESS–PROFICIENT WRITERS
Read the Prompt

Make sure students understand the meanings of significant terms: *mood, figurative language, metaphor, personification.*

Plan Your Writing

- Return to the chart on page 606. Decide on the mood of each work.
- Discuss the details that bring out the mood. Have students circle or list these examples on their charts.

Draft Your Response Provide this template:

Introduction The mood of [title of poem] by [poet] is [adjective from chart]. The mood of [title of vignette] by [author] is [adjective].

Middle paragraphs

- Metaphors are used to create the mood of the poem. [Explain examples.]
- Personification creates the mood of the vignette. [Explain examples.]

Conclusion [Restate the mood of each and explain the effect on you as the reader.]

Writing for Assessment

1. **READ THE PROMPT**

   - Read the prompt aloud. Ask volunteers to identify key words that define the task.
   - Have volunteers read aloud each strategy and identify the part of the chart on page 606 from which they will draw information to implement the strategy.

2. **PLAN YOUR WRITING**

   - Help students analyze each metaphor or example of personification to determine how it supports mood. For example, the metaphor "I am a cluster of bright beads" suggests happiness and brightness.
   - Tell students that for the poem, they should choose only the metaphors that most vividly evoke mood in their minds.

3. **DRAFT YOUR RESPONSE**

   - Remind students to begin each body paragraph with a topic sentence that connects mood and figurative language. For example, "The defiant mood of 'Four Skinny Trees' grows from the specific human traits with which the author personifies the trees."
   - Explain methods of ordering details within each paragraph. Students may wish to follow the order of the original work, cluster similar ideas, or discuss details from the least to the most important.

   R **RESOURCE MANAGER—Copy Master**
   Writing for Assessment p. 158

Assess and Reteach

Assess

R **RESOURCE MANAGER—Copy Masters**
Selection Tests A, B/C pp. 159–160, 161–162

💿 Test Generator CD

Reteach

S **STANDARDS LESSON FILE**
Literature Lesson 36: Mood
Literature Lesson 27: Simile and Metaphor
Literature Lesson 28: Personification
Writing Lesson 29: Comparison-Contrast Essay

Focus and Motivate

OBJECTIVES

- analyze a student model that reflects the key traits of a personal response to a poem
- use the writing process to write a personal response to a poem
- support key points with quotes and details
- revise and edit, using a rubric for a personal response to a poem
- perform an oral interpretation of a poem

WRITER'S ROAD MAP

WRITING PROMPTS 1 AND 2

Help students choose a prompt by brainstorming a list of poems they have read in class or a list of songs they have heard on the radio. For each poem or song, have them tell what the work was about and how it made them feel.

ADDITIONAL PROMPTS

Use these prompts for practice with writing a personal response.

WRITING PROMPT 3

Writing for the Real World Write a movie review for your school newspaper. Explain what the movie is about and your reaction to it.

Subjects to Consider

- an action/adventure movie
- a science fiction/fantasy movie
- a romantic comedy

WRITING PROMPT 4

Writing About Fine Art Write an essay for an art magazine. Describe a painting and explain your response to it. Find your subject in an art book, in this textbook, or on an art museum's Web site.

Ideas to Consider

- a landscape painting
- a portrait painting
- an abstract painting

For additional writing prompts, see

 Write*Smart* CD

 Writing Center at **ClassZone.com**

KEY TRAITS

Review the six *KEY TRAITS*, focusing primarily on ideas and organization. Compare these traits with the rubric on page 614.

Writing Workshop

Personal Response to a Poem

When you respond to a poem, you think about its meaning, but your focus is personal. You discuss your own reactions, feelings, or experiences as well as the language and style of the poem. The **Writer's Road Map** will show you how.

WRITER'S ROAD MAP

Personal Response to a Poem

WRITING PROMPT 1

Writing from Literature Choose a poem that caused strong feelings in you. Write a personal response that explains why the poem made you feel the way you did. Briefly describe the poem so that readers unfamiliar with it can understand your response.

Poems to Consider
- "The Highwayman"
- "Sarah Cynthia Sylvia Stout Would Not Take the Garbage Out"

WRITING PROMPT 2

Writing for the Real World Write an essay for a music magazine that describes your response to a song or a type of music. Give readers specific examples to help them understand why the song or type of music is important to you.

Types of Music to Explore
- rap or hip-hop
- rock
- country

 WRITING TOOLS
For prewriting, revision, and editing tools, visit the **Writing Center** at **ClassZone.com**.

KEY TRAITS

1. IDEAS
- Clearly presents an **overall response** to the work
- Supports key points with **details and quotations**

2. ORGANIZATION
- Identifies the title and author of the work in the **introduction**
- Gives enough **information about the work** for readers to understand the response
- Includes **transitional words and phrases**
- Summarizes the response in a **conclusion**

3. VOICE
- **Tone** is honest and engaging

4. WORD CHOICE
- Uses **literary terms** when describing the work

5. SENTENCE FLUENCY
- Varies **sentence beginnings**

6. CONVENTIONS
- Uses **correct grammar, spelling, and punctuation**

Writing Workshop Resources

 RESOURCE MANAGER UNIT 5

Plan and Teach pp. 163–166
Prewriting–Editing pp. 167–171
Writing Rubric p. 172
Speaking and Listening p. 173
Writing Support p. 174*

STANDARDS LESSON FILE
Writing Lessons 33, 38, 44
Grammar Lesson 1

BEST PRACTICES TOOLKIT

Scaffolding Writing Instruction pp. 43–46*
Analysis Frame: Poetic Language and Style •
Writing Template: Reflective Essay

TECHNOLOGY
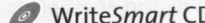 Easy Planner DVD
Writing Center at **ClassZone.com**
Write*Smart* CD

* Resources for Differentiation

Part 1: Analyze a Student Model

WRITING STANDARD
4.A.5.b Explain how the specific language and expression used by the writer affects response

 INTERACTIVE MODEL
CLASSZONE.COM

Kenetha Smithson
Lewiston Middle School

"Sleeping in the Forest"

Some people can't live for even a single night without the Internet or TV. Camping is definitely not for them. For me, though, nothing beats a night outside under the stars. That's why I knew what Mary Oliver was talking about when I read "Sleeping in the Forest." When I go
5   camping, I have some of the same feelings and experiences as the speaker in the poem, even though I don't talk about them in the same way.

Mary Oliver begins her poem by showing the speaker already on the ground, or earth, in the forest. She writes, "I thought the earth / remembered me, she / took me back so tenderly." To Oliver, the earth
10   is a woman with "dark skirts" and pockets full of moss and seeds. Using personification, which means giving human qualities to something that isn't human, Oliver makes the earth seem like an old friend. When I sleep out on the ground, it sometimes feels as if I belong there. Familiar and soft, the earth does feel like a friend.

15   The speaker says that while sleeping in the forest, there is "nothing / between me and the white fire of the stars / but my thoughts." That's how it is when I'm out in the wilderness. I can think better because there are no interruptions from other people and no music or TVs. The speaker uses the simile "light as moths" to show how thoughts float
20   away. This tells exactly how my own thoughts seem to float away or take off into the air because I feel so calm and peaceful.

KEY TRAITS IN ACTION

Introduction identifies the title and author and clearly presents an **overall response** to the poem.

Gives **information about the work** so readers can understand the response. Varied **sentence beginnings** add sophistication.

Uses **literary terms** when describing the work. A simile is a comparison that uses *like* or *as*.

Teach

Part 1: Analyze a Student Model

Have students read the **Student Model** and **Key Traits in Action.** Then discuss the model, helping students identify specific examples of each trait. You may also wish to incorporate the following activities:

- **Sentence Beginnings** Point out that good writers use different sentence beginnings for emphasis and variety. Ask students how the writer emphasizes an important idea in line 14. *(By placing "Familiar and soft" at the beginning, the writer draws attention to these qualities of the earth.)*

Write these sentences on the board and have students rewrite them, beginning with the underlined words:

> I feel at home <u>under the forest canopy</u>.

> The bear was <u>snuffling and snorting</u> as it poked its nose into my knapsack.

> I like to sleep outside the tent <u>because the best part of camping is seeing all the stars</u>.

- **Literary Terms** Explain that using precise literary terms gives readers the sense that the writer really knows what he or she is talking about. Have students name literary terms that could be used to discuss

  — the voice in the poem that talks about sleeping in the forest *(speaker)*

  — a specific description that helps readers see and hear the forest *(image)*

  — how a sleeping person is called "a stone on the riverbed" *(metaphor)*

DIFFERENTIATED INSTRUCTION

FOR ALL STUDENTS
For general guidelines on differentiating writing instruction, see

 BEST PRACTICES TOOLKIT
Scaffolding Writing Instruction
pp. 43–46

FOR ENGLISH LEARNERS
Language: Skill Words Write these terms on the board and review them with students:

- *overall response:* a general feeling or attitude about something. For example, a poem may make you feel happy or sad. You may agree or disagree with the writer's ideas.

- *quotations:* words, phrases, or complete sentences copied exactly from the work. Example: "dark skirts" (line 10)

- *tone:* the writer's attitude toward his or her subject. For example, an essay may be serious or funny, formal or informal. In lines 2–3—"For me, though, nothing beats a night outside under the stars"—the tone is personal and straightforward.

- *literary terms:* words that describe specific devices used by writers to make their work more vivid, interesting, entertaining, or meaningful. Examples: *personification* (line 11), *simile* (line 19)

- **Transitions** Tell students that transitions are like road signs that let readers know where they are and where they're going. Without transitions, an essay would just be a confusing and disorganized collection of ideas. Transitions provide order and structure. For example, when a reader sees the highlighted phrase in line 22, he or she thinks, *Oh, I see, each paragraph is describing something the writer likes about camping. In this paragraph, she's going to describe one more.*

- **Details and Quotations** Point out that an effective response essay needs a good balance of details and quotations. Details make the writer's ideas clear and vivid for the reader. Quotations help the reader understand exactly what the writer is responding to in the poem.

  Read aloud the first part of the sentence that begins in line 25:

  > *Campers hear the little sounds that are hard to hear indoors....*

  Discuss how the details "rustling leaves" and "hooting owls" (line 26) clarify what the "little sounds" are, and how the quotation (lines 26–27) shows the specific part of the poem on which the writer's response is based.

- **Conclusion** Remind students that the conclusion is the last chance for the writer to influence the reader. A good conclusion restates the main points of the essay and explains why the writer feels the way he or she does. A conclusion may even challenge the reader to act or think differently. Discuss how the conclusion in the model accomplishes these purposes.

For interactive student models, see

Write*Smart* CD

Writing Center at **ClassZone.com**

Another great thing about camping is how quiet it is. In the poem, the speaker hears "the small kingdoms breathing / around me." I believe the speaker is describing all of the new worlds that a camper
25 experiences. Campers hear the little sounds that are hard to hear indoors, such as rustling leaves and hooting owls—"the birds / who do their work in the darkness."

In the last lines of the poem, I think the speaker is talking about dreams or a really deep, great sleep. The poem mentions vanishing "into
30 something better." Maybe the "something better" is a good dream. When I'm camping, I think I sleep more deeply in the fresh air. In the morning, I remember many dreams. Sleeping in the forest is like vanishing into a better place.

I believe that people who don't like camping should read this poem.
35 It can help them understand what it feels like to be outside in nature at night. The poem might even convince some people to go camping. Then maybe they could also sleep "as never before," as Oliver says, and get rid of their worries for a little while. Maybe they could even vanish "into something better."

Transitional phrase helps the reader understand how the response is organized.

Details and quotations explain and support the response.

The writer's **tone** is straightforward and thoughtful throughout the essay.

The writer summarizes the response in a satisfying **conclusion.**

2

DIFFERENTIATED INSTRUCTION

FOR ENGLISH LEARNERS

Comprehension: Transitions On the board, copy the sentence that begins in line 7 of the model. Ask students to identify the transition used in writing about the poem. *("Mary Oliver begins her poem")* Then have students work independently to find two other transitions in the model. *(line 22: "Another great thing"; line 28: "In the last lines of the poem")*

R RESOURCE MANAGER—Copy Master
Writing Support p. 174

Part 2: Apply the Writing Process

WRITING STANDARD
4.A.1 Compose texts using prewriting and drafting strategies

PREWRITING

What Should I Do?

1. Create a reading log.
Make a two-column chart. On one side, list words and phrases from the work that caught your attention. On the other side, write your reactions, comments, or questions. When you are finished, (circle) the responses that seem most important to you.

2. Write down your overall response.
Use your circled comments and questions to develop a sentence or two that explains how the work made you feel and why it made you feel that way.

> **TIP** Your response statement doesn't have to be perfect. You can change it when you draft and revise.

3. Look for more support.
Find more words and phrases that affected your response. Examine the poem for images that helped you see or hear what the poet is describing, unusual word choices, or phrases that made you smile or wonder.

What Does It Look Like?

Words/Phrases	My Response
"she / took me back"	I belong there. The earth is like a friend that takes me back.
sleep like "a stone"	When I go camping, I sleep really well.
"floated / light as moths"	What does this mean?
"something better"	Sleep is different outside. It's better & deeper, & I have good dreams.

Working Response:
I know what Mary Oliver is saying in her poem because I know what it's like to sleep on the ground and dream.

Images:
"nothing / between me and the white fire of the stars / but my thoughts": It's so quiet in the forest—no TVs, no music.

"small kingdoms": I hear the insects and little animals, and I know there are other worlds out there.

FOR ENGLISH LEARNERS

Writing an Overall Response Give students the following sentence starters to help them create a working response statement:

- The beginning of the poem made me feel _____. I felt this way because _____.
- The middle of the poem made me feel _____. I felt this way because _____.
- The ending of the poem made me feel _____. I felt this way because _____.
- In general, the poem makes me feel _____.

FOR ADVANCED LEARNERS/PRE–AP

Compare and Contrast Ask students to find a second poem on the same topic. Have them use the Poetic Language and Style analysis frame to write a more complex essay in which they explore how each work made them feel differently and why.

 BEST PRACTICES TOOLKIT—Transparency
Analysis Frame: Poetic Language and Style pp. D23, D40

Practice and Apply

To support students during the writing process, use these copy masters:

R RESOURCE MANAGER—Copy Masters
Prewriting–Editing pp. 167–171
Writing Rubric p. 172
Speaking and Listening p. 173
Writing Support p. 174 *(for English learners)*

Part 2: Apply the Writing Process

PREWRITING

1. **Create a reading log.** Be sure that students use quotation marks around words and phrases taken from the work. Remind students that their responses do not have to be in complete sentences at this point. Help them recognize that each response they circle may become the main idea of a paragraph.

2. **Write down your overall response.** If students are having difficulty with this step, remind them that it is often helpful to talk out their ideas first. Working with partners, have them tell each other how they felt and explain why. Students' partners should advise them as to whether their overall response is clear. If so, students should write down roughly what they said. Remind students of the **TIP** in step 2.

3. **Look for more support.** Remind students that when looking over a poem for the second or third time, they are likely to notice interesting details that they overlooked before. The details that they find will provide development for the body paragraphs of their essays. However, caution students that they should choose only the best examples to include in their essays. After they have listed additional items for more support, they should use a highlighter to mark those details that they want to include in their writing.

For interactive graphic organizers, see

@ Write*Smart* CD

ⓘ Writing Center at **ClassZone.com**

DRAFTING

1. **Develop an informal outline.** Remind students that once they choose a pattern of organization, they must use it throughout the entire essay. Have them study the model outline. Ask: What do all the **A** entries have in common? What do all the **B** entries have in common? (*The A entries give details from the poem. The B entries refer to the writer's response to those details.*)

2. **Make a fresh beginning!** A strong opening makes the reader want to continue reading. Write this sentence on the board:

   The poem I read for my report is "Sleeping in the Forest" by Mary Oliver.

   Ask students why this opening is weaker than the one in the **Student Model**. (*It does not create interest or say anything about the writer's response to the poem. The model's opening has a friendly tone and engages readers' interest with specific references to the Internet, TV, and camping.*)

3. **Clearly explain your response.** Suggest that students review the **Student Model** for examples of explanations of the writer's responses. Draw their attention to lines 3–7, 13–14, 16–18, 20–21, 22–26, 31–33, 35–39. Remind students to refer back to their reading logs as a source of explanations for their own responses.

For personal-response writing templates, see

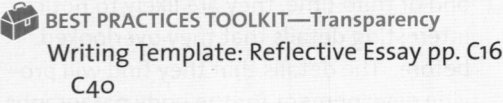
   BEST PRACTICES TOOLKIT—Transparency
     Writing Template: Reflective Essay pp. C16, C40

   WriteSmart CD

   Writing Center at ClassZone.com

DRAFTING

What Should I Do?	What Does It Look Like?

1. Develop an informal outline. Making an outline can help you organize your ideas. This writer organized her response from the beginning to the end of the poem. You can organize your response from the most important idea to the least important idea. You can also briefly summarize the work and then explain your reaction to it.	**I.** Lines 1–5
	  A. The earth "took me back so tenderly."
	  B. The earth seems like an old friend to me, too.
	II. Lines 5–11
	  A. The speaker describes "the white fire of the stars."
	  B. I think the wilderness is calm, peaceful, and beautiful.
	III. Lines 10–14
	  A. The speaker hears "small kingdoms breathing."
	  B. I hear sounds of nature when camping.
	IV. Lines 14–18
	  A. The speaker vanishes "into something better."
	  B. I can sleep well in the fresh air.

2. Make a fresh beginning! Draw your reader in by starting out with a surprising or dramatic statement, an interesting or startling fact, a little bit of humor, or a question.	**A dramatic statement** Some people can't live for even a single night without the Internet or TV. Camping is definitely not for them. **A question** Have you ever slept under the stars?
3. Clearly explain your response. Don't just say, "I liked this" or "I liked that." Explain your responses. The writer of this essay described the memories the poem triggered in her. **TIP** Before you revise, look back at the key traits on page 608 and at the **rubric** and peer-reader questions on page 614.	Maybe the "something better" is a good dream. ⎤ Writer's response When I'm camping, I think I sleep more deeply in the fresh air. In the morning, I remember many dreams. Sleeping in the forest is like vanishing into a better place. ⎤ Reasons for response

612   UNIT 5: APPRECIATING POETRY

DIFFERENTIATED INSTRUCTION

FOR LESS–PROFICIENT WRITERS

Develop an Informal Outline Explain that some type of outline is necessary for all good writing. Without an outline, a writer may forget to include important information. The writer might also discuss ideas in the order in which he or she thinks of them, which could result in a confusing, random order. Provide this frame to help students organize their essays using a least-important-to-most-important pattern.

Opening Paragraph
- Introduce the subject.
- In your thesis, clearly state your overall response to the subject.

Middle Paragraphs (Number will vary.)
- Present the least important part of your response and explain the reasons for it.
- Present a more important part of your response and explain the reasons.
- Present the most important part of your response and explain the reasons.

Concluding Paragraph
- Briefly restate each part of your response.
- Restate in a different way the overall response stated in your thesis.

Be certain students understand that leading up to their most important idea is an effective technique for convincing a reader to agree with their viewpoint.

REVISING AND EDITING

What Should I Do?	What Does It Look Like?

1. Be sure to give enough information.
- Can your reader understand your reaction to the work? Ask a peer reader to underline parts of your response that lack background information.
- Add details and quotations that tell about the work.

See page 614: Ask a Peer Reader

▶ "the ___ breathing / around me."
The speaker hears ~~small kingdoms~~ I believe the
all of the
speaker is describing new worlds, that a camper
experiences. Campers hear the little sounds that
are hard to hear indoors, such as rustling leaves
and hooting owls.

2. Be precise: use literary terms.
- (Circle) literary terms, such as *personification*, *simile*, and *speaker*.
- If you have few or no circles, revise to make your response more specific.

▶ Using personification, which means giving human
qualities to something that isn't human, Oliver
makes the earth seem
~~The earth seems~~ like an old friend.

3. Use different sentence beginnings.
- Draw a box around words you have repeated at the beginnings of sentences.
- Combine, break up, or rewrite these sentences to change the way they start.

▶ In ___ , I think the speaker is talking
~~I think~~ the last two lines of the poem, talk
about dreams or a really deep, great sleep.
The poem mentions
~~I think~~ ~~that's what~~ vanishing "into something
Maybe the
better" means. ~~I think~~ "something better" is a
good dream.

4. Show how your response is organized.
- Highlight transitional words, phrases, or sentences in your response.
- If you have few or no highlights, add transitions. These help your reader by specifying which part of the poem you are discussing or by explaining that you are introducing a new idea.

▶ begins her poem by showing
Mary Oliver ~~shows~~ the speaker   } Tells which part of the poem
already on the ground ...

Another great thing about
camping is how quiet it is. In the   } Introduces new idea
poem, the speaker hears ...

REVISING AND EDITING

1. Be sure to give enough information. Point out that two or three examples are often better than just one. If students find that they need more information, suggest that they look back to their reading logs and to their drafts. They could also reread the poem for details they may have overlooked.

2. Be precise: use literary terms. Have students review the poetry lessons in this unit for terms they might use in their essays. Examples include *imagery*, *personification*, *metaphor*, *simile*, *line*, *stanza*, *rhyme*, *rhythm*, *meter*, *symbol*, *onomatopoeia*, and *alliteration*. Remind them not to confuse the *speaker* of a poem with the *poet*. For example, just because the poet is female, the speaker is not necessarily a "she."

3. Use different sentence beginnings. Have students consider these options for varying sentence beginnings:

- Start with a prepositional phrase, like *in the first stanza* or *under the stars*.
- Swap the order of clauses—*Because I love camping, I love this poem* rather than *I love this poem because I love camping*.
- Move adjectives to the beginning—*Dark and still, the forest allows me to dream*.

4. Show how your response is organized. Remind students that transitions are often useful at the start of a new paragraph. References to line numbers or stanzas make good transitions. *Therefore* is a good transition to a concluding paragraph.

For interactive revision tools, see

⊘ Write*Smart* CD

ⓘ Writing Center at **ClassZone.com**

FOR ENGLISH LEARNERS

Using Different Sentence Beginnings Provide additional opportunities for students to practice sentence beginnings. Help students complete these sentence frames.

- _____ is my favorite sport.
- On _____, I like to sleep late.
- After _____, I like to go to the mall.
- If _____, I will go to the lake on Saturday.
- Because _____, I missed the bus to school.

FOR ADVANCED LEARNERS/PRE–AP

Using Literary Terms Remind students that *simile* and *personification* are types of figurative language, statements that are not meant to be understood literally. Other types include *metaphor*, *hyperbole* (exaggeration), and *apostrophe* (address of an absent person, an idea, or an object). Challenge students to define each term, find three examples of each, place them on index cards including the title and author, and share them with the class.

Preparing to Publish

Support for meeting the goals in the writing rubric is supplied throughout the **Writing Workshop** on pages 608–613.

For Rubric Bank, see

 WriteSmart CD

🛈 Writing Center at ClassZone.com

Assess and Reteach

After reading and assessing students' essays, you might use these lessons to reteach key skills:

5 STANDARDS LESSON FILE
Writing Lesson 33: Writing About Literature
Writing Lesson 44: Using Precise Words
Grammar Lesson 1: Avoiding Sentence Fragments

Apply the Rubric

A strong personal response to a poem . . .

☑ begins by stating the title, the author, and an overall response

☑ contains enough background information for the reader to follow the response

☑ has an honest and consistent tone

☑ is clearly organized and includes transitions

☑ quotes words and phrases from the poem and fully explains the writer's reaction to them

☑ includes literary terms to describe the work

☑ varies sentence beginnings to make ideas flow smoothly

☑ has a conclusion that summarizes the response

Ask a Peer Reader

- Do parts of my response need more background information?
- How could I make my overall response to the poem clearer?
- Where do I need more quotations?

Check Your Grammar

- Avoid dangling modifiers. Make sure that every modifier you use relates to a word in the sentence.

  This phrase dangles. The sentence is missing the word that the phrase should modify.

  > Using personification, the earth seems like an old friend.

  This sentence tells who is using personification.

  > Using personification, Oliver makes the earth seem like an old friend.

  See page R59: Dangling Modifiers

- Correct fragments—groups of words that are punctuated like sentences but are missing a subject, are missing a predicate, or fail to express complete thought.

  > ~~A familiar feeling, like an old friend.~~
  > It feels familiar, like an old friend.

  See page R64: Correcting Fragments

Writing Online

 PUBLISHING OPTIONS
For publishing options, visit the **Writing Center** at ClassZone.com.

ASSESSMENT PREPARATION
For writing and grammar assessment practice, go to the **Assessment Center** at ClassZone.com.

SPEAKING STANDARD
7.A.1 Demonstrate appropriate delivery techniques for oral presentations

SPEAKING AND LISTENING

Oral Interpretation of a Poem

Now that you've written about a poem in your own voice, you can perform one in your own voice too.

Planning the Oral Interpretation

1. **Read the poem aloud.** Listen for places to shout or whisper, mourn or celebrate. Decide when the poem should race or crawl. Think about where you can add body language.

2. **Create your own reading guide.** Use capital letters for words you want to say loudly. Underline words you want to say softly. Add slashes for pauses and hyphens to link words that you plan to run together. You might also try stretching out syllables. Add notes for gestures and facial expressions too.

> I slept /
> as NEVER before, / _a stone_ /   (never: shake head)
> _on the riverbed,_ /
> _nothing_-between-me /
> and the WHITE FIRE of the stars /   (white fire: look up)
> but my thoughts, /
> and they FLOOOATED light as moths   (floated: gently wave arm)

3. **Practice to make it perfect.** Read the poem aloud several times. Then practice your performance for a classmate. Get feedback, adjust, and practice some more.

Performing the Oral Interpretation

1. **Don't be nervous!** Instead, think like an actor and get into your performance. If you're nervous about your classmates' reactions, look just over the tops of their heads.

2. **Find out how you did.** Ask a few classmates for feedback on your performance. Were your volume, pacing, and gestures effective? Think about what you might do differently next time.

See page R80: Evaluate an Oral Interpretation

WRITING WORKSHOP **615**

SPEAKING AND LISTENING

Ask students to read this page to get an overview of how to perform an oral interpretation of a poem. Before students begin working, review this rubric with them so that they understand their goals:

Rubric A strong oral interpretation

- presents a poem that is appropriate to read out loud
- varies tone of voice to reflect the emotion of the lines
- varies pace of delivery to reflect the sense of what is happening
- uses body language, gestures, and facial expressions to enhance the performance
- uses a copy of the poem with reminders on points of delivery
- has been practiced and improved by feedback from others
- is presented with confidence

R RESOURCE MANAGER—Copy Master
Speaking and Listening p. 173

S STANDARDS LESSON FILE
Speaking and Listening Lesson 8: Oral Interpretation

DIFFERENTIATED INSTRUCTION

FOR ALL STUDENTS

Additional Tips Share these tips with students as they prepare for their presentations.

- Take time to reflect on how the poem makes you feel. When you perform the poem, you'll want to use a tone that gives audience members the same feeling.

- When creating your reading guide, remember that the punctuation and capitalization used by the poet can help you determine when to pause, slow down, or speed up, as well as which words to emphasize.

FOR LESS–PROFICIENT WRITERS

Planning an Oral Presentation Explain that poems are meant to be read out loud, but some are more appropriate for this activity than others. Help students select an appropriate example by having them think about these questions:

- Is the poem too long or too short?
- Does the poem provide opportunities to display emotion when performing it?
- Can I pronounce all the words correctly, and do I know what they mean?

As students prepare for their performances, have them ask themselves these questions:

- Do I pause when there are punctuation marks?
- Do I read without pausing at the end of a line if there is no punctuation mark?
- Do I lower my voice at the end of a sentence and raise my voice if there is a question?
- Do I have a plan to control feeling nervous?

WRITING WORKSHOP **615**

Assessment Practice

CHECK READINESS

Read aloud the paragraph under **ASSESS** and stress to students that this is not the full Unit Test but a way for them to check their readiness for it. Then have students examine the skills listed under **REVIEW** and look back in the unit or in the Handbook for any skills they need to study.

READ THE SELECTION

Remind students to keep unit goals in mind as they read each poem, paying particular attention to

- imagery
- figurative language
- sound devices
- their own inferences

To help students focus on **imagery** while reading, encourage them to ask questions such as

- What are some of the vivid images in these poems? To which of my senses do these images appeal?
- How do these images help me understand the poet's purpose and meaning?

ANSWER THE QUESTIONS

Direct students to pages R93–R99 of the Test-Taking Handbook to review test-taking strategies. Remind them not to choose the first alternative that seems to fit when answering a multiple-choice question. Instead, they should read through all the choices, eliminate any that are clearly wrong, and then choose the best answer—the one that is most accurate and complete.

Warn students not to look for patterns in their answers. Although a series of answers sometimes falls into a particular order—such as A, B, C, D—it is only coincidental, not intentional. Each test item should be evaluated independently and answered using evidence from the poem or the student's own knowledge. Answers to previous questions should not influence later choices.

Assessment Practice

ASSESS
The practice test items on the next few pages match skills listed on the Unit Goals page (page 541) and addressed throughout this unit. Taking this practice test will help you assess your knowledge of these skills and determine your readiness for the Unit Test.

REVIEW
After you take the practice test, your teacher can help you identify any skills you need to review.

- Imagery
- Figurative Language
- Sound Devices
- Make Inferences
- Connotation
- Sentence Types
- Active Voice

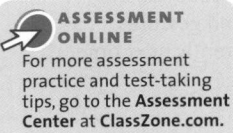

ASSESSMENT ONLINE
For more assessment practice and test-taking tips, go to the **Assessment Center at ClassZone.com.**

Reading Comprehension

DIRECTIONS *Read these poems and answer the questions that follow.*

Ode to enchanted light

Pablo Neruda

Under the trees light
has dropped from the top of the sky,
light
like a green
5 latticework of branches,
shining
on every leaf,
drifting down like clean
white sand.

10 A cicada sends
its sawing song
high into the empty air.

The world is
a glass overflowing
15 with water.

DIFFERENTIATED INSTRUCTION

FOR ENGLISH LEARNERS

Assessment Practice: Work Backwards
Prepare students for the assessment by having them "work backwards," reading the questions before reading the poems. Have pairs follow these steps to learn unfamiliar words in the test directions and questions:

1. Find words you don't recognize and write each one on an index card.
2. Look up the meaning in a dictionary.
3. Write the meaning on the back of the card.

4. Use your word cards to teach and practice the vocabulary with your partner and another pair.

Review Academic Vocabulary List these words on the board: *imagery, simile, metaphor, personification, alliteration.* Work together to review their definitions and discuss examples from the unit.

Snow in the Suburbs

Thomas Hardy

Every branch big with it,
  Bent every twig with it;
  Every fork like a white web-foot;
  Every street and pavement mute:
5 Some flakes have lost their way, and grope back upward, when
Meeting those meandering down they turn and descend again.
  The palings are glued together like a wall,
  And there is no waft of wind with the fleecy fall.

  A sparrow enters the tree,
10   Whereon immediately
  A snow-lump thrice his own slight size
  Descends on him and showers his head and eyes,
    And overturns him,
    And near inurns him,
15   And lights on a nether twig, when its brush
Starts off a volley of other lodging lumps with a rush.

  The steps are a blanched slope,
  Up which, with feeble hope,
  A black cat comes, wide-eyed and thin;
20   And we take him in.

 GO ON

ITEM ANALYSIS

COMPREHENSION AND BRIEF CONSTRUCTED RESPONSE	ITEMS	UNIT PAGES
Imagery	1, 3, 4, 6	546, 549
Figurative Language	5, 7, 8, 10, 12	546, 555, 601
Sound Devices	2, 9, 11, 15	544, 563, 571, 593
Make Inferences	13, 14, 16	555

VOCABULARY	ITEMS	UNIT PAGES
Connotation	1–6	580

WRITING AND GRAMMAR	ITEMS	UNIT PAGES
Sentence Types	1, 4	561, 613
Active Voice	2, 3	581

 MSA PREPARATION

McDougal Littell Assessment System

After checking student readiness with this Assessment Practice, you may administer the complete Unit 5 Test, which matches the structure and format of the MSA.

FOR LESS–PROFICIENT READERS

Assessment Support Consider these options for completing the **Assessment Practice:**

- Read the selections or parts of them aloud to aid in student comprehension.

- Select random questions in the assessment and have students demonstrate how and where to look for the answers.

- Have students record useful test words and definitions in their journals for later reference.

FOR ENGLISH LEARNERS

Vocabulary Support Review this vocabulary before students read the poems:

"Ode to enchanted light"
- *ode,* "lyric poem with a serious tone"
- *enchanted,* "magical"
- *latticework* (line 5), "open framework with a crisscross pattern"
- *cicada* (line 10), "insect that makes a high-pitched droning sound"

"Snow in the Suburbs"
- *mute* (line 4), "silent"
- *meandering* (line 6), "wandering"
- *palings* (line 7), "sticks that form a fence"
- *fleecy* (line 8), "like wool"
- *thrice* (line 11), "three times"
- *inurns* (line 14), "buries"
- *nether* (line 15), "lower"
- *volley* (line 16), "a bursting forth of many things at the same time"
- *blanched* (line 17), "made white"

Comprehension

Model a thinking process for answering multiple-choice questions.

1. **C is correct.** *Lines 3–9 appeal to sight. Lines 10–12 appeal to the sense of hearing. No images in the poem appeal to touch, taste, or smell, making A, B, and D incorrect.*

2. **B is correct.** *The d sound is alliterated in "drifting down." A, C, and D contain no repetition of consonant sounds at the beginnings of words.*

3. **B is correct.** *The word like is used to compare the light to a latticework of tree branches. A is incorrect because it is not a comparison. C is an example of alliteration and does not compare two things using like or as. D is a metaphor.*

4. **C is correct.** *In this image, light is compared to particles of white sand slowly falling down. This image helps readers see how the light looks. A, B, and D are incorrect because they refer to other senses besides sight.*

5. **B is correct.** *In these lines, the world is compared to an overflowing glass with the direct statement "The world is / a glass overflowing." Without the word like or as, this comparison is a metaphor, not a simile as in A. The world is not given human characteristics, so C is incorrect. Nor do the lines contain words that sound like their meanings. Therefore, D is incorrect.*

6. **C is correct.** *A glass overflowing with water suggests abundance and life. It conveys positive feelings. A, B, and D are incorrect because they name negative emotions.*

7. **D is correct.** *The first three lines describe the branches of a tree, heavy with snow. Therefore, within the context of that part of the poem, "fork" refers to a branch with two or more offshoots. A is incorrect because there is no mention of a spider. B is incorrect because it does not fit the context of the poem. The line in which "fork" appears is separated from the reference to streets and pavements by a semicolon, making C also incorrect.*

8. **D is correct.** *In line 4, the streets and pavements are described as "mute" or speechless. This adjective creates the impression of silence. The images in A, B, and C have nothing to do with sound. Therefore, they are incorrect.*

9. **B is correct.** *Line 8 repeats the soft consonant sounds of w and f, emphasizing the softness and silence of the snow falling. A is incorrect, since the rhythm created by the line's sounds is slow. Neither C nor D is supported by the words or sound of the line.*

10. **B is correct.** *Palings is another word for the wood spikes that form a fence. In addition, the word like is used to compare the palings to a wall. A, C, and D are not similes.*

11. **C is correct.** *The rhyme scheme is primarily couplets throughout the poem. A, B, and D do not accurately describe the pattern of rhyme in the poem.*

Comprehension

Comprehension

DIRECTIONS *Answer these questions about "Ode to enchanted light."*

1. The imagery in Neruda's poem appeals primarily to the senses of
   A. taste and sight
   B. touch and taste
   C. sight and hearing
   D. smell and touch

2. Which one of the following lines contains alliteration?
   A. "latticework of branches" (line 5)
   B. "drifting down like clean" (line 8)
   C. "high into the empty air" (line 12)
   D. "a glass overflowing" (line 14)

3. Which one of the following images is an example of a simile?
   A. "light / has dropped from the top of the sky" (lines 1–2)
   B. "light / like a green / latticework of branches" (lines 3–5)
   C. "its sawing song" (line 11)
   D. "The world is / a glass overflowing / with water." (lines 13–15)

4. The image of the light "drifting down like clean / white sand" appeals to the sense of
   A. hearing
   B. smell
   C. sight
   D. taste

5. Which type of figurative language does the author use in lines 13–15?
   A. simile
   B. metaphor
   C. personification
   D. onomatopoeia

6. The image in lines 13–15 suggests that the speaker is responding to the world with
   A. disappointment
   B. confusion
   C. wonder
   D. fear

DIRECTIONS *Answer these questions about "Snow in the Suburbs."*

7. The fork in the simile in line 3 represents
   A. a spider's web
   B. an eating utensil
   C. streets and pavements
   D. a snow-covered tree branch

8. In line 4, personification is used to create an image of a
   A. strong wind
   B. snow-covered tree
   C. beautiful snowdrift
   D. quiet setting

9. The alliteration in line 8 emphasizes

 A. speed

 B. softness

 C. coldness

 D. danger

0. Which of the following is a simile that describes a fence covered with snow?

 A. "Every branch big with it" (line 1)

 B. "The palings are glued together like a wall" (line 7)

 C. "A snow-lump thrice his own slight size" (line 11)

 D. "its brush / Starts off a volley of other lodging lumps with a rush" (lines 15–16)

1. Which statement describes the pattern of rhyme in this poem?

 A. Only the first four lines rhyme.

 B. Every other line rhymes.

 C. Every pair of lines rhymes.

 D. Many lines do not rhyme.

2. Which expression is an example of personification?

 A. "Some flakes have lost their way" (line 5)

 B. "A sparrow enters the tree" (line 9)

 C. "The steps are a blanched slope" (line 17)

 D. "A black cat comes, wide-eyed and thin" (line 19)

DIRECTIONS *Answer this question about both poems.*

13. The two poems suggest that natural elements such as light and snow can

 A. flood natural habitats

 B. destroy animals' food sources

 C. comfort people who are sad

 D. transform a landscape

Brief Constructed Response

14. What can you infer that Neruda is saying about light in "Ode to enchanted light"? Select images from the poem to support your answer.

15. Identify the repetition in lines 13–14 of "Snow in the Suburbs." What is the effect of this repetition?

16. What inference can you make about each poet's response to nature in these poems? Support your answer with details from the poems.

GO ON ➡

12. *A **is correct.** Personification gives human qualities to an inanimate object. In line 5, the snowflakes are described as if they are looking for a particular place. In B and D, the sparrow and cat are described as acting in ways that are normal for them. In C, the steps are compared to another inanimate thing—a slope.*

13. *D **is correct.** In the first poem, the light enchants the landscape, shedding a glow over all it touches. In the second poem, the natural objects become something different under a covering of snow. A is incorrect, since there is no mention of flooding. Neither the snow nor the light is seen as a force of destruction, as in B. There is no evidence to suggest that either speaker is sad, as in C.*

Brief Constructed Response

Evaluate student writing using the Maryland writing rubrics in the back of the book.

Possible responses:

14. *Neruda is saying that light interacts with other parts of nature and contributes to the beauty of the landscape. It creates a latticework out of the tree branches (lines 3–5) and it shines on every leaf (lines 6–7). As the light drifts down, the cicada's song floats up (lines 10–12). All of these elements fill the world with beauty, like a glass overflowing with water (lines 13–15).*

15. *The words and and him are both repeated, as well as the sound "urn." The repetition of sounds and grammatical structure creates an impression of tumbling and rolling. The bird is toppled by the lump of snow and immersed in it.*

16. *Neruda's response is impressionistic and positive. He focuses on the delicate and intangible beauty of light and its power to transform. This is shown through his use of similes and metaphors in lines 3–5, 8–9, and 13–15. Hardy's response is objective and detailed. He uses vivid and concrete images to show how the snowfall affects the landscape and wildlife. He describes the branches as big with snow and the forks of the branches as looking like white web-feet. He says that the palings are glued together and the steps are a blanched slope.*

DIFFERENTIATED INSTRUCTION

FOR ENGLISH LEARNERS

Assessment Support: Make Inferences To help students respond to question 16, complete a chart like this one for each poem.

Images from Neruda Poem	What I infer
"light / has dropped from the top of the sky"	Light is special. It comes directly from the heavens.
"light / like a green / latticework of branches"	Light is delicate and lovely.
"drifting down like clean / white sand"	Light makes everything fresh, clean, and new.
"The world is / a glass overflowing / with water."	Light is life-giving and beautiful.

Vocabulary

1. C is correct. Enchanted *means "bewitched"*
or "placed under a spell," suggesting magi-
cal qualities. A, B, and D do not match this
connotation of enchanted, particularly as it
is developed in the poem.

2. A is correct. *A lattice is a lacy, crisscross*
pattern of thin strips of metal, wood, or
other material. Its structure makes it ap-
pear delicate. C is the opposite of delicacy
and is therefore incorrect. B is incorrect
because a lattice does not afford privacy.
It has open parts that can be seen through.
D is incorrect because a lattice is not trans-
parent, although light can pass through the
open spaces.

3. B is correct. *The sound of sawing is grating*
or harsh. The word scratchy *suggests these*
ideas. A is incorrect because sawing is not
always loud. A harsh grating sound is not
soothing or musical, making both C and D
incorrect.

4. C is correct. *Someone who is mute is un-*
able to talk. He or she is silent or still. A, B,
and D are unrelated to this idea of silence.

5. A is correct. *The snowflakes "grope back*
upward," suggesting that they are uncer-
tain, hesitant, or blinded. Therefore, both
B and D are incorrect. The clumsy, aimless
motion of the snowflakes is the opposite of
elegance, making C incorrect.

6. A is correct. Meandering *means "wander-*
ing slowly and without purpose," or aim-
lessly. Without purpose, progress cannot be
orderly, so B is incorrect. C and D are also
incorrect, as something that is slow cannot
be hasty or rash.

7. D is correct. *Feeble means "weak."*
Weakness might be caused by sadness,
old age, or sickness, but not necessarily.
Therefore, A, B, and C are incorrect.

Vocabulary

DIRECTIONS *Use context clues and your knowledge*
of connotation to answer the following questions.

1. The word *enchanted* in the title of Neruda's
poem suggests that the light is
   A. brilliant
   B. sinister
   C. magical
   D. romantic

2. The word *latticework* in line 5 of "Ode to
enchanted light" has a connotation of
   A. delicacy
   B. privacy
   C. sturdiness
   D. transparency

3. The word *sawing* in line 11 of "Ode to
enchanted light" suggests a sound that is
   A. loud
   B. scratchy
   C. soothing
   D. musical

4. The word *mute* in line 4 of "Snow in the
Suburbs" has a connotation of
   A. illness
   B. darkness
   C. stillness
   D. coldness

5. The word *grope* in line 5 of "Snow in the
Suburbs" has a connotation of
   A. clumsiness
   B. certainty
   C. elegance
   D. aggression

6. The word *meandering* in line 6 of "Snow
in the Suburbs" has a connotation of
   A. aimlessness
   B. orderliness
   C. hastiness
   D. rashness

7. The word *feeble* in line 18 of "Snow in the
Suburbs" has a connotation of
   A. sadness
   B. oldness
   C. sickness
   D. weakness

DIFFERENTIATED INSTRUCTION

FOR ENGLISH LEARNERS

Review Academic Vocabulary Discuss these
definitions:

- *denotation,* "dictionary definition of a word"
- *connotation,* "thoughts or feelings that a
  word brings to mind"

Then write these words and their denotations on the board:

- *gold,* "a soft, yellow metal that is mined
  from the earth or found in rivers or
  streams"

- *moonlight,* "the light reflected from the
  surface of the moon"
- *fleecy,* "covered with the wool of a sheep or
  other animal"
- *blossom,* "a flower"
- *sunny,* "having a lot of sunshine"

List these words in random order on the
board: *soft, happy, delicate, precious, cheerful,*
romantic. Have students match each connotation with the correct word.

MSA SKILLS PRACTICE

Writing & Grammar

DIRECTIONS *Read this passage and answer the questions that follow.*

(1) The Declaration of Independence forever changed American history.
(2) Did you know the colonists listed their complaints against King George in this important document? (3) Freedom from British rule was declared by them.
(4) One year earlier, the colonists had tried to make peace with the king. (5) They outlined their specific pleas in a document known as the Olive Branch Petition.
(6) The king's approval of this document was sought by Congress. (7) After he rejected the petition, the king declared the colonists rebels.

1. How might you revise sentence 2 to make it declarative?

  A. The colonists listed their complaints against King George in this important document.

  B. The colonists listed their complaints against King George in this important document!

  C. Read this important document to find out how the colonists listed their complaints against King George.

  D. Didn't the colonists list their complaints against King George in this important document?

2. Choose the correct way to rewrite sentence 3 by using the active voice.

  A. They declared freedom from British rule.

  B. Freedom from British rule was sought by the colonists.

  C. To gain freedom from British rule was desired by the colonists.

  D. Freedom from British rule was what was declared by them.

3. Choose the correct way to rewrite sentence 6 by using the active voice.

  A. Getting this document approved by the king was wanted by Congress.

  B. An attempt to get this document approved was made by Congress.

  C. Getting approval of this document by the king was attempted by Congress.

  D. Congress sought the king's approval of this document.

4. How might you revise sentence 7 to make it exclamatory?

  A. Did you know that after the king rejected the petition, he declared the colonists rebels?

  B. After he rejected the petition, the king declared the colonists rebels!

  C. The king rejected the petition and declared the colonists rebels.

  D. Find out how the king rejected the petition and declared the colonists rebels.

STOP

621

ANSWERS

Writing & Grammar

1. A *is correct.* *Sentence 2 is a question. To make it a statement, the interrogative phrase "did you know" is dropped and a period is placed at the end.* B *is an exclamation.* C *is an imperative sentence.* D *is a question that is just phrased in a different way from the question in the passage.*

2. A *is correct.* *It is the only sentence in which the subject performs the action.* B, C, and D *are incorrect because the verbs are in the passive voice. Their subjects express the result of the action.*

3. D *is correct.* *The subject* Congress *performs the action of seeking. In* A, B, and C, *the result of the action, getting the document approved, is expressed in the subject.*

4. B *is correct.* *An exclamation point at the end indicates that this sentence expresses strong emotion.* A *is a question,* C *is a declarative sentence, and* D *is an imperative sentence.*

DIFFERENTIATED INSTRUCTION

FOR ENGLISH LEARNERS

Assessment Support: Active and Passive Voice
Before students answer the questions on this page, review active and passive voice.

- A verb is in the **active voice** when its subject performs the action. The verb is also followed by a direct object.

- When a verb is in the **passive voice,** it includes a form of the verb *to be.* The subject does not perform the action but is the result of the action or is acted upon.

Write these examples on the board. Have students identify each sentence as either active or passive and explain why.

  1. The boy caught the ball. *(active)*

  2. The ball was caught by the boy. *(passive)*

  3. The speech was heard by millions of people. *(passive)*

  4. Millions of people heard the speech. *(active)*

  5. The students visited the dairy farm. *(active)*

  6. The dairy farm was visited by the students. *(passive)*

INTRODUCE *MORE GREAT READS*

In Unit 5, students have discussed a number of big questions. Invite students to tell which question they found most intriguing and why. Then focus attention on the three questions that appear on this page. Discuss the recommended books and their summaries, pointing out how each book connects to the related question. Encourage students to choose one or more of these "great reads" to read independently.

ⓘ ClassZone.com

To find additional books that match students' interests and ability levels, visit the Literature Center at **ClassZone.com.**

More Great Reads

UNIT 5

Ideas for Independent Reading

Which questions from Unit 5 made an impression on you? Continue exploring them with these books.

Why do we need memorials?

The Glory Field
by Walter Dean Myers
The Glory Field chronicles milestones in African-American history from the 1700s to the present day through five generations of the Lewis family. Each generation draws strength from the Glory Field, a hallowed plot of land that represents their cherished heritage.

Bull Run
by Paul Fleischman
In this story, characters memorialize the first battle of the Civil War from 16 different perspectives. Together they add an intimate dimension to our nation's bloodiest conflict.

The Monument
by Gary Paulsen
Can the artist behind a monument change you more than the monument itself? When an artist comes to design a war memorial in Rocky's small Kansas town, he becomes Rocky's mentor and opens her eyes to broader horizons.

Whom do you feel closest to?

Our Only May Amelia
by Jennifer L. Holm
Can time and place have an effect on the strength of family ties? You will enjoy reading 12-year-old May Amelia's diary as she gives a candid account of the joys and pains of pioneer life in the late 1800s.

Pink and Say
by Patricia Polacco
Patricia Polacco tells the story of her great-grandfather during the Civil War. Learn why the friendship of an Ohio farm boy and a freed slave has become a story retold through three generations.

Heaven
by Angela Johnson
When deception backfires, who gets hurt? Fourteen-year-old Marley lives in Heaven, Ohio—a perfect, loving community. Then she learns that her parents are not her real parents and that all her life she's lived with deception.

How would you describe yourself?

Rules of the Road
by Joan Bauer
What measurements could you use to describe your character? *Rules of the Road* follows the independent Jenna Boller as she learns what's important in life.

Buddy Love: Now on Video
by Ilene Cooper
When 13-year-old Buddy Love views his life through a camcorder lens, he gains insight into the lives of his family and friends and into his own character. To his delight, he finds his life is infinitely exciting.

The Crane Wife
by Odds Bodkin
Why do people describe themselves in a certain way, hoping to impress others? In this tale of a poor sail maker who saves the life of a beautiful white crane, greed overcomes virtue, and the sail maker must learn a harsh lesson.

UNIT 6

Sharing Our Stories

MYTHS, LEGENDS, AND TALES

623

For help in planning this unit, see

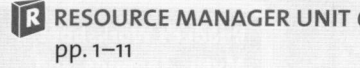 **RESOURCE MANAGER UNIT 6**
pp. 1–11

INTRODUCE THE UNIT

Movies, songs, books, magazines, interviews, blogs—people today have many different ways to share their stories and tell what is important to them. Even though the ways of telling stories have changed through the ages, basic story themes have remained the same, crossing all barriers of time and place. Today we love stories of courage, adventure, justice, love, and humor—just as people of old did. Invite students to think about these ideas as they discuss the pictures on this page. To spark a discussion, ask

- What time period is suggested by each picture? Explain.
- What feeling does each picture create? What details contribute to these feelings?
- If you were going to tell a story about one of the pictures, what would be the theme of the story?
- Is the theme you identified timeless, that is to say, of interest to people in all times and places? Explain.

Discuss reasons why people enjoy sharing stories. Explain that through stories people communicate their values, ideas, fears, and desires. In this unit, students will explore the timeless appeal of **myths, legends,** and **tales.**

About the Art Wassily Kandinsky painted this design for the cover of *Almanach Der Blaue Reiter* in 1911. For more information, see page 652 of the teacher's edition.

UNIT 6
Standards Skills Trace

MARYLAND

SKILLS STRAND	Reader's Workshop: Myths, Legends, and Tales pp. 626–631	Prometheus / Orpheus and Eurydice pp. 632–645	Icarus and Daedalus / Phaëthon, Son of Apollo pp. 646–659	*from* Young Arthur pp. 660–669	*from* Sir Gawain and the Green Knight pp. 670–685
standards	3.A.3.a, 3.A.6.a, 3.A.8.d	1.D.3.b, 1.E.3.a, 3.A.3.a	1.D.3.c, 1.E.3.a, 3.A.6.a, 5.A.2.d	1.D.3.a, 1.E.3.a, 3.A.3.a	1.D.3.c, 1.E.4.d, 3.A.6.a, 5.A.2.d
		Greek Myths *Level: Challenging*	Greek Myths *Level: Challenging*	Medieval Legend *Level: Average*	Medieval Legend *Level: Average*
Literary Analysis	Characteristics of Traditional Tales pp. 626–627, 630–631 Cultural Values in Traditional Tales pp. 628–629, 630–631	Characteristics of Myths pp. 633, 634, 637, 638, 641, 644	Cultural Values in Myths pp. 647, 650, 651, 652, 655, 656, 657	Characteristics of Legends pp. 661, 664, 665, 666, 667	Cultural Values in Legends pp. 671, 672, 675, 676, 679, 680, 682, 683
Reading and Informational Texts	Analyze the Literature pp. 627, 629–631	Monitor pp. 633, 636, 637, 640, 642, 644 Read a Poem p. 643	Identify Cause-and-Effect Relationships pp. 647, 650, 651, 654, 656, 657	Identify Chronological Order pp. 661, 664, 665, 666, 667 Read a Magazine Article p. 669	Predict pp. 671, 675, 677, 678, 680, 682, 683
Vocabulary	Academic Vocabulary pp. 626, 628	Word Acquisition pp. 633, T633, 645 Context Clues p. T633 Latin Roots (*fin*) p. 645	Word Acquisition pp. 647, T647, 658 Context Clues p. T647 Homographs p. 658	Word Acquisition pp. 661, T661, 668 Context Clues p. 661 Compound Words p. 668	Word Acquisition pp. 671, T671, 684 Context Clues p. T671 Easily Confused Words p. 684
Writing, Grammar, and Style			Correct Sentence Structure p. 659 Simple and Compound Sentences p. 659 Independent Clauses p. 659		Correct Sentence Structure p. 685 Complex Sentences p. 685 Dependent Clauses p. 685
Speaking, Listening, Viewing, and Media	Discuss pp. 626–629	Discuss pp. 632, T634–T643, 644 Analyze Visuals pp. 634, 638, T641, T643	Discuss pp. 646, T648–T656, 657 Analyze Visuals pp. 648, T651, 652, 656	Discuss pp. 660, T662–T666, 667 Analyze Visuals p. 662	Discuss pp. 670, T672–T682, 683 Analyze Visuals pp. 672, T677, T681

Assessment-Based Planning: Skills in red are assessed on the Unit 6 Test. **T** = Teacher's Edition page

MARYLAND STANDARDS

For a full listing of state standards see page S1.

1.E.1.b, 3.A.1.b	2.A.4.h, 4.A.2.c	1.D.3.b, 1.E.4.e, 3.A.3.a	1.D.3.c, 1.E.3.a, 3.A.3.a	1.E.3.a, 3.A.6.b	4.A.1, 4.A.2.c, 7.A.1	
Linked selections						**Skills Assessed on the Unit 6 Test:**
from **Crispin: The Cross of Lead** pp. 582–587	**A Medieval Mystery** pp. 692–695	**Brer Possum's Dilemma / Waters of Gold** pp. 696–711	**Sally Ann Thunder Ann Whirlwind** pp. 712–721	**Two Ways to Count to Ten / The Race Between Toad and Donkey** pp. 722–735	**Writing Workshop: Cause-and-Effect Essay** pp. 736–743	**Literary Analysis**
Historical Novel *Level: Average*	Book Review *Level: Average*	Folk Tales *Level: Average*	Tall Tale *Level: Easy*	Fables *Level: Easy*		• Identify and analyze characteristics of myths and legends • Identify cultural values in myths and legends • Identify universal theme
Form (Historical Novel) pp. 686, T688, T689		Characteristics of Folk Tales pp. 697, 698, 701, 702, 707, 708, 709, 710	Characteristics of Tall Tales pp. 713, 716, 718, 719, 720	Universal Theme pp. 723, 724, 726, 727, 728, 729, 730, 732, 733, 734		**Reading and Informational Texts** • Monitor • Identify cause-and-effect relationships • Identify chronological order • Summarize
	Identify Opinions pp. 692, 693, 694 Compare Reactions p. 695 Read a Book Review pp. 693–694	Summarize pp. 697, 700, 704, 706, 710 Review: Predict pp. 700, 705, 707	Visualize pp. 713, 716, 718, 719, 720	Set a Purpose for Reading p. 723	Analyze a Cause-and-Effect Essay pp. 737–738, 742	**Vocabulary** • Understand and use homographs • Understand meanings of compound words
		Word Acquisition pp. 697, T697, 711 Context Clues p. T697 Latin Roots (*primus*) p. 711	Word Acquisition pp. 713, T713, 721 Context Clues p. T713 Dictionary Usage Labels p. 721			**Writing, Grammar, and Style** • Write a cause-and-effect essay • Form compound sentences by combining independent clauses • Form complex sentences by combining dependent and independent clauses • Link causes and effects with transitions • Additional writing and grammar skills
				Write for Assessment p. 735	Write a Cause-and-Effect Essay pp. 736–743 Parallel Sentence Structure p. 742 Cause-Effect Transitions p. 742	
Discuss pp. 686, T691	Discuss pp. 692, T693–T694, 695	Discuss pp. 696, T698–T709, 710 Analyze Visuals pp. 698, 702, T705, T709	Discuss pp. 712, T714–T719, 720 Analyze Visuals pp. 714, T717, T718	Discuss pp. 722, T724–T728, 729, T730–T733, 734 Analyze Visuals pp. 724, 730	Discuss pp. 736–738 Make a Formal Presentation p. 743	

For additional lesson planning help, see **Easy Planner DVD.**

623B

OBJECTIVES

- identify cultural values in myths and legends
- identify and compare universal themes

What can STORIES *teach us?*

Ask students to name favorite stories from movies, TV shows, plays, or books. List students' suggestions on the board. Have students consider why these stories appeal to their generation. How do the stories reflect what is happening in the world around them? What ideas or values do the stories express? As you proceed, discuss how the themes and values of these stories compare to themes and values of stories that have been passed down through their families or cultures.

ACTIVITY Encourage students to jot down notes about their family stories and have volunteers use the notes to share their stories with the class. Guide students to analyze the purpose of the story and to connect the purpose with the lasting appeal that the story has.

CHECK UNDERSTANDING Have students identify the qualities that make a story worthy of passing along from one generation to the next. Which of their own favorite stories will they want to tell to their own children? Why?

Unit Resources

What can STORIES *teach us:*

Many stories do more than simply entertain us. People often tell stories to explain something important or to share different approaches to common experiences. Stories can also express the cultural values of a group of people. Through sharing stories, one generation can teach its values, heritage, and traditions to the next generation.

ACTIVITY Are there any legendary figures in your family line? What stories get passed down from one generation to another or get repeated year after year? In a small group, discuss which family stories mean the most to you and your classmates. Consider the following questions:

- Who told you the story?
- What did you learn from the story?
- Have you told the story to anyone else?

R RESOURCE MANAGER UNIT 6	
BEST PRACTICES TOOLKIT	
S STANDARDS LESSON FILE	

- Easy Planner DVD
- WriteSmart CD
- ClassZone.com
- Audio Anthology CD
- Multi-Language Academic Vocabulary Online
- eEdition CD & Online
- McDougal Littell Assessment System
- Test Generator CD
- MediaSmart DVD

 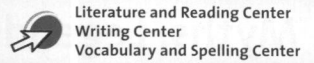
MARYLAND OBJECTIVES

Preview Unit Goals

LITERARY ANALYSIS	• Identify and analyze characteristics of myths, legends, folk tales, and tall tales
	• Identify cultural values in myths and legends
	• Identify and compare universal themes
READING	• Use reading strategies, including predicting, monitoring, and visualizing
	• Identify cause-effect relationships and chronological order
	• Compare reviewer's reaction to a book to one's own reaction
WRITING AND GRAMMAR	• Write a cause-and-effect essay
	• Use correct sentence structure
	• Identify simple and compound sentences
	• Form complex sentences
SPEAKING, LISTENING, AND VIEWING	• Conduct an interview
	• Make a formal presentation
VOCABULARY	• Understand and use homographs
	• Understand the meaning of compound words
ACADEMIC VOCABULARY	• myth • universal theme
	• legend • compound sentences
	• folk tale • complex sentences
	• tall tale • homograph

625

Preview Unit Goals

This page provides an overview of the skills and strategies covered in this unit. Each skill strand is a different color. Remind students that throughout the unit, each skill within a strand matches the color of that strand. Encourage students to consider their ability to use each skill and strategy as they read this page.

Suggest that students copy the Academic Vocabulary terms in their journals and define them in their own words as they read the unit. Encourage students to use these terms as they discuss and write about the selections.

ADDITIONAL UNIT GOALS

These skills will be taught in this unit but are not the major focus of the unit:

Literary Analysis
• Identify characteristics of historical fiction
• Identify theme
• Study a variety of genres: Greek myth, legend, folk tale, tall tale, fable, book review

Reading
• Set a purpose for reading
• Identify opinions
• Summarize
• Compare own reactions to a book to those of reviewers

Writing and Grammar
• Write a compare-and-contrast paper
• Link causes and effects with transitions

Vocabulary
• Understand and use the Latin root *fin* and the Latin word *primus*
• Use correct word from easily confused words
• Use dictionary usage labels

DIFFERENTIATED INSTRUCTION

FOR ENGLISH LEARNERS

Academic Vocabulary Students will study and practice using these terms throughout the unit. Use the Academic Vocabulary copy master to introduce the terms.

1. Read each word aloud and discuss its meaning. Ask students if they have heard any of these words and in what context.

2. Allow students to work in pairs to complete the sentences and the activities. Then discuss students' answers as a class.

Additional Academic Vocabulary Use the second copy master to help students learn other academic vocabulary in the unit.

1. Divide the class into seven groups.

2. Have each group discuss one term, list other forms, and complete the definition.

3. Ask the groups to share their results.

4. Have students complete Part B individually.

📓 **RESOURCE MANAGER—Copy Masters**
Academic Vocabulary p. 9
Additional Academic Vocabulary p. 10

Focus and Motivate

OBJECTIVES

- identify and analyze characteristics of myths, legends, fables, and tall tales
- identify and analyze cultural values in myths and legends
- read a myth, a legend, a fable, and a tall tale

Teach

Part 1: Characteristics of Traditional Stories

Explain to students that reading stories from the oral tradition allows them to make important connections: to the past, to different cultures, to time-honored values, and to friends and family members who also know the stories. Use this activity to help students explore various types of traditional tales:

1. Brainstorm a list of titles of well-known myths, legends, fables, and tall tales.
2. Ask students what traits these traditional tales have in common. Record responses in the center of a Cluster Diagram.
3. In the four outer circles, note which characteristics are particular to myths, legends, fables, and tall tales. Discuss and compare tone, length, characters, and subject matter.
4. Invite students to classify each title from the brainstormed list next to the appropriate type of tale in the diagram.

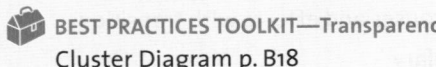 BEST PRACTICES TOOLKIT—Transparency
Cluster Diagram p. B18

Tell students that while many stories are easily classified, some may have elements of more than one type. Read aloud these example story summaries and ask students to identify which types of tales are suggested:

- two hummingbirds discuss how the seasons were created *(myth, fable)*
- a 20-foot-tall buffalo struggles to save a village from drought *(tall tale, legend)*

Reader's Workshop

Myths, Legends, and Tales

Have you heard or read about the foolish grasshopper that refused to plan ahead, or about the legendary king named Arthur? From ancient Greece to medieval England, every culture has its own stories—myths, legends, and tales that have been handed down from one generation to the next. Part of an oral tradition, these tales continue to entertain and teach us hundreds of years after they were first told. By continuing to read, share, and listen to them, we carry on the tradition and keep the past alive.

 MARYLAND OBJECTIVES

LITERATURE STANDARDS
3.A.3.a Distinguish among types of narrative texts
3.A.6.a Analyze universal themes
3.A.8.d Analyze the relationship between structure and the purpose

Part 1: Characteristics of Traditional Stories

Traditional stories may be short or long, inspiring or humorous. They might end with the characters learning a lesson or living "happily ever after." In this unit, you will be reading all types of stories, including the ones shown here.

TYPE OF TALE		CHARACTERISTICS
MYTH A traditional story that was created to explain mysteries of the universe		• Often explains how something connected with humans or nature came to be • Reveals the consequences of both good and bad behavior • Features gods or other beings who have supernatural powers as well as certain flaws
LEGEND A story passed down through many generations that is believed to be based on real people and events		• Tells about a hero or heroine who has unusual powers • Focuses on the hero's or heroine's struggle to defeat a powerful force • Highlights a positive quality or way of behaving
FABLE A brief story that teaches a lesson, or moral, about human nature		• Usually includes animal characters that stand for specific human qualities, such as kindness or dishonesty • Has a moral that is directly stated at the end or indirectly communicated through what happens in the fable
TALL TALE A humorously exaggerated story about impossible events		• Stars a hero or heroine who is larger than life—that is, bigger, stronger, and even louder than a regular person • Uses exaggeration to emphasize the abilities and achievements of the hero or heroine

---

DIFFERENTIATED INSTRUCTION

FOR ALL STUDENTS

For general guidelines on differentiating instruction, see

 BEST PRACTICES TOOLKIT
Differentiated Instruction pp. 31–38

FOR LESS-PROFICIENT READERS

Note Taking For students who need help with note taking, hand out the Note Taking: Characteristics of Traditional Tales copy master and have students read page 626 silently.

Then have students record their notes on the copy master as you discuss the information.

 RESOURCE MANAGER—Copy Master
Note Taking p. 15

Illustrate Tale Have pairs select a scene from the stories on page 627 or from the cluster diagram to illustrate. Encourage students to label the tale's characteristics. Invite volunteers to present their illustrations and explain their labels to the class.

MODEL 1: CHARACTERISTICS OF A FABLE

What human qualities do the fox and the crow display in this fable?

THE **FOX** AND THE **CROW**

Fable by **Aesop**

A crow was sitting on a branch of a tree with a piece of cheese in her beak when a fox observed her and set his wits to work to discover some way of getting the cheese. Coming and standing under the tree, he looked up and said, "What a noble bird I see above me! Her beauty is without
5 equal, the hue of her plumage exquisite. If only her voice is as sweet as her looks are fair, she ought without doubt to be Queen of the Birds."

The crow was hugely flattered by this, and, just to show the fox that she could sing, she gave a loud caw. Down came the cheese, of course, and the fox, snatching it up, said, "You have a voice, madam, I see.
10 What you want are wits."

Flattery is the best persuasion.

Close Read

1. Reread the boxed details. What human qualities does each animal stand for?

2. The moral is directly stated in line 11. In your own words, restate the moral. How does the interaction between the fox and the crow illustrate the moral?

MODEL 2: CHARACTERISTICS OF A TALL TALE

Bess Call is the extraordinary heroine of this tall tale. Here, a stranger from England laughs when "big as life" Bess challenges him to a wrestling match. Will the stranger pay the price?

from **Bess Call**

Tall tale retold by **Robert D. San Souci**

"Humph!" said Bess. "I'll show you a *'real match'*—and no waitin', neither." She rolled up her sleeves and stomped out into the yard.

Back and forth they tussled, making more noise than a boatload of calves on the Hudson. First one, and then the other seemed to get the
5 upper hand, only to find that the edge had slipped over to his or her opponent. The cloud of dust they kicked up covered the sun so that people as far away as Clinton and Cayuga counties reached for their umbrellas thinking unseasonable rain was about to fall.

Their struggles sent them rolling across the yard right up to the fence
10 that separated the farmyard from the road. There Bess took hold of the Englishman one last time and tossed him body, boots, and britches over the fence, where he landed in a muddy ditch.

Close Read

1. In what way is Bess larger than life?

2. One example of humorous exaggeration is boxed. Find another example.

FOR ENGLISH LEARNERS

Language Support: Vocabulary Have students use context clues to determine the meanings of these words that describe the crow in Aesop's fable: *noble* (line 4), *hue* (line 5), *plumage* (line 5), *exquisite* (line 5), *flattered* (line 7). Explain that these words create an ironic, or unexpected, portrait of the crow—a bird more commonly described as *noisy, loud,* or *aggressive.* This irony helps explain why the fox's flattery is so pleasing to the crow.

FOR ADVANCED LEARNERS/PRE–AP

Hypothesize Have students quickwrite a brief continuation to the excerpt from "Bess Call," including an example of a humorous exaggeration or an impossible event. Remind students to develop Bess's qualities as a "larger-than-life" heroine through her words, actions, and interactions with others. Invite volunteers to share their drafts with the class.

MODEL 1: CHARACTERISTICS OF A FABLE

Close Read

1. *Possible answer:* The fox, as hungry to out-smart the crow as he is to take her cheese, represents greed, deceit, and cleverness. The crow's vanity and excessive pride allow her to be tricked—she does not see the fox's ruse behind his compliments.

2. *Possible answer:* "Giving someone a compliment is the best way to get him or her to do what you want." The interaction between the fox and the crow illustrates how the fox's flattery convinces the crow to do what he wants—drop the cheese.

MODEL 2: CHARACTERISTICS OF A TALL TALE

Close Read

1. *Possible answer:* Bess's fierce temper, un-wavering courage, and awesome strength make her a larger-than-life character. Evidence includes Bess's eagerness to fight when angered (lines 1–2), the way she wrestles her opponent relentlessly in the dust (lines 6–8), and her ability to hurl a grown man over a fence (lines 10–12).

2. *Possible answer:* In lines 6–8, the size of the dust cloud Bess and her opponent kick up is greatly exaggerated: it "covered the sun so that people as far away as Clinton and Cayuga counties reached for their umbrellas thinking unseasonable rain was about to fall."

Teach

Part 2: Cultural Values in Traditional Stories

Cultural Values The many elements that define a culture—its attitudes, values, ideals, hopes, fears, language, humor, expectations, rules—are constantly changing and evolving. Stories that reveal details about cultural values are like snapshots in time: they present a picture of the culture's beliefs at the moment they were recorded, and can be preserved for future study or simply for future enjoyment. Use this activity to help students create a snapshot of the culture that currently exists in their classroom:

1. Have students use Think-Pair-Share to answer these questions: *If a new student was joining your English class, what advice would help the student understand how your class behaves and functions? What attitudes and behaviors are rewarded? What traits or actions are discouraged?* For example:

   Classroom Culture

   - Sit in your assigned seat.
   - Sharing your opinions with the class is encouraged and expected.
   - No gum chewing is allowed.
   - Listen when someone else speaks.

   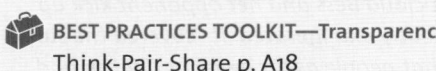 **BEST PRACTICES TOOLKIT—Transparency** Think-Pair-Share p. A18

2. Gather responses from student groups. Discuss what conclusions can be drawn about the values and beliefs of the class.

Traditional Tales The legend of John Henry appealed to railroad workers not only because Henry was a "steel-drivin' man" like them, but also because they admired Henry's character. Ask students which of Henry's personal qualities have universal appeal, even though some of the legend's cultural details are dated.
Possible answers:

- *He cares about his peers (lines 9–11).*
- *He is perceptive and can foresee the future (lines 8–11).*
- *He values dignity and family (line 11).*
- *He is brave and strong (lines 12–13).*

Part 2: Cultural Values in Traditional Stories

One reason for the lasting popularity of many traditional stories is their universal quality. You don't have to be an expert on ancient Greece to understand the moral of an Aesop fable, or know about daily life in 19th-century New York to be amused by "Bess Call."

You can usually appreciate a particular stories without knowing much about the culture or society from which it originally came. But by noticing certain details, you can often draw conclusions about the **cultural values**—the ideals and beliefs—that were honored and upheld by that society or culture. For example, does the story stress the importance of obedience, or does it celebrate those who bend the rules?

Consider the legend of John Henry, a railroad worker and "steel drivin' man" whose job was to drill holes using a hammer and a steel spike. His story was popular among men who worked long days building railroad tracks across the United States after the Civil War. By closely examining the excerpt and asking yourself a few questions, you can learn a great deal about those workers and their concerns.

from

JOHN HENRY

Legend retold by **Mary Pope Osborne**

"I got the best steel driver in the country. His name is John Henry, and he can beat *two* dozen men working together."

"That's impossible," the salesman said. "But if you can prove your hand driller is faster than my steam driller, I'll give you this machine
5 for free."

The boss called to John Henry, "This fellow doubts which of you can drill faster. How about a big contest?"

As John Henry stared at the steam drill, he saw a picture of the future. He saw machines taking over the jobs of the country's finest workers.
10 He saw himself and his friends out of work and begging beside the road. He saw men robbed of their dignity and robbed of their families.

"I'd rather die with my hammer in my hand than let that steam drill run me down," he yelled back. And his boss and friends all cheered.

QUESTIONS TO ASK

Who are the heroes and villains in the story?
The hero is a railroad worker; the villain is a machine.

What attitudes and behaviors are rewarded and admired?
John Henry is rewarded with cheers for taking on the machine. Other workers admire his strength and bravery.

What can you infer about the fears of the country's workers during this time period?
Workers were worried about losing their jobs to machines.

DIFFERENTIATED INSTRUCTION

FOR LESS–PROFICIENT READERS
Note Taking For students who need help with note taking, hand out the Note Taking: Cultural Values in Traditional Tales copy master. Read and discuss the top of page 628. Assist students, as needed, in completing the first item on the copy master. Then have them complete the page independently or in pairs.

RESOURCE MANAGER—Copy Master Note Taking p. 16

FOR ADVANCED LEARNERS/PRE–AP
Make Judgments Ask students to determine the strongest message from the legend of John Henry—a message that will continue to be passed down through the generations, keeping the legend alive. Students may represent this message visually, by writing a motto or moral, or through acting out a scene with a partner. As a class, evaluate the strengths of each student's interpretation.

MODEL 1: CULTURAL VALUES IN A MYTH

The Mexican myth of Quetzalcoatl explains how unhappiness came into the world. In this excerpt, the people—the Toltecs—are still happy.

from
Quetzalcoatl

Mexican myth retold by **Amy Cruse**

But the king-god Quetzalcoatl knew that if his people were to be really happy they must not spend their days in the idle enjoyment of all this loveliness and plenty. They must work, and learn to take a pride in working as well as they possibly could. So he taught them many
5 useful arts—painting and weaving and carving and working in metals. He taught them how to fashion the gold and silver and precious stones which were found in great abundance throughout the country into beautiful vessels and ornaments, and how to make marvelous many-tinted garments and hangings from the feathers of birds. Every one was
10 eager to work, and because each man did his share, there was plenty of leisure for all. No one was in want and no one was unhappy. It seemed as if, for these fortunate Toltecs, the Golden Age had really come.

Close Read

1. What attitudes toward work do you notice in this excerpt? Find specific details to support your answer.

2. Reread lines 4–9. What kinds of skills and products did the people who created this myth value?

MODEL 2: CULTURAL VALUES IN A LEGEND

In this legend, a monster bear called Nyagwahe threatens the peace among the five Iroquois nations. Swift Runner, a weak boy and an unlikely hero, kills the bear. Here, he returns to his village, victorious.

from
Racing the Great Bear

Iroquois legend retold by **Joseph Bruchac**

Then Swift Runner led his people back to the village. He carried with him the teeth of the Nyagwahe, and those who saw what he carried rejoiced. The trails were safe again, and the Great Peace would not be broken. Swift Runner went to his grandmother's lodge and embraced her.
5 "Grandson," she said, "you are now the man I knew you would grow up to be. Remember to use your power to help the people."
So it was that Swift Runner ran with the great bear and won the race. Throughout his long life, he used the teeth of the Nyagwahe to heal the sick, and he worked always to keep the Great Peace.

Close Read

1. What traits does Swift Runner's grandmother display in the boxed text? Draw a conclusion about the attitude the Iroquois people have toward their elders.

2. Reread lines 6–9. What traits or qualities are admired in the Iroquois culture? Support your answer.

MODEL 1: CULTURAL VALUES IN A MYTH

Close Read

1. *Possible answer: The king-god Quetzalcoatl valued work and wished to instill his people with a pride in working (lines 3–4). The Toltec people were eager to do their share of work (lines 9–10) and in return were awarded leisure and happiness (lines 10–12).*

2. *Possible answer: The people who created this myth valued artistic skills such as painting, weaving, carving, and stone and metal work (lines 5–6). The products they created—vessels, ornaments, colorful clothes, and decorations—were both beautiful and functional (lines 7–9).*

MODEL 2: CULTURAL VALUES IN A LEGEND

Close Read

1. *Possible answer: Swift Runner's grandmother, as her dialogue in lines 5–6 reveals, has strong beliefs and expectations; she also cares deeply for her grandson and for her people. The Iroquois value and respect their elders and rely on them for guidance, support, and love.*

2. *Possible answer: The Iroquois culture admires generosity, the ability to heal, and peacekeeping skills. Swift Runner does not hoard the power he gains from the bear's teeth; rather, he is generous with it, using it to heal the sick and to maintain the "Great Peace" (lines 8–9).*

DIFFERENTIATED INSTRUCTION

FOR LESS–PROFICIENT READERS

Analysis Support: Cultural Values Have students reread "Quetzalcoatl," noting a response to each of the **Questions to Ask** from page 628.
Possible answers:

- *heroes/villains: Quetzalcoatl is the hero, who brings happiness; the villain is represented by the idea of idleness*

- *admired attitudes: hard work, pride in industry, skill in creating beautiful things*

- *inferences about fears: the Toltecs fear laziness and unhappiness*

FOR ENGLISH LEARNERS

Language Support: Multiple-Meaning Words
Explain that in "Quetzalcoatl," both the word *share* (line 10) and the word *want* (line 11) have more than one meaning. Tell students that in the myth, *share* means "one's full or fair portion" and *want* means "a lack, or poverty." Have pairs identify one other meaning for each word and use the word in a sentence that shows the second meaning. Ask pairs to share their sentences.

Analysis Support: Traditional Tales Explain that several characteristics from "Racing the Great Bear" are typical of legends. For example, the story features a monster bear and an unlikely hero with special powers. Have student pairs note which details from "Quetzalcoatl" are typical of myths.

Practice and Apply

Part 3: Analyze the Literature

Close Read

1. *Possible answer: Hera is like a human being because she feels jealousy and rage when she suspects that her husband loves someone else. Her strong emotions lead her to take action, and she sets out to discover which nymph is ruining her marriage.*

Part 3: Analyze the Literature

The myths of ancient Greece were first told more than 3,000 years ago. Yet people today still enjoy reading about the powers of mighty gods and goddesses and the daring adventures of heroes. Modern readers can even learn something from these characters' costly mistakes.

In this unit, you will read several Greek myths. Get your first taste of Greek mythology by reading this famous story of unrequited love. What characteristics of a myth do you notice in "Echo"? Through this tale, what do you learn about ancient Greek values?

Echo

Greek myth retold by **Alice Low**

E cho, a beautiful mountain nymph,[1] was a great talker and always had to have the last word. She was a favorite of Artemis, goddess of the hunt. Together they hunted in the woods, swam in mountain pools, and caught fish for meals. But Echo's delightful life was destroyed,
5 all because she tried to protect her friends from Hera's[2] wrath.

One day Hera came spying on a group of nymphs in the woods. She suspected that her husband, Zeus, was in love with one of them and hoped to find out which one he favored.

Echo did not know which nymph was Zeus's favorite, and so she
10 started a conversation with Hera in order to let all the other nymphs escape. "Isn't it lovely here?" she said.

"Yes, indeed," Hera replied, "but I am very busy right now and have no time for talk."

---

1. **nymph:** in Greek mythology, a godlike being that appears as a beautiful young woman in a natural setting.
2. **Hera's:** belonging to Hera, the wife of Zeus, the supreme ruler of Mount Olympus and all the gods and goddesses who live there.

Close Read

1. The ancient Greeks believed that their god acted like regular peop and even experienced human emotions. Consider Hera's feeling and actions in the box lines. In what ways is she like a human being

---

DIFFERENTIATED INSTRUCTION

FOR LESS–PROFICIENT READERS

Language Support The myth "Echo" is introduced as a "famous story of unrequited love." Have small groups decide on a definition for the word *unrequited*. Then see how close the groups' definitions come to the dictionary's definition: "not reciprocated or returned in kind."

FOR ENGLISH LEARNERS

Reading Support: Cultural Values Have student pairs reread lines 9–13. One student should complete an Open Mind organizer for Echo, imagining what thoughts, values, or attitudes are in her mind as she approaches Hera, while the other student completes the organizer for Hera. Then have students compare what they wrote or drew.

🧰 BEST PRACTICES TOOLKIT—Transparency
Open Mind p. D11

FOR ADVANCED LEARNERS/PRE–AP

Synthesize Cultural Values In ancient Greek society, Echo's story served as a cautionary tale for people who might want to thwart the goals of their superiors. Challenge students to re-write the ending so that it reflects different values. For example, Echo might be rewarded for protecting her friends while Hera is punished for her jealousy. Have students share their endings and discuss which version most closely reflects the values of our modern society.

"It seems to me you are busy talking," said Echo, "which is the
15 nicest way to be busy, don't you agree?" She went on and on, and
every time Hera tried to get away from her, Echo asked another
question. By the time Hera got away and ran to the nymphs' pool,
all the nymphs had fled.

"This is *your* doing," said Hera to Echo. "*You* kept talking to let them
20 escape. And I shall punish you for that. You shall never be able to speak
first, but shall only be able to repeat what others say. You shall always
have the last word."

Soon after that, Echo fell in love with a handsome young hunter
named Narcissus.[3] She followed him through the woods, hoping to
25 make him notice her. But she could not speak first and had to wait for
him to speak to her.

One day her chance came. Narcissus became separated from his
friends and called out, "Is anyone here?"
"Here," called Echo.
30 Narcissus could not see her, for she was behind a bush. He shouted,
"Come," thinking she was one of his companions, and she called back,
"Come."

"Let us be together," called Narcissus, for he still could not see anybody.
"Let us be together," called Echo, and she ran up to him with her
35 arms open, ready to embrace him. But Narcissus said cruelly, "Do not
touch me. I would rather perish than let you have power over me."

"Have power over me," said Echo pleadingly, but Narcissus bounded
away, leaving Echo alone and ashamed. Afterward she lived in a cave,
and finally, because of her great grief, she shrank to nothing. The only
40 thing left of her was her voice, which echoed through the mountains,
repeating the words of anyone who called.

---

3. **Narcissus:** a handsome but vain boy known for his cruel rejection of the many nymphs who fell in love with him.

Close Read

2. Why does Hera punish Echo?

3. Think about Echo's behavior and actions, as well as her resulting punishment. What can you infer about the kinds of behavior that the Greeks hoped to discourage by telling this myth?

4. Some myths attempt to explain how something in the world came to be. What natural phenomenon is explained by this myth?

Close Read

2. *Possible answer: Hera punishes Echo for foiling her plan to identify the nymph with whom Zeus is in love. Echo has distracted Hera by talking to her, allowing the other nymphs to escape.*

3. *Possible answers: This myth discourages excessive pride and disrespect for the gods. Echo is overconfident and arrogant—she always has to have the last word (line 2), plots to get in the way of Hera's plan (lines 9–11), and continues to speak when Hera is clearly trying to get away from her (lines 15–17).*

4. *Possible answers: This myth attempts to explain the phenomenon of an echo—why the sound of a person's voice is repeated back when the person calls out in the mountains (lines 39–41).*

Assess and Reteach

Assess

Have students briefly summarize the characteristics and cultural values of the myth "Echo."

Reteach

For students who are unable to apply the workshop skills to "Echo," select from these reteaching options:

1. Review with students their note-taking copy masters. Then have pairs
   - compare the information they recorded
   - explain each term to one another
   - question each other to clarify ideas
   - share their insights and challenges

2. Refer students to a myth, legend, fable, or tall tale with which all students are familiar ("Jack and the Beanstalk," "The Hare and the Tortoise," "Robin Hood"). Have students describe the tale's characteristics, referring to the chart on page 628 as needed. Then have students briefly describe the cultural values (ideals and beliefs) expressed in the story.

DIFFERENTIATED INSTRUCTION

FOR LESS–PROFICIENT READERS

Analysis Support: Traditional Tales Remind students that myths often feature gods or other characters with special powers and traits—as well as certain flaws. Ask students to complete the graphic organizer for the characters of Echo, Hera, and Narcissus.

Character	Special Traits or Powers	Flaws
Echo	beautiful, god-like, shrank to nothing but still repeats others' words	too talkative, disrespectful
Hera	can cast spells, wife of Zeus	jealous, vengeful
Narcissus	handsome hunter	vain, cruel

Focus and Motivate

OBJECTIVES

Literary Analysis
- explore the key idea of **consequences**
- analyze characteristics of Greek myths
- read Greek myths and a poem

Reading
- monitor understanding

Vocabulary
- build vocabulary for reading and writing
- understand and use the Latin root *fin* (also an EL language objective)

SUMMARY

"Prometheus" tells how the Titan Prometheus defies Zeus by giving people fire. As punishment, Zeus has Prometheus chained to a mountain to be continually attacked by vultures. "Orpheus and Eurydice" tells how the musician Orpheus tries to lead his beloved Eurydice out of the underworld. At the last moment, he cannot resist looking back at her. Whispering a sad farewell, Eurydice slips away from him, just as Hades had warned.

Do you THINK
before you act?

Discuss the question and **KEY IDEA** of **consequences.** Challenge students to explain the meaning of "Look before you leap." Ask for examples of characters in books or movies who "leaped before they looked." What were the consequences of their actions? After this discussion, have students work on the **QUICKWRITE** activity.

Selection Resources

Prometheus
Greek Myth Retold by Bernard Evslin

Orpheus and Eurydice
Greek Myth Retold by Olivia Coolidge

Do you THINK
before you act?

MARYLAND OBJECTIVES

READING/LIT STANDARDS
1.E.3.a Select and apply appropriate strategies during reading
3.A.3.a Distinguish among types of narrative texts

KEY IDEA Did you ever make a decision you wished you could take back? If so, then you know that your actions sometimes have **consequences,** or effects, that you didn't bargain for. You're not alone. As you'll see in the Greek myths you're about to read, people have been acting without thinking since ancient times.

QUICKWRITE Think of a risky decision you might make, such as choosing not to study for a test or choosing to make friends with a person outside your group. What are the possible **consequences** of the decision, both negative and positive? Write a short paragraph explaining whether you would be willing to face these consequences.

632

RESOURCE MANAGER UNIT 6
Plan and Teach pp. 17–24
Literary Analysis
Summary pp. 25†*, 26‡*
Characteristics of Myths pp. 27, 28†*
Question Support p. 35*
Reading
Monitoring pp. 29, 30†*
Reading Check p. 34
Reading Fluency p. 36

Vocabulary
Study p. 31*
Practice p. 32
Strategy p. 33
Assessment
Selection Tests A, B/C pp. 37*, 39*
Test Generator CD

BEST PRACTICES TOOLKIT
Differentiated Instruction
pp. 31–38*
Scaffolding Instruction
pp. 43–46*
Graphic Organizers/Strategies
Word Questioning • Read Aloud/Think Aloud • T Chart

Reading Support
Audio Anthology CD*

Technology
Literature and Vocabulary Centers at **ClassZone.com**

WriteSmart CD

---

* Resources for Differentiation   † Also in Spanish   ‡ In Haitian Creole and Vietnamese

LITERARY ANALYSIS: CHARACTERISTICS OF MYTHS

Since ancient times, people have passed down **myths,** or stories that explain mysteries of the universe. Most myths share these characteristics:

- They tell how something came to be, or they reveal the effects of human behavior.
- They feature gods or other beings with supernatural powers. These beings often show such human qualities as anger.

Many famous myths, like the ones you're about to read, were first told in Greece over 3,000 years ago. As you read, note what the myths explain and how the gods act.

READING STRATEGY: MONITOR

The unusual characters, places, and situations in these myths may sometimes distract or confuse you. As you read, try **monitoring,** or checking, your understanding. One way to do this is by asking yourself **questions** about what's going on. If you can't answer, clarify your understanding by reading more slowly, going back, or reading on. Note your questions and the answers in a chart like the one shown.

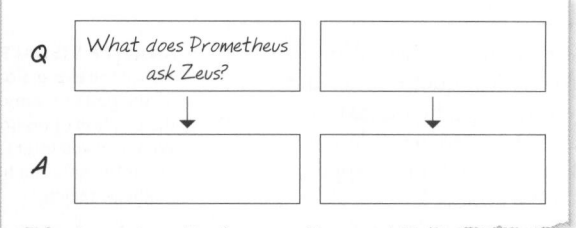

Q | What does Prometheus ask Zeus?

A |

VOCABULARY IN CONTEXT

In the selections, the boldfaced words help tell what happens when the gods are disobeyed. Restate each sentence, using a different word or words for the boldfaced terms.

1. The gods were **infinitely** more powerful than the humans.
2. He had little **aptitude** for following orders.
3. He swore **vengeance** against his enemies.
4. After her son was banished, she was **inconsolable.**
5. She wanted to **ascend** the mountain where the gods lived.

Author Online

Bernard Evslin: Drawn to Myths
In the mid-1960s, Bernard Evslin found his calling retelling myths and legends. His 1986 book *Hercules* won the Washington Irving Children's Book Choice Award.

Bernard Evslin
1922–1993

Olivia Coolidge: Bridging Past and Present
As a child, Olivia Coolidge and her sister made up fairy tales to tell each other. As an adult, Coolidge became a famous reteller of Greek tales and myths.

Olivia Coolidge
born 1908

Background

Zeus, Prometheus, and Hades
The Greek gods were not all equal in power or status. Prometheus was a part of a family of giants, the Titans. Zeus defeated them and became the mighty ruler of all gods. He ordered Prometheus to create humans. Hades, who appears in "Orpheus and Eurydice," was the ruler of the underworld. He, too, answered to Zeus.

 MORE ABOUT THE AUTHOR AND BACKGROUND
To learn more about the authors and the Greek gods, visit the **Literature Center** at **ClassZone.com.**

633

Teach

STANDARDS FOCUS

LITERARY ANALYSIS

● **CHARACTERISTICS OF MYTHS**
Read aloud this example:

> In his underwater palace, the sea-god Poseidon shook with anger and jealousy. His fury rose and rippled through the waters, causing a terrible earthquake.

Ask how Poseidon is like and unlike a human being. What event does his behavior explain? *Possible answer: He has human emotions, like anger, but he also has special abilities—he lives under the sea and can cause an earthquake. His behavior explains why an earthquake occurred.*

CHECK UNDERSTANDING Ask how a myth is different from realistic fiction.

READING STRATEGY

■ **MONITOR**
Ask students to monitor their understanding as they read the **Background** section. Have them share questions they thought about while reading. *Possible answers:*

- *How did Zeus come to rule all the gods?*
- *Why did Prometheus create humans?*
- *Where does Hades rule?*

Answer the questions as a class.

CHECK UNDERSTANDING Ask how questioning can be helpful while reading.

 RESOURCE MANAGER—Copy Master
Monitoring p. 29 (for student use while reading the selections)

VOCABULARY SKILL

▲ **VOCABULARY IN CONTEXT**

DIAGNOSE WORD KNOWLEDGE To determine preteaching needs, have all students complete **Vocabulary in Context.** Check students' answers: **1.** *infinitely = endlessly;* **2.** *aptitude = talent;* **3.** *vengeance = revenge;* **4.** *inconsolable = unable to be comforted;* **5.** *ascend = go up.*

PRETEACH VOCABULARY Use the Vocabulary Study copy master to help students determine the meanings of boldfaced words.

1. Read the first two sentences of the paragraph. Emphasize the boldfaced word.
2. Ask students to think about the way the word is used. Discuss possible meanings for *aptitude,* such as "skill" or "ability."
3. Repeat the procedure for the rest of the paragraph.

RESOURCE MANAGER—Copy Master
Vocabulary Study p. 31

For general guidelines on differentiating vocabulary instruction and for alternative vocabulary activities for students not needing vocabulary preteaching, see

BEST PRACTICES TOOLKIT
Scaffolding Vocabulary Instruction pp. 43–46

ⓘ Vocabulary Center at **ClassZone.com**

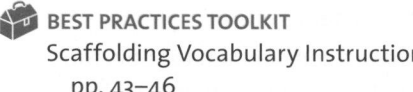

PROMETHEUS

Retold by **Bernard Evslin**

Prometheus was a young Titan, no great admirer of Zeus. Although he knew the great lord of the sky hated explicit questions, he did not hesitate to beard[1] him when there was something he wanted to know.

One morning he came to Zeus and said, "O Thunderer, I do not understand your design. You have caused the race of man[2] to appear on earth, but you keep him in ignorance and darkness."

"Perhaps you had better leave the race of man to me," said Zeus. "What you call ignorance is innocence. What you call darkness is the shadow of my decree. Man is happy now. And he is so framed that he 10 will remain happy unless someone persuades him that he is unhappy. Let us not speak of this again."

But Prometheus said, "Look at him. Look below. He crouches in caves. He is at the mercy of beast and weather. He eats his meat raw. If you mean something by this, enlighten me with your wisdom. Tell me why you refuse to give man the gift of fire." Ⓐ

---

1. **beard:** to confront or defy.
2. **man:** In older translations, the expression *man* was commonly used to refer to all people.

Prometheus Carrying Fire, Jan Cossiers
Prado, Madrid. © Art Resource, New York

BACKGROUND

Friend of Humankind Myths about Prometheus often depict him as a friend to humankind, as does this one. In contrast, the gods and goddesses are often shown to experience conflict and jealousy in their dealings with humans. Prometheus clearly had a soft spot for mortals—and it's no wonder, since he was believed to be their creator. The ancient Roman poet Ovid wrote that Prometheus shaped people out of earth and water, stood them upright, and "commanded [them] to behold the skies."

CULTURAL CONNECTION

Creation Stories Nearly all cultures have stories that tell how people came to exist. The Mayan *Popul Vuh* includes a story in which the gods tried to make humans from clay, but found they talked nonsense and dissolved in water; then they made humans from wood, but found they had hard hearts and no memories; finally, they made humans from corn and water. Ask students what other creation stories they have read or heard about.

FOR ENGLISH LEARNERS

Key Academic Vocabulary Have students use Word Questioning to study these academic vocabulary words: in "Prometheus," *explicit* (line 2) and *capacity* (line 26); in "Orpheus and Eurydice," *visions* (line 30), *rigid* (line 36), *reluctance* (line 62), and *attain* (line 78).

 BEST PRACTICES TOOLKIT—Transparency
Word Questioning p. E9

Options for Reading Read aloud the first Targeted Passage of each selection. Discuss who the characters are. Then have pairs read the rest of each story along with the *Audio Anthology CD*.

Prereading For prereading instruction for English learners, see

 BEST PRACTICES TOOLKIT
Scaffolding Reading Instruction pp. 43–46

FOR ADVANCED LEARNERS/PRE–AP

Pre-AP exercises in the bottom channel provide additional challenge for your advanced students. Use them for small groups or individuals.

ADDITIONAL GUIDELINES

For more help with differentiation and tips for classroom management, see

 BEST PRACTICES TOOLKIT
Differentiated Instruction pp. 31–38

Lines 16–28
DISCUSSION PROMPTS

Use these prompts to help students understand the conflict between Zeus and Prometheus:

Recall Why does Zeus say people were created? *Answer: They were created to worship and admire the gods.*

Analyze What does Prometheus mean when he says that people are "happy as beasts are happy" (line 22)? *Possible answer: He means that without the crafts and knowledge that fire could make possible, people can only be happy in a lowly, survival way, just as the animals are.*

Evaluate Does Zeus make a convincing argument for keeping people ignorant? Explain. *Possible answer: No; he seems to care mostly about how people worship him (lines 26–28). He has no interest in seeing humans reach their full potential.*

Lines 33–36
REINFORCE *KEY IDEA:* CONSEQUENCES

Discuss What does Zeus believe would be the **consequences** of giving people fire? *Possible answer: Zeus thinks that if people have fire, they will become arrogant and behave like they are gods themselves. He fears that people might even attack the home of the gods by storming Olympus (line 36).*

READING STRATEGY

B MONITOR

Possible answer: Prometheus thinks people should have fire; Zeus does not want them to have it.

Have students use a chart like the one on page 633 for their questions. *Possible questions:*

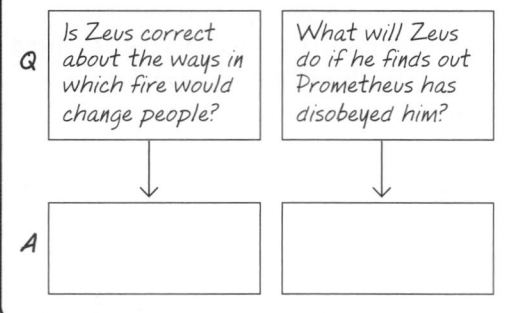

Q	Is Zeus correct about the ways in which fire would change people?	What will Zeus do if he finds out Prometheus has disobeyed him?
	↓	↓
A		

Zeus answered, "Do you not know, Prometheus, that every gift brings a penalty? This is the way the Fates[3] weave destiny—by which gods also must abide. Man does not have fire, true, nor the crafts which fire teaches. On the other hand, he does not know disease, warfare, old age, 20 or that inward pest called worry. He is happy, I say, happy without fire. And so he shall remain."

"Happy as beasts are happy," said Prometheus. "Of what use to make a separate race called man and endow[4] him with little fur, some wit, and a curious charm of unpredictability? If he must live like this, why separate him from the beasts at all?"

"He has another quality," said Zeus, "the capacity for worship. An **aptitude** for admiring our power, being puzzled by our riddles and amazed by our caprice.[5] That is why he was made."

"Would not fire, and the graces he can put on with fire, make him 30 more interesting?"

"More interesting, perhaps, but **infinitely** more dangerous. For there is this in man too: a vaunting pride that needs little sustenance[6] to make it swell to giant size. Improve his lot, and he will forget that which makes him pleasing—his sense of worship, his humility. He will grow big and poisoned with pride and fancy himself a god, and before we know it, we shall see him storming Olympus. Enough, Prometheus! I have been patient with you, but do not try me too far. Go now and trouble me no more with your speculations."

Prometheus was not satisfied. All that night he lay awake making 40 plans. Then he left his couch at dawn and, standing tiptoe on Olympus, stretched his arm to the eastern horizon where the first faint flames of the sun were flickering. In his hand he held a reed filled with a dry fiber; he thrust it into the sunrise until a spark smoldered. Then he put the reed in his tunic and came down from the mountain. **B**

At first men were frightened by the gift. It was so hot, so quick; it bit sharply when you touched it and for pure spite made the shadows dance. They thanked Prometheus and asked him to take it away. But he took the haunch of a newly killed deer and held it over the fire. And when the meat began to sear and sputter, filling the cave with its rich smells, 50 the people felt themselves melting with hunger and flung themselves on the meat and devoured it greedily, burning their tongues.

"This that I have brought you is called 'fire,'" Prometheus said. "It is an ill-natured spirit, a little brother of the sun, but if you handle

aptitude (ăp'tĭ-tood') *n.* natural ability

infinitely (ĭn'fə-nĭt-lē) *adv.* extremely; greatly

● SOCIAL STUDIES CONNECTION

Many settings in Greek myths are real places in Greece.

B MONITOR
Make sure you understand the **conflict** between Prometheus and Zeus. What questions do you have about what has already happened and about what will happen next?

---

3. **the Fates:** in Greek mythology, the three goddesses who decide the course of people's lives.
4. **endow** (ĕn-dou'): to provide with a quality or talent.
5. **caprice** (kə-prēs'): the quality of acting without planning or thinking beforehand.
6. **vaunting pride that needs little sustenance:** boastful pride that needs little support.

DIFFERENTIATED INSTRUCTION

FOR ENGLISH LEARNERS

Vocabulary: Cognates Have students scan "Prometheus" and "Orpheus and Eurydice" for cognates between English and other languages. English-Spanish cognates on page 636 include

- *destiny/el destino* (line 17)
- *separate/separado(a)* (line 23)
- *capacity/la capacidad* (line 26)
- *interesting/interesante* (line 30)
- *giant/gigante* (line 33)
- *humility/la humildad* (line 34)
- *mountain/la montaña* (line 44)
- *cave/la cueva* (line 49)
- *to devour/devorar* (line 51)
- *spirit/el espíritu* (line 53)

Vocabulary: Idioms Help students use context clues to figure out these idioms in "Prometheus":

- *at the mercy of* (line 13), "able to be hurt by"
- *on the other hand* (line 19), "by comparison"
- *improve [one's] lot* (line 33), "make one's life better"

it carefully, it can change your whole life. It is very greedy; you must feed it twigs, but only until it becomes a proper size. Then you must stop, or it will eat everything in sight—and you too. If it escapes, use this magic: water. It fears the water spirit, and if you touch it with water, it will fly away until you need it again."

He left the fire burning in the first cave, with children staring at it 60 wide-eyed, and then went to every cave in the land.

② Targeted Passage

Then one day Zeus looked down from the mountain and was amazed. Everything had changed. Man had come out of his cave. Zeus saw woodmen's huts, farmhouses, villages, walled towns, even a castle or two. He saw men cooking their food, carrying torches to light their way at night. He saw forges[7] blazing, men beating out ploughs, keels, swords, spears. They were making ships and raising white wings of sails and daring to use the fury of the winds for their journeys. They were wearing helmets, riding out in chariots to do battle, like the gods themselves. **C**

Zeus was full of rage. He seized his largest thunderbolt. "So they want 70 fire," he said to himself. "I'll give them fire—more than they can use. I'll turn their miserable little ball of earth into a cinder." But then another thought came to him, and he lowered his arm. "No," he said to himself, "I shall have **vengeance**—and entertainment too. Let them destroy themselves with their new skills. This will make a long, twisted game, interesting to watch. I'll attend to them later. My first business is with Prometheus."

He called his giant guards and had them seize Prometheus, drag him off to the Caucasus,[8] and there bind him to a mountain peak with great chains specially forged by Hephaestus[9]—chains which even a Titan in 80 agony could not break. And when the friend of man was bound to the mountain, Zeus sent two vultures to hover about him forever, tearing at his belly and eating his liver. **D**

Men knew a terrible thing was happening on the mountain, but they did not know what. But the wind shrieked like a giant in torment and sometimes like fierce birds.

Many centuries he lay there—until another hero was born brave enough to defy the gods. He climbed to the peak in the Caucasus and struck the shackles from Prometheus and killed the vultures. His name was Heracles.[10] ◥

---

7. **forges** (fôr´jǐz): places where metal is heated and hammered into shape.
8. **Caucasus** (kô´kə-səs): a mountainous region in southeastern Europe.
9. **Hephaestus** (hǐ-fĕs´təs): the Greek god of fire and metalworking.
10. **Heracles** (hĕr´ə-klēz´): another name for Hercules, a son of Zeus who was famous for his great strength and courage.

● GREEK MYTHS
According to this myth, what event allowed people to build homes, farm, and go to war?

vengeance (vĕn´jəns) *n.* the infliction of punishment in return for an offense

D MONITOR
What does Zeus do to Prometheus, and why? To **clarify** the answer, think about the conflict between the two gods. Then reread lines 77–82.

Lines 39–60
ADDITIONAL TEACHING OPPORTUNITY

Resolving Conflict Explain that the conflicts in a story are often—though not always—resolved, and the way a character decides to resolve a conflict can lead to even more conflicts or problems.

- Ask students how Prometheus resolves his conflict with Zeus. *Possible answer: He ignores Zeus's command and takes fire to the people.*
- Read aloud lines 52–60 and ask students to explain the purpose of Prometheus's instructions. *Possible answer: Prometheus wants to make sure that fire does not destroy the people.*
- What problems might arise from the action Prometheus has taken? *Possible answer: People might begin to overestimate their power, as Zeus predicted. Zeus might decide to punish Prometheus.*

LITERARY ANALYSIS

● GREEK MYTHS

Possible answer: Prometheus's giving people fire made all of these things possible. Once people had fire, they could use it to

- *keep warm inside houses they built, rather than just huddling together in a cave*
- *heat and shape metal to make farm tools, weapons, and armor*

READING STRATEGY

D MONITOR

Possible answers: What Zeus does—Zeus chains Prometheus to a mountain peak and sends two birds of prey to attack his stomach and eat his liver. Why—Prometheus disobeyed Zeus by giving fire to people.

FOR LESS–PROFICIENT READERS
② **Targeted Passage [Lines 59–82]**

This passage presents the climax: after Prometheus gives people fire, Zeus sees how fire has changed human life and vows revenge on Prometheus.

- Where does Prometheus bring the gift of fire?
- How does Zeus find out about Prometheus's gift?
- How does Zeus react to what he sees when he looks down from the mountain?

FOR ADVANCED LEARNERS/PRE–AP

Evaluate Zeus is convinced that humans are doomed to destroy themselves as they develop new skills and make their lives more comfortable. Is this an accurate assessment of human nature? Have students discuss Zeus's opinions in lines 31–38 and 72–76. Then have them make a chart with Zeus's ideas in one column and examples that either support or contradict each idea in the second column.

638 UNIT 6: MYTHS, LEGENDS, AND TALES

ANALYZE VISUALS

Possible answers: The listeners in the painting look as if they could be in a trance. Students may say that they, too, have had the experience of feeling swept away by music.

About the Art *Orpheus in the Underworld* was painted by Louis Jacquesson de la Chevreuse (1839–1901) in the neoclassical style. This art movement emerged in the mid-1700s, after the discoveries at Pompeii and Herculaneum, and it flourished in the 1800s. Neoclassicism celebrated the stories and imagery of ancient Greece and Rome. Figures in neoclassical art looked formal, as they did in the paintings of Pompeii and the statues of ancient Greece. Compare this restrained Orpheus with the robust Prometheus on page 635.

LITERARY ANALYSIS

ⓔ GREEK MYTHS

Possible answers:

- *Orpheus is special because he can create beautiful music.*
- *Line 1 says that the Greeks loved music.*

Orpheus *and* Eurydice

Retold by
Olivia Coolidge

In the legend of Orpheus the Greek love of music found its fullest expression. Orpheus, it is said, could make such heavenly songs that when he sat down to sing, the trees would crowd around to shade him. The ivy and vine stretched out their tendrils. Great oaks would bend their spreading branches over his head. The very rocks would edge down the mountainsides. Wild beasts crouched harmless by him, and nymphs[1] and woodland gods would listen to him enchanted. ⓔ

Orpheus himself, however, had eyes for no one but the nymph, Eurydice.[2] His love for her was his inspiration, and his power sprang from
10 the passionate longing that he knew in his own heart. All nature rejoiced with him on his bridal day, but on that very morning, as Eurydice went down to the riverside with her maidens to gather flowers for a bridal garland, she was bitten in the foot by a snake, and she died in spite of all attempts to save her.

ANALYZE VISUALS
Describe the listeners' expressions. How can you **connect** this ancient scene to your own experience with music?

ⓔ **GREEK MYTHS**
Note what quality makes Orpheus special. According to the first sentence, how much did the Greeks value this quality?

❸ **Targeted Passage**

---

1. **nymphs** (nĭmfs): divine beings represented as beautiful maidens who live in natural places such as trees.
2. **Eurydice** (yŏŏ-rĭd′ĭ-sē).

Orpheus in the Underworld (1863), Louis Jacquesson de la Chevreuse. Oil on canvas, 115 cm × 145 cm. Musée des Augustins. © akg-images

638 UNIT 6: MYTHS, LEGENDS, AND TALES

DIFFERENTIATED INSTRUCTION

FOR LESS–PROFICIENT READERS

❸ **Targeted Passage [Lines 2–14]**

This passage introduces the main character, Orpheus, and the loss that starts the plot's sequence of events—the death of his beloved, Eurydice, on their wedding day.

- How does Orpheus's music affect those who hear it?
- What inspires Orpheus?
- What happens to Eurydice on her wedding day?

FOR ENGLISH LEARNERS

Vocabulary Support Explain that many English words may function as either a noun or a verb. Use Read Aloud/Think Aloud to show students how they might use context clues to figure out whether these words on page 638 are used as a noun (to name something) or as a verb (to perform an action). Then ask students for examples of how each noun could be used as a verb and vice versa.

- *love* (lines 1, 9), noun
- *crowd* (line 3), verb

- *shade* (line 3), verb
- *vine* (line 4), noun
- *bend* (line 4), verb
- *branches* (line 5), noun
- *head* (line 5), noun
- *edge* (line 5), verb
- *power* (line 9), noun

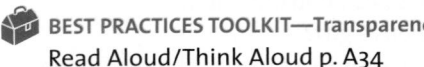 BEST PRACTICES TOOLKIT—Transparency
Read Aloud/Think Aloud p. A34

Orpheus Orpheus's mother was Calliope, the muse of epic poetry. (Muses were minor goddesses who ruled the arts and sciences.) In some stories, his father was Apollo, god of music and the sun; in others, his father was king of the region of Thrace, in southeastern Europe. According to legend, Apollo gave the child Orpheus a lyre (see the picture on page 640) and the muses taught him to play it. It is said that the northern constellation Lyra was placed in the sky as a tribute to Orpheus. In some versions of the Orpheus story, he was torn limb from limb at his death and thrown into the sea; his head later washed ashore on an island, where it was found still singing love songs to his beloved Eurydice.

FOR ENGLISH LEARNERS

Vocabulary: Idioms Help students use context clues to figure out these idioms in "Orpheus and Eurydice":

- *had eyes for no one but* (line 8), "cared about no other person except"
- *in his tracks* (line 22), "right where he was"
- *in vain* (lines 47 and 48), "without success"

Orpheus was **inconsolable.** All day long he mourned his bride, while birds, beasts, and the earth itself sorrowed with him. When at last the shadows of the sun grew long, Orpheus took his lyre and made his way to the yawning cave which leads down into the underworld, where the soul of dead Eurydice had gone.

20　Even grey Charon, the ferryman of the Styx,[3] forgot to ask his passenger for the price of crossing. The dog, Cerberus, the three-headed monster who guards Hades' gate, stopped full in his tracks and listened motionless until Orpheus had passed. As he entered the land of Hades, the pale ghosts came after him like great, uncounted flocks of silent birds. All the land lay hushed as that marvelous voice resounded across the mud and marshes of its dreadful rivers. In the daffodil fields of Elysium[4] the happy dead sat silent among their flowers. In the farthest corners of the place of punishment, the hissing flames stood still. Accursed Sisyphus,[5] who toils eternally to push a mighty rock uphill, sat down and knew not
30　he was resting. Tantalus,[6] who strains forever after visions of cool water, forgot his thirst and ceased to clutch at the empty air.

The pillared hall of Hades opened before the hero's song. The ranks of long-dead heroes who sit at Hades' board looked up and turned their eyes away from the pitiless form of Hades and his pale, unhappy queen. Grim and unmoving sat the dark king of the dead on his ebony throne, yet the tears shone on his rigid cheeks in the light of his ghastly torches. Even his hard heart, which knew all misery and cared nothing for it, was touched by the love and longing of the music. **F**

At last the minstrel came to an end, and a long sigh like wind in pine
40　trees was heard from the assembled ghosts. Then the king spoke, and his deep voice echoed through his silent land. "Go back to the light of day," he said. "Go quickly while my monsters are stilled by your song. Climb up the steep road to daylight, and never once turn back. The spirit of Eurydice shall follow, but if you look around at her, she will return to me."

Orpheus turned and strode from the hall of Hades, and the flocks of following ghosts made way for him to pass. In vain he searched their ranks for a sight of his lost Eurydice. In vain he listened for the faintest sound behind. The barge of Charon sank to the very gunwales[7] beneath

---

3. **Styx** (stĭks): in Greek mythology, the river across which the souls of the dead are transported.
4. **Elysium** (ĭ-lĭz′ē-əm): the home of the blessed, or those who were judged to have lived well, after death.
5. **Sisyphus** (sĭs′ə-fəs): a cruel king of Corinth condemned forever to roll a huge stone up a hill, only to have it fall down again.
6. **Tantalus** (tăn′tə-ləs): a king who, for his crimes, was condemned to stand in water that receded when he tried to drink.
7. **gunwales** (gŭn′əlz): the upper edge of the side of a vessel.

---

inconsolable
(ĭn′kən-sō′lə-bəl) *adj.*
impossible or difficult
to comfort

VISUAL VOCABULARY

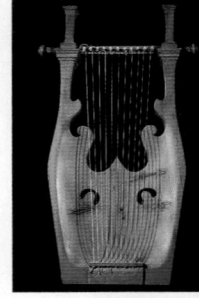

lyre (līr) *n.* an ancient stringed instrument resembling a small harp

④ Targeted Passage

F MONITOR
What **questions** do you have about what the underworld is like? Reviewing what you've read, along with the footnotes, might help you find answers.

READING STRATEGY

F MONITOR

Have students use a chart like the one on page 633 for their questions. *Possible answers:*

Q Is it possible to go in and out of the underworld?	What makes the waters "dreadful" (line 26)?
	↓　　↓
A	

Lines 41–45
REINFORCE *KEY IDEA:* CONSEQUENCES

Discuss If Orpheus disobeys the command of Hades, what will be the **consequences?** *Possible answer: If Orpheus looks back at Eurydice, she will have to return to Hades and the underworld.*

DIFFERENTIATED INSTRUCTION

FOR LESS–PROFICIENT READERS

④ Targeted Passage [Lines 32–45]

This passage presents a turning point in the story: Hades, king of the underworld, tells Orpheus how to bring Eurydice back to the world of the living.

- How does Hades react to Orpheus's music?
- Where does Hades tell Orpheus he may go?
- What does the king tell Orpheus he must not do?
- How is this a turning point in the story?

FOR ENGLISH LEARNERS

Language: Verb Tenses In English, the past tense of a regular verb is formed by adding *-ed,* as in *listened* (line 22). An irregular verb, however, has a unique past-tense form that must be memorized. Have pairs scan "Orpheus and Eurydice" for irregular verbs in the past tense and list them in one column of a T Chart. In the other column, have them write the present tense.

 BEST PRACTICES TOOLKIT—Transparency
T Chart p. A25

Present Tense	Past Tense
forget	forgot (line 20)
come	came (line 24)
sit	sat (line 27)
stand	stood (line 28)
know	knew (line 29)
shine	shone (line 36)
stride	strode (line 46)

⁵⁰ his weight, but no following passenger pressed it lower down. The way from the land of Hades to the upper world is long and hard, far easier to descend than climb. It was dark and misty, full of strange shapes and noises, yet in many places merely black and silent as the tomb. Here Orpheus would stop and listen, but nothing moved behind him. For all he could hear, he was utterly alone. Then he would wonder if the pitiless Hades were deceiving him. Suppose he came up to the light again and Eurydice was not there! Once he had charmed the ferryman and the dreadful monsters, but now they had heard his song. The second time his spell would be less powerful; he could never go again. Perhaps he had lost
⁶⁰ Eurydice by his readiness to believe. **G**

Every step he took, some instinct told him that he was going farther from his bride. He toiled up the path in reluctance and despair, stopping, listening, sighing, taking a few slow steps, until the dark thinned out into greyness. Up ahead a speck of light showed clearly the entrance to the cavern.

At that final moment Orpheus could bear no more. To go out into the light of day without his love seemed to him impossible. Before he had quite **ascended**, there was still a moment in which he could go back. Quick in the greyness he turned and saw a dim shade at his heels, as

G GREEK MYTHS
Recall the rule Hades gave to Orpheus. **Predict** whether Orpheus will obey it.

ascend (ə-sĕnd') *v.* to go or move upward; rise

Orpheus Leading Eurydice from the Underworld (1861), Jean Baptiste Camille Corot. Oil on canvas, 112.3 cm × 137.1 cm. © Museum of Fine Arts, Houston. © The Bridgeman Art Library.

ORPHEUS AND EURYDICE   **641**

Lines 50–68
DISCUSSION PROMPTS
Use these prompts to help students understand what Orpheus experiences as he leaves the underworld:

Intepret How would you describe what Orpheus is feeling as he climbs out of the underworld? *Possible answer: He feels anxious, worried, and hopeless.*

Analyze What words and phrases show how Orpheus is feeling? *Possible answers: "utterly alone" (line 55); "could never go again" (line 59); "toiled up the path in reluctance and despair" (line 62); "could bear no more" (line 66)*

Evaluate Is it worth the risk for Orpheus to check whether Eurydice follows him? Explain. *Possible answers: Yes; if he looks quickly, and if she is not there, he can go back to find her. No; the risk is too great, because disobeying Hades could cause him to lose Eurydice forever.*

LITERARY ANALYSIS

G GREEK MYTHS
Possible answer: Students may predict that, like Prometheus, Orpheus will disobey what the gods told him to do.

ANALYZE VISUALS
About the Art French painter Jean-Baptiste Camille Corot (1796–1875) was known for his misty and finely detailed landscape paintings. Corot painted several scenes from the Orpheus myth. *Orpheus Leading Eurydice from the Underworld* is the largest of these, measuring more than four feet across.

Activity How is this visual interpretation of Orpheus and Eurydice similar to and different from the description in the text? *Possible answers:*
• *Similar—Orpheus with lyre (line 17), pale ghosts (line 24), marshy landscape (line 26), Eurydice follows Orpheus (lines 43–44)*
• *Different—Eurydice in the painting appears to be flesh and blood (Orpheus holds her hand), while in the text she is a mere spirit or "dim shade" (line 69).*

READING STRATEGY

H MONITOR

Possible answer: The "dim shade" is Eurydice. She disappears because Orpheus has disobeyed Hades, and this means she must return to the underworld.

READING STRATEGY

I MONITOR

Possible answer: Orpheus and Eurydice are reunited in death. After Orpheus dies, he goes to the underworld and sees Eurydice again.

SELECTION WRAP–UP

REFLECT Ask students to consider which character expressed a deeper love: Prometheus and his love for humankind, or Orpheus and his love for Eurydice.

★ **CRITIQUE** Ask students to consider what the figures of Zeus and Hades represent in Greek mythology.

READING FLUENCY

Distribute the copy masters and have students work in pairs to practice fluency.

R RESOURCE MANAGER—Copy Master
Reading Fluency p. 36

---

70 indistinct as the grey mist behind her. But still he could see the look of sadness on her face as he sprung forward saying, "Eurydice!" and threw his arms about her. The shade dissolved in the circle of his arms like smoke. A little whisper seemed to say, "Farewell," as she scattered into mist and was gone. **H**

The unfortunate lover hastened back again down the steep, dark path. But all was in vain. This time the ghostly ferryman was deaf to his prayers. The very wildness of his mood made it impossible for him to attain the beauty of his former music. At last, his despair was so great that he could not even sing at all. For seven days he sat huddled together

80 on the grey mud banks, listening to the wailing of the terrible river. The flitting ghosts shrank back in a wide circle from the living man, but he paid them no attention. Only he sat with his eyes on Charon, his ears ringing with the dreadful noise of Styx.

Orpheus arose at last and stumbled back along the steep road he knew so well by now. When he came up to earth again, his song was pitiful but more beautiful than ever. Even the nightingale who mourned all night long would hush her voice to listen as Orpheus sat in some hidden place singing of his lost Eurydice. Men and women he could bear no longer, and when they came to hear him, he drove them away. At last the women

90 of Thrace, maddened by Dionysus[8] and infuriated by Orpheus' contempt, fell upon him and killed him. It is said that as the body was swept down the river Hebrus, the dead lips still moved faintly and the rocks echoed for the last time, "Eurydice." But the poet's eager spirit was already far down the familiar path.

In the daffodil meadows he met the shade of Eurydice, and there they walk together, or where the path is narrow, the shade of Orpheus goes ahead and looks back at his love. ∾ **I**

H MONITOR
Reread lines 66–74. What is the "dim shade" at Orpheus' heels? Why does the shade disappear? If you're not sure, try rereading lines 41–45 and then rereading this passage to **clarify** your understanding.

5 Targeted Passage

I MONITOR
How are Orpheus and Eurydice reunited? If you have any **questions**, review this page.

---

8. **women of Thrace** (thrās), **maddened by Dionysus** (dī'ə-nī'səs): Thrace was a Balkan region colonized by the Greeks; Dionysus was the god of wine.

DIFFERENTIATED INSTRUCTION

FOR LESS–PROFICIENT READERS

5 Targeted Passage [Lines 75–97]

This passage shows the resolution of the story: Orpheus loses Eurydice, dies, and is reunited with her in the underworld.

- What happens when Orpheus goes back to the underworld this time?
- What do the women of Thrace do to Orpheus?
- Where are the "daffodil meadows" (line 95)?
- How is Orpheus's conflict finally resolved?

FOR ENGLISH LEARNERS

Vocabulary: Suffixes Tell students that the suffix -ness changes an adjective to an abstract noun (one that names an idea or something that cannot be touched). Have students identify the parts of these words and then name other words ending in -ness.

- *readiness* (line 60)
- *greyness* (lines 64, 69)
- *sadness* (line 71)
- *wildness* (line 77)

FOR ADVANCED LEARNERS/PRE–AP

Analyze Description How does the author convey the despair that Orpheus feels? Have students reread lines 75–83 and focus on the descriptive language the author uses. Challenge students to create another sentence that could be added to further express Orpheus's feelings.

He felt neither hunger nor thirst, nor wind, nor rain; he felt only the utter agony of his grief for Eurydice.

Orpheus (1618), Marcello Provenzale. © Massimo Listri/Corbis.

Song of Orpheus

William Shakespeare

Orpheus with his lute[1] made trees,
And the mountain tops that freeze,
   Bow themselves when he did sing:
To his music plants and flowers
5 Ever sprung; as sun and showers
   There had made a lasting spring.

Every thing that heard him play,
Even the billows[2] of the sea,
   Hung their heads, and then lay by.
10 In sweet music is such art,
Killing care and grief of heart
   Fall asleep, or hearing, die.

---

1. **lute:** a small, stringed musical instrument with a pear-shaped body.

2. **billows:** huge waves.

ANALYZE VISUALS

About the Art This mosaic by Italian artist Marcello Provenzale depicts the Roman cardinal and art collector Scipione Borghese as Orpheus, charming everyone with his music. Mosaics, which are made of tiny pieces of colored glass or stone, were an important art form in ancient Greece and Rome.

Activity What feeling does this image convey? Based on this, what feeling might the song described in the poem create? *Possible answer: The image conveys a feeling of joyfulness through the happy look of the musician and the contented animals gathered around him. The song will create a feeling of happiness.*

DISCUSSION PROMPTS

Use these prompts to help students understand how Shakespeare expresses the power of music:

Restate How do trees, mountains, and the sea respond to the song of Orpheus? *Possible answer: Trees and mountains bow to his song. Waves in the sea lie down.*

Analyze According to lines 10–12, how can music affect human emotions? *Possible answer: Music can be comforting and transporting to listeners.*

Evaluate Do you agree with the poet's assessment about how music can affect human emotions? Explain. *Some students may say that they have had the experience of feeling comforted or transported when listening to music. Others may say that the poet is exaggerating music's power, or that some music makes people feel sad.*

FOR LESS–PROFICIENT READERS

Comprehension Support Remind students that in poetry, a line may or may not be a sentence. Explain that although line 1 might look like a complete sentence, in fact the sentence continues through line 3, where its meaning becomes clear: Orpheus "made trees ... bow themselves." Have student pairs identify sentences in the poem and the subject and verb of each.

FOR ENGLISH LEARNERS

Comprehension: Cause–Effect Ask students to help you identify the effects of Orpheus's song (lines 1–12) and note them in a cause-effect diagram on the board.

CAUSE

| Orpheus plays his lute. |

EFFECT

| Trees and mountains bow. |

EFFECT

| Plants and flowers grow. |

EFFECT

| The waves of the sea smooth out. |

EFFECT

| Worry and grief are laid aside. |

Practice and Apply

After Reading

For additional support of post-reading questions, use these copy masters:

RESOURCE MANAGER—Copy Masters
Reading Check p. 34 (to check understanding of the selection)
Characteristics of Myths p. 27 (for practice of literary analysis standards focus)
Question Support p. 35 (**After Reading** questions adapted for English learners and less-proficient readers)

Additional selection questions are provided for teachers on page 21.

For additional activities to challenge students, see

Power Thinking at **ClassZone.com**

ANSWERS

Comprehension

1. *At first, people are frightened by the fire and ask Prometheus to take it away.*

2. *Zeus thinks it will be more fun to watch people cause trouble for themselves with fire.*

3. *Hades agrees to return Eurydice because he is so moved by Orpheus's music.*

Literary Analysis

Possible answers:

4. ◼ **STANDARDS FOCUS** *Monitor*
Student pairs should focus on using evidence from the text to answer their remaining questions.

5. *Students should note similarities between the first paragraph of the myth and the Shakespeare poem. They may say that it is easier to visualize the scene with the details from the prose of the myth, such as the trees that crowd Orpheus with shade (line 3) and the plants that "stretched out their tendrils" (line 4).*

6. ● **STANDARDS FOCUS** *Characteristics of Myths* *The passage explains how Prometheus took fire from the sun (lines 42–43), gave it to humans (lines 45–51), and instructed humans on how to handle fire (lines 54–58).*

7. *Rewarded—skill, talent, and obedience; Punished—questioning the gods or going against their wishes; Conclusion—The myths encourage people to be humble and obedient.*

Comprehension

1. **Recall** When Prometheus gives humans fire, what is their first reaction?

2. **Recall** Why does Zeus decide not to punish the humans for having fire?

3. **Clarify** Why does Hades at first agree to return Eurydice to Orpheus?

MARYLAND OBJECTIVES

READING STANDARD
3.A.3.a Distinguish among types of narrative texts

Literary Analysis

4. **Monitor** Review the chart you created as you read. Are there questions you are unsure how to answer? Compare your chart with a classmate's. Together, go over the story to answer any remaining questions.

5. **Compare Literary Works** Compare "Orpheus and Eurydice" to William Shakespeare's "Song of Orpheus" on page 643. Identify the part of the myth the poem describes. Which literary work, the myth or the poem, best helps you **visualize** the scene? Explain your answer with details from the selection you choose.

6. **Analyze Characteristics of Greek Myths** Review lines 39–60 of "Prometheus." Why is this passage important in terms of explaining where fire comes from? Give specific details from the passage to support your answer.

7. **Draw Conclusions** What kind of behavior do you think these myths were meant to encourage? Make a chart and go back through the stories, noting which behaviors are rewarded and which are punished. Then give your conclusions about what kind of behavior the Greeks hoped to encourage in people by telling these myths.

Rewarded	Punished

Extension and Challenge

8. **Inquiry and Research** Zeus and Hades were part of a group of 12 gods who ruled from Mount Olympus. Do research to find out more about the Olympians. Then create a poster that lists all 12 of these gods and goddesses and tells what they were known for.

9. **Big Question Activity** Imagine you could ask Prometheus or Orpheus the Big Question on page 632. Choose one of these characters and write the answer you think he would give on the basis of his experiences.

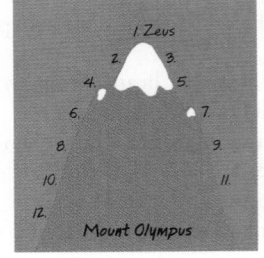

Mount Olympus

RESEARCH LINKS
For more on the Olympians, visit the **Research Center** at **ClassZone.com**.

Extension and Challenge

8. *Students' posters should list all twelve Olympians (Zeus, Hera, Poseidon, Hades, Aphrodite, Apollo, Ares, Artemis, Athena, Hephaestus, Hestia, Hermes) and indicate the significant powers and claims to fame for each. Students might also list Roman names for the Olympians, make note of family relationships among them, and note the symbols associated with them.*

9. *Students should use evidence from the text to support their answers and explain the consequences of the characters' actions.*

Vocabulary in Context

VOCABULARY PRACTICE

Decide whether the words in each pair are synonyms (words that mean the same) or antonyms (words that mean the opposite).

1. aptitude/talent
2. ascend/descend
3. inconsolable/comforted
4. infinitely/barely
5. vengeance/mercy

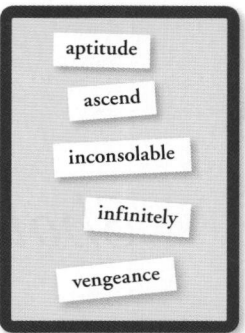

VOCABULARY IN WRITING

In these myths, how do the gods treat people who disobey them? Write a paragraph describing the gods' responses, using two or more vocabulary words. You might start like this.

> **EXAMPLE SENTENCE**
>
> *The gods usually act out some form of **vengeance** against those who disobey them.*

VOCABULARY STRATEGY: THE LATIN ROOT *fin*

The vocabulary word *infinitely* contains the Latin root *fin*, which means "end" or "limit." This root occurs in many English words. To understand the meaning of words with *fin*, use context clues and your knowledge of the root's meaning.

PRACTICE Based on context clues and your knowledge of the root *fin*, write a definition for each boldfaced word.

1. Many contestants spelled words wrong, but at the end of the day Mariah was a **finalist.**
2. I can't give you a **definite** answer until I double-check with Andy.
3. We all have a **finite** number of days in our lives.
4. It's hard for the human mind to understand the **infinity** of the universe.
5. All the performers returned to the stage for the **finale.**

MARYLAND OBJECTIVES

READING STANDARD
1.D.3.b Use word structure to determine meaning

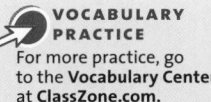
VOCABULARY PRACTICE
For more practice, go to the **Vocabulary Center** at **ClassZone.com.**

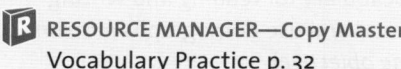

ANSWERS

Vocabulary in Context

VOCABULARY PRACTICE

1. *synonyms*
2. *antonyms*
3. *antonyms*
4. *antonyms*
5. *antonyms*

R RESOURCE MANAGER—Copy Master
Vocabulary Practice p. 32

VOCABULARY IN WRITING

Ask students to recall what happened to Prometheus and Orpheus after they disobeyed the gods. Then suggest that students look at the vocabulary list and consider how each word relates to one or both of these characters' experiences.

VOCABULARY STRATEGY: THE LATIN ROOT *fin* (also an EL language objective)

Help students look for context clues, such as "at the end of the day" and "returned to the stage." Explain that "end" or "limit" can refer to a boundary, such as "*finish* a book" or "*confine* a dog," or it may refer to a level or degree, such as "*fine* poet" or "*fine* dust."

Possible answers:
1. *one of the last contestants;* 2. *final;* 3. *limited;* 4. *endless nature;* 5. *last part of the show*

R RESOURCE MANAGER—Copy Master
Vocabulary Strategy p. 33

i Vocabulary Center at **ClassZone.com**
Additional Vocabulary Activities

Assess and Reteach

Assess

R RESOURCE MANAGER—Copy Masters
Selection Tests A, B/C pp. 37–38, 39–40
Test Generator CD

Reteach

S STANDARDS LESSON FILE
Reading Lesson 2: Monitoring
Vocabulary Lesson 1: Word Parts

DIFFERENTIATED INSTRUCTION

FOR ENGLISH LEARNERS

Vocabulary: Cognates Encourage students who speak Latin-based languages to brainstorm words containing the Latin root *fin,* such as the Spanish cognates *definir, definitivo(a), infinito(a),* and *refinar.*

FOR ADVANCED LEARNERS/PRE–AP

Vocabulary Strategy Have students write a descriptive paragraph about the dilemmas faced by one of the characters in the myths, using three words that contain the Latin root *fin.*

Focus and Motivate

OBJECTIVES

Literary Analysis
- explore the key idea of **limitations**
- identify cultural values in myths
- read Greek myths

Reading
- identify cause-and-effect relationships

Vocabulary
- build vocabulary for reading and writing
- understand and use homographs (also an EL language objective)

Grammar and Writing
- identify simple and compound sentences
- use correct sentence structure
- use writing to analyze literature

SUMMARY

"Icarus and Daedalus" tells of a father and son's flight on homemade wings. Icarus ignores his father's warning about the sun, and his wings melt. In "Phaëthon, Son of Apollo," Phaëthon convinces his reluctant father to let him drive the chariot of the sun. He embarks on a ride so disastrous that Zeus strikes him down. Both disobedient sons fall to their deaths.

Should people always R E A C H *for the stars?*

Discuss the question and the **KEY IDEA**. Ask students to list the risks and benefits of believing there are no **limitations**. What might students tell a friend who wants to pursue a difficult goal? Then have pairs work on the **CHART IT** activity.

Selection Resources

Icarus and Daedalus
Greek Myth Retold by Josephine Preston Peabody

Phaëthon, Son of Apollo
Greek Myth Retold by Olivia Coolidge

Should people always R E A C H *for the stars?*

MARYLAND OBJECTIVES

READING/LIT STANDARDS
1.E.3.a Select and apply appropriate strategies during reading
3.A.6.a Analyze universal themes

KEY IDEA Parents, teachers, and others we admire often proclaim that the only **limitations** placed on what we can achieve are those we place on ourselves. But should we always "reach for the stars" and follow our dream, or should we first consider whether the dream is practical or achievable? The characters in the following selections may provide an answer.

CHART IT In the first column of a chart, list dreams or goals that people often mention. In the second column, list the limits that others sometimes put on those dreams. Then tell whether you think the dream is still worth pursuing.

Dream	Limits	Worth Pursuing?
be an actor	not much money at first and few actors are successful	

646

---

* Resources for Differentiation   † Also in Spanish   ‡ In Haitian Creole and Vietnamese

LITERARY ANALYSIS: CULTURAL VALUES IN MYTHS

Myths of every culture reveal the values of the society in which they were created. These **cultural values** are standards of behavior believed to lead to a good life. In ancient Greece, people entertained one another with stories that celebrated these values:

- Obey your elders.
- Know your place.
- Respect and obey the gods.

Listeners learned important lessons by hearing what happened to characters who upheld—or did not uphold—these values. As you read, notice what happens to each character and decide what values the myth teaches.

READING SKILL: CAUSE AND EFFECT

You'll better understand what happens to characters if you pay attention to the relationship between causes and effects. A **cause** is an event that directly results in a later event, called an **effect**. As you read, record each cause and effect in a graphic. If an effect causes another effect, add squares to your graphic to show the cause-and-effect chain.

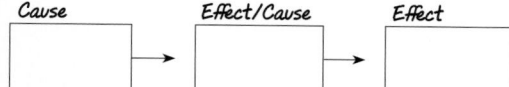

| Cause | → | Effect/Cause | → | Effect |

VOCABULARY IN CONTEXT

In the selections, the boldfaced words help tell what happens when two boys try to follow their dream. Using context clues, write a definition of each.

1. He had to **veer** to the left to avoid a collision.
2. She tried to **dissuade** him from taking such a risk.
3. They made a **rash** decision to ignore the gods' warnings.
4. The boy has a **cunning** plan to outsmart his opponents.
5. The pathway ended in a **precipitous** drop.
6. Being so high up made the climber's head **reel.**
7. They showed no **deference** to the decision makers.
8. He worked to **sustain** his speed.

Author Online

Josephine Preston Peabody: A Born Writer Josephine Preston Peabody's interest in myths and legends frequently influenced her writing, which included poetry and nonfiction. She published *Old Greek Folk Stories Told Anew* in 1897.

Josephine Preston Peabody
1874–1922

Olivia Coolidge: A Lover of the Classics Olivia Coolidge grew up in England, where she learned to share her family's love of history and the classics. She is now one of the best-loved retellers of Greek myths.

Olivia Coolidge
born 1908

Background

Divine Connections In Greek myths, gods and goddesses frequently have human offspring. Many human, or mortal, heroes are related in some way to the gods.

The Story of the Sun God Apollo, who was also called Phoebus Apollo, was the god of the sun. Daily, he pulled the sun into and out of the sky while riding in his chariot.

 MORE ABOUT THE AUTHOR AND BACKGROUND
To learn more about the authors and Greek gods, visit the **Literature Center** at **ClassZone.com.**

647

Teach

STANDARDS FOCUS

LITERARY ANALYSIS

● **CULTURAL VALUES IN MYTHS**

Read aloud this example:

> Instantly Arachne regretted laughing at the goddess Athena—but it was too late. Her human shape slipped away as she felt herself transformed into a spider.

Ask students what cultural value the story might reflect. ***Possible answer:*** *Arachne's fate suggests that respect for the gods was a high cultural value.*

CHECK UNDERSTANDING Ask students to recall a lesson learned by a character in a movie. What value does it illustrate?

READING SKILL

■ **CAUSE AND EFFECT**

Read aloud this example:

> "What a beautiful face," Narcissus thought, as he admired his reflection in the lake. Fascinated, he leaned closer. As he reached out to caress the face, he fell in and drowned.

What happened as a result of Narcissus's love for his own image? ***Possible answer:*** *He drowned.*

CHECK UNDERSTANDING Ask students for an example of a cause-and-effect relationship in another story.

 RESOURCE MANAGER—Copy Master Cause and Effect p. 53 (for student use while reading the selections)

VOCABULARY SKILL

▲ **VOCABULARY IN CONTEXT**

DIAGNOSE WORD KNOWLEDGE To determine preteaching needs, have all students complete **Vocabulary in Context.** Check students' answers. *Possible answers: 1. "swerve";* *2. "prevent"; 3. "careless"; 4. "clever"; 5. "steep";* *6. "feel dizzy"; 7. "respect"; 8. "keep up"*

PRETEACH VOCABULARY Use the Vocabulary Study copy master to help students determine the meaning of each boldfaced word.

1. Read aloud the sentences, emphasizing each boldfaced word.
2. Ask students to think about the way the word *cunning* is used. Discuss possible meanings, such as "clever" or "inventive."
3. Repeat the procedure for each of the other sentences.

RESOURCE MANAGER—Copy Master Vocabulary Study p. 55

For general guidelines on differentiating vocabulary instruction and for alternative vocabulary activities for students not needing vocabulary preteaching, see

BEST PRACTICES TOOLKIT Scaffolding Vocabulary Instruction pp. 43–46

ⓘ Vocabulary Center at **ClassZone.com** Additional Vocabulary Activities

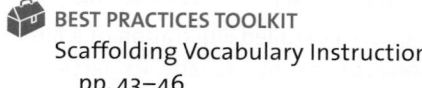

Practice and Apply

ANALYZE VISUALS

Possible answers: The red shape might symbolize the figure's

- heart
- life energy
- creative fire

About the Art This image of Icarus is by French artist Henri Matisse (1869–1954), who was one of the most accomplished painters of the late 19th and early 20th centuries. By about 1940, however, health problems prevented Matisse from painting, and he turned to cut-paper collage—a technique he called "drawing with scissors." His assistants painted the paper with gouache, a thick and brilliantly colored watercolor paint, and then Matisse cut out the shapes. Some of the images, like this one, were small, but in later years Matisse created paper cut-outs that covered entire walls.

ICARUS
and
DAEDALUS

Retold by Josephine Preston Peabody

A mong all those mortals who grew so wise that they learned the secrets of the gods, none was more **cunning** than Daedalus.[1]

He once built, for King Minos of Crete,[2] a wonderful Labyrinth[3] of winding ways so cunningly tangled up and twisted around that, once inside, you could never find your way out again without a magic clue. But the king's favor **veered** with the wind, and one day he had his master architect imprisoned in a tower. Daedalus managed to escape from his cell; but it seemed impossible to leave the island, since every ship that came or went was well guarded by order of the king.

① Targeted Passage

cunning (kŭn'ĭng) *adj.* skillful, clever

veer (vîr) *v.* to change direction; to shift

ANALYZE VISUALS
What might the red shape inside the figure **symbolize?** Explain your thoughts.

---

1. **Daedalus** (dĕd'l-əs).
2. **Crete:** an island in the Mediterranean Sea, southeast of Greece.
3. **Labyrinth** (lăb'ə-rĭnth'): a maze—that is, a complicated network of paths built to cause confusion.

648 UNIT 6: MYTHS, LEGENDS, AND TALES

Icarus, Henri Matisse. Stencil print after a gouache and paper collage. Published in the illustrated book *Jazz,* Editions Tériade, 1947.

DIFFERENTIATED INSTRUCTION

FOR ALL STUDENTS

Enhancing Learning Styles Provide these independent projects for various learning styles.

- **Linguistic** Improvise a dialogue between one of the father-son pairs in the selections.
- **Logical** Draw a detailed illustration of a bird wing, horse, or chariot and label its parts.
- **Visual** Create a Matisse-inspired paper cut-out of a mythical character or setting.

For further details on these projects, see

R RESOURCE MANAGER
Ideas for Extension pp. 46–47

FOR LESS–PROFICIENT READERS

In combination with the *Audio Anthology CD,* use one or more Targeted Passages (pp. 648, 650, 651, 652, 655, 656) to ensure that students focus on key story events, concepts, and skills.

① Targeted Passage [Lines 1–9]

This passage introduces the character of Daedalus, the setting, and the inciting incident: Daedalus has been imprisoned by the king.

- Where does the story take place?
- Who is Daedalus?
- What does King Minos do when he becomes angry with Daedalus?
- Why is it difficult for Daedalus to escape from Crete?

BACKGROUND

A Minoan Maze According to legend, Daedalus was trained as a craftsman by the goddess Athena. It is said that he built the labyrinth for King Minos of Crete to imprison the Minotaur, a terrible monster with the head of a bull and the body of a man. (The words *labyrinth* and *labyrinthine* come from this story.) On Crete, archaeologists have discovered remains of a culture dating to 3000 B.C. and have named it the Minoan civilization, after the legendary King Minos. Among the most interesting Minoan ruins is a palace at the site of Knossos. It is thought that the many rooms and complicated floor plan of this palace inspired the story of Daedalus's labyrinth.

CULTURAL CONNECTION

Flight Myths Many cultures have legends about flying. Emperor Shun of China (c. 2230 B.C.) is said to have used two large reed hats as wings to escape from a burning granary. In Africa, Kibaga was an invisible flying warrior who fought for the king of Uganda. According to South American myths, people used feathered wings similar to those made by Daedalus to leap into the air from tall towers. Invite students to share flying myths from other cultural traditions.

FOR ENGLISH LEARNERS

Options for Reading Have pairs of students take turns reading aloud the sentences on the first page of each myth. Then have them continue reading along as they listen to the *Audio Anthology CD.*

Key Academic Vocabulary Have students use Word Questioning for this academic vocabulary: in "Icarus and Daedalus," *vision* (line 35) and *relax* (line 48); in "Phaëthon, Son of Apollo," *obtain* (line 20) and *seek* (line 113).

 BEST PRACTICES TOOLKIT—Transparency Word Questioning p. E9

Prereading For prereading instruction for English learners, see

 BEST PRACTICES TOOLKIT Scaffolding Reading Instruction pp. 43–46

FOR ADVANCED LEARNERS/PRE–AP

Pre-AP exercises in the bottom channel provide additional challenge for your advanced students. Use them for small groups or individuals.

ADDITIONAL GUIDELINES

For more help with differentiation and tips for classroom management, see

 BEST PRACTICES TOOLKIT Differentiated Instruction pp. 31–38

Ⓐ CULTURAL VALUES

Possible answer: Daedalus shows cleverness.

Lines 27–28
REINFORCE *KEY IDEA:* LIMITATIONS

Discuss Icarus seems to think that if birds aren't careful about flying, he shouldn't have to be, either. How are his **limitations** different from those of a bird, though? *Possible answers: Icarus's wings, unlike a bird's wings, are homemade and could come apart. Icarus has had some instruction in how to use the wings, but he was not born with the ability to fly, as birds are.*

READING SKILL

Ⓑ CAUSE AND EFFECT

Have students use the chart from page 647 to record their answers. *Possible answers:*

Cause	Effect
Icarus is excited about flying for the first time (line 27); he can think only about escaping (line 29).	Icarus forgets his father's warning.

Lines 39–46
DISCUSSION PROMPTS

Use these prompts to help students understand what Icarus experiences:

Interpret What words and phrases express how Icarus feels? *Possible answer: Supported like a "bird in the hollow of a wave" (line 40) or a child "uplifted by his mother" (line 41), he feels only his own "joy" (line 41) and sees all else "vaguely" (line 43). He longs to "quench the thirst of his captivity" (lines 44–45).*

Synthesize What are the dangers of thinking only about how you feel in the moment? Think of a scenario when this might occur. *Possible answer: If you focus only on your feelings in a particular moment, you may be unable to use reason to make wise decisions. This could lead to danger. For example, a surfer might be unable to resist riding a wave that is too big and get pulled under by the current.*

---

10   At length, watching the sea-gulls in the air—the only creatures that were sure of liberty—he thought of a plan for himself and his young son Icarus,[4] who was captive with him. Ⓐ

Little by little, he gathered a store of feathers great and small. He fastened these together with thread, molded them in with wax, and so fashioned two great wings like those of a bird. When they were done, Daedalus fitted them to his own shoulders, and after one or two efforts, he found that by waving his arms he could winnow the air and cleave it,[5] as a swimmer does the sea. He held himself aloft, wavered this way and that with the wind, and at last, like a great fledgling,[6] he learned to fly.

20   Without delay, he fell to work on a pair of wings for the boy Icarus, and taught him carefully how to use them, bidding him beware of rash adventures among the stars. "Remember," said the father, "never to fly very low or very high, for the fogs about the earth would weigh you down, but the blaze of the sun will surely melt your feathers apart if you go too near."

For Icarus, these cautions went in at one ear and out by the other. Who could remember to be careful when he was to fly for the first time? Are birds careful? Not they! And not an idea remained in the boy's head but the one joy of escape. Ⓑ

30   The day came, and the fair wind that was to set them free. The father bird put on his wings, and, while the light urged them to be gone, he waited to see that all was well with Icarus, for the two could not fly hand in hand. Up they rose, the boy after his father. The hateful ground of Crete sank beneath them; and the country folk, who caught a glimpse of them when they were high above the treetops, took it for a vision of the gods—Apollo, perhaps, with Cupid after him.

At first there was a terror in the joy. The wide vacancy of the air dazed them—a glance downward made their brains **reel.**

But when a great wind filled their wings, and Icarus felt himself

40   **sustained,** like a halcyon bird[7] in the hollow of a wave, like a child uplifted by his mother, he forgot everything in the world but joy. He forgot Crete and the other islands that he had passed over: he saw but vaguely that winged thing in the distance before him that was his father Daedalus. He longed for one draft of flight to quench the thirst of his captivity: he stretched out his arms to the sky and made towards the highest heavens.

---

4. **Icarus** (ĭk'ər-əs).
5. **winnow the air and cleave it:** fan the air, as if with wings, and cut through it.
6. **fledgling:** a young bird.
7. **halcyon** (hăl'sē-ən) **bird:** a bird that, according to legend, built a nest on the sea and thus calmed the water.

Ⓐ **CULTURAL VALUES**
A character in a myth often represents one human trait, such as goodness. What trait does Daedalus display?

② **Targeted Passage**

Ⓑ **CAUSE AND EFFECT**
Reread lines 26–29. What causes Icarus to forget his father's warning as soon as he hears it?

reel (rēl) *v.* to feel unsteady or dizzy

sustain (sə-stān') *v.* to keep up; to support

DIFFERENTIATED INSTRUCTION

FOR LESS–PROFICIENT READERS
② Targeted Passage [Lines 10–25]

This passage introduces the main character of Icarus and the story's central conflict: the struggle of Icarus and Daedalus to escape from the island of Crete.

- What is the relationship between Daedalus and Icarus?
- Why does Daedalus make the wings?
- What warning does Daedalus give to Icarus?

FOR ENGLISH LEARNERS
Vocabulary: Idioms Help students use context clues to figure out these idioms in "Icarus and Daedalus":

- *at length* (line 10), "after a while"
- *little by little* (line 13), "gradually"
- *went in at one ear and out by the other* (line 26), "were ignored"

Falling Figure (Icarus) (1944), Henri Matisse. Color lithograph after a paper cut-out and gouache. Published on the back cover of the deluxe art review *Verve* in 1944.

Alas for him! Warmer and warmer grew the air. Those arms, that had seemed to uphold him, relaxed. His wings wavered, drooped. He fluttered his young hands vainly—he was falling—and in that terror he remembered. The heat of the sun had melted the wax from his wings; the feathers were falling, one by one, like snowflakes; and there was none to help. **C**

He fell like a leaf tossed down the wind, down, down, with one cry that overtook Daedalus far away. When he returned, and sought high and low for his poor boy, he saw nothing but the birdlike feathers afloat on the water, and he knew that Icarus was drowned.

The nearest island he named Icaria, in memory of the child; but he, in heavy grief, went to the temple of Apollo in Sicily, and there hung up his wings as an offering. Never again did he attempt to fly. ❧ **D**

❸ Targeted Passage

C CAUSE AND EFFECT
Why does Icarus fall? Add the cause to your graphic.

D CULTURAL VALUES
Explain what this myth suggests about respecting the warnings of elders.

FOR LESS–PROFICIENT READERS
Reading Skill Follow-Up: Cause and Effect Ask students to reread the last three lines and think about the effects of Icarus's death. Have them record these effects in a graphic organizer that shows several effects of a single cause.

🧰 **BEST PRACTICES TOOLKIT—Transparency**
   Cause-and-Effect Diagram pp. B16, B38

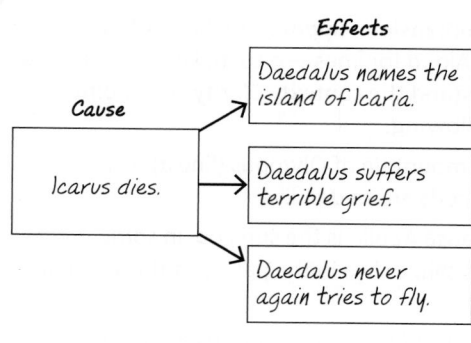

Cause
Icarus dies.

Effects
- Daedalus names the island of Icaria.
- Daedalus suffers terrible grief.
- Daedalus never again tries to fly.

❸ Targeted Passage [Lines 47–56]

This passage presents the climax and resolution of the story: Icarus flies too close to the sun, melting the wax in his wings, and then falls to his death.

- Why does the air grow warmer and warmer?
- What happens to Icarus's wings?
- What happens to Icarus?
- How could Icarus have avoided this fate?

Possible answers:

- *A tense mood is created by the jagged orange shape at the top, the way the rider shields his face, the undulating black lines in the center, the dark blue border, and the green shape in the top left corner that looks like a skull.*

- *A mood of exhilaration is created by the brilliant colors, the soaring horse, the flying cape, and the looseness of the shapes in general—even the tree in the lower left seems to lean in excitement.*

About the Art The Blaue Reiter (Blue Rider) was an association of creative artists who gathered in Germany from 1911 to 1914. Artists in this group used bold, expressive forms and colors. In 1912, the group published an anthology of art, *Almanach Der Blaue Reiter*, which made a lasting impression on 20th-century art. The group's central figure, Russian-born Wassily Kandinsky (1866–1944), painted several different designs for the cover of the anthology. He painted this design in India ink in 1911.

LITERARY ANALYSIS

E CULTURAL VALUES

Possible answers: *Phaëthon is*

- *likely to brag (line 8)*
- *very competitive (line 11)*
- *brave and bold (lines 12–13)*
- *arrogant (lines 14–15)*

Extend the Discussion Notice what Phaëthon tells his comrades in lines 9–11. Why might he make this point? What does it suggest about his ambitions?

Phaëthon, Son of Apollo

Retold by Olivia Coolidge

Though Apollo always honored the memory of Daphne,[1] she was not his only love. Another was a mortal, Clymene,[2] by whom he had a son named Phaëthon.[3] Phaëthon grew up with his mother, who, since she was mortal, could not dwell in the halls of Olympus or in the palace of the sun. She lived not far from the East in the land of Ethiopia, and as her son grew up, she would point to the place where Eos,[4] goddess of the dawn, lighted up the sky and tell him that there his father dwelt. Phaëthon loved to boast of his divine father as he saw the golden chariot riding high through the air. He would remind his comrades of other
10 sons of gods and mortal women who, by virtue of their great deeds, had themselves become gods at last. He must always be first in everything, and in most things this was easy, since he was in truth stronger, swifter, and more daring than the others. Even if he were not victorious, Phaëthon always claimed to be first in honor. He could never bear to be beaten, even if he must risk his life in some **rash** way to win. **E**

1. **Daphne** (dăf'nē): a wood nymph who did not return Apollo's love. She disappeared, and a laurel tree grew in her place.
2. **Clymene** (klī'mə-nē).
3. **Phaëthon** (fā'ə-thŏn').
4. **Eos** (ē'ŏs').

④ **Targeted Passage**

rash (răsh) *adj.* reckless and careless

E CULTURAL VALUES
Reread lines 8–15. What can you **infer** about Phaëthon's personality?

Study of *Almanach Der Blaue Reiter* (1911), Wassily Kandinsk Watercolor, gouache, and black ink. Inv. AM 1994–70. Photo b Philippe Migeat. Musée National d'Art Moderne, Centre George Pompidou, Paris. ©ARS, New York. © CNAC/MNAM/Dis Réunion des Musées Nationaux/Art Resource, New York

652 UNIT 6: MYTHS, LEGENDS, AND TALES

DIFFERENTIATED INSTRUCTION

FOR LESS–PROFICIENT READERS

④ **Targeted Passage [Lines 1–13]**

This passage introduces the main character, Phaëthon, and his central motivation: the desire to be above his peers, and to identify himself with his father, the sun-god Apollo.

- Who are Phaëthon's parents? Are they gods or mortals?
- How does Phaëthon feel about his father?
- How does Phaëthon behave in competitions?

Comprehension Support Use Read Aloud/ Think Aloud for lines 1–9 to make sure students understand the context. Clarify such points as the following:

- The mountain of Olympus (line 4) is where the gods are said to live.
- Because Apollo is the sun god, in some myths he is said to live in the palace of the sun (lines 4–5).
- A chariot (line 8) is a small, two-wheeled vehicle drawn by horses.

- When Phaëthon sees "the golden chariot riding high through the air" (lines 8–9), he is watching the sun rise or set. In Greek myth, Apollo used a chariot to pull the sun across the sky.

Help students identify Greece, Mount Olympus, and Ethiopia on a map.

 BEST PRACTICES TOOLKIT—Transparency Read Aloud/Think Aloud p. A34

BACKGROUND

Demigods In this selection, Phaëthon talks about "other sons of gods and mortal women who ... become gods at last" (lines 9–11). Greek mythology includes a number of half-mortals, or demigods, who came to be worshipped as gods. The best known of these was Dionysus, son of Zeus and the mortal Semele; as an adult, Dionysus became one of the Olympian gods. Several heroes were fathered by gods, including Heracles (Hercules), son of Zeus and the mortal Alcmene. Heracles became a god after his death.

FOR ENGLISH LEARNERS

Vocabulary: Idioms and Sayings Help students use context clues to figure out these idioms and sayings in "Phaëthon, Son of Apollo":

- *by virtue of* (line 10), "because of"
- *a matter of life and death* (line 27), "extremely important"
- *plucked up courage* (lines 46–47), "tried to feel brave"
- *give way* (line 73), "agree to a demand"

FOR ADVANCED LEARNERS/PRE–AP

Explore Hubris Both Icarus and Phaëthon break one of the cardinal rules of ancient Greek society—they forget their place in the social structure that stretches from Zeus to the lowliest beggar. Have students research the idea of hubris, or excessive pride. Ask them to present other myths that illustrate the Greeks' belief that it is dangerous to ignore one's social limitations. Interested students may write original myths with a similar theme.

DISCUSSION PROMPTS

Use these prompts to help students understand Phaëthon's motivations:

Interpret What does Phaëthon want from Epaphos? *Possible answer: He wants Epaphos to treat him as if he is superior.*

Analyze Why is it so important to Phaëthon that people believe Apollo is his father? *Possible answer: He wants to feel special and get a lot of attention and admiration, and he thinks that having a god for a father will ensure this kind of treatment.*

Synthesize What can be the danger of trying to prove your importance to other people? *Possible answer: It can take a lot of time and energy to try to prove your importance to other people; it can also make you seem arrogant. Sometimes it is better to not worry about what other people think and put your time and energy to other uses.*

READING SKILL

F CAUSE AND EFFECT

Have students record their answers in a cause-and-effect chain. *Possible answer:*

Cause	Effect
Apollo likes what he sees in Phaëthon; he is "pleased with his son's beauty and daring" (line 50). →	*He agrees to let Phaëthon have proof of his origin.*

Most of the princes of Ethiopia willingly paid Phaëthon honor, since they admired him greatly for his fire and beauty. There was one boy, however, Epaphos,[5] who was rumored to be a child of Zeus himself. Since this was not certainly proved, Phaëthon chose to disbelieve it and
20 to demand from Epaphos the **deference** that he obtained from all others. Epaphos was proud too, and one day he lost his temper with Phaëthon and turned on him, saying, "You are a fool to believe all that your mother tells you. You are all swelled up with false ideas about your father."

Crimson with rage, the lad rushed home to his mother and demanded that she prove to him the truth of the story that she had often told. "Give me some proof," he implored her, "with which I can answer this insult of Epaphos. It is a matter of life and death to me, for if I cannot, I shall die of shame."

"I swear to you," replied his mother solemnly, "by the bright orb of the
30 sun itself that you are his son. If I swear falsely, may I never look on the sun again, but die before the next time he mounts the heavens. More than this I cannot do, but you, my child, can go to the eastern palace of Phoebus Apollo—it lies not far away—and there speak with the god himself."

The son of Clymene leaped up with joy at his mother's words. The palace of Apollo was indeed not far. It stood just below the eastern horizon, its tall pillars glistening with bronze and gold. Above these it was white with gleaming ivory, and the great doors were flashing silver, embossed with pictures of earth, sky, and sea, and the gods that dwelt therein. Up the steep hill and the bright steps climbed Phaëthon, passing
40 unafraid through the silver doors, and stood in the presence of the sun. Here at last he was forced to turn away his face, for Phoebus sat in state on his golden throne. It gleamed with emeralds and precious stones, while on the head of the god was a brilliant diamond crown upon which no eye could look undazzled.

Phaëthon hid his face, but the god had recognized his son, and he spoke kindly, asking him why he had come. Then Phaëthon plucked up courage and said, "I come to ask you if you are indeed my father. If you are so, I beg you to give me some proof of it so that all may recognize me as Phoebus' son."

50 The god smiled, being well pleased with his son's beauty and daring. He took off his crown so that Phaëthon could look at him, and coming down from his throne, he put his arms around the boy, and said, "You are indeed my son and Clymene's, and worthy to be called so. Ask of me whatever thing you wish to prove your origin to men, and you shall have it." **F**

Phaëthon swayed for a moment and was dizzy with excitement at the touch of the god. His heart leaped; the blood rushed into his face. Now

deference (dĕf′ər-əns) *n.* respect and honor

F CAUSE AND EFFECT
Why does Apollo agree to grant Phaëthon proof of his origin?

---

5. **Epaphos** (ĕp′ə-fəs).

DIFFERENTIATED INSTRUCTION

FOR LESS–PROFICIENT READERS

Comprehension Support Remind students that *Phoebus* (lines 41 and 49) is another name for Apollo. Point out that in lines 32–33, Clymene refers to the sun god as Phoebus Apollo. In ancient Greek, *phoibos* means "shining" or "bright" and was used to refer to Apollo's role as god of the sun.

FOR ENGLISH LEARNERS

Language: Phrasal Verbs Explain that in line 22, *turn on* means "to act hostile toward," while in line 41, *turn away* means "to move back from." Assign pairs other phrasal verbs to look up in a dictionary.

- *grow up* (lines 3, 6)
- *take off* (line 51)
- *let down* (line 86)
- *dry up* (line 98)
- *call upon* (line 105)
- *cast out* (line 108)

FOR ADVANCED LEARNERS/PRE–AP

Analyze Character's Choices What should Phaëthon ask his father to do? Have small groups brainstorm possible requests that Phaëthon could make of his father. What are the pros and cons of each request? Ask students to choose one and predict what would happen if Apollo granted the request.

he felt that he was truly divine, unlike other men, and he did not wish to be counted with men any more. He looked up for a moment at his radiant father. "Let me drive the chariot of the sun across the heavens for one day," he said.

Apollo frowned and shook his head. "I cannot break my promise, but I will **dissuade** you if I can," he answered. "How can you drive my chariot, whose horses need a strong hand on the reins? The climb is too steep for you. The immense height will make you dizzy. The swift streams of air in the upper heaven will sweep you off your course. Even the immortal gods could not drive my chariot. How then can you? Be wise and make some other choice."

The pride of Phaëthon was stubborn, for he thought the god was merely trying to frighten him. Besides, if he could guide the sun's chariot, would he not have proved his right to be divine rather than mortal? For that he would risk his life. Indeed, once he had seen Apollo's splendor, he did not wish to go back and live among men. Therefore, he insisted on his right until Apollo had to give way. **G**

When the father saw that nothing else would satisfy the boy, he bade the Hours[6] bring forth his chariot and yoke the horses. The chariot was of gold and had two gold-rimmed wheels with spokes of silver. In it there was room for one man to stand and hold the reins. Around the front and sides of it ran a rail, but the back was open. At the end of a long pole there were yokes for the four horses. The pole was of gold and shone with precious jewels: the golden topaz, the bright diamond, the green emerald, and the flashing ruby. While the Hours were yoking the swift, pawing horses, rosy-fingered Dawn hastened to the gates of heaven to draw them open. Meanwhile Apollo anointed his son's face with a magic ointment, that he might be able to bear the heat of the fire-breathing horses and the golden chariot. At last Phaëthon mounted the chariot and grasped the reins, the barriers were let down, and the horses shot up into the air.

At first the fiery horses sped forward up the accustomed trail, but behind them the chariot was too light without the weight of the immortal god. It bounded from side to side and was dashed up and down. Phaëthon was too frightened and too dizzy to pull the reins, nor would he have known anyway whether he was on the usual path. As soon as the horses felt that there was no hand controlling them, they soared up, up with fiery speed into the heavens till the earth grew pale and cold beneath them. Phaëthon shut his eyes, trembling at the dizzy, **precipitous** height. Then the horses dropped down, more swiftly than a falling stone, flinging themselves madly from side to side in panic because they were masterless. Phaëthon dropped the reins entirely and clung with all his might to the chariot rail.

---

6. **the Hours:** attendants of Apollo that represented the various hours of the day.

dissuade (dĭ-swād′) *v.* to persuade not to do something

5 Targeted Passage

G CULTURAL VALUES
Reread lines 61–73. What does Apollo request of Phaëthon? What is Phaëthon's reaction? Make a **prediction** about whether Phaëthon's decision will turn out to be a wise one.

precipitous (prĭ-sĭp′ĭ-təs) *adj.* very steep

LITERARY ANALYSIS

G **CULTURAL VALUES**

Possible answer: Apollo wants Phaëthon to reconsider his plea to drive the chariot, but Phaëthon insists upon driving it. Students may predict that for Phaëthon, like Icarus, going against his father's advice will turn out to be unwise.

Lines 87–93
REINFORCE *KEY IDEA*: LIMITATIONS

Discuss As the chariot takes flight, what personal **limitations** does Phaëthon become aware of? *Possible answers: Phaëthon*

- *is too lightweight for the chariot*
- *cannot control the reins*
- *does not know the route*

FOR LESS–PROFICIENT READERS

5 **Targeted Passage [Lines 58–73]**

This passage relates an event that contributes to the rising action of the plot: Phaëthon convinces Apollo to let him drive the chariot of the sun.

- What does Phaëthon ask Apollo to let him do?
- Why does Apollo say it is not a good idea for Phaëthon to drive the chariot?
- What "right" (line 70) does Phaëthon want to prove?

FOR ENGLISH LEARNERS

Vocabulary Support Make sure students understand the parts of the chariot so that they can visualize it accurately. If possible, show students a picture of a chariot and ask them to identify these parts:

- *spokes* (line 76)
- *reins* (line 77)
- *rail* (line 78)
- *pole* (line 78)
- *yokes* (line 79)

Vocabulary: Cognates Spanish speakers may note that the "precious jewels" (lines 80–81) in the chariot pole have Spanish cognates:

- *topaz/el topacio*
- *diamond/el diamante*
- *emerald/la esmerelda*
- *ruby/el rubí*

Students may also note the false cognate *rubio(a),* "blond." Have students scan the myths for more cognates between English and other languages.

About the Art Like the image on page 653, this painting by Kandinsky features one of his favorite visual subjects—a horse and rider. A cavalier is a soldier or knight on horseback.

READING SKILL

H CAUSE AND EFFECT

Have students record their answers in the graphic organizer introduced on page 647.

Possible answers:

Cause		Effect
Phaëthon rides in his father's chariot but loses control of it.	→	The sun burns and dries the earth, creating deserts and shrinking the seas.

LITERARY ANALYSIS

I CULTURAL VALUES

Possible answer: Phaëthon is killed because he is too arrogant to heed his father's advice. The Greeks may have kept his story alive to remind people to be humble and respectful of limits.

SELECTION WRAP–UP

REFLECT Ask students what faults Icarus and Phaëthon displayed and whether they felt sympathy for these characters.

⭐ **CRITIQUE** Ask students whether the myths needed to end with the deaths of Icarus and Phaëthon, or whether the points could still have been made if the characters had survived their ordeals.

READING FLUENCY

Distribute the copy masters and have students work in pairs to practice fluency.

 RESOURCE MANAGER—Copy Master
Reading Fluency p. 61

The Cavalier, Wassily Kandinsky. Staedtische Galerie im Lenbachhaus, Munich, Germany. © ARS, New York. © Giraudon/Art Resource, New York.

ANALYZE VISUALS
Is this painting a good representation of Phaëthon's ride? Why [or] why not?

Meanwhile as they came near the earth, it dried up and cracked apart. Meadows were reduced to white ashes, cornfields smoked and shriveled, 100 cities perished in flame. Far and wide on the wooded mountains the forests were ablaze, and even the snow-clad Alps were bare and dry. Rivers steamed and dried to dust. The great North African plain was scorched until it became the desert that it is today. Even the sea shrank back to pools and caves, until dried fishes were left baking upon the white-hot sands. At last the great earth mother called upon Zeus to save her from utter destruction, and Zeus hurled a mighty thunderbolt at the unhappy Phaëthon, who was still crouched in the chariot, clinging desperately to the rail. The dart cast him out, and he fell flaming in a long trail through the air. The chariot broke in pieces at the mighty blow, 110 and the maddened horses rushed snorting back to the stable of their master, Apollo. **H**

6 Targeted Passage

H CAUSE AND EFFECT
What effects does Phaëthon's chariot ride have on the natural world?

I CULTURAL VALUES
What happens to Phaëthon? Draw a **conclusion** about why the Greeks kept his story alive.

Unhappy Clymene and her daughters wandered over the whole earth seeking the body of the boy they loved so well. When they found him, they took him and buried him. Over his grave they wept and could not be comforted. At last the gods in pity for their grief changed them into poplar trees, which weep with tears of amber in memory of Phaëthon. 〰 **I**

DIFFERENTIATED INSTRUCTION

FOR LESS–PROFICIENT READERS

6 Targeted Passage [Lines 102–111]

This passage shows the climax: Phaëthon has lost control of the chariot of the sun, burning the earth, and Zeus strikes him down.

- Why is the earth getting so hot?
- What does Zeus do to Phaëthon?
- What happens to Apollo's chariot and horses?
- What lesson is suggested by Phaëthon's fate?

Reading Skill Follow-Up: Cause and Effect Ask students to reread lines 105–111 and record causes and effects in the graphic organizer introduced on page 647.

Cause: The earth mother asks Zeus for help.
Effect/Cause: Zeus throws a thunderbolt at Phaëthon.
Effect: Phaëthon falls in a trail of flames.

Comprehension

1. **Recall** Why does Daedalus tell Icarus not to fly too high?

2. **Recall** Why does Phaëthon go to Apollo's palace?

3. **Represent** Make a sketch of Phaëthon in Apollo's chariot. Cite at least three details from the selection that you've shown in your sketch.

Literary Analysis

4. **Analyze Greek Gods** What human qualities do the gods in "Phaëthon" display? In your answer, include concrete details about the gods.

5. **Examine Cause and Effect** Review the graphics you created as you read. Then describe the **limitations** that Daedalus and Apollo tried to place on their sons' plans. What happened when the sons ignored the limitations?

6. **Evaluate a Character** Was Icarus believable to you? Explain whether you think his thoughts and actions are similar to those of a real person. Also tell whether you think people today can relate to someone like Icarus.

7. **Make Inferences** How do you think Daedalus eventually felt about his decision to fly away from Crete? Cite details from the myth in your answer.

8. **Identify Cultural Values** The chart shown lists some of the main values held by the ancient Greeks. Complete a chart like it by citing the line numbers of passages that communicate each value. What other values do you think these myths convey? Add one to your chart, and cite passages to support it.

Values	"Icarus and Daedalus"	"Phaëthon"
Obey your elders.	lines 20–29	
Know your place.		
Respect and obey the gods.		

9. **Draw Conclusions** On the basis of the myths you have read, what conclusions can you draw about the attitude of the ancient Greeks toward human nature? Would you say that their view of people in general is pessimistic, or negative? Explain why or why not, using examples from the selections.

Extension and Challenge

10. **Creative Project: Music** The ancient Greeks often told their myths through songs. Create your own song or rap telling the story of Icarus or Phaëthon. Be sure to base your piece on real details from the myth. Present your piece to the class.

MARYLAND OBJECTIVES

LITERATURE STANDARD
3.A.6.a Analyze universal themes

Practice and Apply

After Reading

For additional support of post-reading questions, use these copy masters:

R RESOURCE MANAGER—Copy Masters

Reading Check p. 58 (to check understanding of the selection)

Cultural Values in Myths p. 51 (for practice of literary analysis standards focus)

Question Support p. 59 (**After Reading** questions adapted for English learners and less-proficient readers)

Additional selection questions are provided for teachers on page 45.

For additional activities to challenge students, see

ⓘ Power Thinking at **ClassZone.com**

ANSWERS

Comprehension

1. *If Icarus flies too high, the sun will melt the wax in his wings.*

2. *Phaëthon wants proof that Apollo is his father.*

3. *Details in students' sketches may include the dropped reins, the steep flight of the horses, Phaëthon clinging to the rail, the great distance from the earth, and the burning cities and forests.*

Literary Analysis

Possible answers:

4. *Apollo can feel romantic love (lines 1–3). He is proud of Phaëthon (line 50), but also disapproves of his son's request and attempts to reason with him (lines 61–67).*

5. ■ **STANDARDS FOCUS** *Cause and Effect When Icarus and Phaëthon ignored the limits their fathers placed on them, they fell to their deaths.*

6. *Icarus was believable and easy to relate to because his enthusiasm for adventure made him reckless, and this is a trait many people share.*

7. *The fact that Daedalus gave up his wings as an offering to a god and never tried to fly again (lines 58–59) indicates that he regretted his decision.*

---

8. ● **STANDARDS FOCUS** *Cultural Values in Myths*

• *"Icarus and Daedalus": Obey elders—lines 20–29; Know your place—lines 47–52; Be clever and bold—lines 10–15*

• *"Phaëthon": Obey elders—lines 61–73; Know your place—lines 87–109; Respect and obey gods—lines 61–73; Be clever and bold—lines 47–54*

9. *Students may say that the Greeks had a pessimistic view of human nature, since both myths emphasize human weakness. Examples might include Icarus's failure to obey his father's instructions and Phaëthon's pride.*

Extension and Challenge

10. *Students' songs should clearly convey the plot of the myth and include details from the reading.*

ANSWERS

Vocabulary in Context

VOCABULARY PRACTICE

1. *(d) wicked*
2. *(c) infuriate*
3. *(a) cooperate*
4. *(d) wide*
5. *(d) distressed*
6. *(c) stare*
7. *(d) tolerance*
8. *(c) whisper*

RESOURCE MANAGER—Copy Master
ocabulary Practice p.

VOCABULARY IN WRITING

Ask students to recall how pride factored into the cause and effect relationships in each myth.

VOCABULARY STRATEGY: HOMOGRAPHS
(also an EL language objective)

Review the basic features of a dictionary entry the headword, numbers and letters that differentiate meanings, and common abbreviations such as *adj.* (for *adjective*) and *ME* (for *Middle English*).

Answers:

1. *n., a piece of meat; v., to cut*
2. *n., a type of soft feather; adv., toward a lower place*
3. *n., a kind of fish; n., an instance of good luck*
4. *n., a sweetened fruit topping; v., to push tightly into place*
5. *n., a spool used for film; v., to fall out of balance*
6. *n., a feeling of horror; n., a spasm caused by contact with an electrical current*

RESOURCE MANAGER—Copy Master
ocabulary trategy p.

ocabulary enter at **ClassZone.com**
Additional ocabulary Activities

Vocabulary in Context

VOCABULARY PRACTICE

For each item, choose the word that differs most in meaning from the other words. Refer to a dictionary if you need help.

1. (a) cunning, (b) clever, (c) resourceful, (d) wicked
2. (a) discourage, (b) prevent, (c) infuriate, (d) dissuade
3. (a) cooperate, (b) sustain, (c) support, (d) uphold
4. (a) steep, (b) sharp, (c) precipitous, (d) wide
5. (a) rash, (b) hasty, (c) impulsive, (d) distressed
6. (a) shift, (b) veer, (c) stare, (d) swerve
7. (a) esteem, (b) honor, (c) deference, (d) tolerance
8. (a) reel, (b) sway, (c) whisper, (d) totter

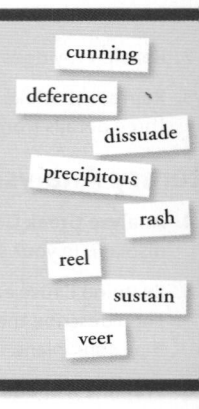

VOCABULARY IN WRITING

What role did pride play in the tragedies of Icarus and Phaëthon? Write a paragraph explaining your thoughts. Use at least two vocabulary words. Here is a sample opening.

> **EXAMPLE SENTENCE**
> *Neither boy showed **deference** to his father.*

VOCABULARY STRATEGY: HOMOGRAPHS

Homographs are words that are spelled the same but have different meanings and origins. Read these dictionary entries for the word *rash*. Notice that *rash* and *rash*, like other homographs, have different etymologies (histories) as well as different meanings. If you see a word used in a way that is unfamiliar to you, check the dictionary to see if it is a homograph.

rash[1] (răsh) *adj.* too hasty and careless [Middle English *rasch*, active]

rash[2] (răsh) *n.* an outbreak on the skin [obsolete French *rache*, sore]

ACTIVITY Use a dictionary to find two or three homographs for each listed word. Write simple definitions that show the differences in meaning for each.

1. chop   3. fluke   5. reel
2. down   4. jam   6. shock

MARYLAND OBJECTIVES

READING STANDARD
1.D.3.c Use resources to confirm definitions

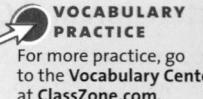
VOCABULARY PRACTICE
For more practice, go to the **Vocabulary Cente** at **ClassZone.com**.

DIFFERENTIATED INSTRUCTION

FOR ENGLISH LEARNERS
Vocabulary Strategy Have students who are more familiar with a non Roman alphabet keep an index card of the nglish alphabet at hand to help navigate alphabetical order in the dictionary. Remind students that bold face words at the upper left or right hand corner of each page indicate the first and last words on that page. onsider having mixed ability pairs work together on the **Vocabulary Strategy** activity.

FOR ADVANCED LEARNERS/PRE–AP
Vocabulary Strategy hallenge students to use multiple meanings of the same homo graph in the same sentence.

I jammed the jars of jam into the box.

Reading-Writing Connection

Deepen your understanding of these myths by responding to the prompts. Then complete the **Grammar and Writing** exercise.

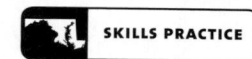

WRITING PROMPTS

A. Short Response: Write a Monologue
If you were Daedalus or Apollo, would you feel your son deserved his fate for not recognizing his **limitations?** Write a **one-paragraph monologue** describing the events of one of the myths from the perspective of the father.

SELF-CHECK

A good monologue will . . .
- include a summary of the myth's plot
- give a believable account of the father's feelings

B. Extended Response: Evaluate Descriptions
Which of the two myths was better at making you see and feel the terrible descent from the sky? Write **two or three paragraphs** evaluating the description in each myth. Then explain which description was more effective and why.

A successful evaluation will . . .
- include a statement that gives your main impression
- support the statement by citing specific details

GRAMMAR AND WRITING

USE CORRECT SENTENCE STRUCTURE An **independent clause** is a group of words that contains a subject and a verb and can stand alone as a sentence. A **simple sentence** contains one independent clause, and a **compound sentence** contains two or more independent clauses joined either by a comma and a coordinating conjunction or by a semicolon.

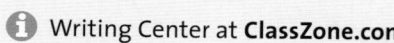
MARYLAND OBJECTIVES

LANGUAGE STANDARD
5.A.2.d Compose simple [and] compound sentences

> Original: Icarus flew too close to the sun. (*A simple sentence contains one independent clause.*)
>
> Revised: Icarus flew too close to the sun, and he fell to his death. (*Two independent clauses joined with a comma and a coordinating conjunction form a compound sentence.*)

PRACTICE Identify each sentence as simple or compound.

1. I told Icarus not to fly too high or low, but he didn't listen to me.
2. The sun's heat melted the glue in his wings.
3. The wings' feathers fell one by one.
4. He wanted to fly high into the sky; this need for freedom cost him his life.
5. Now I am left without my son.

*For more help with independent clauses, see page R63 in the **Grammar Handbook**. For more help with simple and compound sentences, see pages R63–R64 in the **Grammar Handbook**.*

FOR LESS–PROFICIENT WRITERS

For Prompt A:
- Have students choose one father and recall what limits he warned his son about, what the son did, and what happened as a result.
- Help students summarize these events and decide whether the father would feel the son deserved his fate.
- Suggest that students use sensory details and similes, metaphors, or other imaginative comparisons to help express the father's feelings.

For Prompt B:
- Limit the response to two paragraphs.
- Ask students to choose one myth. Help them generate a statement about their impression of the descent described in that myth.
- Have each student list three details that support his or her statement.
- Suggest that students begin by clearly stating their impression, then citing details, and finally explaining why they found those details effective.

Reading-Writing Connection

WRITING PROMPTS

- For **Prompt A,** have students summarize what advice the father gave his son and what the consequences were when the son ignored that advice.
- For **Prompt B,** have students list the details from the myth that describe the character's descent from the sky and evaluate what makes the descriptions effective.

For ideas for writing, see

 Writing Center at **ClassZone.com**

GRAMMAR AND WRITING

Write these sentences on the board. Ask students to identify each as simple or compound.

The myth tells the story of a clever inventor who formed a plan to escape from Crete. *(simple)*

Should he fly closer, or would that be unwise? *(compound)*

Answers:
1. *compound*
2. *simple*
3. *simple*
4. *compound*
5. *simple*

R RESOURCE MANAGER—Copy Master
Use Correct Sentence Structure p. 60

Assess and Reteach

Assess

R RESOURCE MANAGER—Copy Masters
Selection Tests A, B/C pp. 63–64, 65–66

Test Generator CD

Reteach

S STANDARDS LESSON FILE
Reading Lesson 7: Recognizing Cause and Effect
Vocabulary Lesson 20: Homonyms and Homographs
Writing Lesson 8: Sentence Combining (clauses)

Focus and Motivate

OBJECTIVES

Literary Analysis
- explore the key idea of **destiny**
- analyze characteristics of legends
- read a legend and a magazine article

Reading
- identify chronological order

Vocabulary
- build vocabulary for reading and writing
- understand meanings of compound words
  (also an EL language objective)

SUMMARY

This excerpt from *Young Arthur* tells the legend of how the lost heir to Britain's throne discovered his identity. Taken for safekeeping as a baby from his father, King Uther, Arthur grows up ignorant of his royal lineage. On a trip to London with his foster family, Arthur pulls an enchanted sword from a stone—an act possible only for the true king of Britain. His destiny revealed, young Arthur is hailed as king.

Is there a job you were BORN *to do?*

Discuss the question with students. To lead into the *KEY IDEA,* ask students how they would define *destiny.* Do they believe that every person has a destiny? Might some people have more than one? Ask if they think people can make choices that create their destinies— or does destiny choose people? Then have pairs work on the *DISCUSS* activity.

Selection Resources

---

from **Young Arthur**
Medieval Legend Retold by Robert D. San Souci

Is there a job you were BORN *to do?*

MARYLAND OBJECTIVES

READING/LIT STANDARDS
1.E.3.a Select and apply appropriate strategies during reading
3.A.3.a Distinguish among types of narrative texts

KEY IDEA Some people believe that we all have a **destiny,** a predetermined life that we can't change even if we want to. Others think that life is what we make of it. In the legend you're about to read, a kingdom waits to find out which boy is destined to be its king.

DISCUSS With a small group of classmates, discuss whether people are born to do some particular thing. Think of your feelings about your own future, and also consider individuals who have changed history through their dedication to a job or a goal. Be ready to share with the class whether you believe people choose their own destiny or are born to it.

660

RESOURCE MANAGER UNIT 6

Plan and Teach pp. 67–74

Literary Analysis
Summary pp. 75†*, 76‡*
Characteristics of Legends pp. 77, 78†*
Question Support p. 85*

Reading
Chronological Order pp. 79, 80†*
Reading Check p. 84

Vocabulary
Study p. 81*
Practice p. 82
Strategy p. 83

Assessment
Selection Tests A, B/C pp. 87*, 89*
Test Generator CD

BEST PRACTICES TOOLKIT

Differentiated Instruction
pp. 31–38*
Scaffolding Instruction
pp. 43–46*

Graphic Organizers/Strategies
Word Questioning • T Chart •
Reciprocal Teaching

Reading Support
Audio Anthology CD*

Technology
Literature and Vocabulary Centers at **ClassZone.com**

Write*Smart* CD

---

* Resources for Differentiation　　† Also in Spanish　　‡ In Haitian Creole and Vietnamese

LITERARY ANALYSIS: CHARACTERISTICS OF LEGENDS

A **legend** is a story about heroes or heroines that is handed down from the past. Legends often are based on real people and events. However, as the stories pass through the generations, the characters, setting, and events become more imaginary and less factual. For example, the King Arthur legends are probably based on a real-life chieftain who lived in Britain around A.D. 500. In the course of many retellings, the legends' setting changed to the time of knights, 900 years later.

Because of the courage, honor, and fairness King Arthur displayed, he became a model for others to follow. As you read, notice the conflict young Arthur faces and how he proves his goodness.

READING SKILL: CHRONOLOGICAL ORDER

In a legend, events are often presented in **chronological order,** or the order in which they take place. As you read, look for words and phrases that provide clues to this order, such as *when, eventually, this time,* and *in the days that followed.* Mark the sequence of events on a timeline.

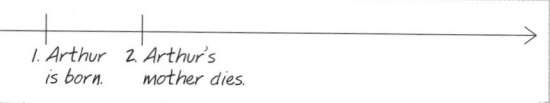

1. Arthur is born. 2. Arthur's mother dies.

VOCABULARY IN CONTEXT

The words in Column A help recreate the world of medieval England. See how many you know by matching each word to the item in Column B that comes closest to its meaning.

Column A	Column B
1. grievous	a. respect
2. homage	b. cringing
3. reclaim	c. boss
4. dismount	d. recover
5. flinching	e. climb down
6. upstart	f. unhappiness
7. melancholy	g. socially climbing
8. taskmaster	h. severe

Author Online

Always a Fan One of the first books Robert D. San Souci ever read was a book about King Arthur, and he remembers being fascinated by dragons and knights. In addition to *Young Arthur,* San

Robert D. San Souci born 1946

Souci has written three other books about the Arthurian legend: *Young Guinevere, Young Lancelot,* and *Young Merlin.* San Souci has also retold the tales and legends of groups ranging from the Alaska Natives to the native Australians.

 MORE ABOUT THE AUTHOR
For more on Robert D. San Souci, visit the **Literature Center** at ClassZone.com.

Background

Pretenders and Kings The Arthur legends paint a vivid picture of the intrigues of medieval life. In the Middle Ages, a king's oldest son was considered the heir to his father's throne. When the enemies of a king wished to take over his kingdom, they might try to kill his son.

Arthurian Legends and Merlin
In the Arthur legends, a magician named Merlin plays an important role. Legends often include unreal or magical people and relate events that could never happen in real life. Some legends also contain magical objects that confer special powers or privileges on their bearers.

Teach

STANDARDS FOCUS

LITERARY ANALYSIS

● CHARACTERISTICS OF LEGENDS

Write this passage on the board:

> In the 1100s, Geoffrey of Monmouth wrote about Merlin, Arthur's adviser. This wise and beloved wizard may have been based on a figure in Welsh history.

Ask: What characteristics of legends are evident in the Merlin story? *Possible answer: It is a very old story, possibly based in history, about an inspiring figure.*

CHECK UNDERSTANDING Ask students to identify other legendary figures, such as Robin Hood and Aladdin, and discuss why they are admired.

READING SKILL

■ CHRONOLOGICAL ORDER

Write this example on the board:

> Lancelot was kidnapped as a baby by the Lady of the Lake. While serving King Arthur, he became known for his bravery. His son, Galahad, ultimately found the Holy Grail.

What words show chronological order? *Answers: as a baby, while, ultimately*

CHECK UNDERSTANDING Ask students to use chronological order and words such as *later* and *next* to summarize a movie.

 RESOURCE MANAGER—Copy Master Chronological Order p. 79 (for student use while reading the selection)

▲ VOCABULARY IN CONTEXT

DIAGNOSE WORD KNOWLEDGE To determine preteaching needs, have all students complete **Vocabulary in Context.** Check students' answers. *(1. h; 2. a; 3. d; 4. e; 5. b; 6. g; 7. f; 8. c)*

PRETEACH VOCABULARY Use the Vocabulary Study copy master to help students determine the meaning of each boldfaced word.

1. Read aloud the first sentence, emphasizing the boldfaced word.

2. Ask students to think about the way the word is used. Discuss possible meanings for *dismount,* such as "get down" or "step off."

3. Repeat the procedure for each of the other sentences.

4. Have students complete the chart in Part B independently.

 RESOURCE MANAGER—Copy Master Vocabulary Study p. 81

For general guidelines on differentiating vocabulary instruction and for alternative vocabulary activities for students not needing vocabulary preteaching, see

BEST PRACTICES TOOLKIT Scaffolding Vocabulary Instruction pp. 43–46

Vocabulary Center at **ClassZone.com** Additional Vocabulary Activities

ANALYZE VISUALS

Possible answers: The young man looks
- *cautious; his posture and facial expression suggest that he is not overly confident.*
- *determined; he has positioned himself carefully to pull out the sword.*
- *sensitive and thoughtful; his face seems to reveal feelings of concern.*

About the Art British artist Walter Crane (1845–1915) was one of the most popular illustrators in the late 19th century. Known for his romantic and finely detailed images, he illustrated children's books about Aladdin, Bluebeard, King Arthur, Robin Hood, and other figures in legend as well as numerous books of fables and fairy tales. Crane also created many political cartoons, posters, and banners to support the struggle for better working conditions.

Lines 5–7
REINFORCE *KEY IDEA:* DESTINY

Discuss What does Merlin say Arthur will do—and when does he say it? How do Merlin's words support the idea of **destiny**? *Possible answer: Even before Arthur was born, Merlin foretold that he would one day be a great king. The fact that Arthur's future role could be known before he was born suggests that it is his destiny—what he was born to do.*

Young Arthur

Retold by Robert D. San Souci

K ing Uther[1] heard the baby's wail and leaped to his feet. There was a sharp rap at the chamber door, and a servant entered grinning happily. "You have a son," he told the king. Uther's joy knew no bounds. When he was ushered into Queen Igerna's[2] bedchamber, Uther looked lovingly at mother and son. "The boy's name shall be Arthur," he declared, "and he shall be a great king. For Merlin [the magician] has foretold that he will one day rule the greatest kingdom under heaven."

But Uther's happiness did not last. His beloved queen died soon after Arthur's birth, and sadness sapped the king's spirit. He lost interest
10 in ruling, and Merlin was unable to rouse him from his **melancholy**.

1. **Uther** (yōō'thər).
2. **Igerna** (ē-gĕr'nə).

ANALYZE VISUALS
Examine the main **character** in this illustration. What kind of personality do you think he might have?

melancholy (mĕl'ən-kŏl'ē) *n.* sadness; depression

Illustration by Walter Crane in *King Arthu Knights* by Henry Gilbert, 1911. © Edw Wallace/Mary Evans Picture Libra

662 UNIT 6: MYTHS, LEGENDS, AND TALES

DIFFERENTIATED INSTRUCTION

FOR ALL STUDENTS
Anchor Activity Provide an opportunity for students to consider how legends are passed down by inviting them to do a live storytelling of *Young Arthur.* Encourage storytellers to emphasize the aspects of the legend they would most want to preserve in oral tradition.

For further details on this project, see

R RESOURCE MANAGER
   Ideas for Extension pp. 72–73

FOR LESS–PROFICIENT READERS
In combination with the *Audio Anthology CD,* use one or more Targeted Passages (pp. 664, 665, 666) to ensure that students focus on key story events, concepts, and skills.

FOR ENGLISH LEARNERS
Options for Reading Read aloud lines 1–21 and check understanding by asking students to identify each character and his or her relationship to Arthur. Then have them continue reading along with the *Audio Anthology CD.*

BACKGROUND

Knighthood and Chivalry In medieval times, a knight (line 20) was a soldier who possessed weaponry and a horse—two signs that he had greater advantages than most people of his time. Often, a knight worked for a wealthy landowner. An aspiring knight might enter his master's house as a child and become an apprentice, known as a page, while he trained for knighthood. Knights became associated with a code of values and ideals known as chivalry. These values included loyalty, courtesy, honor, and valor (bravery). Arthurian legend is one of the best-known sources of lore about knighthood and chivalry.

CULTURAL CONNECTION

Modern-day Knights Today, the sovereign of the United Kingdom bestows honorary knighthood as an award for outstanding achievement. Among the Americans who have received this honor from Queen Elizabeth are film director Steven Spielberg, Microsoft founder Bill Gates, and former mayor of New York Rudy Giuliani. An honorary knight is entitled to use the letters *KBE* after his name, for "Knight Commander of the Most Excellent Order of the British Empire."

FOR ENGLISH LEARNERS

Key Academic Vocabulary Have students use Word Questioning to study this academic vocabulary from the selection: *couple* (line 17), *commit* (lines 94, 102), *approach* (line 106).

 BEST PRACTICES TOOLKIT—Transparency
   Word Questioning p. E9

Prereading For prereading instruction for English learners, see

 BEST PRACTICES TOOLKIT
   Scaffolding Reading Instruction pp. 43–46

FOR ADVANCED LEARNERS/PRE–AP

Pre-AP exercises in the bottom channel provide additional challenge for your advanced students. Use them for small groups or individuals.

ADDITIONAL GUIDELINES

For more help with differentiation and tips for classroom management, see

 BEST PRACTICES TOOLKIT
   Differentiated Instruction pp. 31–38

Ⓐ CHRONOLOGICAL ORDER

Possible answers:

1. *Arthur is born.*
2. *Uther says he will be a great king.*
3. *Arthur's mother dies.*
4. *Merlin offers to take the baby for safekeeping.*

Lines 11–24
DISCUSSION PROMPTS

Use these prompts to help students under-stand Merlin's role in the legend:

Recall In what ways does Merlin serve King Uther? *Possible answer: He gives Uther advice; he fights in battle with Uther; he uses his healing arts on Uther.*

Analyze What evidence suggests how Merlin feels about Arthur? Why might he feel this way? *Possible answer: Merlin is caring and protective, which is shown by his placing of Arthur with good foster parents. He probably cares so much because of his closeness to Uther.*

Evaluate Should Merlin have told the foster parents of Arthur's true identity? Explain. *Possible answers: No; the less they know, the safer Arthur will be. Yes; Arthur's special identity should be known so that he can be carefully guarded.*

Ⓑ LEGENDS

Possible answers:

- *Admirable—Merlin is wise and loyal.*
- *Undesirable—Kay is vain and jealous.*

"Unrest grows throughout the land," Merlin warned. "Your old foes are rising in rebellion. Give the babe into my keeping, for you have enemies even at court." Ⓐ

Anxious for his son's safety, Uther agreed. So Merlin, disguised as a beggar, took the infant Arthur to Sir Ector and his lady, who lived some distance from the court and all its dangers. He told them nothing about the child, save that his name was Arthur. The couple had recently lost their infant son and welcomed Arthur as their own. Soon rebellion divided the kingdom. Uther, **reclaiming** his old spirit, rallied his
20 knights and barons. With Merlin always beside him, he drove back his enemies.

But as Uther celebrated his victory in the town of Verulum,[3] traitors poisoned the town's wells. The king and his loyal followers were stricken. Merlin alone escaped. Though he tried his healing arts on Uther, he was forced to confess, "Sire, there is no remedy."

"Then," said the dying monarch, "I declare that my son shall be king of all this realm after me. God's blessing and mine be upon him." With these words, Uther died.

When the rebels entered Verulum, only Merlin was alive.
30 "Tell us where Uther's son is hidden," they demanded, "so that we can slay him and end Uther's line."

But Merlin vanished before their eyes.

Young Arthur was raised as a son in Sir Ector's house. He learned to read and write alongside his foster brother, Kay, who was four years older. By the time he was fifteen, Arthur was a tall, handsome, quick-witted lad. Though he had great strength, he also had a gentle manner.

Kay, who had recently been knighted, decided to train Arthur in the knightly arts himself. But Kay was vain and jealous of the favor Arthur found with their father, so he was a harsh **taskmaster.** Arthur came
40 away from his lessons in swordsmanship with many bruises and cuts. When he complained, Kay replied, "A knight must be thick-skinned and ready to bear even **grievous** wounds without **flinching.**" Yet if Arthur so much as pricked his brother, Kay would bellow loudly for the physician. Ⓑ

Eventually Kay appointed Arthur his apprentice. This was an honor the younger boy would happily have forgone. However, seeing that Sir Ector wished it so, Arthur sighed and agreed. But he felt in his heart that he already was a knight, though no lord had dubbed him such.

3. **Verulum** (vĕr'ŏŏ-ləm).

Ⓐ CHRONOLOGICAL ORDER
What events have happened so far? Mark the events in order on your timeline.

reclaim (rĭ-klām') *v.* to get back; recover

Ⓘ **Targeted Passage**

taskmaster (tăsk'măs'tər) *n.* a person who sets tasks for others to do

grievous (grē'vəs) *adj.* painful; serious

flinching (flĭn'chĭng) *n.* drawing back from difficulty or danger **flinch** *v.*

Ⓑ LEGENDS
Which of the characters you've met so far represent admirable characteristics and which represent undesirable ones?

DIFFERENTIATED INSTRUCTION

FOR LESS–PROFICIENT READERS

Ⓘ Targeted Passage [Lines 11–31]

This passage explains the context for the legend: the wizard Merlin seeks to protect baby Arthur, heir to the throne, by having him adopted anonymously.

- Why does Merlin bring baby Arthur to Sir Ector and his lady? What does he tell them?
- What happens to Uther?
- What do the rebels want to do to Uther's son? Why?

Comprehension Support Have students review lines 33–48 and formulate impressions of Arthur by recording how they imagine he looks, sounds, and feels. Suggest that they divide a piece of paper into three sections for taking notes, as shown at right.

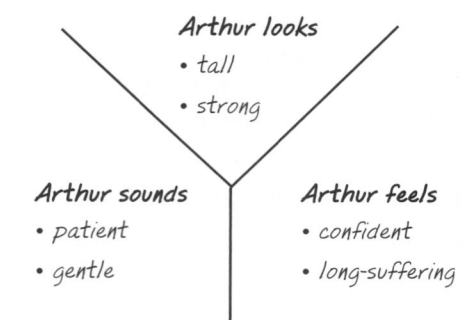

Arthur looks
- *tall*
- *strong*

Arthur sounds
- *patient*
- *gentle*

Arthur feels
- *confident*
- *long-suffering*

Both Arthur and Kay knew it was vital to learn the arts of war. The 50 kingdom was still at the mercy of **upstart** lords who ruled by fire and sword.

The story of Uther's lost son, the true heir to the throne, would have been forgotten but for Merlin. One Christmas Eve, the long-absent magician reappeared and summoned the bishops, lords, and common folk to London's square. There he drove a broadsword halfway into a huge stone. Written on the blade in blazing gold letters were the words: "Whoso pulleth out the sword from this stone is born the rightful King of England." **C**

In the days that followed, knights and barons, cowherds and bakers, an endless parade of would-be kings eagerly pulled at the sword. But 60 none could loosen it, let alone draw it forth.

When they accused Merlin of trickery, he said, "The rightful king has not come. God will make him known at the proper time."

Now it happened that a great tournament[4] was held in London. Among those who came were Sir Ector, Sir Kay, and young Arthur, who served Kay. So eager was the boy to see the jousts[5] that he forgot to pack Kay's sword. There was great upset when the mistake was discovered.

"Woe to you, boy," snarled Kay, "if your error costs me the victory I would otherwise win today!"

Even Sir Ector scolded Arthur and ordered, "Go back directly and 70 fetch the missing sword."

Angry at his carelessness and impatient to see the contests, Arthur started homeward. Then he suddenly reined in his horse.

In the deserted city square was a massive stone with a sword plunged into its center. "Surely that sword is as good as the one left at home," he said. "I will borrow it. When Kay is finished, I will return it to this curious monument."

So saying, he **dismounted,** scrambled up the stone, took the sword handle, and tugged. The sword did not move. Impatient to return to the tournament, he pulled again. This time, the sword slid easily out of the 80 stone. In his haste, he did not notice the words upon the blade. Shoving the weapon into his belt, he remounted and raced to where Sir Kay waited his turn upon the field.

The moment he saw the golden words upon the blade, Kay began to tremble with excitement. When Arthur asked what was amiss, Kay shouted, "Go! Get away! You have caused enough trouble." **D**

But Arthur was curious. So he followed as Kay ran to Sir Ector. "Look, Father!" cried Kay. "Here is the sword of the stone. Therefore, it is I who must be king of all this land!"

---

4. **tournament:** a medieval sporting event in which groups of armored men fought against each other.

5. **jousts:** competitions or combats between two knights on horseback, using lances.

---

upstart (ŭp′stärt′) *adj.* suddenly risen to wealth or power

C CHRONOLOGICAL ORDER
What phrase tells you when Merlin put the sword in the stone? Mark the event on your timeline.

② Targeted Passage

dismount (dĭs-mount′) *v.* to get down or off

D LEGENDS
Why does Kay tell Arthur to get away?

C CHRONOLOGICAL ORDER

Possible answer: "One Christmas Eve" (line 52)

Lines 50–59
REINFORCE KEY IDEA: DESTINY

Discuss What happens when the knights and other people try to pull the sword from the stone? What does this suggest about the uniqueness of **destiny**? *Possible answer: The people cannot pull the sword from the stone. This suggests that personal destiny is unique; you cannot fulfill another person's destiny, no matter how hard you try.*

LITERARY ANALYSIS

D LEGENDS

Possible answer: Kay tells Arthur to get away because he wants people to think that he, Kay, is the rightful king of England, as written on the sword.

FOR LESS–PROFICIENT READERS

② Targeted Passage [Lines 52–82]

This passage presents a turning point: Merlin has put a sword in a stone that only the true heir can remove, and teenage Arthur unwittingly removes it.

- What test does Merlin create?
- What errand does Sir Ector send Arthur to do? How does Arthur complete it?
- Why is Arthur able to pull the sword from the stone?

FOR ADVANCED LEARNERS/PRE–AP

Make Judgments Was Merlin's idea of putting the sword in the stone a good one, or would it have been better for him to simply tell Arthur of his identity? Have students use a two-column chart to analyze the respective merits of each course of action. Then ask students to discuss whether they agree with Merlin's choice and why.

 BEST PRACTICES TOOLKIT—Transparency T Chart p. A25

Sword Test	Telling Arthur
• Provides proof	• Quick, simple
• Offers the thrill of self-discovery	• Kay might stop bossing Arthur sooner
• Dramatic event people will accept as true	• Depends on people believing Arthur's word

When Sir Ector and the others saw the sword and read the golden
90 inscription, they began to shout, "The sword from the stone! The
king's sword!"

Hearing only this much, Arthur thought that he had stolen a king's
weapon. As people hurried excitedly toward Kay, Arthur spurred his horse
away, certain he had committed a great crime.

Looking back, he saw Kay and Sir Ector ride off, surrounded by the
greatest lords of the realm. Were they taking Kay to trial? he wondered.
Had he brought ruin upon Sir Ector's household?

"A true knight would not run away," he said to himself, "and I am a
true knight in my heart." Fearful, but determined to do what was right,
100 the boy wheeled his horse around. **E**

The great square was now filled with people. Just how terrible a crime
had he committed?

Upon the stone stood Kay, holding the sword. The crowd shouted each
time he held the blade aloft. Then silence fell over the throng: Merlin had
appeared at the edge of the square. People stood aside to let the magician
approach the stone.

"Are you the one who pulled the sword from the stone?" Merlin asked.

"I am holding it, am I not?" Kay replied.

"The rightful king could pull it free a hundred times," said Merlin.
110 "Slip the sword into the groove and pull it out again."

With a shrug, Kay reinserted the sword. But when he tried to jerk it
free, it would not budge.

Suddenly all eyes turned toward Arthur, who was pushing his way
through the crowd, bellowing at the top of his lungs. "It wasn't Kay's
fault! I brought him the sword!" Merlin peered closely at Arthur. Then
he smiled and said, "Climb up and draw the sword from the stone."
Uncertainly Arthur clambered up beside Kay. Grasping the pommel,
he easily pulled the sword out.

Then Merlin cried, "This is Arthur, son of Uther Pendragon,[6] Britain's
120 destined king."

An astonished Sir Ector knelt to pay the boy **homage,** followed by
Kay and many others. But all around, there was growing confusion and
dispute. Some cried, "It is the will of heaven! Long live the king!" while
others cried, "It is Merlin's plot to put a beardless boy, a puppet, on the
throne, and so rule the land."

[But] The cries of "Long Live King Arthur!" soon carried the day. ∾ **F**

---

6. **Pendragon** (pĕn-drăg′ən).

❸ Targeted Passage

E LEGENDS
What is Arthur thinking
Make an **inference** abou
his qualities as a persor

VISUAL VOCABULAR

pommel (pŭm′əl) *n.*
a knob on the handle
of a sword

homage (hŏm′ĭj) *n.*
a display of loyalty
and respect

**F CHRONOLOGICAL
ORDER**
After Sir Ector pays
Arthur homage, who
else does? Mark the
final events of the stor
on your timeline.

Lines 92–115
DISCUSSION PROMPTS

Use these prompts to help students understand what kind of person young Arthur is:

Interpret What personal qualities does
Arthur show by returning to the square?
*Possible answer: He shows that he is brave
and honest.*

Analyze Consider Arthur's confused idea of
what is happening. What risks might he believe he is taking by speaking out? *Possible
answer: He may believe that he will be
punished for a crime and that he will disgrace
his family.*

Synthesize How might Arthur's personal
qualities make him a good ruler? *Possible
answer: He is willing to take personal risks for
an ideal, such as honesty; he is brave enough
to stand up for what is right; he has a strong
conscience.*

LITERARY ANALYSIS

E LEGENDS

*Possible answer: Arthur is worried that he
has done something wrong, and that Kay
will take the blame. He is honest and wants
to do what is right.*

READING SKILL

F CHRONOLOGICAL ORDER

*Possible answer: Kay pays homage to Arthur;
then many others in the crowd do the same.*

SELECTION WRAP-UP

REFLECT How did reading about Kay and
Arthur's relationship help you understand
what each boy was like?

★ **CRITIQUE** Does it make the story better to
have Arthur take the sword out of the stone
without being aware of its significance?
Explain.

DIFFERENTIATED INSTRUCTION

FOR LESS-PROFICIENT READERS
❸ Targeted Passage [Lines 92–120]

This passage presents the climax: Kay tries to
pass himself off as the heir, but when Merlin
has both Kay and Arthur try to draw the
sword from the stone, Arthur's identity as the
true heir is revealed.

- Why does Arthur ride away? Why does he
  return?
- What does Merlin tell Kay to do?
- How does Arthur prove his destiny?

FOR ENGLISH LEARNERS
Vocabulary: Idioms and Sayings Explain these
expressions to students, and then help students use them to create original sentences:

- *brought ruin upon* (line 97), "caused
  trouble for"
- *all eyes turned toward* (line 113), "everyone
  watched"

Comprehension

1. **Recall** Why do Uther's enemies want to slay Arthur?

2. **Clarify** Why does Arthur remove the sword from the stone the first time?

3. **Paraphrase** What is written on the sword?

MARYLAND OBJECTIVES

LITERATURE STANDARD
3.A.3.a Distinguish among types of narrative texts

Literary Analysis

4. **Identify Chronological Order** Review the story to make sure you included all its major events on your timeline. Then use your timeline to write a summary of the story.

5. **Examine Characteristics of Legends** Most legends feature a hero or heroine who faces a struggle or conflict. This character often has unusual powers and admirable traits. Note Arthur's conflict, special power, and good traits in a graphic like the one shown.

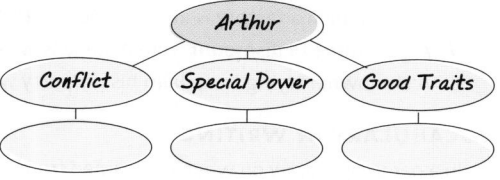

6. **Interpret Theme** Legends communicate their themes not only through the actions of heroes and the consequences the heroes face, but also through the actions of minor characters. Identify the qualities that Kay represents. Then tell whether Kay's behavior pays off in the end. What message about life are readers supposed to learn from Kay's example?

7. **Evaluate a Legend** The story of Arthur has captivated people for generations. What explanation do you have for this? Tell whether you think the legend deserves such wide popularity, and defend your opinion with concrete details from the story.

Extension and Challenge

8. **Big Question Activity** What ideas about **destiny,** or fate, are reflected in this legend? Are they different from or similar to the ideas your group discussed as part of the activity on page 660?

9. **SOCIAL STUDIES CONNECTION** What was life like in Britain during the early Middle Ages? Read "Who Was King Arthur?" on page 669, and then do research on the Internet. Display your answers to the following questions on a poster:

   • How was society organized?
   • Who were the Britons fighting against?
   • What religion was practiced?

> **RESEARCH LINKS**
> For more on Britain during the Middle Ages, visit the **Research Center** at **ClassZone.com.**

Practice and Apply

After Reading

For additional support of post-reading questions, use these copy masters:

R **RESOURCE MANAGER—Copy Masters**
   Reading Check p. 84 (to check understanding of the selection)
   Characteristics of Legends p. 77 (for practice of literary analysis standards focus)
   Question Support p. 85 (**After Reading** questions adapted for English learners and less-proficient readers)

Additional selection questions are provided for teachers on page 71.

ANSWERS

Comprehension

1. *Uther's enemies want to end his line of family rule.*

2. *Arthur removes the sword from the stone to give it to Kay because he has forgotten Kay's sword, and he doesn't want to return home to fetch it.*

3. *The sword says that whoever can pull it out is the rightful king of England.*

Literary Analysis

Possible answers:

4. ■ **STANDARDS FOCUS** *Chronological Order Students' timelines should include all major events; their summaries should present the events in chronological order.*

5. ● **STANDARDS FOCUS** *Characteristics of Legends Conflict: whether to admit that he took the sword; Special Power: the ability to pull the sword from the stone; Good Traits: honesty and bravery*

6. *Kay represents jealousy, meanness, greed, dishonesty, and selfishness. His behavior does not pay off, which suggests that readers should not follow his example.*

7. *Students may say that the legend deserves wide popularity because the elements of suspense, magic, and heroism are compelling; Merlin and Arthur have dramatic and entertaining adventures; and the medieval setting of the legend, with its knights and castles, captures the imagination.*

Extension and Challenge

8. *Students may say that the legend reflects the idea that destiny is determined even before a person is born, as it was for Arthur. They may note that destiny is unavoidable—Arthur fulfills his destiny even though he is raised away from his birthplace—and that it is unique; you cannot adopt another person's destiny, as Kay and the many eager contestants for the sword attempt to do.*

9. **SOCIAL STUDIES CONNECTION** *Students should clearly answer the questions with summaries of factual evidence from more than one reliable source.*

ANSWERS

Vocabulary in Context

VOCABULARY PRACTICE

1. *false;* **2.** *true;* **3.** *true;* **4.** *false;* **5.** *false;*
6. *true;* **7.** *false;* **8.** *true*

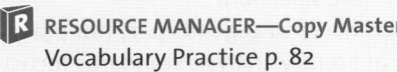 **RESOURCE MANAGER**—Copy Master
Vocabulary Practice p. 82

VOCABULARY IN WRITING

Ask students to recall the significant relationships in Arthur's early life and think about
what impact each had on him. Then have
them review the vocabulary list and identify
words that could be used to describe each
relationship.

VOCABULARY STRATEGY: COMPOUND
WORDS *(also an EL language objective)*

Show students how a compound word can be
broken into shorter base words, such as

task + master = taskmaster

Then show how other compounds can be
made using a base word—for example, *mas-
termind* and *masterpiece.*

Possible answers:
1. *"secret author"*
2. *"play in a rough manner"*
3. *"a layer of rock under the soil"*
4. *"agree to do"*

RESOURCE MANAGER—Copy Master
Vocabulary Strategy p. 83

ⓘ Vocabulary Center at **ClassZone.com**
Additional Vocabulary Activities

Assess and Reteach

Assess

RESOURCE MANAGER—Copy Masters
Selection Tests A, B/C pp. 87–88, 89–90
⊘ Test Generator CD

Reteach

S STANDARDS LESSON FILE
Reading Lesson 6: Recognizing Sequence
and Chronological Order

Vocabulary in Context

VOCABULARY PRACTICE

Show that you understand the vocabulary words by telling whether each
statement is true or false.

1. I am **flinching** when I reach out to hug someone.
2. A sad look or a sigh is often a sign of **melancholy.**
3. It is hard to pay **homage** to someone you don't respect.
4. A **grievous** wound is generally easy to recover from.
5. An **upstart** politician is probably serving a second or third term in office.
6. A foreman in a factory is an example of a **taskmaster.**
7. A good time to **dismount** from a horse is when you are galloping on it.
8. A landowner trying to **reclaim** his property wants to get it back.

dismount
flinching
grievous
homage
melancholy
reclaim
taskmaster
upstart

VOCABULARY IN WRITING

In a paragraph, draw on what you learned from this excerpt from *Young Arthur*
to describe Arthur's early life. Use two or more vocabulary words. You might
start like this.

> **EXAMPLE SENTENCE**
>
> *Kay was a hard* **taskmaster**, *but Arthur's life was not unhappy.*

VOCABULARY STRATEGY: COMPOUND WORDS

Compound words are two or more words combined to have one meaning.
Sometimes, as in the word *taskmaster,* the meaning can be inferred from the
meanings of the two combined words. Other times, though, as with *upstart,*
you may have to look at context clues or even a dictionary.

ACTIVITY Use context clues to figure out the definition of each boldfaced
compound word. Then, write the definition. If you have to, consult a dictionary.

1. The actor had never written a book, so he hired a **ghostwriter** to work
   on his autobiography.
2. The two six-year-old boys love to **roughhouse** when they get together
   to play.
3. To support the huge building, the contractors excavated all the way down
   to **bedrock.**
4. The only way Maura will **undertake** this project is with a lot of support
   from everyone.

MARYLAND OBJECTIVES

READING STANDARD
1.D.3.a Use context to determine
the meanings of words

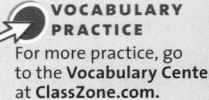

VOCABULARY PRACTICE
For more practice, go
to the **Vocabulary Center**
at **ClassZone.com.**

DIFFERENTIATED INSTRUCTION

FOR ENGLISH LEARNERS
Vocabulary Strategy Make sure students
know how to pronounce the compound
words in the lesson. Point out that although
English—unlike some other languages—has
no rules for which syllable to stress in a
compound word, pronunciation information
can be found in a dictionary. Review how to
interpret stress marks in a dictionary entry.

FOR ADVANCED LEARNERS/PRE-AP
Vocabulary Strategy Challenge students to
use the base words in a compound word to
create as many other compound words as
they can. You might have different pairs of
students work with the same base words and
then compare their lists.

bedrock = bed + rock

- *hotbed*
- *bedside*
- *rockslide*
- *sheetrock*

MAGAZINE ARTICLE Historians disagree on the facts behind King Arthur legends. This magazine article presents some of the theories about Arthur's true home. Decide whether the information in this article matches your own image of Arthur.

Who Was King Arthur?
by Jerry Dunn

King Arthur and his queen, Guinevere, ruled their kingdom in peace from their castle, Camelot. . . . Camelot represents a lost time of innocence and high adventure during the Dark Ages—the period from A.D. 476 to about A.D. 1000. . . .

But did Arthur and his peaceful Camelot ever really exist? Historians say that around A.D. 410, after the Romans left Britain, fierce invaders called Saxons came from Europe, conquering much of England. In the western part of the country, a local chieftain fought the Saxons. He won a great victory at Badon Hill around A.D. 500. According to some scholars, this real-life brave warrior was Arthur.

His triumph brought 12 years of peace. Could this golden age have been Camelot? Some experts say the real Camelot may have been Cadbury Castle in southern England. Here archaeologists found ruins of a fortified tower and what may have been a great hall of timber, all dating from Arthur's time. Other places around England also lay claim to the noble king. For instance Arthur may have fought his last battle in southwestern England at a place called Camlan.

We may never know all the facts about Arthur. Perhaps it doesn't matter. The legend of King Arthur holds its own timeless truths. This is why people have been reciting stories of King Arthur and his Round Table for at least a thousand years.

THE DARK AGES

- Disorder reigned in most of Europe between A.D. 476 and A.D. 1000, the period called the Dark Ages.
- King Arthur and his knights never wore full suits of armor. They lived in the sixth century; full plate armor didn't show up for another 900 years.
- People who lived in what is now England did not speak English. They probably spoke Latin or British, a language from which Welsh developed.
- Disease, poor diet, and frequent wars meant that most people could not expect to live beyond age 30.
- Only monks and some noblemen learned how to read.

READING FOR INFORMATION

This selection provides support for question 9 on page 667. You can also use it as a mini-lesson on reading for information.

DISCUSSION PROMPTS

Use these prompts to help students explore the possible historical context of the Arthurian legend:

Connect Does the fact that there may have been a real King Arthur make the legend more interesting to you? Explain. *Some students may find it amazing that people are still telling stories about someone who may have lived 1,500 years ago. Others may say that the legend is interesting in its own right, and the story has been so heavily fictionalized that any historical roots would be nearly lost.*

Analyze Based on the article, what seems to have made the Dark Ages "dark"? How was Arthur's legendary Camelot a contrast to the Dark Ages? *Possible answer: Warfare, political disorder, low life expectancy, and widespread illiteracy made this time seem dark. Camelot was supposed to have been a secure and peaceful interlude during this grim era.*

Synthesize How would you say the world has improved since the Dark Ages? What threats from that time remain? *Possible answer: Most people today can expect to live long beyond age 30. Many diseases have been curbed by vaccinations and medicine, and literacy is much more common. However, many people today still do not have enough to eat, and many live with the tragedy of war.*

DIFFERENTIATED INSTRUCTION

FOR LESS-PROFICIENT READERS

Comprehension Support Use Reciprocal Teaching to help students understand the historical context of the King Arthur legend. Have students silently read the first two paragraphs of the article and then ask them to summarize, generate questions, clarify, and make predictions about the remainder of the reading.

 BEST PRACTICES TOOLKIT—Transparency
Reciprocal Teaching p. A35

FOR ENGLISH LEARNERS

Vocabulary: Cognates Have small groups scan the article for cognates and report their findings to the class. Spanish cognates in the introductory paragraph include

- *historian/el historiador(a)*
- *to present/presentar*
- *theories/las teorías*
- *to decide/decidir*

Students might also note that Arthur's name has a common Spanish cognate, Arturo.

Comprehension: Sequence Have students create a timeline that shows the dates mentioned in the article. Make sure they understand the designation A.D. Students should be able to show on the timeline what is meant by "the sixth century" and "another 900 years" (mentioned in the second bullet point under **The Dark Ages**).

Focus and Motivate

OBJECTIVES

Literary Analysis
- explore the key idea of **chivalry**
- identify and analyze cultural values in legends
- read a legend

Reading
- predict

Vocabulary
- build vocabulary for reading and writing
- use correct word from easily confused words *(also an EL language objective)*

Grammar and Writing
- use correct sentence structure
- form complex sentences
- use writing to analyze literature

SUMMARY

In this excerpt, the Green Knight bursts into King Arthur's New Year's feast. He challenges any knight to chop off his head and take a return blow in a year and a day. Sir Gawain accepts the task. When the deed is done, the Green Knight picks up his head, reminds Gawain of his promise, and rides off, leaving a stunned court behind him.

Is CHIVALRY *dead?*

Discuss the question and the *KEY IDEA*. Ask students to give examples of behaviors associated with **chivalry**. For example, the photo shows someone sharing an umbrella. List students' ideas on the board and have them add some of these to their *SURVEY* charts.

Selection Resources

---

from **Sir Gawain and the Green Knight**

Medieval Legend Retold by Michael Morpurgo

Is CHIVALRY *dead?*

MARYLAND OBJECTIVES

READING/LIT STANDARDS
1.E.4.d Confirm, refute, or make predictions
3.A.6.a Analyze universal themes

KEY IDEA Back in the ninth century, **chivalry** was a set of rules that gave knights guidance about how to engage in battle, how to serve rulers, and how to behave toward women. Today *chivalry* refers to the personal qualities that were important to knights: bravery, honor, courtesy, and service. In this legend, an act of chivalry gets one knight into a terrible predicament.

SURVEY In our rough-and-tumble modern world, does chivalry still exist? Conduct a survey to find out how often your peers witness people acting chivalrously. Use your results to discuss what modern people are doing well and what they could do better.

	Often	Seldom	Never
Sacrificing for Others			
Keeping Promises			
Being Polite			

670

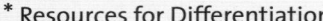

RESOURCE MANAGER UNIT 6

Plan and Teach pp. 91–98

Literary Analysis
Summary pp. 99†*, 100‡*
Cultural Values in Legends pp. 101, 102†*
Question Support p. 109*

Reading
Predict pp. 103, 104†*
Reading Check p. 108

Vocabulary
Study p. 105*
Practice p. 106
Strategy p. 107

Grammar and Writing
Use Correct Sentence Structure p. 111

Assessment
Selection Tests A, B/C pp. 113*, 115*
Test Generator CD

BEST PRACTICES TOOLKIT

Differentiated Instruction pp. 31–38*

Scaffolding Instruction pp. 43–46*

Graphic Organizers/Strategies
T Chart • Word Squares • Read Aloud/Think Aloud • Venn Diagram • Character Map • Plot Diagram • Cause-and-Effect Diagram

Reading Support
Audio Anthology CD*

Technology
Literature and Vocabulary Centers at **ClassZone.com**
Write*Smart* CD

* Resources for Differentiation   † Also in Spanish   ‡ In Haitian Creole and Vietnamese

LITERARY ANALYSIS: CULTURAL VALUES IN LEGENDS

Most popular movies focus on a hero—a person who is unusually brave. Long before people filmed stories or wrote them down, a hero was often the basis for a legend.

In a legend, the hero's main traits usually reflect the **cultural values** of the society, or the standards of behavior the society wants to promote. In medieval Arthurian legends, knights and their code of chivalry represent these ideals, cherished in the Middle Ages:

- Be loyal to those you serve and be courteous to all.
- Always be truthful and keep your word.
- Face danger with courage and show mercy to the weak.

As you read, look for examples of chivalry.

READING STRATEGY: PREDICT

Predicting is making a reasonable guess about what will happen next in a story. To predict, follow these steps:

- Consider what you know about the characters and plot.
- Combine these thoughts with your own experience, and make a logical guess about what might happen next.
- Adjust your prediction as new information is presented.

As you read, track your predictions on a chart.

Text Evidence	Prediction	What Happens
King Arthur wishes for a challenge.		

VOCABULARY IN CONTEXT

The words listed help describe a knight and his challenge. Put each word in the appropriate column of a chart. Then write a definition for each word with which you are familiar.

WORD LIST		
cumbersome	integrity	sever
daunting	lanky	unperturbed
demeaning	revere	

Know Well	Think I Know	Don't Know at All

Author Online

Storyteller with Heart When Michael Morpurgo became a teacher, one of his favorite parts of the job was making up stories for his students. Their interest convinced him that he could become a writer. Now the British author has published over 50 books. In his spare time, Morpurgo runs three farms in England, where kids from the city can stay. In 2003, he was named the third Children's Laureate of England.

Michael Morpurgo
born 1943

Background

The Chivalric Code In the Middle Ages, young men from well-to-do families often became knights. As knights, they served a family of a higher social rank. Knights were expected to be extremely courteous and brave, as well as loyal to their lords.

Knights of the Round Table Stories of Arthur were first told before the age of chivalry, but during the Middle Ages, the stories changed. Arthur and his followers began to be pictured as knights who lived in an ideal kingdom called Camelot. An English writer, Sir Thomas Malory wrote about the Round Table, where the knights sat in perfect equality.

 MORE ABOUT THE AUTHOR AND BACKGROUND
To learn more about Michael Morpurgo and the Round Table, visit the **Literature Center** at **ClassZone.com.**

SIR GAWAIN AND THE GREEN KNIGHT **671**

Teach

STANDARDS FOCUS

● **CULTURAL VALUES IN LEGENDS**

Have students identify heroes of other cultures. Point out how they exemplify different virtues and values. For example, the ancient Greek hero Hercules shows physical strength and courage—traits especially valued by the Greeks in Sparta, who lived in a military society.

CHECK UNDERSTANDING Have students think of contemporary heroes. Ask them what values of 21st-century society are reflected in the behavior of these heroes.

■ **PREDICT**

Read aloud this example:

> The new girl struggled to open her jammed locker. Delmar could tell she was worried about being late to class. Feeling chivalrous, he walked over to her.

What does Delmar do next? What clues lead to this prediction? *Possible answer: He helps the girl open her locker; the word chivalrous is a clue.*

CHECK UNDERSTANDING Have students predict what they will be doing at noon tomorrow and explain their logic. What could happen to change their predictions?

 RESOURCE MANAGER—Copy Master
Predict p. 103 (for student use while reading the selection)

▲ VOCABULARY IN CONTEXT

DIAGNOSE WORD KNOWLEDGE To determine preteaching needs, have all students complete **Vocabulary in Context.** Remind students to look for the definitions of the unknown words as they read the text: *cumbersome* (p. 679), *daunting* (p. 678), *demeaning* (p. 679), *integrity* (p. 680), *lanky* (p. 675), *revere* (p. 680), *sever* (p. 680), *unperturbed* (p. 679).

PRETEACH VOCABULARY Use the Vocabulary Study copy master to help students explore the meaning of each boldfaced word.

1. Read item 1 aloud, emphasizing *cumbersome.*
2. Point out the phrase *hard to handle.* Elicit possible meanings for *cumbersome,* such as "awkward."
3. Discuss which category in Part B *cumbersome* belongs in.
4. Repeat the procedure for items 2–8.

 RESOURCE MANAGER—Copy Master
Vocabulary Study p. 105

For general guidelines on differentiating vocabulary instruction and for alternative vocabulary activities for students not needing vocabulary preteaching, see

BEST PRACTICES TOOLKIT
Scaffolding Vocabulary Instruction pp. 45–46

ℹ Vocabulary Center at **ClassZone.com**

Practice and Apply

ANALYZE VISUALS

Possible answer: Although the knight is carrying a shield and lance, he does not seem ready to do battle. He and his horse are wearing fancy attire, suggesting that they are on their way to a special event.

About the Art Juan Wijngaard (b. 1951) was born in South America and studied in England at the Kingston College of Art and the Royal College of Art. He paints and illustrates books.

LITERARY ANALYSIS

Ⓐ CULTURAL VALUES

Possible answer: People in the Middle Ages valued comradeship, loyalty, and faith.

If students need help ... List the values revealed in this passage in the first column of a two-column chart. Have students work together to find details from the text that support each inference.

Value	Detail from text
comradeship or friendship	The knights are happy to be together.
loyalty	They work together for their king and their kingdom.

Extend the Discussion Based on the description of life in Camelot, what values might Camelot itself represent?

 BEST PRACTICES TOOLKIT—Transparency T Chart p. A25

Sir Gawain
and the
Green Knight

Retold by Michael Morpurgo

It was Christmas time at Camelot, that time of the year when all King Arthur's Knights gathered to celebrate the birth of their Lord and Savior, Jesus Christ. For fifteen joyous days, after holy Mass each morning there was nothing but feasting and dancing and singing, and hunting and jousting too. Jousting was the favorite sport, each Knight striving to unseat the mighty Sir Lancelot—but rarely succeeding of course. And all was done in fun, in a spirit of great comradeship, for they were happy to be all together once more at this blessed time. During the year, these lords were often parted from one another, and from their ladies, as they rode
10 out through the kingdom on their dangerous missions. So this was a time when love and friendship were renewed, a time to celebrate with their young King all their achievements and their great and good purpose: to bring peace to the land, and make of it a kingdom as near to a heaven on earth as had never before been achieved in Britain, or in any other land, come to that. Ⓐ

ANALYZE VISUALS How does the knight in this painting **compare** with your image of a knight?

① **Targeted Passage**

Ⓐ **CULTURAL VALUES** Reread lines 10–15. On the basis of this description, what can you **infer** about the kind of behavior people admired during the Middle Ages?

Illustrations © Juan Wijngaard (1981) from *Sir Gawain and the Green Knight* by Selina Hastings. Reproduced by permission of Walker Books, Ltd., London

672 UNIT 6: MYTHS, LEGENDS, AND TALES

DIFFERENTIATED INSTRUCTION

FOR ALL STUDENTS

Enhancing Learning Styles Provide independent projects for various learning styles.

- **Musical** Compose a song about Gawain and the Green Knight.
- **Visual** Design a personal shield.
- **Kinesthetic** Dramatize a scene from the legend.

For further details on these projects, see

R **RESOURCE MANAGER** Ideas for Extension pp. 96–97

672 UNIT 6: MYTHS, LEGENDS, AND TALES

FOR LESS–PROFICIENT READERS

In combination with the *Audio Anthology CD*, use one or more Targeted Passages (pp. 672, 678, 680–681) to ensure that students focus on key story events, concepts, and skills.

① Targeted Passage [Lines 1–10]

This passage introduces the setting: the story takes place in King Arthur's court at Camelot during the Christmas holiday.

- What is the setting of the legend?
- How do the knights celebrate Christmas?
- How would you describe the relationship of the knights to each other?
- What qualities do King Arthur's knights possess?

BACKGROUND

Sir Lancelot All the knights of the Round Table try to "unseat the mighty Sir Lancelot" (line 6). They rarely succeed due to his military prowess. Sir Lancelot is also known for his love for Guinevere, the king's wife—a circumstance that creates factions and dissent within the ranks of the knights.

Sir Gawain Gawain, the hero of the legend, sits to the left of King Arthur, his uncle, at the Round Table. In the early Arthurian legends, Gawain is a model of courage and loyalty. He is mythically associated with the sun, as his strength is reported to grow stronger at noon each day and then diminish.

Guinevere Many different stories are associated with the "gloriously beautiful" Guinevere (lines 21–22). It is generally held that when her love for Lancelot caused her to betray Arthur, it signaled the beginning of the end for Camelot.

CULTURAL CONNECTION

Stories of Death and Rebirth The story of Sir Gawain takes place around the winter solstice. Many ancient cultures, such as the Celts, celebrated this shortest day of the year as a time when the sun was reborn and the cycle of life set in motion again. The theme of rebirth and renewal is expressed in countless stories across cultures. The Egyptian myth of Osiris tells of a god who is brought back from the dead. As a result, Osiris represents both the afterlife and fertility. In the Hindu tradition, each living being is believed to move through a perpetual cycle of life, death, and reincarnation.

FOR ENGLISH LEARNERS

Options for Reading Read the first Targeted Passage aloud. Make sure students understand the setting of the legend, including the period in history, time of year, and location. Record the names of major characters on the board and explain their relationships to each other. Then have students read the rest of the selection silently as they listen to the *Audio Anthology CD*. Pause the CD frequently to enable students to make predictions.

Key Academic Vocabulary Have students create Word Squares to explore the meaning of the word *challenge* (lines 52, 165, 174, 188).

🧰 BEST PRACTICES TOOLKIT—Transparency
   Word Squares p. E10

Prereading For prereading instruction for English learners, see

🧰 BEST PRACTICES TOOLKIT
   Scaffolding Reading Instruction pp. 43–46

FOR ADVANCED LEARNERS/PRE–AP

Pre-AP exercises in the bottom channel provide additional challenge for your advanced students. Use them for small groups or individuals.

ADDITIONAL GUIDELINES

For more help with differentiation and tips for classroom management, see

🧰 BEST PRACTICES TOOLKIT
   Differentiated Instruction pp. 31–38

Lines 35–39
REINFORCE KEY IDEA: CHIVALRY

Discuss Outward behavior is a way of showing inner values. How does the code of **chivalry** dictate the guests' behavior at the feast? What is revealed about the guests' relationship to the king by this behavior? ***Possible answer:*** *The guests cannot start eating until the king does. Their courtesy shows their respect for and loyalty to King Arthur.*

On New Year's Eve, after evening Mass had been said in the chapel and generous New Year's gifts exchanged, the High King and Guinevere,[1] his Queen, came at last into the great hall where all the lords and ladies were waiting to dine. No one could begin the feasting until they came,
20 of course, so as you can imagine, the lords and ladies cheered them to the rafters when they saw them. Guinevere had never looked so gloriously beautiful as she did that evening, and there were gasps of admiration from around the hall.

With Arthur on one side of her and Gawain[2] on the other, Guinevere sat down at the high table, which was set on a splendid dais draped all about with silk and richly hung with the finest tapestries from Toulouse[3] and Turkestan.[4] Then, with drummers drumming and pipers piping, the servants came in carrying the food on great silver plates, piling each table high with roasted meat, capons and venison and pork, and fish
30 fresh-baked in sea salt, and baskets of crusty bread, and steaming soups too. Truly there was enough to feed five thousand, but there were only five hundred there to eat it. As they poured out the wine and ale, filling every goblet to the brim, the scents of the feast that lay before them filled the air with succulence,[5] and their nostrils too, so that, their appetites whetted, they were all longing now to begin. But the High King and his Queen sat there, not touching their food, or their drink either. Everyone knew that if they did not begin, then out of respect nor could anyone else. And everyone knew also why it was that the king was refusing to let the feast begin.

40 The great hall fell silent as Arthur rose to his feet. "You know the custom," he began. "I will not take one mouthful, or one sip of wine, until I am told of some new and stirring tale, some wonderfully outlandish adventure, some extraordinary feat of arms so far unheard of. And it must be true too. I don't want you to go making it up just so you can get at the food—some of you are good at the tall stories." They laughed at that, but as they looked around, it became clear that none of them had a tale to tell. "What?" cried the High King. "What? Not one of you? Well then, I see we must all go hungry. Such a pity. Isn't it strange how food you cannot eat always smells so wonderful? It needn't be a story,
50 of course. It could be some new happening, some weird and wondrous event. If I can't have a story, then you'd better hope, as I do, that maybe

dais (dāʹĭs) *n.* a raised platform for speakers or honored guests

---

1. **Guinevere** (gwĭnʹə-vîrʹ).
2. **Gawain** (gə-wānʹ).
3. **Toulouse** (tōō-lōōzʹ).
4. **Turkestan** (tûrʹkĭ-stănʹ): During the Middle Ages, trade occurred between Britain and many countries in Asia. Tapestries from the historical region Turkestan were prized objects that only the wealthy could afford.
5. **succulence:** juiciness and tastiness.

FOR ENGLISH LEARNERS

Culture: Connect Explain that the author's purpose in lines 24–31 is to create an impression of a magnificent banquet. The foods that he names are the kinds of dishes that wealthy nobles in the 1300s would have eaten at special dinners. Invite students to make up a menu for a celebration that reflects dishes from their culture. Ask students to share their menus and explain why they chose certain items.

Vocabulary Support Have mixed-ability pairs use context clues to define these phrases:

- *come to that* (line 15), "actually," "in fact"
- *cheered them to the rafters* (lines 20–21), "yelled loudly to show approval"
- *a real head cruncher* (lines 88–89), "a large and destructive weapon"
- *widow maker* (line 93), "a deadly weapon that kills men, leaving their wives as widows"
- *who's in charge here?* (line 101), "who is the leader or king of this place?"

Comprehension: Transitions Explain that the events in the story occur in chronological or time-order sequence. Guide students to identify words and phrases that indicate the sequential relationship of events: *at last* (line 18), *then* (line 27), *as* (line 32), *until* (line 42), *at that very same moment* (line 55). Encourage students to continue looking for transitions such as these as they read.

some stranger will come striding in here right now and challenge us face to face. That would do. I'd be happy with that. Then we could all begin our feasting before the food gets cold." And with that, he sat down. **B**

At that very same moment, just as the High King had finished speaking, they heard a sudden roaring of wind, the rattle of doors and windows shaking, and then outside, the clatter of a horse's hooves on stone. The great doors burst open, and into the hall rode the most awesome stranger anyone there had ever set eyes on. For a start, he was a giant of a man, taller by two heads than any knight there, but not **lanky** and long, not at all. No, shoulder to shoulder he was as broad as any three men stood side by side, and his legs were massive—like tree trunks they were. And you could see the man's arms were about as thick and strong as his legs. But that wasn't all. This giant was green, green from head to toe. Yes, bright green, I tell you, as green as beech leaves in summer when the sun shines through. And when I say the man was green, I don't just mean his clothes. I mean him. His face. Green. His hands. Green. The hair that hung down to his shoulders. Green. Only his eyes, horror of horrors, glowed red, blood red and glaring from under his heavy eyebrows, which were as green as the rest of him. Everyone in that hall simply gaped at him, at his hugeness and his greenness, and at his grimness too, for the man had a thunderous scowl on his face that struck terror into every heart.

Grim he may have been, but the giant was gorgeous too—if such an apparition can ever be said to be gorgeous. He wore a tunic of green velvet with buttons of gleaming gold. Stirrups and spurs were all of gold, both encrusted with the brightest emeralds of the deepest green. And his horse! His warhorse was a monster of a creature—he had to be, just to carry this giant. The horse was green too, green from nose to hoof, from mane to tail. He was pawing at the ground, tossing his head, foaming at his bit; at least the foam was white. And he looked just as bad-tempered as his master. They suited each other, those two. **C**

Yet fierce though he seemed, the Knight in green wore no war helmet and no armor either. He held no shield before him, and carried no spear, not even a sword at his side. Instead, the hand clutching the reins held a sprig of holly—green naturally—which might have been laughable had everyone not already noticed what he was carrying in his other hand. It was an ax, but it was no ordinary battle-ax. This weapon was a real head cruncher, yet the handle was most delicately carved—bright green of course, as was the cord that looped about it and the tassels that hung from it. Only the huge blade itself was not green. Curved like a crescent moon at the cutting edge, it was made of polished steel—a hideous

B PREDICT
Reread lines 40–54. Why does Arthur refuse to let the feast begin? Predict what will happen next.

lanky (lăng'kē) *adj.* tall and thin

C CULTURAL VALUES
Recall what you've learned about knights and chivalry. Does the Green Knight seem like a chivalrous type? As you read, note how chivalry influences his behavior and the reactions of others.

READING SKILL

B PREDICT
Record students' answers in the first two columns of the chart from page 671.
Possible answers:

- *Text Evidence—No one has a tale to tell. Therefore, the feast cannot begin until a stranger issues a challenge.*
- *Prediction—A stranger will walk in and issue a challenge.*

Lines 58–73
DISCUSSION PROMPTS
Use these prompts to help students understand the significance of the Green Knight:

Connect How would you feel at this moment if you were a member of King Arthur's court? *Students might say that they would feel frightened or amazed.*

Analyze What do the lords and ladies think the knight's purpose is? Why? *Possible answer: They think he is there to attack them. His fierce appearance and facial expression suggest this.*

Synthesize What does the color green symbolize? What might that symbolism suggest about the Green Knight's purpose? *Possible answer: The color green might represent nature or life. Perhaps the Green Knight is not as evil as he appears.*

LITERARY ANALYSIS

C CULTURAL VALUES
Possible answer: At first glance, the Green Knight does not appear chivalrous. He bursts into the feast without invitation and looks bad-tempered.

FOR LESS–PROFICIENT READERS
Reading Strategy Follow-Up: Predict

- Have students write clues such as these in their charts from page 671: *The knight is a giant. He is green. He is scowling, but he wears no armor.*

- Use Read Aloud/Think Aloud to model how to use this textual evidence to make predictions about the Green Knight's purpose.

BEST PRACTICES TOOLKIT—Transparency
Read Aloud/Think Aloud p. A34

FOR ADVANCED LEARNERS/PRE–AP
Analyze Point out lines 65–68, in which the presence of the narrator is signaled by the pronoun *I*. Who is this narrator? What is the author's purpose in making readers aware of the narrator in these particular lines? Have small groups discuss their ideas about the role of the narrator in this passage and in the rest of the legend.

DISCUSSION PROMPTS

Use these prompts to help students understand the character of King Arthur:

Recall What had King Arthur said just
before the Green Knight arrived? *Possible
answer: He had wished for a stranger to
come in and challenge the court.*

Contrast In what way is King Arthur's
reaction different from that of the other
knights? *Possible answer: He is not stunned
into silence. He smiles at the Green Knight.*

Synthesize What do you learn about King
Arthur's character from his reaction to the
Green Knight? Explain. *Possible answers:
He has courage and a love of adventure and
novelty. He is gracious and welcoming. In
short, he is a model of chivalry.*

LITERARY ANALYSIS

D CULTURAL VALUES

*Possible answer: In the Middle Ages,
hospitality was very important. Without
knowing who the stranger is, King Arthur
invites him to the feast.*

If students need help . . .

- Remind them that the Green Knight is a
stranger and uninvited. Yet, King Arthur
smiles and immediately asks the Green
Knight to sit down and join the feast.

- Compare the king's behavior with what
might happen if someone intruded on
a wedding reception or private party
today. Help students see the difference
in values shown by the contrast in
behaviors.

---

widow maker if ever there was one. Even
the dogs, usually so fierce with any stranger,
shrank back whining under the tables, their
tails between their legs.

There came no cheery New Year greeting
from this green man, not even a ghost of a
smile. In a thunderous, booming voice as
100 terrifying as the man himself, he said, "So,
who's in charge here?" No one answered him.
"Well, come on. Speak up. Which of you is
the King? It's him I've come to talk to, no
one else." But as he rode around the hall, his
blazing eyes scanning the lords and ladies
on every side, no one spoke up. And you
can understand why. Many of the knights
sitting there in that hushed hall had come
across all kinds of astounding and alarming
110 looking creatures on their quests[6]—dragons
and monsters, goblins and ghouls—but
never anything quite like this. Most sat there
stunned to silence. Others kept quiet out of
respect for their High King, wanting to hear
how he would reply.

No one doubted for a moment that he
would have the courage to speak up, and
so he did. Indeed, as he rose to his feet, he
was smiling broadly. After all, hadn't he just
120 been hoping for such a happening as this?
"Welcome to Camelot, Sir Knight," he began.
"I am the King you are looking for, I think.
My name is Arthur. Believe me, you could
not have arrived at a better moment. So please
dismount and join our New Year's feasting,
and afterward you can tell us perhaps why you
have come here to our court." **D**

The knight in green rode toward the dais and spoke directly to the
High King, but more courteously now. "My thanks, great King. But I
130 will not stay, or keep you from your feasting. I will speak my purpose
plainly. I cannot tell you how honored I am to meet you at last, the great
Arthur, High King of all Britain. I have heard, as all the world has heard,

D CULTURAL VALUES
Reread lines 116–127.
What can you **infer** about
how people in the Middle
Ages believed guests
should be treated?

---

6. **quests:** adventurous journeys made by knights.

DIFFERENTIATED INSTRUCTION

FOR LESS–PROFICIENT READERS
Monitor Comprehension

- Use a Venn Diagram to compare the atmosphere of the hall before the Green Knight
enters (lines 19–39) and after he arrives
(lines 93–115).

- Ask students what they learn about the
Green Knight by noticing how other characters react to him.

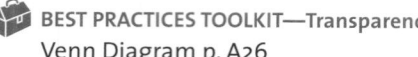 **BEST PRACTICES TOOLKIT—Transparency**
Venn Diagram p. A26

FOR ENGLISH LEARNERS

Language: Phrasal Verbs Give students additional practice in recognizing and defining
phrasal verbs. Remind them that words such
as *up, across,* and *on* can change the meaning
of a verb. Have pairs of students use context
clues, previous knowledge, or a dictionary
to define these phrasal verbs: *come on* (line
102), *speak up* (line 102), *come across* (lines
108–109), *take on* (line 149), *get on* (line 151),
take up (line 165).

ANALYZE VISUALS

Activity Does this Green Knight match your image of him from the description in the text? Why or why not? *Possible answers:*

- *Yes. He is carrying a piece of holly and a crescent-shaped ax. He and his horse are green. Emeralds adorn the bridle of the horse.*
- *No. He looks the same size as the figures behind the table; he is not towering over them as the text describes. His face is not clearly shown to be scowling.*

how you have made of this place the most wondrous kingdom on earth, and gathered around you the most worthy, courageous, and chivalrous knights that ever lived. Looking around me, I begin to wonder whether you deserve this glowing reputation at all. I mean no offense, great King. As you can see from the sprig of holly I carry, I came in peace. If it were otherwise, I'd be armed for a fight, would I not? But you see no armor on me, no helmet, no sword or spear, because it is not war I come for, but sport—well, a sport of sorts, anyway." **E**

E PREDICT
As you read, check your predictions against what actually happens. Did the prediction you made on page 675 come true?

SIR GAWAIN AND THE GREEN KNIGHT **677**

FOR ADVANCED LEARNERS/PRE–AP

Explore Character The narrator describes in great detail what the court sees when they look upon the Green Knight. What does he see and think when he first looks upon them?

- Have students write a brief inner monologue in the voice of the Green Knight, describing his motivation for coming to Camelot, what he expects to find there, and what his first impression is when he looks around the hall at King Arthur's guests.

- Ask students to share their monologues in small groups and to compare and contrast how they portrayed the Green Knight's thoughts. What details in the text helped them develop the voice of the Green Knight?

DISCUSSION PROMPTS

Use these prompts to help students understand the actions of the Green Knight:

Interpret Note that the Green Knight calls the members of King Arthur's court "beardless boys." What reaction does he hope to get from the knights? *Possible answer: He wants to make them angry.*

Analyze Why does the Green Knight want to make the knights feel angry and defensive? *Possible answer: He wants to make sure that someone accepts his challenge.*

Synthesize What do the Green Knight's words in lines 156–157 suggest about the purpose of his "New Year's game"? *Possible answer: The purpose of the game might be to test the bravery and skill of the knights.*

READING STRATEGY

F PREDICT

Record students' predictions in the chart from page 671. *Possible answers:*

- *Text evidence—King Arthur is courageous. Prediction—He will accept the Green Knight's challenge.*

- *Text evidence—The knights of the Round Table are all known for their courage. Prediction—One of Arthur's knights will accept the challenge.*

"If it's jousting you're looking for," the High King replied as politely as his irritation would allow, "or wrestling maybe, then **daunting** though you may look, Sir Knight, you'll find no lack of sport here, I assure you."

"But I joust and wrestle only with men," replied the Green Knight. "I see here nothing but beardless boys. It would be no contest. None of you would stand a chance against me. No, I have in mind something much more testing of a man's courage, and much more interesting for everyone. But I cannot imagine there will be anyone here brave enough to take me on."

150 "We'll see about that," the High King cried, his face flushing with sudden anger at the stranger's insulting tone. "Just get on with it for goodness' sake and tell us what game it is you want to play. Our soup is getting cold."

The Green Knight laughed. "Why don't we just call it a New Year's game," he said. "I don't think any of you will ever have played it before, and nor have I. We'll soon see what stuff your Knights of the Round Table are made of, whether you're all you're cracked up to be." So saying, he held high his great ax. "Here is my battle-ax," he went on. "Is there anyone here in this hall brave enough to take it, I wonder? Whoever does will have 160 one chance, and one chance only, to strike my head from my shoulders. I shall not resist or fight back. I shall not even flinch, I promise."

"Is that the game?" the High King asked, as incredulous as everyone else in the hall.

"Not quite," replied the Green Knight. "Here's how the game goes. If any Knight has the courage to take up the challenge, then he will have to promise, on his honor, that in a year and a day from now he will submit himself to . . . let's call it a return match, shall we? Then it will be my turn to strike the same single blow, and it will be one of you who has to kneel there, bare his neck, and take it—without resisting, without 170 flinching. Well, who dares?" **F**

If there was a hushed silence when he first came into the hall, the place was now as still as death as he glared all around, waiting for someone to speak up. But even the bravest of the Knights lowered their eyes. This was one challenge they all wanted to avoid if they could. The Green Knight wheeled his great warhorse and clattered around the hall, looking down at them, a supercilious sneer on his lips. "I thought so, I thought so," he said, his mocking laughter ringing in the air. "Where's your courage now? Where's that spotless honor, that perfect chivalry I've heard so much about? Is there no one here who has the stomach to take me on?" Still no 180 one spoke. "Chickens, the lot of you. Worse than chickens too. At least

daunting (dôn'tǐng) *adj.* frightening; intimidating **daunt** *v.*

② Targeted Passage

F PREDICT
Use what you know about the **plot** and **characters** to predict what you think will happen next.

DIFFERENTIATED INSTRUCTION

FOR LESS–PROFICIENT READERS

② Targeted Passage [Lines 154–170]

This passage introduces the major conflict: the Green Knight challenges one of the knights to cut off his head.

- What is the first part of the Green Knight's challenge?

- What is the second part of the challenge?

- What seems strange about the Green Knight's proposal?

FOR ENGLISH LEARNERS

Vocabulary: World History Explain that the English word *chivalry* (line 178) comes from the Latin word *caballarius,* meaning "horseman." Chivalry originally referred to the rules governing the behavior of warriors who rode horses, or knights. Point out that the Spanish term for chivalry, *caballería,* has the same roots.

Vocabulary: Idioms and Sayings Have pairs define these expressions from context:

- *what stuff your Knights . . . are made of* (lines 156–157), "what kind of men your Knights are—strong or weak"

- *all you're cracked up to be* (line 157), "as good as you claim to be"

- *has the stomach* (line 179), "is brave enough"

- *short of a miracle* (line 218), "unless something totally unexpected happens"

chickens cluck. I can see I'm in the wrong place. This can't be the court of King Arthur. It's a court of cowards." **G**

Stung to fury now, the High King had had enough. "Cease your insults!" he shouted. "None of us here is frightened of you. We're just speechless at the sheer stupidity of such a ridiculous duel. It's obvious that with an ax like that, whoever strikes the first blow is bound to be the winner. But since you insist upon it and are so brash and rude, I shall take up your challenge myself. So get down off that horse, hand me your ax, and I'll give you what you asked for." And with that, King Arthur sprang down from the dais and strode across the hall toward the Green Knight, who dismounted and at once handed over his ax. "Make yourself ready, then," cried the High King, swinging the ax above his head, testing his grip, feeling the weight and balance of the weapon. The Green Knight looked on. He stood head and shoulders above the King, dwarfing him utterly. **Unperturbed** by the swishing ax, the Green Knight turned down the neck of his tunic and made himself ready.

At that moment, Gawain stood up. "No!" he cried. And leaving the table, he hurried across the hall to his uncle's aid. He bowed low before him. "Let me take your place, Uncle. Give me this fight, please, I beg you. I shall teach this green and haughty man that in a fight there are no Knights braver than your own. It is true that I am no braver than any other man here, I know that, but I am your nephew. Make this an uncle's gift to his nephew. Because the truth is, good Uncle, that if I do lose my life, I would not be much missed compared to you. You are our King, and this is too silly, too **demeaning** a venture for you. Lose you and we lose the kingdom. Lose me and there will always be others to come in my place." **H**

"For goodness' sake, make up your minds," said the Green Knight, shaking his head, "I do not have all day."

Ignoring the man's boorishness, Gawain knelt before the King. "Let me prove myself worthy, Uncle, worthy of being your Knight and your nephew too." There was much applause at this and many loud voices raised in support of Sir Gawain's plea. After thinking for a while, the High King lifted his hand for silence, and taking Gawain's hand, helped him to his feet. "As you wish, Nephew," he said. "There's nothing I'd like better than to separate this man's great green head from his great green shoulders, but I willingly give the task to you. Strike boldly, Nephew. If you do, I really cannot see, short of a miracle, how you will ever have to face him again in a year and a day. Here's the ax. You'll find it a bit heavy and **cumbersome,** but it'll do the job."

G CULTURAL VALUES
On the basis of what you've read so far, is the Green Knight chivalrous? Explain why or why not.

unperturbed
(ŭn'pər-tûrbd') *adj.* not troubled or distressed

demeaning
(dĭ-mē'nĭng) *adj.* lowering one's dignity or standing **demean** *v.*

H CULTURAL VALUES
How does Gawain demonstrate that he is chivalrous? Explain.

cumbersome
(kŭm'bər-səm) *adj.* awkward; hard to manage

G CULTURAL VALUES

Possible answer: The Green Knight is not very chivalrous. At times he speaks courteously to King Arthur—for example, in lines 128–132, he compliments the king. Most of the time, however, he addresses the court rudely. He demands to speak to the person in charge, and he insults the knights by calling them "beardless boys" (line 145) and saying that no one has the courage to take him on (lines 148–149).

If students need help . . . List adjectives describing a chivalrous person (*respectful, courteous, loyal, brave, merciful, just*). Then list adjectives describing the Green Knight's behavior. Compare the two lists.

H CULTURAL VALUES

Possible answer: Sir Gawain demonstrates his chivalry by his loyalty to the king, his humility, and his courage in the face of a frightening challenge.

FOR ADVANCED LEARNERS/PRE–AP
Make Judgments Does the Green Knight have a valid point when he calls the knights of the Round Table "chickens"? Their response to his dare is silence (lines 171–182). King Arthur jumps to their defense in lines 183–187, but how convincing is his explanation? Have students decide whether they think King Arthur's explanation is valid or whether the Green Knight's perception of the knights is accurate. Have students argue their view in an informal class debate.

David and Goliath Line 223 alludes to the battle between the Philistine giant Goliath and the young Israelite David. According to the Bible, Goliath challenged the Israelites. If he could be defeated in single combat, the Philistines would become subjects of the Israelites instead of attacking them. The young boy David came forth, armed only with stones and a slingshot. He knocked Goliath unconscious and then beheaded him with the giant's own sword, thus saving the Israelites.

READING STRATEGY

❶ PREDICT

Record students' answers in the chart from page 671. *Possible answer:*

- *Text evidence—The Green Knight is much larger than Gawain, but Gawain has the ax and will take the first turn. To the court, they seem like David and Goliath. David won that contest.*

- *Prediction—Gawain will chop off the Green Knight's head.*

Lines 228–249
DISCUSSION PROMPTS

Use these prompts to help students understand more about the challenge:

Connect Do you share Gawain's opinion that the game is "foolish"? Why? *Students may say that the game is foolish because there does not seem to be any point to it.*

Analyze Why is the Green Knight pleased that Gawain is to be his opponent? *Possible answer: He has heard others speak about Gawain's courage and integrity, and he admires these qualities.*

Speculate Why might the Green Knight prefer a person with integrity to answer his challenge? *Possible answer: The challenge may have as much to do with character as with physical courage.*

LITERARY ANALYSIS

❶ CULTURAL VALUES

Possible answer: Yes. From the Green Knight's description of Sir Gawain and Gawain's own behavior, it is clear that he is a man of honor. He will keep his promise.

Gawain took the ax from him, gripped it firmly and turned now to face the Green Knight, who stood towering above him, his hands on his hips. To everyone there they looked like David and Goliath—and all were hoping and praying for the same unlikely outcome. "So," said the giant Knight, "so we have a champion at last. Let's get on with it. But before we do I must know your name and make sure we both understand and agree on the rules of the game." ❶

"My name is Sir Gawain, and I already know the rules of your foolish game," came the blunt reply.

230 "Good Sir Gawain, I'm glad it is you," said the Green Knight then, altogether more polite now than he had been so far. "I'll be honored to take the first blow from a knight as noble and worthy as yourself, for you are known and **revered** throughout all Britain as a man of not only the greatest courage, but also the greatest **integrity.** Believe me, you will need both, and in full measure, for what I have in store for you. And just so there can be no misunderstanding, you must promise on your honor, and in the hearing of everyone in this hall, that a year and a day from now you will seek me out and find me so that I can pay you back in kind for whatever you do to me today."

240 "I promise you willingly, on my honor as a Knight of the Round Table," Gawain replied. "But how shall I be able to find you? I don't even know your name or from what part of the country you come. Just tell me, and I'll be there—you have my word." ❶

"Afterward I shall tell you all you need to know," said the Green Knight. "Once you have done your worst, I'll tell you exactly where to come and who I am." And with a smile that sent shivers even into brave Gawain's heart, the Green Knight went on, "I'll be looking forward to you calling on me in a year and a day. I'll be looking forward to it very much indeed."

250 With the smile still on his face, the Green Knight went down on one knee before Gawain and bared his neck. "Do the best you can, Sir Gawain," he said. "Remember, you have only one chance."

"Make your peace with your Maker," Gawain replied, running his finger along the blade.

Then, grasping the handle tight and putting his left foot forward, he took a deep breath and raised the great ax high above his head, the blade flashing blood red in the flames of the fire. Down it came and sliced right through the Green Knight's neck, cutting clean through bone and flesh and skin, **severing** the terrible head entirely and sending

260 it rolling hideously across the floor toward the lords and ladies at their

❶ PREDICT
Reread lines 223–224. How do King Arthur and the others in the hall think the match will turn out? Make your own prediction about the outcome.

revere (rĭ-vîr′) *v.* to honor or worship

integrity (ĭn-tĕg′rĭ-tē) *n.* honesty or sincerity

❶ CULTURAL VALUES
Do you think that others in the hall believe Gawain will keep his promise? Why or why not?

❸ Targeted Passage

sever (sĕv′ər) *v.* to cut off or apart

DIFFERENTIATED INSTRUCTION

FOR ENGLISH LEARNERS
Language: Modifiers Explain that adverbs can modify or tell about verbs. Adverbs often end in -ly. List these examples on the board:

He gripped the ax firmly. (tells how he gripped it)

He promises willingly. (tells in what way he promises)

Have small groups find other -ly adverbs on these pages. Have them explain what each tells about the verb in the sentence.

FOR ADVANCED LEARNERS/PRE–AP
Synthesize Have students collaborate on Character Maps of Gawain, using evidence from lines 197–254. What are his strengths? Does he have any weaknesses? When students have finished their maps, have them discuss how Gawain's encounter with the Green Knight—though frightening and difficult—might make him a better person.

 BEST PRACTICES TOOLKIT—Transparency Character Map p. D8

table. And the blood was not green, as you might have imagined, but bright red like any man's, and it spurted freely from head and body alike.

But instead of toppling over, as everyone expected, that grotesque headless body rose up onto his feet and strode across the floor to where his head lay bleeding, the eyes closed in death. Snatching the baleful[7] head up by the hair, he went straight to his horse, set one foot in the stirrup, and swung himself up easily into his saddle as if nothing at all had happened. Suddenly those eyes opened and glared most horribly around the hall. Everyone was struck dumb with terror.

❸ Targeted Passage

But worse was still to come, for then the mouth began to speak. "Well struck, Sir Gawain. Now I'm afraid you have your side of the bargain to keep, a promise you made freely and openly, in front of everyone here and in front of your King too. You must seek me out and find me at the Green Chapel, a year and a day from now. There I shall repay you, a blow for a blow, as we agreed. I am known everywhere as

---

7. **baleful:** foretelling evil.

FOR LESS–PROFICIENT READERS

❸ Targeted Passage [Lines 255–275]

This passage represents the climax—Sir Gawain's cutting off the Green Knight's head—and the falling action of the story.

- What is the result of Sir Gawain's first blow?
- What happens after the knight picks up his head?
- What does the Green Knight say to Gawain?

FOR ENGLISH LEARNERS

Comprehension: Self-Monitor

1. Pair students. Have them take turns reading lines 230–275 aloud.
2. After students have reread the passage, ask them to summarize what happens, either in outline form or graphically.
3. Have pairs share their summaries and identify similarities and differences.
4. Address discrepancies in a whole-class discussion.

Lines 263–274
DISCUSSION PROMPTS

Use these prompts to help students understand the significance of the outcome:

Connect If you were a member of King Arthur's court, what would you find most horrifying about the Green Knight's behavior after Gawain lops his head off? *Some students may say that the ability of the Green Knight to function without his head is horrifying. Others may say that the fact that the head can speak is the most terrifying.*

Analyze What is revealed about the Green Knight through this event? *Possible answer: He is supernatural.*

Synthesize What do these events mean for Gawain? *Possible answer: Since the Green Knight is still alive, Gawain will have to meet him in a year and a day as promised. Gawain will probably lose his life, since there is no way he could defeat this enormous, supernatural being even if he tried.*

ANALYZE VISUALS

About the Art Juan Wijngaard has included a fool in this illustration of the Sir Gawain legend. Professional jesters, or fools, were common in the royal courts of medieval Europe. They usually wore multicolored costumes including a hood with ears and bells. Fools were allowed to behave in a very unchivalrous manner, even hurling insults at the king. It was their job to amuse the court and perhaps bring good luck.

Activity What is the expression on the onlookers' faces? *Possible answer: They look disgusted.*

K **PREDICT**

Record students' answers in the third column of the chart from page 671.
Possible answer: Gawain is successful and chops off the Green Knight's head. The Green Knight picks it up, reminds Gawain of his pledge, and rides away.

LITERARY ANALYSIS

L **CULTURAL VALUES**

Possible answer: King Arthur wants to lift the mood and distract people's attention from what just happened. The times they lived in were often dangerous and it was important for people to celebrate special occasions even if the future was uncertain.

Epilogue
REINFORCE KEY IDEA: CHIVALRY

Discuss In what ways do both Gawain and the Green Knight demonstrate **chivalry** at the end of the legend? *Possible answer: Gawain keeps his word and goes to the Green Chapel, an act of great courage since he expects to have his head chopped off. The Green Knight shows respect and mercy for Gawain after Gawain has proven himself.*

SELECTION WRAP-UP

REFLECT Have students think about whether Gawain's acceptance of the Green Knight's challenge was a noble or a rash decision.

★ CRITIQUE Have students evaluate how well mood is conveyed throughout the legend and discuss what they might do to intensify the feelings of horror or fear at key moments.

---

the Knight of the Green Chapel. Look into the sky as you go and follow where your eyes and your ears lead you. I shall be waiting. Be sure you come, Sir Gawain, or the world will know you forever as a coward."
He said nothing more, not one goodbye, but turning his horse about,
280 set spurs to his side and galloped from that hall, sparks flying from the horse's hooves as he went. Where he had come from no one knew. Where he went to no one knew. But as you can well imagine, I think, all were glad to see him gone. **K**

It was some time before anyone in the hall found voice to speak, and then it was the High King himself who at last broke the silence. He was as amazed and horrified as everyone else by what they had just witnessed, but he did not like to see his queen and his court so downhearted on this festive evening. "Come on now. Let's not be upset," he said. "After all, this was just such a marvel as we were waiting for, was it not? And
290 marvels like this are as much a part of new year at Camelot as carols and feasting. Like it or not, and I agree it wasn't a very appetizing spectacle, you have to admit we've never seen anything quite like it before, have we? And best of all it means we can now begin our feasting. So hang up your ax, Gawain, somewhere where we can all see it and be reminded of your courage, and come and join us. Let's eat, my friends. Let's drink. Let's be merry." And so they were—all but Gawain, whose thoughts, as ours must now do, ran on ahead of him to New Year's Day a year hence, to the dreaded day when he would meet that Green Knight once again at the Green Chapel. ❧ **L**

Eventually, Sir Gawain did indeed set out to find the Green Chapel and fulfill his promise. On his journey, he encountered three temptations that tested his character. By the time he stood before the Green Knight, he had proven himself a worthy, though not perfect, knight. For this reason, the Green Knight injures Gawain slightly but does not take his life.

K **PREDICT**
Did the prediction you made on page 680 come true? Describe what happened after Gawain struck the Green Knight.

L **CULTURAL VALUES**
What reasons does King Arthur have for choosing this moment to invite his knights to the feast?

DIFFERENTIATED INSTRUCTION

FOR LESS-PROFICIENT READERS

Comprehension Support To help students summarize and review the events in the excerpt, have them work in small groups to complete a Plot Diagram. List the important events on the board and have students place the events in the correct position on the diagram. Go over students' responses.

🛠 BEST PRACTICES TOOLKIT—Transparency
Plot Diagram p. D12

FOR ADVANCED LEARNERS/PRE-AP

Interpret What is the Green Knight's role, or purpose, in the story? One view is that he seeks to uncover the truth; he exposes what is false in people's behavior and in their perceptions of themselves. Ask students to write a statement that explains how the Green Knight's behavior in the court fulfills that role and how he ultimately takes Gawain on a journey to the truth.

Comprehension

1. **Clarify** What has to happen before the feast can begin?

2. **Recall** Whom does the Green Knight come looking for?

3. **Represent** What does the scene in the great hall look like before the Green Knight appears? Make a drawing illustrating the description.

MARYLAND OBJECTIVES

LITERATURE STANDARD
3.A.6.a Analyze universal themes

Literary Analysis

4. **Predict** Review the chart of predictions you made as you read. What events were the most difficult to predict? Why?

5. **Make Inferences About Culture** What details in this legend reflect what people ate, what they wore, and how they celebrated? Tell what you infer about how the wealthy lived during the Middle Ages.

6. **Analyze Suspense** The growing tension, or excitement, that you feel as you read is called suspense. Which passages in this legend were especially suspenseful? Give the line numbers of at least two passages. Then explain your choices.

7. **Draw Conclusions About Cultural Values** People following the code of **chivalry** were expected to demonstrate the qualities shown in the web. Make a similar web and expand it by giving examples from the legend for each type of behavior. What conclusion can you draw about which of these qualities was most important to the people of the Middle Ages?

Loyalty

Honesty

Chivalry

Courage

Courtesy

Knights wait for Arthur to eat first.

8. **Compare and Contrast Legends** How does the king Arthur portrayed by Michael Morpurgo compare with the young Arthur portrayed by Robert D. San Souci in the legend on page 662? Think about characters' attitude toward others, their confidence in themselves, and the courage they display. Decide whether the young Arthur is more similar to or more different from the adult he becomes.

Extension and Challenge

9. **Readers' Circle** Which character is the true hero of this legend? Discuss your thoughts, giving details from the legend to support your opinion.

7. ● **STANDARDS FOCUS** *Cultural Values in Legends* **Loyalty:** *Gawain accepts the challenge for his king.* **Courage:** *Arthur and Gawain are willing to face the Green Knight.* **Honesty:** *Gawain keeps his word and goes to the Green Chapel. Students' conclusions will vary.*

8. *Both the young and the adult Arthur show courage. Both also do what they must, no matter the possible cost. One difference is that the adult Arthur has more confidence and answers to no other knight.*

Extension and Challenge

9. *Students may point to Sir Gawain as the true hero. He shows great courage in meeting the challenge of the Green Knight, when he does not have to do so. He could have let the king follow through, but he shows loyalty to the king in wanting to spare him whatever consequences might result from this encounter.*

Practice and Apply

After Reading

For additional support of post-reading questions, use these copy masters:

R RESOURCE MANAGER—Copy Masters
Reading Check p. 108 (to check understanding of the selection)
Cultural Values in Legends p. 101 (for practice of literary analysis standards focus)
Question Support p. 109 (**After Reading** questions adapted for English learners and less-proficient readers)

Additional selection questions are provided for teachers on page 95.

ANSWERS

Comprehension

1. *Either a wondrous tale must be told or a stranger must issue a challenge to the court.*

2. *The Green Knight is seeking the king.*

3. *Students' drawings should be based on the description given in lines 16–39.*

Literary Analysis

Possible answers:

4. ■ **STANDARDS FOCUS** *Predict* Students may say that Gawain's offer to take his uncle's place was difficult to predict, or they may say that it was difficult to predict that the Green Knight could function without his head.

5. *Students may point to details such as the elaborate jousts, games, dancing, and singing that people engaged in to celebrate Christmas; the generous gift-giving; the richly appointed hall and huge feast; and the description of the Green Knight's apparel and mount as indications of the life of the wealthy in medieval times. Students might infer that though their lives may have lacked some conveniences, the wealthy enjoyed luxuries and entertainment on a fairly lavish scale.*

6. *Lines 55–73 initiate suspense as readers wonder what the Green Knight wants and what he will do to the members of King Arthur's court. Suspense is heightened as Sir Gawain positions the ax in preparation for cutting off the Green Knight's head (lines 250–257).*

Vocabulary in Context

VOCABULARY PRACTICE

1. *large package*
2. *basketball*
3. *sitting calmly*
4. *being criticized publicly*
5. *respect*
6. *cut it off*
7. *honest politician*
8. *climbing a peak*

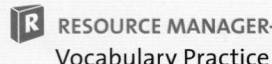 **RESOURCE MANAGER—Copy Master**
Vocabulary Practice p. 106

VOCABULARY IN WRITING

Have students use a flowchart to list the events that occurred after Gawain took up the challenge. Students should then refer to the chart to see which events could be described using a vocabulary word.

VOCABULARY STRATEGY: EASILY CONFUSED WORDS *(also an EL language objective)*

- Before students begin the exercise, read the choices aloud.
- Have students pick out the words that sound familiar and explain what they know about their meanings.

Answers:

1. *envelop*
2. *morale*
3. *thorough*
4. *dessert*
5. *alley*

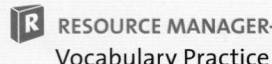 **RESOURCE MANAGER—Copy Master**
Vocabulary Strategy p. 107

🛈 Vocabulary Center at **ClassZone.com**
Additional Vocabulary Activities

Vocabulary in Context

VOCABULARY PRACTICE

Answer the questions to show your understanding of the vocabulary words.

1. Would a large package or one pair of socks more likely be **cumbersome?**
2. In which sport, basketball or football, might it be more important to be **lanky?**
3. If Ann is **unperturbed,** is she sitting calmly or shouting angrily?
4. Would being criticized publicly or being elected class president be more **demeaning?**
5. Would it show respect or disrespect to **revere** a person?
6. Is a telegram sent to **sever** a business deal meant to continue it or cut it off?
7. Who might be a better role model for **integrity,** an honest politician or a popular singer?
8. Which is more **daunting,** climbing a peak or resting in the backyard?

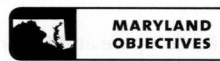

cumbersome
daunting
demeaning
integrity
lanky
revere
sever
unperturbed

VOCABULARY IN WRITING

What happened after Gawain asked to take up the Green Knight's challenge? Describe the events that followed, using three or more vocabulary words. Here is one way you could begin.

> **EXAMPLE SENTENCE**
>
> *Gawain grabbed hold of the* **cumbersome** *battle-ax.*

VOCABULARY STRATEGY: EASILY CONFUSED WORDS

When you first read the vocabulary word *sever,* did you mistake it for *severe?* The words *sever* and *severe* are easy to confuse, especially in writing. Be sure to choose the correct word from confusing pairs, checking spellings and meanings in a dictionary if you are not sure.

ACTIVITY Choose the word in parentheses that correctly completes each sentence. Refer to a dictionary if necessary.

1. The heavy fog seemed to (envelop, envelope) the entire building.
2. After the team lost its first game by 18 points, (moral, morale) among the players dropped dramatically.
3. To get rid of the cooking smells, we gave the room a (through, thorough) airing.
4. Can you really eat (desert, dessert) after that enormous meal?
5. You can get to our garage by driving down the (ally, alley).

MARYLAND OBJECTIVES

READING STANDARD
1.D.3.c Use resources to confirm definitions

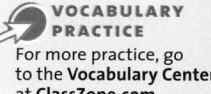 **VOCABULARY PRACTICE**
For more practice, go to the **Vocabulary Center** at **ClassZone.com.**

DIFFERENTIATED INSTRUCTION

FOR ENGLISH LEARNERS

Vocabulary Practice List all of the vocabulary words and their definitions on the board in the order of the sentences. Next to each word, write the two choices from the sentence (*revere: respect or disrespect*). Have students work in pairs, using the clues in the definition to select the correct choice.

FOR ADVANCED LEARNERS/PRE–AP

Vocabulary in Writing Have students use as many vocabulary words as possible to write a short news article that tells of the events in King Arthur's court after Gawain accepts the challenge.

Reading-Writing Connection

Explore this legend further by responding to the prompts. Then complete the **Grammar and Writing** exercise.

SKILLS PRACTICE

WRITING PROMPTS

A. Short Response: Write an Explanation
Why do you think Gawain accepted the Green Knight's challenge? Write a **one-paragraph explanation** of his motivation.

B. Extended Response: Write a Letter
If King Arthur could write a letter to the people of today promoting his **chivalrous** ideals, what would he say? Write a **two- or three-paragraph letter** from Arthur telling why chivalrous behavior makes the world a better place.

SELF-CHECK

A good explanation will . . .
- show an understanding of Gawain's character and the code of chivalry
- explain the causes and effects of his decision

A successful letter will . . .
- be written in the courteous style of a chivalrous leader
- present arguments that are convincing to people

GRAMMAR AND WRITING

USE CORRECT SENTENCE STRUCTURE A **dependent clause** is a group of words that contains a subject and a verb but cannot stand alone as a sentence. Dependent clauses begin with words such as *because, if, that, when, while,* and *who.* When a dependent clause and an independent clause are combined, they form a **complex sentence.**

MARYLAND OBJECTIVES

LANGUAGE STANDARD
5.A.2.d Compose complex sentences

> Original: Gawain accepts the Green Knight's challenge. Because he is brave. (*"Because he is brave" is a dependent clause and cannot stand alone as a sentence.*)
>
> Revised: Gawain accepts the Green Knight's challenge because he is brave. (*The clauses now form a complex sentence.*)

PRACTICE Form a complex sentence by combining the dependent clause with the independent clause.

1. The kingdom would fall. If King Arthur died.
2. Gawain still faces the Green Knight. Even though he is frightened.
3. Gawain must face the Green Knight again a year later. Because he promised he would.
4. Gawain proves to be a good nephew. Who sacrifices himself for his uncle.

*For more help with dependent clauses, see page R64 in the **Grammar Handbook**. For more help with complex sentences, see page R64 in the **Grammar Handbook**.*

FOR LESS-PROFICIENT WRITERS

For Prompt A:
1. Have students reread lines 197–207.
2. Help students list the reasons that Gawain gives for wanting to take the place of his uncle.
3. Help students form a strong topic sentence. Then have them complete their paragraph using details from the list.

For Prompt B:
- Review letter format.
- Limit the letter to one paragraph.
- Give some examples of chivalrous behavior. Discuss how these actions and others help make life better for everyone. Record ideas on the board and suggest that students base their arguments on these ideas.

Reading-Writing Connection

WRITING PROMPTS

- For **Prompt A,** suggest that students use a multiple-causes diagram to analyze Gawain's motives for accepting the challenge.
- For **Prompt B,** students might look back at the **SURVEY** they took before reading (page 670) to remind them of the kinds of behavior considered chivalrous today. Have students think about how each behavior improves people's relationships. Have students list their arguments and choose a logical order before beginning to write.

BEST PRACTICES TOOLKIT—Transparency
Cause-and-Effect Diagram pp. B16, B38

For ideas for writing, see

 Writing Center at **ClassZone.com**

GRAMMAR AND WRITING

Before beginning, read the clauses aloud. Have volunteers identify which one is dependent.

Possible answers:

1. *The kingdom would fall if King Arthur died.*
2. *Even though he is frightened, Gawain still faces the Green Knight.*
3. *Gawain must face the Green Knight again a year later because he promised he would.*
4. *Gawain proves to be a good nephew who sacrifices himself for his uncle.*

RESOURCE MANAGER—Copy Master
Use Correct Sentence Structure p. 111

Assess and Reteach

Assess

RESOURCE MANAGER—Copy Masters
Selection Tests A, B/C pp. 113–114, 115–116

Test Generator CD

Reteach

STANDARDS LESSON FILE
Reading Lesson 1: Predicting
Vocabulary Lesson 21: Homophones and Commonly Confused Words
Writing Lesson 8: Sentence Combining (clauses)

Introduce

Crispin: The Cross of Lead

Historical Novel by Avi

OBJECTIVE

- read historical fiction

Meet Avi

The name *Avi* is one given to the author by his twin sister when they were very young. His real name is a family secret, which he will not divulge, but he willingly talks about the reason he writes. He wants to produce books that make readers feel, think, and even laugh. "I want them [readers] to enjoy a good read." To make sure that his books accomplish this objective, he revises them extensively—by his own count 56 times or more—to get them just right. He also chooses appealing forms of fiction, such as mysteries, adventures, and historical novels, so that there is something to please everyone. "I think you become a writer when you stop writing for yourself . . . and start thinking about readers."

Try a Historical Novel

Historical fiction is set in the past. Authors weave facts about how people lived, what they believed, and what was happening around them into a fictional plot, providing a unique perspective on a moment in history. Some authors focus on specific historical events. For example, *Run, Boy, Run* by Uri Orlev is based on the true story of a Jewish boy who struggled to stay alive in Nazi-occupied Poland. The opening of Oklahoma to homesteaders in 1893 is the setting for *Stop the Train!* by Geraldine McCaughrean. Other novels are tied to locations and eras, rather than events. For example, *Al Capone Does My Shirts* by Gennifer Choldenko is set on the island of Alcatraz in 1935. *The Land* by Mildred Taylor is about the trials of African Americans living in Mississippi in the 1880s.

RESOURCE MANAGER—Copy Master
Historical Fiction p. 117

Avi
born 1937

Other Books by Avi

- *Bright Shadow*
- *The Fighting Ground*
- *The Man Who Was Poe*
- *Midnight Magic*
- *Nothing but the Truth*
- *S.O.R. Losers*
- *The True Confessions of Charlotte Doyle*
- *Wolf Rider*

Meet Avi

Avi notes that reading helped him to become a professional writer: "The more you read, the better your writing can be," he has said. By this measure, it's no surprise Avi is an award-winning writer. He earned a college degree in history and an advanced degree in drama. While working in the New York Public Library's theater collection, he decided to go back to school for an advanced degree in library science.

Avi first wrote plays, but while raising his children, he began writing books for young people. Since then, he has written over 50 books and won many important awards. Avi loves being an author and has said, "To invent the stories that people take to their hearts is, I think, one of the most wonderful things one can do."

Try a Historical Novel

Have you ever wondered what it was like to live in the Middle Ages? Until inventors create a time machine, reading **historical fiction,** or stories that are set in the past, is one of the best ways to find out. Historical fiction can make the past come alive by mixing references to actual people, places, and events with fictional characters and dialogue and other creative details.

Avi's historical fiction has been praised for the accuracy of the historical elements he includes. His 25 years of experience as a research librarian taught him how to find all the details he needs to establish a story's setting in a different time and place.

DIFFERENTIATED INSTRUCTION

FOR LESS–PROFICIENT READERS

Reading Support Before students begin reading, review the teaching notes on pages 687–691 and select those that you think would be most helpful to them. You might read the selection aloud with students and discuss the relevant notes. Stop occasionally to answer questions, give an explanation, or hold a discussion.

Read a Great Book

This story is set in England in the year 1377, when nobles ruled the land and their agricultural workers, the serfs, had almost no rights at all. You are about to read a passage about a young serf named Crispin who is on his way home from his mother's funeral. He is attacked by a group of men for reasons he does not yet understand. He narrowly escapes and hides in the woods overnight, then goes to the village priest for advice on what he should do.

from

CRISPIN
THE CROSS OF LEAD

Near the altar the priest genuflected. I did the same. Then we knelt, facing each other. "Speak low," he said. "There's always Judas lurking. Are you hungry?"

"Yes, Father," I murmured.

From behind the tattered altar cloth he produced a loaf of barley bread and gave it to me. "I was hoping you would come," he said.

I took the heavy bread and began to devour it.

"Where have you been?" he asked.

"In the forest."

10   "Did you know they've been searching for you?"

Read

Read a Great Book

Avi sets his novel in medieval England. At this time, a strictly hierarchical feudal system governed people's lives. As a serf, Crispin is tied to the manor (line 12) upon which he is born. Serfs were under the authority of the lord and could look forward only to a life of drudgery.

By 1377, however, the foundations of feudalism were beginning to crumble. Events such as the Black Death and the Crusades had made serfs more aware of the world beyond the manor boundaries. They had acquired some rights and were starting to see themselves as viable members of society, rather than property to be sold with the land. This larger setting mirrors Crispin's metaphorical journey to self-realization and reinforces Avi's theme about the importance of the individual.

SHARE A READING TIP

Much of this excerpt consists of dialogue. Remind students that in long passages of dialogue, the speakers alternate. If readers can identify the first speaker in a dialogue, they can determine each successive speaker.

SHARE WORD MEANINGS

To *genuflect* (line 1) is to bend the knee or touch one knee to the ground as a sign of reverence. Crispin and the priest are meeting in a church, and they genuflect at the altar to show their respect.

SHARE WORD MEANINGS

In the Bible, Judas Iscariot, one of the twelve apostles, betrayed Jesus to the authorities. For his treachery, he earned 30 pieces of silver. Since that time, the name *Judas* (line 2) has been synonymous with *traitor*.

FOR ENGLISH LEARNERS
Use these options to help English learners enjoy the selection:

Read Aloud Read lines 1–16 aloud to introduce students to the characters of the priest and Crispin, the setting, and the conflict. Then have students continue reading in small groups. Or, read the entire excerpt aloud, pausing to clarify terms, discuss plot developments, or answer questions.

Listen to the *Audio Anthology CD* Have students read along as they listen to the excerpt. Then encourage them to read the text independently. Lead them in a follow-up discussion.

Reciprocal Teaching Make sure students are aware of what has happened to Crispin before the excerpt picks up. Then have students apply the Reciprocal Teaching strategy in small groups to designated passages.

 BEST PRACTICES TOOLKIT—Transparency
Reciprocal Teaching p. A35

SHARE WORD MEANINGS

The *steward* (line 22) of the lord's estate was the most powerful official. He was in charge of collecting rents and taxes and overseeing the running of the manor.

EXPLORE HISTORICAL FICTION

Some characters and events in historical fiction are real. For example, the real Lord Furnival died in 1383, although in the novel he dies a few years earlier. "The wars" (line 26) most likely refer to the Hundred Years' War. This conflict between England and France over the issue of succession to the French throne was fought periodically from 1337 to 1453.

SHARE AN FYI

Serfs' houses were small, usually one room. They had a thatched roof and a wooden frame, which was covered with wattle and daub—a mixture of mud and straw. Because of their simple construction, they were very easy to pull down (lines 42–43).

My mouth full, I nodded.

"Aycliffe claims you stole money from the manor."

"Father," I said, "in all my life, I've never even been there."

"I don't doubt you," the priest said, gently putting his hand to my face to keep me calm. "Most people in the village don't believe the accusation, either. But why does Aycliffe put your name to the crime?"

I told the priest what had happened when I ran from my mother's burial—my fall, my waking to witness the meeting in the clearing, Aycliffe's attempt to kill me.

20 "He said none of this," the priest said.

"It's true."

"What was the thing the steward read?" the priest asked. "He never mentioned that either."

"I don't know," I said. Then I asked, "Who was the man he met?"

"Sir Richard du Brey," the priest said. "He's brought word that Lord Furnival—God keep him well—has returned from the wars. He's ill and expected to die."

"The stranger said Aycliffe must act immediately."

"About what?"

30 I shrugged. "He said, 'Are you not her kin? Do you not see the consequences if you don't?' To which Aycliffe replied, 'A great danger to us all.' Then the man said, 'Precisely. There could be those who will see it so and act accordingly. You'll be placed in danger, too.' It made no sense to me," I said.

The priest pondered the words in silence.

"Father," I said, "what will happen if I'm caught?"

The priest put his hand on my shoulder. "The steward," he said, "has declared you a wolf's head."

"*A wolf's head!*" I gasped, horrified.

40 "Do you understand what it means?"

"That . . . I'm considered not human," I said, my voice faltering. "That anyone may . . . kill me. Is that why they pulled down our house?"

"I suppose."

688

DIFFERENTIATED INSTRUCTION

FOR LESS–PROFICIENT READERS

Reading Support Use a three-column chart such as this one to help students track what is fact and what is fiction.

Element	Historical Fact	Fiction
Setting	• *1377* • *feudal system* • *Great Mortality*	*village church*
Character	*Lord Furnival*	• *parish priest* • *Crispin* • *Aycliffe*
Plot	*inability of a serf to act freely or leave the manor*	• *death of Crispin's mother* • *attempt to kill Crispin* • *declaration of Crispin's outcast status* • *mystery of Crispin's background* • *Crispin's decision to run away*

688 UNIT 6: MYTHS, LEGENDS, AND TALES

"But . . . *why?*"

The priest sat back and gave himself over to thought. In the dim light I studied his face. He seemed distraught, as if the pain of the whole world had settled in his soul.

"Father," I ventured, "is it something about my mother?"

50 He bowed his head. When he looked up it was to gaze at me. "Asta's son, unless you flee, you won't live long."

"But how can I leave?" I said. "I'm bound to the land. They'll never give me permission to go."

He sighed, reached forward, and placed the side of his frail hand aside my face. "Asta's son, listen to me with the greatest care. When I baptized you, you were named . . . Crispin."

"I was?" I cried.

"It was done in secret. What's more, your mother begged me not to tell you or anyone. She chose to simply call you 'Son.'"

60 "But . . . why?" I asked.

He took a deep breath and then said, "Did she tell you anything about your father?"

Once again the priest took me by surprise. "My *father?* Only that he died before I was born. In the Great Mortality," I reminded him. "But what has that to do with my name? Or any of this?"

"Dearest boy," the priest said wearily, "I beg you to find your way to some town or city with its own liberties. If you can stay there for a year and a day, you'll gain your freedom."

"Freedom?" I said. "What has that to do with me?"

70 "You could live by your own choices. As . . . a highborn lord . . . or a king."

"Father," I said, "that's impossible for me. I am what I am. I know nothing but Stromford."

"Even so, you must go. There are cities enough: Canterbury, Great Wexly, Winchester. Even London."

"What . . . what are these places like?"

"They have many souls living there, far more than here. Too many to count. But I assure you they are Christians."

689

EXPLORE HISTORICAL FICTION

The conflicts of characters in historical fiction must be consistent with the setting. A major problem for Crispin is his lack of freedom. He is "bound to the land" (line 52) as all serfs were. His only hope of surviving the attempts to kill him is to evade capture for a year and a day (line 68), the actual law of the time.

Historical fiction also re-creates the social, political, and economic conditions of the time period. Crispin refers to losing his father in the Great Mortality (line 64). This is a reference to the recurrence of the plague or Black Death. After it swept through Europe in 1348, it continued to break out at intervals for years afterwards.

SHARE A READING TIP

In a suspenseful novel, the author often gives clues to hint at what might happen next. This technique increases readers' curiosity and excitement. In lines 56, 61–62, and 70–71, the priest suggests that Crispin's name is significant and that his father might be someone more important than a serf. Point out that the priest says that Crispin could live as a highborn lord or a king if he chose. These hints make readers wonder at the true origins of Asta's son, or Crispin.

EXPLORE HISTORICAL FICTION

One challenge for authors of historical fiction is to create dialogue for their characters that is appropriate for the time period but doesn't discourage modern readers. Avi uses a formal sentence structure and avoids contemporary lingo in the characters' conversation.

Suggest that students use the details in the excerpt to help them imagine being in Crispin's position. Ask them to think about what it would be like to live in England in 1377 without modern conveniences, transportation, or communication. Using text details to spark one's imagination in this way is a key to enjoying historical fiction.

SHARE WORD MEANINGS

The priest tells Crispin to meet him at "Goodwife Peregrine's house" (line 99). *Goodwife* was a title comparable to *Mrs.* in today's society.

SHARE AN FYI

Crispin kisses the priest's hand (line 111) as a mark of respect. Today, kissing the hand of a priest or a higher clergy member's ring is still performed as an act of reverence in some religions.

"Father," I said, "I don't even know where these cities are."

80 "I'm not so certain myself," he admitted. "Follow the roads. Ask for help as you go. God will guide you."

"Is there no other way?"

"You could find an abbey and offer yourself to the church. But it's a grave step, and you're hardly prepared. In any case, you don't have the fees. If I had them, they would be yours. No, the most important thing is for you to get away."

"There's something about my mother that you are keeping from me, is there not?" I said.

He made no reply.

90 "Father . . ." I pressed, "was God angry at her . . . and me?"

He shook his head. "It's not for men to know what God does or does not will. What I do know is that you *must* leave."

Frustrated, I rose up, only to have the priest hold me back. "Your way will be long and difficult," he said. "If you can remain hidden in the forest for another day, I'll find some food to sustain you for a while. And perhaps someone will know the best way to go."

"As you say."

"Your obedience speaks well for you. Come back tomorrow night prepared to leave. Meet me at Goodwife Peregrine's house. I'll ask
100 her to give you some things to protect you on your way."

I started off again.

"And," he added, as if coming to a decision, "when you come . . . I'll tell you about your father."

I turned back. "Why can't you tell me now?"

"Better—safer—to learn such things just before you go. That and my blessing are all I can give."

"Was he a sinner?" I demanded. "Did he commit some crime? Should I be ashamed of him?"

"I'll tell you all I know when you come to Peregrine's. Make sure
110 it's dark so you'll not be seen."

I took his hand, kissed it, then started off, only to have him draw me back again.

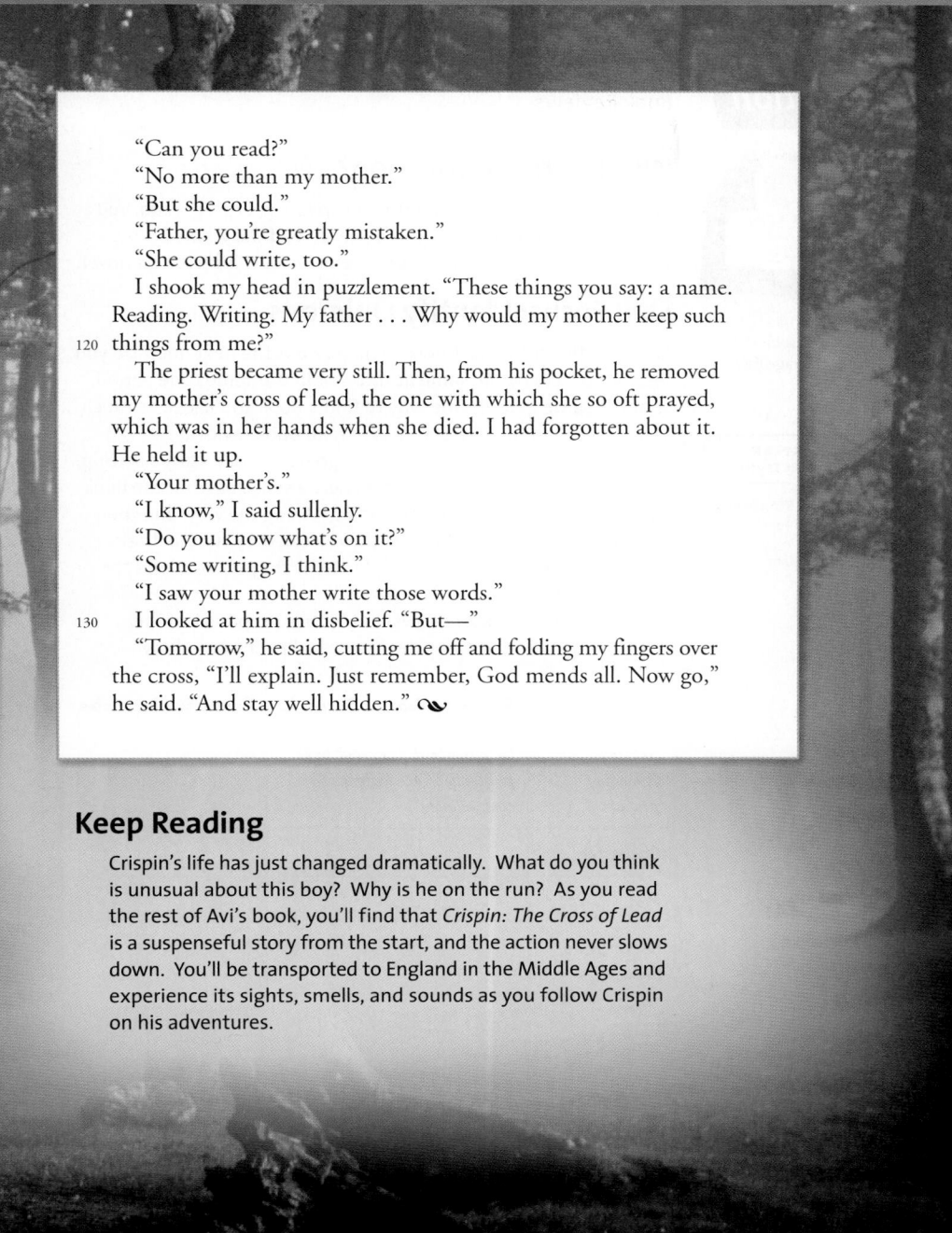

"Can you read?"

"No more than my mother."

"But she could."

"Father, you're greatly mistaken."

"She could write, too."

I shook my head in puzzlement. "These things you say: a name. Reading. Writing. My father . . . Why would my mother keep such
120 things from me?"

The priest became very still. Then, from his pocket, he removed my mother's cross of lead, the one with which she so oft prayed, which was in her hands when she died. I had forgotten about it. He held it up.

"Your mother's."

"I know," I said sullenly.

"Do you know what's on it?"

"Some writing, I think."

"I saw your mother write those words."
130 I looked at him in disbelief. "But—"

"Tomorrow," he said, cutting me off and folding my fingers over the cross, "I'll explain. Just remember, God mends all. Now go," he said. "And stay well hidden." ✑

Keep Reading

Crispin's life has just changed dramatically. What do you think is unusual about this boy? Why is he on the run? As you read the rest of Avi's book, you'll find that *Crispin: The Cross of Lead* is a suspenseful story from the start, and the action never slows down. You'll be transported to England in the Middle Ages and experience its sights, smells, and sounds as you follow Crispin on his adventures.

Discuss

SHARE AN FYI

Crispin is astonished that his mother could read and write (lines 118–120). For serfs to attain any level of literacy was unusual because children worked in the fields from a young age and did not attend school.

Keep Reading

Share these discussion questions with students after they have finished the excerpt. You might use the questions to lead a class discussion or have students form small groups to discuss them.

- Have you read this book? If yes, would you recommend it to others? Why? If no, what questions are you hoping the rest of the book will answer?

- What is the connection between the meeting that Crispin overheard and the declaration by the steward that he is a "wolf's head"?

- Why do you think Crispin's mother did not tell him about his father or the fact that she could read and write? How does Crispin feel when he learns these revelations about his mother?

- Why doesn't the priest tell Crispin the entire truth about his background? What do you think might happen before Crispin is able to get to Goodwife Peregrine's?

- What do you think Crispin will find out about his identity? What details help you make this prediction?

Focus and Motivate

OBJECTIVES

Reading for Information
- identify opinions
- compare your reactions to a book to those of reviewers
- read book reviews

SUMMARY

Both reviews comment favorably on Avi's novel *Crispin: The Cross of Lead,* citing the accurate and vivid depiction of the time period (late 14th century) and the suspenseful plot. Both compare the book to *The Midwife's Apprentice.* While the first review maintains the book's suspense, the second review reveals crucial plot details.

What's the Connection?

Use an Anticipation Guide to prepare students for the book reviews. Write these statements about *Crispin: The Cross of Lead* on the transparency. Have students respond to each statement before and after reading the reviews.

- The setting of the novel shows the author's knowledge of life in medieval England.
- Crispin is an interesting character, but modern readers find little in common with him.
- The plot is exciting and suspenseful.

 BEST PRACTICES TOOLKIT—Transparency
Anticipation Guide p. A14

Teach

Skill Focus: Identify Opinions

Have students consider these questions to evaluate each reviewer's opinion:

- Which statements contain opinion words, such as adjectives or adverbs? What attitudes do these words express?
- Is the overall tone of the review positive or negative?
- Does the reviewer support her opinions with accurate examples or facts?

Possible chart entries appear on page 694.

R RESOURCE MANAGER—Copy Master
Identify Opinions p. 127

A Medieval Mystery
Book Reviews

Use with *Crispin: The Cross of Lead,* page 687.

 MARYLAND OBJECTIVES

INFO TEXT/WRITING STANDARDS
2.A.4.h Distinguish between a fact and an opinion
4.A.2.c Compose to inform

What's the Connection?

Even after reading the scene from *Crispin: The Cross of Lead,* you might not be sure whether you'd like to read the whole book. To reach a decision, read two book reviews of this historical novel.

Skill Focus: Identify Opinions

After you finish a book, how do you pick out the next one? Do you seek out others by the same author, set in the same time period, or of the same genre? One way to find a book you'll love as much as or more than the one before is to read book reviews.

Book reviewers try to provide enough details of a story's setting, characters, and plot to give their readers a sense of what the book offers without giving away the ending. Along the way, and then most strongly toward the end of the review, they sum up their opinions of these elements to explain why they recommend the book—or don't.

As you read the book reviews that follow, keep track of the opinions each reviewer provides in a chart like the one shown.

Opinions About	Review by Rebecca Barnhouse	Review by Cheri Estes
Setting (time and place)	Details about the past are portrayed "accurately and compellingly."	
Character		
Plot		
Other Story Elements		

Selection Resources

R RESOURCE MANAGER UNIT 6
Plan and Teach pp. 119–123

Reading
Summary pp. 125†*, 126‡*
Identify Opinions pp. 127, 129†*
Reading Check p. 131
Compare Your Reactions pp. 128, 130†*
Question Support p. 133*

Assessment
Selection Tests A, B/C pp. 135*, 137*
 Test Generator CD

Reading Support
 Audio Anthology CD*

 BEST PRACTICES TOOLKIT
Anticipation Guide

 * Resources for Differentiation   † Also in Spanish   ‡ In Haitian Creole and Vietnamese

Book Review

Serf on the Run

by Rebecca Barnhouse

Crispin: The Cross of Lead
by Avi   261 pages

In 1377 England, mysteries surround thirteen-year-old Crispin, a serf from a rural village who never knows his own name until his mother dies. Nor does he know just who his mother really was—why she was an outcast or how she learned to read and write. Shortly after her burial, Crispin finds himself pursued by men who mean to kill him for reasons he does not understand. He escapes, only to be captured by a huge juggler named Bear. Bear teaches Crispin to sing and play the recorder, and slowly they begin to get to know one another. When they perform in villages and towns, however, they discover that the hunt for Crispin is still in full swing. For Crispin, this situation makes the question of Bear's trustworthiness vital, for Bear has secrets of his own. **A**

The suspense stays taut until the very end of the book, when Crispin uncovers his identity and then must decide how to act on that information. His journey to selfhood recalls Alice's in Karen Cushman's *The Midwife's Apprentice*. Like Alice, Crispin casts off his timidity to make a place for himself within a society that would discard him. As does Cushman, Avi renders the sights, sounds, and smells of medieval England accurately and compellingly. He shows the pervasiveness of the church in medieval society and, in a subplot, weaves in details about John Ball and the Peasants' Rebellion. Exciting and true to the past, this novel is historical fiction at its finest. **B**

READING FOR INFORMATION   693

F **OCUS ON FORM**
The two selections you are about to read are **book reviews,** short pieces of writing in which a writer describes the main elements of a book and summarizes his or her opinions of the book.

A **BOOK REVIEW**
What details of character, setting, and plot does Rebecca Barnhouse provide?

B **IDENTIFY OPINIONS**
Find the sentences in which Barnhouse states her opinions of *Crispin: The Cross of Lead.* In your own words, write her opinions in the appropriate place in your chart.

Practice and Apply

FOCUS ON FORM
Discuss with students the purpose and characteristics of a book review. This type of writing

- informs and persuades
- includes excerpts and examples from the book
- gives enough detail to interest readers but does not reveal important elements of plot
- often makes comparisons with other works by the same or a different author

Ask students if they have ever read book or movie reviews before and whether they found them helpful.

LITERARY ANALYSIS

A BOOK REVIEW

Possible answer: Barnhouse describes the setting as "1377 England." She introduces the main character, Crispin, and another significant figure, Bear. She provides details such as Crispin's age, his background, Bear's occupation, and their relationship. She explains the major conflict and how it drives the action of the plot.

INFORMATIONAL ANALYSIS

B IDENTIFY OPINIONS
Record students' answers in the chart from page 692. *Possible answers:*

Opinions About	Review by Rebecca Barnhouse
Character	Crispin successfully journeys to selfhood in the course of the novel.
Plot	"The suspense stays taut until the very end of the book."
Other story elements	"This novel is historical fiction at its finest."

If students need help ... Direct them to the second paragraph of the review. Help them find adjectives and adverbs that indicate opinions (*taut, accurately, compellingly, exciting, finest*).

Extend the Discussion Are Barnhouse's opinions supported within the review? Explain.

DIFFERENTIATED INSTRUCTION

FOR LESS–PROFICIENT READERS
Concept Support
- Explain that the first paragraph of each review includes a summary of plot, setting, and character. The second paragraph presents the writer's opinions.
- Have groups of students list the story details provided in the first and second reviews and compare them.
- Ask students which summary is better and why.

FOR ENGLISH LEARNERS
Options for Reading Make sure students understand the term *review*. Explain that in a book review, writers want to share what they think about a book. For their opinions to make sense to people who have not read the book, they must also provide some details about the characters, plot, and setting. Have students read each review along with the *Audio Anthology CD,* or read the reviews together in small groups.

C BOOK REVIEW

*Possible answer: The writer says that the **setting** is 14th-century England. She gives details about Crispin's background, introduces the **characters** of the priest and Aycliffe, and describes Bear's activities. She also identifies the major **conflict** and reveals Crispin's secret, leaving only the success of Crispin's rescue of Bear undisclosed.*

Extend the Discussion Should all of these details have been included? Why or why not?

D IDENTIFY OPINIONS

See below (**Estes review**) for possible answers.

Skill Focus: Identify Opinions

Possible answers for the chart on page 692:

Barnhouse review

- **Setting:** *Details about the past are portrayed "accurately and compellingly."*
- **Character:** *Crispin successfully journeys to selfhood in the course of the novel.*
- **Plot:** *"The suspense stays taut until the very end of the book."*
- **Other story elements:** *"This novel is historical fiction at its finest."*

Estes review

- **Setting:** *The author has "done an excellent job of integrating background and historical information."*
- **Characters:** *The characters evoke "empathy" from the readers.*
- **Plot:** *The book is suspenseful and exciting from start to finish.*
- **Other story elements:** *The story is "meticulously crafted." It includes "adventure, mystery, and action."*

Crispin: The Cross of Lead

by Avi   261 pages

Medieval Adventures Cheri Estes

As with Karen Cushman's *The Midwife's Apprentice*, the power of a name is apparent in this novel set in 14th-century England. "Asta's son" is all the destitute, illiterate hero has ever been called, but after his mother dies, he learns that his given name is Crispin, and that he is
10 in mortal danger. The local priest is murdered before he can tell him more about his background, and Aycliffe, the evil village steward for Lord Furnival, declares that the boy is a "wolf's head," less than human, and that he should be killed on sight. On the run, with nothing to sustain him but his faith in God,
20 Crispin meets "Bear," a roving entertainer who has ties to an underground movement to improve living conditions for the common people. They make

their way to Great Wexly, where Bear has clandestine meetings and Crispin hopes to escape from Aycliffe and his soldiers, who stalk him at every turn.
30 Suspense heightens when the boy learns that the recently deceased Lord Furnival was his father and that Aycliffe is dead set on preventing him from claiming his title. To trap his prey, the villain captures Bear, and Crispin risks his life to save him. **C**

Avi has done an excellent job
40 of integrating background and historical information, of pacing the plot so that the book is a page-turner from beginning to end, and of creating characters for whom readers will have great empathy. The result is a meticulously crafted story, full of adventure, mystery, and action. **D**

C BOOK REVIEW
What do you learn about the book's setting, characters, and plot from Estes's review?

D IDENTIFY OPINIONS
What are Estes's opinions of the setting, plot, and characters of *Crispin: The Cross of Lead?* Add these to your chart. Be sure to put quotation marks around any direct quotations you use.

DIFFERENTIATED INSTRUCTION

FOR LESS–PROFICIENT READERS
Concept Support Return to the chart that students have filled in during their reading. Discuss whether the reviewers agree or disagree in their evaluation of setting, character, plot, and other story elements.

FOR ADVANCED LEARNERS/PRE–AP
Evaluate Ask students to create a checklist that enumerates the elements of a good book review. Provide or have students find other book reviews from a newspaper or magazine. Then have them choose a review and evaluate it to see how well it measures up. Have students read their reviews and discuss their evaluations in small groups.

Comprehension

1. **Recall** Which characters are mentioned in Barnhouse's review? Which are mentioned in Estes's review?

2. **Summarize** Summarize the reasons each reviewer gives for recommending *Crispin: The Cross of Lead*.

Critical Analysis

3. **Compare Opinions** Review the chart you created as you read. Which of Barnhouse's and Estes's opinions are similar to each other's? Which, if any, are different?

4. **Evaluate Book Reviews** A good book review gives details of the story without spoiling the story's suspense. Which of these reviews does a better job of this? Explain.

Read for Information: Compare Your Reactions

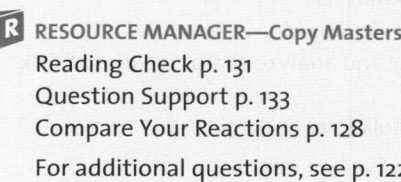

MARYLAND OBJECTIVES

INFO TEXT/WRITING STANDARDS
2.A.4.h Distinguish between a fact and an opinion
4.A.2.c Compose to inform

WRITING PROMPT

Both Rebecca Barnhouse and Cheri Estes recommend *Crispin: The Cross of Lead*. On the basis of what you've read of the novel, do you agree with them? Compare your reactions with theirs, explaining why you agree or disagree.

To answer this prompt, follow these steps:

1. Think about the reactions you had to the setting, characters, and plot you read about in *Crispin: The Cross of Lead* (pages 687–691). Write statements of opinion about each of these elements.

2. Identify each reviewer's opinions of the setting, characters, and plot.

3. Compare your reactions to those of the reviewers to identify which opinions you agree with and which you disagree with.

4. Write an essay in which you compare your reactions to those of the reviewers. Support each comparison with details from the excerpt.

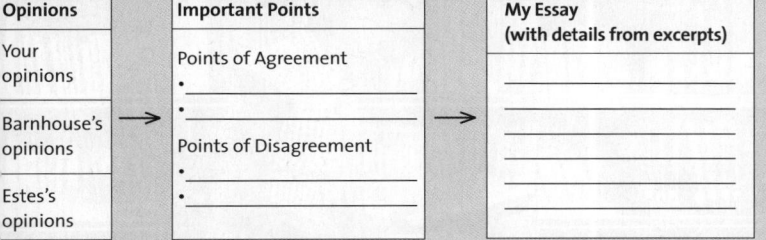

Opinions	Important Points	My Essay (with details from excerpts)
Your opinions	**Points of Agreement** • _____ • _____	_____ _____ _____
Barnhouse's opinions	**Points of Disagreement** • _____	_____ _____ _____
Estes's opinions	• _____	_____ _____

Practice and Apply

For additional support of post-reading questions, use these copy masters:

R RESOURCE MANAGER—Copy Masters
Reading Check p. 131
Question Support p. 133
Compare Your Reactions p. 128

For additional questions, see p. 122.

ANSWERS

Comprehension

1. *Barnhouse mentions Crispin and Bear. Estes mentions Crispin, Bear, the local priest, Aycliffe, and Lord Furnival.*

2. *Possible answer: Barnhouse recommends the novel for its accurate and compelling sensory details and exciting story that is true to the past. Estes recommends the novel because of its historical accuracy, suspenseful pacing, and characters that readers can care about.*

Critical Analysis

Possible answers:

3. ■ **STANDARDS FOCUS** *Identify Opinions*
   Both reviewers agree that setting, plot, and character are skillfully developed. Barnhouse focuses more on the descriptive power of Avi's writing.

4. *Barnhouse's review is superior. She gives enough detail to interest the reader but does not ruin the suspense.*

Read for Information: Compare Your Reactions

Writing Prompt *A strong response will identify reactions and provide details from the novel excerpt in support.*

Assess and Reteach

Assess

R RESOURCE MANAGER—Copy Masters
Selection Tests A, B/C pp. 135–136, 137–138

⊘ Test Generator CD

Reteach

S STANDARDS LESSON FILE
Reading Lesson 5: Distinguishing Fact from Opinion
Reading Lesson 12: Comparing and Contrasting

FOR LESS–PROFICIENT WRITERS

Read for Information

1. Help students express their opinions about the character, plot, and setting based on their own reading of the excerpt.

2. Have students reread the second paragraph of each review.

3. Ask them to choose the reviewer whose opinions most closely match theirs.

4. Have them write a paragraph explaining why they agree with the reviewer.

FOR ADVANCED LEARNERS/PRE–AP

Read for Information After students have completed their essays, invite them to work in groups of three to prepare a panel discussion. Each group member should focus on a different element of the novel (plot, character, or setting) and develop his or her reaction and supporting evidence. Have groups present their ideas and discuss the similarities and differences in their views.

Focus and Motivate

OBJECTIVES

Literary Analysis
- explore the key idea of **lessons**
- identify and analyze characteristics of folk tales
- read a folk tale

Reading
- summarize

Vocabulary
- build vocabulary for reading and writing
- understand and use the Latin word *primus* (also an EL language objective)

SUMMARY

In the first folk tale, kindhearted Brer Possum, against his better judgment, rescues Brer Snake from a pit in the road. Sure enough, Brer Snake ends up biting Brer Possum. In "Waters of Gold," Auntie Lily's kindness to a beggar is rewarded with a bucket of gold coins. Her rich neighbor fakes concern for the beggar, but she gets a bucket of reptiles and insects and then contracts an illness. Humbled, the neighbor is finally inspired to reform her ways.

What can we LEARN *from stories?*

Discuss the question and *KEY IDEA* with students. Challenge students to think of a character from a movie, television program, or story who has taught them **lessons**. Ask volunteers to explain what they learned and why. Then have students complete the *LIST IT* activity.

Selection Resources

Brer Possum's Dilemma
African-American Folk Tale Retold by Jackie Torrence

Waters of Gold
Chinese Folk Tale Retold by Laurence Yep

What can we LEARN *from stories?*

MARYLAND OBJECTIVES

READING/LIT STANDARDS
1.E.4.e Summarize
3.A.3.a Distinguish among types of narrative texts

KEY IDEA You've probably been lectured to many times about things you should and shouldn't do. The problem is, it's easy to forget what you hear in a lecture. But what if you happen to learn **lessons** while being entertained by interesting, even unforgettable, characters? Those lessons may be the ones you carry with you for the rest of your life.

LIST IT On a sheet of notebook paper, list three or four of your favorite stories of all time. What lessons did they teach? Add the lessons to your list, and compare the list to those of your classmates.

Title	Lesson
The Giver	Knowledge comes from experience.

696

RESOURCE MANAGER UNIT 6

Plan and Teach pp. 139–146

Literary Analysis
Summary pp. 147†*, 148‡*
Characteristics of Folk Tales
   pp. 149, 150†*
Question Support p. 157*

Reading
Summarize pp. 151, 152†*
Reading Check p. 156
Reading Fluency p. 158

Vocabulary
Study p. 153*
Practice p. 154
Strategy p. 155

Assessment
Selection Tests A, B/C pp. 159*, 161*
   Test Generator CD

BEST PRACTICES TOOLKIT

Differentiated Instruction
   pp. 31–38*
Scaffolding Instruction
   pp. 43–46*
Graphic Organizers/Strategies
Word Questioning • Words with Multiple Meanings • New Word Analysis • Cause-and-Effect Chain • Venn Diagram

Reading Support
   Audio Anthology CD*

Technology
   Literature and Vocabulary Centers at **ClassZone.com**

   Write*Smart* CD

* Resources for Differentiation   † Also in Spanish   ‡ In Haitian Creole and Vietnamese

696   UNIT 6: MYTHS, LEGENDS, AND TALES

LITERARY ANALYSIS: CHARACTERISTICS OF FOLK TALES

Folk tales are stories that have been handed down through generations by being told out loud. Every culture has its own folk tales, but the stories often share certain characteristics.

- Each character usually represents a specific trait, or quality.
- The plot often centers on events that occur in a set of three.
- Many folk tales teach a lesson, or **moral.**

As you read the selections, pay attention to the way the characters and plot work together to teach a lesson.

READING STRATEGY: SUMMARIZE

When you **summarize** what you've read, you briefly retell the story's main points in your own words, focusing only on the most important details. To help you summarize, use a graphic organizer to record key information as you read each selection.

Title and Culture:	Author:	Setting:
Characters:		
Events:		
Lesson or Moral:		

Review: **Predict**

VOCABULARY IN CONTEXT

Each of the vocabulary words here is in these folk tales. Choose the word that completes each sentence.

WORD	commence	jostling	prime
LIST	humor	perilously	smugly

1. Don't get ahead in life by _____ others out of the way.
2. Sometimes it's better to _____ someone than to argue with him.
3. For the best results, _____ each day with a good attitude.
4. By wanting it all, she came _____ close to losing what she had.
5. Safety should be a _____ concern for all parents.
6. If you accept praise _____, you won't see much of it.

Author Online

Jackie Torrence: The Story Lady
Jackie Torrence was working as a librarian when one day her boss came looking for help: the library's storyteller hadn't shown up, and children were waiting. Torrence

Jackie Torrence 1944–2004

reluctantly took over. She became famous for retelling African-American folk tales, many of which were handed down by her grandfather. Torrence said that "long before TV or radio, all cultures used storytelling to instill values and heritage."

Laurence Yep: Folk Tale Collector
In addition to being an award-winning writer of books for young people, Laurence Yep researches and collects Chinese folk tales. ("Waters of Gold" came to the United States

Laurence Yep born 1948

with Chinese immigrants who settled in California.) He feels that these stories have a "raw power" and mystery that appeal to all ages.

 MORE ABOUT THE AUTHOR
For more on Jackie Torrence and Laurence Yep, visit the **Literature Center** at **ClassZone.com.**

697

Teach

STANDARDS FOCUS

LITERARY ANALYSIS

● **CHARACTERISTICS OF FOLK TALES**

Explain that folk tales are stories for common people. They feature characters who are poor, or animals that act like humans. Magic sometimes enters into the plot. The morals are usually quite straightforward and obvious.

CHECK UNDERSTANDING Have students identify folk tales they have previously read and explain which characteristics these tales illustrate.

READING STRATEGY

■ **SUMMARIZE**

Have students read the first **Author Online** passage. Then read aloud this summary statement: *Jackie Torrence was a librarian who became a famous storyteller.* Discuss the less important details that have been omitted. Then have students read and summarize the second passage. ***Possible answer:*** *Laurence Yep writes young adult books and collects Chinese folk tales.*

CHECK UNDERSTANDING Have students summarize the plot of a movie or television show they have recently seen.

R **RESOURCE MANAGER—Copy Master**
Summarize p. 151 (for student use while reading the selections)

VOCABULARY SKILL

▲ **VOCABULARY IN CONTEXT**

DIAGNOSE WORD KNOWLEDGE To determine preteaching needs, have all students complete **Vocabulary in Context.** Check students' answers. (**1.** *jostling;* **2.** *humor;* **3.** *commence;* **4.** *perilously;* **5.** *prime;* **6.** *smugly*)

PRETEACH VOCABULARY Use the Vocabulary Study copy master to help students explore the meaning of each boldfaced word.

1. Read the first sentence aloud, emphasizing *commence.*

2. Point out the phrase *explaining the background.* Elicit possible meanings for *commence,* such as "start."

3. Have students check their definitions.

4. Repeat the procedure for the rest of the words.

R **RESOURCE MANAGER—Copy Master**
Vocabulary Study p. 153

For general guidelines on differentiating vocabulary instruction and for alternative vocabulary activities for students not needing vocabulary preteaching, see

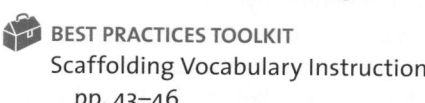 **BEST PRACTICES TOOLKIT**
Scaffolding Vocabulary Instruction pp. 43–46

ⓘ Vocabulary Center at **ClassZone.com**
Additional Vocabulary Activities

ANALYZE VISUALS

Possible answers:

- The animals seem to be talking to each other. The artist suggests this by showing them looking into each other's eyes.

- The possum appears to feel compassion for the snake, suggested by the way he is peering into the hole with a concerned expression on his face.

LITERARY ANALYSIS

Ⓐ FOLK TALES

Possible answers:

- Brer Possum is gentle, kindhearted, and nosy (lines 8–9, 21).

- He thinks and speaks in words (lines 12–14, 19–20, 23).

Extend the Discussion Brer Possum describes some of the snake's traits in line 13. What other traits are associated with snakes?

Brer Possum's Dilemma

Retold by
Jackie Torrence

ANALYZE VISUALS
What human **traits** do the animals in this image suggest? Tell how the artist creates this impression.

Back in the days when the animals could talk, there lived ol' Brer Possum. He was a fine feller. Why, he never liked to see no critters in trouble. He was always helpin' out, a-doin' somethin' for others.

Ever' night, ol' Brer Possum climbed into a persimmon tree, hung by his tail, and slept all night long. And each mornin', he climbed outa the tree and walked down the road to sun 'imself.

One mornin', as he walked, he come to a big hole in the middle of the road. Now, ol' Brer Possum was kind and gentle, but he was also nosy, so he went over to the hole and looked in. All at once, he stepped
10 back, 'cause layin' in the bottom of that hole was ol' Brer Snake with a brick on his back.

Brer Possum said to 'imself, "I best git on outa here, 'cause ol' Brer Snake is mean and evil and lowdown, and if I git to stayin' around 'im, he jist might git to bitin' me."

So Brer Possum went on down the road.

But Brer Snake had seen Brer Possum, and he **commenced** to callin' for 'im.

"Help me, Brer Possum."

Brer Possum stopped and turned around. He said to 'imself, "That's ol'
20 Brer Snake a-callin' me. What do you reckon he wants?"

Well, ol' Brer Possum was kindhearted, so he went back down the road to the hole, stood at the edge, and looked down at Brer Snake.

"Was that you a-callin' me? What do you want?" Ⓐ

① Targeted Passage

commence (kə-mĕns') *v.* to start or begin

Ⓐ FOLK TALES
The characters in folktales may be humans or animals with human characteristics. What human characteristics does Brer Possum have?

DIFFERENTIATED INSTRUCTION

FOR ALL STUDENTS

Interest Stations Create these interest stations and post suggested assignments for students to work on independently:

- **Big Board Book** Adapt one of the tales for young children in an illustrated book.
- **Storytelling Contest** Retell a portion of a tale using storytelling techniques.

For further details on these projects, see

RESOURCE MANAGER
Ideas for Extension pp. 144–145

FOR LESS–PROFICIENT READERS

In combination with the *Audio Anthology CD*, use one or more Targeted Passages (pp. 698, 701, 702, 704, 706) to ensure that students focus on key story events, concepts, and skills.

① Targeted Passage [Lines 1–20]

This passage introduces the characters and foreshadows the conflict: Brer Possum sees Brer Snake trapped in a hole.

- Why does Brer Possum look in the hole? What does he see?

- How does he react to what is in the hole?

- After he walks away, what causes Brer Possum to stop and turn around?

- What do you think he will do next? What character traits support your prediction?

BACKGROUND

Brer The characters in this story are called *Brer.* This title is most likely a shortened version of the word *Brother,* a form of address used in the South.

Possum One of the main characters in this tale is Brer Possum. A possum, or an opossum, is a mammal about the size of a cat. These animals like to climb trees, but unlike Brer Possum, they use their tails to keep their balance, not to hang from branches (lines 4–5). They are not aggressive and have few defense mechanisms other than to hiss or play dead. The expression *to play possum* refers to this behavior; it means "to pretend to be dead or asleep."

CULTURAL CONNECTION

Trickster Tales Around the world, animal characters are often featured in folk tales known as "trickster tales." In trickster tales, a small but clever animal outwits a larger, more powerful opponent. The trickster animal varies according to the culture. The coyote and the raven are tricksters that appear in Native American stories. The fox and the rabbit are tricksters in South American stories. In African stories, the trickster may be a hare, a spider (Ananse), or a tortoise. In the stories of Aesop, from ancient Greece, the trickster may be a fox, a mouse, or a wolf.

FOR ENGLISH LEARNERS

Options for Reading Read the first folk tale aloud, or have students read it along with the *Audio Anthology CD.* Pause frequently to monitor students' comprehension. After reading the first page of "Waters of Gold" aloud, have students use a choral reading strategy or continue reading it along with the *Audio Anthology CD.*

Vocabulary Support Before students read "Brer Possum's Dilemma," have them use a Word Questioning organizer to explore the meaning of the word *dilemma.*

 BEST PRACTICES TOOLKIT—Transparency Word Questioning p. E9

Prereading For prereading instruction for English learners, see

 BEST PRACTICES TOOLKIT Scaffolding Reading Instruction pp. 43–46

FOR ADVANCED LEARNERS/PRE–AP

Pre-AP exercises in the bottom channel provide additional challenge for your advanced students. Use them for small groups or individuals.

ADDITIONAL GUIDELINES

For more help with differentiation and tips for classroom management, see

 BEST PRACTICES TOOLKIT Differentiated Instruction pp. 31–38

B PREDICT

Possible answers:

- *Brer Snake will bite Brer Possum after all.*
- *Brer Snake, desperately needing help, will choose not to bite the kind Brer Possum.*

If students need help ... Use a chart such as this one to help students make their predictions.

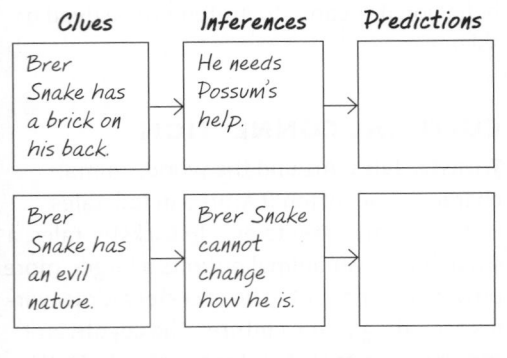

Clues	Inferences	Predictions
Brer Snake has a brick on his back.	He needs Possum's help.	
Brer Snake has an evil nature.	Brer Snake cannot change how he is.	

READING STRATEGY

C SUMMARIZE

Record students' answers in the chart from page 697. *Possible answer:*

- *Events—Brer Possum pushes the brick off Brer Snake with a tree limb. He then uses the branch to lift Brer Snake out of the hole.*

Lines 52–62
REINFORCE *KEY IDEA:* LESSONS

Discuss Based on Brer Possum's behavior so far, what **lessons** has he learned from his past encounters with snakes? *Possible answers: He has learned that snakes will seize any opportunity to bite another creature. He knows that a snake's promise cannot be trusted.*

Brer Snake looked up and said, "I've been down here in this hole for a mighty long time with this brick on my back. Won't you help git it offa me?"

Brer Possum thought.

"Now listen here, Brer Snake. I knows you. You's mean and evil and lowdown, and if'n I was to git down in that hole and git to liftin' that
30 brick offa your back, you wouldn't do nothin' but bite me."

Ol' Brer Snake just hissed.

"Maybe not. Maybe not. Maaaaaaaybe not." **B**

Brer Possum said, "I ain't sure 'bout you at all. I jist don't know. You're a-goin' to have to let me think about it."

So ol' Brer Possum thought—he thought high, and he thought low—and jist as he was thinkin', he looked up into a tree and saw a dead limb a-hangin' down. He climbed into the tree, broke off the limb, and with that ol' stick, pushed that brick offa Brer Snake's back. Then he took off down the road.

40 Brer Possum thought he was away from ol' Brer Snake when all at once he heard somethin'.

"Help me, Brer Possum."

Brer Possum said, "Oh, no, that's him agin."

But bein' so kindhearted, Brer Possum turned around, went back to the hole, and stood at the edge.

"Brer Snake, was that you a-callin' me? What do you want now?"

Ol' Brer Snake looked up outa the hole and hissed.

"I've been down here for a mighty long time, and I've gotten a little weak, and the sides of this ol' hole are too slick for me to climb. Do you
50 think you can lift me outa here?"

Brer Possum thought.

"Now, you jist wait a minute. If'n I was to git down into that hole and lift you outa there, you wouldn't do nothin' but bite me."

Brer Snake hissed.

"Maybe not. Maybe not. Maaaaaaaybe not."

Brer Possum said, "I jist don't know. You're a-goin' to have to give me time to think about this."

So ol' Brer Possum thought.

And as he thought, he jist happened to look down there in that hole
60 and see that ol' dead limb. So he pushed the limb underneath ol' Brer Snake and he lifted 'im outa the hole, way up into the air, and throwed 'im into the high grass.

Brer Possum took off a-runnin' down the road. **C**

Well, he thought he was away from ol' Brer Snake when all at once he heard somethin'.

B PREDICT
The characters disagree about what will happen if Brer Possum helps Brer Snake. From what you know about the characters so far, what do you predict will happen?

C SUMMARIZE
In your graphic organizer, briefly note the events described so far.

DIFFERENTIATED INSTRUCTION

FOR ENGLISH LEARNERS
Vocabulary Support Explain that the author uses contractions, irregular forms of words, double negatives, and even incorrect subject-verb agreement in order to create a certain dialect or form of speech for the narrator and characters. Have mixed-ability groups rewrite these phrases from the tale in conventional English. Ask groups to share their rewritten lines with the class.

- *git it offa me* (lines 25–26)
- *I knows you. You's mean and evil* (line 28)
- *if'n I was to git down in that hole* (line 29)
- *you wouldn't do nothin' but bite me* (line 30)
- *I ain't sure 'bout you at all. I jist don't know.* (line 33)
- *he lifted 'im outa the hole, way up into the air, and throwed 'im into the high grass* (lines 61–62)
- *I done took that brick offa your back* (line 94)

"Help me, Brer Possum."

Brer Possum thought, "That's him agin."

But bein' so kindhearted, he turned around, went back to the hole,
and stood there a-lookin' for Brer Snake. Brer Snake crawled outa the
70 high grass just as slow as he could, stretched 'imself out across the road,
rared up, and looked at ol' Brer Possum.

Then he hissed. "I've been down there in that ol' hole for a mighty
long time, and I've gotten a little cold 'cause the sun didn't shine.
Do you think you could put me in your pocket and git me warm?"

Brer Possum said, "Now you listen here, Brer Snake. I knows you.
You's mean and evil and lowdown, and if'n I put you in my pocket
you wouldn't do nothin' but bite me."

Brer Snake hissed.

"Maybe not. Maybe not. Maaaaaaaybe not."

80 "No, sireee, Brer Snake. I knows you. I jist ain't a-goin' to do it."

But jist as Brer Possum was talkin' to Brer Snake, he happened to git
a real good look at 'im. He was a-layin' there lookin' so pitiful, and Brer
Possum's great big heart began to feel sorry for ol' Brer Snake.

"All right," said Brer Possum. "You must be cold. So jist this once
I'm a-goin' to put you in my pocket." **D**

So ol' Brer Snake coiled up jist as little as he could, and Brer Possum
picked 'im up and put 'im in his pocket.

Brer Snake laid quiet and still—so quiet and still that Brer Possum even
forgot that he was a-carryin' 'im around. But all of a sudden, Brer Snake
90 commenced to crawlin' out, and he turned and faced Brer Possum
and hissed.

"I'm a-goin' to bite you."

But Brer Possum said, "Now wait a minute. Why are you a-goin' to
bite me? I done took that brick offa your back, I got you outa that hole,
and I put you in my pocket to git you warm. Why are you a-goin' to
bite me?"

Brer Snake hissed.

"You knowed I was a snake before you put me in your pocket."

And when you're mindin' your own business and you spot trouble,
100 *don't never trouble trouble 'til trouble troubles you.* ∿ **E**

> **D FOLK TALES**
> Note how many times
> Brer Possum has come to
> help Brer Snake. What
> patterns are developing?

② Targeted Passage

> **E FOLK TALES**
> Reread lines 99–100.
> Sometimes you may
> have to infer the **moral**
> of a folk tale, but in this
> case the moral is stated
> directly. Rephrase it in
> your own words.

DISCUSSION PROMPTS

Use these prompts to help students understand Brer Possum's dilemma:

Connect Think about a time when you had
a hard decision to make. What advice would
you give Brer Possum to help him make a
decision in this situation? *Students may say
that they would tell him to try to foresee
the consequences of each of his choices or to
figure out a way to help Brer Snake without
putting himself in danger.*

Analyze A dilemma is a situation in which
all choices are equally undesirable. What is
Brer Possum's dilemma? Explain. *Possible
answer: Brer Possum is too kindhearted to
ignore someone's need for help. Yet, if he
helps Brer Snake, he may get bitten.*

Evaluate Would you suggest that Brer
Possum trust the snake? Why or why not?
*Possible answer: Probably not. Snakes are
associated with slyness or sneakiness, so Brer
Snake is probably pretending to be more
helpless than he really is.*

LITERARY ANALYSIS

D FOLK TALES

*Possible answer: Brer Possum helps Brer
Snake three times, suggesting the traditional folk tale "set of three." The other pattern
that develops is that Brer Snake asks for
help, Brer Possum has doubts, and then Brer
Possum decides to help Brer Snake anyway.*

LITERARY ANALYSIS

E FOLK TALES

*Possible answers: "Don't go looking for
trouble" or "Don't trust someone whom you
know to be trouble."*

FOR LESS–PROFICIENT READERS

② Targeted Passage [Lines 86–100]

This passage presents the climax of the tale:
Brer Snake says he will bite Brer Possum.

- Why is Brer Snake in Brer Possum's pocket?
- What does Brer Snake say when Brer
  Possum lists the nice things he has done?
- Do you think Brer Snake does bite Brer
  Possum? Why?
- What is the moral of the story?

FOR ADVANCED LEARNERS/PRE–AP

Synthesize What other lesson might be
learned from the experiences of Brer Possum
in this tale? Have students write an original moral for the tale. Encourage them to
imitate the style of the original statement.
Invite them to share their morals in small
groups.

Waters of Gold

Retold by **Laurence Yep**

Many years ago, there lived a woman whom everyone called Auntie Lily. She was Auntie by blood to half the county and Auntie to the other half by friendship. As she liked to say, "There's a bit of Heaven in each of us." As a result, she was always helping people out.

Because of her many kind acts, she knew so many people that she couldn't go ten steps without meeting someone who wanted to chat. So it would take her half the day to go to the village well and back to her home. **F**

Eventually, though, she helped so many people that she had no more
10 money. She had to sell her fields and even her house to her neighbor, a rich old woman. "If you'd helped yourself instead of others, you wouldn't have to do this," the neighbor said **smugly**. "Where are all those other people when you need them?"

"That isn't why I helped them," Auntie Lily said firmly. She wound up having to pay rent for the house she had once owned. She supported herself by her embroidery; but since her eyes were going bad, she could not do very much.

One day an old beggar entered the village. He was a ragbag of a man— a trash heap, a walking pig wallow. It was impossible to tell what color
20 or what shape his clothes had once been, and his hair was as muddy and matted as a bird's nest. As he shuffled through the village gates, he called out, "Water for my feet. Please, water for my feet. One little bowl of water—that's all I ask."

F FOLK TALES
What **trait** do you think Auntie Lily represents?

smugly (smŭg'lē) *adv.* in a self-satisfied way

❸ Targeted Passage

ANALYZE VISUALS
Compare the village in this picture to the village described in the story. In what ways are they similar?

Orchard (2000), Chen Jia Qi. Watercol[...]
Red Lantern Folk Art, Mukashi Collectio[...]
© The Mukashi Collection/SuperStoc[...]

LITERARY ANALYSIS

F FOLK TALES

Possible answers: *Auntie Lily represents generosity or kindness.*

If students need help . . . Use a chart such as this one to help students draw the correct conclusion.

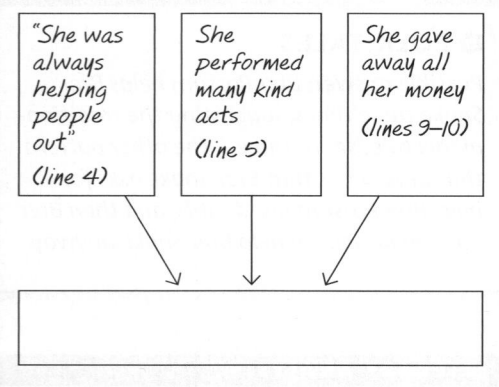

"She was always helping people out" (line 4) → | She performed many kind acts (line 5) → | She gave away all her money (lines 9–10) →

ANALYZE VISUALS

Possible answers: *There are many people out and about in the village in the painting, just as there are in Auntie Lily's village. It looks like a friendly place.*

DIFFERENTIATED INSTRUCTION

FOR LESS–PROFICIENT READERS

❸ Targeted Passage [Lines 1–23]

This passage introduces the setting—a farm community—and the main characters—Auntie Lily, the rich old woman, and the beggar.

- What is Auntie Lily's most important character trait?
- What is the setting of the story? Where does Auntie Lily live?
- What does the beggar want?
- What is likely to happen next?

FOR ENGLISH LEARNERS

Vocabulary: Multiple Meanings Use a multiple-meanings chart to explore the various definitions of *supported* (line 15) and *going* (line 16). Then have students work in small groups to write sentences for each meaning.

 BEST PRACTICES TOOLKIT—Transparency
Words with Multiple Meanings p. E31

DISCUSSION PROMPTS

Use these prompts to help students understand the differences between the two women:

Connect What do you think of the rich old woman's reaction to the beggar's request? *Students will probably say that it would not have cost her anything to give him some water. Her behavior is snobbish and uncaring.*

Analyze What traits does the rich old woman represent? *Possible answer: She represents stinginess and unkindness.*

Synthesize Reread lines 46–47 and 48–49. What is the fundamental difference in attitude between the two women? *Possible answer: The rich old woman sees misfortune as something that is deserved. She believes people bring it on themselves. Auntie Lily thinks that bad luck can happen to anyone.*

READING STRATEGY

G SUMMARIZE

Record students' answers in the chart from page 697. *Possible answer:*

- *Events—The rich woman turns the beggar away, telling him that he is garbage. Auntie Lily gives the beggar a bucket of water.*

Everyone ignored him, pretending to concentrate on their chores instead. One man went on replacing the shaft of his hoe. A woman swept her courtyard. Another woman fed her hens.

The beggar went to each in turn, but they all showed their backs to him.

After calling out a little while longer, the beggar went to the nearest
30 home, which happened to belong to the rich old woman. When he banged at her door, he left the dirty outline of his knuckles on the clean wood. And when the rich woman opened her door, his smell nearly took her breath away.

Now it so happened that she had been chopping vegetables when the beggar had knocked. When the beggar repeated his request, she raised her cleaver menacingly. "What good would one bowl of water be? You'd need a whole river to wash you clean. Go away."

"A thousand pardons," the old beggar said, and shambled on to the next house.

40 Though Auntie Lily had to hold her nose, she asked politely, "Yes?"

"I'd like a bowl of water to wash my feet." And the beggar pointed one grimy finger toward them.

Her rich neighbor had stayed in her doorway to watch the beggar. She scolded Auntie Lily now. "It's all your fault those beggars come into the village. They know they can count on a free meal."

It was an old debate between them, so Auntie Lily simply said, "Any of us can have bad luck."

"Garbage," the rich old woman declared, "is garbage. They must have done something bad, or Heaven wouldn't have let them become beggars."

50 Auntie Lily turned to the beggar. "I may be joining you on the road someday. Wait here."

Much to the neighbor's distress, Auntie Lily went inside and poured water from a large jar in her kitchen into a bucket. Carrying it in both hands, she brought it outside to the beggar and set it down.

The beggar stood on one leg, just like a crane, while he washed one callused, leathery sole over the bucket. "You can put mud on any other part of me, but if my feet are clean, then I feel clean."

As he fussily continued to cleanse his feet, Auntie Lily asked kindly, "Are you hungry? I don't have much, but what I have I'm willing to
60 share." **G**

The beggar shook his head. "I've stayed longer in this village than I have in any other. Heaven is my roof, and the whole world my house."

Auntie Lily stared at him, wondering what she would look like after a few years on the road. "Are you very tired? Have you been on the road for very long?"

④ Targeted Passage

G SUMMARIE
What happens when Auntie Lily and the rich woman encounter the beggar? Record the events in your graphic organizer.

DIFFERENTIATED INSTRUCTION

FOR LESS–PROFICIENT READERS

④ Targeted Passage [Lines 29–54]

This passage develops the plot: the beggar asks for a bucket of water.

- How does the rich old woman treat the beggar?

- What does the rich old woman blame Auntie Lily for? Why?

- What does the woman mean when she says, "Garbage is garbage"?

- How does Auntie Lily treat the beggar?

FOR ENGLISH LEARNERS

Vocabulary Support Have students use New Word Analysis to define these phrases:

- *showed their backs to him* (lines 27–28)

- *joining you* (line 50)

- *on the road* (line 50)

- *the road is on me* (line 66)

 BEST PRACTICES TOOLKIT—Transparency
New Word Analysis p. E8

"No, the road is on me," the beggar said, and held up his hands from his dirty sides. "But thank you. You're the first person to ask. And you're the first person to give me some water. So place the bucket of water by your bed tonight and do not look into it till tomorrow morning." **H**

70 As the beggar shuffled out of the village again, Auntie Lily stared down doubtfully at the bucket of what was now muddy water. Then, even though she felt foolish, she picked it up again.

"You're not really going to take that scummy water inside?" laughed the rich neighbor. "It'll probably breed mosquitoes."

"It seemed important to him," she answered. "I'll **humor** him."

"Humoring people," snapped the neighbor, "has got you one step from begging yourself."

However, Auntie Lily carried the bucket inside anyway. Setting it down near her sleeping mat, she covered the mouth of the bucket with an old,
80 cracked plate so she wouldn't peek into it by mistake, and then she got so caught up in embroidering a pair of slippers that she forgot all about the beggar and his bucket of water.

She sewed until twilight, when it was too dark to use her needle. Then, because she had no money for oil or candles, she went to sleep.

The next morning Auntie Lily rose and stretched the aches out of her back. She sighed. "The older I get, the harder it is to get up in the morning."

Detail from *Spring in the Old Village* (2001), Chen Jia Qi. Watercolor. Red Lantern Folk Art, Mukashi Collection.
© The Mukashi Collection/SuperStock.

H PREDICT
Reread lines 66–69. From what the beggar has said about Auntie Lily, what kind of thing do you predict will happen if she follows his instructions?

humor (hyoo′mər) *v.* to give in to the wishes of

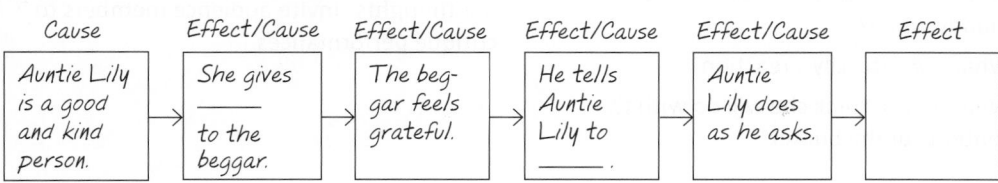

Cause	Effect/Cause	Effect/Cause	Effect/Cause	Effect/Cause	Effect
Auntie Lily is a good and kind person.	She gives ___ to the beggar.	The beggar feels grateful.	He tells Auntie Lily to ___.	Auntie Lily does as he asks.	

She was always saying something like that, but she had never stayed on her sleeping mat—even when she was sick. Thinking of all that day's 90 chores, she decided to water the herbs she had growing on one side of her house.

Her eyes fell upon the beggar's bucket with its covering plate. "No sense using fresh water when that will do as well. After all, dirt's dirt to a plant."

Squatting down, she picked up the bucket and was surprised at how heavy it was. "I must have filled it fuller than I thought," she grunted.

She staggered out of the house and over to the side where rows of little green herbs grew. "Here you go," she said to her plants. "Drink deep."

Taking off the plate, she upended the bucket; but instead of muddy 100 brown water, there was a flash of reflected light and a clinking sound as gold coins rained down upon her plants.

Auntie Lily set the bucket down hastily and crouched, not trusting her weak eyes. However, where some of her herbs had been, there was now a small mound of gold coins. She squinted in disbelief and rubbed her aching eyes and stared again; but the gold was still there.

She turned to the bucket. There was even more gold inside. Scooping up coins by the handful, she freed her little plants and made sure that the stalks weren't too bent.

⑤ **Targeted Passage**

Then she sat gazing at her bucket full of gold until a farmer walked by. 110 "Tell me I'm not dreaming," she called to him.

The farmer yawned and came over with his hoe over his shoulder. "I wish I were dreaming, because that would mean I'm still in bed instead of having to go off to work."

Auntie Lily gathered up a handful of gold coins and let it fall in a tinkling, golden shower back into the bucket. "And this is real?"

The farmer's jaw dropped. He picked up one coin with his free hand and bit into it.[1] He flipped it back in with the other coins. "It's as real as me, Auntie. But where did you ever get that?"

So Auntie Lily told him. And as others woke up and stepped outside, 120 Auntie told them as well, for she still could not believe her luck and wanted them to confirm that the gold was truly gold. In no time at all, there was a small crowd around her. ❶

If the bucket had been filled with ordinary copper cash, that would have been more money than any of them had ever seen. In their wildest dreams, they had never expected to see that much gold. Auntie Lily stared at the bucket uncomfortably. "I keep thinking it's going to disappear the next moment."

❶ **SUMMARIZE**
In your own words, explain what happens to Auntie Lily.

---

1. **bit into it:** Gold is soft, so biting it is a way of testing its authenticity.

Lines 102–108
REINFORCE *KEY IDEA:* LESSONS

Discuss What **lessons** might be learned from this transformation of muddy water into gold?
Possible answers: One lesson might be that kindness to strangers will be rewarded. Another might be to expect the unexpected.

READING STRATEGY

❶ SUMMARIZE

Add students' answers to the chart from page 697. *Possible answer:*

- *Events—The beggar tells Auntie Lily to keep the muddy water overnight. In the morning, the bucket is filled with gold coins.*

If students need help . . .

- Have students work in pairs. Ask one partner to retell what has happened so far while the other records what is said.

- Tell pairs to cross out anything that is not an important event. For example, ideas such as "Auntie Lily is a kind woman" or "The plants bend under the weight of the coins" do not belong.

- Have students record the remaining details in their charts.

DIFFERENTIATED INSTRUCTION

FOR LESS—PROFICIENT READERS
⑤ **Targeted Passage [Lines 92–108]**

This passage presents an important turning point of the tale: Auntie Lily is rewarded for her kindness to the beggar.

- What is in Auntie Lily's bucket instead of muddy water?

- What is Auntie Lily's reaction?

- What do you think she will do with the contents of the bucket?

FOR ADVANCED LEARNERS/PRE–AP

Analyze What is going through Auntie Lily's mind as she pours out the gold coins instead of muddy water? Have students take turns performing monologues in which they act out Auntie Lily's feelings and reveal her thoughts. Invite audience members to critique performances.

The farmer, who had been standing there all this time, shook his head. "If it hasn't disappeared by now, I don't think it will. What are you going to do with it, Auntie?"

Auntie Lily stared at the bucket, and suddenly she came to a decision. Stretching out a hand, she picked up a gold coin. "I'm going to buy back my house, and I'm going to get back my land."

The farmer knew the fields. "Those old things? You could buy a valley full of **prime** land with half that bucket. And a palace with the other half."

"I want what I sweated for." Asking the farmer to guard her bucket, Auntie Lily closed her hand around the gold coin. Then, as the crowd parted before her, she made her way over to her neighbor. **J**

Now the rich old woman liked to sleep late; but all the noise had woken her up, so she was just getting dressed when Auntie knocked. The old woman yanked her door open as she buttoned the last button of her coat. "Who started the riot? Can't a person get a good night's sleep?"

With some satisfaction, Auntie Lily held up the gold coin. "Will this buy back my house and land?"

"Where did you get that?" the old woman demanded.

"Will it buy them back?" Auntie Lily repeated.

The rich old woman snatched the coin out of Auntie Lily's hand and bit into it just as the farmer had. "It's real," the old woman said in astonishment.

"Will it?" Auntie asked again.

"Yes, yes, yes," the old woman said crabbily. "But where did you ever get that much gold?"

When Auntie Lily told her the story and showed her the bucket of gold, the rich old woman stood moving her mouth like a fish out of water. Clasping her hands together, she shut her eyes and moaned in genuine pain. "And I sent him away. What a fool I am. What a fool." And the old woman beat her head with her fists.

That very afternoon, the beggar—the ragbag, the trash heap, the walking pig wallow—shuffled once more through the village gates with feet as dirty as before. As he went, he croaked, "Water for my feet. Please, water for my feet. One little bowl of water—that's all I ask." **K**

This time, people dropped whatever they were doing when they heard his plea. Hoes, brooms, and pots were flung down, hens and pigs were kicked out of the way as everyone hurried to fill a bucket with water. There was a small riot by the village well as everyone fought to get water at the same time. Still others rushed out with buckets filled from the jars in their houses.

---

prime (prīm) *adj.* first in quality or value

J FOLK TALES
Reread lines 129–139. What does Auntie Lily's decision about how to spend her money say about her?

K PREDICT
How do you predict the townspeople will behave now that the beggar has returned?

"Here, use my water," one man shouted, holding up a tub.

170 A woman shoved in front of him with a bucket in her arms. "No, no, use mine. It's purer."

They surrounded the old beggar, pleading with him to use their water, and in the process of **jostling** one another, they splashed a good deal of water on one another and came **perilously** close to drowning the beggar. The rich old woman, Auntie Lily's neighbor, charged to the rescue.

"Out of the way, you vultures," the rich old woman roared. "You're going to trample him." Using her elbows, her feet, and in one case even her teeth, the old woman fought her way through the mob.

No longer caring if she soiled her hands, the old woman seized the 180 beggar by the arm. "This way, you poor, misunderstood creature."

Fighting off her neighbors with one hand and keeping her grip on the beggar with the other, the old woman hauled him inside her house. Barring the door against the rest of the village, she ignored all the fists and feet thumping on her door and all the shouts.

"I really wasn't myself yesterday, because I had been up the night before tending a sick friend. This is what I meant to do." She fetched a fresh new towel and an even newer bucket and forced the beggar to wash his feet.

When he was done, he handed her the now filthy towel. "Dirt's dirt, 190 and garbage is garbage," he said.

However, the greedy old woman didn't recognize her own words. She was too busy trying to remember what else Auntie Lily had done. "Won't you have something to eat? Have you traveled very far? Are you tired?" she asked, all in the same breath.

The old beggar went to the door and waited patiently while she unbarred it. As he shuffled outside, he instructed her to leave the bucket of water by her bed but not to look into it until the morning.

That night, the greedy old woman couldn't sleep as she imagined the heap of shiny gold that would be waiting for her tomorrow. She waited 200 impatiently for the sun to rise and got up as soon as she heard the first rooster crow.

Hurrying to the bucket, she plunged her hands inside expecting to bring up handfuls of gold. Instead, she gave a cry as dozens of little things bit her, for the bucket was filled not with gold but with snakes, lizards, and ants. ⓛ

The greedy old woman fell sick—some said from her bites, some claimed from sheer frustration. Auntie Lily herself came to nurse her neighbor. "Take this to heart: Kindness comes with no price."

The old woman was so ashamed that she did, indeed, take the lesson to 210 heart. Though she remained sick, she was kind to whoever came to her door.

jostling (jŏs'lĭng) *n.* roughly bumping, pushing, or shoving **jostle** *v.*

perilously (pĕr'ə-ləs-lē) *adv.* dangerously

ⓛ **FOLK TALES**
Why do you think the old woman gets this result when she tries to behave like Auntie Lily?

LITERARY ANALYSIS

ⓛ FOLK TALES

Possible answer: The beggar rewards the old woman with lizards, snakes, and ants because even though she did the same things Auntie Lily did, she did them out of greed for gold, and not out of kindness.

Lines 206–210
REINFORCE *KEY IDEA:* LESSONS

Discuss What does Auntie Lily say to her neighbor about kindness? How does the rich old woman show that she has learned her **lesson?** *Possible answer: Auntie Lily tells the rich old woman that "kindness comes with no price." From that time on, the rich old woman is kind to everyone who comes to her door.*

DIFFERENTIATED INSTRUCTION

FOR ENGLISH LEARNERS
Culture: Clarify Explain that *vultures* in line 176 is used figuratively. A vulture is a large bird of prey. By using the word, the old woman is saying that the townspeople are trying to take advantage of the beggar.

Vocabulary: Prefixes List these prefixes and their meanings on the board: *mis-* ("wrongly"); *un-* ("reverse of"); *im-* ("not"). Then have students define *misunderstood* (line 180), *unbarred* (line 196), and *impatiently* (line 200).

FOR ADVANCED LEARNERS/PRE–AP
Analyze Author's Craft The old woman's comment in line 176, in which she calls the people "vultures," is a case of "the pot calling the kettle black." Why? Have students identify other ironies in the story. Ask them to make a chart explaining how this device makes the tale more meaningful.

Detail from *Sunny Spring* (1999), Zhang Min. Watercolor. Red Lantern Folk Art, Mukashi Collection. © The Mukashi Collection/SuperStock.

One day, a leper[2] came into the village. Everyone hid for fear of the terrible disease. Doors slammed and shutters banged down over windows, and soon the village seemed deserted.

Only Auntie Lily and her neighbor stepped out of their houses. "Are you hungry?" Auntie Lily asked.

"Are you thirsty?" the neighbor asked. "I'll make you a cup of tea."

The leper thanked Auntie Lily and then turned to the neighbor as if to express his gratitude as well; but he stopped and studied her. "You're looking poorly, my dear woman. Can I help?"

20   With a tired smile, the rich old woman explained what had happened. When she was finished, the leper stood thoughtfully for a moment. "You're not the same woman as before: You're as kind as Auntie Lily, and you aren't greedy anymore. So take this humble gift from my brother, the old beggar."

With that, the leper limped out of the village; and as he left, the illness fell away from the old woman like an old, discarded cloak. But though the old woman was healthy again, she stayed as kind as Auntie Lily and used her own money as well and wisely as Auntie Lily used the waters of gold. 〰️ Ⓜ️

Ⓜ️ FOLK TALES
What **moral** does this story convey?

---

2. **leper:** a person suffering from the infectious disease of leprosy, which can result in bodily deformities.

FOR LESS–PROFICIENT READERS
Concept Support Help students chart the changes in the rich old woman before and after the beggar's visits. Use the details to develop students' understanding of theme.

FOR ADVANCED LEARNERS/PRE–AP
Interpret When is a beggar not just a beggar? Have students think about the beggar's role in the tale. Has he been sent to test the morality of the characters, as the Green Knight did in the tale of Sir Gawain (page 672)? Have students write a statement explaining their view of the beggar's purpose. Suggest that they reread what the leper says in lines 222–224 for clues.

CULTURAL CONNECTION

Tea To show her hospitality, the rich old woman offers the leper a cup of tea (line 216). In China, tea is usually prepared with boiling water and drunk without milk. In other cultures, tea is also the favored drink, but it may assume different forms. For example, in Tibet, tea is made with butter and salt and kept heated over a fire. In Taiwan, the newest craze is bubble tea, cold flavored tea with tapioca pearls added. Yerba mate is the hot beverage of choice in Uruguay. This is herbal tea drunk out of a gourd with a metal straw.

ANALYZE VISUALS

Activity Ask students how this illustration helps to express how the rich old woman may feel after the leper leaves. ***Possible answer:** The bright colors represent happiness or lightheartedness. The old woman would have felt very relieved at her return to good health.*

LITERARY ANALYSIS

Ⓜ️ FOLK TALES

***Possible answer:** Kindness to others is often rewarded. Greed is always punished.*

If students need help . . . Have them reread lines 222–224. Explain that the leper's words explain why the rich old woman has earned a reward—a cure for her illness.

SELECTION WRAP UP

REFLECT Have students think about the punishment that the old woman suffers. In what way is her illness appropriate? What do students think she learns about misfortune?

⭐ CRITIQUE Have students consider each story's ending and evaluate its importance to the theme.

READING FLUENCY

Distribute the copy masters and have students work in pairs to practice fluency.

Ⓡ RESOURCE MANAGER—Copy Master Reading Fluency p. 158

Practice and Apply

After Reading

For additional support of post-reading questions, use these copy masters:

R **RESOURCE MANAGER—Copy Masters**

Reading Check p. 156 (to check understanding of the selection)

Characteristics of Folk Tales p. 149 (for practice of literary analysis standards focus)

Question Support p. 157 (**After Reading** questions adapted for English learners and less-proficient readers)

Additional selection questions are provided for teachers on page 143.

ANSWERS

Comprehension

1. *Brer Possum meets Brer Snake in the road. Brer Snake is stuck in a hole.*

2. *Brer Possum does not want to help Brer Snake because he knows that Brer Snake is "lowdown" and will probably bite him.*

3. *Auntie Lily had to sell it to her when she had used up all her money helping people.*

Literary Analysis

Possible answers:

4. ■ STANDARDS FOCUS *Summarize Students' summaries should include the important characters and events.*

5. ● STANDARDS FOCUS *Characteristics of Folk Tales Characters Who Represent a Trait: Brer Possum: kindheartedness; Brer Snake: sneakiness; Auntie Lily: selflessness; old woman: greediness. Events That Occur in Sets of Three: Brer Possum helps Brer Snake three times; a beggar (leper) comes to Auntie Lily's village three times. A Moral: Don't go looking for trouble. Kindness will be rewarded.*

6. *"Brer Possum's Dilemma" is a fable. The characters are the possum and the snake. Their actions reveal the moral that people should trust their instincts and not go looking for trouble.*

7. *Both Brer Possum and Auntie Lily are good characters. Both help others out of the goodness of their hearts, even when it seems foolish to do so. However, Brer Possum learns a lesson about evil people, while Auntie Lily teaches a lesson.*

Comprehension

MARYLAND OBJECTIVES

LITERATURE STANDARD
3.A.3.a Distinguish among types of narrative texts

1. **Recall** Where does Brer Possum meet Brer Snake?

2. **Clarify** Why doesn't Brer Possum want to help Brer Snake at first?

3. **Recall** At the beginning of "Waters of Gold," why does the old woman own Auntie Lily's land?

Literary Analysis

4. **Summarize** Review the graphic organizer you created for each tale. Then summarize one of the folk tales in your own words.

5. **Identify Characteristics of Folk Tales** Use a chart like the one shown to identify how each selection demonstrates the main characteristics of a folk tale.

	"Brer Possum"	"Waters of Gold"
Characters Who Represent a Trait	Brer Snake: Sneaky	
Events That Occur in Sets of Three		
A Moral		

6. **Classify a Tale** A fable is a type of folk tale that uses animal characters to teach a **moral** about human nature or the ways of the world. Which of these stories is a fable? Explain your answer.

7. **Compare and Contrast Characters** The characters in folk tales are often thought of as standing for good or evil. Consider the "good" characters in these two tales. Explain how they are alike and how they differ.

8. **Make Judgments** Which story's **lesson** is more useful in your everyday life? Explain your choice.

Extension and Challenge

9. **Reader's Circle** Jackie Torrence inherited "Brer Possum's Dilemma" from her great-grandfather, who had been enslaved. "Waters of Gold" was told by Chinese immigrant communities during the Great Depression. In a group, choose one of the stories and discuss how it might reflect the culture that created it. Questions to consider include the following:

- What do you think life was like for the original tellers of the tale?
- What traits does the story suggest are valuable?
- What traits does the story seem to warn readers about?
- Why might these traits have been significant to the original storytellers and their audiences? Why are they significant to you?

---

8. *Students may say that the lesson about kindness taught by "Waters of Gold" can be applied to many situations in everyday life. There are many opportunities during the course of a single day to show kindness to people, even strangers. The lesson in "Brer Possum's Dilemma" is also helpful, but not in the same way. It does not advise what to do but what not to do. It is a cautionary tale.*

Extension and Challenge

9. *Responses will vary depending on which story is chosen, but for "Brer Possum's Dilemma," discussion could center on the difficulties faced by African Americans under slavery, and contending with racism. For "Waters of Gold," students might focus on the importance of community support in hard times, or the need for immigrants to stick together when someone is in trouble.*

Vocabulary in Context

VOCABULARY PRACTICE

Choose the letter of the item you would associate with each vocabulary word as it is used in these selections.

1. **smugly:** (a) carrying a heavy load, (b) looking pleased with oneself, (c) riding an old bike

2. **prime:** (a) an excellent meal, (b) a small family, (c) a necessary decision

3. **commence:** (a) the opening scene, (b) a large rectangle, (c) a long meeting

4. **jostling:** (a) children laughing, (b) dogs barking, (c) crowds pushing

5. **perilously:** (a) singing in a choir, (b) walking on a tightrope, (c) having lunch

6. **humor:** (a) give in, (b) get angry, (c) get better

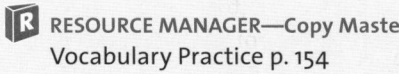

commence
humor
jostling
perilously
prime
smugly

VOCABULARY IN WRITING

Which folk tale character changed more, Brer Possum or the rich old woman in "Waters of Gold"? Using two or more vocabulary words, write several sentences explaining your opinion. Here is a sample opening.

> **EXAMPLE SENTENCE**
>
> At first, the rich old woman **smugly** assumed that she was right.

VOCABULARY STRATEGY: THE LATIN WORD *primus*

The vocabulary word *prime* comes from the Latin word *primus*, which means "first." To determine the meaning of words that come from *primus*, use context clues and your understanding of the root's meaning.

ACTIVITY Choose the word from the web that best completes each sentence. If necessary, consult a dictionary.

1. Before they learned to use fire, early people had a fairly _____ way of life.

2. The first three or four grades of school are called the _____ grades.

3. The highest category of mammals, which includes humans and apes, is called _____.

4. The citizens of the town were _____ from German backgrounds.

5. Some say that our solar system developed from a _____ gas cloud.

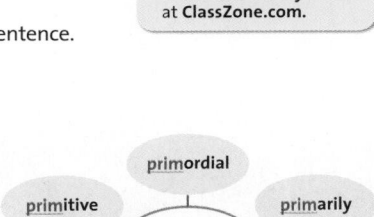

primordial
primitive
primarily
primus
primates
primary
prime

MARYLAND OBJECTIVES

READING STANDARD
1.D.3.b Use word structure to determine meaning

VOCABULARY PRACTICE
For more practice, go to the **Vocabulary Center** at ClassZone.com.

DIFFERENTIATED INSTRUCTION

FOR ENGLISH LEARNERS

Vocabulary Strategy Point out that many of the words derived from *primus* can be matched with similar words in the Spanish language. Have students identify cognates for as many of the choices as they can.

FOR ADVANCED LEARNERS/PRE–AP

Vocabulary Strategy Have students use the dictionary to find additional words that come from *primus*. Have students work in pairs to list as many as they can. Discuss the meanings of the words they discover.

ANSWERS

Vocabulary in Context

VOCABULARY PRACTICE

1. *b*; 2. *a*; 3. *a*; 4. *c*; 5. *b*; 6. *a*

R RESOURCE MANAGER—Copy Master
Vocabulary Practice p. 154

VOCABULARY IN WRITING

Have students skim each selection to help them make their decision. Suggest that they create a "before" and an "after" list before deciding how to express these changes using vocabulary words.

VOCABULARY STRATEGY: THE LATIN WORD

primus (also an EL language objective)

Before students begin the exercise, read the choices aloud and help them identify the part of speech of each word.

Answers:

1. *primitive*
2. *primary*
3. *primates*
4. *primarily*
5. *primordial*

R RESOURCE MANAGER—Copy Master
Vocabulary Strategy p. 155

i Vocabulary Center at **ClassZone.com**
Additional Vocabulary Activities

Assess and Reteach

Assess

R RESOURCE MANAGER—Copy Masters
Selection Tests A, B/C pp. 159–160, 161–162

⊘ Test Generator CD

Reteach

S STANDARDS LESSON FILE
Literature Lesson 29: Symbol and Symbolism
Literature Lesson 13: Theme

Focus and Motivate

OBJECTIVES

Literary Analysis
- explore the key idea of **compatibility**
- analyze characteristics of tall tales
- read a tall tale

Reading
- visualize

Vocabulary
- build vocabulary for reading and writing
- use dictionary usage labels *(also an EL language objective)*

SUMMARY

In this tall tale, Davy Crockett meets Sally Ann Thunder Ann Whirlwind when she frees his head from the crook of a tree. He becomes increasingly enamored with her as he learns that she can do things like ride panthers, tame bears, and laugh the bark off a tree. She is strong, quick, smart, funny, brave—in short, a perfect match for Davy Crockett.

What makes a good COUPLE?

Discuss the question with students. To lead into the **KEY IDEA,** define **compatibility** and ask students what it means to them. List their ideas on the board. Have students keep these details in mind as they complete the **WEB IT** activity. Have students share their webs in small groups.

Selection Resources

Before Reading

Sally Ann Thunder Ann Whirlwind

American Tall Tale Retold by Mary Pope Osborne

What makes a good COUPLE?

MARYLAND OBJECTIVES

READING/LIT STANDARDS
1.E.3.a Select and apply appropriate strategies during reading
3.A.3.a Distinguish among types of narrative texts

KEY IDEA You know who they are. Couples who just seem so right together that they radiate happiness when they walk down the street. Their **compatibility** might come from having similar personalities or interests, or even from respecting each other's differences. In this selection, a character who is larger than life meets her match.

WEB IT In a small group, create an idea web. Fill it with examples of compatible couples in books and movies, as well as those you know from your own life. Then expand the web by including your ideas about what makes the good couples good.

712

RESOURCE MANAGER UNIT 6

Plan and Teach pp. 163–170

Literary Analysis
Summary pp. 171†*, 172‡*
Characteristics of Tall Tales pp. 173, 174†*
Question Support p. 181*

Reading
Visualize pp. 175, 176†*
Reading Check p. 180

Vocabulary
Study p. 177*
Practice p. 178
Strategy p. 179

Assessment
Selection Tests A, B/C pp. 183*, 185*
Test Generator CD

BEST PRACTICES TOOLKIT

Differentiated Instruction
 pp. 31–38*
Scaffolding Instruction pp. 43–46*

Graphic Organizers/Strategies
Draw It • Jigsaw • Cluster Diagram

Reading Support
Audio Anthology CD*

Technology
Literature and Vocabulary Centers at **ClassZone.com**
Write*Smart* CD

* Resources for Differentiation   † Also in Spanish   ‡ In Haitian Creole and Vietnamese

LITERARY ANALYSIS: CHARACTERISTICS OF TALL TALES

A **tall tale** is a humorously exaggerated story about impossible events. Like other folk tales, tall tales were originally passed along by being told out loud. Tall tales share these characteristics:

- They use exaggeration to make difficult situations seem incredible or funny.
- The hero or heroine is often bigger, stronger, and even louder than an ordinary person.
- The setting is usually the American frontier.

As you read, notice how these characteristics apply to "Sally Ann Thunder Ann Whirlwind."

READING STRATEGY: VISUALIZE

Tall tales are often so exaggerated, funny, and action packed that you might be able to **visualize,** or picture, them as cartoons. To try this, look for descriptive details that appeal to your senses of touch, sound, and especially sight. Then picture the characters and action in your mind. Use a chart like the one shown to record descriptive words and phrases in "Sally Ann Thunder Ann Whirlwind."

Character or Event	Descriptive Words or Phrases

VOCABULARY IN CONTEXT

The words listed help add humor to the tall tale. Place each word in the appropriate column in the chart. Use a dictionary to look up the words you don't know.

WORD	forage	oblige
LIST	gigantic	varmint

Know Well	Think I Know	Don't Know

Author Online

Female Heroes
As a child, Mary Pope Osborne says, she was "terrified of little things, like insects and worms and big dogs" and that "it was always a struggle to get over those fears." Now she creates stories with the kind of fearless female heroes that she thinks would have made her "less of a frightened child."

**Mary Pope Osborne
born 1949**

Background

An American Tradition In trying to claim new lands for building and farming, American settlers faced great challenges. Workers tested their endurance through chopping lumber and building railroads. Pioneers faced wild animals and brutal weather, as well as other difficulties. One way of coping with the difficulties life threw their way was to tell tall tales.

Bigger and Better The heroes and heroines of these tall tales were people like the settlers, but they were larger than life and able to handle any hardship that came along. Paul Bunyan and Pecos Bill are two fictional heroes that came out of this tradition. Others, like Davy Crockett, were real people whose adventures were told so many times that they became legendary.

 MORE ABOUT THE AUTHOR AND BACKGROUND
To learn more about Mary Pope Osborne and tall tales, visit the **Literature Center** at **ClassZone.com.**

Teach

STANDARDS FOCUS

LITERARY ANALYSIS

● CHARACTERISTICS OF TALL TALES

Tell students that tall tales, while fictional, have heroes that are based on the lives of real people. Provide examples of tall tales, such as "John Henry" and "Paul Bunyan."

CHECK UNDERSTANDING Have students discuss the heroes' traits in the tall tales that they know.

READING STRATEGY

■ VISUALIZE

Read this example aloud:

> With hands the size of Michigan, she snapped the redwoods as though they were toothpicks, clearing the field in no time. Then, using the comb from her hair, she plowed the earth, kicking a couple of mountains aside first.

Ask students what they "see" as they listen. *Students may respond that they see a huge woman with large hands plucking up trees and moving mountains.*

CHECK UNDERSTANDING Have pairs take turns vividly describing a place, a meal, a person, or an activity. Partners should explain the mental picture created.

 RESOURCE MANAGER—Copy Master
Visualize p. 175 (for student use while reading the selection)

▲ VOCABULARY IN CONTEXT

DIAGNOSE WORD KNOWLEDGE To determine preteaching needs, have all students complete **Vocabulary in Context.** Remind students to look for the definitions of any unknown words as they read: *forage* (p. 718), *gigantic* (p. 719), *oblige* (p. 714), *varmint* (p. 716).

PRETEACH VOCABULARY Use the Vocabulary Study copy master to help students explore the meaning of each boldfaced word.

1. Read the first sentence aloud, emphasizing *gigantic*.
2. Point out the word *mountain*. Elicit possible meanings for *gigantic,* such as "huge."
3. Repeat the procedure for the rest of the passage.

 RESOURCE MANAGER—Copy Master
Vocabulary Study p. 177

For general guidelines on differentiating vocabulary instruction and for alternative vocabulary activities for students not needing vocabulary preteaching, see

📦 **BEST PRACTICES TOOLKIT**
Scaffolding Vocabulary Instruction pp. 43–46

ℹ️ Vocabulary Center at **ClassZone.com**
Additional Vocabulary Activities

ANALYZE VISUALS

Possible answer: The woman is swinging a rope of snakes around with great force, showing that she is fearless and strong.

About the Art Award-winning American artist Michael McCurdy (b. 1942) has had an illustrious career, teaching at various institutions and illustrating more than 200 books, including some that he has written. For the illustrations in "Sally Ann Thunder Ann Whirlwind," he used the technique of wood engraving in which the design is carved onto an end piece of wood, allowing great detail to be shown.

Lines 10–21
DISCUSSION PROMPTS

Use these prompts to help students understand the character of Davy Crockett:

Connect How would you feel if you were Davy Crockett in this situation—with his head stuck in a tree? *Students may say that they would feel panic-stricken.*

Analyze What do you learn about Davy Crockett from his actions in lines 10–13? *Possible answer: He is strong enough to blow the leaves off the trees. He is persistent because he keeps twisting and turning.*

Synthesize How would you describe Davy's initial attitude toward Sally? How might his attitude reflect society's opinion of women at the time the story is set? *Possible answer: He has a superior, or condescending, attitude. At the time the story is set, women were not considered men's equals.*

Sally Ann Thunder Ann Whirlwind

Retold by **Mary Pope Osborne**

One early spring day, when the leaves of the white oaks were about as big as a mouse's ear, Davy Crockett set out alone through the forest to do some bear hunting. Suddenly it started raining real hard, and he felt **obliged** to stop for shelter under a tree. As he shook the rain out of his coonskin cap, he got sleepy, so he laid back into the crotch of the tree, and pretty soon he was snoring.

Davy slept so hard, he didn't wake up until nearly sundown. And when he did, he discovered that somehow or another in all that sleeping his head had gotten stuck in the crotch of the tree, and he couldn't get it out.

10 Well, Davy roared loud enough to make the tree lose all its little mouse-ear leaves. He twisted and turned and carried on for over an hour, but still that tree wouldn't let go. Just as he was about to give himself up for a goner, he heard a girl say, "What's the matter, stranger?"

ANALYZE VISUALS

Examine the woman in the painting. What can you **infer** about her personality?

oblige (ə-blīj') *v.* to force; require

1 Targeted Passage

714 UNIT 6: MYTHS, LEGENDS, AND TALES

DIFFERENTIATED INSTRUCTION

FOR ALL STUDENTS

Integrated Curriculum Have students work in groups to learn more about the events that led to the establishment of the western states between 1775 and 1853. Suggest that they show the results of their research in a color-coded, annotated map of the continental United States or on an annotated timeline.

FOR LESS–PROFICIENT READERS

In combination with the *Audio Anthology CD,* use one or more Targeted Passages (pp. 714, 716, 719) to ensure that students focus on key story events, concepts, and skills.

1 Targeted Passage [Lines 1–13]

This passage establishes the setting, introduces one of the main characters, and presents a conflict: Davy Crockett is stuck in a tree.

- Where is Davy Crockett at the beginning of the story?
- How does Davy get stuck in the tree?
- What does he think is going to happen to him?
- Who discovers Davy? Since this is a tall tale, what kind of character might she be?

Davy Crockett Davy Crockett lived from 1786 to 1836. During his lifetime, he was elected to several political offices and became famous for his "backwoods" humor, his hunting skill, and his stories. To many, he symbolized the best qualities of the frontiersman. As a result, stories grew about him before and after his death in 1836 at the Battle of the Alamo.

Keelboat Tiller Sally Ann Thunder Ann Whirl-wind's arms are described as being "as big as a keelboat tiller's" (lines 15–16). A keelboat tiller is the bar used to steer the huge riverboats, or keelboats, that carried freight along the Ohio and Mississippi rivers.

Mike Fink Sally pays Mike Fink back for trying to scare her. By the time she gets finished with him, he has been knocked "clear across the woods and into a muddy swamp" (line 94). Like Davy Crockett, Mike Fink was an actual person whose life inspired many stories. He piloted keelboats and then turned to trapping. He was known for his shooting ability, his storytelling, and his feistiness.

FOR ENGLISH LEARNERS

Options for Reading Read the first Targeted Passage aloud. Make sure that students understand Davy Crockett's problem and why Sally will be able to help him. Then have students read the rest of the tale in small groups or read along silently with the *Audio Anthology CD*.

Key Academic Vocabulary Have students work in groups to define these words from context: *furthermore* (line 34), *encounter* (line 80), *final* (line 102).

Prereading For prereading instruction for English learners, see

 BEST PRACTICES TOOLKIT
Scaffolding Reading Instruction pp. 43–46

FOR ADVANCED LEARNERS/PRE–AP

Pre-AP exercises in the bottom channel provide additional challenge for your advanced students. Use them for small groups or individuals.

ADDITIONAL GUIDELINES

For more help with differentiation and tips for classroom management, see

BEST PRACTICES TOOLKIT
Differentiated Instruction pp. 31–38

Ⓐ VISUALIZE

Record students' answers in the chart from page 713. **Possible answers:**

Character or Event	Descriptive Words or Phrases
Sally	• "extraordinary" • "tall as a hickory sapling" • "arms as big as a keelboat tiller's"

Ⓑ TALL TALES

Possible answer: *Sally says that she is a "streak of lightning." She is trying to show Davy her speed and power.*

If students need help . . . Remind them that a metaphor is a comparison in which one thing is said to be something else.

Lines 43–45
REINFORCE *KEY IDEA:* COMPATIBILITY

Discuss What has been revealed so far about the **compatibility** of Davy and Sally? *Possible answer: So far it is clear that they both like the outdoors. They are both strong and bold.*

Ⓒ TALL TALES

Possible answer: *Sally can dance a rock to pieces, ride a panther, whip across the Salt River, crack a walnut with her front teeth, and laugh the bark off a pine tree. These descriptions exaggerate her strength, fearlessness, speed, and energetic laugh in a colorful way.*

Even from his awkward position, he could see that she was extra-ordinary— tall as a hickory sapling, with arms as big as a keelboat tiller's. Ⓐ

"My head's stuck, sweetie," he said. "And if you help me get it free, I'll give you a pretty little comb."

"Don't call me sweetie," she said. "And don't worry about giving me
20 no pretty little comb, neither. I'll free your old coconut, but just because I want to."

Then this extraordinary girl did something that made Davy's hair stand on end. She reached in a bag and took out a bunch of rattlesnakes. She tied all the wriggly critters together to make a long rope, and as she tied, she kept talking. "I'm not a shy little colt," she said. "And I'm not a little singing nightingale, neither. I can tote a steamboat on my back, outscream a panther, and jump over my own shadow. I can double up crocodiles any day, and I like to wear a hornets' nest for my Sunday bonnet."

30 As the girl looped the ends of her snake rope to the top of the branch that was trapping Davy, she kept bragging: "I'm a streak of lightning set up edgeways and buttered with quicksilver. I can outgrin, outsnort, outrun, outlift, outsneeze, outsleep, outlie any **varmint** from Maine to Louisiana. Furthermore, *sweetie,* I can blow out the moonlight and sing a wolf to sleep." Then she pulled on the other end of the snake rope so hard, it seemed as if she might tear the world apart. Ⓑ

The right-hand fork of that big tree bent just about double. Then Davy slid his head out as easy as you please. For a minute he was so dizzy, he couldn't tell up from down. But when he got everything going straight
40 again, he took a good look at that girl. "What's your name, ma'am?"

"Sally Ann Thunder Ann Whirlwind," she said. "But if you mind your manners, you can call me Sally."

From then on Davy Crockett was crazy in love with Sally Ann Thunder Ann Whirlwind. He asked everyone he knew about her, and everything he heard caused another one of Cupid's arrows to jab him in the gizzard.

"Oh, I know Sally!" the preacher said. "She can dance a rock to pieces and ride a panther bareback!"

"Sally's a good ole friend of mine," the blacksmith said. "Once I seen her crack a walnut with her front teeth."

50 "Sally's so very special," said the schoolmarm. "She likes to whip across the Salt River, using her apron for a sail and her left leg for a rudder!"

Sally Ann Thunder Ann Whirlwind had a reputation for being funny, too. Her best friend, Lucy, told Davy, "Sally can laugh the bark off a pine tree. She likes to whistle out one side of her mouth while she eats with the other side and grins with the middle!" Ⓒ

Ⓐ **VISUALIZE**
Reread lines 14–16. What words and phrases help you picture Sally in your mind?

② **Targeted Passage**

varmint (vär'mǐnt) *n.* a troublesome person or wild animal

Ⓑ **TALL TALES**
Reread lines 30–36. Notice the **metaphor** Sally uses to describe herself, as well as her other figures of speech. What is she saying about herself?

Ⓒ **TALL TALES**
Reread the peoples' descriptions of Sally, starting with what the preacher says in lines 46–47. Which of her qualities have been exaggerated for humor or emphasis?

DIFFERENTIATED INSTRUCTION

FOR LESS–PROFICIENT READERS

② **Targeted Passage [Lines 17–45]**

This passage develops the main character, Sally, and advances the plot when Davy falls in love with Sally.

- How does the girl respond to Davy at first?
- How does she rescue Davy?
- How does she describe herself?
- How does Davy feel after Sally has freed him? Why does he feel this way?

Reading Strategy Follow-Up: Visualize Have students reread lines 22–55. Ask them to sketch one of the images the words create for them. After students have completed their pictures, have them display their work to the class. Together, find the words and phrases in the text that match what each image shows.

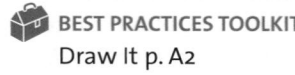

BEST PRACTICES TOOLKIT
Draw It p. A2

According to her friends, Sally could tame about anything in the world, too. They all told Davy about the time she was churning butter and heard something scratching outside. Suddenly the door swung open, and in walked the Great King Bear of the Mud Forest. He'd come to steal one of her smoked hams. Well, before the King Bear could say boo, Sally grabbed a warm dumpling from the pot and stuffed it in his mouth.

The dumpling tasted so good, the King Bear's eyes winked with tears. But then he started to think that Sally might taste pretty good, too. So opening and closing his big old mouth, he backed her right into a corner.

Sally was plenty scared, with her knees a-knocking and her heart a-hammering. But just as the King Bear blew his hot breath in her face, she gathered the courage to say, "Would you like to dance?"

Woman and Bear, © 1991 by Michael McCurdy. From *American Tall Tales* by Mary Pope Osborne. Used by permission of Alfred A. Knopf, an imprint of Random House Children's Books, a division of Random House, Inc.

Lines 56–67
DISCUSSION PROMPTS
Use these prompts to help students understand the reasons that Sally's friends tell stories about her:

Connect How would you feel about Sally if you were her friend? *Students might say that they would feel proud to have such an extraordinary friend who could do just about anything.*

Analyze Why do Sally's friends tell Davy stories such as the one involving the bear? *Possible answers: They want him to know how special she is. The stories are funny and amazing, so people enjoy telling them.*

Synthesize What do you think Davy realizes about Sally after he hears of the incident with the bear? *Possible answer: She is brave, quick-witted, and a good cook. Hearing about this incident might help him realize that she is the one for him.*

ANALYZE VISUALS

Activity Ask students how the impression of movement is created in this image. *Possible answer: The bear is kicking up his leg; Sally's feet aren't even touching the ground. Her pigtails are flying out from around her head.*

FOR ENGLISH LEARNERS

Vocabulary: Prefixes Explain that when *out* is used as a prefix, it means "in a way that goes beyond." Have Jigsaw groups define these words: *outscream* (line 27); *outgrin, outsnort* (line 32); *outrun, outlift, outsneeze, outsleep, outlie* (line 33). Help students understand the humor created by the use of these words.

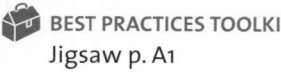 **BEST PRACTICES TOOLKIT**
    Jigsaw p. A1

Culture: Clarify Explain the setting of this tale. It takes place about 200 years ago in the region around the present states of Kentucky and Tennessee. At the time, those territories were still mostly wilderness without large towns, roads, or stores. People who lived in this part of the country needed to be self-reliant and strong. To create an understanding of the setting and the people who lived there, the author uses dialect, or a kind of language used in a certain region.

Vocabulary: Dialect The dialect used in this story includes slang, such as *coconut* (line 20); idioms, such as *made Davy's hair stand on end* (lines 22–23); expressions, such as *knees a-knocking* (line 65); and irregular sentence structures, such as *And don't worry about giving me no pretty little comb, neither* (lines 19–20). Have students work in pairs to find other examples of dialect. Use context clues to help them define the examples.

As everybody knows, no bear can resist an invitation to a square dance, so of course the old fellow forgot all about eating Sally and
70 said, "Love to." **D**

Then he bowed real pretty, and the two got to kicking and whooping and swinging each other through the air, as Sally sang:

> *We are on our way to Baltimore,*
> *With two behind, and two before:*
> *Around, around, around we go,*
> *Where oats, peas, beans, and barley grow!*

And while she was singing, Sally tied a string from the bear's ankle to her butter churn, so that all the time the old feller was kicking up his legs and dancing around the room, he was also churning her butter! **E**
80 And folks loved to tell the story about Sally's encounter with another stinky varmint—only this one was a *human* varmint. It seems that Mike Fink, the riverboat man, decided to scare the toenails off Sally because he was sick and tired of hearing Davy Crockett talk about how great she was.

One evening Mike crept into an old alligator skin and met Sally just as she was taking off to **forage** in the woods for berries. He spread open his

Woman Beating Up Man
© 1991 by Michael McCurdy. From *American Tall Tales* by Mary Pope Osborne. Used by permission of Alfred A. Knopf, an imprint of Random House Children's Books, a division of Random House, Inc.

D VISUALIZE

Have students record their answers in their chart from page 713. **Possible answers:**

- **Event:** *Sally's encounter with the bear*
- **Descriptive Words or Phrases:** *"opening and closing his big old mouth," "knees a-knocking," "heart a-hammering"*

LITERARY ANALYSIS

E TALL TALES

Possible answer: *Sally is presented as quick-thinking and practical. A real person in a dangerous situation would not worry about the butter, however, so this idea is an exaggeration.*

ANALYZE VISUALS

Activity Ask students which details in the picture match their mental image of this event. **Possible answer:** *The details that match include the fact that it is at night, Sally is in control of the situation, she has a basket in which she will put her berries, and she is just about to knock Mike Fink into the swamp.*

D VISUALIZE
Reread lines 65–70. Notice the details that help you visualize Sally as she talks with the bear. Which details help you picture this scene as a cartoon?

E TALL TALES
Reread lines 77–79. What can you **infer** about Sally's intelligence from her actions? How is Sally's intelligence exaggerated?

forage (fôr′ĭj) *v.* to search around for food or other supplies

---

DIFFERENTIATED INSTRUCTION

FOR LESS–PROFICIENT READERS
Concept Support Help students chart the characteristics of a tall tale found in "Sally Ann Thunder Ann Whirlwind."

Exaggeration	Larger-Than-Life Heroine	Setting of the American Frontier
She ties rattlesnakes together to make a rope.	She is as tall as a hickory sapling.	Davy Crockett is alone in the forest on his way to hunt bears.

FOR ADVANCED LEARNERS/PRE–AP
Draw Conclusions Tall tales grew out of the culture of the western frontier. Based on the tale, what are some of the problems that settlers faced as they moved west? Have small groups of students perform short role-plays in which they discuss the challenges of life on the frontier from the perspective of settlers.

gigantic mouth and made such a howl that he nearly scared himself to death. But Sally paid no more attention to that fool than she would have to a barking puppy dog.

However, when Mike put out his claws to embrace her, her anger rose
90 higher than a Mississippi flood. She threw a flash of eye lightning at him, turning the dark to daylight. Then she pulled out a little toothpick and with a single swing sent the alligator head flying fifty feet! And then to finish him off good, she rolled up her sleeves and knocked Mike Fink clear across the woods and into a muddy swamp. **F**

When the fool came to, Davy Crockett was standing over him. "What in the world happened to you, Mikey?" he asked.

"Well, I—I think I must-a been hit by some kind of wild alligator!" Mike stammered, rubbing his sore head.

Davy smiled, knowing full well it was Sally Ann Thunder Ann
100 Whirlwind just finished giving Mike Fink the only punishment he'd ever known.

That incident caused Cupid's final arrow to jab Davy's gizzard. "Sally's the whole steamboat," he said, meaning she was something great. The next day he put on his best raccoon hat and sallied forth[1] to see her.

When he got within three miles of her cabin, he began to holler her name. His voice was so loud, it whirled through the woods like a hurricane.

Sally looked out and saw the wind a-blowing and the trees a-bending. She heard her name a-thundering through the woods, and her heart
110 began to thump. By now she'd begun to feel that Davy Crockett was the whole steamboat, too. So she put on her best hat—an eagle's nest with a wildcat's tail for a feather—and ran outside. **G**

Just as she stepped out the door, Davy Crockett burst from the woods and jumped onto her porch as fast as a frog. "Sally, darlin'!" he cried. "I think my heart is bustin'! Want to be my wife?"

"Oh, my stars and possum dogs, why not?" she said.

From that day on, Davy Crockett had a hard time acting tough around Sally Ann Thunder Ann Whirlwind. His fightin' and hollerin' had no more effect on her than dropping feathers on a barn floor. At least that's
120 what *she'd* tell *you*. He might say something else. ❧

---

1. **sallied forth:** set out.

gigantic (jĭ-găn'tĭk) *adj.*
extremely large

F VISUALIZE
Reread lines 89–94.
Pay attention to the descriptive details in this passage. What do they help you see?

③ Targeted Passage

G TALL TALES
Reread lines 108–112.
Describe Sally's "best hat." Why is the hat so appropriate for a tall-tale heroine like Sally?

SALLY ANN THUNDER ANN WHIRLWIND   **719**

READING STRATEGY

F VISUALIZE
Remind students to use the details they have recorded in their charts. ***Possible answer:*** *Students will probably mention that they can see Sally's eyes flashing, the alligator's head flying, and Mike Fink soaring through the air and landing in a muddy swamp.*

LITERARY ANALYSIS

G TALL TALES
Possible answer: *Sally's hat is an "eagle's nest with a wildcat's tail for a feather." Students might say that since Sally is so big, strong, and daring, it makes sense that she would make a hat out of large and dangerous animals. They might also say that an oversized and ridiculous character should have oversized and ridiculous clothes as well.*

Extend the Discussion What is humorous about Sally's pausing to put on a hat?

Lines 113–120
**REINFORCE *KEY IDEA:*
COMPATIBILITY**

Discuss What kind of life will Davy and Sally have together? Does **compatibility** always lead to complete harmony? Explain. ***Possible answer:*** *Both characters are stubborn and strong. They are bound to clash at times. Compatibility does not guarantee total harmony. It ensures that there is enough common ground to overcome unimportant differences.*

SELECTION WRAP–UP

REFLECT Have students think about which traits of Sally's they admire. How would she fit into today's society?

★ CRITIQUE Ask students to evaluate the author's method of telling about Sally through hearsay—the stories of her friends. Ask students if they would have chosen a similar approach. Why or why not?

FOR LESS–PROFICIENT READERS
③ Targeted Passage [Lines 102–120]
This passage brings the story of Davy Crockett and Sally Ann Thunder Ann Whirlwind to a happy conclusion: they get married.

- What does Davy mean when he says that Sally is "the whole steamboat"?
- How does Sally respond to his proposal of marriage?
- How do you know that Davy has met his match in Sally?

FOR ADVANCED LEARNERS/PRE–AP
Synthesize Davy Crockett obviously feels that Sally is just the woman for him. Would all frontiersmen share his views? Have students reread **Background: An American Tradition** on page 713. Then ask them to write a paragraph in response to this question: *Is Sally the ideal frontier woman? Explain.* Invite students to share their paragraphs in small groups.

Practice and Apply

After Reading

For additional support of post-reading questions, use these copy masters:

RESOURCE MANAGER—Copy Masters
Reading Check p. 180 (to check under-standing of the selection)
Characteristics of Tall Tales p. 173 (for prac-tice of literary analysis standards focus)
Question Support p. 181 (**After Reading** questions adapted for English learners and less-proficient readers)

Additional selection questions are provided for teachers on page 167.

ANSWERS

Comprehension

1. *Davy meets Sally when she helps him free his head from a tree.*

2. *Sally ties a string to the bear so he will help her churn the butter while they dance.*

3. *Mike puts on an alligator skin and waits for Sally in the woods. Sally sees through Mike's trick and sends him flying into the swamp.*

Literary Analysis

Possible answers:

4. ● **STANDARDS FOCUS** *Characteristics of Tall Tales Sally is a typical tall-tale char-acter because she is larger than life. She is physically bigger, as well as braver and more clever than most people. Her appear-ance and actions are exaggerated and are meant to be humorous.*

5. ■ **STANDARDS FOCUS** *Visualize Students' sketches should be based on the details in their charts.*

6. *Davy and Sally make a good couple. Both are larger-than-life characters, and Davy appreciates all the qualities that make Sally unique.*
   - **Event:** *Davy hears that Sally can ride a panther, laugh the bark off a tree, and whip across the Salt River.* **Realization:** *Sally is funny, brave, and strong.*
   - **Event:** *Sally tricks the bear into churning her butter.* **Realization:** *She is quick-witted and courageous.*
   - **Event:** *Sally puts Mike Fink in his place.* **Realization:** *She is handy with her fists.*

Comprehension

1. **Recall** How does Davy Crockett meet Sally?

2. **Clarify** Why does Sally tie a string to the bear's ankle?

3. **Summarize** What happens when Mike Fink tries to scare Sally?

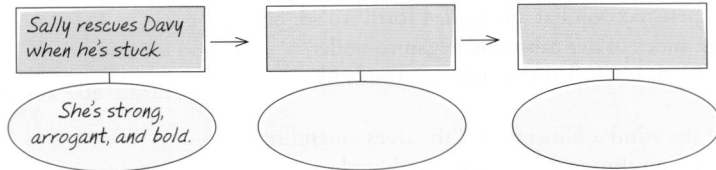

MARYLAND OBJECTIVES

LITERATURE STANDARD
3.A.3.a Distinguish among types of narrative texts

Literary Analysis

4. **Identify Characteristics of Tall Tales** In what ways is Sally a typical tall-tale character? Cite examples from the story.

5. **Visualize** Look at the visualizing chart you made as you read. Choose the character and event you can picture most clearly and sketch him, her, or it. Explain how the sketch reflects the notes in your chart.

6. **Evaluate Characters** Use a diagram to track the events that help Davy discover how **compatible** he and Sally are. For each event, note what Davy discovers about Sally. Are the characters a good couple? Why?

> Sally rescues Davy when he's stuck. → [ ] → [ ]
>
> She's strong, arrogant, and bold.   ( )   ( )

7. **Draw Conclusions** What would make Sally such an appealing character to early American settlers? Explain your answer.

Extension and Challenge

8. **Creative Project: Drama** In groups of two or three, select one of Sally's adventures and write it as a play. Act it out in front of the class. Pay close attention to the vivid and exaggerated details in each incident and find ways to include these details in your performance.

9. 🌐 **SOCIAL STUDIES CONNECTION** Davy Crockett and Mike Fink are examples of real people whose adventures were turned into tall tales. Research one or two of their real-life accomplishments. Do their real roles in the American West resemble the roles they play in "Sally Ann Thunder Ann Whirlwind"?

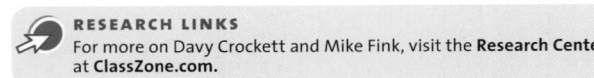

> **RESEARCH LINKS**
> For more on Davy Crockett and Mike Fink, visit the **Research Center** at **ClassZone.com.**

7. *Sally is good-hearted, fun-loving, and clever, which makes her an appealing character. Settlers might also have admired the way she deals with trouble and danger.*

Extension and Challenge

8. *Students' performances should include as many references to the tall tale as possible. Their plays should convey a strong sense of the exaggerations of Sally's character and should include dialogue that matches the style of conversation in the text.*

9. 🌐 **SOCIAL STUDIES CONNECTION**
Students' responses should give specific examples of how the exploits and character-istics of real-life Davy Crockett and Mike Fink match the fictional portrayal of each.

Vocabulary in Context

VOCABULARY PRACTICE

Choose the word from the list that best fits the context of each sentence.

1. We saw an ugly-looking _____ digging around in our yard.
2. It seemed to be trying to _____ for acorns.
3. Its tail was extremely long, and its snout was _____ too.
4. Please _____ him and laugh at his jokes.

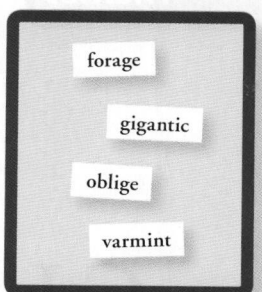

forage

gigantic

oblige

varmint

VOCABULARY IN WRITING

The exaggeration in this tall tale creates humor. Write several sentences that exaggerate the qualities of one or more of the characters. Use at least two of the vocabulary words. Here is an example.

> **EXAMPLE SENTENCE**
>
> Davy's hands were so **gigantic** that they looked like whole sides of beef.

VOCABULARY STRATEGY: DICTIONARY USAGE LABELS

Not all words are appropriate to use in all situations. For example, if you were to look up the vocabulary word *varmint* in a dictionary, you might find the usage label DIALECT at the beginning or end of the entry. This label lets you know that the word is used only in certain regions of the country.

Usage labels may apply to some or all senses of a word. If they relate to only one definition, they are put with that definition. Here are some other usage labels that dictionaries frequently use:

- ARCHAIC or OBSOLETE: a word or meaning that is rarely or never used anymore
- INFORMAL: a word or expression used in everyday speech and writing but not in formal situations
- SLANG: a word or expression that is appropriate in familiar talk with friends

PRACTICE Look up each term in a dictionary and note the usage label you find. If the label applies to only one definition, note that definition as well.

1. legit
2. wishy-washy
3. critter
4. anon
5. lazybones
6. ere

MARYLAND OBJECTIVES

READING STANDARD
1.D.3.c Use resources to gather information about words

VOCABULARY PRACTICE
For more practice, go to the **Vocabulary Center** at **ClassZone.com**.

ANSWERS

Vocabulary in Context

VOCABULARY PRACTICE

1. *varmint;* 2. *forage;* 3. *gigantic;* 4. *oblige*

R RESOURCE MANAGER—Copy Master
Vocabulary Practice p. 178

VOCABULARY IN WRITING

Have students use a Cluster Diagram to record exaggerated details about a character. Then have them decide which ideas might be expressed using the vocabulary words.

BEST PRACTICES TOOLKIT—Transparency
Cluster Diagram p. B18

VOCABULARY STRATEGY: DICTIONARY USAGE LABELS *(also an EL language objective)*

- Write the entry for *legit* on the board to show students where the label will be found.
- Have students work in pairs to look up each word.

Possible answers:

1. *slang*
2. *informal*
3. *informal*
4. *archaic: at once; forthwith*
5. *informal*
6. *archaic*

R RESOURCE MANAGER—Copy Master
Vocabulary Strategy p. 179

i Vocabulary Center at **ClassZone.com**
Additional Vocabulary Activities

Assess and Reteach

Assess

R RESOURCE MANAGER—Copy Masters
Selection Tests A, B/C pp. 183–184, 185–186

Test Generator CD

Reteach

S STANDARDS LESSON FILE
Reading Lesson 2: Monitoring
Vocabulary Lesson 24: Using Dictionaries and Glossaries

Focus and Motivate

OBJECTIVES

Literary Analysis
- explore the key idea of **contests**
- identify theme
- compare universal themes
- read fables

Reading
- set a purpose for reading

Grammar and Writing
- write a compare-contrast response paper
- use writing to analyze literature

SUMMARY

In the first fable, King Leopard decrees that whoever can throw a spear into the air and count to ten before it lands may marry his daughter. No one succeeds until the antelope counts by fives and wins. In the second fable, the toad outwits the donkey to win a 20-mile race. He positions his 20 children, who look just like him, along the mileposts so that they can trick the donkey into thinking that the toad is keeping up with him.

Would you rather be
C L E V E R *or strong?*

Discuss the question with students. Then discuss the *KEY IDEA.* Have students volunteer opinions about the advantages of being clever or being strong in a **contest.** Ask them to consider situations in which a person would have to have one quality or the other. Then have students complete the *QUICKWRITE* and share their responses in small groups.

Selection Resources

Two Ways to Count to Ten
Liberian Fable Retold by Frances Carpenter

The Race Between Toad and Donkey
Jamaican Fable Retold by Roger D. Abrahams

Would you rather be
CLEVER *or strong?*

MARYLAND OBJECTIVES

READING/LIT STANDARDS
1.E.3.a Select and apply appropriate strategies during reading
3.A.6.b Analyze themes across multiple texts

KEY IDEA In every society, athletes come together to try to outrun, outthrow, and outjump one another. When it comes to sports, strength and speed seem to be the point of the game. Can sheer brainpower ever be enough to win such **contests?** The fables you're about to read explore this question.

QUICKWRITE Put yourself in the place of a professional athlete. What would you say it takes to win a championship? Spend a few minutes writing down what you think an athlete might say. Would the manager or coach of the team have the same answer?

722

RESOURCE MANAGER UNIT 6

Plan and Teach pp. 187–194

Literary Analysis
Summary pp. 195†*,196‡*; 201*, 202‡*
Question Support pp. 200*; 204*

Reading
Set a Purpose for Reading pp. 197, 198†*
Reading Check pp. 199; 203

Grammar and Writing
Writing for Assessment p. 205

Assessment
Selection Tests A, B/C
   pp. 207*, 209*
Test Generator CD

BEST PRACTICES TOOLKIT

Differentiated Instruction
   pp. 31–38*

Scaffolding Instruction pp. 43–46*

Graphic Organizers/Strategies
Reciprocal Teaching • New Word Analysis

Reading Support
Audio Anthology CD*

Technology
Literature and Vocabulary Centers at **ClassZone.com**
Write*Smart* CD

---

* Resources for Differentiation   † Also in Spanish   ‡ In Haitian Creole and Vietnamese

LITERARY ANALYSIS: UNIVERSAL THEME

Throughout the world, people speak different languages and have different customs—yet some feelings and experiences are remarkably similar. The selections you're about to read reflect this. They come from different continents but offer a similar **theme,** or message about life. To identify this theme, pay attention to

- the characters and what traits they represent
- the contests
- who wins the contests
- how they win

When a theme appears in the literature of many cultures across many time periods, it's called a **universal theme. Fables,** which are brief stories that teach a lesson, often contain such themes. As you read these two fables, notice that while they share the same universal theme, their stories are not identical. Each expresses the theme in its own way.

READING STRATEGY: SET A PURPOSE FOR READING

When you **set a purpose for reading,** you choose specific reasons for reading one or more works. Your purpose for reading "Two Ways to Count to Ten" and "The Race Between Toad and Donkey" is to identify the universal theme and to find similarities and differences in how the fables express it. As you read the first fable, begin filling in a chart like the one shown.

	"Two Ways to Count to Ten"	"The Race Between Toad and Donkey"
Who are the characters?		
What is the contest and who declares it?		
Who wins the contest? How?		
What do the characters learn?		

Author Online

Francis Carpenter: World Traveler
When Frances Carpenter was young, she and her family traversed the world. Africa, where her geographer father traveled for work, was one of their destinations.

Frances Carpenter
1890–1972

Carpenter used the information gained on these trips in her writing.

Roger D. Abrahams: Legendary Folklorist
Professor Roger D. Abrahams is one of the most respected scholars in the world of folklore. He has written many books about

Roger D. Abrahams
born 1933

the folk tales and legends of Africans and African Americans.

Living Traditions One place Abrahams collected folk tales is Jamaica. This island nation in the West Indies is home to a rich cultural tradition. Many Jamaicans are descendants of enslaved Africans who were taken to the island to work on plantations. The Africans brought their music, stories, and way of life with them. Jamaican life continues to reflect an African influence.

 MORE ABOUT THE AUTHOR
For more on the authors, visit the **Literature Center** at ClassZone.com.

723

Teach

STANDARDS FOCUS

LITERARY ANALYSIS

● UNIVERSAL THEME

Read this example aloud:

> The muscles of the first three contestants rippled and strained as they tried to lift the huge boulder. The rock remained solidly in place. Finally, a frail-looking youth took his turn. Using a lever, he raised the rock just high enough off the ground to collect the prize certificate underneath it. He was soon on his way to the judges' table.

Ask students to express the theme.
Possible answer: Winners are those who use their brains, not their muscles.

CHECK UNDERSTANDING Have students explain how the theme is revealed in the passage above.

READING STRATEGY

■ SET A PURPOSE FOR READING

Suggest that students write this question on a bookmark to stay focused: *What is the theme?*

CHECK UNDERSTANDING Have students read **Author Online** for the purpose of comparing the backgrounds of the two authors.

 RESOURCE MANAGER—Copy Master
Set a Purpose for Reading p. 197 (for student use while reading the fables)

DIFFERENTIATED INSTRUCTION

FOR LESS–PROFICIENT READERS

In combination with the *Audio Anthology CD,* use one or more Targeted Passages (pp. 726, 728, 730, 732, 733) to ensure that students focus on key story events, concepts, and skills.

FOR ENGLISH LEARNERS

Options for Reading Establish the context of each tale by reading the first pages aloud. Then have students either use a Reciprocal Teaching strategy for the remainder of each story or follow along with the *Audio Anthology CD.*

Key Academic Vocabulary Use New Word Analysis to provide instruction and practice for the word *indicate* (line 13) in the second fable.

 BEST PRACTICES TOOLKIT—Transparencies
Reciprocal Teaching p. A35
New Word Analysis p. E8

Prereading For prereading instruction for English learners, see

 BEST PRACTICES TOOLKIT
Scaffolding Reading Instruction pp. 43–46

FOR ADVANCED LEARNERS/PRE–AP

Pre-AP exercises in the bottom channel provide additional challenge for your advanced students. Use them for small groups or individuals.

ADDITIONAL GUIDELINES
For more help with differentiation and tips for classroom management, see

 BEST PRACTICES TOOLKIT
Differentiated Instruction pp. 31–38

LITERARY ANALYSIS

A UNIVERSAL THEME

Possible answer: The setting is a village in Liberia. The villagers are gathering in the Palaver House to listen to the storyteller, who has just arrived.

ANALYZE VISUALS

Possible answer: The spear that the antelope is holding and the garment he is wearing make him appear dignified and strong. His direct gaze makes him seem wise.

Two
Ways to Count to
Ten

Retold by
Frances Carpenter

"Old Tanko has come! The Teller of Good Tales is here!"
The news spread quickly through the Liberian village and in the faraway back country. Men, women, and children came running to the Palaver House, the big "talky-talk" hut which had room for them all. **A**

Everyone in that village knew Old Tanko, the Teller of Good Tales. Everyone there enjoyed his exciting stories. Whenever he wandered into their cluster of grass-roofed huts, they made him welcome.

"Ai, I'll sing you a story," Tanko said that day when he had finished the bowl of soup they set before him. "It will be a strange tale from the long
10 ago." He arranged his white robe and settled himself cross-legged on the earth floor.

The old man placed a very small gourd drum in his lap. And with his bony brown fingers, he began to tap lightly, lightly upon it.

"I had this tale from my grandfather," he began. "He, too, was a great teller of tales."

"What will the tale say to us, Tanko?" The headman of the village was speaking. He had squatted down on the ground, close to the old man.

"It will say there is more than one way to count to ten. It will also tell how, if you can guess the right way, you can even get yourself a king's
20 daughter for your wife."

The people in the talky-talk house nodded to one another. They smiled. It was as if they were thinking, "This will be another good tale." But no one spoke. In silence, they waited for Old Tanko to tell his story.

A UNIVERSAL THEME
What is the **setting** of this fable?

ANALYZE VISUALS
The animals in this tale are **personified,** or given human characteristics. What human traits are suggested by this picture of the antelope?

DIFFERENTIATED INSTRUCTION

FOR ALL STUDENTS
Enhancing Learning Styles Provide independent projects for various learning styles.

- **Analytical** Devise contests to test cleverness.
- **Kinesthetic** Role play characters.
- **Interpersonal** Compare versions of the same tale in small groups.

For further details on these projects, see

R **RESOURCE MANAGER**
Ideas for Extension pp. 192–193

FOR LESS–PROFICIENT READERS
Reading Support

- Explain that this fable is a story within a story. It begins in the narrative present and returns to this time frame at the end. In between, the setting shifts to long ago.
- Point out the extra line spacing that shows the transition from the outer story events to the tale and then back (between lines 25 and 26 and lines 140 and 141).
- Have students look for other clues that indicate the shift, such as transitional words.

BACKGROUND

African Storytellers In the past, storytellers like Old Tanko held essential roles in African life. They preserved the culture's stories, advised the king, passed down the history and lineage of the people, and spread important news.

Palaver House The villagers in the first tale gather in the "Palaver House" (line 4). This refers to a simple structure in the middle of the village in which business is taken care of or meetings are held. The term *palaver* used to refer to negotiations between Europeans and local Africans.

The little drum on the old man's knees soon began to whisper. "Tap! Tap! Tap-tap-tap!" And Tanko in his soft singing voice told this strange tale.

I n the long, long ago, animals were not so different, one from the other. Oh, they had different shapes, just as they do today. But they lived together in friendship and peace. Like people, those of one animal tribe sometimes took their wives from those of a different tribe. Like you
30 and me, in those times beasts could talk. And, like people, they had a king to rule over them.

In the place of this story, the leopard was king. Rich he was, beyond telling. Mighty was he in his power over the other beasts. All the animals obeyed him.

"Whom shall I name to rule after me when I shall die?" King Leopard said one day to his pretty daughter. "I must find one who is wise enough so that he can rule well. Yes, my dear daughter, I must seek out the cleverest beast in our jungle land. I shall make him a prince. He shall have you for his bride. And to me he shall be a son."

40 King Leopard was pleased with his idea, and he planned a great feast. His royal drums carried word of it far and wide through the jungle. And all the animals came.

There were good things to eat. There was plenty to drink. The drums beat. And the guests at King Leopard's feast danced for three days.

At last the king called them to make a huge circle. Stepping into its center, he called his pretty daughter to come to his side. Then he spoke in a loud voice.

"Listen to my words, friends!" he cried. "Someday I must die. Someday another king must rule in my place. I will choose him now from among
50 you, so that he will be ready."

There was a murmur of wonder all through the crowd. The King had to order them to be quiet.

"I shall seek the cleverest among you, for your king must be wise. I shall name him Prince. He shall be to me a son and to my dear daughter a husband. He shall share all my riches. And when I die he shall be your king."

Shouts came from the eager guests at the King's feast. No doubt each animal hoped that the good fortune would be his.

Then King Leopard held up his hunting spear. "Look at this, my
60 people! Watch!" And he flung the spear far up into the air.

"With this spear will I test you," he went on. "He who would be our prince must throw the spear toward the sky. He must send it so high that he can count to ten before it drops down to earth again." **B**

SOCIAL STUDIES CONNECTION

Liberia, a country on the west coast of Africa is home to rain forests filled with elephants, chimpanzees, bush oxen, and antelopes. Leopards, once common there, are in danger of disappearing.

1 Targeted Passage

B UNIVERSAL THEME
Why is King Leopard setting up a contest? In your chart, write down how the contest works.

SOCIAL STUDIES CONNECTION

Liberia In 1821, American officials obtained property on the western coast of Africa to provide a home for freed slaves from the United States. A number of settlements were established, as well as a government, laws, and trade. This territory became known as Liberia, and it was declared an independent republic in 1847.

LITERARY ANALYSIS

B UNIVERSAL THEME

Record students' responses in the chart from page 723. *Possible answers:*

	"Two Ways to Count to Ten"
Who are the characters?	Old Tanko, King Leopard, his daughter,...
What is the contest and who declares it?	King Leopard declares a contest to decide who will marry his daughter. The successful contestant must throw a spear in the air and count to ten before it lands.

Extend the Discussion What does King Leopard's plan reveal about his character?

Lines 61–63
REINFORCE *KEY IDEA:* CONTESTS

Discuss What abilities seem to be required in order to win this **contest?** Explain. *Possible answer: To win the contest, it would seem that the person must be strong, quick, and coordinated.*

DIFFERENTIATED INSTRUCTION

FOR LESS–PROFICIENT READERS
1 Targeted Passage [Lines 48–63]

This passage identifies the basic conflict of the plot: the heir to the throne must first win a contest.

- Why has King Leopard decided to hold a contest?
- What must the contestants do, and what will the winner get?
- What is the contest designed to show, according to the King?

FOR ADVANCED LEARNERS/PRE–AP
Evaluate What does cleverness have to do with throwing a spear in the air and counting to ten? Although the King says that he wants his cleverest subject to win the hand of his daughter, the contest does not appear to test this quality. Does the King know what he is doing or not? Ask students to form an opinion and defend it in an informal class debate.

There was a buzz of talk among all the animals then. This would not be so hard to do, they thought.

One after another, they came forward to try their skill. Each jungle beast danced before King Leopard and his pretty daughter. Each one sang a song that told how well he would rule, if he were chosen.

First to try his luck was the elephant. He was so big that he could push all the other beasts out of his way.

"I must be first," he said to himself. "This task is too easy. Almost any one of us can do it."

The elephant danced clumsily. He was very big and his body was heavy. Then, with his trunk in the air, he trumpeted all the fine deeds he would perform if he were prince. **C**

The great beast threw King Leopard's spear up into the air.

"One! Two! Three!" he began counting. But he spoke slowly, as he did everything else. An elephant cannot easily hurry, you know.

Before the elephant had said, "Four!" the King's spear had dropped to earth. The proud beast hung his head so low that the tip of his trunk dragged on the ground. He knew he had failed.

Next came the bush ox. His wide gray horns swept the other beasts to the side.

"I'll throw the spear up to the sun," the huge animal sang while he danced. "I'll be a strong husband for King Leopard's daughter." **D**

The bush ox picked the spear up in his mouth. With a mighty toss of his great head, he flung it far, far above his spreading horns.

"One! Two! Three! Four!" the bush ox counted more quickly than the elephant. But he, too, was slow. Before he could say "Five," the spear was down on the ground. He went off, ashamed, into the deep jungle.

The chimpanzee was third. He jumped up and down in a merry dance, and King Leopard's daughter laughed at his antics. He beat his hairy chest with his two fists, and he sang of how much he would like to be king in the leopard's place.

The young ape rose up straight on his hind legs. He held the spear in one hand, just like a man. With a twist of his long arm, he threw it up toward the sky.

"One-two-three-four-five-six-seven!" He chattered as fast as he could. The watching animals held their breaths. Surely, with such a quick tongue, the chimpanzee would make the count.

But he did not! He had not even said, "Eight!" before he had caught the spear once more in his hand.

One by one, other animals tried to count to ten while the spear was still up in the air. One by one, they all failed.

C UNIVERSAL THEME
In fables, animal characters often represent human traits. What trait might the elephant represent?

D UNIVERSAL THEME
Why does the bush ox think he would make a good husband?

TWO WAYS TO COUNT TO TEN   **727**

FOR LESS–PROFICIENT READERS

Comprehension Support Help students understand the emergence of theme by having them complete this chart.

- Point out that adjectives describing each contestant give clues to the trait he represents.
- Discuss how each outcome moves closer to success.
- Draw some conclusions about the results so far.

Character	Trait	Outcome
elephant	power	counts to three
bush ox		counts to four
chimpanzee	agility/speed	

LITERARY ANALYSIS

C UNIVERSAL THEME

Possible answer: The elephant might represent power.

If students need help ... Have them reread lines 69–75 and list the adjectives and other details that describe the elephant. Draw inferences from these clues.

LITERARY ANALYSIS

D UNIVERSAL THEME

Possible answer: The bush ox thinks he will be a strong husband for the king's daughter.

Extend the Discussion What are some other folktales that have a similar universal theme?

Lines 77–102
DISCUSSION PROMPTS

Use these prompts to help students predict the results of the contest:

Interpret What does the failure of the elephant and the bush ox suggest about the relationship of strength to success in this contest? *Possible answer: Strength does not seem to be required for success.*

Analyze Why is the contest harder than it seems? *Possible answer: The spear must soar very high in order to allow enough time to count to ten, but no matter how strong the animal is, it appears impossible to do.*

Synthesize Using the title as a clue, how might it be possible to win? *Possible answer: There might be a different and quicker way to count to ten.*

Lines 103–104
REINFORCE *KEY IDEA*: CONTESTS

Discuss What makes a good **contest**? Does this one qualify? *Possible answer: A good contest may be hard, but it should allow real talent and wit to succeed. Using these criteria, this contest seems to be a good one.*

ⓔ UNIVERSAL THEME

Possible answer: The other animals laugh because the antelope is delicate and appears too weak to throw the spear higher than they can, which is what they think he will have to do.

ⓕ UNIVERSAL THEME

Possible answer: King Leopard is just. He does not allow prejudice about the antelope's abilities to keep the antelope out of the contest.

Lines 131–140
DISCUSSION PROMPTS

Use these prompts to help students understand the significance of the contest's outcome:

Connect Did you guess what the antelope would do? What do you think of his strategy? *Students may or may not have guessed what the antelope would do. In either case, they may agree that it is a clever strategy.*

Analyze What qualities of the antelope, in addition to cleverness, are shown by his success? *Possible answer: He is also courageous, imaginative, and daring.*

Evaluate Do you think the king was outwitted? Explain. *Possible answer: The king wanted to test cleverness, so it would seem that he hoped someone might come up with a solution like this.*

SELECTION WRAP–UP

REFLECT Have students think about the lessons that this fable teaches in addition to the theme stated at the end.

⭐ **CRITIQUE** Have students evaluate the choice of the antelope as the animal to win the contest. Ask them what animal they would have chosen and why.

"It seems I must look somewhere else for a prince to rule when I am gone," King Leopard spoke sadly.

Then out from the crowd stepped an antelope.

Beside the elephant, the bush ox, and even the chimpanzee, the young deerlike antelope seemed puny and weak. His legs were long, yet so
110 slender that it was almost a wonder that they would hold up his body. But the antelope spoke bravely.

"Let me try to throw your spear, O King," he cried. "I would like well to marry your pretty daughter."

"Ho! Ho!" The other animals burst into laughter. How could such a weak creature fling the King's spear high enough to say more than two or three words? However could he hope to count up to ten? **ⓔ**

But the antelope would not be turned aside.

"I wish to try," he insisted. And King Leopard nodded his head. He had promised a fair trial for all who wished to take part in this contest.
120 "Who can say what any creature can do until he has tried?" The King spoke to the crowd. "The antelope may throw the spear." So the other beasts were moved back to give him room. **ⓕ**

When the antelope, on his slender legs, danced before the King, the leopard's daughter cried out with pleasure. No one could deny that his steps were more graceful than those of the elephant, or of the bush ox, or the chimpanzee.

Then the antelope threw the spear. With a toss of his head, he flung it far up into the air. Before it could fall to earth, the clever beast called out two words. "Five! Ten!" he cried. "I have counted to ten. King Leopard
130 did not say how the count should be made."

② Targeted Passage

ⓔ UNIVERSAL THEME
Why do the other animals laugh at the antelope?

ⓕ UNIVERSAL THEME
Reread lines 118–122. What do you learn about King Leopard based on his treatment of the antelope?

The leopard laughed then. He nodded his royal head.

"No, I did not say how the count was to be made," he agreed. "And as everyone knows, one can count by fives as well as by ones. The antelope has won the contest. He has proved he is the cleverest of you all. He shall wed my dear daughter. He shall be king when I am gone."

The other animals stared stupidly at the winner. They did not understand yet what had happened. But they could see that the antelope had outwitted the King.

At the wedding feast that King Leopard gave for his daughter, they all
140 cheered for the antelope, their new prince.

Old Tanko put his drum down in his lap.
"Remember this tale, friends," he said to the crowd in the talky-talk hut. "Do not forget that it is not always the biggest nor the strongest, but sometimes the cleverest who wins the prize." ꙮ

DIFFERENTIATED INSTRUCTION

FOR LESS–PROFICIENT READERS

② Targeted Passage [Lines 108–130]

This passage presents the climax of the tale: the antelope steps up and wins the contest.

- How is the antelope different from the other animals that have entered the contest? What is the general opinion about his chance of success?
- How does the antelope count to ten?
- What does the antelope's method of counting show about him?

Comprehension: Clarify Explain that "count by fives" (line 133) refers to the fact that any number that can be divided evenly into another number can be used to count up to the higher figure. For example, there are really three ways to count to ten: by one at a time, two at a time, or five at a time. Have students identify all the ways that might be used to count up to numbers such as 12, 16, or 20.

omprehension

1. **Recall** To whom does Old Tanko tell the fable?

2. **Clarify** Why does King Leopard want a clever husband for his daughter? Describe the contest he creates to find the husband.

3. **Summarize** Summarize what happens when each of the following animals competes: the elephant, the bush ox, the chimpanzee, and the antelope.

terary Analysis

4. **Analyze Characters** Which character in the fable do you think represents wisdom, or good judgment? Which character represents cleverness, or quick, original thinking? Cite evidence from the fable to support your answer.

5. **Identify Theme** Sometimes the theme of a selection must be inferred. Other times, as with this selection, the theme is directly stated. What lines state the theme? Restate the theme in your own words.

6. **Make Judgments** Was King Leopard's contest a good way to find the next king? Explain why.

omparing Universal Themes

Finish filling in the chart column under "Two Ways to Count to Ten." Add information that helped you understand how the fable expresses its theme.

	"Two Ways to Count to Ten"	"The Race Between Toad and Donkey"
Who are the characters?	Old Tanko, King Leopard, King Leopard's daughter, the elephant, the bush ox, the chimpanzee, and the antelope	
What is the contest and who declares it?		
Who wins the contest? How?		
What do the characters learn?		

MARYLAND OBJECTIVES

LITERATURE STANDARD
3.A.6.b Analyze themes across multiple texts

Comparing Universal Themes

■ **STANDARDS FOCUS** *Set a Purpose for Reading*

	"Two Ways to Count to Ten"
Who are the characters?	Old Tanko, King Leopard, King Leopard's daughter, the elephant, the bush ox, the chimpanzee, the antelope
What is the contest and who declares it?	King Leopard declares a contest to decide who will marry his daughter. The successful contestant must throw a spear in the air and count to ten before it lands.
Who wins the contest? How?	The antelope wins the contest. He counts by fives.
What do the characters learn?	The characters learn that it is not always the strongest or the biggest who wins the prize. Sometimes it is the cleverest.

Practice and Apply

After Reading

For additional support of post-reading questions, use these copy masters:

R **RESOURCE MANAGER—Copy Masters**
Reading Check p. 199 (to check understanding of the selection)
Question Support p. 200 (**After Reading** questions adapted for English learners and less-proficient readers)

Additional selection questions are provided for teachers on page 191.

ANSWERS

Comprehension

1. *Old Tanko tells the tale to the villagers.*

2. *Because his daughter's husband will be king, he decides to test the cleverness of possible suitors by having them throw a spear in the air and count to ten before it lands.*

3. *The elephant, the bush ox, and the chimpanzee cannot count to ten fast enough; the spear falls to the ground first. The antelope wins the contest because he counts by fives.*

Literary Analysis

Possible answers:

4. *King Leopard represents wisdom. He knows that a clever king is needed to succeed him (lines 36–38) and plans accordingly, instead of leaving his succession to chance. He shows his wisdom by allowing anyone to take a chance. The antelope is the cleverest. He figures out a way to win the contest.*

5. ● **STANDARDS FOCUS** *Universal Theme* *The theme is stated in lines 143–144. It might be restated as "Brains will win out over brawn."*

6. *Yes. To win the contest, an animal has to have some strength but, more importantly, must be clever, imaginative, daring, and bold—all qualities that a king should have.*

ANALYZE VISUALS

Possible answer: The donkey seems to have a quizzical look on his face, whereas the toad appears to be thinking. Therefore, the toad seems to be the smarter one.

LITERARY ANALYSIS

Ⓐ UNIVERSAL THEME

Possible answer: Donkey knows that his legs are much longer than Toad's. He cannot imagine that the toad has any chance against him.

The RACE Between TOAD and DONKEY

Retold by
Roger D. Abrahams

Ⓞne day, Master King decided to have a race and he would give a big prize to whoever won. Both Toad and Donkey decided to enter, but Toad got Donkey angry with all his boasting about how he'd win.

Now, the race was to be for twenty miles. So when Donkey looked at Toad he wondered out loud how any animal so small and powerless could hope to keep up with him. "I have very long legs, you know, as well as long ears and tail. Just measure our legs, and you'll see why you can't possibly hope to win this race." But Toad was stubborn—and he was smart, too—and he said that he was going to win the race. That just got
10 Donkey more vexed. Ⓐ

❸ Targeted Passage

ANALYZE VISUALS
On the basis of this image, which character would you **infer** is the cleverer of the two? Why?

Ⓐ UNIVERSAL THEME
Note the character who will compete with Donkey. Why does Donkey think he'll win the race?

DIFFERENTIATED INSTRUCTION

FOR LESS–PROFICIENT READERS

❸ Targeted Passage [Lines 1–10]

This passage introduces the major conflict of the story: Donkey and Toad will compete against each other in a race.

- What is the contest in this fable? Who is competing in the contest?
- How does Toad see his chances of winning?
- Why does Donkey expect to win the race?
- How might Toad win the race, even with his short legs?

FOR ENGLISH LEARNERS

Culture: Connect After students have read the first page, they may recognize a familiar plot. The idea of a race being run between two completely dissimilar opponents is found in many stories. Invite students to tell versions of this story that they know.

FOR ADVANCED LEARNERS/PRE–AP

Synthesize Why are stories about contests so popular? Have students brainstorm folk tales, fables, myths, and legends in which a contest is the central event. Have students list each story and name the culture with which it is associated. Have students discuss reasons why many different cultures around the world have stories that are so similar.

732 UNIT 6: MYTHS, LEGENDS, AND TALES

LITERARY ANALYSIS

B UNIVERSAL THEME

Possible answer: Donkey calls Toad a "tricki-fying creature" (line 19). He is afraid that if Toad is given more time he will think of a plan that will help him win.

If students need help . . . Have students use context clues and word parts to define the nonstandard word *trickifying* in line 19.

LITERARY ANALYSIS

C UNIVERSAL THEME

Possible answer: Toad places one of his 20 children at every milepost. They look just like Toad and will make everyone think that Toad is keeping up with Donkey.

Lines 26–30
REINFORCE *KEY IDEA:* CONTESTS

Discuss Does Donkey have the right attitude as he enters the **contest?** Explain. *Possible answer: No. He is not planning to do his best, but thinks he can take his time.*

Lines 31–40
DISCUSSION PROMPTS

Use these prompts to help students understand the ingenuity of Toad's plan:

Connect If you were Donkey, how would you feel at the second milepost? Why? *Students might say that they would be really surprised that Toad had arrived at the same time. They might even begin to worry a bit.*

Analyze What fact is Toad counting on to make his plan successful? *Possible answer: He is counting on the fact that Donkey cannot tell one toad from another.*

Synthesize How do you think the race will end? *Possible answers: It might end with the final toad popping out at mile 20 and claiming victory. Or, Donkey might exhaust himself along the way and fail to finish.*

So Donkey told the king that he was ready to start, but the king said that he had to make the rules first. At each mile every racer had to sing out to indicate he had gotten that far—for the king wanted to know what was happening in the race, you know.

Now Toad is a smart little fellow, and he said to the king that he needed a little time to take care of business, so would he let him have a day or two. And the king said to the two of them, "You must come here first thing tomorrow." Donkey objected, for he knew that Toad was a very trickifying creature, but the king wouldn't listen. **B**

20   Now the toad had twenty children, and they all looked exactly alike. And while Donkey was sleeping, Toad took his twenty children along the racing ground, and at every milepost Toad left one of them. He told them that they must listen for Mr. Donkey, and whenever they heard him cry out, they should do so too. And Toad hid one of his children there behind each of those mileposts. **C**

So the race began the next day. Donkey looked around, and he was so sure in his heart that he was going to beat Toad that he sucked his teeth, *Tche,* to show everyone there how little he thought of Toad. "That little bit of a fellow Toad can't keep up with me. I'll even have a little time to 30   eat some grass along the way. *Tche.*"

So he just went a little way down the road and he stopped and ate some grass. He poked his head through the fence where he saw some good-looking sweet-potato tops and had a taste of some gungo peas. He took more than an hour to get to the first milepost. And as he got there, he bawled out, "Ha, ha, I'm better than Toad." And the first child heard this, and he called, like all toads do:

Jin-ko-ro-ro, Jin-kok-kok-kok.

The sound really surprised Donkey, who of course thought he had gotten there first. Then he thought, "I delayed too long eating that grass. I must 40   run quicker this next mile." So he set off with greater speed, this time stopping only for a minute to drink some water along the way. And as he got to the next post, he bawled out:

Ha! Ha! Ha! I'm better than Toad.

And then the second child called out:

Jin-ko-ro-ro, Jin-kok-kok-kok.

732   UNIT 6: MYTHS, LEGENDS, AND TALES

B UNIVERSAL THEME
Why does Donkey object to Toad's request for more time?

4 Targeted Passage

C UNIVERSAL THEME
How does Toad plan to win the race? As you read, notice how Toad's plan affects Donkey.

DIFFERENTIATED INSTRUCTION

FOR ENGLISH LEARNERS

Comprehension: Cause and Effect Use a diagram such as this one to help students track the effect of Toad's strategy on Donkey.

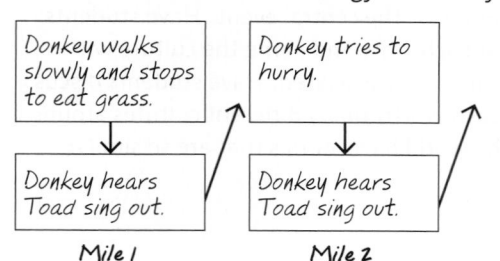

Donkey walks slowly and stops to eat grass. → Donkey hears Toad sing out. *Mile 1* → Donkey tries to hurry. → Donkey hears Toad sing out. *Mile 2*

FOR LESS–PROFICIENT READERS

4 Targeted Passage [Lines 20–25]

This passage explains how Toad plans to win the race: he has his children stand in for him at different mileposts.

• How does the fact that all of Toad's children look alike help Toad's plan?

• What is Toad's purpose in placing each of his children at a milepost?

And Donkey said, "Lord, Toad can really move, for sure. Never mind, there are a lot more miles." So he started, and when he reached the third milepost, he bawled:

Ha! Ha! Ha! I'm better than Toad.

60 And the third child sang:

Jin-ko-ro-ro, Jin-kok-kok-kok.

Now Donkey got very angry when he heard Toad answer him, and he started to smash the toad, but Toad, being a little fellow, hid himself in the grass.

Donkey was then determined to get to the next milepost before Toad, and he took his tail and he switched it like a horsewhip and he began to gallop. And he got to the fourth milepost and he bawled:

Ha! Ha! Ha! I'm better than Toad.

And out came the answer from the fourth child.

When he heard that, he stood there and began to tremble, and he said, "My goodness, what am I going to do? I'm going to have to run so fast I really kick that hard, hard dirt." And he galloped off faster than he ever had before, until he reached the fifth milepost. And now he was very tired, and out of breath. He just barely had enough wind to bawl:

Ha! Ha! Ha! I'm better than Toad.

And then he heard:

Jin-ko-ro-ro, Jin-kok-kok-kok.

This time he was really angry, and he raced on harder than ever. But at each milepost he bawled out the same thing, and at each he heard the same answer. And Donkey got so sad in his mind that he just gave up after a while, sad because he knew he had lost that race.

So through Toad's smartness, Donkey can never be a racer again. **D**
Jack Mandora me no choose one.[1] ~

---

1. **Jack Mandora me no choose one:** Traditionally, Jamaican storytellers make this statement at the end of a tale. In Creole, it means "Don't blame me for the story I've just told."

THE RACE BETWEEN TOAD AND DONKEY   **733**

SOCIAL STUDIES CONNECTION

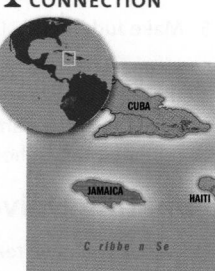

Many Jamaicans speak Creole, which combines elements of English, Spanish, French, and a variety of African languages.

5 Targeted Passage

D UNIVERSAL THEME
Draw a **conclusion** about the lesson or theme of the fable.

SOCIAL STUDIES CONNECTION

Jamaica Some characteristics of Jamaican Creole include dropping the first consonant sound of certain words, such as those beginning with *h*, and pronouncing *th* as *t*, *c* as *cy*, and *v* as *b*. One difficulty with someone trying to learn the language is that there is no standard written form because it is not a recognized dialect. English is still the official language on the island.

LITERARY ANALYSIS

D UNIVERSAL THEME

Remind students to record the theme in their charts. ***Possible answer:*** *It is hard to beat someone who is smarter.*

Extend the Discussion Does this fable send a mixed message? Explain.

SELECTION WRAP—UP

REFLECT Have students think about whether there are any other ways that Toad could have won the race honestly. If not, what should he have done?

⭐ **CRITIQUE** Have students evaluate whether the ending is satisfying. Ask them how they might have concluded the story.

FOR LESS—PROFICIENT READERS

5 Targeted Passage [Lines 60–71]

This passage presents the conclusion of the race: Donkey gives up.

• What does Donkey believe when he hears the toad's call each time?

• How does Donkey respond when he hears Toad's children call out?

• How does Donkey finally lose the race?

Reading Strategy Follow-Up: Set a Purpose for Reading

• Have pairs return to these passages and find the answers to the questions on their chart from page 723: lines 1–14, 20–25, and 60–71.

• Ask students to fill in or revise their chart responses based on their rereading. Have pairs share their details with the class.

FOR ADVANCED LEARNERS/PRE—AP

Make Judgments Does Toad level the playing field, or does he cheat? Have students write an editorial defending or condemning Toad's actions. Ask them to support their ideas with facts, reasons, and examples. Have students present their editorials to the class and invite other students to share their opinions.

Practice and Apply

After Reading

For additional support of post-reading questions, use these copy masters:

 RESOURCE MANAGER—Copy Masters

Reading Check p. 203 (to check understanding of the selection)

Question Support p. 204 (**After Reading** questions adapted for English learners and less-proficient readers)

Additional selection questions are provided for teachers on page 191.

ANSWERS

Comprehension

1. *The race is 20 miles long. At each mile, each racer must sing out to show his progress.*

2. *Toad's children are placed at each milepost. On the day of the race, they sing out at the correct time.*

3. *Students' portraits should show Donkey first looking confident and smug. Then he should appear puzzled, angry, and tired. The final portrait of Donkey should show that he is sad and defeated.*

Literary Analysis

Possible answers:

4. *Donkey represents foolishness. Toad represents craftiness. Students should support their answers with examples from the story.*

5. *No. Toad cheated in order to win the race. He did not actually run it but placed his children along the route.*

6. ● **STANDARDS FOCUS** *Universal Theme Students' responses will vary. They may say that the theme, which expresses the superiority of brains over physical prowess, has been proven true time and again. That is why it is a universal theme.*

After Reading

Comprehension

1. **Recall** What are the rules of the race between Toad and Donkey?

2. **Clarify** What do Toad's children do to help him?

3. **Represent** Draw three profiles of Donkey. Complete each by showing Donkey's expression at the beginning, middle, and end of the race.

Literary Analysis

4. **Identify Characteristics of Fables** What human abilities or traits does Donkey represent? What traits does Toad represent? Give examples from the story to support your answers.

5. **Make Judgments** In your view, did Toad win the contest fairly? Explain.

6. **Evaluate Theme** Recall the theme you identified for this fable. Then think of two other fables, stories, or personal experiences from which you have taken this same message. Why do you think this message has been repeated throughout history and all over the world?

Comparing Universal Themes

Now that you have read both fables, finish filling in your chart. Then state the universal theme the selections share.

	"Two Ways to Count to Ten"	"The Race Between Toad and Donkey"
Who are the characters?	Old Tanko, King Leopard, King Leopard's daughter, the elephant, the bush ox, the chimpanzee, and the antelope	Master King, Toad, Donkey, Toad's 20 children
What is the contest and who declares it?		
Who wins the contest? How?		
What do the characters learn?		
What's the universal theme?		

Comparing Universal Themes

■ **STANDARDS FOCUS** *Set a Purpose for Reading* The third column of students' charts should include the following details for "The Race Between Toad and Donkey":

• ***Who are the characters?*** *Master King, Toad, Donkey, Toad's 20 children*

• ***What is the contest, and who declares it?*** *The contest is a 20-mile race. Master King declares it.*

• ***Who wins the contest? How?*** *The Toad wins the contest. He places his children at the mileposts so that they can sing out and convince Donkey that Toad is keeping up with him. Donkey becomes so discouraged that he gives up.*

• ***What do the characters learn?*** *Toad learns that his brains can help him win out over more powerful rivals.*

• ***What's the universal theme?*** *Cleverness will triumph over strength and size.*

Writing for Assessment

1. READ THE PROMPT

In writing assessments, you will often be asked to compare and contrast two works that are similar in some way, such as the two fables with a similar theme.

PROMPT

While the fables "Two Ways to Count to Ten" and "The Race Between Toad and Donkey" communicate the same universal theme, they express this theme in different ways. In four or five paragraphs, compare and contrast the ways in which the fables convey their message. Cite details from the fables to support your response.

◀ **STRATEGIES IN ACTION**

1. I have to make sure I understand the **message** both fables share.

2. I need to identify the **similarities and differences** in how the fables express the message.

3. I should give examples from the fables to help explain my ideas.

2. PLAN YOUR WRITING

Using your chart, identify the ways each fable conveys the theme. Then think about how you will set up your response.

- Do you want to focus on each fable in a separate paragraph and then write a paragraph comparing them, as shown in the sample outline?

- Do you want to compare each element—characters, contests, and theme—in a separate paragraph and then point out the differences between the stories in another paragraph?

Once you have decided, outline the order of your paragraphs.

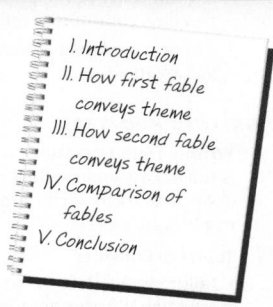

I. Introduction
II. How first fable conveys theme
III. How second fable conveys theme
IV. Comparison of fables
V. Conclusion

3. DRAFT YOUR RESPONSE

Introduction Introduce the fables and tell what universal theme they share. Then state your main idea, which should include an overview of the similarities and differences in the ways the fables convey the theme.

Body Use your chart and outline as a guide to the key points of your comparison. If you're using an outline that's similar to the sample, make sure you discuss the characters, contests, and theme for each selection.

Conclusion Wrap up with a restatement of your main idea and a reminder about how stories from different cultures can have the same theme.

Revision Make sure your sentences vary in structure.

Writing for Assessment

1. **READ THE PROMPT**

- Read the prompt aloud. Ask volunteers to identify words that define the task.

- Work with students to phrase the message in a way that fits both fables.

- Discuss how each fable reveals the message.

2. **PLAN YOUR WRITING**

- Make sure that students' charts are complete before they begin their planning.

- Discuss similarities and differences in how the two fables express the shared message. For example, in the first fable, the antelope wins by using a different but honest strategy. In the second fable, the toad is deceitful as well as clever.

- Compare the two methods of organization. The point-by-point approach will help students focus on specifics and cover each fable thoroughly. It requires strong transitions and a clear plan to avoid repetition. The block method is easier to organize, but students must avoid generalizing.

3. **DRAFT YOUR RESPONSE**

- Tell students to refer to the prompt in their introductory paragraph. For example, they might write, "Although the two fables communicate the same message, they express this message in different ways."

- List transitions on the board that might strengthen the unity within each paragraph and between paragraphs, such as *in addition, unlike, by contrast,* and *similarly.*

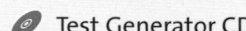 RESOURCE MANAGER—Copy Master
Writing for Assessment p. 205

Assess and Reteach

Assess

 RESOURCE MANAGER—Copy Masters
Selection Tests A, B/C pp. 207–208, 209–210

Test Generator CD

Reteach

STANDARDS LESSON FILE
Literature Lesson 13: Theme

FOR LESS-PROFICIENT WRITERS
Plan Your Writing

- Review completed chart from page 734.

- Help students list how the fables reveal the theme in similar and different ways. For example, both fables center around a contest. In both fables, the strongest and biggest contestants believe they are going to win. In both fables, the smartest wins. Point out that the major difference lies in the way the winner achieves victory.

Draft Your Response Give students a plan for writing their essay.

- The first paragraph will give titles and explain the theme.

- The second paragraph will tell how theme is revealed in the first fable.

- The third paragraph will explain how theme is revealed in the second fable.

- The fourth paragraph will discuss the similarities and the differences identified on the list.

Focus and Motivate

OBJECTIVES

- analyze a student model that reflects the key traits of cause-and-effect writing
- use the writing process to produce a cause-and-effect essay
- link causes and effects with transitions
- revise and edit, using a rubric for cause-and-effect writing
- make a formal presentation

WRITER'S ROAD MAP

WRITING PROMPTS 1 AND 2

Help students choose a prompt by brainstorming events in their lives that caused other events to occur or by reviewing characters from literature whose actions had specific consequences.

ADDITIONAL PROMPTS

Use these prompts for practice with writing cause-and-effect essays:

WRITING PROMPT 3

Writing for the Real World Write a report for your health class that explains the cause-and-effect relationship of specific behaviors.

Subjects to Consider

- sleeping too much or too little
- watching television too much
- exercising too little

WRITING PROMPT 4

Writing from Your Imagination Write an essay about an imaginary event and the possible effects of that event.

Ideas to Consider

- winning a million dollars
- gaining the ability to fly
- becoming invisible
- finding a way to travel through time

For additional writing prompts, see

- WriteSmart CD
- Writing Center at **ClassZone.com**

KEY TRAITS

Review the six **KEY TRAITS,** focusing primarily on ideas and organization. Compare these traits with the rubric on page 742.

Writing Workshop

Cause-and-Effect Essay

One sure lesson in the literature of this unit is that actions have consequences. Make a choice, and results—intended or otherwise—follow. When one thing brings about the next, in literature or in life, that's a cause-and-effect relationship. The **Writer's Road Map** will guide you in writing a cause-and-effect essay.

WRITER'S ROAD MAP
Cause-and-Effect Essay

WRITING PROMPT 1

Writing from the Real World Write an essay about a cause-and-effect relationship that you think is important or interesting. Make sure you can show clearly how one event caused another event to happen.

Topics to Consider

- an event in your life, such as changing schools or moving
- a community development, such as a curfew or a new community center
- a new school policy, such as removing lockers or adding a lounge

WRITING PROMPT 2

Writing from Literature The literature in this unit is full of cause-and-effect relationships. Write an essay that traces a cause-and-effect relationship in a literary work.

Topics to Consider

- failure to heed warnings ("Orpheus and Eurydice," "Icarus and Daedalus," "Phaëthon")
- the consequences of war ("Young Arthur," *Sir Gawain and the Green Knight*)

 WRITING TOOLS
For prewriting, revision, and editing tools, visit the **Writing Center** at ClassZone.com.

KEY TRAITS

1. IDEAS

- Identifies a true **cause-and-effect relationship**
- Presents a **thesis statement** that explains the connection between causes and effects
- Includes **facts, examples,** and other **details** to **support** each cause and effect

2. ORGANIZATION

- Presents causes and effects in a sensible **order**
- Shows the relationship between causes and effects by using **transitions**
- Has an interesting **introduction** and a **conclusion** that summarizes the cause-and-effect relationship

3. VOICE

- Has a **tone** that is appropriate for the audience and purpose

4. WORD CHOICE

- Explains each cause and effect with **precise language**

5. SENTENCE FLUENCY

- Varies **sentence lengths** to add interest and sophistication

6. CONVENTIONS

- Uses **correct grammar, spelling, and punctuation**

Writing Workshop Resources

 RESOURCE MANAGER UNIT 6
Plan and Teach pp. 211–214
Prewriting–Editing pp. 215–219
Writing Rubric p. 220
Speaking and Listening p. 221
Writing Support p. 222*

STANDARDS LESSON FILE
Writing Lessons 16, 19, 21, 30
Speaking and Listening Lesson 4

 **BEST PRACTICES TOOLKIT**
Scaffolding Writing Instruction pp. 43–46*
Sequence Chain/Sequence Circle • Cause-and-Effect Graphics • Writing Templates:
Cause and Effect

TECHNOLOGY
- Easy Planner DVD
- Writing Center at **ClassZone.com**
- WriteSmart CD

* Resources for Differentiation

Part 1: Analyze a Student Model

Zachary Eckler
Robbins Park Charter School

Our Dog Chip

"This is a big decision," my mother said, looking at me with her best mother look. "A dog is a lot of work. For this reason alone, it's going to change your life!"

Because I could see how serious she was, I said, "I know, Mom.
5 You're right." The truth is, however, I didn't know what was ahead. As it turned out, getting our dog Chip caused us a ton of trouble, a whole load of work, and a lot of joy, too.

The trouble came first. We adopted Chip from the nearby shelter when he was two. The woman there told us Chip had had "a couple
10 of failed adoptions." That was code for "trouble," but we didn't know it. Because my sister and I liked Chip, we brought him home. The first night, we learned that Chip didn't care if we called him or not. Accordingly, when he got loose the first time, there was no getting him back. He ran around as long as he wanted. Worse, he found my
15 neighbors' pet rabbit and knocked over its cage. Then he started running down that poor bunny. Dad got there about one second before it was too late. My neighbors weren't too happy. The first week, we also found out how much Chip liked the taste of carpets. Actually, he didn't like the ones that cost $4.98 at Save-a-Buck—no way! He preferred the new
20 living-room carpet. A few days later, he also showed us another great talent he had—he could take bites out of our sofa. For these reasons, I thought Chip might have one more "failed adoption," but somehow we kept him.

KEY TRAITS IN ACTION

Introduction uses dialogue to hook readers.

Thesis statement identifies a true **cause-and-effect relationship** (dog caused trouble, work, and joy).

Transitions signal cause and effect.

Includes **examples** to **support** the first effect (that Chip caused trouble). Uses a variety of **sentence lengths.**

Teach

Part 1: Analyze a Student Model

Have students read the student model and **Key Traits in Action.** Then discuss the model with the class, focusing on specific examples of each trait. You may also wish to incorporate the following activities:

- **Thesis Statement** Write the following weak thesis statement on the board:

  > As it turned out, getting our dog Chip was different than I imagined.

  Ask a student to read this statement and then lines 5–7 of the student model aloud. Ask students to compare the two. **Possible answer:** *The thesis statement on the board does not provide any details about the specific effects of getting the dog. The thesis statement in the model points out three specific effects. The model thesis statement is a road map for organizing the essay that follows.*

- **Examples** To illustrate the use of supporting examples, have students skim the fifth paragraph of the model (page 738, lines 30–39) and locate three specific examples of how Chip brought joy to the writer's family.

  > Example 1: *"he brought my sister and me together" (line 32)*

  > Example 2: *"he gave us all such great greetings" (lines 37–38)*

  > Example 3: *"He could also tell when we were upset and liked to snuggle up and help" (lines 38–39)*

DIFFERENTIATED INSTRUCTION

FOR ALL STUDENTS

For general guidelines on differentiating writing instruction, see

 BEST PRACTICES TOOLKIT
Scaffolding Writing Instruction pp. 43–46

FOR ENGLISH LEARNERS

Language: Skill Words Write these terms on the board and review them with students.

- *cause:* a reason why an event or an action occurs

- *effect:* a result of a previous event or action

- *thesis statement:* a sentence that states the main idea of an essay. In a cause-and-effect essay, the thesis statement might name a cause and several effects, or an effect and several causes.

- *relationship:* the connection between two events. In a cause-and-effect relationship, two events are connected because one causes the other to happen.

- *transition:* word or phrase that shows a relationship between ideas. Transitions that show cause and effect are listed on page 742.

- *order:* the way in which ideas are arranged in an essay. When a writer presents ideas in a logical order, readers are better able to understand the writer's message.

- *tone:* a writer's attitude toward his or her subject. Tone conveys a feeling about the subject that can affect how readers feel about it, too.

- **Precise Language** Display this sentence:

  I had to take Chip out in all kinds of weather.

  Have students compare this sentence to the sentence in lines 27–28. Explain that the details "during rainstorms," "in baking heat," and "in the snow and ice" give readers a more precise understanding of the problems the writer faced. Have students look for precise language in line 26. *("a scoop, gloves, and bags")*

- **Order** Remind students that the order of paragraphs in the model reflects the writer's thesis that the dog caused trouble (paragraph 3), work (paragraph 4), and joy (paragraph 5). Have student pairs find the sequence order in paragraph 5 that shows how the writer's relationship with his sister changed over time. *Possible answer: First, they avoided each other. Then, because of the dog, they worked together and played together. Finally, the writer decided that his sister was not as weird as he thought.*

- **Tone** Explain that a "friendly, conversational tone" reflects how the writer might describe these events to a friend. Ask students to identify words and phrases that contribute to the informal tone in lines 30–39 and suggest more formal ways to phrase the same ideas. *Possible answers:*

  - *"In a funny kind of way" (lines 31–32), "In an unexpected way"*

  - *"I'm all sports and guy stuff and she's all ballet and girl stuff" (lines 32–33), "my main interest is sports while hers is ballet"*

For interactive student models, see

Write*Smart* CD

Writing Center at **ClassZone.com**

Chip caused us a lot of work, too. He has so much energy, and we
25 have a small apartment. So Mom said he had to be walked or run three
times a day. Worse, I had to carry a scoop, gloves, and bags with me.
I had to take Chip out during rainstorms, in baking heat, and in the
snow and ice. When it was late and I just wanted to lie on the sofa,
there was still the evening walk to do.

> Uses **precise language** to describe the second effect (that Chip caused the writer to work hard).

30 Luckily, Chip turned out to be more than a lot of trouble and work.
He actually turned out to be good for our family. In a funny kind of
way, he brought my sister and me together. Because I'm all sports and
guy stuff and she's all ballet and girl stuff, we used to avoid each other.
With the dog, though, we had to work out plans for taking care of him.
35 We played with him together, too. As a result, Chip helped me figure
out that my sister isn't as weird as I thought she was. Also, everybody
in the house loved Chip once he calmed down, because he gave us all
such great greetings. He could also tell when we were upset and liked to
snuggle up and help.

> Presents all three effects in a sensible **order**. The writer uses a friendly, conversational **tone** as he describes the third effect (that Chip brought joy to the family).

40 As it turned out, getting Chip did change my whole life. He made it
harder sometimes and better many other times. Now I know that when
people say that dogs are a lot of work, they're right. Still, because of
the pleasure that results, having a dog is worth it.

> **Conclusion** summarizes the cause-and-effect relationship.

2

DIFFERENTIATED INSTRUCTION

FOR ENGLISH LEARNERS
Comprehension: Transitions

- Refer students to the list of cause-and-effect transitions on page 742. Demonstrate how *if . . . then* is used to show the relationship between two events or actions by writing this sentence on the board:

  If it rains, then the picnic will be postponed.

  Ask students to identify the cause *(rain)* and the effect *(picnic postponed)*.

- Have students work in pairs to write original sentences with *if . . . then*. One student should provide the *if* part of the sentence, and the other student should fill in the *then* part. Students should take turns filling out the parts of the sentences. Have them share their examples with the class.

- To become familiar with the cause-and-effect transitions, ask students to locate transitions from the list used in the model. Keep a list of their responses on the board.

Possible answers: "for this reason" (line 2), "because" (line 4), "because" (line 11), "accordingly" (line 13), "for these reasons" (line 21), "so" (line 25), "because" (line 32), "as a result" (line 35), "because" (line 37)

RESOURCE MANAGER—Copy Master
Writing Support p. 222

WRITING STANDARD
4.A.1. Compose texts using prewriting and drafting strategies

Part 2: Apply the Writing Process

PREWRITING

What Should I Do?	**What Does It Look Like?**

1. Brainstorm to find a topic.
Review the prompts on page 736 and choose the one you prefer. Create a cluster map with a bulleted item from the prompt in the center. Then think of experiences that you have had or read about that relate to that item. Don't edit. Just write!

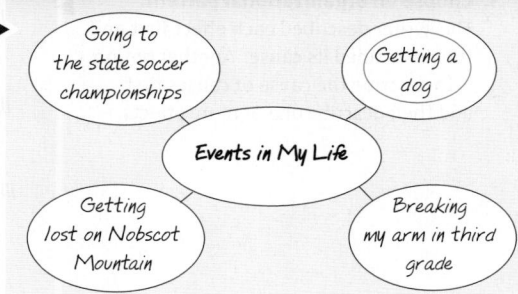

2. Chart the causes and effects.
You might show one cause with several effects or several causes that led to one effect. But remember, just because one event follows another doesn't mean that one event caused the other. "Stacie went out in the rain and caught the flu" is an example of a **false cause.** Not everyone who goes out in the rain gets sick.

Causes	Effects
Dog misbehaves.	→ Trouble
Dog needs to go out.	→ Work
Dog gives great greetings.	→ Joy

3. Write a thesis statement.
Base your thesis on your chart. Zachary Eckler's thesis has three key points: his dog (1) caused him trouble and (2) led to lots of work but (3) made him happy.

Working thesis statement:

Our dog Chip caused trouble at first, and he still needs lots of walks and attention. But he is fun to be around, so I wouldn't trade him for anything.

4. Collect evidence to support each key point.
Evidence is anything that explains, demonstrates, or otherwise clarifies your point. You might include facts, reasons, examples, or other details.

Key point 1: trouble
Evidence:
• almost killed the Hansens' pet rabbit
• chewed our new carpet
• ruined the arm of the living-room sofa

WRITING WORKSHOP **739**

FOR ENGLISH LEARNERS
Writing a Thesis Give students the following sentence starters to help them create a working thesis and gather support for their main ideas:

• My topic is _____.
• If my topic is a cause, three effects are _____, _____, and _____.
• If my topic is an effect, three causes are _____, _____, and _____.

FOR ADVANCED LEARNERS/PRE–AP
Analyze Challenge students to explore the causes and effects of a complex natural phenomenon such as a hurricane. Half of the group should write about causes and the other half effects. Invite them to share their findings with the class.

Practice and Apply

To support students during the writing process, use these copy masters:

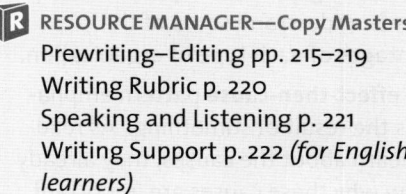 **RESOURCE MANAGER**—Copy Masters
Prewriting–Editing pp. 215–219
Writing Rubric p. 220
Speaking and Listening p. 221
Writing Support p. 222 *(for English learners)*

Part 2: Apply the Writing Process

PREWRITING

1. Brainstorm to find a topic. Be sure students recognize that the more ideas they list during brainstorming, the more likely they are to find a topic that is important and interesting to write about. Once the cluster map is completed, have students work in pairs to determine which topic is best.

2. Chart the causes and effects. Encourage students to experiment with various charts to help them organize ideas.

BEST PRACTICES TOOLKIT—Transparencies
Sequence Chain/Sequence Circle p. B21
Cause-and-Effect Graphics pp. B16, B37–B39

3. Write a thesis statement. Point out that in the model, the writer discusses one cause and three effects. Caution students against a thesis that has either too many causes or too many effects. Help students combine or eliminate ideas if they have too many. Have students return to brainstorming if they have too few. Three is a reasonable number of points to develop in one essay.

4. Collect evidence to support each key point. Direct students to use ideas from their graphic organizers as supporting evidence in their essays. Each key point needs two or three solid details in order to be clear and convincing. Encourage students to find more details than they will actually use and then select the best examples for their essays.

For interactive graphic organizers, see

🔘 Write*Smart* CD
ℹ️ Writing Center at **ClassZone.com**

DRAFTING

1. **Choose an organizational pattern.** Help students understand some of the advantages of each type of organization.

   - The **effect-then-cause** pattern emphasizes the result of something. As readers learn about the causes, they already know why these causes are important.
   - The **cause-then-effect** pattern presents events in the order in which they occurred. Readers see events unfold in a natural way and may feel suspense as they read to learn what happens next.

2. **Tell how and why.** Remind students that readers will not understand cause-and-effect relationships unless they are clearly stated. Display these sentences: *I failed the math test. I didn't understand fractions. I forgot to bring my book home. I didn't do my homework.* Challenge students to combine them into one sentence with the word *because.* (**Possible answer:** *I failed the math test because I didn't understand fractions, I forgot to bring my book home, and I didn't do my homework.*) Discuss how a single transition word instantly clarifies how all the ideas are related. You might also show this graphically:

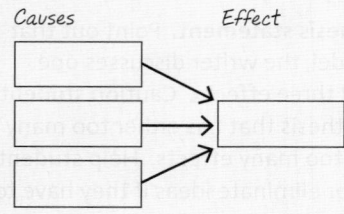

3. **End powerfully.** Tell students that just as they need an effective hook to start their essays, they also need a memorable ending. A good ending is like a reward for readers—they are left with an interesting new insight. Point out the **TIP** provided with step 3.

For cause-and-effect writing templates, see

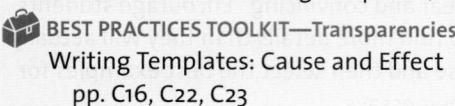

   BEST PRACTICES TOOLKIT—Transparencies
     Writing Templates: Cause and Effect
      pp. C16, C22, C23

  🔘 Write*Smart* CD

  ℹ️ Writing Center at **ClassZone.com**

DRAFTING

What Should I Do?	**What Does It Look Like?**

1. **Choose an organizational pattern.** This writer described each effect first and then explained its cause. Another option is to describe the cause or causes first and then describe one or more effects. ▶	I. Introduction
	  A. Mom said having a dog would be lots of work.
	  B. Thesis: Dog brought us trouble, work, and joy.
	II. Trouble
	  A. Chip almost killed the neighbors' pet rabbit.
	  B. He chewed on the carpet and sofa.
	III. Work
	  A. He has to be walked or run three times a day.
	  B. He needs to go out even if I'm tired or the weather is bad.
	IV. Joy
	  A. My sister and I play with Chip.
	  B. He gives everyone great greetings.
	V. Conclusion
	  A. Chip changed my life.
	  B. Having a dog is worth all the hard work.

2. **Tell how and why.** Don't include examples, facts, and other details just to fill up space. Instead, help your reader understand how and why something happened. ▶	The trouble came first. The first night, we learned that Chip didn't care if we called him or not. Accordingly, when he got loose the first time, there was no getting him back. He ran around as long as he wanted. Worse, he found my neighbors' pet rabbit and knocked over its cage.
3. **End powerfully.** Your conclusion should clearly summarize the cause-and-effect relationship, but it should go further too. It might reflect on the events, show how the topic is important, or include a call to action. **TIP** Before you revise, look back at the key traits on page 736 and at the rubric and peer-reader questions on page 742. ▶	As it turned out, getting Chip did change my whole life. He made it harder sometimes and better many other times. ⎤ Summary Now I know that when people say that dogs are a lot of work, they're right. Still, because of the pleasure that results, having a dog is worth it. ⎤ Significance

---

DIFFERENTIATED INSTRUCTION

FOR LESS–PROFICIENT WRITERS

Choosing an Organizational Pattern Explain that in the student model, the last effect, joy, is really the most important. Suggest that students organize their causes or effects in order of increasing importance.

Introduction
- Identifies the cause-and-effect relationship
- Clearly explains the relationship in a thesis statement
- Hooks the reader

Middle Paragraphs (Number will vary.)
- Each paragraph presents and explains an important cause or effect.
- Most important cause or effect is last.

Conclusion
- Summarizes the cause-and-effect relationship
- Offers a reflection on the importance of the topic
- Makes a memorable final remark

REVISING AND EDITING

What Should I Do?	**What Does It Look Like?**
1. Start out strong. • Use a hook—something special or surprising, like humor, drama, a question, or a quotation—to draw the reader in. • Underline your first sentence or two. If these lines seem ordinary or boring, add fresh details, a question, or a bit of dialogue.	~~My mother said getting a dog was a big decision.~~ "This is a big decision," my mother said, looking at me with her best mother look. "A dog is a lot of work. For this reason alone, it's going to change your life!"
2. Don't be vague. • Make sure you support each key point with evidence. • Don't just state the evidence. Explain it. • Circle your evidence and explanations. If you don't have many circles, see what you can do to tell your reader more.	He has so much energy, and we have a small apartment. So Mom said he had to be walked or run (three times a day). Worse, I had to carry a scoop, gloves, and bags with me. I had to take Chip out during rainstorms, in baking heat, and in the snow and ice.
3. Connect your ideas. • Draw a box around each transition you used. • Ask a peer reader to point out places where the order or organization is unclear. • Add transitions where you need them. **See page 742: Cause-Effect Transitions**	My sister and I used to avoid each other. With the dog, though, we had to work out plans for taking care of him. We played with him together, too. As a result, Chip helped me figure out that my sister isn't as weird as I thought she was.
4. Use long, short, and medium sentences. • Find and [bracket] your longest sentence. Also, look for several short sentences in a row. • Does your essay have too many long, confusing sentences? Does your essay have too many short, immature-sounding sentences? • Revise your essay to vary sentence lengths.	[~~The first week, we also found out how much Chip liked the taste of carpets, but not the kind of carpets that cost $4.98 at Save-a-Buck, no way, he preferred the new living-room carpet.~~] The first week, we also found out how much Chip liked the taste of carpets. Actually, he didn't like the ones that cost $4.98 at Save-a-Buck—no way! He preferred the new living-room carpet.

REVISING AND EDITING

1. **Start out strong.** Ask students to review works they have read that have strong openings. Have them explain what technique each author uses to capture their interest. After sharing some examples, have students review their own introductions. Ask them to write a second introduction and ask a partner which is a better hook.

2. **Don't be vague.** To reinforce the importance of specific explanations, have students examine the third paragraph of the model. Ask them to identify the key point. *(Possible answer: Chip caused a lot of trouble.)* On the board, list evidence found in the paragraph. *Possible answers:*
   - *Chip did not respond when called (line 12).*
   - *Chip chased the neighbor's rabbit (lines 14–16).*
   - *Chip chewed the carpet (line 18).*
   - *Chip took bites out of the sofa (line 21).*

3. **Connect your ideas.** Point out the list of **Cause-Effect Transitions** on page 742. Be sure to emphasize that transitions may be used between paragraphs (to connect main ideas) and within paragraphs (to connect examples and details).

4. **Use long, short, and medium sentences.** Remind students that a complete sentence must have a subject and a verb and must express a complete thought. Ask students to examine the sentence that has been crossed out. It is long because it is a run-on sentence. The corrected version consists of three complete sentences.

For interactive revision tools, see

- WriteSmart CD
- Writing Center at **ClassZone.com**

FOR ENGLISH LEARNERS

Comprehension: Cause-and-Effect Provide sentence frames such as the following to help students show cause-and-effect relationships in their essays.

- Because I was tired, I _____.
- After the alarm sounded, we _____.
- If _____, then I will be glad.
- As a result of tripping on the step, he _____.

- I studied hard for the test; therefore, I felt _____ when I got an A.
- Since the door was locked and I had forgotten my key, I had to _____.

Preparing to Publish

Support for meeting the goals in the writing rubric is supplied throughout the **Writing Workshop** on pages 736–741.

For Rubric Bank, see

 WriteSmart CD

ⓘ Writing Center at **ClassZone.com**

Assess and Reteach

After reading and assessing students' essays, you might use these lessons to reteach key skills:

Ⓢ STANDARDS LESSON FILE

Writing Lesson 30: Cause-and-Effect Essay
Writing Lesson 21: Writing a Thesis Statement
Writing Lesson 16: Cause-and-Effect Order
Writing Lesson 19: Transitions

Apply the Rubric

A strong cause-and-effect essay . . .

☑ introduces and discusses a true cause-and-effect relationship

☑ has a thesis statement that connects causes and effects

☑ includes precise facts or examples to support each cause and effect

☑ is sensibly organized

☑ links causes and effects with transitions

☑ varies sentence lengths

☑ uses a tone that matches the audience and purpose

☑ concludes with a summary of the cause-and-effect relationship

Ask a Peer Reader

• What cause-and-effect relationship does my essay explain?

• Where should I add transitions?

• How could I strengthen my introduction and conclusion?

• Where should I improve my explanations or support?

Cause-Effect Transitions

accordingly	for this reason
as a result	if . . . then
because	so
consequently	therefore

Check Your Grammar

• Remember, *it's* means "it is." The word *its* (without the apostrophe) is a possessive pronoun; *its* shows ownership.

> He found my neighbors' pet rabbit and
>   *its*
> knocked over it's cage.

See page R52: Pronouns

• Be sure elements in your sentences are parallel. For example, when you have items in a series, present them all in the same types of phrases or clauses.

> I had to carry a scoop, gloves, and bring
> bags with me.

See page R64: Parallel Structure

Writing Online

PUBLISHING OPTIONS
For publishing options, visit the **Writing Center** at **ClassZone.com**.

ASSESSMENT PREPARATION
For writing and grammar assessment practice, go to the **Assessment Center** at **ClassZone.com**.

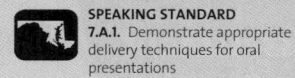

SPEAKING STANDARD
7.A.1. Demonstrate appropriate delivery techniques for oral presentations

Making a Formal Presentation

Now that you have thoroughly explained a cause-and-effect relationship in writing, it's time to educate others.

Planning the Presentation

1. **Decide on your subject.** You might use your essay as the basis of your presentation. If you prefer, you may research a different subject. Your audience will notice your level of enthusiasm, so choose a subject that truly interests you.

2. **Plan the points of your presentation.** Reread your essay or research your topic. Decide which points are most important, and restate them accurately in simple, clear language. You will be talking to audience members, not reading to them. If you include information from books, magazines, newspapers, or other research sources, be sure to cite those sources.

3. **Find or create visuals.** Think about which visuals would make the cause-and-effect relationship clear and intriguing. Consider using photographs, maps, diagrams, charts, graphs, video clips, or music. The writer of the student model included home video footage of his dog, Chip. Audience members saw for themselves how Chip's behavior changed over time.

4. **Develop an outline.** Write down a few words about each of your main points. Note when you will introduce visuals.

5. **Make some practice presentations.** Ask audience members: Was any part of my presentation unclear? Do my pacing, facial expressions, and gestures match my subject matter?

Making the Presentation

1. **Be calm and confident.** If you forget which point is next, glance at your outline. Make sure that everyone can see the visuals.

2. **Reflect.** Think about how well the presentation went and why. Decide what you will do differently next time.

See page R78: Evaluate an Informative Speech

SPEAKING AND LISTENING

Ask students to read this page to get an overview of how to make a formal presentation. Before students begin working, review this rubric with them so that they understand their goals:

Rubric A strong formal presentation

- is based on an interesting topic
- demonstrates your knowledge and enthusiasm about the topic
- is organized so that a listener can easily understand the cause-and-effect relationship
- acknowledges the source of any research
- includes some visuals that enhance the understanding and enjoyment of the audience
- uses appropriate pacing, gestures, and facial expressions
- has been practiced and improved as necessary
- is presented with confidence and pride

R RESOURCE MANAGER—Copy Master
Speaking and Listening p. 221

S STANDARDS LESSON FILE
Speaking and Listening Lesson 4: Informative Speech

DIFFERENTIATED INSTRUCTION

FOR LESS–PROFICIENT WRITERS

Planning the Presentation Explain that the goal is to present information on a subject with a cause-and-effect relationship. Have students use these questions to select appropriate topics:

- Are my classmates likely to find my topic interesting?
- Can I clearly state the cause-and-effect relationship?
- What facts will I need to research in order to make a clear and convincing presentation?

Have students prepare for their presentations by asking themselves these questions:

- Have I done any necessary research and documented my use of sources?
- Are my visuals helpful in illustrating my ideas?
- Are my visuals large enough for the class to see?
- Am I comfortable using my visuals?
- Do I know the material well enough to talk about it and not just read it?

Assessment Practice

CHECK READINESS

Read aloud the paragraph under **ASSESS** and stress to students that this is not the full Unit Test, but a way for them to check their readiness for it. Then have students examine the skills listed under **REVIEW** and look back in the unit or in the Handbook for any they need to study.

READ THE SELECTIONS

Remind students to keep unit goals in mind as they read each passage, paying particular attention to

- characteristics of myths and tales
- cultural values
- chronological order of events
- cause-and-effect relationships

To help students focus on **characteristics of myths and tales** while reading, encourage them to ask questions such as

- What is the relationship between the gods and humans in "The King Who Wished for Gold"?
- What lessons do these stories teach?
- What qualities were valued by each of the cultures from which these stories originated?

ANSWER THE QUESTIONS

Direct students to pages R93–R99 of the Test-Taking Handbook to review test-taking strategies. Remind them not to choose the first alternative that seems to fit when answering a multiple-choice question. Instead, they should read through all the choices, eliminate any that are clearly wrong, and then choose the best answer—the one that is most accurate and complete.

Encourage students to use extra time to check their answers. After completing the test, they should return to questions about which they are unsure. Suggest that they respond to these questions without looking at their previous answers. If their answers do not match, they should study the choices again, being sure to eliminate those that are obviously incorrect. If additional time remains, they should then go on to recheck the rest of the test.

Assessment Practice

Reading Comprehension

DIRECTIONS *Read these selections and answer the questions that follow.*

King Midas had pleased the god Dionysus, and so Dionysus promised to give Midas anything he wished. Midas wished that everything he touched would turn to gold.

from The King Who Wished for Gold

retold by **Anne Rockwell**

As soon as he reached his palace, the king ordered a grand and extravagant feast to be set before him. All kinds of rare and expensive delicacies were prepared because Midas thought, After all, if I am so rich, why should I spare any expense?

And then he sat down to eat.

But the piece of bread he picked up hardened in his hand and turned to gold. Slices of meat became slabs of glimmering gold. He picked up his cup of wine, and slippery liquid gold gagged him so that he could not drink.

10 Poor King Midas realized that for all his newfound wealth he would soon starve to death if he could not eat or drink. Suddenly he hated the gift that he had wanted so much. He lifted his hands toward the sky and said, "Please, Lord Dionysus, forgive me for making such a foolish wish. I beg you, set me free from my own greed and stupidity!"

Dionysus was full of pity for the situation Midas had created for himself. Because he was a kindly and forgiving god, he immediately canceled the charm that had made everything King Midas touched turn to gold.

But he said to him, "Just to be sure that no trace of this charm remains, 20 I want you to go and wash yourself at the source of the River Sardis. Where the spring spouts forth in clouds of spray, scrub your entire body and hair and beard until you wash all the gold away."

King Midas did as the god had told him. Dionysus had been right, for sprinkles of gold spangled the stream when he washed himself in it. To this day, gold flows through that river—the very gold that King Midas washed from himself.

From then on, King Midas was content with his rose garden and never again wished for gold and great wealth.

ASSESSMENT ONLINE
For more assessment practice and test-taking tips, go to the **Assessment Center** at ClassZone.com.

DIFFERENTIATED INSTRUCTION

FOR ENGLISH LEARNERS

Assessment Practice: Work Backwards
Prepare students for the assessment by having them read the questions before reading the text passages. Have pairs follow these steps to learn unfamiliar words in the test directions and questions:

1. Find words you don't recognize and write each one on an index card.
2. Look up the meaning in a dictionary.
3. Write the meaning on the back of the card.

4. Use your word cards to teach and practice the vocabulary with your partner and another pair of students.

Assessment Support: Word Cues Discuss words that show relationships among events. Have students look for them as they read.

- **time order:** *first, then, next, after, finally, soon*
- **cause and effect:** *because, as a result, so, if*

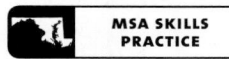
from The Three Wishes

Ricardo E. Alegría

Many years ago, there lived a woodsman and his wife. They were very poor but very happy in their little house in the forest. Poor as they were, they were always ready to share what little they had with anyone who came to their door. They loved each other very much and were quite content with their life together. Each evening, before eating, they gave thanks to God for their happiness.

One day, while the husband was working far off in the woods, an old man came to the little house and said that he had lost his way in the forest and had eaten nothing for many days. The woodsman's wife had little
10 to eat herself, but, as was her custom, she gave a large portion of it to the old man. After he had eaten everything she gave him, he told the woman that he had been sent to test her and that, as a reward for the kindness she and her husband showed to all who came to their house, they would be granted a special grace. This pleased the woman, and she asked what the special grace was.

The old man answered, "Beginning immediately, any three wishes you or your husband may wish will come true."

When she heard these words, the woman was overjoyed and exclaimed, "Oh, if my husband were only here to hear what you say!"
20 The last word had scarcely left her lips when the woodsman appeared in the little house with the ax still in his hands. The first wish had come true.

The woodsman couldn't understand it at all. How did it happen that he, who had been cutting wood in the forest, found himself here in his house? His wife explained it all as she embraced him. The woodsman just stood there, thinking over what his wife had said. He looked at the old man who stood quietly, too, saying nothing.

Suddenly he realized that his wife, without stopping to think, had used one of the three wishes, and he became very annoyed when he
30 remembered all of the useful things she might have asked for with the first wish. For the first time, he became angry with his wife. The desire

GO ON

ITEM ANALYSIS

COMPREHENSION AND BRIEF CONSTRUCTED RESPONSE	ITEMS	UNIT PAGES
Characteristics of Myths and Tales	4, 5, 11, 12	626, 633, 661, 697, 713
Cultural Values	8, 10, 11	628, 647, 671
Chronological Order	2, 6, 9	661
Cause and Effect	1, 3, 7	647

VOCABULARY	ITEMS	UNIT PAGES
Compound Words	1, 2, 3	668
Homographs	4, 5, 6	658

WRITING AND GRAMMAR	ITEMS	UNIT PAGES
Compound Sentences	2, 4	659
Complex Sentences	1, 3	685

FOR LESS–PROFICIENT READERS

Assessment Support Consider these options for completing the **Assessment Practice:**

• Have students "work backwards," reviewing the test questions before reading the passages.

• Select random questions in the assessment and have students demonstrate how and where to look for the answers.

• Ask students to locate unfamiliar vocabulary in the assessment. Elicit the meanings of these words from the class.

• Have students record useful test words and definitions in their journals for later reference.

• Read the selections or parts of them aloud to aid in student comprehension.

McDougal Littell
Assessment System

After checking student readiness with this Assessment Practice, you may administer the complete Unit 6 Test, which matches the structure and format of the MSA.

Comprehension

Model a thinking process for answering multiple-choice questions.

1. **B is correct.** Midas thinks to himself, "If I am so rich, why should I spare any expense?" (lines 3–4). This shows that his motivation is to make use of his wealth. There is no support for A. Midas does not know that his food and drink will turn into gold, so C is also incorrect. He does not invite anyone else to the feast, so D is incorrect.

2. **D is correct.** Lines 6–9 describe how the bread, meat, and wine turn to gold after Midas sits down to eat. A is incorrect because Dionysus does not send Midas to the river until after his food turns to gold. B is incorrect because Midas wishes to be wealthy before he sits down to eat. The fact that no one attends his feast is not related to the question, making C incorrect.

3. **B is correct.** Midas realizes in lines 10–11 that he will starve to death with his golden touch. A is incorrect because there is a chance that Dionysus will be angry about Midas's rejection of his gift. C is incorrect because Midas remembers his love of roses after he rids himself of the gift. D is incorrect because he does not have time to grow bored with the gold before he wants the golden touch removed.

4. **A is correct.** Dionysus bestows the gift and takes it back, proving his supernatural powers. B is incorrect because Dionysus is described as a kind and forgiving god. C is incorrect because his actions do not prove that he will never die. D is incorrect because knowing mortals are foolish is not a characteristic of a myth.

5. **A is correct.** According to lines 24–26, gold can be found in the river in which Midas washed himself. B is not an aspect of the natural world. The natural occurrences in C and D are not mentioned in the myth.

6. **D is correct.** Both show the chronological relationship of events. A is incorrect because after all means "why not." B is incorrect because the verbs are in the past tense but do not show a sequence of events. C is incorrect because before (line 2) is used as a preposition, not an adverb, and but shows contrast, not time order.

for riches had turned his head, and he scolded his wife, shouting at her, among other things, "It doesn't seem possible that you could be so stupid! You've wasted one of our wishes, and now we have only two left! May you grow ears of a donkey!"

He had no sooner said the words than his wife's ears began to grow, and they continued to grow until they changed into the pointed, furry ears of a donkey!

40 When the woman put her hand up and felt them, she knew what had happened and began to cry. Her husband was very ashamed and sorry, indeed, for what he had done in his temper, and he went to his wife to comfort her.

The old man, who had stood by silently, now came to them and said, "Until now, you have known happiness together and have never quarreled with each other. Nevertheless, the mere knowledge that you could have riches and power has changed you both. Remember, you have only one wish left. What do you want? Riches? Beautiful clothes? Servants? Power?"

The woodsman tightened his arm about his wife, looked at the old 50 man, and said, "We want only the happiness and joy we knew before my wife grew donkey's ears."

No sooner had he said these words than the donkey ears disappeared. The woodsman and his wife fell upon their knees to ask forgiveness for having acted, if only for a moment, out of covetousness and greed. Then they gave thanks for all their happiness.

Comprehension

DIRECTIONS *Answer these questions about the excerpt from "The King Who Wished for Gold."*

1. Why does Midas order a large feast?
   A. He wants to eat like the gods.
   B. He thinks he is wealthy enough to spend as much as he wants.
   C. He hopes to see the food and drink become gold treasures.
   D. He wants to share his fortune.

2. What happens after Midas sits down to eat?
   A. Dionysus sends him to the river.
   B. He wishes to be wealthy.
   C. No one attends his feast.
   D. Food turns to gold in his hand.

3. What causes King Midas to hate the gift he had wanted so much?
   A. He wants to please Dionysus.
   B. He realizes he cannot eat or drink.
   C. He remembers that he loves his roses.
   D. He is bored with all of the gold.

746

7. **C is correct.** In lines 28–31, the narrator explains that the woodsman becomes angry when he thinks of all of the useful things his wife might have wished for. A is incorrect because the woodsman and his wife are described as always being willing to share what they have (line 3). B is incorrect because the woodsman is not upset at being home, but at what his wife did to bring him home. D is incorrect because the woodsman wishes to use the reward from the old man wisely.

8. **D is correct.** The woodsman's wish that his wife grow the ears of a donkey is foolish. Although both characters are simple, it is not their simplicity that teaches a lesson, so A is incorrect. B is incorrect because the woodsman appears to work every day. C is incorrect because the woodsman's honesty is not an issue in this tale.

9. **B is correct.** In lines 39–42, the woodsman comforts his wife after she grows donkey ears. A, C, and D all take place before the ears grow.

4. Why is Dionysus' behavior in lines 15–18 characteristic of a Greek myth?

   A. He shows supernatural power.

   B. He becomes extremely angry.

   C. He proves that he is an immortal.

   D. He knows that Midas is a fool.

5. Which aspect of the natural world does this myth explain?

   A. how gold came to be in the river

   B. why rose gardens became popular

   C. why rivers have springs

   D. how thunder forms in the sky

6. Which words in lines 1–9 are clues to the order of events in this myth?

   A. after all, became

   B. ordered, turned

   C. before, but

   D. as soon as, then

DIRECTIONS *Answer these questions about the excerpt from "The Three Wishes."*

7. Which event causes the woodsman to become angry with his wife?

   A. The wife gives food to the old man.

   B. The woodsman is suddenly home.

   C. The wife wastes one of the wishes.

   D. The old man rewards the wife.

8. Which quality does the woodsman stand for in this tale?

   A. simplicity   C. honesty

   B. laziness   D. foolishness

9. After the wife grows donkey ears, the

   A. old man grants three wishes

   B. woodsman comforts his sad wife

   C. wife shares her food

   D. old man knocks on the door

DIRECTIONS *Answer this question about both selections.*

10. Which value is most likely prized by the cultures that gave us these two stories?

    A. Respect your elders.

    B. Be kind to strangers.

    C. Appreciate what you have.

    D. Work steadily toward a goal.

Brief Constructed Response

11. On the basis of "The King Who Wished for Gold," what human traits do you think the ancient Greeks valued?

12. What lessons do King Midas and the couple in "The Three Wishes" learn about happiness and wealth?

GO ON

747

10. **C is correct.** *In both stories, the characters are grateful when their original circumstances are restored. Neither story emphasizes respect for the elderly, eliminating A. The second story does convey the importance of being kind to strangers, but the first story does not, making B incorrect. D is incorrect because none of the characters reaches a goal as a result of hard work.*

Brief Constructed Response

Evaluate student writing using the Maryland writing rubrics in the back of the book.

Possible responses:

11. *The Greeks valued the qualities of wisdom and self-control. These values are revealed through Midas's realization that he has brought misery upon himself through his desire for riches. In lines 12–14, he begs Dionysus to "set me free from my own greed and stupidity."*

12. *Students' responses should show that in both stories, the characters learn that wealth does not bring happiness. King Midas is desperately unhappy, although he is surrounded by gold. He can no longer enjoy the simple and necessary pleasures of life, such as food and drink. Although he relinquishes his wealth at the end of the story, his contentment is vastly greater. He "was content with his rose garden and never again wished for gold and great wealth" (lines 27–28). The woodsman and his wife could have used their last wish to gain beautiful clothes, servants, or riches. Instead, the woodsman looks at his wife and answers for both of them, "'We want only the happiness and joy we knew before my wife grew donkey's ears'" (lines 50–51). They realize through their experiences that even the promise of wealth can cause discord and grief.*

DIFFERENTIATED INSTRUCTION

Midas wants the golden touch.

He thinks riches will make his life happier.

He then finds out that he cannot eat or drink (lines 6–9).

He hates the gift he wanted (lines 11–12).

After the gift is removed, he is content with his rose garden and never wishes for gold again (lines 27–28).

FOR ENGLISH LEARNERS

Assessment Support: Make Inferences To help students respond to question 16, complete a chart like this one for each poem.

This story shows that wealth does not guarantee happiness and, in fact, may lead to misery.

Vocabulary

1. **B is correct.** *Using the parts of the compound word, the definition must be "recently acquired." The first part of the word,* new, *means "recent." The second part,* found, *suggests "acquired."* A, C, *and* D *do not fit into the context of the sentence and cannot be derived from both parts of the compound word.*

2. **A is correct.** *The parts of the compound word as well as the context of the story, in which the woodsman is described as holding an ax and cutting wood, point to the first definition as the correct one. He does not live outdoors, proving* B *to be incorrect. Although he may love nature, there is no proof of that in the story, making* C *incorrect. Although a woodsman could plant trees, the story describes him as cutting them down, making* D *incorrect.*

3. **D is correct.** *The word* over *means "beyond." In the context of the sentence, the definition must be* D. A *and* C *are both incorrect because they do not match the meaning of* over. B *appears to fit the meanings of the two word parts in* overjoyed, *but the meaning "too happy" does not fit the context of the sentence.*

4. **A is correct.** *As used in the story,* last *is an adjective meaning "final" or "coming after all the others." In* B, last *is a verb meaning "endure." In* C, last *means "least desirable." In* D, at long last *means "after a long delay," and* last *functions as a noun.*

5. **C is correct.** *As used in the story,* left *is a verb meaning "departed." In* A, left *is an adverb that refers to a direction. In* B, left *is a noun that refers to a political affiliation. In* D, left *means "allowed to remain."*

6. **C is correct.** *In the story,* still *means "continuing to be present." In* A, still *means "motionless." In* B, still *means "nevertheless." In* D, still *refers to a photograph in which the subjects don't move (as opposed to a video image).*

Vocabulary

DIRECTIONS *Use context clues and your knowledge of compound words to answer the following questions.*

1. Which is the likely definition of the compound word *newfound* in line 10 of "The King Who Wished for Gold"?

   "Poor King Midas realized that for all his <u>newfound</u> wealth he would soon starve to death if he could not eat or drink."

   A. unexpectedly returned
   B. recently acquired
   C. up-to-date
   D. earned

2. In line 1 of "The Three Wishes," the compound word *woodsman* refers to someone who

   A. works in the forest
   B. lives outdoors
   C. loves nature
   D. plants trees

3. Which is the likely definition of the compound word *overjoyed* in line 18 of "The Three Wishes"?

   "When she heard these words, the woman was <u>overjoyed</u> and exclaimed, 'Oh, if my husband were only here to hear what you say!'"

   A. almost happy
   B. too happy
   C. unhappy
   D. extremely happy

DIRECTIONS *Use context clues and your knowledg of homographs to answer the following questions*

> The <u>last</u> word had scarcely <u>left</u> her lips when the woodsman appeared in the little house with the ax <u>still</u> in his hands.

4. Which sentence uses *last* as it is used in line 20 of "The Three Wishes"?

   A. She was the last one out of the pool.
   B. I wonder if that new worker will last.
   C. He is the last person I want to see.
   D. At long last, you may all go home.

5. Which sentence uses *left* as it is used in line 20 of "The Three Wishes"?

   A. According to the map, we turn left.
   B. Liberal groups are sometimes called "the left."
   C. She left the room hastily.
   D. They left the lights on all night.

6. Which sentence uses *still* as it is used in line 21 of "The Three Wishes"?

   A. It felt hotter when the wind died and the air became still.
   B. Still, I can't go shopping until the car is repaired.
   C. The play is still being performed at the 6th Street Theater.
   D. They used a still photograph to promote the movie.

748

DIFFERENTIATED INSTRUCTION

FOR ENGLISH LEARNERS

Review Academic Vocabulary Point out the terms *compound words* and *homographs* in the directions on page 748. Discuss meanings and examples of these terms. Ask students to think of their own examples.

- *compound word*—a word made up of two or more individual words. Examples:
  — houseboat
  — flagpole
  — blueberry
  — bedroom

- *homograph*—a word that is spelled in the same way as another but differs in meaning, origin, and sometimes pronunciation. Examples:
  — Divide the pie so that each person gets a *fair* share.
  — We enjoyed the rides at the *fair*.
  — On what *date* were you born?
  — We have a *date* tree in our backyard.

Writing & Grammar

DIRECTIONS *Read this passage and answer the questions that follow.*

> (1) One of the most famous magicians was Harry Houdini. (2) Whose original name was Erich Weisz. (3) Houdini was born in Hungary in 1874. (4) He later moved to America. (5) Houdini did not get very far in his education. (6) But he loved to read. (7) One day, he read a book by Robert-Houdin, a famous magician. (8) He decided he would be a magician too. (9) He named himself "Houdini" after Robert-Houdin.

1. How might you combine sentence 1 and fragment 2 to form a complex sentence?

   A. One of the most famous magicians was Harry Houdini; Houdini's original name was Erich Weisz.

   B. Harry Houdini's original name was Erich Weisz, and he was one of the most famous magicians.

   C. One of the most famous magicians was Harry Houdini, whose original name was Erich Weisz.

   D. Harry Houdini was one of the most famous magicians, and his original name was Erich Weisz.

2. How might you combine sentences 3 and 4 to form a compound sentence?

   A. Houdini, who was born in Hungary in 1874, later moved to America.

   B. After he was born in Hungary in 1874, Houdini moved to America.

   C. Although he was born in Hungary in 1874, Houdini later moved to America.

   D. Houdini was born in Hungary in 1874; he later moved to America.

3. How might you combine sentences 5 and 6 to form a complex sentence?

   A. Although Houdini did not get very far in his education, he loved to read.

   B. Houdini did not get very far in his education; still, he loved to read.

   C. Houdini did not get very far in his education, but he loved to read.

   D. He loved to read; however, Houdini did not get very far in his education.

4. How might you combine sentences 8 and 9 to form a compound sentence?

   A. Because he decided he would be a magician too, he named himself "Houdini" after Robert-Houdin.

   B. After he decided he would be a magician too, he named himself "Houdini" after Robert-Houdin.

   C. He named himself "Houdini" after Robert-Houdin when he decided he would be a magician too.

   D. He decided he would be a magician too, and he named himself "Houdini" after Robert-Houdin.

STOP

749

ANSWERS
Writing & Grammar

1. **C is correct.** *This sentence has an independent clause and a dependent clause, making it a complex sentence.* A, B, *and* D *are each made up of two independent clauses, making them compound sentences.*

2. **D is correct.** *Two independent clauses are joined by a semicolon to form a compound sentence.* A, B, *and* C *are complex sentences. They include both dependent and independent clauses.*

3. **A is correct.** *The fragment becomes the independent clause, and sentence 5, with the addition of* although, *becomes the dependent clause.* B, C, *and* D *are all compound sentences.*

4. **D is correct.** *The conjunction* and *is used to join the independent clauses in sentences 8 and 9, forming a compound sentence.* A, B, *and* C *are complex sentences. They have dependent clauses beginning with* because, after, *and* when.

DIFFERENTIATED INSTRUCTION

FOR ENGLISH LEARNERS

Assessment Support: Compound and Complex Sentences Review the definition of each type of sentence with students. Discuss how the definitions apply to each example.

- *compound sentence*—combines two independent clauses, or sentences. Some compound sentences are formed with a conjunction such as *and, or,* or *but*. Others are formed with a semicolon. Examples:

  — The woodsman worked, and his wife made the meal.

  — King Midas wanted the golden touch, but he did not think of the consequences.

  — They did not wish for wealth; they felt rich enough already.

- *complex sentence*—has an independent clause and a dependent clause. Dependent clauses cannot stand alone as sentences. They begin with words such as *after, because, when, if, who,* and *which*. Examples:

  — When his food turned to gold, the king realized his foolishness.

  — The woodsman, who loved his wife, felt sorry for her.

Have students pick out other examples of complex sentences in the stories.

In Unit 6, students have discussed a number of big questions. Invite students to tell which question they found most intriguing and why. Then focus attention on the three questions that appear on this page. Discuss the recommended books and their summaries, pointing out how each book connects to the related question. Encourage students to choose one or more of these "great reads" to read independently.

ℹ ClassZone.com

To find additional books that match students' interests and ability levels, visit the Literature Center at **ClassZone.com**.

More Great Reads

UNIT 6

Ideas for Independent Reading

Which of the questions in Unit 6 made an impression on you? Continue exploring them with these books.

Do you think before you act?

Nothing but the Truth
by Avi

In this "documentary novel," 13-year-old Philip Malloy faces dire consequences when he defends his right to freedom of speech. The story is presented through fictional memos, letters, diary entries, and official school documents.

When JFK Was My Father
by Amy Gordon

When 13-year-old Georgia Hughes's family life is changed drastically, she creates a fantasy family in which President Kennedy is her father. What will she do when the time comes to consider reality and leave her fantasies behind?

Honus and Me
by Dan Gutman

Are you willing to risk a guilty conscience? Twelve-year-old Joe Stoshack discovers a baseball card worth half a million dollars—in someone else's attic. As he wrestles with his conscience, will he decide to keep the card?

Should people always reach for the stars?

Purely Rosie Pearl
by Patricia Cochrane

Two young girls—one an optimist and one a pessimist—help each other endure the hardships of the Great Depression. Is either philosophy right, or is the answer somewhere in between?

Through My Eyes
by Ruby Bridges

Could you be optimistic about your future in the face of awful experiences? Learn how Ruby Bridges kept her dreams alive as the only African-American first grader in a newly desegregated school in 1960.

Jazmin's Notebook
by Nikki Grimes

Fourteen-year-old Jazmin has been passed along from one foster home to another. When she is finally given a chance to realize her dream of becoming a writer, will she achieve her goal despite the obstacles?

Is there a job you were born to do?

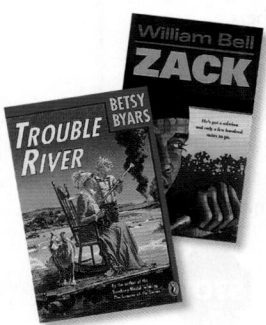

Zack
by William Bell

During a tough year at his new school, Zack discovers that a distant relative of his was a former slave who fought in the American Revolution. What he finds when he researches his family history will surprise you.

Promises to the Dead
by Mary Downing Hahn

Twelve-year-old Jesse promises Lydia, a dying runaway slave, that he will bring her young son Perry to relatives in Baltimore. Along the way, Jesse learns young Perry's true heritage and has to reevaluate everything he's ever known.

Trouble River
by Betsy Byars

Dewey Martin, a 12-year-old boy living in the 1800s, is left behind to tend the family farm while his parents go to Hunter City. Fearing an Indian raid, Dewey, his grandmother, and their dog, Charlie, set off on a small raft on the uncharted Trouble River— the only escape!

UNIT 7

Writing a Life

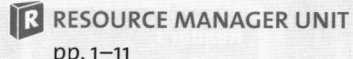

BIOGRAPHY AND AUTOBIOGRAPHY

- In Nonfiction
- In Media
- In Drama
- In Poetry

751

About the Art Francis Criss painted *Alma Sewing* about 1935. For more information, see page 846 of the teacher's edition.

For help in planning this unit, see

RESOURCE MANAGER UNIT 7
pp. 1–11

INTRODUCE THE UNIT

Hopes and dreams, achievements and disappointments, relationships, childhood experiences—authors consider all of these things when they write about a person's life. Invite students to share ideas about the details of people's lives that make interesting stories.

Ask students to keep the idea of life stories in mind as they discuss the pictures on this page. To spark a discussion, ask

- Whose life is being depicted in each picture?
- Based on the details included, what does each picture tell you about the life of the central character?
- What can you tell about the goals, interests, and concerns of the people depicted?
- If you were going to create a picture that represents important details of your own life, what would it show?

Explain that in this unit, students will read **biography** and **autobiography** and explore the choices authors make in deciding how to write about a person's life.

UNIT 7
Standards Skills Trace

MARYLAND

Assessment-Based Planning: Skills in red are assessed on the Unit 7 Test. **T** = Teacher's Edition page

SKILLS STRAND	Reader's Workshop: Biography and Autobiography pp. 754–759	Eleanor Roosevelt pp. 760–775 — Biography Level: Challenging	A First Lady Speaks Out pp. 776–779 — Letter, Autobiography Level: Average	Names/Nombres pp. 780–789 — Personal Essay Level: Challenging	from It's Not About the Bike / from 23 Days in July pp. 790–801 — Autobiography, Nonfiction Account Level: Challenging	from Malcolm X: By Any Means Necessary pp. 802–807 — Biography Level: Average
	1.E.3.a, 3.A.3.a	1.D.3.b, 1.E.3.a, 3.A.3.a	*Linked selections* · 1.E.4.c, 1.E.4.e	1.D.3.a, 1.E.4.f, 3.A.6.a, 5.C.2.c	1.D.3.b, 1.E.3.a, 1.E.4.c	1.E.1.b, 3.A.1.b
Literary Analysis	Biography and Autobiography pp. 754–759	Characteristics of a Biography pp. 761, 762, 765, 767, 769, 772, 773, 774		Characteristics of a Personal Essay pp. 781, 782, 785, 786, 787 · Writer's Message pp. 781, 787	Direct Quotations pp. 791, 792, 795, 796, 798, 800	Form (Biography) p. 802
Reading and Informational Texts	Strategies for Reading Biographies and Autobiographies p. 756 · Analyze the Literature pp. 755, 757–759	Identify Chronological Order pp. 761, 764, 767, 768, 773, 774	Synthesize pp. 776, 777, 778, 779 · Draw Conclusions p. 779 · Read a Letter p. 777 · Read an Autobiography p. 778	Connect pp. 781, 784, 786, 787	Make Inferences pp. 791, 794, 795, 799, 800	
Vocabulary	Academic Vocabulary p. 754	Word Acquisition pp. 761, T761, 775 · Context Clues p. T761 · Latin Roots (*domin*) p. 775		Word Acquisition pp. 781, T781, 788 · Context Clues p. T781 · Connotations and Meaning p. 788	Word Acquisition pp. 791, T791, 801 · Context Clues p. T791 · Base Words p. 801	
Writing, Grammar, and Style				Capitalization of Proper Nouns p. 789		
Speaking, Listening, Viewing, and Media	Discuss pp. 754–757	Discuss pp. 760, T762–T773, 774 · Analyze Visuals pp. 762, T765, 766, T770	Discuss pp. 776, T777–T778, 779	Discuss pp. 780, T782–T786, 787 · Analyze Visuals p. 782	Discuss pp. 790, T792–T799, 800 · Analyze Visuals pp. T792, 796, T798	Discuss pp. 802, T807

1.D.3.b, 1.E.4.e, 3.A.3.a | 2.A.4.a, 2.A.6.b, 4.A.7.a | 2.A.6.b | 1.E.3.a, 3.A.5.a, 5.C.2.c | 3.A.4.b, 3.A.7.c | 4.A.1, 4.A.2.a, 7.A.1

MARYLAND STANDARDS

For a full listing of state standards see page S1.

Linked selections		Media Study: *from* Jackie Robinson pp. 828–831	The Lucy Stone: Champion of Women's Rights pp. 832–843	My Mother Enters the Work Force / Washington Monument by Night pp. 844–849	Writing Workshop: Personal Narrative pp. 850–857
The Noble Experiment pp. 808–821	**Jackie Robinson Makes Headlines** pp. 822–827				
	Historical Sports Articles *Level: Average*				
Autobiography *Level: Average*		Documentary	Drama *Level: Average*	Poems *Level: Average*	
Characteristics of an Autobiography pp. 809, 810, 812, 814, 815, 816, 818, 820			Historical Drama pp. 833, T834, T836, T837, T838, T839, T840, T841	Speaker pp. 845, 846, 847, 849	
Summarize pp. 809, 812, 813, 817, 819, 820	Identify Treatment and Scope pp. 822, 824, 825, 827 Evaluate Texts for Usefulness p. 827 Identify Character-istics of a Historical Sports Article p. T823		Visualize pp. 833, T836, T838, T839, T840, T841	Parapahrase Figurative Language pp. 845, 846, 847, 849	Analyze a Personal Narrative pp. 851–852, 856
Word Acquisition pp. 809, T809, 821 Context Clues p. T809 Latin Roots (*spec*) p. 821		Academic Vocabulary (Video) p. 829	Word Acquisition pp. 833, T833 Context Clues p. T833		
			Punctuation of Titles p. 843		Write a Personal Narrative pp. 850–857 Quotations in Dialogue p. 856 Verb Tenses p. 856
Discuss pp. 808, T810–T819, 820 Analyze Visuals pp. 810, T815, T817	Discuss pp. 822, T823–T826, 827	Discuss pp. 828, 831 Analyze a Documentary pp. 829–831 Plan and Conduct an Interview p. 831	Discuss pp. 832, T834–T841, 842 Analyze Visuals pp. T834, T836, T839, T841	Discuss pp. 844, T846–T848, 849 Analyze Visuals p. 846	Discuss pp. 850–852 Present an Anecdote p. 857

Skills Assessed on the Unit 7 Test:

Literary Analysis
• Identify the form and characteristics of biography and autobiography

Reading and Informational Texts
• Identify chronological order
• Make inferences
• Summarize
• Synthesize
• Identify treatment and scope
• Evaluate texts for usefulness

Vocabulary
• Understand and use Latin roots
• Recognize base words

Writing, Grammar, and Style
• Write a personal narrative
• Capitalize proper nouns correctly
• Punctuate titles with italics and quotation marks
• Additional writing and grammar skills

For additional lesson planning help, see **Easy Planner DVD.**

OBJECTIVES

- establish prior knowledge about characteristics of autobiography
- present a personal narrative

How do we share
OUR STORIES?

Ask students what items they would expect to find in a scrapbook created by a person their age. Why would these items be meaningful to the person? List students' suggestions on the board and help students arrange them into categories such as *friends, family, goals, fun,* and *accomplishments*. Then discuss what items might be found in the scrapbook of an older person or a person living in a different culture.

ACTIVITY Suggest that as they decide on a story to tell, students should consider what they would most like their classmates to know or understand about them. Then they can choose details that emphasize what they want to express. Remind students that even a story from real life should have a beginning, a middle, and an end.

CHECK UNDERSTANDING Have students describe how they can learn about a person by hearing a story from the person's life.

How do we share
OUR STORIES?

Have you ever put together a photo album or scrapbook to help you tell others about an important event in your life? If someone looked through the book without you there to explain it, what would they learn about you? Sharing stories from our lives can help us better understand each other.

ACTIVITY Using words, pictures, or a mix of both, tell your class about a great day you had. As you share your story and listen to the stories told by your classmates, think about the following questions:

- In what ways are other stories similar to yours?
- In what ways are they different?
- What does each story teach you about the person telling it?
- What do your classmates learn about you from your story?

752

Unit Resources

 **RESOURCE MANAGER UNIT 7**

 **BEST PRACTICES TOOLKIT**

S **STANDARDS LESSON FILE**

- Easy Planner DVD
- Write*Smart* CD
- **i** ClassZone.com
- Audio Anthology CD
- **i** Multi-Language Academic Vocabulary Online

- eEdition CD & Online
- **i** McDougal Littell Assessment System
- Test Generator CD
- Media*Smart* DVD

 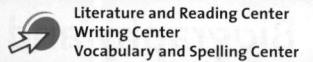

Online **LITERATURE** CLASSZONE.COM — Literature and Reading Center / Writing Center / Vocabulary and Spelling Center

MARYLAND OBJECTIVES

Preview Unit Goals

LITERARY ANALYSIS
- Identify form and characteristics of biography, autobiography, personal essay, and historical drama
- Read and identify characteristics of primary sources and newspaper articles

READING
- Identify chronological order
- Make inferences and draw conclusions
- Summarize
- Identify treatment and scope
- Evaluate texts for usefulness

WRITING AND GRAMMAR
- Write a personal narrative
- Punctuate titles with italics and quotation marks

SPEAKING, LISTENING, AND VIEWING
- Present a personal narrative
- Analyze a documentary
- Plan and conduct an interview

VOCABULARY
- Recognize base words
- Understand and use Latin roots

ACADEMIC VOCABULARY
- biography
- autobiography
- personal essay
- historical drama
- primary sources
- personal narrative

753

Preview Unit Goals

This page provides an overview of the skills and strategies covered in this unit. Color coding is used to identify each skill strand. This color coding is used wherever skills are taught in the unit. Encourage students to consider their ability to use each skill and strategy as they read this page.

Suggest that students copy the **Academic Vocabulary** terms in their journals and define them in their own words as they read the unit. Encourage students to use these terms as they discuss and write about the selections.

ADDITIONAL UNIT GOALS

These skills will be taught in this unit but are not the major focus of the unit:

Literary Analysis
- Identify and analyze speaker
- Identify and understand the role of direct quotations
- Use stage directions
- Evaluate figurative language
- Read and identify characteristics of a personal essay
- Study a variety of genres: biography, autobiography, letter, personal essay, historical drama, newspaper article

Reading
- Use strategies to connect and visualize
- Synthesize
- Analyze a writer's message
- Paraphrase figurative language

Writing and Grammar
- Use dialogue and punctuate it correctly
- Add sensory and descriptive details
- Capitalize proper nouns correctly
- Use verb tenses consistently

Speaking, Listening, and Viewing
- Identify ways information is presented in nonprint sources

Vocabulary
- Understand and use connotative meanings of words

DIFFERENTIATED INSTRUCTION

FOR ENGLISH LEARNERS

Academic Vocabulary Students will study and practice using these terms throughout the unit. Use the Academic Vocabulary copy master to introduce the terms.

1. Read each word aloud and discuss its definition. Ask students if they have heard any of these words and in what context.

2. Allow students to work in pairs to complete the examples and the activities. Then discuss students' answers as a class.

Additional Academic Vocabulary Use this copy master to teach additional academic vocabulary in the unit.

1. Divide the class into four groups. Assign two terms to each group. Have each group discuss their terms and write examples.

2. Have groups share their examples.

3. Have students complete Part B individually.

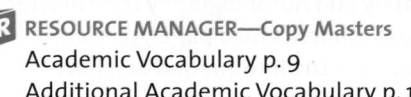 **RESOURCE MANAGER—Copy Masters**
Academic Vocabulary p. 9
Additional Academic Vocabulary p. 10

Focus and Motivate

OBJECTIVES
- identify forms and characteristics of biography and autobiography
- read biography and autobiography

Teach

Part 1: Understanding the Basics

Biography Explain that biographies are often written about famous people. If a person lived many years ago, it can be more difficult to gather information for his or her biography. Use this activity to explore the sources used for the biography of a historical figure:

- Make a two-column chart on the board. Label one column "May be available" and the other "Not available."
- Ask students what resources might be available for a biography of Abraham Lincoln. Review the chart on page 754 and have students give examples of each kind of source. Record their answers in the chart.

May be available	Not available
• letters to and from Lincoln	• interviews with Lincoln and people who knew him
• previous biographies of Lincoln	
• history books	
• diaries kept by Lincoln or his family members	
• interview with historian	

Autobiography Autobiographies are often written by famous people, such as presidents, movie stars, and athletes. Challenge students to think of reasons why an ordinary person might write an autobiography. Make a list of their responses on the board. *(Reasons might include sharing an interesting background, hobby, talent, or travel experience.)*

 BEST PRACTICES TOOLKIT—Transparencies
Analysis Frame: Literary Nonfiction pp. D23, D50, D51

Biography and Autobiography

What was it like to be the first person to set foot on the moon? How did World War II soldiers deal with the horrors of combat while so far away from home? What is an athlete thinking the moment he or she crosses the finish line? We are all curious about other people—about what they do, why they do it, and how they feel. You can satisfy this curiosity by reading biographies and autobiographies.

 MARYLAND OBJECTIVES

READING/LIT STANDARDS
1.E.3.a Select and apply appropriate strategies during reading
3.A.3.a Distinguish among types of narrative texts

Part 1: Understanding the Basics

A **biography** is a story of a person's life told by someone else and written from the third-person point of view. The writer, or **biographer,** usually gets information about the subject by doing detailed research using a number of sources. Sometimes, the biographer might even interview the subject directly.

An **autobiography** is also the story of a person's life, but it is told by that person and is written from the first-person point of view. Although most of the information is from the subject's mind and memories, he or she may still consult others for help in remembering details about his or her life.

Usually, when people talk about biographies or autobiographies, they are referring to whole books about people's lives. However, biographical and autobiographical writing also includes other forms, shown in the chart.

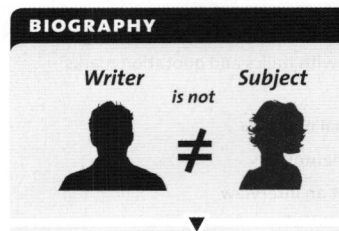

BIOGRAPHY

Writer *is not* Subject

SOURCES
- letters to and from the subject
- interviews with the subject and/or others
- books about the subject
- diaries or journals

FORMS
- biographical books
- encyclopedia entries
- feature articles in newspapers and magazines or on Web sites

AUTOBIOGRAPHY

Writer *is* Subject

SOURCES
- memories
- thoughts and feelings
- family, friends, or associates
- memorabilia

FORMS
- autobiographical books
- diaries and journals
- personal essays
- memoirs

DIFFERENTIATED INSTRUCTION

FOR ALL STUDENTS
For general guidelines on differentiating instruction, see

 BEST PRACTICES TOOLKIT
Differentiated Instruction pp. 31–38

FOR LESS—PROFICIENT READERS
Note Taking For students who need help with note taking, hand out the Note Taking: Biography and Autobiography copy master and have students read page 754 silently. Then discuss the information and have students record notes on the copy master.

 RESOURCE MANAGER—Copy Master
Note Taking p. 15

FOR ENGLISH LEARNERS
Vocabulary Support: Greek Roots Point out the Greek roots in *biography* and *autobiography*. *(auto = self; bio = life; graph = write)* Discuss other English words with these roots, such as *automatic, biology,* and *autograph*.

MODEL 1: BIOGRAPHY

This excerpt is from a biography about Wilbur and Orville Wright, two brothers who invented and flew the first machine-powered airplane.

from
THE WRIGHT BROTHERS

Biography by **Russell Freedman**

Orville was more impulsive, "bubbling over with ideas," according to his niece. Among family and friends, he had a reputation as a tease and a practical joker. Among strangers, however, he seemed uncomfortably shy. He would clam up and fade silently into the background.

5   Orville's greatest pleasure was to take something apart, see how it worked, and put it back together. Wilbur was more of a visionary, fascinated by the big picture rather than its individual parts. He was the one who first dreamed of building an airplane. . . .

Close Read

1. What clues tell you that this is a biography rather than an autobiography?

2. How were Wilbur and Orville different? Cite details to support your answer. Also note who provided the author with some of these details.

MODEL 2: AUTOBIOGRAPHY

Now read this excerpt from the autobiography of a Japanese-American author. What do you learn about her thoughts and feelings?

from
THE INVISIBLE THREAD
Autobiography by **Yoshiko Uchida**

I was born in California, recited the Pledge of Allegiance to the flag each morning at school, and loved my country as much as any other American—maybe even more.

Still, there was a large part of me that was Japanese simply because
5   Mama and Papa had passed on to me so much of their own Japanese spirit and soul. Their own values of loyalty, honor, self-discipline, love, and respect for one's parents, teachers, and superiors were all very much a part of me.

There was also my name, which teachers couldn't seem to pronounce
10 properly even when I shortened my first name to Yoshi. And there was my Japanese face, which closed more and more doors to me as I grew older.

How wonderful it would be, I used to think, if I had blond hair and blue eyes like Marian and Solveig.

Close Read

1. What clues in the boxed sentences signal that this is an autobiography?

2. Name two things you learn about Uchida from her description of her own thoughts and feelings.

MODEL 1: BIOGRAPHY
Close Read

1. ***Possible answer:*** *Orville and Wilbur are described from the third-person point of view, not from the first-person.*

    If students need help . . . Have them paraphrase the first paragraph as if it were an autobiography by Orville Wright.

2. ***Possible answer:*** *Wilbur was more of a dreamer, while Orville liked to find out how things worked. Details include "take something apart" (line 5) to describe what Orville enjoyed and "visionary" (line 6) to describe Wilbur. These details come from the brothers' family and friends (line 2).*

MODEL 2: AUTOBIOGRAPHY
Close Read

1. ***Possible answer:*** *The writer uses the first-person point of view. She expresses her feelings of love (line 2) and her desire to fit in (lines 12–13).*

2. ***Possible answer:*** *She is proud to be an American (lines 1–3). We also learn that she experienced discrimination because of her Japanese heritage. She feels that doors were closed to her because she looked Japanese (lines 10–11).*

FOR ENGLISH LEARNERS

Language Support: First-Person Pronouns
Point out that in autobiographies, the authors refer to themselves and those they know with first-person pronouns *(I, me, my, we, us, our)*. Have students find examples in Model 2.

FOR ADVANCED LEARNERS/PRE–AP

Plan a Biography or Autobiography Allow students to choose one of these activities to explore biography or autobiography:

* Select a famous, interesting person. List all the sources you would use to write this person's biography. Think like a detective!

* Imagine that you are going to write your autobiography. List the events, experiences, and ideas you will write about. Also list any people you might talk to to help you remember events.

Teach

Part 2: Reading Biographies and Autobiographies

Biography Share with students these clues that might suggest a lack of objectivity in a biography:

- praising the subject as the "greatest writer," "best athlete," or "most brilliant scientist"

- using only sources that agree with the biographer's own opinion

- leaving unexplained gaps in the story, such as not telling the reader that the subject spent six months in prison

- writing the biography right after a major event in the subject's life, when the full and most accurate set of facts might not yet be available

- suggesting that this biography is the only one readers would ever need to read on the subject

Ask students to think of a movie based on the life of a famous person. Did they notice any evidence that the presentation was slanted either for or against the subject? Have them explain their answers.

Autobiography Point out to students that there are many reasons why a person would choose to write an autobiography. Here are a few examples:

- to capitalize on his or her fame and make money

- to defend against criticism by telling his or her own side of the story

- to help others understand who he or she is and why he or she has certain beliefs and feelings

- to inspire others to overcome adversity or to achieve their own dreams

- to leave an accurate record of his or her experiences

Invite students to add to the list. Help students identify which reasons for writing an autobiography might lead to a book that is worth reading.

Part 2: Reading Biographies and Autobiographies

Picture yourself standing in front of a shelf at the library, a book in each hand. One is an autobiography of somebody who interests you—perhaps your favorite musician or a former president. The other is a biography of the same person. From which book would you learn more?

You might think that an autobiography is the better source. After all, who knows more about a person's life experiences than that person? Actually, though, each form has strengths and limitations that readers should consider. (Of course, if you want to get a well-rounded picture of a person—and his or her accomplishments and flaws—you should read both forms.)

BIOGRAPHY	AUTOBIOGRAPHY
When you read a biography, you . . .	**When you read an autobiography, you . . .**
• get information from a variety of sources	• get the subject's own interpretation of events
• discover how other people view the subject	• learn the subject's private thoughts and feelings
• might get a more objective picture of the subject's life	• hear the subject's voice and get a sense of his or her personality

Eleanor Roosevelt
by William Jay Jacobs
pages 762–773

The Noble Experiment
by Jackie Robinson as told to Alfred Duckett
pages 810–819

However, you should ask

- How does the writer feel about the subject? A writer's tone or choice of words can reveal his or her personal bias.

- Who are the writer's sources—historians, people close to the subject, the subject, or people who barely knew him or her? A biography is only as reliable as its sources.

- When was this work written? A biography written halfway through the subject's life would be very different from one written 100 years later.

However, you should ask

- Is there another side to the story? Other people in the subject's life might have different recollections or opinions of events.

- Have any details been left out? The subject may have forgotten something or might be leaving out certain details to make himself- or herself look better.

- At what point in the subject's life did he or she write the autobiography? When the subject wrote the work affects what experiences he or she writes about.

DIFFERENTIATED INSTRUCTION

FOR LESS–PROFICIENT READERS

Note Taking For students who need help with note taking, hand out the copy master. Read aloud the information on page 756 about the possible strengths and weaknesses of each type of writing. Have students take notes on the copy master as you read.

 RESOURCE MANAGER—Copy Master
Note Taking p. 16

FOR ENGLISH LEARNERS

Language Support: Objectivity and Bias
Explain that the main idea of page 756 is that readers must analyze biographies and autobiographies to decide whether the information can be trusted. Have mixed language-ability pairs use context clues on the page to define the following terms related to this concept: *well-rounded, objective, bias, reliable, interpretation, opinions.* Ask students to write an original sentence using each word.

MODEL 1: READING A BIOGRAPHY

The actor Christopher Reeve was famous for his 1978 movie role as Superman. This article was published in 1982.

from

Feature article in *Current Biography*

Another outstanding quality is that he [Reeve] brings the same energy and enthusiasm to his recreations that he does to acting: he owns both a $350,000 private plane and a glider; he is an accomplished sailor who, upon completing *Superman,* gathered a six-man crew and sailed
5 a boat from Connecticut to Bermuda; and he has played classical piano since adolescence, usually practicing ninety minutes every day, and also composes music. His hobbies, moreover, include skiing, ice-skating, and playing tennis. But nothing takes precedence over his work, as Aljean Harmetz told readers of the *New York Times* (August 20, 1979), "He
10 thrives on acting. . . ." According to her, Reeve admitted: ". . . [I am] still at the stage where I'm taking care of myself, my career, first."

Close Read

1. Look at the boxed details. How would you describe the author's attitude toward Reeve?

2. What source does the author use for quotes by and about Reeve?

3. Based on this article, how would you describe Reeve?

MODEL 2: READING AN AUTOBIOGRAPHY

In 1995, a fall from a horse left Reeve paralyzed from the neck down, and he died in 2004. In this essay, Reeve reminds people not to let fear take over their lives. Reeve conquered his own fears when he participated in research for spinal cord injuries.

from

LIVING WITHOUT FEAR

Personal essay by **Christopher Reeve**

Of course, the greater difficulty lies in being fearless in surrendering and in giving. I don't want to sound too noble, but I really have been able to say, All right, I've had some setbacks, but look at the other people who have benefited.
5 I recommend you do the same thing because being fearless is not always going to get you exactly where you expect to go. It might take you in a completely different direction. It might not give you what you want, but it can satisfy you to know you did something for the world, for the planet, or even just for your family or your neighbors. And that's enough.

Close Read

1. Describe Reeve's personality at this point in his life. In your opinion, has his attitude toward life changed or stayed the same?

2. What picture do you get of Reeve's life as a whole? Explain how this picture would be different if you had only read one of these excerpts.

MODEL 1: READING A BIOGRAPHY
Close Read

1. *Possible answer: The author has a very favorable attitude toward Reeve. She admires his many talents.*

2. *Possible answer: The source is an article in the* New York Times *written by Aljean Harmetz.*

3. *Possible answer: Reeve is very energetic in all aspects of his life. He has many interests. In addition to acting, he is a skilled sailor and pianist. Although he has a number of different hobbies, he always puts his work first.*

MODEL 2: READING AN AUTOBIOGRAPHY
Close Read

1. *Possible answer: Reeve is fearless, courageous, and realistic. His attitude toward life has changed because he has had to deal with setbacks and limitations. He now thinks more about others than about himself. However, his enthusiasm for life remains strong.*

2. *Possible answer: Reeve experienced great successes as well as great challenges in his life. If I had read only one of the excerpts, I would not have understood either what his life was like before the accident or how the accident changed his outlook on life.*

DIFFERENTIATED INSTRUCTION

FOR ENGLISH LEARNERS

Concept Support: Reading a Biography
Remind students that one of the questions to ask when reading a biography is "When was this work written?" Help students recall that Model 1 was written in 1982, long before the accident in 1995 that changed Reeve's life. Ask students to think of another famous person they know whose biography would be much different if it had been written before a certain date. Have them share their examples.

Concept Support: Reading an Autobiography
Remind students that one of the strengths of an autobiography is that it provides the subject's own interpretation of events. Help students review Model 2 for examples, such as

- Reeve refers to his accident as a "setback" (line 3).
- He feels that his setback has helped other people (lines 3–4).

Practice and Apply

Part 3: Analyze the Literature

Close Read

1. **Possible answer:** *Readers know that this excerpt is from a biography because it is written in the third person. The subject, Rosa Parks, is referred to as "Parks" (line 3), "her" (line 6), and "she" (line 6). Also, the writer quotes Parks's own words on the topic (lines 27–28).*

2. **Possible answer:** *Parks's words are simple, direct, and strong. She says, "No," when asked to move (line 7). Her action of refusing to give up her seat even when threatened with arrest (lines 6–8) shows her courage. The author admires Parks for taking a firm position while noting that other black passengers left the bus.*

3. **Possible answer:** *Parks was brought up by her mother and grandparents. They had taught her that she was not inferior to white people.*

4. **Possible answer:** *Another example of Parks's thoughts and feelings is the statement that "she was uncertain about what exactly had provoked her not to move" (lines 24–25).*

Part 3: Analyze the Literature

In 1955, a 42-year-old African-American woman in Montgomery, Alabama, refused to give up her seat on a public bus. Her action sparked a citywide bus boycott and helped break down the barriers of racial segregation in the South. Her name was Rosa Parks.

The first excerpt is from a biography of Parks; the second is from her autobiography. What do you learn about Parks from each excerpt?

from

ROSA PARKS

Biography by **Mary Hull**

The driver [J. F. Blake] repeated his order: "Look, woman, I told you I wanted the seat. Are you going to stand up?"

In a firm, steady voice, Parks questioned him. "Why should I have to get up and stand? Why should we have to be pushed around?"

5 The driver slammed on the brakes and pulled the bus over to the curb. He walked back to her seat and stood over her. He asked her if she was going to move, and Parks said, "No." He told her he would call the police if she did not move. "Go ahead. You may do that," Parks answered. Blake left the bus angrily and went for the police. Several

10 passengers—all of them black—followed, reluctant to become involved in an incident that invited trouble with whites. While everyone else aboard the bus waited to see what would happen next, Parks looked out the window at Montgomery.

Parks had a right to be scared, for she recognized the driver. Twelve

15 years earlier, she had refused to enter a bus through the rear door and had been evicted from the bus by this same driver. Although Parks had seen him before while waiting at bus stops, she never boarded a bus if she knew he was driving. In all these years she had never forgotten his face. That evening, Parks had not looked at the driver when she boarded,

20 but when he stood over her, there was no mistaking who he was.

Parks's mother and grandparents had always taught her not to regard herself as inferior to whites because she was black, but she admitted that until that fateful December day on the bus "every part of my life pointed to the white superiority and negro inferiority." She was uncertain about

25 what exactly had provoked her not to move on the bus driver's order, but her feet certainly hurt, her shoulders ached, and suddenly everything became too much. "I had had enough," Parks later said. She was tired of giving in. "I wanted to be treated like a human being."

Close Read

1. How can you tell that this excerpt is from a biography? Cite details to support your answer.

2. Consider how the author describes Parks's words and actions in lines 3–13. How does the author seem to feel about Parks?

3. What do you learn about Parks's upbringing from this biography?

4. One of the sources for this biography was Rosa Parks's own autobiography. As a result, the author was able to include details about Parks's thoughts and feelings. One example is boxed. Find one more.

DIFFERENTIATED INSTRUCTION

FOR ENGLISH LEARNERS

Culture: Clarify Be sure students understand that in 1955 in the South, African Americans were required to enter buses through the rear door and sit in the back. That section of a bus is nearer to the exhaust fumes, and the ride is noisier and bumpier. African Americans were also required to stand if a white person needed a seat. If they did not cooperate, they could be arrested and sent to jail.

Now read this excerpt from the beginning of Parks's autobiography. Pay attention to how Parks describes the incident on the bus. Also notice what she reveals about her thoughts and feelings at that time in her life.

from

Rosa Parks:
My Story

Autobiography by **Rosa Parks**
(with Jim Haskins)

One evening in early December 1955 I was sitting in the front seat of the colored section of a bus in Montgomery, Alabama. The white people were sitting in the white section. More white people got on, and they filled up all the seats in the white section. When that happened, we black people
5   were supposed to give up our seats to the whites. But I didn't move. The white driver said, "Let me have those front seats." I didn't get up. I was tired of giving in to white people.
    "I'm going to have you arrested," the driver said.
    "You may do that," I answered.
10 Two white policemen came. I asked one of them, "Why do you all push us around?"
    He answered, "I don't know, but the law is the law and you're under arrest."

For half of my life there were laws and customs in the South that kept African Americans segregated from Caucasians and allowed white
15 people to treat black people without any respect. I never thought this was fair, and from the time I was a child, I tried to protest against disrespectful treatment. But it was very hard to do anything about segregation and racism when white people had the power of the law behind them.
20 Somehow we had to change the laws. And we had to get enough white people on our side to be able to succeed. I had no idea when I refused to give up my seat on that Montgomery bus that my small action would help put an end to the segregation laws in the South. I only knew that I was tired of being pushed around. I was a regular
25 person, just as good as anybody else.

Close Read

1. Reread the boxed sentences. Would you say that this autobiography was written in the 1950s, or later? Explain.

2. How can you tell that the author of the biography used Parks's autobiography as a source? Cite similar details in both excerpts to support your answer.

3. By revealing her thoughts and beliefs in lines 13–25, Parks gives readers a real sense of her personality. How would you describe her? In your opinion, do you get this same sense from reading the biography about her? Support your answer.

Close Read

1. *Possible answer: This autobiography was written later than the 1950s because the boxed sentences refer to the end of segregation laws in the South, which happened years later. The Civil Rights Act was passed in 1965.*

2. **Possible answers:**

Detail	Biography	Autobiography
"You may do that."	line 8	line 9
wonders why black people are "pushed around"	line 4	lines 10–11
"tired of giving in"	lines 27–28	line 7

3. *Possible answer: Parks is a respectful person who wants to be treated with respect. She has the courage to challenge an unfair system. The biography reveals similar qualities, but it also emphasizes her fear of that particular bus driver. The autobiography does not mention her fear.*

Assess and Reteach

Assess

Have students briefly summarize what a biography is and what an autobiography is, and the strengths and weaknesses of each.

Reteach

For students who are unable to apply the workshop skills to the two excerpts, select from these reteaching options:

1. Have students review their note-taking copy masters. Have them select one question for each type of writing. Read aloud lines from each excerpt that will help them answer that question.

2. Have students review the models for this lesson. Remind them that a first-person narrator can express thoughts and feelings. In each part, ask them which model is written in the first person. Have them give an example of a thought or feeling expressed by each narrator.

DIFFERENTIATED INSTRUCTION

FOR ADVANCED LEARNERS/PRE–AP

Make Judgments Have students think about what might have happened if Rosa Parks had not recognized the bus driver as the same one who had evicted her from a bus years earlier. Have those who believe that she would have still refused to give up her seat explain their reasons to the class. Have those who believe that she would have given up her seat explain their reasons as well. Let the class decide which group presents the more convincing argument.

Focus and Motivate

OBJECTIVES

Literary Analysis
- explore the key idea of **duty**
- analyze biography
- read a biography

Reading
- identify chronological order

Vocabulary
- build vocabulary for reading and writing
- understand and use the Latin root *domin* (also an EL language objective)

SUMMARY

In his biography of Eleanor Roosevelt, William Jay Jacobs traces his subject's life from her unhappy childhood to her role as a fighter for the rights of the less fortunate. Jacobs highlights the turning points in her life, including her education at Allenswood Academy, her marriage to Franklin D. Roosevelt, her growing independence when he was struck with polio, and her work as First Lady that continued after his death.

What is your DUTY *to others?*

Discuss the question with students. To lead into the *KEY IDEA,* explain that a **duty** is often something that people think they *should* do. Ask students to think of different reasons someone might feel a sense of duty. Extend the discussion by having students do the *QUICKWRITE* activity.

Selection Resources

R RESOURCE MANAGER UNIT 7

Plan and Teach pp. 17–24

Literary Analysis
Summary pp. 25†*, 26‡*
Biography pp. 27, 28†*
Question Support p. 35*

Reading
Identify Chronological Order
    pp. 29, 30†*
Reading Check p. 34
Reading Fluency p. 36

Vocabulary
Study p. 31*
Practice p. 32
Strategy p. 33

Assessment
Selection Tests A, B/C pp. 37*, 39*
🔘 Test Generator CD

💼 BEST PRACTICES TOOLKIT

Differentiated Instruction
    pp. 31–38*
Scaffolding Instruction
    pp. 43–46*

Graphic Organizers/Strategies
DRTA • Word Questioning •
Think-Pair-Share • Venn Diagram
• Cause-and-Effect Diagram •
T Chart • Jigsaw

Reading Support
🔘 Audio Anthology CD*

Technology
ℹ️ Literature and Vocabulary
    Centers at **ClassZone.com**

🔘 Write*Smart* CD

* Resources for Differentiation   † Also in Spanish   ‡ In Haitian Creole and Vietnamese

---

Eleanor Roosevelt
Biography by William Jay Jacobs

What is your DUTY *to others?*

MARYLAND OBJECTIVES

READING/LIT STANDARDS
1.E.3.a Select and apply appropriate strategies during reading
3.A.3.a Distinguish among types of narrative texts

KEY IDEA There are probably times when you wish you didn't owe anything to anyone. However, like most people, you have responsibilities to many different people. Family members, teachers, classmates, and the teams and other groups you belong to all need you in one way or another. In "Eleanor Roosevelt," you'll learn how a famous first lady's commitment to her **duties** changed history.

QUICKWRITE Make a list of your duties to others. Which of these do you think will most influence the adult you will become? Explore that question in a journal entry, considering career possibilities and other life choices you will be making.

760

LITERARY ANALYSIS: BIOGRAPHY

A **biography** is the story of a person's life told by another person, a biographer. Biographers often reveal their personal opinions of their subject. However, they also balance their opinions with facts and details that

- provide information about the person's life
- reveal important aspects of his or her personality
- show us what others thought of the person
- explain the importance of his or her life and work

As you read "Eleanor Roosevelt," notice how a biography can make you feel about a historical figure.

READING SKILL: IDENTIFY CHRONOLOGICAL ORDER

A biography usually presents events in **chronological order,** or the order in which they happened. Words and phrases such as *then, next, within 18 months, meanwhile, by spring,* and *the first few years* may signal the order of events in this type of work.

As you read "Eleanor Roosevelt," keep track of the order of events on a timeline like the one shown.

> October 11, 1884   Eleanor is 6.
> ├─────────────┼──────────────┤─────────────→
> Eleanor   Elliott and   Eleanor's father
> Roosevelt is born.   Hall are born.   enters sanitarium.

VOCABULARY IN CONTEXT

These headlines describe important moments in Eleanor Roosevelt's life. Use context clues to figure out the meaning of each boldfaced word.

1. Woman from **Prominent** Family Leads by Example
2. First Lady Is **Compassionate** Toward Others
3. **Impoverished** Families Going Hungry in America
4. **Migrant** Workers Search for Jobs
5. Roosevelt Feels **Grave** Obligation to Help
6. Women **Dominate** at Home-Front Meeting
7. **Wavering** Members Convinced to Support War Effort
8. Country **Brooding** at Death of President

Author Online

The Biographer
As an author who wrote more than 30 biographies, William Jay Jacobs said that he was "able to reach a very special audience: young people searching for models. . . ."

William Jay Jacobs
1933–2004

A Strong Role
Model Jacobs admired Eleanor Roosevelt for her strength of character. He noted, "The more I learned about Eleanor Roosevelt, the more I saw her as a woman of courage. She turned her pain to strength."

 MORE ABOUT THE AUTHOR
For more on William Jay Jacobs, visit the **Literature Center** at **ClassZone.com.**

Background

Hard Times Eleanor Roosevelt was first lady of the United States from 1933 to 1945. Her husband, Franklin D. Roosevelt, took office during the Great Depression, a worldwide economic crisis that lasted through most of the 1930s. Millions of Americans were unemployed, penniless, and suffering.

Help on the Way To encourage recovery, the Roosevelt administration introduced programs—such as Social Security and a minimum wage—that still provide relief today. Many of the First Lady's ideas were incorporated into her husband's New Deal programs.

Teach

STANDARDS FOCUS

LITERARY ANALYSIS

● BIOGRAPHY

Remind students that facts can be proven, while opinions express a person's feelings. Ask students to explain which of these is a fact and which is an opinion:

> Eleanor Roosevelt was born in 1884.
> She is a good role model.

Answer: The first is a fact; it can be proven by checking public records. The second is an opinion; it expresses a feeling.

CHECK UNDERSTANDING Ask students to suggest facts and opinions that might be found in a biography.

READING SKILL

■ IDENTIFY CHRONOLOGICAL ORDER

Read aloud these statements:

> Eleanor's parents had two more children after she was born. A little later, her father entered a sanitarium.

Ask which clue words relate to the order of events on the timeline. *Possible answer: After: "Elliott and Hall are born." A little later: "Eleanor's father enters sanitarium."*

CHECK UNDERSTANDING Have students create a timeline for events in this school year.

 RESOURCE MANAGER—Copy Master
Chronological Order p. 29 (for student use while reading the selection)

▲ VOCABULARY IN CONTEXT

DIAGNOSE WORD KNOWLEDGE To determine preteaching needs, have all students complete **Vocabulary in Context.** *Possible answers:*
1. *important* (p. 768); 2. *kind* (p. 771); 3. *poor* (p. 771); 4. *traveling* (p. 771); 5. *serious* (p. 768); 6. *are most important* (p. 767); 7. *undecided* (p. 772); 8. *feeling sad* (p. 768)

PRETEACH VOCABULARY Use the Vocabulary Study copy master to help students predict

meanings for each boldfaced word, using context clues.
1. Read the first sentence in Part A aloud, emphasizing *brooding.*
2. Point out the phrase "after her parents died." Have students suggest possible meanings for *brooding,* such as "unhappy."
3. Repeat the procedure for items 2–8.

 **RESOURCE MANAGER—Copy Master**
Vocabulary Study p. 31

For general guidelines on differentiating vocabulary instruction and for alternative vocabulary activities for students not needing vocabulary preteaching, see

🧰 **BEST PRACTICES TOOLKIT**
Scaffolding Vocabulary Instruction pp. 43–46

ℹ️ Vocabulary Center at **ClassZone.com**
Additional Vocabulary Activities

ANALYZE VISUALS

Possible answer: *She is an older woman who is happy with her life and content with who she is. She has a welcoming smile, and her eyes seem kind. Although she is dressed simply, her well-groomed hair and jewelry suggest she is a regal, dignified woman.*

LITERARY ANALYSIS

A BIOGRAPHY

Possible answer: *An overview quickly introduces why the subject is important and well-known. It also allows Jacobs to contrast Mrs. Roosevelt's adult self with the frightened child she once was, and he introduces an important theme about her strength of character.*

If students need help . . . Ask them to brainstorm all the details about Mrs. Roosevelt that they learn in the overview. Have them consider how these facts set the stage for understanding the rest of the piece.

Extend the Discussion Why do you think Mrs. Roosevelt is "remembered as one of America's greatest women"?

Eleanor Roosevelt

WILLIAM JAY JACOBS

Eleanor Roosevelt was the wife of President Franklin Delano Roosevelt. But Eleanor was much more than just a president's wife, an echo of her husband's career.

Sad and lonely as a child, Eleanor was called "Granny" by her mother because of her seriousness. People teased her about her looks and called her the "ugly duckling.". . .

Yet despite all of the disappointments, the bitterness, the misery she experienced, Eleanor Roosevelt refused to give up. Instead she turned her unhappiness and pain to strength. She devoted her life to helping
10 others. Today she is remembered as one of America's greatest women. **A**

Eleanor was born in a fine townhouse in Manhattan. Her family also owned an elegant mansion along the Hudson River, where they spent weekends and summers. As a child Eleanor went to fashionable parties. A servant took care of her and taught her to speak French.
Her mother, the beautiful Anna Hall Roosevelt, wore magnificent jewels and fine clothing. Her father, Elliott Roosevelt, had his own hunting lodge and liked to sail and to play tennis and polo. Elliott, who loved Eleanor dearly, was the younger brother of Theodore Roosevelt, who in 1901 became president of the United States. The Roosevelt family,
20 one of America's oldest, wealthiest families, was respected and admired.

ANALYZE VISUALS
What can you **infer** about Eleanor Roosevelt from this 1957 photograph taken at her home?

① Targeted Passage

A BIOGRAPHY
Why might Jacobs have chosen to begin with an overview of Mrs. Roosevelt's life?

DIFFERENTIATED INSTRUCTION

FOR ALL STUDENTS

Expert Groups Write these topics on the board and allow individual students or groups to select topics to research.
- Theodore Roosevelt
- polio
- Franklin D. Roosevelt's presidency
- UN Declaration of Human Rights

FOR LESS–PROFICIENT READERS

In combination with the *Audio Anthology CD*, use one or more Targeted Passages (pp. 762, 767, 770, 773) to ensure that students focus on key events, concepts, and skills.

① Targeted Passage [Lines 1–14]

This passage provides an overview of Eleanor Roosevelt's life and gives important details about her childhood.

- Who was Eleanor Roosevelt?
- What were the good things and the bad things about her childhood?
- How did Eleanor Roosevelt respond to the hardships of her life?

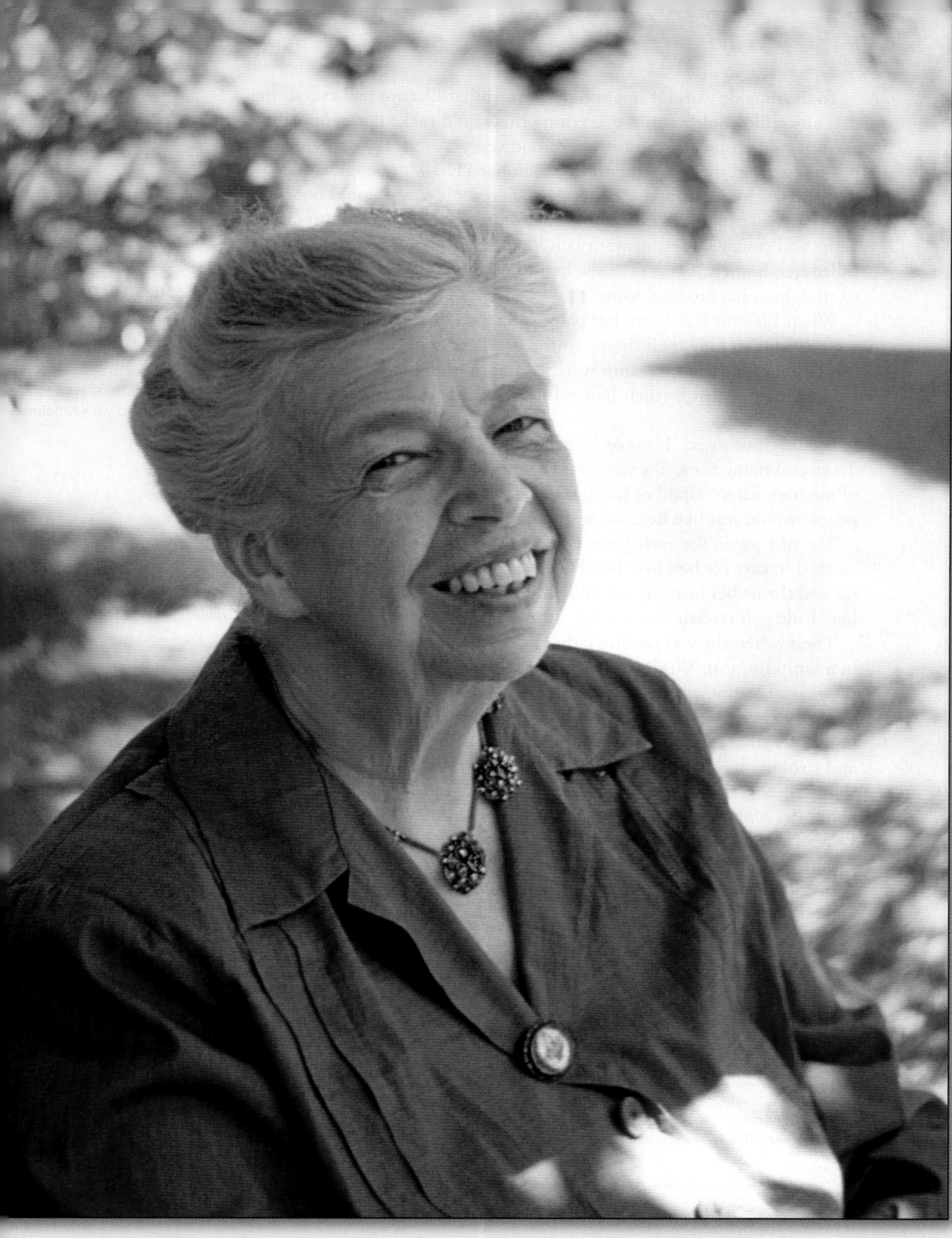

BACKGROUND

The Roosevelt Family The Roosevelts were among the early Dutch settlers of New York, when it was known as New Amsterdam. Claes Martenszen van Rosenvelt came to America from the Netherlands in the 1640s. His name meant "Nicholas, son of Martin of the Rose Field." Descendants of Nicholas's son Johannes included President Theodore Roosevelt and Eleanor Roosevelt's father, Elliott. Descendants of Nicholas's other son, Jacobus, included President Franklin Delano Roosevelt. The Roosevelts were wealthy merchants who invested in industry and owned many acres of land around New York City and along the Hudson River. Family members believed it was their duty to use their wealth in service to others.

FDR's Presidency As the **Background** note on page 761 explains, FDR's presidency coincided with most of the Great Depression. During these bleak years, factories were shut down, banks failed, and families lost their homes; many feared that the country itself was falling apart. In his inaugural address, FDR inspired confidence, stating that "the only thing we have to fear is fear itself." A natural leader, he quickly took action, passing strong, innovative legislation to create jobs and help farmers, small businesses, and the needy. For example, by establishing the Civilian Conservation Corps (CCC), FDR gave nearly 3 million young men a welcome alternative to unemployment: they were given food, housing, uniforms, and wages in exchange for working in national forests. The Public Works Administration (PWA) provided employment on roads, dams, and other public projects.

FOR ENGLISH LEARNERS

Options for Reading Read the first Targeted Passage aloud and ask students what it tells them about Eleanor Roosevelt. Then have students listen to the *Audio Anthology CD.* Use a DRTA strategy to help them read and understand the selection.

Key Academic Vocabulary Use Word Questioning to provide instruction and practice for this academic vocabulary: *team* (lines 106, 108), *recover* (lines 219, 223), *energy* (line 219), *priority* (line 271), *assembly* (lines 311, 324), *convinced* (line 313).

BEST PRACTICES TOOLKIT—Transparencies
Directed Reading-Thinking Activity p. A20
Word Questioning p. E9

Prereading For prereading instruction for English learners, see

BEST PRACTICES TOOLKIT
Scaffolding Reading Instruction pp. 43–46

FOR ADVANCED LEARNERS/PRE–AP

Pre-AP exercises in the bottom channel provide additional challenge for your advanced students. Use them for small groups or individuals.

ADDITIONAL GUIDELINES

For more help with differentiation and tips for classroom management, see

BEST PRACTICES TOOLKIT
Differentiated Instruction pp. 31–38

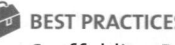

To the outside world it might have seemed that Eleanor had everything that any child could want—everything that could make her happy. But she was not happy. Instead her childhood was very sad.

Almost from the day of her birth, October 11, 1884, people noticed that she was an unattractive child. As she grew older, she could not help but notice her mother's extraordinary beauty, as well as the beauty of her aunts and cousins. Eleanor was plain looking, ordinary, even, as some called her, homely. For a time she had to wear a bulky brace on her back to straighten her crooked spine. **B**

30 When Eleanor was born, her parents had wanted a boy. They were scarcely able to hide their disappointment. Later, with the arrival of two boys, Elliott and Hall, Eleanor watched her mother hold the boys on her lap and lovingly stroke their hair, while for Eleanor there seemed only coolness, distance.

Feeling unwanted, Eleanor became shy and withdrawn. She also developed many fears. She was afraid of the dark, afraid of animals, afraid of other children, afraid of being scolded, afraid of strangers, afraid that people would not like her. She was a frightened, lonely little girl.

The one joy in the early years of her life was her father, who always 40 seemed to care for her, love her. He used to dance with her, to pick her up and throw her into the air while she laughed and laughed. He called her "little golden hair" or "darling little Nell."

Then, when she was six, her father left. An alcoholic, he went to live in a sanitarium[1] in Virginia in an attempt to deal with his drinking problem. Eleanor missed him greatly.

Next her mother became ill with painful headaches. Sometimes for hours at a time Eleanor would sit holding her mother's head in her lap and stroking her forehead. Nothing else seemed to relieve the pain. At those times Eleanor often remembered how her mother had teased her 50 about her looks and called her "Granny." But even at the age of seven Eleanor was glad to be helping someone, glad to be needed—and noticed.

The next year, when Eleanor was eight, her mother, the beautiful Anna, died. Afterward her brother Elliott suddenly caught diphtheria[2] and he, too, died. Eleanor and her baby brother, Hall, were taken to live with their grandmother in Manhattan.

A few months later another tragedy struck. Elliott Roosevelt, Eleanor's father, also died. Within eighteen months Eleanor had lost her mother, a brother, and her dear father. **C**

---

1. **sanitarium** (săn´ĭ-târ´ē-əm): an institution for the care of people with a specific disease or with other health problems.
2. **diphtheria** (dĭf-thîr´ē-ə): a serious infectious disease.

B CHRONOLOGICAL ORDER

Jacobs begins his use of chronological order with Eleanor's birth date. Start adding events to your timeline.

C CHRONOLOGICAL ORDER

Reread lines 52–58. What words and phrases in these paragraphs help you understand the order of events and the passage of time?

DIFFERENTIATED INSTRUCTION

FOR LESS–PROFICIENT READERS

Reading Skill Follow-Up: Chronological Order
Direct students to add the events described in lines 43–65 to their timelines. Point out that in telling when the events happened, the author refers to Eleanor's age rather than to exact dates. Caution students to be careful when inferring dates from such information. For example, Eleanor was six from October 11, 1890, until October 10, 1891, so we do not know exactly what year her father went to the sanitarium.

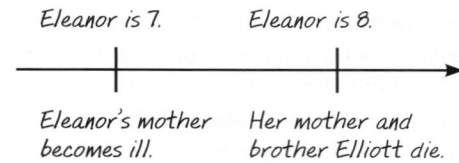

Eleanor is 7.   Eleanor is 8.

Eleanor's mother   Her mother and
becomes ill.   brother Elliott die.

Eleanor Roosevelt with her father, Elliott Roosevelt

For the rest of her life Eleanor carried with her the letters that her
60 father had written to her from the sanitarium. In them he had told her
to be brave, to become well educated, and to grow up into a woman
he could be proud of, a woman who helped people who were suffering.

Only ten years old when her father died, Eleanor decided even then
to live the kind of life he had described—a life that would have made
him proud of her.

*F*ew things in life came easily for Eleanor, but the first few years after
her father's death proved exceptionally hard. Grandmother Hall's
dark and gloomy townhouse had no place for children to play. The family
ate meals in silence. Every morning Eleanor and Hall were expected to
70 take cold baths for their health. Eleanor had to work at better posture
by walking with her arms behind her back, clamped over a walking stick.

Instead of making new friends, Eleanor often sat alone in her room
and read. For many months after her father's death she pretended that
he was still alive. She made him the hero of stories she wrote for school.
Sometimes, alone and unhappy, she just cried.

Some of her few moments of happiness came from visiting her uncle,
Theodore Roosevelt, in Oyster Bay, Long Island. A visit with Uncle Ted meant
playing games and romping outdoors with the many Roosevelt children.

Once Uncle Ted threw her into the water to teach her how to swim,
80 but when she started to sink, he had to rescue her. Often he would read

D BIOGRAPHY
Reread lines 60–62.
According to Jacobs,
how did Eleanor's
father influence her
goals and values?

Activity Have students do a Think-Pair-Share
activity to respond to the photograph of
Eleanor and her father. Encourage them to
think about how different people described
Eleanor as a child and how Eleanor may have
felt about herself. Why was her father so
important in her life? What did he represent
to her?

BEST PRACTICES TOOLKIT—Transparency
Think-Pair-Share p. A18

LITERARY ANALYSIS

D BIOGRAPHY

*Possible answer: He encouraged her to be
brave, to become well educated, and to help
others. Because he had been the person
who most loved her, what he said had a
great influence on her, and she decided to
live the kind of life he described.*

If students need help . . .

- Encourage students to reread lines
  60–62 to see what Eleanor's father wrote
  to her in his letters.
- Have them reread lines 63–65 to find
  out what Eleanor decided to do after her
  father died.

FOR ENGLISH LEARNERS

Comprehension: Compare and Contrast
Read lines 66–84 and use a Venn Diagram to
help students understand what Eleanor's life
was like at her grandmother's house compared to what it was like when she went to
visit her Uncle Ted.

- *Grandmother's house: no place to play,
  harsh and silent, lonely*
- *Uncle Ted's: play games and play outside
  with other children, caring adults*
- *Both: Eleanor enjoyed reading*

 **BEST PRACTICES TOOLKIT—Transparency**
Venn Diagram p. A26

ANALYZE VISUALS

Students' responses should relate the photo-graph to specifics in Jacobs's description of Eleanor Roosevelt at Allenswood. They might say the photo reflects her attention to her physical health and strength and reveals her growing sense of self-confidence.

Lines 100–130
DISCUSSION PROMPTS

Use these prompts to help students under-stand how Eleanor changed during her time at Allenswood Academy:

Connect Why does going into a new environment sometimes inspire people to improve themselves? *Students' responses should show an understanding that going into a new environment can open up new possibilities for people, give them an incen-tive to set new goals, and make them feel hopeful about the future.*

Compare How does Eleanor's life change when she goes to Allenswood? *Possible answer: She learns to take care of herself and grows stronger and healthier. She also makes friends for the first time and grows more con-fident under the guidance of Mademoiselle Souvestre.*

Evaluate Why did Eleanor blossom at Allenswood? *Possible answer: She got away from the difficult circumstances of her child-hood, and for the first time she was valued for her qualities of hard work and intel-ligence. She had reached a time in her life when she decided to take more control of de-fining herself rather than just reacting to the criticisms of others. She also got support and encouragement from an adult she admired.*

---

to the children old Norse[3] tales and poetry. It was at Sagamore Hill, Uncle Ted's home, that Eleanor first learned how much fun it could be to read books aloud.

For most of the time Eleanor's life was grim. Although her parents had left plenty of money for her upbringing, she had only two dresses to wear to school. Once she spilled ink on one of them, and since the other was in the wash, she had to wear the
90 dress with large ink stains on it to school the next day. It was not that Grandmother Hall was stingy. Rather, she was old and often confused. Nor did she show much warmth or love for Eleanor and her brother. Usually she just neglected them.

*J*ust before Eleanor turned fifteen, Grandmother Hall decided to send her to boarding school in England. The school she chose was Allenswood, a private academy for girls located on the outskirts of London.
100 It was at Allenswood that Eleanor, still thinking of herself as an "ugly duckling," first dared to believe that one day she might be able to become a swan.

At Allenswood she worked to toughen herself physically. Every day she did exercises in the morning and took a cold shower. Although she did not like competitive team sports, as a matter of self-discipline she tried out for field hockey. Not only did she make the team but, because she played so hard, also won the respect of her teammates.
110 They called her by her family nickname, "Totty," and showed their affection for her by putting books and flowers in her room, as was the custom at Allenswood. Never before had she experienced the pleasure of having schoolmates actually admire her rather than tease her.

At Allenswood, too, she began to look after her health. She finally broke the habit of chewing her fingernails. She learned to eat nutritious foods, to get plenty of sleep, and to take a brisk walk every morning, no matter how miserable the weather.

Under the guidance of the school's headmistress, Mademoiselle Souvestre (or "Sou"), she learned to ask searching questions and think
120 for herself instead of just giving back on tests what teachers had said.

ANALYZE VISUALS
What **mood** does this photograph of a teenage Eleanor Roosevelt convey?

---

3. **Norse** (nôrs): coming from ancient Scandinavia, the area that is now Norway, Sweden, and Denmark.

766 UNIT 7: BIOGRAPHY AND AUTOBIOGRAPHY

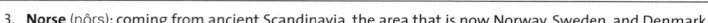

DIFFERENTIATED INSTRUCTION

FOR ENGLISH LEARNERS

Culture: Clarify The allusion to the "ugly duckling" and the "swan" (lines 101–103) refers to the story "The Ugly Duckling" by Hans Christian Andersen. The story is about a swan born among ducks who is called ugly and teased because it is different from the ducks. Eventually, the swan finds its own kind and is seen to be beautiful by those who appreciate swans. Eleanor is hoping that she, too, can find the place where she belongs and can be appreciated for who she is.

Comprehension: Cause and Effect Use a Cause-and-Effect Diagram to help students trace the results of the different activities that Eleanor undertakes when she goes to Allenswood (lines 104–124). Lines 125–126 describe the overall result of these various changes: Eleanor begins to transform her personality. Preceding paragraphs describe causes that lead to Eleanor's transformation.

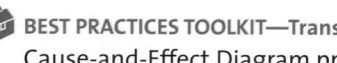 **BEST PRACTICES TOOLKIT—Transparency**
Cause-and-Effect Diagram pp. B16, B38

She also learned to speak French fluently, a skill she polished by traveling in France, living for a time with a French family. Mademoiselle Souvestre arranged for her to have a new red dress. Wearing it, after all of the old, worn dresses Grandmother Hall had given her, made her feel very proud.

Eleanor was growing up, and the joy of young womanhood had begun to transform her personality.

In 1902, nearly eighteen years old, she left Allenswood, not returning for her fourth year there. Grandmother Hall insisted that, instead, she must be introduced to society as a debutante—to go to dances and parties and begin
130 to take her place in the social world with other wealthy young women.

Away from Allenswood, Eleanor's old uncertainty about her looks came back again. She saw herself as too tall, too thin, too plain. She worried about her buckteeth, which she thought made her look horselike. The old teasing began again, especially on the part of Uncle Ted's daughter, "Princess" Alice Roosevelt, who seemed to take pleasure in making Eleanor feel uncomfortable.

Eleanor, as always, did as she was told. She went to all of the parties and dances. But she also began working with poor children at the Rivington Street Settlement House[4] on New York's Lower East Side.
140 She taught the girls gymnastic exercises. She took children to museums and to musical performances. She tried to get the parents interested in politics in order to get better schools and cleaner, safer streets. **E**

Meanwhile Eleanor's life reached a turning point. She fell in love! The young man was her fifth cousin, Franklin Delano Roosevelt. Eleanor and Franklin had known each other since childhood. Franklin recalled how once he had carried her piggyback in the nursery. When she was fourteen, he had danced with her at a party. Then, shortly after her return from Allenswood, they had met by chance on a train. They talked and almost at once realized how much they liked each other.
150 For a time they met secretly. Then they attended parties together. Franklin—tall, strong, handsome—saw her as a person he could trust. He knew that she would not try to **dominate** him. **F**

But did he really love her? Would he always? She wrote to him, quoting a poem she knew: "Unless you can swear, '*For life, for death!*' . . . Oh, never call it loving!"

Franklin promised that his love was indeed "for life," and Eleanor agreed to marry him. It was the autumn of 1903. He was twenty-one. She was nineteen.

On March 17, 1905, Eleanor and Franklin were married. "Uncle Ted,"
160 by then president of the United States, was there to "give the bride away."

---

4. **settlement house:** a place in a poor, neglected neighborhood where services are provided for residents.

E BIOGRAPHY
Reread lines 131–142. Note that Jacobs chooses details that reveal various aspects of Eleanor's personality. What are some of her strengths and weaknesses?

2 Targeted Passage

F CHRONOLOGICAL ORDER
Reread lines 143–152. What words and phrases help you understand the order in which Eleanor and Franklin's relationship progressed?

dominate (dŏm′ə-nāt′)
v. to have control over

ELEANOR ROOSEVELT **767**

Lines 137–142
REINFORCE *KEY IDEA:* DUTY

Discuss Which of Eleanor's **duties** are things she is told to do, and which are things that she does because she believes they are important?
Possible answer: Eleanor goes to parties and dances because her grandmother tells her to, but she works with poor children because she feels she has a duty to help others.

LITERARY ANALYSIS

E BIOGRAPHY

Possible answer: Eleanor's strengths are that she is self-disciplined, relates well to a variety of people, takes care of herself, thinks for herself, and helps those in need. However, her greatest weakness is her low self-esteem.

If students need help . . . Use a T Chart to help students list the aspects of Eleanor's personality that are good for her and for others (strengths) and other aspects that make life challenging (weaknesses). Help students understand that both Eleanor and others perceived her appearance as a weakness, but the real weakness was in how that perception got in the way of her ability to do what she wanted.

BEST PRACTICES TOOLKIT—Transparency T Chart p. A25

READING SKILL

F CHRONOLOGICAL ORDER
Possible answers:
- "meanwhile" (line 143)
- "since childhood" (line 145)
- "when she was fourteen" (lines 146–147)
- "then" (line 147)
- "shortly after" (line 147)
- "for a time" (line 150)
- "then" (line 150)

FOR LESS–PROFICIENT READERS
2 Targeted Passage [Lines 143–159]
This passage describes an important turning point in Eleanor's life: she falls in love with, and marries, Franklin Roosevelt.

- What is the turning point in Eleanor's life?
- How do Franklin and Eleanor know each other?
- What did Franklin like most about Eleanor?
- What did Eleanor need to know before she agreed to marry Franklin?

FOR ENGLISH LEARNERS
Language: Idioms and Sayings Have mixed-ability pairs use context clues to define

- *give the bride away* (line 160), "present the bride to the groom"
- *be the bride at every wedding . . . funeral* (line 162), "be the center of attention"
- *stayed on the sidelines* (lines 183–184), "did not participate"
- *threw herself into* (line 194), "became very involved in"
- *stood up for* (lines 216–217), "defended"

It was sometimes said that the dynamic, energetic Theodore Roosevelt had to be "the bride at every wedding and the corpse at every funeral." And it was certainly true that day. Wherever the president went, the guests followed at his heels.

Before long Eleanor and Franklin found themselves standing all alone, deserted. Franklin seemed annoyed, but Eleanor didn't mind. She had found the ceremony deeply moving. And she stood next to her husband in a glow of idealism—very serious, very **grave**, very much in love.

170 In May 1906 the couple's first child was born. During the next nine years Eleanor gave birth to five more babies, one of whom died in infancy. Still timid, shy, afraid of making mistakes, she found herself so busy that there was little time to think of her own drawbacks.

Still, looking back later on the early years of her marriage, Eleanor knew that she should have been a stronger person, especially in the handling of Franklin's mother, or, as they both called her, "Mammá." Too often Mammá made the decisions about such things as where they would live, how their home would be furnished, how the children would be disciplined. Eleanor and Franklin let her pay for things they could not afford—extra servants, vacations, doctor bills, clothing. She offered, and they accepted.

180 **B**efore long, trouble developed in the relationship between Eleanor and Franklin. Serious, shy, easily embarrassed, Eleanor could not share Franklin's interests in golf and tennis. He enjoyed light talk and flirting with women. She could not be lighthearted. So she stayed on the sidelines. Instead of losing her temper, she bottled up her anger and did not talk to him at all. As he used to say, she "clammed up." Her silence only made things worse, because it puzzled him. Faced with her coldness, her **brooding** silence, he only grew angrier and more distant.

Meanwhile Franklin's career in politics advanced rapidly. In 1910 he was elected to the New York State Senate. In 1913 President Wilson
190 appointed him Assistant Secretary of the Navy—a powerful position in the national government, which required the Roosevelts to move to Washington, D.C. **G**

In 1917 the United States entered World War I as an active combatant. Like many socially **prominent** women, Eleanor threw herself into the war effort. Sometimes she worked fifteen and sixteen hours a day. She made sandwiches for soldiers passing through the nation's capital. She knitted sweaters. She used Franklin's influence to get the Red Cross to build a recreation room for soldiers who had been shell-shocked[5] in combat. . . .

In 1920 the Democratic Party chose Franklin as its candidate for
200 vice-president of the United States. Even though the Republicans won

---

5. **shell-shocked:** affected with a nervous or mental disorder resulting from the strain of battle.

768   UNIT 7: BIOGRAPHY AND AUTOBIOGRAPHY

---

grave (grāv) adj. solemn and dignified

brooding (broo'dĭng) adj. full of worry; troubled **brood** v.

G CHRONOLOGICAL ORDER
The word *meanwhile* indicates that something else happened at the same time. In what ways are the early years of their marriage different for Eleanor and Franklin?

prominent (prŏm'ə-nənt) adj. well-known; widely recognized

READING SKILL

G CHRONOLOGICAL ORDER

Possible answer: *For Eleanor, the time was focused on children (six were born, and one died, between 1906 and 1915) and dealing with her mother-in-law. They were stressful and unhappy years for her because she did not share many of her husband's interests. For Franklin, the time was marked by great success in his career and a growing reputation as a politician.*

If students need help ... Have them review lines 169–187 to find out what the period was like for Eleanor as well as Franklin's reactions to her. Lines 188–192 describe what was happening to Franklin.

DIFFERENTIATED INSTRUCTION

FOR LESS–PROFICIENT READERS
Reading Skill Follow-Up: Chronological Order
Have students update their timelines with the dates mentioned in the biography. Point out that some dates may need to be inferred, for example, "during the next nine years" (line 169). Encourage students to notice the effect that each event had on Eleanor's life. Allow students to share their timelines with a partner. Clarify understanding as needed.

FOR ENGLISH LEARNERS
Vocabulary: Phrasal Verbs Explain that words like *up* and *out* can change the meaning of a verb. Some phrases that combine verbs with such words are colloquial or slang expressions. Assign these phrasal verbs to pairs of students to look up in a dictionary: *bottle up* (line 184), *clam up* (line 185), *drop out* (lines 235–236). Invite volunteers to share the meanings with the class and paraphrase the lines from the biography to show their understanding of how the verbs are used.

768   UNIT 7: BIOGRAPHY AND AUTOBIOGRAPHY

the election, Roosevelt became a well-known figure in national politics. All the time, Eleanor stood by his side, smiling, doing what was expected of her as a candidate's wife.

She did what was expected—and much more—in the summer of 1921 when disaster struck the Roosevelt family. While on vacation Franklin suddenly fell ill with infantile paralysis—polio—the horrible disease that each year used to kill or cripple thousands of children, and many adults as well. When Franklin became a victim of polio, nobody knew what caused the disease or how to cure it.

Franklin lived, but the lower part of his body remained paralyzed. For the rest of his life he never again had the use of his legs. He had to be lifted and carried from place to place. He had to wear heavy steel braces from his waist to the heels of his shoes.

His mother, as well as many of his advisers, urged him to give up politics, to live the life of a country gentleman on the Roosevelt estate at Hyde Park, New York. This time, Eleanor, calm and strong, stood up for her ideas. She argued that he should not be treated like a sick person, tucked away in the country, inactive, just waiting for death to come.

Franklin agreed. Slowly he recovered his health. His energy returned. In 1928 he was elected governor of New York. Then, just four years later, he was elected president of the United States. Ⓗ

Ⓗ BIOGRAPHY
Why was Franklin's illness a turning point for Eleanor?

President Franklin Delano Roosevelt and First Lady Eleanor Roosevelt, April 17, 1938

Lines 204–221
REINFORCE *KEY IDEA*: DUTY

Discuss How would you describe Eleanor's sense of **duty** during this time? *Possible answer: She did what people expected her to do as a political wife, and she also did more than was expected. She not only stood by her husband but also supported his desire to continue his active political life after he became ill.*

LITERARY ANALYSIS

Ⓗ BIOGRAPHY

Possible answer: For perhaps the first time, Eleanor did not go along with what others, especially her mother-in-law, told her to do. Instead, she fought for her beliefs. With Eleanor's encouragement, Franklin remained in politics. Eleanor became First Lady of New York and then of the whole country.

If students need help . . . Remind students that a turning point is an event that marks an important change. Have them read lines 217–224 to see how Eleanor acted differently than she had in the past and to analyze what occurred as a result of those actions.

Extend the Discussion What events in Eleanor's earlier life may explain why she disagreed with Franklin's mother and some advisers about what Franklin should do with his career?

FOR LESS–PROFICIENT READERS
Vocabulary Support Explain that the term *infantile paralysis* is a synonym for *polio*. *Infantile* means "having to do with children." *Paralysis* means "an inability to move." Polio most often struck children, and in the most severe cases, it prevented victims from moving their arms or legs and sometimes interfered with their ability to breathe.

FOR ADVANCED LEARNERS/PRE–AP
Compare and Contrast Have students quick-write about how Franklin's polio affected Franklin and Eleanor. Encourage them to think about how Franklin's physical paralysis seemed to break Eleanor's emotional paralysis, which had kept her from standing up to her mother-in-law and taking charge of her life. Have students consider Eleanor's sense of duty: What was she committed to at this time? Allow students to share their writing with a partner.

Activity What does this photograph tell you about Eleanor Roosevelt's interests?
Possible answer: It shows that she enjoyed helping children and other people less fortunate than she was.

Lines 222–241
DISCUSSION PROMPTS

Use these prompts to help students understand how Eleanor changed as a result of Franklin's illness:

Connect Think about a time when you helped other people. How do these thoughts help you understand Mrs. Roosevelt's reasons for getting involved in politics? *Students' answers should reflect their experiences and connect to the rewards of being useful and helping others.*

Analyze How did Eleanor's desire to "keep Franklin in the public eye" influence her choice of activities? *Possible answer: She got involved in the Democratic Party and traveled around the state of New York making speeches, which helped him as governor of the state.*

Synthesize Women had won the right to vote in 1920. How did this fact affect the kinds of activities that Eleanor became involved in? Give examples from the biography. *Possible answers: Once women had the right to vote, more of them became involved in politics through groups such as the League of Women Voters (line 228) and the Women's Trade Union League (line 230). Eleanor was able to work with groups such as these to try to get laws passed that would improve the lives of women and children (lines 238–241).*

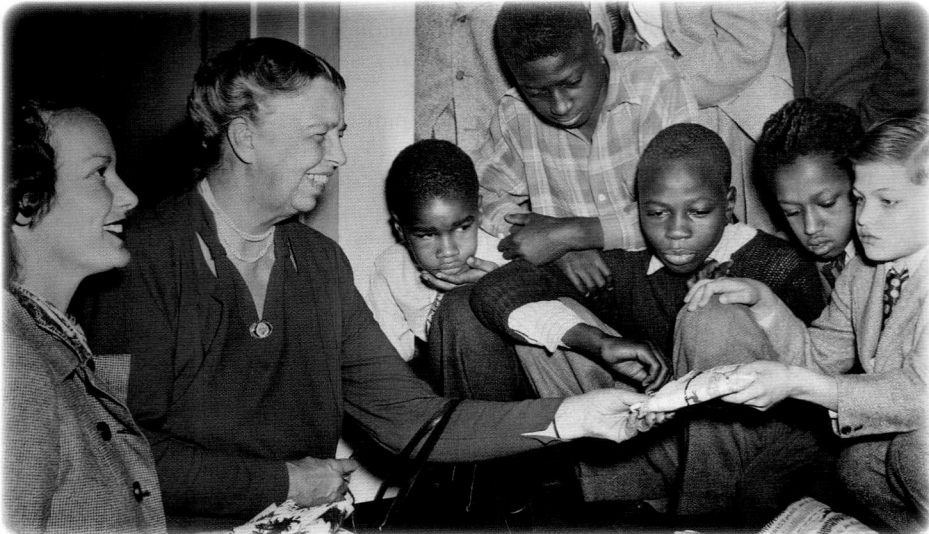

By visiting places such as this school for underprivileged boys, Eleanor Roosevelt raised public awareness of social problems.

Meanwhile Eleanor had changed. To keep Franklin in the public eye while he was recovering, she had gotten involved in politics herself. It was, she thought, her "duty." From childhood she had been taught "to do the thing that has to be done, the way it has to be done, when it has to be done."

With the help of Franklin's adviser Louis Howe, she made fundraising speeches for the Democratic Party all around New York State. She helped in the work of the League of Women Voters, the Consumer's League, and the Foreign Policy Association. After becoming interested
230 in the problems of working women, she gave time to the Women's Trade Union League (WTUL).[6]

③ **Targeted Passage**

It was through the WTUL that she met a group of remarkable women—women doing exciting work that made a difference in the world. They taught Eleanor about life in the slums. They awakened her hopes that something could be done to improve the condition of the poor. She dropped out of the "fashionable" society of her wealthy friends and joined the world of reform—social change.

For hours at a time Eleanor and her reformer friends talked with Franklin. They showed him the need for new laws: laws to get children
240 out of the factories and into schools; laws to cut down the long hours that women worked; laws to get fair wages for all workers.

---

6. **Women's Trade Union League:** an organization founded in 1903 to promote laws to protect the rights of women working in factories and to help establish labor unions for women.

770 UNIT 7: BIOGRAPHY AND AUTOBIOGRAPHY

DIFFERENTIATED INSTRUCTION

FOR LESS–PROFICIENT READERS
③ **Targeted Passage [Lines 222–237]**

This passage describes an important change in Eleanor's life: she became directly involved in politics for the first time.

- Why did Eleanor get involved in politics?
- What did she do to help the Democratic Party?
- What did the women of the WTUL teach Eleanor?
- What did Eleanor do after meeting the women of the WTUL?

FOR ADVANCED LEARNERS/PRE–AP
Synthesize Have students review the author's descriptions of Eleanor's experiences with fashionable society and with social reform work. Invite students to discuss why Eleanor would be more interested in the latter, giving examples from the text to support their opinions.

B y the time that Franklin was sworn in as president, the nation was facing its deepest depression. One out of every four Americans was out of work, out of hope. At mealtimes people stood in lines in front of soup kitchens for something to eat. Mrs. Roosevelt herself knew of once-prosperous families who found themselves reduced to eating stale bread from thrift shops or traveling to parts of town where they were not known to beg for money from house to house.

250 Eleanor worked in the charity kitchens, ladling out soup. She visited slums. She crisscrossed the country learning about the suffering of coal miners, shipyard workers, **migrant** farm workers, students, housewives—Americans caught up in the paralysis of the Great Depression. Since Franklin himself remained crippled, she became his eyes and ears, informing him of what the American people were really thinking and feeling.

Eleanor also was the president's conscience, personally urging on him some of the most **compassionate,** forward-looking laws of his presidency, including, for example, the National Youth Administration (NYA), which provided money to allow **impoverished** young people to stay in school.

260 She lectured widely, wrote a regularly syndicated[7] newspaper column, "My Day," and spoke frequently on the radio. She fought for equal pay for women in industry. Like no other First Lady up to that time, she became a link between the president and the American public.

Above all she fought against racial and religious prejudice. When Eleanor learned that the DAR (Daughters of the American Revolution) would not allow the great black singer Marian Anderson to perform in their auditorium in Washington, D.C., she resigned from the organization. Then she arranged to have Miss Anderson sing in front of the Lincoln Memorial.

Similarly, when she entered a hall where, as often happened in those days, blacks and whites were seated in separate sections, she made it
270 a point to sit with the blacks. Her example marked an important step in making the rights of blacks a matter of national priority.

On December 7, 1941, Japanese forces launched a surprise attack on the American naval base at Pearl Harbor, Hawaii, as well as on other American installations in the Pacific. The United States entered World War II, fighting not only against Japan but against the brutal dictators who then controlled Germany and Italy.

Eleanor helped the Red Cross raise money. She gave blood, sold war bonds. But she also did the unexpected. In 1943, for example, she visited barracks and hospitals on islands throughout the South Pacific. When
280 she visited a hospital, she stopped at every bed. To each soldier she said something special, something that a mother might say. Often, after she left, even battle-hardened men had tears in their eyes. Admiral Nimitz,

---

7. **syndicated** (sĭn′dĭ-kāt′ĭd): sold to many newspapers for publication.

migrant (mī′grənt) *adj.* moving from place to place

compassionate (kəm-păsh′ə-nĭt) *adj.* wanting to help those who suffer

impoverished (ĭm-pŏv′ər-ĭsht) *adj.* very poor **impoverish** *v.*

SOCIAL STUDIES CONNECTION

At the Lincoln Memorial, Marian Anderson performed in front of 75,000 people. Later, in 1943, Anderson performed at Constitution Hall, where she had been denied.

SOCIAL STUDIES CONNECTION

The **Daughters of the American Revolution,** founded in 1890, is a patriotic organization open to women who are direct descendants of those who actively fought for or helped the cause of the American Revolution. Its auditorium, known as Constitution Hall, was built in the late 1920s and is the largest auditorium in the nation's capital.

Marian Anderson's rich contralto voice—most celebrated for bringing the music of Schubert, Schumann, Brahms, Mahler, Verdi, Richard Strauss, and spirituals to life—brought her much fame and respect. However, during the early 1930s, she was more well known in Europe than in the United States because many U.S. concert halls were not open to African Americans. Anderson wanted to rent Constitution Hall for a performance on Easter Sunday in 1939. When the DAR refused to allow Anderson to use the hall, Eleanor Roosevelt and other prominent women resigned from the DAR in protest. In addition to the 75,000 people who witnessed the concert at the Lincoln Memorial, millions listened to it on the radio. Many regard this performance as a milestone of the civil rights movement because of the national attention it focused on the issue of racial segregation.

The DAR has since worked to correct the negative image that resulted from its 1939 actions. Marian Anderson and many other African Americans have performed regularly at the Hall. In January 2005, the U.S. Postal Service dedicated a commemorative stamp to Anderson, and the ceremony was held at Constitution Hall. The head of the DAR expressed regret for the events of 1939.

FOR ENGLISH LEARNERS

Culture: Clarify

- Explain that the term *First Lady* (line 261) refers to the wife of the president of the United States. It is a term that has been used since the late 1800s. Recently, other countries have adopted the term to refer to the wife of their nation's leader.

- Line 269 states that "blacks and whites were seated in separate sections." Clarify that this refers to the practice of racial segregation that was common throughout much of the American South between the late 1870s and the 1950s. Separation of blacks and whites was common in most public facilities, including theaters, rest rooms, drinking fountains, restaurants, and buses.

who originally thought such visits would be a nuisance, became one of her strongest admirers. Nobody else, he said, had done so much to help raise the spirits of the men. ⓘ

By spring 1945 the end of the war in Europe seemed near. Then, on April 12, a phone call brought Eleanor the news that Franklin Roosevelt, who had gone to Warm Springs, Georgia, for a rest, was dead.

As Eleanor later declared, "I think that sometimes I acted as his
290 conscience. I urged him to take the harder path when he would have preferred the easier way. In that sense, I acted on occasion as a spur, even though the spurring was not always wanted or welcome.

"Of course," said Eleanor, "I loved him, and I miss him."

After Franklin's funeral, every day that Eleanor was home at Hyde Park, without fail, she placed flowers on his grave. Then she would stand very still beside him there.

With Franklin dead, Eleanor Roosevelt might have dropped out of the public eye, might have been remembered in the history books only as a footnote to the president's program of social reforms. Instead she
300 found new strengths within herself, new ways to live a useful, interesting life—and to help others. Now, moreover, her successes were her own, not the result of being the president's wife. ⓙ

*I*n December 1945 President Harry S. Truman invited her to be one of the American delegates going to London to begin the work of the United Nations. Eleanor hesitated, but the president insisted. He said that the nation needed her; it was her duty. After that, Eleanor agreed.

In the beginning some of her fellow delegates from the United States considered her unqualified for the position, but after seeing her in action, they changed their minds.
310 It was Eleanor Roosevelt who, almost single-handedly, pushed through the United Nations General Assembly a resolution giving refugees from World War II the right *not* to return to their native lands if they did not wish to. The Russians angrily objected, but Eleanor's reasoning convinced **wavering** delegates. In a passionate speech defending the rights of the refugees she declared, "We [must] consider first the rights of man and what makes men more free—not governments, but man!"

Next Mrs. Roosevelt helped draft the United Nations Declaration of Human Rights. The Soviets wanted the declaration to list the duties people owed to their countries. Again Eleanor insisted that the United
320 Nations should stand for individual freedom—the rights of people to free speech, freedom of religion, and such human needs as health care and education. In December 1948, with the Soviet Union and its allies refusing to vote, the Declaration of Human Rights won approval of the UN General Assembly by a vote of forty-eight to zero.

ⓘ BIOGRAPHY
What does Admiral Nimitz's change in attitude suggest about the quality of the First Lady's work?

ⓙ BIOGRAPHY
Reread lines 297–302. What words and phrases does Jacobs use that give important details about Eleanor?

wavering (wā′vər-ĭng) *adj.* hesitating between two choices **waver** *v.*

DIFFERENTIATED INSTRUCTION

FOR LESS–PROFICIENT READERS

Reading Skill Follow-Up: Chronological Order
As students continue to place dates from the text on their timelines, encourage them to pay attention to the relationship between events and to fill in events between known dates that are identified by other clue words, such as "after retiring" (line 325). Explain that everyone's life includes some events that are milestones or turning points. Invite volunteers to identify milestones in Mrs. Roosevelt's life.

Comprehension Support Help students understand lines 310–324 by explaining that after World War II, the United States and its allies were opposed by the Soviet Union and its allies because the two sides had different ideas about government. The Soviet Union (also referred to as the Soviets or the Russians) supported the spread of communism, which emphasized state control and limited personal freedom. The United States supported democracy and the rights of individuals.

As a delegate to the United Nations, Eleanor Roosevelt defended people's rights and freedoms.

Even after retiring from her post at the UN, Mrs. Roosevelt continued to travel. In places around the world she dined with presidents and kings. But she also visited tenement slums[8] in Bombay, India; factories in Yugoslavia; farms in Lebanon and Israel. **K**

Everywhere she met people who were eager to greet her. Although as a child she had been brought up to be formal and distant, she had grown to feel at ease with people. They wanted to touch her, to hug her, to kiss her.

Eleanor's doctor had been telling her to slow down, but that was hard for her. She continued to write her newspaper column, "My Day," and to appear on television. She still began working at seven-thirty in the morning and often continued until well past midnight. Not only did she write and speak, she taught retarded children and raised money for health care of the poor.

As author Clare Boothe Luce put it, "Mrs. Roosevelt has done more good deeds on a bigger scale for a longer time than any woman who ever appeared on our public scene. No woman has ever so comforted the distressed or so distressed the comfortable."

Gradually, however, she was forced to withdraw from some of her activities, to spend more time at home.

On November 7, 1962, at the age of seventy-eight, Eleanor died in her sleep. She was buried in the rose garden at Hyde Park, alongside her husband.

Adlai Stevenson, the American ambassador to the United Nations, remembered her as "the First Lady of the World," as the person—male or female—most effective in working for the cause of human rights. As Stevenson declared, "She would rather light a candle than curse the darkness." **L**

And perhaps, in sum, that is what the struggle for human rights is all about. ∾

K CHRONOLOGICAL ORDER
Reread lines 303–328. Note the accomplishments that Mrs. Roosevelt achieved after her husband's death. What words and phrases help you figure out the order of the events?

④ Targeted Passage

L BIOGRAPHY
Reread lines 338–350. Why might Jacobs quote two famous people and their thoughts about Mrs. Roosevelt in these last paragraphs?

8. **tenement** (tĕn′ə-mənt) **slums:** parts of a city where poor people live in crowded, shabby buildings.

ELEANOR ROOSEVELT **773**

FOR LESS-PROFICIENT READERS

④ Targeted Passage [Lines 332–352]

This conclusive passage describes Mrs. Roosevelt's final years and sums up her influence.

- How did Mrs. Roosevelt continue to help others as she got older?
- What did Clare Booth Luce and Adlai Stevenson praise Mrs. Roosevelt for doing?
- How old was Eleanor Roosevelt when she died?

FOR ADVANCED LEARNERS/PRE-AP

Synthesize Invite students to use a T Chart to list Clare Booth Luce's and Adlai Stevenson's opinions about Eleanor Roosevelt (column 1) and facts from the biography that support each opinion (column 2). Ask students whether they think these quotations from Luce and Stevenson are good choices for this biography and why.

BEST PRACTICES TOOLKIT—Transparency T Chart p. A25

READING SKILL

K CHRONOLOGICAL ORDER

Possible answers:

- "In December 1945" (line 303)
- "In the beginning" (line 307)
- "after" (line 308)
- "Next" (line 317)
- "In December 1948" (line 322)
- "Even after retiring" (line 325)

LITERARY ANALYSIS

L BIOGRAPHY

Possible answer: The quotations are from people who lived during the same time as Mrs. Roosevelt and show what many of her contemporaries thought of her. They add weight to Jacobs's argument about how important she was, and they help summarize her life.

If students need help . . . Explain that Clare Booth Luce and Adlai Stevenson witnessed Eleanor Roosevelt's work personally. Encourage students to reread their statements.

SELECTION WRAP-UP

REFLECT Have students think about what parts of Mrs. Roosevelt's life made the greatest impression on them. Encourage students to discuss specific events from the biography that impressed them and why.

★ CRITIQUE Ask students to evaluate whether they think the author succeeded in showing why Mrs. Roosevelt is considered "one of America's greatest women."

READING FLUENCY

Distribute the copy master and have students practice fluency.

R RESOURCE MANAGER—Copy Master Reading Fluency p. 36

Practice and Apply

After Reading

For additional support of post-reading questions, use these copy masters:

R RESOURCE MANAGER—Copy Masters
Reading Check p. 34 (to check understanding of the selection)
Biography p. 27 (for practice of literary analysis standards focus)
Question Support p. 35 (**After Reading** questions adapted for English learners and less-proficient readers)

Additional selection questions are provided for teachers on page 21.

For additional activities to challenge students, see

ⓘ Power Thinking at **ClassZone.com**

ANSWERS

Comprehension

1. *Eleanor thought she was unattractive and uninteresting.*

2. *She worked for the poor and for women's rights, racial equality, international peace, and human rights.*

3. *She traveled around the country, talked with people, and reported back to her husband.*

Literary Analysis

Possible answers:

4. ■ **STANDARDS FOCUS** *Identify Chronological Order Students should support their answers with specific evidence from their timelines. They may focus on events of personal importance or on events important in the wider world.*

5. *The comfortable people were those sheltered by privilege or wealth who did not reach out to the needy. She distressed them by working for equality for all people.*

6. *Cause: Eleanor's father . . .; Effect: She helped working women. Cause: Eleanor was teased . . .; Effects: She became frightened and lonely. She wanted to be needed. She worried about her looks.*

7. *Most students will agree. Eleanor cared about the issues facing people all over the world and worked hard at helping nations work together. She was loved and respected by people all over the world.*

After Reading

Comprehension

1. **Recall** Tell how Eleanor felt about herself as a young girl.

2. **Summarize** What are some examples of ways Mrs. Roosevelt helped society?

3. **Clarify** How did Mrs. Roosevelt act as her husband's "eyes and ears" when he was president?

MARYLAND OBJECTIVES

LITERATURE STANDARD
3.A.3.a Distinguish among types of narrative texts

Literary Analysis

4. **Examine Chronological Order** Review the timeline you made. What period do you think contains the most important events in Eleanor Roosevelt's life?

5. **Make Inferences** Reread the quotation by Clare Boothe Luce in lines 338–341. Who were the "comfortable" people, and how did Mrs. Roosevelt "distress" them?

6. **Analyze Cause and Effect** How do you think Eleanor's childhood affected the choices she made later in life? Create a chart to show the effects of these experiences, or causes. Some causes will have more than one effect.

Cause	Effect	Effect
Eleanor's father told her to help people who were suffering.	She worked with poor children.	
Eleanor was teased and made fun of.		

7. **Make Judgments** Adlai Stevenson referred to Mrs. Roosevelt as the "First Lady of the World." Do you agree with this statement? Explain.

8. **Evaluate Biography** Review the bulleted list at the top of page 761. In your opinion, did Jacobs achieve his purpose as a biographer? Provide examples from the text that support your opinion.

Extension and Challenge

9. **Big Question Activity** On page 770, Jacobs writes that Eleanor Roosevelt was taught "'to do the thing that has to be done, the way it has to be done, when it has to be done.'" Think about how this view had an impact on her life. Then reread the journal entry you wrote as part of the **Quickwrite** activity on page 760. Compare your generation's attitude toward **duty** to Eleanor Roosevelt's attitude.

10. 🌐 **SOCIAL STUDIES CONNECTION** In addition to arranging for Marian Anderson to sing at the Lincoln Memorial, Mrs. Roosevelt supported civil rights in other ways. Research to find two more examples of how the First Lady promoted women's rights or racial equality.

↗ **RESEARCH LINKS**
For more on Eleanor Roosevelt's support of civil rights, visit the **Research Center** at ClassZone.com.

---

8. ● **STANDARDS FOCUS** *Biography Jacobs accomplished the goals of a biographer. He provided a complete picture of Eleanor's personality by giving information about her childhood and how it affected her adult choices. He provided quotations that showed what others thought about her. He explained the importance of her work by comparing Eleanor to other first ladies and by giving examples of how she affected the world.*

Extension and Challenge

9. *Students should be able to compare their attitude toward duty with Eleanor Roosevelt's by giving specific details from her life and from their own writing.*

10. 🏆 **SOCIAL STUDIES CONNECTION**

Possible examples: Eleanor helped women and African Americans gain more government jobs and greater access to the president, supported integration in the armed forces and defense industries, and chaired President Kennedy's Commission on the Status of Women.

Vocabulary in Context

VOCABULARY PRACTICE

Note the letter of the item you might associate with each boldfaced word.

1. **prominent:** (a) an unexplored cave, (b) a well-known lawyer, (c) a narrow valley
2. **brooding:** (a) an unhappy person, (b) a late-model car, (c) a small garden
3. **migrant:** (a) a successful business, (b) a bad headache, (c) a traveling worker
4. **grave:** (a) a loud party, (b) a serious illness, (c) a reunion between two brothers
5. **impoverished:** (a) a brick sidewalk, (b) a large grocery store, (c) a poor family
6. **wavering:** (a) a nosy neighbor, (b) a tough decision, (c) the beginning of winter
7. **dominate:** (a) a poorly planned event, (b) an undefeated team, (c) a serious drought
8. **compassionate:** (a) two children playing, (b) an angry crowd, (c) a kind nurse

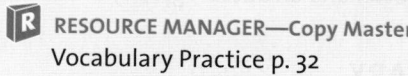

brooding

compassionate

dominate

grave

impoverished

migrant

prominent

wavering

 MARYLAND OBJECTIVES

READING STANDARD
1.D.3.b Use word structure to determine meaning

VOCABULARY IN WRITING

Use three or more vocabulary words to write a paragraph about what Eleanor Roosevelt taught the world. Here is a sample opening sentence.

> **EXAMPLE SENTENCE**
> *Eleanor Roosevelt taught the world that it is important to be* **compassionate**.

VOCABULARY STRATEGY: THE LATIN ROOT *domin*

The vocabulary word *dominate* contains the Latin root *domin*, which means "master" or "rule." This root is found in many English words. To understand the meaning of words with *domin*, you can often use context clues and your knowledge of the root's meaning.

VOCABULARY PRACTICE
For more practice, go to the **Vocabulary Center** at **ClassZone.com**.

PRACTICE Choose a word from the web that best completes each sentence. Use context clues or, if necessary, a dictionary.

1. The king ruled his _____ with fairness and justice.
2. Our boss is very _____ and expects his orders to be taken seriously.
3. In this county, voters for the New Party _____.
4. _____ traits or characteristics may be inherited from one or both parents.
5. The warlord's intent was to gain complete _____ of the country's ports.

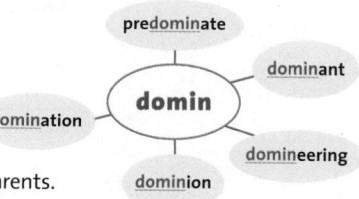

predominate

dominant

domination

domin

domineering

dominion

DIFFERENTIATED INSTRUCTION

FOR ENGLISH LEARNERS

Vocabulary Strategy: The Latin Root *domin*

- Help students identify the part of speech of the missing word in order to narrow their choices (*domination* and *dominion*—nouns; *dominant* and *domineering*—adjectives; *predominate*—verb).
- After students have determined the answer from context clues or a dictionary, point out that certain words are commonly used together—for example, *domineering people* and *dominant traits*.

FOR ADVANCED LEARNERS/PRE–AP

Vocabulary in Writing Have students use as many of the vocabulary words as possible to write a paragraph in the first person by Eleanor Roosevelt about some aspect of her life.

ANSWERS

Vocabulary in Context
VOCABULARY PRACTICE

1. *(b);* 2. *(a);* 3. *(c);* 4. *(b);* 5. *(c);* 6. *(b);* 7. *(b);* 8. *(c)*

R **RESOURCE MANAGER—Copy Master**
Vocabulary Practice p. 32

VOCABULARY IN WRITING

Use a Jigsaw activity to have students review the biography and list ideas that Mrs. Roosevelt taught the world. Then suggest that they discuss how the vocabulary words connect to the items on the list.

BEST PRACTICES TOOLKIT
Jigsaw p. A1

VOCABULARY STRATEGY: THE LATIN ROOT
domin (also an EL language objective)

Have students use context clues to decide which word would fit best in each sentence by thinking of a synonym that would fit in the blank. It is also helpful to determine the part of speech of the missing word. For example, the first sentence requires a noun, and a synonym is "country" or "kingdom."

Answers:
1. *dominion;* 2. *domineering;* 3. *predominate;*
4. *dominant;* 5. *domination*

R **RESOURCE MANAGER—Copy Master**
Vocabulary Strategy p. 33

i Vocabulary Center at **ClassZone.com**
Additional Vocabulary Activities

Assess and Reteach

Assess

R **RESOURCE MANAGER—Copy Masters**
Selection Tests A, B/C pp. 37–38, 39–40

Test Generator CD

Reteach

S **STANDARDS LESSON FILE**
Reading Lesson 6: Recognizing Sequence and Chronological Order
Vocabulary Lesson 10: Latin Roots (active verbs)

ELEANOR ROOSEVELT **775**

Focus and Motivate

OBJECTIVES

Reading for Information
- synthesize
- draw conclusions
- read a letter and an autobiography

SUMMARY

Two primary sources give students an opportunity to learn more about Eleanor Roosevelt. Her letter to the Daughters of the American Revolution protests the organization's treatment of Marian Anderson. In her autobiography, Mrs. Roosevelt describes how her childhood influenced her adult life.

What's the Connection?

Use a Roundtable activity to activate students' prior knowledge about Eleanor Roosevelt. Have groups of students move from station to station to answer these questions:

- Why was Eleanor Roosevelt afraid as a child?
- What role did duty play in her life?
- Who was Marian Anderson? How did Eleanor Roosevelt support her?

 BEST PRACTICES TOOLKIT—Transparency
Roundtable p. A17

Teach

Skill Focus: Synthesize

Explain that synthesizing is like using building blocks. When all the pieces are put together, something new emerges. Give students these suggestions to follow as they read:

- Summarize each selection to make sure you understand its main idea.
- Connect the ideas in each piece to what you already know about the topic.
- Relate the events or ideas in each piece to your personal experience or knowledge.
- Look at the pieces as a group to examine what they tell you about the topic.

Possible chart entries appear on page 778.

 RESOURCE MANAGER—Copy Master
Synthesize p. 47

A First Lady Speaks Out

Letter, page 777

Autobiography, page 778

Use with "Eleanor Roosevelt," page 762.

 MARYLAND OBJECTIVES

READING STANDARDS
1.E.4.c Draw conclusions
1.E.4.e Summarize

What's the Connection?

In "Eleanor Roosevelt," you read William Jay Jacobs's description of Eleanor's life growing up and then as the wife of the president. Now you will have the chance to hear from Mrs. Roosevelt herself as you read a letter she wrote to the Daughters of the American Revolution (DAR) and part of her autobiography.

Skill Focus: Synthesize

Have you ever formed an idea about someone from what one person told you? If so, perhaps your opinion changed once you met him or her for yourself.

When you put together information from more than one source, you **synthesize**. As a result, you gain a better understanding of a subject.

After you read the following letter and autobiography excerpt, you will synthesize the information about Eleanor Roosevelt. Take a moment to think about the impression of the First Lady you formed from Jacobs's biography. Then, as you learn more about her from the following selections, notice whether your idea of Mrs. Roosevelt changes. Doing the following can help:

- Summarize what you learned about Mrs. Roosevelt from reading the biography of her.
- Jot down any additional information you gather about her as you read her letter and autobiography. Feel free to note your own impressions or opinions of her as well.

Record your notes in a chart like the one shown.

Source	Strengths, Weaknesses, Accomplishments, and Other Information
"Eleanor Roosevelt"	She was a sad and lonely child. She devoted her life to helping others.
Letter to the DAR	
Autobiography	

Selection Resources

 RESOURCE MANAGER UNIT 7

Plan and Teach pp. 41–44

Reading
Summary pp. 45†*, 46‡*
Synthesize pp. 47, 49†*
Reading Check p. 51
Draw Conclusions pp. 48, 50†*
Question Support p. 52*

Assessment
Selection Tests A, B/C pp. 53*, 55*
 Test Generator CD

Reading Support
 Audio Anthology CD*

 BEST PRACTICES TOOLKIT

Roundtable • Making Inferences • Word Squares • Cause-and-Effect Chain

* Resources for Differentiation   † Also in Spanish   ‡ In Haitian Creole and Vietnamese

etter to the President General of the aughters of the American Revolution

eanor Roosevelt

anor Roosevelt wrote this letter after the Daughters of the American Revolution rred Marian Anderson's performance at Constitution Hall in Washington, D.C. s. Roosevelt further protested their actions by organizing a performance for rian Anderson in front of 75,000 people at the Lincoln Memorial.

THE WHITE HOUSE
WASHINGTON

February 28, 1939

My dear Mrs. Henry M. Robert Jr.:

I am afraid that I have never been a very useful member of the Daughters of the American Revolution, so I know it will make very little difference to you whether I resign, or whether I continue to be a member of your organization.

However, I am in complete disagreement with the attitude taken in refusing Constitution Hall to a great artist. You have set an example which seems to me unfortunate, and I feel
10 obliged to send in to you my resignation. You had an opportunity to lead in an enlightened way and it seems to me that your organization has failed. **A**

I realize that many people will not agree with me, but feeling as I do this seems to me the only proper procedure to follow. **B**

Very sincerely yours,

Eleanor Roosevelt

Eleanor Roosevelt

A SYNTHESIZE
What event prompted Mrs. Roosevelt to write this letter? In your chart, note what you learn about her from her response to this event.

B LETTER
From Mrs. Roosevelt's closing remark, what do you learn about her personality? Add this to your chart.

READING FOR INFORMATION **777**

Practice and Apply

FOCUS ON FORM
Discuss with students the purpose and the main characteristics of a letter.

- Purpose is to communicate private thoughts, feelings, opinions, and actions of the writer
- Parts of a letter include heading (place and date), salutation or greeting, body, closing, and signature
- Traditionally sent by mail

Ask students to identify the parts of Mrs. Roosevelt's letter.

INFORMATIONAL ANALYSIS

A SYNTHESIZE

Possible answer: *The DAR's refusal to let Marian Anderson perform at Constitution Hall in Washington, D.C., prompted Eleanor Roosevelt to write this letter. Roosevelt was a person who stood up for her beliefs and felt it was her duty to set an example.*

If students need help . . . Use a chart to help students note Mrs. Roosevelt's words and actions and to make inferences about her.

🧰 BEST PRACTICES TOOLKIT—Transparency Making Inferences p. A13

LITERARY ANALYSIS

B LETTER

Possible answer: *She was a strong woman of integrity and character who was concerned with doing what she felt to be right.*

Lines 1–15
ADDITIONAL TEACHING OPPORTUNITY

Evaluate Text and Author's Purpose Explore Eleanor Roosevelt's purpose in writing her letter to the DAR. Ask students to paraphrase her stated message *(she is resigning from the group)* and her hidden agenda *(she is protesting the DAR's racist treatment of Marian Anderson)*. What impact does Eleanor hope her letter will have? Does she truly think that the DAR won't care about her resignation? **Possible answer:** *Eleanor knows that they will hate to lose their most distinguished member, the First Lady. She is using her position's power to protest for a worthy cause.*

READING FOR INFORMATION **777**

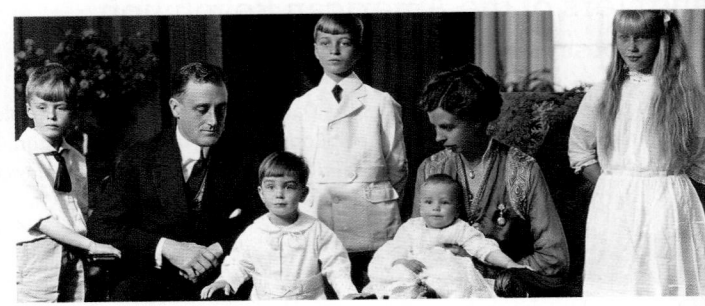

~ FROM ~

THE AUTOBIOGRAPHY OF ELEANOR ROOSEVELT

by Eleanor Roosevelt

C SYNTHESIZE
In "Eleanor Roosevelt," you learned that Eleanor was a lonely child. In your chart, write down additional information about her childhood that you learn from her autobiography.

In the beginning, because I felt, as only a young girl can feel it, all the pain of being an ugly duckling, I was not only timid, I was afraid. Afraid of almost everything, I think: of mice, of the dark, of imaginary dangers, of my own inadequacy. My chief objective, as a girl, was to do my duty. This had been drilled into me as far back as I could remember. Not my duty as I saw it, but my duty as laid down for me by other people. It never occurred to me to revolt. Anyhow, my one overwhelming need in those days was to be approved, to be loved, and I did whatever was required of me, hoping it would bring me nearer to the approval and
10 love I so much wanted. **C**

As a young woman, my sense of duty remained as strict and rigid as it had been when I was a girl, but it had changed its focus. My husband and my children became the center of my life, and their needs were my new duty. I am afraid now that I approached this new obligation much as I had my childhood duties. I was still timid, still afraid of doing something wrong, of making mistakes, of not living up to the standards required by my mother-in-law, of failing to do what was expected of me.

As a result, I was so hidebound by duty that I became too critical, too much of a disciplinarian. I was so concerned with bringing up my
20 children properly that I was not wise enough just to love them. Now looking back, I think I would rather spoil a child a little and have more fun out of it. **D**

D SYNTHESIZE
What new information and insights does Mrs. Roosevelt share about her adulthood? Add these to your chart.

DIFFERENTIATED INSTRUCTION

FOR LESS–PROFICIENT READERS

Vocabulary Support Distribute copies of the Word Squares transparency and have pairs create a word square for *hidebound* (line 18). Encourage them to use context clues to help them predict the meaning of the word before they look it up in a dictionary. Ask volunteers to share their word squares with the class. Discuss the literal meaning related to animals with tight skin and trees with tight bark that impedes growth. Explain that the term came to mean "inflexible" when applied to people.

Comprehension Support In this selection from her autobiography, Eleanor Roosevelt talks about how her childhood influenced her actions as a wife and mother. Use a Cause-and-Effect Chain to help students understand the relationship between childhood causes and adult effects.

 BEST PRACTICES TOOLKIT—Transparencies
Word Squares p. E10
Cause-and-Effect Chain pp. B16, B39

Eleanor felt like an "ugly duckling."

Cause

Effect

She was afraid of being unloved.

Cause

Effect

She did her duty so other people would love her.

Cause

Comprehension

1. **Recall** Why does Mrs. Roosevelt write to Mrs. Henry M. Robert Jr.?

2. **Recall** As a child, why was Eleanor so concerned with doing her duty?

Critical Analysis

3. **Identify Primary Sources** A primary source on Mrs. Roosevelt could be anything she wrote that provides information about her. It could also be a photograph of her or something written about her by someone who knew her. Are the autobiography and letter you just read primary sources on Eleanor Roosevelt? Explain why or why not.

4. **Draw Conclusions from a Letter** What do you learn about Mrs. Roosevelt's character from her letter to Mrs. Henry M. Robert Jr.? Use evidence from the letter to support your answer.

5. **Synthesize** Review the notes in your chart. How did Eleanor's attitude toward duty change over the course of her life? Support your answer.

Read for Information: Draw Conclusions

MARYLAND OBJECTIVES

READING STANDARDS
1.E.4.c Draw conclusions
1.E.4.e Summarize

> **WRITING PROMPT**
>
> In a paragraph, state and support a conclusion about one of these topics:
>
> • the way Eleanor Roosevelt changed over time
> • the kind of person Eleanor Roosevelt was
> • what motivates people to do great things

As you may recall, a **conclusion** is a judgment or belief about something. Following the numbered steps can help you reach and support a conclusion about one of the three topics given above.

1. Review your notes about Mrs. Roosevelt. What do they lead you to conclude? Jot down a conclusion for each topic. Then pick one you think you can best support.

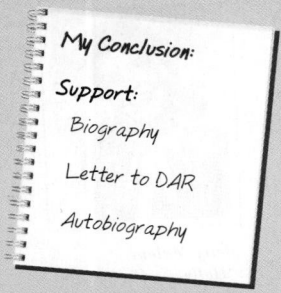

My Conclusion:
Support:
Biography
Letter to DAR
Autobiography

2. Reread the three selections to find details that support your conclusion. If you can't find much support, consider revising your conclusion or picking a different one.

3. Once you have a conclusion you can support well, state it in a topic sentence. Then present the reasons and evidence that support this conclusion.

FOR LESS–PROFICIENT WRITERS

Read for Information

• Divide students into groups based on their chosen topics. Have them brainstorm ideas and discuss their conclusions.

• Assign one or two students in each group to review one selection for evidence to support their conclusion. Direct students to share what they learned with other group members and use the pooled information to write their paragraphs.

FOR ADVANCED LEARNERS/PRE–AP

Read for Information Allow students to expand their writing to more than one paragraph. Encourage students to find an additional letter from Eleanor Roosevelt or another selection from her autobiography that relates to their chosen topic. Have them include evidence from their additional source as well as from the assigned selections when they write their paragraphs.

Practice and Apply

For additional support of post-reading questions, use these copy masters:

R RESOURCE MANAGER—Copy Masters
   Reading Check p. 51
   Question Support p. 52
   Draw Conclusions p. 48
   For additional questions, see p. 43.

ANSWERS

Comprehension

1. *She writes to resign from the DAR in disapproval of their decision to deny Marian Anderson permission to perform.*

2. *She hoped that doing her duty would bring her the approval and love she wanted so badly.*

Critical Analysis

3. *Possible answer: They are primary sources because Eleanor Roosevelt wrote them.*

4. *Possible answers: Eleanor was modest (lines 1–4) and she acted on her beliefs (lines 9–10).*

5. ■ STANDARDS FOCUS *Synthesize*
   Possible answers: In her younger years, Eleanor let others define her duty (lines 6, 14–20). As an older woman, she defined her duty according to her own sense of right and wrong (lines 13–15, 20–22).

Read for Information: Draw Conclusions

Writing Prompt *Students should support their conclusions with evidence from at least two of the selections.*

Assess and Reteach

Assess

R RESOURCE MANAGER—Copy Masters
   Selection Tests A, B/C pp. 53–54, 55–56
⊘ Test Generator CD

Reteach

S STANDARDS LESSON FILE
   Reading Lesson 14: Synthesizing Information
   Reading Lesson 9: Drawing Conclusions

Focus and Motivate

OBJECTIVES

Literary Analysis
- explore the key idea of a **name**
- identify form and characteristics of a personal essay
- analyze the writer's message
- read a personal essay

Reading
- connect

Vocabulary
- build vocabulary for reading and writing
- understand and use connotative meanings of words *(also an EL language objective)*

Grammar and Writing
- capitalize proper nouns correctly
- use writing to analyze literature

SUMMARY

This essay explores the author's adjustment to American society after she and her family move to New York City from the Dominican Republic. The many variations of their names used by the people they meet in America become a symbol of the author's search for her identity.

What does your NAME *really mean?*

Discuss the question and *KEY IDEA* with students. Take a class poll to find out the meanings behind students' **names.** Have students complete the *WEB IT* activity and share their responses in small groups.

Selection Resources

Names/Nombres
Personal Essay by Julia Alvarez

What does your NAME *really mean?*

MARYLAND OBJECTIVES

READING/LIT STANDARDS
1.E.4.f Connect the text to personal experience
3.A.6.a Analyze main ideas

KEY IDEA Parents may choose a **name** for their child because its original meaning is important to them. They might name a new baby after a relative or a famous person. Sometimes parents select a name just because they like the way it sounds. But when it comes to nicknames, adults don't always have control. In "Names/Nombres," author Julia Alvarez writes about how her many nicknames affected her.

WEB IT Create an idea web with your name in the middle. Write down all the names and nicknames you have had throughout your life. Who uses each name and what does that name mean to you?

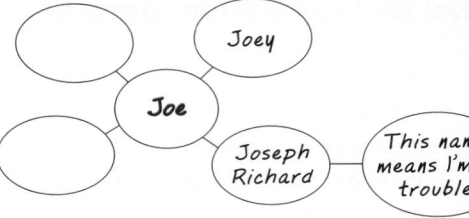

Joey

Joe

Joseph Richard

This name means I'm in trouble.

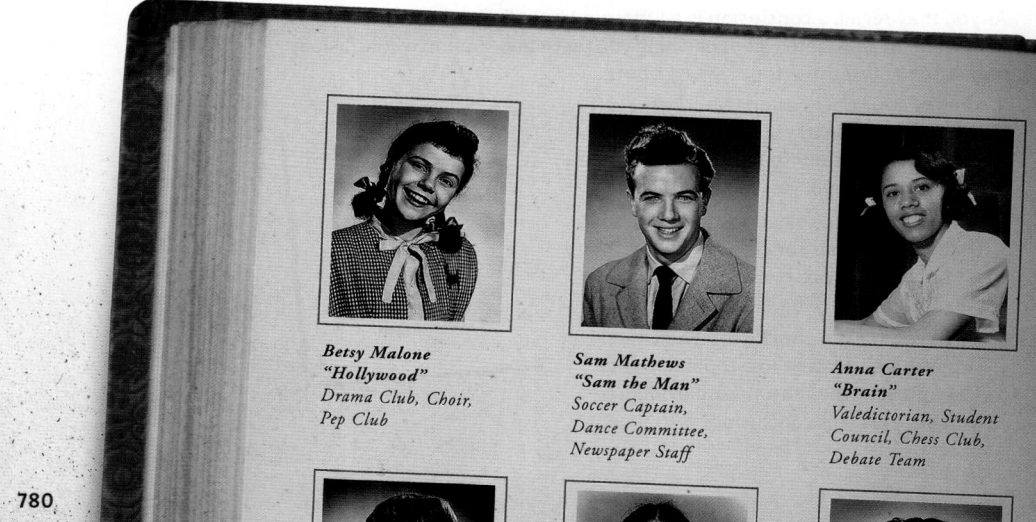

Betsy Malone
"Hollywood"
Drama Club, Choir, Pep Club

Sam Mathews
"Sam the Man"
Soccer Captain, Dance Committee, Newspaper Staff

Anna Carter
"Brain"
Valedictorian, Student Council, Chess Club, Debate Team

780

Selection Resources

R **RESOURCE MANAGER UNIT 7**

Plan and Teach pp. 57–64

Literary Analysis
Summary pp. 65†*, 66‡*
Personal Essay pp. 67, 68†*
Question Support p. 75*

Reading
Connect pp. 69, 70†*
Reading Check p. 74
Reading Fluency p. 77

Vocabulary
Study p. 71*
Practice p. 72
Strategy p. 73

Grammar and Writing
Capitalize Correctly p. 76

Assessment
Selection Tests A, B/C pp. 79*, 81*
 Test Generator CD

🧰 BEST PRACTICES TOOLKIT

Differentiated Instruction pp. 31–38*
Scaffolding Instruction pp. 43–46*

Graphic Organizers/Strategies
Making Inferences • Word Squares • Cluster Diagram • T Chart • Venn Diagram

Reading Support
 Audio Anthology CD*

Technology
ⓘ Literature and Vocabulary Centers at **ClassZone.com**

WriteSmart CD

---

* Resources for Differentiation   † Also in Spanish   ‡ In Haitian Creole and Vietnamese

LITERARY ANALYSIS: PERSONAL ESSAY

A **personal essay** is a form of nonfiction that expresses the writer's thoughts and feelings about one subject. You can understand the **writer's message,** or main point, by paying close attention to the writer's

- use of **anecdotes,** or short accounts of events
- choice of words
- descriptions of thoughts and feelings

As you read "Names/Nombres," pay attention to the anecdotes, thoughts, and feelings Alvarez shares about her name.

READING STRATEGY: CONNECT

Think about the many talks and discussions you have had with your friends. It probably comes naturally to relate to what they're saying. Similarly, you can **connect** with someone's writing by comparing the events described with your own experiences. Connecting can help you better understand both the things you read and your own world.

As you read "Names/Nombres," keep a log to record any connections that you have with the essay.

Julia	Me
Her parents call her "Hoo-lee-tah."	My family calls me "Little Joe."

VOCABULARY IN CONTEXT

The boldfaced words help Julia Alvarez convey her feelings and experiences. Use context clues to figure out what each word means.

1. She noted **ironically** that rain made her think of her former home.
2. Leaving one home for another was exciting but **chaotic.**
3. His **convoluted** answers to my simple questions were frustrating.
4. We wanted to **specify** our choices on the questionnaire.
5. The students wanted to **merge** into their new culture.

Author Online

A Tale of Two Countries
Although Julia Alvarez was born in New York City, she lived in the Dominican Republic until she was ten. When the family returned to New York in 1960 to escape the Dominican dictatorship, Alvarez felt out of place—a foreigner with a different language, name, and way of life.

Julia Alvarez born 1950

A World of Words Alvarez's first years back in New York were tough, but she soon found a way to cope. She started to write stories and poetry. "I could save what I didn't want to lose—memories and smells and sounds, things too precious to put anywhere else," she explained. Alvarez's writings continue to draw on her early memories and immigrant experiences.

 MORE ABOUT THE AUTHOR
For more on Julia Alvarez, visit the **Literature Center** at **ClassZone.com.**

Background

A Troubled History The Dominican Republic is a nation that covers about two-thirds of the island of Hispaniola in the Caribbean Sea. A dictator, General Rafael Trujillo, ruled the nation from 1930 to 1961. Many Dominicans came to the United States—especially New York City—during this violent, unsettling period in Dominican history.

NAMES/NOMBRES   **781**

Teach

STANDARDS FOCUS

LITERARY ANALYSIS

● **PERSONAL ESSAY**

Read aloud this example:

> When I was little, I met an older girl who shared my name. I was fascinated. Did we like the same food? Would I grow up to look like her? After this encounter, I often peered in the mirror, waiting for my features to become hers!

Ask students what this anecdote reveals about the writer as a young girl. ***Possible answers:*** *She thought that people with the same names were alike. She was curious and imaginative.*

CHECK UNDERSTANDING Have students identify the topics of other personal essays they have read.

READING STRATEGY

■ **CONNECT**

Tell students that making connections does not always mean finding similarities. Sometimes recognizing contrasts can lead to deeper insights.

CHECK UNDERSTANDING Have students review **Author Online** and find a difference or similarity that helps them connect to the author's experience.

R **RESOURCE MANAGER—Copy Master**
Connect p. 69 (for student use while reading the selection)

VOCABULARY SKILL

▲ VOCABULARY IN CONTEXT

DIAGNOSE WORD KNOWLEDGE To determine preteaching needs, have all students complete **Vocabulary in Context.** Check students' answers against the definitions in the text:
1. *ironically* (p. 784), 2. *chaotic* (p. 786), 3. *convoluted* (p. 786), 4. *specify* (p. 785), 5. *merge* (p. 785).

PRETEACH VOCABULARY Use the Vocabulary Study copy master to help students explore the meaning of each boldfaced word.

1. Read the first paragraph aloud, emphasizing *convoluted.*
2. Point out the context word "confusing." Elicit possible meanings for *convoluted,* such as "unclear."
3. Repeat the procedure for the rest of the passage.

R **RESOURCE MANAGER—Copy Master**
Vocabulary Study p. 71

For general guidelines on differentiating vocabulary instruction and for alternative vocabulary activities for students not needing vocabulary preteaching, see

 BEST PRACTICES TOOLKIT
Scaffolding Vocabulary Instruction pp. 43–46

 Vocabulary Center at **ClassZone.com**

ANALYZE VISUALS

Possible answer: The blurred brushstrokes and the vivid colors create a strong impression of movement, energy, and activity.

About the Art American artist Patti Mollica is particularly inspired by New York City, the subject of this cityscape. She uses color in original ways to create a feeling of energy and excitement and says that she sees the "world as a mosaic of shapes and color. Even the most mundane sight can be extraordinarily interesting."

LITERARY ANALYSIS

Ⓐ PERSONAL ESSAY

Possible answer: Yes. She describes her last name as an "orchestra of sound" (line 8) and wants to correct the officer's pronunciation.

If students need help . . . In an inferences chart, record details from the text and students' prior knowledge to help them arrive at the correct inference.

Details from essay	What I already know	Inference
"drumroll of the r" (line 7)	A drumroll announces something important or someone special.	The author thinks her name is special. She is proud of it.

Extend the Discussion Why does the author immediately say her name correctly to herself? What thoughts or feelings does this detail reveal?

 BEST PRACTICES TOOLKIT—Transparency Making Inferences p. A13

Names/Nombres

Julia Alvarez

ANALYZE VISUALS
What **mood** do the colors, images, and brushstrokes create in this painting?

When we arrived in New York City, our names changed almost immediately. At Immigration, the officer asked my father, *Mister Elbures,* if he had anything to declare.[1] My father shook his head no, and we were waved through. I was too afraid we wouldn't be let in if I corrected the man's pronunciation, but I said our name to myself, opening my mouth wide for the organ blast of the *a,* trilling my tongue[2] for the drumroll of the *r, All-vah-rrr-es!* How could anyone get *Elbures* out of that orchestra of sound? Ⓐ

At the hotel my mother was *Missus Alburest,* and I was *little girl,*
10 as in, "Hey, little girl, stop riding the elevator up and down. It's *not* a toy."

When we moved into our new apartment building, the super[3] called my father *Mister Alberase,* and the neighbors who became mother's friends pronounced her name *Jew-lee-ah* instead of *Hoo-lee-ah.* I, her namesake, was known as *Hoo-lee-tah* at home. But at school I was *Judy* or *Judith,* and once an English teacher mistook me for *Juliet.*

Ⓐ **PERSONAL ESSAY**
Reread lines 1–8. Consider Alvarez's choice of words and her thoughts at Immigration. Do you think Julia is proud of her last name?

① **Targeted Passage**

---

1. **At Immigration . . . declare:** Immigration is the place where government officials check the documents of people entering a country. People must acknowledge, or declare, certain goods or moneys that they are carrying.

2. **trilling my tongue:** rapidly vibrating the tongue against the roof of the mouth, as in pronouncing a Spanish *r.*

3. **super:** superintendent, or building manager.

West 17th Street, New York City (20th century), Patti Mollica. © Patti Mollica/SuperStock.

DIFFERENTIATED INSTRUCTION

FOR ALL STUDENTS

Enhancing Learning Styles Provide independent projects for various learning styles.

- **Tactile** Find the recipes and make some of the Spanish dishes mentioned in the essay.

- **Linguistic** Prepare an introductory Spanish lesson and record it on audio or videotape.

- **Creative** Organize a portfolio of the styles of the 1950s and 1960s.

FOR LESS–PROFICIENT READERS

In combination with the *Audio Anthology CD,* use one or more Targeted Passages (pp. 782, 785, 786) to ensure that students focus on key events, concepts, and skills.

① **Targeted Passage [Lines 11–15]**

This passage defines the topic of the essay: the many names by which the author is known after she and her family move to America.

BACKGROUND

The 1950s The author and her family moved to the United States during a decade known for its conformity. The increasing popularity of such television shows as *Father Knows Best,* *The Adventures of Ozzie and Harriet,* and *Leave It to Beaver* contributed to a uniform national culture and promoted the ideal of a typical American family.

- What is the author's real name as pronounced by her family?

- What do people at school call her?

- How would you feel if someone pronounced your name differently or called you by another name? How do you think the author feels?

FOR ENGLISH LEARNERS

Key Academic Vocabulary Have students complete Word Squares for these active verbs: *pursue* (line 28), *trace* (line 29), *reveal* (line 40), *transport* (line 56), *located* (line 79).

 BEST PRACTICES TOOLKIT—Transparency
Word Squares p. E10

Prereading For prereading instruction for English learners, see

 BEST PRACTICES TOOLKIT
Scaffolding Reading Instruction pp. 43–46

FOR ADVANCED LEARNERS/PRE–AP

Pre-AP exercises in the bottom channel provide additional challenge for your advanced students. Use them for small groups or individuals.

ADDITIONAL GUIDELINES

For more help with differentiation and tips for classroom management, see

 BEST PRACTICES TOOLKIT
Differentiated Instruction pp. 31–38

REINFORCE *KEY IDEA*: NAME

Discuss Why do you think the author's mother urges her to accept the new versions of her name? *Possible answers: She wants her daughter to fit in. The mother hopes that accepting the new name will help her daughter accept her new life.*

READING STRATEGY

B CONNECT

Have students record their responses in their chart from page 781.

Possible answer:

Julia	Me
Julia feels that her nicknames show her popularity. She likes having a nickname.	My nickname makes me feel special, too.

Lines 16–29
ADDITIONAL TEACHING OPPORTUNITY

Author's Perspective Have students compare how the author's attitude toward her "new names" in high school differs from her point of view when she first arrived in New York City. *(Possible answer: Upon arrival, the author was very proud of her Hispanic names. In high school, she likes her English nicknames because they help her fit in.)* As students continue reading the essay, ask them to consider how the author's **perspective**, or point of view, affects her text. Help students see that her personal feelings about the importance of names strongly influences the message of the essay.

It took a while to get used to my new names. I wondered if I shouldn't correct my teachers and new friends. But my mother argued that it didn't matter. "You know what your friend Shakespeare said, 'A rose by any other name would smell as sweet.'"[4] My family had gotten into the habit of
20 calling any literary figure "my friend" because I had begun to write poems and stories in English class.

By the time I was in high school, I was a popular kid, and it showed in my name. Friends called me *Jules* or *Hey Jude*,[5] and once a group of troublemaking friends my mother forbade me to hang out with called me *Alcatraz*.[6] I was *Hoo-lee-tah* only to Mami and Papi and uncles and aunts who came over to eat *sancocho*[7] on Sunday afternoons—old world folk whom I would just as soon go back to where they came from and leave me to pursue whatever mischief I wanted to in America. JUDY ALCATRAZ: the name on the wanted poster would read. Who would ever trace her to me? **B**

30 My older sister had the hardest time getting an American name for herself because *Mauricia* did not translate into English. **Ironically**, although she had the most foreign-sounding name, she and I were the Americans in the family. We had been born in New York City when our parents had first tried immigration and then gone back "home," too homesick to stay. My mother often told the story of how she had almost changed my sister's name in the hospital.

After the delivery, Mami and some other new mothers were cooing over their new baby sons and daughters and exchanging names and weights and delivery stories. My mother was embarrassed among the Sallys and
40 Janes and Georges and Johns to reveal the rich, noisy name of *Mauricia*, so when her turn came to brag, she gave her baby's name as *Maureen*.

"Why'd ya give her an Irish name with so many pretty Spanish names to choose from?" one of the women asked her.

My mother blushed and admitted her baby's real name to the group. Her mother-in-law had recently died, she apologized, and her husband had insisted that the first daughter be named after his mother, *Mauran*. My mother thought it the ugliest name she had ever heard, and she talked my father into what she believed was an improvement, a combination of *Mauran* and her own mother's name, *Felicia*.

50 "Her name is Mao-ree-shee-ah," my mother said to the group.

"Why, that's a beautiful name," the new mothers cried. "*Moor-ee-sha, Moor-ee-sha*," they cooed into the pink blanket. *Moor-ee-sha* it was when

B CONNECT
You might have listed a nickname for the activity on page 780. Compare how this nickname makes you feel with how Julia's nicknames make her feel.

ironically (ī-rŏn′ĭk-lē) *adv.* in a way that is contrary to what is expected or intended

---

4. **'A rose . . . smell as sweet'**: In Shakespeare's *Romeo and Juliet*, the main characters' families are enemies. But when Romeo and Juliet fall in love, Juliet uses almost these words to say that Romeo is precious to her no matter what his family name is.

5. **Hey Jude**: the title of a hit song by the Beatles in 1968.

6. **Alcatraz** (ăl′kə-trăz′): the name of an island in San Francisco Bay that was once the site of a prison.

7. **sancocho** (säng-kō′chô) *Spanish*: a traditional Caribbean stew of meat and vegetables.

DIFFERENTIATED INSTRUCTION

FOR LESS–PROFICIENT READERS
Reading Strategy Follow-Up: Connect
Discuss the parts of the essay to which students have been able to connect so far. Distribute sticky notes. As students read and make new connections, have them use the notes to jot down words or phrases that will remind them of each connection. After students have finished reading the essay, have them copy the passages into their charts and explain what each connection is.

FOR ADVANCED LEARNERS/PRE–AP
Analyze Symbolism The first two paragraphs on this page describe some of the variations of the author's name and her reaction to them. Ask students to use these details and those from the previous page to explore what the author's name symbolizes to her. Invite students to organize their insights in a chart or diagram and to share their ideas. Then have students use their understanding of the symbolic significance of the name to identify possible themes of the essay.

we returned to the States eleven years later. Sometimes, American tongues found even that mispronunciation tough to say and called her *Maria* or *Marsha* or *Maudy* from her nickname *Maury*. I pitied her. What an awful name to have to transport across borders! **⊙**

My little sister, Ana, had the easiest time of all. She was plain *Anne*— that is, only her name was plain, for she turned out to be the pale, blond "American beauty" in the family. The only Hispanic-seeming thing about 60 her was the affectionate nicknames her boyfriends sometimes gave her. *Anita*, or as one goofy guy used to sing to her to the tune of the banana advertisement, *Anita Banana*.

Later, during her college years in the late 60's, there was a push to pronounce Third World[8] names correctly. I remember calling her long distance at her group house and a roommate answering.

"Can I speak to Ana?" I asked, pronouncing her name the American way.

"Ana?" The man's voice hesitated. "Oh! You must mean *Ah-nah!*"

Our first few years in the States, though, ethnicity was not yet "in." Those were the blond, blue-eyed, bobby-sock years of junior high 70 and high school before the 60's ushered in peasant blouses, hoop earrings, *sarapes*.[9] My initial desire to be known by my correct Dominican name faded. I just wanted to be Judy and **merge** with the Sallys and Janes in my class. But, inevitably, my accent and coloring gave me away.

"So where are you from, Judy?"

"New York," I told my classmates. After all, I had been born blocks away at Columbia Presbyterian Hospital.

"I mean, *originally.*"

"From the Caribbean," I answered vaguely, for if I **specified,** no one was quite sure what continent our island was located on.

80 "Really? I've been to Bermuda. We went last April for spring vacation. I got the worst sunburn! So, are you from Portoriko?"

"No," I shook my head. "From the Dominican Republic."

"Where's that?"

"South of Bermuda."

They were just being curious, I knew, but I burned with shame whenever they singled me out as a "foreigner," a rare, exotic friend.

"Say your name in Spanish, oh, please say it!" I had made mouths drop one day by rattling off my full name, which, according to Dominican custom, included my middle names, Mother's and Father's surnames[10] 90 for four generations back.

---

8. **Third World:** from the developing nations of Latin America, Africa, and Asia.

9. *sarapes* (sə-rä′pāz) *Spanish:* long, blanketlike shawls.

10. **surnames:** last names.

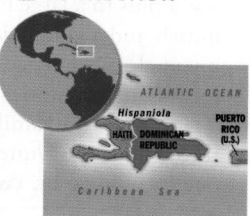

SOCIAL STUDIES CONNECTION

The Dominican Republic

⊙ **PERSONAL ESSAY**
Why do you think Alvarez included this **anecdote** in her personal essay?

② Targeted Passage

merge (mûrj) *v.* to blend together

specify (spĕs′ə-fī′) *v.* to make known or identify

LITERARY ANALYSIS

⊙ PERSONAL ESSAY

Possible answer: This anecdote shows the irony of trying to fit in. Mrs. Alvarez, embarrassed by her baby's real name, invents an "Irish name"; the Americans ask why she didn't choose a "pretty Spanish name" instead. When the truth unfolds, the others love the name "Mauricia," although they mispronounce it.

If students need help . . .

- Encourage students to reread lines 39–41 to see why Mrs. Alvarez felt embarrassed.
- Have them reread lines 51–52 to find out how the Americans react to the true name.

Lines 74–86
DISCUSSION PROMPTS

Use these prompts to help students understand the author's conflict:

Connect How do your experiences help you understand the way the author answers the question of where she is from? *Students may say that in trying to fit in, the author wants to show that she is not much different from her classmates. She also anticipates that her classmates won't know where the Dominican Republic is located.*

Analyze Why is the author shamed by her classmates' curiosity? *Possible answer: It makes her feel singled out as a foreigner.*

Evaluate Do you think the author would have the same reaction to that question if someone asked her today? Explain. *Possible answer: She would not have the same reaction because she feels more comfortable with her identity.*

⊙ SOCIAL STUDIES CONNECTION

The Dominican Republic Since 1996, the Dominican Republic has had a representative democracy with regular elections. Its economy is based on exportation of sugar, coffee, and tobacco, as well as a thriving tourist industry.

FOR LESS–PROFICIENT READERS

② Targeted Passage [Lines 68–73]

This passage presents insights into the thoughts and feelings of the author as a girl who just wanted to fit in.

- What is the popular look when the author is in junior high and high school? Why is that a problem for her?
- How does her feeling about her Dominican name change during this time period? Why?

FOR ENGLISH LEARNERS

Comprehension: Connect Read lines 87–90 aloud. Discuss how the author's full name comes from several generations of her family. Ask volunteers to describe baby-naming traditions in their cultures.

Vocabulary: Idioms and Sayings Have students use context clues to define

- *a push* (line 63), "pressure"
- *gave me away* (line 73), "revealed my secret"
- *made mouths drop* (lines 87–88), "astonished people"

REINFORCE KEY IDEA: NAME

Discuss What function does the author's full name serve? *Possible answer: Her full name ties her to the past—it gives her a history and a very complete identity.*

READING STRATEGY

D CONNECT

Remind students to record their connection in their chart from page 781. *Some students may identify with having a large extended family; others may connect to those classmates with a smaller nuclear family.*

LITERARY ANALYSIS

E PERSONAL ESSAY

Possible answer: Yes. Her high school nickname reminds her of the fun she had in that period of her life.

SELECTION WRAP-UP

REFLECT Have students consider why the author wants to correct teachers and others about the pronunciation of her name during her first years in the United States. What does her name mean to her at that time in her life?

⭐ **CRITIQUE** Ask students to evaluate what the author's stories about her sisters' experiences add to the essay. Have them decide whether or not those anecdotes affect the unity of the essay.

READING FLUENCY

Distribute the copy masters and have students work in pairs to practice fluency.

R RESOURCE MANAGER—Copy Master Reading Fluency p. 77

"Julia Altagracia María Teresa Álvarez Tavares Perello Espaillat Julia Pérez Rochet González." I pronounced it slowly, a name as **chaotic** with sounds as a Middle Eastern bazaar or market day in a South American village.

I suffered most whenever my extended family attended school occasions. For my graduation, they all came, the whole noisy, foreign-looking lot of fat aunts in their dark mourning dresses and hair nets, uncles with full, droopy mustaches and baby-blue or salmon-colored suits and white pointy shoes and fedora hats, the many little cousins who snuck in without tickets. They sat in the first row in order to better understand
100 the Americans' fast-spoken English. But how could they listen when they were constantly speaking among themselves in florid-sounding phrases, rococo consonants, rich, rhyming vowels? Their loud voices carried.

Introducing them to my friends was a further trial to me. These relatives had such complicated names and there were so many of them, and their relationships to myself were so **convoluted.** There was my Tía Josefina, who was not really an aunt but a much older cousin. And her daughter, Aída Margarita, who was adopted, *una hija de crianza.*[11] My uncle of affection, Tío José, brought my *madrina* Tía Amelia and her *comadre* Tía Pilar.[12] My friends rarely had more than their nuclear family[13] to introduce,
110 youthful, glamorous-looking couples ("Mom and Dad") who skied and played tennis and took their kids for spring vacations to Bermuda. **D**

After the commencement ceremony, my family waited outside in the parking lot while my friends and I signed yearbooks with nicknames which recalled our high school good times: "Beans" and "Pepperoni" and "Alcatraz." We hugged and cried and promised to keep in touch.

Sometimes if our goodbyes went on too long, I heard my father's voice calling out across the parking lot. "*Hoo-lee-tah! Vámonos!*"[14] **E**

Back home, my *tíos* and *tías* and *primas*, Mami and Papi, and *mis hermanas* had a party for me with *sancocho* and a store-bought *pudín*,
120 inscribed with *Happy Graduation, Julie.*[15] There were many gifts—that was a plus to a large family! I got several wallets and a suitcase with my initials and a graduation charm from my godmother and money from my uncles. The biggest gift was a portable typewriter from my parents for writing my stories and poems.

Someday, the family predicted, my name would be well-known throughout the United States. I laughed to myself, wondering which one I would go by. ꙮ

---

11. *una hija de crianza* (ōō′nä ē′hä dě krē-än′sä) *Spanish:* a child raised as if one's own.
12. **My uncle of affection . . . Tía Pilar:** My favorite uncle, Uncle José, brought my godmother Aunt Amelia and her close friend Aunt Pilar.
13. **nuclear family:** a family unit consisting of a mother, a father, and their children.
14. *Vámanos* (bä′mä-nôs) *Spanish:* Let's go.
15. **Back home . . . Julie:** Back home, my uncles and aunts and cousins, Mami and Papi, and my sisters had a party for me with a stew and a store-bought pudding, inscribed with *Happy Graduation, Julie.*

chaotic (kā-ŏt′ĭk) *adj.* confused; disordered

③ Targeted Passage

convoluted (kŏn′və-lōō′tĭd) *adj.* difficult to understand; complicated

D CONNECT
Think about how Julia feels when she introduces her family to her friends. What situation have you experienced or read about that can help you understand her feelings?

E PERSONAL ESSAY
Reread lines 112–115. Do you think Julia likes her nickname by the time she graduates from high school? Tell what clues helped you answer this question.

DIFFERENTIATED INSTRUCTION

FOR LESS-PROFICIENT READERS

③ Targeted Passage [Lines 103–111]

This passage presents the contrast in cultures: the author's Dominican family is large and complicated in comparison with the small American families.

- How does the author feel about introducing her friends to her family?
- In what ways is her family different from her friends' families?
- How do you think her friends view her family in comparison to their own?

FOR ADVANCED LEARNERS/PRE-AP

Author's Perspective What does the young Julia Alvarez think about American culture? Explain that an author's **perspective** is the author's attitudes and beliefs as expressed in his or her writing. In "Names/Nombres," Alvarez conveys an opinion about American society through her anecdotes and choice of words. Challenge students to create a letter that Alvarez may have written to a close cousin or friend in the Dominican Republic illustrating her perspective of America.

Comprehension

1. **Clarify** Why does Julia say it is a "trial" to introduce her family?

2. **Summarize** Explain what happens in the hospital when Mauricia is born.

3. **Represent** Review "Names/Nombres" to find all of Julia's names and nicknames. Arrange her names into three categories: (1) those used by her family and friends, (2) those used by strangers, and (3) those used by both.

Literary Analysis

4. **Examine Connections** Review the notes you made in your log while reading "Names/Nombres." What can you learn from Alvarez about your own experiences?

5. **Make Inferences** Reread lines 1–15. Why do you think Alvarez chooses to refer to the mispronunciation of her and her family's names as a changing of their names?

6. **Draw Conclusions** How would you describe Julia's mother, Mrs. Alvarez, on the basis of her words and actions?

7. **Interpret a Personal Essay** In a graphic like the one shown, note clues that contribute to Alvarez's message about **names** and identities. What is the writer's message in "Names/Nombres"? Explain your reasoning based on the information in your graphic.

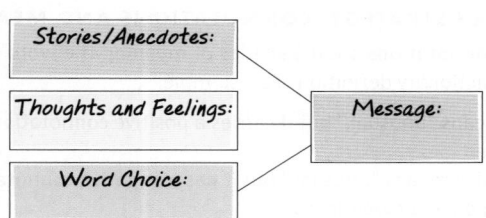

Stories/Anecdotes:

Thoughts and Feelings:

Word Choice:

Message:

Extension and Challenge

8. **Creative Project: Drama** With a partner, role-play a conversation between Eleanor Roosevelt and Julia Alvarez about their experiences with nicknames. Start by reviewing "Eleanor Roosevelt" and "Names/Nombres" to find the nicknames each woman had. Then have them discuss what they think of their nicknames, how their names influenced them, and what advice they have about nicknames.

9. **SOCIAL STUDIES CONNECTION** Julia Alvarez divided her childhood between the United States and the Dominican Republic. Write three questions about the Dominican Republic and research to find the answers. Share the information with the class.

RESEARCH LINKS
For more on the Dominican Republic, visit the **Research Center** at ClassZone.com.

MARYLAND OBJECTIVES

LITERATURE STANDARD
3.A.6.a Analyze main ideas

NAMES/NOMBRES **787**

Practice and Apply

After Reading

For additional support of post-reading questions, use these copy masters:

R RESOURCE MANAGER—Copy Masters
  Reading Check p. 74 (to check understanding of the selection)
  Personal Essay p. 67 (for practice of literary analysis standards focus)
  Question Support p. 75 (**After Reading** questions adapted for English learners and less-proficient readers)

  Additional selection questions are provided for teachers on page 61.

For additional activities to challenge students, see

i Power Thinking at **ClassZone.com**

ANSWERS

Comprehension

1. *The author has so many family members with complex relationships that it takes a long time to introduce them all.*

2. *Alvarez's mother at first lies about the baby's name. When she does tell the other mothers what it is, they think it is beautiful, but they cannot pronounce it.*

3. ***Used by family and friends:** Hoo-lee-tah (line 14), Jules, Hey Jude, Alcatraz (lines 23–25);* ***Used by strangers:** Judith, Juliet (lines 14–15), Julie (line 120);* ***Used by both:** Judy (lines 14, 72)*

Literary Analysis

Possible answers:

4. ■ **STANDARDS FOCUS** *Connect Students' answers will vary and should be based on evidence from the text. Students may say that reading about the author's experiences helped them think about their own names and what they symbolize in a different way.*

5. *The mispronunciations of their names seem to take away their identity.*

6. ***Words:** tells Julia not to correct her teachers and friends (lines 17–18); tells family her story about Mauricia's name (lines 35–36).* ***Actions:** tries to protect Julia (line 24); supports her love of writing (lines 19–21; 123–124).* ***Conclusion:** Mrs. Alvarez is a caring mother who also coped with feeling different.*

---

7. ● **STANDARDS FOCUS** *Personal Essay*
Depending on the anecdotes and the passages chosen, students may interpret the message differently. One view might be that Alvarez feels that some Americans are insensitive to people of other cultures and make them feel like outsiders. Another might be that we have different sides that we show to different people. Being called different names symbolizes the many facets of our personalities.

Extension and Challenge

8. *Students' role plays should accurately reflect the attitudes and experiences of Eleanor Roosevelt and Julia Alvarez. Encourage students to outline important ideas that they wish to include.*

9. **SOCIAL STUDIES CONNECTION**

Students' questions may include some of these: What is the climate of the Dominican Republic? What kind of government does it have now? What are its major industries and economies?

NAMES/NOMBRES **787**

ANSWERS

Vocabulary in Context

VOCABULARY PRACTICE

1. *antonyms*
2. *antonyms*
3. *synonyms*
4. *synonyms*
5. *antonyms*

 RESOURCE MANAGER—Copy Master
Vocabulary Practice p. 72

VOCABULARY IN WRITING

Students can use a Cluster Diagram to list all the different feelings that the author experienced as she tried to find her place in American society. Suggest that students then look at the word list and consider which words can be used to express those feelings.

 BEST PRACTICES TOOLKIT—Transparency
Cluster Diagram p. B18

VOCABULARY STRATEGY: CONNOTATION AND MEANING *(also an EL language objective)*

To help students recognize the connotations of the words, provide them with a synonym for each that has the opposite connotation, such as *hovel, economical, sneaky, blunt, daring,* and so on. Ask students which word they would prefer to have used in a description of themselves.

Answers:
1. *positive*
2. *negative*
3. *positive*
4. *positive*
5. *negative*
6. *negative*
7. *positive*
8. *positive*
9. *positive*
10. *positive*

 RESOURCE MANAGER—Copy Master
Vocabulary Strategy p. 73

ℹ **Vocabulary Center at ClassZone.com**
Additional Vocabulary Activities

Vocabulary in Context

VOCABULARY PRACTICE

Decide whether the words in each pair are synonyms (words that have the same meaning) or antonyms (words that have opposite meanings).

1. chaotic/orderly
2. ironically/predictably
3. specify/identify
4. merge/join
5. convoluted/simple

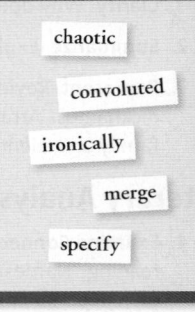

VOCABULARY IN WRITING

How did Julia Alvarez initially want to relate to classmates in the United States? Write a brief paragraph about this, using two or more vocabulary words. Here is an example of how you might begin.

> **EXAMPLE SENTENCE**
> *Julia just wanted to **merge** into classes and everyday activities.*

VOCABULARY STRATEGY: CONNOTATIONS AND MEANING

A word's **connotations** are the shades of meaning the word may take on beyond a dictionary definition. For example,

- *exotic* means "unusual," but it carries a positive connotation of fascination or wonder
- *bizarre* also means "unusual," but it has a negative connotation of strangeness or weirdness

When choosing words in writing, consider their possible connotations. They can affect the way your message is understood.

PRACTICE For each of the following words, tell whether the connotation is positive or negative. Then write a sentence using the word correctly. You may need to use a dictionary.

1. cottage
2. cheap
3. mysterious
4. sincere
5. reckless
6. peculiar
7. funny
8. casual
9. modern
10. strong-willed

 **MARYLAND OBJECTIVES**

READING STANDARD
1.D.3.a Use context to determine the meanings of words

 **VOCABULARY PRACTICE**
For more practice, go to the **Vocabulary Center** at **ClassZone.com**.

DIFFERENTIATED INSTRUCTION

FOR ENGLISH LEARNERS

Vocabulary Strategy Reinforce the idea of connotation by labeling one side of a T Chart "positive or good" and one side "negative or bad." Then offer students these pairs of words: *skinny, slim; careful, fussy; talk, gossip; gaze, glare; shy, fearful.* Help students define each word and then discuss where the word belongs in the T chart and why.

 BEST PRACTICES TOOLKIT—Transparency
T Chart p. A25

FOR ADVANCED LEARNERS/PRE–AP

Vocabulary in Writing Have students expand their paragraph into a journal entry that expresses how Julia Alvarez feels as she tries to make a place for herself in American society. Challenge students to use as many vocabulary words in their entries as possible.

Reading-Writing Connection

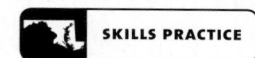

Now that you've read "Names/Nombres," explore the importance of names by responding to these prompts. Then complete the **Grammar and Writing** exercise.

WRITING PROMPTS	SELF-CHECK
A. Short Response: Explore Connections Write **one paragraph** about one of your **names** or nicknames. Using Alvarez's essay as a model, relate an anecdote, or story, that shows how you got the name or that explores your thoughts and feelings about your name.	*A strong response will . . .* • include specific details to describe a revealing event • provide a clear message about your thoughts and feelings toward your name
B. Extended Response: Track Changes Julia Alvarez has had many different names in her life, but she hasn't always felt the same way about them. Write a **two- or three-paragraph explanation** of how her attitude about having different names changes from the beginning to the end of the essay.	*A successful explanation will . . .* • identify Julia's attitude about being called different names • explain why her attitude changes

GRAMMAR AND WRITING

CAPITALIZE CORRECTLY A common noun is a general name for a person, a place, a thing, or an idea *(sister, country, park)* and is usually not capitalized. A **proper noun** is the name of a particular person, place, thing, or idea *(Kathy, Spain, Central Park)* and is always capitalized. Words that indicate family relationships are only capitalized when they are used as names or before names.

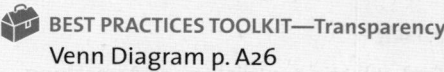 **MARYLAND OBJECTIVES**

LANGUAGE STANDARD
5.C.2.c Use the mechanics of writing correctly

> *Original:* When Julia first arrived in new york, she was known by many different names.
>
> *Revised:* When Julia first arrived in New York, she was known by many different names. (*New York* is a proper noun.)

PRACTICE Correct the capitalization in each of the following sentences.

1. Julia was known as *Hoo-lee-tah* only to her parents and Aunts and Uncles.
2. Mauricia, Julia's Sister, also had many nicknames.
3. Julia knew she had to listen to mother's advice.
4. Julia probably wanted uncle José and aunt Amelia to call her Judy.

For more help with capitalization, see page R51 in the Grammar Handbook.

DIFFERENTIATED INSTRUCTION

FOR LESS—PROFICIENT WRITERS

For Prompt A:
Suggest a flowchart to organize ideas.

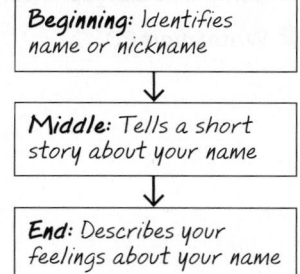

Beginning: Identifies name or nickname

↓

Middle: Tells a short story about your name

↓

End: Describes your feelings about your name

For Prompt B:
• Limit the essay to one paragraph.
• Before students begin to write, list all of the author's names and discuss how she felt about each one.
• Have students choose two names and explain why each was important to her.

Reading-Writing Connection

WRITING PROMPTS

• For **Prompt A,** have students first tell their anecdote to a partner to help them clarify the details they want to include.

• For **Prompt B,** suggest that students record words and phrases from the essay that show the author's attitude toward her different names in the beginning and at the end of the essay. Students might list these details in a Venn Diagram to help them see the change in the author's attitude more clearly.

BEST PRACTICES TOOLKIT—Transparency
Venn Diagram p. A26

For ideas for writing, see

Writing Center at **ClassZone.com**

GRAMMAR AND WRITING

Emphasize that titles such as *aunt, uncle, grandmother,* and *grandfather* are not capitalized after a possessive pronoun. However, they are capitalized when they are used as direct address. Give students this example: "Could you pass me the salt, Uncle?"

Answers:
1. *aunts, uncles*
2. *sister*
3. *Mother's*
4. *Uncle José, Aunt Amelia*

RESOURCE MANAGER—Copy Master
Capitalize Correctly p. 76

Assess and Reteach

Assess

RESOURCE MANAGER—Copy Masters
Selection Tests A, B/C pp. 79–80, 81–82

Test Generator CD

Reteach

STANDARDS LESSON FILE
Vocabulary Lesson 17: Denotation and Connotation

Focus and Motivate

OBJECTIVES

Literary Analysis
- explore the key idea of a **winner**
- identify and understand the role of direct quotations
- read nonfiction

Reading
- make inferences

Vocabulary
- build vocabulary for reading and writing
- recognize base words *(also an EL language objective)*

SUMMARY

In the first selection, cyclist Lance Armstrong describes how a special nurse helped him through his treatment for cancer. In the second selection, journalist John Wilcockson recounts the thrill of seeing Lance Armstrong win his sixth Tour de France victory.

What is a WINNER?

Discuss the question. Then have students volunteer traits of a **winner**. List the traits on the board in a cluster chart. Have students keep these ideas in mind as they discuss the **KEY IDEA.** Then have students complete the **SKETCH IT** activity.

Selection Resources

from **It's Not About the Bike**
Autobiography by Lance Armstrong
with Sally Jenkins

from **23 Days in July**
Nonfiction Account by John Wilcockson

What is a WINNER?

MARYLAND OBJECTIVES

READING STANDARDS
1.E.3.a Select and apply appropriate strategies during reading
1.E.4.c Draw inferences

KEY IDEA You might normally associate a **winner** with a contest, a game, or a sport. But can you also be a winner when you're not competing with other people? If so, how? In the selections you're about to read, you will find out how Lance Armstrong faced two very different challenges and came out a winner in both.

SKETCH IT Do you remember a time in your life when you felt like a winner? Maybe you won a spelling bee or achieved something that no one else ever had. Perhaps you faced a fear or a challenge. Create a sketch of the moment and include a title that describes what is happening. Share your sketch with the class.

790

---

* Resources for Differentiation   † Also in Spanish   ‡ In Haitian Creole and Vietnamese

ELEMENTS OF NONFICTION: QUOTATIONS

Sometimes writers decide that it is best to present information straight from the source. In that case, they use **quotations,** or direct statements from others, which are set off with quotation marks. Quotations can provide

- a clear picture of what a person is like
- an expert opinion to support the writer's ideas
- an eyewitness account that makes a scene come alive

As you read the selections from *It's Not About the Bike* and *23 Days in July*, note how the authors use quotations to help the reader better understand the subjects, setting, and events.

READING SKILL: MAKE INFERENCES

People have many reasons for doing what they do. To understand the behavior of people you read about or encounter in life, it helps to **make inferences,** or make logical guesses based on new clues and what you already know. As you read, make equations to record your inferences about Lance Armstrong.

> Clue + What I Know = Inference

VOCABULARY IN CONTEXT

The following words help tell about Lance Armstrong's victories. See how many you know by choosing the word that best completes each sentence.

WORD LIST	culminate	prestigious	stance
	perception	recessed	terse

1. The athlete's comeback will _____ in a prized medal.
2. His _____, with his feet firmly planted, was one that showed determination.
3. She gave _____, one-word answers to some of his questions.
4. The winner received a _____ award befitting a hero.
5. Special features on the bicycle are _____ in order to aid the cyclist.
6. His nurse spoke with wisdom and _____.

Author On|ine

Against All Odds
Lance Armstrong was a rising star in the world of professional cycling when his life was turned upside down. In 1996, he was diagnosed with cancer and given less than a 50 percent chance

Lance Armstrong born 1971

of survival. He underwent difficult chemotherapy treatments that made him very ill and did not guarantee success. However, Armstrong returned to professional bicycling and won his first Tour de France in 1999. He went on to win again in 2000, 2001, 2002, 2003, and 2004. John Wilcockson captured the moments of the history-making sixth Tour de France win of 2004 in *23 Days in July*.

Then in 2005, Armstrong did the unbelievable once again—he won a seventh Tour de France. After his 2005 win, he announced that he would devote his time and energy to a different kind of challenge: cancer research.

Background

The Tour de France The Tour de France is a 3-week bicycling race that covers about 2,500 miles in France and other European countries.

 MORE ABOUT THE AUTHOR AND BACKGROUND
To learn more about Lance Armstrong and the Tour de France, visit the **Literature Center** at **ClassZone.com.**

791

Teach

STANDARDS FOCUS

ELEMENTS OF NONFICTION

● QUOTATIONS

Read aloud this example:

> When I was ten years old, my Little League coach made a big impresssion on me. On the day of our first game, he told us, "It's not whether you win or lose—it's how you play the game."

Ask students what purpose the quotation serves. *Possible answer: The quotation reveals the coach's values and shows why the narrator was so impressed by him.*

CHECK UNDERSTANDING Have students find significant quotations in a work they have previously read and describe how the author uses them.

READING SKILL

■ MAKE INFERENCES

Have students read **Author Online.** Ask what Armstrong's quick return to racing after battling cancer says about him. *Possible answers: He loves racing; he has inner strength; he is very determined.*

CHECK UNDERSTANDING Have students make inferences about the photograph on page 790.

 RESOURCE MANAGER—Copy Master
Make Inferences p. 95 (for student use while reading the selections)

VOCABULARY SKILL

▲ VOCABULARY IN CONTEXT

DIAGNOSE WORD KNOWLEDGE To determine preteaching needs, have all students complete **Vocabulary in Context.** Check students' answers. *(1. culminate; 2. stance; 3. terse; 4. prestigious; 5. recessed; 6. perception)*

PRETEACH VOCABULARY Use the Vocabulary Study copy master to help students explore the meaning of each boldfaced word.

1. Read the first sentence aloud, emphasizing *culminating.*
2. Point out the phrase "moment of his racing career." Elicit meanings for *culminating,* such as "best."
3. Have students check their definitions against the text in the third column.
4. Repeat the procedure for the rest of the words.

 RESOURCE MANAGER—Copy Master
Vocabulary Study p. 97

For general guidelines on differentiating vocabulary instruction and for alternative vocabulary activities for students not needing vocabulary preteaching, see

 BEST PRACTICES TOOLKIT
Scaffolding Vocabulary Instruction pp. 43–46

ⓘ Vocabulary Center at **ClassZone.com**

ANALYZE VISUALS

Activity Ask students what Lance Armstrong might have been thinking and feeling as this photograph was taken. ***Possible answer:*** *He might have been wondering if he would survive his illness.*

Lines 1–19
REINFORCE *KEY IDEA:*
WINNER

Discuss In what ways is LaTrice Haney a **winner** in Armstrong's eyes? ***Possible answer:*** *He admires the wholehearted way in which she does a very difficult job. She works hard (line 4) and has achieved success in her career at a young age (lines 16–18). Armstrong also admires her gentle, caring approach to people (lines 14, 18–19).*

ELEMENTS OF NONFICTION

A QUOTATIONS

Possible answer: *The quotation explains LaTrice's motivation for doing her job.*

Extend the Discussion What challenges would LaTrice have as a nurse in an oncology unit that she might not have in some other units in the hospital?

It's Not About the Bike

LANCE ARMSTRONG

After his cancer diagnosis, Lance Armstrong launched a relentless attack against his disease with the help of the doctors and nurses at Indiana University Medical Center in Indianapolis. The photo on the right shows Armstrong after chemotherapy treatment.

There are angels on this earth and they come in subtle forms, and I decided LaTrice Haney was one of them. Outwardly, she looked like just another efficient, clipboard-and-syringe-wielding[1] nurse in a starched outfit. She worked extremely long days and nights, and on her off hours she went home to her husband, Randy, a truck driver, and their two children, Taylor, aged seven, and Morgan, four. But if she was tired, she never seemed it. She struck me as a woman utterly lacking in ordinary resentments, sure of her responsibilities and blessings and unwavering in her administering of care, and if that wasn't angelic
10 behavior, I didn't know what was.

Often I'd be alone in the late afternoons and evenings except for LaTrice, and if I had the strength, we'd talk seriously. With most people I was shy and **terse,** but I found myself talking to LaTrice, maybe because she was so gentle-spoken and expressive herself. LaTrice was only in her late 20s, a pretty young woman with a coffee-and-cream complexion, but she had self-possession and **perception** beyond her years. While other people our age were out nightclubbing, she was already the head nurse for the oncology research unit.[2] I wondered why she did it. "My satisfaction is to make it a little easier for people," she said. **A**

20 She asked me about cycling, and I found myself telling her about the bike with a sense of pleasure I hadn't realized I possessed. "How did you start riding?" she asked me. I told her about my first bikes, and the early sense of liberation, and that cycling was all I had done since I was 16. I talked about my various teammates over the years, about their humor and selflessness, and I talked about my mother, and what she had meant to me.

I told her what cycling had given me, the tours of Europe and the extraordinary education, and the wealth. I showed her a picture of

① Targeted Passage

terse (tûrs) *adj.* speaking little; communicating in few words

perception (pər-sĕp'shən) *n.* insight; ability to understand people and situations

A QUOTATIONS
Reread lines 18–19. What does this quotation tell you about LaTrice?

---

1. **syringe-wielding** (sə-rĭnj' wēl'dĭng): holding and using an instrument for giving patients injections.
2. **oncology** (ŏn-kŏl'ə-jē) **research unit:** in a hospital or clinic, the division or section dedicated to the study of cancer.

792 UNIT 7: BIOGRAPHY AND AUTOBIOGRAPHY

DIFFERENTIATED INSTRUCTION

FOR ALL STUDENTS

Learning Center Create a center with resources such as Lance Armstrong's autobiography, articles about previous Tour de France races, and video clips and Web sites on the Tour de France and Lance Armstrong. Provide ideas for independent projects, such as preparing an oral report on bike racing, writing a biography of Armstrong, or compiling facts and figures on the Tour de France.

FOR LESS–PROFICIENT READERS

In combination with the *Audio Anthology CD*, use one or more Targeted Passages (pp. 792, 795, 798) to ensure that students focus on key events, concepts, and skills.

① Targeted Passage [Lines 1–19]

This passage presents the focus of the selection: the gratitude Lance Armstrong feels to the nurse who helped him through his cancer treatments.

- Why does Lance Armstrong call LaTrice an angel?
- How does Lance act differently with LaTrice than he does with other people?
- What is LaTrice's reason for doing such a difficult job?

BACKGROUND

Chemotherapy In this nonfiction account, the author describes receiving chemotherapy for his cancer. He writes, "I lay on my side . . . watching the steady, clear drip-drip of the chemo as it slid into my veins" (lines 75–76). Chemotherapy is the use of strong medications to treat cancer. The medicine is often given intravenously (through the veins) and spreads throughout the body rapidly, killing cancer cells. The drugs used in chemotherapy kill some healthy cells as well. That is why people undergoing this kind of treatment often suffer from side effects such as poor appetite, nausea, dry mouth, and hair loss. In the photo on this page, Lance Armstrong shows this last side effect.

FOR ENGLISH LEARNERS

Key Academic Vocabulary Have small groups use New Word Analysis to learn this vocabulary from the second selection: *intensity* (line 17), *phenomenal* (line 18), *team* (lines 27, 38).

 BEST PRACTICES TOOLKIT—Transparency
New Word Analysis p. E8

Prereading For prereading instruction for English learners, see

 BEST PRACTICES TOOLKIT
Scaffolding Reading Instruction pp. 43–46

FOR ADVANCED LEARNERS/PRE–AP

Pre-AP exercises in the bottom channel provide additional challenge for your advanced students. Use them for small groups or individuals.

ADDITIONAL GUIDELINES

For more help with differentiation and tips for classroom management, see

BEST PRACTICES TOOLKIT
Differentiated Instruction pp. 31–38

B MAKE INFERENCES

Have students record their answers in the form of an equation, as shown on page 791. *Possible answer:*

Clues: She knows he loves cycling. She points to specific places in photographs to get him to talk about cycling.

What I Know: Talking about something I love makes me feel good.

Inference: She wants to take his mind off his sickness and help lift his spirits.

Lines 38–54
DISCUSSION PROMPTS

Use these prompts to help students appreciate how Lance Armstrong feels about his sport:

Connect Think about a passion that you have. How does your experience help you understand Armstrong's feelings about his bike? *Students may say that they, too, care about the equipment that helps them fulfill their passion.*

Analyze What are some of the words and phrases that show how Armstrong feels about his bike? What does this choice of words show? *Possible answer: He uses words and phrases such as "elegant" (line 38), "intimately" (line 42), and "at times I felt melded to it" (lines 43–44). This choice of language shows how much a part of him the bike is.*

Evaluate What does Armstrong say is the price of speed? What is revealed about his character through his willingness to pay this price? *Possible answer: The price of speed is pain. He has determination and endurance.*

C MAKE INFERENCES

Possible answer: Talking about his bike makes Lance feel strong at a time when he is afraid. It also reminds him of his capacity to endure pain in order to reach a goal.

---

my house, with pride, and invited her to come visit, and I showed her snapshots of my cycling career. She leafed through images of me racing
30 across the backdrops of France, Italy, and Spain, and she'd point to a picture and ask, "Where are you here?" **B**

I confided that I was worried about my sponsor, Cofidis,[3] and explained the difficulty I was having with them. I told her I felt pressured. "I need to stay in shape, I need to stay in shape," I said over and over again.

"Lance, listen to your body," she said gently. "I know your mind wants to run away. I know it's saying to you, 'Hey, let's go ride.' But listen to your body. Let it rest."

I described my bike, the elegant high performance of the ultralight tubing and aerodynamic wheels. I told her how much each piece cost, and
40 weighed, and what its purpose was. I explained how a bike could be broken down so I could practically carry it in my pocket, and that I knew every part and bit of it so intimately that I could adjust it in a matter of moments.

I explained that a bike has to fit your body, and that at times I felt melded to it. The lighter the frame, the more responsive it is, and my racing bike weighed just 18 pounds. Wheels exert centrifugal force[4] on the bike itself, I told her. The more centrifugal force, the more momentum. It was the essential building block of speed. "There are 32 spokes in a wheel," I said. Quick-release levers allow you to pop the wheel out and change it quickly, and my crew could fix a flat tire in less than 10 seconds.
50 "Don't you get tired of leaning over like that?" she asked.

Yes, I said, until my back ached like it was broken, but that was the price of speed. The handlebars are only as wide as the rider's shoulders, I explained, and they curve downward in half-moons so you can assume an aerodynamic **stance** on the bike.

"Why do you ride on those little seats?" she asked.

The seat is narrow, contoured to the anatomy, and the reason is that when you are on it for six hours at a time, you don't want anything to chafe your legs. Better a hard seat than the torture of saddle sores. Even the clothes have a purpose. They are flimsy for a reason: to mold
60 to the body because you have to wear them in weather that ranges from hot to hail. Basically, they're a second skin. The shorts have a chamois[5] padded seat, and the stitches are **recessed** to avoid rash. **C**

When I had nothing left to tell LaTrice about the bike, I told her about the wind. I described how it felt in my face and in my hair. I told her about being in the open air, with the views of soaring Alps, and the

---

3. **Cofidis:** the sponsor of the French cycling team that Armstrong then rode for.
4. **centrifugal** (sĕn-trĭf'yə-gəl) **force:** the force that seems to cause a revolving object to move away from the point it revolves around.
5. **chamois** (shăm'ē) **padded:** padded with soft leather made from the skin of goats, sheep, or deer.

B MAKE INFERENCES
Why might LaTrice ask Lance specific questions about his bicycling career?

stance (stăns) *n.* posture; position

recessed (rē'sĕst') *adj.* set-in or set back **recess** v

C MAKE INFERENCES
Why is Lance able to talk so enthusiastically about his bike even though he is seriously ill?

DIFFERENTIATED INSTRUCTION

FOR LESS–PROFICIENT READERS

Reading Skill Follow-Up: Make Inferences
Model how to make inferences by reading a passage of text and thinking aloud. Then have pairs of students read lines 32–37 and use the same strategy to make inferences that answer questions such as *Why is Armstrong so worried about getting out of shape? What will happen if he pushes himself?* Discuss students' responses.

🧰 **BEST PRACTICES TOOLKIT—Transparency**
Read Aloud/Think Aloud p. A34

Vocabulary Support Point out the word *aerodynamic* (lines 39 and 54). Tell students that *aerodynamic* means "designed in a way that decreases wind drag." Explain that the lack of wind resistance results in greater speed with less use of energy. Using the photograph on page 797, explain that aerodynamic designs usually have rounded edges as can be seen in the handlebars and even Armstrong's helmet. Ask students to identify other examples of aerodynamic design.

glimmer of valley lakes in the distance. Sometimes the wind blew as if it were my personal friend, sometimes as if it were my bitter enemy, sometimes as if it were the hand of God pushing me along. I described the full sail of a mountain descent, gliding two wheels only an inch wide. **D**

70 "You're just out there, free," I said.

"You love it," she said.

"Yeah?" I said.

"Oh, I see it in your eyes," she said.

I understood that LaTrice was an angel one evening late in my last cycle of chemo.[6] I lay on my side, dozing on and off, watching the steady, clear drip-drip of the chemo as it slid into my veins. LaTrice sat with me, keeping me company, even though I was barely able to talk.

"What do you think, LaTrice?" I asked, whispering. "Am I going to pull through this?"

80 "Yeah," she said. "Yeah, you are."

"I hope you're right," I said, and closed my eyes again.

LaTrice leaned over to me.

"Lance," she said softly, "I hope someday to be just a figment of your imagination.[7] I'm not here to be in your life for the rest of your life. After you leave here, I hope I never see you ever again. When you're cured, hey, let me see you in the papers, on TV, but not back here. I hope to help you at the time you need me, and then I hope I'll be gone. You'll say, 'Who was that nurse back in Indiana? Did I dream her?'" **E**

It is one of the single loveliest things anyone has ever said to me.

90 And I will always remember every blessed word. ❧

---

6. **chemo** (kē'mō): short for *chemotherapy*.

7. **figment of your imagination:** something not real; a fantasized or made-up image.

Lance Armstrong and LaTrice Haney

D MAKE INFERENCES
Reread lines 63–69. What can you infer about why Lance rides his bike?

2 Targeted Passage

E QUOTATIONS
Reread lines 83–88. Why do you think Armstrong chooses to quote LaTrice here?

FOR LESS–PROFICIENT READERS

2 Targeted Passage [Lines 74–90]

This passage reinforces the main idea of the essay: LaTrice's giving Lance confidence that he will survive and go on to live a full life.

- What is happening to Lance at the time this conversation takes place?
- Why does LaTrice hope she never sees Lance again?
- How do her words make Lance feel?

FOR ADVANCED LEARNERS/PRE–AP

Make Inferences Armstrong chose specific details, quotations, and language (as in line 90) to describe this period in his life. Ask students to put themselves in Armstrong's place as he sat down to write this part of his autobiography. Have them use an Open Mind organizer to suggest how Armstrong may have made some of his literary decisions.

🧰 **BEST PRACTICES TOOLKIT—Transparency**
Open Mind p. D11

D MAKE INFERENCES

Record clues from the text and students' inferences in an equation. ***Possible answer:***

Clues: *Lance describes the feeling of wind in his face and hair (lines 63–64), the views of mountains and lakes (lines 65–66), and the feeling of gliding very fast down a mountain (lines 68–69).*

What I Know: *Being outdoors and moving very fast also give me a sense of freedom.*

Inference: *Biking gives Lance a sense of freedom.*

Lines 74–81
REINFORCE *KEY IDEA*: WINNER

Discuss What qualities does Armstrong need to be a **winner** in the fight against cancer? ***Possible answer:*** *He needs hope, faith, and courage, plus physical strength and endurance.*

ELEMENTS OF NONFICTION

E QUOTATIONS

Possible answer: *The quotation gives a true and vivid account of the moment. Her real words are more touching and powerful than any paraphrasing.*

If students need help . . . Read the original text of lines 83–88 aloud. Then paraphrase LaTrice's words to the class. Ask students how the two versions differ and why her actual words are better.

Lines 63–90
ADDITIONAL TEACHING OPPORTUNITY

Contrast Points of View Explain that informational articles can be written from different points of view. In articles with a **subjective point of view,** the writer includes his or her own opinion—as in personal essays, autobiographies, and editorials. Articles with an **objective point of view** are ideally free of the author's personal opinion; they strictly report facts. Ask students if the viewpoint of *It's Not About the Bike* is subjective or objective *(subjective),* and why.

23
DAYS IN JULY

JOHN WILCOCKSON

Although Armstrong went on to win a seventh Tour de France in 2005, the 2004 race was especially meaningful since no other cyclist had ever won a sixth Tour.

Paris is looking magnificent. Her golden domes and eagles and gilded gates are all glowing in the late-afternoon sunshine. The dark-green plane trees along the Champs-Élysées have been newly trimmed. Rainbows shimmer in the spray from the crystal fountains of the Place de la Concorde.[1] And across the Seine River, the thousand-foot-high Eiffel Tower stands starkly regal against an opaque blue sky.

Another Tour de France has just ended, this one **culminating** in a historical sixth consecutive victory for a long-jawed young man from the lone star state of Texas. He stands now on the top step of the podium,
10 at the finish line on the Champs-Élysées. Dressed in a golden tunic, Lance Armstrong holds a yellow LiveStrong[2] cap over his heart as a full-blooded rendition of the "Star Spangled Banner" rings out, resounding proudly over the russet-brown cobblestones of these Elysian Fields. . . .[3]

At the foot of the yellow steps of the canopied, most **prestigious** viewing stand, Armstrong's coach Chris Carmichael reminds me: "I told you back in March, it wasn't even going to be close. You gotta know the intensity of this guy. Nobody has got his intensity. Nobody. It's just phenomenal." ❶

---

1. **Champs-Élysées** (shän-zā-lē-zā′) . . . **Place de la Concorde** (pläs′ də lä kôN-kôrd′): a famous boulevard and a large plaza in Paris.
2. **LiveStrong:** livestrong.org is the official Web site for the Lance Armstrong Foundation.
3. **Elysian** (ĭ-lĭzh′ən) **Fields:** the English translation of *Champs-Élysées.* In Greek mythology, the Elysian Fields were where good people went after death.

ANALYZE VISUALS

Activity Describe the perspective of this photograph. What effect does this perspective create? *Possible answer: The perspective places the viewer directly behind the riders, seeing what they see as they ride along the Champs-Élysées. The effect is to make the viewer feel as if he or she is doing the victory lap with the cyclists.*

Lines 19–28
REINFORCE *KEY IDEA*:
WINNER

Discuss What makes Armstrong a **winner**? *Possible answers: He is humble even in victory. He acknowledges the support of others. He appreciates his win.*

Armstrong said on the eve of this day, "Winning in '99 was a complete
20 shock and surprise for me. Not that I've gotten used to winning the Tour de France, but I do know what it means and I know what it feels like to ride into the Champs-Élysées. . . . This one is very, very special for me. They're all special, but this one is something that in '99 I never believed possible. I never thought I'd win a second one, or a third, or however many. This one is incredibly special. I'm humbled by it. A lot of people just one month ago thought it wouldn't be possible for me to do it. We tried to stay calm, the team tried to stay calm . . . and we were confident that we had a good chance."

3 Targeted Passage

I think back to December, and remember something Armstrong told
30 me in Austin: "I'm doing three or four hours of exercise every day right now. Yesterday I was in DC, so I got up early—I'd just come back from Europe and had jetlag[4]—and I went down to the gym for an hour and a half . . . yes, lifting weights. It was pouring with freezing rain outside, so I went back to the room, and rode my bike for an hour on the rollers. It's not easy to ride rollers. I hate that." **G**

But he doesn't hate this: homage from a half-million people lining the most glorious boulevard in the world. When he and his U.S. Postal team are introduced by race announcer Daniel Mangeas, as the last team to start their lap of honor around the Champs-Élysées, the modern
40 "anthem" of the British rock group Queen thumps into the balmy Paris air:

G QUOTATIONS
Reread lines 30–35. What do you learn about Armstrong from this quotation?

4. **jet lag:** tiredness and other effects that may be caused by a long flight through several time zones.

ELEMENTS OF NONFICTION

G QUOTATIONS

Possible answer: This quotation shows how dedicated Armstrong is and that he will work hard even when it is not enjoyable.

If students need help . . . Explore the significance of the details in the quotation by completing a chart like this one.

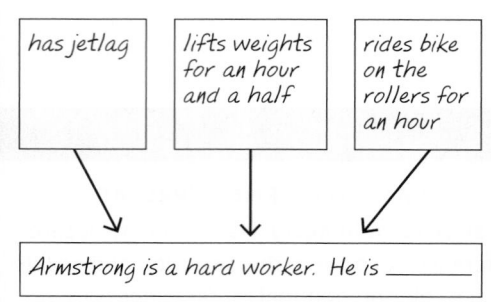

DIFFERENTIATED INSTRUCTION

FOR LESS–PROFICIENT READERS
3 Targeted Passage [Lines 19–28]

This passage presents a quotation that reveals the author's purpose: to show how meaningful Armstrong's victory is.

- Why is this win so special for Armstrong?
- Why does he say he feels humbled by it?
- Was he expected to win? How do you know?

Language: Punctuation Point out the ellipses in lines 22 and 27. Explain that in a direct quotation, an ellipsis indicates that some of the speaker's words have been left out. Tell students that when authors include a direct quotation, they choose the parts that make sense within the context of the article, support the main idea, and are expressed clearly. Discuss why the author includes these parts of Armstrong's quotation.

Armstrong, in yellow, takes a victory lap with his teammates along the Champs-Élysées in Paris.

"We are the champions, my friend. . . . We are the champions. We are the champions. We are the champions . . . of the world."

Girlfriends perch on boyfriends' shoulders to get a better view. Banners unfurl, one saying, "The eyes of Texas are upon you." Thousands of fans from all over the United States line the barriers, most dressed in yellow. Two guys from Texas in the crowd say, "We did it. And next year we'll come again!" . . . **H**

Now they're playing another song over the loudspeakers. Its words float down the boulevard backed by the thumping guitar chords of the champion's 50 gal: "All I want to *do* . . . is have some fun . . ." And Lance *is* having fun. The celebrations will continue all night, maybe for the rest of his life. A life that almost ended in 1996. Six Tour de France wins have come along since then, since his chemo nurse LaTrice gave him that silver cross.

"I really love this event," Armstrong says. "I think it's an epic sport. It's something I will sit around the TV and watch in ten years, and in twenty years." He will always be a fan of the Tour, but right now he's the champion. *Le patron.*[5]

I t's after 7 p.m. and the crowds are starting to leave. One of the last to go is a friendly, middle-aged American. He rolls up his Texas flag, 60 grabs his wife's hand, and, before he walks down the stone steps into the Metro,[6] proclaims to the world, "He's the man!" ∾

H MAKE INFERENCES
Why are the fans dressed in yellow?

---

5. *le patron* (lə pä-trôɴ) *French:* the boss.
6. **Metro:** the Paris subway.

H MAKE INFERENCES

Record students' answers in an equation similar to the one on page 791. *Possible answer:*

Clue: Lance is dressed in yellow.

What I Know: I dress like my favorite athlete when I go to soccer games to show my support.

Inference: The fans are showing their support of Lance.

SELECTION WRAP–UP

REFLECT Have students think about the different sides of Lance Armstrong's personality presented in these two selections. What do students admire most about him?

★ CRITIQUE Have students evaluate whether Wilcockson effectively conveys the excitement of Armstrong's sixth victory in this account. Ask students if he could have organized his article in another way to help readers visualize the moment more clearly.

READING FLUENCY

Distribute the copy masters and have students practice fluency.

R RESOURCE MANAGER—Copy Master
Reading Fluency p. 102

FOR LESS–PROFICIENT READERS

Comprehension Support Help students understand the sequence of events in this nonfiction account by having them work in small groups on a sequence chart. Explain that their charts should reflect the actual order in which events or conversations occurred, not the sequence in which they appear in the text. Tell students that their first box should be labeled "December 2003" and their last "July 25, 2004." Have students compare charts.

FOR ENGLISH LEARNERS

Culture: Clarify Explain that the song "We Are the Champions" (lines 41–42) is often played at sporting events to express the spirit of competition and victory. The song "All I Wanna Do" (line 50) is by American rock musician Sheryl Crow, who was Lance Armstrong's girlfriend during his Tour de France victories in 2004 and 2005.

FOR ADVANCED LEARNERS/PRE–AP

Evaluate Have students write a paragraph in response to this question: *Does the author's obvious admiration for Lance Armstrong subtract from or add to the credibility and value of this account? Explain.* Invite students to compare their responses.

Practice and Apply

After Reading

For additional support of post-reading questions, use these copy masters:

R RESOURCE MANAGER—Copy Masters

Reading Check p. 100 (to check understanding of the selection)

Quotations p. 93 (for practice of elements of nonfiction standards focus)

Question Support p. 101 (**After Reading** questions adapted for English learners and less-proficient readers)

Additional selection questions are provided for teachers on page 87.

For additional activities to challenge students, see

i Power Thinking at **ClassZone.com**

ANSWERS

Comprehension

1. *Armstrong has been diagnosed with cancer and is receiving chemotherapy.*

2. *LaTrice enters his life for a brief time and comforts him. She does her job lovingly and does not ask for anything in return.*

3. *Armstrong was the first person to win the Tour de France six times. Many people thought it was impossible.*

Literary Analysis

Possible answers:

4. ■ **STANDARDS FOCUS** *Make Inferences Students' answers will vary. Many of their inferences will probably remain the same.*

5. *Armstrong says this because LaTrice is really telling him that she hopes he goes into remission. She is also saying that she doesn't expect anything in return for her kindness to him.*

6. *Private: Armstrong thinks deeply about what draws him to his sport. He shares insights about his mother and shows his pride in his house and other aspects of his life. Public: Armstrong is healthy and focused on the goal of winning the Tour de France. Similarities: In both public and private, Armstrong is intense, dedicated to overcoming a challenge, willing to do what it takes to reach a goal, and aware of the help that others give him.*

After Reading

MARYLAND OBJECTIVES

READING STANDARD
1.E.4.c Draw inferences

Comprehension

1. **Recall** In the excerpt from *It's Not About the Bike*, why is Armstrong in the hospital?

2. **Clarify** Why does Armstrong call his head nurse, LaTrice, an "angel"?

3. **Clarify** Reread lines 22–25 in the excerpt from *23 Days in July*. Armstrong says winning the 2004 Tour de France was "incredibly special" to him. Why was it so special?

Literary Analysis

4. **Make Inferences** Review the inference equations that you made while reading. Which, if any, of your inferences have changed? Explain your reasons for either changing an inference or keeping an original inference.

5. **Interpret Meaning** Reread LaTrice's quotation in lines 83–88 of the excerpt from *It's Not About the Bike*. Why does Armstrong say, "It is one of the single loveliest things anyone has ever said to me"?

6. **Compare and Contrast** The autobiography *It's Not About the Bike* shows the private side of Lance Armstrong. On the other hand, John Wilcockson's account portrays Armstrong in public. Use a Y chart like the one shown to compare and contrast the private and public man.

*Private
He describes himself as shy.*

Public

Similarities

7. **Analyze Quotations** On the basis of the quotations in the excerpt from *23 Days in July*, what do you think Wilcockson wants the reader to remember about Armstrong? Cite three quotations to support your opinion.

8. **Draw Conclusions** In 1996, Armstrong beat cancer. In 2004, he became a six-time winner of the Tour de France. Considering what you learned from the selections that you just read, what qualities helped Armstrong win such big victories?

Extension and Challenge

9. **Inquiry and Research** Research the Tour de France and create a tourist's guide to the race. Provide the reader with some historical information, explain the rules of the race, and include a map of the upcoming race.

RESEARCH LINKS
For more on the Tour de France, visit the **Research Center** at ClassZone.com.

---

7. ● **STANDARDS FOCUS** *Quotations Answers will vary, but students may say that the author wants readers to remember Armstrong's determination and intensity.*

8. *Both achievements show his determination, strength, intensity, and willingness to endure pain and discomfort in order to reach a goal.*

Extension and Challenge

9. *Students' guides should contain accurate information in an easy-to-read format. Historical information should include details such as changes that have occurred over the years, the date of the first Tour de France, and origins of the race. Encourage students to use the Internet as a source of information on the Tour de France.*

Vocabulary in Context

VOCABULARY PRACTICE

For each item, choose the word that differs most in meaning from the other words. Refer to a dictionary if you need help.

1. chatty, talkative, terse, gossipy
2. culminate, top, begin, crown
3. awkward, hidden, recessed, inset
4. pose, posture, worry, stance
5. intuition, ignorance, understanding, perception
6. prestigious, notable, honorable, unworthy

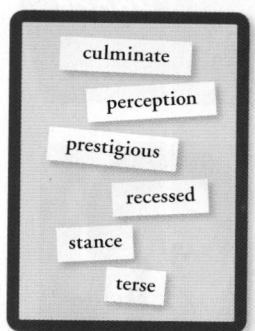

VOCABULARY IN WRITING

Write a paragraph describing how you might have felt if you had been Armstrong entering Paris. Use two or more vocabulary words. You could start like this.

> **EXAMPLE SENTENCE**
>
> *Riding into Paris with my team as the winners of this **prestigious** race was the highlight of my career.*

VOCABULARY STRATEGY: RECOGNIZING BASE WORDS

You already know that to understand an unfamiliar word with affixes, it helps to identify the base word first. Sometimes, though, the spelling of base words is different when affixes are present. The vocabulary word *perception*, for example, is related to *perceive*. In cases where you do not recognize a base word, you may have to rely on context clues to figure out the meaning.

MARYLAND OBJECTIVES

READING STANDARD
1.D.3.b Use word structure to determine meaning

PRACTICE Define each boldfaced word. Then give the base word that each one is related to. Use a dictionary if necessary.

1. Mr. Lewis resented the **intrusion** of noisy neighborhood children into his privacy.
2. The doctor recommended a complete **renunciation** of his patient's lifestyle if she was to become healthy.
3. The severe earthquake did **irreparable** damage to many homes.
4. **Consumption** of several glasses of water a day is a healthy habit.
5. Far from being forced, the audience's loud applause had real **spontaneity**.

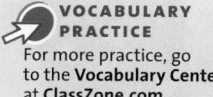

VOCABULARY PRACTICE
For more practice, go to the **Vocabulary Center** at **ClassZone.com**.

OBJECTIVE
- read biography

Meet Walter Dean Myers

Myers, who dropped out of school at the age of 16, has written many books for young adults. He knows that his readers "want an interesting story that touches issues with which they are involved or, at least, concerned." He also knows that they "want to be entertained." In both his fiction and his nonfiction, Myers focuses on values that he hopes will inspire his readers to value themselves.

Try a Biography

The subject of a biography might be a world leader, a famous athlete, a movie star, a musician, an explorer, or a scientist. The person may have lived a long time ago or may still be living. A biography helps the reader get to know the person as well as his or her achievements. Ask students to name some people whose biographies they have read or would like to read. Some works to consider include

- Marc Shapiro's *J. K. Rowling: The Wizard Behind Harry Potter,* about an unemployed single parent who created a world-wide literary phenomenon

- Tricia Andryszewski's *The Amazing Life of Moe Berg: Catcher, Scholar, Spy,* about a baseball player who worked as a spy during World War II

- Carole Ann Camp's *Sally Ride: First American Woman in Space,* about the first female U.S. astronaut

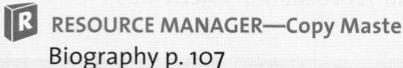 **RESOURCE MANAGER—Copy Master**
Biography p. 107

Malcolm X:
By Any Means Necessary

Biography by Walter Dean Myers

Walter Dean Myers
born 1937

Other Books by Walter Dean Myers

Nonfiction
- *Bad Boy: A Memoir*
- *The Greatest: Muhammad Ali*

Fiction
- *Crystal*
- *The Glory Field*
- *Monster*
- *Scorpions*
- *Somewhere in the Darkness*

Meet Walter Dean Myers

Walter Dean Myers knows what it's like to rise above difficult circumstances. His mother died before he was two years old, and his father, who was very poor, had to give Walter away. Walter's foster mother, Florence Dean, taught him to read, and books soon became a welcome escape for Walter. One of his teachers suggested that he write down his thoughts in the form of poems and stories. Walter began writing then and has never stopped.

Many of the stories Myers writes are based on his childhood in Harlem, on the Upper West Side of Manhattan in New York City. He is also interested in history, which often leads him to write nonfiction books about people or events that grab his attention.

Try a Biography

People are naturally curious about the lives of important, fascinating people. A **biography** is a story of a person's life that is written by someone else. Most biographies are about famous people who changed history or made an impact in other ways. Biographies are often told in chronological order, beginning with the person's childhood and ending with his or her death. The introduction and conclusion of a biography usually highlight the lasting importance of the person.

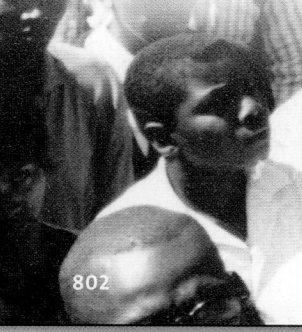

802

 **DIFFERENTIATED INSTRUCTION**

FOR LESS—PROFICIENT READERS

Reading Support Before students begin reading, review the teaching notes on pages 803–807 and select those that you think would be most helpful to them. You might read the selection aloud with students and discuss the relevant notes. Stop occasionally to answer questions, give an explanation, or hold a discussion.

Read a Great Book

Malcolm X was an important figure in the struggle for equal rights for African Americans. The following section from Myers's award-winning biography provides an overview of Malcolm X's life and legacy. You'll read about how Malcolm's experiences shaped him into a leader of the 20th century.

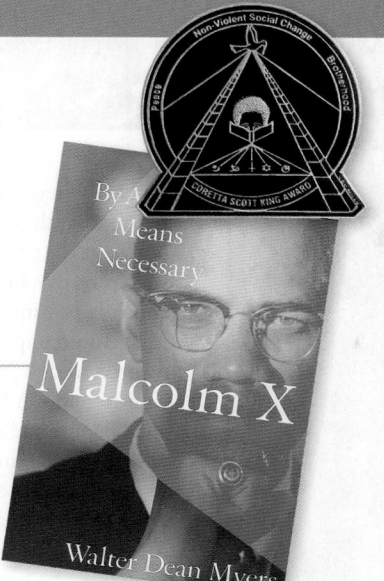

from

Malcolm X:
By Any Means Necessary

Who was Malcolm X, and what is his legacy?

Malcolm's life seems so varied, he did so many things over the far too short thirty-nine years of his life, that it almost appears that there was not one Malcolm at all, but four distinct people. But in looking at Malcolm's life, in examining the expectations against what he actually did, we see a blending of the four Malcolms into one dynamic personality that is distinctively American in its character. For only a black man living in America could have gone through what Malcolm went through.

10   The first Malcolm was Malcolm the child, who lived in Nebraska and Michigan. He lived much like a million other black boys born in the United States. He was loved by two parents, Earl and Louise Little. From them he learned about morality, and decency, and the need to do well in school. His parents gave him a legacy of love, but also a legacy of pride.

Malcolm saw his father, a Baptist minister, at the meetings of the Universal Negro Improvement Association, saw him speaking about the black race, and about the possibility of justice. From what the young Malcolm saw, from what he experienced as a young child,
20   one might have expected him, upon reaching maturity, to become a religious man and an activist for justice, as was his father.

GREAT READS   **803**

Read

Read a Great Book

In an interview, Walter Dean Myers said that "there is no inherent fairness in life, and that ultimately we are our own salvation. It is only when we become spectators, rather than participants, in our lives, that we truly fail." Myers sees Malcolm X as a "participant" who inspired many people and who made a lasting impact on American culture. In writing this biography, Myers concentrates on four distinct stages in the life of Malcolm X. As they read, suggest that students think about what characterizes Malcolm X in each of these stages.

SHARE AN FYI

The subtitle of Myers's biography, *By Any Means Necessary,* also appears in line 79 and is taken from a statement made by Malcolm X in the third stage of his life as a member of the Nation of Islam: "Our objective is complete freedom, justice and equality by any means necessary."

Zoot suit (line 40) is a slang term for a man's suit popular in the 1940s. The trousers had full legs and tight cuffs, and the coat was long with wide lapels and heavily padded, wide shoulders.

Even when Earl Little was killed, Louise Little tried to hold the family together. Malcolm started school and did well. His mother saw to it that he did his assignments, and there was no doubt that Malcolm was bright. Bright children often understand their gifts, and it is possible that Malcolm understood his early on. He said in his autobiography that he had not given a lot of thought to what he wanted to do with those gifts when he was asked by a teacher in the eighth grade. A lawyer, he ventured.

30 Malcolm had not known exactly what he wanted to do with his talents, but he understood that the talents he possessed were valued in his schoolmates. The teacher said to him that it was not practical for him to be a lawyer, because he was black. The teacher probably thought of himself as being a realist. There is no use misleading Malcolm, he probably thought. Where does a black teenaged boy go, to what does he turn if he is not allowed the same avenues of value as his white friends?

The second Malcolm answers that question. The black teenager goes among his own people, and searches among the values of his 40 peers for those he can use. So Malcolm bought the zoot suit, with the gold chain dangling against the pants leg. He bought the wide-brimmed hat and learned the hip jargon of the street, the same way teenagers today buy the gold chains and sneakers that cost enough to feed a family for a week. Malcolm was a human being, and human beings need to be able to look into the mirror and see something that pleases them. . . .

Malcolm said that he wanted to be a lawyer, to use his mind. He was told that no, he couldn't do that because he was black. Perhaps it wouldn't have made any difference what the teacher had said. As 50 was the case with so many black teenagers, Malcolm's family, now with only the mother to support it, would not have been able to afford college for him.

Malcolm toughened himself. Malcolm used his mind. If he couldn't use it to study law, he would use it in street hustles. He used it in making money the way people in the inner cities who don't have "downtown" jobs make money. Eventually he used it to commit burglaries. Some societies never learn that to make a person socially responsible you must first include him or her in your

804

society. Malcolm's career as a petty criminal, much sensationalized
60 in the autobiography he never got to read, ended quickly when he
was caught, tried, and sentenced to eight to ten years in prison.

The second Malcolm, the one using his wits to survive on
the streets, skirting both sides of the law, might have continued
after he was released if it were not for the Nation of Islam. Elijah
Muhammad claimed that he lifted Malcolm up and saved him
from a life of degradation. Nothing was more truthful. The
Nation of Islam, with its strict moral codes, its religion, its
understanding, forgiveness, and even celebration of black men
who had fallen by the wayside, was the garden from which the
70 third Malcolm emerged.

Here now was Malcolm the religious man, the activist, the
thinker, the man who stood up for his people, who confronted the
forces of injustice in America at a time when black people were
being beaten in the streets, were being publicly humiliated and even
killed. Here was a Malcolm who offered himself as the voice of the
defeated, the manliness of a people who badly needed manliness.

And he was a worker. He organized and preached. He cajoled
and threatened. He attacked racism with the biting tone of the
absolute cynic, vowing to attain freedom by any means necessary
80 and with any sacrifice. He understood, as few other leaders did, that
there were people like himself in the streets, and in the prisons, who
had contributions to make. He included people in the struggle for
human rights in America who had never before been included. This
was the third Malcolm.

Malcolm grew. He grew away from the Nation of Islam, and
away from the separatist philosophy of that organization. The
Nation of Islam had returned to him the wings that had been taken
from him because of his color, and Malcolm, the fourth Malcolm,
found himself able to fly.

90 What one would have expected, or at least hoped for, on meeting
the wide-eyed boy in the Pleasant Grove Elementary School, was
that he would one day touch the edge of greatness. It is what we
wish for all children. The fourth Malcolm—the one with his head
slightly bowed as he listened to Jomo Kenyatta, the great African
leader, the one learning firsthand about the liberation of the African

SHARE A READING TIP

Students will notice references to the
Nation of Islam (line 64) and its leader, Elijah
Muhammad. This radical group should not be
confused with the Islamic religion practiced
by Muslims around the world today, and its
prophet, Muhammad.

SHARE AN FYI

Jomo Kenyatta (line 94) became the first
president of Kenya in 1964 after that country
had gained its independence from British rule.

SHARE WORD MEANINGS

Atheism (line 100) means "the belief that there is no God or other supernatural power in the universe."

SHARE A READING TIP

In lines 108–116, Myers begins four consecutive sentences with the words "He spoke." Writers often use this type of repetition to emphasize a point. It also adds a rhythmic quality to the prose.

SHARE AN FYI

Pan-Africanism (line 129) is a movement dedicated to cultivating unity among black people throughout the world.

continent so that he could liberate his own—had touched the edge of that greatness.

Malcolm's life was about growth, about the intensely changing man that moved from thievery to honesty, from being a racial separatist to searching for true brotherhood, and from atheism to Islam.

But his life was also about the return to the idealism of his childhood. The world of the child, before he or she is exposed to racism, before he or she is conditioned to react to the hurts inflicted on him or her, is one of acceptance and love. Malcolm had grown, and in that growing had learned to accept those people, regardless of race or nationality, who accepted and loved him.

Malcolm spoke for the voiceless, for the people from whom not even some black leaders wanted to hear. He spoke for the jobless, and for the homeless. He spoke for the young men whose hard bodies, bodies that could perform miracles on inner-city basketball courts, were not wanted in America's offices. He spoke for the millions of black Americans who saw themselves as a minority in a world in which most of the inhabitants were people of color like themselves. He spoke for the men and women who had to turn too many other cheeks, had to fight off too many insults with nothing but smiles.

Malcolm had walked in their shoes, and they knew it when they heard him speak. . . .

Malcolm, . . . having experienced the same hunger, the same frustrations, even the same jails as poor blacks did, understood something else as well: that all the goals of the mainstream civil rights movement, the civil rights laws, school integration, voting rights, none of these would have meaning if African-Americans still thought of themselves as a racially crippled people, if they still walked with their heads down because they were black.

In the last year of his life, having grown away from the Nation of Islam, and having made a spiritual pilgrimage to Mecca, Malcolm was moving both to a new and an old place. He was moving more solidly into Pan-Africanism, the territory that his father had explored over forty years before.

Malcolm's message is remembered by many people who find comfort and inspiration in it today. One of them is the African-

806

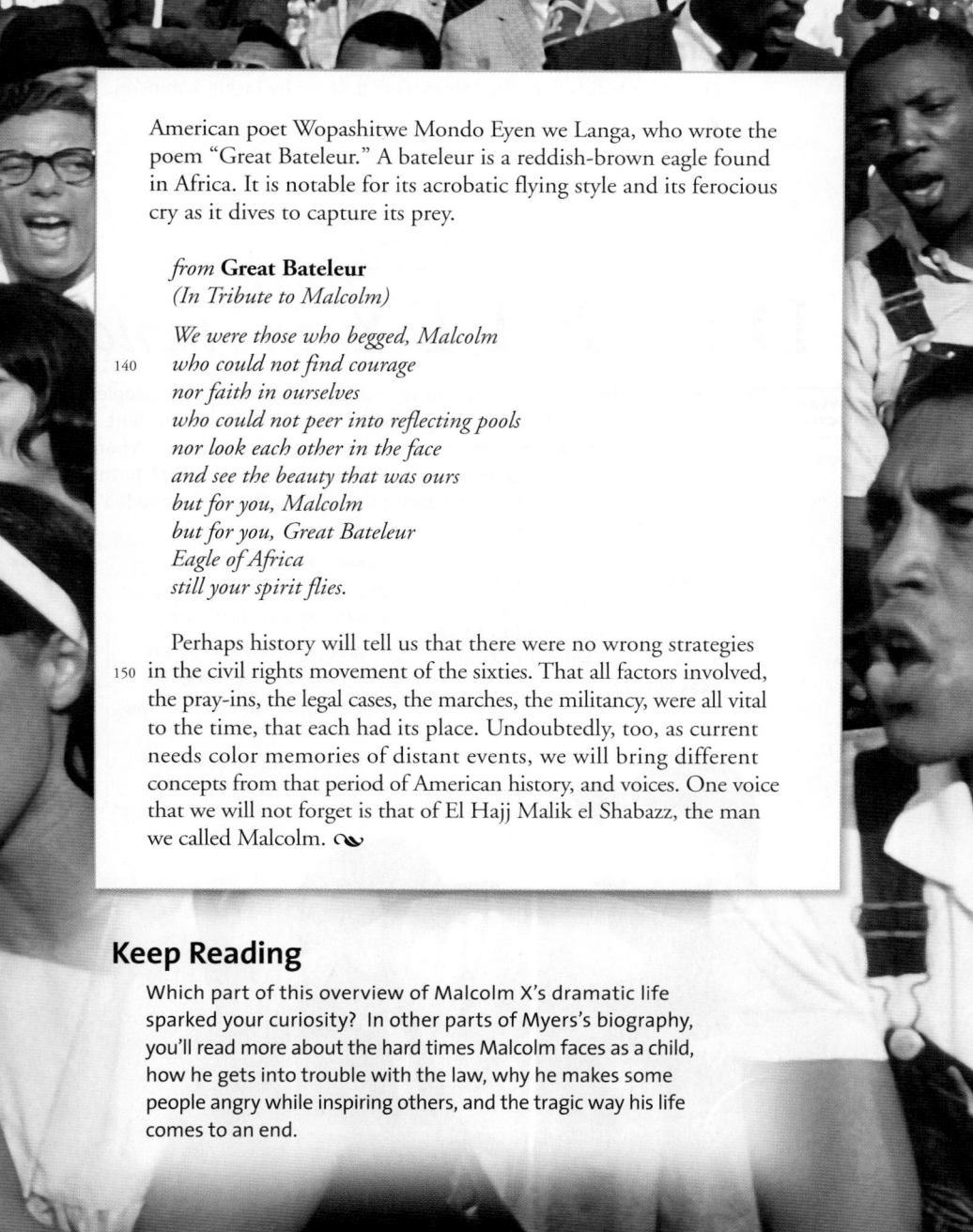

American poet Wopashitwe Mondo Eyen we Langa, who wrote the poem "Great Bateleur." A bateleur is a reddish-brown eagle found in Africa. It is notable for its acrobatic flying style and its ferocious cry as it dives to capture its prey.

from **Great Bateleur**
(In Tribute to Malcolm)

We were those who begged, Malcolm
140 *who could not find courage*
nor faith in ourselves
who could not peer into reflecting pools
nor look each other in the face
and see the beauty that was ours
but for you, Malcolm
but for you, Great Bateleur
Eagle of Africa
still your spirit flies.

Perhaps history will tell us that there were no wrong strategies
150 in the civil rights movement of the sixties. That all factors involved, the pray-ins, the legal cases, the marches, the militancy, were all vital to the time, that each had its place. Undoubtedly, too, as current needs color memories of distant events, we will bring different concepts from that period of American history, and voices. One voice that we will not forget is that of El Hajj Malik el Shabazz, the man we called Malcolm. ∽

Keep Reading

Which part of this overview of Malcolm X's dramatic life sparked your curiosity? In other parts of Myers's biography, you'll read more about the hard times Malcolm faces as a child, how he gets into trouble with the law, why he makes some people angry while inspiring others, and the tragic way his life comes to an end.

Discuss

Keep Reading

Share these discussion questions with students after they have finished the excerpt. You might use the questions to lead a class discussion or have students form small groups to discuss them.

• Have you read this book? If yes, would you recommend it to others? Why? If you haven't read this book, what questions are you hoping the rest of the book will answer?

• If Malcolm X had lived, do you think there would have been a fifth Malcolm? If so, what do you think would have characterized this fifth stage?

• If you could ask Malcolm X a question, what would it be?

• Which character trait of Malcolm X do you find the most admirable? Which do you find the least admirable?

• Do you agree with Myers that Malcolm X touched "the edge of greatness" (line 92)? Why?

Focus and Motivate

OBJECTIVES

Literary Analysis
- explore the key idea of **dignity**
- identify the form and characteristics of autobiography
- read an autobiography

Reading
- summarize

Vocabulary
- build vocabulary for reading and writing
- understand and use the Latin root *spec* (also an EL language objective)

SUMMARY

This excerpt from Jackie Robinson's autobiography tells of the turning point in his career. After a long search, Dodgers president Branch Rickey chooses Robinson to help him achieve his dream of integrating major league baseball. Rickey warns Robinson that it will not be easy to be the first African American on the team and tells him that he will need courage and dignity to endure the insults he is likely to receive.

When is there
DIGNITY *in silence?*

Discuss the question and **KEY IDEA** with students. Use the context to define **dignity**. Ask students to volunteer behaviors that they think make someone worthy of respect and others that do not. Have students complete the **DISCUSS** activity and then ask groups to share their responses.

Selection Resources

The Noble Experiment

From the Autobiography *I Never Had It Made* by Jackie Robinson
as Told to Alfred Duckett

When is there
DIGNITY *in silence?*

MARYLAND OBJECTIVES

READING/LIT STANDARDS
1.E.4.e Summarize
3.A.3.a Distinguish among types of narrative texts

KEY IDEA What do you do when someone yells at you? Some people choose to yell back. Some people explain themselves calmly. But there are times when silence is the most effective response. When does silence give you **dignity,** or make you worthy of respect? In the selection you're about to read, Jackie Robinson tells why he needed to find strength in silence.

DISCUSS With a group, decide the best response to each scenario listed. Should you yell back, explain calmly, or simply stay silent?

Scenario	Response
The principal accuses you of something you didn't do.	
A younger sibling calls you names to make you angry.	
The referee makes a call you think is unfair.	
A friend yells at you for calling a play against him.	

808

RESOURCE MANAGER UNIT 7

Plan and Teach pp. 109–116

Literary Analysis
Summary pp. 117†*, 118‡*
Autobiography pp. 119, 120†*
Question Support p. 127*

Reading
Summarize pp. 121, 122†*
Reading Check p. 126
Reading Fluency p. 128

Vocabulary
Study p. 123*
Practice p. 124
Strategy p. 125

Assessment
Selection Tests A, B/C pp. 129*, 131*

 Test Generator CD

BEST PRACTICES TOOLKIT

Differentiated Instruction pp. 31–38*

Scaffolding Instruction pp. 43–46*

Graphic Organizers/Strategies
New Word Analysis • Whip Around • Cluster Diagram • T Chart • Making Inferences • Spider Map

Reading Support
🖉 Audio Anthology CD*

Technology
ℹ Literature and Vocabulary Centers at **ClassZone.com**

🖉 Write*Smart* CD

---

* Resources for Differentiation   † Also in Spanish   ‡ In Haitian Creole and Vietnamese

LITERARY ANALYSIS: AUTOBIOGRAPHY

An **autobiography** is the story of a person's life as written by that person. The writer

- uses the first-person point of view
- often introduces people who influenced him or her
- shares thoughts and feelings about his or her experiences

Autobiographies not only help you understand a person, but they also help you understand the society in which the person lived. As you read "The Noble Experiment," note what you learn about Jackie Robinson and his times.

READING STRATEGY: SUMMARIZE

When you **summarize,** you briefly restate in your own words the main ideas and important details of something you've read. As you read "The Noble Experiment," note important people and events in a log. Later you can use the log to help you identify the main ideas and summarize the selections.

> *Important Characters*
> - *Branch Rickey—Ohio Wesleyan baseball coach*
> - *Charley Thomas—Player for Ohio Wesleyan*
> -
>
> *Important Events*
> -

VOCABULARY IN CONTEXT

The listed words all help tell about a dramatic turning point in Jackie Robinson's life. See which ones you know well, think you know, or don't know at all. Then place each word in the correct column of a chart like the one shown.

WORD LIST		
camouflage	insinuation	speculate
capitalize	integrated	taunt
disillusionment	retaliate	
eloquence	shrewdly	

Know Well	Think I Know	Don't Know

Author Online

National Hero
Jackie Robinson was the first man at the University of California, Los Angeles, to earn varsity letters in four sports. He then went on to play professional baseball in 1945 in the Negro Leagues.

Jackie Robinson
1919–1972

His talent and extraordinary character were quickly noticed.

In 1947, he joined the Brooklyn Dodgers. Robinson was honored as Rookie of the Year in 1947 and National League Most Valuable Player in 1949. He was inducted into the Baseball Hall of Fame in 1962. With the help of his wife, Rachel, Jackie paved the way for African-American athletes.

Cowriter and Fan Robinson worked on his autobiography with Alfred Duckett, a writer and baseball fan. Active in the civil rights movement, Duckett was a speechwriter for Dr. Martin Luther King Jr.

 MORE ABOUT THE AUTHOR
For more on Jackie Robinson, visit the **Literature Center** at **ClassZone.com**.

Background

Segregated National Pastime In the 1940s, African Americans faced many barriers. Segregation kept African Americans separate from whites in every part of society, including sports. In baseball the Negro League was completely separate from the all-white teams of the Major League. Jackie Robinson would help change that.

Teach

STANDARDS FOCUS

LITERARY ANALYSIS

● AUTOBIOGRAPHY

Explain that most autobiographies focus on significant events in the author's life. Have students review **Author Online** and identify possible events in Jackie Robinson's life that may be included in his autobiography. *Possible answer: Significant events may include earning varsity letters in four sports, playing baseball in the Negro Leagues, joining the Brooklyn Dodgers, and earning various awards.*

CHECK UNDERSTANDING Have students describe autobiographical films or television programs they have seen.

READING STRATEGY

■ SUMMARIZE

Tell students that when they summarize it is important to put ideas into their own words and keep the ideas in the order of the original text.

CHECK UNDERSTANDING Ask pairs to summarize **Author Online.**

 RESOURCE MANAGER—Copy Master
  Summarize p. 121 (for student use while reading the selection)

VOCABULARY SKILL

▲ VOCABULARY IN CONTEXT

DIAGNOSE WORD KNOWLEDGE To determine preteaching needs, have all students complete **Vocabulary in Context.** Remind students to look for the definitions of unknown words as they read the text: *camouflage* (p. 813), *capitalize* (p. 813), *disillusionment* (p. 814), *eloquence* (p. 812), *insinuation* (p. 816), *integrated* (p. 813), *retaliate* (p. 812), *shrewdly* (p. 812), *speculate* (p. 815), *taunt* (p. 818).

PRETEACH VOCABULARY Use the Vocabulary Study copy master to help students explore the meaning of each boldfaced word.

1. Read item 1 aloud, emphasizing *camouflaged*.
2. Point out the context clues "hurt feelings" and "pretending." Discuss possible meanings for *camouflaged,* such as "hid."
3. Have students record their predictions.
4. Repeat the procedure for items 2–10.

 RESOURCE MANAGER—Copy Master
  Vocabulary Study p. 123

For general guidelines on differentiating vocabulary instruction and for alternative vocabulary activities for students not needing vocabulary preteaching, see

🧰 **BEST PRACTICES TOOLKIT**
  Scaffolding Vocabulary Instruction pp. 43–46

ℹ Vocabulary Center at **ClassZone.com**

ANALYZE VISUALS

Possible answer: National attention was focused on Jackie Robinson in 1951.

LITERARY ANALYSIS

Ⓐ AUTOBIOGRAPHY

Possible answer: Robinson wants readers to know about the racism that existed in the society.

Lines 15–22
REINFORCE *KEY IDEA:* DIGNITY

Discuss What does this incident show about the effect of discrimination on a person's **dignity?** *Possible answer: Discrimination makes a person feel inferior and undermines the person's dignity.*

THE NOBLE EXPERIMENT

Jackie Robinson
as Told to Alfred Duckett

In 1910 Branch Rickey was a coach for Ohio Wesleyan. The team went to South Bend, Indiana, for a game. The hotel management registered the coach and team but refused to assign a room to a black player named Charley Thomas. In those days college ball had a few black players. Mr. Rickey took the manager aside and said he would move the entire team to another hotel unless the black athlete was accepted. The threat was a bluff because he knew the other hotels also would have refused accommodations to a black man. While the hotel manager was thinking about the threat, Mr. Rickey came up with a compromise. He suggested
10 a cot be put in his own room, which he would share with the unwanted guest. The hotel manager wasn't happy about the idea, but he gave in. Ⓐ

Years later Branch Rickey told the story of the misery of that black player to whom he had given a place to sleep. He remembered that Thomas couldn't sleep.

"He sat on that cot," Mr. Rickey said, "and was silent for a long time. Then he began to cry, tears he couldn't hold back. His whole body shook with emotion. I sat and watched him, not knowing what to do until he began tearing at one hand with the other—just as if he were trying to scratch the skin off his hands with his fingernails. I was alarmed. I asked
20 him what he was trying to do to himself.

"'It's my hands,' he sobbed. 'They're black. If only they were white, I'd be as good as anybody then, wouldn't I, Mr. Rickey? If only they were white.'"

"Charley," Mr. Rickey said, "the day will come when they won't have to be white."

ANALYZE VISUALS
What might you **infer** from the cover of this 1951 special edition comic book?

❶ **Targeted Passage**

Ⓐ **AUTOBIOGRAPHY**
What does Robinson want the reader to know about the society in which Branch Rickey was coaching?

DIFFERENTIATED INSTRUCTION

FOR ALL STUDENTS

Integrated Curriculum Have mixed-ability groups prepare a multi-media timeline of the steps toward integration in the 1950s and 1960s. Students should include significant events (social studies), speeches and literature (language arts), and songs (music) that mark this era of civil rights activism. Have students present their timelines.

FOR LESS–PROFICIENT READERS

In combination with the *Audio Anthology CD*, use one or more Targeted Passages (pp. 810, 812, 816, 818) to ensure that students focus on key events, concepts, and skills.

❶ **Targeted Passage [Lines 1–11]**

This passage describes the major external conflict in the autobiography: society's discrimination against African Americans.

- How does the hotel management treat Charley Thomas? Why?
- What does Branch Rickey threaten to do?
- What is the compromise that Branch Rickey suggests? What does his action show about him?

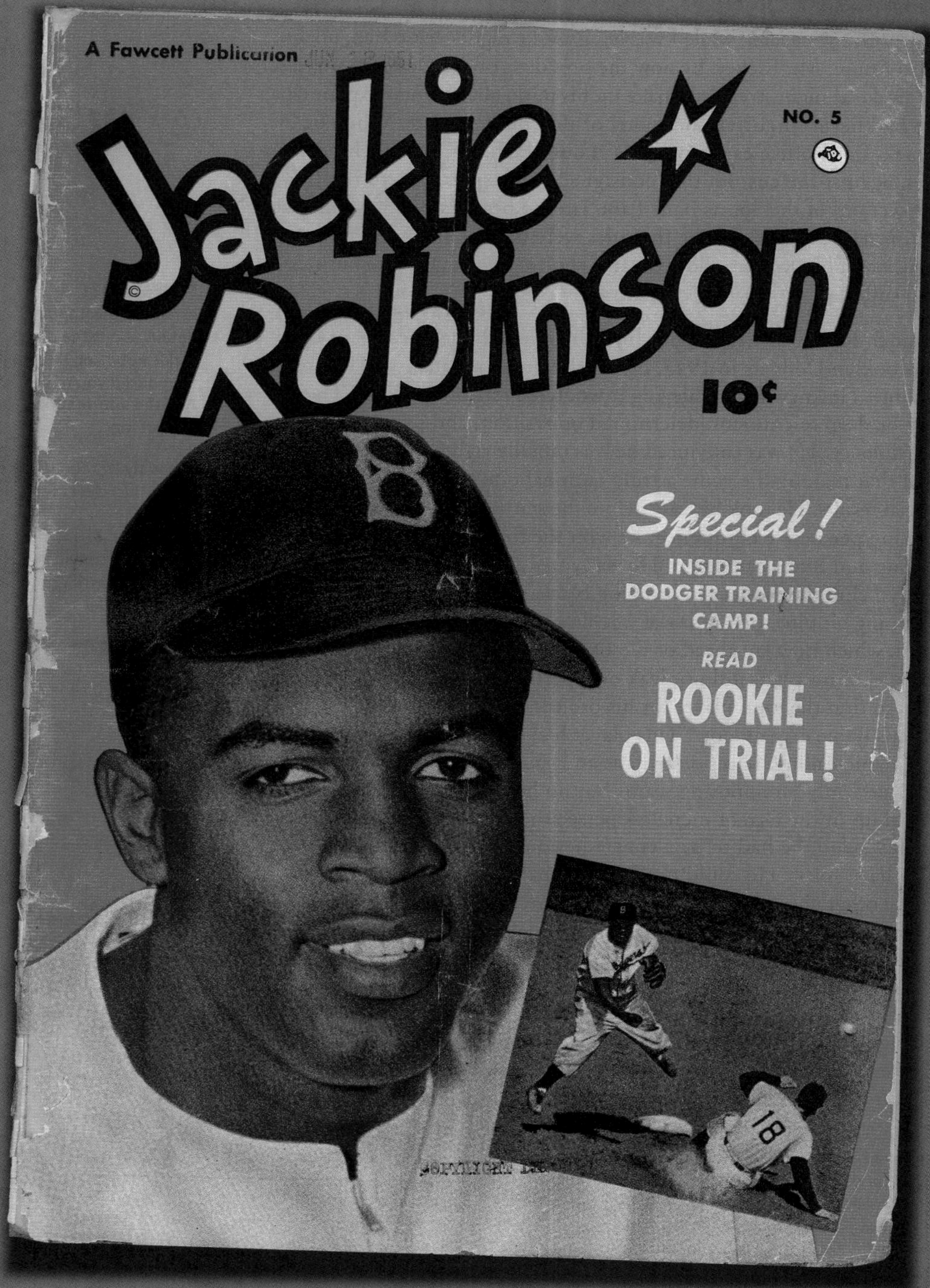

Jackie Robinson

NO. 5

10¢

Special!
INSIDE THE
DODGER TRAINING
CAMP!

READ
**ROOKIE
ON TRIAL!**

BACKGROUND

The Negro Leagues Jackie Robinson was recruited by Branch Rickey from the Kansas City Monarchs in the Negro American League. Robinson had joined the Monarchs in 1945. Several other stars of the African-American teams, such as Satchel Paige, Hank Aaron, and Willie Mays, would eventually join him in the majors, deflecting the fans' attention away from the Negro Leagues. Although there were several leagues between the period of 1920 and the late 1940s, by 1960 the major leagues were racially integrated and the last Negro League had folded.

FOR ENGLISH LEARNERS

Key Academic Vocabulary Have small groups use New Word Analysis to study this academic vocabulary found in the selection: *major* (lines 59, 151), *integrated* (line 78), *conducted* (line 164), *react* (line 171), *investigated* (line 179), *convince* (line 190).

 BEST PRACTICES TOOLKIT—Transparency
New Word Analysis p. E8

Prereading For prereading instruction for English learners, see

 BEST PRACTICES TOOLKIT
Scaffolding Reading Instruction pp. 43–46

FOR ADVANCED LEARNERS/PRE–AP

Pre-AP exercises in the bottom channel provide additional challenge for your advanced students. Use them for small groups or individuals.

ADDITIONAL GUIDELINES

For more help with differentiation and tips for classroom management, see

 BEST PRACTICES TOOLKIT
Differentiated Instruction pp. 31–38

B SUMMARIZE

Have students record their responses in their logs from page 809. **Possible answers:**

Important Characters:
- *Branch Rickey—Ohio Wesleyan baseball coach*
- *Charley Thomas—Player for Ohio Wesleyan*

Important Events:
- *Rickey insists that African-American player Charley Thomas be allowed to stay in the team's hotel.*
- *Thomas despairs over the discrimination he suffers.*
- *Rickey fights for the desegregation of spectators at Sportsman's Park.*

If students need help . . . Ask students what they have learned about Branch Rickey so far. Apply the Whip Around strategy and use students' responses to summarize this part of the text.

 BEST PRACTICES TOOLKIT
Whip Around p. B1

C AUTOBIOGRAPHY

Possible answers: *Jackie Robinson is showing how much thought went into Rickey's plan. He is emphasizing the importance of the selection of the player. He is indirectly revealing the qualities that he possesses and the ideal that he must try to live up to.*

Thirty-five years later, while I was lying awake nights, frustrated, unable to see a future, Mr. Rickey, by now the president of the Dodgers, was also lying awake at night, trying to make up his mind about a new experiment.

He had never forgotten the agony of that black athlete. When he became a front-office executive in St. Louis, he had fought, behind the
30 scenes, against the custom that consigned black spectators to the Jim Crow section[1] of the Sportsman's Park, later to become Busch Memorial Stadium. His pleas to change the rules were in vain. Those in power argued that if blacks were allowed a free choice of seating, white business would suffer. **B**

Branch Rickey lost that fight, but when he became the boss of the Brooklyn Dodgers in 1943, he felt the time for equality in baseball had come. He knew that achieving it would be terribly difficult. There would be deep resentment, determined opposition, and perhaps even racial violence. He was convinced he was morally right, and he **shrewdly**
40 sensed that making the game a truly national one would have healthy financial results. He took his case before the startled directors of the club, and using persuasive **eloquence,** he won the first battle in what would be a long and bitter campaign. He was voted permission to make the Brooklyn club the pioneer in bringing blacks into baseball.

Winning his directors' approval was almost insignificant in contrast to the task which now lay ahead of the Dodger president. He made certain that word of his plans did not leak out, particularly to the press. Next, he had to find the ideal player for his project, which came to be called "Rickey's noble experiment." This player had to be one who could take
50 abuse, name-calling, rejection by fans and sportswriters and by fellow players not only on opposing teams but on his own. He had to be able to stand up in the face of merciless persecution and not **retaliate.** On the other hand, he had to be a contradiction in human terms; he still had to have spirit. He could not be an "Uncle Tom."[2] His ability to turn the other cheek had to be predicated[3] on his determination to gain acceptance. Once having proven his ability as player, teammate, and man, he had to be able to cast off humbleness and stand up as a full-fledged participant whose triumph did not carry the poison of bitterness. **C**

Unknown to most people and certainly to me, after launching a major
60 scouting program, Branch Rickey had picked me as that player. The Rickey talent hunt went beyond national borders. Cuba, Mexico, Puerto Rico, Venezuela, and other countries where dark-skinned people lived

---

1. **consigned . . . to the Jim Crow section:** directed African Americans to sit in a separate section.
2. **"Uncle Tom":** an offensive term for an African-American person seen as trying overly hard to please white people; originally from the novel *Uncle Tom's Cabin*, written in 1851 by Harriet Beecher Stowe.
3. **predicated** (prĕd'ĭ-kā'tĭd): based.

B SUMMARIZE
What are the important details about the people Jackie Robinson has introduced you to so far? Add the information to your log.

shrewdly (shrōōd'lē) *adv.* wisely; in a clever way

eloquence (ĕl'ə-kwəns) *n.* forceful, convincing speech or writing

(2) **Targeted Passage**

retaliate (rĭ-tăl'ē-āt') *v.* to get revenge; get even

C AUTOBIOGRAPHY
Why does Jackie Robinson choose to tell you so much about Branch Rickey's thoughts on the qualities the first major-league black baseball player will have to have?

FOR LESS–PROFICIENT READERS

(2) **Targeted Passage [Lines 35–44]**

This passage identifies Branch Rickey's goal: to make the Brooklyn Dodgers the first integrated baseball team.

- What problems does Branch Rickey expect as he tries to reach his goal?
- Why is he so determined to integrate baseball?
- How do the directors of the Brooklyn Dodgers react?

Reading Strategy Follow-Up: Summarize Tell students that in a long text, it is often helpful to summarize paragraphs or sections. Have students reread lines 45–58. Work together to fill out a Cluster Diagram showing the qualities that Branch Rickey is looking for in his ideal player. Then have pairs summarize or state the main idea of this paragraph in one sentence. Compare summaries.

 BEST PRACTICES TOOLKIT—Transparency
Cluster Diagram p. B18

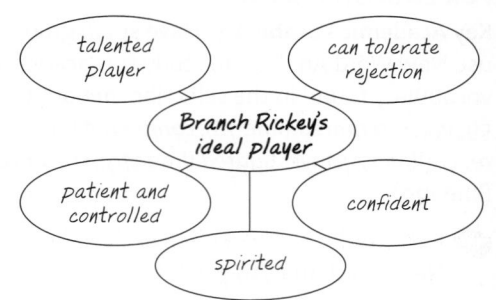

Jackie Robinson in his Kansas City Monarchs uniform shortly before he met Branch Rickey, 1945

had been checked out. Mr. Rickey had learned that there were a number of black players, war veterans mainly, who had gone to these countries, despairing of finding an opportunity in their own country. The manhunt had to be **camouflaged.** If it became known he was looking for a black recruit for the Dodgers, all hell would have broken loose. The gimmick he used as a cover-up was to make the world believe that he was about to establish a new Negro league. In the spring of 1945 he called a press
70 conference and announced that the Dodgers were organizing the United States League, composed of all black teams. This, of course, made blacks and prointegration whites indignant. He was accused of trying to uphold the existing segregation and, at the same time, **capitalize** on black players. Cleverly, Mr. Rickey replied that his league would be better organized than the current ones. He said its main purpose, eventually, was to be absorbed into the majors. It is ironic that by coming very close to telling the truth, he was able to conceal that truth from the enemies of **integrated** baseball. Most people assumed that when he spoke of some distant goal of integration, Mr. Rickey was being a hypocrite on this issue
80 as so many of baseball's leaders had been. **D**

Black players were familiar with this kind of hypocrisy. When I was with the Monarchs, shortly before I met Mr. Rickey, Wendell Smith, then sports editor of the black weekly Pittsburgh *Courier,* had arranged for me and two other players from the Negro league to go to a tryout

camouflage
(kăm′ə-fläzh′) *v.* to disguise or portray falsely in order to conceal

capitalize (kăp′ĭ-tl-īz′) *v.* to take advantage of

integrated (ĭn′tĭ-grā′tĭd) *adj.* open to people of all races and groups
integrate *v.*

D SUMMARIZE
What challenges will face Rickey and any African-American player he chooses?

Lines 59–80
DISCUSSION PROMPTS
Use these prompts to help students understand Rickey's strategy and the possible risks:

Connect Is there a cause you feel strongly about? How do your feelings help you understand Rickey's determination to carry out his plan? *Students may say that they would do whatever it takes to support their cause. Therefore, they understand the lengths that Rickey will go to.*

Analyze What are the possible risks of Rickey's plan? *Possible answer: If public opinion turns against him, he could lose his job. If the plan backfires, integration could be set back even further.*

Evaluate What is your opinion of Branch Rickey? Support your opinion with examples from the text. *Students may say that they admire Rickey's courage and willingness to fight for his principles.*

READING STRATEGY

D SUMMARIZE

Possible answer: There will be public opposition, resentment among people in baseball, and violence. The player will have to face ridicule and resentment.

FOR ENGLISH LEARNERS

Concept Support To help students understand the key ideas of *segregation* (line 73) and *integration* (line 79), draw a continuum. Label the left end "segregation" and the right end "integration." In the middle of the line, write "hiring Jackie Robinson." Explain that *segregation* and *integration* are antonyms, words that have opposite meanings. Have students use context clues and the continuum to define both terms.

hiring Jackie Robinson ⟶

segregation   integration

with the Boston Red Sox. The tryout had been brought about because a Boston city councilman had frightened the Red Sox management. Councilman Isadore Muchneck threatened to push a bill through banning Sunday baseball unless the Red Sox hired black players. Sam Jethroe of the Cleveland Buckeyes, Marvin Williams of the Philadelphia
90 Stars, and I had been grateful to Wendell for getting us a chance in the Red Sox tryout, and we put our best efforts into it. However, not for one minute did we believe the tryout was sincere. The Boston club officials praised our performance, let us fill out application cards, and said, "So long." We were fairly certain they wouldn't call us, and we had no intention of calling them.

Incidents like this made Wendell Smith as cynical as we were. He didn't accept Branch Rickey's new league as a genuine project, and he frankly told him so. During this conversation, the Dodger boss asked Wendell whether any of the three of us who had gone to Boston
100 was really good major league material. Wendell said I was. I will be forever indebted to Wendell because, without his even knowing it, his recommendation was in the end partly responsible for my career. At the time, it started a thorough investigation of my background. **E**

In August 1945, at Comiskey Park in Chicago, I was approached by Clyde Sukeforth, the Dodger scout. Blacks have had to learn to protect themselves by being cynical but not cynical enough to slam the door on potential opportunities. We go through life walking a tightrope⁴ to prevent too much **disillusionment.** I was out on the field when Sukeforth called my name and beckoned. He told me the Brown
110 Dodgers were looking for top ballplayers, that Branch Rickey had heard about me and sent him to watch me throw from the hole. He had come at an unfortunate time. I had hurt my shoulder a couple of days before that, and I wouldn't be doing any throwing for at least a week.

Sukeforth said he'd like to talk with me anyhow. He asked me to come to see him after the game at the Stevens Hotel.

Here we go again, I thought. Another time-wasting experience. But Sukeforth looked like a sincere person, and I thought I might as well listen. I agreed to meet him that night. When we met, Sukeforth got right to the point. Mr. Rickey wanted to talk to me about the
120 possibility of becoming a Brown Dodger. If I could get a few days off and go to Brooklyn, my fare and expenses would be paid. At first I said that I couldn't leave my team and go to Brooklyn just like that. Sukeforth wouldn't take no for an answer. He pointed out that I couldn't play for a few days anyhow because of my bum arm. Why should my team object?

---

4. **walking a tightrope:** maintaining a narrow balance.

814 UNIT 7: BIOGRAPHY AND AUTOBIOGRAPHY

E AUTOBIOGRAPHY
Reread lines 96–103. Notice that Robinson uses first-person pronouns such as *I* and *we*. To whom does the *we* refer?

disillusionment
(dĭs′ĭ-lōō′zhən-mənt) *n.* disappointment; loss of hope

VISUAL VOCABULARY

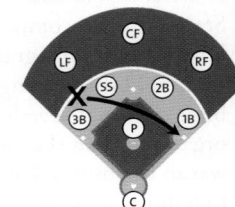

throw from the hole *v.* to throw from deep in the infield (**X**) to first base (**1B**)

DIFFERENTIATED INSTRUCTION

FOR LESS–PROFICIENT READERS

Comprehension Support Robinson says that African Americans have had to walk a "tight-rope" between being cynical but not too cynical (lines 105–107). To help students see Robinson's dilemma, have them complete a T Chart with reasons that support both attitudes. Remind students that the "tightrope" image implies that navigating between the two attitudes is difficult because both are convincing.

Reasons to be cynical	Reasons to be not too cynical
Have often faced "disillusionment"	Need to be open-minded
Need to "protect themselves"	Don't "slam the door on potential opportunities"
Too many "time-wasting experiences"	Sukeforth seems like a "sincere person"

BEST PRACTICES TOOLKIT—Transparency
T Chart p. A25

FOR ADVANCED LEARNERS/PRE–AP

Compare and Contrast On the eve before Robinson is to meet Rickey, both men are full of different emotions: cynicism is about to meet sincerity. Have students compare Robinson's reasons for being cynical with Rickey's motivation for his "noble experiment" by illustrating the thoughts, feelings, and expectations of each man in a separate drawing. Encourage students to add captions, dialogue, and a title. Invite volunteers to explain their illustrations.

Jackie Robinson and Branch Rickey on signing day

I continued to hold out and demanded to know what would happen if the Monarchs fired me. The Dodger scout replied quietly that he didn't believe that would happen.

I shrugged and said I'd make the trip. I figured I had nothing to lose.

130 **B**ranch Rickey was an impressive-looking man. He had a classic face, an air of command, a deep, booming voice, and a way of cutting through red tape and getting down to basics. He shook my hand vigorously and, after a brief conversation, sprang the first question.

"You got a girl?" he demanded.

It was a hell of a question. I had two reactions: why should he be concerned about my relationship with a girl; and, second, while I thought, hoped, and prayed I had a girl, the way things had been going, I was afraid she might have begun to consider me a hopeless case. I explained this to Mr. Rickey and Clyde. **G**

140 Mr. Rickey wanted to know all about Rachel. I told him of our hopes and plans.

"You know, you *have* a girl," he said heartily. "When we get through today, you may want to call her up because there are times when a man needs a woman by his side."

My heart began racing a little faster again as I sat there **speculating**. First he asked me if I really understood why he had sent for me. I told him what Clyde Sukeforth had told me.

F AUTOBIOGRAPHY
Reread lines 135–139. What can you **infer** about Jackie Robinson's personal life and feelings?

speculate
(spĕk′yə-lāt′) *v.* to view or consider different possibilities; to guess what might happen

THE NOBLE EXPERIMENT **815**

"That's what he was supposed to tell you," Mr. Rickey said. "The truth is you are not a candidate for the Brooklyn Brown Dodgers. I've sent
150 for you because I'm interested in you as a candidate for the Brooklyn National League Club. I think you can play in the major leagues. How do you feel about it?"

My reactions seemed like some kind of weird mixture churning in a blender. I was thrilled, scared, and excited. I was incredulous. Most of all, I was speechless.

"You think you can play for Montreal?" he demanded.

I got my tongue back. "Yes," I answered.

Montreal was the Brooklyn Dodgers' top farm club. The players who went there and made it had an excellent chance at the big time.

160 I was busy reorganizing my thoughts while Mr. Rickey and Clyde Sukeforth discussed me briefly, almost as if I weren't there. Mr. Rickey was questioning Clyde. Could I make the grade?

Abruptly, Mr. Rickey swung his swivel chair in my direction. He was a man who conducted himself with great drama. He pointed a finger at me. "I know you're a good ballplayer," he barked. "What I don't know is whether you have the guts."

I knew it was all too good to be true. Here was a guy questioning my courage. That virtually amounted to him asking me if I was a coward. Mr. Rickey or no Mr. Rickey, that was an **insinuation** hard to take. I felt
170 the heat coming up into my cheeks. **G**

Before I could react to what he had said, he leaned forward in his chair and explained.

I wasn't just another athlete being hired by a ball club. We were playing for big stakes. This was the reason Branch Rickey's search had been so exhaustive. The search had spanned the globe and narrowed down to a few candidates, then finally to me. When it looked as though I might be the number-one choice, the investigation of my life, my habits, my reputation, and my character had become an intensified study.

"I've investigated you thoroughly, Robinson," Mr. Rickey said.
180 One of the results of this thorough screening were reports from California athletic circles that I had been a "racial agitator"[5] at UCLA. Mr. Rickey had not accepted these criticisms on face value. He had demanded and received more information and came to the conclusion that if I had been white, people would have said, "Here's a guy who's a contender, a competitor."

After that he had some grim words of warning. "We can't fight our way through this, Robinson. We've got no army. There's virtually nobody on our side. No owners, no umpires, very few newspapermen. And I'm afraid

---

5. **"racial agitator"**: negative term used for someone who tries to stir up trouble between the races.

816 UNIT 7: BIOGRAPHY AND AUTOBIOGRAPHY

---

3 Targeted Passage

insinuation
(ĭn-sĭn′yōō-ā′shən) *n.* a suggestion or hint intended to insult

G AUTOBIOGRAPHY
Reread lines 153–170. What words and phrases help you understand how Robinson felt during his interview with Branch Rickey?

G AUTOBIOGRAPHY

Possible answer: Words and phrases include "weird mixture churning in a blender," "thrilled, scared, and excited," "incredulous," "speechless," "questioning my courage," *and* "hard to take."

Extend the Discussion How do Robinson's feelings change during the interview? Why?

Lines 173–185
DISCUSSION PROMPTS

Use these prompts to help students understand the thought behind the selection of Jackie Robinson:

Connect Think about a time when you had to make a hard decision. How does your experience help you understand Rickey's extensive search for the right candidate? *Students may say that they tried to think of all possible options and consequences before they made their decision, just as Rickey is trying to find all possible players before making his decision.*

Analyze Why is an investigation into Robinson's background necessary? *Possible answer: People will be looking for reasons to criticize the player that Rickey finally chooses. In order for the plan to work, the player has to be someone of great character with a spotless past so that no accusations can be made about him.*

Evaluate Why is the information that Rickey learns about Robinson from UCLA helpful? *Possible answer: He learns that Robinson is "a contender, a competitor" (line 185). In other words, Robinson is a man of strength and conviction who will fight for what he believes in and won't give up.*

DIFFERENTIATED INSTRUCTION

FOR LESS–PROFICIENT READERS
3 Targeted Passage [Lines 148–166]

This passage presents the turning point in Jackie Robinson's career: he is offered a chance to play in the major leagues.

- How does Jackie Robinson feel when he hears what Branch Rickey has in mind for him?

- Why will Robinson start in Montreal?

- Why will he need "guts"?

---

816 UNIT 7: BIOGRAPHY AND AUTOBIOGRAPHY

that many fans will be hostile. We'll be in a tough position. We can win
190 only if we can convince the world that I'm doing this because you're a
great ballplayer and a fine gentleman."

He had me transfixed as he spoke. I could feel his sincerity, and I began
to get a sense of how much this major step meant to him. Because of his
nature and his passion for justice, he had to do what he was doing. He
continued. The rumbling voice, the theatrical gestures were gone.
He was speaking from a deep, quiet strength.

"So there's more than just playing," he said. "I wish it meant only hits,
runs, and errors—only the things they put in the box score. Because you
know—yes, you would know, Robinson, that a baseball box score is a
200 democratic thing. It doesn't tell how big you are, what church you attend,
what color you are, or how your father voted in the last election. It just
tells what kind of baseball player you were on that particular day." **H**

H SUMMARIZE
What does Branch
Rickey really want to
find out about Jackie
Robinson during this
interview? Include these
details in your log.

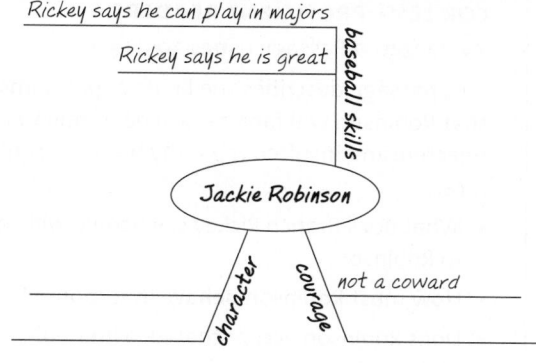

Jackie Robinson crosses the plate after one of his many home-run hits for the Montreal Royals.

THE NOBLE EXPERIMENT   **817**

THE NOBLE EXPERIMENT   **817**

I interrupted. "But it's the box score that really counts—that and that alone, isn't it?"

"It's all that *ought* to count," he replied. "But it isn't. Maybe one of these days it *will* be all that counts. That is one of the reasons I've got you here, Robinson. If you're a good enough man, we can make this a start in the right direction. But let me tell you, it's going to take an awful lot of courage."

He was back to the crossroads question that made me start to get angry
210 minutes earlier. He asked it slowly and with great care.

"Have you got the guts to play the game no matter what happens?"

"I think I can play the game, Mr. Rickey," I said.

The next few minutes were tough. Branch Rickey had to make absolutely sure that I knew what I would face. Beanballs[6] would be thrown at me. I would be called the kind of names which would hurt and infuriate any man. I would be physically attacked. Could I take all of this and control my temper, remain steadfastly loyal to our ultimate aim?

He knew I would have terrible problems and wanted me to know the extent of them before I agreed to the plan. I was twenty-six years old,
220 and all my life—back to the age of eight when a little neighbor girl called me names—I had believed in payback, retaliation. The most luxurious possession, the richest treasure anybody has, is his personal dignity. I looked at Mr. Rickey guardedly, and in that second I was looking at him not as a partner in a great experiment, but as the enemy—a white man. I had a question, and it was the age-old one about whether or not you sell your birthright. ❶

"Mr. Rickey," I asked, "are you looking for a Negro who is afraid to fight back?"

I never will forget the way he exploded.
230 "Robinson," he said, "I'm looking for a ballplayer with guts enough not to fight back."

After that, Mr. Rickey continued his lecture on the kind of thing I'd be facing.

He not only told me about it, but he acted out the part of a white player charging into me, blaming me for the "accident" and calling me all kinds of foul racial names. He talked about my race, my parents, in language that was almost unendurable.

"They'll **taunt** and goad you," Mr. Rickey said. "They'll do anything to make you react. They'll try to provoke a race riot in the ballpark.
240 This is the way to prove to the public that a Negro should not be allowed in the major league. This is the way to frighten the fans and make them afraid to attend the games."

---

6. **beanballs:** pitches thrown purposely at a batter's head.

④ **Targeted Passage**

❶ **AUTOBIOGRAPHY**
Reread lines 218–222. What is most important to Jackie Robinson?

taunt (tônt) v. to make fun of

LITERARY ANALYSIS

❶ AUTOBIOGRAPHY

Possible answer: *His dignity is what is most important to him.*

Extend the Discussion If Robinson accepts Rickey's offer, what will need to become most important to him?

Lines 227–231
REINFORCE *KEY IDEA:* DIGNITY

Discuss What different perceptions of **dignity** do Rickey and Robinson have? ***Possible answers:*** *Rickey's concept of dignity is being "big" enough not to fight back, even when provoked. Robinson's idea of preserving his dignity is to defend it vigorously and physically if necessary.*

DIFFERENTIATED INSTRUCTION

FOR LESS–PROFICIENT READERS

④ **Targeted Passage [Lines 205–231]**

This passage describes the kinds of problems that Robinson will face: he will be humiliated, rejected, and insulted regularly because of his race.

- What does Branch Rickey say people will do to Robinson?
- How must Robinson behave in response?
- Does Robinson accept that idea immediately? Why or why not?

FOR ADVANCED LEARNERS/PRE–AP

Synthesize "I'm looking for a ballplayer with guts enough not to fight back," Rickey tells Robinson (lines 230–231). Have students choose one of these activities to explore Rickey's definition of courage:

- Do a quickwrite to explain how Rickey's definition of courage compares to your own.
- Role-play a conversation between Robinson and Rachel, as he recounts Rickey's ideas.

Jackie makes the big time with the Brooklyn Dodgers.

If hundreds of black people wanted to come to the ballpark to watch me play and Mr. Rickey tried to discourage them, would I understand that he was doing it because the emotional enthusiasm of my people could harm the experiment? That kind of enthusiasm would be as bad as the emotional opposition of prejudiced white fans.

Suppose I was at shortstop. Another player comes down from first, stealing, flying in with spikes high, and cuts me on the leg. As I feel
250 the blood running down my leg, the white player laughs in my face.

"How do you like that, boy?" he sneers. **J**

Could I turn the other cheek? I didn't know how I would do it. Yet I knew that I must. I had to do it for so many reasons. For black youth, for my mother, for Rae, for myself. I had already begun to feel I had to do it for Branch Rickey.

I was offered, and agreed to sign later, a contract with a $3,500 bonus and $600-a-month salary. I was officially a Montreal Royal. I must not tell anyone except Rae and my mother. ∾

J SUMMARIZE
How does Branch Rickey test Jackie Robinson to make sure he is strong enough to succeed with dignity?

THE NOBLE EXPERIMENT   **819**

FOR LESS–PROFICIENT READERS

Comprehension Support Have students work in small groups to review and complete their summary logs. After they have filled in the details, have them write one or two sentences in response to each of these directives:

1. State the most important ideas about Branch Rickey's character.

2. Briefly explain Rickey's plan and describe his ideal player.

3. Tell why Rickey chooses Robinson.

4. Summarize what Rickey says to Robinson about what he should expect.

5. Identify the reasons that Robinson accepts Rickey's offer.

Have groups share their responses. Help them eliminate unnecessary details in preparation for writing their overall summary.

Lines 252–255
REINFORCE *KEY IDEA*: **DIGNITY**

Discuss Whose **dignity** does Robinson agree to uphold when he accepts Rickey's offer? *Possible answer: He will be acting on behalf of African Americans, his family, himself, and Branch Rickey.*

SELECTION WRAP–UP

REFLECT Have students think about what Jackie Robinson gives up and what he gains by accepting Rickey's offer. Is the cost worth the reward?

⭐ **CRITIQUE** Ask students to evaluate whether enough background information on the setting is given for them to understand the enormity of Branch Rickey's action. What else might the author have included?

READING FLUENCY

Distribute the copy masters and have students work in groups to practice fluency.

R RESOURCE MANAGER—Copy Master
Reading Fluency p. 128

Practice and Apply

After Reading

For additional support of post-reading questions, use these copy masters:

R RESOURCE MANAGER—Copy Masters

Reading Check p. 126 (to check understanding of the selection)

Autobiography p. 119 (for practice of literary analysis standards focus)

Question Support p. 127 (**After Reading** questions adapted for English learners and less-proficient readers)

Additional selection questions are provided for teachers on page 113.

For additional activities to challenge students, see

ⓘ Power Thinking at **ClassZone.com**

ANSWERS

Comprehension

1. *The player would have to be able to take abuse, name-calling, and rejection. He also had to be an exceptional ball player.*

2. *The plan would not have worked if revealed ahead of time. Robinson needed to show he was an exceptional ball player first.*

3. *Robinson had been invited to try out for the major leagues before by people who had no intention of hiring him.*

Literary Analysis

Possible answers:

4. ■ **STANDARDS FOCUS** *Summarize*
   Summaries should include Rickey's intentions when recruiting Robinson, what qualities he believed Robinson needed, and Robinson's reaction to being selected.

5. *The society was racist. Details include the incident with Charley Thomas (lines 2–11), the Jim Crow section of Sportsman's Park (line 31), and the tryout with the Boston Red Sox (lines 81–95).*

6. ● **STANDARDS FOCUS** *Autobiography*
   Robinson admires Rickey. His feelings are shown through details about Rickey's experiences and attitudes toward integration and the risks that Rickey was willing to take to make it happen. Robinson also directly describes Rickey as "an impressive-looking man" (line 130) and says that he spoke from a "deep, quiet strength" (line 196).

Comprehension

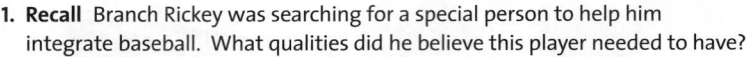

MARYLAND OBJECTIVES

READING STANDARD
1.E.4.e Summarize

1. **Recall** Branch Rickey was searching for a special person to help him integrate baseball. What qualities did he believe this player needed to have?

2. **Clarify** Why was Rickey's search for an African-American player kept secret?

3. **Clarify** Why was Jackie Robinson suspicious of Clyde Sukeforth's invitation to meet with Branch Rickey?

Literary Analysis

4. **Summarize** Review the log you created while reading and cross out details that don't seem as important now. Use the remaining information to write a summary of the selection.

5. **Draw Conclusions** What general statement can you make in regard to the society Jackie Robinson writes about? Cite details to support your answer.

6. **Interpret Autobiography** How does Robinson feel about Branch Rickey? Cite passages from the autobiography that show Robinson's impressions of Rickey.

7. **Analyze Author's Purpose** Why do you think Robinson wanted to share his experience with the public?

8. **Evaluate Title** Do you think "The Noble Experiment" is an appropriate title for this selection? Why or why not?

Extension and Challenge

9. **Readers' Circle** During Jackie Robinson's conversation with Branch Rickey, Robinson asks, "But it's the box score that really counts—that and that alone, isn't it?" Do you agree that the box score is all that counts? With a group, discuss whether we should expect professional athletes to be role models and act with **dignity,** or whether we should only judge them on their athletic performance. Use examples from the selection to support your opinion.

10. **🌎 SOCIAL STUDIES CONNECTION** The 1940s, when Jackie Robinson entered professional baseball, were a dramatic decade. Create a timeline of the era that gives the events in the autobiography and also those in the Eleanor Roosevelt biography beginning on page 762. Then research to find four other events that were happening in the world at the same time. Add these other events to your timeline.

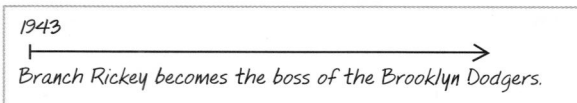

1943

Branch Rickey becomes the boss of the Brooklyn Dodgers.

↻ RESEARCH LINKS
For more on world events in the 1940s, visit the **Research Center** at ClassZone.com.

---

7. *Robinson may have wanted to inspire others to be courageous and to work to bring about justice.*

8. *"The Noble Experiment" is a good title because Rickey's plan was based on a high ideal of trying to end segregation in baseball.*

Extension and Challenge

9. *After students have discussed the question, ask each group to share its ideas with the class. Discuss arguments on both sides and identify the majority view of the class.*

10. **🌎 SOCIAL STUDIES CONNECTION**
    Students' timelines should accurately record the events covered in the texts and should include details related to four other major events, such as World War II, the Cold War, or the first supersonic flight.

Vocabulary in Context

VOCABULARY PRACTICE

Choose the word from the box that is the best substitute for each boldfaced word or term.

1. Branch Rickey **cleverly** devised a cover story to mislead the press.
2. He was accused of trying to **gain advantage** on African Americans.
3. The **lack of hope** African-American baseball players felt about joining the major leagues was based on past experience.
4. Robinson took time to **think** about the outcome of his actions.
5. The true goal of Rickey's plan was to have **desegregated** major leagues.
6. Some players on other teams would **make fun of** Robinson.
7. Robinson was not allowed to **get even.**
8. A sportswriter made a **suggestion** intended to insult Robinson.
9. The minister spoke with **great verbal skill** about the evils of prejudice.
10. Branch Rickey had to **conceal** his plan.

camouflage

capitalize

disillusionment

eloquence

insinuation

integrated

retaliate

shrewdly

speculate

taunt

VOCABULARY IN WRITING

What challenges did Branch Rickey expect Robinson to face during his early baseball career? Using three or more vocabulary words, write a paragraph about them. You could start this way.

> **EXAMPLE SENTENCE**
>
> *Rickey warned Robinson that spectators might* **taunt** *him.*

MARYLAND OBJECTIVES

READING STANDARD
1.D.3.b Use word structure to determine meaning

VOCABULARY STRATEGY: THE LATIN ROOT *spec*

The vocabulary word *speculate* contains the Latin root *spec,* which means "to see" or "to look." This root, which may also be spelled *spect,* is found in many English words. To understand the meaning of words with *spec* or *spect,* you can often use context clues and your knowledge of the root's meaning.

VOCABULARY PRACTICE
For more practice, go to the **Vocabulary Center** at ClassZone.com.

PRACTICE Choose a word from the web that best completes each sentence. Use context clues or, if necessary, a dictionary.

1. The _____ fireworks show thrilled everyone.
2. Interview the witness to get a better _____ on the accident.
3. The health _____ makes sure that all local restaurants are clean.
4. The _____ of speaking before an audience makes me nervous.
5. The police officer carefully removed the blood _____ from the crime scene.

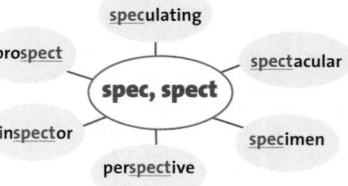

speculating • prospect • spec, spect • spectacular • inspector • perspective • specimen

---

DIFFERENTIATED INSTRUCTION

FOR ENGLISH LEARNERS

Vocabulary Strategy Because *spec* is a Latin root, some Latin-based languages such as Spanish and French have words that are spelled very similarly to those listed here. Point out that the Spanish word *espectacular* is similar to the English word *spectacular.* Have students identify other cognates for the words shown on page 821 and use their knowledge of the meanings to help them complete the exercise.

FOR ADVANCED LEARNERS/PRE–AP

Vocabulary Strategy Have students create a similar web for another Latin root such as *vis* ("to see"), *tract* ("to pull"), or *form* ("to shape"). Ask students to define each word that they create from the root.

ANSWERS

Vocabulary in Context

VOCABULARY PRACTICE

1. *shrewdly*
2. *capitalize*
3. *disillusionment*
4. *speculate*
5. *integrated*
6. *taunt*
7. *retaliate*
8. *insinuation*
9. *eloquence*
10. *camouflage*

R RESOURCE MANAGER—Copy Master
Vocabulary Practice p. 124

VOCABULARY IN WRITING

Encourage students to list the obstacles that Robinson could expect to face. Suggest that they skim pages 816–819. Then have students use vocabulary words to describe three of these challenges in complete sentences before writing their paragraphs.

VOCABULARY STRATEGY: THE LATIN ROOT
spec (also an EL language objective)

Ask students to identify the meanings of the words with which they are familiar. Have them use these words first before examining the remaining sentences and choices.

Answers:

1. *spectacular*
2. *perspective*
3. *inspector*
4. *prospect*
5. *specimen*

R RESOURCE MANAGER—Copy Master
Vocabulary Strategy p. 125

i Vocabulary Center at **ClassZone.com**
Additional Vocabulary Activities

Assess and Reteach

Assess

R RESOURCE MANAGER—Copy Masters
Selection Tests A, B/C pp. 129–130, 131–132
**Test Generator CD

Reteach

S STANDARDS LESSON FILE
Study Skills Lesson 13: Summarizing
Vocabulary Lesson 10: Latin Roots (active verbs)

Focus and Motivate

OBJECTIVES

Reading for Information
- identify treatment and scope
- evaluate texts for usefulness
- read and identify characteristics of an article

SUMMARY

The first article reports on the momentous admission of the first African American to organized baseball as Jackie Robinson is signed up to play with the Montreal Royals. The second article covers a game between the Brooklyn Dodgers and the Pittsburgh Pirates in which Robinson's performance turns the tide in Brooklyn's favor.

What's the Connection?

Use the SQ3R strategy to prepare students for their reading. After distributing copies of the worksheet, have students work together or alone to complete the first steps and read the text. Then ask them to share their summaries in small groups.

 BEST PRACTICES TOOLKIT—Transparency SQ3R p. A23

Teach

Skill Focus: Identify Treatment and Scope

Guide students through the process of identifying the treatment and scope of a text.

- Remind students of the various purposes authors might have—to inform, to persuade, to entertain, or to express thoughts and feelings. Have students think of examples that match each purpose.

- Discuss how tone is revealed through a writer's choice of words and details. One writer might describe a Chihuahua as "a rat with pointy ears," while another calls it "a pint-sized dog with the heart of a lion."

- To help students understand scope, give them some synonyms, such as *range* or *extent*. Ask students to describe the scope of "The Noble Experiment."

Possible chart entries appear on page 826.

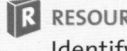 **RESOURCE MANAGER—Copy Master** Identify Treatment and Scope p. 141

Reading for Information

Use with "The Noble Experiment," page 810.

 MARYLAND OBJECTIVES

INFO TEXT/WRITING STANDARDS
2.A.4.a Identify and explain the author's purpose
4.A.7.a Identify sources of information on a given topic

Jackie Robinson Makes Headlines

Historical Sports Articles

What's the Connection?

You have just read Jackie Robinson's autobiography. Now read what newspaper reporters had to say about him during his career.

Skill Focus: Identify Treatment and Scope

Even when the same writing topic is assigned to everyone in your class, each student's paper will be different. This happens because you each make different decisions about how to cover the topic.

The way a topic is handled is called its **treatment.** Treatment includes the form the writer chooses to use, as well as the writer's purpose. Treatment also includes tone, or the writer's attitude toward the subject. For example, here are two ways to treat the same topic: movie ratings.

Movie Ratings	Form	Purpose	Tone
Treatment A	news article	to inform	serious
Treatment B	editorial	to persuade	lighthearted

Another thing that makes each piece of writing different is the writer's **scope**—what he or she focuses on. For example, even two serious articles about movie ratings can still be very different in scope. One might focus on how movie ratings have changed over the years. The other could focus on how inaccurate ratings hurt good movies.

As you read the articles that follow, identify their treatment and scope by answering the questions in this chart.

Element	Questions to Answer	"Montreal Signs Negro Shortstop"	"Robinson Steals Home in Fifth"
Treatment	What form does the writing take?	sports article	sports article
	What is the purpose?		
	What is the tone?		
Scope	What is the topic?		
	What aspects of the topic are covered in the article?		
	How much detail is provided?		

Selection Resources

 RESOURCE MANAGER UNIT 7

Plan and Teach pp. 133–137

Reading
Summary pp. 139†*, 140‡*
Identify Treatment and Scope pp. 141, 143†*
Reading Check p. 145
Evaluate Texts for Usefulness pp. 142, 144†*
Question Support p. 146*

Assessment
Selection Tests A, B/C pp. 147*, 149*

 Test Generator CD

Reading Support

Audio Anthology CD*

 **BEST PRACTICES TOOLKIT**

T Chart • Think-Pair-Share • Read Aloud/ Think Aloud • SQ3R

---

* Resources for Differentiation   † Also in Spanish   ‡ In Haitian Creole and Vietnamese

MONTREAL SIGNS NEGRO SHORTSTOP

Organized Baseball Opens Its Ranks to Negro Player

Jackie Robinson signs with the Montreal Royals. Looking on are Hector Racine, Royals president; Branch Rickey Jr.; and Romeo Gauvreau, Royals vice president.

Robinson Gets Bonus to Sign Ⓐ

MONTREAL, Oct. 23 (AP)—The first Negro player ever to be admitted to organized baseball, Jack Robinson, today put his signature on a contract calling not only for a player's salary, but also a bonus for signing.

Product of a three-year search and $25,000 hunt for Negro diamond talent by the Dodgers, Robinson signed up in a history-making huddle with Hector Racine and Lieut. Col. Romeo Gauvreau, Royals' president and vice president respectively, and Branch Rickey Jr., who heads the Brooklyn farm system.

"Mr. Racine and my father," said young Rickey, "will undoubtedly be severely criticized in some sections of the United States where racial prejudice is rampant. They are not inviting trouble, but they won't avoid it if it comes. Jack Robinson is a fine type of young man, intelligent and college bred, and I think he can take it, too."

DIFFERENTIATED INSTRUCTION

FOR LESS–PROFICIENT READERS
Concept Support Have students read the first four paragraphs with partners. Provide them with small sticky notes. Have them use the sticky notes to label each of these elements of the first article: *headline, subtitle, photograph, caption, lead.* Have them also look for and label the answers to the questions *who, what, when, where, why,* and *how.* Discuss students' placement of the notes.

FOR ENGLISH LEARNERS
Options for Reading To introduce each article, read the lead paragraphs aloud. Then have students use the *Audio Anthology CD* to listen to each article before returning to the text to read independently.

Reading: Predict Before students continue reading the first article, have them predict what the reactions will be to the news of Jackie Robinson's signing. After students listen to the lead in the second article, have them predict what Robinson will do.

FOCUS ON FORM

Discuss the purpose and characteristics of a sports article. Remind students that this type of article is nonfiction and often appears in a separate section of the newspaper devoted to sports coverage.

- Have volunteers read the list of elements aloud.
- Ask students what topics might be covered in a sports article. Have them predict what they will learn from the two articles in this lesson.

LITERARY ANALYSIS

Ⓐ SPORTS ARTICLE
Possible answers: The subtitle reveals that Robinson received a bonus for joining the Montreal team. This implies that Robinson is an exceptional player whom the team was eager to sign.

BACKGROUND

Farm Clubs In the first article, Branch Rickey Jr. is described as the head of the Brooklyn farm system (lines 15–17). Farm clubs are minor league teams, owned or operated by major league teams, that provide a training ground for players. If players are talented, they are brought up to the major league team. Branch Rickey Sr. started the farm club system when he was with the Cardinals as a way to reduce his team's need to buy players in great number. Jackie Robinson began his major league career with the Montreal Royals, one of the Dodgers' farm teams.

B TREATMENT AND SCOPE

Have students record their answers in the chart from page 822. *Possible answer: The author's tone is serious and respectful.*

If students need help . . . Use a T Chart to record words and phrases from lines 1–45 that reveal tone. Use the tone of each to help describe the overall attitude of the writer toward the subject.

Detail from text	Tone
"Robinson signed up in a history-making huddle" (line 11)	awed
"sports writers and photographers assembled" (lines 37–38)	factual
"both he and his father . . . realized the implications and possible reactions" (lines 41–44)	serious

Extend the Discussion Why is the tone fitting for the topic of the article?

 BEST PRACTICES TOOLKIT—Transparency T Chart p. A25

C TREATMENT AND SCOPE

Possible answers: The topic is the precedent-setting event in organized baseball of allowing an African American to play in its ranks. The article covers what happened (lines 2–7), when and where it occurred (line 1), who was involved (lines 11–17), why it was history-making (lines 2–3), why Robinson was chosen (lines 24–27, 68–70), hopes and expectations of Robinson and team officials (lines 27, 29–36, 56–61), and speculations about possible reactions (lines 18–22, 46–55).

Robinson, himself, had little to say. "Of course, I can't begin to tell you how happy I am that I am the first member of my race in organized ball," he declared. "I realize how much it means to me, to my race and to baseball. I can only say I'll do my very best to come through in every manner."

B TREATMENT AND SCOPE

Would you describe the writer's **tone** as respectful, humorous, or something else? Add this description to your chart.

Robinson is seen here as he takes a practice swing.

C TREATMENT AND SCOPE

Identify the **topic** of this article. What aspects of this topic does the reporter focus on? Add this information to your chart.

Implications Are Realized

With sports writers and photographers assembled, young Rickey and Racine made the announcement here. Rickey Jr. went on to explain that both he and his father—who was not present—realized the implications and possible reactions in other quarters of the diamond world. **B**

"It may cost the Brooklyn organization a number of ball players," he said. "Some of them, particularly if they come from certain sections of the South, will steer away from a club with colored players on its roster. Some players now with us may even quit, but they'll be back in baseball after they work a year or two in a cotton mill."

Rickey Sr.'s hunt for Negro talent has produced some twenty-five others he expects to sign to contracts for double-A ball, with the intention of developing them into big leaguers.

On Aug. 29 Robinson was quietly taken to Brooklyn. Rickey Sr. told him what he had in mind, and the broad-shouldered Pasadena, Calif., Negro agreed to sign a contract by Nov. 1.

"Robinson is a good ball player and comes to us highly recommended by our scouts," Racine said. "He will join us at our training camp in Florida next spring." **C**

DIFFERENTIATED INSTRUCTION

FOR LESS–PROFICIENT READERS

Concept Support Review the details that students have recorded in their charts so far about treatment and scope of the first article. Then have students apply a Think-Pair-Share strategy to complete the remaining analysis of the treatment and scope. Have pairs contribute their insights to the class chart.

 BEST PRACTICES TOOLKIT—Transparency Think-Pair-Share p. A18

FOR ENGLISH LEARNERS

Vocabulary Support Make sure students have an understanding of the layout of a baseball field. Briefly review terms such as *infield, outfield,* and *bases.* Draw the four bases on the board and connect them with a line. Explain that the term *diamond* used in lines 10 and 45 refers to the shape formed by the bases.

SPECIAL TO THE NEW YORK TIMES

ROBINSON STEALS HOME IN FIFTH

by Roscoe McGowen

Robinson slides home to win the ball game against Pittsburgh.

PITTSBURGH, June 24—they're never too old to learn something. The 40-year-old Fritz Ostermueller learned tonight at Forbes Field, before 35,331 distressed witnesses, that it is unwise to wind up with Jackie Robinson on third base. **E**

The Negro flash stole home with two out in the fifth inning while ₂₀ the second inning. Dixie Walker

Fritz was going through his full motion to pitch a third ball to Dixie Walker—and that run was enough to win the ball game, although the Brooks went on to outscore the Pirates, 4–2.

At the time Robinson committed his larceny the score was tied, both teams having scored twice in the second inning. Dixie Walker

D SPORTS ARTICLE
Based on the **headline, photo,** and **caption,** what does the article focus on?

E TREATMENT AND SCOPE
Reread lines 2–8. What **tone** does a phrase like "They're never too old to learn something" convey?

LITERARY ANALYSIS

D SPORTS ARTICLE

Possible answer: *The article focuses on the amazing play that Jackie Robinson made in the fifth inning of a baseball game.*

INFORMATIONAL ANALYSIS

E TREATMENT AND SCOPE

Have students record their answers in their chart from page 822. ***Possible answer:*** *The tone conveyed is humorous, mock-dramatic, and may be interpreted as sarcastic.*

If students need help . . . Point out phrases in the article—such as "distressed witnesses" (lines 5–6), "it is unwise to wind up with Jackie Robinson on third base" (lines 6–8), and "Robinson committed his larceny" (lines 17–18)—that also help to show the author's tone.

FOR ENGLISH LEARNERS

Vocabulary: Idioms and Sayings To help students increase their understanding of the second article, use a Read Aloud/Think Aloud strategy on the entire piece. Explain unfamiliar terms as they are encountered—for example, *stole home* (line 9); *going through his full motion* (line 11); *committed his larceny* (lines 17–18); *opened the second* (line 21).

BEST PRACTICES TOOLKIT—Transparency
Read Aloud/Think Aloud p. A34

Comprehension: Concept Support Help students assess the scope of the second article by assigning small groups one paragraph each. Ask them to explain in a brief sentence what they learn from their paragraph. Have groups share their sentences. Record their ideas in the chart from page 822 to identify the aspects of the topic covered by the writer.

F SPORTS ARTICLE

Discuss the information contained in this box score in class. *Possible answer: Students may say that they can learn the batting order, the pitcher's performance, the results of each hit, the duration of the game, and the number of people who attended each game from this box score.*

If students need help . . . Ask a series of specific questions to help them focus on different parts of the box score organizer.

Skill Focus: Identify Treatment and Scope

Possible answers for chart on page 822:

"Montreal Signs Negro Shortstop"
Form: *sports article*
Purpose: *to inform*
Tone: *serious, respectful*
Topic: *precedent-setting event of allowing an African American, Jackie Robinson, to play in organized baseball*
Aspects covered: *what happened, when and where it occurred, why it was history-making, why Robinson was chosen, hopes and expectations of Robinson and team officials, and speculations about possible reactions*
Detail provided: *The article provides many details about the signing event, including historical background and quotations from the people involved.*

"Robinson Steals Home in Fifth"
Form: *sports article*
Purpose: *to inform*
Tone: *humorous, mock-dramatic, sarcastic*
Topic: *Robinson's performance in a baseball game between Pittsburgh and Brooklyn*
Aspects covered: *when the game took place, what the pitcher learned, what Robinson did to ensure the team's win, who else scored for Brooklyn, statistics on the game (all the items in the box score)*
Detail provided: *The article describes in detail what was happening in the game when Robinson stole home (lines 9–13, 17–20). It also describes how the Dodgers scored their first two runs (lines 20–27). The box score provides statistics about the whole game.*

---

opened the second with a long triple to left center and Pee Wee Reese, catching a three-and-one pitch on the fat part of his bat, walloped the ball far over the outer left field barrier for his eighth homer of the campaign.

F SPORTS ARTICLE
A **box score** is a **graphic aid** that uses abbreviations to show at a glance the number of times a player

- was at bat **(ab.)**
- scored a run **(r.)**
- got a hit **(h.)**
- put out another player **(po.)**
- assisted in a play **(a.)**
- made an error **(e.)**

What else can you learn from this box score?

The Box Score

PITTSBURGH		ab.	r.	h.	po.	a.	e.
Rikard	rf	3	0	1	3	0	0
Wiet'nn	2b	4	0	0	3	1	0
Gustine	3b	4	0	0	0	2	0
Kiner	lf	3	1	1	1	0	0
Cox.	ss	3	1	2	2	3	0
Fletcher	1b	4	0	1	5	1	0
W'lake	cf	4	0	0	2	0	0
Howell	c	4	0	1	8	1	0
Oster'ler	p	3	0	1	3	1	0
Sullivan		1	0	0	0	0	0
Total		33	2	7	27	9	0

BROOKLYN		ab.	r.	h.	po.	a.	e.
Stanky	2b	4	0	1	1	4	0
Gionfriddo	lf	4	1	0	3	0	0
Robinson	1b	4	1	1	11	0	0
Furillo	cf	4	0	2	2	0	1
Walker	rf	3	1	1	1	0	0
Reese	ss	4	1	1	3	3	0
Jorgens'n	3b	4	0	2	0	2	0
Hodges	c	3	0	0	5	0	0
Branca	p	4	0	0	1	1	0
Total		34	4	8	27	10	1

Brooklyn	0	2	0	0	1	0	1	0	0	—	4
Pittsburgh	0	2	0	0	0	0	0	0	0	—	2

Runs batted in—Reese 2, Fletcher, Furillo Two-base hit—Rikard. Three-base hit—Walker. Home run—Reese. Stolen bases—Furillo, Robinson, Gionfriddo. Double play—Stanky, Reese and Robinson. Left on bases—Brooklyn 7. Pittsburgh 7. Bases on balls—Off Branca 3. Ostermueller 4. Struck out—By Ostermueller 7. Branca 4. Umpires—Stewart, Ballanfant and Henline. Time of game—2:41. Attendance—35,331. F

DIFFERENTIATED INSTRUCTION

FOR ADVANCED LEARNERS/PRE–AP

Compare and Contrast Pose this question to students: *How has sports reporting changed since the 1940s?* To answer the question, have students bring in sports articles from current newspapers. Ask them to draw up a chart listing the elements of a sports article and then use their chart to compare the recent articles with those from the past. Have them discuss their observations and answers to the question in small groups.

Evaluate Point out examples of figurative language (lines 17–18) and play-on-words (line 7) in the second article. Ask students why the writer might have used these devices and what impact they have on the readers. Have students discuss whether this style is appropriate for a sports article and why.

Comprehension

1. **Recall** What was Jackie Robinson the first African-American person to do?

2. **Summarize** In the article "Montreal Signs Negro Shortstop," Branch Rickey Jr. says that he and his father realize what the reactions to signing Robinson may be. Summarize these possible reactions.

Critical Analysis

3. **Analyze the Lead** Explain what a lead is. Identify the lead in either one of the two sports articles you just read. Then explain how that lead gets its readers' attention.

4. **Compare Treatment and Scope** Using the chart you completed, compare the treatment and scope of the two articles.

Read for Information: Evaluate Texts for Usefulness

MARYLAND OBJECTIVES

INFO TEXT/WRITING STANDARDS
2.A.4.a Identify and explain the author's purpose
4.A.7.a Identify sources of information on a given topic

WRITING PROMPT

Imagine you have chosen one of the following topics for a report:

- box scores and how they have changed over the years
- attitudes toward African-American athletes in the 1940s
- sports reporting

Explain which article you would use as a source of information for this topic and why. If both articles would be useful to you, be sure to explain what each would provide.

To answer this prompt, first identify the topic you would want to focus on. Then follow these steps:

1. Review the chart you filled in. What information does each article provide?

2. In a paragraph, identify the topic you picked, the article(s) you would use for a report on that topic, and a brief explanation as to why the article(s) would be useful to you.

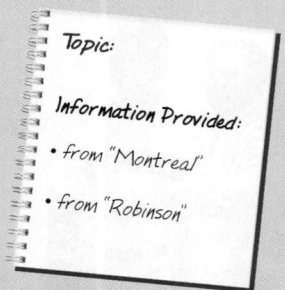

Topic:

Information Provided:
- from "Montreal"
- from "Robinson"

FOR LESS–PROFICIENT WRITERS

Read for Information Help students list the kinds of information they would include for one of the topics (for example, for changes in box scores: facts included, presentation, box scores in the 1940s and now). Have students decide which article contains relevant facts. Then have students write their paragraphs or choose another topic and work through the same process with a partner.

FOR ADVANCED LEARNERS/PRE–AP

Read for Information After completing the prompt, have students continue their research and write a full report on the topic of their choice. Encourage students to use both print and electronic resources and to include charts, graphs, timelines, or other visuals with their text.

Practice and Apply

For additional support of post-reading questions, use these copy masters:

RESOURCE MANAGER—Copy Masters
Reading Check p. 145
Question Support p. 146
Evaluate Texts for Usefulness p. 142

For additional questions, see p. 136.

ANSWERS

Comprehension

1. *Robinson was the first African American to be admitted to organized baseball.*

2. *Reactions to signing Robinson might range from criticism in some parts of the country to some players' steering away from the ball club or even quitting it.*

Critical Analysis

3. *The lead is the first few attention-grabbing sentences of the article. The lead in the first article, lines 1–7, presents surprising facts. The lead in the second article, lines 1–8, first causes readers to wonder who learned something and what was learned and then answers these questions in a dramatic and humorous way.*

4. ■ **STANDARDS FOCUS** *Identify Treatment and Scope Students should note that the form and purpose of both articles are similar. Tone and scope differ.*

Read for Information: Evaluate Texts for Usefulness

Writing Prompt *Students should clearly identify their topic and provide sound reasons for their choice of articles.*

Assess and Reteach

Assess

RESOURCE MANAGER—Copy Masters
Selection Tests A, B/C pp. 147–148, 149–150
Test Generator CD

Reteach

STANDARDS LESSON FILE
Literature Lesson 37: Tone
Research and Study Skills Lesson 6: Evaluating Print Sources

Focus and Motivate

OBJECTIVES

Media Literacy
- analyze a **documentary**
- identify ways that information is presented in nonprint sources
- plan and conduct an interview

SUMMARY

This clip from the A&E Channel's *Biography* series presents a documentary about Jackie Robinson. Using voice-over narration, interviews, archival footage, still photography, and music, the clip tells how Robinson got his start in the major leagues. Viewers learn about the hardships Robinson faced and the importance of his legacy. An interview with Branch Rickey, the Brooklyn Dodgers owner who brought Robinson into the league, describes some of the challenges that both he and Robinson faced.

What makes a person a TRAILBLAZER?

Discuss the question. Clarify the literal definition of a trailblazer: one who creates a path through uncharted territory that others can follow. Ask students to suggest examples of people who have been trailblazers, either figuratively or literally, in a variety of contexts. Have students read the *KEY IDEA* paragraph. Then ask volunteers for examples of personal qualities that enabled Jackie Robinson to lead the way in integrating Major League Baseball during his **remarkable career.**

BACKGROUND

When a professional or college sports team retires a number, no other player on the team can ever wear that number. In 1939 the New York Yankees became the first team in American professional sports to retire a number—Lou Gehrig's number 4. Jackie Robinson's number 42, however, remains the only number retired from an entire professional sport. This singular honor demonstrates the depth of Robinson's contribution, which transcended athletics and helped improve American society.

Media Study

from Jackie Robinson
Documentary on **MediaSmart** DVD

What makes a person a TRAILBLAZER?

MARYLAND OBJECTIVES

INFORMATIONAL TEXT STANDARD 2.A.6.b Analyze structure and features

KEY IDEA Jackie Robinson did more than play baseball. He helped pave the way for racial equality in professional sports. You've read about the key moment in his **remarkable career.** Now watch a documentary that shows the obstacles Jackie Robinson overcame to pave a new path for baseball.

Background

Retiring Number 42 It's common for a professional team to retire the jersey number of an outstanding player. It's quite uncommon to retire a number throughout an entire league. This happened in 1997, when Jackie Robinson's number, 42, was retired to mark the 50th anniversary of breaking the color barrier in baseball. Many baseball greats were at the ceremony to pay tribute to this trailblazer.

This documentary from the A&E Channel's *Biography* series shows how Robinson's courage won him the respect of his teammates and earned him admiration nationwide.

828

Media Study Resources

R **RESOURCE MANAGER UNIT 7**

Plan and Teach pp. 151–154

Media Analysis

Summary pp. 155†*, 156‡*

Viewing Guide p. 157

Close Viewing p. 158

Viewing Activity p. 159

Produce Your Own Media p. 160

S **STANDARDS LESSON FILE**

Media Lessons 4–6: Analyzing Visuals, Sound, and Editing in Film and TV

i Media Center at **ClassZone.com**

MEDIA VIEWING

Media*Smart* DVD

* Resources for Differentiation   † Also in Spanish   ‡ In Haitian Creole and Vietnamese

Media Literacy: Documentary

A **documentary** is a nonfiction film or television production that tells about important people, historic places, or major events. The purpose of a documentary may be to inform, to explain, or to persuade. A documentary that is biographical presents the factual details of a person's life, focusing on major events. Most documentaries use interesting visuals and sounds and are edited to make the information easy to follow.

BASIC FEATURES	STRATEGIES FOR VIEWING	
Visuals To bring a subject to life, a documentary uses **photographs, film, interviews,** or **graphics.**	• Look for **footage** that helps you understand the subject. Footage can include photographs, letters, interviews, news reports, film clips, and even home video movies. Documentary filmmakers use footage to show key information or details about a person, a place, or an event and to give a sense of a particular time. • Pay attention to **interviews.** People who are interviewed can be experts on a topic, or people who are directly involved with the subject of the documentary.	
Sound Many documentaries include **voice-over narration,** which is the voice of an unseen speaker who is heard as the documentary plays. Other sounds include **music, sound effects,** and **dialogue.**	• Listen carefully to the **voice-over narrator.** The voice-over tells viewers why the subject is important and provides clues about how the information is organized. The voice-over may also summarize key scenes or events. • Follow **musical cues.** Music can be used simply to entertain viewers. It can also signal a change in the documentary's setting or changes in mood.	
Editing **Editing** is the process of selecting and arranging visuals and sounds in a way that makes sense and is interesting for viewers.	Pay attention to how the information is presented and **edited.** Most documentaries will show events from beginning to end in a chronological, or time-order, sequence.	

MEDIA STUDY: TEACHING OPTIONS

Teaching Option 1: The Basics (1–2 Days)

1. Begin the Media Study using the material provided on pages 828–829.

2. Show the Introduction on Media*Smart.* Then show the First Viewing. As they watch, have students use the Viewing Guide on page 830, along with the corresponding copy master on page 157 of the Resource Manager. Discuss their responses.

3. Return to the pupil edition for the extension activities on page 831.

Teaching Option 2: In-Depth Study (2–3 Days)

1. Begin the Media Study using pages 828–829.

2. Show the Introduction and First Viewing from Media*Smart.*

3. Continue on Media*Smart* with the Media Lessons, using the teacher notes available in the Resources section.

4. Show the Guided Analysis presentation. Have students record their observations on the Student Viewing Guide available in the Resources section from Media*Smart.*

5. Return to the pupil edition, page 831.

MEDIA LITERACY

Review the definition of a *documentary* and ask students for examples. For each documentary cited, ask students to explain what made it effective. List on the board any responses that students generate. Then discuss the chart on page 829.

• **Visuals** Make sure students understand the difficulties that documentary filmmakers often face when collecting images to tell a story. First they assemble all available film, photographs, recorded interviews, and graphics related to a topic. Then they must select and sequence parts of these visuals in a way that clearly presents the documentary's message.

• **Sound** Point out that in addition to introducing and summarizing, the voice-over narrator also provides a "bridge" between content segments. Explain that, unlike clips of existing footage and interviews, the voice-over script is completely under the filmmaker's control, and he or she can use it to help make connections and transitions.

Ask students to think about the ways that sound influences and enhances their perception of an image. Have them consider how the crack of a bat and the roar of a crowd can help bring to life a photograph of a baseball player's swing.

• **Editing** Explain that the editor of a documentary must assemble and present sounds and images in a coherent, seamless, and visually entertaining manner. Editors often insert generic images strictly for visual interest, such as the railroad footage used to signify travel in the *Biography* clip.

S STANDARDS LESSON FILE

Media Lesson 4: Analyzing Visuals in Film and TV

Media Lesson 5: Analyzing Sound in Film and TV

Media Lesson 6: Analyzing Editing in Film and TV

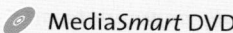 Media*Smart* DVD

Practice and Apply

VIEWING GUIDE

1. As students prepare to view the clip, tell them that they will be asked to identify techniques the filmmaker used to convey historical information. Encourage them to watch and listen for the following elements:

   - the use of **footage**, including archival film, still images, and **interviews**
   - how the **voice-over narration** helps organize, connect, and summarize information, and how **musical cues** help signal changes in setting
   - the way that **editing** defines sequence and makes the presentation interesting

2. Some students may have difficulty focusing on the technical aspects of the documentary. Suggest that they first listen to the clip without viewing the picture. Once they've become familiar with the content and analyzed the use of music, have them view the clip. Ask them to look for ways in which the editor used visuals to make the presentation more interesting.

R RESOURCE MANAGER—Copy Masters
Viewing Guide p. 157
Close Viewing p. 158
Viewing Activity p. 159

MediaSmart DVD

ANSWERS

FIRST VIEWING: Comprehension

1. *Robinson's closest friend during his first year with the Dodgers was shortstop Harold "Pee Wee" Reese.*

2. *Possible answer: The most important thing a person can do in life is try to have a positive effect on other people.*

CLOSE VIEWING: Media Literacy

Possible answers:

3. *Big-band swing provides a musical cue for the 1947 World Series footage. The music is upbeat and historically appropriate, and it may evoke feelings of nostalgia in older viewers.*

MediaSmart DVD
- **Video Clip:** *Jackie Robinson*
- **Genre:** Documentary
- **Running Time:** 8 minutes

830

Viewing Guide for
Jackie Robinson

Today, all athletes have an equal chance to play in professional sports, but there was a time when Jackie Robinson was the only African-American athlete out in the field. As you view the documentary, pay attention to the comments of those who knew and worked with Robinson. They will help you understand why he is considered a hero by so many people.

To continue exploring the features of a documentary, answer the following questions.

NOW VIEW

FIRST VIEWING: Comprehension

1. **Recall** Who is the player who became Jackie Robinson's friend during Robinson's first year with the Dodgers?

2. **Clarify** The documentary ends with this quotation from Jackie Robinson: "A life is not important except in the impact it has on other lives." In your own words, explain what this means.

CLOSE VIEWING: Media Literacy

3. **Examine Musical Cues** Describe the music that is used during the footage of the 1947 World Series. What kind of **mood**, or feeling, does the music create?

4. **Analyze Interviews** Andrew Young, a civil rights leader, explains why he admires Jackie Robinson. Based on the interview, what do you think Young wants today's viewers to admire about Jackie Robinson?

5. **Evaluate Footage** The documentary uses such footage as interviews, photographs, and video. Which of these features helped you understand most about the impact of "The Noble Experiment"? Explain.

4. *Andrew Young wants viewers to admire Robinson's self-control, his professionalism, and his respect for the game and for his opponents.*

5. *Interviews: These help viewers understand the impact Jackie Robinson had on others. For example, Andrew Young says that Robinson "was a pioneer" and "symbolized . . . the gentleman athlete."*
Photographs: The photo of Robinson on the cover of Time *magazine demonstrates that "his achievement impressed all Americans."*

Video: The archival film sequences help viewers gain a better understanding of the era in which Robinson played—he is the only African-American player on the field and in the dugout. His impact on the game is shown in the reactions of fans who cheer for him and swarm around him for autographs.

Write or Discuss

Analyze the Documentary The television documentary clip you've just viewed shows highlights of Jackie Robinson's life and baseball career. What new information did you learn about Jackie Robinson from the documentary? Think about

- the interviews with Rachel Robinson, Andrew Young, Branch Rickey, and Jackie Robinson himself
- the film footage that shows Jackie Robinson as a player, the Brooklyn fans, and the 1947 World Series
- the voice-over narration that provides details of key events in Robinson's life

Produce Your Own Media

Record an Interview Imagine you're creating a documentary about someone you think is an everyday hero. Make plans for an **interview.** If you don't have direct contact with a hero, create a list of jobs that you think involve heroism and courage. Then get permission to find and interview someone whose job you have listed.

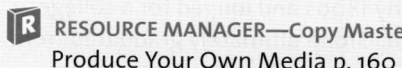

MEDIA TOOLS
For help with interviewing, visit the **Media Center** at ClassZone.com.

HERE'S HOW Use the tips and the student model to help you prepare for and carry out an interview session.

- Do some research about your interview subject. Then contact the person and arrange an interview. Arrange to have an adult accompany you for this session.
- Make a list of questions you'd like to ask. Organize those questions into a key-word outline. For example, questions about the subject's childhood and education could be listed under the key word "Background."
- During the interview, listen to the person's responses and ask follow-up questions. Refer to your key-word outline for question ideas.

STUDENT MODEL

> QUESTIONS
>
> Background
> Where did you grow up?
> Who was your hero when you were young?
>
> Earliest Success
> What was the first project you really felt successful doing?
> How did you feel about being given greater responsibility?
>
> Favorite Activities
> What do you like to do most in your spare time?
> Do you have a favorite book?

Tech Tip
If available, use an audio or video recorder to tape the interview.

Write or Discuss

Analyze the Documentary In their responses, students should address some of the techniques used in the documentary: footage (including photographs, film, interviews, and graphics), voice-over narration, musical cues, sound effects, and editing. Make sure that students understand the decisions that the editor had to make when selecting and sequencing visuals and sound for the documentary.

Produce Your Own Media

Rubric A strong interview should contain

- a well-chosen subject
- thoughtful questions
- an organized key-word outline
- insightful follow-up questions

 RESOURCE MANAGER—Copy Master
Produce Your Own Media p. 160

MediaSmart DVD

MEDIA STUDY WRAP–UP

Summarize Ask students to summarize the techniques documentary filmmakers use to present information. Have them provide specific examples of different types of footage and explain the interrelationship of visuals and sound. Ask them to explain the role of a voice-over narrator. Prompt them, if necessary, to focus on decisions an editor must make when selecting and arranging sounds and images.

RETEACH

STANDARDS LESSON FILE
Media Lesson 4: Analyzing Visuals in Film and TV
Media Lesson 5: Analyzing Sound in Film and TV
Media Lesson 6: Analyzing Editing in Film and TV

Focus and Motivate

OBJECTIVES

Literary Analysis
- explore the key idea of **change**
- identify form and characteristics of a historical drama
- read a historical drama
- use stage directions

Reading
- visualize

Vocabulary
- build vocabulary for reading and writing

Grammar and Writing
- punctuate titles correctly
- use writing to analyze literature

SUMMARY

This historical drama tells how the young Lucy Stone rebelled against the limits faced by girls in the early 1800s and longed for a college education. Stone ultimately graduated from Oberlin College and became a prominent orator and women's rights activist.

How can we CHANGE *what's wrong?*

Discuss the question and **KEY IDEA** with students. Tell them that Martin Luther King Jr. once said, "Freedom is never voluntarily given by the oppressor; it must be demanded by the oppressed." Ask students if they think it is possible to **change** the world for the better without making demands and causing trouble. Have students use this quotation as a starting point for the **DISCUSS** activity.

Selection Resources

Lucy Stone: Champion of Women's Rights
Drama by Claire Boiko

How can we CHANGE *what's wrong?*

MARYLAND OBJECTIVES

READING/LIT STANDARDS
1.E.3.a Select and apply appropriate strategies during reading
3.A.5.a Use structural features to distinguish among types of plays

KEY IDEA It's not easy to **change** what is wrong or unfair. Those people who fought to end slavery, those who helped women get the right to vote, and those who protected children from harmful working conditions were considered troublemakers by many in their day. Yet their victories made the world a better place. In this play, you'll learn about one such person.

DISCUSS List people who fought for change in order to make the world a better place. Discuss whether these people might have achieved the same results if they hadn't upset anyone.

In the Spirit of Dr. Martin Luther King, Jr.: FIGHT RACISM, POVERTY & WAR!

832

 **RESOURCE MANAGER UNIT 7**

Plan and Teach pp. 161–168

Literary Analysis
Summary pp. 169†*, 170‡*
Historical Drama pp. 171, 172†*
Question Support p. 177*

Reading
Visualize pp. 173, 174†*
Reading Check p. 176

Vocabulary
Study p. 175*

Grammar and Writing
Punctuate Titles Correctly p. 178
Assessment
Selection Tests A, B/C pp. 179*, 181*
Test Generator CD

 BEST PRACTICES TOOLKIT

Differentiated Instruction pp. 31–38*

Scaffolding Instruction pp. 43–46*
Graphic Organizers/Strategies
Word Questioning • New Word Analysis

Reading Support
Audio Anthology CD*

Technology
Literature and Vocabulary Centers at **ClassZone.com**

WriteSmart CD

---

* Resources for Differentiation   † Also in Spanish   ‡ In Haitian Creole and Vietnamese

LITERARY ANALYSIS: HISTORICAL DRAMA

Historical dramas are plays that take place in the past and are based on real events. In many of these plays, like the one you're about to read, the characters are also based on real historical figures. The dialogue and the action, however, are mostly created by the playwright. As you read *Lucy Stone: Champion of Women's Rights,* look for details and dialogue that tell you about Lucy and the time in which she lived.

READING STRATEGY: VISUALIZE

When you watch a play being performed, you can see the stage, the costumes, and the actors' movements. When you read a play, **visualizing** these elements, or forming a mental picture of them, can help you understand the setting and the action.

As you read, examine the **stage directions** carefully. These instructions to the actors, director, and reader are in parentheses and contain details that help you create mental pictures. Record the details in a chart. Then sketch the pictures you form in your mind.

Details from Stage Directions	Mental Picture
"Two Women, wearing shabby farm clothing with aprons, enter, followed by Man, wearing somber clothes of the early 1800s."	

VOCABULARY IN CONTEXT

The boldfaced words help describe the feelings of Lucy Stone and her family. To see how many of the words you know, substitute a different word or words for each term.

1. He was **aghast** at what he heard.
2. She was seen as the **agitator** in the family.
3. She was **bemused** by her friend's sudden secretiveness.
4. The grandfather was the **patriarch** of the whole clan.
5. He bowed his head **piously** to pray.
6. Don't **squander** your money on unnecessary things.
7. She didn't want to be **subservient** to anyone.
8. "No way!" Lucy cried **vehemently.** "I won't do it!"

Author Online

On Stage and Off
Claire Boiko has been performing in, producing, and writing plays since she earned a drama degree in 1946. For two years during the Korean War, she served as an entertainment and music technician for the U.S. Army. Many of the historical pageants Boiko has written were coauthored by her husband, a history teacher.

Claire Boiko
born 1925

> **MORE ABOUT THE AUTHOR**
> For more on Claire Boiko, visit the
> **Literature Center** at ClassZone.com.

Background

Fighting for Her Rights Lucy Stone was born in Massachusetts in 1818. At that time, women did not have the same rights as men. They were not allowed to vote or own property. In many places, they were not allowed to attend college. However, Stone was determined to fight for women's rights, even as a young woman. She attended Oberlin College, the first college in the United States to admit both men and women.

A Vision for Change Stone married Henry Blackwell, an antislavery activist, in 1855, but she did not take his last name. This was a radical idea for a woman at that time. In 1869, Stone helped create the American Woman Suffrage Association, which fought for women's right to vote.

833

Teach

STANDARDS FOCUS

LITERARY ANALYSIS

● HISTORICAL DRAMA

Read aloud this example:

> **Frederick Douglass.** You ask me to accept laws that keep black and white separate. But I cannot. As a slave I fought slavery; as a free man I will fight for equality for all people.

Ask students what they can learn about Douglass from this dialogue. ***Possible answer:*** *Readers learn about his historical time and about his beliefs and feelings.*

CHECK UNDERSTANDING Ask students how televised historical dramas can help viewers understand historical figures.

READING STRATEGY

◼ VISUALIZE

Read aloud this example:

> By the dim light of her oil lamp, Lucy peered into the barn and saw the lambs all piled together, sleeping peacefully.

Ask students which details help them create a mental image of this scene. ***Possible answers:*** *the dim light, the oil lamp, the pile of sleeping lambs*

CHECK UNDERSTANDING Ask students what descriptive details they would use to help a reader visualize their classroom.

 RESOURCE MANAGER—Copy Master
Visualize p. 173 (for student use while reading the selection)

VOCABULARY SKILL

▲ VOCABULARY IN CONTEXT

PRETEACH VOCABULARY To preteach vocabulary, use the Vocabulary Study copy master, which provides a teacher-directed activity. Supply these definitions as needed:

aghast (ə-găst′) *adj.* shocked; amazed
agitator (ăj′ĭ-tā′tər) *n.* someone who upsets others
bemused (bĭ-myo͞ozd′) *v.* bewildered; confused
patriarch (pā′trē-ärk′) *n.* male leader of a family group

piously (pī′əs-lē) *adv.* with religious devotion; virtuously
squander (skwŏn′dər) *v.* waste
subservient (səb-sûr′vē-ənt) *adj.* in a position of having to serve others
vehemently (vē′ə-mənt-lē) *adv.* with strong emotion

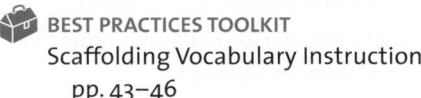 **RESOURCE MANAGER—Copy Master**
Vocabulary Study p. 175

For general guidelines on differentiating vocabulary instruction and for alternative vocabulary activities for students not needing vocabulary preteaching, see

🧰 **BEST PRACTICES TOOLKIT**
Scaffolding Vocabulary Instruction
pp. 43–46

ℹ️ Vocabulary Center at **ClassZone.com**
Additional Vocabulary Activities

ANALYZE VISUALS

About the Art Nothing is known about the girl depicted by American portraitist Eastman Johnson (1824–1906) in *The Girl I Left Behind Me*. However, because the title comes from a soldiers' marching song and because Johnson witnessed battles in the Civil War—and made this painting not long after fighting ended—it has been suggested that the young, spirited figure represents the United States after the war. The painting was apparently close to the artist's heart; though he exhibited it at major shows, he never sold it, but kept it for himself.

Activity Ask students what their impression is of the girl in the painting. What details create that impression? *Possible answer: She is smart and independent.*

- *Her expression is serious and capable.*
- *She holds books and may be wearing an academic robe.*
- *Her posture is firm, though the wind blows her hair and garments.*
- *She stands alone but looks sure and steady in her dark, cloudy surroundings.*

LITERARY ANALYSIS

● **HISTORICAL DRAMA**

Based on the introduction (*"In the early 1800s, . . ."*), how do you think 16-year-old Lucy's ideas might have been affected by the changing times? *Possible answer: Knowing that women were beginning to be educated and to ask for equality might have made Lucy want these things for herself. The changing times provided hope that the situation of women would change.*

L U C Y
STONE
CHAMPION OF WOMEN'S RIGHTS

Claire Boiko

CHARACTERS

Two Women, narrators	**Bowman,** Lucy's brother
Man, narrator	**Eliza,** Lucy's sister
Hannah Stone	**Rhoda,** Lucy's sister
Francis Stone	**Luther,** Lucy's brother
Lucy Stone, their daughter, 16	**Sarah,** Lucy's sister
Aunt Sally	**Henry Brown Blackwell**

In the early 1800s, women were considered inferior to men. Women did not enjoy the rights they have today, such as the right to vote. It was difficult for them to get an education. But times were starting to change. Women began to go to college. They also began to organize to demand more equality. This play is about Lucy Stone, a pioneer of the women's rights movement.

The Girl I Left Behind Me (1870–1875), Eastman Johnson. Smithsonian American Art Museum, Washington, D.C. Photo © Smithsonian American Art Museum, Washington, D.C./Art Resource, New York.

DIFFERENTIATED INSTRUCTION

FOR ALL STUDENTS

Enhancing Learning Styles Provide independent projects for various learning styles.

- **Visual** Draw a storyboard of the drama.
- **Verbal** Create and perform a monologue that expresses a character's thoughts.
- **Logical** Make a chart that compares the viewpoints of different characters.

For further details on these projects, see

 RESOURCE MANAGER
Ideas for Extension pp. 166–167

FOR LESS–PROFICIENT READERS

In combination with the *Audio Anthology CD*, use one or more Targeted Passages (pp. 836, 840, 841) to ensure that students focus on key events, concepts, and skills.

FOR ENGLISH LEARNERS

Key Academic Vocabulary Have students use Word Questioning to learn and practice these words found in the drama: *persist* (lines 9, 243), *legal* (line 13), *notion* (lines 94, 168), *approach* (lines 109, 170), *conclude* (line 173), *founded* (line 333), *partners* (line 342).

 BEST PRACTICES TOOLKIT—Transparency
Word Questioning p. E9

Lines 7–9
REINFORCE *KEY IDEA*: CHANGE

Discuss Can just one person **change** the world? Explain. *Possible answer: One person can make a big difference. However, the person's efforts usually need the help of other people to achieve success.*

Lines 16–26

LITERARY ANALYSIS

● HISTORICAL DRAMA

What do the Man's words (lines 16–20, 24–26) reveal about Lucy Stone's era? *Possible answer: The Man expresses the ideas of those who opposed women's rights and believed women were inferior.*

Lines 37–44

READING STRATEGY

■ VISUALIZE

Use the stage directions in lines 37–44 to visualize the characters. What details help you create a mental image? Add details and sketches to your chart. *Possible answer: Lucy runs fast and laughs as she speaks. Luther limps and whines. Aunt Sally sits in a comfortable chair, knits, and yawns.*

ANALYZE VISUALS

About the Art American painter George Inness (1825–1894) is remembered for his romantic images of landscapes in the rural northeastern United States.

Before rise:[1] Two Women, *wearing shabby farm clothing with aprons, enter, followed by* Man, *wearing somber clothes of the early 1800s.*

1st Woman. We come from the shadows of time to remind you—men and women both— of how things used to be.

2nd Woman. If the world is a better place for women now, it is because of the courage and persistence of one young girl—Lucy Stone.

10 **1st Woman.** In the early nineteenth century, when Lucy was growing up, girls weren't educated beyond the sixth grade.

2nd Woman. A husband had the legal right to beat his wife.

1st Woman. And women had *no* legal rights!

Man (*vehemently*). Education? Legal rights? For women? Never! Why, they are the inferior sex. A woman must be **subservient** to her husband in all things. 'Twas ever thus and 20 shall always be so. Subject closed!

2nd Woman. Subject closed. Until Lucy Stone.

1st Woman. Lucy Stone, champion of women's rights.

Man (*shaking head*). Lucy Stone. She's nothing but an **agitator**! A disturber of the natural order! (*They exit.*)

Time: *a summer evening, 1834.*

Setting: *the parlor of the Stone farmhouse, West Brookfield, Massachusetts. A settle*[2] 30 *stands in front of large fireplace, up center. Behind settle is a metal oil can. A table with oil lamp and three chairs stand left, before curtained window. An easy chair stands up right, beside which is a knitting basket. Against wall right is a small settle. Exit down right leads outside, exit down left leads to rest of house.*

Detail of *Old Homestead* (about 1877), George Inness. Oil on canvas. The Haggin Museum, Stockton, California (1943.56.10).

At rise:[3] Aunt Sally *is seated in easy chair knitting. After a moment she yawns, rubs her eyes, and puts down her knitting.* Lucy, *a bright,* 40 *lively, 16-year-old girl, runs in right, followed by her older brother* Luther, *who limps.* Lucy *stops center, turns to* Luther.

Lucy (*laughing*). Slowpoke. I beat you again.

Luther (*whining*). It's not fair, Lucy. I stubbed my toe.

Lucy. You always have an excuse, Luther. Why don't you admit I'm a faster runner?

Luther. Because it's not right for a girl to run faster than a boy. You're a freak, Lucy Stone.

50 **Lucy** (*shrugging*). I'd rather be a freak than a bad loser.

Aunt Sally. Here now, you two. Stop your quarreling.

Luther (*complaining*). I'm going to soak my poor sore toe. It's all swollen. I'll never race with you again, Lucy.

① Targeted Passage

1. **before rise:** before the curtain rises.
2. **settle:** a long wooden bench with a high back.
3. **at rise:** as the curtain rises.

DIFFERENTIATED INSTRUCTION

FOR LESS–PROFICIENT READERS

① Targeted Passage [Lines 10–41]

This passage introduces the historical context for the drama, its setting, and the main character, Lucy.

- How much education did girls receive in Lucy's time? What rights did women have?
- Where and in what year does the audience first meet Lucy?
- How old is Lucy? What is she doing as she comes onstage?

Comprehension Support To help students visualize the action, sketch a diagram of the stage on the board and explain that stage directions are given from the position of an actor who is onstage and facing the audience. "Left" means the actor's left; therefore, the chairs that "stand left" (line 32) are on the audience's right, and when Lucy "runs in right" (line 40) she appears to the audience's left. Help students visualize *up center* (line 30), *up right* (line 33), *down right* (line 35), *down left* (line 36).

BACK OF THE STAGE		
up right	up center	up left
right	center	left
down right	down center	down left

AUDIENCE

Lucy (*laughing*). Well, don't, then. Go race with the other slowpokes—the *boys*. (Luther *scowls and limps off left.*)

50 **Aunt Sally** (*shaking her head*). Lucy, Lucy. What's to become of you? Look at you, all tousled like a dog caught in the brambles.

Lucy (*tossing her head*). I like being tousled, Aunt Sally. It makes me feel alive—not like a wax dummy of a girl in a frilly dress.

Aunt Sally. I've been meaning to speak to you. You're sixteen years old, no longer a child. Young men'll be looking you over soon, for marriage.

70 **Lucy** (*defiantly*). Looking me over? You mean like a prize cow? (*opens her mouth wide*) Checking to see if my teeth are good, and if I'm strong enough to work the fields?

Aunt Sally (*briskly*). Don't be pert[4] with me, young lady. You've got to start thinking about marriage. It's the only way for a woman.

Lucy (*sharply*). Well, it's not the way for *this* woman. I've seen the mean way men treat their wives around here. They work them until they're ready to drop, and then complain that 80 they aren't young and pretty anymore. Why, if a man did that to his hired hand, he'd be brought up on charges.

Aunt Sally (*sighing*). That's the way of the world. You can't change it.

Lucy. I can change it for me. (*tossing her head*) I just won't marry.

Aunt Sally (*firmly*). Oh, yes, you will. You don't want to end up an old maid, like me. A left-over person of no use to anyone. (Lucy *runs to her.*)

90 **Lucy** (*hugging her*). Aunt Sally, don't say that! You're not a left-over person. Why, I don't know what we'd do without you. You have character!

Aunt Sally (<u>*bemused*</u>). Where do you get your notions, child? I declare there's not another like

---

4. **pert:** too bold in speech or action.

---

you in the state of Massachusetts. All that fire and spunk is wasted on a girl. What a pity you weren't a boy!

Lucy (*defiantly*). I like being a girl. I wouldn't be a boy for all the tea in China.

100 **Aunt Sally** (*sighing*). Be that as it may— (*She rises, crosses to window, and peers out.*) The sun's going down. You'd best fill the lamp. Your father wants everyone gathered here at sundown. He has something to tell us. (*shivering*) It's a bit cold. I'll get my shawl. (*She exits left.* Lucy *takes metal oil can from behind settle, fills the lamp on table, and lights it.* Bowman *enters left, carrying a Bible. He approaches* Lucy *hesitantly.*)

110 **Bowman.** Lucy?

Lucy (*looking up*). Yes, Bowman? (*spying Bible*) Ah—you want a little help with your Bible lesson again?

Bowman. I'd be obliged, Lucy. I'm to read the lesson this Sunday and I don't want to make a fool of myself. You're the only one in the family who can help me. Pa's too busy, and Ma doesn't know much.

Lucy (*hotly*). Ma knows a good deal, Bowman, 120 even if it's not from books. If you had to work from sunup to sundown and raise children to boot, you wouldn't have much time for book learning either.

Bowman (*taken aback*). I suppose not. I never thought about it. (*opens Bible and indicates place*) I've tried to read these words, but I stumble on them.

Lucy (*reading clearly*). "Then came the daughters of Zelophehad, the son of Hepher, 130 the son of Gilead, the son of Machir, the son of Manasseh, of the families of Manasseh the son

---

LUCY STONE: CHAMPION OF WOMEN'S RIGHTS **837**

FOR ENGLISH LEARNERS

Vocabulary Support Use New Word Analysis to teach these expressions:

- *the way of the world* (lines 83–84), "reality"
- *old maid* (line 88), "unmarried woman"
- *[not] for all the tea in China* (lines 98–99), "nothing could persuade me"
- *a good deal* (line 119), "a lot"
- *to boot* (lines 121–122), "in addition"

 **BEST PRACTICES TOOLKIT—Transparency** New Word Analysis p. E8

FOR ADVANCED LEARNERS/PRE–AP

Analyze Similes Have students consider the similes in lines 62, 64–65, and 70 and reflect on what the similes used by the characters reveal about their setting. Challenge students to express the same ideas in original language that reflects a modern setting.

Character's simile	My simile
You mean like a prize cow? (lines 69–70)	You mean like a sports car?

Lines 73–82

LITERARY ANALYSIS

● **HISTORICAL DRAMA**

What does the conversation between Aunt Sally and Lucy in lines 73–82 tell you about the choices women had at the time? *Possible answer: Women didn't have many choices. Aunt Sally says marriage is "the only way for women." Lucy says that no matter how hard a woman works for her husband, she has fewer rights than a hired hand.*

Lines 114–125
DISCUSSION PROMPTS

Use these prompts to help students understand how gender affects Lucy's family relationships:

Connect Lucy says that her mother "knows a good deal . . . even if it's not from books." What things that you consider important are not learned from books? *Students may say that many practical skills and social skills are learned from experience and from other people, rather than from books.*

Analyze Compare Lucy and Bowman's different views of their mother. How might you explain the difference? *Possible answer: Because she is a girl, Lucy has thought more about the duties and limits in women's lives. This greater awareness may help her to value her mother's abilities.*

Synthesize How does having "never thought about" a situation allow it to continue unchanged? *Possible answer: If you never think about a situation, you cannot really know how you feel about it or determine whether it should be changed. Therefore, the situation is likely to continue unchanged.*

LUCY STONE **837**

● HISTORICAL DRAMA

What details and dialogue in lines 146–167 help you imagine what people's lives were like in Lucy's time? **Possible answers:**

- *Props such as the handbell and the lamp that needs to be lit are from another era.*
- *The children are called from their work in the barn by a bell.*
- *Lucy has been taught that "a woman must submit to her husband in all things."*
- *People go to college to study Greek and Latin—and college is but a dream for a bright girl like Lucy.*

Lines 161–167

READING STRATEGY

■ VISUALIZE

How do the stage directions in lines 161–167 help you create a mental image of Lucy as she speaks? Add details and sketches to your chart. **Possible answers:**

- *When Lucy speaks "insistently," she might lean forward and speak in a voice that conveys her frustration.*
- *When she speaks "firmly," she might put her hands on her hips and use a serious tone.*
- *When she speaks "dreamily," she may have a faraway gaze that reveals her longing for education.*

If students need help . . . Have volunteers read aloud the dialogue in lines 161–167, expressing the feelings suggested by the stage directions.

Lines 184–188
REINFORCE *KEY IDEA:* CHANGE

Discuss Lucy's mother tells her that fixing the problems of the world "isn't [her] burden." Whose responsibility is it to **change** the world for the better? *Possible answer: It is everyone's responsibility. If you think of the world's problems as someone else's burden, they will never get better.*

---

of Joseph; and these are the names of his daughters: Mahlah, Noah, and Hoglah, and Milcah, and Tirzah." There. That's not so hard, is it?

Bowman (*admiringly*). You read that every bit as well as Reverend Blagdon. You'd make a mighty fine preacher—if only you were a boy.

Lucy (*angrily*). I could do a thousand wonderful
140 things, if only I were a boy. Why shouldn't I go to school, learn a profession—even preach, if I want to? Answer me that, Bowman!

Bowman (*backing away, alarmed*). Don't take it out on me, Lucy. I didn't make the world the way it is.

(Hannah Stone *enters left, carrying a handbell.*)

Hannah. Oh, there you are, Bowman. Will you please go out to the barn and ring the bell to call the other children? Your father has something to
150 tell everyone. And Bowman—tell them to hurry. You know how your father hates to be kept waiting. (*She hands the bell to* Bowman.)

Bowman. I'll make them hustle, Ma. Don't worry. (*He exits right.*)

Hannah (*to Lucy*). Thank you for lighting the lamp, Lucy dear. (*offstage sound of bell ringing*)

Lucy (*thoughtfully*). Mama—I've been thinking . . .

Hannah (*sighing*). Oh, Lucy. I wish you wouldn't.
160 . . . Every time you think, it means trouble.

Lucy (*insistently*). But that's just it, Mama. I must think. My mind won't let me stop. Here on the farm I feel as if I'm starving. (*firmly*) Mama— is it true that a woman must submit to her husband in all things? (*pause, then dreamily*) If I could only go to college, I could study Greek and Latin and decide for myself.

Hannah (*aghast*). Oh, Lucy! What a notion. Your father would never hear of it.

170 **Lucy.** But what if I approached him in a calm, logical manner? I would say, "Father, you must be aware that I am the equal of any of the boys in this family. Do you not conclude that I am worthy of an education?" (Hannah, *shaking her head, puts her arm around* Lucy's *shoulder.*)

Hannah (*gently*). When you were first born, I looked at your sweet face, so like a flower, and I wept. Yes, I wept because you were a girl, and a woman's life is so hard. Why must you make
180 it even harder by defying the way things are?

Lucy. Because all around me I see bright women with fine minds reduced to a kind of slavery. (*fiercely*) It isn't right, Mama! It just isn't fair!

Hannah (*reasoning with her*). But my dear child, it isn't your burden. It isn't up to you to turn the world upside down.

Lucy (*strongly*). But somebody must. Why shouldn't I be the one? (Bowman *enters, followed by* Eliza, Rhoda, Luther, *and* Sarah.
190 *They ad lib boisterously.*)[5]

Bowman. Here they are, Ma. (*smiling*) They were frisky as spring lambs, but I brought them into the fold. (*The girls and* Lucy *sit on settle right; the boys sit on chairs at table left.* Hannah *sits on settle upstage.* Aunt Sally *enters, adjusting her shawl.*)

Aunt Sally (*anxiously*). Am I late?

Hannah. Not at all, Sally.

Eliza. What do you reckon Papa wants to tell us?

Luther (*sourly*). He's probably got a complaint
200 about how we did the haying.

Rhoda (*teasingly*). Well, Luther, you did lean on your pitchfork more than usual.

Bowman. Seemed to me, Papa was almost happy when I saw him in the field. He nearly smiled at me.

---

5. **ad lib boisterously:** make up dialogue on the spot, in a loud manner.

DIFFERENTIATED INSTRUCTION

FOR ENGLISH LEARNERS

Vocabulary: Suffixes Remind students that the suffix *-ful* means "full of." A word that ends in *-ful*, such as *wonderful* (line 139), is an adjective. When the suffix *-ful* is combined with the suffix *-ly*, as in *thoughtfully* (line 157), the resulting word is an adverb. Have students analyze the word parts in *scornfully* (line 297) and *beautiful* (line 341) and ask them to explain how they can identify the part of speech each word represents.

Language: Conversational English Patterns Explain to students that in conversational English it is common to start a sentence with a conjunction in order to emphasize the words that follow. Lucy tries to add emphasis when she argues with her mother by beginning her sentences with *But* (lines 161, 170, and 187) and *Because* (line 181). Read aloud these sentences to convey the emphasis and have students scan the drama for other uses of this pattern in conversational English.

Detail of *A Musical Evening* (19th century), Thomas Webster. Oil on canvas, 50.5 cm × 60.5 cm. Private collection. © Phillips, The International Fine Art Auctioneers/Bridgeman Art Library.

Sarah (*in mock surprise*). Pa nearly smiled? Sakes alive. The world is coming to an end! (*All laugh uproariously.*)

Hannah. Hush, children. (*looks off left*) Here
210 comes your father, now. (*Laughter stops abruptly. Children rise, as Francis Stone, a stern* **patriarch**, *enters left, crosses to stand in front of the upstage settle. Girls curtsey, boys bow and are seated.*)

Francis (*clearing his throat*). I'm a man of few words, and I'll not make a book of the matter at hand. This concerns Bowman and Luther— and the rest of you as well.

Bowman and Luther (*exchanging worried*
220 *looks*). Us?

Francis. It seems that Bowman and Luther have high ambitions. They want to go to college. (*All buzz with excitement. Francis holds up his hand for silence.*) I have taken the matter under consideration. (*pauses*) They may go, even though it means you girls will have to double up on the work. I expect we can do without the boys while they get their education.

(*Girls groan. Francis* looks at them sharply.)

230 **Bowman** (*excitedly*). Thank you, Papa, thank you.

Luther (*happily*). That is mighty good news, Papa. Will you pay for the books, too?

Francis. I reckon so. It's worth the expense to have educated men in the family.

Aunt Sally (*aside*). Humph. Educated "men," is it?

Lucy (*rising*). Papa! (Hannah *tries to hush her.*)

Francis (*impatiently*). Not now, Lucy. Whatever
240 it is can wait. It's time for you to do the evening chores, now.

Lucy (*persistently*). But, Papa—(Francis *waves her aside.*)

Hannah (*nervously*). Come along, children. There are things for us to do. Lucy, dear. Do come with me. (Lucy *shakes her head. All exit left, except* Lucy, *who faces her father with determination.*)

Francis (*sternly*). Well, Lucy? What is it?

ANALYZE VISUALS

About the Art The English painter Thomas Webster (1800–1886) was renowned for his images of everyday life. Before the 1800s, most paintings had been portraits of wealthy aristocrats or heroic scenes from history.

Activity Ask students to imagine that this painting shows a scene from a performance of *Lucy Stone*. Would they change anything about the costumes, props, set, or position of the actors? Why? *Students might suggest*

- *giving the older woman at left knitting to do, like Aunt Sally*

- *moving the father to the center and the mother to the side, to reflect their relative importance*

- *adding a handbell and an oil lamp, because they are mentioned in the stage directions*

- *grouping the characters by sex, as mentioned in the stage directions*

Lines 210–214

READING STRATEGY

■ **VISUALIZE**

Use the stage directions in lines 210–214 to visualize how the family behaves when Francis Stone enters the room. What does your mental image suggest about his importance in the family? *Possible answer: Francis Stone is the most important person in the family. When he enters the room, people stop laughing and stand up; the boys bow and the girls curtsey before being seated again.*

Lines 221–235

LITERARY ANALYSIS

● **HISTORICAL DRAMA**

What elements in lines 221–235 are likely to be based on historical fact? What elements might be creations of the playwright? *Possible answers:*

- *It is historical fact that people once believed it was important to "have educated men in the family" and that girls should work to make that happen.*

- *The dialogue and the action would have been made up by the playwright.*

FOR LESS–PROFICIENT READERS

Reading Strategy Follow-Up: Visualize Have students use the stage directions in lines 210–214 to create a mental picture of Francis entering the room. Then record the details and sketch a picture in the chart introduced on page 833.

FOR ADVANCED LEARNERS/PRE–AP

Analyze Dialogue Draw students' attention to Aunt Sally's "aside" in lines 236–237. Although Aunt Sally had tried to convince Lucy to be obedient and accept her limits as a girl, this line suggests that she may also be dissatisfied with how things are. Have students quickwrite a monologue of Aunt Sally's private thoughts as she observes this scene.

Lines 280–300
DISCUSSION PROMPTS

Use these prompts to help students explore Lucy's conflict with her father:

Connect If you were Lucy, what would you say to argue your case about going to college? *Students may say that she (Lucy) should have the same rights in the family as the brothers, and that she would make good use of an education.*

Analyze Francis says that if he educated his daughter, he'd "be a laughingstock." What does this reveal about him? *Possible answer: Francis is concerned that other people would think him wasteful and foolish if he sent his daughter to college. He is, however, eventually persuaded by Lucy.*

Evaluate How does the playwright show Lucy's intelligence? *Possible answer: In this scene, Lucy shows her ability to think and reason. Because she knows that her father does not want to spend money on her education, she convinces him that he won't have to spend money—just lend it to her.*

Lines 283–285
READING STRATEGY

■ VISUALIZE

Read the stage directions in lines 283–285 and then try to picture Lucy's movements. What do they suggest about how she feels? *Possible answer: Lucy is frustrated— she "buries her face in her hands"—but her mind is made up. She tries to give herself courage by drawing "a deep breath" and then speaks calmly and firmly.*

Lines 301–308
LITERARY ANALYSIS

● HISTORICAL DRAMA

What words and phrases make Francis Stone's dialogue sound right for the historical setting? *Possible answer: Old-fashioned words and phrases include*

- *"pestiferous" (line 302)*
- *"get you from this house" (line 304)*
- *"fripperies" (line 307)*
- *"draw up the note" (line 308)*

---

250 **Lucy.** Papa, I will do the evening chores. But the matter I wish to discuss cannot wait.

Francis (*annoyed*). I declare, girl, you are like a burr under my hide. Very well, speak up.

Lucy (*taking a deep breath*). Papa, you hate waste, don't you?

Francis (*__piously__*). Waste not, want not. That is what I always say.

Lucy. Well, if there were someone in this family brighter by far than Bowman and
260 Luther, wouldn't it be a waste for that person not to go to college?

Francis (*briskly*). Yes, but there is no such person. What is your point?

Lucy (*firmly*). But there *is* such a person . . . Me!

Francis (*astonished*). You?

Lucy. If you'd paid attention, Papa, you'd know that I learn faster, read better, and think more clearly than the boys. (*pleading*) Oh, Papa. I want to go to college so much. There's a col-
270 lege in Ohio, called Oberlin, that will admit women. Please, Papa, please let me go there!

Francis (*furiously*). Are you daft?[6] You want me to **squander** my money on a girl? Why, the minute you get yourself a husband—if ever a flibbertigibbet[7] like you could get one—you'll turn your back on your so-called education and where will I be? Shortchanged by a mere female.

Lucy (*firmly*). No, Papa. I would never do such a thing.

280 **Francis** (*angrily*). I will not spend a penny to educate a girl. It's unnatural. I'd be a laughingstock. Go now—do your chores. (*He starts to exit down left.* Lucy *buries her face in her hands, then takes a deep breath*

and speaks with calm determination.)

Lucy. Papa—I have a proposition for you.

Francis (*turning back*). Have you, now? And what sort of proposition could *you* possibly have?

290 **Lucy.** Don't the banks lend money upon a note for security? If I were to give *you* a note stating that I would pay you back every penny for my education, would you lend me the money?

Francis (*in disbelief*). Lend you money? And how, pray tell, would you ever pay me back?

Lucy. I could teach the lower grades.

Francis (*scornfully*). At a dollar a week, it would take you years to repay me.

Lucy (*defiantly*). If it takes me till I'm ninety—
300 so be it. I will repay you every cent.

Francis (*impatiently*). You are the most pestiferous[8] girl ever born. You never let a man be. It would be worth my while to give you a loan just to get you from this house. (*thinks for a moment.*) Very well. You'll get your tuition and not a penny more. Nothing for books, nor for food, nor for any of your female fripperies.[9] I'll draw up the note in the morning.

Lucy (*with deliberate irony*). Thank you, Papa.
310 It is more than generous of you.

Francis. Go do your chores. And blow out the lamp. I'll not have oil wasted in this house (*He stalks off left.*)

Lucy (*crossing to table, aside*). I'll teach every minute the sun shines. I'll rise at five and gather nuts and berries to sell for my books. I'll work till midnight sewing and mending. I'll work and study until my eyes grow dim. (*drawing lamp close*) I'll snuff this flame,

---

6. **daft:** crazy.
7. **flibbertigibbet** (flĭb′ər-tē-jĭb′ĭt): a silly, scatterbrained person.
8. **pestiferous** (pĕ-stĭf′ər-əs): troublesome.
9. **fripperies** (frĭp′ə-rēz): showy clothes.

DIFFERENTIATED INSTRUCTION

FOR LESS–PROFICIENT READERS
② Targeted Passage [Lines 280–306]

This passage presents the climax of the drama: Lucy confronts her father about his lack of support for her education and gains his permission to enter college.

- Why doesn't Francis want to pay for Lucy's education?
- How does Lucy convince her father to give her the money for tuition?
- How does Lucy plan to pay back the loan?

FOR ADVANCED LEARNERS/PRE–AP

Visualize Drama Have pairs of students write additional stage directions for the scene between Lucy and Francis (lines 252–313) that tell where they move as they speak. Lucy might follow Francis as she pleads; he might advance upon her in anger; or they might turn their backs in frustration or thought. Have students use terms such as *stage left, up left,* and *down left* in their stage directions, and invite them to perform the scene for the class.

320 Papa. But inside my mind there is a flame glowing more radiant by the hour. And that flame, Papa, I promise you, will *never* go out! (*She blows out lamp, and as stage darkens, spotlight shines on* Lucy, *who faces audience with a triumphant smile. Two Women enter.*)

1st Woman. Lucy Stone kept her promise and more. She graduated from Oberlin College and was the first woman in the state of Massachusetts to earn a college degree.

330 **2nd Woman.** She sounded a trumpet call for the women's rights movement, lecturing to all who would hear her.

1st Woman. She founded her own paper, the *Woman's Journal,* in Boston, and called for the First National Woman's Rights Convention in 1850. (*Henry Brown Blackwell enters, bows.*)

Henry. And she was the first married woman to keep her own name. Oh, yes. Despite Aunt Sally's fears, Lucy was married. For there were 340 men in those days who appreciated such a rare and beautiful spirit, men who wanted their wives to be equal partners in every way. I know, because I am the man who married Lucy Stone—Henry Brown Blackwell. (*He crosses to* Lucy *and takes her arm. Two Women cross to stand beside* Lucy *and* Henry. *Other female cast members enter and join them.*)

1st Woman. And now, because of Lucy Stone and others inspired by her example, the 350 Nineteenth Amendment to the Constitution of the United States of America, passed by Congress in 1919, declares . . .

All (*together*). "The rights of citizens of the United States to vote shall not be denied or abridged by the United States or by any state on account of sex."

2nd Woman. And the words of Thomas Jefferson in the Declaration of Independence now include the other half of the human race.

360 **All** (*together*). "We hold these truths to be self-evident . . .

Henry. That all men—

All Women. And women—

All. Are created equal, that they are endowed by their Creator with certain unalienable rights;[10] that among these are life, liberty—

Lucy (*proudly*). And the pursuit of happiness!" (*curtain*)

(3) Targeted Passage

Lucy Stone, about 1875

---

10. **endowed . . . rights:** given, by God, certain rights that cannot be taken away.

FOR LESS–PROFICIENT READERS

(3) Targeted Passage [Lines 327–356]

This passage shows the resolution of the drama: the narrators tell how Lucy became a voice for women's rights and how the U.S. Constitution was amended to give women the right to vote.

- How was Lucy Stone a "first" in history?
- What were some of Lucy's accomplishments?

- What constitutional amendment was passed in 1919? What right did it extend to women?

Reading Strategy Follow-Up: Visualize Have students use the stage directions in lines 345–347 to visualize Lucy, Henry, the Women, and other female cast members. Ask them to imagine the postures of the people and the expressions on their faces. Then have them record the details and sketch a picture in the chart introduced on page 833.

Lines 337–344

LITERARY ANALYSIS

● HISTORICAL DRAMA

How does this passage (lines 337–344) combine historical fact with drama created by the playwright? *Possible answer: You can assume it is true that Lucy married Henry and kept her name. However, Henry's words are the invention of the playwright.*

Lines 345–360

READING STRATEGY

■ VISUALIZE

Based on the stage directions in lines 345–360, try to visualize the group. How does this image help to show how Lucy's ideas were accepted over time? *Possible answer: Over time, more and more people came to agree with Lucy's belief that women should have the same rights as men. Seeing the cast gather and speak together helps to represent this idea.*

ANALYZE VISUALS

Activity Look at the photograph of Lucy Stone. How would you describe her? *Possible answer: She looks smart and determined.*

SELECTION WRAP–UP

REFLECT Ask students how well they think Lucy Stone handled the conflicts she had with her family.

★ CRITIQUE Ask students to evaluate the effectiveness of the unison readings on the last page. How would the scene feel different if just one character spoke the lines?

Practice and Apply

After Reading

For additional support of post-reading questions, use these copy masters:

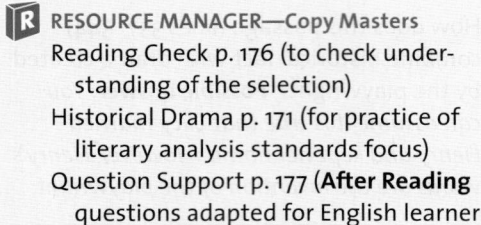

RESOURCE MANAGER—Copy Masters

Reading Check p. 176 (to check understanding of the selection)

Historical Drama p. 171 (for practice of literary analysis standards focus)

Question Support p. 177 (**After Reading** questions adapted for English learners and less-proficient readers)

Additional selection questions are provided for teachers on page 165.

ANSWERS

Comprehension

1. *Lucy says she will never marry because she sees the men around her treat their wives terribly.*

2. *Lucy promises to pay her father back if he lends her enough money to go to college.*

3. *Lucy lectured about women's rights, founded a newspaper (the* Woman's Journal*), organized the first national women's rights convention, and helped women win the right to vote.*

Literary Analysis

Possible answers:

4. ■ **STANDARDS FOCUS** *Visualize Students may say that they visualized characters more clearly, based on what the stage directions said about how they moved and spoke. Words and phrases will vary.*

5. *Lucy means that women had no legal rights of their own. They had to do as their husbands said, and many faced lives of never-ending work.*

6. *Aunt Sally—thinks Lucy is reckless but admires her spirit;* **Mother**—*pities Lucy and wishes she would behave;* **Father**—*thinks Lucy is foolish and pesky*

7. ● **STANDARDS FOCUS** *Historical Drama Fact—Lucy graduated from Oberlin College;* **Fiction**—*the argument Lucy and Luther had about running*

8. *Mother and Aunt Sally seem resigned and agree that it is better to be a boy. Lucy prefers being a girl and takes negative ideas*

Comprehension

1. **Clarify** Why does Lucy say that she will never marry?

2. **Recall** What deal does Lucy make with her father?

3. **Summarize** What did Lucy go on to do after she finished college? In your own words, summarize her accomplishments.

Literary Analysis

4. **Visualize** Look over the sketches you made as you read. Which were you able to visualize more clearly, the play's characters or its setting? Which words and phrases helped you to form such a vivid mental picture?

5. **Draw Conclusions** Reread lines 181–183. In light of how women were treated in the early 1800s, what does Lucy mean when she says that women were "reduced to a kind of slavery"?

6. **Compare Characters** How does each member of Lucy's family respond to her? Create a spider map like the one shown to explore how each character reacts to Lucy's confidence, strength, and intelligence.

7. **Analyze Historical Drama** Historical drama is usually a mix of fact and fiction. Facts can be confirmed by a reliable source, such as an encyclopedia. Find one example of factual information in the play and one example of a conversation or situation that was probably created by the playwright.

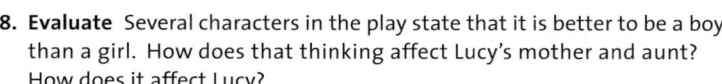

Aunt Sally

• Bowman depends on her.
• Luther feels jealous of her.

Siblings

Lucy Stone

Father

Mother

8. **Evaluate** Several characters in the play state that it is better to be a boy than a girl. How does that thinking affect Lucy's mother and aunt? How does it affect Lucy?

Extension and Challenge

9. **Creative Project: Drama** Lucy discusses the role of girls and women with various people in this play. Work with a partner to choose one of these conversations and act it out for the class.

10. **SOCIAL STUDIES CONNECTION** Lucy Stone founded the American Woman Suffrage Association (AWSA). Research AWSA's history. What **change** was it fighting for? Did it succeed? Share your findings with the class.

RESEARCH LINKS
For more on AWSA, visit the **Research Center** at ClassZone.com.

---

about girls as a challenge; she wants to do things boys can do.

Extension and Challenge

9. *Possibilities for scenes would include Lucy's conversations with Aunt Sally (lines 60–99), Bowman (lines 110–145), Hannah (lines 157–188), and Francis (lines 250–313). Students should use movements, facial expressions, and tone of voice to help convey the thoughts and feelings suggested by the dialogue.*

10. **SOCIAL STUDIES CONNECTION**
Students' reports should use facts and other evidence to clearly state AWSA's goals and achievements. When reporting findings to the class, students should explain the cause-and-effect relationship between AWSA's work and women gaining the right to vote in the United States, as well as how long the suffrage movement worked toward that goal.

Reading-Writing Connection

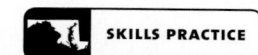

Demonstrate your understanding of *Lucy Stone: Champion of Women's Rights* by responding to these prompts. Then complete the **Grammar and Writing** exercise.

WRITING PROMPTS	SELF-CHECK

A. Short Response: Analyze Issues
If Lucy Stone were alive today, which national or world issues might concern her? In **one paragraph,** describe one or two current problems Stone might work to **change.**

▶

An effective analysis will . . .
- identify a problem Stone might fight to solve
- use examples from the play to explain why the issues would bother Stone

B. Extended Response: Write a Letter
Write a **two- or three-paragraph letter** to Lucy Stone, updating her on the progress the women's rights movement has made. Make sure to clearly describe how things are different for American women today.

▶

A strong letter will . . .
- address Stone directly and clearly explain your purpose
- tell the rights women have and give details of what has changed

GRAMMAR AND WRITING

PUNCTUATE TITLES CORRECTLY The punctuation you use in titles shows what kind of work you are writing about. Use **quotation marks** to set off the titles of shorter works, such as short stories, tall tales, essays, articles, and poems. Use **italics** (or underlining) for titles of longer works, such as books, plays, magazines, newspapers, movies, and TV series.

> Original: The poem Jabberwocky is my favorite.
>
> Revised: The poem "Jabberwocky" is my favorite.

MARYLAND OBJECTIVES

LANGUAGE STANDARD
5.C.2.c Use the mechanics of writing correctly

PRACTICE Correctly punctuate the titles in the following sentences.

1. Little Women is an example of a book with strong women characters.
2. Mary Pope Osborne's tall tale Sally Ann Thunder Ann Whirlwind also features a strong woman.
3. Newspapers, such as the Chicago Tribune, often devote whole sections to news about women.
4. Oprah Winfrey, who hosts The Oprah Winfrey Show, is one of the wealthiest entertainers in the world.

*For more help with punctuating titles, see page R50 in the **Grammar Handbook.***

DIFFERENTIATED INSTRUCTION

FOR LESS–PROFICIENT WRITERS

For Prompt A:

1. Ask students to recall an issue that concerned Stone and find an example in the play that shows why it bothered her.
2. Help students identify a similarity between this issue and a modern one.
3. Have them summarize what bothered Stone in her day, citing evidence, and use this summary to explain why she might also be troubled by the contemporary issue.

For Prompt B:

Help students write a thesis statement on the progress of the movement and identify three examples. Have them begin the letter by clearly stating the relationship between the movement and the progress made, then give examples, and then offer a conclusion.

Reading-Writing Connection

WRITING PROMPTS

- For **Prompt A,** have students focus on finding examples in the play that reveal what kind of issues concerned Stone. Ask them how these issues might be reflected in a national or world concern today.

- For **Prompt B,** have students make a list of changes that have occurred in American women's lives in the last century. Encourage them to explain the significance of these changes and how the changes show that progress has been made.

For ideas for writing, see

Writing Center at **ClassZone.com**

GRAMMAR AND WRITING

Write these sentences on the board. Ask students to punctuate the titles correctly.

> The book Caddie Woodlawn tells about a strong-willed pioneer girl. *(Caddie Woodlawn)*
>
> Chicago is my favorite poem. *("Chicago")*

Answers:

1. *Little Women*
2. "*Sally Ann Thunder Ann Whirlwind*"
3. *Chicago Tribune*
4. *The Oprah Winfrey Show*

RESOURCE MANAGER—Copy Master
Punctuate Titles Correctly p. 178

Assess and Reteach

Assess

RESOURCE MANAGER—Copy Masters
Selection Tests A, B/C pp. 179–180, 181–182

Test Generator CD

Reteach

STANDARDS LESSON FILE
Literature Lesson 24: Elements of Drama

OBJECTIVES

Literary Analysis
- explore the key idea of **perseverance**
- identify and analyze speaker
- read poetry

Reading
- paraphrase figurative language

SUMMARY

"My Mother Enters the Work Force" and "Washington Monument by Night" are poems that commemorate perseverance. In "My Mother," the speaker tells how a woman paid her own way through business school by working as a seamstress. In "Washington Monument," the speaker muses about the dedication of soldiers who fought during the eight years of the American Revolution.

Why should you keep T R Y I N G ?

Discuss the question. Ask students what would happen if they never used **perseverance** to follow their dreams. What might happen if they did try? Ask them to think of a person they know who worked hard to achieve something that was important to him or her. What did this person learn from the experience? Where did the person's efforts lead? Have students use this discussion as a starting point for the **WEB IT** activity.

My Mother Enters the Work Force
Poem by Rita Dove

Washington Monument by Night
Poem by Carl Sandburg

Why should you keep TRYING?

LITERATURE STANDARDS
3.A.4.b Analyze language
3.A.7.c Analyze figurative language

KEY IDEA Heroes are not necessarily people who are perfect or who never fail. Often they are the people who keep trying until they are successful. This quality is called **perseverance,** and the people in the poems you're about to read share it. Their successes can show us the value of trying over and over again.

WEB IT Create an **idea web** that shows some people you consider heroes. Expand the web by adding the challenges they have faced and the successes they have achieved.

My Heroes — sister — She has dyslexia. — She graduated from college.

844

Selection Resources

RESOURCE MANAGER UNIT 7

Plan and Teach pp. 183–190

Literary Analysis
Speaker pp. 191, 192†*
Question Support p. 195*

Reading
Understand Figurative Language
pp. 193, 194†*
Reading Fluency p. 196

Assessment
Selection Tests A, B/C pp. 197*, 199*
 Test Generator CD

BEST PRACTICES TOOLKIT

Differentiated Instruction
pp. 31–38*

Graphic Organizers/Strategies
Jigsaw • Sequence Circle •
Read Aloud/Think Aloud •
Think-Pair-Share

Reading Support
⌀ Audio Anthology CD*

Technology
ⓘ Literature Center at
ClassZone.com

⌀ WriteSmart CD

* Resources for Differentiation   † Also in Spanish

LITERARY ANALYSIS: SPEAKER

The **speaker** of a poem is the voice who "talks" to the reader through the poem's words. The speaker and the poet aren't necessarily the same person.

You might think of the speaker as a character in a very short play. The speaker walks onto a dark stage, says his or her lines (the poem), and exits. There are no props, scenery, or lighting. The speaker's words provide everything you need to know about the feelings, ideas, and experiences he or she is sharing. As you read "My Mother Enters the Work Force" and "Washington Monument by Night," watch for clues that tell you who the speaker is and what he or she thinks of the subject of the poem.

READING STRATEGY: UNDERSTAND FIGURATIVE LANGUAGE

Poems often use **figurative language,** or words that mean something other than their "real" meaning. For example, in "Washington Monument by Night," Sandburg describes the monument this way:

A lean swimmer dives into night sky,

Sandburg does not really mean a person is leaping into the sky. Instead, he's using words in an imaginative way. The words create a dramatic effect and emphasize how the monument soars above everything else.

If you restate figurative language in your own words, or **paraphrase** it, you can often better understand a poem's main ideas. As you read each poem, keep a chart of the figurative language in the poem and your paraphrases.

Figurative Language	Paraphrase
Lines 1–3: "The path to ABC Business School / was paid for by a lucky sign: / ALTERATIONS, QUALIFIED SEAMSTRESS INQUIRE WITHIN."	The mother just happened to see a sign for a job that gave her money to go to business school.

Author Online

Rita Dove: People's Poet Rita Dove served as poet laureate, or the representative poet, of the United States from 1993 to 1995. Her poems reflect experiences of the many whose stories haven't always been heard.

Rita Dove
born 1952

Carl Sandburg: People's Voice Carl Sandburg, recognized as a poet to use the language of the people, honored both the great heroes of U.S. history and the everyday heroes who make the country work.

Carl Sandburg
1878–1967

 MORE ABOUT THE AUTHOR For more on these poets, visit the **Literature Center at ClassZone.com.**

Background

An Eight-Year Conflict One of the poems you are about to read refers to the Revolutionary War, which lasted from 1775 to 1783. A low point for the American troops occurred during the winter of 1777 and 1778. Led by General George Washington, the ragtag soldiers camped out at Valley Forge, Pennsylvania. They had little food or warm clothing, and disease was widespread.

845

Teach

STANDARDS FOCUS

LITERARY ANALYSIS

● SPEAKER

Read aloud this example:

The old tree sighed softly under foot,

whispering secrets long forgotten.

Beneath its canopy, I found my perch,

my friend, my shoulder to lean on.

Ask students who is the speaker of the poem. ***Possible answer:*** *The speaker is most likely a boy or girl who climbs a tree.*

CHECK UNDERSTANDING Ask how a poem's speaker is like the narrator of a story.

READING STRATEGY

■ UNDERSTAND FIGURATIVE LANGUAGE

Write this example on the board:

Nine days they walked across the prairie

While the ocean of grasses rose and fell,

Churned by the summer wind.

Ask students to paraphrase the example. ***Possible answer:*** *As some people walk across a prairie, wind moves the grass in a way that looks like waves on an ocean.*

CHECK UNDERSTANDING Ask students how they go about rephrasing a challenging passage in their own words.

 RESOURCE MANAGER—Copy Master Understand Figurative Language p. 193 (for student use while reading the poems)

DIFFERENTIATED INSTRUCTION

FOR ALL STUDENTS

For general guidelines on differentiating instruction, see

 BEST PRACTICES TOOLKIT Differentiated Instruction pp. 31–38

FOR LESS–PROFICIENT READERS

Comprehension Support Divide students into mixed-ability Jigsaw groups. Have them read stanzas of the poems. Ask them to discuss the parts that they have trouble understanding and share ideas about what each poem is saying. After they read aloud to the class, encourage students to ask questions that help clarify their understanding of the poems and the figurative language.

BEST PRACTICES TOOLKIT Jigsaw p. A1

FOR ENGLISH LEARNERS

Options for Reading Have students read along with the *Audio Anthology CD,* listening for pauses and emphases. Then have pairs of students take turns reading the poems aloud to each other.

FOR ADVANCED LEARNERS/PRE–AP

Pre-AP exercises in the bottom channel provide additional challenge for your advanced students. Use them for small groups or individuals.

Lines 12–19
REINFORCE *KEY IDEA:*
PERSEVERANCE

Discuss How do the words *path* (line 12) and *journey* (line 19) help the speaker convey the mother's **perseverance?** *Possible answer: Traveling on a path or making a journey requires time and commitment.*

LITERARY ANALYSIS

Ⓐ SPEAKER

Possible answer: The speaker is the daughter or son of the mother in the poem.

READING STRATEGY

Ⓑ UNDERSTAND FIGURATIVE LANGUAGE

Possible answer: The mother spends her evenings sewing at home on taffeta and velvet. The sewing machine makes a repetitive sound that sounds like "and now and now."

ANALYZE VISUALS

Possible answer: Like the mother, the woman in the painting looks skillful, thoughtful, knowledgeable, intelligent, and determined.

About the Art *Alma Sewing* is by American painter Francis Criss (1901–1973). Criss combined realistic details with unusual visual elements that give his work a modern feel: moody shadows, striking blocks of color, and bold, almost abstract forms. Criss's housekeeper is said to have been the model for this portrait. Look closely to see a self-portrait of the artist in the reflection on the lamp.

MY MOTHER **ENTERS** THE
WORK FORCE

RITA DOVE

The path to ABC Business School
was paid for by a lucky sign:
ALTERATIONS, QUALIFIED SEAMSTRESS INQUIRE WITHIN.
Tested on sleeves, hers
5 never puckered—puffed or sleek,
leg-o'-mutton or raglan—[1]
they barely needed the damp cloth
to steam them perfect. Ⓐ

Those were the afternoons. Evenings
10 she took in piecework,[2] the treadle machine
with its locomotive whir
traveling the lit path of the needle
through quicksand taffeta
or velvet deep as a forest.
15 *And now and now* sang the treadle,
I know, I know. . . . Ⓑ

And then it was day again, all morning
at the office machines, their clack and chatter
another journey—rougher,
20 that would go on forever
until she could break a hundred words
with no errors—ah, and then

no more postponed groceries,
and that blue pair of shoes!

Ⓐ SPEAKER
The title of the poem gives a good clue about the speaker. Who is "telling" this poem?

Ⓑ UNDERSTAND FIGURATIVE LANGUAGE
In your own words, restate what the speaker is describing in lines 9–16.

ANALYZE VISUALS
How does the woman in this painting **compare** with your mental image of the mother in the poem?

---

1. **leg-o'-mutton or raglan:** types of sleeves. A leg-of-mutton sleeve is wide at the top and narrow at the bottom. A raglan sleeve is cut so that it continues up to the collar.
2. **piecework:** work paid for according to the amount done, not the time it takes.

846 UNIT 7: BIOGRAPHY AND AUTOBIOGRAPHY

Alma Sewing (about 1935), Francis Criss. Oil on canvas, 33″ × 45″. High Museum of Art, Atlanta, Georgia.

DIFFERENTIATED INSTRUCTION

FOR LESS–PROFICIENT READERS

Review Onomatopoeia Remind students that the use of words that sound like what they mean, such as *buzz* and *thwack,* is known as onomatopoeia. Have students reread "My Mother Enters the Work Force" to find examples:

- *whir* (line 11)
- *clack* (line 18)
- *chatter* (line 18)

Ask students what other onomatopoeic words they could use to describe images in each poem.

Concept Support Have students help you complete a Sequence Circle showing how the mother spends her mornings, afternoons, and evenings. Discuss how this daily cycle of efforts shows her perseverance.

 BEST PRACTICES TOOLKIT—Transparency
Sequence Circle p. B21

FOR ENGLISH LEARNERS

Vocabulary: Cognates Have students scan the poems for cognates, words that are similar to words in other languages. Spanish cognates include

- *perfect/perfecto(a)* (page 846, line 8)
- *locomotive/la locomotora* (page 846, line 11)
- *pair/el par* (page 846, line 24)
- *republic/la república* (page 848, line 10)
- *soldier/el soldado* (page 848, line 13)
- *to button/abotonar* (page 848, line 18)

BACKGROUND

Sewing Work Working with fabric—from spinning yarn to sewing clothes—has been so closely identified with women's labor that unmarried women used to be called "spinsters." Throughout history, women were often the ones who made their family's clothing. Because many women grew up learning these skills, sewing for other people was a common way for them to earn extra money. Sewing is time-consuming, requires a lot of attention, and usually doesn't pay much; as a result, it was often done by people who didn't have a lot of options. It is no wonder that the mother in Rita Dove's poem wanted an office job instead. In recent years, more and more of the garments sold in the United States have been made overseas.

FOR LESS–PROFICIENT READERS

Comprehension Support Use Read Aloud/ Think Aloud for lines 17–24 to help students understand what the mother works toward during her mornings.

- Remind them of the mention of ABC Business School (line 1).

- Make sure they understand the use of the multiple-meaning word *break* (line 21, used to mean "outdo," as in "break a record") and explain that it refers to taking a typing test.

- Ask students why the mother might no longer have to postpone buying groceries (line 23).

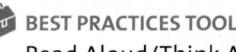 **BEST PRACTICES TOOLKIT—Transparency** Read Aloud/Think Aloud p. A34

FOR ADVANCED LEARNERS/PRE–AP

Analyze Sensory Details Have students review lines 9–14 and notice how the author uses details that appeals to the senses:

- sound ("locomotive whir," line 11)
- sight ("lit path," line 12)
- touch ("velvet deep as a forest," line 14)

Ask students to create an original description, using sensory details, that relates to one of the poems or to the act of writing a poem.

Lines 8–11
DISCUSSION PROMPTS

Use these prompts to help students explore the meaning of "the republic is a dream" (line 10):

Connect Think about the people in your idea web (page 844). What dreams did they have? *Students' answers should reflect the idea that "dreams" means personal goals.*

Analyze What was the dream of soldiers in the American Revolution? Why was it just a dream? *Possible answer: They dreamed that the war would end with an independent American republic. Because the republic did not yet exist, it was still a dream.*

Synthesize What traits do the monument and George Washington share in common? *Possible answer: Both are strong, stand alone, endure over time, and inspire others to fight for freedom.*

848

WASHINGTON MONUMENT BY NIGHT

CARL SANDBURG

1
The stone goes straight.
A lean swimmer dives into night sky,
Into half-moon mist.

2
Two trees are coal black.
5 This is a great white ghost between.
It is cool to look at.
Strong men, strong women, come here. **C**

3
Eight years is a long time
To be fighting all the time.

4
10 The republic is a dream.
Nothing happens unless first a dream.

5
The wind bit hard at Valley Forge one Christmas.
Soldiers tied rags on their feet.
Red footprints wrote on the snow . . .
15 . . . and stone shoots into stars here
. . . into half-moon mist tonight.

6
Tongues wrangled dark at a man.
He buttoned his overcoat and stood alone.
In a snowstorm, red hollyberries, thoughts,
        he stood alone.

7
20 Women said: He is lonely
. . . fighting . . . fighting . . . eight years . . .

8
The name of an iron man goes over the world.
It takes a long time to forget an iron man. **D**

9
. . .   .
25 . . .   .

C UNDERSTAND FIGURATIVE LANGUAGE
In your chart, tell what surrounds the monument and what color the monument is.

D SPEAKER
Is the speaker someone who lived during Washington's time or someone who lives in the present time of the poem? Tell how you know.

SELECTION WRAP–UP

★ **CRITIQUE** Have students evaluate whether Sandburg was effective in conveying the visual impact of the monument and what it represents.

READING FLUENCY

Distribute the copy masters and have students work in groups to practice fluency.

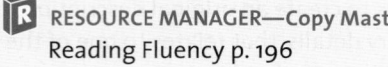 **RESOURCE MANAGER—Copy Master**
Reading Fluency p. 196

DIFFERENTIATED INSTRUCTION

FOR LESS–PROFICIENT READERS

Reading Skill Follow-Up: Understand Figurative Language Have students use Think-Pair-Share to paraphrase this figurative language in the chart from page 845:

- "the wind bit hard" (line 12), *fierce wind*
- "footprints wrote on the snow" (line 14), *footprints left tracks in the snow*
- "stone shoots into stars" (line 15), *stars surround the monument at night*

BEST PRACTICES TOOLKIT—Transparency
Think-Pair-Share p. A18

FOR ADVANCED LEARNERS/PRE–AP

Analyze Language Ask students to think about how the effect of the poem might have been different if it had been about the Washington monument by day. Have them write a new version of lines 2–5 that create an image of the monument by day. Invite them to read their lines aloud to the class and discuss how the effect and the mood are different.

Comprehension

1. **Recall** How does the mother in "My Mother Enters the Work Force" pay for business school?

2. **Clarify** How does the mother's life change in lines 21–24 of "My Mother Enters the Work Force"?

3. **Clarify** Who is the "man" in stanzas 6, 7, and 8 in "Washington Monument by Night"?

Literary Analysis

4. **Understand Figurative Language** Compare the paraphrases you wrote with those of a partner. How are your paraphrases similar or different?

5. **Analyze Speaker** What is the speaker's opinion of her mother in "My Mother Enters the Work Force"? Support your answer with words and phrases from the poem.

6. **Interpret** What does the last stanza in "Washington Monument by Night" suggest about the "iron man"?

7. **Compare and Contrast Character** Both the mother in "My Mother Enters the Work Force" and the man in "Washington Monument by Night" **persevered** in the face of huge obstacles. What other similarities do they share? What are their differences? Use a Venn diagram like the one shown to compare and contrast the two people.

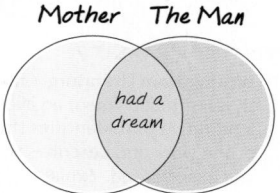

Mother The Man

had a dream

8. **Evaluate Figurative Language** Is line 5 of "Washington Monument by Night" a good description of the Washington Monument? Refer to evidence in the poem and to the photograph on page 848 to support your opinion.

Extension and Challenge

9. **Big Question Activity** Review the Big Question on page 844 and the idea web that you made as part of the **Web It** activity. Write a journal entry that explains how you think each hero in your web would answer the Big Question. Then write a response for the mother in "My Mother Enters the Work Force" and the man in "Washington Monument by Night."

10. **Creative Project: Art** Carl Sandburg's poem describes a monument to the man in the poem. Now sketch a monument in honor of the speaker's mother in "My Mother Enters the Work Force." List the materials you would use to make the monument. In a short dedication speech, explain your reasons for the monument's design, why you chose the colors you did, and how the materials reflect the mother's personality.

MY MOTHER ENTERS . . . / WASHINGTON MONUMENT . . . **849**

---

10. *In their monuments students may choose to incorporate items mentioned in the poem, such as the sewing machine, the blue shoes, and fabrics that would remind viewers of the mother's work. Their dedication speeches should clearly explain why they made the choices they did and reflect an understanding of the mother's efforts as described in the poem.*

Assess and Reteach

Assess

R **RESOURCE MANAGER—Copy Masters**
Selection Tests A, B/C pp. 197–198, 199–200

💿 Test Generator CD

Reteach

S **STANDARDS LESSON FILE**
Literature Lessons 18, 27
Research and Study Skills Lesson 12

 MARYLAND OBJECTIVES

LITERATURE STANDARD
3.A.7.c Analyze figurative language

Practice and Apply

After Reading

For additional support of post-reading questions, use these copy masters:

R **RESOURCE MANAGER—Copy Masters**
Speaker p. 191 (for practice of literary analysis standards focus)
Question Support p. 195 (**After Reading** questions adapted for English learners and less-proficient readers)

Additional selection questions are provided for teachers on page 187.

ANSWERS

Comprehension

1. *The speaker's mother works at a shop as a seamstress and does piecework at home.*

2. *The mother becomes an office worker and is able to earn more money.*

3. *The man is George Washington.*

Literary Analysis

Possible answers:

4. *Answers will vary. Students should note that although they use different words, the general ideas are similar.*

5. ● **STANDARDS FOCUS** *Speaker The speaker admires the mother. The speaker praises the mother's skill—the sleeves she sewed "never puckered" and looked "perfect." The words "path" and "journey" honor the mother's persistence.*

6. *The repeated ellipses in the last stanza suggest that as time marches on, the legacy of George Washington endures.*

7. *Mother: did sewing work, went to school. Man (Washington): was a soldier, fought for his country. Both: admirable, determined, had a goal*

8. ■ **STANDARDS FOCUS** *Understand Figurative Language It is a good description because it makes an impact and conveys the monument's size and color.*

Extension and Challenge

9. *Mother: might say that you must work hard to achieve goals; that things don't happen overnight, but with time and effort you can succeed. Man: might say that you must commit yourself to a goal while it is still only a dream, or that dream will never come true.*

Focus and Motivate

OBJECTIVES

- analyze a student model that reflects the key traits of a personal narrative
- use the writing process to produce a personal narrative
- add sensory and descriptive details
- use dialogue
- revise and edit, using a rubric for a strong personal narrative
- punctuate dialogue correctly
- use verb tenses consistently
- present an anecdote

WRITER'S ROAD MAP

WRITING PROMPTS 1 AND 2

Help students choose a prompt by brainstorming memorable events in their lives or by reviewing stories with characters whose experiences are similar to their own.

ADDITIONAL PROMPTS

Use these prompts for practice in writing different kinds of personal narrative:

WRITING PROMPT 3

Writing for the Real World Write a personal narrative for your special memories scrapbook. Focus on a specific event and explain why it was important to you.

Ideas to Consider
- a reunion
- a vacation
- a holiday tradition

WRITING PROMPT 4

Writing from Media Select a movie or television character whose experience reminds you of an experience in your own life. Write about this connection.

Possible Subjects
- a character who faced a difficult decision
- a character who learned from a mistake
- a character who lost a friend

For additional writing prompts, see

 WriteSmart CD

 Writing Center at **ClassZone.com**

KEY TRAITS

Review the six **KEY TRAITS,** focusing mainly on ideas and organization. Compare these traits with the rubric on page 856.

Writing Workshop

Personal Narrative

Although few people have a life story like Jackie Robinson's or Eleanor Roosevelt's, every life is filled with stories to share. You have them too, and chances are you tell them every day, informally or in bits and pieces. Follow the **Writer's Road Map** to learn how to turn these stories into personal narratives.

WRITER'S ROAD MAP
Personal Narrative

WRITING PROMPT 1

Writing from Your Life Write a narrative that describes a special event in your life. Include details that help your reader understand what the event was like. Be sure to explain why the event was important to you.

Events to Consider
- your first day in a new place
- going to a different school or to camp
- winning a game or learning a skill

WRITING PROMPT 2

Writing from Literature Choose a literary work that reminded you of an event in your life. Write a narrative that identifies the title and author of the work and describes the similar event that you experienced. Explain why the event was important to you.

Events and Literary Works to Consider
- a time when you felt different or out of place ("Names/Nombres")
- an accomplishment by a family member ("My Mother Enters the Work Force")

 WRITING TOOLS
For prewriting, revision, and editing tools, visit the **Writing Center** at **ClassZone.com.**

KEY TRAITS

1. IDEAS
- Focuses on a **single experience**
- Re-creates the event with **descriptive details** and **dialogue**

2. ORGANIZATION
- Gets the reader's attention with an interesting **introduction**
- Makes the **order of events** clear by using transitional words and phrases
- Concludes by summarizing the **significance** of the event

3. VOICE
- Uses the **active voice**

4. WORD CHOICE
- Brings the event alive for the reader by using **sensory language**

5. SENTENCE FLUENCY
- Uses a variety of **sentence types** (statements, questions, commands, and exclamations)

6. CONVENTIONS
- Uses **correct grammar, spelling, and punctuation**

Writing Workshop Resources

 RESOURCE MANAGER UNIT 7
Plan and Teach pp. 201–204
Prewriting–Editing pp. 205–209
Writing Rubric p. 210
Speaking and Listening p. 211
Writing Support p. 212*

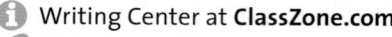 **STANDARDS LESSON FILE**
Writing Lessons 35, 39, 48
Grammar Lesson 17

BEST PRACTICES TOOLKIT
Scaffolding Writing Instruction pp. 43–46*
Writing Template • Round Robin

TECHNOLOGY
Easy Planner DVD
Writing Center at **ClassZone.com**
WriteSmart CD

* Resources for Differentiation

Part 1: Analyze a Student Model

WRITING STANDARD
4.A.2.a Compose to express personal ideas

Michelle Gruneisen
St. Columban School

The Secret Kitten

"So how exactly are we going to do this?" I asked.

My friend Amy and I were sitting in the front room of her house, bored stiff. It was a hot summer day, and Amy's bellyaching about giving up her cute, cuddly, purring kittens had gotten her wheels turning.

5   "I don't know how," said Amy, "but we have to hide at least one kitten."

Amy's parents had decided to give her last two of the original five kittens away, claiming that Amy already had two cats and that was enough. Amy, however, was determined to keep at least one.

10   "I know! How about underground?" I suggested playfully.

"No!" she replied passionately. "Cave-ins would be bad! What about in my shed?"

"Amy, dear, sharp objects and kittens don't mix," I shot back.

"Okay," she said meekly. "How about in my closet?"

15   "Now that's an idea!" I said with enthusiasm.

Straightaway, we went to work. We cleared out old toys and games and made room for the litter box and food dishes. Next, we made sure that every shelf was stable, and we made a soft bed for the kitten. We even spread out Amy's clothes to muffle any sound the kitten emitted.
20   In addition, we made a schedule to exercise and groom the kitten. We cleaned off the rust from the screen latch and oiled the window crank, making it easy to get the kitten from Amy's room to Amy's yard without being noticed.

KEY TRAITS IN ACTION

Introduction grabs the reader's attention by introducing characters and including **descriptive details.**

Uses realistic **dialogue** and a variety of **sentence types.**

Focuses on a **single experience** (trying to hide the kitten).

Teach

Part 1: Analyze a Student Model

Have students read the student model and **Key Traits in Action.** Then discuss the model with the class, pointing out specific examples of each trait and building on what students have already noted. You may also wish to incorporate these activities:

- **Introduction** Ask students to read lines 1–4 and describe how this introduction grabs their attention. What details are interesting? How does the introduction make them want to keep reading by raising questions in their minds?

- **Sentence Types** Explain that some sentences make a simple statement (declarative), while others ask questions (interrogative), give commands (imperative), or express strong emotions (exclamatory). Write these sentences on the board:

  "I have an idea."

  "We could hide one underground."

  "That is not a good idea."

  "There could be a cave-in."

  "We could hide one in my shed."

Ask a student to compare the sentences on the board with lines 10–12 of the student model. How do the sentences in the model differ from those on the board? ***Possible answer: The sentences on the board are all declarative. The model has a variety of sentence types, which makes the narrative more realistic and interesting.***

FOR ALL STUDENTS

For general guidelines on differentiating writing instruction, see

 BEST PRACTICES TOOLKIT
Scaffolding Writing Instruction
pp. 43–46

FOR ENGLISH LEARNERS

Language: Skill Words Write these terms on the board and review them with students:

- *single experience:* one event that happens in a short period of time

- *descriptive details:* words or phrases that help a reader picture what is happening

- *dialogue:* words and phrases that are the exact ones spoken by the people in the narrative (*She said, "I want a kitten!"* instead of *She said she wanted a kitten.*)

- *significance:* why the event is important to the person writing the narrative

- *active voice:* way of writing in which the subject performs an action (*We cleared out old toys and games* [line 16] instead of *Old toys and games were cleared out*)

- *sensory language:* words or phrases that appeal to a reader's sense of sight, hearing, taste, touch, or smell. Examples: in line 4, *cuddly* (touch) and *purring* (hearing); in line 25, *white paws* (sight)

- **Active Voice** Explain that verbs can be in either the active or the passive voice. A verb is active when the subject of the sentence performs the action. A verb is passive when the subject receives the action. Write this sentence on the board: *At least one kitten has to be hidden by us.* Ask students to compare this sentence to lines 5–6 of the model. *(The statement on the board is in the passive voice. The subject* kitten *receives the action of being* hidden. *The model uses the active voice. The subject* we *performs the action* have *to hide.)* Discuss how the active voice adds directness and power to the narrative.

Have students rewrite these sentences in the active voice:

  The closet was cleaned out by us.

  A female kitten was chosen by Amy.

- **Significance** Point out that a personal narrative has many of the same elements as a story: characters, a plot with a problem to be solved, and a resolution. One difference is that in a personal narrative, readers expect the writer to explain why he or she decided to tell the story—in other words, why the story is significant.

Have students read over the model without the last paragraph. Ask them to identify the characters, problem, and resolution. Since the resolution is clear before the last paragraph, ask students to explain the purpose of the last paragraph. ***Possible answer:*** *The last paragraph explains the significance of the narrative. The writer is telling this story because it had a funny, ironic ending that made it memorable.*

Ask students to state the significance in the writer's life of a true story they have read, such as the excerpt from *An American Childhood* (page 120) or "Encounter with Martin Luther King Jr." (page 260).

For interactive student models, see

🖉 Write*Smart* CD

ℹ️ Writing Center at **ClassZone.com**

By the following week, all that was left to do was choose the kitten.
25 Amy decided on a female kitten with white paws, smoky black and gray fur, and eyes like deep pools of crystal-clear water. It was that same day that her parents made the announcement.

> **Order of events** is clear. **Sensory language** helps the reader imagine the kitten.

I was over at her house in the front room; we were plotting about our secret kitten when her parents came in. Her mom had an expression
30 of suppressed joy, and her dad looked quite proud of himself.

"Well, Amy," her mom started. "We've made a decision."

Had they found out about our plan? Did they find homes for both kittens already? So many thoughts raced through my head. It seemed as though the moment would never end.

> Uses the **active voice.** Dramatic questions help make the narrative suspenseful.

35 Her dad continued, "We've decided that you may keep one more kitten!"

Amy and I looked at each other in wonderment. Amy was happy, sad, and frustrated all at once. Somehow she managed a smile. I felt like crying and laughing at once.

40 We had done all that work and planning for nothing, but Amy got what she wanted. Looking back, I realize that our plan never would have worked, but it would have been fun trying!

> Concludes with a reflection on the event's **significance**.

2

DIFFERENTIATED INSTRUCTION

FOR ENGLISH LEARNERS

Comprehension: Transitions Check to make sure students understand transitional words and phrases that indicate a sequence of events, such as *first, next, then, soon,* and *suddenly.* If necessary, use this activity to illustrate the concept of sequence:

1. Write a brief paragraph on the board that describes something you did that morning. Include appropriate sequence words.

2. Read the paragraph aloud. Underline the sequence words.

   First, I went to homeroom. *Then* I had English class. *After that,* I went to math.

3. Ask student volunteers to use sequence words to describe what they do when the dismissal bell rings.

4. Use the copy master for further practice.

📘 RESOURCE MANAGER—Copy Master
Writing Support p. 212

Part 2: Apply the Writing Process

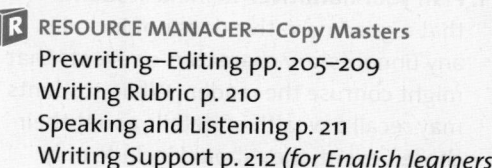

WRITING STANDARD
4.A.1. Compose texts using prewriting and drafting strategies

Practice and Apply

To support students during the writing process, use these copy masters:

R RESOURCE MANAGER—Copy Masters
Prewriting–Editing pp. 205–209
Writing Rubric p. 210
Speaking and Listening p. 211
Writing Support p. 212 *(for English learners)*

Part 2: Apply the Writing Process

PREWRITING

What Should I Do?	What Does It Look Like?

1. Analyze the prompt.
Read the prompt carefully. (Circle) the word that names the type of writing you must produce. <u>Underline</u> words and phrases that tell what you must include.

▶ **WRITING PROMPT** Write a (narrative) that <u>describes a special event in your life.</u> Include <u>details that help your reader understand what the event was like.</u> Be sure to <u>explain why the event was important to you.</u>

2. Think of an event to share.
This writing has to come from your own past, so make a list of memory triggers: people, places, times, and events that might bring back the stories of your life.

▶

Memory Triggers	Specific Memory
summers at Camp Far Winds	learning to swim
(my best friend, Amy)	(our secret kitten)
baseball teams	my grand slam
our family pets	when Muffin ran away

3. Consider your audience and purpose.
Make a chart to show who you think will read your narrative, what your purpose for writing is (stated in the prompt), and what the event meant to you.

TIP Is the event you chose too personal to share with your teacher or classmates? Choose a new event from the list you generated in Step 2.

▶

Audience	Purpose	Significance
classmates, teacher	describe a special event	seemed so important at the time, but didn't matter in the end

4. Use your descriptive powers.
Use descriptive words and phrases to help your reader understand important parts of your narrative.

▶ *cleared out toys and games* — **Hiding the Kitten** — *made a soft bed* / *fixed the window so that kitten could get in and out*

PREWRITING

1. **Analyze the prompt.** Have students work in pairs to identify three key words from the prompt that tell them what must be included in their narratives. *(Possible answers: describes, details, explain)*

2. **Think of an event to share.** Encourage students to recall stories they have heard other people—parents, grandparents, friends, coaches, or neighbors—tell about them. They can use the special event in one of these stories as the basis for telling the story from their own point of view. Suggest some graphic organizers students can use to generate ideas.

3. **Consider your audience and purpose.** When students think of ideas for their narratives, they should ask themselves if they would find each story interesting as a listener. Since their audience is primarily their classmates, they should consider what story their classmates might enjoy. Be sure to point out the **TIP** in step 3.

4. **Use your descriptive powers.** Write this sentence on the board: *Amy decided to keep the female kitten.* Then have students read lines 25–26 from the model. Ask them to identify the words that make the sentence from the model more descriptive than the one on the board. *(Possible answers: white paws, smoky black and gray fur, eyes like deep pools of crystal-clear water)* Have students brainstorm other words that could be used to enhance the description of the cat.

For interactive graphic organizers, see

WriteSmart CD

Writing Center at ClassZone.com

FOR ENGLISH LEARNERS

Think of an Event to Share Have students use these sentence starters to help them focus their ideas before they begin writing:

• My narrative is about _____.
• The people in my story are _____.
• My narrative begins when _____.
• My narrative ends when _____.

Students should work in pairs and take turns asking each other questions that will help the writer add details and revise his or her ideas.

FOR ADVANCED LEARNERS/PRE–AP

Consider Your Audience and Purpose Ask students to exchange copies of their narratives with the explanation of what the event meant to them blocked out. Students should read their partner's narrative and write their own idea of what the event might have meant. Then students should compare ideas. Ask them to explain which explanation of the event's significance they like better and why.

DRAFTING

1. Plan your narrative. Remind students that a good narrative does not include any unnecessary characters or events that might confuse the reader. While students may recall a wealth of details about their chosen event, they should include only those that help readers understand what happened.

2. Set the scene in your introduction. Help students understand the importance of background information in a narrative. In some stories the time of day might be most important. In others, the season or the year might be most important. Have students review the model. Ask them when the story happened and why it is important. *(It is summer, and Amy is bored and cranky.)* Have them explain why readers do not need to know the time of day or the year.

3. Tell who said what to whom. Be sure that when students use dialogue, they include appropriate dialogue tags (*she said, he exclaimed,* and so on). Dialogue tags serve the following purposes:

- They help the reader follow the conversation.
- They provide clues to the tone of voice used by the speaker.
- They provide opportunities to vary sentence structure.

Have students look at lines 10–15 and write down the dialogue tags. *(I suggested playfully, she replied passionately, I shot back, she said meekly, I said with enthusiasm)* Discuss which purposes are served by each tag.

Ask students to write three sentences with dialogue tags that they could use in their narratives. One tag should appear at the beginning of the sentence, one in the middle, and one at the end.

For a personal narrative writing template, see

📦 **BEST PRACTICES TOOLKIT—Transparency**
Writing Template: Personal Narrative pp. C16, C18

✐ Write*Smart* CD

ℹ️ Writing Center at **ClassZone.com**

DRAFTING

What Should I Do?

1. Plan your narrative.
An engaging personal narrative often has many of the same elements as a terrific short story, such as plot, characters, dialogue, and suspense. To make sure that your narrative is well organized, make a story map. Be sure it includes your characters and the setting. Be sure, too, that you have a clear sequence of events. Most narratives are told in **chronological order,** also called time order. If you want, you can work in a **flashback** (an event that took place before the start of the story).

See page 26: Plot at a Glance

2. Set the scene in your introduction.
Use your introduction to tell basic information, such as who, where, and when. Every reader requires a little background, but not every story has to give the same kind of background. Here the writer vividly relates how Amy came up with the idea of the secret kitten.

3. Tell who said what to whom.
Be sure to include dialogue to make your characters sound like real people taking part in real events.

TIP Before revising, look back at the key traits on page 850 and at the rubric and peer-reader questions on page 856.

What Does It Look Like?

Title: The Secret Kitten

Setting: Amy's house

Characters: Amy, her parents, me

Plot Summary: Amy and I make plans to hide a kitten, and then her parents give her the kitten after all.

Sequence of Events:

1. We decide to hide one kitten in the closet.
2. We clean and prepare.
3. We decide which kitten to keep.
4. Amy's parents announce she can have one more kitten.

Significance: We couldn't believe that we had done all that for nothing!

From prewriting notes . . .
My friend Amy got an idea
. . . to draft
My friend Amy and I were sitting in the front room of her house, bored stiff. It was a hot summer day, and Amy's bellyaching about giving up her cute, cuddly, purring kittens had gotten her wheels turning.

From prewriting notes . . .
We talked over places to keep the kitten.
. . . to draft
"I know! How about underground?" I suggested playfully.
"No!" she replied passionately. "Cave-ins would be bad! What about in my shed?"

DIFFERENTIATED INSTRUCTION

FOR LESS—PROFICIENT WRITERS

Plan Your Narrative To help students organize the elements of their narratives, provide the following frame and explain that it represents the organization of the model:

First paragraphs
- Identify characters.
- Tell where and when story takes place.
- Focus a single experience.

Middle paragraphs
- Tell what happens first.
- Tell what happens next.
- Tell what happens last.
- Include dialogue and sensory details.

Last paragraphs
- Refer again to main characters.
- Refer again to the single experience.
- Tell why the event was important to you.

REVISING AND EDITING

What Should I Do?	What Does It Look Like?
1. Make sure the sequence is clear. • Ask a peer reader to <u>underline</u> parts of your narrative that are out of order or that do not lead clearly from one step to the next. • Add transitions, move text, or revise the narrative to make the sequence clear. **See page 856:** Ask a Peer Reader	Her mom had an expression of suppressed joy. I was over at her house in the front room; we were plotting about our secret kitten when Her parents came in.
2. Add sensory language or other descriptive details. • Circle words that tell how something looked, sounded, felt, tasted, or smelled. • If you have few or no circles, revise to make your response more detailed.	*a female* Amy decided on ~~the kitten she wanted~~. with white paws, smoky black and gray fur, and eyes like deep pools of crystal-clear water.
3. Use the active voice. • Draw a box around sentences in the passive voice (*The kitten was hidden by us*). • Change inappropriate uses of the passive voice to the active voice (*We hid the kitten*).	We cleared out Old toys and games ~~got cleared out~~. We made A schedule to exercise and groom the kitten was made. Had they found out about our plan? ~~Had our plan been found out about by them?~~
4. Reflect on the experience. • [Bracket] parts of your narrative that tell what you learned from the experience, why you chose it, or even why—as the writer of the student model concluded—it seemed more important than it really was. • Be sure that your narrative explains what the experience meant to you.	We had done all that work and planning for nothing, but [Amy got what she wanted.] Looking back, I realize that our plan never would have worked, but it would have been fun trying!

DIFFERENTIATED INSTRUCTION

FOR ENGLISH LEARNERS

Vocabulary: Sensory Words Place students in Round-Robin groups of three or four. Have students take turns reading aloud a brief scene from his or her personal narrative, after which other group members brainstorm descriptive words that could be added to appeal to the senses of sight, smell, taste, touch, or hearing.

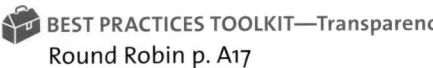

BEST PRACTICES TOOLKIT—Transparency
Round Robin p. A17

REVISING AND EDITING

1. **Make sure the sequence is clear.** Remind students that unless they have intentionally included a flashback, the narrative should describe events in chronological order. Suggest that students review their narratives and ask themselves after each event, "Then what happened?" If the next section answers the question, their work is in a logical sequence.

2. **Add sensory language or other descriptive details.** Point out that vivid descriptive details help draw readers into a story. Visual images are the most common, but students should also strive to appeal to the other senses. Warn students, however, that too many descriptive details may distract readers from the main point.

3. **Use the active voice.** If students are having trouble removing the passive voice from their writing, have them locate the subject of the sentence and place it before the verb. Refer students back to the model for examples of the active voice.

4. **Reflect on the experience.** Explain to students that this part of the narrative is essential. It is the reason why the narrative has been written in the first place. For students having trouble with the reflection, use these prompts:

   • Did you learn something about yourself as a result of the event?
   • Did you learn something about other people?
   • Did you learn something about life?
   • How did you feel at the end? Happy? Sad? Explain why you felt this way.

For interactive revision tools, see

📀 Write*Smart* CD

ℹ️ Writing Center at **ClassZone.com**

Preparing to Publish

Support for meeting the goals in the writing rubric is supplied throughout the **Writing Workshop** on pages 850–855.

For Rubric Bank, see

 WriteSmart CD

 Writing Center at **ClassZone.com**

Assess and Reteach

After reading and assessing students' narratives, you might use these lessons to reteach key skills:

S STANDARDS LESSON FILE

Writing Lesson 35: Personal Narrative

Writing Lesson 39: Elaborate with Sensory Details

Writing Lesson 48: Writing Dialogue

Grammar Lesson 17: Mixing Verb Tenses

Preparing to Publish — Personal Narrative

Apply the Rubric

A strong personal narrative . . .

☑ captures the reader's attention with an interesting introduction

☑ focuses on a single experience

☑ makes the order of events clear by using transitional words and phrases

☑ re-creates the event with dialogue, sensory language, and descriptive details

☑ uses the active voice

☑ uses a variety of sentence types (statements, questions, commands, and exclamations)

☑ concludes by reflecting on the significance of the experience

Ask a Peer Reader

- What kinds of descriptive details or dialogue should I add?

- What could I do to make the sequence clearer?

- Where in my conclusion do I reflect on why the experience is important to me?

Check Your Grammar

- When you write dialogue, enclose each speaker's exact words in quotation marks. Begin a new paragraph each time the speaker changes.

> "Amy, dear, sharp objects and kittens don't mix," I shot back.
> "Okay," she said meekly." How about in my closet?"

- Use a comma to separate a speaker's words from a description of who is speaking. If the speaker's words end with a question mark or an exclamation point, no comma is needed.

> "Well, Amy ," her mom started.
> "Now that's an idea!" I said.

See pages R49–R50: Quick Reference: Punctuation

- Use the same verb tense to show two or more actions that occur at the same time.

> We cleared out old toys and make made room for the litter box and food dishes.

See page R56: Verb Tense

Writing Online

 PUBLISHING OPTIONS
For publishing options, visit the **Writing Center** at **ClassZone.com**.

ASSESSMENT PREPARATION
For writing and grammar assessment practice, go to the **Assessment Center** at **ClassZone.com**.

DIFFERENTIATED INSTRUCTION

FOR ALL STUDENTS

Gallery Walk Consider this publishing option:

1. Have each student print out a clean copy of his or her narrative and decorate it with a frame of colored paper, glitter, pictures cut from magazines, and so on.

2. Arrange the pictures on one or more walls.

3. Distribute sticky notes. Have each student read several framed narratives in the gallery, write compliments on the sticky notes, and attach them to the narratives.

SPEAKING STANDARD
7.A.1. Demonstrate appropriate delivery techniques for oral presentations

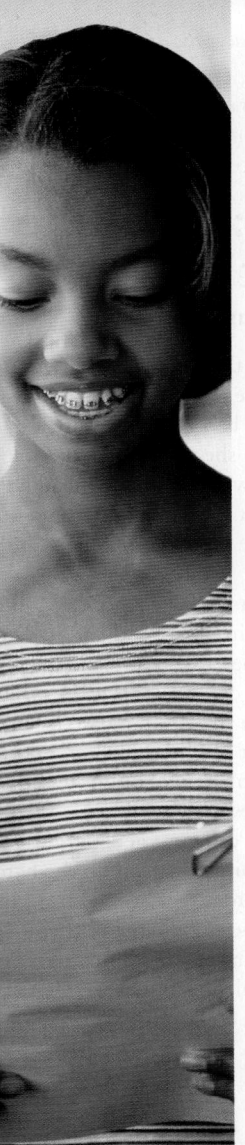

Presenting an Anecdote

In this unit, you've read some big stories about fascinating lives. Now it's your turn to tell a little story, or anecdote, from your own life.

Preparing the Anecdote

1. **Choose part of your narrative to share.** Find the best part of your personal narrative—the part that's funniest, liveliest, most dramatic, or most surprising. Pull it out for shaping into an anecdote, which is a brief story that you might tell a friend.

2. **Add and subtract.** Decide what you need to add, such as humor or drama, to punch up your story for a face-to-face audience. Alternatively, you may want to shorten or tighten your story. Be sure that your anecdote clearly specifies the setting—where and when the event took place. Remember, your audience is listening, not reading. They can't slow down your pace or go back and reread.

3. **Consider your tone.** You might want to make formal language more conversational, long sentences shorter, or complicated descriptions simpler.

4. **Practice and refine.** Consider learning your anecdote by heart so that you don't have to rely on notes. Tell your anecdote to a friend or family member, and get feedback on how to improve your performance.

Presenting the Anecdote

1. **Act out the parts.** Create a different voice for each character. Consider changing stances, gestures, and facial expressions for each character.

2. **Watch your pacing.** You might pause once or twice to make your anecdote suspenseful. If possible, have a friend in the audience signal to let you know whether to speed things up or slow them down.

3. **Take a bow.** Don't just trail off at the end. Finish with confidence. Afterward, ask audience members whether any parts of your anecdote were unclear.

See page R80: Evaluate a Descriptive Speech

SPEAKING AND LISTENING

Ask students to read this page to get an overview of how to tell an anecdote from one's own life. Before students begin working, review this rubric with them so that they understand their goals:

Rubric A strong anecdote

- contains the most entertaining or interesting part of the written narrative
- clearly states where and when the event took place
- is told with good pacing—neither too slow nor too fast
- uses pauses where appropriate to build suspense or check audience reaction
- includes the use of appropriate gestures, facial expressions, and tone of voice
- has been carefully rehearsed but sounds as if the speaker is talking to a friend
- is presented with confidence

 RESOURCE MANAGER—Copy Master
Speaking and Listening p. 211

DIFFERENTIATED INSTRUCTION

FOR LESS–PROFICIENT WRITERS

Preparing an Anecdote Ask students to identify two sections of their personal narrative that are likely to be the most entertaining for an audience. To help them determine which section is better suited to be presented as an anecdote, have them think about these questions:

- Does this section contain a humorous, dramatic, or interesting event?

- What would I need to add to help the audience understand the anecdote?
- What details are not essential?

As students prepare for their performances, have them ask themselves these questions:

- What gestures, tone of voice, and facial expressions should I use for the dialogue?
- Where should I pause for dramatic effect?
- Have I practiced enough so that I can deliver my performance without notes?

Assessment Practice

CHECK READINESS

Read aloud the paragraph under **ASSESS** and stress to students that this is not the full Unit Test but a way for them to check their readiness for it. Then have students examine the skills listed under **REVIEW** and look back in the unit or in the Handbook for any skills they need to study.

READ THE SELECTION

Remind students to keep unit goals in mind as they read the passage, paying particular attention to

- form and characteristics of biography
- chronological order
- making inferences

To help students focus on characteristics of **biography** while reading, encourage them to ask questions such as

- Whom is the excerpt about?
- Who is the author of the excerpt?
- What point of view does the author use?
- How does the author present the subject's thoughts and feelings?
- In what order does the author describe events?

ANSWER THE QUESTIONS

Direct students to pages R93–R99 of the Test-Taking Handbook to review test-taking strategies. Remind students not to choose the first alternative that seems to fit when answering a multiple-choice question. Instead, they should read through all the choices, eliminate any that are clearly wrong, and then choose the best answer—the one that is most accurate and complete.

Encourage students to skim the questions that follow the passage before they begin reading. It may be helpful for students to jot down key points that are asked for in the questions. This will help them focus their reading so that they can quickly identify the most important information as they read.

Assessment Practice

Reading Comprehension

DIRECTIONS   *Read the following selection and then answer the questions.*

The world-famous pilot Amelia Earhart worked as a volunteer nurse in Toronto, Canada, during World War I. There, she developed her lifelong interest in flying.

from East to the Dawn: The Life of Amelia Earhart

Susan Butler

When Amelia had spare time, she headed for the stables, and it was through her riding that she got her first exposure to airplanes. She was riding a horse named Dynamite, whom she had "gentled" with a combination of horsemanship and apples, when she was joined by three air force officers. They were so impressed by how well she controlled her mount—famous for bucking off a colonel—that they asked her to go out to Armour Heights, an airfield at the edge of the city, to watch how they controlled their planes.

Amelia had seen planes before. She saw her first at a fair in Des Moines
10 when she was ten, but "it was a thing of rusty wire and wood and looked not at all interesting." The chances are, it was the same first plane that Clarence Chamberlin, who also grew up to be a crack pilot, saw in his home town of Denison, Iowa, at about the same time—an old-style pusher, with the pilot sitting out front "on a sort of birdcage seat," and the propeller and engine in the rear. He too had been "frankly unimpressed . . quite willing to let anyone take such fool chances who would."

But ten years had passed. These planes were a different generation; now they were beautiful: "They were full sized birds that slid on the hard-packed snow and rose into the air with an extra roar that echoed from the
20 evergreens that banked the edge of the field." She stood close to them—so close that the propellers threw snow in her face, and "I felt a first urge to fly." She tried to get permission to go up, but failed—"not even a general' wife could do so—apparently the only thing she couldn't do." So she did "the next best thing" and got to know the fliers.

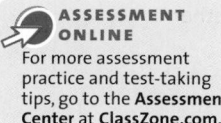

ASSESSMENT ONLINE
For more assessment practice and test-taking tips, go to the **Assessment Center** at **ClassZone.com**.

DIFFERENTIATED INSTRUCTION

FOR ENGLISH LEARNERS

Assessment Practice: Active Reading Strategies   Remind students to use active reading strategies, asking questions as they read and making notes on scrap paper.

- Students can check their understanding by asking questions such as "What did he or she do? Why?"
- They can jot down their impressions of people and events, noting descriptive words that the author uses.

- Students can check comprehension by stopping after every few paragraphs and summarizing what they have read.

Vocabulary Support   Review this vocabulary before students read the selection:

- *crack* (line 12), "expert"
- *pusher* (line 14), "a plane with the propeller and engine located behind the pilot"
- *propeller* (line 15), "a set of blades that spin through the air to move a plane forward"
- *stunt* (line 27), "fancy trick"

One day she had a chance to test her faith in planes, not by flying but by standing in the path of one. It was at a Toronto fair, and the pilots, war aces, were giving exhibitions of stunt flying. She and a girlfriend were standing in the middle of a clearing off by themselves in order to see better. The pilot began diving at the crowd. She would never forget what
30 happened next.

"He was bored. He had looped and rolled and spun and finished his little bag of tricks, and there was nothing left to do but watch the people on the ground running as he swooped close to them." Then he started diving at the two girls off in the clearing. "I remember the mingled fear and pleasure which surged over me as I watched that small plane at the top of its earthward swoop. Common sense told me that if something went wrong with the mechanism, or if the pilot lost control, he, the airplane and I would be rolled up in a ball together. I did not understand it at the time but I believe that little red airplane said something to me as
40 it swished by." Her friend ran off. Amelia didn't; she was fascinated.

GO ON

ITEM ANALYSIS

COMPREHENSION AND BRIEF CONSTRUCTED RESPONSE	ITEMS	UNIT PAGES
Biography	1, 5, 6, 11	754, 756, 761, 802
Chronological Order	3, 4, 10	761
Make Inferences	9, 11, 12	791
Summarize	2, 7, 8	809

VOCABULARY	ITEMS	UNIT PAGES
Latin Roots	1, 2, 3	775, 821
Base Words	4, 5, 6, 7	801

WRITING AND GRAMMAR	ITEMS	UNIT PAGES
Proper Nouns	1, 2, 3	789
Italics and Quotation Marks	4, 5	843

FOR LESS–PROFICIENT READERS

Assessment Support Consider these options for completing the **Assessment Practice:**

- Have students "work backwards," reviewing the questions before reading the passage.

- Select random questions in the assessment and have students demonstrate how and where to look for the answers.

- Ask students to locate unfamiliar vocabulary in the assessment. Elicit the meanings of these words from the class.

- Have students jot down useful test words and definitions for later reference.

- Read the selection or parts of it aloud to aid in student comprehension.

FOR ENGLISH LEARNERS

Review Academic Vocabulary List these words on the board: *biography, chronological order, infer, summarize.* Work together to review their definitions and discuss examples from the unit.

MSA PREPARATION

McDougal Littell
Assessment System

After checking student readiness with this Assessment Practice, you may administer the complete Unit 7 Test, which matches the structure and format of the MSA.

Comprehension

Model a thinking process for answering multiple-choice questions.

1. **B *is correct.*** *A biography is the story of someone's life told by someone else, so the use of the third-person pronoun* she *is a clue that this is a biography.* A, C, *and* D *can be eliminated because these elements may be present in either autobiography or biography, through the use of quotations and primary sources.*

2. **B *is correct.*** A *is incorrect because there is no indication in the passage that the officers had tried to tame a wild horse or that they were embarrassed.* C *and* D *are incorrect because the excerpt does not include any information about Earhart's motives for riding the horse.*

3. **B *is correct.*** *Except for a jump back in time to describe Amelia's first sight of a plane, the events are in chronological order.* A *can be eliminated because the events are not presented in random order but instead follow Earhart's growing interest in planes.* C *is incorrect because readers don't know the importance of each event to Earhart.* D *can be eliminated because readers don't know the order in which the author learned about the events.*

4. **D *is correct.*** *All of these words and phrases indicate the passage of time.* A *is incorrect because, while the phrases all relate to time, "spare time" and "one day" tell nothing about the order of events.* B *and* C *can be eliminated because none of these words and phrases relates to time order.*

5. **C *is correct.*** *This quotation expresses an urge that would become a future career goal for Earhart.* A *is incorrect because Earhart's horsemanship does not relate to her future as a pilot.* B *is incorrect because it merely says that Earhart saw her first plane when she was ten, without indicating that the event shaped her future.* D *shows that Earhart wanted to have a good view of the airshow, but it does not convey any impact that the event had on her future.*

Comprehension

DIRECTIONS *Answer these questions about the excerpt from* East to the Dawn: The Life of Amelia Earhart.

1. Which statement is a clue that this is a biography and not an autobiography?
   - **A.** The author reveals the thoughts and feelings of Amelia Earhart.
   - **B.** The author uses the word *she* to refer to Amelia Earhart.
   - **C.** The author reveals the thoughts and feelings of other people.
   - **D.** The author includes dialogue throughout the excerpt.

2. Which statement best summarizes lines 1–8?
   - **A.** Embarrassed that Earhart could tame a wild horse better than they could, three air force officers showed off their flying skills.
   - **B.** Impressed with Earhart's ability to control a wild horse, three air force officers invited her to watch them fly.
   - **C.** Earhart tamed a wild horse so that she might be invited to see the newest planes.
   - **D.** Earhart was afraid of airplanes and decided to tame a wild horse to prove that she was brave.

3. Events in this excerpt are presented in
   - **A.** random order
   - **B.** mostly chronological order
   - **C.** the order of their importance to Earhart
   - **D.** the order in which the author learned about them

4. Which words or phrases in the excerpt help you understand the order in which events happen?
   - **A.** spare time, first exposure, one day
   - **B.** chances, different generation, next best thing
   - **C.** stood close, in order to, also
   - **D.** before, ten years had passed, what happened next

5. Which quotation from the excerpt gives you an important clue about Amelia Earhart's future?
   - **A.** "She was riding a horse named Dynamite, whom she had 'gentled' with a combination of horsemanship and apples. . . ."
   - **B.** "Amelia had seen planes before. She saw her first at a fair in Des Moines when she was ten. . . ."
   - **C.** "She stood close to them—so close that the propellers threw snow in her face, and 'I felt a first urge to fly.'"
   - **D.** "She and a girlfriend were standing in the middle of a clearing off by themselves in order to see better."

6. You learn about Amelia Earhart's thoughts and feelings in this excerpt mostly from
   - **A.** direct quotations from her
   - **B.** the author's opinions of her
   - **C.** facts about her accomplishments
   - **D.** quotations from people who knew her

---

6. **A *is correct.*** *The author quotes Earhart directly in lines 10–11, 18–20, 21–24, and 31–40.* B *is incorrect because the author does not express her own opinions of Earhart.* C *is incorrect because facts about a person's accomplishments (such as taming the horse) do not necessarily reveal the person's thoughts and feelings.* D *is incorrect because most of the quotations in the excerpt are from Earhart.*

7. **D *is correct.*** A *is incorrect because Earhart had not fallen in love with planes ten years earlier.* B *provides supporting details, not a summary.* C *is also a detail, not a summary, and it is incorrect because nowhere in the excerpt is it stated that Earhart "knew she could never fly."*

8. **C *is correct.*** A *is incorrect because Amelia was fascinated, not scared.* B *is incorrect because the pilot did not lose control of the plane.* D *is incorrect because Earhart was not fearful, but instead watched the plane with pleasure.*

7. Which statement best summarizes lines 17–24?

A. Ten years after she first fell in love with airplanes, Amelia Earhart saw the beautiful new airplanes and enjoyed the way they roared off the field.

B. The latest airplanes were beautiful, large machines that roared when they took off, kicked up snow with the propellers, and slid on snow when they landed.

C. Although she was fascinated with the latest airplanes, Amelia Earhart knew she could never fly them because even a general's wife could not get permission to fly.

D. Amelia Earhart loved watching the beautiful new planes and wanted to fly; when she was unable to get permission to go up in them, she befriended the fliers instead.

8. Which statement best summarizes lines 31–40?

A. The pilot was bored, so he started to do more tricks and scared the two young women in the field.

B. The pilot lost control of the plane and it started to swoop down toward Earhart, who did not move.

C. After the pilot had run out of stunts and started diving at people, he dove at the two girls; Earhart stood watching, spellbound, and her friend ran away.

D. Earhart's friend ran away after the pilot of the stunt plane threatened the crowd at the fair, but Earhart froze in fear as the plane dove at her.

9. Which qualities can you infer Earhart has from her reaction to the diving plane?

A. pride and defiance

B. foolishness and immaturity

C. level-headedness and reliability

D. curiosity and courageousness

10. Which list presents the main events in this excerpt in chronological order?

A. Earhart met air force pilots; she saw her first plane; she stood in the path of a diving plane.

B. Earhart tamed a horse; she saw her first plane; she watched stunt flying.

C. Earhart saw her first plane; she watched air force pilots; she stood in the path of a diving plane.

D. Earhart tamed a horse; she went to a fair; she met war pilots.

Brief Constructed Response

11. What can you infer about the biographer's opinion of Amelia Earhart?

12. What can you infer from Earhart's explanation in lines 38–40 that, "I did not understand it at the time but I believe that little red airplane said something to me as it swished by"?

GO ON

861

9. D is correct. A, B, and C can be eliminated because they are not supported by the details used to describe the incident.

10. C is correct. A and B are incorrect because Earhart saw her first plane before she met air force pilots and tamed a horse. D is incorrect because she went to a fair before she tamed a horse.

Brief Constructed Response

Evaluate student writing using the Maryland writing rubrics in the back of the book.

Possible responses:

11. *The biographer admires her subject. In this excerpt she highlights many of Earhart's positive qualities. Students might give examples such as these:*

- **Skill:** *She could tame a wild horse (lines 1–8).*

- **Determination:** *When she couldn't get permission to fly, she befriended the fliers (lines 20–24).*

- **Daring:** *She stood in the path of a diving plane (lines 31–36).*

- **Intelligence:** *She understood instinctively the dangers of flying (lines 36–38).*

12. *When reflecting back on this event, Earhart was aware that it helped spark her desire to become a pilot. Before that, she knew she wanted to go up in a plane (line 22), but as she stood in the path of this little red airplane, she realized that she wanted to be the one who could make a plane loop and roll and dive.*

DIFFERENTIATED INSTRUCTION

FOR ENGLISH LEARNERS

Organize Information To help students respond to question 11, have them use a Cluster Diagram to list examples that show Earhart's positive qualities. Have partners work together to make inferences about the biographer's opinion.

BEST PRACTICES TOOLKIT—Transparency
Cluster Diagram p. B18

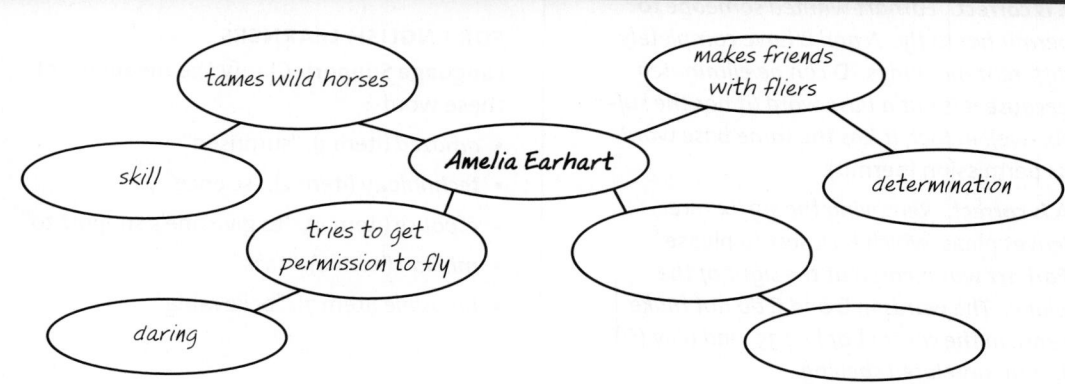

Vocabulary

1. **A is correct.** Amelia's ability with the horses was "pressed into" the minds of the air force officers. The context suggests that the officers were amazed she could control a horse that had bucked a colonel. While the experience did influence the officers to invite Earhart to the airfield, we can eliminate B because it does not relate to the detail about the colonel. C and D are incorrect because they have negative connotations, and it is clear from the context that the officers had a positive reaction to Earhart.

2. **B is correct.** We can eliminate A, C, and D because these all refer to living beings, and the planes mentioned in line 17 are machines that are the result of technological advances.

3. **B is correct.** As the plane prepared to swoop down over Earhart, she felt a sudden increase of both fear and pleasure. We can eliminate A because marched does not suggest the image of rising from below. C is incorrect because settled presents the image of descending from above. D is incorrect because Earhart's emotions did not increase and decrease in waves; they simply increased.

4. **D is correct.** Removing the suffix -ure from exposure shows that it is closest to expose. The words in A, B, and C have different spellings, and their meanings do not fit with the context of line 2.

5. **A is correct.** Removing the suffix -ation leaves combin, which is closest to combine. B and C can be eliminated because the words have significantly different spellings. D can be eliminated because the meaning of comb does not fit the context of line 4.

6. **C is correct.** Earhart wanted someone to permit her to fly. A and B have completely different meanings. D can be eliminated because it is not a base word (it has the suffix -ive); in fact, it has the same base word as permission (permit).

7. **A is correct.** Removing the suffix -ure leaves pleas, which is closest to please. Earhart was pleased at the sight of the plane. The words in B and C do not make sense in the context of line 35, and play (D) has an unrelated spelling.

Vocabulary

DIRECTIONS *Use context clues and the definitions of the Latin words and roots to answer the following questions.*

1. The prefix *im-* means "into," and the Latin word *premere* means "to press." What is the most likely meaning of *impressed* as it is used in line 5?
   - **A.** amazed
   - **B.** influenced
   - **C.** annoyed
   - **D.** pressured

2. The Latin root *gen* means "to be produced." What is the most likely meaning of the word *generation* as it is used in line 17?
   - **A.** a group of people born at about the same time
   - **B.** new technology developed from earlier models
   - **C.** a stage in the life cycle of an organism
   - **D.** time between the birth of parents and the birth of their children

3. The Latin word *surgere* means "to rise." What is the most likely meaning of *surged* as it is used in line 35?
   - **A.** marched in columns
   - **B.** increased suddenly
   - **C.** settled gradually
   - **D.** flowed in waves

DIRECTIONS *Use your knowledge of base words to answer the following questions.*

4. The word *exposure* is used in line 2. What is the base word of *exposure*?
   - **A.** espouse
   - **B.** explode
   - **C.** expound
   - **D.** expose

5. The word *combination* is used in line 4. What is the base word of *combination*?
   - **A.** combine
   - **B.** combat
   - **C.** combust
   - **D.** comb

6. The word *permission* is used in line 22. What is the base word of *permission*?
   - **A.** mission
   - **B.** permeate
   - **C.** permit
   - **D.** permissive

7. The word *pleasure* is used in line 35. What is the base word of *pleasure*?
   - **A.** please
   - **B.** plausible
   - **C.** plead
   - **D.** play

DIFFERENTIATED INSTRUCTION

FOR ENGLISH LEARNERS

Language Support Clarify the meanings of these words:

- *amazed* (item 1), "surprised"
- *technology* (item 2), "science"
- *espouse* (item 4), "to give one's support to"
- *mission* (item 6), "task"
- *plausible* (item 7), "believable"

Review Academic Vocabulary Write this academic vocabulary from page 862 on the board and have groups brainstorm what they know about each topic:

- *context clues* (first direction line)
- *prefix* (item 1)
- *Latin root* (item 2)
- *base word* (second direction line; items 4–7)

Writing & Grammar

DIRECTIONS *Read the passage and answer the questions that follow.*

> (1) Throughout the years, women have excelled in the field of aviation. (2) In 1912, harriet quimby became the first woman to fly across the english channel. (3) Nine years later, Bessie Coleman became the world's first licensed African-American aviator. (4) In 1935, amelia earhart became the first person to fly solo across the Pacific ocean. (5) Women reached another milestone on june 17, 1983, when astronaut Sally Ride became the first U.S. woman in space. (6) The book At the Controls: Women in Aviation has more on this subject. (7) Also check Aviation History magazine for an article entitled Lady Lindy: The Remarkable Life of Amelia Earhart.

1. Which nouns should be capitalized in sentence 2?

  A. harriet, quimby

  B. harriet, quimby, woman

  C. english channel

  D. harriet, quimby, english channel

2. Which nouns should be capitalized in sentence 4?

  A. amelia, earhart, person

  B. amelia, earhart, ocean

  C. amelia

  D. person, ocean

3. Which noun should be capitalized in sentence 5?

  A. june

  B. woman

  C. astronaut

  D. space

4. Choose the correct way to punctuate the title in sentence 6.

  A. *At the Controls: Women in Aviation*

  B. "At the Controls: Women in Aviation"

  C. "At the Controls": *Women in Aviation*

  D. *"At the Controls: Women in Aviation"*

5. Choose the correct use of italics and quotation marks for the titles in sentence 7.

  A. *Aviation History* and *Lady Lindy: The Remarkable Life of Amelia Earhart*

  B. *Aviation History* and "Lady Lindy: The Remarkable Life of Amelia Earhart."

  C. "Aviation History" and "Lady Lindy: The Remarkable Life of Amelia Earhart"

  D. "Aviation History" and *Lady Lindy: The Remarkable Life of Amelia Earhart*

STOP

ANSWERS
Writing & Grammar

1. **D** *is correct.* A, B, *and* C *can be eliminated because none of these choices includes all of the proper nouns in sentence 2. The word* woman, *as in B, is almost always used as a common noun and not capitalized.*

2. **B** *is correct. It is more complete than* C. A *and* D *can be eliminated because each contains the word* person, *which should not be capitalized because it is not a proper noun.*

3. **A** *is correct. The names of months of the year should be capitalized.* B, C, *and* D *are common nouns and therefore should not be capitalized.*

4. **A** *is correct. Book titles should be italicized.* B, C, *and* D *are incorrect because they include quotation marks, which are not used around book titles.*

5. **B** *is correct. Magazine titles should be in italics, and titles of articles should be enclosed in quotation marks.* A *incorrectly uses italics for both the magazine title and the article title.* C *incorrectly uses quotation marks for both titles.* D *incorrectly uses quotation marks for the magazine title and italics for the article title.*

DIFFERENTIATED INSTRUCTION

FOR ENGLISH LEARNERS

Assessment Support: Proper Nouns Remind students that a common noun is a general name for a person, place, thing, or idea and is not usually capitalized. A proper noun is the name of a particular person, place, thing, or idea and is always capitalized. Have students sort the following words into common and proper nouns and ask them to capitalize the proper nouns: *chicago, brother, uncle jim, aviator, des moines, lake.*

Common Nouns	Proper Nouns
brother	Chicago
aviator	Uncle Jim
lake	Des Moines

UNIT 7

More Great Reads

Ideas for Independent Reading

Which of the questions in Unit 7 made an impression on you? Continue exploring them with these books.

What is your duty toward others?

Lyddie
by Katherine Paterson

When her family loses their farm, 14-year-old Lyddie Worthen risks everything and takes a job in a Massachusetts mill. Under the worst possible working conditions, she succeeds in overcoming adversity through the strength of her character.

Across Five Aprils
by Irene Hunt

This historical novel centers on the divided loyalties of the Creightons during the Civil War. Jethro is left behind to run the family farm, but he is not spared the horrors of war as experienced from the home front.

The Greatest: Muhammad Ali
by Walter Dean Myers

This biography traces the life of boxer Muhammad Ali from his childhood through his present-day struggles with Parkinson's disease. Along the way, he fights racism, stands up for his beliefs, and becomes a hero to millions.

When is there dignity in silence?

Touching Spirit Bear
by Ben Mikaelsen

Families have rules, schools have rules, and societies have rules. Fifteen-year-old Cole Matthews has always had trouble with those rules. Can he change his destructive path while living alone on a remote island?

On the Way Home
by Laura Ingalls Wilder

Finding strength in writing, Laura Ingalls Wilder captures in her diary the landscapes, cultures, and people she encounters as her family travels from South Dakota to Missouri in the late 1800s.

Homeless Bird
by Gloria Whelan

What is it like to live in a society where how you are treated depends on your gender? In modern-day India, 13-year-old Koly must marry a 16-year-old boy from a distant village. When he dies, Koly is alone in an unfamiliar city.

How can we change what's wrong?

Beyond the Burning Time
by Kathryn Lasky

What would it take to make you stand alone? In a New England village during colonial times, 12-year-old Mary Chase must defend her mother against the community's accusations of witchcraft.

The Golden Compass
by Philip Pullman

Fairy tales and legends allow you to imagine yourself saving the world. In the first book of a trilogy, the adventurer Lyra holds the future of the world and all of its inhabitants in her hands.

Under the Blood-Red Sun
by Graham Salisbury

Life is normal for 13-year-old Tomi Nakaji. Then, on December 7, 1941, Japanese planes bomb Pearl Harbor and Tomi's world turns into a nightmare.

UNIT 8

Face the Facts

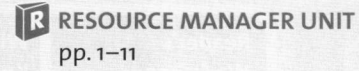

INFORMATION, ARGUMENT, AND PERSUASION

- In Nonfiction
- In Media

865

About the Art This image of the surface of Mars appears with the article "Why We Shouldn't Go to Mars." See page 932.

For help in planning this unit, see

R RESOURCE MANAGER UNIT 8
pp. 1–11

INTRODUCE THE UNIT

When U.S. astronauts landed on the moon in 1969, the event was covered around the world on TV and in print media. Despite the evidence of live images, photographs, and detailed text reports, however, some people refused to believe that the event really took place. For them, the evidence was not enough to prove that the claims were true. Ask students how people evaluate information to determine whether it is true or false. What sources do people trust most? What kinds of details are convincing?

Ask students to keep these ideas in mind as they discuss the pictures on this page. To spark a discussion, ask

- What does each image depict? (Make sure students understand that the larger picture is a computer-generated image of the surface of Mars.)
- Do both images depict reality? Explain.
- Which image would you use on the cover of a report about the U.S. space agency, NASA? Why?
- Which image would you use to accompany an article about the importance of going to Mars? What message does your choice convey?

Explain that in this unit, students will read selections that use facts for the purposes of **informing, argument,** and **persuasion.** Students will discover how to determine what is true, what is false, and what is open to debate.

UNIT 8
Standards Skills Trace

MARYLAND

SKILLS STRAND	Reader's Workshop: Reading for Information pp. 868–871 *1.E.4.a, 2.A.2.a, 2.A.2.b*	What Do You Know About Sharks? pp. 872–883 Magazine Article Level: Easy *1.D.3.c, 2.A.2.a, 2.A.2.b, 5.C.2.a*	Great White Sharks pp. 884–893 Magazine Article Level: Average *1.D.3.b, 2.A.4.h, 2.A.6.d*	Like Black Smoke: The Black Death's Journey / A World Turned Upside Down: How the Black Death Affected Europe pp. 894–907 Magazine Articles Level: Average *1.D.3.c, 1.E.3.a, 2.A.3.a, 2.A.3.b*	Media Study: News Reports pp. 908–911 TV Newscast Clip, Web News Report *2.A.6.b*	Reader's Workshop: Argument and Persuasion pp. 912–917 *2.A.6.d, 2.A.6.f*
Reading and Informational Texts	Use Text Features pp. 868, 871 Identify Main Ideas and Supporting Details pp. 870, 871 Take Notes pp. 870–871 Identify Topic Sentences p. 870 Analyze the Literature pp. 869, 871	Use Text Features pp. 873, 874, 875, 877, 878, 879, 880, 881 Outline a Text pp. 873, 875, 876, 877, 881	Identify Fact and Opinion pp. 885, 888, 889, 890, 892 Recognize Author's Bias pp. 885, 887, 891, 892 Review: Compare-and-Contrast Organization pp. 885, 887	Compare Patterns of Organization pp. 895, 899, 900, 901, 903, 904, 905 Set a Purpose for Reading pp. 895, 896, 902 Review: Interpret Graphic Aids pp. 895, 897, 898, 904, 905		Argument and Persuasion pp. 912–917 Analyze the Literature pp. 913, 915–917
Vocabulary	Academic Vocabulary pp. 868, 870	Word Acquisition pp. 873, T873, 882 Context Clues p. T873 Content-Specific Words p. 882	Word Acquisition pp. 885, T885, 893 Context Clues p. T885 Prefixes and Latin Roots (*vert*) p. 893	Word Acquisition pp. 895, T895, 906 Context Clues p. T895 Specialized Vocabulary p. 906	Academic Vocabulary (News Report) p. 909	Academic Vocabulary pp. 912, 914
Writing, Grammar, and Style		Appositive Phrases p. 883 Commas in Appositive Phrases p. 883		Write for Assessment p. 907		
Speaking, Listening, Viewing, and Media	Discuss pp. 868–870	Discuss pp. 872, T874–T880, 881	Discuss pp. 884, T886–T891, 892 Analyze Visuals pp. 886, T889	Discuss pp. 894, T896–T900, 901, T902–T904, 905 Analyze Visuals pp. 896, T900, 903	Discuss pp. 908, 911 Compare News Reports for Newsworthiness pp. 909–910 Make a Reporter's Guidebook p. 911	Discuss pp. 912–915

Assessment-Based Planning: Skills in red are assessed on the Unit 8 Test. **T** = Teacher's Edition page

MARYLAND STANDARDS

For a full listing of state standards see page S1.

1.D.3.a, 2.A.6.d, 2.A.6.f, 5.C.2.a	1.D.3.b, 1.E.3.a, 2.A.6.d	1.D.3.c, 2.A.6.b, 2.A.6.f, 5.C.2	2.A.6.f	4.A.1, 4.A.2.d, 7.A.1
Pro Athletes' Salaries Aren't Overly Exorbitant / Do Professional Athletes Get Paid Too Much? pp. 918–927 Editorials *Level: Average*	**Why We Shouldn't Go to Mars** pp. 928–935 Magazine Article *Level: Challenging*	**Remarks at the Dedication of the Aerospace Medical Health Center** pp. 936–943 Speech *Level: Challenging*	**Media Study: Persuasive Techniques in Commercials** pp. 944–947 TV Commercials	**Writing Workshop: Persuasive Essay** pp.948–955
Argument pp. 919, 920, 921, 922, 923, 925	Counterargument pp. 929, 931, 933, 934	Persuasive Techniques pp. 937, 939, 940, 941		Analyze a Persuasive Essay pp. 949–950, 954
Evaluate Reasoning pp. 919, 920, 921, 924, 925	Take Notes pp. 929, 932, 934	Strategies for Reading a Speech pp. 938, 939, 940, 941		
Word Acquisition pp. 919, T919, 926	Word Acquisition pp. 929, T929, 935	Word Acquisition pp. 937, T937, 942	Academic Vocabulary (TV Commercial) p. 945	
Word Questioning Map p. T919	Context Clues p. T929	Context Clues p. T937		
Idioms p. 926	Greek Roots (*aut*) p. 935	Acronym p. 942		
Commas After Introductory Words and Phrases and in a Series p. 927		Colons p. 943		Write a Persuasive Essay pp. 948–955 Supporting Evidence pp. 948, 951, 952 Interrogative Pronouns p. 954
Discuss pp. 918, T920–T924, 925	Discuss pp. 928, T930–T933, 934 Analyze Visuals p. 930	Discuss pp. 936, T938–T940, 941	Discuss pp. 944, 947 Analyze Persuasion in TV Advertising pp. 945–946 Identify a Target Audience p. 945 Design a Print Ad p. 947	Discuss pp. 948–950 Deliver a Persuasive Speech p. 955

Skills Assessed on the Unit 8 Test:

Reading and Informational Texts
- Identify main ideas and supporting details
- Recognize author's bias
- Identify facts and opinions
- Use text features to locate and comprehend information
- Identify and compare patterns of organization (cause and effect, chronological order)
- Understand elements of an argument
- Analyze persuasive techniques

Vocabulary
- Understand and use Latin roots and words
- Understand and use prefixes
- Define idioms by using context clues

Writing, Grammar, and Style
- Write a persuasive essay
- Use commas correctly (in appositive phrases, in a series, after introductory words)
- Use colons correctly (in lists and formal greetings, between numerals in the time)
- Additional writing and grammar skills

For additional lesson planning help, see **Easy Planner DVD.**

OBJECTIVES

- establish prior knowledge about evaluating information
- write a persuasive paragraph

Can you BELIEVE
everything you read?

Ask students how they would feel if something they read about and believed was later shown to be false. What can be learned from such an experience?

ACTIVITY Brainstorm sources and list students' ideas on the board. Suggest that students think about sources that relate to their interests and activities, such as places to find information about sports, entertainment, and hobbies. Then have students answer the questions on page 866. When students write their paragraphs, remind them to include reasons and examples.

CHECK UNDERSTANDING Ask students how they can tell if a source of information is reliable and accurate.

Unit Resources

866

Can you BELIEVE
everything you read?

All around you are sources of information—newspapers, books, magazines, and the Internet, to name a few. You may also get information from television, radio, billboards, product labels, and people you know. But can you **believe** all of it? It is important to learn to evaluate the information you receive so that you can know what to believe and what not to believe.

ACTIVITY What do you know? How did you come to know it? Think about all the sources of information you encounter in a day. Make a list of the sources, and then answer the following questions:

- How useful is the information you get from each source?
- Which source do you depend on most often?
- Is the information from that source always accurate?

After answering these questions, write a paragraph encouraging people to use your favorite source for information.

Dog Enrolls in College

August 9   Dr. Zachary Lynch, veterinarian at Zach's General Store, thought that someone had made a mistake when he was asked to help conduct physicals for incoming freshmen at the local community...

Two-Headed Turtle Talks Twice As Muc...

August 9   In recent scientists have been observ language habits of the r discovered two-headed turt turtle, which was found nest a small island off the coast c Bora, seemed somewhat disor...

R RESOURCE MANAGER UNIT 8

BEST PRACTICES TOOLKIT

S STANDARDS LESSON FILE

- Easy Planner DVD
- Write*Smart* CD
- ClassZone.com
- Audio Anthology CD
- Multi-Language Academic Vocabulary Online

- eEdition CD & Online
- McDougal Littell Assessment System
- Test Generator CD
- Media*Smart* DVD

 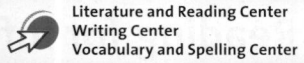
 MARYLAND OBJECTIVES

Preview Unit Goals

READING
- Identify main idea and supporting details
- Identify fact and opinion
- Identify and use text features to locate and comprehend information
- Understand elements of an argument
- Analyze persuasive techniques
- Evaluate reasoning

WRITING AND GRAMMAR
- Write a persuasive essay
- Use commas and colons correctly

SPEAKING, LISTENING, AND VIEWING
- Deliver a persuasive speech
- Compare how different media cover the same event
- Recognize and analyze persuasive techniques in television advertising
- Identify target audience

VOCABULARY
- Use word roots and prefixes to help determine the meanings of words
- Use context clues to understand idioms

ACADEMIC VOCABULARY
- fact
- opinion
- text features
- argument
- persuasive techniques
- reasoning

867

Preview Unit Goals

This page provides an overview of the skills and strategies covered in this unit. Make sure students are aware of the color coding that identifies each skill strand. This color coding is used wherever skills are taught in the unit. Encourage students to consider their ability to use each skill and strategy as they read this page.

Suggest that students copy the Academic Vocabulary terms in their journals and define them in their own words as they read the unit. Encourage students to use these terms as they discuss and write about the selections.

ADDITIONAL UNIT GOALS

These skills will be taught in this unit but are not the major focus of the unit:

Elements of Nonfiction
- Interpret graphic aids
- Study a variety of genres: magazine article, editorial, speech

Reading
- Set a purpose for reading
- Read a speech aloud
- Identify topic sentence
- Recognize and analyze author's bias
- Take notes in a graphic organizer, outline, or other format
- Outline a text
- Identify and compare patterns of organization (cause-and-effect, chronological order)
- Analyze an argument

Writing and Grammar
- Write a compare-contrast essay

Speaking, Listening, and Viewing
- Identify characteristics of newsworthiness in a news report
- Create a reporter's guidebook
- Design a print ad

Vocabulary
- Understand and use content-area and specialized vocabulary
- Understand origins and meanings of acronyms

DIFFERENTIATED INSTRUCTION

FOR ENGLISH LEARNERS

Academic Vocabulary Students will study and practice using these terms throughout the unit. Use the Academic Vocabulary copy master to introduce the terms.

1. Read each word aloud and discuss the example. Ask if students have heard any of these words and, if so, in what context.

2. Allow students to work in pairs to complete the definitions and the activities. Then discuss students' answers as a class.

Additional Academic Vocabulary Use the second copy master to teach *counterargument, acronyms, outline, graphic aids, appositive, bias, loaded language,* and *overgeneralization.*

1. Have partners work together to complete the definitions. Then have students complete the sentences and Part B individually.

2. Have students share their work.

R RESOURCE MANAGER—Copy Masters
Academic Vocabulary p. 9
Additional Academic Vocabulary p. 10

867

Focus and Motivate

OBJECTIVES

- identify main ideas and supporting details
- identify topic sentences
- take notes in a graphic organizer, an outline, or another format
- identify and use text features (title, headings, subheadings, graphic aids, captions) to locate and comprehend information

Teach

Part 1: Get the Big Picture

Preview Text Features Tell students they will preview the workshop as if it is an article that they will report on. Use the PLAN process to show students how to use text features to plan their reading.

1. **P—Preview** content and structure: Begin a Cluster Diagram by writing the workshop title in the center circle (*Reading for Information*). Then add a circle for the first main heading (*Part 1: Get the Big Picture*). Add another circle for the first subheading (*Model: Text Features*).

2. **L—Locate** visual information: Have students locate any graphic aids and note each one in a circle connected to the appropriate head.

3. **A—Add** information as you read: Have students scan the article, looking for boldfaced words. Add the words to a circle near the related head.

4. **N—Note** your reflections on the information: As you add information to the organizer, include these symbols to note students' reactions to the text:

   X = familiar information
   ? = unfamiliar information
   + = interesting or important
   ! = surprising or amazing

   Tell students that the symbols will help them decide which parts of the text they should spend the most time studying.

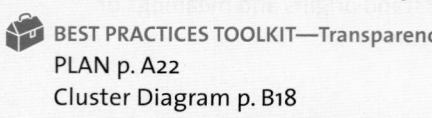 **BEST PRACTICES TOOLKIT—Transparencies**
PLAN p. A22
Cluster Diagram p. B18
Analysis Frame: Persuasion pp. D23, D46

Reading for Information

In today's information age, knowledge is power. Facts and figures on just about any subject, from consumer products to Jupiter's moons, are virtually at your fingertips. How do you find the information you're looking for? What are the best ways to understand and remember what you read? Learning a few simple strategies now can give you an edge and empower you for a lifetime.

 **MARYLAND OBJECTIVES**

READING/INFO TEXT STANDARDS
1.E.4.a Identify and explain the main idea
2.A.2.a Analyze print features
2.A.2.b Analyze graphic aids

Part 1: Get the Big Picture

Flipping through a newspaper or surfing the Web can be an overwhelming experience. That's because information overload can keep you from knowing where to begin. To help readers get their bearings and quickly see what a text is about, many writers use **text features,** or special design elements. Text features include headings, subheadings, boldfaced type, and captions. These elements all serve as road signs, guiding you through a text and pointing out key ideas.

Just as you would look at a road map before driving to a new place, you may also find it helpful to **preview** a text before you start to read it carefully. Notice how much you can tell about this article by scanning the text features.

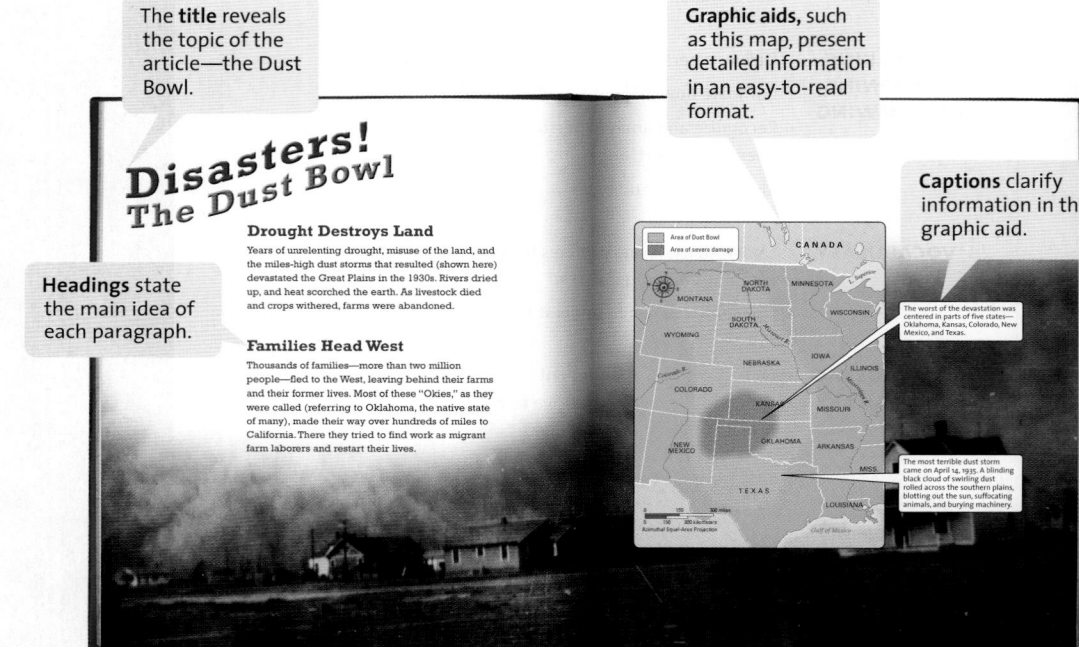

The **title** reveals the topic of the article—the Dust Bowl.

Graphic aids, such as this map, present detailed information in an easy-to-read format.

Captions clarify information in the graphic aid.

Headings state the main idea of each paragraph.

Disasters! The Dust Bowl

Drought Destroys Land
Years of unrelenting drought, misuse of the land, and the miles-high dust storms that resulted (shown here) devastated the Great Plains in the 1930s. Rivers dried up, and heat scorched the earth. As livestock died and crops withered, farms were abandoned.

Families Head West
Thousands of families—more than two million people—fled to the West, leaving behind their farms and their former lives. Most of these "Okies," as they were called (referring to Oklahoma, the native state of many), made their way over hundreds of miles to California. There they tried to find work as migrant farm laborers and restart their lives.

868

DIFFERENTIATED INSTRUCTION

FOR ALL STUDENTS

For general guidelines on differentiating instruction, see

 BEST PRACTICES TOOLKIT
Differentiated Instruction pp. 31–38

FOR LESS–PROFICIENT READERS

Note Taking Distribute the copy master. Read and discuss the first three paragraphs on page 868. Assist students in completing the first two items on the copy master. Then

have students read the rest of the page and take notes on the specific text features.

 RESOURCE MANAGER—Copy Master
Note Taking p. 15

Illustrate Text Features Have students work in small groups to create a sketch that shows typical text features of an article. The sketch may include two pages. Students can draw boxes and lines to represent text and graphics. Have them label each feature.

Quickly skim the text features of this article. After seeing these features, what information do you think the article will provide? Now read the passage closely and answer the questions.

from
EARTHQUAKES
Reference article in **Popular Science Almanac**

. . . Earth's crust isn't just one solid piece, like an eggshell. Instead, it's broken up into different pieces, called plates. . . .

5 . . . Plate movement is responsible for earthquakes as well as volcanoes. See, Earth's plates are constantly growing at one end, getting consumed at the other, shifting alongside other

10 plates, and pushing headlong into others. All of this causes a tremendous amount of pressure build-up. Rocks are rigid. Since they don't break easily, they resist this pressure for a long,

15 long time. But after a while, something's got to give. Rapid movement of massive blocks of rock releases the tension . . . at least for the time being.

The San Andreas Fault in California falls at the boundary of two tectonic plates. The slipping of these plates is often the cause of earthquakes in the region.

Anatomy of an Earthquake

A **FAULT** is the break in the rock where the movement that caused the earthquake occurred.

The **EPICENTER** is the area on the surface directly above the focus.

AFTERSHOCKS are little earthquakes that follow the initial one. They can go on for days.

The **FOCUS** of an earthquake is its underground point of origin. It's where the most rock movement occurs.

Close Read

1. If you were doing a report on the parts of an earthquake, would this article help you? Explain your answer.

2. Name two things you learn about earthquakes from the caption and the photograph.

3. Review the graphic aid at the bottom of this article. In your own words, describe the information it presents.

READER'S WORKSHOP **869**

MODEL: TEXT FEATURES
Close Read

1. ***Possible answer:*** *Yes. The title, "Earthquakes," indicates that the article addresses the right topic for the report. The title of the graphic aid, "Anatomy of an Earthquake," is directly related to the topic of the report.*

2. *Students may mention that the San Andreas Fault is in California, that it is at the boundary of two tectonic plates, and that when these plates slip, they cause earthquakes in the region.*

3. ***Possible answer:*** *The diagram and its labels define three terms that describe parts of an earthquake—fault, epicenter, and focus. Another label tells what aftershocks are.*

FOR ENGLISH LEARNERS

Vocabulary: Idioms Use context clues to teach the meaning of the following idioms used on page 868: *at your fingertips* ("easily available"); *give you an edge* ("give you an advantage"); *get the big picture* ("understand the entire situation"); *information overload* ("too much information"); *get their bearings* ("figure out where they are or what the situation is").

FOR ADVANCED LEARNERS/PRE–AP

Identify and Explain Text Features on Web Pages Have students read the workshop independently. Assign pairs to analyze the text features they find in Web articles. Have them use a T Chart to note the text features that they find and to explain the purpose of each feature. Ask students to highlight special features that appear on Web pages, such as links.

Text Features in Web Articles	
Feature	Purpose of Feature

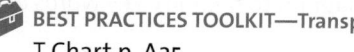 **BEST PRACTICES TOOLKIT—Transparency**
T Chart p. A25

Teach

Part 2: Read for Understanding

Main Idea Discuss with students how to find the main idea of a paragraph when it is not stated in the text. Distribute copies of the Main Idea and Details chart. Have students reread the second paragraph of the "Earthquakes" article on page 869, covering up the first sentence, which states the main idea. Tell students they can use this strategy to infer the main idea:

1. Look for the most important details. Write each important detail in the chart.

2. Ask yourself what one idea about earthquakes the details seem to support. Try to express that idea by summarizing the details in one sentence.

3. Discuss your summary sentence with a partner or group and adjust it as necessary to express the main idea of the paragraph.

Main Idea	Detail Notes
	1.
	2.
	3.

 BEST PRACTICES TOOLKIT—Transparency
Main Idea and Details p. B6

Take Notes After students read the outline, have them suggest graphic organizers they could use to take notes on an article (for example, Cluster Diagram, Main Idea and Details, Spider Map).

• Have small groups each select a graphic organizer and use it to take notes on the "Earthquakes" article.

• Have the groups compare the information they listed in their organizers.

• Discuss the pros and cons of each format. Have students consider ease of use, clarity of presentation, and level of detail included.

Point out that students' choice of organizer may vary according to their purpose for reading. If they are reading to gather specific information for a research paper, they may want to use an outline, to accommodate several levels of detail. If they are reading for more general information, they can use an organizer such as a Cluster Diagram to organize key words or concepts.

Part 2: Read for Understanding

Text features may be the road signs guiding you through a text, but your final destination is not just the end of the selection or page. It's arriving at an understanding of what you've read. The following strategies can help you reach that destination without running into roadblocks:

IDENTIFY THE MAIN IDEAS

To really understand a text, you first need to know how to find its main ideas. **Main ideas** are the most important ideas about a topic that a writer wants to communicate to readers. **Supporting details,** such as facts and examples, help to explain or elaborate on the main ideas. Most of the time, the main idea of a paragraph is directly stated in a **topic sentence,** which is usually located at the beginning or end of that paragraph. Consider this example from the article you just read.

> . . . Plate movement is responsible for earthquakes as well as volcanoes. See, Earth's plates are constantly growing at one end, getting consumed at the other, shifting alongside other plates, and pushing headlong into others. . . .

This **topic sentence** states the main idea of one paragraph in the article: the cause of earthquakes.

This **supporting detail** further explains what plate movement is and how it can cause earthquakes.

Sometimes the main idea is **implied**—suggested but not directly stated. In such a case, you have to **infer** it by asking yourself: What do all the supporting details add up to?

TAKE NOTES

Taking notes as you read can help you identify the main ideas and supporting details in a text and remember them after you've finishing reading. The key to good note taking is learning to zero in on the important information and restate it in your own words. You can take notes in a **graphic organizer,** an **outline,** or a variety of other formats.

To create a formal outline like this one, use Roman numerals to label the main ideas and capital letters to label the supporting points.

Earthquakes

I. Caused by movement of plates (pieces of the earth's crust)
   A. Plates hit each other.
   B. Movement causes pressure on rocks.
   C. Tension is released when rock shifts.
II. Anatomy of an earthquake
   A. Focus is the point where rock shifts underground.
   B. Epicenter is the point on surface above focus.

DIFFERENTIATED INSTRUCTION

FOR LESS–PROFICIENT READERS

Note Taking For students who need help with note taking, hand out the second copy master before beginning the preview. Then have students record their notes on the copy master as you discuss the information.

 RESOURCE MANAGER—Copy Master
Note Taking p. 16

FOR ADVANCED LEARNERS/PRE–AP

Outline Text Have students create an outline for Part 2 of the Reader's Workshop. Then have students compare their outlines to check main ideas and details.

Part 3: Analyze the Text

Read this article about the *Titanic*, the famous ship that sank in 1912. Preview the article and answer the first **Close Read** question. Then read the article more closely, using the other questions to help you take notes.

What's Eating the *Titanic*?

SCIENCE WATCH

The world's most famous sunken wreck becomes a gift for deep-sea scientists.

Oceanographer Robert Ballard is returning to the *Titanic*, but it's not the same sunken ship he found in 1985. The deep ocean has been steadily destroying the once-great cruise liner, and scientists say the process is unlike any they've ever seen. "Even if we could stop it, I
5 wouldn't," says scientist Charles Pellegrino. "The *Titanic* is becoming something that belongs to biology."

The ship has attracted all kinds of hungry deep-sea life. Other critters (including tourists) are steadily chomping away at the ship too. Here's your guide to the wreck's undoing.

THE CULPRITS	THE DESTRUCTION	AN END IN SIGHT?
Mollusks and microorganisms that stirred up from the ocean floor when the ship first hit bottom	Worms munched on softer woods, while microorganisms ate some clothes and other fabrics. By the time scientists arrived to survey the ship, only the hard woods, such as mahogany, remained.	The worms moved on—the worst is done.
Bacteria from the ocean floor	Living off the sulfur in steel, bacteria also remove iron for housing and get rid of the rest. Bacteria have sucked over 1,000 tons of iron from the ship.	The bacterial colonies are growing, and half the steel could be gone by 2204.
The elements, such as water pressure, salt, and icebergs	Water pressure damaged parts of the ship when it sank. Salt slowly eats away at the hull, while gravel from icebergs overhead rains down on the deck.	Some suggest saving specific parts of the *Titanic* by bringing them on shore.
Tourists, pirates, and explorers attracted by profit and the popularity of *Titanic* TV specials	Small submarines are used to explore the site of the wreck. Careless piloting of these submarines has caused some damage to the hull and the deck.	The government has rules for protecting sunken ships, but it does not have the power to enforce them.

Close Read

1. Preview the title, the subtitle, and the headings in the chart. What do you think this article will be about?

2. The main idea of the first paragraph is listed in the outline shown. In your notebook, record two supporting details.

> I. Scientists see the *Titanic's* destruction as an opportunity for study.
>   A.
>   B.

3. The second paragraph and the chart present another main idea listed by Roman numeral II. One supporting detail has been filled in. Complete the outline by adding other details.

> II. Many culprits are causing the destruction.
>   A. Mollusks and microorganisms
>   1. Worms ate softer woods
>   2. Microorganisms ate fabrics
>   3. Worst damage is done

DIFFERENTIATED INSTRUCTION

FOR LESS–PROFICIENT READERS

Infer Main Idea Point out that the main idea of the first paragraph, shown in the outline, is not stated in the text. Have students reread and discuss the last two sentences of the paragraph. Guide them to focus on these key details: the speaker is a scientist; he doesn't want to stop the destruction; he says the ship "belongs to biology." Lead students to infer that the scientist is interested in studying the processes that are destroying the *Titanic*.

FOR ENGLISH LEARNERS

Concept Support: Vocabulary Explain that *critters* (line 8) is slang for creatures. To help students define *culprits,* have them read across each row of the chart. Use sentence frames to show what each culprit does:

Mollusks and microorganisms _____ woods and fabrics. *(ate)*

Bacteria _____ iron from the ship. *(removed/sucked)*

Guide students to infer that *culprits* means "those who are guilty of doing something."

Practice and Apply

Part 3: Analyze the Text
Close Read

1. *Possible answer:* The article will be about the destruction of the wreck of the Titanic and why it is a "gift" to scientists.

2. *Possible answer:*
   A. *Steady destruction by deep ocean*
   B. *Unique process to be studied*

3. *Possible answer:*
   B. *Bacteria*
      1. *Destruction: bacteria destroyed tons of iron*
      2. *End in sight: half the steel gone by 2204*
   C. *Elements*
      1. *Destruction: water pressure, salt, and gravel from icebergs damaged parts of the ship*
      2. *End in sight: could bring some parts on shore*
   D. *People*
      1. *Destruction: small submarines collide with the hull and deck*
      2. *End in sight: destruction will continue*

Assess and Reteach

Assess

Have students briefly summarize how to use text features and note taking to read for information.

Reteach

For students who are unable to apply the workshop skills, try these reteaching options:

1. Review with students the note-taking copy masters for this lesson. Have pairs
   - compare the information they recorded
   - explain each term to one another, using their own words
   - question each other to clarify understanding
   - share their insights and challenges with the class

2. Refer students to an article the class has read recently. Help them use text features to tell what the article is about. Write the topic on the board. Then help students identify the main idea and supporting details and outline them.

Focus and Motivate

OBJECTIVES

Elements of Nonfiction
- explore the key idea of how appearances can **deceive**
- identify and use text features to locate and comprehend information
- read a magazine article

Reading
- outline a text
- identify main ideas and supporting details

Vocabulary
- build vocabulary for reading and writing
- understand and use content-area vocabulary *(also an EL language objective)*

Grammar and Writing
- use commas in appositive phrases
- use writing to analyze literature

SUMMARY

The article presents facts about the importance of sharks to the environment, their size, the threat they pose to people, the way they hunt and eat, their physiology, and their relationship to other aquatic creatures.

Can appearances DECEIVE?

Discuss the question and *KEY IDEA.* Ask students for examples of sayings that suggest that appearances can **deceive**. *(Don't judge a book by its cover. Beauty is only skin deep.)* Discuss the consequences of trusting appearances. Have students keep these ideas in mind as they complete the *DISCUSS* activity.

Selection Resources

What Do You Know About Sharks?
Magazine Article by Sharon Guynup

Can appearances DECEIVE?

MARYLAND OBJECTIVES

INFORMATIONAL TEXT STANDARDS
2.A.2.a Analyze print features
2.A.2.b Analyze graphic aids

KEY IDEA Cute doesn't always mean cuddly, and frightening doesn't always mean vicious. Appearances can **deceive,** as you will find out when you read "What Do You Know About Sharks?"

DISCUSS How much do you really know about sharks? Copy the chart shown here, and decide whether each statement is true or false. Then gather with others in a small group and share your answers. Does everyone agree on the "facts"?

Statement	True or False?
1. The great white is the largest shark.	
2. Most sharks are dangerous to humans.	
3. Sharks lived at the time of dinosaurs.	

872

 **RESOURCE MANAGER UNIT 8**

Plan and Teach pp. 17–24

Elements of Nonfiction
Summary pp. 25†*, 26‡*
Text Features pp. 27, 28†*
Question Support p. 35*

Reading
Outline pp. 29, 30†*
Reading Check p. 34
Reading Fluency p. 37

Vocabulary
Study p. 31*
Practice p. 32
Strategy p. 33

Grammar and Writing
Use Commas in Appositive Phrases p. 36

Assessment
Selection Tests A, B/C pp. 39*, 41*
 Test Generator CD

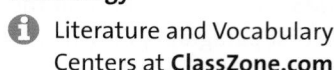 **BEST PRACTICES TOOLKIT**

Differentiated Instruction pp. 31–38*
Scaffolding Instruction pp. 43–46*

Graphic Organizers/Strategies
Jigsaw • New Word Analysis • Read Aloud/Think Aloud • Cause-and-Effect Diagram • Classification Chart

Reading Support
🖭 Audio Anthology CD*

Technology
ⓘ Literature and Vocabulary Centers at **ClassZone.com**

🖭 Write*Smart* CD

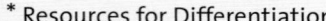

* Resources for Differentiation   † Also in Spanish   ‡ In Haitian Creole and Vietnamese

ELEMENTS OF NONFICTION: TEXT FEATURES

Writers use design elements called **text features** to organize text and to point out key ideas and important information. Some of the most common text features include

- titles
- sidebars
- captions
- subheadings
- graphic aids
- bulleted lists

As you read, use the notes in the margins as a guide to help you identify these features. Ask yourself how each text feature helps you understand what you are reading.

READING SKILL: OUTLINE

To help yourself keep track of the **main ideas** and **supporting details** in a text, create an **outline.** To take notes in outline form, follow these guidelines:

- Use the text features to identify the article's main ideas.
- Use a roman numeral to label each main idea.
- Under each main idea, add supporting details. Label each with a capital letter.

> **"What Do You Know About Sharks?"**
>
> I. Protection
>
> A. Sharks could vanish from ocean.
>
> B. Without sharks, other species would overpopulate.
>
> II. Kinds of Sharks

VOCABULARY IN CONTEXT

The boldfaced words helped Sharon Guynup share her knowledge of sharks and the sea. Use context clues to figure out what each word means.

1. Fish and whales are **aquatic** creatures.
2. The ocean is one kind of **ecosystem.**
3. A terrible disease can **decimate** a species.
4. The **carcass** of a half-eaten sea lion washed ashore.
5. Light will **diffuse** as it enters the water.
6. A life jacket increases a swimmer's **buoyancy.**

Author Online

Animal Lover
Sharon Guynup (gī'nəp) has found a way to combine her two loves, writing and the environment. She completed a master's degree in journalism from New York University's Science

Sharon Guynup
born 1958

and Environmental Reporting program and continues to write articles about animals and the environment. Her work has appeared in national science magazines, in newspapers, and on the Web. Guynup also produces *State of the Wild,* a yearly review of the condition of the world's wildlife and lands.

> **MORE ABOUT THE AUTHOR**
> To learn more about Sharon Guynup, visit the **Literature Center** at ClassZone.com.

Background

An Ocean of Knowledge How do we know so much about sharks? People who study fish and how they live and grow in their environment are called ichthyologists (ĭk'thē-ŏl'ə-jĭsts). Their work in laboratories, in museums, at universities, and on research ships provides information about over 300 species of sharks. "What Do You Know About Sharks?" gives information about sharks in general, as well as facts about specific species.

Teach

ELEMENTS OF NONFICTION

● TEXT FEATURES

Review the function of each text feature listed by asking students to explain where it might be found and to tell what kind of information it might contain.

CHECK UNDERSTANDING Have students identify an example of each text feature on pages 872–873.

READING SKILL

■ OUTLINE

Have students complete this outline based on the **Background** paragraph:

Learning About Sharks

 I. Ichthyologists

  A. They study how fish live and grow in their environment.

  B.

 II. "What Do You Know About Sharks?"

Possible answer: B. They work in laboratories, in museums, at universities, and on research ships.

CHECK UNDERSTANDING Have students explain one advantage of using an outline method of taking notes.

 RESOURCE MANAGER—Copy Master
Outline p. 29 (for student use while reading the selection)

▲ VOCABULARY IN CONTEXT

DIAGNOSE WORD KNOWLEDGE To determine preteaching needs, have all students complete **Vocabulary in Context.** Remind students to look for the definitions of the unknown words as they read the text: *aquatic* (p. 874), *ecosystem* (p. 874), *decimate* (p. 874), *carcass* (p. 877), *diffuse* (p. 878), *buoyancy* (p. 880).

PRETEACH VOCABULARY Use the Vocabulary Study copy master to help students explore the meaning of each boldfaced word.

1. Read the first set of sentences aloud, emphasizing *aquatic.*
2. Point out the phrase "die if removed from water." Elicit possible meanings for *aquatic,* such as "needing water."
3. Have students record their definitions in the chart.
4. Repeat for the rest of the words.

 RESOURCE MANAGER—Copy Master
Vocabulary Study p. 31

For general guidelines on differentiating vocabulary instruction and for alternative vocabulary activities for students not needing vocabulary preteaching, see

 BEST PRACTICES TOOLKIT
Scaffolding Vocabulary Instruction pp. 43–46

ⓘ Vocabulary Center at **ClassZone.com**

ELEMENTS OF NONFICTION

Ⓐ TEXT FEATURES

Possible answer: This article will give information about sharks.

Extend the Discussion What is the effect of phrasing the title as a question?

BACKGROUND

Food Chains A food chain, as mentioned in line 5, shows how energy moves from one living thing to another in the form of food. Most food chains have only four or five levels.

Lines 4–10
DISCUSSION PROMPTS

Use these prompts to help students understand the importance of sharks to other ocean life:

Connect What do you know about food chains in addition to what you have read in this article? *Students may have other facts to add from their science studies.*

Analyze If the population of one level on a food chain increases, what happens to the other levels? *Possible answer: The populations above them on the food chain would increase, but the populations below them would decrease.*

Synthesize In what ways might the disappearance of sharks affect humans? *Possible answers: Humans might not be able to obtain seafood. Overpopulation of some species and underpopulation of others might lead to changes in the quality of the ocean's water and environment. Land animals, affected by the loss of certain foods, might also disappear.*

Ⓐ **TEXT FEATURES**
The **title** often helps readers identify an article's main idea. What kind of information do you think this article will present?

Targeted Passage ①

aquatic (ə-kwăt′ĭk) *adj.* growing or living in the water

ecosystem (ē′kō-sĭs′təm) *n.* a physical environment, such as an ocean, and the community of things that live in it

decimate (dĕs′ə-māt′) *v.* to kill or destroy a large part of

WHAT DO YOU KNOW ABOUT SHARKS? Ⓐ

SHARON GUYNUP

They're ferocious predators. They haunt us in nightmares. But the scariest thing about sharks may be that they're vanishing from the world's oceans. . . .

Why do sharks need protection? Sharks are top predators in the **aquatic** food chain—a web that interconnects all organisms, in which smaller creatures become food for larger predators. Without sharks, the ocean's delicate **ecosystem** would be disrupted. Species that sharks devour, like seals, for example, would overpopulate and in turn **decimate** other species, like
10 salmon. Read the following questions and answers to learn more about the world's most fear-inspiring fish.

Nurse Shark
Nurse sharks are sluggish bottom dwellers found in the Atlantic Ocean. They're usually not dangerous and are one of the few sharks that breathe by pumping water through their gills while lying motionless. They sometimes suck in prey as well.

Wobbegong Shark
Wobbegongs are found resting on the sea floor in shallow waters of the Ind[...] Pacific and the Red Sea. The barbels fringe of flesh around their mouths, a[...] feelers that act as camouflage.

874 UNIT 8: INFORMATION, ARGUMENT, AND PERSUASION

DIFFERENTIATED INSTRUCTION

FOR ALL STUDENTS
Integrated Curriculum Have students make a connection to math by compiling statistics related to the disappearance of sharks in the world's oceans. Explain that overfishing, pollution, and other factors have affected the shark population in the past decade. Ask students to present their data in graphs or tables to show the trend.

FOR LESS—PROFICIENT READERS
In combination with the *Audio Anthology CD,* use one or more Targeted Passages (pp. 874, 880) to ensure that students focus on key facts, concepts, and skills.

① **Targeted Passage [Lines 1–10]**
This passage presents a main idea of the article: sharks are vital members of the ocean's food chain and must be protected.

- What is happening to the number of sharks in the ocean?
- Where are sharks in the food chain?
- What would happen if sharks could not fill their role in the food chain?

What Are Sharks? **B**

Sharks are fish with skeletons made of rubbery cartilage (tough, flexible tissue) instead of bone. They're cold-blooded (unable to generate their own body heat), breathe through gills (respiratory organs), and have a two-chambered heart. Though most live in warm seas, the Greenland shark thrives in frigid Arctic seas. **C**

What's the Largest Shark? The Smallest?

Weighing in at 15 tons and stretching up to 14 meters (46 feet) long, the whale shark is the world's largest fish—bigger than a school bus! Nine hundred meters (2,953 feet) below the ocean surface lives the smallest shark: the dwarf shark. An adult measures only 25 centimeters (10 inches) long!

Are All Sharks Dangerous to People?

Most sharks are harmless. "Out of 375 shark species, only two dozen are in any way really dangerous to us," says Robert Hueter, director of the Center for Shark Research at Mote Marine Laboratory. Still, scientists don't know for sure why sharks sometimes attack humans. One theory: sharks may mistake the sound of swimming humans for that of injured fish—which are easy prey.

Goblin Shark
Goblin sharks feature needle-like teeth. They're rarely spotted—only 36 specimens have been counted—most found in waters deeper than 1,150 feet. Scientists think they inhabit seas from Europe to Australia.

Hammerhead Shark
Hammerheads inhabit shorelines and deep seas worldwide. The head, or cephalofoil, provides greater maneuverability—and enlarged nostrils and eyes at the ends of their "hammer" receive more information giving them a hunting advantage. **D**

B OUTLINE
Each orange question is a **subheading** that introduces a new main idea. State each main idea as a phrase and add it to your outline.

C OUTLINE
What are the important details in this paragraph? Add them to your outline.

D TEXT FEATURES
Sidebars are set off from the main article—usually on the side or bottom of the page—and provide additional information. You can read sidebars at any time. What information does this sidebar give you?

Ⓔ TEXT FEATURES

Possible answer: The subheading "Where Do Most Shark Attacks Happen?" suggests that the following section will tell where swimmers are most at risk.

BACKGROUND

Jaws The "*Jaws* flicks" (line 34) are a series of movies involving attacks on humans by great white sharks. The first *Jaws* film, directed by Steven Spielberg, was released in 1975. It shattered box-office records and increased many people's fear and loathing of sharks.

Sidebar
REINFORCE *KEY IDEA*: DECEIVE

Discuss What does the appearance of the whale shark suggest about its nature? What fact proves that this impression of the shark is **deceiving**? *Possible answer: The whale shark's enormous size suggests that it is dangerous to humans. However, because it eats tiny plankton, it is not a threat to humans.*

Lines 36–46
DISCUSSION PROMPTS

Use these prompts to help students understand the threat posed by sharks:

Connect Did you think the number of shark attacks was higher or lower than 100 each year? *Students may say that they thought the number was much higher.*

Analyze How do you think the frequency of shark attacks on humans compares to the rate of fatalities caused by other accidents, such as those involving cars? *Possible answer: Car or other accidents cause many more deaths each year. According to the World Health Organization, there are over 1 million traffic fatalities a year worldwide.*

Evaluate Why does the writer include the information on the strength of the shark's bite in this section? *Possible answers:*

- *It is a reminder that sharks are not harmless; they are powerful creatures that should be treated with respect.*
- *It is the kind of information that most readers would find interesting. Also, the comparison to the weight of a car is something that readers can relate to.*

Ⓔ TEXT FEATURES
Preview the **subheadings** on these pages. Which section will tell you where swimmers are most at risk?

Which Shark Is the Most Dangerous to Humans? Ⓔ

30 "In terms of fatal attacks, it's a tossup between the great white, the tiger, and the bull shark," Hueter says. People fear the massive great white the most because of its size—up to 6.4 meters (21 feet) long—and its large razor-like teeth, not to mention the terror stirred up by *Jaws* flicks. But great whites usually inhabit deep seas—not shallow waters where people swim. Worldwide, fewer than 100 human attacks by all shark species are reported each year.

Where Do Most Shark Attacks Happen?

Florida leads the world in shark bites, with 22 to 25 reported incidents each year. But, claims Hueter, they're not repeated
40 shark attacks—usually a single bite. . . . "Most really bad attacks occur off the coasts of California, Hawaii, Australia, and South Africa," Hueter says.

Just How Powerful Is a Shark's Bite?

Scientists built a "shark-bite meter" that measures the jaw strength of one species, the dusky shark. It exerts 18 tons of pressure per square inch on a victim. That's like being crushed beneath the weight of ten cars!

Whale Shark
The largest fish in the sea—whale sharks—are very docile. They feed on plankton, tiny drifting animals. They swim with their enormous mouths open, filtering food from the water with 15,000 tiny teeth.

Leopard Shark
Leopard sharks are commonly found near shore, often in large schools along the Pacific coast from Oregon to Mexico. They feed on small fish and crustaceans and are generally harmless.

DIFFERENTIATED INSTRUCTION

FOR ENGLISH LEARNERS
Language: Punctuation Point out the dashes in lines 32 and 33. Tell students that dashes usually set off information that helps explain, emphasize, or reinforce an idea already stated in the sentence. For example, in lines 32–33, the measurements of the great white shark are given. Have students point out other sentences on these pages in which the dash is used. Discuss what the information set off by dashes adds to their comprehension.

FOR ADVANCED LEARNERS/PRE–AP
Synthesize After a shark attack, people in coastal areas such as Florida often stay away from the beaches, creating problems for the recreation industry. Have students create a poster on behalf of the Florida tourism board that corrects misconceptions about sharks. Invite students to share their posters with the class.

What Do Sharks Eat?

Sharks chow down on what they can when they can—usually smaller animals from shrimp and fish to turtles and seabirds. Some, like the bull shark, consume large mammals like
50 sea lions or dolphins; others, like the whale shark, eat only plankton, tiny drifting animals. And tiger sharks devour just about anything—mammal <u>carcasses</u>, tin cans, plastic bags, coal, and even license plates have been found inside their stomachs! **F**

How Do Sharks Find Prey?

Sharks can hear a wide range of sounds but are attracted by bursts of sound—like those made by an injured fish—or occasionally humans romping in water. At close range, sharks also sense vibration with their lateral line, a sensory system that runs from head to tail on each side of a shark's body.
60 Inside the lateral line, which helps a shark maintain balance as well as detect sound, are canals filled with fluid and tiny "hair cells." Sound causes the liquid to vibrate, alerting the shark to the presence of another creature. This sense allows sharks to hunt even in total darkness.

Brushing and Flossing

Sharks continually lose their teeth, but some species grow new teeth as often as every week to replace worn or lost ones. During their lifetime, some species shed 30,000 teeth. Shark teeth vary according to what's on the menu:

top: nurse shark teeth, which chew up shellfish

middle: tiger shark teeth, which crunch everything from fish and birds to tin cans and other garbage

bottom: mako shark teeth, which grind up squid and big fish like tuna and mackerel **G**

carcass (kär'kəs) *n.* the dead body of an animal

F OUTLINE
How many details about what sharks eat have you included in your outline? Remember, you can include as many lettered details as you need.

G TEXT FEATURES
Graphic aids are visuals, such as graphs, photographs, and maps, that provide more information on a topic. What information do you get from looking at these photographs that you don't get from the text?

F OUTLINE

Have students add their answers to their outlines. ***Possible answers:***

VIII. What Sharks Eat

A. *Sharks eat what is available.*

B. *Most eat smaller animals, ranging from shrimp and fish to turtles and seabirds.*

C. *Some sharks eat large mammals like sea lions or dolphins.*

D. *Others eat just plankton, tiny animals that float in the sea.*

E. *Tiger sharks eat anything, including pieces of metal, carcasses, and plastic.*

G TEXT FEATURES

Possible answer: *The photographs provide information about the different types of teeth that sharks have. They show that sharks' teeth differ widely, from many rows of even teeth, to sharp, pointy, needlelike teeth.*

Extend the Discussion What determines the shape of each shark's teeth?

FOR LESS–PROFICIENT READERS

Reading Skill Follow-Up: Outline

1. Work together to create phrases for each subheading on this page. Have students use these as main ideas in their outlines.
2. Have students work in pairs to identify the important details that belong under each Roman numeral.
3. Compare details and then record them on the class outline.

Comprehension Support Explain that signal words show relationships between facts. Read lines 55–64 aloud, pointing out the words and phrases that indicate contrast (*but,* line 55), elaboration (*also,* line 58), spatial relationships (*inside,* line 60), and cause and effect (*causes,* line 62). Have students identify signal words in the sidebar text and explain the relationship that each indicates.

BEST PRACTICES TOOLKIT—Transparency
Read Aloud/Think Aloud p. A34

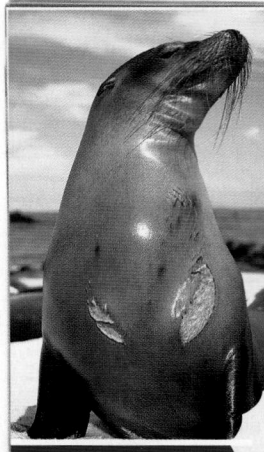

What's a "Feeding Frenzy"?

Sharks usually travel solo, but if one finds easy prey, an excited, competitive swarm of sharks may join in the feast, biting anything that lies in its path.

How Do Sharks Breathe?

70   A shark usually swims with its mouth open to force oxygen-rich water to pass over a set of gills housed in a cavity behind its head—a process known as ramjet ventilation. Gill flaps called lamellae absorb and help **diffuse** oxygen into the shark's bloodstream. Lamellae also help sharks expel carbon dioxide, a gaseous waste product of breathing, from the bloodstream.

diffuse (dĭ-fyōōz′) v. to spread out or through

H TEXT FEATURES
A **caption** is the text that provides information about a graphic aid. How does this caption support your understanding of the photo and reinforce the article?

Shark Attack
This sea lion managed to survive a vicious shark attack. **H**

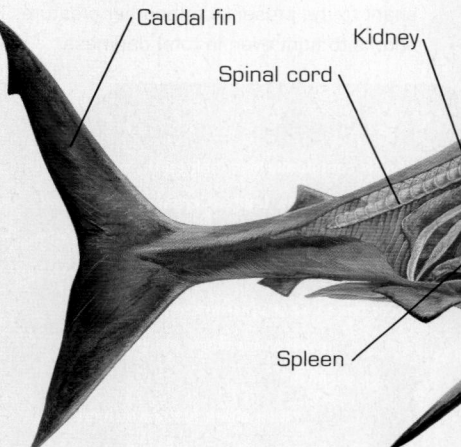

Caudal fin

Kidney

Spinal cord

Spleen

Top-Powerful Tail
Since its upper lobe is larger than the lower one, the great white's thrashing tail movements drive the shark forward and push its head down. This nosedive is countered by the fish's wedge-shaped head and its pectoral fins, which lift the front end.

DIFFERENTIATED INSTRUCTION

FOR LESS—PROFICIENT READERS

Comprehension Support Tell students that making a simple diagram can sometimes help them understand what they are reading. Have students work in pairs to create a flow chart that shows the shark's respiration process (lines 69–77). Have pairs share their charts.

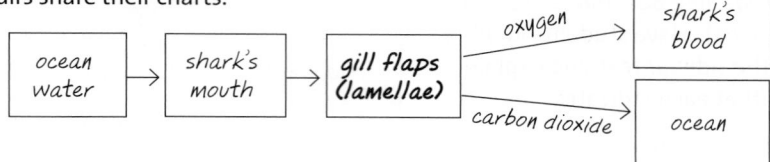

FOR ENGLISH LEARNERS
Vocabulary Support

- Define challenging key words in the first paragraph of the sidebar text that accompanies the illustration: *lobe, thrashing, nosedive, countered.*

- Provide a think-aloud using the key words to explain that the shark's tail pushes the front end down while the shape of its head and its fins lift the front end up. The result is that the shark can swim in a straight line.

Are Sharks Smart?

80 Experiments show that sharks recognize and remember shapes and patterns. Using shark snacks as rewards, scientists have taught lemon sharks to swim through mazes, ring bells, and press targets. "Although we learn new things about sharks every day, there's still a lot we don't know about them," says Hueter.

Great White Shark

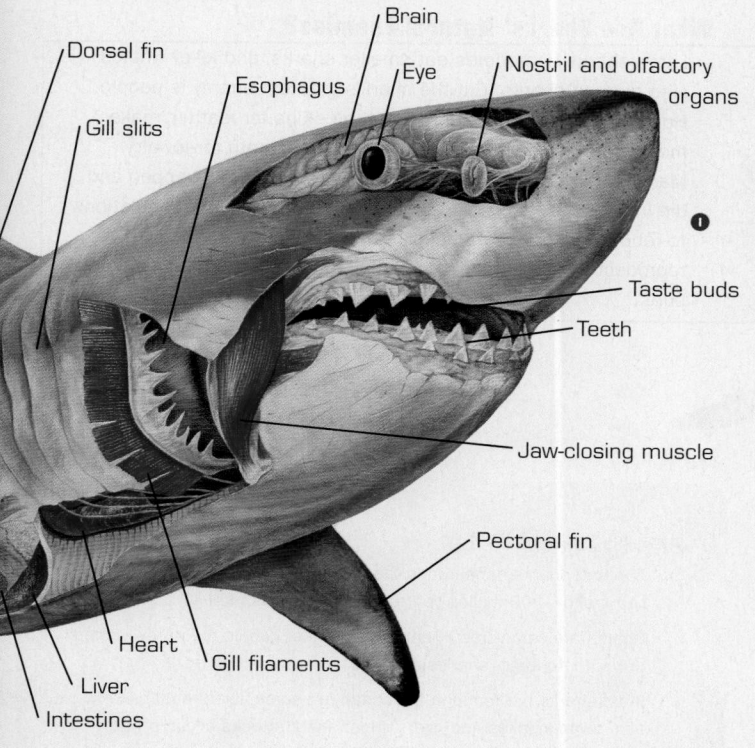

Dorsal fin

Brain

Esophagus

Eye

Nostril and olfactory organs

Gill slits

Taste buds

Teeth

Jaw-closing muscle

Pectoral fin

Heart

Gill filaments

Liver

Intestines

❶ **TEXT FEATURES**
Use the **labels** on the illustration to identify the spinal cord, kidney, and brain.

Sandpaper Skin
Rough and tough, shark skin is made of hard, platelike scales, like tiny teeth pointing backward.

Gills
Water flows in the mouth and over blood-rich gill filaments. Some dissolved oxygen passes into the bloodstream before the water flows out through gill slits.

FOR ADVANCED LEARNERS/PRE–AP

Draw Conclusions How important is it to know whether sharks can remember and recognize shapes and patterns? Have students imagine that they are in charge of funding shark research projects such as those described on this page (lines 78–81). The group seeking funding wants to continue testing sharks' intelligence. Have students write a letter that grants or denies the group's request and explains why they made the decision.

ELEMENTS OF NONFICTION

❶ TEXT FEATURES

Have students describe where each part of the shark is located. *Possible answers:*

• *The spinal cord is along the back.*

• *The kidneys are above the spleen.*

• *The brain is behind the eye.*

If students need help . . . Say each word aloud and have students point to its position on the diagram.

Lines 84–89
REINFORCE KEY IDEA: DECEIVE

Discuss Humans appear less threatening than sharks. How is this appearance **deceiving?** *Possible answer: Humans are a great threat to the shark population. They kill many sharks—not with ferocious-looking teeth, but with technology that allows them to overfish the oceans.*

SELECTION WRAP-UP

REFLECT Have students think about how their perceptions of sharks have changed after reading this article. Which facts did they find particularly interesting?

★ **CRITIQUE** Have students evaluate the effectiveness of the text features. Would they have included any others? Would they have eliminated any? Which features were most helpful to readers?

READING FLUENCY

Distribute the copy masters and have students work in pairs to practice fluency.

> ℝ RESOURCE MANAGER—Copy Master
> Reading Fluency p. 37

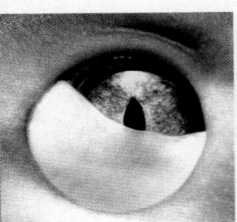

Shark Eyes

Sharks have good eyesight and can see colors. Their eyes are protected by a nictitating (nĭk'tĭ-tā'tĭng) membrane that moves up and down like an eyelid.

What Are Sharks' Natural Enemies?

Targeted Passage ②

Large sharks sometimes eat smaller sharks, and killer whales also dine on sharks. But the shark's greatest enemy is people. Humans kill sharks for food, use their skins for leather, make medicine from their liver oil, and use shark teeth for jewelry. Many sharks are killed senselessly for sport or get trapped and die in fishing nets. And it takes a long time for shark populations to rebound. Most shark species take ten years to reach reproductive age and produce small litters of less than a dozen pups.

90

buoyancy (boi'ən-sē) *n.* the ability to remain afloat in liquid

❶ TEXT FEATURES
The Bite-Size Facts are organized in a **bulleted list.** Why do you think writers use bulleted lists to present information?

Bite-Size Facts

- The first sharks appeared in the ancient oceans about 400 million years ago—200 million years before the dinosaurs!

- Sharks are carnivores (meat-eaters). Most gobble their prey whole or rip it into large, shark-size bites.

- Most sharks are found in the ocean but some, like the bull shark, also swim in lakes and rivers. Most shark attacks occur in warm waters—20° to 30°C (68° to 86°F).

- Sharks lack the inflatable swim bladder that allows bony fish to control **buoyancy**. Most sharks must swim endlessly. If they stop, they sink to the bottom and may drown from a lack of water flowing over the gills. ❶

DIFFERENTIATED INSTRUCTION

FOR LESS-PROFICIENT READERS

② Targeted Passage [Lines 83–91]

This passage completes the thought begun in the first paragraph: sharks are vanishing because of humans.

- Why do humans kill sharks?

- How do the reproductive patterns of sharks contribute to their decrease in population?

- How do you think the writer feels about human predators?

FOR ENGLISH LEARNERS

Comprehension: Cause and Effect

- Point out that the writer chose to start her article by identifying an effect. Have students reread lines 1–3. Ask them what the effect or result is.

- Point out that the causes of this effect are not presented until the last part of the article.

- Complete a multiple causes chart to help students see the relationship between the two parts of the text.

> 🧰 BEST PRACTICES TOOLKIT—Transparency
> Cause-and-Effect Diagram (Multiple Causes) pp. B16, B37

Comprehension

MARYLAND OBJECTIVES

INFORMATIONAL TEXT STANDARD
2.A.2.a Analyze print features

1. **Recall** What does the author think is the scariest thing about sharks?

2. **Clarify** What place do sharks hold in the aquatic food chain?

3. **Represent** Draw a simple illustration of a shark. Label its tail, dorsal fin, pectoral fins, and gill slits.

Critical Analysis

4. **Identify Text Features** Locate the photograph of the shark's eye on page 880 and the text features that are used with it. What do you learn from the photograph alone? What does the text add to your understanding of the photograph?

5. **Compare Outlines** Compare the outline you made while reading this article to one created by a classmate. Which main ideas and supporting details did you both have? Which were different?

6. **Analyze Author's Purpose** What do you think is the author's main purpose for writing "What Do You Know About Sharks?" Explain how the text features help Guynup achieve this purpose.

7. **Draw Conclusions** Do appearances **deceive** when it comes to sharks? Use a chart like the one shown to list facts supporting both of the opinions given. Use information from your outline, or return to the article if necessary. Be prepared to defend your conclusion in class.

Opinion 1: Sharks Are Very Dangerous	Opinion 2: Sharks Are Mostly Harmless
A dusky shark's bite is like being crushed beneath the weight of ten cars.	

Extension and Challenge

8. **Creative Project: Art** Work with a partner to create a poster illustrating the truth about sharks. Use your outline to help you remember the information that is important to include.

9. **Big Question Activity** Review the chart you made as part of the **Discuss** activity on page 872. After reading "What Do You Know About Sharks?" have you changed your mind about whether any of the statements are true or false? Next to each answer you want to change, record the information from the article that supports your new view.

Opinion 2: Sharks Are Mostly Harmless

- Nurse sharks are sluggish and not usually dangerous.
- Leopard sharks feed on small fish and crustaceans.
- Out of 375 shark species, only about 24 are dangerous.
- Great whites usually inhabit deep seas far away from people.
- Fewer than 100 shark attacks are reported each year.

Students may conclude that sharks are mostly harmless.

Extension and Challenge

8. Students' posters should include accurate facts presented in an organized and readable way.

9. **False.** Whale sharks are the largest (line 19).

    False. Only about 24 of 375 shark species are dangerous (line 24).

    True. Sharks appeared about 200 million years before the dinosaurs (bulleted list).

Practice and Apply

After Reading

For additional support of post-reading questions, use these copy masters:

R RESOURCE MANAGER—Copy Masters
Reading Check p. 34 (to check understanding of the selection)
Text Features p. 27 (for practice of elements of nonfiction standards focus)
Question Support p. 35 (**After Reading** questions adapted for English learners and less-proficient readers)

Additional selection questions are provided for teachers on page 21.

ANSWERS

Comprehension

1. *The scariest thing is that sharks are disappearing from the oceans.*

2. *Sharks are at the top of the food chain.*

3. *Encourage students to return to pages 878–879 and use the information in the diagram to help them with their own sketch.*

Critical Analysis

Possible answers:

4. ● **STANDARDS FOCUS** *Text Features* The *graphic aid* shows the location of the nictitating membrane and how it functions. The *caption* explains the purpose of the membrane and sharks' vision capacity.

5. ■ **STANDARDS FOCUS** *Outline* Students may alter their main idea phrases after comparing outlines with a partner. They may also decide to eliminate some details or add others.

6. *The purpose of the article is to present accurate information about sharks. The text features help Guynup achieve her purpose by organizing information in a way that is easy for readers to understand. Graphic aids present information that she might not have been able to convey in words alone.*

7. *Students' charts may include these ideas:*

    Opinion 1: Sharks Are Very Dangerous

    - *Sharks may mistake humans for injured fish and attack.*
    - *Great whites have razorlike teeth.*
    - *Goblin sharks have needlelike teeth.*
    - *Sharks eat meat.*

ANSWERS

Vocabulary in Context

VOCABULARY PRACTICE

1. *desert*
2. *overhunting*
3. *fan*
4. *raft*
5. *dead*
6. *fish tank*

 RESOURCE MANAGER—Copy Master
Vocabulary Practice p. 32

VOCABULARY IN WRITING

Have students review how each vocabulary word is used in the text to help them think of questions.

VOCABULARY STRATEGY: CONTENT-SPECIFIC WORDS (also an EL language objective)

Remind students to match the words they know first. That narrows down the number of choices for the unfamiliar terms.

Answers:

1. *f*
2. *d*
3. *b*
4. *a*
5. *c*
6. *e*

 RESOURCE MANAGER—Copy Master
Vocabulary Strategy p. 33

ℹ **Vocabulary Center at ClassZone.com**
Additional Vocabulary Activities

Vocabulary in Context

VOCABULARY PRACTICE

Answer the questions to show your understanding of the vocabulary words.

1. Which is an example of an **ecosystem,** a desert or a gymnasium?
2. Which would be more likely to **decimate** a species, overhunting or rain?
3. If you wanted to **diffuse** air in a room, would you use a vacuum or a fan?
4. Which has **buoyancy,** a boulder or a raft?
5. If something is a **carcass,** is it alive or dead?
6. Would a person who liked **aquatic** things more likely own a fish tank or a cactus?

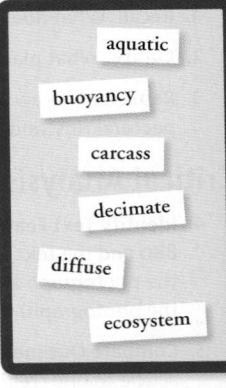

aquatic

buoyancy

carcass

decimate

diffuse

ecosystem

VOCABULARY IN WRITING

What else do you want to know about sea animals? Write several questions, using at least three vocabulary words. Here is an example.

> **EXAMPLE SENTENCE**
>
> *How do animals in the shark's __ecosystem__ protect themselves?*

VOCABULARY STRATEGY: CONTENT-SPECIFIC WORDS

Whenever you study a specific subject or explore an area of interest, you are likely to encounter new words that are directly related to that subject. For example, in this article about sharks, you learned that the word *aquatic* refers to things that grow or live in the water. By learning content-specific words, you'll be better able to understand, discuss, and write about the subject yourself.

PRACTICE Match the word in the first column with its definition in the second column. Refer to a dictionary or science textbook if you need help.

1. tsunami   a. having to do with the sea or the things in it
2. current   b. animals with soft bodies and often hard shells
3. mollusks   c. large brown seaweed
4. marine   d. ocean stream that moves continuously in one direction
5. kelp   e. hard-shelled animals with jointed body and legs
6. crustaceans   f. destructive wave caused by an underwater earthquake

 **MARYLAND OBJECTIVES**

READING STANDARD
1.D.3.c Use resources to confirm definitions

 **VOCABULARY PRACTICE**
For more practice, go to the **Vocabulary Center** at **ClassZone.com.**

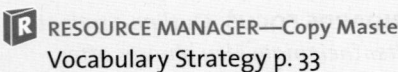 *DIFFERENTIATED INSTRUCTION*

FOR ENGLISH LEARNERS
Vocabulary Strategy Divide students into groups. Have each group find the definition(s) of one of the words. Ask groups to record their definitions on the board. Then have students match the word with the correct choice.

FOR ADVANCED LEARNERS PRE AP
Vocabulary in Writing Have students write a question using each vocabulary word. Then ask them to exchange questions and do research to find the answers. Have students present their information in class.

Reading-Writing Connection

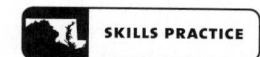

Increase your understanding of "What Do You Know About Sharks?" by responding to these prompts. Then complete the **Grammar and Writing** exercise.

WRITING PROMPTS	SELF-CHECK
A. Short Response: Write Informational Text Rewrite the information in the caption for "Shark Eyes" on page 880 so that it is organized in a question-answer format. Use the organization of the article as a model.	***Strong informational text will . . .*** • include a subheading in the form of a question • provide a clear main idea and at least two details
B. Extended Response: Write a Summary When you write a summary, you restate the main ideas and the most important details of a selection in your own words. Use your outline to help you write a **two- or three-paragraph summary** of "What Do You Know About Sharks?"	***A successful summary will . . .*** • provide a one-sentence overview of the article • include only the most important details

GRAMMAR AND WRITING

MARYLAND OBJECTIVES

LANGUAGE STANDARD
5.C.2.a Use commas correctly

USE COMMAS CORRECTLY Commas are used to make the meanings of sentences clear by setting off certain elements. One such element is an **appositive.** An appositive is a noun or pronoun that explains, identifies, or renames the noun or pronoun it follows. Sometimes the appositive has a modifier. This is called an **appositive phrase.**

Original:	The tiger shark a ferocious predator will eat just about anything.
Revised:	The tiger shark, a ferocious predator, will eat just about anything. (*Insert a comma before and after the appositive phrase "a ferocious predator."*)

PRACTICE In the following sentences, add commas where necessary.

1. Great white sharks the most fearsome fish usually live in deep seas.
2. The whale shark the world's largest fish eats plankton.
3. Humans the shark's greatest enemy kill sharks for leather.
4. The nurse shark a slow bottom dweller is not usually dangerous.

For more help with punctuating appositive phrases, see page R61 in the ***Grammar Handbook.***

FOR LESS–PROFICIENT WRITERS

For Prompt A:
Help students create subheadings in the form of a question. Then help students write their main idea statements before having them finish their paragraphs with the important details.

For Prompt B:
• Help students write a main idea statement.

• Have pairs write a one-sentence summary of an assigned section of their outline. Have them contribute their statements to a class summary.

Reading-Writing Connection

WRITING PROMPTS

• For **Prompt A,** students might begin their questions with the word *How*.

• For **Prompt B,** students might find it helpful to use a classification chart to help them see the relationships of the facts on their outline. Encourage students to group main ideas under more general headings, such as *Physical Characteristics*, so that they are able to cover all of the important information in the article in just two or three paragraphs.

BEST PRACTICES TOOLKIT—Transparency
Classification Chart p. B17

For ideas for writing, see

i Writing Center at **ClassZone.com**

GRAMMAR AND WRITING

Tell students that most appositives add information but do not affect the main idea of a sentence. The commas indicate that they are not essential parts of the sentence.

Possible answers:
1. *Great white sharks, the most fearsome fish, usually live in deep seas.*
2. *The whale shark, the world's largest fish, eats plankton.*
3. *Humans, the shark's greatest enemy, kill sharks for leather.*
4. *The nurse shark, a slow bottom dweller, is not usually dangerous.*

R RESOURCE MANAGER—Copy Master
Use Commas in Appositive Phrases p. 36

Assess and Reteach

Assess

R RESOURCE MANAGER—Copy Masters
Selection Tests A, B/C pp. 39–40, 41–42

CD Test Generator CD

Reteach

S STANDARDS LESSON FILE
Informational Texts Lesson 1: Text Features
Reading Lesson 4: Recognizing Main Idea and Supporting Details
Research and Study Skills Lesson 15: Outlining Your Reading
Grammar Lesson 20: Missing or Misplaced Commas

Focus and Motivate

Great White Sharks
Magazine Article by Peter Benchley

OBJECTIVES

Elements of Nonfiction
- explore the key idea of what is **accurate**
- identify fact and opinion
- read a magazine article

Reading
- recognize and analyze author's bias

Vocabulary
- build vocabulary for reading and writing
- understand and use prefixes (*ab-, a-, extra-, extro-, re-, trans-, tra-*) and the Latin root *vert* (also an EL language objective)

SUMMARY

In this article, Peter Benchley corrects erroneous facts about the great white shark that he included in his novel *Jaws*. He also shares new facts that have been discovered in recent years. He argues for the need to prevent the extinction of this magnificent animal.

Can you tell **FACT** *from fiction?*

Discuss the question and the ***KEY IDEA***. Challenge students to explain the saying "Don't believe everything you read." Ask them what their attitude should be toward facts they are not sure are **accurate**. Then have students complete the ***LIST IT*** activity and share their results in small groups.

Can you tell FACT *from fiction?*

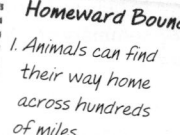

MARYLAND OBJECTIVES

INFORMATIONAL TEXT STANDARDS
2.A.4.h Distinguish between a fact and an opinion
2.A.6.d Analyze the author's position for bias

KEY IDEA Artists and writers often use what they know to be true about the world to create imaginary scenerios that can seem more real than life itself. But how do you know when a work of fiction is technically **accurate** and when it's not? Peter Benchley has made a name for himself by dealing in both facts and fiction about great white sharks.

LIST IT Choose a movie you have seen or a book you have read that features animals or natural events. For each movie or book, make a list of some of the details that were included, explaining whether they're true or not.

Homeward Bound
1. Animals can find their way home across hundreds of miles.
2.
3.
4.

884

Selection Resources

* Resources for Differentiation   † Also in Spanish   ‡ In Haitian Creole and Vietnamese

ELEMENTS OF NONFICTION: FACT AND OPINION

Even informational text can include opinions. Be sure you can tell the difference between facts and opinions.

- A **fact** is a statement that can be proved. To prove, or verify, a fact, you might use personal observations, eyewitness accounts, a reliable print or online source, a scientific experiment, or a discussion with an expert.
- An **opinion** is a statement that can't be proved because it expresses a person's beliefs, feelings, or thoughts.

As you read Peter Benchley's article, decide which of his statements are facts and which are opinions.

READING SKILL: RECOGNIZE AUTHOR'S BIAS

Writers' experiences and beliefs often affect their attitude about their topic. This creates a **bias** for or against what they're writing about. One way writers reveal their bias is through **loaded language,** or words that suggest a strong positive or negative feeling. As you read, record the loaded language in a chart like the one shown. Use the clues the language provides to identify the author's bias.

Loaded Language	Possible Author's Bias
"most wonderful of natural-born killers"	Benchley is impressed by sharks' survival instincts.

Review: **Compare-and-Contrast Organization**

VOCABULARY IN CONTEXT

The boldfaced words help Peter Benchley share facts and feelings about great white sharks. Use context clues to figure out the meaning of each word.

1. Humans **demonize** an innocent creature out of fear.
2. The tourist gave **anecdotal** evidence instead of hard facts.
3. We finally reached a **consensus** after a loud debate.
4. The evidence was subject to close **scrutiny.**
5. Most scary movies are based on our **visceral** fears.
6. The scientist interviewed two **prospective** assistants.
7. The test errors were caused by **inadvertence** to detail.
8. The trial was a **travesty** because the jury was biased.

Author Online

The *Jaws* Sensation
Peter Benchley is best known for his novel *Jaws,* which is about the hunt for a great white shark that killed several people in a beach community. *Jaws* stayed on the bestseller list for 40 weeks. In 1975, Steven Spielberg turned it into one of the top-grossing movies at the time. It was also nominated for an Academy Award for Best Picture. Benchley went on to write other novels and screenplays with the ocean as the setting, as well as nonfiction works about the ocean.

Peter Benchley
1940–2006

Regrets In the 1970s, when Benchley wrote *Jaws,* little was known about great white sharks. His description of them as vicious man-eaters frightened many people out of the water and triggered an aggressive shark hunt. Benchley, always fascinated by the ocean, spent a great deal of his life exploring it. He came to discover that much of what he wrote was incorrect. He was outspoken in his regrets for helping to create this hysteria. Benchley noted, "For every human being killed by a shark, roughly ten million sharks are killed by humans."

 MORE ABOUT THE AUTHOR
For more on Peter Benchley, visit the **Literature Center** at ClassZone.com.

GREAT WHITE SHARKS 885

Teach

ELEMENTS OF NONFICTION

● **FACT AND OPINION**
Read aloud these examples:

1. *Jaws* is about a great white shark that killed several people in a beach community.
2. The book stayed on the bestseller list for 40 weeks.
3. The book is better than the movie.

Ask students to identify each statement as fact or opinion. *Possible answer: The first two statements are facts. The third is an opinion.*

CHECK UNDERSTANDING Have students find examples of facts and opinions in nonfiction works they have read.

READING SKILL

■ **RECOGNIZE AUTHOR'S BIAS**
Read aloud this example:

> The beautiful shark glided gracefully through the water.

Ask students to identify the loaded language. *Possible answer:* Beautiful *and* gracefully *are both loaded words.*

CHECK UNDERSTANDING Have students describe the writer's bias in the above example.

 RESOURCE MANAGER—Copy Master
Recognize Author's Bias p. 55 (for student use while reading the article)

VOCABULARY SKILL

▲ **VOCABULARY IN CONTEXT**
DIAGNOSE WORD KNOWLEDGE To determine preteaching needs, have all students complete **Vocabulary in Context.** Remind students to look for the definitions of the unknown words as they read the text: *demonize* (p. 887), *anecdotal* (p. 887), *consensus* (p. 888), *scrutiny* (p. 889), *visceral* (p. 890), *prospective* (p. 891), *inadvertence* (p. 891), *travesty* (p. 891).

PRETEACH VOCABULARY Use the Vocabulary Study copy master as follows:

1. Read item 1 aloud, emphasizing *anecdotal.*
2. Point out the phrase "share their stories." Elicit possible meanings for *anecdotal,* such as "based on people's stories."
3. Have students record their predicted definitions in the chart.
4. Repeat the procedure. Remind students to revise their definitions as they read.

 RESOURCE MANAGER—Copy Master
Vocabulary Study p. 57

For general guidelines on differentiating vocabulary instruction and for alternative vocabulary activities for students not needing vocabulary preteaching, see

 BEST PRACTICES TOOLKIT
Scaffolding Vocabulary Instruction pp. 43–46

ⓘ Vocabulary Center at **ClassZone.com**

GREAT WHITE SHARKS **885**

Practice and Apply

ANALYZE VISUALS

Possible answer: The appearance of the shark suggests that it is powerful. Based on the look of its teeth, it probably attacks and eats large sea animals.

BACKGROUND

The Great White Shark The great white is found mostly in warmer waters. While the underside of the shark is white, the rest of it may be gray, blue, or brown. This coloration is helpful when the shark is stalking prey. From above, the shark's dark coloring blends in with the deeper water and the ocean floor. From below, the white underbelly mimics the sunlit surface.

GREAT WHITE SHARKS

PETER BENCHLEY

ANALYZE VISUALS
What might you **infer** about the great white shark from this photograph?

DIFFERENTIATED INSTRUCTION

FOR ALL STUDENTS

Learning Center With students' help, set up a learning center on marine life. Stock it with books, videos, and pictures that cover a wide range of sea creatures. Provide a variety of projects that students may complete independently, such as painting a sea life mural, writing an illustrated report on a species, or organizing pictures and facts into a glossary.

FOR LESS–PROFICIENT READERS

In combination with the *Audio Anthology CD,* use one or more Targeted Passages (pp. 887, 891) to ensure that students focus on key facts, concepts, and skills.

FOR ENGLISH LEARNERS

Options for Reading Read the first Targeted Passage aloud. Make sure students understand Benchley's purpose in this article. Have students read the rest of the article silently along with the *Audio Anthology CD.*

Key Academic Vocabulary Have students work in small groups to define these words using context clues: *decline* (line 27), *contact* (line 36), *integral* (line 41), *attitude* (line 60), *environment* (line 141).

Prereading For prereading instruction for English learners, see

 BEST PRACTICES TOOLKIT
Scaffolding Reading Instruction pp. 43–46

C onsidering the knowledge accumulated about great whites in the past 25 years, I couldn't possibly write *Jaws* today—not in good conscience anyway. Back then, it was generally accepted that great whites were anthropophagous—they ate people by choice. Now we know that almost every attack on a human is an accident. The shark mistakes the human for its normal prey.

Back then, we thought that once a great white scented blood, it launched a feeding frenzy that inevitably led to death. Now 10 we know that nearly three-quarters of all bite victims survive, perhaps because the shark recognizes that it has made a mistake and doesn't return for a second bite.

Back then, we believed that great whites attacked boats. Now we know that their sensory systems detect movement, sound, and electrical fields, such as those caused by metal and motors, in water, and when they approach a boat, they're merely coming to investigate. Granted, investigation by a 3,000-pound animal can wreak havoc.[1]

Finally, back then, it was OK to **demonize** an animal, 20 especially a shark, because man had done so since the beginning of time, and, besides, sharks appeared to be infinite in number. **A**

No longer. Today we know that these most wonderful of natural-born killers, these exquisite creatures of evolution, are not only *not* villains, they are victims in danger of—if not extinction quite yet—serious, perhaps even catastrophic, decline. Much of the evidence is **anecdotal.** Fishermen and naturalists are seeing fewer great whites, and in most places those they are seeing are younger and smaller. **B**

---

1. **wreak havoc:** bring about great destruction.

① **Targeted Passage**

demonize (dē′mə-nīz′) *v.* to give evil, demonic qualities to

A **COMPARE AND CONTRAST** What is Benchley comparing and contrasting in the previous four paragraphs?

anecdotal (ăn′ĭk-dōt′l) *adj.* based on observations rather than scientific analysis

B **RECOGNIZE AUTHOR'S BIAS** Reread lines 23–27. What examples of **loaded language** do you find here? Record them in your chart.

Lines 1–7
REINFORCE *KEY IDEA:* ACCURATE

Discuss What impression of great white sharks is not **accurate?** *Possible answer: Sharks do not attack humans deliberately. In fact, they attack only if they believe that humans are other prey.*

READING SKILL: *Review*

A COMPARE AND CONTRAST

Possible answer: Benchley is contrasting what was believed about sharks at the time he wrote Jaws *with what is known about them now.*

Extend the Discussion How does the author use the phrase *back then* as a transition to organize his ideas?

READING SKILL

B RECOGNIZE AUTHOR'S BIAS

Record students' answers in the chart from page 885. Use the answers to identify the author's bias. *Possible answers:*

Loaded Language	Possible Author's Bias
"most wonderful," "exquisite," "not villains," "victims," "catastrophic decline"	These words indicate Benchley's admiration for the sharks and his strong feeling that they need to be saved.

If students need help . . . Complete a Drawing Conclusions chart using these statements to help students recognize the author's bias:

- *Benchley calls the sharks "wonderful" and "exquisite."*
- *Benchley says that they are not villains.*
- *Benchley is afraid that sharks may become extinct.*

 BEST PRACTICES TOOLKIT—Transparency Drawing Conclusions p. A28

FOR LESS–PROFICIENT READERS

① **Targeted Passage [Lines 1–27]**

This passage establishes the author's bias: he feels strongly that sharks have been misunderstood and need to be protected.

- What did Benchley believe about great white sharks when he wrote *Jaws*?
- What does he know about the sharks now?
- What is the danger to great white sharks?

FOR ADVANCED LEARNERS/PRE–AP

Pre-AP exercises in the bottom channel provide additional challenge for your advanced students. Use them for small groups or individuals.

ADDITIONAL GUIDELINES

For more help with differentiation and tips for classroom management, see

 BEST PRACTICES TOOLKIT Differentiated Instruction pp. 31–38

C FACT AND OPINION

Possible answer:

- **Facts:** *Scientists estimate that the population of some shark species has dropped by 80 percent. They believe that the rate of reproduction is lower than the rate of death.*

- **Bias:** *Benchley uses words such as "grace," "power," and "remarkably fragile" to show that his sympathy lies with the sharks.*

Lines 59–67
ADDITIONAL TEACHING OPPORTUNITY

Author's Perspective Remind students that an author's perspective, or how the writer views a topic, is influenced by his or her experiences, feelings, values, and beliefs. Peter Benchley included misinformation in his novel that led to an inaccurate perception of sharks. Ask students how he feels about that now and how this feeling influences this article. **Possible answer:** *He feels guilty. He tries to justify the harm that his novel may have done by saying it led to a greater interest in sharks. Throughout the article, he works hard to include the truth about sharks and correct people's perception of them. His perspective influences the content and tone of his article.*

---

consensus (kən-sĕn′səs)
n. general agreement

C FACT AND OPINION
Reread lines 30–37. Which statements can be verified, or proved? Where do you see evidence of bias?

---

30 Scientists estimate that, worldwide, populations of some species of sharks have dropped by 80 percent. Though precise numbers of white sharks aren't known, there is a growing **consensus** that they are not reproducing at a rate sufficient to maintain the population. What *is* known now is that great white sharks—scarce by nature and growing scarcer thanks to contact with man—are, for all their grace and power and manifest menace, remarkably fragile. . . . **C**

Nowadays more people are coming to respect and appreciate sharks for what they are: beautiful, graceful,
40 efficient, and, above all, integral members of the ocean food chain. In large measure the change is due to television and the abundance of films documenting not only the glories from sharks but also the dangers to them from longlines, nets, and the odious practice of finning— slicing the fins off sharks to sell in Asian markets, then tossing the living
50 animals overboard to die. Gradually governments and individuals are learning that while a dead shark may bring ten or twenty or even fifty dollars to a single fisherman, a live shark can be worth thousands of dollars more in tourist revenue to a community. Divers will fly halfway around the world to see white sharks.

Immodestly I claim some credit
60 for the change in attitude. For while the *Jaws* phenomenon was blamed for distorting the public's view of sharks and causing sporadic outbreaks of macho mayhem,[2] it also generated a fascination with and, over time, an affection for sharks that had not existed before.

Shark finning in the Pacific Ocean

This 17-foot great white shark was caught in the Atlantic Ocean. It weighed a record-breaking 3,500 pounds.

---

2. **sporadic outbreaks of macho mayhem:** occasional wild flare-ups of people trying to show their superiority over sharks by attacking and killing them.

DIFFERENTIATED INSTRUCTION

FOR LESS-PROFICIENT READERS

Reading Skill Follow-Up: Recognize Author's Bias Have students write these statements in the **Possible Author's Bias** column of the chart: *Benchley believes great white sharks are among nature's most magnificent creatures. He blames humans for destroying shark populations.* Have pairs work together to identify words and phrases from lines 30–50 that support each statement and add them to the **Loaded Language** column.

FOR ENGLISH LEARNERS

Vocabulary Support Have mixed-ability pairs define the following words and phrases using context clues:

- *scented* (line 8), "smelled"
- *granted* (line 17), "it's true"
- *thanks to* (lines 35–36), "as a result of"
- *manifest menace* (line 37), "obvious danger"
- *odious* (line 47), "disgusting"

- *apex predators* (line 72), "animals at the top of the food chain"
- *pup* (line 77), "give birth to [baby sharks]"
- *fully armed and ready to rumble* (line 80), "able to hunt their own food"
- *widely circulated* (line 96), "sent to many people"
- *adage* (line 116), "saying"

These days I receive more than a thousand letters a year from youngsters who were not alive when *Jaws* appeared, and all of them, without exception, want to know more about sharks in general and great whites in particular.

A great white shark in South Africa jumps out of the water to attack a seal.

Great white sharks are among the true apex predators in the ocean. The largest predatory fish in the world, they have few natural enemies. And so, in balanced nature, there are not very many great whites, and the number grows or shrinks depending on availability of food. They breed late in life and pup relatively few. Again, nobody knows exactly how many, but seven or eight seems to be a safe average. The youngsters appear alive, four or five feet long, weighing 50–60 pounds, fully armed and ready to rumble. Still, many don't survive the first year because other sharks, including great whites, will eat them. **D**

Of all the infuriating unknowns about great white sharks, none is more controversial than size. How big can they grow to be? Fishermen from Nova Scotia to South Australia, from Cape Town to Cape Cod claim to have encountered 25-footers, 30-footers, even 36-footers. Usually the proof offered is that the beast was "bigger than the boat." There have been reports of a 23-footer in the waters off Malta and a 21-foot, 7,000-pounder off Cuba, but none has held up under **scrutiny**. The largest

D FACT AND OPINION
Reread lines 72–82. What methods would you use to verify these facts?

scrutiny (skrōōt′n-ē) *n.* close examination or study

ANALYZE VISUALS

Activity Ask students to describe the qualities of the great white shark based on this photograph. *Possible answers: The shark is powerful, agile, quick, and deadly.*

ELEMENTS OF NONFICTION

D FACT AND OPINION

Possible answers: Reliable print and online sources, scientific experiments, and expert discussions could be used to verify the facts.

Lines 83–90
REINFORCE *KEY IDEA*: ACCURATE

Discuss Why is it difficult to obtain **accurate** measurements of the great white shark? *Possible answers: It is not easy to get close to a shark. People's perceptions vary. The only truly accurate way to measure a shark may be to capture it first.*

FOR LESS–PROFICIENT READERS

Comprehension Support Complete a Spider Map with the information in lines 72–82 to help students understand the relationships among facts in this passage. Place the word *shark* in the center and terms such as *predator* and *reproductive patterns* on the legs. Then have students volunteer facts or details that develop each characteristic.

 **BEST PRACTICES TOOLKIT—Transparency**
Spider Map p. B22

FOR ENGLISH LEARNERS

Vocabulary: Cognates The word *predator* (line 72) is similar to the Spanish word *depredador*. Ask students to work in small groups to complete Word Squares that explore the meaning of this key word ("animals that live by preying upon others"). Have students use their knowledge of the cognate or a dictionary. Remind students to look for additional cognates as they read the article.

BEST PRACTICES TOOLKIT—Transparency
Word Squares p. E10

ⒺFACT AND OPINION

Possible answer:

- **Fact:** *No great white shark longer than 19.5 feet has ever been validated.*
- **Opinion:** *The media are irritating because of their stubborn reluctance to stick to the truth when reporting the size of sharks.*

If students need help . . .

- Remind them that opinions are statements that express personal feelings or make judgments.
- Read the paragraph aloud, using your voice to express Fergusson's irritation and sarcasm.

Lines 124–134
DISCUSSION PROMPTS

Use these prompts to help students understand how much is known about sharks:

Connect Do you think that people should learn as much as possible about sharks? Why? *Students may say that knowing more will enable people to help sharks survive.*

Analyze How is most information about sharks collected? *Possible answer: Divers, guides, and naturalists gather data about sharks from their observations of and experiences with the animals.*

Synthesize On the basis of this paragraph, what conclusion can you draw about people's understanding of sharks? *Possible answers: Knowledge about sharks is growing, but there is much more to learn.*

ⒺFACT AND OPINION
Notice that Benchley quotes an expert in this paragraph. But even experts communicate both facts and opinions. Reread lines 94–101. What part of Fergusson's statement is a fact and what part is an opinion?

visceral (vĭs′ər-əl) *adj.*
instinctive

---

generally accepted catch—made by lasso, of all things—was a shark 19.5 feet long. The largest great white shark ever caught on rod and reel weighed 2,664 pounds.

According to British biologist Ian Fergusson, chairman of the Shark Trust, no great white shark longer than 19.5 feet has ever been validated, and in a widely circulated e-mail, he expressed irritation at "this stubborn reluctance by some elements of the media to accept the facts and even more of a reluctance to accept that a 16-foot, 4500-pound white shark is big, very big, 100 and should need no further exaggeration to impress even the most discerning of viewers when seen up close." Ⓔ

I can attest that underwater, cruising toward you out of the gloom with the serene confidence of the invincible, a 12-foot great white looks like a locomotive with malice in mind. . . .

At the moment science accepts about 400 species of sharks, but the number changes as new species are discovered. Of all known species, only four attack human beings with any frequency: bull sharks, tiger sharks, oceanic whitetips, and great whites.

110 In Australia, between 1876 and 1999, 52 attacks by great whites were recorded, and of them 27 were fatal. In the Mediterranean Sea since 1900 there have been 23 reliably recorded encounters with great whites, including one in 1909 in which the remains of two adults and a child were found inside a single 15-foot-long female shark caught off Augusta, Sicily.

The old adage is true: A swimmer has a better chance of being struck by lightning than killed by a shark. And around the world many, many more people die every year from bee stings, snakebites, falling off ladders, or drowning in bathtubs 120 than from shark attack. None of which, to be sure, detracts from the ghastly, **visceral** horror of being eaten by a huge fish, but all of which should give some comfort to the recreational swimmer. . . .

More and more these days it is the naturalists and field operators, guides and dive masters who are contributing to the accumulation of practical knowledge about great whites. To cite just one example: Until recently scientists thought that the scars that mar nearly every

---

DIFFERENTIATED INSTRUCTION

FOR LESS–PROFICIENT READERS
Concept Support Create a large chart on the board with three categories of facts: "Facts That Tell What Has Happened," "Facts That Tell What Is Happening," and "Facts That Identify Something That Exists or Can Be Observed." Have groups work together to identify the facts from assigned portions of the text, keeping in mind these three categories. Review the facts identified by each group and add them to the chart.

FOR ADVANCED LEARNERS/PRE–AP
Synthesize It is well known that fish stories are often exaggerated, so why is Ian Fergusson so irritated? Have students reread lines 94–101, keeping in mind the context of the entire article. Have pairs list reasons why his irritation is justified in view of the possible consequences of exaggerating the size of great white sharks. Have students share their lists in small groups.

mature shark were acquired either from prey that fought back
30 or from ritual biting by **prospective** mates. Now there is
eyewitness testimony of aggressive social interaction[3] between
sharks and also of spectacular threat displays that take the
place of major—potentially fatal—encounters with other
white sharks. **F**

A caged diver in South Australia comes face to face with a great white shark.

So we are learning—bit by bit, anecdote by anecdote—more
and more about these magnificent predators. We must hope
that we're learning enough to save them before, through
ignorance and **inadvertence,** we destroy them.

Great white sharks have survived, virtually unchanged,
40 for millions of years. They are as perfectly in tune with their
environment as any living thing on the planet. For them to be
driven to extinction by man, a relative newcomer, would be
more than an ecological tragedy; it would be a moral **travesty. G**

---

3. **aggressive social interaction:** contact that is combative even though there is no actual
intent to fight.

---

prospective
(prə-spĕk'tĭv) *adj.* likely
to be or become

**F RECOGNIZE
AUTHOR'S BIAS**
Reread lines 130–134.
What does the word
spectacular reveal about
Benchley's attitude
toward sharks' behavior?

inadvertence
(ĭn'əd-vûr'tns) *n.* a lack of
attention; carelessness

travesty (trăv'ĭ-stē) *n.*
a degraded or grotesque
likeness

**G RECOGNIZE
AUTHOR'S BIAS**
Identify the **loaded
language** in the last two
paragraphs. Why do
you think Benchley uses
loaded language here?

2 **Targeted Passage**

F RECOGNIZE AUTHOR'S BIAS

Have students record their answers and
the quotation in their charts. *Possible
answer:*

- *Loaded Language: "spectacular threat
displays"*

- *Possible Author's Bias: Benchley
finds even sharks' aggressive behavior
fascinating.*

READING SKILL

G RECOGNIZE AUTHOR'S BIAS

Have students record their answers in their
charts. *Possible answers:*

- *Loaded Language: "magnificent,"
"ignorance," "inadvertence," "perfectly,"
"driven to extinction," "relative newcomer," "ecological tragedy," "moral travesty"*

- *Possible Author's Bias: He uses loaded
language to leave a powerful last impression on his readers.*

SELECTION WRAP–UP

REFLECT Ask students whether they think
Peter Benchley should feel guilty about the
novel he wrote. Are fiction writers obliged to
base their stories on solid facts?

★ **CRITIQUE** Have students evaluate how
effectively this article corrects some of the
myths about sharks. What else could Benchley
have included to fulfill his purpose?

FOR LESS–PROFICIENT READERS

2 Targeted Passage [Lines 135–143]

This passage reinforces the main idea of this
article: it is up to people to save the sharks.

- Why does Benchley think it is important
to learn more about sharks as quickly as
possible?

- Compared to sharks, how long have
humans been living on the earth?

- How does Benchley feel about what
humans are doing to sharks?

FOR ENGLISH LEARNERS

Comprehension: Task Support Point out that
what someone knows can influence how
they feel about a topic, an event, or a person.
Have students reread lines 1–29 and 105–120.
Have them identify three facts that have
influenced Benchley's positive opinion about
sharks. Ask students to share their facts.

Practice and Apply

After Reading

For additional support of post-reading questions, use these copy masters:

R RESOURCE MANAGER—Copy Masters

Reading Check p. 60 (to check understanding of the selection)

Fact and Opinion p. 53 (for practice of elements of nonfiction standards focus)

Question Support p. 61 (**After Reading** questions adapted for English learners and less-proficient readers)

Additional selection questions are provided for teachers on page 47.

ANSWERS

Comprehension

1. *Twenty-five years passed between the time Benchley wrote* Jaws *and the time he wrote the article.*

2. *Sharks breed late in life and have only a few pups at a time. Many don't survive their first year because adult sharks eat the pups.*

3. **Possible answers:** *Sharks can detect movement, sound, and electrical fields in the water. The largest great white shark ever validated was 19.5 feet long.*

Critical Analysis

Possible answers:

4. ● STANDARDS FOCUS *Fact and Opinion*

   • **Statistics:** *Of 52 recorded great white shark attacks in Australia between 1876 and 1999, 27 were fatal. In the Mediterranean Sea, 23 great white shark encounters have been recorded since 1900.*

   • **Fact:** *It is unlikely that a great white will fatally attack a human.*

5. ● STANDARDS FOCUS *Fact and Opinion*
   Benchley's **prediction** *is that great white sharks will become extinct.*

6. ■ STANDARDS FOCUS *Recognize Author's Bias*

   • **Bias:** *Great white sharks are fascinating and in great danger of extinction.*

   • **Reason:** *Benchley is fascinated with the ocean and has spent much of his life exploring it. He feels responsible for the decline of the great white population.*

Comprehension

1. **Recall** How many years passed between the time the author wrote *Jaws* and the time he wrote the article?

2. **Clarify** Why are there naturally so few great white sharks?

3. **Summarize** What are two facts about great white sharks?

Critical Analysis

4. **Identify Fact** Statistics are facts expressed in numbers. Reread lines 110–115 and identify the statistics. On the basis of the statistics in this paragraph, what factual statement can you make about the likelihood of a great white shark fatally attacking a human?

5. **Examine Opinion** A **prediction** is an opinion about something that will happen in the future. Reread lines 135–143. What does Benchley predict will happen to the great white shark if something isn't done?

6. **Analyze Author's Bias** Review the chart you made while reading. Identify Benchley's attitude toward his subject. On the basis of the information in the chart and what you know from the biography on page 885, why do you think Benchley feels as he does about great whites?

7. **Compare and Contrast Articles** Review "Great White Sharks" and "What Do You Know About Sharks?" to find ways they are similar and different. Then use a Venn diagram like the one shown to record your answers.

"What Do You Know About Sharks?"   "Great White Sharks"

Extension and Challenge

8. **SCIENCE CONNECTION** Review the article and choose three facts about great white sharks. For each fact, find two reliable sources, such as an encyclopedia, an atlas, or an almanac, that verify it. Present your findings to the class.

9. **Creative Response: Screenplay** Benchley compares and contrasts the beliefs about great white sharks at the time he wrote *Jaws* with the knowledge available now. Use the facts that are now known to write a movie scene that features an accurate portrayal of a great white shark.

MARYLAND OBJECTIVES

INFORMATIONAL TEXT STANDARD
2.A.4.h Distinguish between a fact and an opinion

---

7. *Possible answers:*

   • **"What Do You Know About Sharks?":** *organized with headings; includes graphic aids, sidebars, and other text features; covers different kinds of sharks; objective tone*

   • **Both:** *describe sharks; blame humans for the decline in population; include photographs*

   • **"Great White Sharks":** *uses comparison and contrast; covers only the great whites; subjective tone*

Extension and Challenge

8. **SCIENCE CONNECTION**
   Students should indicate what sources they used and which facts they verified.

9. *Students' movie scenes should be based on facts from the text and should include dialogue or narration as well as action.*

Vocabulary in Context

VOCABULARY PRACTICE

Decide whether the words in each pair are synonyms (words with the same meaning) or antonyms (words with opposite meanings).

1. consensus/disagreement
2. inadvertence/inattention
3. visceral/analytical
4. demonize/praise
5. travesty/distortion
6. scrutiny/observation
7. anecdotal/scientific
8. prospective/unexpected

VOCABULARY IN WRITING

Review your list from the activity on page 884. Using three or more vocabulary words, describe one of the movies or books. Here is a sample beginning.

> **EXAMPLE SENTENCE**
>
> *The spider's __visceral__ needs caused it to bite Peter Parker.*

VOCABULARY STRATEGY: PREFIXES AND THE LATIN ROOT *vert*

The vocabulary word *inadvertence* contains the Latin root *vert*, which means "turn." This root, sometimes spelled *vers(e)*, is combined with various prefixes to form simple English words. To understand the meanings of words with *vert* or *vers(e)*, use the meaning of the root and the prefixes it is used with.

PRACTICE Combine a prefix from the chart with *vert* or *vers(e)* to form words to complete each of these sentences. Note that some prefix spellings vary.

1. If you back up a car, you put it in _____.
2. A person who is very outgoing is known as a(n) _____.
3. If you don't want to watch a scary movie, you can _____ your eyes.
4. To cross a desert, you must _____ a lot of sand.

Prefixes Used with *vert*, *vers(e)*	Meaning
ab-, a-	away from
extra-, extro-	outside
re-	again; back
trans-, tra-	across

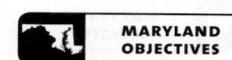
MARYLAND OBJECTIVES

READING STANDARD
1.D.3.b Use word structure to determine meaning

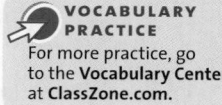
VOCABULARY PRACTICE
For more practice, go to the **Vocabulary Center** at **ClassZone.com**.

GREAT WHITE SHARKS **893**

ANSWERS

Vocabulary in Context
VOCABULARY PRACTICE

1. *antonyms*
2. *synonyms*
3. *antonyms*
4. *antonyms*
5. *synonyms*
6. *synonyms*
7. *antonyms*
8. *antonyms*

R RESOURCE MANAGER—Copy Master
Vocabulary Practice p. 58

VOCABULARY IN WRITING

Students might find it helpful to brainstorm movie details with a partner before writing their sentences.

VOCABULARY STRATEGY: PREFIXES AND THE LATIN ROOT *vert* (also an EL language objective)

- Suggest that students create a list of possible words from the chart before they begin to fill in the blanks.
- Remind students to use context clues to help them decide which word should be used.

Possible answers:
1. *reverse;* 2. *extrovert;* 3. *avert;* 4. *traverse*

R RESOURCE MANAGER—Copy Master
Vocabulary Strategy p. 59

i Vocabulary Center at **ClassZone.com**
Additional Vocabulary Activities

Assess and Reteach

Assess

R RESOURCE MANAGER—Copy Masters
Selection Tests A, B/C pp. 63–64, 65–66

⊘ Test Generator CD

Reteach

S STANDARDS LESSON FILE
Reading Lessons 5, 17
Vocabulary Lessons 4, 10

DIFFERENTIATED INSTRUCTION

FOR ENGLISH LEARNERS

Vocabulary Strategy Create a word bank for students from the prefixes listed and the root *vert*. Before students begin the exercise, work together to define the words from the bank based on the meanings of the prefix and root. Then have students work in pairs to complete the sentences.

FOR ADVANCED LEARNERS/PRE–AP

Vocabulary in Writing Have students write a movie or book review using as many vocabulary words as possible. In their review, they should analyze the accuracy of the facts included in the work and how the facts contribute to or detract from the overall impact of the plot or characterization.

GREAT WHITE SHARKS **893**

Focus and Motivate

OBJECTIVES

Elements of Nonfiction
- explore the key idea of **disease**
- identify and compare patterns of organization (cause-and-effect, chronological order)
- interpret graphic aids (map, bar graph)
- read magazine articles

Reading
- set a purpose for reading

Vocabulary
- build vocabulary for reading and writing
- understand and use specialized vocabulary *(also an EL language objective)*

Grammar and Writing
- write a compare-contrast essay

SUMMARY

"Like Black Smoke" tells how the bubonic plague spread from wild rodents in Asia to human populations in western Europe, moving along trade routes via fleas and ships. "A World Turned Upside Down" tells how depopulation brought far-reaching social and economic change, especially by contributing to the decline of the feudal system.

How do we fight
DISEASE?

Discuss the question and the **KEY IDEA**. Note **disease**-prevention measures that are common today, such as vaccinating infants or staying home from school or work when sick. Then have students work on the **LIST IT** activity.

Selection Resources

Like Black Smoke:
The Black Death's Journey
Magazine Article by Diana Childress

A World Turned Upside Down:
How the Black Death Affected Europe
Magazine Article by Mary Morton Cowan

How do we fight
DISEASE?

MARYLAND OBJECTIVES

READING/INFO TEXT STANDARDS
1.E.3.a Select and apply appropriate strategies during reading
2.A.3.a Analyze the organizational patterns of texts

KEY IDEA Each year, doctors and scientists learn more about how communities can stay healthy and prevent **disease**. But people didn't always know what we know now. The articles you are about to read tell about a time during the Middle Ages when the bubonic plague affected so many people that it changed a society.

LIST IT What can each of us do to encourage good health for ourselves and others? Make a list of at least five guidelines that people can follow to prevent contagious diseases from spreading. Be ready to explain why you included each guideline.

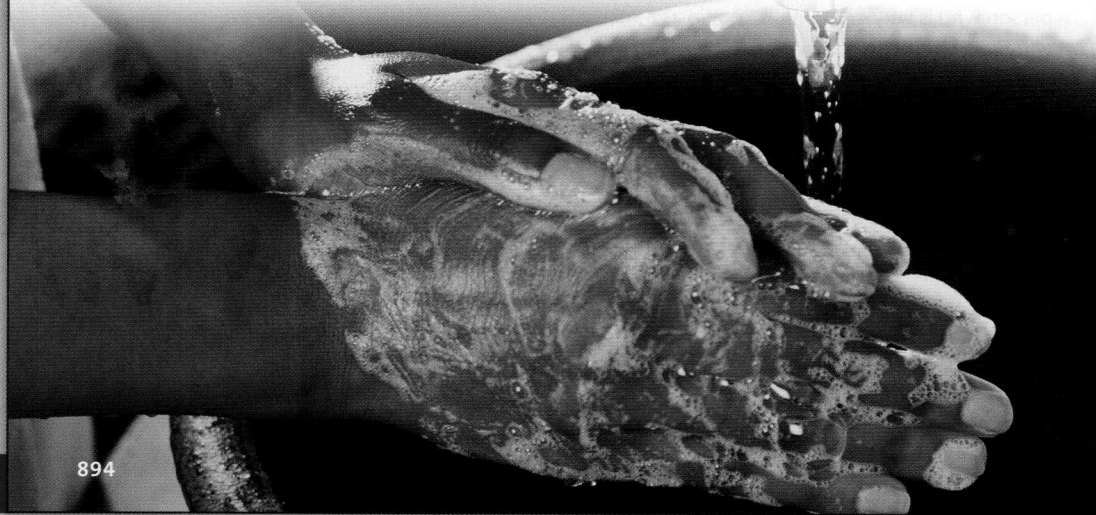

894

 **RESOURCE MANAGER UNIT 8**

Plan and Teach pp. 67–74
Elements of Nonfiction
Summary pp. 75†*, 76‡*; 81†*, 82‡*
Question Support pp. 80*; 84*

Reading
Set a Purpose for Reading pp. 77, 78†*
Reading Check pp. 79; 83

Vocabulary
Study p. 85*
Practice p. 86
Strategy p. 87

Grammar and Writing
Writing for Assessment p. 89

Assessment
Selection Tests A, B/C pp. 91*, 93*
Test Generator CD

BEST PRACTICES TOOLKIT
Differentiated Instruction pp. 31–38*

Scaffolding Instruction pp. 43–46*

Graphic Organizers/Strategies
Word Questioning • Read Aloud/ Think Aloud • Timeline • Draw It • Comparison Matrix • T Chart

Reading Support
Audio Anthology CD*

Technology
Literature and Vocabulary Centers at **ClassZone.com**

WriteSmart CD

---

* Resources for Differentiation   † Also in Spanish   ‡ In Haitian Creole and Vietnamese

ELEMENTS OF NONFICTION: PATTERNS OF ORGANIZATION

Nonfiction writers use a **pattern of organization** to help them explain key points. Here are two common patterns:

- **Cause-and-effect organization** points out the relationship between an event and its cause or effect. Signal words and phrases, such as *caused, because,* and *led to,* may indicate a cause or an effect.

- **Chronological order** organizes events according to when they happened. Signal words include *after* and *the following* and phrases that give specific times or dates.

As you read, decide how each article's pattern of organization helps the author explain her main points.

READING STRATEGY: SET A PURPOSE FOR READING

As you read these two articles, look for similarities and differences in the information the articles contain and the ways they are organized. A chart like the one shown can help you identify these similarities and differences.

	"Like Black Smoke"	"A World Turned Upside Down"
Purpose		
Main Idea and Supporting Details		
Type of Organization		

Review: Interpret Graphic Aids

VOCABULARY IN CONTEXT

The following words help provide information about the bubonic plague. See which ones you already know. Place each word in the correct column of a chart like the one shown.

WORD LIST			
	artisan	cope	rampage
	bacterium	disarray	recurrence
	chronicle	hierarchy	

Know Well	Think I Know	Don't Know at All

Author Online

Diana Childress: History Lover Award-winning author Diana Childress has written numerous books and articles for young people, most of them based on her favorite subject— history.

Diana Childress born 1940

Mary Morton Cowan: Many Talents Articles aren't the only thing Mary Morton Cowan writes for young people. She also writes folk tales, historical plays, photo essays, and puzzles.

Mary Morton Cowan born 1939

 MORE ABOUT THE AUTHOR For more on the authors, visit the **Literature Center** at **ClassZone.com.**

Background

Devastation in the Middle Ages The Middle Ages lasted from about A.D. 500 to A.D. 1500. One of the most significant events of this time period was the spread of the bubonic plague, or the Black Death. Those who caught the disease suffered fever and painful swellings, called buboes, in the lymph glands. The buboes, from which the disease gets its name, were followed by black spots on the skin. Next came a severe, bloody cough, and after that— death. At the time, no one knew what caused the disease.

STANDARDS FOCUS

ELEMENTS OF NONFICTION

● PATTERNS OF ORGANIZATION

Read aloud this example:

> Tasting cookie dough or cake batter can lead to infection by *Salmonella enteritidis* because this bacterium may be present in uncooked eggs.

How is the information organized? ***Possible answer:*** *It is organized by cause and effect; the words* lead to *and* because *are clues.*

CHECK UNDERSTANDING Have students read the **Background** information on page 895 and identify how it is organized.

READING STRATEGY

■ SET A PURPOSE FOR READING

Remind students that people read for various purposes. They may read to compare and contrast points of view, to understand a historical figure, or to find out about an event. Tell students that formulating a question about what they want to learn can help them set a purpose.

CHECK UNDERSTANDING Ask students how reading for information is different from reading just for fun.

 RESOURCE MANAGER—Copy Master Set a Purpose for Reading p. 77 (for student use while reading the selections)

VOCABULARY SKILL

▲ VOCABULARY IN CONTEXT

DIAGNOSE WORD KNOWLEDGE To determine preteaching needs, have all students complete **Vocabulary in Context.** Remind them to look for the vocabulary words and their definitions as they read the articles.

PRETEACH VOCABULARY Use the Vocabulary Study copy master to help students determine the meaning of each boldfaced word.

1. Read aloud the paragraph, emphasizing the boldfaced words.

2. Ask students to think about the way each word is used. Discuss possible meanings for *bacterium,* such as "germ" or "disease-causing agent."

3. Repeat the procedure for the remaining boldfaced words.

 RESOURCE MANAGER—Copy Master Vocabulary Study p. 85

For general guidelines on differentiating vocabulary instruction and for alternative vocabulary activities for students not needing vocabulary preteaching, see

📦 **BEST PRACTICES TOOLKIT** Scaffolding Vocabulary Instruction pp. 43–46

ℹ️ Vocabulary Center at **ClassZone.com** Additional Vocabulary Activities

Practice and Apply

ANALYZE VISUALS

Possible answers: The people are

- digging graves
- transporting coffins
- placing coffins in graves

About the Art Like the image on page 900, this miniature is an illumination—a painting in a book or manuscript that is painted in colors and, usually, gold. Illuminations were an important art form in Europe from at least the 500s. Some of the most beautiful illuminations were made from the 1200s through the 1400s. After that time, fewer books were made and illustrated by hand because the invention of the printing press made mass production possible.

READING STRATEGY

A SET A PURPOSE FOR READING

Possible answer: The title and subheadings suggest that the article will trace the path of the plague as it spread from its "eastern beginnings" across Asia and the Mediterranean, then continuing along trade routes.

ANALYZE VISUALS
What are the individuals in this image doing?

A SET A PURPOSE FOR READING
Read the title and scan the **subheadings.** What do you expect to learn from this article?

Burying plague victims in coffins at Tournai in 1349. Illumination from the *Annals of Gilles de Muisit* (1352). The Granger Collection, New York.

Like Black Smoke
The Black Death's Journey
Diana Childress

"We see death coming into our midst like black smoke," wrote the poet Jeuan Gethin,[1] when plague invaded Wales in March 1349. This "rootless phantom which has no mercy" was especially frightening for those who witnessed it because they knew it was somehow contagious, but no one could halt or explain its relentless spread across Europe.

Eastern Beginnings

The earliest evidence of the Black Death lies in a cemetery in what was once a prosperous town near Lake Issyk-Kul[2] on the fabled Silk Road[3] in Central Asia. An unusually large number of graves there are dated 1338 and 1339. Three headstones mentioning the cause of death provide a clue about why
10 so many people died: the plague.

Did the Black Death originate near Issyk-Kul? No one knows for sure. Most medieval writers say that the plague began in the East. They name places like Cathay (China), India, and Turkey. Modern historians agree that

---

1. **Jeuan Gethin** (yā′ən gĕth′ĭn).
2. **Lake Issyk-Kul** (ĭ′sĭk-kŭl′).
3. **Silk Road:** an important trade route on which both goods and ideas were exchanged between China and the countries of western Europe.

DIFFERENTIATED INSTRUCTION

FOR ALL STUDENTS

Anchor Activity Allow students to explore how bacteria continue to affect human health by inviting them to research bacterial diseases that occur in the United States today. After students complete their research, lead a discussion of ways to prevent bacterial infection. For further details on this project, see

 RESOURCE MANAGER
Ideas for Extension pp. 72–73

FOR ENGLISH LEARNERS

Vocabulary: Cognates Point out these Spanish cognates in "Like Black Smoke":

- *bubonic plague* (**Background,** page 895), *peste bubónica*
- *contagious* (line 4), *contagioso*
- *epidemic* (line 14), *epidemia*
- *bacteria* (lines 16, 27), *bacterias*
- *germ* (line 21), *germen*
- *infect* (line 26), *infectar*
- *contaminate* (line 50), *contaminar*
- *pestilence* (line 97), *pestilencia*

Key Academic Vocabulary

Have students use Word Questioning to study this academic vocabulary in "Like Black Smoke": *region* (lines 16, 65), *theory* (line 20), *major* (line 55), *area* (lines 80, 118), and *annual* (line 96).

 BEST PRACTICES TOOLKIT—Transparency
Word Questioning p. E9

Prereading For prereading instruction for English learners, see

BEST PRACTICES TOOLKIT
Scaffolding Reading Instruction pp. 43–46

the epidemic started in Asia—more specifically, somewhere on the central steppes[4] or in the Himalayan lowlands on the border of India and China. In both regions, the plague **bacterium,** *Yersinia pestis,*[5] has long thrived among wild marmots, ground squirrels, and gerbils.

On the Move

How did the disease travel from wild rodents to humans? According to early accounts, before the Black Death broke out, earthquakes, floods, and
20 famines devastated Asia. One theory is that these disasters drove wild animals into villages and towns in search of food. Fleas then spread plague germs to rats. . . .

When rats died of the plague, their fleas hunted for new hosts. Since rats nested in the adobe (sun-dried brick) walls and thatched roofs of medieval houses, the next meal for these fleas often came from people. . . .

The disease spread more easily if an infected person's lungs started filling up with plague bacteria. Then, every cough and sneeze spewed germs into the air, spreading pneumonic plague[6]
30 directly to others.

If they are not among the lucky few who recover, people and rats soon die of the plague, but infected fleas can lurk in a rat's nest, barnyard manure, or bedding and
40 clothing for many months without eating. A medieval writer was not far wrong when he wrote that "even the houses or clothes of the victims could kill."

. . . Cloth, grain, furs, and hides kept in rat-infested warehouses soon became delayed-action "plague bombs" waiting to go off. An account tells

bacterium (băk-tîr′ē-əm) *n.* the singular form of *bacteria,* microscopically small living things that may cause disease

① Targeted Passage

Fleas infect rats with *Yersinia pestis,* the plague bacterium. Rats spread the disease to humans. Once human lungs fill with plague bacteria, the germ becomes airborne every time a person coughs or sneezes.

Ⓑ INTERPRET GRAPHIC AIDS How does this illustration **clarify** your understanding of how people caught the disease?

---

4. **steppes:** treeless plains in southeastern Europe and in Asia.
5. *Yersinia pestis* (yər-sĭn′ē-ə pĕst′ĭs).
6. **pneumonic** (nŏŏ-mŏn′ĭk) **plague:** the most contagious and deadly form of the Black Death.

READING SKILL: *Review*

Ⓑ INTERPRET GRAPHIC AIDS

Possible answer: The aid helps to clarify

- *which creature first had the plague (flea)*
- *how the disease spread from one host to the next—from fleas to rats, rats to humans, and humans to humans through the air*
- *that the plague is caused by a bacterium*

Extend the Discussion The existence of bacteria was not observed until more than 300 years later (by Anton van Leeuwenhoek after he developed improvements in the microscope). What explanations do you imagine people in the 1300s might have had for where the disease came from?

FOR LESS–PROFICIENT READERS

In combination with the *Audio Anthology CD,* use one or more Targeted Passages (pp. 897, 899, 900, 903, 904) to ensure that students focus on key events, concepts, and skills.

① Targeted Passage [Lines 14–30]

This passage introduces the author's purpose: to explain where and how the Black Death originated and spread.

- Where is the plague believed to have originated?
- How might the plague have spread from wild animals to people?
- How did the plague spread through the air?

FOR ADVANCED LEARNERS/PRE–AP

Pre-AP exercises in the bottom channel provide additional challenge for your advanced students. Use them for small groups or individuals.

ADDITIONAL GUIDELINES

For more help with differentiation and tips for classroom management, see

 BEST PRACTICES TOOLKIT Differentiated Instruction pp. 31–38

Lines 53–63
DISCUSSION PROMPTS

Use these prompts to help students understand why the plague spread where it did:

Interpret What does the writer mean when she says that travelers "'carried' the Black Death in their baggage" (lines 53–54)? ***Possible answer:*** *As people traveled, they spread germs, though they did not intend to.*

Analyze What role did trade play in the spread of the plague? ***Possible answer:*** *Merchants and traders spread the disease along their trade routes as they traveled over land (across the Mongol Empire) and by sea (in the Crimea and the Mediterranean).*

Synthesize How do people today try to reduce the risk of travel-related disease? ***Possible answer:*** *Today, people can get information from their governments and their doctors about what diseases they might encounter in another country. For some diseases, they can be given vaccinations or preventive medications.*

READING SKILL: *Review*

C INTERPRET GRAPHIC AIDS

Possible answer: *The map shows that the plague first spread westward and eventually afflicted three continents.*

---

50 how four soldiers learned the hard way about contaminated goods. Looting houses in a deserted town, they stole a fleece off a bed and later slept under it. They were dead by morning.

Commercial caravans, Mongol armies, and other wayfarers[7] "carried" the Black Death in their baggage as they crisscrossed Asia. By 1345, it had traveled from Issyk-Kul to Sarai and Astrakhan,[8] the major cities of the Golden Horde[9] (a part of the Mongol Empire that is today southwestern Russia).

From Asia to the Mediterranean

At the time, Italian merchants from Genoa and Venice had established trading posts at Kaffa, a city on the Crimean Peninsula that juts out into
60 the Black Sea. Since the mid-1200s, their galleys had transported Asian horses, furs, and slaves to Syria and Egypt and silks and spices to Italy. When plague began to spread to the Crimea, many of the Europeans tried to escape by sea, but the Black Death sailed with them.

---

7. **commercial caravans . . . wayfarers:** Commercial caravans are bands of merchants or traders traveling together for safety. Mongols had a large empire covering most of Asia and eastern Europe. Wayfarers are generally people who travel on foot.

8. **Sarai** (sä-rī') **. . . Astrakhan** (ăs'trə-kăn').

9. **Golden Horde:** a name for the Mongol army.

C INTERPRET GRAPHIC AIDS
According to the map, in what direction did the Black Death first travel? Note how many continents were affected.

DIFFERENTIATED INSTRUCTION

FOR LESS–PROFICIENT READERS

Review Interpret Graphic Aids Remind students that graphic aids can express complex information in a clear and easy-to-understand way. Have students work in pairs to explain to each other what the red arrows on the map mean. Ask them to express their understanding in complete sentences, as in "The plague spread from Barcelona to Paris, and then from Paris to London."

Comprehension Support Use Read Aloud/Think Aloud for lines 53–64. Tell students that as you read each place name, you

- look for it on the map
- put one finger on the name and use another finger to trace the arrow to the next place

Explain that if you cannot find a place on the map, you skip over it and look for the next one.

 BEST PRACTICES TOOLKIT—Transparency
Read Aloud/Think Aloud p. A34

FOR ENGLISH LEARNERS

Vocabulary Support Help students use context clues to understand these expressions, and then work together to use them in new sentences:

- *not far wrong* (lines 43–44), "basically accurate"
- *learned the hard way* (line 50), "made a terrible mistake"
- *petered out* (line 110), "came to an end"
- *full circle* (line 112), "back to where it started"

The following summer, plague broke out in Constantinople. From there, it crossed the Mediterranean region. That fall, ships brought the plague to Alexandria, Egypt, one arriving with only 45 of its original crew of 332 men still alive. Another fleet came to Messina, Sicily, its crew so ill that a <u>chronicle</u> reports that the men had "sickness clinging to their very bones." **D**

The epidemic reached Genoa on New Year's Eve 1347 aboard three galleys laden with spices from the East. On discovering that many seamen were sick, the Genoese chased the ships from the port with "burning arrows and engines of war." Plague-ridden rats, however, had already jumped ship. The galleys sailed off along the coast of France, still hoping to find a place to sell their deadly merchandise.

Following the Trade Routes

Following 14th-century trade routes, the Black Death swept across Europe, North Africa, and the Middle East. After it assaulted the seaports, smaller boats carried it to neighboring towns and to river ports far inland. It could not be stopped. Although some towns refused entry to travelers from infected areas, and people learned to mistrust "plague goods," few noticed the dead rats, and no one thought of the fleas.

Reports of plague in 1348 show how the circles of infection widened. In the east, it hit Cyprus, Aleppo, Damascus, Jerusalem, and even pilgrims

chronicle (krŏn′ĭ-kəl)
n. a record of historical events in the order in which they took place

D PATTERNS OF ORGANIZATION
Reread lines 64–69. What phrases help you follow this paragraph's pattern of organization?

2 Targeted Passage

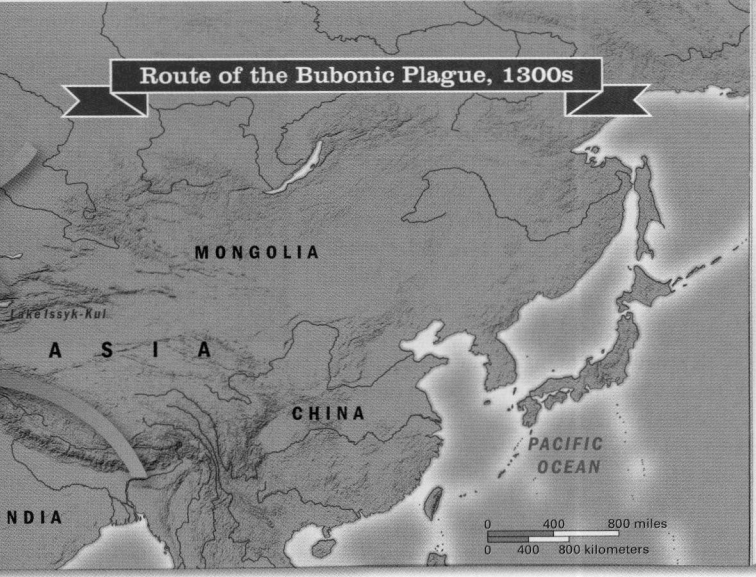

Route of the Bubonic Plague, 1300s

MONGOLIA

Lake Issyk-Kul

ASIA

CHINA

PACIFIC OCEAN

INDIA

0   400   800 miles
0   400   800 kilometers

LIKE BLACK SMOKE: THE BLACK DEATH'S JOURNEY **899**

ELEMENTS OF NONFICTION

D PATTERNS OF ORGANIZATION

Possible answer: Phrases that help the reader follow the pattern of chronological order include

- *"the following summer" (line 64)*
- *"that fall" (line 65)*

Lines 70–81
REINFORCE *KEY IDEA*: DISEASE

Discuss How did people try to stop the spread of the **disease?** Why were their efforts unsuccessful? *Possible answer: People tried to stop ships, travelers, and foreign goods from entering their areas. However, rats and fleas carrying the disease still moved freely. People did not understand that rats and fleas carried the disease.*

BACKGROUND

Place Names Some place names have changed since the 1300s. The city of Kaffa is located in what is now Ethiopia. The city of Constantinople was renamed Istanbul in 1930 by the Republic of Turkey.

FOR LESS–PROFICIENT READERS

2 Targeted Passage [Lines 64–81]

This passage explains how ships and trade routes helped spread the plague throughout the Middle East, Europe, and North Africa.

- How was the plague brought to the Mediterranean region?
- What role did ship rats play in the spread of the plague?
- What routes did the plague follow as it spread?

FOR ENGLISH LEARNERS

Vocabulary: Phrasal Verbs Explain that while the verb *break* usually means "to separate into pieces," the phrasal verb *break out* has a different meaning. Assign pairs these verbs to look up in a dictionary, and then have them share their definitions:

- *broke out* (line 64), "developed quickly"
- *run aground* (line 100), "been stranded"
- *closed in on* (line 107), "moved toward"

Reading Comprehension: Sequence Have student pairs create timelines of the years mentioned on pages 898–900. Next to each year, have them write the place(s) associated with that year. Then have students use their timelines alongside the map on pages 898–899 to trace the course of the plague during those years.

 BEST PRACTICES TOOLKIT—Transparency Timeline p. B23

DISCUSSION PROMPTS

Use these prompts to help students understand the westward spread of the plague:

Restate How did weather affect the spread of the plague in England? *Possible answer: During a mild winter, fleas and rats thrived. It was also wet, so people stayed indoors, breathing contaminated air.*

Infer In one town, people wrote wills at 30 times the normal yearly rate. What does this fact suggest about their understanding of the plague? *Possible answer: They knew that it was spreading and they expected that they might not survive.*

Synthesize Note the means by which the plague spread. How might these be controlled now? *Possible answer: Today, people know more about how disease can spread. People have access to better medications, disinfectants, and pest control.*

ELEMENTS OF NONFICTION

E PATTERNS OF ORGANIZATION

Possible answer: Words that signal the pattern of chronological organization include "In 1350" (line 103), "The following year" (line 104), "In 1353" (lines 106–107), and "Finally" (line 110). The subheading indicates that it will tell how the spread of the disease ended.

ANALYZE VISUALS

Activity What details in this image help you understand what is happening in it? *Possible answers: The monks are covered in spots. The priest's hat, gesture, and separateness show that he is an authority figure.*

SELECTION WRAP–UP

⭐ **CRITIQUE** Ask students which image or graphic aid contributed most to their understanding of the article.

---

visiting Mecca. From Genoa and Venice it crept down the Italian boot toward Florence and Rome. Going west, it struck Marseilles, Tunis, and Barcelona. By June, the epidemic was storming Paris, causing the French royal family to flee to Rouen,[10] where it soon followed. That summer, it overran Germany, Poland, and Hungary and crossed the channel to southern England.

90   Winter did not slow its progress. The weather was unusually mild and wet, perhaps warm enough for fleas living on house rats to remain active. Huddled indoors, people were also exposed to air contaminated both by those suffering from pneumonic plague and by the dust from rodent droppings.

As the disease moved northward through England, citizens of Lincoln wrote wills at 30 times the normal annual rate. At first, the Scots avoided the plague, but when they assembled troops to invade England, pestilence[11] struck, perhaps imported by soldiers from France.

The Black Death landed in Scandinavia on a ship carrying wool from
100   London to Norway. The ship had run aground near Bergen because all the crew had died. From there, plague spread across Norway, into Sweden, and across the Baltic Sea to Russia.

The Journey Ends

Targeted Passage ❸

In 1350, plague peaked in Scotland and Scandinavia, while in southern Spain, it killed King Alfonso XI of Castile. The following year, it stretched to Greenland, where it helped wipe out the Norwegian colony, and to Yemen, at the tip of the Arabian peninsula. In 1353, it closed in on Moscow, killing both the patriarch of the Russian church and the grand duke of Muscovy.

rampage (răm'pāj') *n.* a wild or violent outbreak

❸ **PATTERNS OF ORGANIZATION**
Reread lines 103–119. Which words signal the pattern of organization? How does the final subheading reinforce this organization?

110   Finally, the Black Death petered out somewhere in Kiev, having come almost full circle back to Kaffa. During its long **rampage**, between one-third and one-half of the population of Europe, North Africa, and the Middle East died. No natural disaster before or since has caused such devastation of human life over such a large area. It was one of the greatest catastrophes in human history. ❸

A priest blesses plague-infected monks. Illumination from *Omne Bonum* (about 1370), Jacobus Anglicus. Ms. Royal 6, E VI, fol. 301. © British Library/akg-images.

---

10. **Rouen** (rōō-än'): a city in France, about 84 miles northwest of Paris.

11. **pestilence** (pĕs'tə-ləns): any disease that spreads rapidly and causes many deaths.

DIFFERENTIATED INSTRUCTION

FOR LESS–PROFICIENT READERS

❸ **Targeted Passage [Lines 103–119]**

This passage explains how the plague ended and describes the devastating impact it had on the population.

• Did the plague affect only poor people? How do you know?

• When and where did the plague come to an end?

• What effect did the plague have on the population of the areas it affected?

FOR ADVANCED LEARNERS/PRE–AP

Explore Personification How does the writer make the plague seem like an evil villain? Prompt students to explain how vivid verbs help create this personification: *crept* (line 84), *struck* (line 85), *storm[ed]* (line 86), *followed* (line 87), *overran* (line 88), and *crossed* (line 88). Challenge them to describe another natural disaster using personification.

The flood raged across the town, chasing people from their homes.

Comprehension

1. **Recall** Where do most historians think the Black Death started?

2. **Recall** How did boats spread the disease?

3. **Summarize** Summarize how the plague spread from rodents to people.

Critical Analysis

4. **Identify Fact or Opinion** Reread the last statement in the article. Is this sentence a fact or an opinion? Explain why you think so.

5. **Examine Cause and Effect** Reread lines 49–52. Which of the soldiers' actions probably led to their deaths? Explain.

6. **Analyze Author's Purpose** What do you think are the main points Childress wants readers to learn from this article? Explain your reasoning.

7. **Evaluate Events** Create a timeline of the key events that contributed to the spread of the Black Death. Which event do you think was most critical? Support your choice with details from the article.

Comparing Patterns of Organization

In your chart complete the column labeled "Like Black Smoke." Add information that helps you understand how the article is organized.

MARYLAND OBJECTIVES

INFORMATIONAL TEXT STANDARD
2.A.3.a Analyze the organizational patterns of texts

	"Like Black Smoke"	"A World Turned Upside Down"
Purpose		
Main Idea and Supporting Details	Black Death travels from the East.	
Type of Organization		

Practice and Apply

After Reading

For additional support of post-reading questions, use these copy masters:

RESOURCE MANAGER—Copy Masters
Reading Check p. 79 (to check understanding of the selection)
Question Support p. 80 (**After Reading** questions adapted for English learners and less-proficient readers)

Additional selection questions are provided for teachers on page 71.

ANSWERS

Comprehension

1. *The Black Death may have started near Lake Issyk-Kul on the Silk Road in Asia.*

2. *Boats (especially merchant ships) transported the plague from one city to another.*

3. *Disasters in Asia may have caused wild animals to go to towns to find food. Their fleas jumped onto rats and gave plague germs to city rats. When the rats died, these infected fleas jumped onto people. The infected people coughed and sneezed, causing germs to spread through the air.*

Critical Analysis

Possible answers:

4. *Students may say that considering the number of people who died, the sentence is a fact.*

5. *Stealing and using the fleece probably led to the soldiers' deaths, as there were probably infected fleas living on it.*

6. *Childress wants readers to understand where the plague came from, how it spread, and what happened when it spread.*

7. ● **STANDARDS FOCUS** *Patterns of Organization Answers will vary. Students may say that the disasters in Asia were most crucial because they caused wild animals to flee to cities. Some may cite the ships that transported infected rats to other countries. Others may blame the mild winters that allowed fleas to remain active.*

Comparing Patterns of Organization

■ **STANDARDS FOCUS** *Set a Purpose for Reading*
Possible answers:

	"Like Black Smoke"
Purpose	To explain how plague began and spread
Main Idea and Supporting Details	• Black Death travels from the East. • starts in Asia • spreads from rodents to people • follows trade routes to Mediterranean • sweeps across Europe, North Africa, and Middle East
Type of Organization	Chronological

Detail of *Triumph of Death* (1597), Jan Brueghel. Oil on canvas, 119 cm × 164 cm. Steiermärk. Landesmuseum Johanneum. © akg-images.

A WORLD TURNED UPSIDE DOWN: HOW THE BLACK DEATH AFFECTED EUROPE

Mary Morton Cowan

A SET A PURPOSE FOR READING
Reread lines 1–4. **Paraphrase** the main idea that this article will explore.

hierarchy (hī′ə-rär′kē) *n.* an organization of people according to rank

Substantial changes in population often have dramatic effects on society. The bubonic plague, which in just four years killed up to one-third of the people in Europe, almost literally turned Europe's social structure upside down. **A**

Life in the Middle Ages centered around a **hierarchy** called the feudal system. Noble lords lived in castles or manors, which were surrounded by acres of land. The nobles depended on peasants to farm their land. In turn, peasants received protection, shelter, and a small plot of land to plant their own crops. According to the Christian church, the feudal system was God's
10 plan, and no one questioned the authority of the church. **B**

In the 300 years before the Black Death, the European population tripled. Additional land was cultivated, but food was still scarce. Some peasants left

902 UNIT 8: INFORMATION, ARGUMENT, AND PERSUASION

Lines 2–4
REINFORCE *KEY IDEA*: DISEASE

Discuss If one-third of the people in Europe died from bubonic plague, how were those who survived this **disease** probably affected by the loss? *Possible answers:*

- *People probably lost family members, friends, and neighbors.*
- *They probably saw areas depopulated and heard of more deaths (and perhaps saw more burials) than they could count.*
- *There probably weren't enough people left to do work that needed to be done.*
- *People were probably afraid that plague would return.*

DIFFERENTIATED INSTRUCTION

FOR LESS–PROFICIENT READERS
Comprehension Support Use Draw It to help students understand the hierarchy explained in lines 5–10. Talk as you illustrate the elements described, and have students read along to give you cues for what to draw next. You might draw a castle at the top of the board with stick figures (peasants) and a few huts at the bottom. A church at the side could represent the authority of the church.

BEST PRACTICES TOOLKIT
Draw It p. A2

FOR ENGLISH LEARNERS
Vocabulary: Cognates English has many cognates with other languages, especially those that are Latin based. English–Spanish cognates in line 1 include

- *substantial/sustancial*
- *dramatic/dramático(a)*
- *effects/los efectos*
- *society/la sociedad*

Ask students to look for other cognates as they read this article.

ANALYZE VISUALS
What might the skeletons in this painting **symbolize,** or stand for?

for a better life in the city, where merchants and craftsmen were beginning to thrive. The now-crowded cities, however, could not handle the overflow of unskilled laborers.

After gunpowder was invented, the lords had found it harder to defend their castles. They also experienced some bad harvests, and many had to **cope** with the consequences of a war between France and England. Yet, they remained in control.

cope (kōp) *v.* to struggle with and act to overcome

20 Then, without warning, the Black Death swept through Western Europe, killing 25 million people. Some families were wiped out. Large estates were left without heirs. Survivors moved in and claimed any property they could find. Cities and towns lost people by the thousands. Monasteries,[1] which previously had as many as 150 monks, now had only seven or eight. In all, thousands of villages were abandoned. **B**

Agriculture was also in **disarray**. The tools and land were there, but suddenly the workers were missing. Food prices dropped, and there was even a surplus of food where once many had barely had enough to stay alive.

30 Because workers were scarce, peasants who survived the plague now had bargaining power for the first time. Resentment among the working class led to violence and revolt in the centuries that followed, as Europe teetered between the old feudal system and a new economic system.

④ **Targeted Passage**

B PATTERNS OF ORGANIZATION
Reread lines 20–25. What effects of the Black Death does the author give?

disarray (dĭs′ə-rā′) *n.* a state of disorder; confusion

---

1. **monasteries:** buildings where religious men called monks live, work, and pray together.

ANALYZE VISUALS
Possible answers: The skeletons might symbolize the unavoidability of death, disease, or people's fear of death.

About the Art The Brueghels were a family of Flemish painters. Jan Brueghel's (1568–1625) early work was largely devoted to flowers and still lifes, earning him the nickname Velvet. Later, he became known for his intricate landscapes. This is a copy he made of a work by his father, Pieter Brueghel the Elder.

ELEMENTS OF NONFICTION

B PATTERNS OF ORGANIZATION
Possible answers: The Black Death killed 25 million people in western Europe, reduced populations in cities and towns, and eliminated some villages entirely.

Lines 20–29
DISCUSSION PROMPTS
Use these prompts to help students understand the impact of the plague:

Connect Think about a time when you heard about a large-scale disaster. How do those thoughts help you imagine the feelings of survivors of the plague? *Students may say they felt shocked, sad, and numb.*

Analyze What words and phrases express the shocking effects of the plague? *Possible answers: "without warning" (line 20), "swept through" (line 20), "disarray" (line 26), "suddenly" (line 27)*

Evaluate What feeling does the phrase "the workers were missing" convey? *Possible answer: It conveys a feeling that things are wrong or unnatural. People who have always been there are suddenly gone.*

FOR LESS–PROFICIENT READERS
④ **Targeted Passage [Lines 20–33]**

This passage summarizes some of the fundamental effects of the plague on western European society.

- What impact did the death toll of the plague have on estates, cities, and villages?

- What happened to the food supply in the aftermath of the plague?

- How did life change for peasants who survived the plague? Why?

Comprehension Support Have students create a Comparison Matrix to organize the changes identified on pages 902–903.

Factor	Before Plague	After Plague
nobles	controlled all	had less power
peasants	had little power	could bargain
economy	feudal	changing
population	growing fast	lost one-third
food	scarce	surplus
cities	overcrowded	less populated

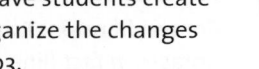 BEST PRACTICES TOOLKIT—Transparency
Comparison Matrix p. A24

904 UNIT 8: INFORMATION, ARGUMENT, AND PERSUASION

ELEMENTS OF NONFICTION

ⓒ PATTERNS OF ORGANIZATION

Possible answers:

- *"Because" (line 30)*
- *"led to" (line 32)*
- *"caused" (line 35)*

READING SKILL: *Review*

ⓓ INTERPRET GRAPHIC AIDS

Answer: *about 75 million*

If students need help . . . Point out that the label for the *y*-axis says that the population is noted in millions. Therefore, 75 means 75 million.

SELECTION WRAP–UP

REFLECT What surprised you most about how population loss affected society in the Middle Ages?

⭐ **CRITIQUE** Ask students to evaluate whether the writer provided enough background information to help them understand the impact of the plague on Europe.

Targeted Passage ⑤

artisan (är'tĭ-zən) *n.* a person who is skilled in a trade

ⓒ **PATTERNS OF ORGANIZATION**
Reread lines 30–45. What clue words help you recognize the pattern of organization?

recurrence (rĭ-kûr'əns) *n.* the act of happening again; return

ⓓ **INTERPRET GRAPHIC AIDS**
What was the population of western Europe in the early 1300s?

The shortage of skilled craftsmen caused an industrial crisis. Unlike agricultural workers, craftsmen require long apprenticeships, and now
40 there were few replacements when any skilled **artisan** died. Reduced production forced prices of saddles, farm tools, and other goods to soar. ⓒ
This depopulation crisis, however, encouraged technological developments. The most notable labor-
50 saving invention was the printing press, developed around 1450. One such press replaced hand-copying by hundreds of scribes.[2]

Survivors of the plague use a printing press to copy manuscript.

Illumination from *Chants royaux* (about 1500). Bibliothèque Nationale. © akg-images/VISIOARS.

T he Black Death affected the entire medieval social structure. When the pestilence returned a few years later, people were even more terrified. Its unpredictable **recurrence** in the following decades was enough to keep Europeans in constant fear. A mood of gloom swept
60 across Europe, and many began to question the authority of the church. In fact, they began to have doubts about their entire world view. Yet, it was this questioning that led to far-reaching reforms in religion, art, medicine, and science. Without a doubt, the Black
70 Death forever changed Europe's economic and social structure.

---

2. **scribes:** people whose job was to copy manuscripts.

Population of Western Europe Before and After the Bubonic Plague

Population (millions)

75

50

25

ⓓ 0

1300s   1400s

Time Period

Detail of *Danse Macabre. Pope* (1500s), Bernt Notke. Oil on canvas, 160 cm × 750 cm. St. Nicholas' Church, Art Museum of Estonia, Tallinn, Estonia. © Bridgeman Art Library.

DIFFERENTIATED INSTRUCTION

FOR LESS–PROFICIENT READERS

⑤ Targeted Passage [Lines 34–54]

This passage explains how depopulation due to the plague transformed the European economy.

- What impact did the plague have on the population of skilled workers?
- Why did the price of commercial goods rise after the plague?
- How did the invention of the printing press save labor?

FOR ENGLISH LEARNERS

Comprehension: Transitions Explain that the phrases *in fact* (line 63) and *without a doubt* (line 69) are transitions that are used to add emphasis. Ask students if they can name other transitions that add emphasis. Have students help you create original sentences about the plague that use emphasis transitions such as *indeed* and *certainly*.

FOR ADVANCED LEARNERS/PRE–AP

Make Judgments What was the most significant change caused by the plague? Ask pairs or small groups to formulate an answer based on the information in the text and their own knowledge. Have each pair or group present its opinion, along with supporting evidence.

Comprehension

1. **Recall** How long did it take for the bubonic plague to wipe out one-third of Europe's population?

2. **Recall** Why did the depopulation of Europe encourage technological developments?

3. **Summarize** What was life like in Europe in the Middle Ages before the Black Death swept through?

 **MARYLAND OBJECTIVES**

INFORMATIONAL TEXT STANDARD
2.A.3.a Analyze the organizational patterns of texts

Critical Analysis

4. **Identify Author's Main Idea** Writers choose the details that will best support the main idea they want to convey. What main idea is Cowan supporting in this article?

5. **Examine Cause and Effect** Why did food prices drop after the Black Death swept through western Europe?

6. **Analyze Graphic Aids** What information does the bar graph on page 904 give you that the text does not?

7. **Evaluate** What were some positive changes caused by the spread of this deadly disease?

Comparing Patterns of Organization

Now that you've read both articles, finish filling in your chart. Then use the chart to help you identify each article's pattern of organization.

	"Like Black Smoke"	*"A World Turned Upside Down"*
Purpose		
Main Idea and Supporting Details	Black Death travels from the East.	Plague reversed Europe's social structure.
Type of Organization		

Comparing Patterns of Organization

■ **STANDARDS FOCUS** *Set a Purpose for Reading*
Possible answers:

	"A World Turned Upside Down"
Purpose	To explain how the plague changed Europe
Main Idea and Supporting Details	Plague reversed Europe's social structure. • strict feudal hierarchy before plague • 25 million western Europeans killed • surviving peasants had bargaining power • labor-saving technologies created • authority of church questioned
Type of Organization	Cause and effect

Practice and Apply

After Reading

For additional support of post-reading questions, use these copy masters:

R **RESOURCE MANAGER—Copy Masters**
　Reading Check p. 83 (to check understanding of the selection)
　Question Support p. 84 (**After Reading** questions adapted for English learners and less-proficient readers)

　Additional selection questions are provided for teachers on page 71.

ANSWERS

Comprehension

1. *It took four years for the plague to kill one-third of the population.*

2. *Because the population was reduced, labor-saving devices that allowed fewer people to do more work became essential.*

3. *Before the plague, life centered on the feudal system. Lords lived in castles, and peasants worked the land in exchange for shelter and protection. Europe was overpopulated and food was scarce. Some people went to cities to find work, and cities became crowded.*

Critical Analysis
Possible answers:

4. *Cowan is supporting the main idea that the plague caused widespread social and economic changes in Europe.*

5. ● **STANDARDS FOCUS** *Patterns of Organization* *So many people died that there was too much food. The prices dropped so that people would buy more food.*

6. *The bar graph tells the total population of western Europe before and after the plague. The text tells only how many people died.*

7. *Some positive changes that came about as a result of the plague were the invention of the printing press and other technological developments as well as reforms in religion, art, and medicine that came from a distrust of old authorities.*

ANSWERS

Vocabulary in Context

VOCABULARY PRACTICE

1. *clock*
2. *artisan*
3. *caretaker*
4. *hierarchy*
5. *class*
6. *pandemonium*
7. *renounce*
8. *cope*

 RESOURCE MANAGER—Copy Master
Vocabulary Practice p. 86

VOCABULARY IN WRITING

Ask students to recall the effects of the Black Death on European society and the death toll of the disease.

VOCABULARY STRATEGY: SPECIALIZED VOCABULARY *(also an EL language objective)*

Tell students that specialized vocabulary in science sometimes has Greek and Latin word parts. For example:

- *antibiotic,* a medicine against infection (*anti* = "against"; *bio* = "life")
- *pandemic,* a widespread disease (*pan* = "all")

Ask what other forms of the specialized vocabulary on page 906 students know, such as *viral* (from *virus*) or *sterilize* (from *sterile*).

Answers:
1. *f;* 2. *a;* 3. *g;* 4. *d;* 5. *c;* 6. *e;* 7. *b*

 **RESOURCE MANAGER—Copy Master**
Vocabulary Strategy p. 87

ⓘ Vocabulary Center at ClassZone.com
Additional Vocabulary Activities

Vocabulary in Context

VOCABULARY PRACTICE

In each item, choose the word that differs most in meaning from the other words. Refer to a dictionary if you need help.

1. (a) record, (b) listing, (c) chronicle, (d) clock
2. (a) artisan, (b) police officer, (c) firefighter, (d) sanitation worker
3. (a) turmoil, (b) commotion, (c) caretaker, (d) disarray
4. (a) hierarchy, (b) anarchy, (c) chaos, (d) disorganization
5. (a) class, (b) frenzy, (c) rampage, (d) uproar
6. (a) bacterium, (b) germ, (c) pandemonium, (d) microorganism
7. (a) reappearance, (b) renounce, (c) repetition, (d) recurrence
8. (a) instruct, (b) teach, (c) cope, (d) educate

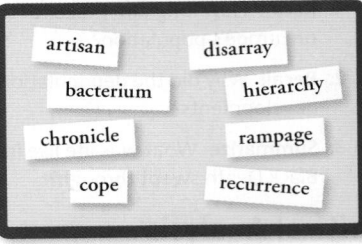

artisan   disarray
bacterium   hierarchy
chronicle   rampage
cope   recurrence

VOCABULARY IN WRITING

Pretend you are a survivor of the Black Death. Using three or more vocabulary words, write about how your life has changed. You could start like this.

> **EXAMPLE SENTENCE**
> *I survived the plague, but my whole life is in **disarray**.*

VOCABULARY STRATEGY: SPECIALIZED VOCABULARY

Recognizing a word that is often associated with disease or its prevention or treatment can help you better understand issues related to health.

PRACTICE Match the word in the first column with its definition in the second column. Refer to a dictionary or a science textbook if you need help.

1. virus   **a.** medicine for treating infections caused by bacteria
2. antibiotic   **b.** free from germs
3. pandemic   **c.** substance used to build immunity to a disease
4. inoculation   **d.** process of administering a vaccine
5. vaccine   **e.** decrease or disappearance of symptoms of a disease
6. remission   **f.** very small particle that can cause many types of disease
7. sterile   **g.** a very widespread or worldwide epidemic

MARYLAND OBJECTIVES

READING STANDARD
1.D.3.c Use resources to confirm definitions

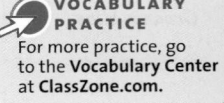

VOCABULARY PRACTICE
For more practice, go to the **Vocabulary Center** at ClassZone.com.

DIFFERENTIATED INSTRUCTION

FOR ENGLISH LEARNERS

Vocabulary Support Since specialized vocabulary in science often has Greek or Latin roots, ask students who speak Latin-based languages if they can identify cognates for any of the specialized vocabulary on page 906, such as the Spanish *el antibiótico* and *la inoculación.* Suggest that students try to learn unfamiliar specialized vocabulary by writing it down and drawing a visual cue next to the word, such as a sketch of a hypodermic needle for *vaccine.*

FOR ADVANCED LEARNERS/PRE–AP

Vocabulary Strategy Specialized vocabulary is used in many fields, from oceanography to culinary arts, architecture to information science. Have students choose a field that uses specialized vocabulary and create a glossary of ten words from that field. Suggest that they include pronunciation information as well as a definition for each word. Invite students to share their glossaries.

Writing for Assessment

1. READ THE PROMPT

In writing assessments, you might be asked to compare and contrast two informational texts that have a similar subject but differ in other ways.

PROMPT

In four or five paragraphs, compare and contrast "Like Black Smoke" and "A World Turned Upside Down." Be sure to identify the purpose, the main idea, and the pattern of organization of each article. Support your response with details from the two articles.

◄ **STRATEGIES IN ACTION**

1. I have to note **similarities** and **differences** between the two articles.

2. I must **tell** each **author's point** and **reason** for writing. I must **tell** how the ideas are organized.

3. I should **give examples** from each article to prove my points.

2. PLAN YOUR WRITING

Review the chart you filled out on page 905. Use the chart to help you identify how the articles are alike and different. Write a position statement that conveys your main idea about how the articles compare. Then think about how to best present and support the similarities and differences.

- Review the articles to find examples and details that support the similarities and differences.

- Create an outline to organize your ideas. The sample outline shows one way to organize your paragraphs.

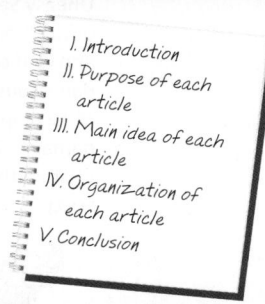

I. Introduction
II. Purpose of each article
III. Main idea of each article
IV. Organization of each article
V. Conclusion

3. DRAFT YOUR RESPONSE

Introduction Introduce the topic mentioned in the prompt. Include your position statement.

Body Use your chart and outline as guides to writing the key points of your comparison. Support your points with details from the selections.

Conclusion Leave your readers with a final thought about why the authors used different patterns of organization when writing about a similar subject.

Revision Use words that make your ideas clear. Proofread your response.

FOR LESS–PROFICIENT WRITERS

Draft Your Response

- To help students focus before writing, record similarities and differences on the board.

- Discuss which details relate to the author's purpose and the main idea of each article. Provide this writing template to help students structure their responses:

Introduction
Give titles and authors, identify the topic covered, and state the main idea.

Middle Paragraphs
In one paragraph, explain the similarities. In the other, explain the differences.

- State one similarity or difference at a time.
- Support each idea with specific details.

Conclusion
Explain how the similarities and differences between the two articles help readers understand the subject in different ways.

Writing for Assessment

1. **READ THE PROMPT**

- Read the prompt aloud. Ask volunteers to identify key terms and describe the task in their own words.

- Discuss the second **Strategy in Action.** Ask students to recall the purpose they set for reading and what they learned as they read.

2. **PLAN YOUR WRITING**

- Students can use a T Chart with the column headings "Similarities" and "Differences" to organize their details.

- Have students summarize their main idea in a clear position statement. Give them an example, such as "Although both articles describe the impact of the plague, one focuses on the path the disease took and the other focuses on its social consequences."

- Give students this alternative outline:
  First paragraph: introduction
  Second paragraph: compare similarities
  Third paragraph: compare differences
  Fourth paragraph: conclusion

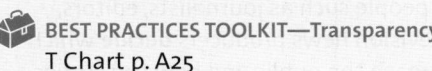 BEST PRACTICES TOOLKIT—Transparency
T Chart p. A25

3. **DRAFT YOUR RESPONSE**

- Remind students to use transitional words and sentences to highlight comparisons.

- Suggest that students exchange drafts. Have peer readers evaluate the organization and supporting details.

[R] RESOURCE MANAGER—Copy Master
Writing for Assessment p. 89

Assess and Reteach

Assess

[R] RESOURCE MANAGER—Copy Masters
Selection Tests A, B/C pp. 91–92, 93–94

Test Generator CD

Reteach

[S] STANDARDS LESSON FILE
Informational Texts Lessons 2, 4, 21, 24
Writing Lesson 29

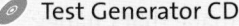

Focus and Motivate

OBJECTIVES

Media Literacy

- explore the key concept of **deciding** what stories are newsworthy
- view a news report to identify characteristics of newsworthiness
- compare how different media cover the same event
- create a reporter's guidebook

SUMMARY

The newscast from *ABC World News Tonight* covers the damage inflicted on areas of Florida by Hurricane Charley in 2004. It includes footage taken of the damage, a reporter on the scene, and interviews with people who lost their homes. Accompanying the newscast is an online news report about Hurricane Frances.

What DECISIONS *shape the news?*

Discuss the question. Explain that in the news media, people such as journalists, editors, and television news producers **decide** which stories reach the public and how the stories are told. Ask students to think about the news outlets that compete for their attention each day, such as national and cable networks, local TV stations, radio, newspapers, and Weblogs. After they read the *KEY IDEA* paragraph, ask volunteers to rate the reliability of these sources and to offer reasons for their opinions.

BACKGROUND

Hurricane Charley began in the Caribbean as a tropical depression on August 9, 2004. It quickly reached hurricane status and struck Cuba with 120-mile-per-hour winds on the evening of August 12. The hurricane reached Florida's Gulf coast the next day with winds of more than 145 miles per hour. The more than $14 billion in property damage that Charley caused made it the third most costly hurricane in U.S. history. Only Hurricane Katrina, which devastated the Gulf region in 2005, and Hurricane Andrew, which struck Florida in 1992, surpassed it. As with most natural disasters, Hurricane Charley received extensive media attention.

Media Study

News Reports

TV Newscast Clip / Web News Report on  **MediaSmart** DVD

What DECISIONS *shape the news?*

MARYLAND OBJECTIVES

INFORMATIONAL TEXT STANDARD
2.A.6.b Analyze structure and features

KEY IDEA The news is a flow of information that doesn't stop. Today's fresh news reports compete for space with updated details of news that happened yesterday. What helps journalists choose what to publish each day? You'll examine two news forms to discover who **decides** what news is reported and why.

Background

Uneasy Seasons The hurricane seasons of 2004 and 2005 were difficult ones for millions of people who live along the Atlantic and Gulf coastal regions of the United States. In two of the most dangerous and destructive seasons on record, Florida, Louisiana, Mississippi, Texas, and other coastal states suffered major damage. The TV newscast in this lesson deals with Hurricane Charley, the first of four major hurricanes that battered Florida in 2004. The Web news report deals with Hurricane Frances.

908

Media Study Resources

R RESOURCE MANAGER UNIT 8

Plan and Teach pp. 95–98

Media Analysis
Summary pp. 99†*, 100‡*
Viewing Guide p. 101
Close Viewing p. 102
Viewing Activity p. 103
Produce Your Own Media p. 104

S STANDARDS LESSON FILE

Media Lesson 8: Understanding the Basics of News Reporting
Media Lesson 9: Analyzing TV News
Media Lesson 10: Analyzing Print and Online News

 Media Center at **ClassZone.com**

MEDIA VIEWING
Media*Smart* DVD

---

* Resources for Differentiation   † Also in Spanish   ‡ In Haitian Creole and Vietnamese

Media Literacy: Newsworthiness

Newsworthiness is the importance of an event or action that makes it worthy of media reporting. Each day, journalists such as news editors decide which news stories will appear in newspapers, on newscasts, and online. Certain factors guide journalists in choosing a report and in shaping its details.

KEY FACTORS OF NEWSWORTHINESS

Timeliness is the quality of being current. The public is always eager for the latest news reports.

Proximity is the nearness of an event to a particular city, region, or country. Most people are more interested in stories that take place locally.

Widespread impact is said to belong to any event with a far-reaching effect. The more people the event could affect, the more likely it is to be newsworthy.

Uniqueness is a quality of news reports about very uncommon events or circumstances.

Human interest characterizes stories that cause readers or viewers to feel emotions such as happiness, anger, or sadness. People are interested in learning news about other people.

Compelling video and **photographs** grab people's attention. In a sense, visual images can place viewers right at the scene of an event.

STRATEGIES FOR VIEWING

In general, understand that the more factors of newsworthiness that a story has, the more attention-getting and long lasting the news report might be.

- Consider the **purposes** behind a report. The primary purpose of news is to inform. Another purpose is to present the advertisements that pay for published or broadcast news.

- Ask yourself: What people or groups are affected by the report? Does the report appeal to the emotions? How does this news affect my world?

- Be aware that the dramatic, attention-getting wording often appears in the **lead,** the opening sentences of a news story.

MEDIA STUDY **909**

MEDIA STUDY: TEACHING OPTIONS

Teaching Option 1: The Basics (1–2 Days)

1. Begin the Media Study using the material provided on pages 908–909.

2. Show the Introduction on Media*Smart.* Then show the First Viewing. As they watch, have students use the Viewing Guide on page 910, along with the corresponding copy master on page 101 of the Resource Manager. Discuss their responses.

3. Return to the pupil edition for the extension activities on page 911.

Teaching Option 2: In-Depth Study (2–3 Days)

1. Begin the Media Study using pages 908–909.

2. Show the Introduction and First Viewing from Media*Smart.*

3. Continue on Media*Smart* with the Media Lessons, using the teacher notes available in the Resources section.

4. Show the Guided Analysis presentation. Have students record their observations on the Student Viewing Guide available in the Resources section from Media*Smart.*

5. Return to the pupil edition, page 911.

Teach

MEDIA LITERACY

Review the definition of *newsworthiness.* Explain that not every story that receives media coverage is worthy of such attention. Ask students for examples of current news topics that they consider newsworthy, and others that they consider less than newsworthy. List these stories and their sources. Then discuss the chart on page 909.

- **Timeliness** Point out that the most timely news stories usually appear on the front page of a newspaper or in the first few minutes of a news program. Work with students to list some of the most timely news stories of the week.

- **Widespread Impact** Ask students to give an example of something in the news that affects many people, such as a natural disaster, a political event, or a health issue.

- **Human Interest** This could be a tale of heroism, a personal tragedy, or gossip about a celebrity. Have students think of events or situations that could be newsworthy as human interest stories.

- **Proximity** Talk about local news stories. Ask students to explain why they do or do not find stories that take place locally more newsworthy than other news stories.

- **Uniqueness** Explain that stories in this category are often told mainly for their entertainment or shock value. Ask students what scenarios might make for unique news stories.

- **Compelling Video/Photographs** Have students look at the stills on page 909 and explain why they are compelling and newsworthy. For example, the bent trees show how powerful the wind is, and the ruins of a home convey the devastation.

S STANDARDS LESSON FILE
> Media Lesson 8: Understanding the Basics of News Reporting
> Media Lesson 9: Analyzing TV News
> Media Lesson 10: Analyzing Print and Online News

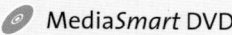 Media*Smart* DVD

Practice and Apply

VIEWING GUIDE

1. As students prepare to view the clip and read the Web news report, tell them that they will be asked to identify key factors of newsworthiness that characterize the pieces. Encourage students to watch and listen for these elements:

   - the use of **compelling video** and **photographs** to convey the strength of and the devastation caused by Hurricane Charley and Hurricane Frances
   - quotations and facts that add **human interest** and cause people to feel strong emotions about what has happened
   - information that helps viewers or readers understand the **widespread impact** of the hurricanes' destruction

2. Some students might want to view the clip and the Web news report more than once. Encourage them to watch or read each piece once straight through without taking any notes. Then have them watch or read a second time and take notes on details that make the story newsworthy. Students can make a chart to organize the factors of newsworthiness.

R RESOURCE MANAGER—Copy Masters
Viewing Guide p. 101
Close Viewing p. 102
Viewing Activity p. 103

MediaSmart DVD

ANSWERS

FIRST VIEWING: Comprehension

1. *Possible answer: There is total destruction everywhere. Buildings and entire neighborhoods are reduced to piles of rubble, and people are without electricity or running water.*

2. *The hurricane caused between $4 billion and $8 billion in damage.*

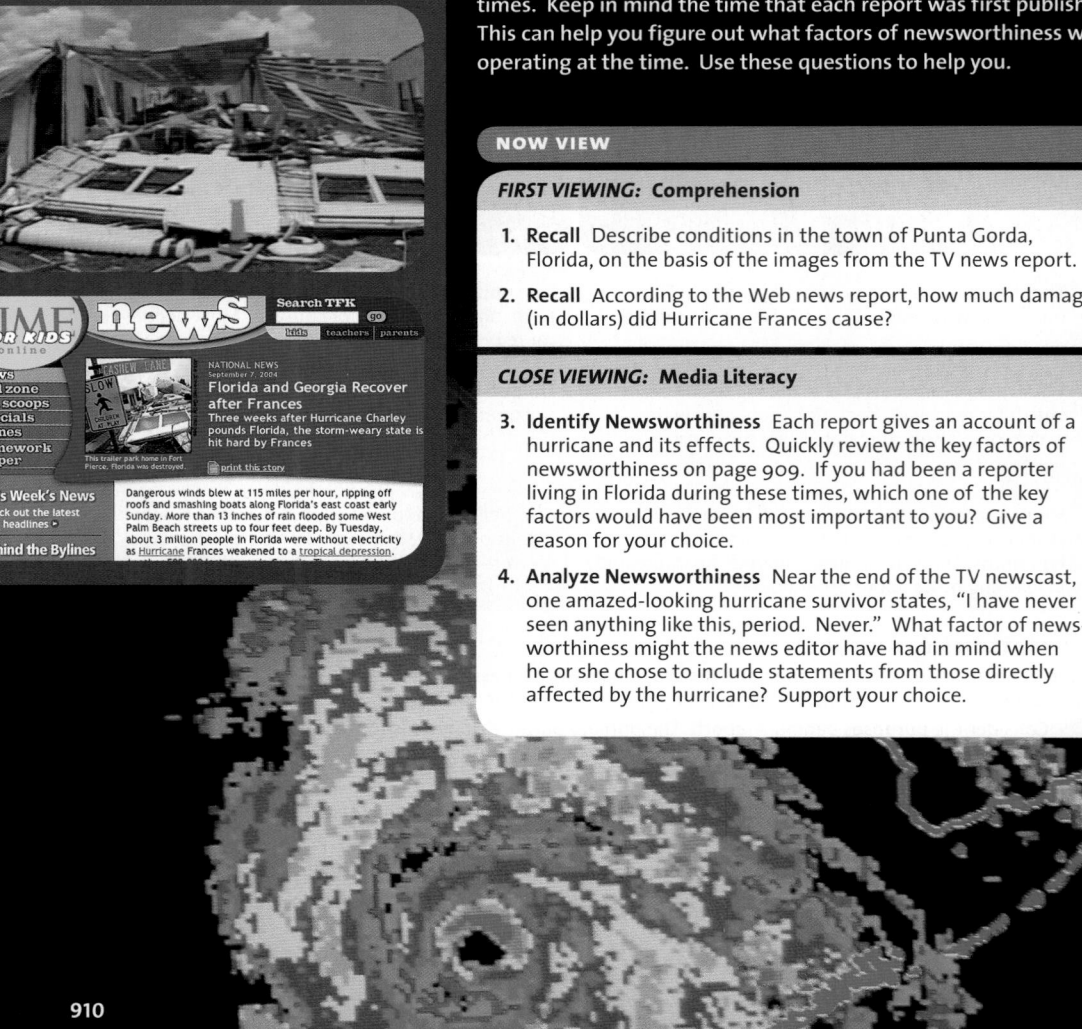

MediaSmart DVD
- **News Format 1:** "Hurricane Charley"
- **Genre:** TV newscast
- **Running Time:** 3.5 minutes

- **News Format 2:** "Florida and Georgia Recover After Frances"
- **Genre:** Web news report

910

Viewing Guide for
News Reports

The ABC network news report was first broadcast shortly after Hurricane Charley had struck a Florida town called Punta Gorda. The Web news report was published three weeks later, when Florida was struck by Hurricane Frances.

Watch the TV newscast clip and read the Web report a few times. Keep in mind the time that each report was first published. This can help you figure out what factors of newsworthiness were operating at the time. Use these questions to help you.

NOW VIEW

FIRST VIEWING: Comprehension

1. **Recall** Describe conditions in the town of Punta Gorda, Florida, on the basis of the images from the TV news report.

2. **Recall** According to the Web news report, how much damage (in dollars) did Hurricane Frances cause?

CLOSE VIEWING: Media Literacy

3. **Identify Newsworthiness** Each report gives an account of a hurricane and its effects. Quickly review the key factors of newsworthiness on page 909. If you had been a reporter living in Florida during these times, which one of the key factors would have been most important to you? Give a reason for your choice.

4. **Analyze Newsworthiness** Near the end of the TV newscast, one amazed-looking hurricane survivor states, "I have never seen anything like this, period. Never." What factor of newsworthiness might the news editor have had in mind when he or she chose to include statements from those directly affected by the hurricane? Support your choice.

CLOSE VIEWING: Media Literacy

Possible answers:

3. *It would be most important to use compelling video and pictures. These visual images would get people's attention, show exactly what the hurricanes have done, and indicate how much help the victims need.*

4. *The news editor wanted to add human interest and get viewers to feel sadness and fear for the victims. The statements all show some type of suffering or difficulty caused by the hurricane.*

Write or Discuss

Compare Newsworthiness Now that you've examined two news reports about hurricanes, think about how the two are alike or different. Which of the key factors of newsworthiness do you think might have led journalists to publish each report? Briefly explain the reasons for your choices. Think about the factors that make a news event worth reporting.

- Timeliness
- Widespread impact
- Human interest
- Proximity
- Uniqueness
- Compelling video or photographs

Produce Your Own Media

Make a Reporter's Guidebook Use recent news reports and photographs to present what you've learned about the key factors of newsworthiness. Begin by gathering three days' worth of newspaper clippings and Web news reports. (Be sure you have permission to take clippings and to make copies.) Skim the reports. Using sticky notes, label the stories (or photographs) with the factors you find, such as timeliness, widespread impact, and so on.

HERE'S HOW In a small group, follow these steps to assemble the guidebook:
- Use construction paper and paper fasteners to form the basic booklet. Choose a different color to represent each factor of newsworthiness.
- Start each section with a cover sheet that presents a key factor and its definition.
- Look over the clippings and photographs more carefully. Select the best examples for each section of the guide.
- Paste the clippings into the appropriate sections.

> **MEDIA TOOLS**
> For help with creating a reporter's guidebook, visit the **Media Center** at **ClassZone.com**.

STUDENT MODEL

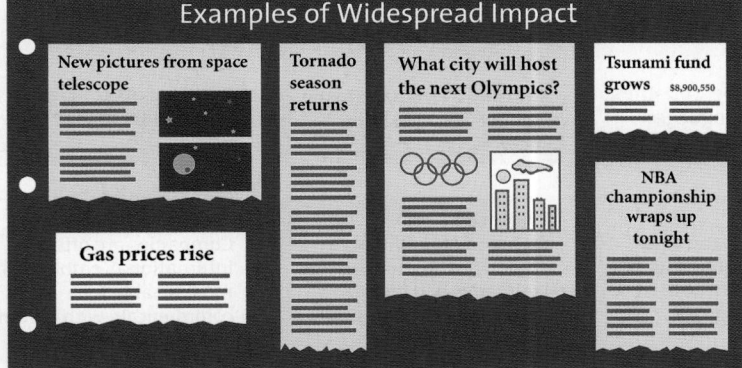

Examples of Widespread Impact

- New pictures from space telescope
- Tornado season returns
- What city will host the next Olympics?
- Tsunami fund grows $8,900,550
- NBA championship wraps up tonight
- Gas prices rise

Tech Tip
You can use a word-processing program to create cover sheets for the key factors.

Assess and Reteach

Write or Discuss

Compare Newsworthiness In their responses, students should show that they understand the factors of newsworthiness that guided the decisions made by the journalists who created the pieces. Students should give specific examples that indicate the events described in each piece are newsworthy. For example, the newscast about Hurricane Charley features extensive video of the damage, and this video places viewers at the center of the devastation. The Web article gives readers a brief and timely report on the facts. Both pieces are surveys of the damage caused by hurricanes. The newscast uses more images and uses the words of survivors to give the human-interest side of the story. The Web article gives more of a timely overview of the facts.

Produce Your Own Media

Rubric A strong reporter's guidebook should contain

- an interesting selection of newsworthy newspaper clippings and Web news reports
- clippings organized properly according to newsworthiness
- a cover sheet that begins each section about each key factor

R RESOURCE MANAGER—Copy Master
Produce Your Own Media p. 104

⊘ Media*Smart* DVD

MEDIA STUDY WRAP–UP

Summarize Newsworthiness Ask students to summarize the key factors of newsworthiness. Prompt them to identify these factors in the newscast about Hurricane Charley and the Web report on Hurricane Frances. Encourage students to discuss the kinds of decisions editors and journalists must make in deciding what news is reported and how it is reported.

RETEACH

S STANDARDS LESSON FILE
Media Lesson 8: Understanding the Basics of News Reporting
Media Lesson 9: Analyzing TV News
Media Lesson 10: Analyzing Print and Online News

Focus and Motivate

OBJECTIVES

- understand elements of an argument (claim, support)
- analyze persuasive techniques (appeals by association, emotional appeals, loaded language)

Teach

Part 1: What Is an Argument?

Claim Point out that a claim cannot simply be a statement of fact, because a fact cannot be argued. For example, "Crunchy Puffs is a breakfast cereal" is a fact. However, the statement that this cereal is "an important part of a nutritious breakfast" is a claim that can be argued. It calls out for supporting information: Why are they an important part of breakfast? What makes them nutritious?

Display these examples of claims:

- Middle school students with jobs should set aside 20 percent of their earnings for college.
- If you like fashion, friends, and fun, you'll love the Farley School of Design.

For each claim, ask students: Is this claim stated directly or implied? If implied, what exactly is the claim? What kinds of reasons and facts could support this claim?

Support Tell students that support is what persuades readers to accept a writer's claim. Besides facts, statistics, and examples, support may include anecdotes and quotations from ordinary people or from experts.

Help students analyze the argument outlined on page 912. Discuss each reason and its supporting evidence and have students decide whether it is convincing. *Possible answers:*

- *Reason 1: This reason is not very convincing, because what other countries do is not neces-sarily right for the United States.*
- *Reason 2: This reason is more convincing, but the cause-and-effect relationship is not certain. It's possible that students who excel in school overall may be more likely to take electives like foreign languages.*
- *Reason 3: This reason is very convincing, especially for students who are interested in business careers.*

MARYLAND OBJECTIVES

INFORMATIONAL TEXT STANDARDS
2.A.6.d Analyze the author's argument
2.A.6.f Analyze language and other techniques intended to persuade

Argument and Persuasion

Have you ever tried to count the number of persuasive messages you see and hear each day? Letters to the editor, billboards, slogans on the back of your cereal box—persuasive messages are everywhere. In this workshop, you will learn how to analyze the arguments at the heart of these messages and recognize the techniques that are used to persuade you. Armed with this knowledge, you can make up your own mind about messages and ideas that matter.

Part 1: What Is an Argument?

When you hear the word *argument,* you might think of a fight between two people, complete with differences of opinion, angry shouting, and hurt feelings. In formal speaking and writing, however, an argument is not emotional. It is a claim supported by reasons and evidence.

A **claim** is a writer's position on a problem or an issue. A claim might be stated directly, as in this example: "Crunchy Puffs are an important part of a nutritious breakfast." Sometimes a writer's claim is implied, as in this slogan "Juan for Student Council—Let the Good Times Roll." The slogan suggests that if Juan is elected, everyone at school will have more fun.

The strength of an argument depends not on the claim but on the **support,** or the reasons and evidence that are used to prove the claim. Evidence can take many forms, including facts, statistics, and examples.

Look closely at the elements of an argument in this example.

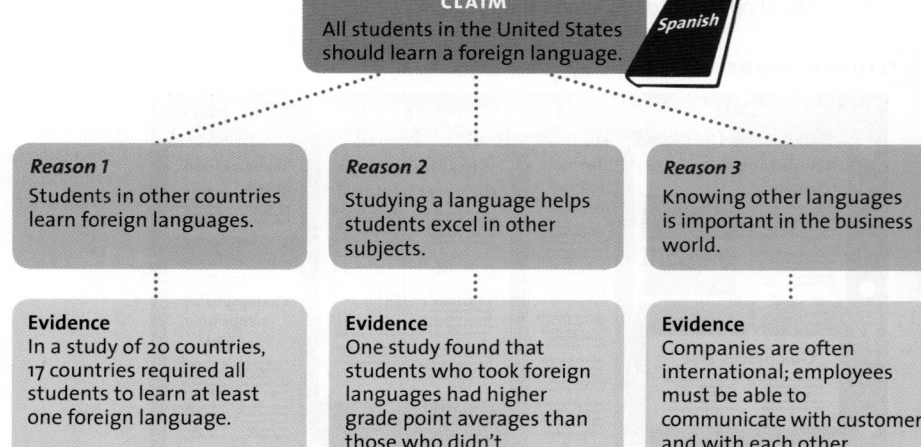

CLAIM
All students in the United States should learn a foreign language.

Reason 1	*Reason 2*	*Reason 3*
Students in other countries learn foreign languages.	Studying a language helps students excel in other subjects.	Knowing other languages is important in the business world.
Evidence In a study of 20 countries, 17 countries required all students to learn at least one foreign language.	**Evidence** One study found that students who took foreign languages had higher grade point averages than those who didn't.	**Evidence** Companies are often international; employees must be able to communicate with customers and with each other.

912 UNIT 8: INFORMATION, ARGUMENT, AND PERSUASION

DIFFERENTIATED INSTRUCTION

FOR ALL STUDENTS

For general guidelines on differentiating instruction, see

 BEST PRACTICES TOOLKIT
Differentiated Instruction pp. 31–38

FOR LESS–PROFICIENT READERS

Note Taking Hand out the copy master and have students read the first paragraph on page 912 silently. Then, as you discuss the parts of an argument, have students record notes on the copy master.

 RESOURCE MANAGER—Copy Master
Note Taking p. 107

Analysis Support: Argument Have students check whether a claim can be argued by (1) making sure it is not simply a statement of fact, and (2) trying to think of an opposing viewpoint. For example, an opposing view-point to the example claim is that U.S. stu-dents do not need to learn foreign languages.

As you read this article about the importance of exercise, try to identify the claim. What is the author urging you to do or believe? What reasons and evidence help the author make her case?

Why Work Out?

Magazine article by **Erica Cheng**

"You don't need to exercise—you look fine the way you are."
You've probably heard comments like this one before. Maybe you yourself have even reassured a friend or an acquaintance with these words of encouragement. After

5 all, the message we see and hear constantly is that exercise is the key to looking like the models on the covers of fitness magazines. So if you are generally happy with the way you look, why bother working out?

Exercise does burn calories and help you build stronger,
10 more defined muscles. Changes in your physical appearance may be the easiest to see, but they are certainly not the most important. Here are a few *real* reasons to work up a sweat:

Raw power. You don't have to be an action hero to find out how satisfying it feels to push yourself and achieve
15 more than you ever thought you could. Regular exercise pays off in greater strength, endurance, and agility— whether your goal is to swim faster, pedal farther, or cross the finish line in record time.

Mood enhancement. When you exercise, your body
20 generates endorphins—chemicals that help you feel content and peaceful, even if you had previously been feeling down. In fact, in one recent study, people who were anxious, lonely, or depressed got the biggest boost from a good workout.

25 **Pure fun.** Exercising does not have to be a chore, especially since there are so many exciting activities that you can choose from. Snowboarding. Judo. Trampoline. Hip-hop. Kickboxing. Dodge ball. If you find something you love to do, you'll be more likely to stick with it. And
30 when you're strong, happy, and having a good time, who even cares about how you look?

Close Read

1. Think about the title of this article and reread lines 9–12. What claim is the author making?

2. In the boxed paragraph, the author explains that exercise can have a positive effect on a person's mood. What evidence does she offer to support this reason?

3. In your own words, summarize the other two reasons that the author uses to support her position, or claim.

MODEL: THE ELEMENTS OF AN ARGUMENT

Close Read

1. *Possible answer: The author is making the claim that people should work out and that there are many good reasons to do so beyond improved physical appearance.*

2. *Possible answer: The author points out that exercise makes the body generate endorphins, which help people feel content and peaceful. She notes that this effect of exercise was confirmed by a recent study.*

3. *Possible answer:*
   - *Exercise helps people build strength, endurance, and agility.*
   - *Exercise can be fun, especially if people choose something that they like to do.*

FOR ENGLISH LEARNERS

Concept Support: Argument Have student pairs study the elements of an argument by imitating a paragraph in the example. Allow time for them to choose a paragraph, examine its structure, identify useful words and phrases, and then create a paragraph on a new subject that uses these elements.

Word power. *You don't have to be a great writer to find out how satisfying it feels to keep a journal.*

FOR ADVANCED LEARNERS/PRE–AP

Analyze Argument Have students practice using the elements of an argument by writing letters to you that attempt to persuade you to change something about the class. Remind them to anticipate your objections and provide answers for them. Suggest that they start by making an outline.

I. *Ms. Levy should assign less homework.*

   A. *If students had less homework, they would go to bed earlier and be more alert in class.*

BEST PRACTICES TOOLKIT—Transparency
Outline p. B19

Teach

Part 2: What Really Persuades You?

Appeals by Association Point out that the type of persuasive technique used depends on the audience. For example, an ad campaign that uses the testimonial technique to remind people to drink water might show a celebrity happily drinking water. The intended audience would be people who admire and want to be like that celebrity. For each example of appeal by association on page 914, ask students

- Who is the intended audience?
- What do the users of this persuasive technique want the audience to do?

Ask students for examples of appeals by association from television, magazines, or other media sources.

Emotional Appeals Use this exercise to help students analyze emotional appeals. Read each example and then ask what kind of emotional appeal is being used.

- "You're right, Mr. Hu, I don't have my homework. I knew you would notice—you're so observant." *(appeal to vanity)*
- "Mr. Hu, I know I don't have my homework, but my dog was sick and I missed the bus today." *(appeal to pity)*
- "No, I don't have my homework, Mr. Hu. Did you know that my aunt is the new principal? She'll be reviewing your salary increase for next year." *(appeal to fear)*

Loaded Language Ask students to choose a product that could appear in advertising. Then have them brainstorm strongly positive words that could be associated with that product, as well as strongly negative words that could be applied to a competing product. Record the words in a Two-Column Chart.

Super Paper Towels	Competing Product
strong	disappointing
fresh	wasteful
"more for your money"	falls apart

 **BEST PRACTICES TOOLKIT—Transparency** Two-Column Chart p. A25

Part 2: What Really Persuades You?

Do you wear a brand of jeans because they're comfortable, or because everyone else is wearing them? Did you donate money to an animal shelter because you have a passion for saving animals, or because the photograph of a puppy on the shelter's brochure captured your heart?

People aren't always logical. Emotion can play a key role in decision-making. That's why writers and speakers use **persuasive techniques,** or methods that are intended to sway people's feelings and actions. The following techniques can give a strong argument extra punch. Be aware, however, that they are often used to disguise flaws in a weak argument.

Appeals by Association	*Emotional Appeals*	*Loaded Language*
Link an idea or a product to something or someone positive or influential	Use strong feelings, rather than facts, to persuade	Uses words with strongly positive or negative associations
Bandwagon Appeal Taps into people's desire to belong	**Appeal to Pity** Taps into people's compassion for others	**Words with Positive Associations** Call up favorable images, feelings, or experiences
See the movie and discover the surprise ending that everybody's talking about.	Won't you give this abandoned puppy a home? 	Start your day with Morning Glory's refreshing, all-natural juice. 
Testimonial Uses celebrities or satisfied customers to persuade	**Appeal to Fear** Preys upon people's fear for their safety	**Words with Negative Associations** May bring to mind unpleasant images, feelings, or experiences; often create a sense of distrust or unease
As an Olympic athlete, I need all the energy I can get. That's why I drink Quench-Ade.	Is your home safe? ProAlarm Systems— because you shouldn't take any chances.	Who wants to hear the same tired, stale ideas? We need a candidate with a fresh vision.
Transfer Connects a product, a candidate, or a cause with a positive image or idea	**Appeal to Vanity** Uses flattery to win people over	
A vote for Proposition 43 is a vote for freedom. ☑ VOTE YES TO 43!	Bring your creativity and intelligence to our team. Join the yearbook staff!	

DIFFERENTIATED INSTRUCTION

FOR LESS–PROFICIENT READERS

Note Taking For students who need help with note taking, hand out the second copy master. Read and discuss the first two paragraphs on page 914. Assist students as needed in completing the first item on the copy master. Then have students read the rest of the page and take notes on the various types of persuasive techniques.

 RESOURCE MANAGER—Copy Master Note Taking p. 108

FOR ADVANCED LEARNERS/PRE–AP

Synthesize: Advertisement Have students choose one persuasive technique discussed on page 914 to use in creating a poster that promotes a campaign or a product. Invite them to present their advertisements to the class and then have the class identify which persuasive technique was used.

MODEL 1: PERSUASION IN TEXT

The author of this editorial argues that playing video games can have some significant harmful effects. What techniques does the author use to persuade you to adopt his position?

from

Break the Addiction!

Editorial by **Ethan Flemming**

Hours disappear, and you don't notice. You spend all your money buying more. You think it's an effective way to relieve stress but you end up cutting yourself off from family, friends, and reality.

5 What started in living rooms across the country as a few hours here and there has become an alarming widespread problem—a population addicted to video games. In fact, the average eighth-grade boy spends 23 hours a week playing video games, while the average eighth-grade girl spends 12 hours.

You may think that video games are just harmless fun, but studies
10 tell a more disturbing story. Some studies have concluded that excessive playing can decrease attention spans, dull imaginations, and create serious social problems. At least 60 percent of games are violent, and most teenagers cite those as their favorites. Repeatedly seeing violent situations unfold on a TV screen can take its toll. After all, such games
15 glamorize violent behavior and paint an unrealistic picture of the world.

Close Read

1. What emotion is the author appealing to in this editorial? Explain how the author might want readers to react to his message.

2. One example of loaded language is boxed. Find two additional examples.

MODEL 2: PERSUASION IN ADVERTISING

If you've turned on the television or skimmed a magazine recently, you know that persuasive techniques are used to sell all kinds of products, from soap to video games. What techniques do you notice in this ad?

RAGING TYPHOONS—
VENOMOUS SNAKES—
BLOODTHIRSTY PIRATES—

Are **YOU** tough enough to take on the elements—and survive?

STRANDED

DON'T MISS THE MOST EXCITING VIDEO GAME TO HIT THE STORES
THIS YEAR—THE ONE THAT EVERYBODY'S TALKING ABOUT!

Close Read

1. Explain how this ad tries to appeal to your vanity.

2. Name at least one other persuasive technique used in the ad. Support your answer with details.

MODEL 1: PERSUASION IN TEXT

Close Read

1. *Possible answer: The author is appealing to readers' fears. The author might want readers to stop playing video games.*

2. *Possible answers:*
   - *"alarming" (line 5)*
   - *"disturbing" (line 10)*
   - *"serious social problems" (line 12)*

MODEL 2: PERSUASION IN ADVERTISING

Close Read

1. *Possible answer: The ad appeals to vanity by asking if the reader is "tough enough" to play the game. The advertiser hopes that readers will want to prove their toughness by buying the game and meeting the challenge.*

2. *Possible answer: Two other persuasive techniques are*
   - *words with positive associations: "the most exciting video game"*
   - *bandwagon appeal: "the [game] that everybody's talking about"*

DIFFERENTIATED INSTRUCTION

FOR LESS–PROFICIENT READERS

Analysis Support: Persuasion Have students analyze the excerpt from "Break the Addiction!" to find phrases and images that appeal to fear and to explain why they are effective. For example, "Hours disappear, and you don't notice" (line 1) suggests to readers that something bad may be happening that they are not even aware of.

FOR ENGLISH LEARNERS

Language Support For the excerpt from "Break the Addiction!" have students use context clues to determine the meanings of the phrasal verbs *end up* (lines 2–3) and *cut off* (line 3) and the metaphors *take a toll* (line 14) and *paint an unrealistic picture* (line 15). Discuss how these words appeal to fear by creating a sense of threat. Ask what other common verbs and metaphors create a similar feeling.

Practice and Apply

Part 3: Analyze the Text

Close Read

1. *Possible answer: Goodall claims that people have reasons to feel hopeful about the state of the world.*

2. *Possible answer: Positive words include*
   - *"amazing brains" (line 10)*
   - *"[technology has] greatly benefited" (line 11)*
   - *"awesome problem-solving ability" (line 14)*
   - *"environmentally friendly" (line 15)*
   - *"nature is amazingly resilient" (line 21)*
   - *"land can . . . blossom again" (lines 22–23)*

3. *Possible answer: Goodall says that "hundreds of industries and businesses" have already begun to "adopt new 'green' ethics" (lines 16–17).*

Part 3: Analyze the Text

In this essay, British scientist Jane Goodall shares her outlook on the future of the earth. Originally famous for studying the behaviors of chimpanzees in Africa, Goodall now travels around the world, speaking to people about the importance of protecting the environment. Read Goodall's essay, and then examine the public service ad that follows. What argument does each text present? What techniques does each use to persuade you?

THE PROMISE

Nonfiction article by **Jane Goodall**

As we begin the 21st century, it is easy to be overwhelmed by feelings of hopelessness. We humans have destroyed the balance of nature: forests are being destroyed, deserts are spreading, there is terrible pollution and poisoning of air, earth, water. Climate is changing, people are starving.
5   There are too many humans in some parts of the world, overconsumption in others. There is human cruelty to "man" and "beast" alike; there is violence and war. Yet I do have hope. Let me share my four reasons.

Firstly, we have at last begun to understand and face up to the problems that threaten the survival of the earth. And we are problem-
10 solving creatures. Our amazing brains have created modern technology, much of which has greatly benefited millions of people around the globe. Sadly, along with our tendency to overreproduce, it has also resulted in massive destruction and pollution of the natural world. But can we not use our awesome problem-solving ability to now find more
15 environmentally friendly ways to conduct our business? Good news—it's already happening as hundreds of industries and businesses adopt new "green" ethics.[1] And we must play our part—in our billions we must adopt less-harmful lifestyles. Refuse to buy products from companies, corporations, that do not conform to new environmental standards. We
20 *can* change the world.

Second, nature is amazingly resilient.[2] Given the chance, poisoned rivers can live again. Deforested land can be coaxed—or left—to blossom again. Animal species, on the verge of extinction, can sometimes be bred and saved from a few individuals.

---

1. **"green" ethics:** rules and guidelines that require businesses to use resources, machines, and procedures that are not harmful to the environment.
2. **resilient:** flexible.

Close Read

1. Reread the first paragraph. What is Goodall's claim?

2. In the boxed examples of loaded language, Goodall uses negative words to describe the world's problems. However, she also uses positive words to explain why she still has hope. Find four examples.

3. Goodall's first reason for hope is that humans have already begun to solve some of the problems affecting our environment. What evidence does she give to back up this reason?

DIFFERENTIATED INSTRUCTION

FOR LESS–PROFICIENT READERS

Analysis Support: Argument Have students complete a Classification Chart like the one on page 912 to identify Goodall's claim and supporting evidence. If they have difficulty, suggest that they look for signal words such as *firstly* and *second*.

 BEST PRACTICES TOOLKIT—Transparency
Classification Chart p. B17

FOR ENGLISH LEARNERS

Language Support: Prefix *over-* Point out the words *overconsumption* (line 5) and *over-reproduce* (line 12). Explain that their common prefix *over-* means "too much." Discuss how Goodall uses these words to show that the world's problems are partly due to human excess. Ask how she explores this idea in the second paragraph. You may also mention how *overwhelmed* (line 1) expresses the feeling that these problems are too much to handle—and how Goodall refutes this idea throughout the article.

25   My third reason for hope lies in the tremendous energy, enthusiasm, and commitment of young people around the world. Young people want to fight to right the wrongs, for it will be their world tomorrow—they will be the ones in leadership positions, and they themselves will be parents. . . .

    My fourth reason for hope lies in the indomitable[3] nature of the
30 human spirit. There are so many people who have dreamed seemingly unattainable dreams and, because they never gave up, achieved their goals against all the odds, or blazed a path along which others could follow.

    So let us move into the next millennium with hope—with faith in
35 ourselves, in our intelligence, in our indomitable spirit. Let us develop respect for all living things. Let us try to replace violence and intolerance with understanding and compassion and love.

---

3. **indomitable:** incapable of being defeated; unconquerable.

Close Read

4. Summarize the other reasons that Goodall gives to support her claim.

Close Read

1. Examine the text and the photographs at the top of this ad. What emotional appeal is being used?

2. How does this ad use the technique of transfer?

3. What claim is being made in this ad? (Think about what the ad is trying to convince you to do.)

Close Read

4. ***Possible answer:*** *Goodall says that*
- *nature is resilient—land and species can sometimes be saved*
- *young people are energetic and enthusiastic*
- *people have achieved many other amazing things*

Close Read

1. ***Possible answer:*** *The text and photographs use an appeal to fear. The words* pollution *and* destruction *and the related images create a sense of threat.*

2. ***Possible answer:*** *This ad uses the technique of transfer by connecting a desire to help the earth with what consumers purchase.*

3. ***Possible answer:*** *The ad puts forth the claim that "buying green" will help save the earth from pollution and destruction.*

Assess and Reteach

Assess

Have students briefly explain how "The Promise" uses argument and persuasion.

Reteach

For students who are unable to apply the workshop skills to the Goodall article and the public service ad, select from these reteaching options:

1. Review with them the note-taking copy masters for this lesson. Have pairs
- compare the information they recorded
- explain their understandings of claims, evidence, and persuasive techniques to one another, using their own words
- question each other to clarify understanding
- share their insights and challenges with the class

2. Have students reread **Model 1** on page 915 and identify the claim, reasons, and persuasive techniques. Suggest that they use the chart on page 914 to help them classify the techniques.

DIFFERENTIATED INSTRUCTION

FOR ENGLISH LEARNERS

Analysis Support: Persuasion Clarify how these multiple-meaning words are used in the public service ad:

- *to buy* can mean "to accept as truthful"
- *green* can mean "supportive of environmental causes"

Have small groups discuss their impressions of the images and text, and what feelings are appealed to. Ask them to compare the first two panels with the last panel. Then invite the groups to share their ideas.

FOR ADVANCED LEARNERS/PRE–AP

Persuasive Speaking Have students use "The Promise" as a starting point for exploring persuasive speaking. Ask small groups to divide the article into sections and have group members take turns reading aloud, using voice, facial expression, gestures, and eye contact to emphasize key points and persuasive techniques. Have students discuss what they noticed as they listened.

Focus and Motivate

OBJECTIVES

Elements of Nonfiction
- explore the key idea of **salaries**
- analyze the elements of an argument (claim, support, counterargument)
- analyze an argument
- read editorials

Reading
- evaluate reasoning

Vocabulary
- build vocabulary for reading and writing
- define idioms by using context clues (*also an EL language objective*)

Grammar and Writing
- use commas correctly (items in a series, introductory phrases)
- use writing to analyze literature

SUMMARY

The first writer believes that athletes should be paid high salaries because they generate a lot of revenue. The second writer believes that players' salaries are outrageous, making a sad commentary on our social values.

Are people paid FAIRLY?

Discuss the question and the **KEY IDEA.** Ask students whether **salaries** are a reflection of people's worth. Have students debate this question before beginning the **DISCUSS** activity.

Selection Resources

Pro Athletes' Salaries Aren't Overly Exorbitant
Editorial by Mark Singletary

Do Professional Athletes Get Paid Too Much?
Editorial by Justin Hjelm

Are people paid FAIRLY?

MARYLAND OBJECTIVES

INFORMATIONAL TEXT STANDARDS
2.A.6.d Analyze the author's argument
2.A.6.f Analyze language and other techniques intended to persuade

KEY IDEA The president of the United States earns $400,000 a year. A Wall Street stock trader can earn even more, while a first-year New York City policeman earns less than $20,000. Is this fair? In the editorials that follow, two writers offer opposite opinions about the multimillion-dollar **salaries** today's professional athletes make.

DISCUSS With a group of classmates, examine this chart of average annual salaries. If it were up to you, how would the salaries be different? Talk about who you think deserves more, who could do with a little less, who is paid the right amount, and why.

AVERAGE ANNUAL SALARIES	
Retail Salesperson $22,540	**Firefighter** $38,810
Kindergarten Teacher $43,530	**Registered Nurse** $52,810
Computer Programmer $65,170	**Airline Pilot** $129,230
Surgeon $182,690	**Major League Baseball Player** $2,376,580

Source: "November 2003 National Occupational Employment and Wage Estimates," U.S. Department of Labor: Bureau of Labor Statistics

918

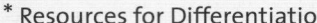 **RESOURCE MANAGER UNIT 8**

Plan and Teach pp. 109–116

Elements of Nonfiction
Summary pp. 117†*, 118‡*
Argument pp. 119, 120†*
Question Support p. 127*

Reading
Evaluate Reasoning pp. 121, 122†*
Reading Check p. 126

Vocabulary
Study p. 123*
Practice p. 124
Strategy p. 125

Grammar and Writing
Use Commas Correctly p. 129

Assessment
Selection Tests A, B/C pp. 131*, 133*

Test Generator CD

BEST PRACTICES TOOLKIT
Differentiated Instruction
   pp. 31–38*
Scaffolding Instruction
   pp. 43–46*

Graphic Organizers/Strategies
New Word Analysis • Cluster Diagram

Reading Support
Audio Anthology CD*

Technology
Literature and Vocabulary Centers at **ClassZone.com**

Write*Smart* CD

---

* Resources for Differentiation   † Also in Spanish   ‡ In Haitian Creole and Vietnamese

ELEMENTS OF NONFICTION: ARGUMENT

An **argument** expresses a position on an issue or problem and provides support for that position. Strong arguments have the following elements:

- a **claim,** which is the writer's main idea or position
- **support,** or reasons and evidence that back up the claim
- **counterarguments,** which are arguments made to address points that someone with an opposing view might raise

As you read, identify the elements in each argument.

READING SKILL: EVALUATE REASONING

When you analyze an argument, it is important to look for fallacies, or **errors in reasoning,** like those explained below:

- An **overgeneralization** is a statement about a group of people or things that is much too broad to be true. "All teenagers love to listen to loud music" is an overgeneralization, because not all teenagers do.
- A **single-cause fallacy** suggests there is only one cause for something when there are actually several. "The only reason people go to the beach is to swim" is a single-cause fallacy. People might go to sunbathe or to hang out with friends.

As you read, use a chart to record errors in reasoning.

Example of Error	Type of Error/Explanation
"… the players are selfish …" (line 10)	Overgeneralization

VOCABULARY IN CONTEXT

The boldfaced words help these authors construct their arguments. To see how many you know, substitute a different word or phrase for each boldfaced term.

1. Star Player's **Compensation** Shoots Up to $15 Million
2. **Brevity** of Pitcher's Career Caused by Arm Injury
3. Umpire Call Challenged by **Dissenter**
4. Coach's **Entitlement** to Special Treatment Questioned
5. **Appalling** Brawl in Bleachers Injures 20
6. **Voracious** Fans Can't Get Enough of Home Team

Author Online

Mark Singletary: Veteran Publisher
Mark Singletary is president and publisher of New Orleans Publishing Group, which prints business-related journals. What does Singletary say about professional athletes' salaries? "More power to 'em."

Mark Singletary born 1952

Justin Hjelm: Student Journalist
While attending Westmont College in California, Justin Hjelm (yĕlm) knew that the best way to make his views known was to write about them. Hjelm's editorial is an example of how students can make their voices heard.

Justin Hjelm born 1983

 MORE ABOUT THE AUTHOR For more on the authors, visit the **Literature Center** at **ClassZone.com.**

Background
Weighing In on Heavy Salaries Frequently when athletes' salaries make the news, editorials start appearing in many publications. "Pro Athletes' Salaries Aren't Overly Exorbitant" appeared in *New Orleans CityBusiness.* "Do Professional Athletes Get Paid Too Much?" was published in Westmont College's campus newspaper, the *Horizon.*

919

Teach

Practice and Apply

New Orleans
CITY BUSINESS

A player signs autographs for die-hard fans before the 75th Major League Baseball All-Star Game.

Pro Athletes' Salaries Aren't Overly Exorbitant[1] Ⓐ

MARK SINGLETARY

I am going to try and make a point about the salaries that professional athletes get to play their games. I think I'm moving into a very solid "more power to 'em" position. I guess until recently I've thought the players were a bit selfish and their salaries would lead to the failure of professional sports.

Of course, the players are selfish and ultimately professional sports will fail or have to be restructured significantly. Who knows when that time will come? Ⓑ

But the players are no more selfish than the owners who pay the salaries. And the owners are no more selfish than the television and radio networks that pay outlandish sums to broadcast 20 the games.

All of us are looking for something. The games work best when those willing to pay match up evenly with what the others have to sell.

I've always thought of myself as the kind of guy who would give his left arm or eye or big toe to have a chance to play any of the major league sports. Now I think I can honestly 30 say that I would give up a lot, but

---

1. **exorbitant** (ĭg-zôr′bĭ-tənt): exceeding all bounds of custom or fairness.

not everything, to have the chance to play one big game.

Pause and reflection make me think now that it would still be awesome to train hard, make a major league roster and spend an entire season with the team, but at some point the fun might turn into work.

I would probably begin to think that if I was good enough to make the squad, then I would deserve to be paid the same as my teammates. And if by chance I would happen to be star quality and could reasonably assume that coming to see me play was a big deal, then I might end up asking for a little more than the average player gets.

Also, when I read the sports or business pages of the newspaper, I see that television networks pay huge sums to broadcast my games. When I go to work, I realize that other companies want to name our stadium, promote our schedule and decorate our arena with their advertisements.

The historical argument for paying exorbitant salaries to athletes is the **brevity** of their careers. All of these athletes are a busted knee, concussion or torn rotator cuff[2] away from the end of their career, and very few sports offer guaranteed contracts that go beyond the season when the injury occurs.

Our fans are important to the economic health of our ball club. My teammates and I are responsible for

finding and keeping fans. If I am a star, it can rightly be assumed the fans come to see me play. **C**

70 When the fans come to see the stars perform, the value of the franchise[3] increases. I'm pretty smart and understand all this and how it relates to me. I also know what I make and how that relates to others that play my game.

So, it seems to me that even though I love the game, even though just playing the game is huge **compensation** and very, very 80 satisfying, I want things to be fair.

Fair is fair. And fair is that the athletes deserve what the fans are willing to pay.

The owners probably don't care what the athletes make, as long as they can pass the cost on to sponsors and ticket buyers. The intelligence in sports ownership is the ability to predict exactly where the fans and 90 sponsors lose interest.

Until that time, it seems fair to allocate as much as possible to the players that make the games entertaining. It's also the only way to win consistently in modern, major league sports. The smartest in all the groups are not only taking as much and passing along as much as possible, but they are also looking toward the 100 future to see when it all ends. **D**

So, everyone benefits right up until the time that no one benefits.

---

2. **concussion ... rotator cuff:** A concussion is an injury to the brain caused by a fall or a blow to the head. A rotator cuff is the muscle and tendon that support the shoulder joint, a place of common injury among baseball pitchers.

3. **franchise:** a team that is a member of a professional sports league.

C EVALUATE REASONING
Reread lines 64—69. Do you think Singletary's statement is a **single-cause fallacy?** Explain.

compensation
(kŏm'pən-sā'shən) *n.* payment

1 Targeted Passage

brevity (brĕv'ĭ-tē) *n.* shortness

D ARGUMENT
Reread lines 91–100, which contain Singletary's main **claim.** Paraphrase, or restate, his claim.

Lines 33–55
DISCUSSION PROMPTS

Use these prompts to help students understand the writer's reasoning process:

Connect Do you agree that playing on a major sports team would turn into work? *Students might say that the need to put forth effort on a regular basis would make it work. Others might say that doing something one loves is not work.*

Analyze What does the writer think the transition from fun to work justifies? *Possible answer: He thinks it is a reason to ask for more money.*

Synthesize What is the relationship between advertisers and athletes? How should this affect the athletes' salaries? *Possible answer: The athletes attract advertisers, so their salaries should include a share of the money that advertisers pay.*

READING SKILL

C EVALUATE REASONING

Record students' answers in the chart from page 919. *Possible answer:*

Example of Error	Type of Error/ Explanation
Players are responsible for bringing people to games (lines 65–69).	Single-cause fallacy— Fans might go to games because they love the sport, because they like to go with friends or family, or because they are loyal to a certain team.

ELEMENTS OF NONFICTION

D ARGUMENT

Possible answer: Professional sporting events generate a lot of money, and most of that money should be used to pay the players' salaries, since they are the ones who make the games fun to watch.

FOR LESS–PROFICIENT READERS

1 Targeted Passage [Lines 81–90]

This passage summarizes the basis of the writer's argument: as long as the money comes in, players should be paid high salaries.

- Where does the money to pay high salaries come from?
- What are the owners' attitudes toward the high salaries? Why?
- What is the only thing that will stop players from getting high salaries?

FOR ADVANCED LEARNERS/PRE–AP

Pre-AP exercises in the bottom channel provide additional challenge for your advanced students. Use them for small groups or individuals.

ADDITIONAL GUIDELINES

For more help with differentiation and tips for classroom management, see

 BEST PRACTICES TOOLKIT
Differentiated Instruction pp. 31–38

DO PROFESSIONAL ATHLETES GET PAID TOO MUCH?

JUSTIN HJELM
Staff Reporter

YES. When asked in the early twenties what justified him making more money than the President of the United States, Babe Ruth[1] replied "Well, I had a better year."

For nearly a century, superstar athletes have demanded and received salaries grossly out of proportion with the average income of their times. What makes modern times different and more disturbing is that even the role players in professional sports are pulling in an exorbitant amount of money.

Fifty years ago, only the 40-home-run outfielder would make a huge salary. Now, however, the utility infielder who comes in as a defensive replacement three times a week makes ten times more than the average working man. **E**

Nolan Ryan[2] broke ground in 1979, becoming the first athlete to receive a $1-million-a-year contract. It took over a century for baseball to reach this milestone income figure, and just 25 years later a $1 million contract offer is considered an insult.

---

1. **Babe Ruth:** a baseball player from 1914 to 1935, considered by many to be the best baseball player in the history of the sport.
2. **Nolan Ryan:** a baseball pitcher from 1966 to 1993 who held over 50 major-league records.

E ARGUMENT
"Athletes have always made a lot of money"—that's the argument Hjelm anticipates in lines 6–21. What is his **counterargument?**

ELEMENTS OF NONFICTION

E ARGUMENT

Possible answer: Hjelm concedes that star athletes have always earned a lot of money, but he points out that today even substitute players (who might work only three times a week) make ten times more than the average worker.

Extend the Discussion Why is the writer's counterargument effective?

DIFFERENTIATED INSTRUCTION

FOR LESS—PROFICIENT READERS
Reading Skill Follow-Up: Evaluate Reasoning

- Tell students that overgeneralizations often contain signal words such as *all, none, never, everyone,* and *always.*
- Explain that substituting a word such as *some, sometimes, few,* or *often* limits the statement and makes it logical.
- Display these statements. Have pairs identify and rewrite overgeneralizations.

No player deserves a high salary.

Everyone benefits under the present system.

Athletes are some of the wealthiest people in our nation.

All young people who play sports want to become professional athletes.

Some games are entertaining to watch.

FOR ENGLISH LEARNERS
Vocabulary Support Have mixed-ability pairs use context clues to define this vocabulary:

- *role players* (line 12), "players who are not stars but just fill out the roster"
- *utility infielder* (lines 17–18), "a player who substitutes for the team's star players in the infield as needed"
- *unchecked* (line 30), "without any limits"
- *raking in seven-figure salaries* (line 41), "being paid at least $1,000,000 per year"

The contracts of professional athletes
30 have gone unchecked for too long,
and now athletes are among the
wealthiest people in our nation.

Athletes are paid far too much
for simply playing games. Essentially,
as anyone can tell you, sports
are entertainment. We pay to see
these athletes perform at the
highest level. **F**

It is a sad commentary on our
40 societal values that these entertainers
are raking in seven-figure salaries
while teachers, police officers, and fire
fighters make less than one percent
of the income of some athletes.
Entertainment is a necessary thing,
but it is not needed nearly as much as
countless other occupations are.

What kind of message are we
sending our children with these
50 backward values?

From the perspective of a young
person, sports seem like the better
and easier path. Would a child rather
play basketball and make millions
or go to school for years and end up
making $50,000 a year?

Dissenters will say that it is not
that cut and dried,[3] and they are
probably right. Making a professional
60 sporting league is exceptionally
difficult. But fewer and fewer kids
are realizing this.

One only needs to look as far as
the NBA draft[4] for proof of this.

Athlete: Babe Ruth
Sport: Baseball
Team: New York Yankees
Contract Year: 1921
Contracted Salary: $39,638
Salary Adjusted to 2004 Dollars: $418,303

② Targeted Passage

Athlete: Jackie Robinson
Sport: Baseball
Team: Brooklyn Dodgers
Contract Year: 1947
Contracted Salary: $8,500
Salary Adjusted to 2004 Dollars: $72,002

Athlete: Bill Russell
Sport: Basketball
Team: Boston Celtics
Contract Year: 1956
Contracted Salary: $19,500
Salary Adjusted to 2004 Dollars: $135,425

Athlete: Nolan Ryan
Sport: Baseball
Team: Houston Astros
Contract Year: 1979
Contracted Salary: $1,100,000
Salary Adjusted to 2004 Dollars: $2,862,121

F ARGUMENT
Reread lines 33–38.
What is Hjelm's **claim**
about the salaries of
professional athletes?
As you continue to
read, note how Hjelm
supports his claim.

dissenter (dĭ-sĕn'tər) *n.*
one who disagrees or
holds a different opinion

---

3. **cut and dried:** simple

4. **NBA draft:** the process by which teams in the National Basketball Association select, or draft,
players. Generally, the teams with the worst records from the preceding year get the top draft choices.

F ARGUMENT

*Possible answer: His claim is that "athletes
are paid far too much for simply playing
games."*

Lines 39–47
REINFORCE KEY IDEA: SALARIES

Discuss According to the writer, what should
salaries reflect? *Possible answer: He implies
that salaries should reflect the contributions
that individuals make to society.*

Lines 48–64
DISCUSSION PROMPTS

Use these prompts to help students understand the writer's reasoning process:

Connect If you were an athlete, would you
be tempted to start playing professionally
as soon as possible? Why? *Students may say
that they would be tempted by the possibility
of making so much money.*

Analyze What message does the writer feel
that athletes' salaries send to the youth of
today? *Possible answer: The message is that
money is all-important. The more money
a person earns, the more worthwhile the
person is.*

Evaluate How does this message influence
the decisions that young athletes make?
Why does the writer view these decisions
negatively? *Possible answer: He sees many
young athletes skipping college and going
right into the NBA draft. Many do not make
it, and then they are left without a college
education.*

FOR LESS–PROFICIENT READERS

② Targeted Passage [Lines 33–47]

This passage presents the basis of the writer's
argument: athletes are just entertainers who
do not deserve such high salaries.

- How much do teachers and police officers
  make in comparison to athletes?
- What does the writer think about this contrast in pay? Why?

FOR ENGLISH LEARNERS

Vocabulary Support Have pairs continue using
context clues to define this vocabulary:

- *early entrants* (line 67), "high school athletes
  who skip college to enter the NBA draft at a
  young age"
- *egos* (line 77), "feelings of self-importance"
- *lockout* (line 81), "situation in which games
  are suspended and players are not paid"
- *crying poverty* (line 82), "claiming not to have
  enough money to live"

FOR ADVANCED LEARNERS/PRE–AP

Make Judgments Both writers seem sincere,
but their ways of expressing their views and
organizing their editorials differ. Ask students
which writer they would invite to speak at their
annual sports banquet and why. Have students
create an imaginary invitation to the writer of
their choice, explaining the reasons that he has
been invited to their school.

![icon] **MATH CONNECTION**

How much more was Alex Rodriguez's contracted salary in 2004 than Kenny Anderson's was in 1999?

Athlete: Kenny Anderson
Sport: Basketball
Team: Boston Celtics
Contract Year: 1999
Contracted Salary: $5,845,000
Salary Adjusted to 2004 Dollars: $6,627,374

Athlete: Alex Rodriguez
Sport: Baseball
Team: New York Yankees
Contract Year: 2004
Contracted Salary: $21,726,881

A decade ago, a high school player skipping college was a rarity. In 1994, you could count the early entrants on one hand. Now, however, there are numerous high schoolers declaring for 70 the draft every year, some of whom do not even get drafted. These players forfeit their college eligibility and will struggle for years to make an NBA team. After that, without a college education, they struggle to find a decent job.

Also troubling are the egos of the athletes receiving these giant paychecks. They have no ability to 80 relate to the public. During the NBA lockout in 1998-99, players were crying poverty. **G**

Kenny Anderson, then a guard for the Boston Celtics, complained of not being able to afford the insurance on his eight cars. The sense of **entitlement** that these athletes have is **appalling.** They play a game that

many would play for meal money and 90 get paid like royalty, and then have the gall to whine that they are not paid enough.

It's startling that people have blasé[5] attitudes about $100 million contracts. Eight-figure deals are not something to be yawned at, but with their current frequency, it is becoming that way. Athletes are paid far too much for what they do, 100 but I believe that society is more at fault for this than the athletes themselves are.

We simply put too much importance on entertainment, and with this statement I condemn myself and the rabidity[6] with which I follow sports. The once tightly controlled finances of the sporting world have been torn apart and the winds of greed and America's 110 **voracious** thirst for entertainment have scattered the pieces so that they can never be put together again.

 Targeted Passage

G EVALUATE REASONING Reread lines 77–82. What **overgeneralization** does Hjelm make about professional athletes? Explain.

entitlement (ĕn-tīt′l-mənt) *n.* the state of having a right or claim to something

appalling (ə-pô′lĭng) *adj.* outrageous; terrible **appall** *v.*

voracious (vô-rā′shəs) *adj.* possessing an insatiable desire; greedy

---

5. **blasé** (blä-zā′): unconcerned; uninterested.
6. **rabidity:** craziness or unreasonable extremeness.

Comprehension

1. **Recall** What does Singletary believe about the future of professional sports?

2. **Clarify** Why does Hjelm place some of the blame for athletes' high salaries on himself as a sports fan and on society as a whole?

MARYLAND OBJECTIVES

INFORMATIONAL TEXT STANDARD
2.A.6.f Analyze language and other techniques intended to persuade

Critical Analysis

3. **Identify a Counterargument** Reread lines 10–20 of the first editorial. What counterargument does Singletary offer to oppose the notion that pro athletes are selfish?

4. **Analyze an Argument** Think about the **claim** that Hjelm presents in "Do Professional Athletes Get Paid Too Much?" Complete the graphic by listing three reasons or examples Hjelm uses to **support** his claim.

Claim: "Athletes are paid far too much for simply playing games." (lines 33–34)

Support:　Support:　Support:

5. **Evaluate Reasoning** Examine the errors in reasoning you noted as you read. Suggest how Singletary and Hjelm might each reword his statements to correct these errors and make his argument stronger.

6. **Make Judgments** Which of these editorials did you find more convincing? Explain your answer, citing specific lines you found especially effective.

Extension and Challenge

7. **Speaking and Listening** Work with classmates to set up a panel discussion about the **salaries** of professional athletes. Each panelist should play the role of a different character: a team owner, a professional athlete, a sports broadcaster, and a fan. A moderator can take questions from the audience, and the panelists should respond as they think their characters would.

8. **MATH CONNECTION** Using Babe Ruth's salary adjusted to 2004 dollars, how much more money did Alex Rodriguez make in 2004 than Babe Ruth did in 1921? What percentage increase is this? You can find these numbers in the sidebars on pages 923 and 924.

$$\% \text{ increase} = \frac{\text{amount of increase}}{\text{lower salary in 2004 dollars}}$$

Practice and Apply

After Reading

For additional support of post-reading questions, use these copy masters:

R RESOURCE MANAGER—Copy Masters
Reading Check p. 126 (to check understanding of the selection)
Argument p. 119 (for practice of elements of nonfiction standards focus)
Question Support p. 127 (**After Reading** questions adapted for English learners and less-proficient readers)

Additional selection questions are provided for teachers on page 113.

ANSWERS

Comprehension

1. *Singletary thinks that "ultimately professional sports will fail or have to be restructured significantly" (lines 11–13).*

2. *Hjelm thinks that society puts too much emphasis on entertainment, and he himself contributes to this problem by being such a rabid sports fan.*

Critical Analysis

Possible answers:

3. *Singletary argues that players are no more selfish than the owners or the networks that pay so much to be able to broadcast the games.*

4. ● **STANDARDS FOCUS** *Argument*
Support: Even today's "role players" make ten times what the average working person makes (lines 10–21).

Support: People in more important professions—such as teachers, police officers, and firefighters—make less than 1 percent of what some players make (lines 39–47).

Support: The number of teenagers skipping college to go straight to the draft has risen sharply since 1994 as a result of the huge increase in salaries (lines 66–76).

---

5. ● **STANDARDS FOCUS** *Evaluate Reasoning Students should note that overgeneralizations can be amended by inserting words such as* some, few, *and* several. *Single-cause fallacies should be adjusted to include additional causes.*

6. *Students should choose one or the other and give specific examples from the text to support their view.*

Extension and Challenge

7. *Students should present arguments from the perspective of each character.*

8. **MATH CONNECTION**
21,726,881 minus 418,303 equals 21,308,578. This number divided by 418,303 equals 50.94, or about 5,000 percent.

Vocabulary in Context

VOCABULARY PRACTICE

1. *false*
2. *true*
3. *true*
4. *true*
5. *false*
6. *false*

 RESOURCE MANAGER—Copy Master
Vocabulary Practice p. 124

VOCABULARY IN WRITING

Have students brainstorm reasons to support their choice first. They may wish to organize these reasons in a Cluster Diagram or in a list. Then have them choose the vocabulary words that will help them express their points.

📁 **BEST PRACTICES TOOLKIT—Transparency**
Cluster Diagram p. B18

VOCABULARY STRATEGY: IDIOMS *(also an EL language objective)*

Tell students that context clues are most helpful in figuring out the meaning of idiomatic expressions.

Possible answers:

1. *keep quiet*
2. *making him conceited*
3. *shabby*
4. *point out exactly*
5. *agree*
6. *paid too much*

 **RESOURCE MANAGER—Copy Master**
Vocabulary Strategy p. 125

ℹ️ **Vocabulary Center at ClassZone.com**
Additional Vocabulary Activities

Vocabulary in Context

VOCABULARY PRACTICE

Decide whether each statement is true or false.

1. A **dissenter** is usually a person who goes along with what others think.
2. Someone with a **voracious** appetite for sports often goes to several games a week.
3. An **appalling** situation is one that shocks and depresses you.
4. If you do volunteer work, you don't expect **compensation** for your services.
5. The author of a 3,400-page book should be praised for her **brevity**.
6. Meek, humble people usually feel a strong sense of **entitlement**.

VOCABULARY IN WRITING

Choose an athlete or other professional who you think either deserves or does not deserve a high salary. Write a paragraph explaining your opinion, using two or more vocabulary words. You might start like this.

> **EXAMPLE SENTENCE**
>
> *Since she was voted Most Valuable Player three years in a row, this player's **compensation** makes sense.*

VOCABULARY STRATEGY: IDIOMS

Idioms are common expressions that mean something different from the meaning of the individual words in them. For example, the expression *cut and dried*, which appears on page 923, means "simple," not "sliced into pieces and dried."

READING STANDARD
1.D.3.a Use context to determine the meanings of words

PRACTICE Define the italicized idiom in each sentence.

1. To get along with Madeline, you need to learn to *hold your tongue*.
2. All those compliments are *going to Sam's head*.
3. After he lost his job, Mr. Murphy looked a bit *down at the heels*.
4. I can't quite *put my finger on* why she makes me so angry.
5. It is a good idea for business partners to *see eye to eye* on most things.
6. The rumor is that Jake *paid through the nose* for that car.

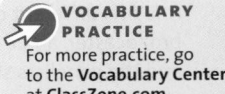

VOCABULARY PRACTICE For more practice, go to the **Vocabulary Center** at **ClassZone.com**.

DIFFERENTIATED INSTRUCTION

FOR ENGLISH LEARNERS

Vocabulary Strategy Collect a list of additional idioms, either ones that students have heard or sayings that are used frequently in everyday conversation. Write each on the board in a sentence. Then have small groups each take some of the expressions and create flash cards with the definitions on the back. Have groups take turns quizzing each other.

FOR ADVANCED LEARNERS/PRE–AP

Vocabulary in Writing Have students write a speech expressing their opinion about a player who does or does not deserve an exorbitant salary. Encourage students to incorporate as many vocabulary words as possible. Have students give their speeches to the class.

Reading-Writing Connection

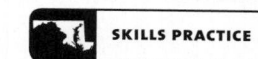

Demonstrate your understanding of these editorials by responding to the prompts. Then complete the **Grammar and Writing** exercise.

WRITING PROMPTS	SELF-CHECK
A. Short Response: Write a Letter Write a **one-paragraph letter** to the editor of *New Orleans CityBusiness* or the *Horizon* in response to one of the selections. Explain whether you agree or disagree with the writer's opinion. Remember to keep your audience in mind as you write.	*A strong letter will . . .* • point out any errors in reasoning • provide one more claim to support the argument or one brief counterargument
B. Extended Response: Explore the Key Idea Select one of the athletes listed in the sidebar on pages 923 and 924. In a **two- or three-paragraph response**, construct an argument that expresses why you think that person's **salary** is fair or unfair.	*A successful response will . . .* • have one primary claim • use adequate support, including factual examples • include a counterargument

GRAMMAR AND WRITING

 **MARYLAND OBJECTIVES**

LANGUAGE STANDARD
5.C.2.a Use commas correctly

USE COMMAS CORRECTLY Be sure to use commas correctly after **introductory words and phrases** and when listing **items in a series.** Place commas immediately after introductory words such as *Finally* and *Afterwards* and after introductory phrases that contain prepositional phrases. Also place a comma after every item in a series except the last one. (A series consists of three or more items.)

Original: During their careers athletes face injuries stiff competition and a lot of pressure to prove themselves.

Revised: During their careers, athletes face injuries, stiff competition, and a lot of pressure to prove themselves.

PRACTICE In each sentence, add commas where they are needed.

1. In recent years athletes' salaries have greatly increased.
2. Babe Ruth Jackie Robinson and Nolan Ryan deserved good salaries.
3. Within the sports community it is well known how much money owners make from sponsors.
4. The owners the networks and the sponsors are all making money.

*For more help with punctuating introductory words and phrases and items in a series, see page R49 in the **Grammar Handbook**.*

FOR LESS–PROFICIENT WRITERS

For Prompt A:

• Provide a model of correct letter format.
• Have students choose an editorial and list the reasons for their support.
• Help students write their topic sentence.

For Prompt B:

• Limit the assignment to one paragraph.
• Lead the class in brainstorming why an athlete's salary might be fair or unfair.
• Have students choose their athlete and decide their position on his salary.
• Help students express a claim.
• Have students choose reasons from the class discussion that support their view.

Reading-Writing Connection

WRITING PROMPTS

• For **Prompt A,** have students first decide with which editorial they agree or disagree. Before they write their letters, have them return to the chart or reread the editorial to identify errors or additional points that they might make.

• For **Prompt B,** suggest that students brainstorm ideas in pairs before organizing the ideas graphically or in an outline.

For ideas for writing, see

ℹ️ Writing Center at **ClassZone.com**

GRAMMAR AND WRITING

Have students compare the two examples to identify where commas were added.

Answers:

1. *In recent years, athletes' salaries have greatly increased.*
2. *Babe Ruth, Jackie Robinson, and Nolan Ryan deserved good salaries.*
3. *Within the sports community, it is well known how much money owners make from sponsors.*
4. *The owners, the networks, and the sponsors are all making money.*

📋 RESOURCE MANAGER—Copy Master
Use Commas Correctly p. 129

Assess and Reteach

Assess

📋 RESOURCE MANAGER—Copy Masters
Selection Tests A, B/C pp. 131–132, 133–134

💿 Test Generator CD

Reteach

📄 STANDARDS LESSON FILE
Informational Texts Lesson 13: Types of Faulty Reasoning
Informational Texts Lesson 14: Elements of an Argument
Vocabulary Lesson 22: Idioms
Grammar Lesson 20: Missing or Misplaced Commas

OBJECTIVES

Elements of Nonfiction
- explore the key idea of **priorities**
- understand elements of an argument: counterargument
- read a magazine article

Reading
- take notes in a graphic organizer, outline, or other format

Vocabulary
- build vocabulary for reading and writing
- understand and use the Greek root *aut* (also an EL language objective)

SUMMARY

Writer Gregg Easterbrook argues against President George W. Bush's stated goal of beginning a people-to-Mars space program. While conceding that the idea is exciting, Easterbrook concludes that with our present state of technology, a Mars program would be impractical and much too expensive, given all the other demands on taxpayer dollars.

Do we have our PRIORITIES *straight?*

Discuss the question and the *KEY IDEA* with students. Ask them to give examples of how they set **priorities** for their schoolwork, free time, and spending money. List students' ideas on the board and have them refer to the ideas during the *ROLE-PLAY.*

Why We Shouldn't Go to Mars
Magazine Article by Gregg Easterbrook

Do we have our PRIORITIES *straight?*

MARYLAND OBJECTIVES

READING/INFO TEXT STANDARDS
1.E.3.a Select and apply appropriate strategies during reading
2.A.6.d Analyze the author's argument

KEY IDEA As a seventh grader, you may have many obligations to juggle—homework, sports or hobbies, time with friends and family, and maybe even an afterschool job. Deciding on **priorities,** or what is most important, can be a difficult task. Setting priorities can be tough for nations and societies too. You're about to read one writer's ideas of what our national priorities should and should not be.

ROLE-PLAY With a group, create a panel discussion in which each student represents a different demand on one seventh grader's time. (The list of obligations in the paragraph above can give you ideas.) Each person should argue why his or her demand deserves to be a priority. Then decide as a group which two demands should be at the top of the priority list.

1. Dinner with my family
2. Homework
3. Band practice
4. Gemma's party

928

* Resources for Differentiation   † Also in Spanish   ‡ In Haitian Creole and Vietnamese

ELEMENTS OF NONFICTION: COUNTERARGUMENT

A strong counterargument is an important part of any argument. A **counterargument** anticipates what "the other side" might say and answers possible objections with reasons and evidence.

As you can probably guess from this article's title, author Gregg Easterbrook believes that sending astronauts on a mission to Mars is a mistake. Rather than ignoring those who disagree with him, Easterbrook states his opponents' views and then tells why he disagrees. As you read, search for examples of this technique.

READING SKILL: TAKE NOTES

When you **take notes,** you record a text's most important information in a way that is easy to refer to later. The form your notes take will depend on what you're reading and why you're reading it.

In an article like this one, where the author states his opinion in the title, you can expect the main ideas to be the reasons for his opinion. The evidence he gives for this opinion are the details. As you read, note the main reasons and evidence as shown.

> *Why Easterbrook Thinks We Shouldn't Go to Mars*
> • *It's too expensive.*
>   *—It would cost #600 billion in today's money.*

VOCABULARY IN CONTEXT

The boldfaced words help Easterbrook make his case for not sending people to Mars. To see how many you know, match each vocabulary word in Column A to the word or phrase in Column B that is closest in meaning.

Column A	Column B
1. amenable	a. tempting
2. exhilarating	b. agreeable
3. tantalizing	c. self-running
4. automated	d. reasonableness
5. proponent	e. supporter
6. rationality	f. thrilling

Author Online

A Wide World of Writing Before he became a full-time writer and editor, Gregg Easterbrook worked as a bus driver and a used-car salesman. Now a senior editor of *The New Republic*, Easterbrook has contributed to *Time, Newsweek*, and ESPN.

**Gregg Easterbrook
born 1953**

Background

The Red Planet The United States and the former Soviet Union began attempting flights to Mars in the early 1960s. In 1965, the first successful mission was completed when a U.S. spacecraft flew by Mars and sent 22 photos back to Earth. Since then, extensive space missions have revealed that Mars is rocky, cold, and sterile. Humans have never gone to Mars, and scientists still aren't sure if there has ever been life there.

Mission to Mars? In 2004, President George W. Bush announced a new space exploration program. Gregg Easterbrook responded to this announcement by writing the article "Why We Shouldn't Go to Mars" for *Time* magazine.

 MORE ABOUT THE AUTHOR AND BACKGROUND To learn more about Gregg Easterbrook and the space exploration program, visit the **Literature Center** at ClassZone.com.

Teach

ELEMENTS OF NONFICTION

● COUNTERARGUMENT

Read aloud this example:

> "Mom, this computer has special features that will help me with my schoolwork, and I've found a part-time job to help pay for it."

Ask: What arguments from his mother is the speaker anticipating? *Possible answer: The speaker anticipates the arguments that buying the computer isn't necessary and that it is too expensive.*

CHECK UNDERSTANDING Ask students to name a school rule they would like to change and then think of reasons both for and against changing it.

READING SKILL

■ TAKE NOTES

Tell students that when they take notes, they should look for

• main ideas in headings and topic sentences

• terms in boldface type, dates, and details that support the main ideas

CHECK UNDERSTANDING Have students take notes on the **Background** section and share the most important ideas.

R **RESOURCE MANAGER—Copy Master** Take Notes p. 147 (for student use while reading the selection)

▲ VOCABULARY IN CONTEXT

DIAGNOSE WORD KNOWLEDGE To determine preteaching needs, have all students complete **Vocabulary in Context.** Check students' answers (**1.** *b*; **2.** *f*; **3.** *a*; **4.** *c*; **5.** *e*; **6.** *d*).

PRETEACH VOCABULARY Use the Vocabulary Study copy master to help students explore the meaning of each boldfaced word.
  1. Read item 1 aloud, emphasizing *amenable*.

2. Point out the clue "able to survive." Discuss possible meanings for *amenable*, such as "agreeable."

3. Repeat the procedure for each of the other sentences.

4. Have students enter their predicted meanings in the chart. After reading, they can add meanings based on the selection.

 RESOURCE MANAGER—Copy Master Vocabulary Study p. 149

For general guidelines on differentiating vocabulary instruction and for alternative vocabulary activities for students not needing vocabulary preteaching, see

 BEST PRACTICES TOOLKIT Scaffolding Vocabulary Instruction pp. 43–46

❶ Vocabulary Center at **ClassZone.com** Additional Vocabulary Activities

ANALYZE VISUALS

Possible answers: The placement of the planets in relation to each other creates a feeling of order and serenity. The differences in color, size, and features lend an air of mystery and wonder.

About the Art From top to bottom, the planets in this montage are Mercury, Venus, Earth, Mars, Jupiter, Saturn, Uranus, and Neptune. The perspective is looking toward the sun. If the sun were included, it would be at the top of the picture, beyond Mercury. The planets farthest from the sun are at the bottom of the picture.

The Mercury image was taken by *Mariner 10,* the Venus image by *Magellan,* the Earth image by *Galileo,* and the Mars image by *Viking.* The Jupiter, Saturn, Uranus, and Neptune images were all taken by *Voyager.*

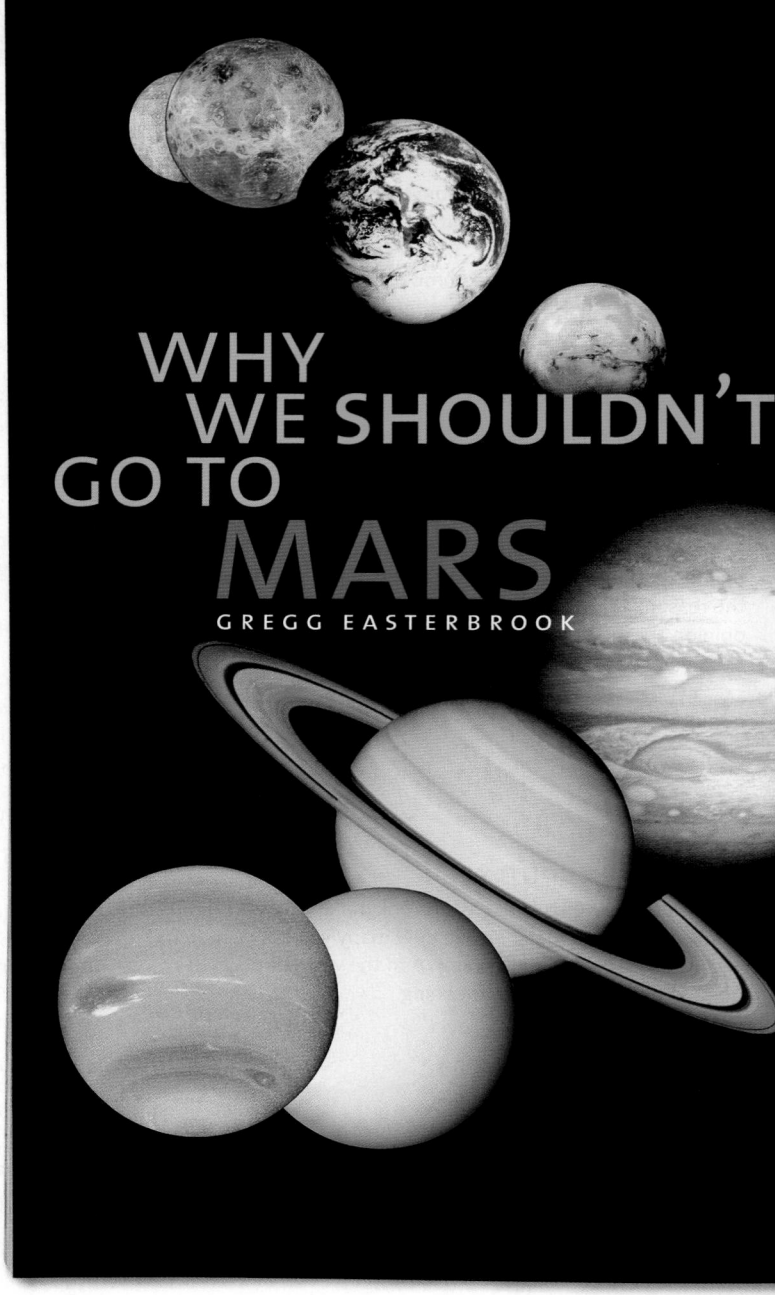

ANALYZE VISUALS
This picture of the planets combines photographs taken by different spacecraft. Pluto is not shown because no spacecraft has yet visited it. As a whole, what **mood** does this image convey?

WHY WE SHOULDN'T GO TO MARS

GREGG EASTERBROOK

DIFFERENTIATED INSTRUCTION

FOR ALL STUDENTS

Enhance Learning Styles Provide independent projects for various learning styles.

- **Linguistic** Write a poem or song to express an opinion about space exploration.
- **Analytic** Report on details of a Mars trip.
- **Spatial/Visual** Create a cartoon expressing an opinion about Mars exploration.

For further details on these projects, see

 RESOURCE MANAGER
Ideas for Extension pp. 140–141

FOR LESS—PROFICIENT READERS

In combination with the *Audio Anthology CD,* use one or more Targeted Passages (pp. 930, 933) to ensure that students focus on key facts, concepts, and skills.

① **Targeted Passage [Lines 1–16]**

This passage introduces the idea of sending people to Mars and sets out three reasons why the argument is faulty.

- What is the idea or argument with which Easterbrook disagrees?

- Why does he point out that many people already lived in the area that Lewis and Clark explored?

- What does Easterbrook imply about the places and things that might be found by sending people to Mars?

- What fact does he provide about the cost of sending people to Mars?

"Two centuries ago, Meriwether Lewis and William Clark left St. Louis to explore the new lands acquired in the Louisiana Purchase,"[1] George W. Bush said, announcing his desire for a program to send men and women to Mars. "They made that journey in the spirit of discovery. . . . America has ventured forth into space for the same reasons."

Yet there are vital differences between Lewis and Clark's expedition and a Mars mission. First, Lewis and Clark were
10 headed to a place **amenable** to life; hundreds of thousands of people were already living there. Second, Lewis and Clark were *certain* to discover places and things of immediate value to the new nation. Third, the Lewis and Clark venture cost next to nothing by today's standards. In 1989 NASA estimated that a people-to-Mars program would cost $400 billion, which inflates to $600 billion today. The Hoover Dam cost $700 million in today's money, meaning that sending people to Mars might cost as much as building about 800 new Hoover Dams. A Mars mission may be the single
20 most expensive nonwartime undertaking in U.S. history. **Ⓐ**

The thought of travel to Mars is **exhilarating.** Surely men and women will someday walk upon that planet, and surely they will make wondrous discoveries about geology[2] and the history of the solar system, perhaps even about the very origin of life. Many times I have stared up at Mars in the evening sky—in the mountains, away from cities, you can almost see the red tint—and wondered what is there, or was there.

But the fact that a destination is **tantalizing** does not mean the journey makes sense, even considering the human
30 calling to explore. And Mars as a destination for people makes absolutely no sense with current technology.

---

1. **Louisiana Purchase:** an area extending from the Mississippi River to the Rocky Mountains, purchased from France in 1803.
2. **geology:** the scientific study of the history and structure of the earth.

① Targeted Passage

amenable (ə-mē′nə-bəl) *adj.* open; agreeable

Ⓐ COUNTERARGUMENT
A **false analogy** is a comparison that doesn't hold up because of an important difference between the two subjects. How does Easterbrook prove that likening a Mars mission to Lewis and Clark's expedition is a false analogy?

exhilarating (ĭg-zĭl′ə-rā′tĭng) *adj.* stimulating; making one feel thrilled or inspired **exhilarate** *v.*

tantalizing (tăn′tə-lī′zĭng) *adj.* tempting but out of reach **tantalize** *v.*

BACKGROUND

The Lewis and Clark Expedition In 1802, President Thomas Jefferson began to make plans to send an expedition to explore the uncharted territory of the West. In 1803, the United States acquired much of this territory through the Louisiana Purchase. In that same year, Congress gave approval for the expedition. The funding approved for Lewis and Clark's Corps of Discovery amounted to $2,500. The actual cost eventually reached $38,722. In addition to the leaders, Meriwether Lewis and William Clark, about 30 other persons belonged to the permanent group that made up the Corps of Discovery. The expedition set out in May 1804 and traveled over 8,000 miles in nearly two and a half years. They dispelled the myth of finding a "northwest passage"—a river or a series of connected waterways that would make travel to the Pacific easier. In addition to mapping the territory, the expedition studied and recorded information about plants and wildlife.

ELEMENTS OF NONFICTION

Ⓐ COUNTERARGUMENT

Possible answers: Easterbrook cites this evidence for a false analogy:

- *Lewis and Clark's journey was to a place amenable to human life; the Mars mission is not.*
- *Lewis and Clark were certain to discover places and things of value to the country; a Mars mission is not.*
- *Lewis and Clark's expedition was inexpensive; a Mars mission will be hugely expensive.*

FOR ENGLISH LEARNERS
Options for Reading Read the first Targeted Passage aloud. Make sure students understand why the comparison between Lewis and Clark's expedition and a people-to-Mars mission doesn't hold up. Then have students listen to the *Audio Anthology CD.* Use a DRTA strategy to help students read and understand the selection. Pause frequently to enable students to take notes.

Key Academic Vocabulary Use New Word Analysis to provide instruction for this vocabulary: *estimate* (line 15), *technology* (lines 31, 55, 62, 75), *evidence* (line 46).

 BEST PRACTICES TOOLKIT—Transparencies
DRTA p. A20
New Word Analysis p. E8

Prereading For prereading instruction for English learners, see

 BEST PRACTICES TOOLKIT
Scaffolding Reading Instruction pp. 43–46

FOR ADVANCED LEARNERS/PRE–AP
Analyze Easterbrook describes his own fascination with Mars in lines 21–27. Ask students how his tone changes in lines 28–31 and what effect this has on his argument.

ADDITIONAL GUIDELINES
For more help with differentiation and tips for classroom management, see

 BEST PRACTICES TOOLKIT
Differentiated Instruction pp. 31–38

Lines 40–53
DISCUSSION PROMPTS

Use these prompts to help students understand Easterbrook's objections to a Mars mission:

Recall What does Easterbrook say about traveling to Mars with our current technology? *Answer: He says that sending people to Mars makes no sense with our current technology (lines 30–31).*

Analyze What scientific activities could humans do on Mars that automated devices cannot do? *Possible answer: Humans could do nothing beyond what automated devices are already doing.*

Evaluate What effect might a people-to-Mars mission have on the amount of scientific information being gathered by space exploration? Explain. *Possible answer: It would actually decrease the amount of information being gathered, because the huge costs would require unmanned missions to be cut. Further, it wouldn't supply any new information that the unmanned missions can't supply.*

READING SKILL

B TAKE NOTES

Possible answers:

Why Easterbrook Thinks We Shouldn't Go to Mars

• *Getting equipment from Earth to low-Earth orbit is too expensive.*

—*It would require either a tax hike or a cut to social programs.*

• *No new knowledge would be gained.*

—*Astronauts on Mars could do little more than analyze rocks.*

—*Rocks can be analyzed by automated probes at lower cost and with no risk to human life.*

Left, NASA artist's concept of the Mars Exploration Rover, which landed on Mars in 2004; *right,* computer-generated image of the surface of Mars.

automated (ô′tə-mā′tĭd) *adj.* able to function with little or no assistance from people **automate** *v.*

B TAKE NOTES
In this paragraph, what are the main reasons Easterbrook gives for not sending a person to Mars? Jot them down in your notes.

Present systems for getting from Earth's surface to low-Earth orbit[3] are so fantastically expensive that merely launching the 1,000 tons or so of spacecraft and equipment a Mars mission would require could be accomplished only by cutting health-care benefits, education spending or other important programs—or by raising taxes. Absent some remarkable discovery, astronauts, geologists and biologists once on Mars could do little more than analyze rocks and feel awestruck
40 beholding the sky of another world. Yet rocks can be analyzed by **automated** probes without risk to human life, and at a tiny fraction of the cost of sending people. **B**

It is interesting to note that when President Bush unveiled his proposal, he listed these recent major achievements of space exploration: pictures of the rings of Saturn and the outer planets, evidence of water on Mars and the moons of Jupiter, discovery of more than 100 planets outside our solar system and study of the soil of Mars. All these accomplishments came from automated probes or automated space telescopes. Bush's
50 proposal, which calls for "reprogramming" some of NASA's present budget into the Mars effort, might actually lead to a reduction in such unmanned science—the one aspect of space exploration that's working really well.

Rather than spend hundreds of billions of dollars to hurl tons toward Mars using current technology, why not take

---

3. **low-Earth orbit:** a region roughly 200 to 500 miles above Earth, the easiest area to reach in space and the area from which scientists hope to launch future space missions.

DIFFERENTIATED INSTRUCTION

FOR LESS–PROFICIENT READERS

Note Taking For students who need help with note taking, hand out copies of the Main Idea and Details chart. Read and discuss the information on page 932. Assist students as needed in completing the chart.

 BEST PRACTICES TOOLKIT—Transparency
Main Idea and Details p. B6

FOR ENGLISH LEARNERS

Vocabulary: Prefixes List these prefixes and their meanings on the board: *ex-* ("out"); *dis-* ("opposite"); *re-* ("back"). Then have students define *expensive* (line 33), *exploration* (lines 45, 53), *discovery* (lines 38, 47), *reprogramming* (line 50), and *reduction* (line 52). Point out that the quotation marks around *reprogramming* indicate an unusual usage of the term. In this case it means "reallocating."

Mars, the Red Planet

a decade—or two decades, or however much time is required—researching new launch systems and advanced propulsion? If new launch systems could put weight into orbit affordably, and if advanced propulsion could speed up that long, slow transit to Mars, then the dream of stepping onto the Red Planet might become reality. Mars will still be there when the technology is ready.

Space-exploration **proponents** deride as lack of vision the mention of technical barriers or the insistence that needs on Earth come first. Not so. The former is **rationality,** the latter the setting of priorities. If Mars proponents want to raise $600 billion privately and stage their own expedition, more power to them; many of the great expeditions of the past were privately mounted. If Mars proponents expect taxpayers to foot their bill, then they must make their case against the many other competing needs for money. And against the needs for health care, education, poverty reduction, reinforcement of the military and reduction of the federal deficit,[4] the case for vast expenditures to go to Mars using current technology is very weak. **C**

The drive to explore is part of what makes us human, and exploration of the past has led to unexpected glories. Dreams must be tempered by realism, however. For the moment, going to Mars is hopelessly unrealistic.

---

4. **federal deficit:** a shortage of funds caused by the government's spending more than it collects in taxes.

proponent (prə-pō′nənt) *n.* a person who supports something

rationality (răsh′ə-năl′ĭ-tē) *n.* reasonableness

C COUNTERARGUMENT
Easterbrook's opponents could claim that he has a "lack of vision" because he is against a Mars mission. Reread lines 63–75. What is his counterargument to this possible criticism?

2 Targeted Passage

Lines 54–62
REINFORCE KEY IDEA: PRIORITIES

Discuss What **priorities** does Easterbrook think must be considered in planning the technology for sending people to Mars? What important point does he make about taking time to work on the technology? *Possible answer: He suggests that instead of rushing the process, we should take time to develop affordable launch systems. He makes the point that Mars will still be there when the technology is ready to send people to study it.*

ELEMENTS OF NONFICTION

C COUNTERARGUMENT
Possible answer: Easterbrook argues that his position shows "rationality" and "the setting of priorities," not a lack of vision.

SELECTION WRAP–UP

REFLECT Have students reflect on Easterbrook's position on sending people to explore Mars. Do they agree or disagree?

⭐ CRITIQUE Ask students to evaluate the writer's use of counterargument. Does it effectively make his case? Why or why not?

READING FLUENCY

Distribute the copy masters and have students work in pairs to practice fluency.

R RESOURCE MANAGER—Copy Master
Reading Fluency p. 154

FOR LESS–PROFICIENT READERS

2 Targeted Passage [Lines 63–79]

This passage summarizes the writer's main points and restates his main idea: space exploration must be approached realistically.

- What two opposing viewpoints does the writer set out in this passage?
- What facts and ideas are repeated?
- What effect is created by the writer's admission that exploration is part of what makes us human and has led to past glories?

FOR ADVANCED LEARNERS/PRE–AP

Analyze Arguments Does Easterbrook's article appeal more to the reader's emotions or to reason? Have students use a Two-Column Chart to list examples of the two types of appeal. Then have them discuss their conclusions in small groups.

 BEST PRACTICES TOOLKIT—Transparency
Two-Column Chart p. A25

Appeals to Reason	Appeals to Emotions
costs (lines 15–20, 32–37, 49–53, 66–75)	fear (lines 49–53)
technology (lines 40–42, 58–61)	

Practice and Apply

After Reading

For additional support of post-reading questions, use these copy masters:

RESOURCE MANAGER—Copy Masters
Reading Check p. 152 (to check understanding of the selection)
Counterargument p. 145 (for practice of elements of nonfiction standards focus)
Question Support p. 153 (**After Reading** questions adapted for English learners and less-proficient readers)

Additional selection questions are provided for teachers on page 139.

ANSWERS

Comprehension

1. *A Mars mission would cost about $600 billion—the equivalent of the cost to build roughly 800 new Hoover Dams (lines 16–19).*

2. *Easterbrook speculates that humans will make discoveries on Mars about geology, the history of the solar system, and the origin of life (lines 23–25).*

3. *Easterbrook says that health care, education, poverty reduction, military reinforcement, and deficit reduction are more important priorities (lines 72–74).*

Critical Analysis

Possible answers:

4. ■ **STANDARDS FOCUS** *Take Notes*
Students' summaries should include the following points: sending people to Mars would (1) be too expensive, (2) require better technology than we have today, and (3) pose unnecessary risk to human life, because automated probes already provide the same information humans could gather.

5. ● **STANDARDS FOCUS** *Counterargument*
Easterbrook offers the counterargument that the advancements noted in lines 45–48 were all accomplished using automated technology, not astronauts. The proposed Mars mission might actually hurt the space program by cutting the budget for this successful technology.

6. *Students' charts should include clear examples of evidence and reasons for their reactions.*

After Reading

Comprehension

1. **Recall** How does the cost of a Mars mission compare to the cost of the Hoover Dam?

2. **Recall** In what areas does Easterbrook suggest that "wondrous discoveries" might one day be made on Mars?

3. **Clarify** What national issues does Easterbrook suggest are more important than sending U.S. astronauts to Mars?

Critical Analysis

4. **Summarize Notes** What are three main reasons Easterbrook gives for believing that the government should not send people to Mars? If you can't find the answer in your notes, look for it in the article. Then revise your notes so that they include this important information.

5. **Identify a Counterargument** Reread lines 43–53. Easterbrook's opponents argue that sending astronauts on missions is necessary in order to make achievements in space exploration. What counterargument does Easterbrook offer in response?

6. **Evaluate Support** Easterbrook supports his argument with evidence. Which pieces of evidence did you find most, or least, convincing? Pick at least two and list them in a chart. Then describe your reaction to the evidence.

Evidence	My Reaction
Lewis and Clark's expedition cost very little, while a Mars mission will cost $600 billion.	I think $600 billion seems like way too much money! We could put that money to better use.

Extension and Challenge

7. **Readers' Circle** When deciding about how to spend taxpayers' money, Easterbrook says, "needs on Earth come first." Discuss whether you agree with Easterbrook's opinion about what our national **priorities** should be.

8. **SCIENCE CONNECTION** Do some research on past automated Mars missions. Consider the following questions:

- What was the name of the spacecraft that first orbited Mars?
- What year did a U.S. craft first land on the planet?
- What do you think is the best thing that Mars probes have discovered?

RESEARCH LINKS
For more on Mars, visit the **Research Center** at ClassZone.com.

934 UNIT 8: INFORMATION, ARGUMENT, AND PERSUASION

Extension and Challenge

7. *Responses will vary. Students' opinions should be supported by reasons or evidence.*

8. **SCIENCE CONNECTION**
Responses will vary. Students' research should provide facts and details documented by sources; opinions should be supported by reasons or evidence.

Vocabulary in Context

VOCABULARY PRACTICE

Choose the letter of the item most closely associated with each vocabulary word.

1. **tantalizing:** (a) an old pair of tennis shoes, (b) the smell of chocolate-chip cookies baking, (c) a statement about an overdue bill

2. **amenable:** (a) an easygoing person, (b) a dilapidated car, (c) a protest march

3. **automated:** (a) a soccer ball, (b) a robot, (c) a birthday party

4. **exhilarating:** (a) a brisk walk on a beach, (b) a large herd of cattle, (c) a low hedge

5. **proponent:** (a) part of an airplane, (b) leader of a voting drive, (c) carton of unworn gloves

6. **rationality:** (a) a new shopping center, (b) a letter from an old friend, (c) a well thought-out plan

amenable
automated
exhilarating
proponent
rationality
tantalizing

VOCABULARY IN WRITING

What issues or projects do you think our government should invest money in? Choose one and explain your opinion about it, using at least two vocabulary words. You might start like this.

> **EXAMPLE SENTENCE**
>
> I am a strong **proponent** of our government's working to eliminate hunger around the world.

MARYLAND OBJECTIVES

READING STANDARD
1.D.3.b Use word structure to determine meaning

VOCABULARY STRATEGY: THE GREEK ROOT *aut*

The vocabulary word *automated* contains the Greek root *aut,* which means "self." This root, and the related prefix *auto-,* is found in a number of English words. Use your understanding of the root's meaning, as well as context clues, to figure out the meanings of words formed from *aut.*

PRACTICE Choose a word from the web that best completes each sentence. If you need help, check a dictionary.

1. A genuine _____ by Abraham Lincoln is worth a lot of money.
2. How often are planes flown on _____?
3. Because of _____, many jobs can be done more quickly and with less effort.
4. Countries that are _____ are governed by their own people.
5. _____ limits its sufferers' ability to communicate with others.

VOCABULARY PRACTICE
For more practice, go to the **Vocabulary Center** at **ClassZone.com.**

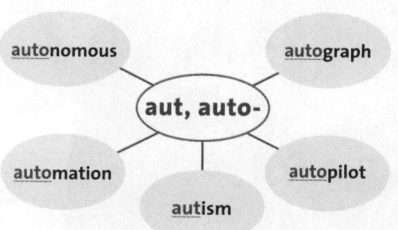

autonomous · autograph · aut, auto- · automation · autism · autopilot

---

DIFFERENTIATED INSTRUCTION

FOR ENGLISH LEARNERS

Vocabulary Strategy Note that the Spanish cognate *automatizar* is similar to the English word *automate.* Point out that many of the words derived from *aut* can be matched with similar words in the Spanish language. Have students identify cognates for as many of the choices as they can (*autonomous/autónomo, autograph/autógrafo, autism/autismo*).

FOR ADVANCED LEARNERS/PRE–AP

Vocabulary Strategy Have students work in pairs to brainstorm additional words that come from *aut.* Discuss the meanings of the words and then challenge students to write a claim statement for an argument using each of the words.

ANSWERS

Vocabulary in Context

VOCABULARY PRACTICE

1. *b;* **2.** *a;* **3.** *b;* **4.** *a;* **5.** *b;* **6.** *c*

R RESOURCE MANAGER—Copy Master
Vocabulary Practice p. 150

VOCABULARY IN WRITING

Have students create a list of issues or projects in which government should invest money. Then they can choose the one that they feel deserves the most support. Suggest that they think about the reasons for their choice before they explain their opinion using vocabulary words.

VOCABULARY STRATEGY: THE GREEK ROOT
aut (also an EL language objective)

- Before students begin the exercise, read the choices aloud.

- Help students identify the part of speech of each word.

Answers:
1. autograph
2. autopilot
3. automation
4. autonomous
5. autism

R RESOURCE MANAGER—Copy Master
Vocabulary Strategy p. 151

i Vocabulary Center at **ClassZone.com**
Additional Vocabulary Activities

Assess and Reteach

Assess

R RESOURCE MANAGER—Copy Masters
Selection Tests A, B/C pp. 155–156, 157–158

◎ Test Generator CD

Reteach

S STANDARDS LESSON FILE
Informational Texts Lesson 13: Types of Faulty Reasoning
Informational Texts Lesson 14: Elements of an Argument
Vocabulary Lesson 9: Greek Roots and Combining Forms

Focus and Motivate

OBJECTIVES

Elements of Nonfiction
- explore the key idea of **inspire**
- analyze persuasive techniques (appeal to authority, logical appeal, appeal by association, emotional appeal)
- read a speech

Reading
- read a speech aloud

Vocabulary
- build vocabulary for reading and writing
- understand origins and meanings of acronyms *(also an EL language objective)*

Grammar and Writing
- use colons correctly (formal greetings, numerals, lists)
- use writing to analyze literature

SUMMARY

In this speech, President Kennedy discusses how medical space research will benefit all people. He explains that it will lead to more information about the environment, new ways to diagnose and treat illnesses, and new technology to protect people against the hazards of life. He concludes by inviting everyone to be a part of this great space endeavor.

What INSPIRES *people?*

Discuss the question with students. Have them list people or ideas that **inspire** them. Ask volunteers to share what is on their lists before introducing the *KEY IDEA*. Then have students complete the *QUICKWRITE* activity.

Selection Resources

RESOURCE MANAGER UNIT 8

Plan and Teach pp. 159–166

Elements of Nonfiction
Summary pp. 167†*, 168‡*
Persuasive Techniques pp. 169, 170†*
Question Support p. 177*

Reading
Reading a Speech pp. 171, 172†*
Reading Check p. 176
Reading Fluency p. 179

Vocabulary
Study p. 173*
Practice p. 174
Strategy p. 175

Grammar and Writing
Use Colons Correctly p. 178

Assessment
Selection Tests A, B/C pp. 181*, 183*
⊘ Test Generator CD

🧰 BEST PRACTICES TOOLKIT
Differentiated Instruction pp. 31–38*
Scaffolding Instruction pp. 43–46*

Graphic Organizers/Strategies
Word Squares • Venn Diagram • Cluster Diagram

Reading Support
⊘ Audio Anthology CD*

Technology
ℹ Literature and Vocabulary Centers at **ClassZone.com**
⊘ Write*Smart* CD

* Resources for Differentiation   † Also in Spanish   ‡ In Haitian Creole and Vietnamese

---

Remarks at the Dedication of the Aerospace Medical Health Center
Speech by John F. Kennedy

What INSPIRES *people?*

MARYLAND OBJECTIVES

INFORMATIONAL TEXT STANDARDS
2.A.6.b Analyze structure and features
2.A.6.f Analyze language and other techniques intended to persuade

KEY IDEA It's sometimes hard to do the right thing, especially if you feel as if you're doing it all alone. Every once in a while, a leader emerges who can **inspire** people to break through their fear and preoccupation to make our society the best it can be. You're about to read a speech by one such leader—President John F. Kennedy.

QUICKWRITE Think about a time when someone convinced you to make a change or take an action. Write a journal entry telling why you felt inspired.

936

ELEMENTS OF NONFICTION: PERSUASIVE TECHNIQUES

Advertisers, politicians, and writers often try to influence or persuade us to support their product, beliefs, or position on an issue. Common **persuasive techniques** include

- referring to the opinion of an expert (appeal to authority)
- appealing to common sense (logical appeal)
- appealing to the desire to belong (appeal by association)
- evoking strong feelings (emotional appeal)

As you read President Kennedy's speech, identify the persuasive techniques he uses.

READING STRATEGY: READING A SPEECH

After reading the **speech** silently, read it aloud. If you listen closely, you will be able to hear the techniques and strategies Kennedy uses to keep the listeners' interest. Use a chart to note examples of the strategies.

Strategies	Examples from the Speech
Sound devices such as rhythm, repetition, and alliteration	first paragraph: repeats "era" three times
Organization that makes the speech easy to follow	
Concrete examples that connect to the audience's lives	

VOCABULARY IN CONTEXT

The boldfaced words helped Kennedy communicate the importance of space research. Restate each sentence using a different word or words for the boldfaced term.

1. It is a **partisan** law that only benefits the rich.
2. This is a noble **endeavor** that will eventually succeed.
3. The pilot observed the spacecraft on **radar.**
4. She experienced **disorientation** in the space lab.
5. Exercise helped the patient increase his **metabolism.**
6. He has a temporary **impairment** and needs to use crutches.
7. Cheap land was a great **impetus** for the new settlers.
8. Studying the chart is a **tedious** task.

Author Online

U.S. President John F. Kennedy, the 35th president of the United States, set out to lead the way into a future filled with scientific discoveries and improvements in society. Wanting to bring democracy and freedom to the world, Kennedy asked that all American citizens join him in this New Frontier.

John F. Kennedy
1917–1963

A Race to Space In 1957, the country then known as the Soviet Union launched *Sputnik I,* the first satellite to orbit the earth. The Soviet Union and the United States were bitter enemies, and after becoming president in 1961, Kennedy was determined to equal and even surpass the Soviets' knowledge of space. He said, "No nation which expects to be the leader of other nations can expect to stay behind in this race for space." In a session before Congress in 1961, Kennedy called for plans to send astronauts to the moon. The United States achieved this goal on July 20, 1969.

An Inspirational Speaker A line from Kennedy's inaugural address is often quoted: "Ask not what your country can do for you—ask what you can do for your country." You are about to read the speech he made on November 21, 1963. The following day, November 22, 1963, John F. Kennedy was assassinated.

 MORE ABOUT THE AUTHOR For more on John F. Kennedy, visit the **Literature Center** at **ClassZone.com.**

937

Teach

STANDARDS FOCUS

ELEMENTS OF NONFICTION

● **PERSUASIVE TECHNIQUES**

Read these examples aloud:

1. "The space program depends on the support of far-sighted Americans like you."
2. "This product has been approved by NASA scientists."

Ask students to identify the appeal used in each example. *Possible answers: Item 1 is an appeal by association. Item 2 is an appeal to authority.*

CHECK UNDERSTANDING Have students find advertisements that illustrate each persuasive technique described.

READING STRATEGY

■ **READING A SPEECH**

Explain that unlike readers, people listening to a speech cannot go back to reread or clarify details. Therefore, to help listeners remember important ideas, speakers often repeat key points. They also use transitions and other cues to let listeners know what is coming next.

CHECK UNDERSTANDING Have students identify other techniques that speakers might use.

 RESOURCE MANAGER—Copy Master Reading a Speech p. 171 (for student use while reading the selection)

VOCABULARY SKILL

▲ **VOCABULARY IN CONTEXT**

DIAGNOSE WORD KNOWLEDGE To determine preteaching needs, have all students complete **Vocabulary in Context.** Check students' answers. *(Possible answers:* **1.** *one-sided;* **2.** *activity;* **3.** *a device using radio waves;* **4.** *confusion;* **5.** *internal health;* **6.** *handicap;* **7.** *motivation;* **8.** *boring)*

PRETEACH VOCABULARY Use the Vocabulary Study copy master to help students explore the meaning of each boldfaced word.

1. Read the first two sentences aloud, emphasizing *endeavor.*
2. Point out the word *mission.* Elicit possible meanings for *endeavor,* such as "job."
3. Repeat for the rest of the passage.
4. Have students match words with meanings in Part B.

 **RESOURCE MANAGER—Copy Master** Vocabulary Study p. 173

For general guidelines on differentiating vocabulary instruction and for alternative vocabulary activities for students not needing vocabulary preteaching, see

 BEST PRACTICES TOOLKIT Scaffolding Vocabulary Instruction pp. 43–46

🛈 Vocabulary Center at **ClassZone.com** Additional Vocabulary Activities

READING STRATEGY

A READ A SPEECH

Record students' answers in the chart from page 937. *Possible answer:*

Strategies	Examples from the Speech
Sound devices such as rhythm, repetition, and alliteration	first paragraph: repeats "era" three times (lines 6, 7, 8); uses alliteration in "pathfinders and pioneers" (line 10)

Extend the Discussion Why is repetition an effective technique for speakers?

BACKGROUND

Aerospace Medical Center The School of Aviation Medicine (line 12) began as the Air Service Medical Research Laboratory in 1918. It was created to study the effects of flight on the human body. In 1959, it became the key component of the new Aerospace Medical Center at Brooks Air Force Base.

Project Mercury President Kennedy refers to Project Mercury in line 62. This was the first series of U.S. space flights with astronauts aboard. The project ran from 1961 to 1963. Alan Shepard Jr. rode in the first space capsule. His flight lasted 15 minutes. The flight of L. Gordon Cooper Jr. was the last and the longest in the series. Cooper orbited for 34 hours.

Lines 15–20
REINFORCE *KEY IDEA:* INSPIRE

Discuss How have the people mentioned in these lines **inspired** others? *Possible answers: They were pioneers in the air. They helped others envision what might be possible. They pushed the boundaries.*

Remarks at the Dedication of the Aerospace Medical Health Center

President John F. Kennedy

Mr. Secretary, Governor, Mr. Vice President, Senator, Members of the Congress, members of the military, ladies and gentlemen:

For more than 3 years I have spoken about the New Frontier. This is not a **partisan** term, and it is not the exclusive property of Republicans or Democrats. It refers, instead, to this Nation's place in history, to the fact that we do stand on the edge of a great new era, filled with both crisis and opportunity, an era to be characterized by achievement and by challenge. It is an era which calls for action and for the best efforts of all those who would test the unknown and the uncertain in every phase of human

10 **endeavor**. It is a time for pathfinders and pioneers. **A**

I have come to Texas today to salute an outstanding group of pioneers, the men who man the Brooks Air Force Base School of Aerospace Medicine and the Aerospace Medical Center. It is fitting that San Antonio should be the site of this center and this school as we gather to dedicate this complex of buildings. For this city has long been the home of the pioneers in the air. It was here that Sidney Brooks, whose memory we honor today, was born and raised. It was here that Charles Lindbergh and Claire Chennault,[1] and a host of others, who, in World War I and World War II and Korea, and even today have helped demonstrate American mastery of the skies, trained at Kelly

20 Field and Randolph Field,[2] which form a major part of aviation history. And in the new frontier of outer space, while headlines may be made by others in other places, history is being made every day by the men and women of the Aerospace Medical Center, without whom there could be no history.

Many Americans make the mistake of assuming that space research has no values here on earth. Nothing could be further from the truth. Just as the wartime development of **radar** gave us the transistor, and all that it made possible, so research in space medicine holds the promise of

partisan (pär′tĭ-zən) *adj.* relating to or in support of one political party

endeavor (ĕn-dĕv′ər) *n.* purposeful or serious activity; enterprise

A READ A SPEECH
Reread lines 3–10. Speech writers often use **repetition** and **alliteration,** or the repetition of consonant sounds at the beginning of words, to create memorable phrases. Find an example of both.

radar (rā′där) *n.* a method of detecting distant objects through the use of radio waves

Targeted Passage

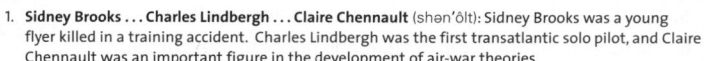

---

1. **Sidney Brooks . . . Charles Lindbergh . . . Claire Chennault** (shən′ôlt): Sidney Brooks was a young flyer killed in a training accident. Charles Lindbergh was the first transatlantic solo pilot, and Claire Chennault was an important figure in the development of air-war theories.
2. **Kelly Field and Randolph Field:** airfields in the San Antonio area where many military pilots were trained.

DIFFERENTIATED INSTRUCTION

FOR ALL STUDENTS

Anchor Activity Provide opportunities for independent learning on the topic of space. Have individual students or groups research space program achievements for one of the decades from the 1960s to the present. For further details on this project, see

R RESOURCE MANAGER
Ideas for Extension pp. 164–165

FOR LESS–PROFICIENT READERS

① Targeted Passage [Lines 24–50]

This passage presents Kennedy's claim (that medical space research will benefit people on Earth) and his first supporting example.

- What mistake or counterargument about space research does Kennedy refute?
- What will scientists learn from examining an astronaut's reactions to space?
- How will a solution to the problem of exhaust gases in space help cities on Earth?

substantial benefit for those of us who are earthbound. For our effort in
30 space is not, as some have suggested, a competitor for the natural resources that we need to develop the earth. It is a working partner and a coproducer of these resources. And nothing makes this clearer than the fact that medicine in space is going to make our lives healthier and happier here on earth.

I give you three examples: first,
40 medical space research may open up new understanding of man's relation to his environment. Examinations of the astronaut's physical, and mental, and emotional reactions can teach us more about the differences between normal and abnormal, about the causes and effects of **disorientation**, about changes in **metabolism** which could result in extending the life span. When you study the effects on our astronauts of exhaust gases which can contaminate their environment, and you seek ways to alter these gases so as to reduce their toxicity, you are working on problems similar to those we face in our great urban centers
50 which themselves are being corrupted by gases and which must be clear. **B**

And second, medical space research may revolutionize the technology and the techniques of modern medicine. Whatever new devices are created, for example, to monitor our astronauts, to measure their heart activity, their breathing, their brain waves, their eye motion, at great distances and under difficult conditions, will also represent a major advance in general medical instrumentation. Heart patients may even be able to wear a light monitor which will sound a warning if their activity exceeds certain limits. An instrument recently developed to record automatically the impact of acceleration upon an astronaut's eyes will also be of help to small
60 children who are suffering miserably from eye defects, but are unable to describe their **impairment**. And also by the use of instruments similar to those used in Project Mercury, this Nation's private as well as public nursing services are being improved, enabling one nurse now to give more critically ill patients greater attention than they ever could in the past. **C**

And third, medical space research may lead to new safeguards against hazards common to many environments. Specifically, our astronauts will need fundamentally new devices to protect them from the ill effects of

① Targeted Passage

disorientation
(dĭs-ôr′ē-ĕn-tā′shən) *n.* mental confusion or impaired awareness

metabolism
(mĭ-tăb′ə-lĭz′əm) *n.* all the processes a living thing uses to continue to grow and live

B READ A SPEECH
In lines 38–50, President Kennedy supports the **claim** he made in lines 34–37. What words introduce his first example? Watch for where he repeats the phrase in later paragraphs.

impairment
(ĭm-pâr′mənt) *n.* the condition of being damaged, injured, or harmed

C PERSUASIVE TECHNIQUES
Reread lines 58–61. Notice President Kennedy refers to "small children who are suffering." What persuasive technique is he using?

FOR ENGLISH LEARNERS
Key Academic Vocabulary Have students use Word Squares to define these nouns: *research* (line 24), *resources* (line 31), *environment* (line 41).

 BEST PRACTICES TOOLKIT—Transparency
Word Squares p. E10

Prereading For prereading instruction for English learners, see

 BEST PRACTICES TOOLKIT
Scaffolding Reading Instruction pp. 43–46

FOR ADVANCED LEARNERS/PRE–AP
Compare and Contrast Are astronauts the new pioneers, and is space the new frontier, as President Kennedy suggests? Have students compare the pioneers who explored the Western frontier in the 1800s and the astronauts who explore space. Suggest they use a Venn Diagram to organize their ideas. Then have students share their ideas in small groups.

 BEST PRACTICES TOOLKIT—Transparency
Venn Diagram p. A26

Lines 24–37
DISCUSSION PROMPTS
Use these prompts to help students understand President Kennedy's point of view on space exploration:

Connect Do you think space exploration should be encouraged? Why or why not? *Students' answers will vary but should be supported by logical reasons.*

Analyze Why might people be opposed to spending tax money on the space program? *Possible answer: They might believe that tax money should be spent on natural resources to develop the earth.*

Evaluate Identify the claim that President Kennedy makes. Do you think he has other reasons for promoting space exploration? Why does he present this one? *Possible answer: President Kennedy claims that research in space medicine will benefit everyone. He could make other claims about the importance of space exploration, but this one can be supported with concrete examples and is bound to appeal to many, especially the health professionals in his audience.*

READING SKILL

B READ A SPEECH
Record students' examples in the second row of the chart. *Possible answers:*

- *lines 38–39: "I give you three examples: first, medical space research may . . ."*
- *line 51: "And second, medical space research may . . ."*
- *line 65: "And third, medical space research may . . ."*

If students need help . . . Have them identify the signal words *first*, *second*, and *third* (lines 38, 51, 65). Point out that each cue is followed by an additional example.

ELEMENTS OF NONFICTION

C PERSUASIVE TECHNIQUES
Possible answer: He uses an emotional appeal by referring to the children.

Extend the Discussion When is an emotional appeal appropriate and effective?

READING STRATEGY

D READ A SPEECH

Record students' examples in the third row of the chart. *Possible answers:*

- *Solving the problem of exhaust gases in a space environment will help take care of similar problems in cities.*
- *Instruments that record the effects of acceleration on astronauts' eyes will help children suffering from eye defects.*
- *Devices to protect astronauts from the effects of radiation will lead to safeguards against environmental hazards.*

READING STRATEGY

E READ A SPEECH

Possible answer: The word areas *and the phrases "there will be," "must go on," and "that much" are repeated in this paragraph.*

ELEMENTS OF NONFICTION

F PERSUASIVE TECHNIQUES

Possible answer: He calls upon the listeners to support the endeavor as members of "this Nation" and as Americans.

SELECTION WRAP–UP

⭐ **CRITIQUE** Have students evaluate the effectiveness of the conclusion of the speech. What are its strengths? What would students add, if anything?

READING FLUENCY

Distribute the copy masters and have students work in pairs to practice fluency.

🅡 RESOURCE MANAGER—Copy Master
Reading Fluency p. 179

D READ A SPEECH
What three **concrete examples** does President Kennedy give to connect the technical issues of space exploration to people's everyday lives?

impetus (ĭm′pĭ-təs) *n.* a driving force; a motivation

tedious (tē′dē-əs) *adj.* tiresome; boring

E READ A SPEECH
What words or phrases are repeated in this paragraph?

F PERSUASIVE TECHNIQUES
In this paragraph, President Kennedy appeals to people's desire to belong. To what group does he hope people feel an association or loyalty?

---

radiation which can have a profound influence upon medicine and man's relations to our present environment. **D**

70　Here at this center we have the laboratories, the talent, the resources to give new **impetus** to vital research in the life centers. I am not suggesting that the entire space program is justified alone by what is done in medicine. The space program stands on its own as a contribution to national strength. And last Saturday at Cape Canaveral I saw our new Saturn C-1 rocket booster,[3] which, with its payload,[4] when it rises in December of this year, will be, for the first time, the largest booster in the world, carrying into space the largest payload that any country in the world has ever sent into space.

　I think the United States should be a leader. A country as rich and powerful as this which bears so many burdens and responsibilities, which
80　has so many opportunities, should be second to none. And in December, while I do not regard our mastery of space as anywhere near complete, while I recognize that there are still areas where we are behind—at least in one area, the size of the booster—this year I hope the United States will be ahead. And I am for it. We have a long way to go. Many weeks and months and years of long, **tedious** work lie ahead. There will be setbacks and frustrations and disappointments. There will be, as there always are, pressures in this country to do less in this area as in so many others, and temptations to do something else that is perhaps easier. But this research here must go on. This space effort must go on. The conquest of space must
90　and will go ahead. That much we know. That much we can say with confidence and conviction. **E**

　Frank O'Connor, the Irish writer, tells in one of his books how, as a boy, he and his friends would make their way across the countryside, and when they came to an orchard wall that seemed too high and too doubtful to try and too difficult to permit their voyage to continue, they took off their hats and tossed them over the wall—and then they had no choice but to follow them.

　This Nation has tossed its cap over the wall of space, and we have no choice but to follow it. Whatever the difficulties, they will be overcome.
100　Whatever the hazards, they must be guarded against. With the vital help of this Aerospace Medical Center, with the help of all those who labor in the space endeavor, with the help and support of all Americans, we will climb this wall with safety and with speed—and we shall then explore the wonders on the other side. **F**

　Thank you.

---

3. **booster:** a rocket used to launch a spacecraft.
4. **payload:** the load carried by a rocket or other vehicle.

DIFFERENTIATED INSTRUCTION

FOR LESS–PROFICIENT READERS
Reading Strategy Follow-Up: Read a Speech
Have students work in pairs. Assign each pair a paragraph. Have them take turns reading the paragraph aloud to each other and listening for the strategies described in the chart from page 937. Have students record what they find on sticky notes next to their paragraph. Ask pairs to read their paragraphs aloud and share their details before adding them to the chart.

FOR ENGLISH LEARNERS
Comprehension: Task Support Check students' comprehension of President Kennedy's central argument by completing a summary chart.

Claim: Medicine in space will make people's lives better.
Example 1:
Example 2:
Example 3:
Summary:

Comprehension

1. **Recall** Who is in the audience that President Kennedy is speaking to?

2. **Clarify** Why does President Kennedy believe the United States needs to be a leader?

3. **Summarize** According to President Kennedy, what are three ways that medical research in space can make life on Earth better?

Critical Analysis

4. **Identify Audience** Reread lines 11–23. What does President Kennedy say to the audience members to make a strong connection with them?

5. **Identify a Counterargument** Reread lines 24–37. President Kennedy anticipates that his opponents will argue that research in space medicine competes for the natural resources we need to develop the earth. What counterargument does President Kennedy give?

6. **Examine Persuasive Techniques** Which of the four persuasive techniques listed on page 937 do you think President Kennedy uses most successfully? Give an example of how he uses this technique to **inspire** people.

7. **Evaluate a Speech** Review the chart that you made while you read. Explain the effect each strategy had on you. Was President Kennedy successful in keeping your interest? Why or why not?

8. **Compare Nonfiction** Both Gregg Easterbrook, author of "Why We Shouldn't Go To Mars," and President Kennedy try to influence people's beliefs about funding space-related programs. Use a Y chart to compare and contrast Easterbrook's and President Kennedy's reasons for their differing opinions.

Easterbrook
A mission to Mars will not give us things we can use on Earth.

President Kennedy
Space exploration will make our lives better.

Similarities

Extension and Challenge

9. **SCIENCE CONNECTION** Search the Internet for three everyday products that resulted from space-related research. Share your findings with the class.

 RESEARCH LINKS
For more on space research, visit the **Research Center** at ClassZone.com.

8. *Possible answers:*

- **Easterbrook:** *Sending people to Mars will not be of value to people on Earth. Current technology is too expensive and would take money from other programs. Mars missions should be privately funded.*

- **President Kennedy:** *Space research has value on Earth. Space research does not take money from other programs but produces more resources. The Saturn C-1 booster is proof of the space program's success.*

- **Similarities:** *Exploration and research in the past have "led to unexpected glories" such as the Lewis and Clark expedition and the wartime development of radar.*

Extension and Challenge

9. **SCIENCE CONNECTION**
Have students include explanations of how the products evolved from space research.

Practice and Apply

After Reading
For additional support of post-reading questions, use these copy masters:

R **RESOURCE MANAGER—Copy Masters**
Reading Check p. 176 (to check understanding of the selection)
Persuasive Techniques p. 169 (for practice of elements of nonfiction standards focus)
Question Support p. 177 (**After Reading** questions adapted for English learners and less-proficient readers)

Additional selection questions are provided for teachers on page 163.

ANSWERS
Comprehension

1. *The audience includes several federal and state officials and elected representatives and the men and women of the Aerospace Medical Center (lines 1–2).*

2. *The United States should be a leader because it is rich and powerful (lines 78–80).*

3. *Medical space research can help people improve their environment, develop new medical technology, and protect against the hazards of the environment.*

Critical Analysis
Possible answers:

4. *Kennedy compliments members of the audience, associating them with leaders in their fields and implying that they all are pioneers who are making history.*

5. *Kennedy responds that research in space medicine produces resources for Earth and will make our lives happier and healthier.*

6. ● **STANDARDS FOCUS** *Persuasive Techniques* *Students may say that appeals to emotion are used most effectively, including appeals to pity (small children with eye defects), fear (the hazard of radiation), and hope for the future (the New Frontier).*

7. ■ **STANDARDS FOCUS** *Reading a Speech* *Yes. The sound devices focus attention, the organization is clear and easy to follow, and the examples are relevant to people's lives. In addition, the use of direct address draws listeners in.*

ANSWERS

Vocabulary in Context

VOCABULARY PRACTICE

1. *endeavor*
2. *tedious*
3. *impairment*
4. *partisan*
5. *impetus*
6. *radar*
7. *disorientation*
8. *metabolism*

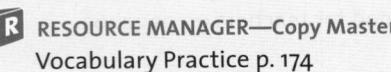 **RESOURCE MANAGER—Copy Master**
Vocabulary Practice p. 174

VOCABULARY IN WRITING

Have students review the speech and decide on a reason. Have them brainstorm ideas about why it was convincing before they choose vocabulary words and write their paragraphs.

VOCABULARY STRATEGY: ACRONYMS (also an EL language objective)

Have students work in pairs to look up the words.

Answers:

1. *d (Organization of Petroleum Exporting Countries)*
2. *e (light amplification by stimulated emission of radiation)*
3. *c (National Aeronautics and Space Administration)*
4. *b (United Nations International Children's Emergency Fund)*
5. *a (personal identification number)*

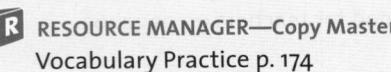 **RESOURCE MANAGER—Copy Master**
Vocabulary Strategy p. 175

ⓘ Vocabulary Center at **ClassZone.com**
Additional Vocabulary Activities

Vocabulary in Context

VOCABULARY PRACTICE

Choose the word from the list that best completes each sentence.

1. Sending people to the moon was a difficult _____ .
2. I would rather do anything else than that _____ job.
3. The wrestler used his _____ as an excuse to forfeit the match.
4. The senator was not reelected because of his _____ voting record.
5. The quest for advancement in medicine was a(n) _____ for space research.
6. The plane flew under the _____.
7. The astronaut's _____ grew worse as the rocket disappeared into space.
8. It is important to have a healthy _____ to live and grow.

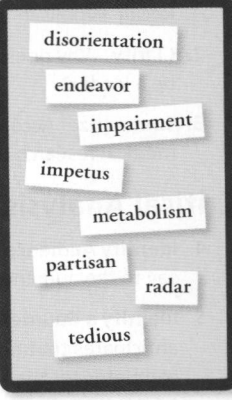

disorientation
endeavor
impairment
impetus
metabolism
partisan
radar
tedious

VOCABULARY IN WRITING

Which of President Kennedy's reasons for continuing the space program did you think was most convincing? Write a paragraph explaining your opinion, using at least three vocabulary words. You might begin this way.

> **EXAMPLE SENTENCE**
>
> I think improving the health of people on Earth is a great **impetus** for space research.

VOCABULARY STRATEGY: ACRONYMS

Acronyms are words that are formed from the first letters or syllables of other words. The vocabulary word *radar*, for example, is formed from the opening letters of <u>ra</u>dio <u>de</u>tection <u>a</u>nd <u>r</u>anging. As time passes and an acronym takes on its own meaning, its origin in many cases becomes less important.

PRACTICE Using a dictionary, match each acronym with the description of what it stands for. Then provide the actual words from which each acronym is formed.

1. OPEC   a. a safeguard to protect people's identity
2. laser   b. group that helps children around the world
3. NASA   c. group that works on aerospace development
4. UNICEF   d. group of countries that produce and sell oil
5. PIN   e. a very intense beam of light

 **MARYLAND OBJECTIVES**

READING STANDARD
1.D.3.c Use resources to gather further information about words

 **VOCABULARY PRACTICE**
For more practice, go to the **Vocabulary Center** at **ClassZone.com.**

DIFFERENTIATED INSTRUCTION

FOR ENGLISH LEARNERS

Vocabulary Practice Divide the vocabulary words into two groups according to whether they complete one of the first four sentences or one of the last four. Then have students take one group of words at a time and work on the corresponding sentences in pairs. Have pairs share their responses.

FOR ADVANCED LEARNERS/PRE–AP

Vocabulary Strategy Have small groups of students find additional acronyms and the words they represent. Then have students create crossword puzzles using the original phrases or names as clues. Have groups exchange puzzles and try to complete each other's.

Reading-Writing Connection

Explore the ideas presented in President Kennedy's speech by responding to these prompts. Then complete the **Grammar and Writing** exercise.

WRITING PROMPTS	SELF-CHECK

A. Short Response: Write a Letter
Write a **one-paragraph letter** to a congressional representative or senator arguing your position on funding space research with tax dollars.

▶

A strong letter will . . .
- clearly state your opinion and give specific reasons
- use a persuasive technique
- address opposing views

B. Extended Response: Write a Speech
Imagine that not long from now you're asked to give a speech at your class's graduation ceremony. Write a **two- or three-paragraph speech** to **inspire** your classmates to rise to a challenge.

▶

A strong response will . . .
- explain a challenge and its importance
- use a persuasive technique to inspire your audience

GRAMMAR AND WRITING

MARYLAND OBJECTIVES

LANGUAGE STANDARD
5.C.2. Apply standard English punctuation

USE COLONS CORRECTLY Colons have many uses. They indicate that a **list** follows (*I need to get the following groceries: bread, milk, and butter*). They are used after a **formal greeting** in a business letter (*Dear Madam:*). They also are used **between numerals** in expressions of time (*5:45*). When using a colon to introduce a list, avoid placing the colon directly after a verb or a preposition.

Original: Our new school provides: better opportunities, newer computers, and many activities.

Revised: Our new school provides the following: better opportunities, newer computers, and many activities. (*Inserting* the following *makes use of the colon correct.*)

PRACTICE In the following sentences, insert or delete colons where needed.

1. Some of the activities include the following an art club and a school newspaper.
2. We will meet at 11 00 A.M. today to discuss more of these activities.
3. We should be proud of: the support we've received, the high quality of our students, and the new facilities.
4. Please join me at 1 30 P.M. tomorrow to celebrate our new school.

For more help with using colons correctly, see page R50 in the ***Grammar Handbook.***

FOR LESS–PROFICIENT WRITERS

For Prompt A:
- Help students brainstorm reasons for and against continuing to fund space research. List the reasons in a two-column chart.
- Help students write their topic sentences. Then have them choose two or three reasons from the list as support.
- Discuss and list transitions that will help students unify their ideas, such as *in addition, furthermore,* and *also.*

For Prompt B:
- Limit the assignment to one paragraph.
- Suggest that students choose any context for their speeches. They might be giving a pregame speech to their sports team, encouraging classmates to join a project, or urging a friend to run for a class office.
- Have students identify what they want done and why before they write their speeches. Students may wish to work together or alone.

Reading-Writing Connection

WRITING PROMPTS
- For **Prompt A,** students might brainstorm their reasons first, using a Cluster Diagram, before they put them into a logical and effective order.
- For **Prompt B,** students might find it helpful to review the organization of President Kennedy's speech. Remind them to keep the attention of their listeners by using repetition and specific examples that will be meaningful to the lives of their audience.

BEST PRACTICES TOOLKIT—Transparency
   Cluster Diagram p. B18

For ideas for writing, see

ℹ Writing Center at **ClassZone.com**

GRAMMAR AND WRITING
Explain that a colon should not be used between a verb and its object or between a preposition and its object.

Possible answers:
1. *Some of the activities include the following: an art club and a school newspaper.*
2. *We will meet at 11:00 A.M. today to discuss more of these activities.*
3. *We should be proud of the support we've received, the high quality of our students, and the new facilities.*
4. *Please join me at 1:30 P.M. tomorrow to celebrate our new school.*

R RESOURCE MANAGER—Copy Master
   Use Colons Correctly p. 178

Assess and Reteach

Assess

R RESOURCE MANAGER—Copy Masters
   Selection Tests A, B/C pp. 181–182, 183–184
Test Generator CD

Reteach

S STANDARDS LESSON FILE
   Informational Texts Lesson 15: Persuasive Techniques

OBJECTIVES

Media Literacy

- explore the key concept of how persuasive techniques are used to **sell** products
- view two television advertisements to recognize and analyze persuasive techniques
- identify a target audience
- design a print ad

SUMMARY

Two commercials show how advertisers use various persuasive, visual, and sound techniques to sell products. In the Mountain Dew commercial, fast music plays as a parking valet drives recklessly through a parking garage, a can of Mountain Dew fueling his exhilaration. In the Kibbles 'n Bits commercial, two dogs walk down the street. The terrier jumps over the bulldog, excitedly repeating that they're having Kibbles 'n Bits for dinner.

How do you S E L L *an idea?*

Discuss the question. To help students explore the **KEY IDEA**, ask them about ads they've seen recently. What is each ad trying to **sell**? What techniques do advertisers use to make their products seem appealing? Discuss the creative use of language, images and visual techniques, and music and sound effects.

BACKGROUND

The creation of a mainstream TV commercial is a complicated and expensive process. A typical ad campaign can cost millions. A commercial usually begins with creative people at an ad agency brainstorming ideas. The creative team puts together rough drawings and a script to present to advertising account managers and to the client who is selling the product. The concept goes through many editorial stages before actors are hired and production begins. When an ad is completed—if not before—it goes through test-marketing, after which more changes are made. Finally, time slots are purchased for the ad. An ad will run for as long as it seems to be effective in selling the product.

Media Study

Persuasive Techniques in Commercials

TV Commercials on  **MediaSmart** DVD

How do you SELL *an idea?*

MARYLAND OBJECTIVES

INFORMATIONAL TEXT STANDARD
2.A.6.f Analyze language and other techniques intended to persuade

KEY IDEA From the latest gadgets to the trendiest pair of shoes, advertisers want you to buy their products. They will use many persuasive tools to get your attention. In this lesson, you'll watch two TV commercials that will help you explore the techniques advertisers use to **sell** practically everything.

Background

To Buy or Not to Buy Ads are everywhere. They're on trains, buses, buildings, and even stadium walls. Think about the **logos,** the symbols or names of companies, that appear on your clothes and shoes. Right now, you may be a walking advertisement.

Each year, companies spend billions of dollars on TV commercials that showcase products and services. The first TV commercial you'll view is for Mountain Dew, a popular soft drink. The second commercial is for Kibbles 'n Bits, a well-known brand of dog food.

944

Media Study Resources

R RESOURCE MANAGER UNIT 8

Plan and Teach pp. 185–188

Media Analysis
Summary pp. 189†*, 190‡*
Viewing Guide p. 191
Close Viewing p. 192
Viewing Activity p. 193
Produce Your Own Media p. 194

S STANDARDS LESSON FILE

Media Lesson 13: Understanding the Basics of Advertising
Media Lesson 15: Analyzing Persuasive Techniques in Advertising
Media Lesson 16: Evaluating Ads

 Media Center at **ClassZone.com**

MEDIA VIEWING
Media*Smart* DVD

---

* Resources for Differentiation   † Also in Spanish   ‡ In Haitian Creole and Vietnamese

Media Literacy: Persuasion in Advertising

Advertisers carefully design TV ads with a specific audience in mind. A **target audience** is one that sponsors want to persuade. Members of a target audience share certain features, such as age, gender, ethnic background, values, or lifestyle. Advertisers rely on certain **persuasive techniques,** which are methods used to convince a target audience to buy products. Here are some things to think about when you're analyzing TV commercials.

STRATEGIES FOR ANALYZING TV COMMERCIALS

Persuasive Techniques

- Notice how some ads use words to appeal to your sense of reason, while other ads appeal to your emotions. **Emotional appeals** create strong feelings, such as happiness, sadness, or excitement. For example, if a commercial makes you laugh, chances are you'll remember the product and the commercial.
- Watch for ads that tell viewers that everyone is using their product. The **bandwagon** technique appeals to people's desire to fit in or be accepted.
- Listen for **repetition.** Repeated words help viewers remember a product.

Visual Techniques

- Notice the use of **color.** Colors can create certain feelings about a product. For example, blue is often used to create a fresh or peaceful feeling.
- Think about how commercials are **edited.** Each shot is carefully selected and arranged to create a persuasive effect. The **pace,** or length of time each shot stays on the screen, is often designed to express excitement.

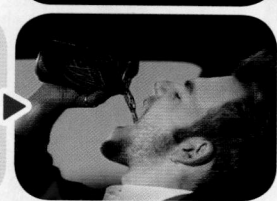

Sound Techniques

- Pay attention to the **music.** For example, an upbeat, popular song might be used to make a product seem exciting.
- Listen for **sound effects,** such as the screeching of tires, the sizzling of a burger, or the popping and fizzing of a soft drink. Sound effects are often used to make a product more appealing or to grab viewers' attention.
- Listen closely to what the voice in the commercial (called a **voice-over**) is saying. The details that viewers hear about a product are just as important as the carefully designed images.

MEDIA STUDY **945**

MEDIA STUDY: TEACHING OPTIONS

Teaching Option 1: The Basics (1–2 Days)

1. Begin the Media Study using the material provided on pages 944–945.
2. Show the Introduction on Media*Smart.* Then show the First Viewing. As they watch, have students use the Viewing Guide on page 946, along with the corresponding copy master on page 191 of the Resource Manager. Discuss their responses.
3. Return to the pupil edition for the extension activities on page 947.

Teaching Option 2: In-Depth Study (2–3 Days)

1. Begin the Media Study using pages 944–945.
2. Show the Introduction and First Viewing from Media*Smart.*
3. Continue on Media*Smart* with the Media Lessons, using the teacher notes available in the Resources section.
4. Show the Guided Analysis presentation. Have students record their observations on the Student Viewing Guide available in the Resources section from Media*Smart.*
5. Return to the pupil edition, page 947.

Teach

MEDIA LITERACY

Review the definitions of *target audience* and *persuasive techniques* and ask students to recall moments from particularly interesting and persuasive TV ads. Ask: What made those ads memorable and effective for you? On the board, list the answers they generate, such as *good music, humor, convincing pictures or video, sound effects,* and *action.* Then discuss the chart on page 945.

- **Persuasive Techniques** Work with students to brainstorm advertising scenarios that appeal to emotion, reason, or the desire to be accepted. For example, an ad for a medication that uses charts and medical terminology appeals to reason, while an ad that shows video images of people dancing, smiling, and having fun appeals more to emotion. An ad that uses the bandwagon appeal might show a middle school student, an astronaut, an artist, and a retired person all listening to the same kind of portable music device.

- **Visual Techniques** Discuss how color and pacing can be used to move viewers. For example, an ad with bright yellow tones might create a happy feeling, while red might suggest passion or drama. An ad that uses blue tones might be edited at a slow pace to emphasize the peaceful feeling.

- **Sound Techniques** Discuss the range of sound effects and music that students hear in commercials. Ask what sounds they associate with ads for certain food or beverage items, such as the crunch of chips or the sound of beverages being opened and poured. What effect are these sounds supposed to have on viewers? Also discuss how an advertiser might use music to appeal to different target audiences.

S STANDARDS LESSON FILE

Media Lesson 13: Understanding the Basics of Advertising
Media Lesson 15: Analyzing Persuasive Techniques in Advertising
Media Lesson 16: Evaluating Ads

Media*Smart* DVD

VIEWING GUIDE

1. As students prepare to view the clips, tell them that they will be asked to identify persuasive techniques the advertisers used to appeal to target audiences. Encourage them to watch and listen for the following elements:

   - **repetition** to encourage viewers to re-member a product
   - careful **editing** to express a particular emotion
   - **music** and **sound effects** to create a par-ticular mood and make an impression

2. After students view the clips once, you might want to help them focus on visual techniques by having them watch the clips without sound. Students can pay attention to the images on the screen to figure out what ideas they convey. To help them pay more attention to music and sound, have them listen to the clips without watching the images.

R RESOURCE MANAGER—Copy Masters
   Viewing Guide p. 191
   Close Viewing p. 192
   Viewing Activity p. 193

MediaSmart DVD

ANSWERS

FIRST VIEWING: Comprehension

1. *In the Mountain Dew commercial, a young parking valet drives away in a car owned by a man in a suit. He drives fast and reck-lessly through the parking garage, jumps to the roof of another building, and drinks Mountain Dew. In the dog food commer-cial, a bulldog and a terrier walk home next to each other. The terrier jumps back and forth over the bulldog's back and promises they will eat Kibbles 'n Bits when they get home. The commercial shows images of the food and its ingredients.*

2. **Possible answer:** *The music is loud and has a lot of energy. Viewers can hear the sound of brakes squealing and the car landing on the pavement.*

- **MediaSmart** DVD
  - **Commercial 1:** "Mountain Dew"
  - **Commercial 2:** "Kibbles 'n Bits"
  - **Genre:** Advertisement

946

CLOSE VIEWING: Media Literacy
Possible answers:

3. *The fast-paced editing goes with the way the boy is driving the car and gives viewers the idea that people who drink Mountain Dew are exciting, fast, and energetic.*

4. *The music creates an image of youth, reck-lessness, excitement, and energy.*

Viewing Guide for
TV Commercials

The first TV commercial is a Mountain Dew ad that begins at the entrance of a parking lot. As you view the ad, pay attention to music and sound effects. The second commercial is entitled "Spike and Speck II." The ad follows two dogs on their way to dinner. Notice persuasive techniques that help make this commercial memorable.

   To help you analyze how persuasive techniques are used in TV commercials, view each ad more than once and answer the following questions.

NOW VIEW

FIRST VIEWING: Comprehension

1. **Summarize** Describe what happens in each commercial.

2. **Recall** Describe the music and sound effects that are used in the Mountain Dew ad.

CLOSE VIEWING: Media Literacy

3. **Analyze Visual Techniques** The Mountain Dew ad uses fast-paced **editing**. What is the effect of using this technique?

4. **Analyze Sound Techniques** Music is often used to create an image for a product. For example, the use of classical music can create an image of elegance and class. What kind of image do you think the **music** creates in the Mountain Dew ad?

5. **Evaluate Persuasive Techniques** Do you think the technique of **repetition** is effective in the Kibbles 'n Bits commercial? Why or why not? Think about the following:

   - how repetition may affect viewers' memories
   - the kind of emotional appeal advertisers might be making by using a repeated word or phrase.

5. *Yes, the repetition helps viewers remember the name of the dog food. When viewers are at the store, they can easily recall the name of the food described in the commer-cial. The way the terrier repeats "it's Bits" also suggests the dog's enthusiasm for the product, and viewers may want their dogs to feel a similar excitement about their food.*

Write or Discuss

Evaluating TV Commercials Consider the commercials in this lesson. Which one do you think is more effective at grabbing your attention and helping you remember the product? As part of your response think about

- how the visual elements help the product stand out
- how the sound techniques trigger certain emotions
- how the persuasive techniques influence how you feel about the product

Produce Your Own Media

Designing a Print Ad Imagine that you are part of an advertising team whose job it is to create a magazine **print ad** for a major company. In small groups, choose one product from the list and create your own print ad.

- Turbo Racer (video game)
- Raisin Oatbran O's (healthy cereal)
- Zoom (running shoes)
- Dazzle (toothpaste)
- Pep (energy snack bar)
- Essence (bottled water)

> **MEDIA TOOLS**
> For help with designing print ads, visit the **Media Center** at ClassZone.com.

HERE'S HOW Before you create your ad, consider where you will place the product and how much space it will take up on the page. To help you create the ad, think about the following suggestions:

- Determine who will be the target audience—for example, teens, athletes, parents, or young children.
- Use persuasive techniques that will make your ad more appealing.
- Use visual techniques, such as color, that will draw attention to your product.

STUDENT MODEL

Tech Tip

Search the Internet for clip art and other images that can be used in your ad.

Assess and Reteach

Write or Discuss

Evaluating TV Commercials In their evaluations, students should show an understanding of persuasive, sound, and visual techniques and how these techniques are used to create an effective advertisement. Students should be specific about what elements are present in each commercial and why one commercial might be more effective than the other. For example, a student might note that the dog food commercial makes use of repetition and uses vivid images of the product. The Mountain Dew commercial, on the other hand, does not feature the actual product as often. It uses music, sound, and fast-paced editing to create a certain mood. The advertisers are equating the product with a particular lifestyle.

Produce Your Own Media

Rubric A strong print ad should have

- a clear target audience
- persuasive language that makes the ad appealing
- visual elements that help the product stand out

R **RESOURCE MANAGER—Copy Master**
Produce Your Own Media p. 194

MediaSmart DVD

MEDIA STUDY WRAP–UP

Ask students to summarize the techniques television advertisers use to sell their products to target audiences. Have them describe persuasive, visual, and sound techniques. In talking about persuasive techniques, students should touch on the use of emotional appeals, the bandwagon approach, and repetition. When talking about visual and sound techniques, students should discuss the use of color, editing for pace, music, sound effects, and voice-over. Have them provide specific examples of techniques from the commercials they viewed.

RETEACH

S **STANDARDS LESSON FILE**
Media Lesson 13: Understanding the Basics of Advertising
Media Lesson 15: Analyzing Persuasive Techniques in Advertising
Media Lesson 16: Evaluating Ads

Focus and Motivate

OBJECTIVES

- analyze a student model that reflects the key traits of persuasive writing
- use the writing process to produce a persuasive essay
- revise and edit, using a rubric for persuasive writing
- deliver a persuasive speech

WRITER'S ROAD MAP

WRITING PROMPTS 1 AND 2

Help students choose a prompt by reviewing topics from the unit or brainstorming issues from the school or local newspaper. Point out that these issues often bring out strong feelings on both sides. Students' essays must show respect for opposing viewpoints.

ADDITIONAL PROMPTS

Use these prompts for practice with writing persuasive essays:

WRITING PROMPT 3

Writing for the Real World Write a persuasive essay for your school newspaper. Your essay should include convincing details to support your position.

Subjects to Consider
- a proposal to lengthen the school day
- a proposal to change the school dress code
- a proposal to eliminate field trips

WRITING PROMPT 4

Writing from Your Life The town council has asked you to give a speech before their next vote. In order to be persuasive, you must include convincing reasons.

Ideas to Consider
- a curfew for persons under age 16
- a skateboarding ban on public sidewalks
- a proposal to close the public library on weekends

For additional writing prompts, see

 WriteSmart CD

 Writing Center at **ClassZone.com**

KEY TRAITS

Review the six **KEY TRAITS,** focusing primarily on ideas and organization. Compare these traits with the rubric on page 954.

Writing Workshop

Persuasive Essay

The writers in this unit have explored real-life issues and taken firm, clear positions on them. Taking a stand, however, was only the beginning of what they did. To persuade, they also gave reasons, explained and supported their ideas, and used logical arguments. The **Writer's Road Map** will show you how to do the same.

WRITER'S ROAD MAP

Persuasive Essay

WRITING PROMPT 1

Writing for the Real World Have you ever been treated unfairly? Have you noticed injustices you want to speak up about? Choose an issue you feel strongly about. Write a persuasive essay in which you explain the issue and attempt to persuade your reader to agree with your point of view.

Issues to Explore
- school locker searches
- discrimination in various forms
- banning junk food on school property

WRITING PROMPT 2

Writing from Literature Sometimes you read something that gives you a whole new way to think about an issue. Using a selection in this unit as a springboard, write a persuasive essay about an issue that interests you.

Issues to Explore
- salaries of professional athletes ("Do Professional Athletes Get Paid Too Much?")
- funding for space travel ("Why We Shouldn't Go to Mars")

WRITING TOOLS
For prewriting, revision, and editing tools, visit the **Writing Center** at ClassZone.com.

KEY TRAITS

1. IDEAS
- Presents a **thesis statement** that makes a **claim** about a clearly identified issue
- Uses convincing details to **support** the position
- Answers **opposing arguments** and counterclaims

2. ORGANIZATION
- Explains the issue in a memorable **introduction**
- Uses **transitions** to create a consistent **organizational pattern**
- Concludes by **summarizing** the position or issuing a **call to action**

3. VOICE
- Reflects the writer's **commitment** to his or her ideas

4. WORD CHOICE
- Uses **persuasive language** effectively

5. SENTENCE FLUENCY
- Varies **sentence lengths** and **structures**

6. CONVENTIONS
- Uses **correct grammar, spelling, and punctuation**

Writing Workshop Resources

RESOURCE MANAGER UNIT 8
Plan and Teach pp. 195–198
Prewriting–Editing pp. 199–203
Writing Rubric p. 204
Speaking and Listening p. 205
Writing Support p. 206*

STANDARDS LESSON FILE
Writing Lessons 19, 22, 34, 40, 47
Speaking and Listening Lesson 1

BEST PRACTICES TOOLKIT
Scaffolding Writing Instruction pp. 43–46*
Persuasive Writing Template: Proposal

TECHNOLOGY
- Easy Planner DVD
- Writing Center at **ClassZone.com**
- WriteSmart CD

* Resources for Differentiation

Part 1: Analyze a Student Model

WRITING STANDARD
4.A.2.d Compose to persuade

Mehmet Alzein
Rockland Junior High School

Homework: Let's Do One Thing at a Time

My literature book weighs almost five pounds. My social studies book weighs three pounds. Carrying home a stack of books each night is hard work. I also have so many assignments that I have trouble keeping track of them all. That is why teachers in English, math,
5 science, and social studies should each give homework only once every four nights. That way, backpacks will be lighter, students can give their full attention to just one subject per night, and teachers can assign more in-depth work.

The most obvious reason for giving homework in just one subject
10 per night is the weight of textbooks. Studies have shown that heavy backpacks can be painful and harmful. Overloaded packs can even cause students to fall. Our school nurse says that children are having back pain at earlier and earlier ages because of heavy backpacks. She recommends using bags with wheels instead, but they are expensive. If
15 teachers rotated nights for homework, each student would carry home materials for just one subject per night. Students would avoid back injuries and pain.

A second reason for giving homework in just one subject per night is that students can focus all their attention on that subject.
20 Students shouldn't race through four or more assignments. Instead, they should concentrate on just one. Students who have more time are able to do better work. They can plan, research, review, revise, or double-check their assignments.

KEY TRAITS IN ACTION

Introduction is unusual and memorable.

Thesis statement presents a **claim** (also called an opinion or a position) on a clearly defined issue.

Convincing details **support** each reason and show the writer's **commitment** to his idea.

Transitions help the reader see the **organizational pattern**.

Teach

Part 1: Analyze a Student Model

Have students read the **Student Model** and **Key Traits in Action.** Then discuss the model with the class, focusing on specific examples of each trait. You may also wish to incorporate the following activities:

- **Thesis Statement** Tell students that a strong thesis statement lets readers know exactly what the essay will be about. Help them analyze the highlighted thesis statement (lines 4–8) by asking these questions:

  What basic issue does the writer intend to discuss? *(homework in English, math, science, and social studies)*

  What is the writer's claim about this issue? *(Homework in each subject should be given only once every four nights.)*

  How does the second sentence help organize the rest of the essay? *(It lists three reasons to support the writer's opinion. These reasons will be explored in the body of the essay.)*

- **Support** Write this sentence on the board: *I don't like carrying a heavy backpack every night.* Ask students to compare it to lines 10–13 of the model. Which provides better support for the writer's claim? How does the model show a greater commitment to the writer's idea? *(The model is more convincing because it uses two sources, studies and the nurse. It shows commitment because the writer has taken time to research the issue rather than just stating a personal opinion.)*

DIFFERENTIATED INSTRUCTION

FOR ALL STUDENTS
For general guidelines on differentiating writing instruction, see

 BEST PRACTICES TOOLKIT
Scaffolding Writing Instruction
pp. 43–46

FOR ENGLISH LEARNERS
Language: Skill Words Write these terms on the board and review them with students:

- *thesis statement:* in a persuasive essay, one or two sentences that state the writer's opinion on a topic and briefly give reasons

- *convincing details:* facts, examples, reasons, and research that persuade the reader to agree with the writer's position

- *commitment:* the feeling that the writer has studied his or her topic and feels strongly about it

- *transitions:* words or phrases that connect one idea to another (for example, *a second reason* [line 18]; *another argument* [line 36])

- *organizational pattern:* the particular order in which information is presented

- *call to action:* writing that encourages readers to do something specific

- **Opposing Arguments** Point out that the topics discussed in persuasive essays have reasons both for and against. The writer of the model does not ignore opposing arguments. Help students locate these two opposing arguments in the model:

  "They say students will have to juggle many assignments in college and the working world." (lines 32–33)

  "Another argument against rotating assignments is that it is better to review material every night." (lines 36–37)

  Be sure students notice that the writer does not make fun of opposing views, but rather reasons against them. Discuss how the writer refutes each opposing argument. *(Argument 1: Students have time to learn "juggling" skills in high school. It is not worth risking injury. Argument 2: If students focus on one class at a time, they will learn to concentrate.)*

- **Sentence Structures** Write this sentence on the board: *These skills are not worth the cost of injuring a student's back.* Ask students to compare it to line 35 of the model. Explain that the question in the model is rhetorical—the answer is assumed to be obvious. Have them discuss why the question is a more effective choice in the essay. *(The question provides variety in sentence structure. Also, it emphasizes the writer's commitment to the thesis and presents the idea in a more engaging and persuasive manner. Most readers would not want to answer yes to the question, so the writer's point is proved.)*

- **Call to Action** Remind students that the purpose of a persuasive essay is to convince someone to agree with the writer's position. Ask: To whom is the model essay directed? What action is urged? *(The essay addresses teachers and urges them to start rotating homework assignments immediately.)*

For interactive student models, see

- WriteSmart CD
- Writing Center at **ClassZone.com**

A third reason for limiting homework to just one subject per
25 night is that teachers can give longer, more in-depth assignments. For
example, a student might read a whole chapter of a science textbook
instead of just one section. Reading everything at once will help
students see how the material is related from section to section. A
student might also read, outline, and answer questions on the same
30 night.

Some people argue that students should have several assignments
each night. They say students will have to juggle many assignments in
college and in the working world. These skills, however, do not need
to be taught in junior high; there is time for that in high school.
35 Also, are these skills worth the cost of injuring a student's back?

Another argument against rotating assignments is that it is better to
review material every night. If teachers always expect nightly reviews of
every subject, however, students will never learn to concentrate on just
one thing for a long time. As it is, students are always flipping channels.
40 They instant-message several kids at once. Students already know how
to bounce from one thing to the next. Let's focus on one class at a time
so we learn to concentrate, too.

For all these reasons, teachers should start rotating homework
assignments immediately. Rotating assignments in the four major
45 subject areas will result in healthier students and better thinkers.

> Another **transition** introduces the third reason.

> The writer answers **opposing arguments** and counterclaims that opponents might have. He also varies **sentence lengths** and **structures** effectively.

> The writer uses **persuasive language,** including lively words (*flipping, bounce, focus, concentrate*) and examples from his everyday life.

> A strongly stated **call to action** and a brief **summary** conclude the essay.

2

950 UNIT 8: INFORMATION, ARGUMENT, AND PERSUASION

DIFFERENTIATED INSTRUCTION

FOR ENGLISH LEARNERS

Comprehension: Transitions Display the outline for a persuasive argument and a list of appropriate transitional phrases—*the first reason, the second reason, the third reason,* and so on. Have pairs use the information to write a paragraph with transitions.

We should paint the classroom walls yellow.
 —It is a bright color.
 —Yellow reminds me of the sun.
 —Yellow makes me feel happy.

Possible answer: The first reason to paint the classroom yellow is that it is a bright color. The second reason is that yellow reminds me of the sun. A third reason is that yellow makes me feel happy.

For further practice with transitions, use

 RESOURCE MANAGER—Copy Master
Writing Support p. 206

Part 2: Apply the Writing Process

WRITING STANDARD
4.A.1 Compose texts using prewriting and drafting strategies

PREWRITING

What Should I Do?

1. Analyze the prompt.
Read the prompt carefully. (Circle) the type of writing you must do. Underline other important details, such as information about your purpose and audience. Make notes to help you understand and interpret the prompt.

2. List issues that matter to you.
You must show your strong commitment to your ideas, so write about an issue you truly care about.

TIP Be sure there are two sides to the topic you choose. You can't write a persuasive essay if everybody already agrees with you.

3. Write a thesis statement.
In persuasive writing, your thesis is the claim you are making, and it belongs in your introduction. You can revise your thesis as you draft and edit your essay.

4. Decide on your reasons and support.
You need strong, clear reasons for your opinion. Reasons aren't enough to persuade, though. In addition, you need explanations, evidence, facts, or statistics that help your reader understand why, how, and what for.

What Does It Look Like?

WRITING PROMPT Choose an issue you feel strongly about. Write a persuasive essay in which you explain the issue and attempt to persuade your reader to agree with your point of view.

The audience is not specified, so I must be writing for my teacher and classmates.

Issues I Care About
price of tickets for sports events
too much homework every night and too many books to carry
school starting way too early
cheating (one-sided issue: nobody supports cheating)

Working thesis statement:
We should rotate homework so we have assignments in English, math, science, and social studies once every four nights.

Reason	Support
heavy textbooks	all books + all notebooks = back pain, injuries, falls
concentrate on one thing	more time to research, study, review, revise
teachers able to give longer, tougher assignments	helps students see how ideas are related

FOR ENGLISH LEARNERS
Write a Thesis Statement Give students the following sentence frames to help them create a working thesis and gather support for their main arguments:

- My topic is _____.
- My opinion about this topic is _____.
- One reason for my opinion is _____.
- Some facts to support my first reason are _____.
- A second reason for my opinion is _____.

FOR ADVANCED LEARNERS/PRE–AP
Write for Publication Suggest that students take a stand on a controversial issue important to young people. Be sure that some will argue for and others will argue against. Encourage students to submit their completed essays to the school or local newspaper, to the school administration, or to local government officials. Post published essays as well as any responses that might be received.

Practice and Apply

To support students during the writing process, use these copy masters:

R RESOURCE MANAGER—Copy Masters
Prewriting–Editing pp. 199–203
Writing Rubric p. 204
Speaking and Listening p. 205
Writing Support p. 206 *(for English learners)*

Part 2: Apply the Writing Process

PREWRITING

1. Analyze the prompt. Be sure students understand what the prompt is asking them to produce. Four key action words are *choose, write, explain,* and *persuade.* Remind them that their teacher and their classmates are the intended audience.

2. List issues that matter to you. Point out that if students convey their enthusiasm for their topic to the audience, they are more likely to be persuasive. Encourage students to work together with brainstorming diagrams or other organizers to help them generate ideas. Remind students of the **TIP** in step 2.

3. Write a thesis statement. Have students work in pairs to get feedback on their working thesis statements, keeping these questions in mind:

Is the topic for the paper clear?
Is the topic interesting?
Is the writer's claim about the topic clear?
What evidence could the writer use to be persuasive?

4. Decide on your reasons and support. Make a variety of resources available to students. They might need to consult encyclopedias or other reference books or do some online research. Also suggest that students interview a person with specialized knowledge about their topic.

For interactive graphic organizers, see

Write Smart CD

Writing Center at **ClassZone.com**

DRAFTING

1. Plan your organization. Help students understand some of the advantages and challenges of each type of organization.

- **Pattern 1** presents all the reasons for without interruption. However, a reader might think of reasons against and not learn how the writer counters those arguments until later in the essay.

- **Pattern 2** gives immediate responses to each reason against. This organization is more direct, but the writer must be sure that all the reasons for, which are scattered throughout the essay, are clearly emphasized.

2. Use persuasive language. Advise students to avoid personal references to those who may disagree with their position. They can do this by concentrating on reasons. Provide these examples of personal references to avoid:

- All those who disagree with my position are stupid.
- Only a fool would disagree with my conclusion.
- There must be something wrong with anyone who cannot understand my point.

3. Provide supporting evidence. Remind students to present any facts, quotations, or statistics accurately.

4. Answer each opposing argument fully and completely. Have students work in small groups. As each student reads his or her draft aloud, have the other students make a list of opposing arguments raised. Have them discuss whether or not each argument is effectively countered. Where necessary, ask them to make suggestions for improvement.

For persuasive writing templates, see

- BEST PRACTICES TOOLKIT—Transparency
  Writing Template: Proposal pp. C16, C37
- WriteSmart CD
- Writing Center at ClassZone.com

What Should I Do?

1. Plan your organization.
You can organize your ideas by explaining all your reasons and then dealing with the opposing reasons (pattern 1). Another approach is to discuss both sides of each point or reason as you present it (pattern 2).

2. Use persuasive language.
No one needs to shout to persuade, but your sentences should sound firm and strong. They should say, between the lines, "I'm sure" or "I know." Notice how the writer states his ideas with confidence and certainty.

3. Provide supporting evidence.
Explain your reasons. You can use examples, statistics, quotations, and facts. You can quote or describe the ideas of experts.

4. Answer each opposing argument fully and completely.
Explain why you disagree with opposing viewpoints. Help your reader dismiss the ideas that might cause disagreement.

What Does It Look Like?

PATTERN 1

A. Arguments for
1. lighter backpacks
2. longer, more in-depth assignments

B. Arguments against
1. juggling assignments prepares kids for college, work
2. important to review material every night

PATTERN 2

A. Lighter backpacks
1. for: avoid injuries
2. against: use wheeled bags to avoid injuries

B. In-depth assignments
1. for: can see how ideas are related
2. against: important to review teaching every night

If teachers rotated nights for homework, each student would carry home materials for just one subject per night. Students would avoid back injuries and pain.

For all these reasons, teachers should start rotating homework assignments immediately.

Studies have shown that heavy backpacks can be painful and harmful. Our school nurse says that children are having back pain at earlier and earlier ages because of heavy backpacks.

Opposing argument: Kids have to learn to organize. These skills do not need to be taught in junior high. There is time for that in high school.

---

952   UNIT 8: INFORMATION, ARGUMENT, AND PERSUASION

DIFFERENTIATED INSTRUCTION

FOR LESS—PROFICIENT WRITERS

Provide Supporting Evidence Explain that an essay will be more effective if it uses various types of supporting evidence, including examples, statistics, quotations, facts, and ideas of experts. Place these sentences on the board and ask students to identify what type of evidence each one is:

- 75 percent of students responding to the survey are opposed to Saturday detention. (statistic)

- My older brother works on Saturdays and would not be able to serve a detention without losing money. (example)

- Mr. Brady, the principal, stated, "Saturday detention will reduce the number of discipline problems." (quotation)

- Central School tried Saturday detention, but there were so many problems that they went back to after-school detention. (fact)

REVISING AND EDITING

What Should I Do?	What Does It Look Like?
1. Correct circular reasoning. Circular reasoning is supporting a statement by merely repeating it in different words. Ask a peer reader to point out examples of circular reasoning. Add facts and reasons to support your statements. See page 954: More Errors in Reasoning	▶ *A third reason for limiting homework to just one subject per night is that ~~limited homework is better~~: teachers can give longer, more in-depth assignments.*
2. Make sure your support makes sense and is fully explained. • (Circle) the facts, examples, and other details you used to support each reason. • If you don't have many circles, decide what you can do to tell your reader more.	▶ *Another argument against rotating assignments is that it is better to review material every night. If teachers always expect nightly reviews of every subject, however,* (students will never learn to concentrate) *on just one thing for a long time. As it is, students are always flipping channels. They instant-message several kids at once. Students already know how to bounce from one thing to the next. Let's focus on one class at a time so we learn to concentrate, too.*
3. Revise for more persuasive language. • Use precise words instead of vague ones, such as *really* and *very*. • Hold your reader's attention by asking a question or making a suggestion.	▶ *~~Maybe these skills aren't really that important.~~ Are these skills worth the cost of injuring a student's back?*
4. Craft a strong ending. • Include a call to action that tells your reader what he or she should do. • You may also want to make your point one more time in a brief summary statement.	▶ *For all these reasons, teachers should ~~maybe think about what I'm saying here,~~ start rotating homework assignments immediately.* *Rotating assignments in the four major subject areas ~~is the best idea for students and teachers~~. will result in healthier students and better thinkers.*

REVISING AND EDITING

1. **Correct circular reasoning.** Suggest that students look at **More Errors in Reasoning** on page 954. Discuss why this example is faulty reasoning: *I use Brand X toothpaste and I had no cavities at my last check-up.* Ask students to recall other examples from ads or commercials.

2. **Make sure your support makes sense and is fully explained.** Caution students that when they tell the reader more, they must provide additional support for their reasons and not irrelevant details. Students also need to guard against providing so many details that the most important point becomes overshadowed.

3. **Revise for more persuasive language.** For practice, have students revise these sentences to make them more precise and persuasive:

   The price of the tickets is kind of high. (*A price of $50 per ticket is too high for most students.*)

   Increasing taxes might be a good thing. (*Is keeping taxes low more important than funding a summer program for youth?*)

4. **Craft a strong ending.** Remind students that the purpose of a persuasive essay is not only to convince the reader to agree with a position, but also to get the reader to act on his or her beliefs. Discuss appropriate actions that a persuasive essay might encourage—such as voting, attending a meeting, writing a letter, changing a behavior, or convincing others.

For interactive revision tools, see

🖉 Write*Smart* CD

ℹ Writing Center at **ClassZone.com**

FOR ENGLISH LEARNERS

Revise for More Precise Language Provide additional practice by using these examples of vague wording and the accompanying frames for revision:

• The problem is bad.

   _____ is a serious problem because _____.

• Someone should do something about it.

   _____ should _____ the broken swings in the playground.

• A lot of people feel the same way that I do.

   _____ believe(s) that _____ should be done.

• All the cool kids think that it would be great.

   _____, who is an expert on _____, believes that _____ would solve the problem.

Preparing to Publish

Support for meeting the goals in the writing rubric is supplied throughout the **Writing Workshop** on pages 949–953.

For Rubric Bank, see

💿 Write*Smart* CD

ℹ️ Writing Center at **ClassZone.com**

Assess and Reteach

After reading and assessing students' descriptive essays, you might use these lessons to reteach key skills:

S STANDARDS LESSON FILE

Writing Lesson 19: Transitions
Writing Lesson 22: Writing Introductions
Writing Lesson 34: Persuasive Writing
Writing Lesson 40: Elaborate with Facts and Statistics
Writing Lesson 47: Finding a Voice

Preparing to Publish — Persuasive Essay

Apply the Rubric

A strong persuasive essay . . .

☑ has a thesis statement that takes a clear stand on an issue

☑ presents reasons and convincing details that support the thesis

☑ organizes points clearly and links them with transitions

☑ answers opponents' arguments and counterclaims

☑ reflects the writer's strong beliefs

☑ uses persuasive and accurate language

☑ varies sentence lengths and structures

☑ concludes with a summary or a call to action

Ask a Peer Reader

• How can I state my thesis more clearly?

• How could I make my arguments more persuasive?

• Where have I made mistakes in reasoning?

More Errors in Reasoning

False cause: thinking that one event led to another just because the second event followed the first ("Draper School rotates assignments, and they beat us in the spelling bee.")

Either/or fallacy: a statement that suggests there are only two choices available ("Either we accept my plan, or students will suffer.")

Check Your Grammar

The pronouns *who* and *whom* can be confusing. If you can substitute the subject pronoun *he, she,* or *they* for the interrogative word, use *who.*

> Who wants to carry such a heavy backpack?
> She wants to carry such a heavy backpack.

If you can answer a question with the object pronoun *him, her,* or *them,* use *whom,* not *who.*

> Whom do you know with back pain?
> I know her.

See page R54: Interrogative Pronouns

Writing Online

PUBLISHING OPTIONS
For publishing options, visit the **Writing Center** at **ClassZone.com.**

ASSESSMENT PREPARATION
For writing and grammar assessment practice, go to the **Assessment Center** at **ClassZone.com.**

SPEAKING STANDARD
7.A.1 Demonstrate appropriate delivery techniques for oral presentations

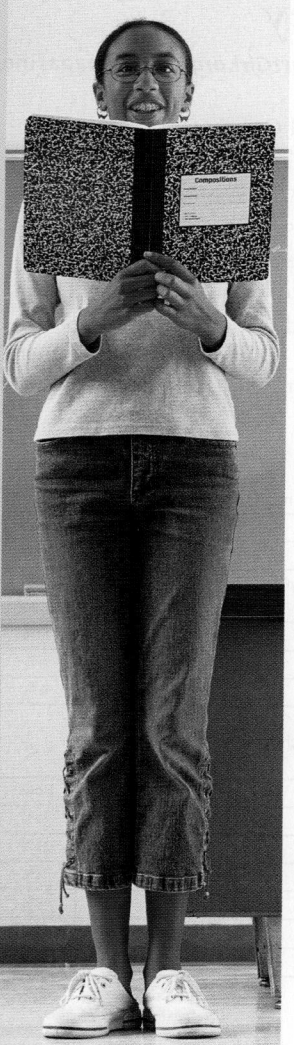

Delivering a Persuasive Speech

Follow these steps to turn your essay into a persuasive speech.

Planning the Speech

1. **Make notes on your essay.** Mark the points you want to make in your speech. Try out different ways of stating them persuasively.
2. **Write your script.** Start with a strong introduction. Begin with an interesting little story, some startling statistics, or a bit of humor. Then state your opinion. Continue with strong, well-supported reasons. Wrap it up with a brief summary and a powerful call to action.
3. **Create a visual aid.** Put your main points on a poster—or prepare transparencies or screens for use with an overhead projector or a power presentation. Remember that as you display each point, you'll need to present the information that explains and supports it.

Backpack Safety

- Heavy backpacks cause injuries.
- No one should carry more than 25 pounds.

4. **Use strong, positive language.** Your audience should know how you feel about the topic, why you feel that way, and what you want others to do.

Delivering the Speech

1. **Show your commitment.** As much as possible, look your audience in the eye. Use a tone that shows you are confident and serious.
2. **Use pauses and a varied pace.** Add more power to your speech by pausing briefly after important points or slowing down to deliver your most important lines.

   See page R79: Evaluate a Persuasive Speech

SPEAKING AND LISTENING

Ask students to read this page to get an overview of how to deliver a persuasive speech.

Before students begin working, review this rubric with them so that they understand their goals:

Rubric An effective persuasive speech

- introduces the topic in a way that grabs the attention of the audience
- clearly states an opinion and the reasons for that opinion
- calls on the audience to take some specific action as a result of the presentation
- uses a visual aid to highlight each major point
- uses convincing language
- is presented in a tone that conveys the speaker's commitment to the issue
- emphasizes key points with appropriate pauses and gestures
- appeals to the audience by making eye contact with as many people as possible
- is presented with confidence

R RESOURCE MANAGER—Copy Master
Speaking and Listening p. 205

S STANDARDS LESSON FILE
Speaking and Listening Lesson 1: Preparing and Presenting a Speech

DIFFERENTIATED INSTRUCTION

FOR LESS—PROFICIENT WRITERS

Planning the Speech Help students identify the most persuasive points from their essays to use in their speeches. Have them read the opening line of the **Student Model:** "My literature book weighs almost five pounds." Discuss why this would make a good opening for a speech. *Possible answer: It contains a startling fact that will get the attention of the audience.*

As students prepare for their presentations, have them ask themselves these questions:

- Are my visual aids attractive and easy to read?
- Are all of my main points covered by the visual aids?
- Do I avoid placing too much information on any one slide, transparency, or poster?
- Do I know what I want to say as I present my visuals aids?

Assessment Practice

CHECK READINESS

Read aloud the paragraph under **ASSESS** and stress to students that this is not the full Unit Test but a way for them to check their readiness for it. Then have students examine the skills listed under **REVIEW** and look back in the unit or in the Handbook for any skills they need to study.

READ THE SELECTIONS

Remind students to keep unit goals in mind as they read each passage, paying particular attention to

- elements of an argument
- fact and opinion
- text features
- main idea and supporting details

To help students focus on **fact and opinion** while reading, encourage them to ask questions such as

- Can this statement be proved?
- How might the statement be proved?
- Do the author's statements show evidence of bias?
- Does the author's language reveal strong positive or negative feelings?

ANSWER THE QUESTIONS

Direct students to pages R93–R99 of the Test-Taking Handbook to review test-taking strategies. Remind students not to choose the first alternative that seems to fit when answering a multiple-choice question. Instead, they should read through all the choices, eliminate any that are clearly wrong, and then choose the best answer—the one that is most accurate and complete.

Encourage students to take a few moments to plan their written responses before they actually begin writing. The time they spend thinking and planning will result in more focused and better-organized responses. Also point out that students should proofread their writing when they have finished. This will help them spot any errors they may have made while hurrying to complete a timed test.

ASSESS
The practice test items on the next few pages match skills listed on the Unit Goals page (page 867) and addressed throughout this unit. Taking this practice test will help you assess your knowledge of these skills and determine your readiness for the Unit Test.

REVIEW
After you take the practice test, your teacher can help you identify any skills you need to review.

- Elements of an Argument
- Fact and Opinion
- Text Features
- Main Idea and Supporting Details
- Idioms
- Prefixes and Latin Roots and Words
- Commas
- Colons

ASSESSMENT ONLINE
For more assessment practice and test-taking tips, go to the **Assessment Center** at ClassZone.com.

Reading Comprehension

DIRECTIONS *Read these selections and answer the questions that follow.*

Teen Reading Survey

SmartGirl.org online magazine

Reading Habits: Respondent Behavior and Opinion

The survey showed that

- Many teens enjoy reading and often do read for pleasure; 43% of teens surveyed said that most often they read for the fun of it.
- There was a significant difference, however, between boys and girls; 50% of girls said they read for pleasure, while only 32% of boys did.

While teens appear to enjoy reading, they find that they often do not have the time to do so. Other reasons given for not reading or not reading more: they found reading boring and prefer watching television or movies; they
10 lack good reading materials.

Survey Results

SmartGirl asked: Which statement below do you agree with most?

Statement	Total	Girls	Boys
I read constantly for my own satisfaction, and I love it.	26%	31%	18%
I don't have much time to read for pleasure, but I like to when I get a chance.	46%	49%	40%
I only read what I'm supposed to for school.	16%	12%	22%
I don't read books much at all.	7%	4%	11%
No answer	6%	4%	9%

20 *SmartGirl* asked: Most often, the reason I read is . . . (Please choose the best answer from this selection).

Statement	Total	Girls	Boys
Just for the fun of it	43%	50%	32%
Because I have to for school	19%	17%	22%
Because I get bored and have nothing else to do	12%	13%	11%
To learn new things on my own	12%	10%	15%
I don't really read much	5%	3%	8%
Because my parents encourage me to	4%	3%	4%

DIFFERENTIATED INSTRUCTION

FOR ENGLISH LEARNERS

Assessment Practice: Active Reading Strategies Tell students that they can focus their reading by skimming the questions first, before they read the passage. These tips can help them implement the strategy:

- Jot down line numbers and key terms referred to in the questions.
- While reading the passage, pay special attention to the line numbers or sections that the questions ask about.

Vocabulary Support Review these idioms before students read the selection:

- *make up* (line 8), "create"
- *know it by heart* (line 14), "have it memorized"
- *carry on* (line 34), "continue"

Take a Book Wherever You Go

Joan Aiken

If you were going to sail round the world alone in a small boat, and could take only one of these things to amuse you, which would you choose: a big iced cake, a beautiful picture, a book, a pack of cards, a paintbox (and paper), a pair of knitting needles and wool, a musical box, a harmonica . . . ? It would be a hard choice. Myself, I wouldn't want the cake; I'd eat it too fast. Nor the cards; they might blow away. Nor the wool; in case it got wet. The harmonica would be better than the musical box, for one could make up one's own tunes. I wouldn't take the picture, for I could look at the sea. Nor the paintbox, because in the end I'd use up
10 all the paper. So the last choice would be between the harmonica and the book. And I'm pretty sure I'd choose the book.

One book! I can hear someone say. But if you were sailing round the world, you'd have read it a hundred times before the trip was over. You'd know it by heart.

And I'd answer, Yes, I might read it a hundred times; yes, I might know it by heart. *That wouldn't matter.* You don't refuse to see your friend, or your mother, or your brother, because you have met them before. You don't leave home because you know what's there.

A book you love is like a friend. It is like home. You meet your friend a
20 hundred times. On the hundred-and-first meeting you can still say, "Well, I never realized you knew that!" You go home every day; after ten years you can still say, "I never noticed how beautiful the light is, when it shines on that corner."

There is always something new to find in a book, however often you read it.

When you read a story you do something that no animal can, however well trained; only man can do it; you are stepping out of your own mind into someone else's. You are listening to the thoughts of another person. While doing this, you are making your own mind work. And making
30 your own mind work is the most interesting thing there is to do.

So I'd sit in my boat and read that book over and over. First I'd think about the people in the story, why they acted the way they did. Then I

ITEM ANALYSIS

COMPREHENSION AND BRIEF CONSTRUCTED RESPONSE	ITEMS	UNIT PAGES
Elements of an Argument	6, 7, 9	913, 919, 929
Fact and Opinion	3, 4, 8	885
Text Features	1, 5, 11	868, 873
Main Idea and Supporting Details	2, 10, 12	870, 873

VOCABULARY	ITEMS	UNIT PAGES
Idioms	1, 2, 3, 4	926
Prefixes and Latin Roots and Words	5, 6, 7	893

WRITING AND GRAMMAR	ITEMS	UNIT PAGES
Commas	2, 3, 5	883, 927
Colons	1, 4, 5	943

MSA PREPARATION

McDougal Littell
Assessment System

After checking student readiness with this Assessment Practice, you may administer the complete Unit 8 Test, which matches the structure and format of the MSA.

Comprehension

Model a thinking process for answering multiple-choice questions.

1. **D is correct.** *A survey is a report based on information gathered, so the words "present statistics" are a clue to the correct answer. A is incorrect because the title of the survey does not include movies. B and C can be eliminated because the title of the survey does not refer to book sales or to other teen interests and activities.*

2. **A is correct.** *The first bulleted item states the overall findings of the survey. B and D are incorrect because they are supporting details for why some students do not read. C is incorrect because it is a supporting detail for the main idea.*

3. **B is correct.** *The word* should *is a clue that this is an opinion. A, C, and D can be eliminated because they are all survey results, so they are facts, not opinions.*

4. **C is correct.** *The percentage and the statement are included in the second survey chart (line 28). A is incorrect because the survey does not address the quality of books written for teens. B and D can be eliminated because they are statements that cannot be proved.*

5. **D is correct.** *The subheading "Survey Results" introduces the charts below. A is incorrect because the title refers to the entire article. B is incorrect because the first subheading introduces the text in lines 2–10. C is incorrect because the bulleted list does not introduce anything; it presents information.*

6. **C is correct.** *The author compares a book to a friend and to a home, describing the continuing satisfaction and pleasure that each brings (lines 19–25 and 40–41). A, B, and D can be eliminated because none of these claims is stated or even implied in the passage.*

7. **A is correct.** *Lines 24–25 state the author's reason why a book would be the best choice. B, C, and D can be eliminated because the author does not refer to any of these reasons in the passage.*

---

might wonder why the writer wrote that particular story. Then I might carry on the story in my mind, after the end. Then I'd go back and read all my favorite bits and wonder why I liked them best. Then I'd read all the rest and look for things that I hadn't noticed before. Then I'd list the things I'd learned from the book. Then I'd try to imagine what the writer was like, from the way he's written his story. . . . It would be like having another person in the boat.

40 A book you love is a friend; it's a familiar place where you can go when you choose. It's something of your own, for no two people read the same book in the same way.

If every single person in the world had a book, just one book (they'd have to be able to read it, of course) we'd have a lot less trouble, I'm sure.

Just one book apiece. That shouldn't be too hard to manage.

How shall we start?

Comprehension

DIRECTIONS *Answer these questions about "Teen Reading Survey."*

1. The title "Teen Reading Survey" tells you that this selection will most likely
   A. compare books and movies for teens
   B. analyze book sales in the teen market
   C. list teens' favorite interests and activities
   D. present statistics about teens' reading habits

2. Which statement from lines 1–10 expresses the main idea of the survey results?
   A. "Many teens enjoy reading and often do read for pleasure."
   B. "They lack good reading materials."
   C. "50% of girls said they read for pleasure, while only 32% of boys did."
   D. "They found reading boring and prefer watching television or movies."

3. Which statement is an opinion based on information gathered in the survey?
   A. Many teens think that they have little time to read for pleasure.
   B. Boys should spend more time reading.
   C. Ten percent of girls read to learn new things on their own.
   D. More boys than girls read only what is required for school.

4. Which statement is a fact based on information from the survey?
   A. Many teens do not read because there are few good books written for them.
   B. Teens should not wait for an adult to encourage them to read.
   C. Of the teens who responded, 4% read because their parents encourage them to.
   D. Parents need to be more involved in getting their teens to read.

958

---

8. **D is correct.** *The statement can be proved. It is common knowledge that animals cannot read. A, B, and C are incorrect because these statements cannot be proved. A is a prediction about the difficulty of the choice, B is a comparison, and the phrase "most interesting" in C is a clue that this is an opinion.*

9. **B is correct.** *The author concedes that she might read the book a hundred times, but insists that that would be a good thing. A, C, and D can be eliminated because the author makes no mention of these possibilities.*

MSA SKILLS
PRACTICE

5. Which text feature introduces the two charts?

   A. the title of the article

   B. the subheading in line 1

   C. a bulleted list

   D. the subheading in line 11

DIRECTIONS *Answer these questions about "Take a Book Wherever You Go."*

6. By choosing to take a book on her trip, the author is making which claim?

   A. A book is easy to carry on a trip.

   B. There are many kinds of books that appeal to different people.

   C. A book will provide the most satisfaction and pleasure.

   D. Books are inexpensive to replace.

7. Which reason does the author give to support her claim?

   A. Every time you read a book, you can discover something new.

   B. Reading a book would make the trip seem shorter.

   C. By reading, you could learn how to write your own book.

   D. You could learn a book so well that you could discuss it later with your friends.

8. Which statement from the essay is a fact?

   A. "It would be a hard choice."

   B. "A book you love is like a friend."

   C. "And making your own mind work is the most interesting thing there is to do."

   D. "When you read a story you do something that no animal can. . . ."

9. What counterargument does the author address in lines 12–18?

   A. She would probably stop reading the book before she got to the end of it.

   B. She would have to read the book over and over again on such a long trip.

   C. The book would probably fall apart before the trip was done.

   D. She would regret her choice and wish she had the harmonica.

DIRECTIONS *Answer this question about both selections.*

10. Which idea about reading do both selections convey?

   A. Reading is enjoyable.

   B. Reading is necessary to succeed.

   C. Reading is unlike any other activity.

   D. Reading is like talking to a friend.

Brief Constructed Response

11. Read the subheading in line 1 of "Teen Reading Survey." Which two categories of reading habits are covered in the survey? Which chart covers which category?

12. Discuss the main idea of "Take a Book Wherever You Go." What details does the author use to support this idea?

GO ON

959

---

10. A *is correct.* *It is the only idea that is conveyed by both selections. B and C can be eliminated because these ideas do not appear in either selection. D is an idea conveyed in the second selection, but it does not appear in the first selection.*

Brief Constructed Response

Evaluate student writing using the Maryland writing rubrics in the back of the book.

Possible responses:

11. *The survey covers the respondents' reading behaviors and their opinions about reading. The first chart deals with behavior, and the second chart deals with opinions about why reading is valuable.*

12. *Students may respond that reading is the most interesting way to spend time. Some students may write that everyone should be reading a book, or that if everyone loved reading, there would be less trouble in the world. Students may cite these supporting details:*

- *Reading gives you lasting pleasure (lines 15–18).*
- *You can find something new in a book each time you read it (lines 24–25).*
- *Reading is interesting—it makes your mind work because you are trying to understand another person's thoughts (lines 26–30).*
- *You learn new things from reading (lines 36–37).*
- *A reader can develop a relationship with a book that makes it seem like an old friend (lines 40–41).*

DIFFERENTIATED INSTRUCTION

FOR ENGLISH LEARNERS

Organize Information To help students respond to question 12, have them use a graphic organizer to list main ideas and details. Have students agree on the main idea. Then ask them to add supporting details.

BEST PRACTICES TOOLKIT—Transparency
Main Ideas and Details p. C6

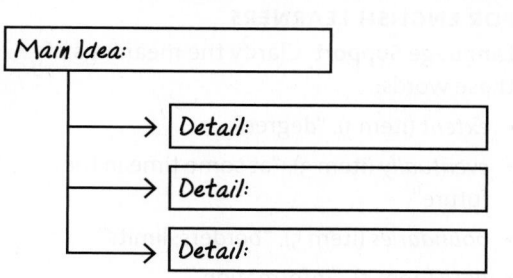

Vocabulary

1. **B is correct.** A is incorrect because it simply repeats the idea already expressed in the sentence by the word *much*. C *and* D *are incorrect because they do not make sense in the context of the survey.*

2. **B is correct.** *We can eliminate* A *and* D *because "my own" suggests something related to one's self, and neither of these choices relates to that idea. In choosing between* B *and* C, *the phrase "one's own efforts" is more relevant to learning new things than one's house, so* C *is incorrect.*

3. **C is correct.** A *is incorrect because location does not relate to why it would be bad to run out of paper.* B *is incorrect because the words "the end" do not suggest something that will happen soon.* D *is incorrect because it does not make sense in the context.*

4. **C is correct.** A *can be eliminated because it doesn't make sense; if you read the book just one time, obviously you've learned to read.* B *and* D *can be eliminated because reading a book a hundred times wouldn't be likely to produce either of these results.*

5. **C is correct.** A, B, *and* D *are all possible meanings of* survey, *but the context, which includes charts containing different viewpoints, points to* C *as the correct answer.*

6. **C is correct.** *Based on the fact that 43 percent of teens surveyed read for pleasure (line 3), they seem to enjoy the activity.* A, B, *and* D *can be eliminated because they do not make sense if they are used in the sentence in place of* appear. Seem *does make sense in the sentence.*

7. **D is correct.** *The author is suggesting a goal that she would like to see accomplished—making sure every person has a book and knows how to read it.* A, B, *and* C *are all possible meanings of* manage, *but none of these makes sense in the context of the sentence.*

Vocabulary

DIRECTIONS *Use context clues and your knowledge of idioms to answer the following questions.*

1. In line 18 of "Teen Reading Survey," the idiom "at all" means
   A. often
   B. to any extent
   C. considering everything
   D. to the degree expected

2. In line 26 of "Teen Reading Survey," the idiom "on my own" means
   A. in a short time
   B. by one's own efforts
   C. at one's own house
   D. with guidance

3. In line 9 of "Take a Book Wherever You Go," the idiom "in the end" means
   A. somewhere
   B. soon
   C. eventually
   D. maybe

4. In lines 14 and 16 of "Take a Book Wherever You Go," the idiom "by heart" means
   A. learned to read
   B. felt deeply
   C. memorized word for word
   D. understood meanings

DIRECTIONS *Use context clues and your knowledge of prefixes and Latin words to answer the following questions.*

5. The Latin prefix *super-* means "over," and the Latin word *videre* means "to look." What is the meaning of the word *survey* as it is used in the title "Teen Reading Survey"?
   A. a careful inspection
   B. the determination of an area's boundaries
   C. a collection of data or viewpoints
   D. an outline of a subject

6. The Latin prefix *ad-* means "toward," and the Latin word *parere* means "to show." The most likely meaning of *appear* as it is used in line 7 of "Teen Reading Survey" is
   A. show up
   B. exist
   C. seem
   D. intend

7. The word *manage* comes from the Latin word *manus*, which means "hand." The most likely meaning of *manage* as it is used in line 45 of "Take a Book Wherever You Go" is to
   A. continue to get along
   B. direct business affairs
   C. control the use of
   D. succeed in accomplishing

DIFFERENTIATED INSTRUCTION

FOR ENGLISH LEARNERS

Language Support Clarify the meanings of these words:

- *extent* (item 1), "degree"
- *eventually* (item 3), "at some time in the future"
- *boundaries* (item 5), "borders; limits"
- *data* (item 5), "information"

Review Academic Vocabulary Write this academic vocabulary from page 960 on the board and have groups brainstorm what they know about each topic:

- *context clues* (first direction line)
- *idioms* (second direction line)
- *Latin prefix* (item 5)

Writing & Grammar

DIRECTIONS *Read this section from a letter and answer the questions that follow.*

> Dear Student
>
> (1) This Friday is the last day of school. (2) As a result we will be having a small party. (3) The party a hot dog lunch will be held in the cafeteria. (4) However, when school lets out at 335 P.M., please behave. (5) Do not run, push, or yell. (6) Students who violate these rules are subject to the following a call to parents a meeting with the principal or other disciplinary action.

1. Choose the correct way to punctuate the formal greeting.

   A. Dear Student!   **C.** Dear Student:

   B. Dear Student;   **D.** Dear Student.

2. Choose the correct way to punctuate sentence 2 with a comma.

   A. As a result we will be having a small, party.

   B. As a result we will, be having a small party.

   C. As a result we will be having a small party.

   D. As a result, we will be having a small party.

3. Choose the correct way to punctuate the appositive phrase in sentence 3.

   A. The party a hot, dog lunch, will be held in the cafeteria.

   B. The party, a hot dog lunch, will be held in the cafeteria.

   C. The party a hot dog lunch will be held, in the cafeteria.

   D. The party a hot dog lunch, will be held in the cafeteria.

4. Chose the correct place to insert a colon in sentence 4.

   A. 335 P.M.:   **C.** please:

   B. 3:35 P.M.   **D.** However:

5. Choose the correct way to punctuate sentence 6 with a colon and commas.

   A. Students who violate these rules are subject to the following: a call, to parents, a meeting with the principal or other disciplinary action.

   B. Students who violate these rules are subject to: the following a call to parents, a meeting with the principal, or other disciplinary action.

   C. Students who violate these rules are: subject to the following, a call to parents, a meeting with the principal, or other disciplinary action.

   D. Students who violate these rules are subject to the following: a call to parents, a meeting with the principal, or other disciplinary action.

STOP

961

ANSWERS
Writing & Grammar

1. **C *is correct.*** A, B, and D *are incorrect because a colon should be used after a formal greeting in a business letter.*

2. **D *is correct.*** *The introductory phrase "As a result" should be set off with a comma. A is incorrect because an adjective should not be set off by a comma from the noun it modifies. B is incorrect because a comma should not separate the parts of a verb. C can be eliminated because it does not correctly identify the introductory phrase.*

3. **B *is correct.*** *The phrase "a hot dog lunch" explains the noun "party," so it should be set off with commas. A is incorrect because the commas do not set off the complete appositive phrase. C is incorrect because the phrase "in the cafeteria" does not explain, identify, or rename a noun, so it is not an appositive. D can be eliminated because the comma does not set off an explanatory noun, pronoun, or phrase; instead, it incorrectly separates the subject ("party") and the verb ("will be held").*

4. **B *is correct.*** *A colon should be used between numerals to separate the hours and the minutes in expressions of time. The colon is placed incorrectly in A, C, and D.*

5. **D *is correct.*** *The colon separates the phrase "the following" and the items to which this phrase refers. Commas are correctly used to separate the three items that follow the colon. A is incorrect because the commas are placed incorrectly. B and C are incorrect because they do not place the colon after "the following."*

DIFFERENTIATED INSTRUCTION

FOR ENGLISH LEARNERS

Assessment Support: Punctuation Review with students the uses of commas and colons. Have students punctuate these examples and explain their choice of punctuation and placement:

1 OO P.M.

I like to read books magazines and newspapers.

Dear Sir

The dog a black poodle was waiting on the porch.

I need the following supplies paint paper brushes and a bucket.

More Great Reads

UNIT 8

Ideas for Independent Reading

Which of the questions in Unit 8 made an impression on you? Continue exploring them with these books.

Can appearances deceive?

Buffalo Gals: Women of the Old West
by Brandon Marie Miller

This book makes history "come alive" through journal entries, letters, and songs. Learn about the many experiences of these strong, fearless women and the difficulties they faced as they took care of their children and homes.

The Contender
by Robert Lipsyte

An African-American high-school dropout living in Harlem in the 1960s, during the civil rights movement, struggles to prove himself through the rigor and discipline of boxing. He wonders whether he has the heart of a contender—inside and outside the ring.

The Tulip Touch
by Anne Fine

Who might deceive you? Advertisers? Friends? When Natalie meets her neighbor, a girl named Tulip, she becomes a willing pawn in Tulip's wicked deceits. When the lies turn dangerous, can Natalie escape?

How do we fight disease?

Fever 1793
by Laurie Halse Anderson

In this novel, 14-year-old Mattie Cook's day in 18th-century Philadelphia begins with her coffeehouse chores and ends with an epidemic of yellow fever. Does Mattie become a statistic of this outbreak?

Lost in the War
by Nancy Antle

Events like war are often a kind of disease. Thirteen-year-old Lisa Grey is too young to remember her father, who was killed in Vietnam. But she relives the war every day through her mom, who suffers from posttraumatic stress disorder.

Snake Dreamer
by Priscilla Galloway

Disease can be physical or mental. Sixteen-year-old Dusa suffers from nightmares of writhing snakes. When her mother takes her to a sleep-disorder clinic in Greece, things become even more frightening.

What inspires people?

Walks Alone
by Brian Burks

It's how we overcome challenges that can make us heroes. It's 1879, and 15-year-old Walks Alone watches the massacre of her tribe during a raid. Her loss and the challenges that follow teach her courage and hope.

Passage to Freedom
by Ken Mochizuki

Japanese diplomat Chiune Sugihara watched Nazi forces invade Europe at the start of World War II. Jewish citizens were applying for visas in order to leave, but for many there were no visas. Inspired to help, Sugihara risked much to grant visas to as many as 10,000 Jews.

Bound for the North Star: True Stories of Fugitive Slaves
by Dennis Brindell Fradin

The former slaves described in these 12 stories of heroic escapes have inspired movies and books. These stories continue to inspire readers to fight against cruelty worldwide.

962 UNIT 8: INFORMATION, ARGUMENT, AND PERSUASION

The Power of Research

9

POCKET GUIDE

SHELLS

RESEARCH WORKSHOPS

- **Research Strategies**
- **Writing Research Reports**

963

For help in planning this unit, see

RESOURCE MANAGER UNIT 9
pp. 1–7

INTRODUCE THE UNIT

This unit is divided into two workshops. The **Research Strategies Workshop,** beginning on page 966, introduces students to strategies they can use to find answers to both academic and everyday questions. Students learn about a variety of electronic and print resources. They also have the chance to do hands-on activities that help them become familiar with these research tools.

The **Writing Workshop** begins on page 984. This workshop provides a framework for students to apply the strategies they have learned to a specific academic purpose. Students are guided through a step-by-step process that helps them write their own research report.

UNIT 9
Standards Skills Trace

1.E.2.a, 4.A.7.b

MARYLAND

SKILLS STRAND

Research Strategies Workshop
pp.966–983

Reading and Informational Texts	Plan and Focus Research pp. 967–968
	Clarify Research Goals and Develop Research Questions p. 968
	Take Notes p. 968
	Use the Internet to Research a Topic pp. 969–971, 982
	Navigate Relevant Internet Sites p. 971
	Evaluate Print and Nonprint Information pp. 972–973
	Use Evaluation Criteria to Evaluate a Web Site p. 973
	Use Library or Media Center Resources pp. 974–975, 983
	Choose and Evaluate Sources pp. 976–980, 982
	Distinguish Between Primary and Secondary Sources p. 976
	Use Parts of a Book to Locate Information p. 977
	Collect Data for a Report by Conducting Interviews, Field Research, and Observations p. 981
	Understand Library Classification Systems (Dewey Decimal System, Library of Congress System) p. 983
Vocabulary	Academic Vocabulary pp. 969, 971, 974, 975, 976–977, 978, 982
Speaking, Listening, Viewing, and Media	Discuss pp. 966, T967–T983

Assessment-Based Planning: Skills in red are assessed on the Unit 9 Test. **T** = Teacher's Edition page

MARYLAND STANDARDS
For a full listing of state standards see page S1.

SKILLS STRAND

Writing Workshop: Research Report
pp. 984–999

Skills Assessed on the Unit 9 Test:

Reading and Informational Texts
• Analyze and evaluate a research report

SKILLS STRAND	
Reading and Informational Texts	Analyze a Research Report pp. 985–987, 998
Writing, Grammar, and Style	Write a Research Report pp. 984–999
	Find and Narrow a Research Topic p. 988
	Locate and Evaluate Sources p. 989
	Make Source Cards p. 990
	Take Notes p. 991
	Summarize and Paraphrase Information p. 991
	Quote Directly and Avoid Plagiarism p. 992
	Write a Thesis Statement p. 993
	Organize and Outline Information p. 993
	Document Sources p. 995
	Prepare a Works Cited List pp. 995, 998
	Format a Research Report pp. 985, T985
Speaking, Listening, Viewing, and Media	Discuss pp. 984, T985–T987, 998
	Create a Multimedia Report p. 999

Research and Study Skills
• Use the Internet to select and navigate relevant sites
• Use library and reference sources
• Distinguish between primary and secondary sources
• Evaluate Web sites and other sources of information
• Collect data for a report

Writing, Grammar, and Style
• Narrow a research topic
• Take notes and document sources
• Organize information for a report
• Summarize and paraphrase information to avoid plagiarism
• Prepare a Works Cited list
• Use transitions to connect ideas
• Support ideas with reasons
• Additional writing and grammar skills

@ For additional lesson planning help, see **Easy Planner DVD.**

963B

OBJECTIVES

- establish prior knowledge about **research** strategies
- discuss possible sources of information

How can I find ANSWERS?

After students have read the paragraph, divide them into small groups and give each group a telephone book. Ask the groups to explore the various types of information contained in this commonplace resource. What kinds of questions could they answer by using the white pages? the yellow pages? What other sections are included in the book? How is it organized? Have students share their insights. Then point out that the more they know about the sources available to them, the easier it will be for them to **research** and find the answers they need.

ACTIVITY Give students examples of questions they might include in the chart.

- **Home:** What will the weather be like today?
- **School:** What is the capital of South Korea?
- **Other places:** How many shoe stores does this mall have?

Then have students work in small groups to complete the chart. Review the sources of information that students list. Help them classify sources that are reliable and those that might not be as credible.

CHECK UNDERSTANDING Have students summarize the steps they take to find answers to some common questions.

Unit Resources

How can I find ANSWERS?

You do research every day. You find out the weather report, movie times, and game scores. Maybe you also locate the lowest price for an item or the best Web site for keeping up with music. Every time you track down information, even in the phone book or on TV, you are doing research. In this unit, you'll learn to sharpen your skills to answer harder questions.

ACTIVITY List some research questions you answer at home, at school, and in other places. Tell where you get answers.

	Questions	Where I Find Answers
Home		
School		
Other places		

LITERATURE CLASSZONE.COM

Literature and Reading Center
Writing Center
Vocabulary and Spelling Center

 MARYLAND OBJECTIVES **Preview Unit Goals**

DEVELOPING RESEARCH SKILLS	• Plan research
	• Develop research questions
	• Use library and media center resources
	• Evaluate information and sources, including nonfiction books, periodicals, and Web sites
	• Collect your own data
WRITING	• Write a research report
	• Narrow your research topic
	• Locate and evaluate sources
	• Take notes
	• Make source cards
	• Summarize and paraphrase
	• Quote directly and avoid plagiarism
	• Document sources
	• Prepare a Works Cited list
	• Format your paper
SPEAKING, LISTENING, AND VIEWING	• Create a multimedia report
ACADEMIC VOCABULARY	• research topic • plagiarism
	• research report • documentation
	• sources • Works Cited
	• source cards • multimedia report

965

Preview Unit Goals

As students look at the unit goals, point out that they will be exposed to some different kinds of skills than in previous units. Suggest that they review all the items under **Developing Research Skills** and **Writing**. Which skills have they used in the past? Which skills are new to them? Students might record in their journals any questions they have about the unfamiliar skills and then look for answers as they read the unit.

Suggest that students also write the Academic Vocabulary terms in their journals and define them as they read the unit. Encourage students to use these terms when they discuss their research and writing.

ADDITIONAL UNIT GOALS

These skills will be taught in this unit but are not the major focus of the unit:

Developing Research Skills
• Clarify research goal
• Get overview of topic
• Use the Internet, including searching the Web, using keywords, conducting advanced searches, and conducting library catalog searches
• Select relevant sites from search engine results and explore those sites
• Evaluate information based on currency, authorship, publisher, credibility of author or publisher, and relevance
• Use reference works, newspapers, periodicals, fiction and nonfiction books, audio and video resources, e-resources, and an online catalog
• Use primary and secondary sources
• Use databases
• Use parts of a book
• Evaluate newspapers and periodicals
• Conduct interviews, field research, surveys, and questionnaires

Writing
• Write a thesis statement
• Organize and outline information

DIFFERENTIATED INSTRUCTION

FOR ENGLISH LEARNERS
Academic Vocabulary Use the Academic Vocabulary copy master to introduce the vocabulary words, including *research report* and *documentation*.

1. Read each word and the sample sentence aloud. Encourage students to volunteer their own examples.
2. Allow students to work in pairs to complete the definitions on the copy master and answer the questions.
3. Reconvene to review students' responses.

Additional Academic Vocabulary Use the second copy master to help students study these terms from the unit: *catalog, database, keyword, menu, search engine,* and *Web site.* Have students take turns reading aloud the terms and definitions. Then have students work individually to complete the sentences in the chart and the word squares in Part B. Discuss answers as a class.

RESOURCE MANAGER—Copy Masters
Academic Vocabulary p. 6
Additional Academic Vocabulary p. 7

965

OBJECTIVES

Developing Research Skills
- explore the key idea of **research**
- plan research
- use the Internet
- evaluate information
- use the library or media center
- choose and evaluate sources
- collect data through interviews and field research

Research Strategies Workshop

Tell students that in this section of the unit, they will be learning about resources and techniques that will help them research many kinds of questions. Explain that once they know the basics of the research process, they will be able to apply this process to all areas of their lives.

Where do I look for INFORMATION?

Discuss the question and the **KEY IDEA.** Ask students if they have heard this saying: "Give a man a fish, and he eats for a day. Teach a man to fish, and he eats for a lifetime." Ask students how this saying might apply to the key idea of **research.** *(Possible answer: If you give someone an answer, it will help him or her with one particular question. By teaching someone how to research questions, however, you help him or her to find many answers.)* Have students work on the **QUICKWRITE** and share their ideas in small groups.

Research Workshop Resources

Where do I look for INFORMATION?

MARYLAND OBJECTIVES

WRITING STANDARD
4.A.7.b *Use various information retrieval sources to obtain information*

KEY IDEA Finding answers isn't always easy, especially since many questions have more than one answer. This unit will help you answer **research** questions in efficient and reliable ways. You will learn how and where to look, as well as how to look critically at everything you find.

QUICKWRITE In this unit, you will follow a group of students as they look for information about different kinds of collections. Begin by putting yourself in the same situation. Imagine that your school puts on a collectors' show each year. You want to participate, but what will you display? Working alone or with a partner, list several types of collections that you would like to learn more about.

Annual Collectors' Show

Saturday, May 7
Grant Middle School
2118 Catalpa Street
10:00 A.M. to 4:00 P.M.

RESOURCE MANAGER UNIT 9

Plan and Teach pp. 9–11, 14
Write Research Questions p. 15
Examine Search Engine Results p. 16
Navigate Web Sites p. 17
Evaluate Web Sites p. 18
Use Library and Media Center Sources p. 19
Use Parts of a Book to Find Information p. 20

Evaluate Nonfiction Books p. 21
Evaluate Newspapers and Periodicals p. 22

STANDARDS LESSON FILE
Research and Study Skills Lessons 1–8
Speaking and Listening Lesson 1

BEST PRACTICES TOOLKIT

Differentiated Instruction pp. 31–38*

Graphic Organizers/Strategies
Reciprocal Teaching • Cluster Diagram • Main Idea and Details • Classification Chart • KWL • Jigsaw Reading • Two-Column Chart • Spider Map • Round Robin • New Word Analysis

Technology
- Easy Planner DVD
- Write*Smart* CD

* Resources for Differentiation

Planning Your Research

Good research begins with a reading and thinking stage. Don't just jump in. Stop and think about what you want to accomplish.

SET A GOAL

What do you want to learn from your research? Start by listing your general and specific goals.

> *General goal:* How can I figure out something I would like to collect?
>
> *Questions:*
> - *What especially interests me?* I like baseball, bugs, rocks, and camping.
> - *Do any of my interests lead to collections?* I could collect baseball cards, certain kinds of bugs, or different kinds of rocks.
>
> *Specific goal:* I want to learn more about collecting baseball cards.

GET AN OVERVIEW

After you set a goal, it's time to understand your topic better.

- **Talk to people.** Look for a person who knows about your topic. Talking to him or her may give you lots of ideas.
- **Use the Internet.** For example, if you type the words *baseball cards* into a search engine, you will probably get a few million hits. Look at the first ten entries or so. They may give you ideas for more specific terms to use.
- **Visit the library.** Is there a reference book or an encyclopedia article on your topic? These sources will give you an overview.
- **Talk with a librarian.** He or she may be able to suggest books, magazines, and online sources.

NARROW YOUR FOCUS

Big topics are harder to manage than smaller, more specific ones. Once you decide on a specific topic, you might brainstorm ways to narrow it. The result of your brainstorm might look like this.

Topic	More Specific	Even More Specific
baseball cards	baseball cards from a specific time period	baseball cards of a specific team or player

---

Teach

Planning Your Research

SET A GOAL

- Point out that all the examples in this unit relate to collecting various items such as baseball cards, seashells, and so forth. The Annual Collector's Show sign on page 966 introduces this theme. Make sure students understand that the process of writing a research paper can be applied to any topic, not just collecting.
- Explain that taking time to list possible topics at the start of a research project can help students make the best choices.

GET AN OVERVIEW

- Ask students how they might find a person who knows about baseball cards (for example, by visiting a store where the cards are sold).
- Tell students that this preliminary research helps them figure out whether they want to pursue a particular topic, and if so, which aspect they would like to explore.

NARROW YOUR FOCUS

Give students another topic and have them suggest ways to narrow it down. For example:
- **Topic:** music
- **More Specific:** classical music, folk music, contemporary music
- **Even More Specific:** Mozart, American folk music in the 1960s, hip-hop

---

DIFFERENTIATED INSTRUCTION

FOR ALL STUDENTS
Enhance Learning Styles This workshop can be adapted to suit various learning styles.

- **Visual** Have students produce an illustrated manual of research techniques.
- **Analytical** Have students chart or outline the major ideas in the workshop.
- **Interpersonal** Have small groups apply a Reciprocal Teaching strategy.

BEST PRACTICES TOOLKIT—Transparency
Reciprocal Teaching p. A35

FOR LESS–PROFICIENT READERS
Concept Support

- Have small groups review "Like Black Smoke" (page 896). The topic is the Black Death. Ask each group to identify two or three more specific topics based on their reading.
- Record groups' topics in a Cluster Diagram.
- Explain that by spending a small amount of time narrowing a topic, students will save a lot of time when they begin their research.

BEST PRACTICES TOOLKIT—Transparency
Cluster Diagram p. B18

FOR ENGLISH LEARNERS
Vocabulary: Jargon Explain that there are many specialized words related to computers and the Internet. Some familiar words are used in different ways in this context. Point out the word *hits* under **Get an Overview.** Tell students that when talking about the Internet, *hits* means "results" or "choices." Students may find it helpful to keep an ongoing list of terms associated with the Internet and computers.

WRITE RESEARCH QUESTIONS

- Divide students into small groups. Have them think of three or four additional research questions they might ask to find out more about Seattle Mariners baseball cards. Students might include questions such as these: *What are the rarest Seattle Mariners baseball cards? What is the best place to obtain Seattle Mariners baseball cards?*

- Have groups volunteer their questions. Write them on the board.

- Explain that the key term is the word or phrase that is the focus of a question. Work together to identify key terms in each group's questions.

- Tell students that when they begin their research, these key terms might help them locate information in the index of a book. They might also find these terms helpful as keywords when searching the Internet or a library catalog.

R RESOURCE MANAGER—Copy Master
Write Research Questions p. 15

GET READY TO TAKE NOTES

- Be sure students understand that for most research reports, using note cards will be the most efficient method of taking notes.

- Point out that charts that organize information into categories or main ideas and details can also be helpful.

BEST PRACTICES TOOLKIT—Transparencies
Main Idea and Details p. B6
Classification Chart p. B17

S STANDARDS LESSON FILE
Research and Study Skills Lesson 1:
    Research Questions and Topic
Research and Study Skills Lesson 8: Source
    Cards and Note Cards

WRITE RESEARCH QUESTIONS

Let's say you have a narrow topic—for example, Seattle Mariners baseball cards. A good next step is to develop questions to guide your research.

Research questions are big questions about your topic. They can't be answered with just a yes or a no. They sum up what you want to know about your topic. After you write your research questions, highlight key terms in them.

> - When did people first start collecting Seattle Mariners baseball cards?
> - What determines the prices and values of these cards?
> - What are some interesting stories about collectors and Mariners cards?

Use the questions and the terms to focus your research.

GET READY TO TAKE NOTES

As you get started on your research, the more organized you are, the better off you will be. When you do research for a class assignment, one of the best ways to take notes is by using note cards. You will learn more about note cards on page 991.

For other kinds of research, you might use different note-taking tools, such as charts or lists. Think about the kinds of information you need and the format that would work best to keep you organized. For instance, you might create a chart of terms used by baseball card collectors.

Term	Meaning
Star cards	cards of the best-known players—can be expensive
Common cards	cards of lesser-known players—cheaper, but very important to collectors who want all the cards of a certain team
Insert cards	cards with special designs that are placed into some packs
Memorabilia cards	insert cards that either are autographed by the players or contain fragments of equipment used by the players, such as pieces of bats, jerseys, or caps

---

DIFFERENTIATED INSTRUCTION

FOR LESS-PROFICIENT READERS

Concept Support Remind students that they should gather some information about a topic before narrowing the focus. This information can also help them form good research questions. If they know a little about a topic, then they can figure out what additional facts they want to learn. Explain that they should use the words *who, what, when, where, why,* and *how* to help them generate questions. Suggest that they use a KWL chart to record research questions.

Know	Want to Know	Learned
Some people collect Seattle Mariners baseball cards.	How old is the oldest Seattle Mariners card? Which cards are the most valuable? What makes them valuable?	

BEST PRACTICES TOOLKIT—Transparency
KWL: Know, Want to Know, Learned p. A21

Using the Internet

When you use the World Wide Web, you are also using the Internet, a huge system of linked computers. The Web includes hundreds of millions of Web sites and billions of Web pages.

SEARCH THE WEB

Begin your search by going to one or more search engines. **Search engines** are Web sites that locate information based on titles, keywords, and content. There are many to choose from, and each yields different information.

USE KEYWORDS

A **keyword** is the term or phrase that you enter into a search engine. The best keywords are very specific, like those you highlighted on page 968.

Suppose you want to learn more about collecting bracelets that people wear to show their support for a cause. Here's what may happen if you use a search engine.

YOU TYPE IN...	YOU GET...	THIS IS...
bracelet	4,120,000 results	too broad, but perhaps you see the word *awareness* a lot
+bracelet +awareness	324,000 results	still too broad, but now you see *nonprofit,* so you try *+bracelets +nonprofit*

ADVANCED SEARCHES

Some search engines let you make a search more specific by using the word *AND, NOT,* or *OR*. Other search engines let you use plus and minus signs. Here are some examples:

- *bracelet NOT charm* (This eliminates results about charm bracelets.)
- *+bracelet +nonprofit +"Lance Armstrong"* (This finds only pages that mention all three terms.)
- *bracelet AND "Race for the Cure"* (This finds only pages that mention both terms.)

LIBRARY CATALOG SEARCHES

Library search engines tend to be different from commercial search engines. A good way to get started searching on them is to explain your topic to a reference librarian and ask for help in identifying key terms.

ACADEMIC VOCABULARY FOR THE INTERNET
Here are terms that you will use when discussing the Internet:

- World Wide Web
- Web site
- keyword
- home page
- URL (uniform resource locator, also called a Web address)
- search engine
- menu
- hyperlink
- icon

 TIP Use quotation marks to enclose words that go together as one term. For example, instead of *Lance Armstrong*, type in *"Lance Armstrong."*

DIFFERENTIATED INSTRUCTION

FOR ADVANCED LEARNERS/PRE–AP

Define Academic Vocabulary Have students work in pairs or small groups. Assign each group different terms from the list of **Academic Vocabulary for the Internet.** Have them use the information in the text, their own knowledge, and additional resources to teach the word or phrase to the class and illustrate its meaning through a series of examples, pictures, or additional facts.

Using the Internet

ACADEMIC VOCABULARY FOR THE INTERNET

Record the list of terms on the board. Ask students if they can define any of them. Revise definitions as students encounter the terms on pages 969–971.

SEARCH THE WEB

- With students, brainstorm a list of search engines (Google, Yahoo!, Lycos, Ask Jeeves).
- Have Jigsaw groups locate different search engines and describe the format of each.

USE KEYWORDS

Have each Jigsaw group use a different search engine and enter keywords related to collectible items, such as *bracelet* or *cancer bracelet*. Have groups compare their first few results for each keyword.

BEST PRACTICES TOOLKIT
Jigsaw Reading p. A1

ADVANCED SEARCHES

- Point out the **TIP**. Have students return to the keywords they used in the previous activity and insert quotation marks around *cancer bracelet* or other phrases before entering them. Students should see a decrease in the number of results, or hits.
- Clarify that the plus sign (+) tells a search engine that the following word or phrase is required in all hits. The minus sign (–) indicates that the following word or phrase must not appear in any hits.
- Brainstorm additional searches using *and, not, or,* or plus and minus signs.

LIBRARY CATALOG SEARCHES

Tell students that an online catalog in a library allows them to search by subject or keyword as well as by author or title. Ask students how many of them have used a library catalog and what kind of search they performed.

S STANDARDS LESSON FILE
Research and Study Skills Lesson 3: Using Reference and Search Tools

EXAMINE SEARCH ENGINE RESULTS

- Remind students that the more focused and narrow their search is, the more relevant their results will be.

- Explain that search engines organize their results differently. Some may present sites in order of popularity. Because millions of people use the Internet for many different reasons, the most popular site is not necessarily the most helpful for research purposes.

- Make sure students understand the **TIP**. Point out that sites ending in *.edu, .gov,* or *.org* are often reliable sources of information. The meanings of these abbreviations are explained on page 982.

- Identify helpful examples of *.edu, .gov,* and *.org* sites for students, including the Smithsonian sites (www.si.edu and www.smithsonianeducation.org/students) and the NASA site (www.nasa.gov). Note that NASA also has a site for students in grades 5–8, as well as several sites in Spanish.

Close Read

1. *Possible answer: The term "rock collecting" was used. The search could be narrowed by inserting* and *or* not, *by using plus and minus signs, or by identifying specific rocks or fossils.*

2. *Students may say that they would click first on the fourth site, "Start Rock Collecting." It is aimed at someone who wants to begin rock collecting and offers links to other sites with more specific content.*

3. *Possible answer: The "Rock Collecting at Amazon" link would provide information about books on rock collecting and how to buy them.*

If students need help ... Read the description of each Web site aloud and analyze why it seems promising or why it might not be an appropriate choice.

RESOURCE MANAGER—Copy Master
Examine Search Engine Results p. 16

One search can bring up millions of results. For example, a rock collector who types in *rocks* could get information on everything from Red Rocks Community College to a database of rock music downloads. A more manageable search might begin with *"rock collecting"* or *rock* NOT *music* or *+collecting +rocks +minerals.*

Follow these guidelines for examining the results that pop up:

1. Don't just click on the first result. The page that the search engine lists first may not be the most useful source for you.

2. Read the description of each page, including the Web address. The abbreviation at the end of the domain name in the Web address tells you about the page's source. For example, names of U.S. government domains end in *.gov.* Names of school sites contain *.edu.*

3. If a description seems to match your goal or keywords, click on it. If not, either go to the next description or think of ways to make your search terms better and try again.

TRY IT OUT! *Select Search Engine Results*

Entering *"rock collecting"* in a search engine led to these results (and more than 30,000 others). Which ones would you click on? Why?

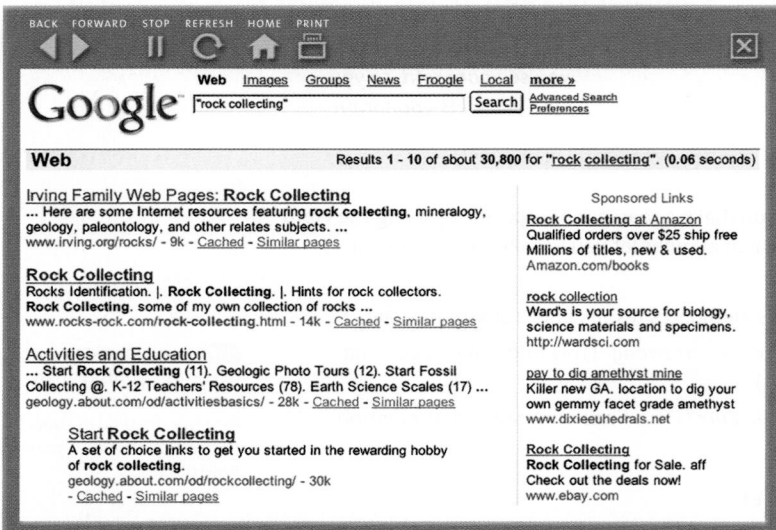

TIP The most common ending in domain names is *.com.* Sites with *.com* in their names are generally personal sites or product sites. Domains with names that end in *.org* often belong to nonprofit organizations, including some libraries.

Close Read

1. What term was used in this search? How could you narrow the search even more?

2. Which of these results would you click on first? Why?

3. The "sponsored links" are paid for by businesses. They want to sell their products on the Web. Predict what you would find at one of the sponsored links on this page.

DIFFERENTIATED INSTRUCTION

FOR LESS–PROFICIENT READERS

Concept Support Have students work in small groups at the computer and experiment with keywords for the topic of rock collecting. Have students use a Two-Column Chart to identify each keyword they use and the number of results it calls up. Have students share their charts and discuss what they learned.

 BEST PRACTICES TOOLKIT—Transparency
Two-Column Chart p. A25

FOR ENGLISH LEARNERS

Oral Language Explain to students how the various suffixes of Web site addresses are pronounced in spoken English.

Suffix	Pronunciation
.com	"dot com"
.org	"dot org" or "dot o-r-g"
.edu	"dot e-d-u"
.gov	"dot guv"

EXPLORE A WEB SITE

Web sites have many special features.

- **Home page** A home page is the "first" page of a Web site—a title page and table of contents all in one. It welcomes you to the site, provides general information, and helps you get where you want to go.

- **Menus** These can run across the top, along the sides, or across the bottom of pages. They tell you what pages or sections the site has and can keep you from getting lost as you explore the site. Many sites also include **hyperlinks** (underlined or boldfaced words) and **icons** (small pictures or symbols). Clicking on any of these takes you to other pages or to different sites.

- **Sponsor or creator** A site should tell you who created it.

- **Credits** Many sites include information about who created them and when they were last updated.

TRY IT OUT! **Navigate a Web Site**

Look at the information on this Web page about collecting.

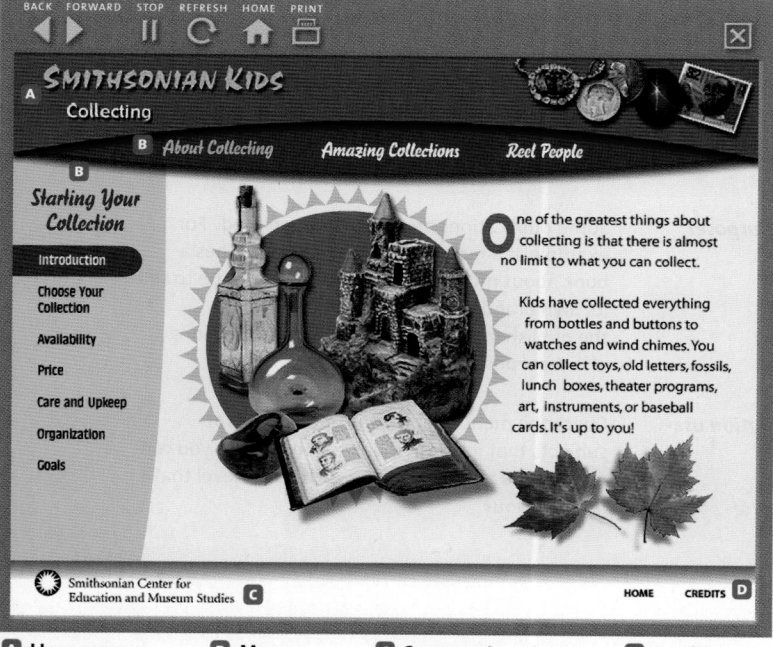

A **Home page**   B **Menus**   C **Sponsor/creator**   D **Credits**

Close Read

1. Where are the menus on this page?

2. What would you click on to get ideas about different kinds of collections?

3. Where would you click to find out who created this site and when it was last updated? Why is that information important?

DIFFERENTIATED INSTRUCTION

FOR LESS–PROFICIENT READERS

Comprehension Support Have groups input a Web address, such as one for the Smithsonian or NASA cited on page 970 of the teacher's edition. Ask them to locate the site's home page. Then have students create an oversize mock-up of the page on poster paper. Ask them to label each feature of the home page using the terms and information from page 971.

FOR ADVANCED LEARNERS/PRE–AP

Design a Home Page Have students create the first page of a personal Web site. Ask them to include graphics and text. Their home page should have at least one menu, several hyperlinks and icons, a description of the site, and the identity of the creator. Have students share their home pages in small groups.

EXPLORE A WEB SITE

Use the example on page 973 to give students additional practice in identifying parts of a Web page.

- **Home Page** Have students look at the home page on page 973 and read the text describing the site. Ask them what kind of information they will learn from visiting this site.

- **Menus** Have students identify the menus on the derekshirts.com Web page. Explain that the major sections of the site are listed across the top of the page. The specific pages within the "See My Collection" section are listed down the left side. All of the sections are accessible through hyperlinks.

- **Sponsor or Creator** Ask students who created the Web site. Have students explain whether or not derekshirts.com would be a good source if they wanted to find out more about T-shirt collecting.

- **Credits** Point out the dates at the bottom of the example. The derekshirts.com site was last updated in 2000. Ask students how they could find more information about the creator of the site. (**Possible answer:** *by clicking on the "About Derek" hyperlink*)

Close Read

1. **Possible answer:** *The menus appear across the top of the page and down the left side.*

2. **Possible answer:** *Clicking on "Amazing Collections" would give examples of different collections. The link "Choose Your Collection" might also give some ideas about what to collect.*

3. **Possible answer:** *The link "Credits" at the bottom of the page would provide information about the creators of the site and the last update. This information allows users to decide whether or not the site is a valid source for their purposes.*

S STANDARDS LESSON FILE
Research and Study Skills Lesson 4: Using a Web Site for Research

R RESOURCE MANAGER—Copy Master
Navigate Web Sites p. 17

Evaluating Information

Have volunteers read each entry in the chart aloud. Discuss the important ideas presented.

Date Tell students that as a general rule, they should choose the material with the most recent date. Exceptions include authoritative sources, such as well-known encyclopedias, that present basic facts unlikely to change over time, such as the dates of historical events and primary source material.

Author Ask students where they might look in a book to find information about the author. Where is that information found on a Web site? How else could students use the Internet to find information about an author? *Possible answers: In a book, information about the author might appear on the dust jacket or at the beginning or end of the book. On a Web site, there might be a page that tells about the author. An Internet search on the author's name may also yield information.*

Publisher Tell students that the organization that sponsors a Web site is the equivalent of a book's publisher. Write these suffixes on the board: *.com, .org, .edu, .gov.* Have students explain what they can infer about the sponsor of each site from its suffix.

Purpose Tell students that the home page of a Web site will often give them clues about the site's purpose. They should read the text and examine the menus carefully. Is the purpose to share information or to sell something? If the site's purpose is to sell a product or to promote a particular point of view, it may present facts in a biased way. Commercial sites may not present unbiased or accurate information. Remind students that the most useful sites for research purposes are those that are objective and factual.

Usefulness Explain that making a habit of checking menus and tables of contents first will help students determine whether a source is appropriate for their needs—before they waste a lot of time reading information that is not useful.

S STANDARDS LESSON FILE
Research and Study Skills Lesson 6:
  Evaluating Print Sources
Research and Study Skills Lesson 7:
  Evaluating Electronic Sources

Evaluating Information

Not all sources of information are created equal. To be sure the sources you choose are trustworthy, you must evaluate them first. That means asking and answering questions about each source you find. These evaluation guidelines apply to all sources—books, magazines, newspapers, Web sites, and even personal interviews.

WHAT TO ASK	WHY IT MATTERS
What is the date of the information?	For some topics—especially in science, medicine, technology, and sports—up-to-the-minute information is especially important. Even when an event happened long ago, up-to-date sources often contain the latest findings and insights.
Who is the author?	Some authors are experts on their topics. Some aren't. Look for information on the author's other books, education, job or profession, and awards. Is he or she an authority on this topic?
Who is the publisher?	Some publishers are more reliable and careful than others. For example, university presses tend to produce reliable books. Tabloid newspapers such as the *National Enquirer* can be far less reliable. A reference librarian can help you find reliable sources.
What is the purpose?	Some publications are one-sided or biased. For example, if a model-train company publishes a book about model trains, its purpose may be to sell its own brand. Look for information about the publisher and the author. Draw conclusions about purpose.
Is this information useful to me?	Check the menu or the table of contents for subjects that interest you. Also, make sure you can understand the source. Is it written at a level that's right for you?

DIFFERENTIATED INSTRUCTION

FOR LESS–PROFICIENT READERS

Concept Support Divide students into small groups. Provide each group with one reliable source and one source that is not credible. The unreliable source might be an article from a tabloid or from a personal Web site. Sources can be the same for each group. Ask groups to decide which of the two is not trustworthy and explain why. Discuss their evaluations.

FOR ADVANCED LEARNERS/PRE–AP

Evaluate Sources Have students locate two reliable sources on any subject. These sources should be different media. Have students present their sources in small groups and explain why they are reliable. Encourage other group members to challenge the reliability of each source so that the presenting student can defend his or her evaluation.

EVALUATE A WEB SITE

Publishing a book usually involves an author and editors. Many books are fact-checked and updated regularly. The Web is different. A personal Web site is usually the work of just one individual. Not all personal Web sites are unreliable, but be cautious. Ask yourself these questions:

- **Who created the site?** Is there a way to contact that person or group?

- **Why was the site created?** Is the site designed to give you information, to entertain you, or to sell you something? Some sites are created for more than one purpose.

- **Does the site contain problems?** Do you notice misspelled words, grammatical errors, or broken hyperlinks?

- **Does the author of the site seem knowledgeable about the topic?** Could you find more or better information in another source, such as an encyclopedia?

See page 982: Checklist for Evaluating a Source

TIP Even reputable publishers and Web sites sometimes publish incorrect information. Use a variety of sources when you do research.

TRY IT OUT! *Examine a Web Site*

This is an example of a personal Web site. What do you think is useful here? What problems do you see?

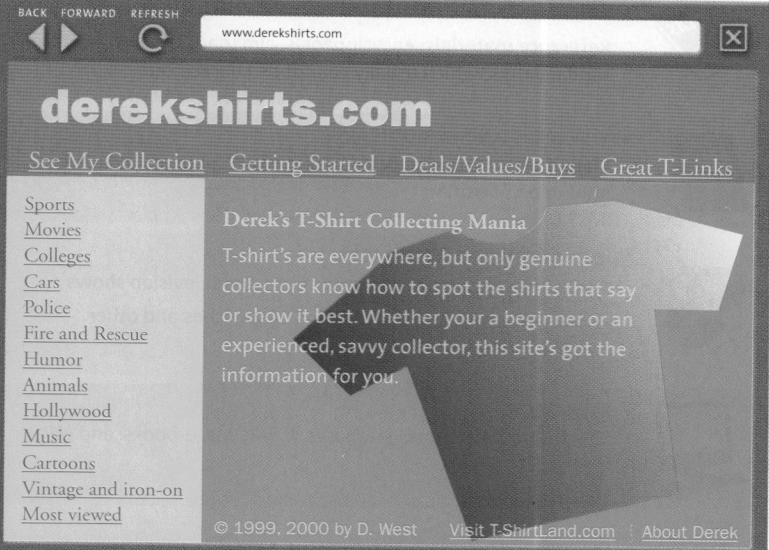

Close Read

1. Who created this site?
2. What is the purpose of this site?
3. When was the site last updated? How do you know?
4. What problems do you notice?

DIFFERENTIATED INSTRUCTION

FOR LESS–PROFICIENT READERS

Concept Support Reinforce the importance of the information on this page by working together to evaluate several Web sites on a particular subject. Use the checklist on page 982 to guide students in determining whether each site is a good source of information.

FOR ADVANCED LEARNERS/PRE–AP

Evaluate Web Sites Have students work together to create a bulletin board of tips for identifying good Web sites. Tips should be based on the criteria outlined on page 973 as well as information from other sources. Students should also include examples to illustrate each point they make.

EVALUATE A WEB SITE

Remind students that anyone can create a Web site that says anything. Therefore, it is up to the user to evaluate each Web site before relying on its information.

Authorship Generally, it is a good idea to avoid personal Web sites unless the author is an expert in the field and has the credentials to prove it. Have students volunteer the kinds of credentials they might look for. **(Possible answers:** *association with a respected educational institution, a position with a national or well-known organization, degrees and experience that can be verified)*

Purpose Have students return to their Jigsaw groups and locate three home pages: one for a site that entertains, one that informs, and one that persuades or sells. Have groups share their home pages.

Problems Discuss the conclusions users can draw from these kinds of sloppy errors.

Author's Knowledge As students know, one of the first steps in the research process is to obtain an overview of the subject from a respected encyclopedia or reference book. That information will help students determine if later sources are on the right track. As the *TIP* points out, it is important to verify information by checking a number of sources. These sources should agree on major facts. If not, more research is required to determine which sources can be trusted.

Close Read

1. *Possible answer: Derek West created the site.*

2. *Possible answer: The purpose of the site is to provide information about collecting T-shirts.*

3. *Possible answer: The site was last updated in 2000. The date appears at the bottom of the page.*

4. *The site has not been updated recently. Also, students might point out that there are two misspellings. "T-shirt's" should be "T-shirts," and "your" should be "you're." The misspellings may mean that the site as a whole is sloppy and the information it contains may not be accurate.*

R RESOURCE MANAGER—Copy Master
Evaluate Web Sites p. 18

Using the Library or Media Center

ACADEMIC VOCABULARY FOR THE LIBRARY

Read the terms aloud. Have students explain what they know about each. Remind students to look for definitions as they read the text.

LIBRARY AND MEDIA CENTER RESOURCES

Before students read this section of the text, ask them to identify resources that they might find in their school or local library. Record their responses on a Spider Map. (Label the legs *books, reference works, newspapers and periodicals, audio and video resources,* and *e-resources*.) Add details to the map during discussion of the text.

 BEST PRACTICES TOOLKIT—Transparency
Spider Map p. B22

Books Have students identify some fiction and nonfiction books that they have read. Ask them which they would most likely use for a research report and why.

Reference Have students describe the kinds of information that they would find in an ency-clopedia, an almanac, and an atlas.

Newspapers and Periodicals Explain that libraries do not have space to keep years' worth of past newspapers and magazines. Instead, past issues are photographed, and reduced-size images are stored on microfilm or microfiche. The film or transparency can be read with a special machine in the library.

Audio and Video Resources Tell students that audio or video recordings of interviews, speeches, and so on can be valid sources of information.

E-Resources Define each term for students.

- A **database** is a collection of information in electronic form that can be easily searched.
- A **CD-ROM** is a compact disk that can store information.
- An **e-book** is a book in electronic form.
- **MP3 files** contain songs or other audio data.

R RESOURCE MANAGER—Copy Master
Use Library and Media Center Sources
p. 19

ACADEMIC VOCABULARY FOR THE LIBRARY

You will use these terms when doing research in the library or media center:

- reference section
- primary source
- secondary source
- table of contents
- bibliography
- index
- catalog
- database

Using the Library or Media Center

Libraries have sections for adults, for children, and often for young adults or teens. In addition, most libraries have several other areas:

- meeting and study rooms
- special sections (such as ones for business, local history, and genealogy)
- special resources (such as maps)
- computer terminals

LIBRARY AND MEDIA CENTER RESOURCES

BOOKS

Fiction: Works of fiction come from writers' imaginations, although the writers may base their works on real people and events. Novels and short stories are works of fiction.

Nonfiction: Nonfiction is writing that tells about real people, places, and events. Biographies, diaries, newspaper and magazine articles, essays, and true-life adventure stories are examples of nonfiction.

REFERENCE

Reference desk: a place to ask for help with your research

Reference materials: encyclopedias, almanacs, atlases, and similar works, which usually cannot be checked out

NEWSPAPERS AND PERIODICALS

Magazines and newspapers: current issues, plus past issues in print or on microfilm

AUDIO AND VIDEO RESOURCES

DVDs: documentaries and other films and television shows

Audio resources: audio recordings of speeches and other events, audio books, and audio CDs

E-RESOURCES

Electronic collections: databases, CD-ROMs, e-books, and MP3s

---

DIFFERENTIATED INSTRUCTION

FOR LESS–PROFICIENT READERS

Comprehension Support Arrange for small groups of students to take tours of the school library. Provide them with a worksheet that asks them to name an example of each of these resources: nonfiction book, fiction book, encyclopedia series, atlas, newspaper, periodi-cal, database, DVD, CD-ROM.

FOR ADVANCED LEARNERS/PRE–AP

Synthesize Information Have students visit the school library to study and take note of its resources and layout. Then have students create a labeled map of the school library and its contents. Encourage them to be detailed and precise.

THE LIBRARY CATALOG

An online library **catalog** is a complete index of a library's or library network's holdings. If you have questions about accessing the catalog, or if you want tips on more efficient searching, ask a reference librarian.

There are at least four ways to search a library catalog:

- **Author** Check to see whether you should type the first name first (for example, *Juan Gutierrez*) or the last name first (*Gutierrez, Juan*).

- **Title** You do not need to type in beginning words such as *A, An,* or *The.*

- **Subject** You may need to try a variety of words to get to your subject. For example, some systems may not respond to the subject word *seashells.* Instead, they may use *shells.*

- **Keyword** You can try various keywords, or you can ask a reference librarian for help.

TRY IT OUT! **Search a Library Catalog**

To get to a catalog page, you might do a subject search for the term *shells.* That search would probably give you a list of subcategories, such as "Shells—Caribbean Sea" and "Shells in Art." The catalog page below is for the subcategory "Shells—Collection and Preservation."

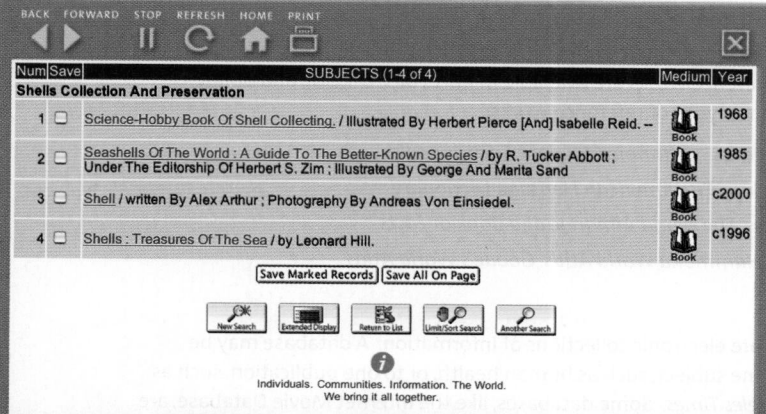

Close Read

1. Which book has information about both shells and collecting? How do you know?

2. Are these books or periodicals? How do you know?

DIFFERENTIATED INSTRUCTION

FOR ENGLISH LEARNERS

Vocabulary Support Have mixed-ability groups define these and other specialized terms as they are used in the pupil edition using context clues, prior knowledge, and a dictionary. Discuss their definitions.

- *online,* "on a computer"
- *catalog,* "listing of books and other resources"
- *network,* "group of libraries"
- *system,* "kind of computer program"
- *subcategory,* "smaller part of a category or group"

FOR ADVANCED LEARNERS/PRE–AP

Compare and Contrast Have students use both the keyword and the subject search to locate information on the same topic. Ask them to compare and contrast their results. Then discuss the advantages of each type of search.

THE LIBRARY CATALOG

Before students read this section, divide them into Round Robin groups and have them compile a written list of what they know about the library catalog. Ask a member of each group to read the list aloud.

 BEST PRACTICES TOOLKIT—Transparency
   Round Robin p. A17

Author Tell students that they must know the correct spelling of an author's name. Otherwise, they may be told that there are no books by that author in the library. If this happens, they can try a different spelling or ask a librarian for help with the spelling.

Title This search option should be used only if students have a specific book in mind. For a general search, it is not as helpful as a subject or keyword search.

Subject Explain that there are specific subject headings (such as *History, Computer Science,* and *Music*) recognized by the library catalog system. If users do not phrase the subject correctly, they may be referred to subject headings with a similar spelling—or the search might fail. Tell students that a librarian can help them locate lists of appropriate subject headings.

Keyword Tell students that keyword searches are a good place to begin. Suggest that they add terms each time to narrow down the number of results. Also, encourage students to think of synonyms for their keywords to see if they can improve their searches.

Close Read

1. *Possible answer: The first book on the list has the words* shell *and* collecting *in the title.*

2. *Possible answer: The symbol and the word* Book *in the "Medium" column identifies each of these sources as a book.*

If students need help . . . Discuss the different parts of the catalog page and each entry. Explain that if students wanted to learn more about the contents of each book, they could click on the title.

 STANDARDS LESSON FILE
   Research and Study Skills Lesson 2: Using Library Catalogs

Choosing and Evaluating Sources

PRIMARY AND SECONDARY SOURCES

Primary Sources Point out to students that some primary sources are more objective and accurate than others. For example, a memoir or autobiography may contain opinions as well as facts. A persuasive speech may contain bias.

Secondary Sources Tell students that secondary sources often combine information from primary sources and other secondary sources. Ask students to identify some advantages and some disadvantages of using secondary sources in their research. *(Possible answers: Advantages: Secondary sources often provide interpretation and analysis of events or topics. They offer a compilation of facts from many sources. They may be easier to find. Disadvantages: The author may have drawn inaccurate conclusions that he or she presents as facts.)*

REFERENCE WORKS

- Divide students into small groups. Give each group a different reference work.
- Have each group chart the key features of their reference work and offer examples of the kinds of questions it could answer.

 STANDARDS LESSON FILE
Research and Study Skills Lesson 5: Using Primary and Secondary Sources

DATABASES

- Ask a volunteer to read the text aloud.
- List some popular databases for students on the board: *Web Music Database, USA Sports Monitor, InfoTrac Junior Edition, Lands and Cultures.* Explain that some, such as Britannica Online and InfoTrac, have information on a variety of subjects. Others are more specialized.

Choosing and Evaluating Sources

The many different departments and resources in your local library can seem confusing. Be sure to ask a librarian for guidance.

PRIMARY AND SECONDARY SOURCES

All sources are either primary or secondary. This chart shows the difference.

PRIMARY SOURCES	SECONDARY SOURCES
Definition: firsthand accounts created by people who took part in or witnessed events	**Definition:** records of events created by people who were not directly involved in or present at the events
Examples: letters, diaries, photographs, autobiographies, interviews, speeches, birth certificates, census reports, first-person newspaper and magazine articles	**Examples:** textbooks, reference books, biographies, third-person newspaper and magazine articles

REFERENCE WORKS

The best place to get an overview of a topic is often a library's reference section. Reference works are available in print, on CD-ROM, and online. Here are some types of reference works:

- **Encyclopedias:** *Britannica Student Encyclopedia*
- **Dictionaries:** *The American Heritage Dictionary*
- **Almanacs:** *The World Almanac and Book of Facts*
- **Atlases:** *Hammond World Atlas, Goode's World Atlas*

DATABASES

Databases are electronic collections of information. A database may be specific to one subject, such as human health, or to one publication, such as the *Los Angeles Times.* Some databases, like the Internet Movie Database, are free. Many others, including InfoTrac, require paid subscriptions. Your school media center or your local library probably subscribes to many databases, which you can browse for free.

DIFFERENTIATED INSTRUCTION

FOR ENGLISH LEARNERS

Vocabulary: Cognates Point out that *primary, secondary,* and *reference* are similar to the Spanish words *primario, secundario,* and *referencia.* Have small groups apply New Word Analysis to help them define these terms from the text: *primary source, secondary source,* and *reference work.* Students should use context clues as well as their understanding of the cognates.

 BEST PRACTICES TOOLKIT—Transparency
New Word Analysis p. E8

FOR ADVANCED LEARNERS/PRE–AP

Synthesize Have students work in small groups to develop a user's guide to several reference works and significant databases. Their guides should include publication details for the sources, including the titles of Web sites and their addresses, and briefly describe their usefulness and the kind of information they contain. Encourage students to organize their entries in a logical way.

NONFICTION BOOKS

One of the best ways to get in-depth information about a topic is to check out a nonfiction book. Certain parts of a book can help you decide whether the book is right for your research.

1. Read the **title** and **subtitle** to get a general idea of the subject matter.

2. Check out the **copyright page** for the copyright date. The latest date is the one you should focus on. Is the book recent enough for your topic?

3. Read the **table of contents** for an overview. This page can also tell you whether the book contains a **bibliography** (a list of the sources used) or a list of **further reading**. Another useful feature in many books is a **glossary,** which is an alphabetical list of specialized terms, with definitions.

4. Look in the **index** for specific terms and topics that interest you. See how many pages include your topic. If the index lists just a page or two, the book may only mention your topic rather than explain it.

> **TIP** Are there whole books written on your exact topic? Then your topic may be too broad.

TRY IT OUT! *Examine the Parts of a Book*

Which parts of a book are shown here?

Close Read

1. How does the subtitle help you understand what the book is about?

2. Does this book contain information about collecting post cards? How about autographs? How do you know?

3. How up-to-date is this information? How do you know?

NONFICTION BOOKS

Have students use the illustration on this page to identify the parts of the book.

Title Ask students for the title of the book *(You Can Collect!)*. Have them identify the other information included on the title page *(author, publisher)*. Remind students that not all books include a subtitle, although this book has one—*A Beginner's Guide*.

Copyright Page Have students find this book's date of publication *(2008)*. Point out that earlier editions may have sold out or been updated.

Table of Contents Point out that this is only Part 1 of the table of contents. Ask students questions about the table of contents, such as how many pages are devoted to toy collecting *(74)* or where the chapter containing information about rock collections begins *(page 167)*.

Bibliography, Further Reading, Glossary Some books contain one or more of these sections. Explain to students that a bibliography or a list of books for further reading might give them ideas of other sources that they could use for their research. A glossary is useful in more technical or specialized works because it defines difficult terms that are not used in everyday conversation.

Index Tell students that they can scan the index of a possible source to see how much information it contains on their topic. Remind them that an index is organized alphabetically.

Have a volunteer read the **TIP** aloud. Point out that examining the table of contents of a book can help students narrow their focus.

 **RESOURCE MANAGER**—Copy Master
Use Parts of a Book to Find Information
p. 20

Close Read

1. *Possible answer: The subtitle indicates that this is a book for someone who is just starting to collect.*

2. *Possible answer: Yes. The table of contents includes a section on collecting post cards and other souvenirs. The index refers to information about autographs on page 224.*

3. *Possible answer: The book's copyright date is 2008. The books in the list of further reading date from 2003 to 2005. As of 2008, this book's information is up to date.*

DIFFERENTIATED INSTRUCTION

FOR LESS–PROFICIENT READERS

Comprehension Support Have students work in small groups. Distribute a nonfiction book to each group. Ask students to create illustrated charts of the significant features, using the boldfaced terms on page 977 as a guide.

Concept Support Have students use their nonfiction books from the previous activity to compare and contrast the table of contents with the index. They should examine the organization of both parts, the kind of information included, and the purpose. Have students present their information in a T Chart.

 BEST PRACTICES TOOLKIT—Transparency
T Chart p. A25

EVALUATE NONFICTION BOOKS

- Distribute appropriate nonfiction books from the school library to pairs of students. Also give pairs sticky notes.

- Read aloud and discuss the text that follows each bullet point.

- Then have pairs identify these parts of their books with sticky-note labels: *copyright date, bibliography, endnotes, appendix, preface, author information.*

- Have each pair draw a conclusion about whether the book would be a good source to use for information on a related topic. Ask pairs to present their insights to the class.

 **RESOURCE MANAGER—Copy Master**
Evaluate Nonfiction Books p. 21

Close Read

1. *Possible answer: This book tells how to collect political campaign buttons and includes a price guide.*

2. *Possible answer: The author appears qualified to write on this topic because he has been a collector for many years. He has written other books on the subject, and parts of his collection are in important museums.*

3. *Possible answer: According to the back cover, this fourth edition of the book has been "completely updated for 2008." Researchers should always remember to check for the latest edition.*

4. *Possible answer: Before deciding whether this book is useful for them, researchers should check the table of contents, the index, and the bibliography and the glossary (if they are included in the book).*

EVALUATE NONFICTION BOOKS

To be sure a nonfiction book is right for your purposes, ask these questions:

- **What is the most recent copyright date?** Check the **copyright notice,** which is usually on the back side of the title page. Have there been many updates and printings? That is often a sign that the book is reliable.

- **Is this a well-researched book?** Look for the author's sources. Is there a **bibliography,** a list of works the author consulted? Are there **footnotes, endnotes,** or **cross-references** that help you understand how the author got information? Is there an **appendix** of additional material, such as maps, tables, or charts?

- **What does the book say about the author?** Look for information about the author on the book jacket, at the beginning of the book, and at the end. Check the **preface** too. In this short introductory essay you may find clues to the author's background and a statement of his or her purpose.

TRY IT OUT! *Examine a Nonfiction Book*

Use what you have learned about nonfiction books to decide whether this book is a good source for someone who wants to learn more about collecting buttons.

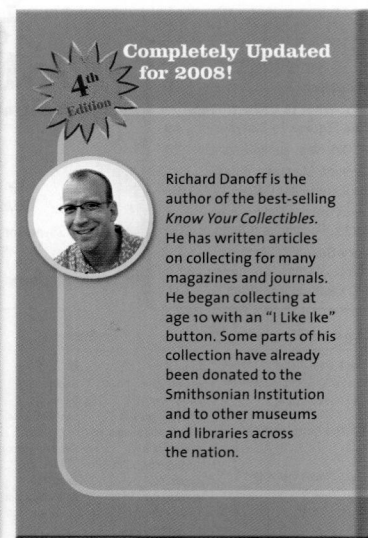

Close Read

1. What is this book about?

2. Why is the author qualified or not qualified to write about the topic?

3. How recent is the information in the book? How do you know?

4. What other parts of the book should someone look at to be sure it's suitable for his or her research? (Hint: See page 977.)

DIFFERENTIATED INSTRUCTION

FOR ADVANCED LEARNERS/PRE-AP
Evaluate Nonfiction

- Have pairs create an evaluation checklist for a nonfiction book based on the criteria listed in the text.

- Ask them to locate a nonfiction book related to a topic in which they are interested.

- Have them evaluate the book using their checklist.

- Have students share their evaluations with the class.

NEWSPAPERS AND PERIODICALS

Newspapers are publications that contain news and advertising and that are published very frequently, in most cases daily or weekly. Publications that are issued on a regular basis of more than one day apart are called **periodicals.** Magazines are a common type of periodical.

- **Newspapers** *Seattle Times, Boston Globe, St. Louis Post-Dispatch, Houston Chronicle, Miami Herald, Sacramento Bee*
- **Magazines** *Time, Teen Ink, Next Step, Skateboarder, Newsweek, Odyssey, New York Times Upfront*

One of the best ways to search for articles on your topic is by using a database of newspaper and magazine articles, such as InfoTrac. The page below comes from InfoTrac Junior Edition, a database aimed at students in grades 5–12.

TRY IT OUT! *Finding a Newspaper or Magazine Article*

A keyword search for *collecting autographs* brought up these results on InfoTrac Junior Edition. Clicking on the title of a document or on the "Check Out" link brings up the text of the entire article.

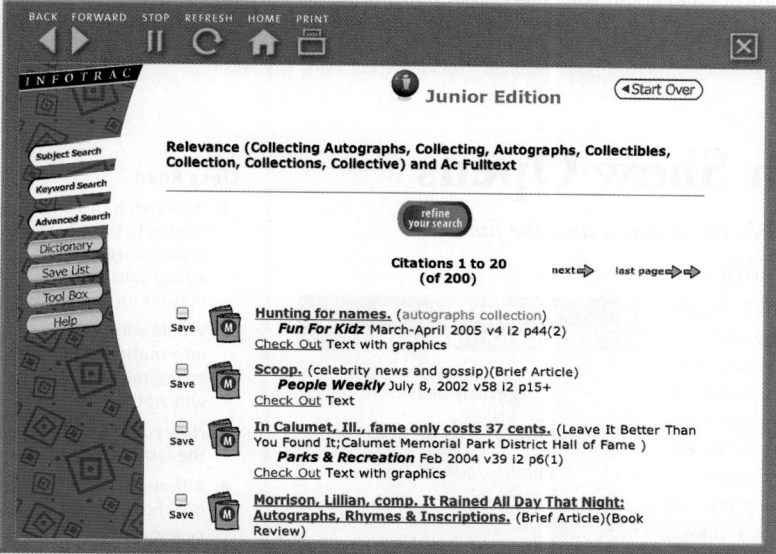

Close Read

1. If you were hunting for information on collecting autographs, which result would you click on first? Why?

2. These results are arranged by relevance, or how well they are related to the user's search terms. What does that tell you about the entries near the end of the list?

3. What could you click on to improve your search?

NEWSPAPERS AND PERIODICALS

- Have students read the first paragraph and discuss the differences between newspapers and periodicals.

- If possible, distribute samples of newsmagazines, such as *Newsweek* or *Time*, and daily newspapers to groups of students. Discuss the various elements of each type of publication. Point out that both magazines and newspapers may have feature articles or essays. These may express opinions, as opposed to presenting facts.

- Ask groups to compare and contrast the organization, kinds of topics, and content of the news articles in newspapers and magazines. Have groups share what they discover.

Close Read

1. *Possible answer: The first article, "Hunting for Names," is about autograph collections and seems directly related to the topic.*

2. *Possible answer: The entries at the end of the list are less relevant. They will probably not be useful sources of information about the topic.*

3. *Possible answer: Clicking on "refine your search" or "advanced search" would allow someone to reword his or her search in order to bring up more relevant results.*

If students need help . . . Discuss the parts of the screen and the information included in each entry.

DIFFERENTIATED INSTRUCTION

FOR LESS–PROFICIENT READERS

Comprehension Support Arrange for small groups to visit the library for the purpose of using the periodical and newspaper searching system with the librarian's help. Create a list of keywords that groups might use, such as *collecting shells, valuable baseball cards, rare stamps,* and so on. Have groups locate one article on their subject. After all students have completed the assignment, discuss and list the steps they followed in their searches.

FOR ENGLISH LEARNERS

Comprehension: Self-Monitor Have students review the previous pages and place sticky notes next to ideas that they find confusing. Then have them meet with partners to discuss and clarify these concepts. Discuss students' remaining questions in class.

EVALUATE NEWSPAPERS AND PERIODICALS

Reliability Gather a collection of newspapers and magazines, including both respected sources and more frivolous ones. Present them one at a time to the class. Ask students to raise their hands if the source is reliable. Then discuss the clues that led students to their conclusions.

Date Tell students that whether they use current articles or those from past publications depends on their topic and their approach. For example, the topic of cancer research could be approached from a historical perspective (requiring some older sources) or from a purely scientific one (requiring the latest information).

Author Reinforce the idea that if an article appears in a respected publication, the author is most likely reliable. Students could also ask a librarian or teacher about the author.

Factual Sources Remind students that one way to verify information is to find more than one source that presents similar facts.

Close Read

1. *Possible answer: The article describes an autograph show and explains the kind of information the show offers to beginning autograph collectors. Therefore, it is likely to be useful to someone who wants to learn more about collecting autographs.*

2. *Possible answers:*
   - *Yes. The information appears in a respected newspaper and quotes the museum director, who probably knows a great deal about the exhibit.*
   - *No. Newspapers make many mistakes because stories are written with tight deadlines and little time for research. Also, the museum director's opinions may be biased.*

3. *Possible answer: The facts could be checked by visiting, calling, or e-mailing the museum, by visiting the museum's Web site, or by finding another article about the show.*

4. *Possible answer: Readers who have questions about something in the article could contact the newspaper or the museum.*

RESOURCE MANAGER—Copy Master
Evaluate Newspapers and Periodicals p. 22

EVALUATE NEWSPAPERS AND PERIODICALS

Newspaper and magazine articles can be a good source of concise information. Your library may offer some of them in hard copies and many others online, on microfilm, or on microfiche. Once you find an article, you should evaluate it before you use it. Ask yourself these questions:

- **Is the source well-known and respected?** Most large-circulation newspapers and many national magazines are reliable. Avoid newspapers and magazines that cover mostly celebrity gossip, fad diets, UFOs, and similar topics.

- **When was it published?** Up-to-date is great, but not always best. For example, if you're researching the first moon landing, a newspaper article from 1969 could be your best source.

- **Who is the author?** Staff writers and contributing editors for major newspapers and magazines tend to be reliable. Some articles include notes about the authors' qualifications and previous publications.

- **Can the facts be verified?** Does the author give sources for the facts?

TRY IT OUT! *Examine a Newspaper Article*

Ask questions about the author and about the facts and other content to evaluate this article.

from the **Springfield Courier**

Autograph Show Opens

Exhibit features the rich, the famous, and the faded

BY TAISHA JACKSON, STAFF WRITER

The autographs of John F. Kennedy, Rosa Parks, and Tiger Woods will be on display for the next six weeks at the Ritter Museum's first-ever autograph show. Visitors will see those signatures and almost 1,200 others on letters, photographs, books, and documents.

Other highlights include a football signed by Joe Montana, a movie poster signed by Harrison Ford, and a very rare document with George Washington's signature.

Museum director Marcia Fiore calls this show a must for anyone interested in collecting. "There's a ton of stuff here for the beginning collector," she adds.

Among the displays for beginners are a timeline of collecting history, tips **See AUTOGRAPHS, page A6**

WHAT MAKES AN AUTOGRAPH VALUABLE?

Age/rareness

Popularity/"fickle factor"

Quality/condition

Close Read

1. How well is this article related to the research topic "collecting autographs"? Give reasons for your answer.

2. Would you call the information in this article reliable? Why or why not?

3. How could you check the facts in this article?

4. Although they are not shown here, the newspaper's and museum's e-mail addresses appear at the end of the article. Why is this important?

DIFFERENTIATED INSTRUCTION

FOR ENGLISH LEARNERS
Language Support: Bias

- Provide small groups with two newspaper articles each: an editorial and a news article. Be sure that the editorial uses emotionally loaded words to express its author's point of view.

- Have students identify words in both articles that express emotion or bias. Remind them to look for cognates.

- Ask students to explain which article would be the better source for unbiased facts.

FOR ADVANCED LEARNERS/PRE–AP
Demonstrate Have students reteach the ideas on this page in an interesting way. They might choose one of these approaches:

- Use the text information to evaluate two articles, including one that is not credible.

- Create a "how-to" video that explains how these evaluation tools should be implemented.

- Develop an oral presentation that uses graphic organizers and other visual aids.

Collecting Your Own Data

Although the library and the Internet are good resources, they are not the only places to get information. When you conduct an interview or learn by observation, you are doing original research.

INTERVIEWS

Interviews can be excellent means of gathering information. First, they provide primary-source information. Second, they can give you new insights into your topic or even whole new ways of looking at it.

You might interview someone who has in-depth knowledge of your topic. An interview can take place in person, or it can be conducted by telephone, e-mail, or letter. The most important part of an interview is preparing for it. Specific questions, prepared and thought through in advance, are a must.

See pages R81–R82: Conducting an Interview

FIELD RESEARCH AND OBSERVATION

When you observe with a research goal in mind, you are doing **field research.** For example, if you want to know more about teddy bear collecting, you might do field research at a flea market that attracts teddy bear collectors. In that case, your field research might include creating a chart of available items and their prices. Or you might visit a museum if you want to learn about certain kinds of butterflies or about life during the European Middle Ages. Observations that you make and carefully record in these places are also field research.

> *Notes on Visit to Winston County Flea Market, 5/21/2008*
>
> - *132 booths/tables/displays, only 4 with teddy bears*
> - *military-themed bears: army, navy, marines, air force*
> - *teddy bears with brand-name labels; also teddy bears that are sold along with children's books*
> - *koala, panda, and other "bears"*
> - *prices ranging from #1 to #1,500 (for a teddy bear from the 1950s)*
> - *bears vary by clothing, ribbons, other accessories; some bears for holidays (Valentine's Day) or occasions (graduation)*

DIFFERENTIATED INSTRUCTION

FOR LESS–PROFICIENT READERS
Concept Support

- As a class, develop questions that an interviewer might ask someone about his or her hobbies or favorite pastime.

- Have students copy the questions onto individual index cards.

- Have pairs interview each other using the questions and recording the responses.

- Have students orally summarize what they learn from their interviews.

FOR ADVANCED LEARNERS/PRE–AP

Research Have students choose a school or community activity or exhibit that they would like to research and report on. For example, students might investigate another class's fundraising car wash event or the local library's display of quilts. Ask students to visit the activity or exhibit and do field research. Have them use their field research to develop an oral or written report for the class.

Collecting Your Own Data

INTERVIEWS

Suggest that students keep these interviewing tips in mind:

- Do research ahead of time about the person to be interviewed or the topic to be discussed. Knowing something about the topic or person will enable you to ask better questions, save time in the interview, and show that you are serious about wanting to learn more.

- Write each question on a separate index card with space to record the response. Or, ask permission to audio- or videotape the interview. Put questions in order before the interview, but be flexible about following new lines of thought.

- If anything is confusing, clarify it immediately with the person being interviewed. If the interview is not taped, take a few minutes to summarize important ideas before ending the interview.

- Ask for suggestions for sources of further information, such as books or other people who might be willing to be interviewed.

- If conducting the interview by e-mail, be sure to use formal language and correct sentence structure in all correspondence.

Encourage students to consult pages R81–R82 of the Handbook for additional ideas.

FIELD RESEARCH AND OBSERVATION

Have students read through the sample field notes.

- Point out that the facts recorded during the visit to the flea market include statistics (numbers) and specific details.

- Have students work in small groups to draw some conclusions about teddy bear collecting from the information presented in this field observation.

S STANDARDS LESSON FILE
Speaking and Listening Lesson 1: Interview

Research Tips and Strategies

Web Know-How

- Divide students into five groups. Assign each group one of the Web tools (**Search Engines, Metasearch Tools,** and so on).
- Have each group look up the example Web sites in its assigned category and explore how these sites work.
- Ask groups to report back to the class on how the sites work and what kinds of research they would best support.

Checklist for Evaluating a Source

Point out the checklist, which summarizes what students learned on pages 972–980. Suggest that they copy it into their notebooks for future reference when choosing resources.

Understanding Web Addresses

.COM Tell students that some *.com* sites can be valuable sources of information. For example, *www.britannica.com* provides access to reference works as well as Web sites.

.EDU Although some *.edu* sites give practical information about the educational institutions that sponsor them, others can be helpful sources for students doing research. For example, *sunsite.berkeley.edu/KidsClick!/* is a searchable directory of Web sites reviewed for kids by librarians.

.GOV For information about the government, these are the sites to visit. Sites such as *www.kids.gov* and *bensguide.gpo.gov* are specially designed to help students access all sorts of Web pages and facts about different government agencies.

.MIL Most departments in the military branch of the government maintain their own sites. Students can find out more about various armed services by visiting sites such as *www.army.mil* and *www.af.mil*.

.NET Within some of the sites ending in *.net,* there may be useful information. For example, the site *eelink.net* helps students find facts about environmental issues on the Web. Tell students to check out these sites if the initial description on the home page looks promising.

.ORG These sites can be very helpful to researchers. For example, *www.ipl.org* is the Internet Public Library, an extensive resource on many topics.

Research Tips and Strategies

Web Know-How

To search the Web, you have to know what tools to use. Keep these options in mind.

Search Engines

You can and should use more than one search engine. Here are a few to try:

- Ask Jeeves for Kids (ajkids.com)
- Google (google.com)
- Yahoo! (search.yahoo.com)

Metasearch Tools

A metasearch engine combines results from a number of search engines.

- Dogpile (dogpile.com)
- Metacrawler (go2net.com)

Directories

Directories arrange Internet resources into subject categories.

- LookSmart directory (looksmart.com)
- Yahoo! Directory (dir.yahoo.com)

Virtual Libraries

Use a virtual library to find information in encyclopedias, directories, and indexes.

- Internet Public Library (ipl.org)
- Librarians' Index to the Internet (lii.org)

Other Web Resources

- Our Nation's Library: The Library of Congress (loc.gov)
- Databases: ProQuest K-12, InfoTrac Junior Edition

Checklist for Evaluating a Source

- ☑ The information is clearly related to your topic.
- ☑ The author is qualified to write about the topic.
- ☑ The information is up-to-date.
- ☑ The information is trustworthy because it has been reviewed and/or updated or it has been developed and posted by a reliable institution, such as a U.S. government agency.
- ☑ The facts can be verified in at least one other source.
- ☑ The writing is at your level. It isn't for little kids, and it isn't for scholars.

Understanding Web Addresses

The abbreviations in Web addresses give clues about who created the site and why.

WEB ABBREVIATIONS AND MEANINGS

.COM	commercial—information about products; some personal sites; some combinations of products and information, such as World Book Online
.EDU	education—information about schools, classes, schedules, and campus life; may also include students' personal sites
.GOV	U.S. government—official sites of the White House, the Library of Congress, and many government agencies
.MIL	U.S. military—official sites of the armed forces and related agencies
.NET	network—product information and sales
.ORG	organizations—charities, libraries, and other nonprofit organizations; also political parties

DIFFERENTIATED INSTRUCTION

FOR LESS–PROFICIENT READERS

Comprehension Support Use a graphic organizer to reinforce students' understanding of the steps of the research process.

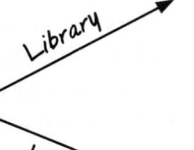

- Decide on topic.
- Read to get an overview.
- Narrow focus.
- Develop research questions.
- Find and evaluate sources.

Library →

- Use online catalog or periodical search system.
- Check reference materials.
- Locate nonfiction books.
- Find newspaper and magazine articles.
- Use electronic resources.

Internet →

- Choose search engine.
- Enter keywords.
- Identify credible sites.

Library Literacy

Almost all libraries and media centers arrange **fiction** by authors' last names. In general, for **nonfiction**, school media centers and public libraries use the Dewey decimal system, and university and research libraries use the Library of Congress system.

DEWEY DECIMAL SYSTEM

000–099	General works
100–199	Philosophy and psychology
200–299	Religion
300–399	Social sciences
400–499	Language
500–599	Natural sciences and mathematics
600–699	Technology (applied sciences)
700–799	Arts and recreation
800–899	Literature and rhetoric
900–999	Geography and history

LIBRARY OF CONGRESS SYSTEM

A	General works	M	Music
B	Philosophy, psychology, religion	N	Fine arts
		P	Language and literature
C–D	History		
E–F	American history	Q	Science
G	Geography, anthropology, recreation	R	Medicine
		S	Agriculture
		T	Technology
H	Social sciences	U	Military science
J	Political science	V	Naval science
K	Law	Z	Bibliography and library science
L	Education		

DIFFERENTIATED INSTRUCTION

FOR ADVANCED LEARNERS/PRE–AP

Chart Assign pairs or groups of students one of the major categories in the Dewey Decimal system (general works, philosophy and psychology, and so on). Ask them to create posters that graphically illustrate the subdivisions that organize the volumes within each broad category. For example, the literature category includes American (810s), English (820s), literatures of the Germanic languages (830s), and so on. Display students' posters around the room.

Library Literacy

Bring in several nonfiction books from the school library and present them to the class. Show the call number and relate it to the Dewey Decimal system used by the school library.

Focus and Motivate

OBJECTIVES

- analyze a student model that reflects the key traits of a research report
- use the writing process to produce a research report
- revise and edit, using a rubric
- create and present a multimedia report

Writing Workshop

In this part of the unit, students will learn the specific steps involved in developing and writing a research paper.

WRITER'S ROAD MAP

WRITING PROMPTS 1 AND 2

Help students choose a topic by listing works of fiction and nonfiction read in class this year and developing questions related to them. Or, to generate topics related to real-world issues, have students finish this sentence: "Inquiring minds want to know how _____."

ADDITIONAL PROMPTS

Use these prompts for more practice:

WRITING PROMPT 3

Writing About History Write a research report that explores an event in history and its consequences for people today.

Possible Subjects
- dismantling of the Berlin Wall
- first successful moon landing
- passage of the 19th Amendment (suffrage for women)

WRITING PROMPT 4

Writing for the Real World Write a research report about a current world problem.

Possible Subjects
- global warming
- destruction of the South American rain forests
- infectious diseases in Africa

For additional writing prompts, see

- WriteSmart CD
- Writing Center at **ClassZone.com**

KEY TRAITS

Review the six **KEY TRAITS** with students, emphasizing ideas and organization. Compare the traits with the rubric on page 998.

Writing Workshop

Research Report

When you write a formal research report, you draw information from many sources and put it together in a way that is your own. In the process, you show what you have learned about a topic and present your own ideas about it. The **Writer's Road Map** will show you how.

WRITER'S ROAD MAP

Research Report

WRITING PROMPT 1

Writing from Literature Develop a specific question about a work of fiction or nonfiction that you read this year. Write a research report that explores that question in detail. Your report should present information from at least three sources as well as your own ideas. Include a list of the sources you used.

Topics to Consider
- How did Jackie Robinson change baseball? ("The Noble Experiment")
- What was it like to be a knight? (*Sir Gawain and the Green Knight*)

WRITING PROMPT 2

Writing from the Real World Is there a question or topic that you have always wanted to know more about? Write a research report that investigates it. Your report should present information from at least three sources. It should also include your own ideas. Finish with a list of the sources you used.

Topics to Consider
- How does the human brain store information?
- Can tsunamis be predicted and prevented?

 RESEARCH TOOLS
For research tools and citation guidelines, go to the **Research Center** at ClassZone.com.

KEY TRAITS

1. IDEAS
- Presents a **thesis statement** that identifies the controlling idea of the report
- Supports the thesis with **evidence**, such as facts, statistics, examples, and expert opinions
- Combines information from **multiple sources** and includes **quotations** and **paraphrases**
- Includes the **writer's own ideas**

2. ORGANIZATION
- Follows a clear **organizational pattern**
- Connects ideas with **transitions**
- Includes a strong **introduction** and a satisfying **conclusion**

3. VOICE
- Maintains a serious, formal **tone**

4. WORD CHOICE
- Uses **precise words** to explain ideas

5. SENTENCE FLUENCY
- Varies the **lengths of sentences**

6. CONVENTIONS
- Uses **correct grammar, spelling, and punctuation**
- **Credits sources**
- Uses **correct formats and style**

Writing Workshop Resources

 RESOURCE MANAGER UNIT 9
Plan and Teach pp. 9, 12–14
Prewriting–Editing pp. 23–32
Publishing with Technology p. 33
Writing Support p. 34*

 STANDARDS LESSON FILE
Writing Lessons 1–2, 12, 21–23, 26, 40–41
Research and Study Skills Lessons 8–11
Media Lesson 22

BEST PRACTICES TOOLKIT
Scaffolding Writing Instruction pp. 43–46*
Cluster Diagram • KWL • Two-Column Chart
• Jigsaw Reading • Microtheme • Storyboard

TECHNOLOGY
- Easy Planner DVD
- Writing Center at **ClassZone.com**
- WriteSmart CD

* Resources for Differentiation

Part 1: Analyze a Student Model

WRITING STANDARD
4.A.2.c Compose to inform

Latushkin 1

Alex Latushkin
Ms. Tokoyuni
English 7
12 March 2008

A Short, Hard Life

What was it like to be alive during the Middle Ages? Movies and
television shows have led many people to imagine handsome young
knights dodging swords, arrows, and axes as they storm a castle.
However, most Europeans of the time were peasants, not knights, and
5   their lives were anything but glamorous. Peasants were at the bottom of
the social order during the European Middle Ages, so they struggled to
survive, had few comforts, and lived short lives.

For the typical peasant, each day was a struggle. Peasants had to
grow or raise their own food and make everything they needed to live,
10 including their clothes, blankets, and tools. In addition, in return for
protection, they had to grow grain for their lord, or landowner. Farming
was backbreaking work in the Middle Ages because peasants had only
basic tools, such as plows and pitchforks, instead of machinery (Hackett
254). If there was a flood or drought, if some crops froze, or if pests
15 ate the crops, the peasants didn't have enough to eat. Sometimes, when
there was war, invaders burned their fields and homes.

A peasant's struggle to survive did not end with growing crops.
Peasants "had few rights and were almost completely at the mercy of
their lords" (Deliyannis). Besides growing food for their lord, they had
20 to do services for him. For example, they might have to build roads or
cut wood for him. They even had to fight sometimes, although they

KEY TRAITS IN ACTION

Uses headers and margins required by teacher.

Exciting **introduction** grabs the reader's attention.

Clear **thesis statement** gives the most important idea and shows how the report will be organized.

Uses **precise words** and varies **sentence lengths** throughout.

WRITING WORKSHOP   **985**

Teach

Part 1: Analyze a Student Model

Have students read the **Student Model** and **Key Traits in Action.** Then discuss the model with the class, pointing out specific examples of each trait and building on what students have already noted. You may also wish to incorporate the following activities:

- **Introduction** Explain that a strong introduction also provides a context for the topic of the report. This writer mentions some general aspects of the Middle Ages, such as battles, knights, and castles, before he narrows his focus.

  Help students identify the strengths of this introduction by asking these questions:

  How does the writer capture the attention of readers? (**Possible answer:** *He asks a thought-provoking question [line 1].*)

  What is the purpose of the second sentence? (**Possible answer:** *to engage readers by drawing upon their prior knowledge*)

  What is the effect of placing the thesis statement at the end of the introduction? (**Possible answer:** *The focus of the report is fresh in readers' minds as they begin reading the next paragraph.*)

- **Sentence Variety** Write these sentences on the board:

  Farming was backbreaking work. Peasants had only basic tools. There were floods and droughts. Sometimes crops froze. Pests ate crops. Then peasants starved.

  Read the sentences aloud. Then read the corresponding sentences in the model (lines 11–15). Ask students to compare the effect of both. (**Possible answer:** *The sentences on the board are short and choppy. The varied sentence lengths in the model help hold readers' attention and create a smoother flow. The writing in the model also seems more sophisticated, making the writer sound confident and knowledgeable.*)

DIFFERENTIATED INSTRUCTION

FOR ALL STUDENTS
For general guidelines on differentiating writing instruction, see

BEST PRACTICES TOOLKIT
Scaffolding Writing Instruction
pp. 43–46

FOR ENGLISH LEARNERS
Language: Skill Words Review these terms:

- *thesis statement:* in a research report, one or two sentences that explain the content of the report and its organization

- *multiple sources:* more than one primary or secondary source that provide information about the topic of a research report

- *quotations:* sentences or phrases that are taken directly from a source and presented within quotation marks

- *paraphrase:* information from a source that is stated in the writer's own words

- *to credit sources:* to identify where facts, examples, or ideas were found

- *format:* how the parts of a research report are arranged on the pages

WRITING WORKSHOP   **985**

- **Charts** Have students study the chart. Point out that the writer could have included the information in a series of sentences instead of using a visual aid. Ask students to explain the chart verbally. *(Possible answer: A loaf of bread cost a quarter of a penny. Half a penny bought a dozen eggs. An ax cost four pennies. A pound of candles cost six pennies.)*

  Discuss why the chart is a more effective way to present this information. Then point out how the writer introduces it and summarizes its significance, tying it into his report. He also keeps the chart small, minimizing the interruption of the text.

- **Multiple Sources** Explain that the writer uses parenthetical documentation to identify the source of each fact. The author's last name (or a shortened version of the title) and the page number are given in parentheses at the end of the sentence in which the fact appears.

  Have students list the sources that the writer has cited in his paper. *(Deliyannis, Singman, Hackett, "Middle Ages")*

  Ask students which sentence includes facts from more than one source. How do they know? *(Possible answer: The sentence in lines 39–41 includes facts from more than one source. Three sources are included in the parenthetical documentation.)*

Latushkin 2

did not have training or good weapons. Peasants also had to make other payments to their lord, such as for using his mill to grind their grain. Finally, peasants had to pay one-tenth of everything they produced to the
25 church (Singman 100). All this work and all these costs made life hard. No wonder Hackett says that peasants "worked from sunrise to sunset" (158).

> **Transitions** show how ideas are related.

Even though some peasants earned a little money through their labor, they still struggled. According to Singman, in England in the late 1200s, some peasants could earn about 1 d. (one English penny) per
30 day (59). As this chart shows, that didn't buy much.

Some Thirteenth-Century Prices			
1 loaf of bread	1/4 d.	1 dozen eggs	1/2 d.
1 ax	4 d.	1 pound of candles	6 d.

Source: Singman 60.

> This student used a chart to show a large amount of information in a small space.

In other words, a peasant could work all day for just four loaves of bread.

Peasants who survived had few comforts, because "most medieval homes were cold, damp, and dark" ("Middle Ages"). A peasant's home
35 was just a hut with a place for a fire in the middle (Hackett 158). Pigs and chickens might live in the house with the family. The floor was dirt or clay, and there was not much light or heat. People didn't have beds. Instead, they slept on sacks of straw on the floor. For furniture, there might have been a stool, a bench, and maybe a table (Singman 84-85). A peasant's
40 diet was simple: bread, beans, chicken, eggs, vegetables (such as cabbage and onions), and perhaps milk and cheese (Deliyannis; "Middle Ages"; Singman 70). Only "the fortunate peasant" might have a cow (Hackett 159).

> Weaves together information from **multiple sources** and **credits** each one properly.

DIFFERENTIATED INSTRUCTION

FOR ENGLISH LEARNERS

Comprehension: Transitions Explain to students that a research report might use all sorts of transitions, depending upon how the writer chooses to organize his or her facts. Use the **Student Model** to help students review the different kinds of transitions.

- What are some words or phrases that the writer uses to point out differences? *(Possible answers: "however," "not," "but" [lines 4–5]; "instead" [line 37]; "compared with today" [line 45])*

- What are some words or phrases that the writer uses to show cause-and-effect relationships? *(Possible answers: "so" [line 6], "because" [line 12], "if" [line 14], "although" [line 21], "even though" [line 27])*

- What are some words that the writer uses to show a time-order or sequential relationship in lines 47–53? *(Possible answers: "during" [line 47], "before" [lines 48, 49], "after" [line 52])*

- What are some words or phrases that the writer uses to develop main ideas in lines 8–11 and in lines 17–23? *(Possible answers: "including," "in addition" [line 10]; "besides" [line 19]; "for example" [line 20]; "even" [line 21]; "also" [line 22]; "such as" [line 23])*

Latushkin 3

Compared with today, people in the Middle Ages had short lives.
45 They faced "malnutrition, poor hygiene, parasitic infections, and disease" (Hackett 158). Singman explains that during the 1200s, one child out of every six died before his or her first birthday (18). Many others died before they became adults. Deliyannis says the average life span was 30 years in the 900s. Old age was especially hard on peasants.
50 Singman believes that many old peasants had to beg to survive (31). After a lifetime of hard work, it must have been terrible to beg for a crust of bread.

Although many films and television shows make life in the European Middle Ages seem exciting and glamorous, the peasants
55 probably had a different view of things. Their lives were short and hard, and their crops meant far more to them than any castle did.

> Provides a direct **quotation** and an expert opinion as **evidence.** The serious **tone** is appropriate for the subject matter.

> Writer reflects on what he has learned and includes **his own idea** about it.

> Thoughtful **conclusion** refers back to the introduction and summarizes what the writer learned.

Latushkin 4

Works Cited

Deliyannis, Deborah Mauskopf. "Middle Ages." <u>World Book Online Reference Center</u>. 2005. World Book. 25 Feb. 2008 <http://www.worldbookonline.com/wb/Article?id=ar360060>.

Hackett, Jeremiah, ed. <u>Medieval Europe, 814-1350</u>. World Eras 4. Detroit: Gale, 2002.

"The Middle Ages: Homes." <u>Learner.org</u>. Annenberg/CPB. 6 Mar. 2008 <http://www.learner.org/exhibits/middleages/homes.html>.

Singman, Jeffrey L. <u>Daily Life in Medieval Europe</u>. Westport: Greenwood, 1999.

> Online encyclopedia

> Reference book

> Reliable Web site

> Book

- **Quotations** Point out how the writer weaves the quotation (lines 46–47) into the text of his paper. He places it in the framework of his sentence. Explain that direct quotations should be used sparingly. As a rule, use a quotation only when paraphrasing the idea would make it less effective, less clear, or less striking.

- **Original Ideas** Explain that a good research paper includes inferences, conclusions, and summaries of the evidence presented. Ask students how they know which ideas in the model are the writer's own. (*Possible answer: His own ideas are not documented.*)

- **Works Cited** Tell students that every research paper should have a Works Cited page. This is a separate page at the end of the research report that lists all of the sources the writer used in preparing his or her paper. The sources included on the Works Cited page should all appear in parenthetical documentation within the paper at least once.

Ask students how the Works Cited page is organized. (*Possible answer: The sources are listed in alphabetical order, either by author or by title. A title is used only when a work does not have a distinct author.*)

Ask students why a Works Cited list is helpful to readers of research reports. (*Possible answers: It shows the sources used by the writer. It gives ideas for further reading. It allows readers to check facts for accuracy and bias.*)

For interactive student models, see

*Write*Smart CD

Writing Center at **ClassZone.com**

FOR LESS–PROFICIENT READERS

Language Support Students may be confused between the homonyms *site* (as in "Web site") and *cite* (as in "Works Cited"). Explain that the verb *cite* means "to mention as support or evidence." The noun *site* usually means "a place," but in the context of the Internet it means "a collection of information published as text and graphics in a set of linked Web pages."

FOR ENGLISH LEARNERS

Comprehension: Transitions Have students use the appropriate transitions to connect these ideas in a short paragraph:

Our class wanted to raise money. We decided to sell wrapping paper.

Each student sold five rolls. We would reach our goal.

Some customers bought several rolls. They gave extra money to our fund.

The fund drive was completed. We donated the money to our local soup kitchen.

*Possible answer: Our class wanted to raise money, **so** we decided to sell wrapping paper. **If** each student sold five rolls, we would reach our goal. Some customers bought several rolls. They **also** gave extra money to our fund. **After** the fund drive was completed, we donated the money to our local soup kitchen.*

For further practice with transitions, use

 **RESOURCE MANAGER—Copy Master** Writing Support p. 34

WRITING WORKSHOP **987**

Practice and Apply

To support students during the writing process, use these copy masters:

R RESOURCE MANAGER—Copy Masters
Prewriting–Editing pp. 23–32
Publishing with Technology p. 33
Writing Support p. 34 *(for English learners)*

Part 2: Apply the Writing Process

PREWRITING

1. Find a topic. Have students work in pairs to brainstorm topics. Suggest that they create a list of topics or questions or use a Cluster Diagram to record their ideas.

BEST PRACTICES TOOLKIT—Transparency
Cluster Diagram p. B18

2. Narrow the topic. Have students locate some information on the topic in which they are interested. They might read an encyclopedia article or browse through the table of contents of a nonfiction book. Suggest that students use this information to help them identify a focus.

3. Ask research questions. Tell students that beginning their research process without questions is like driving across the country without a map. They are bound to get lost and take many wrong turns, wasting both time and energy.

Have students write a question about their topic beginning with each of these words: *who, what, when, where, how,* and *why.* Have students share their questions in small groups to get ideas about other types of questions they might ask. Explain that as they learn more about their topic, they will think of additional questions. At some point, they may need to select a few of their best questions and set aside the rest to keep their focus narrow.

R RESOURCE MANAGER—Copy Masters
Narrow a Research Topic p. 23
Ask Research Questions p. 24

For interactive graphic organizers, see

🖉 Write*Smart* CD

ℹ️ Writing Center at **ClassZone.com**

Part 2: Apply the Writing Process

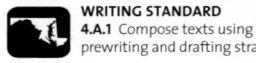

WRITING STANDARD
4.A.1 Compose texts using prewriting and drafting strate...

PREWRITING

What Should I Do?	*What Does It Look Like?*
1. Find a topic. Make a list of topics that you want to research and write about. If your teacher has assigned you a specific subject area, generate ideas and questions based on that. If your teacher has told you to choose your own topic, think about what you have learned this year in school or on your own. For example, you may want to explore a topic or idea from literature, science, or social studies. Circle the most interesting words and ideas on your list.	▶ I liked learning about (medieval Europe) in social studies class and English class this year. kinds of weapons that knights used kings and queens, knights, archers, monks, (peasants) <u>Crispin: The Cross of Lead</u> is about a peasant accused of murder. What was it like to live in a medieval village? What did everyday people eat, drink, and wear? TV shows and movies make medieval times seem exciting. Were they?
2. Narrow the topic. Most topics that leap to mind are too broad. Keep "reducing" your topic until you have something that you can cover in the number of pages your teacher has assigned. **See page 967:** Narrow Your Focus	▶ LIVING IN THE MIDDLE AGES THE FEUDAL SYSTEM Classes of Feudal Society Peasants/Commoners daily life of peasants
3. Ask research questions. What do you want to know about your topic? List some questions that will help guide your research.	▶ My Research Questions 1. What work did peasants do? 2. Were they more like slaves or more like farmers? 3. What were their homes like? 4. What did they do besides work?

DIFFERENTIATED INSTRUCTION

FOR LESS–PROFICIENT WRITERS

Find a Topic Help students implement the **Prewriting** steps described on this page.

1. Provide students with a complete set of topics drawn from the writing prompts on page 984 or other sources.

2. Briefly examine each topic and discuss ways that it might be approached.

3. Have each student choose two topics. Help students find related encyclopedia articles and then have them read about both topics before making a final choice.

Ask Research Questions Remind students to use a KWL chart or other graphic organizer to record what they already know about their topics. Gathering information this way will help them think of research questions.

 BEST PRACTICES TOOLKIT—Transparency
KWL: Know, Want to Know, Learned
p. A21

RESEARCHING

What Should I Do?

1. Find possible sources.
One of the best places to start is an encyclopedia, whether in print, online, or in CD-ROM form. You may have to look up a broad topic, such as "Middle Ages," in order to find a subsection about a narrow topic, such as "peasants." Ask a librarian for help.

After you have examined some reference materials, you will have a better idea of what **keywords** to type into an online catalog or search engine. Specific keywords will help you find just the right books, Web sites, and other sources.

What Does It Look Like?

Sources	My Comments
General Encyclopedias	
"Middle Ages" <u>World Book Online</u>	interesting; good facts
"Middle Ages" <u>World Book</u> (print)	not a lot about peasants
Library Reference Books	
<u>Encyclopedia of the Middle Ages</u> (Ref 940.1 ENC)	really hard to understand!
<u>Medieval Europe, 814–1350</u> (Ref 940.14 MED)	good info; I can understand this
Other Library Materials	
<u>Life in the Middle Ages: The Serf</u> (J VIDEO 909.07 SERF)	video from children's room
<u>Daily Life in Medieval Europe</u> (940.1 S617)	terrific source: lots of facts, illustrations, explanation
Web Sites	
"The Middle Ages"	terrific; I bookmarked this
"The Middle Ages: Life of a Medieval Peasant"	easy to read; reliable?

2. Evaluate each source.
Decide whether each source is worth using or has a problem. Sources with problems might include

- a Web site that does not show who created it
- a book or Web site that is too simple or too complicated for your needs

See pages 973 and 976–980 for evaluation guidelines.

Rejected Sources

<u>Encyclopedia of the Middle Ages</u>: too specific for my topic

<u>Life in the Middle Ages</u> video: for younger students; should use sources from Teen and Adult Nonfiction sections instead

"The Middle Ages: Life of a Medieval Peasant" Web site: no author given, so information may not be reliable

RESEARCHING

1. Find possible sources. Suggest that students also return to their research questions for ideas of keywords that they might use to locate sources. Tell them to circle key terms in the questions and use these to create keywords. For example, from the research questions on page 988, students might develop the keywords *medieval peasants, medieval peasants' homes,* and *medieval farming techniques and tools.* Remind students to also look for possible keywords among the entries brought up by the library catalog or Web search engine.

Tell students to keep track of all the promising sources that they come across, whether or not they are ready to use them. Suggest that they use a Two-Column Chart such as the one on page 989. They should record all information that will help them locate the source again, such as the titles, authors, and call numbers of books; the locations and titles of articles; and the URLs of Web sites.

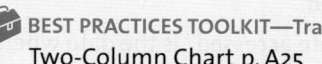 BEST PRACTICES TOOLKIT—Transparency Two-Column Chart p. A25

2. Evaluate each source. Review the general criteria for evaluating sources on page 972 as well as the specific guidelines for each type of source. Then have students bring in all the materials that they have gathered so far. Circulate around the room, quickly checking their sources and allowing them a chance to ask any questions that they have.

Remind students that in addition to being credible, their sources must contain information that will help them answer their specific research questions.

R RESOURCE MANAGER—Copy Master Find Sources p. 25

FOR ENGLISH LEARNERS

Task Support Help students locate and use audio versions of printed texts such as reference works or nonfiction books. Also suggest books with good visuals: illustrations, diagrams, cutaways, and so on.

FOR ADVANCED LEARNERS/PRE–AP

Find Possible Sources Challenge students to locate and use one of these types of sources in their research reports:

- documentary or film
- correspondence or personal interview with an expert in the field
- primary source such as a diary, a speech, an eyewitness account, or a letter

3. **Make source cards.** Tell students that if they are interested in a source, they should create a source card immediately, before they start to take notes. Their cards need not be in any particular order but will probably reflect the sequence in which they locate and use each source.

Explain that students should follow the format for each type of source exactly. Later, when it is time to create their Works Cited lists, all the information will be readily available on the cards. Draw students' attention to these conventions:

- The author's last name appears first, followed by a comma, and then the first name.
- Periods are used to separate each element of the entry.
- Titles of books, magazines, and Web sites are underlined.
- Titles of articles are placed in quotation marks.
- The call number of nonfiction books is recorded.
- The "date accessed" is the date when the student visited a particular Web site.

Point out the additional bibliographic forms on page 998 so that students know where to look if they have sources other than those described on this page, such as a CD-ROM encyclopedia, a magazine or newspaper article, an interview, a book with an editor, or a motion picture.

RESEARCHING

What Should I Do?

3. **Make source cards.**
   Write the information below on each card. Then number the card in the top right-hand corner.

Online encyclopedia
- author (if given) and title of article
- date of publication or posting (if given)
- publisher and date accessed
- URL

Print or CD-ROM encyclopedia
- author (if given) and title of article
- name and year of encyclopedia
- if a CD-ROM, the term *CD-ROM* and place of publication and publisher

World Wide Web site
- author (if given) and title of Web page or article
- publication information for a print version (if there is one)
- date created or posted (if given)
- name of institution or organization responsible for the site
- date accessed
- URL

Book
- author or editor and title
- place of publication and publisher
- year of publication
- library call number

See page 998: Citing Other Types of Sources

What Does It Look Like?

Online encyclopedia

Deliyannis, Deborah Mauskopf. "Middle Ages." World Book Online Reference Center. 2005. World Book 25 Feb. 2008 <http://www.worldbookonline.com/wb/Article?id=ar360060>.

(1)

Print encyclopedia

Lyon, Bryce. "Middle Ages." The World Book Encyclopedia. 2000 ed.

(2)

World Wide Web site

"The Middle Ages: Homes." Learner.org. Annenberg/CPB. 6 Mar. 2008 <http://www.learner.org/exhibits/middleages/homes.html>.

(3)

Book

Singman, Jeffrey L. Daily Life in Medieval Europe. Westport: Greenwood, 1999. 940.1 S617

(4)

DIFFERENTIATED INSTRUCTION

FOR LESS–PROFICIENT READERS
Make Source Cards

- Place students in Jigsaw groups and assign each group one of the sample entries on this page or page 998.
- Have students copy their entries onto sheets of large poster paper.
- Have them label each part of the entry using the information on the left side of page 990.
- Have groups explain their entries. Display posters around the room.
- After students have presented their labeled entries, have individuals create their own source cards.
- Have students reassemble in their groups and check each other's cards against the labeled entries displayed around the room.

 **BEST PRACTICES TOOLKIT**
Jigsaw Reading p. A1

RESEARCHING

What Should I Do?

4. Take notes.
As you read your sources, look for information that answers your questions and makes you think of new questions. Use this information to create note cards.

Each card should include the following:

- a specific heading
- the source number (from its source card)
- the fact or idea that you want to include in your report
- a page number if one is available

5. Record information accurately.
There are three different ways to capture a piece of information:

- You can **quote** the text, which means **copying it exactly.** Put quotation marks around what you write.
- You can **paraphrase** the text, which means **restating the ideas in your own words.** A paraphrase captures all the ideas of the original passage and is about the same length as it.
- You can **summarize** the text, which means **recording only the most basic ideas** in it. Because a summary does not include unnecessary details, it is shorter than the original passage.

What Does It Look Like?

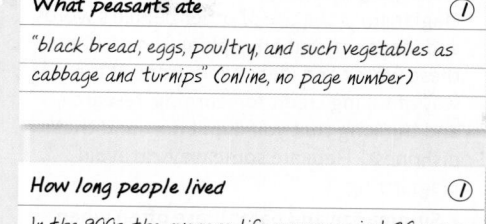

What peasants ate ①

"black bread, eggs, poultry, and such vegetables as cabbage and turnips" (online, no page number)

How long people lived ①

In the 900s, the average life span was just 30 years (online, no page number).

Original source

Each house was a simple single-room, single-story, high-roofed structure. At the center of the room was an open-hearth fire on the packed-earth floor; it vented through a hole in the roof.

Hackett, Jeremiah, ed., Medieval Europe, 814–1350

Paraphrase

Peasants' homes ⑤

A peasant's home was just one room with high walls, a roof, and a dirt floor. Each home had a fireplace in the middle and an opening in the roof to let the smoke out (158).

Summary

Peasants' homes ⑤

A peasant's home was just a hut with a place for a fire in the middle (158).

4. Take notes. Tell students it is a good idea to skim a source first before taking notes.

Explain that only one fact or idea should be written on each note card. That way, facts can be easily moved around or eliminated when it is time to organize or write the paper.

Encourage students to make each note card self-sufficient. In other words, each card should include all the information necessary to understand the fact. For the same reason, students should avoid unclear pronoun references. For example, the note "it dramatically affected the average life span of peasants" is confusing because there is no clear antecedent for *it*.

Urge students not to worry about keeping their note cards in the order in which they wrote them. Later in the process, they will choose the best way to organize their facts.

5. Record information accurately. Tell students that it is important to copy names, dates, and other specific details accurately onto the note card. The note-taking process is meant to eliminate the need to return to sources for information.

Remind students that direct quotations should be reserved for very significant ideas or memorable phrasing.

Tell students that they might summarize when they want to provide background information or a context for more interesting or more significant details to come. Have students read lines 34–35 in the **Student Model** in which the summary from this page appears. The writer does not want to waste space describing the roof or walls. Rather, he wants to give a general impression of the house and follow it up with details that he thinks are more important, such as the fact that livestock share the living space.

Students should paraphrase, however, when they are taking notes on major ideas that need to be developed with examples, reasons, facts, statistics, or other details.

R RESOURCE MANAGER—Copy Masters
Paraphrase and Summary 1 p. 26
Paraphrase and Summary 2 p. 27

FOR LESS–PROFICIENT WRITERS

Record Information Have students read the second paragraph of "Great White Sharks" on page 887 and then classify these notes:

- In the past, we believed that once a shark smelled blood, there would be a feeding frenzy. Now we know that most shark bites are not fatal because the shark realizes its mistake and goes away. *(paraphrase)*
- Contrary to previous beliefs, most shark victims survive because the shark does not return for a second bite. *(summary)*

- "a feeding frenzy that inevitably led to death" *(quotation)*

Take Notes Give students additional practice in taking notes. Have them turn to a passage in a nonfiction selection such as "What Do You Know About Sharks?" (page 874). Have students work in small groups to take notes on this passage using both the paraphrasing and the summarizing method. Record different groups' examples on the board. Choose or put together the best paraphrase and the best summary to serve as models.

6. **Avoid plagiarism.** Review the explanation and examples on page 992. Then have students exchange sets of note cards with a partner. Ask students to review the note cards, keeping the questions listed below in mind. Suggest that students flag questionable note cards with sticky notes before returning them to their partners.

- **Does each note card have a source number on it?**

  Presenting someone else's ideas as your own is plagiarism. These ideas might be facts, observations, inferences, conclusions, examples, reasons, anecdotes, comparisons, sayings, or data. All such ideas must be documented. This means that note cards must have a source number and usually a page number as well. Failure to document leads readers to believe that the ideas are those of the person writing the paper. Plagiarism can happen on purpose, which is dishonest, but it can also happen by mistake if the writer is not careful.

- **Does the note sound as if a seventh grader wrote it?**

  If the note is not in quotation marks but uses high-level vocabulary or language, it probably has not been paraphrased. As the **TIP** indicates, using someone else's exact words without putting them into quotation marks and citing the source is plagiarism.

- **Is material from an online source paraphrased, summarized, or presented in quotations?**

  Although online sources might give permission to duplicate their material, that does not mean that the information can be copied into a research paper without acknowledging the source or paraphrasing the text. Writers of research papers must tell their readers where they found all their information.

R RESOURCE MANAGER—Copy Masters
Avoid Plagiarism 1 p. 28
Avoid Plagiarism 2 p. 29

RESEARCHING

What Should I Do?

6. **Avoid plagiarism.**
   Plagiarism is the use of other people's words and ideas without an explanation of where these words and ideas came from. It is a way of taking credit for learning, research, and thinking that you didn't do—and that's dishonest. Here are some ways to avoid plagiarizing:

   - **Summarize and paraphrase often when taking notes.** This will help you avoid lifting other people's words and ideas when you draft.
   - **Don't rely heavily on one source.** The more you read from many authors, the more likely you are to see a bigger picture—and start developing your own ideas and opinions.
   - **Put all your sources away when you draft.** At that time, use only your note cards.

   TIP When you use specific phrases that someone else wrote, you must credit the source. For example, if your source uses the phrase "the fortunate peasant" and you use that phrase without citing the source, you are plagiarizing.

What Does It Look Like?

Original source

Children have weak immune systems, and the high incidence of disease and limited medical knowledge of the period meant that many children never reached adulthood. During the thirteenth century, about one child in six may have died in the first year, one in four by age five; perhaps two-thirds lived to age twenty.
Singman, Jeffrey L., Daily Life in Medieval Europe

Plagiarized

In the thirteenth century, about one child in six may have died in its first year.

Correctly documented

Singman explains that during the 1200s, one child out of every six died before his or her first birthday (18).

Original source

The fortunate peasant might have a cow tethered at the base of the garden grazing on the naturally growing grasses.
Hackett, Jeremiah, ed., Medieval Europe, 814–1350

Plagiarized

The fortunate peasant might have a cow tied up at the edge of the garden.

Correctly documented

Only "the fortunate peasant" might have a cow (Hackett 159).

DIFFERENTIATED INSTRUCTION

FOR LESS–PROFICIENT WRITERS

Avoid Plagiarism List these examples on the board. Ask small groups to decide whether or not they would need to document each one. Discuss students' responses.

1. You completely rewrite an idea from a source in your own words. You even change the sentence structure.

2. You draw a conclusion or make an observation based on research you have included in your paper.

3. You borrow an example from a source to use as an example in your own paper.

4. You take the statistics or data from a chart, but you use a different kind of chart and put the facts in a different order.

5. You tell about a personal experience in your introduction.

6. You interview a friend to get information about your topic.

*(**Possible answers:** Documentation is necessary for examples 1, 3, 4, and 6. It is not necessary for examples 2 and 5.)*

RESEARCHING

What Should I Do?

7. Write your thesis.
Ask yourself: What are the answers to my research questions? What main point do I want to make about my topic? Remember, your thesis doesn't have to be perfect right now. You can revise it later.

TIP Your thesis is the governing idea of your whole report. In other words, the thesis tells your reader what information you will discuss and how the parts of your discussion will be arranged.

8. Organize and outline your report.
Sort your note cards into piles, with each pile having a similar main idea. Next, put the piles in a logical order—maybe from earliest event to latest or from simplest idea to most complicated.

The key ideas you have discovered and organized will be the basic entries in your outline.

TIP You can create a formal outline, as shown here. Or if you prefer, you can create a graphic organizer or group the ideas into questions and answers.

What Does It Look Like?

> **Answers to Some of My Research Questions**
> • Peasants didn't have a life of their own. They had to do what their lord wanted.
> • They farmed—long, hard work!
> • Their homes were small and basic and had farm animals in them (yuck).
> • Peasants didn't live long.

↓

> **Working thesis statement:**
> Peasants had to do what their lord wanted, worked hard, had bad homes, and didn't live long.

> **The Hard Lives of Peasants**
> I. Introduction
>   A. Interesting "hook"
>   B. My thesis
> II. Body
>   A. Peasants had to grow or make everything.
>   B. They had to do extra jobs for their lord.
>   C. They could earn money but couldn't buy much.
>   D. They had terrible homes.
>   E. They didn't live long.
> III. Conclusion
>   A. It was tough to be a peasant.
>   B. People don't know what it was really like.

FOR ENGLISH LEARNERS

Task Support Have students use these frames to help them define their thesis:

1. The topic of my report is _____.
2. My report will explain _____, _____, and _____ about my topic.
3. I want readers to understand _____ when they read my report.

FOR ADVANCED LEARNERS/PRE–AP

Organize and Outline Your Report Have students use a Microtheme outline to help them develop and organize the ideas for each part of their papers. The Microtheme outline prompts students to consider options for the introduction, formulate a thesis statement, list main ideas and supporting evidence, and develop a strong conclusion.

BEST PRACTICES TOOLKIT—Transparency
Microtheme p. C13

7. Write your thesis. Suggest that students use these additional steps to help them formulate their thesis statements:

1. Read through all note cards. Jot down main ideas covered by your research.
2. Decide on the purpose of your paper. How do these main ideas fit into what you want to accomplish?
3. Keeping in mind your main ideas and your purpose, draft a thesis statement.

Have students exchange their working thesis statements with a partner. Have students critique each other's statements, keeping the **TIP** in mind.

R RESOURCE MANAGER—Copy Master
Write a Thesis Statement p. 30

8. Organize and outline your report. Tell students that they will choose one method of organization to present their major ideas. The details within individual paragraphs may be ordered in different ways, however. For example, a paper on the life of a knight might use classification to organize major ideas such as the knight's military, economic, and social obligations. Within the paragraphs, however, cause and effect or comparison and contrast could be used to organize specific facts.

Ask students to look back at the **Student Model.** What overall pattern of organization does the writer use? *(Possible answer: He uses classification, exploring each major aspect of a peasant's life in turn.)* What is one other method he uses to organize facts within the second paragraph? *(Possible answer: cause and effect)*

As students write their outlines, they may need to reorganize their papers. Remind them that as the **TIP** suggests, they may find it helpful to use a graphic organizer such as a flowchart or a classification chart instead of an outline format.

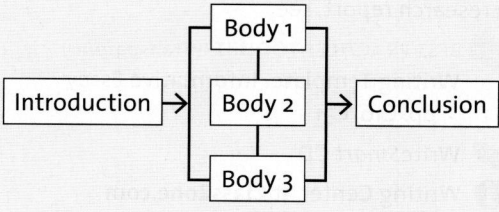

DRAFTING

1. **Begin your first draft.** To help students with this process, make these suggestions:

- If you are comfortable with a computer, use word processing to write your draft. That way, corrections and insertions can be done easily.

- Include all parts of your paper in your first draft. Do not skip over sections. However, if you cannot think of good opening sentences for your introduction, insert your thesis statement and make a note to return to the introduction later.

- Be careful to document your sources in your first draft. Mistakes occur when you try to retrace your steps and insert them later.

- Keep your note cards in piles that are organized according to your outline. Begin a new paragraph each time you discuss a different aspect of your major idea or move on to a new pile of note cards.

- You may not need all of your notes. Do not throw note cards away, however, until the final paper is completed.

2. **Weave in sources as you draft.** After students have finished a first draft, have them work in small groups and peer review each other's drafts, looking specifically for introductory phrases or follow-up remarks. Encourage students to make suggestions for places to insert these phrases.

3. **Consider creating a graphic.** Discuss the types of information that might be presented in a graphic organizer, such as statistics in a graph, dates and events on a timeline, steps of a process in a sequence chart, and locations on a map. Be sure to point out the **TIP**, and have students locate the source line for the sample chart on page 994 ("Source: Singman 60").

For a writing template that can be adapted to a research report, see

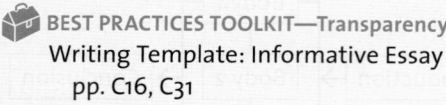 **BEST PRACTICES TOOLKIT**—Transparency
  Writing Template: Informative Essay
      pp. C16, C31

WriteSmart CD

Writing Center at **ClassZone.com**

DRAFTING

What Should I Do?	What Does It Look Like?
1. **Begin your first draft.** Use your outline and note cards to tell your reader what you learned.	*Peasants were at the bottom of the social order in the Middle Ages. They had to grow or raise their own food and make everything they needed to live. Farming was very hard work in the Middle Ages (Hackett 254). Sometimes there was too much rain. Other times there wasn't enough.*
2. **Weave in sources as you draft.** Don't just plop ideas from your note cards straight into your paper. Instead, introduce them with phrases such as "Singman believes," "Deliyannis says," and "According to Hackett." Another way to weave in sources is to follow them with comments or conclusions of your own.	*According to Singman,* ∧*In England in the late 1200s, some peasants could earn about 1 d. (one English penny) per day (~~Singman~~ 59).* *Deliyannis says* ∧*The average life span was 30 years in the 900s. Old age was especially hard on peasants.* *Singman believes that* ∧*Many old peasants had to beg to survive (~~Singman~~ 31). After a lifetime of hard work, it must have been terrible to beg for a crust of bread.*
3. **Consider creating a graphic.** A chart, a graph, a diagram, or another graphic organizer can give your reader a great deal of information in a small space. **TIP** Add a source line that tells where you found any facts or figures that you are using.	**Some Thirteenth-Century Prices** *1 loaf of bread: 1/4 d.* *1 dozen eggs: 1/2 d.* *1 ax: 4 d.* *1 pound of candles: 6 d.* *Source: Singman 60.*

DIFFERENTIATED INSTRUCTION

FOR LESS—PROFICIENT WRITERS
Write a First Draft

- Explain that each new paragraph in a research report signals discussion of another main idea or important aspect of the topic.

- Have students look at the model outline on page 993. Explain that each point under II corresponds to a paragraph in the **Student Model.** Each of these major points represents a pile of note cards.

- Remind students that each paragraph must have a topic sentence. A topic sentence states the main idea of the paragraph. It is not a fact taken from a source.

- Have students work in pairs to identify the topic sentence in each body paragraph of the **Student Model.** Discuss what makes each example a good topic sentence.

DRAFTING

What Should I Do?

4. Document your sources.
Show the source of each idea in parentheses at the end of the sentence. This is called **parenthetical documentation** and usually includes an author's last name and a page number, like this: (Hackett 254). Here are some exceptions:

- **Author already mentioned in sentence**—use only the page number: (158)

- **Web site (no page numbers)**—use only the author's name: (Deliyannis)

- **Web site, article, or book with no author named**—use a short form of the title: ("Middle Ages")

- **More than one source supporting an idea**—separate the citations of the sources with semicolons: (Deliyannis; "Middle Ages"; Singman 70)

5. Make a Works Cited list.
Put your source cards in alphabetical order by the authors' last names. (If there is no author, alphabetize by title.) Follow the examples shown here. For situations not shown, see page 998 of this book or the *MLA Handbook for Writers of Research Papers.*

What Does It Look Like?

> Finally, peasants had to pay one-tenth of everything they produced to the church (Singman 100).

Basic documentation: author and page number

> All this work and all these costs made life hard. No wonder Hackett says that peasants "worked from sunrise to sunset" (158).

Author mentioned in sentence

> A peasant's diet was simple: bread, beans, chicken, eggs, vegetables (such as cabbage and onions), and perhaps milk and cheese (Deliyannis; "Middle Ages"; Singman 70).

Information from three sources

Works Cited

Deliyannis, Deborah Mauskopf. "Middle Ages." *World Book Online Reference Center.* 2005. World Book. 25 Feb. 2008. <http://www.worldbookonline.com/wb/Article?id=ar360060>.

Hackett, Jeremiah. *Medieval Europe, 814–1350.* World Eras 4. Detroit: Gale, 2002.

"The Middle Ages: Homes." *Learner.org.* Annenberg/CPB. 6 Mar. 2008 <http://www.learner.org/exhibits/middleages/homes.html>.

4. Document your sources. Point out that parenthetical documentation is placed before the period at the end of a sentence. Most sentences in the body of a research report should have documentation unless they state the writer's original ideas or very well-known facts, such as the fact that Abraham Lincoln was the president of the United States during the Civil War.

5. Make a Works Cited list. Remind students that this is a separate page at the end of the report. Point out that in each entry, every line after the first is indented. Otherwise, the information is identical to what is recorded on the source cards.

Circulate to check the basic format of each student's Works Cited list.

FOR LESS-PROFICIENT WRITERS
Document Your Sources

- Have students exchange papers and highlight the parenthetical documentation in each sentence, including the author's name if it appears in the sentence.

- To help students focus on one section at a time, have them cover sections they are not reading with a blank sheet of paper.

- Allow time for students to ask questions and revise their papers after they have been returned.

FOR ENGLISH LEARNERS

Task Support Record several examples of bibliographic entries on the board, including two written by authors with the same last name but different first names. Also include two or three sources without authors but with different articles (*A, The*) as the first word of the title. Have students work in small groups to alphabetize the entries. Review their lists and make sure they understand why certain entries would be placed before others.

REVISING AND EDITING

1. **Improve your introduction.** Remind students that the introduction has a variety of functions. It must interest the reader, provide a context for the topic, and define the contents of the paper.

   Have students think about why they were drawn to their topic in the beginning. What question prompted them to choose the topic? What event triggered their interest? What did they already know that made them anxious to learn more? Have students use their own motivations as a starting point for creating interesting introductions.

   Have students craft final versions of their thesis statements. A thesis statement often comes at the end of the introductory paragraph. It leads readers directly into the body of the paper, where the writer will provide support for the thesis.

2. **Use transitions to connect ideas.** Have students read several paragraphs of their reports aloud to a partner to help them hear where they need additional transitions. Remind them that transitions can be placed in the middle or at the end of a sentence as well as at the beginning.

3. **Delete unnecessary information.** Remind students that each paragraph should have a strong topic sentence that states the main idea. Placing the topic sentence at the beginning of the paragraph will help them to include only those facts that develop the main idea. Have students highlight their topic sentences. Then have them check each detail against that main idea.

   Have students return to their thesis statements. Are there any paragraphs that do not support or develop the thesis? If so, they may need to be eliminated as well.

REVISING AND EDITING

What Should I Do?	What Does It Look Like?
1. Improve your introduction. • Highlight your introduction. • Ask yourself: Will this beginning interest my reader? Why or why not? • Consider starting with a vivid description, a surprising question, or a short and thought-provoking quotation.	▶ *What was it like to be alive during the Middle Ages? Movies and television shows have led many people to imagine handsome young knights dodging swords, arrows, and axes as they storm a castle. However, most Europeans of the time were peasants, not knights, and their lives were anything but glamorous. Peasants were at the bottom of the social order in the Middle Ages.*
2. Use transitions to connect ideas. • Because a research report is longer than an essay or a narrative, it's especially important to have a clear organizational pattern. • Circle the transitional words, phrases, and sentences in your report. If you don't have very many circles, add some transitions to help your reader understand how ideas are related.	▶ *For example,* (Besides) *growing food for their lord, peasants had to do services for him.* They *might have to build roads or cut wood for him. They even had to fight sometimes,* (although) *they did not have training or good weapons.* *also* *Peasants had to make other payments to their lord,* (such as) *for using his mill to grind their grain.*
3. Delete unnecessary information. • Reread your report. Are there parts that are unrelated to your thesis? • Revise or delete these passages to make your report clear and to the point.	▶ *They even had to fight sometimes, although they did not have training or good weapons.* ~~I saw a movie once that showed peasants using clubs and pitchforks as weapons, which was pretty gross. It was a good movie because it was very exciting, and also I learned some things about medieval times.~~

DIFFERENTIATED INSTRUCTION

FOR LESS-PROFICIENT WRITERS

Improve Your Introduction Display these examples and have students discuss which introduction would grab their interest and why.

- The night our dog Rex got sprayed by a skunk, we could have smelled him a mile and a half away—literally! That's how far the odor from a skunk's spray can travel.

- Skunks can discharge an oily liquid that causes severe eye inflammation. The odor from this liquid can be detected from a distance of one and a half miles.

FOR ADVANCED LEARNERS/PRE-AP

Improve Your Introduction Challenge students to experiment with introductions. They might begin with a short anecdote, a startling fact, or even an analogy relevant to their topic. Encourage them to read the opening paragraphs of famous speeches, letters, or nonfiction articles to get some different ideas about how to interest readers in their reports.

REVISING AND EDITING

What Should I Do?	*What Does It Look Like?*

4. Strengthen your support.
- Ask a peer reader to read your draft and [bracket] parts that lack support.
- Add facts, details, and examples where they are needed. Be sure to document where each came from.

See page 998: Ask a Peer Reader

▶

> , including their clothes, blankets, and tools.
> [Many peasants struggled to survive. They had to grow or raise their own food and make everything they needed to live. Farming was very hard work in the Middle Ages] because peasants had only basic tools, such as plows and pitchforks, instead of machinery (Hackett 254).

5. Improve sentence quality.
- Skim your report again, this time looking at sentence lengths. Do you have many short sentences in a row? Do you have long sentences that are hard to understand?
- Combine choppy sentences and break up droning sentences to make your report smooth and easy to read.

▶

> ~~Sometimes there was too much rain. Other times there wasn't enough. Some years the weather was too cold. Other years there were lots of bugs. During those times, there wasn't enough food.~~
> If there was a flood or drought, if some crops froze, or if pests ate the crops, the peasants didn't have enough to eat.

6. Craft a strong ending.
Don't waste your conclusion by repeating what you have already written. Even though you don't need new ideas at this point, you do need fresh words.

TIP One way to create a strong ending is to return to an image or idea from the beginning of the report.

▶

> ~~The Middle Ages was not a great time to be a peasant. The lives of peasants were short and hard. All they did was farm and work for the lord.~~
> Although many films and television shows make life in the European Middle Ages seem exciting and glamorous, the peasants probably had a different view of things. Their lives were short and hard, and their crops meant far more to them than any castle did.

4. Strengthen your support. Explain to students that each judgment statement in a research report must be supported with evidence. Point out this sentence under **What Does It Look Like?:** "Farming was very hard work in the Middle Ages." This statement is unconvincing until the writer adds the reasons why farming was such hard work.

Suggest that students review their unused note cards. They may see some facts that could be used to support the ideas in their papers.

5. Improve sentence quality. Review these methods that students might use to vary their sentence structures:

- Combine two short sentences using a comma and a conjunction or a semicolon.
- Use subordinate clauses.
- Break up a long sentence into two shorter ones.

6. Craft a strong ending. Draw students' attention to the **TIP**. Explain that they can elaborate on that original image or make more sense of it, now that readers have more information. Tell students that they might also choose to incorporate a particularly powerful quotation or develop conclusions based on their research.

For interactive revision tools, see

- **WriteSmart** CD
- Writing Center at **ClassZone.com**
- **RESOURCE MANAGER**—Copy Master Proofreading and Editing p. 32

FOR ENGLISH LEARNERS

Improve Sentence Quality Work with students to help them combine these sentences. Remind them that they can put two sentences together using a comma and a conjunction, such as *and, but,* or *or.* Or, if the subject of the sentences is the same, they can combine the verbs.

The first encyclopedia had many articles. There were none on my topic. *(The first encyclopedia had many articles, but there were none on my topic.)*

I checked another encyclopedia. I found good information. *(I checked another encyclopedia and found good information.)*

At the library, I could look for a book. I could visit the World Wide Web. *(At the library, I could look for a book, or I could visit the World Wide Web.)*

Preparing to Publish

Support for meeting the goals in the writing rubric is supplied throughout the **Writing Workshop** on pages 984–997.

 RESOURCE MANAGER—Copy Master
Ask a Peer Reader p. 31

For Rubric Bank, see

 WriteSmart CD

 Writing Center at **ClassZone.com**

Citing Other Types of Sources

Draw students' attention to the different types of formats listed. Add a book with two authors to the list:

Book with two authors
Tartaglino, Anna Cazzini, and Nanda Torcellan. Medieval Paris. New York: Raintree, 2001.

Formatting a Research Report

Share with students these formatting guidelines for the final research report:

- Leave one-inch margins at the top, bottom, and sides of each page (except for page numbers).
- On separate lines, type your name, your teacher's name, the class, and the date at the top left of the first page.
- On each page, type your last name and the page number one-half inch from the top, aligned at the right-hand corner.
- Double-space all text, including quotations and the list of works cited.
- Indent paragraphs one-half inch (or five spaces) from the left margin.
- Indent block quotations one inch (or ten spaces) from the left margin.
- Begin your Works Cited list on a separate page and indent the second and subsequent lines of entries one-half inch (or five spaces). End each entry with a period.

Have students check the *MLA Handbook for Writers of Research Papers* for additional formatting guidelines.

 Preparing to Publish **Research Report**

Apply the Rubric

A strong research report . . .

☑ has an exciting or thought-provoking introduction
☑ has a clear thesis statement
☑ supports the thesis with evidence
☑ follows a logical pattern of organization and uses transitions
☑ uses information from three or more sources and credits them completely and correctly
☑ includes the writer's own ideas
☑ is appropriately serious and formal
☑ employs precise words and varied sentence lengths
☑ has a fresh, interesting conclusion

Ask a Peer Reader

- Where should I add support?
- How can I do a better job of weaving in my supporting information?
- Where have I made mistakes in documenting my sources?

Citing Other Types of Sources

When writing your source cards and Works Cited list, you may need to use these formats.

CD-ROM encyclopedia
"Middle Ages." Britannica Student Encyclopedia. 2004 ed. CD-ROM. Chicago: Encyclopaedia Britannica, 2004.

Magazine or newspaper article
Hilton, R. H. "The Ties That Bound: Peasant Families in Medieval England." History Today Dec. 1986: 52.

Interview you conducted with an expert
Kurland, Sari. Personal interview. 1 Mar. 2008.

Book with editor
Schetter, Daniela, ed. Everyday Life in Medieval Times. Westport: Greenwood, 2005.

Film or documentary
The Merchant. Dir. Ashleigh V. Denneth. Videocassette. Schlessinger Media, 2002.

For more citation guidelines, see the *MLA Handbook for Writers of Research Papers*.

Writing Online

PUBLISHING OPTIONS
For publishing options, visit the **Writing Center** at **ClassZone.com.**

ASSESSMENT PREPARATION
For writing and grammar assessment practice, go to the **Assessment Center** at **ClassZone.com.**

Assess and Reteach

After reading and assessing students' reports, you might use these lessons to reteach key skills:

 STANDARDS LESSON FILE
Writing Lesson 1: Finding a Writing Idea
Writing Lesson 2: Limiting or Expanding a Topic
Writing Lesson 12: Topic Sentence and Supporting Details
Writing Lesson 21: Writing a Thesis Statement
Writing Lesson 22: Writing Introductions
Writing Lesson 23: Writing Conclusions
Writing Lesson 26: Coherence in Compositions
Writing Lesson 40: Elaborate with Facts and Statistics
Writing Lesson 41: Creating Visuals
Research and Study Skills Lesson 8: Source Cards and Note Cards
Research and Study Skills Lesson 9: Avoiding Plagiarism
Research and Study Skills Lesson 10: Paraphrasing
Research and Study Skills Lesson 11: Summarizing

SPEAKING STANDARD
7.A.1 Demonstrate appropriate delivery techniques for oral presentations

Creating a Multimedia Report

Now that you're an expert on the subject you researched, you can create a multimedia report that will inform and educate others.

Planning the Presentation

1. **Review your report with an eye for sights and sounds.** Mark parts of your findings that would lend themselves to pictures, photographs, drawings, musical accompaniment, or sound effects.

2. **Make a rough outline.** This should be an ordered list of what your audience will see and hear, including narration.

3. **Create a storyboard.** Sketch out, screen by screen, what your audience will see and hear.

(Sound: Whoosh of arrows)

(Sound: Horses and knights charging; shouting)

Producing the Presentation

1. **Create or collect the parts of your show.** Gather images or draw them. Scan or download them into a computer. Record or download your music and sound effects too.

2. **Put it together.** Use an editing software program to put the parts of your multimedia presentation into sequence. Create a title screen that includes your name. Include a final screen that credits the sources of your words, sounds, and images.

WRITING WORKSHOP   **999**

PUBLISHING WITH TECHNOLOGY

Ask students to read this page to get an overview of how to create a multimedia report. Students who choose this option should then familiarize themselves with the software program they will use to put together their presentation by taking advantage of the tutorial option that is usually included.

Before students begin working, review this rubric with them so that they understand their goals:

Rubric A strong multimedia report

- has narration or text that conveys accurate information
- incorporates vivid images such as pictures, photographs, or drawings
- is accompanied by appropriate sound effects or music
- is effectively and logically organized
- includes a title screen and a credit screen

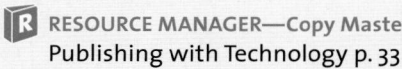 **RESOURCE MANAGER—Copy Master**
Publishing with Technology p. 33

 **STANDARDS LESSON FILE**
Media Lesson 22: Creating a Power Presentation

DIFFERENTIATED INSTRUCTION

FOR LESS–PROFICIENT WRITERS

Planning the Presentation Have students review the **Student Model** and discuss which parts might lend themselves to images and sound effects. Then help students choose parts of their own reports to include in their multimedia presentations. Remind them to pick main ideas that can be easily illustrated or accompanied by sound effects. Have students transfer these ideas to their storyboards.

BEST PRACTICES TOOLKIT—Transparency
Storyboard p. C11

Producing the Presentation

- Have partners explain their storyboards to each other. Have students evaluate these points as they listen: *Is the text or commentary clear and informative? Are the images vivid and appropriate? Where could music or sound effects be added?*

- Allow time for students to revise their work based on their partners' suggestions.

- Pair computer-proficient students with less experienced partners to download, scan, and edit their multimedia reports.

Student Resource Bank

Reading any text—short story, poem, magazine article, newspaper, Web page—requires the use of special strategies. For example, you might plot the events of a short story on a diagram, while you may use text features to spot main ideas in a magazine article. You also need to identify patterns of organization in the text. Using such strategies can help you read different texts with ease and also help you understand what you're reading.

1 Reading Literary Texts

Literary texts include short stories, novels, poems, and dramas. Literary texts can also be biographies, autobiographies, and essays. To appreciate and analyze literary texts, you will need to understand the characteristics of each type of text.

1.1 READING A SHORT STORY
Strategies for Reading

- Read the title. As you read the story, you may notice that the title has a special meaning.
- Keep track of events as they happen. Plot the events on a diagram like this one.

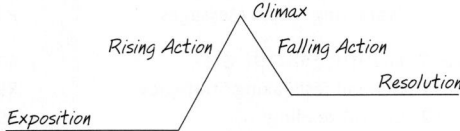

- From the details the writer provides, **visualize** the characters. **Predict** what they might do next.
- Look for specific adjectives that help you visualize the **setting**—the time and place in which events occur.

1.2 READING A POEM
Strategies for Reading

- Notice the **form** of the poem, or the number of its lines and their arrangement on the page.
- Read the poem aloud a few times. Listen for **rhymes** and **rhythms.**
- **Visualize** the images and comparisons.
- **Connect** with the poem by asking yourself what message the poet is trying to send.
- Create a word web or another **graphic organizer** to record your reactions and questions.

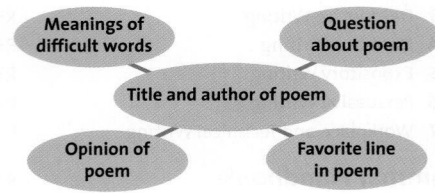

1.3 READING A PLAY
Strategies for Reading

- Read the stage directions to help you **visualize** the setting and characters.
- **Question** what the title means and why the playwright chose it.
- Identify the main conflict (struggle or problem) in the play. To **clarify** the conflict, make a chart that shows what the conflict is and how it is resolved.
- **Evaluate** the characters. What do they want? How do they change during the play? You may want to make a chart that lists each character's name, appearance, and traits.

1.4 READING LITERARY NONFICTION
Strategies for Reading

- If you are reading a biography, an autobiography, or another type of biographical writing, such as a diary, a memoir, or letters, use a family tree or word web to keep track of the people mentioned.
- When reading an essay, **evaluate** the writer's ideas. Is there a clear main idea? Does the writer use appropriate details to support a main idea?

2 Reading Informational Texts: Text Features

An **informational text** is writing that provides factual information. Informational materials, such as chapters in textbooks and articles in magazines, encyclopedias, and newspapers, usually contain elements that help the reader recognize their purpose, organization, and key ideas. These elements are known as **text features.**

2.1 UNDERSTANDING TEXT FEATURES

Text features are design elements of a text that indicate its organizational structure or otherwise make its key ideas and information understandable. Text features include titles, headings, subheadings, boldface type, bulleted and numbered lists, and graphic aids, such as charts, graphs, illustrations, and photographs. Notice how the text features help you find key information on the textbook page shown.

A The **title** identifies the topic.

B A **subheading** indicates the start of a new topic or section and identifies the focus of that section.

C **Questions** may be used to focus your understanding of the text.

D A **bulleted list** shows items of equal importance.

E **Graphic aids,** such as illustrations, photographs, charts, diagrams, maps, and timelines, often make ideas in the text clearer.

F A **caption,** or the text that accompanies a graphic aid, gives information about the graphic aid that isn't necessarily obvious from the image itself.

PRACTICE AND APPLY

1. What is the first subhead following the title?

2. Reread the Essential Question. Identify one lasting contribution of Roman culture.

3. What activity does the mosaic portray? What do you learn from the caption?

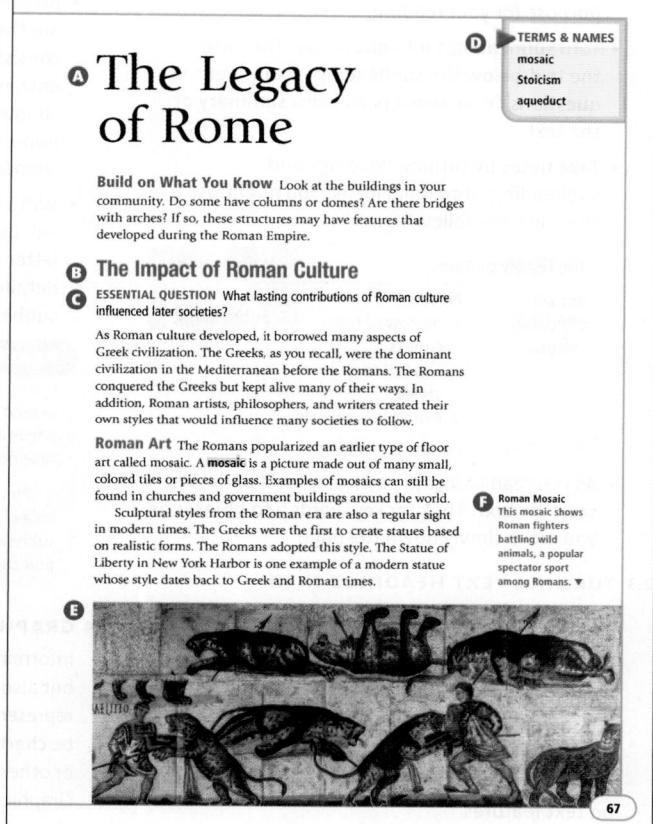

A The Legacy of Rome

D ▶ TERMS & NAMES
mosaic
Stoicism
aqueduct

Build on What You Know Look at the buildings in your community. Do some have columns or domes? Are there bridges with arches? If so, these structures may have features that developed during the Roman Empire.

B The Impact of Roman Culture

C ESSENTIAL QUESTION What lasting contributions of Roman culture influenced later societies?

As Roman culture developed, it borrowed many aspects of Greek civilization. The Greeks, as you recall, were the dominant civilization in the Mediterranean before the Romans. The Romans conquered the Greeks but kept alive many of their ways. In addition, Roman artists, philosophers, and writers created their own styles that would influence many societies to follow.

Roman Art The Romans popularized an earlier type of floor art called mosaic. A **mosaic** is a picture made out of many small, colored tiles or pieces of glass. Examples of mosaics can still be found in churches and government buildings around the world.

Sculptural styles from the Roman era are also a regular sight in modern times. The Greeks were the first to create statues based on realistic forms. The Romans adopted this style. The Statue of Liberty in New York Harbor is one example of a modern statue whose style dates back to Greek and Roman times.

F **Roman Mosaic** This mosaic shows Roman fighters battling wild animals, a popular spectator sport among Romans. ▼

67

ANSWERS

1. *The Impact of Roman Culture*

2. *mosaic art*

3. *Possible answer: The mosaic portrays men fighting animals. The caption explains that battling wild animals was a popular spectator sport among the Romans.*

Students' outlines will vary. They should follow the format on page R4 and should include a main idea for each Roman-numeral entry, a subheading for each capital letter entry, and a detail(s) for each numbered entry. The following is an example of a partial outline:

I. *The Black Death's Journey*

  A. *Eastern beginnings*

    1. *Evidence near Lake Issyk-Kul*

    2. *Origins of the plague in Asia*

  B. *On the move*

    1. *Spread of disease*

      a. *natural disasters*

      b. *wild animals and rats*

      c. *airborne disease*

    2. *Black Death across Asia*

      a. *Mongol armies carry disease*

      b. *disease spreads to Golden Horde*

  C. *From Asia to the Mediterranean*

    1. *Kaffa, a major trading post*

    2. *Escape from Crimea*

    3. *Plague breaks out in Constantinople and Mediterranean region*

    4. *Epidemic reaches Genoa, Italy in 1347*

2.2 USING TEXT FEATURES

You can use text features to locate information, to help you understand it, and to take notes. Just use the following strategies when you encounter informational text.

Strategies for Reading

- **Preview** the text by looking at the title, headings, and subheadings to get an idea of the main concepts and the way the text is organized.

- Before you begin reading the text more thoroughly, **skim** it—read it quickly—to get an overview.

- Read any **questions** that appear at the end of a lesson or chapter. Doing this will help you set a purpose for your reading.

- Turn subheadings into questions. Then use the text below the subheadings to answer the questions. Your answers will be a **summary** of the text.

- **Take notes** by turning headings and subheadings into main ideas. You might use a chart like the following.

The Legacy of Rome		Main heading
Impact of Roman culture	Notes: 1. borrowed from Greeks 2. created their own styles 3. example is mosaic	Subheading

- As you read to locate particular facts or details, **scan** the text. Look for key words and phrases as you move slowly down the page.

2.3 TURNING TEXT HEADINGS INTO OUTLINE ENTRIES

After you have read a selection at least once, you can use text features to take notes in outline form. The following outline shows how one student used text headings from the sample page on page R3. Study the outline and use the strategies that follow to create an outline based on text features.

I. Legacy of Rome   **Main heading** roman numeral entry

  A. Impact of Roman culture   **Subheading** capital letter entry

    1. Roman Art

      a. mosaic   **Detail** number entry

      b. sculpture

  B.

    1.

    2.

Strategies for Using Text Headings

- Preview the headings and subheadings in the text to get an idea of what different kinds there are and what their positions might be in an outline.

- Be consistent. Note that subheadings that are the same size and color should be used consistently in Roman-numeral or capital-letter entries in the outline. If you decide that a chapter heading should appear with a Roman numeral, then that's the level at which all other chapter headings should appear.

- Write the headings and subheadings that you will use as your Roman-numeral and capital-letter entries first. As you read, fill in numbered details from the text under the headings and subheadings in your outline.

Reread "Like Black Smoke: The Black Death's Journey," pages 896–900. Use text features in the selection to take notes in outline form.

Preview the subheadings in the text to get an idea of the different kinds. Write the headings and subheadings you are using as your Roman-numeral and capital-letter entries first. Then fill in the details.

2.4 GRAPHIC AIDS

Information is communicated not only with words but also with graphic aids. **Graphic aids** are visual representations of verbal statements. They can be charts, webs, diagrams, graphs, photographs, or other visual representations of information. Graphic aids usually make complex information easier to understand. For that reason, graphic aids are often used to organize, simplify, and summarize information for easy reference.

Graphs

Graphs are used to illustrate statistical information. A **graph** is a drawing that shows the relative values of numerical quantities. Different kinds of graphs are used to show different numerical relationships.

Strategies for Reading

Ⓐ Read the title.

Ⓑ Find out what is being represented or measured.

Ⓒ In a circle graph, compare the sizes of the parts.

Ⓓ In a line graph, study the slant of the line. The steeper the line, the faster the rate of change.

Ⓔ In a bar graph, compare the lengths of the bars.

A **circle graph,** or **pie graph,** shows the relationships of parts to a whole. The entire circle equals 100 percent. The parts of the circle represent percentages of the whole.

MODEL: CIRCLE GRAPH

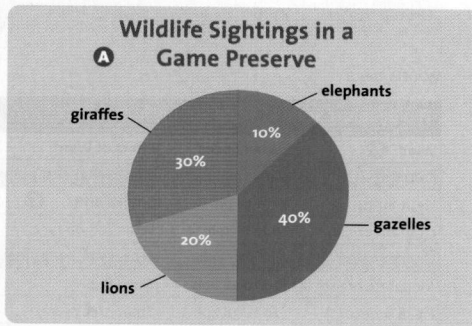

Line graphs show changes in numerical quantities over time and are effective in presenting trends such as world population growth. A line graph is made on a grid. Here, the vertical axis indicates quantity, and the horizontal axis shows years. Points on the graph indicate data. The line that connects the points highlights a trend or pattern.

MODEL: LINE GRAPH

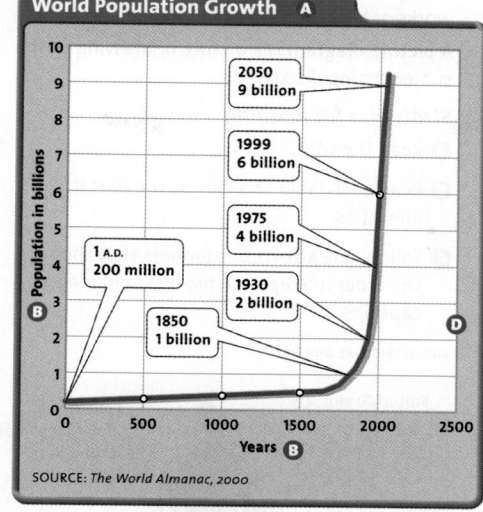

SOURCE: *The World Almanac, 2000*

In a **bar graph,** vertical or horizontal bars are used to show or compare categories of information, such as voting trends. The lengths of the bars indicate the quantities.

MODEL: BAR GRAPH

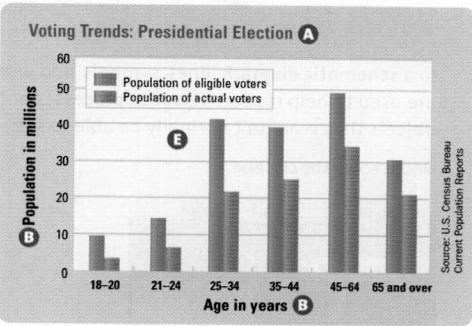

WATCH OUT! Evaluate carefully the information presented in graphs. For example, circle graphs show major factors and differences well but tend to reduce the importance of smaller factors and differences.

Diagrams

A **diagram** is a drawing that shows how something works or how its parts relate to one another.

A **picture diagram** is a picture or drawing of the subject being discussed.

Strategies for Reading

(A) Read the title.

(B) Read each label and look at the part it identifies.

(C) Follow any arrows or numbers that show the order of steps in a process, and read any captions.

MODEL: PICTURE DIAGRAM

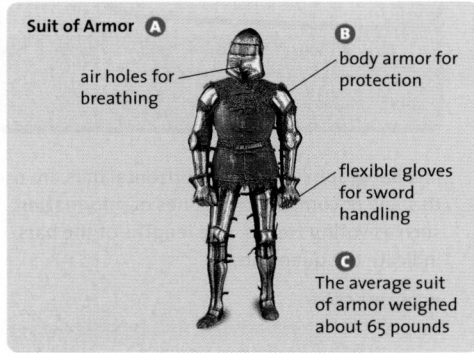

Suit of Armor (A)

air holes for breathing

(B) body armor for protection

flexible gloves for sword handling

(C) The average suit of armor weighed about 65 pounds

In a **schematic diagram,** lines, symbols, and words are used to help readers visualize processes or objects they wouldn't normally be able to see.

MODEL: SCHEMATIC DIAGRAM

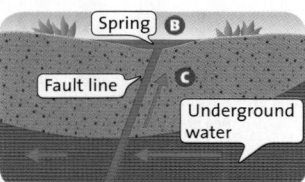

Spring (B)

Fault line

(C)

Underground water

Oasis (A)
An oasis is a fertile or green spot in the midst of a desert.

Charts and Tables

A **chart** presents information, shows a process, or makes comparisons, usually in rows or columns.

A **table** is a specific type of chart that presents a collection of facts in rows and columns and shows how the facts relate to one another.

Strategies for Reading

(A) Read the title to learn what information the chart or table covers.

(B) Study column headings and row labels to determine the categories of information presented.

(C) Look down columns and across rows to find specific information.

MODEL: CHART

Size of Selected Civilizations (A)		
Civilization	(B) Dates	Size (est.) millions of sq. miles
Persia	559–330 B.C.	(C) 2.0
Rome	27 B.C.–A.D. 476	3.40
Mongol	1206–1368	11.7
Aztec	1325–1521	0.2
United States	1776	3.7

MODEL: TABLE

The Beaufort Scale of Wind Strength (A)		
Wind (B)	Wind Speed	Effect of Wind
Calm (0)	Less than 1 kph	smoke rises straight up.
Light air (1)	1 to 5 kph	Smoke drifts. (C)
Light breeze (2)	6 to 11 kph	Wind felt on face.
Gentle breeze (3)	12 to 19 kph	Leaves and twigs move.
Moderate breeze (4)	20 to 28 kph	Flags flap.
Fresh breeze (5)	29 to 38 kph	Small trees sway.
Strong breeze (6)	39 to 49 kph	Large branches move.
Moderate gale (7)	50 to 61 kph	Whole trees sway.
Fresh gale (8)	62 to 74 kph	Twigs break off trees.
Strong gale (9)	75 to 88 kph	Branches break off trees.
Whole gale (10)	89 to 102 kph	Trees uprooted.
Storm (11)	103 to 117 kph	Widespread damage.
Hurricane (12)	More than 117 kph	Destruction.

Maps

A **map** visually represents a geographic region, such as a state or country. It provides information about areas through lines, colors, shapes, and symbols. There are different kinds of maps.

- **Political maps** show political features, such as national borders.

- **Physical maps** show the landforms in areas.

- **Road or travel maps** show roads and highways.

- **Thematic maps** show information on a specific topic, such as climate, weather, or natural resources.

Strategies for Reading

Ⓐ Read the title to find out what kind of map it is.

Ⓑ Read the labels to get an overall sense of what the map shows.

Ⓒ Look at the **key** or **legend** to find out what the symbols and colors on the map stand for.

MODEL: PHYSICAL MAP

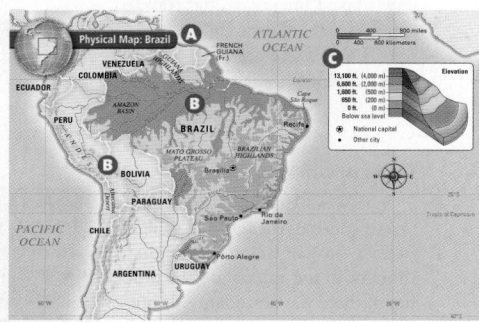

MODEL: THEMATIC MAP

PRACTICE AND APPLY

Use the graphic aids shown on pages R5–R7 to answer the following questions:

1. According to the circle graph, were there more elephants than lions at the game preserve?

2. How many years did it take to double the world population from 1 billion to 2 billion?

3. According to the bar graph, does the number of actual voters equal the number of eligible voters in any age group?

4. What important feature is part of the helmet of a suit of armor?

5. According to the diagram of an oasis, how does water get to the surface of the ground?

6. Which civilization controlled the largest amount of territory according to the chart?

7. Using the table, find the wind speed that is strong enough to make whole trees sway.

8. Are there mountains over 13,000 feet high in Brazil?

9. Using the key on the climate map of Brazil, determine whether the driest area is in the eastern or western part of the country.

PRACTICE AND APPLY

ANSWERS

1. *no*

2. *80 years*

3. *no*

4. *air holes for breathing*

5. *Underground water travels through a fault line to the surface, creating a spring.*

6. *the Mongols*

7. *a moderate gale with wind speeds of 50–61 mph*

8. *no*

9. *eastern part of the country*

3 Reading Informational Texts: Patterns of Organization

Reading any type of writing is easier once you recognize how it is organized. Writers usually arrange ideas and information in ways that best help readers see how they are related. There are several common patterns of organization:

- main idea and supporting details
- chronological order
- cause-effect organization
- compare-and-contrast organization

3.1 MAIN IDEA AND SUPPORTING DETAILS

Main idea and supporting details is a basic pattern of organization in which a central idea about a topic is supported by details. The **main idea** is the most important idea about a topic that a particular text or paragraph conveys. **Supporting details** are words, phrases, or sentences that tell more about the main idea. The main idea may be directly stated at the beginning and then followed by supporting details, or it may be merely implied by the supporting details. It may also be stated after it has been implied by supporting details.

Strategies for Reading

- To find a stated main idea in a paragraph, identify the paragraph's topic. The topic is what the paragraph is about and can usually be summed up in one or two words. The word, or synonyms of it, will usually appear throughout the paragraph. Headings and subheadings are also clues to the topics of paragraphs.

- Ask: What is the topic sentence? The topic sentence states the most important idea, message, or information the paragraph conveys about this topic. It is often the first sentence in a paragraph; however, it may appear at the end.

- To find an implied main idea, ask yourself: Whom or what did I just read about? What do the details suggest about the topic?

- Formulate a sentence stating this idea and add it to the paragraph. Does your sentence convey the main idea?

Notice how the main idea is expressed in each of the following models.

MODEL: MAIN IDEA AS THE FIRST SENTENCE

When the nomads of Africa began using camels around 300 A.D., trade across the Sahara became easier. — **Main idea**

The donkeys, horses, and oxen that had been used previously could not travel far without stopping for food and water. Camels, on the other hand, could cover 25 miles in a day and often go for two weeks without water. — **Supporting details**

MODEL: MAIN IDEA AS THE LAST SENTENCE

The new trade routes passed through lands occupied by the Soninke people. These farming people referred to their chief as ghana. Soon the land came to be known as the kingdom of Ghana. The tribal chiefs taxed the goods that traveled across their territory. — **Supporting details**

By the eighth century, trade had made Ghana a rich kingdom. — **Main idea**

MODEL: IMPLIED MAIN IDEA

The West African savannas and forests south of the savanna were rich in gold. No salt was available there, though. In the Sahara, on the other hand, there was abundant salt but no gold. Traders brought salt south through the desert and traded it for gold mined from the forests. — **Implied main idea: Gold and salt were two important items that were traded in West Africa.**

Read each paragraph, and then do the following:

1. Identify the main idea in the paragraph, using one of the strategies discussed on the previous page.

2. Identify whether the main idea is stated or implied in the paragraph.

> Home is where the heart is. There's no place like it. I love my home with a ferocity totally out of proportion to its appearance or location. I love dumb things about it: the hot-water heater, the plastic rack you drain dishes in, the roof over my head, which occasionally leaks. And yet it is precisely those dumb things that make it what it is—a place of certainty, stability, predictability, privacy, for me and for my family. It is where I live. What more can you say about a place than that? That is everything.
>
> —Anna Quindlen, "Homeless"

> Some boys taught me to play football. This was fine sport. You thought up a new strategy for every play and whispered it to the others. You went out for a pass, fooling everyone. Best, you got to throw yourself mightily at someone's running legs. Either you brought him down or you hit the ground flat out on your chin, with your arms empty before you. It was all or nothing. If you hesitated in fear, you would miss and get hurt: you would take a hard fall while the kid got away, or you would get kicked in the face while the kid got away. But if you flung yourself wholeheartedly at the back of his knees—if you gathered and joined body and soul and pointed them diving fearlessly—then you likely wouldn't get hurt, and you'd stop the ball. Your fate, and your team's score, depended on your concentration and courage. Nothing girls did could compare with it.
>
> —Annie Dillard, *An American Childhood*

3.2 CHRONOLOGICAL ORDER

Chronological order is the arrangement of events in the order in which they happen. This type of organization is used in short stories and novels, historical writing, biographies, and autobiographies. To show the order of events, writers use order words such as *before, after, next,* and *later* and time words and phrases that identify specific times of day, days of the week, and dates, such as *the next morning, Tuesday,* and *on July 4, 1776.*

Strategies for Reading

- Look in the text for headings and subheadings that may indicate a chronological pattern of organization.

- Look for words and phrases that identify times, such as *in a year, three hours earlier, in 202 B.C.,* and *the next day.*

- Look for words that signal order, such as *first, afterward, then, during,* and *finally,* to see how events or steps are related.

- Note that a paragraph or passage in which ideas and information are arranged chronologically will have several words or phrases that indicate time order, not just one.

- Ask yourself: Are the events in the paragraph or passage presented in time order?

Notice the words and phrases that signal time order in the first two paragraphs of the following model.

> **MODEL**
> **A Butterfly Gets Its Wings**
> How does a butterfly get its wings? During its life, the butterfly goes through different growth stages. [Events] There are four main stages altogether: 1) the egg, 2) the caterpillar, 3) the pupa, and 4) the adult. The ancient Greeks called this whole process *metamorphosis,* a word we still use today.
> At first, [Order words and phrases] the butterfly is a single slimy egg, no larger than a fingertip. The baby insect grows within the egg until it is ready to hatch. For most types of butterflies, this first stage lasts about 10 days. When [Time words and phrases] the egg cracks open, a caterpillar crawls out.

ANSWERS

1. *Possible answers: First paragraph: Home is where the heart is. Second paragraph: Learning how to play football was more exciting for the narrator than anything girls played.*

2. *In the first paragraph, the main idea is stated. In the second paragraph, the main idea is implied.*

1. *Possible answers: "in the second stage,"*
   "during its life," "once," "for the last time,"
   "in the third stage," "immediately," "then,"
   "after," "finally," "in a short time"

2. *The four growth stages include the egg, the*
   caterpillar, the pupa, and the adult.

3. *A butterfly begins its life in the form of a*
   single, slimy egg.

In the second stage, the caterpillar spends most of its time eating and growing. As the caterpillar becomes bigger, it sheds its spiky or fuzzy skin. This process is called *molting*. A caterpillar molts several times during its life. Once the caterpillar has shed its skin for the last time, it becomes a pupa.

In the third stage, the pupa immediately grows a hard shell called a *chrysalis*. Then, inside the chrysalis, the pupa goes through the changes that will make it a butterfly. The pupa's hormones turn its body into wings, antennas, and other butterfly parts. After all the changes are complete, the shell splits open. A butterfly is ready to make its entrance.

Finally, the adult butterfly breaks from the chrysalis. Its body, however, doesn't look quite right. It's all soft and wrinkly. As air and blood are pumped through the butterfly's body, it starts to look more like its usual self. In a short time, the butterfly is ready to try out its new wings. With a few flutters, it's off and away!

PRACTICE AND APPLY

Refer to the preceding model to do the following:

1. List at least six words in the last three paragraphs that indicate time or order.

2. What does the writer call the four main parts in the life of a butterfly?

3. In what form does a butterfly begin its life?

3.3 CAUSE-EFFECT ORGANIZATION

Cause-effect organization is a pattern of organization that shows causal relationships between events, ideas, and trends. Cause-effect relationships may be directly stated or merely implied by the order in which the information is presented. Writers often use the cause-effect pattern in historical and scientific writing. Cause-effect relationships may have several forms.

One cause with one effect

Cause ▶ Effect

One cause with multiple effects

Multiple causes with a single effect

A chain of causes and effects

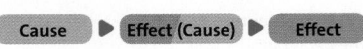

Strategies for Reading

- Look for headings and subheadings that indicate a cause-effect pattern of organization, such as "Effects of Food Allergies."

- To find the effect or effects, read to answer the question, What happened?

- To find the cause or causes, read to answer the question, Why did it happen?

- Look for words and phrases that help you identify specific relationships between events, such as *because, since, had the effect of, led to, as a result, resulted in, for that reason, due to, therefore, if . . . then,* and *consequently.*

- Look closely at each cause-effect relationship. Do not assume that because one event happened before another, the first event caused the second event.

- Use graphic organizers like the diagrams shown to record cause-effect relationships as you read.

Notice the words that signal causes and effects in the following model.

> **MODEL**
> **How a Tsunami Forms**
> Tsunami is a word that brings fear to people who live near the sea. Also known in English as a tidal wave, a tsunami is a huge ocean wave caused by an underwater volcanic eruption or earthquake. | **Effect** / **Signal words**
> An earthquake or the explosion of a volcano on the ocean floor creates massive waves of energy. These energy waves spread out in widening circles, like waves from a pebble dropped into a pond. | **Cause** / **Cause** / **Effect**

As the tsunami nears the shore, it begins to scrape along the ocean bottom. This friction causes the waves in the front to slow down. As a result, the waves traveling behind begin piling up and growing higher. This increase in height can happen very quickly—by as much as 90 feet in 10 or 15 minutes.

The effects of a tsunami can include the death of many people and the destruction of ships, buildings, and land along the shore. An especially dangerous situation may occur when the first part of a tsunami to hit the shore is the trough, or low point, rather than the crest of a wave. This trough sucks all the water away from the shore and may attract curious people on the beach. Within a few minutes, however, the crest of the wave will hit and may drown the onlookers. The most destructive tsunami ever recorded struck the Indonesian island of Sumatra, in 2004. It left more than 200,000 people dead.

PRACTICE AND APPLY

1. Use the pattern of a chain of causes and effects, illustrated on page R10, to make a graphic organizer showing the causes and effects described in the text.

2. List three words that the writer uses to signal cause and effect in the last two paragraphs.

3.4 COMPARE-AND-CONTRAST ORGANIZATION

Compare-and-contrast organization is a pattern of organization that provides a way to look at similarities and differences in two or more subjects. A writer may use this pattern of organization to compare the important points or characteristics of two or more subjects. These points or characteristics are called **points of comparison.** The compare-and-contrast pattern of organization may be developed in either of two ways:

Point-by-point organization—The writer discusses one point of comparison for both subjects, then goes on to the next point.

Subject-by-subject organization—The writer covers all points of comparison for one subject and then all points of comparison for the next subject.

Strategies for Reading

- Look in the text for headings, subheadings, and sentences that may suggest a compare-and-contrast pattern of organization, such as "Plants Share Many Characteristics," to help you identify where similarities and differences are addressed.

- To find similarities, look for words and phrases such as *like, similarly, both, all, every, also,* and *in the same way.*

- To find differences, look for words and phrases such as *unlike, but, on the other hand, more, less, in contrast,* and *however.*

- Use a graphic organizer, such as a Venn diagram or a compare-and-contrast chart, to record points of comparison and similarities and differences.

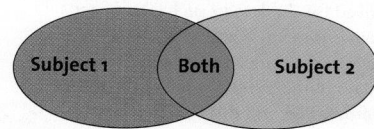

	Subject 1	Subject 2
Point 1		
Point 2		
Point 3		

Read the following models. As you read, use the signal words and phrases to identify the similarities and differences between the subjects and how the details are organized in each text.

MODEL 1

Living in Outer Space

Ten . . . nine . . . eight . . . The date is December 21, 1968.

Seven . . . six . . . five . . . Alongside a launch gantry at Cape Kennedy, Florida, a huge Saturn V rocket stands fueled and ready for blastoff, hydrogen vapor steaming from its rocket motors.

Four . . . three . . . two . . . At the top of the rocket sits the *Apollo 8* command module, the capsule that will ferry astronauts Frank Borman, James A. Lovell Jr., and William A. Anders to the moon and back.

One . . . zero . . . Liftoff! The Saturn's powerful engines roar to life, and another exciting chapter

READING HANDBOOK **R11**

PRACTICE AND APPLY

ANSWERS

1. *Students should create a graphic organizer that shows a chain of causes and effects.* ***Possible answers: Cause:*** *earthquake or volcano occurs in ocean;* ***Effect (Cause):*** *waves spread out;* ***Effect (Cause):*** *tsunami scrapes along shore bottom;* ***Effect (Cause):*** *friction slows down front waves;* ***Effect (Cause):*** *the back waves grow higher;* ***Effect:*** *enormous wave crashes ashore*

2. ***Possible answers:*** *"causes," "as a result," "the effects"*

in the history of the United States space program begins.

Today, that same *Apollo 8* command module is one of the most popular attractions at the Henry Crown Space Center at the Museum of Science and Industry in Chicago. For six days in 1968, this cone-shaped capsule was home to the first humans to leave the security of Earth's orbit and venture out to visit another heavenly body.

Museum visitors, especially young people accustomed to space travel in the shuttle era, are often amazed at the cramped quarters within the capsule, and they wonder just how three adults lived for six days in such a compact environment. Space travel has come a long way since those pioneering days of the 1960s. Some of the main ==similarities== and ==differences== relate to living quarters and food.

> **Comparison words and phrases**

==Today's shuttle crews== have both a flight deck and a lower crew-quarters deck in which to move around. ==The Apollo crews,== ==however,== were pretty much confined to their metal-and-fabric flight couches, although there was a little stretching room beneath the couches and around the hatch area that led to the Lunar Excursion Module.

> **Contrast words and phrases**

> **Subjects**

Mealtime is a highlight of anyone's day, including every astronaut's. Early space travelers were limited to puréed foods squeezed out of toothpaste tubes and juices in plastic bags. Shuttle crews, on the other hand, enjoy a much more appetizing diet. It's still not exactly fine dining, but at least the food is served on trays, is eaten with utensils, and includes healthy snacks, like fresh fruit.

At the end of a working "day" in space, all astronauts are ready for some rest. In *Apollo,* the crew simply drifted off to sleep on their couches. Aboard the shuttle, crew members sleep in special sleep restraints. Some sleep horizontally, while others opt for a vertical snooze. In zero gravity, position doesn't matter!

The United States has continued to develop the space program. The lessons learned during the first three decades of space flight are making life in the alien environment beyond Earth's atmosphere much more pleasant for a new generation of space explorers.

MODEL 2

To compare the two types of energy, we must first understand what energy is. Energy is the ability to do work. That doesn't just mean work as in homework or yard work. Energy comes in many forms, such as a rock falling off a cliff, a moving bicycle, or the stored energy in food. With all these forms, ==there are only two main types of energy, potential and kinetic. These are the energies of rest and motion.==

> **Subjects**

Potential energy is the energy an object has stored up based on how high up it is or how much it weighs. For instance, suppose two kids weigh the ==same== and climb a tree. If they are on different branches, the kid on the higher branch has ==more== potential energy than the kid on the lower branch. ==However,== if one kid weighs more than the other, and they both sit at the same height, the heavier kid has more potential energy than the lighter kid.

> **Comparison words and phrases**

> **Contrast words and phrases**

If the kids jump out of the tree, their potential energy becomes kinetic energy. This kind comes from the motion of an object. Kinetic energy increases with the speed of an object. When the kids jump, their speed increases as they fall. They have more kinetic energy when they are falling faster than they do when they first jump and are falling more slowly. Also, the more mass an object has, the more kinetic energy it has. Even if both kids jump at the exact same time, the one with more mass will always have more kinetic energy.

These two kids probably knew they were using a lot of energy, but they would probably be surprised to know how much work they had been doing.

PRACTICE AND APPLY

Refer to the preceding models to answer the following questions:

1. Which model is organized by subject? Which model is organized by points of comparison?

2. Identify two words or phrases in each model that signal a compare-and-contrast pattern of organization.

3. List two points that the writer of each model compares and contrasts.

4. Use a Venn diagram or a compare-and-contrast chart to identify two or more points of comparison and the similarities and differences shown in one of the two models.

3.5 PROBLEM-SOLUTION ORDER

Problem-solution order is a pattern of organization in which a problem is stated and analyzed and then one or more solutions are proposed and examined. This pattern of organization is often used in persuasive writing, such as editorials or proposals.

Strategies for Reading

- Look for an explanation of the problem in the first or second paragraph.
- Look for words, such as *problem* and *reason*, that may signal an explanation of the problem.
- To find the solution, ask: What suggestion does the writer offer to solve the problem?
- Look for words, such as *propose, conclude,* and *answer,* that may signal a solution.

MODEL

I love baseball, but I won't be going to any major-league games, and I won't be rooting for the local major-league team. The reason is simple. There is no local major-league team in North Dakota. There's none in South Dakota or in Montana or even in Wyoming. The closest major-league team is the Minnesota Twins, and that's over 240 miles away!

The problem is that getting a major-league team costs money. Any city that wants a team has to have enough money to build a stadium. The city also has to have a big enough population to support the team. Fargo is the biggest city in North Dakota, and it only has about 91,484 people. That's not enough to support a major-league franchise. Sports stadiums often hold more people than Fargo has!

Even though the towns around here aren't exactly huge, there are a lot of die-hard baseball fans like my friends and me. So here's my plan. Why couldn't a couple of towns get together to build a stadium and start a team? For example, Moorhead, Minnesota, is right next to Fargo. They already share the same airport, and the metropolitan area has about 174,367 people. That might be enough to support a team. If it's not, then maybe Grand Forks, or even Aberdeen, could join in too.

People might say that there would be a problem naming a team that is supported by cities in two or three different states. I think baseball fans would be so happy to have a team, they wouldn't really care what it was called.

If enough people wrote to the Fargo and Moorhead city governments, maybe the idea could be put on the ballot. Major-league baseball is supposed to be our national pastime. Shouldn't we be a part of it too?

PRACTICE AND APPLY

Reread the model and then answer the following questions:

1. According to the model, what is the cause of the problem?

2. What solution does the writer offer? What words are a clue?

PRACTICE AND APPLY

ANSWERS

1. *Model 1 is organized by points of comparison. Model 2 is organized by subject.*

2. *Possible answers: Model 1: "both," "although," "on the other hand," "while"; Model 2: "than," "both," "also," "same," "the larger of the two," "always"*

3. *Possible answers: Model 1: the size of the living quarters, the quality of the food, the shuttle's sleeping accommodations; Model 2: the relationship of height, weight, speed to each type of energy*

4. *Students should create a Venn diagram or a compare-and-contrast chart like the examples on page R11. Possible answers:*

- *Model 1: Apollo Crew (1968)—Living quarters: metal-and-fabric flight couches. Meals: pureed foods squeezed out of tubes and juice in plastic bags. Sleeping accommodations: slept on couches with no room to move or spread out. Shuttle crews (today)—Living quarters: separate flight deck and lower crew-quarters deck. Meals: food served on trays, eaten with utensils, and includes healthy snacks. Sleeping accommodations: use sleep restraints that allow crew to sleep horizontally or vertically.*

- *Model 2: Potential energy—based on height and weight; heavier objects have more potential energy. Kinetic energy—based on the motion of an object; energy increases with the speed of an object. Similarities—The heavier the object, the greater the energy.*

PRACTICE AND APPLY

ANSWERS

1. *Fargo does not have a large enough population to financially support a major-league franchise.*

2. *The writer proposes that the town of Fargo and nearby towns such as Moorhead, Grand Forks, and Aberdeen combine to help finance and support a new baseball team. The words "here's my plan" provide a clue to the reader.*

PRACTICE AND APPLY

ANSWERS

1. *The graphic is the logo used by the organization featured in the article.*

2. *Lauren Beckham*

3. *The caption and photograph explain that City Year now offers a program called "Young Heroes" for middle school students.*

4 Reading Informational Texts: Forms

Magazines, newspapers, Web pages, and consumer, public, and workplace documents are all examples of informational materials. To understand and analyze informational texts, pay attention to text features and patterns of organization.

4.1 READING A NEWSPAPER ARTICLE

Because people often skim newspapers, newspaper publishers use devices to attract attention to articles.

Strategies for Reading

A "Teen Rap" is the name of a **column,** a type of article that appears regularly in a newspaper and is usually written by the same person.

B Notice whether **graphic aids** or **quotations** attract your attention.

C Once you decide that you're interested in the article, read the **title** and other **headings** to find out more about its topic and organization.

D Notice whether the article has a **byline,** a line naming the author.

E A **caption** accompanying a graphic aid may provide information or examples that add to the meaning of the article.

PRACTICE AND APPLY

1. How does the circle graphic relate to the title?

2. Who wrote the article?

3. What does the photograph with its caption tell you?

A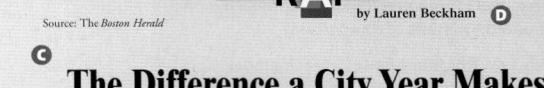

Source: The *Boston Herald*

D by Lauren Beckham

C

The Difference a City Year Makes

What kind of person gets up at the break of dawn, spends all day tutoring teenagers, cleaning up former crack houses, or teaching kids to read and write—all in the name of community service?

The kind who joins City Year.

B Hundreds of young adults come together in Boston for CYZYGY, City Year's Annual Convention of Idealism, to show community leaders, business people and—most importantly—other young adults that community service, though difficult, is rewarding to both those who give and those who receive.

E Two participants in a Winter Wonderland camp for young children displaced by Hurricane Katrina.

Barnes Middle School in East Boston, mentoring and tutoring at-risk boys in a remedial class.

"I could say that it was a challenge but that's what I needed," said the Dorchester teen. "And they needed me. I'm proud to be part of their accomplishments."

Samuels plans to attend Bunker Hill Community College next year and then pursue a bachelor's degree in child psychology. Meanwhile, he is looking forward to the CYZYGY conference.

"Hopefully in the next five years we'll have, instead of eight City Year sites, 15 to 20," he said. "CYZYGY will show Boston that young people are coming together and giving back."

B "Young people are coming together and giving back"

When Anthony Samuels of Dorchester graduated from Melrose High School last year, he had a specific plan.

"I was ready to give back to my community," Samuels, 19, said. "When I learned about City Year, I jumped right in."

Samuels spends his days at the Umana

4.2 READING A TEXTBOOK

Each textbook that you use has its own system of organization based on the content in the book. Often an introductory unit will explain the book's organization and special features. If your textbook has such a unit, read it first.

Strategies for Reading

Ⓐ Before you begin reading the lesson or chapter, read any **questions** that appear at the end of it. Then use the questions to set your purpose for reading.

Ⓑ **Read slowly and carefully** to better understand and remember the ideas presented in the text. When you come to an unfamiliar word, first try to figure out its meaning from **context clues.** If necessary, find the meaning of the word in a **glossary** in the textbook, or in a dictionary. Avoid interrupting your reading by constantly looking up words in a dictionary.

*For more information on context clues and glossaries, see the **Vocabulary and Spelling Handbook,** pages R68 and R72.*

Ⓒ Use the book's special features, such as sidebars, to increase your understanding of the text. A **sidebar** is a short presentation of additional information. It is usually set off in a box on the page.

Ⓓ Take notes as you read. Use text features such as **subheadings** and boldfaced terms to help you organize your notes. Record your notes in graphic organizers, such as cause-effect charts, to help you clarify relationships among ideas.

Primary Source Ⓒ

Background: One of the most important Stoic thinkers of the Roman era was the scholar and politician Marcus Tullius Cicero (106–43 B.C.). He stressed the importance of citizenship and believed that Romans should work for the good of each other and Rome.

from "On Duty"
By Marcus Tullius Cicero
Translated by Walter Miller

As the Stoics hold, everything that the earth produces is created for man's use; and as men, too, are born for the sake of men, that they may be able mutually to help one another ... we ought to ... contribute to the general good by an interchange of acts of kindness, by giving and receiving, and thus by our skill, our industry, and our talents to cement human society more closely together, man to man.

DOCUMENT–BASED QUESTION
What are ways that people can demonstrate good citizenship, according to Cicero?

Ⓑ **Philosophy and Citizenship** The Romans borrowed much of their philosophy from the Greeks. The philosophy of **Stoicism** was especially influential in Rome. It was developed by the Greek philosopher Zeno. Stoicism stressed the importance of virtue, duty, and endurance in life. These were all values that many Romans prized.

The beliefs of Stoicism helped create a strong sense of citizenship in Rome. Citizenship refers to the relationship individuals have with their country. As part of this relationship, a country provides protection and security for its citizens. In return, citizens are expected to take an active part in society in order to strengthen their country. Today, these aspects of Stoicism are viewed by many as necessary qualities for being a good citizen.

Ⓓ **Roman Language** Another lasting aspect of Roman culture was its language, known as Latin. Because the Romans conquered most of Europe, Latin is the basis for several European languages. These include Spanish, Italian, French, Portuguese, and Romanian. In addition, more than half of the words in English have a basis in Latin. What's more, Latin was the official language of the Roman Catholic Church into the 20th century.

Ⓐ **REVIEW** What influence did Latin have on the larger world?

PRACTICE AND APPLY

Reread the textbook page and answer the following questions:

1. How would you find the definition of *philosophy*?
2. How does the sidebar add to the text?
3. Use the text to answer the Review question.

PRACTICE AND APPLY
ANSWERS

Possible answers:

1. *One way to find the meaning of an unfamiliar word is to use context clues. Another way to find the definition of a word is to look it up in a glossary or dictionary.*

2. *The sidebar provides additional background information about the philosopher Marcus Tullius Cicero, an important Stoic thinker.*

3. *Latin is the basis for several European languages, including Spanish, Italian, French, Portuguese, and Romanian. In addition, more than half of the words in English have a basis in Latin.*

PRACTICE AND APPLY

ANSWERS

1. *Touch the STOP/CLEAR pad. Touch the TIMER CLOCK pad. Enter the time of day. Press the TIMER CLOCK pad again to set the time.*

2. *Touch the STOP/CLEAR pad when "EE" appears on the screen. Repeat steps 1–3 to set the clock.*

4.3 READING A CONSUMER DOCUMENT

Consumer documents are printed materials that accompany products and services. They usually provide information about the use, care, operation, or assembly of the products they accompany. Some common consumer documents are contracts, warranties, manuals, instructions, and schedules.

Strategies for Reading

Ⓐ Read the heading to see what information the document covers. Read the **subheadings** to learn what process each section of the instructions explains.

Ⓑ Read the directions all the way through at least once.

Ⓒ Look for **numbers** or **letters** that indicate the order in which the steps should be followed. Or look for signal words such as *first* and *finally* to see the order in which the steps should be followed.

Ⓓ Words that appear in **all capital letters** are often names or labels that appear on the device you are being shown how to use. If there is an illustration or diagram, try to match the words in the instructions to words or symbols in the graphic aid.

Ⓔ Look for **verbs that describe actions** you should take, such as *plug, touch, enter,* and *press.*

Ⓕ Pay attention to **warnings** or **notes** that describe problems.

PRACTICE AND APPLY

Reread the microwave instructions and explain how to solve the following problems:

1. The clock needs to be reset after a power outage.

2. The clock was incorrectly set at 14:30.

MICROWAVE INSTRUCTIONS
Ⓐ **Before Operating**

Ⓑ 1. Plug the power cord into a three-pronged electrical outlet.

Ⓒ 2. Display panel will light up and flash 00:00. Touch STOP/CLEAR pad.

3. Set the clock.

Ⓓ Touch STOP/CLEAR pad when the oven is first plugged in, or after the electrical power has been interrupted.

Ⓐ **Setting the Clock**

Procedure

Ⓔ 1. Touch TIMER CLOCK pad.

2. Enter the time of day. For example, if it is 10:30, touch the number pads 1030 and "10:30" will appear.

3. Press the TIMER CLOCK pad again to set the time.

Note You can select any time of the day from 1:00–12:59. To reset Clock, repeat steps 1 through 3 above. If incorrect time (for example, 8:61 or 13:00, etc.) is entered, "EE" will appear on display. Touch STOP/CLEAR pad and program correctly.

Canceling a Program

- To reset, or cancel, a cooking program as it is being entered, touch STOP/CLEAR pad once.

- To stop the oven while it is operating, touch STOP/CLEAR pad once. Do not open the door without pressing STOP/CLEAR pad.

- An entire cooking program (one stage or multiple stages) can be canceled after the oven has started cooking. This can be done by touching STOP/CLEAR pad twice.

Ⓕ **Note** See page 10 to create your own cooking programs.

Power Levels

Most foods can be cooked at full power (P-HI). However, for best results, some foods require a lower cooking power. Some foods such as tender cuts of meat can be cooked only with a lower power. Before setting any power level, the POWER LEVEL pad must be touched, followed by desired number. See chart.

1	2	3
4	5	6
7	8	9
POWER LEVEL	0	TIMER CLOCK
STOP CLEAR		START

POWER	Touch POWER LEVEL pad, then	Display
100%	Touch Power Level pad once more.	P-HI
90%	Touch number pad 9.	P-90
80%	Touch number pad 8.	P-80
70%	Touch number pad 7.	P-70
60%	Touch number pad 6.	P-60
50%	Touch number pad 5.	P-50
40%	Touch number pad 4.	P-40
30%	Touch number pad 3.	P-30
20%	Touch number pad 2.	P-20
10%	Touch number pad 1.	P-10

Note Choose P.30 for thawing or defrosting foods.

4.4 READING A PUBLIC DOCUMENT

Public documents are documents that are written for the public to provide information that is of public interest or concern. These documents are often free. They can be federal, state, or local government documents. They can be speeches or historical documents. They may even be laws, posted warnings, signs, or rules and regulations.

Strategies for Reading

Ⓐ The **shapes** of signs help convey their messages.

- circle—railroad
- diamond—warning
- square—information
- rectangle (vertical)—regulations, such as speed limits, lane markings, parking restrictions

Ⓑ The **colors** of signs have specific meaning.

- yellow—warning
- orange—construction
- green—information
- white—regulations

Ⓒ The **symbols,** or pictures, used on signs give specific information that anyone can usually understand.

SIGNS IN A DRIVER EDUCATION PAMPHLET

Signs

1. Ⓐ
2. Ⓒ
3. Ⓑ
4. KEEP LEFT RIGHT

PRACTICE AND APPLY

Refer to the signs shown to answer the following questions:

1. How do you know that the first sign is a warning sign as well as a railroad sign? What warning does it give?

2. If you had just moved to a new town, how would the second sign help you?

3. What does the third sign tell a driver?

4. If you are walking on the right side of a path and see the fourth sign, what should you do?

PRACTICE AND APPLY

ANSWERS

1. *The sign is yellow, which indicates it is a warning sign, and the circular shape lets drivers know it is a railroad sign. The sign is warning drivers that a railroad crossing is ahead and that they should watch for trains.*

2. *It is an informational sign that tells drivers that a train station is nearby.*

3. *The sign lets drivers know that there is construction ahead and that drivers should reduce their speed and watch for workers on the road.*

4. *You should cross over to the left side of the path where pedestrians are supposed to walk.*

PRACTICE AND APPLY

ANSWERS

1. *Middleton Park District*
2. *volunteers*
3. *an adult*
4. *Touch the door to see if it is hot.*
5. *You should make sure the playroom is clean, wipe tabletops clean with a damp sponge, and turn off the lights.*

Workplace documents are materials that are produced or used within a workplace, usually to aid in the functioning of a business. These may be documents generated by a business to monitor itself, such as minutes of a meeting or a sales report. These documents may also explain company policies, organizational structures, and operating procedures. Workplace documents include memos, business letters, job applications, and résumés.

Strategies for Reading

A Read the title and any subtitles to see what information the document covers.

B Determine who needs to read the document. Look for clues to see if it applies to you.

C Look for subheadings to identify main ideas and topics and to determine how the document is organized.

D Read the document slowly and carefully, as it may contain details that should not be overlooked.

E Notice how to contact the creator of the document. You will need this information to clear up anything you don't understand.

F Take notes to help you remember what actions are required.

PRACTICE AND APPLY

Reread the document and answer the questions:

1. What organization created the document?
2. Who needs to read the document?
3. Who should accompany children onto the playground?
4. If there is a fire, what should you do before opening a door?
5. What three things should you do before leaving for the day?

OPERATING PROCEDURES

"Little Folks" Play Group **A**

Middleton Park District

Notice to Volunteers
Safety Guidelines **B**

We're glad you have volunteered to help with our Saturday morning play group for children ages 2–5. To keep our space clean and safe and our children happy, we all must follow these safety rules.

Staffing **C**
- An adult must be in the playroom at all times.
- Children who go outside to the playground must be accompanied by an adult.

Emergencies **C**
- In case of emergency, dial 911 on the phone in the kitchen.
- In case of fire, evacuate the children through the main door or the emergency exit. Before opening a door, touch it to see if it is hot. A fire extinguisher is located next to the emergency exit.

Cleanup **C**
- Make sure the playroom is clean at the end of the day. Put all toys in the toy chests.
- Wipe tabletops clean with a damp sponge.
- Turn off the lights as you leave.

This document was prepared by the Middleton Park District. If you have questions or concerns, contact the Program Coordinator. **E**

4.6 READING ELECTRONIC TEXT

Electronic text is any text that is in a form that a computer can store and display on a screen. Electronic text can be part of Web pages, CD-ROMs, search engines, and documents that you create with your computer software. Like books, Web pages often provide aids for finding information. However, each Web page is designed differently, and information is not in the same location on each page. It is important to know the functions of different parts of a Web page so that you can easily find the information you want.

Strategies for Reading

A Look at the **title** of a page to determine what topics it covers.

B For an online source, such as a Web page or search engine, note the **Web address,** known as a **URL** (Universal Resource Locator). You may want to make a note of it if you need to return to that page.

C Look for a **menu bar** along the top, bottom, or side of a Web page. Clicking on an item in a menu bar will take you to another part of the Web site.

D Notice any hyperlinks to related pages. **Hyperlinks** are often underlined or highlighted in a contrasting color. You can click on a hyperlink to get to another page—one that may or may not have been created by the same person or organization.

E For information that you want to keep for future reference, save documents on your computer or print them. For online sources, you can pull down the **Favorites** or **Bookmarks** menu and bookmark pages so that you can easily return to them or print the information you need. Printing the pages will allow you to highlight key ideas on a hard copy.

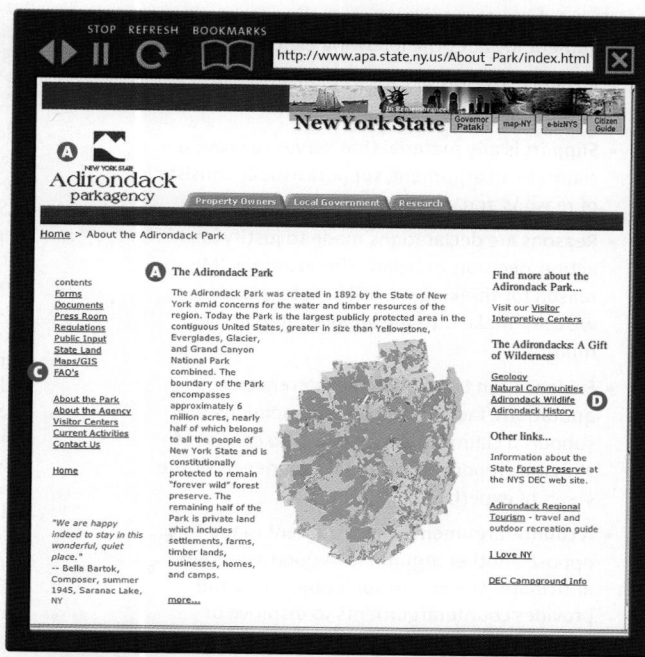

PRACTICE AND APPLY

1. What is the URL of the Web page shown?
2. Which links would you click on to find out about recreation in the park?
3. What would you do if you had questions that weren't answered by information on the site?

PRACTICE AND APPLY

ANSWERS

1. *http://www.apa.state.ny.us/About_Park/Index.html*
2. *To find information about recreation in the park, click on "Visitor Centers" and "Current Activities" links.*
3. *Click on the "Contact Us" link.*

ANSWERS

*Students should create a chart like the one on page R20. The chart should include details similar to the ones below. **Possible answers:***

***Claim:** You can do more than you think to make an important contribution to an older person's life.*

***Reason:** Even spending an hour a week can mean a lot to an older person.*

***Evidence:** An older person may have trouble stooping down to pick up objects. You can help an older person find things. And by helping, you are reminding the person that he or she is not forgotten.*

***Evidence:** It can be hard for an older person to reach up high. By helping put away groceries and other heavy objects, you are helping the person feel that he or she can still keep up with life's challenges.*

***Evidence:** Older people have lived a long life and have had many experiences. By listening to an older person's stories, you can show the person that he or she is contributing to your life.*

***Counterargument:** It's easy to talk yourself out of volunteering your time by saying, "I only have an hour a week. What good would that do?" Never underestimate how much good you can do even in a little bit of time.*

5 Reading Persuasive Texts

5.1 ANALYZING AN ARGUMENT

An **argument** expresses a position on an issue or problem and supports it with reasons and evidence. Being able to analyze and evaluate arguments will help you distinguish between claims you should accept and those you should not. A sound argument should appeal strictly to reason. However, arguments are often used in texts that also contain other types of persuasive devices. An argument includes the following elements:

- A **claim** is the writer's position on an issue or problem.

- **Support** is any material that serves to prove a claim. In an argument, support usually consists of reasons and evidence.

- **Reasons** are declarations made to justify an action, decision, or belief—for example, "My reason for thinking we will be late is that we can't make it to the appointment in five minutes."

- **Evidence** can be the specific references, quotations, facts, examples, and opinions that support a claim. Evidence may also consist of statistics, reports of personal experience, or the views of experts.

- A **counterargument** is an argument made to oppose another argument. A good argument anticipates the opposition's objections and provides counterarguments to disprove or answer them.

Claim	I think I should be allowed to watch more TV.
Reason	TV can provide opportunities for learning and enjoyment.
Evidence	TV can take you to faraway places and can bring art, music, and science right into your home.
Counterargument	Some people think TV is really bad for kids, but those people are looking at only the worst part of TV, not the best.

Read the following editorial and use a chart like the one shown to identify the claim, reason, evidence, and counterargument.

Important Hours
by Gina Maraini

"The Golden Years." That is what some people call old age. They think it is a time of peace and relaxation. But many old people spend time alone. Some cannot get out of their homes because of illness. "What can I do?" you ask. You can do more than you think to make an important contribution to an older person's life. Even spending an hour a week can mean a lot to an older neighbor who lives alone.

Some kids might say that they can only do good for an older person if they have lots of time and lots of patience. It's easy to talk yourself out of volunteering your time by saying, "I only have an hour a week. What good would that do?" Never underestimate just how much good you can do even in a little bit of time.

Sometimes things happen that seem unimportant to a kid but can really be a problem to an old person. If a small object like a pen or pencil slides under furniture, an older person often is not able to stoop down and pick it up. But they feel embarrassed to ask for help. So, the pen stays there. Sometimes it gets forgotten about and becomes lost. You can help that older person find these things. And by helping, you are reminding that person that he or she is not forgotten about either.

Sometimes it is hard for an older person to reach up high. Putting things away, like groceries, becomes a problem. Often the older person gets tired and gives up. You can help to put groceries and other heavy objects away. And by doing that, you are helping that older person feel like he or she can still keep up with life's challenges.

One of the most important things you can do for a senior citizen who lives alone is to give that person someone to talk to. Old people, who have lived long lives and had many experiences, have stories to tell that you can learn a lot from. And it is important for you to say so, too. That way, you can show the older person that he or she is contributing to your life.

You can make a real contribution to an older person's life. Even if you only have an hour to spend, you can help an older person feel cared about and important. Find ways to reach out, whether through volunteer organizations or just by being aware of who is alone in your neighborhood. And always remember: as much as you give, you get back so much more, simply by knowing the difference that you have made.

5.2 RECOGNIZING PERSUASIVE TECHNIQUES

Persuasive texts typically rely on more than just the **logical appeal** of an argument to be convincing. They also rely on ethical and emotional appeals and other **persuasive techniques**—devices that can convince you to adopt a position or take an action.

Ethical appeals establish a writer's credibility and trustworthiness with an audience. When a writer links a claim to a widely accepted value, the writer not only gains moral support for that claim but also establishes a connection with readers. For example, with the following appeal, the writer reminds readers of a value they should accept and links a claim to it: "Most of us agree that we should protect our natural resources, but we don't invest a lot of time or money to preserve them."

The chart shown here explains several other means by which a writer may attempt to sway you to adopt his or her position. Learn to recognize these techniques, and you are less likely to be influenced by them.

Persuasive Technique	Example
Appeals by Association	
Bandwagon appeal Suggests that a person should believe or do something because "everyone else" does	Every day more buyers are enjoying the conveniences of catalog shopping.
Testimonial Relies on endorsements from well-known people or satisfied customers	Todd Marshall, star of stage and screen, buys his shoes at Fine Footwear. Shouldn't you?
Snob appeal Taps into people's desire to be special or part of an elite group	Be among the first to enjoy the upgraded facilities at Spring Lake Fitness Center.
Appeal to loyalty Relies on people's affiliation with a particular group	Say *Yes!* to your community—support the campaign to build a new library!
Emotional Appeals	
Appeals to pity, fear, or vanity Use strong feelings, rather than facts, to persuade	We need to keep the homeless shelter open— think how you would feel if you had no place to go.
Word Choice	
Glittering generality A generalization that includes a word or phrase with positive connotations, to promote a product, person, or idea.	Buying handmade jewelry from the Hang Up helps support small-town America.

PRACTICE AND APPLY

ANSWERS

Possible answers:

- **Appeals by Association—bandwagon appeal:** *"join the leaders in your community and many of your neighbors who have already put their support behind Victor Velazquez";* **testimonial:** *"Local businesswoman Janice Wu is behind Victor Velazquez all the way"*

- **Emotional Appeals—appeals to pity, fear, or vanity:** *"a dinosaur who's stuck in the past or someone who's courageously facing the future";* *"Why settle for Jill Jolsen, who hasn't lifted a finger to help this community?"*

- **Word Choice—glittering generality:** *"once-in-a-lifetime chance to change this town"*

Identify the persuasive techniques used in this model.

Vote for Velazquez!

Whom do you want to represent you in Congress—a dinosaur who's stuck in the past or someone who's courageously facing the future? Why settle for Jill Jolsen, who hasn't lifted a finger to help this community? Don't let her slick ads fool you. Instead, join the leaders in the community and many of your neighbors who have already put their support behind Victor Velazquez. Local businesswoman Janice Wu is behind Velazquez all the way—she says he will bring new jobs and fresh ideas that will really work. Don't miss this once-in-a-lifetime chance to change this town. Vote for Velazquez!

5.3 ANALYZING LOGIC AND REASONING

While persuasive techniques may sway you to side with a writer, they should not be enough to convince you that an argument is sound. To determine the soundness of an argument, you really need to examine the argument's claim and support and the logic or reasoning that links them. To do this, it is helpful to identify the writer's mode of reasoning.

The Inductive Mode of Reasoning

When a writer leads from specific evidence to a general principle or generalization, that writer is using **inductive reasoning.** Here is an example of inductive reasoning.

SPECIFIC FACTS

Fact 1 Turtles are the only reptiles that have a shell.

Fact 2 The green turtle, a sea turtle, can swim almost 20 miles an hour.

Fact 3 Snapping turtles have powerful, sharp-edged jaws and are aggressive when attacked.

GENERALIZATION

Turtles have a variety of protective strategies.

Strategies for Determining the Soundness of Inductive Arguments

Ask yourself the following questions to evaluate an inductive argument:

- **Is the evidence valid and sufficient support for the conclusion?** Inaccurate facts lead to inaccurate conclusions.

- **Does the conclusion follow logically from the evidence?** From the facts listed above, the conclusion that *all* turtles have a wide variety of protective strategies would be too broad a generalization.

- **Is the evidence drawn from a large enough sample?** Even though there are only three facts listed above, the sample is large enough to support the claim. If you wanted to support the conclusion that only turtles have a variety of protective strategies, the sample is not large enough.

The Deductive Mode of Reasoning

When a writer arrives at a conclusion by applying a general principle to a specific situation, the writer is using **deductive reasoning.** Here's an example.

| Being exposed to loud noise over a long period will damage a person's hearing. | General principle or premise |

| I listen to my stereo at its highest setting for hours every day. | Specific situation |

| I will have some hearing loss. | Specific conclusion |

Strategies for Determining the Soundness of Deductive Arguments

Ask yourself the following questions to evaluate a deductive argument:

- **Is the general principle actually stated, or is it implied?** Note that writers often use deductive reasoning in arguments without stating the general principles. They just assume that readers will recognize and agree with the principles. So you may want to identify the general principle for yourself.

- **Is the general principle sound?** Don't just assume the general principle is sound. Ask yourself whether it is really true.

- **Is the conclusion valid?** To be valid, a conclusion in a deductive argument must follow logically from the general principle and the specific situation.

The following chart shows two conclusions drawn from the same general principle.

All seventh-graders are going to the zoo next week.	
Accurate Deduction	**Inaccurate Deduction**
Laura is in the seventh grade; therefore, Laura is going to the zoo next week.	Laura is going to the zoo next week; therefore, Laura is in the seventh grade.

Laura may be going to the zoo with her family or friends.

PRACTICE AND APPLY

Identify the mode of reasoning used in the following paragraph.

> In science class, I learned what different substances do for the human body. Protein aids growth and repairs muscles. Fruits and vegetables provide critical vitamins, and calcium strengthens bones. Carbohydrates supply energy to the body. Clearly, a balanced diet is important for good health.

PRACTICE AND APPLY

ANSWER

The paragraph uses inductive reasoning.

Identifying Faulty Reasoning

Sometimes an argument at first appears to make sense but isn't valid because it is based on a fallacy. A **fallacy** is an error in logic. Learn to recognize these common fallacies.

TYPE OF FALLACY	DEFINITION	EXAMPLE
Circular reasoning	Supporting a statement by simply repeating it in different words	I'm tired because **I don't have any energy.**
Either/or fallacy	A statement that suggests that there are only two choices available in a situation that really offers more than two options	**Either** we raise taxes, **or** we close the parks.
Oversimplification	An explanation of a complex situation or problem as if it were much simpler than it is	Getting a good grade in Mrs. Raimi's class depends on **whether she likes you.**
Overgeneralization	A generalization that is too broad. You can often recognize overgeneralizations by the use of words such as *all, everyone, every time, anything, no one,* and *none.*	You **never** get me anything I want.
Hasty generalization	A conclusion drawn from too little evidence or from evidence that is biased	She left after fifteen minutes. **She must not like us.**
Stereotyping	A dangerous type of overgeneralization. Stereotypes are broad statements about people on the basis of their gender, ethnicity, race, or political, social, professional, or religious group.	**All rock stars** are self-centered.
Attacking the person or name-calling	An attempt to discredit an idea by attacking the person or group associated with it. Candidates often engage in name-calling during political campaigns.	The **narrow-minded** senator opposes recycling.
Evading the issue	Responding to an objection with arguments and evidence that do not address its central point	Yes, I broke my campaign promise not to raise taxes, **but higher taxes have led to increases in police patrols and paved highways.**
False cause	The mistake of assuming that because one event occurred after another event in time, the first event caused the second one to occur	John didn't get his homework done because he had to take the dog for a walk.

Look for examples of logical fallacies in the following argument. Identify each one and explain why you identified it as such.

Dear Editors:

There has been a lot of talk about students' lack of concern for the appearance of our school. Nobody gets rid of his or her trash properly and everyone writes graffiti on the walls. But if the school seemed more worth caring about, students would take better care of it. Most of the school is very old. The halls are dark and the walls are dingy because the maintenance staff has been on strike for several weeks. The old-fashioned school board said that an entirely new building wasn't needed. So only a new gym was added. It is clean and bright because students have kept it that way. Either we build a new school, or it will be destroyed in three years.

5.4 EVALUATING PERSUASIVE TEXTS

Learning how to evaluate persuasive texts and identify bias will help you become more selective when doing research and also help you improve your own reasoning and arguing skills. **Bias** is an inclination for or against a particular opinion or viewpoint. A writer may reveal a strongly positive or negative opinion on an issue by presenting only one way of looking at it or by heavily weighting the evidence on one side of the argument. The presence of the following is often a sign that a writer is biased:

Loaded language consists of words with strongly positive or negative connotations that are intended to influence a reader's attitude.

EXAMPLE: *Barbara Larsen is the best choice for student council president because she has fresh ideas and fantastic people skills.* (*Fresh* and *fantastic* have very positive connotations.)

Propaganda is any form of communication that is so distorted that it conveys false or misleading information. Some politicians create and distribute propaganda. Many logical fallacies, such as name-calling, the either/or fallacy, and false causes, are often used in propaganda. The following example shows an oversimplification. The writer uses one fact to support a particular point of view but does not reveal another fact that does not support that viewpoint.

EXAMPLE: *Since the new park opened, vandalism in the area has increased by 10 percent. Clearly, the park has had a negative impact on the area.* (The writer does not include the fact that the vandalism was caused by people who were not drawn into the area by the park.)

For more information on logical fallacies, see **Identifying Faulty Reasoning,** *page R24.*

Strategies for Evaluating Evidence

It is important to have a set of standards by which you can evaluate persuasive texts. Use the questions below to help you critically assess facts and opinions that are presented as evidence.

- **Are the facts presented verifiable?** Facts can be proved by eyewitness accounts, authoritative sources such as encyclopedias and almanacs, experts, or research.

- **Are the opinions presented well informed?** Any opinions offered should be supported by facts, be based on research or eyewitness accounts, or be the opinions of experts on the topic.

- **Is the evidence thorough?** Thorough evidence leaves no reasonable questions unanswered. If a choice is offered, background for making the choice should be provided. If taking a side is called for, all sides of the issue should be presented.

- **Is the evidence biased?** Be alert to evidence that contains loaded language or other signs of bias.

- **Is the evidence authoritative?** The people, groups, or organizations that provided the evidence should have credentials that support their authority.

PRACTICE AND APPLY

ANSWERS

1. *Possible answer: Overgeneralization:* "Nobody gets rid of his or her trash properly and everyone writes graffiti on the walls." *Explanation: The writer uses words such as* nobody *and* everyone *to make broad generalizations about people.*

2. *Possible answer: Hasty generalization:* "If the school seemed more worth caring about, students would take better care of it." *Explanation: The statement presents a biased point of view based on one person's opinion.*

3. *Possible answer: False cause:* "The halls are dark and the walls are dingy because the maintenance staff has been on strike for several weeks." *Explanation: The writer makes the assumption that one event (the strike) caused another (the condition of the building) but does not consider other causes.*

4. *Possible answer: Attacking the person or name-calling:* "old-fashioned school board" *Explanation: The writer uses negative language to discredit the board.*

5. *Possible answer: Either/or fallacy:* "Either we build a new school, or it will be destroyed in three years." *Explanation: The statement does not take into account other alternatives.*

PRACTICE AND APPLY

ANSWERS

Possible answers:

Facts: The Students' League is hosting a demonstration against Representative Sharon Bullhorn on Saturday. Last week, Representative Bullhorn voted against raising the minimum wage.

Opinion: "If she did [care], she would have helped pass the much-needed minimum wage increase, so that preteens and teens could earn the money they deserve."

Elements of bias: "Obviously Representative Bullhorn doesn't care about young people."

PRACTICE AND APPLY

ANSWER

Students' responses will vary, but they should evaluate the strength of the claim, the evidence supporting the claim, and the counterarguments.

Possible answer: The writer presents a clear thesis and offers a logical and effective solution to help maintain a safe learning environment. The evidence the writer provides in support of video monitoring is adequate, accurate, and appropriate. He or she also anticipates counterclaims and addresses concerns about maintaining students' privacy. For the most part, this person's argument is strong. However, the writer's proposal is undermined at the end by faulty reasoning; specifically, the use of name-calling, generalization, and false cause. The closing statements weaken what would otherwise be a strong proposal.

• **Is it important that the evidence be current?**
Where timeliness is crucial, as in the areas of medicine and technology, the evidence should reflect the latest developments in the areas.

PRACTICE AND APPLY

Read the argument below. Identify the facts, opinion, and elements of bias.

> Let your voice be heard. The Students' League is hosting a demonstration against U.S Representative Sharon Bullhorn on Saturday. Just last week, Representative Bullhorn voted against raising the minimum wage. Obviously Representative Bullhorn doesn't care about young people. If she did, she would have helped pass the much-needed minimum wage increase, so that preteens and teens could earn the money they deserve.

Strategies for Determining a Strong Argument

Make sure that all or most of the following statements are true:

• The argument presents a claim or thesis.

• The claim is connected to its support by a general principle that most readers would readily agree with. Valid general principle: *It is the job of a school to provide a well-rounded physical education program.* Invalid general principle: *It is the job of a school to produce healthy, physically fit people.*

• The reasons make sense.

• The reasons are presented in a logical and effective order.

• The claim and all reasons are adequately supported by sound evidence.

• The evidence is adequate, accurate, and appropriate.

• The logic is sound. There are no instances of faulty reasoning.

• The argument adequately anticipates and addresses reader concerns and counterclaims with counterarguments.

PRACTICE AND APPLY

Use the preceding criteria to evaluate the strength of the following proposal.

MODEL

Summary of Proposal

I propose that our school install video cameras in halls, lunchrooms, and other public areas to monitor students' activities.

Need

The halls and public areas of our school are not well supervised because of a shortage of security staff. Last month, three students were hurt in fights on school property.

Proposed Solution

Installing video monitors in the halls and public areas of the school will create a safe environment for students at a reasonable cost.

There is good evidence that video monitoring works. Westview School has monitored its students for over a year. In that time there has not been one incident of fighting or damage to property.

People who are against video monitoring don't agree. They say that monitoring violates students' rights to privacy.

In my opinion, junior high students need to act like responsible adults. We need guidelines and monitoring to show us where the limits are and to help us learn to act responsibly on our own.

Not only does video monitoring work, but installing the equipment can lower supervisory costs in the long run. Only eight cameras would be needed, installed in the two main hallways, the lunchroom, and the auditorium. The total cost would be around $16,000. I believe the money can be found in the general school budget.

What idiot would not support video monitoring of students?

It would be a crime not to have video monitoring.

Most school officials only care about their jobs and not what's good for students. I say to those school officials who do care: Either install video cameras or wait for more students to be injured.

---

6 Adjusting Reading Rate to Purpose

You may need to change the way you read certain texts in order to understand what you read. To adjust the way you read, you first need to be aware of what you want to get out of what you are reading. Then you can adjust the speed at which you read in response to your purpose and the difficulty of the material.

Determine Your Purpose for Reading

You read different types of materials for different purposes. You may read a novel for enjoyment. You may read a textbook unit to learn a new concept or to master the content for a test. When you read for enjoyment, you naturally read at a pace that is comfortable for you. When you read for information, you need to read material more slowly and thoroughly. When you are being tested on material, you may think you have to read fast, especially if the test is being timed. However, you can actually increase your understanding of the material if you slow down.

Determine Your Reading Rate

The rate at which you read most comfortably is called your **independent reading level.** It is the rate that you use to read materials that you enjoy. To learn to adjust your reading rate to read materials for other purposes, you need to be aware of your independent reading level. You can figure out your reading level by following these steps:

1. Select a passage from a book or story you enjoy.
2. Have a friend or classmate time you as you begin reading the passage silently.
3. Read at the rate that is most comfortable for you.
4. Stop when your friend or classmate tells you one minute has passed.
5. Determine the number of words you read in that minute and write down the number.
6. Repeat the process at least two more times, using different passages.
7. Add the numbers and divide the sum by the number of times your friend timed you.

Reading Techniques for Informational Material

You can use the following techniques to adapt your reading for informational texts, to prepare for tests, and to better understand what you read:

- **Skimming** is reading quickly to get the general idea of a text. To skim, read only the title, headings, graphic aids, highlighted words, and first sentence of each paragraph. Also, read any introduction, conclusion, or summary. Skimming can be especially useful when taking a test. Before reading a passage, you can skim questions that follow it in order to find out what is expected and better focus on the important ideas in the text.

  When researching a topic, skimming can help you decide whether a source has information that is related to your topic.

- **Scanning** is reading quickly to find a specific piece of information, such as a fact or a definition. When you scan, your eyes sweep across a page, looking for key words that may lead you to the information you want. Use scanning to review for tests and to find answers to questions.

- **Changing pace** is speeding up or slowing down the rate at which you read parts of a particular text. When you come across familiar concepts, you might be able to speed up without misunderstanding them. When you encounter unfamiliar concepts or material presented in an unpredictable way, however, you may need to slow down to understand the information.

WATCH OUT! Reading too slowly can affect your ability to understand what you read. Make sure you aren't just reading one word at a time. Practice reading phrases.

PRACTICE AND APPLY

Find an article in a magazine or textbook. Skim the article. Then answer the following questions:

1. What did you notice about the organization of the article from skimming it?
2. What is the main idea of the article?

PRACTICE AND APPLY

ANSWER

Accept answers that provide an accurate description of the article's organization and its main idea.

Writing is a process, a journey of discovery in which you can explore your thoughts, experiment with ideas, and search for connections. Through writing, you can explore and record your thoughts, feelings, and ideas for yourself alone or you can communicate them to an audience.

> **WRITING TOOLS**
> Go to the **Writing Center** at **ClassZone.com** for interactive models, publishing ideas, and other support.

1 The Writing Process

The writing process consists of the following stages: prewriting, drafting, revising and editing, proofreading, and publishing. These are not stages that you must complete in a set order. Rather, you may return to an earlier stage at any time to improve your writing.

1.1 PREWRITING

In the prewriting stage, you explore what you want to write about, what your purpose for writing is, whom you are writing for, and what form you will use to express your ideas. Ask yourself the following questions to get started.

Topic	• Is my topic assigned, or can I choose it? • What would I be interested in writing about?
Purpose	• Am I writing to entertain, to inform, to persuade, or for some combination of these purposes? • What effect do I want to have on my readers?
Audience	• Who is the audience? • What might the audience members already know about my topic? • What about the topic might interest them?
Format	• Which format will work best? Essay? Poem? Speech? Short story? Article? Research paper?

Find Ideas for Writing

• Browse through magazines, newspapers, and Web sites.

• Start a file of articles you want to save for future reference.

• With a group, brainstorm as many ideas as you can. Compile your ideas into a list.

• Write down anything that comes into your head.

• Interview someone who is an expert on a particular topic.

• Use a cluster map to explore subordinate ideas that relate to a general topic.

Organize Ideas

Once you've chosen a topic, you will need to compile and organize your ideas. If you are writing a description, you may need to gather sensory details. For an essay or a research paper, you may need to record information from different sources. To record notes from sources you read or view, use any or all of these methods:

• **Summarize:** Briefly retell the main ideas of a piece of writing in your own words.

• **Paraphrase:** Restate all or almost all of the information in your own words.

• **Quote:** Record the author's exact words.

Depending on what form your writing takes, you may also need to arrange your ideas in a certain pattern.

*For more information, see the **Writing Handbook**, pages R34–R41.*

1.2 DRAFTING

In the drafting stage, you put your ideas on paper and allow them to develop and change as you write. You don't need to worry about correct grammar and spelling at this stage. There are two ways that you can draft:

Discovery drafting is a good approach when you are not quite sure what you think about your subject. You just start writing and let your feelings and ideas lead you in developing the topic.

Planned drafting may work better if you know that your ideas have to be arranged in a certain way, as in a research paper. Try making a writing plan or an informal outline before you begin drafting.

1.3 REVISING AND EDITING

The revising and editing stage allows you to polish your draft and make changes in its content, organization, and style. Use the questions that follow to spot problems and determine what changes would improve your work:

- Does my writing have a **main idea** or central focus? Is my thesis clear?

- Have I used **precise** nouns, verbs, and modifiers?

- Have I included **adequate detail** and **evidence?** Where might I include a telling detail, revealing statistic, or vivid example?

- Is my writing **unified?** Do all ideas and supporting details help explain my main idea?

- Is my writing clear and **coherent?** Do sentences connect to one another smoothly and logically?

- Have I used a consistent **point of view?**

- Do I need to add **transitional words, phrases,** or sentences to explain relationships among ideas?

- Have I used a **variety of sentence types?** Are they well constructed? What sentences might I combine to improve the rhythm of my writing?

- Have I used a **tone** appropriate for my audience and purpose?

1.4 PROOFREADING

When you are satisfied with your revision, proofread your paper for mistakes in grammar, usage, and mechanics. You may want to do this several times, looking for a different type of mistake each time. Use the following questions to help you correct errors:

- Have I corrected any errors in **subject-verb agreement** and **pronoun-antecedent agreement?**

- Have I double-checked for errors in **confusing word pairs,** such as *it's/its, than/then,* and *too/to?*

- Have I corrected any **run-on sentences** and **sentence fragments?**

- Have I followed rules for **correct capitalization?**

- Have I used **punctuation marks** correctly?

- Have I checked the **spellings of all unfamiliar words** in the dictionary?

TIP If possible, don't begin proofreading just after you've finished writing. Put your work away for at least a few hours. When you return to it, you will find it easier to identify and correct mistakes.

For more information, see the Grammar Handbook and the Vocabulary and Spelling Handbook, pages R46–R75.

Use the proofreading symbols in the chart to mark changes on your draft.

Proofreading Symbols	
∧ Add letters or words.	/ Make a capital letter lowercase.
⊙ Add a period.	¶ Begin a new paragraph.
≡ Capitalize a letter.	↗ Delete letters or words.
⊂ Close up space.	∿ Switch the positions of letters or words.
∧ Add a comma.	

1.5 PUBLISHING AND REFLECTING

Always consider sharing your finished writing with a wider audience. Reflecting on your writing is another good way to finish a project.

Publishing Ideas

- Post your writing on a Weblog.

- Create a multimedia presentation and share it with classmates.

- Publish your writing in a school newspaper, local newspaper, or literary magazine.

- Present your work orally in a report, speech, reading, or dramatic performance.

Reflecting on Your Writing

Think about your writing process and whether you would like to add what you have written to your writing portfolio. You might attach a note in which you answer questions like these:

- Which parts of the process did I find easiest? Which parts were more difficult?

- What was the biggest problem I faced during the writing process? How did I solve the problem?

- What changes have occurred in my writing style?

- Have I noticed any features in the writing of published authors or my peers that I can apply to my own work?

1.6 PEER RESPONSE

Peer response consists of the suggestions and comments you make about the writing of your peers and also the comments and suggestions they make about your writing. You can ask a peer reader for help at any time in the writing process.

Using Peer Response as a Writer

- Indicate whether you are more interested in feedback about your ideas or about your presentation of them.

- Ask questions that will help you get specific information about your writing. Open-ended questions that require more than yes-or-no answers are more likely to give you information you can use as you revise.

- Give your readers plenty of time to respond thoughtfully to your writing.

- Encourage your readers to be honest.

Being a Peer Reader

- Respect the writer's feelings.

- Offer positive reactions first.

- Make sure you understand what kind of feedback the writer is looking for, and then respond accordingly.

For more information on the writing process, see the **Introductory Unit,** *pages 16–19.*

2 Building Blocks of Good Writing

Whatever your purpose in writing, you need to capture your reader's interest and organize your thoughts clearly.

2.1 INTRODUCTIONS

An introduction should present a thesis statement and capture your reader's attention.

Kinds of Introductions

There are a number of ways to write an introduction. The one you choose depends on who the audience is and on your purpose for writing.

Make a Surprising Statement Beginning with a startling statement or an interesting fact can arouse your reader's curiosity about a subject, as in the following model.

> **MODEL**
>
> Bats may seem like a nuisance, but not as much as the many pounds of insects a colony of bats can eat in one night. Despite their ugly faces and all the scary stories about them, bats are very important and useful animals.

Provide a Description A vivid description sets a mood and brings a scene to life for your reader.

Here, details about wild geese swimming in an unfrozen river during the winter set the tone for an essay about water pollution.

> **MODEL**
>
> The temperature is 15 degrees. Drifts of snow hide picnic tables and swings. In the middle of the park, however, steam rises from a lake where Canada geese swim. It sounds beautiful, but the water is warm because it has been heated by a chemical plant upriver. In fact, the geese should have migrated south by now.

Ask a Question Beginning with a question can make your reader want to read on to find out the answer. The following introduction asks what two seemingly different things have in common.

> **MODEL**
>
> What do billiard balls and movie film have in common? It was in an effort to find a substitute for ivory billiard balls that John Hyatt created celluloid. This plastic substance was also used to make the first movies.

Relate an Anecdote Beginning with an anecdote, or brief story, can hook your reader and help you make a point in a dramatic way. The following anecdote introduces a humorous story about a childhood experience.

MODEL

When I was younger, my friends and I would rub balloons in our hair and make them stick to our clothes. Someone once said, "I get a charge out of this," not knowing that we were really generating static electricity.

Address the Reader Speaking directly to your reader establishes a friendly, informal tone and involves the reader in your topic.

MODEL

Learn the latest dances from a famous video choreographer. Come to the community center for a free dance lesson on Saturday night at 6 P.M.

Begin with a Thesis Statement A thesis statement expressing a main idea may be woven into both the beginning and the end of a piece of nonfiction writing.

MODEL

Unlike the strategically planned warfare in today's world, warfare in medieval times was unsophisticated and included many primitive weapons.

TIP To write the best introduction for your paper, you may want to try more than one of the methods and then decide which is the most effective for your purpose and audience.

2.2 PARAGRAPHS

A paragraph is made up of sentences that work together to develop an idea or accomplish a purpose. Whether or not it contains a topic sentence stating the main idea, a good paragraph must have unity and coherence.

Unity

A paragraph has unity when all the sentences support and develop one stated or implied idea. Use the following technique to create unity in your paragraphs:

Write a Topic Sentence A topic sentence states the main idea of the paragraph; all other sentences in the paragraph provide supporting details. A topic sentence is often the first sentence in a paragraph, as shown in the model that follows. However, it may also appear later in a paragraph or at the end, to summarize or reinforce the main idea.

MODEL

Flying a hot-air balloon looks fun, but it requires a good mathematician to fly one safely. Since a balloon is controlled by heating and cooling the air inside the balloon, the pilot must know the temperature of the air outside it and how high he or she plans to fly in order to calculate the maximum weight the balloon can carry. If the pilot doesn't do the math correctly, the balloon could crash.

TIP Paying attention to topic sentences when you read literature can help you craft your own topic sentences. Notice the use of strong topic sentences in "The Noble Experiment" on pages 810–819. For example, the fourth paragraph on page 812 begins, "Winning his directors' approval was almost insignificant in contrast to the task which now lay ahead of the Dodger president." The rest of the paragraph then explains that task in detail.

Coherence

A paragraph is coherent when all its sentences are related to one another and each flows logically to the next. The following techniques will help you achieve coherence in paragraphs:

- Present your ideas in the most logical order.
- Use pronouns, synonyms, and repeated words to connect ideas.
- Use transitional words to show relationships among ideas.

In the model shown here, the writer used several techniques to create a coherent paragraph.

MODEL

Before you buy a backpack, you should make sure it fits you and will last a long time. First, check the seams to be sure they are zigzag stitched and not single-row stitched. Next, check that the zippers are covered by flaps so your homework doesn't get wet when it rains. Finally, make sure that the bottom of the backpack rests comfortably on your hips.

2.3 TRANSITIONS

Transitions are words and phrases that show connections between details. Clear transitions help show how your ideas relate to one another.

Kinds of Transitions

The types of transitions you choose depend on the ideas you want to convey.

Time or Sequence Some transitions help to clarify the sequence of events over time. When you are telling a story or describing a process, you can connect ideas with such transitional words as *first, second, always, then, next, later, soon, before, finally, after, earlier, afterward,* and *tomorrow.*

MODEL

Long before mountain bikes were made, bicycles were much less comfortable. The first cycle, which actually had four wheels, was made in 1645 and had to be walked. Later, two-wheeled cycles with pedals were called boneshakers because of their bumpy ride.

Spatial Order Transitional words and phrases such as *in front, behind, next to, along, nearest, lowest, above, below, underneath, on the left,* and *in the middle* can help your reader visualize a scene.

MODEL

The audience entered the theater from the back. The stage was in front, and fire exits were located to the right and left of the stage.

Degree of Importance Transitional words such as *mainly, strongest, weakest, first, second, most important, least important, worst,* and *best* may be used to rank ideas or to show degrees of importance.

MODEL

My strongest reason for going on the canoeing trip would be not hearing my little brother and sister squabbling over the TV. My weakest reason for going is that there is nothing better to do.

Compare and Contrast Words and phrases such as *similarly, likewise, also, like, as, neither ... nor,* and *either ... or* show similarity between details. *However, by contrast, yet, but, unlike, instead, whereas,* and *while* show difference. Note the use of transitions showing contrast in the model.

MODEL

While my local public library is a quieter place to study than home, I don't always get much done in the library. I'm so used to the cheerful chatter of my baby brother that, by contrast, the stillness of the library makes me sleepy.

TIP Both *but* and *however* can be used to join two independent clauses. When *but* is used as a coordinating conjunction, it is preceded by a comma. When *however* is used as a conjunctive adverb, it is preceded by a semicolon and followed by a comma.

EXAMPLE

A greenbottle fly is small, but its eyes contain many lenses.

You can try to quietly sneak up on a fly with a swatter; however, the fly, with its compound eyes, will still be able to see the motion of the swatter.

Cause-Effect When you are writing about a cause-effect relationship, use transitional words and phrases such as *since, because, thus, therefore, so, due to, for this reason,* and *as a result* to help explain that relationship and make your writing coherent.

MODEL

Because we missed seven days of school as a result of snowstorms, the school year will be extended. Therefore, we will be in school until June 17.

2.4 CONCLUSIONS

A conclusion should leave readers with a strong final impression.

Kinds of Conclusions

Good conclusions sum up ideas in a variety of ways. Here are some techniques you might try.

Restate Your Thesis A good way to conclude an essay is by restating your thesis, or main idea, in different words. The following conclusion restates the thesis introduced on page R31.

MODEL

It may be hard to imagine that ladders, bows, and catapults were once used in battle; yet these primitive weapons accomplished the attackers' main goal—to get a castle's inhabitants to surrender.

Ask a Question Try asking a question that sums up what you have said and gives your reader something new to think about. This question concludes a piece of persuasive writing and suggests a course of action.

MODEL

If tutoring a student in writing, reading, or math can help you do better in these subjects yourself, shouldn't you take advantage of the opportunities to tutor at Western Elementary School?

Make a Recommendation When you are persuading your audience to take a position on an issue, you can conclude by recommending a specific course of action.

MODEL

Since learning a foreign language gives you a chance to expand your world view and make new friends, register for one of the introductory courses that start next fall.

Offer an Opinion Leave your reader with something to think about by offering your personal opinion on the topic. The following model offers an opinion about medieval warfare.

MODEL

Even though the tools used in medieval times seem primitive today, warfare is serious and deadly business, no matter what century you're in.

End with the Last Event If you're telling a story, you may end with the last thing that happens. Here, the ending includes an important moment for the narrator.

MODEL

As I raced down the basketball court in the final seconds of the game, I felt as alone as I did on all those nights practicing by myself in the driveway. My perfect lay-up drew yells from the crowd, but I was cheering for myself on the inside.

2.5 ELABORATION

Elaboration is the process of developing an idea by providing specific supporting details that are relevant and appropriate to the purpose and form of your writing.

Facts and Statistics A fact is a statement that can be verified, and a statistic is a fact expressed as a number. Make sure the facts and statistics you supply are from reliable, up-to-date sources.

MODEL

Rhode Island is the smallest state in area; however, it is not the smallest in population. According to the U.S. Census Bureau, its population was estimated to be 1,080,632 in 2004. There are fewer people living in Alaska, Delaware, Montana, North Dakota, South Dakota, Vermont, and Wyoming.

Sensory Details Details that show how something looks, sounds, tastes, smells, or feels can enliven a description, making readers feel they are actually experiencing what you are describing. Which senses does the writer appeal to in the following model?

WRITING HANDBOOK   **R33**

I was nervous during my math test last week. Chewing on my pencil left my mouth feeling dry and flaky. My palms were sweating so much, they left stains on the pages. The ticking of the clock seemed like the beating of a drum inside my head.

Incidents From our earliest years, we are interested in hearing "stories." One way to illustrate a point powerfully is to relate an incident or tell a story, as shown in the example.

MODEL

People who are afraid of heights tend to panic even in perfectly safe situations. When my friend Jill and I rode to the top floor of a shopping mall, I enjoyed the view from the glass-enclosed elevator, but Jill's face was pale and her hands trembled.

Examples An example can help make an abstract idea concrete or can serve to clarify a complex point for your reader.

MODEL

The origins of today's professional sporting events in the United States can be traced to countries all over the world. For example, hockey is believed to have been influenced by the Irish game of hurling which included a stick and a square wooden block.

Quotations Choose quotations that clearly support your points, and be sure that you copy each quotation word for word. Remember always to credit the source.

MODEL

After the tragic events that come to pass in Rod Serling's teleplay *The Monsters Are Due on Maple Street*, the narrator says to the audience, "The tools of conquest do not necessarily come with bombs and explosions and fallout. There are weapons that are simply thoughts, attitudes, prejudices—to be found only in the minds of men. For the record, prejudices can kill and suspicion can destroy."

3 Descriptive Writing

Descriptive writing allows you to paint word pictures about anything, from events of global importance to the most personal feelings. It is an essential part of almost every piece of writing.

RUBRIC: Standards for Writing

Successful descriptive writing should

- have a clear focus and sense of purpose
- use sensory details and precise words to create a vivid image, establish a mood, or express emotion
- present details in a logical order

For more information, see **Writing Workshop: Descriptive Essay,** *pages 158–165.*

3.1 KEY TECHNIQUES

Consider Your Goals What do you want to accomplish with your description? Do you want to show why something is important to you? Do you want to make a person or scene more memorable? Do you want to explain an event?

Identify Your Audience Who will read your description? How familiar are they with your subject? What background information will they need? Which details will they find most interesting?

Think Figuratively What figures of speech might help make your description vivid and interesting? What simile or metaphor comes to mind? What imaginative comparisons can you make? What living thing does an inanimate object remind you of?

Gather Sensory Details Which sights, smells, tastes, sounds, and textures make your subject come alive? Which details stick in your mind when you observe or recall your subject? Which senses does it most strongly affect?

You might want to use a chart like the one shown here to collect sensory details about your subject.

Sights	Sounds	Textures	Smells	Tastes

Organize Your Details Details that are presented in a logical order help the reader form a mental picture of the subject. Descriptive details may be organized chronologically, spatially, by order of impression, or by order of importance.

3.2 OPTIONS FOR ORGANIZATION

Option 1: Spatial Order Choose one of these options to show the spatial order of elements in a scene you are describing.

For more information, see Transitions, page R32.

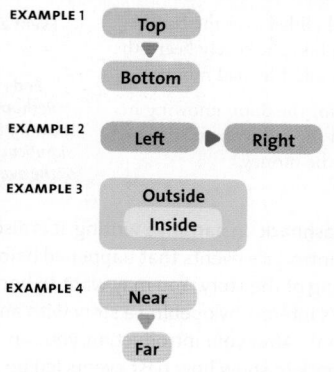

MODEL

The room was quiet—too quiet. To my left loomed the big white refrigerator. To my right squatted the gas stove, blue pilots glowing. Straight ahead sat the huge island. Cutting board, knife, and half-chopped carrot lay abandoned upon it now. Stepping cautiously to the right of the island, I came in view of the oven. That's where I froze. The oven door was open. A faint, white light pulsed and flickered high in one corner.

Option 2: Order of Impression Order of impression is the order in which you notice details.

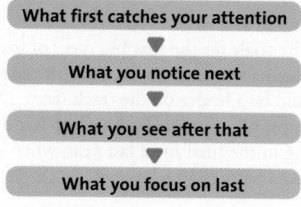

MODEL

As she lost her balance on the slippery pebbles, her first thought was that she was going to sprain her ankle and be swept away by the surf. Her heart beat rapidly, but before she knew it, she was sitting in the sand while the warm surf rolled in, almost covering her. She realized that the water was not going to reach beyond her shoulders and that she was safe. Then, suddenly, she felt the tug of the water in the other direction as the undertow flowed back, sweeping the sand from under her as it went. As soon as the water had receded she scrambled to her feet.

TIP Use transitions that help readers understand the order of the impressions you are describing. Some useful transitions are *after, next, during, first, before, finally,* and *then.*

Option 3: Order of Importance You can use order of importance as the organizing structure for a description.

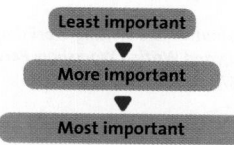

MODEL

I think our school should offer karate as part of the gym program. There are several reasons this is a good idea. First, karate is fun, and anyone can learn to do it. Many students who want to learn martial arts can't afford to because private lessons are so expensive. Karate is also a great form of exercise. It improves strength, coordination, and grace. The most important reason, though, is that learning karate makes students more confident and gives them skills that can help them throughout life.

For more information, see Transitions, page R32.

Option 4: Chronological Order You can use chronological order as the organizing structure for a description. See section 4.2 on page R36 for an example of how this is done.

4 Narrative Writing

Narrative writing tells a story. If you write a story from your imagination, it is a fictional narrative. A true story about actual events is a nonfictional narrative. Narrative writing can be found in short stories, novels, news articles, personal narratives, and biographies.

> **RUBRIC: Standards for Writing**
>
> **A successful narrative should**
>
> - hook the reader's attention with a strong introduction
> - include descriptive details and dialogue to develop the characters, setting, and plot
> - have a clear beginning, middle, and end
> - have a logical organization, with clues and transitions that help the reader understand the order of events
> - maintain a consistent tone and point of view
> - use language that is appropriate to the audience
> - demonstrate the significance of events or ideas

*For more information, see **Writing Workshop: Short Story**, pages 420–427, and **Writing Workshop: Personal Narrative**, pages 850–857.*

4.1 KEY TECHNIQUES

Identify the Main Events What are the most important events in your narrative? Is each event needed to tell the story?

Describe the Setting When do the events occur? Where do they take place? How can you use setting to create mood and to set the stage for the characters and their actions?

Depict Characters Vividly What do your characters look like? What do they think and say? How do they act? What details can show what they are like?

TIP Dialogue is an effective means of developing characters in a narrative. As you write dialogue, choose words that express your characters' personalities and that show how the characters feel about one another and about the events in the plot.

4.2 OPTIONS FOR ORGANIZATION

Option 1: Chronological Order One way to organize a piece of narrative writing is to arrange the events in chronological order, as shown.

EXAMPLE

Roger walked into the store where he had seen the fancy new bikes.

"Can I help you?" the salesperson asked. Roger pointed toward the bikes against a wall.

As his hand glided over the handle-bars on the bike, he barely heard the salesperson ask if he had money.

Roger ran for the door, knowing he had to find the old woman who had given him the money.

Introduction
Characters and setting

▼

Event 1

▼

Event 2

▼

End
Perhaps showing the significance of the events

Option 2: Flashback In narrative writing, it is also possible to introduce events that happened before the beginning of the story. You may want to hook your reader's interest by opening a story with an exciting event. After your introduction, you can use a flashback to show how past events led up to the present situation or to provide background about a character or event. Use clue words such as *last summer, as a young girl, the previous school year,* and *his earliest memories* to let your reader know that you are interrupting the main action to describe earlier events.

Notice how the flashback interrupts the action in the model.

MODEL

At the trials for the first big meet of the school year, Shayna was eager to prove to the coach that she could be a leader on the track team. During warm-ups, her mind drifted back to her disastrous showing in the final meet last year, when she had dropped a baton in a relay race.

Option 3: Focus on Conflict When a fictional narrative focuses on a central conflict, the story's plot may be organized as in the following example.

EXAMPLE

A kind stranger gives Roger money he doesn't really deserve. Roger decides he will buy a bike with the money. In the store the bikes are lined up in a row, beautiful, shiny, and bright.

> **Describe main characters and setting.**

Roger is struggling with spending the stranger's money on a fancy bike that he really doesn't need.

> **Present conflict.**

- A salesperson walks up to Roger.
- Roger explains that he is looking at a 12-speed, super-lightweight bike.
- The salesperson tells Roger that the bike is very expensive and asks if he has enough money.

> **Relate events that make conflict complex and cause characters to change.**

Roger realizes that he shouldn't spend the money needlessly and runs out of the store in search of the stranger. He plans to return the money.

> **Present resolution or outcome of conflict.**

5 Expository Writing

Expository writing informs and explains. You can use it to explain how to cook spaghetti, to explore the origins of the universe, or to compare two pieces of literature. There are many types of expository writing. Think about your topic and select the type that presents the information most clearly.

5.1 COMPARISON AND CONTRAST

Compare-and-contrast writing examines the similarities and differences between two or more subjects. You might, for example, compare and contrast two short stories, the main characters in a novel, or two movies.

RUBRIC: Standards for Writing

Successful compare-and-contrast writing should

- hook the reader's attention with a strong introduction
- clearly identify the subjects that are being compared and contrasted
- include specific, relevant details
- follow a clear plan of organization
- use language and details appropriate to the audience
- use transitional words and phrases to clarify similarities and differences

For more information, see **Writing Workshop: Comparison-Contrast Essay,** *pages 286–293,* **Writing Workshop: Interpretive Essay,** *pages 524–531,* **Writing Workshop: Personal Response to a Poem,** *pages 608–615, and* **Writing Workshop: Cause-and-Effect Essay,** *pages 736–743.*

Options for Organization

Compare-and-contrast writing can be organized in different ways. The examples that follow demonstrate point-by-point organization and subject-by-subject organization.

Option 1: Point-by-Point Organization

EXAMPLE

I. Similarities in Appearance   **Point 1**

   Subject A. Domestic honeybees are about five-eighths of an inch long.

   Subject B. Africanized bees, contrary to rumor, are about the same size.

II. Differences in Temperament   **Point 2**

   Subject A. Domestic honeybees are bred to be gentle.

   Subject B. The Africanized bee is a "wild" bee that is quick-tempered around animals and people.

Option 2: Subject-by-Subject Organization

EXAMPLE

I. Domestic Honeybees   **Subject A**

   Point 1. Domestic honey-bees are about five-eighths of an inch long.

   Point 2. Domestic honeybees are bred to be gentle.

II. Africanized Bees   **Subject B**

   Point 1. Africanized bees are about five-eighths of an inch long.

   Point 2. The Africanized bee is a "wild" bee that is quick-tempered around animals and people.

*For more information, see **Writing Workshop: Comparison-Contrast Essay,** pages 286–293.*

5.2 CAUSE AND EFFECT

Cause-effect writing explains why something happened, why certain conditions exist, or what resulted from an action or a condition. You might use cause-effect writing to explain a character's actions, the progress of a disease, or the outcome of a war.

> **RUBRIC: Standards for Writing**
>
> **Successful cause-effect writing should**
>
> - hook the reader's attention with a strong introduction
> - clearly state the cause-and-effect relationship
> - show clear connections between causes and effects
> - present causes and effects in a logical order and use transitions effectively
> - use facts, examples, and other details to illustrate each cause and effect
> - use language and details appropriate to the audience

*For more information, see **Writing Workshop: Cause-and-Effect Essay,** pages 736–743.*

Options for Organization

Your organization will depend on your topic and your purpose for writing.

Option 1: Effect-to-Cause Organization If you want to explain the causes of an event, such as the threat of Africanized bees to commercial beekeeping, you might first state the effect and then examine its causes.

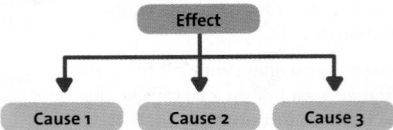

Option 2: Cause-to-Effect Organization If your focus is on explaining the effects of an event, such as the appearance of Africanized bees in the United States, you might first state the cause and then explain the effects.

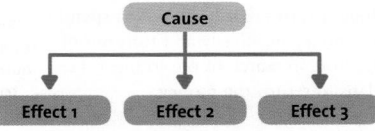

Option 3: Cause-Effect Chain Organization Sometimes you'll want to describe a chain of cause-and-effect relationships to explore a topic such as the myths about the Africanized honeybee.

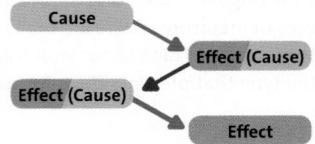

TIP Don't assume that a cause-effect relationship exists just because one event follows another. Look for evidence that the later event could not have happened if the first event had not caused it.

5.3 PROBLEM-SOLUTION

Problem-solution writing clearly states a problem, analyzes the problem, and proposes a solution to the problem. It can be used to identify and solve a conflict between characters, investigate global warming, or tell why the home team keeps losing.

> **RUBRIC: Standards for Writing**
>
> **Successful problem-solution writing should**
>
> - hook the reader's attention with a strong introduction
> - identify the problem and help the reader understand the issues involved
> - analyze the causes and effects of the problem
> - include quotations, facts, and statistics
> - explore possible solutions to the problem and recommend the best one(s)
> - use language, details, and a tone appropriate to the audience

Options for Organization

Your organization will depend on the goal of your problem-solution piece, your intended audience, and the specific problem you have chosen to address. The organizational methods that follow are effective for different kinds of problem-solution writing.

Option 1: Simple Problem-Solution

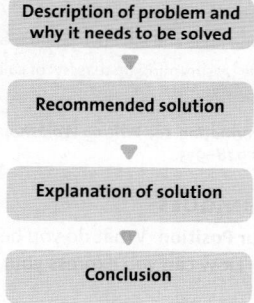

```
Description of problem and
why it needs to be solved
        ▼
Recommended solution
        ▼
Explanation of solution
        ▼
     Conclusion
```

Option 2: Deciding Between Solutions

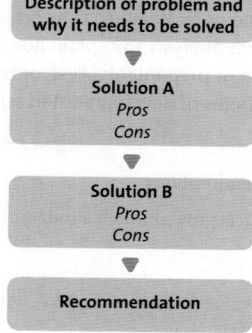

```
Description of problem and
why it needs to be solved
        ▼
     Solution A
        Pros
        Cons
        ▼
     Solution B
        Pros
        Cons
        ▼
   Recommendation
```

5.4 ANALYSIS

In writing an analysis, you explain how something works, how it is defined, or what its parts are.

> **RUBRIC: Standards for Writing**
>
> **A successful analysis should**
>
> - hook the reader's attention with a strong introduction
> - clearly define the subject and its parts
> - use a specific organizing structure to provide a logical flow of information
> - show connections among facts and ideas through transitional words and phrases
> - use language and details appropriate for the audience

Options for Organization

Organize your details in a logical order appropriate to the kind of analysis you're writing. Use one of the following options:

Option 1: Process Analysis A process analysis is usually organized chronologically, with steps or stages in the order in which they occur. You might use a process analysis to explain how to program a cell phone or prepare for a test, or to explain the different stages of development in an insect's life.

> **MODEL**
>
> Insect metamorphosis   **Introduce process.**
>
> Many insects grow through a four-   **Give background.**
> step cycle.
>
> Step 1 egg
> Step 2 larva
> Step 3 pupa   **Explain steps.**
> Step 4 adult

Option 2: Definition Analysis You can organize the details of a definition analysis in order of importance or impression. Use a definition analysis to explain a quality (such as excellence), the characteristics of a limerick, or the characteristics of insects.

> **MODEL**
>
> What is an insect?
>
> An insect is a small animal with   **Introduce term and definition.**
> an external skeleton, three body
> segments, and three pairs of legs.
>
> Feature 1: external skeleton   **Explain features.**
>
> Feature 2: three body segments
>
> Feature 3: three pairs of legs

Option 3: Parts Analysis The following parts analysis explains the main parts of an insect..

> **MODEL**
>
> An insect's body is divided into three   **Introduce subject.**
> main parts.
>
> Part 1: The head includes eyes, mouth,
> and antennae.
>
> Part 2: The thorax has the legs and   **Explain parts.**
> wings attached to it.
>
> Part 3: The abdomen contains organs
> for digesting food, eliminating waste,
> and reproducing.

6 Persuasive Writing

Persuasive writing allows you to use the power of language to inform and influence others. It includes speeches, persuasive essays, newspaper editorials, advertisements, and critical reviews.

> **RUBRIC: Standards for Writing**
>
> **Successful persuasive writing should**
>
> - hook the reader's attention with a strong introduction
> - state the issue and the writer's position
> - give opinions and support them with facts or reasons
> - have a reasonable and respectful tone
> - answer opposing views
> - use sound logic and effective language
> - conclude by summing up reasons or calling for action

*For more information, see **Writing Workshop: Persuasive Essay,** pages 948–955.*

6.1 KEY TECHNIQUES

Clarify Your Position What do you believe about the issue? How can you express your opinion most clearly?

Know Your Audience Who will read your writing? What do they already know and believe about the issue? What objections to your position might they have? What additional information might they need? What tone and approach would be most effective?

Support Your Opinion Why do you feel the way you do about the issue? What facts, statistics, examples, quotations, anecdotes, or expert opinions support your view? What reasons will convince your readers? What evidence can answer their objections?

Ways to Support Your Argument	
Statistics	facts that are stated in numbers
Examples	specific instances that explain points
Observations	events or situations you yourself have seen
Anecdotes	brief stories that illustrate points
Quotations	direct statements from authorities

*For more information, see **Identifying Faulty Reasoning**, page R24.*

Begin and End with a Bang How can you hook your readers and make a lasting impression? What memorable quotation, anecdote, or statistic will catch their attention at the beginning or stick in their minds at the end? What strong summary or call to action can you conclude with?

MODEL

Beginning

If you want to spend an evening with your neighbors, seeing a live performance or shopping for homemade crafts, will you come to the community center? Probably not. It's too hot!

End

Many people put hours and weeks into providing our town with entertainment. Often only a few people attend these events at the community center because the building is too hot on summer evenings. One "cool" solution would be to purchase an air-conditioning system.

6.2 OPTIONS FOR ORGANIZATION

In a two-sided persuasive essay, you want to show the weaknesses of other opinions as you explain the strengths of your own.

Option 1: Reasons for Your Opinion

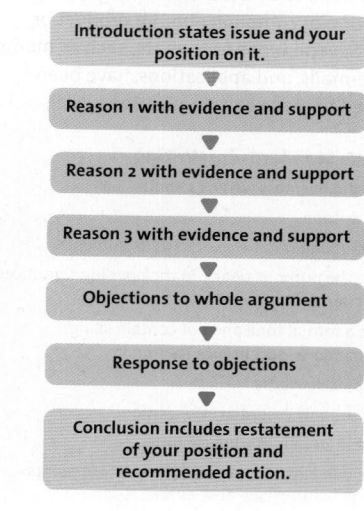

Introduction states issue and your position on it.

▼

Reason 1 with evidence and support

▼

Reason 2 with evidence and support

▼

Reason 3 with evidence and support

▼

Objections to whole argument

▼

Response to objections

▼

Conclusion includes restatement of your position and recommended action.

Option 2: Point-by-Point Basis

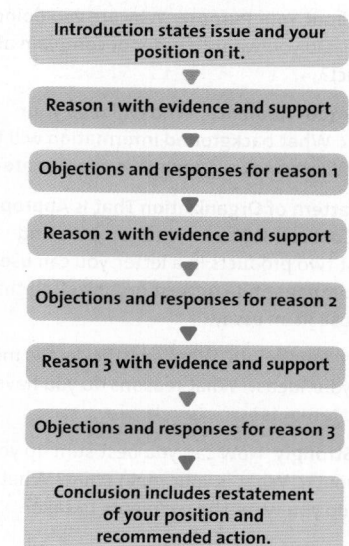

Introduction states issue and your position on it.

▼

Reason 1 with evidence and support

▼

Objections and responses for reason 1

▼

Reason 2 with evidence and support

▼

Objections and responses for reason 2

▼

Reason 3 with evidence and support

▼

Objections and responses for reason 3

▼

Conclusion includes restatement of your position and recommended action.

7 Workplace and Technical Writing

Business writing is writing done in a workplace to support the work of a company or business. You may need to do business writing to request information or complain about a product or service. Several types of formats, such as memos, letters, e-mails, and applications, have been developed to make communication easier.

> **RUBRIC: Standards for Writing**
>
> **Successful business writing should**
>
> - be courteous
> - use language that is geared to its audience
> - state the purpose clearly in the opening sentences or paragraph
> - have a formal tone and not contain slang, contractions, or sentence fragments
> - use precise words
> - present only essential information
> - present details in a logical order
> - conclude with a summary of important points

7.1 KEY TECHNIQUES OF WORKPLACE WRITING

Think About Your Purpose Why are you doing this writing? Do you want to order or complain about a product?

Identify Your Audience Who will read your writing? What background information will they need? What tone or language is appropriate?

Use a Pattern of Organization That Is Appropriate to the Content If you have to compare and contrast two products in a letter, you can use the same compare-and-contrast organization that you would use in an essay.

Support Your Points What specific details might clarify your ideas? What reasons do you have for your statements?

Finish Strongly How can you best sum up your statements? What is your main point? What action do you want the recipients to take?

Revise and Proofread Your Writing Just as you are graded on the quality of an essay you write for a class, you will be judged on the quality of your writing in the workplace.

7.2 MATCHING THE FORMAT TO THE OCCASION

E-mail messages, memos, and letters have similar purposes but are used in different situations. The chart shows how each format can be used.

Format	Occasion
Memo	Use to send correspondence **inside** the workplace only.
E-mail message	Use to send correspondence **inside or outside** the company.
Letter	Use to send correspondence **outside** the company.

TIP Memos are often sent as e-mail messages in the workplace. Remember that both require formal language and standard spelling, capitalization, and punctuation.

Technical writing is used for detailed instructions or descriptions of items and processes. It is important to a variety of fields, such as science, government, and industry. Technical writing is used to present information in such a way that the reader can use it to complete a task, such as performing an experiment, assembling an object, or using a tool.

At work, at school, or in everyday life you may have to use technical writing to leave instructions for another person.

> **RUBRIC: Standards for Writing**
>
> **Instructions should**
>
> - present only essential information
> - present steps in a logical order
> - include sentences that are short and simple
> - include definitions of unfamiliar terms if necessary
> - use transitions and/or numbered steps
> - use verbs that describe actions
> - use the present tense

7.3 KEY TECHNIQUES OF TECHNICAL WRITING

Think About Your Organization As you write, make sure you are presenting your information in a sensible order. For example, you would probably list any necessary tools and materials early on. Then you would present the steps in the order in which they should be followed.

Keep Your Audience in Mind Make sure you explain to readers unfamiliar with the activity or process what they need to know. Sometimes making a comparison to something the reader is familiar with can help. Graphics, such as pictures and maps, can also help make instructions easier to understand.

Use Transitions as Needed Transitions such as *first, next, after,* and *last* and numbered steps can make the order of steps clear and guide your reader from one step to the next.

Review Your Ending You can simply end with the last step, or you can end by describing the result or outcome of following the directions.

Evaluate Your Instructions Have a friend follow your instructions to make sure they are clear.

7.4 FORMATS

Business letters usually have a formal tone and a specific format as shown below. The key to writing a business letter is to get to the point as quickly as possible and to present your information clearly.

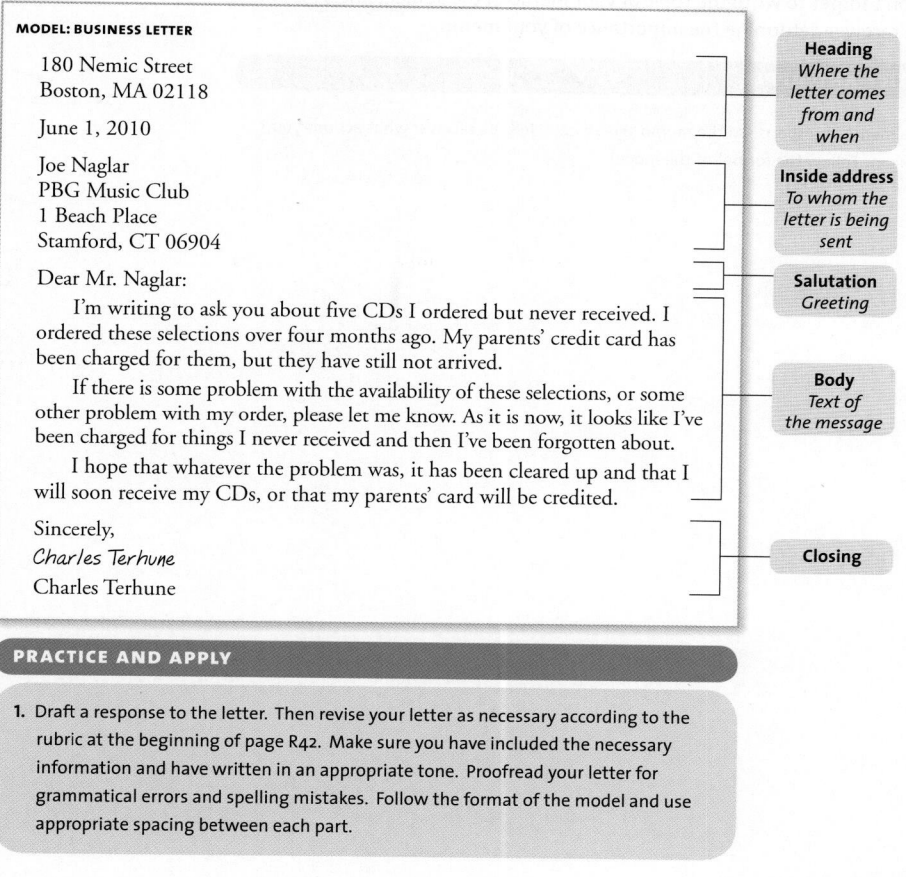

MODEL: BUSINESS LETTER

180 Nemic Street
Boston, MA 02118

June 1, 2010

Joe Naglar
PBG Music Club
1 Beach Place
Stamford, CT 06904

Dear Mr. Naglar:

    I'm writing to ask you about five CDs I ordered but never received. I ordered these selections over four months ago. My parents' credit card has been charged for them, but they have still not arrived.

    If there is some problem with the availability of these selections, or some other problem with my order, please let me know. As it is now, it looks like I've been charged for things I never received and then I've been forgotten about.

    I hope that whatever the problem was, it has been cleared up and that I will soon receive my CDs, or that my parents' card will be credited.

Sincerely,
Charles Terhune
Charles Terhune

Heading
Where the letter comes from and when

Inside address
To whom the letter is being sent

Salutation
Greeting

Body
Text of the message

Closing

PRACTICE AND APPLY

1. Draft a response to the letter. Then revise your letter as necessary according to the rubric at the beginning of page R42. Make sure you have included the necessary information and have written in an appropriate tone. Proofread your letter for grammatical errors and spelling mistakes. Follow the format of the model and use appropriate spacing between each part.

WRITING HANDBOOK **R43**

PRACTICE AND APPLY

ANSWER

Students' responses will vary. Each letter should include a heading, an inside address, a salutation, a body, and a closing. Students should provide an explanation for the missing CDs, such as a shortage of supply. They should provide a formal apology and a solution to the problem, such as crediting the account and shipping the CDs immediately.

R44 WRITING HANDBOOK

PRACTICE AND APPLY

ANSWER

Students' responses will vary. Each memo should include a heading and body. Students' replies should indicate that they have shipped the CDs and have credited the account.

Memos are often used in workplaces as a way of sending information in a direct and concise manner. They can be used to announce or summarize meetings and to request actions or specific information.

MODEL: MEMO

To: Grace Brodsky
From: Joe Naglar
Subject: customer complaint
Date: June 10, 2010

Please read the attached letter. Then review the original order from Charles Terhune. Send a letter of apology and the CDs he ordered as soon as possible. Do not charge him for two of the CDs, and credit his parents' account.

Heading
Receiver's name
Sender's name
Topic of memo
Complete date

Body

TIP Don't forget to write the topic of your memo in the subject line. This will help the receiver determine the importance of your memo.

PRACTICE AND APPLY

Write a memo in response to the memo shown here. Tell the receiver what actions you have taken. Follow the format of the model.

MODEL: INSTRUCTIONS

How to Prove That Rusting Is a Chemical Reaction That Causes Heat

You can do a simple experiment that shows that rusting is a chemical reaction that produces heat.

You will need:

- a pad of steel wool
- vinegar
- a small bowl
- a thermometer
- a large glass jar with a lid

1. Place the thermometer in the jar and put the lid on the jar.
2. After five minutes, record the temperature while the thermometer is still in the jar.
3. Fill the small bowl with vinegar.
4. Soak the steel-wool pad in the vinegar for two minutes.
5. Remove the lid from the jar, and wrap the steel-wool pad around the bulb of the thermometer. Put the lid back on the jar.
6. After five more minutes, record the temperature again while the thermometer is still in the jar.

Notice that the temperature has risen a few degrees. The vinegar removes a coating from the steel wool. As a result the iron in the steel-wool pad starts to rust. The rusting is caused by the interaction of iron and oxygen. This chemical reaction releases heat, causing the temperature reading on the thermometer to rise.

PRACTICE AND APPLY

Think about something you might want someone else to do because you won't be at home, such as do laundry or prepare dinner. Use the rubric at the bottom of page R42 to write instructions. Be sure to include the following:

- an opening statement that describes what needs to be done
- a list of tools and materials needed to perform the task
- the steps needed to perform the task
- transition words and/or numbered steps if order is important
- any special notes or warnings about a tool or step in the process

PRACTICE AND APPLY

ANSWER

Students' responses will vary. The instructions should provide a brief opening statement with an explanation of the task, a list of materials or tools, and the steps needed to perform the task. Encourage students to present the steps in a logical order and to provide only essential information.

Writing that has a lot of mistakes can confuse or even annoy a reader. A business letter with a punctuation error might lead to a miscommunication and delay a reply. Or a sentence fragment might lower your grade on an essay. Paying attention to grammar, punctuation, and capitalization rules can make your writing clearer and easier to read.

Quick Reference: Parts of Speech

PART OF SPEECH	FUNCTION	EXAMPLES
Noun	names a person, a place, a thing, an idea, a quality, or an action	
Common	serves as a general name, or a name common to an entire group	poet, novel, love, journey
Proper	names a specific, one-of-a-kind person, place, or thing	Jackson, Pleasant Street, Statue of Liberty
Singular	refers to a single person, place, thing, or idea	shark, planet, flower, truth
Plural	refers to more than one person, place, thing, or idea	sharks, planets, flowers, truths
Concrete	names something that can be perceived by the senses	snake, path, Philadelphia, damage
Abstract	names something that cannot be perceived by the senses	intelligence, fear, joy, loneliness
Compound	expresses a single idea through a combination of two or more words	girlfriend, father-in-law, Christmas Eve
Collective	refers to a group of people or things	army, flock, class, species
Possessive	shows who or what owns something	Strafford's, Bess's, children's, witnesses'
Pronoun	takes the place of a noun or another pronoun	
Personal	refers to the person making a statement, the person(s) being addressed, or the person(s) or thing(s) the statement is about	I, me, my, mine, we, us, our, ours, you, your, yours, she, he, it, her, him, hers, his, its, they, them, their, theirs
Reflexive	follows a verb or preposition and refers to a preceding noun or pronoun	myself, yourself, herself, himself, itself, ourselves, yourselves, themselves
Intensive	emphasizes a noun or another pronoun	(same as reflexives)
Demonstrative	points to one or more specific persons or things	this, that, these, those
Interrogative	signals a question	who, whom, whose, which, what
Indefinite	refers to one or more persons or things not specifically mentioned	both, all, most, many, anyone, everybody, several, none, some
Relative	introduces an adjective clause by relating it to a word in the clause	who, whom, whose, which, that

PART OF SPEECH	FUNCTION	EXAMPLES
Verb	expresses an action, a condition, or a state of being	
Action	tells what the subject does or did, physically or mentally	run, reaches, listened, consider, decides, dreamed
Linking	connects the subject to something that identifies or describes it	am, is, are, was, were, sound, taste, appear, feel, become, remain, seem
Auxiliary	precedes the main verb in a verb phrase	be, have, do, can, could, will, would, may, might
Transitive	directs the action toward someone or something; always has an object	The storm **sank** the ship.
Intransitive	does not direct the action toward someone or something; does not have an object	The ship **sank.**
Adjective	modifies a noun or pronoun	**strong** women, **two** epics, **enough** time
Adverb	modifies a verb, an adjective, or another adverb	walked **out, really** funny, **far** away
Preposition	relates one word to another word	at, by, for, from, in, of, on, to, with
Conjunction	joins words or word groups	
Coordinating	joins words or word groups used the same way	and, but, or, for, so, yet, nor
Correlative	used as a pair to join words or word groups used the same way	both . . . and, either . . . or, neither . . . nor
Subordinating	introduces a clause that cannot stand by itself as a complete sentence	although, after, as, before, because, when, if, unless
Interjection	expresses emotion	wow, ouch, hurrah

Quick Reference: The Sentence and Its Parts

The diagrams that follow will give you a brief review of the essentials of a sentence and some of its parts.

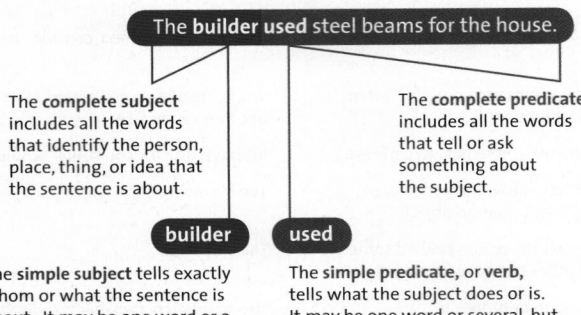

The **builder used** steel beams for the house.

The **complete subject** includes all the words that identify the person, place, thing, or idea that the sentence is about.

The **complete predicate** includes all the words that tell or ask something about the subject.

builder

used

The **simple subject** tells exactly whom or what the sentence is about. It may be one word or a group of words, but it does not include modifiers.

The **simple predicate,** or **verb,** tells what the subject does or is. It may be one word or several, but it does not include modifiers.

Every word in a sentence is part of a complete subject or a complete predicate.

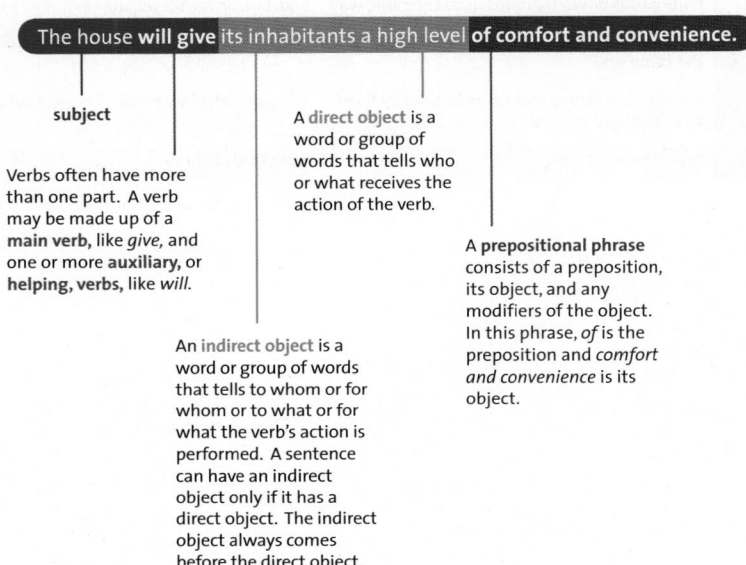

The house **will give** its inhabitants a high level **of comfort and convenience.**

subject

Verbs often have more than one part. A verb may be made up of a **main verb,** like *give,* and one or more **auxiliary,** or **helping, verbs,** like *will.*

A direct object is a word or group of words that tells who or what receives the action of the verb.

A **prepositional phrase** consists of a preposition, its object, and any modifiers of the object. In this phrase, *of* is the preposition and *comfort and convenience* is its object.

An indirect object is a word or group of words that tells to whom or for whom or to what or for what the verb's action is performed. A sentence can have an indirect object only if it has a direct object. The indirect object always comes before the direct object.

Quick Reference: Punctuation

MARK	FUNCTION	EXAMPLES
End Marks period, question mark, exclamation point	ends a sentence	We can start now. When would you like to leave? What a fantastic hit!
period	follows an initial or abbreviation **Exception:** postal abbreviations of states	Mrs. Dorothy Parker, McDougal Littell Inc., C. P. Cavafy, P.M., A.D., lb., oz., Blvd., Dr. NE (Nebraska), NV (Nevada)

period	follows a number or letter in an outline	I. Volcanoes
		  A. Central-vent
		    1. Shield

Comma	separates part of a compound sentence	I had never disliked poetry, but now I really love it.
	separates items in a series	She is brave, loyal, and kind.
	separates adjectives of equal rank that modify the same noun	The slow, easy route is best.
	sets off a term of address	Maria, how can I help you? You must do something, soldier.
	sets off a parenthetical expression	Hard workers, as you know, don't quit. I'm not a quitter, believe me.
	sets off an introductory word, phrase, or dependent clause	Yes, I forgot my key. At the beginning of the day, I feel fresh. While she was out, I was here. Having finished my chores, I went out.
	sets off a nonessential phrase or clause	Ed Pawn, the captain of the chess team, won. Ed Pawn, who is the captain, won. The two leading runners, sprinting toward the finish line, finished in a tie.
	sets off parts of dates and addresses	Mail it by May 14, 2010, to the Hauptman Company, 321 Market Street, Memphis, Tennessee.
	follows the salutation and closing of a letter	Dear Jim, Sincerely yours,
	separates words to avoid confusion	By noon, time had run out. What the minister does, does matter. While cooking, Jim burned his hand.
Semicolon	separates items that contain commas in a series	We spent the first week of summer vacation in Chicago, Illinois; the second week in St. Louis, Missouri; and the third week in Albany, New York.
	separates parts of a compound sentence that are not joined by a coordinating conjunction	The last shall be first; the first shall be last. I read the Bible; however, I have not memorized it.
	separates parts of a compound sentence when the parts contain commas	After I ran out of money, I called my parents; but only my sister was home, unfortunately.

For more help with punctuation, see

 GRAMMAR FOR WRITING
pp. 248–275

MARK	FUNCTION	EXAMPLES
Colon	introduces a list	Those we wrote were the following: Dana, John, and Will.
	introduces a long quotation	Abraham Lincoln wrote: "Four score and seven years ago, our fathers brought forth on this continent a new nation. . . ."
	follows the salutation of a business letter	To Whom It May Concern: Dear Leonard Atole:
	separates certain numbers	1:28 P.M., Genesis 2:5
Dash	indicates an abrupt break in thought	I was thinking of my mother—who is arriving tomorrow—just as you walked in.
Parentheses	enclose less important material	It was so unlike him (John is always on time) that I began to worry. The last World Series game (did you see it?) was fun.
Hyphen	joins parts of a compound adjective before a noun	The not-so-rich taxpayer won't stand for this!
	joins parts of a compound with *all-, ex-, self-,* or *-elect*	The ex-firefighter helped rescue him. Our president-elect is self-conscious.
	joins parts of a compound number (to ninety-nine)	Today, I turned twenty-one.
	joins parts of a fraction	My cup is one-third full.
	joins a prefix to a word beginning with a capital letter	Which Pre-Raphaelite painter do you like best? It snowed in mid-October.
	indicates that a word is divided at the end of a line	How could you have any reasonable expect-ations of getting a new computer?
Apostrophe	used with *s* to form the possessive of a noun or an indefinite pronoun	my friend's book, my friends' books, anyone's guess, somebody else's problem
	replaces one or more omitted letters in a contraction or numbers in a date	don't (omitted *o*), he'd (omitted *woul*), the class of '99 (omitted *19*)
	used with *s* to form the plural of a letter	I had two A's on my report card.
Quotation Marks	set off a speaker's exact words	Sara said, "I'm finally ready." "I'm ready," Sara said, "finally." Did Sara say, "I'm ready"? Sara said, "I'm ready!"
	set off the title of a story, an article, a short poem, an essay, a song, or a chapter	I like Paulsen's "Dirk the Protector" and Poe's "Annabel Lee." I like Ritchie Valens's "La Bamba."
Ellipses	replace material omitted from a quotation	"When in the course of human events . . . and to assume among the powers of the earth. . . ."
Italics	indicate the title of a book, a play, a magazine, a long poem, an opera, a film, or a TV series, or the name of a ship	*Holes, The Monsters Are Due on Maple Street, Newsweek,* the *Odyssey, Madame Butterfly, Gone with the Wind, Seinfeld, Titanic*

Quick Reference: Capitalization

CATEGORY	EXAMPLES
People and Titles	
Names and initials of people	Amy Tan, W. H. Auden
Titles used before a name	Professor Holmes, Senator Long
Deities and members of religious groups	Jesus, Allah, Buddha, Zeus, Baptists, Roman Catholics
Names of ethnic and national groups	Hispanics, Jews, African Americans
Geographical Names	
Cities, states, countries, continents	Philadelphia, Kansas, Japan, Europe
Regions, bodies of water, mountains	the South, Lake Baikal, Mount Everest
Geographic features, parks	Great Basin, Yellowstone National Park
Streets and roads, planets	318 East Sutton Drive, Charles Court, Jupiter, Pluto
Organizations, Events, Etc.	
Companies, organizations, teams	Ford Motor Company, Boy Scouts of America, St. Louis Cardinals
Buildings, bridges, monuments	Empire State Building, Eads Bridge, Washington Monument
Documents, awards	Declaration of Independence, Stanley Cup
Special named events	Mardi Gras, World Series
Government bodies, historical periods and events	U.S. Senate, House of Representatives, Middle Ages, Vietnam War
Days and months, holidays	Thursday, March, Thanksgiving, Labor Day
Specific cars, boats, trains, planes	Porsche, *Carpathia*, *Southwest Chief*, Concorde
Proper Adjectives	
Adjectives formed from proper nouns	French cooking, Spanish omelet, Edwardian age, Western movie
First Words and the Pronoun *I*	
First word in a sentence or quotation	This is it. He said, "Let's go."
First word of sentence in parentheses that is not within another sentence	The spelling rules are covered in another section. (Consult that section for more information.)
First words in the salutation and closing of a letter	Dear Madam, Very truly yours,
First word in each line of most poetry Personal pronoun *I*	Then am I A happy fly If I live Or if I die.
First word, last word, and all important words in a title	*The Call of the Wild*, "Take Me Out to the Ball Game"

For more help with capitalization, see

 GRAMMAR FOR WRITING
pp. 228–247

For more help with nouns, see

GRAMMAR FOR WRITING
pp. 34–55

For more help with pronouns, see

GRAMMAR FOR WRITING
pp. 56–89

1 Nouns

A **noun** is a word used to name a person, a place, a thing, an idea, a quality, or an action. Nouns can be classified in several ways.

*For more information on different types of nouns, see **Quick Reference: Parts of Speech**, page R46.*

1.1 COMMON NOUNS

Common nouns are general names, common to entire groups.

1.2 PROPER NOUNS

Proper nouns name specific, one-of-a-kind people, places, and things.

Common	Proper
leader, park, forest, mountain	Sequoya, Sierra Nevada, Giant Forest, Mount Whitney

*For more information, see **Quick Reference: Capitalization**, page R51.*

1.3 SINGULAR AND PLURAL NOUNS

A noun may take a singular or a plural form, depending on whether it names a single person, place, thing, or idea or more than one. Make sure you use appropriate spellings when forming plurals.

Singular	Plural
tourist, city, mouse	tourists, cities, mice

*For more information, see **Forming Plural Nouns**, page R74.*

1.4 POSSESSIVE NOUNS

A **possessive noun** shows who or what owns something.

*For more information, see **Forming Possessives**, page R74.*

2 Pronouns

A **pronoun** is a word that is used in place of a noun or another pronoun. The word or word group to which the pronoun refers is called its **antecedent.**

2.1 PERSONAL PRONOUNS

Personal pronouns change their form to express person, number, gender, and case. The forms of these pronouns are shown in the following chart.

	Nominative	Objective	Possessive
Singular			
First person	I	me	my, mine
Second person	you	you	your, yours
Third person	she, he, it	her, him, it	her, hers, his, its
Plural			
First person	we	us	our, ours
Second person	you	you	your, yours
Third person	they	them	their, theirs

2.2 AGREEMENT WITH ANTECEDENT

Pronouns should agree with their antecedents in number, gender, and person.

If an antecedent is singular, use a singular pronoun.
> EXAMPLE: *Rachel wrote a **detective story.** It has a surprise ending.*

If an antecedent is plural, use a plural pronoun.
> EXAMPLES: *The **characters** have their motives for murder.*
> *Javier loves **mysteries** and reads them all the time.*

The gender of a pronoun must be the same as the gender of its antecedent.
> EXAMPLE: *The **man** has to use all his wits to stay alive and solve the crime.*

The person of the pronoun must be the same as the person of its antecedent. As the chart in Section 2.1 shows, a pronoun can be in first-person, second-person, or third-person form.
> EXAMPLE: ***You** want a story to grab your attention.*

GRAMMAR PRACTICE

Rewrite each sentence so that the underlined pronoun agrees with its antecedent.

1. The story "Dark They Were, and Golden-Eyed" tells about a man who travels to Mars and <u>its</u> life.

2. Harry has a feeling of dread, but he ignores <u>them</u>.

3. The colonists began to change, but <u>he</u> didn't notice anything odd.

4. Harry's fears were coming true, and <u>it</u> was hard to ignore.

5. When you finish this story, <u>we</u> might wonder if it could really happen.

2.3 PRONOUN FORMS

Personal pronouns change form to show how they function in sentences. The three forms are the subject form, the object form, and the possessive form. For examples of these pronouns, see the chart in Section 2.1.

A **subject pronoun** is used as a subject in a sentence.

EXAMPLE: A Christmas Carol *tells about Ebenezer Scrooge. He visits his past.*

Also use the subject form when the pronoun follows a linking verb.

EXAMPLE: *The first ghost was he.*

An **object pronoun** is used as a direct object, an indirect object, or the object of a preposition.

SUBJECT   OBJECT

He will lead them to us.

OBJECT OF PREPOSITION

A **possessive pronoun** shows ownership. The pronouns *mine, yours, hers, his, its, ours,* and *theirs* can be used in place of nouns.

EXAMPLE: *This money is mine.*

The pronouns *my, your, her, his, its, our,* and *their* are used before nouns.

EXAMPLE: *Scrooge thanked the spirits for their help.*

WATCH OUT! Many spelling errors can be avoided if you watch out for *its* and *their.* Don't confuse the possessive pronoun *its* with the contraction *it's,* meaning "it is" or "it has." The homonyms *they're* (a contraction of *they are*) and *there* ("in that place" or an expletive) are often mistakenly used for *their.*

TIP To decide which pronoun to use in a comparison, such as "He tells better tales than (I *or* me)," fill in the missing word(s): *He tells better tales than I tell.*

GRAMMAR PRACTICE

Write the correct pronoun form to complete each sentence.

1. Charles Dickens wrote *A Christmas Carol* when (he, him) was 31 years old.

2. This work of (him, his) was written in only a few weeks.

3. Dickens wrote other novels about Christmas. All of (their, his) dates of composition are from the 1840s.

4. (Them, They) have rather serious themes mixed with some humor.

5. When William Makepeace Thackeray, a fellow writer, reviewed *A Christmas Carol,* he said that (its, his) publication was a national benefit.

2.4 REFLEXIVE AND INTENSIVE PRONOUNS

These pronouns are formed by adding *-self* or *-selves* to certain personal pronouns. Their forms are the same, and they differ only in how they are used.

A **reflexive pronoun** follows a verb or preposition and reflects back on an earlier noun or pronoun.

EXAMPLES: *He likes himself too much.*
She is now herself again.

Intensive pronouns intensify or emphasize the nouns or pronouns to which they refer.

EXAMPLES: *They themselves will educate their children.*
You did it yourself.

GRAMMAR PRACTICE

ANSWERS

1. *The story "Dark They Were, and Golden-Eyed" tells about a man who travels to Mars and <u>his</u> life.*

2. *Harry has a feeling of dread, but he ignores <u>it</u>.*

3. *The colonists began to change, but <u>they</u> didn't notice anything odd.*

4. *Harry's fears were coming true, and <u>they</u> were hard to ignore.*

5. *When you finish this story, <u>you</u> might wonder if it really could happen.*

GRAMMAR PRACTICE

ANSWERS

1. *he*

2. *his*

3. *their*

4. *They*

5. *its*

WATCH OUT! Avoid using *hisself* or *theirselves*. Standard English does not include these forms.

NONSTANDARD: *Alex dedicated hisself to learning the magician's secrets.*

STANDARD: *Alex dedicated himself to learning the magician's secrets.*

2.5 DEMONSTRATIVE PRONOUNS

Demonstrative pronouns point out things and persons near and far.

	Singular	Plural
Near	this	these
Far	that	those

2.6 INDEFINITE PRONOUNS

Indefinite pronouns do not refer to specific persons or things and usually have no antecedents. The chart shows some commonly used indefinite pronouns.

Singular	Plural	Singular or Plural	
another	both	all	none
anybody	few	any	some
no one	many	more	most
neither			

TIP Indefinite pronouns that end in *one*, *body*, or *thing* are always singular.

INCORRECT: *Did everybody play their part well?*

If the indefinite pronoun might refer to either a male or a female, *his or her* may be used to refer to it, or the sentence may be rewritten.

CORRECT: *Did everybody play his or her part well?*
Did all the students play their parts well?

2.7 INTERROGATIVE PRONOUNS

An **interrogative pronoun** tells a reader or listener that a question is coming. The interrogative pronouns are *who, whom, whose, which,* and *what.*

EXAMPLES: *Who is going to rehearse with you?*
From whom did you receive the script?

TIP *Who* is used as a subject; *whom,* as an object. To find out which pronoun you need to use in a question, change the question to a statement.

QUESTION: *(Who/Whom) did you meet there?*
STATEMENT: *You met (?) there.*

Since the verb has a subject (*you*), the needed word must be the object form, *whom.*

EXAMPLE: *Whom did you meet there?*

WATCH OUT! A special problem arises when you use an interrupter, such as *do you think,* within a question.

EXAMPLE: *(Who/Whom) do you think will win?*

If you eliminate the interrupter, it is clear that the word you need is *who.*

2.8 RELATIVE PRONOUNS

Relative pronouns relate, or connect, adjective clauses to the words they modify in sentences. The noun or pronoun that a relative clause modifies is the antecedent of the relative pronoun. Here are the relative pronouns and their uses.

	Subject	Object	Possessive
Person	who	whom	whose
Thing	which	which	whose
Thing/Person	that	that	whose

Often, short sentences with related ideas can be combined by using a relative pronoun to create a more effective sentence.

SHORT SENTENCE: *Poe wrote "Annabel Lee."*

RELATED SENTENCE: *"Annabel Lee" is a well-known poem in American literature.*

COMBINED SENTENCE: *Poe wrote "Annabel Lee," which is a well-known poem in American literature.*

Write the correct form of each incorrect pronoun.

1. Whom has read "Dark They Were, and Golden-Eyed"?
2. Colonists whom travel to Mars realize they can't go home.
3. Nobody knows what they will do.
4. Each person is changing, but they don't worry about it.
5. Harry hisself doesn't believe what is happening.

2.9 PRONOUN REFERENCE PROBLEMS

The referent of a pronoun should always be clear. Avoid problems by rewriting sentences.

An **indefinite reference** occurs when the pronoun *it, you,* or *they* does not clearly refer to a specific antecedent.

UNCLEAR: *My aunt hugged me in front of my friends, and it was embarrassing.*

CLEAR: *My aunt hugged me in front of my friends, and I was embarrassed.*

A **general reference** occurs when the pronoun *it, this, that, which,* or *such* is used to refer to a general idea rather than a specific antecedent.

UNCLEAR: *Jenna takes acting lessons. This has improved her chances of getting a part in the school play.*

CLEAR: *Jenna takes acting lessons. The lessons have improved her chances of getting a part in the school play.*

Ambiguous means "having more than one possible meaning." An **ambiguous reference** occurs when a pronoun could refer to two or more antecedents.

UNCLEAR: *Tony talked to Fred and said that he could meet us later.*

CLEAR: *Tony talked to Fred and said that Fred could meet us later.*

Rewrite the following sentences to correct indefinite, ambiguous, and general pronoun references.

1. During the *Titanic*'s maiden voyage, they hit an iceberg and sank in less than three hours.
2. Jack Thayer talked to Milton Long and said that he was traveling home to the States.
3. The *Titanic* split in two in its last moments. This made each half plunge to the bottom of the ocean.
4. In the article, it said that many lifeboats were only half full.

3 Verbs

A **verb** is a word that expresses an action, a condition, or a state of being.

*For more information, see **Quick Reference: Parts of Speech**, page R47.*

3.1 ACTION VERBS

Action verbs express mental or physical activity.

EXAMPLE: *Mr. Cho slept with the window open.*

3.2 LINKING VERBS

Linking verbs join subjects with words or phrases that rename or describe them.

EXAMPLE: *When he awoke the next morning, his bed was wet from the rain.*

3.3 PRINCIPAL PARTS

Action and linking verbs typically have four principal parts, which are used to form verb tenses. The principal parts are the **present,** the **present participle,** the **past,** and the **past participle.**

Action verbs and some linking verbs also fall into two categories: regular and irregular. A **regular verb** is a verb that forms its past and past participle by adding *-ed* or *-d* to the present form.

GRAMMAR PRACTICE
ANSWERS

1. *Who has read "Dark They Were, and Golden-Eyed"?*
2. *Colonists who travel to Mars realize they can't go home.*
3. *Nobody knows what he or she will do.*
4. *Everyone is changing, but they don't worry about it.*
5. *Harry himself doesn't believe what is happening.*

GRAMMAR PRACTICE
ANSWERS

1. *The Titanic hit an iceberg during its maiden voyage and sank in less than three hours.*
2. *Jack Thayer was traveling home to the States when he talked to Milton Long.*
3. *The Titanic split in two in its last moments. The split made each half plunge to the bottom of the ocean.*
4. *The article states that many lifeboats were only half full.*

For more help with verbs, see

GRAMMAR FOR WRITING
pp. 90–123

Present	Present Participle	Past	Past Participle
jump	(is) jumping	jumped	(has) jumped
solve	(is) solving	solved	(has) solved
grab	(is) grabbing	grabbed	(has) grabbed
carry	(is) carrying	carried	(has) carried

An **irregular verb** is a verb that forms its past and past participle in some other way than by adding *-ed* or *-d* to the present form.

Present	Present Participle	Past	Past Participle
begin	(is) beginning	began	(has) begun
break	(is) breaking	broke	(has) broken
go	(is) going	went	(has) gone

3.4 VERB TENSE

The **tense** of a verb indicates the time of the action or the state of being. An action or state of being can occur in the present, the past, or the future. There are six tenses, each expressing a different range of time.

The **present tense** expresses an action or state that is happening at the present time, occurs regularly, or is constant or generally true. Use the present part.

> NOW: *That snow looks deep.*
> REGULAR: *It snows every day.*
> GENERAL: *Snow falls.*

The **past tense** expresses an action that began and ended in the past. Use the past part.

> EXAMPLE: *The storyteller finished his tale.*

The **future tense** expresses an action or state that will occur. Use *shall* or *will* with the present part.

> EXAMPLE: *They will attend the next festival.*

The **present perfect tense** expresses an action or state that (1) was completed at an indefinite time in the past or (2) began in the past and continues into the present. Use *have* or *has* with the past participle.

> EXAMPLE: *Poetry has inspired many readers.*

The **past perfect tense** expresses an action in the past that came before another action in the past. Use *had* with the past participle.

> EXAMPLE: *He had built a fire before the dog ran away.*

The **future perfect tense** expresses an action in the future that will be completed before another action in the future. Use *shall have* or *will have* with the past participle.

> EXAMPLE: *They will have read the novel before they see the movie version of the tale.*

TIP A past-tense form of an irregular verb is not used with an auxiliary verb, but a past-participle main irregular verb is always used with an auxiliary verb.

> INCORRECT: *I have saw her somewhere before.* (*Saw* is the past-tense form of an irregular verb and shouldn't be used with *have*.)
> CORRECT: *I have seen her somewhere before.*
> INCORRECT: *I seen her somewhere before.* (*Seen* is the past participle of an irregular verb and shouldn't be used without an auxiliary verb.)

3.5 PROGRESSIVE FORMS

The progressive forms of the six tenses show ongoing actions. Use forms of *be* with the present participles of verbs.

> PRESENT PROGRESSIVE: *She is rehearsing her lines.*
> PAST PROGRESSIVE: *She was rehearsing her lines.*
> FUTURE PROGRESSIVE: *She will be rehearsing her lines.*
> PRESENT PERFECT PROGRESSIVE: *She has been rehearsing her lines.*
> PAST PERFECT PROGRESSIVE: *She had been rehearsing her lines.*
> FUTURE PERFECT PROGRESSIVE: *She will have been rehearsing her lines.*

WATCH OUT! Do not shift from tense to tense needlessly. Watch out for these special cases.

• In most compound sentences and in sentences with compound predicates, keep the tenses the same.

> INCORRECT: *His boots freeze, and he shook with cold.*
> CORRECT: *His boots freeze, and he shakes with cold.*

- If one past action happens before another, do shift tenses.

  INCORRECT: *They wished they started earlier.*

  CORRECT: *They wished they had started earlier.*

GRAMMAR PRACTICE

Rewrite each sentence, using a form of the verb in parentheses. Identify each form that you use.

1. Some medical developments (begin) with the space age—for example, laparoscopy and robotics.

2. Both of these areas (grow) and (advance) the field of surgery.

3. In the 1990s "robotic assistants" (help) in surgery.

4. People (come) to expect simpler procedures because of these new techniques.

5. Some day other procedures that avoid cutting into tissue (develop).

Rewrite each sentence to correct an error in tense.

1. I seen a movie about the cobra and its natural enemy, the mongoose.

2. Most snakes hide and avoided people.

3. The cobra raised its head when it seeks out its next victim.

4. Both the male and female protected their eggs and will attack an approaching intruder.

5. The venom of a cobra was deadly and kills a human being within a few hours.

3.6 ACTIVE AND PASSIVE VOICE

The voice of a verb tells whether its subject performs or receives the action expressed by the verb. When the subject performs the action, the verb is in the **active voice.** When the subject is the receiver of the action, the verb is in the **passive voice.**

Compare these two sentences:

ACTIVE: *Lois Lowry wrote The Giver.*

PASSIVE: *The Giver was written by Lois Lowry.*

To form the passive voice, use a form of *be* with the past participle of the verb.

WATCH OUT! Use the passive voice sparingly. It can make writing awkward and less direct.

AWKWARD: *The Giver is a novel that was written by Lois Lowry.*

BETTER: *Lois Lowry wrote the novel* The Giver.

There are occasions when you will choose to use the passive voice because

- you want to emphasize the receiver: *The king was shot.*

- the doer is unknown: *My books were stolen.*

- the doer is unimportant: *French is spoken here.*

4 Modifiers

Modifiers are words or groups of words that change or limit the meanings of other words. Adjectives and adverbs are common modifiers.

4.1 ADJECTIVES

Adjectives modify nouns and pronouns by telling which one, what kind, how many, or how much.

WHICH ONE: *this, that, these, those*
EXAMPLE: *That bird is a scarlet ibis.*

WHAT KIND: *small, sick, courageous, black*
EXAMPLE: *The sick bird sways on the branch.*

HOW MANY: *some, few, ten, none, both, each*
EXAMPLE: *Both brothers stared at the bird.*

HOW MUCH: *more, less, enough*
EXAMPLE: *The bird did not have enough strength to remain perched.*

4.2 PREDICATE ADJECTIVES

Most adjectives come before the nouns they modify, as in the examples above. A **predicate adjective,** however, follows a linking verb and describes the subject.

EXAMPLE: *My friends are very intelligent.*

Be especially careful to use adjectives (not adverbs) after such linking verbs as *look, feel, grow, taste,* and *smell.*

EXAMPLE: *The bread smells wonderful.*

GRAMMAR HANDBOOK **R57**

GRAMMAR PRACTICE

ANSWERS

1. *Some medical developments <u>began</u> with the space age—for example, laparoscopy and robotics. (past tense)*

2. *Both of these areas <u>have grown</u> and <u>have advanced</u> the field of surgery. (present perfect tense)*

3. *In the 1990s "robotic assistants" <u>helped</u> in surgery. (past tense)*

4. *People <u>have come</u> to expect simpler procedures because of these new techniques. (present perfect tense)*

5. *Some day other procedures that avoid cutting into tissue <u>will be developed</u>. (future tense)*

ANSWERS

1. *I <u>saw</u> a movie about the cobra and its natural enemy, the mongoose.*

2. *Most snakes hide and <u>avoid</u> people and other animals.*

3. *The cobra <u>raises</u> its head when it seeks out its next victim.*

4. *Both the male and female <u>protect</u> their eggs and will attack an approaching intruder.*

5. *The venom of the cobra <u>is</u> deadly and can kill a human being within a few hours.*

For more help with modifiers, see

G GRAMMAR FOR WRITING
pp. 124–149

4.3 ADVERBS

Adverbs modify verbs, adjectives, and other adverbs by telling where, when, how, or to what extent.

WHERE: *The children played outside.*

WHEN: *The author spoke yesterday.*

HOW: *We walked slowly behind the leader.*

TO WHAT EXTENT: *He worked very hard.*

Adverbs may occur in many places in sentences, both before and after the words they modify.

EXAMPLES: *Suddenly the wind shifted.*

The wind suddenly shifted.

The wind shifted suddenly.

4.4 ADJECTIVE OR ADVERB?

Many adverbs are formed by adding *-ly* to adjectives.

EXAMPLES: *sweet, sweetly; gentle, gently*

However, *-ly* added to a noun will usually yield an adjective.

EXAMPLES: *friend, friendly; woman, womanly*

4.5 COMPARISON OF MODIFIERS

Modifiers can be used to compare two or more things. The form of a modifier shows the degree of comparison. Both adjectives and adverbs have **comparative** and **superlative** forms.

The **comparative form** is used to compare two things, groups, or actions.

EXAMPLES: *His father's hands were stronger than his own.*

His father was more courageous than the other man.

The **superlative form** is used to compare more than two things, groups, or actions.

EXAMPLES: *His father's hands were the strongest in the family.*

His father was the most courageous of them all.

4.6 REGULAR COMPARISONS

Most one-syllable and some two-syllable adjectives and adverbs have comparatives and superlatives formed by adding *-er* and *-est*. All three-syllable and most two-syllable modifiers have comparatives and superlatives formed with *more* or *most*.

Modifier	Comparative	Superlative
small	smaller	smallest
thin	thinner	thinnest
sleepy	sleepier	sleepiest
useless	more useless	most useless
precisely	more precisely	most precisely

WATCH OUT! Note that spelling changes must sometimes be made to form the comparatives and superlatives of modifiers.

EXAMPLES: *friendly, friendlier* (Change *y* to *i* and add the ending.)

sad, sadder (Double the final consonant and add the ending.)

4.7 IRREGULAR COMPARISONS

Some commonly used modifiers have irregular comparative and superlative forms. They are listed in the following chart. You may wish to memorize them.

Modifier	Comparative	Superlative
good	better	best
bad	worse	worst
far	farther *or* further	farthest *or* furthest
little	less *or* lesser	least
many	more	most
well	better	best
much	more	most

4.8 PROBLEMS WITH MODIFIERS

Study the tips that follow to avoid common mistakes:

Farther and **Further** Use *farther* for distances; use *further* for everything else.

Double Comparisons Make a comparison by using *-er/-est* or by using *more/most*. Using *-er* with *more* or using *-est* with *most* is incorrect.

INCORRECT: *I like her more better than she likes me.*

CORRECT: *I like her better than she likes me.*

Illogical Comparisons An illogical or confusing comparison results when two unrelated things are compared or when something is compared with itself. The word *other* or the word *else* should be used when comparing an individual member to the rest of a group.

ILLOGICAL: *The narrator was more curious about the war than any student in his class.* (implies that the narrator isn't a student in the class)

LOGICAL: *The narrator was more curious about the war than any other student in his class.* (identifies that the narrator is a student)

Bad vs. Badly *Bad*, always an adjective, is used before a noun or after a linking verb. *Badly*, always an adverb, never modifies a noun. Be sure to use the right form after a linking verb.

INCORRECT: *Ed felt badly after his team lost.*

CORRECT: *Ed felt bad after his team lost.*

Good vs. Well *Good* is always an adjective. It is used before a noun or after a linking verb. *Well* is often an adverb meaning "expertly" or "properly." *Well* can also be used as an adjective after a linking verb when it means "in good health."

INCORRECT: *Helen writes very good.*

CORRECT: *Helen writes very well.*

CORRECT: *Yesterday I felt bad; today I feel well.*

Double Negatives If you add a negative word to a sentence that is already negative, the result will be an error known as a double negative. When using *not* or *-n't* with a verb, use *any-* words, such as *anybody* or *anything*, rather than *no-* words, such as *nobody* or *nothing*, later in the sentence.

INCORRECT: *We haven't seen nobody.*

CORRECT: *We haven't seen anybody.*

Using *hardly, barely,* or *scarcely* after a negative word is also incorrect.

INCORRECT: *They couldn't barely see two feet ahead.*

CORRECT: *They could barely see two feet ahead.*

Misplaced Modifiers Sometimes a modifier is placed so far away from the word it modifies that the intended meaning of the sentence is unclear. Prepositional phrases and participial phrases are often misplaced. Place modifiers as close as possible to the words they modify.

MISPLACED: *We found the child in the park who was missing.*

CLEARER: *We found the child who was missing in the park.* (The child was missing, not the park.)

Dangling Modifiers Sometimes a modifier doesn't appear to modify any word in a sentence. Most dangling modifiers are participial phrases or infinitive phrases.

DANGLING: *Looking out the window, his brother was seen driving by.*

CLEARER: *Looking out the window, Josh saw his brother driving by.*

GRAMMAR PRACTICE

Choose the correct word or words from each pair in parentheses.

1. When Ellis Island opened, it was the (larger, largest) port of entry to the United States.

2. In the 1980s, the facility underwent the (greatest, most greatest) restoration ever performed.

3. The restoration project (bad, badly) needed funds.

4. The project didn't have (no, any) funding until fundraising efforts began in 1982.

5. In 1990, the (grandly, grand) reopening was received (good, well.)

GRAMMAR PRACTICE

Rewrite each sentence that contains a misplaced or dangling modifier. Write "correct" if the sentence is written correctly.

1. We traveled to Yellowstone Park with many tourists.

2. Driving our car, the mother bear growled.

3. We took pictures of the bears in the camper.

4. My brother and I went for a hike, but we got lost.

5. Taping our adventures, we had lots of film.

GRAMMAR PRACTICE

ANSWERS

1. *largest*
2. *greatest*
3. *any*
4. *badly*
5. *grand; well*

GRAMMAR PRACTICE

ANSWERS

1. *Correct*
2. **Possible answer:** *The mother bear growled as we drove by in our car.*
3. **Possible answer:** *We took pictures of the bears while we were inside the camper.*
4. *Correct*
5. **Possible answer:** *We had lots of film to tape our adventures.*

For more help with the sentence and its parts, see

GRAMMAR FOR WRITING
   pp. 4–33

For more help with prepositional phrases and appositives, see

GRAMMAR FOR WRITING
   pp. 155–157, 255

5 The Sentence and Its Parts

A **sentence** is a group of words used to express a complete thought. A complete sentence has a subject and a predicate.

*For more information, see **Quick Reference: The Sentence and Its Parts**, page R48.*

5.1 KINDS OF SENTENCES

There are four basic types of sentences.

Type	Definition	Example
Declarative	states a fact, a wish, an intent, or a feeling	Gary Soto understands youths.
Interrogative	asks a question	Did you read "Seventh Grade"?
Imperative	gives a command or direction	Read the story.
Exclamatory	expresses strong feeling or excitement	The story is great!

5.2 COMPOUND SUBJECTS AND PREDICATES

A compound subject consists of two or more subjects that share the same verb. They are typically joined by the coordinating conjunction *and* or *or*.

> **EXAMPLE:** *A short story or novel will keep you engaged.*

A compound predicate consists of two or more predicates that share the same subject. They too are usually joined by a coordinating conjunction: *and, but,* or *or*.

> **EXAMPLE:** *The class finished all the poetry but did not read the short stories.*

5.3 COMPLEMENTS

A **complement** is a word or group of words that completes the meaning of the sentence. Some sentences contain only a subject and a verb. Most sentences, however, require additional words placed after the verb to complete the meaning of the sentence. There are three kinds of complements: direct objects, indirect objects, and subject complements.

Direct objects are words or word groups that receive the action of action verbs. A direct object answers the question *what* or *whom*.

> **EXAMPLES:** *The students asked many questions.* (Asked what?)
> *The teacher quickly answered the students.* (Answered whom?)

Indirect objects tell to whom or what or for whom or what the actions of verbs are performed. Indirect objects come before direct objects. In the examples that follow, the indirect objects are highlighted.

> **EXAMPLES:** *My sister usually gave her friends good advice.* (Gave to whom?)
> *Her brother sent the store a heavy package.* (Sent to what?)

Subject complements come after linking verbs and identify or describe the subjects. A subject complement that names or identifies a subject is called a **predicate nominative.** Predicate nominatives include **predicate nouns** and **predicate pronouns.**

> **EXAMPLES:** *My friends are very hard workers.*
> *The best writer in the class is she.*

A subject complement that describes a subject is called a **predicate adjective.**

> **EXAMPLE:** *The pianist appeared very energetic.*

6 Phrases

A **phrase** is a group of related words that does not contain a subject and a predicate but functions in a sentence as a single part of speech.

6.1 PREPOSITIONAL PHRASES

A **prepositional phrase** is a phrase that consists of a preposition, its object, and any modifiers of the object. Prepositional phrases that modify nouns or pronouns are called **adjective phrases.** Prepositional phrases that modify verbs, adjectives, or adverbs are **adverb phrases.**

> **ADJECTIVE PHRASE:** *The central character of the story is a villain.*
> **ADVERB PHRASE:** *He reveals his nature in the first scene.*

6.2 APPOSITIVES AND APPOSITIVE PHRASES

An **appositive** is a noun or pronoun that identifies or renames another noun or pronoun. An **appositive phrase** includes an appositive and modifiers of it. An appositive usually follows the noun or pronoun it identifies.

An appositive can be either **essential** or **nonessential**. An **essential appositive** provides information that is needed to identify what is referred to by the preceding noun or pronoun.

> **EXAMPLE:** *The book is about the author Dave Barry.*

A **nonessential appositive** adds extra information about a noun or pronoun whose meaning is already clear. Nonessential appositives and appositive phrases are set off with commas.

> **EXAMPLE:** *The book, an autobiography, tells how he began writing.*

7 Verbals and Verbal Phrases

A **verbal** is a verb form that is used as a noun, an adjective, or an adverb. A **verbal phrase** consists of a verbal along with its modifiers and complements. There are three kinds of verbals: **infinitives, participles,** and **gerunds.**

7.1 INFINITIVES AND INFINITIVE PHRASES

An **infinitive** is a verb form that usually begins with *to* and functions as a noun, an adjective, or an adverb. An **infinitive phrase** consists of an infinitive plus its modifiers and complements.

> **NOUN:** *To know her is my only desire.* (subject)
> *I'm planning to walk with you.* (direct object)
> *Her goal was to promote women's rights.* (predicate nominative)
> **ADJECTIVE:** *We saw his need to be loved.* (adjective modifying *need*)
> **ADVERB:** *She wrote to voice her opinions.* (adverb modifying *wrote*)

Because *to,* the sign of the infinitive, precedes infinitives, it is usually easy to recognize them. However, sometimes *to* may be omitted.

> **EXAMPLE:** *Let no one dare [to] enter this shrine.*

7.2 PARTICIPLES AND PARTICIPIAL PHRASES

A **participle** is a verb form that functions as an adjective. Like adjectives, participles modify nouns and pronouns. Most participles are present-participle forms, ending in *-ing,* or past-participle forms ending in *-ed* or *-en.* In the examples below, the participles are highlighted.

> **MODIFYING A NOUN:** *The dying man had a smile on his face.*
> **MODIFYING A PRONOUN:** *Frustrated, everyone abandoned the cause.*

Participial phrases are participles with all their modifiers and complements.

> **MODIFYING A NOUN:** *The dogs searching for survivors are well trained.*
> **MODIFYING A PRONOUN:** *Having approved your proposal, we are ready to act.*

7.3 DANGLING AND MISPLACED PARTICIPLES

A participle or participial phrase should be placed as close as possible to the word that it modifies. Otherwise the meaning of the sentence may not be clear.

> **MISPLACED:** *The boys were looking for squirrels searching the trees.*
> **CLEARER:** *The boys searching the trees were looking for squirrels.*

A participle or participial phrase that does not clearly modify anything in a sentence is called a **dangling participle.** A dangling participle causes confusion because it appears to modify a word that it cannot sensibly modify. Correct a dangling participle by providing a word for the participle to modify.

> **DANGLING:** *Running like the wind, my hat fell off.* (The hat wasn't running.)
> **CLEARER:** *Running like the wind, I lost my hat.*

7.4 GERUNDS AND GERUND PHRASES

A **gerund** is a verb form ending in *-ing* that functions as a noun. Gerunds may perform any function nouns perform.

> **SUBJECT:** *Running is my favorite pastime.*
> **DIRECT OBJECT:** *I truly love running.*

For more help with verbals and verbal phrases, see

 GRAMMAR FOR WRITING
pp. 168–183

GRAMMAR PRACTICE

ANSWERS

1. *Possible answer: I read Jackie Robinson's autobiography to learn more about segregation in baseball.*

2. *Possible answer: Researching one afternoon at the library, I found several books and articles about him.*

3. *Possible answer: Opposition to Robinson died down shortly after his first season with the Dodgers.*

4. *Possible answer: Robinson played his entire major-league career with the same team, the Dodgers.*

5. *Possible answer: Robinson went on to become one of the most popular Dodger players, earning a place in the Baseball Hall of Fame.*

For more help with clauses, see

G GRAMMAR FOR WRITING
pp. 186–205

INDIRECT OBJECT: *You should give* running *a try.*
SUBJECT COMPLEMENT: *My deepest passion is* running.
OBJECT OF PREPOSITION: *Her love of* running *keeps her strong.*

Gerund phrases are gerunds with all their modifiers and complements.

SUBJECT: *Wishing on a star never got me far.*
OBJECT OF PREPOSITION: *I will finish before leaving the office.*
APPOSITIVE: *Her avocation, flying airplanes, finally led to full-time employment.*

GRAMMAR PRACTICE

Rewrite each sentence, adding the type of phrase shown in parentheses.

1. I read Jackie Robinson's autobiography. (infinitive phrase)

2. I found several books and articles about him. (participial phrase)

3. Opposition to Robinson died down. (prepositional phrase)

4. Robinson played his entire major-league career with the same team. (appositive phrase)

5. Robinson went on to become one of the most popular Dodger players. (gerund phrase)

8 Clauses

A **clause** is a group of words that contains a subject and a predicate. There are two kinds of clauses: independent clauses and subordinate clauses.

8.1 INDEPENDENT AND SUBORDINATE CLAUSES

An **independent clause** can stand alone as a sentence, as the word *independent* suggests.

INDEPENDENT CLAUSE: *I read "Amigo Brothers."*

A sentence may contain more than one independent clause.

EXAMPLE: *I finished dinner, and I read the story.*

In the preceding example, the coordinating conjunction *and* joins two independent clauses.

For more information, see **Coordinating Conjunction,** page R47.

A **subordinate (dependent) clause** cannot stand alone as a sentence. It is subordinate to, or dependent on, an independent clause.

EXAMPLE: *After I finished dinner, I read "Amigo Brothers."*

The highlighted clause cannot stand by itself.

8.2 ADJECTIVE CLAUSES

An **adjective clause** is a subordinate clause used as an adjective. It usually follows the noun or pronoun it modifies.

EXAMPLE: *Felix and Antonio are the boys who are the main characters in "Amigo Brothers."*

Adjective clauses are typically introduced by the relative pronouns *who, whom, whose, which,* and *that.*

For more information, see **Relative Pronouns,** page R54.

EXAMPLE: *The story, which takes place in New York, is about a boxing tournament.*

An adjective clause can be either essential or nonessential. An **essential adjective clause** provides information that is necessary to identify the preceding noun or pronoun.

EXAMPLE: *The boys had to make a decision that might change their lives.*

A **nonessential adjective clause** adds additional information about a noun or pronoun whose meaning is already clear. Nonessential clauses are set off with commas.

EXAMPLE: *The boys, who fought each other, wanted to remain friends.*

8.3 ADVERB CLAUSES

An **adverb clause** is a subordinate clause that is used to modify a verb, an adjective, or an adverb. It is introduced by a subordinating conjunction.

For examples of subordinating conjunctions, see **Noun Clauses,** page R63.

Adverb clauses typically occur at the beginning or end of sentences.

MODIFYING A VERB: *When we need you, we will call.*

MODIFYING AN ADVERB: *I'll stay here where there is shelter from the rain.*

MODIFYING AN ADJECTIVE: *Roman felt as good as he had ever felt.*

TIP An adverb clause should be followed by a comma when it comes before an independent clause. When an adverb clause comes after an independent clause, a comma may not be needed.

8.4 NOUN CLAUSES

A **noun clause** is a subordinate clause that is used as a noun. A noun clause may be used as a subject, a direct object, an indirect object, a predicate nominative, or the object of a preposition. Noun clauses are introduced either by pronouns, such as *that, what, who, whoever, which,* and *whose,* or by subordinating conjunctions, such as *how, when, where, why,* and *whether.*

For more subordinating conjunctions, see **Quick Reference: Parts of Speech,** page R47.

TIP Because the same words may introduce adjective and noun clauses, you need to consider how a clause functions within its sentence. To determine if a clause is a noun clause, try substituting *something* or *someone* for the clause. If you can do it, it is probably a noun clause.

EXAMPLES: *I know whose woods these are.*
("I know *something.*" The clause is a noun clause, direct object of the verb *know.*)

Give a copy to whoever wants one. ("Give a copy to *someone.*" The clause is a noun clause, object of the preposition *to.*)

GRAMMAR PRACTICE

Add descriptive details to each sentence by writing the type of clause indicated in parentheses.

1. Some students volunteer at animal shelters. (adjective clause)

2. They help take care of dogs and cats. (adverb clause)

3. The veterinarian tries to explain to the students. (noun clause)

4. Many people appreciate the students. (adjective clause)

5. I plan to work at the shelter. (adverb clause)

9 The Structure of Sentences

When classified by their structure, there are four kinds of sentences: simple, compound, complex, and compound-complex.

9.1 SIMPLE SENTENCES

A **simple sentence** is a sentence that has one independent clause and no subordinate clauses.

EXAMPLES: *Sam ran to the theater.*
Max waited in front of the theater.

A simple sentence may contain a compound subject or a compound verb.

EXAMPLES: *Sam and Max went to the movie.* (compound subject)

They clapped and cheered at their favorite parts. (compound verb).

9.2 COMPOUND SENTENCES

A **compound sentence** consists of two or more independent clauses. The clauses in compound sentences are joined with commas and coordinating conjunctions (*and, but, or, nor, yet, for, so*) or with semicolons. Like simple sentences, compound sentences do not contain any subordinate clauses.

EXAMPLES: *Sam likes action movies, but Max prefers comedies.*

The actor jumped from one building to another; he barely made the final leap.

GRAMMAR PRACTICE

ANSWERS

1. ***Possible answer:*** *Students who want school credit volunteer at animal shelters.*

2. ***Possible answer:*** *They help take care of dogs and cats when the shelters are understaffed.*

3. ***Possible answer:*** *The veterinarian tries to explain to students how to care for sick animals.*

4. ***Possible answer:*** *Many people appreciate the students who donate their time each week.*

5. ***Possible answer:*** *When soccer season ends, I plan to work at the shelter.*

For more help with the structure of sentences, see

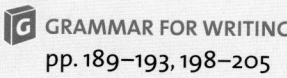 GRAMMAR FOR WRITING
pp. 189–193, 198–205

For more help with writing complete sentences, see

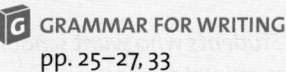 **GRAMMAR FOR WRITING**
pp. 25–27, 33

WATCH OUT! Do not confuse compound sentences with simple sentences that have compound parts.

EXAMPLE: *The actor knew all the lines but didn't play the part well.*
(Here *but* joins parts of a compound predicate, not a compound sentence.)

9.3 COMPLEX SENTENCES

A **complex sentence** consists of one independent clause and one or more subordinate clauses.

EXAMPLES: *One should not complain unless one has a better solution.*
Mr. Neiman, who is an artist, sketched pictures until the sun went down.

9.4 COMPOUND-COMPLEX SENTENCES

A **compound-complex sentence** contains two or more independent clauses and one or more subordinate clauses. Compound-complex sentences are, simply, both compound and complex. If you start with a compound sentence, all you need to do to form a compound-complex sentence is add a subordinate clause.

COMPOUND: *All the students knew the answer, yet they were too shy to volunteer.*
COMPOUND-COMPLEX: *All the students knew the answer that their teacher expected, yet they were too shy to volunteer.*

9.5 PARALLEL STRUCTURE

When you write sentences, make sure that coordinate parts are equivalent, or **parallel,** in structure.

NOT PARALLEL: *Erin loved basketball and to play hockey.* (*Basketball* is a noun; *to play hockey* is a phrase.)
PARALLEL: *Erin loved basketball and hockey.* (*Basketball* and *hockey* are both nouns.)
NOT PARALLEL: *He wanted to rent an apartment, a new car, and traveling around the country.* (*To rent* is an infinitive, *car* is a noun, and *traveling* is a gerund.)

PARALLEL: *He wanted to rent an apartment, to drive a new car, and to travel around the country.* (*To rent, to drive,* and *to travel* are all infinitives.)

🔟 Writing Complete Sentences

Remember, a sentence is a group of words that expresses a complete thought. In writing that you wish to share with a reader, try to avoid both sentence fragments and run-on sentences.

10.1 CORRECTING FRAGMENTS

A **sentence fragment** is a group of words that is only part of a sentence. It does not express a complete thought and may be confusing to a reader or listener. A sentence fragment may be lacking a subject, a predicate, or both.

FRAGMENT: *Waited for the boat to arrive.* (no subject)
CORRECTED: *We waited for the boat to arrive.*
FRAGMENT: *People of various races, ages, and creeds.* (no predicate)
CORRECTED: *People of various races, ages, and creeds gathered together.*
FRAGMENT: *Near the old cottage.* (neither subject nor predicate)
CORRECTED: *The burial ground is near the old cottage.*

In your writing, fragments may be a result of haste or incorrect punctuation. Sometimes fixing a fragment will be a matter of attaching it to a preceding or following sentence.

FRAGMENT: *We saw the two girls. Waiting for the bus to arrive.*
CORRECTED: *We saw the two girls waiting for the bus to arrive.*

10.2 CORRECTING RUN-ON SENTENCES

A **run-on sentence** is made up of two or more sentences written as though they were one. Some run-ons have no punctuation within them. Others may have only commas where conjunctions or stronger punctuation marks are necessary. Use your judgment in correcting run-on sentences, as you have choices. You can change a run-on to two sentences if the thoughts are not closely connected. If the thoughts are closely related, you can keep the run-on as one sentence by adding a semicolon or a conjunction.

> RUN-ON: *We found a place for the picnic by a small pond it was three miles from the village.*
>
> MAKE TWO SENTENCES: *We found a place for the picnic by a small pond. It was three miles from the village.*
>
> RUN-ON: *We found a place for the picnic by a small pond it was perfect.*
>
> USE A SEMICOLON: *We found a place for the picnic by a small pond; it was perfect.*
>
> ADD A CONJUNCTION: *We found a place for the picnic by a small pond, and it was perfect.*

WATCH OUT! When you form compound sentences, make sure you use appropriate punctuation: a comma before a coordinating conjunction, a semicolon when there is no coordinating conjunction. A very common mistake is to use a comma alone instead of a comma and a conjunction. This error is called a **comma splice.**

> INCORRECT: *He finished the job, he left the village.*
>
> CORRECT: *He finished the job, and he left the village.*

11 Subject-Verb Agreement

The subject and verb in a clause must agree in number. Agreement means that if the subject is singular, the verb is also singular, and if the subject is plural, the verb is also plural.

11.1 BASIC AGREEMENT

Fortunately, agreement between subjects and verbs in English is simple. Most verbs show the difference between singular and plural only in the third person of the present tense. In the present tense, the third-person singular form ends in *-s.*

Present-Tense Verb Forms

Singular	Plural
I sleep	we sleep
you sleep	you sleep
she, he, it sleeps	they sleep

11.2 AGREEMENT WITH *BE*

The verb *be* presents special problems in agreement, because this verb does not follow the usual verb patterns.

Forms of *Be*

Present Tense		Past Tense	
Singular	Plural	Singular	Plural
I am	we are	I was	we were
you are	you are	you were	you were
she, he, it is	they are	she, he, it was	they were

11.3 WORDS BETWEEN SUBJECT AND VERB

A verb agrees only with its subject. When words come between a subject and a verb, ignore them when considering proper agreement. Identify the subject, and make sure the verb agrees with it.

> EXAMPLES: *A story in the newspapers tells about the 1890s.*
>
> *Dad as well as Mom reads the paper daily.*

11.4 AGREEMENT WITH COMPOUND SUBJECTS

Use plural verbs with most compound subjects joined by the word *and.*

> EXAMPLE: *My father and his friends play chess everyday.*

To confirm that you need a plural verb, you could substitute the plural pronoun *they* for *my father and his friends.*

If a compound subject is thought of as a unit, use a singular verb. Test this by substituting the singular pronoun *it.*

> EXAMPLE: *Peanut butter and jelly [it] is my brother's favorite sandwich.*

For help with subject-verb agreement, see

 GRAMMAR FOR WRITING
pp. 206–227

Use a singular verb with a compound subject that is preceded by *each*, *every*, or *many a*.

    EXAMPLE: *Each novel and short story seems grounded in personal experience.*

When the parts of a compound subject are joined by *or*, *nor*, or the correlative conjunctions *either . . . or* or *neither . . . nor*, make the verb agree with the noun or pronoun nearest the verb.

    EXAMPLES: *Cookies or ice cream is my favorite dessert.*

    Either Cheryl or her friends are being invited.

    Neither ice storms nor snow is predicted today.

11.5 PERSONAL PRONOUNS AS SUBJECTS

When using a personal pronoun as a subject, make sure to match it with the correct form of the verb *be*. (See the chart in Section 11.2.) Note especially that the pronoun *you* takes the forms *are* and *were*, regardless of whether it is singular or plural.

WATCH OUT! *You is* and *you was* are nonstandard forms and should be avoided in writing and speaking. *We was* and *they was* are also forms to be avoided.

    INCORRECT: *You was a good student.*

    CORRECT: *You were a good student.*

    INCORRECT: *They was starting a new school.*

    CORRECT: *They were starting a new school.*

11.6 INDEFINITE PRONOUNS AS SUBJECTS

Some indefinite pronouns are always singular; some are always plural.

Singular Indefinite Pronouns			
another	either	neither	one
anybody	everybody	nobody	somebody
anyone	everyone	no one	someone
anything	everything	nothing	something
each	much		

    EXAMPLES: *Each of the writers was given an award.*

    Somebody in the room upstairs is sleeping.

Plural Indefinite Pronouns			
both	few	many	several

    EXAMPLES: *Many of the books in our library are not in circulation.*

    Few have been returned recently.

Still other indefinite pronouns may be either singular or plural.

Singular or Plural Indefinite Pronouns		
all	more	none
any	most	some

The number of the indefinite pronoun *any* or *none* often depends on the intended meaning.

    EXAMPLES: *Any of these topics has potential for a good article.* (any one topic)

    Any of these topics have potential for good articles. (all of the many topics)

The indefinite pronouns *all*, *some*, *more*, *most*, and *none* are singular when they refer to quantities or parts of things. They are plural when they refer to numbers of individual things. Context will usually give a clue.

    EXAMPLES: *All of the flour is gone.* (referring to a quantity)

    All of the flowers are gone. (referring to individual items)

11.7 INVERTED SENTENCES

A sentence in which the subject follows the verb is called an **inverted sentence.** A subject can follow a verb or part of a verb phrase in a question, a sentence beginning with *here* or *there,* or a sentence in which an adjective, an adverb, or a phrase is placed first.

    EXAMPLES: *There clearly are far too many cooks in this kitchen.*

    What is the correct ingredient for this stew?

    Far from the embroiled cooks stands the master chef.

TIP To check subject-verb agreement in some inverted sentences, place the subject before the verb. For example, change *There are many people* to *Many people are there.*

11.8 SENTENCES WITH PREDICATE NOMINATIVES

In a sentence containing a predicate noun (nominative), the verb should agree with the subject, not the predicate noun.

EXAMPLES: *The speeches of Martin Luther King Jr. are a landmark in American civil rights history.* (*Speeches* is the subject—not *landmark*—and it takes the plural verb *are.*)

One landmark in American civil rights history is the speeches of Martin Luther King Jr. (The subject is *landmark*—not *speeches*—and it takes the singular verb *is.*)

11.9 *DON'T* AND *DOESN'T* AS AUXILIARY VERBS

The auxiliary verb *doesn't* is used with singular subjects and with the personal pronouns *she, he,* and *it.* The auxiliary verb *don't* is used with plural subjects and with the personal pronouns *I, we, you,* and *they.*

SINGULAR: *She doesn't know Martin Luther King's famous "I Have a Dream" speech.*

Doesn't the young woman read very much?

PLURAL: *We don't have the speech memorized.*

Don't speakers usually memorize their speeches?

11.10 COLLECTIVE NOUNS AS SUBJECTS

Collective nouns are singular nouns that name groups of persons or things. *Team,* for example, is the collective name of a group of individuals. A collective noun takes a singular verb when the group acts as a single unit. It takes a plural verb when the members of the group act separately.

EXAMPLES: *Our team usually wins.* (The team as a whole wins.)

Our team vote differently on most issues. (The individual members vote.)

11.11 RELATIVE PRONOUNS AS SUBJECTS

When the relative pronoun *who, which,* or *that* is used as a subject in an adjective clause, the verb in the clause must agree in number with the antecedent of the pronoun.

SINGULAR: *I didn't read the **poem** about fireflies that was assigned.*

The antecedent of the relative pronoun *that* is the singular *poem;* therefore, *that* is singular and must take the singular verb *was.*

PLURAL: ***Mary Oliver and Pat Moran,** who are very different from each other, are both outstanding poets.*

The antecedent of the relative pronoun *who* is the plural compound subject *Mary Oliver and Pat Moran.* Therefore *who* is plural, and it takes the plural verb *are.*

GRAMMAR PRACTICE

Locate the subject of each verb in parentheses in the sentences below. Then choose the correct verb form.

1. In "Zebra" one (learn, learns) how John Wilson and Adam become friends.

2. John (tell, tells) Adam that he has an idea for a summer art class.

3. Many of Adam's classmates (think, thinks) that the summer art class will be fun.

4. Some (go, goes) to camp during the summer months, while others just (hang, hangs) around.

5. Among psychologists, many (believe, believes) that making art is good therapy.

6. Even you (has, have) a chance to be a good artist.

7. Does anyone else (want, wants) to take this class?

8. Objects in the attic, such as a broken umbrella, (is, are) good materials for making sculptures.

9. There (is, are) many beautiful objects made from old things.

10. Each of the students (leave, leaves) the class having learned something special.

GRAMMAR PRACTICE

ANSWERS

1. *learns*
2. *tells*
3. *think*
4. *go; hang*
5. *believe*
6. *have*
7. *want*
8. *are*
9. *are*
10. *leaves*

The key to becoming an independent reader is to develop a tool kit of vocabulary strategies. By learning and practicing the strategies, you'll know what to do when you encounter unfamiliar words while reading. You'll also know how to refine the words you use for different situations—personal, school, and work.

Being a good speller is important when communicating your ideas in writing. Learning basic spelling rules and checking your spelling in a dictionary will help you spell words that you may not use frequently.

VOCABULARY PRACTICE
For more practice, go to the **Vocabulary Center** at ClassZone.com.

1 Using Context Clues

The context of a word is made up of the punctuation marks, words, sentences, and paragraphs that surround the word. A word's context can give you important clues about its meaning.

1.1 GENERAL CONTEXT

Sometimes you need to determine the meaning of an unfamiliar word by reading all the information in a passage.

> The sweater was of *inferior* quality. It was torn and had several buttons missing.

You can figure out from the context that *inferior* means "poor or low."

1.2 SPECIFIC CONTEXT CLUES

Sometimes writers help you understand the meanings of words by providing specific clues such as those shown in the chart.

1.3 IDIOMS, SLANG, AND FIGURATIVE LANGUAGE

An **idiom** is an expression whose overall meaning is different from the meaning of the individual words. **Slang** is informal language in which made-up words and ordinary words are used to mean something different from their meanings in formal English. **Figurative language** is language that communicates meaning beyond the literal meaning of the words. Use context clues to figure out the meanings of idioms, slang, and figurative language.

> *Button your lip* about the party. (idiom; means "keep quiet")

> That's a really *bad* jacket; I want one. (slang: means "good-looking, excellent")

> My brother had tried to make dinner. The kitchen was *a battleground of dirty dishes, stains, spills, and potato peels.* (figurative language; battleground, dirty dishes, stains, spills, and potato peels represent a messy scene)

Specific Context Clues

Type of Clue	Key Words/ Phrases	Example
Definition or restatement of the meaning of the word	or, which is, that is, in other words, also known as, also called	Most chemicals are *toxic*, or **poisonous.**
Example following an unfamiliar word	such as, like, as if, for example, especially, including	*Amphibians*, such as **frogs and salamanders,** live in the pond by our house.
Comparison with a more familiar word or concept	as, like, also, similar to, in the same way, likewise	Like the rest of my *frugal* family, I always **save** most of the money I earn.
Contrast with a familiar word or experience	unlike, but, however, although, on the other hand, on the contrary	I wish I had more *ingenuity* in making money instead of simply relying on the **same old** baby-sitting jobs.
Cause-and-effect relationship in which one term is familiar	because, since, when, consequently, as a result, therefore	Because the chemicals are *flammable,* the scientists wear special **fire-resistant** clothing.

For more information, see **Vocabulary Strategy: Context Clues,** pages 225 and 354, **Vocabulary Strategy: Idioms,** page 278, and **Vocabulary Strategy: Literal and Figurative Meanings,** page 506.

2 Analyzing Word Structure

Many words can be broken into smaller parts. These word parts include base words, roots, prefixes, and suffixes.

2.1 BASE WORDS

A **base word** is a word part that by itself is also a word. Other words or word parts can be added to base words to form new words.

For more information, see Vocabulary Strategy: Recognizing Base Words, page 801.

2.2 ROOTS

A **root** is a word part that contains the core meaning of the word. Many English words contain roots that come from older languages such as Greek, Latin, Old English (Anglo-Saxon), and Norse. Knowing the meaning of the word's root can help you determine the word's meaning.

Root	Meaning	Example
photo (Greek)	light	photography
therm (Greek)	heat	thermometer
cred (Latin)	believe	credit
mot (Latin)	move	motion
hēadfod (Old English)	head, top	headfirst

For more information, see Vocabulary Strategy: Word Roots, pages 40, 90, 256, 324, 464, 645, 775, 821, 893, and 935.

2.3 PREFIXES

A **prefix** is a word part attached to the beginning of a word. Most prefixes come from Greek, Latin, or Old English.

Prefix	Meaning	Example
mal-	bad or wrong	**mal**function
micro-	small or short	**micro**scope
semi-	half	**semi**circle

For more information, see Vocabulary Strategy: Prefixes, pages 70, 373, 893.

2.4 SUFFIXES

A **suffix** is a word part that appears at the end of a root or base word to form a new word. Some suffixes do not change word meaning. These suffixes are

- added to nouns to change the number of persons or objects
- added to verbs to change the tense
- added to modifiers to change the degree of comparison

Suffix	Meaning	Examples
-s, -es	to change the number of a noun	lock + s = locks
-d, -ed, -ing	to change verb tense	stew + ed = stewed
-er, -est	to indicate comparison in modifiers	mild + er = milder soft + est = softest

Other suffixes can be added to the root or base to change the word's meaning. These suffixes can also determine a word's part of speech.

Suffix	Meaning	Example
-er	one who does	teacher
-able	capable of	readable
-ly	in what manner	slowly

For more information, see Vocabulary Strategy: Suffixes That Form Adjectives, page 127.

2.5 CONTENT-AREA VOCABULARY

Knowing the meaning of Greek, Latin, and Anglo-Saxon word parts can help you figure out the meaning of content-area vocabulary.

Word Part	Meaning	Example
derm	skin	dermatologist
logy	study of	astrology
bio	life	biography
hydr	water	hydrant
hypo	below, beneath	hypodermic
vid/vis	to see	visual
fract	to break	fraction

Etymology Have students research the etymology of the following words:

- *union*
- *vitality*
- *abolish*
- *voracious*
- *propeller*
- *cherish*
- *taut*

3 Understanding Word Origins

Strategies for Understanding Unfamiliar Words

- Look for any prefixes or suffixes. Remove them so that you can concentrate on the base word or the root.

- See if you recognize any elements—prefix, suffix, root, or base—of the word. You may be able to guess its meaning by analyzing one or two elements.

- Think about the way the word is used in the sentence. Use the context and the word parts to make a logical guess about the word's meaning.

- Look in a dictionary to see whether you are correct.

PRACTICE AND APPLY

Use the strategies in this section and the vocabulary lessons in this book to help you figure out the meanings of the following content-area words.

forefathers	vision	microfilm
biology	fracture	import
auditory	ecology	hypothermia

3.1 ETYMOLOGIES

Etymologies show the origin and historical development of a word. When you study a word's history and origin, you can find out when, where, and how the word came to be.

> ge•om•e•try (jē-ŏm'i-trē) *n., pl.* -tries **1.** The mathematics of the properties, measurement, and relationships of points, lines, angles, surfaces, and solids. **2.** Arrangement. **3.** A physical arrangement suggesting geometric lines and shapes. [from Greek *geōmetriā,* from *geōmetrein,* to measure land].

3.2 WORD FAMILIES

Words that have the same root make up a word family and have related meanings. The following chart shows a common Greek and a common Latin root. Notice how the meanings of the example words are related to the meanings of their roots.

Latin Root	*sens:* "sense or feel"
English	**sensory** relating to the senses
	sensitive responsive to sensations
	sensation a perception or feeling

Greek Root	*ast(e)r:* "star"
English	**asteroid** a small object in outer space
	asterisk a star-shaped punctuation mark
	astronomy the study of outer space

3.3 FOREIGN WORDS

The English language includes words from diverse languages, such as French, Dutch, Spanish, Italian, and Chinese. Many words have stayed the way they were in their original languages.

French	Dutch	Spanish	Italian
ballet	boss	canyon	diva
vague	caboose	rodeo	cupola
mirage	dock	bronco	spaghetti

4 Synonyms and Antonyms

4.1 SYNONYMS

A **synonym** is a word with a meaning similar to that of another word. You can find synonyms in a thesaurus or a dictionary. In a dictionary, synonyms are often given as part of the definition of the word. The following word pairs are synonyms:

satisfy/please   occasionally/sometimes

rob/steal   schedule/agenda

*For more information, see **Vocabulary Strategy: Use the Best Synonym,** page 487.*

4.2 ANTONYMS

An **antonym** is a word with a meaning opposite that of another word. The following word pairs are antonyms:

accurate/incorrect   similar/different

fresh/stale   unusual/ordinary

*For more information, see **Vocabulary Strategy: Antonyms As Context Clues,** page 59.*

5 Denotation and Connotation

5.1 DENOTATION

A word's dictionary meaning is called its **denotation.** For example, the denotation of the word *thin* is "having little flesh; spare; lean."

5.2 CONNOTATION

The images or feelings you connect to a word add a finer shade of meaning, called **connotation.** The connation of a word goes beyond its basic dictionary definition. Writers use connotations of words to communicate positive or negative feelings.

Positive	Negative
slender	scrawny
thrifty	cheap
young	immature

Make sure you understand the denotation and connotation of a word when you read it or use it in your writing.

*For more information, see **Vocabulary Strategy: Denotations and Connotations,** pages 336, 580, and 788.*

6 Analogies

An **analogy** is a comparison between two things that are similar in some way but are otherwise not alike. Analogies are sometimes used in writing when unfamiliar subjects or ideas are explained in terms of familiar ones. Analogies often appear on tests as well. In an analogy problem, the analogy is expressed using two groups of words. The relationship between the first pair of words is the same as the relationship between the second pair of words. Some analogy problems are expressed like this:

love : hate :: war: _____
a. soldier b. peace c. battle d. argument

Follow these steps to determine the correct answer:

- Read the problem as "*love* is to *hate* as **war** is to...."

- Ask yourself how the words *love* and *hate* are related. (*Love* and *hate* are antonyms.)

- Ask yourself which answer choice is an antonym of *war.* (*Peace* is an antonym of *war,* therefore *peace* is the best answer.)

*For more information, see **Vocabulary Strategy: Analogies,** page 116.*

7 Homonyms, Homographs, and Homophones

7.1 HOMONYMS

Homonyms are words that have the same spelling and sound but have different meanings.

> *The snake shed its skin in the shed behind the house.*

Shed can mean "to lose by natural process," but an identically spelled word means "a small structure."

Sometimes only one of the meanings of a homonym may be familiar to you. Use context clues to help you figure out the meaning of an unfamiliar word.

7.2 HOMOGRAPHS

Homographs are words that are spelled the same but have different meanings and origins. Some are also pronounced differently, as in these examples.

> *Please close the door. (clōz)*
> *That was a close call. (clōs)*

If you see a word used in a way that is unfamiliar to you, check a dictionary to see if it is a homograph.

*For more information, see **Vocabulary Strategy: Homographs,** page 658.*

7.3 HOMOPHONES

Homophones are words that sound alike but have different meanings and spellings. The following homophones are frequently misused:

it's/its   they're/their/there

to/too/two   stationary/stationery

Many misused homophones are pronouns and contractions. Whenever you are unsure whether to write *your* or *you're* and *who's* or *whose*, ask yourself if you mean *you are* and *who is/has*. If you do, write the contraction. For other homophones, such as *fair* and *fare*, use the meaning of the word to help you decide which one to use.

8 Words with Multiple Meanings

Some words have acquired additional meanings over time that are based on the original meaning.

> I had to be replaced in the *cast* of the play because of the *cast* on my arm.

These two uses of *cast* have different meanings, but both of them have the same origin. You will find all the meanings of *cast* listed in one entry in the dictionary.

For more information, see **Vocabulary Strategy: Words with Multiple Meanings,** *page 238.*

9 Specialized Vocabulary

Specialized vocabulary is special terms suited to a particular field of study or work. For example, science, mathematics, and history all have their own technical or specialized vocabularies. To figure out specialized terms, you can use context clues and reference sources, such as dictionaries on specific subjects, atlases, or manuals.

For more information, see **Vocabulary Strategy: Specialized Vocabulary,** *page 906.*

10 Using Reference Sources

10.1 DICTIONARIES

A **general dictionary** will tell you not only a word's definitions but also its pronunciation, parts of speech, and history and origin.

❶ **tangible** (tăn′jə-bəl) ❷ *adj.* ❸ **1a.** Discernible by the touch; palpable. **b.** Possible to touch. **c.** Possible to be treated as fact; real or concrete. ❹ **2.** Possible to understand or realize. **3.** Law that can be valued monetarily [Late Latin *tangibilis,* from Latin *tangere,* to touch] ❺

❶ Entry word
❷ Pronunciation
❸ Part of speech
❹ Definitions
❺ Etymology

A **specialized dictionary** focuses on terms related to a particular field of study or work. Use a dictionary to check the spelling of any word you are unsure of in your English class and other classes as well.

For more information, see **Vocabulary Strategy: Dictionary Usage Labels,** *page 721.*

10.2 THESAURI

A **thesaurus** (plural, *thesauri*) is a dictionary of synonyms. A thesaurus can be especially helpful when you find yourself using the same modifiers over and over again.

10.3 SYNONYM FINDERS

A **synonym finder** is often included in word-processing software. It enables you to highlight a word and be shown a display of its synonyms.

10.4 GLOSSARIES

A **glossary** is a list of specialized terms and their definitions. It is often found in the back of a book and sometimes includes pronunciations. Many textbooks contain glossaries. In fact, this textbook has three glossaries: the **Glossary of Literary Terms,** the **Glossary of Reading & Informational Terms,** and the **Glossary of Vocabulary in English & Spanish.** Use these glossaries to help you understand how terms are used in this textbook.

For more information, see **Vocabulary Strategy: Using Reference Aids,** *page 266.*

11 Spelling Rules

11.1 WORDS ENDING IN A SILENT *E*

Before adding a suffix beginning with a vowel or *y* to a word ending in a silent *e*, drop the *e* (with some exceptions).

> **amaze + -ing = amazing**
> **love + -able = lovable**
> **create + -ed = created**
> **nerve + -ous = nervous**

Exceptions: *change + -able = changeable; courage + -ous = courageous*

When adding a suffix beginning with a consonant to a word ending in a silent *e,* keep the *e* (with some exceptions).

late + -ly = lately
spite + -ful = spiteful
noise + -less = noiseless
state + -ment = statement

Exceptions: *truly, argument, ninth, wholly, awful,* and others

When a suffix beginning with *a* or *o* is added to a word with a final silent *e,* the final *e* is usually retained if it is preceded by a soft *c* or a soft *g.*

bridge + -able = bridgeable
peace + -able = peaceable
outrage + -ous = outrageous
advantage + -ous = advantageous

When a suffix beginning with a vowel is added to words ending in *ee* or *oe,* the final silent *e* is retained.

agree + -ing = agreeing   free + -ing = freeing
hoe + -ing = hoeing   see + -ing = seeing

11.2 WORDS ENDING IN Y

Before adding most suffixes to a word that ends in *y* preceded by a consonant, change the *y* to *i.*

easy + -est = easiest
crazy + -est = craziest
silly + -ness = silliness
marry + -age = marriage

Exceptions: *dryness, shyness,* and *slyness*

However, when you add *-ing,* the *y* does not change.

empty + -ed = emptied   but
empty + -ing = emptying

When adding a suffix to a word that ends in *y* preceded by a vowel, the *y* usually does not change.

play + -er = player
employ + -ed = employed
coy + -ness = coyness
pay + -able = payable

11.3 WORDS ENDING IN A CONSONANT

In one-syllable words that end in one consonant preceded by one short vowel, double the final consonant before adding a suffix beginning with a vowel, such as *-ed* or *-ing.* These are sometimes called 1+1+1 words.

dip + -ed = dipped   set + -ing = setting
slim + -est = slimmest   fit + -er = fitter

The rule does not apply to words of one syllable that end in a consonant preceded by two vowels.

feel + -ing = feeling   peel + -ed = peeled
reap + -ed = reaped   loot + -ed = looted

In words of more than one syllable, double the final consonant when (1) the word ends with one consonant preceded by one vowel and (2) when the word is accented on the last syllable.

be•gin´   per•mit´   re•fer´

In the following examples, note that in the new words formed with suffixes, the accent remains on the same syllable:

be•gin´ + -ing = be•gin´ning = beginning
per•mit´ + -ed = per•mit´ted = permitted

Exceptions: In some words with more than one syllable, though the accent remains on the same syllable when a suffix is added, the final consonant is nevertheless not doubled, as in the following examples:

tra´vel + er = tra´vel•er = traveler
mar´ket + er = mar´ket•er = marketer

In the following examples, the accent does not remain on the same syllable; thus, the final consonant is not doubled:

re•fer´ + -ence = ref´er•ence = reference
con•fer´ + -ence = con´fer•ence = conference

11.4 PREFIXES AND SUFFIXES

When adding a prefix to a word, do not change the spelling of the base word. When a prefix creates a double letter, keep both letters.

dis- + approve = disapprove
re- + build = rebuild
ir- + regular = irregular
mis- + spell = misspell
anti- + trust = antitrust
il- + logical = illogical

When adding *-ly* to a word ending in *l,* keep both *l*'s. When adding *-ness* to a word ending in *n,* keep both *n*'s.

careful + -ly = carefully
sudden + -ness = suddenness
final + -ly = finally
thin + -ness = thinness

11.5 FORMING PLURAL NOUNS

To form the plural of most nouns, just add -s.

prizes   dreams   circles   stations

For most singular nouns ending in *o*, add -s.

solos   halos   studios   photos   pianos

For a few nouns ending in *o*, add -es.

heroes   tomatoes   potatoes   echoes

When the singular noun ends in *s, sh, ch, x,* or *z,* add -es.

waitresses   brushes   ditches
axes   buzzes

When a singular noun ends in *y* with a consonant before it, change the *y* to *i* and add -es.

army—armies   candy—candies
baby—babies   diary—diaries
ferry—ferries   conspiracy—conspiracies

When a vowel (*a, e, i, o, u*) comes before the *y,* just add -s.

boy—boys   way—ways
array—arrays   alloy—alloys
weekday—weekdays   jockey—jockeys

For most nouns ending in *f* or *fe,* change the *f* to *v* and add -es or -s.

life—lives   calf—calves   knife—knives
thief—thieves   shelf—shelves loaf—loaves

For some nouns ending in *f,* add -s to make the plural.

roofs   chiefs   reefs   beliefs

Some nouns have the same form for both singular and plural.

deer   sheep   moose   salmon   trout

For some nouns, the plural is formed in a special way.

man—men   goose—geese
ox—oxen   woman—women
mouse—mice   child—children

For a compound noun written as one word, form the plural by changing the last word in the compound to its plural form.

stepchild—stepchildren   firefly—fireflies

If a compound noun is written as a hyphenated word or as two separate words, change the most important word to the plural form.

brother-in-law—brothers-in-law
life jacket—life jackets

11.6 FORMING POSSESSIVES

If a noun is singular, add *'s.*

mother—my mother's car   Ross—Ross's desk

Exception: The *s* after the apostrophe is dropped after *Jesus', Moses',* and certain names in classical mythology *(Zeus').* These possessive forms can thus be pronounced easily.

If a noun is plural and ends with *s,* just add an apostrophe.

parents—my parents' car
the Santinis—the Santinis' house

If a noun is plural but does not end in *s,* add *'s.*

people—the people's choice
women—the women's coats

11.7 SPECIAL SPELLING PROBLEMS

Only one English word ends in -sede: *supersede.* Three words end in -ceed: *exceed, proceed,* and *succeed.* All other verbs ending in the sound "seed" are spelled with -cede.

concede   precede   recede   secede

In words with **ie** or **ei,** when the sound is long *e* (as in *she*), the word is spelled *ie* except after *c* (with some exceptions).

i before *e*	thief	relieve	field
	piece	grieve	pier
except after *c*	conceit	perceive	ceiling
	receive	receipt	
Exceptions:	either	neither	weird
	leisure	seize	

🔢 Commonly Confused Words

WORDS	DEFINITIONS	EXAMPLES
accept/except	The verb *accept* means "to receive or believe"; *except* is usually a preposition meaning "excluding."	Did the teacher **accept** your report? Everyone smiled for the photographer **except** Jody.
advice/advise	*Advise* is a verb; *advice* is a noun naming that which an *adviser* gives.	I **advise** you to take that job. Whom should I ask for **advice?**
affect/effect	As a verb, *affect* means "to influence." *Effect* as a verb means "to cause." If you want a noun, you will almost always want *effect.*	How deeply did the news **affect** him? The students tried to **effect** a change in school policy. What **effect** did the acidic soil produce in the plants?
all ready/already	*All ready* is an adjective meaning "fully ready." *Already* is an adverb meaning "before or by this time."	He was **all ready** to go at noon. I have **already** seen that movie.
desert/dessert	*Desert* (dĕz´ərt) means "a dry, sandy, barren region." *Desert* (dĭ-zûrt´) means "to abandon." *Dessert* (dĭ-zûrt´) is a sweet, such as cake.	The Sahara, in North Africa, is the world's largest **desert.** The night guard did not **desert** his post. Alison's favorite **dessert** is chocolate cake.
among/between	*Between* is used when you are speaking of only two things. *Among* is used for three or more.	**Between** ice cream and sherbet, I prefer the latter. Gary Soto is **among** my favorite authors.
bring/take	*Bring* is used to denote motion toward a speaker or place. *Take* is used to denote motion away from such a person or place.	**Bring** the books over here, and I will **take** them to the library.
fewer/less	*Fewer* refers to the number of separate, countable units. *Less* refers to bulk quantity.	We have **less** literature and **fewer** selections in this year's curriculum.
leave/let	*Leave* means "to allow something to remain behind." *Let* means "to permit."	The librarian will **leave** some books on display but will not **let** us borrow any.
lie/lay	To *lie* is "to rest or recline." It does not take an object. *Lay* always takes an object.	Rover loves to **lie** in the sun. We always **lay** some bones next to him.
loose/lose	*Loose* (lōōs) means "free, not restrained"; *lose* (lōōz) means "to misplace or fail to find."	Who turned the horses **loose?** I hope we won't **lose** any of them.
passed/past	*Passed* is the past tense of *pass* and means "went by." *Past* is an adjective that means "of a former time." *Past* is also a noun that means "time gone by."	We **passed** through the Florida Keys during our vacation. My **past** experiences have taught me to set my alarm. Ebenezer Scrooge is a character who relives his **past.**
than/then	Use *than* in making comparisons; use *then* on all other occasions.	Ramon is stronger **than** Mark. Cut the grass and **then** trim the hedges.
two/too/to	*Two* is the number. *Too* is an adverb meaning "also" or "very." Use *to* before a verb or as a preposition.	Meg had **to** go **to** town, **too.** We had **too** much reading **to** do. **Two** chapters is **too** many.
their/there/they're	*Their* means "belonging to them." *There* means "in that place." *They're* is the contraction for "they are."	**There** is a movie playing at 9 P.M. **They're** going to see it with me. Sakara and Jessica drove away in **their** car after the movie.

*For more information, see **Vocabulary Strategy: Easily Confused Words,** page 684.*

Effective oral communication occurs when the audience understands a message the way the speaker intends it. Good speakers and listeners do more than just talk and hear. They use specific techniques to present their ideas effectively, and they are attentive and critical listeners.

1 Speech

In school, in business, and in community life, a speech is one of the most effective means of communicating.

1.1 AUDIENCE, PURPOSE, AND OCCASION

Delivering a speech is an opportunity to share your ideas. Before you begin to prepare a speech, you will need to know *why* you are making the presentation and to *whom* you are presenting it. Understanding your purpose, the background and interests of your audience, and the occasion will help you select an appropriate focus and organizational structure for your speech.

- **Know Your Audience** What kind of group are you presenting to? Fellow classmates? A group of teachers? What are their interests and backgrounds? Understanding their different points of view can help you organize the information so that they understand and are interested in it.

- **Understand Your Purpose** Keep in mind your purpose for speaking. Are you trying to persuade the audience to do something? Perhaps you simply want to entertain them by sharing a story or experience. Your purpose directly affects your tone. Decide whether you'll best accomplish your purpose by being serious or humorous.

- **Know the Occasion** Are you speaking at a special event? Is it formal? Will others be giving speeches besides you? Knowing what the occasion is will help you choose the proper language and the right length for the event.

1.2 WRITING YOUR SPEECH

Once you understand your purpose and audience, you are ready to write your speech. Use the following guidelines to help you:

- **Create a Unified Speech** Do this first by organizing your speech into paragraphs, each of which develops a single main idea. Then make sure that just as all the sentences in a paragraph support the main idea of the paragraph, all the paragraphs in your speech support the main idea of the speech.

- **Clarify Your Ideas** Make sure that you show clear relationships between ideas. Transition words can help listeners follow your ideas.

*For more information on transitions, see the **Writing Handbook**, page R32.*

- **Use Appropriate Language** The subject of your speech—and the way you choose to present it—should match your audience, your purpose, and the occasion. You can use informal language, such as slang, to share a story with your classmates. For a persuasive speech in front of a school assembly, use formal, standard American English. If you are giving an informative presentation, be sure to explain any terms that the audience may not be familiar with.

- **Provide Evidence** Include relevant facts, statistics, and incidents; quote experts to support your ideas and opinions. Elaborate—provide specific details, perhaps with visual or media displays—to clarify what you are saying.

- **Arrange Details and Evidence Effectively** In a good presentation, your main thesis statement should be supported by clearly stated evidence. The evidence can be presented as details, reasons, descriptions, or examples. Use the following chart to help you arrange your ideas.

Introduction	• Focus on one strong example or statistic. • Make sure your evidence is intense or even surprising, so that it grabs the audience's attention.
Main Body	• Try to provide at least one piece of evidence for every new idea you introduce. • Define unfamiliar terms clearly. • When possible, include well-labeled diagrams or illustrations.
Conclusion	• Leave your audience with one strong piece of evidence or a powerful detail.

• **Use Figurative Language** To help your audience follow the main ideas of your speech, be sure to draw attention to important points with similes, metaphors, and sensory images.

• **Use Precise Language** Use precise language to convey your ideas, and vary the structure and length of your sentences. You can keep the audience's attention with a word that brings out strong emotion. You can use a question or interjection to make a personal connection with the audience.

• **Start Strong, Finish Strong** As you begin your speech, consider using a "hook"—an interesting question or statement to capture your audience's attention. At the end of the speech, restate your main ideas simply and clearly. Perhaps conclude with a powerful example or anecdote to reinforce your message.

• **Revise Your Speech** After you write your speech, revise, edit, and proofread it as you would a written report. Use a variety of sentence structures to achieve a natural rhythm. Check for correct subject-verb agreement and consistent verb tense. Correct run-on sentences and sentence fragments. Use parallel structure to emphasize ideas. Make sure you use complete sentences and correct punctuation and capitalization, even if no one else will see it. Your written speech should be clear and error free. If you notice an error in your notes during the speech, you may not remember what you actually wanted to say.

1.3 DELIVERING YOUR SPEECH

Confidence is the key to a successful presentation. Use these techniques to help you prepare and present your speech:

Prepare

• **Review Your Information** Reread your notes and review any background research. You'll feel more confident during your speech.

• **Organize Your Notes** Some people prefer to write down only key points. Others prefer the entire script. Write each main point, or each paragraph, of your speech on a separate numbered index card. Be sure to include your most important evidence and examples.

• **Plan Your Visual Aids** If you are planning on using visual aids, such as slides, posters, charts, graphs, video clips, overhead transparencies, or computer projections, now is the time to design them and decide how to work them into your speech.

Practice

• **Rehearse** Rehearse your speech several times, possibly in front of a practice audience. Maintain good posture by standing with your shoulders back and your head up. If you are using visual aids, arrange them in the order in which you will use them. Adapt your rate of speaking, pitch, and tone of voice to your audience and setting. Glance at your notes to refresh your memory, but avoid reading them word for word. Your style of performance should express the purpose of your speech. Use the following chart to help you.

Purpose	Pace	Pitch	Tone
To persuade	fast but clear	even	urgent
To inform	using plenty of pauses	even	authoritative
To entertain	usually building to a "punch"	varied to create characters or drama	funny or dramatic

- **Use Audience Feedback** If you had a practice audience, ask them specific questions about your delivery: Did I use enough eye contact? Was my voice at the right volume? Did I stand straight, or did I slouch? Use the audience's comments to evaluate the effectiveness of your delivery and to set goals for future rehearsals.

- **Evaluate Your Performance** When you have finished each rehearsal, evaluate your performance. Did you pause to let an important point sink in or use gestures for emphasis? Make a list of the aspects of your presentation that you will try to improve for your next rehearsal.

Present

- **Begin Your Speech** Try to look relaxed and smile.

- **Make Eye Contact** Try to make eye contact with as many audience members as possible. This will establish personal contact and help you determine if the audience understands your speech.

- **Remember to Pause** A slight pause after important points will provide emphasis and give your audience time to think about what you're saying.

- **Speak Clearly** Speak loud enough to be heard clearly, but not so loud that your voice is overwhelming. Use a conversational tone.

- **Maintain Good Posture** Stand up straight and avoid nervous movements that may distract the audience's attention from what you are saying.

- **Use Expressive Body Language** Use facial expressions to show your feelings toward your topic. Lean forward when you make an important point; move your hands and arms for emphasis. Use your body language to show your own style and reflect your personality.

- **Watch the Audience for Responses** If they start fidgeting or yawning, speak a little louder or get to your conclusion a little sooner. Use what you learn to evaluate the effectiveness of your speech and to decide what areas need improvement for future presentations.

Respond to Questions

Depending on the content of your speech, your audience may have questions. Follow these steps to make sure that you answer questions in an appropriate manner:

- Think about what your audience may ask and prepare answers before your speech.

- Tell your audience at the beginning of your speech that you will take questions at the end. This helps avoid audience interruptions that may make your speech hard to follow.

- Call on audience members in the order in which they raise their hands.

- Repeat each question before you answer it to ensure that everyone has heard it. This step also gives you time to prepare your answer.

2 Different Types of Oral Presentations

2.1 INFORMATIVE SPEECH

When you deliver an informative speech, you give the audience new information, provide a better understanding of information, or enable the audience to use the information in a new way. An informative speech is presented in an objective way.

*For more information, see **Speaking and Listening: Making a Formal Presentation,** page 743.*

Use the following questions to evaluate the presentation of a peer or a public figure, or your own presentation.

> **Evaluate an Informative Speech**
> - Did the speaker explain the purpose of the presentation?
> - Did the speaker take the audience's previous knowledge into consideration?
> - Did the speaker cite a variety of sources for the information?
> - Did the speaker communicate the information objectively?
> - Did the speaker explain technical terms?
> - Did the speaker use visual aids effectively?

2.2 PERSUASIVE SPEECH

When you deliver a persuasive speech, you offer a thesis or clear statement on a subject, you provide relevant evidence to support your position, and you attempt to convince the audience to accept your point of view.

*For more information, see **Speaking and Listening: Delivering a Persuasive Speech**, page 955.*

Use the following questions to evaluate the presentation of a peer or a public figure, or your own presentation.

Evaluate a Persuasive Speech

- Did the speaker present a clear thesis or argument?
- Did the speaker anticipate and address audience concerns, biases, and counterarguments?
- Did the speaker use sound logic and reasoning in developing the argument?
- Did the speaker support the argument with convincing evidence, examples, facts, expert opinions, and quotations?
- Did the speaker hold the audience's interest with an effective voice, facial expressions, and gestures?
- Is your reaction to the speech similar to other audience members'?

2.3 DEBATE

A debate is a balanced argument covering both sides of an issue. In a debate, two teams compete to win the support of the audience. In a formal debate, two teams, each with two members, present their arguments on a given proposition or policy statement. One team argues for the proposition or statement and the other argues against it. Each debater must consider the proposition closely and must research both sides of it. To argue persuasively either for or against a proposition, a debater must be familiar with both sides of the issue.

Use the following guidelines to evaluate a debate.

Evaluate a Team in a Debate

- Did the team prove that a significant problem does or does not exist?
- How did the team convince you that the proposition is or is not the best solution to the problem?
- How effectively did the team present reasons and evidence supporting the case?
- How effectively did the team respond to arguments made by the opposing team?
- Did the speakers maintain eye contact and speak at an appropriate rate and volume?
- Did the speakers observe proper debate etiquette?

PRACTICE AND APPLY

View a political debate for a school, local, state, or national election. Use the preceding criteria to evaluate it.

2.4 NARRATIVE SPEECH

When you deliver a narrative speech, you tell a story or present a subject using a story-type format. A good narrative keeps an audience informed and entertained. It also allows you to deliver a message in a creative way.

Use the following guidelines to evaluate a speaker or your own presentation.

Evaluate a Narrative Speech

- Did the speaker choose a setting that makes sense and contributes to a believable narrative?
- Did the speaker locate incidents in specific places?
- Does the plot flow well?
- Did the speaker use words that convey the appropriate mood and tone?
- Did the speaker use sensory details that allow the audience to experience the sights, sounds, and smells of a scene and the specific actions, gestures, and thoughts of the characters?
- Did the speaker use a range of narrative devices to keep the audience interested?
- Is your reaction to the presentation similar to other audience members'?

2.5 DESCRIPTIVE SPEECH

Description is part of most presentations. In a descriptive speech, you describe a subject that you are personally involved with.

Use the following questions to evaluate a speaker or your own presentation.

Evaluate a Descriptive Speech
- Did the speaker make clear his or her point of view toward the subject being described?
- Did the speaker use sensory details, figurative language, and factual details?
- Did the speaker use tone and pitch to emphasize important details?
- Did the speaker use facial expressions to emphasize his or her feelings toward the subject?

For more information, see **Speaking and Listening: Presenting an Anecdote,** page 857.

2.6 ORAL INTERPRETATION

When you read a poem, play, or story aloud, your voice can bring the literature to life.

Oral Reading

An oral reading can be a monologue, during which you assume the voice of a character, the narrator, or the speaker in a poem. Or it may be a dialogue, during which you take the roles of two or more characters. Use the following techniques when giving an oral reading:

- **Speak Clearly** As you speak, pronounce your words carefully and clearly.
- **Control Your Volume** Make sure that you are loud enough to be heard but do not shout.
- **Pace Yourself** Read at a moderate rate, but vary your pace if it seems appropriate to the emotions of the character or to the action.
- **Vary Your Voice** Use a different voice for each character. Stress important words and phrases. Use your voice to express different emotions.

For more information, see **Speaking and Listening: Producing a Radio Dramatization,** page 165, and **Speaking and Listening: Oral Interpretation of a Poem,** page 615.

Dramatic Reading

In a dramatic reading, several speakers participate in the reading of a play or other work. Use the following techniques in your dramatic reading:

- **Prepare** Rehearse your material several times. Become familiar with the humorous and serious parts of the script. Develop a special voice that fits the personality of the character you portray.
- **Project** As you read your lines, aim your voice toward the back of the room to allow everyone to hear you.
- **Perform** React to the other characters as if you were hearing their lines for the first time. Deliver your own lines with the appropriate emotion. Use not only hand gestures and facial expressions but also other body movements to express your emotions.

For more information, see **Speaking and Listening: Dramatizing a Short Story,** page 427.

Use the following questions to evaluate an artistic performance by a peer or public presenter, a media presentation, or your own performance.

Evaluate an Oral Interpretation
- Did the speaker speak clearly?
- Did the speaker maintain eye contact with the audience?
- Did the speaker project his or her voice without shouting?
- Did the speaker vary the rate of speech appropriately to express emotion, mood, and action?
- Did the speaker use a different voice for the character(s)?
- Did the speaker stress important words or phrases?
- Did the speaker use voice, tone, and gestures to enhance meaning?

PRACTICE AND APPLY

Listen to an oral reading by a classmate or view a dramatic performance in a theater or on television. Use the preceding criteria to evaluate it.

2.7 ORAL SUMMARY

An oral summary includes the main ideas of a book or article. It also includes the most important details or evidence.

Use the following questions to evaluate a speaker or your own presentation.

Evaluate an Oral Summary

- Did the speaker introduce the subject clearly?
- Did the speaker present the main ideas early in the presentation?
- Did the speaker discuss the supporting details?
- Did the speaker show the audience that he or she really understood the piece?

PRACTICE AND APPLY

Listen as a classmate delivers an oral summary of a book or an article. Use the preceding criteria to evaluate the presentation.

3 Other Types of Communication

3.1 CONVERSATION

Conversations are informal, but they are important means of communicating. When two or more people exchange messages, it is equally important that each person contribute and actively listen.

3.2 GROUP DISCUSSION

Successful groups assign a role to each member. These roles distribute responsibility among the members and help keep discussions focused.

Role	Responsibilites
Chairperson	• Introduces topic • Explains goal or purpose • Participates in discussion and keeps it on track • Helps resolve conflicts • Helps group reach goal
Recorder	• Takes notes on discussion • Reports on suggestions and decisions • Organizes and writes up notes • Participates in discussion
Participants	• Contribute relevant facts or ideas to discussion • Respond constructively to one another's ideas • Reach agreement or vote on final decision

Guidelines for Discussion

- Be informed about the topic.
- Participate in the discussion.
- Ask questions and respond appropriately to questions.
- Don't talk while someone else is talking.
- Support statements and opinions with facts and examples.
- Listen attentively; be courteous and respectful of others' viewpoints.
- Work toward the goal; avoid getting sidetracked by unrelated topics.

3.3 INTERVIEW

An **interview** is a formal type of conversation with a definite purpose and goal. To conduct a successful interview, use the following guidelines:

Prepare for the Interview

- Select your interviewee carefully. Identify who has the kind of knowledge and experience you are looking for.
- Set a time, a date, and a place. Ask permission to tape-record the interview.
- Learn all you can about the person you will interview or the topic you want information on.

- Prepare a list of questions. Create questions that encourage detailed responses instead of yes-or-no answers. Arrange your questions in order from most important to least important.
- Arrive on time with everything you need.

Conduct the Interview

- Ask your questions clearly and listen to the responses carefully. Give the person whom you are interviewing plenty of time to answer.
- Be flexible; follow up on any responses you find interesting.
- Avoid arguments; be tactful and polite.
- Even if you tape an interview, take notes on important points.
- Thank the person for the interview, and ask if you can call with any follow-up questions.

Follow Up on the Interview

- Summarize your notes or make a written copy of the tape recording as soon as possible.
- If any points are unclear or if information is missing, call and ask more questions while the person is still available.
- Select the most appropriate quotations to support your ideas.
- If possible, have the person you interviewed review your work to make sure you haven't misrepresented what he or she said.
- Send a thank-you note to the person in appreciation of his or her time and effort.

*For more information, see **Speaking and Listening: Conducting an Interview,** page 293.*

Evaluate an Interview

You can determine how effective your interview was by asking yourself these questions:

- Did you get the type of information you were looking for?
- Were your most important questions answered to your satisfaction?
- Were you able to keep the interviewee focused on the subject?

---

4 Active Listening

Active listening is the process of receiving, interpreting, evaluating, and responding to a message. Whether you listen to a class discussion or a formal speech, use the following strategies to get as much as you can from the message.

Listening with a Purpose		
Situation	**Reason for Listening**	**How to Listen**
A friend tells a funny story.	enjoyment	Maintain eye contact; react to the joke.
You're watching a TV show called "Wolves of the Tundra."	for enjoyment, to learn something new	Listen for ideas that interest you or add to your knowledge.

Before Listening

- Learn what the topic is beforehand. You may need to read background information about the topic or learn new terms in order to understand the speaker's message.
- Think about what you know or want to know about the topic.
- Have a pen and paper to take notes.
- Establish a purpose for listening.

While Listening

- Focus your attention on the speaker. Your facial expressions and body language should demonstrate your interest in hearing the topic. Try to ignore uncomfortable room temperature and noise.
- Listen for the speaker's purpose (usually stated at the beginning), which alerts you to main ideas.
- To help you understand the speaker's message, listen for words or phrases that signal important points, such as *to begin with, in addition, most important, finally,* and *in conclusion.*
- Listen carefully for explanations of unfamiliar terms. Use these terms to help you understand the speaker's message.
- Listen for ideas that are repeated for emphasis.

- Take notes. Write down only the most important points.

- If possible, use an outline or list format to organize main ideas and supporting points.

- Note comparisons and contrasts, causes and effects, or problems and solutions.

- As you take notes, use phrases, abbreviations, and symbols to keep up with the speaker.

- To aid your understanding, note how the speaker uses word choice, voice pitch, posture, and gestures to convey meaning.

After Listening

- Ask questions to clarify anything that was unclear or confusing.

- Review your notes right away to make sure you understand what was said.

- Summarize and paraphrase the speaker's ideas.

- You may also wish to compare your interpretation of the speech with the interpretations of others who listened to it.

4.1 CRITICAL LISTENING

Critical listening involves evaluating a spoken message to judge its accuracy and reliability. You can use the following strategies as you listen to messages from public speakers:

- **Determine the Speaker's Purpose** Think about the background, viewpoint, and possible motives of the speaker. Separate facts from opinions. Listen carefully to details and evidence that a speaker uses to support the message.

- **Listen for the Main Idea** Figure out the speaker's main message before allowing yourself to be distracted by seemingly convincing facts and details.

- **Recognize the Use of Persuasive Techniques** Pay attention to a speaker's choice of words. Speakers may present information in a particular way to persuade you to buy a product or accept an idea. Persuasive devices such as glittering generalities, either/or reasoning, and bandwagon or snob appeal may represent faulty reasoning and provide misleading information.

*For more information, see **Recognizing Persuasive Techniques,** page R21.*

- **Observe Nonverbal Messages** A speaker's gestures, facial expressions, and tone of voice should reinforce the message. If they don't, you should doubt the speaker's sincerity and his or her message's reliability.

- **Give Appropriate Feedback** An effective speaker looks for verbal and nonverbal cues from you, the listener, to see how the message is being received. For example, if you understand or agree with the message, you might nod your head. If possible, during or after a presentation, ask questions to check your understanding.

4.2 VERBAL FEEDBACK

At times you will be asked to give direct feedback to a speaker. You may be asked to evaluate the way the speaker delivers the presentation as well as the content of the presentation.

Evaluate Delivery

- Did the speaker articulate words clearly and distinctly?
- Did the speaker pronounce words correctly?
- Did the speaker vary his or her rate?
- Did the speaker's voice sound natural and not strained?
- Was the speaker's voice loud enough?

Evaluate Content

Here's how to give constructive suggestions for improvement:

Be Specific Don't make statements like "Your charts need work." Offer concrete suggestions, such as "Please make the type bigger so we can read the poster from the back of the room."

Discuss Only the Most Important Points Don't overload the speaker with too much feedback about too many details. Focus on important points, such as

- Is the topic too advanced for the audience?
- Are the supporting details well organized?
- Is the conclusion weak?

Give Balanced Feedback Tell the speaker not only what didn't work but also what did work: "Consider dropping the last two slides, since you covered those points earlier. The first two slides got my attention."

Every day you are exposed to hundreds of images and messages from television, radio, movies, newspapers, and the Internet. What is the effect of all this media? What do you need to know to be a smart media consumer? Being media literate *means that you know what media products are, who created them, and what they mean. It means that you are able to analyze and evaluate media messages and how they influence you and your world. To become media literate, you'll need the tools to study media messages.*

MEDIA TOOLS

For more information, visit the **Media Center** at **ClassZone.com.**

❶ Five Core Concepts in Media Literacy

from The Center for Media Literacy

The five core concepts of media literacy provide you with the basic ideas you can consider when examining media messages.

All media messages are "constructed." All media messages are made by someone. In fact, they are carefully thought out and researched and have attitudes and values built into them. Much of the information that you use to make sense of the world comes from the media. Therefore, it is important to know how a medium is put together so you can better understand the message it conveys.

Media messages are constructed using a creative language with its own rules. Each means of communication—whether it is film, television, newspapers, magazines, radio, or the Internet—has its own language and design. Therefore, the message must use the language and design of the medium that delivers the message. Thus, the medium actually shapes the message. For example, a horror film may use music to heighten suspense, or a newspaper may use a big headline to signal the importance of a story. Understanding the language of each medium can increase your enjoyment of it as well as help you recognize any subtle attempt to persuade you.

Different people experience the same media messages differently. Personal factors such as age, education, and experience will affect the way a person responds to a media message. How many times has your interpretation of a film or book differed from that of a friend? Everyone interprets media messages differently.

Media have embedded values and points of view. Media messages carry underlying values, which are purposely built into them by the creators of the message. For example, a commercial's main purpose may be to persuade you to buy something, but the commercial may also aim to convince you that the product is important to a particular way of life. Understanding not only the main message but also any other points of view will help you decide whether to accept or reject the message.

Most media messages are constructed to gain profit and/or power. The creators of media messages often provide a commodity, such as information or entertainment, in order to make money. The bigger the audience, the more the media outlet can charge for advertising. Consequently, media outlets want to build large audiences in order to bring in more revenue from advertising. For example, a television network will create programming to appeal to the largest audience possible, in the hope that the viewer ratings will attract more advertising dollars.

2 Media Basics

2.1 MESSAGE

When a film or TV show is created, it becomes a media product. Each media product is created to send a **message,** or an expression of a belief or opinion, that serves a specific purpose. In order to understand the message, you will need to deconstruct it.

Deconstruction is the process of analyzing a media presentation. To analyze a media presentation you will need to ask why and how it was created, who created it, and whom it is trying to influence.

2.2 AUDIENCE

A **target audience** is the specific group of people that a product or presentation is aimed at. The members of a target audience usually share certain characteristics, such as age, gender, ethnic background, values, or lifestyle. For example, a target audience may be kids ages 11 to 14 who like to eat hamburgers.

Are you done yet?
Super-sized for super taste!
Hungry Boy Burgers
Get 2 for 99¢ for a short time only.

Demographics are the characteristics of a population, including age, gender, profession, income, education, ethnicity, and geographical location. Media decision makers use demographics to shape their content to suit the needs and tastes of a target audience.

2.3 PURPOSE

The **purpose,** or intent, of a media presentation is the reason it was made. All media products—from news programs to video games—are created for a specific purpose. Identifying why a media product was invented is the first step in understanding how it can influence you. The following chart shows purposes of different media products.

Purposes of Media Products	
Purpose	**Example**
Inform	news reports and articles, public service announcements, some Web sites
Persuade	advertisements, editorials, reviews, political cartoons
Entertain	most TV shows, films, recorded music; video games; most talk shows

Most media products have more than one purpose. For example, TV commercials are often entertaining, but their main purpose is to persuade you to buy something. If you aren't aware of all of a media products' purposes, you may become influenced without knowing it. This chart shows some examples.

Main and Other Purposes in Media		
Media Product	**Main Purpose**	**Other Purposes**
Sports coverage	To entertain	To inform you about sports or athletes
Advertisement	To persuade	To entertain you; to inform you about a product
News broadcast	To inform	To persuade you that an issue or idea is important

2.4 TYPES AND GENRES OF MEDIA

The term *media* refers to television, newspapers, magazines, radio, movies, and the Internet. Each is a **medium** or means for carrying information, entertainment, and advertisements to a large audience.

Each type of media has different characteristics, strengths, and weaknesses. The following chart shows how several types of media deliver their messages.

Type of Media	Characteristics
Newspaper Article	• Provides detailed information and dramatic photographs • Use **headlines** and **subheads** to give main ideas • Can't be updated until next edition or next day
Television News Report	• Uses an **announcer,** or "anchor," to guide viewers through the news report • Uses **video footage** to bring news to life or clarify what happened • Uses **graphics** to give information at a glance • Can be updated quickly
Documentary	• Tells about historic people and places, major events, and important social, political, or environmental issues • Uses **footage,** or shots of photographs, interviews, news reports, and film clips, to help viewers understand the subject • Features **interviews** of experts or people directly involved with the subject • Uses a **voice-over narrator,** the voice of an unseen speaker, who tells viewers why the subject is important and how the information about the subject is organized
Web Site	• Gives in-depth information on specialized subjects • Uses **text, still images,** and **video** • Allows users to select the information they want to receive by clicking on links • Allows users to see when the site was last updated • Can be updated quickly

*For more information, see **Types of Media**, page 10.*

2.5 PRODUCERS AND CREATORS

People who control the media are known as **gatekeepers.** Gatekeepers decide what information to share with the public and the ways it will be presented. The following diagram gives some examples.

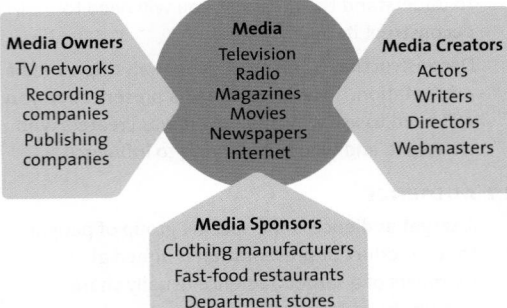

Media Owners
TV networks
Recording companies
Publishing companies

Media
Television
Radio
Magazines
Movies
Newspapers
Internet

Media Creators
Actors
Writers
Directors
Webmasters

Media Sponsors
Clothing manufacturers
Fast-food restaurants
Department stores

Media sponsors are companies that pay for their products to be advertised. It's important to be aware of sponsors and other gatekeepers, because they control much of what you see and hear. For example, if a soft-drink company sponsors a TV show, you probably won't see or hear about competing brands of soft drinks on that show.

2.6 INFLUENCE OF MEDIA

Everywhere you go, you're bombarded by the media—advertisements, newspapers, magazines, radio, and television. Different kinds of media are all competing for your attention, telling you, "Buy this product. Listen to this music. Read this story. Look at this image. Think about this opinion." The creators of these media products are selling messages. But they may also be sending subtle messages about values that they want you to believe in. For example, a car ad is meant to sell a car, but if you look closer, you will see that it is using a set of values, such as a luxurious lifestyle, to make the car attractive to the target audience. One message of the ad is that if you buy the car, you'll have the luxurious lifestyle. The other message is that the luxurious lifestyle is good and desirable. TV shows, movies, and news programs also convey values and beliefs.

Media can also shape your opinions about the world. For example, news about crime shapes our understanding about how much and what type of crime is prevalent in the world around us. TV news items, talk show interviews, and commercials may shape what we think of a political candidate, a celebrity, an ethnic group, a country, or a regional area. As a result, our knowledge of someone or someplace could be completely based on the information we receive from the television.

3 Film and TV

Films and television programs come in a variety of types. Films include comedies, dramas, documentaries, and animated features. Televison programs cover dramas, sitcoms, talk shows, reality shows, newscasts, and so on. Producers of films and producers of television programs rely on many of the same elements to make the action and settings seem real and to also affect the emotions of their audiences. Among these elements are scripts, visual and sound elements, special effects, and editing.

3.1 SCRIPT AND WRITTEN ELEMENTS

The writer and editor develop a story for television or film using a script and storyboard. A **script** is the text or words of a film or television show. A **storyboard** is a device used to plan the shooting of a movie or TV show. A storyboard is made up of drawings and brief descriptions of what is happening in each shot of a scene. The drawings of a storyboard help a director visualize how a finished scene might look before the scene is filmed. The following storyboard shows some scenes that a student created.

Shot 1
Marty is speeding down the street.

Shot 2
The hand moves on the clock.

*For more information, see **Media Study: Produce Your Own Media,** page 153.*

3.2 VISUAL ELEMENTS

Visual elements in film and television include camera shots and angles. A **camera shot** is a single, continuous view taken by a camera. A **camera angle** is the angle at which the camera is positioned during the recording of a shot or image. Each azis carefully planned to create an effect. The chart shows what different shots are used for.

Camera Shot/Angle	Effect
Establishing shot introduces viewers to the location of a scene, usually by presenting a wide view of an area	establishes the setting of a film
Close-up shot shows a close view of a person or object	helps to create emotion and make viewers feel as if they know the character
Medium shot shows a view wider than a close-up but narrower than an establishing or long shot	shows part of an object, or a character from the knees or waist up
Long shot gives a wide view of a scene, showing the full figure(s) of a person or group and the surroundings	allows the viewer to see the "big picture" and shows the relationship between characters and the environment
Reaction shot shows in some way what he or she sees	allows the viewer to see how the subject feels in order to create empathy in the viewer
Low-angle shot looks up at an object or person	makes a character, object, or scene appear more important or threatening
High-angle shot looks down on an object or person	makes a character, object, or scene seem weak or unimportant
Point-of-view (POV) shot shows a part of the story through a character's eyes	helps viewers identify with that character

3.3 SOUND ELEMENTS

Sound elements in film and television include music, voice-over, and sound effects.

Music may be used to set the mood and atmosphere in a scene. Music can have a powerful effect on the way viewers feel about a story. For example, fast-paced music helps viewers feel excited during an action scene.

Voice-over is the voice of the unseen commentator or narrator of a film, TV program, or commercial.

Sound effects are the sounds added to films, TV programs, and commercials during the editing process. Sound effects, such as laugh tracks or the sounds of punches in a fight scene, can create humor, emphasize a point, or contribute to the mood.

3.4 SPECIAL EFFECTS

Special effects include computer-generated animation, manipulated video images, and fast- or slow-motion sequences in films, TV programs, and commercials.

Animation on film involves the frame-by-frame photography of a series of drawings or objects. When these frames are projected—at a rate of 24 per second—the illusion of movement is achieved.

A **split screen** is a special-effects shot in which two or more separate images are shown in the same frame. One example is when two people, actually a distance apart, are shown talking to each other.

3.5 EDITING

Editing is the process of selecting and arranging shots in a sequence. Moviemakers put shots together in ways that help you follow the action of a story. The editor decides which scenes or shots to use, as well as the length of each shot, the number of shots, and their sequence.

Cut is the transition from one shot to another. To create excitement, editors often use quick cuts, which are a series of short shots strung together.

Dissolve is a device in which one scene fades into another.

Fade-in is a device in which a white or black shot fades in to reveal the beginning of a new scene.

Fade-out is a device in which a shot fades to darkness to end a scene.

Jump cut is an abrupt and jarring change from one shot to another. A jump cut shows a break in time.

Pace is the length of time each shot stays on the screen and the rhythm that is created by the transitions between shots. Short, quick cuts create a fast pace in a story. Long cuts slow down a story.

4 News

The **news** is information on events, people, and places in your community, the region, the nation, and the world. It can be found in local newspapers, newscasts, online wire services, magazines, and documentaries. Because it's impossible to publish all the news that happens in one day in any one source, journalists have to make decisions about which stories will appear in newspapers and on newscasts. They use several factors to help them choose stories.

4.1 CHOOSING THE NEWS

Newsworthiness is the importance of an event or action that makes it worthy of media reporting. Journalists and their editors often use the following criteria in determining which stories should make the news:

Timeliness is the quality of being very current. Timely events usually take priority over previously reported events. For example, a car accident with deaths will be timely on the day it occurs. Because of its timeliness it may be on the front page of a newspaper or may be the lead story on a newscast.

Widespread impact is a characteristic of an event that could affect a number of people. The more widespread the impact of an event, the more likely it is to be newsworthy.

Proximity measures the nearness of an event to a particular city, region, or country. People tend to be more interested in stories that take place close to where they live and that thus may affect them directly.

Human interest is a quality of stories that cause readers or listeners to feel emotions such as happiness, anger, or sadness. People are interested in reading stories about other people.

Uniqueness is the condition of being the only one of a kind. Unique or uncommon events or circumstances are likely to be interesting to an audience.

Compelling video and **photographs** grab people's attention and stay in their minds.

4.2 REPORTING THE NEWS

While developing a news story, a journalist makes a variety of decisions about how to construct the story, such as what information to include and how to organize it. The following elements are commonly used in news stories:

5 *W*'s and *H* are the six questions reporters answer when writing news stories—*who, what, when, where, why,* and *how.* It is a journalist's job to answer these questions in any type of news report. These questions also provide a structure for writing and editing a story.

Inverted pyramid is the means of organizing information according to importance. In the inverted-pyramid diagram below, the most important information (the answers to the 5 *W*'s and *H*) appears at the top of the pyramid. The less important details appear at the bottom. Not all stories are reported using the inverted-pyramid form. The form remains popular, however, because it helps a reader to get the important information without reading the entire story. Notice the following example.

> Soft-drink makers announced that they would work to limit the availability of soft drinks in schools around the country.
>
> The industry feels it needs to help fight childhood obesity.
>
> The president of the Soft Drink Association formally announced the new policy last week.

Angle or slant is the point of view from which a story is written. Even an objective report must have an angle.

Consider these two headlines that describe the same house fire.

Family Heirlooms Destroyed in Fire

Firefighters Slow to Respond to Fire

The first headline focuses on a fact. The second headline focuses on an opinion and has a negative slant.

Standards for News Reporting

The ideal of journalism is to present news in a way that is objective, accurate, and thorough. The best news stories contain the following elements:

- **Objectivity** The story takes a balanced point of view on the issues. It is not biased, nor does it reflect a specific attitude or opinion.

- **Accuracy** The story presents factual information that can be verified.

- **Thoroughness** The story presents all sides of an issue. It includes background information, telling *who, what, when, where, why,* and *how.*

Balanced Versus Biased Reporting

Objectivity in news reporting can be measured by how balanced or biased the story is.

Balanced reporting represents all sides of an issue equally and fairly.

A balanced news story

- represents people and subjects in a neutral light

- treats all sides of an issue equally

- does not include inappropriate questions, such as "Will you seek counseling after this terrible tragedy?"

- does not show stereotypes or prejudice toward people of a particular race, gender, age, religion, or other group
- does not leave out important background information that is needed to establish a context or perspective

Biased reporting is reporting in which one side is favored over another or in which the subject is unfairly represented. Biased reporting may show an overly negative view of a subject, or it may encourage racial, gender, or other stereotypes and prejudices. Sometimes biased reporting is apparent in the journalist's choice of sources.

Sources are the people interviewed for the news report and also any written materials and documents the journalist used for background information. From each source, the journalist gets a different point of view. To decide whether news reporting is balanced or biased, you will need to pay attention to the sources. Consider a news story on a new snack food, for instance. If the journalist's only source is a representative from the company that made the snack, the report may be biased. But if the journalist also includes the perspective of someone neutral, such as a scientist who is studying the nutritional value of the snack, the report may be more balanced. The following chart shows which sources are reliable.

Sources for News Stories	
Reliable Sources	**Weak Sources**
• experts in a field • people directly affected by the reported event (eyewitnesses) • published reports that are specifically mentioned or shown	• unnamed or anonymous sources • people who are not involved in the reported event (for example, people who heard about a story from a friend) • research, data, or reports that are not specifically named or are referred to only in vague terms (for example, "Research shows that …")

5 Advertising

Advertising is a sponsor's paid use of various media to promote products, services, or ideas. Some common forms of advertising are shown in the chart.

Type of Ad	Description
Billboard	a large outdoor advertising sign
Print ad	typically appears in magazines and newspapers; uses eye-catching graphics and persuasive copy
Flyer	a print ad that is circulated by hand or mail
Infomercial	an extended ad on TV that usually includes detailed product information, demonstrations, and testimonials
Public service announcement	a message aired on radio or TV to promote ideas that are considered to be in the public interest
Political ad	broadcast on radio or TV to promote political candidates
Trailer	a short film promoting an upcoming movie, TV show, or video game

Marketing is the process of transferring products and services from producer to consumer. It involves determining the packaging and pricing of a product, how it will be promoted and advertised, and where it will be sold. One way companies market their products is by becoming media sponsors.

Sponsors pay for their products to be advertised. These companies hire advertising agencies to create and produce specific campaigns for their products. They then buy television or radio airtime or magazine, newspaper, or billboard space to feature ads where the target audience is sure to see them. Because selling time and space to advertisers produces much of the income the media need to function, the media need advertisers just as much as advertisers need the media.

Product placement is the intentional and identifiable featuring of brand-name products in movies, television shows, video games, and other media. The intention is to have viewers feel positive about a product because they see a favorite character using it. Another purpose may be to promote product recognition.

5.1 PERSUASIVE TECHNIQUES

Persuasive techniques are the methods used to convince an audience to buy a product or adopt an idea. Advertisers use a combination of visuals, sound, special effects, and words to persuade their target audience. Recognizing the following techniques can help you evaluate persuasive media messages and identify misleading information:

Emotional appeals use strong feelings, such as fear and pity, rather than facts to persuade consumers. An example is, "Is your home safe? ProAlarm Systems will make sure it is."

Bandwagon appeals use the argument that a person should believe or do something because "everyone else" does. These appeals take advantage of people's desire to be socially accepted by other people. An example of a bandwagon appeal is "More and more people are making the switch to Discountline long-distance service."

Slogans are memorable phrases used in advertising campaigns. Slogans substitute catchy phrases for facts.

Logical appeals rely on logic and facts, appealing to a consumer's reason and his or her respect for authority. Two examples of logical appeals are expert opinions and product comparison.

Celebrity ads use one of the following two categories of spokesperson:

• **Celebrity authorities** are experts in a particular field. Advertisers hope that audiences will transfer the respect or admiration they have for the person to the product. For example, a famous chef may endorse a particular brand of cookware. The manufacturers of the cookware want you to think that it is a good product because a cooking expert wouldn't endorse pots and pans that didn't perform well.

• **Celebrity spokespeople** are famous people who endorse a product. Advertisers hope that audiences will associate the product with the celebrity.

Product comparison is comparing between a product and its competition. Often mentioned by name, the competing product is portrayed as inferior. The intended effect is for people to question the quality of the competing product and to believe the featured product is better.

6 Elements of Design

The design of a media message is just as important as the words are in conveying the message. Like words, visuals are used to persuade, inform, and entertain.

Graphics and images, such as charts, diagrams, maps, timelines, photographs, illustrations, and symbols, present information that can be quickly and easily understood. The following basic elements are used to give meaning to visuals:

Color can be used to highlight important elements such as headlines and subheads. It can also create mood, because many colors have strong emotional or psychological impacts on the reader or viewer. For example, warm colors are often associated with happiness and comfort. Cool colors are often associated with feelings of peace and contentment or sometimes with sadness.

Lines—strokes or marks—can be thick or thin, long or short, and smooth or jagged. They can focus attention and create a feeling of depth. They can frame an object. They can also direct a viewer's eye or create a sense of motion.

Texture is the surface quality or appearance of an object. For example, an object's texture can be rough, wet, or shiny. Texture can be used to create contrast. It can also be used to make an object look "real." For example, a pattern on wrapping paper can create a feeling of depth even though the texture is only visual and cannot be felt.

Shape is the external outline of an object. Shapes can be used to symbolize living things or geometric objects. They can emphasize visual elements and add interest. Shapes can symbolize ideas.

Notice how this movie poster uses design elements.

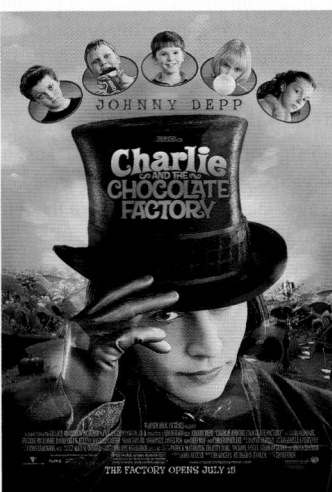

Lines The reader's eyes are led upward from the main image by the top hat, to the smaller images at the top of the poster.

Color Bright pinks, blues, and yellows suggest that the film may tell a happy story.

Shape The circles at the top of the poster add interest and also help to tell who the other characters in the movie are.

7 Evaluating Media Messages

By looking closely at media products, you can see how their messages influence your opinions and your buying habits. Here are six questions to ask about any media message:

Who made—and who sponsored—this message, and for what purpose? The source of the message is a clue to its purpose. If the source of the message is a private company, that company may be trying to sell you a product. If the source is a government agency, that agency may be trying to promote a program or particular point of view. To discover the purpose, think about why its creator paid for and produced the message.

Who is the target audience and how is the message specifically tailored to it? Think about the age group, ethnic group, gender, and/or profession the message is targeting. Decide how it relates to you.

What are the different techniques used to inform, persuade, entertain, and attract attention? Analyze the elements, such as humor, music, special effects, and graphics, that have been used to create the message. Think about how visual and sound effects, such as symbols, color, photographs, words, and music, support the purpose behind the message.

What messages are communicated (and/or implied) about certain people, places, events, behaviors, lifestyles, and so forth? The media try to influence who we are, what we believe in, how we view things, and what values we hold. Look or listen closely to determine whether certain types of behavior are being depicted and if judgments or values are communicated through those behaviors. What are the biases in the message?

How current, accurate, and believable is the information in this message? Think about the reputation of the source. Note the broadcast or publication date of the message and whether the message might change quickly. If a report or account is not supported by facts, authoritative sources, or eyewitness accounts, you should question the message.

What is left out of this message that might be important to know? Think about what the message is asking you to believe. Also think about what questions come to mind as you watch, read, or listen to the message.

Strategies and Practice for State and Standardized Tests

The test items in this section are modeled after test formats that are used on many state and standardized tests. The strategies presented here will help you prepare for these tests. This section offers general test-taking strategies and tips for answering multiple-choice items, as well as short-response and extended-response questions in critical reading and writing. It also includes guidelines and samples for essay writing. For each test, read the tips in the margin. Then apply the tips to the practice items. You can also apply the tips to Assessment Practice Tests in this book.

❶ General Test-Taking Strategies

- Arrive on time and be prepared. Be sure to bring either sharpened pencils with erasers or pens—whichever you are told to bring.

- If you have any questions, ask them before the test begins. Make sure you understand the test procedures, the timing, and the rules.

- Read the test directions carefully. Look at the passages and questions to get an overview of what is expected.

- Tackle the questions one at a time rather than thinking about the whole test.

- Look for main ideas as you read passages. They are often stated at the beginning or the end of a paragraph. Sometimes the main idea is implied.

- Refer back to the reading selections as needed. For example, if a question asks about an author's attitude, you might have to reread a passage for clues.

- If you are not sure of your answer, make a logical guess. You can often arrive at the correct answer by reasoning and eliminating wrong answers.

- As you fill in answers on your answer sheet, make sure you match each test item to its numbered space on the answer sheet.

- Don't look for patterns in the positions of correct choices.

- Only change an answer if you are sure your original choice is incorrect. If you do change an answer, erase your original choice neatly and thoroughly.

- Check your answers and reread your essay.

2 Critical Reading

As you advance through middle school and into high school, you will be exposed to different types of writing, both fiction and nonfiction. You will read novels, persuasive essays, poems, historical documents, and scientific or technical information. Tests will measure your ability to read and analyze these kinds of writings. Test selections can range in length from 100 words to 500 or 600 words.

Directions: Read the selection and then answer the questions on the following page.

SELECTION

On Friday I had my last day at Happy Valley Elementary School. On Saturday the moving truck came and took all our stuff to Hoboken, New Jersey, and we left our house in Happy Valley forever. On Sunday, our first day in the new house, the temperature was one hundred degrees Fahrenheit—the beginning of the hottest heat wave ever recorded in Hoboken in the month of June for 120 years.

One hundred and twenty years ago was when our Hoboken house had been built. This is what my parents did. They gave up a modern house in Happy Valley, New Jersey—a house with a front yard, a backyard, and trees,
10 on a street with similar houses and similar trees—to move to a brick house with no front yard, practically no backyard, and no trees, on a street with guys sitting on the steps and spitting on the sidewalk, and cars and buses running right past our door. And the Hoboken house was in rotten condition and cost three times as much as we got for our Happy Valley house.

My parents said we were going to fix up the house and have an "urban lifestyle." This is what an urban lifestyle is: My bike was stolen the first hour we were in town. And it was one hundred degrees Fahrenheit. My mother said she didn't want me growing up in a suburb. She said life was real in cities. I went upstairs to sit in my crummy 120-year-old room.

20 My father climbed the stairs to my room. "Egad! It's hot as an oven in here, old pal," he said.

My father says things like "egad" and "odds bodkin." They have no meaning. I simply tolerate these weirdnesses, along with so many things my parents do.

"Sorry about your bike, old man," my father said.

He calls me *old man,* also *old chap*. There is no explanation for this.

"We'll get you another bike, I promise," he said. "But could you possibly wait until your birthday? There are a lot of expenses fixing up the new house."

This was great. I could have a bike for my birthday, instead of some other present, which I would have gotten if I was not to get a bike, which I would
30 not be getting if the one I already had hadn't been stolen, which it probably would not have been if we had not moved to Hoboken, which was not my idea in the first place. . . .

Tips: Reading Text

1 Before you begin reading a passage, skim the questions that follow it to focus your reading.

2 Look for key ideas as you read. Change is a key idea in this passage. It is expressed in the opening lines.

3 Pay attention to the connotation of words. The examples that the narrator uses to define an "urban lifestyle" give the expression a negative connotation.

4 Draw conclusions. The narrator isn't happy with the move, but he tells his father that everything is fine. He probably doesn't want to hurt his father's feelings.

"That will be fine, Dad," I said.

"Good show, old man," my father said. "Now about this room. I don't see how you can stand it. Maybe you'd like us to drag your mattress into our room, where it's nice and cool." ──④

My parents' bedroom had a little dinky air conditioner that puffed air about three degrees cooler than what was outside. It was pathetic.

"I'll be fine here, Dad," I said.

40 "Good lad. Now do you want to help us scrape paint off the woodwork or just explore around?"

"I think I'll do some exploring," I said.

—from *Looking for Bobowicz*
Daniel Pinkwater

Directions: Answer these questions about the selection from *Looking for Bobowicz*.

① [stem]

1. What can you infer about the narrator from his description of the two houses in lines 8–19?

   A He is unhappy about moving.

   B He wants to run away.

   C He is spoiled.

   D He likes city life. ──④

2. Which statement best describes the *theme* of this passage? ②

   A Suburban life is better than city life.

   B Parents don't listen to their children.

   C Crime is a big part of urban life.

   D Change is difficult to accept.

3. In this passage, the narrator and his parents have different feelings about

   ③ [choices]

   A household chores

   B the benefits of city life

   C the importance of honesty

   D family finances

4. The summer heat wave in this passage symbolizes the ──⑤

   A danger of the city

   B narrator's intense feelings

   C run-down house

   D father's enthusiasm

Tips: Multiple Choice

A multiple-choice question consists of a stem and a set of choices. The stem is in the form of a question or an incomplete sentence. One of the choices correctly answers the question or completes the sentence. Many tests offer four answer choices, but no matter how many choices are given, you can use the same strategies to guide you to the best answer.

① Read the stem carefully and try to answer the question before you look at the choices.

② Pay attention to key words in the stem. They may direct you to the correct answer. Note that question 2 is looking for the *theme*, or main idea, of the passage.

③ Don't jump to conclusions about the correct answer until you've read all of the choices. In question 3, you might decide to stop at choice A, because the narrator does talk about the modern house he moved out of and the 120-year-old house he lives in now, but that is not the correct answer.

④ After reading all of the choices, eliminate any that you know are incorrect. In question 1, you can safely eliminate choice D, because the narrator expresses his strong dislike of city life throughout the passage.

⑤ Some questions ask you to interpret a symbol.

Answers: **1.** A, **2.** D, **3.** B, **4.** B

3 Vocabulary

Most standardized tests include items that ask about the meanings of words. Some questions might refer to a passage you just read, while others might provide a sentence or paragraph of context followed by the answer choices.

1. Which of the following words from the passage on pages R94–R95 has a negative connotation? ❶
   - **A** stuff (line 2)
   - **B** modern (line 8)
   - **C** egad (line 20)
   - **D** dinky (line 37)

2. Which word from the passage comes from the Latin root meaning "city"?
   - **A** house (line 3)
   - **B** street (line 10)
   - **C** sidewalk (line 12)
   - **D** urban (line 15) ❷

3. Which line from the passage contains a simile? ❸
   - **A** "She said life was real in cities." (lines 18–19)
   - **B** "It's hot as an oven in here, old pal" (lines 20–21)
   - **C** "Good show, old man" (line 34)
   - **D** "It was pathetic." (line 38)

4. Read this dictionary entry for the word *chap*. Which noun definition represents the meaning of *chap* as used in line 25 of the passage?

> **DEFINITION**
>
> *n.* **1.** The roughening of the skin caused especially by cold. **2.** (*Chiefly Brit.*) fellow. **3.** The face.

   - **A** *n.* meaning 1
   - **B** *n.* meaning 2
   - **C** *n.* meaning 3
   - **D** *v.* meaning 1 ❹

❹ Writing and Grammar

You will be asked to write essays and even research papers in middle school. When it comes to writing, good ideas aren't enough. You need to know how to express them. That requires knowledge of English grammar, sentence structure, and usage. To measure that skill, many standardized tests ask you to identify errors or to improve sentences and paragraphs.

> **Directions:** Read this passage and then answer the questions.

PASSAGE

❶   (1) On May 1 and October 1 you might see two or three moving trucks on a single city block. (2) These are the busiest moving days of the year. (3) The longest trucks are usually from companies that supply movers and sturdy packing boxes. (4) You have to reserve these trucks weeks in advance. (5) They won't be available. (6) Professional movers use thick pads <u>for furniture protection from scratches</u>. (7) Sometimes people try to save money by renting a truck and moving himself. (8) Their things often get broken because they aren't packed properly.

1. The correct coordinating conjunction to join sentences 4 and 5 is

❸
- **A**   but
- **B**   for
- **C**   or
- **D**   while

2. What is the best way to rewrite the underlined part of sentence 6?

❷
- **A**   to protect furniture from scratches
- **B**   for scratch protection on furniture
- **C**   for the protection of furniture from scratches
- **D**   in order to protect from scratches on furniture

❹ **3.** What change, if any, should be made to sentence 7?
- **A**   Change *try* to *trying*
- **B**   Change *renting* to *getting*
- **C**   Change *himself* to *themselves*
- **D**   Make no change ❻

❺ **4.** What change, if any, should be made to sentence 8?
- **A**   Change *their* to *there*
- **B**   Change *broken* to *broke*
- **C**   Change *aren't* to *are'nt*
- **D**   Make no change ❻

Tips: Grammar

❶ Read the entire passage to grasp its overall meaning. Pay particular attention to any underlined parts.

❷ Before choosing a revision, read through all of the choices to decide which one is best. Your selection should produce a sentence that is grammatically correct.

❸ If you are asked to combine sentences, think about how the ideas relate to each other. When you understand the connection between the thoughts, you will know how to join them. The word *but* (choice A) can be used to show how two different ideas are related, but it is not the right word to use to join sentences 4 and 5.

❹ Some items will test your knowledge of language conventions. Make sure that pronouns agree with antecedents and that verbs agree with subjects.

❺ Some items will also test your knowledge of commonly confused words. In test item 4, choice A is a possible revision. Read sentences carefully to determine how each word is used before deciding which choice is best.

❻ In test items 3 and 4, choice D says, "Make no change." Choose this answer only if the sentence is correct as it is originally written.

Answers: 1. C, **2.** A, **3.** C, **4.** D

5 Responding to Writing Prompts

Not all tests are multiple choice. Sometimes you have to develop your ideas into a paragraph or a short essay. You might be asked to interpret, summarize, or react to a reading selection.

> **Directions:** Reread the selection from *Looking for Bobowicz* on pages R94–R95 and follow the directions for the short and extended responses.

SHORT RESPONSE

Write a well-organized paragraph comparing and contrasting the narrator's old and new homes.

> **SAMPLE SHORT RESPONSE**
>
> The narrator's two homes are very different. **❶** In Happy Valley he lived on a tree-lined street in a quiet suburb. In Hoboken he lives in a noisy urban neighborhood where bicycles get stolen. The house in Happy Valley was modern and was surrounded by greenery. The house in Hoboken is an old, run-down building surrounded by busy streets. **❷** The name Happy Valley suggests a cool, rural locale that is free from the stifling heat and close quarters of Hoboken.

EXTENDED RESPONSE

Discuss in two or three paragraphs what the narrator's mother means when she says life is "real" in cities.

> **SAMPLE EXTENDED RESPONSE**
>
> When the narrator's mother says life is real in cities, she probably means that the city is a reflection of life itself. **❸**
>
> Variety is what makes a city real. As you travel through a big city you can hear many languages being spoken, and you can sample foods from different parts of the world. You can rub shoulders with executives on one street and panhandlers on the next. You find people living in penthouses, modest homes, and public housing. You see mosques, churches, and synagogues. **❹**
>
> The challenges of urban life are also very real. **❸** People in cities, including children, learn to cope with overcrowding, noise, air pollution, traffic, and crime. **❺**

Tips: Responding to Writing Prompts

Tips: Responding to Writing Prompts

❶ Short-response prompts are often fact based rather than interpretive. Get right to the point in your answer, and stick to the facts.

❷ Make sure that you write about the assigned topic. Support your answer with details from the passage, such as a quotation, a paraphrase, or an example.

❸ When you are writing an extended response, build your paragraphs around clear topic sentences that will pull your ideas together.

❹ If you are asked to interpret a passage, don't just copy the author's words. Try to express the ideas in your own words. Express your ideas clearly so that the reader understands your viewpoint.

❺ Proofread your response for errors in capitalization, punctuation, spelling, or grammar.

6 Writing an Essay

Many tests will ask you to read a prompt and write an essay in response to it. You might be asked to write a narrative, persuasive, or expository essay. You might be asked to write a story, summarize an article, or respond to a piece of writing. It is important to read the prompt carefully and look for direction words that tell you what to write about. Because of the time constraints, an impromptu essay will not be polished. It will represent a first draft. Even so, it should be complete. Essays are scored on the following criteria:

- **Focus** Establish a point of view in the opening paragraph. Stay with that topic throughout the essay.

- **Organization** Maintain a logical progression of ideas.

- **Support for ideas** Use details and examples to develop an argument or line of thinking.

- **Style/word choice** Use words accurately and vary sentences.

- **Grammar** Use standard English and proofread for errors.

Writing Prompt

In 2004, a bill was introduced to the California legislature that proposed lowering the voting age to 14. Under the "Training Wheels for Citizenship" concept, votes cast by 14- and 15-year-olds would be counted as one-fourth of a full vote, and those cast by 16- and 17-year-olds would be counted as one-half. Write a persuasive essay of four or five paragraphs supporting or rejecting this idea.

SAMPLE PERSUASIVE ESSAY

Lowering the voting age is not a good idea, especially if our votes wouldn't count as full votes. A lot of high school students aren't interested in politics. It seems that many adults aren't either, because less than half of them vote in most elections. Teenagers are focused on getting into college. Events on Capitol Hill seem a long way off. Most of us probably wouldn't vote even if we could. **❶ ❷**

Voter independence is another issue. I generally listen to my parents, but sometimes they have their ideas and I have mine. If I were allowed to vote, I'm afraid they would try to influence my decision. Voting is supposed to be private, but my mom can always get the truth out of me.

As for counting our votes as fractions of a vote, that is an insult. For teenagers to have an impact on an election, four times as many of us would have to vote. It's almost un-American, because our nation was founded on the idea that everyone's vote has the same weight, whether we are rich or poor.

A lot of political issues affect young people. Most of the people living in poverty, for example, are kids. And of course the government pays more attention to the needs of people who vote. But money also influences government policies, and money is one thing young people don't have. **❸**

In conclusion, young people lack the interest, the independence, and the economic power to make a difference in the voting booth. **❹**

Tips: Writing an Essay

Before you begin writing, take a minute or two to gather your thoughts. You don't need to prepare a complete outline, but write the main points you want to make. In the essay here on lowering the voting age, the lack of interest, independence, and equality of voters are key issues.

❶ When writing a persuasive essay, state your point of view in the introduction.

❷ Facts and examples make your writing come to life, no matter what the topic is. Use them in the body of your essay to clarify your points and to strengthen your arguments. The writer of this essay uses statistics to demonstrate voter apathy among adults.

❸ Try to consider the opposing point of view and respond to it. In the sample essay, the student notes that "the government pays more attention to the needs of people who vote."

❹ Make sure your essay has a conclusion, even if it's just a single sentence. A conclusion pulls your ideas together and lets the reader know you have finished.

❺ Allow time to reread what you have written. If you have to make a correction, do so neatly and legibly.

Act An act is a major division within a play, similar to a chapter in a book. Each act may be further divided into smaller sections, called scenes. Plays can have as many as five acts. *The Monsters Are Due on Maple Street* by Rod Serling has two acts.

Adventure Story An adventure story is a literary work in which action is the main element. An **adventure novel** usually focuses on a main character who is on a mission and is facing many challenges and choices.

Alliteration Alliteration is the repetition of consonant sounds at the beginning of words. Note the repetition of the *b* sound in these lines.

> Crusts of black burned buttered toast,
> Gristly bits of beefy roasts . . .
> —Shel Silverstein, "Sarah Cynthia Sylvia Stout Would
> Not Take the Garbage Out"

See pages 544, 594.

Allusion An allusion is a reference to a famous person, place, event, or work of literature. In the essay "The Only Girl in the World for Me," Bill Cosby makes an allusion to the poet John Keats.
See page 496.

Analogy An analogy is a point-by-point comparison between two things that are alike in some respect. Often, writers use analogies in nonfiction to explain unfamiliar subjects or ideas in terms of familiar ones.
See also **Extended Metaphor; Metaphor; Simile.**

Anecdote An anecdote is a short account of an event that is usually intended to entertain or make a point. In "Names/Nombres," Julia Alvarez uses an anecdote about arriving at the immigration office to show how her name began changing once she entered the United States.
See page 781.

Antagonist The antagonist is a force working against the protagonist, or main character, in a story, play, or novel. The antagonist is usually another character but can be a force of nature, society itself, or an internal force within the main character. In Michael Morpurgo's retelling of "Sir Gawain and the Green Knight," the Green Knight is the antagonist.
See page 671.
See also **Protagonist.**

Assonance Assonance is the repetition of vowel sounds within nonrhyming words. An example of assonance is the repetition of the *i* sound in the following line.

> is a diamond blind in the black belly of coal
> —Lucille Clifton, "the earth is a living thing"

Author's Perspective An author's perspective is the unique combination of ideas, values, feelings, and beliefs that influences the way the writer looks at a topic. **Tone,** or attitude, often reveals an author's perspective. Peter Benchley writes "Great White Sharks" from a perspective that reflects his fascination with the sea and his regret that his novel *Jaws* caused misconceptions about sharks.
See page 885.
See also **Author's Purpose; Tone.**

Author's Purpose A writer usually writes for one or more of these purposes: to express thoughts or feelings, to inform or explain, to persuade, and to entertain. For example, in his "Remarks at the Dedication of the Aerospace Medical Health Center," President John F. Kennedy's purpose was to persuade Americans that the United States should lead the world in space research.
See also **Author's Perspective.**

Autobiography An autobiography is a writer's account of his or her own life. In almost every case, it is told from the first-person point of view. Generally, an autobiography focuses on the most significant events and people in the writer's life over a period of time. Lance Armstrong's *It's Not About the Bike* is an autobiography.
See pages 8, 754, 792.
See also **Memoir.**

Ballad A ballad is a type of narrative poem that tells a story and was originally meant to be sung or recited. Because it tells a story, a ballad has a setting, a plot, and characters. **Folk ballads** were composed orally and handed down by word of mouth from generation to generation. "The Highwayman" by Alfred Noyes is an example of a **literary ballad,** which takes its form from the folk ballad but is not composed orally.

Biography A biography is the true account of a person's life, written by another person. As such, biographies are usually told from a third-person point of view. The writer of a biography usually researches his or her subject in order to present accurate information. The best biographers strive for honesty and balance in their accounts of their subjects' lives. William Jay Jacobs's "Eleanor Roosevelt" is an example of a biography.

Cast of Characters In the script of a play, a cast of characters is a list of all the characters in the play, usually in order of appearance. It may include a brief description of each character.

Character Characters are the people, animals, or imaginary creatures who take part in the action of a work of literature. Like real people, characters display certain qualities, or **character traits,** that develop and change over time, and they usually have **motivations,** or reasons, for their behaviors.

> **Main character:** Main characters are the most important characters in literary works. Generally, the plot of a short story focuses on one main character, but a novel may have several main characters.
>
> **Minor characters:** The less important characters in a literary work are known as minor characters. The story is not centered on them, but they help carry out the action of the story and help the reader learn more about the main character.
>
> **Dynamic character:** A dynamic character is one who undergoes important changes as a plot unfolds. The changes occur because of the character's actions and experiences in the story. The changes are usually internal and may be good or bad. Main characters are usually, though not always, dynamic.
>
> **Static character:** A static character is one who remains the same throughout a story. The character may experience events and have interactions with other characters, but he or she is not changed because of them.

See pages 5, 24, 176, 183.

See also **Characterization; Character Traits.**

Characterization The way a writer creates and develops characters is known as characterization. There are four basic methods of characterization:

- The writer may make direct comments about a character through the voice of the narrator.
- The writer may describe the character's physical appearance.
- The writer may present the character's own thoughts, speech, and actions.

- The writer may present thoughts, speech, and actions of other characters.

See pages 178, 241, 255, 259.

See also **Character; Character Traits.**

Character Traits Character traits are the qualities shown by a character. Traits may be physical (brown eyes) or expressions of personality (shyness). Writers reveal the traits of their characters through methods of characterization. Sometimes writers directly state a character's traits, but more often readers need to infer traits from a character's words, actions, thoughts, appearance, and relationships. Examples of words that describe traits include *courageous, humble, generous,* and *wild.*

Climax The climax stage is the point of greatest interest in a story or play. The climax usually occurs toward the end of a story, after the reader has understood the **conflict** and become emotionally involved with the characters. At the climax, the conflict is resolved and the outcome of the plot usually becomes clear.

See pages 26, 574.

See also **Plot.**

Comedy A comedy is a dramatic work that is light and often humorous in tone, usually ending happily with a peaceful resolution of the main conflict.

Conflict A conflict is a struggle between opposing forces. Almost every story has a main conflict—a conflict that is the story's focus. An **external conflict** involves a character who struggles against a force outside him- or herself, such as nature, a physical obstacle, or another character. An **internal conflict** is one that occurs within a character.

Examples: In Rudyard Kipling's "Rikki-tikki-tavi," the mongoose Rikki is in conflict with the cobras Nag and Nagaina. In Robert D. San Souci's retelling of *Young Arthur,* Arthur is torn between wanting to escape punishment when he thinks he has stolen the king's sword and wanting to accept responsibility as a true knight should.

See pages 5, 24, 63, 74, 661.

See also **Plot.**

Connotation A word's connotations are the ideas and feelings associated with the word, as opposed to its dictionary definition. For example, the word *mother,* in addition to its basic meaning ("a female parent"), has connotations of love, warmth, and security.

Couplet A couplet is a rhymed pair of lines. A couplet may be written in any rhythmic pattern.

> Masons, when they start upon a building,
> Are careful to test out the scaffolding;
> —Seamus Heaney, "Scaffolding"

See also **Stanza.**

Critical Essay *See* **Essay.**

Denotation A word's denotation is its dictionary definition.
See also **Connotation.**

Description Description is writing that helps a reader to picture events, objects, and characters. To create descriptions, writers often use **imagery**—words and phrases that appeal to the reader's senses.

Dialect A dialect is a form of a language that is spoken in a particular place or by a particular group of people. Dialects may feature unique pronunciations, vocabulary, and grammar. For example, when Antonio and Felix speak to each other in Piri Thomas's story "Amigo Brothers," they use dialect that reflects their Puerto Rican community in New York. Their dialect includes informal grammar and slang words drawn from both American Spanish and English.

> "Same here. It ain't natural not to think about the fight. I mean, we both are *cheverote* fighters, and we both want to win."

Dialogue Dialogue is written conversation between two or more characters. Writers use dialogue to bring characters to life and to give readers insights into the characters' qualities, traits, and reactions to other characters. In fiction, dialogue is usually set off with quotation marks. In drama, stories are told primarily through dialogue.

Diary A diary is a daily record of a writer's thoughts, experiences, and feelings. As such, it is a type of autobiographical writing. The terms *diary* and *journal* are often used synonymously.

Drama A drama, or play, is a form of literature meant to be performed by actors in front of an audience. In a drama, the characters' dialogue and actions tell the story. The written form of a play is known as a script. A script usually includes dialogue, a cast of characters, and stage directions that give instructions about performing the drama. The person who writes the drama is known as the playwright or dramatist.

Dynamic Character *See* **Character.**

Epic Poem An epic poem is a long narrative poem about the adventures of a hero whose actions reflect the ideals and values of a nation or a group of people.

Essay An essay is a short work of nonfiction that deals with a single subject. There are many types of essays. An **expository essay** presents or explains information and ideas. A **personal essay** usually reflects the writer's experiences, feelings, and personality. A **persuasive essay** attempts to convince the reader to adopt a certain viewpoint. A **critical essay** evaluates a situation or a work of art.
See pages 8, 494, 757.

Exaggeration An extreme overstatement of an idea is called an exaggeration. It is often used for purposes of emphasis or humor. In "Sally Ann Thunder Ann Whirlwind," Mary Pope Osborne exaggerates Sally's size, strength, and cleverness to create a humorous, memorable impression of the character.

Exposition Exposition is the first stage of a typical story plot. The exposition provides important background information and introduces the setting and the important characters. The conflict the characters face may also be introduced in the exposition, or it may be introduced later, in the rising action.
See pages 26, 31.
See also **Plot.**

Expository Essay *See* **Essay.**

Extended Metaphor An extended metaphor is a figure of speech that compares two essentially unlike things at some length and in several ways. It does not contain the word *like* or *as*.
See also **Metaphor.**

External Conflict *See* **Conflict.**

Fable A fable is a brief tale told to illustrate a moral or teach a lesson. Often the moral of a fable appears in a distinct and memorable statement near the tale's beginning or end. "The Race Between Toad and Donkey" by Roger D. Abrahams is an example of a fable from Jamaica.
See also **Moral.**

Falling Action The falling action is the stage of the plot in which the story begins to draw to a close. The falling action comes after the climax and before the resolution. Events in the falling action show the results of the important decision or action that happened at the climax. Tension eases as the falling action begins; however, the final outcome of the story is not yet fully worked out at this stage.

See page 26.

See also **Climax; Plot.**

Fantasy Fantasy is a type of fiction that is highly imaginative and portrays events, settings, or characters that are unrealistic. The setting might be a nonexistent world, the plot might involve magic or the supernatural, and the characters might have superhuman powers.

Farce Farce is a type of exaggerated comedy that features an absurd plot, ridiculous situations, and humorous dialogue. The main purpose of a farce is to keep an audience laughing. Comic devices typically used in farces include mistaken identity, wordplay (such as puns and double meanings), and exaggeration.

Fiction Fiction is prose writing that tells an imaginary story. The writer of a fictional work might invent all the events and characters or might base parts of the story on real people and events. The basic elements of fiction are plot, character, setting, and theme. Fiction includes both short stories and novels.

See also **Novel; Short Story.**

Figurative Language In figurative language, words are used in an imaginative way to express ideas that are not literally true. "Tasha's money is burning a hole in her pocket" is an example of figurative language. The sentence does not really mean that Tasha's pocket is on fire. Instead, it means that Tasha is anxious to spend her money. Figurative language is used for comparison, emphasis, and emotional effect.

See pages 546, 555, 601.

See also **Metaphor; Onomatopoeia; Personification; Simile.**

First-Person Point of View *See* **Point of View.**

Flashback In a literary work, a flashback is an interruption of the action to present events that took place at an earlier time. A flashback provides information that can help a reader better understand a character's current situation.

Example: In "The Last Dog," Katherine Paterson uses flashback to explain how Brock became interested in the "ancient fictions" and the world outside the dome.

Foil A foil is a character who provides a striking contrast to another character. By using a foil, a writer can call attention to certain traits possessed by a main character or simply enhance a character by contrast. In Avi's "What Do Fish Have to Do with Anything?" the mother acts as a foil to the main character, Willie.

Folklore The traditions, customs, and stories that are passed down within a culture are known as its folklore. Folklore includes various types of literature, such as legends, folk tales, myths, trickster tales, and fables.

See **Fable; Folk Tale; Myth.**

Folk Tale A folk tale is a story that has been passed from generation to generation by word of mouth. Folk tales may be set in the distant past and involve supernatural events. The characters in them may be animals, people, or superhuman beings. "Waters of Gold" is an example of a folk tale.

Foreshadowing Foreshadowing occurs when a writer provides hints that suggest future events in a story. Foreshadowing creates suspense and makes readers eager to find out what will happen. For example, in the myth "Icarus and Daedalus," Daedalus' warnings about flying close to the sun hint at Icarus' fate.

Form The structure or organization of a work of writing is often called its form. The form of a poem includes the arrangement of its words and lines on the page.

Free Verse Poetry without regular patterns of rhyme and rhythm is called free verse. Some poets use free verse to capture the sounds and rhythms of ordinary speech. The poem "The Names" by Billy Collins is written in free verse.

> Yesterday, I lay awake in the palm of the night.
> A soft rain stole in, unhelped by any breeze,
> And when I saw the silver glaze on the windows,
> I started with A, with Ackerman, as it happened,
> Then Baxter and Calabro, . . .
> —Billy Collins, "The Names"

See pages 542, 549.

See also **Rhyme.**

Genre The term *genre* refers to a category in which a work of literature is classified. The major genres in literature are fiction, nonfiction, poetry, and drama.

Haiku Haiku is a form of Japanese poetry in which 17 syllables are arranged in three lines of 5, 7, and 5 syllables. The rules of haiku are strict. In addition to following the syllabic count, the poet must create a clear picture that will evoke a strong emotional response in the reader. Nature is a particularly important source of inspiration for Japanese haiku poets, and details from nature are often the subjects of their poems.

> On sweet plum blossoms
> The sun rises suddenly.
> Look, a mountain path!
>
> —Bashō

Hero A hero is a main character or protagonist in a story. In older literary works, heroes tend to be better than ordinary humans. They are typically courageous, strong, honorable, and intelligent. They are protectors of society who hold back the forces of evil and fight to make the world a better place. In modern literature, a hero may simply be the most important character in a story. Such a hero is often an ordinary person with ordinary problems.

Historical Dramas Historical dramas are plays that take place in the past and are based on real events. In many of these plays, the characters are also based on real historical figures. The dialogue and the action, however, are mostly created by the playwright.

Historical Fiction A short story or a novel can be called historical fiction when it is set in the past and includes real places and real events of historical importance. The novel *Crispin: The Cross of Lead* by Avi is an example of historical fiction.
See page 686.

Humor Humor is a quality that provokes laughter or amusement. Writers create humor through exaggeration, amusing descriptions, irony, and witty and insightful dialogue. In his essay "The Only Girl in the World for Me," Bill Cosby uses humor to tell the story of the absurd things he did to impress his first girlfriend.
See pages 496, 593.

Hyperbole Hyperbole is a figure of speech in which the truth is exaggerated for emphasis or humorous effect.

Idiom An idiom is an expression that has a meaning different from the meaning of its individual words. For example, "to go to the dogs" is an idiom meaning "to go to ruin."

Imagery Imagery consists of words and phrases that appeal to a reader's five senses. Writers use sensory details to help the reader imagine how things look, feel, smell, sound, and taste.

> When the sun paints the desert
> with its gold,
> I climb the hills.
> Wind runs round boulders, ruffles
> my hair. . . .
>
> —Pat Mora, "Gold"

See pages 546, 549, 559.

Internal Conflict *See* **Conflict.**

Interview An interview is a conversation conducted by a writer or reporter, in which facts or statements are elicited from another person, recorded, and then broadcast or published. This book includes an interview with Ray Bradbury.
See page 462.

Irony Irony is a contrast between what is expected and what actually exists or happens. The last line of Dorothy Parker's "Song for an April Dusk," which changes the meaning of the poem, is an example of irony.
See page 509.

Journal *See* **Diary.**

Legend A legend is a story handed down from the past about a specific person, usually someone of heroic accomplishments. Legends usually have some basis in historical fact. *Young Arthur* by Robert D. San Souci is an example of a legend.

Limerick A limerick is a short, humorous poem composed of five lines. It usually has the rhyme scheme *aabba*, created by two rhyming couplets followed by a fifth line that rhymes with the first couplet. A limerick typically has a sing-song rhythm.

> There was an old man with a light,   *a*
> Who was dressed in a garment of white;   *a*
> He held a small candle,   *b*
> With never a handle,   *b*
> And danced all the merry long night.   *a*
>
> —Edward Lear

Lyric Poetry Lyric poetry is poetry that presents the personal thoughts and feelings of a single speaker. Most poems, other than narrative poems, are lyric poems. Lyric poetry can be in a variety of forms and cover many subjects, from love and death to everyday experiences. Mary Oliver's "Sleeping in the Forest" is an example of a lyric poem.

Memoir A memoir is a form of autobiographical writing in which a writer shares his or her personal experiences and observations of significant events or people. Often informal or even intimate in tone, memoirs usually give readers insight into the impact of historical events on people's lives. *An American Childhood* by Annie Dillard is a memoir.

See page 119.

See also **Autobiography.**

Metaphor A metaphor is a comparison of two things that are basically unlike but have some qualities in common. Unlike a simile, a metaphor does not contain the word *like* or *as.* In "The Delight Song of Tsoai-Talee," the speaker of the poem compares himself to different things in nature, including "a feather on the bright sky" and "the hunger of a young wolf."

See pages 546, 601.

See also **Extended Metaphor; Figurative Language; Simile.**

Meter In poetry, meter is the regular pattern of stressed (ˊ) and unstressed (˘) syllables. Although poems have rhythm, not all poems have regular meter. Each unit of meter is known as a **foot** and is made up of one stressed syllable and one or two unstressed syllables. Notice the meter marked in the following lines.

> The wind was a torrent of darkness among the gusty trees.
> The moon was a ghostly galleon tossed upon cloudy seas.
> —Alfred Noyes, "The Highwayman"

See pages 544, 571.
See also **Rhythm.**

Minor Character *See* **Character.**

Mood Mood is the feeling or atmosphere that a writer creates for the reader. Descriptive words, imagery, and figurative language all influence the mood of a work. In "Dark They Were, and Golden-Eyed," Ray Bradbury creates a mood of fearfulness and dread.

See pages 438, 445, 601.
See also **Tone.**

Moral A moral is a lesson that a story teaches. A moral is often stated at the end of a fable. For example, the stated moral of the Liberian fable "Two Ways to Count to Ten" is "It is not always the biggest nor the strongest, but sometimes the cleverest who wins the prize."
See also **Fable.**

Motivation *See* **Character.**

Myth A myth is a traditional story that attempts to answer basic questions about human nature, origins of the world, mysteries of nature, and social customs. For example, "Prometheus" is a Greek myth that explains how humans received the gift of fire.

Narrative Nonfiction Narrative nonfiction is writing that reads much like fiction, except that the characters, setting, and plot are real rather than imaginary. Narrative nonfiction includes autobiographies, biographies, and memoirs. *Exploring the Titanic* by Robert D. Ballard is an example of narrative nonfiction.

Narrative Poetry Poetry that tells a story is called narrative poetry. Like fiction, a narrative poem contains characters, a setting, and a plot. It might also contain such elements of poetry as rhyme, rhythm, imagery, and figurative language. Ernest Lawrence Thayer's "Casey at the Bat" is a narrative poem.

Narrator The narrator is the voice that tells a story. Sometimes the narrator is a character in the story. At other times, the narrator is an outside voice created by the writer. The narrator is not the same as the writer.

An **unreliable narrator** is one who tells a story or interprets events in a way that makes readers doubt what he or she is saying. An unreliable narrator is usually a character in the story. The narrator may be unreliable for a number of different reasons. For example, the narrator may not have all the facts or may be too young to understand the situation.
See also **Point of View.**

Nonfiction Nonfiction is writing that tells about real people, places, and events. Unlike fiction, nonfiction is mainly written to convey factual information. Nonfiction includes a wide range of writing—newspaper articles, letters, essays, biographies, movie reviews, speeches, true-life adventure stories, advertising, and more.

Novel A novel is a long work of fiction. Like a short story, a novel is the product of a writer's imagination. Because a novel is considerably longer than a short story, a novelist can develop the characters and story line more thoroughly.
See also **Fiction.**

Ode An ode is a type of lyric poem that deals with serious themes, such as justice, truth, or beauty.

Onomatopoeia Onomatopoeia is the use of words whose sounds echo their meanings, such as *buzz, whisper, gargle,* and *murmur.* In "Amigo Brothers," the word *bong* is used to indicate the bell sounding at the beginning and end of each round of the boxing match.

> *Bong! Bong! Bong!* **The bell sounded over and over again.**
> —Piri Thomas, "Amigo Brothers"

Oral Literature Oral literature consists of stories that have been passed down by word of mouth from generation to generation. Oral literature includes folk tales, legends, and myths. In more recent times, some examples of oral literature have been written down or recorded so that the stories can be preserved.

Personal Essay *See* **Essay.**

Personification The giving of human qualities to an animal, object, or idea is known as personification. In "Rikki-tikki-tavi," for example, the animals are personified. They have conversations with each other as if they were human.

> **"Don't kill me," said Chuchundra, almost weeping. "Rikki-tikki, don't kill me!"**
> **"Do you think a snake killer kills muskrats?" said Rikki-tikki scornfully.**
> —Rudyard Kipling, "Rikki-tikki-tavi"

See pages 74, 546.
See also **Figurative Language.**

Persuasive Essay *See* **Essay.**

Play *See* **Drama.**

Playwright *See* **Drama.**

Plot The series of events in a story is called the plot. The plot usually centers on a **conflict,** or struggle, faced by the main character. The action that the characters take to solve the problem builds toward a climax in the story. At this point, or shortly afterward, the problem is solved and the story ends. Most story plots have five stages: exposition, rising action, climax, falling action, and resolution.
See pages 5, 26, 31.
See also **Climax; Exposition; Falling Action; Rising Action.**

Poetry Poetry is a type of literature in which words are carefully chosen and arranged to create certain effects. Poets use a variety of sound devices, imagery, and figurative language to express emotions and ideas.
See also **Alliteration; Assonance; Ballad; Free Verse; Imagery; Meter; Narrative Poetry; Rhyme; Rhythm; Stanza.**

Point of View Point of view refers to how a writer chooses to narrate a story. When a story is told from the **first-person** point of view, the narrator is a character in the story and uses first-person pronouns, such as *I, me,* and *we.* In a story told from the **third-person** point of view, the narrator is not a character. Third-person narration makes use of pronouns such as *he, she, it,* and *they.* A writer's choice of narrator affects the information readers receive.

It is also important to consider whether a writer is writing from a **subjective** or an **objective** point of view. When writing from a subjective point of view, the writer includes personal opinions, feelings, and beliefs. When writing from an objective point of view, the writer leaves out personal opinions and instead presents information in a straightforward, unbiased way.
See pages 176, 217, 227.
See also **Narrator.**

Prop The word *prop,* originally an abbreviation of the word *property,* refers to any physical object that is used in a drama. In the play based on Charles Dickens's *A Christmas Carol,* the props include a turkey and a dove.

Prose The word *prose* refers to all forms of writing that are not in verse form. The term may be used to describe very different forms of writing—short stories as well as essays, for example.

Protagonist A protagonist is the main character in a story, play, or novel. The protagonist is involved in the main conflict of the story. Usually, the protagonist undergoes changes as the plot runs its course. In "A Retrieved Reformation" by O. Henry, Jimmy Valentine is the protagonist.

Radio Play A radio play is a drama that is written specifically to be broadcast over the radio. Because the audience is not meant to see a radio play, sound effects are often used to help listeners imagine the setting and the action. The stage directions in the play's script indicate the sound effects.

Recurring Theme *See* **Theme.**

Refrain A refrain is one or more lines repeated in each stanza of a poem.

See also **Stanza.**

Repetition Repetition is a technique in which a sound, word, phrase, or line is repeated for emphasis or unity. Repetition often helps to reinforce meaning and create an appealing rhythm. Note how the use of repetition in the following lines emphasizes the rhythm of battle.

> Cannon to right of them,
> Cannon to left of them,
> Cannon in front of them
> —Alfred, Lord Tennyson, "The Charge of the Light Brigade"

See page 129.

See also **Alliteration; Sound Devices.**

Resolution *See* **Falling Action.**

Rhyme Rhyme is the repetition of sounds at the end of words. Words rhyme when their accented vowels and the letters that follow have identical sounds. *Cat* and *hat* rhyme, as do *feather* and *leather.* The most common type of rhyme in poetry is called **end rhyme,** in which rhyming words come at the ends of lines. Rhyme that occurs within a line of poetry is called **internal rhyme.** The following lines include examples of end rhyme.

> 'Twas brillig, and the slithy toves
> Did gyre and gimble in the wabe:
> All mimsy were the borogroves,
> And the mome raths outgrabe.
> —Lewis Carroll, "Jabberwocky"

See pages 129, 544, 571, 592.

Rhyme Scheme A rhyme scheme is a pattern of end rhymes in a poem. A rhyme scheme is noted by assigning a letter of the alphabet, beginning with *a,* to each line. Lines that rhyme are given the same letter.

> It was many and many a year ago,   *a*
>   In a kingdom by the sea,   *b*
> That a maiden there lived whom you may know   *a*
>   By the name of Annabel Lee;   *b*
>   —Edgar Allan Poe, "Annabel Lee"

See pages 563, 567.

Rhythm Rhythm is a pattern of stressed and unstressed syllables in a line of poetry. Poets use rhythm to bring out the musical quality of language, to emphasize ideas, and to create moods. Devices such as alliteration, rhyme, assonance, and consonance often contribute to creating rhythm.

See pages 129, 544.

See also **Meter.**

Rising Action The rising action is the stage of the plot that develops the **conflict,** or struggle. During this stage, events occur that make the conflict more complicated. The events in the rising action build toward a **climax,** or turning point.

See page 26.

See also **Plot.**

Scene In drama, the action is often divided into acts and scenes. Each scene presents an episode of the play's plot and typically occurs at a single place and time.

See also **Act.**

Scenery Scenery is a painted backdrop or other structures used to create the setting for a play.

Science Fiction Science fiction is fiction in which a writer explores unexpected possibilities of the past or the future, using known scientific data and theories as well as his or her creative imagination. Most science fiction writers create believable worlds, although some create fantasy worlds that have familiar elements. Ray Bradbury, the author of "Dark They Were, and Golden-Eyed," is a famous writer of science fiction.

See also **Fantasy.**

Screenplay A screenplay is a play written for film.

Script The text of a play, film, or broadcast is called a script.

Sensory Details Sensory details are words and phrases that appeal to the reader's senses of sight, hearing, touch, smell, and taste. Note the sensory details in the following line. These details appeal to the senses of touch and smell.

> There was a cool breeze blowing and a sweet smell of mesquite fruit in the air, but I didn't appreciate it.
> —Marta Salinas, "The Scholarship Jacket"

See also **Imagery.**

Setting The setting of a story, poem, or play is the time and place of the action. Sometimes the setting is clear and well-defined. At other times, it is left to the reader's imagination. Elements of setting include geographic location, historical period (past, present, or future), season, time of day, and culture.
See pages 5, 24, 43.

Short Story A short story is a work of fiction that centers on a single idea and can be read in one sitting. Generally, a short story has one main conflict that involves the characters and keeps the story moving.
See also **Fiction.**

Simile A simile is a figure of speech that makes a comparison between two unlike things using the word *like* or *as*.

> The fingers were all there, but <u>like dead leaves that never fell</u>, the ring and little fingers were rigid and curled, the others barely moved.
> —Chaim Potok, "Zebra"

See pages 184, 546.
See also **Figurative Language; Metaphor.**

Sonnet A sonnet is a poem that has a formal structure, containing 14 lines and a specific rhyme scheme and meter. The sonnet, which means "little song," can be used for a variety of topics.
See also **Rhyme Scheme.**

Sound Devices Sound devices are ways of using words for the sound qualities they create. Sound devices can help convey meaning and mood in a writer's work. Some common sound devices include **alliteration, assonance, meter, onomatopoeia, repetition, rhyme,** and **rhythm.**
See pages 544, 563, 593.
See also **Alliteration; Assonance; Meter; Onomatopoeia; Repetition; Rhyme; Rhythm.**

Speaker In poetry the speaker is the voice that "talks" to the reader, similar to the narrator in fiction. The speaker is not necessarily the poet. For example, in Carl Sandburg's "Washington Monument by Night," the experiences described may or may not have happened to the poet.
See pages 509, 542, 563, 845.

Speech A speech is a talk or public address. The purpose of a speech may be to entertain, to explain, to persuade, to inspire, or any combination of these purposes. President John F. Kennedy's speech "Remarks at the Dedication of the Aerospace Medical Health Center" was written and delivered in order to persuade his audience.
See pages 8, 937.

Stage Directions In the script of a play, the instructions to the actors, director, and stage crew are called the stage directions. Stage directions might suggest scenery, lighting, sound effects, and ways for actors to move and speak. Stage directions often appear in parentheses and in italic type.

> (*As soon as* Scrooge *shouts, the* girl *and the* carolers *vanish and* Cratchit *begins to close up the shop.*)
> —Frederick Gaines, *A Christmas Carol*

See pages 7, 387.

Stanza A stanza is a group of two or more lines that form a unit in a poem. Each stanza may have the same number of lines, or the number of lines may vary.
See also **Couplet; Form; Poetry.**

Static Character *See* **Character.**

Stereotype In literature, characters who are defined by a single trait are known as stereotypes. Such characters do not usually demonstrate the complexities of real people. Familiar stereotypes in popular literature include the absent-minded professor and the busybody.

Structure The structure of a work of literature is the way in which it is put together. In poetry, structure involves the arrangement of words and lines to produce a desired effect. One structural unit in poetry is the stanza. In prose, structure involves the arrangement of such elements as sentences, paragraphs, and events. "Dark They Were, and Golden-Eyed," for example, has a circular structure, in which the end mirrors the beginning.

Style A style is a manner of writing. It involves how something is said rather than what is said. For example, "A Day's Wait" by Ernest Hemingway is written in a style that makes use of vivid verbs, precise nouns, long descriptive sentences, and realistic dialogue.

Surprise Ending A surprise ending is an unexpected plot twist at the end of a story. The surprise may be a sudden turn in the action or a piece of information that gives a different perspective to the entire story. The short story writer O. Henry is famous for using this device.
See page 228.

Suspense Suspense is a feeling of growing tension and excitement felt by a reader. Suspense makes a reader curious about the outcome of a story or an event within a story. A writer creates suspense by raising questions in the reader's mind. The use of **foreshadowing** is one way that writers create suspense.

See pages 73, 89, 99.

See also **Foreshadowing.**

Symbol A symbol is a person, a place, an object, or an activity that stands for something beyond itself. For example, a flag is a colored piece of cloth that stands for a country. A white dove is a bird that represents peace.

Example: In "What Do Fish Have to Do with Anything?" by Avi, money represents happiness, opportunity, and freedom to Willie's mother.

See pages 339, 583.

Tall Tale A tall tale is a humorously exaggerated story about impossible events, often involving the supernatural abilities of the main character. Stories about folk heroes such as Pecos Bill and Paul Bunyan are typical tall tales.

Teleplay A teleplay is a play written for television. In a teleplay, scenes can change quickly and dramatically. The camera can focus the viewer's attention on specific actions. The camera directions in teleplays are much like the stage directions in stage plays.

See page 135.

Theme A theme is a message about life or human nature that the writer shares with the reader. In many cases, readers must infer what the writer's message is. One way of figuring out a theme is to apply the lessons learned by the main characters to people in real life. For example, a theme of "A Crush" by Cynthia Rylant is that simple acts of kindness can make a positive difference in people's lives.

Recurring themes are themes found in a variety of works. For example, authors from different backgrounds might express similar themes having to do with the importance of family values. **Universal themes** are themes that are found throughout the literature of all time periods. For example, *The Lord of the Rings* contains a universal theme relating to the hero's search for truth, goodness, and honor.

See pages 5, 304, 327, 364.

See also **Moral.**

Third-Person Point of View *See* **Point of View.**

Title The title of a piece of writing is the name that is attached to it. A title often refers to an important aspect of

the work. For example, the title "The War of the Wall" refers to Lou and the narrator's conflict with the "painter lady."

Tone The tone of a literary work expresses the writer's attitude toward his or her subject. Words such as *angry, sad,* and *humorous* can be used to describe different tones. For example, the tone of Dave Barry's essay "Breaking the Ice" is humorous.

See pages 438, 495.

See also **Author's Perspective; Mood.**

Tragedy A tragedy is a dramatic work that presents the downfall of a dignified character or characters who are involved in historically or socially significant events. The events in a tragic plot are set in motion by a decision that is often an error in judgment on the part of the hero. Succeeding events are linked in a cause-and-effect relationship and lead inevitably to a disastrous conclusion, usually death. William Shakespeare's *Romeo and Juliet* is a famous tragedy.

Traits *See* **Character.**

Turning Point *See* **Climax.**

Understatement Understatement is a technique of creating emphasis by saying less than is actually or literally true. It is the opposite of **hyperbole,** or exaggeration. Understatement is often used to create a humorous effect.

Universal Theme *See* **Theme.**

Unreliable Narrator *See* **Narrator.**

Voice The term *voice* refers to a writer's unique use of language that allows a reader to "hear" a human personality in the writer's work. Elements of style that contribute to a writer's voice can reveal much about the author's personality, beliefs, and attitudes.

See page 18.

Word Choice The success of any writing depends on the writer's choice of words. Words not only communicate ideas but also help describe events, characters, settings, and so on. Word choice can make a writer's work sound formal or informal, serious or humorous. A writer must choose words carefully depending on the goal of the piece of writing. For example, a writer working on a science article would probably use technical, formal words; a writer trying to establish the setting in a short story would probably use more descriptive words.

See also **Style.**

Almanac *See* **Reference Works.**

Analogy An analogy is a comparison between two things that are alike in some way. Often, writers use analogies in nonfiction to explain an unfamiliar subject or idea by showing how it is like a familiar one.

Argument An argument is speaking or writing that expresses a position on a problem and supports it with reasons and evidence. An argument often takes into account other points of view, anticipating and answering objections that opponents might raise.
See also **Claim; Counterargument; Evidence.**

Assumption An assumption is an opinion or belief that is taken for granted. It can be about a specific situation, a person, or the world in general. Assumptions are often unstated.

Author's Message An author's message is the main idea or theme of a particular work.
See also **Main Idea; Theme,** *Glossary of Literary Terms, page R109.*

Author's Perspective *See Glossary of Literary Terms, page R100.*

Author's Position An author's position is his or her opinion on an issue or topic.
See also **Claim.**

Author's Purpose *See Glossary of Literary Terms, page R100.*

Autobiography *See Glossary of Literary Terms, page R100.*

Bias In a piece of writing, the author's bias is the side of an issue that he or she favors. Words with extremely positive or negative connotations are often a signal of an author's bias.

Bibliography A bibliography is a list of related books and other materials used to write a text. Bibliographies can be good sources for further study on a subject.
See also **Works Consulted.**

Biography *See Glossary of Literary Terms, page R100.*

Business Correspondence Business correspondence is written business communications such as business letters, e-mails, and memos. In general, business correspondence is brief, to the point, clear, courteous, and professional.

Cause and Effect Two events are related by cause and effect when one event brings about, or causes, the other. The event that happens first is the **cause;** the one that

follows is the **effect.** Cause and effect is also a way of organizing an entire piece of writing. It helps writers show the relationships between events or ideas.
See also **False Cause,** *Reading Handbook, page R24.*

Chronological Order Chronological order is the arrangement of events by their order of occurrence. This type of organization is used in fictional narratives and in historical writing, biography, and autobiography.

Claim In an argument, a claim is the writer's position on an issue or problem. Although an argument focuses on supporting one claim, a writer may make more than one claim in a text.

Clarify Clarifying is a reading strategy that helps readers understand or make clear what they are reading. Readers usually clarify by rereading, reading aloud, or discussing.

Classification Classification is a pattern of organization in which objects, ideas, and/or information are presented in groups, or classes, based on common characteristics.

Cliché A cliché is an overused expression. "Better late than never" and "hard as nails" are common examples. Good writers generally avoid clichés unless they are using them in dialogue to indicate something about a character's personality.

Compare and Contrast To compare and contrast is to identify the similarities and differences of two or more subjects. Compare and contrast is also a pattern of organizing an entire piece of writing.

Conclusion A conclusion is a statement of belief based on evidence, experience, and reasoning. A valid conclusion is one that logically follows from the facts or statements upon which it is based.

Connect Connecting is a reader's process of relating the content of a text to his or her own knowledge and experience.

Consumer Documents Consumer documents are printed materials that accompany products and services. They usually provide information about the use, care, operation, or assembly of the product or service they accompany. Some common consumer documents are applications, contracts, warranties, manuals, instructions, labels, brochures, and schedules.

Context Clues When you encounter an unfamiliar word, you can often use context clues to understand it. Context clues are the words or phrases surrounding the word that provide hints about the word's meaning.

Counterargument A counterargument is an argument made to oppose another argument. A good argument anticipates opposing viewpoints and provides counterarguments to disprove them.

Credibility Credibility is the believability or trustworthiness of a source and the information it provides.

Critical Review A critical review is an evaluation or critique by a reviewer, or critic. Types of reviews include film reviews, book reviews, music reviews, and art show reviews.

Database A database is a collection of information that can be quickly and easily accessed and searched and from which information can be easily retrieved. It is frequently presented in an electronic format.

Debate A debate is basically an argument—but a very structured one that requires a good deal of preparation. In school settings, debate usually is a formal contest in which two opposing teams defend and attack a proposition.
See also **Argument.**

Deductive Reasoning Deductive reasoning is a way of thinking that begins with a generalization, presents a specific situation, and then moves forward with facts and evidence toward a logical conclusion. The following passage has a deductive argument embedded in it: "All students in the math class must take the quiz on Friday. Since Lana is in the class, she had better show up." This deductive argument can be broken down as follows: generalization: All students in the math class must take the quiz on Friday; specific situation: Lana is a student who is in the math class; conclusion: Therefore, Lana must take the math quiz.
See also **Analyzing Logic and Reasoning,** *Reading Handbook, pages R22–R25.*

Dictionary *See* **Reference Works.**

Draw Conclusions To draw a conclusion is to make a judgment or arrive at a belief based on evidence, experience, and reasoning.

Editorial An editorial is an opinion piece that usually appears on the editorial page of a newspaper or as part of a news broadcast. The editorial section of the newspaper presents opinions rather than objective news reports.
See also **Op/Ed Piece.**

Either/Or Fallacy An either/or fallacy is a statement that suggests that there are only two choices available in a situation when in fact there are more than two.
See also **Identifying Faulty Reasoning,** *Reading Handbook, page R24.*

Emotional Appeals Emotional appeals are messages that create strong feelings to make a point. An appeal to fear is a message that taps into people's fear of losing their safety or security. An appeal to pity is a message that taps into people's sympathy and compassion for others to build support for an idea, a cause, or a proposed action. An appeal to vanity is a message that attempts to persuade by tapping into people's desire to feel good about themselves.
See also **Recognizing Persuasive Techniques,** *Reading Handbook, pages R21–R22.*

Encyclopedia *See* **Reference Works.**

Essay *See Glossary of Literary Terms, page R102.*

Evaluate To evaluate is to examine something carefully and to judge its value or worth. Evaluating is an important skill. A reader can evaluate the actions of a particular character, for example. A reader can also form opinions about the value of an entire work.

Evidence Evidence is a specific piece of information that supports a claim. Evidence can take the form of a fact, a quotation, an example, a statistic, or a personal experience, among other things.

Expository Essay *See* **Essay,** *Glossary of Literary Terms, page R102.*

Fact Versus Opinion A fact is a statement that can be proved, or verified. An opinion, on the other hand, is a statement that cannot be proved because it expresses a person's beliefs, feelings, or thoughts.
See also **Generalization; Inference.**

Fallacy A fallacy is an error of reasoning. Typically, a fallacy is based on an incorrect inference or a misuse of evidence.
See also **Either/Or Fallacy; Logical Appeal; Overgeneralization.**
See also **Identifying Faulty Reasoning,** *Reading Handbook, page R24.*

Faulty Reasoning *See* **Fallacy.**

Feature Article A feature article is a main article in a newspaper or a cover story in a magazine.

Generalization A generalization is a broad statement about a class or category of people, ideas, or things based on a study of, or a belief about, some of its members.
See also **Overgeneralization; Stereotyping.**

Government Publications Government publications are documents produced by government organizations. Pamphlets, brochures, and reports are just some of the many forms these publications take. Government publications can be good resources for a wide variety of topics.

Graphic Aid A graphic aid is a visual tool that is printed, handwritten, or drawn. Charts, diagrams, graphs, photographs, and maps are examples of graphic aids.
See also **Graphic Aids,** *Reading Handbook, pages R4–R7.*

Graphic Organizer A graphic organizer is a "word picture"—a visual illustration of a verbal statement—that helps a reader understand a text. Charts, tables, webs, and diagrams can all be graphic organizers. Graphic organizers and graphic aids can look the same. However, graphic organizers and graphic aids do differ in how they are used. Graphic aids help deliver important information to students using a text. Graphic organizers are actually created by students themselves. They help students understand the text or organize information.

Historical Documents Historical documents are writings that have played a significant role in human events. The Declaration of Independence, for example, is a historical document.

How-To Book A how-to book explains how to do something—usually an activity, a sport, or a household project.

Implied Main Idea *See* **Main Idea.**

Index The index of a book is an alphabetized list of important topics covered in the book and the page numbers on which they can be found. An index can be used to quickly find specific information about a topic.

Inductive Reasoning Inductive reasoning is the process of logical reasoning that starts with observations, examples, and facts and moves on to a general conclusion or principle.
See also **Analyzing Logic and Reasoning,** *Reading Handbook, pages R22–R25.*

Inference An inference is a logical guess that is made based on facts and one's own knowledge and experience.

Informational Text Informational text is writing that provides factual information. It often explains an idea or teaches a process. Examples include news reports, a science textbook, software instructions, and lab reports.

Internet The Internet is a global, interconnected system of computer networks that allows for communication through e-mail, listservs, and the World Wide Web. The Internet connects computers and computer users throughout the world.

Journal A journal is a periodical publication issued by a legal, medical, or other professional organization. The term may also be used to refer to a diary or daily record.

Loaded Language Loaded language consists of words with strongly positive or negative connotations, intended to influence a reader's or listener's attitude.

Logical Appeal A logical appeal is a way of writing or speaking that relies on logic and facts. It appeals to people's reasoning or intellect rather than to their values or emotions. Flawed logical appeals—that is, errors in reasoning—are called logical fallacies.
See also **Fallacy.**

Logical Argument A logical argument is an argument in which the logical relationship between the support and claim is sound.

Main Idea The main idea is the central or most important idea about a topic that a writer or speaker conveys. It can be the central idea of an entire work or of just a paragraph. Often, the main idea of a paragraph is expressed in a topic sentence. However, a main idea may just be implied, or suggested, by details. A main idea is typically supported by details.

Make Inferences *See* **Inference.**

Monitor Monitoring is the strategy of checking your comprehension as you read and modifying the strategies you are using to suit your needs. Monitoring often includes the following strategies: questioning, clarifying, visualizing, predicting, connecting, and rereading.

Narrative Nonfiction *See Glossary of Literary Terms, page R105.*

News Article A news article is writing that reports on a recent event. In newspapers, news articles are usually brief and to the point, presenting the most important facts first, followed by more detailed information.

Nonfiction *See Glossary of Literary Terms, page R105.*

Op/Ed Piece An op/ed piece is an opinion piece that typically appears opposite ("op") the editorial page of a newspaper. Unlike editorials, op/ed pieces are written and submitted by readers.

Organization *See* **Pattern of Organization.**

Overgeneralization An overgeneralization is a generalization that is too broad. You can often recognize overgeneralizations by the appearance of words and phrases such as *all, everyone, every time, any, anything, no one,* or *none.* An example is "None of the city's workers really cares about keeping the environment clean." In all probability, there are many exceptions. The writer can't possibly know the feelings of every city worker.
See also **Identifying Faulty Reasoning,** *Reading Handbook, page R24.*

Overview An overview is a short summary of a story, a speech, or an essay.

Paraphrase Paraphrasing is the restating of information in one's own words.
See also **Summarize.**

Pattern of Organization The term *pattern of organization* refers to the way ideas and information are arranged and organized. Patterns of organization include cause-and-effect, chronological, compare-and-contrast, classification, and problem-solution, among others.
See also **Cause and Effect; Chronological Order; Classification; Compare and Contrast; Problem-Solution Order; Sequential Order.**
See also **Reading Informational Texts: Patterns of Organization,** *Reading Handbook, pages R8–R13.*

Periodical A periodical is a magazine or other publication that is issued on a regular basis.

Personal Essay *See* **Essay,** *Glossary of Literary Terms, page R102.*

Persuasion Persuasion is the art of swaying others' feelings, beliefs, or actions. Persuasion normally appeals to both the mind and the emotions of readers.
See also **Emotional Appeals; Loaded Language; Logical Appeal.**
See also **Recognizing Persuasive Techniques,** *Reading Handbook, pages R21–R22.*

Predict Predicting is a reading strategy that involves using text clues to make a reasonable guess about what will happen next in a story.

Primary Source *See* **Sources.**

Prior Knowledge Prior knowledge is the knowledge a reader already possesses about a topic. This information might come from personal experiences, expert accounts, books, films, and other sources.

Problem-Solution Order Problem-solution order is a pattern of organization in which a problem is stated and analyzed and then one or more solutions are proposed and examined.

Propaganda Propaganda is a form of communication that may use false or misleading information.

Public Documents Public documents are documents that were written for the public to provide information that is of public interest or concern. They include government documents, speeches, signs, and rules and regulations.
See also **Government Publications.**

Reference Works Reference works are sources that contain facts and background information on a wide range of subjects. Most reference works are good sources of reliable information because they have been reviewed by experts. The following are some common reference works: encyclopedias, dictionaries, thesauri, almanacs, atlases, and directories.

Review *See* **Critical Review.**

Rhetorical Questions Rhetorical questions are those that have such obvious answers that they do not require a reply. Writers often use them to suggest that their claim is so obvious that everyone should agree with it.

Scanning Scanning is the process used to search through a text for a particular fact or piece of information. When you scan, you sweep your eyes across a page, looking for key words that may lead you to the information you want.

Secondary Source *See* **Sources.**

Sequential Order Sequential order is a pattern of organization that shows the order of steps or stages in a process.

Setting a Purpose The process of establishing specific reasons for reading a text is called setting a purpose. Readers can look at a text's title, headings, and illustrations to guess what it might be about. They can then use these guesses to figure out what they want to learn from reading the text.

Sidebar A sidebar is additional information set in a box alongside or within an article. Popular magazines often make use of sidebars.

Signal Words In a text, signal words are words and phrases that help show how events or ideas are related. Some common examples of signal words are *and, but, however, nevertheless, therefore,* and *in addition.*

Sources A source is anything that supplies information. **Primary sources** are materials written by people who witnessed or took part in an event. Letters, diaries, autobiographies, and speeches are primary sources. Unlike primary sources, **secondary sources** are made by people who were not directly involved in an event or present when it occurred. Encyclopedias, textbooks, biographies, and most newspaper and magazine articles are examples of secondary sources.

Speech *See Glossary of Literary Terms, page R108.*

Stereotyping Stereotyping is a dangerous type of overgeneralization. It can lead to unfair judgments of people based on their ethnic background, beliefs, practices, or physical appearance.

Summarize To summarize is to briefly retell the main ideas of a piece of writing in one's own words.
See also **Paraphrase.**

Support Support is any information that helps to prove a claim.

Supporting Detail *See* **Main Idea.**

Synthesize To synthesize information means to take individual pieces of information and combine them in order to gain a better understanding of a subject.

Text Features Text features are elements of a text, such as boldface type, headings, and subheadings, that help organize and call attention to important information. Italic type, bulleted or numbered lists, sidebars, and graphic aids such as charts, tables, timelines, illustrations, and photographs are also considered text features.

Thesaurus *See* **Reference Works.**

Thesis Statement A thesis statement is the main proposition that a writer attempts to support in a piece of writing.

Topic Sentence The topic sentence of a paragraph states the paragraph's main idea; all other sentences in the paragraph provide supporting details.

Visualize Visualizing is the process of forming a mental picture based on written or spoken information.

Web Site A Web site is a collection of "pages" on the World Wide Web, usually devoted to one specific subject. Pages are linked together and accessed by clicking hyperlinks or menus, which send the user from page to page within a Web site. Web sites are created by companies, organizations, educational institutions, branches of the government, the military, and individuals.

Workplace Documents Workplace documents are materials that are produced or used within a work setting, usually to aid in the functioning of the workplace. They include job applications, office memos, training manuals, job descriptions, and sales reports.

Works Cited The term *works cited* refers to a list of all the works a writer has referred to in his or her text. This list often includes not only books and articles but also Internet sources.

Works Consulted The term *works consulted* refers to a list of all the works a writer consulted in order to create his or her text. It is not limited just to those cited in the text.
See also **Bibliography.**

accommodations (ə-kŏm′ə-dā′shənz) *n.* rooms and food, especially in a hotel or on a ship or train
  alojamiento *s.* habitaciones para que duerman y coman viajeros en hoteles, barcos o trenes

accost (ə-kôst′) *v.* to approach a person and speak unpleasantly or aggressively
  importunar *v.* acercarse a una persona y hablarle de modo desagradable o agresivo

adjoining (ə-joi′nĭng) *adj.* next to or in contact with **adjoin** *v.*
  colindante *adj.* al lado; contiguo **colindar** *v.*

aghast (ə-găst′) *adj.* struck by terror or amazement
  aterrado *adj.* espantado; sobresaltado

agile (ăj′əl) *adj.* quick and light in movement
  ágil *adj.* que puede moverse con facilidad

agitator (ăj′ĭ-tā′tər) *n.* someone who stirs up people to support a cause
  agitador *s.* persona que exhorta a apoyar una causa

agonizing (ăg′ə-nī′zĭng) *adj.* resulting in great pain or deep sadness **agonize** *v.*
  angustioso *adj.* que produce mucho dolor o tristeza **angustiar** *v.*

amenable (ə-mē′nə-bəl) *adj.* open; agreeable
  dispuesto *adj.* que está de acuerdo

anecdotal (ăn′ĭk-dōt′l) *adj.* based on observations rather than scientific analysis
  anecdótico *adj.* basado en observaciones más que en análisis científico

anonymous (ə-nŏn′ə-məs) *adj.* having an unknown or withheld name
  anónimo *adj.* de nombre desconocido u oculto

antagonism (ăn-tăg′ə-nĭz′əm) *n.* hostility; unfriendliness
  antagonismo *s.* hostilidad; oposición

appalling (ə-pô′lĭng) *adj.* outrageous; terrible **appall** *v.*
  terrible *adj.* espantoso; atroz

aptitude (ăp′tĭ-tōōd′) *n.* natural ability
  aptitud *s.* habilidad natural

aquatic (ə-kwăt′ĭk) *adj.* growing or living in the water
  acuático *adj.* que crece o vive en el agua

aroma (ə-rō′mə) *n.* a smell; odor
  aroma *s.* olor, generalmente agradable

artisan (är′tĭ-zən) *n.* a person who is skilled in a trade
  artesano *s.* persona que hace objetos a mano siguiendo un método tradicional

ascend (ə-sĕnd′) *v.* to go or move upward; rise
  ascender *v.* subir

assent (ə-sĕnt′) *n.* agreement
  asentimiento *s.* acuerdo

automated (ô′tə-mā′tĭd) *adj.* able to function with little or no assistance from people **automate** *v.*
  automatizado *adj.* que funciona por su cuenta con poca ayuda humana **automatizar** *v.*

bacterium (băk-tîr′ē-əm) *n.* the singular form of *bacteria*, microscopically small living things that may cause disease
  bacteria *s.* organismo microscópico que puede causar enfermedades

balk (bôk) *v.* to refuse to move or act
  resistirse *v.* rehusarse

barrage (bə-räzh′) *n.* a rapid, heavy attack
  descarga *s.* sucesión rápida de golpes o balas

barren (băr′ən) *adj.* empty; lacking interest or charm
  estéril *adj.* vacío; sin interés o encanto

beckon (bĕk′ən) *v.* to summon or call, usually by a gesture or nod
  llamar *v.* atraer con un gesto

bedlam (bĕd′ləm) *n.* a noisy confusion
  pandemonio *s.* confusión y ruido

bemused (bĭ-myōōzd′) *adj.* confused
  desconcertado *adj.* confuso

brevity (brĕv′ĭ-tē) *n.* shortness
  brevedad *s.* concisión

brooding (brōō′dĭng) *adj.* full of worry; troubled **brood** *v.*
  inquietante *adj.* perturbador; preocupante **inquietar** *v.*

brusque (brŭsk) *adj.* abrupt or blunt in speaking
  brusco *adj.* abrupto o contundente al hablar

buoyancy (boi′ən-sē) *n.* the ability to remain afloat in liquid
  flotabilidad *s.* capacidad de flotar en un líquido

camouflage (kăm′ə-fläzh′) *v.* to disguise or portray falsely in order to conceal
  camuflar *v.* disfrazar o disimular

capitalize (kăp′ĭ-tl-īz′) v. to take advantage of
  capitalizar v. sacar provecho

carcass (kär′kəs) n. the dead body of an animal
  cadáver s. esqueleto de animal muerto

cascade (kă-skād′) n. a waterfall or something that resembles a waterfall
  cascada s. caída de agua

chafe (chāf) v. to irritate by rubbing
  rozar v. frotar e irritar

chaotic (kā-ŏt′ĭk) adj. confused; disordered
  caótico adj. confuso; desordenado

cherish (chĕr′ĭsh) v. to care for deeply
  apreciar v. querer; valorar

chronicle (krŏn′ĭ-kəl) n. a record of historical events in the order in which they took place
  crónica s. registro de sucesos históricos en el orden en que se dan

claret (klăr′ĭt) adj. dark red
  granate adj. color vino tinto

clarity (klăr′ĭ-tē) n. clearness of mind
  claridad s. lucidez

cohort (kō′hôrt′) n. a companion or associate
  compinche s. compañero o socio

commence (kə-mĕns′) v. to start or begin
  comenzar v. empezar

compassionate (kəm-păsh′ə-nĭt) adj. wanting to help those who suffer
  compasivo adj. que siente pena por los que sufren y desea ayudar

compensation (kŏm′pən-sā′shən) n. payment
  remuneración s. pago

compulsory (kəm-pŭl′sə-rē) adj. forced; required
  obligatorio adj. forzoso

consensus (kən-sĕn′səs) n. general agreement
  consenso s. acuerdo general

consolation (kŏn′sə-lā′shən) n. a comfort
  consuelo s. alivio

contemplate (kŏn′təm-plāt′) v. to consider carefully and at length
  contemplar v. considerar con atención

contorted (kən-tôr′tĭd) adj. twisted or strained out of shape **contort** v.
  contorsionado adj. torcido **contorsionar** v.

contour (kŏn′tŏŏr′) n. the outline of a figure or body
  contorno s. conjunto de líneas que limitan una figura

conventional (kən-vĕn′shə-nəl) adj. usual; traditional
  convencional adj. usual; tradicional

converge (kən-vûrj′) v. to come together
  convergir v. unirse

convivial (kən-vĭv′ē-əl) adj. enjoying the company of others; sociable
  cordial adj. sociable; simpático

convoluted (kŏn′və-lōō′tĭd) adj. difficult to understand; complicated
  enrollado adj. difícil de entender; complicado

cope (kōp) v. to struggle with and overcome
  superar v. hacer frente y vencer

copious (kō′pē-əs) adj. more than enough; plentiful
  copioso adj. abundante

covey (kŭv′ē) n. a small group or flock of birds, especially partridges or quail
  nidada s. grupo de aves, especialmente de perdices o codornices

cower (kou′ər) v. to crouch or shrink down in fear
  encogerse v. doblarse con miedo

croon (krōōn) v. to sing softly
  canturrear v. cantar suavemente

culminate (kŭl′mə-nāt′) v. to reach the highest point or degree
  culminar v. llegar a su momento o grado más alto

cumbersome (kŭm′bər-səm) adj. awkward; hard to manage
  incómodo adj. pesado y difícil de manejar

cunning (kŭn′ĭng) adj. skillful, clever
  astuto adj. ingenioso, listo

cunningly (kŭn′ĭng-lē) *adv.* in a clever way that is meant to trick or deceive
　astutamente *adv.* de modo ingenioso con el fin de engañar

currency (kûr′ən-sē) *n.* money
　moneda *s.* dinero

cynically (sĭn′ĭ-kəl-lē) *adv.* in a way that shows mistrust in the motives of others
　cínicamente *adv.* con desconfianza de los motivos ajenos

daunting (dôn′tĭng) *adj.* frightening; intimidating **daunt** *v.*
　sobrecogedor *adj.* desalentador; asustador **sobrecoger** *v.*

decimate (dĕs′ə-māt′) *v.* to kill or destroy a large part of
　diezmar *v.* matar o destruir una gran parte

decoy (dē′koi′) *n.* a person or thing used to distract others or lead them in a different direction
　señuelo *s.* persona o cosa que se usa para distraer o desviar

deference (dĕf′ər-əns) *n.* respect and honor
　deferencia *s.* respeto y honor

defiant (dĭ-fī′ənt) *adj.* willing to stand up to opposition; bold
　desafiante *adj.* que confronta oposición

demeaning (dĭ-mē′nĭng) *adj.* lowering one's dignity or standing **demean** *v.*
　degradante *adj.* que reduce la dignidad o posición de una persona **degradar** *v.*

demonize (dē′mə-nīz′) *v.* to give evil, demonic qualities to
　demonizar *v.* atribuir características muy negativas

despair (dĭ-spâr′) *v.* to lose hope
　desesperar *v.* perder la esperanza

detached (dĭ-tăcht′) *adj.* separated; disconnected **detach** *v.*
　separado *adj.* alejado; distanciado **separar** *v.*

devastating (dĕv′ə-stā′tĭng) *adj.* very effective in causing pain or destruction **devastate** *v.*
　devastador *adj.* que causa gran dolor o destrucción **devastar** *v.*

diffuse (dĭ-fyōōz′) *v.* to spread out or through
　difundir *v.* difuminar; diseminar

disarray (dĭs′ə-rā′) *n.* a state of disorder; confusion
　desorganización *s.* desorden; confusión

disciplinarian (dĭs′ə-plə-nâr′ē-ən) *n.* someone who enforces strict discipline, or rules
　ordenancista *s.* persona que impone reglas estrictas de orden y disciplina

discreetly (dĭ-skrēt′lē) *adv.* in a manner that shows caution and good judgment
　discretamente *adv.* de modo moderado y sensato

disembodied (dĭs′ĕm-bŏ′dēd) *adj.* separated from or lacking a body **disembody** *v.*
　incorpóreo *adj.* que no tiene cuerpo

disillusionment (dĭs′ĭ-lōō′zhən-mənt) *n.* disappointment; loss of hope
　desilusión *s.* decepción; pérdida de la esperanza

dismay (dĭs-mā′) *n.* distress caused by trouble or something unexpected
　consternación *s.* angustia por problemas o por sucesos inesperados

dismount (dĭs-mount′) *v.* to get down or off
　desmontarse *v.* bajarse

disorientation (dĭs-ôr′ē-ĕn-tā′shən) *n.* mental confusion or impaired awareness
　desorientación *s.* confusión mental

dispel (dĭ-spĕl′) *v.* to get rid of
　disipar *v.* hacer desaparecer

dissenter (dĭ-sĕn′tər) *n.* one who disagrees or holds a different opinion
　disidente *s.* el que no está de acuerdo o tiene una opinión distinta

dissuade (dĭ-swād′) *v.* to persuade not to do something
　disuadir *v.* convencer de no hacer algo

dominate (dŏm′ə-nāt′) *v.* to have control over
　dominar *v.* mandar

dwindle (dwĭn′dl) *v.* to become less, until little remains
　disminuir *v.* reducir hasta que no queda casi nada

eavesdrop (ēvz′drŏp′) *v.* to listen secretly to a private conversation of others
　fisgonear *v.* escuchar en secreto conversaciones privadas

ecosystem (ē′kō-sĭs′təm) *n.* a physical environment, such as an ocean, and the community of things that live in it
　ecosistema *s.* ambiente físico, como un océano, y las comunidades que viven en él

eloquence (ĕl'ə-kwəns) *n.* forceful, convincing speech or writing
  elocuencia *s.* facultad de hablar o escribir de modo convincente

elusive (ĭ-lōō'sĭv) *adj.* tending to elude capture
  evasivo *adj.* escurridizo; difícil de capturar

eminent (ĕm'ə-nənt) *adj.* famous; well-respected
  eminente *adj.* muy famoso

endeavor (ĕn-dĕv'ər) *n.* purposeful or serious activity; enterprise
  empeño *s.* esfuerzo serio y resuelto

entitlement (ĕn-tīt'l-mənt) *n.* the state of having a right or claim to something
  derecho *s.* prerrogativa o atribución

epidemic (ĕp'ĭ-dĕm'ĭk) *n.* an outbreak of a disease that spreads quickly among many people
  epidemia *s.* enfermedad que ataca a mucha gente al mismo tiempo

evasive (ĭ-vā'sĭv) *adj.* tending or trying to avoid
  evasivo *adj.* que tiende a evitar

evidently (ĕv'ĭ-dənt-lē) *adv.* obviously; clearly
  evidentemente *adv.* obviamente; claramente

excess (ĭk-sĕs') *adj.* too much or too many
  excesivo *adj.* que tiene demasiado

exhilarating (ĭg-zĭl'ə-rā'tĭng) *adj.* stimulating; making one feel thrilled or inspired **exhilarate** *v.*
  estimulante *adj.* tonificante; que hace sentir entusiasmo **estimular** *v.*

exuberantly (ĭg-zōō'bər-ənt-lē) *adv.* in a manner showing enthusiasm or joy
  exuberantemente *adv.* con mucho entusiasmo o alegría

falsify (fôl'sə-fī') *v.* to make false by adding to or changing
  falsificar *v.* falsear

ferocity (fə-rŏs'ĭ-tē) *n.* fierceness; extreme intensity
  ferocidad *s.* fiereza; extrema intensidad

fester (fĕs'tər) *v.* to become an increasing source of irritation or poisoning
  enconarse *v.* volverse más irritante o venenoso

feverishly (fē'vər-ĭsh-lē) *adv.* in a way marked by intense emotion or activity
  febrilmente *adv.* con intensa emoción o actividad

flail (flāl) *v.* to wave wildly
  agitar *v.* ondear fuertemente

fledgling (flĕj'lĭng) *n.* a young bird that has recently grown its flight feathers
  polluelo *s.* pichón que acaba de echar plumas

flimsy (flĭm'zē) *adj.* not solid or strong
  ligero *adj.* insubstancial; débil

flinching (flĭn'chĭng) *n.* drawing back from difficulty or danger **flinch** *v.*
  reculada *s.* titubeo; vacilación **recular** *v.*

forage (fôr'ĭj) *v.* to search around for food or other supplies
  hurgar *v.* buscar lo que se necesita, especialmente alimento

foray (fôr'ā') *n.* a trip into an unknown area
  incursión *s.* viaje a un territorio desconocido

forerunner (fôr'rŭn'ər) *n.* person or thing that came before
  precursor *s.* persona o cosa que precede algo que se desarrollará más tarde

foresighted (fôr'sī'tĭd) *adj.* having the ability to anticipate the future and prepare for it
  visionario *adj.* que anticipa el futuro y se prepara

forlorn (fər-lôrn') *adj.* appearing lonely or sad
  desdichado *adj.* de aspecto triste y solo

frail (frāl) *adj.* delicate; weak and fragile
  frágil *adj.* delicado; débil

fray (frā) *n.* a fight; a heated dispute
  refriega *s.* lucha

gait (gāt) *n.* a manner of walking or moving on foot
  paso *s.* modo de andar

gaunt (gônt) *adj.* thin and bony
  enjuto *adj.* delgado y huesudo

genially (jēn'yəl-lē) *adv.* in a pleasant, friendly manner
  cordialmente *adv.* de modo amistoso

ghastly (găst'lē) *adj.* terrifyingly horrible
  espantoso *adj.* horrendo

gigantic (jī-găn'tĭk) *adj.* extremely large
  gigantesco *adj.* enorme

glinty (glĭn'tē) *adj.* sparkling
  destellante *adj.* brillante

grave (grāv) *adj.* solemn and dignified
  grave *adj.* solemne y digno

grievous (grē′vəs) *adj.* painful; serious
  penoso *adj.* doloroso; serio

grimace (grĭm′ĭs) *v.* to twist one's face to show pain or disgust
  hacer una mueca *v.* retorcer la cara de dolor o desagrado

heady (hĕd′ē) *adj.* tending to make one feel really happy or excited
  embriagador *adj.* emocionante; vertiginoso

hierarchy (hī′ə-rär′kē) *n.* an organization of people according to rank
  jerarquía *s.* organización por rango

homage (hŏm′ĭj) *n.* a display of loyalty and respect
  homenaje *s.* demostración de lealtad y respeto

humor (hyōō′mər) *v.* to give in to the wishes of
  llevar la corriente *v.* acceder; satisfacer

hustle (hŭs′əl) *v.* to gain by energetic effort
  conseguir *v.* obtener con mucho esfuerzo

impairment (ĭm-pâr′mənt) *n.* the condition of being damaged, injured, or harmed
  deterioro *s.* daño o herida

impasse (ĭm′păs′) *n.* a situation in which no progress can be made; a deadlock
  impasse s. situación en que no se avanza; punto muerto

impetus (ĭm′pĭ-təs) *n.* a driving force; a motivation
  ímpetu *s.* fuerza motriz; motivación

impoverished (ĭm-pŏv′ər-ĭsht) *adj.* very poor **impoverish** *v.*
  empobrecido *adj.* muy pobre **empobrecer** *adj.*

improbable (ĭm-prŏb′ə-bəl) *adj.* not likely
  improbable *adj.* poco probable

improvise (ĭm′prə-vīz′) *v.* to make up on the spur of the moment, without preparation
  improvisar *v.* inventar en el momento

inadvertence (ĭn′əd-vûr′tns) *n.* a lack of attention; carelessness
  inadvertencia *s.* descuido; omisión

incoherent (ĭn′kō-hîr′ənt) *adj.* confused; lacking logical connections
  incoherente *adj.* confuso; carente de conexiones lógicas

inconsolable (ĭn′kən-sō′lə-bəl) *adj.* impossible or difficult to comfort
  inconsolable *adj.* que no se puede consolar

incredulously (ĭn-krĕj′ə-ləs-lē) *adv.* in a way that shows doubt or disbelief
  incrédulamente *adj.* con incredulidad

incriminate (ĭn-krĭm′ə-nāt′) *v.* to cause to appear guilty
  incriminar *v.* hacer parecer culpable

indefinitely (ĭn-dĕf′ə-nĭt-lē) *adv.* for an unlimited length of time
  indefinidamente *adv.* por un tiempo ilimitado

inevitably (ĭn-ĕv′ĭ-tə-blē) *adv.* unavoidably; without fail
  inevitablemente *adv.* que no se puede evitar; sin falta

infinitely (ĭn′fə-nĭt-lē) *adv.* extremely; greatly
  infinitamente *adv.* sumamente; enormemente

infuriated (ĭn-fyŏŏr′ē-ā′tĭd) *adj.* very angry **infuriate** *v.*
  enfurecido *adj.* furioso **enfurecer** *v.*

inscription (ĭn-skrĭp′shən) *n.* something written, carved, or engraved on a surface
  inscripción *s.* cosa escrita, tallada o gravada en una superficie

insinuation (ĭn-sĭn′yōō-ā′shən) *n.* a suggestion or hint intended to insult
  insinuación *s.* manera sutil de insultar

insolently (ĭn′sə-lənt-lē) *adv.* boldly and insultingly
  insolentemente *adv.* de modo grosero

integrated (ĭn′tĭ-grā′tĭd) *adj.* open to people of all races and groups **integrate** *v.*
  integrado *adj.* abierto a personas de todas las razas o grupos étnicos **integrar** *v.*

integrity (ĭn-tĕg′rĭ-tē) *n.* honesty or sincerity
  integridad *s.* honestidad o sinceridad

intricate (ĭn′trĭ-kĭt) *adj.* arranged in a complex way; elaborate
  intrincado *adj.* presentado de una manera compleja; elaborado

ironically (ī-rŏn′ĭk-lē) *adv.* in a way that is contrary to what is expected or intended
  irónicamente *adv.* de manera contraria a lo esperado

jauntily (jôn′tə-lē) *adv.* in a light and carefree way
  gallardamente *adv.* de manera ligera y despreocupada

jostling (jŏs′ə-lĭng) *n.* roughly bumping, pushing, or shoving **jostle** *v.*
    empujón *s.* empellón **empujar** *v.*

languish (lăng′gwĭsh) *v.* to remain unattended or be neglected
    languidecer *v.* debilitarse o perder fuerza por abandono

lanky (lăng′kē) *adj.* tall and thin
    largirucho *adj.* alto y flaco

linger (lĭng′gər) *v.* to continue to stay; delay leaving
    vacilar *v.* quedarse; tardar en partir

masterpiece (măs′tər-pēs′) *n.* a great work of art
    obra maestra *s.* obra de arte magistral

melancholy (mĕl′ən-kŏl′ē) *n.* sadness; depression
    melancolía *s.* tristeza; depresión

merge (mûrj) *v.* to blend together
    combinarse *v.* unirse

metabolism (mĭ-tăb′ə-lĭz′əm) *n.* all the processes a living thing uses to continue to grow and live
    metabolismo *s.* conjunto de procesos que se producen en las células de los seres vivos

migrant (mī′grənt) *adj.* moving from place to place
    migratorio *adj.* que se muda de un sitio a otro

mistrust (mĭs-trŭst′) *v.* to think of without confidence or trust
    desconfiar *v.* no tener confianza

moderate (mŏd′ər-ĭt) *adj.* not excessive or extreme; average
    moderado *adj.* mediano; módico

muse (myōōz) *v.* to say thoughtfully
    contemplar *v.* decir de modo pensativo

novelty (nŏv′əl-tē) *n.* something new, original, or unusual
    novedad *s.* algo nuevo, original o inusual

oblige (ə-blīj′) *v.* to force; require
    obligar *v.* forzar; requerir

optimistic (ŏp′tə-mĭs′tĭk) *adj.* hopeful about the future
    optimista *adj.* con esperanzas del futuro

partisan (pär′tĭ-zən) *adj.* relating to or in support of one political party
    partidario *adj.* que apoya un partido político

patriarch (pā′trē-ärk′) *n.* a male head of a family
    patriarca *s.* hombre jefe de familia

pendulum (pĕn′jə-ləm) *n.* a weight hung so that it can swing freely, sometimes used in timing the workings of certain clocks
    péndulo *s.* cuerpo que oscila libremente usado para regular el movimiento de las manecillas de los relojes

pensively (pĕn′sĭv-lē) *adv.* thoughtfully
    pensativamente *adv.* reflexivamente

perception (pər-sĕp′shən) *n.* insight; ability to understand people and situations
    percepción *s.* comprensión; capacidad de entender personas y situaciones

perfunctorily (pər-fŭngk′tə-rĭ-lē) *adv.* in a mechanical or unconcerned way
    mecánicamente *adv.* superficialmente; como por obligación

perilously (pĕr′ə-ləs-lē) *adv.* dangerously
    arriesgadamente *adv.* peligrosamente

perpetual (pər-pĕch′ōō-əl) *adj.* continual; unending
    perpetuo *adj.* eterno; sin fin

piously (pī′əs-lē) *adv.* religiously; in a manner showing reverence or respect
    piadosamente *adv.* devotamente; de modo reverente y respetuoso

portly (pôrt′lē) *adj.* stout or overweight
    corpulento *adj.* grueso o con exceso de peso

posterity (pŏ-stĕr′ĭ-tē) *n.* future generations
    posteridad *s.* generaciones futuras

precipitous (prĭ-sĭp′ĭ-təs) *adj.* very steep
    escarpado *adj.* muy pendiente

predatory (prĕd′ə-tôr′ē) *adj.* given to stealing from or hurting others for one's own gain
    rapaz *adj.* propenso a robar o hacer daño por beneficio propio

preoccupied (prē-ŏk′yə-pīd′) *adj.* lost in thought; distracted
    absorto *adj.* ensimismado; distraído

presentable (prĭ-zĕn′tə-bəl) *adj.* fit to be seen by people
    presentable *adj.* en condiciones de ser visto

prestigious (prĕ-stē'jəs) *adj.* having a high reputation
  prestigioso *adj.* que tiene renombre o importancia

prime (prīm) *adj.* first in quality or value
  óptimo *adj.* de primera calidad o valor

prominent (prŏm'ə-nənt) *adj.* well-known; widely recognized
  prominente *adj.* bien conocido; reconocido en muchas partes

prophecy (prŏf'ĭ-sē) *n.* a prediction of the future
  profecía *s.* predicción del futuro

proponent (prə-pō'nənt) *n.* a person who supports something
  defensor *s.* el que apoya una posición

prospective (prə-spĕk'tĭv) *adj.* likely to be or become
  potencial *adj.* posible

punctual (pŭngk'chōō-əl) *adj.* on time; prompt
  puntual *adj.* a tiempo

puny (pyōō'nē) *adj.* weak and small
  enclenque *adj.* débil y raquítico

quiver (kwĭv'ər) *v.* to shake with a slight, rapid movement
  temblar *v.* vibrar con un movimiento rápido y sutil

radar (rā'där) *n.* a method of detecting distant objects through the use of radio waves
  radar *s.* método de detectar objetos distantes por medio de ondas de radio

rampage (răm'pāj') *n.* a wild or violent outbreak
  alboroto *s.* tumulto violento

rash (răsh) *adj.* reckless and careless
  precipitado *adj.* impetuoso e imprudente

rationality (răsh'ə-năl'ĭ-tē) *n.* reasonableness
  racionalidad *s.* lógica; conformidad con la razón

raucous (rô'kəs) *adj.* loud and harsh-sounding
  escandaloso *adj.* fuerte y estridente

recede (rĭ-sēd') *v.* to become fainter or more distant
  desvanecerse *v.* alejarse

recessed (rē'sĕst') *adj.* set-in or set back **recess** *v.*
  empotrado *adj.* metido en la pared **empotrar** *v.*

reclaim (rĭ-klām') *v.* to get back; recover
  recuperar *v.* recobrar

recurrence (rĭ-kûr'əns) *n.* the act of happening again; return
  reaparición *s.* repetición; regreso

redeem (rĭ-dēm') *v.* to set free
  redimir *v.* liberar

redundant (rĭ-dŭn'dənt) *adj.* not needed; more than necessary
  redundante *adj.* más de lo necesario

reel (rēl) *v.* to feel unsteady or dizzy
  tambalearse *v.* sentirse mareado

rehabilitate (rē'hə-bĭl'ĭ-tāt') *v.* to restore to useful life, as through therapy and education
  rehabilitar *v.* restaurar a través de terapia y educación

renounce (rĭ-nouns') *v.* to give up
  renunciar *v.* dejar o abandonar

reproof (rĭ-prōōf') *n.* criticism for a fault
  reprobación *s.* crítica por una falta

reservoir (rĕz'ər-vwär') *n.* a place where anything is collected and stored
  depósito *s.* lugar de almacenamiento

retaliate (rĭ-tăl'ē-āt') *v.* to get revenge; get even
  vengarse *v.* tomar represalias

retort (rĭ-tôrt') *v.* to reply sharply
  replicar *v.* contestar con brusquedad

retribution (rĕt'rə-byōō'shən) *n.* punishment for bad behavior
  castigo *s.* pena al que ha cometido una falta

revelation (rĕv'ə-lā'shən) *n.* something made known
  revelación *s.* algo que se da a conocer

revere (rĭ-vîr') *v.* to honor or worship
  venerar *v.* honrar o adorar

revert (rĭ-vûrt') *v.* to return to a former condition
  revertir *v.* regresar a una condición anterior

revive (rĭ-vīv') *v.* to return to life or consciousness
  revivir *v.* recobrar la conciencia; despertarse

righteous (rī'chəs) *adj.* based on one's sense of what is right
  recto *adj.* correcto; honrado

saunter (sôn'tər) *v.* to stroll in a casual manner
   pasear *v.* caminar lentamente

scrutiny (skrōōt'n-ē) *n.* close examination or study
   examen *s.* estudio detallado

sever (sĕv'ər) *v.* to cut off or apart
   cortar *v.* separar

shanty (shăn'tē) *n.* a rundown house; a shack
   choza *s.* casucha

sheepishly (shē'pĭsh-lē) *adv.* with a bashful or embarrassed look
   tímidamente *adv.* con una expresión tímida o avergonzada

shrewdly (shrōōd'lē) *adv.* wisely; in a clever way
   astutamente *adv.* inteligentemente; con astucia

shuffle (shŭf'əl) *v.* to slide the feet along the ground while walking
   arrastrar los pies *v.* rozar el suelo con los pies al caminar

simultaneously (sī'məl-tā'nē-əs-lē) *adv.* at the same time
   simultáneamente *adv.* al mismo tiempo

singe (sĭnj) *v.* to burn lightly
   chamuscar *v.* quemar en la superficie

slack (slăk) *adj.* not firm or tight; loose
   flojo *adj.* fláccido

smugly (smŭg'lē) *adv.* in a self-satisfied way
   presumidamente *adv.* con satisfacción vanidosa

snag (snăg) *v.* to catch and tear
   enganchar *v.* agarrarse y romperse

somber (sŏm'bər) *adj.* serious; gloomy
   sombrío *adj.* serio; triste

specify (spĕs'ə-fī') *v.* to make known or identify
   especificar *v.* detallar o identificar

speculate (spĕk'yə-lāt') *v.* to view or consider different possibilities; to guess what might happen
   especular *v.* pensar en distintas posibilidades; imaginar lo que puede pasar

spherical (sfîr'ĭ-kəl) *adj.* having the shape of a sphere or round ball
   esférico *adj.* con forma de esfera o de pelota

squander (skwŏn'dər) *v.* to waste
   derrochar *v.* malgastar

stance (stăns) *n.* posture; position
   postura *s.* posición

subservient (səb-sûr'vē-ənt) *adj.* humble and obedient
   obsequioso *adj.* humilde y obediente

subtly (sŭt'lē) *adv.* not obviously; in a manner hard to notice or perceive
   sutilmente *adv.* veladamente; con discreción

suppressing (sə-prĕ'sĭng) *n.* keeping in; holding back **suppress** *v.*
   inhibidor *s.* supresor **inhibir** *v.*

sustain (sə-stān') *v.* to keep up; to support
   sustentar *v.* preservar; mantener

tantalizing (tăn'tə-lī'zĭng) *adj.* tempting but out of reach **tantalize** *v.*
   tentador *adj.* que inspira interés sin satisfacer **tentar** *v.*

taskmaster (tăsk'măs'tər) *n.* a person who sets tasks for others to do
   supervisor *s.* persona que reparte tareas

taunt (tônt) *v.* to make fun of
   burlar *v.* provocar con burlas; ridiculizar

taut (tôt) *adj.* not loose or flabby
   tirante *adj.* tenso; terso

tawny (tô'nē) *adj.* a warm, sandy shade of brownish orange
   leonado *adj.* color pardo rojizo

tedious (tē'dē-əs) *adj.* tiresome; boring
   tedioso *adj.* aburrido

terse (tûrs) *adj.* speaking little; communicating in few words
   seco *adj.* lacónico; que se comunica con pocas palabras

threshold (thrĕsh'ōld') *n.* a doorway or entrance
   umbral *s.* entrada

torrent (tôr'ənt) *n.* a violent, rushing stream
   torrente *s.* corriente rápida y veloz

trance (trăns) *n.* a condition of daydreaming or being unconscious of one's surroundings
   trance *s.* ensoñación; ensimismamiento

transition (trăn-zĭsh′ən) *n.* change from one place or condition to another
   transición *s.* cambio de un lugar o situación a otros

translucent (trăns-lōō′sənt) *adj.* allowing light to pass through
   translúcido *adj.* que deja pasar la luz

travesty (trăv′ĭ-stē) *n.* a degraded or grotesque likeness
   parodia *s.* imitación burlesca de una cosa seria; distorsión

unbridled (ŭn-brīd′ld) *adj.* lacking restraint or control
   desenfrenado *adj.* sin restricciones

unison (yōō′nĭ-sən) *n.* harmony or agreement; as with one voice
   unísono *s.* armonía o acuerdo; dicho con una voz

unperceived (ŭn-pər-sēvd′) *adj.* not seen or noticed
   desapercibido *adj.* no visto

unperturbed (ŭn′pər-tûrbd′) *adj.* not troubled or distressed
   impasible *adj.* que no se molesta

upstart (ŭp′stärt′) *adj.* suddenly risen to wealth or power
   advenedizo *adj.* arribista

urgency (ûr′jən-sē) *n.* a condition of pressing importance; necessity
   urgencia *s.* gran necesidad

usher (ŭsh′ər) *v.* to guide in a certain direction
   conducir *v.* llevar en cierta dirección

valiant (văl′yənt) *adj.* brave; courageous
   valiente *adj.* valeroso

varmint (vär′mĭnt) *n.* a troublesome person or wild animal
   alimaña *s.* persona o animal que causa problemas

veer (vîr) *v.* to change direction; to shift
   virar *s.* cambiar de dirección; dar un viraje

vehemently (vē′ə-mənt-lē) *adv.* forcefully
   vehementemente *adv.* de modo apasionado

venerable (věn′ər-ə-bəl) *adj.* deserving respect because of age, character, or importance
   venerable *adj.* que merece respeto por edad, carácter o importancia

vengeance (věn′jəns) *n.* the infliction of punishment in return for an offense
   venganza *s.* imposición de castigo por una ofensa

vile (vīl) *adj.* disgusting; unpleasant
   repugnante *adj.* desagrable; asqueroso

virtuous (vûr′chōō-əs) *adj.* morally good; honorable
   virtuoso *adj.* de buen carácter moral; honorable

visceral (vĭs′ər-əl) *adj.* instinctive
   visceral *adj.* instintivo

voracious (vô-rā′shəs) *adj.* possessing an insatiable desire; greedy
   voraz *adj.* que tiene un deseo insaciable; glotón

wavering (wā′vər-ĭng) *adj.* hesitating between two choices **waver** *v.*
   vacilante *adj.* que duda entre dos alternativas **vacilar** *v.*

wince (wĭns) *v.* to draw back, as in pain or distress
   estremecerse *v.* encogerse o contraerse por dolor

writhe (rīth) *v.* to twist or move painfully
   retorcerse *v.* contorsionarse de dolor

Pronunciation Key

Symbol	Examples	Symbol	Examples	Symbol	Examples
ă	at, gas	m	man, seem	v	van, save
ā	ape, day	n	night, mitten	w	web, twice
ä	father, barn	ng	sing, hanger	y	yard, lawyer
âr	fair, dare	ŏ	odd, not	z	zoo, reason
b	bell, table	ō	open, road, grow	zh	treasure, garage
ch	chin, lunch	ô	awful, bought, horse	ə	awake, even, pencil, pilot, focus
d	dig, bored	oi	coin, boy		
ĕ	egg, ten	ŏŏ	look, full	ər	perform, letter
ē	evil, see, meal	ōō	root, glue, through		
f	fall, laugh, phrase	ou	out, cow		
g	gold, big	p	pig, cap		
h	hit, inhale	r	rose, star		
hw	white, everywhere	s	sit, face		
ĭ	inch, fit	sh	she, mash		
ī	idle, my, tried	t	tap, hopped		
îr	dear, here	th	thing, with		
j	jar, gem, badge	th	then, other		
k	keep, cat, luck	ŭ	up, nut		
l	load, rattle	ûr	fur, earn, bird, worm		

Sounds in Foreign Words

Symbol	Examples
KH	*German* i**ch**, au**ch**; *Scottish* lo**ch**
N	*French* e**n**tre, bo**n**, fi**n**
œ	*French* f**eu**, c**œu**r; *German* sch**ö**n
ü	*French* **u**tile, r**u**e; *German* gr**ü**n

Stress Marks

ˈ This mark indicates that the preceding syllable receives the primary stress. For example, in the word *language*, the first syllable is stressed: lăngˈgwĭj.

ˌ This mark is used only in words in which more than one syllable is stressed. It indicates that the preceding syllable is stressed, but somewhat more weakly than the syllable receiving the primary stress. In the word *literature*, for example, the first syllable receives the primary stress, and the last syllable receives a weaker stress: lĭtˈər-ə-chŏŏrˌ.

Adapted from *The American Heritage Dictionary of the English Language,* fourth edition. Copyright © 2000 by Houghton Mifflin Company. Used with the permission of Houghton Mifflin Company.

Index of Skills

A

Abbreviations, 826, R83
  periods in, R49
  postal, R49
  Web, 970, 982
Academic vocabulary, 5, 6, 7, 8, 10, 23,
  175, 303, 437, 541, 625, 753, 867,
  965, 969, 974. *See also* Specialized
  vocabulary.
Acronyms, 942
Act (in a play), 7, R100, R107
Active listening, R82–R83
Active voice, 581, 616, R57
Adjective clauses, R46, R54, R62, R67
Adjective phrases, R60
Adjectives, 127, 440, 594, R2, R47, R57–
  R59, R61, R66
  versus adverbs, R58, R59
  avoiding too many, 467
  commas and, R49
  compound, R50
  precise, 529, R29
  predicate, R57
  proper, R51
  sensory, R33–R34
Adventure stories or novels, 89, 92, R100
Adverb clauses, R62–R63
Adverb phrases, R60
Adverbs, 467, 529, R32, R47, R58, R61, R66
  versus adjectives, R58, R59
Advertising, 4, 10, 979, R84, R90–R91
  billboard, R90
  celebrities in, 914, R91
  flyer, R90
  infomercial, R90
  marketing, R90
  persuasive techniques in, 10, 915, 944–
    947, R91
  political ad, R90
  print ad, 947, R90
  product placement, R90–R91
  public service announcement, R90
  sponsors, R90
  television commercials, 946, 947, R90
  trailer, R90
  types of, R90
Affixes. *See* Prefixes; Suffixes.
Agreement
  pronoun-antecedent, 91, 166, 426, R29,
    R52–R53, R97
  subject-verb, 465, 475, 532, R29, R65–
    R67, R77
Alliteration, 544, 545, 547, 593, 596, 599,
  618, 619, 937, 938, R100, R107,
  R108. *See also* Sound devices.

Allusions, 498, R100
Almanacs, 892, 974, 976, R25, R113. *See also*
  References.
Ambiguous pronoun references, R55
Analogy, 116, 323, R71, R100, R110. *See also*
  Rhetorical devices.
  false, 931
Analysis, writing, 279, 325, 561, 843, R39–
  R40
  definition analysis, R40
  parts analysis, R40
  process analysis, R40
Anecdotes, 781, 785, 787, 789, 857, R30,
  R41, R77, R100
Angle, in news reporting, R89
Animation, R88
Antagonist, R100
Antecedent-pronoun agreement, 91, 166, 426,
  R29, R52–R53, R97
Antonyms, 15, 59, 116, 238, 645, 788, 893,
  R70, R71
Apostrophes, 71, 742, R50, R74
Appeals
  by association, 937, 940, R21
  to authority, 914, 937
  bandwagon, 914, 945, R21, R83, R91
  emotional, 914, 917, 937, 945, 946, R21,
    R91, R111
  ethical, R21
  to fear, 914, R21, R91, R111
  logical, 937, R21, R22–R25, R91, R112
  to loyalty, 940, R21
  to pity, 914, R21, R91, R111
  to vanity, 914, 915, R21, R111
Applications, job, R18, R114
Appositives and appositive phrases, 883, R61,
  R62
Approaches to literature. *See* Literary criticism.
Arguments, 8, 912–913, 919, R20, R110.
  See also Appeals; Persuasive techniques;
  Persuasive writing.
  analysis of, 919–925, 937–941, R22–R26
  claims, 912, 913, 919, 920, 921, 923, 925,
    927, R20, R26
  counterarguments, 919, 922, 925, 927,
    929–934, 941, 943, 948, 952, R20,
    R26, R79, R111
  deductive, R23, R111
  elements of, 912–917, 956
  evidence, 912, 916, R20, R22, R25, R26
  faulty, R24, R25, R26, R83
  general principle, R23
  inductive, R22, R112
  logical, 948, R21, R22–R25, R26, R112
  opposing. *See* counterarguments, *above.*
  reasons, R20, R26

  strategies for determining strong, 914, 919,
    R22–R26
  strategies for reading, 912–913, R20–R21
  support, 912, 913, 916, 919, 923, 925,
    927, 934, R20
  writing, 685, 927, 948–954, R40–R41,
    R99
Art. *See* Visuals.
Articles (written). *See* Feature articles;
  Magazine articles; News articles;
  Newspapers, articles in.
Articulation. *See* Speaking strategies.
Artistic effects. *See* Media presentations.
Assessment practice, 166–171, 294–299,
  428–433, 532–537, 616–621, 744–749,
  858–863, 956–961, R93–R99
  reading comprehension, 166–169,
    294–297, 428–431, 532–535, 616–
    619, 744–747, 858–861, 956–959,
    R94–R95
  vocabulary, 170, 298, 432, 536, 620, 748,
    862, 960, R96
  writing, 169, 171, 297, 299, 431, 433,
    535, 537, 619, 621, 747, 749, 861,
    863, 959, 961, R97–R99
  writing and grammar, 171, 299, 433, 537,
    621, 749, 863, 961, R97
Assonance, R100, R107, R108
Assumptions, 509, R10, R23, R24, R38,
  R110
Atlases, 892, 974, 976, R72, R113. *See also*
  References.
Attitudes, comparing, 49, 308, 505, 507, 513,
  757, 774
Audience, 7, 710, 941, R28, R102
  media, 10, 151, 152, 417, 945, 947, R84,
    R85, R92
  speaking and listening, 743, 857, 925, 937,
    955, 999, R76, R77, R78, R79
  target, 945, 947, R85, R92
  writing, 16, 288, 289, 526, 853, 927, 943,
    951, R28, R29, R33, R34, R39, R41,
    R42, R43
Authority. *See* Arguments; Sources.
Author's background, 31, 43, 63, 73, 92, 99,
  119, 129, 135, 183, 217, 227, 241, 259,
  269, 281, 311, 327, 339, 363, 374, 381,
  387, 445, 467, 481, 488, 495, 509, 515,
  549, 555, 563, 571, 583, 593, 601, 633,
  647, 661, 671, 686, 697, 713, 723, 761,
  781, 791, 802, 809, 833, 845, 873, 885,
  895, 919, 929, 937
  influence of, 978
Author's intent. *See* Author's purpose.

353, 363, 372, 381, 384, 387, 414,
445, 463, 467, 473, 481, 486, 495,
501, 505, 509, 513, 515, 519, 549,
552, 555, 560, 563, 569, 571, 579,
583, 587, 593, 599, 601, 606, 633,
644, 647, 657, 661, 667, 671, 683,
697, 710, 713, 720, 723, 729, 734,
761, 774, 781, 787, 791, 800, 809,
820, 833, 842, 845, 849
Literary criticism
author's style, 467, 470, 473, 481, 485,
486, 495, 498, 505, 513
cultural context. *See* Cultural values.
historical context, 549, 551, 552
Literary elements and devices. *See also*
Characters; Conflict; Plot; Poetic
elements and devices; Point of view;
Settings; Theme.
allusions, R100
assonance, R100, R107, R108
character foils, R103
characterization, 69, 178–180, 241–249,
250–255, 260–265, 281–285, 475
characters, 11, 178, 183–205, 277, 294,
579, 671, 697, 723, R101, R102,
R103, R108
comic relief. *See* Humor.
conflict, 5, 24–31, 63–69, 80, 84, 88, 99,
110, 112, 113, 129, 132, 135–149,
306, 316, 323, 327, 328, 332, 420–
426, 481, 484, 485, 527, 571, 577,
636, 637, 661, 667, R2, R37, R101,
R102, R106, R107
dialect, 282, 406, 485, 721, R102
dialogue, 7, 135, 151, 245, 315, 325,
387, 417, 420–427, 459, 463, 467,
468, 470, 473, 525–528, 581, 737,
741, 829, 833, 850–856, R36, R80,
R101, R102, R103, R104, R108,
R110
diction. *See* Word choice.
epic characteristics, R102
exaggeration, 495, 593, 626, 627, 713,
716, 718, 720, 721, R102, R103,
R104, R109
extended metaphors, R102
figurative language, 206, 294, 531, 544,
546, 547, 555–560, 561, 601–606,
607, 616, 845–849, R34, R68, R77,
R80, R102, R103, R105, R106, R108
flashbacks, 43, 58, 854, R36, R103
foreshadowing, 73, 76, 89, 106, 115,
149, 463, R103, R109
form, 6, 135, 209 , 211, 357 , 477, 488,
509, 510, 512, 513, 515, 542–543,
547, 549, 555, 563, 583, 589, 593,
693, 754, 756, 777, 822, 823, R2,
R14–R19, R28, R103
humor, 438, 494, 495–505, 507,
509–513, 520, 593–599, 612, 626,
627, 713, 716, 721, 741, 824, 857,

955, R30–R31, R76, R80, R88, R92,
R101, R102, R103, R104, R109
hyperbole, R104, R109
imagery, 6, 440, 441, 544, 546, 547, 549,
550, 551, 552, 561, 616, R33–R34,
R102, R104, R106
irony, 237, 509–513, 519, R104
metaphors, 546, 555–560, 561, 601, 602,
606, 716, R34, R77, R102, R105
meter, 544, 571–579, R105, R108
mood, 234, 427, 438–439, 440, 442,
443, 445–463, 468, 520–523, 524–
528, 532, 544, 545, 549, 551, 560,
578, 601–606, 607, 652, 766, 782,
829, 830, 930, R30, R34, R36, R79,
R80, R88, R91, R105, R107, R108
narrators, 176–177, 178, 180
onomatopoeia, 593–599
personification, 546, 555–560, 601, 606,
613, R106
point of view, 5, 8, 176–177, 205,
217–224, 227–237, 269–277, 294,
335, 372, 423, 754, 809, 814, 976,
R100, R106
repetition, 129, 133, 512, 544, 545, 560,
566, 568, 587, 593, 599, 602, 937,
938, 945, 946, R107
rhyme, 6, 129, 132, 488, 510, 513, 540,
542, 543, 544, 545, 547, 549, 563–
569, 593, 598, 599, R2, R102, R103,
R104, R105, R107, R108
rhyme scheme, 563–569, 598, R104,
R107, R108
rhythm, 6, 129, 132, 281, 442, 488, 509,
512, 542, 543, 544, 545, 547, 549,
560, 571–579, 593–599, 937, R2,
R29, R77, R88, R102, R103, R104,
R105, R107, R108
setting, 5, 24–25, 43–58, 119–126, 166,
R36
similes, 206, 294, 546, 547, 555–560,
585, 609, R34, R77, R96, R105,
R108
sound devices, 6, 129, 133, 544, 545,
547, 563, 587, 593–599, 616, 937,
R106, R108
speaker, 6, 205, 285, 305, 325, 380,
381, 382, 383, 384, 467, 468, 470,
509, 513, 519, 542, 543, 547, 552,
555, 558, 559, 560, 563–569, 829,
845–849, 856, R50, R76, R78, R79,
R80, R81, R82, R83, R86, R105,
R108, R112
stanzas, 6, 133, 384, 509, 510, 513, 542,
543, 545, 547, 563–569, 849, R107,
R108
style, 440–441, 467–473, 481–486,
515–519
suspense, 26, 73–89, 106, 108, 111, 115,
129, 132, 133, 683, 695, 852, 854,
857, R84, R103, R109

symbols, 339–353, 355, 384, 414, 428,
583–587, 648, 903, R109
theme, 5, 305–309, 311–323, 327–335,
363–372, 387–414, 428
themes, recurring, 381–384
themes, universal, 723–734, 735, R109
tone, 18, 417, 418, 438–443, 495–505,
507, 509, 510, 524, 526, 529, 530,
532, 608, 610, 614, 736, 738, 742,
756, 822, 824, 857, 955, 984, 987,
R29, R30, R31, R36, R39, R40, R41,
R42, R43, R76, R77, R78, R79, R80,
R83, R100, R101, R105, R109
tragedy, R109
word choice, 123, 438, 439, 440, 441,
445, 454, 463, 467, 473, 495, 499,
501, 504, 505, 515, 531, 532, 611,
756, 781, 782, 787, R21, R29, R83,
R109
Literary nonfiction, 8, 118, 258, 268, 356,
494, 502, 760, 778, 780, 790, 802,
808, 858, 913, 916, 957. *See also*
Narrative nonfiction.
strategies for reading, R2
Literary techniques. *See* Literary elements and
devices.
Loaded language, 885, 887, 891, 914, 915,
916, R25, R112
Logic. *See* Arguments; Reasoning.
Logical appeals, 937, R21, R22–R25, R91,
R112
Logical argument, 948, R21, R22–R25, R26,
R112
Logical fallacy. *See* Fallacy.
Lyric poetry, 555–560, R105, R106

M

Magazine articles, 8, 10, 209, 337, 462, 524,
608, 669, 754, 912, 974, 976, 979,
998, R112, R114
strategies for reading, 972, R3, R14
Magazines, 8, 423, 743, 843, 915, 947, 967,
972, 979, R28, R50, R84, R85, R86,
R88, R90, R113. *See also* References.
Main characters, 5, 178, 183, 205, 224, 249,
334, 662, R100, R101
Main ideas, 8, R29
identifying, R8
implied, R8
summarizing, R28
and supporting details, 956, R8–R9, R31
Making inferences. *See* Inferences, making.
Manuals (instruction), 8, R16
Maps, 588, 743, 868, 877, 898, 974, 978,
R3, R7, R43, R91, R112
Margins, 985
Media, 4, 10. *See also* Advertising; Films;
Media elements and techniques; Media
genres and types; Media messages;
Viewing skills and strategies.

Novellas, 4, 5
Novels, 4, 5, 92, 374, 488, 686, 974, R2, R9,
    R27, R36, R94, R100, R101, R103,
    R104, R105, R106
    in verse, 488–493

O

Objections, anticipating, 929, R20, R41,
    R110
Objective pronoun case, 117, R52
Objectivity, R89
Objects
    direct, R48, R53, R60, R61, R63
    indirect, R48, R53, R60, R62, R63
    of prepositions, R53, R62, R63
    use of *whom* as, in sentence, R54
Ode, R106
Online catalog, 969, 975, 989
Online information. *See* Internet; Web sites.
Onomatopoeia, 545, 593, 594, 599, R106,
    R108
Op-ed pieces, R113. *See also* Editorials.
Opinion statement. *See* Persuasion.
Opinions
    in conclusions, R33
    evaluating, R25–R26
    expert, 791, 984, R25, R79, R91
    versus facts, 956, 476–479, 881, 885–
        892, 901, 956, R41, R81, R83, R89
    identifying, 692–695
    supporting, R20
Opposing argument. *See* Counterarguments.
Opposing viewpoint. *See* Counterarguments.
Oral interpretation, 427, 615, R80
Oral presentations. *See also* Speaking
    strategies.
    debate, R79, R111
    oral interpretation, 427, 615, R80
    panel discussions, 925, 928
    props in, 427
Oral tradition, R106
    ballads, 579, R100
    fables, 305, 626, 627, 628, 710, 723,
        724, 727, 729, 733, 734, 735, R102,
        R103, R105
    folk tales, 480, 697–710, 745
    legends, 626, 628, 629, 660, 661–667,
        671–683, R103, R104
    myths, 626, 629, 630, 633–644, 647–
        657, 744, R103, R105, R106
    tall tales, 626, 627, 712, 744, 843, R109
Order of importance, R32, R35
Order of impression, R35
Organizational patterns. *See* Patterns of
    organization.
Organizing. *See* Graphic organizers; Patterns
    of organization.
Origin of words, 658, 711, 942. *See also*
    Word roots.

Outlines, 873–881
    drafting from, 17, 993–994, R28
    for taking notes, R4
Overgeneralization, 919, 920, 924, R24,
    R113, R114
Oversimplification, R24, R25
Overview, 507, 735, 762, 883, 967, 976,
    977, R4, R93, R113

P

Pace, R27
Pacing. *See* Speaking strategies.
Panel discussions, 925, 928
Paragraphs, R31–R32
    coherence of, R29, R31–R32
    organizing, R31–R32, R35
    topic sentence in, 71, 215, 479, 779, 870,
        R8, R31, R98, R114
    transitions in, R29, R31, R35
    unity of, R29, R31
Parallelism, 742, R64, R77
    as a rhetorical device, R77
Paraphrasing, 667, 845, 849, 902, 920, 921,
    984, 991, 992, R28, R83, R98, R113.
    See also Plagiarism.
Parentheses, 135, 833, 995, R50, R51, R108
Parenthetical documentation, 995
Participles and participial phrases, R55, R56,
    R61
    dangling, 614, R59
    misplaced, R59
    past, R55, R56, R57
    present, R55, R56
Parts analysis, R40
Parts of a book, 977
Parts of speech. *See also specific part of speech.*
    reference chart of, R46
Passive voice, 581, R57
Past participle verb forms, R55, R56, R57
Patterns of organization, 158, 286, 740, 895,
    948, 949, 952, 984, 996, 998, R2,
    R8–R13, R42, R113
    analysis of, 895–905, 907
    cause-effect, 166, 428, 736–742, 744,
        R10–R11, R32–R33
    chronological, 99–115, 661–667, 744,
        761, 764, 767, 768, 773, 774, 802,
        829, 854, 858, 895, R8, R9–R10, R35,
        R36, R40, R110, R113
    classification, R110, R113
    comparison-contrast, R11–R13, R32
    deductive, R23, R111
    inductive, R22, R112
    main idea and supporting details, 956,
        R8–R9, R31
    order of importance, R32, R35
    order of impression, R35
    point-by-point, 287, 290, 323, R11–R13,
        R37, R41, R100
    problem-solution, R13, R39, R113

reasons for opinion, 952, R20, R26
sequential, R9, R16, R32
spatial order, 162, R32, R35
subject-by-subject, 290, R11–R13, R38
Peer response, R30
Performing arts. *See* Drama.
Periodicals, 974, 975, 979, 980, R112, R113.
    See also Magazines; Newspapers.
Periods, 561, R29, R49
    in abbreviations, R49
    with quotation marks, 325, 530
Personal essay, 754, 781–787, R102
Personal narratives, writing, 850–856, R36–
    R37. *See also* Narrative writing.
Personification, 546, 555–560, 601, 606, 613,
    R106
Perspective, author's, 356, 359, 361, R100.
    See also Point of view.
Persuasive essay, 948–954, R40–R41, R94,
    R99, R102
Persuasive techniques, 912–917, 937–941,
    948–954, R20–R26. *See also* Persuasion.
    appeals by association, R21
    appeals to fear, pity, or vanity, 914, 915,
        R21, R91, R111
    appeals to loyalty, 940, R21
    bandwagon appeals, 914, 945, R21, R83,
        R91
    celebrity ads, 914, R91
    emotional appeals, 914, 917, 937, 945,
        946, R21, R91, R111
    ethical appeals, R21
    evaluating, 919–925, R25–R26
    glittering generality, R21, R83
    loaded language, 885, 887, 891, 914, 915,
        916, R25, R112
    logical appeals, 937, R21, R22–R25, R91,
        R112
    slogans, R91
    snob appeal, R21, R83
    testimonials, 914, R21, R90
    transfer, 914, 917
    word choice in, R21
Persuasive writing. *See also* Arguments.
    essay, 948–954, R40–R41, R94, R99,
        R102. *See also* Expository writing.
    key techniques, 948, R40–R41
    opinion statement, 948, 949, R33
    options for organizing, 952, R20, R26
    rubric for, 954
Photographs, 15, 99, 103, 184, 203, 282,
    520–523, 743, 762, 766, 769, 829, 830,
    869, 877, 881, 886, 909, 911, 917, 930,
    976, 999, R3, R4, R14, R86, R89, R91,
    R92, R112, R114
Phrases
    adjective, R60
    adverb, R60
    appositive, 883, R61, R62
    gerund, R61–R62
    infinitive, R59, R61

interrogative, R46, R54
nominative, 117, R52, R60
objective, 117, R52, R53
personal, R46, R51, R52, R53, R66, R67
possessive, 742, R52, R53, R54
predicate, R60
reference problems, R55
reflexive, R46, R53
relative, 954, R46, R54, R62, R67
second-person, R52
as subject of sentence, 117, R53
third-person, 227, R52
verb agreement with, R66
Proofreading, 17, 19, 907, R29, R42, R43, R77, R98, R99. *See also* Revising and editing.
of test responses, R98, R99
Propaganda, R25, R113
Props, 427, 531, R106
Prose, 488, R103, R106, R108
Protagonist, R100. R104, R106. *See also* Hero.
Public documents, R17, R113. *See also* Editorials; Government publications; Nonfiction, types of; Speech.
strategies for reading, R17
Public service announcements, R85, R90
persuasion in, 917
Publishing, 17, 164, 165, 292, 426, 530, 531, 614, 742, 856, 954, 998, R29
Punctuation, R29, R49–R50
apostrophes, 71, 742, R50, R74
colons, 943, 956, R50
commas, 140, 164, 225, 292, 325, 355, 530, 659, 856, 883, 927, 956, R32, R49, R61, R62, R63, R65
dashes, 225, R50
in dialogue, 325, 467, 856
ellipses, R50
end marks, 60, 325, R49
exclamation points, 561, 856, R49
hyphens, R50, R74
italics, 7, 135, 843, 858, R50, R108, R114
parentheses, 135, 833, 995, R50, R51, R108
periods, 325, 530, 561, R29, R49
question marks, 561, 856, R49
quick reference chart, R49–R50
quotation marks, 325, 530, 694, 791, 843, 856, 858, 969, 991, R50
semicolons, 60, 659, 995, R32, R49, R63, R65

Q

Qualities of a character. *See* Character traits.
Questioning, 17, R2, R112. *See also* Monitoring.
Question marks, 561, 856, R49
in dialogue, 856
Questions, R30, R33. *See also* Interviews; Research; Sentences.

rhetorical, R113
as text feature, 588, 589, R3, R4, R15
Quick reference charts
capitalization, R51
parts of speech, R46
punctuation, R49
sentence and its parts, R48
Quickwriting, 62, 108, 216, 258, 310, 338, 466, 548, 562, 632, 722, 760, 936, 966. *See also* Freewriting.
Quotation marks, 858, R50
commas with, 325, 530, 856
to enclose Internet search terms, 969
periods with, 325, 530, 856
to set off direct quotations, 530, 694, 991
to set off speaker's exact words, 325, 791, 856, R50
with titles, 843, R50
Quotations, 8, 15, 99, 791–800, R14, R28. *See also* Plagiarism; Works cited.
capitalization in, R51
colon to introduce, R50
in elaboration, 117, 257, 292, 524, 525, 527, 528, 591, 608, 610, 613, 791, 952, 984, 987, R34, R39, R41, R79, R82, R98, R111
ellipses in, R50
interpreting, 102, 114, 792, 795, 796, 798, 800, 830
in introduction, 291, 741, 996
punctuating, 325, 530, 694, 791, 856, 991, R50

R

Radio plays, 165, R106
Reading comprehension, assessment practice, 166–169, 294–297, 428–431, 532–535, 616–619, 744–747, 858–861, 956–959, R94–R95
Reading for information. *See also* Informational texts; Reading skills and strategies.
citing evidence, R20, R22, R25, R26
compare and contrast, R11–R13
critical reviews, R40, R111
drawing conclusions, R22, R23
electronic text, R19
feature articles, 4, 8, 209, 211, 215, 754, R112
identifying main ideas, R8, R9
magazine articles, 8, 10, 209, 337, 462, 524, 608, 669, 754, 972, 974, 976, 979, 998, R3, R14, R112, R114
making generalizations, 126
memoirs, 119, 269, 277, 279, 754, R2, R105
news articles, 4, 8, R14
political cartoons, R85
primary sources, 108, 779, 974, 976, 981, R114
process description, R18

supporting an opinion, R20, R25
synthesizing, 208–215, 776–779, R114
timeline, 99, 106, 109, 111, 115, 661, 664, 665, 666, 667, 761, 764, 774, 820, 901, R3, R91, R114
Reading log, 611
Reading rate, R27
Reading skills and strategies
analyzing sequence, 387–414
author's perspective, 356, 359, 361, R100
bias in, 885, 887, 888, 891, R25, R26, R92
cause and effect, 119–126, 166, 269–277, 363–372, 428, 647–657, 744
chronological order, 661–667, 761–774
clarifying, 12, 213, 515, 516, 517, 518, 633, 637, 642, 897, R2, R15, R110, R112
compare and contrast, 311–323, 428, R11–R13
connecting, 31–39, 259–265, 588–591, 781–787, R2
details in, R8, R18
distinguishing fact from opinion, 476–479
drawing conclusions, 215, 776–779, R22, R23
evaluating, R2, R25–R26
graphic aids in, R4–R7, R14, R16
identifying sequence, 43–58, 166, R16
implied main ideas, R8
main idea, 8, R8, R9
making inferences, 12, 14, 39, 58, 63, 66, 67, 68, 69, 110, 112, 115, 123, 125, 126, 186, 191, 193, 217–224, 232, 235, 236, 245, 246, 247, 250, 252, 254, 255, 256, 265, 273, 279, 285, 294, 323, 327, 335, 339–353, 372, 384, 414, 428, 453, 456, 457, 460, 463, 501, 505, 515, 519, 522, 555–560, 577, 606, 616, 657, 666, 683, 730, 774, 787, 791–800, 848, 858, R112
monitoring, 12, 13, 327–335, 515–519, 593–599, 633–644, R112
note taking, 929–934, R4
outlines, 873–881
pace, R27
paraphrasing, 667, 845, 849, 902, 920, 921, 984, 991, 992, R28, R83, R98, R113
patterns of organization, 158, 286, 740, 895–905, 907, 948, 949, 952, 984, 996, 998, R2, R8–R13, R42, R113
predicting, 12, 14, 60, 73–89, 227–237, 307, 502, 634, 641, 655, 671–683, 700, 705, 707, 892, 970, R2, R112, R113
previewing, 12, 589, 868, 871, 876, R4
rate, R27
reading poetry, 129–133, 281–285, 509–513, 571–579
reading science fiction, 445–463

Page numbers that appear in italics refer to biographical information.

ACKNOWLEDGMENTS

UNIT 1

Hill and Wang: "The Last Cover," from *The Pride of Lions and Other Stories* by Paul Annixter. Copyright © 1960 by Hill and Wang, renewed copyright © 1988 by Hill and Wang. Reprinted by permission of Hill and Wang, a division of Farrar, Straus and Giroux, LLC.

Brandt & Hochman: Excerpt from "The Third Wish," from *Not What You Expected: A Collection of Short Stories* by Joan Aiken. Copyright © 1974 by Joan Aiken. Reprinted by permission of Brandt & Hochman, Inc.

Harcourt: "Seventh Grade," from *Baseball in April and Other Stories* by Gary Soto. Copyright © 1990 by Gary Soto. Reprinted by permission of Harcourt, Inc.

Scholastic: "The Last Dog" by Katherine Paterson. Copyright © 1999 by Minna Murra, Inc. Published in *Tomorrowland: 10 Stories about the Future* compiled by Michael Cart. Copyright © 1999 by Michael Cart. Reprinted by permission of Scholastic, Inc.

ABC: Excerpts from "'Spot' Goes High-Tech" by Jackie Judd, from ABCNEWS.com. Copyright © 2002 by ABCNews Internet Ventures. Courtesy of ABCNEWS.com.

Hill and Wang: "Thank You, M'am," from *Short Stories* by Langston Hughes. Copyright © 1996 by Ramona Bass and Arnold Rampersad. Reprinted by permission of Hill and Wang, a division of Farrar, Straus and Giroux, LLC.

Harvard University Press: "If I can stop one heart from breaking," from *The Poems of Emily Dickinson*, edited by Thomas H. Johnson. Copyright © 1951, 1955, 1979, 1983 by the President and Fellows of Harvard College. Reprinted by permission of the publishers and the Trustees of Amherst College.

Farrar, Straus and Giroux: Excerpt from *Holes* by Louis Sachar. Copyright © 1998 by Louis Sachar. Jacket design by Vladimir Radunsky from *Holes* by Louis Sachar. Jacket art and design copyright © 1998 by Vladimir Radunsky. Reprinted by permission of Farrar, Straus and Giroux, LLC.

Scholastic: Excerpts from *Exploring the Titanic* by Robert D. Ballard. Copyright © 1988 by Ballard & Family. Reprinted by permission of Scholastic, Inc.

HarperCollins Publishers: Excerpt from *An American Childhood* by Annie Dillard. Copyright © 1987 by Annie Dillard. Reprinted by permission of HarperCollins Publishers.

The Estate of Rod Serling: "The Monsters Are Due on Maple Street" by Rod Serling. Copyright © 1960 by Rod Serling. Copyright © 1988 by Carolyn Serling, Jody Serling, and Anne Serling Sutton. Reprinted by permission of Code Entertainment and Carol Serling, on behalf of the Estate of Rod Serling.

Daniel Briney: Excerpts from "The Unnatural Course of Time" by Daniel Briney, from CultureDose.net. Copyright © 2002 by Daniel Briney. Reprinted with permission.

UNIT 2

Scholastic: Excerpt from "An Hour with Abuelo," from *An Island Like You: Stories of the Barrio* by Judith Ortiz Cofer. Copyright © 1995 by Judith Ortiz Cofer. Reprinted by permission of Scholastic, Inc.

Gish Jen: Excerpt from "The White Umbrella" by Gish Jen. Copyright © 1984 by Gish Jen. First published in *the Yale Review*. Reprinted by permission of the author.

Random House Children's Books: Excerpt from "Kitty and Mack: A Love Story," from *145th Street: Short Stories* by Walter Dean Myers. Copyright © 2000 by Walter Dean Myers. Used by permission of Random House Children's Books, a division of Random House, Inc.

Curtis Brown: "Birthday Box" by Jane Yolen, from *Birthday Surprises: Ten Great Stories to Unwrap*, published by Morrow Junior Books. Copyright © 1995 by Jane Yolen. Reprinted by permission of Curtis Brown, Ltd.

Alfred A. Knopf: "Zebra," from *Zebra and Other Stories* by Chaim Potok. Copyright © 1998 by Chaim Potok. Used by permission of Alfred A. Knopf, an imprint of Random House Children's Books, a division of Random House, Inc.

Naomi Shihab Nye: "The Rider" by Naomi Shihab Nye, first published in *Invisible*. Reprinted by permission of the author.

The Washington Post: Excerpts from "The Collected Grief of a Nation; An Exhibit of Mementos from the Vietnam Wall" by Judith Weinraub, from *the Washington Post*. Copyright © 1992 by the Washington Post. Reprinted with permission.

National Park Service: Mrs. Eleanor Wimbish Letter to Her Son, William "Billy" Stocks. Reprinted by permission of the National Park Service, Vietnam Veterans Memorial Collection.

Bilingual Press/Editorial Bilingüe: "The Scholarship Jacket" by Marta Salinas, from *Nosotras: Latina Literature Today* (1986), edited by María del Carmen Boza, Beverly Silva, and Carmen Valle. By permission of Bilingual Press/Editorial Bilingüe, Arizona State University, Tempe, AZ.

Philomel Books: "The Three-Century Woman" by Richard Peck, from *Second Sight: Stories for a New Millennium*. Copyright © 1999 by Richard Peck. Reprinted by permission of Philomel Books, a division of Penguin Putnam Books for Young Readers.

Farrar, Straus and Giroux: "Charles," from *The Lottery* by Shirley Jackson. Copyright © 1948, 1949 by Shirley Jackson, renewed © 1976, 1977 by Laurence Hyman, Barry Hyman, Mrs. Sarah Webster, and Mrs. Joanne Schnurer. Reprinted by permission of Farrar, Straus and Giroux, LLC.

Random House: Excerpt from *The Heart of a Woman* by Maya Angelou. Copyright © 1981 by Maya Angelou. Used by permission of Random House, Inc.

Estate of Martin Luther King Jr.: Excerpt from Crusade for Citizenship Mass Meeting, February 12, 1958. Copyright © 1958 by Martin Luther King Jr. Copyright renewed © 1991 by Coretta Scott King. Reprinted by arrangement with the Estate of Martin Luther King Jr., c/o Writers House as agent for the proprietor New York, NY.

Wylie Agency: "It Was a Long Time Before," from *Storyteller* by Leslie Marmon Silko. Copyright © 1981 by Leslie Marmon Silko. Reprinted with permission of the Wylie Agency, Inc.

Susan Bergholz Literary Services: "Abuelito Who," from *My Wicked Wicked Ways* by Sandra Cisneros. Copyright © 1987 by Sandra Cisneros. Published by Third Woman Press and in hardcover by Alfred

A. Knopf. Reprinted by permission of Susan Bergholz Literary Services, New York and Third Woman Press. All rights reserved.

UNIT 3

HarperCollins Publishers: "The Lion and the Mouse," from *Fables of Aesop* retold by Frances Barnes-Murphy. Copyright © 1994 by Frances Barnes-Murphy. Used by permission of HarperCollins Publishers.

Curtis Brown: "Little Sister" by Nikki Grimes. First appeared in *Something On My Mind* published by Peter Smith Publisher. Copyright © 1978 by Nikki Grimes. Reprinted by permission of Curtis Brown, Ltd.

Piri Thomas: Excerpt from *Stories from El Barrio* by Piri Thomas. Copyright © 1978 by Piri Thomas. Reprinted by permission of the author.

Pantheon Books: "The War of the Wall," from *Deep Sightings and Rescue Missions* by Toni Cade Bambara. Copyright © 1996 by the Estate of Toni Cade Bambara. Used by permission of Pantheon Books, a division of Random House, Inc.

Time: "Back to the Wall," from *People Weekly,* May 27, 2004. Copyright © 2004 by People Weekly. Used by permission of Time, Inc. All rights reserved.

Candlewick Press: "What Do Fish Have to Do With Anything?" from *What Do Fish Have to Do With Anything? and Other Stories* by Avi. Copyright © 1994 by Avi. Used by permission of Candlewick Press.

Random House: "Homeless," from *Living Out Loud* by Anna Quindlen. Copyright © 1987 by Anna Quindlen. Used by permission of Random House, Inc.

Scholastic: "A Crush," from *A Couple of Kooks and Other Stories About Love* by Cynthia Rylant. Copyright © 1990 by Cynthia Rylant. Published by Orchard Books/Scholastic, Inc. Used by permission.

Houghton Mifflin Company: Excerpt from *The Giver* by Lois Lowry. Copyright © 1993 by Lois Lowry. Reprinted by permission of Houghton Mifflin Company. All rights reserved.

Harvard University Press: "Spring Harvest of the Snow Peas," from *To Be the Poet* by Maxine Hong Kingston, pp. 86–87, Cambridge, Mass., Harvard University Press. Copyright © 2002 by Maxine Hong Kingston. Reprinted by permission of the publisher.

BOA Editions: "Eating Alone," from *Rose* by Li-Young Lee. Copyright © 1986 by Li-Young Lee. Reprinted with the permission of the author and BOA Editions, Ltd., www.BOAEditions.org.

University of Minnesota Press: *A Christmas Carol* by Charles Dickens, adapted by Frederick Gaines, from *Five Plays from the Children's Theatre Company of Minneapolis,* published by the University of Minnesota Press. Copyright © 1975 by Frederick Gaines. All rights reserved.

David A. Perdue: *A Christmas Carol Review* by David A. Perdue, from the Charles Dickens Page. Used by permission of the author.

UNIT 4

Bantam Books: Excerpt from "One Ordinary Day, with Peanuts," from *Just An Ordinary Day: The Uncollected Stories* by Shirley Jackson. Copyright © 1979 by the Estate of Shirley Jackson. Used by permission of Bantam Books, a division of Random House, Inc.

Don Congdon Associates: "Dark They Were, and Golden-Eyed" as "The Naming of Names," from *Thrilling Wonder Stories* by Ray Bradbury. Copyright © 1949 by Standard Magazines, renewed 1976 by Ray Bradbury. Reprinted by permission of Don Congdon Associates, Inc.

The Charlotte Observer: Excerpt from "Ray Bradbury, Science Fiction Supernova, Has Little Use for the Internet" by Sandy Hill, the *Charlotte Observer,* October 12, 1997. Copyright © 1997 by the *Charlotte Observer.* Reprinted with permission of the *Charlotte Observer.*

Scribner: "A Day's Wait," from *The Short Stories of Ernest Hemingway.* Copyright 1933 by Charles Scribner's Sons. Copyright © 1961 by Mary Hemingway. Reprinted with permission of Scribner, an imprint of Simon & Schuster Adult Publishing Group.

Alfred A. Knopf Children's Books: Excerpt from *The People Could Fly: American Black Folktales* by Virginia Hamilton. Text copyright © 1985 by Virginia Hamilton. Reprinted by permission of Alfred A. Knopf Children's Books, a division of Random House, Inc.

Scholastic: "Fields of Flashing Light" and "Wild Boy of the Road," from *Out of the Dust* by Karen Hesse. Copyright © 1997 by Karen Hesse. Published by Scholastic Press/Scholastic, Inc. Reprinted by permission.

Doubleday: Excerpt from *Love and Marriage* by Bill Cosby. Copyright © 1989 by Bill Cosby. Used by permission of Doubleday, a division of Random House, Inc.

Crown Publishers: "Breaking the Ice," from *Dave Barry Is Not Making This Up* by Dave Barry. Copyright © 1994 by Dave Barry. Used by permission of Crown Publishers, a division of Random House, Inc.

Viking Penguin: "One Perfect Rose" by Dorothy Parker, from *The Portable Dorothy Parker,* edited by Brendan Gill. Copyright © 1926, copyright renewed © 1954 by Dorothy Parker. Used by permission of Viking Penguin, a division of Penguin Group (USA), Inc.

National Association for the Advancement of Colored People: "Song for an April Dusk" by Dorothy Parker, from *Dorothy Parker: Complete Poems.* Copyright © 1999 by The NAACP. The publisher wishes to thank the National Association for the Advancement of Colored People for this use of Dorothy Parker's work.

Liveright Publishing: "maggie and milly and molly and may," from *Complete Poems: 1904–1962* by E. E. Cummings, edited by George J. Firmage. Copyright © 1956, 1984, 1991 by the Trustees for the E. E. Cummings Trust. 1904 "who are you,little i?" from *Complete Poems: 1904–1962* by E. E. Cummings, edited by George J. Firmage. Copyright © 1963, 1991 by the Trustees for the E. E. Cummings Trust. "old age sticks," from *Complete Poems: 1904–1962* by E. E. Cummings, edited by George J. Firmage. Used by permission of Liveright Publishing Corporation.

UNIT 5

Henry Holt and Company: Excerpt from "A Minor Bird," from *The Poetry of Robert Frost,* edited by Edward Connery Lathem. Copyright © 1956 by Robert Frost. Copyright © 1928, 1969 by Henry Holt and Company. Reprinted by permission of Henry Holt and Company, LLC.

Arnold Adoff: "Under the Back Porch" by Virginia Hamilton. Copyright © 1992, 1999 by Virginia Hamilton Adoff. Copyright © 2006 by Arnold Adoff, Executor of the Estate of Virginia Hamilton Adoff. Used by permission.

Scribner: "Faults" by Sara Teasdale, from *The Collected Poems of Sara Teasdale.* Copyright © 1937 by the Macmillan Company. Reprinted with the permission of Scribner, an imprint of Simon & Schuster Adult Publishing Group.

Harvard University Press: "A word is dead" and "Fame is a bee," from *The Poems of Emily Dickinson,* edited by Thomas H. Johnson. Copyright © 1951, 1955, 1979, 1983 by the President and Fellows of Harvard College. Reprinted by permission of the publishers and the Trustees of Amherst College.

HarperCollins Publishers: "Cynthia in the Snow," from *Bronzeville Boys and Girls* by Gwendolyn Brooks. Copyright © 1956 by Gwendolyn Brooks Blakely. Used by permission of HarperCollins Publishers.

Harcourt: Excerpt from "Ode to Mi Gato," from *Neighborhood Odes* by Gary Soto. Copyright © 1992 by Gary Soto. Reprinted by permission of Harcourt, Inc. This material may not be reproduced in any form or by any means without the prior written permission of the publisher.

Harcourt: "Primer Lesson," from *Slabs of the Sunburnt West* by Carl Sandburg. Copyright © 1922 by Harcourt, Inc., and renewed 1950 by Carl Sandburg. Reprinted by permission of the publisher. This material may not be reproduced in any form or by any means without the prior written permission of the publisher.

Sterling Lord Literistic: "The Names" by Billy Collins. Copyright © 2002 by Billy Collins. Reprinted by permission of Sll/Sterling Lord Literistic, Inc.

Copper Canyon Press: "the earth is a living thing," from *The Book of Light* by Lucille Clifton. Copyright © 1993 by Lucille Clifton. Reprinted with the permission of Copper Canyon Press, P.O. Box 271, Port Townsend, WA 98368-0271.

Little, Brown and Company: "Sleeping in the Forest," from *Twelve Moons* by Mary Oliver. Copyright © 1972, 1973, 1974, 1976, 1977, 1978, 1979 by Mary Oliver. By permission of Little, Brown and Company, Inc.

Curtis Brown: "Gold" by Pat Mora, first appeared in *Home: A Journey Through America*, published by Silver Whistle Books. Copyright © 1998 by Pat Mora. Reprinted by permission of Curtis Brown, Ltd.

Faber and Faber: "Scaffolding," from *Death of a Naturalist* by Seamus Heaney. Copyright © 1966 by Seamus Heaney. Reprinted by permission of Faber and Faber, Ltd.

HarperCollins: "The World Is Not a Pleasant Place to Be," from *My House* by Nikki Giovanni. Copyright © 1972 by Nikki Giovanni. Reprinted by permission of HarperCollins Publishers.

Hugh Noyes: "The Highwayman," by Alfred Noyes. Reprinted by permission of Hugh Noyes for the Society of Authors as the Literary Representative of the Estate of Alfred Noyes.

HarperCollins Publishers: One haiku by Basho, from *The Essential Haiku: Versions of Basho, Buson & Issa*, edited and with an introduction by Robert Hass. Copyright © 1994 by Robert Hass. Reprinted by permission of HarperCollins Publishers.

HarperCollins Publishers: "Fireflies," from *Joyful Noise* by Paul Fleischman. Text copyright © 1988 by Paul Fleischman. Used by permission of HarperCollins Publishers.

Henry Holt and Company: "Fireflies in the Garden," from *The Poetry of Robert Frost* edited by Edward Connery Lathem. Copyright 1956 by Robert Frost. Copyright 1928, 1969 by Henry Holt and Company. Reprinted by permission of Henry Holt and Company, LLC.

HarperCollins Children's Books: "Sarah Cynthia Sylvia Stout Would Not Take the Garbage Out," from *Where the Sidewalk Ends* by Shel Silverstein. Copyright © 2004 by Evil Eye Music, Inc. Reprinted with permission from the Estate of Shel Silverstein and HarperCollins Children's Books.

N. Scott Momaday: "The Delight Song of Tsoai-talee," from *The Gourd Dancer* by N. Scott Momaday. Copyright © 1976 by N. Scott Momaday. Reprinted by permission of the author.

Susan Bergholz Literary Services: "Four Skinny Trees," from *The House on Mango Street* by Sandra Cisneros. Copyright © 1984 by Sandra Cisneros. Published by Vintage Books, a division of Random House, Inc., and in hardcover by Alfred A. Knopf in 1994. Reprinted by permission of Susan Bergholz Literary Services, New York. All rights reserved.

UNIT 6

Philomel Books: "Bess Call," from *Cut From the Same Cloth* by Robert D. San Souci. Copyright © 1993 by Robert D. San Souci. Used by permission of Philomel Books, a division of Penguin Young Readers Group, a member of Penguin Group (USA) Inc., 345 Hudson Street, New York, NY 10014. All rights reserved.

Scholastic: "Racing the Great Bear," from *Flying with the Eagle, Racing the Great Bear* by Joseph Bruchac. Copyright © 1993 by Joseph Bruchac. Reprinted by permission of Scholastic Inc.

Simon & Schuster Books for Young Readers: "Echo," from *The Macmillan Book of Greek Gods and Heroes* by Alice Low. Copyright © 1985 by Macmillan Publishing Company. Reprinted with the permission of Simon & Schuster Books for Young Readers, an imprint of Simon & Schuster Children's Publishing Division.

Scholastic: Excerpt from *The Greek Gods* by Bernard Evslin. Copyright © 1966 by Scholastic, Inc. Reprinted by permission of Scholastic, Inc.

Houghton Mifflin Company: "The Great Musician" and "Phaëthon, Son of Apollo," from *Greek Myths* by Olivia E. Coolidge. Copyright © 1949 by Olivia E. Coolidge. Copyright renewed © 1977 by Olivia E. Coolidge. Adapted by permission of Houghton Mifflin Company. All rights reserved.

Barbara S. Kouts Literary Agent: *Young Arthur* by Robert D. San Souci. Copyright © 1977 by Robert D. San Souci. Reprinted by permission of Barbara S. Kouts Literary Agent.

National Geographic Society: Excerpts from "Looking for King Arthur" by Jerry Dunn, from *National Geographic World*, March 1997. Copyright © 1997 by National Geographic. Reprinted with permission from the National Geographic Society.

Candlewick Press: *Sir Gawain and the Green Knight* by Michael Morpurgo. Text copyright © 2004 by Michael Morpurgo. Reproduced by permission of the publisher Candlewick Press, Inc., Cambridge, MA., on behalf of Walker Books Ltd., London.

Hyperion: Excerpt from *Crispin: The Cross of Lead* by Avi. Copyright © 2002 by Avi. Reprinted by permission of Hyperion, an imprint of Disney Children's Book Group, LLC.

Rowman & Littlefield Publishing Group: "Crispin: The Cross of Lead" book review by Rebecca Barnhouse, from *Voya*, Vol. 25, No. 2, June 2002. Copyright © 2002 by Rowman & Littlefield Publishing Group. Reprinted with permission.

Reprint Management Services: "Crispin: The Cross of Lead" book review by Cheri Estes, from *School Library Journal*, Vol. 48, No. 6, June 2002. Copyright © 2002 by School Library Journal. Reprinted with permission.

Lori Seals: "Brer Possum's Dilemma" by Jackie Torrence. Copyright © by Jackie Torrence. Used by permission of Lori Seals for the Estate of Jackie Torrence.

Curtis Brown: "Waters of Gold," from *Tongues of Jade* by Laurence Yep, published by HarperCollins. Text copyright © 1991 by Laurence Yep. Reprinted by permission of the author.

Alfred A. Knopf: "Sally Ann Thunder Ann Whirlwind," from *American Tall Tales* by Mary Pope Osbourne. Copyright © 1991 by Mary Pope Osbourne. Illustrations copyright © 1991 by Michael McCurdy. Used by permission of Alfred A. Knopf, an imprint of Random House Children's Books, a division of Random House, Inc.

Doubleday: "Two Ways to Count to Ten," from *African Wonder Tales* by Frances Carpenter Huntington. Copyright © 1963 by Frances Carpenter Huntington. Used by permission of Doubleday, a division of Random House, Inc.

Pantheon Books: "The Race Between Toad and Donkey," from *Afro-American Folktales,* edited by Roger D. Abrahams. Copyright © 1985 by Roger D. Abrahams. Used by permission of Pantheon Books, a division of Random House, Inc.

UNIT 7

Holiday House: Excerpt from *The Wright Brothers: How They Invented the Airplane* by Russell Freedman. Copyright © 1991 by Russell Freedman. Reprinted by permission of Holiday House, Inc.

Simon & Schuster Books for Young Readers: Excerpt from *The Invisible Thread* by Yoshiko Uchida. Copyright © 1991 by Yoshiko Uchida. Reprinted with the permission of Simon & Schuster Books for Young Readers, an imprint of Simon & Schuster Children's Publishing Division.

H. W. Wilson Company: Excerpt from "Christopher Reeve," from *Current Biography.* Copyright © 1982 by the H. W. Wilson Company. Reprinted by special arrangement with the H. W. Wilson Company.

Dial Books for Young Readers: Excerpt from *Rosa Parks: My Story* by Rosa Parks with Jim Haskins. Copyright © 1992 by Rosa Parks. Used by permission of Dial Books for Young Readers, a division of Penguin Young Readers Group, a Member of Penguin Group (USA), Inc., 345 Hudson Street, New York, NY 10014. All rights reserved.

Atheneum Books for Young Readers: Excerpts from "Eleanor Roosevelt," from *Great Lives: Human Rights* by William Jay Jacobs. Copyright © 1990 by William Jay Jacobs. Reprinted with the permission of Atheneum Books for Young Readers, an imprint of Simon & Schuster Children's Publishing Division.

Susan Bergholz Literary Services: "Names/Nombres" by Julia Alvarez, first published in *Nuestro,* March 1985. Copyright © 1985 by Julia Alvarez. Reprinted by permission of Susan Bergholz Literary Services, New York. All rights reserved.

G. P. Putnam's Sons: "Chemo," from *It's Not About the Bike* by Lance Armstrong. Copyright © 2000 by Lance Armstrong. Used by permission of G. P. Putnam's Sons, a division of Penguin Group (USA), Inc.

Da Capo Press: Excerpt from *23 Days in July* by John Wilcockson. Copyright © 2004 by John Wilcockson. Reprinted by permission of Da Capo Press, a member of Perseus Books, LLC.

CMG Worldwide: Excerpt from *I Never Had It Made* by Jackie Robinson as told to Alfred Duckett. Copyright © 1972 by Jackie Robinson and Alfred Duckett. Copyright © Rachel Robinson by CMG Worldwide, www.JackieRobinson.com. Reprinted by permission of CMG Worldwide.

Excerpt from *Malcolm X: By Any Means Necessary* by Walter Dean Myers. Copyright © 1993 by Walter Dean Myers. TM 2005 Malcolm X by CMG Worldwide, Inc. www.CMGWorldwide.com.

The New York Times: Excerpt from "Montreal Signs Negro Shortstop," from *the New York Times.* Copyright © 1945 by the New York Times Co. Reprinted by permission.

The New York Times: Excerpts from "Robinson Steals Home in Fifth" by Roscoe McGowen, from *the New York Times.* Copyright © 1947 by the New York Times Co. Reprinted with permission.

PLAYS: "Lucy Stone, Champion of Women's Rights" by Claire Boiko, from *Plays of Great Achievers.* Reproduced with the permission of PLAYS, the Drama Magazine for Young People/Sterling Partners, Inc., P.O. Box 600160, Newton, MA 02460.

W. W. Norton & Company: "My Mother Enters the Work Force," from *On the Bus with Rosa Parks* by Rita Dove. Copyright © 1999 by Rita Dove. Used by permission of W. W. Norton & Company, Inc.

Harcourt: "Washington Monument by Night," from *Slabs of the Sunburnt West* by Carl Sandburg. Copyright © 1922 by Harcourt, Inc., and renewed 1950 by Carl Sandburg. Reprinted by permission of the publisher. This material may not be reproduced in any form or by any means without the prior written permission of the publisher.

UNIT 8

Popular Science: Adaptation of "What's Eating the Titanic?" by Gregory Mone, from *Popular Science,* July 2004. Copyright © 2004 by Popular Science. Reprinted with permission.

Sharon Guynup: Excerpts from "What Do You Know About Sharks?" by Sharon Guynup, from *Science World.* Copyright © 2001 by Scholastic, Inc. Reprinted by permission of the author.

National Geographic Society: Excerpts from "Great White Sharks" by Peter Benchley, from *National Geographic,* April 2000. Copyright © 2000 by National Geographic. Reprinted with permission from the National Geographic Society.

Cobblestone Publishing: "Like Black Smoke—The Black Death's Journey" by Diana Childress, from *CALLIOPE,* March 2001. Copyright © 2001 by Cobblestone Publishing, 30 Grove Street, Suite C, Peterborough, NH 03458. All rights reserved. Used by permission of Carus Publishing Company.

Cobblestone Publishing: "A World Turned Upside Down: How the Black Death Affected Europe" by Mary Morton Cowan, from *CALLIOPE,* March 2001. Copyright © 2001 by Cobblestone Publishing, 30 Grove Street, Suite C, Peterborough, NH 03458. All rights reserved. Used by permission of Carus Publishing Company.

D. Mark Singletary: "Pro Athletes' Salaries Aren't Overly Exorbitant" by Mark Singletary, from *New Orleans CityBusiness,* March 25, 2002. Copyright © 2002 by D. Mark Singletary. Reprinted with permission.

Justin Hjelm: "Do Professional Athletes Get Paid Too Much?" by Justin Hjelm, from *the Horizon.* Copyright © 2004 by Justin Hjelm. Used by permission of the author.

Time: "Why We Shouldn't Go to Mars" by Gregg Easterbrook, from *Time,* January 26, 2004. Copyright © 2004 by TIME, Inc. Reprinted by permission.

The editors have made every effort to trace the ownership of all copyrighted material found in this book and to make full acknowledgment for its use. Omissions brought to our attention will be corrected in a subsequent edition.

ART CREDITS

CONSULTANTS

Title page © Getty Images; Photo © Duane McCubrey; Photo © Mark Schmidt; Photo © Bruce Forrester; Photo © McDougal Littell; Photo © Howard Gollub; Photo © Tamra Stallings; Photo © Mark Schmidt; Photo © Robert J. Marzano; Photo © McDougal Littell; Photo © Dawson & Associates Photography; Photo © Gitchell's Studio; Photo © Michael Romeo; Photo © Monica Ani; Photo © William McBride; Photo © Bill Caldwell; Photo © Gabriel Pauluzzi; Photo © Steven Scheffler.

TABLE OF CONTENTS

Contents in Brief verso *top* An Imprint of HarperCollins Publishers. Illustration © 1997 by Jerry Pinkney; *bottom* From *The People Could Fly* Illustrations © 1985 by Leo and Diane Dillon. Used by permission of Alfred A. Knopf, an imprint of Random House Children's Books, a division of Random House, Inc.; **recto** *top* © Detlev Van Ravensway/Photo Researchers, Inc.; *bottom* © Photo by Sharon Hoogstraten; *bottom left* Plate 57 from *A Field Guide to the Shells of the Atlantic and Gulf Coasts and the West Indies* © 1995 by R. Tucker Abbott and Violet French Morris. Reprinted by permission of Houghton Mifflin Company. All rights reserved; *bottom right* From *Shells* © 2004 Quantum Publishing Ltd., London; **Unit 1 verso** *left* Illustration by Erika O'Rourke/Elm Studios; *right* right © Artville; **recto** *top* Courtesy American Library Association; *bottom left* From *North by Night* by Katherine Ayers. Cover illustration by Jeff Barson. Used by permission of Yearling Books, a division of Random House, Inc.; *bottom right* Cover from *Bearstone* by Will Hobbs. Jacket illustration © 1989 by Patricia Mulvihill. Used with the permission of Macmillan Publishing Company; **Unit 2 verso** *left* Library of Congress; *right, Boy with Orange,* Murray Kimber. © Murray Kimber/Illustrationworks.com; **recto** *left* Jacket of *The Midwife's Apprentice* by Karen Cushman. © 1995, Clarion Books, New York; **Unit 3 verso** *left* © Adrian Arbib/Alamy Images; *right* Detail of *Birds XII* (2003), Barbara Weldon. Oil, gold leaf, and wax on canvas; **recto** *top* Courtesy American Library Association; *bottom left* Cover of *Wolf Shadows* by Mary Casanova. Cover art © 1997 by Dan Brown. Reprinted by permission of Hyperion Books for Children; **Unit 4 verso** *right* © Andrew Judd/Masterfile; *left* © Ferdinando Scianna/Magnum Photos; **recto** *left* Cover from *Shabanu* by Suzanne Fisher Staples. Cover photograph © Jim Zuckerman/Corbis. Used by permission of Random House Publishers; *right* Cover of *A Long Way from Chicago* by Richard Peck. Cover illustration © Steve Cieslawski, 2004. Cover design by Lori Thoorn. Reprinted by permission of Penguin Modern Classics, a division of Penguin Group (USA) Inc., 345 Hudson Street, New York, 10014. All rights reserved; **Unit 5 verso** *left* © The Image Bank/Getty Images; *right, Dragon,* Greg Spalenka. © Greg Spalenka; **recto** *left* Cover of *The Monument* by Gary Paulsen. Jacket illustration © 1991 by Nan Parson. Used by permission of Delacorte Press, New York; **Unit 6 verso** *left, Falling Figure (Icarus)* (1944), Henri Matisse. Color lithograph after a paper cut-out and gouache. Published on the back cover of the deluxe art review *Verve* © 2007 Succession H. Matisse, Paris/Artists Rights Society (ARS), New York; *right* Illustration © Juan Wijngaard (1981) from *Sir Gawain and the Green Knight* by Selina Hastings. Reproduced by permission of Walker Books, Ltd., London; **recto** *top* Courtesy American Library Association; *bottom left* Cover of *Jazmin's Notebook* by Nikki Grimes. Cover illustration ©1998 by Eric Velasquez. Reprinted by permission of Penguin Putnam, New York; *bottom right* Cover of *Trouble River* by Betsy Byars. Cover illustration © 1997 Robert McGinnis. Published by Puffin Books, a division of Penguin Putnam Books for Young Readers, New York. All rights reserved; New York; **Unit 7 verso** *left* © Marvin Koner/Corbis; *right* AP/Wide World Photos; *bottom* Courtesy American Library Association; **recto** *left* Cover of *Beyond the Burning Time* by Kathryn Lasky. © 1994 by Kathryn Lasky. Cover art by David Shannon. Published by permission of

Scholastic, Inc.; **Unit 8 verso** *left* © Jeff Rotman/Alamy Images; *right* © Stephen Frink Collection/Alamy Images; **recto** *left* Cover of *Bound for the North Star* by Dennis Brindell Fradin. Jacket illustration from the Underground Railroad Quilt, courtesy of the Oberlin Senior Center. Photo by Judith Bloom Fradin. Published by Clarion Books, an imprint of Houghton Mifflin Company, New York; **Unit 9** *left* © Photo courtesy of Seattle Public Library; *right* © Photo by Sharon Hoogstraten; *inset left* Plate 57 from *Shells* © 1995 by R. Tucker Abbott and Violet French Morris. A Peterson Field Guide. Used by permission of Houghton Mifflin Company, New York; *inset right* From *Shells* © 2004 Quantum Publishing Ltd., London.

THE POWER OF IDEAS

1 *left* From *The People Could Fly* Illustrations © 1985 by Leo and Diane Dillon. Used by permission of Alfred A. Knopf, an imprint of Random House Children's Books, a division of Random House, Inc.; *top right* © 2008 by Universal Studios Licensing LLLP. Courtesy of Universal Studios Licensing LLLP. All rights reserved; *bottom right* © Joseph Sohm; Visions of America/Corbis; **2** *left* An Imprint of HarperCollins Publishers. Illustration © 1997 by Jerry Pinkney; *right* © Alan Powdrill/Getty Images; **7** *left* © Images.com/Corbis; *right* AP/Wide World Photos; **8** *top to bottom* © Bettmann/Corbis; © Bill Pierce/Time Life Pictures/Getty Images; © Corbis; © Photographer's Choice/Getty Images; © Judith Collins/Alamy; **10** *top to bottom* © 2008 by Universal Studios Licensing LLLP. Courtesy of Universal Studios Licensing LLLP. All rights reserved; Courtesy of ABC NEWS; © CBS Photo Archive; *Kibbles n' Bits Commercial* © Del Monte corporation; The Granger Collection, New York; **11** © Garry Hunter/Getty Images; **16** *left* © Jose Luis Pelaez, Inc./Corbis; *center* © Yellow Dog Productions/Getty Images; *right, inset left* © Time Life Pictures/Getty Images; *right, inset right* © 2005 The Summer Northwestern; **17** © Siede Preis/Photodisc Green/Getty Images; **18** © Sam Barricklow/Workbookstock.com; **19** *left* © Image Source/Getty Images; *center* © Rob Brimson/Getty Images; *right* © Flying Colours, Ltd./Getty Images.

UNIT 1

21 *left* © William Low; *right* © Galen Rowell/Corbis; **22–23** © Paul Edmondson/Corbis; **22** *left* From *The Black Stallion* by Walter Farley. Cover art © 2002 by John Rowe. Used by permission of Random House; *right* © Kelly Reno/Photofest; **30** © Ed Bock/Corbis; **31** Courtesy of Gary Soto; **33** © Lisa Pines/Getty Images; **35** © Elizabeth Knox/Masterfile; **36** *left* © Jose Luis Pelaez, Inc./Corbis; *center* © Royalty-Free/PictureQuest; **42** *background* © Doug Wilson/Corbis; *center* © PhotoDisc; **43** © Samantha Loomis Paterson; **45** Illustration by Erika O'Rourke/Elm Studios; **46** © Javier Larrea/Age Fotostock America, Inc.; **49–57** Illustrations by Erika O'Rourke/Elm Studios; **62** © David M. Grossman/Workbookstock.com; **63** © Corbis; **67** *Gamin* (1929), Augusta Savage. Painted plaster, 9 × 5 3/4" × 4 3/8". Gift of Benjamin and Olya Margolin © Smithsonian American Art Museum, Washington, D.C./Art Resource, New York; **72** *center* © Marc Romanelli/Getty Images; *background* © Artbeats; **73** © Getty Images; **75** An Imprint of HarperCollins Publishers. Illustration © 1997 by Jerry Pinkney **76** © Jeremy Horner/Corbis; **77** *top* © GeoNova, LLC; *bottom* An Imprint of HarperCollins Publishers. Illustration © 1997 by Jerry Pinkney; **78, 82, 85, 86** An Imprint of HarperCollins Publishers. Illustration © 1997 by Jerry Pinkney; **92** *top* © Les Cunliffe/Age Fotostock America, Inc.; *center* © Carla Sachar; **92–93** © Jeff Hunter/Getty Images; **93** *top* Courtesy American Library Association; *bottom* From *Holes* by Louis Sachar. Cover illustration by Vladimir Radunsky. Reprinted by permission of Yearling Books, a division of Random House, Inc.; **94–95** © Royalty-Free/Corbis; **96–97** © Digital Vision/Getty Images; **98** *background* © C. Lee/Photolink/Getty Images; *center* © Richard Cummins/Corbis; **99** © Bettmann/Corbis; **103** *top* ©

Don Lynch Collection; *frame* © Kimbell Art Museum/Corbis; *bottom* © From the Collections of the University of Pennsylvania Archives; *frame* © Kimbell Art Museum/Corbis; **106** Museum of Science and Industry, Chicago; **107** *top right* The Granger Collection, New York; *frame* © Kimbell Art Museum/Corbis; **111** © The National Archives of the United Kingdom; **115** 20th Century Fox/Paramount © Photofest; **118** © S. Beaudet/zefa; **119** © Jerry Bauer; **124** © Helen Norman/Corbis; **128** © Joe Robbins/Getty Images; **129** HUP Thayer, Ernest L. (1), Courtesy of the Harvard University Archives; **133** © Bettmann/Corbis; **134** © Enrique Algarra/Age Fotostock America, Inc.; **135** © Bettmann/Corbis; **137** *Empire of Lights* (1954), René Magritte. Oil on canvas, 146 cm x 114 cm. Musée d'Art Moderne, Brussels. © Phototheque R. Magritte/ADAGP, Paris/Art Resource, New York/© 2007 C. Herscovici, Brussels/Artists Rights Society (ARS), New York; **139, 140, 143, 144, 147** © CBS Photo Archive; **150** © MCA/Universal Pictures/Courtesy Everett Collection; **151** *top* © 2008 by Universal Studios Licensing LLLP. Courtesy of Universal Studios Licensing LLLP. All rights reserved; *center* © MCA/Universal Pictures/Courtesy Everett Collection; *bottom* © 2008 by Universal Studios Licensing LLLP. Courtesy of Universal Studios Licensing LLLP. All rights reserved; **152** *top left, bottom left* © 2008 by Universal Studios Licensing LLLP. Courtesy of Universal Studios Licensing LLLP. All rights reserved; *background* © A & J Verkaik/Corbis; **155** © MCA/Universal Pictures/courtesy The Everett Collection; **158, 164** © Craig Aurness/Corbis; **165** © Jim Cummins/Corbis; **172** *top left* From *The Ghost in the Tokaido Inn* by Dorothy and Thomas Hooble. Cover illustration © Gregg Call, 2000. Used by permission of Penguin Putnam, Inc.; *top right* From *No Man's Land* by Susan Bartoletti. Jacket painting © 1999 by David Shannon. Used by permission of Blue Sky Press, a division of Scholastic, Inc.; *center left* Cover from *Bearstone* by Will Hobbs. Jacket illustration © 1989 by Patricia Mulvihill. © 1989 by Macmillan Publishing Company. Reprinted with the permission of Atheneum, an imprint of Simon & Schuster Children's Division; *center right* Cover from *Nobody's Daughter* by Susan Beth Pfeffer. © 1995 by Susan Beth Pfeffer. Cover illustration by Bill Farnsworth. Reprinted by permission of Delacorte Press, New York.

UNIT 2

173 *left, Bernadita* (1922), Robert Henri. Oil on canvas, 24⅛″ × 20⅛″. Gift of the San Diego Wednesday Club. © San Diego Museum of Art (1926:138); *right* © Michael Goldman/Taxi/Getty Images; **174–175** © 20th Century Fox/ZUMA/Lucasfilm Ltd./Photofest; **182** *background* © Getty Images/Royalty Free; *center* © Alexander Walter/Getty Images; **183** © Bettmann/Corbis; **185** *background* © James Gritz/Getty Images; *center* © Joshua Sheldon/Getty Images; **189** © Alan Powdrill/Getty Images; **192** © Peter Finger/Corbis; **195** © GeoNova, LLC; **197** *background* © Joe Raedle/Getty Images; *center left, center right* AP/Wide World Photos; **199** © Royalty-Free/Corbis; **203** © Alamy Images; **204** © Thinkstock/Getty Images; **205, 209** AP/Wide World Photos; **210, 211** © Nathan Benn/Corbis; **214** *top* © David J. and Janice L. Frent Collection/Corbis; *bottom, left* © Leif Skoogfors/Corbis; *bottom right* © Corbis Sygma; **216** © Alan Schein Photography/Corbis; **217** © David H. Wells; **226** AP/Wide World Photos; **227** © Bettmann/Corbis; **229** *Tides of Memory* (1936), Norman Rockwell. Oil on board, 18¾″ × 15¼″. Collection of Mr. and Mrs. Norman Rockwell. Reproduced by permission of the Norman Rockwell Family Agency, Inc. Photo courtesy of the Norman Rockwell Museum at Stockbridge, Massachusetts; **234** *Hill, Main Street, Gloucester* (1916), John Sloan. Oil on canvas, 25 3/4″ x 39 7/8″. Littlejohn Collection, The Parrish Art Museum, Southampton, New York, 1961.3.208; **240** © Reuters/Corbis; **241** *top, bottom* AP/Wide World Photos; **246** Library of Congress, Prints and Photographs Division; **247** © Beth Reitmeyer/McDougal Littell; **248** © Photodisc Blue/Getty Images; **250** © Images.com/Corbis; **258** Louis Lanzano/AP/Wide World Photos; **259** © Frederick M. Brown/Getty Images; **261** *inset* © Bettmann/Corbis; *background* © Reg Lancaster/Express/Getty Images; **262** *left, right* Library of Congress; *center* © Bettmann/Corbis; **263** *left, right* © Bettmann/Corbis; *center* Library of Congress; **268** Photo by Sharon Hoogstraten; **269** ©

C.E. Mitchell/stockphoto.com; **274** © Peter Weimann/Animals Animals–Earth Scenes; **280** © Walter Hodges/Corbis; **281** *top* © Nancy E. Crampton; *bottom* © Gene Blevins/Corbis; **284** © Chris Dyball/Getty Images; **286, 292** © Joseph Sohm; ChromoSohm Inc./Corbis; **293** © Jeff Greenberg/Age Fotostock America, Inc.; **300** *top left* Cover of *Getting Near to Baby* by Audrey Couloumbis. Cover art © 1999 by Ian Schoenherr. Used by permission of G. P. Putnams Sons, a division of Penguin Putnam Books Young Readers Group, a member of Penguin Group (USA) Inc., 345 Hudson Street, New York, 10014. All rights reserved; *top right* From *The Birthday Room* by Kevin Henkes. © 1999 by Kevin Henkes. Cover reprinted by permission of HarperCollins Publishers, Inc.; *center right* Jacket of *The Midwife's Apprentice* by Karen Cushman. © 1995, Clarion Books, New York; *bottom left* Jacket cover from *Spider Boy* by Ralph Fletcher. Used by permission of Random House Children's Books, a division of Random House, Inc.; *bottom right* From *Spinners* by Donna Jo Napoli and Richard Tchen. Cover art © 1999 by Donna Diamond. Used by permission of Dutton Children's Books, a division of Penguin Young Readers Group, a member of Penguin Group (USA) Inc., 345 Hudson Street, New York, 10014. All rights reserved.

UNIT 3

301 *left* Detail of *Birds XII* (2003), Barbara Weldon. Oil, gold leaf, and wax on canvas; *right* © Adrian Arbib/Alamy Images; **302** *left* Cover from *The Wonderful Wizard of Oz,* 100th Anniversary Edition by L. Frank Baum. Illustrated by W. W. Denslow. © 2000 HarperCollins Publishers, Inc.; *right* © MGM/The Kobal Collection; **304** *left, Faith Ringgold* (1977), Alice Neel. Oil on canvas, 48″ × 36″. Private collection. © 2004 Estate of Alice Neel/Courtesy Robert Miller Gallery, New York/Philadelphia Museum of Art, Special Exhibition (Accession: *The Art of Alice Neel,* Page 150, Plate 70); *right, Mighty Casey Advancing to the Bat* (1912), Dan Sayre Groesbeck. From illustration series for *Casey at the Bat* by Phineas Thayer. Mary Evans Picture Library; **310** *background* © Getty Images; *front* © Royalty-Free/Corbis; **311** © Nic Paget-Clarke; **314** © GeoNova, LLC; **323** AP/Wide World Photos; **326** © Jim West/The Image Works, Inc.; **327** © Schomburg Center for Research in Black Culture, New York Public Library/Art Resource, New York; **329** *Harlem Street Scene* (1942), Jacob Lawrence. Gouache on paper, 21″ × 20 3/4″. Private collection. © The Jacob and Gwendolyn Lawrence Foundation/Art Resource, New York. Artists Rights Society (ARS), New York; **334** © Bettmann/Corbis; **337** *World Wall: A Vision of the Future Without Fear.* With Judith Baca. © SPARC www.sparcmurals.org; **338** © Alex James Photographic/Getty Images; **339** Courtesy of the author; **341** *Gregory. Los Angeles, March 31st 1982* (1982), David Hockney. Composite Polaroid. 14 1/2″ × 13 1/4″. © David Hockney/The David Hockney No. 1 U.S. Trust; **347** © 2002 Gueorgui Pinkhassov/Magnum Photos; **350** *Celia. Los Angeles, April 10th 1982* (1982), David Hockney. Composite Polaroid. 18″ × 30″. © David Hockney/The David Hockney No. 1 U.S. Trust; **357** © Bill Pierce/Time Life Pictures/Getty Images; **358** © Jeff Dunn/PictureQuest; **360** Gloria H. Chomica/Masterfile; **362** © Cassy Cohen/PhotoEdit; **363** © Margaret Miller/Courtesy Simon & Schuster; **365** © Bill Firestone; **368** *left* © Comstock Images/Alamy Images; *center* © John McAnulty/Corbis; *right* © Richard Cummins/Corbis; **371** © Bill Firestone; **374** *top* © Les Cunliffe/Age Fotostock America, Inc.; *bottom* © Courtesy of the author; **374–375** © Hulton-Deutsch Collection/Corbis; **375** *top* Courtesy American Library Association; *bottom* Cover illustration by Cliff Nelson from *The Gift,* Lois Lowry. © 1993 Houghton Mifflin. A Bantam Book, June 1999. New York, New York; **376–377** © Horace Bristol/Corbis; **378–379** © Laurence Mouton/PhotoAlto; **380** © Al Petteway /National Geographic Image Collection; **381** *top* © Christopher Felver/Corbis; *bottom* © 2002 Margaretta K. Mitchell; **386** © Thierry Dosogne/iconica Limited; **387** The Granger Collection, New York; **388, 389, 391, 393, 395, 397, 403, 404, 407, 408, 409, 411** © 2003 Michael Rasbury/Louisiana Tech University School of Performing Arts; **413, 414** The Granger Collection, New York; **416** © Bettmann/Corbis; **417** *top* © Bettmann/Corbis; *center* © John Springer

UNIT 4

UNIT 5

UNIT 6

623 *left* Study of *Almanach Der Blaue Reiter* (1911), Wassily Kandinsky. Watercolor, gouache, and black ink. Inv. AM 1994-70. Photo by Philippe Migeat. Musée National d'Art Moderne, Centre Georges Pompidou, Paris. © CNAC/MNAM/Dist. Réunion des Musées Nationaux/Art Resource, New York © 2007 Artists Rights Society (ARS), New York/ADAGP, Paris; *right* © Jim Zuckerman/Corbis; **624** © Tom Smart/Liaison/Getty Images; **632** © Paul A. Souders/Corbis; **633** *top* Courtesy of the author; *bottom* Courtesy of Julian Coolidge; **636** © GeoNova, LLC; **640** Museo della Civilta Romana, Rome. © Dagli Orti/The Art Archive; **646** © JupiterImages/Creatas/Royalty-Free; **647** *top* © The Schlesinger Library, Radcliffe Institute, Harvard University. http://www.radcliffe.edu/schles; *bottom* Courtesy of Julian Coolidge; **649** *The Fall of Icarus* (1944),Henri Matisse. Color lithograph after paper cut-out and gouache. Published in Verve in 1944. © 2007 Succession H. Matisse, Paris/Artists Rights Society (ARS), New York; **651** *Falling Figure (Icarus)* (1944), Henri Matisse. Color lithograph after a paper cut-out and gouache. Published on the back cover of the deluxe art review Verve © 2007 Succession H. Matisse, Paris/Artists Rights Society (ARS), New York; **653** *Study of Almanach Der Blaue Reiter* (1911), Wassily Kandinsky. Watercolor, gouache, and black ink. Inv. AM 1994-70. Photo by Philippe Migeat. Musée National d'Art Moderne, Centre Georges Pompidou, Paris. © CNAC/MNAM/Dist. Réunion des Musées Nationaux/Art Resource, New York © 2008 Artists Rights Society (ARS), New York/ADAGP, Paris; **656** *The Cavalier*, Wassily Kandinsky. Staedtische Galerie im Lenbachhaus, Munich, Germany © Giraudon/Art Resource, New York © 2008 Artists Rights Society (ARS), New York/ADAGP, Paris; **660** © Mason Morfit/Workbookstock/Jupiterimages Corporation; **661** © Robert D. San Souci; **666** © Arte & Immagini srl/Corbis; **669** © Francis G. Mayer/Corbis; **670** © Kelvin Murray/Getty Images; **671** © David Levenson/Getty Images; **674** © Heritage-Images/The Image Works, Inc.; **686** *top left* © Les Cunliffe/Age Fotostock America, Inc.; *bottom left* Photo by Russ Wright; courtesy of the author; **686–687** © Robert Estall/Corbis; **687** *top* Courtesy American Library Association; *bottom* Cover image from *Crispin, The Cross of Lead* by Avi. © 2002. Reprinted with permission of Hyperion Books for Children, New York, New York; **688–689** © Bruno Morandi/Age Fotostock America, Inc.; **690–691** © Santiago Yaniz/Age Fotostock America, Inc.; **693** Dover Publications; **694** Cover image from *Crispin, The Cross of Lead* by Avi. © 2002. Reprinted with permission of Hyperion Books for Children, New York, New York; **696** © Digital Vision/Getty Images; **697** *top* Courtesy of the author; *bottom* Courtesy of Laurence Yep; **699** Illustration by Ingrid Hess; **712** *foreground* © Eric and David Hosking/Corbis; *background* © PhotoDisc; **713** © 2003 Paul Coughlin; **722** © Warner Brothers Entertainment Inc. All Rights Reserved; **723** *top* Sophia Smith Collection, Smith College/Smithsonian Institution; *bottom* University of Pennsylvania Center for Folklore and Ethnography; **725** Collage created by Celia Jordan; *background* © Gallo Images/Corbis; *center* © Paul A. Souders/Corbis; **726** © GeoNova, LLC; **731** *background* © David Reddick/Workbookstock. com; *left* © Tracy Kahn Photography, Inc./Workbookstock.com; *right* © Image Source/Workbookstock.com; **733** © GeoNova, LLC; **736, 742** © J. David Andrews/Masterfile; **743** © Zigy Kaluzny/Getty Images; **750** *top left* Cover of *Nothing But the Truth* by Avi. Cover design by Hilary Zarycky. © 2003 by HarperCollins Publishers, Inc. Reprinted by permission; *top right* Cover of *Honus & Me* by Dan Gutman. Cover art © 2003 by Steve Chorney. Cover © 2003 by HarperCollins Publishers Inc. Reprinted by permission; *center left* From *Through My Eyes* by Ruby Bridges. Published by Scholastic Press, a division of Scholastic, Inc. Jacket image © UPI/Bettmann/Corbis; *center right* Cover of *Jazmin's Notebook* by Nikki Grimes. Cover illustration ©1998 by Eric Velasquez. Reprinted by permission of Penguin Putnam, New York; *bottom left* Cover of *Trouble River* by Betsy Byars. Cover illustration © 1997 Robert McGinnis. Published by Puffin Books, a division of Penguin Putnam Books for Young Readers, New York; *bottom right* Cover of Zack by William Bell. © 1998 by William Bell. Cover illustration © 1998 by Kadir Nelson. Cover design by Steve

Scott. Reprinted by permission of Aladdin Paperbacks, an imprint of Simon & Schuster Children's Publishing Division, New York.

UNIT 7

751 *left,* Detail of *Alma Sewing* (about 1935), Francis Criss. Oil on canvas, 33″ × 45″. High Museum of Art, Atlanta, Georgia. Purchase with funds from the Fine Art Collectors, Mr. and Mrs. Henry Schwob, the Director's Circle, Mr. and Mrs. John L. Huber, High Museum of Art Enhancement Fund, Stephen and Linda Sessler, the J.J. Haverty Fund, and through prior acquisitions. 2002.70; *right* © Jim Cornfield/Corbis; **752** girls Photos © Amy Carneghi; daisies © Bezkorovayny Dmitry/ShutterStock; peanuts © Neil Webster/ShutterStock; glove © PhotoDisc; popcorn © Scott Rothstein/ShutterStock; **752–753** © Photo by Sharon Hoogstraten; grass © Donna Middlemiss/ShutterStock; boys Photo © Erik Koelle; **753** baseball, bat © PhotoDisc; **756** *left* © Marvin Koner/Corbis; *right* © Bettmann/Corbis; **759** © Reuters/Corbis; **760** © Viviane Moos/Corbis; **761** Reprinted with the permission of Atheneum Books for Young Readers, an imprint of Simon and Schuster Children's Publishing Division from the author photograph in *Great Lives: Human Rights* by William Jay Jacobs. Charles Scribner's Sons, New York, 1990; **763** © Marvin Koner/Corbis; **765, 766** © Corbis; **769, 770** © Bettmann/Corbis; **771** © Hulton Archive/Getty Images; **773** The Granger Collection, New York; **777, 778** © Bettmann/Corbis; **780** *left, center* © SuperStock, Inc./SuperStock; *right* © Michael Rougier/Getty Images; **781** © The Boston Globe/www.Merlin-Net.com; **785** © GeoNova, LLC; **790** South Bend Tribune/AP/Wide World Photos; **791** © Duomo/Corbis; **793** © James Startt; **795** Courtesy LaTrice Haney; **797, 798–799** AP/Wide World Photos; **800** © AFP/Getty Images; **802** *top left* © Les Cunliffe/Age Fotostock America, Inc.; *center left* © Jerry Bauer; **802–803** AP/Wide World Photos; **803** *left* From *By Any Means Necessary* by Malcolm X. Cover photograph © John Launois/Black Star. Used with permission of the publisher Scholastic, Inc., New York; *right* Courtesy American Library Association; **804–805** © Bruce Davidson/Magnum Photos; **806–807** © James P. Blair/National Geographic Image Collection; **808** AP/Wide World Photos; **809** © Bettmann/Corbis; **811** Library of Congress Serial and Government Publications Division, LC-USZC4-6144 DLC; **813** *left* Library of Congress Prints and Photographs Division, LC-USZ62-119886 DLC; *right* © Barros & Barros/Getty Images; **815** *left* National Archives; *right* © Lake County Museum/Corbis; **817** *left* © Bettmann/Corbis; *right* © PhotoDisc/Getty Images; **819** *left* © Bettmann/Corbis; *right* © Blank Archives/Getty Images; *inset* Library of Congress, Prints and Photographs Division; **823, 824** AP/Wide World Photos; **825** © Bettmann/Corbis; **828** © Getty Images; **829** Footage from *Biography: Jackie Robinson,* A & E Television Networks; **830** *top left, bottom left* Footage from *Biography: Jackie Robinson,* A & E Television Networks; *background* © Jerry Driendl/Getty Images; **832** AP/Wide World Photos; **833** Courtesy Patricia Boiko; **841** © The Schlesinger Library, Radcliffe Institute, Harvard University; *frame* © 1996 Image Farm, Inc. All rights reserved; **844** © Bettmann/Corbis; **845** *top* © Fred Viebahn; *bottom* © Bettmann/Corbis; **847** *Alma Sewing* (about 1935), Francis Criss. Oil on canvas, 33″ × 45″. High Museum of Art, Atlanta, Georgia. Purchase with funds from the Fine Art Collectors, Mr. and Mrs. Henry Schwob, the Director's Circle, Mr. and Mrs. John L. Huber, High Museum of Art Enhancement Fund, Stephen and Linda Sessler, the J.J. Haverty Fund, and through prior acquisitions. 2002.70; **848** © Sylvia Offe/Getty Images; **850, 856** © Jason Ernst/Age Fotostock America, Inc.; **857** Hunter Freeman/Getty Images; **864** *top left* Cover of *The Greatest Muhammad Ali* by Walter Dean Myers. © 2001 Scholastic, Inc., New York; *top right* From *Beyond the Burning Time* by Kathryn Lasky. Cover illustration by David Shannon. Reprinted by permission of Scholastic, Inc.; *center left* Cover of *Homeless Bird* by Gloria Whelan. Jacket illustration © 2000 by Robert Crawford. Jacket design by Alison Donalty. © 2000 by HarperCollins Publishers; *center right* Jacket of *Touching Spirit Bear* by Ben Mikaelsen. Cover art by Cliff Nielsen. Cover design by Hilary Zarycky. © 2002 by HarperCollins Publishers, Inc.; *bottom left* Cover of *Beyond the Burning Time* by Kathryn Lasky. ©1994 by Kathryn Lasky. Cover art by David Shannon. Published by permission of Scholastic, Inc.; *bottom right* Jacket cover from *Under the Blood-Red Sun* by Graham Salisbury. Used by permission of Random House Children's Books, a division of Random House, Inc.

UNIT 8

865 *left* © Detlev Van Ravensway/Photo Researchers, Inc.; *right* NASA Dryden Flight Research Center (NASA-DFRC); **866** *left* © Cynthia Pringle/Corbis; *right* © Steve Cole/Getty Images (Royalty-Free); **866–867** © Royalty Free/Artbeats; **868** *background* NOAA George E. Marsh Album/AP/Wide World Photos; *right* © GeoNova, LLC; **869** *top* © D. Parker/Photo Researchers, Inc.; *bottom* Illustration by Raymond Turvey; **871** Raul Touzon/Getty Images; **872** © Ralph A. Clevenger/Corbis; **873** Courtesy of the author; **874** *left* © Jeff Rotman/Alamy Images; *right* © Gary Bell/oceanwideimages.com; **874–875** *bottom* © Raul Touzon/Getty Images; **875** *left* © David Shen/SeaPics.com; *right* © Fred Bavendam/Minden Pictures; **876** *left* © Douglas D. Seifert/Getty Images; *right* © Kelvin Aitken/marinethemes.com; *bottom* © Raul Touzon/Getty Images; **877** *top* © Bob Cranston/SeaPics.com; *center, bottom* © Kelvin Aitken/marinethemes.com; **878** *top* © Tui De Roy/Minden Pictures; **878–879** Illustration by Stuart Jackson-Carter/The Art Agency; **880** © Jeff Rotman/Alamy Images; **884** © James O'Mara/Getty Images; **885** © Yvonne Hemsey/Getty Images; **886** © Stephen Frink Collection/Alamy Images; **888** *top* © Brandon Cole/www.brandoncole.com; *bottom* © Bettmann/Corbis; **889** © C. and M. Fallows/oceanwideimages.com; **891** © Jeff Rotman/Getty Images; **894** © Steve Mason/Getty Images; **895** *top* © Courtesy of Diana Childress; *bottom* Courtesy of the author; **897** Illustration by Stephen R. Wagner; **898–899** © GeoNova, LLC; **908** AP/Wide World Photos; **909** *left, right* Courtesy of ABC NEWS; **910** *top* Courtesy of ABC NEWS; *background* AP/Wide World Photos; **910** *center* © 2005 Time Inc.; *inset* © Jose Jimenez/Getty Images; **913** © Rick Gomez/Masterfile; **915** © Royalty-Free/Corbis; **917** *top* © Bruce Forster/Getty Images; *center* © James P. Blair/Getty Images; *bottom* © Kelvin Murray/Getty Images; **918** © Big Cheese Photo/PictureQuest; **919** *top* Courtesy of Mark Singletary; *bottom* Courtesy of Justin Hjelm; **920** © Getty Images; **922** © Photographer's Choice/Getty Images; **923** *top* © Getty Images; *top center* © MLB Photos via Getty Images; **923** *bottom center* © NBAE 2002 Photo by NBAP/NBAE/Getty Images; *bottom* © Focus on Sport/Getty Images; **924** *left* © Nat Butler/NBAE/Getty Images; *right* AP/Wide World Photos; **928** © Patrick Olear/PhotoEdit; **929** © Courtesy of Random House; **930** NASA Jet Propulsion Laboratory; **932** *left* NASA Jet Propulsion Laboratory; *right* © Detlev Van Ravensway/Photo Researchers, Inc.; **933** *left* © U.S. Geological Survey/Photo Researchers, Inc.; *right* © NASA/Roger Ressmeyer/Corbis; **936** AP/Wide World Photos; **937** © Bettmann/Corbis; **938** The Granger Collection, New York; **939** © Corbis; **945** Mountain Dew's *Parking Attendant* © Pepsi-Cola Company; **946** *top left* Mountain Dew's *Parking Attendant* © Pepsi-Cola Company; *bottom left, Kibbles n' Bits Commercial* © Del Monte corporation; **948, 954** © Alain Choisnet/Getty Images; **955** *left* © Sean Justice/Getty Images; *right* © Photodisc Green/Getty Images (Royalty-Free); **962** *top left* Cover of *Walks Alone,* © 1998 by Brian Burks, reproduced by permission of Harcourt, Inc. This material may not be reproduced in any form or by any means without the prior written permission of the publisher; *top right* Cover of *Buffalo Gals, Women of the Old West* by Brandon Marie Miller. Cover image by Nebraska State Historical Society, Lincoln, Nebraska. © 1995 by Lerner Publications Company, Minneapolis, Minnesota; *center left* Cover of *Lost in the War* by Nancy Antle. © 1998 Nancy Antle. Cover design by Lynne Yeamans and Galen Smith. Cover photo courtesy of Eade Yeamans. © 2000 Published by Puffin Books, a division of Penguin Putnam Books for Young Readers, New York; *center right* Cover of *Fever 1793* by Laurie Halse Anderson. Cover illustration © 2000 by Lori Earley. Published by Aladdin Paperbacks, an imprint of Simon & Schuster Children's Publishing Division; *bottom left* Cover of *Bound for the North Star* by Dennis Brindell Fradin. Jacket illustration from the Underground Railroad Quilt, courtesy of the Oberlin Senior Center. Photo by Judith Bloom Fradin. Published by Clarion Books, an imprint of Houghton Mifflin Company, New York; *bottom right* Cover of *Walks Alone* by

Brian Burks. © 1998 by Brian Burks. Cover illustration © 1998 by Terry Hoff. Published by Harcourt, Inc., New York.

UNIT 9

963 *left* © George Grall/National Geographic Image Collection; *right* © Photo by Sharon Hoogstraten; *center* Plate 57 from *A Field Guide to the Shells of the Atlantic and Gulf Coasts and the West Indies* © 1995 by R. Tucker Abbott and Violet French Morris. Reprinted by permission of Houghton Mifflin Company. All rights reserved; *inset right* From *Shells* © 2004 Quantum Publishing Ltd. London.; **964** © Photo by Sharon Hoogstraten; **966** © Brand X Pictures/Alamy Images; **970** © Google; **971** Smithsonian Institution, www.SmithsonianEducation.org; **975** Courtesy of Minuteman Library Network; **978** © Richard Levine/Alamy Images; **979** From *Info Trac,* by Gale Group. Reprinted by permission of the Gale Group; **983** © Photo courtesy of Seattle Public Library; **984, 998** © Sam Barricklow/Workbookstock.com; **999** © Ian Shaw/Getty Images.

STUDENT RESOURCE BANK

R3 Mosaic with circus scene: fight with leopards. Galleria Borghese, Rome, Italy. © Scala/Art Resource, New York; **R6** *Armor* (1400 or later). Italian. Steel, brass, textile, H. 66.5 in. (168.9 cm.). Bashford Dean Memorial Collection. Gift of Helen Fahnestock Hubbard, in memory of her father, Harris C. Fahnestock, 1929. (29.154.3) © Metropolitan Museum of Art/Art Resource, New York; **R7** GeoNova, LLC; **R14** *left* © City Year; *right* AP/Wide World Photos; **R15** Bust of Cicero (0-100). © Araldo de Luca/Corbis; **R19** © 2003 New York State Adirondack Park Agency. All rights reserved; **R85** © Stockbyte Photography/Veer; **R92** © Warner Bros./The Kobal Collection.

BACK COVER

© Photodisc/Getty Images

ARS Electronic Restrictions↑
The multimedia product and its contents are protected under copyright law. Any theatrical, televised, or public display or performance, including transmission of any image over a network, excepting a local area network is prohibited by law, as is the preparation of any derivative work, including the extraction in whole or in part of any images without the permission of Artists Rights Society (ARS), New York.

Reproduction, including downloading of Ernst, Miro, Dali, Matisse, Kandinsky, Lawrence, and Giacometti works is prohibited by copyright laws and international conventions without the express written permission of Artists Rights Society (ARS), New York.

McDougal Littell has made every effort to locate the copyright holders of all copyrighted material in this book and to make full acknowledgment for its use. Omissions brought to our attention will be corrected in a subsequent edition.

MARYLAND VOLUNTARY STATE CURRICULUM FOR READING/ENGLISH LANGUAGE ARTS

1.0 General Reading Processes

1.A Phonemic Awareness: Students will master the ability to hear, identify, and manipulate individual sounds in spoken words by the end of grade one.

Maryland has no Indicator for this topic at this grade level.

1.B Phonics: Students will apply their knowledge of letter/sound relationships and word structure to decode unfamiliar words.

Maryland has no Indicator for this topic at this grade level.

1.C Fluency: Students will read orally with accuracy and expression at a rate that sounds like speech.

1.C.1   Read orally at an appropriate rate
      1.C.1.a   Read familiar text at a rate that is conversational and consistent
1.C.2   Read grade-level text with both high accuracy and appropriate pacing, intonation, and expression
      1.C.2.a   Apply knowledge of word structures and patterns to read with automaticity
      1.C.2.b   Demonstrate appropriate use of phrasing
            1.C.2.b.1   Attend to sentence patterns and structures that signal meaning in text
            1.C.2.b.2   Use punctuation cues to guide meaning and expression
            1.C.2.b.3   Use pacing and intonation (emphasis on certain words) to convey meaning and expression
            1.C.2.b.4   Adjust intonation and pitch (rise and fall of spoken voice) appropriately
      1.C.2.c   Increase sight words read fluently

1.D Vocabulary: Students will use a variety of strategies and opportunities to understand word meaning and to increase vocabulary.

1.D.1   Develop and apply vocabulary through exposure to a variety of texts
      1.D.1.a   Acquire new vocabulary through listening to, independently reading, and discussing a variety of literary and informational texts
      1.D.1.b   Discuss words and word meanings daily as they are encountered in texts, instruction, and conversation
1.D.2   Apply a conceptual understanding of new words
      1.D.2.a   Classify and categorize increasingly complex words into sets and groups
      1.D.2.b   Explain relationships between and among words
1.D.3   Understand, acquire, and use new vocabulary
      1.D.3.a   Use context to determine the meanings of words
      1.D.3.b   Use word structure to determine the meanings of words
      1.D.3.c   Use resources to confirm definitions and gather further information about words
      1.D.3.d   Use new vocabulary in speaking and writing to gain and extend content knowledge and clarify expression

1.E Comprehension: Students will use a variety of strategies to understand what they read (construct meaning).

1.E.1   Apply comprehension skills through exposure to a variety of texts, including traditional print and electronic texts
      1.E.1.a   Listen to critically, read, and discuss texts representing diversity in content, culture, authorship, and perspective, including areas, such as race, gender, disability, religion, and socioeconomic background
      1.E.1.b   Read a minimum of 25 self-selected and/or assigned books or book equivalents representing various genres
      1.E.1.c   Discuss reactions to and ideas/information gained from reading experiences with adults and peers in both formal and informal situations
1.E.2   Use strategies to prepare for reading (before reading)
      1.E.2.a   Select and apply appropriate strategies to prepare for reading the text

1.E.3   Use strategies to make meaning from text (during reading)
    1.E.3.a   Select and apply appropriate strategies to make meaning from text during reading
1.E.4   Use strategies to demonstrate understanding of the text (after reading)
    1.E.4.a   Identify and explain the main idea
    1.E.4.b   Identify and explain information directly stated in the text
    1.E.4.c   Draw inferences and/or conclusions and make generalizations
    1.E.4.d   Confirm, refute, or make predictions and form new ideas
    1.E.4.e   Summarize or paraphrase
    1.E.4.f   Connect the text to prior knowledge or personal experience

2.0 Comprehension of Informational Text: Students will read, comprehend, interpret, analyze, and evaluate informational texts.

2.A Comprehension of Informational Text

2.A.1   Apply comprehension skills by selecting, reading, and interpreting a variety of print and electronic informational texts
    2.A.1.a   Read, use, and identify the characteristics of primary and secondary sources of academic information
    2.A.1.b   Read, use, and identify the characteristics of workplace and other realworld documents
    2.A.1.c   Select and read to gain information from personal interest materials, such as books, magazines, cookbooks, catalogs, web sites, and other online materials
2.A.2   Analyze text features to facilitate understanding of informational texts
    2.A.2.a   Analyze print features that contribute to meaning
    2.A.2.b   Analyze graphic aids that contribute to meaning
    2.A.2.c   Analyze informational aids that contribute to meaning
    2.A.2.d   Analyze organizational aids that contribute to meaning
    2.A.2.e   Analyze online features that contribute to meaning
    2.A.2.f   Analyze the relationship between the text features and the content of the text as a whole
2.A.3   Apply knowledge of organizational patterns of informational text to facilitate understanding
    2.A.3.a   Analyze the organizational patterns of texts
    2.A.3.b   Analyze the contribution of the organizational pattern
    2.A.3.c   Use organizational pattern to locate specific information
2.A.4   Analyze important ideas and messages in informational texts
    2.A.4.a   Identify and explain the author's/text's purpose and intended audience
    2.A.4.b   Identify and explain the author's argument, viewpoint, or perspective
    2.A.4.c   State and support main ideas and messages
    2.A.4.d   Summarize or paraphrase
    2.A.4.e   Identify and explain information not related to the main idea
    2.A.4.f   Explain relationships between and among ideas
    2.A.4.g   Synthesize ideas from text
    2.A.4.h   Distinguish between a fact and an opinion
    2.A.4.i   Explain how someone might use the text
    2.A.4.j   Connect the text to prior knowledge or experience
2.A.5   Analyze purposeful use of language
    2.A.5.a   Analyze specific word choice that contributes to the meaning and/or creates style
    2.A.5.b   Analyze specific language choices to determine tone
    2.A.5.c   Analyze repetition and variation of specific words and phrases that contribute to meaning
2.A.6   Read critically to evaluate informational text
    2.A.6.a   Analyze the extent to which the text fulfills the reading purpose
    2.A.6.b   Analyze the extent to which the structure and features of the text clarify the purpose and the information
    2.A.6.c   Analyze the text and its information for reliability
    2.A.6.d   Analyze the author's argument or position for clarity and/or bias
    2.A.6.e   Analyze additional information that would clarify or strengthen the author's argument or viewpoint
    2.A.6.f   Analyze language and other techniques intended to persuade the reader

3.0 Comprehension of Literary Text: Students will read, comprehend, interpret, analyze, and evaluate literary texts.

3.A Comprehension of Literary Text

3.A.1   Apply comprehension skills by reading and analyzing a variety of self-selected and assigned literary texts

    3.A.1.a   Listen to critically, read, and discuss a variety of literary texts representing diverse cultures, perspectives, ethnicities, and time periods

    3.A.1.b   Listen to critically, read, and discuss a variety of literary forms and genres

3.A.2   Analyze text features to facilitate understanding of literary texts

    3.A.2.a   Analyze text features that contribute to meaning

3.A.3   Analyze elements of narrative texts to facilitate understanding and interpretation

    3.A.3.a   Distinguish among types of narrative texts

    3.A.3.b   Analyze the conflict and the events of the plot

    3.A.3.c   Analyze details that provide information about the setting, the mood created by the setting, and ways in which the setting affects characters

    3.A.3.d   Analyze characterization

    3.A.3.e   Analyze relationships between and among characters, setting, and events

    3.A.3.f   Analyze the actions of the characters that serve to advance the plot

    3.A.3.g   Analyze conflicts that motivate characters and those that advance the plot

    3.A.3.h   Analyze the author's approach to issues of time in a narrative

    3.A.3.i   Analyze the point of view

    3.A.3.j   Analyze the interactions among narrative elements and their contribution to meaning

3.A.4   Analyze elements of poetry to facilitate understanding and interpretation

    3.A.4.a   Use structural features to distinguish among types of poetry

    3.A.4.b   Analyze language and structural features to determine meaning

    3.A.4.c   Analyze sound elements of poetry that contribute to meaning

    3.A.4.d   Analyze other poetic elements, such as setting, mood, tone, etc. that contribute to meaning

3.A.5   Analyze elements of drama to facilitate understanding and interpretation

    3.A.5.a   Use structural features to distinguish among types of plays

    3.A.5.b   Analyze the action of individual scenes and acts and its relationship to the plot

    3.A.5.c   Analyze how stage directions affect dialogue, characters, and plot

3.A.6   Analyze important ideas and messages in literary texts

    3.A.6.a   Analyze main ideas and universal themes

    3.A.6.b   Analyze similar themes across multiple texts

    3.A.6.c   Summarize or paraphrase

    3.A.6.d   Reflect on and explain personal connections to the text

    3.A.6.e   Explain the implications of the text for the reader and/or society

3.A.7   Analyze the author's purposeful use of language

    3.A.7.a   Analyze how specific language choices contribute to meaning and create style

    3.A.7.b   Analyze language choices that create tone

    3.A.7.c   Analyze figurative language that contributes to meaning and/or creates style

    3.A.7.d   Analyze imagery that contributes to meaning and/or creates style

    3.A.7.e   Analyze elements of style and their contribution to meaning

3.A.8   Read critically to evaluate literary texts

    3.A.8.a   Analyze the plausibility of the plot and the credibility of the characters

    3.A.8.b   Analyze the extent to which the text contains ambiguities, subtleties, or contradictions

    3.A.8.c   Analyze the relationship between a literary text and its historical and/or social context

    3.A.8.d   Analyze the relationship between the structure and the purpose of the text

4.0 Writing: Students will compose in a variety of modes by developing content, employing specific forms, and selecting language appropriate for a particular audience and purpose.

4.A Writing

4.A.1   Compose texts using the prewriting and drafting strategies of effective writers and speakers

    4.A.1.a   Use a variety of selfselected prewriting strategies to generate, select, narrow, and develop ideas

        4.A.1.a.1   Evaluate topics for personal relevance, scope, and feasibility

        4.A.1.a.2   Begin a coherent plan for developing ideas

        4.A.1.a.3   Explore and evaluate relevant sources of information

    4.A.1.b   Select, organize, and develop ideas appropriate to topic, audience, and purpose

        4.A.1.b.1   Organize information logically

        4.A.1.b.2   Use techniques, such as graphic organizers and signal words to complete and clarify organizational structures

        4.A.1.b.3   Verify the effectiveness of paragraph development by modifying topic, support, and concluding sentences as necessary

4.A.2   Compose oral, written, and visual presentations that express personal ideas, inform, and persuade

    4.A.2.a   Compose to express personal ideas by experimenting with a variety of forms and techniques suited to topic, audience, and purpose in order to develop a personal style and a clear, intentional, and consistent voice and tone

    4.A.2.b   Describe in prose and/or poetic forms to clarify, extend, or elaborate on ideas by using evocative language and appropriate organizational structure to create a dominant impression

    4.A.2.c   Compose to inform using relevant support and a variety of appropriate organizational structures and signal words within and between paragraphs

    4.A.2.d   Compose to persuade by supporting, modifying, or disagreeing with a position, using effective rhetorical strategies

        4.A.2.d.1   Write an assertion and use evidence that appeals to audience emotion, reasoning, or trust

        4.A.2.d.2   Organize ideas to construct a logical progression

        4.A.2.d.3   Use diction and syntax that is sincere, honest, and trustworthy

        4.A.2.d.4   Use connotation, repetition, parallelism, and figurative language to control audience emotion and reaction

        4.A.2.d.5   Use authoritative citations when effective and document appropriately

    4.A.2.e   Use writing-to-learn strategies, such as reflective and metacognitive writing to set goals, make discoveries, and make connections among learned ideas

    4.A.2.f   Manage time and process when writing for a given purpose

4.A.3   Compose texts using the revising and editing strategies of effective writers and speakers

    4.A.3.a   Revise texts for clarity, completeness, and effectiveness

        4.A.3.a.1   Eliminate redundant and irrelevant words and ideas

        4.A.3.a.2   Clarify meaning through the placement of antecedents, modifiers, connectors, and transitional devices

        4.A.3.a.3   Clarify the relationships among ideas through coordination and subordination that are purposeful, logical, succinct, and balanced

        4.A.3.a.4   Clarify meaning and purpose by using active voice and consistent person, number, tense, and mood

        4.A.3.a.5   Vary sentence types and lengths to clarify and extend meaning and to develop style

    4.A.3.b   Use suitable traditional and electronic resources to refine presentations and edit texts for effective and appropriate use of language and conventions, such as capitalization, punctuation, spelling, and pronunciation

        4.A.3.b.1   Self edit

        4.A.3.b.2   Peer edit

        4.A.3.b.3   Dictionary

        4.A.3.b.4   Thesaurus

        4.A.3.b.5   Spell checker

        4.A.3.b.6   Language handbook

        4.A.3.b.7   Grammar checker

        4.A.3.b.8   Style book

    4.A.3.c   Prepare the final product for presentation to an audience

4.A.4 Identify how language choices in writing and speaking affect thoughts and feelings
- 4.A.4.a Use precise word choice, formal to informal, based on audience, situation, or purpose
- 4.A.4.b Make effective decisions regarding word choice according to connotative and denotative meanings
- 4.A.4.c Consider how readers or listeners might respond differently to the same words

4.A.5 Assess the effectiveness of choice of details, organizational pattern, word choice, syntax, use of figurative language, and rhetorical devices in the student's own composing
- 4.A.5.a Assess the effectiveness of diction that reveals his or her purpose
  - 4.A.5.a.1 Language appropriate for a particular audience
  - 4.A.5.a.2 Language suitable for a given purpose
  - 4.A.5.a.3 Words/phrases/ sentences that extend meaning in a given context
- 4.A.5.b Explain how the specific language and expression used by the writer or speaker affects reader/listener response
- 4.A.5.c Evaluate the use of transitions in a text

4.A.6 Evaluate textual changes in a work and explain how these changes alter tone, clarify meaning, address a particular audience, or fulfill a purpose
- 4.A.6.a Alter the tone of one's own writing by revising its diction for a specific purpose and/or audience
- 4.A.6.b Justify revisions in syntax and diction from a previous draft of his or her same text by explaining how the change affects meaning

4.A.7 Locate, retrieve, and use information from various sources to accomplish a purpose
- 4.A.7.a Identify, evaluate, and use sources of information on a selfselected and/or given topic
- 4.A.7.b Use various information retrieval sources (traditional and/or electronic) to obtain information on a selfselected and/or given topic
- 4.A.7.c Use appropriate note taking procedures, organizational strategies, and proper documentation of sources of information
  - 4.A.7.c.1 Appropriate strategies for taking notes
    - 4.A.7.c.1.a Appropriate strategies for organizing source information or notes
    - 4.A.7.c.1.b Information to include or exclude when using a note taking method
    - 4.A.7.c.1.c Advantages, disadvantages, or limitations of a given strategy or procedure for recording or organizing information
    - 4.A.7.c.1.d Advantages, disadvantages, or limitations of sources of information, such as bias, accuracy, availability, variety, currency
  - 4.A.7.c.2 Use a recognized format for documentation, such as MLA
- 4.A.7.d Synthesize information from two or more sources to fulfill a self-selected or given purpose
- 4.A.7.e Use a recognized format to credit sources when paraphrasing, summarizing, and quoting to avoid plagiarism

5.0 Controlling Language: Students will control language by applying the conventions of standard English in speaking and writing.

5.A Grammar

5.A.1 Recognize elements of grammar in personal and academic reading

5.A.2 Apply knowledge of grammar concepts and skills to control oral and written language
- 5.A.2.a Consider the meaning, position, form, and function of words when identifying and using grammatical concepts, such as verbal and verbal phrases (gerunds, participles, and infinitives), reflexive and intensive pronouns, progressive forms of verbs, and active and passive voice
- 5.A.2.b Combine and expand sentences by incorporating subjects, predicates, and modifiers and by logically coordinating, subordinating, and sequencing ideas
- 5.A.2.c Differentiate grammatically complete sentences from nonsentences, including comma splices
- 5.A.2.d Compose simple, compound, complex, and compound-complex sentences using independent, dependent, restrictive, and nonrestrictive clauses; transitions; conjunctions; and appropriate punctuation to connect ideas

5.B Usage

5.B.1   Recognize examples of conventional usage in personal and academic reading
5.B.2   Comprehend and apply standard English usage in oral and written language

    5.B.2.a   Apply appropriate subject/verb agreement, such as agreement involving words of amount, time, and money
    5.B.2.b   Apply consistent and appropriate use of the person, number, and case of pronouns; pronoun/antecedent agreement; special pronoun problems, such as who - whom, and incomplete constructions; active and passive voice; and verbal and verbal phrases
    5.B.2.c   Recognize and correct common usage errors, such as misplaced and dangling modifiers; incorrect use of verbs; double negatives; and commonly confused words, such as accept - except
    5.B.2.d   Use available resources to correct or confirm editorial choices
    5.B.2.e   Explain editorial choices

5.C Mechanics

5.C.1   Explain and justify the purpose of mechanics to make and clarify meaning in academic and personal reading and writing
5.C.2   Apply standard English punctuation and capitalization in written language

    5.C.2.a   Use commas and semicolons correctly, such as in a compound sentence joined by a conjunctive adverb
    5.C.2.b   Use an apostrophe to designate possession with indefinite pronouns and adjectives
    5.C.2.c   Use the mechanics of writing correctly
    5.C.2.d   Use a colon to introduce a list

5.C.3   Explain editorial choices involving mechanics

5.D Spelling

5.D.1   Recognize conventional spelling in and through personal and academic reading
5.D.2   Apply conventional spelling in written language

    5.D.2.a   Use conventional spelling in personal writing
    5.D.2.b   Develop self-monitoring strategies for frequently misspelled words
    5.D.2.c   Use suitable traditional and electronic resources as a spelling aid

5.D.3   Maintain a personal list of words to use in editing original writing

5.E Handwriting

5.E.1   Produce writing that is legible to the audience

    5.E.1.a   Write fluidly and legibly in manuscript and cursive
    5.E.1.b   Use word processing technology when appropriate

6.0 Listening: Students will demonstrate effective listening to learn, process, and analyze information.

6.A Listening

6.A.1   Apply and demonstrate listening skills appropriately in a variety of settings and for a variety of purposes

    6.A.1.a   Use criteria to evaluate oral presentations, such as purpose, delivery techniques, content, visual aids, body language, and facial expressions
    6.A.1.b   Gather information from listening to a speaker
    6.A.1.c   Use memory techniques for various listening tasks

6.A.2   Apply comprehension and literary analysis strategies and skills for a variety of listening purposes and settings

    6.A.2.a   Ask relevant questions concerning the speaker's content, delivery, and purpose
    6.A.2.b   Determine a speaker's purpose and viewpoint
    6.A.2.c   Interpret the speech or performance or presentation
    6.A.2.d   Make inferences or draw conclusions based on the presentation
    6.A.2.e   Provide constructive feedback to speakers concerning the coherence and logic of a speech's content and delivery as well as its overall impact upon the listeners

7.0 Speaking: Students will communicate effectively in a variety of situations with different audiences, purposes, and formats.

7.A Speaking

7.A.1 Demonstrate appropriate organizational strategies and delivery techniques to plan for a variety of oral presentation purposes

- 7.A.1.a Select the purpose and format for an oral presentation
- 7.A.1.b Evaluate the needs and perspectives of the audience
- 7.A.1.c Anticipate and effectively answer listener concerns and counter arguments through the inclusion and arrangement of details, reasons, examples, and other elements
- 7.A.1.d Use a variety of organization structures, such as narrative, cause and effect, chronological order, description, main idea and detail, problem/solution, question/answer, comparison and contrast, and contrast that are appropriate to the purpose and topic

Open-Ended Rubric

Score	Response
3	**The response demonstrates an understanding of the complexities of the text.** • Addresses the demands of the question • Effectively uses text-relevant information to clarify or extend understanding
2	**The response demonstrates a general understanding of the text.** • Partially addresses the demands of the question • Uses text-relevant information to show understanding
1	**The response demonstrates a minimal understanding of the text.** • Minimally addresses the demands of the question • Uses minimal information to show some understanding of the text in relation to the question
0	**The response is completely incorrect, irrelevant to the question, or missing.**

CORRELATION TO MARYLAND VOLUNTARY STATE CURRICULUM FOR READING/ENGLISH LANGUAGE ARTS

1.0 General Reading Processes

1.A Phonemic Awareness: Students will master the ability to hear, identify, and manipulate individual sounds in spoken words by the end of grade one.

Maryland has no Indicator for this topic at this grade level.	

1.B Phonics: Students will apply their knowledge of letter/sound relationships and word structure to decode unfamiliar words.

Maryland has no Indicator for this topic at this grade level.	

1.C Fluency: Students will read orally with accuracy and expression at a rate that sounds like speech.

1.C.1	Read orally at an appropriate rate	
	1.C.1.a Read familiar text at a rate that is conversational and consistent	All reading selections can be used to meet this standard.
1.C.2	Read grade-level text with both high accuracy and appropriate pacing, intonation, and expression	
	1.C.2.a Apply knowledge of word structures and patterns to read with automaticity	All reading selections can be used to meet this standard.
	1.C.2.b Demonstrate appropriate use of phrasing	
	1.C.2.b.1 Attend to sentence patterns and structures that signal meaning in text	All reading selections can be used to meet this standard.
	1.C.2.b.2 Use punctuation cues to guide meaning and expression	All reading selections can be used to meet this standard.
	1.C.2.b.3 Use pacing and intonation (emphasis on certain words) to convey meaning and expression	All reading selections can be used to meet this standard.
	1.C.2.b.4 Adjust intonation and pitch (rise and fall of spoken voice) appropriately	All reading selections can be used to meet this standard.
	1.C.2.c Increase sight words read fluently	All reading selections can be used to meet this standard.

1.D Vocabulary: Students will use a variety of strategies and opportunities to understand word meaning and to increase vocabulary.

1.D.1	Develop and apply vocabulary through exposure to a variety of texts	
	1.D.1.a Acquire new vocabulary through listening to, independently reading, and discussing a variety of literary and informational texts	15, 31-38, 40, 43-57, 59, 63-68, 70, 73-88, 90, 99-114, 116, 119-125, 127, 135-148, 183, 205-206, 217, 224-225, 227, 237-238, 241, 255-256, 265-266, 269, 277-278, 311, 323-324, 327, 335-336, 339, 353-354, 363, 372-373, 387, 445, 463-464, 467, 473-474, 481, 486-487, 495, 501, 505-506, 570, 572-574, 579-580, 633-637, 643-645, 647, 657-658, 661, 667, 671, 683-684, 697, 710-712, 720, 761, 774-775, 781, 787-788, 790-795, 800-801, 809, 820-821, 833, 873, 881-882, 885, 892-893, 895, 905-906, 919-921, 925-926, 929, 934-935, 937, 941-942

1.D.1.b	Discuss words and word meanings daily as they are encountered in texts, instruction, and conversation	31-38, 40, 43-57, 59, 63-68, 70, 73-88, 90, 183-203, 206, 217-223, 225, 227-236, 238, 241-248, 256, 311-322, 324, 327-334, 336, 339-352, 354, 363-371, 373, 445-461, 464, 467-472, 474, 481-485, 487, 633-642, 645, 647-651, 658, 661-666, 668, 672-682, 697-701, 711-712, 714-721
1.D.2	Apply a conceptual understanding of new words	
1.D.2.a	Classify and categorize increasingly complex words into sets and groups	474, 906
1.D.2.b	Explain relationships between and among words	59, 116, 225, 278, 298, 336, 431, 487, 536, 580, 619, 658, 747, 788, 926, 959
1.D.3	Understand, acquire, and use new vocabulary	
1.D.3.a	Use context to determine the meanings of words	31, 40, 43, 59, 63, 70, 90, 99, 116, 119, 127, 135, 183, 206, 217, 223, 225, 227, 238, 241, 256, 259, 266, 278, 298, 311, 324, 327, 336, 339, 354, 363-371, 373, 387, 432, 445, 464, 467, 474, 481, 487, 495, 506, 536, 571, 580, 594, 633, 645, 647, 658, 661, 668, 671, 684, 697, 711, 713, 721, 748, 761, 775, 781, 788, 791, 801, 809, 821, 833, 845, 862, 873, 882, 885, 893, 895, 919, 926, 929, 935, 937, 942, 960
1.D.3.b	Use word structure to determine the meanings of words	40, 70, 90, 127, 170, 256, 324, 373, 464, 645, 668, 711, 748, 775, 801, 821, 862, 893, 935, 960
1.D.3.c	Use resources to confirm definitions and gather further information about words	206, 238, 266, 278, 336, 474, 487, 506, 580, 599, 658, 668, 684, 711, 721, 882, 906, 942
1.D.3.d	Use new vocabulary in speaking and writing to gain and extend content knowledge and clarify expression	40, 59, 70, 90, 116, 127, 206, 225, 238, 256, 266, 278, 324, 336, 354, 373, 464, 474, 487, 506, 580, 645, 658, 684, 711, 720, 775, 788, 801, 821, 882, 893, 906, 926, 935, 942

1.E Comprehension: Students will use a variety of strategies to understand what they read (construct meaning).

1.E.1	Apply comprehension skills through exposure to a variety of texts, including traditional print and electronic texts	
1.E.1.a	Listen to critically, read, and discuss texts representing diversity in content, culture, authorship, and perspective, including areas, such as race, gender, disability, religion, and socioeconomic background	119-125, 468-472, 509-511, 549, 563, 566, 781-786
1.E.1.b	Read a minimum of 25 self-selected and/or assigned books or book equivalents representing various genres	4-11, 24-29, 32-38, 44-57, 61, 64-68, 74-88, 93-97, 100-114, 120-125, 130-132, 136-148, 166-172, 184-204, 208-213, 218-223, 228-236, 242-249, 260-264, 270-276, 281-283, 294-300, 306, 312-322, 328-334, 337, 340-352, 356, 364-371, 375, 381-382, 388-413, 428-433, 441, 446-462, 468-472, 476, 482-485, 489, 496-500, 502-504, 510-512, 515-517, 532-538, 541-547, 550-551, 553, 555-558, 563-565, 567-568, 572-578, 583-585, 588, 593-597, 601-603, 616-622, 625-631, 634-643, 648-651, 662-666, 669, 672-682, 687, 692-693, 698-701, 714-719, 722, 729, 744, 750, 753-759, 762-773, 776-777, 782-786, 792-799, 803, 810-819, 822-824, 834-841, 845-847, 858-864, 874-880, 886-891, 896-901, 920-924, 930-933, 938-940, 956, 962
1.E.1.c	Discuss reactions to and ideas/information gained from reading experiences with adults and peers in both formal and informal situations	224, 237

1.E.2	Use strategies to prepare for reading (before reading)	
	1.E.2.a Select and apply appropriate strategies to prepare for reading the text	11-15, 31-39, 43-58, 63-69, 73-89, 99-115, 119-126, 129-133, 135-149, 183-203, 205, 208-215, 217-224, 227-237, 241-255, 259-265, 269-277, 281-285, 311-323, 327-335, 339-353, 356-361, 363-372, 381-384, 387-412, 414, 445-461, 463, 467-473, 476-479, 481-486, 495-505, 509-513, 515-519, 542-543, 547-552, 555-560, 562-569, 571-579, 583-586, 588-591, 593-599, 601-606, 633-642, 644, 647-657, 661-667, 671-683, 692-695, 697-701, 710, 712, 714-720, 722, 724-734, 761-774, 776-779, 781-787, 800, 809-820, 822-827, 832-842, 845-849, 868-872, 874-881, 885-892, 895-905, 919-925, 934, 937-941, 957-958, 968, 989-995
1.E.3	Use strategies to make meaning from text (during reading)	
	1.E.3.a Select and apply appropriate strategies to make meaning from text during reading	11-15, 30-39, 42-43, 58, 62-69, 72-73, 89, 98-115, 118-126, 128-135, 149, 154-157, 173-962
1.E.4	Use strategies to demonstrate understanding of the text (after reading)	
	1.E.4.a Identify and explain the main idea	8, 15, 481, 588, 607, 735, 809, 845, 869, 871, 873-881, 905, 958-959, R2-R86
	1.E.4.b Identify and explain information directly stated in the text	869-871, 873-881, 905, 958-959
	1.E.4.c Draw inferences and/or conclusions and make generalizations	12-14, 39, 58, 63-69, 100-115, 120-126, 130-133, 149, 184-203, 215, 217-224, 228-236, 242-248, 250-255, 265, 277, 285, 296-297, 323, 335, 339-353, 372, 384, 414, 430-431, 446-461, 463, 473, 501, 505, 519, 555-558, 560, 569, 606, 619, 644, 657, 683, 720, 774, 779, 787, 791-799, 820, 842, 881
	1.E.4.d Confirm, refute, or make predictions and form new ideas	12-14, 227-237, 307-309, 671-683, 698-701
	1.E.4.e Summarize or paraphrase	39, 58, 69, 115, 208-215, 224, 237, 323, 473, 481-486, 501, 513, 532-533, 579, 587, 667, 695, 697-701, 710, 720, 729, 774, 776-778, 787, 809-820, 827, 842, 845-849, 858-859, 883, 892, 901-905, 934, 941
	1.E.4.f Connect the text to prior knowledge or personal experience	11-12, 30-39, 42, 58, 62, 72, 98, 118, 126, 128, 134, 174-175, 182, 216, 226, 240, 258-265, 268, 280, 302-303, 310, 326, 338, 353, 362, 380, 386, 436, 444, 466, 480, 486, 494, 508, 514, 540-541, 548, 554, 560, 562, 570, 582, 592, 600, 624, 632, 646, 659, 667, 670, 696, 712, 722, 752-753, 760, 774, 780-787, 790, 808, 820, 832, 844, 866, 872, 884, 894, 918, 928, 934, 936

2.0 Comprehension of Informational Text: Students will read, comprehend, interpret, analyze, and evaluate informational texts.

2.A Comprehension of Informational Text

2.A.1	Apply comprehension skills by selecting, reading, and interpreting a variety of print and electronic informational texts	
	2.A.1.a Read, use, and identify the characteristics of primary and secondary sources of academic information	108, 753, 976-981
	2.A.1.b Read, use, and identify the characteristics of workplace and other realworld documents	209-211, 337, 462, 477-478, 588, 591, 669, 823-827, 868-869, 871, 873-881, 886-891, 896-900, 902-904, 914-915, 920-924, 929, 938-940, 958-959, 969, 976, 978, R17, R42, R43
	2.A.1.c Select and read to gain information from personal interest materials, such as books, magazines, cookbooks, catalogs, web sites, and other online materials	209-211, 337, 462, 477-478, 588, 591, 669, 823-827, 874-880, 886-891, 896-900, 902-904, 929, 979

2.A.2 Analyze text features to facilitate understanding of informational texts	
2.A.2.a Analyze print features that contribute to meaning	209-211, 337, 462, 477-478, 588, 591, 669, 823-827, 868-869, 871, 873-881, 886-891, 896-900, 902-904, 929, 958-959, 969-970, 977-978
2.A.2.b Analyze graphic aids that contribute to meaning	100, 103, 105, 120, 260, 502, 588, 762, 766, 796, 810, 825-826, 868-869, 871, 873-881, 896, 902-905, 930
2.A.2.c Analyze informational aids that contribute to meaning	588, 825-826, 868-869, 871, 873-881, 902-905, 977
2.A.2.d Analyze organizational aids that contribute to meaning	12, 588, 591, 823-826, 868-869, 871, 873-881, 894, 896-905, 937-941, 958-959, 970, 977
2.A.2.e Analyze online features that contribute to meaning	969, 971, 977
2.A.2.f Analyze the relationship between the text features and the content of the text as a whole	895-905
2.A.3 Apply knowledge of organizational patterns of informational text to facilitate understanding	
2.A.3.a Analyze the organizational patterns of texts	39, 44-57, 69, 71, 89, 100-114, 205, 239, 241-255, 277, 285-286, 312-323, 353, 381-385, 430-431, 495-507, 513, 519, 560, 579, 588, 591, 601-607, 644, 683, 691-695, 710, 722, 724-735, 796-799, 822-827, 842, 849, 868-869, 871, 873-881, 886-892, 895-905, 907, 937-941, 958-959, 970, 977
2.A.3.b Analyze the contribution of the organizational pattern	895-905, 907
2.A.3.c Use organizational pattern to locate specific information	895-905
2.A.4 Analyze important ideas and messages in informational texts	
2.A.4.a Identify and explain the author's/text's purpose and intended audience	588, 822-827, 881, 901, 937-941
2.A.4.b Identify and explain the author's argument, viewpoint, or perspective	154-157, 356, 692-693, 822-827, 885
2.A.4.c State and support main ideas and messages	115, 208-215, 501, 695, 774, 776-778, 787, 809-819, 827, 860, 883, 892, 901, 905, 934, 941
2.A.4.d Summarize or paraphrase	115, 208-215, 501, 695, 774, 776-778, 787, 809-819, 827, 860, 883, 892, 901, 905, 934, 941
2.A.4.e Identify and explain information not related to the main idea	588, 822-827, 881, 901
2.A.4.f Explain relationships between and among ideas	154-156, 692-693, 885
2.A.4.g Synthesize ideas from text	208, 989-995
2.A.4.h Distinguish between a fact and an opinion	476, 692, 885
2.A.4.i Explain how someone might use the text	972-973, 982, 989-993
2.A.4.j Connect the text to prior knowledge or experience	12, 98, 118, 258, 268, 760, 780, 790, 808, 832, 872, 884, 918, 928, 936
2.A.5 Analyze purposeful use of language	
2.A.5.a Analyze specific word choice that contributes to the meaning and/or creates style	501, 787, 822-827, 937-941, R21
2.A.5.b Analyze specific language choices to determine tone	8, 438, 439, 494-505, 822-827

2.A.5.c	Analyze repetition and variation of specific words and phrases that contribute to meaning	936-941
2.A.6	Read critically to evaluate informational text	
2.A.6.a	Analyze the extent to which the text fulfills the reading purpose	495, 501, 505, 895, 901, 905, R15, R27
2.A.6.b	Analyze the extent to which the structure and features of the text clarify the purpose and the information	829, 895-905, 908, 937-941
2.A.6.c	Analyze the text and its information for reliability	695, 842, 885-892, 972, 982
2.A.6.d	Analyze the author's argument or position for clarity and/or bias	476-479, 692-693, 695, 884-892, 901, 915, 919-925, 929, 934, 937, 958-959, 972-973
2.A.6.e	Analyze additional information that would clarify or strengthen the author's argument or viewpoint	776, 778, 875
2.A.6.f	Analyze language and other techniques intended to persuade the reader	885-891, 912-913, 915-917, 919-925, 937-941, 945

3.0 Comprehension of Literary Text: Students will read, comprehend, interpret, analyze, and evaluate literary texts.

3.A Comprehension of Literary Text

3.A.1	Apply comprehension skills by reading and analyzing a variety of self-selected and assigned literary texts	
3.A.1.a	Listen to critically, read, and discuss a variety of literary texts representing diverse cultures, perspectives, ethnicities, and time periods	63-68, 73-89, 183-203, 205, 217-223, 387-412, 414, 486, 509-513, 549-552, 570, 572-574, 579, 644, 661-667, 671-682, 712, 714-720, 761-774
3.A.1.b	Listen to critically, read, and discuss a variety of literary forms and genres	27, 32-38, 44-57, 64-68, 74-88, 93-97, 130-132, 136-148, 166-168, 181, 184-204, 218-223, 228-236, 242-248, 250-254, 270-276, 282-284, 294-296, 307-309, 312-322, 328-334, 337, 340-352, 357-360, 364-371, 375-379, 382-383, 388-428-430, 442-443, 446, 468-472, 482-485, 489-493, 510-512, 516-518, 532-533, 550-551, 556-559, 564-568, 572-578, 584-586, 594-598, 602-605, 616-617, 634-643, 648-656, 662-666, 669, 672-682, 687-691, 693, 698-709, 714-719, 724-728, 730-733, 745-746, 834-841, 846-848, 858-859, 957-958
3.A.2	Analyze text features to facilitate understanding of literary texts	
3.A.2.a	Analyze text features that contribute to meaning	6-7, 135-149, 281-285, 386, 388-412, 509-514, 516-518, 542-543, 547, 549-552, 554, 556-559, 563-569, 582, 584, 833-841
3.A.3	Analyze elements of narrative texts to facilitate understanding and interpretation	
3.A.3.a	Distinguish among types of narrative texts	4-5, 24-27, 31-39, 43-58, 63-69, 73-89, 166-168, 176-182, 184-203, 216, 218-224, 226, 228-237, 240, 242-255, 296-297, 304-310, 312-323, 326, 328-336, 362, 364-372, 445-461, 463, 467-473, 480, 482-486, 626-629, 633-642, 644-645, 648-657, 661-667, 670, 672-683, 697-710, 713-720, 722, 724-735, 745-746, 756-757, 761, 809
3.A.3.b	Analyze the conflict and the events of the plot	24-27, 31-39, 43-58, 63-69, 73-89, 99-114, 129-132, 135-149, 168-169, 570, 572-579
3.A.3.c	Analyze details that provide information about the setting, the mood created by the setting, and ways in which the setting affects characters	24-25, 27, 43-58, 129-133, 327-334

3.A.3.d	Analyze characterization	69, 133, 178-181, 183-203, 205, 241-255, 281-285, 296-297, 363-372, 463, 466-473, 475, 657
3.A.3.e	Analyze relationships between and among characters, setting, and events	24-25, 27, 43-58, 63-69, 74-88, 133, 135-149, 166-168, 257, 327-334, 353, 363-371, 667
3.A.3.f	Analyze the actions of the characters that serve to advance the plot	43-58, 63-69, 135-149, 327-334, 353, 363-371, 667
3.A.3.g	Analyze conflicts that motivate characters and those that advance the plot	63-69, 74-88, 135-148, 166-168
3.A.3.h	Analyze the author's approach to issues of time in a narrative	43-58, 73-89, 135-148
3.A.3.i	Analyze the point of view	176-177, 181, 205, 217-224, 227-237, 268-269, 285, 296-297, 372
3.A.3.j	Analyze the interactions among narrative elements and their contribution to meaning	43-58, 63-69, 135-149, 224, 237, 438-444, 446-461, 463, 507, 534-535, 600, 602-607
3.A.4 Analyze elements of poetry to facilitate understanding and interpretation		
3.A.4.a	Use structural features to distinguish among types of poetry	4, 6, 129-133, 281-285, 509-513, 515-518, 542-543, 547, 549-552, 555-560, 563-570, 572-579, 583-586, 592, 594-599
3.A.4.b	Analyze language and structural features to determine meaning	6, 281-285, 509-513, 542-543, 547, 563-569, 845
3.A.4.c	Analyze sound elements of poetry that contribute to meaning	129, 544, 563, 570, 593
3.A.4.d	Analyze other poetic elements, such as setting, mood, tone, etc. that contribute to meaning	438-443, 508-513, 514-519, 544-547, 549, 552, 555, 560, 571, 579, 600-607
3.A.5 Analyze elements of drama to facilitate understanding and interpretation		
3.A.5.a	Use structural features to distinguish among types of plays	135-148, 833-842
3.A.5.b	Analyze the action of individual scenes and acts and its relationship to the plot	7, 135-149, 387-412, 833-841
3.A.5.c	Analyze how stage directions affect dialogue, characters, and plot	7, 135-149, 387-412, 833-841
3.A.6 Analyze important ideas and messages in literary texts		
3.A.6.a	Analyze main ideas and universal themes	69, 304-309, 311-323, 327-335, 353, 363-372, 380-385, 387-412, 414, 417, 430-431, 486, 519, 552, 626-631, 647-657, 667, 671-683, 697-710, 722-735, 745-746, 781
3.A.6.b	Analyze similar themes across multiple texts	69, 304-305, 381-385, 519, 697-710, 722, 724-735
3.A.6.c	Summarize or paraphrase	481-486, 667, 697-701, 710
3.A.6.d	Reflect on and explain personal connections to the text	11-12, 30-39, 42, 58, 62, 69, 72, 98, 118, 128, 134, 174-175, 182, 216, 226, 240, 268, 280, 302-303, 310, 326, 338, 353, 362, 380, 386, 436, 444, 466, 480, 486, 494, 508, 514, 540-541, 548, 554, 560, 562, 570, 582, 592, 600, 624, 632, 645, 659, 667, 670, 696, 722, 752-753, 760, 774, 844, 866, 872, 918, 928, 934, 936
3.A.6.e	Explain the implications of the text for the reader and/or society	509-512, 552
3.A.7 Analyze the author's purposeful use of language		
3.A.7.a	Analyze how specific language choices contribute to meaning and create style	339, 381, 439-441, 445-461, 463, 467-473, 495-505, 508, 510-513, 515-519, 546-547, 549-552, 555-561, 583, 585, 599, 601-607, 617, 619, 845-849
3.A.7.b	Analyze language choices that create tone	439, 442-443, 507, 534-535

3.A.7.c	Analyze figurative language that contributes to meaning and/or creates style	546-547, 555-561, 585, 601-607, 618-619, 845-849
3.A.7.d	Analyze imagery that contributes to meaning and/or creates style	381, 440-441, 495-505, 546, 549-552, 599, 618-619
3.A.7.e	Analyze elements of style and their contribution to meaning	339-353, 381, 384, 414, 430-431, 440-441, 445-461, 463, 467-473, 481-486, 495-505, 509-513, 515-519, 521, 546-547, 549-552, 555-560, 583-586, 599, 601-607, 618-619, 626-627, 845-849
3.A.8	Read critically to evaluate literary texts	
3.A.8.a	Analyze the plausibility of the plot and the credibility of the characters	178-181, 241-248, 250-255, 281-285, 296-297, 657
3.A.8.b	Analyze the extent to which the text contains ambiguities, subtleties, or contradictions	5-7, 24-27, 89, 129-132, 135-148, 176-181, 304-309, 372, 463, 475, 505, 507, 560, 593-599, 626-631, 633-642, 657, 659, 662-667, 697-710, 712, 714-720, 746-747, 774, 833-841
3.A.8.c	Analyze the relationship between a literary text and its historical and/or social context	63-68, 73-89, 183-203, 205, 217-223, 387-412, 414, 486, 509-513, 549-552, 570, 572-574, 579, 644, 661-667, 671-682, 712, 714-720, 761-774
3.A.8.d	Analyze the relationship between the structure and the purpose of the text	5-7, 24-27, 89, 129-132, 135-148, 176-181, 304-309, 593-599, 626-631, 633-642, 661-667, 697-710, 712, 714-720, 745-746, 833-841

4.0 Writing: Students will compose in a variety of modes by developing content, employing specific forms, and selecting language appropriate for a particular audience and purpose.

4.A Writing

4.A.1	Compose texts using the prewriting and drafting strategies of effective writers and speakers	
4.A.1.a	Use a variety of selfselected prewriting strategies to generate, select, narrow, and develop ideas	
4.A.1.a.1	Evaluate topics for personal relevance, scope, and feasibility	17, 19, 161, 289, 385, 423, 527, 611, 739, 853, 951, 967, 988
4.A.1.a.2	Begin a coherent plan for developing ideas	16-17, 19, 161, 286, 289, 385, 423, 475, 479, 507, 527, 607, 611, 695, 735, 739, 843, 853, 907, 948, 951, 967-968, 988-993
4.A.1.a.3	Explore and evaluate relevant sources of information	969-974, 976-978, 982-983
4.A.1.b	Select, organize, and develop ideas appropriate to topic, audience, and purpose	
4.A.1.b.1	Organize information logically	17, 162-163, 257, 290, 292, 385, 423-424, 479, 507, 527-528, 607, 612-613, 735, 740-742, 854-855, 907, 952, 989-993, 996-997
4.A.1.b.2	Use techniques, such as graphic organizers and signal words to complete and clarify organizational structures	17, 162, 257, 385, 423, 507, 527-528, 607, 612, 735, 740, 854, 907, 952, 989-993
4.A.1.b.3	Verify the effectiveness of paragraph development by modifying topic, support, and concluding sentences as necessary	17, 19, 162-164, 290, 292, 424-426, 479, 507, 527, 529-530, 607, 613-614, 740-742, 854-856, 954, 996-998
4.A.2	Compose oral, written, and visual presentations that express personal ideas, inform, and persuade	

4.A.2.a	Compose to express personal ideas by experimenting with a variety of forms and techniques suited to topic, audience, and purpose in order to develop a personal style and a clear, intentional, and consistent voice and tone	19, 40, 163, 207, 216, 239, 258, 291, 310, 338, 355, 420, 425, 427, 463, 465-466, 474-475, 529, 548, 562, 685, 843, 849-850, 853-856, 936
4.A.2.b	Describe in prose and/or poetic forms to clarify, extend, or elaborate on ideas by using evocative language and appropriate organizational structure to create a dominant impression	41, 69, 71, 90, 116-117, 158, 161-164, 207, 238, 336, 513, 560, 580, 586, 599, 668
4.A.2.c	Compose to inform using relevant support and a variety of appropriate organizational structures and signal words within and between paragraphs	163, 215, 225, 286, 289-293, 385, 465, 507, 524, 591, 613, 695, 736, 739-742, 779, 796-799, 801, 827, 883, 984, 988-998
4.A.2.d	Compose to persuade by supporting, modifying, or disagreeing with a position, using effective rhetorical strategies	
4.A.2.d.1	Write an assertion and use evidence that appeals to audience emotion, reasoning, or trust	70, 927, 942-943, 948, 951-955
4.A.2.d.2	Organize ideas to construct a logical progression	948, 952
4.A.2.d.3	Use diction and syntax that is sincere, honest, and trustworthy	163, 291, 425, 529
4.A.2.d.4	Use connotation, repetition, parallelism, and figurative language to control audience emotion and reaction	161-162, 424-425, 560, 581, 854-855
4.A.2.d.5	Use authoritative citations when effective and document appropriately	994-995, 998
4.A.2.e	Use writing-to-learn strategies, such as reflective and metacognitive writing to set goals, make discoveries, and make connections among learned ideas	850, 853-855
4.A.2.f	Manage time and process when writing for a given purpose	169, 257, 296-297, 385, 430-431, 507, 534-535, 607, 619, 735, 747, 860, 907, 958-959
4.A.3 Compose texts using the revising and editing strategies of effective writers and speakers		
4.A.3.a	Revise texts for clarity, completeness, and effectiveness	
4.A.3.a.1	Eliminate redundant and irrelevant words and ideas	996-997
4.A.3.a.2	Clarify meaning through the placement of antecedents, modifiers, connectors, and transitional devices	91, 163, 170, 207, 239, 279, 290, 292, 298, 385, 426, 465, 475, 507, 529, 613-614, 741-742, 853, 856, 953-954, 996-997
4.A.3.a.3	Clarify the relationships among ideas through coordination and subordination that are purposeful, logical, succinct, and balanced	529, 607, 659, 996-997
4.A.3.a.4	Clarify meaning and purpose by using active voice and consistent person, number, tense, and mood	91, 171, 207, 239, 426, 475, 536, 581, 620, 742, 855-856, 954
4.A.3.a.5	Vary sentence types and lengths to clarify and extend meaning and to develop style	163, 425, 529, 613, 685, 741, 996-997

4.A.3.b	Use suitable traditional and electronic resources to refine presentations and edit texts for effective and appropriate use of language and conventions, such as capitalization, punctuation, spelling, and pronunciation	
4.A.3.b.1	Self edit	164, 165, 257, 291, 292, 425, 426, 529, 530, 613, 614, 741, 742, 855, 856, 953, 954
4.A.3.b.2	Peer edit	164, 257, 292, 426, 530, 614, 742, 856, 927, 954
4.A.3.b.3	Dictionary	Revision opportunities can be found on the following pages: 164, 257, 292, 325, 426, 530, 614, 742, 789, 843, 856, 883, 927, 943, 954
4.A.3.b.4	Thesaurus	Revision opportunities can be found on the following pages: 164, 257, 292, 325, 426, 530, 614, 742, 789, 843, 856, 883, 927, 943, 954
4.A.3.b.5	Spell checker	Revision opportunities can be found on the following pages: 164, 257, 292, 325, 426, 530, 614, 742, 789, 843, 856, 883, 927, 943, 954
4.A.3.b.6	Language handbook	Revision opportunities can be found on the following pages: 164, 257, 292, 325, 426, 530, 614, 742, 789, 843, 856, 883, 927, 943, 954
4.A.3.b.7	Grammar checker	Revision opportunities can be found on the following pages: 164, 257, 292, 325, 426, 530, 614, 742, 789, 843, 856, 883, 927, 943, 954; Also see opportunities to revise grammar on pages: 41, 60, 71, 91, 117, 207, 239, 279, 325, 355, 415, 465, 475, 561, 581, 659, 685, 789, 843, 883, 927, 943
4.A.3.b.8	Style book	Revision opportunities can be found on the following pages: 164, 257, 292, 325, 426, 530, 614, 742, 789, 843, 856, 883, 927, 943, 954
4.A.3.c	Prepare the final product for presentation to an audience	15, 17, 165, 239, 355, 427, 475, 685, 743, 843, 857, 927, 943, 955, 994-995, 998
4.A.4	Identify how language choices in writing and speaking affect thoughts and feelings	
4.A.4.a	Use precise word choice, formal to informal, based on audience, situation, or purpose	161-162, 164, 291, 424-425, 529, 531, 581, 613, 853, 855, 952-953
4.A.4.b	Make effective decisions regarding word choice according to connotative and denotative meanings	161-162, 164, 291, 424-425, 529, 613, 853, 855, 952-953
4.A.4.c	Consider how readers or listeners might respond differently to the same words	17, 165, 291, 427, 529, 743, 857, 955
4.A.5	Assess the effectiveness of choice of details, organizational pattern, word choice, syntax, use of figurative language, and rhetorical devices in the student's own composing	
4.A.5.a	Assess the effectiveness of diction that reveals his or her purpose	
4.A.5.a.1	Language appropriate for a particular audience	158, 257, 286, ,291, 385, 420, 507, 607, 608, 735, 736, 850, 907, 948, 984
4.A.5.a.2	Language suitable for a given purpose	158, 257, 286, 385, 420, 507, 607, 608, 735, 736, 850, 907, 948, 984
4.A.5.a.3	Words/phrases/ sentences that extend meaning in a given context	158, 161, 279, 613, 853, 855

	4.A.5.b	Explain how the specific language and expression used by the writer or speaker affects reader/listener response	18, 41, 60, 71, 91, 117, 158, 164, 207, 239, 279, 286, 292, 325, 355, 415, 420, 426, 465, 475, 524, 530, 560, 581, 608, 614, 659, 685, 736, 742, 789, 843, 850, 856, 883, 927, 943, 948, 954, 984, 998
	4.A.5.c	Evaluate the use of transitions in a text	18, 41, 60, 71, 91, 117, 158, 164, 207, 239, 279, 286, 292, 325, 355, 415, 420, 426, 465, 475, 524, 530, 560, 581, 608, 614, 659, 685, 736, 742, 789, 843, 850, 856, 883, 927, 943, 948, 954, 984, 998
4.A.6		Evaluate textual changes in a work and explain how these changes alter tone, clarify meaning, address a particular audience, or fulfill a purpose	
	4.A.6.a	Alter the tone of one's own writing by revising its diction for a specific purpose and/or audience	291, 529
	4.A.6.b	Justify revisions in syntax and diction from a previous draft of his or her same text by explaining how the change affects meaning	163, 291, 425, 613, 855, 953
4.A.7		Locate, retrieve, and use information from various sources to accomplish a purpose	
	4.A.7.a	Identify, evaluate, and use sources of information on a selfselected and/or given topic	827, 969-970, 972-973, 976, 978, 980-982, 989-993
	4.A.7.b	Use various information retrieval sources (traditional and/or electronic) to obtain information on a selfselected and/or given topic	968-971, 974-977, 982
	4.A.7.c	Use appropriate note taking procedures, organizational strategies, and proper documentation of sources of information	
	4.A.7.c.1	Appropriate strategies for taking notes	
	4.A.7.c.1.a	Appropriate strategies for organizing source information or notes	154, 208, 356, 588, 692, 766, 822, 968, 989-993
	4.A.7.c.1.b	Information to include or exclude when using a note taking method	154, 356, 972
	4.A.7.c.1.c	Advantages, disadvantages, or limitations of a given strategy or procedure for recording or organizing information	154, 208, 356, 588, 692, 766, 822
	4.A.7.c.1.d	Advantages, disadvantages, or limitations of sources of information, such as bias, accuracy, availability, variety, currency	972-973, 978-980, 982
	4.A.7.c.2	Use a recognized format for documentation, such as MLA	994-995, 998
	4.A.7.d	Synthesize information from two or more sources to fulfill a self-selected or given purpose	994-995
	4.A.7.e	Use a recognized format to credit sources when paraphrasing, summarizing, and quoting to avoid plagiarism	989-995, 998

5.0 Controlling Language: Students will control language by applying the conventions of standard English in speaking and writing.

5.A Grammar

5.A.1	Recognize elements of grammar in personal and academic reading	415, 659, 685, 954
5.A.2	Apply knowledge of grammar concepts and skills to control oral and written language	
	5.A.2.a Consider the meaning, position, form, and function of words when identifying and using grammatical concepts, such as verbal and verbal phrases (gerunds, participles, and infinitives), reflexive and intensive pronouns, progressive forms of verbs, and active and passive voice	581, 621
	5.A.2.b Combine and expand sentences by incorporating subjects, predicates, and modifiers and by logically coordinating, subordinating, and sequencing ideas	163, 355, 425, 529, 659
	5.A.2.c Differentiate grammatically complete sentences from nonsentences, including comma splices	41, 60, 415, 614
	5.A.2.d Compose simple, compound, complex, and compound-complex sentences using independent, dependent, restrictive, and nonrestrictive clauses; transitions; conjunctions; and appropriate punctuation to connect ideas	163-164, 290, 292, 355, 385, 415, 507, 529-530, 561, 613, 659, 685, 741-742, 853, 883, 927, 996-997

5.B Usage

5.B.1	Recognize examples of conventional usage in personal and academic reading	91, 207, 426, 475, 742, 856, 954
5.B.2	Comprehend and apply standard English usage in oral and written language	
	5.B.2.a Apply appropriate subject/verb agreement, such as agreement involving words of amount, time, and money	465, 475, 537
	5.B.2.b Apply consistent and appropriate use of the person, number, and case of pronouns; pronoun/antecedent agreement; special pronoun problems, such as who - whom, and incomplete constructions; active and passive voice; and verbal and verbal phrases	91, 117, 171, 426, 581, 621, 855, 954
	5.B.2.c Recognize and correct common usage errors, such as misplaced and dangling modifiers; incorrect use of verbs; double negatives; and commonly confused words, such as accept - except	41, 60, 91, 207, 239, 279, 292, 426, 465, 475, 614, 742, 856, 954
	5.B.2.d Use available resources to correct or confirm editorial choices	R46-R67
	5.B.2.e Explain editorial choices	17, 19, 164, 292, 426, 530, 614, 742, 856, 954, 998

5.C Mechanics

5.C.1	Explain and justify the purpose of mechanics to make and clarify meaning in academic and personal reading and writing	17, 19, 164, 292, 426, 530, 614, 742, 856, 954, 998
5.C.2	Apply standard English punctuation and capitalization in written language	

5.C.2.a	Use commas and semicolons correctly, such as in a compound sentence joined by a conjunctive adverb	164, 292, 530, 883, 927
5.C.2.b	Use an apostrophe to designate possession with indefinite pronouns and adjectives	71, 171, 742
5.C.2.c	Use the mechanics of writing correctly	71, 164, 171, 292, 325, 530, 742, 789, 843, 856, 862, 883, 927, 943
5.C.2.d	Use a colon to introduce a list	943
5.C.3	Explain editorial choices involving mechanics	17, 19, 164, 292, 426, 530, 614, 742, 856, 954, 998

5.D Spelling

5.D.1	Recognize conventional spelling in and through personal and academic reading	R72-R75
5.D.2	Apply conventional spelling in written language	
5.D.2.a	Use conventional spelling in personal writing	R72-R75
5.D.2.b	Develop self-monitoring strategies for frequently misspelled words	R72-R75
5.D.2.c	Use suitable traditional and electronic resources as a spelling aid	R72-R75
5.D.3	Maintain a personal list of words to use in editing original writing	R72-R75

5.E Handwriting

5.E.1	Produce writing that is legible to the audience	
5.E.1.a	Write fluidly and legibly in manuscript and cursive	All writing exercises can be used to meet this standard.
5.E.1.b	Use word processing technology when appropriate	All writing exercises can be used to meet this standard.

6.0 Listening: Students will demonstrate effective listening to learn, process, and analyze information.

6.A Listening

6.A.1	Apply and demonstrate listening skills appropriately in a variety of settings and for a variety of purposes	
6.A.1.a	Use criteria to evaluate oral presentations, such as purpose, delivery techniques, content, visual aids, body language, and facial expressions	R83
6.A.1.b	Gather information from listening to a speaker	293, R82-R83
6.A.1.c	Use memory techniques for various listening tasks	R82-R83
6.A.2	Apply comprehension and literary analysis strategies and skills for a variety of listening purposes and settings	
6.A.2.a	Ask relevant questions concerning the speaker's content, delivery, and purpose	743, 857, 955, R83
6.A.2.b	Determine a speaker's purpose and viewpoint	743, 955, R82-R83
6.A.2.c	Interpret the speech or performance or presentation	615, 743, R82-R83

6.A.2.d	Make inferences or draw conclusions based on the presentation	743, 955, R82-R83
6.A.2.e	Provide constructive feedback to speakers concerning the coherence and logic of a speech's content and delivery as well as its overall impact upon the listeners	615, 857, 743, 857, 955, R83

7.0 Speaking: Students will communicate effectively in a variety of situations with different audiences, purposes, and formats.

7.A Speaking

7.A.1	Demonstrate appropriate organizational strategies and delivery techniques to plan for a variety of oral presentation purposes	
7.A.1.a	Select the purpose and format for an oral presentation	743, 857, 955
7.A.1.b	Evaluate the needs and perspectives of the audience	743, 857, 955
7.A.1.c	Anticipate and effectively answer listener concerns and counter arguments through the inclusion and arrangement of details, reasons, examples, and other elements	743, 955
7.A.1.d	Use a variety of organization structures, such as narrative, cause and effect, chronological order, description, main idea and detail, problem/solution, question/answer, comparison and contrast, and contrast that are appropriate to the purpose and topic	743, 857, 955